DATE DUE			
REF.	REF.	REF.	REF.
	REF.	REF.	
	REF.	REF.	

AMERICAN INSECTS

**A handbook of the insects of
America north of Mexico**

Ross H. Arnett, Jr., Ph.D.

Research Taxonomist
Florida State Collection of Arthropods
Gainesville, Florida

VNR VAN NOSTRAND REINHOLD COMPANY
—————————————————————— New York

Manufactured in the United States of America

Published by Van Nostrand Reinhold Company Inc.
115 Fifth Avenue
New York, New York 10003

Van Nostrand Reinhold Company Limited
Molly Millars Lane
Wokingham, Berkshire RG11 2PY, England

Van Nostrand Reinhold
480 La Trobe Street
Melbourne, Victoria 3000, Australia

Macmillan of Canada
Division of Canada Publishing Corporation
164 Commander Boulevard
Agincourt, Ontario M1S 3C7, Canada

15 14 13 12 11 10 9 8 7 6 5 4 3

Library of Congress Cataloging in Publication Data

Arnett, Ross H.
 American Insects.

 Includes index.
 1. Insects –United States. 2. Insects—Canada.
I. Title.
QL474.A76 1985 595.7097 84-15320
ISBN 0-442-20866-9

To Mary, my wife,

and

Ross, Michael, Mary Anne, Barbara, Frances,
Joseph, Bernadette, and Matthew,
my children,

All of whom spent their summers with me in the
field helping gather data for this book

Foreword

Publications that enable the nonspecialist to identify and gain access to information on insects across the broad spectrum of this diverse and abundant group of organisms are very useful, very difficult to prepare, and rather infrequently attempted. This attempt by Dr. Arnett to bridge the gap between identification manuals and the source literature is one of the most successful. It will undoubtedly be enthusiastically welcomed by the many persons who need to identify, and to obtain certain basic information about, flies one day, beetles the next, and so on.

To accomplish a publication of this nature requires an unusually broad taxonomic outlook as well as knowledge, hour upon hour in the trenches of taxonomic literature, successful personal experience in basic taxonomic research, and a peculiar integument that will enable an author to recover quickly from the occasional pointed barbs of colleagues whose "special group" has had to be treated in a new way.

The source of a synthesis such as this, alpha level systematics, is largely a world of specialists, and to transfer such knowledge into a handbook useful to nonspecialists is a unique undertaking. Taxonomic specialists are indebted to generalists for making their specialized studies useful to a broader audience. Likewise, the generalists are dependent on the specialists, for only accumulations of year-in, year-out dedicated taxonomic study can produce basic classifications. Thus the users of this volume benefit not only from Dr. Arnett's endeavors and those of his many colleagues who have directly contributed information and reviewed the manuscript, but also from the efforts of current and previous generations of taxonomists.

As one of my main interests and responsibilities is to ensure the production of basic and applied taxonomy for the nontaxonomist user as well as for taxonomists, I am very pleased to see this fine distillation of the fruits of basic research. Also, as Dr. Arnett has been a long-time cooperator with the U.S. Department of Agriculture's insect and mite taxonomic unit, we are especially gratified that we can point to this significant volume as one of the many results of our relationship.

This brief attempt to relate the reader to the origin and process of production of this work would be very incomplete without noting that neither the special nor general studies would be possible without the magnificent research collections that taxonomists are so fortunate to have for study and reference, especially those of the National Collection at the Smithsonian Institution.

Lloyd Knutson

Chairman
Insect Identification and Beneficial
 Insect Introduction Institute
Agricultural Research Service
U.S. Department of Agriculture
Beltsville, Maryland

Preface

The final form of this book was conceived while I was teaching at Purdue University. There I became impressed with the need for an accurate way to "spot" identify (identify on sight) the common insects of all orders. I also realized that this would be an impossible task. To do so, one would first have to have a vast collection of insects, a library full of literature, an unfailing memory, and years of experience with the local fauna. Without these resources, a great many spot *mis*identifications would continue to go undetected year after year. Nevertheless, fortified by this original incentive, I have attempted to compile in a single reference book a tool that will be useful to those working without a major collection and library. To do so, however, I needed the facilities of a great museum and library. Fortunately, I was able to work at the museum I know best, the institution where I started my professional career and where I retain the title of Cooperating Scientist: the Systematic Entomology Laboratory of the United States Department of Agriculture at the National Museum of Natural History in Washington and the Agricultural Research Center, Beltsville, Maryland. The final manuscript was completed at this institution and at the laboratory of Insect Control and Research, Baltimore. With the help of these facilities, the various curators of the insect collections, and approximately seventy reviewers, the book has at last been completed.

Attention was given during the course of writing to the needs of users who would like to have a general knowledge of insect life without becoming overwhelmed by the vast number of insect species. Many people need to know about kinds of insects without being bogged down by the enormous number of minute species, most of which even many entomologists have never seen. The needs of agriculture extension agents, pest control operators, pest management field scouts, teachers, advanced horticulturists, as well as the curious public are best served by providing a usable guide that gives sizes, shapes, color patterns, and salient features of some species of each major family, by pointing out those groups most likely to be encountered, and by bypassing obscure groups for immediate consideration. At the same time, this book makes it impossible for its users to overlook the existence of any family, genus, or group of species because they are all listed.

What started out to be an apparently easy task, considering the wealth of literature on insects, occupied much of the author's time for over 10 years, during which period he was unable to continue research on his favorite groups of beetles. It also required the aid of many friends and colleagues, specialists who would corroborate details that were beyond the author's personal experience. For this help I am very grateful. Every author has certain misgivings about accepting such aid, not only because of the infringement upon other people's time, but also because no specialist will agree exactly with another's treatment of the subject. The individuals acknowledged here have helped with the project, but they are not responsible for my treatment of any section. I only hope that the end result is enough to reward them with the satisfaction that the users of the book are sharing in their knowledge.

The art work comes either from existing literature or from original drawings by the author and his daughter, Frances X. Armstrong, and his son, Michael J. P. Arnett. Many of the photographs were taken from specimens in the author's collection, the National Museum of Natural History, or Florida State Collection of Arthropods. A great number of the Lepidoptera specimens in the collection of Professor John G. Franclemont were photographed by John Edward Rawlins, Cornell University. Professor Michael Kosztarab, Virginia Polytechnic Institute, supplied photographs of scale insects. Photographs of equipment were supplied by the American Biological Supply Co., Baltimore; BioQuip Products, Santa Monica; and Ward's Natural Science Establishment, Rochester.

I am indebted to the following individuals for helping in many ways with this book. Dr. Robert E. Woodruff, Florida State Collection of Arthropods, made specimens available to me for illustrations and helped in other ways. Dr. E. V. Komarek, Executive Secretary of the Tall Timbers Research Station at Tallahassee, provided me with a fellowship and a place to work during the early phase of the writing. Theodore J. Spilman, Systematic Entomology Laboratory, United States Department of Agriculture, devoted a great many

hours helping me find specimens, locate publications, and most of all, encouraged me with friendship and critical analysis of ideas and concepts. Another close friend, Dr. Eugene J. Gerberg, not only provided me with space to work and live during the final stages of the writing but gave me many helpful suggestions and criticisms. Special thanks go to Timothy T. Matson, my nephew, an amateur naturalist and at the time a student at Cornell University, for his helpful suggestions and comments on the use of the book by young amateurs; to Professor Michael Kosztarab, for his special help with the Homoptera; and to Dr. Tim L. McCabe, New York State Museum, Science Service, Albany, for help in locating certain literature and for the use of the museum collection.

As has been the pattern for many years, my friends and colleagues at the Systematic Entomology Laboratory, United States Department of Agriculture, and the Department of Entomology, Smithsonian Institution—both organizations at the National Museum of Natural History, Washington—have helped in various ways, some by reading portions of the text and others by supplying information, checking specimens and names, and in many other ways throughout the duration of the project. I am grateful for their help and the help of other specialists, as listed below, at other institutions.

The following individuals reviewed or otherwise helped with the order sections:

Collembola: Professor José A. Mari Mutt, University of Puerto Rico, Mayaguez; Professor J. T. Salmon, Waikanae, New Zealand; and Professor Kenneth Christiansen, Grinnell College, Grinnell, Iowa.

Protura: Professor José A. Mari Mutt, University of Puerto Rico.

Microcoryphia, Thysanura, and Entotrophi: Dr. Pedro Wygodzinsky, American Museum of Natural History, New York.

Entotrophi: Dr. Charles L. Remington, Peabody Museum, Yale University, New Haven.

Ephemeroptera: Professor William J. Peters, Florida A&M University, Tallahassee; Professor George F. Edmunds, Jr., University of Utah, Salt Lake City; and Professor W. Patrick McClaffery, Purdue University, West Lafayette, Indiana.

Odonata: Professor Minter J. Westfall, Jr., University of Florida, Gainesville; Professor George H. Bick, Gainesville; and Dr. Oliver S. Flint, Jr., Smithsonian Institution, Washington.

Plecoptera: Professor Richard W. Bauman, Brigham Young University, Provo; Professor Kenneth W. Stewart, North Texas State University, Denton, Texas; and Robert H. Boyle, Cold Spring, New York.

Grylloblattodea, Orthoptera, Phasmatodea, Dictyoptera, Isoptera, Dermaptera, Zoraptera, and Psocoptera: Dr. Ashley B. Gurney and Dr. David Nickle, U.S. Department of Agriculture; and Jacques R. Helfer, Mendocino, California.

Orthoptera: Professor Thomas J. Walker, University of Florida, Gainesville.

Dictyoptera, Blattaria: Dr. Lewis M. Roth, U.S. Army Natick Laboratories, Natick, Massachusetts.

Embioptera: Dr. Edward S. Ross, California Academy of Sciences, San Francisco.

Psocoptera: Professor Edward L. Mockford, Illinois State University, Normal.

Mallophaga: Dr. Robert C. Dalgleish, Huyck Preserve, Rensselaerville, New York.

Anoplura: Professor Ke Chung Kim, Pennsylvania State University, University Park.

Hemiptera: Dr. Jon Herring and Thomas J. Henry, U.S. Department of Agriculture, Washington; Dr. Richard C. Froeschner, Smithsonian Institution, Washington; and Dr. Frank Mead, Division of Plant Industry, Gainesville, Florida.

Homoptera: Professor Michael Kosztarab, Virginia Polytechnic Institute (who furnished a great amount of unpublished data for this section); Dr. Avas Hamon, Division of Plant Industry, Gainesville, Florida; Dr. Manya Stoetzel, Dr. James P. Kramer, Suco Nakahara, and Dr. Douglass R. Miller, U.S. Department of Agriculture, Washington and Beltsville; and Dr. Lois O'Brien, Florida A&M University, Tallahassee.

Thysanoptera: Professor Thomas H. Wilson, Judson College, Marion, Alabama; and Suco Nakahara, U.S. Department of Agriculture, Beltsville.

Neuroptera: Dr. Olivier S. Flint, Jr., Smithsonian Institution, Washington; Dr. Lionel Strange, Division of Plant Industry, Gainesville, Florida; and Professor Phillip A. Adams, California State University, Fullerton.

Coleoptera: Professor N. M. Downie, Lafayette, Indiana, and Theodore J. Spilman, U.S. Department of Agriculture, Washington.

Trichoptera: Professor Norman H. Anderson, Oregon State University, Corvallis; Dr. Olivier S. Flint, Jr., Smithsonian Institution, Washington; and Professor Glenn B. Wiggans, University of Toronto.

Lepidoptera: Professor John G. Franclemont, Cornell University, Ithaca; Dr. Eugene G. Munroe, Entomology Research Institute, Ottawa; Professor Jerry Powell, University of California, Berkeley; Dr. John B. Heppner, Division of Plant Industry, Gainesville, Florida; Dr. Donald R. Davis, Smithsonian Institution; Dr. Douglas C. Ferguson, Dr. Ronald W. Hodges, and Dr. Robert W. Poole, U.S. Department of Agriculture, Washington.

Mecoptera: Professor George W. Byers, University of Kansas, Lawrence.

Hymenoptera: Professor Howard E. Evans, Colorado State University, Fort Collins; Dr. Henry K. Townes, American Entomological Institute, Gainesville, Florida; Dr. Arnold S. Menke and Dr. David R. Smith, U.S. Department of Agriculture, Washington; Dr. John K. Bouseman, Illinois Natural History Survey, Urbana; and Dr. Karl V. Krombein, Smithsonian Institution, Washington.

Diptera: Dr. Paul Arnaud, Jr., California Academy of Sciences, San Francisco; the late Professor John N. Belkin, University of California, Los Angeles; Dr. Ray-

mond J. Gagné, Dr. Richard H. Foote, Dr. Lloyd Knutson, Dr. Curtis W. Sabrosky, George C. Steyskal, Dr. F. Christian Thompson, Dr. D. Dee Wilder, and Dr. Willis W. Wirth, U.S. Department of Agriculture; Dr. Wayne N. Mathis, Smithsonian Institution, Washington; and Dr. Howard Weems, Jr., Division of Plant Industry, Gainesville, Florida.

Siphonaptera: Professor Allen H. Benton, Jr., State University College, Fredonia; Professor Cluff E. Hopla, University of Oklahoma, Norman; and Professor Robert E. Lewis, Iowa State University, Ames.

Dr. J. Richard Gorham, Food and Drug Administration, Washington, provided information about beneficial insects.

My sincere thanks to all of these scientists. Without their help, this book would have been impossible.

The user may find mistakes in spite of the combined efforts of all involved. My wife, Mary, has spent many tedious hours finding and eliminating many of these, plus many hours compiling and typing the massive index; I am grateful for this help and for over 40 years of love and devoted help of all sorts. The author assumes the responsibility for all errors and hopes that none is serious. Corrections and additions will be welcomed as they are noted.

Ross H. Arnett, Jr.
Gainesville, Florida

NOTICE

Users of this book should know that the classification of insects, especially at the generic and specific level, changes rather rapidly each year with the discovery of new species and new information about known species that accrues from the continued collecting of additional specimens. Consequently, the author is publishing all such changes that come to his attention in the journal *Insecta Mundae*. This series may be consulted in many major libraries or private copies may be obtained. Consult your librarian or write to the author for further information.

This book will serve as a general taxonomic introduction for the proposed series of publications dealing with the genera and species of the insect fauna of North America, a project sponsored by The Entomological Society of America, in which Dr. Arnett actively participates.

DR. MICHAEL KOSZTARAB

Professor of Systematic Entomology
Virginia Polytechnic Institute and State University
Blacksburg, Virginia

Special Instructions for the Use of This Book

1. Each section is arranged so that topics follow the same sequence. See the first chapter for details about the order of the descriptive data. The classification system that follows the introductory material is arranged according to what is presumed to be the correct phylogeny.

2. Common names of species of insects are written with capital initial letters, for example, Baboon Beetle. This name, which refers to a particular species for which a Latin name is available, is listed in the classification section. Common names of groups of insects are written entirely in lower case, for example, flies, bugs, ants, and the like.

3. Large orders with many families and synonyms of family names appear in a table of classification followed by a list of all family-name taxa arranged alphabetically. This table may be used instead of the general index at the end of the book for the rapid location of a name. The number of the family is given in both the table and the index, enabling one to turn quickly to the proper section.

4. Each order, each family, and each genus has been given a number. Because there are approximately 22,000 names cited in this book, a simple system has been devised for quick reference in the index. For example, *Platypedia,* 21.13.21 indicates that this genus is in order 21, family 13 of that order, and genus 21 of that family. It is the genus *Platypedia* Uhler and contains the species *Platypedia aroelata* Uhler (Orchard Cicada). Both the specific name and the common name of this species are cited under the same number. Unnumbered names—for example, subfamily names—are cited by giving the genus number that immediately follows the name—for example, Phymatinae, *supra* 20.16.1. This system simplifies finding a name on pages with a long list of names.

5. If a species is discussed within a genus, the generic name is centered, followed by information about the genus, followed by the included species. If no species is cited (except in monobasic genera), the generic name is placed in square brackets along with the generic number, followed by the author name and the number of species included in the genus, for example, [21.13 *Lasiochilus* Reuter (7 spp.)]. In the case of monobasic genera, the species name is always cited.

6. Distribution is cited by regional numbers and state and province codens as shown in the map and coden list of Figs. 1.1. and 1.2 in Chap. 1. If a species is found throughout an entire region—say, northeastern North America—the states and provinces are not cited; instead, it is noted as (1) n.e. NA; if the species is not found in northeastern Canada, except perhaps in southern Ontario, the range is cited as (1) n.e. US. When the species is found only in part of a region, the states and/or province codens are cited along with the region number, for example, (1) PA, NJ, MD. If the species is found throughout the United States and Canada, the range may be cited as (1), (2), (3), (4), (5). If the species is found in all of one region, but not in all regions, the range is cited, as for example, (1), (2), (3), (5). Various combinations are given that best and most accurately describe the range.

7. All pest species that have been given a common name are cited under the correct genus with the common name in parentheses, for example, *M. persicae* (Sulzer) (Green Peach Aphid). Other common species are also given a common name.

Contents

Foreword by *Lloyd Knutson* v

Preface vii

Part I: Introduction
 1. General considerations 3
 2. Insect classification and systematics 10
 3. Identification features 20
 4. Insect ecology, behavior, and distribution 24
 5. Insect collecting 31
 6. The orders of insects 53

Part II: The insect fauna of America, north of Mexico
 1. Collembola—Springtails and Allies 67
 2. Protura—Proturans 73
 3. Entotrophi—Entotrophs 75
 4. Microcoryphia—Bristletails 78
 5. Thysanura—Silverfish and Allies 80
 6. Ephemeroptera—Mayflies 82
 7. Odonata—Dragonflies and Damselflies 92
 8. Plecoptera—Stoneflies 104
 9. Embioptera—Webspinners 111
 10. Phasmatodea—Walkingsticks 113
 11. Orthoptera—Grasshoppers, Katydids, and Crickets 116
 12. Grylloblatodea—Rock Crawlers 138

 13. Dermaptera—Earwigs 139
 14. Dictyoptera—Mantids and Cockroaches 143
 15. Isoptera—Termites 152
 16. Zoraptera—Angel Insects 156
 17. Psocoptera—Barklice and Booklice 157
 18. Mallophaga—Biting Lice 162
 19. Anoplura—Sucking Lice 166
 20. Hemiptera—Bugs 170
 21. Homoptera—Cicadas, Hoppers, Whiteflies, Aphids, and Scale Insects 207
 22. Thysanoptera—Thrips 243
 23. Neuroptera—Dobsonflies, Lacewings, Antlions, and Allies 249
 24. Coleoptera—Beetles, Weevils, and Stylopids 263
 25. Hymenoptera—Wasps, Ants, and Bees 402
 26. Trichoptera—Caddisflies 471
 27. Lepidoptera—Moths, Skippers, and Butterflies 484
 28. Mecoptera—Scorpionflies and Allies 636
 29. Diptera—Flies and Keds 640
 30. Siphonaptera—Fleas 709

Glossary 715

Index 723

MAGNA EST VERITAS

For want of me the world's course will not fail!
When all its work is done, the lie shall rot;
The truth is great, and shall prevail,
When none cares whether it prevails or not.

Coventry Patmore

Part I
Introduction

1
General Considerations

This book combines the features of a field book, an identification manual, and an abbreviated catalog of the insects of the United States and Canada arranged in the most modern *published* classification available. Its main purposes are as follows:

1. To list and describe many species that might be encountered by the general collector and about which there is enough published information to enable their identification by a nonspecialist.
2. To account for all species of North American (north of Mexico) insects by listing and describing each order, keying each family, and listing each genus and the number of known species in each genus for the area covered.
3. To give general bibliographic references to every taxon included by listing books, monographs, and catalogs.
4. To illustrate most features used in the identification keys.
5. To provide general biological information and distribution for the taxa in the area covered.

Because of these objectives, special keys and, in some cases, identification tables were either prepared or adapted for this book. Highly technical features of the anatomy and complicated anatomical terms have been avoided wherever possible. It will soon become apparent as the book is used that not many insects are as easy to "spot" identify as most birds. Almost always a hand lens is needed (to replace the bird student's binoculars), and often specimens must be examined under a microscope. However, once experience with the local fauna is gained, it will become possible to make some sight identifications, at least to family, and in certain large-sized insects, to genus and even species.

Identification is an important process—in fact, one of the most important steps in any scientific investigation of animal or plant life. Therefore, this book places considerable stress on identification; it is recommended that users take the time to read all identification instructions so that they can learn how to distinguish between those common insects that may be recognized easily and those that may be identified only by a specialist.

The introductory chapters (1 through 6) provide the preliminary steps and information needed for the identification and study of insects. The rationale for each is explained in the following paragraphs.

DISTINGUISHING INSECTS FROM OTHER ANIMALS

One must be sure that the specimen to be identified is an insect, not a spider or some other kind of animal. Also, one must know the life stage of the specimen under study. Detailed treatment of the immature stages is not provided here, but keys to the immature stages of a few orders are given. Chapter 2 discusses the place of insects in the classification scheme of living organisms and also provides some basic information about the field of *systematics*. To manage a seemingly bewildering mass of insect species (well over a million species in the world), one can assign them to genera, families, and orders. One must become accustomed to using these group names. Although common names are given for ready reference, one must advance in the study of insects (or any other kind of animal or plant) to the use of Latin names. Doing so soon becomes as easy as using English names if the principles of naming are understood. All these factors are involved in distinguishing insects as a group.

INSECT FEATURES USEFUL FOR IDENTIFICATION

The structure of insects is complicated and usually unfamiliar to most people. However, certain obvious features can be used for identification without resorting to all the technical details that entomologists need for a scientific classification. The correct identification of many insects does not always require the high power of a microscope. The structural features needed for this purpose are discussed in Chap. 3.

ENVIRONMENT AND DISTRIBUTION OF INSECTS

Even though everywhere we turn insects seem to be present, we must know more about their habits, habitats, and distribution before many groups can be collected

and studied. In the strictest sense, there is no such thing as a rare species. Any species must be relatively common someplace in order for its members to find mates, reproduce, and survive the vicissitudes of the environment. As is true of all kinds of organisms, each species has a unique habitat and distribution range. The ecology, distribution, and speciation of insects is briefly discussed in Chap. 4.

METHODS OF INSECT STUDY

Unlike the study of birds and even of plants, the study of insects usually requires that they be collected and preserved for later identification and distribution research or kept alive in captivity for behavioral and other biological observations. Most insects may be sight identified to order and many to family while still alive and active, but species identification usually requires immobility of the specimen and its magnification. The best way to begin any study of insects, therefore, is to make a collection. Before starting, however, certain objectives must be determined and understood, and the tools and techniques available must be known. These matters are discussed in detail in Chap. 5.

THE ORDERS OF INSECTS

The bulk of this book (Part II) consists of a detailed discussion of the orders of insects and the species assigned to each order. Chapter 6 contains a key to all orders (Table 6.2) and some hints for "spot" identification so that the user may learn how to identify any specimen encountered very quickly. Once the order is known, it is a simple matter to turn to the applicable section of Part II and work from there.

First, one must know the difference between *identifying* insects and *classifying* them. To identify is to find the correct name of a group; to classify is to place or arrange it in a system that reflects its probable evolution. The latter is the practice of the science of systematics, discussed in Chap. 2, whereas identification is the acceptance of the results of the systematic studies of others. The methods for making identifications will be discussed in a later section in this chapter.

Each order section in Part II contains the same sequence of information:

1. Latin name of the order
2. Common name of the order
3. Introductory paragraph on the general features of the order
4. Meaning of the order name and other names that might apply to it
5. General biology of the order
6. Formal description, or *diagnosis*, of the characteristics of the members of the order, starting with the range of the physical size of the species, either in terms of its body length or wingspan, followed by its color, shape, body texture, and features of the head, thorax—including legs and wings, if the latter are present—and abdomen
7. Brief discussion of the immature stages of the species

8. Similar insects and how they are distinguished
9. Type of metamorphosis
10. Habits and habitats, including ecology and physiology in some cases
11. Reproductive behavior, i.e., courtship patterns, if known, and other data
12. Methods of collecting and preserving.
13. Methods of rearing
14. Distribution in the world and in the United States and Canada, the total number of species, and the number of species recorded in the United States and Canada.
15. Notes on the identification of families, genera, and species
16. Economic importance, i.e., role as a pest or benefactor in ecological cycles.

These introductory statements are followed by general notes on the classification of the order. Each order section includes a key to the families; in the larger orders, an index to the families; and in some large orders, a table of the families, with emphasis on features used for sight identification. Keys to the genera of a few orders are also provided.

Each order section lists, and often gives a diagnosis for, all taxa—that is, suborders, superfamilies, families, subfamilies (in some cases, tribes), and genera. The fact that all valid generic names are included (although usually not their synonyms) enables the user to determine the proper place in the classification of insect names that may appear in general books, textbooks, research papers, and other nontaxonomic works. In most cases, subgenera are also listed but not numbered. Each genus is followed by an indication of the number of species in the genus. If there is only a single species (that is, if the genus is *monobasic* in the United States and Canada), the name and author (that is, the individual who named the species) is given (the author name is included as a bibliographic aid). If there is a generally accepted common name for the species, it is given after the Latin name.

Species are described in some detail if they are of general interest, sufficiently common, of economic importance, or representative of their group. Size, shape, color, and other features of each species are described as an aid for spot identification; biological details are often included.

Illustrations are identified by a figure number that includes the order number first; for example, 29.1 indicates the first figure in Order No. 29. For about 350 of the species, reference is made to another of the author's books *Guide to Insects* (see the bibliography at the end of this chapter), using the notation (A&J 150) or the like, where the number indicates the number of the color photo in the Guide.

The distribution of the species is indicated by a simple code. The United States and Canada are divided into five major regions (Fig. 1). All of the states of the United States (except Hawaii) and the provinces of Canada are given two-letter codens (see the list of abbreviations in Table 1.1). In the case of the United States, these are the codens assigned by the United States Postal Service. Figure 2 shows them arranged from west to east by re-

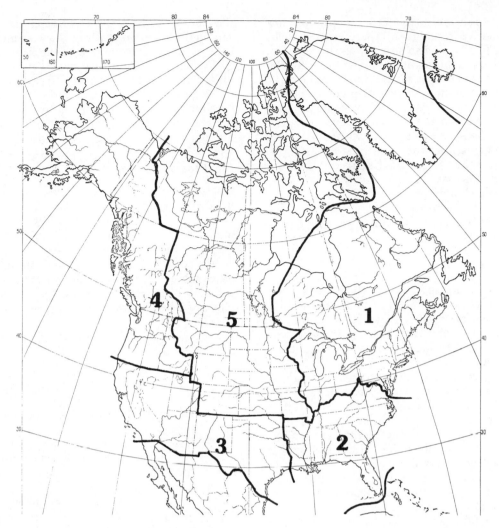

Fig. 1. Map of North America showing the five areas used for recording genera and species distribution.

gion numbers. To record the distribution of a species, the region number is given, in parentheses, followed by the appropriate codens; if the species is distributed throughout an entire region, generalized geographical indications are given. One example of a distribution citation: *(1) NY, VT, NH, MA, NJ, MD, DE, DC; (2) VA, NC.* Another example: *(1) n.e. NA; (2) s.e. US* (northeastern North America; southeastern United States.)

(1) WI MI ON PQ NB NS NF NY VT NH ME MA CT
 RI IL IN OH PA NJ MD DE DC

(2) KY WV VA TN NC AR LA MS AL GA SC FL

(3) CA AZ NM OK TX NV UT

(4) BC WA OR ID AK AI

(5) AB SK MB MT ND MN WY SD NE IA CO KS MO

Fig. 2. The state and province codens by regions used to record distribution.

SPECIES IDENTIFICATION

As stated above, a major purpose of this book is to give information needed to make identifications of the insects found in the United States and Canada, but a word of caution is necessary. Because of the great number of species of insects, it is usually difficult to identify accurately any but those that are well-known and distinctly shaped and marked unless the identifier is a specialist in the group. Therefore, all identifications made with the aid of this book should be considered tentative and subject to verification by a specialist or by the use of the available technical literature. With experience, one soon learns the common species of a particular region.

To use this book properly, one must become familiar with the system designed for it. It is as simple as a plant guide or a bird guide, except for the limitations imposed by the great number of species involved. Obviously, with approximately 90,000 species living in the United States and Canada, only a small portion of them can be described and named in a single volume; actually, this book contains less than 10 percent of the total. However, those species that are illustrated and described show much of the diversity of the fauna. Thus, even if the

specimen at hand is not described, named, or illustrated here, a relative is, and it will therefore be possible to identify it to family, and in some cases, to genus and to species. Further identification may be made by consulting the literature cited in the references given at the end of each order. Minute species of Diptera, Hymenoptera, Coleoptera, Hemiptera, and Homoptera are difficult to identify, even to family. Most species under 5 mm are nearly impossible to identify without considerable experience or without the aid of a specialist.

Only adults of the species are described. Most adult insects—but not all—have wings, and wings are never present during their immature stages. Except for casual identification, most insect specimens should be mounted on an insect pin, preserved in alcohol, or mounted on microscope slides.

Preliminary Identification

Making an identification is similar to the process a physician uses to diagnose an illness. The physician looks for symptoms; the taxonomist looks for features. The combined symptoms enable the physician to identify the disease; the combined features enable the taxonomist to identify the insect.

The first step is to "run" the specimen through the key to orders found in Chap. 6, a chapter that serves as an introduction to the classification system. Then turn to the specific order section indicated. The diagnosis found there will help verify whether the identification of the order is correct. If the specimen doesn't fit the diagnosis, return to the key to orders in Chap. 6, and try again. Once the correct order has been determined, turn to the table of families and the family key. Repeat the process to learn the correct name of the family.

For those not familiar with the use of identification keys, here are brief instructions. First turn to any of the order sections in Part II and examine its key to families. A key is composed of "couplets" (rarely, "triplets"), all of which are numbered and each half of which describes alternative insect features. Look at the specimen to be identified and decide which of the two alternatives corresponds with its features. The number that appears at the end of the alternative that fits the specimen indicates the next couplet to be consulted. Repeat the process for this new couplet and for all subsequent couplets until an alternative is reached that has a family name at the end. The process of identification is then complete. Note that from the second couplet on, a number in parentheses appears after the couplet number, e.g., 6(3). The number in parentheses indicates the previous couplet read, thereby making it easy to backtrack in case an error was made or one is suspected.

In large orders such as the Coleoptera, Lepidoptera, Diptera, and Hymenoptera, determining the correct family will be much more difficult than determining the correct order, with many more chances for error. It will be necessary to check specimens against the illustrations. In most cases—Coleoptera excepted—characteristics of *wing venation* must be used. Study the section on wing venation carefully; learn how to identify the veins and match the specimen with the illustrations and the features listed in the key. Sometimes it will be necessary in the beginning to draw the wing and label the veins to assure that they agree with the key.

When the family has been determined, check the diagnosis with the specimen. It will be impossible to make further identification with this book alone if the specimen you have is not illustrated and described in the text or in the few orders where keys to the genera are given.

Final Identification

Once a collection has been sorted and identified to family, certain groups may be of more interest than others. One may wish to concentrate on these and store the remainder for others to study and identify. Various revisionary works, available in the large libraries, must be consulted for further identification of these groups. Since the use of this literature often requires a large vocabulary of technical terms, the reader is referred to the glossary listed in the Bibliography at the end of this chapter.

Some additional ways to make final identifications are as follows:

1. Compare the specimens to be identified with specimens whose correct identification is already established.
2. Obtain the help of other collectors who know the species involved.
3. Use the reference collections of large museums (see page 42 for more details about contacting specialists).
4. Check a catalog of the species of the group. To do so, first identify the specimen to genus. If only a single species has been previously assigned to that genus, it is probable that the specimen belongs to that species. Other genera may be represented by only a single species in the locality in which the specimen was found. The specimen may therefore be tentatively assumed to be of that species, but it should be compared with the description of that species before it can be positively identified. Since the distribution ranges of most species are poorly known, it is possible for many specimens to be noted for the first time in any given region.
5. Finally, it is always necessary to use keys and descriptions of the species before the specimen can be correctly named.

To verify an identification is a complicated procedure reserved for the specialist. A *verified identification* (or *vouchering* as it is sometimes termed) is one in which the specimen has been compared with the specimen that was originally named, that is, the *holotype* (or *type specimen* as it is sometimes called). Since these holotypes—one for each species—are scattered in various museums and collections throughout the world, it is obviously impossible to verify all identifications in this manner. Specialists often find it necessary to travel to museum after museum, studying holotype after holotype. It is for this reason that beginners must get speci-

mens verified (vouchered) by specialists. (See page 42 for the procedure for doing so.)

The beginner who does not fully realize the importance of this identification process should be reminded that the correct name of the insect is the only means of gaining access to the literature that has already been gathered and recorded about the species and of adding any new information to that literature. Since the number of species involved is so vast, the correct name of each is vital.

THE NUMBER OF INSECTS COMPARED TO PLANTS AND OTHER ANIMALS

One might think that we have placed too much emphasis on the mere number of species of insects. The fact is that among the multitudinous species of living organisms in the world, both plant and animal, insects predominate as far as the number of species is concerned if not the number of individual organisms (probably bacteria represent the greatest number of the latter). It is not the number of species that is important, however, but rather their diversity, as we shall discuss later. Since it is difficult to rank living organisms by their degree of diversity, and since, as systematists, we are not interested in the *amount* of diversity, but the *kind*, no attempt will be made to rank groups by this criterion.

Unfortunately, in our quest for pure knowledge, disproportionate emphasis has been placed upon the study of certain groups at the expense of others. For example, the relatively few vertebrate animals and the modest group of species known as bacteria have received the attention of the majority of biologists. The remaining species of animals and plants, representing the large majority have been woefully neglected because there are relatively few botanists, invertebrate zoologists, and entomologists to concentrate on them.

Figure 3 shows the relative proportions of the number of species of the major groups of living organisms. The sizes of the circles are proportionate to the number of known species of each. It is apparent from this illustration that the dominant group consists of the arthropods, that most of the arthropods are insects, and furthermore, that most of the insects are beetles. One can only conclude that the creative processes of evolution seemingly favor beetles.

One can only guess how many persons in the world today carry on systematic studies of plants and animals. Perhaps in round numbers there may be 100,000 serious students. If so, a similar conservative estimate of the number of persons studying Coleoptera would be 2,000. Such figures indicate that only 2 percent of all researchers are studying 20 percent of all living organisms.

Table 1.2 shows the estimated number of species of insects in the world, the exact number of genera and species of insects recorded in the United States and Canada, and the number of species named in this book. If one studies these figures carefully, several things become clear. First of all, there are probably fewer species of insects in the United States and Canada than most estimates predict. Second, considering how relatively well known the species of North America are, and

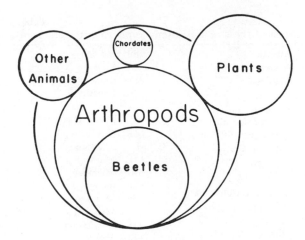

Fig. 3. The relative size, in number of described species, of the major groups of organisms. Each circle represents the percentage of species of each group. The area of the largest circle equals 100 percent of the species. Each of the other circles represents a percentage of the largest circle.

considering our very poor present knowledge of the insects of tropical regions, the number of species in the world might easily be double that already catalogued. We don't know and we may never find out, considering the current rate of worldwide habitat destruction.

To philosophize a bit, one might ask what difference such knowledge would make to the world now or in the future. A possible answer might take the form of two questions. What if there had been no Louis Pasteur to study bacteria? What if there had been no Beethoven, no Rembrandt, no Dickens? Many esoterically valuable things would have remained unknown to us. Isn't it important for us to know as much as possible?

THE SELECTION OF TAXA

It is exceedingly difficult to determine which species can be properly termed "common." As explained previously, every species is common somewhere and rare or absent elsewhere. Only through considerable experience with a local fauna can one guess what to expect while collecting. Amateur collectors often look for "rare" species. Once a "rare" species has been found, however, a place where it *is* common is soon learned, and it may no longer be considered rare. Therefore, whether a species is thought rare or common was not one of the criteria for selecting it for inclusion in this book.

With the awareness that the specialist—because of his experience, and with an abundance of specimens and literature around him—will question any selection for a book such as this, the decision was made to include the following categories to the extent that such was practical:

1. All orders in the world (30 orders by the classification used here)
2. All North American families, with a key to the North American families of each order, and with a description of most of these families, especially if they contain species with the following characteristics:

Table 1.1 Abbreviations

Most of these abbreviations apply to distribution statements; those for states follow the United States Postal Service codens.

AB	Alberta	IN	Indiana	NB	New Brunswick	PQ	Quebec
AK	Alaska	KS	Kansas	NC	North Carolina	RI	Rhode Island
AL	Alabama	KY	Kentucky	ND	North Dakota	s.	southern part
AR	Arkansas	L.	Length	NE	Nebraska	SC	South Carolina
AZ	Arizona	LA	Louisiana	n.e.	northeastern part	SD	South Dakota
BC	British Columbia	MA	Massachusetts	NF	Newfoundland	s.e.	southeastern part
c.	central part	MB	Manitoba	NH	New Hampshire	SK	Saskatchewan
CA	California	MD	Maryland	NJ	New Jersey	s.w.	southwestern part
CO	Colorado	ME	Maine	NM	New Mexico	TN	Tennessee
CT	Connecticut	MI	Michigan	NS	Nova Scotia	TX	Texas
DC	District of Columbia	mm	millimeter	NV	Nevada	US	United States
DE	Delaware	MN	Minnesota	n.w.	northwestern part	UT	Utah
e.	eastern part	MO	Missouri	NY	New York	VA	Virginia
FL	Florida	MS	Mississippi	OH	Ohio	VT	Vermont
GA	Georgia	MT	Montana	OK	Oklahoma	w.	western part
IA	Iowa	MX	Mexico	ON	Ontario	WA	Washington
ID	Idaho	n.	northern part	OR	Oregon	WI	Wisconsin
IL	Illinois	NA	North America,	PA	Pennsylvania	WV	West Virginia
			including Mexico	Pl.	Plate	WY	Wyoming

(a) Species that are over 7 mm in length
(b) Species that are economic pests or biologically important
(c) Species that commonly frequent flowers and foliage or appear around lights at night.

3. All genera represented in the United States and Canada. For those genera that are monotypic in this region (there may be more than one species in the genus elsewhere) the species is named; for all other genera, the number of species is cited.

Table 1.2 Number of Species of Insects

Orders	Estimated No. of Species in the World	Recorded No. of Species in U.S. and Canada	Recorded No. of Families in U.S. and Canada	Recorded No. of Genera in U.S. and Canada	No. of Species Treated in This Book
1. Collembola	6,000	677	7	74	59
2. Protura	260	20	3	9	20
3. Entotrophi	659	64	4	19	8
4. Microcoryphia	250	20	2	12	20
5. Thysanura	320	18	3	12	18
6. Ephemeroptera	2,000	611	17	59	29
7. Odonata	4,870	407	11	83	75
8. Plecoptera	1,550	465	9	88	39
9. Embioptera	150	10	3	6	10
10. Phasmatodea	2,000	29	4	10	7
11. Orthoptera	12,500	1,080	11	223	162
12. Grylloblattodea	20	10	1	1	1
13. Dermaptera	1,100	20	5	12	11
14. Dictyoptera	5,500	69	6	41	40
15. Isoptera	1,900	44	4	18	14
16. Zoraptera	24	2	1	1	2
17. Psocoptera	2,500	245	24	56	27
18. Mallophaga	5,000	943	8	116	54
19. Anoplura	500	56	9	17	18
20. Hemiptera	50,000	3,587	40	630	391
21. Homoptera	32,000	6,359	38	894	632
22. Thysanoptera	4,000	694	5	138	18
23. Neuroptera	4,670	349	15	61	37
24. Coleoptera	290,000	23,701	113	3,145	1,750
25. Hymenoptera	103,000	17,777	70	2,034	988
26. Trichoptera	7,000	1,261	18	141	62
27. Lepidoptera	112,000	11,286	75	2,332	2,027
28. Mecoptera	480	68	5	10	9
29. Diptera	98,500	16,914	108	2,222	1,106
30. Siphonaptera	2,259	325	7	66	31
TOTAL	751,012	87,107	626	12,530	7,719

This generic checklist not only gives the number of genera and species described and recorded for the region but provides a complete list of names in one place as well. Thus, if the user finds a name in the literature—for example, in a field book, a general article, a textbook, or similar nontaxonomic work—it will be possible to find out where the organism belongs in our present classification.

4. All species that
 (a) have been given a common name
 (b) are economic pests
 (c) are representative of genera that might be commonly collected
 (d) are illustrated in the text but not described therein.

NUMBERING SYSTEM

To aid in finding names on a page, all orders, families, and genera are numbered. These numbers, which are used in the index, conform to the following system:

1. All orders are numbered in sequence as they appear in the book. These numbers serve as the chapter numbers for Part II (for example: Order 13. DERMAPTERA).
2. All families are numbered in the same way (for example: 4. ROMALEIDAE).
3. Suborders, subfamilies, and tribes are *not* numbered. The family numbers follow in sequence throughout the entire order.
4. All genera are numbered in sequence under each family, and the family number is included as a part of the genus number (for example: 4.1 *Dracottettix* Bruner).
5. The number of species assigned to each genus is given, but the species themselves are not numbered. If species are listed, only the generic initial is given. In the index, the species is assigned the generic number.

With this system, one may locate any species in the index by looking up the order, family, and genus number; for example, the Little Wingless Grasshopper, *Gym-noscirtetes pusillus* Scudder, is cited in the index as 11.5.79. The method quickly places each species and each genus into the classification scheme without having to cite the name of the order and family and allows each genus to be assigned a unique number. This system is much faster than citing a page number, which would require that the page be searched for the name.

As with any numbering system, the inherent weakness of this one is future change. As a self-contained system, it has a practical value, however, and will require only minimal modification as classifications change. (Large orders, particularly the four major orders—Coleoptera, Lepidoptera, Hymenoptera, and Diptera, are subject to the greatest change.)

Bibliography

(See end of order section for specific works on that order.)

Arnett, Ross H., Jr., and Jacques, Richard L., Jr. 1981. *Simon and Schuster's Guide to insects*. New York: Simon and Schuster, 512 pp.

Bland, Roger G., and Jacques, H. E. 1978. *How to know the insects*, 3rd ed. Dubuque: Wm. C. Brown Co., xi + 409 pp.

Borror, Donald J.; Delong, Dwight, M.; and Triplehorn, Charles A. 1981. *An introduction to the study of insects*, 5th ed. New York: Saunders College Publishing, xii + 828 pp.

Borror, Donald J., and White, Richard E. 1970. *A field guide to the insects of America north of Mexico*. Boston: Houghton Mifflin Co., xi + 404 pp.

Brues, Charles T.; Melander, A. L.; and Carpenter, Frank M. 1964. Classification of insects. *Bull. Mus. of Comp. Zool.*, vol. 108, 917 pp.

Grzimek, Bernard 1975. *Grzimek's animal life encyclopedia*. Insects, vol. 2. New York: Van Nostrand Reinhold Co., 643 pp.

Hollis, D., ed. 1980. *Animal identification, a reference guide*. Insects, vol. 3. London: British Museum (Natural History), viii + 160 pp.

de la Torre-Bueno, J. R. 1937. *A glossary of entomology*, ix + 336 pp. [Available from College Park, MD: Entomological Society of America.]

Powell, Jerry A., and Hogue, Charles L. 1979. *California insects*. Berkeley: University of California Press, x + 388 pp.

Richards, O. W., and Davies, R. G. 1977. *Imm's General textbook of entomology*. 10th ed. *Structure, physiology and development*, vol. I, viii + pp. 1–418; *Classification and biology*, vol. II, viii + pp. 421–1354. London: Chapman Hall.

2
Insect Classification and Systematics

INSECT CLASSIFICATION

Although insects exhibit more diversity than any other group of organisms (as might be expected, considering their great diversity of habitats and the huge number of species that have evolved), their body systems differ little from those of other animals except in details. Twelve features of these systems (numbered and in capital letters in the following discussion) are used to distinguish adult insects from their relatives, such noninsect groups as spiders, crustaceans, and others. Since not all distinguishing features are external, it is necessary to make dissections to find some of them.

The following discussion defines both the phylum Arthropoda and the superclass Hexapoda. Details of the external features will be given in the next chapter.

Phylum Arthropoda

All arthropods share the feature of having an exoskeleton composed of chitin and sclerotin—a complex proteinlike chemical—and sometimes other chemical materials such as calcium (lacking in all insects). The most distinctive feature, however, is their segmented appendages, that is, appendages divided into parts separated by joints. These parts are moved either by muscles that are contained within each one (making it a *true segment*) or by tendonlike connections attached to internal muscles at the base of the series of segmentlike parts. These connections are called *merons*, and this term is added to the name of those parts that are not true segments, merely segmentlike.

In insects, for example, the series of parts that make up the tarsi are not true segments and are therefore termed *tarsomeres*. Frequently, the series of parts that comprise antennal segments are not true segments and should therefore be termed *antennameres*. However, since these parts are true segments in some cases, for the sake of consistency, the term *antennal segments* is usually employed throughout this book.

Approximately 14 classes are assigned to the phylum Arthropoda. They are distinguished mainly on the basis of the specialization of body regions, the number and distribution of the appendages of the body regions, and the structure of these appendages.

Because of the insects, the phylum Arthropoda is the largest of them all by hundreds of thousands of species. In brief, examples of arthropods are as follows: Class *Trilobita*, extinct marine arthropods; class *Crustacea*, a large group comprised of such animals as lobsters, crabs, and sowbugs; class *Diplopoda*, the millipedes, similar to centipedes; class *Pauropoda*, minute soil-inhabiting arthropods; class *Symphyla*, represented by the Garden Centipede, which is not a true centipede but only resembles that group; class *Chilopoda*, the true centipedes; class *Xiphosura*, the Horseshoe Crab; class *Arachnida*, the spiders, ticks, mites, scorpions, and others; class *Pentastomida*, the tounge worms, a group of degenerated parasitic arthropods; class *Pycnogonida*, the sea spiders, a peculiar marine group resembling spiders, but with all their body parts in their legs; the *Tardigrada*, or water bears, a group of minute animals found in both terrestrial and aquatic habitats; and finally, the class *Insecta*, the insects and their relatives, now placed in the superclass Hexapoda, along with the class Entognatha. Further details about the noninsect Arthropoda may be found in books on zoology.

Superclass Hexapoda

This superclass, as mentioned above, is composed of two classes, both sharing the following features:

They have an (1) EXOSKELETON composed of chitin and sclerotin, as do all Arthropoda (Fig. 4). Most of this outer shell is nonliving. Muscles are attached, as in the Arthropoda, to the inside of this skeleton. Hence, they function somewhat differently than human muscles. The exoskeleton is moved by the contraction of the muscles attached to the internal surface of the next segment instead of to a central bone as in vertebrates. It must be mentioned, however, that internal projections, called *apodemes*, also anchor muscles; their function is very similar to that of bone in the vertebrates. The exoskeleton also provides a seal for the body cavity and prevents the leaking of body fluids. It varies from very thin and soft to extremely hard and is covered with an

Fig. 4. Diagram of the integument of an insect, showing layers and accessory structures.

oily or waxy material that is impervious to fluids and gases.

It is the exoskeleton, of course, that determines the (2) SIZE of insects. The body reaches its maximum size at the same time that it becomes sexually mature and ceases to molt. No further growth takes place except for the springtails. This stage, for most species of insects, is marked by the presence of functional wings. The smallest known insect is about 0.25 mm in length, or one one-hundredth of an inch. As a rule, however, insects are not much smaller than 1 mm. The largest are about 16 cm, or a little over 6 in., although some moths have wingspans greater than 16 cm. Most large insects do not exceed 8 cm (about 3 in.). A considerable number of species measure between 1 to 4 cm (approximately ½ to 1½ in.), but most are less than 7 mm (a little more than ¼ in.) in length.

The exoskeleton is typically divided into three major (3) BODY REGIONS—the head, thorax (including legs and wings), and abdomen (Fig. 5). This division is one of the most distinctive features of insects, and very few exceptions exist. Only in certain parasitic forms have these body regions been so highly modified as to be indistinct.

The thorax of insects bears the locomotive appendages: the wings and the legs. This, too, is one of the

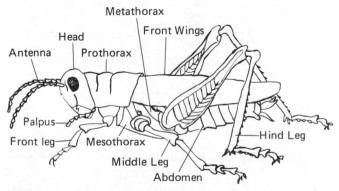

Fig. 5. External view of a grasshopper to illustrate the principal external structures of an insect.

most distinctive features of insects. Usually there are (4) THREE PAIRS OF LEGS. In a few species, the legs may be reduced in size or absent, or only the front legs may be missing because of some adaptive modification. The legs vary considerably from group to group because they are specialized for various uses in addition to locomotion. They may be used for grasping prey, digging, swimming, or other activities.

Only a very few groups of animals have wings and are capable of sustained flight. Structures permitting flight are present only in a few mammals, poorly developed in certain fish, but well-developed in most birds and insects. Insects usually have (5) TWO PAIRS OF WINGS, although some have only ONE PAIR OF WINGS, and a few have NO WINGS. Four of the primitive orders and the three ectoparasitic orders—Mallophaga, Anoplura, and Siphonaptera—are always wingless. Some species of almost all other orders of insects lack wings in the adult stage because of some special adaptation. *All sexually immature individuals lack functional wings.*

All insects have an (6) ABDOMEN LACKING *FUNCTIONAL* LEGS IN THE ADULT STAGE. A few species have the rudiments of abdominal legs as adults, but these are never used for locomotion. Many larvae have *unsegmented* abdominal legs (caterpillars, etc.). Adults of some orders have terminal abdominal appendages of various shapes that are used for grasping, egg laying, and sense detection. These are described in the order section to which the insect belongs.

The (7) MOUTHPARTS of insects are basically mandibulate, that is, the principal part consists of a pair of *mandibles* used for feeding (see illustrations at the introduction of each order). Other arthropods have either mandibles or *chelicerae* (pinchers), or both. The chelicerae, also called *claws* (such as those of a lobster), are modifications of leg parts. No insect has chelicerae, but in exactly the same way, their mouthparts are actually modified legs of the head segments. Several pairs of these, modified in various ways, form the group of structures we call the mouthparts. They may be adapted for biting and chewing, or for lapping, sucking, and piercing. Each of these types is described in the diagnosis of the orders. In those insects that do not feed as adults, the mouthparts are either reduced and functionless or absent entirely.

The circulatory system of insects is termed *open* because there are no blood vessels. Taking the place of vessels are *open sinuses*. The fluid within the insect's body circulates more or less haphazardly through these cavities. However, there is a dorsal tube, called the *heart*, that is open at both ends (Fig. 6). Muscles are attached to the sides of this tube. Inside it are valves, and along the side of part of the tube are small openings. When the tube is flattened by the contraction of the muscles, blood is forced out the anterior end of the tube. When the muscles relax, blood flows back into the tube from the posterior end and through the holes in the side of the tube. This action circulates the blood and sets up a very low blood pressure that causes a flow of blood across the brain and into the ventral part of the body. Body movement itself aids this flow of fluid. However, be-

Fig. 6. Heart or dorsal aorta of an insect: (a) aorta, (h) heart, (m) muscle, and (o) ostia. Arrows show usual direction of hemolymph flow.

cause oxygen is usually not carried in the blood, there is no need for a more extensive circulatory system, and considering the number and great activity of insects, the system obviously works efficiently.

The respiratory system consists of a series of open tubes called (8) TRACHEAE, through which gases diffuse (Fig. 7). Visible only by dissection, they run through the body and open at its surface through holes called *spiracles*. Tracheae are found in all but certain very small, primitive insects. Insects share this feature with only a few other arthropods, such as the Onychophora (usually considered a separate phylum), myripods (centipedes, millipedes, and pauropods), and spiders.

Insects are *homothermic*, or cold-blooded. A few insects (for example, some moths) are able to raise their body temperature above that of the environment by

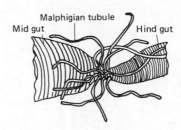

Fig. 8. Excretory system of an insect showing part of mid and hind gut and Malphigian tubules.

short, rapid wing vibrations, or *wing trembling*. The energy required by the muscles to do this causes them to warm, which in turn increases body temperature. Ordinarily, insects are inactive when the air temperature drops below 10°C. Unless its body is warmed by radiation or by muscular activity, the insect remains inactive until warm weather returns.

Excretion in almost all species is by means of (9) MALPIGHIAN TUBES, which collect waste material from the circulatory system and then discharge it into the hind portion of the digestive tract. These structures (Fig. 8) are visible only by dissection.

The sensory receptor organs are numerous and diverse. The most evident and characteristic are the (10) SINGLE PAIR OF ANTENNAE, or feelers (Fig. 9). These are of various lengths and shapes. Their surface is covered with microscopic sensory receptors. Similar structures are found on the palpi (part of the mouthparts).

The (11) EYES are of two types (Fig. 10): the paired *compound eyes* and the simple *ocelli*. Compound eyes are usually present except for some specialized species. The species of many orders have three small ocelli in addition to compound eyes. These are usually located on the top of the head, but they may be hidden (in the case of many moths) near the compound eyes, partially covered by scales. Instead of three ocelli, typical of some grasshoppers, there may be only two, or even only one—for a few species of beetles; most beetles lack ocelli altogether.

Fig. 7. Respiratory system of an insect showing trachea, air sacs, and spiracle opening.

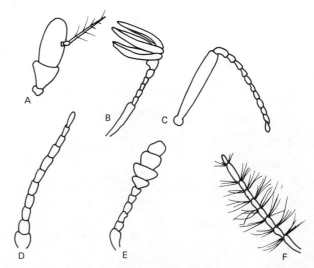

Fig. 9. Some types of insect antennae: (A) aristate, (B) lamellate, (C) elbowed, (D) filiform, (E) clavate, and (F) plumose.

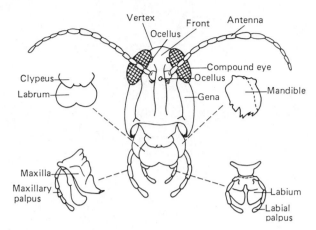

Fig. 10. The head and mouthparts of a grasshopper, representing a typical insect with biting mouthparts.

The endocrine and reproductive systems are well developed in insects. Most insect species undergo some (12) TYPE OF METAMORPHOSIS, usually *complete*—or *holometabolous*—*metamorphosis*, which is controlled by endocrine gland secretions. The four largest orders—the Coleoptera, Hymenoptera, Lepidoptera, and Diptera—as well as a few of the smaller orders (see Table 2.1) undergo complete metamorphosis, that is, they pass through the egg, larval, and pupal stages before becoming adults. As explained below, not all insects undergo this type of metamorphosis, and therefore, this feature is characteristic rather than definitive of the class because it is a feature of the majority of the species. All insects have the sexes separate, that is, none is hermaphroditic. Some lack males, making parthenogenetic reproduction by the female the only means of reproducing. Other species during their complicated life cycles may reproduce sexually (biparental) at times and partheongenetically at other times.

Gradual metamorphosis (termed *paurometabolous metamorphosis*) is a feature of many orders (see Table 2.1). It is characterized by egg, nymphal, and adult stages.

Those orders with naiads instead of nymphs are sometimes referred to as undergoing *hemimetabolous metamorphosis*. The naiad is an aquatic nymph. Species without external metamorphosis are said to be *ametabolous*.

Metamorphic Stages

Eggs With few exceptions, insects begin their life as a fertilized egg. The eggs of parthenogenetic species are unfertilized but may develop into males or females. In certain groups, because of a specialized habit, the eggs are retained and hatch within the abdomen of the female. The larvae of some flies, for example, develop internally, and by the time they leave the female they are nearly fully developed. Many insects lay their eggs in cracks, crevices, under bark, in soil, and other secluded places in an attempt to hide them from predators. Others, especially leaf-feeding species, lay their eggs exposed on the food plant. Still others lay eggs in a mass and secrete a protective case around them. The eggs of some species are distinctive in shape, surface sculpturing, and color (Fig. 11). They vary in size from species to species. Because of the secretive egg-laying habits of most species, relatively few eggs have been described. Anytime one happens to see eggs being laid, the adult and the eggs may be associated. Photographs of these known eggs provide valuable scientific records. This is an area of study that is open to anyone willing to spend the time and effort, and all such data will contribute to our present meager knowledge of the egg stage. Eventually, enough may be learned about eggs to permit identification at least of major groups.

Nymphs, Naiads, and Larvae The major feeding stage of insects is the stage that hatches from the egg. These immature insects lack functional wings. The term *nymph* (Fig. 12) is applied to those immature stages that resemble the adult stage except for wings and size. Nymphs may have external wing pads—small flaps that eventually develop into the wings of the adult—which gradually enlarge as the nymph grows. Molting takes

Table 2.1 Insect Orders and Their Type of Metamorphosis

Ametabolous (No external metamorphosis)	Hemimetabolous (Gradual metamorphosis with a naiad)	Paurometabolous (Gradual metamorphosis with a nymph)	Holometabolous (Complete metamorphosis)
Collembola	Ephemeroptera	Grylloblattodea	Neuroptera
Protura	Odonata	Orthoptera	Coleoptera
Entotrophi	Plecoptera	Phasmatodea	Trichoptera
Microcoryphia		Dictyoptera	Lepidoptera
Thysanura		Isoptera	Mecoptera
Mallophaga		Dermaptera	Hymenoptera
Anoplura		Embioptera	Diptera
		Zoraptera	Siphonaptera
		Psocoptera	
		Hemiptera	
		(Orders with a prepupal and pupal stage):	
		Homoptera	
		Thysanoptera	

Fig. 11. A few types of insect eggs: (a) water bug, (b) tree cricket; (c) butterfly, and (d) true bug.

Fig. 13. The naiad of a damselfly.

place several times, the outer integument being shed when the next, expandable skin develops beneath. In this manner, growth is able to take place within the protective exoskeleton. The number of molts, usually four to six, varies with the species. Some species may molt many times during a long period of development. The term *instar* is applied to the time period between molts; the length of the instars varies with the kind of insect and the availability of food.

Sometimes the term *naiad* is used to indicate a nymph specialized for aquatic life (Fig. 13). Naiads differ considerably from the adult stage. The classical meaning of

Fig. 12. The nymph of a true bug.

the term *naiad* (a sea nymph) perfectly fits this stage; it is used in this book for the nymphs of Odonata, Ephemeroptera, and Plecoptera, even though many specialists object to the term, preferring the terms *nymph* or *larva*.

The most complicated type of metamorphosis, complete or holometabolous metamorphosis, provides for a more thoroughgoing change from the immature stages to adulthood. The larva is a very different individual from the adult of the same species and may live a very different life in a distinct habitat of its own. The larval stage is the active feeding stage; it is specially adapted to finding and consuming food. Since these adaptive features involve all parts of the body, there is little physical similarity between this stage and the adult. Indeed, larvae are controlled by a distinct set of genes; another set that will be used to regulate the adult is stored within the larval cells in a state of quiescence. Larvae vary considerably from order to order (Fig. 14). For example, larvae usually have mandibulate mouthparts even though as adults (Lepidoptera and Diptera, for example) they may have sucking or other types of mouthparts. Unlike nymphs and naiads, they show no external evidence of wings. Their eyes are usually simple, and the antennae are small. Many have abdominal legs (unsegmented); others are legless. The shape of the larva is characteristic for many families, and the larvae of many groups (especially Lepidoptera) may be identified to species. Even so, probably only about 10 percent of the larvae of insects are known. As is true of eggs, this stage needs to be studied. Unfortunately, space considerations prohibit a discussion of details in this book. It should be noted, however, that in certain groups—especially Diptera, Coleoptera, and Lepidoptera—the larval and adult classification are correlated as much as possible. Some entomologists place considerable weight on larval features in constructing a classification of the order (particularly Coleoptera). One must remember that very di-

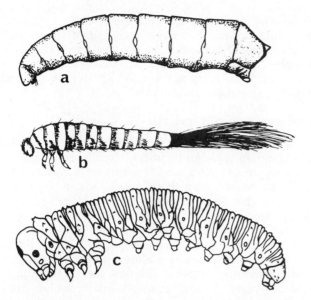

Fig. 14. Examples of larvae of the Holometabola: (a) fly larva (maggot), (b) beetle larva (dermestid), and (c) sawfly larva. (From USDA publication).

verse groups may be adapted to very similar habitats and develop similar larval structures to live in these habitats. This fact may obscure the true relationship of these species.

Pupae Considerable structural reorganization is necessary during the transformation of larvae into adults. The wings develop; the mouthparts and alimentary canal usually need to change to accommodate a change of feeding habits; and the reproductive system, copulatory organs, and egg laying apparatus—obviously not needed by the larvae— must now form. For this transformation, a special "resting" stage has evolved between the larval and the adult stages. This stage is termed the *pupal stage* (Fig. 15). The pupa is usually externally inactive, that is, it does not move about because it no longer feeds, although movement is possible as a reaction to being disturbed. (Some pupae of aquatic insects—for example, mosquitoes—are capable of swimming to avoid predators.) Most pupae are enclosed in some kind of a covering: Moths spin a cocoon; beetles form a pupal cell in

Fig. 15. A pupa of a beetle.

the ground or under bark; flies secrete a puparium as an outer covering; and so forth. After an appropriate period of time, the fully developed adult emerges. Very little is known about the pupal stages of most insects. In some groups, pupae can be identified to family, and sometimes to genus, but seldom to species. To learn more about pupae, the discarded pupal skin, cocoon, or other pupal remains should be retained with adult insect specimens obtained through rearing.

Metamorphosis of Wingless Orders The primitive wingless orders show very little external change as they grow in size; they are ametabolous (a somewhat misleading description because some change does take place as they grow). True insects do not add segments to the body after emergence from the egg. Postembryonic change other than in size is not noticeable even in those primitive forms in which the reproductive system is developing and sexual differentiation is taking place. After the sexually mature (adult) stage is reached, molting no longer takes place.

Adult Stage The remainder of this book pertains to the adult, with only casual remarks, at most, about immature stages. Newly emerged from the last skin, or from the pupa, adults of many insects may not yet have fully developed wings. A brief period of time is spent "inflating" the wings and allowing them to dry. At the same time, the insect may void various metabolic waste material stored during the transformation stage. It is then ready to feed (some, however, do not feed in the adult stage) and search for or attract a mate.

INSECT TAXA

The classification of organisms used by systematic biologists is arbitrary. Species are arranged in a way that is primarily intended to provide a means of reference to them. Most modern classifications also reveal something about the evolution of the species. We frequently say that one group is "related" to another group, and this relationship is indicated by the proximity of one group to another in a linear classification list, which also gives some idea of the similarity of one group to another. This grouping, however, cannot show the evolution of the taxa, as explained later (see the section on Insect Systematics).

Scientific Names of Insects

It has already been pointed out that insects belong to the phylum Arthropoda and the superclass Hexapoda, the two classes of which comprise the Insecta, or insects proper. The major division within each class is the order, and this is further divided. Such classification terms— phylum, superclass, class, order, etc.—are called *categories*. Organisms are assigned to categories by ranking them in various groups called *taxa* (singular, *taxon*). The most generally used categories within the order (see Table 2.2) are *family, subfamily, tribe, genus* (pl. *genera*), and *species* (pl. also *species*). Other divisions such as *suborder* (occasionally *infraorder*) and *superfamily* may be used. In reference to these names, one should note that superfamily names always end in *-oidea;* family

Table 2.2 Categories and Examples of Taxa

Category	Taxon
Kingdom	Animalia
Phylum (pl. phyla)	Arthropoda
Class	Insecta
Order	Coleoptera
Family	Oedermer*idae*
Subfamily	Oxycopiinae
Tribe	Oxycopiini
Genus (pl. genera)	*Oxycopis*
Specific name	*notoxoides*
Species and author	*Oxycopis notoxoides* (Fabricius)
Common name	Southern Pollen Beetle

names, in *-idae;* subfamily names, in *-inae;* and tribe names, in *-ini.*

One or more species may be assigned to a genus. Technically speaking, a *specific name* standing alone refers only to a taxon, not to a species. A particular species can be referred to only by a combination of the generic name and the specific name. Thus we can talk about *Oxycopis notoxoides*, but not about *Oxycopis* (the genus) or about *notoxoides* (the specific name) unless we are talking about the name itself and not the insect. If we wish to refer to specimens that we know are members of the genus *Oxycopis* without mentioning the specific name, we may say *Oxycopis sp.*, "*sp.*" being the abbreviation for *species* in the singular. If we mean more than one species, we can indicate the plural as *Oxycopis spp.* Another way to indicate the species belonging to a genus is to say the "species of *Oxycopis*." We cannot correctly refer simply to the genus when we mean the species of a genus, although this is often done in print, for example, by saying "oxycopis" to mean the species of that genus, using the generic name as a common name, or, as another example, using "drosophila" to mean the fruit fly *Drosophila melanogaster.* Obviously, a genus without species does not exist since a genus is only a category to which species are assigned.

The hierarchy of categories and an example of a taxon for each are shown in Table 2.2. Note the difference between the specific name and the species name; as explained previously, a species name must include a generic name. The generic name is always capitalized; the specific name is never capitalized even when it is a proper name Latinized (for example: *davidi*, not *Davidi*). In the example of *Oxycopis notoxoides* in Table 2.2, the original author (describer) was a famous eighteenth-century entomologist, J. Fabricius. His name is included, as are authors' names throughout this book, as an abbreviated way of giving a bibliographic reference. Any such name and original reference may be looked up in one of the available catalogs of insects. The author's name in this case is in parentheses to indicate that the species was originally assigned to a genus different from the one indicated. If it were still assigned to its original genus, no parentheses would be used.

Classification of an insect means placing a species in its proper place in the taxonomic scheme by assigning it to the right genus, the genus to the right family, and so on. This procedure, as explained in Chap. 1, is not to be confused with the identification (or determination) of a species. One should not say that one is classifying a species when one actually means that one is identifying a species. Classifying is the chore of the specialist engaged in systematic research.

Common Names of Insects

No formal rules have been established for the selection of a common name for an insect. Usually the names vary from region to region, and several names may apply to the same insect. Often these names indicate a group of species rather than a single species. However, many large, showy insects have common names that may appear to be more permanently established than their scientific names. A good example is the Monarch Butterfly, whose common name is almost universally used, but whose scientific name has changed several times in the past 200 years. Another example is the common group name *ladybug*, applied to all species of the beetle family Coccinellidae. It is apparent that common names apply to all taxa, regardless of category, and not just to species.

No current list of common names, however, is complete, uniform, or universally acceptable. Some new names have been designated for use in this book. The rules for forming common names used here are the following:

1. A name standing alone indicates the order. Thus "fly" means a member of the order Diptera.
2. If the name is used as a part of another name, it means that the insect is not a member of that order. For example, a "firefly" is not a fly, but a beetle, order Coleoptera, and a "lightningbug" is not a true bug, order Hemiptera, but also a beetle. Therefore, its name should not be written as two words "lightning bug" because this would imply that it is a member of the order Hemiptera, which is not the case.
3. Common names, to be effective, are kept as short as possible, usually only three words at the most.

All common names commonly applied to the insects of the United States (excluding Hawaii) and Canada are listed in this book because of their frequent appearance in pest control literature or in news releases. Some of the species listed, however, are not truly common and may be of little economic importance. Some are improperly named—that is, for example, they may be called "Western" and occur in the East, and so on—but until they are properly renamed, and perhaps even after that, as with scientific names, they remain in the literature. Many very common species that might well have common names are included in this book under their Latin names only because no common names have been previously used in the literature. Those species not described in this book but for which common names are available are listed in their proper place in the classification of Part II. As noted in the Special Instructions, the common names of species, but not of other taxa, are cited with capitalized initial letters.

Rules of Scientific Nomenclature

The Latin names of insects are used for universal stability of nomenclature and as key words for reference purposes. They do not change as more becomes known about the insects in question. Although common names may sometimes seem to be more stable, in certain cases this is the fault of catalogs that do not fully document name changes. In rare cases it is necessary to "freeze" a scientific name arbitrarily—that is, to apply a name counter to the rules of nomenclature (to be described)—in order to reinforce the stability of the nomenclature. Because of these problems, one will notice, when one examines any insect catalog or classification list, that synonyms appear after the names of many species. Synonyms are created by naming, unknowingly, the same species more than once. The descriptions of species found in entomological literature do not always give enough details to permit insect identification by description alone. It is usually not until type specimens are studied that it is realized that more than one name applies to the same species.

Formal rules are followed in applying scientific names. These rules, established by the International Commission of Zoological Nomenclature, are universally applied to animals by scientists all over the world. Although it is necessary to modify the rules from time to time to accommodate new cases or complexities, they remain basically the same. The intent of the rules is to provide one name, and one valid name only, for each animal species. As previously noted, some insects have been named more than once. The rules require that the oldest validly proposed name to be used and that the others be regarded as junior synonyms. The application of this "law of priority," as it is called, accounts for much of the complexity of the rules, but ultimately the correct name is located and applied.

Pronunciation of Scientific Names

All scientific names of plants and animals are formed from Latin words or words from other languages that have been Latinized. They are not pronounced, however, in the same way as classical Latin words. In general, the words are pronounced as if they were English words. The few exceptions to this rule are explained here:

1. There is no letter "w" in the Latin alphabet, but certain Latinized English words contain it, for example, "*Walesiomorphus*." In those special cases, the "w" is pronounced as in English.
2. All syllables are pronounced: for example, Wes-tri-ni-á-na, which happens to be accented on the penultimate syllable. In words of more than two syllables that are derived from Latin words with a "short" vowel, the accent falls on the antepenult, for example, Chry-so-mél-i-dae and Xy-lo-sté-a-na. Since there is no simple way to determine this vowel quantity, it is best to pronounce the word in the way that is easiest and has the most pleasant sound, for example, Co-rýd-a-lus, instead of Co-ry-dál-us.

3. Consonants are pronounced as in English except for the following: "ch" is always pronounced as "k"; "th" as in "*th*ought" rather than in "*th*is"; "ct" as "t" in "ten." For example, Ctenophora is pronounced Te-nof-or-a. For words beginning with "Gn," the "g" is silent; with "Mn," the "m" is silent; with "Ps," the "p" is silent; and with "pt," the "p" is silent.
4. Diphthongs "ae" and "oe" both have the sound of long "e"; other diphthongs follow English. For example, Oedemeridae is pronounced e-de-mér-i-de.
5. Vowels are almost always pronounced as in English.

To determine its exact pronunciation, one must know the classical origin of a word, but common sense in syllabication, ease of utterance, and euphonious sound are the best guides. Usually one cannot learn to pronounce such words correctly unless they are first heard, but the way in which they are pronounced by others varies considerably from place to place. It is helpful, therefore, to break them down into syllables and slowly pronounce each. Soon the words will flow naturally.

INSECT SYSTEMATICS

Systematics is the study of plants and animals from the standpoint of their kinds, their origins, and their evolution from those origins to the present time. This science makes use of any available data—anatomical, physiological, ecological, genetic, behavioral, or paleontological—that can be applied to kinds rather than just processes. These data are used to determine the reality of our concepts of the particular species of plants and animals that we perceive. *Phylogenetic systematics* (also termed *cladistics*) is based on our knowledge of the processes of evolution through time and space. If it were not for this unifying principle, there would be no such science. There is, however, another approach to systematics, *phenetics* (also called *numerical taxonomy*), whose techniques, especially the mathematical analysis of characteristics, are applied without reference to phylogeny in an attempt to stabilize biological classification. These two approaches are in conflict.

One might say that the crux of *taxonomy* (that is, classification) is based on the names of organisms, for with these, whether accurately or inaccurately applied, one is able to store, associate, and retrieve information. At the same time, one might say that the crux of the *systematics* is the origin, evolution, and variation of each species, but this is based on what is said under the taxonomic name given to that species. It follows, then, that attention must be given to the taxon species.

Types of Species

One might concede that there are two types of species: those that are described in the literature and labeled in collections and those that actually exist in nature. By "in nature," we mean those that are alive (or were once alive)

and reproducing. We must admit that the former type of species is dealt with in most cases; at the same time, it is the latter type of species that we hope we are dealing with. Systematics is a fascinating science because it has all the elements of a good detective story. A body is discovered (in this case, a specimen from the field), and the systematic detective sets about to learn what this body represents. He may follow false clues for a while for want of sufficient information (in this case, the scarcity of literature), but eventually, through continuing exploration and study, he discovers the true nature of the body. Because there are countless bodies and few detectives, the solutions to identity problems have taken a long time. Many bodies remain in the morgue (museum) waiting to be studied, while many others have been put aside with tentative names (the "tentative identification" mentioned in the previous chapter) until they can be studied in detail.

It is the natural species that we are most interested in. As in the Biblical story of Genesis, species start with a breeding pair (in some cases, since sexuality has been lost through time, other complex processes take place that will not be discussed here). Our Adam and Eve are the beginnings of the human species. Their origin, however, was from other pairs of breeding individuals, back to the point where the first breeding species literally arose from the dust as the Biblical account maintains. We might go on to discuss the details of the evolutionary process, but this subject is far too complex to be treated here. Suffice it to say, however, that individual variations and the genes that control these variations (ultimately, the genetic code of the DNA molecule) are responsible for all changes in the offspring of the original pair of the evolving species. Minute differences merely keep the species as a whole pliable. Gross differences are another matter. If the gross differences are sufficient to prevent cross breeding, a different species has evolved. This process has been taking place from the beginning so that today the number of species on earth is vast.

It is apparent that the natural species referred to here consist of individuals in a *breeding population*. The task of the systematist is to learn about the breeding population. In most cases, there will be more than one of these populations. It could be experimentally determined if each of these populations is capable of interbreeding—a nearly sure test of their sameness. Generally speaking, however, a careful study of the anatomy of the individuals representing the populations will be logically sufficient to predicate their sameness. Once a significant number of populations has been observed, there is good reason to believe that the particular species in question is natural and has been properly recognized. If further study reveals the isolating mechanisms—that is, the factors that prevent interbreeding with another natural species—it becomes possible to deduce something about the evolutionary mechanisms involved. When these data are compared with those for other extant species, and, rarely with those for extinct species, some reliable knowledge of the phylogeny of the species can be achieved.

The term *species* (meaning natural species) may be defined as a series of interbreeding populations in time and space that are reproductively isolated from other interbreeding populations in time and space. It is in this sense that we apply the term to a representative of one of the natural breeding populations as a means of making an accurate identification.

Two additional terms should be considered, *variation* and *diversity*.

Variation As used here, the term *variation* refers to the individual differences found within a species. These can include differences in size, shape, color, and even the presence or absence of certain structures. The nature of variation in insects will be discussed in the next chapter.

Diversity The term *diversity*, as applied in the study of systematics, is quite distinct from variation. It does not mean, as is sometimes supposed, differences between species. It would be incorrect to say that a large group (that is, a taxon with many species) is very diverse, whereas a small group is not, because this would be the same as saying that there are many or few species in a taxon—a statement that has little significance. The term is correctly used only when it conveys the presence of a wide range of body types and systems in a taxon. It is best applied to the higher taxa. A large genus such as the beetle genus *Apion* (with over 1100 species recorded in the world) is not diverse—that is, it shows little diversity—because its species are so anatomically similar that they are difficult to differentiate. On the other hand, the large family Curculionidae, to which the genus *Apion* belongs, shows great diversity of body types. In size, they range from the minute to the giant; some are round; some are flat; some have extremely long snouts (head extended into a narrow tube) and others extremely short ones; and so forth. The term *diversity* is useful only when applied in a comparative sense. Members of the fly family Tipulidae are not diverse when compared to members of the beetle family Staphylinidae, yet both families have a great number of species.

Subspecies This taxon is difficult to define because it has so many denotations. Variations within species have led many authors of entomological articles to divide species into subspecies, often as a means of identifying more or less isolated populations. This practice is not universally accepted (some researchers are strongly opposed to it), but it has the approval of the International Commission of Zoological Nomenclature, and many subspecies have been named. Most uses of the subspecies taxon require that it reflect different distribution ranges as well as differences in morphological features (often a difference of color).

No other term to indicate taxa within a species has nomenclature approval, although a number of terms are used to indicate population differences, the most popular term today being *cline*. Differences in populations arise as a species gradually varies throughout its geographical range. These populations are commonly referred to in relation to their restricted distribution and are not given Latin names. In the past, however, variations such as

these were known as *varieties, races, forms,* or *aberrations,* names that are no longer applied.

BIBLIOGRAPHY

Arnett, Ross H., Jr. 1970. The type locality and the study of natural populations. *Ent. News,* 81: 95–100.

Borror, Donald J. 1960. *Dictionary of word roots and combining forms.* Palo Alto: Mayfield Publ. Co., v + 134 pp.

Hennig, Willi, Adrian C. Pont (ed.), and Dieter Schlee 1981. *Insect phylogeny.* New York: John Wiley and Sons, xxiii + 514 pp.

Jeffery, Charles 1977. *Biological nomenclature.* 2nd ed. New York: Crane, Russak & Co., viii + 72 pp.

Peterson, Alvah 1962. *Larvae of insects. Lepidoptera and Hymenoptera,* part I, 315 pp., 1960. *Coleoptera, Diptera, Neuroptera, Siphonaptera, Mecoptera, Trichoptera,* part II, 416 pp.

Stoll, R. N., *et al.* 1964. *International code of zoological nomenclature* (*adopted by the XV International Congress of Zoology*). London: International Trust for Zoological Nomenclature, xix + 176 pp.

Wiley, E. O. 1981. *Phylogenetics: the theory and practice of phylogenetic systematics.* New York: John Wiley and Sons, xv + 439 pp.

3
Identification Features

A number of special terms must be applied to insect parts to provide the precision necessary for accurate description and to ensure brevity in identification tables, keys, and descriptions. Insect parts are homologous from order to order but are variously modified within each order. This chapter provides a general discussion of these parts. *At the beginning of each insect order section in Part II, the reader will find a figure illustrating a representative of that order and labeling its basic parts.* At the end of the book is a glossary of the terms used throughout, with cross-references to the text illustrations. Proper use of the book will require frequent reference to these illustrations and the glossary.

MAJOR BODY REGIONS

Insects, like earthworms, are segmented animals, but not all their segments are as easy to see as those of earthworms. The insect body, as already described, is divided into three major regions: the *head*, the *thorax*, and the *abdomen* (see Fig. 5). Each segment is organized in a fairly uniform manner. The integument of an insect is made up of plates of sclerotin. These plates are either articulated (jointed) to each other, or they are more or less solidly fused together. Because of the great variety of insects and their proliferating adaptive structures, the ways these plates are fused or articulated provides a great diversity of parts, many of them extremely useful for description and identification.

The basic arrangement of each body segment, in its simplest form, is found in the segments of the abdomen. The four basic plates, called *sclerites*, are as follows: (1) *tergum* (pl. *terga*), the dorsal or top plate; (2) two *pleura* (singular, *pleuron*), one on each side of the segment; and (3) the *sternum* (pl. *sterna*), or bottom plate (Fig. 16). The groove between these plates, or the line where the plates meet, is called a *suture*. When appendages such as the legs (see cx, signifying the *coxa*, or basal leg segment) are present on a segment they are found between the bottom of the pleura and the sterna. However, the pleuron of most insects, being fused with the sternum, is obscure.

The Head

The segments of the head are fused to such an extent that they can no longer be seen except in the embryo, and even there they are not too apparent. Nevertheless, the various appendages roughly represent the head segments. The head appendages start with the *labrum* (see Fig. 10), or the upper lip that serves as the front cover for the mouthparts. The labrum is articulated on the front of the head to a region termed the *clypeus* and is variously modified throughout the orders. Also in this region is located the single pair of *antennae*. The shape and number of antennal segments (sometimes termed antennameres) vary greatly from order to order. These sensory structures are also very diverse within some orders as well as within families. This variation provides useful features for identification purposes (see Fig. 9). *Compound eyes* are usually located above or behind the antennae. In many groups, one to three *ocelli* (singular *ocellus*), small simple eyes, are located between or above the compound eyes and antennae. (See Fig. 9.) Neither these nor the antennae are true appendages; rather, they are sense organs, specialized regions of the surface of the integument.

The front part of the head, above the clypeus, is called the *front* (sometimes termed frons). The two sides

Fig. 16. Diagram of an arthropod segment: (T) tergum, (Pl) pleuron, (Cx) coxa, and (Stn) sternum.

20

of the head are the *genae*. The top of the head is the *vertex*. Behind the labrum, attached to the genae, is a pair of *mandibles*. These are followed by the *maxillae*, also paired structures, usually with *maxillary palpi* (singular palpus), segmented sensory-bearing structures. The compliment of mouthparts is completed by the hind cover or lower lip, the *labium*. This is also a paired structure, but the two parts have fused to form a single appendage. The labium also bears a pair of palpi, the *labial palpi*. These structures (Fig. 10) are typical of a grasshopper, or most beetles. Modifications of these appendages occur by the elongation of various parts into tubes and *stylets* (long knifelike structures) used for piercing and sucking—the type of mouthparts found in many other orders. Some insects lack mouthparts or have them greatly reduced and nonfunctional in the adult stage.

The head is loosely articulated to the thorax, as a rule, so that it has at least some, often considerable, freedom of movement, depending upon the habits of the group. Some insects have the head sunken into the thorax to such an extent that it can barely turn, but it is never solidly fused to the thorax. One can always determine where the head ends and the thorax begins.

The Thorax

The thorax is composed of three more or less distinct segments. Since it contains all of the locomotion muscles, it is usually much larger than the head and sometimes than the abdomen. The front segment, termed the *prothorax*, bears the first pair of legs. The middle segment, the *mesothorax*, bears the front pair of wings and the middle pair of legs. The hind segment, the *metathorax*, bears the hind legs and the hind pair of wings. (See Fig. 5.) The top surface of the prothorax is called the *pronotum;* of the mesothorax, the *mesonotum;* and of the metathorax, the *metanotum.* The combined mesothorax and metathorax is frequently referred to as the *pterothorax* because it bears the wings. Usually, a portion of the metanotum is rather distinctly marked off between the wing bases and more or less prominent; this is called the *scutellum.* It is variously shaped, but most often triangular. Many other parts of the sclera of the thorax have been named and described, especially for the Diptera, where these parts are extensively used in identification keys and descriptions. A pair of *spiracles*, openings into the tracheal system, are located on the anterior edge of the meso- and metathorax (Fig. 17).

Wings and Wing Veins

The wings are perhaps the most frequently used structures for the identification of all the large orders of insects except the beetles. The wing consists of a double layer of thin sclerotin formed as an expansion of the thoracic integument. Between the layers are enlarged channels, the wing *veins*. These channels, formed from tracheae during the nymphal or larval stage, are arranged in a systematic way with a distinct and uniform pattern accruing to each species, each vein traceable to and homologous with the veins of other species and other

Fig. 17. Diagram of the body wall of an insect showing a spiracle (Sp) opening and the junction of a trachea (Tra).

orders. Even though the fully formed adult wing is primarily a nonliving structure, an active circulation of blood continues in the wings of the species of most orders. Sense organs are located on the wings of most species, with the associated nerves running to the central nervous system of the insect. In the higher orders, each major wing vein has a name and its branches are numbered. Short veins connecting the main veins, called the *cross veins*, are sometimes named. These names are abbreviated and numbered according to a system devised by two famous entomologists, Comstock and Needham; the system has been modified by recent students of the evolution of insect wings.

The main *veins* and *cells* of the prototype of winged insects are identified in Fig. 18A and B. Starting with the leading edge of the wing, these veins are as follows: C, *costa*; Sc, *subcosta*; R, *radius*, a branched vein in

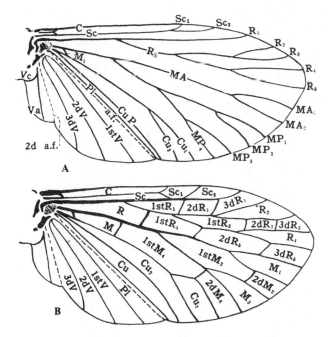

Fig. 18. Prototype of primitive winged insects: (A) the wing veins, and (B) the wing cells. The anterior media (MA) which is no longer present in extant insects, and the posterior media (MP), are shown. In many modern orders, the media (M) is no longer termed MP (see text). Other features include: (Pl) plica vein, (CuP) cubital plica, (a.f.) anal fold, (V) vannal vein, (Va) vena arcuata, and (Vc) vena cardinalis (the last two correspond to the jugal veins of some authors).

modern insects, many species exhibiting R_1, Rs (*radial sector*), R_2, R_3, R_4, and R_5, although these branches are sometimes fused, e.g., R_{4+5}, etc.; M, *median*, which in the primitive state consisted of an anterior median (MA) and a posterior median (MP), but in extant insects, the MA has disappeared, leaving only the MP, which is usually treated as M_1, M_2, etc., although these too may fuse; CuP, *cubital plical;* Pl, *plical;* and V, *vannals,* each with a separate number, 1st V, 2nd V, etc. Unfortunately, recent authors refer to the plical and vannals as A, or *anals.* The anals are used in keys, and this practice is followed throughout this book. Other changes are discussed in the appropriate order section.

The cross veins that are named are designated by lower-case letters, as follows: h, *humeral;* r, *radial;* r-m, *radial-median;* m, *median;* and m-cu, *mediocubital.* Cells take their name from the preceding vein (see Fig. 18B).

Some insects have greatly reduced venation. If a vein has dropped out entirely, as determined by a comparative study, its nonappearance on the wing signifies that fact; a fusion, e.g., R_{4+5}, is not indicated. The lower orders—for example, the Odonata—have wings with a very large number of cross veins. These are not named, but sometimes the number of cross veins between two major veins, or the pattern the veins make, offer characteristics useful for identification of families, and so on.

The Legs

Insect legs, even though they may become highly modified for specialized use, all have the same fundamental parts (Fig. 19). These are, from the base to the apex, as follows: *coxa* (pl. *coxae*), *trochanter, femur* (pl. *femora*), *tibia* (pl. *tibiae*), and *tarsus* (pl. *tarsi*). The tarsus usually has from three to five tarsomeres, never more, rarely less. The last tarsomere usually has two claws as appendages, and, in addition, it may have a median sensory hair, a pad, or *pulvillus,* and certain other modifications. The claws may be absent in some groups. Certain parts, moreover, may be so fused or reduced that they are not readily apparent. Legs may have various *spines* (rigid bristles) and *setae* (hairlike, flexible bristles) along their sides or at the end of a segment near a joint or articulation. These may be regularly placed or randomly distributed. The end of the tibia frequently bears two stout setae referred to as the *tibial spurs.* The many leg modifications are illustrated throughout this book.

Fig. 20. The structure of the abdomen of a female insect.

The Abdomen

The abdomen, which best illustrates the segmented arthropod body arrangement, is very distinct in almost all species. The usual number of visible segments is seven or eight, but there are actually eleven segments. The first may be obscure because of the way it is attached to the thorax, and the last three are usually modified to form part of the copulatory structures. Most of the visible portion of the abdomen is tergum and may be covered by the wings when they are folded back at rest. The ventral portion is visible, and the segments may be easily counted by turning the insect over. At the point where the tergum and the sternum join, there is a narrow, more or less membranous, area, the *pleuron.* Usually located in each pleuron of all segments, except the tenth and eleventh, is a *spiracle* opening into the *abdominal tracheae.* The species of many of the more primitive orders of insects have a pair of terminal abdominal *cerci* (s. *cercus*) and often a median terminal *caudal filament.* Males of most of the higher orders have highly modified copulatory apparatus, and females often have elaborate, specialized ovipositors (including *claspers*) at the end of the abdomen. (See Fig. 20.)

Insects are very different internally from the vertebrate animals, with which most people are more familiar. Muscles of insects occur in sheets rather than bundles and are anchored to the body wall, as explained previously, instead of to bones; nevertheless, a partial internal skeleton exists. Certain parts of the external skeleton have internal projections, or apodemes, to which some of the larger muscles are attached.

A digestive tract is usually present (Fig. 21), but some adult insects may lack a complete alimentary canal simply because they do not feed during the adult stage.

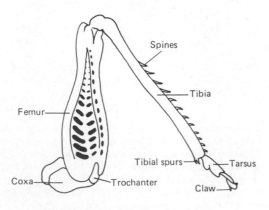

Fig. 19. Parts of the leg of an insect.

Fig. 21. Diagram of the digestive tract of an insect.

The construction of the alimentary canal is as varied as are the feeding habits. Insects that feed on leaves have, as one would expect, an intestine with numerous folds to increase the digestive surface. Aphids and other insects that feed on liquids have a filtering system to rid the tract of excess water. The carnivorous species have relatively less digestive surface because of the nature of fleshy food.

The structure and physiology of the remaining body systems is beyond the scope of this book.

VARIATION IN APPEARANCE

Size is usually recorded as the length of the body from the head (without antennae) to the end of the abdomen (without ovipositors, etc.), but insects are subject to more intraspecific variation than many other animal groups. For some species, their diet as larvae or nymphs determines their size as adults, so much so that one specimen may be twice the size of another; in rare cases, even more of a size difference is possible. Only rarely, therefore, is size alone a determining characteristic useful for identification. However, if a long series of specimens (ten or more) are consistently larger or smaller than another series of similar, but presumed different, species, the size ranges of the two may well be considered a useful identification feature.

Living or freshly killed specimens make much better study material, of course, than those that have dried or been preserved in liquid since they give a truer picture of the living insect. Preservation by drying may cause specimens to shrink; or liquid may cause them to swell. Often there may be considerable color change; greens may change to brown or even red or pink, and so on.

As a rule, a considerable range of color and color pattern is noted within a species. In certain groups, individuals of a species may show a complete range of color from all one color—for example, black—through a series of spots or stripes of another color—for example, red— to all this second color. Some common species of ladybird beetles show this tendency. If one had only the two extremes in a collection, one might reasonably think that two different species were involved. Obviously color cannot be used as an identification key unless an extended series of specimens is available. For some insects, however—as for example, many moths and butterflies—color patterns serve as very useful identification tools.

Sometimes the age of an individual specimen may be a variation factor. The collector should realize that if newly emerged specimens are collected, they might not have their full adult color. Newly emerged, pale or brownish insects are called *tenerals*. They usually have softer bodies because their external covering is not fully formed and their full complement of melanin, the black pigment, has not been deposited. Collectors should keep these specimens alive for a few hours until they reach their normal color. (It might be noted in passing that tenerals often make good fish bait.)

Other factors affecting color include geographical distribution—which usually means genetic variation of populations within a species—and environmental factors such as water, temperature, or food. Color or structural differences that can be attributed to geographical distribution, are often called *clines*, as previously mentioned. It should be noted, however, that individuals from humid regions tend to be darker in color than those from dry regions. Sometimes the failure to consider this kind of variation has resulted in double-naming (synonyms). Additional study has revealed seasonal broods with color differences. Freaks (individuals malformed as a result of accidents or genetic malfunction) are rarely found. Aberrations may include branched antennae, bisexual apparatus (nonfunctional genitalia) in individuals known thus as *gynandromorphs*, deformed legs, and other anomalies that are usually recognized as being just that. Single specimens are sometimes described and given a scientific name, but additional specimens are never found. Perhaps these are anomalies, but they remain in our literature, seemingly forever. It also appears likely that natural hybrids have been found and named as species or subspecies.

BIBLIOGRAPHY

Richards, O. W., and Davies, R. G. 1977. *Imms' general textbook of entomology.* 10th ed. *Structure, physiology and development*, vol. I. London: Chapman and Hall, viii + 418 pp.

Snodgrass, Robert E. 1935. *Principles of insect morphology.* New York: McGraw-Hill Book Co., ix + 667 pp.

de la Torre-Bueno, J. R. 1937. *A glossary of entomology.* College Park, MD: Entomological Society of America, ix + 336 pp.

4
Insect Ecology, Behavior, and Distribution

Insects are usually found where they feed, mate, or move from one breeding ground to another. Only a few species have migratory flights similar to those of birds, but all species have dispersal migrations at some time during their life cycle in a persistent attempt to populate new areas. Most insects do most of their feeding during their immature stages. Since these stages tend to be more secretive, they are seldom observed. Adults, on the other hand, are very much apparent as they go about the process of mating and egg laying. In Part II, which comprises the bulk of this book, the habits and habitats of the species of each family are given. Some general statements may be made, however, about the places insects live and how they behave. Their habitats are summarized in Table 4.1, which should give some helpful suggestions about places to look for particular kinds of insects.

FEEDING HABITATS

Roots, stems, leaves, flowers, seeds, and fruits of flowering plants are good places to look for many species of insects. These are the feeding sites of most of our economically important species. No flowering plant is without its pests, but not very many insects are known to feed on algae, moss, or ferns. Many species feed on and live within many kinds of fungi.

Carnivorous species of insects may be found preying upon the plant-feeding species, just as carnivorous mammals prey upon vertebrate herbivores. Other predatory species are found in the soil, in humus, under bark, and in aquatic habitats.

Saprophagous insects aid bacteria and fungi in the detritus cycle by feeding on dead plants and animals and animal dung. The saprophages are in turn preyed upon so that any of these microhabitats provide a lively exchange of species.

Ectoparasitic insects (lice, fleas, and a few others) are found on almost all kinds of birds and mammals. Internal parasitic larvae of insects are common among other insect species, but only a few have invaded the interior of vertebrates. Several groups of flies are nasal and intestinal parasites. Thousands of species of fly and wasp larvae are internal parasites of other insect larvae.

Stored plant and animal products are infested by many species, particularly beetles and moths, where they cause great economic loss.

Finally, a long list of species of several orders invade the nests of reptiles, birds, and mammals, as well as the nests of social insects. There they occupy various niches—some as invaders, some as tolerated guests, and still others as welcome additions to the colony. In fact, some of these species are even cultivated by their hosts. The study of these insects is a fascinating facet of entomology still to be thoroughly investigated. Whenever a nest of a social insect is opened, careful attention should be given to searching out these guests.

BEHAVIOR

Mating and Egg Laying

The mating period of adult insects is often very short. As explained previously, the adult stage of holometabolous insects is often lived in a very different habitat from that of the larvae. In fact, the genes that function in these two stages are quite different. Many insects observe a courtship pattern prior to mating. The pattern may differ from species to species within the same group and sometimes becomes rather intricate. Mating may take place during flight, on flowers and vegetation, or on the cocoon or pupal skin at the time the female emerges. Relatively few comparative studies have been made of these procedures.

Egg laying is briefly discussed in Chap. 2, and the habits of some of the orders will be treated in more detail later. Phytophagous insects usually lay their eggs on the food plant of the young, but not always. Sometimes the eggs are placed in a protected place for incubation. When the young hatch, they must wander about in search of their food. This behavior is particularly true of soil inhabiting species.

Table 4.1 Insect Habitats

(A) *Ground*

1. On surface
 (a) Beneath stones and wood (A* & I**: Collembola, Grylloblattodea, Dictyoptera, Dermaptera, Zoraptera, Coleoptera, Hymenoptera)
 (b) In rotting plant material (A & I: Collembola, Protura, Entotrophi, Microcoryphia, Thysanura, Embioptera, Psocoptera, Coleoptera, Diptera)
 (c) Open soil (A & I: Orthoptera; I: Neuroptera; A: Coleoptera, Hymenoptera)
 (d) Snow (A & I: Collembola; A: Plecoptera, Mecoptera)
2. Beneath surface
 (a) In loose stones and gravel (A & I: Dictyoptera; A: Coleoptera, Hymenoptera)
 (b) In wet, upland, and desert soil (A & I: Protura, Entotrophi, Isoptera, Embioptera, Coleoptera)

(B) *Aquatic and semiaquatic*

1. Beneath surface along margins of bodies of water (A & I: Orthoptera, Coleoptera; I: Ephemeroptera, Odonata, Plecoptera, Trichoptera, Neuroptera, Diptera)
2. Intertidal (A & I: Hemiptera, Coleoptera; I: Diptera)
3. On surface and diving beneath surface (A & I: Collembola, Coleoptera, Hemiptera, Homoptera; I: Neuroptera, Diptera)
4. Flying near water (A: Ephemeroptera, Odonata, Plecoptera, Neuroptera, Trichoptera, Diptera, Hymenoptera, Lepidoptera)

(C) *In association with other animals or their by-products*

1. Dung (A & I: Coleoptera, Diptera, Lepidoptera)
2. Carrion (A & I: Coleoptera, Diptera, Lepidoptera)
3. Nests of vertebrates (A & I: Coleoptera, Hymenoptera, Lepidoptera)
4. Ectoparasites (A & I: Mallophaga, Anoplura, Hemiptera; A: Coleoptera, Siphonaptera, Diptera)

(D) *In other animals as parasites* (A & I: Coleoptera; I: Diptera, Hymenoptera)

(E) *In stored animal products* (A & I: Coleoptera, Lepidoptera)

(F) *In association with plants*

1. Fungus and moss (A & I: Psocoptera, Collembola, Diptera, Coleoptera)
2. Stems, foliage, and flowers (A & I: Orthoptera, Phasmatodea, Dermaptera, Thysanoptera, Hemiptera, Homoptera, Neuroptera, Mecoptera, Coleoptera, Diptera, Lepidoptera, Hymenoptera)
3. Seeds (A & I: Coleoptera, Hymenoptera, Hemiptera)
4. Sap (A & I: Coleoptera, Diptera, Lepidoptera)
5. Under bark (A & I: Microcoryphia, Thysanura, Isoptera, Dermaptera, Embioptera, Psocoptera, Dictyoptera, Hemiptera, Coleoptera, Hymenoptera)
6. In roots (A & I: Coleoptera; I: Lepidoptera)
7. Galls (I: Homoptera, Lepidoptera, Diptera, Hymenoptera)
8. Wood
 (a) In living wood (A & I: Coleoptera; I: Lepidoptera, Hymenoptera)
 (b) In rotting wood (A & I: Zoraptera, Coleoptera; I: Hymenoptera)
9. Stored plant products (A & I: Coleoptera, Lepidoptera)

(G) *Nest makers* (A & I: Coleoptera [rarely], Isoptera, Hymenoptera)

*Adult
**Immature

Seasonal Changes

Most insects complete their life cycle during the spring and summer. The overwinter stage varies from species to species. Some may hibernate as eggs, with fully developed larvae usually ready to hatch as soon as favorable conditions develop in the spring. Others pass the winter as pupae, the adults emerging in the spring. A surprising number hibernate as adults, particularly beetles. Many common moths and butterflies, however, spend the winter hidden under leaves and in cervices; they may suddenly appear on warm days in midwinter. Eggs may remain unhatched for a year or more, awaiting proper conditions. The larvae of wood borers and root borers may take more than one year to mature; sometimes many years are needed, as is true of the famous Seventeen-year Locust. Some buprestid beetle larvae are known to take up to 12 or more years to reach the pupal stage.

Insect Sounds

As a part of courtship patterns, many species of insects emit deliberate sounds for communication in addition to their incidental random noises such as hums and buzzes. Of course, the very loud noise produced by cicadas, crickets, katydids, grasshoppers, and related insects is well known even to the casual listener. Less noticed, or completely overlooked, is the very low-intensity sound produced by many beetles as well as other insects. It cannot be heard by human beings unless they are very close to the singing insect. Unfortunately, these sounds can be recorded only by using very expensive special equipment. Once on tape and properly amplified, the sounds of some insects prove to be of different kinds, showing that they have several "words" in their "vocabulary." Insect sounds are usually produced by rubbing one part against another—an action called *stridulation*. The quality and intensity of the sound is dependent upon the structure of the surface of both the *file* and the *scraper*—the first being the stationary part; the second, the part moved. Many stridulating insects have a hollow body area covered by a tympanic membrane to amplify the sound. Sound may also be produced by air movement, as it is in vertebrates. For example, the Madagascaran Cockroach, *Gromphadorhina laevigata* Saussaure and Zehntn, produces sound by forcing air out through the second pair of spiracles. Other methods of sound production—including tapping, scratching with legs, clicking wings, and so on—exist. In addition to singing to attract a mate, it is known that warning noises are given, and parents may call their larvae by making such sounds.

Light Production

A few insects—particularly the fireflies (which are adult beetles), a few click beetles, the larvae of several kinds of beetles, and certain fly larvae—produce light. Its purpose is either to attract mates or to attract prey.

Migration and Dispersal

Not very many insects actually migrate, although this phenomenon is a well-known characteristic of monarch

butterflies and a few other species. All insects, as all plants and animals, have a dispersal stage. This usually occurs after mating and before egg laying. When large numbers of insects are flying in this way, it appears to be a migration, but it is not one in the same sense as a migration of birds.

DISTRIBUTION

As previously discussed, each species has a definite distribution or range, this being the geographical area in which it lives. The species is adapted to particular ecological situations within this range. For most species, only part of the available habitat is actually occupied by the species, even the so-called overabundant pest species. Obviously, the ranges are spotty, rather than solidly distributed throughout a particular *biome* (the biomes in the U.S. and Canada will be described later). Many species are found in more than one biome. Consequently, a species may be found over a great geographical area and still occupy only a total of a few acres of land or water. Such a distribution is probably true of most insect species, making the terms "common" and "rare" of no more than relative value in describing the abundance of a particular species. These facts, combined with the short life span of many adults, account for the difficulty in learning more about insect habits and emphasize the need for keeping careful records of all field observations.

When distribution statements are made or maps constructed to show the range of a species, it is not possible to include all details. Maps cannot show habitats or the distribution of habitats. Distributions given in a text may indicate that a species is widespread and common, but collecting experience might show that it is not "common" until one knows exactly where to look for it. Conversely, so-called "rare" species must be common somewhere or they would soon become extinct. Thus, all maps, ranges, and abundance statements made here must be understood in this context.

Insect Enemies

All species of insects are subject to parasites and predators, although some species seem to be well protected. Various devices and maneuvers are used to avoid predation and parasitization, including cryptic coloration, protective resemblance, hiding in dark cracks and crevices, and confining activities to the night. The ability of some species to sting and bite provides a degree of protection that is respected by animal as well as human predators. The bites and stings of insects are seldom serious enough to stop the avid collector, however. Parasitized insects are abundant, so much so that those attempting to rear the larva of a beautiful moth to the adult stage may be rewarded instead with a small collection of parasitic flies or wasps. It is well to remember that all aspects of nature are interesting, and it is quite possible that these disappointing parasites may never have been recorded!

Other means of protection are used by certain insects. It is well known that many beetles will fold up their legs when disturbed and drop from wherever they are resting. This form of defense is taken advantage of when a collector uses a beating net. Most species fly instead of dropping—an obvious means of escape. Feigning death is a deception practiced by some. A few species bleed at the joints; the fluid extruded is irritating to prospective predators. In still other cases, poisonous substances are discharged to ward off enemies, sometimes as a gas (see bombardier beetles, 4.4 *Brachinus* spp.). A few groups of beetles secrete a blistering agent. All of these forms of protection tax the ingenuity of predators, parasites, and would-be collectors.

Environmental Factors

Extremes of weather are natural deterrents to insect activity. One does not expect to find many insects about on cold, wet, windy days. Conversely, on calm, warm, sunny days during the height of the flower blooming season, many insects are on the wing and present many opportunities for observation and capture. Insects are always present in some form the year around, however, and they abound in all but the extreme polar regions. Very few species inhabit the ocean.

The effect of man's environmental pollution on insect life has not been very well documented. Habitat destruction, of course, has caused the extermination of thousands of species. Few have been missed except by systematists and ecologists. Obviously, insecticides have killed more than insect pests. Predators and parasites may have suffered more from these pesticides than the pests themselves, for the latter have managed to build up their resistance as fast as the dose is increased. Some heavily polluted areas, especially aquatic habitats, are known to be completely devoid of insect life where it was once abundant. With the extermination of the insects, many other organisms, including fish and other aquatics, lose their food supply and are destroyed.

Endangered Species

Hundreds of species of insects, including many of great beauty, have become extinct because of ecological changes brought about by the building of cities, dams, and other activities concomitant with the spread of civilization. Few cases are documented because such changes usually take place before biologists have a chance to study the affected areas. An exception is the mosquito fauna of Panama, where it appears that many species of sabethine mosquitoes became extinct with the flooding of the Gatun River valley to make Gatun Lake in the center of the isthmus. No one knows how many of the species we continue to carry in our catalogs of plants and animals are actually extinct. Although we now have laws regulating the collecting of plants and animals, it is extremely doubtful if any insect species has been exterminated solely by being captured for collections. More than likely the opposite is true. Amateurs and professionals both, upon becoming aware of the scarcity of a species, are now much more inclined to take steps to prevent its extermination by demanding habitat preservation.

The recovery of a damaged ecosystem is remarkably fast, at least so far as insects and plants are concerned. Therefore, one of the best (if not *the* best) ways to pre-

Table 4.2 Comparison of Faunal Zones, Regions, and Biomes*

Faunal Zones	Regions	Biomes
Arctic Hudsonian Canadian	Boreal	Tundra Coniferous forest or taiga
Transition Alleghanian	Transition	Deciduous forest
Upper Sonoran Carolinian	Upper Austral	Grassland and desert scrub Deciduous forest (part)
Lower Sonoran Austroriparian	Lower Austral	Desert scrub and chaparral Deciduous forest (part)
Tropical	Tropical	Tropical rain forest

*Based on the U.S. Biological Survey's "Fourth Provisional Zone Maps of North America," 1910, by C. Hart Merriam, Vernon Bailey, E. W. Nelson, and E. A. Preble, and on *The ecology of North America*, 1963, by V. E. Shelford.

serve our wildlife is to leave it alone. Let the weeds grow. Stop mowing so much grass (a measure that also saves energy). A few choice weeds in the back yard will attract many species of butterflies, and so on. The resulting increase in insect life will provide food for many birds. A true "balance of nature" requires weeds and bugs as well as the birds and the bees.

COLLECTING AREAS

We know that each species has its own peculiar habitat, but the habitats for the majority of insect species are unknown. It follows, then, that much of our insect collecting is a matter of luck. Nevertheless, some knowledge of ecology can be helpful in selecting places to collect.

Different *biomes*—major vegetation areas, defined by their complement of plant species—have similar assemblages of characteristic insect species. Although biomes are defined on the basis of their plant cover, it is easy to see that they might also be defined by the insects that inhabit them; one might expect as much, considering the coevolution of the two groups. Some authors use the system devised in 1910 by Merriam, Bailey, Nelson, and Preble for fauna zones, and others, including this book, use that devised by Shelford. Table 4.2 compares the terms used in the two systems. The biomes are shown in Fig. 22. The following brief notes are intended as clues to what insects one should look for in each of the biomes of North America.

1. *Ocean:* Few insect species spend their entire life in the ocean. One exception is the bug (Hemiptera), *Halobates sericeus* Eschscholtz, found off the coast of California and across the Pacific. Many other species of aquatic bugs are found along the shore of the ocean; representatives of other orders of insects are intertidal. The orders of insects living in marine habitats are these: Collembola, Thysanura, Hemiptera, Trichoptera, Diptera, and Coleoptera.
2. *Oceanic islands:* Hawaii is politically a part of North America, but not ecologically. Other than some of the economically important species, the insect fauna of Hawaii and other oceanic islands is very different from that of mainland North

America. The study of the insects of these islands, how they were populated, and their evolution is a subject that cannot be covered in a book of this size.

3. *Tundra:* The insect fauna of northern Canada and Alaska—that area beyond the treeline, the Arctic polar region (Fig. 23)—is limited to a few

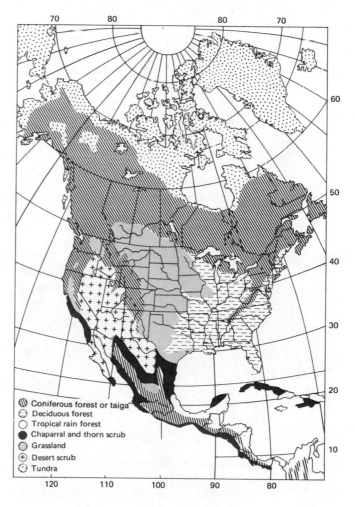

Fig. 22. Map of the biomes of North America.

Legend:
- Coniferous forest or taiga
- Deciduous forest
- Tropical rain forest
- Chaparral and thorn scrub
- Grassland
- Desert scrub
- Tundra

Fig. 23. Tundra.

Fig. 25. Grassland, showing ungrazed land (left) and overgrazed land (right).

species, but these may be abundant in individuals. Butterflies are common. Mosquitoes and other biting flies occur in vast swarms during the brief summer period. Collembola are abundant in the soil and on the sparse vegetation. A few species of beetles have been recorded.

4. *Coniferous forest* (*taiga*): Much of northern North America is covered by forests of pine, spruce, and other conifers (Fig. 24). These forests are composed of large stands of single or very few species. The diversity of the insect fauna is very limited because of the limited number of habitats available. The species are largely wood boring beetles, needle feeding moth caterpillars, plant eating wasp caterpillars, and parasitic wasps. Open areas and lakes provide breeding grounds for flies, especially mosquitoes and black flies. Some tips for the collector are these: newly cut wood attracts many species of beetles; fire attracts certain species of beetles; open areas in the forest and at the forest edge provide interfaces that often abound with many species.

5. *Deciduous forests:* A great variety of plants comprise the temperate forest, dominated by

those deciduous trees that lose their leaves in winter. This diversity results in a much richer insect fauna than is found in the coniferous forest. One may expect to find many leaf eating moths and butterflies, leaf mining moths and flies, aphids, ants, and leaf beetles along with the allied plant and animal groups that together comprise this biome. Complex ecosystems intertwine throughout, including communities in the leaf litter found on the forest floor. Where swampy areas and meandering streams are found in the forest, even more insect life may be expected.

6. *Grasslands:* Almost all natural midwestern grasslands and prairies have been destroyed by the plow or by cattle grazing (Fig. 25). The natural insect fauna is almost overlooked because of the abundance of pest species that accompany civilization in these regions. A typical grassland insect is the grasshopper, of which there are many species. As their name suggests, many of these orthopterans are native grass feeders. Their destruction of forage and grain plants is merely a change of food plants from those that previously grew wild in these regions. Along with these insects, the grasslands harbor harvester ants, caterpillars known as armyworms, leafhoppers, and predators of many kinds that attack these hordes. In terms of individuals, the population density of grasslands is very high, but the diversity of species may not be as great as in some of the other biomes.

7. *Desert scrub, chaparral, and thorn scrub:* The western arid or desert regions are very diverse and harbor a great variety of insects. Almost all groups are represented despite the scarcity of inhabitable areas. True desert—for example, the Sonoran Desert (Fig. 26)—have many interesting adaptations for overcoming the severity of the climate—excessive lack of water and ex-

Fig. 24. Coniferous forest or taiga.

Fig. 26. Desert scrub in the front ranges of Mount Lemon, Arizona, in the background, and true Sonoran Desert in the foreground.

Fig. 27. Tropical rain forest.

tremes of temperature. The rainy period, which is limited to only a few days or a few weeks during the year, is the best time for collecting. Flowers come suddenly into blossom and attract a great variety of insects day and night. UV-blacklight collecting is very productive at these times. Beating branches and searching the desert floor with a light helps to round out a representative collection of species. Chaparral and thorn scrub regions are not true desert areas; rather, they are characterized by seasonal, if limited, rainfall and larger trees and shrubs. These areas have a fauna similar to that of the desert.

8. *Tropical rain forests:* The true tropical rain forest of the United States occurs only in very limited areas in southern Florida. The only other tropical part of the United States is near Brownsville, Texas, but no forest remains. Tropical insects, well known for their brilliant colors, fantastic shapes, and giant size, often stray into the extreme southern parts of the United States. A few of the species are established. Many are listed in this book, but because of their limited distribution, they are seldom seen by the ordinary collector. A few miles south of the border into Mexico, dense forests (Fig. 27) may be found that exhibit the characteristic diversity of tropical plant life, with its hundreds of ecological niches for myrids of insect species. A few temperate rain forests occur in the United States, the most extensive being on the Olympic Peninsula, in Washington state (Fig. 28). The insect fauna in this region is relatively sparse.

9. *Mountains:* Insects of the very high mountains are much more numerous than one might imagine (Fig. 29). Some very unique insects are resident in these habitats. For example, the rare rock-crawlers (Grylloblattodea) are found high above the treeline among the rocks at the edges of glaciers and in the sparse vegetation of these tundralike areas. Numerous species of butterflies are seen in the alpine meadows during the

few weeks of summer. Some of these have a complex interrelationship with ants and lupines. The springtails (Collembola) are at home in this country and form an important food source for some of the other insects there. These isolated mountain tops seem to be extensions of the arctic biome.

10. *Inland waters:* The aquatic insects of lakes, ponds, pools, streams, swamps, marshes, and bogs (Fig. 30) include all species of entire orders (Odonata, for example) and entire families (Dytiscidae, etc.), not to mention one or two species of particular groups. Almost every order of insects has some aquatic members, their immature stages being modified for aquatic living, and the adults of many others enter water for egg laying or feeding. Orders in which all species are aquatic (with one or two exceptions) in the nymphal (naiad) stage include, in addition to the damselflies and dragonflies—the Odonata mentioned above—the mayflies (Ephemeroptera) and stoneflies (Plecoptera). Other groups will be pointed out in Part II.

Fig. 28. Rain Forest on the Olympic Peninsula, Washington.

Fig. 29. Mountain vegetation.

Places Forbidding Collecting

National Parks and most state parks and preserves are closed to insect collectors as well as other collectors of natural history specimens. Under very special circumstances, permits may be obtained by specialists to collect in specified areas designated by the director or resident naturalists.

The importance of conserving insect species is a result of our knowledge of the complex ecosystems that keep any habitat functioning properly. To upset or remove even a single species from a system through the use of chemicals, other control methods, or just for the sport of collecting will bring about unforeseen changes. Although it is true that there is a great natural fluctuation of species from season to season and year to year, our knowledge does not presently permit us to state with certainty which species should be left unaffected by man and which may be safely exterminated, if, indeed, it were possible to be that selective. Naturalists will understand that it is not just the large and obvious plants and animals in any biome that comprise the ecosystem, but that every species involved is in a delicate balance with all the others. When this balance is disturbed, for whatever cause, changes may be expected. Some may be minor and recovery will be rapid; others will prove to be drastic and irreversible. When the latter happens, a part of our world is changed and another part lost forever. Greed in collecting is a sign of poor sportsmanship,

Fig. 30. Pond in deciduous forest area.

and the greedy should be punished. It is far better to follow the rules of the sport and practice preservation and conservation.

BIBLIOGRAPHY

Alcock, John 1979. *Animal behavior*. 2nd ed. Sunderland, Mass.: Sinauer Assoc. Inc., xii + 532 pp.

Askew, R. R. 1971. *Parasitic insects*. London: Heinemann Educational Books, xvii + 316 pp.

Busnel, R. G. (ed.) 1963. *Acoustic behaviour of animals*. New York: Elsevier Publ. Co., xx + 933 pp.

Clausen, Curtis P. 1940. *Entomophagous insects*. New York: McGraw-Hill, x + 688 pp.

Price, Peter W. 1975. *Insect ecology*. New York: John Wiley and Sons, xii + 514 pp.

Shelford, Victor E. 1963. *The ecology of North America*. Urbana: University of Illinois Press, xxii + 610 pp.

Wigglesworth, Vincent B. 1964. *The life of insects*. London: Weidenfeld and Nicolson, xii + 360 pp.

Wilson, Edward O. 1971. *The insect societies*. Cambridge: Harvard University Press, x + 548 pp.

5
Insect Collecting

In the preceding chapters, emphasis has been placed on the collecting of insects. Probably, most professional entomologists started their study of insects by collecting them. At the beginning, only simple tools are required; as the collection enlarges, more specialized equipment is added. From the study of the foregoing chapters, it should be apparent that a goal should be set before proceeding further. Many insect collections have been started and then discarded without contributing much, if anything, to the knowledge of the collector. It should be remembered that the collection is only a beginning, not an end in itself. A knowledge of the complex and fascinating habits of the living insect should be the ultimate goal.

GOALS, REQUIREMENTS, AND OBLIGATIONS

There are six reasons for maintaining an insect collection, as follows:

1. *As a laboratory record of field work:* No collector can know even a fraction of the species encountered during any field excursion. As specimens are collected, field observations should be written into a notebook in such a way that they can be accurately associated with the species involved, once these are identified.
2. *As a study of variation:* The individuals of a population and the populations of a species both exhibit variations. In order to know a species, this variation needs to be studied and recorded. To do so, a series of individuals must be collected and preserved so that measurements and other observations of the variations may be made.
3. *As a study of distribution:* A knowledge of the distributional range of a species enlarges our understanding of the variation, perhaps of the hybridization, and, ultimately, of the speciation of insects in general. Collecting specimens from many areas makes this kind of study possible. Usually the work of many collectors is necessary before much can be learned about the range of a particular species.
4. *As a reservoir for morphological studies:* Most insect species are known from only a few specimens; many are still undescribed. The greatest immediate use of any collection is to provide a stock of specimens needed for morphological studies. No matter how small the collection, it will be of value to someone making a taxonomic study of the groups represented if it has been carefully prepared and adequately labeled.
5. *As stock for other specialists:* Every collector will soon want to add specimens from other areas by exchanging specimens with other collectors. A supply of common local species can be used for this purpose.
6. *As study material for the beginner:* The novice will find it easier to learn about the insects of his area by making a collection of the insects he has *personally observed in the field.* A collection should be started from these insects that have been studied while still alive in their natural habitat. So far as possible, it should be more than a general collection of specimens attracted to lights at night, or specimens obtained by sweeping over vegetation. This type of mass collecting is a good way to build a working collection, but it must not stop there. Specimens that have been observed as living organisms carrying on some phase of their complicated life processes will be remembered much longer because of these very associations. Any collection becomes more meaningful as soon as the student overcomes the urge to grab before observing.

The six important requirements and obligations that must be met by collectors before their collections can become of real value to themselves or to others are as follows:

1. *Proper handling in the field:* Use the right killing agent; store specimens in a manner that will assure complete preservation; keep careful field notes. Unless these precautions are taken, the specimens will be worthless and should not have been collected at all.
2. *Proper preservation:* Each specimen should be mounted with all possible care, using the most reliable techniques. If a specimen is worth the

trouble to collect, it is worth the effort of proper mounting and preservation.

3. *Correct attribution of data:* All precautions must be taken to insure that field data are associated with their respective specimens in such a way that no possibility of data switching exists. A specimen without, or with incorrect, data has no scientific value.

4. *Orderly storage for accessibility:* Specimens should be stored in a way that permits easy access for study, sorting, and arranging.

5. *Uniform mounting for ease in handling and storing:* Specimens should be mounted uniformly in accordance with a standard system to permit their easy transfer from one collection to another. The standard procedures described here are used throughout the world so that any worker anywhere can use the specimens so prepared without difficulty. Although a great variety of storage containers are commercially available, relatively few are used by the major collections of this country. The collector will do well to consider a uniform storage system right from the start. To do so will save time as the collection grows because boxes and cabinets can be expanded without having to repin major portions of the collection.

6. *Adequate protection:* The collection must be constantly maintained since many dangers threaten one that is neglected; for example, insect pests (dermestid beetles), mold, dust, heat, and breakage by careless handling. Instructions for maintenance follow. Any specimens that are the basis of published records, however, should be deposited in a museum or university collection where they will be available to other workers for study.

FIELD RECORDS

Detailed field notes are of great importance to the serious collector because the scientific value of a collection depends upon them. A notebook should always be taken into the field to record all pertinent data. The idea that such data can be recalled once back home is usually mistaken. More than likely, forgotten details will make it necessary to return to the same place (if that is possible). To prevent this from happening, it is best to devise a suitable checklist to be consulted in the field. This can be a printed form fitted into a small ring binder, or simply a reminder card listing the items to look for.

Whatever method is used, it is necessary to establish some key numbering system to correlate the field notes with the specimens. The system most frequently used identifies any given field trip or collecting station with a lot number. Each vial or storage container used for that trip or station is assigned that number; details about the specimens collected are given a subnumber. Thus, on trip number 391, a collection made on dogbane, say, would be given the subnumber 391–1. Specimens collected in another environment would be marked 391–2, and so on. Numbers should be written with alcohol-resistant ink or typed using an alcohol-resistant ribbon and the label placed inside the container with the specimens. It

is always a good idea to add the locality as well in case the notes should be lost before the specimens are mounted. Other systems are used, of course; the important thing is to make sure all data are properly correlated with the specimens. Many collectors make photocopies of their field notes for deposit in a safe place.

METHODS OF INSECT CAPTURE

The materials needed for collecting insects are simple and inexpensive. Some of the more general techniques for luring and capturing insects will be discussed here, with emphasis on those materials and techniques that are particularly useful for the general collector. A little experience will help each student to develop more refined techniques. Those wishing to specialize in certain groups of insects will need to study the references listed. A checklist of necessary items (all of which are described in the text) appears in Table 5.1. The absolutely basic items are a killing jar, insect pins, and storage boxes, which are used to kill, preserve, and store specimens, respectively. All additional equipment is a refinement of these basic requirements.

Nets

Several types of nets are used for capturing active insects. An air net (Fig. 31) is made of lightweight, sturdy material that will not damage delicate Lepidoptera, Hymenoptera, Diptera, and similar insects as they struggle within it. A heavier netting may be used to capture beetles, grasshoppers, and other hard-bodied insects. A net made of muslin or one protected by a muslin apron is used when collecting in heavy vegetation and for sweeping across fields and bramble patches. Commercial nets with strong handles and rings are available for this purpose, although nets may be homemade if desired. (See Fig. 32.)

A useful aid when using the sweep net is a *separator box* (Fig. 33). This is made of ¾-in. plywood approximately 15 in. on all sides, the top of which slides open to permit the user to empty the contents of the sweep net. A circular hole the size of a Mason jar metal ring is cut on the side of the box, near the top; the ring is nailed in place around this hole; and a Mason jar is screwed into the ring. This forms a window to which the insects in the plant debris in the box will fly, thus separating them from the debris. Two more Mason jar rings soldered together will allow the separator box jar, once removed, to be connected to a killing jar of the same size. A third jar will then be needed to replace the original jar on the box. After the most active insects have been captured by this method, it will be necessary to dump out and sort the contents of the box for additional specimens. Others that remain on the sides of the box may be easily captured.

Netting techniques require practice. The proper use of the air net will depend upon the habits of the insects being captured. Once the specimens are inside the net, flop the end over the ring to close the net.

Beating nets are made of a single piece of cloth held taut by crossed poles (Fig. 34). They are placed under a branch or limb to catch insects that will drop when their resting place is struck with a heavy stick or metal rod.

A wide assortment of aquatic nets (Fig. 35) is com-

Table 5.1 Checklist of Entomological Equipment for Field Trips and Laboratory Use

For Capturing Insects

Air net	Mason's hammer or	Alcohol and vials
Sweep net	heavy screwdriver	Berlese funnels
Separator box	Ground traps	Record book and pen
Beating net	Aspirator	Field bag
Aquatic net	Forceps	
UV "black" light	Geologist's or mason's	
and sheet, *or*	hammer	
UV light trap	Small water color brush	

Killing Equipment

Cyanide or ethyl acetate	Paper or cellophane envelopes
metal-cap killing jars of 2¼-	Barber's fluid
to 5⅜-in. diameter	KAAD
Vials (3- or 4-dram) with neo-	Plaster of Paris
prene stoppers	Sawdust
Test tubes (1 × 8 in.) with cork	Potassium cyanide
stoppers	Ethyl acetate
	Ether or chloroform

For Rearing

1-quart jars	Plastic Petri dishes
Cages	Plastic refrigerator jars
Blotting or filter paper	

Mounting and Storage Equipment

Flat, white enamel sorting pan	Pen holder, points (or nibs), or
Insect pins (assorted size: 2,	Rapidograph No. 000
3) and pin holders	Glue
Insect boxes or drawers	Relaxing jar
"Protem" block	Pinning forceps
Step block	Point punch
Ledger 100-percent rag paper	Spreading board
India ink	Drying cabinet
	PDB or similar fumigant

For Identifications, Including Dissection Materials

Hand lens or binocular	Syracuse or USDA Plant	Bleach
microscope and light	Quarantine watch	Scissors
L-cork, with plasticine	glasses	Beaker
Dissecting needles (fine)	Microscope slides	(50-cc)
Medicine dropper	Slide boxes or trays	Gage's
Alcohol lamp	Cover slips (size No. 2,	stain
Tripod	13 mm round)	Eosin stain
Wire screen	Fine jeweler's forceps	Acid–
Canada balsam or	Dropping bottles for:	alcohol
Euparal	distilled water	
Hoyer's mounting	80-percent alcohol	
media	95-percent alcohol	
KOH	100-percent alcohol	
Stender jars	carbo-xylene	
Glacial acetic acid	xylene	
Clove oil		

Fig. 31. Long-handled air net useful for collecting high-flying butter-flies. (*Courtesy of American Biological Supply Co.*)

pating the reactions of insects in the field soon becomes second nature to the avid collector.

UV Black Lights

Capturing insects that are attracted to lights at night is one of the best ways to add to a collection. Porch lights and other lights around buildings are favorite collecting sites. Ultraviolet (UV) black lights are commercially available either in portable light fixtures or mounted in specially designed traps that may be left outside all night (Fig. 36). Because insects see well in the upper end of the light spectrum, the blue wave lengths of these bulbs at-

mercially available. These are constructed to drag across the bottom of a body of water or to stretch across a stream. Dip nets of various sizes are often desirable. One of the handiest nets of this type is a wire mesh tea strainer; another is a larger kitchen strainer.

After some experience, collectors learn the habits of insects and catch on to the proper technique to collect them. One must know exactly which species of insects will drop into a killing jar, which will fly away when disturbed, which will crawl under stones, and so on. Antici-

Fig. 32. Details for construction of combined air and sweeping net.

Sliding top

Hole surrounded
by mason jar
ring

$\frac{3}{4}$″ Plywood construction

Mason jar rings glued top to top.

Fig. 33. Separator box.

Fig. 35. One type of aquatic scrapper net.

tract many species in addition to those that would come to ordinary light bulbs of a lower wave length. (It is well known that orange light will not attract insects and hence the use of these bulbs as porch lights.) Two types of UV bulbs are available. The one that is very dark (so-called *black light*) is less satisfactory, not because of limited attractive power but because of possible damage to the human eye. The lighter type (of a lower wave length) can be used more safely. It may be hung in front of a white sheet suspended over a branch, clothesline, or on a knock-down frame built specially to hold it. Many kinds of insects, particularly moths and beetles, will be attracted to the light and come to rest on the sheet, where they may be captured directly in a killing jar. Since some insects will drop to the ground, letting a part of the sheet cover a portion of the ground beneath the light will capture more specimens. [Note: Unfortunately, the country mercury vapor lights now so common around homes and farms, meant to frighten off intruders, attract insects in great numbers. Hundreds of billions are lured each year from their food plants and die without reproducing. Many of our most attractive and beneficial species are nearing extinction as a result. This needless slaughter, as well as energy waste, should be discouraged by every means possible. The least that could be done is to change

from high-wave-length mercury vapor bulbs to low-wave-length orange bulbs.]

Bait

Bait of various kinds is used as lures. One of the most popular is a thick mixture of fermenting bananas, brown sugar, and beer. Painted in patches on trunks and fence posts at night this attracts many moths and other insects. A fisherman's headlamp is used to find the insects at the bait, leaving both hands free to make the capture.

Other materials to use as bait are carrion, which attracts many kinds of beetles and flies, and dung for flies, dung beetles, and sometimes even butterflies, wasps, and other insects. Soapy water and drying laundry have been observed as attractants of various species, including some thought to be very rare.

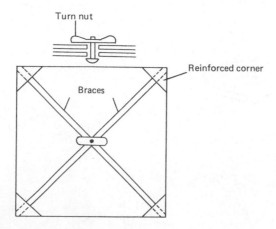

Turn nut

Reinforced corner

Braces

Fig. 34. Details for construction of beating net.

Fig. 36. Portable light trap that may be used on house current or batteries. (*Courtesy of Ward's Science Establishment, Inc.*)

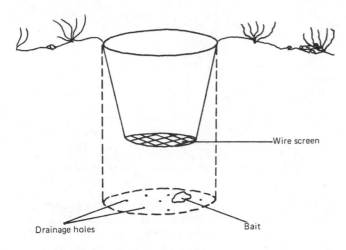

Fig. 37. A bait trap.

Fig. 39. Berlese funnel.

Traps

In addition to the light traps already referred to, other types of traps include pans (sometimes painted yellow inside) or similar vessels filled with antifreeze (an odorless liquid killing agent and preservative) and sunk into the ground so that walking insects will fall into them. Traps made from tin cans can be baited with carrion (Fig. 37). (Note: These must be emptied frequently because they easily fill with water and the trapped insects will rot.) A very useful trap for flying insects is the Malaise trap (Fig. 38), which is available commercially. Made of netting, it is erected much the same as a tent and placed across a fly-way such as a sunny path in a woods or woodland glade. Many interesting species will soon find their way in but not their way out.

Berlese Funnel

This apparatus (Fig. 39) will yield small and seldom seen species, particularly tiny beetles. Funnels are easily made from galvanized iron, 10 to 14 in. in diameter at the top and some 15 in. long. The spout of the funnel should taper to a tubular piece several inches long and about $\frac{1}{2}$

Fig. 38. A Malaise trap. (*Courtesy of BioQuip Products*)

or $\frac{3}{4}$ in. in diameter. A stand is constructed to hold the funnel over a jar of 70-percent ethyl or 80-percent isopropyl (rubbing) alcohol. Screens of fine enough mesh (for example, hardware cloth) to hold back debris but coarse enough to admit insects are inserted into the bottom of the funnel. The nature of the debris will determine the screening. Sometimes it will be necessary to sift the debris to remove the large leaves, stones, and so on, but leave the finer material containing the insects. Leaf mold, decayed wood particles, humus, rotting plant material, and similar vegetation are placed in the funnel. Heat is then applied to its top by means of an electric light bulb suspended overhead. As the material dries, the insects work down toward the bottom and eventually fall into the alcohol, where they are killed and preserved. It will take from two to several days, depending upon the density of the material, to complete the process. One advantage of this apparatus is that it can be used in the winter, trapping many hibernating species.

Other Methods of Capture

A mason's hammer or sturdy screwdriver is useful for breaking up logs and digging in soil. A garden trowel or even a shovel may sometimes be useful, but the hammer or screwdriver is the most frequently used tool of this sort, having the advantage of adding less weight to the collecting kit.

Forceps are used for picking up small specimens. They should have broad, flexible ends and be handled carefully to prevent specimen damage. Actually, so few species of insects are harmful to human beings that fingers make one of the best and safest tools for handling them; in fact, they are usually superior to forceps except for reaching into deep cracks and crevices.

A water color brush is used to pick up extremely small specimens by wetting the brush in alcohol in a vial, touching the specimen, and dipping the brush back into the alcohol. A finger moistened with saliva is an excellent substitute for the water color brush and often easier to apply.

Aspirators (Fig. 40) are special devices used to suck up small insects—particularly flies or tiny beetles on collecting sheets, in beating nets, or on leaves or flowers. These can be made or purchased from supply companies.

Fig. 40. An aspirator for capturing small insects.

KILLING METHODS

Cyanide Jars

The use of potassium cyanide killing jars is dangerous. Unfortunately, nothing else yet meets all the requirements of a killing agent so well as cyanide. Although it has some very undesirable qualities when used to kill insects, it is extremely quick. It will kill most insects in a matter of seconds (except for weevils, which seem to be able to close their spiracles and remain for days unharmed by this deadly gas). The advantage of this rapid kill is that specimens can be added to the jar in such rapid succession that previously captured specimens have no time to escape. The extremely poisonous nature of potassium cyanide is reason enough for the difficulty in obtaining it commercially, and no one should use it without adequate training. There are other disadvantages. Specimens killed in cyanide have a tendency to become rigid and brittle when mounted. A few insects, moreover, are discolored by the gas, or their color is changed.

Cyanide jars may be homemade from ordinary food jars. Most olive jars are very useful because they are the same diameter throughout. It is best to use jars with threaded metal tops (as opposed to those with crimped edges) that screw off with a half turn or more. Such jars require the use of only one hand, the fingers easily turning the top at the same time as they hold the jar itself. A crimped top jar may jiggle open in transport, a danger not worth risking. Jars with necks narrower than the body are less desirable because dead insects tend to stick inside, making them difficult to remove.

The cyanide jar is made by placing a layer of potassium cyanide about 1 in. deep at its bottom (Fig. 41). This is tamped down by the smooth end of a dowel or similar instrument until it is firmly packed. Obviously, this operation should take place in a well ventilated room, or better, outdoors (but not in the wind). Work over newspapers so that any spilled particles can be safely discarded. Make sure that no cyanide adheres to the end of the dowel. Next, tamp in a layer of fine, dry sawdust of about the same thickness over the cyanide. It is now necessary to mix a thin batch of plaster of Paris, thin enough so that the mixture will drop off the end of a teaspoon, but not so thin that it is actually runny, much

Fig. 41. Details for construction of cyanide killing jar.

less watery. A $\frac{1}{2}$- to $\frac{3}{4}$-in. layer of this is then poured on top of the sawdust, making sure that the entire surface is covered. The jar may be sharply tapped to make the plaster flow evenly on top so that it is free of holes or bubbles. Leave the cover off the jar for six to eight hours (do not leave it in the sun) so that the plaster will dry without sweating. Moisture will slowly work down to the cyanide as the jar ripens. As soon as the moisture reaches the cyanide, hydrogencyanic gas will be generated, and the jar will be charged and ready to use. Thereafter, the addition of moisture from the bodies of the insects and from the atmosphere will keep the jar working. Be sure to wash your hands after making one of these jars, and make sure no cyanide has been spilled.

Ethyl Acetate Jars

A safer jar may be made by using ethyl acetate as the killing agent (Fig. 42). Its disadvantage is that it is much slower to kill. A partial remedy is to add a small amount of ethyl ether, but this should be used sparingly because it causes specimens to become greasy. One advantage of ethyl acetate is that specimens killed by it and stored in Barber's Fluid (to be discussed) remain flexible after being mounted instead of becoming brittle as cyanide-killed specimens do. Ethyl acetate, moreover, also serves as a preservative. Some collectors store, as well as collect, specimens in tubes containing ground cork charged with ethyl acetate. However, since green specimens tend to turn red in this material, these tubes must be used with caution. This material is also difficult to purchase; ordinarily, it must be obtained through an institution.

An ethyl acetate jar may be constructed from the same type food jar described above. More sawdust instead of the cyanide is used. It must be tamped down before the plaster of Paris is poured on. If you wish, a small cork may be placed in the center of the surface of

Fig. 42. Details for construction of ethyl acetate jar.

the sawdust and the plaster poured around it. Once the plaster has set, the cork may be removed, the acetate poured into the jar to saturate the sawdust, and the cork replaced to prevent any of the sawdust from falling out or insects from entering the chamber. (Sawdust is not always necessary; the plaster will absorb the ethyl acetate.) A few strips of paper toweling should be placed in the jar to absorb the excess moisture that is sure to accumulate from the insects' bodies.

Other Methods

A modification of this jar will accommodate other killing agents, such as chloroform or ether, but these are not recommended. Almost all insects may be placed directly into 70-percent ethyl alcohol or 80-percent isopropyl (rubbing) alcohol without damage. Even moths and hairy bees collected in alcohol may be recovered as fairly good specimens if a small amount of detergent is added to the alcohol used in the sorting tray. If such moths and bees, upon removal from the tray, are air dried—especially by a slight breeze, as from a slow fan—their scales and hair will not mat (see section on Mounting Insects Collected in Alcohol).

FIELD STORAGE

Storage Containers

The proper field treatment of insects is vital to their final value as specimens. As soon as an insect expires in the killing jar, or as soon afterward as possible, it should be transferred to a storage container. Butterflies and moths are often stored in paper triangles (Figs. 43 and 44), in glassine envelopes, or between thin layers of cellucotton. Various kinds of boxes are useful for storing dried specimens. Paper pill boxes (Fig. 45) and small plastic boxes may be recommended, but specimens must be kept dry and treated to prevent the growth of mold. Crystalline chlorocresol (available commercially) can be sprinkled into the box to keep specimens relaxed and prevent mold. Specimens preserved in this way may be handled without fear of breakage; they will be ready for mounting on insect pins without first being placed in a relaxing jar (Fig. 46). Since dried-out specimens become brittle, they must be placed in a humid relaxing chamber for several hours (48 or more) before they can be pinned.

Another storage container often used in the field is a numbered vial containing either one of the killing and

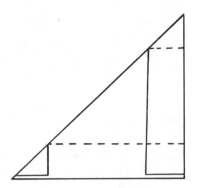

Fig. 44. Folded paper triangle.

storage fluids described in the next section or ground cork saturated with ethyl acetate. (The latter may be preferred because specimens preserved in liquid may lose their color; with the former, the fats dissolving out of the body by the alcohol will dry on the surface of the mounted specimens.) The 4-dram vial with neoprene stopper (No. 0) is the most useful for storing specimens in the field since it holds alcohol without leakage and without danger of its top coming off in the collecting bag, a common occurrence with corked or screw-top vials.

Specimens with hairlike setae or pile should be wrapped in absorbent tissue before being stored in cardboard or wooden field boxes.

Field Storage in Liquids

Dietrich's modification of Barber's fluid[1] or Peterson's modification[2] (for use when tissue mounts are desired) are efficient mediums for storing adult specimens. Usually insects stored in these fluids are relaxed, degreased, and ready for mounting. Any further degreasing required can be done in chloroform or ethyl ether. The genital structures of fresh, or even dried, specimens are extruded after being placed in these liquids.

Larvae of moths, butterflies, and beetles are better perserved by yet another fluid, KAAD, developed by Peterson.[3] Larvae may be killed by dropping them di-

[1]Dietrich's modificaton of Barber's Fluid:

Ethyl alcohol (95%)	265 parts (42%)	840 cc
Water (distilled, deionized)	245 (38%)	760
Ethyl acetate	95 (15%)	300
Benzol (Benzene)	35 (5%)	100
		2000 (approx. ½ gal)

Note: (if benzol separates out, add more alcohol)

[2]Peterson's modification of Barber's fluid (mix in the order given, stirring each time for a clear mixture):

Benzol	16 parts	18 cc
Alcohol (95%)	34	38
Ethyl acetate	10	12
Triton X155	13	15
Water	27	30
		113

[3]KAAD constituents:

Kerosene	1 part
95% ethyl or isopropyl alcohol	7–10
Glacial acetic acid	2
Dioxane	1

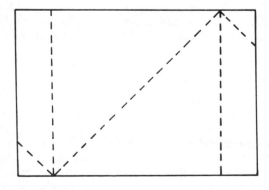

Fig. 43. Fold marks for constructing paper triangle.

Fig. 45. Cross section of paper pill box showing how insects collected in the field may be simply and safely stored.

Fig. 47. The proper way to mount small insects on pins.

rectly into this fluid in the field or by placing them in hot water. They should be kept in this mixture for at least 30 minutes, but not more than 4 hours, before being removed to 70-percent ethyl alcohol.

Drying in Wet Climates

Specimens stored in paper triangles or pill boxes must be dried by the application of heat. A simple drying oven may be devised by placing a screen-covered chamber over a cardboard box in which an electric light bulb serves as the heat source. The arrangement must allow for a dry air flow throughout the chamber. Since the dried specimens will be very brittle, they must be carefully stored in boxes with moth crystals or phenol crystals to prevent the growth of mold. If, as an alternative to drying, the chemical chlorocresol is used, the specimens should be checked regularly to see that no mold is growing. Chlorocresol should always be used with caution.

Transporting Live Insects

Collectors may wish to bring living insects in from the field for further study or to rear or breed. To do so successfully, the following precautions must be taken:

1. The insects must be prevented from drying out in their cages.
2. They must be kept away from direct sunlight lest they be killed by the heat.
3. They must be provided with a resting surface that is natural for the species.
4. A sufficient supply of oxygen must be assured by regulating the openings in the top or cover of the container, keeping in mind that the air must circulate, without drying.
5. Predatory and cannibalistic insects must be kept apart.

Live insects should be transported with as little shock by jarring as possible, and in the shortest possible time. Suitable rearing jars should be prepared in advance to receive the specimens. Most entomologists start with quart fruit jars, placing a layer of soil in the bottom to retain moisture and a stick or twig to provide a resting place. Solid lids are replaced with coverings of fly screen

Fig. 46. Cross section of a metal relaxing jar.

or gauze. Too much food should be avoided and uneaten portions removed. Watch for growth of mold, a sign of too much moisture. Other usable receptacles are plastic refrigerator jars or similar, inexpensive containers, including those made of paper. Sometimes a larger container is necessary. These are available commercially, some of them collapsible and easily stored.

Since food of many insects is unknown, those attempting to rear such insects must do a considerable amount of experimentation. The time will be well spent if only because of the new information acquired. Whenever possible, food should be brought in from the field.

PREPARATION OF INSECT COLLECTIONS

Types of Insect Pins

Standard-length insect pins of various diameters are used for mounting insects (Fig. 47). Available in several grades, these pins may be obtained from any of a number of biological supply companies. Only rust- and acid-resistant pins with secure heads should be used unless the specimens are to be kept for just a short time—as for certain types of surveys, student study material, and so on. Poorer quality pins tend to have points that buckle when pushed into any but the softest pinning surfaces. In especially humid climates, stainless steel pins must be substituted even though they are not as strong as varnished pins. For easy handling, no pin smaller than a No. 2 should be used; No. 3 is preferred. Since it is necessary to handle very small pins with extreme care, preferably with pinning forceps, it is usually better to glue small specimens to a point.

Specimens that have been allowed to dry must be relaxed before they can be pinned. Freshly caught insects, on the other hand, can be easily mounted on the spot. They will dry in place on the pin, and no further preservation will be needed (other than protection from museum pests).

Relaxing Methods

Specimens (especially hairy and scaly ones) may be relaxed in a humid chamber (Fig. 46) or by placing them in Barber's Fluid or very hot (but not boiling) water. A large crock or metal can with a tight, but easily removed, cover may be employed as the relaxing jar. Its bottom should be filled with sand (the best way) or paper toweling kept saturated with water and an aluminum wire screen placed over the wet area so as to prevent the speci-

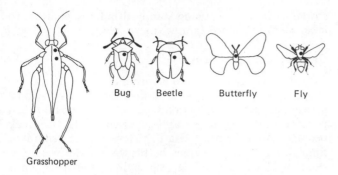

Bug Beetle Butterfly Fly

Grasshopper

Fig. 48. Position of pin hole for proper mounting of common insect orders.

Fig. 49. Pinning step block used to regulate the height of specimens and labels on an insect pin.

mens from coming into direct contact with it. Some carbolic acid crystals should be added to prevent the growth of mold. Although relaxing in such a jar may take several days, it is the best method for moths, butterflies, skippers, hairy bees and flies, and so on. A special relaxing fluid that is simetimes faster and less likely to damage delicate specimens may be used instead.[1]

If very old specimens that have been kept in papers, boxes, or metal containers are relaxed by any of the methods described here, they may fall apart, either because they were attacked by mold when stored or because they rotted as they dried. If the specimens are valuable, they can be repaired by careful gluing, using a binocular microscope to match up the parts. Specimens from tropical areas are often subject to this disintegration, and great care must be taken in handling them.

Mounting on Pins

The position for inserting the insect pin is illustrated in Fig. 48. This differs according to the structure of the insect. The specimen is first pierced and then positioned on the pin at a standard height. Use of a pinning step block (Fig. 49) assures this uniformity. Once the specimen is nearly in position, the head of the pin is inserted in the hole at the lowest level of the block that will, in effect, place the specimen at the highest level when it is turned over.

Once the specimen has been pinned, special attention must be given to the arrangement of its parts. Insects that fold their legs into grooves on the sterna or bend their heads down against the underside of the thorax must be positioned so that these parts may be seen when dry, by extending them with the aid of fine forceps or an insect pin; otherwise, the specimens will be almost unidentifiable and would have to be relaxed in order for these parts to be seen—obviously a needless waste of time. Large specimens full of eggs or food should be cut open, their contents removed, and the hole filled with absorbent cotton. This precaution keeps them from be-

coming greasy and helps minimize any change in color. Very small specimens may be glued to a triangular-shaped point (see Fig. 47). (Care must be taken that none of the glue covers any parts needed for making an indentification.) Points may be cut out of a good grade of drawing paper, either with scissors or with special punches made for this purpose (Fig. 50). The glue may be a water-soluble milk glue, a gum arabic glue called Dietrich's mounting glue,[1] plastic cement that has been diluted with ethyl acetate, or polyvinyl acetate (Gelva U-25®) dissolved in alcohol. Milk glue has the advantage of easily dissolving in water if the specimen has to be removed. Any of these glues, however, will dissolve in Barber's fluid or its modifications.

Mounting Specimens Collected in Alcohol

Beetles and other large, hard-bodied insects may be mounted directly from the alcohol in which they were collected. However, if moth scales are present, as they usually are in light-trap collections, they should be removed by washing the beetles in a solution of weak alcohol, water, and a mild detergent. Soft-bodied specimens collected in the alcohol, on the other hand, always require additional treatment. One of the best methods is to transfer the specimens from the alcohol to cellosolve (ethylene glycol monoethyl ether), which may be obtained from a biological supply company, and leave them in this solution for several hours (12 to 24). Then they are transferred to xylene for one or two hours to a full day (no more). Once removed from this solution and mounted on pins with parts arranged, they will dry in a few minutes and present a very clean, well preserved collection.

Specimens preserved in formalin may be freshened by placing them in 10-percent citric acid and then warming in an oven or by immersing them in a 0.5-percent solution of trisodium phosphate for 24 hours. In both cases, wash them in water and degrease before mounting.

[1]Relaxing fluid constituents:

Ethyl alcohol (75%)	106 cc
Distilled water	28
Benzol	14
Ethyl Acetate	36
	184

[2]Dietrich's mounting glue:

Gum arabic	60 grams
Sugar	30 grams
Carbolic acid	2 cc
Ethyl alcohol (95%)	8 cc

Dissolve the gum arabic and sugar separately in as little water as possible; then mix the two together and strain through fine muslin. Dissolve the carbolic acid in the alcohol, and slowly mix in the other ingredients while stirring continually. The end product should be of the consistency of a thick syrup; if too thin, remove the excess water by heating slowly.

Fig. 50. Triangular points for mounting small insects—(A) round base; (B) square base—and a point punch. (*Courtesy of BioQuip Products*)

Wing Spreading

It is customary to spread the wings of butterflies, moths, and skippers, as well as many orthopterans, to display their shape, venation, and color patterns. The specimens must be relaxed first and a pin passed through their thorax; the pin is then pushed into the cork in the grooved center of a spreading board (Fig. 51). The wings are spread to either side of the groove and held with pins at their base until strips of cellophane or tracing paper can be pinned over them to hold them in place. The edges of the strips are folded first to keep them from cutting into the wings. Once everything is properly in place—including the abdomen and antennae, which may have to be supported by crossed pins—the pinning boards are placed in a drying cabinet, or other warm, dry place, to set. After two or three days, the specimens will be dry and rigid and may be removed from the boards for labeling and storing.

Dragonflies, damselflies, antlions, and a few other kinds of insects with long fragile abdomens are placed in cellophane envelopes to dry, with wings folded together over the body. In very humid areas, they must be dried in a paper triangle, which also serves to hold the parts in place. When dry, they are transferred to a transparent envelope held in shape by insertion of a 3 × 5 file card. The name of the insect as well as the collecting data may be typed on the card. Such envelopes may be

stored in file boxes, using standard index separators to label them by genus, family, and other taxa.

Cleaning the Specimens

Two things may happen to a specimen that will obscure characteristics needed for identification. It may become greasy because of the breakdown of body fats that then penetrate the integument and cover the body, or it may become dusty because left uncovered for a length of time. Dust may sometimes be blown off, but usually it sticks to the body surface, especially if the specimen is greasy. Other means are therefore needed to clean such specimens. Small, inexpensive ultrasonic cleaners similar to those used by jewelers are very useful for this purpose. The insect, still on its pin but with labels removed, is merely dipped into the water in the basin of the cleaner for several seconds until the dust or any other debris is loosened and floats away. Beetles that cover themselves with a layer of mud may also be cleaned by this method.

It may be necessary to use other methods to remove grease. Dietrich's modification of Barber's fluid is useful for this purpose. Specimens may be soaked in it until saturated, then placed in absolute alcohol, and finally into either xylene or ethyl ether. They must not be left too long in these solutions, and some experimentation may be necessary to find the best way to treat any particular group of insects. Once cleaned, the specimens will regain their flexibility and look very lifelike.

Labeling Specimens

Data labels (Fig. 52) are attached to the pin below the specimen or placed in the storage vials or storage envelopes. Their purpose is to let other collectors know the exact place the specimen was found and to associate the appropriate field data with it. Usually three labels are used: (1) a locality label, (2) an ecological label, and (3) an identification label.

Locality Label The locality label should record as much information in as much detail in as little space as possible. It must give the exact location at which the specimen was taken, usually in four printed lines and in the following order: (1) country; (2) state or province; (3)

Fig. 51. A spreading board illustrating the way to spread Lepidoptera and other insects.

Fig. 52. Sample of insect data labels (actual size).

county, or similar political subdivision or nearest permanent geographical feature (for example, river, mountain, etc.); (4) nearest permanently named population center with compass directions from this place (for example, 5 miles n.w., etc.). As shown by the following examples, the data need not be separated into four lines but should always be arranged for maximum compactness:

B.W.I., Grand Cayman Is.	U.S.A., Indiana
Boatswain Point	Tippecanoe Co.
Lime Tree Estate	Lafayette, 1 mile s.w.
	nr. Wabash River
U.S.A., Arizona	Ecuador, Guayas
Santa Cruz Co.	3 k s. Empalme
Pajarito Mts.	Grassy area nr.
Pena Blanca Canyon	stream

Some collectors add the latitude and longitude, taken from Geological Survey maps or by a sextant, to the labels. This will enable another collector to return to within a few feet of the exact spot the specimen was collected.

Ecological Data Label A second label is attached below the locality label (on pins, at a height regulated by the step block). This label is an abbreviated statement of the ecological features of the area in which the specimen was collected (as recorded in the field notebook). If a lot number system is used, the lot number is included. This label may also be divided into four lines: (1) the lot number, with subnumber if there is one; (2) the date; (3) the name of the collector; and (4) a simple statement about the habitat or conditions under which the specimen was taken. Blank spaces (indicated by the lines in the samples below) may be left for numbers and dates, which are added by hand, using India ink:

Lot. no. _____	Lot no. 938
June_____, 19___	June 23, 1968
T. P. Jones	T. P. Jones
At UV light	On oak leaves

The ecological data labels should also be as small as possible. They may be hand inked or printed. Custom printed labels are available from biological supply companies or directly from local printers if needed in large enough quantities to make them worthwhile (Fig. 53). The data may first be typed using a carbon ribbon. The printer will then make a plate, reducing the typewriter size to about one-third its original size. Printing should be done on a rag-content ledger paper. If the label is handwritten, use a No. 000 Rapidograph pen with India ink or any very fine dip pen; these may be obtained at art supply stores.

If the data recorded in the lot book are too extensive to put on these labels, as they usually are, then it is a good idea to compile summary sheets of localities and abstracted ecological data. These may be duplicated and deposited with specimens that are sent to other collections or loaned to specialists for study.

Fig. 53. Sample of ecological data labels (actual size).

Identification Label The third label—the identification label—is placed on the pin below the other two in such a way that it may be easily read. Ideally, every specimen should have one of these labels, but unless you are a specialist on the group, you will find it too time-consuming to write one for every specimen. Specialists often have identification labels printed in advance. Like the other labels, they usually consist of four lines:

1. The generic name spelled out, never just its initial even though use of it might save time and space
2. The specific name
3. The author's name (that is, the describer)
4. The name of the identifier

Sometimes the date (year) of the identification is included for historical reference, as testimony to the reliability of the name on the label. For example, if the identification was made before the publication of a monograph on the group, the name on the label might be a synonym of the name in current use.

ARRANGING AND STORING INSECT COLLECTIONS

Storage Containers

After specimens are mounted and labeled, they must be arranged and stored for ready access. Many beginners use cigar boxes for storage. These make excellent containers if a proper pinning bottom is provided and if they are kept fumigated. Although the bottom may be lined with corrugated cardboard, this is a temporary substitute for the almost universally used polyethylene sheets now available from supply companies. Styrofoam should not be used because the fumigant will melt it. Eventually, however, wooden insect boxes (Fig. 54) with tightly fitting covers or standard-size insect drawers (Fig. 55) will be needed for the safe storage of the collection. The system the collector chooses will depend upon one's budget. One should study supply company catalogs and select a standard system. The most elaborate system—that used by museums—consists of glass-topped drawers with pinning trays (Fig. 56) to hold the specimens of a single species (these trays come in a range of sizes).

Fig. 54. Standard-size wooden insect box. (*Courtesy of American Biological Supply Co.*)

Fig. 56. Assorted size trays for the Cornell drawer. (*Courtesy of American Biological Supply Co.*)

As additional species are incorporated into the collection, the trays may be moved without having to repin major portions of the collection as one is forced to do with insect boxes.

Fumigants

The collection must be fumigated from time to time to prevent pest invasion and destruction. Even though tightly covered boxes and drawers help prevent such destruction, chemical fumigants are still necessary. All boxes and drawers must be inspected at least once a year and the fumigant replaced as needed. Paradichlorobenzene (PDB) or a mixture of this with the naphthalene flakes commonly used as a clothes moth repellent has long been the standard fumigant. Since the former kills and the latter repells, a mixture of the two in equal parts is quite satisfactory. These fumigants must be packaged to prevent them from being able to move around when the box is moved and thus damage the specimens.

Arrangement Sequence

Specimens in a collection are usually arranged in a catalog sequence—order by order, family by family within each order, genus and species within each family, and so on. The order in which descriptions are given in this

book follows that of the latest catalogs. One should remember, however, that this order may change from time to time as new information becomes available. To keep it up to date requires continued rearranging of the collection.

A pair of pinning forceps (Fig. 57) is useful for safely moving specimens from place to place in boxes or trays. L-corks are used to hold pins with mounted specimens (Fig. 58) so that they may be examined with a hand lens or microscope. A lump of plasticine (Fig. 59) makes possible an even better adjustment of specimens. A pinhead may be inserted into the placticine on an L-cork so that its specimen may be exposed for ventral surface viewing.

Important as identifications are, it must be understood that not every insect can be identified to species, even by the most advanced insect taxonomists. As explained in the first chapter, there will always be some specimens that must be turned over to specialists for identification. Some insect groups are still so poorly known, however, that the species cannot be accurately identified by anyone. These groups are the ones that we say "need revision"; identification must wait until some researcher becomes sufficiently interested in them to make a special study.

CONTACTING SPECIALISTS FOR IDENTIFICATIONS

Before you contact a specialist, your specimens must be properly mounted, labeled, and sorted to groups. Specimens should never be sent to anyone without prior arrangements. A specialist cannot be expected to spend hours making identifications without expecting a profit from his work. He may use the data on the labels in future publications. It is customary for him to retain up to

Fig. 55. Standard-size drawer (Cornell University) for insect pining trays. (*Courtesy of American Biological Supply Co.*)

Fig. 57. Insect pinning forceps. (*Courtesy of BioQuip Products*)

Fig. 58. "L" cork used to hold pinned specimens in various positions for microscope examination.

50% of the specimens he identifies. He should always receive all specimens of a series. It is scientifically dishonest to retain part of a series thinking that they may be identified when the others are returned. Often a specialist can separate two or more species, and even genera, from a series that seems to be all one species. The following rules should be observed to the letter:

1. Do not assume that a specialist is desirous of more specimens for their own sake; usually he is interested only in establishing new records or additional species. The specialist is doing you a favor by spending valuable time to make identifications. At consultant wages, this could be very expensive. Therefore, a request for identification is equivalent to asking for a substantial donation.
2. Never ship specimens for identification without making prior, detailed arrangements with the specialist, including:
 (a) Return shipping costs
 (b) Time that specimens are to be returned
 (c) Specimens to be retained as identification fee
 (d) Disposition of type specimens
3. All specimens submitted for identification must be
 (a) Properly prepared and preserved.
 (b) Provided with exact locality data.
 (c) Sorted to group.
4. Never send bulk collections or unsorted collections with a request that the material be picked over to find things of interest.
5. Remember that a refusal to make identifications of large masses of material does not necessarily indicate a lack of interest, but sometimes just a lack of time or facilities.
6. Under certain circumstances a specialist may request a fee for providing an identification. This

practice has become nearly universal for court cases, commercial activities such as pest control operations, or environmental impact studies. Make sure that both you and the specialist agree upon the fee, if any, before the identifications are made.

MICROSCOPE SLIDES OF INSECTS AND INSECT PARTS

As your study of insects becomes more specialized, more refined techniques must be employed in examining the details needed for identifications. Dissections of genitalia, wings, legs, and mouthparts may be necessary. Permanent slides of these parts may be made and retained in the collection pertaining to the specimen. Each order of insects requires certain techniques that are peculiar to that group, and it must be treated accordingly. Slide making involves a variety of procedures, certain of which are basic to all groups. The materials needed for dissections are listed in Table 5.1.

Genitalia Slides

The most frequently dissected parts are those that comprise the genital or copulatory apparatus of both sexes. (Since the male structures tend to be the most varied, however, they are the ones most frequently used for identifications.) These dissections may involve not only the genitalia proper, but any segments of the abdomen that may be modified. Slides or other preparations should include all such parts. Several layers of sclerotized structures at the end of the abdomen are usually involved. Sometimes it is advantageous to dissect the membranes that hold these layers together and thus separate the individual segments, but this operation is not necessary if the genital tube can be drawn out to prevent the overlapping of parts. Associated with these hard parts are muscles and ducts. These softer parts are frequently destroyed in the preparation of a slide, resulting in the loss of features that might be useful in classification, particularly in the case of the female reproductive tract. Therefore, a preliminary study of the entire anatomy of the reproductive system of each group should be made to determine the features that might be useful.

Each specimen must be relaxed after its labels have been removed (these are saved, of course, and replaced on the pin after the dissection has been completed). The genitalia is removed either by pulling it out of the end of the abdomen or by cutting off the end entirely. Large specimens may be held between the thumb and forefinger under the low power of a binocular microscope or a magnifying glass and the genitalia extracted with dissecting needles made from finely ground insect pins.[1] Specimens too small to hold in the fingers must be dissected in a watch glass containing alcohol or distilled water. Before removing the structures from the abdo-

Fig. 59. "L" cork with plastocine to hold the insect pin.

[1]The pins are inserted into dissecting needle handles obtained from a commercially manufactured set, the heavy needles themselves being discarded. A small, fine-grain grinding stone must be placed on the stage of a binocular microscope. While keeping an eye on the tip of the pin, make continuous quarter turns to grind a fine point with square sides. Such a point will allow you to cut with the dissecting needle as well as tease away parts.

men, note and record their position *in situ*. Care must be taken not to cut or pierce the structures with the pin. Thoroughly relaxed specimens will be easy to handle. The genitalia will pull out to a position where they may be cut off with fine scissors or with a dissecting needle. Very small genitalia will prove troublesome to handle, however, and it may be necessary to devise special methods to remove them. Avoid using a pipette for parts handling because small parts tend to stick inside the tube. Number the specimen and the genitalia with the same number to keep them properly associated.

Treatment and Storage of Dissected Parts

Several dissections made at one time may be stored in separate watch glasses. The larger Syracuse watch glasses are satisfactory for moth dissections; parts from smaller insects should be dissected in the 28-mm diameter watch glass of the U.S. Department of Agriculture, Plant Quarantine (obtainable from commercial supply houses). If muscle and membrane obscure the details of the parts, they may be removed by soaking the genitalia at room temperature in a 5-percent solution of potassium hydroxide (KOH) or by heating in this solution. Heating will make it more concentrated, and it must be diluted.

To prevent damage, small, delicate structures should be soaked in cold KOH. If these small parts need to be stained, Gage's stain is recommended.[1] The parts are removed from the KOH first into distilled water and then into acid-alcohol (100 cc of 70-percent ethyl alcohol with 1 cc of concentrated hydrochloric acid added or three parts of 50-percent ethyl alcohol and one part of glacial acetic acid). This solution stops the action of the KOH and somewhat expands the structures. The parts are then removed to a watch glass containing diluted Gage's stain. If the specimens have not been completely neutralized, the Gage's stain will not take. Staining time varies from a few minutes to 12 hours, depending upon the structures to be stained. Washing in water will remove any excess stain. Dissection may take place either before or after staining, whichever is more convenient. Only those parts that cannot be easily seen need be separated by pulling out the tube. Preliminary sketches may be necessary for each step unless the structures are already well known. Sometimes it is an advantage to postpone dissecting until after the parts have been cleaned in xylene. These measures are determined only through practice.

After washing, place the parts in 95-percent alcohol (for very delicate specimens, a weaker alcohol may be necessary as a first step and higher concentrations worked up to in stages). The parts are then removed to carbo-xylene (one part of melted carbolic acid and three parts of xylene). This solution must be colorless, indicating

that it is dry. As water is absorbed by the solution, it turns red and must be discarded. If delicate specimens will not tolerate its violence, 100-percent (absolute) alcohol should be substituted. After the specimens have been dried by this treatment, place them in xylene. (If not completely dehydrated, they will turn milky and must be returned to the carbo-xylene or alcohol and again dehydrated.) After a few minutes in the xylene, they will be ready for mounting in Canada Balsam on a standard microscope slide. The length of time a specimen should be kept in each solution can be determined only by experience. In general, 5 minutes in each should be sufficient. Some indication of the action taking place can be determined by watching the convection currents. When these stop, the change is nearly complete. If there is little to prevent the solution's free penetration of the specimen, much less time will be necessary for each step. Sometimes it is necessary to puncture a specimen to get adequate penetration. Unless all water is removed, the specimen will be distorted and nearly useless. If all water has been removed, the xylene will "clear" the specimen and it will be sufficiently translucent for its parts to be easily seen.

Mounting Dissected Parts

It is best to center mounted specimens on the slide. To do so, first trace an outline of the slide on a 3 × 5 card and draw two diagonal lines from opposite corners of the outline. The slide must be protected with a coverslip to prevent dust from adhering to the sticky balsam. If desired, the coverslip may also be outlined on the card to help determine the amount of balsam that should be placed on the slide. (Never use too much.) After the parts have been placed in the balsam and properly oriented, dip the coverslip in xylene and wipe it off with a clean cloth. Then touch a drop of xylene to the under surface of the slip and place the slip over the balsam. The balsam should fill the entire area beneath the slip but not run out at the ends. If it doesn't flow to the edges of the slip, add a small amount of xylene to the edges with fine forceps. Usually this will cause the slip to press down on the balsam and make it fill the area. The slide may be dried on a warming plate.

If drawings are to be made of dissections, it may be well to leave the coverslip off the slide until after the drawings are completed, but it should be attached as soon as possible. The balsam may be softened with xylene at any time parts must be moved to make a structure visible.

Treatment of Immature Stages, Wings, and Other Small Parts

The procedures outlined above are the basic ones for making dissections and mounts of any insect part—mouthparts, legs, wings, immature stages, or whatever. If a structure is too thick for an ordinary balsam mount, it may be necessary to jack up the coverslip with small pieces of celluloid. These can be easily cut out and inserted in the balsam (usually arranged in the shape of a triangle) before the coverslip is added.

[1] Gage's stain:

Acid fuchsin	0.5 g
10-percent hydrochloric acid	25.0 cc
Distilled water	300.0 cc

Add 10 cc of concentrated HCL (s. g., 1.18) to 90 cc of distilled water, making a 10-percent solution. When stain is used, dilute this stock solution by adding one drop of stain to five drops of water.

Wing mounts can be simplified by placing the wings directly into 95-percent alcohol. Since they need a minimum of dehydrating, they should be moved into carboxylene and xylene before being mounted in balsam. Small wings with faint veins may be stained with eosin stain in water or alcohol. Beetle wings must be treated somewhat differently. Beetles fold their wings in particular patterns, many of which remain unknown. The wings should be kept in their original folded position. Sketches can be made of the fold as seen through the transparent wing. As they are unfolded in the alcohol wash, the direction of the fold should be noted. When finally unfolded, they should be mounted in the same manner as similar wings. Lepidoptera wings should be bleached in ammonium hydroxide to remove their color and scales so that their venation may be observed.

Special techniques have been developed for certain groups of insects using other mounting media. One of these—Hoyer's modification of Berlese's solution—is used for mosquito larvae and sometimes for large insect parts.[1] This solution dries slowly under the coverslip. Some entomologists leave the coverslip off until the specimen is dry and then place a slight amount of the solution on the slip. A faster method of mounting can be achieved by placing specimens directly into cellusol. After the specimen has been completely penetrated—which can take from 2 hours to overnight—it is removed from the cellusol and permanently mounted in euparal, as it would be in balsam. These substances can be obtained commercially.

The immature stages of most insects may be stored in fluid after they have been killed and fixed in KAAD (see previous discussion). Some small larvae however, may be studied more easily if mounted on slides. Each group requires special techniques even if the same materials are used.

PREPARING SPECIMENS FOR CHROMOSOME COUNTS

Since chromosome counts of insects are difficult to make, these data are available for relatively few species. However, they do provide useful information about the species of groups that are otherwise difficult to identify. Not all insects show meiotic patterns in their tissues as adults, meiosis having been completed during the pupal stage in both sexes. One group in particular, however, continues to exhibit meiosis as adults—the Coleoptera. Most male beetles, if not all, continue to exhibit spermatogenesis as adults. Their testes are easily located in the dorsum of the abdomen and make good chromosome smash slides.

Specimens to be used for chromosome counts should either be fixed immediately in the field or slides should be prepared directly from live material. Meiosis is known to cease shortly after a specimen has been disturbed. Live specimens should be fixed in the field in the following manner. Hold the specimen in one hand and raise its elytra with fine forceps so that a part of one side of the abdomen can be opened by pulling open the terga. Do not detach the abdomen if that can be avoided. Drop the specimen immediately into a vial containing the fixer. After about one to three hours, remove the specimen from the fixer and place it in 70-percent alcohol, making sure to label the storage vial.

Fixers may often be used several times. If Carnoy's A is decided upon, however, it must be mixed fresh each day.[2] Newcomer's Fixing Fluid will presumably keep indefinitely.[3]

If living insects are used to make chromosome counts, place them in water alive; if fixed specimens are used, place them in 70-percent alcohol. If the sex can be determined externally, open the dorsum of the abdomen of a male; if not, check the internal genitalia. The glistening silver bodies lying just beneath the dorsal surface are the testes. Remove them and tease them apart on a microscope slide to which a drop of Aceto-orcein stain has been added.[4]

As soon as the stain completely covers the testes, cover with a coverslip, place a piece of blotting paper or paper toweling over the slide, and press down and squash the testes. Make sure that the follicles burst open. In the meantime, preserve the specimen in alcohol so that it may be associated with the chromosome count slide. Next remove the blotting paper and, with forceps, lift the coverslip just enough to again flood the testes with stain. Heat the slide slightly for a moment over an alcohol flame to help the stain penetrate the cells. After about one-half hour of staining, remove the coverslip and place both slide and coverslip in absolute alcohol in a closed Petri dish for several minutes. When the slide is removed, any excess alcohol or stain should be wiped away from the area of the testes, a drop of euparal added, and the coverslip replaced. As soon as the euparal dries, the slide may be examined under the oil immersion lens of a microscope for suitable meiotic configurations to be drawn or photographed. Note that the cells are in various stages of division. First division cells are easier to count than second division cells because their chromo-

[1] Hoyer's modification of Berlese's solution:

Distilled water	50 g
Gum Arabic (clear)	30
Chloral hydrate	200
Glycerine	20

Mix materials at room temperature in the sequence listed. Allow to stand until clear. (Sometimes it is necessary to filter the solution.)

[2] Carnoy's A:

Glacial acetic acid	1 part
Absolute ethyl alcohol	3 parts

[3] Newcomer's Fixing Fluid:

Isopropyl alcohol	6 parts
Propionic acid	1 part
Ether (petroleum)	1 part
Acetone	1 part
Dioxane	1 part

[4] Aceto-orcein stain:

Orcein	1 to 2 g
Acetic acid	45 cc
Distilled water	55 ml

Add the orcein to hot acetic acid. When cool, add the distilled water and filter.

somes are larger. Examine several cells to verify the count and determine the chromosome morphology.

ILLUSTRATING SPECIMENS

Scientific illustration is a special field reserved for those capable of drawing well. The simpler techniques, however, can be mastered by almost anyone with brief instruction and a little practice. Drawings may be used (1) as a study aid, since if one must draw what is seen, more careful observations will have to be made; (2) for the preparation of reports of all types; and (3) as a teaching aid. Illustrating techniques are especially useful in entomology because of the small size of most insects. A number of books are available that treat basic drawing techniques in detail.

Several aids may be used when drawing directly from specimens under a microscope. Specimens mounted on microscope slides may be projected with a microslide projector. Their outlines may then be traced on paper and the details filled in after these have been studied under the microscope. Many drawings in this book were made by first photographing the specimen and then projecting the negative for an outline drawing that was completed by referring to the specimen under a microscope. Attaching a camera lucida to a microscope is a useful way to draw directly from the microscope. Ocular grids and quadrille paper also offer quick and cheap ways to make accurate outlines.

Although photographs of excellent quality may be made quite cheaply, they will never replace drawings as a means of illustrating insect parts. The small size of insects makes it impossible for photographs to reveal many anatomical details. Scanning-electron photomicrographs of surface structures, setae, and other features greatly enhance descriptions, however. These, of course, are available only at large research centers.

SUGGESTIONS FOR FURTHER STUDY

The Two Types of Scientific Observation

As generally understood, experimentation is the measurement of phenomena rates, that is, something is happening that can be measured. In experimentation, most of the factors affecting the course of the phenomenon are stabilized, and only one or a few of the nonstabilized ones need to be measured. Such is the method in physical, chemical, and most physiological experiments. Conversely, direct observation is a tabulation or record of phenomena as they occur unchanged in the field or the laboratory. Refined experimentation of all kinds is based first upon direct observations and second upon hypotheses drawn from these observations. Observations made in the field that do not involve experimentation are termed *anecdotical* because they can not be *repeated*, the crux of all experimental methods. An example of an anecdotical observation is given in the excerpt that follows:

Facts Vs Ideas in Observation[1]

The following examples illustrate two types of observation and reporting. The first example is direct and factual. The reporter draws no conclusions. His conclusions are reserved for the dis-

cussion to follow. His observations are not colored by ideas as to why the wasp does certain things. In the second example, the author adds conclusions which are not supported by observation, but which to the author seem to be the reasons behind these actions, or are based on facts and data not here given or referred to. These conclusions are underscored in the quotations.

Making such statements is a common procedure in biological writing. These statements are easily inserted and difficult to recognize. Many of them are passed on as factual and are often thought to be based on a series of observations and tests by subsequent writers using such information as textbook material. Actually much of our biological information is passed on from book to book, added to and changed by this writer and that until there is almost hopeless confusion in separating fact from ideas and errors.

"My friend John called me over to a nearby field one day to see an object that was an orange and black thing that looks like a wasp. It has a body about three-fourths of an inch long. It was carrying a caterpillar about an inch and a quarter long. He carried it for awhile and then stopped and started to dig. I suddenly realized that he was uncovering a hole *he had dug before*. He took rocks and dirt from the hole in the earth, and then he climbed in his hole and dragged the caterpillar in with him. Soon he came out and threw dirt in his hole and proceeded to pack it with his head. Then he picked up rocks in his mouth and put them in his hole and kept doing this 'til he ran out of dirt and then he started to dig with his front four feet until he got enough to fill the hole. Then he proceeded to fit rocks in his hole and what he didn't need he threw in the weeds and flew away."—Written by an eleven year old boy.

The following account is based on the description in *Social Life among the Insects* by William M. Wheeler and refers to a solitary digger wasp of the genus *Sphex*.

"After mating, the female digs a slanting or perpendicular tunnel in sandy soil and enlarges its lower end to form a chamber. This completed, she closes the entrance to the tunnel and flies into the air, circling over the burrow in what is called a "flight of orientation" or "locality study" *because it enables her to fix in her senses the exact position of the burrow in relation to the surroundings*. Now she goes off in search of her prey, which is a particular species of hairless caterpillar. When she finds one of these, she stings it, chews its neck, and sucks some of its blood without, however, killing it. Then she drags it to the entrance of her burrow. After opening up the entrance and a *preliminary inspection*, she takes the caterpillar down into the chamber and fastens a single egg to the surface of its skin, comes out and closes up the burrow, which she leaves, *never to return*. As soon as the next egg matures, she repeats the performance. The egg hatches into a larva, which, after eating the caterpillar, spins a cocoon, pupates, and emerges as an adult wasp."—From Mayor, *General Biology*, pp. 394–396, 1952, with permission of The Macmillan Co.

The first quotation comes from an inexperienced child; the second from a famous professor. The first is an exact account of an observation; The second is an annotated account of the same observation combined with explanations and suppositions. The first, given the proper setting, might be set up as an experiment. Observations made in the field are basically no different from those made in a laboratory since both fundamentally entail the gathering of data. Laboratory instruments may have greater sensitivity, but sensitive instruments may also be used in the field. Field observations of changing situations may be measured, and, if compared with similar observations made elsewhere, are in effect repeated, and therefore, repeatable. Careful plan-

[1]From Arnett, Ross H., Jr. 1955. *Principles of Biology*, Rochester: St. John Fisher College, pp. 2–3.

ning of field work is very necessary, however, if field observations are to yield data scientifically comparable to those acquired by laboratory experimentation. Field work involves open systems. Controls, one of the essential elements of experimentation, can be readily achieved by testing two noncommunicating natural systems with nearly identical characteristics. In field biology, we are usually concerned with natural populations. Testing two independent populations of the same, or presumed to be the same, species will therefore serve as the systems control, although it is preferable to test a larger number of such populations whenever possible. The experimental study of populations under these conditions can yield valuable systematic data.

A species cannot be fully understood without a detailed knowledge of its life system. Such a system encompasses a subject population and its total effective environment, that is, all those external agencies that influence the population, including man. The various genotypes of the individuals that make up the population, and the environmental influences they encounter determine the ultimate characteristics of the population, that is, its rates of birth, death, and dispersal. The systematist is interested in those aspects of population ecology that shed light on the origin and evolution of the species being investigated.

Keeping these principles in mind, the student of systematic entomology has several courses of action to follow. First, he may enlarge his collections through exchanges. Second, he may decide to conduct some original research.

ENLARGING A COLLECTION

Exchanges

As a collection grows, one needs to contact other collectors. Many entomological societies, both local and international, disseminate membership lists, newsletters, and other publications that are helpful to beginners as well as advanced students. (See the list of selected American societies at the end of this chapter.) One of the best ways to add more species to a collection is through exchanges of surplus specimens with members of these societies.

Shipping Specimens

Empty cigar boxes with polyethylene foam glued into the bottom make good containers for shipping very fragile specimens. Pin the specimens into the box, and fit a piece of corrugated cardboard snugly inside on top of the pins. Put a tab pull on the cardboard so that it may be easily removed. Then cover it with a loose layer of paper toweling or wads of newspaper so that everything will be held securely in place when the cover is closed. Wrap the box in paper, mark the top, and place it in a larger cardboard box with at least 4 inches of loose packing material around each side to act as a cushion. Tie the outer carton securely with string or seal it with strong tape. Usually, it is not necessary to wrap the outer box, but make sure that the mailing label and fragile labels show plainly. Dried insect specimens can be marked "Scientific Study Material" and qualify for a special reduced postal rate. Check with the post office for details.

Population Samples

Insects in a collection are representatives of the species and the various breeding (natural) populations that constitute the living components of each. An insect collection, then, provides a means of storing accurate information about the species. This information takes three forms: (1) The data that may be gathered from an examination of the specimens themselves (for example, morphological data); (2) the data recorded on the labels and in the lot record book; and (3) the data that may be deduced from the arrangement of the specimens in the collection, that is, from their classification.

The collector should pay particular attention to the relative efficiency of the various sampling methods since the value of a collection depends upon the care taken in collecting and recording the data. Each population sample should be separately stored and provided with the following notes:

1. The environmental situation at which the collection was made, including the date and time of day.
2. The method of collection
3. Locality data as detailed as possible (for possible repetition of field experiment)
4. The participants involved.

As the investigation proceeds, the collector should ask himself the following questions:

1. Is the collecting method likely to give a random sample or does it bias the data?
2. Is there any evidence to explain why the specimen captured happened to be in the habitat found?
3. Is there anything about the physiological structure or the behavior of the specimen that indicates the presence of adaptive structures or behavior of evolutionary significance?
4. If the species exhibits variation, is it a true sample of the variation, or is the collection biased toward a particular variation?
5. Is there any indication of evolutionary selection value in the variations?
6. What information does the specimen provide about the life system?

Specimens collected in the manner just described may be thought of as data files; in other words, they are collected not for their own sake as individual objects but as representatives of whole populations and species. As a species becomes better known, it becomes increasingly less necessary to store specimens for any other reason. Ideally, after species and variants have been cultured and made readily available for laboratory study and the data about them has been published in journals and books, specimen files become of less importance, except as a check on the literature. Most species, however, do not lend themselves to culturing; samples of these species must therefore be filed in museum collections.

New Storage Methods

The customary standard for storing insect collections requires that research specimens be pinned in insect trays, which are then arranged in drawers in pest-proof cabinets. New patterns of investigation, however, have brought about changes in this storage technique. Some of the basic classifications now being proposed (for example, the suborders and superfamilies of the Lepidoptera) require a knowledge of the internal anatomy of the species. Specimens have to be dissected in order to obtain this knowledge, and dried specimens are not easily dissected. The alternative is to store all but the smallest specimens in vials of alcohol; even the latter can be stored in small vials inside larger ones. Lepidoptera may be stored in alcohol (although this will make them more difficult to identify using current descriptions) or pinned; both methods are recommended when preparing research—as opposed to display—specimens of this order.

RESEARCH PROJECTS

The biggest difficulty in undertaking a research project is finding out what is already known. The great volume of scientific literature stored in specialized libraries throughout the world is hard to get at and explore. A considerable amount of training and experience is necessary, moreover, to make use of this knowledge. Otherwise, a so-called "research" project may be no more than a useless duplication of work already accomplished, particularly if it is in the field of insect taxonomy. (Only a very advanced and specialized amateur should attempt taxonomic research.) Nevertheless, before attempting any project, you should make a literature search, first by consulting the references given in this book and then by referring to the various abstracting journals and similar literature.

The possibility of discovering new information about the insects of the world is so great that only an enthusiastic interest and careful preparation are needed to contribute to the body of knowledge now available.

Two main approaches to insect research are categorized below, each with a list of possible projects:

I. Studies Requiring the Identification of Many Species (Taxonomic Studies):
 A. Ecological survey of:
 1. A single habitat
 2. Food chains
 3. Phytophagous insects on a particular plant
 4. Predators of phytophagous insects
 5. Pollinators
 6. Parasites of phytophagous insects
 7. Decomposers in a habitat
 B. Systematic survey of:
 8. A particular group (family, genus) of species in a particular area
 9. The species of a genus throughout the world, in a particular country, or in a particular biome
II. Studies Requiring the Identification of One or a Few Species Only (Morphological and Physiological Studies):

A. Population survey of:
 10. The range of a given species by season
 11. The crossbreeding of two or more populations of a species
 12. The fluctuation of population numbers from season to season
B. Life history studies of (rearing):
 13. A particular species
 14. Genetic variation
C. Morphology of:
 15. A particular species
 16. A particular part found in a genus, family, or order
D. Physiology of:
 17. A species
 18. A function
E. Behavior patterns of:
 19. A species
 20. A function

Note that some of these studies require extensive collecting; others, acute observation; and still others, critical experimentation and interpretation of results. The three prerequisites for all of them are as follows: (1) adequate background information, (2) limitation of the size of the project to what can be accomplished within a reasonable time, and (3) acquisition of tools and materials needed to do the work properly. Beginners who select too big a project and attempt to do it without the necessary background information can always expect less meaningful results. The tools and materials needed for most of these projects are simple and inexpensive, and their design and development are part of the fun.

REARING INSECTS

Much current research in entomology requires the culturing (rearing) of insect species to fill the many gaps in our knowledge of insect life systems, habits, and habitats. Although the life cycles of many species are known, those of most species have yet to be studied. A more thorough acquaintance with the immature stages would immensely help our understanding of the complexities of insect classification and might even lead to new methods of controlling some of the pest species. Each order section in Part II discusses a few techniques for rearing members of that order, particularly the raising of immature stages to the adult stage so that they may be better associated. Most of the rearing currently being done is confined to aquatic species, Lepidoptera, and parasitic Hymenoptera and Diptera.

Often no more rearing equipment is required than items that can be found around the home. Used jars and cans, flower pots, and plastic refrigerator dishes can all be useful. Herbivorous insects may be raised on covered potted plants, or on fresh leaves from a host plant. Insects dependent upon animal life are more difficult to rear, and the equipment required is correspondingly more elaborate. In all cases, a certain amount of improvisation will be necessary; one will have to develop one's own methods as circumstances dictate.

The increased interest in insect zoos, both public and private, has expanded the amount of information

available. Most keepers of public insect zoos are eager to share rearing experiences with visitors. No doubt, as techniques become better known, more literature on the subject will be published. The following generalizations should be thought of as pointers for getting started:

1. Detailed records should be kept; observations should be recorded daily. The length of time each stage lasts, the time of year changes of stage take place, and the times of moulting must all be noted.
2. Samples of each stage must be preserved and properly associated with the adults. Whenever there is any question about the identification of a species, separate rearings are in order. Obviously, individuals hatched from the eggs of a single female may be reared together (unless, of course, the species is cannibalistic).
3. Foliage feeders are usually reared on potted plants that are covered with netting or screening or in tin cans or glass jars that contain leaves taken from appropriate food plants.
4. Stem and root borers of herbaceous plants are best reared in the field but can be induced to infest potted plants. Field plants must be covered with netting to confine newly emerged adults.
5. Bark and wood boring insects are reared in the appropriate wood, cut to a convenient size and stored in a cardboard box. The box must be checked periodically (sometimes for a matter of years) for the emergence of adults.
6. Insects that live under loose, dead bark are often predators and prove more difficult to rear than borers. They should be isolated in the field with a food supply to maintain them until they transform. If they are reared in a terrarium, suitable prey must be collected to keep them alive.
7. Beetles and moths that infest stored products or seed are the easiest insects to rear. They must be kept in glass jars partly filled with the product or seed. Moisture and mold control must be maintained. Processed foods such as flour must usually be fortified with yeast or other vitamin-rich substances.
8. Soil-inhabiting insects may be reared in terraria or covered jars. Since many of them are predators, the soil used must contain sufficient micro-fauna to satisfy their nutritional requirements.
9. Predators are often the most difficult insects to rear because of the trouble in obtaining a proper food supply. A well-balanced terrarium might sustain them for a short while, but their voracious appetites will eventually require that additional food be added, either insects from other cultures or insects captured in the field. Some predators can be kept alive with bits of meat, but this method is usually not very successful.
10. Rearing parasitic insects presents the extreme example of complicated procedures. Most of them are so poorly known that it is necessary to experiment with each species to find a suitable rearing method. Since both the host and the

Fig. 60. A terrarium with details for construction: (A) assembled parts, and (B) details of corner pieces.

parasite have their own special needs, very few parasitic insects are kept in culture.
11. A basic rule in experimenting with rearing procedures is to simulate natural conditions as closely as possible. All factors controlling the life processes of a particular species must be kept in balance—food, water, temperature, and protection from mold, disease organisms, and predators. Light is a factor in determining the length of the life cycle of some species. Dormancy and the arousal from dormancy are necessary to many species in temperate climates. The more that is known about the life cycle of the species in the wild, the more the chance of success in rearing it in the laboratory.
12. A terrarium is a very useful apparatus for rearing and observing insects (Fig. 60). Glass aquaria may be used as terraria. Should a large number be needed, they can be built inexpensively of wood, glass, and a few pieces of bent tin. A convenient size (inside dimensions) is 19 in. long, 15 in. wide, and 17 in. high. The base is made of $\frac{3}{4}$-in. plywood, sanded all around. Four pieces of thin (20-gauge) galvanized iron about 14 in. long and $1\frac{1}{2}$ in. wide are bent at right angles down their middle, lengthwise, to form the angle-irons that support the glass walls at the four corners. The lower end of each angle iron is cut along the bend for a distance of $\frac{1}{2}$ in. so that the ends can be folded back at right angles and attached by nails to the corners of the plywood base (Fig. 60B). The glass walls rest on the bottom of the inside of the box, their lower edge held in place with a strip of wood. The angle-irons have slits at the top for a distance of 1 in., and a strip of metal about $\frac{1}{8}$ in. wide is removed along the slit. The ends thus formed are bent inward and over the glass walls to hold them securely in place at the top. The glass top rests at each corner on the folded-over ends of the angle-irons, leaving a little space for ventilation. The plywood portions are given two coats of black asphalt paint. It may be necessary to cover the top with gauze or screen if the occupants are particularly ac-

tive. A thin strip of vaseline around the top may also help keep the insects inside.

13. Plastic refrigerator dishes are particularly useful for rearing foliage-feeding larvae. Fresh food may be added frequently (usually daily) and any uneaten food removed.

14. It may be necessary to keep pupae out of doors during the winter to insure the proper tempera-

Table 5.2 Companies Offering Collecting Equipment, Supplies, Specimens, or Food

AMERICAN BIOLOGICAL SUPPLY CO. 1330 Dillon Heights Ave. Baltimore, MD 21228 (Entomological equipment)	BIO QUIP, INC. P.O. Box 61 Santa Monica, CA 90406 (Entomological equipment)
BIO-SERV, INC. 466 Prospect Ave. Little Silver, NJ 07739 (Insect food)	CAROLINA BIOLOGICAL SUPPLY CO. Burlington, NC 27215 (Live insects)
GENERAL BIOLOGICAL SUPPLY HOUSE, INC. 8200 South Hoyne Ave. Chicago, IL 60620 (Live insects)	INSECT CONTROL AND RESEARCH, INC. 1330 Dillon Heights Ave. Baltimore, MD 21228 (Live insects)
RINCON-VITOVA, INC. P.O. Box 475 Rialto, CA 92376 (Live predators)	SELPH'S CRICKET RANCH, INC. Box 2123 DeSoto Station Memphis, TN 38102 (Live crickets)
WARD'S NATURAL SCIENCE ESTABLISHMENT, INC. P.O. Box 1712 Rochester, NY 14603 (Entomological equipment)	CALIFORNIA GREEN LACEWINGS P.O. Box 2495 Merced, CA 95340 (Catalog available)
NATURAL PEST CONTROLS 9397 Premier Way Sacramento, CA 95826	BIOLOGICAL CONTROL SERVICES PROGRAM 3288 Meadowview Road Sacramento, CA 95832 (For list of suppliers of beneficial insects)

Table 5.3 Some American Entomological Societies

AMERICAN ENTOMOLOGICAL SOCIETY 1900 Race St. Philadelphia, PA 19103 (Publs: *Entomological News;* Transactions; Memoirs)	PACIFIC COAST ENTOMOLOGICAL SOCIETY California Academy of Sciences Golden Gate Park San Francisco, CA 94118 (Publ: *Pan-Pacific Entomologist*)
ENTOMOLOGICAL SOCIETY OF AMERICA 4603 Calvert Road College Park, MD 20740 (Publs: Bulletin; Annals; *Environmental Entomology; Journal of Economic Entomology;* Miscellaneous publications)	ENTOMOLOGICAL SOCIETY OF CANADA 1320 Carling Ave. Ottawa, ON KIZ 7K9, CANADA (Publs: Bulletin; *Canadian Entomologist;* Memoirs; Proceedings)
ENTOMOLOGICAL SOCIETY OF WASHINGTON Department of Entomology Smithsonian Institution Washington, DC 20560 (Publs: Proceedings; Memoirs)	FLORIDA ENTOMOLOGICAL SOCIETY P.O. Box 12425, University Station Gainesville, FL 32604 (Publ: *Florida Entomologist*)
KANSAS ENTOMOLOGICAL SOCIETY Department of Entomology Kansas State University Manhattan, KS 66506 (Publ: Journal)	NEW YORK ENTOMOLOGICAL SOCIETY c/o Waksman Institute of Microbiology Rutgers University New Brunswick, NJ 08903 (Publ: Journal)
CAMBRIDGE ENTOMOLOGICAL CLUB 19 Divinity Avenue Cambridge, MA 02138 (Publ: *Psyche*)	

Table 5.4 Some Antiquarian Book Dealers

BOOK DIVISION Bio Quip Products P.O. Box 61 Santa Monica, CA 90406	WELDON AND WESLEY, LTD. Lytton Lodge, Codicote, nr. Hitchin, Herts, SG4 8TE ENGLAND
BERNARD QUARITCH, LTD. 5-8 Lower John St. Golden Square London W1R 4AY, ENGLAND	E. W. CLASSEY LTD. P.O. Box 93 Faringdon, Oxon. SN77DR, England
RUDOLPH WM. SABBOT Natural History Books 5239 Tendilla Avenue Woodland Hills, CA 91364	SCIENCES NAT 2, rue Andre Mellenne Venette, 60200 Compiegne FRANCE FLORA AND FAUNA PUBLICATIONS 4300 NW 23rd Ave., Suite 100 Gainesville, FL 32606
JULIAN J. NADOLNY 121 Hickory Hill Road Kensington, CT 06037	

ture. Exposure to rain and snow may also be needed to maintain the proper moisture. If refrigerator space is available, it may be possible to keep them there, but the moisture must be controlled. Larvae often make a pupal cell in soil. After pupation is complete, the pupae may be removed from the soil and placed in sphagnum moss where they can be watched for emergence activity.

15. Care must be taken not to expose jars or cans to the direct rays of the sun because of the heat and moisture condensation these will cause.
16. Fungus (mold) is the worst enemy of laboratory reared-insects. Debris must be continually removed and the soil must be sterilized to prevent fungal spores.

Several commercial organizations supply food for rearing insects. Others supply living insects of certain species for rearing. The names of these organizations may be obtained from county extension agents or biological supply houses. A number of companies offering collecting equipment, supplies, specimens, or food are listed in Table 5.2.

SOURCES OF ENTOMOLOGICAL INFORMATION

Many major publishers in the United States, Canada, the United Kingdom, and Europe publish books and monographs on insects. Their names will be found in the various bibliographies throughout this volume. Some offer academic discounts for books purchased directly from them, provided they are ordered on institutional stationery.

Most entomological literature is published by entomological societies or by museums, universities, and similar research institutions. Throughout the world there are more than 100 entomological societies and over 260 serial publications devoted exclusively to entomology and many more that publish occasional entomological studies. A complete catalog of the societies and serial publications of the world can be found in the *Naturalists' Directory of Insects and Identifiers* (*International*), available in libraries or from the publisher. It should be noted that society addresses often change with the election of new officers. A list of selected American entomological societies appears in Table 5.3.

Used book dealers (more properly referred to, perhaps, as antiquarian book dealers) carry many items in stock and many of them will offer to search for publications upon request. A list of selected dealers appears in Table 5.4.

Only a few major libraries have first-rate collections of entomological books, journals, and separates. Among these are those located in the following cities, either at museums or universities, or, less often, in public facilities:

Cambridge, MA: Harvard University
New Haven, CT: Yale University
New York, NY: American Museum of Natural History
Ithaca, NY: Cornell University
Philadelphia, PA: Philadelphia Academy of Natural Sciences
Beltsville, MD: United States Department of Agriculture
Washington, DC: Smithsonian Institution
Raleigh, NC: North Carolina State University
Gainesville, FL: Florida State Collection of Arthropods
Chicago, IL: Field Museum of Natural History
Columbus, OH: Ohio State University
Lawrence, KS: University of Kansas
Austin, TX: University of Texas
Seattle, WA: University of Washington
San Francisco, CA: California Academy of Sciences
Berkeley, CA: University of California
Los Angeles, CA: University of California

BIBLIOGRAPHY

Arnett, Ross H., Jr. 1947. A technique for staining, dissecting, and mounting the male genitalia of beetles. *Coleopt. Bull.*, 1: 63–66, illus.

Arnett, Ross H., Jr. 1969. Storage and retrieval of information from insect specimens. *Entom. News*, 80: 197–205.

Arnett, Ross H., Jr. 1970. *Entomological information storage and retrieval.* Gainesville, FL: Flora and Fauna Publications, xiii + 210 pp.

Humason, G. L. 1962. *Animal tissue techniques.* San Francisco: W. H. Freeman Co., xv + 468 pp.

Lutz, Frank E., *et al.* 1937. *Culture methods for invertebrate animals.* New York: Dover Publ., Inc. xxxii + 590 pp.

Martin, J. E. H. 1977. *The insects and arachnids of Canada. Collecting, preparing, and preserving insects, mites, and spiders,* part 1. Publ. 1643, Canada Department of Agriculture, 182 pp.

Oldroyd, H. 1958. *Collecting, preserving, and studying insects.* London: Hutchinson and Co., Ltd., 327 pp.

Papp, C. S. 1963. *An introduction to scientific illustration.* Published by author: Riverside, Calif., 212 pp.

Peterson, A. 1955. *A manual of entomological techniques.* Published by author: Columbus, Ohio, v + 367 pp.

Southwood, T. R. E. 1966. *Ecological methods with particular reference to the study of insect populations.* London: Methuen and Co., Ltd., xviii + 391 pp.

Zweifel, F. W. 1961. *A handbook of biological illustrations.* Phoenix Science Series, PSS 510, xv + 131 pp.

6
The Orders of Insects

The classification of insect orders used in this book is given in Table 6.1. Compiled from several sources, it is believed to be an arrangement generally acceptable today. The accompanying technical Key to the Orders has been used by students for many years. So far as is known, this key will "work" for any insect on earth. For those just beginning, however, some time-saving hints for a "spot" (or sight) identification of the orders are listed below. They are based on the characteristics of *the adults only*.

If an insect is or has:

1. Four large wings covered with minute, dustlike scales, see Order No. 27, LEPIDOPTERA (butterflies, skippers, and moths).
2. (a) Front wings that are hardened instead of transparent and that form a cover for the transparent hind wings and (b) an abdomen without large terminal forceps, see Order No. 24, COLEOPTERA (beetles and weevils).
3. Similar to above, but (a) the wing covers are short and (b) the abdomen exhibits forceps, see Order No. 13, DERMAPTERA (earwigs). (If lacking forceps, it is probably a staphylinid beetle.)
4. Similar to 2 above, but (a) the apical half of the front wing is more or less transparent, or at least thinner, and exhibits veins, and (b) there are sucking mouthparts, see Order No. 20, HEMIPTERA (true bugs).
5. (a) Only two flying wings, both transparent with conspicuous veins (and possibly colored markings), and (b) abdomen without long apical filaments, see Order No. 29, DIPTERA (flies).
6. Four more or less transparent wings, but front wings somewhat thickened, and:
 (a) Hind wings that fold fanlike and hind legs that are enlarged for jumping, see Order No. 11, ORTHOPTERA (grasshoppers and crickets).
 (b) Similar to (a), but with large front legs for grasping prey instead of jumping hind legs,

see Order No. 14, DICTYOPTERA (praying mantids).
 (c) Similar to (a), but no enlarged legs, a flattened body, and long antennae, see Order No. 14, DICTYOPTERA (cockroaches).
 (d) Similar to (a), but body greatly elongate, resembling a stick, and legs not enlarged, see Order No. 10, PHASMATODEA (walkingsticks).
7. Four transparent wings of the same texture and:
 (a) All four similar, held out horizontally to the sides, and incapable of being folded back over the long, thin abdomen, see Order No. 7, ODONATA (dragonflies).
 (b) All four similar, held vertically over long, thin abdomen, but since the thorax is angled backward, wings appear to fold over abdomen, see Order No. 7, ODONATA (damselflies).
 (c) Front wings much larger than hind wings and held vertically over an abdomen that has two or three very long terminal filaments, see Order No. 6, EPHEMEROPTERA (mayflies).
 (d) Similar to (c), except that wings are held horizontally and close over an abdomen that lacks abdominal filaments; leg bases are close together, see Order No. 23, NEUROPTERA (antlions, lacewings, dobsonflies, and so on).
 (e) Similar to (d), except for the presence of two or three short terminal filaments and widely separated leg bases, see Order No. 8, PLECOPTERA (stoneflies).
 (f) Hind wings considerably smaller than front wings, with few cross veins and not held rooflike over abdomen; mouthparts not piercing (but possibly elongate, for sucking); head loosely joined to thorax, see Order No. 25, HYMENOPTERA (wasps, ants, and bees).
 (g) Wings held rooflike over the abdomen; head

Table 6.1 Insect Orders

Superclass HEXAPODA		
Extant Orders	**Common Names of Orders**	**Extinct Orders**

Class ENTOGNATHA

1. Collembola	*Springtails*	
2. Protura	*Proturans*	
3. Entotrophi	*Entotrophs*	

Class INSECTA

Subclass *Archaeognatha*

4. Microcoryphia	*Bristletails*	"Monura"

Subclass *Dicondylia*
 Superorder *Thysanura*

5. Thysanura	*Silverfish and allies*	

 Superorder *Pterygota*

 Division *Palaeoptera*

6. Ephemeroptera	*Mayflies*	Paleodictyoptera
7. Odonata	*Dragonflies, damselflies*	Megasecoptera
		Diaphanopterodea

 Division *Neoptera* (Protodonata)

 Subdivision *Polyneoptera*

8. Plecoptera	*Stoneflies*	
9. Embioptera	*Webspinners*	
10. Phasmatodea	*Walkingsticks*	Protorthoptera
11. Orthoptera	*Grasshoppers, katydids, crickets*	Miomoptera
		Caloneurodea
12. Grylloblattodea	*Grylloblattids*	
13. Dermaptera	*Earwigs*	
14. Dictyoptera	*Mantids, cockroaches*	Protelytroptera
15. Isoptera	*Termites*	

 Subdivision *Paraneoptera*

16. Zoraptera	*Angel Insects*	

 Subdivision *Acercaria*

 Section *Psocodea*

17. Psocoptera	*Barklice and booklice*	
18. Mallophaga	*Chewing lice*	
19. Anoplura	*Sucking lice*	

 Section *Condylognatha*

20. Hemiptera	*Bugs*	
21. Homoptera	*Cicadas, hoppers, whiteflies, aphids, scales*	
22. Thysanoptera	*Thrips*	

 Subdivision *Holometabola*

 Section *Neuropterida* — Glosselytrodea

23. Neuroptera	*Fishflies, lacewings, snakeflies, antlions*	
24. Coleoptera	*Beetles, weevils, stylopids*	

 Section *Panorpida*

25. Hymenoptera	*Wasps, ants, bees*	

 Subsection *Amphiesmenoptera*

26. Trichoptera	*Caddisflies*	
27. Lepidoptera	*Moths, skippers, butterflies*	

 Subsection *Antliophora*

28. Mecoptera	*Scorpionflies and allies*	
29. Diptera	*Flies, keds*	
30. Siphonaptera	*Fleas*	

large and closely compressed to the thorax; sucking–piercing mouthparts, see Order No. 21, HOMOPTERA (cicadas, aphids, scale insects, and so on).

(h) Head prolonged into a beak, but with chewing-type mouthparts, see Order No. 28, MECOPTERA (scorpionflies and allies).

8. Wings other than those found in preceding orders, see orders with sucking mouthparts or under 7 mm (about ¼ in.) in length.

(a) Wings with fringes of long hairlike setae; sucking mouthparts; very small (length, usually 0.5–2.0 mm), see Order No. 22, THYSANOPTERA (thrips).

(b) Wings similar, with few veins, deciduous, and present only while swarming (otherwise wingless); mouthparts for chewing; length, 3–10 mm, but usually under 7 mm (except for wingless queen), see Order No. 15, ISOPTERA (termites).

(c) Length under 3 mm, see illustrations of Order No. 16 ZORAPTERA (zorapterans).

(d) Length under 5 mm, see illustrations of Order No. 17, PSOCOPTERA (barklice).

(e) Length under 7 mm, see illustrations of Order No. 9, EMBIOPTERA (webspinners).

(f) Wing surface with fine hairlike setae; long antennae; similar to moths, see Order No. 26, TRICHOPTERA (caddisflies).

9. Wingless as adult, but with a distinctive shape: if 0.5–6 mm in length and the mouthparts are chewing, see Order No. 18, MALLOPHAGA, chewing lice; if mouthparts are sucking, see Order No. 19, ANOPLURA (sucking lice); if compressed (flattened side-to-side), with jumping hind legs, see Order No. 30, SIPHONOPTERA (fleas). (*Note:* Certain members of other orders are also wingless as adults but almost always

their shape is similar to that of the winged species, for example, bedbugs, sheep keds, etc.)

(a) Usually with scales and long abdominal filaments and usually over 7 mm in length, see Order No. 4, MICROCORYPHIA (bristletails) and Order No. 5, THYSANURA (silverfish and allies).

(b) Usually without scales; usually with abdominal jumping apparatus; length usually 1–3 mm but usually under 7 mm, see Order No. 1, COLLEMBOLA (springtails).

(c) Very small and slender, length 0.6–1.5 mm, see Order No. 2, PROTURA (proturans).

(d) Long and slender, length under 7 mm; two abdominal filaments or forceps, see Order No. 3, ENTOTROPHI (entotrophs).

(e) Length 15–30 mm, found only in n.w. U.S. and Canada in mountains, see Order No. 12, GRYLLOBLATTODEA (rock crawlers).

10. Ectoparasitic habits, length never over 10 mm, rarely over 6 mm, and:

(a) Flattened side-to-side (compressed), with jumping hind legs, see Order No. 30, SIPHONAPTERA (fleas).

(b) Flattened top-to-bottom (depressed); ectoparasites of birds and some mammals, see Order No. 18, MALLOPHAGA (chewing lice).

(c) Flattened; ectoparasites of mammals, see Order No. 19, ANOPLURA (sucking lice).

BIBLIOGRAPHY

Henning, Willi 1981. *Insect phylogeny.* New York: John Wiley and Sons, xxii + 514 pp.

Kristensen, Niels P. 1981. Phylogeny of insect orders. *Ann. Rev. Ent.* 26: 133 157.

Wootton, Robin J 1981. Palaeozoic insects. *Ann. Rev. Ent.* 26:319–344.

Key to the Extant and Extinct Orders of Insects

A. *Adults and Immatures*

1.	Wings entirely absent externally or represented at most by immovable external wing pads (immatures of all insects and some adults) .	*2*
	At least one pair of wings present, movable upon the thorax, usually with at least one vein and a distinct membrane; mesothoracic wing often greatly modified to form veinless *elytron* (adults of the majority of insects; subimago of Ephemeroptera) .	*43*
2(1).	External wing pads present, at least as caudolateral prolongations of mesonotum or metanotum or both; appendages usually well developed	*3*
	No indication of external wing pads; appendages conspicuous, reduced or completely absent .	*5*
3(2).	External genitalia developed as articulating lobes, processes, or rods surrounding the reproductive opening or withdrawn into a genital pouch (adults of some Holometabola and a few Acercaria) .	*24*
	External genitalia developed at most as broad, thick, nonarticulating lobes; reproductive opening absent (immatures) .	*4*
4(3).	Anal and mouth openings absent; body more or less mummylike; appendages included in sheaths, usually nonfunctional; adult structures often visible under the external covering; wing pads often extending to ventral surface (pupae of Holometabola and some Acercaria) .	*KEY C*

A. *Adults and Immatures (Contd.)*

Anal and mouth openings present; body not mummylike; appendages free and functional; wing pads always dorsal or dorsolateral (naiads and nymphs of Polyneoptera and Acercaria) .. **21**

5(2). Mouthparts composed of greatly elongated bristles held in a long or short, usually segmented beak or coiled within body when retracted; body may be covered by scalelike waxy secretion or woolly material (scale insects, aphids, and other homopterous forms) **21. HOMOPTERA**

Mouthparts never in the form of elongated bristles that are either coiled in body or held in a segmented beak (shorter than bristles); body seldom covered by waxy or woolly secretions **6**

6(5). Thoracic legs entirely absent **7**

Thoracic legs present at least as paired lobes **9**

7(6). Several sclerotized abdominal sternites with median unpaired or paired birth pores; body surrounded by unsclerotized exuviae (females of the majority of stylopids) **24. COLEOPTERA**

Abdomen without such birth pores; body may be covered by larval exuviae but these are usually at least partially sclerotized **8**

8(7). Body completely covered by distinctly segmented, shell-like, uniformly sclerotized and pigmented cuticle (larval exuviae); no indication of functional mouthparts, mouth, or anus, or developing adult within (puparia of flies) *KEY C*

Body with at least some membranous areas; mouthparts fully exposed, partially withdrawn or reduced; mouth and anus usually functional (larvae and larviform females of Holometabola) .. *KEY B*

9(6). Body caterpillarlike, usually cylindrical; abdomen with paired, ventrolateral short stubby "prolegs" on some or majority of segments (larvae of some Holometabola) *KEY B*

Body not caterpillarlike; abdomen without paired, ventrolateral "prolegs" but sometimes with small appendages on proximal segments, or large ones laterally or distally ... **10**

10(9). Venter of abdomen with appendages present on at least some of the first 6 segments; mandibulate mouthparts more or less retracted into head; only their tips visible in some forms (Entognatha and Archaeognatha) **18**

Venter of abdomen without appendages on proximal segments; if mouthparts are mandibulate, they are fully exposed and not retracted into head; haustellate mouthparts may be retracted **11**

11(10). Body mummylike; appendages included in sheaths, nonfunctional, usually appressed (pupae of wingless Holometabola) *KEY C*

Body not mummylike; appendages free and usually projecting from body **12**

12(11). Antennae with at least 7 distinct segments, usually long and conspicuous **24**

Antennae with at most 5 distinct segments, often short or partially hidden in recess of head but sometimes exposed, long, and bristlelike **13**

13(12). All tarsi with 5 distinct tarsomeres **14**

No tarsus with more than 4 tarsomeres **16**

14(13). Mouthparts mandibulate (females of stylopids) **24. COLEOPTERA**

Mouthparts haustellate .. **15**

15(14). Metathorax well developed; metapleuron greatly expanded; legs fitted for jumping and body strongly compressed, that is, flattened from side to side (fleas) **30. SIPHONAPTERA**

Metathorax greatly reduced; metapleuron very short; body rarely moderately compressed (wingless flies) **29. DIPTERA**

16(13). Body louselike, small and depressed (flattened dorsoventrally); legs modified for clinging to hairs or feathers; specialized claw and processes of tibia or tarsus; ectoparasites of warmblooded vertebrates in all stages (lice) **17**

Body not louselike, extremely varied in form; legs not modified for clinging to hairs or feathers; rarely ectoparasites on warmblooded vertebrates (larvae and larviform females of Holometabola) *KEY B*

17(16). Sucking mouthparts; claws large **19. ANOPLURA**

Chewing mouthparts; claws small **18. MALLOPHAGA**

18(10). Antenna not developed as such; first 3 abdominal segments with nonsegmented or 2-segmented small ventral appendages (proturans) **2. PROTURA**

Antenna conspicuous; abdominal appendages otherwise **19**

19(18). Six or fewer abdominal segments, with segmentation often indistinct; first abdominal segment always with a forked or simple sucker midventrally, 3rd with or without a catch mechanism, 4th and 5th with or without a spring (springtails) ... **24. COLLEMBOLA**

A. *Adults and Immatures* (*Contd.*)

Ten to 12 distinct abdominal segments; proximal to 7th segment with small styli; no sucker, catch, or spring apparatus **20**

20(19). Abdomen ending in at least 1 median and 2 lateral many-segmented appendages; body usually covered with small scales; mouthparts with tips exposed (silverfish, bristletails) **4. MICROCORYPHIA** and **5. THYSANURA**

Abdomen without median caudal appendage and with or without lateral caudal appendages; body never scaly; mouthparts completely withdrawn into head except for palpi (japygids, compodeids) **3. ENTOTROPHI**

21(4). Labium greatly elongated, hinged transversely and folded as a mask hiding remaining mouthparts (naiads of dragonflies and damselflies) **7. ODONATA**

Labium without median transverse hinge and not folded as a mask over remaining mouthparts ... **22**

22(21). Tracheal gills in the form of platelike, featherlike, fingerlike, or simple processes present on abdomen, thorax, or head **23**

Tracheal gills entirely absent ... **24**

23(22). Tarsi with one claw each; tracheal gills on lateral margins of abdominal tergites only; wing pads usually very conspicuous; usually 3 long terminal processes on abdomen (naiads of mayflies) **6. EPHEMEROPTERA**

Tarsi with 2 claws each; tracheal gills usually on the venter of thorax or on base of mouthparts, legs, or on last segment of abdomen; wing pads usually very inconspicuous, developed merely as caudolateral expansions of metanotum and mesonotum (naiads of stoneflies) **8. PLECOPTERA**

24(22), Mouthparts mandibulate, frequently atrophied but, in that case, segmented palps
(12), distinct ... **25**
(3). Mouthparts haustellate, frequently hidden but, in that case, palps, if present, not segmented .. **40**

25(24). Abdomen *either* strongly constricted at its base and joining the thorax by a narrow stalk (petiole) *or* with a deep dorsal excision so that it joins the thorax by a thin but wide connection (ants, velvet ants, and other wingless forms) **25. HYMENOPTERA**

Abdomen broadly joined to thorax both horizontally and vertically **26**

26(25). Head capsule hypognathous, produced into a long ventral snout with mouthparts at its tip and back (wingless scorpionflies) **28. MECOPTERA**

Head capsule not produced into a long ventral snout **27**

27(26). Basal tarsomere of front tarsus enlarged and greatly swollen (embiids, webspinners) ... **9. EMBIOPTERA**

Basal tarsomere of front tarsus not greatly swollen, although it may be elongate **28**

28(27). Tarsi with 5 distinct tarsomeres ... **29**

Tarsi with 4 tarsomeres or less .. **31**

29(28). Pronotum very short, inconspicuous, and much shorter on middorsal line than mesonotum (some caddisflies) **26. TRICHOPTERA**

Pronotum well developed, conspicuous, and usually at least as long on middorsal line as mesonotum ... **30**

30(29). Cercus present, segmented or unsegmented **35**

Cercus absent (some beetles with reduced elytra and hind wings, beaver parasite) ... **24. COLEOPTERA**

31(28). Cercus absent; pronotum usually much shorter than mesonotum or middorsal line (barklice, booklice, psocids) **17. PSOCOPTERA**

Cercus present; pronotum longer than mesonotum on middorsal line **32**

32(31). Compound eye absent or greatly reduced in size and number of facets; thorax and abdomen often very soft and unpigmented; if well pigmented, then stubs of broken wings present or head extremely large **33**

Compound eye always present, with numerous and well developed facets; body usually at least well pigmented and without stubs of broken wings **37**

33(32). Tarsi with 4 tarsomeres (basal tarsomere may be partially subdivided ventrally); cercus usually segmented; if nonsegmented, then short and without an apical bristlelike appendage (termites, white ants) **15. ISOPTERA**

Tarsi with 2 or 3 tarsomeres; cercus nonsegmented and either long and incurved apically or short and with an apical bristlelike appendage **34**

34(33). Tarsi with 2 tarsomeres; cercus short and with a conspicuous bristlelike appendage apically (zorapterans) **16. ZORAPTERA**

Tarsi with 3 tarsomeres; cercus long and forcepslike; its apex incurved and without bristlelike appendage (earwigs) **13. DERMAPTERA**

A. *Adults and Immatures (Contd.)*

35(30). Body elongate with cylindrical thorax; prothoracic legs not raptorial; head prognathous or hypognathous, never covered by pronotum; coxal not enlarged .. 36

Body ovate and usually strongly depressed, but if elongate, front legs raptorial; head opisthognathous and usually covered by pronotum; coxal very large ...
.. **14. DICTYOPTERA**

36(35). Cercus long and 8- or 9-segmented; body ± 25 mm in length
.................................... **12. GRYLLOBLATTODEA**

Cercus short and unsegmented; body usually more than 25 mm in length
... **10. PHASMATODEA**

37(32). Either hind femur elongated and thickened for jumping, or front leg or all legs thickened and flattened and provided with processes for digging, or front legs distinctly different in form from the others; tarsi with 3 or 4 tarsomeres, rarely with 5 or 2 (grasshoppers, cave crickets, etc.) **11. ORTHOPTERA**

None of the legs modified for jumping or digging and all essentially the same in form; tarsi always with 3 tarsomeres 38

38(37). Cercus many-segmented and usually very long (stoneflies, some naiads, and some adults) .. **8. PLECOPTERA**

Cercus nonsegmented and usually incurved apically 39

39(38). Cercus long and usually strongly sclerotized and polished (earwigs)
... **13. DERMAPTERA**

Cercus short and inconspicuous, not heavily sclerotized or polished (timemas) .
... **10. PHASMATODEA**

40(24). Mouthparts in the form of a proboscis coiled under head; body densely covered with overlapping scales (females of some moths) **27. LEPIDOPTERA**

Mouthparts not in the form of a coiled proboscis; body rarely covered with small, nonoverlapping scales .. 41

41(40). Last tarsomere (pretarsus) swollen, bladderlike, or hooflike, without strong sclerotized claws; mouthparts an asymmetrical cone (thrips)
.. **22. THYSANOPTERA**

Last tarsomere (pretarsus) not bladderlike, with distinct claws 42

42(41). Pronotum distinct, well developed, and usually at least as long as mesonotum middorsally; mouthparts usually composed of elongated bristles held in a segmented beak; palpus absent (nymphs and some brachypterons and apterous bugs) ...
... **20. HEMIPTERA**

Pronotum very short, usually not visible dorsally and much shorter than mesonotum middorsally; mouthparts enclosed in a nonsegmented beak; palpus present (wingless flies, louseflies) **29. DIPTERA**

43(1). Mesothoracic wing reduced to club- or paddle-shaped knob projecting out from body; metathoracic wing extremely broad and radially folded; metanotum extremely developed (males of stylopids) **24. COLEOPTERA**

Mesothoracic wings not reduced to club- or paddle-shaped knobs that project out from body; metathoracic wing otherwise developed; metathorax may be enlarged but never as much as in preceding case 44

44(43). Mesothoracic wing horny, leathery, or parchmentlike, at least at base, and distinctly different in texture of membrane from the metathoracic wing when latter is present (care must be exercised in intrepreting, as coloration and vestiture may obscure the texture) 45

Mesothoracic wing not horny, leathery, or parchmentlike, usually membranous and transparent, but may be covered with scales or hairlike setae or pigmented; always essentially similar in texture of membrane to metathoracic wing when latter is present 49

45(44). Mesothoracic wing without distinct veins, sometimes greatly reduced in length or fused with its mate along straight line middorsally over the abdomen; metathoracic wing, when present, folded transversely or radially and usually tucked under mesothoracic wing in repose 46

Mesothoracic wing with definite veins, often reduced in size but never fused; metathoracic wing, when present, usually folded longitudinally 47

46(45). Cercus present, developed as long movable forcepslike appendage; metathoracic wing folded radially (earwigs) **13. DERMAPTERA**

Cercus absent; metathoracic wing, when present, folded transversely (beetles) ..
... **24. COLEOPTERA**

47(45). Mouthparts haustellate, composed of greatly elongate bristles enclosed in a jointed labium (true bugs) **20. HEMIPTERA**

Mouthparts mandibulate .. 48

48(47). Meso- and metathoracic wings similar in length and width and neither folded in vannal area (termites, white ants) **15. ISOPTERA**

A. *Adults and Immatures (Contd.)*

Metathoracic wing usually very different in form from mesothoracic, with a broad, longitudinally folding vannal area (grasshoppers, crickets)
.. **11. ORTHOPTERA**

49(44). Only mesothoracic wings fully developed; metathoracic sometimes present as stubs or completely absent ... **50**
Both mesothoracic and metathoracic wings present, although latter sometimes considerably reduced ... **52**

50(49). Pronotum greatly reduced, usually invisible from above, and at most represented by a narrow transverse necklike area; mouthparts haustellate, enclosed in a non-segmented labium or greatly reduced; abdomen without apical processes (two-winged flies) .. **29. DIPTERA**
Pronotum well developed and conspicuous dorsally; mouthparts always reduced; abdomen with apical process or long filaments **51**

51(50). Mesothoracic wing with many longitudinal and cross veins; apex of abdomen with a pair of long, many-segmented filaments (some mayflies)
...................................... **6. EPHEMEROPTERA**
Mesothoracic wing with only one or two veins; apex of abdomen with a single median or a pair of lateral unsegmented processes (males of scale insects) ...
...................................... **21. HOMOPTERA**

52(49). Wings entirely or largely covered with overlapping scales; body covered with similar or greatly elongated scales; mouthparts usually a proboscis coiled under head, sometimes reduced (butterflies, skippers, and moths)
...................................... **27. LEPIDOPTERA**
Wings and body not covered with overlapping scales but sometimes with long hairlike setae or patches of nonoverlapping scales; mouthparts never in form of coiled proboscis ... **53**

53(52). Both pairs of wings long and narrow and quite thick, with 1 or 2 veins or none, and with long marginal fringes of hairlike setae; tarsi ending in a bladder and without conspicuous sclerotized claws; mouthparts an asymmetrical cone (thrips)
...................................... **22. THYSANOPTERA**
Without such a combination of characteristics; wings sometimes as above but tarsi do not end in a bladder ... **54**

54(53). Mouthparts haustellate, composed of elongate bristles enclosed in a segmented labium; palps absent (true bugs, aphids, cicadas, leafhoppers, etc.) **55**
Mouthparts mandibulate or greatly reduced and not enclosed in a jointed labium **56**

55(54). Mouthparts originating from anterior of head **20. HEMIPTERA**
Mouthparts originating from posterior of head **21. HOMOPTERA**

56(54). Antenna short, inconspicuous, bristlelike; wings incapable of being flexed flat over abdomen and normally held vertically above the body or stretched out horizontally (Paleoptera) ... **57**
Antenna usually long and conspicuous, never bristlelike; wings normally capable of being flexed over or against the abdomen **58**

57(56). Meso- and metapleural sutures running caudodorsad from base of leg (reverse of normal); pronotum greatly reduced, forming a narrow transverse necklike part; wings with a *nodus*, an emargination and thickening at the middle of the anterior margin; metathoracic wing as large or larger than mesothoracic; legs with conspicuous rows of stiff erect spines (dragonflies and damselflies)
...................................... **7. ODONATA**
Meso- and metapleural sutures running cephalodorsad from base of leg (normal); pronotum well developed; wings without a nodus; metathoracic wing much smaller than mesothoracic; legs without conspicuous rows of spines (mayflies)
...................................... **6. EPHEMEROPTERA**

58(56). Wings net-veined with many longitudinal veins and at least 12 cross veins **59**
Wings not net-veined or veinless; few longitudinal veins and usually less than 12 cross veins ... **64**

59(58). Head produced into a long ventral snout with mandibulate mouthparts at its apex; males sometimes with conspicuous genitalia folded forward over the abdomen (scorpionflies) **28. MECOPTERA**
Head normal, or if hypognathus, then mandibles arise near the compound eyes .. **60**

60(59). Cercus absent (dobson flies, snakeflies, lacewings, antlions, etc.)
...................................... **23. NEUROPTERA**
Cercus present ... **61**

61(60). All tarsi with 5 distinct tarsomeres (preying mantids, cockroaches)
...................................... **14. DICTYOPTERA**
All tarsi with apparently 4 tarsomeres or less **62**

62(61). Mesothoracic and metathoracic wings long and narrow and approximately equal

A. *Adults and Immatures (Contd.)*

size; metathoracic wings not folded in vannal area (termites, white ants)
.. **15. ISOPTERA**

Mesothoracic and metathoracic wings of unequal size and different in form; meta- thoracic wings usually much broader and longitudinally folded in vannal area **63**

63(62). Hind femur elongated and thickened for jumping, or front leg, and sometimes other legs, thickened and modified for digging; mouthparts always well devel- oped (grasshoppers, crickets) **11. ORTHOPTERA**

Leg segments unmodified for jumping or digging; mouthparts usually greatly re- duced (stoneflies) **8. PLECOPTERA**

64(58). Body and wings covered with fine whitish powder (dustywings)
.. **23. NEUROPTERA**

Neither body nor wings covered with fine whitish powder **65**

65(64). Abdomen constricted into a slender stalk where it joins the thorax or with a deep dorsal excision at this point, leaving a shallow but broad connection (wasps, bees, ants, etc.) **25. HYMENOPTERA**

Abdomen broadly joined to the thorax, laterally as well as dorsoventrally **66**

66(65). Tarsi with 5 distinct tarsomeres ... **67**

Tarsi with apparently 4 tarsomeres or less **69**

67(66). Pronotum well developed and at least as long middorsally as the meso- and meta- notum combined (preying mantids) **14. DICTYOPTERA**

Pronotum reduced and much shorter middorsally than meso- and metanotum combined ... **68**

68(67). Ventral portion of mesoepisternum narrow; mesothoracic wing frequently densely clothed with long hairlike setae; wings with generalized venation (caddisflies)
.. **26. TRICHOPTERA**

Ventral portion of mesoepisternum broad; mesothoracic wing never densely clothed with long hairlike setae; wings with specialized venation (sawflies, horntails, etc.)
.. **25. HYMENOPTERA**

69(67). Hind femur lengthened and thickened for jumping, or front leg, and sometimes other legs, thickened and modified for digging (crickets, etc.)
.. **11. ORTHOPTERA**

Leg segments unmodified for jumping or digging **70**

70(69). Metathoracic wing with a broad, longitudinally folded vannus, usually marked by a distinct anal notch (some stoneflies) **8. PLECOPTERA**

Metathoracic wing without a distinct (or folding) vannus and without an anal notch ... **71**

71(70). Mesothoracic and metathoracic wings approximately equal in size and similar in form ... **72**

Metathoracic wing distinctly shorter and somewhat different in form from meso- thoracic ... **73**

72(71). Basal tarsomere of front tarsus greatly enlarged and swollen (webspinners)
.. **9. EMBIOPTERA**

Basal tarsomere of front tarsus not elongated or swollen (termites, white ants) .
.. **15. ISOPTERA**

73(71). Pronotum as long or longer than mesonotum middorsally and fully exposed; cer- cus present and nonsegmented but with a conspicuous bristlelike apical process (zorapterans) **16. ZORAPTERA**

Pronotum very short, necklike, and much shorter than mesonotum middorsally; cercus absent (booklice, barklice) **17. PSOCOPTERA**

B. *Larvae and Larviform Females of Holometabola*

1. Paired thoracic legs present on at least two segments, often reduced in size and segmentation ... **2**

Paired thoracic legs entirely absent; a median, simple, or forked process may be present ... **17**

2(1). Paired "prolegs" present on 2 or more abdominal segments from 1 to 8, never fringed but often reduced to peglike structures; body form caterpillarlike **3**

Paired "prolegs" present at most on abdominal segment 8 and those following but usually completely absent; various lateral or dorsal processes sometimes present, sometimes fringed; body form not caterpillarlike **5**

3(2). Five or fewer pairs of "prolegs," always absent from 2nd segment and each usually with a crown of hooklets at apex (caterpillars) **27. LEPIDOPTERA**

Six to 10 pairs of "prolegs," usually present on 2nd segment, but never with a crown of hooklets ... **4**

B. *Larvae and Larviform Females of Holometabola (Contd.)*

4(3). Stemmata either absent or one on each side of head; "prolegs" on segment 2 to 7 or 2 to 6 and terminal (sawflies) **25. HYMENOPTERA**

Stemmata always present, with 7 or more on each side of head; "prolegs" on segments 1 to 8 or 3 to 8 (mecopterans) **28. MECOPTERA**

5(2). Head prognathous (directed forward), its dorsal surface only slightly longer than its ventral ... **6**

Head hypognathous (directed ventrad), its dorsal surface much longer than its ventral ... **11**

6(5). Legs with 2 distinct claws each .. **7**

Legs with only 1 claw each; a stout spine at base may appear to be another claw but differs in structure ... **9**

7(6). Labrum and clypeus exposed and visible from above **23. NEUROPTERA**

Labrum and clypeus not exposed and not visible from above **8**

8(7). Mandible and maxilla grooved and apposed dorsoventrally to form a sucking tube on each side; maxillary palpus always absent **23. NEUROPTERA**

Mandible and maxilla separate, not forming a sucking tube; mandible in some forms grooved mesally; maxillary palpus always present (beetles) **24. COLEOPTERA**

9(6). Mouthparts needlelike, forming a median "beak" several times as long as head (spongilla flies) **23. NEUROPTERA**

Mouthparts of the normal mandibulate type, not forming an elongate beak ... **10**

10(9). Apex of abdomen with a pair of "hooks," one on each side dorsally over an "anal leg"; body often in a case; aquatic (caddisworms) **26. TRICHOPTERA**

Apex of abdomen without "hooks" dorsally as above; recurved spines sometimes present, but anal leg then not developed (beetles) **24. COLEOPTERA**

11(5). Prothoracic leg distinctly shorter than the mesothoracic and usually than the metathoracic (if in a case made of conifer needles or leaves, *see* Lepidoptera) **12**

Prothoracic leg of the same size and structure as the mesothoracic; the metathoracic may be reduced ... **13**

12(11). Apex of abdomen with a pair of "hooks," one on each side dorsally over an "anal leg"; body often in a case; aquatic (caddisworms) **26. TRICHOPTERA**

Apex of abdomen without "hooks" as described above; terrestrial (mecopterans) .. **28. MECOPTERA**

13(11). Labrum with a protruding spinneret; antenna arising from membranous area above base of mandible (caterpillars) **27. LEPIDOPTERA**

Labrum without a protruding spinneret; antenna arising from sclerotized portion of head capsule adjacent to mandible **14**

14(13). Thoracic legs segmented and elbowed at two or more joints (beetles) **24. COLEOPTERA**

Thoracic legs, if segmented, not elbowed at two or more joints **15**

15(14). Claws present on thoracic legs **25. HYMENOPTERA**

Claws absent on thoracic legs .. **16**

16(15). One pair of thoracic spiracles (beetles) **25. COLEOPTERA**

Two pairs of thoracic spiracles **25. HYMENOPTERA**

17(1). Head indistinct, not sclerotized or pigmented **18**

Distinct sclerotized head present, usually pigmented but sometimes unpigmented, partially sclerotized, or deeply embedded in thorax **19**

18(17). Mouthparts composed chiefly of a pair (sometimes fused) of vertically moving mouth-hooks but sometimes completely absent; spiracles absent, or one pair on thorax and from one pair on subterminal abdominal to one on every abdominal segment 1 through 8 (flies) **29. DIPTERA**

Mouthparts, not as above, may be reduced to opposable, horizontally moving mandibles or to sclerotized plates or sensoria around mouth opening; spiracles on 1 to 3 thoracic segments and on 5 to 8 abdominal segments **25. HYMENOPTERA**

19(17). Labium with a protruding spinneret or antenna inserted in membrane near base of mandible (caterpillars) **27. LEPIDOPTERA**

Labium without a protruding spinneret and antenna inserted on sclerotized part of head near or away from mandible **20**

20(21). Abdomen with 10 segments, the last with a pair of ventral clawlike processes, *and* body with dorsal bristles on each segment usually becoming progressively longer caudally (fleas) **30. SIPHONAPTERA**

Abdomen with 10 segments or less; if 10-segmented, pair of ventral clawlike processes and body with dorsal bristles not present as above **21**

B. *Larvae and Larviform Females of Holometabola (Contd.)*

21(20). Abdomen usually with either 8 or 9 distinct segments or segmentation indistinct (flies) .. **29. DIPTERA**

Abdomen usually with 10 distinct segments 22

22(21). Second thoracic segment with a "breast bone" (gall midges) ... **29. DIPTERA**

Second thoracic segment without a "breast bone" 23

23(22). Maxillary palpus with 2 or more segments; thorax with 1 pair of spiracles (beetles) ... **24. COLEOPTERA**

Maxillary palpus unsegmented, frequently reduced to a sensorium; thorax with 1 or 2 pairs or spiracles .. 24

24(23). Pleura of abdominal segments subdivided (beetles) **24. COLEOPTERA**

Pleura of abdominal segments undivided **25. HYMENOPTERA**

C. *Pupae of Holometabola and some Acercaria*

1. Body enclosed in sclerotized, pigmented larval exuviae that hide the true pupa within; neither distinct body regions, mouthparts, nor appendage cases visible externally (puparia) **29. DIPTERA**

Body regions distinct and appendage cases usually visible externally; if located within larval exuviae, the latter not sclerotized nor pigmented, *nor* is a distinct head capsule present .. 2

2(1). Mandible strong, sclerotized, well pigmented, and articulated at its base with pupal integument; appendages free, never glued to body wall (decticuous pupa) ... 3

Mandible, if discernible, not articulated and not functional; appendages either free or glued to body wall (adecticuous pupa) 6

3(2). Pronotum well developed and usually as long as mesonotum 4

Pronotum much shorter than mesonotum 5

4(3). Head hypognathous and elongated into a ventrally directed beak cephalad of compound eyes, with mandibulate mouthparts at tip **28. MECOPTERA**

Head prognathous and normal; mouthparts sometimes greatly elongated in front of head capsule .. **23. NEUROPTERA**

5(3). Abdomen with paired plates bearing recurved hooks on dorsum of proximal segments; apex of abdomen frequently with platelike, triangular, or fingerlike processes; fingerlike or filamentous gills often present on thorax or abdomen **26. TRICHOPTERA**

Abdomen never with recurved hooks on dorsum of proximal segments; no sclerotized anal process or gills of any kind **27. LEPIDOPTERA**

6(2). Mouthparts with distinct mandibles that are usually short and triangular in shape or sickle-shaped and elongate .. 7

Mouthparts either haustellate, without such mandibles, or no mouthparts discernible at all .. 9

7(6). Metanotum several times as long as pronotum and mesonotum combined (stylopids) .. **24. COLEOPTERA**

Metanotum, at most, slightly longer than pronotum and mesonotum combined 8

8(7). Pronotum at least as long as mesonotum on middorsal line **24. COLEOPTERA**

Pronotum much shorter than mesonotum on middorsal line **25. HYMENOPTERA**

9(6). Body strongly compressed (flattened from side to side) **30. SIPHONAPTERA**

Body of various shapes but never strongly compressed 10

10(9). Mouthparts completely absent or greatly reduced **21. HOMOPTERA**

Mouthparts with at least some parts plainly visible 11

11(10). Mouthparts in the form of a short asymmetrical cone on caudoventral surface of head .. **22. THYSANOPTERA**

Mouthparts short or long but not asymmetrical 12

12(11). One pair of wing pads, with a small second pair sometimes developed but not hidden by the first **29. DIPTERA**

Two pairs of wing pads, with the first pair covering most of the second **27. LEPIDOPTERA**

D. *Extinct Insects*

1. Wingless; somewhat resembles Thysanura; about 10 mm (also extinct Collembola and Thysanura) (Permian) **MONURA**

Winged .. 2

2(1). Wings without basal folding mechanism, or if wings capable of folding over abdomen, cerci longer than body .. 3

D. *Extinct Insects* (*Contd.*)

	Wings with basal folding mechanism and capable of folding over abdomen; cerci not longer than abdomen ...	*7*
3(2).	Wings with posterior media and anterior cubitus	*4*
	Wing without posterior media and anterior cubitus (Pennsylvanian to Permian) **PROTODONATA**	
4(3).	Mouthparts mandibulate, without beak	*5*
	Mouthparts with prominent beak (Pennsylvanian to Permian) Extinct **HEMIPTERA**	
5(4).	Wings with fine, irregular, or reticulated crossveins (Pennsylvanian to Permian) ... **PALAEODICTYOPTERA**	
	Wings with distinct, not irregular or reticulate, crossveins	*6*
6(5).	With median caudal filament (Pennsylvanian) .. Extinct **EPHEMEROPTERA**	
	Without median caudal filament (Pennsylvanian to Permian) **DIAPHANOPTERODEA** and **MEGASECOPTERA**	
7(2).	Mesothoracic wings tegmens or elytra	*8*
	Mesothoracic wings membranous	*10*
8(7).	Mesothoracic wing with conspicuous precostal area; subcosta and posterior cubitus following submarginally distal half of wing (Permian to Jurassic) **GLOSSELYTRODEA**	
	Mesothoracic wing with small precostal area at most; without submarginal veins	*9*
9(8).	Elytra with reduced, weak venation; anal area of metathoracic wing much larger than remainder of wing (Permian) **PROTELYTROPTERA**	
	Front wing with normally developed venation; anal area of mesothoracic wing small (Pennsylvanian to Permian) **PROTORTHOPTERA**	
10(7).	Meso- and metathoracic wings with similar shape and venation (Pennsylvanian to Permian) **CALONEURODEA**	
	Metathoracic wing with much larger anal area and more anal veins than mesothoracic wing ...	*11*
11(10).	Prothoracic paranotal lobes of adults always present and independent of each other; anal area of metathoracic wing with not more than 6 veins; nymphs aquatic (Permian) **MIOMOPTERA** and Extinct **PLECOPTERA**	
	Prothoracic paranotal lobes of adults, when present, fused together; anal area of metathoracic wing with several more than 6 veins; nymphs terrestrial (Pennsylvanian to Permian) **PROTORTHOPTERA**	

Part II
The Insect Fauna of America, North of Mexico

The classification of all organisms considered to be "insects" in the usual sense, as they occur in the United States and Canada, is the subject of Part II. A discussion of the taxonomy and systematics involved will be found in Chap. 2 of Part I.

Superclass HEXAPODA

Class ENTOGNATHA

The three orders included in this class (Collembola, Protura, and Entotrophi) are closely similar to true insects, but because of the structure of their heads and mandibles, they are no longer treated as Insecta but placed in this separate class.

Order 1

COLLEMBOLA (Springtails and Allies)

Springtails are very primitive hexapods that are exceedingly abundant, but because of their small size and obscure habits, they are seldom collected and studied. Their presence is most noticeable when they cover the surface of snow or ponds. The diligent collector will find many interesting species in soil, forest litter, or decaying wood, under bark, and in fungi. They usually have a very simple life cycle, with little change in their appearance from the time they hatch from eggs to the time they reach sexual maturity in the adult stage. They continue to molt after they have reached adulthood.

The name of their order is derived from two Greek words—*coll*, to glue, and *embolos*, a peg—and refers to the tubelike appendage on the first abdominal segment. The terminal abdominal segments are often modified into a forklike apparatus, the *furcula*, that is flexed ventrally and held by the catch, or *tenaculum*, which releases the furcula with a snap that propels the insect violently forward. Species that do not exhibit this structure cannot properly be called "springtails."

Diagnosis: L. 0.25–10 mm (most species 1-3 mm); body elongate or subglobular and soft. Color usually whitish or gray, but some purple, blue, green, orange, and yellow. Antennae usually short, with four to six segments. Eyes small, with no more than eight facets in each eye patch. *Pseudocelli*—smooth, thin areas of cuticle usually outlined by a rim or ring of granules—are located on the head and body of Onychiuridae. They are not true ocelli but probably control the release of hemolymph as a repellent to predators. Some species have a postantennal organ located between each antenna and each eye, the exact nature of which is not known. Mouthparts of the biting type, sometimes modified for sucking or filtering, recede somewhat into the head. Wingless. Legs slender, small, without specialized modifications. Abdomen with five or six visible segments, or with segments obscure, usually equipped with the jumping apparatus described previously. The first abdominal segment with ventral tube is equipped with a membranous

tip, a universal and diagnostic feature of Collembola. (See Fig. 1.1)

The immature stages resemble the adult stage in all external details.

Springtails can be confused with wingless Psocoptera—especially those found in bird nests—but these have longer antennae and true compound eyes, and, of course, no jumping apparatus or ventral tube. Those species of Collembola that do not jump might be confused with lice, but Collembola are not flattened, not ectoparasitic, and usually soft-bodied. The soil proturans are more slender and do not have antennas as soil Collembola do. The diplurans have two anal cerci instead of the jumping mechanism.

Metamorphosis: Gradual, or ametabolous. Molting takes place six to eight times, sexual maturity being reached after the fifth molt. A few adults have rather strikingly different features that enable them to be distinguished from the immatures. Nothing has been reported about the morphology of the eggs.

Habits and habitats: The various species are found throughout the year in the adult or immature stages in both fresh water and marine habitats, in soil (subterranean forms), leaf mold, on decaying plant and animal material, in bird nests, and on growing leaves in moist areas. They occur abundantly in all forests, less abundantly in grasslands. They apparently feed on bacteria, fungi, pollen, lichens, and decaying vegetation and carrion. A few are carnivores. Sometimes they are found in great numbers on stagnant water, and they are well-known on the eternal shows of glaciers, where apparently they feed on algae.

The slender species (Arthropleona) that live above ground are very different from those that live deep in the soil. As a rule, the former are relatively large and possess long antennae and legs and usually a well-developed jumping apparatus. They may be rather brightly colored. Some have scales and most have setae. Their eyes are highly developed, usually eight

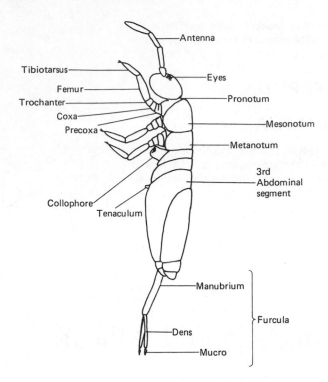

Fig. 1.1. General anatomy of a springtail.

to each eye patch. The subterranean species are ordinarily much smaller—under 1 mm in length in most species—with short antennae and legs and the jumping apparatus greatly reduced or entirely absent. The eyes of the species are also greatly reduced or absent. Their bodies are pale and without pigment.

The globose species (Symphypleona) live in very moist habitats or in caves and appear to be more active jumpers as a consequence of their well-developed furculae. Their bodies tend to be pigmented, and the eye patch is often relatively large. They usually show striking sexual dimorphism and complex behavior.

Reproductive behavior: Even though these hexapods are considered to be primitive, certain features of their known reproductive habits indicate that they are advanced members of an ancient order. Sperm transfer seems to follow the indirect method used by many aquatic forms. Most species do not form pairs. Instead, males deposit a number of stalked droplets of sperm on the ground for wandering females to find and harvest with their slitlike genital openings. Some species, however, have been observed to temporarily pair and conspicuously touch each other, the female being more or less directed to the sperm droplets by the male. In the presumably more advanced Sminthuridae, the males appear to be able to see females at a distance as great as 2 cm. The male approaches the female and grasps her with his antennae to test whether she is sexually mature. If she passes this test, the male stays with her, but she pays no attention to his behavior. He proceeds to plant several stalked sperm droplets in a semicircle around her so that she is trapped into coming into contact with them. If she is carrying eggs that are ready to be laid, she promptly harvests one of the droplets, thus ensuring the eggs' fertilization.

Although this behavior occurs in what might be taken as an advanced group, the otherwise primitive species, *Podura aquatica* (see genus 1.1)—which lives by the thousands on the surface of weedy ponds—not only builds a fence of stalked sperm droplets around the female, but proceeds to shove her toward the fence to force her to take his sperm.

Finally, members of the genus *Sminthirides* (7.1) and related genera show sexual dimorphism. The males are much smaller than the females (one-half to one-eighth as large). Their antennae are developed into clasping organs with which they cling to the female and are carried about for days. Eventually, the female puts him down. He then deposits a sperm droplet and with great effort pulls the female over the spot so that she comes in contact with the sperm and is fertilized.

Collecting and preserving: Springtails are collected with a Berlese funnel from leaf mold, humus, decaying vegetation, moss, margins of bodies of water, and from water and snow. Soil forms may be attracted to soda water poured into the soil. Specimens should be placed directly into 80-percent alcohol. They may be mounted on slides at any time thereafter.

Rearing: Springtails are usually abundant in moss and may be kept in covered finger bowls or covered teraria where they will feed on decaying vegetation and fungi. Special culture jars may be made by adding carbon black (also known as "animal black") to plaster of Paris (one part carbon black to 10 parts of plaster of Paris). Water is added to the mixture, which is then poured into a 9-oz culture jar. Granulated yeast is used as food. Unicellular green algae is preferred by some species. A small quantity of decayed leaves (kept at a temperature of 60° to 70°C for 12 hours prior to use) may be added as a diet supplement.

Distribution: Cosmopolitan; approximately 6,000 species in the world (Salmon, in litt.) with 677 species in 74 genera in the U.S. and Canada.

Identification: The genera and species cannot be identified with certainty without a good compound microscope and slide mounted specimens. However, some of the largest and most common species can be tentatively identified by shape and color. The discussion here covers all of the families, the genera that are known to occur in the U.S. and Canada, and some of the most common species. It is likely—judging from the limited distribution records for most species—that intensive collecting in any one area will probably reveal many more species than the literature indicates. Now that the species in the U.S. and Canada have been monographed (see Christiansen and Bellinger, 1980), it is a simpler matter to identify collected specimens.

Economic importance: Occasionally the number of Collembola in greenhouses reaches pest proportions.

CLASSIFICATION

Authorities generally agree that the order is divided into two suborders based on body shape and abdominal segmentation, as described in the accompanying Key to the families. The monograph by Christiansen and Bellinger (1980) recognizes seven families in the United States and Canada, this classification being used here.

Key to the Families of Colembola

1. Body elongate, cylindrical or flattened dorsoventrally or laterally; thoracic and abdominal segmentation more or less distinct; furcula present, rudimentary, or absent (see Fig. 1.3) (Suborder Arthropleona) .. *2*

 Body globose; thoracic and abdominal segments 1 through 4 fused, with segments 5 and 6 usually forming a small papilla; furcula always well developed (see Fig. 1.1) (Suborder Symphypleona) .. *7*

2(1). First thoracic segment dorsally distinct and with dorsal setae (Section Poduromorpha) . *3*

 First thoracic segment dorsally indistinct and frequently not visible dorsally (see Fig. 1.1) (Section Entomobryomorpha) .. *4*

3(2). Dentes of furcula (see Fig. 1.6) more than 3 times as long as manubrium (base of furcula) and distal rings of granules .. **1. Poduridae**

 Dentes absent or relatively shorter and not ringed *6*

4(2). Antennal segment 3 much shorter than segment 4 *5*

 Antennal segment 3 much longer than segment 4 (Subfamily Tomocerinae)
 .. **5. Entomobryidae**

5(4). Abdominal segment 4 middorsally usually much longer than segment 3. (Subfamilies Oncopodurinae, Entomobryinae, Cyphoderinae, and Paronellinae) **5. Entomobryidae**

 Abdominal segment 4 middorsally subequal to or shorter than segment 3; postantennal organ almost always present .. **4. Isotomidae**

6(3). Pseudocelli present, at least on antennal base or dorsum of 5th abdominal segment; almost always without functional furcula **3. Onychiuridae**

 Pseudocelli absent; furcula absent or short, never reaching beyond end of abdomen
 .. **2. Hypogastruridae**

7(1). Antenna much shorter than head **6. Neelldae**

 Antenna subequal to head or longer **7. Sminthuridae**

Suborder ARTHROPLEONA

Five of the families and the majority of the species of North American Collembola belong to this suborder, the most diverse of the group. The linear shape and distinct abdominal segmentation are obvious recognition features. Two sections, not perfectly distinct, comprise the suborder. They are (1) Section Poduromorpha, with the families Poduridae, Hypogastruridae, and Onychiuridae, and (2) Section Entomobryomorpha, with the families Isotomidae and Entomobryidae.

Section Poduromorpha

1. PODURIDAE (Water Springtail Family)

Only one species is known:

1.1 *Podura* Linnaeus

P. aquatica Linnaeus (Water Springtail). L. ±1.3 mm. Dark blue to reddish brown; furcula very long, flattened, adapted for jumping on water. On the surface of fresh water ponds throughout North America.

2. HYPOGASTRURIDAE (Elongate-Bodied Springtail Family)

L. 0.8–3 mm. Body elongate; abdominal segments distinct; prothorax well-developed, with setae; eyes present or absent; furcula short or absent.

This family is divided into two subfamilies, with a total of 20 genera and 194 described species in U.S. and Canada. The species are frequently common and difficult to separate.

Subfamily Hypogastrurinae

2.1 *Hypogastrura* Bourlet

This genus is divided into four subgenera with species as follows: *Hypogastrura* s. str. (41 spp.); *Ceratophysella* Börner (20 spp.); *Michellania* Wray (8 spp.); *Schoettella* Schäffer (4 spp.). Perhaps the most commonly seen species is the following:

H. (*H.*) *nivicola* (Fitch) (Snowflea). L. ±2 mm. Dark indigo blue throughout. This species is often found in very large numbers on snow in late winter during a thaw. Attracted to maple sap, it is a pest in buckets of sap during the harvest. (1) n.e. NA; (2) VA, NC; (3) n. CA; (4) Pacific n.w.; (5) n. central states. [See (Fig. 1.2).]

The remaining species of this genus are more local in distribution:

[2.2 *Schaefferia* Absolon with two subgenera: *Schaefferia* s. str. (1 sp., *S. cheoha* Wray) and *Typhlogastrura* Bonet (3 spp.); 2.3 *Mesachorutes* Absolon, subgenus *Denigastrura* Stach (1 sp., *M. thomomys* (Chamberlain)); 2.4 *Knowltonella* Wray (1 sp., *K. idahoensis* Wray); 2.5 *Triacanthella* Schäffer (1 sp., *T. copelandi* (Wray)); 2.6 *Microgastrura* Stach (1 sp., *M. minutissma* (Mills)); 2.7 *Stenogastrura* Christiansen and Bellinger (1 sp., *S. hiemalis* Christiansen and Bellinger);

Fig. 1.2.

2.8 *Xenylla* Tullberg (14 spp.); 2.9 *Acherontiella* Absolon (1 sp., *A. sabina* Bonet); 2.10 *Willemia* Börner (7 spp.); 2.11 *Tafallia* Bonet (2 spp.)]

Subfamily Neanurinae

2.12 *Anurida* Laboulbene

Body form slender with a clearly unlobed sixth abdominal segment; furcula usually absent; fourth antennal segment with well-developed, blunt setae of various sizes. There are four subgenera: *Anurida* s. str. (10 spp.); *Anuridella* Willem (1 sp., *A. calcarata* (Denis)); *Micranurida* Börner (4 spp.); and *Protechorutes* Cassagnau (1 sp., *A. bicolor* Christiansen and Bellinger).

A. (A.) maritima (Guérin) (Seashore Springtail). L. 3–3.5 mm. Dark, uniform blue. Mouthparts functional, sucking. This species lives in the intertidal zone of the seashore and feeds on dead crustaceans and molluscs. During high tide, they find refuge in air-filled pockets in the cracks and crevices of rocks. (See Fig. 1.3.) (1) n.e. NA; (4) BC.

The remaining species of the remaining genera of this family are more local in distribution; many no doubt are abundant and widespread, but the published records are few.

[2.13 *Brachystomella* Agren (4 spp.); 2.14 *Friesea* Dalla Torre (14 spp.); 2.15 *Morulina* Börner (7 spp.); 2.16 *Neanura* MacGillivray: sub-

Fig. 1.3.

genera *Crossodonthina* Yosii (3 spp.); *Lathriopyga* Caroli (1 sp., *N. setosa* Canby); *Lobella* Börner (1 sp., *N. ambigua* Christiansen and Bellinger); *Neanura* s. str. (12 spp.); 2.17 *Odontella* Schaeffer: subgenera *Odontella* s. str. (8 spp.); *Xenyllodes* Axelson (1 sp., *O. armata* (Axelson)); 2.18 *Oudemansia* Schott (1 sp., *O. georgia* Christiansen and Bellinger); 2.19 *Paranura* Axelson (5 spp.)]

2.20 *Pseudachorutes* Tullberg

This genus is divided into the following subgenera: *Pseudachorudina* Stach (2 spp.), and *Pseudachorutes* s. str. (13 spp.). The following is an example:

P. (Pseudachorutes) simplex Maynard. L. ±2 mm. Grayish blue to blue with granular pigment scattered pale spots. (See Fig. 1.4.) (1) IL, IN, NY; (2) WV, KY, TN.

Fig. 1.4.

3. ONYCHIURIDAE (Blind Springtail Family)

L. 1.2–.0 mm. Elongate, slender, similar to the Hypogastruridae except that nearly all species are white, all are blind, and the furcula is usually absent. There are 66 species in four genera known in the U.S.A. and Canada.

[3.1 *Lophognathella* Börner (1 sp., *L. choreutes* Börner); 3.2 *Sensiphorura* Rusek (1 sp., *S. marshalli* Rusek)]

3.3 *Onychiurus* Gervais

All of the species in this genus lack a furcula, all are white, and all have four or more papillae in an apical organ on the third antennal segment. (See Fig. 1.5.) The 41 species are assigned to subgenera as follows: *Archaphorura* Bagnall (4 spp.); *Protaphorura* Absolon (23 spp.); *Onychiurus* s. str. (15 spp.). Most species appear to be rather local, as well as northern, in distribution. Several are found in caves; a few are littoral. At least nine species are reported in the literature as *O. fimetarius* Linnaeus, but no North American species are in this group. All species in the "*fimetarius*" group lack anal spines. The following is perhaps closest to being the widespread species of the literature:

O. (O.) pseudofimetarius Folsom. L. ±1.5 mm. White. Body elliptical. Fourth antennal segment without apical bulb or blunt setae; apical organ of third antennal segment with five guard setae. Integumentary granulation slightly coarser

Fig. 1.5 Head of *Onychiurus gervais*, showing apical organ on third antennal segment and postantennal organ: (c) sense club, (r) sense rod, and (p) paddle-shaped sensilla. (*Redrawn from Christiansen and Vellinger, 1980*)

around some pseudocelli and on the front of the head than elsewhere. Sometimes found in caves; scattered distribution. (1) n. central states.

[3.4 *Tullbergia* Lubbock; subgenera *Metaphorura* Stach (1 sp., *T. knowltoni* Wray); *Neonaphorura* Bagnall (1 sp., *T. howdeni* Wray); *Tullbergia* s. str. (21 spp.)]

Section Entomobryomorpha

4. ISOTOMIDAE (Smooth Springtail Family)

L. 0.7–6.0 mm. Body elongate and clearly segmented; prothorax reduced and membranous; scales absent; antennae never annulated, each segment distinct. The classification of the family is uncertain, with little agreement on the arrangement of the genera. Due to this confusion, it is difficult to tell what species may be regarded as "common."

The 170 known species are assigned to genera as follows:

[4.1 *Tetracanthella* Schött (6 spp.); 4.2 *Uzelia* Absolon (2 spp.); 4.3 *Anurophorus* Nicolet: subgenera *Anurophorus* s. str. (5 spp.); *Pseudanurophorus* Stach (2 spp.); 4.4 *Micranurophorus* Bernard (1 sp., *M. musci* Bernard); 4.5 *Coloburella* Latzel: subgenera *Coloburella* s. str. (1 sp., *C. octogeneria* (Mills and Schmidt)); *Paranurophorus* Denis (1 sp., *C. simplex* (Denis)); 4.6 *Stachanorema* Wray (2 spp.); 4.7 *Weberacantha* Christiansen (1 sp., *W. octa* Christiansen); 4.8 *Isotomodes* Linnaniemi (4 spp.); 4.9 *Dagamaea* Yosii (1 sp., *D. tenuis* (Folsom)); 4.10 *Folsomides* Stach (4 spp.); 4.11 *Bonetrura* Christiansen and Bellinger (1 sp., *B. boneti* Yosii) 4.12 *Proisotoma* Börner: subgenera *Appendisotoma* Stach (8 spp.); *Proisotoma* s. str. (11 spp.); *Ballistura* Börner (14 spp.); 4.13 *Archisotoma* Linnaniemi (1 sp., *A. besselsi* (Packard); 4.14 *Cryptopygus* Willem (9 spp.); 4.15 *Folsomia* Willem (26 spp.); 4.16 *Metisotoma* Maynard (1 sp., *M. grandiceps* (Reuter)); 4.17 *Microsotoma* Ballinger (1 sp., *M. achromata* Bellinger); 4.18 *Isotomiella* Bagnall (1 sp., *I. minor* (Schäffer)); 4.19 *Axelsonia* Börner (1 sp., *A. tubifera* Strenzke)]

4.20 *Isotomurus* Börner

This genus is divided into two subgenera: *Hydroisotoma* Stach (1 sp., *I. schaefferi* (Krausbauer)) and *Isotomurus* s. str. (7 spp.). Perhaps the most common species of the family is the following (although there is some question as to its identity, the literature records it as *I. palustris* (Muller):

Fig. 1.6.

I. (*I.*) *tricolor* (Packard). L. ±2.5 mm. Usually yellowish or greenish with blue, purple, or black spots. A very abundant species found on the surface of water, on the vegetation along the shores of lakes, ponds, pools, and streams. (See Fig. 1.6.) (1), (2), (3), (4), (5). Widespread.

[4.21 *Agrenia* Börner (1 sp., *A. bidenticulata* (Tullberg); 4.22 *Semicerura* Maynard (2 spp.).]

4.23 *Isotoma* Bourlet

This large genus contains the following subgenera: *Isotoma* s. str. (3 spp.); *Desoria* Nicolet (41 spp.); *Panchaetoma* Bagnall (1 sp., *I.* (*P.*) *communa* MacGillivray) *Myopia* Christiansen and Bellinger (1 sp., *I.* (*M.*) *alaskana* Christiansen and Bellinger); *Vertagopus* Börner (6 spp.); *Pseudiostoma* Handschin (2 spp.); *Cheirotoma* Bagnall (1 sp., *I.* (*C.*) *spatulata* Chamberlain). All species of this genus have a well-developed furcula, with 15 or more ventral setae on the manubrium and a mucro with three or more teeth. One species, *I.* (*Cheirotoma*) *spatulata* Chamberlain, lives in termite nests in (3) CA; (4) OR. A common species is as follows:

I. (*I.*) *viridis* Bourlet. L. ±6 mm (sometimes larger). Color extremely variable, taking almost any hue except uniform black or blue-black; also variably patterned. Extremely common throughout North America, especially in eastern two-thirds of the U.S. (1), (2), (3), (4), (5).

5. ENTOMOBRYIDAE (Slender Springtail Family)

L. 1.0–6.0 mm (rarely, to 10 mm). Very distinctive because of the large fourth abdominal segment, which is usually at least twice the length, and usually more, of the third segment as viewed dorsally; in some species, however, these two segments may be about equal. Antennae are long, and the last two segments in some species (Tomocerinae) are ringed (see Fig. 1.7), making them seem to be composed of a large number of subsegments; prothorax is reduced. The family is divided into four subfamilies, with a total of 138 species in U.S. and Canada.

Fig. 1.7.

Subfamily Entomobryinae

[5.1 *Corynothrix* Tullberg (1 sp., *C. borealis* Tullberg)]

5.2 *Orchesella* Templeton

The fourth abdominal segment is less than twice as long as the third. Antennae with basal subsegments of the second segment, and sometimes the first, and the fourth segment, and sometimes the third, showing distinct annulation or setal whorling. There are 14 species in the U.S. and Canada.

Orchesella folsomi Maynard. L. ±1.8 mm. Pale yellow to blackish purple. Antennae six-segmented. This is a woods species or found on sphagnum moss in woodland pools. (See Fig. 1.8.) (1) n.e. NA; (2) VA, NC, TN; (5) MO, IA, KS.

O. ainsliei Folsom (Slender Sphagnum Springtail) is a closely related species found in much the same localities as the preceding. (See A&J 1.)

[5.3 *Entomobrya* Rondani subgenera: *Calx* Christiansen (1 sp., *E. sabulicola* Mills), *Drepanura* Schött (2 sp.), *Entomobrya* s. str. (26 spp.), *Entomobryoides* Maynard (4 spp.), *Homidia* Börner (2 spp.), and *Mesentotoma* Salmon (1 sp., *E. laguna* Bacon); 5.4 *Sinella* Brook (15 spp.); 5.5 *Janetschekbrya* Yosii (1 sp., *J. arida* Christiansen and Bellinger); 5.6 *Willowsia* Shoebotham (2 spp.); 5.7 *Seira* Lubbock (4 spp.); 5.8 *Lepidocyrtus* Bourlet (15 spp.); 5.9 *Heteromurus* Wankel (1 sp., *H. nitidus* (Templeton))]

Paronellinae

[5.10 *Salina* MacGillivray (3 spp.)]

Oncopodurinae

[5.11 *Harlomillsia* Bonet (1 sp., *H. oculata* (Mills)); 5.12 *Oncopodura* Carl and Lebedinsky (6 spp.)]

Tomocerinae

5.13 *Tomocerus* Nicolet

Adults and large nymphs belonging to species of this genus have the last two segments of the antennae very flexible and whorled and the fourth segment much shorter than the third. (See Fig. 1.7.). The species live in very diverse habitats, including caves.

The 16 species from U.S. and Canada are assigned to subgenera as follows: *Pogonognathellus* Paclt (5 spp.); *Pluto-*

Fig. 1.8.

murus Yosii (4 spp.); *Tomocerina* Yosii (3 spp.); *Tomocerus* s. str. (2 spp.); *Tomolonus* Mills (1 sp., *T. reductus* Mills); and *Lethemurus* Yosii (1 sp., *T. missus* Mills).

A species typical of the genus is the following:

T. (*Pogonognathellus*) *flavescens* Tullberg. L. ±6 mm (sometimes up to 10 mm). Silvery gray to lead-colored, yellow or brownish, or grayish blue. Body without scales; pigment, when present, usually uniformly distributed. This large species, although typical, probably represents a complex of species. It has been observed under stones and logs, in huge numbers on moist ground, in gardens, and under boards in greenhouses; it probably inhabits many other environments, including caves. (1), (2), (3), (4), (5), throughout NA.

Suborder SYMPHYPLEONA

The remaining two families, Sminthuridae and Neelidae, comprise the "globular" Collembola. The body is "swollen," the first four abdominal segments being completely fused. Other body segments may be obscurely delimited, but the furcula and tenaculum are always well developed. The integument is smooth, setae are relatively sparse, and body scales are absent.

6. NEELIDAE (Short-horned Springtail Family)

Members of this family have antennae shorter than the head; eyes are absent. The seven species are all very small, ranging in size from 0.27 to 0.7 mm. The group is poorly known but has been collected in rotting wood, wooded areas, and caves.

[6.1 *Neelus* Folsom: subgenera: *Megalothorax* Willem (3 spp.); *Neelides* Caroli (3 spp.); and *Neelus* s. str. (1 sp., *N. murinus* Folsom)]

7. SMINTHURIDAE (Globular Springtail Family)

L. 0.4–2.7 mm., but rarely over 1.3 mm. Body subglobose, with abdominal segments indistinct; shape similar in all species. Antennae longer than the head; eyes present. A total of 99 known species in the U.S. and Canada. Most species seem to have limited distribution. They are found in moist environments, including caves.

The family is divided into four subfamilies, as follows:

Subfamily Sminthuridinae

[7.1 *Sminthurides* Börner: subgenera: *Sphaeridia* Linnaniemi (2 spp.); *Denisiella* Folsom and Mills (1 sp., *S. sexpinnatus* Denis); *Sminthurides* s. str. (13 spp.); *Stenacidia* Börner (1 sp., *S. violaceus* Reuter [US?])]

Subfamily Katianninae

[7.2 *Collophora* Richards (1 sp., *C. quadrioculata* (Denis))]

7.3 *Arrhopalites* Börner

Eyes small. Antennae of male, unlike *Sminthurides*, are not modified for clasping. Adult females have well-developed subanal appendages. Twelve species are known in the U.S. and Canada. Most species are white and have rather restricted distribution.

A. pygmaeus (Wankel). L. ±1.5 mm. White to yellowish brown over entire body; legs and antennae pale. Antennae with setae of fourth segment three times as long the diameter of segment. Common and widely distributed. (1) n.e. NA; (2) s.e. U.S.; (3) NM, TX.

Fig. 1.9.

[7.4 *Sminthurinus* Börner: subgenera: *Katiannina* Maynard and Downs (1 sp., *S. macgillivrayi* (Banks)); *Polykatianna* Salmon (4 spp.); and *Sminthurinus* s. str. (7 spp.)]

Subfamily Sminthurinae

[7.5 *Vesicephalus* Richards (2 spp.)]

7.6 *Bourletiella* Banks

Fourth antennal segment subdivided; fifth and sixth abdominal segments separate (as in all Sminthrinae). Most species are marked with various colors. In length they are hardly 1 mm, the maximum being under 2 mm. The subgenera are: *Bourletiella* s. str. (7 spp.); *Deuterosminthurus* Börner (7 spp.); *Heterosminthurus* Stach (2 spp.); *Prorastriopes* Delamare (1 sp., *B. coalingaensis* Snider); *Pseudobourletiella* Stach (1 sp., *B. spinata* (MacGillivray)).

B. (*B.*) *hortensis* (Fitch) (Seedling Springtail). L. Female, ±1.8 mm; male ±1.2 mm. Mottled blue to purple brown; area between eyes pale or bright yellow to orange; abdomen with scattered pale spots, sometimes large and regularly arranged, with venter pale. It is a well-known pest, often damaging seedlings. Very common, especially in the spring and early sum-

Fig. 1.10.

mer. (See Fig. 1.9 for dorsal and Fig. 1.10 for lateral view.) (1) n.e. NA; (2) VA, NC, SC.

[7.7 *Sphyrotheca* Börner (3 spp.); 7.8 *Neosminthurus* Mills (3 spp.); 7.9 *Sminthurus* Latreille: subgenera: *Allacma* Börner (1 sp., *S. purpurescens* (MacGillivray)) and *Sminthurus* s. str. (11 spp.)]

Subfamily Dicyrtominae

[7.10 *Dicyrtoma* Bourlet: subgenera: *Bothriovulsus* Richards (1 sp., *D. pineolae* (Wray)); *Dicyrtoma* s. str. (5 spp.); *Dicyrtomina* Börner (3 spp.); and *Ptenothrix* Börner (10 spp.)]

BIBLIOGRAPHY

Christiansen, K. 1964. Bionomics of Collembola. *Ann. Rev. Ent.* 9: 147–148.

Christiansen, K., and Bellinger, P. F. 1980. *The Collembola of North America north of the Rio Grande.* Part 1, *Introduction, Genera, Families Poduridae and Hypogastruridae*, pp. 1–386; Part 2, *Families Onychiuridae and Isotomidae*, pp. 387–784; Part 3, *Family Entomobryidae*, pp. 385–1042; Part 4, *Families Neelidae and Sminthiridae* (Glossary, Bibliography, and Index), pp. 1043–1322. Grinnell College, Grinnell, Iowa.

Maynard, E. A. 1951. A monograph of the Collembola or springtail insects of New York State. Ithaca: Cornell U. Press, xii + 339 pp.

Salmon, J. T. 1964. An index to the Collembola. 2 vol. Wellington, New Zealand: Royal Soc. New Zealand, 644 pp.

Scott, H. G. 1961. Collembola: pictorial key to the Nearctic genera. *Ann. Ent. Soc. America*, 54(1):104–113.

Order 2

PROTURA (Proturans)

Proturans are seldom collected except by specialists. The order, not recognized until 1907, remains poorly known even with the current interest in soil biology. For example, the eggs have not been discovered, and although individuals are probably abundant and widespread, they have never been reported for many regions of North America and other parts of the world. The discerning collector might therefore succeed in making some interesting discoveries about these puzzling hexapods.

Proturans lack antennae and are blind; however, other

senses are sufficiently acute to enable them to survive in their soil habitat. The appendages of the first thoracic segment, the front legs, serve as antennae and are projected forward and upward in the manner of true antennae.

The name *Protura* is a combination of the Greek words for "first," *proto-*, and "tail," *-ura*, probably selected as an indication of the primitive nature of the group. The abdomen has retained small appendages on the first three segments, a further sign of the early stage of hexapod evolution that this order represents.

Diagnosis: L. 0.6–2.5 mm. Soft-bodied; elongate; shape similar to that of some of the smallest, white onychiurid springtails; white or pale amber. The mouthparts are of a primitive sucking type, that is, the mandibles are long and thin but do not form a sucking tube such as that found in the winged insects. Wingless. Second and third pairs of legs are short and without apparent special modification. The abdomen lacks cerci but has a well-developed telson; three basal segments (sometimes two) with paired appendages. These hexapods might be confused with some of the minute collembolans, but the peculiar position of the front pair of legs will permit correct identification. (See Fig. 2.1. for general anatomy.)

Metamorphosis: As with the other three primitive wingless orders, metamorphosis is gradual, although the nymphs add an abdominal segment with each molt.

Habits and habitats: Proturans live in moist habitats such as moldy soil around roots. They have been separated in Berlese funnels from leaf humus, dead leaves, moss, lichens, and from under the bark of rotting logs. Some have been collected in subterranean mammal nests. Apparently, however, they are always associated with fungus. They feed by piercing fungi mycelia, from which they suck the cell contents. The species living around roots feed on the fungi associated with vascular plant roots. The effect of this feeding has yet to be determined.

Collecting and preserving: Proturans are collected with a Berlese funnel from moist humus, bark, rotting wood, decaying vegetation, or debris from under stones. Preserve in 80-percent alcohol and mount on slides.

Rearing: No information is available on the rearing of Proturans.

Distribution: A complete catalog of the species was published in 1964 (Tuxen) listing the 260 species that have been discovered worldwide. Twenty species in nine genera have been recorded in the U.S. and Canada. Keys for the identification of the species can be found in this catalog but are difficult to use; only carefully prepared specimens are identifiable.

CLASSIFICATION

The order Protura is divided into four families, three of which have been recognized in North America—Eosentomidae, Protentomidae, and Acerentomidae. The fourth family, Sinentomidae, is known only in China. The genera of the world are treated in Nosek (1978). This classification is followed here for the North American species. Because of their restricted known distribution, all 20 species and nine genera in Canada and the U.S. are listed here. There is little or no information about their abundance. A Key to the Families follows:

Key to the Families of Protura

1. Mesothorax and metathorax with dorsal spiracles **1. Eosentomidae**
 Spiracles not developed ... *2*
2(1). At least 2 pairs of abdominal appendages with terminal vesicle **2. Protentomidae**
 Only the 1st pair of abdominal appendages with terminal vesicle **3. Acerentomidae**

Superfamily **EOSENTOMOIDEA**

1. EOSENTOMIDAE

This family contains one genus only, as follows:

[1.1 *Eosentomon* Berlese (7 spp.: *E. rostratum* Ewing, (2) TN, NC; *E. vermiforme* Ewing, (1) IL; (2) MD, VA; (3) TX, AR; *E. wheeleri* Silvestri, (1) NY; *E. pusillum* Ewing, (2) FL; *E. yosemitense* Ewing, (3) CA; *E. christianseni* Bonet, (1) MA; *E. pallidum* Ewing, (1) IL, IN; (2) KY, MD, GA; and *E. turneri* Bonet, (2) GA, FL)]

Superfamily **ACERENTOMOIDEA**

2. PROTENTOMIDAE

Subfamily Hesperentominae

[2.1 *Hesperentomon* Price (1 sp., *H. macswaini* Price, (3) CA)]

Subfamily Protentominae

[2.2 *Proturentomon* Silvestri (1 sp., *P. iowaense* Wormersley, (5) IA); 2.3 *Protentomon* Ewing (1 sp., *P. transitans* Ewing, (2) MD)]

3. ACERENTOMIDAE

[3.1 *Acerentulus* Berlese (1 sp., *A. confinis* (Berlese), (5) IA); 3.2 *Amerentulus* Tuxen (1 sp., *A. americanus* (Ewing), (2) MD); 3.3 *Acerella* Berlese (3 spp.: *A. canadensis* (Tuxen), Richmond Mts., Canada; *A.*

condei (Tuxen), Richmond Mts., Canada; and *A. barberi* (Ewing), (2) MD (see Fig. 2.1)); 3.4 *Nipponentomon* Imadate and Yosii (3 spp.: *N. andrei* (Ewing), (4) UT; *N. californicum* (Hilton), (3) CA; and *N.*

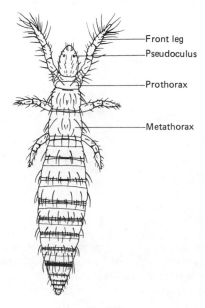

Fig. 2.1.

aureitarsus (Ewing), (2) VA); 3.5 *Gracilentulus* Tuxen (1 sp.; *G. floridanus* (Ewing), (2) FL)]

BIBLIOGRAPHY

Nosek, J. 1973. *The European Protura.* Geneva: Museum d'Historie Naturelle, 345 pp.

Nosek, J. 1978. Key and diagnosis of Protura genera of the world. *Annot. Zool. Bot. Bratislava,* vol. 122, pp. 1–59.

Tuxen, S. L. 1960. Ontogenie und phylogenie bezogen auf die apterygoten Insecten. *Zool. Ang.,* 164: 359–365.

Tuxen, S. L. 1964. *The Protura, a revision of the species of the world with keys for determination.* Paris: Herman, 360 pp.

Order 3

ENTOTROPHI (Entotrophs)

The entotrophs are very distinctive and easily recognized but do not look very much like the true insects. At first sight, they might be confused with centipedes, but as they have only three pairs of legs, they are definitely hexapods. Recently, this order has been called the *Diplura* (from *diplo*, two or double, and *ura*, tail), because they have two terminal cerci or, in some species, forceps; the name Entotrophi (from *ento*, within, and *trophi*, food, in reference to the mouthparts), however, is the correct one.

Species of this order might be confused with Microcoryphia and Thysanura, but the presence of two cerci or forceps in contrast to the three caudal filaments of the latter readily distinguishes the groups.

Diagnosis: L. 2–50 mm, but usually less than 10 mm. Soft-bodied; shape elongate, slender, slightly flattened, without scales. Pale brown, with the end of the abdomen of some species darkened. Head large; antennae longer than the head and stout, with an indefinite number of segments; eyes and ocelli absent. Mouthparts of the biting type but deeply recessed into the head. Wingless. Legs short, slender, and unmodified. The abdomen is long and slender, with a pair of prominent terminal cerci of several segments or with a pair of unsegmented forceps; abdominal segments 1 through 7 or 2 through 7 have small, paired, styletlike appendages. (See Fig. 3.1 for general body form.)

Immature stages resemble adults, but they have fewer antennal segments. Their metamorphosis is gradual.

Habits and habitats: These very fragile, secretive hexapods are commonly found in decaying vegetation, in damp soil, under logs and stones, or in caves. Some feed on vegetable matter; others are carnivorous and eat springtails, mites, and other small, soil-inhabiting arthropods.

Reproductive behavior: Entotrophs reproduce by the same primitive means as the springtails. The male places sperm droplets on a stalk in the vicinity of the female but wanders away without making any attempt to induce her to gather the sperm. After the female is fertilized, she digs a hole in the ground, crawls inside, and deposits her eggs on a stalk in this nesting chamber. Whether she stays with the eggs or leaves them to their fate is unknown.

Collecting and preserving: Entotrophs are best collected by hand or from Berlese funnel material and preserved in 80-percent alcohol. If they are mounted on microscope slides, the mounting media should be one of the water-soluble solutions.

Rearing: Nothing is known about rearing these species.

Distribution: The 659 described species are widely distributed throughout the world. So far, only 64 species in 19 genera have been recorded in the U.S. and Canada. The published information on this group is widely scattered. The monograph by Paclt (1957) summarizes the previous literature, but recent papers have shown its classification to be confused. Most of the North American species listed in Paclt are cited only as "U.S.A.".

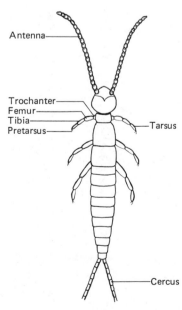

Fig. 3.1.

Identification: Although these species are larger than many of the other primitive hexapods, they are difficult to identify. There is no work dealing with the species of the U.S. and Canada, although a key to the genera is included in Paclt (1957). Smith (1960) contains the most useful work on the Projapygidae and Anajapygidae, but these account for only a small part of the species.

Economic importance: A few species are reported as minor economic pests in gardens.

CLASSIFICATION

The four families of the U.S. and Canada may be distinguished by using the accompanying Key.

Keys to the Families of Entotrophi

1. Cercus forcepslike, one-segmented, heavily sclerotized and darkly pigmented **4. Japygidae**
Cercus filiform, many-segmented, poorly sclerotized and not pigmented *2*
2(1). Cercus short, its basal segments wider than long *3*
Cercus long, its basal segments longer than wide **1. Campodeidae**
3(2). Antennae with hairlike setae-bearing spots (trichobothria) on segments 3 through 7; first abdominal sternum without appendages **2. Procampodeidae**
Antennae without hairlike setae-bearing spots (trichobothria) on segment 3; first abdominal sternum with appendages **3. Anajapygidae**

The following genera and species occur in the U.S. and Canada.

1. CAMPODEIDAE (Slender Entotroph Family)

L. 8–10 mm. Body elongate; head without eyes; abdomen with 10-segmented cerci. Thirty-four species are found in the U.S. and Canada, but most of these are known only from the type specimens, and details about their distribution are not available.

Subfamily Campodeinae

1.1 *Campodea* Westwood

Eleven species in three subgenera as follows:

Subgenus *Campodes* s. str. (6 spp.), of which the following is an example:

C. (*C.*) *folsomi* Silvestri. This species is apparently widespread and is thought to be the most common one in the U.S. and Canada. Found under stones in damp woodland and in humus throughout the year. (See Fig. 3.2.)

The two other subgenera are subgenus *Hypercampa* Silvestri (1 sp., *C. essigi* Silvestri) and subgenus *Monocampa* Silvestri (1 sp., *C. morgani* Silvestri, and 3 doubtful spp.).

[1.2 *Litocampa* Silvestri: subgenera: *Litocampa* s. str. (3 spp.) and *Tychocampa* Paclt (1 sp., *L. henroti* (Condé)); 1.3 *Meiocampa* Silvestri: subgenera: *Meiocampa* s. str. (4 spp.) and *Remycampa* Condé (1 sp., *M. spenceri* (Silvestri)); 1.4 *Tricampa* Silvestri; subgenus *Tricampa* s. str. (1 sp., *T. rileyi* (Silvestri)); 1.5 *Eumesocampa* Silvestri: subgenera: *Eumesocampa* s. str. (2 spp.) and *Mimocampa* Paclt (1 sp., *E. vandykei* (Silvestri)); 1.6 *Haplocampa* Silvestri (3 spp.); 1.7 *Metriocampa* Silvestri: subgenera *Metriocampa* s. str. (2 spp.) and *Holocampa* Paclt (4 doubtful spp.)]

Subfamily Plusiocampinae

1.8 *Plusiocampa* Silvestri

One species, as follows:

P. cookei (Packard). Found in caves. (See Fig. 3.3.) (2) TN.

2. PROCAMPODEIDAE (Procampodeid Entotroph Family)

[2.1 *Procampodea* Silvestri (1 sp., *P. macswaini* Condé and Pagés, (3) CA)]

Fig. 3.2.

Fig. 3.3. (*Courtesy of Thomas C. Barr, Jr.*)

Fig. 3.4.

Fig. 3.5.

3. ANAJAPYGIDAE (Anajapygid Entotroph Family)

[3.1 *Anajapyx* Silvestri (1 sp., *A. hermosa* Smith, (3) CA)] Note that *A. vesiculosus* Silvestri, from Europe, is a similar species (Fig. 3.4).

4. JAPYGIDAE (Earwiglike Entotroph Family)

Members of this family are distinctive in having the apical filaments replaced by a pair of forceps in the adult stage. There are 28 species in nine genera in the U.S. and Canada.

Subfamily Japyginae

[4.1 *Japyx* Haliday (5 spp.); 4.2 *Dipljapyx* Silvestri (2 spp.); 4.3 *Metajapyx* Silvestri (8 spp.); 4.4 *Eojapyx* Smith (1 sp., *E. pedis* Smith, (5) MO)]

4.5 *Catajapyx* Silvestri

One species, as follows:

C. *diversiunguis* (Silvestri). L. 8–10 mm. Elongate, pale tan, with central portion of each abdominal segment darker

and apical segment dark brown, with a pair of stout forceps. Soil-inhabiting species. (See Fig. 3.5 and A&J 4.)

[4.6 *Occasjapyx* Silvestri (2 spp., (3) CA)]

Subfamily Evalljapyginae

[4.7 *Evalljapyx* Silvestri (4 spp., (3) CA, AZ)]

Subfamily Parajapyginae

[4.8 *Parajapyx* Silvestri (3 spp., (2) GA, GL, AL); 4.9 *Miojapyx* Ewing (2 spp., (2) SC; (3) TX)]

BIBLIOGRAPHY

Palct, J. 1957. Diplura. *Genera Insectorum*. Fascicule 212: 123 pp. 37 figs.

Remington, C. L. 1954. *Ann. Ent. Soc. America*, 47: 277–286.

Silvestri, F. 1949. Japygidarum et Projapygidarum catalogus. *Boll. Lab. Ent. Agar. Portici.* 9: 40–75.

Smith, L. M. 1960. The family Projapygidae and Anajapygidae (Diplura) in North America. *Ann. Ent. Soc. America*. 53: 575–583 (25 figs.)

Smith, L. M. and C. L. Bolton 1964. Japygidae of North America, 9. The genus *Metajapyx*. *Journ. Kansas Ent. Soc.* 37: 126–138.

Class INSECTA

The remaining 27 orders are considered to be true insects.

Subclass ARCHAEOGNATHA

The order that follows is the only order of the subclass Archaeognatha (*archae*, "ancient," and *gnatha*, "mouth"). A fossil from the Lower Permian deposits in southwest Siberia called *Ḍasyleptus brongniarti* Sharov and additional specimens found in the United States have been assigned to the extinct order Monura. Although recorded in the literature as a separate order related to Thysanura and associated with the family Machilidae, this classification has not been generally accepted, and at the present time the order is not considered distinct from the order Microcoryphia.

Order 4

MICROCORYPHIA (Bristletails)

[= Thysanura *in part*]

These arthropods are considered the most primitive of the true insects. The name is derived from the Greek—*micro*, "small," and *coryphia*, "head"—and refers to the primitive type of head (the mandible moves vertically on the head and is equivalent to the swing of a walking leg).

Diagnosis: L. 10–12 mm; body soft, with flexible integument; white, gray, or yellowish gray to brown; body somewhat flattened, with pigmented scales. Mouthparts primitive, mandibles long, with a single condyle and a molar area well separated from the terminal incisor. Large compound eyes, meeting dorsally; ocelli present. Thorax strongly arched. Abdominal segments 2 through 9 with ventral styles and 1 through 7 usually with one or two pairs of exsertile vesicles. Median apical filament much longer than the lateral cerci. (See Fig. 4.1 for general body form.)

Immature stages resemble the adult with no noticeable external metamorphosis.

This group, once considered a part of the order Thysanura, is now placed in a separate subclass of the insects, the Archaeognatha, a classification based primarily on the structure of the mandibles, but also on features of the eyes (for example, the ommatidium is primitive, resembling that of the Collembola, with only a single-layered retina and other details).

Habits and habitats: These species are found by day hiding in rock crevices or under bark. They feed at night on algae, lichens, and vegetable debris. They are frequently found on rocks near the shore, above the high tide mark, or in other rocky situations, particularly shortly after dusk. They may be recognized by their ability to jump.

Collecting and preserving: Bristletails are separated from litter with a Berlese funnel or collected directly into 80-percent alcohol. Preservation in alcohol is better than pinning or mounting on microscope slides.

Rearing: As yet, species of this order have not been reared in captivity.

Distribution: According to specialists, there are about 250 species throughout the world, but they are poorly known and probably many more remain to be discovered. There is no complete catalog of the described species in print. Twenty species in 12 genera are known to occur in the U.S. and Canada.

Identification: Except for Wygodzinsky and Schmidt (1980), no keys for the easy identification of the species are readily available. The literature is widely scattered.

Economic importance: Bristletails are of no known economic importance.

The following discussion includes all recorded species known to occur in the United States and Canada. Several species recorded in the literature are omitted here because they two families in this order may be distinguished by the accompanying Key to the Families.

Key to the Families of Microcoryphia

Midventral sterna of proximal abdominal segments well developed, at least one-half of appendage length .. **1. Machilidae**
Midventral sterna of all abdominal segments poorly developed, at most one-quarter of appendage length .. **2. Meinertellidae**

Fig. 4.1.

1. MACHILIDAE (Jumping Bristletail Family)

L. ±12 mm. Brownish. Body elongate, convex, and covered with scales. Eyes large, compact, and contiguous dorsally; ocelli present. Tarsomeres 3-3-3. Cerci shorter than caudal filament. The jumping bristletails are found in leaf litter, under bark, among rocks along the seashore, or in old stone walls.

The following 8 genera and 14 species occur in the U.S. and Canada:

[1.1 *Petridiobus* Paclt (1 sp., *P. arcticus* (Folsom), (4) AK); 1.2 *Pedetontus* Silvestri, (1 sp., *P. saltator* Wygodzinsky and Schmidt, (1) MA, CT, NJ, PA); 1.3 *Mesomachilis* Silvestri, (1 sp., *M. nearcticus* Sil-

vestri, (3) CA); 1.4 *Mixomachilis* Paclt (1 sp., *M. remingtoni* Paclt, (3) CA)]

1.5 *Petrobius* Leach

Petrobius brevistylis Carpenter. L. ±12 mm. Brown. Common in rocky cliffs along the coast, usually 5 to 20 ft above tide line. (See Fig. 4.1.) (1) NB, NS, ME, MA, NH, RI.
 P. maritimus Leach. (1) NS [Note: this species is confused in the literature]
 P. californicus Silvestri. (3) CA.
 P. superior Silvestri. (4) OR.
 P. submutans Silvestri. (4) OR.
 P. persquamosus Silvestri. (3) CA.
 P. calcaratus Silvestri. (5) CO.

[1.6 *Trigoniophthalmus* Verhoff (1 sp., *T. alternatus* Silvestri, (1) CT, NY, NJ, PA, MD [introduced]); 1.7 *Machilis* Latreille (1 sp., *M. strenuva* Silvestri, (3) CA); 1.8 *Neomachilis* Silvestri (1 sp., *N. halophilus* Silvestri, (3) CA)]

2. MEINERTELLIDAE (Rock Bristletail Family)

L. 10–12 mm. Similar in appearance to the preceding family; poorly defined. Only six species are assigned here, as follows:

[2.1 *Machilinus* Silvestri (2 spp., *M. nevadensis* Sweetman, (4) NV, and *M. aurantiacus* (Schött), (3) CA); 2.2 *Machiloides* Silvestri (2 spp., *M. banksi* Silvestri, (2) VA, and *M. petauristes* Wygodzinsky and Schmidt, (1) NJ); 2.3 *Neomachilellus* Wygodzinsky (1 sp., *N.* sp. [undescribed, from s.e. US]); 2.4 *Hypomachilodes* Silvestri (1 sp., *H. texanus* Silvestri, (3) TX)]

BIBLIOGRAPHY

Wygodzinsky, Pedro and Kathleen Schmidt 1980. Survey of the Microcoryphia (Insecta) of the northeastern United States and adjacent provinces of Canada. American Mus. Novitatis. No. 2701, 17 pp.

Subclass DICONDYLIA

All remaining orders are assigned to this subclass.

Superorder THYSANURA

Only a single order appears in this superorder. It comprises the last of the wingless insects. All other wingless species are presumed to be derived from winged ancestors.

Order 5

THYSANURA (Silverfish and Allies)

The silverfish and their allies, sometimes referred to as *Zygentoma*, are an interesting group of true insects, probably the most advanced of the existing primitive orders of wingless insects. Their name is taken from the Greek: *thysan*, a fringe, and *ura*, tail.

Diagnosis: L. 2–20 mm. Body soft, with flexible integument; shape flattened or convex, with or without scales. White, gray, brown, or ground color. Mouthparts with biting mandibles and two condyles. Antennae short, to nearly as long as the body, with many segments. Compound eyes small or absent, never meeting dorsally; ocelli absent, except in one family. Abdomen with short styli on segments 2 through 9, but sometimes absent on some segments. Median apical abdominal filament usually only slightly longer than the lateral cerci. (See Fig. 5.1 for general body form.) The advanced structure of the mandibles shows this group to be very distinct from the Microcoryphia. Their resemblance is thought to be superficial only.

Immature stages resemble the adults; there is no noticeable external metamorphosis.

Habits and habitats: The common species in domestic situations feed on starchy materials and may be able to withstand considerable drying. However, most species remain hidden under bark or in leaf litter and require relatively high humidity. Some species are subterranean or live in caves; others are found in ant and termite nests. They are all vegetable feeders.

Collecting and preserving: As with the Microcoryphia.

Rearing: Silverfish are easy to rear in large jars of starchy material such as oatmeal or flour with yeast added. They need slight moisture, but mold must be prevented.

Distribution: Three hundred and twenty species are recorded in the literature as occurring throughout the world, but there is no recent complete catalog of them. Eighteen species in 12 genera occur in the U.S. and Canada.

The literature on this order is also scattered and not readily available. However, keys to the species of Lepismatidae (see Wygodzinsky, 1961) are available. All species in the three families recorded in the U.S. and Canada are included here. These families may be distinguished by the accompanying Key.

Key to the Families of Thysanura

1.	Ocelli present; 5 tarsomeres	1. **Lepidotrichidae**
	Ocelli absent; 3 or 4 tarsomeres ..	*2*
2(1).	Compound eyes present; body always with scales	3. **Lepismatidae**
	Compound eyes absent; body with or without scales	2. **Nicoletiidae**

1. LEPIDOTRICHIDAE (Forest Silverfish Family)

L. ±12 mm. Reddish, elongate, flat body without scales. Eyes and ocelli present; tarsomeres 5-5-5; abdominal cerci about as long as the caudal filament. This family is represented in the U.S. by only one species, as follows:

1.1 *Tricholepidion* Wygodzinsky

Tricholepidion gertschi Wygodzinsky. L. ±12 mm. Features same as in the family description. Found under bark of Douglas fir logs. (3) n. CA.

2. NICOLETIIDAE (Subterranean Silverfish Family)

L. 4–10 mm. Pale, elongate, flat (or rarely, oval) body with or without scales. Eyes absent; tarsomeres 4-4-4. Abdominal cerci about as long as the caudal filament. These insects are found in soil, caves, burrows, and ant and termite nests. The family is widespread with many genera occurring in the Old World.

[2.1 *Battigrassiella* Paclt (1 sp., *B. wheeleri* (Escherich), (3) TX); 2.2 *Nicoletia* Gervais, (2 spp., *N. tergata* Mills, (2) FL, and *N. ruckeri* Sil-

Fig. 5.1.

Fig. 5.2.

vestri, (3) TX); 2.3 *Texoreddellia* Wygodzinsky (1 sp., *T. texensis* Ulrich, (3) TX)]

3. LEPISMATIDAE (Silverfish and Firebrat Family)

L. 8–20 mm. Brown, tan, or silver gray. Elongate, flat body with scales. Eyes small with separate elements; no ocelli; with three or four tarsomeres. Abdominal cerci shorter than the caudal filament. The silverfish and firebrats are found in warm places, including human habitations. Some of the 13 species that occur in the U.S. and Canada are very common and widely distributed. The two cosmopolitan species described below are minor pests:

[3.1 *Acrotelsa* Escherich, (1 sp., *A. collaris* (Fabricius), (2) FL); 3.2 *Allacrotelsa* Silvestri [=*Stachisma* Wygodzinsky] (1 sp., *A. spinulata* (Packard), (2) TN, SC, FL, AR; (3) OK, TX, AZ, CA; (4) WA, OR)]

3.3 *Ctenolepisma* Escherich

Five species, extreme southern in distribution, except for the following:

C. lineata (Fabricius): subsp. *pilifera* Lucas (Four-lined Silverfish). L. ±15 mm. Color variable but usually with a basic silvery sheen and with four dark lines extending lengthwise on the dorsal surface of the body. Known from (1) s. central Canada and n.e. U.S. from MA s. to (2) TN, GA; (3) AZ, CA; (4) OR, NV.

C. longicaudata Eschscholtz (Long-tailed Silverfish). L. 13–15 mm. Pale, unpigmented. Antennae and filaments longer than the body. Found in houses. (2) NC s. to FL, w. to LA; (3) s. CA; (5) MO.

C. ciliata (Dufour). (3) CA.
C. diversisquamis Silvestri. (2) FL.
C. targionii (Grassi and Rovelli). (2) SC.

3.4 *Lepisma* Linnaeus

One species, as follows:

L. saccharina Linnaeus (Silverfish). L. ±12 mm. Uniformly slate gray. The species occurs in habitations but has been recorded in the wild in extreme southern Florida. It feeds on starchy materials, including wall paper glue, book bindings, and photographs. Cosmopolitan. (See Fig. 5.2 and A&J 3.)

[3.5 *Leucolepisma* Wall, (1 sp., *L. arenaria* Wall, (3) AZ, CA; (4) NV); 3.6 *Mirolepisma* Silvestri, (1 sp., *M. deserticola* Silvestri, (3) AZ, CA); 3.7 *Stylifera* Stach (1 sp., *S. gigantea* Escherich, (2) FL)]

3.8 *Thermobia* Bergroth

Two species, as follows:

T. domestica (Packard) (Firebrat). L. ±12 mm. Gray, with tufts of brown setae. Found throughout North America in habitations where it is warm and humid. Introduced.

T. campbelli (Barnhart). (1) OH, PA.

BIBLIOGRAPHY

Paclt, J. 1963. Thysanura fam. Nicoletiidae. Genera Insectorum, fasc. 216e, 58 pp.
_____. 1967. Thysanura fam. Lepidotrichidae, Maindroniidae, Lepismatidae. General Insectorum, fasc. 218e, 86 pp.
Remington, C. L. 1954. The suprageneric classification of the order Thysanura (Insecta). *Ann. Ent. Soc. America.* 47: 277–286.
Wygodzinsky, P. 1961. On the surviving representative of the Lepicto-trichidae (Thysanura), *Ann. Ent. Soc. America.* 54: 621–627.
_____. 1963. On J. Paclt's Nicoletiidae (Thysanura) in Genera Insectorum, *Ann. Mag. Nat. Hist.* (13) 6: 265–269.
_____. 1972. A review of the silverfish (Lepismatidae, Thysanura) of the United States and Caribbean area. *American Mus. Novit.* No. 2481, 26 pp.

The remaining orders are called the *winged insects* even though some of the species and three entire orders—the Mallophaga, Anoplura, and Siphonaptera—are wingless. It is thought, however, that this wingless condition is a secondary trait and that the species evolved from winged ancestors.

The wings of insects show a remarkable progression of characteristics. Wing veins are arranged in a similar pattern throughout all the orders and provide one of the clearest demonstrations of evolution by a comparative study. The terminology for wing veins and cells is more or less uniform, although a different nomenclature was formerly used for some groups, especially the Hymenoptera and the Diptera. If some of the older literature is referred to, it will be necessary to learn the terms for these particular groups. The modern literature follows the Comstock-Needham system of nomenclature, with some recent improvements. For proper use of the family keys that follow, it will be necessary to review the terms for wing veins and cells as explained in the introduction.

Division **PALAEOPTERA**

Two extant orders—the Ephemeroptera and the Odonata—and three extinct orders belong to this division. The wings of its members are incapable of folding back over the abdomen, unlike those of all other orders of winged insects, because of the lack of certain sclera at their base. At best, the wings are held at rest by touching one another above the thorax. In the damselflies (as in the Neoptera), the thorax is tilted back to allow the wings to lie in repose over the abdomen without folding.

Extinct Order **PALEODICTYOPTERA**

This extinct order, well known from the Pennsylvanian period, is less abundant in Permian strata. Although the group shows considerable variation in wing structure and size, there is no doubt about its relationship to the extant order of the Palaeoptera. All known species are reported to have sucking mouthparts, a certain indication that they do not represent the primitive ancesters of the Ephemeroptera or Odonata. All species seem to have some form of prothoracic lobe or spines. Those with large lateral lobes are of particular interest because these lobes are doubtlessly homologs of meso- and metathoracic wings.

Extinct Order **MEGASECOPTERA**

This extinct order is less well known than the preceding, but fossils from both the Pennsylvania and Permian periods have been studied. They are closely related to the Paleodictyoptera, being distinguished mainly by their narrow wing bases. These insects had primitive sucking mouthparts.

Extinct Order **DIAPHANOPTERODEA**

Members of this extinct order from the Permian period were capable of folding their wings over the abdomen, but this characteristic was developed independently of the Neoptera. Their exact morphological structure has not been worked out in detail.

Order 6

EPHEMEROPTERA (Mayflies)

The mayflies are the oldest of the winged insects to survive to the present day. The living species represent an ancient group that is unique among living insects in that they molt after reaching the first winged or subimaginal stage. The aquatic naiads present quite a different appearance from the delicate adults. Because many of the adults are extremely short-lived, or "ephemeral," they are given the scientific name, *ephemeroptera*, from *ephemero-*, "lasting a day," and *pteron*, "winged." The adult stage usually lasts only from a few minutes to several days. The adults do not feed; their mouthparts are vestigial. Mayflies are seldom noticed by the general public except when large numbers of their crushed bodies become a nuisance along rivers and on highways. The adults have long been such favorite bait for fishermen that many of the artificial flies used in fly fishing are imitations of either the adult or the naiad.

The presence of mayflies is usually an indicator of the absence of pollution because their naiads usually will not tolerate polluted bodies of water. In a few cases, however, they have successfully inhabited polluted areas. Knowledge of the species present at a particular body of water may sometimes be used as an indicator of the degree of its pollution. Unfortunately, many species of mayflies are becoming nearly extinct as a result of the extensive contamination of our waterways.

Diagnosis: L. 1–30 mm. Soft-bodied, with a cylindrical, elongate shape. Antennae short and setalike. Two pairs of delicate, triangularly-shaped wings as a rule, the front pair large,

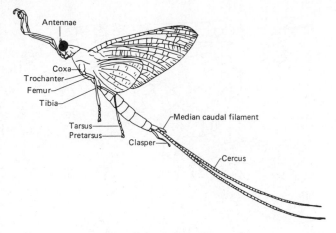

Fig. 6.1. (*Redrawn from Burks, 1953*)

with many veins, and the hind pair smaller, sometimes reduced, or, in a few species, absent; wings held vertically over the body when not in use. Legs long, slender, and unmodified except that the front pair are usually noticeably longer than the others. Abdomen usually as long as or longer than the body, with two or three long caudal filaments. Mouthparts not functional, but of the biting type. (See Fig. 6.1 for general body form as exemplified by *Hexagenia limbata* Serville.)

Metamorphosis: Hemimetabolous, with egg, naiad, and adult stages. Eggs are small, a few having specific features.

The naiads are of various shapes, most of them broad, and have functional gills along the sides of the abdomen. (See Fig. 6.2.) Their mouthparts are well developed for chewing aquatic vegetation, detritus, and sometimes dead animal matter; some are carnivorous. Molting is frequent, often as many as 20 to 60 times before the adult stage is reached.

Adult mayflies are distinguished from the stoneflies (Plecoptera), to which they bear a superficial resemblance, by the presence of long and thin caudal filaments and by the wing position. Some resemble certain ichneumon wasps because these caudal filaments may be confused with the ovipositors of the latter, but the presence of a great number of cross veins in their wings quickly separates the two groups.

Habits and habitats: Naiads live in fresh water streams, ponds, and lakes. This stage lasts from a few weeks to a year (rarely to four years), during which time the naiads feed on

Fig. 6.2.

plant and animal materials. They eventually transform into subimagos, rise to the water surface enveloped in an air bubble, and emerge. These preadults are able to fly to a nearby bush or tree, where another molt usually takes place and the true adults (imagos) appear. Fertilization and egg laying take place soon thereafter.

Reproductive behavior: Mating takes place in a variety of ways. In many species, emerging males grab the slightly later emerging females by means of their elongate front legs that reach up from beneath. Their abdomen clasps the female and mating takes place on the wing. Most noticeable, however, are the swarms of males of many other species that perform a mating dance. The males fly vertically into the air a few feet and then fall with wings outstretched, only to repeat this action again and again. When females enter the swarm, they are grasped by the males, and mating takes place as the pair leaves the swarm. In one species, *Dolania americana*, a different ritual occurs. The female subimagos emerge after the males but do not molt to imagos. Instead, they fly in an almost level, slightly undulating pattern one to two meters above the water, occasionally rising upwards for a few meters and then returning to a more level course. As soon as the female subimagos are seen, the males increase the speed of their flight and race in pursuit.

The female lays eggs immediately, dropping balls or packets of several hundred eggs as she hovers over the water. Sometimes she flies directly into the water and dies. After she hits the water surface, the eggs are released from her floating body. The fertilized female of a few species actually enters the water to deposit her eggs, attaching them to stones, moss, fallen leaves, or some other substrate. She dies as soon as she finishes laying them. Several species—for example, *Cailibaetis floridanus* Banks—retain the eggs and give birth to six to several hundred naiads as they fly over the water. The living naiads drop into the water and sink to the bottom. Males die as soon as fertilization has been completed; the female, usually as soon as her eggs are laid.

Naiad structure and ecology: Many naiads prefer flowing water, particularly trout streams (perhaps it is the trout that prefer streams with naiads, but the majority of mayflies are warm water species). All species occur in fresh, more or less unpolluted water. Temperature seems to be an essential factor in the distribution of any particular species; some prefer cool waters, others, warmer, and so on. The structure of the naiad varies according to its habitat.

Those naiads that are swimmers are elongate, slender, with slender legs and undulating, floating gills along the abdomen; they have ciliated cerci and a terminal filament. This type of naiad is characteristic of species of Leptophlebiidae, Siphlonuridae, and a few Baetidae.

Flowing water naiads are flattened, short, with large heads, dorsal eyes, and flattened and ciliated legs with very broad femora; their gills are lateral and their caudal filaments short. They cling to stones in shallow streams. Species of Oligoneuriidae and *Baetisca* Walsh are of this type. The latter are modified by having the mesonotum expanded into a shield that completely covers the thorax and one to five of the abdominal terga plus part of the sixth (see Fig. 6.3).

Crawling naiads have more robust legs. Since their cilia entrap mud, they are hidden on the bottom of the body of water in which they live. Naiads of Caenidae and *Potamanthus verticalis* (Say) are of this type.

Fig. 6.3.

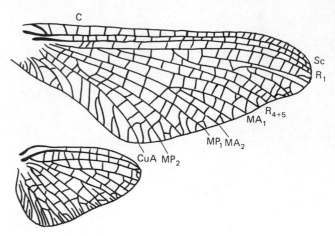

Fig. 6.4.

Burrowing naiads form galleries or U-shaped tunnels in mud, sand, or clay. These species are cylindrical, with somewhat enlarged, forward projecting heads and mandibles modified for tube building. The gills are folded over the back; caudal filaments are long, with cilia on each side. These species usually spend more than one year as naiads. The naiads of *Hexagenia* spp. are of this type.

Both naiads and adults are important food sources for other aquatic animals, particularly fish.

Collecting and preserving: These insects are collected with nets, either as naiads that may be reared or as adults. The cast skins of the naiads should be associated with the emerged adults. Both are best preserved in 95-percent alcohol, not pinned. Because of the water content of naiads, it is necessary to drain off the initial preservative and replace with fresh alcohol after a few days. Other solutions for preservation may be used in the field but should be replaced with 80-percent alcohol for permanent storage.

Rearing: Although rearing species in colonies from egg to egg is rarely possible, naiads may be collected and placed in rearing cups so that they may be associated with their adult stage. Plastic drinking cups may be cut and fitted for this purpose. Two large squares should be cut out of the lower half of each cup, one on each side, and the interior lined with nylon mesh to the top. A large circle is cut out of the lid and nylon mesh glued in its place. Several cups are floated half submerged in water by inserting them into a board through holes of the right diameter to maintain them in such a position. The board is tied to a stake in the water or to a tree trunk. Naiads are placed one per cup into these cages. If naiads with black wing pads are selected, only a few days wait will be necessary before the subimago emerges. Shortly thereafter the adult will emerge. The cast skin of the naiad and the adult can then be carefully transferred to an alcohol vial for storage.

Distribution: Of the approximately 2,000 described species, 611 in 59 genera occur in the U.S. and Canada, with some species found in every region and others with a very restricted distribution. Although no world catalog is available, the work by Edmunds, *et al.* (1976), lists all species in the U.S. and Canada.

Identification: Adults are identified mainly by the different arrangements of wing veins [see Fig. 6.4 for arrangement in *Isonychia bicolor* (Walker)] and by features of the male copulatory organs. Color may distinguish certain species, but its variability precludes its being depended upon for more than preliminary spot identifications. Naiads are sometimes easier to identify, but at best they are usually recognizable only to genus.

Economic importance: Other than providing a considerable amount of fish food, mayflies are of no economic importance.

CLASSIFICATION

The order has been divided into two suborders, and several superfamilies are recognized, six of which are found in the U.S. and Canada, as listed in Table 6.1. Recent researchers recognize 17 families of mayflies in the U.S. and Canada. The

Table 6.1 Families of Mayflies in the U.S. and Canada

Suborder SCHISTONATA (Splitback Mayflies)

Superfamily BAETOIDEA
1. SIPHLONURIDAE (Primitive Minnow Mayfly Family)
2. METRETOPODIDAE (Cleftfooted Minnow Mayfly Family)
3. AMETROPODIDAE (Sand Minnow Mayfly Family)
4. BAETIDAE (Small Minnow Mayfly Family)
5. OLIGONEURIIDAE (Brushlegged Mayfly Family)
6. HEPTAGENIIDAE (Flatheaded Mayfly Family)

Superfamily LEPTOPHLEBIOIDEA
7. LEPTOPHLEBIIDAE (Pronggill Mayfly Family)

Superfamily EPHEMEROIDEA (Burrowing and Tusked Mayflies)
8. BEHNINGIIDAE (Tuskless Burrower Mayfly Family)
9. POTAMANTHIDAE (Hacklegill Mayfly Family)
10. POLYMITARCYIDAE (Pale Burrower Mayfly Family)
11. EPHEMERIDAE (Common Burrower Mayfly Family)
12. PALINGENIIDAE (Spinyheaded Burrower Mayfly Family)

Suborder PANNOTA Fusedback Mayflies

Superfamily EPHEMERELLOIDEA
13. EPHEMERELLIDAE (Spiny Crawler Mayfly Family)
14. TRICORYTHIDAE (Little Stout Crawler Mayfly Family)

Superfamily CAENOIDEA
15. NEOEPHEMERIDAE (Large Squaregill Mayfly Family)
16. CAENIDAE (Small Squaregill Mayfly Family)

Superfamily PROSOPISTOMATOIDEA (Shieldback Mayflies)
17. BAETISCIDAE (Armored Mayfly Family)

following discussion lists all these families and their respective genera, including the number of species in each. Only locally prevalent species representing the most common families will be described and illustrated here. The common names are those used by entomologists, not necessarily those of fishermen.

A key to the families of naiads is provided as well as to the families of adult Ephemeroptera.

Key to the Families of Ephemeroptera

1.	Wings with only 3 or 4 longitudinal veins posterior to R_1 (Fig. 6.5); body black (5.1 *Lachania*) ...**5. Oligoneuriidae**	
	Wings with more than four longitudinal veins; color various	*2*
2(1).	Males with penes longer than forceps; female with antennae arising from prominent anterolateral projections **8. Behningiidae**	
	Males with penes shorter than forceps; antennae of female not inserted as in preceding	*3*
3(4).	Wing with bases of MP_2 and CuA not sharply bent toward CuP, or unforked, or atrophied basally; hind wing of some very small, or absent, or with MA forked or not [see Fig. 6.4 for notation] ...	*8*
	Wing with bases of MP_2 and CuA bent sharply toward CuP; hind wing with MA not forked, but with numerous veins and cross veins	*4*
4(3).	Hind wing with prominent costal projection near base and 1A in front wing not forked; hind wing with fork of MP beyond middle; basal costal cross veins weak or atrophied ... **15. Neoephemeridae**	
	Hind wing without prominent costal projection near base, or 1A in front wing forked; hind wing with fork of MP in basal half of wing; basal costal cross veins well developed	*5*
5(4).	Middle and hind legs of male, and all legs of female, atrophied beyond trochanters **10. Polymitarcyidae**	
	All legs well developed in both sexes	*6*
6(5).	Wings with 1A forked near wing margin **9. Potamanthidae**	
	Wings with 1A not forked; 3 or more veinlets extending from 1A to hind margin of wing ..	*7*
7(6).	Male pronotum short and about 3 times as wide as long; penes of male long and tubular; female with caudal filaments shorter than body **12. Palingeniidae**	
	Pronotum of male no more than twice as wide as long; penes of male not long and tubular; female with caudal filaments longer than body **11. Ephemeridae**	
8(3).	Hind wings present, but may be very small	*11*
	Hind wings absent ..	*9*
9(8).	Abdomen with 2 caudal filaments; wings with bases of MA_2 and MP_2 atrophied and 1 or 2 short marginal veinlets between main longitudinal veins **4. Baetidae**	
	Abdomen with 3 caudal filaments; bases of MA_2 and MP_2 usually well developed and without short marginal veinlets between main longitudinal veins ,...............	*10*
10(9).	Wing with MP_2 and $1MP_1$ extending less than three-fourths of the distance to wing base; male genital forceps 2- or 3-segmented; thorax usually black or gray; (in part) **14. Tricorythidae**	
	Wing with MP_2 and $1MP_1$ extending to wing base; male genital forceps one-segmented; thorax usually brown **16. Caenidae**	
11(8).	Wing with cubital intercalaries a series of veinlets, often forked or sinuate, extending from CuA to hind margin of wing; MA in hind wing usually forked; 4 hind tarsomeres Some **5. Oligoneuriidae** and some **1. Siphlonuridae**	
	Cubital intercalaries not as above; MA in hind wing forked or unforked; 4 or 5 hind tarsomeres ..	*12*
12(11).	Abdomen with 3 well-developed caudal filaments	*13*
	Abdomen with 2 well-developed caudal filaments, the median filament being very short or absent ..	*16*
13(12).	Hind wing small, with 1 or 2 unbranched veins only, the costal projection long and somewhat recurved (in part) **14. Tricorythidae**	
	Hind wing larger, with 1 or more branched veins and costal projection not as in the preceding ..	*14*
14(13).	Wing with 2 somewhat parallel cubital intercalaries; 1A attached to hind margin of wing by a series of veinlets **3. Ametropodidae**	
	Wing with cubital intercalaries not as in the preceding	*15*
15(14).	Wing with some short, basally marginal veinlets along outer margin **13. Ephemerellidae**	
	Wing without basally detached marginal veinlets along outer margin **7. Leptophlebiidae**	
16(12).	Wing with cubital intercalaries absent and 1A extending to outer margin; hind wing with many long, free marginal veinlets **17. Baetiscidae**	
	Wing with cubital intercalaries present and 1A extending to hind margin; hind wing not as in the preceding ...	*17*

Key to the Families of Ephemeroptera (*Contd.*)

17(16). Wing with 1 or 2 short basally detached marginal veinlets between main longitudinal veins and with bases of MA$_2$ and MP$_2$ atrophied **4. Baetidae**

Wing with marginal veinlets basally attached to other veins, and MA$_2$ and MP$_2$ attached basally ... *18*

18(17). Hind legs with 5 distinct tarsomeres; wing with 2 parallel pairs of cubital intercalaries; (in part) .. **6. Heptageniidae**

Hind legs with apparently 4 tarsomeres, the basal one more or less fused to tibiae; wing with 1 or 2 pairs of cubital intercalaries *19*

19(18). Front tarsi of males three times as long as tibiae; eyes contiguous or nearly so; females with apical and basal abdominal segments subequal to middle segments in length and width, and the subgenital plate evenly convex, not notched **2. Metretopodidae**

Front tarsi of males twice as long as tibiae; eyes separated dorsally by a distance equal to twice the width of median ocellus; female with abdomen long and slender, the apical segments more elongate and slender than basal segments, and the subgenital plate with a median notch; (Pseudironinae) **6. Heptageniidae**

Key to the Families of Naiads

1. Dorsal surface of body with an undivided sclerite covering all of the thorax and abdomen to segment 6, including all gills **17. Baetiscidae**

Dorsal surface of body without such a sclerite; pronotum, mesonotum, wing pads and at least 1 pair of abdominal gills visible from above *2*

2(1). Mandibles with long, slender process projecting in front of head capsule *3*

Mandibles without such a process ... *7*

3(2). Gills on abdominal segments 2 through 7 not fringed; (in part) .. **7. Leptophlebiidae**

Gills on abdominal segments 2 through 7 fringed *4*

4(3). Tibiae and tarsi cylindrical; abdominal gills lateral **9. Potomanthidae**

Tibiae and tarsi more or less distinctly flattened; abdominal gills dorsal *5*

5(4). Apex of hind tibia produced into an acute point ventrally; mandibular process curved dorsad distally ... *6*

Apex of hind tibia rounded; mandibular process horizontal or curved ventrad distally .. **10. Polymitarcidae**

6(5). Mandibular tusks with a distinct dorsolateral keel more or less toothed, with a line of spurs along toothed edge **12. Palingeniidae**

Mandibular tusks more or less circular in cross section, without a distinct toothed keel .. **11. Ephemeridae**

7(2). Head and prothorax each with anterolateral dorsal spiculose lobe .. **8. Behningiidae**

Head and prothorax without such lobes *8*

8(7). Front legs with 2 rows of long setae on inner surface; gill tuft present at base of maxillae *9*

Front legs without such setae on inner surface; no gill tuft at base of maxillae *10*

9(8). Gills of abdominal segment 1 ventral; no gill tufts at base of front coxae **5. Oligoneuriidae**

Gills of abdominal segment 1, dorsal; gill tufts present at base of front coxae (1.7 *Isonychia*) ... **1. Siphlonuridae**

10(8). Gills of abdominal segment 2 covering, at least in part, succeeding gills *11*

Gills of abdominal segment 2 either absent or not covering any succeeding gills *13*

11(10). Gills of abdominal segment 2 triangular or oval, not meeting on midline **14. Tricorythidae**

Gill of abdominal segment 2 quadrate, fused with or closely approximated on midline *12*

12(11). Mesonotum with projecting anterolateral lobe; gills of abdominal segment 2 fused on midline ... **15. Neoephemeridae**

Mesonotum without such lobe; gills of abdominal segment 2 approximated but not fused on midline ... **16. Caenidae**

10(10). Gills absent on abdominal segment 2 **13. Ephemerellidae**

Gills present on abdominal segment 2 *14*

14(13). Body distinctly flattened dorsoventrally *15*

Body more or less cylindrical .. *16*

15(14). Abdominal gills ending in a filament or point; (in part) **7. Leptophlebiidae**

Abdominal gills with dorsal portion platelike and ventral portion filamentous **6. Heptageniidae**

16(14). Claw of front leg different in structure from those of mid leg or hind leg *17*

Claws of all legs similar in structure *18*

Key to the Families of Naiads (*Contd.*)

17(16). Claw of front leg with series of long, slender denticles **3. Ametropodidae**
Claw of front leg bifid **2. Metretopodidae**
18(16). Abdominal gills ending in a filament or point; (in part) **7. Leptophlebiidae**
Abdomen with platelike gills *19*
19(18). Three well-developed tails; antennae shorter than twice the head width
.. **1. Siphlonuridae**
Two or 3 well-developed tails; if 3 tails present, then antennae two to three times the
head width .. **4. Baetidae**

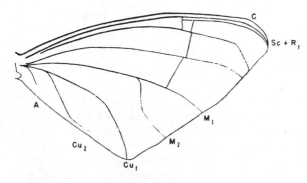

Fig. 6.5.

Suborder SCHISTONOTA (Splitback Mayflies)

Superfamily BAETOIDEA

1. SIPHLONURIDAE (Primitive Minnow Mayfly Family)

L. 9–13 mm. Abdomen with two or three caudal filaments; four hind tarsomeres; front wing with veins M and Cu parallel; costal cross vein usually present; ocelli small. The family contains eight genera and 81 species widely distributed in the U.S. and Canada. The naiads inhabit small, rapid streams among pebbles or shallow, quiet, well-aerated streams; some inhabit swamps and forest pools.

Subfamily Siphlonuridae

[1.1 *Ameletus* Eaton (31 spp.); 1.2 *Edmundsius* Day (1 sp., *E. agilis* Day); 1.3 *Parameletus* Bengtsson (4 spp.); 1.4 *Siphlonisca* Needham (1 sp., *S. aerodromia* Needham); 1.5 *Siphlonurus* Eaton (17 spp.)]

Subfamily Acanthametropodinae

[1.6 *Acanthametropus* Tshernova (1 sp., *A. pecatonica* (Burks))]

Subfamily Isonychiinae

1.7 *Isonychia* Eaton

Members of this genus are called *white-legged mayflies*. There are 25 species, of which the following is an example:

I. bicolor (Walker). L. 9–16 mm. Body dark reddish, fading laterally to olive-brown with some yellowish markings; eyes large and red; wings (see Fig. 6.4) grayish or bluish; middle and hind legs white. Adults emerge mid-June to July. Naiads frequent medium to large gravel-bottomed rivers in fairly swift current. Common. (1) n.e. U.S.; (2) s.e. U.S.

2. METRETOPODIDAE (Cleftfooted Minnow Mayfly Family)

[2.1 *Metretopus* Eaton (1 sp., *M. borealis* Eaton); 2.2 *Siphloplecton* Clemens (5 spp.)]

3. AMETROPODIDAE (Sand Minnow Mayfly Family)

Naiads inhabit stream bottoms on rocks and sand or on vegetation. This family contains only three species, but they are widely distributed throughout U.S. and Canada.

[3.1 *Ametropus* Albarda (3 spp.)]

4. BAETIDAE (Small Minnor Mayfly Family)

L. 3–7 mm (rarely to 10 mm). Usually two pair of wings, but some species reported with only one; hind wings reduced; two caudal filaments; three hind tarsomeres; male with turbanate compound eyes (that is, the upper half enlarged and divided from the lower half, resembling a turban); costal cross veins usually present. Ten genera and 147 species are found in the U.S. and Canada, widely distributed. Naiads are often warm water species, but some are found in a wide variety of other habitats, including several that tolerate polluted water.

[4.1 *Apobaetis* Day (1 sp., *A. indeprensus* Day)]

4.2 *Baetis* Leach

This genus contains 59 species of which the following two are common:

B. pygmaeus (Hagen). L. 3–5 mm. Dark brown to black, with legs white except at base; abdomen white or yellowish with black stigmatic markings. Naiads live in shallow, sluggish streams on marginal vegetation. Adults emerge mid-August to mid-September. (1) n.e. NA; (5) MO.
B. spinosus McDunnough. L. 4–5 mm. Head dark brown to black with yellow-brown markings; antennae light gray-brown to yellow apically; thorax black, laterally yellow-brown to dark; legs yellow to white; abdomen white, stained with tan or black. Naiads inhabit slow to swift streams, especially those having submerged vegetation. Adults emerge throughout the year. (See Fig. 6.6.) (1) n.e. NA; (2) s.e. U.S.

[4.3 *Baetodes* Needham and Murphy (2 spp.)]

4.4 *Callibaetis* Eaton (Flecked Mayflies)

Of the 23 species in this genus that exist in the U.S. and Canada, the following two are the ones likely to be collected:

Fig. 6.6. (*Redrawn from Berner, 1950*)

Fig. 6.7. (*Redrawn from Berner, 1950*)

C. ferrugineus (Walsh). L. 7–9 mm. Color variable; head and thorax often light brown with very small, darker brown spots and white markings; legs pale buff; abdomen light brown, with sides and venter having darker markings and small spots. Naiads live on vegetation in still water. Adults emerge mid-April to late September. (1) n.e. NA; (5) IA, MO.

C. pretiosus Banks. L. 8–10 mm. Female with brown stripe on front wing; male with darkened thorax and darkened abdominal segments. Naiads are found in roadside ditches, ponds, or lakes. Adults emerge throughout the year. (1) n.e. NA; (2) s.e. U.S.

[4.5 *Centroptilum* Eaton (24 spp.); 4.6 *Cloeon* Leach (12 spp.); 4.7 *Dactylobaetis* Traver and Edmunds (2 spp.); 4.8 *Heterocloen* McDunnough (3 spp.); 4.9 *Paracloeodes* Day (2 spp.); 4.10 *Pseudocloeon* Klapalek (19 spp.)]

5. OLIGONEURIIDAE (Brushlegged Mayfly Family)

The five species in this family are assigned to two genera in a single subfamily Oligoneuriinae. The adults have reduced wing venation. The naiads inhabit moderate to rapid streams in sand or under rocks. The species are found throughout central and s.w. U.S. and central Canada.

Subfamily Oligoneuriinae

[5.1 *Lachlania* Hagen (3 spp.) (see Fig. 6.5); 5.2 *Homoeoneuria* Eaton (2 spp.)]

6. HEPTAGENIIDAE (Flatheaded Mayfly Family)

L. 4.14 mm. This family is similar to the Siphlouridae except that it exhibits five hind tarsomeres. The wing venation is distinctive (see Fig. 6.7). The naiads are usually found under stones or logs in shallow, rapid streams or in lakes. There are 133 species in 12 genera in the U.S. and Canada, widely distributed.

Subfamily Heptageniinae

[6.1 *Cinygma* Eaton (3 spp.); 6.2 *Cinygmula* McDunnough (11 spp.); 6.3 *Epeorus* Eaton: subgenera: *Iron* Eaton (17 spp.) and *Ironopsis* Travers (2 spp.); 6.4 *Heptagenia* Walsh (36 spp.); 6.5 *Ironodes* Traver (6 spp.); 6.6 *Rhithrogena* Eaton (21 spp.); 6.7 *Stenacron* Jenson (7 spp.)]

6.8 *Stenonema* Traver

L. 7–9 mm. Yellow head with black markings; body and legs yellow with black markings. Naiads live in rivers and lakes.

Adults emerge from May through August. Twenty-four species are found throughout eastern North America, of which the following is an example:

S. modestrum (Banks). L. 8–10 mm. Head deep orange-brown; antennae pale yellow; thorax red-brown with white and yellow markings; abdomen light yellow with orange-markings. Naiads are found in gravel riffles of medium to large streams where current is swift and depth is 6 inches or less. Adults emerge June to mid-August. (See Fig. 6.7) (3) AZ, NM, TX; (4) ID, UT; (5) CO.

Subfamily Arthropleinae

[6.9 *Arthroplea* Bengtsson (1 sp., *A. bipunctata* McDunnough)]

Subfamily Pseudironinae

[6.10 *Pseudiron* McDunnough (2 spp.)]

Subfamily Anepeorinae

[6.11 *Anepeorus* McDunnough (2 spp.)]

Subfamily Spinadinae

[6.12 *Spinadis* Edmunds and Jensen (1 sp., *S. wallacei* Edmunds and Jensen)]

Superfamily LEPTOPHLEBIOIDEA

7. LEPTOPHLEBIIDAE (Prongill Mayfly Family)

L. 4–8 mm (rarely 12 mm). This family is similar to the Siphlouridae except that the Cu vein is bent (see Fig. 6.8), and the caudal filaments are often noticeably longer than the body. The costal cross veins are present but sometimes faint. Naiads prefer crevices under rocks, logs, and sticks in slow streams or rivers or in shallow, rapid streams. There are 70 species in eight genera widely distributed throughout the U.S. and Canada.

[7.1 *Choroterpes* Eaton (12 spp.); 7.2 *Habrophlebia* Eaton (1 sp., *H. vibrans* Needham); 7.3 *Habrophlebiodes* Ulmer (4 spp.); 7.4 *Homothraulus* Demoulin (1 sp., unnamed)]

7.5 *Leptophlebia* Westwood

There are ten species in this genus, of which the following is an example:

L. nebulosa Walker. (See Fig. 6.8 for wing venation.) (1) n.e. NA.

7.6 *Paraleptophlebia* Lestage

This genus contains 33 species, many of them widely distributed. The following species is common:

Fig. 6.8.

P. adoptiva (McDunnough). L. 7–8 mm. Head and thorax dark brown; abdomen lighter brown; wings with brown longitudinal veins. Naiads frequent shallow, gravel-bottomed streams of various sizes. Adults emerge May to July. (1) n.e. NA; (2) s.e. U.S.

[7.7 *Thraulodes* Ulmer (5 spp.); 7.8 *Traverella* Eaton (4 spp.)]

Superfamily EPHEMEROIDEA (Burrowing and Tusked Mayflies)

8. BEHNINGIDAE (Tuskless Burrower Mayfly Family)

This family is represented in the U.S. and Canada by the single species that follows:

8.1 *Dolania* Edmunds and Traver

D. americana Edmund and Traver. Naiads burrow in sand in rivers. (2) s.e. U.S.

9. POTAMANTHIDAE (Hacklegill Mayfly Family)

This family contains one genus and eight species, all confined to eastern and central North America. The naiads live on the bottom of fast-flowing streams in silt and sand or beneath stones.

9.1 *Potamanthus* Picet

There are eight species in this genus, including the following:

P. verticalis (Say). Common. (1) n.e. U.S.; (2) s.e. U.S.

10. POLYMITARCYIDAE (Pale Burrower Mayfly Family)

This family contains six species in three genera in the U.S. and Canada. The naiads are found in swift streams in tubular burrows or in clay banks of large rivers.

Subfamily Polymitarcyinae

[10.1 *Ephoron* Williamson (2 spp.)]

Subfamily Campsurinae

[10.2 *Campsurus* Eaton (1 sp., *C. decoloratus* [Hagen]); 10.3 *Tortopus* Needham and Murphy (3 spp.)]

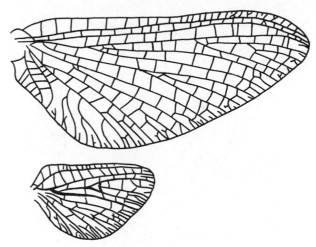

Fig. 6.9.

11. EPHEMERIDAE (Common Burrower Mayfly Family)

L. 10–30 mm (rarely larger). The family is best recognized by its large bodily size and the strongly divergent M and Cu veins in its front wings. Naiads burrow in sand and silt in streams and lakes. The 13 species are assigned to three genera. Some species occur in every part of the U.S. and Canada.

11.1 *Ephemera* Linnaeus

This genus contains seven species in the U.S. and Canada, a common one being the following:

E. simulans Walker. L. 10–14 mm. Dark with lighter prothorax; wings (Fig. 6.9) with dark mottling. Naiads are found in streams and lake bottoms composed of sand and gravel, but sometimes silt and mud. Adults emerge from June to mid-July. (1) n.c. NA; (2) VA.

11.2 *Hexagenia* Walsh

The five species that occur in the U.S. and Canada all belong to the subgenus *Hexagenia* s. str. The following are common:

H. limbata (Serville) (Giant Mayfly). L. 18–30 mm. Yellow with brown prothorax and abdominal stripes; wings dark. Naiads burrow in muddy bottoms of streams and lakes to depth of 60 ft. Adults emerge mid-June to mid-September. This species is also known as the Green Bay Fly because of the hordes of adults that once emerged from Green Bay of Lake Michigan and covered the city of Green Bay, Wisconsin, before lake pollution greatly reduced their populations. (See Fig. 6.1.) Common. (1) n.e. U.S.

H. bilineata (Say). L. 14–18 mm. Much darker but otherwise similar to the preceding species. Naiads frequent large rivers. Adults emerge June to mid-September. (See A&J 5.) Common. (2) s.e. U.S.

[11.3 *Litobranchia* McCafferty (1 sp., *L. recurvata* (Morgan))]

12. PALINGENIIDAE (Spinyheaded Burrower Mayfly Family)

Two species are assigned to this family:

[12.1 *Pentagenia* Walsh (2 supp.)]

Fig. 6.11.

Fig. 6.10.

Suborder **PANNOTA (Fusedback Mayflies)**

Superfamily **EPHEMERELLOIDEA**

13. EPHEMERELLIDAE (Spiny Crawler Mayfly Family)

L. 5–12 mm. This family is similar to the Gray Drake family (Siphlouridae), but the cross veins are always absent and three caudal filaments are always present. There are 81 species in eight genera, some of them occurring in all parts of the U.S. and Canada. Naiads are found in a wide variety of habitats but are especially well represented in trout streams and are frequently used as bait for trout.

13.1 *Ephemerella* Walsh

There are twenty-eight species in this genus, including the following:

E. subvaria McDunnough. L. 9–12 mm. Body dark olive brown to black; head reddish-yellow; wings blue with veins amber. Naiads live in gravel riffles in streams of all sizes. Adults emerge from late April to mid-June. (1) n.e. NA.

E. invaria (Walker). A similar species. (See Fig. 6.10 for wing venation.) (1) n.e. NA; (2) s.e. U.S.; (5) n. central states.

[13.2 *Attenella* Edmunds (4 spp.); 13.3 *Caudatella* Edmunds (5 spp.); 13.4 *Dannella* Edmunds (2 spp.); 13.5 *Drunella* Edmunds (15 spp.); 13.6 *Eurylophella* Tiensuu (12 spp.); 13.7 *Serratella* Edmunds (14 spp.); 13.8 *Timpanoga* Needham (1 sp., *T. hecuba* (Easton)).

14. TRICORYTHIDAE (Little Stout Crawler Mayfly Family)

This family contains two genera with 21 species in the U.S. and Canada. Naiads are found in large rivers and streams on sticks and logs or in sand, silt, or algae.

14.1 *Tricorythodes* Ulmer

This genus contains 13 species of which the following is a common representative:

T. stygiatus McDunnough. Hind wings absent. (1) n.e. NA; (2) s.e. U.S. (See Fig. 6.11 for wing venation.)

[14.2 *Lephohypes* Easton (8 spp.)]

Superfamily **CAENOIDEA**

15. NEOEPHEMERIDAE (Large Squaregill Mayfly Family)

This family contains only four species, all assigned to the following genus:

15.1 *Neoephemera* McDunnough

Three of the species are confined to the southeast U.S. The following is widespread:

N. bicolor McDunnough. (1) n.e. NA; (5) n. central states.

16. CAENIDAE (Small Squaregill Mayfly Family)

L. 2–6 mm (rarely larger). Front wings only; three caudal filaments; hind legs with four tarsomeres; ocelli half as large as the compound eyes; costal cross veins absent. This family contains two genera and 18 species.

Naiads are found in flowing streams near the edge in sand and silt (*Brachycercus* Curtis) or in ponds (*Caenis* Stephens) throughout the U.S. and Canada.

16.1 *Brachycercus* Curtis

Five species are assigned to this genus, of which the following is a common representative.

B. lacustris (Needham). L. 6–7 mm. Head brown with small, irregular light brown to yellow markings; thorax brown to dark brown; legs grayish-white; wings light with brown or

Fig. 6.12.

purplish-brown veins; abdomen grayish-white above with anterior portion having dark transverse bands. Naiads frequent silt and leaves in brackwater areas. Adults emerge late July to early August. (1) n.e. NA; (5) n. central U.S.

[16.2 *Caenis* Stephens (13 spp.)]

Superfamily PROSOPISTOMATOIDEA (Shieldback Mayflies)

17. BAETISCIDAE (Armored Mayfly Family)

This family contains 12 species in a single genus.

17.1 *Baetisca* Walsh

Naiads frequent small to moderate-size streams and edges of lakes having some wave action. The species occur in all of the U.S. except the Southwest.

B. laurentina McDunnough. (See Fig. 6.3 for naiad and Fig. 6.12 for wing venation.)

BIBLIOGRAPHY

Berner, Lewis 1950. The mayflies of Florida. Univ. of Florida Studies, Biol. Sci. Ser., (4(4) xii + 267 pp.

Burks, B. D. 1953. The mayflies or Ephemeroptera of Illinois. *Bull. Illinois Nat. Hist. Surv.*, 26(1) vi + 216 pp.

Edmunds, George F., Jr.; Jensen, Steven L.; and Berner, Lewis 1976. *The mayflies of North and Central America.* Minneapolis: University of Minnesota Press, x + 330 pp.

Klots, Elsie B. 1966. *The new field book of freshwater life.* New York: G. P. Putnam's Sons. (Mayflies, pp. 190–197.)

Leonard, Justin W., and Leonard, Fannie A. 1962. *Mayflies of Michigan trout streams.* Bloomfield Hills: Cranbrook Inst. of Sci., x + 139 pp. (Color illus.)

McCafferty, W. Patrick 1981. *Aquatic entomology, the fisherman's and ecologists' illustrated guide to insects and their relatives.* Science Books International, xv + 448 pp.

Merritt, R. W., and Cummins, K. W. eds. 1978. *An introduction to the aquatic insects of North America.* Dubuque: Kendall/Hunt Publ. Co., xiii + 441 pp. (Ephemeroptera, pp. 57–80, by G. F. Edmunds, Jr.)

Specimens of very large extinct dragonflies are known from the Upper Carboniferous through the Permian periods. These Protodonata closely resemble modern Odonata except for differences in their wing venation. The fossils lack the arculus, nodus, and pterostigma, but the wing articulation is much the same. The head is large, and massive mandibles are present. The structure of the legs resembles that of modern dragonflies, that is, they form a basket for capturing prey, indicating that their feeding habits were much the same as those of present-day odonates. Naiads are not known.

Order 7

ODONATA (Dragonflies and Damselflies)

The dragonflies and damselflies represent the first really successful group of flying insects as well as the end of the ancient Paleoptilota line of development. Long a favorite of poets and artists, these graceful and elusive insects charm every outdoorsman. They not only present a challenge in their capture but defy their collectors to preserve their beauty. Unfortunately, their body color patterns are not stable, and thus an exquisite, vibrant, flying individual becomes a drab and lifeless specimen in a collection. These creatures, the second order of the primitive winged insects, retain many ancient features, especially in their wing venation. Specialized features such as the forward placement of the legs of the adult to form an air scoop for catching prey, their very large, acute eyes, and their courtship and mating habits, however, all combine to manifest the modern advances of this fascinating group of insects.

The name of the order is derived from a Greek word, *odontos*, meaning "toothed," and refers to the large mandibles of the adult. In addition to the usual common names, these insects are often called "devil's darning needles," "snake doctors," and "mosquito hawks."

Odonata are aquatic insects. Their naiads are similar to those of the Ephemeroptera, but instead of eating mainly vegetable matter as mayfly naiads do, odonate naiads are all carnivorous. Their prey consists of any moving object not too large to be seized by their prehensile mouthparts. The adults also are carnivorous and capture a variety of insects on the wing.

Diagnosis: Wingspread 20–190 mm. Body thin and flexible, with large spines or setae, without scales, but with a very fine pile or bloom of microsetae. Shape elongate and cylindrical. Color varied, the body generally dull brown or black, with white, blue, green, or red markings; the wings usually transparent, sometimes with white, red, brown, or black markings (rarely, entirely dark or dark green). Head large, with a very slim neck that gives it great ability to turn and move. Antennae short, resembling setae. Mouthparts large, well-developed, and of the chewing type. Compound eyes very large with thousands of facets; three ocelli. Thorax very large and filled with wing muscles. Wings always much narrower than long; hind wings the same or very similar to the front wings, being as large or larger; both pairs with many cross veins. Legs long and slender and fitted with long spines, and the front legs usually modified for capturing prey by being shorter, the other legs more elongate and forming a basket for holding prey to permit feeding during flight. Abdomen cylindrical, long, and slender, with small apical cerci used during mating and egg laying. The copulatory organs of the male are located beneath the second abdominal segment, a position that accounts for the placing of the tip of the female abdomen in this region during mating. (See Fig. 7.1 for the general body form of an adult damselfly.)

The naiads are aquatic and very different in appearance from the adult. (See Fig. 7.2 for general body form of naiad damselfly; Fig. 7.3 for that of naiad dragonfly.) Their heads are large, well-developed mouthparts, fitted for their predacious life. The labium is modified to form a "labial mask," a large ventral structure on the head that shoots outward in front of the head to capture prey. When the mask is withdrawn, the captive creature is stuffed between the waiting mandibles and devoured. External wing pads are evident during the later naiad stages. Respiration is by means of either external gills— located at the tip of the abdomen in damselfly naiads—or rectal gills—located internally in the rectal chamber in dragonfly naiads. Water for respiration in the latter case is taken into the rectum by muscular expansion of the cavity. Contraction expels the deoxygenated water. When violently contracted, a threatened dragonfly naiad is able to escape from a predator by jet propulsion.

Adult dragonflies and damselflies are easily distinguished by their wing shape from mayflies, stoneflies, and most neuropterans. When not in use, stonefly wings are held in contact with, and parallel to, the abdomen, moreover, a position quite distinct from the wing position of damselflies and dragonflies. Damselflies are able to hold their wings closed together over, and at about a 30-degree angle to, the thorax, or nearly in repose over the abdomen. The backward tilt of the wings is achieved by the angled dorsal portion of the thorax, not by wing hinges. This structure is thought to be an adaptation to prevent these weak flyers from being blown about in the wind. Dragonflies, on the other hand, rest with their wings held outstretched and horizontal to the body. Their front and hind wings are dissimilar in shape, the hind wings being broader at

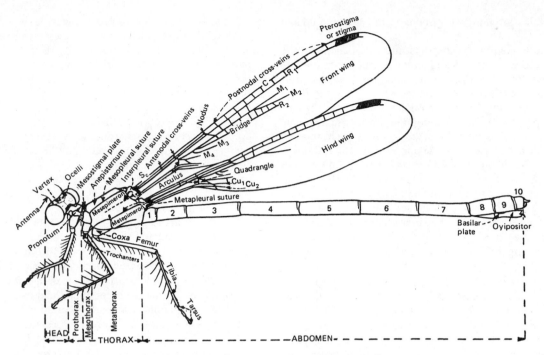

Fig. 7.1. Adult damselfly (*From Garman, 1927*)

the base than the front wings. Some neuropterans—ant lion and owl-fly adults, in particular—are very similar in appearance to dragonflies, but these neuropterans have conspicuous antennae, which are as long as, or much longer than, the head as well as enlarged at the tip.

Metamorphosis: Hemimetabolous. Eggs are laid in water and develop into a naiad, the aquatic nymph. Eggs are of various shapes and show some specific differences. They hatch in three to five weeks (rarely in so short a time as one week), depending upon the temperature of the water in which they are deposited. The naiad stage may last for many months or as long

as several years, with 10 or 15 instars. At maturity, the naiad crawls out of the water onto the stem of an aquatic plant. The adult then emerges from the naiad skin, dries its wings, and flies away to seek a mate.

Habits and habitats: The naiads are predacious and always aquatic. They live in a variety of habitats; some are climbers, ascending stems and camouflaging themselves by lying parallel to the stems so that their green and brown stripes blend in with the vegetation; others are sprawlers, spreading out and blending in with the bottom where they lie in wait of passing

Fig. 7.2. Naiad damselfly (*From Garman, 1927*)

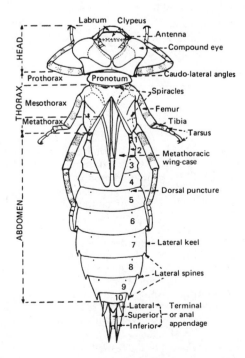

Fig. 7.3. Naiad dragonfly (*From Garman, 1927*)

prey; still others are burrowers, living in the bottom mud and silt.

The adults frequent waterways and are a characteristic feature of fresh water ponds and strems. Airborne dragonflies are aggressive, freewheeling predators and can be seen capturing relatively large insects while on the wing. Often they fly an established route, alighting first on one tree trunk, then on another, or perhaps on stones along the shore or in a stream, proceeding along the shore for several hundred feet, then returning to repeat this patrol in the opposite direction. Damselflies, on the other hand, flit about grassy areas or among reeds and cattails. Their flight is slower and more erratic. Both kinds of odonates may stray away from bodies of water in their search for prey. Some dragonflies range great distances and have been observed far out to sea as well as in desert regions. Some species are even seen in cities, where they are often attracted to macadam parking lots, apparently confusing these with bodies of water.

Reproductive behavior: Mating takes place while perched on stems in the case of damselflies and a few dragonflies, but most dragonflies mate on the wing, the males and females flying in tandem. Egg laying follows, often while the male is still attached, and observes a definite pattern according to the species. Most female libellulines dip the tip of their abdomen in water to deposit their eggs. Aeschnids implant eggs in underwater vegetation. Zygopterans are climbers or crawlers, depositing eggs in submerged plants or sticks, etc. These variations have been the subject of recent research, but much remains to be learned about the habits of individual species.

Collecting and preserving: Use the same methods for Odonata as for Ephemeroptera. Since the adults are rarely attracted to light at night, however, their capture is more difficult. Adults are usually stored in $3\frac{1}{4} \times 5\frac{3}{4}$-in. cellophane envelopes (into which a 3×5-in. data card is inserted) instead of alcohol. Naiads are preserved in 80-percent alcohol.

Rearing: The life cycle of these insects is rather long. Since they are predators, it is difficult to rear them in any numbers. As a rule, the older naiads are collected and confined in small individual wire cages and placed in water tanks until the adults emerge. The skin of the naiad is kept with the adult for specific association.

Distribution: The 4,870 known species range from the arctic to the tropics, including even desert regions where they are always looking for new bodies of water to inhabit. Four hundred and three species in 83 genera have been collected in the U.S. and Canada. They are abundant around nearly all bodies of water except for those so heavily polluted that aquatic organisms are unable to survive.

Identification: Identification of adults to species is based upon featurs of wing venation, the structure of male and female genital organs, and wing and body color. There are many common, strikingly marked species in every region that one can learn to sight identify very quickly. These can form the nucleus of an interesting collection and provide fascinating records of field observations.

The two major groups—the Anisoptera (dragonflies) and the Zygoptera (damselflies)—are distinguished as follows: All dragonflies hold their wings out from the body; the hind wings are broader near the base than the front wings; the eyes of the adults are not farther apart than the diameter of one of them. Most damselflies, on the other hand, hold their wings, when at rest, over the abdomen; their front and hind wings are nearly the same shape, each with narrow bases; the eyes of the adults are widely separated and somewhat stalked.

Economic importance: No known species of Odonata is a pest. On the contrary, their role in aquatic ecosystems is important both in their adult and naiad stages. As predators, they function as population regulators. Some attempts have been made to use the adults to control adult mosquitoes, but this effort has been unsuccessful in keeping down either pest- or disease-carrying mosquitoes.

CLASSIFICATION

All families of Odonata that occur in the U.S. and Canada are described here, as well as most common species. Any single locality will have at least 15 or 20 commonly observed species, and often many more, flying along sunny ponds and slow moving streams. Many species are very widely distributed. The order in North America is divided into two suborders—the Anisoptera and the Zygoptera—and 11 families. See the accompanying Key to the Families.

Key to the Families of Odonata

Adults

1. Front and hind wings nearly similar in shape, their greatest width nearly or quite the same (see Fig. 7.20); wings inclined upward in repose; compound eyes very broadly separated by more than their horizontal diameter and directed laterally; anal appendages of male always 4 in number, 2 superior and 2 inferior. (Damselflies). **Suborder ZYGOPTERA** *2*
Front and hind wings dissimilar in shape, with hind wings broader at base than front wings (see Fig. 7.4); wings usually held horizontally in repose; compound eyes usually convergent or contiguous on top of head; anal appendages of male usually 3 in number, 2 superior and a single broad inferior. (Dragonflies) **Suborder ANISOPTERA** *5*

2(1). Antenodal cross veins, numerous; wings not stalked **8. Calopterygidae**
Antenodal cross veins, two; wings stalked *3*

3(2). Vein M_3 rises nearer arculus than nodus; short intercalary sectors running to wing margin between veins M_3 and adjacent principal veins **9. Lestidae**
Vein M_3 rises nearer nodus than arculus; intercalary sectors absent *4*

4(3). Anal vein absent or greatly reduced; Cu_2 absent or at most only as long as one cell; quadrangle cell somewhat rectangular **10. Protoneuridae**
Anal vein and Cu_2 of normal length; quadrangle cell distinctly trapezoidal
.. **11. Coenagrionidae**

5(1). Triangles about equally distant from arculus in front and hind wings and similarly shaped *6*
Triangles nearer arculus in hind than in front wing and of different shape *9*

6(5). Stigma with brace vein at its inner end .. **7**
Stigma without brace vein at its inner end **2. Cordulegasteridae**

7(6). Front wing with anal vein apparently forked before triangle **1. Petaluridae**
Front wing with anal vein extending directly to hind angle of triangle **8**

8(7). Eyes widely separated on top of head **3. Gomphidae**
Eyes meeting on top of head **4. Aeshnidae**

9(5). Anal loop compact, a little longer than wide, with included cells not in 2 rows and not separated by a distinct bisector or mid-rib; bordering basal portion of vein Cu₂ straight; triangle of hind wing remote from arculus; arculus with long stalked sectors; more than two cubito-anal cross-veins present **5. Macromiidae**
Anal loop elongate, becoming foot-shaped, divided lengthwide into 2 rows of cells by bisector or mid-rib; bordering basal portion of vein Cu₂ sinuous; triangle of hind wing close to arculus; 1 or 2 cubito-anal cross-veins present **10**

10(9). Anal loop somewhat foot-shaped, but with little development of toe; males with auricles on sides of 2nd abdominal segment; adjacent inner margin of hind wing notched **6. Corduliidae**
Anal loop distinctly foot-shaped as a rule, with well-developed toe; male without auricles on 2nd abdominal segment; inner margin of hind wing rounded **7. Libellulidae**

Naiads

1. Anus surrounded by 3 stiff pointed valves; head not markedly wider than thorax and abdomen. (Dragonflies, **Suborder ANISOPTERA**) **2**
Anus surrounded by 3 external gills; head wider than thorax and abdomen. (Damselflies, **Suborder ZYGOPTERA**) ... **8**

2(1). Mentum of labium (including lateral lobes) flat, or nearly so, without stout setae **3**
Mentum of labium (including lateral lobes) spoon-shaped, covering face to base of antennae, and armed with stout setae ... **5**

3(2). Antennae with 6 to 7 segments; 3 tarsomeres; front tarsus with 2 tarsomeres in a few species .. **4**
Antennae with 4 segments; front and middle tarsus with 2 tarsomeres; hind tarsus with 3 tarsomeres .. **3. Gomphidae**

4(3). Antennae short, thick, and heavily setiferous; abdominal segments 2 (or 3) to 9 with pair of laterodorsal tufts of long black bristles **1. Petaluridae**
Antennae slender and bristlelike; abdominal segments without laterodorsal tufts **4. Aeshnidae**

5(2). Labium with large irregular teeth on distal edge of lateral lobe; mentum with median cleft .. **2. Cordulegastridae**
Labium with distal edge of lateral lobe entire or with small, even-sized crenulations or teeth; mentum without median cleft .. **6**

6(5). Head with prominent, almost erect, thick frontal horn between base of antennae, its width at base distinctly less than its length; metasternum with broad mesal tubercle near posterior margin; legs very long, with apex of each hind femur reaching to or beyond apex of abdominal segment 8 **5. Macromiidae**
Head without prominent frontal horn; metasternum without tubercle near posterior margin; legs shorter, with apex of each hind femur usually not reaching to apex of abdominal segment 8 ... **7**

7(6). Lateral caudal appendages usually more than half as long as inferior appendages; lateral spines of abdominal segment 9 longer than its dorsal length; middorsal hooks on abdomen often cultriform **6. Corduliidae**
Lateral caudal appendages usually not more than half as long as inferior appendages; if lateral spines of segment 9 are longer than its middorsal length, then middorsal hooks on abdomen are not cultriform but more spinelike, or stubby, or altogether absent ... **7. Libellulidae**

8(1). Antennae approximately equal in length; mentum entire or with closed median cleft .. **9**
Antennae unequal in length, the first being as long as the other 6 combined; mentum with deep, open median cleft **8. Calopterygidae**

9(8). Basal half of labium greatly narrowed and stalklike; lateral lobes with distal margin deeply cut by 2 or 3 incisions; median cleft present and closed **9**
Basal half of labium not greatly narrowed; lateral lobes not deeply cleft; median cleft absent ... **10**

10(9). Prementum with one seta; palpi with 3 to 5 setae; basal portion of gills thickened and darkened, apical portion thinner and more lightly pigmented, nodus distinct **10. Protoneuridae**
Prementum usually with 3 to 5 setae or none (if only one present, gills not as above and 6 palpal setae usually present); palpi with no or as many as 6 setae; as above, with notus only partly delineated, or, if distinct, with only 3 or 4 premental setae) **11. Coenagrionidae**

Suborder ANISOPTERA (Dragonflies)

This suborder is adequately defined in the key. Its members are easily distinguished from the Zygoptera both as adults and as naiads. There are 280 species of dragonflies assigned to seven families in the U.S. and Canada, in contrast to 123 species of damselflies assigned to four families.

1. PELATURIDAE (Grayback Family)

Only two, seldom collected species of this family occur in the U.S., as follows:

1.1 *Tachopteryx* Selys

T. thoreyi Hagen. Wingspread: 100–110 mm. Grayish brown with blackish stripes on the sides. Adults on the wing from early April to mid-August and most often seen in open woods. Uncommon. (1) MI, NY, NH, MA, IN, OH, PA; (2) MD, NC, SC, TN, KY, FL, AL; (3) OK, TX; (5) MO.

1.2 *Tanypteryx* Kennedy

T. hageni Selys. Wingspread: 115–125 mm. Black with light spots on the thorax and abdomen. Rare. (3) CA; (4) BC, WA, OR, NV.

2. CORDULEGASTERIDAE (Biddie Family)

Wingspread: 70–120 mm. Eyes separated or meeting at a single point on the top of the head; head blackish with front greenish or yellowish; thorax brown or blackish with a pair of oblique pale stripes at the front and two wide stripes on each side; wings hyaline, but in some species smoky; stigma without a brace vein, the absence of which is characteristic of this family and of the Libellulidae, the common skimmers. At least one species is represented in each of the major regions of the U.S., usually found along woodland streams. There is one genus only.

2.1 *Cordulegaster* Leach

This genus contains seven species, of which the following are fairly common and the rest only locally abundant:

C. maculatus Selys. Wingspread: 80–100 mm. Entire top of front surface much darker than anterior surface; abdomen usually with lateral yellow spots. (1) n.e. NA; (2) s.e. U.S.; (3) TX.

C. dorsalis Hagen. Similar to the preceding but abdomen with dorsal yellow spots. (See A&J 8.) (3) CA; (4) AK, BC, NV, UT.

3. GOMPHIDAE (Clubtail Family)

Wingspread: 38–116 mm. Black and yellow, or greenish. Eyes widely separated dorsally; apical segments of the abdomen of the male more or less enlarged (hence their common name); both wing triangles about equally distant from the arculus and similarly shaped. Clubtails—unlike Aeshnidae, the darners—spend little time flying. They are usually found resting, well camouflaged, on vegetation along streams, brooks, some ponds, and margins of some lakes. Males do not accompany the female during egg laying. Eighty-six species in 11 genera occur in the U.S. and Canada, the largest genus being *Gomphus*, which is divided into five subgenera.

3.1 *Progomphus* Selys

All four U.S. species lack cross veins in the small triangle of the front wing. The most widespread is *P. obscurus* Rambur, which may be recognized by its greenish yellow color, beautifully striped with brown.

[3.2 *Gomphoides* Selys (=*Phyllogomphoides* Belle, 1970) (2 spp.); 3.3 *Aphylla* Selys (2 spp.)]

3.4 *Hagenius* Selys

One species only, as follows:

H. brevistylus Selys (Black Clubtail). Wingspread: 95–115 mm (see Fig. 7.4). Black, with blackish wing veins; head, thorax, front edge of wing, and some abdominal segments marked with yellow. This is the largest dragonfly in North America. Its naiads are large, flattened, formidable creatures living along the edges of large woodland streams. Common throughout (1) n.e. NA; (2) s.e. U.S.; (3) OK; (5) MB, MN, KS, MO.

3.5 *Ophiogomphus* Selys

All 14 species in the U.S. and Canada have clear wings. Grayish-green or yellowish-green and blackish colored, these species can be found flying along the margins of open, grassy streams. Most of them occur in the northeast U.S. and adjacent Canada.

3.6 *Dromogomphus* Selys

The three species found in the U.S. and Canada are easily recognized by their extremely long hind femora, which are armed with strong spines. The wings are hyaline with some yellow on the front edge; the head is yellow or green with yellow markings. Mainly s.e. U.S. but also n.e. U.S.

3.7 *Lanthus* Needham

The two species in this genus are small and black, with distinct, narrow yellow lines. They occur in the eastern U.S. and nearby Canada.

3.8 *Octogomphus* Selys

One species only, *O. specularis* Hagen, which occurs along the West Coast (See A&J 6.)

3.9 *Gomphus* Leach

The 53 species in this genus are assigned to the following five subgenera: *Gomphus* s. str. (17 spp.), *Arigomphus* Needham (7 spp.), *Gomphurus* Needham (14 spp.), *Hylogomphus* Need-

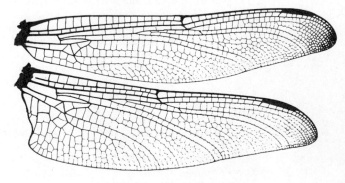

Fig. 7.4. (*From Garman, 1927*)

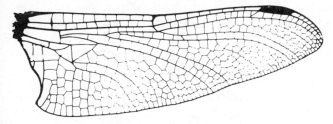

Fig. 7.5. (*From Garman, 1927*)

ham (4 spp.), and *Stylurus* Needham (11 spp.). The genus is recognized by the short spines on the hind femora, the lack of cross veins in the triangle of the wing, and an indistinct or totally absent anal loop. [The wing venation of *Gomphus spicatus* Hagen (e. NA) is shown in Fig. 7.5.]

[3.10 *Erpetogomphus* Selys (5 spp.); 3.11 *Stylogomphus* Fraser (1 sp., *S. albistylus* (Hagen))]

4. AESHNIDAE (Darner Family)

Wingspread: 55–90 mm, although that of *Anax strenuus* Hagen (the Giant Hawaiian Dragonfly) is much larger. Dark brown, with greenish or bluish markings; compound eyes meet dorsally; both wings with triangles as in the Gomphidae. There are 11 genera and 34 species in the U.S. and Canada, of which the genus *Aeshna* contains the most species.

4.1 *Aeshna* Fabricius

Members of this genus are recognized by their pale face, the black T spot on the blue upper surface of their frons, and the two rows of blue spots on each side of their abdomen. The 19 species found in the U.S. and Canada are widely distributed but in rather restricted habitats. They include the following:

A. verticalis Hagen (Eastern Blue Darner). Windspread: 85–100 mm. Dark brown to blackish, with green, blue, and a few yellow markings. Hind edge of base of hind wing angled. Adults fly from mid-June to mid-October. (1) n.e. NA, s. to (2) NC, w. to (5) MN, IA.

4.2 *Anax* Leach

Four species of very large darners belong to this genus; the following species is common:

A. junius Drury (Big Green Darner). Wingspread: 90–110 mm. Thorax and head are bright green; round, black spot in

Fig. 7.6.

Fig. 7.7. (*From Garman, 1927*)

front of eyes surrounded by a yellow ring and then a dark blue ring. Hind edge of base of hind wing rounded, resembling a target (Fig. 7.6). These tireless darners fly in circles over ponds and lakes or wander over roads and meadows, especially during hours when other insects swarm. They enter the swarm to feed. They often fly over desert areas after rains. Adults fly from March to October. They are found throughout NA, Asia, and the Pacific Islands.

[4.3 *Basiaeschna* Selys (1 sp., *B. janata* (Say)); 4.4 *Boyeria* McLachlan (2 spp.); 4.5 *Coryphaeschna* Williamson (1 sp., *C. ingens* (Rambur)]

4.6 *Epiaeschna* Hagen

One species, as follows:

E. heros (Fabricius) (Smoky-winged Darner). Wingspread: 100–120 mm. Body brown; wings smoky; front of head with T-shaped spot; hind edge of wing base as in *Aeshna*. Adults fly from early March to October. (See Fig. 7.7.) (1) n.e. NA; (2) s.e. US; (3) OK, TX; (5) MO.

[4.7 *Gomphaeschna* Selys (2 spp.); 4.8 *Gynacantha* Rambur (1 sp., *G. nervosa* Rambur); 4.9 *Nasiaeschna* Selys (1 sp., *N. pentacantha* Rambur); 4.10 *Oplonaeschna* Selys (1 sp., *O. armata* (Hagen)); 4.11 *Triacanthagyna* Selys (1 sp., *T. trifida* Rambur)]

5. MACROMIIDAE (Belted Skimmer Family)

Wingspread: 50–120 mm. Eyes in contact above, each with a large, rounded tubercle on the hind border at the outer side. Triangles in front wing and hind wing different in shape and position; wings clear or darkened but without markings. Legs long. Body brown or blackish, marked with yellow. There are 11 species in two genera in the U.S. and Canada.

Fig. 7.8. (*From Garman, 1927*)

5.1 *Didymops* Rambur

Large brown dragonflies without metallic reflections. There are two species, one of which, *D. floridensis* Davis, is confined to (2) FL.

D. transversa Say (Belted Skimmer). Wingspread: 68–72 mm. Brown body; head with yellow markings; wings (Fig. 7.8) stained with brown across extreme base at front, with brown to yellowish veins. Adults fly from early March in the South to August in the North. Although these interesting creatures are difficult to capture, they follow a routine flight pattern, and the collector who awaits their return to a certain spot is often rewarded with a specimen. (1) n.e. NA; (2) s.e. US; (3) OK, TX.

5.2 *Macromia* Rambur

This genus contains nine species found locally throughout most of North America. The following is a far western species:

M. magnifica MacLachlan (Magnificent Skimmer). Wingspread: 85–95 mm. Head yellow; face with two black crossbands; thorax brown with brownish-yellow stripes; wings (Fig. 7.9) hyaline, with bright yellow costa and brown or black stigma; abdomen half-ringed with dull yellow above, black below. Adults fly from early June to September. (3) CA, AZ; (4) BC, WA, NV.

M. taeniolata Rambur. (1) southern n.e. US; (2) s.e. US; (3) TX; (5) IA.

6. CORDULIIDAE (Green-eyed Skimmer Family)

Windspread: 45–105 mm. Some brilliantly metallic, some brownish, usually without markings; eyes, in life, bright green, with low tubercle on the hind border at the outer side; anal loop of hind wing club-shaped but not reaching hind margin. Many species have wing markings. The 49 species of this family are assigned to eight genera. They are mostly found along streams, in swamps, or about ponds.

6.1. *Epicordulia* Selys

One species, as follows:

E. princeps Hagen (Water Prince). Wingspread: 75–105 mm. Brown spots on wings usually distinctive, but may be reduced. Adults fly from mid-May to mid-September; strong flyer along muddy, cattail banks. (See Fig. 7.10.) (1) n.e. NA; (2) KY, VA, TN, NC, LA, MS, AL; (3) OK, TX; (5) MN, NE, IA, MO.

[6.2 *Cordulia* Leach (1 sp., *C. shurtleffi* Scudder); 6.3 *Dorocordulia* Needham (2 spp.); 6.4 *Helocordulia* Needham (2 spp.)]

6.5 *Neurocordulia* Selys

Moderate-size, brown dragonflies without metallic coloration; triangle of front wing three-celled, of hing wing two-celled. Most of the six species are confined to the southeastern United States.

N. yamaskanensis Provancher. Brown spot at base of hind wing. (1) n.e. NA.

6.6 *Somatochlora* Selys

Clear-winged dragonflies whose dark brown bodies give off metallic reflections. Apex of abdominal segment 2 exhibits a pale ring. This is one of the largest genera of Odonata, with 25 species in the U.S. and Canada. Most of the species are found in northeastern North America; with only two species known in the southeastern U.S.

S. tenebrosa Say. Wingspread: 70–90 mm. Dark brown with coppery reflections from head and thorax; front yellowish, with blaskish hairs; labrum orange-edged and crossed with black. This species is distinguished from the others of its genus by the elbowed caudal appendages of the male and by the very long, strongly compressed, and downwardly directed ovipositor of the female. Adults usually fly at twilight. (1) n.e. NA; (2) s.e. US; (5) IA, MO.

Fig. 7.9.

Fig. 7.10.

6.7 *Tetragoneuria* Hagen

The ten species of this genus are easily spotted by their wing markings. Some exhibit one spot at the base, one in the middle, and one at the tip of the wing; others have olive or dull yellow markings.

T. canis MacLachlan (Dog's Head). Wingspread: 60–62 mm. Brown with yellowish markings; thorax with white hairs on front, tawny hairs on side; wing color variable, from clear to smoky brown. (1) WI, ON, PQ, NB, NS, NY, NH, ME, CT, PE; (3) CA, OK; (4) BC, WA, OR.

[6.8 *Williamsonia* Davis (2 spp.)]

7. LIBELLULIDAE (Common Skimmer Family)

Wingspread: 20–105 mm. Easily recognized by "boot" in hind wing that nearly reaches the wing's hind margin and by rounded basal structure of that margin. Stigma without brace vein; eyes always in contact at top of head, frequently broadly joined; color various on body, but not many species with metallic coloration. Many species have markings on their wings. This is the largest family of Odonata, with 28 genera and 91 species in the U.S. and Canada.

[7.1 *Belonia* Kirby (2 spp.); 7.2 *Brachymesia* Kirby (3 spp.); 7.3 *Brechmorhoga* Kirby (1 sp., *B. mendax* Hagen); 7.4 *Cannaphila* Kirby (1 sp., *C. funerea* (Carpenter))]

7.5 *Celithemis* Hagen

All eight species assigned to this genus have wing markings distinctive of the species; front yellowish. They are found in eastern North America only.

C. elisa Hagen. Wingspread: 54–56 mm. A small, rounded spot on the wings between large basal spot and the stigma. (See Fig. 7.11.) (1) n.e. NA; (2) s.e. US; (3) OK, TX; (5) MN, KS, MO.

C. eponina Drury. Wingspread 64–68 mm. Wings yellow with basal spot extending to middle of wing; middle band present; without definite apical spot. Adults fly around ponds. (See Fig. 7.12.) (1) n.e. NA; (2) s.e. US; (3) OK, TX; (5) MN, NE, IA, KS, MO.

C. fasciata Kirby. Wingspread 58–64 mm. Wings clear, with three well-defined bands. (1) IN (2) s.e. US; (3) OK, TX.

[7.6 *Dythemis* Hagen (3 spp.)]

Fig. 7.11.

Fig. 7.12.

7.7 *Erythemis* Hagen

Three species are assigned to this genus. The following is widespread:

E. simplicicollis Say (Green Jacket). Wingspread 60–66 mm. Wings without markings; front of head and thorax bright green; abdomen half-ringed with black and green. Adults in flight throughout the year in the south. (1) n.e. NA; (2) s.e. US; (3) CA, AZ, OK; (4) WA, OR, NV, UT; (5) MT, MN, NE, IA, KS, MO.

[7.8 *Erythrodiplax* Brauer (4 spp.); 7.9 *Idiataphe* Cowley (1 sp., *I. cubensis* Scudder); 7.10 *Ladona* Needham (3 spp.); 7.11 *Lepthemis* Hagen (1 sp., *L. vesiculosa* Fabricius)]

7.12 *Leucorrhinia* Brittinger

Of the seven species assigned to this genus, the following is a common, easily recognized one:

L. intacta Hagen (Johnny White-face). Wingspread: 46–50 mm. Front of head white; conspicuous dorsal twin spot on abdominal segment 7 in the male and on several segments in the female; wings without markings. Common around farm ponds in mid-April to mid-August. (1) n.e. NA; (2) TN; (4) BC, WA, OR, NV, UT; (5) AB, MB, ND, SD.

7.13 *Libellula* Linnaeus

The 18 members of this genus are called Pond Skimmers. The genus can be recognized by features of the wing venation; in particular, the arculus is at or very close to the second antenodal cross vein, a feature that distinguishes the genus from *Plathemis*, in which the arculus is nearly midway between the first and second antenodal cross veins. The front wing triangle is straight or very slightly convex on the outer side. The abdomen of both sexes tapers from front to rear, with that of the male bare on the underside of segment 1 and that of the female slowly tapered to the rear on the side margins of the middle segment.

L. luctuosa Burmeister (Widow). Wingspread: 72–80 mm. The basal portions of the wings are dark brown or black, with the outer portions clear except in old males; the middle portion is chalky white; the tip, especially of males, is often smoky brown. Found at ponds. (See Fig. 7.13.) (1) n.e. NA; (2) s.e. US; (3) NM, OK, TX; (5) NM, SD, NE, IA, KS, MO.

L. forensis Hagen (Western Widow). Wingspread: 38–40 mm. Wings with characteristic brown and black markings;

Fig. 7.13.

Fig. 7.15.

thorax dull brown. Adults fly June to mid-September. (See Fig. 7.14 and A&J 9.) (3) CA, AZ; (4) BC, WA, OR, UT; (5) MT, NE, CO.

L. saturata Uhler (Southwestern Big Red). Wingspread: 41–45 mm. Red all over, including legs and wing veins, with brown eyes and occiput. Adults fly from mid-May to early October. (See Fig. 7.15.) (3) CA, AZ, OK, TX; (4) ID, NV, UT; (5) MT, WY, CO, KS, MO.

L. pulchella Drury (Ten-spot). Wingspread: 84–92 mm. Wings spotted with brown at base, mid-wing, and apex, with ten chalky white spots between brown spots. Adults fly from April to October. (1) n.e. NA; (2) s.e. US; (3) s.w. US; (4) n.w. US; BC; (5) n. central US; MB.

L. quadrimaculata Linnaeus (Four-spot). Wingspread: 66–72 mm. Head with yellow and brown markings; front and hind wings spotted at base and at nodus, the two spots connected by a yellow streak that runs along the anterior portion to the wing tip. Adults fly from May through September. (1) n.e. NA; (3) AZ, NM; (4) n.w. NA; (5) n. central NA.

L. semifasciata Burmeister (Amber-spot). Wingspread: 96–105 mm. Wings brown and white with amber wing tips. Adults active from April to December, usually near woodland brooks: (1) n.e. US, ON; (2) s.e. US; (3) TX.

[7.14 *Macrodiplax* Brauer (1 sp., *M. balteata* Hagen); 7.15 *Macrothemis* Hagen (2 spp.); 7.16 *Miathyria* Kirby (1 sp., *M. marcella* Selys); 7.17

Micrathyria Kirby (1 sp., *M. hageni* Kirby); 7.18 *Nannothemis* Brauer (1 sp., *N. bella* (Uhler); 7.19 *Orthemis* Hagen (1 sp., *O. ferruginea* Fabricius); 7.20 *Pachydiplax* Brauer (1 sp., *P. longipennis* (Burmeister)); 7.21 *Paltothemis* Karsch (1 sp., *P. lineatipes* Karsch)]

7.22 *Pantala* Hagen

This genus contains two species, the following of which occurs throughout the world; the other species, *P. hymenaea* Say, which has a large brown spot near the broadly rounded anal angle of the hind wings, occurs in most of the U.S. and southern Canada.

P. flavescens Fabricius (Globe Trotter). Wingspread: 72–84 mm. Front of head yellow to reddish; thorax yellowish with black ridges and hairy; wings without markings, broad at base, and more or less pointed apically; abdomen basally black, with caudal appendages yellow. Adults are attracted to fires; they have been found far out to sea as well. Occurring throughout the world, they fly all year long in warmer regions.

[7.23 *Perithemis* Hagen (3 spp.)]

7.24 *Plathemis* Hagen

This genus is very similar to *Libellula* Linnaeus. Its two species are distinguished from *Libellula* by an arculus that is more nearly midway between the first and second antenodal cross veins. The two species known as white tails, are *P. subornata* Hagen, found in the western U.S. and B.C., and the following:

P. lydia Drury (White-tailed Skimmer). Wingspread: 60–70 mm. Males easily recognized by their white abdomen and white wings with central black cross band. Females resemble *Libellula pulchella* closely, but their smaller size and the row of oblique yellow spots on each side of the abdomen distinguish them from the latter. (See Fig. 7.16 and A&J 8.) (1) n.e. NA; (2) s.e. US; (3) CA, MN, TX; (4) BC, WA, ID, UT; (5) MN, NE, IA, CO, KS, MO.

[7.25 *Pseudoleon* Kirby (1 sp., *P. superbus* Hagen)]

7.26 *Sympetrum* Newman

The 13 species of this genus, known as the *topers*, are usually red and fly in the autumn. The following species is typical:

S. semicinctum Say. Wingspread: 36–46 mm. Abdomen red; basal half of wings yellowish, with colored area rounded

Fig. 7.14.

Fig. 7.16.

Fig. 7.18.

externally and darkest toward margins. Adults fly from mid-June to late October. (1) n.e. NA; (2) WV, VA, TN, NC.

[7.27 *Tauriphila* Kirby (2 spp.)]

7.28 *Tramea* Hagen

The seven species assigned to this genus are known as saddle bags. All are conspicuously marked with bands of brown across the base of the hind wing. The species occur throughout the U.S., a common one being *T. onusta* Hagen (Fig. 7.17).

Suborder ZYGOPTERA (Damselflies)

Damselflies are usually smaller than dragonflies and weaker flyers; they are also not as well known. The 120 species are assigned to four families.

8. CALOPTERYGIDAE (Broad-winged Damselfly Family)

Wingspread: 56–80 mm. Wings with many cross veins basal to the nodus; wings tapered gradually to the base; body metallic. The family contains eight species assigned to two genera.

8.1 *Calopteryx* Charpentier

[=*Agrion*]

Five species belong to this striking genus, of which the following two are common:

C. maculata Beauvois (Black-wing). Wingspread: 56–60 mm. Metallic blue or green; wings of male black and of female dark gray with a white stigma. (See Fig. 7.18 and A&J 11.) (1) n.e. NA.

C. aequabile Say. (See Fig. 7.19.) (1) n.e. NA.

8.2 *Hetaerina* Hagen

This genus has three species. Their wings, which are narrower than those of the preceding genus, are clear, with the basal spot ruby in the male and diffuse reddish or amber in the female.

H. americana Fabricius (American Ruby Spot). Wingspread: 56–60 mm. Body reddish; base of male wings with bright red spots; base of female wings with dull reddish brown spot. (See Fig. 7.20 and A&J 10.) (1) n.e. NA.

Fig. 7.17.

Fig. 7.19.

Fig. 7.20.

9. LESTIDAE (Stalked-winged Damselfly Family)

Wingspread: 32–64 mm. wings stalked, with only two cross veins basal to nodus. Unlike other damselflies, members of this family hold their wings outstretched horizontally to the body when at rest. There are two genera and 18 species in the U.S. and Canada.

9.1 *Archilestes* Selys

The two species in this genus are not only larger than the species of *Lestes*, they are the largest in the Nearctic damselflies, their wingspread being over 60 mm. The adults commonly hang on leaves and stems of willow and alder to sun themselves. They fly from September to November.

A. grandis (Rambur). Transcontinental from (1) PA to (3) n. CA, but absent in Atlantic and Gulf Coastal plains.

A. californica MacLachlan. (3) CA; (4) WA, OR.

9.2 *Lestes* Leach

The 16 species of this genus are all very similar and can be distinguished only by technical differences. They are quite common throughout the U.S. and Canada. The following species is typical:

L. uniguiculatus Hagen. Wingspread: 36–44 mm. Dull brown (female) or metallic green and blue with blue eyes (male). The adults are found around marshy areas during July and August. The females lay eggs in aerial parts of plants growing in ponds and pools. (See Fig. 7.21 for wing venation.)

10. PROTONEURIDAE (Tropical Damselfly Family)

This group is tropical with two species reaching as far north as Texas.

[10.1 *Neoneura* Selys (1 sp., *N. aaroni* Calvert); 10.2 *Protoneura* Selys (1 sp., *P. cara* Calvert)]

11. COENAGRIONIDAE (Narrow-winged Damselfly Family)

[= Agrionidae of authors]

Wingspread: 20–45 mm. Wings, with two cross veins basal to the nodus, are held together over the abdomen when not in flight. This family is easily separated from the Lestidae by the difference in the wing venation indicated in the key to the family; otherwise, they are very similar. Most species are black marked with blue, although some exhibit other colors.

All 92 species in 14 genera assigned to this family are so similar that they can be distinguished only by technical features of wing venation, genital apparatus, and the like.

[11.1 *Amphiagrion* Selys (3 spp.); 11.2 *Anomalagrion* Selys (1 sp., *A. hastatum* (Say); 11.3 *Apanisagrion* Kennedy (1 sp., *A. lais* Selys)]

11.4 *Argia* Rambur (Incl. *Hyponeura* Selys)

This genus contains 27 species distinguished locally by color patterns, but, as a group, the structure of the male terminal abdominal appendages is needed to distinguish the species.

The adults are found mostly along streams or flying low over sunny places along roads or hard paths, around clay banks, or over logs or rocks near or in streams. Unlike most other members of the order, the females lay their eggs in wet wood in a stream. Oviposition usually occurs in tandem, but the female occasionally oviposits alone. Some even enter the water to do so. The following species is very common throughout e. North America.

A. fumipennis violacea Hagen (Violet Dancer). Wingspread: 40–44 mm. Dark brown to dull violet or purple. Adults fly during June to October. (See Fig. 7.22.) n. NA.

[11.5 *Argiallagma* Selys (1 sp., *A. pallidulum* Calvert); 11.6 *Chromagrion* Needham (1 sp., *C. conditum* (Hagen)); 11.7 *Coenagrion* Kirby (3 spp.)]

Fig. 7.21.

Fig. 7.22.

Fig. 7.23. (*From Garman, 1927*)

11.8 *Enallagma* Selys

This is the largest genus of the family with 34 species in the U.S. and Canada. As is the case with the other genera, the species are all very similar in appearance. In the field, local species can be distinguished by color differences, but unfortunately these colors fade soon after death. The following two species are common:

E. civile Hagen (Civil Bluet). Wingspread: 34–40 mm. Body blue and black. (See Fig. 7.23 for tip of abdomen.) Adults fly from April through September. (See A&J 12.) NA.

E. ebrium Hagen (Common Bluet). Wingspread: 30–36 mm. Body blue, black, and yellow. Adults fly from May to September. (1) ME; (4) WA.

[11.9 *Hesperagrion* Calvert (1 sp., *H. heterodoxum* (Selys))]

11.10 *Ischnura* Charpentier

The 13 species assigned to this genus are rather colorfully marked. The following species is a typical example:

I. verticalis Say (Common Forktail). Windspread: 22–34 mm. Body black or dark metallic green, pale green, orange, and black; tip of abdomen sometimes blue. Adults fly from mid-May to late September. (1) n.e. NA; (2) s.e. US.

[11.11 *Nehalennia* Selys (3 spp.); 11.12 *Neoerythromma* Kennedy (1 sp., *N. cultellatum* Hagen); 11.13 *Telebasis* Selys (2 spp.); 11.14 *Zoniagrion* Kennedy (1 sp., *Z. exclamationis* (Selys)]

BIBLIOGRAPHY

Corbet, P. S. 1963. *A biology of dragonflies.* Chicago: Quadrangle Books, xvi + 247 pp.

Garman, P. 1927. The Odonata or dragonflies of Connecticut. *Connecticut State Geological and Natural History Survey Bulletin*, 39, 331 pp.

Gloyd, L. K., and Wright, M. 1959. *Freshwater biology*, edited by W. T. Edmondson. New York: John Wiley, pp. 917–940.

Merritt, R. W., and Cummins, K. W., eds. 1978. *An introduction to the aquatic insects of North America.* Dubuque: Kendall/Hunt Publ. Co., xiii + 441 pp. (Odonata, by M. J. Westfall, pp. 81–93.)

Needham, J. E., and Westfall, M. J. 1955. *A manual of the dragonflies of North America (Anisoptera).* Berkeley: Univ. of California Press, xii + 615 pp.

Pennak, R. W. 1953. *Fresh-water invertebrates of the United States.* New York: Ronald Press, ix + 769 pp.

Robert, Adrien. 1963. *Les libellules du Québec.* Service de la Faune, Vol. 1, 223 pp.

Smith, R. F., and Pritchard, A. E. 1956. *Aquatic Insects of California*, edited by R. L. Usinger. Berkeley: Univ. of California Press, pp. 106–153.

Walker, E. M. 1953. *The Odonata of Canada and Alaska.* Vol. I: Part I, General; Part II, The Zygoptera damselflies. Toronto: Univ. of Toronto Press, 292 pp.

Walker, E. M. 1958. *The Odonata of Canada and Alaska.* Vol. 2: Anisoptera. Toronto: Univ. of Toronto Press, 318 pp.

Walker, E. M., and Corbet, P. S. 1975. *The Odonata of Canada and Alaska.* Vol. 3: Part II, The Anisoptera-three families. Toronto: Univ. of Toronto Press, 308 pp.

Division NEOPTERA

This division includes all insects with wing base structures that permit the wings to be folded back over the abdomen when not in use. As previously explained, it also includes those wingless orders that are presumed to be derived from winged ancestors.

Exactly how the remaining 22 orders are to be arranged is the subject of considerable speculation. The fossil record sheds little light on the matter. The classification chosen here follows that of Martynov with a few modifications for the sake of consistency. The scientific basis of these subdivisions and

sections is too problematic and complicated to recount here and may be subject to modification in the future. For present purposes, the Neoptera is divided into the following subdivisions: (1) the Polyneoptera, roughly equivalent to the "Orthopteroid" insects and the Plecoptera; (2) the Paraneoptera, erected to show the distinctness of the Zoraptera; (3) the Acercaria, the licelike insects and the great mass of sucking insects—bugs, thrips, and the like; and (4) the Holometabola, which constitutes the most advanced insects and by far the majority of the species.

Subdivision POLYNEOPTERA

Order 8
PLECOPTERA (Stoneflies)

Since stoneflies, as an order, form a group with rather obscure habits, they are likely to be overlooked by the general collector. As many as a third of the species emerge, mate, feed, and die during the winter months when most collectors are indoors. It can prove a challenge, however, to tramp through the snow in search of those species and to track down the habitats of the other species that become adults during the summer months as well. Because of their dependence upon flowing fresh water during their immature life, some members of the order are threatened by the pollution of our streams, although they exhibit considerable variation in their sensitivity to pollutants.

The name, Plecoptera, is based on the Greek word, *plecto*, meaning "plaited," and refers to the way the adult folds its wings together over its abdomen. The common name, *stonefly*, refers to the fact that many live under stones and rocks while they are naiads. Other naiads are to be found in submerged masses of dead leaves and twigs or the rotting limbs of trees that have fallen into a stream.

The immature stage—termed *naiad* here, for the sake of consistency, instead of *nymph*, as many authors prefer—is more similar in appearance to the adult than those of the Odonata and Ephemeroptera. In fact, the adult retains much of the shape of the naiad, discarding, in most cases, only the external gills and adding wings. Remnants of these gills can be found on some adults. The immature stage is certainly intermediate between that of the Odonata, which is very different from the adult, and that of the Orthoptera, which is decidedly similar to the adult in both appearance and habits. It is because of its wing venation and other morphological features, including those of the naiads, that this order is assigned close to the Orthoptera. The adults remain near the water from which they emerge. They are rather feeble flyers.

Diagnosis: Length: 3–50 mm. Body leathery; shape elongate, flattened; brown or black, sometimes yellowish or greenish. Antennae long, multisegmented, simple. Compound eyes small to moderate; either two or three ocelli, or ocelli absent. Mouthparts usually weak and often nonfunctional. Wings [see Fig. 8.1 for those of *Phasganophora capitata* (Pictet)] well developed, elongate, with many veins and cells; both pairs capable of being folded back over the abdomen, the hind pair being somewhat shorter and much broader than the front pair. Legs stout and widely separated laterally. Abdomen with short, dragonflies are, to ensure the correlation of the cast skin of the

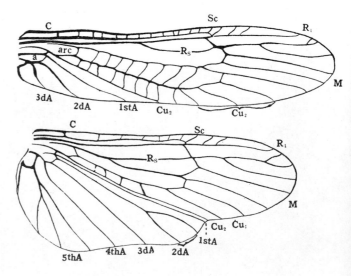

Fig. 8.1. (*From Needham and Claassen, 1925*)

104

Fig. 8.2.

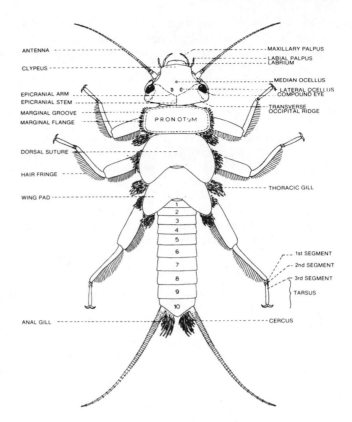

Fig. 8.3. (*From Bauman, Gaufin, and Surdick, 1977*)

single-segmented to very long, many-segmented cerci [see Fig. 8.2 for those of *Perlinella ephyra* (Newman)]; median filament absent.

The eggs apparently vary in shape and shell texture from species to species. Those of some are spindle-shaped, whereas others have numerous filaments with flared tips to hold them in crevices, and so on. In ovipositing, the female dips her abdomen into water and the eggs are washed off and float to the bottom. Those that are sticky adhere to the bottom and probably to aquatic vegetation, logs, and debris as well.

Naiads have filamentous tracheal gills, usually arranged in tufts near the base of the legs, on the neck, on the first two or three abdominal segments, and at the top of the abdomen; these gills are absent in some species. Wing pads are present. Body broad; legs wide apart; antennae shorter than those of the adult; legs with two tarsal claws; abdomen with two caudal filaments. (See Fig. 8.3 for the general body form of a mature naiad.) The so-called "white nymph" favored by fishermen is the naiad that has just emerged from its molted skin and has not yet hardened and received its full color.

Adult stoneflies are distinguished from the mayflies, dragonflies, and damselflies by their long antennae and wing shape, and from other winged insects by their widespread legs and caudal filaments.

Metamorphosis: Hemimetabolous; naiads take one to three years to develop, passing through as many as 22 instars.

Habits and habitats: Naiads crawl on the bottom of a body of water or on stones and logs; they seldom swim. They are found in leaf packs or hiding under rocks and stones in torrents as well. They make excellent trout bait. Many species are detritus feeders; the naiads of most Perlodidae and Perlidae, however, are predacious.

An interesting phenomenon that has recently received considerable study is termed "behavioral drift." It has been observed in a number of groups—for example, Ephemerop-

tera, Plecoptera, Trichoptera, Diptera, and even Coleoptera—and is a form of diel periodicity, responsive to the 24-hour light/dark cycle. It has been noted that the drift of insects in water increases at night, the greatest amount in the hour after sunset. Naiads and larvae float downstream in large numbers during this period. This drift peaks again in some species just before sunrise. The extent of the drifting varies with the species. Apparently, the insects use their ocelli to detect light changes; one study has suggested that there is more drift on dark nights than moonlit nights. This downstream drifting appears to be a mechanism for the dispersal of the naiads and larvae to insure adequate food supplies as well as the occupation of new habitats. It may be countered in some species by the migration upstream of the adults for egg laying.

The adults may be found resting on trees and bushes near shore, or on bridges, in the spring and summer and on snow near open flowing streams in the winter.

Reproductive behavior: The newly emerged winged adults fly or crawl about the shore in search of a mate. Males of some species drum on the substrate to attract a female. Mating takes place on land or in vegetation near the ground instead of in flight. Many adults do not feed and are short-lived. After mating, the female drops eggs into the water at random or, rarely, in loose packets. A single female may lay as many as 6,000 eggs.

Collecting and preserving: In general, the same techniques should be used as for collecting Ephemeroptera and Odonata, although adults may be collected from bushes, grass, branches of trees, on bridges, stones, and even snow. In fact, winter is the only season for collecting adults of many species.

Rearing: The naiads may be collected when nearly ready for adult emergence and confined in screened "pillows," much as

naiad with the adult. Because of the length of the life cycle and the necessity of fresh, usually cold, running water and special food requirements, the rearing of eggs or young naiads is difficult, if not impossible.

Distribution: About 1550 species have been described throughout the world, most species being found in the cooler regions of the earth. The 465 species in 88 genera recorded in the U.S. and Canada are found in all regions but again are most abundant in the mountainous areas of the northern parts.

Notes on identification: The characteristics used for specific identification in this group are extremely variable. They are best studied locally with large series so that the variation of the species can be observed. The family classification has changed considerably over the years, but the work by Zwick (1973) has done much to stabilize it. Recent monographic works provide useful aids for identification.

Economic importance: A few adults are plant feeders, and some species have been known to damage fruit trees by feeding on their buds in the winter or early spring. The naiads and some adults are an important source of fish food. The emergence of *Pteronarcys californica*, the Salmonfly, attracts thousands of anglers from all over the United States to Montana and other western states and, of course, contributes to the economy of those regions.

CLASSIFICATION

The placing of this order in the Polyneoptera near the orthopteroid insects is relatively recent and subject to considerable debate. Likewise, the placing of all species in a single suborder, Arctoperlaria, is a change from the old classification employing two suborders, Setipalpia and Filipalpia, now believed to be an unnatural dichotomy.

The order consists of nine families in the U.S. and Canada. These families may be distinguished by use of the accompanying Key.

Key to the Families of Plecoptera

Adults

1. Cerci usually short, no longer than greatest width of pronotum, or if longer, then anal area of front wing with 2 or more full rows of cross veins; paraglossae and glossae of about equal length ... **2**
 Cerci much longer than greatest width of pronotum; paraglossae much longer than glossae **7**

2(1). Abdominal sterna with branched gill remnants; anal area of front wing entirely without or with only 1 row of cross veins ... **3**
 Anterior abdominal sterna without branched gill remnants; anal area of front wing with 2 or more full rows of cross veins **5. Pteronarcyidae**

3(2). Ocelli, 2; shape, cockroachlike; front wing with 10 or more costal cross veins **6. Peltoperlidae**
 Ocelli, 3; front wing usually with less than 10 costal cross veins (except *Isocapnia*) **4**

4(3). Tarsus with 2nd tarsomere much shorter than 1st **5**
 Tarsus with 2nd tarsomere at least as long as 1st **2. Taeniopterygidae**

5(4). Wings not rolled; 2nd anal vein of front wing forked; cerci 1-segmented. **1. Nemouridae**
 Wings rolled around body, or if not, 2nd anal vein of front wing simple; cerci either 1-segmented or with 4 or more segments ... **6**

6(5). Wings rolled around body; 2nd anal vein of front wing forked; cerci 1-segmented **4. Leuctridae**
 Wings not rolled; 2nd anal vein of front wing simple; cerci with at least 4 segments **3. Capniidae**

7(1). Branched gill remnants absent from thorax; cubitoanal cross vein of front wing, if present, usually separated from anal cell by more than its own length **8**
 Branches of gill remnants at lower angles of thorax; cubitoanal cross vein of front wing usually either in anal cell or separated from it by no more than its own length **9. Perlidae**

8(7). Pronotum nearly rectangular, with corners acute or narrowly rounded; fork of 2nd anal vein of front wing included in anal cell so that its 2 branches leave cells separately **7. Perlodidae**
 Pronotum ellipsoidal; 2nd anal vein of front wing either not forked or forked beyond anal cell, except in *Kathroperla* spp., which have fork at margin of cell or included in it **8. Chloroperlidae**

Naiads

1. Paraglossae and glossae of about equal length **2**
 Paraglossae much longer than glossae ... **7**

2(1). Abdomen without branched gills on ventral side **3**
 Branched gills on ventral side of abdominal segments 1, 2, and sometimes 3 **1. Pteronarcyidae**

3(2). Ocelli, 2; thoracic sterna produced posteriorly into thin plates overlapping posterior segments; broad, flattened, roachlike shape **6. Peltoperlidae**
 Ocelli, 3; thoracic sterna not produced posteriorly to overlap posterior segments; shape not roachlike ... **4**

Key to the Families of Plecoptera (*Contd.*)

Naiads

4(3). Second tarsomere much shorter than 1st **5**
Second tarsomere at least as long as 1st **2. Taeniopterygidae**
5(4). Stout; hind wing pads strongly diverging from axis of body **1. Nemouridae**
Cylindrical elongate; hind wing pads nearly parallel with axis of body **6**
6(5). Abdominal segments 1 to 9 divided laterally by membranous fold **3. Capniidae**
Abdominal segments 1 to 7 at most divided laterally by membranous fold
.. **4. Leuctridae**
7(1). Profusely branched gills at lower angles of thorax **9. Perlidae**
Branched gills absent from thorax ... **8**
8(7). Body usually pigmented in distinct pattern; cerci usually as long as or longer than abdomen; pads of hind wing set at angle from body; gills absent or simple on submentum, thorax, or abdomen .. **7. Perlodidae**
Body almost concolorous, without pattern; cerci not over three-fourths length of abdomen; hind wing pads nearly parallel to body (except *Kathroperla* spp.); external gills entirely absent .. **8. Chloroperlidae**

Suborder **ARCTOPERLARIA**
Group **EUHOLOGNATHA**
Superfamily **NEMOUROIDEA**

1. NEMOURIDAE (Spring Stonefly Family)

L. 6–15 mm (most species under 10 mm). Brown or blackish. Front wing with a curved cross vein reaching front vein at apical third (see Fig. 8.4 for wing of *Prostoia besametsa* Ricker). Tarsi with second tarsomere much shorter than first and third; one-segmented cerci very short. The naiads are dull to dark brown, stout-bodied with many spines and setae; they live in fastmoving, rocky creeks where they feed on leaves and detritus. Adults emerge from April through August at different latitudes and elevations. The family contains 58 species in 12 genera in the U.S. and Canada.

Subfamily Amphinemurinae

[1.1 *Amphinemura* Ris (13 spp.); 1.2 *Mulenka* Ricker (11 spp.)]

Subfamily Nemourinae

[1.3 *Lednia* Ricker (1 sp., *L. tumana* (Ricker)); 1.4 *Nemoura* Latreille (4 spp.); 1.5 *Ostrocerca* Ricker (6 spp.); 1.6 *Paranemoura* Needham and Claassen (1 sp., *P. perfecta* (Walker)); 1.7 *Podmosta* Ricker (5 spp.); 1.8 *Prostoia* Ricker (3 spp.; see Fig. 8.4); 1.9 *Shipsa* Ricker (1 sp., *S. rotunda* (Claassen))]

1.10 *Soyedina* Ricker

This genus contains seven species distributed across northern North America, of which the following is an example:

S. vallicularia (Wu) (Threadtailed Stonefly). L. 11–13 mm. Cerci one-segmented; wings not rolled around body when at rest; second tarsomere much stouter than others. Adults emerge

April through May. (See Fig. 8.5.) (1) NY, NJ, PA, MD; (2) VA, NC.

[1.11 *Visoka* Ricker (1 sp., *V. cataractae* (Neave)); 1.12 *Zapada* Ricker (8 spp.)]

2. TAENIOPTERYGIDAE (Winter Stonefly Family)

L. 10–25 mm (most species 10–15 mm). Dark brown or blackish. Antennae very long; all tarsomeres of about same length; cerci very short. Naiads have divergent wing pads and live in rivers feeding on plant material. Adults emerge in mid-January through mid-April. They may feed on flowers. The family contains 25 species divided into two subfamilies, as follows.

Subfamily Brachypterinae

[2.1 *Bolotoperla* Freison (1 sp., *B. rossi* (Ricker)); 2.2 *Doddsia* Needham and Claassen (1 sp., *D. occidentalis* (Banks); 2.3 *Oemopteryx* Klapalek (4 spp.)]

Fig. 8.5. (*From Needham and Claassen, 1925*)

Fig. 8.4. (*From Bauman, 1975*)

2.4 *Strophopteryx* Frison

This genus contains seven species, all of them confined to eastern North America. The following is an example:

S. fasciata (Linneaus). L. 10–15 mm. Cerci with one to three segments; second tarsomere equal to others. Adults emerge from February to May and crawl on stones, fenceposts, and rails, especially if painted white. (1) n.e. NA; (2) VA, NC.

[2.5 *Taenionema* Banks (8 spp.)

Subfamily **Taeniopteryginae**

[2.6 *Taeniopteryx* Pictet (9 spp.)]

3. CAPNIIDAE (Small Winter Stonefly Family)

L. 3–15 mm (most species less than 12 mm; many under 7 mm). Blackish; wings with few cross veins. Middle tarsomere very short; cerci very long. Naiads have cerci at least half as long as body to as long as body and live in creeks; adults emerge from November through March. Most of the species occur in northern North America. The family contains 129 species in 9 genera.

3.1 *Allocapnia* Claassen

This genus, containing 38 species, is found in eastern North America. The following is one example of the many closely allied species.

A. pygmaea (Linnaeus). L. 3–7 mm. Found on snow, white posts, sides of buildings, tree trunks, and stones, especially near the lake shores. Adults emerge February through April. (See Fig. 8.6 for wing venation.) (1) n.e. NA.

[3.2 *Bolshecapnia* Ricker (4 spp.); 3.3 *Capnia* Pictet (50 spp.); 3.4 *Eucapnopsis* Okamoto (1 sp., *E. brevicauda* (Claassen)); 3.5 *Isocapnia* Banks (11 spp.); 3.6 *Mesocapnia* Rauser (11 spp.); 3.7 *Nemocapnia* Banks (1 sp., *N. carolina* Banks); 3.8 *Paracapnia* Hanson (3 spp.); 3.9 *Utacapnia* Gaufin (10 spp.)]

4. LEUCTRIDAE (Rolled-winged Winter Stonefly Family)

L. 6–13 mm (usually not over 10 mm). Some species reddish-brown; others brown to blackish. Wings rolled tightly to

Fig. 8.6. (*From Needham and Claassen, 1925*)

Fig. 8.7. (*From Needham and Claassen, 1925*)

body when at rest (Fig. 8.7); front wing without subapical anterior cross vein. Cerci and second tarsal segment very short. Naiads have wing pads parallel to body axis and live in creeks. Adults fly from December through August. There are 45 species in 7 genera.

Subfamily **Leuctrinae**

[4.1 *Despaxia* Ricker (1 sp., *D. augusta* Banks)]

4.2 *Leuctra* Stephens

This genus, containing 21 species, is found in eastern North America.

L. hamula (Claassen. L. 7.5–9 mm. Brown to dark brown; legs dark brown; wings slightly smoky. (See Fig. 8.7.) (1) n.e. NA.

[4.3 *Moselia* Ricker (1 sp., *M. infuscata* (Claassen)); 4.4 *Paraleuctra* Hansen (7 spp); 4.5 *Zealeuctra* (8 spp.); 4.6 *Megaleuctra* Neave (5 spp.); 4.7 *Perlomyia* Banks (2 spp.)]

Group SYSTELLOGNATHA
Superfamily PTERONARCYOIDEA

5. PTERONARCYIDAE (Giant Stonefly Family)

L. 38–63 mm. Body brownish or grayish. Anal area of front wing with two or more rows of cross veins. The naiads inhabit small brooks, streams, and rivers where they feed on plant material. The nocturnal adults emerge from June to August and do not feed. There are three genera and ten species in the U.S. and Canada.

There are three genera and ten species of the U.S. and Canada.

[5.1 *Allonarcys* Needham and Claassen (4 spp.); 5.2 *Pteronarcella* Banks (2 spp.)]

5.3 *Pteronarcys* Newman

The genus contains four species in the U.S. and Canada, of which the first of the following is the largest known stonefly.

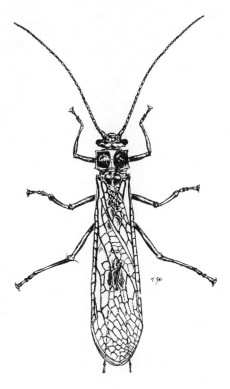

Fig. 8.8.

P. dorsata Say (Giant Stonefly). Widespread: 70–106 mm. Adults emerge in June and July. (See Fig. 8.8.) (1) n.e. NA.

P. californica Newport (Salmonfly). (3) CA, AZ, NM; (4) BC, WA, OR, ID, UT; (5) MT, WY, CO.

Superfamily PELTOPERLOIDEA

6. PELTOPERLIDAE (Roachlike Stonefly Family)

L. 9–30 mm. Head with two ocelli only; anal region of front wing without cross veins; cerci short. Body of the naiads somewhat roachlike in appearance. The family contains five genera and 13 species in the U.S. and Canada.

Subfamily Peltoperlinae

[6.1 *Peltoperla* Needham (1 sp., *P. arculata* Needham; see Fig. 8.9 for naiad)]

6.2 *Sierraperla* Jewett

This genus contains only the following species:

S. cora Needham and Smith. Wingspread: 34–49 mm. Brown to dark brown; wings lightly to heavily infuscated. (See Fig. 8.10 and A&J 13.) (3) CA; (4) NV.

[6.3 *Soliperla* Ricker (4 spp.); 6.4 *Tallaperla* Starke and Stewart (1 sp., *T. maria* (Needham and Smith)); 6.5 *Viehoperla* Ricker (1 sp., *V. ada* (Needham and Smith)); 6.6 *Yoroperla* Ricker (2 spp.)]

Superfamily PERLOIDEA

7. PERLODIDAE (Predatory Stonefly Family)

L. 6–20 mm, or rarely larger. Pronotum rectangular. Perlodinae species are brownish; Isoperlinae, yellowish or greenish. Naiads lack gills and are waxy smooth; they live in

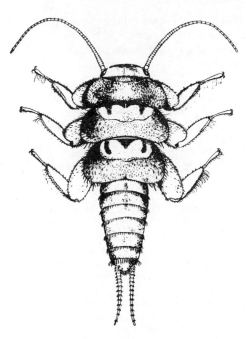

Fig. 8.9. (*From Claassen, 1931*)

rivers, usually in quiet waters, but some in faster moving, erosional waters; omnivores or predatory. Adults emerge in April, May, or June. The family contains 98 mostly uncommon species, assigned to 23 genera. They are widely distributed throughout the U.S. and Canada.

Subfamily Isoperlinae

[7.1 *Calliperla* Banks (1 sp., *C. luctuosa* (Banks)]

7.2 *Isoperla* Banks

This is one of the largest genera of the order with 50 species in the U.S. and Canada. The following are abundant species:

Fig. 8.10. (*From Needham and Claassen, 1925*)

I. confusa Frison (Green-winged Stonefly). L. 8–10 mm. Orange-yellow with black markings. Naiads live in clumps of fallen leaves. Adults emerge in late March to mid-April. (1) IL, IN.

I. bilineata (Say). L. 10–12 mm. Yellowish-green to whitish-green. Wings without dark veins. Naiads are found in most large rivers unpolluted enough to sustain fish. Adults emerge in late March to mid-May. (1) n.e. US; (2) s.e. US.

[7.3 *Rickera* Jewett (1 sp., *R. venusta* Jewett); 7.4 *Cascadoperla* Szezythko and Stewart (1 sp., *C. trictura* [Hoppe])]

Subfamily Perlodinae

[7.5 *Arcynopteryx* Klapalek (1 sp., *A. compacta* (MacLachlan); 7.6 *Chernokrilus* Ricker (3 spp.); 7.7 *Cultus* Ricker (4 spp.); 7.8 *Diploperla* Needham and Claassen (2 spp.); 7.9 *Diura* Billberg (2 spp.); 7.10 *Helopicus* Ricker (2 sp.); 7.11 *Hydroperla* Frison (2 spp.); 7.12 *Isogenoides* Klapalek (9 spp.); 7.13 *Kogotus* Ricker (3 spp.); 7.14 *Malirekus* Ricker (1 sp., *M. hastatus* (Banks)); 7.15 *Megarcys* Klapalek (5 spp.); 7.16 *Oroperla* Needham (1 sp., *O. barbara* (Needham)); 7.17 *Osobenus* Ricker (1 sp., *O. yakimae* (Hoppe)); 7.18 *Perlinoides* Needham and Claassen (1 sp., *P. aurea* (Smith)); 7.19 *Pictetiella* (1 sp., *P. expansa* (Banks)); 7.20 *Remenus* Ricker (1 sp., *R. bilobatus* (Needham and Claassen)); 7.21 *Setvena* Ricker (1 sp., *S. bradleyi* (Smith)); 7.22 *Skwala* Ricker (2 spp.); 7.23 *Yugus* Ricker (3 spp.)]

8. CHLOROPERLIDAE (Green Stonefly Family)

L. 6–24 mm (most species under 15 mm). Yellowish, greenish, bright green, or black. Anterior margin of the pronotum broadly rounded or oval; second tarsomere short, about equal in length to others. Naiads have short cerci, rounded wing pads, no external gills. They are tubular-shaped, with bristles adapted for burrowing, and live in creeks. The adults fly from May to September. The family in the U.S. and Canada is composed of 57 species in ten genera and two subfamilies.

Subfamily Chloroperlinae

8.1 *Alloperla* Banks

This is the largest genus of the family with 17 species. The following are representative of both the family and genus:

A. atlantica Baumann. L. 6.5–9 mm. Bright green without dark or pale stripes or spots. Adults emerge from May through July, resting on foliage, mostly near streams; diurnal. (1) n.e. US; (2) VA, NC, SC, GA.

[8.2 *Hastaperla* Ricker (3 spp.); 8.3 *Neaviperla* Ricker (1 sp., *N. forcipata* (Neave)); 8.4 *Rasvena* Ricker (1 sp., *R. terna* (Frison)); 8.5 *Suwallia* Ricker (4 spp., including *S. marginata* (Banks); (see Fig. 8.11); 8.6 *Sweltsa* Ricker (23 spp.); 8.7 *Triznaka* Ricker (3 spp.)]

Subfamily Paraperlinae

[8.8 *Kathroperla* Banks (1 sp., *K. perdita* Banks); 8.9 *Paraperla* Banks (2 spp.); 8.10 *Utaperla* Ricker (2 spp.)]

9. PERLIDAE (Common Stonefly Family)

L. 8–44 mm (many species over 20 mm). Many are yellowish or brownish. Front wing with many cross veins; hind wing wide. Thorax beneath with profusely branched gill remnants at the posterior angles of the pro- and mesothoracic segments. Naiads are often patterned in brown and yellow; their body is flattened. They live on the bottom and are predacious. Adults

Fig. 8.11.

of various species appear from April to as late as September; they do not feed. The family is divided into two subfamilies and three tribes, with a total of 30 species in 12 genera.

Subfamily Acroneuriinae
Tribe Acroneuriini

[9.1 *Acroneuria* Pictet (12 spp.); 9.2 *Attaneuria* Ricker (1 sp., *A. ruralis* (Hagen)); 9.3 *Beloneura* Needham and Claassen (3 spp.); 9.4 *Doroneuria* Needham and Claassen (2 spp.); 9.5 *Eccoptura* Klapalek (1 sp., *E. xanthenes* (Newman)); 9.6 *Hesperoperla* Banks (2 spp.); 9.7 *Perlesta* Banks (2 spp.)]

9.8 *Perlinella* Banks

This genus contains three species, all in the eastern United States. The following is an example of the genus and this family.

P. ephyra (Newman). L. 9–16 mm. Dark brown with cloudy to smoky wings. (See Fig. 8.2.) (1) n.e. US; (2) VA, NC.

Subfamily Perlinae
Tribe Neoperlini

[9.9 *Neoperla* Needham (2 spp.)]

Tribe Perlini

[9.10 *Claassenia* Wu (1 sp., *C. sabulosa* (Banks); 9.11 *Paragnetina* Klapalek (5 spp.); 9.12 *Phasganophora* Klapalek (1 sp., *P. capitata* (Pictet)) [See Fig. 8.1])]

BIBLIOGRAPHY

Bauman, Richard W. 1975. Revision of the stonefly family Nemouridae (Plecoptera): a study of the world fauna at the generic level. *Smithsonian Contributions to Zoology*, No. 211, 74 pp.

Bauman, Richard W.; Gaufin, Arden R.; and Surdick, Rebecca F. 1977. The Stoneflies (Plecoptera) of the Rocky Mountains. *Mem. American Ent. Soc.*, 31, 208 pp.

Claassen, Peter W. 1939. A catalogue of the Plecoptera of the world. *Cornell Univ. Agric. Exp. Stat. Mem.*, 232, 235 pp.

Fiance, S. D. 1977. The genera of eastern North American Chloroperlidae (Plecoptera): key to larval stages. *Psyche*, 84: 308–316.

Frison, Theodore H. 1935. The stoneflies, or Plecoptera of Illinois. *Illinois Nat. Hist. Surv. Bull.*, 20(4), v + 281–471. [Reprinted by Entomological Reprint Specialists, 1975.]

Hitchcock, Stephen W. 1974. The Plecoptera or stoneflies of Connecticut. *Guide to the insects of Connecticut*, VII. Connecticut Dept. of Environ. Prot., 262 pp.

Hynes, H. B. N. 1976. Biology of Plecoptera. *Annual Rev. Ent.*, 21: 135–153.

Illies, J. 1966. Katalog der rezenten Plecoptera. *Das Tierreich*, 82. Berlin: Walter de Gruyter and Co., 632 pp.

Jewett, Stanley G., Jr. 1959. The stoneflies (Plecoptera) of the Pacific Northwest. *Oregon State Mon. Ent.*, 95 pp.

Jewett, Stanely G., Jr. 1960. The stoneflies (Plecoptera) of California. *Bull. California Insect Survey*, 6(6): 125–177.

Leiser, Eric and Boyle, Robert H. 1982. *Stoneflies for the angler.* New York: Alfred A. Knopf, 174 pp.

Merritt, R. W. and Cummins, K. W., eds. 1978. *An introduction to the aquatic insects of North America.* Dubuque: Kendall/Hunt Publ. Co., xiii + 441 pp. (Plecoptera, pp. 105–118, by P. P. Harper).

Needham, J. G. and Claassen, Peter W. 1925. A monograph of the Plecoptera or stoneflies of America north of Mexico. *Thomas Say Foundation, Ent. Soc. America,* publ. No. 2, 397 pp.

Ricker, W. E. 1976. Origin of stonefly names proposed by Ricker and collaborators. *Perla*, 2: 5–19.

Stark, Bill P. and Gaufin, Arden R. 1976. The Nearctic genera of Perlidae (Plecoptera). *Misc. Publ. Ent. Soc. America*, 10(1): 1–77.

Stark, B. P. and Gaufin, A. R. 1979. The stoneflies (Plecoptera) of Florida. *Trans. American Ent. Soc.*, 104: 391–433.

Stark, B. P. and Stewart, K. W. 1981. The Nearctic genera of Peltoperlidae (Plecoptera). *Journ. Kansas Ent. Soc.*, 54: 285–311.

Szcytko, S. W. and Stewart, K. W. 1979. The genus *Isoperla* (Plecoptera) of western North America; holomorphology and systematics; and a new stonefly genus *Cascadoperla. Memoirs American Ent. Soc.*, 32: 1–120.

Usinger, Robert L., ed. 1956. *Aquatic insects of California.* Berkeley: Univ. of California Press, 508 pp. (Plecoptera, pp. 155–181, by Stanley G. Jewett, Jr.).

Zwick, Peter. 1973. Insecta: Plecoptera. Phylogenetisches system und katalog. *Das Tierreich,* Lieferung 94. Berlin: Walter de Gruyter, xxxvii + 465 pp.

Order 9

EMBIOPTERA (Webspinners)

These secretive insects are noted for their ability to spin labyrinths of silken galleries in which they live gregariously. They have no real social structure, a colony usually consisting of a single female and her brood of developing young. It is the weblike galleries that give them their common name, webspinners. They are also called embiids or Embiidina, this Latin name coming from *embios*, meaning "lively" or "embodied with life."

Most adult males have two pairs of nearly equally long wings, which are not shed like those of termites. In a gallery, they are folded forward while the male moves backward thereby minimizing friction against the gallery walls. During flight, on the other hand, they are stiffened by blood pressure in sinuslike veins. Such wing specialization is found in no other insect group.

Webspinner galleries are found in the soil, crevices, in loose debris, and in and under bark. The adults and nymphs primarily eat dead leaves, lichen, and bark surfaces. They are not active fliers, but some males may fly to lights at night.

Diagnosis: L. 4–7 mm (a few as long as 22 mm). Body soft; shape elongate and cylindrical; usually pale tan to black. Antennae slender with 9 to 36 or more segments and much longer than the head. Mouthparts of nymphs and adult females adapted for chewing vegetation; those of males for clasping females during mating. The males (Fig. 9.1) may or may not have wings; the nymphlike females are always wingless (Fig. 9.2). Veins of the wings are long, with very few cross veins; the radius is thickened as a blood sinus. Legs are short, all stages of all species having the first tarsomere of the front legs enlarged because of the presence of many silk glands; spinning tarsi, the most distinctive features of the order are present in all species. The abdomen is slender, with the cerci in both sexes short and basically two-segmented. The nymphs closely resemble adult females. Although webspinners bear some resemblance to adult stoneflies, their wings have few cross veins and their enlarged front tarsomere quickly distinguishes them from all other similar insects.

Fig. 9.1.

Fig. 9.2.

Metamorphosis: Paurometabolous.

Habits and habitats: The silk galleries, which serve as protective coverage during development and while foraging for food, are primarily constructed in forest debris, usually close to the trunks of trees. Because the corridors are narrow, escape from a predator encountered at the end of a passage is best effected by rapid retreat into the interior, a habit to which these insects are particularly well adapted.

Reproductive behavior: Males of most species fly during the day in search of females. Adult males never eat and die soon after mating; females may live at least six months. Because of the gregarious nature of these insects, a colony may persist for a considerable period of time by generational overlap; usually however, there is a single generation per year with no overlap.

Collecting and preserving: Search out webs in their habitat. Specimens are preserved in 80% alcohol.

Rearing: Webspinners are easily cultured, but unless males are reared, the varous species are not easily identified. Plastic vials 4 to 6 in. long with snap-on lids may be used. A large circular vent is punched out of the center of the lid and a circular piece of fly screen glued over the opening. The tube or jar is filled with bark flakes or crumpled dead leaves found at the nesting site. Specimens introduced into the container immediately spin new gallery webs. They will eat any kind of bark or dead leaves. Fresh lettuce periodically added will sustain a culture that has become crowded. The bottom of the rearing chamber must be kept moist.

Distribution: Most of the 150 described species (and many more remain to be described) are tropical. Six genera with ten species are established in the southern U.S., with one species living as far north as South Carolina and another ranging into southwestern Utah.

Note on identification: Since the best identification features are found in the mandibles, wing venation, and copulatory organs of adult males, it is necessary to rear specimens to associate males, females, and nymphs.

Economic importance: These rare species are of no economic importance.

CLASSIFICATION

Three families of webspinners occur in the U.S. See the accompanying Key.

Key to the Families of Embioptera

1. Female and immatures with basal hind tarsomere with two small ventral pads (*Gynembia tarsalis* Ross, a parthenogenetic species; male unknown); (in part) ... **2. Oligotomidae**
 Females, males, and immatures with basal hind tarsomere without ventral pad or with only 1 small pad ... *2*
2(1). Front wing with R_{4+5} branched; left cercus 2-segmented **3. Oligembiidae**
 Front wing with R_{4+5} unbranched; if wings absent, then left cercus not segmented *3*
3(2). Mandible without inner apical denticles **1. Anisembiidae**
 Mandible with distinct apical denticles; (in part) **2. Oligotomidae**

1. ANISEMBIIDAE

[1.1 *Chelicerca* Ross (1 sp., *C. rubra* (Ross), (3) CA, AZ; (4) UT); 1.2 *Anisembia* Krauss (1 sp., *A. texana* (Melander), (3) TX). (Note: *Chelicerca davisi* Ross may occur in (3) TX as stray from Mexico)]

2. OLIGEMBIIDAE

[= Teratembiidae]

[2.1 *Oligembia* Davis (4 spp.: *O. hubbardi* (Hagen), (2) FL; *O. melanura* Ross, (2) LA, (3) TX; *O. lobata* Ross, (3) TX (Note: *O. excisa* Ross may occur in CA, from Guatemala; *O. nigrina* Ross reported in (1) NJ, from Venezuela; *O. vandykei* Ross, (2) SC, FL, MS, LA (Note: *O. gigantea* Ross reported in (1) DC, from Venezuela)]

3. OLIGOTOMIDAE

[3.1 *Oligotoma* Westwood (2 spp.: *O. saundersii* (Westwood), (2) FL, (3) TX (see Fig. 9.1 for adult male and Fig. 9.2 for adult female), and *O. nigra* Hagen, (3) CA, AZ, TX); 3.2 *Gynembia* Ross (1 sp., *G. tarsalis* Ross, (3) CA, AZ)]

3.3 *Haploembia* Verhoeff

One species only, which is widespread:

H. solieri (Rambur) L. 4–7 mm. Elongate, cylindrical, slightly flattened; antennae filiform. (2) FL, LA; (3) CA, AZ, TX. (See A&J 38.)

BIBLIOGRAPHY

Ross, E. S. 1940. Revision of the Embioptera of North America. *Ann. Ent. Soc. America,* 33: 629–676, 50 figs.

———. 1944. A revision of the Embioptera, or webspinners of the New World. *Proc. United States Nat. Mus.,* 94(3175): 401–504.

———. 1970. Biosystematics of the Embioptera. *Ann. Rev. Ent.,* 15: 157–172.

Note: After this text was in page proof, the following revision was published, resulting in numerous name changes:

Ross, E. S. 1984. A synopsis of the Embiidina of the United States. *Proc. Ent. Soc. Washington,* 86: 82–93.

Extinct Order PROTORTHOPTERA

The Protorthoptera are represented by numerous fossils found in Mississippian (Upper Carboniferous) and Permian period rock. Few complete specimens are known, most of the fossils consisting of front wings. These resemble the wings of Orthoptera in that they are thickened and probably were not the primary flying wings. They retained the filiform cerci of the Palaeoptera. Some have paranotal lobes on the prothorax. One group, formerly considered to be a separate order, the Protoperlaria, have aquatic immatures with lateral abdominal gills similar to those of Plecopteran naiads. At the same time, terrestrial nymphs are known that are believed to belong to the Protorthoptera.

The legs of these insects are variously modified; some of them have raptorial legs. Until a more complete set of specimens has been found, their classification will continue to remain speculative.

Extinct Order MIOMOPTERA

Members of this order, found in Mississippian through Permian period rock, are small, with nearly homonomous wings of reduced venation, biting mouthparts, and distinct cerci. This order is probably parallel to, rather than more advanced than, the Protorthoptera, even though most of the known fossils are of the Permian rather than the Mississippian period. The order may have given rise to the sucking-mouthpart insects.

Extinct Order CALONEURODEA

These insects are known from about the same time as the Protorthoptera and the Miomoptera; that is, they are Mississippian and Permian. They differ from the other two extinct orders as well as the Orthoptera and Plecoptera by having slender homonomous wings with small anal areas. They retain cerci and filiform antennae. Although the relationship is obscure, it is generally believed that they are related to the Orthoptera.

Order 10

PHASMATODEA (Walkingsticks)

[= Phasmida]

Certainly, few other groups of insects have evolved such a remarkable degree of protective resemblance as these. Most of the species are found in tropical rain forests and show a great diversity of form. Although we call them walkingsticks, in many parts of the world phasmids are better known as leaf insects or stick insects. Their Latin name, Phasmatodea, means an apparition or specter, alluding, no doubt, to their camouflage. Their resemblance to their habitat clearly indicates where they live—in trees and bushes, especially the foliage of large tropical forest trees.

Walkingsticks might be confused with the mantids, but all lack raptorial front legs.

Diagnosis: L. 10–70 mm or more. Body leathery or hard. Shape greatly elongate, either cylindrical [native species (see Fig. 10.1)] or flattened and resembling leaves (some tropical species). Body mostly green or brown; wings, when present, transparent and often with green veins or dark. Antennae usually long, with 8 to 80 segments; mouthparts of the biting type. All but one of the native species wingless. Legs long and slender and not enlarged for jumping, digging, or capturing prey. Abdomen long and slender, with the hind part of the male's fitted with clasping appendages.

The nymphs are hard to distinguish from the adults except by their rudimentary copulatory organs. Eggs are usually distinctly shaped and resemble seeds.

Metamorphosis: Paurometabolous, with nymphs that pass through few instars.

Habits and habitats: All species feed on leaves, mostly at night. During the day, they hide by resting on twigs that they closely resemble (see Fig. 10.1). This camouflage seems to protect them from bird and animal predators. One species, the

Fig. 10.1.

Two-striped Walkingstick, secretes a vapor or milky fluid that provides a good defense against predatory insects and perhaps birds. If this substance gets in a person's eyes, it can be very uncomfortable. Some are thought to sting, but this is a misconception.

Reproductive behavior: Many species of phasmids are parthogenetic, the males being completely unknown, or, in some cases, extremely rare, with as few as one male per 1,000 females. The nymphs, unlike those of all other insects, can regenerate their legs. In fact, they frequently break off their legs, a process termed *autotomy*, at a specific point between the trochanter and femur. New legs are then regenerated during the nymphal stage. There are very few nymphal molts, only two in some species. Males are smaller than females. In mating, the male holds the female's abdomen by a pair of terminal claspers. Eggs are laid as copulation takes place, the eggs dropping to the forest floor. Winter months are generally spent in the egg stage.

Collecting and preserving: Nymphs and adults are easily shaken or beaten from trees or bushes, usually dropping to the ground where they may be captured. Adults may be pinned. Their bodies should be supported while they are drying. Extra crossed pins must be placed in the box or tray to keep specimens from swinging on the original pin.

Rearing: Nymphs are easily reared in cages where they can be fed fresh leaves from host trees. Any eggs laid in the cages will hatch the following spring.

Distribution: Most of the 2000 or more species live in the Indo-Malayan region. Only 29 species in 10 genera are known in the U.S., and most of these are confined to the extreme southern portion.

Notes on identification: The identification of the species requires considerable study of their anatomy using fairly high magnification. Keys to the species in the U.S. can be found in Helfer (1963).

Economic importance: These insects are never abundant enough to do any serious damage to forest foliage.

CLASSIFICATION

The species found in the U.S. are assigned to four families in nine genera. See the Key to the Families.

Key to the Families of Phasmatodea

1. Tarsi with 3 tarsomeres ... **3. Timemidae**
 Tarsi with 5 tarsomeres .. *2*
2(1). Mesothorax four or more times as long as prothorax; meso- and metatibiae not deeply emarginate ventrally at apex ... *3*
 Mesothorax never more than three times as long as prothorax; meso- and metatibae broadly and deeply emarginate ventrally at apex, thus forming a cavity to receive base of tarsi when in repose .. **4. Pseudophasmatidae**
3(2). Wings absent; 1st abdominal segment transverse or only slightly longer than wide, much shorter than metanotum **1. Heteronemiidae**
 Adults with short wings; first abdominal segment as long as or longer than metanotum, or at least much longer than wide; head with 2 stout spines on vertex; thorax and legs often spinous ... **2. Phasmatidae**

Suborder ANAREOLATEA

1. HETERONEMIIDAE (Common Walkingstick Family)

All species of this family are wingless. There are 20 species in seven genera.

Subfamily Heteronemiinae

Tribe Heteronemiini

[= Bacunculinae]

[1.1 *Pseudosermyle* Caudell (2 spp.); 1.2 *Sermyle* Stål (1 sp., *S. mexicana* (Saussure)); 1.3 *Manomera* Rehn and Hebard (2 spp.)]

1.4 *Diapheromera* Gray

This is the largest genus of the family, having 10 species that occur throughout the southern U.S. The following is also commonly collected in the Northeast:

Diapheromera femorata (Say) (Common Walkingstick). L. 65–100 mm. Hind femora of both sexes with a subapical spine on underside; middle femora of the male thicker than the

Fig. 10.2.

Fig. 10.3.

hind one. Common from August to October on leaves of oak, black locust, and wild cherry, especially on young, isolated trees along fence rows or on bushes. (See Fig. 10.2 and A&J 31.) (1) n.e. US; (2) s.e. US; (3) AZ, TX, OK.

[1.5 *Megaphasma* Caudell (1 sp., *M. denticrus* (Stål)); 1.6 *Heteronemia* Gray (2 spp.)]

Fig. 10.4.

Fig. 10.5.

Subfamily Pachymorphinae

Tribe Ramulini

[1.7 *Parabacillus* Caudell (2 spp.)]

2. PHASMATIDAE (Winged Walkingstick Family)

[= Phibalosominae]

Only one species of Phasmatodea in the U.S. has wings; as follows:

Subfamily Cladomorphinae

Tribe Hesperophasmatini

2.1 *Aplopus* Gray

One species, as follows:

A. mayeri Claudell (Mayer's Walkingstick). L. 80–130 mm. Winged. Common on bay cedar and other shore vegetation. (See Fig. 10.3.) (2) s. FL, FL Keys.

Suborder AREOLATAE

3. TIMEMATIDAE (Timema Family)

Very different in appearance from the preceding walkingsticks, these insects are relatively short and stout. They are green, brown, or even pinkish. Only one genus is found in the U.S.

3.1 *Timema* Scudder

Six species, of which the following is an example:

T. californica Scudder (California Timemas). L. 12–25 mm. Green, brown, or pinkish. Found on such plants as *Cea-*

nothus spp. (Redroot), *Cercocarpus* spp. (Mountain Mahogany), and others, as well as trees such as firs. They are collected by beating this vegetation. (See A&J 32.) (3) CA.

4. PSEUDOPHASMATIDAE (Striped Walkingstick Family)

[= Anisomorphinae]

Subfamily Pseudophasmatinae
Tribe Anisomorphini

Only one genus is found in the U.S., as follows:

4.1 *Anisomorpha* Brunner

Two species, as follows:

A. ferruginea (Beauvois). L. 30–36 mm. Stripes pale and inconspicuous. (1) IL; (2) VA, FL; (3) TX.

A. buprestoides (Stoll). L. 40–80 mm. Male (Fig. 10.4) brownish-yellow; female (Fig. 10.5) brown; median dorsal stripe and each side with a dark stripe. Found on grass or bushes all year. Defensive glands under pronotum squirt a thick milky fluid at predators. (2) s.e. GA; FL.

BIBLIOGRAPHY

Bedford, G. O. 1978. Biology and ecology of the Phasmatodea. *Ann. Rev. Ent.*, 23: 125–149.

Bradley, J. C. and Galil, B. S. 1977. The taxonomic arrangement of the Phasmatodea with keys to the subfamilies and tribes. *Proc. Ent. Soc. Washington*, 79: 176–208.

Helfer, J. R. 1963. *How to know the grasshoppers, cockroaches, and their allies.* Dubuque: W. C. Brown Co., vi + 353 pp.

Order 11

ORTHOPTERA (Grasshoppers, Crickets, and Katydids)

Sound production by animals is not as universal as one might think. We know that the vertebrates are outstanding sound producers, especially birds. Many members of the Orthoptera are rivals of the birds and far outnumber them in species as well as individuals. Although the quality of their song is debatable, the whirr and chirr of katydids and field and tree crickets are unforgetable sounds that are as much a part of summer as the wind in the trees and the splashing of water. Summer katydids replace the sound of spring frogs. Grasshoppers too are a part of the summer chorus, but their songs are not so well known. Crickets are so well thought of that they occupy a significant place in our poetic literature and art. Grasshoppers are cast into metal wind vanes, such as the one atop Boston's Faneuil Hall, or adopted as a colophon, such as that adopted by Old Sturbridge Village, Connecticut (Fig. 11.1). A grasshopper appeared on the heraldic crest of Sir Thomas Gresham, a London banker in the mid-sixteenth century. An ancient Greek symbol denotes that they sprang from the soil of Athens. Unfortunately, grasshoppers are often very destructive and universally despised by farmers. As a result of their despoilations, they found a place in the Bible; they are the locusts of the Old Testament that devastated Egypt.

The Latin name for this order of insects, Orthoptera, is derived from the Greek *orthos* and *pteron*, meaning "straight wings." In addition, they have many common names, among them the locust referred to above and the common name bush crickets (our katydids) used in Europe and Africa. Some of the

Fig. 11.1.

older literature divides the Orthoptera or "Saltoria," that is, the jumping Orthoptera, into two major groups: the Ensifera—the various kinds of cave crickets, katydids, and true crickets (those Saltoria with swordlike ovipositors)—and The Caelifera—the short-horned grasshoppers, grouse locusts, and others.

Hordes of grasshoppers clean fields of crops to this day and cause disastrous famines in many parts of the world. Accounts of their activities form a substantial part of the world's entomological literature.

Most species of Orthoptera are large enough to be easily seen, but they are not so easily collected because of their ability to jump as well as to fly. Some are very colorful, especially those grasshoppers with colored hind wings. Although Orthoptera are found in many habitats—including caves, various aquatic

environments, and even glaciers—they are best known as part of the grassland biome.

Diagnosis: L. 5–150 mm (most species between 10–50 mm, but some 150 mm or perhaps even more, with a few very small, under 5 mm). They are leathery bodied, sometimes hard, elongate, and cylindrical (see Fig. 2.2 in Part I, Chap. 2.) The antennae are usually long (sometimes much longer than the body) and slender and are often composed of many (an indefinite number) antennal segments. The mouthparts (see Fig. 2.7 in Chap. 2) are fitted for biting. Most species are plant eaters but some are predators. The front wings, which are somewhat thickened, serve more as covers for the hind wings than as flight equipment. They are often fitted with scraper and file, spines, or teeth that are used for sound production. The hind wings are thin, membranous, and fold fanlike beneath the front wings when not in use. Some Orthoptera are wingless as adults. The front and middle legs are moderate in size and often have spines. The front pair may be modified with scooplike spines to equip them for digging or scratching in the soil. Some species have earlike organs on the front tibia for sound reception. The hind legs of most species are much larger than the others, with the basal part (femur) enlarged because of the large muscles. Such legs enable these insects to hop and hence the common name, grasshopper. The tibiae are correspondingly elongated but not enlarged. The abdomen is cylindrical and usually has seven complete segments, the others being modified for copulation and egg laying. The female ovipositor (see Fig. 11.2 for that of a grasshopper) is often greatly elongate, occasionally nearly as long as the remainder of the abdomen (in the katydids and crickets) and sometimes even longer.

The nymphs are almost always terrestrial (a few rare exceptions are aquatic) and resemble the adult except for their lack of wings. The small wing pads gradually develop into the adult wings. After several molts (usually five), the wings and sex organs have fully developed, and the adult is formed.

The Orthoptera may sometimes be confused with cockroaches, mantids, walkingsticks, and earwigs. They are so very similar to these insects that they were all once grouped together in a single order. The distinctive shape of the Orthoptera and their enlarged hind leg serve as the best distinguishing features.

Metamorphosis: Paurometabolous, with terrestrial eggs, nymphs, and adults.

Habits and habitats: Grasshoppers, katydids, and crickets are found feeding on vegetation, usually in open fields. The cave and camel crickets (the more primitive members of the order) are predacious and hunt at night. Some species of crickets and katydids are found in trees and bushes. One small group, the Pygmy Mole Crickets (Tridactylidae), are aquatic, with their hind legs fitted for swimming.

Reproductive behavior: Many species of Orthoptera

Fig. 11.2.

produce sound for the purpose of attracting the opposite sex. This familiar chirr is produced when the *file*, a row of pegs or teeth on the overlapping front wing, is rubbed across the *scraper*, or stridulatory ridge on the upper posterior margin of the underlying front wing. The noise produced is amplified by a tightly stretched circular surface that forms a drumhead on the underlying front wing. Moreover, a resonating chamber is formed between the wings and the abdomen when the latter is depressed for sound production. Usually, only males produce sound, but in some species the female may do so as well. Grasshoppers also produce sound simply by clicking their wings together.

In order for the sound to achieve its purpose, the females must be able to hear it. The auditory organs of katydids and crickets are located on the anterior tibiae near the tibial-femoral joint. Here the cuticle is thin enough to form a tympanic membrane beneath which are air-filled enlargements of the trachea. The auditory organs of grasshoppers are located on the first tergum of the abdomen. Stridulatory sounds vary considerably in frequency (or pitch), from low sounds in the 3 kHz range to ultrasonic 100 kHz. Not only must the female be able to hear, she must also be able to determine the direction from which the sound came if she is to locate her potential mate. In addition, the sound of each species must be distinct enough from that of other species to offer an isolating mechanism; normally, the female will respond only to the song of males of her own species. The sound differences may be very subtle. Indeed, it has been shown that the tree crickets form a large complex of species virtually indistinguishable morphologically, but quite recognizable by the sound they produce, although human beings may not always be able to detect the difference. Copulation consists of the male's attaching a spermatophore to the outside of the female genital aperture, there being no intromittent organs or penis in most male crickets and katydids. The eggs are fertilized during the egg laying process from the sperm released from the spermatophore and stored in the female spermatheca, a storage sac at the end of the oviduct. Eggs of grasshoppers are inserted into the soil by the female ovipositor; those of katydids and crickets are laid in a variety of places, including grass, reeds, galls on willows, stems of plants, bark of trees and shrubs, and even within leaves between the upper and lower epidermis.

Collecting and preserving: A few orthopterans are attracted to light at night and to bait. Others may be collected by sweeping and beating vegetation. Specimens may be mounted on pins. Their wings (usually only the left one) may be spread if they have a color pattern and dried on a spreading board. Large specimens should be eviscerated and the abdomen filled with cotton. When pinned into an insect box, two pins should be placed on each side of the abdomen to prevent its turning if the specimen loosens on the pin. Legs should be closed (not spread) and positioned as close to the body as possible.

Rearing: Many species may be kept in cages and reared by feeding them the proper vegetation. Often lettuce is sufficient. Some are rather host specific and must be fed a particular host plant. Moist sandy soil in the bottom of the cage will provide a place for egg laying for most species of grasshoppers and crickets. Some species, for example, the Field Cricket, are raised commercially for fish bait, bird and reptile food, and laboratory experiments.

Distribution: Orthoptera are distributed throughout the world, most of the 12,500 species being found in tropical grass-

Fig. 11.3. Swarming adult locusts darken the sky. (*Courtesy of African Anti-locust Research Centre*)

Fig. 11.4. Hoppers (nymphs) of the migratory locust eat everything in sight. (*Courtesy of Shell Photographic Union, London*)

lands. There are 1080 species in 223 genera living in the U.S. and Canada.

Notes on identification: Although the number of species is rather large, it is not difficult to build up an accurately identified local collection because of the distinctive shapes and color markings of these insects. Since most Orthoptera are over 7 mm in length, they may be identified with fairly low magnification. Of the 601 species of grasshoppers in the U.S. and Canada, over 200 belong to the genus *Melanoplus*. Since the other genera of the family have relatively few species, the species are easier to identify. The katydid family, Tettigoniidae, has 243 species; the Gryllacrididae, 129 species; and the Gryllidae, 96 species. The species of these families are difficult to separate without technical keys. The remaining six families

have relatively few species. Most of the commonly collected species, other than Acrididae, are described in the following pages.

Economic importance: Several species of grasshoppers become abundant enough each year to cause severe damage to crops and grassland if not controlled. The principle states affected are those in the northern plains from eastern Washington to western Minnesota and south to northern Texas. There is usually less damage in most of the other western states. In the East, several species are garden pests. Actually, all vegetable-feeding species are destructive to some degree. The locusts of the Bible, *Schistocerca gregaria* (see genus 5.114), may become

Table 11.1 Table of families

Family	Antennae	Wings	Legs	Other features
1. Tetrigidae	Short, about one-half length of body	Hidden under pronotum	Tarsomeres 2-2-3	Pronotum projects behind over abdomen
2. Eumastacidae	Short, hardly longer than head	Wingless	Slender	Head long, narrow, pointed
3. Tanaoceridae	Nearly as long as body	Wingless	Stout; hind femora enlarged, about as long as abdomen	Tympanal organs absent
4. Romaleidae	Short, about one-half length of body	Hind wings usually colorful	Tibia usually with two apical immovable spurs	Very large grasshoppers, often marked with bright colors
5. Acrididae	Short, about one-half length of body	Usually well-developed, some with colorful hind wings	Stout; hind femora enlarged, about as long as abdomen	The most numerous Orthoptera
6. Tridactylidae	Short, about one-half length of body; 12 or fewer segments	With brown and black markings	Front legs enlarged for digging	Very small, 4–10 mm in length; often swimmers
7. Tettigoniidae	Long, usually much longer than body	Large, green; usually extend well beyond abdomen; a few short or absent	Tarsomeres 4-4-4; hind femora longer than abdomen	Auditory organs at base of front tibia; ovipositor usually large
8. Prophalangopsidae	Long, usually about length of body	Short, about one-half length of body	Short and stout	Bulky insects resembling Decticinae of the Tettigoniidae
9. Gryllacrididae	Long as body or longer	Absent or very much reduced	Hind legs very large; tarsomeres usually 4-4-4	Gray or brown in color; body hump-backed
10. Gryllidae	Long as body or longer	Bent sharply at sides; front wings often shortened; fitted for stridulation	Tarsomeres 3-3-3	Ovipositors usually long, conspicuous
11. Gryllotalpidae	Short, less than one-half length of body	Short; appressed to abdomen	Front legs enlarged for digging	Digging habit and large size diagnostic

so extremely abundant (see Figs. 11.3 and 11.4) that they darken earth and sky when they migrate across the landscape to feed on all green plants in their path.

CLASSIFICATION

The classification followed here is essentially that of Rehn and Grant (1961). The generic arrangement has been taken from various sources, including some unpublished lists. Many other arrangements have been proposed in recent years, but none has really received general acceptance. As more information becomes available about the Orthoptera of the world, further changes are bound to be made and more subgroups added to the classification.

The list of families that appears in Table 11.1 gives comparative recognition features for those that occur in the United States and Canada. Additional features appear in the accompanying Key to the Families.

Key to the Families of Orthoptera

1. Prothoracic legs not fossorial (fitted for digging) *2*
 Prothoracic legs fossorial; front tibiae short and broadened, with conspicuous spines or processes ... *7*
2(1). Antennae much shorter than body and relatively heavy; tympanal organ, when present, at base of abdomen .. *3*
 Antennae usually as long as, or longer than, body and relatively slender; tympanal organ, when present, at base of protibia ... *8*
3(2). Pronotum extending over entire abdomen or beyond; pretarsus without arolium; front and middle tarsi with only 2 visible tarsomeres; hind tarsi with 3 tarsomeres **1. Tetrigidae**
 Pronotum much shorter, never extending over entire abdomen; pretarsus with arolium; tarsi with tarsomeres 3-3-3 ... *4*
4(3). First abdominal segment with tympanal organs *5*
 First abdominal segment without tympanal organs *6*
5(4). Hind tibia with both inner and outer immovable spines at tip (Fig. 11.5); prosternum usually with median tubercle **4. Romaleidae**
 Hind tibia with only the inner immovable spine at tip, the outer one absent; prosternum with or without median tubercle **5. Acrididae**
6(4). Antennae shorter than front femur **2. Eumastacidae**
 Antennae longer than front femur **3. Tanaoceridae**
7(1). Tarsomeres 3-3-3; antenna multisegmented; length over 12 mm **1. Gryllotalpidae**
 Tarsomeres 2-2-1 or 2-2-0; antenna composed of 12 or fewer elongate segments; length under 12 mm .. **6. Tridactylidae**
8(2). Middle tarsus always, and front and hind tarsus usually, with 4 tarsomeres; ocelli usually present; ovipositor sword-shaped .. *10*
 Tarsomeres 3-3-3; ocelli present or absent; ovipositor usually cylindrical or slender ... *9*
9(8). First apparent hind tarsomere not subdivided; ovipositor cylindrical, spear, or needle-shaped .. **10. Gryllidae**
 First apparent hind tarsomere subdivided indistinctly into 2 tarsomeres; ovipositor not as above .. **8. Prophalangopsidae**
10(8). Wings present, sometimes abbreviated; front tibia with auditory organ at base **7. Tettigoniidae**
 Wings usually absent (present in *Camystonotus*); front tibia without auditory organ **9. Gryllacrididae**

Fig. 11.5.

1. TETRIGIDAE (Grouse Locust, or Pygmy Grasshopper, Family)

L. 6–16 mm. The posteriorly projecting pronotum extending over the abdomen and covering the wings easily identifies members of this family. The relatively small adults hibernate in the winter. There are 29 species in the U.S. and Canada, many of them restricted to the southern U.S. but several common in the northeastern and central states. The family is divided into two subfamilies and six genera.

Subfamily Tetriginae

[1.1 *Nomotettix* Morse (4 spp.)]

1.2 *Tetrix* Latreille

The eight species of this genus are very similar, among them:

T. subulata (Linnaeus) (Granulated Grouse Locust). L. 7–14 mm. Color pattern variable. Found in low-lying wet woods and along the margins of bogs and lakes throughout the year. (See Fig. 11.6.) (1) n.e. NA, s. to NJ; (4) Pacific n.w. mountains.

[1.3 *Neotettix* Hancock (3 spp.); 1.4 *Paratettix* Bolivar (7 spp.)]

Fig. 11.6.

Subfamily Batrachideinae

[1.5 *Tettigidea* Scudder (6 spp.)]

1.6 *Paxilla* Bolivar

One species only, as follows:

P. obesa (Scudder) (Obese Pgymy Grasshopper). L. 9–12 mm. Chocolate-brown and shining; dorsal surface and lower third of lateral lobes of pronotum and lower part of front often pale brown; pronotum with a median carina, viewed from the side, and broadly arched; surface rather coarsely and sparsely punctate. Occurs where pitcher plants grow. (See Fig. 11.7.) (2) s.e. US.

2. EUMASTACIDAE (Monkey Grasshopper Family)

The 12 species in this family found in the U.S. are wingless and are confined to the Southwest. Other species occur in tropical regions. They frequent bushes and trees.

Subfamily Morseinae

[2.1 *Morsea* Scudder (5 spp.); 2.2 *Psychomastax* Rehn and Hebard (5 spp.); 2.3 *Eumorsea* Hebard (2 spp.)]

Fig. 11.7.

3. TANAOCERIDAE (Desert Long-horned Grasshopper Family)

Only three species of these nocturnal, wingless grasshoppers are found in the U.S., all confined to the southwestern states. They are best collected at night on desert vegetation.

[3.1 *Tanaocerus* Bruner (2 spp.); 3.2 *Mohavacris* Rehn (1 sp., *M. timberlakei* Rehn)]

4. ROMALEIDAE (Lubber Grasshopper Family)

L. 18–80 mm. Most species of this family are large, have shortened wings, and are often marked with bright colors. The group is poorly represented in the U.S.; only one species is found outside the western states. The classification is complex because of the large number of tropical species; the nine species north of Mexico undoubtedly are northern range extensions.

Tribe Dracotettigini

[4.1 *Dracotettix* Bruner (2 spp., CA)]

Tribe Phrynotettigini

[4.2 *Phrynotettix* Glover (2 spp.); 4.3 *Tytthotyle* Scudder (1 sp., *T. maculata* (Bruner)]

Tribe Spaniacrini

[4.4 *Spaniacris* Hebard (1 sp., *S. deserticola* (Brunner))]

Tribe Romaleini

4.5 *Romalea* Serville

One species only, as follows:

R. guttata (Latreille) [= *R. microptera* (Beauvois)] (Eastern Lubber Grasshopper). L. 45–75 mm. Black with broad yellow markings on body and red markings on wings. Common June to late November as adults. This species often used in biology classes. (See Fig. 11.8.) (2) s.e. US.

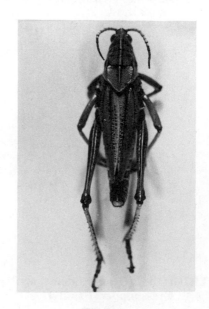

Fig. 11.8.

4.6 *Taeniopoda* Stål

One species only, as follows:

T. eques (Burmeister) (Horse Lubber). L. 38–64 mm. Body black and shiny; marked with margins of yellow to orange; veins of front wings outlined in yellow; hind legs rosy-red with black borders. Although this species prefers arid regions, it is found as far east as the edge of the range of *Romalea guttata*, which it resembles. Both species feed on a variety of plants along roadsides. (See A&J 15.) (3) AZ, TX.

Tribe Brachystolini

4.7 *Brachystola* Scudder

B. magna (Girard) (Lubber Grasshopper). L. 38–80 mm. One of the largest species in the U.S.; grayish-green to brown; front wings pink. Adults from August to October. (See Fig. 11.9.) (3) AZ, TX; (5) MT, ND, MN.

5. ACRIDIDAE (Short-horned Grasshopper Family)

L. 9–80 mm (most species, 15–30 mm). Most grasshoppers (=locusts) in the U.S. and Canada belong to this large family of 548 species in 114 genera. Of these, 209 species belong to the genus *Melanoplus*. The family is divided into five subfamilies as indicated by the accompanying key.

Subfamily Gomphocerinae (Tooth-legged Grasshoppers)

Males of this subfamily "sing" during the day except for a few species that have secondarily lost the pegs on the hind femora. Front wings are rounded at the apex and without prominent crossbands, but may be spotted.

5.1 *Chloealtis* Harris

Five species, including the following:

C. conspersa Harris (Sprinkled Locust). L. 15–28 mm. Male usually light brown, always with a broad, shining black bar that wholly covers the lateral lobes of the pronotum; front wing without spots or with a few faint dusky ones; hind tibiae red or yellowish; knees black. Female varies from dull clay-yellow to dark brown, with front wing usually more or less sprinkled with black spots and sides of pronotum with only traces of the dark bar. Front wing covers only half the abdomen of the female but reaches nearly to the tip in the male. Found in thickets on the borders of open woods, in grassy plots

Fig. 11.9.

Fig. 11.10.

alongside fences, and often along the banks of streams in woodland pastures. (1) n.e. NA; (2) WV, VA, KY, VA, TN, NC, SC; (3) OK; (4) BC; (5) n. Central States and Provinces.

[5.2 *Chrysochraon* Fisher (1 sp., *C. petraea* (Gurney, Strohecker, and Helfer)); 5.3 *Chorthippus* Fieber (1 sp., *C. curtipennis* (Harris)); 5.4

Key to the Subfamilies of Acrididae

1. Prosternum without spine or tubercle between front legs *2*
 Prosternum with distinct conical or cylindrical tubercle between front legs (Fig. 11.10); face vertical or nearly so; pronotum with dorsal surface flattened, never strongly crested, tuberculate, or rugose; wings, when present, transparent, never with contrasting colors .. **Cyrtacanthacridinae** and **Melanoplinae**

2(1). Front more or less oblique, usually meeting vertex at acute angle; foveolae usually absent or invisible from above; median carinae of pronotum never raised in form of crest or cut by more than one sulcus ... *3*
 Front nearly vertical and rounded at its junction with vertex; foveolae present and visible from above; median carina of pronotum often more or less crested and usually cut by more than one sulcus; wings usually both brightly colored and with black band **Oedipodinae**

3(2). Row of stridulatory pegs on inner face of male hind femora; face (side view) strongly slanted to vertical; hind wings usually transparent, some banded, and two species black, pink, or reddish ... **Gomphocerinae**
 Without rows of stridulatory pegs; face moderately to strongly slanted; hind wings transparent or only faintly tinged with color and without dark or smoky band .. **Acridinae**

Fig. 11.11.

Fig. 11.12. (*From Blatchley, 1920*)

Stenobothrus Fisher, subgenus *Bruneria* McNeill (3 spp.); 5.5 *Aeropedellus* Hebard (2 spp.); 5.6 *Philbostroma* Scudder (1 sp., *P. quadrimaculatum* (Thomas)); 5.7 *Esselenia* Hebard (1 sp., *E. vanduzeei* (Hebard)); 5.8 *Orphulella* Giglio-Tos (2 spp.); 5.9 *Dichromorpha* Morse (2 spp.); 5.10 *Eritettix* Bruner (3 spp.); 5.11 *Opeia* McNeill (2 spp.); 5.12 *Amphitornus* McNeill (1 sp., *A. coloradus* (Thomas)); 5.13 *Rhammatocerus* Saussure (1 sp., *R. viatoria* (Saussure)); 5.14 *Psoloessa* Scudder (2 spp.); 5.15 *Horesidotes* Scudder (1 sp., *H. cinereus* (Scudder)); 5.16 *Eupnigodes* McNeil (2 spp.); 5.17 *Ageneotettix* McNeil (2 spp.); 5.18 *Aulocara* Scudder (3 spp.); 5.19 *Heliaula* Scudder (1 sp., *H. rufa* (Scudder)); 5.20 *Boopedon* Thomas (4 spp.); 5.21 *Amblytropidia* Stål (1 sp., *A. mysteca* (Saussure)); 5.22 *Syrbula* Stål (3 spp.)]

5.23 *Mermiria* Stål

Four species, including the following:

M. texana Bruner. Head and pronotum with sharply contrasting dark brown and yellow stripes and a dark brown stripe along the dorsal midline. (See Fig. 11.11.) (3) AZ, NM, TX; (5) CO.

[5.24 *Pseudopomala* Morse (1 sp., *P. brachyptera* (Scudder))]

5.25 *Achurum* Saussure

The three species of this genus are very slender and slant-faced; the following are examples:

A. sumichrasti Saussure (Sumichrast's Toothpick Grasshopper). L. 38–45 mm. Yellowish-to-greenish-brown with brown stripes on the head and pronotum. Wings pointed at the tip. Adults and nymphs found on coarse grass, usually with body parallel to the grass blade. Adults fly in June and July. (3) AZ, NM, TX.

A. carinatum (Walker). (See Fig. 11.12.) (2) MS, AL, GA, SC, FL.

[5.26 *Paropomala* Scudder (3 spp.); 5.27 *Prororcorpha* Rehn (1 sp., *P. snowi* (Rehn)); 5.28 *Cordillacris* Rehn (2 spp.); 5.29 *Acantherus* Scudder (1 sp., *A. piperatus* Scudder)]

5.30 *Acrolophitus* Thomas

Four species, including the following:

A. maculipennis (Scudder). L. 23–43 mm. Mottled gray-green and ivory; front wings mottled with gray and black; hind wings black. (See Fig. 11.13.) (3) s. AZ, s. NM; w. TX.

5.31 *Bootettix* Bruner

One species, as follows:

B. argentatus Bruner. Olive green. Found on creosote bushes. (See Fig. 11.14) (3) CA, AZ, NM, TX; (4) UT, NV.

[5.32 *Stethophyma* Fisher (3 spp.)]

Subfamily Acridinae

Only one species of this subfamily occurs in the U.S. and Canada.

5.33 *Metaleptea* Brunner

M. brevicornis (Johnson) (Short-horned Grasshopper). L. 19–35 mm. Green, brown, or a combination of both; brownish beneath. Hind wing of male with a large transparent area near front margin; front wings reaching beyond tip of abdomen. Nymphs and adults common in wet areas on sedges and grasses near water, including seacoasts. (1) n.e. US; (2) s.e. US; (3) TX.

Subfamily Oedipodinae (Band-winged Grasshoppers)

Most species of this subfamily, as may be deduced from the common name, have brightly colored hind wings with a marginal or submarginal band. The peg is absent between the front legs. Otherwise they look very much like the Spur-throated Grasshoppers (Cyrtacanthacridinae). The pronotum has a

Fig. 11.13.

Fig. 11.14.

Fig. 11.15.

median keel. A few species have clear hind wings. They make a crackling sound when they fly.

5.34 *Arphia* Stål

This genus contains 12 rather large, stout species with a keeled pronotum that is raised in a distinct crest and is usually entire, that is, not interrupted by a transverse groove. The hind wings are banded. The species are difficult to distinguish without technical keys. The following is a common representative:

A. sulphurea (Fabricius) (Sulphur-winged Locust). L. 17–22 mm. Dark brown, nearly black, to a pale brown. Front wings of males often with a pale yellowish band along the hind margin; those of the female lighter colored. Hind wings with basal two-thirds a bright sulphur-yellow and outer third with a dusky curved band, from which a distinct dark ray runs nearly to base of wing near the front margin. Common in dry upland pastures and meadows, along roadsides, and on gravelly and rocky slopes. Nymphs overwinter; adults are most abundant in June. (1) n.e. NA; (2) s.e. US; (5) NE.

5.35 *Chortophaga* Saussure

Two species, the following of which is common:

C. viridifasciata (DeGeer) (Green-striped Grasshopper).

[5.36 *Chimarocephala* Scudder (1 sp., *C. pacifica* (Thomas)); 5.37 *Encoptolophus* Scudder (4 spp.)]

5.38 *Camnula* Stål

One species, as follows:

C. pellucida (Scudder) (Clear-winged Grasshopper). L. 17–32 mm. Light brown with reddish-brown face; antennae yellowish at base, with apical half dusky; a dark triangular spot behind the eye and an oblong black spot on the lateral lobe of the front dorsal part of the pronotum; front wing smokey-brown, with several darker rounded spots on the sides, these separated by lighter yellowish blotches; dorsal surface usually with a dull yellow stripe along the overlapping margins; hind wings transparent, with dark wing veins; hind tibia yellowish. Nymphs and adults sometimes migrate in large numbers, although for rather short distances, and may cause considerable damage to grassy regions. June-August. (1) n.e. NA; (2) VA; (3) TX, CA.

5.39 *Hippiscus* Saussure

Two species, the more common of which is the following:

H. rugosus (Scudder) (Wrinkled Grasshopper). L. 28–51 mm. Brown, with brownish-yellow abdomen; front wing with large dark spots; hind wing pale yellow or orange with dark submarginal band. Inner apical spur of hind tibia more than twice as long as outer spur. Pronotum front half and hind half in lateral view about equal in length, separated by dorsal groove of the disk. Adults fly from June into November in grassy areas, especially in open woods. (See Fig. 11.15.) (1) n.e. US; (2) s.e. US; (3) AZ, TX, OK; (5) MT, CO, IA, NE, MO.

[5.40 *Pardalophora* Saussure (4 spp.); 5.41 *Xanthippus* Saussure (10 spp.); 5.42 *Cratypedes* Thomas (1 sp., *C. neglectus* (Thomas)); 5.43 *Sticthippus* Scudder (1 sp., *S. californicus* Scudder); 5.44 *Agymnastus* Scudder (2 spp.)]

5.45 *Leprus* Saussure

Seven species, of which the following is common:

L. cyaneous Cockerell (Cockerell's Blue-winged Grasshopper). L. 37–45 mm. Hind wing with blue disc. (See Fig. 11.16.) (3) AZ, NM, TX; (5) CO.

[5.46 *Tropidolophus* Thomas (1 sp., *T. formosus* (Say))]

5.47 *Dissosteira* Scudder

Four species, one of which, *D. longipennis* (Thomas)—the High Plains Grasshopper—is destructive to range grasses. It is similar to the following widespread species:

D. carolina (Linnaeus) (Carolina Grasshopper). L. 24–52 mm. Usually dull ashy-brown but also light grayish-yellow to bright reddish to dark brown, sprinkled with numerous small dusky spots, particularly on pronotum and front wing. Hind wings black except for pale greenish-yellow margin. Pronotum with median ridge about equally high in front of dorsal groove as behind. This species is the one most frequently seen flying from July through October in towns, in open fields, along grassy roads, and in cultivated areas. They are strong but somewhat erratic fliers. When handled, they "spit tobacco juice,"

Fig. 11.16.

that is, empty the contents of their crop. (See Fig. 11.17.) (1) n.e. NA; (2) s.e. US; (3) s.w. NA; (4) Pacific n.w. (5) Central NA.

5.48 *Spharagemon* Scudder

This genus contains eight species, all very similar, with hind wings yellow with a black to brown marginal band. They "crackle" in flight, that is, their wings rub together to make a crackling sound, which accounts for their Latin generic name. One or more of these species is found throughout Canada and the U.S., of which the following is typical:

S. collare (Scudder) (Mottled Sand Grasshopper). L. 30–38 mm. Gray to brown. Hind wings yellow with black margin. Hind tibiae partly to entirely orange or red. Adults are found in open fields of mixed vegetation from June to October. (See A&J 19.) (1) n.e. NA; (2) s.e. NA; (3) OK, TX, AZ; (5) AB, MT, CO.

[5.49 *Scirtetica* Saussure (2 spp.); 5.50 *Microtes* Scudder (1 sp., *M. nubila* (Scudder); 5.51 *Lactista* Saussure (2 spp.); 5.52 *Platylactista*

Hebard (1 sp., *P. azteca* (Saussure)); 5.53 *Tomonotus* Saussure (1 sp., *T. ferruginosus* Bruner); 5.54 *Derotmena* Scudder (4 spp.); 5.55 *Trepidulus* McNeill (2 spp.); 5.56 *Rehnita* Hebard (2 spp.); 5.57 *Trachyrhachis* Scudder (6 spp.); 5.58 *Metator* McNeill (2 spp.); 5.59 *Mestobregma* Scudder (4 spp.); 5.60 *Psinidia* Stål (2 spp.)]

5.61 *Conozoa* Saussure

Three species, including the following:

C. wallula (Scudder). (Wallula Grasshopper). L. 25–35 mm. Hind wing yellow with black band and spur; hind tibia reddish with pale ring and blackish at base varying to yellowish. (See Fig. 11.18.) (3) CA; (4) WA, OR, UT; (5) WY.

5.62 *Trimerotropis* Stal

A large genus with 49 species that are usually smaller than those of preceding genera. The pronotal ridge is usually faint or entirely absent on the posterior half of the pronotum. The front wings have dark markings. Most of the species are western, a few southern, and only four occur in the northeastern U.S. The following are examples, but technical keys are necessary to identify the species:

T. albolineata (Brunner) (White-lined Grasshopper). L. 26–35 mm. Brownish to rusty-red; front wings with dark spots; hind wings yellow without pronounced dark band; hind femora with dark spots and with a white line along the lower portion. Usually seen on trees and shrubs in sandy areas, it blends in with the substrate when it drops to the ground. (See A&J 17.) (3) s. CA, AZ.

T. helferi Strohecker (Helfer's Dune Grasshopper). L. 19–30 mm. This rare species may be recognized by the unusual erect pubescence covering the body. Found on beaches and dunes along the coast of (3) n. CA.

T. verruculatus (Kirby) (Cracker Grasshopper). L. 21–30 mm. Dark gray, often almost black. Front wings dark brown or black, sometimes without spots, but often with pale crossbar anterior to middle and another behind. Hind wings with basal third or more transparent with a yellowish tinge, with curved brownish bar faint, narrow across wing. This northern

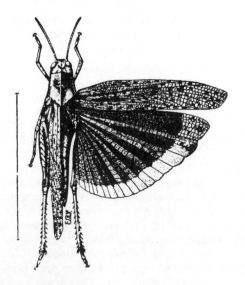

Fig. 11.17. (*From Blatchley, 1920*)

Fig. 11.18.

Fig. 11.19.

species is sometimes placed in genus 5.65 *Circotettix*. A noisy, cracking species, it occurs in rocky places. (1) n.e. NA.

T. fontana Thomas (Fontana Grasshopper). L. 23–35 mm. Blackish, varying to brownish, pinkish, or yellowish; front wing with distinct bands; hind wing yellow to pale greenish; hind tibiae blue, pale near base. (See Fig. 11.19.) (3) CA, AZ; (5) MT, WY, CO.

[5.63 *Hadrotettix* Scudder (1 sp., *H. trifasciatus* (Say)); 5.64 *Shotwellia* Gurney (1 sp., *S. isleta* Gurney); 5.65 *Circotettix* Scudder (9 spp.); 5.66 *Aerochoreutes* Rehn (1 sp., *A. carlinianus* (Thomas)); 5.67 *Anconia* Scudder (3 spp.); 5.68 *Coniana* Caudell (1 sp., *C. snowi* Caudell); 5.69 *Heliastus* Saussure (4 spp.); 5.70 *Xeracris* Caudell (1 sp., *X. minimus* (Scudder)); 5.71 (Number not used); 5.72 *Cibalacris* Hebard (1 sp., *C. parviceps* (Brunner))]

Subfamily Melanoplinae (Spur-throated Grasshoppers)

·This is the largest subfamily with 39 genera and 309 species, most of them belonging to the genus *Melanoplus*. Species of this subfamily may be recognized by the peg or spine located between the front pair of legs. Front of head at only a slight slant; hind wings transparent; pronotum without a median keel. Except for the species of the genus *Melanoplus*, most species are found in the southwestern U.S.; others occur on mountain tops; relatively few are widely distributed.

[5.73 *Leptysma* Stål (2 spp.); 5.74 *Stenacris* Walker [=*Opshomala* Serville] (1 sp., *S. vitreipennis* (Marschall)); 5.75 (Number not used); 5.76 *Prorocorypha* Rehn (1 sp., *P. Snowi* Rehn); 5.77 *Eremiacris* Hebard (3 spp.); 5.78 *Clematodes* Scudder (1 sp., *C. larreae* Scudder)]

5.79 *Gymnoscirtetes* Scudder

The two species of this genus are wingless. The one cited below is the more common; the other, *G. morsei* Hebard, is found only in a single locality, De Funiak Springs, FL.

G. pusillus Scudder (Little Wingless Grasshopper). L. 12.5–22 mm. Greenish-yellow with brown areas; sides with a broad, shining blackish-brown stripe that extends from eyes back along the upper halves of lateral lobes of pronotum to beyond middle of abdomen; wingless. Common in some marshy pine barrens on sedges and other undergrowth. (2) GA, FL.

[5.80 *Netrosoma* Scudder (2 spp.); 5.81 *Phaedrotettix* Scudder (3 spp.); 5.82 *Paraidemona* Brunner (4 spp.); 5.83 *Phaulotettix* Scudder (2 spp.); 5.84 *Agroecotettix* Bruner (1 sp., *A. modestus* Hebard); 5.85 *Conalcaea* Scudder (4 spp.); 5.86 *Hypochlora* Brunner (1 sp., *H. alba* (Dodge)); 5.87 *Campylacantha* Scudder (1 sp., *C. olivacea* Rehn and Hebard); 5.88 *Chloroplus* Hebard (1 sp., *C. cactocaetes* Hebard)]

5.89 *Aeolophides* Caudell

This genus of five small species, all very similar, is common in the western U.S. The following is typical:

A. tenuipennis (Scudder) (Narrow-winged Bush Grasshopper). L. 14–28 mm. Brownish, lighter ventrally; hind, tibia purple, blue, or red; body marked with a few dark spots. Adults found on saltbush and other desert shrubs. (3) s. CA, AZ, NM; (5) UT, ID.

[5.90 *Oedaleonotus* Scudder (7 spp.); 5.91 *Hesperotettix* Scudder (7 spp.); 5.92 *Eotettix* Scudder (3 spp.); 5.93 *Paratylotropidia* Scudder (3 spp.)]

5.94 *Melanoplus* Stål

L. 9.5–44 mm (most species about 25–30 mm). Brown with dark marks; diagonal whitish mark on the side of the metathorax; underside of hind femora usually reddish or yellow; a black band often extending back from the eye onto the side of the pronotum. The species can be identified only by use of technical keys based mainly on features of the male genitalia. Of the 209 species, the following may be taken as typical.

M. bivittatus (Say) (Two-striped Grasshopper). L. 25–40 mm. Usually brown, pale ventrally, but also varying to yellow-brown or even greenish; hind tibia variable from red to purple; two pale dorsal lateral stripes from eye to tip of front wings. May be very destructive. (See Fig. 11.20.) (1) n.e. NA; (2) s.e. US (not in extreme south); (3) s.w. US; (4) Pacific n.w.; (5) Central States).

Fig. 11.20.

Fig. 11.21.

M. femurrubrum (De Geer) (Red-legged Grasshopper). L. 19–26 mm. Brownish, yellowish, reddish, hind tibia red to yellowish. Very common in fields, pastures, meadows, lawns, in woods, and in arid regions around irrigation ditches. Adults fly from June to December; often a destructive pest and also the intermediate host of *Choanotaenia infundibulum* (Poultry Tapeworm) and other parasitic worms; should not be eaten unless thoroughly cooked. (See Fig. 11.21.) (1) n.e. NA; (2) s.e. US; (3) s.w. US; (4) Pacific n.w.; (5) n. Central States.

M. differentialis (Thomas) (Differential Grasshopper). L. 30–45 mm. Brown to yellow, with spotting above; hind femur marked with black herringbone pattern. Common, nonmigrating, but very destructive species that feeds on grass and forage crops. (See A&J 18.) (1) n.e. NA; (2) s.e. US; (3) s.w. US; (4) Pacific n.w. (5) n. Central States).

Note: Because of their destructive habits, several other species have been given common names often found in the literature: *M. packardi* Scudder—Packard Grasshopper; *M. rugglesi* Gurney—Nevada Sage Grasshopper; *M. sanguinipes* (Fabricius)—Migratory Grasshopper (not to be confused with the African Migratory Locust); *M. devastator* Scudder—Devastating Grasshopper; and *M. spretus* (Walsh)—Rocky Mountain Grasshopper.

[5.95 *Dendrotettix* Riley (3 spp.); 5.96 *Appalachia* Rehn and Rehn (2 spp.)]

5.97 *Zubovskya* Dovnar-Zapolskij

One species, as follows:

Z. glacialis (Scudder) (Wingless Mountain Grasshopper). L. 14–25 mm. Olive to brownish dorsally; yellow ventrally; male with broad, dull, dark stripes on head and thorax; hind tibia bluish to brown. Adults are found in weedy places and on trees on high mountain peaks. (1) n.e. US; (4) OR.

[5.98 *Podisma* Berthold (1 sp., *P. hesperus* (Hebard)); 5.99 *Asemoplus* Scudder (3 spp.); 5.100 *Argiacris* Hebard (1 sp., *A. rehni* Hebard); 5.101 *Bradynotes* Scudder (8 spp.)]

5.102 *Phoetaliotes* Scudder

One species, as follows:

P. nebrascensis (Thomas) (Large-headed Grasshopper). L. 21–30 mm. Brown; head and pronotum usually pale dor-

sally; hind tibia blue to purple; wings short (common) or long (uncommon). Found on grasses and prairie plants. (1) IL, IN; (3) s.w. US; (4) Pacific n.w.; (5) n. Central States and adjacent Canada.

[5.103 *Paroxya* Scudder (3 spp.)]

5.104 *Aptenopedes* Scudder

Four species of this genus occur in the U.S. and Canada. Although all have slanted faces, they belong in this subfamily. The wings are short; eyes are about twice as long as wide. The following species is common:

A. sphenarioides Scudder (Linear-winged Grasshopper). L. 16–35 mm. Green or brown, with some specimens reddish dorsally; yellow stripes extend from the eyes to the front wing and down the middle of the abdomen; ventrally dull yellow; hind tibia blue green or pink. Found on low vegetation in open pine woods. Adults fly from March to November. (2) GA, FL, AL.

5.105 *Poecilotettix* Scudder

Of the three assigned species, the following is the most common:

P. pantherina (Walker) (Panther-spotted Grasshopper). L. 25–30 mm. Light green; head, pronotum, and legs marked with small black and white spots; antennae black, with alternate segments ringed with white. Occurs on various plants belonging to the family Compositae in arid regions. (See A&J 16.) (3) AZ.

5.106 *Dactylotum* Charpentier

Two species (sometimes treated as subspecies) occur in this genus, both of them brightly colored and among the most beautiful of insects:

D. bicolor variegatum (Scudder) (Rainbow Grasshopper). L. 20–35 mm. Bluish with bold red and yellow markings. Wings short, not extending over the abdomen. Occurs in desert grasslands, especially on gravely soil, rarely on forage crops. Adults occur from June to October. (See Fig. 11.22 and A&J 21.) (3) AZ, NM, TX.

D. pictum (Thomas) (Pictured Grasshoppers). L. 21–32 mm. Marked with bands of black and yellow with orange and pink in the yellow. (3) n. TX, n.e. NM; (5) UT, WY, MT.

[5.107 *Buckellacris* Rehn and Rehn (3 spp.); 5.108 *Prumnacris* Rehn and Rehn (1 sp., *P. rainierensis* Caudell); 5.109 *Nisquallia* Rehn (1 sp., *N. olympica* Rehn); 5.110 *Barytettix* (Scudder) (2 spp.); 5.111

Fig. 11.22.

Fig. 11.23.

Fig. 11.25.

Aidemona Brunner (1 sp., *A. azteca* (Saussure)); 5.112 *Aztecacris* Roberts (1 sp., *A. gloriosus* (Hebard)); 5.113 *Hebardacris* Rehn (1 sp., *H. albida* (Hebard))]

Subfamily Cyrtacanthacridinae (Migratory Bird Locusts)

There is only one genus in this subfamily, as follows:

5.114 *Schistocerca* Stål

L. 24–70 mm (large species usually 40–60 mm). The 12 species assigned to this genus are characterized by a mesosternum with lateral lobes longer than wide; wings transparent; second tarsomere one-half length of first; hind tibiae with numerous spines in regular rows on each side. The following three species are representative:

S. americana (Drury) (American Bird Grasshopper). L. 35–55 mm. Brown with yellow stripes dorsally; paler ventrally; hind tibiae red. Adults fly June to November in North and throughout year in South. Adults often destructive; migratory phase occurs often. (See Fig. 11.23.) (1) n.e. A; (2) s.e. US; (5) n. Central States.

S. damnifica (Saussure) (Mischievous Bird Grasshopper). L. 25–40 mm. Brownish-red dorsally, paler ventrally, with pale dorsal stripe on head and pronotum; hind tibia brown. Adults common in July to November. (See Fig. 11.24.) (1) IL, IN, OH, PA; (2) s.e. US.

S. nitens nitens (Thunberg) [= *S. vaga* Scudder] (Vagrant Grasshopper). L. 40–70 mm. Grayish or brownish; pale stripe dorsally on middle of head and pronotum; hind femur with distinct crossbands. Common, sometimes destructive. (See Fig. 11.25.) (3) CA, AZ, NM; (5) NV.

Note: *S. gregaria* (Forskål) is the Desert Locust of Africa, the species frequently referred to in the Bible and certainly one of the most destructive insects in the world. (See Fig. 11.26 for the female.) A similar species, *S. paranensis* (Burmeister), is a destructive swarming species in South America.

6. TRIDACTYLIDAE (Pygmy Mole Cricket Family)

L. 4–10 mm. Dark brown; front tibia fitted for digging; hind tarsus with swimming plates. The two species of this fam-

Fig. 11.24.

Fig. 11.26. (*Courtesy of Shell Photographic Service, London*)

ily dig in moist sand near waters of streams, rivers, lakes, and ponds. They apparently use the swimming plates to form a platform on the water surface to help them jump from the water, but they do not swim.

6.1 *Neotridactylus* Gunther

One species, as follows:

N. apicalis (Say) (Large Sand Cricket). L. 6–10 mm. (1) n.e. NA; (2) s.e. US; (3) s.w. US.

6.2 *Ellipes* Scudder

One species, as follows:

E. minuta (Scudder) (Smaller Sand Cricket). L. 4–5 mm. (1) NJ, PA, MD; (2) s.e. US; (3) s.w. US.

7. TETTIGONIIDAE (Long-horned Grasshopper, or Katydid, Family)

L. 15–75 mm (most species, 35–50 mm). Antennae usually much longer than the body; wings broad; many species bright green, often brown, rarely pink; nocturnal; males produce characteristic stridulatory sounds. The family in North America is divided into seven subfamilies, which may be distinguished by the accompanying key. There are 49 genera and 243 species.

Key to the Subfamilies of Tettigoniidae

1. Head globose, not usually slanted or frontally flattened; front tibiae in section approximately square in distal portion; dorsal surface flat or slightly concave, not convex; proximal tarsomere cylindrical, not laterally sulcate; ovipositor usually short and upturned; flattened laterally, with margins usually crenulate; prosternum unarmed **Phaneropterinae**
Without the preceding combination of characters *2*

2(1). Antennal sockets strongly margined, produced, especially on internal dorsal margins; thoracic auditory spiracle small, inconspicuous, not hidden by pronotum . **Pseudophyllinae**
Antennal sockets not strongly margined and especially not on internal margins; thoracic auditory spiracle large, conspicuous, elongate, and, in most species, often wholly or partially concealed by pronotum *3*

3(2). Prosternum unarmed; small, delicate, highly agile and usually arboreal and epiphyllic; greenish or greenish yellow in coloration **Meconematinae**
Prosternum armed or not; combination of characters not as above *4*

4(3). Front tibiae bearing a single apical spur on posterior margin of dorsal surface; fastigium of vertex ranging from width of 1st antennal segment to half width of same; hind basal tarsomere with plantula in most species that is one-half length of tarsomere *5*
Lacking at least two of the preceding characters *6*

5(4). Plantula of hind tarsus very well developed; fastigium of vertex broad, in most species at least as broad as antennal scape; coloration highly variable but most species not concolorous .. **Decticinae**
Plantula of hind tarsus either knob-like, scarcely more developed than adjacent pulvillus, or virtually absent; fastigium of vertex broad or narrow **Tettigoniinae**

6(4). Hind tibiae without apical spurs on dorsal surface; large, with elongate spurs on ventral surface of front and middle tibiae; stout teeth on ventral surface of front and hind femora ... **Saginae**
Hind tibiae with at least 1 external apical spur on dorsal surface; if not, then posterior portion of lateral lobe of pronotum modified *7*

7(6). Front tibiae usually bearing 5 to 7 long, movable, outwardly opposing spines, the longest of which in many species being as long as or longer than the combined lengths of first 2 tarsomeres; fastigium of vertex narrow, strongly compressed laterally, its greatest width less than that of 1st antennal segment in most species and barely projected above same, and usually sulcate ... **Listroscelinae**
Front tibiae of most species with spines not unusually lengthened and not as long as or longer than first 2 tarsomeres combined; fastigium of vertex variable in width and not sulcate ... *8*

8(7). Front and middle femora unarmed; fastigium of vertex broad, obtuse, with cephalic ventral portion not produced or forming a hook; small species; stridulatory activity diurnal to crepuscular ... **Conocephalinae**
Front and middle femora armed, often with quite large teeth; fastigium of vertex conical, often forming an elongate cone with a tubercle at its base; large species; stridulatory activity crepuscular and nocturnal **Copiphorinae**

Subfamily Phaneropterinae (Bush and Round-headed Katydids)

Fifty-six species are assigned to this subfamily in the U.S. and Canada. These include vegetarian, bush- and tree-dwelling Katydids that are sometimes wingless and have long antennae. They are green, brownish, or sometimes pinkish. The tympanic membranes on the anterior tibiae are entirely uncovered. The prosternum is spineless and the hind wings are usually longer than the front wings.

7.1 *Amblycorypha* Stål

The eight species assigned to this genus comprise the Round-headed Katydids. Top of the head rounded, strongly deflexed, and more than twice as broad as the first antennal segment; front wings distinctly wider at the middle than at the apex; hind femora reaching to at least the apical fourth of the front wing. They include the following:

A. oblongifolia (De Geer) (Oblong-winged Katydid). L. 21–25 mm. Bright pea-green; legs yellowish or brownish green.

Fig. 11.27.

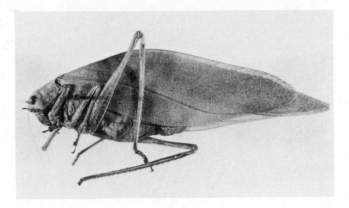

Fig. 11.28.

(Note: Some rare individuals pink.) Stridulating area of male front wing large, exceeding that of the pronotal disk. Common on flowers of goldenrod and other composites along fences and at the edge of thickets, especially where damp. Eggs, laid in the ground, take two to three years to hatch. (1) n.e. NA; (2) s.e. US, except GA and FL; (3) TX; (5) CO.

A. floridana Rehn and Hebard (Round-headed Katydid). L. 30–35 mm. Green (some individuals pink); similar to preceding species but the stridulatory disk of the male is smaller, approximately the size of the pronotal disk. (See Fig. 11.27.) Common in (2) FL, AL; (3) TX.

7.2 *Arethaea* Stål

The 14 species of this genus are elongate and very slender. Front of the head flat, perpendicular; antennae very long, extending nearly twice the distance of the wings; hind femora well over twice the length of the abdomen; eyes oblong-oval, nearly twice as long as wide.

A. gracilipes papago (Hebard) (Papago Thread-legged Katydid). L. 30–35 mm. Green body, with colored stripe on side of abdomen. Found on grass and weeds along roadsides and in meadows; attracted to lights at night. (See A&J 25.) Common (3) AZ, CA.

[7.3 *Dichopetala* Brunner (7 spp.)]

7.4 *Insara* Walker

This genus includes six rather uncommon species recognized by green body with dark green and white spots. Found on various desert plants. Confined to (3) s.w. US.

I. elegans Scudder (Mesquite Katydid). L. 28–30 mm. Light green body and darker green front wings marked by eight white bands. Found on mesquite trees, creosote bushes, and other desert plants. (See A&J 23.) (3) s.w. US.

[7.5 *Inscudderia* Caudell (3 spp.)]

7.6 *Microcentrum* Scudder

Hind femora stout and short, not reaching beyond apical third of the front wing; disk of pronotum flat with rounded or subacute margins. There are five species, the following two of which are common:

M. retinerve (Burmeister) (Smaller Angular-winged Katydid). L. 20–26 mm. Front margin of the pronotum squarely truncate; body pale green, with head and ventral surface tinged with yellow. Found on trees and shrubs. (1) s. IN, s. OH, s. PA, s. NJ, MD; (2) s.e. US to s. GA; (3) OK, TX, NM, AZ; (5) KS, NE.

M. rhombifolium (Saussure) (Broad-winged Katydid). L. 50–65 mm. Green, front margin of the pronotum sinuate, and with more or less distinct median tooth; front wing is broad and leaflike. Common on many kinds of plants and trees; often destructive. Eggs are glued in double rows on the sides of slender twigs previously roughened with the jaws; egg laying takes place in September. Nymphs hatch in May; first adults are heard in July. This species is often confused with *Pterophylla camellifolia* (Fabricius), the True Katydid, but its song is much different—a "tic" repeated 8 to 20 times at the rate of about four per second. (See Fig. 11.28 and A&J 24.) (1) IN, OH, NY, PA, NJ, MD; (2) s.e. US; (5) UT, CO, KS.

[7.7 *Montezumina* Hebard (1 sp., *M. modesta* (Brunner); 7.8 *Phaneroptera* Audinet-Serville (1 sp., *P. quadripunctata* (Brunner)); 7.9 *Phrixa* Stål (1 sp., *P. maya* (Saussure and Pictet)); 7.10 *Platylyra* Scudder (1 sp., *P. californica* Scudder)]

7.11 *Scudderia* Stål

The seven species of this genus are often called the Bush Katydids. Front wing distinctly shorter than hind wing, long, and narrow, being only slightly broader at middle than at apex; middle femora without ventral spines. The species are difficult to distinguish except by using technical characters of the male abdomen; the following species is representative.

S. furcata Brunner (Fork-tailed Bush Katydid). L. 36–40 mm. Green, sometimes tinged with brown. Common on grasses, shrubs, and trees, usually at the edges of meadows, forests, and marshes. This is the most common and widespread species in NA. (Fig. 11.29 and A&J 22.) (1) n.e. NA; (2) s.e. US, s. to c. FL; (3) s.e. US; (4) Pacific n.w.; (5) n. Central States.

[7.12 *Stilpnochlora* Stål (1 sp., *S. couloniana* (Saussure); 7.13 *Turpilia* Stål (1 sp., *T. rostrata* (Rehn and Hebard))]

Subfamily **Pseudophyllinae** (True Katydids)

[=Pterophyllinae]

These large insects rarely fly but plane from bushtop to bushtop. The five species are easily recognized by the broad margin of the front wings with coarse cross-veins.

Fig. 11.29.

Fig. 11.31.

[7.14 *Lea* Caudell (1 sp., *L. floridensis* (Beutenmuller)); 7.15 *Paracyrtophyllus* Caudell (2 spp.)]

7.16 *Pterophylla* Kirby

This genus contains two species distinguished by features of the male genitalia. Disk of pronotum only slightly longer than wide, the lateral lobe subquadrate or deeper than long; front wing broadly oval. The most widespread species follows:

P. camellifolia (Fabricius) (True Katydid). L. 45–55 mm. Front wings dark green; rest of body paler green. The nocturnal song is well-known as "katy-did, katy-didn't." Both sexes stridulate from midsummer until the first frost. (See Fig. 11.30.) (1) n.e. NA; (2) s.e. US; (3) TX; (5) AR, KS.

Subfamily Copiphorinae (Cone-heads)

The head of the species in this subfamily is prolonged at the front to form a cone, or at least a knob; ovipositor long and sword-shaped; green or brown.

[7.17 *Belocephalus* Scudder (4 spp.); 7.18 *Bucrates* Burmeister (1 sp., *B. malivolans* (Scudder))]

7.19 *Neoconocephalus* Karny

There are 14 species assigned to this genus. Cone of the head much longer than wide; ovipositor very long, longer than abdomen.

N. ensiger (Harris) (Sword-bearing Katydid). L. 24–30 mm. Green, rarely brown; front wings long and narrow; ovipositor very long and swordlike. Common in cornfields. Males stridulate day and night. (See Fig. 11.31.) (1) n.e. US; (2) VA, NC; (3) TX; (5) ND, SD, IA, MO.

[7.20 *Pyrgocorypha* Stål (1 sp., *P. uncinata* (Harris))]

Subfamily Conocephalinae (Meadow Katydids)

The species of this subfamily are small, usually 15–35 mm in length, but make up for it by being loud diurnal singers. The forward top of the head projects as a rounded tubercle with concave sides The species are difficult to distinguish without technical keys.

7.21 *Conocephalus* Thumberg

Nineteen species are assigned to this genus, the following being representative:

C. fasciatus (De Geer) (Slender Meadow Katydid). L. 15–20 mm. Green and brown; prosternal spines short or absent. Found in grass and weeds in damp areas. (1) n.e. NA; (2) s.e. US; (3) TX; (5) e. MT, ND, MN, e. WY, SD, NE, IA, e. CO, KS, MO.

[7.22 *Odontoxiphidium* Morse (1 sp., *O. apterum* Morse)]

7.23 *Orchelimum* Serville

The 19 species assigned to this genus are over 18 mm in length. All are distinguished by features of the male genitalia. The prosternum is armed with long, slender spines. The following is a representative and common species:

Fig. 11.30.

Fig. 11.32.

O. vulgare Harris (Common Meadow Katydid). L. 30–35 mm. Green with brown and tan markings; prosternum with long slender spines. Found in clumbs of tall grass. (See Fig. 11.32.) (1) n.e. NA; (2) KY, WV, VA, TN, NC, SC, GA; (5) MT, ND, MN, WY, SD, NE, IA, CO, KS, MO.

Subfamily Listroscelinae

This subfamily contains only the following genus with two species that resemble species of the subfamily Decticinae.

7.24 *Neobarrettia* Rehn

Two uncommon species, including the following:

N. spinosa (Caudell). (See Fig. 11.33.) (3) NM, TX; (5) KS.

Subfamily Decticinae (Shield-backed Katydids)

L. 13–85 mm (most species under 50 mm). These insects look more like Crickets than Katydids. They usually have short wings and are brown or black. They may bite if handled; in fact, in Europe they are known as Wart Biters. Several species are of economic importance. Most species are found in the western U.S.

[7.25 *Acrodectes* Rehn and Hebard (1 sp., *A. philophagus* Rehn and Hebard)]

7.26 *Anabrus* Haldeman

The four species assigned to this genus are similar in appearance and best distinguished by features of the male cerci. The following is the most common:

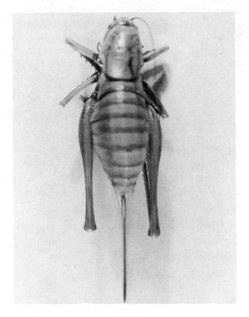

Fig. 11.34.

A. simplex Haldeman (Mormon Cricket). L. 24–62 mm. Pronotum more than one-third length of the body (ovipositor excluded), with shiny surface; body dark brown or black to yellowish or green, sometimes irregularly mottled. May be a crop pest and cause great damage. (See Fig. 11.34.) (3) CA, AZ, NM, OK, TX; (4) BC, WA, OR, ID, NV, UT; (5) n. Central States.

[7.27 *Apote* Scudder (2 spp.); 7.28 *Atelophus* Scudder (8 spp.)]

7.29 *Atlanticus* Scudder

There are nine species assigned to this genus, the female with a straight ovipositor and the male with the front wing shorter than the pronotum. Prosternum usually armed with a pair of spines; lateral lobes of the prothorax longer than deep, in contrast to those of the large western genus *Idiostatus* (7.36) that are as deep as long. Species are identified by features of the genitalia. Two common species follow:

A. gibbosus Scudder (Scudder's Decticid). L. 25–35 mm. Brown with darker sides; female with long, swordlike ovipositor. (2) NC, SC, GA, FL.

A. americanus (Saussure). (See Fig. 11.35.)

Fig. 11.33.

Fig. 11.35.

[7.30 *Capnobotes* Scudder (8 spp); 7.31 *Clinopleura* Scudder (4 spp.); 7.32 *Cyrtophyllicus* Hebard (1 sp., *C. chlorum* Hebard); 7.33 *Decticita* Hebard (3 spp.); 7.34 *Eremopedes* Cockerell (12 spp.); 7.35 *Idionotus* Scudder (7 spp.); 7.36 *Idiostatus* Pictet (24 spp.); 7.37 *Inyodectes* Rentz and Birchim (4 spp.); 7.38 *Metrioptera* Wesmael (2 spp.)]

7.39 *Neduba* Walker

Members of this genus have moderately large to large pronotal disks, especially those of the subgenus *Aglaothorax* Caudell; apex of the posterior tibia with two spurs in contrast to the species of *Atlanticus*, which have six spurs; ovipositor of the female curved upward and minutely serrated. The genus contains 11 species, of which the following is an example.

N. carinata Walker (Carinated Shield-back Katydid). L. 20–40 mm. Brownish body; pronotum is striped or mottled with light tan; wings vestigial. Found on bushes, shrubs, or trees. (See A&J 26.) (3) CA; (4) OR, WA, BC.

[7.40 *Pediodectes* Rehn and Hebard (9 spp.)]

7.41 *Peranabrus* Scudder

One species only, as follows:

P. scabricollis (Thomas) (Coulee Cricket). L. 28–50 mm. Dark brown or reddish-brown, with margins of the pronotum yellow and legs and ventral surface yellowish-brown; pronotum rough, with low, rounded median ridge; hind femur nearly reaching the apex of the abdomen (exclusive of ovipositor). This species is sometimes very destructive to crops. (See Fig. 11.36.) (4) BC, ID; (5) AB, MT.

[7.42 *Plagiostira* Scudder (3 spp.); 7.43 *Platycelis* Fieber (1 sp., *P. tessellata* (Charpentier)); 7.44 *Platyoplus* Tinkham (1 sp., *P. gilaensis* Tinkham); 7.45 *Steiroxys* Herman (4 spp.); 7.46 *Zacycloptera* Caudell (1 sp., *Z. atripennis* Caudell)]

Subfamily Saginae

One introduced species, as follows:

7.47 *Saga* Charpentier

S. pedo (Pallas) (Matriarchal Katydid). (1) MI.

Fig. 11.36.

Fig. 11.37.

Subfamily Meconematinae

One introduced species, as follows:

7.48 *Meconema* Audinet-Serville

M. thalassinum (De Deer) (Drumming Katydid). (1) NY.

Subfamily Tettigoniinae

Only one species is assigned to this subfamily in the U.S. It is closely related to the Decticinae but distinguished by its pronotum, which does not extend to the abdomen, and by the large size of the free plantula. Other species in this subfamily occur in the Old World.

7.49 *Hubbellia* Hebard

H. marginifera (Walker) (Big Green Pine-tree Katydid) [=*H. praestans* Hebard]. L. 36–90 mm. Green, with dorsal brown markings on head and pronotum; front wings with lower margins yellow in female and white in male. Found high in conifers. (See Fig. 11.37.) (2) FL.

8. PROPHALANGOPSIDAE (Hump-winged Cricket Family)

This rare family contains only four species in the entire world, two of which occur in western North America, as follows:

8.1 *Cyphoderris* Uhler

The two species are distinguished by features of the male genitalia.

C. monstrosa Uhler (Hump-winged Cricket). L. 21–25 mm. Brown, with black and pale yellowish or pinkish-buff markings. Males with palpus of apical lobe of genitalia terminal. Males stridulate. Found near timber line on branches or trunks of trees and can be orchard pests. (4) BC, WA, OR, ID; (5) AB, SK, CO, NY.

C. buckelli Hebard (Buckell's Hump-winged Cricket). L. 18–22 mm. Similar to preceding, but palpus of male genitalia subapical, not extending beyond tip. (4) BC, WA, ID.

9. GRYLLACRIDIDAE (Ground and Camel Crickets)

L. 7–50 mm (usually under 20 mm.) All species are wingless or at most with vestiges of wings. Gray, brown, or black in color, and without sound-producing structures. The group as a whole is rather poorly known. Its three subfamilies with 20 genera and 129 species are distinguished by the accompanying Key.

Key to the Subfamilies of Gryllacrididae

1. Antennae nearly or actually contiguous at base **Rhaphidophorinae**
 Antennae separated at base by distance equal to or greater than length of 1st antennal segment ... *2*

2(1). Tarsomeres lobed and somewhat flattened; hind femora extending beyond apex of abdomen .. **Gryllacridinae**
 Tarsomeres not lobed, somewhat compressed; hind femora not extending beyond apex of abdomen .. **Stenopelmatinae**

Subfamily **Gryllacridinae** (Leaf-rolling Crickets)

The following two genera are reported in the U.S. and Canada:

9.1 *Camptonotus* Uhler

One species, as follows:

C. carolinensis (Gerstaeker) (Leaf-rolling Cricket). L. 12–15 mm. Body reddish-brown; antennae very long. This species usually makes a nest by rolling a leaf and fastening the roll with silken threads spun from its mouth glands; reportedly, bladder-nut pods are sometimes used instead of rolled leaves. These nocturnal insects feed on aphids. (See Fig. 11.38.) (1) IN, OH, PA, NJ, MD, DE, DC; (2) s.e. US.

[9.2 *Cnemotettix* Caudell (1 sp., *C. pulvillifer* Caudell). (Some authors place this genus in a separate subfamily, Henicinae)]

Subfamily **Stenopelmatinae** (Jerusalem or Sand Crickets)

This is a group of four nocturnal species that are common west of the Rocky Mountains.

9.3 *Stenopelmatus* Burmeister

Of the four species, the following is common:

S. fuscus Haldeman (Jerusalem Cricket). L. 30–50 mm. Brown with black bands on abdominal segments. This common species bites and is sometimes a pest. (See Fig. 11.39 and A&J 27.) (3) CA, AZ, NM; (4) BC, WA, OR, ID, NV, UT; (5) AB, SK, MB, MT, SD, CO.

Subfamily **Rhaphidophorinae**

This, the largest subfamily, includes the camel crickets and the true cave crickets. Although it is divided into four tribes, most species belong to a single genus, *Ceuthophilus* (9.10).

Tribe **Rhaphidophorini**

[9.4 *Diestrammena* Bruner (1 sp., *D. apicalis* Brunner)]

9.5 *Tachycines* Adelung

One species only, as follows:

T. asynamorous Adelung (Greenhouse Stone Cricket). L. 14–16 mm. Brownish-yellow with pronounced brown mottling; front tibia with a small spine between pair of large ventral spurs at the apex. Pest in greenhouses in U.S.; also reportedly common in basements and warm garages. (See Fig. 11.40.)

Tribe **Gammarotettigini**

[9.6 *Gammarotettix* Brunner (3 spp.); 9.7 *Tropidischia* Scudder (1 sp., *T. xanthostoma* (Scudder))]

Fig. 11.38.

Fig. 11.39.

Fig. 11.40.

Tribe **Dolichopodini** (True Cave Crickets)

One genus, as follows:

9.8 *Hadenoecus* Scudder

L. 11–20 mm. Body slender; antennae very long, 80–100 mm; eyes small, and narrowly triangular; maxillary palpi very long, nearly as long as body; front femora more than twice as long as pronotum; tibiae more or less round in cross section. Of the three species found in caves in the southeastern U.S., the following is common:

H. subterraneus (Scudder) (Common Cave Cricket). L. 16–20 mm. Pale yellowish-brown; eyes black; dorsal seg-

ments of abdomen often with more or less transverse brownish blotches. (2) s.e. US.

Tribe **Ceuthophilini**

Although this is the largest group, with 114 species, most are rather rare and seldom collected without a special effort. The majority are found west of the Mississippi.

[9.9 *Pristoceuthophilus* Rehn (8 spp.)]

9.10 *Ceuthophilus* Scudder

The ninety-one species in this genus are difficult to distinguish except with technical keys based on features of the male genitalia. Many are western, but others, including the following, are found east of the Mississippi.

C. uhleri Scudder (Uhler's Camel Cricket). L. 13–16 mm. Pale reddish-brown or clay yellow, irregularly flecked with fuscus. Found from July to November in dry woods under logs. (See Fig. 11.41.) (1) IN, OH, NY, PA, MD; (2) KY, WV, VA, TN, NC, AR, SC, GA.

C. gracillipes (Haldeman). (See Fig. 11.42.)

[9.11 *Udeopsylla* Scudder (1 sp., *U. robusta* (Haldeman)); 9.12 *Styracosceles* Hubbell (3 spp.); 9.13 *Rhachocnemis* Caudell (1 sp., *R. validus* (Scudder)); 9.14 *Phrixocnemis* Scudder (1 sp., *P. truculentus* Scudder); 9.15 *Daihiniodes* Hebard (2 spp.); 9.16 *Daihiniella* Hubbell (1 sp., *D. bellicosum* (Scudder)); 9.17 *Daihinia* Haldeman (1 sp., *D. brevipes* Haldeman); 9.18 *Ammobaenetes* Hubbell (3 spp.); 9.19

Key to the Subfamilies of Gryllidae

1. Tarsi compressed, with 2nd tarsomere minute, compressed *2*
 Tarsi with 2nd tarsomere distinct, somewhat flattened, heart-shaped *5*
2(1). Body subspherical, wingless; pronotum covering top of head and eyes; eyes very small; hind femur ovate and very strongly enlarged; hind tibia armed dorsally with only a few movable spines ... **Myrmecophilinae**
 Body more elongate, usually winged; top of head and eyes not covered by pronotum; eyes well-developed; hind femur more elongate and not exceptionally enlarged *3*
3(2). Hind tibia armed dorsally on both margins with minute teeth, but without spines; body covered with translucent scales; pronotum of male usually prolonged backward; species either wingless or most males with short membranous front wings **Mogoplistinae**
 Hind tibia armed dorsally with 2 rows of spines; body not covered with scales; pronotum not prolonged backward in either sex; front wings always present, sometimes much shortened .. *4*
4(3). Head short, vertical or nearly so; hind tibia rather stout, armed with stout spines without teeth between them; ocelli present; color black or brown *6*
 Head elongate, horizontal; hind tibia slender, armed with delicate spines (in *Oecanthus*, not in *Neoxabea*) with minute teeth between them; ocelli absent; color white or pale green .. **Oecanthinae**
5(1). Hind tibia armed dorsally with 2 rows of spines without intervening teeth and with only 2 apical spurs on inner side; ovipositor in eastern species compressed and distinctly upcurved ... **Trigonidiinae**
 Hind tibia armed dorsally with 2 rows of spines with small teeth between them and with 3 apical spurs on both outer and inner sides; ovipositor in eastern species subcylindrical and slightly upcurved ... **Eneopterinae**
6(4). Hind tibia with long, movable, pilose spines; maxillary palpi with apical segment at least twice length of penultimate; hind tarsus in eastern species with basal tarsomere unarmed dorsally; smaller body (length, less than 12 mm) *7*
 Hind tibia with stout, immovable spines; maxillary palpi with apical segment not more than one-third longer than penultimate; hind tarsus with basal tarsomere serrate dorsally on both margins; larger body (length, rarely under 14 mm); (in part) **Gryllinae**
7(6). Pronotum with lower front angle of lateral lobes rounded; front wing of male with tympanum; hind tibia armed dorsally with 4 spines on each margin and with 3 subapical spurs on each side ... **Nemobiinae**
 Pronotum with lower front angle of lateral lobes rectangular or acute; front wing of male without tympanum; hind tibia armed dorsally with 3 spines on each margin and with only 2 subapical spurs on inner side; (in part) **Gryllinae**

Typhloceuthophilus Hubbell (1 sp., *T. floridanus* Hubbell); 9.20 *Macrobaenetes* Tinkham (1 sp., *M. valgum* (Strohecker))]

10. GRYLLIDAE (Cricket Family)

L. 2–30 mm. Many species of true crickets are only 6–12 mm in length. The family is divided into seven subfamilies, with 96 species assigned to 26 genera, all having fewer than 14 described species. However, such genera as *Cycloptilum*, *Gryllus*, and probably others, have more species biologically distinguished by differences in sound production (which create reproductive barriers) than by obvious morphological differences. The subfamilies are identified by the accompanying Key (see p. 134).

Subfamily Myrmecophilinae (Ant-loving Crickets)

The members of this subfamily are very small (L. 2–4 mm) and wingless. They are found in ants' nests.

[10.1 *Myrmecophila* Latreille (4 spp.)]

Subfamily Mogoplistinae (Scaly Crickets)

The 13 species assigned to this subfamily are also small (L. 5–7 mm, but up to 15 mm in one species). The scale-covered body is diagnostic. Most species are found in the tropics.

[10.2 *Cycloptiloides* Sjostedt (1 sp., *C. americanus* (Saussure)); 10.3 *Cycloptilum* Scudder (10 spp.); 10.4 *Oligacanthopus* Rehn and Hebard (1 sp., *O. prograptus* Rehn and Hebard); 10.5 *Hoplosphyrum* Rehn and Hebard (1 sp., *H. boreale* (Scudder))]

Subfamily Gryllinae (Field and House Crickets)

These are the most familiar and most abundant crickets. Their well known songs are the subject of poetry and fable. Several closely related species belonging to several genera are assigned to this subfamily.

10.6 *Acheta* Linnaeus

One species only, the worldwide domestic cricket:

A. domesticus (Linnaeus) (House Cricket). L. 10–18 mm. Light brown or yellowish. Introduced from Europe and often found overwintering in homes in the eastern U.S. May be fed and kept in cages to sing. (See Fig. 11.43.)

[10.7 *Anurogryllus* Saussure (2 spp.); 10.8 *Gryllita* Hebard (1 sp., *G. arizonae* Hebard); 10.9 *Gryllodes* Saussure (1 sp., *G. sigillatus* (Walker))]

Fig. 11.42.

10.10 *Gryllus* Linnaeus

There are 14 described species in this genus and others yet to be described. The species are very similar and may be distinguished only by examining highly technical features; no adequate identification key has been published. The species often appear under the single name, *Gryllus* (or *Acheta*) *assimilis* (Fabricius), but this species occurs only in south Florida. Some species are reared commercially for fish bait and laboratory animals. They are easily reared at home if fed lettuce, bread, and bone meal.

G. assimilis (Fabricius) (Field Cricket). L. 20–29 mm. Black; most of the area around the eyes light yellow-brown; hind wings never shorter than the front wings. (See Fig. 11.44 and A&J 29.)

[10.11 *Miogryllus* Saussure (3 spp.); 10.12 *Valifictorus* Randel (1 sp., *V. micado* (Saussure)). Note: *Teleogryllus oceanicus* (LeGuillou) is related to our mainland crickets; it is found in Hawaii, where, oddly enough, it is called the Oceanic Field Cricket, although it is certainly not aquatic.]

Subfamily Nemobiinae (Ground Crickets)

L. 7–13 mm. Reddish-brown to black and sometimes striped. Found along roads and pastures and open woods.

10.13 *Allonemobius* Hebard

Seven species, the following of which is common:

A. fasciatus (De Geer) (Striped Ground Cricket). L. 7–12 mm. Back reddish-brown; back part of the head with four dark

Fig. 11.41.

Fig. 11.43.

Fig. 11.44.

stripes. Males sing from July until frost. (See 11.45.) (1) n.e. US; (2) s.e. US; (5) Plains states.

[10.14 *Eunemobius* Hebard (3 spp.); 10.15 *Hygronemobius* Hebard (1 sp., *H. alleni* (Morse); 10.16 *Neonemobius* Hebard (5 spp.); 10.17 *Pictonemobius* Vickery and Johnstone (1 sp., *P. ambitiosus* (Scudder))]

Subfamily Oecanthinae (White Tree Crickets)

These are pale green species, lacking ocelli. They are loud singers, their song differences being one means of separating the species, of which many are closely similar. Two genera, as follows:

[10.18 *Neoxabea* Kirby (3 spp.)]

10.19 *Oecanthus* Serville

This genus contains 15 described species, but more remain undescribed. The following is the species most commonly identified in collections:

O. fultoni Walker (Snowy Tree Cricket). L. 12–15 mm. Pale green with yellow head and antennal bases. This species, found commonly on shrubs, is carnivorous and feeds on aphids

Fig. 11.45. (*From Hebard, 1934*)

Fig. 11.46. (*From Hebard, 1934*)

but may damage bushes by laying eggs under the bark of young stems and twigs. It is also called the Temperature Cricket because air temperature may be roughly computed by counting the number of chirps per minute, dividing this number by 4 and adding 40 for degrees Fahrenheit or dividing it by 6 for degrees Celsius. Throughout the U.S. (See A&J 28.)

Two closely related species have been given common names: *O. nigricornis* Walker (Black-horned Tree Cricket) (Fig. 11.46.) and *O. quadripunctatus* Beutenmuller (Four-spotted Tree Cricket).

Subfamily Trigonidiinae (Winged Bush Crickets)

The species assigned here are small (L. 5–7 mm), sometimes common, often brightly colored, but rarely collected.

[10.20 *Anaxipha* Saussure (7 spp., including *A. scia* Hebard, (2) FL [see Fig. 11.47]); 10.21 *Cyrtoxipha* Saussure (4 spp.); 10.22 *Falcicula* Rehn (1 sp., *F. hebardi* Rehn)]

10.23 *Phyllopalpus* Uhler

One species, as follows:

P. pulchellus Uhler (Red-headed Bush Cricket). L. 6–7 mm. Head and pronotum red, the latter with yellow on sides;

Fig. 11.47. (*From Blatchley, 1920*)

Fig. 11.48.

Fig. 11.49.

remainder black and brown. Found on low shrubs, small trees, and grass. (1) IN, OH, PA, NY, NJ, ND, DE, DC; (2) s.e. US.

Subfamily Eneopterinae (Larger Brown Bush Crickets)

L. 23–30 mm. There are a few common species among the nine assigned to this subfamily, but they are seldom collected. The species are eastern.

[10.24 *Hapithus* Uhler (2 spp.)]

10.25 *Orocharis* Uhler

Six species are included in this genus, the following of which is rather common:

O. saltator Uhler (Jumping Bush Cricket). L. 14–16 mm. Almost uniformly reddish-brown as a rule, with the front of the head flecked with darker brown, but sometimes grayish and more or less marked with brown spots; ocelli very small and widely separated; pronotum thickly pubescent. Found in dense woods, thickets along streams, and orchards and yard shrubs. (1) NJ, MD, DE, DC; (2) s.e. US; (3) TX; (5) NE.

[10.26 *Tafalisca* Walker (1 sp., *T. lurida* Walker)]

11. GRYLLOTALPIDAE (Mole Cricket Family)

L. 20–40 mm. Brown with some dark markings or pinkish-brown. Front tibia and tarsus fitted for rapid burrowing into loose soil and sand. All seven species are included in the following two subfamilies:

Subfamily Gryllotalpinae

The genera of this subfamily are united by the presence of three or four tibial dactyls (fingerlike processes) on the front legs and a short process on the front trochanter. They are distinguished on the basis of the arrangement of the dactyls (heavy digging spines) as follows:

11.1 *Gryllotalpa* Latreille

Front tibiae with four dactyls; hind femora shorter than pronotum; hind tibiae with several spines on the inner margins. This genus includes only the following species:

G. gryllotalpa (Linnaeus) (European Mole Cricket). L. 35–40 mm. Reddish or brownish-yellow, tinged with tan above and pale brownish-yellow beneath. Ocelli very small, sub-

rotund; antennae and pronotum about the same length; front wings short, pointed, and about one-half as long as abdomen; hind wings fully developed. Introduced species. (1) n.e. US; (2) s.e. US.

11.2 *Neocurtilla* Kirby

Very similar to *Gryllotalpa* but hind tibiae lack spines on the inner margins. Includes three species, of which the following is common and well known.

N. hecadactyla (Perty) (Common Mole Cricket). L. 20–30 mm. Brown with black markings; body covered with a fine pile; nocturnal. Found near margins of lakes, ponds, and streams. Common, but seldom seen. (1) n.e. US; (2) s.e. US. (See Fig. 11.48 and A&J 30.)

Subfamily Scapteriscinae

11.3 *Scapteriscus* Scudder

Two dactyls on front tibia; hind tibia usually longer than pronotum. Three species, all in the southeastern U.S., including:

S. acletus Rehn and Hebard (Southern Mole Cricket). L. 26–36 mm. Brownish to pinkish-buff with dark pattern on the pronotum. May be a pest in vegetable gardens. (2) NC, SC, LA, MS, AL, GA, FL; (3) TX.

S. vicinus Scudder (Changa). (See Fig. 11.49.) (2) SC, GA, FL.

S. abbreviatus Scudder (Short-winged Mole Cricket). (2) FL.

BIBLIOGRAPHY

Ball, E. D., *et al.* 1942. The grasshoppers and other Orthoptera of Arizona. *Univ. Ariz. Agric. Exp. Sta. Tech. Bull.* 93, pp. 257–373.

Blatchley, W. S. 1920. *Orthoptera of Northeastern America.* 784 pp. (Out-of-print.)

Cohn, Theodore J. 1965. The arid-land Katydids of the North American genus *Neobarrettia* (Orthoptera: Tettigoniidae): their systematics and a reconstruction of their history. Misc. Publ. Mus. Zool., Univ. Michigan, No. 126, 179 pp.

Froeschner, R. C. 1954. The grasshoppers and other Orthoptera of Iowa. *Iowa State College Journ. Sci.*, 29: 163–354.

Hebard, M. 1934. The Dermaptera and Orthoptera of Illinois. *Ill. Nat. Hist. Sur. Bull.* 20(3): iv + 125–279 pp.

Helfer, J. R. 1963. *How to know the grasshoppers, cockroaches, and their allies.* Dubuque: W. C. Brown Co., vi + 353 pp.

Hubbell, T. H. 1936. A monographic revision of the genus *Ceuthophilus* (Orthoptera, Gryllacrididae, Rhaphidophorinae). *Univ. Florida Pub. Biol. Sci. Ser.* 2(1): 1–551.

Otte, Daniel 1981. *The North American grasshoppers.* Vol. 1, Acrididae, Gomphocerinae and Acridinae. Cambridge: Harvard University Press, ix + 275 pp.

Rehn, James A. G., and Grant, Harold J., Jr. 1959. Review of the Romaleinae. *Proc. Acad. Nat. Sci.* Philadelphia, 111: 109–271.

———. 1960. A new concept involving the subfamily Acridinae (Orthoptera: Acridoidea). *Trans. American Ent. Soc.*, 86: 173–185.

———. 1961. A new monograph of the Orthoptera of North America (North of Mexico). Vol. 1, Acridoidea in part, covering the Tetrigidea, Eumastacidae, Tanaoceridae, and Romaleinae of the Acrididae. *Monograph, Academy of Nat. Sci.*, Philadelphia, No. 12, 257 pp.

Rentz, David C., and Birchim, James D. 1968. Revisionary studies in the Nearctic Decticinae. *Mem. Pacific Coast Ent. Soc.*, vol. 3, 173 pp.

Order 12

GRYLLOBLATTODEA (Rock Crawlers)

This small group of 20 species represents the last of an ancient line of insect development that probably links together many of the following orders of insects known as the orthopteroids, although currently there is little evidence for this assumption. Their Latin name implies that they look like a combination of a cricket and a cockroach, and they were so named to show their relationship to these two groups, but the matter is far from settled. Their English common name refers to their wingless condition and the fact that they live among rocks, usually at high altitudes in Siberia, Japan, and North America, the only regions of the world where they have been found.

Diagnosis: L. 14–30 mm. Body leathery; shape elongate and cylindrical; pale brown or gray, covered with a fine pubescence; antennae long and slender, with 23 to 40 segments; eyes small or absent; mouthparts with simple mandibles for biting; wingless; legs slender and unmodified; abdomen oval and cylindrical, with two moderately sized cerci of eight to nine segments; female ovipositor nearly as long as the cerci.

The nymphs resemble the adults except for the developed reproductive organs. There are eight nymphal instars. The last nymphal stage is pure white in color, except for the eyes. In this unpigmented stage, the nymph has probably never been exposed to light and represents a transformation stage during which adult features develop. The complete life history of these insects is poorly known, but it is established that they need several years to mature.

Both nymphs and adults might be confused with those of certain crickets, or particularly with the phasmid genus *Timema*. The large head, long antennae, and rather long, multisegmented cerci are distinguishing features.

Metamorphosis: Paurometabolous, with terrestrial eggs, nymphs, and adults.

Habits and habitats: Both adults and nymphs feed chiefly on the debris of insects that have died on the snow fields at high altitudes. They are seldom collected, probably because they are nocturnal and by day are usually concealed in crevices in cold wet gravel or under the snow. Living as they do at altitudes from 3,500 to over 10,000 feet among rocks, especially at the edges of glaciers, their optimum temperature is about the freezing point, i.e., 0°C. They are said to burrow several feet into cracks and crevices during warm periods. Some species are known to inhabit caves.

Reproductive behavior: Unknown.

Collecting and preserving: Hand collect at night in the restricted habitat and preserve in 80-percent alcohol.

Rearing: Method unknown.

Distribution: The 20 species are known in Siberia, Japan, and northern North America. Ten described species occur in the U.S. and Canada, all members of the single family and genus listed below:

Economic importance: None

Fig. 12.1.

1. GRYLLOBLATTIDAE (Rock Crawler Family)

1.1 *Grylloblatta* Walker

Ten species, including the following:

G. campodeiformis Walker (Northern Rock Crawler). L. 10–30 mm. Amber-yellow, with appendages somewhat lighter in color. Occurs in rocks near glaciers. (See Fig. 12.1 and A&J 14.) (4) BC; (5) AB, MT, WY.

BIBLIOGRAPHY

Gurney, A. B. 1953. Recent advances in the taxonomy and distribution of *Grylloblatta* (Orthoptera: Grylloblattidae). *Journ. Washington Acad. Sci.* 43: 325–332.

Kamp, J. W. 1963. Descriptions of two new species of Grylloblattidae and of the adult of *Grylloblatta barberi*, with an interpretation of their geographical distribution. *Ann. Ent. Soc. America.* 56: 53–68.

———. 1970. The cavernicolous Grylloblattoidea of the western United States. *Ann. Speleology.* 25: 223–230.

Order 13

DERMAPTERA (Earwigs)

Earwigs have short wing covers and well-developed and usable forceps at the apex of the abdomen. The latter easily serve as a feature to distinguish them from beetles with short wing covers. The earwigs owe their common name to a mistaken notion that they may enter a person's ear. (In this context, "wig"— short for "perwig"—means "to scold.") The Latin name, Dermaptera, on the other hand, refers to the thickened or "skinlike" front wings. Naturalists usually first notice earwigs when they infest flowers or invade camping tents or sleeping bags. They live in humid places, under bark or in soil, cracks, or similar locations. Species in the U.S. and Canada are omnivorous, but some tropical species are ectoparasites and others carnivorous.

Diagnosis: L. 4–25+ mm. Body leathery to hard; shape elongate and somewhat flattened; brownish to black in color, sometimes with reddish markings. Except for the grasshoppers, these insects are much harder than those previously described. The antennae are simple, about half the length of the body, with 6 to 15 segments. The mouthparts have mandibles for biting. Some species are wingless, but most have short front wings that do not cover the abdomen; the hind wings (Fig. 13.1) fold fanlike beneath the front pair when the insects are at rest. The legs are moderate in size and without specialized features. Since the abdomens of males (Fig. 13.2) and females (Fig. 13.3) have terminal forceps of different shapes, this dissimilarity is useful for distinguishing the sexes as well as the species.

Some female earwigs tend their egg clutches and young nymphs in small nests in the ground, from which they repel all intruders including their mates. The eggs are licked almost constantly while the embryo is developing, presumably to prevent the growth of fungus on their surface, although this fact has never really been verified. The young nymphs soon stray away and become independent of their mother. Some semisocial activity occurs among the adults during the breeding season.

Fig. 13.1.

Metamorphosis: Paurometabolous, with egg, nymphal, and adult stages.

Collecting and preserving: Use the same techniques described for Orthoptera.

Rearing: May be kept in a terrarium if provided with soil and suitable vegetable matter for food.

Distribution: Although most of the approximately 1100 species live in tropical regions, 20 species in 12 genera occur in the U.S., including several that range into temperate states.

Economic importance: Some species infest garden flowers.

CLASSIFICATION

The classification followed here is that used by Hans Reichardt in his catalog of the New World Dermaptera. There is no comprehensive work treating this order. The order is represented in the U.S. and Canada by five families, which may be distinguished by the accompanying Key. There are no satisfactory identification keys for the species, and the literature is widely scattered.

Key to the Families of Dermaptera in the United States and Canada

1. Second tarsomere simple, cylindrical, not prolonged beneath 3rd segment *2*
 Second tarsomere prolonged beneath 3rd segment *4*
2(1). Antennal segments 4 to 6, taken together, seldom longer than basal segment; antennae with 15 to 30 segments; body more or less flattened; 9 to 25+ mm in length *3*
 Antennal segments 4 to 6; taken together, longer than basal segment; antennae with 11 to 15 segments; usually dark; winged; 4 to 10 mm in length **3. Labiidae**
3(2). Adults wingless; male forceps asymmetrical, with right forcep more strongly curved than left .. **1. Carcinophoridae**
 Adult winged; male forceps symmetrical **2. Labiduridae**
4(1). Second tarsomere with elongate lobe extending beneath 3rd; body stout; 20 to 25 mm in length .. **4. Chelisochidae**
 Second tarsomere heart-shaped, extending beneath 3rd but more or less bilobed; 8 to 12 mm in length .. **5. Forficulidae**

1. CARCINOPHORIDAE
(Red-legged Earwig Family)

Subfamily Carcinophorinae

Five species of this family occur in the U.S., as follows:

[1.1 *Gonolabis* Burr (1 sp., *G. azteca* Dohrn [FL])]

1.2 *Euborellia* Burr

Three species, of which the following is the most common:

E. annulipes (Lucas). L. 9–13 mm. Wingless; antennae with 15 to 16 segments. Probably cosmopolitan, but found in the southern U.S. in debris and litter; may enter houses. (See Fig. 13.2 for the male and Fig. 13.3 for the female.)

[1.3 *Anisolabis* Fieber (1 sp., *A. maritima* [Géné])]

2. LABIDURIDAE
(Long-horned Earwig Family)

One cosmopolitan species in this family, as follows:

2.1 *Labidura* Leach

L. riparia (Pallas). L. 18–25 mm. Emits a foul odor. Found along oceans and rivers. (See Fig. 13.4 for male.) (2) FL.

3. LABIIDAE (Little Earwig Family)

Members of this family are seldom seen, although nine species occur in the U.S.

Fig. 13.3.

Subfamily Spongiphorinae

[3.1 *Vostox* Burr (2 spp.); 3.2 *Spongovostox* Burr (1 sp., *S. apicedentatus* Caudell); 3.3 *Laprobia* Hincks (2 spp.)]

Subfamily Labiinae

3.4 *Labia* Leach

Three species in the U.S., of which the following is the most abundant and widespread:

L. minor (Linnaeus). L. 4–7 mm. Dull black, pubescent, with pale legs. Said to be common on flowers and flying around

Fig. 13.2.

Fig. 13.4.

Fig. 13.5.

Fig. 13.7.

manure piles throughout the U.S. (See Fig. 13.5 for male nymph.)

[3.5 *Marava* Burr (1 sp., *M. arachidis* Yersin)]

4. CHELISOCHIDAE (Black Earwig Family)

One species only in the U.S., introduced into California from the Pacific region, probably during World War II.

4.1 *Chelisoches* Scudder

C. morio (Fabricius). L. 16–20 mm. Black or brown. (See Fig. 13.6 for male; Fig. 13.7 for female.)

5. FORFICULIDAE (Common Earwig Family)

Four species of this, the largest family of earwigs, occur in the U.S., of which one is regarded as a pest.

5.1 *Doru* Burr

Three species in the U.S., including the following:

D. aculeatum (Scudder) (Spine-tailed Earwig). L. 10–12 mm. Brownish with pale markings. Common (1) n.e. US; (2) s.e. US. (See Fig. 13.8 for male; Fig. 13.9 for female.)

Fig. 13.8.

Fig. 13.6.

Fig. 13.9.

Fig. 13.10.

Fig. 13.11.

U.S. in 1912 but now widely, if spottily, distributed. (See Fig. 13.10 for male; Fig. 13.11 for female.)

D. taeniatum (Dorhn). Similar to preceding. (1) coastal n.e. US; (2) coastal s.e. US; (4) AZ, CA.

5.2 *Forficula* Linnaeus

One species in the U.S., as follows:

F. auricularia Linnaeus. L. 11–18 mm. Blackish-brown with wing covers and legs pale. Sometimes a garden pest that feeds on petals of flowers, especially roses. Introduced into the

BIBLIOGRAPHY

Helfer, J. R. 1963. *How to know the grasshoppers, cockroaches, and their allies.* Dubuque: W. C. Brown Co., vi + 353 pp.

Reichardt, Hans 1968. *Catalogue of New World Dermaptera (Insecta).* Part I: Introduction and Pygidicranoidea. Papeis Avulsos Zool. S. Paulo, 21 (19): 183–193; Part II: Labioidea, Carcinophoridae. Ibid, 22 (5): 35–46; 1970, Part III: Labioidea, Labiidae. Ibid, 23 (10): 83–109.

These small fossil insects, known only from the Permain, are relatives of the Dictyoptera (cockroaches) with the front wing thickened to form a tegmina or elytra. The venation is greatly reduced and faint in the front wing, but present. The hind wing is large, and probably fanlike, with the anal area expanded. The antennae are short, being no longer than the head and the thorax combined, and there is no existing evidence of abdominal cerci.

Order 14

DICTYOPTERA (Mantids and Cockroaches)

Although at first one might suppose that the much disliked cockroach and the beloved praying mantid have little in common, current studies reveal that the two groups are closely allied, with several linking primitive traits. These include similar wing venation and biting mouthparts of the same type, as well as other features. Aside from such technical details, however, they must be separately described. Their ordinal name, Dictyoptera, meaning "net-winged," refers to their wing venation.

There are 69 species in 41 genera in the U.S.A. and Canada.

Suborder **MANTODEA (Mantids)**

Diagnosis: L. 10–160 mm. Body leathery; shape elongate and cylindrical (some tropical species, however, have broad expansions on the thorax and legs, similar to the leaf insects, Phasmida, giving them a flattened appearance). Species in the U.S. and Canada usually green in color, with others gray, brown, or a mixture of green and gray; antennae long and slender with many segments; biting mouthparts; front wings somewhat thickened, serving as covers for membranous hind wings; legs long and slender; abdomen enlarged.

The most distinctive feature of the mantids is the front pair of legs, which are modified for capturing prey. The femora are enlarged because of the raptorial muscles, with large spines arranged along the inside to impale prey while it is eaten (see Fig. 14.1). This feature distinguishes mantids from almost all other insects. Some Neuroptera also have raptorial front legs, as do some Hemiptera, but these groups are easily recognized by their very different wing venation. Both pairs of Neuroptera wings are transparent and have relatively fewer closed cells, and the hind wings do not fold fanlike as those of the Mantids do. The raptorial Hemiptera have shorter, more compact bodies, and their front wings are thickened only on the basal half.

Metamorphosis: Paurometabolous, with egg, nymphal, and adult stages.

Reproductive behavior: Most mantids seen in the field are females, usually with eggs developing in the enlarged abdomen. The numerous eggs are laid in large cases made of a paperlike material and glued to a twig or small branch (rarely to the side of a building). Nymphs overwinter in this egg case and emerge early in the spring. They are carnivorous and will eat one another if kept in a confined area. The adult female has the macabre habit of immediately eating the male (shown in Fig. 14.1) as soon as courtship and mating are over, although in natural surroundings the male sometimes escapes.

Habits and habitats: Mantids are found on bushes and occasionally on the sides of buildings where they alight after being attracted to lights at night. They will stalk flying insects or almost any moving insect large enough to attract their attention. They have exceptionally good eyesight for an insect and will sit motionless on a twig until an insect flies or crawls within range of their deadly front legs. These lash out with extreme accuracy, and in a flash they clamp the prey between the femora and the tibiae and quickly devour it while it is still struggling to escape.

Collecting and preserving: Adults may be hand captured on bushes and around lights at night. They will attempt to bite, but they are harmless. Once they have been killed, the contents of the abdomen should be removed and the cavity filled with cotton to avoid greasy specimens and aid in color preservation. When pinned, they should be supported by stiff paper beneath

Fig. 14.1. (*Courtesy of James L. Cox and* Insect World Digest)

the body to prevent it from drooping. When dry, this may be removed. Large specimens should be supported by pins at each side of the body to prevent them from swinging and damaging nearby specimens.

Rearing: Female mantids will form an egg case on a twig in a cage. They must be fed living flies or other suitable living insects until the egg case is complete. Usually the female dies after egg laying. The egg cases may be kept outside until the following spring when insect food again becomes available. After the eggs have hatched, the young nymphs must be provided with plenty of food or they will feed upon one another; they may also be isolated in individual cages.

Distribution: Recent workers recognize eight families of mantids, but only one of these, the Mantidae, occurs in North America. In all, there are about 1,500 species, most of them tropical in distribution. Since only five of the 20 species in 12 genera recorded in the U.S. and Canada are commonly found, only these are described here.

Economic importance: Mantids, because of their predatory habits, are welcomed in gardens with the hope that they will consume many, if not all, garden pests. In fact, these insects are sold in garden shops and other stores as a means of biological control of such pests. In actual practice, they are of relatively little value for this purpose because there are never enough of them to be effective. Even if there were, their predatory activities would bring an end to their food supply, and they would soon starve.

CLASSIFICATION

1. MANTIDAE (Mantids)

Subfamily Eremiaphilinae

[1.1 *Mantoida* Newman (1 sp., *M. maya* Saussure and Zehntner)]

Subfamily Amelinae

[1.2 *Yersiniops* Hebard (2 spp.); 1.3 *Litaneutria* Saussure (2 spp.)]

Subfamily Oligonicinae

[1.4 *Oligonicella* Giglio-Tos (2 spp.); 1.5 *Thesprotia* Stål (1 sp., *T. graminis* (Scudder))]

Fig. 14.2.

Fig. 14.3.

1.6 *Iris* Saussure

One species, as follows:

I. oratoria (Linnaeus) (Mediterranean Mantis). L. 45–55 mm. Usually green with brownish dorsal markings; hind wings often reddish with dark "eye spots." Attracted to lights at night. Introduced in 1933, it is found on vegetation. (See Fig. 14.2 for male; Fig. 14.3 for female; Fig. 14.4 for egg case.) (3) s. CA.

Subfamily Liturgousinae

[1.7 *Gonatista* Saussure (1 sp., *G. grisea* (Fabricius) (Lichen mantid))]

Subfamily Mantinae

1.8 *Stagmomantis* Saussure

Three species, of which the following is common:

S. carolina (Johannson) (Carolina Mantis). L. 45–60 mm. Green or brown, mottled with darker brown. This is the most common native mantis. (See Fig. 14.5 for male; Fig. 14.6 for egg case.) (1) MD; (2) s.e. US.

1.9 *Mantis* Linnaeus

One species only, as follows:

M. religiosa Linnaeus (European Mantis). L. 45–65 mm. Green to brown, with the green of front wing gradually merging with the brown of hind wing. Introduced in 1899, it is now common in many parts of the U.S. and commercially available. (See Fig. 14.7 for male; Fig. 14.8 for egg case.)

Fig. 14.4.

Fig. 14.5.

Fig. 14.7.

1.10 *Tenodera* Burmeister

Three species, of which the following two are common:

T. aridifolia sinensis Saussure (Chinese Mantis). L. 75–105 mm. Green of front wings sharply confined to front (costal) area; body sometimes laterally brownish; hind wings with heavy dark markings. Found on vegetation; egg cases are placed on stems of weeds or bushes. Introduced into the eastern U.S. in 1896 and now widespread throughout the country by commercial sale of egg masses. (See Fig. 14.9 for female; Fig. 14.10 for egg case.)

T. angustipennis Saussure (Narrow-winged Mantis). L. 70–105 mm. Green front (costal) margin of front wings sharply confined; hind wings narrower than front and lightly marked with black. Introduced in 1926 and now widespread throughout the U.S. (See Fig. 14.11 for male; Fig. 14.12 for egg case.)

Subfamily Photininae

[1.11 *Brunneria* Saussure (1 sp., *B. borealis* Scudder)]

Subfamily Vatinae

[1.12 *Phyllovates* Kirby (1 sp., *P. chlorophaea* (Blanchard)); 1.13 *Pseudovates* Saussure (1 sp., *P. arizonae* Hebard)]

Suborder BLATTARIA (Cockroaches)

Diagnosis: L. 2.5–60+ mm. Body leathery and rarely hardened; shape flattened and more or less oval. Cockroaches (often called water bugs or roaches) are usually dark reddish-brown, a few are black, and some are green; still other colors are found in tropical species. The antennae are long and slender with a great number of segments. Mouthparts are of the biting type. Usually both sexes are winged, with the front wings thickened and covering the hind wings when not in use. (See Fig. 14.13). Some species have shortened wings, and some species are entirely wingless. The legs are slender and usually not greatly elongate. A few uncommon species have enlarged hind femora. The abdomen is similar to that of the mantids, including the ovipositor valves for egg case formation. The eggs are

Fig. 14.6.

Fig. 14.8.

Fig. 14.9.

Fig. 14.11.

laid in smaller egg packets (oothecae), which may be carried by the female externally or internally, or are either lightly attached to leaves or other surfaces, or deposited in debris, where they hatch in several weeks. Those that carry the oothecae internally (all Blaberidae) give birth to their young alive.

The shape of cockroaches readily distinguishes these insects from their relatives, the mantids. They are well known as scavengers in homes, restaurants, and other public places where they can find moisture, warmth, and organic debris to feed upon. In the wild, they live a similar existence as scavengers in forest litter, and some feed on wood. They are nocturnal but are often attracted to lights at night. The household species often migrate from one building to another when the population builds up.

Metamorphosis: Paurometabolous, with egg, nymphal, and adult stages.

Collecting and preserving: Use the same techniques for cockroaches as for Orthoptera. Wild species are often attracted to lights at night; others may be obtained from leaf litter in forests and other habitats. Household species may be trapped by using commercial roach traps.

Rearing: Cockroaches may be reared in jars provided with food material. They must be supplied with moisture and warmth as well as a place to hide during the day.

Distribution: About 4,000 species of cockroaches occur throughout the world, most of them tropical. There are 49 species in 29 genera in the U.S. and Canada, most of them southern in distribution.

Economic importance: As pests in homes and buildings, they cause considerable concern. Since they are scavengers, however, they are, in fact, beneficial insects and have seldom been associated with disease transmission even though health officials treat them as a health hazard. Usually only under the most severe stress conditions—such as extreme poverty, riot and war, or epidemics—do they transmit diseases by becoming carriers of disease infested filth. They are extremely difficult to control except by constant cleaning up of all organic mate-

Fig. 14.12.

Fig. 14.10.

Fig. 14.13. (*From Blatchley, 1920*)

rial that might serve as a food source. Even then, they can be repeatedly introduced into homes and restaurants through groceries and packing cases or by direct migration from one building to another. For this reason, even periodic application of chemical agents is seldom effective.

Notes on identification: The literature on cockroaches is widely scattered. There is no comprehensive treatment of the species, except for those considered to be household pests.

Household Cockroaches: The four species of cockroaches that commonly invade homes and public buildings where food is handled are easily distinguished by the accompanying key.

Key to the Species of Household Cockroaches

1.	Adults with wings entire ...	*2*
	Adults with wings very short, not covering the abdomen, or entirely absent; black or dark brown. (Oriental Roach) **Blatta orientalis Linnaeus**	
2(1).	Tan or light brown ..	*3*
	Dark brown body; base of front wings pale or yellowish, forming a transverse narrow band; females and nymphs with a 2nd band posterior to the basal band. (Brown-banded Cockroach) ... **Supella longipalpa (Fabricius)**	
3(2).	Pronotum with 2 mid-lateral dark longitudinal stripes; female carries egg case at end of abdomen almost until hatching occurs (German Cockroach) **Blattella germanica (Linnaeus)**	
	Pronotum with a dark central spot on pale background; front wings glossy and reddish brown; large (25–45 mm). (American Cockroach) **Periplaneta americana (Linnaeus)**	

Further details about these cockroaches as well as some of the more common wild cockroaches, are given in the following discussion.

CLASSIFICATION

The family classification of the Blattaria that is based on recent studies of wing venation, fossil specimens, and the genitalia has yet to reach the point of congruity. The accompanying key to all genera of Blattaria with species established in the U.S. and Canada will take the place of the usual Key to the families.

Superfamily BLATTOIDEA

2. CRYPTOCERCIDAE (Brown-hooded Cockroach Family)

2.1 *Cryptocercus* Scudder

One species only, as follows:

C. punctulatus Scudder (Brown-hooded Cockroach). L. 24–29 mm. Black or dark brown, shining; pronotum thickened and projecting forward over the head to form a hood; wingless. Lives in wet rotten wood; feeds on wood. The most primi-

Key to the Genera of Blattaria*

1.	Ventral margins of all femora supplied with numerous spines	*2*
	Ventral margins of femora unarmed, with only a few distal spines, or only posterior femora armed with spines ...	*16*
2(1).	Ventro-anterior margin of front femora with row of spines that either decrease gradually in size and length toward apex or are of nearly equal length throughout	*3*
	Ventro-anterior margin of anterior femora with row of heavy basal spines followed by row of more slender, shorter apical spines	*11*
3(2).	Front wings reduced or not; if latter, then with longitudinal discoidal (cubital) sections extending to apex of front wings ...	*4*
	Front wings not reduced, with discoidal (cubital) sections oblique and extending to hind margin of front wings .. **5.10 Supella**	
4(3).	Ventro-anterior margin of front femora with 2 heavy apical spines	*5*
	Ventro-anterior margin of front femora with 3 heavy apical spines	*7*
5(4).	Front wing much reduced; body above blackish, with numerous light yellowish markings ... **6.7 Nauphoeta**	
	Front wings reduced or not, but body above without this color	*6*
6(5).	Hind wings with costal veins strongly clubbed apically **5.9 Cariblatta**	
	Hind wings with costal veins normal, not clubbed apically **5.3 Symploce**	
7(4).	Front and hind wings reduced or not; if latter, then discoidal (cubital) sections not angulate near base; antennae not densely hairy basally	*8*
	Front and hind wings fully developed, with discoidal (cubital) sections strongly angulate near base; antennae densely hairy basally **5.4 Pseudomops**	
8(7).	Male with subgenital plate symmetrical; styles elongate, straight, slender symmetrical processes; female with subgenital plate valvate	*9*
	Male with subgenital plate strongly asymmetrical; styles relatively short and heavy, symmetrical or not; female with subgenital plate simple, not valvate **5.1 Blattella**	
9(8).	Terminal pad between claw (arolia) present; size medium to large (over 24 mm)	*10*
	Terminal pad between claw absent; size medium (under 24 mm) **3.1 Blatta**	

Key to the Genera of Blattaria (*Contd.*)

10(9). Front wing represented by subquadrate pads, with inner (sutural) margins weakly overlapping .. **3.4 Eurycotis**

Front wing represented by small, rounded, trigonal, lateral pads... **3.3 Neostylopyga**

Front and hind wings fully developed, extending beyond apex of abdomen **3.2 Periplaneta**

11(2). Four basal tarsomeres, each with a ventral pad *12*

Fourth tarsomere only with a ventral pad *15*

12(11). Ventro-anterior margin of front femora with 3 apical spines *13*

Ventro-anterior margin of front femora with only 1 apical spine .. **6.3 Phoetalia Stål**

13(12). Tarsal claws symmetrical .. *14*

Tarsal claws strongly asymmetrical **5.11 Latiblattella**

14(13). Male with 6th dorsal abdominal segment bearing toward the middle, at specialization of 6th and 7th segments, 2 minute, chitinous projections armed dorso-median with elongate delicate teeth; styles of subgenital plate not flexed, of very unequal bulk; female with general color solid, shining blackish brown, legs yellowish orange **5.2 Ischnoptera**

Male with dorsal surface of abdomen either specialized or not but never showing armed projections or character of specialization just mentioned; styles of subgenital plate slender, deflexed, cylindrical processes, with rounded apices, right slightly longer; female with general color never solid, shining blackish brown with legs yellowish orange .. **5.5 Parcoblatta**

15(11). Front wings fully developed (male), considerably reduced but not truncate (female); pronotum shining blackish brown, margined laterally and anteriorly with buff **5.8 Euthlastoblatta**

Front wings considerably reduced, truncate, in both sexes; pronotum buffy, disk submarginally bordered, rather narrowly, with blackish brown and median anchor-shaped marking **5.8 Euthlastoblatta** [= *Aglaopteryx*]

16(1). Subgenital plate absent; apical portion of abdomen covered by the protruded 7th dorsal and 6th ventral abdominal sclera; wingless **2.1 Cryptocercus**

Subgenital plate present; apical portion of abdomen not covered; male with at least front wing rudiments ... *17*

17(16). Front and hind wings not reduced, anal section of hind wings folding fanwise; general surface hairless ... *18*

Front and hind wings reduced or not; some species with wings completely absent, but if hind wings present, anal field not folded fanwise; general surface usually hairy *25*

18(17). Fourth tarsomere only with a ventral pad; hind wings with an intercalated triangle or appendicular field .. *19*

Four basal tarsomeres each with a ventral pad; wings without an intercalated triangle or appendicular field .. *21*

19(18). Front femur with 3 spines on ventral margin and 2 spines at the tip... **5.12 Ectobius**

Front femur with a single elongate apical spine *20*

20(19). Tarsal claws single but asymmetrical; hind wing with an intercalated triangle of length equal to not more than one-third total wing length **5.7 Chorisoneura**

Tarsal claws equal but with 2 microscopic teeth on each internal margin; hind wing with a reflexed appendicular field of length equal to approximately one-half total wing length .. **5.6 Plectoptera**

21(18). Pad between claws present; size medium (under 30 mm); pronotum produced posteriorly obtuse-angulate, apex rounded .. *22*

Pad between claws absent; size extremely large (over 40 mm); pronotum subelliptical .. **6.1 Blaberus**

22(21). General color brown .. *23*

General color light Paris green; front wings not pitted **6.5 Panchlora**

23(22). Large (L. 38–50 mm); hind margin of middle and hind femora each with 1 short apical spine only; front femur with a row of short, fine spines **6.6 Leucophaea**

Small (L. 16–24 mm) ... *24*

24(23). Front wing light brown; pronotum dark brown, pale in front; basal fourth of front wing with numerous small round pits, many in double rows; front femur bordered with stiff hairs and single stout spine at base **6.4 Pycnoscelus**

Pronotum and front wing pale brownish; pronotum with dark central blotch, with intricate pale markings, and a dark band at each side; basal third of discoidal vein of hind wing pigmented brown **6.7 Nauphoeta**

25(17). Tarsomeres with pads ... *26*

Tarsomeres without pads ... *27*

26(25). Front wing not reaching to middle of abdomen; pad between claws absent; size large (L. over 30 mm) **6.2 Hemiblabera**

Key to the Genera of Blattaria (*Contd.*)

Front and hind wings extending beyond apex of abdomen; pad present between claws; size small (under 7 mm) **4.4 Holocompsa**

27(25). Middle and hind femora with a disto-genicular spine *28*

Middle and hind femora without a disto-genicular spine; body very hairy **4.2 Eremoblatta**

28(27). Pad between claws extremely small or absent; male with fully developed front wings; size small to medium (over 5 mm); not found in ants' nests *29*

Pad large; male with front wings reduced; size minute (under 3 mm); found in ants' nests .. **6.8 Attaphila**

29(28). Ocelli absent; male with styles of subgenital plate small; female without transverse clypeal swelling; subgenital plate valvular **4.3 Compsodes**

Ocelli large (male) or ocellar spots present, usually weakly defined (female); male with styles absent from subgenital plate; female with transverse clypeal swelling; subgenital plate simple .. **4.1 Arenivaga**

*Adapted from Rehn, 1950.

tive cockroach known, their newly hatched nymphs resemble termites, probably their distant relatives. (See Fig. 14.14 for adult.) Occurs in mountainous terrain. Uncommon. (1) NY, PA, MD; (2) KY, WV, VA, TN, NC, GA; (3) CA; (4) WA, OR.

3. BLATTIDAE (American Cockroach Family)

Subfamily Blattinae

3.1 *Blatta* Linnaeus

One species, as follows:

B. orientalis Linnaeus (Oriental Cockroach). L. 18–30 mm. This pest (see Key to Household Cockroaches) prefers warm, moist locations in homes and restaurants and is seldom found outdoors. Cosmopolitan. (See Fig. 14.15.)

3.2 *Periplaneta* Burmeister

Four species, as follows:

P. americana (Linnaeus) (American Cockroach). L. 27–45 mm. A common pest (see Key to Household Cockroaches) except in northern regions with extremely cold weather. This large insect is the cockroach most often seen in stress areas (city slums, etc.), frequently migrating from building to building. Cosmopolitan. (See Fig. 14.16.)

P. brunnea Burmeister (Brown Cockroach). L. 25–33 mm. Front wings glossy reddish-brown. Pronotum with darker central markings more diffuse than in the preceding species. Found both in homes and in the wild. (2) FL; (3) TX.

Fig. 14.15.

P. australasiae (Fabricius) (Australian Cockroach). L. 23–29 mm. Front wings reddish-brown with conspicuous yellow stripes at sides in front; pronotum yellowish with base and one or two large, distinct blackish-brown spots. Found in homes and gardens and in the wild, often in pitcher plants. (2) FL.

Fig. 14.14.

Fig. 14.16.

Fig. 14.17.

P. fuliginosa (Serville) (Smoky-brown Cockroach). L. 24–33 mm. Entirely blackish-brown, shining. Occurs in the wild but near towns, now common in homes. (2) FL, AL, MS, LA; (3) TX.

3.3 *Neostylopyga* Shelford

One species, as follows:

N. rhombifolia (Stoll) (Harlequin Cockroach). L. 20–26 mm. Dorsally blackish with numerous light yellowish markings that distinguish it from all other U.S. species; front wings greatly reduced. Introduced; a household pest in Asia and Mexico, but not the U.S. (3) s. AZ, s. CA.

Subfamily Polyzosteriinae

[3.4 *Eurycotis* Stål (2 spp.)]

Superfamily BLABEROIDEA

4. POLYPHAGIDAE (Desert Cockroach Family)

Subfamily Polyphaginae

4.1 *Arenivaga* Rehn

Often common around sand dunes at night in little burrows resembling tiny mole runs. Seven species, including the following:

A. bolliana (Saussure) (Boll's Sand Cockroach). L. 15–24 mm. Female black with pronotum usually brown in front; male brown; front femur hairy at base; female wingless. Found in wood rat nests. (See Fig. 14.17.) (3) TX.

[4.2 *Eremoblatta* Rehn (1 sp., *E. subdiaphana* (Scudder)); 4.3 *Compsodes* Hebard (2 spp.)]

Subfamily Holocompsinae

[4.4 *Holocompsa* Burmeister (2 spp.)]

5. BLATTELLIDAE (German Cockroach Family)

Subfamily Blattellinae

5.1 *Blattella* Caudell

Two species in U.S. and Canada, as follows:

B. germanica (Linnaeus) (German Cockroach). L. 10–13 mm. Markings on pronotum described for household cockroaches are distinctive for this species. A major household pest in many areas; secreted fluid leaves a characteristic odor indicative of their presence. Cosmopolitan.

Fig. 14.18.

B. vaga Hebard (Field Cockroach). L. 8.5–11.5 mm. Similar in appearance to the preceding except olive green with a black face. Found around irrigated areas, sometimes around water pipes in homes. (3) TX, AZ.

[5.2 *Ischnoptera* Burmeister (1 sp., *I. deropeltiformis*[Brunner]); 5.3 *Symploce* Hebard (1 sp., *S. capitata* (Saussure)); 5.4 *Pseudomops* Serville (1 sp., *P. septentrionalis* Hebard)]

5.5 *Parcoblatta* Hebard

Twelve species, of which the following is the most common:

P. pensylvanica (De Geer) (Pennsylvania Wood Cockroach). L. 12–18 mm. Light brown, shining, uniformly colored. Common in woods in the north; sometimes a pest in homes. (See Fig. 14.18.) (1) n.e. NA; (2) s.e. US; (3) TX.

Several other species of this genus are common in woods but are not known to invade homes.

Subfamily Plectopterinae

[5.6 *Plectoptera* Saussure (1 sp., *P. poeyi* (Saussure)); 5.7 *Chorisoneura* Brunner (1 sp., *C. texensis* Saussure and Zehntner); 5.8 *Euthlastoblatta* Hebard [=*Aglaopteryx* Hebard] (2 spp.); 5.9 *Cariblatta* Hebard (1 sp., *C. lutea* (Saussure and Zehntner))]

5.10 *Supella* Shelford

One species only, as follows:

S. longipalpa (Fabricius) (Brown-banded Cockroach). L. 10–14 mm. The wing bands described for household cockroaches serve to distinguish this species. Often a house pest but not as common as other household species. Cosmopolitan. (See Fig. 14.19 for female and A&J 37.)

[5.11 *Latiblattella* Hebard (2 spp.)]

Subfamily Ectobiinae

5.12 *Ectobius* Stephens

One species only, as follows:

E. lapponicus (Linnaeus) (Mediterranean Cockroach). L. 8–9 mm. Glossy light yellowish-brown with numerous darker spots. Introduced in 1951 from Europe. (1) MA.

Fig. 14.19.

6. BLABERIDAE (Ovoviviparous Cockroach Family)

Subfamily Blaberinae

6.1 *Blaberus* Serville

One species only, as follows:

B. craniifer Burmeister (Death's Head Cockroach). L. 42–60 mm. Pronotum dull yellowish with central black-brown markings suggesting a "death's head"; front wings brown, yellowish at the base. Our largest species, often used as a laboratory animal, but only by federal permit. Found under boards and in other hiding places. (See Fig. 14.20.) Common in tropical America and now established in (2) s. FL.

[6.2 *Hemiblabera* Saussure (1 sp., *H. tenebricosa* Rehn and Hebard); 6.3 *Phoetalia* Stål [=*Leurolestes* Rehn and Hebard] (1 sp., *P. pallidus* (Brunner))]

Subfamily Pycnoscelinae

6.4 *Pycnoscelus* Scudder

One species, as follows:

P. surinamensis (Linnaeus) (Surinam Cockroach). L. 16–23 mm. Front wings light brown; pronotum dark brown, pale in front. Obligatorily parthenogenetic (no males known). Sometimes a pest in greenhouses. Found in the wild in litter

and debris. (2) FL, AL, MS, LA; (3) TX; elsewhere in greenhouses.

Subfamily Panchlorinae

6.5 *Panchlora* Burmeister

One species, as follows:

P. nivea (Linnaeus) (Cuban Cockroach). L. 12–18 mm. Pale green; top of head, pronotum, and front half of front wings pale; front wings usually with a small brown spot about one-third of the way from the apex. Often found on bunches of bananas throughout the U.S.; now known to be established in (2) FL and (3) Brownsville, TX.

Subfamily Oxyhaloinae

6.6 *Leucophaea* Brunner

One species only, as follows:

L. maderae (Fabricius) (Madeira Cockroach). L. 38–53 mm. Glossy pale brown with darker markings on wings and pronotum. Adults stridulate; also emit offensive odor when disturbed. Found in the wild in tropical regions; feeds on bananas. Established in the U.S. in (1) New York City.

6.7 *Nauphoeta* Burmeister

One species only, as follows:

N. cinerea Saussure (Cinereous Cockroach). L. 23–24 mm. Pronotum and front wings pale brownish; pronotum with dark central blotch with intricate pale markings, and a dark band at each side. Occurs in grain storage and processing plants. (2) FL.

[*Gromphadorhina* Brunner]

The following species and related species of this genus are of considerable interest because of their ability to hiss. By expelling air through their spiracles, they make a distinctly audible sound when handled or otherwise disturbed. As a result of this

Fig. 14.20.

Fig. 14.21. (*Courtesy of William J. Yurkiewicz and* Insect World Digest.)

Fig. 14.22.

ability and their large size and rugged looks, these insects (see Fig. 14.21) are now displayed in insect zoos and have made several TV appearances. Although no species of the genus has yet become established in the U.S., it seems certain that the

following species, available only by federal permit, will soon find its way into our environment as an established group.

G. laevigata Saussure and Zehntner (Madagascaran Cockroach). L. ±60 mm. (See Fig. 14.22.)

Subfamily Attaphilinae
6.8 *Attaphila* Wheeler

One species only, as follows:

A. fungicola Wheeler (Atta Ant Cockroach). L. 2.5–2.7 mm. Pronotum hairy; amber yellow to brownish; front wings reduced in male, absent in female. Lives in Atta Ant nests. (3) TX.

BIBLIOGRAPHY

Cornell, P. B. 1968. *The Cockroach*. London: Hutchinson, 391 pp.

Helfer, J. R. 1963. *How to know the grasshoppers, cockroaches, and their allies*. Dubuque: W. C. Brown Co., vi + 353 pp.

Rehn, J. W. H. 1950. A key to the genera of North American Blattaria, including established adventives. *Ent. News*, 61: 64–67.

Roth, Louis M. 1970. Evolution and taxonomic significance of reproduction in Blattaria. *Annual Rev. Ent.*, vol. 15, pp. 75–96.

Order 15

ISOPTERA (Termites)

Termites have a bad reputation among most homeowners because a few species can cause great economic loss by destroying wooden structures. This reputation is unfortunate because it obscures the fact that termites comprise an important part of the detritus cycle, without which the recycling of valuable nutrients would be slowed. Wood and other cellulose materials are indigestible by most animals; when broken down by the symbiotic protozoa and bacteria found in the alimentary tract of termites, however, these materials become a great source of simple sugars that are essential to the metabolism of these insects. These remarkable insects have attained great biological success in many tropical and subtropical regions by a combination of this ability and their advanced social life.

The name of their order, Isoptera, means simply that both pairs of wings, unlike the wings of ants, are of the same shape and appearance. Although termites are often called White Ants, this is a misnomer. They are not always white, and they have no direct relationship or even close similarity to ants. Because of their superficial resemblance to ants, however, swarms of the latter in the spring and fall are often thought to be termite swarms. As a result, owners of buildings, fearing the

worst, often take the unwarranted precaution of treating uninfested wood with chemicals to kill nonexistent enemies.

Termite colonies are well organized and divided into distinct castes, that is, specialized groups of individuals that work at specific tasks. Except when swarming, they are confined to their nests and to runways they have hollowed out through soil or wood. These tunnels are constructed from a paperlike material made by the worker termites, a caste that is seen only when the nests or tunnels are disturbed. Termites never go out in the open to forage as do ants.

Diagnosis: L. 3–10 mm. Soft-bodied; shape elongate, cylindrical, with only slight constrictions between the thorax and abdomen (unlike ants, which have a very deep constriction of the abdomen). The body is usually pale in North American species (but may be dark in certain exotic species); the wings are darker in color, with brown veins; the head is brownish. Antennae are short, usually not much longer than the head, with 9 to 30 or more segments. Mouthparts have large mandibles for biting, and those of the soldier caste are often elongate and require a greatly enlarged head to accommodate the large mandibular muscles. Both pairs of wings, when pres-

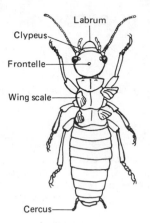

Fig. 15.1.

ent, are large and almost exactly alike. Usually, termites are wingless. When wings develop, they are used to fly a short distance during the swarming period and then break off at the base. The legs are short without any special modifications. The abdomen of the workers and soldiers is simple, cylindrical, somewhat oval. The abdomen of the queen may become enormous when filled with eggs. All termites have very short inconspicuous terminal cerci. (See Fig. 15.1 for general body form of an adult worker termite.)

One of the easiest ways to tell termite swarms from ant swarms is by comparing their wings. Termite wings have long, slightly curved veins with no or very few cross veins (see Fig. 15.5). Ant wings (see Fig. 25.1) are very different and cannot be confused.

Metamorphosis: Paurometabolous, with egg, nymphal, and adult stages. The nymphs look very much like the adults except that the young queens are very large and the males, as well as the young queens, develop wings during the swarming period. Social hormones secreted by the queen prevent transformation of the nymphs into reproductives, therefore only a few individuals in any colony are sexually mature, usually just one female, the queen (enlarged with eggs in Fig. 15.2), and several males. If the queen is removed from the colony, the absence of her hormones permits nymphal transformation into supplemental reproductives.

The termite colony: A new colony is established by a single pair after a swarming flight. Pairing takes place during

Fig. 15.2.

the swarming, after which the pair digs a nuptial chamber in the soil where their mating takes place. These pioneers become the king and queen of the new colony. Termite colony organization differs considerably from species to species, although the castes and duties remain essentially the same. There is a strict division of labor. At first, the reproductive pair must do all of the work of tending to the young, but give it up as soon as this chore can be taken over by the newly developed workers. These nymphlike adults are of both sexes but are incapable of reproduction. Instead, they gather food, feed the reproductives and soldiers, and build and enlarge the nest. Not all species produce true workers, however. Some produce a type of nymph that serves as a worker but is capable, at any time, of developing into a winged reproductive, soldier, or supplementary reproductive. Other species produce two kinds of workers, a large male and a smaller female, both adult in appearance and incapable of reproduction. The soldier caste also varies. Some species have large soldiers that have developed from small workers and small soldiers that have developed from nymphs. The soldiers' task is to guard the nest by frightening intruders with their large mandibles. One group of termites also has a caste called *nasutes*, which are able to defend the nest by extruding an irritating substance from a pore in the end of their snouts formed by the elongation of the head. Termites with this caste are found in the U.S. only in the southwestern desert region. The fourth major caste, found only in some species, is that of the supplementary reproductive, which differs from the king and queen in size and serves only as a replacement in case of the death of one or both of the royal pair.

Collecting and preserving: All formative stages and all castes of termites should be removed from a nest by carefully dissecting it. At the same time, one should look for beetles and other insects that live in the nest as guests. Keeping a record of the date, time of day, and weather conditions during termite swarms will provide valuable data for research studies. All termites may be preserved in 80-percent alcohol.

Rearing: Termites may be reared in old boards and logs laid over soil. Some species will infest bails of old paper. Since termites are very high in protein—about 68 percent—compared to ordinary hamburger—only about 15 percent—they could easily become an excellent source of protein in protein-starved countries. Not only are they good to eat, they might even become a gourmet food in the U.S. if they were properly served in expensive restaurants. Should this fad develop, rearing techniques will certainly become more refined.

Distribution: About 1900 species of termites are catalogued, including 61 species known as fossils. Forty-four species in 18 genera are recorded in the U.S., almost all of them in the southern states.

Notes on identification: The species can be identified only by examining technical characteristics under relatively high magnification. Although no comprehensive monograph is available, there is an abundance of literature for a detailed study of these insects.

Economic importance: Termites cause untold amounts of monetary damage to wooden structures. Some species bore into the wood from the ground beneath, whereas others penetrate the wood directly after swarming. In both cases, unless careful inspection is made, the damage will go undetected until the wooden structure, internally weakened beyond repair, must be replaced at considerable expense. Chemical control can effectively kill a termite colony in soil. If found in time, their

infestation of the wood in buildings may also be treated. The best control, however, is through prevention—using a type of construction that will prevent the termites from reaching the wood. Special training is necessary for the proper application of these controls. Buyers of buildings are advised to have them inspected and certified termite-free before purchase and building contractors must be trained to take the proper precautions.

CLASSIFICATION

Four of the five termite families occur in the U.S. and Canada (A very primitive family, Mastotermitidae, lives only in Australia; its single species is very closely related to cockroaches.) These four families may be identified by the accompanying Key.

Key to the Families of Isoptera

1. Front wing scales short, not reaching base of hind wing scale; wings not reticulate **4. Termitidae**
 Front wing scales overlapping at least the base of hind wing scale; wings reticulate *2*
2(1). Ocelli absent ... **1. Hodotermitidae**
 Ocelli present .. *3*
3(2). Fontanelle (a frontal pore on the head) present **3. Rhinotermitidae**
 Frontanelle absent ... **2. Kalotermitidae**

Soldiers, Nasutes, and Workers

1. Head produced into a noselike process; mandibles rudimentary (nasutes) **4. Termitidae**
 Head without such a process *2*
2(1). Head small; mandibles small, not projecting anteriorly (cannot be keyed to family) **Workers**
 Head large; mandibles very large and projecting anteriorly (soldiers) *3*
3(2). Cercus relatively long, 4-segmented **1. Hodotermitidae**
 Cercus short, 2-segmented *4*
4(3). Fontanelle (a frontal pore on the head) present *5*
 Fontanelle absent ... **2. Kalotermitidae**
5(4). Pronotum flat, without anterolateral lobe **3. Rhinotermitidae**
 Pronotum saddle-shaped, with anterolateral lobe **4. Termitidae**

1. HODOTERMITIDAE (Rotten-wood Termite Family)

Subfamily Termopsinae

The three species in one genus that are assigned to this family occur in western and southwestern states and colonize dead wood.

1.1 *Zootermopsis* Emerson

Three species, including the following:

Z. angusticollis (Harger) (Pacific Dampwood Termite). This is the most likely pest species in the Pacific Northwest. It can live in wood that is out of contact with the ground if the wood is moist. (See A&J 39.)

2. KALOTERMITIDAE (Powder-post Termite Family)

Members of this family are also termed Dry-wood Termites and Damp-wood Termites. It is the largest family in the U.S.; with 18 species in eight genera, all confined to the South and Southwest. Several species are of considerable economic importance. All species nest in dry wood, damp wood, and wood not in contact with soil.

[2.1 *Pterotermes* Holmgren (1 sp., *P. occidentis* (Walker); 2.2 *Marginitermes* Krishna (1 sp., *M. hubbardi* (Banks)); 2.3 *Paraneotermes* Light (1 sp., *P. simplicicornis* (Banks))]

2.4 *Incisitermes* Krishna

Nine species, of which the following is a pest.

I. minor (Hagen) (Western Drywood Termite). Found in (3) CA, AZ; (4) WA; (5) UT.

[2.5 *Kalotermes* Hagen (1 sp., *K. approximatus* Snyder); 2.6 *Neotermes* Holmgren (2 spp.); 2.7 *Calcaritermes* Snyder (1 sp., *C. nearcticus* (Snyder)); 2.8 *Cryptotermes* Banks (2 spp.)]

3. RHINOTERMITIDAE (Subterranean Termite Family)

The nine species assigned to this family nest in soil. Several of them are significant pests.

Subfamily Heterotermitinae

3.1 *Reticulitermes* Holmgren

The six species assigned to this genus include the most common and destructive in the U.S., among them the following:

R. flavipes (Kollar) (Eastern Subterranean Termite). Found throughout the eastern U.S. and west of the Rocky Mountain area.

R. hesperus Banks (Western Subterranean Termite). Replaces *R. flavipes* in the western U.S. (See A&J 40.)

[3.2 *Heterotermes* Froggatt (1 sp., *H. aureus* [Snyder])]

Subfamily Rhinotermitinae

3.3 *Prorhinotermes* Silvestri

One species only, as follows:

P. simplex (Hagen) (Florida Damp-wood Termite). L. 5–9 mm (incl. wings). This large species resembles *Reticulitermes flavipes* (Kollar). It is confined to s. FL. (See Fig. 15.3 for worker; Fig. 15.4 for soldier.)

Fig. 15.5.

Fig. 15.3.

Fig. 15.6.

Subfamily Coptotermitinae

3.4 *Coptotermes* Wasmann

One species only, as follows:

C. formosanus Shiraki (Formosan Subterranean Termite). Introduced into the southern U.S., this species may become a serious pest. (2) SC, FL, LA; (3) TX.

4. TERMITIDAE (Desert Termite Family)

This family contains 11 U.S. species, all found in the Southwest. Also called Soldierless Termites and Nasutiform Termites, they nest in soil under rotting wood, cow chips, or in wood in soil. Sometimes they damage buildings.

Subfamily Amitermitinae

[4.1 *Anopolotermes* Fritz Mueller (1 sp., *A. fumosus* (Hagen)); 4.2 *Amitermes* Silvestri (8 spp.)]

4.3 *Gnathamitermes* Light

Two species, including the following:

G. tubiformans (Buckley) (Tube-forming Desert Termite). L. 5–5.5 mm (Soldier). Brown; soldier with gray abdomen, white legs, mandibles reddish brown. A subterranean termite that feeds on roots of grass and other vegetation and constructs thin-walled tubes over vegetation, it is also common in dried cow manure. (See Fig. 15.5 for a winged specimen.) (3) w. TX.

Subfamily Nasutitermitinae

4.4 *Nasutitermes* Dudley

One species only, as follows:

N. corniger (Motschulsky) (Tropical Nasutiform Termite). L. 6–8 mm. Reddish-brown or yellowish-brown. Of interest because it is one of the few U.S. species with the nasute caste, this species, and others of its subfamily, lack protozoa in their gut, harboring in their place certain kinds of bacteria that serve the same purpose, that of digesting cellulose. (See Fig. 15.6 for a nasute.) (2) FL; (3) TX.

[4.5 *Tenuirostritermes* Holmgren (2 spp.)]

Fig. 15.4.

BIBLIOGRAPHY

Arauja, R. L. 1977. *Catalogo dos Isoptera do Novo Mondo*. Rio de Janeiro: Acad. Brasileira des Ciencas, 92 pp.

Helfer, J. R. 1963. *How to know the grasshoppers, cockroaches, and their allies*. Dubuque: W. C. Brown Co., vi + 353 pp.

Hickin, Norman E. 1971. *Termites, a world problem*. London: Hutchinson & Co., 232 pp.

Krishna, K., and Weesner, F. M., eds. 1969–1970. *Biology of Termites*. Vol. 1, xiv + 600 pp; vol. 2, 600 pp. New York: Academic Press.

Snyder, T. E. 1949. *Catalog of the termites (Isoptera) of the world*. Smithsonian Misc. Collect. Vol. 112, 490 pp.

Snyder, T. E. 1956. *Annotated, subject-heading bibliography of termites 1350* B.C. *to 1954* A.D. Smithsonian Misc. Collect. Vol. 130, 305 pp.

Snyder, T. E. 1961. *Supplement to the annotated, subject-heading bibliography of termites 1955 to 1960*. Smithsonian Misc. Collect. Vol. 143, no. 3, 137 pp.

Snyder, T. E. 1968. *Second supplement to the annotated, subject-heading bibliography of termites 1961–1965*. Smithsonian Misc. Collect. Vol. 152, 188 pp.

Order 16

ZORAPTERA (Angel Insects)

These insects, not discovered until 1913, are found in little, gregarious clusters hidden under bark, in decaying wood, and often in sawdust piles. Although not much is known about their habits, they appear to eat fungi and perhaps mites.

Their name means "purely wingless," from the Latin *zoro* (pure) and *optera* (wingless). There is no indication why they are so-called except that only wingless individuals were known when the order was first discovered. Their common name, "Angel Insects," is taken from the Zoroastrian belief (an ancient Persian religion) that man's fate after death will depend on the good and evil in his life, the pure attaining the angelic state.

Diagnosis: L. 2–2.5 mm. Body soft; shape elongate, cylindrical; very pale tan to brownish. Antennae short, bead-like, with nine segments; biting mouthparts. Wings present on some individuals, absent on others of both sexes. Winged forms darker and apparently swarm, dropping wings after swarming. Front wings somewhat larger than hind; venation reduced to a few veins and no cross veins. Winged forms with compound eyes; wingless forms blind. Legs moderate, slender, without special modifications. Abdomen oval, cylindrical, with short, obscure terminal cerci. (See Fig. 16.1 for general body form of winged adult.)

Nymphs closely resemble the wingless adults.

Metamorphosis: Paurometabolous, with eggs that hatch into nymphs. The adult stage is reached after several months.

Collecting and preserving: Specimens are found by searching through sawdust piles, rotten wood, and under bark. They are preserved in 80-percent alcohol.

Rearing: It is reported that colonies may be reared in suitable sawdust.

Distribution: Twenty-four species have been described, all in the single family and genus listed below. They are found in North and South America, Africa, Hawaii, Samoa, Fiji, East Indies, and Sri Lanka.

Economic importance: These rare insects are never pests.

Fig. 16.1.

Fig. 16.2.

Although obviously a part of the detritus cycle, their role certainly is not very significant.

CLASSIFICATION

1. ZOROTYPIDAE (Angel Insect Family)

One genus in the U.S., as follows:

1.1 *Zorotypus* Silvestri

Two species, as follows:

Z hubbardi Caudell (Hubbard's Angel Insect). L. 2–2.5 mm. (1) PA, MD; (2) s.e. US; (3) TX; (5) MO. (See Fig. 16.2 for wingless adult.)

Z snyderi Caudell (Snyder's Angel Insect). L. 2–2.5 mm. Robust, cylindrical; brown to dark brown or blackish; head rather small; antennae short, nine-segmented; thorax with three distinct segments; legs short, rather stout; wings on thoracic segments are widely separated at the base, hind wings smaller than front wings, both with reduced venation. Frequently found in old sawdust piles. (See A&J 41.) (3) s. FL (also West Indies, Hawaii, East Indies, Sri Lanka, and w. Africa).

BIBLIOGRAPHY

Gurney, A. B. 1938. A synopsis of the order Zoraptera, with notes on the biology of *Zorotypus hubbardi* Caudell. *Proc. Ent. Soc. Washington*, 40(3): 57–87.

Riegal, Garland T. and Ferguson, M. B. 1960. New state records of Zoraptera. *Ent. News.* 71(8): 213–216.

Order 17

PSOCOPTERA (Booklice and Barklice)

These insects are usually very small and soft-bodied, with rather long antennae. Either wings have reduced venation with very few cells or they are absent. Sometimes the older ordinal name, Corrodentia, is used for this group, but Psocoptera is more often considered correct.

The formation of the name Psocoptera is rather odd. Its first part comes from the Greek word, *psokos*, meaning "rubbed small," hence "gnawed." This is combined with the Greek word for wing, *pteron*, which has nothing to do with the first part. The "psoco" obviously refers to the insect's manner of eating.

Booklice are often found in old books, among old papers, and in certain kinds of stored food such as cereals. They may become exceedingly abundant in closed buildings where there is plentiful food, for example, in the libraries of schools closed during the summer. Should they be mistaken for parasitic lice when discovered after the schools reopen, all manner of unnecessary concern may result.

Barklice, as their common name implies, are found on the bark and leaves of trees where they feed on algae, lichens, and organic debris. On rare occasions, they can become a pest by their sheer abundance in granaries, houses, and packing materials; in humid regions, they can become pests of insect collections. Once while studying tropical insects, the author experienced this type of nuisance; before his eyes, hungry barklice began to eat away parts of mounted mosquitoes as they were being examined under a microscope lens. It was necessary to keep the insect boxes closed at all times and well charged with a strong fumigant. Barklice are common scavangers in bird nests (where they are often confused with bird lice) and also in beehives, wasp's nests, and caves.

Diagnosis: L. 1.5–5 mm (rarely less than 1 mm or as large as 10 mm). Oval; pale or dusky; antennae long and slender, extending at least half the length of the body and often as long or longer than the body, with 12 to 20 or more segments. Mouthparts of the biting, mandibulate type (see Fig. 17.1 for those of a book louse). Wings various; rarely reduced in size or absent; the front pair larger than the hind pair and both membranous; venation with few or no cross veins. Legs moderate, not modified for special functions, although some are capable of jumping. Abdomen oval, without cerci. (See Fig. 17.2 for the general body form of a winged adult booklouse.)

The nymphs resemble the adults. They are often gregarious and found close to the adults.

Fig. 17.1.

Although these lice are sometimes confused with parasitic lice by the novice, the resemblance is only superficial even though they are closely related; none of the Psocoptera are ectoparasitic, and only rarely do they infest mammal hair.

Metamorphosis: Paurometabolous, with egg, nymphal, and adult stages.

Habits and habitats: In addition to the habits and habitats already mentioned, it is interesting to note that these rather obscure, usually overlooked insects are among the first to invade new islands, and no doubt they are a part of any pioneering fauna in disturbed areas.

Reproductive behavior: The coxae contain organs (Pearman's) that are presumably intended for stridulatory sound

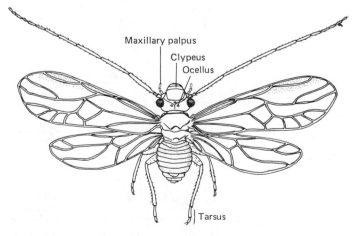

Fig. 17.2.

production, perhaps for use during courtship. In addition, a ticking noise has been described in adult female trogiids that is caused by the underside of the apex of the abdomen being struck against the surface. The purpose of this noise has not been described, but it is possible that it functions as a sex attractant. A courtship pattern has been observed in some species. The male either faces the female or approaches from behind, circles her, and finally backs under her from the front. Copulation takes place with the transfer of sperm in a spermatophore. Eggs, which are laid on the substrate or under leaves, may be covered with silk or an encrustation of debris. Some species lay their eggs singly and others lay them in groups. A few species are viviparous; others are parthenogenetic in some or all of their distribution range. Facultative parthogenesis has been reported.

Collecting and preserving: Psocoptera are far more abundant than their presence in collections would indicate. They are difficult to identify without the aid of a microscope and technical literature. By beating branches of trees—especially conifers, bushes, and foliage, particularly the bark of fallen branches—many specimens may be gathered. Abandoned bird and mammal nests are also worthy of attention, and shaded stone outcrops and stone and cement bridges harbor various species. A camel's hair brush dipped in alcohol or an aspirator is needed to pick up these tiny insects. Species in leaf and bark litter can be separated with a Berlese funnel or by using a sieve. Specimens should be preserved in 80-percent alcohol. Before specific identification can be made, it will often be necessary to mount dissected specimens on microscope slides.

Rearing: Very little information is available about rearing specimens, but it is likely that they will thrive in jars containing debris of various sorts, especially bark with algae collected at the site; yeast might also be added to the jar. The humidity must be kept at 70 to 90 percent.

Distribution: About 2500 species have been described, most of them found in tropical regions, with 245 named species in 56 genera in the U.S. and Canada. Many more species remain to be described and many more records are yet to be published on the Pscoptera of North America.

Notes on identification: The classification of the group on a worldwide basis has received some attention in the past few years, but much remains to be done before a comprehensive monograph of North American species can be prepared. The literature is scattered. Some of the larger works are listed in the Bibliography, and some of these refer to shorter works on specific genera.

Economic importance: As stated above, Psocoptera have been implicated as pests but certainly their depredations are of no great economic significance. No doubt they are an important part of the detritus cycle.

CLASSIFICATION

According to the most recent classification, there are 22 families grouped in three suborders in the U.S. and Canada. The following key to these families has been compiled from the notes given in Smithers (1972). All known North American genera are subsequently listed and assigned to the families indicated by Smithers. However, this classification differs greatly from the textbook treatment usually followed in the two countries. No doubt further changes will be made.

Key to the Families of Psocoptera

1.	Legs with 3 tarsomeres; antennae with more than 20 segments; labial palpi with 2 segments; ocelli separate or absent (Trogiomorpha)	2
	Legs with 3 tarsomeres; antennae with 11 to 17 segments; labial palpi one- or 2-segmented; ocelli separate (Troctomorpha)	5
	Legs with 2 or 3 tarsomeres; antennae with less than 14 segments; labial palpi 1-segmented; ocelli grouped (Psocomorpha)	6
2(1).	Ocelli absent; wings absent or rudimentary (Group Atropetae)	2. Trogiidae
	Ocelli present; wings present	3
3(2).	Front wings usually acuminate, clothed with scales (Group Atropetae)	1. Lepidopsocidae
	Front wings rounded, without scales	4
4(3).	Hind wing with M simple (Group Atropetae)	3. Psoquillidae
	Hind wing with M branched (Group Psocatropetae)	4. Psyllipsocidae
5(1).	Head long; ocelli separate (Group Amphientometae)	5. Amphientomidae
	Head short; body depressed; ocelli close together but not grouped on a tubercle (Group Nanopsocetae)	6. Liposcelidae
	Head medium length; body not depressed; ocelli widely spaced (Group Nanopsocetae)	7. Pachytroctidae
6(1).	Head long, vertical; claws straight, with a preapical tooth (Group Epipsocetae)	8. Epipsocidae
	Head usually short, transverse; claws with or without a preapical tooth	7
7(6).	Claws curved, with a preapical tooth	8
	Claws without a preapical tooth	9
8(7).	Legs with 2 tarsomeres	14
	Legs with 3 tarsomeres	18
9(7).	Labial palpi protruding, triangular	11
	Labial palpi ovoid	10
10(9).	Front and hind wings with reduced venation	19. Archipsocidae
	Front and hind wings with complete venation	18. Pseudocaeciliidae

Key to the Families of Psocoptera (*Contd.*)

11(9).	Front wings with M two-branched or unbranched **13. Polypsocidae**
	Front wing with M three-branched, or sometimes with more branches *12*
12(11).	Wings broad, costal margin thickened and densely hairy between base of pterostigma and wing apex ... **12. Amphipsocidae**
	Wings not particularly broad and without costal margin thickened; 1 row of setae on wing veins only ... *13*
13(12).	Pterostigma free; branches of veins in front wing with 1 row of setae **10. Caeciliidae**
	Pterostigma with veins running from posterior margin usually to Rs; front wings with veins (except Cu_2) setose, with 1 row of setae not crossing one another **11.Stenopsocidae**
	Pterostigma more or less rectangular **16. Ectopsocidae**
14(8).	Front wing with M and Cu_{1a} fused for some distance **23. Psocidae**
	Front wing without such a junction ... *15*
15(14).	Front wing with vein M three-branched *16*
	Front wing with vein M two-branched *17*
16(15).	Pulvillus narrow ... **14. Lachesillidae**
	Pulvillus filamentous (Subfamily Peripsocinae):............ **15. Peripsocidae**
	Pulvillus long, fine, slightly expanded (20.2 *Palmicola* and 20.3 *Reuterella*) **20. Elipsocidae**
17(15).	Areola postica absent (20.4 *Nepiomorpha*) **20. Elipsocidae**
	Areola postica present **17. Hemipsocidae**
18(8).	Wings with a mottling of irregularly confluent, small, dark marks **24. Myopsocidae**
	Wings without preceding pattern ... *19*
19(18).	Front wing's vein Cu_2 with setae ... *20*
	Front wing's vein Cu_2 without setae **21. Philotarsidae**
20(19).	Front wing with Rs and M joined by a cross vein **9. Ptiloneuridae**
	Front wing with Rs and M fused for a distance (20.1 *Elipsocus*) **20. Elipsocidae**

Suborder TROGIOMORPHA

Group ATROPETAE

1. LEPIDOPSOCIDAE (Scaly-winged Barklice Family)

Subfamily Lepidopsocinae

The five species representing this family in the U.S. and Canada have scales on their wings; usually there are wing markings; antennae are very long.

1.1 *Echmepteryx* Aaron

Three species, of which the following is common:

E. hageni (Packard) (Scaly-winged Barklouse). L. 1.5–5 mm. Brown; head grayish with brown markings; brown scales on thorax and front wings. Found on tree trunks and branches, they run rapidly and will take flight to escape capture. Most specimens are females. (1) n.e. US. (See A&J 42.)

[1.2 *Pteroxanium* Enderlein (1 sp., *P. kelloggi* (Ribaga))]

Subfamily Lepolepidinae

[1.3 *Lepolepis* Enderlein (1 sp., *L. occidentalis* Mockford)]

2. TROGIDAE (Granary Booklice Family)

Subfamily Trogiinae

[2.1 *Cerobasis* Kolbe (4 spp.)]

2.2 *Lepinotus* Heyden

Three species, of which the following two are commonly collected:

L. reticulatus Enderlein (Reticulate Winged Booklouse). Very common as a stored product pest.

L. inquilinus Heyden (Granary Booklouse). Found in granaries and houses, this species can be a pest because of its sheer abundance. There is some evidence that it may damage stored grain.

[2.3 *Myrmicodipnella* Enderlein (1 sp., *M. aptera* Enderlein)]

2.4 *Trogium* Illiger

One species, as follows:

T. pulsatorium (Linnaeus) (Larger Pale Booklouse). A common species in human habitations and nests of wasps and bees; widely dispersed by man.

3. PSOQUILLIDAE (Bird Nest Barklice Family)

Frequently found in bird nests, these barklice also occur on bark, human habitations, and elsewhere.

[3.1 *Psoquilla* Hagen (1 sp., *P. marginepunctata* Hagen); 3.2 *Rhyopsocus* Hagen (4 spp.)]

Group PSOCATROPETAE

4. PSYLLIPSOCIDAE (Cave Barklice Family)

This small family occurs in caves, in human habitations, and in tropical regions, especially in termite nests.

[4.1 *Dorypteryx* Aaron (2 spp.); 4.2 *Psocatropes* Ribaga (2 spp.)]

Fig. 17.3.

Fig. 17.4.

4.3 *Psyllipsocus* Selys-Longchamps

Two species, of which the following is widespread in the U.S.:

P. ramburii Selys-Longchamps. Occurs throughout the world; found in caves, leaf litter, mines, and human habitations; associated with man. (See Fig. 17.3.)

[4.4 *Speleketor* Gurney (sp., *S. flocki* Gurney)]

Suborder TROCTOMORPHA

Many of the species in this suborder are wingless and have been omitted from the family key.

Group AMPHIENTOMETAE

5. AMPHIENTOMIDAE (Tropical Barklice Family)

This rather large tropical family is characterized by its 15-segmented antennae, each segment secondarily annulated. Only two species are found in North America.

Subfamily Amphientominae

[5.1 *Pseudoseopsis* Badonnel (1 sp., *P. hellmani* Mockford and Gurney. (3) TX)]

5.2 *Stimulopalpus* Enderlein

One species, as follows:

S. japonicum Enderlein. Found on cement and stone surfaces. (1) OH, PA, MD, DC; (2) WV, VA, KY, TN, NC, SC.

Group NANOPSOCETAE

6. LIPOSCELIDAE (Booklice Family)

Thirty species of this large family occur in the U.S. and Canada:

Subfamily Embidopsocinae

[6.1 *Belaphotroctes* Roesler (5 spp.); 6.2 *Embidopsocus* Hagen (3 spp.)]

Subfamily Liposcelinae

6.3 *Liposcelis* Motschulsky

Twenty-two species, of which the following is an example:

L. bostrychophilus Badonell (Booklouse). This is the common, wingless species found in old books and damp places in houses. Several other species are common in houses. (See Fig. 17.4.)

7. PACHYTROCTIDAE (Thick Barklice Family)

[7.1 *Tapinella* Enderlein (2 spp.); 7.2 *Nanopsocus* Pearman (1 sp., *N. oceanicus* Pearman)]

Suborder PSOCOMORPHA

This suborder, the largest of the three, contains the remaining 17 families. The antennae of these species are usually shorter, although some are very long (as many as 13 segments). Most of the species mentioned here are winged.

Group EPIPSOCETAE

8. EPIPSOCIDAE (Damp Barklice Family)

Subfamily Epipsocinae

[8.1 *Epipsocus* Hagen (2 spp.)]

9. PTILONEURIDAE (Hairy-veined Barklice Family)

[9.1 *Ptiloneura* Enderlein (1 sp., unnamed) (3) s. AZ)]

Group CAECILIETAE

10. CAECILIIDAE (Lizard Barklice Family)

This large family is widely distributed throughout the world. North American species are assigned to the following genus:

10.1 *Caecilius* Curtis

Twenty-five species, including the following:

C. manteri Sommerman. (1) CT. (See Fig. 17.5.)

11. STENOPSOCIDAE (Narrow Barklice Family)

Most species of this family are Old World; one species occurs in the U.S.

[11.1 *Graphopsocus* Kolbe (1 sp., *G. cruciatus* (Linnaeus))]

Fig. 17.5.

12. AMPHIPSOCIDAE (Hairy-winged Barklice Family)

The single species found in North America occurs on vegetation.

Subfamily Dasydemellinae
Tribe Dasydemellini

[21.1 *Nepiomorpha* Pearman (1 sp., *N. peripsocoides* Mockford)]

13. POLYPSOCIDAE (Gnawing Barklice Family)

The habitat of most of the species assigned to this family is unknown. Of the 18 species in the world, only the following occurs in the U.S.

13.1 *Polypsocus* Hagen

One species, as follows:

P. corruptus (Hagen). On leaves of herbaceous plants, shrubs, and understory trees in deciduous forests and occasionally on foliage of hemlock and other conifers in mixed forests. (1) n.e. US; .s.e. US; (3) CA; (4) WA, OR.

Group HOMILOPSOCIDEA
14. LACHESILLIDAE (Fateful Barklice Family)

Two genera only, with species found in leaf litter, dried leaves, bark, and sometimes in stored products and buildings.

14.1 *Lachesilla* Westwood

Twenty-six species, the following being very common in barns and houses:

L. pedicularia (Linnaeus) (Cosmopolitan Grain Barklouse). Cosmopolitan.

[14.2 *Anomopsocus* Roesler (1 sp., *A. amabilis* (Walsh) [See Fig. 17.6.])]

15. PERIPSOCIDAE (Stout Barklice Family)

This rather large family is represented in the U.S. by the following genus:

Subfamily Peripsocinae

[15.1 *Peripsocus* Hagen (11 spp.)]

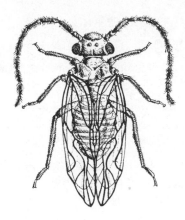

Fig. 17.6.

16. ECTOPSOCIDAE (Outer Barklice Family)

Nine species, as follows:

[16.1 *Ectopsocopis* Badonnel (1 sp., *E. cryptomeriae* (Enderlein)); 16.2 *Ectopsocus* McLachlan (8 spp.)]

17. HEMIPSOCIDAE (Leaf Litter Barklice Family)

[17.1 *Hemipsocus* Selys-Longchamp (2 spp.)]

18. PSEUDOCAECILIIDAE (False Lizard Barklice Family)

Subfamily Pseudocaeciliinae

[18.1 *Pseudocaecilius* Enderlein (3 spp.)]

19. ARCHIPSOCIDAE (Ancient Barklice Family)

[19.1 *Archipsocus* Hagen (5 spp.); 19.2 *Archipsocopsis* Badonel (4 spp.)]

20. ELIPSOCIDAE (Elliptical Barklice Family)

This family contains a number of genera with a sufficiently wide variety of featurs to make it difficult to define. The Key to the Families lists these genera and hence is essentially a key to the genera listed below.

Subfamily Elipsocinae

[20.1 *Elipsocus* Hagen (6 spp.)]

Subfamily Pseudopsocinae

[20.2 *Palmicola* Mockford (2 spp.); 20.3 *Reuterella* Enderlein (1 sp., *R. helvimacula* Enderlein)]

Subfamily Nepiomorphinae

[20.4 *Nepiomorpha* Pearman (1 sp., *N. peripsocoides* Mockford)]

21. PHILOTARSIDAE (Loving Barklice Family)

[21.1 *Aaroniella* Mockford (3 spp.); 21.2 *Philotarsus* Kolbe (2 spp.)]

22. MESOPSOCIDAE (Middle Barklice Family)

[22.1 *Mesopsocus* Enderlein (3 spp.)]

Group PSOCETAE
23. PSOCIDAE (Common Barklice Family)

This large family contains 62 species in the U.S. and Canada. They are found on bark and on rocks.

Subfamily Amphigerontiinae

[23.1 *Amphigerontia* Kolbe (4 spp.); 23.2 *Blaste* Kolbe (9 spp.); 23.3 *Blastopsocus* Roesler (5 spp.)]

Subfamily Cerastipsocinae
Tribe Cerastipsocini

[23.4 *Cerastipsocus* Kolbe (2 spp.)]

Tribe Metylophorini

[23.5 *Metylophorus* Pearman (3 spp.)]

Subfamily Psocinae

[23.6 *Camelopsocus* Mockford (5 spp.); 23.7 *Hyalopsocus* Roesler (2 spp.); 23.8 *Psocidus* Pearman (10 spp.); 23.9 *Psocus* Latreille (2 spp.); 23.10 *Trichadenotecnum* Enderlein (13 spp.); 23.11 *Indiopsocus* Mockford (5 spp.); 23.12 *Ptycta* Enderlein (2 spp.)]

24. MYOPSOCIDAE (Mouselike Barklice Family)

[24.1 *Lichenomima* Enderlein (11 spp.); 24.2 *Myopsocus* Hagen (1 sp., *M. antillanus* (Mockford))]

BIBLIOGRAPHY

Gurney, A. B. 1950. Corrodentia. From *Pest Control Technology* (Entomological Section, pp. 129–163). New York: National Pest Control Assn.

Mockford, E. L. 1951. The Psocoptera of Indiana. *Proc. Indiana Acad. Sci.*, 60: 192–204.

———. 1967. The electrentomoid psocids (Psocoptera). *Psyche*, 74: 118–165.

———. 1965–1969. The genus *Caecilius* (Psocoptera: Caeciliidae). *Trans. American Ent. Soc.* Part I, v. 91: 121–166; Part II, v. 92: 133–174; Part III, v. 95: 77–151.

———. 1978. A generic classification of family Amphipsocidae (Psocoptera: Caecilietae). *Trans. American Ent. Soc.* v. 104: 139–190.

Smithers, Courtenay N. 1965. A bibliography of the Psocoptera (Insecta). *Australian Zoologist*, 13(2): 137–209.

———. 1967. A catalog of the Psocoptera of the world. *Australian Zoologist*, 14(1): 1–145.

———. 1972. The classification and phylogeny of the Psocoptera. *Australian Museum, Memoir 14*, 351 pp.

Order 18

MALLOPHAGA (Chewing Lice)

Certainly it was no great evolutionary problem for certain barklice (Psocoptera) of long ago to evolve from scavengers on debris in bird nests to creatures living as ectoparasites on the birds themselves. These chewing lice, which now feed on their bird hosts and on some mammals, are placed in this separate order because of their specialized adaptation for ectoparasitic life. A study of the classification of these insects and that of their bird hosts shows some interesting parallels and has led entomologists and ornithologists to believe that as the bird groups evolved, so did the lice—a one-sided "coevolution."

The Latin name of the order is derived from the Greek words *mallos*, meaning "wool," and *phagus*, meaning "to eat." Thus, they were once believed to be wool eaters and were so named because the first kinds described were found in the fur of mammals.

The degree of host specificity—that is, obligate association of louse host taxa—varies greatly, although the restriction of one species of louse to one host species is commonly the case. Mallophaga spend their lives on the feathers or hair of the host and do not live long if removed from the host. Some of them apparently feed on blood exclusively; many others appear to be omnivorous, feeding on the feathers, hair, skin, blood, seba-cious fluids, or even other ectoparasites on the host. Their affinity for blood appears to have evolved independently of the blood-feeding Anoplura, or sucking lice, which are discussed in the next section.

Diagnosis: L. 0.5–6 mm (rarely as long as 10 mm). Body flattened; shape oval or elongate; pale tan, some with yellowish markings, or with dark brown or black bands. Head larger than thorax; antennae short, never more than half the length of head, not more than five-segmented; eyes very small or absent. Never any evidence of wings; legs reduced, stout, modified to attach to feathers or fur; abdomen simple, without cerci.

The eggs are usually attached to feathers or fur, often with surface sculpturing or plumelike processes. The nymphs resemble the adults and have the same habits.

The Mallophaga may be confused with several other groups, notably the Psocoptera, from which they can be readily distinguished by the differences in the antennae: short, with five or fewer segments in the Mallophaga; long, with ten or more segments in the Psocoptera. The eyes of the former are much reduced whereas those of the latter are relatively large. Chewing lice also have six or fewer spiracles whereas Psocoptera have seven or more. The Anoplura are also similar, but they have a

much smaller head, sucking mouthparts, and are all confined to mammal hosts.

Metamorphosis: Paurometabolous, with egg, nymphal, and adult stages.

Habits and habitats: Mallophaga probably infest all species of birds and 20 percent of the taxa of mammals, but not on Monotremata, Insectivora, Dermoptera, most Primates, Edentata, Lagomorpha, and Pholidota. The latter have different kinds of insects as ectoparasites (see Anoplura and Diptera).

Reproductive behavior: Eggs are singly attached to the hair or feathers of the host by a drop of water-impervious glue. The base of the egg and the feather or hair shaft is surrounded by this glue. The nymphs hatch from the egg and join the adults in feeding. They molt as growth takes place but change little in appearance.

Collecting and preserving: To collect Mallophaga, the living, or freshly killed, vertebrate host must be very carefully examined. Sometimes the lice will leave the host as it cools after death. A freshly killed bird or small mammal placed in a plastic bag may yield specimens. The lice and eggs collected from the bag should be placed in 80-percent alcohol. Specimens should be kept in this storage media until they are macerated and cleared; they are then mounted venter up on microscope slides for identification and study.

Rearing: Although possible, rearing is unnecessary since specimens may be collected from a host for experimental work or life history studies.

Distribution: There are approximately 5,000 described species of lice in the world, of which 943 species in 116 genera are recorded as infesting birds and mammals in (or visiting) the U.S. and Canada.

Identification notes: Identification of the species of Mallophaga requires an examination of a variety of anatomical features that are visible only by using a compound microscope. It is therefore necessary to mount specimens carefully on microscope slides. It is important also to identify, and record, the host.

Economic importance: Mallophaga do not infest man and are not involved in human disease transmission. They are of veterinary medical importance, however. Massive infestations can be lethal to young fowl and cause a drop-off of egg laying capacity among hens. Similar effects occur among other domestic animals as well as wild species.

CLASSIFICATION

The Mallophaga classification parallels that of bird hosts but very little that of mammal hosts. One must, however, be knowledgeable about the classification and identification of both groups. Unfortunately, since these associations have not always been recorded, there is a lack of host data in the older literature; some of the early host records, moreover, are inaccurate. Recent workers have done much to correct this situation. There are no comprehensive keys to the lice of the U.S. and Canada; what literature does exist is widely scattered in a variety of publications. The order is divided into three suborders and ten families. Families found in the U.S. and Canada may be identified by the Key to the Families.

Key to the Families of Mallophaga
(Adapted from key by Robert C. Dalgleish, *in litt.*)

1.	Maxillary palpi absent; 3rd antennal segment not pedunculate	**2**
	Maxillary palpi present; 3rd antennal segment pedunculate (Amblycera)	**4**
2(1).	Mandibles at end of long proboscis (Rhynchophthirina; in Africa and East Indies only) ...**Haematomyzidae**	
	Mandibles not at end of long proboscis (Ischnocera)	**3**
3(2).	One tarsal claw on all legs**2. Trichodectidae**	
	Two tarsal claws on all legs**1. Philopteridae**	
4(1).	Spiracles on segments III–VII (5 pair) ..	**5**
	Spiracles on segments III–VIII (6 pair)	**7**
5(4).	Meso- and metathoracic legs each with 1 tarsal claw	**6**
	Meso- and metathoracic legs each with 2 tarsal claws**8. Trimenoponidae**	
6(5).	Prothoracic leg with 1 tarsal claw (in Chile only)**Abrocomophagidae**	
	Prothoracic leg without a tarsal claw (Glirocolinae)**4. Gyropidae**	
7(4).	Meso- and metathoracic legs each with 1 tarsal claw	**8**
	Meso- and metathoracic legs each with 2 tarsal claws	**9**
8(7).	All legs with simple, unmodified tarsal claws (Protogyropinae)**4. Gyropidae**	
	Prothoracic leg and tarsal claw modified for clasping hair (Gyropinae) **4. Gyropidae**	
9(7).	Meso- and metanotum separate ...	**10**
	Meso- and metanotum fused ..	**11**
10(9).	Tergum I fused with metanotum**3. Boopidae**	
	Tergum I not fused with metanotum**6. Menoponidae**	
11(10).	Tergum I fused with metanotum**7. Ricinidae**	
	Tergum I not fused with metanotum**5. Laemobothriidae**	

Suborder ISCHNOCERA

The antennae of this suborder are filiform and exposed. The following two families—Philopteridae and Trichodectidae—are assigned here.

1. PHILOPTERIDAE (Bird Lice Family)

This very large family with 500 species and 61 genera contains several poultry pests.

[1.1 *Acidoproctus* Piaget (2 spp.); 1.2 *Acutifrons* Guimaraes (2 spp.)]

Fig. 18.1.

1.3 *Anaticola* Clay

Five species, of which the following two are common:

A. anseris (Linnaeus) (Slender Goose Louse).

A. crassicornis (Scopoli) (Slender Duck Louse). (See Fig. 18.1.)

[1.4 *Anatoecus* Cummings (5 spp.); 1.5 *Aquanirmus* Clay and Meinertzhagen (6 spp.); 1.6 *Ardeicola* Clay (15 spp.); 1.7 *Bruelia* Keler (62 spp.)]

1.8 *Campanulotes* Keler

One species, as follows:

C. bidentatus compar (Burmeister) (Small Pigeon Louse).

[1.9 *Carduiceps* Clay and Meinertzhagen (4 spp.)]

1.10 *Chelopistes* Keler

Two species, of which the following is common:

C. meleagridis (Linnaeus) (Large Turkey Louse). (See Fig. 18.2)

[1.11 *Cirrophthirius* Timmermann (1 sp., *C. testudinarius* (Children)); 1.12 *Colinicola* Carriker (4 spp.); 1.13 *Coloceras* Taschenberg (3 spp.)]

1.14 *Columbicola* Ewing

Seven species, of which the following is common:

C. columbae (Linnaeus) (Slender Pigeon Louse).

[1.15 *Craspedonirmus* Thompson (2 spp.); 1.16 *Craspedorrhynchus* Keler (11 spp.)]

Fig. 18.2.

1.17 *Cuclotogaster* Carriker

Two species, of which the following is common:

C. heterographis (Nitzsch) (Chicken Head Louse).

[1.18 *Cuculicola* Clay and Meinertzhagen (2 spp.); 1.19 *Cuculoecus* Ewing (3 spp.); 1.20 *Cummingsiella* Ewing (4 spp.); 1.21 *Degeeriella* Neuman (11 spp.); 1.22 *Docophoroides* Giglioli (5 spp.); 1.23 *Episbates* Harrison (1 sp., *E. pederiformis* (Dufour)); 1.24 *Esthiopterum* Harrison (1 sp., *E. brevicephalus* (McGregor)); 1.25 *Falcolipeurus* Bedford (5 spp.); 1.26 *Fulicoffula* Clay and Meinertzhagen (9 spp.)]

1.27 *Goniocotes* Burmeister

Six species, of which the following is common:

G. gallinae (De Geer) (Fluff Louse).

1.28 *Goniodes* Nitzsch

Twenty species, of which the following are common:

G. gigas (Taschenberg) (Large Chicken Louse).

G. dissimilis Denny (Brown Chicken Louse).

[1.29 *Haffneria* Timmerman (1 sp., *H. grandis* (Piaget)); 1.30 *Halipeurus* Thompson (14 spp.); 1.31 *Harrisoniella* Bedford (3 spp.); 1.32 *Ibidoecus* Cummings (6 spp.); 1.33 *Incidifrons* Ewing (5 spp.); 1.34 *Lagopoecus* Waterston (9 spp.)]

1.35 *Lipeurus* Nitzsch

Four species, of which the following are common:

L. caponis (Linnaeus) (Wing Louse).

L. numidae (Denny) (Slender Guinea Louse).

[1.36 *Lunaceps* Clay and Meinertzhagen (4 spp.); 1.37 *Mulcticola* Clay and Meinertzhagen (1 sp., *M. macrocephalus* (Kellogg)); 1.38 *Naubates* Bedford (3 spp.); 1.39 *Neophilopterus* Cummings (1 sp., *N. heteropygus* (Nitzsch)); 1.40 *Numidilipeurus* Tendeiro (1 sp., *N. lawrensis* Bedford); 1.41 *Ornithobius* Denny (6 spp.)]

1.42 *Oxylipeurus* Mjöberg

Nine species, of which the following is common:

O. polytrapezius (Burmeister) (Slender Turkey Louse).

[1.43 *Paraclisis* Timmermann (3 spp.); 1.44 *Pectinopygus* Mjöberg (12 spp.); 1.45 *Penenirmus* Clay and Meinertzhagen (10 spp.); 1.46 *Perineus* Harrison (4 spp.); 1.47 *Philoceanus* Kellog (5 spp.); 1.48 *Philopterus* Nitzsch (30 spp.); 1.49 *Physconelloides* Ewing (6 spp.); 1.50 *Picicola* Clay and Meinertzhagen (5 spp.); 1.51 *Pseudonirmus* Mjöberg (1 sp., *P. gurlti* (Taschenberg)); 1.52 *Quadraceps* Clay and Meinertzhagen (49 spp.); 1.53 *Rallicola* Johnston and Harrison (11 spp.); 1.54 *Rhynonirmus* Thompson (3 spp.); 1.55 *Rotundiceps* Edwards (1 sp., *R. cordatus* (Osborn)); 1.56 *Saemundssonia* Tinnermann (52 spp.); 1.57 *Strigiphilus* Mjöberg (13 spp.); 1.58 *Sturnidoecus* Eichler (7 spp.); 1.59 *Trabeculus* Rudow (5 spp.); 1.60 *Trogoninirmus* Eichler (1 sp., *T. eleganus* Emerson); 1.61 *Vernoniella* (2 spp.)]

2. TRICHODECTIDAE (Mammal Chewing Lice Family)

This family contains species that parasitize mammals instead of birds. Although some infest domestic animals, they are usually of little medical importance. There are 137 species in 10 genera reported in the U.S. and Canada.

Fig. 18.3.

2.1 *Bovicola* Ewing

Twelve species, of which the following are common:

B. equi (Denny) (Horse Chewing Louse).

B. caprae (Gurlt) (Goat Chewing Louse).

B. limbatus (Gervais) (Angora Goat Chewing Louse).

B. bovis (Linnaeus) (Cattle Chewing Louse). (See Fig. 18.3.)

B. ovis (Schrank) (Sheep Chewing Louse).

[2.2 *Eutrichophilus* Mjöberg (1 sp., *E. setosus* (Giebel))]

2.3 *Felicola* Ewing

Three species, of which the following is common:

F. subrostratus (Burmeister) (Cat Louse).

[2.4 *Geomydoecus* Ewing (102 spp.); 2.5 *Lutridia* Keler (1 sp., *L. exilis* (Nitzsch)); 2.6 *Neotrichodectes* Ewing (7 spp.); 2.7 *Stachiella* Keler (4 spp.); 2.8 *Suricatoecus* Bedford (2 spp.)]

2.9 *Trichodectes* Nitzsch

Three species, of which the following is common:

T. canis (De Geer) (Dog Chewing Louse).

[2.10 *Tricholipeurus* Bedford (2 spp.)]

[HEPTASOGASTERIDAE]

A family of about 18 genera found only in South America on the wingless avian family Tinamidae.

Suborder AMBYLCERA

Members of this suborder have somewhat clubbed antennae, which are usually concealed in grooves on the underside of the head. Six families are assigned here.

3. BOOPIDAE (Marsupial Chewing Lice Family)

3.1 *Heterodoxus* Le Souëf and Bullen

One species, as follows:

H. spiniger (Enderlein) (Australian Dog Louse). This species has apparently transferred from Australian marsupials to domestic dogs and has become widely distributed.

4. GYROPIDAE (Guinea Pig Lice Family)

The following four genera and four species have been recorded in the U.S. and Canada:

4.1 *Gliricola* Mjöberg

One species, as follows:

G. porcelli (Schrank) (Guinea Pig Louse).

4.2 *Gyropus* Nitzsch

One species, as follows:

G. ovalis Burmeister (Oval Guinea Pig Louse).

[4.3 *Macrogyropus* Ewing (1 sp., *M. dicotylis* (Macalister); 4.4 *Pitrufquenia* Marelli (1 sp., *P. coypus* Marelli)]

5. LAEMOBOTHRIIDAE (Hawk Lice Family)

This family infests birds of prey and some water fowl. One genus only in the U.S. and Canada, as follows:

5.1 *Laemobothrion* Nitzsch

Eight species, of which the following is common:

L. maximum Scopolli (Hawk Louse). L. 6.5–11 mm. Each side of the head has prominent enlargements in front of the eyes near the base of the antennae. Ectoparasitic on hawks and osprey. Throughout NA. (See A&J 43.)

6. MENOPONIDAE (Poultry Lice Family)

This large family infests many kinds of birds and includes some common pests of poultry. The 260 species are assigned to 35 genera.

[6.1 *Actornithophilus* Ferris (25 spp.); 6.2 *Amyrsidea* Ewing (7 spp.); 6.3 *Ancistrona* Westwood (1 sp., *A. vagelli* (Fabricius); 6.4 *Ardeiphilus* (1 sp., *A. floridae* Tuff); 6.5 *Austromenopon* Bedford (24 spp.); 6.6 *Bonomiella* Conci (2 spp.); 6.7 *Ciconiphilus* Bedford (5 spp.); 6.8 *Clayia* Hopkins (1 sp., *C. theresae* Hopkins); 6.9 *Colpocephalum* Nitzsch (25 spp.); 6.10 *Comatomenopon* Uchida (5 spp.); 6.11 *Cuculiphilus* (3 spp.); 6.12 *Dennyus* Neumann (6 spp.); 6.13 *Eidmaniella* Keler (4 spp.); 6.14 *Eucolpocephalum* Bedford (1 sp., *E. femorale* (Piaget); 6.15 *Eureum* Nitzsch (4 spp.); 6.16 *Fregatiella* Ryan and Price (1 sp., *F. aurifasciata* (Kellogg)); 6.17 *Gruimenopon* Clay and Meinertzhagen (1 sp., *G. canadense* Edwards); 6.18 *Helenomus* Ferris (1 sp., *H. assimilis* (Piaget)); 6.19 *Hohorstiella* Eichler (3 spp.); 6.20 *Holomenopon* Eichler (9 spp.); 6.21 *Kurodaia* Uchida (11 spp.); 6.22 *Longimenopon* (3 spp.); 6.23 *Machaerilaemus* Harrison (5 spp.)]

6.24 *Menacanthus* Neuman

Of the forty-one species in the U.S. and Canada assigned to this genus, the following is common:

M. stramineus (Nitzsch) (Chicken Body Louse).

6.25 *Menopon* Nitzsch

Two species, of which the following is common:

M. gallinae (Linnaeus) (Shaft Louse). L. 1.5–2 mm. Pale yellow. Found on chickens, ducks, and pigeons. Cosmopolitan. (See Fig. 18.4.)

[6.26 *Myrsidea* Waterston (30 spp.); 6.27 *Nosopon* Hopkins (1 sp., *N. lucidum* (Rudow)); 6.28 *Numidicola* Ewing (1 sp., *N. antennatus* (Kellogg and Paine)); 6.29 *Osborniella* Thompson (2 spp.); 6.30 *Piagetiella* Grosse (4 spp.); 6.31 *Plegadiphilus* Bedford (2 spp.); 6.32 *Procellariphaga* Eichler (12 spp.); 6.33 *Pseudomenopon* Mjöberg (12 spp.); 6.34 *Somaphantus* (1 sp., *S. lusius* Paine)]

Fig. 18.4.

6.35 *Trinoton* Nitzsch

Four species, of which the following two are common:

T. querquedulae (Linnaeus) (Large Duck Louse).

T. anserinus (Fabricius) (Goose Body Louse).

7. RICINIDAE (Hummingbird Lice Family)

These lice are found on hummingbirds and many passerine birds.

[7.1 *Ricinus* De Geer (29 spp.); 7.2 *Trochiliphagus* (1 sp., *T. ochoterenai* (Zavaletta); 7.3 *Trochiloecetes* Paine and Mann (2 spp.)]

8. TRIMENOPONIDAE (Marsupial Lice Family)

Members of this family occur on rodents and marsupials in South America. Only one species occurs in North America, as follows:

8.1 *Trimenopon* Cummings

One species, as follows:

T. hispidum (Burmeister) (Guinea Pig Louse).

[ABROCOMOPHAGIDAE]

One species, *Abrocomophaga chilensis* Emerson and Price, found on the rat chinchilla in Chile.

Suborder RHYNCHOPHTHIRINA

There is only one family with two species in this order. The head is prolonged into a rostrum, with the mandibles on the apex. Because these lice are blood-sucking insects, they are often considered to be a connecting link between the Mallophaga and the Anoplura. Some authors, therefore, consider the two orders to be a single order, the PHTHIRAPTERA, which is given the common name, Animal Lice.

[HAEMATOMYZIDAE]

These lice do not occur in the U.S. or Canada except in zoos. The following two species belong to the genus *Haematomyzus* Piaget: *H. elephatis* Piaget (Elephant Louse) and *H. hopkinsi* Clay (Wart Hog Louse).

BIBLIOGRAPHY

Emerson, K. C. 1972. *Checklist of the Mallophaga of North America (north of Mexico)*. Part 1. Suborder Ischnocera; Part 2. Suborder Amblycera; Part 3. Mammal Host List; Part 4. Bird Host List. Dugway, Utah: Desert Test Center, Dugway Proving Ground.

Kim, K. C. and H. W. Ludwig. 1978. Phylogenetic relationships of parasitic Psocodea and taxonomic position of Anoplura. *Ann. Ent. Soc. America*, 71:910–920.

Order 19

ANOPLURA (Sucking Lice)

The sucking lice are closely related to both the chewing lice and the Psocoptera and are even more specialized as ectoparasites than the former. All pierce the skin of their mammal hosts and feed by sucking blood, their mouthparts and head structure being highly modified and specialized for this function.

The ordinal name is derived from the two Greek words, *anoplos,* meaning "unarmed," and *ura,* meaning "tail." This refers to the lack of cerci or external copulatory structures.

Diagnosis: L. 0.5–5 mm. Dorso-ventrally flattened, oval, or circular; pale, sometimes with brownish or gray pigment. Head small, narrower than thorax; antennae about the length of head, with three to five segments; mouthparts piercing-sucking type; thorax about the same length as the head; wings entirely lacking. Legs short, inwardly bent, and fitted for climbing and grasping hair, with large apical claw that can be folded in to surround the shaft of hair. Abdomen oval, nine-segmented, unmodified, without cerci. The Anoplura are readily distinguished from the Mallophaga by the features given in the preceding section.

The nymphs resemble the adults and live on the same host with the parents.

Metamorphosis: Paurometabolous, with egg, nymphal, and adult stages.

Habits and habitats: All Anoplura are parasitic on the

skin of placental mammals. These insects rarely leave their host and die within a short time if they are removed or if the host dies. All species glue their eggs to the hair of the host except for one, *Pediculus humanus humanus,* the Body Louse. Each species is host specific. Transfer from one individual to another is effected almost entirely by body contact, although some lice hosted by human beings may be transferred by clothing or bedding.

Reproductive behavior: Other than their egg laying habits, little is known about the reproductive behavior of lice.

Collecting and preserving: Anoplura are collected and preserved in the same manner as the Mallophaga.

Rearing: Sometimes it is necessary to rear lice for medical experiments. They must be reared on the living host. The Body Louse, *Pediculus humanus humanus,* has been successfully reared on rabbits, however, in the laboratory of Insect Control and Research in Baltimore, MD.

Distribution: About 500 species of sucking lice are known. Fifty-six species in 17 genera have been recorded on the mammals of North America. There are many undescribed species.

Economic importance: Infestation with lice involves far more than the nuisance of their bites. They are vectors of numerous diseases of animals, including human beings. Such diseases as relapsing fever, trench fever, and particularly typhus—all transmitted by the Body Louse, *Pediculus humanus humanus*—have been responsible for more changes in human history than any other single causative agent (see also the discussion of mosquito-borne and flea-borne diseases). Louse infestation is generally the result of crowded conditions and poor sanitation. During wartime, outbreaks of these diseases have resulted in the illness and death of countless troops as well as members of the civilian population. It is reported that in Russia alone during the revolution of 1917–1922, ten million people became ill with typhus and three million died of it.

CLASSIFICATION

No comprehensive work on the Anoplura of North America is available as yet. Many changes in the classification in recent years have resulted in an unsettled family scheme, but recently Kim and Ludwig (1978) recognized 15 families throughout the world, nine of them in the U.S. and Canada, as indicated by the accompanying key.

Key to the Families of Anoplura
(Adapted from Kim and Ludwig, 1978)

1. Head with distinct eyes or subacute ocular points on lateral margins posterior to antennae *2*
 Head without external evidence of eyes or prominent ocular points . *5*
2(1). Head with prominent ocular points but without eyes; all legs subequal in size and shape, each tibia with a distal process . **3. Haematopinidae**
 Head with eyes with distinct lens but without ocular points . *3*
3(2). Head long and slender, much longer than thorax; abdomen narrowly elliptic, with small tuberculiform paratergites on abdominal segments 3 through 8 **4. Pecaroecidae**
 Head about as long as thorax; abdomen oval or elliptic, with paratergites as sclerotized caps or lobes . *4*
4(3). Compact body less than twice as long as wide; thorax very wide; abdomen short, as wide as thorax at base and narrower toward apex, with prominent, tubercular lateral lobes; front legs slender; middle and hind legs very stout, each with a stout claw **9. Pthiridae**
 Slender, with body more than twice as long as wide; abdomen long, wider than thorax, with paratergites as sclerotized caps or lobes . **8. Pediculidae**
5(1). Head and thorax thickly covered with setae; abdomen thickly covered with setae of various shapes and sizes including scales and spines; spiracular atrium tubular
 . **1. Echinophthiriidae**
 Head and thorax with only a few setae; abdomen without scales; spiracular atrium bulbous *6*
6(5). Front legs smallest; middle legs usually subequal to hind legs in size and shape or at least somewhat larger than front legs, each with larger and stouter claw; second abdominal segment without detached ventral plate . *7*
 Front legs subequal to middle legs in size and shape, both more slender and smaller than hind legs, and with acuminate claw; second abdominal segment usually with pair of small, sclerotized, detached ventral plates, or, if these plates absent, either antennae with less than 5 segments and abdomen without tergal and sternal plate, or basal segment of antennae ventrally with a heavily sclerotized plate bearing 3 to 5 large thornlike structures
 . **5. Enderleinellidae**
7(6). Abdomen with distinct paratergites, apically free from the body; front coxae mesally close together . *8*
 Abdomen without distinct paratergites, or at most with small tubercles posterior to each spiracle; front coxae widely separated from each other **2. Linognathidae**
8(7). Sternum of abdominal segment 2 extended laterally on each side to articulate with corresponding paratergal plates; hind legs largest, stout, each with a stout and blunt claw
 . **6. Hoplopleuridae**
 Sternum of abdominal segment 2 narrow, not extending laterally; middle legs usually subequal to hind legs in size and shape; very diverse group **7. Polyplacidae**

The following classification of families includes all of those recognized throughout the world. All are represented in the U.S. on zoo animals, but only those that are numbered have species that infest animals indigenous to the U.S. and Canada.

1. ECHINOPHTHIRIIDAE (Seal Louse Family)

Members of this family infest seals, sea lions, walrus, and river otter. Three of the five genera and three of the 12 species are found in the U.S. and Canada.

[1.1 *Antarctophthirus* Enderlein (1 sp., *A. callorhini* (Osborn)); 1.2 *Echinophthirius* Giebel (1 sp., *E. phocae* (Lucas)); 1.3 *Proechinophthirus* Ewing (1 sp., *P. fluctus* (Ferris))]

2. LINOGNATHIDAE (Pale Louse Family)

Sixty-nine species are assigned to this family throughout the world. They parasitize domestic animals, including those listed below, as well as wild cows, deer, giraffes, dogs, and hyraxes.

2.1 *Linognathus* Enderlein

Of the 51 species assigned to this genus, only four have been recorded in the U.S. and Canada. The following three are common on domestic animals:

L. stenopsis (Burmeister) (Goat Sucking Louse).

L. setosus (Olfers) (Dog Sucking Louse).

L. vituli (Linnaeus) (Longnosed Cattle Louse).

[2.2 *Solenopotes* Enderlein (3 spp.)]

[MICROTHORACIIDAE]

Four species in the single genus *Microthoracius* Fahrenholz are parasites of camels and llamas.

3. HAEMATOPINIDAE (Ungulate Louse Family)

Several species of this family are pests of domestic animals, as well as of wild cows, deer, pigs, horses, and zebras. Only the following genus with 22 species has been described for the world.

3.1 *Haematopinus* Leach

Four species in the U.S. and Canada, as follows:

H. suis (Linnaeus) (Hog Louse).

H. asini (Linnaeus) (Horse Sucking Louse).

H. eurysternus (Nitzsch) (Short Nosed Cattle Louse).

H. quadripertusus Fahrenholz (Cattle-tail Louse).

4. PECAROECIDAE (Pecarry Louse Family)

Only one species in this family as follows:

4.1 *Pecaroecus* Babcock and Ewing

P. javalii Babcock and Ewing. Parasitic on pecarries in the southwestern U.S. and Mexico.

5. ENDERLEINELLIDAE (Squirrel Louse Family)

The eight species assigned to this family infest rodents and squirrels in the U.S. and Canada. There are five genera and 49 species in the world.

5.1 *Enderleinellus* Fahrenholz

This genus contains 43 species, with seven species recorded in the U.S.

[5.2 *Microphthirus* Ferris (1 sp., *M. uncinatus* Ferris)]

6. HOPLOPLEURIDAE (Armored Louse Family)

Members of this large family (132 species in the world) are ectoparasites of rodents, pikas, moles, and shrews.

Subfamily Hoplopleurinae

[117 species in the world, including 6.1 *Hoplopleura* Enderlein (9 spp.)]

Subfamily Haematopinoidinae

6.2. *Haematopinoides* Osborn

One species only, as follows:

H. squamosus Osborn. Found on species of *Geomys* (gophers).

7. POLYPLACIDAE (Spiny Rat Louse Family)

Most of the species of this large family (175 species in the world) parasitize rodents; some parasitize rabbits, hares, or monkeys. North American genera follow.

7.1 *Polyplax* Enderlein

Three species in the U.S. and Canada, of which the following is common:

P. spinulosa (Burmeister) (Spined Rat Louse). (See Fig. 19.1.)

[7.2 *Fahrenholzia* Kellogg and Ferris (4 spp.); 7.3 *Neohaematopinus* Mjoeberg (12 spp.)]

7.4 *Haemodipus* Enderlein

One species, as follows

H. ventricosus (Denny) (Rabbit Louse).

Fig. 19.1.

Fig. 19.2.

8. PEDICULIDAE (Body Louse Family)

Two species, one with two subspecies as described below. They occur on New World monkeys, gibbons, great apes, and man.

8.1. *Pediculus* Linnaeus

P. humanus humanus Linnaeus (Body Louse). This subspecies infests fibers of clothing and attacks the body to feed on blood and then returns to the clothing. Also called the "cootie," it transmits typhus and relapsing fever. (See Fig. 19.2 and A & J 44.)

P. humanus capitis De Geer (Head Louse). This subspecies infests the hairs of the head, to which it glues its eggs. Transmission is by direct contact or from eggs on fallen hair. There is no known morphological difference between it and *P. humanus humanus*.

[HAMOPHTHIRIIDAE]

One species only in this family in the genus *Hamophthirius* Mjoeberg: *H. galeopitheci* Mjoeberg. Found on flying lemurs.

[HYBOPHTHIRIDAE]

One species only in this family in the genus *hybophthirus* Enderlein: *H. orycteropodis* Enderlein. Found on aardvarks.

[NEOLINOGNATHIDAE]

Two species in the genus *Neolinognathus* Bedford. Found on the Elephant Shrew.

Fig. 19.3.

[PEDICINIDAE]

Sixteen species assigned to the genus *Pedicinus* Gervais. Parasites of Old World monkeys.

[RATEMIIDAE]

Two species in the single genus *Ratemia* Fahrenholz. Found on zebras and asses.

9. PTHIRIDAE (Pubic Louse Family)

Two species in the world, one infesting man and the other the gorilla, in the following single genus:

9.1 *Pthirus* Leach

One cosmopolitan species infests human beings, as follows:

P. pubis (Linnaeus) (Pubic Louse or Crab Louse). Lives on the hairs of the pubic area and armpits of the body; may infest beards and eye brows. It is transmitted only by body contact because it never leaves these body regions. (See Fig. 19.3.)

BIBLIOGRAPHY

Buxton, P. A. 1946. *An account of the lice which infest man, their medical importance and control.* London: Edward Arnold and Co., 104 pp.

Ferris, G. F. 1951. The sucking lice. *Pacific Coast Ent. Soc. Mem.* 1, x + 320 pp.

Kim, K. C., and Ludwig, H. W. 1978. The family classification of Anoplura. *Systematic Ent.,* 3: 249–284.

Order 20

HEMIPTERA (Bugs)

This large group is often commonly referred to as the plant bugs or true bugs. Some entomologists unite Hemiptera with the Homoptera, the succeeding order, and refer to these two groups as the suborders Heteroptera and Homoptera.

Bugs are found throughout the world. They are abundant in numbers of species and individuals in both tropical and temperate regions. Many are serious crop pests and vectors of plant and animal diseases.

Most Hemiptera are easily recognized by the formation of the front pair of wings (as exemplified by those of the Miridae, Fig. 20.1). The basal portion of the wing is generally thickened to form a wing cover, but the apical portion is thin, membranous, and usually transparent. It is this particular structure that is referred to by the Latin name for this order, from *hemi,* meaning "half," and *pteron,* meaning "wing." The wings are held at rest with the apical portion crossing, an additional recognition mark. The triangular portion of the thorax exposed between the bases of the wings, the *scutellum,* is also a distinctive feature of the Hemiptera, but one that is shared with the Coleoptera. Hemiptera mouthparts are elongate, forming a beak that is used for piercing and sucking liquids. Most species are phytophagous and imbibe plant juices, but several zoophagous species feed on blood or body fluids.

Individuals of these insects are among the most abundant kinds seen in open fields, particularly on grasses; others are found on bushes and trees. A large number of species are aquatic.

Diagnosis: L. 1.0–50 mm (rarely larger in tropical species). Soft to hard bodied; shape of considerable variation, usually somewhat flattened, oval, or elongate cylindrical. A wide range of colors is found, including some of the most brilliant greens, reds, blues, and yellows; however, like most insects, most species of this order are dark. The head is bent down in front, with elongate, sucking mouthparts that extend backward between the legs when not in use; the antennae are short and slender, with at most only four or five segments. The wings are usually no longer than the abdomen and cover it when not in flight. A few species have short wings, and some are wingless as adults; hence, it is not always easy to distinguish nymphs from wingless adults without a careful examination of the dorsal surface of the abdomen, as discussed later on.

The basal, hardened portion of the front wing (Fig. 20.1) is termed the *corium*; the apical, membranous portion, the *membrane.* The triangular area, when present, at the tip of the corium is the *cuneus,* and the oblong basal part along the inner

Fig. 20.1. (*Courtesy of John N. Belkin*)

edge is the *clavus.* All are important terms in the descriptions of Hemiptera families. The legs are slender, with the front legs sometimes raptorial and the middle and/or hind legs sometimes fitted for swimming by the presence of a fringe of long hairs and a flattened, paddlelike shape. In some species, the hind femora is enlarged for jumping. The abdomen of the adults sometimes has complex terminal copulatory appendages, which are at least partially withdrawn into the abdomen if not entirely concealed; cerci are absent. (See Fig. 20.2 for principal body parts.)

Both the aquatic and the terrestrial nymphs closely resemble the adults. Terrestrial nymphs have two or three pairs of odor glands near the middle of the dorsum of the abdomen that open through pores surrounded by modified exoskeleton. The most obvious difference between adults and nymphs, of course, except in apterous forms, is the absence of functional wings. Wing pads appear in the early instars and increase in size through successive molts. There are four, five, or sometimes more molts, depending upon the species.

Hemiptera and many Homoptera species closely resemble each other, but the wings of species of Homoptera do not have the basal half of the wing thickened, and they hold their wings rooflike over the abdomen instead of flat with wing tips crossed as the Hemiptera do. Other differences include the way the mouthparts arise from the head. In the Hemiptera, the proboscis appears to originate from the front or ventral part of the head, except in some water bugs whose inflexed head brings the insertion of the mouthparts against the front coxae; in the Homoptera, the proboscis seems to come from the back of the head between the front legs.

Metamorphosis: Paurometabolous, with egg, nymphal, and adult stages present.

Habits and habitats: The general habit of feeding on plant juices is characteristic of most terrestrial species of Hemiptera.

Fig. 20.2. (*Drawings by H. H. Knight, from Blatchley, 1926*)

A considerable number, however, are predatory on other insects, spiders, and various other invertebrates. A few of these have developed blood-sucking habits and feed on large animals, including man and domestic animals. One family, the Cimicidae (20), including the infamous Bed Bug and other species, are ectoparasites of mammals and birds and live exclusively on their blood. As a result, several species have become important vectors of serious human diseases. Even some plant-feeding species will occasionally pierce the skin and appear to draw blood; such bites are usually defensive and not for feeding.

Terrestrial species have a distinctive smell because of a substance produced in glands on the dorsal side of the abdomen in nymphs and in the metathorax of the adults. This substance seems to repel ants and other possible predators. It is poisonous and often lethal if squirted onto the integument of other insects because its fat-dissolving chemical, tridecane, can destroy the waxy protective covering on the surface of the integument.

The only insects found living in the open ocean far out at sea (that is, past the intertidal zone) are the marine Water Striders (*Halobates* spp.), members of the family Gerridae (27). Why only this single genus of insects has produced exclusively marine species is one of the mysteries of evolution.

Reproductive behavior: Eggs may be laid conspicuously on open surfaces or more or less out of harms way in cracks or crevices or actually imbedded in plant tissues. Many plant-juice feeders will also suck eggs of other insects, including other Hemiptera. Nymphs are frequently—in fact, usually—found with the adults. Mating takes place as groups of nymphs and adults are feeding.

Ordinarily, copulation is effected by the insertion of the male's intromittent organ into the female's genital orifice. The mating behaviour of the bed bugs—the Cimicidae (20)—however, is unique. The male organ punctures the body wall of one of the abdominal segments of the female. Sperm are placed in a sac, the *spermalege,* which is not connected to the reproductive system of the female. Instead, the spermatozoa leave this sac and actually migrate through the body cavity, eventually reaching the seminal conceptacles located at the lower end of the oviducts. Here they are stored for a later fertilization of the eggs. This method of fertilization, referred to as *traumatic insemination,* also occurs in Polyctenidae, (19), Anthocoridae (21), and the exotic family Plokiophilidae.

Collecting and preserving: Beating vegetation, using a sweep net over fields, seining through water, and UV lights at night will yield a great number of species of bugs. Adults may be mounted on insect pins. Nymphs and very soft-bodied species should be preserved in 80-percent alcohol. The colors of most species will be preserved, but green specimens tend to turn brown.

Rearing: Plant-feeding species are easily reared by feeding them their host plant. Most species will feed on a variety of plants; some are host specific. Predatory species are more difficult to rear. Predatory aquatic species, which make interesting additions to aquaria, must be provided with living aquatic food.

Distribution: The approximate count of Hemiptera species for the world is 50,000, but many species in tropical regions remain to be described, and even in temperate regions more species are discovered each year. There are 3,587 species in 630 genera presently recorded in the U.S. and Canada.

Notes on identification: Special structures of the front wing have already been named, and their characteristics are used in the identification tables and keys. The identification of some groups of Hemiptera is difficult without a good library, although families are relatively easy to identify. Many species found in the eastern U.S. may be identified by referring to Blatchley (1926). Other comprehensive works are useful for many families. Species in the large families, such as Miridae (23), are not easily identified without the aid of a specialist. Many common species found locally can be recognized by their size, shape, and often their color pattern alone and may be correctly spot-identified once compared with previously identified specimens.

Economic importance: Hemiptera of many families, but particularly the Miridae (23), are notorious crop pests. They weaken plants by their injurious bites and, in addition, transmit plant diseases. On the other hand, some predatory species of certain families like the Pentatomidae (3)—a family that also includes plant pests—are beneficial because they help keep down populations of other noxious insects. A few, such as the Bed Bug and some members of the Reduviidae (17), transmit diseases contractable by human beings. The order probably ranks fourth among the economically destructive orders.

CLASSIFICATION

This large order is divided into two suborders and 40 distinct families in the U.S. and Canada, as shown in the following Key to the Families and Tables 20.1 and 20.2. Superfamily names are used by some authors, but this practice has yet to find general acceptance.

Key to the Families of Adult Hemiptera

1. Head very broad and short, with posterior part, including compound eyes, flattened and overlapping pronotum ... **36. Corixidae**
 Head not like the preceding and not broadly overlapping pronotum................. *2*

2(1). Body more or less globular, beetlelike; front wings without membrane, greatly thickened, meeting each other along straight line and covering entire abdomen; labium arising apparently from prothorax and sheathed at base by extensions of propleura........ ..**35. Pleidae**
 Body and front wings not like the preceding; labium not sheathed by propleura....... *3*

3(2). Hind leg without claws and with tibia and tarsus flattened and provided with long fringes; middle leg with normal claws; front wings with distinct membrane and tightly covering the strongly convex abdomen **34. Notonectidae**
 Hind leg claws similar to those of middle leg; front wings with distinct membrane flexed flat over abdomen and usually with tips overlapping; front wing usually thickened at base and membranous apically, or wing may be absent *4*

4(3). Antennae shorter than head and usually hidden in lateral or ventral grooves below eye *5*
 Antennae longer than head and usually exposed *9*

5(4). Ocelli present ..,.... *6*
 Ocelli absent .. *7*

6(5). Antennae hidden in grooves below strongly protuberant eye; front legs raptorial with femora very broad and grooved for reception of curved tibiae ... **40. Gelastocoridae**
 Antennae exposed; eye not strongly protuberant; front legs not raptorial, similar to middle legs ... **41. Ochteridae**

7(5). Membrane of front wing without veins; apex of abdomen without protruding appendage ... **39. Naucoridae**
 Membrane of front wing with a network of veins; apex of abdomen with protruding appendage, either short and straplike or long and slender *8*

8(9). Apical abdominal appendage short, flat, and retractile; hind leg flattened and fringed ... **38. Belostomatidae**
 Apical abdominal appendage long, slender, and nonretractile; hind leg not flattened and not fringed .. **37. Nepidae**

9(4). Compound eye absent; combs of short spinulets, or small spines, present on at least head and scape of antennae **19. Polyctenidae**
 Compound eye present; combs not developed *10*

10(9). Front legs with claws arising in a longitudinal cleft of tarsus *11*
 Front leg with claws arising at apex of uncleft tarsus *12*

11(10). Hind femora extending well beyond apex of abdomen, and base of middle legs closer to hind legs than to front legs **28. Gerridae**
 Hind femora extending slightly, if at all, beyond apex of abdomen, or legs evenly spaced ... **29. Veliidae**

12(11). Body and legs linear and head at least as long as entire thorax **27. Hydrometridae**
 Body and legs varied; if linear, then head shorter than entire thorax *13*

13(12). Body clothed with dense, short, velvety hydrofuge pile, at least ventrally; both clavus and membrane clear and veinless; small semiaquatic bugs with cursorial legs *14*
 Body not clothed with fine hydrofuge pile; terrestrial *15*

14(12). Labium 4-segmented; 2 tarsomeres; body stout, legs short **31. Hebridae**
 Labium 3-segmented; 3 tarsomeres, basal tarsomere very short; body slender, legs elongate .. **30. Mesoveliidae**

15(13). Antennae 5-segmented; scutellum very large, sometimes nearly covering entire abdomen ... *16*
 Antennae 4-segmented; scutellum moderate or large, sometimes concealed *19*

16(15). Front legs raptorial; femora enlarged; (in part) **18. Nabidae**
 Front legs with slender femora ... *17*

17(16). Tibiae with several rows of spinulets **1. Cydnidae**
 Tibiae with slender bristles only ... *18*

18(17). Scutellum large, almost completely covering corium and reaching, or almost reaching, end of abdomen ... **2. Thyreocoridae**
 Scutellum much smaller, not reaching end of abdomen **3. Pentatomidae**

19(18). Hemelytron and/or pronotum with lacelike or honeycomblike sculpturing. *20*
 Hemelytron and pronotum without lacelike or honeycomblike sculpturing *21*

20(19). Ocelli present; pronotum not extending over scutellum **10. Piesmatidae**
 Ocelli absent; pronotum extending over scutellum **14. Tingidae**

21(19). Body greatly flattened dorsoventrally ... *22*
　　　　 Body not greatly flattened dorsoventrally *23*

22(21). Labium 3-segmented; 3 tarsomeres **20. Cimicidae**
　　　　 Labium 4-segmented; 2 tarsomeres **13. Aradidae**

23(21). Antennal scape and pedicel very short and thick, flagellar segments very slender; 3 tarsomeres; labium 3-segmented; ocelli present; very small (3.5 mm or less) *24*
　　　　 Without preceding combination of characteristics *26*

24(23). Head including eyes, pronotum, front wings, and front legs very spiny
　　　　 ...**32. Leptopodidae**
　　　　 Head, eyes, pronotum, front wings, and front legs not spiny *25*

25(24). Eye lobe overlapping anterolateral angle of pronotum............ **26. Schizopteridae**
　　　　 Eye lobe not overlapping anterolateral angle of pronotum **25. Dipsocoridae**

26(23). Ocelli absent ... *27*
　　　　 Ocelli present ... *31*

27(26). Labium 4-segmented, elongate, and straight at base *28*
　　　　 Labium 3-segmented, short, and curved at base *34*

28(27). Hemelytron with cuneus; corium with distinct subapical marginal fracture, wing bent down beyond fracture ... **23. Miridae**
　　　　 Hemelytron without cuneus; corium without fracture, wing not bent down. *29*

29(28). Front femora swollen; (in part) **7. Lygaeidae**
　　　　 Front femora not swollen ... *30*

30(29). Pronotum with sharp lateral margin **8. Pyrrhocoridae**
　　　　 Pronotum with rounded lateral margin **9. Largidae**

31(26). Middle and hind tarsi with 1 or 2 tarsomeres; small or minute sizes *32*
　　　　 Middle and hind tarsi with 3 tarsomeres; size varied *34*

32(31). Hemelytron with cuneus **22. Microphysidae**
　　　　 Hemelytron without cuneus ... *33*

33(32). Front leg raptorial; femora and tibiae enlarged; pronotum lobed; hemelytron entirely membranous; labium 3-segmented **15. Enicocephalidae**
　　　　 Front femora and front tibiae not enlarged; pronotum not lobed; hemelytron thickened except on posterior part of apex **11. Thaumastocoridae**

34(31, Hemelytron with cuneus; size, usually 2–3 mm *35*
　27). Hemelytron without cuneus; size varies *36*

35(34). Labium 3-segmented **21. Anthocoridae**
　　　　 Labium 4-segmented (Isometopinae) **23. Miridae**

36(35). Labium 3-segmented ... *37*
　　　　 Labium 4-segmented ... *40*

37(36). Labium long, straight **33. Saldidae**
　　　　 Labium short, curved at base *38*

38(37). Prosternum without groove for reception of labium; (in some) **18. Nabidae**
　　　　 Pronotum with groove for reception of labium *39*

39(38). Front femora greatly enlarged, more or less triangular in outline; apical antennal segment swollen **16. Phymatidae**
　　　　 Front femora at most moderately enlarged, not triangular; apical antennal segment not swollen; (in part) **17. Reduviidae**

40(36). Arolia absent; (in part) .. **18. Nabidae**
　　　　 Arolia present ... *41*

41(40). Body and appendages linear sometimes stout and heavily spined; scape of antennae very long and clubbed apically, terminal flagellar segment spindle-shaped
　　　　 ... **12. Berytidae**
　　　　 Body and appendage shape varied; antennae not like the preceding *42*

42(41). Membrane of hemelytron with only 4 or 5 veins; (in part) **7. Lygaeidae**
　　　　 Membrane of hemelytron with numerous veins *43*

43(42). Metathoracic ostiolar openings absent or greatly reduced. **6. Rhopalidae**
　　　　 Metathoracic ostiolar openings large and conspicuous *44*

44(43). Bucculae not extending backward beyond bases of antennae; interocular distance greater than basal width of scutellum **5. Alydidae**
　　　　 Bucculae extending backward beyond bases of antennae; interocular space not as great as basal width of scutellum .. **4. Coreidae**

1. CYDNIDAE (Burrower Bug Family)

Diagnosis: L. 3–8 mm. Black or reddish-brown bugs with front tibiae flattened and spined, fitted for digging. Scutellum is large but does not cover wings. Thirty-six species assigned to the following subfamilies and genera.

Subfamily Sehirinae

1.1. *Sehirus* Amyot and Serville

One species in the U.S. and Canada, as follows:

S. cinctus (Palisot de Beauvois). L. 4–7 mm. Shining black to blue-black or dark reddish-brown; narrow white margins

along body. Adults active from April to August. Found on milkweed, wild cherry, timothy, blue grass, wild plum, nettles, mint, and other low vegetation. (See Fig. 20.3.) (1) n.e. NA; (2) s.e. US; (3) s.w. US; (4) Pacific n.w.; (5) n. Central States.

Subfamily Cydninae

[1.2 *Microporus* Uhler (2 spp.); 1.3 *Melanaethus* Uhler (11 spp.); 1.4 *Pangaeus* Stål (5 spp.); 1.5 *Cyrtomenus* Amyot and Serville (2 spp.); 1.6 *Tominotus* Mulsant and Ray (4 spp.); 1.7 *Dallasiellus* Berg (6 spp.)]

Subfamily Amnestinae

1.8 *Amnestus* Dallas

Five species in the U.S., of which the following is a common representative:

A. spinifrons (Say). L. 3.2–4.2 mm. Chestnut-brown, wings paler; antennae and ventral surface reddish-brown; legs dull yellow. Adults active from May to October. Found on

Fig. 20.3. (*From Blatchley, 1926*)

Fig. 20.4. (*From Blatchley, 1926*)

herbage in low moist ground or under decaying wood. (See Fig. 20.4) (1) n.e. US; (2) s.e. US; (3) TX; (5) KS.

2. THYREOCORIDAE (Negro Bug Family)

[= Corimelaenidae]

Diagnosis: L. 3–6 mm. This family resembles beetles. Greatly enlarged scutellum that covers wings and abdomen; shining black, sometimes purplish, bronze, or greenish, rarely marked with white, yellowish-white, or orange-red. Thirty

Table 20.1 The Families of the Hemiptera of the U.S. and Canada

Suborder DIPSOCOROMORPHA

1. Cydnidae (Burrower Bug Family)
2. Thyreocoridae (Negro Bug Family)
3. Pentatomidae (Stink Bug Family)
4. Coreidae (Squash Bug Family)
5. Alydidae (Broad Headed Bug Family)
6. Rhopalidae (Scentless Plant Bug Family)
7. Lygaeidae (Seed Bug Family)
8. Pyrrhocoridae (Cotton Stainer Family)
9. Largidae (Red Bug and Ant Mimic Bug Family)
10. Piesmatidae (Ash-gray Leaf Bug Family)
11. Thaumastocoridae (Royal Palm Bug Family)
12. Berytidae (Stilt Bug Family)
13. Aradidae (Flat Bug Family)
14. Tingidae (Lace Bug Family)
15. Enicocephalidae (Unique-headed Bug Family)
16. Phymatidae (Ambush Bug Family)
17. Reduviidae (Assassin and Thread-legged Bug Family)
18. Nabidae (Damsel Bug Family)
19. Polyctenidae (Bat Bug Family)
20. Cimicidae (Bed Bug Family)
21. Anthocoridae (Minute Pirate Bug Family)
22. Microphysidae (Minute Bladder Bug Family)
23. Miridae (Plant Bug Family)
24. Dipsocoridae (Ground Bug Family)
25. Schizopteridae (Jumping Soil Bug Family)

Suborder NEPOMORPHA

26. Hydrometridae (Marsh Treader Bug Family)
27. Gerridae (Water Strider Bug Family)
28. Veliidae (Smaller Water Strider Bug Family)
29. Mesoveliidae (Water Treader Bug Family)
30. Hebridae (Velvet Water Bug Family)
31. Leptopodidae (Spiny-legged Bug Family)
32. Saldidae (Shore Bug Family)
33. Notonectidae (Backswimmer Bug Family)
34. Pleidae (Pigmy Backswimmer Bug Family)
35. Corixidae (Waterboatman Bug Family)
36. Nepidae (Waterscorpion Bug Family)
37. Belostomatidae (Giant Water Bug Family)
38. Naucoridae (Creeping Water Bug Family)
39. Gelastocoridae (Toad Bug Family)
40. Ochteridae (Velvety Shore Bug Family)

Table 20.2 Family Groups of the Hempitera

NOTE: The following families (all very small, usually under 3 mm) are omitted from these tables but they are treated in the text and family key: (10) Piesmatidae; (11) Thaumastocoridae; (15) Enicocephalidae; (19) Polyctenidae; (22) Microphysidae; (24) Dipsocoridae; (25) Schizopteridae; (30) Hebridae; and (31) Leptopodidae.

1. *The short-horned bugs:* Bugs with antennae shorter than head and concealed, or nearly so, beneath the head.
 - 1.1 *Short-horned water bugs:* Bugs that live in and rarely leave the water. (See Table A.)
 - 1.2 *Short-horned shore bugs:* Bugs that live near the water; ocelli present. (See Table B.)
2. *The long-horned bugs:* Bugs with antennae at least as long as the head and prominent, rarely concealed under the head [see Phymatidae (16) for exception].
 - 2.1 *Semiaquatic long-horned bugs:* Bugs that live on or near the water. (See Table C.)
 - 2.2 *Terrestrial bugs:* Bugs with four-segmented antennae (minute intermediate segments between principle segments not counted). (See Table D.)
 - 2.3 *Stink Bugs and allies:* Bugs with five-segmented antennae. (See Table E.)

Table A Short-horned Water Bugs

Family	Front Legs	Appearance	Length (mm)
(35) Corixidae	One tarsomere, scoop-shaped	Oval, surface with fine transverse lines; middle legs long; wings without differentiated texture; beak short and broad	3–11
(33) Notonectidae	Two tarsomeres, not raptorial	Elongate, wedge-shaped; dorsal surface convex, keeled; swim upside down; hind legs long	1.8–15.5
(34) Pleidae	Not raptorial	Small, oval; hind legs no longer than others	1.5–2.5
(37) Belostomatidae	Raptorial	Very large; middle and hind legs about the same length	25–60
(38) Naucoridae	Raptorial	Broadly oval; front femora enlarged; middle and hind legs slender	6–15
(36) Nepidae	Raptorial; tarsi one-segmented	Oval or elongate, with long caudal breathing tube (16–44 mm)	18–46

Table B Short-horned Shore Bugs

Family	Antennae	Front Legs	Proboscis	Length (mm)
(39) Gelastocoridae	Hidden	Raptorial	Short	5–10
(40) Ochteridae	Exposed	Not raptorial	Long	4–5

Table C Semiaquatic Long-horned Bugs

Family	Ocelli	Antennae	Tarsi	Hind Femora	Shape, Length (mm)
(27) Gerridae	Present	Stout	Tip of last segment cleft	Extended beyond abdomen	Slender, 5–15 mm
(28) Velidae	Absent	Stout	Same as above	About even with abdominal apex	Elongate, oval, 2–5 mm
(26) Hydrometridae	Absent	Slender	Tip of last segment entire	Somewhat shorter than abdomen	Very slender, 7–11 mm
(29) Mesoveliidae	Present	Slender	Tip of last segment entire	About even with abdominal apex	Oval, 2–4 mm
(32) Saldidae	Present	Stout	Tip of last segment entire	Shorter than abdomen	Oval, 3–6 mm

Table D Terrestrial Bugs with Four-segmented Antennae

Family	Ocelli	Front Wings	Proboscis	Other Features	Length (mm)
(20) Cimicidae	Absent	Absent or vestigial	Four-segmented	Wingless; ecto-parasites of birds, mammals	3–6
(21) Anthocoridae	Present	Cuneus present	Three-segmented	Tarsi three-segmented	2–5
(23) Miridae	Absent	Cuneus present	Four-segmented	Tarsi three-segmented	2–10
(18) Nabidae	Present	Cuneus absent	Four-segmented	Front legs slender, used to grasp prey	7–11
(17) Reduviidae	Usually present	Cuneus absent	Three-segmented	Front femora sometimes greatly thickened	7–36
(16) Phymatidae	Present	Cuneus absent	Three-segmented	Front legs raptorial	5–12
(14) Tingidae	Absent	Cuneus absent	Four-segmented	Pronotum with process extending over scutellum	3–5
(13) Aradidae	Absent	Cuneus absent	Four-segmented	Very flat; tarsi two-segmented	3–11
(7) Lygaeidae	Usually present	Cuneus absent; four to five veins only	Four-segmented	Tarsi three-segmented	2–20
(12) Berytidae	Present	Cuneus absent	Four-segmented	First segment of antennae long, enlarged apically; legs very long; body slender	5–9
(9) Largidae	Absent	Cuneus absent; many veins	Four-segmented	Pronotum rounded laterally; some antlike	7–18
(8) Pyrrhocoridae	Absent	Without cuneus	Four-segmented	Pronotum margined laterally	8–18
(4) Coreidae	Present	Cuneus absent; many veins	Four-segmented	Head narrow, shorter than pronotum; dark colors	10–20
(6) Rhopalidae	Present	Cuneus absent; many veins	Four-segmented	Head narrower than prono-tum; pale colors	5.5–14
(5) Alydidae	Present	Cuneus absent; many veins	Four-segmented	Head about as wide as pronotum	10–18

Table E Stink Bugs and Allies (with Five-Segmented Antennae)

Family	Scutellum	Tibiae	Special Features	Length (mm)
(3) Pentatomidae, Scutellerinae	Very large, rounded posteriorly, covering most of abdomen	With stout setae only	Scutellum reaching tip of abdomen	8–10
Pentatominae	Triangular, not covering abdomen	With small setae only	Many species with sharp lateral pronotal spines; tarsi two and three segmented	6–23
Acanthosominae, Tessaratominae, Asopinae	Very large, rounded posteriorly, covering most of abdomen	With small setate only	Small, brownish, rare	3–7
(1) Cydnidae	Triangular, not covering abdomen	With large spines	Black; pronotum with nearly straight sides, margined; tarsi three-segmented	3–8
(2) Thyreocoridae	Very large, rounded posteriorly, covering most of abdomen	With large spines	Black; pronotum with sides arcuate, not margined	3–6

species are known in southern Canada and the U.S. They are difficult to identify as to species. The following three genera are not assigned to subfamilies.

2.1 *Galgupha* Amyot and Serville

Six species in the U.S., of which the following is common:

G. atra Amyot and Serville. L. 4.6–6 mm. Shining black with weak punctations dorsally. In summer, this species is found on grass and weeds in moist soil along roads, edges of woods and streams; in autumn, under leaves and fallen masses of grass; in winter, under logs, roots, or under leaves of mullein. (1) n.e. US; (2) s.e. US; (3) OK, TX, NM, AZ; (4) WA; (5) n. Central States.

2.2 *Cydnoides* Malloch

Six species in the U.S., all western except for one that extends into (2) FL.

2.3 *Cormelaena* White

Eighteen species in the U.S. and Canada, of which the following is common:

C. pulicaria (Germar) (Negro Bug). L. 3–3.5 mm. Black with front wings margined with pale yellow that broadens at the base. Found on flowers, Wild Plum, Jersey Tea, Spanish Needles, *Veronica* spp., Smartweed, Tanzy, Red Clover, and grass of various species; sometimes a pest on berries. Adults, which are active in spring and summer, may be found in April under dead leaves along fence rows. (See Fig. 20.5.) Very common throughout US and s. Canada. (1), (2), (3), (4), (5).

3. PENTATOMIDAE (Stink Bug Family)

[=Scutelleridae; Acanthosomatidae; Podopidae]

Diagnosis: L. 6–23 mm (many species of moderate to large size, that is, over 7 mm). Large scutellum and broad body—usually with a broad pronotum having sharp, even-pointed lateral margins—makes this family rather easy to sight identify. Usually green or brown in color, sometimes marked with bright red and other colors, stink bugs are either plant feeders of some economic importance or are predacious and prey upon insects and insect eggs. Some species are beneficial, therefore, by helping keep down crop pest populations.

Seventy-six genera and 247 species are known in the U.S. and Canada. The family is divided into the five subfamilies listed below. The identification of western species is difficult because the literature is widely scattered.

Fig. 20.5. (*Courtesy of J. E. V. Gerberg*)

Subfamily Scutellerinae

Tribe Tetyrini

3.1 *Tetyra* Fabricius

Four species, the following of which is of economic importance:

T. bipunctata (Herrich-Schaeffer) (Shieldbacked Pine Seedbug).

[3.2 *Pachycoris* Burmeister (1 sp., *P. torridus* (Scopoli)); 3.3 *Chelysoma* Bergroth (1 sp., *C. guttatum* (Herrich-Schaeffer)); 3.4 *Camirus* Stål (2 spp.); 3.5 *Acantholomidea* Sailer [=*Acantholoma* Stål (preoccupied)] (2 spp.); 3.6 *Diolcus* Mayr (2 spp.); 3.7 *Stethaulax* Bergroth (1 sp., *S. marmoratus* Say); 3.8 *Sphyrocoris* Mayr (2 spp.); 3.9 *Homaemus* Dallas (5 spp.); 3.10 *Symphylus* Dallas (1 sp., *S. carribeanus* Kirkaldy)]

Tribe Odontotarsini

3.11 *Eurygaster* Laporte

Four species, including the following:

E. alternata (Say). L. 7.5–9 mm. Dull yellow marked with numerous fuscous punctures that form short oblique lines on the scutellum. (See Fig. 20.6.) (1) n.e. US; (3) CA, NM; (4) BC, WA, OR; (5) n. Central States.

[3.12 *Fokkeria* Schouteden (1 sp., *F. producta* (Van Duzee)); 3.13 *Phimodera* Germar (3 spp.); 3.14 *Euptychodera* Bergroth (1 sp., *E. corrugata* (Van Duzee)); 3.15 *Vanduzeeina* Schouteden (5 spp.)]

Subfamily Pentatominae

Tribe Podopini

[3.16 *Oncozygia* Stål (1 sp., *O. clavicornis* Stål); 3.16a *Neapodops* Slater and Baranowski (1 sp., *N. floridanus* Slater and Baranowski)]

3.17 *Amaurochrous* Stal

[=*Podops* Laporte]

Five species, of which the following is common:

A. cinctipes (Say). L. 6–6.5 mm. Pronotum with tooth near humeral angle; dull greenish brown to yellowish brown. Found on grasses and sedges in damp places. (1) n.e. US; (2) s.e. US; (5) n. Central States.

[3.18 *Weda* Schouteden (4 spp.); 3.19 *Notopodops* Barber and Sailer (1 sp. *N. omani* Barber and Sailer); 3.20 *Allopodops* Harris and Johnson (1 sp., *A. mississippiensis* Harris and Johnson)]

Tribe Discocephalini

[3.21 *Platycarenus* Fieber (2 spp.); (*Dryptocephala* Laporte may occur in s. TX; species not given); 3.22 *Lineostethus* Rucker (1 sp., *L. tenebricornis* (Rucker))]

Fig. 20.7. (*From Blatchley, 1926*)

Tribe Sciocorini

[3.23 *Sciocoris* Fallen (1 sp., *S. microphthalmus* Flor; see Fig. 20.7)]

Tribe Mecidini

[3.24 *Mecidea* Dallas (1 sp., *M. longula* Stål)]

Tribe Halyini

3.25 *Brochymena* Amyot and Serville

Twenty-three species, of which the following are common:

B. quadripustulata (Fabricius) (Rough Stink Bug). L. 14–18 mm. Shallow groove on underside of abdomen; proboscis extending back to the hind coxae; broad, rough surface; reddish-brown, resembling the bark on which it is found. Feeds on foliage, especially of apple, cherry, and wild grape, but also of various trees and shrubs including beech and oak; sometimes preys on soft-bodied insects. Adults active from February through November. (1), (2), (3), (4), (5), especially in the north.

B. cariosa Stål. L. 17–19 mm. Blackish, feebly shining; pronotum and scutellum thickly marked with intermixed coarse and fine punctures and with numerous smooth, elevated, more or less reticulated yellow spaces. (See Fig. 20.8.) (2) s.e. US; (3) TX.

Tribe Pentatomini

[3.26 *Holcostethus* Fieber (7 spp.)]

Fig. 20.6. (*Courtesy of J. E. V. Gerberg*)

Fig. 20.8.

3.27 *Trichopepla* Stål

Eight species, including the following:

T. semivittata (Say). L. 6–8 mm. Dull brownish-yellow, marked with many brownish-gray punctations. Feeds on umbelliforous plants, especially wild carrot and button snakeroot. (1) n.e. US; (2) s.e. US; (5) ND, MN, SD, NE, IA, KS, MO.

[3.28 *Rhytidolomia* Stål (6 spp.)]

3.29 *Chlorochroa* Stål

[=*Pitedia* Amyot]

Four species, of which the following is common throughout the northern U.S.:

C. uhleri (Stål). L. 11–15 mm. Bright green, with yellow side margins and a yellow tip to the scutellum. Found on juniper. (1) n.e. NA; (3) CA; (4) Pacific n.w.; (5) n. Central States.

C. ligata (Say) (Conchuela). w. US

C. sayi Stål (Say's Stink Bug). Often a pest on cotton. (See Fig. 20.9.) w. US.

C. persimilis Horvath. May be a synonym of *C. uhleri* (Stål). e. US.

[3.30 *Carpocoris* Kolenati (2 spp.); 3.31 *Moromorpha* Rolston (1 sp., *M. tetra* (Walker))]

3.32 *Mormidea* Amyot and Serville

Five species, of which the following is common:

M. Lugens (Fabricius). L. 6–7 mm. Dull grayish-yellow with black on head, apical third of pronotum, and all of scutellum, which is narrowly margined with white; basal three antennal segments pale. Adults from May to October on mullein; hibernates under the leaves; feeds on many other plants. Very common. (1) n.e. NA; (2) s.e. US; (3) TX, OK; (5) n. Central States, e. of Rocky Mts.

Fig. 20.9.

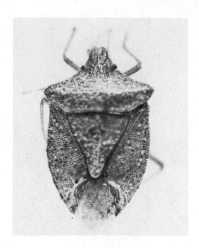

Fig. 20.10.

3.33 *Oebalus* Stål

[=*Solubea* Bergroth]

Two species, of which the following is of economic importance:

O. pugnax (Fabricius) (Rice Stink Bug).

3.34 *Euschistus* Dallas

Eighteen species, including the following:

E. servus (Say) (Brown Stink Bug). L. 12.5–15 mm. Brown, mottled with dark brown; punctations medium sized. Found on cotton. (See Fig. 20.10.) Common throughout the U.S. (1), (2), (3), (4), (5).

E. impunctiventris (Stål) (Western Brown Stink Bug).

E. tristigmus (Say) (Dusky Stink Bug).

[3.35 *Padaeus* Stal (1 sp., *P. trivittatus* Stål); 3.36 *Proxys* Spinola (2 spp.)]

3.37 *Coenus* Dallas

Two species, of which the following is common:

C. delius (Say). L. 4.5–6 mm. Straw-yellow with distinct black punctations. Found in dry fields and pastures from March through October, usually on grass. (1) n.e. US.

[3.38 *Hymenarcys* Amyot and Serville (5 spp.); 3.39 *Aelia* Fabricius (1 sp., *A. americana* Dallas); 3.40 *Neottiglossa* Kirby (5 spp.)]

3.41 *Cosmopepla* Stål

Five species, including the following:

C. bimaculata (Thomas). L. 5–7 mm. Shining black with bright red or yellowish stripes on pronotum and two red spots on scutellum near tip. Found on foliage and flowers of oats, mullein, Bouncing Bet, Greater Ragweed, goldenrod, Wild Columbine, and mints. Adult from May to October. (See Fig. 20.11.) Common throughout the U.S. (1), (2), (3), (4), (5).

[3.42 *Eysarcoris* Hahn (1 sp., *E. intergressus* Uhler); 3.43 *Menecles* Stål (1 sp., *M. insertus* (Say)); 3.44 *Prionosoma* Uhler (1 sp., *P. podopioides* Uhler)]

Fig. 20.11. (*From Blatchley, 1926*)

3.45 *Thyanta* Stål

Fourteen species, of which the following is common:

T. accerra McAtee (Red-shouldered Stink Bug).

[3.46 *Chlorocoris* Spinola (5 spp.); 3.47 *Loxa* Amyot and Serville (2 spp.)]

3.48 *Murgantia* Stål

Four species, of which the following is very common:

M. histrionica (Hahn) (Harlequin Bug; also called the Calico Bug, Fire Bug, and other common names). L. 9–11.5 mm. Shining black or deep blue, with prominent red markings. Damages cabbage and related plants, both wild and cultivated. Eggs are white with two black bands and a white spot and look like small barrels, laid in double rows. Adults hibernate. (See Fig. 20.12 and A & J 62.) (1) n.e. US; (2) s.e. US; (3) TX, CA; (5) ND, MN, SD, NE, IA, CO, KS, MO. (A&J 62).

[3.49 *Vulsirea* Spinola (1 sp., *V. violacea* Fabricius)); 3.50 *Runibia* Stål (1 sp., *R. proxima* (Dallas))]

3.51 *Nezara* Amyot and Serville

One species, as follows:

N. viridula (Linnaeus) (Southern Green Stink Bug). L. 14–17 mm. Green, tinged with reddish yellow or yellow. Pest of vegetable crops. (2) s.e. US; (3) TX.

3.52 *Acrosternum* Fieber

Three species, of which the following is common:

A. hilare (Say) (Green Stink Bug). L. 14–19 mm. Green; margins of head, pronotum, and abdomen yellowish. Found on vegetation near woodlands. Sometimes a pest of orchard fruits

Fig. 20.12.

Fig. 20.13. (*From Blatchley, 1926*)

and soybeans. (See Fig. 20.13.) Occurs throughout the U.S. (1), (2), (3), (4), (5).

3.53 *Banasa* Stål

Nine species, of which the following is common:

B. calva (Say). L. 11.5–12 mm. Greenish-yellow; each abdominal segment ventrally with a lateral black spot. Found on various deciduous trees. Adults from June to October. Occurs throughout the U.S. but more common in the North. (1), (2), (3), (4), (5).

[3.54 *Piezodorus* Fieber (3 spp.); 3.55 *Arvelius* Spinola (1 sp., *A. albopunctatus* (DeGeer)); 3.56 *Neopharnus* Van Duzee (1 sp., *N. fimbriatus* Van Duzee); 3.57 *Dendrocoris* Bergroth (6 spp.); 3.58 *Odmalea* Bergroth (1 sp., *O. schaefferi* (Barber)); 3.59 *Brepholoxa* Van Duzee (1 sp., *B. heidemanni* Van Duzee)]

Tribe Edessini

[3.60 *Edessa* Fabricius (2 spp.)]

Subfamily Tessaratominae

[3.61 *Piezosternum* Amyot and Serville (1 sp., *P. subulatum* Thunberg)]

Subfamily Acanthosomatinae

[3.62 *Elasmucha* Stål [=*Meadorus* Mulsant and Rey] (1 sp., *E. lateralis* (Say))]

3.63 *Elasmostethus* Fieber

Three species, of which the following is common:

E. atricornis (Van Duzee). L. 9–10 mm. Antennae black throughout; humeral angles black; pronotal punctures fine. Found on spikeweed in July and August. (1) n.e. NA.

Subfamily Asopinae
Tribe Discocerini
3.64 *Stiretrus* Laporte

One species, as follows:

S. anchorago (Fabricius) (Anchor Stink Bug). L. 8–11 mm. Blue and white or yellow and orange and red on black; although color markings are variable, color pattern of scutellum always forms an anchor, if sometimes obscure. Predacious, feeding on the larvae of beetles, butterflies, and moths. (See Fig. 20.14 and A&J 61.) (1) n.e. US; (2) s.e. US; (5) ND, MN, SD, NE, IA, CO KS, MO. (A&J 61).

Fig. 20.14.

Tribe Asopini

[3.65 *Heterosceloides* Schouteden (1 sp., *H. lepida* (Stål))]

3.66 *Alcaeorrhynchus* Bergroth

Two species, of which the following is common:

A. grandis Dallas (Predatory Stink Bug). L. 16–25 mm. Double spines on the humeral angles; brown with dark bands on legs and dark spots along margins of abdomen. Preys on various soybean pests; also reported on eggplant and shrubs near streams and marshes. (2) LA, MS, AL, FL; (3) TX.

[3.67 *Oplomus* Spinola (3 spp.)]

3.68 *Perillus* Stål

Six species, of which the following is common:

P. bioculatus (Fabricius) (Two-spotted Stink Bug). L. 8.5–12 mm. Brightly marked with the scutellum, corium, and thorax margined with red, yellow, white, or orange; color extremely variable. Predacious; an important predator upon the Colorado Potato Beetle, *Leptinotarsa decemlineata* (Say). (See Fig. 20.15 for bug feeding on beetle eggs). Occurs throughout the U.S. where the beetle is found. (1), (2), (3), (4), (5).

[3.69 *Andrallus* Bergroth (1 sp., *A. spinidens* Fabricius); 3.70 *Rhacognathus* Fieber (1 sp., *R. americanus* Stål); 3.71 *Euthyrhynchus* Dallas (1 sp., *E. floridanus* (Linnaeus)); 3.72 *Mineus* Stål (1 sp., *M. strigipes* (Herrich-Schaeffer))]

3.73 *Apateticus* Dallas

Six species, including the following:

A. cynicus (Say). L. 15–20 mm. Dull clay-yellow, thickly marked with small reddish or fuscous punctures; pronotum

Fig. 20.15.

Fig. 20.16.

with two or three greenish dots behind the front angles; abdomen yellow, thickly marked with fine reddish punctures. (See Fig. 20.16.) (1) n.e. US; (2) s.e. US; (3) AZ, TX; (5) CO.

3.74 *Podisus* Herrich-Schaeffer

Ten species, of which the following are common:

P. maculiventris (Say) (Spined Soldier Bug). L. 11–13.5 mm. Sharp spine on each side of pronotum; light brown, sometimes marked with purplish-red. Predatory and found on tall weeds in alluvial soils along streams and in dense woodlands. Adults active from May to October. (See A&J 63.) Very common throughout the U.S. (1), (2), (3), (4), (5).

P. acutissimus Stål. (See Fig. 20.17.) (3) AZ, TX; (5) CO.

[3.75 *Zicrona* Amyot and Serville (1 sp., *Z. caerulea* (Linnaeus)); 3.76 *Picomerus* Amyot and Serville (1 sp., *P. bidens* (Linnaeus), introduced)]

4. COREIDAE (Squash Bug Family)

This large family, mainly tropical, includes 33 genera and 120 species in the U.S. and Canada.

L. 10–20 mm (some exotic species to 40 mm). Body brown to dark brown, sometimes with white or pale stripes. Membrane

Fig. 20.17.

of front wing with numerous veins; margin of the abdomen of many species raised, with the wings lying in the depression that is formed. Several of the genera (for example *Leptoglossus* and others) have species with the hind tibiae enlarged and flattened into broad paddles; others have a similarly enlarged antennal segment (for example, *Chariesterus*). The scent glands are well developed and can secrete an unpleasant odor similar to that of stink bugs. All are plant feeders. The only serious pest is the Squash Bug, and that is seldom abundant enough to cause extensive damage, except locally.

Subfamily Merocorinae

[4.1 *Merocoris* Perty (1 sp., *M. typhaeus* (Fabricius))]

Subfamily Coreinae

Tribe Acanthocephalini

4.2 *Acanthocephala* Laporte

Six species in two subgenera, *Acanthocephala* s. str. and *Metapodiessa* Kirkaldy. The following are common:

A. terminalis (Dallas) (Leaf-footed Bug). L. 10–20 mm. Dark brown; head narrower than pronotum; hind tibiae expanded and leaflike. Found on trees, shrubs, and weeds. (See A & J 60.) (1) n.e. US; (2) s.e. US; (3) OK, TX; (5) KS, CO.

A. femorata (Fabricius). L. 25–28 mm. Dark chestnut or fuscous-brown, thickly clothed above and beneath with fine, appressed, yellowish hairlike setae; membrane blackish-brown; tip of scutellum greenish-yellow. Hind femora of male extremely stout, curved, armed beneath with two rows of short tubercles or teeth, the median one of outer row long, curved, acute; hind femora of female more slender, with teeth on apical half of outer row regular and longer than those of male. (See Figure 20.18 for male; Fig. 20.19 for female.) (2) NC, AR, LA, MS, AL, GA, SC, FL; (3) TX, OK.

Tribe Anisoscelini

[4.3 *Chondrocera* Laporte (1 sp., *C. laticornis* Laporte)]

4.4 *Leptoglossus* Guerin

Ten species, of which the following are common:

L. phyllopus (Linnaeus) (Eastern Leaf-footed Bug). L. 18–20 mm. Chestnut-brown with three narrow stripes on head,

Fig. 20.19.

and side margins of pronotum dull yellow; front wings with ivory-white straight cross-bar. Found on cotton, fruit, and truck crops; rarely of economic importance. (See Fig. 20.20.) (1) NY, PA, NJ, DE, MD; (2) s.e. US; (5) MO.

L. clypealis Heidemann. Similar to preceeding; front wing with zig-zag cross-bar. (See Fig. 20.21.) (3) s.w. US; (4) OR, UT, (5) CO.

[4.5 *Narnia* Stål (5 spp. in subgenus *Narnia* s. str. and *Xerocoris* Van Duzee)]

Tribe Leptoscelini

[4.6 *Phthia* Stål (1 sp., *P. picta* (Drury)); 4.7 *Amblyomia* Stål (1 sp., *A. bifasciata* Stål)]

Tribe Mictini

4.8 *Thasus* Stål

One species as follows:

T. acutangulus Stål. L. 35–40 mm. Dark brown; front wings with veins orange-yellow; antennae variegated red and dark brown; males with enlarged hind femora. Found on mesquite. (See Fig. 20.22.) (3) AZ. NM.

[4.9 *Mozena* Amyot and Serville, subgenus *Mozena* s. str. (6 spp.); subgenus *Rhombogaster* Dallas (1 sp., *M. obesa* Montandon); 4.10 *Capaneus* Stål, subgenus *Xuthus* Stål (1 sp., *C. auriculatus* Stål), subgenus *Rhyparopharus* Stål (2 spp.); 4.11 *Archimerus* Burmeister (4 spp.); 4.12 *Mamurius* Stål (1 sp., *M. mopsus* Stål); 4.13 *Hymeniphera* Laporte (1 sp., *H. lobata* (Burmeister)); 4.14 *Euthochtha* Mayr (1 sp., *E. galeator* (Fabricius))]

Fig. 20.18.

Fig. 20.20.

Fig. 20.21.

Tribe Corecorini

[4.15 *Corecoris* Hahn (3 spp.); 4.16 *Sephina* Amyot and Serville (3 spp.)]

Tribe Chariesterini

[4.17 *Chariesterus* Laporte (4 spp.)]

Tribe Chelinidini

4.18 *Chelinidea* Uhler

Four species, including the following:

C. vittiger Uhler. L. 11–15 mm. Light yellow; head dark brown with wide median yellow stripe; scutellum and posterior portion of pronotum dark. Introduced as a pest of opuntia cactus. (See Fig. 20.23.) (2) s.e. US; (3) s.w. US.

Tribe Coreini

[4.19 *Madura* Stål (1 sp., *M. perfida* Stål); 4.20 *Margus* Dallas (3 spp.); 4.21 *Namacus* Amyot and Serville (1 sp., *N. annulicornis* Stål); 4.22 *Scolopocerus* Uhler (3 spp.); 4.23 *Nissoscolopocerus* Barber (1 sp., *N. apiculatus* Barber); 4.24 *Catorhintha* Stål (6 spp.); 4.25 *Ficana* Stål (1 sp., *F. apicalis* (Dallas)); 4.26 *Cimolus* Stål (1 sp., *C. obscurus* Stål)]

4.27 *Anasa* Amyot and Serville

Seven species, of which the following two are very common:

A. tristis (DeGeer)(Squash Bug). L. 13–18 mm. Pronotum and basal half of front wings speckled with brown; side-margins

Fig. 20.22.

Fig. 20.23.

of pronotum yellowish; hind femora spineless. Eggs oval, pale-yellowish to dark, laid in irregular clusters, usually on underside of leaves. Active from May into October on squash; adults hibernate under rubbish and loose bark. (See Fig. 20.24.) Occurs throughout NA (1) (2) (3) (4) (5).

A. armigera (Say) (Horned Squash Bug). L. 13–17 mm. Similar to the preceding; spines of head very prominent; head without pale line; basal segment of antennae with large black dots. Found on wild cucumber; sometimes a pest on cultivated cucumbers. (1) n.e. US; (2) s.e. US; (3) OK, TX; (5) MN, IA, KS.

[4.28 *Zicca* Amyot and Serville (1 sp., *Z. taeniola* Dallas); 4.29 *Hypselonotus* Hahn (2 spp.); 4.30 *Paryphes* Burmeister (1 sp *P. rufoscutellatus* (Gray))]

Tribe Discogastrini

[4.31 *Saxius* Stål (1 sp., *S. jurgiosus* Stål)]

Subfamily Pseudophloeinae

[4.32 *Ceraleptus* Costa (2 spp.); 4.33 *Coriomeris* Westwood (2 spp.)]

5. ALYDIDAE (Broad-headed Bug Family)

[=Coriscidae]

L. 10–18 mm. Very similar to Rhopalidae (6) but usually slender, elongate, with large heads; some species broad. The

Fig. 20.24. (*From Blatchley, 1926*)

best way to distinguish this family is by the distance between the eyes, which is greater than the width of the scutellum. Scent glands are present. There are 11 genera and 29 species in the U.S. and Canada, none of which is very common or a pest in North America. They feed on vegetation.

Subfamily Micrelytrinae

5.1 *Protenor* Hagland

Two species, including the following:

P. belfragei Hagland. L. 12–15 mm. Slender. Uncommon. (1) n.e. US; (5) ND, MN, SD, IA, NE, KS.

[5.2 *Darmistus* Stål (3 spp.); 5.3 *Cydamus* Stål (2 spp.); 5.4 *Esperanza* Barber (1 sp., *E. texana* Barber)]

Subfamily Leptocorisinae

[5.5 *Stenocris* Burmeister (2 spp.)]

Subfamily Alydinae

[5.6 *Hyalymenus* Amyot and Serville (6 spp.); 5.7 *Megalotomus* Fieber (1 sp., *M. quinquespinosus* (Say)); 5.8 *Burtinus* Stål (1 sp., *B. notatipennis* Stål)]

5.9 *Alydus* Fabricius

Six species including the following:

A. conspersus (Montandon). L. 10–12 mm. Brownish-yellow; head, apical third of pronotum, and femora black; basal segment of tarsi yellow; membrane of front wing with scattered brown spots. Found on plants in dry sandy places. Adults active in July and August. (1) n.e. NA; (2) TN; (3) n. TX; (4) WA.

[5.10 *Tollius* Stål (4 spp.)]

5.11 *Stachyocnemus* Stål

Two species, including the following:

S. apicalis (Dallas). L. 7–8 mm. Broad. Occurs only in sandy regions and feeds on foliage of shrubs and trees. Uncommon but found locally throughout NA. (1), (2), (3), (4), (5).

6. RHOPALIDAE (Scentless Plant Bug Family)

[= Corizidae]

L. 5.5–14 mm. Features as in key; scent glands absent. Numerous veins in the membrane of the front wing distinguish these species from the Pyrrhocoridae, which also lack scent glands. The 36 species are assigned to 9 genera as follows.

Subfamily Rhopalinae

Tribe Niesthrini

[6.1 *Niesthrea* Spinola (2 spp.); 6.2 *Arhyssus* Stål (14 spp.)]

Tribe Rhopalini

6.3 *Liorhyssus* Stål

One species, as follows:

L. hyalinus (Fabricius) (Hyaline Grass Bug). L. 5.5–6.5 mm. Varies from black to reddish to pale yellow; lateral

Fig. 20.25. (*From Blatchley, 1926*)

margins of pronotum broadly pale yellow; apex of corium often reddish. Found on weeds and grass. (1) NY, MA, PA, NJ, MD, DE; (2) s.e. US; (3) CA, AZ, NM; (5) ND, MN, NE, IA, CO, WY.

Tribe Harmostini

6.4 *Harmostes* Burmeister

Eight species, including the following:

H. reflexulus (Say). L. 7.5–9 mm. Greenish-yellow to pale reddish-brown, usually with scattered brown spots on body. Found on flowers of Compositae on borders of meadows and streams. Adults active in July and August; overwinter under mullein leaves, logs, and other hiding places. (See Fig. 20.25.) Occurs throughout the U.S. (1), (2), (3), (4), (5).

[6.5 *Aufeius* Stål (1 sp., *A. impressicollis* Stål)]

Tribe Chorosimini

[6.6 *Xenogenus* Berg (1 sp., *X. extensum* Distant)]

Tribe Maccevethini

6.7 *Stictopleurus* Stål

Five species, including the following:

S. crassicornis (Linnaeus). L. 6–8.5 mm. Brownish or grayish-yellow; usually sprinkled or clouded with brown; head yellow, with a black spot. Found in spring on foliage of trees and shrubs along thickets and edges of woods; in late summer and early fall, on weeds and in timothy fields, espcially in old fields; overwinter, under cover on ground and under bark. (1) n.e. US; (4) Pacific n.w.; (5) n. Central States.

Subfamily Serinethinae

6.8 *Leptocoris* Hahn

Two species, of which the following is the most common:

L. trivittatus (Say). (Boxelder Bug). L. 11–13.5 mm. Black with reddish-orange markings; head black; thorax with central and lateral reddish-orange stripes. Feeds on seeds of Boxelder; hibernates in houses as well as under boards, loose bark, and similar places; not destructive. (See Fig. 20.26.) Occurs throughout NA. (1), (2), (3), (4), (5).

[6.9 *Jadera* Stål (2 spp.)]

Fig. 20.26. (*From Blatchley, 1926*)

7. LYGAEIDAE (Seed Bug Family)

L. 2–20 mm. Body hard; head with ocelli usually present; antennae inserted between and below middle of eyes; membrane of front wing with five distinct veins and usually only one closed cell. The majority of the 295 species in the U.S. and Canada feed on seeds, but a few are sap feeders, a few are predacious, and some are of economic importance. One, the infamous Chinch Bug, is a pest of corn and other grain crops and causes great economic loss. There are over 2630 species in the world.

Subfamily Lygaeinae

[7.1 *Craspeduchus* Stål (1 sp., *C. uhleri* Stål); 7.2 *Lygaeospilus* Barber (3 spp.)]

7.3 *Lygaeus* Fabricius

Six species, of which the following is common:

L. kalmii Stål (Small Milkweed Bug) L. 10–12 mm. Black with red markings on head, thorax, and front legs, the latter in the form of an irregular "X." Adults from February through October on Milkweed. (See Fig. 20.27 and A & J 57.) Occurs throughout the U.S. (1), (2), (3), (4), (5).

[7.4 *Melanocoryphus* Stål (7 spp.); 7.5 *Melanopleurus* Stål (3 spp.); 7.6 *Ochrimnus* Stål (1 sp., *O. mimudus* Stål); 7.7 *Ochrostomus* Stål (9 spp.)]

Fig. 20.27.

Fig. 20.28.

7.8 *Oncopeltus* Stål

Seven species, the most common of which is the following:

O. fasciatus (Dallas) (Milkweed Bug) L. 17–18 mm. Black with orange Y-shaped spot on head and margins of thorax, and bands across wings. Found on milkweed; easily reared on milkweed seeds in small cages. (See Fig. 20.28). (1) n.e. US; (2) s.e. US; (3) s.w. US; (5) SD, MN, IA, KS, MO.

[7.9 *Orsillacis* Barber (1 sp., *O. producta* Barber)]

Subfamily Orsillinae

Tribe Orsillini

[7.10 *Belonochilus* Uhler (1 sp., *B. numenius* Say)]

7.11 *Nysius* Dallas

Eleven species, of which the following is common:

N. raphanus Howard (False Chinch Bug). General feeder, and sometimes a pest of fruits and in gardens.

[7.11a Xyonysius Ashlock and Lattin (3 spp.); 7.12 *Ortholomus* Stål (6 spp.)]

Subfamily Ischnorhynchinae

[7.13 *Kleidocerys* Stephens (8 spp.)]

Subfamily Cyminae

Tribe Cymini

[7.14 *Arphnus* Stål (2 spp.); 7.15 *Cymus* Hahn (7 spp.)]

Subfamily Blissinae

7.16 *Blissus* Burmeister

Fourteen species, many of which are of economic importance. The best known are the following:

B. leucopterus leucopterus (Say)) (Chinch Bug). L. 3.8–4.2 mm. Black; body thickly clothed with fine, appressed pubescence; wings milky-white, with veins tinged with yellow; apex of corium with large black spot. Of great economic importance as a pest of corn, grain, and other plants. (See Fig. 20.29.) (1) n.e. NA, (2) s.e. US; (3) s.e. US, in grain; (4) Pacific n.w., in grain; (5) n. Central States.

Fig. 20.29.

B. leucopterus hirtus Montandon (Hairy Chinch Bug).

B. occiduus Barber (Western Chinch Bug).

B. insularis Barber (Southern Chinch Bug).

[7.17 *Ischnodemus* Fieber (15 spp.)]

Subfamily Geocorinae

Tribe Geocorini

7.18 *Geocoris* Fallen

Twenty-three species, of which the following are common:

G. bullatus Say (Bigeyed Bug) L. 3–3.5 mm. Grayish, tinged with yelled; eyes prominent, projecting posteriorly. Runs on ground beneath clumps of weeds and sparse grass, especially in sandy places, in woods, and near streams. Overwinters beneath logs and vegetation. Occurs throughout the U.S. (1), (2), (3), (4), (5).

G. pallens Stål (Western Bigeyed Bug).

[7.19 *Hypogeocoris* Montandon (4 spp.)]

Subfamily Bledionotinae

Tribe Pamphantini

[7.20 *Pamphantus* Stål (1 sp., *P. elegantulus* Stal)

Subfamily Oxycareninae

[7.21 *Crophius* Stål (9 spp.); 7.22 *Dycoderus* Uhler (1 sp., *D. picturatus* Uhler)]

Subfamily Pachygronthinae

Tribe Pachygronthini

[7.23 *Oedancala* Amyot and Serville (3 spp.); 7.24 *Pachygrontha* Germar (1 sp., *P. compacta* Distant)]

Tribe Teracriini

[7.25 *Phlegyas* Stål (2 spp.)]

Subfamily Heterogastrinae

[7.26 *Heterogaster* Schilling (2 spp.)]

Subfamily Rhyparochrominae

Tribe Plinthisini

[7.27 *Plinthisus* Stephens (4 spp.)]

Tribe Lethaeini

[7.28 *Cistalia* Stål (2 spp.); 7.29 *Cryphula* Stål (5 spp.) 7.30 *Valtissius* Barber (1 sp., *V. diversus* Distant); 7.31 *Xestocoris* Van Duzee (1 sp., *X. nitens* Van Duzee)]

Tribe Antillocorini

[7.32 *Antillocoris* Kirkaldy (5 spp.); 7.33 *Botocudo* Kirkaldy (2 spp.); 7.34 *Cligenes* Distant (1 sp., *C. distinctus* Distant)]

Tribe Drymini

[7.35 *Drymus* Fieber (2 spp.); 7.36 *Eremocoris* Fieber (10 spp.); 7.37 *Gastrodes* Westwood (5 spp.); 7.38 *Scolopostethus* Fieber (5 spp.); 7.39 *Thylochromus* Barber (1 sp., *T. nitidulus* Barber); 7.40 *Togodolentus* Barber (1 sp., *T. wrighti* Van Duzee)]

Tribe Ozophorini

[7.41 *Ozophora* Uhler (9 spp.)]

Tribe Udeocorini

[7.42 *Neosuris* Barber (2 spp.); 7.43 *Tempyra* Stål (2 spp.)

Tribe Myodochini

[7.44 *Kolenetrus* Barber (1 sp., *K. plenus* Distant); 7.45 *Ereminellus* Harrington (2 spp.); 7.46 *Caenopamera* Barber (1 sp., *C. forreri* Distant); 7.47 *Volonetus* Barber (1 sp., *V. puberulus* Stål); 7.48 *Ptochiomera* Say (1 sp., *P. nodosa* Say); 7.49 *Carpilis* Stål (3 spp.); 7.50 *Sisamnes* Distant (2 spp.); 7.51 *Prytanes* Distant (6 spp.); 7.52 *Paromius* Fieber (1 sp., *P. longulus* (Dallas)); 7.53 *Pseudopachybrachius* Malipatil (2 spp.); 7.54 *Slaterobius* Harrington (2 spp.); 7.55 *Ligyrocoris* Stål (11 spp.); 7.56 *Froeschneria* Harrington (2 spp.); 7.57 *Perigenes* Distant (2 spp.); 7.58 *Zeridoneus* Barber (3 spp.); 7.59 *Pseudopamera* Distant (6 spp.); 7.60 *Pseudocnemodus* Barber (1 sp., *P. canadensis* Provancher); 7.61 *Ashlockaria* Harrington (2 spp.); 7.62 *Zeropamera* Barber (1 sp., *Z. nigra* Barber); 7.63 *Cnemodus* Herrich-Schaeffer (3 spp.); 7.64 *Neopamera* Harrington (5 spp.); 7.65 *Heraeus* Stål (9 spp.)]

7.66 *Myodocha* Latreille

Two species of which the following is common.

M. serripes Olivier. L. 8–9.5 mm. Head and neck elongate; shining black with reddish-brown or pale yellow marking. Found on grass and low plants; hibernates along margins of woods under bark annd litter; sometimes a pest of strawberries. (See Fig. 20.30.) (1) n.e. NA; (2) s.e. US; (5) ND, MN, SD, NE, IA, KAS, MO.

Fig. 20.30. (*From Blatchley, 1926*)

Fig. 20.31. (*From Blatchley, 1926*)

Fig. 20.32.

Tribe Rhyparochromini

[7.67 *Dieuches* Dohn (1 sp., *D. occidentalis* Torre-Bueno); 7.68 *Peritrechus* Fieber (4 spp.); 7.69 *Uhleriola* Horvath (1 sp., *U. floralis* (Uhler))]

Tribe Megalonotini

[7.70 *Megalonotus* Fieber (1 sp., *M. chiragrus* (Fabricius)); 7.71 *Sphragisticus* Stål (2 spp.)]

Tribe Gonianotini

[7.72 *Delochilocoris* Bergroth (2 spp.); 7.73 *Emblethis* Fieber (1 sp., *E. vicarius* Horvath); 7.74 *Malezonotus* Barber (7 spp.); 7.75 *Trapezonotus* Fieber (4 spp.)]

8. PYRRHOCORIDAE (Red Bug and Cotton Stainer Family)

L. 8–18 mm. Similar in appearance to Milkweed Bug, Lygaeidae (7). Ocelli absent; scent glands absent, or nearly so, the greatly reduced opening behind the base of the middle legs. All seven species belong to the following genus:

8.1 *Dysdercus* Amyot and Serville

D. suturellus (Herrich-Schaeffer) (Cotton Stainer). L. 11–17 mm. Dark brown; head, base of antennae, femora, and scutellum bright red; wings with pale yellow margins. Pest of cotton; also found on hisbiscus, oranges, *Solanum* spp., and many other plants. (See Fig. 20.31 and A & J 58.) (2) s. e. U.S.

D. andreae (Linnaeus) (St. Andrew's Cotton Bug). L. 8–11.5 mm. Corium red, narrowly margined with white, usually with a large transverse dark spot on apical third. (See Fig. 20.32 and A & J 59.) (2) s. FL.

D. mimulus Hussey (Arizona Cotton Stainer). Similar to *D. suturellus* but found in (2) s. FL; (3) s.w. U.S.

[Note: *Pyrrhocoris apterus* (Linnaeus) was reported in NJ many years ago, but that record has never been confirmed.].

9. LARGIDAE (Red Bug and Ant Mimic Bug Family)

L. 7–18 mm. Front wing membrane with seven or eight branching veins arising from the two large basal cells; ocelli absent.

Subfamily Larginae
[=Euryophthalminae]

9.1 *Largus* Burmeister
[=*Euryophthalmus* Laporte]

Eight species, of which the following are common:

L. succinctus (Linnaeus) (Red Bug). L. 14–17 mm. Adults black, marked with reddish-yellow; nymphs a brilliant steel-blue with red legs. Found on oak, wax-myrtle, other woodland foliage, and sometimes on weeds. (See Fig. 20.33.) (1) NY. NJ. PA. MD; (2) s.e. US; (3) OK, TX, NM, AZ; (5) NE, IA, KS, CO, MO.

L. cinctus (Herrich-Schaeffer). (3) s.w. US; (4) OR, NV; (5) CO.

[9.2 *Stenomacra* Stål (2 spp.); 9.3 *Acinocoris* Hahn (1 sp., *A. lunaris* (Gmelin))]

9.4 *Arhaphe* Herrich-Schaeffer

Five species of which the following is common:

A. cicindeloides (Walker). L. 8–10 mm. Black with

Fig. 20.33.

Fig. 20.34. (*From Blatchley, 1926*)

Fig. 20.35. (*From Blatchley, 1926*)

yellowish-white markings on thorax, wings, and abdomen. Feeds on weeds. (See Fig. 20.34.) (2) s.w. US.

[9.5 *Japetus* Distant (1 sp., *mimeticus* (Barber))]

10. PIESMATIDAE (Ash-gray Leaf Bug Family)

L. 2.5–3.5. Legs with two tarsomeres; ocelli present; pronotum with five raised longitudinal ridges. One genus only, as follows:

10.1 *Piesma* Le Peletier and Serville

Ten species; of which the following is common:

P. cinereum (Say) Found on pigweed and many other plants. Occurs throughout the U.S. (1), (2), (3), (4), (5).

11. THAUMASTOCORIDAE (Royal Palm Bug Family)

One species only, as follows:

Subfamily Xylastodorinae

11.1 *Xylastodoris* Barber

X. luteolus Barber. L. 2–3 mm. Body flattened. Lives in fronds of Royal Palms; sometimes a pest. (2) s. FL.

12. BERYTIDAE (Stilt Bug Family)

[=Neididae]

L. 5–9 mm. Some resemble crane flies; legs very long; front legs lack grasping ability of front legs of thread-legged bugs. Unlike marsh treader bugs, Hydrometridae (26), which some species resemble, they are not water treaders. First antennal segment very long. The 14 species are assigned to 8 genera, as follows:

Subfamily Metacanthinae

[12.1 *Aknisus* McAtee (2 spp.)]

12.2 *Jalysus* Stål

Five closely similar species, the following of which are common:

J. wickhami Van Duzee (Spined Stilt Bug). L. 7–9 mm. Dull reddish brown to brownish yellow marked with grayish brown. Found on weeds and underbrush of woodlands and

on tall grasses about edges of ponds and fields from May through October; overwinters under logs, mullein leaves, and other cover. Very common. (1), (2), (3), (4), (5).

J. spinosus (Say). Similar to the preceding. Common. (See Fig. 20.35.) (1) n.e. US; (2) s.e. US.

[12.3 *Protacanthus* Uhler (1 sp., *P. decorus* Uhler); 12.4 *Pronotacantha* Uhler (1 sp., *P. annulata* Uhler); 12.5 *Acanthophysa* Uhler (2 spp.)]

Subfamily Berytinae

12.6 *Neides* Latreille

One species, as follows:

N. muticus (Say) (Common Stilt Bug). L. 9–10 mm. Elongate, with very long legs; pale yellow, with distal ends of tibiae, tarsi, and fourth antennal segment, which is somewhat thickened, dark brown to black. Found on weeds, especially Orange Hawkweed, in fields and pastures. (1), (2), (3), (4), (5).

[12.7 *Berytinus* Kirkaldy (1 sp., *B. minor* Herrich-Schaeffer)]

13. ARADIDAE (Flat Bug Family)

L. 3–11 mm. Oval, very flat; dark brown or black. The reddish, wingless nymphs resemble Bed Bugs. They feed on fungus on dead wood and under bark. Of the 104 species in 10 genera, most belong to the genus *Aradus*.

Subfamily Aradinae

13.1 *Aradus* Fabricius

Seventy-eight species, including the following:

A. robustus Uhler (Flat Bug). L. 5.5–7 mm. Dark ash-gray or dark brown with paler wing veins; thickly covered above with large, dense, flat granules. Found under bark of red and black oaks. Very common. (1) n.e. NA; (5) MN, SD, NE, IA, KS, MO.

A. acutus Say. (See A&J 56.)

Subfamily Calisiinae

[13.2 *Calisius* Stål (2 spp.); 13.3 *Aneurus* Curtis (7 spp.)]

Subfamily Carventinae

[13.4 *Acaricoris* Harris and Drake (1 sp., *A. ignotus* Harris and Drake); 13.5 *Proxius* Stål (2 spp.)]

Subfamily Mezirinae

[13.6 *Mezira* Amyot and Serville (7 spp.); 13.7 *Neuroctenus* Fieber (4 spp.); 13.8 *Nannium* Bergroth (1 sp., *N. pusio* Heidemann); 13.9 *Notapictinus* Usinger and Matsuda (1 sp., *N. aurivillii* (Bergroth)); 13.10 *Aphleboderrhis* Stål (1 sp., *A. pubescens* Walker)]

14. TINGIDAE (Lace Bug Family)

L. 3–5 mm. Front wings and prothorax expanded and pitted with the appearance of fine lace; ocelli absent. These species are plant juice feeders and are pests of many plants. They are usually found on the underside of leaves. The eggs are often placed near the leaf veins. Some species hibernate as adults. There are about 1,820 species in the world, of which 157 are found in the U.S. and Canada, assigned to the following 23 genera.

Subfamily Tinginae

Tribe Tingini

[14.1 *Acalypta* Westwood (9 spp.); 14.2 *Acanthocheila* Stål (1 sp., *A. exquisita* Uhler); 14.3 *Alveotingis* Osborn and Drake (3 spp.); 14.4 *Atheas* Champion (5 spp.); 14.5 *Calotingis* Drake (1 sp., *C. knighti* Drake); 14.6 *Corythaica* Stål (4 spp.)]

14.7 *Corythucha* Stål

This is the largest genus in North America, with 51 species. The following are some of the common species:

C. arcuata (Say) (Oak Lace Bug). L. 3–3.5 mm. Black; legs and antennae dull yellow; pale preapical cross bar on front wings dark brown. Found on foliage of oak and sometimes maple, apple, chestnut, and roses; often a pest. Hibernates under bark. Occurs throughout the U.S. (1), (2), (3), (4), (5).

C. ciliata (Say) (Sycamore Lace Bug). L. 3–7 mm. Body black; antennae and legs yellowish; upper surface milky-white with prominent grayish-brown spot on elytra. Adults from April through October. A pest on Sycamore leaves; overwinters under bark. (See A&J 55.) (1) n.e. US; (2) s.e. US; (5) MN, NE, IA, KS, MO.

C. bellula Torre-Bueno. L. ±2 mm. (See Fig. 20.36.) (1) n.e. U.S.; (2) s.e. U.S. (Fig. 20.36).

C. morrilli Osborn and Drake (Morrill Lace Bug).

C. celtidis Osborn and Drake (Hackberry Lace Bug).

C. cydoniae (Fitch) (Hawthorn Lace Bug).

C. gossypii (Fabricius) (Cotton Lace Bug).

C. marmorata (Uhler) (Chrysanthemum Lace Bug).

C. ulmi Osborn and Drake (Elm Lace Bug).

[14.8 *Dichocysta* Champion (1 sp., *D. pictipes* Champion); 14.9 *Dictyla* Stål (4 spp.); 14.10 *Galeatus* Curtis (1 sp., *G. spinifrons* (Fallen))]

14.11 *Gargaphia* Stål

Fifteen species, several of which are of economic importance.

G. tiliae (Walsh) (Basswood Lace Bug). L. 4–5 mm. Pale white; head with five spines. Found on leaves of Basswood and

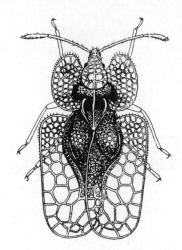

Fig. 20.36. (*Courtesy of J. E. V. Gerberg*)

sometimes Redbud, Sycamore, and Wild Cherry. (1) n.e. US; (2) s.e. US; (3) AZ, TX, OK; (5) NE, KS, MO.

G. solani Heidemann (Eggplant Lace Bug).

[14.12 *Hesperotingis* Parshley (9 spp.); 14.13 *Leptodictya* Kirkaldy (6 spp.); 14.14 *Leptopharsa* Stål (7 spp.); 14.15 *Leptoypha* Stål (9 spp.); 14.16 *Melanorhopala* Stål (3 spp.); 14.17 *Phymacysta* Monte (1 sp., *P. tumida* (Champion)); 14.18 *Physatocheila* Fieber (5 spp.); 14.19 *Pseudacysta* Blatchley (1 sp., *P. perseae* (Heidemann))]

14.20 *Stephanitis* Stål

Four species, of which the following are of some economic importance:

S. pyrioides Scott (Azalea Lace Bug).

S. rhododendri Horvath (Rhododendron Lace Bug).

14.21 *Teleonemia* Costa

Fourteen species, of which the following may be in the U.S. on Lantana.

T. scrupulosa Stål (Lantana Lace Bug).

[14.22 *Tingis* Fabricius (1 sp., *T. auriculata* (Costa))]

Tribe Ypsotingini

[14.23 *Dictyonota* Curtis (2 spp.)]

15. ENICOCEPHALIDAE (Unique-headed Bug Family)

L. 2–5 mm. Head constricted between eyes, then enlarged before pronotum; Predacious. Sometimes these bugs swarm and resemble swarms of small flies. There are six species in the following two genera:

[15.1 *Hymenocoris* Uhler (1 sp., *H. formicina* (Uhler))]

15.2 *Systelloderes* Blanchard

Five species, of which the following is representative:

S. biceps (Say). Rare. (1) n.e. US; (2) s.e. US; (3) AZ, NM, TX; (5) UT.

16. PHYMATIDAE (Ambush Bug Family)

L. 5–12 mm. These predacious insects hide in flowers, blending in by virtue of their matching colors, until a bee or

Fig. 20.37. (*Courtesy of J. E. V. Gerberg*)

Fig. 20.38.

other insect comes to gather pollen and nectar. They grasp their prey (often much larger than they are) with their raptorial front legs and hold on bulldog style while sucking it dry. The 22 species are assigned to the following two genera:

Subfamily Phymatinae
16.1 *Phymata* Latreille

Fourteen species. Scutellum triangular and shorter than the pronotum.

P. americana Melin (Ambush Bug). L. 8–9 mm. Yellow with brown or black marking. Adults from May through September. Predacious, hiding in flowers of goldenrod, Boneset, and others. (See A&J 54.) Occurs throughout the U.S. (1), (2), (3), (4), (5).

P. erosa (Linnaeus). (See Fig. 20.37.) (1); (2); (3); (4) NV, UT; (5) MN, IA, CO, KS, MO.

Subfamily Macrocephalinae
16.2 *Macrocephalus* Swederus

Eight species. Scutellum narrowly U-shaped and much longer than the thorax, reaching the end of the abdomen. Most species are in (3) s.w. US but two occur in (2) s.e. US

M. cimicoides Swederus. L. 9–11 mm. Scutellum with a smooth, yellowish, calloused median carina or elevation, widest posteriorly and reaching middle of scutellum or beyond; hind lobe of pronotum bicarinate, with its humeral angles notched. (2) NC, GA, FL, AL, MS, LA; (3) TX, AZ, CA.

17. REDUVIIDAE
(Assassin and Thread-legged Bug Family)

L. 7–36 mm. Prosternum grooved to receive the relatively short beak when not in use; brown, but some species brightly colored; abdomen of female usually broader than that of male. Some species are very long, slender, with long legs and antennae, and resemble small walkingsticks (Phasmatodea); these are called the thread-legged bugs. The species are either predatory or bloodsucking. There are 39 genera and 106 species in the U.S. and Canada.

Subfamily Apiomerinae

[17.1 *Apiomerus* Hahn (2 spp.)]

Subfamily Ectrichodiinae

[17.2 *Rhiginia* Stål (1 sp., *R. cinctiventris* (Stål)]

Subfamily Emesinae
17.3 *Emesaya* McAtee and Malloch

Six species, of which the following is typical:

E. brevipennis (Say) (Thread-legged Bug). L. 33–37 mm. Very slender, elongate, with long legs; front legs raptorial; dark brown. Feeds on small insects. (See Fig. 20.38.) Occurs throughout the U.S.

17.4 *Empicoris* Wolff

Six species, including the following:

E. rubromaculatus (Blackburn) (Thread Bug). L. 5–5.5 mm. Head with lateral ridges. (1) IN; (2) VA, FL, MS; (3) CA.

[17.5 *Gardena* Dohrn (2 spp.); 17.6 *Ghilianella* Spinola (1 sp., *G. productilis* Barber); 17.7 *Ischnonyctes* Stål (1 sp., undetermined; (2) LA); 17.8 *Metapterus* Costa (7 spp.); 17.9 *Ploiaria* Scopoli (12 spp.); 17.10 *Stenolemoides* McAtee and Malloch (3 spp.)]

Subfamily Harpactorinae
17.11 *Acholla* Stål

One species only, as follows:

A. multispinosa (DeGeer). L. 12–16 mm. Dark brown to yellowish brown; legs vaguely ringed with brown and yellow; abdomen with margins marked with pale yellow; body covered with gray pubescence. Found on foliage of shrubs and herbs along roadsides and pathways of open woods, especially on *Crataegus* spp. Adults present from June to October. (1) n.e. US; (2) s.e. US; (2) s.e. US; (3) AZ; (5) CO.

17.12 *Arilus* Hahn

One species only, as follows:

A. cristatus (Linnaeus) (Wheel Bug). L. 28–36 mm. Pronotum with a semi-circular crest with 8 to 12 stout tubercles resembling half a wheel with cogs; uniformly dark grayish brown; body with thick, short, grayish pubescence. Predacious on insects; occasionally bites man. (See Fig. 20.39.) (1) IL, IN, PA, NJ, MD, DE; (2) s.e. US.

[17.13 *Atrachelus* Amyot and Serville (1 sp., *A. cinereus* (Fabricius); 17.14 *Castolus* Stål (1 sp., *C. ferox* (Banks)); 17.15 *Doldina* Stål (2 spp.); 17.16 *Fitchia* Stål (2 spp.)]

Fig. 20.39.

17.17 *Pselliopus* Bergroth

Three species, including the following:

P. cinctus (Fabricius). L. 12–13 mm. Dull orange; head and front lobe of the pronotum marked with black and white; legs and first two segments of antennae with black and white bands. Predacious upon insects; found on shrubs and other vegetation, particularly in meadows. (See Fig. 20.40 and A&J 53.) (1) n.e. NA; (2) s.e. US.

[17.18 *Repipta* Stål (1 sp., *R. taurus* (Fabricius)); 17.19 *Rhynocoris* Hahn (4 spp.); 17.20 *Rocconota* Stål (1 sp., *R. annulicornis* (Stål))]

17.21 *Sinea* Amyot and Serville

Four species, including the following:

S. diadema (Fabricius) (Spined Assassin Bug). L. 12–14 mm. Body bright red to dark brown; lobe of pronotum black; wings black with yellowish markings; legs and tip of beak black. Adults active June through October. Found on weeds and grasses along roadsides and fallow fields in summer and on flowers of Compositae in autumn. (See Fig. 20.41.) Very common throughout the U.S. (1), (2), (3), (4), (5).

17.22 *Zelus* Fabricius

Seven species, including the following:

Z. exsanguis (Stål). L. 15–17 mm. Greenish-yellow in life, fading to dull straw-yellow in collections; second antennal

Fig. 20.40.

Fig. 20.41. (*From Blatchley, 1926*)

segment long, nearly half length of first. Found on small trees and shrubs in upland woods from May through September. (1) n.e. US; (2) s.e. US; (4) Pacific n.w. (5) n. Central States.

Z. renardii Kolenati (Leafhopper Assassin Bug). A southwestern U.S. species introduced into Hawaii for pest control.

Z. longipes (Linnaeus). (See Fig. 20.42) (2) s.e. US; (3) TX.

Subfamily Microtominae

[17.23 *Homalocoris* Perty (1 sp., *H. minutus* Mayr); 17.24 *Microtomus* Illiger (1 sp., *M. purcis* (Drury))]

Subfamily Piratinae

17.25 *Melanolestes* Stål

Two species, the following of which is common:

M. picipes (Herrich-Schaeffer). L. 15–20 mm. Black or reddish-black; antennae and legs with reddish tinge; female nearly wingless. Predacious. Found beneath stones, under loose bark, or in piles of weeds. Overwinters in dry upland woods, fields, and under logs. (1) n.e. US; (2) s.e US; (2) s.w. US; (5) MN, SD, NE, IA, KS, MO.

[17.26 *Rasahus* Amyot and Serville (1 sp., *R. biguttatus* (Say)); 17.27 *Sirthenea* Spinola (1 sp., *S. carinata* (Fabricius))]

Subfamily Reduviinae

[17.28 *Pseudozelurus* Lent and Wygodninsky (1 sp., *P. arizonicus* (Banks))]

17.29 *Reduvius* Fabricius

One species, as follows:

R. personatus (Linnaeus) (Masked Hunter; also Kissing Bug). L. 17–20 mm. Nearly uniformly black with reddish tinge; pale markings on legs; body of nymph with bristly hairlike setae that gather dust, thereby accounting for the common name Masked Hunter. Feeds on Bed Bugs and other insects in houses.

Fig. 20.42.

Fig. 20.43.

Attracted to lights during June and July. It is known to bite humans, sometimes on the lips (which swell greatly) and hence the other common name, Kissing Bug. (See Fig. 20.43.) (1) n.e. US; (2) s.e. US; (5) MN, SD, NE, IA, KS, MO.

[17.30 *Zeluroides* Lent and Wygodzinsky (1 sp., *Z. americanus* Lent and Wygodzinsky)]

Subfamily Saicinae

[17.31 *Oncerotrachelus* Stål (2 spp.); 17.32 *Saica* Amyot and Serville (1 sp., *S. fuscovittata* Barber)]

Subfamily Stenopodinae

[17.33 *Ctenotrachelus* Stål (1 sp., *C. shermani* Barber)]

17.34 *Narvesus* Stål

One species, as follows:

N. carolinensis Stål. (See Fig. 20.44.) (1) NJ; (2) s.e. US; (3) AZ, TX.

[17.35 *Oncocephlus* Klug (3 spp.); 17.36 *Pnirontis* Stål (5 spp.); 17.37 *Pygolampis* Germar (2 spp.)]

Subfamily Triatominae

[17.38 *Paratriatoma* Barber (1 sp., *P. hirsuta* Barber)]

Fig. 20.44.

17.39 *Triatoma* Laporte

Twelve species, some of which are important as disease vectors. The following are examples:

T. sanguisuga (LeConte) (Bloodsucking Conenose). L. 16–21 mm. Dark brown to black with reddish-yellow markings; antennae with scattered bristly hairs. Predacious; in homes, feeds on Bed Bugs but also bites human beings and other mammals; vector of Chagas Disease, which has been reported in the southwestern U.S. (1) IL, IN, PA, NJ, MD; (2) s.e. US; (3) TX, OK; (5) KS, MO.

T. protracta (Uhler) (Western Bloodsucking Conenose).

T. rubrofasciatus (DeGeer) (Large Kissing Bug).

T. gerstaecheri (Stål). (See Fig. 20.45.) (3) TX.

18. NABIDAE (Damsel Bug Family)

L. 7–11 mm. Front femora enlarged; pronotum two-lobed; ocelli present; usually brown, some yellowish, a few black with yellow legs; wingss fully developed to very short. Predacious. There are 11 genera and 48 species, as follows:

Subfamily Prostemminae

[18.1 *Pagasa* Stål (3 spp.); 18. 2 *Phorticus* Stål (2 spp.); 18. 3 *Alloeorrhynchus* Fieber (7 spp.)]

Subfamily Nabinae

Tribe Nabini

[18.4 *Arachnocoris* Scott (3 spp.)]

18.5 *Nabis* Latreille

Eleven species, some common ones being as follows:

N. americoferus Carayon (Common Damsel Bug). L. 6–9 mm. Dull gray-yellow; head and front lobe of pronotum with an obscure median dark stripe; hind lobe usually with five vague dusky stripes; elytra with numerous small, brownish-gray dots. Found on grasses and weeds in meadows and old fields from May to October. Overwinters under dead leaves along roadsides and cultivated fields. (See Fig. 20.46.) Very common throughout the U.S. (1), (2), (3), (4), (5).

N. capsiformis Germar (Pale Damsel Bug).

N. alternatus Parshley (Western Damsel Bug).

Fig. 20.45.

Fig. 20.46. (*From Blatchley, 1926*)

18.6 *Nabicula* Kirby

One species, as follows.

N. subcoleopteratus Kirby. L. 9–11 mm. Resembles ants or certain beetles. Shining black; sides of head behind eyes gradually converging obliquely backward; antennae and legs pale brownish-yellow. Abundant in grasses and weeds in fields from June through August, often on goldenrod. (See Fig. 20.47.) (1) n.e. US; (5) MN, NE, IA, KS, CO.

[18.7 *Hoplistoscelis* Reuter (5 spp.); 18.8 *Lasiomerus* Reuter (4 spp.); 18.9 *Dolichonabis* Reuter (3 spp.); 18.10 *Metatropiphorus* Reuter (2 spp.)]

Tribe Gorpini

[18.11 *Carthasis* Champion (7 spp.)]

19. POLYCTENIDAE (Bat Bug Family)

L. 3.5–4.5 mm. These bat ectoparasites, which resemble staphylinid beetles, are extremely rare. The two species are listed below.

19.1 *Hesperoctenes* Kirkaldy

H. eumops Ferris and Usinger. (3) CA.

H. hermsi Ferris and Usinger. (3) TX.

Fig. 20.47.

20. CIMICIDAE (Bed Bug Family)

L. 3–6 mm. Ectoparasites of mammals and birds as bloodsuckers. Their hosts include chickens, swallows, hawks, owls, condors, and human beings. There are seven genera and 14 species represented in the U.S. and Canada.

Subfamily Primicimicinae

[20.1 *Primicimex* Barber (1 sp., *P. cavernis* Barber)]

Subfamily Cimicinae

20.2 *Cimex* Linnaeus

Seven species, of which the most infamous follows:

C. lectularius Linnaeus (Bed Bug). L. 4–5 mm. Ectoparasite of man, chickens, and other mammals and birds. Flat; reddish-brown. In order for the nymphs to mature, they must suck blood during each of their five nymphal instars. The bug frequently makes several punctures, resulting in swellings at each. Since their salivary fluid is not immediately irritating, the bites go unnoticed for awhile. The nymph and adult leave the host after feeding and hide out of the way of harm. These insects, as do other blood-feeding parasites, have certain bacteria in their body to supply them with essential vitamin B that would otherwise be lacking in their blood as a nutrient; these bacteria are passed on from adult to nymphs through the eggs. During times of human stress, Bed Bugs may become very abundant. The number of nymphs and adults feeding at night may be large enough to cause lethargy in the host. They have been implicated, but without conclusive evidence, in the transmission of at least 25 diseases. Cosmopolitan. (See Fig. 20.48.)

20.3 *Oeciacus* Stål

One species, as follows:

O. vicarius (Swallow Bug). L. 4–4.6 mm. covered with long, silky, pale hairlike setae. Feeds on swallows, particularly Cliff Swallows. Occurs throughout NA. (1), (2), (3), (4), (5).

Subfamily Haematosiphoninae

20.4 *Haematosiphon* Champion

One species, as follows:

H. inodorus (Duges). L. 4–4.5 mm. The long labium distinguishes this species from the Bed Bug. It feeds on owls,

Fig. 20.48. (*From Blatchley, 1926*)

eagles, and the California Condor, as well as chickens. (3) s. w. U.S.).

[20.5 *Cimexopsis* List (1 sp., *C. nyctalus* List); 20.6 *Synxenoderus* List (1 sp., *S. comosus* List); 20.7 *Hesperocimex* List (2 spp.)]

21. ANTHOCORIDAE (Minute Pirate Bug Family)

L. 2–5 mm. These minute, flattened bugs are easily confused with many other small bugs but usually may be distinguished by the faint or obsolete veins in the membrane of the front wing. The 24 genera include 85 species in the U.S. and Canada, many of them rather common on flowers and trees; others live under bark, in fungus, and even in nests of mammals and birds. Some use the peculiar method of insemination found in the Cimicidae (20) (see introduction to this order).

Subfamily Anthocorinae

Tribe Anthocorini

[21.1 *Melanocoris* Champion (2 spp.); 21.2 *Elatophilus* Reuter (4 spp.); 21.3 *Temnostethus* Fieber (2 spp.); 21.4 *Coccivora* McAtee and Mallock (1 sp., *C. californica* McAtee and Malloch); 21.5 *Anthocoris* Fallen (14 spp.); 21.6 *Tetraphleps* Fieber (5 spp.); 21.7 *Acompocoris* Reuter (2 spp.)]

Tribe Oriini

[21.8 *Orius* Wolff (7 spp.); 21.9 *Paratriphleps* Champion (1 sp., *P. laeviusculus* Champion); 21.10 *Macrotracheliella* Champion (4 spp.); 21.11 *Montandoniola* Poppius (1 sp., *M. moraguesi* (Puton))]

Subfamily Lasiochilinae

[21.12 *Plochiocoris* Champion (1 sp., *P. comptulus* Drake and Harris); 21.13 *Lasiochilus* Reuter (7 spp.)]

Subfamily Lycotocorinae

Tribe Lyctocorini

21.14 *Lyctocoris* Hahn

Nine species, the following being a common example:

L. campestris (Fabricius). L. ±3.5 mm. Found in houses, granaries, and the nests of birds and mammals; they may bite. (See Fig. 20.49.) Occurs throughout the U.S. (1), (2), (3), (4), (5).

Tribe Xylocorini

[21.15 *Xylocoris* Dufour (8 spp.)]

Fig. 20.49. (*From Blatchley, 1926*)

Tribe Scolopini

[21.16 *Scoloposcelis* Fieber (5 spp.); 21.17 *Calliodis* Reuter (2 spp.); 21.18 *Nidicola* Harris and Drake (1 sp., *N. marginata* Harris and Drake); 21.19 *Lasiochiloides* Champion (1 sp., *L. socialis* Drake and Harris)]

Tribe Cardiastethini

[21.20 *Physopleurella* Reuter (1 sp., *P. floridana* Blatchley); 21.21 *Amphiareus* Distant (1 sp., *A. constrictus* (Stål)); 21.22 *Alofa* Herring (1 sp., *A. sodalis* (White)); 21.23 *Cardiastethus* Fieber (3 spp.); 21.24 *Dufouriellus* Van Duzee (1 sp., *D. ater* (Dufour))]

22. MICROPHYSIDAE (Minute Bladder Bug Family)

L. 1–1.5 mm. One rare species, as listed below.

22.1 *Mallochiola* Bergroth

M. gagates (McAtee and Malloch). Habitat unknown. (1) MD, DC.

23. MIRIDAE (Plant Bug Family)

L. 2–10 mm. Front wings with a cuneus (see Fig. 20.1); membrane with one or two cells; ocelli absent (except in the Isometopinae). This is the largest family of the Hemiptera, with 1,777 species in 207 genera in the U.S. and Canada, or slightly under 50 percent of the total order. The genera and species are difficult to identify even with the available technical literature (see Fig. 20.2). The following list of genera highlights the species that are of economic interest. Many species are plant juice feeders, and a large number are predacious. The Isometopinae (often treated as a separate family) includes eight species with ocelli and jumping hind legs; they are predators.

Subfamily Isometopinae

Tribe Diphlebini

[23.1 *Diphleps* Bergroth (1 sp., *D. unica* Bergroth)]

Tribe Isometopini

[23.2 *Corticoris* McAtee and Malloch (4 spp.); 23.3 *Lidopus* Gibson (1 sp., *L. heidemann* Gibson)]

23.4 *Myiomma* Puton

One species, as follows:

M. cixiforna (Uhler). The most widespread species of the subfamily. Found on bark and dead limbs of scale infested trees; predacious. (1) MI, NY, PA, NJ, MD; (2) VA.

[23.5 *Wetmorea* McAtee and Malloch (1 sp., *W. notabilis* McAtee and Malloch)]

Subfamily Cylapinae

[23.6 *Cylapus* Say (1 sp., *C. tenuicornis* Say); 23.7 *Fulvius* Stål (2 spp.); 23.8 *Peritropis* Uhler (2 spp.)]

Subfamily Deraeocorinae

Tribe Clivinemini

[23.9 *Bothynotus* Fieber (5 spp.); 23.10 *Clivinema* Reuter (10 spp.); 23.11 *Largidea* Van Duzee (10 spp.)]

Tribe Hyaliodini

23.12 *Hyaliodes* Reuter

Three species, of which the following is representative:

H. vitripennis (Say). L. 4.5–4.8 mm. Hind margin of pronotum straight or nearly so; front wings glassy with dark brown markings. Found on grape vines and Jewelweed (Touchme-not); feeds on aphids. May to September. (1) n.e. US; (2) s.e. US; (3) TX.

Tribe Deraeocorini

[23.13 *Deraeocapsus* Knight (2 spp.)]

23.14 *Deraeocoris* Kirschbaum

This is a large genus of mostly predacious bugs with 56 species. The following is an example.

D. nebulosus (Uhler). L. 3.5–4 mm. Olive-yellow with black markings; membrane of front wing with two brown spots. Found on White Oak and other trees as well as shrubs. Very common. (1) n.e. US; (2) s.e. US; (3) OK, TX; (5) CO, KS, MO.

[23.15 *Diplozona* Van Duzee (1 sp., *D. collaris* Van Duzee); 23.16 *Eurychilopterella* Reuter (3 spp.); 23.17 *Eustictus* Reuter (21 spp.); 23.18 *Hesperophylum* Reuter and Poppius (2 spp.)]

Tribe Termatophylini

[23.19 *Conocephalocoris* Knight (1 sp., *C. nasicus* Knight)]

Subfamily Bryocorinae

Tribe Bryocorini

[23.20 *Caulotops* Bergroth (2 spp.); 23.21 *Cyrtocapsus* Reuter (1 sp., *C. caligineus* Stål)]

23.22 *Halticotoma* Townsend

Five species, of which the following is common:

H. valida Townsend (Yucca Plant Bug). L. ±3.5 mm. Head, pronotum, and legs orange to red; hemelytra bluish-black. Found on Yucca. (1) IL, IN, OH, PA, NJ, MD, DE, DC; (2) s.e. US; (3) CA, AZ, OK, TX; (5) UT, CO.

[23.23 *Hemisphaerodella* Reuter (1 sp., *H. mirabilis* Reuter); 23.24 *Hesperolabops* Kirkaldy (1 sp., *H. gelastops* Kirkaldy); 23.25 *Monalocoris* Dahlbom (2 spp.)]

23.26 *Pycnoderes* Guérin-Méneville

Ten species, of which the following is of some economic importance:

P. quadrimaculatus Guerin-Meneville (Bean Capsid).

[23.27 *Sixeonotus* Reuter (17 spp.)]

Subfamily Dicyphinae

23.28 *Cyrtopeltis* Fieber

Six species, of which the following are of economic importance:

C. notatus (Distant) (Suckfly). Pest of tobacco. (2) s.e. US.

C. modestus (Distant) (Tomato Bug). Pest of tomatoes (2) MS, FL; (3) CA, TX.

23.29 *Dicyphus* Fieber

Twenty-one species, of which the following is representative:

D. famelicus Uhler. L. 4.5–5 mm. Pale greenish or straw-yellow, shining; front wings with red lines and streaks; eyes separated from pronotum by a space equal to dorsal width of an eye. Found on Flowering Raspberry. (1) n.e. NA; (2) VA, NC.

[23.30 *Macrolophus* Fieber (4 spp.)]

Subfamily Phylinae

Tribe Phylini

[23.31 *Amblytylus* Fieber (1 sp., *A. nasutus* (Kirschbaum)); 23.32 *Ankylotylus* Knight (1 sp., *A. pallipes* Knight); 23.33 *Atomoscelis* Reuter (1 sp., *A. modestus* (Van Duzee)); 23.34 *Atractotomus* Fieber (13 spp.); 23.35 *Beamerella* Knight (2 spp.); 23.36 *Beckocoris* Knight (1 sp., *B. laticephalus* Knight); 23.37 *Brachyceratocoris* Knight (1 sp., *B. nevadensis* Knight)]

23.38 *Chlamydatus* Curtis

Twenty-two species, including the following common one:

C. associatus (Uhler) (Ragweed Plant Bug). Found on ragweed and other plants throughout NA. (1), (2), (3), (4), (5).

[23.39 *Campylomma* Reuter (1 sp., *C. verbasci* (Meyer); 23.40 *Conostethus* Fieber (1 sp., *C. americanus* Knight); 23.41 *Criocoris* Fieber (2 spp.); 23.42 *Europiella* Reuter (37 spp.); 23.43 *Heidemanniella* Poppius (1 sp., *H. scutellaris* Poppius); 23.44 *Hoplomachidea* Reuter (1 sp., *H. consors* (Uhler)); 23.45 *Hoplomachus* Fieber (1 sp., *H. affiguratus* (Uhler)); 23.46 *Icodema* Reuter (1 sp., *I. nigrolineatum* (Knight)); 23.47 *Keltonia* Knight (4 spp.); 23.48 *Lepidopsallus* Knight (18 spp.); 23.49 *Megalopsallus* Knight (7 spp.); 23.50 *Merinocapsus* Knight (1 sp., *M. ephedrae* Knight); 23.51 *Microphylellus* Reuter (18 spp.); 23.52 *Microphylidea* Knight (2 spp.); 23.53 *Mineocapsus* Knight (1 sp., *M. minimus* Knight); 23.54 *Monosynamma* Scott (1 sp., *bohemani* (Fallen)); 23.55 *Myochroocoris* Reuter (1 sp., *M. griseolus* Reuter); 23.56 *Nevadocoris* Knight (3 spp.); 23.57 *Nicholia* Knight (1 sp., *N. eriogoni* Knight); 23.58 *Oncotylus* Fieber (1 sp., *O. guttalatus* Uhler); 23.59 *Phyllopidea* Knight (4 spp.); 23.60 *Phymatopsallus* Knight (20 spp.); 23.61 *Plagiognathus* Fieber (78 spp.); 23.62 *Plesiodema* Reuter (1 sp., *P. sericea* (Heidemann)); 23.63 *Psallus* Fieber (38 spp.)]

23.64 *Pseudatomoscelis* Poppius

One species, as follows:

P. seriatus (Reuter) (Cotton Fleahopper). L. ±3.5 mm. Second antennal segment with distinct black spots; hemelytra with silvery silky pubescence grouped into small clusters, arising from these spots. Found on cotton, also Croton, Evening Primrose, Goatweed, Sage Weed, Horsemint, and many other weeds. (See Fig. 20.50.) (1) IL, IN, PA, NJ; (2) KY, NC, LA, MS, AL, FL; (3) CA, AZ, TX; (5) UT, MN, CO, NE.

[23.65 *Ranzovius* Distant (1 sp., *R. moerens* Reuter); 23.66 *Reuteroscopus* Kirkaldy (5 spp.)]

23.67 *Rhinacloa* Reuter

Four species; the following name is in the literature:

R. forticornis Reuter (Western Plant Bug). Although given a common name and presumed to be an economic pest, H. H. Knight believed this species to be predacious. Found on a wide variety of weedy plants.

[23.68 *Rhinocapsus* Uhler (3 spp.)]

Fig. 20.50. (*From Knight, 1968*)

23.69 *Spanagonicus* Berg

One species, as follows:

S. albofasciatus (Reuter) (Whitemarked Fleahopper). Injurious to grass, the damage being especially noticeable on golf greens. (1) NJ, PA, MD; (2) s.e. US; (3) CA, AZ, TX; (5) MO.

[23.70 *Sthenarus* Fieber (5 spp.); 23.71 *Tannerocoris* Knight (1 sp., *T. sarcobati* Knight); 23.72 *Tuponia* Reuter (3 spp.); 23.73 *Tytthus* Fieber (7 spp.)]

Tribe Hallodapini

[23.74 *Chaetophylidea* Knight (1 sp., *C. moerens* (Reuter)); 23.75 *Coquillettia* Uhler (23 spp.); 23.76 *Orectoderus* Uhler (4 spp.); 23.77 *Pronotocrepis* Knight (3 spp.); 23.78 *Teleorhinus* Uhler (7 spp.)]

Tribe Oncotylini

[23.79 *Lopus* Hahn (1 sp., *L. decolor* (Fallen)); 23.80 *Macrotylus* Fieber (14 spp.); 23.81 *Megalocoleus* Reuter (1 sp., *M. molliculus* (Fallen))]

Subfamily Orthotylinae
Tribe Halticini

[23.82 *Anapus* Stål (1 sp., *A. americanus* Knight)]

23.83 *Halticus* Hahn

Three species, including the following:

H. bractatus (Say) (Garden Fleahopper). L. 3–4 mm. Black, with fine pale spots; extremities of legs and antennae pale. Females are of two types—a long-winged form, with straight sides, similar to the male, and a short-winged, round form. Males have long wings. Legs and antennae long. This species feeds on a wide variety of garden and truck crop vegetables and many weeds. (See Fig. 20.51 for male; Fig. 20.52 for short-winged females.) (1) n.e. NA; (2) s.e. US; (3) TX, OK; (5) ND, MN, SD, NE, IA, KS, MO.

[23.84 *Orthocephalus* Fieber (2 spp.); 23.85 *Scalponotatus* Kelton (2 spp.); 23.86 *Slaterocoris* Wagner (43 spp.)]

Tribe Orthotylini

[23.87 *Argyrocoris* Van Duzee (1 sp., *A. scurrilis* Van Duzee); 23.88 *Ballella* Knight (1 sp., *B. basicornis* Knight); 23.89 *Bifidungulus* Knight (2 spp.); 23.90 *Blepharidopterus* Kolenati (1 sp., *B. angulatus* Fallen); 23.91 *Brachynotocoris* Reuter (1 sp., *B. puncticornis* Reuter)]

Fig. 20.51. (*From Knight, 1968*)

23.92 *Brooksetta* Kelton

Fifteen species, of which the following is common.

B. althaeae (Hussey) (Hollyhock Plant Bug).

[23.93 *Ceratopidea* Knight (1 sp., *C. daleae* Knight); 23.94 *Cyrtorhinus* Fieber (1 sp., *C. caricis* (Fallen); 23.95 *Daleapidea* Knight (2 spp.); 23.96 *Diaphnidia* Uhler (2 spp.)]

23.97 *Diaphnocoris* Kelton

Four species, of which the following is of economic importance:

D. chlorionis (Say) (Honeylocust Plant Bug). L. 3.5–4 mm. Elongate-oval; pale green or greenish-yellow, fading to straw-yellow; pubescence of upper surface black; antennae and membrane of front wings entirely pale. Found on Honey Locust; also reported as a pest of beets. (1) n.e. NA; (3) CA.

[23.98 *Dichaetocoris* Knight (12 spp.); 23.99 *Fieberocapsus* Carvalho and Southwood (1 sp., *F. flaveolus* Reuter); 23.100 *Globiceps* LePeletier and Serville (3 spp.)]

23.101 *Hadronema* Uhler

Twelve species, of which the following is a common representative:

Fig. 20.52. (*From Knight, 1968*)

H. militare Uhler. L. 5–6 mm. Grayish-blue with distinct white lateral wing margins and pale hind margins of pronotum. Common on prairie grasses. (1) MI, NY, IN; (5) MT, ND, MN, WY, SD, NE, IA, CO, KS, MO.

[23.102 *Hesperocapsus* Knight (15 spp.); 23.103 *Heterocordylus* Fieber (2 spp.); 23.104 *Heterotoma* Latreille (1 sp., *H. meriopterum* (Scopoli); 23.105 *Hyalochloria* Reuter (1 sp., *H. caviceps* Reuter); 23.106 *Ilnacora* Reuter (14 spp.); 23.107 *Ilnacorella* Knight (3 spp.); 23.108 *Labopidea* Uhler (7 spp.)]

23.109 *Labopidicola* Kelton

Five species, of which the following is common:

L. allii Knight (Onion Plant Bug). Both long and short winged forms are known. Pest of onions, cultivated and wild.

23.110 *Lopidea* Uhler

This is an extremely large genus of 101 species, which are distinguished on the basis of the structure of the male genitalia. Some of the following species are of economic importance:

L. robiniae (Uhler). L. 6.5–6.8 mm. Dull orange to orange-red with black stripes. found on Black Locust. Active June through August. (1) n.e. NA; (2) s.e. US; (5) MN, IA, NE, CO, KS, MO.

L. media (Say). L. 5.6–5.7 mm. Bright red to orange-red with black stripes. Found on goldenrod. Active June through July. (1) n.e. NA; (2) s.e. US; (5) ND, MN, SD, NE, CO, KS, MO.

L. confluenta (Say). (See Fig. 20.53 for female.)

L. dakota Knight (Caragana Plant Bug).

L. davisi Knight (Phlox Plant Bug).

[23.111 *Lopidella* Knight (1 sp., *L. flavoscuta* Knight); 23.112 *Macrotyloides* Van Duzee (2 spp.); 23.113 *Mecomma* Fieber (4 spp.); 23.114 *Melanotrichus* Reuter (30 spp.); 23.115 *Noctuocoris* Knight (1 sp., *N. fumidus* Van Duzee); 23.116 *Orthotylus* Fieber (45 spp.); 23.117 *Paraproba* Distant (5 spp.); 23.118 *Parthenicus* Reuter (68 spp.); 23.119 *Pseudopsallus* Van Duzee (3 spp.); 23.120 *Reuteria* Puton (8 spp.); 23.121 *Saileria* Hsiao (1 sp., *S. bella* (Van Duzee)); 23.122 *Sericophanes* Reuter (8 spp.); 23.123 *Squamocoris* Knight (2 spp.); 23.124 *Texocoris* Schaffner (1 sp., *T. secludis* Schaffner)]

Tribe Pilophorini

[23.125 *Alepidia* Reuter (2 spp.); 23.126 *Alepidiella* Poppius (1 sp., *A. heidemanni* Poppius); 23.127 *Pilophorus* Hahn (45 spp.); 23.128

Pseudoxenetus Reuter (2 spp.); 23.129 *Renodaeus* Distant (1 sp., *R. texanus* Knight)]

Tribe Ceratocapsini

[23.130 *Ceratocapsus* Reuter (65 spp.); 23.131 *Pamillia* Uhler (4 spp.); 23.132 *Pilophoropsis* Poppius (3 spp.); 23.133 *Schaffneria* Knight (5 spp.)]

Tribe Labopini

[23.134 *Labopella* Knight (1 sp., *L. claripennis* Knight); 23.135 *Labops* Burmeister (8 spp.)]

Tribe Semiini

[23.136 *Semium* Reuter (2 spp.)]

Tribe Systellonotini

[23.137 *Cyrtopeltocoris* Reuter (10 spp.)]

Subfamily Mirinae

Tribe Mirini

[23.138 *Acetropis* Fieber (1 sp., *A. americana* Knight)]

23.139 *Adelphocoris* Reuter

Three species, as follows:

A. rapidus (Say) (Rapid Plant Bug). L. 7–8 mm. Dark brown with dull, pale yellowish margins of front wings; antennae alternately black and light yellow; pronotum with two dark spots. Feeds on *Rumex* spp.; sometimes a pest of cotton and legumes. (See Fig. 20.54.) (1) n.e. US; (2) s.c. US; (5) ND, MN, SD, NE, IA, KS, MO.

A. lineolatus (Goeze) (Alfalfa Plant Bug).

A. superbus (Uhler) (Superb Plant Bug).

[23.140 *Agnocoris* Reuter (4 spp.); 23.141 *Allorhinocoris* Reuter (2 spp.); 23.142 *Bolteria* Uhler (14 spp.); 23.143 *Calocoris* Fieber (5 spp.); 23.144 *Calyptodera* Van Duzee (1 sp., *C. robusta* Van Duzee); 23.145 *Camptozygum* Reuter (1 sp., *C. aequale* Villers))]

23.146 *Closterocoris* Uhler

One species only, as follows:

C. amoenus (Provancher). L. 6–8 mm. Body narrow and elongate; eyes some distance from pronotal collar; pronotum

Fig. 20.53. (*From Knight, 1968*)

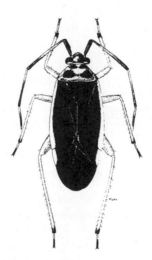

Fig. 20.54. (*From Knight, 1968*)

triangular and collar region flattened; tarsi with first tarsomere elongated. (See A&J 50.) (3) CA.

[23.147 *Coccobaphes* Uhler (1 sp., *C. sanguinareus* Uhler); 23.148 *Creontiades* Distant (3 spp.); 23.149 *Cyphopelta* Van Duzee (1 sp., *C. modesta* Van Duzee)]

Tribe **Hersoniini**

[23.150 *Paradacerla* Carvalho and Usinger (2 spp.); 23.151 *Paraxenetus* Reuter (1 sp., *P. guttulatus* (Uhler); 23.152 *Barberiella* Poppius (1 sp., *B. formicoides* Poppius)]

23.153 *Dacerla* Bergroth

Two species, including the following:

D. mediospinosa Signoret (Ant Bug). L. 4–6 mm. Shape antlike; pronotum with raised posterior margin forming spine-like projection. Yellow; head dark brown; apical half of front wings dark. Found on lupines with ants. (See A&J 52.) (3) CA.

[23.154 *Dagbertus* Distant (2 spp.); 23.155 *Derophthalma* Berg (1 sp., *D. variegata* (Blatchley)); 23.156 *Dichrooscytus* Fieber (30 spp.); 23.157 *Ecertobia* Reuter (1 sp., *E. decora* Reuter); 23.158 *Ectopiocerus* Uhler (1 sp., *E. anthracinus* Uhler); 23.159 *Ganocapsus* Van Duzee (1 sp., *G. filiformis* Van Duzee); 23.160 *Garganus* Stål (3 spp.); 23.161 *Irbisia* Reuter (15 spp.); 23.162 *Klopicoris* Van Duzee (1 sp., *K. phorodendronea* Van Duzee); 23.163 *Lampethusa* Distant (2 spp.)]

23.164 *Lygidea* Reuter

Nine species, the following of which is of economic importance:

L. mendax Reuter (Apple Red Bug). L. 6.3–6.5 mm. Orange-red with dark brown to black markings; wing margins nearly parallel. Found on cultivated apple, crataegus, and other rosaceous trees and shrubs. June through July. (1) n.e. US.

23.165 *Lygocoris* Reuter

Thirty-eight species, the following of which are of economic interest:

L. caryae (Knight) (Hickory Plant Bug).

L. communis (Knight) (Pear Plant Bug).

23.166 *Lygus* Hahn

Thirty-four species, of which the following is an important plant pest:

L. lineolaris (Palisot de Beauvois). (Tarnished Plant Bug). L. 5–6 mm. Yellowish-brown with brown and black mottling; scutellum with broad yellow Y-marking. Abundant as pest on nursery stock, ornamental plants, cultivated crops, preferring Compositae and Umbelliferae. June through Sept. Very abundant throughout NA. (1), (2), (3), (4), (5).

23.167 *Metriorrhynchomiris* Kirkaldy

[= *Horcias* Distant of some authors]

Three species, the following being of interest:

M. dislocatus (Say). L. ±6.5 mm. Usually reddish-orange with large black spot on base of scutellum and black stripes on wings, but color extremely variable. Found on *Smilacina racemosa*, *Geranium maculatum*, *Scrophularia* spp., and other plants, especially in shaded areas. April to July. (See A&J 51.) (1) n.e. US; (2) s.e. US; (3) TX; (5) MN, IA, MO.

[23.168 *Neoborella* Knight (2 spp.); 23.169 *Neoborops* Uhler (1 sp., *N. vigilax* Uhler); 23.170 *Neocapsus* Distant (1 sp., *N. cuneatus* Distant)]

23.171 *Neurocolpus* Reuter

Fourteen species, the following being a common representative:

N. nubilus (Say) (Clouded Plant Bug). L. 6.5–7 mm. Antennae with flattened hairs on first segment; bright reddish-tan to yellow-brown; front wings with very small yellow spots. Found on buttonbush and many other plants. June to August. (1) n.e. NA; (2) s.e. US; (3) NM, OK, TX; (5) CO, KS, MO.

[23.172 *Notholopus* Bergroth (1 sp., *N. californicus* Knight); 23.173 *Orthops* Fieber (1 sp., *O. scutellatus* (Uhler); 23.174 *Pachypeltocoris* Knight (1 sp., *P. conspersus* Knight); 23.175 *Pallacocoris* Reuter (1 sp., *P. suavis* Reuter); 23. 176 *Phytocoris* Fallén (198 spp.); 23.177 *Pinalitus* Kelton (6 spp.); 23.178 *Platylygus* Van Duzee (6 spp.); 23.179 *Plesiocoris* Fieber (1 sp., *P. rugicollis* (Fallén))]

23.180 *Poecilocapsus* Reuter

Two species, of which the following is a pest:

P. lineatus (Fabricius) (Four-lined Plant Bug). L. 7–7.5 mm. Bright green with four broad black stripes on pronotum and wings, usually with a large black spot in cuneus of front wings. Found on a great variety of plants; often a pest of garden crops. (See Fig. 20.55) (1) n.e. NA; (4) Pacific n.w.; (5) n. central states.

[23.181 *Polymerus* Hahn (42 spp.); 23.182 *Proba* Distant (3 spp.); 23.183 *Pycnocoris* Van Duzee (1 sp., *P. ursinus* Van Duzee); 23.184 *Rhasis* Distant (1 sp., *R. laeviscutatus* (Knight)); 23.185 *Salignus* Kelton (1 sp., *S. distinguendus* (Reuter)); 23.186 *Stenotus* Jakovlev (1 sp., *S. binotatus* (Fabricius)); 23.187 *Sittocapsus* Knight (1 sp., *S. franseriae* Knight)]

23.188 *Taedia* Distant

Twenty-six species, the following being of some economic importance:

T. hawleyi (Knight) (Hop Plant Bug).

[23.189 *Taylorilygus* Leston (1 sp., *T. pallidulus* (Blanchard))]

Fig. 20.55. (*From Blatchley, 1926*)

23.190 *Tropidosteptes* Uhler

[= *Xenoborus* Reuter]

Thirty-six species, the following being of some economic importance:

T. amoenus Reuter (Ash Plant Bug). This species and most others in this genus feed on Ash. Its form and color are extremely variable.

Tribe Pithanini

[23.191 *Mimoceps* Uhler (1 sp., *M. insignis* Uhler); 23.192 *Pithanus* Fieber (1 sp., *P. maerkelii* (Herrich-Schaeffer))]

Tribe Stenodemini

[23.193 *Actitocoris* Reuter (1 sp., *A. signatus* Reuter); 23.194 *Chaetofoveolocoris* Knight (1 sp., *C. hirsuta* Knight); 23.195 *Collaria* Provancher (3 spp.); 23.196 *Dolichomiris* Reuter (1 sp., *D. linearis* Reuter)]

23.197 *Leptopterna* Fieber

Two species, the following being of economic importance:

L. dolabrata (Linnaeus). L. 7–9 mm. Color varies from yellow-orange to reddish-brown in males and pale green to nearly white with two black stripes on pronotum of females; wings short in females. Pest of blue grass and timothy. Eggs overwinter in stems of grasses and are hence widely distributed by livestock hay. Introduced from Europe. (See Fig. 20.56.) (1) n.e. NA; (2) s.e. US; (5) CO, KS, MO.

[23.198 *Litomiris* Slater (7 spp.); 23.199 *Megaloceroea* Fieber (1 sp., *M. recticornis* (Geoffroy)); 23.200 *Porpomiris* Berg (2 spp.)]

23.201 *Stenodema* Laporte

Six species, the following being a common one:

S. trispinosa (Reuter). L. 6.8–7.5 mm. Three spines on underside of hind femora. Found on grasses in moist meadows. July to August, and later; may overwinter as adults. (1) n.e. NA; (4) Pacific n.w.; (5) n. central states.

[23.202 *Teratocoris* Fieber (6 spp.); 23.203 *Trigonotylus* Fieber (18 spp.)]

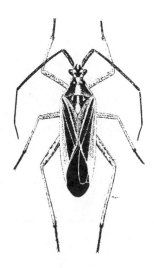

Fig. 20.56. (*From Knight, 1968*)

Fig. 20.57.

Tribe Resthenini

[23.204 *Oncerometopus* Reuter (8 spp.); 23.205 *Opistheurista* Carvalho (1 sp., *O. clandestina* (Van Duzee))]

23.206 *Prepops* Reuter

Thirty-five species, including the following:

P. fraternus (Knight). Found on sumac. (See Fig. 20.57.) (1) n.e. US.

24. DIPSOCORIDAE (Ground Bug Family)

L. 0.75–1.7 mm. Head and tibiae with long bristles. These tiny insects, which live beneath dead leaves along the margins of streams and lakes, run quickly when disturbed. There are five species in two genera as follows:

24.1 *Ceratocombus* Signoret

Three species, as follows:

C. vagans McAtee and Malloch. Locally distributed. (1) n.e. US; (2) s.e. US.

C. latipennis Uhler. (3) NM; (5) MO.

C. hesperus McAtee and Malloch. (3) CA.

24.2 *Cryptostemma* Herrich-Schaeffer

Two species, known only from (2) GA; (3) CA.

25. SCHIZOPTERIDAE (Jumping Soil Bug Family)

L. 0.8–2 mm. Second antennal segment twice as long as first; otherwise similar to the preceding family, with which it is often combined. The family is largely tropical. They live in damp soil and leaf litter, jumping when disturbed. There are 3 species, very rare, with very restricted distribution, as indicated below.

Subfamily Hypselosomatinae

25.1 *Glyptocombus* Heideman

G. saltator Heidemann. (1) MI, MD; (2) TN.

Subfamily Schizopterinae

[25.2 *Corixidea* Reuter (1 sp., *C. major* McAtee and Malloch, (2) TN); 25.3 *Schizoptera* Fieber (1 sp., *S. bispina* McAtee and Malloch, (2) FL, in Spanish Moss)]

Suborder NEPOMORPHA

26. HYDROMETRIDAE (Marsh Treader Bug Family)

L. 7–11 mm. Very slender; long legs; long head with eyes about midway between base and apex. These aquatic bugs resemble tiny walkingsticks; they are able to walk on the surface of small ponds or may be found on aquatic vegetation. One genus, with nine species.

26.1 *Hydrometra* Latreille

H. martini Kirkaldy. L. 8–11 mm. Dark or reddish brown with vague pale markings. They feed on small insects and crustaceans. (See Fig. 20.58.) (1) n.e. NA; (2) s.e. US; (3) AZ, TX.

27. GERRIDAE (Water Strider Bug Family)

L. 2.5–15 mm. These bugs can hardly be mistaken for any other insect. Their characteristic shape, long legs, and darting motions over the surface of a pond or stream are familiar to anyone who even casually watches fresh water life. Water Striders often jump up in the air, and, landing again, make dimples in the water's surface without breaking it (See Fig. 20.59). Since their hairy legs are normally not wetable, the slight pressure of their body does not break the surface film. They seldom fly; instead, they move about on their middle and hind pair of legs, holding the front pair up to grasp either living or dead insects and other aquatics upon which they feed. Both winged and wingless adults of the same species occur in the same populations. Eggs are laid at, or just beneath, the surface of the water on any solid object. They hibernate during the winter but sometimes become active on warm winter days and may be seen swimming. The 45 species are assigned to eight genera, as follows.

Subfamily Gerrinae

[27.1 *Limnogonus* Stål (1 sp., *L. franciscanus* (Stål)); 27.2 *Neogerris* Matsumura (1 sp., *N. hesione* (Kirkaldy))]

27.3 *Gerris* Fabricius

This is the largest genus of the family, with 15 species; it is also the largest in terms of the physical size of its species, all of

Fig. 20.59. (*Courtesy of O. Wilford Olsen and* Insect World Digest)

them measuring over 10 mm; other species in the family range from 2.5 to 5 mm. The abdomen of this genus is elongate; that of other genera, short. Identification of the species requires technical keys. The following is a common species:

G. remigis Say. L. 11–15 mm. Dark brown to black with yellow or orange stripe down middle of anterior lobe of pronotum. Adults active from March to October on surface of streams, rivers, ponds, and lakes. (See Fig. 20.60 and A&J 48.) Very common throughout NA. (1), (2), (3), (4), (5).

[27.4 *Limnoporus* Stål (4 spp.)]

Subfamily Halobatinae

27.5 *Halobates* Eschscholtz

One species only near the U.S., but several other species in the Pacific Ocean, with a total of 42 species in the world. Since the only insects to be found on the ocean beyond the shoreline belong to this group, these are the only truly marine insects; many other species representing several insect orders live in salt water, but always at or very close to the shore.

H. sericeus Eschscholtz (Pacific Pelagic Water Strider). L. 3.5–6.5 mm. Black, but appears gray because of covering pile;

Fig. 20.58. (*From Blatchley, 1926*)

Fig. 20.60.

abdomen short; front legs short; middle legs longest. This is the most abundant of the five open ocean species and occurs throughout the Pacific.

Subfamily Rhagadotarsinae

[27.6 *Rheumatobates* Bergroth (8 spp.)]

Subfamily Trepobatinae

[27.7 *Metrobates* Uhler (6 spp.); 27.8 *Trepobates* Uhler (9 spp.)]

28. VELIIDAE (Smaller Water Strider Bug Family)

L. 2–4 mm. Some of these insects resemble Water Striders (Gerridae), but others are broader, with much shorter legs. The middle pair of legs are about equidistant from front and hind legs. Thirty-five species are assigned to the following five genera.

Subfamily Rhagoveliinae

[28.1 *Trochopus* Carpenter (1 sp., *T. plumbeus* Uhler))]

28.2 *Rhagovelia* Mayr

Nine species, of which the following is representative:

R. obesa Uhler. L. 3–4 mm. Black with basal third of first antennal segment pale yellowish-white. Adults found from July to October in schools on surface of rapid streams in sheltered spots and eddies. (See Fig. 20.61 for male; Fig. 20.62 for female.) (1) n.e. NA; (2) s.e. US; (5) MN.

Subfamily Microveliinae

[28.3 *Husseyella* Herring (1 sp., *H. turmalis* Drake and Harris)]

28.4 *Microvelia* Westwood

This is the largest genus, with 19 species. A common species follows.

M. americana (Uhler). L. 2–2.5 mm. Abdomen with large silver patches of hair. Found along banks of sluggish streams and ponds, submerged sticks, floating vegetation, and sides of springs. (1) n.e. NA; (2) s.e. US; (5) CO, KS, MO.

Subfamily Veliinae

[28.5 *Paravelia* Breddin (5 spp.)]

Fig. 20.61. (*From Blatchley, 1926*)

Fig. 20.62. (*From Blatchley, 1926*)

29. MESOVELIIDAE (Water Treader Bug Family)

L. 2–4 mm. Semiaquatic bugs found on the surface of ponds and sometimes lakes, living in areas of dense surface vegetation. They are green or brown with yellow markings and resemble Miridae (23) with long legs. Five species are assigned to the following three genera.

29.1 *Mesovelia* Mulsant and Rey

Three species, of which the following is the most widespread:

M. mulsanti White. L. ±3 mm. Found throughout the U.S. (1), (2), (3), (4), (5).

[29.2 *Macrovelia* Uhler (1 sp., *M. hornii* Uhler); 29.3 *Oravelia* Drake and Chapman (1 sp., *O. pege* Drake and Chapman)]

30. HEBRIDAE (Velvet Water Bug Family)

L. Less than 3 mm. Body densely covered with pubescence. They walk on the surface of pond water or on floating mats of vegetation. Most are rare, at least in collections, but are widely distributed. The 15 species are assigned to two genera, as follows:

[30.1 *Hebrus* Curtis (12 spp.)]

30.2 *Merragata* White

Three species, of which the following is relatively common and widespread:

M. hebriodes White. (1) n.e. US; (2) s.e. US; (5) CO, KS, MO.

31. LEPTOPODIDAE (Spiny-legged Bug Family)

Only one species of this family occurs in the U.S., as follows:

31.1 *Patapius* Horvath

P. spinosus (Rossi). L. 3–3.5 mm. Spines on the head, thorax, and front legs. Predacious. Introduced. (3) CA.

32. SALDIDAE (Shore Bug Family)

L. 3–6 mm. Large flylike eyes and head, often with stout antennae, and black or brown body with white markings distinguish this family, which somewhat resemble tiger beetles both in shape and habit. Long spines absent. These tiny predacious bugs are found along grassy shores, often digging

holes and spending part of their life underground. Salt and brackish marshes may contain great numbers of them; others live on stones in streams and marshes near springs. The 76 species found in the U.S. and Canada are assigned to the following 11 genera.

Subfamily Chiloxanthinae

[32.1 *Enalosalda* Polhemus and Evans (1 sp., *E. mexicanum* (Van Duzee)); 32.2 *Chiloxanthus* Reuter (1 sp., *C. stellata* (Curtis)); 32.3 *Pentacora* Reuter (5 spp.)]

Subfamily Saldinae

[32.4 *Saldoida* Osborn (3 spp.); 32.5 *Lampracanthia* Reuter (1 sp., *L. crassicornis* (Uhler)); 32.6 *Calacanthia* Reuter (1 sp., *C. trybomi* (Sahlberg)); 32.7 *Teloleuca* Reuter (2 spp.); 32.8 *Salda* Fabricius (12 spp.); 32.9 *Ioscytus* Reuter (5 spp.)]

32.10 *Saldula* Van Duzee

Thirty-four species, of which the following is a common representative:

S. pallipes (Fabricius). L. 4–5 mm. Black, usually with pale yellow or white marking on front wing but sometimes entirely black. May to August along shores of streams or on rocks in streams. Occurs throughout the U.S. (1), (2), (3), (4), (5).

[32.11 *Micracanthia* Reuter (11 spp.)]

33. NOTONECTIDAE (Backswimmer Bug Family)

L. 1.8–15.5 mm. These insects resemble a boat, their legs being the oars. They swim with their dark ventral surface up (that is, on their backs) with their wings serving as the bottom of the boat. Their back is light in color, making them less visible from below in their inverted position. The hind pair of legs are much longer than the others. Backswimmers rest at the surface, usually with their head down and their abdomen piercing the water film to allow air to pass through the pile covered channel from the abdominal tip to spiracles on the thorax. Backswimmers prey on other small, aquatic animals and will inflict a painful bite if handled. Not only are they good swimmers—less erratic than Water Boatmen (35)—they also fly and are attracted to lights at night. Males have a stridulatory apparatus probably used to attract females and communicate during courtship. Both the stridulatory structures and features of the male genitalia serve for accurate identification of the species. Three genera and 35 species occur in the U.S. and Canada, as follows.

Subfamily Anisopinae

33.1 *Buenoa* Kirkaldy

Fifteen species in the U.S., mostly in the Southwest. Front wings lack pubescence; antennae three-segmented. The following is a common species:

B. margaritacea Torre-Bueno. L. 6–8 mm. Pearly-white to pale straw-yellow above; scutellum orange-yellow (preserved specimens darken); body slender. Adults frequent ponds and large water tanks. Found throughout the U.S. (1), (2), (3), (4), (5).

Subfamily Notonectinae

33.2 *Martarega* White

One species only, *M. mexicana* Truxal, reported from (3) AZ.

33.3 *Notonecta* Linnaeus

Nineteen species. Front wings pubescent; antennae four-segmented, the apical segment much shorter than the preceding segment.

N. undulata Say (Backswimmer). L. 18–20 mm. Black and white with black scutellum. Found in weedy ponds and streams from May to August in the North but throughout the year in warmer regions. (See Fig. 20.63 and A&J 49.) This is the most common species, found throughout the U.S. (1), (2), (3), (4), (5).

N. insulata Kirby. L. 12–16 mm. Head and pronotum pale greenish-yellow; scutellum and part of pronotum black; wings pale grayish or dull whitish to yellowish with black crossbar beyond midwing, distally with traces of reddish to orange. Found in pools. (1) n.e. NA; (5) MO.

N. indica Linnacus. (See Fig. 20.64.) (3) s.w. US; (4) OR, NV, UT.

34. PLEIDAE (Pigmy Backswimmer Bug Family)

L. ±2.5 mm. Similar to backswimmers but lack a fringe of hair on the hind tibiae and tarsi; abdomen without a keel on the midline; all legs subequal in length. Predacious. Two genera and seven species, as follows:

34.1 *Neoplea* Esaki and China

Five species, including the following:

N. striola. Found in pools with abundant aquatic vegetation. (1) n.e. NA; (2) s.e. US.

[34.2 *Paraplea* Esaki and China (2 spp.)]

35. CORIXIDAE (Water Boatman Bug Family)

L. 3–11 mm. Proboscis unsegmented; wings same texture throughout, some without differentiated membrane on front wings. These water bugs swim through the water and feed or rest on the bottom or on aquatic plants. They take air directly into the thoracic spiracles when they come up to the surface, where they float in a horizontal position. Males make sounds by rubbing their front legs against the front of their head. Some species are vegetarians; others are predacious. A few have been known to eat small particles of solid food, the only bugs known to consume other than liquid substances. The female fastens her eggs on submerged objects but does not insert them into vegetation. They are attracted to lights at night. Certain tropical species—for example, some species of *Ahautlea* (35.7)—are so

Fig. 20.63. (*Courtesy of J. E. V. Gerberg*)

Fig. 20.64.

Fig. 20.65. (*Courtesy of Kurzius and* Insect World Digest)

abundant that they and their eggs are gathered for human food and frequently constitute a substantial part of the food of birds. With 19 genera and 122 species in the U.S. and Canada, this is the largest family of water bugs. The species are all very similar and can be distinguished mainly by structures of the male genitalia and other technical characteristics.

Subfamily Micronectinae

[35.1 *Tenagobia* Bergroth (1 sp., *T. mexicana* Deay)]

Subfamily Cymatiinae

[35.2 *Cymatia* Flor (1 sp., *C. americana* Hussey)]

Subfamily Corixinae
Tribe Glaenocorisini

[35.3 *Glaenocorisa* Thomson (1 sp., *G. quadrata* Walley); 35.4 *Dasycorixa* Hungerford (3 spp.)]

Tribe Graptocorixini
35.5 *Graptocorixa* Hungerford

Six species, including the following:

G. *abdominalis* (Say). (See Fig. 20.65.) (3) CA, AZ; (4) UT.

[35.6 *Neocorixa* Hungerford (1 sp., *N. snowi* Hungerford)]

Tribe Corixini

[35.7 *Ahautlea* de la Llave [=*Kirzousacorixa* Hungerford] (2 spp.); 35.8 *Arctocorisa* Wallengren [=*Arctocorixa* of authors] (4 spp.); 35.9 *Callicorixa* White (5 spp.); 35.10 *Cenocorixa* Hungerford (10 spp.); 35.11 *Centrocorisa* Lundblad (1 sp., *C. kollarii* (Fieber)); 35.12 *Corisella* Lundblad (4 spp.)]

35.13 *Hesperocorixa* Kirkaldy

Eighteen species, of which the following is common:

H. *interrupta* (Say). L. 9–11 m. Yellowish brown; eight to ten broad, dark bands across pronotum; zigzag patterns on wings. Adults present from April to November (See Fig. 20.66.) (1) n.e. NA; (2) VA, NA, SC, GA; (5) NE, IA, MO.

[35.14 *Morphocorixa* Jaczewski (2 spp.); 35.15 *Palmocorixa* Abbott (3 spp.); 35.16 *Pseudocorixa* Jaczewski (1 sp., *P. beameri* (Hungerford)); 35.17 *Ramphocorixa* Abbott (2 spp.)]

35.18 *Sigara* Fabricius

There are forty-six species in this genus, which is divided into several subgenera. Lateral lobes of the prothorax elongate [except for *S. ornata* (Abbott)]. Front tibiae with a few small apical spines, those of the male carinate dorsally, often with an apical pad. Hind femora ventrally pubescent on at least the basal third and often more, the bare portion with scattered spines. Upper surface with from two or three spines to two or three longitudinal rows of spines. The following species is widely distributed:

S. *alternata* (Say). L. 5.5–6.9 mm. Brown with reddish tinge; pronotum crossed by eight or nine narrow brown bands—some of them only across median portion of disk but others complete, with distal ones tending to coalesce along lateral edge; clavus banded with alternate light and dark stripes of equal width; corial pattern much broken, giving a mealy appearance of light and dark lines scattered, wavy, and broken; dark color tending to coalesce on inner distal angle of corium; membrane separated from corium by a pale line, with pattern similar to that of corium; embolium, head, legs, and margins of venter pale; area around coxae and basal segments of abdomen

Fig. 20.66.

smoky to black. Occurs throughout NA, except far north. (1), (2), (3), (4), (5).

[35.19 *Trichocorixa* Kirkaldy (11 spp.)]

36. NEPIDAE (Waterscorpion Bug Family)

L. 18–46 mm, with breathing tube 16–44 mm. Front legs raptorial; abdomen with long breathing tube. These are sluggish creatures that crawl but do not swim, often remaining motionless for hours on the muddy, leaf-covered bottom of their favorite pond; they rarely fly to lights at night. Their eggs, usually placed on submerged objects rather than vegetation, are furnished with filaments at one end, the number varying with the genus. They will bite if handled. The 13 species in the U.S. and Canada are assigned to three genera, as follows.

Subfamily Ranatrinae

36.1 *Ranatra* Fabricius

Long and slender with hind coxae close together. Species of this widespread genus stridulate by rubbing their front coxae against the body. There are ten species, of which the following is a common example:

R. americana Montandon. L. 23–30 mm. Brownish with banded legs. (See Fig. 20.67 for adult and Fig. 20.68 for details of grasping front legs. (1) n.e. NA; (2) s.e. US.

Subfamily Nepinae

Tribe Nepini

36.2 *Nepa* Linnaeus

These bugs are broader than the species of *Ranatra* and somewhat resemble the Giant Water Bug (37). One species, as follows:

N. apiculata Uhler. L. 18–20 mm. Grayish brown. Occurs in ponds and slow moving streams. (See Fig. 20.69.) (1) n.e. US; (2) s.e. US.

Tribe Curictini

36.3 *Curicta* Stål

The surface of these bugs appears to be covered with warts. Two species, including the following:

C. drakei Hungerford. (See Fig. 20.70.) (3) AZ.

Fig. 20.68. (*Courtesy of Kurzius and* Insect World Digest)

37. BELOSTOMATIDAE (Giant Water Bug Family)

L. 25–60 mm. Their broad, flat hind legs and flat body, with a keel in the middle underneath, well fit these bugs for aquatic locomotion. Their sharp hooked front legs and short, powerful beak make them formidable predators. They lurk on muddy bottoms of ponds, often concealing themselves under mud or leaves, ready to dart out after some prey. They are known to attack and suck the blood of fishes and can thus be pests in fish hatcheries. They are often called Electric-light Bugs because at night adults frequent electric lights near ponds and pools. They may bite if handled. Giant Water Bugs abound in the tropics where they may reach a length of over 100 mm. The family is represented in the U.S. and Canada by 20 species in three genera, as follows:

Subfamily Lethocerinae

37.1 *Lethocerus* Mayr

Five species, of which the following is common.

L. americanus (Leidy) (Giant Water Bug). L. 50–60 mm. Brown, with dark brown markings on legs. Adults from May to October. Rarely seen except at street lights; dredging deep ponds will bring them up. (See Fig. 20.71.) (1) n.e. NA; (5) n. central states.

Fig. 20.67.

Fig. 20.69.

Fig. 20.70.

Subfamily Belostomatinae

[37.2 *Abedus* Stål (6 spp.)]

37.3 *Belostoma* Latreille

Nine species, of which the following is very common:

B. fumineum Say. L. 20–25 mm. Light brown; legs with darker markings. They live among weeds of muddy-bottomed ponds. Female lays her eggs on the back of the male. Adults fly from May to October. (See A&J 46.) Occurs throughout NA. (1), (2), (3), (4), (5).

38. NAUCORIDAE (Creeping Water Bug Family)

L. 6–15 mm. Greatly enlarged raptorial front legs; no ocelli; tarsi with two tarsomeres and with long claws on middle and hind tarsi; wings without veins; legs not adapted for swimming. Five genera and 19 species occur in the U.S. and Canada.

Subfamily Limnocorinae

[38.1 *Usingerina* LaRivers (1 sp., *U. moapensis* LaRivers); 38.2 *Limnocoris* Stål (1 sp., *L. lutzi* LaRivers)]

Fig. 20.71. (*From Britton, 1923*)

Fig. 20.72.

Subfamily Naucorinae

38.3 *Pelocoris* Stål

Three species, of which the following is common:

P. femoratus (Palisot-Beauvois). L. 9–11.5 mm. Eyes not prominent; pronotum shiny, greenish-yellow, marked with many dark olive spots; front wings dark brown with light shoulder area. Crawls on submerged plants. (See Fig. 20.72.) (1) n.e. US; (2) s.e. US; (5) ND, SD, MN, NE, IA, MO.

Subfamily Ambryinae

38.4 *Ambrysus* Stål

Thirteen species, all of which occur in the southwestern U.S. Anterior margin of pronotum deeply concave. The following species are common:

A. pudicus Stål (See A&J 47.) (3) s.w. US; (5) WY.

A. signoreti Stål. (See Fig. 20.73.) (3) CA, AZ, NM; (5) CO. ·

Subfamily Cryphocricinae

38.5 *Cryphocricos* Signoret

One species only, as follows:

C. hungerfordi Usinger. Found in swiftly flowing streams. (3) s.e. TX.

Fig. 20.73.

Fig. 20.74. (*From Blatchley, 1926*)

39. GELASTOCORIDAE (Toad Bug Family)

L. 5–10 mm. These bugs resemble tiny toads and hop away or crouch down when disturbed. Eyes large and bulging; front legs short; predacious. The seven species are assigned to two genera, as follows:

Subfamily **Gelastocorinae**

39.1 *Gelastocoris* Kirkaldy

Two species, as follows:

G. oculatus (Fabricius) (Toad Bug). L. 5–6 mm. Front tarsi with two claws; yellow to nearly black. (See Fig. 20.74.) Occurs throughout the U.S. (1), (2), (3), (4), (5).

G. rotundatus Champion. (3) AZ, NM.

Subfamily **Nerthrinae**

39.2 *Nerthra* Say

Front tarsi with a single claw. Five species occur in the western and southeastern U.S., including the following:

N. stygica Say. L. 5.3–5.5 mm. (2) GA, FL.

40. OCHTERIDAE (Velvety Shore Bug Family)

L. 4–5 mm. Oval; black; tarsomere formula, 2–2–3; beak long, slender, reaching hind coxae; antennae short, exposed, inserted beneath eyes; two ocelli; legs slender, fitted for running. Lives in vegetation along shores of streams and ponds. One genus with seven species, of which the most common is probably the following:

40.1 *Ochterus* Latreille

O. americanus (Uhler). (1) n.e. US; (2) s.e. US; (3) TX.

BIBLIOGRAPHY

Blatchley, W. S. 1926. *Heteroptera or true bugs of Eastern North America.* 1116 pp., 205 figs., 12 pls.

Britton, W. E., *et al.* 1923. *The Hemiptera or sucking insects of Connecticut.* Connecticut State Geol. Nat. Hist. Serv., 807 pp.

Carayon, J. 1972. Caracteres systematiques et classification des Anthocoridae (Hemiptera). *Ann. Soc. Entom. France*, 8: 309–359.

Carvalho, J. C. 1957. *Catalogo dos Mirideos do Mundo.* Part I, Subfamilies Cylapinae, Deraeocorinae, Bryocorinae. v. 44, pp. 1–158; 1958. Part II, Subfamily Phylinae, v. 45, pp. 1–216; 1958. Part III, Subfamily Orthotylinae, v. 47, pp. 1–161; 1959. Part IV, Subfamily Mirinae, v. 48, pp. 1–384; 1960. Part V, Bibliography and General Index, v. 51, pp. 1–194. Arquivos do Museu Nacional. Brazil.

Chopra, N. P. 1967. Higher classification of the family Rhopalidae (Hemiptera). *Trans. R. Ent. Soc. London*, 119 (12): 363–399.

———. 1968. A revision of the genus *Arhyssus* Stål. *Ann. Entom. Soc. America*, 61(3): 629–655.

Drake, C. J., and Chapman, H. C. 1953. Preliminary report on the Pleidae (Hemiptera) of the Americas. *Proc. Biol. Soc. Washington*, 66: 53–59.

Drake, Carl J., and Ruhoff, Florence A. 1965. Lacebugs of the world: a catalog (Hemiptera: Tingidae). *United States Nat. Mus. Bull.* 213, viii+634 pp.

Emsley, M. G. 1969. The Schizopteridae (Hemiptera: Heteroptera) with descriptions of new species from Trinidad. *Mem. American Ent. Soc.* No. 25, 154 pp.

Froeschner, Richard C. 1960. Cydnidae of the Western Hemisphere. *Proc. United States Nat. Mus.*, v. 111 (No. 3430), pp. 337–680.

Harrington, B. Jane. 1980. A generic level revision and cladistic analysis of the Myodochini of the world (Hemiptera, Lygaeidae, Rhyparochrominae). *Bull American Mus. Nat. Hist.* v. 167(2): 49–116.

Harris, Halbert M. 1928. A monographic study of the hemipterous family Nabidae as it occurs in North America. *Ent. Americana*, 9(1,2): 1–97.

Henry, T. J. 1980. Review of *Lidopus* Gibson and *Wetmorea* McAtee and Malloch, descriptions of three new genera and two new species, and key to New World genera (Hemiptera: Miridae: Isometopinae). *Proc. Ent. Soc. Washington*, 82(2): 178–194.

Herring, Jon L. 1976. Keys to genera of Anthocoridae of America north of Mexico, with description of a new genus (Hemiptera: Heteroptera). *Florida Entom.* 59(2): 143–150.

Hungerford, H. B. 1948 (reprint 1977). *The Corixidae of the Western Hemisphere.* Los Angeles: Entomological Reprint Specialists, viii+827 pp.

Kelton, Leonard A. 1980. *The insects and Arachnids of Canada.* Part 8: The plant bugs of the Prairie Provinces of Canada: Heteroptera: Miridae. Canada Agriculture, 408 pp.

Knight, Harry H. 1968. Taxonomic review: Miridae of the Nevada test site and the Western United States. *Science Bull. Brigham Young Univ.*, Biol. Series, v. 9(3): vii+282 pp.

McAtee, W. L. 1919. Key to the Nearctic species of Piesmatidae (Heteroptera). *Bull. Brooklyn Ent. Soc.* 14: 80–83.

Menke, Arnold S. 1979. The semiaquatic and aquatic Hemiptera of California. *Bull. Calif. Insect Survey*, v. 21, xi+166 pp.

Ryckman, Raymond E. 1962. Biosystematics and hosts of the *Triatoma protracta* Complex in North America (Hemiptera: Reduvidae) (Rodentia: Cricetidae). *Univ. Calif. Publ. Entom.* 27(2): 93–240.

Slater, J. A., and Baranowski, R. M. 1978. *How to know the true bugs.* Dubuque: Wm. C. Brown Co., x+256 pp.

Smith, C. L., and Polhemus, J. T. 1978. The Veliidae of America north of Mexico—keys and check list. *Proc. Entom. Soc. Washington.* 80(1): 56–68.

Todd, Edward L. 1955. A taxonomic revision of the family Gelastocoridae (Hemiptera). *Univ. Kansas Sci. Bull.* 37 (No. 11): 277–473.

de la Torre-Bueno, J. R. 1939. A synopsis of the Hemiptera-Heteroptera of America North of Mexico. Part I. Families Scutelleridae, Cydnidae, Pentatomidae, Aradidae, Dysodiidae and Termitaphididae. *Ent. Americana*, 19: 141–304.

———. 1941. A synopsis of the Hemiptera-Heteroptera of America

North of Mexico, Part II. Families Coreidae, Alydidae, Corizidae, Neididae, Pyrrhocoridae, and Thaumastotheriidae. *Ent. Americana*, 21: 41–122.

Usinger, Robert L. 1944. The Triatominae of North and Central America and the West Indies and their public health significance. *Publ. Health Bull.* No. 288, iv+83 pp.

———. 1945. Classification of the Enicocephalidae. *Ann. Entom. Soc. Amer.* 38: 321–342.

———. 1966. Monograph of Cimicidae. Thomas Say Foundation, v. 7, xi+585 pp.

Van Duzee, Edward P. 1917. *Catalogue of the Hemiptera of America north of Mexico excepting the Aphididae, Coccidae and Aleurodidae.* Berkeley: University of California Press, xiii+902 pp.

Wygodzinsky, Petr. 1949. *Elenco sistematico de los Reduviiformes Americanos.* Monografia no. 1, Instituto de Medicina Regional. Tucuman, 102 pp.

Order 21

HOMOPTERA

(Cicadas, Leafhoppers, Aphids, Scale Insects, and Allies)

Some of the primitive Homoptera are of very much the same appearance as the Hemiptera, although some other species are hardly even recognizable as insects. Several distinctive features to be described subsequently are shared by many of the diverse forms assigned here. Individuals of many species are exceedingly abundant. As a group, the homopterans are perhaps the most detrimental order of insects, not only because of the economic loss they cause by damaging crops and ornamental plants but because they are vectors of plant pathogens.

One of their ordinal features is reflected in their Latin name, *homo,* meaning "same," and *pteron,* "wing." This refers to the more or less uniform structure of the front wings, which are generally membranous and thin or, at most, only slightly thickened throughout, as opposed to the basal thickening of the front wings of the Hemiptera. Although this wing type is found in many other insect groups, none of the other orders combine it with this wing shape and venation (Fig. 21.1) or with piercing–sucking mouthparts. Although the order is basically winged, many species are wingless throughout the adult stage, having secondarily lost their wings during their long evolution; it is therefore necessary to consider several other features in order to define the order. Fortunately, the several body types represented (and illustrated) in this section are very distinctive.

All Homoptera are plant-juice feeders, although a few tiny leaf-hoppers may sometimes mistake an arm for a plant and inadvertently, or so it would seem, inject some saliva as they bite; the bite can be momentarily painful. There is no evidence that they actually suck blood, however, and very likely they are unable to. It is certain that no Homopteran sucks blood of any animal as a food source.

Diagnosis: L. 1 55 mm (rarely, to 100 mm, or more, in some tropical species). Body of many species soft but others thickened and leathery, sometimes with spines, setae, or with a secreted waxy covering. (See Fig. 21.29). Most species are green

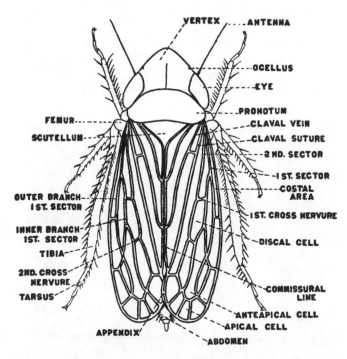

Fig. 21.1. (*From Britton, 1923*)

or brown, but some, particularly tropical species, are brightly colored, marked with red, yellow, black, white, blue, and so on. The head is bent down (except in scale insects) and does not move very much. The antennae—ordinarily 3- to 10-segmented, but some 11-, 12-, or 13-segmented—are bristlelike and short—commonly shorter than the head but in some, longer than the head; in some female scale insects, they are absent. The mouthparts, modified for piercing-sucking, arise from the hind portion of the head. The wings, if they are present, are more or less of a uniform texture, with reduced venation, and are held at rest tentlike over the abdomen. The males of all scale insects that have wings have two pairs, the hind pair greatly reduced. The legs, when present, are moderate in length and often exhibit heavy spines; the hind legs, although not greatly enlarged for jumping, are often used for this purpose (especially those of leafhoppers, and the like). Tarsi have one, two, or three tarsomeres only. The abdomen is not provided with cerci, although the basal segment of a few is modified for sound production (see cicadas). On their fifth or sixth abdominal segment, many aphids—for example, the rose aphid *Macrosiphum rosae* [Aphididae (19.122)] (Fig. 21.2)—have paired, short, tubelike structures, called *cornicles*, through which they secrete a defensive fluid. At first sight, leafhoppers and other Homoptera might be confused with Hemiptera, but the position of their beak readily distinguishes them. Aphids might be confused with barklice, but the latter have chewing mouthparts.

The nymphs of most families closely resemble the adults.

Metamorphosis: Paurometabolous, usually with eggs (some species are ovoviviparous) and nymphal (some with prepupal as well as pupal) and adult stages. The prepupal and pupal stages of male scale insects resemble those found in some thrips.

Habits and habitats: The long, coiled mouthparts of most species penetrate into the phloem and xylem—the food- and water-conducting tissues—of a plant; those of others act as cell bursters in leaf tissues. The proboscis of most scale insects affixes itself to a plant in a manner similar to that of an oil derrick and pump, allowing both the nymphs and adults to feed on the plant's liquid carbohydrates. Homopterans are never found far from their host plants, all parts of which they infest—

roots, stems, leaves, flowers, and fruits. Some species of aphids, as well as male scale insects, lack mouthparts and do not feed as adults. There are no predacious or true aquatic members of the order. Some species are attracted to lights at night.

Reproductive behavior: Species may be biparental or parthenogenetic. The males of some species—certain cicadas—attract females by sound production. Courtship patterns have been little studied.

Economic importance: All groups of Homoptera contain species that are economically significant, as will be discussed in detail later. The cicada, [Cicadidae (13)], or seventeen-year locust, loudly announce their presence shortly after emergence from the soil with a shrill, midsummer song; after copulation, the female inserts her eggs into twigs of young fruit trees, causing them serious damage, just one example of the type of injury that can occur to a plant in addition to that caused by juice sucking. To get an idea of the great abundance of certain species of this order—such as spittle bugs[Cercopidae (12)] or leafhoppers [Cicadellidae (14)]—one need only use a sweep net across any field in summer; thousands of individuals will be captured in a few sweeps. Although treehoppers [Membracidae (15)] come in bizarre shapes, especially tropical species, they are very rarely pests. Some species of the superfamily Fulgoroidea can be equally bizarre and pests as well. The heads of some of its members are grossly enlarged, a famous case being that of an insect from the South American tropics called the Peanut Bug (Fig. 21.3), or sometimes the Lanternfly because it was once thought to be luminescent. Jumping plantlice [Psyllidae (17)], the whiteflies [Aleyrodidae (18)], aphids [superfamily Aphidoidea], and the scale insects [superfamily Coccoidea] are almost all very damaging plant pests. In addition to sapping the strength of plants by sucking their juices, they also transmit viral plant diseases that thrive on the weakened plants.

Collecting and preserving: Some cicadas are attracted to lights at night, but those that rest high in trees will be difficult to collect. (The author has seen people in Japan capture unwary cicadas from top branches by touching them with a sticky substance at the tip of a long bamboo pole; other people have been known to shoot cicadas with very fine bird shot.) Sweeping fields, beating vegetation, and searching flowers and foliage will yield other representatives of the order. Scale insects and whiteflies must be collected with care. A frequent custom is to remove a sample of the infested plant and preserve it with the insects attached. Because many species are host specific, it is important to keep detailed records of the host plants for all aphids, whiteflies, and scale insects. Hard-bodied Homoptera may be pinned, if they are large enough, or glued to triangular points, if they are small. Soft-bodied aphids, scale insects, and whiteflies may be preserved in 80-percent alcohol; for purposes of identification, they may be, and often must be, mounted on

Fig. 21.2. (*Courtesy of O. Wilford Olsen and* Insect World Digest)

Fig. 21.3. (*After Comstock*)

microscope slides. Scale insects also require special techniques for detailed studies and identification. For many of these insects—with the exception of the Cicadidae, some Cicadellidae, the Membracidae, and the Fulgoroidea—a high-magnification microscope is necessary for accurate identification.

Rearing: Many species, especially aphids and scale insects, are easily reared on potted plants.

Distribution: Approximately 32,000 species of this order have been described throughout the world, with 6,359 of these in 894 genera recorded in the U.S. and Canada. Many new species are described each year, and much remains to be known about the vast number of tropical species, many of which are undescribed.

Identification: The identification of Homoptera does not come easily. Because of the great number of species, their relatively small size (for the most part), and the lack of readily available literature, this group is particularly difficult, even for specialists.

CLASSIFICATION

The order Homoptera is divided into three suborders, as follows:

1. Suborder COLEORRHYNCHA (Primitive Homopterans)—These insects are very primitive, resembling some of the fossil Palaeozoic protohemipterans. There are about 20 species, found only in Australia, New Zealand, and South America.
2. Suborder AUCHENORRHYNCHA (Cicadas, Leafhoppers, and allies)—These insects have tarsi with three tarsomeres; their mouthparts arise from the back, lower surface of the head; their antennae are usually short and bristle-like. (See Fig. 21.4.)
3. Suborder STERNORRHYNCHA (Jumping Plantlice, Aphids, Whiteflies, and Scale Insects)—These insects have only one or two tarsomeres (some scales have no legs at all); their mouthparts, if visible, seem to arise between the front coxae; their antennae can be an unsegmented tubercle or filiform and moderately long. (See Fig. 21.5 for the general morphology of scale insects.)

The North American families of the last two suborders are listed in Table 21.1. These families are grouped in nine superfamilies, as defined by the accompanying Key to the Superfamilies.

Key to the Superfamilies of Homoptera of the U.S. and Canada

1. Legs absent or reduced; when present, tarsi with one or two tarsomeres; reduced body regions and segments usually indistinct; body often covered with secretions in the form of scale (females and sedentary nymphs of the scale insects) Superfamily **COCCOIDEA**
 Legs present and distinct; body region and segments usually distinct; body sometimes covered with secretions, but not in the form of a scale **2**

2(1). Labium arising distinctly from head; tarsi with three tarsomeres; antennae with bristlelike flagellum, usually short .. **3**
 Labium arising apparently between or behind the front coxae and not continuous with head; tarsi with two tarsomeres or none; antenna threadlike, often long, never bristlelike .. **9**

3(2). Tegula (a small scale between pronotum and base of front wing) present Superfamily **FULGOROIDEA**
 Tegula absent ... **4**

4(3). Middle coxae elongate, similar to front coxae and inserted some distance from midline .. Superfamily **FULGOROIDEA**
 Middle coxae shorter than front coxae and inserted near midline **5**

5(4). Three ocelli Superfamily **CICADOIDEA**
 Two ocelli, or ocelli absent .. **6**

6(5). Pronotum extending over abdomen and hiding the scutellum (Superfamily **MEMBRACOIDEA**) 15. Membracidae
 Pronotum not extending over abdomen and not hiding scutellum **7**

7(6). Posterior border of pronotum produced into a broadly rounded median lobe (Superfamily **MEMBRACOIDEA**) 16. Aetalionidae
 Posterior border of pronotum straight or emarginate; if produced into a median lobe, the latter emarginate ... **8**

8(7). Hind tibiae with one or two toothlike projections on shaft and an apical crown of denticles, all immovable Superfamily **CERCOPOIDEA**
 Hind tibiae with rows of articulated spines or bristles on shaft Superfamily **CICADELLOIDEA**

9(2). Tarsi, when present, with one or two tarsomeres and with one claw on each; females and some males wingless, other males with one pair of wings Superfamily **COCCOIDEA**
 Tarsi with two tarsomeres and with two claws each; two pairs of wings in winged individuals .. **10**

10(9). Hind legs with femora thickened, saltatorial; antennae five- to ten-segmented, the last segment with two fine apical bristles Superfamily **PSYLLOIDEA**
 Hind legs with femora slender, not saltatorial; antennae three- to seven-segmented, the last segment without two fine apical bristles **11**

Key to the Superfamilies of Homoptera of the U.S. and Canada (*Contd.*)

11(10). Wings opaque, subequal; tarsomeres subequal, usually a strong empodium present; body of adult usually covered with fine powdery white wax; anal aparatus, the opening of which is the vasiform orifice, with an operculum and a lingula Superfamily **ALEYRODOIDEA**
Wings transparent and hind wings considerably smaller; basal tarsomere usually reduced, empodium usually absent; body not covered with fine powdery wax but sometimes with woolly wax; cornicles often present on abdomen of aphids Superfamily **APHIDOIDEA**

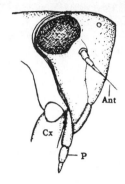

Fig. 21.4. (*Courtesy of E. J. Gerberg*)

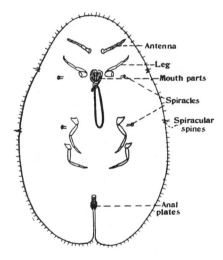

Fig. 21.5. (*From Britton, 1923*)

Table 21.1 Families of the Homoptera of the U.S. and Canada

Suborder AUCHENORRHYNCHA

Superfamily FULGOROIDEA

 1. CIXIIDAE (Cixiid Planthopper Family)
 2. DELPHACIDAE (Delphacid Planthopper Family)
 3. FULGORIDAE (Fulgorid Planthopper Family)
 4. ACHILIDAE (Archilid Planthopper Family)
 5. TROPIDUCHIDAE (Tropiduchid Planthopper Family)
 6. ISSIDAE (Issid Planthopper Family)
 7. ACANALONIIDAE (Acanaloniid Planthopper Family)
 8. FLATIDAE (Flatid Planthopper Family)
 9. DERBIDAE (Derbid Planthopper Family)
10. KINNARIDAE (Kinnarid Planthopper Family)
11. DICTYOPHARIDAE (Dictyopharid Planthopper Family)

Table 21.1 Families of the Homoptera (*Contd.*)

Superfamily CERCOPOIDEA

12. CERCOPIDAE (Spittle Bug Family)

Superfamily CICADOIDEA

13. CICADIDAE (Cicada Family)

Superfamily CICADELLOIDEA

14. CICADELLIDAE (Leafhopper Family)

Superfamily MEMBRACOIDEA

15. MEMBRACIDAE (Treehopper Family)
16. AETALIONIDAE (Aetalionid Treehopper Family)

Suborder STERNORRHYNCHA

Superfamily PSYLLOIDEA

17. PSYLLIDAE (Jumping Plantlice Family)

Superfamily ALEYRODOIDEA

18. ALEYRODIDAE (Whitefly Family)

Superfamily APHIDOIDEA

19. APHIDIDAE (Aphid Family)
20. ADELGIDAE (Pine and Spruce Adelgid Family)
21. PHYLLOXERIDAE (Phylloxerid Family)

Superfamily COCCOIDEA

22. ORTHEZIIDAE (Ensign Scale Insect Family)
23. MARGARODIDAE (Giant Scale Insect Family)
24. PUTOIDAE (Giant Mealybug Family)
25. PSEUDOCOCCIDAE (Mealybug Family)
26. COCCIDAE (Soft Scale Insect Family)
27. ACLERDIDAE (Flat Grass Scale Insect Family)
28. DACTYLOPIIDAE (Cochineal Scale Insect Family)
29. KERMESIDAE (Gall-like Scale Insect Family)
30. CRYPTOCOCCIDAE (Bark Crevice Scale Insect Family)
31. ERIOCOCCIDAE (Felt Scale Insect Family)
32. TACHARDIIDAE (Lac Scale Insect Family)
33. LECANODIASPIDIDAE (False Pit Scale Insect Family)
34. CEROCOCCIDAE (Ornate Pit Scale Insect Family)
35. ASTEROLECANIIDAE (Pit Scale Insect Family)
36. CONCHASPIDIDAE (False Armored Scale Insect Family)
37. PHOENICOCOCCIDAE (Palm Scale Insect Family)
38. DIASPIDIDAE (Armored Scale Insect Family)

Table 21.2 Superfamilies of Auchenorrhyncha

Superfamily	Antennae	Ocelli	Hind tibiae	Special features
Cicadoidea	Between eyes	3	Spines in rows at apex	Usually large; wings entirely membranous
Membracoidea	Between eyes	2	Spines or spinelike setae usually in rows	Pronotum prolonged over abdomen, often with horns, stout spines, etc.
Cercopoidea	Between eyes	2	One or two spinelike seta on shaft; apex with several spines	Hind coxae short and cone-shaped
Cicadelloidea	Between eyes	2	Rows of many spinelike setae on shaft; none at apex	Hind coxae transverse
Fulgoroidea	Below eyes	2 (rarely, 3)	Rows of few spines on shaft (or none); apex with several spines	Middle coxae elongate, widely separated; front wings with tegulae

Suborder AUCHENORRHYNCHA

Diagnosis: L. 2–150 mm. In addition to the features noted in the preceding discussion, the metapleura of these insects are relatively well developed; the female usually has a well-developed ovipositor for laying her eggs in plant tissue. Most species are active, with well-developed wings. The suborder is divided into five superfamilies, whose characteristics are briefly described in Table 21.2.

Superfamily FULGOROIDEA (Planthoppers)

L. 2–20 mm (some tropical species over 100 mm). The eleven families recognized in this superfamily are of diverse body form. Eyes, antennae, and ocelli are located laterally. The front and sides of the head and the clypeus often have three carinae. Many of the species are difficult to distinguish except by examining the characteristics of the male genitalia.

Planthoppers are abundant in the tropics. All are plant-juice feeders and when abundant enough transmit plant pathogens. Little is known of their host plant preferences, but these include herbaceous plants, grasses, shrubs, and trees. Often the eggs are laid in the twigs of shrubs and trees.

The nymphs are often, and the adults seldom, covered with wax. They are frequently found with the adults. They prefer herbaceous plants and must migrate to their preferred host from the site of egg-laying.

The accompanying Key will distinguish the families that occur in the U.S. and Canada.

Key to the Families of Fulgoroidea

1. Hind tibiae with a broad apical spur nearly as long as first tarsomere, inserted inside apical rim of tibiae and movable in life; wings well-developed or short **2. Delphacidae**
Hind tibiae without apical spur as just described *2*

2(1). Anal area of hind wing with many cross veins between anal veins **3. Fulgoridae**
Anal area of hind wing without cross veins *3*

3(2). Hind tarsi with second tarsomere with apex rounded with an apical spur on each side ... *4*
Hind tarsi with second tarsomere with apex straight across or emarginate and with a row of apical spurs *9*

4(3). Clavus of front wing either granulate with numerous small secretory pores, or base of costa strongly bent; wings longer than body, held almost vertical to body when at rest, usually wedge-shaped, mothlike **8. Flatidae**
Clavus of front wing not granular, without small secretory pores, base of costa not strongly bent; wings various *5*

5(4). Scutellum with apex separated by a distinct transverse groove **5. Tropiduchidae**
Scutellum without a transverse groove *6*

6(5). Front wings large, very broad, oval, with costal margin rounded, longer than body, costal area reticulate, without cross veins, basal cell large; hind tibiae without lateral spines except for a crown of spines at apex **7. Acanaloniidae**
Front wings thick, leathery, sometimes of roughened consistency, and when well-developed, oval, convex, covering body laterally (Issinae) but often shorter than abdomen (Caliscelinae), with many cross veins in costal area, basal cell very small or obscure, base of costa gradually curved; hind tibiae often with spines on sides in addition to apical ones **6. Issidae**

9(3). Apical segment of labium very short, not more than $1\frac{1}{2}$ times as long as wide **9. Derbidae**
Apical segment of labium more than twice as long as wide, usually longer *10*

10(9). Species in NA somewhat flattened; folded front wings markedly overlapping at apex, basal half of costal area usually without cross veins; claval suture short, ending just beyond halfway, not reaching wing margin but making a distinct angle **4. Achilidae**

Key to the Families of Fulgoroidea (*Contd.*)

Species not particularly flattened; folded front wing usually not overlapping; claval suture otherwise ... *11*

11(10). Head prolonged anteriorly into a long, slender, beaklike structure (spp. of *Scolops*); if not so prolonged, then front with 2 or 3 longitudinal carinae (in addition to lateral carinae) or with tegulae of wings absent and claval suture obscure; median ocellus absent from front .. **11. Dictyopharidae**

Head not particularly prolonged in front; front either without carinae or with median carinae only; tegulae of wing present; median ocellus usually present *12*

12(11). Veins of front wing usually with pustules or granules; abdominal terga 6 to 8 rectangular ... **1. Cixiidae**

Veins of front wing without pustules or granules; abdominal terga 6 to 8 V-shaped, with wax-secreting pores .. **10. Kinnaridae**

1. CIXIIDAE (Cixiid Planthopper Family)

L. 3–10 mm. Body often somewhat flattened, broad; head short, at most only slightly extended anteriorly; antennae two-segmented with apical flagellum; usually three ocelli; both pairs of wings usually relatively large, held rooflike over abdomen when at rest. Legs with long hind tibiae and only a few or no lateral spines, but with a circle of apical spines on the hind tibiae. Adults are good jumpers and feed on trees and shrubs. They overwinter as nymphs in the soil and feed on roots of grasses and other plants. There are 13 genera and 172 species in the U.S. and Canada, as follows.

Tribe Cixiini

[1.1 *Pintalia* Stål (3 spp.)]

1.2 *Oliarus* Stål

Fifty-one species, including the following:

O. cinnamomeus Provancher (Huckleberry Planthopper). L. 6–7 mm. Blackish, with narrow pale front margin on front wings. Occurs in bogs. Uncommon. (See Fig. 21.6) (1) n.e. US.

[1.3 *Monorachis* Uhler (1 sp., *M. sordulentus* Uhler); 1.4 *Myndus* Stål (34 spp.); 1.5 *Cixius* Latreille (25 spp.); 1.6 *Oecleus* Stål (40 spp.); 1.7 *Microledrida* Fowler (3 spp.); 1.8 *Platycixius* Van Duzee (1 sp., *P. calvus* Van Duzee); 1.9 *Nymphocixia* Van Duzee (1 sp., *N. unipunctata* Van Duzee)]

Tribe Bothriocerini

[1.10 *Bothriocera* Burmeister (10 spp.); 1.11 *Oliaronus* Ball (1 sp., *O. tontonus* Ball)]

2. DELPHACIDAE (Delphacid Planthopper Family)

[= Araeopidae]

L. 2–9 mm. Body usually elongate, almost parallel-sided; brown; head usually short, sometimes as long as body; head

Fig. 21.6.

carinae may be indistinct; antennae simple, short; pronotum usually collarlike; mesonotum triangular. Front wings often short with reduced venation; hind wings sometimes reduced. Ovipositor of female long, curved, sword-shaped. Sexes sometimes very different. These species are frequently found on grasses and sedges in humid habitats, especially on grassy meadows near streams. Some species are of economic importance, especially in tropical regions. The 26 genera and 145 species are classified as follows.

Subfamily Asiracinae

[2.1 *Copicerus* Swartz (1 sp., *C. irroratus* Swartz); 2.2 *Pentagramma* Van Duzee (3 spp.)]

Subfamily Delphacinae

Tribe Alohini

[2.3 *Stobaera* Stål (8 spp.)]

Tribe Tropidocephalini

[2.4 *Liburniella* Crawford (1 sp., *L. ornata* Stål); 2.5 *Eurysa* Fieber (2 spp.)]

Tribe Araeopini

[2.6 *Laccocera* Van Duzee (5 spp.); 2.7 *Achorotile* Fieber (2 spp.); 2.8 *Phyllodictus* Ball (3 spp.); 2.9 *Phyllodinus* Van Duzee (1 sp., *P. nervatus* Van Duzee); 2.10 *Stenocranus* Fieber (7 spp.); 2.11 *Kelisia* Fieber (4 spp.); 2.12 *Megamelus* Fieber (10 spp.); 2.13 *Bakerella* Crawford (1 sp., *B. maculata* Crawford); 2.14 *Bostaera* Ball (1 sp., *B. nasuta* Ball); 2.15 *Saccharosydne* Kirkaldy (1 sp., *S. saccharivora* Westwood); 2.16 *Dicranotropis* Fieber (1 sp., *D. incerta* Van Duzee); 2.17 *Euidella* Puton (5 spp.)]

2.18 *Peregrinus* Kirkaldy

One species, as follows:

P. maidis Ashmead (Corn Hopper). L. 4–5 mm. A pest of corn in the U.S., Canada, and throughout the world. (1), (2), (3), (4), (5).

[2.19 *Pissonotus* Van Duzee (19 spp.); 2.20 *Megamelanus* Ball (8 spp.); 2.21 *Kormus* Fieber (1 sp., *K. californicus* Crawford); 2.22 *Prokelisia* Osborn (4 spp.); 2.23 *Chloriona* Fieber (1 sp., *C. slossoni* Ball); 2.24 *Criomorphus* Curtis (2 spp.); 2.25 *Liburnia* Stål (5 spp.); 2.26 *Delphacodes* Fieber (48 spp.)]

3. FULGORIDAE (Fulgorid Planthopper Family)

L. 1–8+ mm. Usually reddish, but of various brilliant colors in tropical species; head may be produced; front large,

usually quadrangular, with well-elevated lateral margins; usually two ocelli, located between eye and antennal base; thorax large, with pronotum sometimes transverse; mesonotum triangular. Wings large with many cross veins. Some species secrete a large amount of wax in the form of filaments. This family includes the famous Peanut Bug referred to before. Host plant preferences are knwon for only a few species. The group is mostly tropical but is represented in the U.S. and Canada by 15 species in 7 genera.

Subfamily Poiocerinae
Tribe Poicerini

[3.1 *Poblicia* Stål (4 spp.); 3.2 *Calyptoproctus* Spinola (1 sp., *C. marmoratus* Spinola); 3.3 *Cyrpoptus* Stål (5 spp.)]

3.4 *Alphina* Stål

One species, as follows:

A. glauca (Metcalf). L. 10–15 mm. Brownish gray. Common at lights in southwestern canyons. (2) MS; (3) AZ, TX.

Subfamily Amyclinae
Tribe Amyclini

[3.5 *Amycle* Stål (2 spp.); 3.6 *Scolopsella* Ball (1 sp., *S. reticulata* Ball); 3.7 *Rhabdocephala* Van Duzee (1 sp., *R. brunnea* Van Duzee)]

4. ACHILIDAE (Achilid Planthopper Family)

L. 3–14 mm. Brown or tan, sometimes green, a few species black. Proboscis often long, five-segmented, with apical segment very long, reaching the apex of hind coxae, or short, only as long as the clypeus; two ocelli. Hind tibiae with or without spine in basal half. Abdomen without wax pores and basal processes. Many species live in coniferous forests in North America. Nymphs of these species live under loose bark and in rotten logs. They may feed on fungi. Poorly represented in the U.S. and Canada, with 46 species in three genera as follows.

Subfamily Achilinae

[4.1 *Catonia* Uhler (33 spp.); 4.2 *Uniptera* Ball (1 sp., *U. ampliata* Ball); 4.3 *Epiptera* Metcalf (12 spp.)]

5. TROPIDUCHIDAE
(Tropiduchid Planthopper Family)

L. 7–9 mm. Body slender; greenish, yellowish, or brownish. Head narrow, usually projecting forward; anterior margin of vertex often with a thick callus; two ocelli, usually in front of compound eyes; scutellum with apex set apart by a distinct transverse groove. Hind trochanter usually directed posteriorly. Abdomen large, somewhat flattened. This large tropical family is represented in the U.S. by only three species, as follows.

Subfamily Tambiniinae
Tribe Tambiniini

[5.1 *Neurotneta* Guérin-Méneville (1 sp., *N. sponsa* Guérin-Méneville) (2) FL; 5.2 *Pelitropis* Van Duzee (1 sp., *P. rotulata* Van Duzee, (2) NC, FL, MS); 5.3 *Monopsis* Spinola (1 sp., *M. tabida* Spinola, (2) FL)]

Fig. 21.7.

6. ISSIDAE (Weevillike Planthopper Family)

L. 3–8 mm. Body compact, often slightly compressed; dull brown to nearly black. Head produced in some species to form a short weevillike snout; ocelli present or absent; antennal flagellum unsegmented. Front legs of some species enlarged with leaflike femora and tibiae; hind tarsi with second tarsomere having a spine on each side. Both adults and nymphs live on trees or on grasses. This is a large tropical family with 127 species in 23 genera represented in the U.S. and Canada.

Subfamily Caliscelinae
Tribe Caliscelini
6.1 *Fitchiella* Van Duzee

Eight species, including the following:

F. robertsoni Fitch. L. ±6 mm. Brownish with black dots. (See Fig. 21.7.)

6.2 *Bruchomorpha* Newman

Twenty species, of which the following is common:

B. dorsata Fitch. L. ±5 mm. Body with coppery reflections. (See Fig. 21.8.)

6.3 *Aphelonema* Uhler

Fifteen species, of which the following is representative:

A. histrionica Stål. L. 7–8 mm. Two parallel dorsal lines and broader stripes on the side of the abdomen. (See Fig. 21.9.)

Fig. 21.8.

Fig. 21.9.

Tribe Ommatidiotini

6.4 *Asarcopus* Horvath

One species only, as follows:

A. palmarum Horvath (Date Bug). L. ±7 mm.

[6.5 *Papagona* Ball (2 spp.)]

Subfamily Issinae

Tribe Hysteropterini

[6.6 *Euthiscia* Van Duzee (1 sp., *E. tuberculata* Van Duzee); 6.7 *Traxus* Metcalf (1 sp., *T. fulvus* Metcalf); 6.8 *Hysteropterum* Amyot and Serville (11 spp.); 6.9 *Dictyonia* Uhler (1 sp., *D. obscura* Uhler); 6.10 *Misodema* Melichar (1 sp., *M. reticulata* Melichar); 6.11 *Neaethus* Stål (18 spp.); 6.12 *Dictyssa* Melichar (15 spp.); 6.13 *Dictyonissus* Uhler (2 spp.); 6.14 *Dictyobia* Uhler (4 spp.); 6.15 *Dictyssonia* Ball (1 sp., *D. beameri* Ball); 6.16 *Dyctia* Uhler (7 spp.); 6.17 *Danepteryx* Uhler (5 spp.); 6.18 *Osbornia* Ball (2 spp.)]

Tribe Issini

[6.19 *Ulixes* Stål (1 sp., *U. scutatus* Walker); 6.20 *Tylanira* Ball (1 sp., *T. bifurea* Ball)]

Tribe Thioniini

[6.21 *Thionia* Stål (6 spp.); 6.22 *Picumma* Stål (3 spp.)]

Subfamily Tonginae

[6.23 *Tylana* Stål (1 sp., *T. ustulata* Uhler)]

7. ACANALONIIDAE
(Acanaloniid Planthopper Family)

L. 10–12 mm. Usually greenish, yellowish, sometimes with brown markings; front wings very broad, oval, without many cross veins in costal area; head usually narrower than pronotum or mesonotum. First segment of antennae collarlike, second subglobular. Hind tarsi with second tarsomere having a spine on each side. Usually found on grasses, this small group, has only one genus and 18 species in the U.S. and Canada.

7.1 *Acanalonia* Spinola

Eighteen species, of which the following is common:

A. bivittata Say. L. 10–12 mm. Pale green or greenish yellow. (1) n.e. NA; (2) s.e. US; (5) ND, MN, NE, IA, KS, MO.

8. FLATIDAE (Flatid Planthopper Family)

L. 8–15 mm. Mothlike with wedge shape; brownish or pale green, often brilliantly colored in the tropics. Head with two ocelli; antennal flagellum unsegmented; hind tibiae with spines on sides in addition to apical spines, but without a movable spur. Tarsi with first tarsomere short or very short and second tarsomere short or very short, with a spine on each side. Sexual dimorphism is common. Adults and nymphs are gregarious. Nymphs have long waxy filament on body. This group feeds on sap of shrubs, trees, and vines in wooded areas. This large family contains 14 genera and 33 species in the U.S. and Canada.

Subfamily Flatinae

Tribe Flatini

[8.1 *Hesperophantia* Kirkaldy (1 sp., *H. ricanioides* Spinola)]

Tribe Nephesini

[8.2 *Leptormenis* Melichar (1 sp., *L. relicta* Fabricius); 8.3 *Acrophaea* Melichar (4 spp.)]

8.4 *Anormenis* Melichar

Two species, of which the following is common:

A. septentrionalis Spinola. L. 10–12 mm. Light green to nearly white. (1) NY, PA, NJ, DE, MD; (5) MN, NE, IA, MO.

[8.5 *Antillormenis* Fennah (1 sp., *A. contaminata* Uhler); 8.6 *Ormenoides* Melichar (2 spp.); 8.7 *Melormenis* Metcalf (2 spp.)]

8.8 *Metcalfa* Caldwell and Martorell

One species, as follows:

M. pruinosa (Say) (Citrus Planthopper). L. 5–8 mm. Bluish, appearing to be covered with powder; eyes and parts of body beneath powder are light brown. A pest of citrus fruit as well as many woody plants, this species lays its eggs in small twigs, sometimes stunting new growth. (See A&J 73.) (1) n.e. US; (2) s.e. US; (3) s.w. US.

[8.9 *Ormenaria* Metcalf and Bruner (1 sp., *O. rufifascia* Walker)]

Tribe Selizini

[8.10 *Mistharnophantia* Kirkaldy (6 spp.); 8.11 *Cyarda* Walker (3 spp.)]

Subfamily Flatoidinae

[8.12 *Flatoides* Guérin-Méneville (2 spp.); 8.13 *Flatoidinus* Melichar (5 spp.); 8.14 *Atracodes* Melichar (2 spp.)]

9. DERBIDAE (Derbid Planthopper Family)

L. 8–11 mm. Delicate, mothlike insects; yellow, brown, or cream; head more or less compressed; antennae often flattened, short; vertex and frons usually greatly reduced; compound eyes very large; two ocelli, usually prominent, located in front of compound eyes. Legs slender, often elongate. Hind tarsi with second tarsomere large, with row of spines at apex; abdomen usually small. These insects feed on woody fungi growing on rotting logs or on flowering plants, including trees, particularly willow, oak, and hickory. This large family contains 47 species in 14 genera in the U.S. and Canada.

Subfamily Zoraidinae

Tribe Sikaianini

[9.1 *Euklastus* Metcalf (1 sp., *E. harti* Metcalf); 9.2 *Mula* Ball (1 sp., *M. resonans* Ball); 9.3 *Mysidia* Westwood (1 sp., *M. mississippiensis* Dozier)]

Tribe **Cenchreini**

[9.4 *Patara* Westwood (1 sp., *P. vanduzeei* Ball); 9.5 *Syntames* Fowler (3 spp.); 9.6 *Neocenchrea* Metcalf (1 sp., *N. heidemanni* Ball); 9.7 *Dysimia* Muir (1 sp., *D. maculata* Muir); 9.8 *Cedusa* Fowler (16 spp.); 9.9 *Sayiana* Ball (1 sp., *S. sayi* (Ball))]

Tribe **Otiocerini**

[9.10 *Amalopota* Van Duzee (2 spp.); 9.11 *Anotia* Kirby (7 spp.)]

9.12 *Otiocerus* Kirby

There are nine species in this genus throughout the eastern U.S. and Canada, the following of which is the largest:

O. kirbyi Fitch. L. 10–11 mm. Pale yellow to whitish, with vitta on front wing from apex of clavus to costal margin. (1) NY.

9.13 *Apache* Kirkaldy

One species, as follows:

A. degeeri (Kirby). L. 11 mm. Reddish to dark red; front wings with a short whitish line beyond apex of clavus. Widely distributed. (1), (2), (3), (4), (5).

[9.14 *Shellenius* Ball (2 spp.)]

10. KINNARIDAE (Kinnarid Planthopper Family)

L. 3–4 mm. Pale, without dark spots on wings. Labium nearly reaches apex of abdomen, with long apical segment; compound eyes wider than long; three ocelli; antennae short, second segment usually globose, rarely elongate. Wings usually somewhat rounded, very clear and glassy. Most species are tropical, but five species occur in the U.S., as follows:

[10.1 *Oeclidius* Van Duzee (5 spp.)]

11. DICTYOPHARIDAE (Dictyopharid Planthopper Family)

L. 8–12 mm. Green or brown; head of most adults prolonged anteriorly into long slender, beaklike structure, but that of others as in key to family. Apex of front wing usually narrow, with reticulate network of small veins; hind wing large, small, or absent. Legs usually slender, elongate. Most adults and nymphs feed on grasses in damp meadows. Moderately large family with 16 genera and 64 species in the U.S. and Canada. (See Fig. 21.10 for general features.)

Subfamily Dictyopharinae

Tribe Dictyopharini

[11.1 *Nersia* Stål (2 spp.); 11.2 *Mitrops* Fennah (1 sp., *M. dioxys* Walker); 11.3 *Rhynchomitra* Fennah (3 spp.); 11.4 *Phylloscelis* Germar (5 spp.)]

11.5 *Scolops* Schaum

Thirty-two species, of which the following is common:

S. sulcipes Say (Meadow Planthopper). L. 10–12 mm. Brown. Common in grassy meadows. (2) s.e. US.

S. angustatus Uhler.

Subfamily Orgeriinae

Tribe Orgeriini

[11.6 *Orgamara* Ball (3 spp.); 11.7 *Deserta* Ball and Hartzell (4 spp.); 11.8 *Yucanda* Ball and Hartzell (3 spp.); 11.9 *Orgerius* Stål (1 sp., *O.*

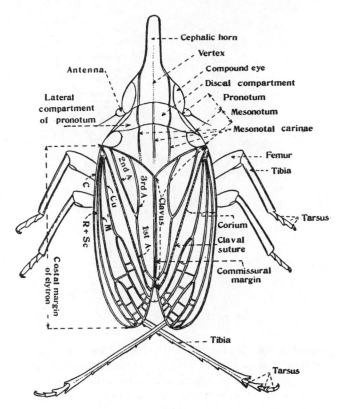

Fig. 21.10. (*From Britton, 1923*)

rhyparus Stål); 11.10 *Parorgerius* Melichar (1 sp., *P. minor* Ball); 11.11 *Acinaca* Ball and Hartzell (1 sp., *A. lurida* Ball and Hartzell); 11.12 *Aridia* Ball and Hartzell (3 spp.); 11.13 *Timodema* Ball (1 sp., *T. miracula* Ball); 11.14 *Ticida* Uhler (1 sp., *T. cingulata* Uhler); 11.15 *Loxophora* Van Duzee (2 spp.); 11.16 *Timonidia* Ball and Hartzell (1 sp., *T. solitaria* Ball and Hartzell)]

Superfamily CERCOPOIDEA

One family only, as follows:

12. CERCOPIDAE (Spittle Bug Family)

L. 5–20 mm (usually not more than 15 mm). Most species brown or gray, some tropical species brightly colored; head usually narrower than pronotum; antennae short, bristlelike, inserted in front of compound eyes; two ocelli on vertex; pronotum usually large, flat or convex; scutellum as long as or longer than pronotum in most species. Front wings longer than body, often very thick, leathery, venation often obscured; hind wings usually large; hind coxae often short and conical, laterally dilated; hind femora and tibiae usually elongate, adapted for leaping; hind tibiae with one or two stout marginal spines and usually with single or double row of circlets of spines at apex. (See Fig. 21.11 for general features.)

Eggs are laid in the stems or sheaths of grasses and other plants where they overwinter. The nymphs, which appear in the spring, are often so abundant that their "spittle," the secreted froth in which they hide, will wet the clothing of someone crossing their habitat. The spittle appears to be effective in protecting this stage of the bugs. Adults are often called "froghoppers" because they have a vague resemblance to frogs and are strong jumpers. Most species suck sap from herbaceous

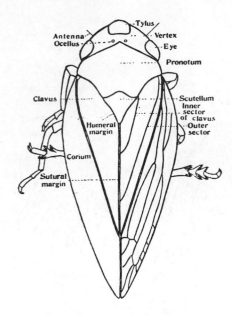

Fig. 21.11. (*From Britton, 1923*)

plants, but some feed on trees. They are of varying economic importance, some species doing considerable damage to crops such as pecans, cotton, clover, alfalfa, and even pine.

The family is large but represented by only seven genera and 54 species in the U.S. and Canada.

Subfamily Cercopinae
Tribe Cercopini
12.1 *Prosapia* Fennah

One species, as follows:

P. bicincta Say (Two-lined Spittle Bug). L. 8–10 mm. Dark, nearly black, with two narrow orange bands across front wings. Common in the Southeast, sparse in the Northeast. Extends into the tropics. The species has been divided into four subspecies, *P. b. bicincta* s.str.; *P. b. angustata* Walker; *P. b. bifascia* Walker, and *P. b. ignipecta* Fitch. (1) n.e. US; (2) s.e. US; (5) IA, KS, MO.

Subfamily Aphrophorinae
Tribe Ptyelini

[12.2 *Philaronia* Ball (2 spp., 6 subspp.)]

Tribe Lepyroniini
12.3 *Lepyronia* Amyot and Serville

Four species, one of which, *L. coleoptrata* Linnaeus, is questionable. The following is a widespread representative:

L. quadrangularis Say. L. 8–10 mm. Brown, with two oblique brown bands across front wings. (1) n.e. NA; (2) s.e. US; (3) NM, TX; (4) UT; (5) AB, MB, MN, SD, NE, IA, CO, KS, MO.

12.4 *Philaenus* Stål

Three species, including the following:

P. leucophthalmus Linnaeus, divided into 12 subspecies, including *P. l. spumarius* Linnaeus (Meadow Spittle Bug): L.

6–8 mm. Brownish with paler mottled markings. (1) n.e. US; (2) s.e. US; (3) CA; (4) UT; (5) ND, SD. (See A & J 70.)

P. lineatus Linnaeus (Lined Spittle Bug). (1) n.e. NA.

12.5 *Aphrophora* Germar

Fourteen species, of which the following are common:

A. parallela Say (Pine Spittle Bug). (1) n.e. NA; (5) AB, SK, MN.

A. saratogensis (Fitch) (Saratoga Spittle Bug). (1) n.e. NA; (2) s.e. US; (3) CA; (4) BC.

[12.6 *Omalaphora* Matsumura (1 sp., *O. salicis* DeGeer, (1) n.e. US)]

Subfamily Clastopterinae
Tribe Clastopterini
12.7 *Clastoptera* Germar

Thirty-two species and 11 subspecies. Several species of economic importance are as follows:

C. achatina Germar (Pecan Spittle Bug). (1) n.e. US; (2) s.e. US; (3) CA, NM, TX; (5) CO, KS, IA, MO.

C. obtusa Say (Alder Spittle Bug). Divided into three subspecies. (1) n.e. NA; (2) s.e. US; (3) TX; (5) AB, CO, KS, MO.

C. proteus Fitch (Dogwood Spittle Bug). Divided into four subspecies. (1) n.e. NA; (2) s.e. US; (3) TX; (4) WA, UT; (5) CO, KS, IA, MO.

C. saintcyri Provancher (Heath Spittle Bug). Divided into two subspecies. (1) n.e. NA; (2) s.e. US; (3) CA; (5) CO.

C. xanthocephala Germar (Sunflower Spittle Bug). Divided into two subspecies. (1) n.e. NA; (2) s.e. US; (3) s.w. US; (5) CO, KS, IA, MO.

Superfamily CICADOIDEA

One family only, as follows:

13. CICADIDAE (Cicada Family)

L. 23–55 mm. Head wide and blunt; antennae short, inserted on front of head between compound eyes; three ocelli close together, forming a triangle; compound eyes large, colored; body green, brown, often with black markings. Wings large, transparent brown, black, or green; hind wings smaller than front wings, veins not reaching wing margin, sometimes with brown or black spots. Front femora enlarged, often armed with teeth; middle coxae short, inserted close together.

Members of this family are best known for the characteristic song of each species made by male stridulation. Sound-producing organs are located on venter at base of abdomen in most species. Others make sound by wing banging. Both males and females of a few species produce sound by tapping costal margins of front wings.

Eggs are laid in twigs of trees, causing them to wilt, droop down, and eventually fall to the ground. This natural pruning process usually results in better foliage growth the following year, although young trees may be killed. One of the mysteries of natural processes is why the eggs are laid high in the tree since the newly hatched nymphs must drop or fall with the twig to the

Fig. 21.12.

ground, then dig their way into the soil, down to the tree roots where they feed.

All species have a long life cycle of four or more years; three North American species have a 17-year cycle; three have a 13-year cycle. These species occur in broods that emerge in different years. The 17-year cycle species have 13 broods; the 13 year cycle species, five broods. Each of these has a different geographic range. Emerging broods may contain two or three different species. When the last nymphal stage is reached, the nymphs crawl out of the soil and complete their transformation to the adult stage on the trunk of a tree. The emergent adult leaves its last nymphal shell clinging to the bark. After inflating and drying its wings, it flies high into the branches. The males sing only during the daytime, often just before sunset.

Twenty-two genera and 166 species occur in the U.S. and Canada.

Subfamily Tibiceninae

Tribe Zammarini

[13.1 *Odopoea* Stål (1 sp., *O. fumestra* Walker); 13.2 *Zammara* Amyot and Serville (1 sp., *Z. smaragdina* Walker)]

Tribe Tibicenini

[13.3 *Diceroprocta* Stål (22 spp., and 9 subspecies)]

13.4 *Tibicen* Latreille

Thirty species and 15 subspecies, of which the following are common:

T. canicularis Harris (Dog-day Cicada). L. 50–60 mm. Green. Song is characteristic of hot summer days, the time of heat waves in the North, but foreshadows the coming of autumn, after which they become silent. Nymphal stage last 2 to 5 years. Since broods overlap, adults are present each year. (See A & J 65.) (1) n.e. NA; (2) s.e. US; (3) TX; (5) CO, KS, MO.

T. resh Haldeman. (See Fig. 21.12.) (2) AR, LA, MS, AL; (3) s.w. US; (4) UT; (5) KS, MO.

T. similaris Smith and Grossbeck (See Fig. 21.13.) (2) s.e. US.

T. superbus Fitch. (See Fig. 21.14.) (2) AR; (3) NM, OK, TX; (5) KS, MO.

[13.5 *Cornuplura* Davis (2 spp., (3) s.w. US); 13.6 *Cacama* Distant (5 spp., (3) s.w. US; (4) UT; (5) CO)]

Tribe Fidicinini

[13.7 *Proarna* Stål (1 sp., *P. championi* Distant, (3) s.w. US; 13.8 *Beameria* Davis (2 spp., (3) s.w. US; (5) CO, KS)]

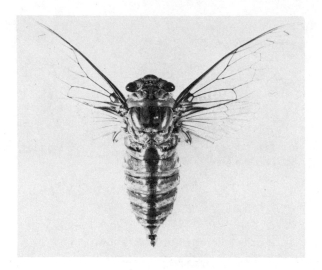

Fig. 21.13.

13.9 *Pararina* Distant

One species, as follows:

P. puella Davis. (See Fig. 21.15.) (2) LA; (3) AZ, TX, OK.

Tribe Hyantiini

13.10 *Quesada* Distant

One species, as follows:

Q. gigas Olivier (See Fig. 21.16.) (3) s.w. US.

Subfamily Cicadinae

Tribe Cicadini

[13.11 *Neocicada* Kato (1 sp., *N. hieroglyphica* Say, (1) n.e. US; (2) s.e. US; (5) KS, MO); 13.12 *Cicada* Linnaeus (2 spp., *C. chisos* Davis, (3) TX; *C. guttata* Foerster, questionable record)]

Subfamily Tibicininae

Tribe Carinetini

[13.13 *Herrera* Distant (1 sp., *H. ancilla* Stål, (3) s.e. US)]

Tribe Tibicinini

[13.14 *Tibicinoides* Distant (4 spp., (3) s.w. US; (4) UT; (5) MT, CO, KS); 13.15 *Okanagana* Distant, 51 spp., 14 subspp.); 13.16 *Okanagodes* Davis (2 spp., 2 subspp., (3) s.e. US; (4) UT); 13.17 *Clidophleps* Van Duzee (6 spp., 2 subspp., (3) CA)]

Fig. 21.14.

Fig. 21.15.

Fig. 21.17.

13.18 *Magicicada* Davis

Three species, the following being best known:

M. septendecim Linnaeus (Periodical Cicada). L. 27–33 mm (17-year race); 19–27 mm (13-year race). Body dark; eyes and principal wing veins red. Studies show that a complex of biological species is included under this one name. Often called locusts, a name properly applied to certain Orthoptera (some grasshoppers), these insects are well known by their sound if not on sight. Two races are common in various parts of the eastern U.S. The 17-year race (so-called because the nymph takes 17 years to mature) occurs in n. US from the Mississippi River e. and from s. NY s. to n. GA and MS. The 13-year race occurs throughout the s.e. U.S., extending into (3) TX, OK and (5) MO and reaching as far north as central IL. Their broods emerge in different parts of this range in different years according to a predictable schedule. There are 30 broods whose distribution and emergence dates have been plotted. Of the 18 distinct broods (13 for the 17-year and 5 for the 13-year race) some have discontinuous distribution. When a brood is due to emerge, young trees—which may be killed by the great number of eggs laid in their twigs—must be covered in advance. Since more than one brood may be in an area, adults appear oftener than every 13 or 17 years but never in as great numbers as the main brood. (See Fig. 21.17 and A & J 66.)

Tribe Cicadettini

[13.19 *Cicadetta* Kolenati (4 spp., 2 subspecies, (2) s.e. U.S.; (5) MO)]

Subfamily Tettigadinae

[13.20 *Tettigades* Amyot and Serville (1 sp., *T. mexicana* Distant, (3) AZ)]

Subfamily Platypediinae

13.21 *Platypedia* Uhler

Twenty-three species and 5 subspecies found in (3) s.w. U.S.; (4) Pacific n.w.; (5) MT, WY, CO, NE, SD. The following is representative:

P. areolata Uhler (Orchard Cicada). L. 18–23 mm. (3) CA; (4) Pacific n.w.; (5) MT, CO.

[13.22 *Neoplatypedia* Davis (2 spp., (3) CA, AZ; (4) OR, UT, ID)]

Superfamily CICADELLOIDEA

One family only, as follows:

14. CICADELLIDAE (Leafhopper Family)

[= Jassidae]

L. 3–12 mm (some to 22 mm). Green, brown, often with bright color markings; head usually with two ocelli well-separated from the compound eyes. Front wing thickened, with claval area and corium. Both long-wing and short-wing forms occur in some species. Hind legs fitted for jumping.

Leafhoppers (also called Sharpshooters and Doggers) are very abundant in numbers of individuals and species. With more than 20,000 species worldwide, this is the largest family of the Homoptera. There are 2507 species in 225 genera in the U.S. and Canada, with many subfamilies and tribes as indicated below. They are very difficult to identify.

Many species are pests of many cultivated plants, and probably all plants are infested with one or more species. They suck plant juices and leave white or yellowish spots on the leaves. Their egg laying process, in which the ovipositor is inserted into plant tissue, plugs the conductive tissues of stalks and veins and causes leaves to curl and brown. They also excrete a honeydew on which sooty mold grows, interfering with photosynthesis. Some species are known to be vectors of plant diseases.

There may be more than one generation per year. Most species have five nymphal instars. They overwinter as eggs or as adults.

Subfamily Ledrinae
Tribe Xerophloeini

[14.1 *Xerophloea* Germar (13 spp.)]

Subfamily **Dorycephalinae**

Tribe **Dorycephalini**

[14.2 *Dorycephalus* Kouchakewitch (subgenus *Dorycephalus* s. str., 4 spp.; *Atlenuipyga* Oman, 4 spp.); 14.3 *Neoslossonia* Van Duzee (1 sp., *N. putnami* (Osborn))]

Subfamily **Hecalinae**

Tribe **Hecalini**

[14.4 *Hecullus* Oman (2 spp.); 14.5 *Hecalus* Stål (2 spp.); 14.6 *Memnonia* Ball (5 spp.); 14.7 *Parabolocratus* Fieber (21 spp.); 14.8 *Dicyphonia* Ball (5 spp.); 14.9 *Spangbergiella* Signoret (3 spp.)]

Subfamily **Megophthalminae**

Tribe **Megophthalmini**

[14.10 *Brenda* Oman (1 sp., *B. arborea* (Ball)); 14.11 *Tiaja* Oman (6 spp.)]

Subfamily **Agalliinae**

Tribe **Agalliini**

[14.12 *Agalliopsis* Kirkaldy (subgenus *Agalliopsis* s. str., 5 spp.; subgenus *Agallaria* Oman, 10 spp.)]

14.13 *Agallia* Curtis

Nine species, including the following:

A. quadripunctata Provancher. (See Fig. 21.18.) (1) n.e. US; (2) s.e. US; (3) CA, NM; (4) Pacific n.w.; (5) MN, SD, NE, IA, CO, KS, MO.

[14.14 *Ceratagallia* Kirkaldy (25 spp.)]

14.15 *Aceratagallia* Kirkaldy

Two subgenera: *Ionia* Ball (1 sp., *A. trianata* (Ball)) and *Aceratagallia* s. str., with 28 species, the following being of economic importance:

A. (A.) sanguinolenta (Provancher) (Clover Leafhopper)

Subfamily **Macropsinae**

Tribe **Macropsini**

[14.16 *Oncopsis* Burmeister (15 spp.)]

Fig. 21.18. (*From Britton, 1923*)

14.17 *Macropsis* Lewis

Thirty-nine species, the following being of economic importance:

M. trimaculata (Fitch) (Plum Leafhopper).

Subfamily **Idiocerinae**

Tribe **Idiocerini**

[14.18 *Idiocerus* Lewis (73 spp.)]

Subfamily **Iassinae**

Tribe **Gyponini**

[14.19 *Dragonana* Ball and Reeves (1 sp., *D. dracontea* (Gibson)); 14.20 *Prairiana* Ball (12 spp.); 14.21 *Negosiana* Oman (5 spp.); 14.22 *Gyponana* Ball: 2 subgenera: *Gyponana* s. str. (70 spp.) and *Rugosana* DeLong (9 spp.); 14.23 *Hamana* DeLong (5 spp.); 14.24 *Acusana* DeLong (11 spp.); 14.25 *Gypona* Germar (8 spp.); 14.26 *Marganana* DeLong (1 sp., *M. suilla* (Ball)); 14.27 *Polana* DeLong (1 sp., *P. quadrinotata* (Spångberg)); 14.28 *Ponana* Ball: 2 subgenera: *Ponana* s. str. (20 spp.) and *Bulbana* DeLong (4 spp.)]

Tribe **Iassini**

14.29 *Stragania* Stål

Twenty-two species, of which the following is of economic importance:

S. robusta (Uhler) (Robust Leafhopper).

[14.30 *Pachyopsis* Uhler (1 sp., *P. laetus* Uhler)]

Subfamily **Penthimiinae**

Tribe **Penthimiini**

[14.31 *Penthimia* Germar (2 spp.)]

Subfamily **Koebeliinae**

Tribe **Koebeliini**

[14.32 *Koebelia* Baker (4 spp.)]

Subfamily **Coelidiinae**

Tribe **Coelidiini**

[14.33 *Coelidia* Germar (5 spp.)]

Tribe **Tinobregmini**

[14.34 *Tinobregmus* Van Duzee (5 spp.)]

Subfamily **Nioniinae**

Tribe **Nioniini**

[14.35 *Nionia* Ball (1 sp., *N. palmeri* (Van Duzee))]

Subfamily **Aphrodinae**

Tribe **Aphrodini**

[14.36 *Aphrodes* Curtis (6 spp.)]

Subfamily **Xestocephalinae**

Tribe **Xestocephalini**

[14.37 *Xestocephalus* Van Duzee (14 spp.)]

Subfamily **Neocoelidiinae**

Tribe **Neocoelidiini**

[14.38 *Neocoelidia* Gillette and Baker (23 spp.); 14.39 *Paracoelidea* Baker (3 spp.)]

Fig. 21.19. (*From U.S. Dept. Agric.*)

Subfamily Tettigellinae
Tribe Proconiini

[14.40 *Aulacizes* Amyot and Serville (2 spp.); 14.41 *Homalodisca* Stål (4 spp., including *H. triquetra* (Fabricius) [Fig. 21.19]); 14.42 *Oncometopia* Stål (3 spp.); 14.43 *Cuerna* Melichar (16 spp.)]

Tribe Tettigellini

[14.44 *Ciminius* Metcalf and Bruner (3 spp.); 14.45 *Tylozygus* Fieber (4 spp.); 14.46 *Plesiommata* Provancher (2 spp.)]

14.47 *Draeculacephala* Ball

Sixteen species, of which the following are common:

D. mollipes (Say) (Watercress Sharpshooter).

D. minerva Ball (Grass Sharpshooter).

D. sp. (See Fig. A & J 72.)

D. angulifera (Walker). (See Fig. 21.20.)

14.48 *Carneocephala* Ball

Eight species, of which the following is of economic interest:

C. flaviceps (Riley) (Yellowheaded Leafhopper).

[14.49 *Helochara* Fitch (2 spp.); 14.50 *Hortensia* Metcalf and Bruner (1 sp., *H. similis* (Walker))]

14.51 *Graphocephala* Van Duzee

Five species, of which the following is common and attractive:

G. coccinea (Forster) (Candy-stripe Leafhopper). L. 8–9 mm. Green with red markings. Common on blackberry and various cultivated ornamentals. Widespread throughout (1), (2), (3), (4), (5). (See Fig. A & J 71.)

[14.52 *Hordnia* Oman (2 spp.); 14.53 *Sibovia* China (1 sp., *S. occatoria* (Say)); 14.54 *Colimona* Oman (2 spp.); 14.55 *Marathonia* Oman (1 sp., *M. marathonensis* Olsen); 14.56 *Decua* Oman (2 spp.); 14 57 *Manzutus* Oman (2 spp.); 14.58 *Neokolla* Melichar (3 spp.); 14.59 *Keonella* Oman (5 spp.)]

Tribe Evacanthini

[14.60 *Evacanthus* Peletier and Serville (2 spp.)]

Fig. 21.20. (*From Beirne, 1956*)

Tribe Errhomenellini

[14.61 *Errhomus* Oman (3 spp.); 14.62 *Carsonus* Oman (6 spp.); 14.63 *Pagaronia* Ball (4 spp.); 14.64 *Friscanus* Oman (1 sp., *F. friscanus* (Ball)); 14.65 *Thatuna* Oman (1 sp., *T. gilletti* Oman); 14.66 *Lystridea* Baker (2 spp.)]

Subfamily Cicadellinae
Tribe Alebrini

[14.67 *Alebra* Fieber (1 sp., *A. albostriella* (Fallen)); 14.68 *Protalebra* Baker (3 spp.)]

Tribe Dikraneurini

[14.69 *Alconeura* Ball and DeLong (21 spp.); 14.70 *Dikraneura* Hardy (25 spp.); 14.71 *Notus* Fieber (2 spp.); 14.72 *Forcipata* DeLong and Caldwell (10 spp.); 14.73 *Kunzeana* Oman (12 spp.); 14.74 *Dikrella* Oman (14 spp.); 14.75 *Idona* DeLong (1 sp., *I. minuenda* (Ball)); 14.76 *Dikraneuroidea* Lawson (1 sp., *D. beameri* Lawson)]

14.77 *Empoasca* Walsh

This very large genus is divided into the following subgenera: *Kybos* Fieber (45 spp.); *Hebata* DeLong (29 spp.), and *Empoasca* s. str. (103 spp.). The following species are of economic interest:

E. fabae Harris (Potato Leafhopper). L. 5–7 mm. Pale green. A pest of potatoes, beans, clover, and alfalfa that migrates north in the spring. (1) n.e. NA; (2) s.e. US; (3) central CA.

E. maligna (Walsh) (Apple Leafhopper).

E. stevensi Young (Steven's Leafhopper).

E. solana DeLong (Southern Garden Leafhopper).

E. abrupta DeLong (Western Potato Leafhopper).

Tribe Jorumini

[14.78 *Joruma* McAtee (2 spp.)]

Tribe Cicadellini

[14.79 *Cicadella* Dumeril (10 spp.); 14.80 *Typhlocybella* Baker (2 spp.)]

14.81 *Typhlocyba* Germar

Eighty-two species, the following being of economic interest:

T. *pomaria* McAtee (White Apple Leafhopper).

T. *rosae* (Linnaeus) (Rose Leafhopper).

T. *prunicola* (Edwards) (Prune Leafhopper).

14.82 *Erythroneura* Fitch

Three hundred and seventy species in this gigantic genus, of which the following two are common, but many others are abundant as well:

E. *tricincta* Fitch (Threebanded Leafhopper).

E. *ziczac* Walsh (Virginia Creeper Leafhopper).

[14.83 *Hymetta* McAtee (7 spp.)]

Subfamily Deltocephalinae
Tribe Cochlorhinini

[14.84 *Eulonus* Oman (1 sp., *E. almus* Van Duzee); 14.85 *Drionia* Ball (1 sp., *D. nigra* Ball); 14.86 *Cochlorhinus* Uhler (6 spp.); 14.87 *Calonia* Beamer (1 sp., *C. signata* (Ball)); 14.88 *Huleria* Ball (1 sp., *H. quadripunctata* Ball); 14.89 *Penehuleria* Beamer (1 sp., *P. acuticephala* Beamer)]

Tribe Scaphytopiini

[14.90 *Japananus* Ball (1 sp., *J. hyalinus* (Osborn)); 14.91 *Ascius* DeLong (1 sp., *A. triangularis* DeLong)]

14.92 *Scaphytopius* Ball

This genus is divided into the following three subgenera: *Convelinus* Ball (19 spp.); *Scaphytopius* s. str. (6 spp.); *Cloanthanus* Ball (47 spp.). The following is a common species:

S. *loricatus* (Van Duzee) (Yellow-faced Leafhopper).

Tribe Acinopterini
14.93 *Acinopterus* Van Duzee

Twenty-three species, of which the following is common:

A. *angulatus* Lawson (Angulate Leafhopper).

Tribe Balcluthini

[14.94 *Nesosteles* Kirkaldy (9 spp.)]

14.95 *Balclutha* Kirkaldy

Seven species, of which the following are common:

B. *hospes* Kirkaldy (Little Green Leafhopper).

B. *beardsleyi* Namba (Beardsley Leafhopper).

Tribe Macrostelini

[14.96 *Baldulus* Oman (3 spp.)]

14.97 *Macrosteles* Fieber

This genus is divided into the following three subgenera: *Davisonia* Dorst (5 spp.), *Sonronius* Dorst (3 spp.), and *Macrosteles* s. str. (17 spp.). The following is a common species on ornamental plants:

M. *fascifrons* (Stål) (Aster Leafhopper).

Tribe Deltocephalini

[14.98 *Prescottia* Ball (2 spp.)]

14.99 *Scaphoideus* Uhler

Forty-seven species, of which the following is a pest:

S. *luteolus* Van Duzee (White-banded Elm Leafhopper).

[14.100 *Cantura* Oman (3 spp.); 14.101 *Osbornellus* Ball (26 spp.); 14.102 *Spathanus* DeLong (5 spp.); 14.103 *Omanana* DeLong (2 spp.); 14.104 *Knullana* DeLong (1 sp., *K. huachuca* DeLong); 14.105 *Allygus* Fieber (1 sp., *A. mixtus* (Fabricius)); 14.106 *Chlorotettix* Van Duzee (45 spp.); 14.107 *Doleranus* Ball (3 spp.)]

14.108 *Colladonus* Ball

Thirty-one species, of which the following are common:

C. *clitellarius* (Say) (Saddled Leafhopper).

C. *montanus* (Van Duzee) (Mountain Leafhopper).

[14.109 *Nigridonus* Oman (1 sp., *N. illumina* Ball); 14.110 *Caladonus* Oman (1 sp., *C. coquilletti* Van Duzee); 14.111 *Idiodonus* Ball (12 spp.); 14.112 *Nurenus* Oman (1 sp., *N. snowi* Ball); 14.113 *Neodonus* DeLong and Hershberger (1 sp., *N. piperatus* DeLong and Hershberger); 14.114 *Bonneyana* Oman (3 spp.); 14.115 *Floridonus* Oman (1 sp., *F. taxodii* Sanders and DeLong); 14.116 *Zabrosa* Oman (1 sp., *Z. sexpunctata* (Beamer)); 14.117 *Eusama* Oman (1 sp., *E. amanda* Ball); 14.118 *Cetexa* Oman (1 sp., *C. graecula* Ball); 14.119 *Fridonus* Oman (1 sp., *F. concanus* Oman); 14.120 *Gloridonus* Ball (4 spp.); 14.121 *Ballana* DeLong (70 spp.); 14.122 *Limbanus* Oman (3 spp.); 14.123 *Allygianus* Ball (3 spp.); 14.124 *Allygiella* Oman (1 sp., *A. clathratus* Ball), 14.125 *Pasadenus* Ball (5 spp.); 14.126 *Mesamia* Ball (16 spp.); 14.127 *Twiningia* Ball (19 spp.); 14.128 *Fitchana* Oman (3 spp.); 14.129 *Sobata* Oman (1 sp., *S. palliolata* Ball); 14.130 *Bandara* Ball (4 spp.); 14.131 *Danbara* Oman (1 sp., *D. aurata* Ball); 14.132 *Atanus* Oman (2 spp.); 14.133 *Ollarianus* Ball (9 spp.); 14.134 *Aligia* Ball (32 spp.); 14.135 *Eutettix* Van Duzee (34 spp.); 14.136 *Eusora* Oman (2 spp.); 14.137 *Crassana* DeLong and Hershberger (1 sp., *C. goniana* (Ball)); 14.138 *Norvellina* Ball (30 spp.); 14.139 *Aplanus* Oman (2 spp.); 14.140 *Paraphlepsius* Baker (63 spp.); 14.141 *Phlepsanus* Oman (3 spp.); 14.142 *Texananus* Ball, with 3 subgenera: *Texananus* s. str. (28 spp.), *Excultanus* Oman (4 spp.), and *Iowanus* Ball (6 spp.); 14.143 *Orientus* DeLong (1 sp., *O. ishidae* (Matsumura)); 14.144 *Dorydiella* Baker (2 spp.); 14.145 *Dixianus* Ball (1 sp., *D. utahnus* (Ball)); 14.146 *Lycioides* Oman (8 spp.); 14.147 *Tropicanus* DeLong (2 spp.)]

14.148 *Opsius* Fieber

One species, as follows:

O. *stactogalus* Fieber (Tamarix Leafhopper).

14.149 *Circulifer* Zakhvatkin

One species, as follows:

C. *tenellus* (Baker) (Beet Leafhopper).

[14.150 *Fieberiella* Signoret (1 sp., *F. florii* Stål)); 14.151 *Cicadula* Zetterstedt (14 spp.); 14.152 *Calanana* DeLong (3 spp.); 14.153 *Paluda* DeLong (2 spp.); 14.154 *Elymana* DeLong (6 spp.); 14.155 *Euscelidius* Ribaut (1 sp., *E. schenkii* (Kirschbaum)); 14.156 *Thamnotettix* Zetterstedt (1 sp., *T. simplex* (Herrich-Schaeffer)); 14.157 *Doliotettix* Ribaut (1 sp., *D. pallens* (Zetterstedt)); 14.158 *Macustus* Ribaut (1 sp., *M. grisescens* (Zetterstedt)); 14.159 *Streptanus* Ribaut (2 spp.); 14.160 *Extrusanus* Oman (2 spp.); 14.161 *Frigartus* Oman (1 sp., *F. frigidus* (Ball)); 14.162 *Remadosus* Ball (2 spp.); 14.163 *Athysanus* Burmeister (1 sp., *A. argentatus* (Fabricius)); 14.164 *Limotettix* Sahlberg (9 spp.)]

14.165 *Scleroracus* Van Duzee

Twenty-one species, of which the following is common.

S. vaccinii (Van Duzee) (Blunt-nosed Cranberry Leaf-hopper).

14.166 *Exitianus* Ball

Two species, of which the following is of economic importance:

E. exitiosus (Uhler) (Gray Lawn Leafhopper).

[14.167 *Stirellus* Osborn and Ball (9 spp.); 14.168 *Penestirellus* Beamer and Tuthill (1 sp., *P. catalinus* Beamer and Tuthill); 14.169 *Gillettiella* Osborn (3 spp.); 14.170 *Kinonia* Ball (1 sp., *K. elongata* Ball); 14.171 *Hardya* Edwards (1 sp., *H. dentata* (Osborn and Ball)); 14.172 *Stenometopiellus* Haupt (1 sp., *S. cookei* (Gillette)); 14.173 *Doratura* Sahlberg (1 sp., *D. stylata* (Boheman)); 14.174 *Driotura* Osborn and Ball (6 spp.); 14.175 *Athysanella* Baker, subgenus *Athysanella* s. str. (22 spp.); subgenus *Amphipyga* Osborn (25 spp.); subgenus *Brachydella* Ball and Beamer (1 sp., *B. abdominalis* Ball and Beamer); subgenus *Gladionura* Osborn (32 spp.); subgenus *Pedumella* Ball and Beamer (2 spp.); 14.176 *Menosoma* Ball (2 spp.); 14.177 *Paramesus* Fieber (1 sp., *P. obtusifrons* Stål); 14.178 *Pasaremus* Oman (1 sp., *P. concentricus* (Van Duzee)); 14.179 *Palus* DeLong and Sleesman (7 spp.); 14.180 *Orocastus* Oman (1 sp., *O. perpusillus* Ball and DeLong; 14.181 *Auridius* Oman (3 spp.); 14.182 *Mocuellus* Ribaut (3 spp.); 14.183 *Psammotettix* Haupt (10 spp.); 14.184 *Hebexa* Oman (1 sp., *H. incognita* Oman); 14.185 *Arthaldeus* Ribaut (1 sp., *A. pascuellus* (Fallen)); 14.186 *Sorhoanus* Ribaut (9 spp.); 14.187 *Giprus* Oman (7 spp.); 14.188 *Cazenus* Oman (7 spp.); 14.189 *Laevicephalus* DeLong (18 spp.); 14.190 *Lemellus* Oman (1 sp., *L. bimaculatus* Gillette and Baker); 14.191 *Verdanus* Oman (1 sp., *V. evansi* (Ashmead)); 14.192 *Diplocolenus* Ribaut (1 sp., *D. configuratus* (Uhler)); 14.193 *Cribrus* Oman (2 spp.); 14.194 *Aflexia* Oman (1 sp., *A. rubranura* (DeLong)); 14.195 *Flexamia* DeLong (27 spp.); 14.196 *Secopennis* DeLong and Steesman (1 sp., *S. slossonae* (Ball)); 14.197 *Alapus* DeLong and Sleesman (7 spp.); 14.198 *Latalus* DeLong and Sleesman (3 spp.); 14.199 *Errastunus* Ribaut (2 spp.); 14.200 *Pinumius* Ribaut (1 sp., *P. sexmaculatus* (Gillette and Baker)); 14.201 *Quontus* Oman (4 spp.); 14.202 *Rosenus* Oman (4 spp.); 14.203 *Hebecephalus* DeLong (16 spp.); 14.204 *Pazu* Oman (1 sp., *P. balli* (Beamer)); 14.205 *Telusus* Oman (2 spp.); 14.206 *Peconus* Oman (1 sp., *P. scriptanus* (Oman)); 14.207 *Commellus* Osborn and Ball (4 spp.); 14.208 *Cabrulus* Oman (3 spp.); 14.209 *Crumbana* Oman (1 sp., *C. arundineus* (Crumb)); 14.210 *Haldorus* Oman (1 sp., *H. australis* (DeLong)); 14.211 *Deltocephalus* Burmeister (27 spp.); 14.212 *Umoka* Lawson (1 sp., *U. ornata* (Gillette)); 14.213 *Polyamia* DeLong (30 spp.)]

14.214 *Endria* Oman

Four species, of which the following is common:

E. inimica (Say) (Painted Leafhopper).

[14.215 *Lonatura* Osborn and Ball (12 spp.); 14.216 *Mexara* Oman (1 sp., *M. atascasus* (Ball)); 14.217 *Deltella* Oman (1 sp., *D. decisus* (DeLong)); 14.218 *Daltonia* Oman (1 sp., *D. estacadus* (Ball)); 14.219 *Amblysellus* Sleesman (1 sp., *A. curtisii* (Fitch))]

14.220 *Graminella* DeLong

Thirteen species, of which the following are common:

G. nigrifrons (Forbes) (Blackfaced Leafhopper).

G. sonorus (Ball) (Lesser Lawn Leafhopper).

[14.221 *Destria* Oman (2 spp.); 14.222 *Deltanus* Oman (1 sp., *D. texanus* (Osborn and Ball)); 14.223 *Amplicephalus* DeLong (6 spp.); 14.224 *Sanctanus* Ball (10 spp.); 14.225 *Arundanus* DeLong (15 spp.)]

Superfamily MEMBRACOIDEA

Two families (distinguished in the Key to the Superfamilies).

15. MEMBRACIDAE (Treehopper Family)

L. 5–13 mm (rarely over 12 mm). Green, brown, or black, sometimes brightly colored in tropical species. The highly modified prothorax is characteristic of this family. The pronotum extends back over the abdomen and is variously modified; it may be humpbacked, thornlike, or with bizzare enlargements and branches. Two ocelli. Antennae short, hair-like, inserted below and in front of the compound eyes. Both pairs of wings membranous, concealed by the pronotum. Hind legs slightly enlarged for jumping; hind tibiae often with three longitudinal rows of small setae and a transverse row of spurs; tarsi with three tarsomeres. (See Fig. 21.21 for general features.)

This is a large group, with over 2400 species in the world. Common on trees, shrubs, and field vegetation, most species are host specific; they are sap feeders on trees and shrubs. Some nymphs feed on grasses and herbaceous plants. The nymphs, usually gregarious, are often attended by ants for the honeydew they excrete.

There are 56 genera and 258 species in the U.S. and Canada.

Subfamily Centrotinae
Tribe Platycentrini

[15.1 *Platycentrus* Stål (2 spp.); 15.2 *Tylocentrus* Van Duzee (2 spp.)]

Subfamily Nessorhininae
Tribe Nessorhinini

[15.3 *Callicentrus* Stål (1 sp., *C. bonasia* Fabricius)]

Subfamily Membracinae
Tribe Hoplophorionini
15.4 *Umbonia* Burmeister

One species, as follows:

U. crassicornis Amyot and Serville (Thorn Bug). L. ±5 mm. Yellow; pronotum is modified into a thornlike projection, which is dark at the apex. Sometimes a pest in resort areas because pronotal thorns injure bare feet. (1) OH; (2) s.e. US. (See A&J 67.)

[15.5 *Platycotis* Stål (3 spp.); 15.6 *Leioscyta* Fowler (3 spp.); 15.7 *Campylenchia* Stål (2 spp.)]

Fig. 21.21. (*From Britton, 1923*)

15.8 *Enchenopa* Amyot and Serville

Two species, of which the following is common:

 E. binotata (Say) (Two-marked Treehopper).

[15.9 *Membracis* Fabricius (2 spp.)]

Tribe Hypsoprorini

[15.10 *Philya* Walker (2 spp.); 15.11 *Hypsoprora* Stål (2 spp.); 15.12 *Scalmophorus* Fowler (1 sp., *S. minutus* Ball)]

15.13 *Sphongophorus* Fairmaire

All species of this genus are ornate. (See A&J 68, 69.) One species in the U.S., as follows:

 S. mexicana (Guerin-Meneville) (Sponged Treehopper).

Tribe Centrodontini

 All species of this tribe are found on Cresote Bush in (3) s.w. US, n. Mexico, and Baja California.

[15.14 *Centrodontus* Funkhouser (2 spp.); 15.15 *Multareoides* Cook (3 spp.); 15.16 *Multareis* Goding (1 sp., *M. cornutus* Goding)]

Subfamily Darninae
Tribe Darnini

[15.17 *Taunaya* Fonseca (2 spp.); 15.18 *Darnis* Fabricius (1 sp., *D. lateralis* Coquebert); 15.19 *Stictopelta* Stål (5 spp.)]

Subfamily Smiliinae
Tribe Acutalini

[15.20 *Acutalis* Fairmaire (4 spp.)]

Tribe Micrutalini

[15.21 *Micrutalis* Fowler (7 spp.)]

Tribe Ceresini

[15.22 *Ilithucia* Stål (1 sp., *I. pacificata* Buckton); 15.23 *Ceresa* Amyot and Serville (3 spp.)]

15.24 *Stictocephala* Stål

Sixteen species, of which the following is a common example:

 S. bisonia Kopp and Yonke (Buffalo Treehopper). L. 7–9 mm. Green or yellowish-green. Since its eggs are laid in the bark and twigs of fruit trees, this species is of some economic importance. The nymphs feed on herbaceous vegetation in orchards and fields. Common (1), (2), (3), (4), (5).

[15.25 *Tortistilus* Caldwell (9 spp.)]

15.26 *Spissistilus* Caldwell

Nine species, the following of which is common:

 S. festinus (Say) (Three-cornered Alfalfa Treehopper).

[15.27 *Anisostylus* Caldwell (4 spp.); 15.28 *Stictolobus* Metcalf (3 spp.); 15.29 *Vestistilus* Caldwell (2 spp.); 15.30 *Trichaetipyga* Caldwell (1 sp., *T. juniperina* Ball); 15.31 Parantonae Fowler (1 sp., *P. hispida* Van Duzee)]

Tribe Amastrini

[15.32 *Bajulata* Ball (1 sp., *B. bajula* [Goding])]

15.33 *Vanduzeea* Goding

Five species, of which the following is common:

 V. segmentata (Fowler) (Van Duzee Treehopper).

[15.34 *Amastris* Stål (2 spp.)]

Tribe Smilini

[15.35 *Carynota* Fitch (4 spp.)]

15.36 *Glossonotus* Bulter

Six species, of which the following is common:

 G. crataegi (Fitch) (Quince Treehopper).

[15.37 *Heliria* Stål (12 spp.); 15.38 *Helonica* Ball (1 sp., *H. excelsa* (Fairmaire)); 15.39 *Palonica* Ball (4 spp.); 15.40 *Telamona* Fitch (26 spp.); 15.41 *Telonaca* Ball (2 spp.); 15.42 *Telamonanthe* Baker (2 spp.)]

15.43 *Antianthe* Fowler

One species only, as follows:

 A. expansa (Germar) (Solanaceous Treehopper).

[15.44 *Atymna* Stål (6 spp.); 15.45 *Cyrtololus* Goding (40 spp.); 15.46 *Ashmeadea* Goding (1 sp., *A. carinata* (Stål)); 15.47 *Grandolobus* Ball (1 sp., *G. grandis* Van Duzee)]

15.48 *Thelia* Amyot and Serville

Two species, of which the following is common:

 T. bimaculata Fabricius (Locust Treehopper). L. 10–11 mm. This extremely abundant species occurs only on locust, where it is attended by ants. (1) n.e. US; (2) s.e. US.

[15.49 *Ophiderma* Fairmaire (14 spp.); 15.50 *Smilia* Germar (2 spp.); 15.51 *Xantholobus* Van Duzee (12 spp.)]

Tribe Polyglyptini

[15.52 *Publilia* Stål (5 spp.); 15.53 *Bryantopsis* Ball (1 sp., *B. ensigera* Ball); 15.54 *Entylia* Germar (5 spp.)]

Subfamily Stegaspinae
Tribe Microcentini

[15.55 *Microcentrus* Stål (6 spp.); 15.56 *Dontonodus* Funkhouser (1 sp., *D. schaefferi* Goding)]

16. AETALIONIDAE (Aetalionid Treehopper Family)

 L. 7–30 mm. Brown, reddish brown, or black. This family is worldwide in distribution, but most of the 50 species occur in tropical North and South America. Only one species reaches the U.S., as follows:

[16.1 *Aetalion* Latreille (1 sp., *A. nervosopunctatum* Signoret) (3) AZ.]

Suborder STERNORRHYNCHA

This large suborder contains the scale insects and related families, including the large family Aphididae. They are small in size and usually have long and filiform antennae, although these may be greatly reduced in some of the scale insects. Their legs are well developed, rudimentary, or entirely lacking. The beak, if present, seems to arise between the front coxae. The wings may or may not be present; if present, they are thin, with reduced venation. Wings are present in some scale insect males,

Table 21.2 Superfamilies of Sternorrhyncha

Family	Tarsi	Antennae	Special features of adults
Psylloidea	Two-segmented	Usually ten- or eleven-segmented; as few as five segments occasionally.	L. 2–5 mm. Resemble tiny cicadas. Hind legs fitted for jumping; both sexes winged as adults; wings held rooflike over body when at rest.
Aleyrodoidea	Two-segmented	Usually seven-segmented.	L. 2–3 mm. Resemble tiny moths. Adults with four wings; two ocelli.
Aphidoidea	Two-segmented	Usually three- or six-segmented.	Many have cornicles on the abdomen; some wingless.
Coccoidea	Usually one-segmented	Varies from rudimentary tubercle to eleven-, twelve-, or thirteen-segmented.	Male with one pair of functional wings; female wingless, often legless; sedentary forms attached to host plant.

but only the first pair is developed (the hind pair being reduced to halterlike structures), which might lead to some confusion with the Diptera.

The group is one of great economic importance. Not only do they multiply in large numbers, they are difficult to control because of the protection they receive from their waxy coatings and the fact that they are transported worldwide with plant material. Many of them are host specific.

There are four superfamilies, as listed in Table 21.2, and 22 families in the U.S. and Canada.

Superfamily PSYLLOIDEA

One family only, as follows:

17. PYSLLIDAE (Jumping Plantlice Family)

[= Chermidae]

L. 2–5 mm. Some of these tiny insects resemble miniature cicadas. Head with three ocelli, beak short; three-segmented; antennae slender or rather stout, usually 10-segmented, sometimes less. Tarsi with two tarsomeres and terminal tarsomere with two claws; hind legs modified for jumping. Four wings present.

The eggs are stalked; some are laid on plant surfaces and others in plant tissue. The nymphs pass through five instars; some of them on the plant surface and some in galls. Some excrete honeydew and are attended by ants.

Although some species secrete a wax that forms a woolly covering, they are different from woolly aphids described below. Most species are host specific and of some economic importance. They are involved in the transmission of plant diseases.

There are 28 genera and 257 species in the U.S. and Canada.

Subfamily Liviinae
Tribe Liviini

[17.1 *Livia* Latreille (5 spp.)]

Tribe Aphalarini

[17.2 *Aphalara* Foerster, subgenus *Aphalara* s. str. (17 spp.); 17.3 *Anomocera* Crawford (2 spp.); 17.4 *Aphalaroida* Crawford (5 spp.); 17.5 *Craspedolepta* Enderlein (41 spp.)]

Subfamily Pauropsyllinae

[17.6 *Gyropsylla* Tuthill (1 sp., *G. ilicis* Ashmead); 17.7 *Heteropsylla* Crawford (2 spp.); 17.8 *Calophya* Loew (5 spp.)]

Subfamily Carsidarinae

[17.9 *Rhinopsylla* Riley (3 spp.)]

Subfamily Triozinae
17.10 *Trioza* Foerster

Forty-two species, of which the following is a pest:
 T. diospyri (Ashmead) (Persimmon Psylla).

17.11 *Paratrioza* Crawford

Six species, of which the following is of economic importance:
 P. cockerelli (Sulc) (Tomato Psyllid; also Potato Psyllid).

[17.12 *Kuwayama* Crawford (1 sp., *K. medicaginis* (Crawford)); 17.13 *Neotriozella* Crawford (4 spp.); 17.14 *Metatriozoa* Tuthill (1 sp., *M. pubescens* Tuthill); 17.15 *Leuronota* Crawford (2 spp.); 17.16 *Ceropsylla* Riley (1 sp., *C. sideroxyli* Riley); 17.17 *Hemitrioza* Crawford (2 spp.); 17.18 *Levidea* Tuthill (1 sp., *L. lineata* Tuthill)]

Subfamily Psyllinae
Tribe Pachypsyllini

[17.19 *Crawfordiella* Van Duzee (1 sp., *C. mira* (Crawford)); 17.20 *Tetragonocephala* Crawford (1 sp., *T. flava* Crawford)]

17.21 *Pachypsylla* Riley

Seven species, of which the following is a pest:
 P. celtidismamma Riley (Hackberry Nipplegall Maker). L. ±3 mm. Produces galls on the leaves of Hackberry (*Celtis occidentalis*).

Tribe Euphyllurini

[17.22 *Katacephala* Crawford (1 sp., *K. grandiceps* Crawford); 17.23 *Euphyllura* Foerster (7 spp.)]

Tribe Arytainini

17.24 *Euphalerus* Schwarz (7 spp.); 17.25 *Arytaina* Foerster (13 spp.); 17.26 *Psyllopsis* Loew (3 spp.)]

Fig. 21.22. *(From Britton, 1923)*

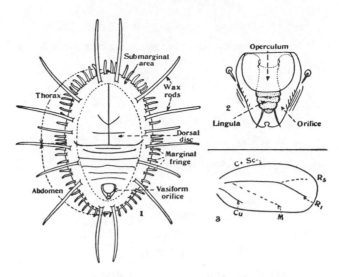

Fig. 21.23. *(From Britton, 1923)*

Tribe Psyllini

17.27 *Psylla* Geoffroy

Sixty-five species, of which the following are of economic importance:

P. pyricola Foerster (Pear Psylla). L. ±2.5 mm. Reddish crimson with brownish-black markings; bronzy eyes. Serious pest of pears. (See Fig. 21.22.)

P. negundinis Mally (Boxelder Psyllid).

P. mali (Schmidberger) (Apple Sucker).

P. buxi (Linnaeus) (Boxwood Psyllid).

P. uncatoides (Ferris and Klyver) (Acacia Psyllid).

[17.28 *Spanioneura* Foerster (1 sp., *S. fonscolombii* Foerster)]

Superfamily ALEYRODOIDEA

One family only, as follows:

18. ALEYRODIDAE (Whitefly Family)

L. 2–3 mm. Adults with four wings that are transparent, white and clouded or mottled with spots or bands. The wings and body are covered with a whitish powder. Head with two ocelli near compound eyes; antennae usually seven-segmented. Tarsi with two tarsomeres, the apical one with two claws and an empodium between the claws. (See Fig. 21.23 for general body structures.)

The adults of most species are unknown. The nymphs, which resemble certain scale insects, secrete a wax in forms that vary according to the species. All species feed on leaves of plants; many of them are therefore of economic importance. Many are found on house plants, where they are relatively easy to control.

The classification of the genera is based on the structure of the fourth instar nymph, which forms a pupa. There are 1156 species in the world, of which 19 genera and 99 species have been recorded in the U.S. and Canada; the remainder are mainly tropical.

Subfamily Aleyrodinae

18.1 *Aleurocanthus* Quaintance and Baker

One species only, a pest of citrus, as follows:

A. woglumi Ashby (Citrus Blackfly).

[18.2 *Aleurochiton* Tullgren (1 sp., *A. forbesii* (Ashmead)); 18.3 *Aleurocybotus* Quaintance and Baker (2 spp.); 18.4 *Aleuroglandulus* Bondar (1 sp., *A. emmae* Russell); 18.5 *Aleurolobus* Quaintance and Baker (1 sp., *A. solitarius* Quaintance and Baker); 18.6 *Aleuroparadoxus* Quaintance and Baker (3 spp.); 18.7 *Aleuroplatus* Quaintance and Baker (14 spp.); 18.8 *Aleuropleurocelus* Drews and Sampson (8 spp.)]

18.9 *Aleurothrixus* Quaintance and Baker

Three species, of which the following is common:

A. floccosus (Maskell) (Woolly Whitefly).

[18.10 *Aleurotulus* Quaintance and Baker (1 sp., *A. nephrolepidus* (Quaintance))]

18.11 *Aleyrodes* Latreille

Ten species, of which the following is common:

A. shizuokensis Kuwana (Oxalis Whitefly)]

18.12 *Bemisia* Quaintance and Baker

The following two species occur in the U.S. and Canada.

B. giffardi (Kotinsky) (Giffard's Whitefly).

B. tabaci (Gennadius) (Sweetpotato Whitefly).

[18.13 *Crenidorsum* Russel (1 sp., *C. commune* Russell)]

18.14 *Dialeurodes* Cockerell

The following four species occur in the U.S. and Canada.

D. citrifolii (Morgan) (Cloudywinged Whitefly).

D. citri (Ashmead) (Citrus Whitefly).

D. kirkaldyi (Kotinsky) (Kirkaldy's Whitefly).

D. chittendeni Laing (Rhododendron Whitefly).

18.15 *Pealius* Quaintance and Baker

The following three species of the genus occur in the U.S. and Canada:

> *P. azaleae* (Baker and Moles) (Azalea Whitefly).
>
> *P. maskelli* (Bemis).
>
> *P. hibisci* (Kotinsky) (Hibiscus Whitefly).

18.16 *Tetraleurodes* Cockerell

Thirteen species, of which the following is common:

> *T. mori* (Quaintance) (Mulberry Whitefly).

18.17 *Trialeurodes* Cockerell

Twenty-nine species, of which the following are common:

> *T. coryli* Britton. (See Fig. 21.23).
>
> *T. vittata* (Quaintance) (Grape Whitefly).

T. floridensis (Quaintance) (Avocado Whitefly).

T. abutilonea (Haldeman) (Banded-winged Whitefly).

T. packardi (Morrill) (Strawberry Whitefly).

T. vaporariorum (Westwood) (Greenhouse Whitefly). L. ±1.5 mm. White, covered with white, waxy powder. Pest in greenhouses and of house plants and, during the summer, on vegetables. Cosmopolitan. (See A&J 74.)

Subfamily Aleurodicinae

[18.18 *Aleurodicus* Douglas (1 sp., *A. dispersus* Russell; 18.19 *Paraleyrodes* Quaintance (1 sp., *P. perseae* (Quaintance))]

Superfamily APHIDOIDEA

There are three families in this superfamily, as noted in the accompanying key.

Key to the Families of Aphidoidea of the U.S. and Canada

1. Front wings with 4 to 5, rarely 6, veins behind stigma extending to wing margin; cornicles usually present; ninth abdominal tergum modified into a cauda; antennae usually 6-segmented . **19. Aphididae**
 Front wings with only 3 veins behind the stigma extending to wing margin; cornicles and cauda not developed; antennae 3 to 5 segmented . **2**
2(1). Wings at rest held rooflike over abdomen; front wing with Cu₁ and Cu₂ separate at base; wingless forms covered with waxy material . **20. Adelgidae**
 Wings at rest held horizontal; front wing with Cu₁ and Cu₂ stalked at base; wingless forms usually not covered with waxy material . **21. Phylloxeridae**

19. APHIDIDAE (Plantlice)

L. 1–5 mm. Usually pale or greenish; antennae with four- to six-segments; wings transparent and sometimes marked; hind wings always smaller than front wings; many species wingless. (See Fig. 21.24 for general body features.)

These are among the most injurious insect pests, as well as the most numerous of all insects. Aphids usually have a pair of cornicles on the fifth or sixth abdominal segment and a cauda, or tail—the features that best characterize the family. The cornicles secrete a defensive fluid. Honeydew, which is excreted by the anus, represents excess food filtered through the digestive tract and voided in large quantities onto leaf surfaces or the ground. It is sticky; when it dries, it forms a film upon which sooty mold grows. It also attracts ants, some of which are known to "herd" aphids to their food plant and protect them from predators in return for the honeydew they excrete.

Perhaps the most interesting feature of these insects is their remarkable life cycle. This is characterized by a series of parthenogenetic generations followed by a biparental generation. Even within the series of parthenogenetic generations, there is often an alternation of wingless and winged forms. One part of the life cycle may require an herbaceous plant while another part requires a hardwood host. These biological deviations lead to considerable complexity. The following two examples may serve to explain some of the complexities of these cycles.

Two principal types of life cycle involve differences in host plant requirement. The first type involves only one host plant; these insects are monophagous. They overwinter as eggs and hatch in the spring when flower and leaf buds begin to open.

The nymphs develop into wingless females that are capable of reproducing parthenogenetically. The offspring from these wingless females continue to reproduce parthenogenetically for

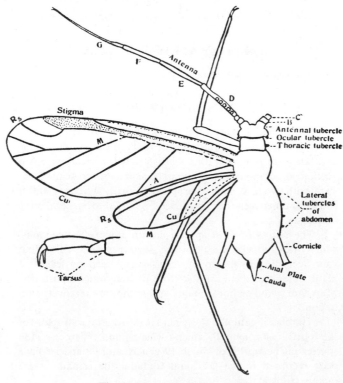

Fig. 21.24. (*From Britton, 1923*)

as many generations as conditions (weather, food supply, etc.) permit. When winged females are produced, they migrate to new host plants of the same species to start new colonies. As winter or other adverse conditions approach, sexual forms of both sexes are produced. These mate and the females lay eggs on the host plant. This stage overwinters, and the cycle begins again in the spring. This life cycle is typical of most of the aphid species. Its many variations depend upon the species involved.

The second major type of cycle involves an alternation of hosts as well as an alternation of generations. The first host, or *primary host*, supports a series of parthenogenetically produced aphids, beginning with the nymphs that hatch from the overwintering eggs. Early in the cycle, winged parthenogenetic females develop. These migrate to another host, called the *secondary host*, where a new colony of the species is established. A series of wingless and winged generations take place here until autumn. Then winged forms of both sexes develop. Both migrate back to the primary host plant. The winged, parthenogenetic females produce wingless sexual females that then mate with the males. Each fertilized female lays two to six eggs. The eggs overwinter, and the nymphs that hatch in the spring produce the new cycle.

Several things are accomplished by this complicated cycle. First, it provides an easy and rapid way to increase the number of individuals. Since these fragile insects are vulnerable to many environmental factors—lack of food, bad weather, and many predators—a large number of individuals is needed for the population to survive. The elimination of wings during part of the cycle is a protective device to prevent the insects from being blown away. There is no need for wings when there is no need to fly. Wings are developed only when needed for migration or mate searching.

There are a number of variations of this cycle. Some species infest a considerable number of plants rather than a single host or at most two hosts. Some cycles incorporate ovovivipary, the production of eggs that hatch within the female body or immediately after extrusion. Obviously, this is an easy way to protect eggs from predators.

It is well known that ants are often associated with aphids. They are attracted to the sticky, sweet honeydew the aphid excretes from its anus. (These excretions may drop on automobiles parked under trees infested with aphids, much to the annoyance of the owners.) Aphids are sometimes dependent upon ants for their existence. Their autumn eggs are stored and cared for during the winter by the ants. When the eggs hatch in the spring, the ants carry the nymphs to the roots of various host plants. Later, the ants transport their "cattle" to the roots of other plants. Other species "herd" their "cattle" to leaves of host plants.

Some aphids produce plant galls. These species are placed in a separate subfamily, the Pemphiginae. They usually lack cornicles, but wax glands are often present. The sexual forms do not feed; their mouthparts are reduced or absent. Nearly all species have two host plants, but the gall-forming stage produces galls on only one host.

At the present time there are 224 genera, 40 subgenera, and 1351 species of aphids recorded in the U.S. and Canada. About 80 species are pests of food crops and ornamental plants.

Very technical characteristics must be examined for the specific identification of aphids. Since many species are host specific, one might assume that the species on a particular host is one of the species recorded; it will not necessarily be one of the species named below because several species of aphids may infest a single plant species. Since there is always the possibility of establishing new host records, those interested in learning more about these fascinating creatures should dig into the technical literature.

No generally accepted supergeneric classification is available at the present time; therefore, the following list of genera (from Smith and Parron, 1978) could not be assigned to subfamilies and tribes. This list provides the species name and the common name of representative pest species as well as the number of species recorded in the U.S. and Canada for each genus.

Alphabetical List of the Genera of Aphididae

19.1 *Acuticauda* Hille Ris Lambers (2 spp.).

19.2 *Acrythosiphon* Mordvilko: two subgenera: *Acyrthosiphon* s. str. (17 spp.) and *Metopolophium* Mordvilko (8 spp.).

A. solani (Kaltenbach) (Foxglove Aphid).

A. caraganae (Cholodkovsky) (Caragana Aphid).

A. porosum (Sanderson) (Yellow Rose Aphid).

A. pisum (Harris) (Pea Aphid).

19.3 *Alloambria* Richards (1 sp., *A. caudata* Richards).

19.4 *Aloephagus* Essig (1 sp., *A. myersi* Essig).

19.5 *Alphitoaphis* Hottes (1 sp., *A. lonicericola* (Williams)).

19.6 *Ambaraphis* Richard (1 sp., *A. costalis* Richards).

19.7 *Amphicercidus* Oestlund (2 spp.).

19.8 *Amphorophora* Buckton (19 spp.).

19.9 *Anconatus* Buckton (2 spp.).

19.10 *Aniferella* Richards (1 sp., *A. bostoni* Richards).

19.11 *Anoecia* Koch (6 spp.).

19.12 *Anthracosiphon* Hille Ris Lambers (1 sp., undescribed).

19.13 *Anuraphis* Del Guercio (2 spp.) [belongs to subfamily Pemphiginae].

A. maidiradicis (Forbes) (Corn Root Aphid). This is a serious pest of corn and of weeds in and near infested corn fields. Ants tend to black eggs and move the nymphs and adults from host to host.

19.14 *Aphidopsis* Scudder (1 sp., *A. margarum* Scudder).

19.15 *Aphis* Linnaeus (150 spp.).

A. pomi DeGeer (Apple Aphid). Monophagus species, generally distributed in apple growing regions where it feeds on the leaves of apple trees.

A. hederae Kaltenbach (Ivy Aphid).

A. gossypii Glover (Melon Aphid; Cotton Aphid).

A. illinoisensis Shimer (Grapevine Aphid).

A. craccivora Koch (Cowpea Aphid).

A. nasturtii Kaltenbach (Buckthorn Aphid).

A. fabae Scopoli (Bean Aphid).

A. nerii Fonscolombe (Oleander Aphid).

A. middletonii (Thomas) (Erigeron Root Aphid).

A. salicariae Koch (Willow Aphid). (See A&J 75)

A. viburniphila Patch (Viburnum Aphid).

A. forbesi Weed (Strawberry Root Aphid).

A. citricola van der Goot (Spirea Aphid).

19.16 *Aphthargelia* Hottes (1 sp., *A. symphoricarpi* (Thomas)).

19.17 *Appendiseta* Richards (1 sp., *A. robiniae* (Gillette)).

19.18 *Asiphonaphis* Wilson and Davis (2 spp.).

19.19 *Aspidaphis* Gillette (1 sp., *A. adjuvans* (Walker)).

19.20 *Aspidaphium* Boerner (2 spp.).

19.21 *Atarsaphis* Takahashi (1 sp., *A. agrifoliae* (Ferris)).

19.22 *Atarsos* Gillette (1 sp., *A. grindeliae* Gillette).

19.23 *Atheroides* Haliday (1 sp., *A. serrulatus* Haliday).

19.24 *Aulacorthum* Mordvilko: two subgenera: *Aulacorthum* s. str. (4 spp.) and *Neomyzus* van der Goot (1 sp., *A. circumflexum* (Buckton) (Crescent-marked Lily Aphid)).

19.25 *Betulaphis* Glendenning (5 spp.).

19.26 *Bipersona* Hottes (2 spp.).

19.27 *Boernerina* Bramstedt: two subgenera: *Boernerina* s. str. (1 sp., *B. variabilis* Richards) and *Boernerinella* Hille Ris Lambers and Hottes (1 sp., *B. occidentalis* Hille Ris Lambers and Hottes).

19.28 *Brachycaudus* van der Goot: four subgenera: *Brachycaudus* s. str. (1 sp., *B. helichrysi* (Kaltenbach)), *Acaudus* van der Goot (3 spp.), *Appelia* Boerner (2 spp.), and *Thuleaphis* Hille Ris Lambers (2 spp.).

B. persicae (Passerini) (Black Peach Aphid).

B. cardui (Linnaeus) (Thistle Aphid).

19.29 *Brachycolus* Buckton (2 spp.).

B. tritici Gillette (Western Wheat Aphid).

B. heraclei Takahashi (Celery Aphid).

19.30 *Brachycorynella* Aizenberg (1 sp., *B. asparagi* (Mordvilko)).

19.31 *Brachysiphum* van der Goot (1 sp., *B. hyperici* (Monell)).

19.32 *Brachyungius* Das (1 sp., *B. bonnevillensis* (Knowlton)).

19.33 *Braggia* Gillette and Palmer (7 spp.).

19.34 *Brevicoryne* Das (3 spp.).

B. brassicae (Linnaeus) (Cabbage Aphid).

19.35 *Bursaphis* Baker (1 sp., *B. solitaria* Baker).

19.36 *Byrsocrytoides* Dzhibladze (1 sp., *B. polumomo* (Stroyan)).

19.37 *Cachryphora* Oestlund (2 spp.).

19.38 *Calaphis* Walsh (14 spp.).

19.39 *Callaphis* Walker (1 sp., *C. juglandis* (Goeze)).

19.40 *Callipterenella* van der Goot (1 sp., *C. callipterus* (Hartig)).

19.41 *Canadaphis* Essig (1 sp., *C. carpenteri* Essig).

19.42 *Capitophorus* van der Goot (12 spp.).

19.43 *Carolinaia* Wilson (3 spp.).

19.44 *Catamergus* Oestlund (2 spp.).

19.45 *Cavariella* Del Guercio: two subgenera: *Cavariella* s. str. (11 spp.) and *Cavaraiellia* Heinze (1 sp., *C. aquatica* (Gillette and Bragg)).

19.46 *Cedoaphis* Oestlund (2 spp.).

19.47 *Cerpegillettea* Granovsky (3 spp.).

19.48 *Cerataphis* Lichtenstein (3 spp.).

C. orchidearum (Westwood) (Fringed Orchid Aphid).

19.49 *Ceruraphis* Boerner (2 spp.).

C. viburnicola (Gillette) (Snowball Aphid).

19.50 *Chaetosiphon* Mordvilko: two subgenera: *Chaetosiphon* s. str. (1 sp., *C. scalaris* Richards) and *Pentatrichopus* Boerner (6 spp.)

C. fragaefolii (Cockerell) (Strawberry Aphid)

19.51 *Chaitophorus* Koch (31 spp.).

19.52 *Chromaphis* Walker (1 sp., *C. juglandicola* (Kaltenbach) (Walnut Aphid)).

19.53 *Cinara* Curtis (152 spp.).

C. fornacula Hottes (Green Spruce Aphid).

C. laricis (Walker) (Larch Aphid).

C. atlantica (Wilson) (Carolina Conifer Aphid).

C. strobi (Fitch) (White Pine Aphid).

19.54 *Colopha* Monell (1 sp., *C. ulmicola* (Fitch) (Elm Cockscomb-gall Aphid), a gall-making species found on elm and witch hazel).

19.55 *Coloradoa* Wilson (5 spp.).

19.56 *Cornaphis* Gillette (1 sp., *C. populi* Gillette).

19.57 *Cryptaphis* Hille Ris Lambers (2 spp.).

19.58 *Cryptomyzus* Oestlund (2 spp.).

C. ribis (Linnaeus) (Current Aphid).

19.59 *Ctenocallis* Klodnitzki (1 sp., *C. setosus* (Kaltenback)).

19.60 *Decorosiphon* Boerner (1 sp., *D. corynothrix* Boerner).

19.61 *Delphiniobium* Mordvilko (1 sp., *D. canadensis* (Robinson)).

19.62 *Diphyllaphis* Takahashi (1 sp., *D. microtrema* Quednau).

19.63 *Diuraphis* Aizenberg: 2 subgenera: *Diuraphis* s. str. (1 sp., *D. mexicana* (Baker)) and *Holcaphis* Hille Ris Lambers (3 spp.).

19.64 *Drepanaphis* Del Guercio: 2 subgenera: *Drepanaphis* s. str. (18 spp.) and *Shenahweum* Hottes and Frison (1 sp., *D. minuta* Davis).

D. acerifoliae Thomas (Painted Maple Aphid).

19.65 *Drepanosiphum* Koch (5 spp.).
19.66 *Durocapillata* Knowlton (1 sp., *D. utahensis* Knowlton).
19.67 *Dysaphis* Boerner: 2 subgenera: *Dysaphis* s. str. (7 spp.) and *Pomaphis* (3 spp.).

D. plantaginea Passerini (Rosy Apple Aphid). Polyphagous species that feeds on the leaves of apple trees and the weed, Narrow-leaved Plantain. It has the typical two-host life cycle.

D. tulipae (Fonscolombe) (Tulip Bulb Aphid).

D. apiifolia (Rusty Banded Aphid).

19.68 *Echinaphis* (Cockerell (1 sp., *E. rohweri* Cockerell).
19.69 *Elatobium* Mordvilko (1 sp., *E. abietinum* (Walker) (Spruce Aphid)).
19.70 *Eoessigia* David, Rajasingh, and Narayanan (1 sp., *E. longicauda* Richards).
19.71 *Eomacrosiphon* Hille Ris Lambers (1 sp., *E. nigromaculosum* (MacDougall)).
19.72 *Epameibaphis* Oestlund (3 spp.).
19.73 *Ericaphis* Boerner (1 sp., *E. scammelli* (Mason)).
19.74 *Eriosoma* Leach: subgenera: *Eriosoma* s. str. (5 spp.) and *Schizoneura* Hartig (2 spp.).

E. pyricola Baker and Davidson (Woolly Pear Aphid).

E. lanigerum (Hausmann) (Woolly Apple Aphid).

E. americanum (Riley) (Woolly Elm, Aphid).

19.75 *Essigella* Del Guercio (21 spp.).
19.76 *Eucallipterus* Schouteden (1 sp., *E. tiliae* (Linnaeus)).
19.77 *Euceraphis* Walker (6 spp.).
19.78 *Eulachnus* Del Guercio (4 spp.).
19.79 *Euthoracaphis* Takahashi (1 sp., *E. umbellulariae* (Essig)).
19.80 *Fagiphagus* Smith (1 sp., *F. imbricator* (Fitch) (Beech Blight Aphid)).
19.81 *Fimbriaphis* Richards (6 spp.).
19.82 *Flabellomicrosiphum* Gillette and Palmer (2 spp.).
19.83 *Forda* von Heyden (2 spp.).
19.84 *Fullawaya* Essig (8 spp.).
19.85 *Geoica* Hart (4 spp.).
19.86 *Geopemphigus* Hille Ris Lambers (1 sp., *G. floccosus* (Moreira)).
19.87 *Georgiaphis* Maxon and Hottes (2 spp.).
19.88 *Geranchon* Scudder (1 sp., *G. petrorum* (Scudder)).
19.89 *Glabromyzus* Richard (4 spp.).
19.90 *Glendenningia* MacGillivray (1 sp., *G. philadelphi* MacGillivray).

19.91 *Glyphina* Koch (4 spp.).
19.92 *Grylloprociphilus* Smith and Pepper (1 sp., *G. frosti* Smith and Pepper).
19.93 *Gypsoaphis* Oestlund (1 sp., *G. oestlundi* Hottes).
19.94 *Hamamelistes* Shimer (1 sp., *H. spinosus* Shimer).
19.95 *Hayhurstia* Del Guercio (1 sp., *H. atriplicis* (Linnaeus)).
19.96 *Hoplochaitophorus* Granovsky (3 spp.).
19.97 *Hormaphis* Osten-Sacken (1 sp., *H. hamamelidis* (Fitch)).
19.98 *Hyadaphis* Kirkaldy (2 spp.).
19.99 *Hyalomyzus* Richards (5 spp.).
19.100 *Hyalopteroides* Theobald (1 sp., *H. humilis* (Walker)).
19.101 *Hyalopterus* Koch (2 spp.).

H. pruni (Geoffroy) (Mealy Plum Aphid).

19.102 *Hyperomyzus* Boerner: 2 subgenera: *Hyperomyzus* s. str. (2 spp.) and *Neonasonovia* Hille Ris Lambers (10 spp.).
19.103 *Hysteroneura* Davis (1 sp., *H. setariae* (Thomas) (Rusty Plum Aphid)).
19.104 *Idiopterus* Davis (1 sp. *I. nephrelepidis* Davis) (Fern Aphid)).
19.105 *Illinoia* Wilson: 4 subgenera: *Illinoia* s. str. (31 spp.), *Amphorinophora* MacGillivray (1 sp., *I. crystleae* Smith and Knowlton), *Masonaphis* Hille Ris Lambers (9 spp.), and *Oestlundia* Hille Ris Lambers (3 spp.).
19.106 *Iowana* Hottes (1 sp., *I. frisoni* Hottes).
19.107 *Iziphya* Nevsky (12 spp.).
19.108 *Jacksonia* Theobald (1 sp., *J. papillata* Theobald).
19.109 *Kakimia* Hottes and Frison (23 spp.).

K. houghtonensis (Troop) (Gooseberry Witchbroom Aphid).

19.110 *Kaltenbachiella* Shouteden (1 sp., *K. ulmifusa* Walsh and Riley).
19.111 *Lachnochaitophorus* Granovsky (2 spp.).
19.112 *Lachnus* Burmeister (3 spp.).
19.113 *Landisaphis* Knowlton and Ma (1 sp., *L. davisi* Knowlton and Ma).
19.114 *Linosiphon* Boerner (1 sp., *L. sanguinarium* (Hottes and Frison)).
19.115 *Liosomaphis* Walker (1 sp., *L. berberidis* (Kaltenbach)).
19.116 *Lipamyzodes* Heinze (1 sp., *L. matthiolae* (Doncaster)).
19.117 *Lipaphis* Mordvilko (1 sp., *L. erysimi* (Kaltenbach) (Turnip Aphid)).
19.118 *Longicaudus* van der Goot (1 sp., *L. trirhodus* (Walker)).
19.119 *Longistigma* Wilson (2 spp.).

L. caryae (Harris). This large species (l. up to 6 mm) feeds on bark of hickory, maple and other forest trees.

19.120 *Macchiatiella* Del Guercio (1 sp., *M. rhamni* (Fonscolombe)).

19.121 *Macrosiphoniella* Del Guercio (14 spp.).

M. sanborni (Gillette) (Chrysanthemum Aphid).

19.122 *Macrosiphum* Passerini: 3 subgenera: *Macrosiphum* s. str. (55 spp.), *Neocorylobium* MacGillivray (3 spp.), and *Sitobion* Mordvilko (17 spp.).

M. avenae (Fabricius) (English Grain Aphid).

M. luteum (Buckton) (Orchid Aphid).

M. scoliopi (Monell) (Western Lily Aphid).

M. rosae (Linnaeus) (Rose Aphid). (See Fig. 21.2).

M. liriodendri (Monell) (Tuliptree Aphid).

M. euphorbiae (Thomas) (Potato Aphid).

M. lilii (Monell) (Purplespotted Lily Aphid).

19.123 *Maculolachnus* Gaumont (2 spp.).

19.124 *Mastopoda* Oestlund (1 sp., *M. pteridis* Oestlund).

19.125 *Megoura* Buckton (1 sp., *M. viciae* Buckton).

19.126 *Megourina* Hille Ris Lambers (1 sp., *M. lagacei* Hille Ris Lambers).

19.127 *Megouroparsus* Smith and Heie (2 spp.).

19.128 *Melanaphis* van der Goot (2 spp.).

M. bambusae (Fullaway).

M. sacchari (Zehntner) (Sugarcane Aphid).

19.129 *Melanocallis* Oestlund (1 sp., *M. caryaefoliae* (Davis)).

19.130 *Melaphis* Walsh (1 sp., *M. rhois* (Fitch)).

19.131 *Meliarhizophagus* Smith (1 sp., *M. fraxinifolii* (Riley)).

19.132 *Microlophium* Mordvilko (2 spp.).

19.133 *Microparsus* Patch (3 spp.).

19.134 *Microsiphoniella* Hille Ris Lambers (4 spp.).

19.135 *Mindarus* Koch (4 spp.).

M. abietinus Koch (Balsam Twig Aphid).

19.136 *Misturaphis* Robinson (1 sp., *M. shiloensis* Robinson).

19.137 *Monellia* Oestlund (5 spp.).

M. costalis (Fitch) (Blackmargined Aphid).

19.138 *Monelliopsis* Richards (5 spp.).

19.139 *Mordvilkoja* Del Guercio (1 sp., *M. vagabunda* (Walsh) (Poplar Vagabond Aphid)).

19.140 *Muscaphis* Boerner (1 sp., *M. musci* Boerner).

19.141 *Myzaphis* van der Goot (3 spp.).

19.142 *Myzocallis* Passerini: 3 subgenera: *Myzocallis* s. str. (4 spp.), *Lineomyzocallis* Richards (15 spp.), and *Neomyzocallis* Richards (5 spp.).

M. coryli (Goetze) (Filbert Aphid).

19.143 *Myzodium* Boerner (2 spp.).

19.144 *Myzus* Passerini: 2 subgenera: *Myzus* s. str. (9 spp.) and *Nectarosiphon* Schouteden (8 spp.).

M. persicae (Sulzer) (Green Peach Aphid).

M. cerasi (Fabricius) (Black Cherry Aphid).

M. ornatus Laing (Ornate Aphid).

M. ascalonicus Doncaster (Shallot Aphid).

M. ligustri (Mosley) (Privet Aphid).

19.145 *Nasonovia* Mordvilko: 2 subgenera: *Nasonovia* s. str. (2 spp.) and *Neokakimia* Doncaster and Stroyan (1 sp., *N. saxifragae* (Doncaster and Stroyan)).

N. lactucae (Linnaeus) (Sow Thistle Aphid).

19.146 *Nearctaphis* Shaposhnikov (15 spp.).

N. bakeri (Cowen) (Clover Aphid).

19.147 *Neoamphorophora* Mason (1 sp., *N. kalmiae* Mason).

19.148 *Neophyllaphis* Takahashi (2 spp.)..

N. araucariae Takahashi (Araucaria Aphid).

19.149 *Neoprociphilus* Patch (1 sp., *N. aceris* (Monell)).

19.150 *Neosymydobius* Baker (8 spp.).

19.151 *Neotoxoptera* Theobald (3 spp.).

N. formosana (Takahashi) (Onion Aphid).

N. violae (Pergande) (Violet Aphid).

19.152 *Nevadaphis* Drews (1 sp., *N. sampsoni* Drews).

19.153 *Obtusicauda* Soliman: 2 subgenera: *Obtusicauda* s. str. (12 spp.) and *Artemisaphis* Knowlton and Roberts (1 sp., *O. artemisicola* Williams).

19.154 *Oestlundiella* Granovsky (1 sp., *O. flava* (Davidson)).

19.155 *Ovatus* van der Goot (6 spp.).

O. crataegarius (Walker) (Mint Aphid).

19.156 *Pachypappa* Koch (3 spp.).

19.157 *Paducia* Hottes and Frison (1 sp., *P. antennatum* (Patch)).

19.158 *Palaeoaphis* Richards (1 sp., *P. archimedia* Richards).

19.159 *Papulaphis* Robinson (1 sp., *P. sleesmani* (Pepper)).

19.160 *Paracolopha* Hille Ris Lambers (1 sp., *P. morrisoni* (Baker)).

19.161 *Patchia* Baker (2 spp.).

19.162 *Pemphigus* Hartig (19 spp.).

P. bursarius (Linnaeus) (Lettuce Root Aphid).

P. populivenae Fitch (Sugar Beet Root Aphid).

P. populitransversus Riley (Poplar Petioleball Aphid).

P. populiramulorum Riley (Poplar Twig Gall Aphid).

19.163 *Pentalonia* Coquerel (1 sp., *P. nigronervosa* Coquerel) (Banana Aphid).

19.164 *Pentamyzus* Hille Ris Lambers (1 sp., *P. graminis* Hille Ris Lambers).

19.165 *Periphyllus* van der Hoeven (8 spp.).

P. lyropictus (Kessler) (Norway Maple Aphid).

P. negundinis (Thomas) (Boxelder Aphid).

19.166 *Phloeomyzus* Horvath (2 spp.).

19.167 *Phorodon* Passerini (1 sp., *P. humuli* (Schrank) (Hop Aphid)).

19.168 *Phyllaphis* Koch (3 spp.).

19.169 *Picturaphis* Blanchard (1 sp., *P. brasiliensis* (Moreira)).

19.170 *Placoaphis* Richards (1 sp., *P. siphunculata* Richards).

19.171 *Pleotrichophorus* Boerner (51 spp.).

19.172 *Prociphilus* Koch: 3 subgenera: *Prociphilus* s. str. (8 spp.), *Neoparacletus* (1 sp., *P corrugatans* (Sirrine), and *Paraprociphilus* Mordvilko (1 sp., *P. tessallatus* (Fitch)).

P. tessallatus (Fitch) (Wooly Alder Aphid). This species secretes long, fine strands of wax. It is both monophagus and polyphagus, some staying an alder only and others migrating to maple.

19.173 *Protopterocallis* Richards (1 sp., *P. canadensis* Richards).

19.174 *Pseudacaudella* Boerner (1 sp., *P. rubida* (Boerner)).

19.175 *Pseudambia* Richards (1 sp., *P. longirostris* Richards).

19.176 *Pseudasiphonaphis* Robinson (1 sp., *P. corni* (Tissot)).

19.177 *Pseudocercidis* Richards (1 sp., *P. rosae* Richards).

19.178 *Pseudoepameibaphis* Gillette and Palmer (5 spp.).

19.179 *Pseudopterocomma* MacGillivray (2 spp.).

19.180 *Pseudoregma* Doncaster (1 sp., *P. panicola* (Takahashi)).

19.181 *Pterocallis* Passerini (3 spp.).

19.182 *Pterocomma* Buckton (12 spp.).

19.183 *Rhodobium* Hille Ris Lambers (1 sp., *R. porosum* (Sanderson)).

19.184 *Rhopalomyzus* Mordvilko: 2 subgenera: *Rhopalomyzus* s. str. (2 spp.) and *Judenkoa* Hille Ris Lambers (1 sp., *R. lonicerae* (Siebold)).

19.185 *Rhopalosiphoninus* Baker: 2 subgenera: *Rhopalosiphoninus* s. str. (3 spp.) and *Myzosiphon* Hille Ris Lambers (2 spp.).

19.186 *Rhopalosiphum* Koch (13 spp.).

R. maidis (Fitch) (Corn Leaf Aphid).

R. fitchii (Sanderson) (Apple Grain Aphid).

R. rufiabdominalis (Sasaki) (Rice Root Aphid).

R. nymphaeae (Linnaeus) (Waterlily Aphid).

19.187 *Saltusaphis* Theobald (2 spp.).

19.188 *Sanbornia* Baker (1 sp., *S. juniperi* Pergande).

19.189 *Sarucallis* Shinji (1 sp., *S. kahawaluokalani* (Kirkaldy) (Crapemyrtle Aphid).

19.190 *Sbenaphis* Scudder (1 sp., *S. ?quesneli* Scudder)). The name of this fossil species may not be valid.

19.191 *Schizaphis* Boerner: 3 subgenera: *Schizaphis* (6 spp.), *Euschizaphis* Hille Ris Lambers (2 spp.), and *Paraschizaphis* Hille Ris Lambers (2 spp.).

S. graminum (Rondani) (Green Bug).

19.192 *Schizolachnus* Mordvilko (6 spp.).

19.193 *Schizoneurata* Hille Ris Lambers (1 sp., *S. tissoti* Hille Ris Lambers).

19.194 *Schoutedenia* Ruebsaamen (1 sp., *S. viridis* (van der Goot)).

19.195 *Semiaphis* van der Goot (1 sp., *S. dauci* (Fabricius)).

19.196 *Sipha* Passerini: 2 subgenera: *Sipha* s. str. (3 spp.) and *Rungsia* Mimeur (1 sp., *S. elegans* Del Guercio).

S. flava (Forbes) (Yellow Sugarcane Aphid).

19.197 *Siphonatrophia* (2 spp.).

19.198 *Siphonophoroides* Buckton (4 spp.).

19.199 *Smynthurodes* Westwood (1 sp., *S. betae* Westwood).

19.200 *Stagona* Koch (3 spp.).

19.201 *Stegophylla* Oestlund (5 spp.).

19.202 *Subacyrosiphon* Hille Ris Lambers (1 sp., *S. cryptobium* Hille Ris Lambers).

19.203 *Subsaltusaphis* Quednau (3 spp.).

19.204 *Symydobius* Mordvilko (2 spp.).

19.205 *Takecallis* Matsumura (3 spp.).

19.206 *Tamalia* Baker (3 spp.).

19.207 *Tetraneura* Hartig: 2 subgenera: *Tetraneura* s. str. (1 sp., *T. ulmi* (Linnaeus)) and *Tetraneurella* Hille Ris Lambers (2 spp.).

19.208 *Thecabius* Koch: 2 subgenera: *Thecabius* s. str. (1 sp., *T. affinis* (Kaltenbach)) and *Parathecabius* Boerner (5 spp.).

19.209 *Therioaphis* Walker (4 spp.).

T. maculata (Buckton) (Spotted Alfalfa Aphid).

T. trifolii (Monell) (Yellow Clover Aphid).

T. riehmi (Boerner) (Sweetclover Aphid).

19.210 *Thripsaphis* Gillette: 3 subgenera: *Thripsaphis* s. str. (1 sp., *T. ballii* (Gillette)), *Peltaphis* Frison and Ross (1 sp., *T. hottesi* Frison and Ross), and *Trichocallis* Boerner (10 spp.).

19.211 *Tiliphagus* Smith (1 sp., *T. lycoposugus* Smith).

19.212 *Tinocallis* Matsumura (2 spp.).

 T. ulmifolii (Monell) (Elm Leaf Aphid).

 T. kahawaluokalani (Kirkaldy) (Crapemyrtle Aphid).

19.213 *Titanosiphon* Nevsky (1 sp., *T. artemisiae* (Koch)).

19.214 *Toxoptera* Koch (2 spp.).

 T. citricida (Kirkaldy) (Brown Citrus Aphid).

 T. aurantii (Fonscolombe) (Black Citrus Aphid).

19.215 *Toxopterella* Hille Ris Lambers: 2 subgenera: *Toxopterella* s. str. (2 spp.) and *Sorbobium* MacGillivray and Bradley (1 sp., *T. drepanosiphoides* MacGillivray and Bradley).

19.216 *Trama* von Heyden (1 sp., *T. rara* Mordvilko).

19.217 *Tuberculatus* Mordvilko: 3 subgenera: *Tuberculatus* s. str. (2 spp.), *Pacificallis* Richards (7 spp.), and *Tuberculoides* van der Goot (1 sp., *T. annulatus* (Hartig)).

19.218 *Tuberolachnus* Mordvilko (1 sp., *T. salignus* (Gmelin)).

19.219 *Uroleucon* Mordvilko: 4 subgenera: *Uroleucon* s. str. (34 spp.), *Lambersius* Olive (23 spp.), *Satula* Olive (1 sp., *U. brachychaeta* (Olive)), and *Uromelan* Mordvilko (14 spp.).

 U. rudbeckiae (Fitch) (Goldenglow Aphid).

19.220 *Utamphorophora* Knowlton (5 spp.).

19.221 *Vesiculaphis* Del Guercio (1 sp., *V. caricis* (Fullaway)).

19.222 *Wahlgreniella* Hille Ris Lambers (3 spp.).

19.223 *Xerophilaphis* Nevsky (1 sp., *X. tetrapteralis* (Cockerell)).

19.224 *Zyxaphis* Knowlton (10 spp.).

20. ADELGIDAE (Pine and Spruce Adelgid Family)

[= Chermidae]

L. 2–3 mm. Front wing with reduced venation; antennae three-segmented in wingless females, four-segmented in sexual forms, and five-segmented in winged females; abdomen without cornicles. Wingless females and nymphs covered with waxy flocculence. This small group is confined to conifers, feeding on needles, twigs, or on the galls they form. Most species alternate their coniferous hosts, but the primary host is always a spruce. There are two genera and 22 species in the U.S. and Canada.

20.1 *Adelges* Vallot

Ten species, the following of which are pests:

 A. cooleyi (Gillette) (Cooley Spruce Gall Adelgid).

 A. abietis (Linnaeus) (Eastern Spruce Gall Adelgid).

 A. piceae (Ratzeburg) (Balsam Woolly Adelgid).

20.2 *Pineus* Shimer

Twelve species, the following of which are pests:

 P. strobi (Hartig) (Pine Bark Adelgid).

 P. pinifoliae (Fitch) (Pine Leaf Adelgid).

21. PHYLLOXERIDAE (Phylloxerid Family)

L. 2–3 mm. Venation of front wing reduced; antennae three-segmented (rarely, four-segmented), with or without a short terminal process. Abdomen without cornicles; anus absent (thus no excretion of honeydew). Wingless parthenogenetic females are usually not covered with waxy flocculence. Sexual males and females are wingless, and sexual females each lay only one overwintering egg. These species may have a complex life cycle and produce both bisexual and parthenogenetic generations. They may produce galls on both leaves and roots of their host plant. The females are all egg producers rather than oviparous. One genus with 29 species has been recorded in the U.S. and Canada, as follows.

21.1 *Phylloxera* Fonscolombe

Of the 29 species, the following are pests:

 P. vitifoliae Fitch (Grape Phylloxera). Found on grape leaves.

 P. notabilis Pergande (Pecan Leaf Phylloxera).

 P. devastatrix Pergande (Pecan Phylloxera).

Superfamily COCCOIDEA

The 17 families that belong to this superfamily are collectively called scale insects. Except for the adult males, they are all wingless and sometimes legless. The tarsi of those that have legs feature only one or two tarsomeres. The body regions are usually fused and usually covered, as are the eggs of the female, with a waxy secretion that forms a scale, feltlike sac, cottony wax threads, or similar cover. (See Fig. 21.25 for scale formation from exuvia.)

The newly hatched nymphs, or "crawlers," have legs and are active; in many species, however, these are soon lost, and the nymphs, like the adult females, are sedentary. Most adult males are winged and bear little resemblance to the females and nymphs. Prepupal and pupal stages are usually undergone before the adult stage. The males have no functional mouthparts.

Some of the most serious agricultural pests belong to this large group. Most species live on the leaves, stems, and fruit of plants; a few infest the roots of their hosts. Since most species remain fixed on their host during most of their life cycle, many of these pests are worldwide in distribution, having been transported with fruit or nursery stock. A few species are beneficial because of the products obtained from the waxy secretion. The Lac Insect [Tachardiidae (32)] produces a resinous substance used in the preparation of shellac. Some produce natural dyes [Dactylopiidae (28) and Kermesidae (29)].

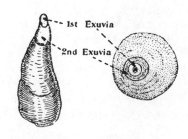

Fig. 21.25. (*From Britton, 1923*)

The life cycle of scale insects is much simpler than that of aphids. Eggs are usually laid by the female at the fixed site of her feeding station; in some cases, nymphs are produced instead of eggs. Female armored scales are fertilized by active males equipped with a long copulatory organ capable of reaching under her scale cover. Although most males are winged, some are not; all, however, have well-developed legs.

The eggs hatch into nymphs with legs, antennae, and functional mouthparts. At this stage, the nymph is able to crawl about on the host plant, the principal means of dispersal for the species. They soon settle down, insert their long, internally coiled mouthparts deep into the vascular tissue of the plant, and remain in place through two to four nymphal molts. Males become quiescent during the second instar but form a "cocoon," a sort of special scale within or beneath which they transform— by a process similar to the pupal transformation of the higher insects—into a two-winged adult. They emerge, find a female, and the cycle is repeated.

Two major types of scale insects are distinguished by their protective cover. Unarmored scales do not form a hard scale but secrete a soft waxy covering instead. The modified types known as armored scales [Diaspididae (38)] produce a hard scale that is detached from the body and has a different consistency, incorporating exuvae.

Collecting, preserving, and identifying scale insects. The insects may be collected intact from the host plant. Small pieces of leaves or bark may be placed in coin envelopes or in paper sacks; most should be placed in vials of 75-percent alcohol. Data of the time and place of collection, the name of the plant, and the plant parts infested should be recorded. If the plant cannot be identified at the time of collection, suitable botanical specimens must be taken as well, including both leaves and flowers.

Preliminary identification may be made by observing the field appearance of scale characteristics, comparing the specimens with previously identified ones. For a final identification, however, specimens must be prepared and mounted on microscope slides. The insect must be removed from its covering beforehand by heating it in a small, covered crucible filled three-quarters full with 10-percent potassium hydroxide (KOH) solution (see Chap. 5 for details about the use of KOH). After heating, transfer the insect to a small watch glass for dissection. Remove the scale cover, rupture the anterior part of the body with the edge of a probe, and press out the body contents with a spatula until the specimen appears as a clear, membranous sack. Then place it in distilled water after washing away any excess KOH, and stain it with a 5-percent aqueous acid fuchin stain. Dehydrate and mount permanently on a glass slide. The slide should be marked with the name of the plant sample and filed in a microscope slide box or cabinet.

The special terminology needed to describe the detailed anatomy of the scale insects for identification appears in Fig. 21.5. The accompanying Key to the Families of Coccoidea of the U.S. and Canada is based on the features of adult females.

Key to the Families of Coccoidea
(Slightly modified from Howell and Williams, 1976)

1. Abdominal spiracles present (family group Archaeococcoidea) *2*
 Abdominal spiracles absent (family group Neococcoidea) *3*

2(1). Anal ring distinct, with numerous pores and six long setae; eyes usually stalked; antennae with three to eight segments **22. Ortheziidae**
 Anal ring reduced, with no pores or setae, or pores on internal portion of tube; eyes rarely stalked; antennae with one to thirteen segments **23. Margarodidae**

3(1). A large dorsal spine present near center of abdomen; anterior spiracles much larger than posterior ones; brachial plates present on dorsum near spiracles ... **32. Tachardiidae**
 No large dorsal spine near center of abdomen; spiracles about equal in size; brachial plates absent .. *4*

4(3). Anal opening covered with two triangular anal plates (absent in *Physokermes*) that usually form an operculum; abdomen with a well-developed anal cleft
 .. **26. Coccidae**
 Never more than one anal plate covering anal opening, although sometimes sclerotized plates laterad and anteriad of anal opening are present; anal cleft, if present, usually not well-developed .. *5*

5(4). A triangular or oval anal plate covering anal opening; furrows or ridges present on caudal margin .. **27. Aclerdidae**
 No anal plate covering anal opening unless, rarely, a single dorsal triangular-shaped plate covers it; furrows or ridges not present on caudal margin *6*

6(5). Cluster pore plate present just below each posterior thoracic spiracle; anal ring surrounded with short, stout setae **30. Cryptococcidae**
 Cluster pore plate absent; anal ring not surrounded with short, stout setae *7*

7(6). Figure-eight-shaped pores present on dorsum *8*
 Figure-eight-shaped pores absent from dorsum; figure-eight-shaped tubular ducts rare; if present, dermal covering always with small irregularities *11*

8(7). Figure-eight-shaped pores on dorsum and in a submarginal band on venter; ventral tubular ducts scattered over body; antennae with one to nine segments *9*
 Figure-eight-shaped pores restricted to dorsum; ventral tubular ducts forming a submarginal band around body; antennae with five segments; (in part)
 .. **29. Kermesidae**

9(8). Antennae with 1 to 9 segments ; ventral bilocular pores and sclerotized anal plate present
 .. *10*

Key to the Families of Coccoidea (*Contd.*)

Antennae with 1 segment; ventral bilocular pores and sclerotized anal plate absent **35. Asterolecaniidae**

10(9). Antennae with 1 segment, with an associated cluster of 5 to 7 locular pores; triangular-shaped sclerotized plate lying over anal opening **34. Cerococcidae**

Antennae with 7 to 9 segments, without an associated cluster of 5 to 7 locular pores; sclerotized plate lying over anal opening not triangular-shaped, much wider than long .. **33. Lecanodiaspididae**

11(7). Locular pores in clusters, with a common tubular duct, and scattered over dorsum; numerous thick, truncate setae on body; anal opening usually appears as a transverse slit .. **28. Dactylopiidae**

Pores not arranged as above; setae usually not truncate, though sometimes blunt; anal opening variable .. *12*

12(11). Abdomen terminating in a compound pygidium or pygidiumlike area; body covered with a secreted, thin, shieldlike scale .. *13*

Abdomen without posterior segments fused to form a pygidium; body not covered by thin, shieldlike scale ... *14*

13(12). Beak one-segmented; legs absent or reduced to remnants; antennae one-segmented; multilocular pores absent; a pygidium formed of the fused terminal abdominal segments, contrasting with the anterior segments of the abdomen; dorsal ocellar eyespots absent; scale covering constructed around the first and second molted skin ... **38. Diaspididae**

Beak 2-segmented; legs present; antennae 3- or 4-segmented; multilocular pores present; pygidial segments less completely fused; dorsal ocellar eyespots present; scale covering without the exuviae of earlier molts **36. Conchaspididae**

14(12). Small irregularities present on dermal covering; legs absent; figure-eight shaped tubular ducts on dorsum and venter (very small); anal ring simple, with 0 to 2 setae and no pores .. **37. Phoenicoccidae**

Dermal covering without irregularities; legs usually present; figure-eight-shaped tubular ducts absent; anal ring variable .. *15*

15(14). Dorsal ostioles, ventral circuli, and trilocular pores usually present; usually with 1 to 18 pair of cerarii; anal ring with inner and outer layers of pores; tubular ducts not invaginated ... *17*

Without dorsal ostioles, cerarii, circuli, and trilocular pores; invaginated tubular ducts present; anal ring variable .. *16*

16(15). Tubular ducts, when present, scattered over venter of body; anal ring usually with pores and setae; microtubular ducts present; usually with protruding anal lobes **31. Eriococcidae**

Tubular ducts arranged in a ventral submarginal band; anal ring simple, without pores and setae; microtubular ducts absent; without distinctly protruding anal lobes; (in part) ... **29. Kermesidae**

17(15). Cerarius nearest antenna with 5 or more cerarian setae; cerarii often with tubular ducts ... **24. Putoidae**

Cerarius nearest antenna absent or with fewer than 5 cerarian setae; cerarii without tubular ducts .. **25. Pseudococcidae**

ARCHAECOCCOIDEA (Primitive Coccoids)

This family group name is used for two families that occur in the U.S. and Canada: Ortheziidae (22) and Margarodidae (23). The adult females of these families retain primitive features such as abdominal spiracles, which are often concealed by thick body setae and usually lack tubular ducts. The males usually have multifaceted compound eyes.

22. ORTHEZIIDAE (Ensign Scale Insect Family)

Females with abdominal spiracles; anal opening surrounded by sclerotized anal ring with six long setae and many pores; antennae with three to eight segments and apex bearing an elongate thick setae; eyes often bulging and on eye stalk; legs usually as long as body. The females are covered with white wax, their eggs being carried in a sac made of wax plates attached to their abdomen. Four genera and 34 species are recorded in the U.S. and Canada.

22.1 *Orthezia* Bosc

Twenty-seven species, of which the following is a pest:

O. insignis Brown (Greenhouse Orthezia). An introduced species found in greenhouses as a pest on the leaves and shoots of many kinds of plants.

[22.2 *Arctorthezia* Cockerell (3 spp.); 22.3 *Newsteadia* Green (2 spp.); 22.4 *Nipponorthezia* Kuwana (2 spp.)]

23. MARGARODIDAE (Giant Scale Insect Family)

L. 3–35 mm. Adult female with two to eight abdominal spiracles; anal ring absent; anal duct tube well-developed in some species but without setae. Antennae with six to thirteen

segments; beak usually present, usually with one to three segments. Legs usually present, with five segments; tarsi with two tarsomeres in some species, sometimes with numerous setae; front legs adapted for digging in the soil in certain species. Some species form cysts, called ground pearls, during their development. These are used as beads in some parts of the world. Their nymphs may remain quiescent for several years in drought areas. The family is sometimes called the "Ground Pearl Family." There are 11 genera and 42 species in the U.S. and Canada.

Subfamily Xylococcinae

Tribe Xylococcini

[23.1 *Xylococculus* Morrison (4 spp.)]

Tribe Matsucoccini

23.2 *Matsucoccus* Cockerell

Fourteen species, of which the following are pests:

M. *resinosae* Bean and Godwin (Red Pine Scale).

M. *acalyptus* Herbert (Pinyon Pine Scale).

M. *bisetosus* Morrison (Two Seta Pine Scale).

M. *gallicolus* Morrison (Gall Pine Scale).

M. *vexillorum* Morrison (Prescott Pine Scale).

Subfamily Steingeliinae

Tribe Steingeliini

[23.3 *Stomacoccus* Ferris (2 spp.)]

Subfamily Margarodinae

Tribe Kuwaniini

[23.4 *Neosteingelia* Morrison (1 sp., *N. texana* (Morrison)); 23.5 *Kuwania* Cockerell (1 sp., *K. quercus* Kuwania)]

Tribe Margarodini

23.6 *Margarodes* Guilding

Nine species, of which the following are pests:

M. *laingi* (Jakubski).

M. *meridionalis* Morrison.

Subfamily Monophlebinae

Tribe Iceryini

[23.7 *Crypticerya* Cockerell (1 sp., *C. rosae* (Riley and Howard))]

23.8 *Icerya* Signoret

Two species, the following of which is of economic importance:

I. *purchasi* Maskell (Cottony Cushion Scale). L. 6–8 mm. An introduced species and a major pest of citrus trees and fruit until brought under control by the introduction of a species of Ladybird Beetles from Australia that prey on scale insects. (See Fig. 21.26 and A&J 76.)

[23.9 *Steatococcus* Ferris (3 spp.)]

Subfamily Pityococcinae

Tribe Pityococcini

[23.10 *Pityococcus* McKenzie (3 spp.); 23.11 *Desmococcus* McKenzie (2 spp.)]

Fig. 21.26. (*Courtesy of M. Kosztarab*)

NEOCOCCOIDEA

These are known as the advanced scale insects and consist of the remaining 15 families that occur in the U.S. and Canada. The females lack abdominal spiracles, but tubular ducts are usually present. Males lack faceted compound eyes.

24. PUTOIDAE (Giant Mealybug Family)

Members of this family resemble the adult females of the next family, the Mealybugs. They possess 17 or 18 pairs of large cerarii (clusters of pores and setae that serve as the base of the waxy filaments produced along the body margin), each usually on a well-developed sclerotized plate with more than five conical setae. Legs large, robust. Antennae normally with nine segments, sometimes only eight. Adult males rarely lack wings and have five to seven pairs of simple eyes. The third antennal segment is usually five times longer than wide. There is only one genus and 20 species of this family in the U.S. and Canada.

24.1 *Puto* Signoret

Twenty species, the following of which is of economic importance:

P. *sandini* Washburn (Spruce Mealybug).

25. PSEUDOCOCCIDAE (Mealybug Family)

These scale insects secrete a covering of waxy material that gives them the appearance of being "mealy." The body of the female is more or less elongate. Antennae one- to nine-segmented; legs usually five-segmented, but sometimes reduced or absent; anal ring with six or more setae and one to three rows of pores. The family is characterized by its ostioles, trilocular pores, and circular cerarii. Mealybugs infest all parts of plants. Many species live in temperate climates and many infest greenhouses. This, the second largest family of scale insects with over 1100 species, includes 45 genera and 280 species in the U.S. and Canada. The supergeneric classification is uncertain. The following list of genera, arranged alphabetically, includes generally recognized species of economic importance, but there are additional species that commonly infest commercially valuable plants.

[25.1 *Amonostherium* Morrison and Morrison (2 spp.); 25.2 *Anthelococcus* McKenzie (1 sp., *A simondsi* McKenzie); 25.3 *Anisococcus* Ferris (8 spp.)]

25.4 *Antonina* Signoret

Five species, the following of which is of economic importance:

A. graminis (Maskell) (Phodesgrass Mealybug).

[25.5 *Antoninoides* Ferris (1 sp., *A. parrotti* Cockerell); 25.6 *Brevennia* Goux (1 sp., *B. rehi* (Lindinger)); 25.7 *Chnaurococcus* Ferris (2 spp.); 25.8 *Cataenococcus* Ferris (2 spp.); 25.9 *Chorizococcus* McKenzie (26 spp.); 25.10 *Circaputo* McKenzie (1 sp., *C. hirsutus* McKenzie); 25.11 *Crisircoccus* Ferris (2 spp.); 25.12 *Cryptoripersia* Cockerell (3 spp.); 25.13 *Cucullococcus* Ferris (1 sp., *C. vaccinii* Ferris); 25.14 *Discococcus* Ferris (6 spp); 25.15 *Distichlicococcus* Ferris (6 spp.)]

25.16 *Dysmicoccus* Ferris

Twenty-nine species, the following of which are pests:

D. boninsis (Kuwana) (Gray Sugarcane Mealybug).

D. brevipes (Cockerell) (Pineapple Mealybug).

D. wistariae (Green) (Taxus Mealybug).

[25.17 *Ehrhornia* Ferris (1 sp., *E. cupressi* (Ehrhorn)); 25.18 *Eurycoccus* Ferris (4 spp.)]

25.19 *Ferrisia* Fullaway

Four species, the following of which is a pest:

F. virgata (Cockerell) (Striped Mealybug).

[25.20 *Ferrisicoccus* Ezzat and McConnell (1 sp., *F. angustus* Ezzat and McConnel); 25.21 *Heliococcus* Sulc (7 spp.); 25.22 *Heterococcus* Ferris (3 spp.); 25.23 *Humococcus* Ferris (8 spp.); 25.24 *Hypogeococcus* Rau (2 spp.); 25.25 *Misericoccus* Ferris (1 sp., *M. arenarius* (Doane and Steinweden)]

25.26 *Nipaecoccus* Sulc

Three species, the following of which is a pest:

N. nipae (Maskell) (Coconut Mealybug).

[25.27 *Oracella* Ferris (1 sp., *O. acuta* (Lobdell)); 25.28 *Paludicoccus* Ferris (1 sp., *P. distichlium* (Kuwana); 25.29 *Paracoccus* Ezzat and McConnell (1 sp., *P. solani* Ezzat and McConnel); 25.30 *Paradoxococcus* McKenzie (1 sp., *P. mcdanieli* McKenzie); 25.31 *Peliococcus* Borchsenius (2 spp.)]

25.32 *Phenacoccus* Cockerell

Thirty-four species, of which the following are pests:

P. aceris (Signoret) (Apple Mealybug).

P. dearnessi King (Two Circuli Mealybug).

P. gossyppi Townsend and Cockerell (Mexican Mealybug).

P. minimus Tinsley (Minimus Mealybug).

P. solani Ferris (Solanum Mealybug).

25.33 *Planococcus* Ferris

Three species, the following of which is a pest:

P. citri Risso (Citrus Mealybug). A greenhouse pest in temperate regions, but a pest of citrus, avocado, oleander, and coffee in tropical and subtropical regions.

[25.34 *Pseudantonina* Green (3 spp.)]

25.35 *Pseudococcus* Westwood

Twenty species, the following of which are pests:

P. maritimus (Ehrhorn) (Grape Mealybug).

P. longispinus (Targioni-Tozetti) (Longtailed Mealybug).

P. comstocki (Kuwana) (Comstock Mealybug).

P. calceolariae (Maskell) (Citrophilus Mealybug). (A&J 77).

P. obscurus Essig (Obscure Mealybug).

P. importus McKenzie (Imported Mealybug).

P. microcirculus McKenzie (Orchid Mealybug).

[25.36 *Pygmaeococcus* McKenzie (1 sp., *P. morrisoni* McKenzie); 25.37 *Radicoccus* Hambleton (1 sp., *R. kelloggi* (Ehrhorn))]

25.38 *Rhizoecus* Kuenckel d'Herculais

Twenty-eight species, the following of which are of economic importance:

R. falcifer Kuenckel d'Herculais (Ground Mealybug).

R. americanus (Hambleton) (American Ground Mealybug).

R. floridanus Hambleton (Florida Ground Mealybug).

R. kondonis Kuwana (Kondo Ground Mealybug).

R. dianthi Green (Pritchard Ground Mealybug).

25.39 *Saccharicoccus* Ferris

One species, as follows:

S. sacchari (Cockerell) (Pink Sugarcane Mealybug).

[25.40 *Scaptococcus* McKenzie (2 spp.); 25.41 *Spilococcus* Ferris (23 spp.); 25.42 *Stemmatomeinx* Ferris (4 spp.); 25.43 *Syrmococcus* Ferris (2 spp.); 25.44 *Tridiscus* Ferris (3 spp.); 25.45 *Trionymus* Berg (21 spp.)]

26. COCCIDAE (Soft Scale Insect Family)

Adult females have an anal cleft and usually anal plates; the anal ring has pores and either no or one to twelve (usually 6) setae. The beak is one-segmented; antennae, five- to nine-segmented. These insects are pests of fruit and ornamental trees, in greenhouses, and on house plants. They comprise a very large family with over 1,000 species in 22 genera; 92 species are recorded in the U.S. and Canada.

26.1 *Ceroplastes* Gray

Eleven species, the following of which are of economic importance:

C. floridensis Comstock (Florida Wax Scale).

C. cirripediformis Comstock (Barnacle Scale).

C. rubens Maskell (Red Wax Scale).

C. ceriferus (Fabricius) (Indian Wax Scale). Found on holly, as in Fig. 21.27.

C. sinensis Del Guercio (Chinese Wax Scale).

[26.2 *Ceroplastodes* Cockerell (3 spp.); 26.3 *Eriopeltis* Signoret (2 spp.)]

Fig. 21.27. (*From U.S. Dept. Agric.*)

26.4 *Coccus* Linnaeus

Eight species, the following of which are pests:

C. *viridis* (Green) (Green Scale).

C. *pseudohesperidum* (Cockerell) (Orchid Soft Scale).

C. *pseudomagnoliarum* (Kuwana) (Citricola Scale).

C. *hesperidum* Linnaeus (Brown Soft Scale).

C. *elongatus* (Signoret) (Long Brown Scale).

26.5 *Eucalymnatus* Cockerell

One species, as follows:

E. *tessellatus* (Signoret) (Tessellated Scale).

26.6 *Eulecanium* Cockerell

Five species, the following of which are of economic importance:

E. *caryae* (Fitch) (Large Hickory Lecanium).

E. *cerasorum* (Cockerell) (Calico Scale).

[26.7 *Inglisia* Maskell (2 spp.)]

26.8 *Kilifia* DeLotto

Two species, the following of which is of economic importance:

K. *acuminata* (Signoret) (Acuminate Scale).

[26.9 *Lichtensia* Signoret (2 spp.); 26.10 *Luzulaspis* Cockerell (4 spp.)]

26.11 *Mesolecanium* Cockerell

Two species, the following of which is of economic importance:

M. *nigrofasciatum* (Pergande) (Terrapin Scale).

26.12 *Neolecanium* Parrott

Two species, the following of which is of economic importance:

N. *cornuparvum* (Thro) (Magnolia Scale).

26.13 *Parasaissetia* Takahashi

One species, as follows:

P. *nigra* (Nietner) (Nigra Scale).

26.14 *Parthenolecanium* Sulc

Seven species, the following of which are pests:

P. *fletcheri* Cockerell (Fletcher Scale).

P. *corni* Bouche (European Fruit Lecanium).

P. *persicae* (Fabricius) (European Peach Scale).

P. *quercifex* (Fitch) (Oak Lecanium).

[26.15 *Philephedra* Cockerell (1 sp., *P. ephedrae* Cockerell)]

26.16 *Physokermes* Targioni-Tozzetti

Six species, the following of which are pests:

P. *piceae* (Schrank) (Spruce Bud Scale).

P. *hemicryphus* (Dalman). Found on spruce, as in Fig. 21.28.

26.17 *Protopulvinaria* Cockerell

Two species, both of which are pests:

P. *pyriformis* (Cockerell) (Pyriform Scale).

P. *mangiferae* (Green) (Mango Shield Scale).

26.18 *Pseudophilippia* Cockerell

One species, as follows:

P. *quaintancii* Cockerell (Wolly Pine Scale).

26.19 *Pulvinaria* Targioni-Tozzetti

Seventeen species, the following of which are of economic importance:

P. *acericola* (Walsh and Riley) (Cottony Maple Leaf Scale).

P. *psidii* Maskell (Green Shield Scale).

P. *floccifera* (Westwood) (Cottony Camellia Scale).

P. *hydrangeae* Steinweden (Cottony Hydrangea Scale).

P. *vitis* (Linnaeus) (Cottony Grape Scale).

P. *innumerabilis* (Rathvon) (Cottony Maple Scale). L. 5–7 mm. One of the largest scale insects attacking ornamental trees throughout the U.S. Found on silver maple in Fig. 21.29.

Fig. 21.28. (*Courtesy of M. Kosztarab*)

Fig. 21.29. (*From U.S. Dept. Agric.*)

26.20 *Saissetia* Deplanches

Four species, as follows:

 S. coffeae (Walker) (Hemispherical Scale).

 S. oleae (Olivier) (Black Scale).

 S. neglecta De Lotto (Caribbean Black Scale).

 S. miranda (Cockerell and Parrott) (Mexican Black Scale).

26.21 *Sphaerolecanium* Sulc

One species, as follows:

 S. prunastri (Fonscolombe) (Globose Scale).

26.22 *Toumeyella* Cockerell

Nine species, the following of which are pests:

 T. liriodendri (Gmelin) (Tuliptree Scale). (See Fig. 21.30.)

 T. parvicornis (Cockerell) (Pine Tortoise Scale). (See Fig. 21.31.)

 T. pini (King) (Striped Pine Scale).

[Note: The Chinese Wax Scale (*Ericerus pela* Chavannes) also belongs to this family. Known for the pure white wax it secretes, it is sometimes used to produce special candles in China and Japan but does not occur in the U.S. or Canada.]

Fig. 21.30. (*From U.S. Dept. Agric.*)

Fig. 21.31. (*Courtesy of Frank W. Mead*)

27. ACLERIDAE
(Flat Grass Scale Insect Family)

This is a small family of flattened scale insects that live under the leaf sheaths and in the crowns of grasses and related plants. Their short anal cleft is partly covered by a single anal plate, and the posterior apex of the abdomen is sclerotized and has a series of furrows or ridges. Legs are absent or greatly reduced. Some species are covered with wax; most are naked. The family is represented throughout the world, but only the following genus occurs in U.S. and Canada:

[27.1 *Aclerda* Signoret (15 spp.)]

28. DACTYLOPIIDAE
(Cochineal Scale Insect Family)

The adult female has a five-locular disc and clusters of pores scattered over the body, most of which have one or more associated invaginated tubular ducts. The large, thick setae have truncate tips. Antennae are six- or seven-segmented, the segments short. The legs are short. The anal ring is thin or absent, without pores. Both the body and the eggs are covered with white waxy secretions. When preserved, these insects cause alcohol to turn red. The species feed on cactus of the genera *Opuntia* and *Nopalea* and have been used for the biological control of cactus.

28.1 *Dactylopius* Costa

Five species, the following of which is of interest:

 D. coccus Costa (Cochineal Insect). This is the source of cochineal dye, a bright red natural dye for which the insects are often cultivated in Mexico.

29. KERMESIDAE
(Gall-like Scale Insect Family)

The dorsal dermal covering of the adult female folds ventrally under the body and hardens with age, becoming ball-

like or gall-like. Antennae of young females (before forming the "gall") are usually six-segmented. The legs are small. The labium is long and slender and three-segmented. Anal ring without pores, often without setae. Most species feed on oaks, a few on chinquapin. Some species produce galls. The family is represented in the U.S. and Canada by the following genera:

29.1 *Kermes* Boitard

Twenty-five species. [Note *K. ilicis* Linnaeus lives on oak in southern Europe where it is famous as the source of a dye.]

[29.2 *Ollifiella* Cockerell (1 sp., *O. cristicola* Ferris; found in leaf galls)]

30. CRYPTOCOCCIDAE
(Bark Crevice Scale Insect Family)

Adult females: L. 0.6–1.0 mm. Antennae one- to six-segmented; legs reduced or absent. Spiracles surrounded by a sclerotized area, with associated five-locular disc pores. A cluster pore plate posterior of each hind spiracle. Anal ring heavily sclerotized and usually with four to six setae. This very small, poorly known family, has one genus and two species in the U.S. and Canada, both of economic importance.

30.1 *Cryptococcus* Douglas

C. fagisuga Lindinger (Beech Scale).

C. williamsi Kosztarab and Hale (Sugar Maple Scale).

31. ERIOCOCCIDAE
(Felt Scale Insect Family)

Adult females are varied in structure and best characterized by the couplet in the Key to the Families. Although many species are host specific, others feed on a variety of host plants. Some are of economic importance. There are 9 genera and 53 species in the U.S. and Canada.

[31.1 *Apezococcus* Ferris (1 sp., *A. idiastes* Ferris); 31.2 *Atriplicia* Cockerell and Rohwer (1 sp., *A. gallicola* Cockerell and Rohwer); 31.3 *Cornoculus* Ferris (2 spp.)]

31.4 *Eriococcus* Targioni-Tozzetti

Twenty-nine species, the following of which are of economic interest:

E. araucariae (Maskell) (Norfolk Island Pine Felt Scale).

E. azaleae Comstock (Azalea Bark Scale).

E. gillettei Tinsley (Gillette Felt Scale).

E. coccineus Cockerell (Cactus Felt Scale).

E. insignis Newstead (Remarkable Felt Scale).

E. quercus (Comstock) (Oak Felt Scale).

31.5 *Gossyparia* Signoret

One species, as follows:

G. spuria (Modeer) (European Elm Scale).

[31.6 *Hypericicoccus* Williams (1 sp., *H. hyperici* (Ferris)); 31.7 *Oregmopyga* Hoy (6 spp.); 31.8 *Ovaticoccus* Kloet (9 spp.); 31.9 *Spiroporococcus* Miller (3 spp.)]

32. TACHARDIIDAE (Lac Scale Insect Family)

[= Kerridae, Lacciferidae]

The adult female is globular or pear-shaped. Antennae one- to seven-segmented. Legs vestigial or absent. Labium one- or two-segmented with ten to twelve setae. Brachial plates near spiracles and a dorsal spine anterior to the anal ring, the latter with pores and as many as ten long setae. Female secretes a resinous test or covering that contains openings originating near the anterior spiracles and the anal process. A few species are useful sources of certain commercial products. For example, shellac is made from the resinous test of the Lac Insect (*Laccifer lacca* Linnaeus). This species lives on the small branches of several tropical trees, partucularly various figs (*Ficus* spp.). It does not occur in the U.S. Another species is used for the production of certain medicines in Mexico, and others are used for dyes. Of this small family with about 65 species in the world, only six occur in the U.S.

[32.1 *Tachardiella* Cockerell (6 spp.)]

33. LECANODIASPIDIDAE
(False Pit Scale Insect Family)

Adult females have an anal cleft. Antennae two- to seven-segmented; labium one- or two-segmented. Anal ring with two to three rows of pores and six to eighteen setae. All adults and eggs are enclosed in a waxy test. Of the 71 species in the world, only five occur in the U.S. and Canada.

33.1 *Lecanodiaspis* Targioni-Tozzetti

Five species, the following of which is an example:

L. prosopidis Maskell. Found on azalea stems and other plants. (See Fig. 21.32 for adult females and nymphs; Fig. 21.33 for pits and depressions on stems.)

34. CEROCOCCIDAE
(Ornate Pit Scale Insect Family)

Adult females have a shieldlike anal plate. Antennae are reduced to stubs with setaceous and fleshy setae. Labium three-

Fig. 21.32. (*Courtesy of M. Kosztarab*)

Fig. 21.33. (*Courtesy of M. Kosztarab*)

segmented with eight to twelve setae. Legs usually absent, at most stublike. Anal ring with six to ten setae. Adult females and their eggs covered with a waxy papery test. This small family is represented in U.S. and Canada by only one genus with five species.

[34.1 *Cerococcus* Comstock (5 spp.)]

35. ASTEROLECANIIDAE
(Pit Scale Insect Family)

Adult females lack an anal plate and the anal lobes are usually rounded. Antennae normally one-segmented. Labium often close to the center of the body; one- or two-segmented, small, conical, or cordate, with either no or as many as 14 setae. Legs reduced or bsent. Anal ring with two to four setae. There are about 200 species of these insects in the world, some of them pests of ornamental trees and shrubs since they produce pits or galls on twigs. There are 29 species in the U.S. and Canada, as follows.

35.1 *Asterolecanium* Targioni-Tozzetti

Twenty-six species, the following of which are pests and produce ringlike swellings or other deformations on plants:

A. variolosum (Ratzeburg) (Golden Oak Scale).

A. pustulans (Cockerell) (Oleander Pit Scale).

[35.2 *Mycetococcus* Ferris (1 sp., *M. ehrhorni* (Cockerell)); 35.3 *Pollinia* Targioni-Tozzetti (1 sp., *P. pollini* (Costa)); 35.4 *Sclerosococcus* Mckenzie (1 sp., *S. bromeliae* McKenzie)]

36. CONCHASPIDIDAE
(False Armored Scale Insect Family)

These insects resemble the species of the family of Armored Scales (38), but the female test lacks exuviae. Antennae usually four-segmented; labium three-segmented with 18 to 20 setae; legs four-segmented. Abdominal segments 7 through 11 form a false pygidium but without lobes and plates on the margin. The few commercial pests of this small family feed on bark, stems, and leaves of plants. Only one species occurs in the U.S.

[36.1 *Conchaspis* Cockerell (1 sp., *C. angraeci* Cockerell)]

37. PHOENICOCOCCIDAE
(Palm Scale Insect Family)

Adult female body membranous, elongate, or pear-shaped, often with irregular papillae on surface, covered with a mass of waxy filaments. Antennae reduced, unsegmented, with invaginated apex containing five sensory setae. Legs absent. Labium one- or two-segmented, usually with 10 setae. Male wingless and body of some species not clearly divided into three body regions. Only one species in the U.S. and the world.

[37.1 *Phoenicococcus* Cockerell (1 sp., *P. marlatti* (Cockerell) (Red Date Scale)]

38. DIASPIDIDAE
(Armored Scale Insect Family)

Adult females are covered with a wax test that rests tentlike over the body and not attached. The test is composed of molted skins, excretions, and wax. Antennae, eyes, and legs reduced or absent. Labium one-segmented. This is the largest family of scales with over 1500 species in more than 350 genera, many of which are of great economic importance. The 194 species in the U.S. and Canada are assigned to the following 85 genera.

38.1 *Abgrallaspis* Balachowsky

Nine species, the following of which are pests:

A. cyanophylli (Signoret) (Cyanophyllum Scale).

A. ithacae (Ferris) (Hemlock Scale).

38.2 *Acutaspis* Ferris

Five species, the following of which is a pest:

A. perseae Ferris (Redbay Scale).

[38.3 *Ancepaspis* Ferris (2 spp.); 38.4 *Andaspis* MacGillivray (2 spp.); 38.5 *Annulaspis* Ferris (1 sp., *A. polysgona* Ferris); 38.6 *Aonidia* Targioni-Tozzetti (3 spp.)]

38.7 *Aonidiella* Maskell

Five species, the following four of which are of economic interest and the fifth an important pest:

A. aurantii (Maskell) (California Red Scale).

A. inornata McKenzie (Inornate Scale).

A. citrina (Coquillett) (Yellow Scale).

A. taxus Leonardi (Asiatic Red Scale).

A. orientalis (Newstead) (Oriental scale).

[38.8 *Aonidomytilus* Leonardi (12 spp.); 38.9 *Aspidaspis* Ferris (4 spp.)]

38.10 *Aspidiella* Berlese and Leonardi

One species, as follows:

A. sacchari (Cockerell) (Sugarcane Scale).

38.11 *Aspidiotus* Bouché

Six species, the following of which are pests:

A. destructor Signoret (Coconut Scale).

A. nerii Bouché (Oleander Scale).

38.12 *Aulacaspis* Cockerell

One species, as follows:

A. rosae (Bouché) (Rose Scale).

38.13 *Carulaspis* MacGillivray

Two species, the following of which are of economic interest:

C. juniperi Bouché (Juniper Scale).

C. minima (Targioni-Tozzetti) (Minute Cypress Scale).

38.14 *Chionaspis* Signoret

Twenty species, the following of which are of economic importance:

C. corni Cooley (Dogwood Scale).

C. americana Johnson (Elm Scurfy Scale).

C. heterophyllae Cooley (Pine Scale).

C. furfura (Fitch) (Scurfy Scale).

C. pinifoliae Fitch (Pine Needle Scale). Found on pine needles.

[38.15 *Chortinaspis* Ferris (6 spp.)]

38.16 *Chrysomphalus* Ashmead

Three species, the following two of which are common:

C. dictyospermi (Morgan) (Dictyospermum Scale).

C. aonidum (Linnaeus) (Florida Red Scale).

[38.17 *Circulaspis* MacGillivray (3 spp.)]

38.18 *Clavaspis* MacGillivray

Eleven species, the following of which is of economic importance:

C. herculeana (Doane and Hadden) (Herculean Scale).

38.19 *Comstockiella* Cockerell

One species, as follows:

C. sabalis (Comstock) (Palmetto Scale).

[38.20 *Crassaspis* Ferris (1 sp., *C. multipora* (Ferris)); 38.21 *Crenulaspidiotus* MacGillivray (1 sp., *C. mini* Davidson); 38.22 *Cupidaspis* MacGillivray (2 spp.); 38.23 *Dactylaspis* Ferris (1 sp., *D. lobata* Ferris)]

38.24 *Diaspidiotus* Leonardi

Twelve species, the following of which are of economic importance:

D. uvae (Comstock) (Grape Scale).

D. ancylus (Putnam) (Putnam Scale).

D. osborni (Newell and Cockerell) (Osborn Scale).

38.25 *Diaspis* Costa

Thirteen species, the following of which are pests:

D. echinocacti (Bouché) (Cactus Scale).

D. bromeliae (Kerner) (Pineapple Scale).

D. boisduvalli Signoret (Boisduval Scale).

38.26 *Duplaspidiotus* MacGillivray

Two species, the following of which is of economic importance:

D. claviger (Cockerell) (Camellia Mining Scale).

38.27 *Dynaspidiotus* Thiem and Gerneck

One species, as follows:

D. britannicus (Newstead) (Holly Scale).

38.28 *Epidiaspis* Cockerell

Four species, the following of which is a pest:

E. leperii (Signoret) (Italian Pear Scale).

[38.29 *Exuviaspis* Ferris (1 sp., *E. enceliae* Ferris); 38.30 *Ferrisidea* Borchsenius (1 sp., *F. magna* (Ferris)]

38.31 *Fiorinia* Targioni-Tozzetti

Five species, the following of which are pests:

F. fioriniae (Targioni-Tozzetti) (Fiorinia Scale).

F. externa Ferris (Elongate Hemlock Scale).

F. theae Green (Tea Scale).

[38.32 *Fissuraspis* Ferris (1 sp., *F. ulmi* (Hoke)]

38.33 *Furcaspis* Lindinger

One species, as follows:

F. biformis (Cockerell) (Red Orchid Scale).

[38.34 *Furchadaspis* MacGillivray (1 sp., *F. zamiae* (Morgan); 38.35 *Genaparlatoria* MacGillivray (1 sp., *G. pseudaspidiotus* (Lindinger)); 38.36 *Geodiaspis* Tippins and Howell (1 sp., *G. arundinariae* Tippins and Howell); 38.37 *Gymnaspis* Newstead (1 sp., *G. aechmeae* Newstead); 38.38 *Haliaspis* Takagi (6 spp.)]

38.39 *Hemiberlesia* Cockerell

Eight species, the following of which are pests:

H. lataniae (Signoret) (Latania Scale).

H. rapax (Comstock) (Greedy Scale).

[38.40 *Hemigymnsapis* (1 sp., *H. jessopae* Davidson and Miller)]

38.41 *Howardia* Berlese and Leonardi

One species, as follows:

H. biclavis (Comstock) (Mining Scale).

38.42 *Ischnaspis* Douglas

One species, as follows:

I. longirostris (Signoret) (Black Thread Scale).

[38.43 *Kuwanaspis* MacGillivray (3 spp.); 38.44 *Lapazia* Ferris (1 sp., *L. obscura* Howell and Beshear)]

38.45 *Lepidosaphes* Shimer

Sixteen species, many of them of economic interest:

L. ulmi (Linnaeus) (Oyster Shell Scale). This very common scale insect on many ornamental and fruit trees is one species that may be recognized by its characteristic shape, which is that of an oyster shell.

L. gloveri (Packard) (Glover Scale).

L. conchiformis (Gmelin) (Fig. Scale).

L. camelliae Hoke (Camellia Scale).

L. tokionis (Kuwana) (Croton Mussel Scale).

L. beckii (Newman) (Purple Scale).

[38.46 *Leucaspis* Targioni-Tozzetti (1 sp., *L. portaeureae* Ferris); 38.47 *Lindingaspis* MacGillivray (2 spp.)]

38.48 *Lopholeucaspis* Balachowsky

Two species, the following of which is a pest:

L. japonica (Cockerell) (Japanese Maple Scale).

38.49 *Melanaspis* Cockerell

Fifteen species, the following of which are pests:

M. tenebricosa (Comstock) (Gloomy Scale).

M. obscura (Comstock) (Obscure Scale).

[38.50 *Morganella* Cockerell (2 spp.); 38.51 *Mycetaspis* Cockerell (4 spp.); 38.52 *Nelaspis* Hall (1 sp., *N. crookiae* Ferris); 38.53 *Neopinnaspis* McKenzie (1 sp., *N. harperi* McKenzie); 38.54 *Nicholiella* Ferris (1 sp., *N. bumeliae* Ferris); 38.55 *Niveaspis* MacGillivray (1 sp., *N. ilicis* (Hoke))]

38.56 *Nuculaspis* Ferry

Four species, the following of which is a pest:

N. californica (Coleman) (Black Pineleaf Scale).

[38.57 *Odonaspis* Leonardi (7 spp.); 38.58 *Opuntiaspis* Cockerell (1 sp., *O. carinata* (Cockerell)); 38.59 *Palinaspis* Ferris (1 sp., *P. quohoqiformis* (Merrill)); 38.60 *Pallulaspis* Ferris (1 sp., *P. ephedrae* Ferris)]

38.61 *Parlatoreopsis* Lindinger

Two species, the following of which is a pest:

P. chinensis (Marlatt) (Chinese Obscure Scale).

38.62 *Parlatoria* Targioni-Tozzetti

Nine species, the following of which are of economic interest:

P. camelliae Comstock (Camellia Parlatoria Scale).

P. pergandii Comstock (Chaff Scale).

P. theae Cockerell (Tea Parlatoria Scale).

P. lleae (Colvee) (Olive Scale).

P. blanchardi (Targioni-Tozzetti) (Parlatoria Date Scale).

[38.63 *Pelliculaspis* Ferris (1 sp., *P. celtis* McDaniel)]

38.64 *Pinnaspis* Cockerell

Three species, two of which are pests:

P. strachani (Cooley) (Lesser Snow Scale).

P. aspidistrae (Signoret) (Fern Scale).

[38.65 *Poliaspis* Maskell (1 sp., *P. cycadis* Comstock); 38.66 *Praecocaspis* Ferris (1 sp., *P. diversa* Ferris); 38.67 *Protodiaspis* Cockerell (6 spp.)]

38.68 *Pseudaonidia* Cockerell

Three species, all of which are pests:

P. duplex (Cockerell) (Camphor Scale).

P. paeonia (Cockerell) (Peony Scale).

P. trilobitiformis (Green) (Trilobe Scale).

38.69 *Pseudaulacaspis* Hempel

Three species, the following of which are pests:

P. cockerelli (Cooley) (False Oleander Scale).

P. pentagona (Targioni-Tozzetti) (White Peach Scale).

[38.70 *Pseudischnaspis* Hempel (1 sp., *P. bowreyi* (Cockerell)); 38.71 *Pseudodiaspis* Cockerell (1 sp., *P. larreae* (Cockerell))]

38.72 *Pseudoparlatoria* Cockerell

Three species, the following of which is of economic importance:

P. parlatorioides (Comstock) (False Parlatoria Scale).

38.73 *Quadraspidiotus* MacGillivray

Nine species, the following of which are pests:

Q. perniciosus Comstock (San Jose Scale). Perhaps the most serious pest of apples and other orchard crops as well as many ornamental trees, this was introduced into San Jose, CA, in 1880 and is difficult to control. Fruit is attacked only on trees that are very heavily infested, but the presence of the insects on the bark and leaves weakens the tree and degrades the fruit.

Q. ostreaeformis (Curtis) (European Fruit Scale).

Q. forbesi (Johnson) (Forbes Scale).

Q. juglansregiae (Comstock) (Walnut Scale).

[38.74 *Quernaspis* Ferris (3 spp.); 38.75 *Radionaspis* Ferris (1 sp., *R. indica* (Marlatt)); 38.76 *Rhizaspidiotus* MacGillivray (1 sp., *R. dearnessi* (Cockerell)); 38.77 *Rugaspidiotus* MacGillivray (3 spp.)]

38.78 *Selenaspidus* Cockerell

Three species, the following of which is a pest:

S. articulatus (Morgan) (Rufous Scale).

[38.79 *Situlaspis* MacGillivray (4 spp.); 38.80 *Stramenaspis* Ferris (1 sp., *S. kelloggi* (Coleman)); 38.81 *Targionia* Signoret (2 spp.); 38.82 *Tsugaspidiotus* Takahashi and Takagi (1 sp., *T. pseudomeyeri* (Kuwana))]

38.83 *Unaspis* MacGillivray

Two species, both of which are pests:

U. citri (Comstock) (Citrus Snow Scale).

U. euonymi (Comstock) (Euonymus Scale). (See Fig. 21.34 for female scales and male cocoons.)

[38.84 *Velataspis* Ferris (3 spp.); 38.85 *Xerophilaspis* Cockerell (1 sp., *X. prosopidis* Cockerell)]

BIBLIOGRAPHY

Crawford, D. L. 1914. Monograph of the jumping plant lice or Psyllidae of the New World. *U. S. Nat. Mus. Bull.* 85: 185 pp.

DeLong, D. M. 1948. The leafhoppers, or Cicadellidae, of Illinois. *Illinois Nat. Hist. Surv. Bull.,* 24(2): 91–376 pp.

Ferris, G. F. 1937–1955. *Atlas of the scale insects of North America.* Vols. 1–7. Stanford Univ. Press. 1187 pp.

Hottes, F. C., and Frison, T. H. 1931. The plant lice, or Aphididae, of Illinois. *Illinois Nat. Hist. Surv. Bull.* 19(3): 121–447 pp.

Howell, J. O., and Williams, M. L. 1976. An annotated key to the families of Scale Insects (Homoptera: Coccoidea) of America, north of Mexico, based on characteristics of adult females. *Ann. Ent. Soc. Amer.* 69: 181–189.

Hoy, J. M. 1963. A catalogue of the Eriococcidae (Homoptera: Coccoidea) of the World. *Bull. N. Z. Dept. Sci. Ind. Res.* 150: 1–260.

Kosztarab, M. 1968. Cryptococcidae, a new family of the Coccoidea (Homoptera). *Virginia Journ. Sci.* 19: 12.

_____ . 1974. An annotated list of generic names of the Scale Insects (Homoptera: Coccoidea), Second Supplement. *U.S. Dept. Agric. Misc. Publ.* No. 1285. 22 pp.

McKenzie, H. L. 1967. *Mealybugs of California, with taxonomy,* biology and control of North American species. Berkeley: University of California Press. 526 pp.

Metcalf, Z. P. 1923. A key to the Fulgoridae of eastern North America with descriptions of new species. *Journ. Elisha Mitchel Soc.* 38 (3–4): 139–230 (70 pls.).

Miller, D. R., and Kasztarab, M. 1979. Recent advances in the study of scale insects. *Ann. Rev. Ent.* 24: 1–27.

Morrison, H. 1925. Classification of Scale Insects of the subfamily Ortheziinae. *Journ. Agric. Res.* 30 (2): 97–154.

_____ . 1952. Classification of the Ortheziidae. *U.S. Dept. Agric. Tech. Bull.* No. 1052, 80 pp.

Morrison, H., and Morrison, E. R. 1966. An annotated list of generic names of the Scale Insects (Homoptera: Coccoidea). *U.S. Dept. Agric. Misc. Publ.* No. 1015, 206 pp.

Oman, P. W. 1949. The Nearctic leafhoppers (Homptera: Cicindellidae), a generic classification and checklist. *Ent. Soc. Wash. Mem.* No. 3.

Osborn, H. 1940. The Membracidae of Ohio. *Ohio Biol. Surv. Bull.* 7(2): 51–101.

Russell, L. M. 1970. Additions and corrections to an annotated list of generic names of the scale insects (Homoptera: Coccoidea). *U.S. Dept. Agric. Misc. Publ.* No. 1015 (Supplement), iv+ 13 pp.

Smith, Clyde F., and Parron, Carol S. 1978. An annotated list of Aphididae (Homoptera) of North America. *Tech. Bull. No. 255.* N.C. Agric. Exp. Stat. viii+428 pp.

Tuthill, L. D. 1943. The psyllids of America north of Mexico. *Iowa St. Coll. J. Sci.,* 17: 443–660.

Williams, D. J. 1969. The family-group names of the Scale Insects (Hemiptera: Coccoidea). *Bull. British Mus. Nat. Hist. (Entomology).* 23(8): 315–341.

Williams, M. L., and Kosztarab, M. 1972. The Coccidae of Virginia. *Virginia Polytech. Inst. and State Univ. Res. Div. Bull.* 74: 215 pp.

Order 22

THYSANOPTERA (Thrips)

Thrips are very small, usually concealed insects that can often be found in flower blossoms or on the underside of leaves, under bark, and a variety of other habitats. Most any flower head thumped against a white cloth or handkerchief will expose numerous tiny thrips and their nymphs. Some cause damage to flower parts and growing shoots, but others are predacious on mites and small insects and are therefore beneficial.

The Latin name comes from the Greek word, *thysanos,* meaning a "fringe" or "tassel," which refers to the long hairs fringing both pairs of wings. The exact relationship of this group of insects to other orders is not certain, but they have features similar to the previous few orders plus those of the Hemiptera and Homoptera and appear to be somewhat advanced over these large groups of plant feeders. Among the several features that link them with the Hemiptera–Homoptera is the lack of abdominal cerci. The presence of a pupal stage places them close to the Holometabolous orders, along with certain Homoptera that have a pupalike stage. It is doubtful if there is any phylogenetic connection between these orders and the primitive Holometabola, however; it is more likely that the "pupa" stage of these successful groups developed parallel to that of the Holometabola.

Diagnosis: L. 0.5–14 mm (but usually 1–2 mm). Soft bodied; adults more heavily chitinized than nymphs; shape elongate, cylindrical, usually only slightly flattened but some flattened dorsoventrally (these live under bark and in grasss leaf axils). Usually black, but may be gray, brown, or yellowish and sometimes marked with black, red, or white. Antennae short, sometimes as long as head and thorax but usually shorter. Right mandible vestigial, but other mouthparts elongate into stylets fitted for piercing plant tissue or sucking blood of mites and small insects or plant sap. Either wingless or with two pairs of

Fig. 22.1. (*From Univ. Calif. Exp. Sta.*)

Fig. 22.3. (*From Dyadechko, 1977*)

very narrow wings with veins greatly reduced or absent, each with a fringe surrounding both margins or only the hind margin. The legs are short and slender, unmodified except for the tarsi. The tarsi of species of the suborder Terebrantia have two tarsomeres. Those of the suborder Tubulifera have the front tarsi with a single tarsomere and the middle and hind tarsi with two tarsomeres. In many species of Tubulifera, a tooth is located on the inner side of the front tarsus. This tooth is strongly developed in the males. In some species, it is located at the apex of the tarsus.

Attachment devices are seen on the tarsi of all species, both in the nymph and the adult. These consist of lobes modified as a special bladder that is joined to claws modified as a plate. The bladder is supported by a base, from which a chitinized thickening extends into the tarsus. Muscles are attached to the base to make it movable. In use, the bladder is inflated with hemolymph so that the base can be held firmly to the surface of a plant.

The abdomen is one of two types: Either the terminal segment is not tubular and divided ventrally, with major setae not ovoid and with platelets in both sexes and a sawlike ovipositor in the female, or the terminal abdominal segment is tubular, with major setae on platelets attached to the apex in both sexes and the female without an ovipositor. These

abdominal features are used to divide the group into two suborders, the Terebrantia [see Fig. 22.1 (*T. inconsequens*, 4.52)] and the Tubulifera [see Fig. 22.2 (*L. vaneecki*, 5.49)].

Eggs are usually large, reniform or oblong and oval, with or without a micropyle. Their surface is smooth. Only a few eggs—sometimes about a fifth the size of the female—are formed at a time. Nymphs (often referred to as larvae) resemble the adults except that they lack wings. Wing pads become evident in later instars.

Thrips might be confused with small flies, wasps, and even certain beetles were it not for the four distinctively fringed wings that distinguish members of this order from all other groups.

Metamorphosis: Paurometabolous, but modified to resemble holometabolism. In the Terebrantia, the third instar nymph (or larva) forms a prepupa, but it is still capable of feeding. The fourth instar is more pupalike and may even form a cocoon. In the Tubulifera, the fifth instar is a pupa incapable of feeding [see Fig. 22.3 (*T. Tabaci*, 4.53)]. In all cases, however, the nymphs and pupae greatly resemble the adult (see Fig. 22.4 (*H. femoratis*, 4.5)].

Habits and habitats: In addition to frequenting flower heads, some species are found under bark, on leaves and fruit, in leaf litter, moss, and flower bulbs, and in the leaf axils of grasses and similar plants. A large number of species suck plant juices from the leaves and young shoots of trees and shrubs particularly. A considerable number of species feed on eggs and larvae of various kinds of insects, on mites, and even on nematodes.

Fig. 22.2. (*From Calif. Dept. Agric.*)

Fig. 22.4. (*From Florida Dept. Agric.*)

Others feed on fungi and algae in rotting wood and on the juices oozing from decomposing wood. Among the phytophagous species, most thrips feed on a great variety of plants; some are restricted to a few species; only a few are plant host specific. Female thrips hibernate.

Reproductive behavior: Eggs are laid on leaves, flower scales, and the bark of trees and shrubs. Males are unknown in many species; in others, they are rare. Reproduction by parthenogenesis is common.

Collecting and preserving: Examining flowers, leaves, and other plant parts and shaking or beating flower heads, leaves, grasses, or branches over a piece of white cloth are good ways to collect specimens of thrips. They are common in leaf litter, under bark, and in grass clumps, especially in the latter throughout the year. The use of a Berlese funnel or similar device can prove very effective. Another approach is to place fresh plant material in plastic bags, which are then tied tightly. After several days when the material has wilted, the bags are opened and the scattering thrips captured with a small brush moistened in glycerine and dipped into alcohol. The thrips are then placed in 60- or 70-percent alcohol or in a solution containing eight parts of 95-percent alcohol, five parts distilled water, and one part glycerine and glacial acetic acid. If the latter solution is used, the specimens should be transferred to 60- or 70-percent alcohol after a few months, where they may be stored indefinitely. Eventually, however, they must be mounted on microscope slides since the various structures used in the keys for identification must be as clearly visible as possible.

Rearing: Large test tubes with moist soil in the bottom may be used as rearing tubes. Plant material from the thrips' habitat should be inserted along with nymphs and adults and the tube plugged with cotton. After some time, the nymphs will appear between the soil and the side of the tube, where their transformation to the adult stage may be observed.

Distribution: There are approximately 4,000 species found throughout the world; 694 of these species in 138 genera are described and recorded in the U.S. and Canada.

Identification: The identification of thrips requires a fairly high magnification microscope and a detailed knowledge of their anatomy. The literature on the species is scattered, but the fauna is well known. The works listed in the Bibliography offer identification keys for a majority of the species found in the U.S. and Canada, and the bibliographies in these works give references to even more detailed works. Unfortunately, this group has attracted few students, and there is a pressing need for more specialists. A major contribution to entomology can be made by collecting specimens and recording accurate plant host data and other details about habitats.

Economic importance: Many phytophagous species are harmful to cereal crops, field crops, fruits, and garden flowers. Many other species, the carnivorous ones, play an important role in checking the populations of pest mites on cotton and other crops. Their exact effect on any given ecosystem has not been adequately assessed.

CLASSIFICATION

The order as represented in the U.S. and Canada is divided into two easily recognized suborders and five families. The accompanying key will be helpful in sorting specimens to family.

Key to the Families

1. Terminal abdominal segment tubular; females without ovipositor (suborder Tubulifera) .. **5. Phlaeothripidae**
 Terminal abdominal segment rounded or conical; females with ventral surface of last visible abdominal segment longitudinally divided, usually with long-toothed ovipositor (suborder Terebrantia) ... *2*
2(1). Antennae always 9-segmented, segments 3 and 4 with flat, longitudinal sensoria; wings relatively broad and rounded apically; ovipositor curved upward distally **1. Aeolothripidae**
 Antenna 6- to 9-segmented, segments 3 and 4 with projecting sensoria or with flat, rounded sensoria; wings narrow and usually pointed apically; ovipositor, when present, curved downward apically ... *3*
3(2). Sensoria of antennal segments 3 and 4 projecting as slender, simple, or forked cones **4. Thripidae**
 Sensoria of antennal segments 3 and 4 either projecting as short, blunt cones or flat *4*
4(3). Antennae 8-segmented, sensoria of segments 3 and 4 large, flat apical areas **2. Merothripidae**
 Antennae 9-segmented, sensoria of segments 3 and 4 small, circular areas forming band around apex .. **3. Heterothripidae**

Suborder TEREBRANTIA

Apical segment of the abdomen is rounded or conical; segment 10 of the female is divided, usually with a long ovipositor. The front wings, if present, have veins.

Superfamily AEOLOTHRIPOIDEA

1. AEOLOTHRIPIDAE (Predacious Thrips Family)

Most of the species in this family are predacious.

Subfamily Melanthripinae

[1.1 *Ankothrips* Crawford, subgenus *Ankothrips* s. str. (7 spp.); 1.2 *Dactuliothrips* Moulton (4 spp.); 1.3 *Melanthrips* Haliday (3 spp.)]

Subfamily Aeolothripinae
Tribe Orothripini

[1.4 *Erythrothrips* Moulton (4 spp.); 1.5 *Orothrips* Moulton (3 spp.); 1.6 *Stomatothrips* Hood (4 spp.)]

Tribe **Franklinothripini**

1.7 *Franklinothrips* Back

One species only, as follows:

F. vespiformis (Crawford) (Vespiform Thrips).

Tribe **Aeolothripini**

[1.8 *Aeolothrips* Haliday (31 spp.)]

2. MEROTHRIPIDAE (Jumping Thrips Family)

Members of this family have enlarged front and hind femora. Most species occur in fungi or in debris and under bark.

Subfamily **Erotidothripinae**

[2.1 *Merothrips* Hood (4 spp.)]

Superfamily THRIPOIDEA

3. HETEROTHRIPIDAE (Tree Thrips Family)

These species, seldom collected, live on various trees and flowers.

Tribe **Heterothripini**

[3.1 *Heterothrips* Hood (20 spp.); 3.2 *Oligothrips* Moulton (1 sp., *O oreios* Moulton)]

4. THRIPIDAE (Thrips Family)

The 264 species in 50 genera are commonly collected on flowers and leaves.

Subfamily **Panchaetothripinae**

[4.1 *Anisopilothrips* Stannard and Mitri (1 sp., *A. venustulus* (Priesner))]

4.2 *Caliothrips* Daniel

Seven species, the following of which is a common pest:

C. fasciatus (Pergande) (Bean Thrips).

[4.3 *Dinurothrips* Hood (2 spp.)]

4.4 *Heliothrips* Haliday

One species, as follows:

H. haemorrhoidalis (Bouche) (Greenhouse Thrips).

4.5 *Hercinothrips* Bagnall

One species, as follows:

H. femoralis (Reuter) (Banded Greenhouse Thrips). (See Fig. 22.4.)

[4.6 *Parthenothrips* Uzel (1 sp., *P. dracaenae* (Heeger)); 4.7 *Monilothrips* Moulton (1 sp., *M. kempi* Moulton)]

4.8 *Selenothrips* Karny

One species, as follows:

S. rubrocinctus (Giard) (Redbanded Thrips).

Subfamily **Thripinae**

Tribe **Dendrothripini**

4.9 *Dendrothrips* Uzel

One species, as follows:

D. ornatus (Jablonowski) (Privet Thrips).

[4.10 *Leucothrips* Reuter (3 spp.); 4.11 *Pseudodendrothrips* Schmutz (1 sp., *P. mori* (Niwa))]

Tribe **Sericothripini**

4.12 *Sericothrips* Haliday

Of this large genus with 36 species, the following is a pest:

S. variabilis (Beach)) (Soybean Thrips).

[4.13 *Zonothrips* Priesner (1 sp., *Z. osmundae* Crawford); 4.14 *Drepanothrips* Uzel (1 sp., *D. reuteri* Uzel)]

4.15 *Scirtothrips* Shull

Fifteen species, of which the following is a pest:

S. citri (Moulton)) (Citrus Thrips).

[4.16 *Sericopsothrips* Hood (1 sp., *S. palloris* Hood)]

Tribe **Chirothripini**

[4.17 *Chirothrips* Haliday (26 spp.)]

4.18 *Limothrips* Haliday

Three species, of which the following is a pest:

L. cerealium (Halium) (Grain Thrips).

Tribe **Thripini**

Subtribe **Aptinothripina**

4.19 *Anaphothrips* Uzel

Fifteen species, the following of which is common and sometimes a pest:

A. obscurus (Müller) (Grass Thrips).

[4.20 *Apterothrips* Bagnall (1 sp., *A. secticornis* (Trybom)); 4.21 *Aptinothrips* Haliday (2 spp.); 4.22 *Arpediothrips* Hood (1 sp., *A. mojave* Hood); 4.23 *Baileyothrips* Kono and O'Neill (1 sp., *B. arizonensis* (Morgan)); 4.24 *Bregmatothrips* Hood (3 spp.); 4.25 *Chaetanaphothrips* Priesner (1 sp., *C. orchidii* (Moulton)); 4.26 *Chilothrips* Hood (3 spp.); 4.27 *Kurtomathrips* Moulton (2 spp.); 4.28 *Oxythrips* Uzel (6 spp.); 4.29 *Prosopoanaphothrips* Moulton (1 sp., *P. reticulatus* (Moulton)); 4.30 *Prosopothrips* Uzel (1 sp., *P. cognatus* Hood); 4.31 *Psilothrips* Hood (2 spp.); 4.32 *Caprithrips* Faure (1 sp., *C. insularis* Beshear); 4.33 *Tmetothrips* Amyot and Serville (1 sp., *T. subapterus* (Haliday)); 4.34 *Salpingothrips* Hood (1 sp., *S. aimotofus* Kudo)]

Subtribe **Thripina**

[4.35 *Baliothrips* Uzel (1 sp., *B. dispar* (Haliday)); 4.36 *Catinathrips* O'Neill (2 spp.); 4.37 *Ceratothrips* Reuter (2 spp.); 4.38 *Ctenothrips* Franklin (2 spp.); 4.39 *Dorcadothrips* Priesner (1 sp., *D. walteri* (Crawford)); 4.40 *Echinothrips* Moulton (3 spp.)]

4.41 *Frankliniella* Karny

This large genus of 40 species has several pest species.

F. tritici (Fitch) (Flower Thrips).

F. occidentalis (Pergande) (Western Flower Thrips).

F. vaccinii Morgan (Blueberry Thrips).

F. fusca (Hinds) (Tobacco Thrips).

[4.42 *Iridothrips* Priesner (1 sp., *I. iridis* (Watson) (Iris Thrips); 4.43 *Isoneurothrips* Bagnall (1 sp., *I. australis* Bagnall)]

4.44 *Microcephalothrips* Bagnall

Two species, the following of which is a pest:

M. abdominalis (Crawford) (Composite Thrips).

[4.45 *Mycterothrips* Trybom (4 spp.); 4.46 *Odontothrips* Amyot and Serville (2 spp.); 4.47 *Pezothrips* Karny (1 sp., *P. dianthi* (*Priesner*)); 4.48 *Plesiothrips* Hood (7 spp.); 4.49 *Pseudothrips* Hinds (2 spp.); 4.50 *Rhaphidothrips* Uzel (1 sp., *R. longistylosus* Uzel)]

4.51 *Scolothrips* Hinds

Four species, of which the following is predacious:

S. sexmalculatus (Pergande) (Six-spotted Thrips).

4.52 *Taeniothrips* Amyot and Serville

Ten species, of which the following is a pest:

T. inconsequens (Uzel) (Pear Thrips). (See Fig. 22.1.)

4.53 *Thrips* Linnaeus

Thirty-four species, of which the following are pests:

T. tabaci Lindeman (Onion Thrips). (See Fig. 22.3 for second pupal stages.)

T. nigropilosus Uzel (Chrysanthemum Thrips).

T. simplex (Morison) (Gladiolus Thrips). (See Fig. 22.5).

[4.54 *Toxonothrips* Moulton (1 sp., *T. gramineae* (Moulton)]

Fig. 22.5. (*From Utah Agric. Exp. Sta.*)

Suborder TUBULIFERA

The apical segment of the abdomen of both sexes is tubular, but the female lacks an ovipositor, and segment 10 is never divided. Wings, if present, lack veins. Only one large family (that indicated below) is found in the U.S. and Canada. Only a few of its species are pests; some are beneficial as predators.

Superfamily PHLAEOTHRIPOIDEA

5. PHLAEOTHRIPIDAE
(Tube-tailed Thrips Family)

There are 348 species in 77 genera known to occur in the U.S. and Canada.

Subfamily Idolothripinae

[5.1 *Allothrips* Hood (4 spp.); 5.2 *Atractothrips* Hood (1 sp., *A. bradleyi* Hood); 5.3 *Barythrips* Hood and Williams (1 sp., *B. sculpticauda* Hood and Williams); 5.4 *Bolothrips* Priesner (7 spp.); 5.5 *Ceuthothrips* Hood (1 sp., *C. timuqua* Hood); 5.6 *Cryptothrips* Uzel (6 spp.); 5.7 *Diceratothrips* Bagnall (5 spp.); 5.8 *Diopsothrips* Hood (1 sp., *D. louisianae* Hood); 5.9 *Elaphrothrips* Buffa (7 spp.); 5.10 *Gastrothrips* Hood (4 spp.); 5.11 *Illinothrips* Stannard (1 sp., *I. rossi* Stannard); 5.12 *Megalothrips* Uzel (3 spp.); 5.13 *Megathrips* Targioni-Tozzetti (3 spp.); 5.14 *Nesothrips* Kirkaldy (1 sp., *N. brevicollis* (Bagnall)); 5.15 *Oedaleothrips* Hood (8 spp.); 5.16 *Parallothrips* Hood (1 sp., *P. thomasi* Hood); 5.17 *Priesneriella* Hood (1 sp., *P. citricauda* Hood); 5.18 *Pygidiothrips* Hood (1 sp., *P. seminole* Hood); 5.19 *Pygothrips* Hood (3 spp.); 5.20 *Rhaebothrips* Karny (1 sp., *R. lativentris* Karny); 5.21 *Sporothrips* Hood (1 sp., *S. amplus* (Hood)); 5.22 *Syncerothrips* Hood (1 sp., *S. harti* Hood); 5.23 *Scotothrips* Priesner (1 sp., *S. claripennis* (Moulton))]

Subfamily Phlaeothripinae

[5.24 *Amynothrips* O'Neill (1 sp., *A. andersoni* O'Niell); 5.25 *Acanthothrips* Uzel (4 spp.); 5.26 *Acrosothrips* Stannard (1 sp., *A. asymmetricus* (Watson)); 5.27 *Adreanothrips* Hood (18 spp.); 5.28 *Agrothrips* Jacot-Guillarmod (5 spp.); 5.29 *Aleurodothrips* Franklin (1 sp., *A. fasciapennis* (Franklin)); 5.30 *Amphibolothrips* Buffa; two subgenera: *Stephanothrips* Trybon (6 spp.) and *Trachythrips* Hood (5 spp.); 5.31 *Antillothrips* Stannard (1 sp., *A. cingulatus* (Hood)); 5.32 *Bagnalliella* Karny (8 spp.); 5.33 *Cephalothrips* Uzel (2 spp.); 5.34 *Chirothripoides* Bagnall (1 sp., *C. dendropogonus* Watt); 5.35 *Diphyothrips* Stannard (1 sp., *D. morainensis* Stannard); 5.36 *Docessissophothrips* Bagnall (1 sp., *D. richardsi* (Stannard)); 5.37 *Erkosothrips* Stannard (4 spp.); 5.38 *Eschatothrips* Stannard (1 sp., *E. barythripoides* (Watson)); 5.39 *Eurythrips* Hinds (14 spp.); 5.40 *Glyptothrips* Hood (2 spp.); 5.41 *Goniothrips* Hood (1 sp., *g. denticornis* Hood)]

5.42 *Gnophothrips* Hood and Williams

One species, as follows:

G. fuscus (Morgan) (Slash Pine Flower Thrips).

5.43 *Gynaikothrips* Karny

One species, as follows:

G. ficorum (Marchal) (Cuban Laurel Thrips).

5.44 *Haplothrips* Amyot and Serville

This genus is divided into four subgenera—*Haplothrips* s. str., subgenus *Karnyothrips* Watson, subgenus *Leptothrips* Hood, and subgenus *Neoheegeria* Schmutz—but its 50 species are not all assigned to these subgenera (see Stannard, 1957).

[5.45 *Hindsiothrips* Stannard (2 spp.); 5.46 *Hoplandrothrips* Hood (27 spp. in two subgenera: *Hoplandrothrips* s. str. and *Phloeobiothrips* Hood); 5.47 *Hoplothrips* Amyot and Serville (=*Phlaothrips* Haliday) (35 spp.); 5.48 *Hyidiothrips* Hood (1 sp., *H. atomarius* Hood)]

5.49 *Liothrips* Uzel

Thirty-five species, the following of which are of economic interest:

L. vaneecki Priesner (Lily Bulb Thrips). (See Fig. 22.2)

L. floridensis (Watson) (Camphor Thrips).

[5.50 *Lispothrips* Reuter (5 spp.); 5.51 *Lissothrips* Hood (3 spp.); 5.52 *Macrophthalmothrips* Karny (1 sp., *M. helenae* Hood); 5.53 *Malacothrips* Hinds (3 spp.); 5.54 *Neothrips* Hood (1 sp., *N. corticis* Hood); 5.55 *Neurothrips* Hood (1 sp., *N. magnafemoralis* Hinds); 5.56 *Phrasterothrips* Priesner (1 sp., unnamed in (2) FL); 5.57 *Phthirothrips* Priesner (1 sp., *morgani* Hood); 5.58 *Plectrothrips* Hood (3 spp.); 5.59 *Podothrips* Hood (1 sp., *P. semiflavus* Hood); 5.60 *Poecilothrips* Uzel (2 spp.); 5.61 *Polyphemothrips* Schmutz (14 spp. in two subgenera: *Adelothrips* Hood and *Polyphemothrips* s. str.); 5.62 *Preeriella* Hood (2 spp.); 5.63 *Rhopalothrips* Hood (1 sp., *R. bicolor* Hood (3) ?AZ); 5.64 *Scopaeothrips* Crawford (2 spp.); 5.65 *Sophiothrips* Hood (1 sp., *S. spadix* (Hood)); 5.66 *Stictothrips* Hood (1 sp., *S. maculatus* Hood); 5.67 *Symphyothrips* Hood and Williams (1 sp., *S. punctatus* Hood and Williams); 5.68 *Mixothrips* Stannard (1 sp., *M. craigheadi* Stannard); 5.69 *Nanothrips* Faure (1 sp., *N. bicolor* (Watson and Preer); 5.70 *Strepterothrips* Hood (1 sp., *S. floridanus* Hood); 5.71 *Thorybothrips* Priesner (1 sp., *T. yuccae* Moulton); 5.72 *Torvothrips* Johnsen (1 sp., *T. kosztarabi* Johnson); 5.73 *Treherniella* Watson (1 sp., *T. amplipennis* (Morgan)); 5.74 *Trichinothrips* Bagnall (1 sp., *T. pusillus* (Hood)); 5.75 *Tylothrips* Hood (1 sp., *T. bruesi* Hood); 5.76 *Williamsiella* Hood (1 sp., *W. bicoloripes* Hood); 5.77 *Zaxenothrips* Crawford (3 spp.)]

BIBLIOGRAPHY

Dyadechko, N. P. 1977. *Thrips or fringe-winged Insects* (Thysanoptera) *of the European part of the USSR*. New Delhi: Amerind Publ. Co., 344 pp.

Jacot-Guillarmod, C. F. 1970–1978. Catalogue of the Thysanoptera of the world. *Ann. Cape Prov. Mus. (Nat. Hist.)*. 1970, 7(1): iii+216 pp; 1971, 7(2): 217–515; 1974; 7(3): 517–976; 1975; 7(4): 977–1255; 1978, 7(5): 1257–1556.

Sakimura, K. and O'Neill, 1979. *Frankiniella,* redefinition of genus and revision of *Minuta* group species (Thysanoptera: Thripidae). *U.S. Dept. Agric. Tech. Bull.* 1572, 49 pp.

Stannard, Lewis J., Jr. 1957. The phylogeny and classification of the North American genera of the suborder Tubulifera (Thysanoptera). *Ill. Biol. Mon.* No. 25. Urbana: Univ. Ill. Press, 200 pp.

——. Two new and two rare tubuliferous Thrips, recorded principally from Illinois (Thysanoptera, Phlaeothripidae). *Proc. Ent. Soc. Washington.* 60(6): 271–275.

——. New genera and species of Thysanoptera (Tubulifera: Phliaeothripidae) from Illinois and Alabama. *Ill. State Acad. Sci. Trans.* 56(3): 134–138.

——. The Thrips, or Thysanoptera of Illinois. *Bull. Ill. Nat. Hist. Survey.* 29(4): 215–552.

Wilson, Thomas H. 1975. A monograph of the subfamily Panchaetothripinae (Thysanoptera: Thripidae). *Memoirs Amer. Ent. Inst.* No. 23, 354 pp.

Extinct Order GLOSSELYTRODEA

Most of the presently known fossils of this order occur in Permian deposits, with a few from the Triassic. The front wing is membranous in some and hardened, elytralike, in others, but with parallel veins and many cross veins retained by the latter. Although no immatures have been found, it has been assumed—because of their similarity in structure to the Neuroptera and Coleoptera—that their metamorphosis was holometabolous and that they are primitive members of the subdivision Holometabola. This assumption, however, has not been accepted by all authors.

Order 23

NEUROPTERA (Dobsonflies, Lacewings, Antlions, and Allies)

This is the most primitive order of insects with complete metamorphosis. Compared to most other orders of the Holometabola, there are relatively few species in this diverse group. Their primitive features are of interest to insect evolutionists because they give clues to the origin of the rest of the Holometabola, which includes the majority, by far, of all insect species, and, in fact, of all animal species. The Neuroptera may not constitute a single order. Many entomologists divide them into three separate orders, which are here treated as suborders. In spite of their interesting structure and habits, the Neuroptera are not very well known by the general entomologists, and there are few specialists on the group.

One member of the order, the Dobsonfly, is frequently come across by children and fisherman, and sometimes even by householders. They fly to lights at night and remain near them during the day. The males in particular appear fearsome because of their long and savage-looking mandibles. They usually cause great concern among those who see them for the first time, but they are not aggressive. Once this fact is understood, they may well excite enough interest for the discoverer to wish to learn more. The larva of the Dobsonfly, known as a Hellgrammite, is often used as fish bait.

As with most of the orders of the Holometabola, the form of the wing is the basis for the Latin name of the order. The Greek word *neuron* means "sinew" (not "nerve," as is sometimes supposed), and, of course, *pteron* means "wing." The Latin name is generally assumed to refer to the netlike arrangement of the veins and cross veins of the wings, from an old usage of the word *nervation* (or *neuration*), meaning "strengthening by sinews." This order was named long before nerves as a tissue were understood.

Most species of Neuroptera are carnivorous in the larval stage and some in the adult stage; other adults feed on nectar and pollen. Most species are terrestrial. The aquatic larvae are usually bottom dwellers, where they capture various aquatic organisms. Members of one family feed exclusively on freshwater sponges. The terrestrial larvae of Planipennia have a variety of habits, and most (including the sponge feeders) have specially modified mandibles (see Fig. 23.1; ventral view, right, dorsal view, left). These are channeled to suck body fluids from their prey. Their digestive tracts are incomplete in that the alimentary canal is not connected in the middle; hence, they

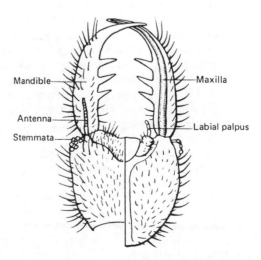

Fig. 23.1. (*Courtesy of John N. Belkin*)

Fig. 23.2.

Fig. 23.3.

cannot pass solid excrement during their larval life. Most adults, except for the ascalaphids, are not strong flyers. Although some resemble dragonflies, their flight resembles that of a damselfly. Adults are usually found near their larval habitat.

Diagnosis: Wingspan 5–160 mm. Body soft-textured; shape various, but elongate, cylindrical, usually with long, narrow, simple abdomen. Most species are dull brown, with some green, others black, and some tropical species with colorful wing markings. The antennae are various, usually long and many-segmented, but some of them short and not much longer than the head and thorax, rarely pectinate. The mouthparts of adults and some larvae are either the normal chewing-biting type or the sucking type already mentioned for some larvae. The two pair of very similar wings, which are usually longer than the abdomen, are held over the abdomen when not in use. The legs are well-developed. Some species have raptorial front legs resembling those of the preying mantids. The abdomen of the adult is without cerci, although claspers, ovipositors, hair pencils, and other modifications may be present. (See Fig. 23.2 for general body features of the male.)

The larvae are very different in appearance from the adult, being of various shapes from short and oval to elongate. (See Fig. 23.3 for dorsal view of the head.) They are somewhat flattened. The abdomen of the larvae of Megaloptera have a terminal pair of prolegs. The mature larvae form pupae. Those of Megaloptera form in the ground under a stone or log. In a few species, they are attached to leaves. The last instar larva of Planipennia spins a light cocoon of silk as a pupation chamber. The adults either emerge from the pupa cell in a couple of weeks or remain as pupae over the winter.

Neuroptera may be confused with several other groups of insects. Some of them resemble Dragonflies, as already mentioned but are easily distinguished by their long antennae and type of wing venation. Others may be confused with Stoneflies, but the latter are much flatter and their leg attachments are widely separated and have three tarsomeres. The mouthparts quickly distinguish Neuroptera from any of the Homoptera they may resemble because the latter have long piercing-sucking

mouthparts that are directed backward between the front legs. The short antennae and type of wing venation distinguish the raptorial species from the Mantids. Caddisfly adults have hairy wings and fewer cross veins, which should keep them from being confused with most Neuroptera.

Metamorphosis: Holometabolous, with egg, larvae, pupae, and adult stages.

Habits and habitats: The methods of feeding and types of food vary greatly throughout this order. Sialidae adults may be found on shore plants beside slowly flowing water near their larval habitat. Both stages are predacious, the adults feeding on small insects that alight nearby. As previously mentioned, adult Corydalidae usually frequent lights at night. Sisyridae, the Spongilla flies, inhabit only freshwater lakes, the habitat of their hosts, the freshwater sponges. Adults are rare but may be obtained by rearing the larvae on sponges. The strange snakeflies—of very ancient origin, known from fossils as far back, perhaps, as the Carboniferous period—stalk prey in much the same manner as a snake. When an insect is within reach, the snakefly suddenly flexes its long neck and, with open jaws, seizes it. Their larvae, which hatch from eggs laid under bark, have a similar neck and feed in much the same manner. They either live under the bark or in tunnels of wood-borer insects. The larvae of the remaining families are terrestrial and prey on a wide variety of insects and other invertebrates. Those of the antlions (Myrmeleontidae, *Myrmeleon* spp.) are well-known for their sand traps and frequently capture ants that fall into them. The larvae of Chrysopidae are well known egg, aphid, and scale insect feeders and are sometimes used for the biological control of certain crop pests. The larvae of both Chrysopidae and Hemerobiidae often feed on aphids and are sometimes called aphidlions.

Reproductive behavior: The large mandibles of the male Dobsonfly are used to "capture" females as part of the mating behavior. Ascalaphidae males, whose flight resembles that of damselflies, further enhance this ritual by capturing a female in flight and holding her much as the male damselfly does.

Collecting and preserving: A number of species are attracted to lights at night, but since they do not fly very far, collecting lights must be placed in a variety of habitats to get representative species. Beating vegetation will yield some of the less common species. The best way to preserve these insects is by pinning them with their wings set on a spreading board as is done with moths and butterflies. Some may be safely stored in 80-percent alcohol prior to mounting but this is not recommended for Planipennia. Larvae are best preserved in 80-percent alcohol.

Economic importance: The predacious habits of the

Fig. 23.4. (*Courtesy of Dwight Kuhn and* Insect World Digest)

Fig. 23.5. (*Courtesy of Dwight Kuhn and* Insect World Digest)

members of this order make them of considerable interest to specialists in biological control. Some species are being mass reared and released in crop fields to control small insect pests such as aphids (see larva feeding on aphid in Fig. 23.4). The unassessed value of the group as a whole in keeping down phytophagous insect populations is undoubtedly very great.

Rearing: Some species, such as many Chrysopidae, may be reared in the larval stage on the eggs of moths. Both the eggs of Lacewings and the eggs of grain pest moths may be obtained from commercial sources. Interesting experiments may be conducted to determine the effect that the introduction of predators has on the populations of the stored grain pests. Quantitative results may be obtained by making grid counts of the eggs of the prey and introducing a known number of Lacewing eggs (Since these are on long stalks as shown in Fig. 23.5, they may be easily counted). Aquatic species may be reared in much the same manner as stoneflies or dragonflies.

Distribution: The most recent count indicates that there are approximately 4,670 species in the world. They occur in almost all regions, from tropical rain forests, to deserts, to temperate and even Arctic areas. The 349 species in 61 genera that live in North America have not been as well studied as one might expect, considering the small number of species involved and the relatively large size of many of the species. However, recent interest in the order may result in more comprehensive revisions than have been attempted of late.

CLASSIFICATION

The various families are easy to recognize, as shown by Table 23.1 and the accompanying key to the three suborders—Megaloptera, Raphidiodea, and Planipennia. The literature needed to make identifications to species is not readily available, but discussion that follows includes keys to most of the genera that occur in the U.S. and Canada.

Key to the Suborders of Neuroptera*

1. Hind wings broad at base (see Fig. 23.7), usually distinctly larger than the front wings, and with enlarged anal area; longitudinal veins, as a rule, not forked at tips; pronotum subquadrate in dorsal view; larvae aquatic, with biting mouthparts and labrum distinct, maxillary palpi present, and abdomen with lateral filaments. (Suborder) **MEGALOPTERA**
Hind wings narrow at base (see Fig. 23.15), small, not distinctly larger than front wings; longitudinal veins forked at tip, or if not, then either venation is greatly reduced and wings covered with whitish powder or pronotum is elongate; larvae terrestrial, with sucking mandibles, or if aquatic (Sisyridae), associated with fresh water sponges, and lateral filaments absent *2*

2(1). Prothorax elongate and cylindrical (as long as, or longer than, meso- and metathorax combined) and front legs simple; larvae terrestrial with biting mouthparts; labrum distinct; maxillary palpi present. (Suborder) **RAPHIDIODEA**
Prothorax short, not as long as meso- and metathorax combined, or if so (Mantispidae), then front legs raptorial; larvae terrestrial or aquatic; labrum absent or fused with head capsule; mandible and maxilla interlocked to form sucking tube; maxillary palpi absent (if aquatic, see Sisyridae). (Suborder) **PLANIPENNIA**

*Suborders often treated as separate orders.

Table 23.1 Family Features of the Neuroptera

Family	Ocelli	Antennae	Prothorax	Wings
Suborder Megaloptera				
1. Sialidae	Absent	Long, filiform	Broad	Hind wings broader than front wings
2. Corydalidae	Present	Long, filiform, serrate or pectinate	Broad	Hind wings broader than front wings
Suborder Raphidiodea				
3. Raphidiidae	Present	Moderate	Long	With stigma; cross vein at basal side of stigma
4. Inocellidae	Absent	Moderately long, filiform	Long	With stigma; no cross vein at basal side of stigma
Suborder Planipennia				
5. Coniopterygidae	Absent	Long, filiform	Broad	Few veins and cross veins; powdery scales
6. Ithonidae	Absent	Long, filiform	Broad	Front wing with Sc separate from R apically
7. Mantispidae	Absent	Short, stout	Long, front legs raptorial	With few cross veins, including costal region
8. Hemerobiidae	Absent	Long, filiform	Broad	Broad, with costal cross vein branched on front wings
9. Chrysopidae	Absent	Long, filiform	Broad	Broad, with costal cross veins unbranched; green
10. Dilaridae	Absent	Male pectinate	Broad	Front wing with basal costal cross vein straight and simple
11. Berothidae	Absent	Long, filiform	Broad	Front wing with some costal cross veins distinctly forked
12. Polystoechotidae	Absent	Long, filiform	Broad	Front wing with Sc fused to R_1 apically.
13. Sisyridae	Absent	Long, filiform	Broad	Broad, with relatively few cross veins
14. Myrmeleontidae	Absent	Moderate, clubbed	Broad	Narrow, with many cross veins and branched along margin
15. Ascalaphidae	Absent	Very long, clubbed	Broad	Narrow, relatively few branches along margin; stigma present.

Suborder MEGALOPTERA

This small group is cosmopolitan in distribution, with about 200 species in the world. The two extant families listed in the key are generally recognized. In addition, one extinct family has been described, Permosialidae, from the Upper Permian of Russia.

Key to the Families of Megaloptera

1. Ocelli absent; fourth tarsomere bilobed; submentum and gula with parallel sides; small black species; larvae with caudal segment of abdomen greatly elongated and setaceous; lateral filaments on abdomen unsegmented **1. Sialidae**

Ocelli present; fourth tarsomere simple; submentum and gula Y-shaped; large grey or black species with mottled or white-banded wings; larvae without elongated caudal segment, but with forked structures (prolegs) with prominent hooks **2. Corydalidae**

1. SIALIDAE (Alderfly Family)

The alderflies have only the following single genus in the U.S. and Canda:

1.1 *Sialis* Latreille

Twenty-three species in the U.S. and Canada, the following of which is typical:

S. infumata Newman (Smoky Alderfly). L. 13–18 mm. Wings smoky. Commonly found resting on alders near stream banks. Adults fly during May and June. (1) n.e. NA; (2) s.e. US.

2. CORYDALIDAE (Dobsonfly Family)

This family is most abundant in eastern Asia but also occurs in North and South America, Africa, Australia, and New Zealand. There are about 80 species, of which 22 in 6 genera occur in the U.S. and Canada. See the accompanying keys to the genera of adults and larvae.

Key to the Genera of Adult Corydalidae of the U.S. and Canada
(Modified from Chandler, in Usinger, 1956.)

1. Mandibles large, not concealed by labrum **2.1 Corydalus**
 Mandibles smaller, nearly covered by labrum *2*

2(1). Cell A_1 closed distally by anterior fork of vein A_2, which fuses with vein A_1 for short distance so that vein A_1 appears 3-branched; radial sector with only 3 forks; R_3 and R_4 fused for nearly ½ their length. .. *3*
 Cell A_1 closed distally by cross vein from A_1 to A_2; A_1 2-branched; radial sector with 4 to 5 forks ... *4*

3(2). Antennae of male moniliform, as long as body, with numerous erect hairs in band around each segment; R_3 and R_4 with cross vein beyond fork. **2.4 Neohermes**
 Antennae of both sexes filiform, ½ to nearly as long as body, without erect hairs; R_3 and R_4 without cross vein beyond fork **2.6 Protochauliodes**

4(2). Second anal cell not reaching fork of second anal vein; R_5 never forked; antennae either serrate or pectinate ... *5*
 Second anal cell with end closed by posterior branch of second anal vein; R_5 forked near middle; antennae filiform **2.3 Dysmicohermes**

5(4). Anterior ocellus small, rounded, more than twice its diameter from posterior ocelli; costal cells about as long as broad; fork of second anal vein well beyond cross vein between first and second anal vein; black species **2.5 Nigronia**
 Anterior ocellus large, not rounded, not twice its long diameter from others; cross vein between first and second anal vein at or beyond fork of the second; grey, mottled species .. **22. Chauliodes**

Key to the Genera of Larval Corydalidae of the U.S. and Canada
(Modified from Chandler, in Usinger, 1956.)

1. First 7 abdominal segments with large tuft of filamentous gills at base of each lateral gill process; patch of hydrofuge pile on ventral side of 9th and 10th segments **2.1 Corydalus**
 Without filamentous gills at base of lateral gill process; no hydrofuge pile on 9th and 10th segments ... *2*

2(1). Eighth abdominal segment with spiracles at end of long contractile respiratory tubes that extend well past end of terminal claws **2.2 Chauliodes**
 Eighth abdominal segment with spiracles at end of respiratory tubes too short to reach middle of 9th segment ... *3*

3(2). Spiracles of 8th abdominal segment small and anteromesad to lateral gill processes; lateral wings of submentum pointed at apex (*D. crepusculus*) **2.3 Dysmicohermes**
 Spiracles of 8th abdominal segment larger than those of anterior segments and posteromesad to lateral gill processes; lateral wings of submentum with apex emarginate ... *4*

4(3). Lateral gill processes short, ½ as wide as abdominal segments (longer in early instars); spiracle of 8th abdominal segment large, situated on short respiratory tube, about as long as wide ... **2.3 Dysmicohermes**
 Lateral gill processes longer, at least as long as width of abdominal segments; spiracles of 8th segment smaller ... *5*

5(4). Spiracles of 8th abdominal segment at end of a short, tapered respiratory tube, about 1½ times as long as wide; clypeus narrower than base of vertex where joined **2.5 Nigronia**
 Spiracles of 8th abdominal segment on posterior edge of 8th segment without respiratory tube; clypeus as wide as base of vertex **2.4 Neohermes** and **2.6 Protochauliodes**

The dobsonflies, or fishflies as they are sometimes called, are divided into six genera, as follows.

Subfamily Corydalinae

2.1 *Corydalus* Latreille

The two species of this genus have the hind corners of the head sharply angled, for example:

C. cornutus Linnaeus (Dobsonfly). L. 100–140 mm. Dull grey; mandibles of male about half length of body; female with short mandibles. Larvae, called Hellgrammites, make good bass bait. Adults fly in July and August. (See Fig. 23.6 for head of the male) (1) n.e. NA: (2) s.e. US.

Subfamily Chauliodinae

2.2 *Chauliodes* Latreille

Two species, known as fishflies. Brownish gray with white spots or bands and with serrate or pectinate antennae; hind corners of the head rounded.

C. rastiicornis Rambur (Fishfly). L. 30–50 mm. Wings pale; antennae pectinate. Adults fly May to July near lakes and large streams. Common. (1) n.e. NA; (2) s.e. US.

[2.3 *Dysmicohermes* Munroe (5 spp.); 2.4 *Neohermes* Banks (5 spp.)]

2.5 *Nigronia* Banks

Two species, the following being an example:

N. serricornis (Say) (Dark Fishfly). L. 20–30 mm. Wings blackish with white markings; antennae serrate. Uncommon. (See Fig. 23.7.) (1) n.e. US; (2) s.e. US.

[2.6 *Protochauliodes* Van derWeele (6 spp.)]

Suborder RAPHIDIODEA

The snakeflies, as the members of this group are popularly known, are among the most peculiar of the Neuroptera. They are primarily Holarctic in distribution, with a few representatives in Mexico. They are entirely absent, so far as present information indicates, from the Ethiopian and Australian Regions. In North America, they are confined to the area west of the eastern slopes of the Rocky Mountains. Of the eight known fossil families, the Permoraphidiidae comes from the Lower Permian of Kansas and the Alloraphidiidae from the Cretaceous of Labrador.

There is no key available to distinguish the larvae of the two families shown in the accompanying key to the families. Apparently the characters given in the Key to the Suborders of Neuroptera apply only to the family Raphidiidae.

Key to the Families of Raphidiodea of the U.S. and Canada

1. Ocelli present; front wing with pterostigma bordered proximally by a veinlet . **3. Raphidiidae**
Ocelli absent; front wing with pterostigma not bordered proximally by a veinlet . **4. Inocelliidae**

Fig. 23.6.

3. RAPHIDIIDAE (Snakefly Family)

This family contains two genera, both represented in the U.S. and Canada, with 18 species widely distributed throughout the Rocky Mountains, Great Basin, and Pacific Coast states. About 5 species of the Miocene are known from the Florissant shales in Colorado.

3.1 *Raphidia* Linnaeus

Fourteen species, including the following:

R. adnixa (Hagen). L. 12–14 mm. Wings clear; adults predacious; larvae predacious. Uncommon. (See Fig. 23.8.) (5) Western Mountain States.

[3.2 *Alena* Navas (4 spp.)]

4. INOCELLIIDAE (Square-headed Snakefly Family)

This family has two genera, one in the Nearctic Region and *Fibla* Navas, confined to Europe except for a fossil species of the Miocene known from the Florissant shales of Colorado.

4.1 *Inocellia* Schneider

One species, as follows:

I. inflata Hagen. (4) Pacific n.w.

Fig. 23.8.

Fig. 23.7.

Suborder PLANIPENNIA

This is the largest suborder of the Neuroptera. The larvae are all characterized by suctorial jaws composed of mandibles and maxillae, by the absence of maxillary palpi, and by the modification of the Malpighian tubules in the third instar to form silk-secreting organs. Both the larvae and adults are predacious on such insects as aphids and scale insects, and most are terrestrial.

The suborder is worldwide in distribution. The accompanying Key to the Families omits several extant families not found in the Nearctic Region, namely, Nemopteridae, Psychopsidae, Osmylidae, Neurorthidae, and Nymphidae. Several fossil families have also been omitted.

Key to the Major Families of Planipennia of the U.S. and Canada

1. Wings covered with whitish powder; veins and cross veins few in number, radial sector at most only forked; very small (wingspan 3–10 mm); slender, pale-colored **5. Coniopterygidae**

 Wings not covered with whitish powder; veins and cross veins usually abundant, radial sector with several branches or forks *2*

2(1). Prothorax more or less elongate; front legs raptorial **7. Mantispidae**

 Prothorax short; front legs simple, never raptorial *3*

3(2). Antennae at least thickly cylindrical, variable in length, usually gradually enlarged distad, or filiform and strongly clavate at apex; wings with at least disc densely and reticulately veined; Sc and R_1 coalesced apically *4*

 Antennae never thickly cylindrical enlarged toward apex, or clavate; moniliform or filiform, rarely pectinate .. *5*

4(3). Antennae short, about as long as head and thorax; wings usually with an elongate narrow cell immediately behind point of coalescence of Sc and R_1 **14. Myrmeleontidae**

 Antennae very elongate, slender, and strongly clavate apically; wings without elongate hypostigmatic cell behind point of coalescence of Sc and R_1 **15. Ascalaphidae**

5(3). Males with antennae pectinate; female with long, conspicuous ovipositor **10. Dilaridae**

 Antennae not pectinate in either sex; females without long ovipositor. *6*

6(5). Front wings with 2 or more sectors or branches arising from R_1 **8. Hemerobiidae**

 Front wings with only single radial sector, all branches of Rs arising from 4th vein ... *7*

7(6). Front wings with humeral cross vein recurrent and branched *8*

 Front wings with humeral cross vein not recurrent and simple *9*

8(7). Wings with only one discal and one marginal distinct gradate series of cross veins; costal and marginal areas with many forked veinlets; radial sector with 10 to 15 branches; wings mainly dark; rather large nocturnal species with wingspan varying from 40 to 75 mm ..**12. Polystoechotidae**

 Wings with disc provided with many irregularly arranged cross veins, not forming a gradate series and not sharply differentiated from costal and marginal area, which are without many forked veinlets; Sc and R_1 not coalesced apically; radial sector 5–6 branched; wing veins white; smaller species with wingspan under 40 mm **6. Ithonidae**

9(7). Front wings falcate, outer margin concave; costal cross veins forked ... **11. Berothidae**

 Front wings not falcate, outer margin convex; costal veins usually simple. *10*

10(9). Front wings with few elongate radial and medial cells, branching pattern dichotomous; wing margins with trichosors; small enlargement or expansion of marginal vein between veinlets present between terminations of veins; membrane with microtrichia, translucent ... **13. Sisyridae**

 Front wings with numerous polygonal radial and pseudomedial cells; trichosors absent; membrane glassy transparent, without microtrichia **9. Chrysopidae**

Key to the Major Families of Larvae of the U.S. and Canada

1. Tarsus with 2 claws .. *2*

 Tarsus with 1 claw; aquatic feeders on fresh water sponges **13. Sisyridae**

2(1). Mandibles with teeth, usually 3, along mesal margin; antennae and labial palpi very small *3*

 Mandibles without teeth on sesal margin; antennae and labial palpi conspicuous *4*

3(2). Dorsocaudal margin of head bilobed; lateral projections on thoracic and abdominal segments prominent; caudal abdominal segment somewhat cone-shaped; prothoracic and first 2 abdominal spiracles on dorsal aspect, remainder on ventral aspect; collected from trees, especially pines, low vegetation, or among stones **15. Ascalaphidae**

 Dorsocaudal margin of head not bilobed; lateral projections on thoracic and abdominal segments absent or inconspicuous; caudal segment not cone-shaped; live in dry soil, where some dig pits **14. Myrmeleontidae**

4(2). Mandibles and maxillae curved medially and usually as long or longer than head ... *7*

 Mandibles and maxillae straight and usually shorter than head *5*

Key to the Major Families of Larvae of the U.S. and Canada (*Contd.*)

5(4). Thorax much shorter than abdomen and usually not as wide **6**
Thorax as long or longer and as wide or wider than abdomen; antennae usually 2-segmented with distal segment longer than first; labial palpi prominent and apparently 3-segmented as a rule with distal segment large and clavate; body spindleshaped and bent; length under 3 mm ... **5. Coniopterygidae**

6(5). Abdomen 3 to 4 times as long as thorax; 6 or more segmented antennae with proximal and penultimate segments much longer than segments 2 to 4; empodia absent or inconspicuous on tarsi; body elongated and narrow; live under bark of fallen trees ..
.. **10. Dilaridae**
Abdomen less than 3 times length of thorax; antennae 3-segmented; distinct empodia present on all tarsi especially in 1st instar; hypermetamorphic, with first instar somewhat thysanuriform and late instars C-shaped with diameter of midabdominal segments enlarged; some live among, and on, spider eggs **7. Mantispidae**

7(4). No trumpet-shaped empodia between paired tarsal claws, except in first instar of some species ... **8. Hemerobiidae**
Distinct trumpet-shaped empodia between paired tarsal claws; setiferous tubercles (verrucae) usually present on lateral margins of most thoracic and abdominal segments
.. **9. Chrysopidae**

Superfamily CONIOPTERYGOIDEA

5. CONIOPTERYGIDAE (Dusty-Wings Family)

L. ±3 mm. Wings and body covered with whitish, powdery exudation. Antennae filiform, 16- to 43-segmented; ocelli lacking; eyes large. Eggs are laid in trees infested with aphids, scale insects, or mites, on which the larvae prey. There are 28 species in 7 genera in the U.S. and Canada, with a total of 240 species in the world. Although generally believed to be rare, they are at times rather common, if easily overlooked.

Subfamily Aleuropteryginae

Tribe Aleuropterygini

[5.1 *Aleuropteryx* Löw (3 spp., (3) s.w. US)]

Tribe Fontenelleini

[5.2 *Helicoconis* Enderlein (4 spp., (1) WI, MI, PA, ME, (3) CA); 5.3 *Neoconis* Enderlein (2 spp., (3) AZ, TX)]

Subfamily Coniopteryginae

Tribe Coniopterygini

[5.4 *Coniopteryx* Curtis (9 spp., throughout US and Canada); 5.5 *Parasemidalis* Enderlein (1 sp., *P. fuscipennis* (Reuter), (2) FL, MS; (3) AZ, CA)]

Tribe Conwentziini

5.6 *Conwentzia* Enderlein

Four species, as follows:

C. barretti (Banks). (3) CA.

C. californica Meinander. (3) AZ, CA; (4) WA; (5) WY, CO, UT.

C. pineticola Enderlein. (1) n.e. NA; (2) VA, NC, FL.

C. psociformis (Curtis). Introduced from Europe. (1) NJ, OH.

[5.7 *Semidalis* Enderlein (5 spp.)]

Superfamily OSMYLOIDEA

6. ITHONIDAE (Mothlike Netwing Family)

L. 21–40 mm. Head small. Wings with veins many branched. Larvae subterranean, scarabaeoid. Probably vegetarians, feeding on roots in sandy soil. Only eight species known, of which only one is known in the U.S.

6.1 *Oliarces* Banks

One species, as follows:

O. clara Banks. L. 21–35 mm. Dark brown or black; wings milky, shiny; sides of thorax with tufts of black setae. Adults fly at midday in April and May. Larvae live in roots under trees or shrubs. Rare. (3) CA, AZ.

Superfamily MANTISPOIDEA

7. MANTISPIDAE (Mantislike Lacewing Family)

L. 20–35 mm. Prothorax elongate; front pair of legs modified for capturing prey, resembling those of Preying Mantis. Larvae undergo hypermetamorphosis and are parasitic on spider egg masses and predators on subterranean larvae of Scarabeidae, Noctuidae, and certain social wasps. Some adults mimic wasps. There are 18 species in the U.S., mostly in the South, and two subfamilies as indicated by the accompanying key.

Key to the Subfamilies of Mantispidae

1. Front tarsi with two terminal claws; pronotum not greatly elongate **Platymantispinae**
Front tarsi with only one terminal claw; pronotum greatly elongate **Mantispinae**

Subfamily Platymantispinae

Two genera of this subfamily are found in the U.S., each in a different tribe. The Nearctic representatives of this group are confined largely to the arid Southwest and are evidently derivatives of the Neotropical fauna there.

Key to the Genera of Platymantispinae

1. Front tibiae prolonged into a digitiform process, tarsi arising anterior to this process; front tarsi with 4 tarsomeres; front femora armed below with small denticulations (Platymantispini) .. **7.1 Plega**
 Front tibiae not prolonged into digitiform process; front tarsi with 5 tarsomeres, tarsi arising from apex of tibiae; front femora armed below with relatively large toothlike dentations (Nolimini) ... **7.2 Nolima**

Tribe **Platymantispini**

[7.1 *Plega* Navás (4 spp.)]

Tribe **Nolimini**

[7.2 *Nolima* Navás (2 spp.)]

Subfamily **Mantispinae**

This subfamily is represented by four genera in the Nearctic Region, as indicated by the accompanying key. The species are scattered throughout the U.S., some Neotropical in origin and others with their closest affinities in the Old World.

Key to the Genera of Mantispinae of the U.S. and Canada

1. Wings with radial cells long and narrow, particularly basal 2; pronotum with neither strong transverse rugae or sudden and strong constrictions, or both **2**
 Wings with radial cells not long and narrow, basal 2 relatively broad; pronotum without either strong transverse rugae or sudden constrictions **3**
2(1). Pronotum with strong transverse rugae and prominent but flattened pronotal tubercles; wings with anterior protion not fuscous and with pterostigma thickened **7.6 Entanoneura**
 Pronotum with abrupt and strong constrictions but without strong transverse rugae; pronotal tubercles low and rounded; wings with anterior portion fuscous, pterostigma not greatly thickened ... **7.5 Climaciella**
3(1). Pronotum with evident transverse rugae, but without short, stiff setae. **7.4 Mantispa**
 Pronotum without evident transverse rugae, but with short, stiff setae ... **7.3 Mantispilla**

Fig. 23.9.

[7.3 *Mantispilla* Enderlein (2 spp.)]

7.4 *Mantispa* Illiger

Six species, including the following:

M. interrupta Say. (See Fig. 23.9.) (1) n.e. U.S.

7.5 *Climaciella* Enderlein

One species, as follows:

C. brunnea (Say). L. 25–30 mm. Brownish; wings clear. Adults found on vegetation; larvae parasitic on spider eggs. Rare (2) s.e. U.S.; (3) s.w. U.S.

[7.6 *Entanoneura* Enderlein (1 sp., *E. floridana* (Banks)]

Superfamily **HEMEROBIOIDEA**

8. HEMEROBIIDAE (Brown Lacewing Family)

Length: 6–12 mm. This cosmopolitan family of moderate-sized insects resemble green lacewings except for their wing color, which is brownish. Most of the 50 species recorded in the U.S. are western in distribution, but some commonly occur in the east. Adults and larvae are predacious, feeding on aphids, mealybugs, and mites. They are common inhabitants of forests. There are eight genera, as indicated by the accompanying key.

Key to the Genera of Hemerobiidae of the U.S. and Canada

1. Front wing with humeral vein recurrent .. **3**
 Front wing with humeral vein straight, not recurrent **2**
2(1). Front wing with 3 or more branches to radial sector; costal cross vein mostly forked, set closely together in pterostigmatic region; one to 3 cross veins present; hind wings never rudimentary ... **8.7 Micromus**
 Front wing with only 2 braches to radial sector; costal cross veins mostly simple, not set closely together in pterostigmatic region; about 5 cross veins between Sc and R; one complete series of gradate cross veins; hind wings often rudimentary **8.8 Psectra**
3(1). Front wing with 5 or more radial sector braches (rarely 3; see *M. minor*) **8.5 Megalomus**
 Front wing with less than 5 branches to Rs **4**

Key to the Genera of Hemerobiidae of the US. and Canada (*Contd.*)

4(3). Hind wing with MP forked well beyond origin of MA **5**

Hind wing with MP forked approximately as far out as, or slightly basal of origin of MA
.. **6**

5(4). Front wing with basal cross vein between R and M situated before or at origin of first branch of Rs; more than 5 cross veins in outer gradate series of cross veins
.. **8.1 Hemerobius**

Front wing with basal cross vein between R and MP situated at or beyond first fork of MP; only upper 4 of outer gradate series of cross veins present; Rs with only 2 or 3 branches; hind wing with no outer cross veins present **8.4 Sympherobius**

6(4). Front wing with only one accessory branch arising from Cu_1 between lowest cross vein of inner gradate series and basal cross vein connecting M with Cu_1; subcostal area with 2 cross veins in basal third and at least 1 in pterostigmatic region; Rs with 3 or 4 branches; hind wing with basal cross vein between R_1 and Rs situated beyond separation of MP from Rs ... **8.6 Boriomyia**

Front wing with several accessory branches arising from Cu_1 between lowest cross vein of inner gradate series and basal cross vein connecting M with Cu_1; subcostal area with only 1 basal and usually 1 apical cross vein; Rs with 3 or 4 branches **7**

7(6). Front wing broad, with wide costal area; Rs normally with 4 branches; hind wing with basal cross vein between R_1 and Rs situated beyond separation of MA from Rs; males with anal plates apparently triangular in lateral aspect, with acute toothed process projecting below lower margin; females with lobes of 9th sternum elongate and upturned. .. **8.3 Wesmaelius**

Front wing more elongate, with relatively narrow costal area; Rs normally with only 3 branches (rarely 4); hind wing with basal cross vein between R_1 and Rs (if present) situated before separation of MA from Rs; males with anal plates in lateral aspect more or less parallel-sided basally, and more elongate; females with lobes of ninth sternum short and rounded .. **8.2 Kimminsia**

8.1 *Hemerobius* Linnaeus

Twelve species, the following being a common example:

H. pacificus Banks. L. ±10 mm. Wings brownish; eyes dark; apical posterior margin of front wing nearly straight. (See A&J 80.) (3) TX, NM, AZ, CA; (4) OR, WA; (5) CO, WY, UT, NV.

[8.2 *Kimminsia* Killington (10 spp.); 8.3 *Wesmaelius* Kruger (1 sp., *W. longifrons* (Walker)]

8.4 *Sympherobius* Banks

This, the largest genus, has 15 species in the U.S., the most common of which appears to be the following:

S. barberi (Banks). (Barber's Brown Lacewing). L. 12–15 mm. Brown. Front wings spotted with gray; each with a recurrent humeral vein, not more than four outer gradate cross veins, and radial cross vein absent. (2) s.e. US; (3) TX, NM, AZ.

[28.5 *Megalomus* Rambur (4 spp.); 8.6 *Boriomyia* Banks (2 spp.); 8.7 *Micromus* Rembur (5 spp.); 8.8 *Psectra* Hagen (1 sp., *P. diptera* (Burmeister)]

9. CHRYSOPIDAE (Green Lacewing Family)

L. 10–25 mm. Body and wings green, rarely brown; wings transparent; eyes sometimes golden. These well-known insects are now reared commercially for the biological control of aphids. The adults and larvae of some are predacious; others are nectar or pollen feeders. The group has a world-wide distribution except that no indigenous species appear to be present in New Zealand. There are 87 species in 13 genera recorded from the U.S. and Canada. Identification of some genera is difficult and depends upon genitalic disection; these are not included in the accompanying Key.

Key to Common Genera of Chrysopidae of the U.S. and Canada

1. Front wing (Fig. 23.10) with median loop (MP_{3+4}) joining cross vein instead of MP_{1+2}; cell 1st M_2 equal or subequal to cell 1st M_4 .. **2**

Front wing with median loop (MP_{3+4}) joining MP_{1+2} and enclosing a small elongate cell (1st M_2), which is only about ½ or less, size of 1st M_4 **3**

2(1). Wings with veinlets on outer and posterior margins forked; green species.
.. **9.2 Leucochrysa**

Wings with veinlets on outer and posterior margins mostly simple; dark brown species with salmon or orange markings; 14 mm or more in length **9.1 Nothochrysa**

3(1). Front wings with gradate series consisting of only a few veins, usually 3 to 5 brown cross veins; hind wings with only 1 series of gradate cross veins; predominantly brown or reddish brown in color, with wing veins spotted with brown; small species, 10–14 mm in length.
.. **9.8 Eremochrysa**

Front wings with gradate series consisting of more cross veins (from 4 to 9) and green or brown in color; hind wings with 2 series of gradate cross veins; predominantly green in color (various yellowish or reddish discolorations frequent; but specimens rarely as dark brown as preceeding species); large species, 13–18 mm in length. **4**

Key to Common Genera of Chrysopidae of the U.S. and Canada (*Contd.*)

4(3). Antennae with bases distant from one another, separated by as much as width of basal segment and often outwardly bowed; males usually with front provided with interantennal protuberance bearing a tuft of brown setae apically, or with face frequently sunken or concave below antennae .. **9.3 Meleoma**

Antennae spproximate at base, not as widely separated as preceding species and not markedly bowed outwardly; males without interantennal protuberance on front, or front concave below antennae .. **5**

5(4). Antennae much longer than wings; pterostigma with brown dot**9.4 Nodita**

Antennae shorter, or only slightly longer, than wings; pterostigma without brown dot .. **9.5 Chrysopa**

[9.1 *Nothochrysa* McLachlan (1 sp., *N. californica* Banks); 9.2 *Leucochrysa* Banks (2 spp.); 9.3 *Meleoma* Fitch (9 spp.); 9.4 *Nodita* Navás (7 spp.); 9.5 *Nacarina* Navás (1 sp.); 9.6 *Nineta* Navás (2 spp.); 9.7 *Suarius* Navás (4 spp.); 9.8 *Mallada* Navás (4 spp.)]

9.9 *Chrysopa* Leach

This, the largest genus of the family, is divided into two subgenera (sometimes treated as genera): *Chrysoperla* Steinman (16 spp.) and *Chrysopa* s. str. (19 spp.). The best known species follow:

C. (*Chrysopa*) *oculata* Say. (Golden-eye Lacewing). L. 15–22 mm. Green, with pale green wings (see Fig. 23.10); eyes golden. Adults are found on foliage and come to lights at night. Eggs are held upright on long stalks attached to leaves. Adults fly May to September. (1) n.e. NA; (2) s.e. US; (3) CA, OK, TX; (4) WA, OR; (5) ND, MN, SD, NE, IA, KS, MO.

C. (*Chrysoperla*) *carneia* Stephens. L. 15–22 mm. Similar to the preceding with pale green wing veins and golden eyes but distinguishable absence of black band on vertex of head. This species is more widespread than the former, being found throughout North America and in many other parts of the world (See A&J 78.)

[9.10 *Abachrysa* Banks (1 sp., *A. eureka* Banks)); 9.11 *Chrysopiella* Banks (4 spp.); 9.12 *Eremochrysa* Banks: Two subgenera: *Eremochrysa* s. str. (7 spp.) and *Lolochrysa* Banks (6 spp.); 9.13 Pimachrysa Adams (4 spp.)]

Superfamily BEROTHOIDEA

10. DILARIDAE (Pleasing Lacewing Family)

Male antennae pectinate; female ovipositor protruding. Larvae live under bark of dead trees and probably feed on beetle eggs and larvae. Their eggs are not stalked. The only two species of this family in the Nearctic fauna are exceedingly rare; there are several Old World genera and species.

10.1 *Nallachius* Navas

Two species, including the following:

N. americanus (McLachlan). (2) KY, VA.

11. BEROTHIDAE (Beaded Lacewing Family)

Representatives of the Berothidae are present in every region of the world. The Nearctic Region has 10 rare and poorly known species. The females have enlarged scales on the thorax and hind wings.

11.1 *Lomamyia* Banks

Ten species, including the following:

L. flavicornis Walker. Widely distributed in the eastern part of U.S. (Fig. 23.11).

L. texana Banks. Known from (3) s.w. US.

12. POLYSTOECHOTIDAE (Giant Lacewing Family)

The relatively large size (L. 35–75 mm) and characteristic venation immediately differentiate the members of this family from all other North American Planipennia. The disc of the wing is provided with only one distinct and simple gradate series of cross veins, this being distinct from the costal and marginal areas, which have many forked veinlets. The larvae are terrestrial and predacious. These rare nocturnal insects are confined entirely to the New World; only the following two species occur in the U.S.

[13.1 *Polystoechotes* Burmeister (1 sp., *P. punctatus* [Fabricius], (3) CA); 13.2 *Platystoechotes* Carpenter (1 sp., *P. lineatus* Carpenter)]

13. SISYRIDAE (Spongillafly Family)

L. 6–8 mm. These small insects resemble brown lacewings. Adults are found near lakes, on wharves or nearby vegetation; larvae live in and feed upon the fresh water sponge, *Spongilla fragilis*, among others. Two genera, each with three species, are

Fig. 23.10.

Fig. 23.11.

distributed throughout the eastern U.S. and the Pacific Northwest (two records from California) in and near lakes and streams harboring the fresh water sponge.

[13.1 *Climacia* McLachlan (3 spp.)]

13.2 *Sisyra* Burmeister

Three species, of which the following is common:

S. vicaria Walker (Common Spongefly). L. 6–8 mm. Common in lakes. (1) n.e. US.

Superfamily MYRMELEONTOIDEA

14. MYRMELEONTIDAE (Antlion Family)

This family, the dominant one of the order, is probably better known from its familiar larval forms, called antlions, rather than from the slender, delicate adult lacewing. It reaches its optimum development in the more arid areas throughout the world. Most species are nocturnal or crepuscular and frequently come to UV lights at night.

These large insects (40–80 mm) not only resemble damselflies but fly as feebly as the latter. They are easily distinguished by their prominent, clubbed, and short (about the length of head and thorax) antennae; wings are transparent or mottled with brown or black. The larvae are voracious predators that hide under bits of debris in woods and attack passing insects. Some are called doodlebugs. In sandy regions, some species dig

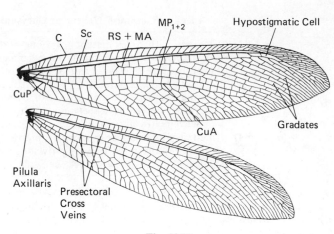

Fig. 23.12.

a shallow cone-shaped pit and wait at its bottom for an ant (hence their common name) to slip on the loose sand and fall in, only to be immediately devoured.

The family consists of four distinct subfamilies (one of which, the Palparinae, does not occur in the New World) with nearly a dozen tribes (a number of which are absent in the Nearctic Region). Since the Nearctic fauna (79 species in 13 genera) is chiefly a northward extension of the Neotropical fauna, the southwestern states contain the greatest number of genera and species found in the U.S. and Canada.

Key to the Subfamilies of Myrmeleontidae of the U.S. and Canada

1. Hind femur with an elongate sense hair near base; male with a dorsal, eversible, and long-haired sac at anterolateral margin of intersegmental membrane between abdominal segments 6 and 7; pretarsal claws strongly arched near base **Acanthaclisinae**
 Hind femur without an elongate sense hair; male without eversible sac between abdominal segments 6 and 7; pretarsal claws nearly straight *2*

2(1). Hind wing with 4 or more presectoral cross veins; vein 2A in front wing runs close to 1A for a short distance and then bends at a sharp angle toward 3A; relative position of radial sector to cubital fork of front wing about the same as that between radial sector and medial fork in hind wing .. **Myrmeleontinae**
 Hind wing with 1 or 2 presectoral cross veins (Fig. 23.12); vein 2A of front wing runs in a fairly even curve and is connected to third anal by a short cross vein or connected to it for a short distance; relative position of radial sector to cubital fork of front wing usually different from that between radial sector and medial fork in hind wing
 .. **Dendroleontinae**

Subfamily Dendroleontinae

The most primitive representatives of the Nearctic Myrmeleontids are referable to this subfamily. The venational characteristics of the members of this group are far less constant than those of the other two subfamilies. The group is essentially American;

only a few species are known in Europe and Asia, and possibly in South America, although several striking species of the typical tribe occur in Australia. The subfamily is divisible into three tribes, distinguishable able by means of the accompanying Key.

Key to the Tribes of the Subfamily Dendroleontinae of the U.S. and Canada

1. Vein 2A of front wing runs in a fairly even curve toward 3A; pilula axillaris—a small, stalked tuft of setae located basal to vein 3A (see Fig. 23.12)—often present in male *2*
 Vein 2A of front wing runs close to vein 1A for a short distance and then bends at sharp angle toward 3A; pilula axillaris absent **Glenurini**

2(1). Tibial spurs as long as front coxa; male 9th sternite divided **Dendroleontini**
 Tibial spurs much shorter than front coxa; male 9th sternite not divided
 .. **Brachynemurini**

Tribe Dendroleontini

The tribe has only one genus in the Nearctic Region, with two species.

14.1 *Dendroleon* Brauer

Of the two species, the following is well-known:

D. obsoletus (Say). (Spottedwinged Antlion).

Tribe **Brachynemurini**

The majority of the North American species are referable to this tribe, which has four genera, as indicated by the accompanying Key.

Key to the Genera of the Tribe Brachynemurini of the U.S. and Canada

1. Tibial spurs present, or CuA of hind wing runs along the posterior branch of MP$_2$ for a short distance ... **2**
 Tibial spurs absent; CuA of hind wing bends to hind margin near medial fork **3**
2(1). Wings narrow with relatively sparse venation; legs short and relatively thick, with front femur less than 1.5 times longer than front coxa **14.3 Gnopholeon**
 Wings broader with denser venation; legs longer and relatively slender, with front femur over 1.5 times longer than front coxa. **14.2 Brachynemurus**
3(1). Wings narrow with relatively sparse venation **14.5. Tyttholeon**
 Wings broad with denser venation **14.4 Menkeleon**

14.2 *Brachynemurus* Hagen

This, the largest genus of the tribe, has 50 closely similar species. The Nearctic species are divided into several groups (see Stange, 1970). The following are typical of the genus:

B. ferox (Walker). L. 30–43 mm. Adults brownish gray to gray; body dark; tibial spurs very evident, equal to the basal tarsomere of the hind legs or the basal 2 tarsomeres of the middle leg and front leg; distal tarsomere longer than the basal 3 tarsomeres. (See A&J 79.) (3) CA, AZ, NM; (4) OR; (5) UT, WY.

B. nebulosus (Olivier). L. 18–34 mm. Similar to preceding, with tibial spurs absent (See Fig. 23.13.) (1) WI, NY, IL, OH, PA, NJ; (2) NC, LA, GA, FL; (3) OK, TX; (5) MN, NE.

[14.3 *Gnopholeon* Stange (2 spp.); 14.4 *Menkeleon* Stange (1 sp., *M. bellula* (Banks)); 14.5 *Tyttholeon* Adams (1 sp., *T. puerilis* Adams)]

Fig. 23.13.

Tribe **Glenurini**

In the Nearctic Region, this tribe is represented by four very distinct genera, as indicated in the accompanying Key. Several other tribes occur in the tropics.

Key to the Genera of the Tribe Glenurini of the U.S. and Canada

1. Legs very slender, femora cylindrical, front femur about twice as long as front coxae, and longer than height of thorax; pronotum usually longer than broad **2**
 Legs not particularly slender, femora somewhat thickened, front femur less than twice as long as front coxa, and not longer than height of thorax; pronotum usually broader than long ... **3**
2(1). Hind wings with large dark spot near apex, and broadest at or beyond rhegma, a small area in the front wing where small branches of Rs + MA, MP, and CuA curve together beneath the stigma .. **14.8 Glenurus**
 Hind wings without large spot, and broadest somewhat before rhegma
 ... **14.9 Eremoleon**
3(1). Front wing with 2 series of costal cells for part way; venation dense and irregular
 ... **14.7 Puren**
 Front wing with only 1 series of costal cells; venation open and regular.
 ... **14.6 Psammoleon**

[14.6 *Psammoleon* Banks (5 spp.); 14.7 *Puren* Navás (1 sp., *P. inscriptus* [Hagen]; 14.8 *Glenurus* Hagen (3 spp.); 14.9 *Eremoleon* Banks (2 spp.)]

Subfamily **Myrmeleontinae**

This, the most specialized subfamily, contains only the nominate genus.

Tribe **Myrmeleontini**

[14.10 *Myrmeleon* Linnaeus (7 spp.)]

Subfamily **Acanthaclisinae**

Three genera and six species of this subfamily occur within the confines of the U.S. (see the accompanying Key).

Key to the Genera of the Subfamily Acanthaclisinae of the U.S. and Canada

1. Front wings with only one series of costal cells; apical field scarcely widened beyond stigma; labial palpi with apical segment scarcely pedicellate; tibial spurs bent at an angle
 ... **14.11 Paranthaclisis**

Key to the Genera of the Subfamily Acanthaclisinae of the U.S. and Canada (*Contd.*)

Front wings with two series of costal cells for most of length; apical field distinctly widened beyond stigma; labial palpi with apical segment long and pedicellate; tibial spurs simply curved, not bent at an angle ... **2**

2(1). Hind wings with distinct Banksian line, a prominent longitudinal line in the wing formed by the bending of the branches of MP$_2$ **14.12 Heoclisis**

Hind wings without Banksian line **14.13 Vella**

[14.11 *Paranthaclisis* Banks (3 spp.); 14.12 *Heoclisis* Navás (1 sp., *H. americana* (Drury)); 14.13 *Vella* Navas (3 spp.)]

15. ASCALAPHIDAE (Owlfly Family)

Probably the most highly developed group of the Planipennia, these are diurnal or crepuscular insects with a strong, musklike odor, and, like their analogues in the Lepidoptera, the butterflies, they have developed long knobbed antennae. In many species, the eyes are divided into two parts by a groove.

L. 40–80 mm. Antennae clubbed and nearly as long as the body but otherwise resemble those of damselflies. When at rest on small twigs, adults apply head, wings, and antennae closely to the twigs and elevate the abdomen to resemble a branch. Larvae hide under debris to prey upon other insects.

The family is divisible into three subfamilies, one of which, the Albardiinae, does not occur in the Nearctic Region, being confined wholly to Brazil. The other two groups have representatives in all, or practically all, of the faunal regions of the world (see the accompanying Key). The family is predominantly Old World, however, and only two genera and six species occur in the U.S. and Canada.

Key to the Subfamilies of Ascalaphidae of the U.S. and Canada

1. Eyes entire, not divided into 2 parts by a groove **Haplogleniinae**

Eyes divided into 2 parts by a groove **Ascalaphinae**

Fig. 23.14.

Fig. 23.15.

Subfamily Haplogleniinae

This group is represented in the Nearctic region by only one genus, as follows:

15.1 *Neuroptynx* MacClendon

Two species, including the following:

N. appendiculatus (Fabricius). (Fig. 23.14.) (3) s.w. US.

Subfamily Ascalaphinae

Representatives of one genus of this subfamily occur in the U.S. Although the range of the five species is considerably wider than that of the species of the preceding subfamily, they are nevertheless largely southern in distribution.

15.2 *Ululodes* Currie

Five species, the following of which is probably the most common:

U. arizonensis Banks. L. ±45 mm. Abdomen as long as the wings; stigma dark; wings of female with dusky patches. Often attracted to lights at night. (Fig. 23.15.) (3) s.w. US.

BIBLIOGRAPHY

Adams, P. A. 1967. A review of the Mesochysinae and Nothochrysinae (Neuroptera: Chrysopidae). *Bull Mus. Comp. Zool.* 135: 215–238.

Agnew, C. W., Sterling, W. L. and Dean, D. A. 1981. Notes on the Chrysopidae and Hemerobiidae of Eastern Texas with keys for their identification. *Suppl. Southwest. Ent.* No. 4, 20 pp.

Aspoeck, U. 1975. The present state of knowledge on the Raphidioptera of America (Insecta: Neupteriodea). *Polskie Pismo Ent.* 45: 537–546.

Banks, N. 1903. A revision of Nearctic Chrysopidae. *Trans. Ent. Soc. America.* 29: 137–162, 1 pl.

Banks, N. 1906. A revision of the Nearctic Coniopterygidae. *Proc. Ent. Soc. Washington.* 8: 77–86, pls. vi–vii.

Banks, N. 1907. Catalogue of the Neuropteriod Insects of the United States. *American Ent. Soc.,* Philadelphia. 53 pp.

Banks, N. 1927. Revision of Nearctic Myrmeleontidae. *Bull. Mus. Comp. Zool.* 68: 84 pp., 4 pls.

Belkin, J. N. 1954. Additional records of *Oliarces clara* in California and Arizona (Neuroptera, Ithonidae). *Bull. S. California Acad. Sci.* 53: 65–68.

Bram, R. A., and Bickley, W. E. 1963. The green lacewings of the genus *Chrysopa* in Maryland (Neuroptera: Chrysopidae). *Bull. Univ. Maryland Agric. Exper. Stat.* A-124. 18 pp.

Bickley, W. E., and MacLeod, E. G. 1956. A synopsis of the Nearctic Chrysopidae with a key to the genera (Neuroptera). *Proc. Ent. Soc. Washington.* 58: 177–202.

Carpenter, F. M. 1936. Revision of the Nearctic Raphidiodea (recent and fossil). *Proc. American Acad. Arts and Sci.* 71: 89–157, 25 figs., 13 text figs.

Carpenter, F. M. 1940. A revision of the Nearctic Hemerobiidae, Berothidae, Sisyridae, Polystoechotidae, and Dilaridae (Neuroptera). *Proc. American Acad. Arts and Sci.* 74: 193–280, 103 figs.

Davis, K. c. 1903. Sialididae of North and South America. *New York State Museum Bull.* 68: 442–486, pls. ii–iii.

Froeschner, R. C. 1947. Notes and keys to the Neuroptera of Missouri. *Ann. Ent. Soc. America.* 40: 123–136, 20 figs.

Gurney, A. B. 1947. Notes on Dilaridae and Berothidae, with specieal reference to the immature stages of the Nearctic genera (Neuroptera). *Psyche.* 54: 145–169, 22 figs.

Meinander, M. 1972. A revision of the family Coniopterygidae (Plannipennia). *Acta Zool. Fennica.* 136: 1–357.

Nakahara, Waro. 1965. Contribution to the knowledge of the Hemerobiidae of Western North America (Neuroptera). *Proc. United States Nat. Mus.* v. 116 (No. 3503): 205–222.

Parfin, S. I., and Gurney, A. B. 1956. The spongillaflies, with special reference to those of the western hemisphere (Sisyridae, Neuroptera). *Proc. United States Nat. Mus.* 105: 421–529, 24 figs., 3 pls.

Rehn, J. W. H. 1939. Studies in North American Mantispidae (Neuroptera). *Trans. Ent. Soc. America.* 65:237–263, 22 figs.

Stange, L. A. 1970. Revision of the ant-lion tribe Brachynemurini of North America (Neuroptera: Myrmeleontidae). *Univ. California Pub. Ent.* 55: 1–192 pp.

Tauber, C. A. 1969. Taxonomy and biology of the lacewing genus *Meleoma* (Neuroptera: Chrysopidae). *Univ. California Pub. Ent.* 58: 1–94.

Order 24

COLEOPTERA

(Beetles, Weevils, and Stylopids)

This, the largest order of the animal kingdom, has approximately as many species as the entire plant kingdom, including the algae and fungi. The number of species, however, is only a part of the story of this remarkable order. There is almost as much diversity in several of the larger families of beetles as is found in the entirety of most other orders. Beetles occupy all terrestrial and fresh water habitats; some are ectoparasitic (a few of them are occasionally found in the lower digestive tract of higher animals); some are endoparasites of other insects as larvae and as adult females. It is their ability to occupy the gamut of terrestrial and fresh water ecological niches that accounts for their diversity.

Their name, Coleoptera (Greek, *koleos,* meaning "sheath," and *pteron,* meaning "wing"), refers to the formation of the front pair of wings into hardened wing covers under which the hind pair of wings are folded when not in use. This one feature—which affords protection through the hard cover, on the one hand; and the ability to fold the flying wings, on the other—may be the major reason for their successful evolution throughout past geological ages.

Besides this feature, most species have developed the ability to crawl into almost all known habitats. Actually, the wings are used much less often than those of most other flying insects. Although their primary function is to provide rapid transit from place to place as with other species, they have the added feature of combining distance with powers of penetration. Wingless species cannot move rapidly over great distances; other winged insects are hampered by the delicate nature of their wings. One might compare the airplane and the automobile; combine the two and call the results a beetle.

Diagnosis: L. 0.025 to 150 mm, usually 2 to 20 mm. Body usually hard, but may be leathery, frequently elongate, cylindrical, hemispherical, or slightly to extremely flattened. (See Fig. 24.1 for general body regions of the adult.) The females of some species resemble larvae rather than adults. A very large number of species are black or dark brown, but certain groups—particularly leaf beetles, longhorn beetles, ladybugs, and a few other families—have many brightly colored species. The colors are usually red or yellow, but many are marked with blue or green. The head is usually short except for the weevils and some

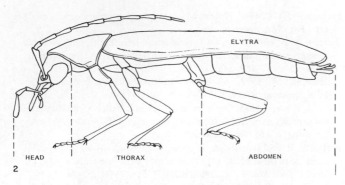

Fig. 24.1. General body form of adult beetle.

Fig. 24.3. Head, ventral view: (Ge) gena, (g.s.) gular suture, (Gu) gula, (Lb) labium, (Md) mandible, and (Mx) maxilla.

species of certain other families, whose heads are elongated into a snout, sometimes extremely so. The antennae have various shapes that are useful as identification features (See Fig. 24.2) Usually, they are composed of a scape—or basal segment—a pedicel—or second segment—and flagellomeres—the following nine units. Generally, however, they are referred to in the literature as basically eleven-segmented, it being understood that the apical units are not true segments. The number of apical units may be greatly increased in a few groups such as certain Cerambycidae, or it may be reduced.

The mouthparts are almost always of the biting type with well-developed mandibles (See Fig. 24.3), but some rare species in the Australian region have piercing-sucking mouthparts. Sometimes certain parts that are elongate for sucking nectar resemble the mouthparts of moths, but the mandibles are always retained and are functional. The elytra are modified front, or mesothoracic, wings that cover, or at least partly cover, the abdomen; they meet at the center and usually do not overlap. The flight wings—metathoracic wings—are almost always folded under the elytra when not in use. The folding is not random; on the contrary, it is uniform and specific for each family, but varies, as does the wing venation, from family to family. Beetle legs are modified in many different ways—for

digging, swimming, running, grasping, not to mention other activities. Their various characteristics are useful for identification of families and sometimes genera. The number of tarsomeres (Fig. 24.4) varies from family to family (see the section on Identification). The abdomen of most species is covered by the elytra except during flight. Some groups (for example, the Staphylinidae) have shortened elytra that leave the abdomen exposed. Beetles do not have cerci; their copulatory apparatus is withdrawn into the abdomen and not normally visible.

The larvae are of various shapes and have biting mouthparts. Although their abdomen lacks prolegs, ambulatory tubercles in some species assist locomotion. Many larvae have terminal abdominal cercilike structures, which are sometimes developed into pinchers. Usually, the thoracic legs are well developed, but in some species—especially the wood boring types—they are reduced or absent. The pupae are very poorly known.

Beetles are easily distinguished from other orders of insects by their elytra. Although earwigs may be confused with some Staphylinidae, earwigs have large forceps (cerci) at the end of the abdomen, and these are always lacking in adult beetles. A few of the Hemiptera resemble beetles in shape and in the hardening of the front wings or by the extension of the

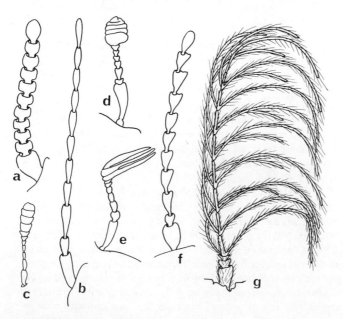

Fig. 24.2. Antennae: (a) moniliform, (b) filiform, (c) clavate, (d) capitate, (e) lamellate, (f) serrate, and (g) plumose.

Fig. 24.4. Tasi: (a) pentamerous tarsus, (b) dorsal view of pseudo-pentamerous tarsus, (c) lateral view of pseudopentamerous tarsus, and (e) tarsus fitted for swimming.

scutellum over the abdomen, but the sucking mouthparts of the Hemiptera easily distinguish the two groups. Cockroaches at first glance might be confused with beetles, but their wings differ considerably from the beetle elytra and their hind wings do not fold.

Metamorphosis: Holometabolous, with eggs of various sizes and shapes, a series of larval instars, pupae, and completely transformed (except for a few larviform females) adults.

Habits and habitats: Beetle larvae and most adults consume large amounts of food because of their relatively high metabolic rate. Larvae are found in soil from deep in the ground to near the surface where they feed either on living plant tissue (roots) or dead plant material and occasionally on animal inhabitants. They also bore into all parts of living plants and into dead wood and feed upon all kinds of stored organic material, including seeds, flowers, clothing, and meat products. Some of them are carnivorous and live in humus and forest litter where they attack and consume other insects and various terrestrial invertebrates. Still others inhabit the nests of insects, birds, and mammals, including the houses and buildings of man.

Adults usually live above ground, but many species live under bark and a number of them bore into wood. They visit flowers and feed upon nectar and pollen or the flower itself. In fact, a large part of the evolution of flower parts is the result of beetle activity during the early history of floral evolution. A large number of species are leaf feeders, and a few are ectoparasites (a few rare cases of rectal parasitism have been reported). The larvae of Meloidea, and the adult females of Stylopidae are endoparasites of other insects. The very large number of species that are scavengers—feeding on fecal material, carrion, or decaying vegetable matter—are an important factor in the detritus cycle. Several groups are aquatic both as larvae and as adults, some of them carnivorous and others plant eaters.

Reproductive behavior: Compared to those of other groups of insects the courtship and egg-laying habits of beetles have received relatively little attention. It is known that many species have courtship sequences prior to copulation, some of them using their antennae in various ways to sense the presence of the other and even to flog one another in various sequences. As a rule, the male mounts the back of the female and, to make her accept him, frequently nips at the back of her head. The use of pheromones in sex attraction has been reported in a number of groups. Many families of beetles have mating calls produced by the stridulation of various parts. In a few groups, the call is rather highly developed, but since its invariably low-intensity sound ranges into very high frequencies—usually above the human auditory range—it often goes unnoticed by the entomologist. Egg laying habits vary, of course, with the food requirements of the larvae. In general, eggs are deposited in cracks and crevices but also in plant stems, flowers, and elsewhere.

Collecting and preserving: Beetles may be collected almost anywhere. They are attracted in large numbers to UV lights at night. Beating vegetation, including bushes and trees, yields many kinds. Carrion, dung, decaying vegetation, and aquatic habitats also offer many representatives. Most species can be killed in cyanide jars, but weevils in particular seem to resist that deadly gas. Although ethyl acetate sometimes causes slight color changes, it may be used safely. Isopropyl alcohol is suitable for all species, but large specimens so treated may turn greasy when they dry. Beetles may be stored indefinitely in alcohol, but they

are more easily studied (except for very small specimens) when they are mounted on insect pins and arranged boxes or trays. By virtue of the number of species, they are the dominant part of any collection and are probably the easiest of any of the insect orders to prepare properly for display and study.

Rearing: Beetles may be reared in much the same way as Lepidoptera. Plant feeding groups must be supplied, of course, with the proper vegetable matter. Wood boring beetles will eventually emerge from wood sections stored for long periods of time, sometimes after several years. Although aquatic species are difficult to rear, the same techniques used for other aquatic insects will yield some specimens. The easiest to rear are the species that infest stored products. Flour beetles—the Tenebrionid genus *Tribolium*, for example—are raised routinely for genetic studies. The techniques for doing so have been published.

Distribution: Approximately 290,000 species of beetles have been described and catalogued, and many new species are added to the list each year. The 23,701 species and 3145 genera in the U.S. and Canada comprise about 30 percent of all insect species recorded in the region.

Notes on identification: To make identifications even to family, a careful study of the antennae and legs is necessary. The various types of both these parts are described in detail in the keys and tables. The number of tarsomeres on each leg is an important feature since it varies from group to group, although never exceeding five. The size and shape of each tarsomere provides additional identification features. Keys, tables, and descriptions include a formula that indicates the number of tarsomeres on each pair of legs. Thus, the numbers 5-5-5, in that order, indicate that the front, middle, and hind legs have five tarsomeres apiece. Another common formula for beetle tarsi, 5-5-4, is termed *heteromerous*. Although the formula for leaf beetles would appear at first sight to be 4-4-4, close examination shows that a very small fourth segment is concealed within the base of the cordate (heart-shaped) third segment; the correct formula is therefore 5-5-5. Each feature must be examined very carefully for accurate keying. When specimens are pinned, it is important to arrange the legs in a position that allows the parts to be counted easily. The antennae also must be free of obstruction. Some species have special grooves under the head into which their antennae are placed for protection when not in use. To ensure that the antennae dry in a position that permits them to be seen, they must be teased out while the beetle is still fresh or relaxed.

Economic importance: A considerable number of beetles (but fewer perhaps than the Lepidoptera) are crop pests, their total annual damage costing growers and distributers billions of dollars. Not only do they damage plants during the growing season, but certain species infest stored produce in warehouses and homes. Many species are pests of forest trees, some spreading fungus and viral plant diseases. Often unnoticed, however, is the beneficial effect they have in the detritus cycle as mentioned above. Beetles considered to be pests are singled out in the text that follows.

CLASSIFICATION

The tremendous number of species of beetles tends to overwhelm one even when trying to identify them only to family. The accompanying key is broken into sections to try to simplify its use. It should be helpful to know that certain families are

much more commonly collected than others. If these large families are recognized, much time can be saved in making identifications. Once their characteristics have been learned, it is fairly easy to eliminate a lot of keying. The twelve most common and species-abundant families are the following: 4. *Carabidae,* 24. *Staphylinidae,* 30. *Scarbaeidae,* 46. *Buprestidae,* 48. *Elateridae,* 56. *Cantharidae,* 67. *Cleridae,* 80. *Coccinellidae,* 87. *Tenebrionidae,* 106. *Cerambycidae,* 107. *Chrysomelidae,* and 113. *Curulionidae.* They account for approximately 70 percent of all beetle species, including most of the economically important ones. Most of the remaining species belong to just fourteen more families, whereas the rest of them occur in 87 families.

The classification of the families in Table 24.1 is based on adult features. Some recent authors have arranged the families in accordance with features found in the larvae instead. This approach may indicate some evolutionary relationships, but in view of the practical need for identification, the author believes that the supergeneric classification should be based on adult features. Moreover, the family arrangement given here follows certain traditional arrangements that allow families to be recognized by sight. An index to the families of the U.S. and Canada by their scientific names in given in Table 24.2 and by their common names in Table 24.3.

The genera listed for each family has been revised and updated from the author's book on beetles (Arnett, 1960). In each case, the distribution is shown for the species represented if there is not one or more species found in each of the five regions of the U.S. and Canada.

Table 24.1 Classification of the Families of Coleoptera in the U.S. and Canada

Suborder ARCHOSTEMATA

 1. CUPEDIDAE (Reticulated Beetle Family)

Suborder ADEPHAGA

 2. RHYSODIDAE (Wrinkled Bark Beetle Family)
 3. CICINDELIDAE (Tiger Beetle Family)
 4. CARABIDAE (Ground Beetle Family)
 5. AMPHIZOIDAE (Trout-stream Beetle Family)
 6. HALIPLIDAE (Crawling Water Beetle Family)
 7. DYTISCIDAE (Predacious Diving Beetle Family)
 8. NOTERIDAE (Burrowing Water Beetle Family)
 9. GYRINIDAE (Whirligig Beetle Family)

Suborder MYXOPHAGA

 10. SPHAERIIDAE (Minute Bog Beetle Family)
 11. HYDROSCAPHIDAE Skiff (Beetle Family)

Suborder POLYPHAGA

 Series STAPHYLINIFORMIA

 Superfamily HYDROPHILOIDEA

 12. HYDROPHILIDAE (Water Scavenger Beetle Family)
 13. LIMNEBIIDAE (Minute Moss Beetle Family)
 14. GEORYSSIDAE (Mud-baked Beetle Family)

 Superfamily STAPHYLINOIDEA

 15. PTILIIDAE (Feather-winged Beetle Family)
 16. LIMULODIDAE (Horseshoe Crab Beetle Family)
 17. DASYCERIDAE (Minute Scavenger Beetle Family)
 18. LEPTINIDAE (Mammal Nest Beetle Family)
 19. LEIODIDAE (Round Fungus Beetle Family)
 20. SCYDMAENIDAE (Antlike Stone Beetle Family)
 21. SILPHIDAE (Carrion Beetle Family)
 22. LEPTODIRIDAE (Small Carrion Beetle Family)
 23. SCAPHIDIIDAE (Shining Fungus Beetle Family)
 24. STAPHYLINIDAE (Rove Beetle Family)
 25. PSELAPHIDAE (Antloving Beetle Family)

 Superfamily HISTEROIDEA

 26. HISTERIDAE (Clown Beetle Family)
 27. SPHAERITIDAE (False Clown Beetle Family)

 Series SCARABAEIFORMIA

 Superfamily SCARABAEOIDEA

 28. LUCANIDAE (Stag Beetle Family)
 29. PASSALIDAE (Peg or Bess Beetle Family)
 30. SCARABAEIDAE (Lamellicorn Beetle Family)

 Superfamily DASCILLOIDEA

 31. EUCINETIDAE (Plate-thigh Beetle Family)
 32. HELODIDAE (Marsh Beetle Family)
 33. CLAMBIDAE (Minute Beetle Family)
 34. DASCILLIDAE (Soft-bodied Plant Beetle Family)

 Series ELATERIFORMIA

 Superfamily BYRRHOIDEA

 35. BYRRHIDAE (Pill Beetle Family)

 Superfamily DRYOPOIDEA

 36. PSEPHENIDAE (Water Penny Beetle Family)
 37. BRACHYPSECTRIDAE (Texas Beetle Family)
 38. PTILODACTYLIDAE (Toed-winged Beetle Family)
 39. RHIPICERIDAE (Cicada Parasite Beetle Family)
 40. CALLIRHIPIDAE (Cedar Beetle Family)
 41. CHELONARIIDAE (Turtle Beetle Family)
 42. HETEROCERIDAE (Variegated Mud-loving Beetle Family)
 43. LIMNICHIDAE (Minute Marsh-loving Beetle Family)
 44. DRYOPIDAE (Long-toed Water Beetle Family)
 45. ELMIDAE (Drive or Riffle Beetle Family)

 Superfamily BUPRESTOIDEA

 46. BUPRESTIDAE (Metallic Wood-boring Beetle Family)

 Superfamily ELATEROIDEA

 47. CEBRIONIDAE (Robust Click Beetle Family)
 48. ELATERIDAE (Click Beetle Family)
 49. THROSCIDAE (False Metallic Wood-boring Beetle Family)
 50. CEROPHYTIDAE (Rare Click Beetle Family)
 51. PEROTHOPIDAE (Beech-tree Beetle Family)
 52. EUCNEMIDAE (False Click Beetle Family)

Table 24.1 (*Contd.*)

Superfamily CANTHAROIDEA

53. TELEGEUSIDAE (Long-lipped Beetle Family)
54. PHENGODIDAE (Glowworm Beetle Family)
55. LAMPYRIDAE (Firefly Beetle Family)
56. CANTHARIDAE (Soldier Beetle Family)
57. LYCIDAE (Net-winged Beetle Family)
58. MICROMALTHIDAE (Telephone-pole Beetle Family)

Series BOSTRICHIFORMIA

Superfamily DERMESTOIDEA

59. DERODONTIDAE (Tooth-necked Fungus Beetle Family)
60. NOSODENDRIDAE (Wounded-tree Beetle Family)
61. DERMESTIDAE (Skin Beetle and Larder Beetle Family)

Superfamily BOSTRICHOIDEA

62. PTINIDAE (Spider Beetle Family)
63. ANOBIIDAE (Drug-store and Death-watch Beetle Family)
64. BOSTRICHIDAE (Horned Powder-post Beetle Family)
65. LYCTIDAE (Powder-post Beetle Family)

Series CUCUJIFORMIA

Superfamily CLEROIDEA

66. TROGOSSITIDAE (Bark-gnawing Beetle Family)
67. CLERIDAE (Checkered Beetle Family)
68. MELYRIDAE (Soft-winged Flower Beetle Family)

Superfamily LYMEXYLOIDEA

69. LYMEXYLIDAE (Ship-timber Beetle Family)

Superfamily CUCUJOIDEA

70. NITIDULIDAE (Sap-feeding Beetle Family)
71. RHIZOPHAGIDAE (Root-eating Beetle Family)
72. CUCUJIDAE (Flat Bark Beetle Family)
73. SPHINDIDAE (Dry-fungus Beetle Family)
74. CRYPTOPHAGIDAE (Silken Fungus Beetle Family)
75. LANGURIIDAE (Lizard Beetle Family)
76. EROTYLIDAE (Pleasing Fungus Beetle Family)
77. PHALACRIDAE (Shining Flower Beetle Family)
78. CERYLONIDAE (Minute Bark Beetle Family)
79. CORYLOPHIDAE (Minute Fungus Beetle Family)
80. COCCINELLIDAE (Ladybird Beetle Family)

81. ENDOMYCHIDAE (Handsome Fungus Beetle Family)
82. LATHRIDIIDAE (Minute Brown Scavenger Beetle Family)
83. BIPHYLLIDAE (False Skin Beetle Family)
84. BYTURIDAE (Fruitworm Beetle Family)

Superfamily TENEBRIONOIDEA

85. MONOMMATIDAE (Opossum Beetle Family)
86. CEPHALOIDAE (False Longhorned Beetle Family)
87. TENEBRIONIDAE (Darkling Beetle Family)
88. ALLECULIDAE (Comb-clawed Bark Beetle Family)
89. LAGRIIDAE (Long-jointed Beetle Family)
90. SALPINGIDAE (Narrow-waisted Bark Beetle Family)
91. MYCETOPHAGIDAE (Hairy Fungus Beetle Family)
92. CIIDAE (Minute Tree-fungus Beetle Family)
93. COLYDIIDAE (Cylindrical Bark Beetle Family)
94. PYROCHROIDAE (Fire-colored Beetle Family)
95. OTHNIIDAE (False Tiger Beetle Family)
96. PROSTOMIDAE (Jugular-horned Beetle Family)
97. OEDEMERIDAE (Pollen-feeding Beetle Family)
98. MELANDRYIDAE (False Darkling Beetle Family)
99. MORDELLIDAE (Tumbling Flower Beetle Family)
100. RHIPIPHORIDAE (Wedge-shaped Beetle Family)
101. MELOIDAE (Blister Beetle Family)
102. ANTHICIDAE (Antlike Flower Beetle Family)
103. PEDILIDAE (False Antlike Flower Beetle Family)
104. EUGLENIDAE (Antlike Leaf Beetle Family)

Series STREPSIPTERIFORMIA

Superfamily STYLOPOIDEA

105. STYLOPIDAE (Parasitic Beetle Family)

Series CHRYSOMELIFORMIA

Superfamily CHRYSOMELOIDEA

106. CERAMBYCIDAE (Longhorned Beetle Family)
107. CHRYSOMELIDAE (Leaf Beetle Family)

Superfamily CURCULIONOIDEA

108. BRUCHIDAE (Pea and Bean Weevil Family)
109. ANTHRIBIDAE (Fungus Weevil Family)
110. BRENTHIDAE (Straight-snouted Weevil Family)
111. PLATYPODIDAE (Ambrosia Beetle Family)
112. SCOLYTIDAE (Bark Beetle Family)
113. CURCULIONIDAE (Snout Beetle and True Weevil Family)

Table 24.2 Index to the Families of Coleoptera

Acanthoceridae; *see* Scarabaeidae (30)
Acanthocnemidae; *see* Phloeophilidae (not Nearctic)
Aculagnathidae; not Nearctic
Adephaga; *supra* 2
Aderidae; *see* Euglenidae (104)
Adimeridae; *see* Colydiidae (93)
Aegialitidae; *see* Salpingidae (90)
Aglycyderidae; *see* Curculionidae (113)
Agyrtidae; *see* Silphidae (21)
Alleculidae, 88
Allocorynidae; *see* Curculionidae (113)
Amphizoidae, 5
Anistomidae; *see* Leiodidae (19)

Anobiidae, 63
Anthicidae, 102
Anthribidae, 109
Apionidae; *see* Curculionidae, 113
Archeocrypticidae; *see* Tenebrionidae (87)
Archostemata; *supra* 1
Artematopidae; *see* Dascillidae (34)
Artematopoidea; *see* Dascilloidea (*supra* 31)
Aspidiphoridae; *see* Sphindidae (73)
Attelabidae; *see* Curculionidae (113)

Belidae; *see* Curculionidae
Biphyllidae; 83

Table 24.2 (*Contd.*)

Boganiidae; not Nearctic
Boridae; *see* Salpingidae (90)
Bostrichidae, 64
Bostrichiformia; *supra* 59
Bostrichoidea; *supra* 62
Bostrychidae; *see* Bostrichidae (64)
Brachypsectridae, 37
Brathinidae; *see* Staphylinidae (24)
Brenthidae, 110
Brentidae; *see* Brenthidae (110)
Bruchelidae; *see* Bruchidae (108)
Bruchidae, 108
Buprestidae, 46
Buprestoidea; *supra* 46
Byrrhidae; 35
Byrrhoidea; *supra* 35
Byturidae, 84

Callirhipidae, 40
Calyptomeridae; *see* Clambidae (33)
Cantharidae, 56
Cantharoidea; *supra* 53
Carabidae, 4
Carabiformia; *see* Adephaga (*supra* 2)
Caraboidea; *see* Adephaga (*supra* 2)
Catapochrotidae; *see* Cryptophagidae (74)
Cavognathidae; *see* Boganiidae (not Nearctic)
Cebrionidae, 47
Cephaloidae, 86
Cerambycidae, 106
Ceratocanthidae; *see* Scarabaeidae (30)
Cerophytidae, 50
Cerylonidae, 78
Chaetosomatidae; *see* Cleridae (67)
Chalcodryidae; not Nearctic
Chauliognathidae; *see* Cantharidae (56)
Chelonariidae, 41
Chrysomelidae, 107
Chrysomeloidea; *supra* 106
Cicindelidae, 3
Ciidae, 92
Cisidae; *see* Ciidae (92)
Clambidae, 33
Clavicornia; *see* Cucujoidea (*supra* 70)
Cleridae, 67
Cleroidea, *supra* 66
Cneoglossidae; *see* Dascillidae (34)
Coccinellidae, 80
Colydiidae, 93
Cononotidae; *see* Salpingidae (90)
Corylophidae, 79
Cossyphodidae; *see* Tenebrionidae (87)
Cryptophagidae, 74
Cryptophilidae; *see* Cryptophagidae (74)
Cucujidae, 72
Cucujiformia; *supra* 66
Cucujoidea; *supra* 70
Cupedidae, 1
Cupediformia; *see* Archostemata (*supra* 1)
Cupedoidea; *see* Archostemata (*supra* 1)
Curculionidae, 113
Curculionoidea; *supra* 109
Cyathoceridae; *see* Lepiceridae (not Nearctic)
Cyphonidae; *see* Helodidae (32)

Dacoderidae; *see* Salpingidae (90)
Dascillidae, 34

Dascilloidea; *supra* 31
Dasyceridae, 17
Dasytidae; *see* Melyridae (68)
Dermestidae, 61
Dermestoidea; *supra* 59
Derodontidae, 59
Diphyllostomatidae; *see* Scarabaeidae (30)
Discolomidae; not Nearctic
Disteniidae; *see* Cerambycidae (106)
Drilidae; not Nearctic
Dryopidae, 44
Drypoidea; *supra* 36
Dytiscidae, 7

Ectrephidae; *see* Anobiidae (63)
Elacatidae; *see* Othniidae (95)
Elateridae, 48
Elateriformia; *supra* 35
Elateroidea, *supra* 47
Elmidae, 45
Elminthidae; *see* Elmidae (45)
Empelidae; *see* Clambidae (33)
Endomychidae, 81
Erotylidae, 76
Eucinetidae, 31
Eucinetoidea; *see* Dascilloidea (*supra* 31)
Eucnemidae, 52
Euglenidae, 104
Eulichadidae; *see* Ptilodactylidae (38)
Eurypogonidae; *see* Dascillidae (34)

Georyssidae, 14
Geotrupidae; *see* Scarabaeidae (30)
Glaphyridae; *see* Scarabaeidae (30)
Gnostidae; *see* Anobiidae (63)
Gyrinidae, 9

Haliplidae, 6
Helodidae, 32
Helotidae; not Nearctic
Hemipoplidae; *see* Cucujidae (72)
Heteroceridae, 42
Heteromera; *see* Tenebrionoidea (*supra* 85)
Heterotarsidae; *see* Tenebrionidae (87)
Histeridae, 26
Histeroidea, *supra* 26
Hobartiidae; *see* Boganiidae (not Nearctic)
Homalisidae; *see* Lycidae (57)
Hybosoridae; *see* Scarabaeidae (30)
Hydraenidae; *see* Limnebiidae (13)
Hydrochidae; *see* Hydrophilidae (12)
Hydrophilidae, 12
Hydrophiloidea; *supra* 12
Hydroscaphidae, 11
Hydrobiidae; not Nearctic
Hygrobiidae; not Nearctic
Hylophilidae; *see* Euglenidae (104)
Hyprcopridae; *see* Rhizophagidae (71)

Inopeplidae; *see* Cucujidae (72)
Ithyceridae; *see* Curculionidae (113)

Jacobsoniidae, not Nearctic

Karumiidae; *see* Dascillidae (34)

Largriidae, 89
Lamingtoniidae; not Nearctic

Table 24.2 (*Contd.*)

Lampyridae, 55
Languriidae, 75
Lathridiidae, 82
Latrochidae; *see* Limnichidae (43)
Leiodidae, 19
Lepiceridae; not Nearctic
Leptinidae, 18
Leptodiridae, 22
Limnebiidae, 13
Limnichidae, 43
Limulodidae, 16
Lophocateridae; *see* Trogossitidae (66)
Lucanidae, 28
Lutrochidae; *see* Limnichidae (43)
Lycidae, 57
Lyctidae, 65
Lymexylidae, 69
Lymexylonidae; *see* Lymexylidae (69)
Lymexyloidea; *supra* 69

Malachiidae; *see* Melyridae (68)
Megalopodidae; *see* Chrysomelidae (107)
Melandryidae, 98
Melasidae; *see* Eucnemidae (52)
Meloidae, 101
Melyridae, 68
Merophysiidae; *see* Lathridiidae (82)
Merycidae; *see* Colydiidae (93)
Micromalthidae, 58
Micropeplidae; *see* Staphylinidae (24)
Microsporidae; *see* Sphaeriidae (10)
Monoedidae; *see* Colydiidae (93)
Monommatidae, 85
Monommidae; *see* Monommatidae (85)
Monotomidae; *see* Rhizophagidae (71)
Mordellidae, 99
Murmidiidae; *see* Cerylonidae (78)
Mycetaeidae; *see* Endomychidae (81)
Mycteridae; *see* Salpingidae (90)
Mycetophagidae, 91
Mylabridae; *see* Bruchidae (108)
Myxophaga; *supra* 10

Nemonychidae; *see* Anthribidae (109)
Nilionidae; not Nearctic
Nitidulidae, 70
Nosodentridae, 60
Noteridae, 8

Ochodaeidae; *see* Scarabaeidae (30)
Oedemeridae, 97
Omethidae; *see* Cantharidae (56)
Ommadidae; *see* Cupedidae (1)
Omophronidae; *see* Carabidae (4)
Orthoperidae; *see* Corylophidae (79)
Ostomidae; *see* Trogossitidae (66)
Othniidae, 95
Oxycorynidae; *see* Curculionidae (113)

Parnidae; *see* Dryopidae (44)
Passalidae, 29
Passandridae; *see* Cucujidae (72)
Paussidae; *see* Carabidae (4)
Pedilidae, 103
Peltidae; *see* Trogossitidae (66)
Perimylopidae; not Nearctic

Perothopidae, 51
Petriidae; not Nearctic
Phaenocephalidae; not Nearctic
Phalacridae, 77
Phenogodidae, 54
Phloeophilidae; not Nearctic
Phloeostichidae; *see* Cucujudae, 72
Phloiophilidae; *see* Phloeophilidae (not Nearctic)
Phreatodytidae; *see* Noteridae, 8
Phycosecidae; not Nearctic
Plastoceridae; *see* Elateridae (48)
Platypodidae, 111
Platypsyllidae; *see* Leptinidae (18)
Pleocomidae; *see* Scarabaeidae (30)
Polyphaga; *supra* 12
Propalticidae; not Nearctic
Prostomidae, 96
Proterhinidae; *see* Curculionidae (113)
Protocucujidae; not Nearctic
Pselaphidae, 25
Psephenidae, 36
Pterogeniidae; not Nearctic
Ptiliidae, 15
Ptilodactylidae, 38
Ptinidae, 62
Pyrochroidae, 94
Pythidae; *see* Salpingidae (90)

Rhinomaceridae; *see* Anthribidae (109)
Rhipiceridae, 39
Rhipiphoridae, 100
Rhizophagidae, 71
Rhychitidae; *see* Curculionidae (113)
Rhysodidae, 2

Salpingidae, 90
Sandalidae; *see* Callirhipidae (40)
Sarothriidae; *see* Jacobsoniidae (not Nearctic)
Scaphidiidae, 23
Scarabaeidae, 30
Scarabaeiformia; *supra* 28
Scarabaeoidea; *supra* 28
Scirtidae; *see* Helodidae (32)
Scolytidae, 112
Scraptiidae; *see* Melandryidae (98)
Scydmaenidae, 20
Serropalpidae; *see* Melandryidae (98)
Silphidae, 21
Silvanidae; *see* Cucujidae (72)
Spercheidae; *see* Hydrophilidae (12)
Sphaeriidae, 10
Sphaeriiformia; *see* Myxophaga (*supra* 10)
Sphaerioidea; *see* Myxophaga (*supra* 10)
Sphaeritidae, 27
Sphaerosomatidae; *see* Endomychidae (81)
Sphaerosomidae; *see* Endomychidae (81)
Sphindidae, 73
Staphylinidae, 24
Staphyliniformia; *supra* 12
Staphylinoidea; *supra* 15
Strepsiptera; *see* Stylopidae (105)
Strepsipteriformia; *supra* 105
Stylopidae, 105
Stylopoidea; *supra* 105
Syncalpytidae; *see* Byrrhidae (35)
Synchroidae; *see* Melandryidae (98)
Synteliidae; not Nearctic

Table 24.2 (Contd.)

Telegeusidae, 53
Telephoridae; *see* Cantharidae (56)
Temnochilidae; *see* Trogossitidae (66)
Tenebrionidae, 87
Tenebrionoidea; *supra* 85
Tentyriidae; *see* Tenebrionidae (87)
Tetraphaleridae; *see* Cupedidae (1)
Tetratomidae; *see* Melandryidae (98)
Thoricitidae; *see* Dermestidae (61)
Throscidae, 49
Torridincolidae; not Nearctic

Trachypachidae; *see* Carabidae (2)
Tretothoracidae; *see* Salpingidae (90)
Trictenotomidae; not Nearctic
Trogidae; *see* Scarabaeidae (30)
Trogositidae; *see* Trogossitidae (66)
Trogossitidae, 66

Urodonidae; *see* Bruchidae (108)

Xylophilidae; *see* Euglenidae (104)

Zopheridae; *see* Tenebrionidae (87)

Table 24.3 Index to the Common Names of Beetle Families

Ambrosia beetle family; *see* Platypodidae (111)
Antblood beetle family; *see* Dermestidae (61)
Antlike flower beetle family; *see* Anthicidae (102)
Antlike leaf beetle family; *see* Euglenidae (104)
Antlike stone beetle family; *see* Scydmaenidae (20)
Antloving beetle family; *see* Pselaphidae (25)
Antsucking beetle family; *see* Aculagnathidae (not Nearctic)

Bark beetle family; *see* Scolytidae (112)
Bark-gnawing beetle family; *see* Trogossitidae (66)
Bean weevil family; *see* Bruchidae (108)
Beech-tree beetle family; *see* Perothopidae (51)
Bess beetle family; *see* Passalidae (29)
Blister beetle family; *see* Meloidae (101)
Burrowing water beetle family; *see* Noteridae (8)

Carrion beetle family; *see* Silphidae (21)
Cedar beetle family; *see* Callirhipidae (40)
Checkered beetle family; *see* Cleridae (67)
Cicada parasite beetle family; *see* Rhipiceridae (39)
Click beetle family; *see* Elateridae (48)
Clown beetle family; *see* Histeridae (26)
Comb-clawed beetle family; *see* Alleculidae (88)
Crawling water beetle family; *see* Haliplidae (6)
Cylindrical bark beetle family; *see* Colydiidae (93)

Darkling beetle family; *see* Tenebrionidae (87)
Deathwatch beetle family; *see* Anobiidae (63)
Drive beetle family; *see* Elmidae (45)
Drug-store beetle family; *see* Anobiidae (63)
Dry-fungus beetle family; *see* Sphindidae (73)

False antloving flower beetle family; *see* Pedilidae (103)
False blister beetle family; *see* Oedemeridae (97)
False click beetle family; *see* Eucnemidae (52)
False clown beetle family; *see* Sphaeritidae (27)
False darkling beetle family; *see* Melandryidae (98)
False firefly beetle family; *see* Drilidae (not Nearctic)
False ladybird beetle family; *see* Nilionidae (not Nearctic)
False long-horned beetle family; *see* Cephaloidae (86)
False metallic wood-boring beetle family; *see* Throscidae (49)
False skin beetle family; *see* Biphyllidae (83)
False snout beetle family; *see* Jacobsoniidae (not Nearctic)
False tiger beetle famiy; *see* Othniidae (95)
Feather-winged beetle family; *see* Ptiliidae (15)
Fire-colored beetle family; *See* Pyrochroidae (94)
Firefly beetle family; *see* Lampyridae (55)
Flat bark beetle family; *see* Cucujidae (72)
Flat-horned beetle family; *see* Carabidae (4), Paussidae (not Nearctic)
Fruitworm beetle family; *see* Byturidae (84)
Fungus weevil family; *see* Anthribidae (109)

Glowworm beetle family; *see* Phengodidae (54)
Ground beetle family; *see* Carabidae (4)

Hairy fungus beetle family; *see* Mycetophagidae (91)
Handsome fungus beetle family; *see* Endomychidae (81)
Horned powder-post beetle family; *see* Bostrichidae (64)
Horseshoe crab beetle family; *see* Limulodidae (16)

Jugular-horned beetle family; *see* Prostomidae (96)

Ladybird beetle family; *see* Coccinellidae (80)
Lamellicorn beetle family; *see* Scarabaeidae (30)
Larder beetle family; *see* Dermestidae (61)
Leaf beetle family; *see* Chrysomelidae (107)
Lively ant-guest beetle family; *see* Tenebrionidae (87), Cossyphodinae
Lizard beetle family; *see* Languriidae (75)
Long-horned beetle family; *see* Cerambycidae (106)
Long-jointed beetle family; *see* Lagriidae (89)
Long-lipped beetle family; *see* Telegeusidae (53)
Long-toed water beetle family; *see* Dryopidae (44)

Mammal nest beetle family; *see* Leptinidae (18)
Marsh beetle family; *see* Helodidae (32)
Metallic sap beetle family; *see* Helotidae; (32) not Nearctic
Metallic wood-boring beetle family; *see* Buprestidae (46)
Minute bark beetle family; *see* Cerylonidae (78)
Minute beetle family; *see* Clambidae (33)
Minute bog beetle family; *see* Sphaeriidae (10)
Minute brown scavenger beetle family; *see* Lathridiidae (82)
Minute fungus beetle family; *see* Corylophidae (79)
Minute marsh-loving beetle family; *see* Limnichidae (43)
Minute moss beetle family; *see* Hydraenidae (13)
Minue scavenger beetle family; *see* Dasyceridae (17)
Minute tree fungus beetle family; *see* Ciidae (92)
Mud-backed beetle family; *see* Georyssidae (14)

Narrow-waisted bark beetle family; *see* Salpingidae (90)
Net-winged beetle family; *see* Lycidae (57)

Opossum beetle family; *see* Monommatidae (85)

Parasitic beetle family; *see* Stylopidae (105)
Pea and been weevil family; *see* Bruchidae (108)
Peg beetle family; *see* Passalidae (29)
Pill beetle family; *see* Byrrhidae (35)
Pleasing fungus beetle family; *see* Erotylidae (76)
Plate-thigh beetle family; *see* Eucinetidae (31
Pollen feeding bettle family; *see* Oedemeridae (97)
Powder-post beetle family; *see* Lyctidae (65)
Predacious diving beetle family; *see* Dytiscidae (7)

Table 24.3 (*Contd.*)

Rare click beetle family; *see* Cerophytidae (50)
Reticulated beetle family; *see* Cupedidae (1)
Riffle beetle family; *see* Elmidae (45)
Robust click beetle family; *see* Cebrionidae (47)
Root-eating beetle family; *see* Rhizophagidae (71)
Round fungus beetle family; *see* Leiodidae (19)
Rove beetle family; *see* Staphylinidae (24)

Sap-feeding beetle family; *see* Nitidulidae (70)
Sap-flow beetle family; *see* Synteliidae (not Nearctic)
Savage beetle family; *see* Carabidae (4), Omophroninae
Shining flower beetle family; *see* Phalacridae (77)
Shining fungus beetle family; *see* Scaphidiidae (23)
Ship-timber beetle family; *see* Lymexylidae (69)
Silken fungus beetle family; *see* Cryptophagidae (74)
Skin beetle family; *see* Dermestidae (61)
Skiff beetle family; *see* Hydroscaphidae (11)
Small carrion beetle family; *see* Leptodiridae (22)
Snout beetle family; *see* Curculionidae (114)
Soft-bodied plant beetle family; *see* Dascillidae (34)
Soft-winged flower beetle family; *see* Melyridae (68)
Soldier beetle family; *see* Cantharidae (56)
Spider beetle family; *see* Ptinidae (62)
Squeaker beetle family; *see* Hygrobiidae (not Nearctic)

Stag beetle family; *see* Lucanidae (28)
Straight-snouted weevil family; *see* Brentidae (110)

Telephone-pole beetle family; *see* Micromalthidae (58)
Termitelike beetle family; *see* Dascillidae, Karumiinae, not Nearctic (34)
Texas beetle family; *see* Brachypsectridae (37)
Tiger beetle family; *see* Cicindelidae (3)
Toad beetle family; *see* Cyathoceridae (not Nearctic)
Toed-winged beetle family; *see* Ptilodactylidae (38)
Tooth-necked fungus beetle family; *see* Derodontidae (59)
Tropical log beetle family; *see* Discolomidae (not Nearctic)
Trout-stream beetle family; *see* Amphizoidae (5)
True weevil family; *see* Curculionidae (113)
Tumbling flower beetle family; *see* Mordellidae (99)
Turtle beetle family; *see* Chelonariidae (41)

Variegated mud-loving beetle family; *see* Heteroceridae (42)

Water penny beetle family; *see* Psephenidae (36)
Water scavenger beetle family; *see* Hydrophilidae (12)
Wedge-shaped beetle family; *see* Rhipiphoridae (100)
Weevil family; *see* Curculionidae (113)
Whirligig beetle family; *see* Gyrinidae (9)
Wounded-tree beetle family; *see* Nosodendridae (60)
Wrinkled bark beetle family; *see* Rhysodidae (2)

I. Key to the Suborders of Coleoptera of the World

1. Hind coxae immovably fused to metasternum, completely dividing first visible abdominal sternum (See Fig. 24.5); notopleural sutures nearly always present (See Fig. 24.6) but absent in some Dytiscidae if first abdominal sternum is hidden by large coxal plates (see Fig. 24.7) that cover all but two abdominal sterna, and notopleural suture is present; *see* Haliplidae (See Key III) ... **ADEPHAGA**

Fig. 24.5. Abdomen, ventral view showing (S) sternum.

Fig. 24.6. Prothorax, ventral view, showing notopleural sutures: (cx. c.) coxal cavity, (Epm) epimeron, (Eps) episternum, (Msth) mesothorax, (np.s.) notopleural suture; (pl.s.) pleural suture, (plst.s.) pleurosternal suture, (Prnt) pronotum, and (Stn) sternum.

Fig. 24.7. Abdomen, ventral view, showing enlarged coxal plates.

I. Key to the Suborders of Coleoptera of the World (*Contd.*)

Hind coxae not fused to metasternum and not dividing first visible abdominal sternum (see Fig. 24.19); notopleural sutures present or absent *2*

2(1). Pronotum without notopleural sutures. (See Key IV.)**POLYPHAGA**

3(2). Antennae filiform (see Fig. 24.26); wings with apex spirally rolled in repose; all species over 7 mm. in length. (1. *Cupedidae*) **ARCHOSTEMATA**

Antennae clavate to capitate (see Fig. 24.2c and 24.2d); wings with apex folded in repose, never rolled; very small beetles, 0.5–1.5 mm in length. (See Key III.) ... **MYXOPHAGA**

**II. Key to the Families of Suborder Adephaga
in the U.S. and Canada**

1. Hind coxae greatly expanded, covering at least first 3 visible abdominal sterna
... **6. Haliplidae**
Hind coxae not expanded, not covering first visible abdominal sternum *2*

2(1). Hind legs fitted with long setae or spines for swimming; prosternum prolonged to the rear, more or less as a keel; body and appendages usually very streamlined for aquatic life ... *3*
Hind legs without long swimming setae; prosternum not particularly modified as a keel; body and appendages not streamlined for aquatic life *6*

3(2). Eyes divided on each side into 2 isolated eyes **9. Gyrinidae**
Eyes entire ... *4*

4(3). Scutellum completely concealed by bases of elytra *5*
Scutellum fully visible (see also couplet 5) **7. Dytiscidae**

5(4). Hind tarsi with 2 slender, curved claws of equal length; posterior margin of hind tarsi uniform; anterior tibiae frequently with strong recurved spur at outer apical angle (except *Notomicrus*) .. **8. Noteridae**
Hind tarsi each with one thick, straight claw; hind margin of hind tarsomeres produced into lobes (see Fig. 24.4e); anterior tibiae without recurved spines or spurs (Laccophilinae) (see also couplet 4) **7. Dytiscidae**

6(2). Antennae moniliform; prothorax elongate and deeply grooved. **2. Rhysodidae**
Antennae various, never moniliform; prothorax never with deep grooves *7*

7(6). Body without prominent sensory setae; hind coxae extending laterally to lateral margin of abdomen; aquatic ... **5. Amphizoidae**
Body with prominent sensory setae; hind coxae usually extending laterally only 4/5 of distance to lateral margin of abdomen; if meeting margin of abdomen (rare), always with prominent sensory hairs; terrestrial ... *8*

8(7). Antennae arising on front between eyes, above and closer together than bases of mandibles; clypeus produced laterally over bases of antennae; mandibles long, with long teeth (see Fig. 24.8); legs long, armed with long hairlike setae or spines; often brightly colored
... **3. Cicindelidae**

Fig. 24.8. Head: (Cpl) cplyeus, (Fr) front, (Lbr) labrum, (Md) mandible, and (Vx) vertex.

Antennae arising on sides of head directly between eyes and bases of mandibles; mandibles not particularly long or armed with long teeth; legs usually not particularly long or armed with long hairlike setae or long spines; generally dull colored, or marked with orange
... **4. Carabidae**

**III. Key to the Families of Suborder Myxophaga
in the U.S. and Canada**

1. Abdomen with 3 visible sterna; hind coxae very large, contiguous; elytra entire; antennae eleven-segmented ... **10. Sphaeriidae**
Abdomen with 6 to 7 visible sterna; hind coxae smaller, well separated; elytra trunctate, exposing at least 2 abdominal terga; antennae 9-segmented **11. Hydroscaphidae**

IV. Key to the Families of Suborder Polyphaga
in the U.S. and Canada

[*Note:* For ease in using an otherwise unwieldily lengthy key, the key to the suborder Polyphaga is divided into parts as indicated below. These parts usually constitute an unnatural division and do not correspond with the series and superfamilies established in the classification. If a family keys out in more than one part, a cross-reference to the additional part or parts is indicated.]

Key to the Parts of Suborder Polyphaga

1. Laviform: Adult females larviform, lacking wings and elytra, but sexually mature and full grown .. **KEY E**
 With elytra, usually entire, but may be reduced, exposing the abdomen to varying degrees; usually with fully developed flying wings. *2*

2(1). Musciform: Male resembling small flies; elytra reduced to fleshy flaps; hind wings as wide as long with reduced venation; pro-, meso-, and metathorax distinct; antennae 4- to 7-segmented, with 1 or several segments prolonged into a long lateral process; females all endoparasitic (see also Key E) **105. Stylopidae**
 Body various; elytra may be reduced but cover at least part of pterothorax and usually part or all of abdomen; prothorax distinct, but meso- and metathorax united; antennae various; females not endoparasitic .. *3*

3(2). Antennae lamellate: Last 3 to 7 segments enlarged on one side to form lamellate club (see Fig. 24.2e) that usually can be opened and closed; legs usually armed with spines fitted for digging; tarsomeres (with rare exceptions) 5-5-5, with front tarsi sometimes reduced or absent .. **KEY C**
 Antennae not lamellate, or if lamellate (rare) with many more than 5 segments; tarsomeres 5-5-5, with 4th minute, hidden in bilobed 3rd *4*

4(3). Short elytra exposing much of abdomen, with three or more terga entirely sclerotized instead of membranous or semimembranous as in most species **KEY B**
 Elytra usually covering abdomen entirely, or nearly so, with at most two abdominal terga exposed when in normal position, or if more exposed, terga not heavily sclerotized *5*

5(4). Antennae short, with segment 6 modified to form a cupule, followed by 3 to 5 segments forming a pubescent, sometimes asymmetrical club (see Fig. 24.9); maxillary palpi usually longer than antennae and slender [if antennae and maxillary palpi are subequal, see Dryopidae (44); if only last segment of maxillary palpi greatly elongate, see Telegeusidae (53); if ligula elongate, see Meloidae (101)] **KEY A**
 Antennae without a distinct cupule; maxillary palpi not longer than antennae *6*

Fig. 24.9. Antenna showing cupule (c). **Fig. 24.10.** Geniculate antenna.

6(5). Tarsomeres 5-5-5, but 4th minute, hidden in bilobed 3rd and fused immovably to 5th (see Fig. 24.4b), and 3rd usually densely pubescent beneath; if 4th small but not hidden, with gular sutures confluent on median line [see Platypodidae (111) and some Scolytidae (112)]; head often prolonged into a beak; antennae geniculate (see Fig. 24.10), clavate (see Fig. 24.2c), capitate (see Fig. 24.2d), or greatly elongate **KEY J**
 Tarsi otherwise; gular sutures separate ... *7*

7(6). Tarsomeres clearly 5-5-5, although 1 or more may be very small but never hidden by a bilobed 3rd .. *9*
 Tarsomeres fewer than 5-5-5 .. *8*

Key to the Parts of Suborder Polyphaga (*Contd.*)

8(7). Tarsomeres 5-5-4 (next to last may be very short (rare) so that hind tarsi appear to have 3 tarsomeres and others 4; in very exceptional cases, front tarsi with 5 tarsomeres and both other pairs with 4)); abdomen with 5 visible sterna [Leiodidae (19) and Staphylinidae (24) are heteromerous but have 6 visible abdominal sterna or short elytra] **KEY F**
Tarsomeres fewer than 5-5-4 (All tarsi with fewer than 5 tarsomeres, or at least more than 1 pair with fewer than 5) ... **KEY G**

Fig. 24.11. Clubbed antenna.

Fig. 24.12. Coxal cavities: (a) globose, (b) traverse, (c) conical, and (d) flat. (Cx) coxa, (Fr), front, (PN), pronotum.

9(7). Abdomen with 3 visible sterna: First sternum very long; antennae apparently with only 3 segments, all but the 2 basal ones fused into a large club-shaped mass (see Fig. 24.11); small in size (L. 2–3 mm) and associated with ants' nests (genus *Gnostus*) **62. Ptinidae**
Abdomen with 5 visible sterna [rarely 4; see *Colon* in Leptodiridae (22)]: Front coxae globose (see Fig. 24.12a), transverse (see Fig. 24.12b), or conical (see Fig. 24.12c) and small or prominent .. **KEY H**
Abdomen with 6 or 7 visible sterna: Front coxae flat and rounded (see Fig. 24.12d), or globose (see Fig. 24.12a), small, and usually not prominent **KEY I**
Abdomen with 7 or 8 visible sterna: Front coxae conical, prominent, usually large (see Fig. 24.12c) .. **KEY D**

A. Key to the Hydrophiloidea

1. Six or seven visible abdominal sterna; antennae with five-segmented, pubescent club **13. Limnebiidae**
Five visible abdominal sterna; antennae with three pubescent segments beyond cupule (see Fig. 24.9) .. *2*

2(1). Tarsomeres apparently 4-4-4; front coxae very large, concealing sterna; first two visible abdominal sterna connate **14. Georyssidae**
Tarsomeres 5-5-5 but some males 4-5-5 or 5-4-4; front coxae smaller, not covering sterna; first two visible abdominal sterna usually free **12. Hydrophilidae**

B. Key to the Families with Short Elytra

1. Abdomen flexible, not enlarged apically, parallel or tapering with 5 to 8 freely movable sterna; antennae with variable number of segments, usually 11; tarsomeres with many combinations; species usually small in size but occasionally large, slender *2*
Abdomen not flexible, very much wider than prothorax, and swollen, oval, with segments anchylosed; usually 3 to 6 visible sterna; antennae often with fewer than 11 segments; tarsi 3-segmented; species small or minute in size (L. 0.05–5.5 mm; avg. 1.5 mm) but robust **25. Pselaphidae**

B. Key to the Families with Short Elytra (*Contd.*)

2(1). Abdomen with 5 visible sterna .. *3*

Abdomen with 6 to 8 visible sterna .. *4*

3(2). Three abdominal terga exposed, heavily sclerotized; antennae distinctly capitate (see also Keys F, G, and H) (Carphalinae) **70. Nitidulidae**

Elytra greatly reduced, exposing entire abdomen; antennae pectinate (see also Key F) **100. Rhipiphoridae**

Wings absent; elytra short; jugum with 2 long processes projecting forward nearly as far as tips of mandibles (see Fig. 24.13); extremely flat species **96. Prostomidae**

Fig. 24.13. Head, ventral view.

4(2). Heteromerous; abdomen soft; head deflexed, much broader than pronotum, with latter narrowed in front (see also Key F) **101. Meloidae**

Tarsomeres usually not 5-5-4; if 5-5-4, not with preceding combination of characteristics *5*

5(4). Maxillary palpi flabellate; hind wings with series of radiating veins (see also Keys D and H) .. **69. Lymexylonidae**

Maxillary and labial palpi greatly lengthened, with last segment nearly as long as antennae (see also Key D) ... **53. Telegeusidae**

Palpi normal ... *6*

6(5). Antennae inserted at sides of front and anterior to eyes, or if inserted between eyes, with elytra exposing all abdominal terga **24. Staphylinidae**

Antennae inserted at upper part of front or at base of the frontal lobe (see also Key D) ... *7*

Antennae reduced to 3 segments; eyes absent; flattened; beaver ectoparasites (*Platypsyllus*) .. **18. Leptinidae**

7(6). Antennae 12-segmented, flabellate (see Fig. 24.2g) (see also Key D) **54. Phengodidae**

Antennae 11-segmented, filiform, serrate, or flabellate (see also Key D). **56. Cantharidae**

C. Key to the Families of Scarabaeoidea

[*Note:* In a few rare cases, the antennae of some Scarabaeidae are not lamellate to the usual degree; also in those few rare cases in which the antennae of some Hydrophilidae (12) are somewhat lamellate, the maxillary palpi are longer than the antennae; the antennae of some Gyrinidae (9) are somewhat lamellate, in which cases the eyes are divided.]

1. Plates of antennal club flattened and capable of closing. **30. Scarabaeidae**

Plates of antennal club not capable of close apposition, and usually not flattened *2*

2(1). Antennae straight, usually curled when at rest; large, flattened species with deeply striate elytra .. **29. Passalidae**

Antennae of most genera geniculate; if not, species not large and flattened and elytra not deeply striate .. **28. Lucanidae**

D. Key to the Families of Cantharoidea and Lymexylonoidea

[*Note:* The species *Thylodrias contractus* Motschulsky (Dermestidae) will key here because of the seven visible abdominal sterna, but the presence of a median ocellus distinguishes it from all the following families, which lack ocelli.]

1. Middle coxae distant; epipleural fold absent (see Fig. 24.14a); elytra usually with reticulate sculpture; no phosphorescent organs; species usually flat, widened behind, and often with bold color pattern. .. **57. Lycidae**

Middle coxae contiguous or nearly so; epipleural fold distinct (see Fig. 24.14b); elytra not reticulate and sometimes greatly reduced in size (see also Key B) *2*

2(1). Antennae inserted at sides of front, anterior to eyes *3*

Antennae inserted at upper part of front or at base of the frontal lobe; phosphorescent organs often present .. *4*

D. Key to the Families of Cantharoidea and Lymexylonoidea (*Contd.*)

3(2). Maxillary palpi flabellate; eyes almost meeting in front; elytra very short; hind wings with series of radiating veins (see also Key B) **69. Lymexylonidae**
Maxillary and labial palpi greatly lengthened, with last segment nearly as long as antennae; slender, depressed species, elytra extending to middle of abdomen in female (see also Key B) .. **53. Telegeusidae**

4(2). Head more or less completely covered by prothorax; metepisterna not sinuate on inner side (see Fig. 24.14b, Eps₃) .. **55. Lampyridae**
Head not all covered by prothorax; metepisterna sinuate on inner side (see Fig. 24.14c); antennae of male sometimes flabellate ... *5*

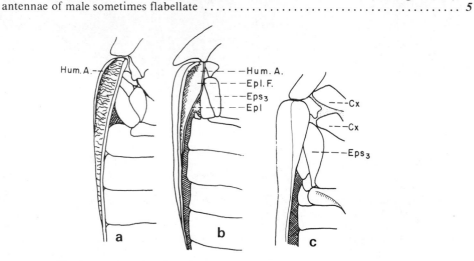

Fig. 24.14. Ventral surface showing humeral regoin: (Cx) coxa, (Epl) epipleura, (Epl. F.) epipleural fold, (Eps₃) metepisternum, and (Hum. A.) humeral angle.

5(4). Antennae 12-segmented, flabellate; elytra short (see also Keys B and E). **54. Phengodidae**
Antennae 11-segmented, filiform, serrate, or flabellate; elytra entire or short (see also Key B) ... **56. Cantharidae**

E. Key to the Families with Larviform Females

1. Female endoparasitic on other insects; all appendages lacking, very simple organization (see also Key IV) .. **105. Stylopidae**
Female free-living; appendages present ... *2*

2(1). Head more or less completely retracted within prothorax; legs larviform, bearing single claw ... **54. Phengodidae**
Head prominent, not retracted; legs of normal form with 2 tarsal claws *3*

3(2). Narrow, somewhat compressed species **100. Rhipiphoridae**
Broad, somewhat depressed species (see also Keys H and I). **61. Dermestidae**

F. Key to the Families of Tenbrionoidea and other Heteromera

1. Front coxal cavities closed behind (see Fig. 24.15a) *2*
Front coxal cavities open behind (see Fig. 24.15b) *8*

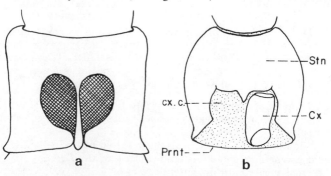

Fig. 24.15. Ventral view of prosternum showing coxal cavities: (a) front coxal cavities closed behind, and (b) front coxal cavities open behind, (Cx) coxa, (Cx. C.) coxal cavity, (Prnt) pronotum, (Stn) sternum.

F. Key to the Families of Tenbrionoidea and other Heteromera (*Contd.*)

2(1). Tarsal claws simple .. *3*
Tarsal claws pectinate; usually elongate, convex, rather soft-bodied, and often thinly silky-pubescent species of small or moderate size; prothorax widened behind
...**88. Alleculidae**

3(2). Abdominal sterna all freely movable, that is, membrane visible between segments *4*
First 2 to 4 of the 6 visible abdominal sterna more closely united, more or less fused or immovable, that is, no membrane visible between segments, a simple suture *7*

4(3). Antennae 11-segmented .. *5*
Antennae 10-segmented .. *6*

5(4). Prothorax quadrate, not wider than head; narrow-bodied species **95. Othniidae**
Prothorax greatly expanded at sides, much wider than head, antennae capitate, with club two-segmented (see also Keys G and H) **7. Rhizophagidae**

6(4). Elytra entire; small (L. 1.5–3 mm), convex species **73. Sphindidae**
Elytra of males truncate, exposing pygidium; small (L. 1.5–3 mm), flattened species, (see also Keys G and H) **71. Rhizophagidae**

7(3). Penultimate tarsomere (at least) spongy pubescent beneath; front coxae globose, projecting from coxal cavity; slender, elongate, usually hairy, sometimes metallic in color; last antennal segment often several times as long as preceding one
.. **89. Lagriidae**
Penultimate tarsomere not spongy pubescent beneath; front coxae globose, usually not projecting from cavities **87. Tenebrionidae**

8(1). Antennae geniculate (see Fig. 24.10); elytra truncate behind, exposing 2 abdominal terga (see also Key H) .. **26. Histeridae**
Antennae not geniculate .. *9*

9(8). Head not strongly or suddenly narrowed or constricted behind eyes,... *10*
Head strongly and suddenly constricted behind eyes; or, if more gradually narrowed, tarsal claws pectinate .. *17*

10(9). Tarsal claws simple, cleft, toothed, or appendiculate *11*
Tarsal claws with fleshy lobe, often pectinate **86. Cephaloidae**

11(10). Pronotum usually widest anteriorly, always without margins; tarsi with at least penultimate tarsomere dilated and tomentose beneath...........**97. Oedemeridae**
Pronotum widest near center, or basally, usually with margins; tarsomeres dilated or not .. *12*

12(11). Antennae received in grooves in underside of prothorax; moderately sized (L. 5–12 mm), oval, flattened species with head partly concealed in prothorax; legs retractile ...
.. **85. Monommidae**
Antennae free, not received in grooves *13*

13(12). Prothorax with lateral margins, at least basally *15*
Prothorax not margined laterally, narrowed behind, its disc without impressions *14*

14(13). Five visible abdominal sterna **90. Salpingidae**
Six visible abdominal sterna, the first 2 immovably united (Aegialitinae)
.. **90. Salpingidae**

15(13). Mesepimera not reaching coxae (see Fig. 24.16a); coxal cavities entirely surrounded by sterna (male Cryptophagini) (see also Key H) **74. Cryptophagidae**
Mesepimera reaching coxae (see Fig. 24.16d) *16*

16(15). Metasternum long; metepimera usually visible; prothorax widened near center or toward base, its disc usually with basal impressions; tarsal claws sometimes cleft or appendiculate; elongate or broadly oval species **78. Melandryidae**
Metasternum quadrate; metepimera hidden by elytra; small, flattened species (see also Keys G and H) .. **72. Cucujidae**

17(9). Prothorax with sharp lateral margins, at least basally *18*
Prothorax rounded at sides, without sharp lateral margins *20*

18(17). Antennae filiform ... *19*
Antennae pectinate (male) or subserrate (female); tarsal claws serrate or toothed; elytra covering abdomen (see also couplet 20 and Key E). **100. Rhipiphoridae**

19(18). Abdomen with last dorsal segment forming pronounced prolongation; body more or less compressed laterally and arched; abdomen with segments tightly overlapping
.. **99. Mordellidae**
Abdominal segments loosely joined together, none prolonged; body not compressed laterally .. **98. Melandryidae**

20(19). Base of prothorax narrower than elytra *21*
Base of prothorax as wide as elytra; body broad, much narrowed behind; elytra usually shortened and narrowed behind; antennae pectinate in male, often serrate in female; females sometimes very degenerate (see also couplet 19 and Key E)
.. **100. Rhipiphoridae**

F. Key to the Families of Tenbrionoidea and other Heteromera (*Contd.*)

21(20). Hind coxae transverse, not prominent (see Fig. 24.12b); tarsal claws usually simple ... *22*
Hind coxae transverse, large and prominent tarsal claws often cleft or toothed *24*

22(21). Eyes more or less emarginate; hind coxae contiguous or nearly so *23*
Eyes elliptical, entire; hind coxae usually well seperated **102. Anthicidae**

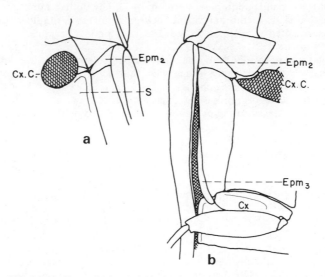

Fig. 24.16. Ventral view of humeral region showing epimeron: (a) mesepimera not reaching coxa, and (b) mesepimera reaching coxa; (Cx) coxa; (Cx. C.) coxal cavity, (Epm$_2$) mesepimeron, (Epm$_3$) metepimeron, (S) sternum.

23(22). Tarsomeres clearly 5-5-4; body elongate; abdominal segments all free. ... **103. Pedilidae**
Tarsomeres apparently 4-4-3, with penultimate extremely minute; body more oval than preceding; first 2 visible abdominal sterna immovably united **104. Euglenidae**

24(22). Tarsal claws simple; head horizontal; antennae serrate, ofen pectinate in male; body flattened; moderate-sized species (L. 6–20 mm) **94. Pyrochroidae**
Tarsal claws toothed or cleft; head deflexed, with front vertical; elytra sometimes shortened; body usually more or less cylindrical; moderate-sized or large species (L. 3–30 mm; usually 10–15 mm) **101. Meloidae**

G. Key to the Families with Tarsomeres Less than 5-5-4

[*Note:* Tarsomeres in the Lyctidae (57) appear to be 4-4-4 but are actually 5-5-5; the first is very minute and easily overlooked. The Lyctidae may key to either Mycetophagidae (91) or Colydiidae (93) but may be distinguished from the former by their elongate rather than oval shape, and from the latter by their incomplete elytral striae formed by rows of punctures. Tarsomeres in the Leiodidae (19) may be 4-4-4, 5-4-4, 4-4-5, 4-4-3, or 3-3-3, but this family has six visible abdominal sterna and should therefore be keyed in family Key I. One genus, *Octhebis,* of Limnebiidae (13) might also be keyed in the present section because the maxillary palpi are shorter than the antennae and the tarsomeres are apparently 4-4-4 or 3-3-3; actually, they are 5-5-5, the first and/or second or third being greatly reduced (see Key A).]

1. Tarsomeres 4-4-4 (anterior legs with 3 tarsomeres in males of some Mycetophagidae) *2*
Tarsomeres 3-3-3 (sometimes apparently 2-2-2, the 1st being minute and concealed by tibiae) ... *13*

2(1). Wings fringed with long hairlike setae, which can usually be seen beneath elytra; very small, highly convex species ... *3*
Wings not fringed ... *4*

3(2). Hind coxae in contact, with plates at least partially covering femora ... **33. Clambidae**
Hind coxae separated, transverse, not laminate **78. Corylophidae**

4(2). Abdominal sterna all free and movable; all sutures complete *5*
Sterna 1 to 4 firmly united and immovable; sutures may be incomplete *10*

G. Key to the Families with Tarsomeres Less than 5-5-4 (*Contd.*)

5(4). First tarsomere dilated, overlapping the very minute 2nd and 3rd tarsomeres part of the
 long 4th; elongate species with costate elytra (Monoedinae) (see also couplets 10 and 17)
 ... **93. Colydiidae**
 First tarsomere not dilated .. **6**

6(5). Front coxae transverse (see Fig. 24.12b); fungus beetles (Cylocephalinae) (see also Key H)
 ... **70. Nitidulidae**
 Front coxae globose or oval ... **7**

7(6). Front coxae globose (see Fig. 24.12a) **8**
 Front coxae oval (see Fig. 24.12d) .. **9**

8(7). Tarsi slender, with 3rd tarsomere distinct but shorter than 2nd (see also couplet 15) ...
 ... **81. Endomychidae**
 Tarsi slender, with 3rd tarsomere subequal to 2nd and 4th; pronotum without lateral
 grooves (male *Platycholeus*) (see also Keys H and I). **22. Leptodiridae**
 Tarsi with 3rd tarsomere fused to base of 4th **14**

9(7). Head more or less concealed by projecting prothorax; last tarsomere usually very long;
 body cylindrical ... **92. Ciidae**
 Head free, not covered by prothorax **11**

10(4). Antennae thickened, with 2- or 3-segmented club; tibiae simple, not dilated or spinose; not
 aquatic (see also couplets 5 and 17) **93. Colydiidae**
 Antennae with large serrate, 7-segmented club; front and middle tibiae dilated and armed
 with rows of spines; small (L. 4–6 mm), subaquatic species **42. Heteroceridae**

11(9). Body oval, depressed **91. Mycetophagidae**
 Body elongate ... **12**

12(11). Procoxal cavities open behind (some Cucujini) (see also Keys F and H) **72. Cucujidae**
 Procoxal cavities closed behind (see also Keys F and H). **71. Rhizophagidae**

13(1). Wings with a fringe of long harlike setae (see Fig. 24.17) **15. Ptiliidae**
 Wings not fringed, or at most with a short fringe **14**
 Wings absent; species horse-shoe shaped **16. Limulodidae**

Fig. 24.17. Antenna.

Fig. 24.18. Tarsus of Coccinellidae (80)
and Endomychidae (81).

14(8). Second tarsomere dilated and the 3rd really consisting of 2 tarsomeres, the small, true 3rd
 being fused with the base of the 4th, which thus appears to be the 3rd (see Fig. 24.18)
 ... **15**

14(13). Second tarsomere not dilated .. **16**

15(14). Tarsal claws usually dilated or toothed at base; 1st visible abdominal sternum with curved
 coxal lines; mesepimeron tringular; rounded, convex, usually brightly spotted species
 ... **80. Coccinellidae**
 Tarsal claws simple; 1st visible abdominal sternum without coxal lines; mesepimeron
 quadrangular; oblong or oval species, often with striking color pattern and usually
 living in fungi (see also couplet 8) **81. Endomychidae**

16(14). Elytra entire ... **17**
 Elytra truncate, exposing last abdominal segment (see also Keys F and H) (*Smicrips* spp.)
 ... **71. Rhizophagidae**

17(16). Abdominal sterna all free .. **18**
 Basal 3 visible sterna connate (see also couplets 5 and 10) **19**

18(17). Procoxal cavities open behind and contiguous **17. Dasyceridae**
 Procoxal cavities closed behind **82. Lathridiidae**

19(17). Apical segment of maxillary palpi not needlelike **93. Colydiidae**
 Apical segment of maxillary palpi needlelike **78. Cerylonidae**

H. Key to the Pentamerous Families with Five Visible Abdominal Sterna

1. Front coxae globose (see Fig. 24.12a), flat and rounded (see Fig. 24.12d), or transverse (see Fig. 24.12b), usually only barely projecting from coxal cavities *2*
 Front coxae more or less conical and prominent (see Fig. 24.12c) *12*

2(1). Front coxae transverse, more or less cylindrical *3*
 Front coxae globose, or flat and rounded .. *15*

3(2). Hind coxae grooved to receive femora ... *4*
 Hind coxae flat and not grooved ... *10*

4(3). Strongly convex species with more or less retractile legs; tibiae dilated and usually grooved near outer end to receive tarsi ... *5*
 Slightly convex, oval species with nonretractile, slender legs *8*

5(4). Antennae inserted at sides of head .. *6*
 Antennae inserted on front; head retracted; 3rd tarsomere lobed; thorax margined; oval species ... **41. Chelonariidae**

6(5). Head prominent; mentum large, elongate, and subelliptical; tarsomeres not lobed
 .. **60. Nosodendridae**
 Head retracted; mentum small and quadrate *7*

7(6). Clypeus not distinct from front ... *9*
 Clypeus separated from front by fine epistomal sulcus **43. Limnichidae**

8(4). Claws very large; moderate-sized (L. 3–7 mm), aquatic or subaquatic species
 .. **44. Dryonidae**
 Claws not enlarged; mandibles prominent; terrestrial species **34. Dascillidae**

9(7). Antennae capitate (*Orphilus* spp.) **61. Dermestidae**
 Antennae clavate **35. Byrrhidae**

10(3). Antennae geniculate, very strongly clavate or capitate; elytra shortened, leaving 2 terga uncovered; all tibiae usually dilated, front ones usually not connate; head very much narrower than pronotum; (see also couplet 22 and Key F) **26. Histeridae**
 Antennae straight, not geniculate ... *11*

11(10). Tarsi more or less dilated, first tarsomere not shortened, fourth very small; elytra frequently extending to apex of abdomen *12*
 Tarsi slender, first tarsomere may be extremely short so that tarsomeres appear to be 4-4-4; elytra entire, never truncate **66. Trogossitidae**

12(11). Maxillae with well-developed inner and outer lobes *13*
 Maxillae with only a single lobe; species found on sap and fruit (see also triplet 14 and Key B) (Nitidulinae, Meligethinae, and Cryptarchinae) **70. Nitidulidae**

13(12). Antennae clavate or capitate; elytra usually not covering apex of abdomen *14*
 Antennae filiform; elytra entirely covering abdomen; moderately large (L. 5–20 mm), elongate beetles (see also couplet 40 and Key J) **106. Cerambycidae**
 Antennae serrate in females at least, males often pectinate; head deflexed; moderate in size (L. 7–12 mm); elytra covering abdomen **38. Ptilodactylidae**

14(13). Antennae 11-segmented, with 3-segmented club; labrum free; body without dense pubescence (see also couplet 12 and Keys F and G) **70. Nitidulidae**
 Body with dense, long pubescence; otherwise very similar to the preceding
 .. **84. Byturidae**
 Antennae 10-segmented, with 2-segmented club; labrum fused with clypeus (see also Keys F and G) ... **71. Rhizophagidae**

15(2). First 2 or 3 sterna fused or immovably united *16*
 All sterna free, or at least separated by equally distinct sutures, except in very rare cases
 .. *17*

16(15). First 2 sterna connate, with suture between them very weak; antennae serrate, very rarely pectinate in male; tarsomeres with membranous lobes beneath; last tarsomere not lengthened; claws moderate or small; antecoxal piece more or less distinct (see Fig. 24.19) ... **46. Buprestidae**
 First 3 sterna connate; antennae slender, slightly thickened externally; last tarsomere greatly elongate, with large claws; antecoxal piece absent **45. Elmidae**
 First 3 sterna connate; antennae with first segment long and stout, pectinate in males, serrate in females; last tarsomere not greatly elongate, with moderate claws; hind trochanters very long ... **50. Cerophytidae**

17(15). Prosternum prolonged behind into a median process that is received in mesosternum (see Fig. 24.20) ... *18*
 Prosternum without such a process; if so (rare), it is not received in mesosternum *21*

18(17). Prothorax loosely joined to mesothorax and freely movable, its hind angles usually produced (see Fig. 24.20); prosternal spine loosely received in a fossa in mesosternum (see Fig. 24.20); front coxal cavities lateral to spinasternum *19*
 Prothorax firmly attached, not movable; front coxal cavities partly covered by spinasternum laterally ... **49. Throscidae**

H. Key to the Pentamerous Families with Five Visible Abdominal Sterna (*Contd.*)

19(18). Labrum visible, free; antennae arising near eyes under frontal margin; last 2 sterna connected by membranous suture; prosternum usually lobed in front; species often capable of moving prothorax by its basal joint producing a click (see also Key I) **48. Elateridae**

Labrium concealed; no membranous fold between last 2 sterna; prosternum not lobed in front; antennae inserted on front between eys; received in transverse grooves on front; species not able to click ... *20*

 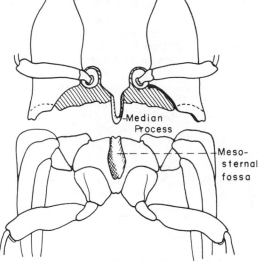

Fig. 24.19. Ventral view of metasternum showing antecoxal piece (Ant. Cx. P.).

Fig. 24.20. Ventral view of thoracic sterna showing prosternal process.

20(19). Claws simple ... **52. Eucnemidae**
Claws pectinate ... **51. Perothopidae**

21(17). Hind coxae contiguous **77. Phalacridae**
Hind coxae not contiguous, although very closely approximate in certain very much flattened species ... *22*

22(21). Elytra shortened, leaving 2 segments of abdomen exposed; antennae geniculate, very strongly clavate or capitate; tibiae compressed, front pair usually toothed; hard-bodied, smooth, shining species that are small, convex or much flattened, rarely elongate (see also couplet 10 and Key F) **26. Histeridae**
Elytra entire or nearly covering propygidium and usually pygidium *23*

23(22). Middle coxal cavities closed externally by sterna (see Fig. 24.15a) *24*
Middle coxal cavities open externally, not closed by meeting of meso- and metasterna (see Fig. 24.15b); body elongate, usually greatly flattened (see also Keys F and G) **72. Cucujidae**

24(23). Prosternum not prolonged behind; small (L. 2–3 mm), oval, coarsely punctate species with 4th tarsomere short and third bilobed **83. Biphyllidae**
Prosternum prolonged behind, meeting mesosternum *25*

25(24). Front coxal cavities open behind (see Fig. 24.15b); small or minute species (L. 0.5–3 mm), usually with angular anterior margins on pronotum and blunt, small lateral teeth; or if front coxal cavities are closed behind, then larger (L. +5 mm), more elongate species, usually with some evidence of lateral teeth on prothorax (see also Key F) **74. Cryptophagidae**
Front coxal cavities closed behind (see Fig. 24.15a); without thoracic teeth; antennae with abrupt club; moderate-sized species (L. 7–15+ mm), usually black with orange markings (Dacninae) (see also Key J) **76. Erotylidae**

26(1). Hind coxae dilated into plates that are grooved for reception of femora *27*
Hind coxae not dilated, not grooved for reception of femora *32*

27(26). Front coxal cavities closed behind (see Fig. 24.15a); 2 lateral ocelli .. **59. Derodontidae**
Front coxal cavities open behind (see Fig. 24.15b); ocelli present or absent *28*

28(27). Antennae with last 3 segments much enlarged, forming a strong club; scales usually on body (see also couplet 36 and Keys E and I) **61. Dermestidae**
Antennae not capitate ... *29*

H. Key to the Pentamerous Families with Five Visible Abdominal Sterna (*Contd.*)

29(28). Tarsi with long hairy pad (onychium) between claws; tibial spurs present; head prominent, porrect; antennae usually flabellate in male, often with more than 11 segments **38**
Onychium not developed ... **30**

30(29). Tibial spurs present .. **32. Helodidae**
Tibial spurs absent ... **31**

31(30). Prosternum large, area between coxae and head being nearly as long as wide; head erect; body depressed **37. Brachypsectridae**
Prosternum short, head reaching coxae when head in deflexed position; oval or cylindrical species .. **63. Anobiidae**

32(26). First tarsomere very short and indistinctly separated from 2nd **33**
First tarsomere distinct; if very short (rare), then 1st visible abdominal sternum not elongate and head not deflexed .. **34**

33(32). First visible abdominal sterna elongate, always much longer than 2nd; antennae with distinct 2-segmented club; small (L. 1–7 mm), elongate beetles with prominent head not covered by prothorax ... **65. Lyctidae**
First visible abdominal sternum not elongate; antennal club 3- or 4- segmented; head usually deflexed (except Psoinae) and protected by prothorax; declivity of elytra usually toothed or spined; elongate, more or less cylindrical species **64. Bostrichidae**

34(32). Hind coxae flat or oval, not extending more than slightly below base of abdomen **35**
Hind coxae prominent internally, extending well below abdomen **39**

35(34). Fourth tarsomere extremly short, not visible from above; usually brightly colored (Karynetinae) (see also couplet 37 and Key I) **67. Cleridae**
Fourth tarsomere not abnormally short .. **36**

36(35). Antennae 11-segmented, with solid club consisting of 3 almost entirely fused segments; length less than 2.0 mm; tufts of golden hairlike setae at sides of prothorax or beneath body; species live in ants' nests (Thorictini) (see couplet 32 and Key I) **61. Dermestidae**
Segments of antennal club not fused, or antennae with fewer segments, or without club ... **37**

37(36). Trochanters normal (Clerinae) (see also couplet 35 and Key I) **67. Cleridae**
Trochanters elongate (see Fig. 24.21) **62. Ptinidae**

Fig. 24.21. Leg showing elongate trochanter (t).

Fig. 24.22. Head and thorax: (Mx.Pl.) maxillary palpi, and (S₁) prosternum.

38(29). Tarsomeres lobed beneath **39. Rhipiceridae**
Tarsomeres not lobed beneath **40. Callirhipidae**

39(34). Antennae capitate ... **42**
Antennae not capitate, usually simple .. **40**

40(30). Prothorax very large, oval, longer than elytra; hind coxae very large, almost dividing 1st sternum; antennae very short; hind legs greatly thickened; (see also couplet 13 and Key J) ... **106. Cerambycidae**
Not as just described .. **41**

41(40). Antennae not flabellate; palpi normal; shape not extremely long and narrow (see also Key I) ... **68. Melyridae**
Antennae of female flabellate, of male serrate; male palpi greatly modified (see Fig. 24.22); female palpi normal; extremely long and narrow species (see also Key I) **69. Lymexylidae**

42(39). Elytra truncate ... **27. Sphaeritidae**
Elytra entire ... **43**

H. Key to the Pentamerous Families with Five Visible Abdominal Sterna (*Contd.*)

43(42). Procoxal cavities closed behind; dorsal surface pubescent; length less than 3 mm (*Colon* spp.) (see also Keys G and I) **22. Leptodiridae**

Procoxal cavities open behind; dorsal surface glabrous; length over 6 mm (Agyrtini) (see also Key I) ... **21. Silphidae**

I. Key to the Families of Pentamera with Six or Seven Visible Abdominal Sterna

1. Front coxae rounded (see Fig. 24.12d) or globose (see Fig. 24.12a), small, not prominent .. *2*

Front coxae conical, prominent, usually large (see Fig. 24.12c) *5*

2(1). Last tarsomere not excessively lengthened; tarsal claws not enlarged *3*

Last tarsomere greatly lengthened; tarsal claws very large; first 3 visible abdominal sterna connate; aquatic species **36. Psephenidae**

3(2). Prosternum prolonged behind into a process received in a notch in mesosternum; prothorax loosely attached to mesothorax *4*

Prosternum without such backwardly directed process; eyes very small or absent; species found in nests of rodents (see also Key B) **18. Leptinidae**

4(3). Labrum fused with clypeus; antennae distant at base; tibial spurs well developed **47. Cebrionidae**

Labrum free; tibial spurs very weak (see also Key H) **48. Elateridae**

5(1). Abdomen with 6th visible sternum conical and as long as 3 preceding segments combined .. **23. Scaphidiidae**

Abdomen with 6th visible segment not conical nor excessively lengthened. *6*

6(5). Hind coxae large, forming broad oblique plates that reach side margin of body and cover most of 1st sternum ... **31. Eucinetidae**

Hind coxae simple, not forming broad oblique plates *7*

7(6). Hind coxae flat, not prominent, covered by femora in repose; first posterior tarsomere usually very short and indistinct (see also Key H) **67. Cleridae**

Hind coxae prominent, at least internally *8*

8(7). Hind coxae widely separated .. *9*

Hind coxae approximate or contiguous *10*

9(8). Eyes absent (Catopocerini) (see also couplet 15 and Keys G and H) **22. Leptodiridae**

Eyes present, coarsely granulated; small (L. less than 3 mm), more or less ovate species .. **20. Scymaenidae**

Eyes present; abdomen with 7 visible sterna; small, elongate species with narrow elytra (*Thylodrias contractus*) (see also Keys E and H) **61. Dermestidae**

10(8). Tibial spurs large; antennae gradually thickened, clavate or capitate; hind tarsi slender, not widened; species usually found on carrion *11*

Tibial spurs small or indistinct .. *12*

11(10). Elytra that embrace sides, smooth and shiny; appendages capable of being retracted; deflexed head and thorax with abdomen capable of forming a ball ... **19. Leiodidae**

Elytra flat, somewhat truncate; appendages long and not capable of forming a ball ... *15*

12(10). Front coxae with distinctly exposed trochantin (see Fig. 24.23); small (L. 3–7 mm), usually soft-bodied species (see also Key H) **68. Melyridae**

Front coxae without visible trochantin *13*

Fig. 24.23. Front coxal area showing exposed trochantin (Trn), procoxa (Cx₁), elytra (Ely), pronotum (Prn), and prosternum (S₁).

I. Key to the Families of Pentamera with Six or Seven Visible Abdominal Sterna (*Contd.*)

13(12). Two ocelli present; maxillary palpi simple; body more or less ovate (*Brathinus* spp.) ...
.. **27. Staphylinidae**
 Ocelli absent; maxillary palpi often modified; body elongate *14*

14(13). Elytra shortened, exposing several abdominal segments; maxillary palpi simple in both
 sexes; very small species (L. ±2 mm) **58. Micromalthidae**
 Elytra entire; maxillary palpi of male flabellate (see also Keys D and H)
.. **69. Lymexylondiae**

15(11). Antennae clavate, with segment 8 somewhat smaller and narrower than segment 7 or 9;
 small species (L. 3–5 mm) (see also couplet 9 and Keys G and H) **22. Leptodiridae**
 Antennae clavate or capitate, with segment 8 subequal to 7 and 9; usually large beetles (L.
 8–20 mm) (see also Key H) **21. Silphidae**

J. Key to the Families with Pseudotetramerous Tarsomeres

1. Head not prolonged into a beak; gular sutures double (see Fig. 24.3), at least before and
 behind; pleurosternal sutures of prothorax distinct *2*
 Head usually prolonged in front of eyes and snoutlike (see Fig. 24.24); gular sutures
 confluent along median line or obsolete; pleurosternal suture present or absent;
 antennae usually geniculate; palpi usually rigid *6*

Fig. 24.24. General features of snoutlike head.

2(1). Antennae filiform or nearly so ... *3*
 Antennae distinctly clavate .. *4*

3(2). Oval, compact species; antennae and body usually with scales; elytra shortened, exposing
 pygidium; antennae eleven-segmented, serrate, rarely pectinate; head prolonged into
 broad snout ... **108. Bruchidae**
 If oval, compact species, then without preceding combination of characteristics *5*

4(2). Procoxal cavities narrowly open behind; somewhat elongate, cylindrical species
.. **25. Languriidae**
 Procoxal cavities closed behind; more oval, somewhat depressed species (Erotylinae and
 Triplacinae) (see also Key H) **76. Erotylidae**

5(3). Antennae usually long or greatly developed, frequently inserted on frontal prominences;
 front often vertical, large, and quadrate; pronotum rarely margined; tibial spurs well
 developed; usually rather large, elongate or oblong species with parallel sides and
 pubescent upper surface (see also Key H) **106. Cerambycidae**
 Antennae moderate or short, not inserted on frontal prominences; front small, oblique,
 sometimes greatly inflexed; prothorax most frequently margined; tibial spurs usually
 absent; body usually glabrous above and often rather oval in form
.. **107. Chrysomelidae**

J. Key to the Families with Pseudotetramerous Tarsomeres (*Contd.*)

6(1). Beak extremely short and broad, scarcely developed; tibiae with series of teeth externally or front tibiae anteriorly produced, forming stout curved process at apex; antennae short with broad club; small, oval, cylindrical species **7**

Beak of variable length, usually at least longer than broad; tibiae simple, without teeth externally or process at apex; antennae clubbed or not **8**

7(6). First anterior tarsomere shorter than 2nd, 3rd, and 4th combined; eyes oval, emarginate or divided; head narrower than prothorax **112. Scolytidae**

First anterior tarsomere very long, longer than 2nd, 3rd, and 4th combined; head broader than prothorax; eyes rounded **111. Platypodidae**

8(6). Antennae straight without distinct club, but with outer segments often more or less thickened; beak present in female at least and pointing directly forward; body very slender and elongate **110. Brentidae**

Antennae straight or geniculate, always with distinct club **9**

9(8). Palpi flexible; antennal club rarely compact; beak always short and broad; labrum present; thorax with transverse raised line either ante basal or basal
... **109. Anthribidae**

Palpi rigid; antennal club usually compact; labrum absent except in subfamily Rhinomacerinae, which have long, well-developed beak; beak variable in length, often long and curved downward .. **113. Curculionidae**

Suborder ARCHOSTEMATA

One family, as follows:

1. CUPEDIDAE (Reticulated Beetle Family)

Length: 7–25 mm. Body elongate, somewhat depressed and covered with broad scales; rows of closely placed, square punctures on elytra. Adults and larvae found in logs of oak, chestnut, and pine with adults sometimes found swarming in sunlit woods. There are five species in the U.S. and Canada, as follows:

1.1 *Cupes* Fabricius

Four species [(1), (2), (3), (5)], of which the following is common:

C. concolor Westwood (Mottled Cupes). L. 7–11 mm. Yellowish brown; elytra mottled by irregular pattern of interrupted, narrow, darker lines of scale. Larvae bore into pine and oak. Found in dead wood and under bark. (See Fig. 24.25.) (1) MI, NY, IN, PA, DE, MD; (2) SC, GA, FL.

Fig. 24.25.

1.2 *Priacma* LeConte

One species, as follows:

P. serrata (LeConte). (3) CA; (4) BC, WA, OR, ID; (5) MT.

Suborder ADEPHAGA

First abdominal sternum cut through by the hind coxae; tarsi with five tarsomeres; antennae simple, rarely clubbed. For identification of the families of Adephaga, see Table 24.4.

The following eight families belong in this suborder.

2. RHYSODIDAE (Wrinkled Bark Beetle Family)

Length: 5–8 mm. Head deeply grooved; antennae beadlike; pronotum with deep grooves; dark brown or black and shiny. The family contains eight species in the U.S. and Canada.

[2.1 *Omoglymmius* Ganglbauer [=*Rhysodes* of authors] (2 spp.: *O. americanus* Laporte, (1) WI, MI, ON, IL, IN, OH, PA, NJ, MA; (2) KY, TN, VA, NC, AR, LA, MS, AL, FL; (5) MN, NE, IA, KS, MO; and *O. hamatus* LeConte, (3) CA, AZ; (4) WA, OR, ID)]

2.2 *Clindium* Kirby

The six species found in the U.S. and Canada, in (1), (2), (3), and (5) are assigned to the subgenus *Arctoclinidium* Bell, of which the following is a common representative:

C. sculptile Newman. L. 5.5–7.5 mm. Elytra with intervals narrower than deep intervening grooves; male with front tibia distinctly toothed. (See Fig. 24.26.) (1) NY, IN, OH, PA, NJ, DE, MD, DC; (2) KY, WV, VA, TN, NC, SC, AL, GA; (5) MO.

3. CICINDELIDAE (Tiger Beetle Family)

Length: 6–24 mm. Body elongate, cylindrical; usually brightly colored; mandibles large; eyes very large; legs long, with heavy spines.

Larvae have large heads and prominent jaws and live in vertical burrows dug in sandy soil. Their body forms a plug at the top of the tunnel, where they await the passing of an insect, worm, or similar creature of the right size. With jaws open, they leap their body length out of the tunnel, grasp their prey, and consume it while it is still alive. (See Fig. 24.27.)

Table 24.4 Identification of the Families of Adephaga

Family	Principal feature	Habitat and Distribution
Rhysodidae (2)	Antennae beadlike	Under bark; mostly eastern U.S.
Cicindelidae (3)	Mandibles large; body with long, erect setae; usually bright colored	Often in sandy areas; generally distributed
Carabidae (4)	Large hind trochanters; usually black, with few erect setae	Almost all species terrestrial; common under logs, stones, near water; generally distributed
Amphizoidae (5)	Resemble Carabidae but lack erect setae	Aquatic; Pacific Coast States east to Colorado, Montana
Haliplidae (6)	Hind coxal plates nearly cover abdominal sterna; length: 2–6 mm.	Aquatic; generally distributed
Dytiscidae (7)	Streamlined, with legs modified for swimming; scutellum usually present.	Aquatic; generally distributed
Noteridae (8)	Similar to Dytiscidae but lack scutellum; L. 1.2–5.5 mm.	Aquatic; eastern and southern U.S.
Gryinidae (9)	Two pairs of eyes; antennae clubbed; streamlined, with legs fitted for swimming.	Aquatic; generally distributed.

Adults of many species are found actively pursuing prey in sunny, sandy glades. They tear their victums apart and consume them as rapidly as the larvae do. Sometimes adults occur in great numbers and destroy nearly all suitable victims that wander near them (see Fig. 24.28.)

There are 108 species in the U.S. and Canada.

Fig. 24.26.

Fig. 24.27.

Subfamily **Cicindelinae**

Tribe **Megacephalini**

Subtribe **Omina**

[3.1 *Amblychila* Say (5 spp. (3), (5))]

3.2 *Omus* Eschscholtz

Fifteen species—(3), (4)—including the following:

O. dejeani Reiche (Dejean's Omus). L. 15–21 mm. Black; elytra with numerous very large scattered pits among smaller punctures; remainder of body nearly smooth. (See A&J 83.) Adults will bite if handled. Found in rotten stumps. (4) BC, WA, OR.

Subtribe **Megacephalina**

[3.3 *Megacephala* Latreille (2 spp. (1), (2), (3), (4), (5))]

Tribe **Cicindelini**

Subtribe **Cicindelina**

3.4 *Cicindela* Linnaeus

The 86 species in the U.S. and Canada are assigned to the following subgenera: *Cicindela* s. str.; *Cicindelidia* Rivalier; *Habroscelimorpha* Dokhtourow; *Eunota* Rivalier; *Microthylax* Rivalier; *Opilidia* Rivalier; *Brasiella* Rivalier; *Cylindera* Westwood; *Ellipsoptera* Doktourow; and *Dromochorus* Guerin. Many species are common, including the following:

C. (Cicindela) repanda Dejean (Bronze Tiger Beetle). L. 12–13 mm. Bronze brown; humeral crescent complete. (See A&J 81.) Occurs on sand and gravel banks and other sandy places. (1) n.e. NA; (2) s.e. US; (5) n. Central States.

C. (Cicindela) formosa generosa Dejean (Noble Tiger Beetle). L. 16.5–18 mm. Bronze brown on greenish copper, with

Fig. 24.28.

Fig. 24.29.

middle band of elytra turned strongly backward, color variable. (1) n.e. US; (2) KY, WV, VA, TN, AR, LA, MS; (5) IA, MO.

C. (Cicindela) splendida Hentz (Splendid Tiger Beetle). L. 12–15 mm. Elytral margins metallic blue or green, strongly contrasting with brillant copper red or malachite green disk of the elyta. (See A&J 82.) Usually found in sandy areas, particularly in evergreen forests. (1) WI, IL, IN, PA, MD, DC; (2) KY, WV, VA, TN, NC, AR, LA, MS, AL, GA, SC; (3) OK, TX; (5) MN, WY, NE, IA, CO, KS, MO.

C. (Cicindela) sexguttata Fabricius (Six-spotted Tiger Beetle). L. 10–14 mm. Brilliant metallic green or violet; elytra with six white spots, or fewer, rarely more. Adults hibernate and appear in spring and early summer. Common along paths and open sandy areas in woods and along roadways. (1) n.e. US; (2) s.e. US; (3) NM, OK, TX; (5) MN, SD, NE, IA, KS, MO.

C. (Habroscelimorpha) dorsalis Say (White Beach Tiger Beetle). L. 13–15 mm. Elytra predominantly white; head, thorax, abdomen, and legs metallic green. Common in white sandy areas. (1) NY, MA, CT, RI, NJ, DE, MD; (2) VA, NC, SC, GA, FL, LA, MS, AL; (3) TX.

C. (Cylindera) unipunctata Fabricius. L. 16–18 mm. Dull brown dorsally, dark blue ventrally; elytra rough with green pits and a triangular marginal white dot. (See Fig. 24.29.) (1) n.e. US; (2) s.e. Us; (5) IA, MO.

4. CARABIDAE (Ground Beetle Family)

Length: 2–85 mm (usually 4–12 mm). As a group, the ground beetles are a dull black, although some are bluish or greenish, a few are marked with red or white, and some are red, tan, or brown. Their shape is characteristic of the family—elongate, somewhat flattened, with more or less parallel sides, often with the pronotum narrower than the elytra. The elytra is usually entire. The legs are long, with the large hind trochanter extending nearly to, and sometimes beyond, the hind margin of the second abdominal sternum.

The family is abundant both in species and individuals. Most species are predacious as adults and larvae. Adults are found under logs or stones, on grassy ground, or along the shore of ponds and streams. They rarely fly, but some are attracted to lights at night and to sugar bait.

Ground beetles are difficult to identify to species without technical descriptions that use the number and position of setae on the head and thorax, the shape of the legs, and the structure and sculpturing of the elytra.

The family is divided into four subfamilies, 20 supertribes, and 42 tribes. Some classifications include the Cicindelidae and Rhysodidae as supertribes of the Carabidae, to which they certainly are closely related, and the tribe Trachypachini as a separate family—the Trachypachidae. Since these assignments are not consistent with the rest of the classification of the order, however, the traditional arrangement is retained here. There are 168 genera and 2271 species recorded in the U.S. and Canada. Only a very few of these are described here, but those that are represent some of the most commonly collected species.

Subfamily Trachypachinae

Tribe Trachypachini

[4.1 *Trachypachus* Motschulsky (3 spp. (3), (4), (5))]

Subfamily Omophroninae

Tribe Omophronini

4.2 *Omophron* Latreille

L. 5–8 mm. Oval with variegated black or green markings. Adults found in burrows in mud or sand in moist situations, usually along shores of lakes, ponds, or streams. They may be driven to the surface by throwing water on the soil containing their burrows. Of the eleven species, the following are common representatives:

O. americanum DeJean (Hunch-backed Beetle). L. 6–7 mm. Elytra with 15 striae; thorax with pale side margins; mouthparts, legs, and sides of elytra yellow, with three spots protruding into black or green of elytra. (See A&J 85.) Common in ponds. (1) NF, NS, PE, NB, PQ, ON, NH, MA, CT, NY, NJ, PA, DE, MD; (2) VA, NC, SC, FL, AL, MS, LA, AR, TN; (3) OK, TX, NM, AZ:; (4) UT, ID; (5) AB, SA, MB, ND, SD, MN, NE, IA, CO, OK.

[*O. tesselatum* Say. Very similar to the preceding. (See Fig. 24.30.) (1) n.e. US; (2) VA, KY; (3) s.e. US; (5) n. Central States.

Subfamily Paussinae

Supertribe Metriitae

Tribe Metriini

[4.3 *Metrius* Eschscholtz (2 spp. (3), (4))]

Supertribe Brachinitae

Tribe Brachinini

4.4 *Brachinus* Weber

The species of this genus are noted for their ability to spray a defensive, irritating gas at would-be predators. They are recognized by the square-cut apices of the elytra. Of the 48 species in the U.S. and Canada, the following is a common representative.

Fig. 24.30.

B. fumans Fabricius (Bombardier Beetle). L. 11–12.5 mm. Head and thorax orange; elytra dull blue, with sides nearly parallel. Gregarious in the spring. Eggs are laid in mud cells built by the female on stems, twings, or stones. The larvae parasitize pupae of aquatic beetles. Found under logs and stones, usually in damp woods. (1), (2), (3), (4), (5), generally distributed.

Supertribe Paussitae

Tribe Ozaenini

[4.5 *Goniotropis* Gray (1 sp., *G. parca* LeConte (3) AZ); 4.6 *Pachyteles* Perty (1 sp., *P. testacea* Horn (3) AZ)]

Subfamily Carabinae

Supertribe Nebriitae

Tribe Opisthiini

[4.7 *Opisthius* Kirby (1 sp., *O. richardsoni* Kirby (3) NM, CA; (4) OR, WA, BC, AK, NV, UT, ID; (5) NW, YU, AB, SA,MT,WY,CO))]

Tribe Nebriini

[4.8 *Leistus* Froelich (4 spp. (1), (3), (4)); 4.9 *Pelophila* Dejean (2 spp. (1), (4))]

4.10 *Nebria* Letreille

Forty-three species, found along the margins of cold streams, the following being common:

N. pallipes Say. L. 10–12 mm. Black; head with two vague, dull red spots between eyes; apices of elytra broadly rounded. Restricted to wet places in forested regions or under stones near running water. (1) n.e. US; (2) KY, WV, VA, TN, NC, SC.

Tribe Notiophilini

[4.11 *Notiophilus* Dumeril (15 spp.)]

Supertribe Carabitae

Tribe Carabini

Species are large, predatory beetles, often brightly colored with green, blue, or purple; some have red spots.

4.12 *Carabus* Linnaeus

Thirteen species, including the following:

C. vinctus Weber. L. 21–25 mm. Elytra with dull satiny luster, bronzed, but not strongly so. A common species found in damp woodlands, often hiding under bark. (1) ON, NY, PA, DE, IN; (2) NC, SC, GA, FL. (See Fig. 24.31.)

4.13 *Calosoma* Weber

Thirty-nine species, the following being representative:

C. scrutator Fabricius (Caterpillar Hunter). L. 25–36 mm. Elytra metallic green or violet. Found in fields; often attracted to street lights at night. (1) n.e. US; (2) s.e. US; (3) s.w. US; (5) CO, IA, KS, NK, MO, SD.

C. calidum Fabricius (Fiery Hunter). L. 19–24 mm. Side margin of pronotum broadened behind and upturned; pits of elytra red or green, large, nearly touching the striae. (See Fig. 24.32.) Occurs in fields and gardens where it feeds on cutworms and other larvae. (1) n.e. US; (2) KY, TN, VA, NC, GA; (3) NM; (4) BC, WA; (5) NW, MB, SA, AB, CO, IA, KS, MT, NK, ND, SD.

Tribe Cychrini

These sometimes very common beetles are large, black, and often rather colorful, the edge of their bodies being marked with violet or purple. The head is long, with long narrow mandibles. They feed on snails in most woods and similar places.

[4.14 *Sphaeroderus* Dejean (6 spp. (1), (2), (5)); 4.15 *Cychrus* Fabricius (3 spp. (3), (4), (5))]

4.16 *Scaphinotus* Latreille

Forty-nine species occur in the U.S. and Canada, of which the following are common:

S. elevatus Fabricius, with five subspecies as follows: *S. e. elevatus* s. str. (1) NY, MA, DE; (2) NC, SC, FL, AR, AL; (3) TX, NM; (5) MB, SD, MN, NE, CO, IA, KS; *S. e. neomexicanus* VanDyke (3) NM; *S. e. tenebricosus* Roeschke (2) NC, SC; *S. e. coloradensis* VanDyke (3) NM; (5) CO, NE; and *S. e. lengi* VanDyke (2) VA. (See Fig. 24.33.)

S. viduus Dejean. L. 18–33 mm. Black, dorsally bluish, purple, or coppery; pronotum with broad, laminate lobes on posterior lateral margin. Feeds on snails. (1) NB, PQ, NH, VT, OH, PA; (2) NC, FL.

S. angulatus Harris (Snail Eating Ground Beetle). L. 16–30 mm. Black; elytra somewhat metallic purple; head about twice as long as broad and much narrower than pronotum; pronotum with side margins in front of hind angles posteriorly divergent; elytra 14-striate. Feeds on snails. (4) BC, WA, OR.

S. angusticollis Mannerheim (Narrow Snail Eater). L. 16–24 mm. Black with brownish red on elytra and head; pronotum and elytral margin somewhat greenish; elytra slightly sculptured with about 20 striae; both maxillary and labial palpi

Fig. 24.31.

Fig. 24.32.

Fig. 24.33.

each with apical segment enlarged and spoon-shaped. Occurs in forests, where adults feed on snails and slugs. (See A&J 84.) (3) CA; (4) AK, BC, WA, OR.

Supertribe Loriceritae

Tribe Loricerini

[4.17 *Loricera* Latreille (3 spp. (1), (3), (4), (5))]

Supertribe Elaphritae

Tribe Elaphrini

The species belonging to this tribe stridulate, squeaking when held. Most species are found near water.

[4.18 *Diacheila* Motschulsky (2 spp. (1), (4), (5)); 4.19 *Blethisa* Bonelli (5 spp. (1), (4), (5))]

4.20 *Elaphrus* Fabricius

Seventeen species, including the following:

E. ruscarius Say. L. 7–8 mm. Resembles the tiger beetle. Dull brass dorsally; metallic green ventrally; legs reddish brown; body with large "pock-marks." (See Fig. 24.34.) Found on mud flats or other muddy areas along the shores of streams, ponds, and bogs. (1) ON, DE; (2) SC; (3) TX; (5) SD.

Supertribe Scarititae

Tribe Promecognathus

[4.21 *Promecognathus* Chaudoir (2 spp. (3), (4))]

Tribe Scaritini

4.22 *Pasimachus* Bonelli

Ten species, including the following:

P. depressus Fabricius. L. 23–26 mm. Black; pronotum and elytra margined with blue. Found in sandy regions where it preys on caterpillars. (1) NY, NJ, PA; (2) NC, SC, FL.

4.23 *Scarites* Fabricius

Three species, including the following:

S. subterraneus Fabricius. L. 20–22 mm. Shiny black; head with two deeply impressed grooves on front half. Feigns death by holding body rigid. Common in gardens. (1) ON, PA, DE; (2) SC, FL; (3) CA; (5) SD.

4.24 *Dyschirius* Bonelli

Fifty-six species, found in wet sand banks bordering streams. Usually seen running about at night, they will emerge during the day if water is poured over the sand. The following is an example:

Fig. 24.34. **Fig. 24.35.**

D. integer LeConte. L. 3–5 mm. (1) NF, NY; (3) CA; (4) AK; (5) SD.

4.25 *Clivina* Latreille

Twenty four species, found on mud flats and shores of streams, the following of which is a pest:

C. impressifrons LeConte (Slender Seedcorn Beetle). L. 6–6.5 mm. Uniformly reddish brown. Sometimes found in damp areas in fields and known to feed on sprouting seeds of corn. (See Fig. 24.35.) (1) NY, IN, DE; (2) KY; (5) SD, IA, KS.

[4.26 *Halocoryza* Alluaud (1 sp., *H. arenaria* Darlington (2) FL); 4.27 *Schizogenius* Putzeys (24 spp.); 4.28 *Oxydrepanus* Putzeys (1 sp., *O. rufus* Putzeys (2) FL); 4.29 *Ardistomis* Putzeys (5 spp. (1), (2), (3)); 4.30 *Aspidoglossa* Putzeys (1 sp., *A. subangulata* Chaudoir)]

Tribe Morionini

[4.31 *Morion* Latreille (2 spp. (1), (2), (3), (5))]

Supertribe Broscitae

Tribe Broscini

[4.32 *Miscodera* Eschscholtz (1 sp., *M. arctica* Paykull (1) NF, LB, PQ, ON, ME, NH, NY, WI; (4) WA, BC, AK; (5) AB, SA, MB, NW, YU, MT); 4.33 *Broscodera* Lindroth (1 sp., *B insignis* Mannerheim (4) OR, BC, AK); 4.34 *Zacotus* LeConte (1 sp., *Z. matthewsi* LeConte (3) CA; (4) OR, WA, BC, AK, ID; (5) MT)]

Supertribe Psydritae

Tribe Nomiini

4.35 *Nomius* Laporte

One species, as follows:

N. pygmaeus (Dejean) (Stink Beetle). L. 6–8 mm. Chestnut brown to dull black. The foul smell emitted when this beetle is handled accounts for its common name. Found under stones and at lights at night. (1) PQ, ON, MI, DE; (2) SC, GA; (3) CA; (4) AB, MB.

Tribe Psydrini

[4.36 *Psydrus* LeConte (1 sp., *P. piceus* LeConte (1) PQ, ON; (3) CA, AZ; (4) OR, WA, BC; (5) AB, MB.

Supertribe Trechitae

Tribe Trechini

[4.37 *Trechoblemus* Ganglbaur (1 sp., *T. westcotti* Barr (4) OR); 4.38 *Pseudanophthalmus* Jeannel (89 spp. (1), (2)); 4.39 *Nelsonites* Valentine (2 spp. (2)); 4.40 *Neaphaenops* Jeannel (1 sp., *N. tellkampf* Erichson (2) KY); 4.41 *Xenotrechus* Barr and Krekeler (2 spp. (5) MO); 4.42 *Aphanotrechus* Barr (1 sp., *A. virginicus* Barr (2) VA); 4.43 *Darlingtonea* Valentine (1 sp., *D. kentuckensis* Valentine (2) KY); 4.44 *Ameroduvalius* Valentine (1 sp., *A. jeaneli* Valetine (2) KY); 4.45 *Trechus* Clairville (38 spp.)]

Tribe Pogonini

[4.46 *Thalassotrechus* VanDyke (1 sp., *T. baebarae* Horn (3) CA); 4.47 *Pogonus* Dejean (1 sp., *P. texanus* Chaudoir (3) TX); 4.48 *Pogonistes* Chaudoir (1 sp., *P. planatus* Horn (3) CA); 4.49 *Diplochaetus* Chaudoir (2 spp. (1), (2), (3))]

Tribe Gehringiini

[4.50 *Gehringia* Darlington (1 sp., *G. olympica* Darlington (4) OR, WA, BC; (5); MT, AB)]

Fig. 24.36.

Fig. 24.37.

Tribe Bembidiini

[4.51 *Mioptachys* Bates (1 sp., *M. flavicauda* Say (1) PA; (2)WV, SC, LA; (5) SD); 4.52 *Tachyta* Kirby (5 spp.); 4.53 *Elaphropus* Motschulsky (31 spp.); 4.54 *Pericompus* LeConte (3 spp. (1), (2), (3)); 4.55 *Tachys* Stephens (12 spp.); 4.56 *Paratachys* Casey (18 spp. (1), (2), (3), (5)); 4.57 *Porotachys* Netolitzky (1 sp., *P. bisulcatus* Nicolay (1) NY); 4.58 *Polyderis* Motschulsky (3 spp. (1), (2), (3), (5)); 4.59 *Micratopus* Casey (1 sp., *M. aenescens* LeConte (2) GA); 4.60 *Anillodes* Jeannel (2 spp., (3) CA); 4.61 *Troglanillus* Jeannel (1 spl., *T. valentinei* Jeannel (2) AL); 4.62 *Anillinus* Casey (12 spp. (1), (2), (3), (5)); 4.63 *Anillaspis* Casey (2 spp. (3)); 4.64 *Horologion* Valentine (1 sp., *H. speokites* Valentinre (2) WV); 4.65 *Phrypeus* Casey (1 sp., *P. rickseckeri* Hayward (3) CA; (4) OR, BC); 4.66 *Asaphidion* des Gozis (3 spp. (1), (4), (5))]

4.67 *Bembidion* Latreille

L. 3–6 mm. Very difficult to identify to species, these beetles are found on mud flats, sand banks along streams, or sometimes in dry fields and woods. There are 255 species in the U.S. and Canada. (See Fig. 24.36 for *B. lenae* Csiki.)

Supertribe Patrebitae

Tribe Patrobini

[4.68 *Diplous* Motschulsky (4 sp. (1), (3), (4), (5)); 4.69 *Platidiolus* Chaudoir (1 sp., *P. vandykei* Kurnakow (4) WA, BC, AK; (5) AB); 4.70 *Patrobus* Dejean (6 spp.); 4.71 *Platypatrobus* Darlington (1 sp., *P. lacustris* Darlington (1) PQ, ON, ME, NH, VT; (5) NW, AB)]

Supertribe Pseudomorphitae

Tribe Pseudomorphini

[4.72 *Pseudomorpha* Kirby (19 spp. (2), (3))]

Supertribe Pterostichitae

Tribe Pterostichini

(These very abundant species are found in desert regions and elsewhere.

[4.73 *Sericoda* Kirby (4 spp.)]

4.74 *Agonum* Bonelli

There are 115 species in this genus, including the following:

A. cupripenne Say. L. 7.5–9.5 mm. Shiny; head and pronotum green or blue; elytra disc reddish or coppery, sharply delimited laterally by green, blue, or bronze; ventrally black with black legs. Found in fields and near water. (1) NS, PA, DE; (2) NC; (4) OR, BC; (5) SD, KS.

A. maculicolle Dejean (Tule Beetle). L. 7–9 mm. Found, among other plants, near the large bulrush, tule (*Scirpus* spp.), that grows in its range. (3) CA; (4) OR.

[4.75 *Olisthopus* Dejean (6 spp. (1), (2)); 4.76 *Colpodes* MacLeay (1 sp., *C. buchanani* Hope (4) OR))]

4.77 *Platynus* Bonelli

Many of the 55 species assigned to this genus are found under stones and logs but are also attracted in large numbers to sugary moth bait.

[4.78 *Anchonoderus* Reiche (2 spp., (3) TX); 4.79 *Atranus* LeConte (1 sp., with 2 subspp.: *A. pubescens* Dejean (1) PQ, ON, NH, NY, IN, DC; (2) WV, VA, SC and *A. p. pallescens* Casey (1) PA); 4.80 *Lachnophorus* Dejean (1 sp., *L. elegantulus* Mannerheim (3) TX, AZ, CA); 4.81 *Euphorticus* Horn (2 spp. (2), (3)); 4.82 *Ega* Laporte (2 spp., (2), (3), (5)); 4.83 *Myas* Dejean (2 spp. (1), (2)); 4.84 *Stomis* Schellenberg (1 sp., *S. pumicata* Panzer (1) PQ)]

4.85 *Pterostichus* Bonelli

L. 7–24 mm. Common throughout the year (when warm enough) under stones and similar hiding places. The 234 species are very similar and difficult to identify (See Fig. 24.37 for *P. mutus* Say.)

[4.86 *Abacidus* LeConte (6 spp., (1), (2), (3), (5)); 4.87 *Abax* Bonelli (1 sp., *A. parallelepipedus* Piller and Mitterpacher (1) NS); 4.88 *Evarthrus* LeConte (43 spp., (1), (2), (3), (5)); 4.89 *Loxandrus* LeConte (62 spp., (1); (2); a few (3) TX, OK; a few (5) IA, KS, MO); 4.90 *Oxycrepis* Reiche (1 sp., *O. intercepta* Chaudoir (3) TX); 4.91 *Synchus* Gyllenhal (2 spp.); 4.92 *Pristonychus* Dejean (2 spp., (1), (3), (4)); 4.93 *Calathus* Bonelli (10 spp.)]

Tribe Zobrini

[4.94 *Disamara* Lindroth (1 sp., *D. arenaria* (LeConte) (1) PQ, ON, MI, VT, NH, NY); 4.95 *Amara* Bonelli (132 spp.)]

Supertribe Panagaeitae

Tribe Panagaeini

[4.96 *Panageus* Latreille (3 spp.); 4.97 *Micrixys* LeConte (1 sp., *M. distincta* Haldeman (3) TX)]

Supertribe Callistitae

Tribe Callistini

4.98 *Chlaenius* Bonelli

This group of moderately large ground beetles are usually brightly colored, pubescent, and foul-smelling. The 50 species in the U.S. and Canada include the following:

C. pensylvanicus Say (Say's Ground Beetle). L. 10–12 mm. Dorsal surface green; head and pronotum bright green and shiny, the latter with lateral margins brownish; elytra darker green; legs, palpi, and antennae reddish brown; elytra with striae fine and distinctly punctate and intervals between striae flat and densely and finely punctate. Found under stones in woodlands and along fence rows or in grass in wet areas. (1) n.e. NA; (2) s.e. US; (4) Pacific n.w.; (5) AB, SA, MB, MT, SD, MN, CO, IA, KS.

C. sericeus Foerster (Green Ground Beetle). L. 13–17 mm. Body elongate-oval, convex; bright green, sometimes with bluish tinge; antennae usually pale but with darker apex; legs pale; ventral surface nearly black; otherwise similar to the preceding. Adults common. (A&J 86). (See Fig. 24.38.) (1) n.e. NA; (2) s.e. US; (3) s.w. US; (4) BC, WA, OR, NV, UT, ID; (5) n. Central States.

Fig. 24.38. Fig. 24.39.

Fig. 24.40. Fig. 24.41.

Tribe Oodini

[4.99 *Oodes* Bonelli (4 spp. (1), (2), (3), (5)); 4.100 *Stenocrepis* Chaudoir (7 spp. (1), (2), (3), (5)); 4.101 *Anatrichus* LeConte (3 spp. (1), (2), (3)); 4.102 *Evolenes* LeConte (1 sp., *E. exarata* Dejean (2) SC, GA, FL, AL); 4.103 *Dercylinus* Chaudoir (1 sp., *D. impressus* LeConte (2) LA)]

Tribe Licinini

[4.104 *Diplocheila* Brulle (8 spp.)]

4.105 *Dicaelus* Bonelli

Fourteen species, occurring in (1), (2), (3), (5), including the following:

D. dilatus Say. L. 20–25 mm. Black; pronotum about one and one-half times as wide as long; elytra with deep striae. (See Fig. 24.39.) Found under stones and logs in woods.

[4.106 *Licinus* Latreille (1 sp., *L. silphoides* Rossi (1) MA); 4.107 *Badister* Clairville (15 spp.)]

Supertribe Harpalitae

Tribe Harpalini

[4.108 *Xestonotus* LeConte (1 sp., *X. lugubris* Dejean (1) NS, PQ, ON, MI, NY, MA, PA; (5) SD, IA; 4.109 *Nottobis* Perty (7 spp. (1), (3), (5))]

4.110 *Anisodactylus* Dejean

Members of this genus are often common and are found under stones, in leaf litter, and under logs, especially in dry, open upland woods. There are 33 species in the U.S. and Canada.

4.111 *Geopinus* LeConte

One species, as follows.

G. incrassatus Dejean (Burrowing Ground Beetle). L. 13–17 mm. Pale reddish brown; front tibiae modified for digging; elytra with at least the inner stria darker; pronotum with a more or less pronounced central cloud. Burrows in sand and often under logs partly buried in sand; sometimes attracted to lights. (See Fig. 24.40.) (1) PQ, ON, NY, IN, DE, DC; (2) SC, AR; (5) SA, MB, SD, MN, IA, KS.

[4.112 *Amphasia* Newman (2 spp., (1), (2), (5)); 4.113 *Dicheirus* Mannerheim (5 spp. (3), (4))]

4.114 *Stenolophus* Stephens

Forty-one species, the following of which are representative:

S. comma Fabricius. L. 5.5–8 mm. Body reddish brown; pronotum pale, sometimes with a darker center; elytra with discal spot reaching the base for its entire width, or truncate, but not extending forward along the suture. Common at lights at

night. (1) NF, PQ, ON, NY, MA, DE; (2) SC; (3) TX, AZ; (4) UT, BC; (5) AB, SA, MB, SD.

S. plebejus Dejean. Similar to the preceding. (See Fig. 24.41.)

S. lecontei (Chaudoir) (Seed-corn Beetle). Similar to the preceding, but discal black spot of elytra is prolonged along suture toward the base. Feeds on planted corn seeds, damaging them before they sprout. Attracted to lights at night. (1) PQ, ON, WI, DE; (2) SC, AR; (3) OK; (5) KS.

[4.115 *Bradycellus* Erichson (54 spp.); 4.116 *Amerinus* Casey (3 spp. (1), (2)); 4.117 *Trichocellus* Ganglbauer (2 spp. (1), (3), (4), (5)); 4.118 *Acupalpus* Latreille (19 spp.), 4.119 *Polpochila* Solier (3 spp. (3)); 4.120 *Pogonodaptus* Horn (1 sp., *P. mexicanus* (Bates) (3) TX); 4.121 *Piosoma* LeConte (1 sp., *P. setosum* LeConte (3) NM, AZ; (4) BC; (5) AB, SA, SD, CO); 4.122 *Euryderus* LeConte (1 sp., *E. grossus* Say (1) ON, OH; (3) TX, AZ; (4) OR, WA, BC; (5) AB, MB, SD, MN, NE, CO, IA); 4.123 *Harpalobrachys* Tschitscherine (1 sp., *H. leiroides* Motschulsky (4) AK; (5) NW)]

4.124 *Harpalus* Latreille

The 97 species in the U.S. and Canada are very difficult to identify. Most are 7 to 15 mm in length, rather broad, with a square pronotum. The following is representative:

H. pensylvanicus DeGeer. Common under logs and litter, especially at edges of cultivated fields. Attracted to lights at night. Abundant. (See Fig. 24.42.) (1) n.e. NA; (2) s.e. US; (3) s.w. US; (4) Pacific n.w.; (5) MB, MT, ND, MN, WY, SD, NE, IA, CO, KS, MO.

[4.125 *Episcopellus* Casey (1 sp., *E. autumnalis* Say (1) ON, NY, MA, IN, PA, DC; (2) SC); 4.126 *Selenophorus* Dejean (39 spp.); 4.127 *Discoderus* LeConte (24 spp. (1), (2), (3), (5)); 4.128 *Hartonymus* Casey (2 spp. (1), (2), (3), (5)); 4.129 *Stenomorphus* Dejean (3 spp. (2), (3)); 4.130 *Ambylgnathus* Dejean (3 spp. (2), (3)); 4.131 *Gynandropus*

Fig. 24.42.

Dejean (2 spp., (1), (2)); 4.132 *Harpalellus* Lindroth (1 sp., *H. basilaris* Kirby (1) NS, PQ, ON; (4) Pacific n.w.; (5) NW, YU, AB, SA, MB, SD, CO); 4.133 *Aztecarpalus* Ball (1 sp., *A. schaefferi* Ball (3) TX); 4.134 *Trichotichnus* Morawitz (3 spp. (1), (2), (5)); 4.135 *Catacanthus* Dejean (4 spp. (1), (2), (3), (5))]

Supertribe Ctenodactylitae

Tribe Ctenodactylini

[4.136 *Leptotrachelus* Latreille (3 spp. (1), (2), (3), (5))]

Supertribe Lebiitae

Tribe Perigonini

[4.137 *Perigona* Laporte (1 sp., *P. nigriceps* Dejean (1) PQ, IN, NH, NJ, DC; (2) NC, SC, FL, AL; (3) CA)]

Tribe Masoreini

[4.138 *Tetragonoderus* Dejean (4 spp., (1), (2), (3))]

Tribe Pentagonicini

[4.139 *Pentagonica* Schmidt-Goebel (4 spp., (1), (2), (3))]

Tribe Odacanthini

[4.140 *Colliuris* DeGeer (3 spp., (1), (2), (3), (5))]

Tribe Lebiini

Members of this tribe are rather different from other members of the family in that many are nocturnal, arboreal, and may be colorfully marked. A few are found on plants during the day.

[4.141 *Cymindis* Latreille (6 spp.); 4.142 *Apenes* LeConte (3 spp. (1), (2), (3)); 4.143 *Pinacodera* Schaum (16 spp. (1), (2), (3), (5)); 4.144 *Phloeoxena* Chaudoir (1 sp., *P. signata* Dejean (2) NC, SC, GA, FL, AL, LA)); 4.145 *Somotrichus* Seidlitz (1 sp., *S. unifasciatus* Dejean (4) WA? (introduced, may not be established)); 4.146 *Coptodera* Dejean (1 sp., *C. aerata* Dejean (1) IN, DE; (2) VA, SC, FL, AL); 4.147 *Callida* Latreille and Dejean (12 spp.); 4.148 *Infernophilus* Larson (1 sp., *I. castaeneus* Horn (3) CA; (4) NV); 4.149 *Lecalida* Casey (2 spp. (3) AZ); 4.150 *Inna* Putzeys (1 sp., *I. texana* Schaeffer (3) TX); 4.151 *Agra* Fabricius (1 sp., *A. oblongopunctata* Chevrolat (3) TX); 4.152 *Eucaerus* LeConte (1 sp., *E. varicornis* LeConte (2) FL, AL, LA); 4.153 *Euproctinus* Leng and Mutchler (2 spp. (2), (3)); 4.154 *Onota* Chaudoir (1 sp., *O. floridana* Horn (2) FL); 4.155 *Cylindronotum* Putzeys (1 sp., *C. seneum* Putzeys (3) TX); 4.156 *Tecnophilus* Chaudoir (2 spp. (3), (4), (5)); 4.157 *Plochionus* Dejean (4 spp. (1), (2), (3)); 4.158 *Nemotarsus* LeConte (1 sp., *N. elegans* LeConte (1) IL, MD; (2) SC; (5) IA)]

4.159 *Lebia* Latreille

Fifty-one species, including the following:

L. grandis Hentz. L. 8.5–10.5 mm. Head and pronotum reddish yellow; elytra entirely dark blue; antennae yellowish brown; legs yellowish; ventrally yellowish brown except abdomen is black. Nocturnal. Found on foliage and flowers in summer and under stones and dead leaves in spring and fall. Feeds on eggs of other insects as well as small insects. (See Fig. 24.43.) (1) n.e. NA; (2) s.e. US; (3) TX; (5) SD, MN, NE, KS, MO.

[4.160 *Dromius* Bonelli (2 spp.); 4.161 *Apristus* Chaudoir (13 spp.); 4.162 *Axinopalpus* LeConte (11 spp.); 4.163 *Microlestes* Schmidt-Goebel (7 spp.); 4.164 *Metabletus* Schmidt-Goebel (1 sp., *M. americanus* Dejean (1) NF, LB, PQ, ON, NH; (3) AZ; (4) BC, AK; (5) NW, YU, AB, SA, MD, SD, CO)]

Fig. 24.43. Fig. 24.44.

Supertribe Dryptitae
Tribe Zuphiini

[4.165 *Pseudaptinus* Laporte (10 spp. (2), (3)); 4.166 *Zuphium* Latreille (5 spp. (1), (2), (3), (5))]

Tribe Galeritini
4.167 *Galerita* Fabricius

Seven species, occurring in (1), (2), (3), (5), including the following:

G. janus Fabricius. L. 17–22 mm. Head strongly rounded behind eyes; black with red spot on front; pronotum reddish brown; elytra black; legs and large basal segment of antennae reddish brown, remaining segments dark; ventral surface dark. Found under stone piles along fence rows and in open woodland. (See Fig. 24.44.) (1) n.e. NA; (2) s.e. US; (3) TX, AZ; (5) SD, MN, NE, IA, CO, KS, MO.

Supertribe Anthiitae
Tribe Helluonini

[4.168 *Helluomorphoides* Ball (7 spp. (1), (2), (3), (5))]

5. AMPHIZOIDAE (Trout-stream Beetle Family)

Length: 11–16 mm. Similar in appearance to some ground beetles. Both larvae and adults are semiaquatic. There is one genus, as follows:

5.1 *Amphizoa* LeConte

Four species—found in (3), (4), (5)—the following of which is typical:

A. lecontei Matthew. (See Fig. 24.45.) (3) AZ; (4) BC, WA, OR, ID, UT; (5) AB, MT, WY.

Fig. 24.45.

6. HALIPLIDAE (Crawling Water Beetle Family)

Length: 2–6 mm. Its oval shape, distinctive markings, and extremely large hind coxal plates covering most of the abdomenal sterna distinguish this family from all others. Although the legs have a fringe of long swimming hairs, these beetles seldom swim; instead, they crawl along the bottom where they feed on vegetation. There are 70 species in the U.S. and Canada, as follows:

6.1 *Haliplus* Latreille

The 46 species are assigned to three subgenera: *Haliplus* s. str., *Paraliaphilus* Guignot, and *Liaphlus* Guignot. The following is typical of the genus:

H. (*Liaphlus*) *fasciatus* Aubé. L. 4–4.5 mm. Yellowish, with large black spots on the elytra; elytra sutural black stripe broad basally, reaching to the first row of large, deep punctures; apex of elytra produced into a short, rounded lobe. (See Fig. 24.46.) Common in ponds. (1) n.e. US; (2) KY, VA, NC, AL, AR, GA, SC; (5) KS, MO.

[6.2 *Peltodytes* Regimbart: subgenus *Neopeltodytes* Sato (19 spp.); 6.3 *Apteralipus* Chandler (1 sp., *A. parvulus* Roberts (3) CA; (4) WA, OR); 6.4 *Brychius* Thomson (4 spp. (1), (3), (4), (5))]

7. DYTISCIDAE (Predacious Diving Beetle Family)

Length: 1–40 mm (usually 5–25 mm). These truly aquatic insects are not only capable swimmers, their streamlined shape and swimming legs make them easily recognized. The palpi are much shorter than the antennae, distinguishing them from the Hydrophilidae, which they otherwise resemble. Usually the species are black, but some have yellow, green, bronze, or brownish stripes, spots, or bands. The scutellum is hidden in a few species.

Both larvae, called water tigers, and adults are found in ponds and streams where they prey upon other insects and various small aquatic animals. Their large mandibles are channeled and used for sucking instead of biting. Their legs are fitted with two claws. They are long lived, often hibernating in bottom mud over winter. Many species are attracted to lights at night.

Special structures permit breathing under water. Spiracles on the apex of the abdomen of both larvae and adults are enlarged. When at rest, they hang head down in the water with the abdominal spiracles breaking the water surface. When the adults dive, a fresh supply of air is carried under the elytra to be used during a relatively long submergence.

Adults discharge defensive fluids from glands located behind the head and from anal glands to afford protection from predatory fish. Eggs are either dropped into water as females swim or are glued in rows on leaves of aquatic plants (for example, by *Colymbetes* spp.). There are 475 species assigned to 42 genera, arranged as follows:

Subfamily Laccophilinae

Tribe Laccophilini

[7.1 *Laccophilus* Leach (14 spp.); 7.2 *Laccodytes* Regimbart (1 sp., *L. pumilio* LeConte (2) FL))]

Subfamily Hydroporinae

Tribe Vatellini

[7.3 *Derovatellus* Sharp (1 sp., *D. lentus* Wehncke: subspecies *D. floridanus* Fall (2) FL))]

Tribe Hydrovatini

[7.4 *Hydrovatus* Motschulsky (7 spp. (1), (2), (3))]

Tribe Pachydrini

[7.5 *Desmopachria* Babington (8 spp.); 7.6 *Pachydrus* Sharp (1 sp., *P. obniger* Chevrolat (2) GA, FL)]

Tribe Bidessini

[7.7 *Amarodytes* Regimbart (11 spp.); 7.8 *Anodocheilus* Babington (1 sp., *A. exiguus* Aube (2) GA, FL); 7.9 *Bidessonotus* Regimbart (3 spp. (1), (2), (3)); 7.10 *Liodessus* Guignot (5 spp. (1), (2), (3), (5)); 7.11 *Bidessus* Sharp (1 sp., *B. apicatus* Clark (2) FL); 7.12 *Neobidessus* Young (3 spp. (2), (3)); 7.13 *Neoclypeodytes* Young (9 spp. (3), (4))]

Tribe Celinini

[7.14 *Celina* Aubé (9 spp. (1), (2), (3), (5))]

Tribe Hydroporini

[7.15 *Hygrotus* Stephens (52 spp.); 7.16 *Hydroporus* Schellenberg (128 spp.); 7.17 *Deronectes* Sharp (21 spp.); 7.18 *Deuteronectes* Guignot (2 spp. (2), (3)); 7.19 (11 spp. (1), (3), (4), (5)); 7.20 *Laccornis* Des Gozis (4 spp. (1), (2), (4), (5)); 7.21 *Haideoporus* Young and Longley (1 sp., *H. texanus* Young and Longley); 7.22 *Hydrotrupes* Sharp (1 sp., *H. palpalis* Sharp (3) CA; (4) OR); 7.23 *Agabinus* Crotch (2 spp. (3), (4))]

Subfamily Colymbetinae

Tribe Agabini

[7.24 *Agabus* Leach (82 spp.); 7.25 *Carrhydrus* Fall (1 sp., *C. crassipes* Fall); 7.26 *Ilybius* Erichson (14 spp.)]

Tribe Agabetini

[7.27 *Agabetes* Crotch (1 sp., *A. acuductus* Harris (1) IN, MA; (2) GA, FL)]

Tribe Matini

[7.28 *Matus* Aubé (4 spp. (1), (2), (3))]

Tribe Copelatini

[7.29 *Copelatus* Erichson (8 spp. (1), (2), (3), (5))]

Tribe Coptotomini

[7.30 *Coptotomus* Say (6 spp.)]

Fig. 24.46.

Fig. 24.47.

Tribe Colymbetini

[7.31 *Neoscutopterus* Balfour-Browne (2 spp. (1), (4), (5)); 7.32 *Rhantus* Boisduval and Lacordaire (10 spp.); 7.33 *Colymbetes* Clairville (9 spp. (1), (3), (4), (5)); 7.34 *Hoperius* Fall (1 sp., *H. planatus* Fall (1) MD; (2) AR)]

Subfamily Dytiscinae
Tribe Dytiscini
7.35 *Dytiscus* Linnaeus

Eleven species, including the following:

D. harrisi Kirby. L. 30–40 mm. Tarsal spurs slender; pronotum margined with yellow anteriorly, posteriorly, and laterally; elytra margined with yellow and obliterated apically, but with a subapical, oblique yellow cross-bar. Three basal tarsomeres of the male front tarsi modified to form an adhesive, cuplike disc that aids in holding onto female during copulation. Adults and larvae predacious. (See Fig. 24.47.) (1) WI, ON, PQ, NY, IN; (4) BC; (5) AB, MB, MN, NT.

Subfamily Hydaticinae
Tribe Hydaticini

[7.36 *Acilius* Leach (7 spp.)]

Tribe Thermonectini

[7.37 *Hydaticus* Leach (6 spp.)]

7.38 *Thermonectus* Dejean

Six brightly marked species, found in (1), (2), (3), (5). The following is an example:

Fig. 24.48. (*Courtesy of Kurzius and* Insect World Digest)

T. marmoratus Hope. L. 9–10 mm. Body yellow with black markings; head with black base and small black spot on front; thorax with black disk with two yellow spots in center; elytra with irregular network of black. (See Fig. 24.48 for swimming beetle and A&J 87.) (3) CA, AZ.

[7.39 *Graphoderus* Dejean (5 spp.)]

Tribe Eretini

[7.40 *Eretes* Laporte (1 sp., *E. sticticus* Linnaeus (2) FL; (3) CA, AZ, OK; (5) KS)]

Subfamily Cybisterinae

[7.41 *Megadytes* Sharp (1 sp., *M. fraternus* Sharp (2) FL; (3) CA); 7.42 *Cybister* Curtis (4 spp. (1), (2), (3), (5))]

8. NOTERIDAE (Burrowing Water Beetle Family)

Length: 1.2–3.5 mm. Unlike the Dytiscidae, which they resemble, these beetles lack a visible scutellum. Their habits also differ in that their larvae burrow into the mud. The 17 species are assigned to 6 genera, most of them found in the southern U.S.

Tribe Notomicrini

[8.1 *Notomicrus* Sharp (2 spp. (2))]

Tribe Suphisini

[8.2 *Suphis* Aubé (1 sp., *S. inflatus* LeConte (2) LA, FL); 8.3 *Suphisellus* Crotch (6 spp. (1), (2), (3))]

Tribe Noterini

[8.4 *Pronoterus* Sharp (1 sp., *P. semipunctatu* LeConte (1) MI?; (2) FL); 8.5 *Mesonoterus* Sharp (1 sp., *M. addendus* Blatchley (2) FL)]

Tribe Hydrocanthini
8.6 *Hydrocanthus* Say

Six species are found in (1), (2), (3), including the following:

H. iricolor Say. (See Fig. 24.49.) (1) n.e. US; (2) VA, KY, TN, NC, SC; (3) CA?

9. GYRINIDAE (Whirligig Beetle Family)

Length: 3–15 mm. body black, streamlined, fitted for swimming; head with each compound eye divided, permitting vision above and below water surface; antennae short, clubbed; front legs long; hind legs short, flat, paddlelike. The common name of these beetles describes their habit of swimming in circles or zigzagging when disturbed. Both adults and larvae are

Fig. 24.49.

Fig. 24.50.

predacious. When handled, they secrete odors; some smell like apples; other have a foul smell. The family contains 58 species in three genera in the U.S. and Canada. All are externally very similar, and most can be identified to species only by an examination of the male genitalia.

Subfamily Enhydrinae

Tribe Enhydrini

(=Dineutini)

9.1 *Dineutus* MacLeay

Fifteen large species (L. 9–15 mm) with concealed scutellum. Occurs in (1), (2), (3). The following is typical:

D. nigrior Roberts. Found in schools on surface of large streams and lakes (See Fig. 24.50.) (1) n.e. US.

Subfamily Gyrininae

9.2 *Gyrinus* Geoffroy

Forty species, ranging in length from 4 to 7 mm, with exposed scutellum; otherwise very similar to the preceding species. Also found in schools on surface of lakes and rivers. The following is common:

G. limbatus Say. L. 3.5–4.5 mm. (See A&J 88.) (1) IN, PA; (2) FL.

Subfamily Orectochilinae

9.3 *Gyretes* Brulle

Three species with fringe of hairs dorsally along margin of body. L. 3–5 mm. Found in (2), (3).

Suborder MYXOPHAGA

This suborder, based on features described in the Key to Suborders, contains two families that occur in the U.S. and Canada and another family, Torridincolidae, found in Brazil. Although some authors include the family Micromalthidae, these tiny beetles do not exhibit all features of the suborder and need further study. Until then, the family is retained in the Polyphaga.

10. SPHAERIIDAE (Minute Bog Beetle Family)

Length: 0.5–0.75 mm. These obscure beetles resemble Orthoperidae but may be distinguished from other families by the comparatively large and prominent head, the capitate antennae, the large posterior coxae, and the unequal length of the visible abdominal sterna. They are semiaquatic and found under stones, in moss in bogs, and in mud. One genus and two species occur in the U.S., as follows:

[10.1 *Sphaerius* Waltl (2 spp., *S. texanus* Matthews (3) TX, and *S. politus* Horn (3) CA)]

11. HYDROSCAPHIDAE (Skiff Beetle Family)

Length: ±1.5 mm. These small beetles resemble some Staphylinidae but are distinguished by the presence of a distinct notopleural suture. The hind femora are partially covered by a platelike projection of the hind coxae. There is one species, as follows:

11.1 *Hydroscapha* LeConte

H. natans LeConte. Often found in hot springs. (3) s. CA, AZ; (4) NV.

Suborder POLYPHAGA

All remaining families of beetles, which represent the majority of the species, are included in this suborder, which is further divided into series and superfamilies as indicated in Table 24.1.

The hind margin of the first abdominal sternum is entire, not cut through by the hind coxae (See Fig. 24.19). Tarsomeres are usually 5-5-5 (although the fourth may be hidden in the lobe of the third), 5-5-4, 4-4-4, 3-3-3, or rarely with a different combination of segments. Antennae vary from family to family, a feature useful for family recognition in some cases. Most species have five visible abdominal sterna, but some have more. Do not count those that have been modified as copulatory organs; these may protrude slightly but are usually hidden within the last sternum and tergum.

In order to identify beetle families, one must become familiar with a variety of characteristics that are often somewhat obscurely described in the indentification keys because of the great variation in the same feature from family to family. To help identify specimens to family, Table 24.5 groups families by their characteristics. It should be pointed out, however, that there is little relationship between these groupings and the phylogenetic classification of the suborder.

Series STAPHYLINIFORMIA

Superfamily HYDROPHILOIDEA

12. HYDROPHILIDAE (Water Scavenger Beetle Family)

Length: 1–40 mm. Body usually black, broadly oval, with legs fitted for swimming. Most members of this family are aquatic, but one group, Sphaeridiinae, live in dung and moist earth. Maxillary palpi of aquatic members longer than their short, clavate antennae, which are usualy hidden beneath the head. Many species are scavengers and feed on plant material; some prey on snails and other invertebrates. The giant larvae of some species are the dragons of many freshwater pools and streams. Their agressive habits are apparent when they are introduced into an aquarium. After they have eaten everything else in sight, they eat each other. These larvae may be distinguished from the Dyticidae larvae by their single claw. The family contains 284 species in the U.S. and Canada.

Table 24.5 Table of Polyphaga Family Group

[*Note:* The names of most families appear in capital letters to indicate that all species in those families possess these features. Only some species of those family names in lower-case possess the features indicated. Families in which all species are 5 mm or less in length are preceded by an asterisk (*). All families of Polyphaga found in the U.S. and Canada are arranged in the sequence of their formal classification pages that follow.]

1. *Larvae resembling, sexually mature adult females without elytra and wings: see* STYLOPIDAE (parasites), PHENGODIDAE (fitted with light organs), some Rhipiphoridae, and some *Dermestidae.

2. *Antennae short and maxillary palpi usually longer than antennae; segment 6 of latter modified to form a cuplike base for a three- to five-segmented pubescent club: see* most HYDROPHILIDAE (aquatic; a few terestrial species have slightly longer antennae), *Hydraenidae, and *Georyssidae.

3. *Elytra short, not covering at least 2, usually more, abdominal terga: see* STAPHYLINIDAE, PSELAPHIDAE, HISTERIDAE (antennae elbowed), SCAPHIDIIDAE (shiny, abdomen pointed), some Nitidulidae (antennae clubbed), some Rhipiphoridae (antennae pectinate, body wedge-shaped), some Meloidae (tarsi 5-5-4), some Lymexylonidae (hind wings large, not foldable), most Telegeusidae (maxillary and labial palpi greatly elongate), one * Leptinidae (beaver ectoparasite), most Phengodidae (antennae plumose), some Silphidae, a few Cantharidae, and if hind wings are large and fan-shaped, and they resemble flies, males of *STYLOPIDAE.

4. *Antennal Club composed of lamellate plates: see* SCARABAEIDAE, Passalidae, and Lucanidae.

5. *Abdomen with 7 or 8 visible sterna: see* LAMPYRIDAE (usually with light organs), CANTHARIDAE, LYCIDAE, some Lymexylidae, Telegeusidae, Phengogidae, and one *Dermestidae (elongate).

6. *Tarsi 4-4-4: see* COLYDIDAE (elongate), MYCETOPHAGIDAE (oval), ENDOMYCHIDAE (with 2 longitudinal grooves on pronotum; tarsi appear to be 3-3-3), HETEROCERIDAE (antennae with 7-segmented, serrate club), some Rhizophagidae, some Erotylidae, rarely Nitidulidae (*Cybocephalus*), *Ciidae (head hidden by prothorax), *Corylophidae (abdomen with 6 visible sterna; head hidden by prothorax), Cerylonidae (apical segment of maxillary palpi needlelike), *Clambidae.

7. *Tarsi apparently 3-3-3: see* COCCINELLIDAE (oval, usually brightly colored with spots), ENDOMYCHIDAE (with 2 longitudinal grooves on pronotum; tarsi usually actually 4-4-4, 3rd segment minute), *Ptiliidae (wings featherlike), *Limulodidae (shaped like horseshoe crab), *Rhizophagidae, *Lathridiidae, and *Dasyceridae.

8. *Tarsi 5-5-5, but 4th segment small to minute, usually hidden in the bilobed 3rd segment; antennae not elbowed: see* CHRYSOMELIDAE, most CERAMBYCIDAE (some with short antennae have distinct 5-5-5 tarsi), BRUCHIDAE (seed-shaped), Languriidae, and some Erotylidae.

9. *Head elongate, produced into a snout; antennae elbowed; tarsi 5-5-5, but 4th segment minute, hidden in the bilobed 3rd segment: see* ANTHRIBIDAE, Brentidae (with snout projecting straight forward), Platypodidae, SCOLYTIDAE, and CURCULIONIDAE. (Note: Some species of other families may have an elongate head, but their antennae are not elbowed, and their tarsi are not as just described.)

10. *Tarsi 5-5-5 and Abdomen with 6 visible sterna: see* PSEPHENIDAE (larst tarsal segment very long and claws large), CERBRIONIDAE (resemble click beetles), SILPHIDAE (on carrion), *SCYDMAENIDAE (antlike), *Micromalthidae, some *Leptinidae (in rodent nests), some Elateridae (with clicking mechanism), SCAPHIDIIDAE (5th sternum long and conical; 6th, minute), *Eucinetidae, some Cleridae (brightly colored), some Melyridae (body soft), Callirhipidae, and some Lymexylidae.

11. *Tarsi 5-5-4: see* TENEBRIONIDAE (usually black, hard-bodied), ALLECULIDAE (with comb claws), OTHNIIDAE (resemble tiger beetles), SALPINGIDAE (sometimes flattened), LAGRIIDAE (usually with last antennal segment elongate), CEPHALOIDAE (tarsal claws with fleshy lobes beneath), OEDEMERIDAE (pronotum widest anteriorly), MONOMMATIDAE (oval, antennae clubbed), MELANDRYIDAE (pronotum with basal impressions), RHIPIPHORIDAE (wedge-shaped, antennae pectinate or serrate), MORDELLIDAE (wedge-shaped, abdomen with last segment elongate, pointed), ANTHICIDAE (eyes elliptical, entire, small; pronotum sometimes with a horn), PEDILIDEAE (eyes emarginate), PYROCHROIDAE (antennae serrate or pectinate, body flattened), MELOIDAE (tarsal claws toothed), *Sphindidae, *Euglenidae (tarsi appear to be 4-4-3), a few Nitidulidae (antennae clubbed), a few *Rhizophagidae, a few Histeridae (oval, compact), some *Cryptophagidae, a few Cucujidae (very flat).

12. *Tarsi 5-5-5 and Abdomen with 5 visible sterna:*
 (A) *Body hard, usually shiny, metallic colored, with various markings: see* BUPRESTIDAE.
 (B) *With functional prothoracic clicking mechanism: see* ELATHERIDAE. *With rudimentary, nonfunctional clicking mechanism; elongate, resembling that of click beetles, often with head deflexed: see* THROSCIDAE, Cerophytidae, Perothopidae, EUCNEMIDAE, and Dascillidae.
 (C) *Body very flat; many species under 5 mm: see* CUCUJIDAE.
 (D) *Body soft; antennae not clubbed: see* MELRIDAE and Lymexylidae (antennae serrate; maxillary palpi flabellate).
 (E) *Antennae clubbed: see* DERMESTIDAE (oval or elongate oval), Nosodendridae (oval, black, elytra with tufts of hair in rows), ANOBIIDAE (club elongate), BOSTRICHIDAE (cylindrical, hard body, with horns and rasplike tubercles), LYCTIDAE (antennal club 2-segmente), TROGOSSITIDAE (flattened, oval, or elongate), CLERIDAE (brightly colored), NITIDULIDAE (elongate oval, somewhat flattened, usually marke), EROTYLIDAE (marked with red, somewhat flattened), LEIODIDAE (convex, shiny, contractile), SILPHIDAE (associated with carrion), Byturidae (segments 2 and 3 of tarsi lobed), *Rhizophagidae (antennal club 1- or 2-segmented), *Phalacridae.
 (F) *Antennae not clubbed: see* SPHAERITIDAE (resemble Histeridae, but truncate elytra cover all but last abdominal segment), BYRRHIDAE (body oval, convex; head deflexed; resemble seeds or dark colored pills), PTILODACTYLIDAE (antennae with segments 4 through 10 each with a supernumerary, long basal process), DRYOPIDAE (claws very long), ELMIDAE (aquatic or subaquatic), Rhipiceridae (resemble click beetles but with lamellate antennae), Brachypsectridae (similar to the preceding; antennae serrate), Derodontidae (pronotum with lateral teeth), some Cerambycidae (large; pronotum usually with lateral teeth; see Prioninae), some Staphylinidae (6 mm or less; antlike; see *Brathinus*).
 (G) *Not over 5 mm in length: see* *Chelonariidae (compact; turtlelike in shape), *LEPTODIRIDAE (resemble small Silphidae), *PTINIDAE (resemble spiders), *CRYPTOPHAGIDAE, *Limnichidae, *Helodidae, and *Biphyllidae.

Subfamily Helophorinae

[12.1 *Helophorus* Fabricius (31 spp.)]

Subfamily Epimetopinae

[12.2 *Epimetopus* Lacordaire (2 spp. (3) AZ, TX)]

Subfamily Hydrochinae

[12.3 *Hydrochus* Leach (23 spp.)]

Subfamily Hydrophilinae

[12.4 *Tropisternus* Solier (17 spp.); 12.5 *Dibolocelus* Regimbart (2 spp. (1), (2), (3))]

12.6 *Hydrophilus* Geoffroy

Three species, including the following:

H. triangularis Say. L. 34–37 mm. Olive black, elongate, moderately convex; sterna with a spinelike keel. Often attracted to lights at night. (1) n.e. US; (2) s.e. US; (3) s.w. US; (4) Pacific n.w.; (5) ND, KS, NE.

12.7 *Hydrochara* Berthold

Four species, including the following:

H. obtusatus Say. L. 13–16 mm. Black; sides of each abdominal segment with small, reddish yellow spot; elongate, oval; prosternum with a keel. Found in leaf-filled pools, mudholes, or large ponds with vegetation. (1) n.e. US; (2) s.e. US; (4) BC, WA; (5) ND, NE, MO.

12.8 *Hydrobiomorpha* Blackburn

One species, as follows:

H. casta (Say). (See Fig. 24.51.) (2) LA, MS, AL, FL.

Subfamily Chaetarthriinae

[12.9 *Chaetarthria* Stephens (15 spp.)]

Subfamily Berosinae

[12.10 *Berosus* Leach (29 spp.); 12.11 *Hemiosus* Sharp (2 spp.)]

Fig. 24.51.

Subfamily Hydrobiinae
Tribe Hydrobiini

[12.12 *Derallus* Sharp (1 sp., *D. altus* LeConte (1) IL, NJ; (2) LA, FL; (3) TX); 12.13 *Laccobius* Erichson (15 spp.)]

12.14 *Hydrobius* Leach

Three species, of which the following is common:

H. fuscipes Linnaeus. L. 6.5–8 mm. oblong, convex; pitch black above, shiny, somewhat paler beneath; thorax finely punctate; elytra striated, with some striae indistinct at base; striae closely punctate, the intervals flat, not densely punctate. Often found in debris along the beach of lakes. (See A&J 89.) (1), (3), (4), (5).

[12.15 *Sperchopsis* LeConte (1 sp., *S. tesselatus* Ziegler (1), (2), (5)); 12.16 *Ametor* semenov (2 spp. (3), (4)); 12.17 *Paracymus* Thomson (14 spp.); 12.18 *Crenitis* Bedel (12 spp. (1), (3), (4), (5)); 12.19 *Anacaena* Thomson (3 spp.)]

Tribe Helocharini

[12.20 *Enochrus* Thomson (20 spp.); 12.21 *Helochares* Mulsant (3 spp.); 12.22 *Helobata* Bergroth (1 sp., *H. striata* Brulle (2) LA, FL); 12.23 *Helocombus* Horn (1 sp., *H. bifidus* LeConte (1), (2) GA, FL); 12.24 *Cymbiodyta* Bedel (22 spp.)]

Subfamily Sphaeridiinae
Tribe Sphaeridiini

[12.25 *Sphaeridium* Fabricius (3 spp.); 12.26 *Dactylosternum* Wollaston (4 spp.); 12.27 *Phaenonotum* Sharp (2 spp. (1), (2))]

Tribe Cercyonini

[12.28 *Pelosoma* Mulsant (1 sp., *P. capillatum* Mulsant (3) AZ, TX); 12.29 *Oosternum* Sharp (3 spp. (1), (2))]

12.30 *Cercyon* Leach

Thirty-three species, including the following:

C. praetextatus Say. (See Fig. 24.52.)

[12.31 *Omicrus* Sharp (1 sp., *O. palmarum* Schwartz (3) FL)]

Tribe Megasternini

[12.32 *Cryptopleurum* Mulsant (5 spp. (1), (3), (4)); 12.33 *Megasternum* Mulsant (2 spp. (3), (4)); 12.34 *Pemelus* Horn (1 sp., *P. costatus* LeConte (1) DC; (2) TN)]

Fig. 24.52.

13. LIMNEBIIDAE (Minute Moss Beetle Family)

Length: 1.2–1.7 mm. Similar to the Hydrophilidae in shape and color. Six or seven abdominal sterna are visible as oppose to the five of Hydrophilidae. Found in matted vegetation along margins of streams and in sphagnum moss near shores of bogs. There are 36 species in two subfamilies as follows:

Subfamily Hydraeninae

[13.1 *Ochthebius* Leach (23 spp.); 13.2 *Hydraena* Kugelann (6 spp. (1), (2))]

Subfamily Limnebiinae

[13.3 *Limnebius* Leach (7 spp. (1), (3), (4))]

14. GEORYSSIDAE (Mud-backed Beetle Family)

Length: 1.5–3 mm. These beetles somewhat resemble certain snout beetles, but the head is not elongated to form a beak. Their habitat is along the margins of streams, in sand, or in mud, with which they are often coated.

Two species, as follows:

14.1 *Georissus* Latreille

G. pusillus LeConte. (1) NY, CT, ME; (4) BC, WA, OR, ID; (5) NE, ND.

G. californicus LeConte. (3) CA; (4) ID.

Superfamily STAPHYLINOIDEA

15. PTILIIDAE (Feather-winged Beetle Family)

Length: 0.25–1.0 mm. Oval; antennae clavate with whorls of pubescence; elytra entire; hind wings with fringe of long hair (See Fig. 24.17). Found in fungus, rotting wood, humus, and dung. There are 107 species in 22 genera in the U.S. and Canada.

Subfamily Nanosellinae

[15.1 *Nanosella* Motschulsky (2 spp. (1) OH; (2) GA); 15.2 *Throscoptilium* Barber (1 sp., *T. duryi* Barber (1) OH); 15.3 *Porophila* Dybas (1 sp., *P. malkini* Dybas (4) OR) 15.4 *Suturella* Dybas (1 sp., *S. microcephala* Dybas (1) PA); 15.5 *Hydnosella* Dybas (1 sp., *H. globitheca* Dybas (1) IN)]

Subfamily Ptiliinae
Tribe Ptiliini

[15.6 *Nossidium* Erichson (3 spp., distribution uncertain); 15.7 *Actidium* Matthews (6 spp. (3) CA, TX; (4) BC); 15.8 *Motschulskium* Matthews (1 sp., *M. sinuatocolle* Matthews (1) CA); 15.9 *Micridium* Motschulsky (1 sp., *M. lineatum* LeConte (2) LA, AL); 15.10 *Dilinium* Casey (1 sp., *D. rhodeanum* Casey (1) RI); 15.11 *Ptilium* Erichson (13 spp. (1), (3), (4)); 15.12 *Ptenidium* Erichson (13 spp. (1), (2), (3)); 15.13 *Ptiliola* Haldeman (2 spp., distribution uncertain)]

Tribe Acratrichini

[15.14 *Pteryx* Matthews (4 spp., distribution uncertain); 15.15 *Ptinellodes* Mathews (1 sp., *P. lecontei* Gemminger and Harold (2) GA, FL; (5) MN); 15.16 *Ptiliopycna* Casey (1) MI); 15.17 *Ptiliodina* Casey (1)

RI)); 15.18 *Acratrichis* Motschulsky (43 spp.); 15.19 *Smicrus* Matthews (1 sp., *S. americanus* Casey (3) TX); 15.20 *Ptinella* Motschulsky (2 spp. (1) IN; (2) GA, FL; (5) MN); 15.21 *Nephanes* Thomson (7 spp. (1), (2), (4), (5)); 15.22 *Actinopteryx* Matthews (1 sp., *A. fuciocola* Allibert (2) VA, FL)]

16. LIMULODIDAE (Horseshoe Crab Beetle Family)

Length: 0.7–3.2 mm. Horseshoe-crab-shpaed; antennae clavate; elytra truncate. Found in ant nests. These are five species, as follows:

[16.1 *Limulodes* Matthews (4 spp. (1), (2), (3)); 16.2 *Paralimulodes* Brunch (1 sp., *P. wasmanni* Brunch (2) AL)]

17. DASYCERIDAE (Minute Scavenger Beetle Family)

Length: 1–3 mm. Procoxal cavities open behind and contiguous.

17.1 *Dasycerus* Brong

There are two species in the U.S. and Canada, as follows:

D. carolinensis Horn. (2) NC, GA; (3) CA.

D. angulicollis Horn. (3) CA.

18. LEPTINIDAE (Mammal Nest Beetle Family)

Length: 2–5 mm. Ectoparasites of various mammals, particularly beaver. There are four species in the U.S. and Canada, as follows.

[18.1 *Leptinus* Mueller (1 sp., *L. testaceous* Mueller (See Fig. 24.53) (1), (4), (5)); 18.2 *Leptinillus* Horn (2 spp., *L. validus* Horn (1) ON and *L. aplodontiae* Ferris (3) CA)]

18.3 *Platypsyllus* Ritsema

One species, as follows:

P. castoris Ritsema (Beaver Parasite). L. 2–3 mm. Flattened, louse-shaped; reddish brown to dark brown; antennae short with an apical club; eyes absent; elytra short; wings absent; legs short with spines. Ectoparasite of beavers, the larvae and adults spending most of their lives in the fur of the host, feeding upon epidermal material or exudates from the skin through lesions caused by biting. The larvae leave the host

Fig. 24.53.

to pupate in the earth of the beaver lodge. (1) n.e. NA, wherever beaver live. (See A&J 90.)

19. LEIODIDAE (Round Fungus Beetle Family)

Length: 1.5–6.5 mm. Strongly convex and shiny, black or dark brown; no pubescence on body; usually contractile and capable of rolling into a ball. The family contains 137 species in the U.S. and Canada.

Subfamily Leiodinae

[19.1 *Triarthron* Maerkel (2 spp. (1), (3), (4)); 19.2 *Hydnobius* Schmidt (16 spp. (1), (3), (4), (5)); 19.3 *Leiodes* Latreille (23 spp.); 19.4 *Anogdus* LeConte (3 spp.); 19.5 *Cainosternum* Notman (1 sp., *C. imbricatum* Notman (1) NY); 19.6 *Colenis* Erichson (1 sp., *C. impunctata* LeConte (1) MI; (2) LA, FL); 19.7 *Neocyrtusa* Brown (13 spp. (1), (2), (3), (4)); 19.8 *Ecarinosphaerula* Hatch (1 sp., *E. ecarinata* Horn (3) CA; (4) NV)]

Subfamily Agathidiinae

[19.9 *Anisotoma* Panzer (13 spp. (1), (2), (3), (4)); 19.10 *Agathidium* Panzer (41 spp.); 19.11 *Stetholiodes* Fall (1 sp., *S. laticollis* Fall (1) IN); 19.12 *Aglyptinus* Cockerell (1 sp., *A. laevis* (LeConte) (1), (2)); 19.13 *Lionothus* Brown (1 sp., *L. ulkei* Brown (1) DC); 19.14 *Caenocyrta* Brown (1 sp., *C. picipennis* (LeConte) (1), (4)); 19.15 *Apheloplastus* Brown (1 sp., *A. egenus* (LeConte) (1), (2)); 19.16 *Isoplastus* Horn (1 sp., *I. fossor* Horn (1)]

Subfamily Glacicaricolinae

[19.17 *Glacicavicola* Westcott (1 sp., *G. bathysciuides* Westcott (4) ID)]

Subfamily Catopocerinae

[19.18 *Catopocerus* Motschulsky (14 spp. (1), (2), (3), (4))]

20. SCYDMAENIDAE (Antlike Stone Beetle Family)

Length: 1–5 mm. Somewhat antlike in shape, oval, shiny, brown to reddish; antennae slightly clavate. Abundant in humus near base of trees and also under bark, stones, logs, in moss, in treeholes, and in ant and termite nests. There are 181 species in the U.S. and Canada.

Subfamily Scydmaeninae

Tribe Lophioderini

[20.1 *Lophioderus* Casey (8 spp., (2), (3), (4))]

Tribe Euconnini

[20.2 *Euconnus* Thompson: 5 subgenera: *Euconnus* s. str., *Microscydmus* Saulcy and Croiss, *Psomophus* Casey, *Xestophus* Casey (1 sp., *E. salinator* (LeConte) (1); (2) FL, TN; (5) IA), and *Scopophus* Casey (27 spp.); 20.3 *Napochus* Thomson (82 spp.); 20.4 *Noctophus* Casey (1 sp., *N. schmitti* Casey (2) NC, SC, FL); 20.5 *Drastophus* Casey (1 sp., *D. laevicollis* Casey (3) CA; (4) BC); 20.6 *Pycnophus* Casey (1 sp., *P. rasus* (LeConte) (1), (5) IA)]

Tribe Opresini

[20.7 *Opresus* Casey (4 spp.); 20.8 *Delius* Casey (1 sp., *D. robustulus* Casey (1), (2)); 20.9 *Neladius* Casey (1 sp., *N. tenuis* Casey (1), (2))]

Tribe Neuraphini

[20.10 *Stenichnus* Thomson: 2 subgenera: *Chrtoscydmus* Motschulsky and *Brachycepsis* Brendel (21 spp.); 20.11 *Catalinus* Casey (1 sp., *C. angustus* (LeConte) (3) CA)]

Tribe Cephenniini

[20.12 *Cephennium* Mueller and Kunze (3 spp.)]

Tribe Eutheliini

[20.13 *Eutheia* Stephens (3 spp. (1), (4)); 20.14 *Veraphis* Casey (8 spp. (1), (3), (4), (5)); 20.15 *Euthiodes* Brendel (1 sp., *E. latus* Brendel (1), (2), (5))]

Tribe Chevrolatiini

[20.16 *Chevrolatia* Duval (2 spp. (1), (2))]

Tribe Leptoscydmini

[20.17 *Leptoscydmus* Casey (2 spp. (1), (2), (5))]

Tribe Scydmaenini

[20.18 *Scydmaenus* Latreille (11 spp. (1), (2), (3), (5)); 20.19 *Acholerops* Casey (2 spp. (1), (2)); 20.20 *Ceramphis* Casey (1 sp., *c. deformata* (Horn) (3) CA, AZ)]

Subfamily Clidicinae
Tribe Clidicini

[20.21 *Papusus* Casey (1 sp., *P. macer* Casey (3) CA)]

21. SILPHIDAE (Carrion Beetle Family)

Length: 10–35 mm. Body black or dark brown, rarely metallic blue or green, frequently with orange or reddish markings; elytra entire, or truncate, exposing one or more abdominal terga; antennae clavate or capitate; front coxae prominent. These common beetles are usually seen on carrion, although some, especially *Nicrophorus* spp., are attracted to lights at night. There are 42 species in the U.S. and Canada.

Subfamily Pterolominae
Tribe Pterolomini

[21.1 *Pteroloma* Gyllenhal: 2 subgenera: *Pteroloma* s. str. and *Apteroloma* Hatch (6 spp. (3), (4))]

Tribe Lyrosomini

[21.2 *Lyrosoma* Mannerheim (1 sp., *L. opacum* Mannerheim (4) AK)]

Subfamily Agyrtinae
Tribe Agyrtini

[21.3 *Pelatines* Cockerell (1 sp., *P. latus* Mannerheim (4), (5) AB); 21.4 *Agyrtes* Froelich (2 spp. (3) CA; (4))]

Tribe Necrophilini

[21.5 *Necrophilus* Latreille (2 spp. (1), (2), (3), (4))]

Superfamily Silphinae
Tribe Necrodini

[21.6 *Necrodes* Leach (1 sp., *N. surinamensis* Fabricius (1), (2), (4), (5))]

Tribe Silphini
21.7 *Silpha* Linnaeus

Twelve species, including the following:

S. lapponica Herbst (Common Carrion Beetle). L. 12–13 mm. Body dark brown to black; head and pronotum black with conspicuous pale yellow pubescence; elytra with prominent

Fig. 24.54.

tubercles. Common on carrion. (See A&J 92.) (1) n.e. US; (2) s.e. US; (3) TX; (5) n. Central States.

S. americana Linnaeus. (See Fig. 24.54.) (1) n.e. NA; (2) s.e US; (3) TX; (5) NE, IA.

[21.8 *Blitophaga* Reitter (2 spp. (4), (5))]

Subfamily Nicrophorinae
Tribe Nicrophorini
21.9 *Nicrophorus* Fabricius

Commonly called Sexton Beetles, these insects bury small carcasses to feed on them underground, thereby preventing flesh flies from laying their eggs on them. The sensory pits in the enlarged portion of the antennae are doubtless olfactory and explain how the adults can so quickly locate carrion and outwit the flies. Even if fly larvae happen to develop however, the sexton beetle larvae eat them. There are 15 species, including the following:

N. investigator Zetterstedt. L. 18–22 mm. Black with orange markings; pronotum black; elytra with four orange spots; body elongate, convex. Adults found on carrion. (See A&J 91.) (1) n.e. US; (3) CA, AZ, NM; (4) Pacific n.w.; (5) MN.

N. americanus Olivier. Rare. (See Fig. 24.55.) (1) n.e. US; (2) s.e. US; (3) TX; (5) NE, MO.

Tribe Lendomini [from Mycetophagidae]

[21.10 *Lendomus* Casey (1 sp., *L. politus* Casey (1) PQ)]

22. LEPTODIRIDAE (Small Carrion Beetle Family)

Length: 2–5 mm. These beetles resemble silphidae but are smaller and somewhat more convex. The eighth antennal segment is much smaller in diameter than the seventh or ninth. Many species have cross-striations on thorax and abdomen. They are found on carrion, fungi, and ant and mammal nests, usually as scavengers. There are 89 species in the U.S. and Canada.

Fig. 24.55.

Fig. 24.56.

Subfamily Bathysciinae

[22.1 *Platycholeus* Horn (2 spp. (3) CA; (4) WA, OR, NV)]

Subfamily Catopinae
Tribe Nemadini

[22.2 *Nemadus* Thomson (11 spp.); 22.3 *Dissochaetus* Reitter (3 spp. (1), (2), (3), (5))]

Tribe Ptomaphagini

[22.4 *Echinocoleus* Horn (1 sp., *E. setiger* Horn (3) AZ); 22.5 *Ptomaphagus* Illiger (24 spp.); 22.6 *Adelopsis* Portevin (1 sp., *A. mitchellensis* (Hatch) (2) NC)]

Tribe Catopini
22.7 *Catops* Paykull

Ten species, including the following:

C. basilaris Say. Common on carcasses and other ill-smelling matter. (See Fig. 24.56.) (1) n.e. US; (2) s.e. US; (3) s.w. US; (5) n. Central States and Provinces.

[22.8 *Prionochaeta* Horn (1 sp., *P. opaca* Say (1) n.e. US); 22.9 *Catoptrichus* Murray (1 sp., *C. frankenhaeuseri* Mannerheim (4) AK, BC, WA, OR, ID)]

Subfamily Coloninae

[22.10 *Colon* Herbst (35 spp. (1), (2), (4))]

23. SCAPHIDIIDAE (Shining Fungus Beetle Family)

Length: 2–7 mm. Oval, convex, long-legged, black, very shiny beetles, some with red spots on elytra; head small; abdomen pointed; elytra truncate. They are found in fungus, dead wood, rotting leaves, and under bark. There are 54 species in the U.S. and Canada.

Tribe Scaphidiini

[23.1 *Scaphium* Kirby (1 sp., *S. castanipes* Kirby (5) MN)]

23.2 *Scaphidium* Olivier

Three species, including the following:

S. quadriguttatum piceum Melsheimer. L. 5–6 mm. Black; elytral striae distinct. (See Fig. 24.57.) (1) IN, RI; (5) IA.

[23.3 *Cyparium* Erichson (3 spp. (1), (2), (3))]

Tribe Scaphisomini

[23.4 *Scaphisoma* Leach (28 spp.); 23.5 *Eubaeocera* Cornell (20 spp. (1), (2), (3), (5)); 23.6 *Toxidium* LeConte (2 spp. (1), (2), (5))]

Fig. 24.57.

24. STAPHYLINIDAE (Rove Beetle Family)

Length: 1–20 mm. The short elytra of almost all its species, which usually expose form to six abdominal terga, characterize this large family. Most species are narrow, parallel-sided; the head is usually porrect; the antennae are filiform or clavate. The body is usually black or brown, some species having white or red markings. The abdomen is flexible. Tarsomeres are variable (often 5-5-5, but with many other combinations).

Although most of the common species are found on carrion, a great number prefer fungi, and some are represented in almost every other terrestrial habitat as well. They are difficult to identify, although keys to the subfamilies are easy to use (see the one here) and key to the genra are available (see Arnett, 1961 and Moore and Legner, 1974). The literature on the species is widely scattered.

There are 3187 species in 315 genera in the U.S. and Canada. The large subfamily Aleocharinae is poorly known and identifications are nearly impossible; no suitable key to its genera exists at the present time. Only a very few of the common species are described and illustrated here.

Key to the Subfamilies of Staphylinidae

1.	Elytra entire; tarsomeres 5-5-5; head with pair of ocelli between hind margins of eyes .. **Brathininae**	
	Elytra short, exposing at least 3 abdominal terga; tarsomeres 5-5-5 or less; ocelli usually absent, or if present, see couplet 6 ...	*2*
2(1).	Antennae inserted on surface of head between anterior margin of eyes; apical segment of maxillary palpi sublate ...	*3*
	Antennae inserted at front or side margin of head	*4*
3(2).	Hind coxae small, separated .. **Steninae**	
	Hind coxae large, contiguous **Aleocharinae**	
4(2).	Antennae with 9 segments; hind coxae separated **Micropeplinae**	
	Antennae with 10 or 11 segments; hind coxae contiguous	*5*
5(4).	Labial palpi with apical segment large, semilunar **Oxyporinae**	
	Labial palpi with apical segment not similunar	*6*
6(5).	Head with pair of ocelli between hind margins of eyes	*7*
	Head without ocelli ...	*8*
7(6).	Five tarsomeres ... **Omaliinae**	
	Two or 3 tarsomeres ... **Leptotyphlinae**	
8(6).	Abdomen with 7 visible sterna **Oxytelinae**	
	Abdomen with 6 visible sterna ..	*9*
9(8).	Labrum with anterior margin having 2 long anteriorly directed processes with setae within .. **Megalopsidiinae**	
	Labrum without processes ..	*10*
10(9).	Antennae 10-segmented .. **Hypocyphtinae**	
	Antennae 11-segmented ...	*11*
11(10).	Maxillary palpi with last segment longer than next to last, slightly arcuate, with oblique, elongate, concave truncation **Pinophilinae**	
	Maxilary palpi otherwise ...	*12*
12(11).	Metasternum with expanded plate covering part of hind femora **Trichopseniinae**	
	Metasternum without such plates; hind femora exposed	*13*
13(12).	Maxillary palpi with 1st segment elongate, at least ½ as long as second **Euaesthetinae**	
	Maxillary palpi with 1st segment short, not more than ⅓ as long as second	*14*
14(13).	Abdomen without double margin ...	*15*
	Abdomen with prominent double margin	*17*
15(14).	Hypomeron not visible from side (*Sepedophilus* (24.181)) **Tachyporinae**	
	Hypomeron at least partly visible from side	*16*
16(15).	Front coxae small, globular, without transverse or diagonal groove on front face .. **Lispininae**	
	Front coxae large, elongate, with transverse or diagonal groove on front face **Osoriinae**	
17(13).	Front coxae small, globular **Piestinae**	
	Front coxae large, elongate ...	*18*
18(17).	Elytra long, completely covering 1st tergum **Proteininae**	
	Elytra shorter, not completely covering 1st tergum	*19*
19(18).	Abdomen with 4 or 5 basal terga, each with a diagonal impressed line from near middle of front margin to each apical angle; pronotum and elytra costate **Pseudopsinae**	
	Abdomen without impressed lines ...	*20*

Key to the Subfamilies of Staphylinidae (*Contd.*)

20(19). Head constricted behind eyes, forming distinct neck clearly visible from above *21*
 Head converging to base, without neck visible from above 27

21(20). Small sclerite present at front margin of prosternum **Xantholininae**
 Neck plate sclerite absent .. 22

22(21). Maxillary palpi with last segment less than ½ as long as next to last segment, usually little
 longer than width of next to last segment and usually subulate or papilliform *23*
 Maxillary palpi with last segment at least ½ as long as next to last, subulate only in
 Heterothops (24.24) ... *24*

23(22). Antennal fossae closer to mandibular fossae than to each other **Paederinae**
 Antennal fossae about as close to each other as to mandibular fossae **Diochinae**

24(22). Pronotum with front angles produced anteriorly beyond front lateral angle of proster-
 num; pronotal margin apparently single, hypomeron not or imcompletely margined
 along inner side ... **Quediinae**
 Pronotum with front angles not produced; pronotal margin not produced; pronotal
 margin double, hypomeron completely margined along inner side 25

25(24). Pronotum with lateral marginal lines separate throughout **Xanthopyginae**
 Pronotum with lateral marginal lines united behind front angles 26

26(25). Antennal fossae closer to eyes than to each other **Staphylininae**
 Antennal fossae closer to each other than to eyes **Platyprosopinae**

27(20). Antennae with segment 3 through 11 filamentous 28
 Antennae not filamentous .. 29

28(27). Anterior tarsi very slender ... **Habrocerinae**
 Anterior tarsi broadly dilated **Trichophyinae**

29(27). Elytral epipleuron delimited by a carina *30*
 Elytral epipleuron not delimited by a carina **Phleoocharinae**

30(29). Pronotal epimeron delimited by a distinct suture **Olisthaerinae**
 Pronotal epimeron not delimited by a suture **Tachyporinae**

The following generic catalog is that of Moore and Legner (1975). These authors omit tribes and have rearranged the subfamilies so that some of the former tribes have been elevated to subfamily rank. Since this is the only complete catalog of the species at the present time, it may serve as a reference to the existing literature of the group, but it should be remembered that it reflects the biases of the authors. The numerous undefined subgenera are omitted.

Subfamily Staphylininae

[24.1 *Belonuchus* Nordman (11 spp. (1), (2), (3)); 24.2 *Beeria* Hatch (1 sp., *B. punctata* Hatch (4) OR); 24.3 *Cafius* Curtis (10 spp. (1), (2), (3), (4)); 24.4 *Erichsonius* Fauvel (9 spp.); 24.5 *Gabrius* Curtis (25 spp); 24.6 *Gabronthus* Tottenham (1 sp., *G. thermarum* Aubé (1) DC; (5) MO); 24.7 *Hesperus* Fauvel (4 spp. (1), (2), (3), (5)); 24.8 *Laetulonthus* Moore and Legner (1 sp., *L. laetulus* Say (1) IN; (2) GA; (3) TX); 24.9 *Neobisnius* Ganglbauer (17 spp.); 24.10 *Ocypus* Samouelle (4 spp. (1), (2), (3), (4)); 24.11 *Ontholestes* Ganglbauer (3 spp. (1), (4))]

24.12 *Philonthus* Curtis

One hundred and forty-three species, including the following:

P. politus Linnaeus. L. 9.5–15 mm. Black, shiny; elytra bronze, sparely pubescent; apical segment of male abdomen with a V-shaped notch. Found in dung. (1) n.e. US; (2) AL; (3) CA; (4) Pacific n.w.

24.13 *Staphylinus* Linnaeus

Thirty-three species, the following of which are common:

S. maculosus Gravenhorst. L. 18–25 mm. Dark brown; elytra and abdomen dorsally marked with brownish spots. (See Fig. 24.58.) Found on carrion. (1) n.e US.

S. violaceus Gravenhorst. (Violet Rove Beetle). L. 12–14 mm. Elongate, rather slender; black and shiny; head, thorax,

and elytra dark violet-blue or coppery; antennae pitch black, slightly longer than head; pronotum as wide as head and as wide

Fig. 24.58.

as long, with curved sides; surface coarsely and rather sparsely punctured but with a distinct, smooth median line; elytra dense-ly punctuate, sparsely pubescent. Found on fungi, carrion, and beneath bark and logs. (See A&J 93.) (1) n.e. US; (2) NC.

Subfamily Xanthopyginae

24.14 *Creophilus* Samouelle

One species, as follows:

C. maxillosus (Linnaeus) (Hairy Rove Beetle). L. 12–21 mm. Stout, black, shiny body; abdominal segments 2 and 3, and sometimes 4, with a band of yellowish hair similar to that of the elytra. Very common at the first sign of the decay of a dead animal. Probably cosmopolitan. (See Fig. 24.59.)

[24.15 *Hadrotes* Maeklin (1 sp., *H. crassus* Mannerheim (3) CA; (4) Pacific n.w.); 24.16 *Thinopinus* LeConte (1 sp., *T. pictus* LeConte (3) CA; (4) Pacific n.w.); 24.17 *Trigonopselaphus* Gemminger and Harold (1 sp., *T. subcoeruleus* LeConte (3) TX); 24.18 *Tympanophorus* Nordman (1 sp., *T. puncticollis* Erichson (1) PQ, MI; (4) BC); 24.19 *Xanthopygus* Kraatz (1 sp., *X. cacti* Horn (3) AZ)]

Fig. 24.59.

Subfamily Quediinae

[24.20 *Acylophorus* Nordman (17 spp.); 24.21 *Anaquedius* Casey (1 sp., *A. vernix* LeConte (1) WI, LB; (2) NC, LA); 24.22 *Atanygnathus* Jacobson (3 spp. (1), (2), (3)); 24.23 *Hemiquedius* Casey (1 sp., *H. ferox* LeConte (1) WI, NS; (2) LA, FL); 24.24 *Heterothops* Stephens (17 spp. (1), (3), (4), (5)); 24.25 *Quedius* Stephens (86 spp.)]

Subfamily Diochinae

[24.26 *Diochus* Erichson (5 spp. (1), (2), (3), (5)); 24.27 *Ophioomma* Notman (1 sp., *O. rufa* Notman (2) FL)]

Subfamily Platyprosopinae

[24.28 *Platyprosopus* Mannerheim (1 sp., *P. texanus* Moore (3) TX)]

Subfamily Xantholininae

[24.29 *Atrecus* Jacquelin du Val (6 spp. (1), (2), (3), (4)); 24.30 *Gyrohypnus* Samouelle (1 sp., *G. fulgidus* Fabricius (1) (4)); 24.31 *Habrolinus* Casey *(1 sp.,* H. tahoensis Casey (3) CA); 24.32 *Hesperolinus* Casey (7 spp. (3), (4)); 24.33 *Hyponygrus* Tottenham (24 spp.); 24.34 *Leiolinus* Casey (2 spp. (4)); 24.35 *Leptacinus* Erichson (5 spp.); 24.36 *Lissohypnus* Casey (1 sp. (3) TX); 24.37 *Lithocharodes* Sharp (3 spp. (1), (2), (3)); 24.38 *Megalinus* Mulsant and Rey (6 spp. (1), (3), (4), (5)); 24.39 *Microlinus* Casey (1 sp., *M. pusio* LeConte (2) SC, FL)); 24.40 *Nematolinus* Casey (1 sp., *N. longicollis* LeConte (1) RI; (5) MO); 24.41 *Nudobius* Thomson (9 spp.); 24.42 *Oligolinus* Casey (1 sp., *O. floridanus* LeConte (2) FL); 24.43 *Parothius* Casey (1 sp., *P. californicus* Mannerheim (3) CA; (4) BC, WA, OR); 24.44 *Saurohypnus* Sharp (1 sp., *S. scutellaris* Sharp (3) TX); 24.45 *Stenistoderus* Jacquelin du Val (1 sp., *S. rubripennis* LeConte (1) IN, OH; (3) TX; (5) IA); 24.46 *Stictolinus* Casey (4 spp. (1), (3), (4)); 24.47 *Xestolinus* Casey (3 spp. (3), (4), (5)); 24.48 *Acalophaena* Sharp (1 sp., *A. compacta* Casey (3) AZ; (4) NV); 24.49 *Achenomorphus* Motschulsky (1 sp., *A. corticinus* Gravenhorst (1) IN, PA; (2) FL; (5) IA); 24.50 *Acrostilicus* Hubbard (1 sp., *A. hospes* Hubbard (2) FL); 24.51 *Astenus* Dejean (24 spp.); 24.52 *Biocrypta* Casey (2 spp. (2), (3)); 24.53 *Dacnochilus* LeConte (2 spp. (2), (3)); 24.54 *Echiaster* Erichson (2 spp. (1), (2), (3)); 24.55 *Homaeotarsus* Hochhuth (36 spp); 24.56 *Lathrobium* Gravenhorst (100 spp.); 24.57 *Lissobiops* Casey (1 sp., *L. serpentinum* LeConte (2) NC, AL); 24.58 *Lithocharis* Dejean (12 spp.); 24.59 *Lobrathium* Mulsant and Rey (66 spp.); 24.60 *Medon* Stephens (52 spp. (1), (3), (4), (5)); 24.61 *Megastilicus* Casey (1 sp., *M. formicarius* Casey (1) IN, MA); 24.62 *Neomedon* Sharp (2 spp. (3)); 24.63 *Ochthephilum* Stephens (6 spp. (1), (3)); 24.64 *Orus* Casey (1), (3), (4), (5)); 24.65 *Pachystilicus* Casey (2 spp. (3), (4), (5)); 24.66 *Paederopsis* Wasmann (1 sp., *P. gloydi* Kistner (3) AZ); 24.67 *Paederus* Fabricius (15 spp.); 24.68 *Rugilus* Samouelle (12 spp.); 24.69 *Scopaeus* Erichson (41 spp.); 24.70 *Stamnoderus* Sharp (3 sp. (2)); 24.71 *Stilicolina* Casey (5 spp. (1), (2), (3)); 24.72 *Stilicopsis* Sachse (2 spp. (1), (2)); 24.73 *Stilomedon* Sharp (1 sp., *S. tabacinum* Casey (3) AZ); 24.74 *Sunius* Curtis (28 spp. (1), (2), (3),(4)); 24.75 *Thinocharis* Kraatz (5 spp. (1), (2), (3)); 24.76 *Xenomedon* Fall (1 sp., *X. formicarium* Fall (3) s. CA)]

Subfamily Pinophilinae

[24.77 *Araeocerus* Nordmann (2 spp. (3)); 24.78 *Lathropinus* Sharp (1 sp., *L. picipes* Erichson (2) VA, NC, SC, GA, FL); 24.79 *Palaminus* Erichson (14 spp. (1), (2), (3)); 24.80 *Pinophilus* Gravenhorst (12 spp. (1), (2), (3), (5))]

Subfamily Micropeplinae

[24.81 *Kalissus* LeConte (1 sp., *K. nitidus* LeConte (4) BC, WA); 24.82 *Micropeplus* Latreille (10 spp.)

Subfamily Pseudopsinae

[24.83 *Pseudopsis* Newman (4 spp. (3), (4), (5))]

Subfamily Piestinae

[24.84 *Asemobius* Horn (1 sp., *A. caelatus* Horn (3) CA; (4) WA); 24.85 *Charhyphus* Sharp (2 spp. (1), (2), (3), (5)); 24.86 *Hypotelus* Erichson (2 spp. (2), (3)); 24.87 *Piestus* Gravenhorst (1 sp., *P. extimus* Sharp (3) AZ); 24.88 *Siagonium* Kirby and Spence (3 spp.); 24.89 *Trigonurus* Mulsant (7 spp. (3), (4)); 24.90 *Zalobius* LeConte (2 spp. (3), (4))]

Subfamily Lispininae

[24.91 *Clavilispinus* Bernhauer (5 spp. (1), (2), (3), (4)); 24.92 *Eleusis* Laporte (2 spp. (1), (3), (5)); 24.93 *Lispinus* Erichson (1 sp., *L. aequipunctatus* LeConte (3) AZ, NM); 24.94 *Nacaeus* Blackwelder (2 spp. (1), (2), (3)); 24. 95 *Renardia* Motschulsky (2 spp. (1), (3), (4)); 24.96 *Thoracophorus* Motschulsky (4 spp. (1), (2), (3), (5))]

Subfamily Osoriinae

[24.97 *Fenderia* Hatch (1 sp., *F. capizzii* Hatch (3) CA; (4) WA, OR); 24.98 *Neotrochus* Blackwelder (4 spp. (1), (2), (3)); 24.99 *Osorius* Latreille (9 spp. (1), (2), (3), (5))]

Subfamily Proteininae

[24.100 *Megarthrus* Curtis (6 spp.); 24.101 *Proteinus* Latreille (8 spp. (1), (3), (4), (5))]

Subfamily Omaliinae

[24.102 *Acidota* Stephens (3 spp. (1), (4)); 24.103 *Acrulia* Thomson (1 sp., *A. tumidula* Maeklin (4) AK, BC, WA); 24.104 *Amphicroum* Kraatz (3 spp. (3), (4)); 24.105 *Anthobium* Samouelle (12 spp. (2), (3), (4), (5)); 24.106 *Anthophagus* Gravenhorst (1 sp., unnammed (3) CA); 24.107 *Arpedium* Erichson (7 spp. (1), (5)); 24.108 *Artochia* Casey (2 spp. (3)); 24.109 *Boreaphilus* Sahlberg (3 spp. (1), (4)); 24.110 *Elonium* Leach (12 spp. (1), (3), (4), (5)); 24.111 *Ephelinus* Cockerell (5 spp.)); 24.112 *Eudectus* Redtenbacher (1 sp., *E. crassicornis* LeConte (2) LA); 24.113 *Eusphalerum* Kraatz (27 spp.); 24.114 *Haida* Keen (1 sp., *H. keeni* Keen (4) Pacific n.w.); 24.115 *Hapalarea* Thomson (9 spp. (1), (3), (4), (5)); 24.116 *Lesteva* Latreille (2 spp. (1), (4)); 24.117 *Mathrilaeum* Moore (2 spp. (3), (4)); 24.118 *Micralymma* Westwood (4 spp. (1)); 24.119 *Microedus* LeConte (7 spp. (1), (4), (5)); 24.120 *Occiephelinus* Hatch (1 sp., *O. vandykei* Hatch (4) WA); 24.121 *Olophrum* Erichson (9 spp. (1), (4)); 24.122 *Omalium* Gravenhorst (20 spp.); 24.123 *Orobanus* LeConte (7 spp. (3), (4), (5)); 24.124 *Orochares* Kraatz (1 sp., *O. angustata* Erichson (1) MA); 24.125 *Paradeliphrum* Hatch (2 spp. (3), (4), (5)); 24.126 *Pelecomalium* Casey (12 spp. (3), (4)); 24.127 *Phalaeopterus* Motschulsky (14 spp. (3), (4), (5)); 24.128 *Phloeonomus* Heer (3 spp. (4), (5)); 24.129 *Porrhodites* Kraatz (1 sp., *P. fenestralis* Zetterstedt (1) LB, MI; (3) CA; (4) AK, BC; (5) CO); 24.130 *Psephidonus* Gistel (12 spp.); 24.131 *Pseudohaida* Hatch (2 spp. (4)); 24.132 *Pycnoglypta* Thomson (1 sp., *P. lurida* Gyllenhal (1) MA; (2) NC; (4) BC, OR); 24.133 *Subhaida* Hatch (1 sp., *S. rainieri* Hatch (4) WA); 24.134 *Tanyrhinus* Mannerheim (1 sp., *T. singularis* Mannerheim (3) CA; (4) AK, BC, WA, OR); 24.135 *Trigonodemus* LeConte (2 spp. (1), (4)); 24.136 *Unamis* Casey (5 spp. (3), (4)); 24.137 *Vellica* Casey (1 sp., *V longipennis* Casey (3) CA; (4) BC); 24.138 *Xenicopoda* Moore and Legner (1 sp., *X. helenae* Moore and Legner (3) CA); 24.139 *Xylodroomus* Heer (3 spp. (1), (3), (4))]

Subfamily Brathininae

24.140 *Brathinus* LeConte

Three species are found in (1), (3), including the following:

B. nitidus LeConte (Grass-root Beetle). L. ±6 mm. Tan; body elongate, somewhat antlike; antennae long, reaching nearly to end of elytra; elytra entire; legs long. Found among the roots of grass growing near water. Rare. (1) NS, PQ.

Subfamily Oxytelinae

[24.141 *Anotylus* Thomson (16 spp.); 24.142 *Aploderus* Stephens (7 spp. (3), (4); 24.143 *Apocellus* Erichson (9 spp.); 24.144 *Bledius* Samouelle (103 spp.); 24.145 *Carpelimus* Leach (79 spp.); 24.146 *Coprophilus* Latreille (2 spp. (4)); 24.147 *Deleaster* Erichson (3 spp.(1), (3), (4), (5)); 24.148 *Manda* Blackwelder (1 sp., *M. nearctica* Moore (2) FL); 24.149 *Microbledius* Herman (4 spp. (2), (3), (5)); 24.150 *Neoxus* Herman (1 sp., *N. crassicornis* Casey (3) TX); 24.151 *Ochthephilus* Mulsant and Rey (3 spp. (1), (3), (4), (5)); 24.152 *Oxytelus* Gravenhorst (2 spp.); 24.153 *Platystethus* Mannerheim (3 spp. (1), (3), (4)); 24.154 *Psamathobledius* Herman (1 sp., *P. punctatissimus* LeConte (2) MD, FL; (3) CA); 24.155 *Syntomium* Curtis (4 spp. (1), (4)); 24.156 *Teropalpus* Soiler (1 sp., *T. lithocharinus* LeConte (3) CA; (4) WA); 24.157 *Thinobius* Kiesenwetter (24 spp. (1), (3), (4)); 24.158 *Thinodromus* Kraatz (5 spp. (1), (2), (3), (4))]

Subfamily Oxyporinae

[24.159 *Oxyporus* Fabricius (11 spp. (1), (2), (3), (5))]

Subfamily Megalopsidiinae

[24.160 *Megalopinus* Eichelbaum (2 spp. (1), (2))]

Subfamily Euaesthetinae

[24.161 *Edaphus* Motschulsky (1 sp., *E. nitidus* Motschulsky (1) IL, PA, DC; (2) MS); 24.162 *Euaesthetus* Gravenhorst (18 spp. (1), (2), (3), (4)); 24.163 *Stictocranius* LeConte (1 sp., *S. puncticeps* LeConte (1) PA, DC: (2) NC; (4) OR))]

Subfamily Leptotyphlinae

[24.164 *Cainotyphlus* Coiffait (2 spp. (3) CA); 24.165 *Heteroleptotyphlus* Coiffait (2 spp. (3) CA); 24.166 *Homeotyphlus* Coiffait (1 sp., *H. maritimus* Coiffait (3) CA); 24.167 *Neoleptotyphlus* Coiffait (1 sp., *N. californicus* Coiffait (3) CA); 24.168 *Prototyphlus* Coiffait (1 sp., *P. gigas* Coiffait (3) CA); 24.169 *Telotyphlus* Coiffait (2 spp. (3) CA); 24.170 *Xenotyphlus* Coiffait (3) CA)]

Subfamily Phloeocharinae

[24.171 *Rimulincola* Sanderson (1 sp., *R. divalis* Sanderson (2) AR); 24.172 *Ecbletus* Sharp (1 sp., *E. leechi* Moore (3) CA); 24.173 *Vicelva* Moore and Legner (1 sp., *V. vandykei* Hatch (4) WA, OR)]

Subfamily Olisthaerinae

[24.174 *Olisthaerus* Dejean (2 spp. (1), (3), (4))]

Subfamily Tachyporinae

[24.175 *Bolitobius* Leach (4 spp. (1), (4)); 24.176 *Bryoporus* Kraatz (2 spp. (1), (2), (3), (4)); 24.177 *Cilea* Jacquelin du Val (1 sp., *C. silphoides* Linnaeus (4) BC, WA, OR); 24.178 *Coproporus* Kraatz (8 spp.)); 24.179 *Lordithon* Thomson (29 spp.); 24.180 *Mycetoporus* Mannerheim (22 spp.); 24.181 *Sepedophilus* Gistel (22 spp. (1), (2), (3), (4)); 24.182 *Tachinomorphus* Kraatz (4 spp. (3) AZ); 24.183 *Tachinus* Gravenhorst (40 spp.); 24.184 *Tachyporus* Gravenhorst (18 spp.)]

Subfamily Habrocerinae

[24.185 *Habrocerus* Erichson (3 spp. (1), (3), (4), (5))]

Subfamily Trichophyinae

[24.186 *Trichophya* Mannerheim (3 spp. (1), (3), (4), (5))]

Subfamily Trichopseniinae

[24.187 *Trichopsenius* Horn (5 spp. (1), (2), (3), (4)); 24.188 *Xenistusa* LeConte (2 spp. (2) FL; (3) TX))]

Subfamily Hypocyphtinae

[24.189 *Anacyptus* Horn (1 sp., *A. testaceus* LeConte (2) NC, FL, AR; (3) AZ; (5) MN); 24.190 *Cypha* Samouelle (4 spp. (1), (4), (5))]

Subfamily Steninae

[24.191 *Dianous* Samouelle (2 spp. (1), (4), (5)); 24.192 *Stenus* Latreille (197 spp.)]

Subfamily Aleocharinae

[24.193 *Acrimea* Casey (3 spp. (4)); 24.194 *Aleochara* Gravenhorst (93 spp.); 24.195 *Aleodorus* Say (3 spp.); 24.196 *Alisalia* Casey (7 spp. (1), (2), (3)); 24.197 *Amarochara* Thomson (4 spp. (1), (5)); 24.198 *Amblopusa* Casey (2 spp. (3), (4)); 24.199 *Amischa* Thomson (14 spp. (1), (2), (3), (5)); 24.200 *Aneurota* Casey (1 sp., *A. sucifrons* Casey (2) FL); 24.201 *Anomognathus* Solier (1 sp., *A. cuspidata* Erichson (1) OH, NY); 24.202 *Apimela* Mulsant and Rey (3 spp. (3)); 24.203 *Apteronina* Wasmann (1 sp., *A. schmitti* Wasmann (5) CO); 24.204 *Asthenesita* Casey (1 sp., *A. pallens* Casey (2) FL); 24.205 *Atheta* Thomson (536 spp.); 24.206 *Autalia* Samouelle (4 spp. (1), (3), (4)); 24.207 *Bamona* Sharp (1 sp., *B. falliana* Casey (2) NC; (3) CA); 24.208 *Beyeria* Fenyes (1 sp., *B. vespa* Fenyes (3) AZ); 24.209 *Blepharhymenus* Solier (21 spp. (3), (4), (5)); 24.210 *Bolitochara* Mannerheim (17 spp. (1), (3), (4), (5)); 24.211 *Borboropora* Kraatz (1 sp., *B. quadriceps* LeConte (1) NY, PA; (2) WV); 24.212 *Brachyusa* Mulsant and Rey (1 sp., *B. raptoria* Wollaston (NA, locality?)); 24.213 *Bryobiota* Casey (1 sp., *B. bicolor* Casey (3) CA; (4) BC); 24.214 *Bryothinusa* Casey (1 sp., *B. catalinae* Casey (3) s. CA); 24.215 *Calodera* Mannerheim (1 sp., *C. infuscata* Blatchley (1) IN); 24.216 *Cordalia* Jacobs (1 sp., *C. obscura* Gravenhorst (1) NY, PA); 24.217 *Crataraea* Thomson (3 spp. (1), (2), (3), (5)); 24.218 *Crimalia* Casey (1 sp., *C. quadriceps* Casey (2) MS); 24.219 *Cyphea* Fauvel (1 sp., *C. wallisi* Fenyes (5) MB); 24.220 *Decusa* Casey (1 sp., *D. expansa* LeConte (5) CO); 24.221 *Deinopsis* Matthews (1 sp., *D. americana* Kraatz (1) IN; (2) VA, FL, LA); 24.222 *Devia* Blackwelder (1 sp., *D. prospera* Erichson (1) MA; (3) CA; (4) AK); 24.223 *Diaulota* Casey (4 spp. (3), (4)); 24.224 *Diestota* Mulsant and Rey (4 spp. (2), (3)); 24.225 *Diglotta* Champion (1 sp., *D. pacifica* Fenyes (3) s. CA); 24.226 *Dinardilla* Wasmann (1 sp., *D. liometopi* Wasmann (5) CO); 24.227 *Dinocoryna* Casey (6 spp. (2), (3), (5)); 24.228 *Doliponta* Blackwelder (1 sp., *D. veris* Fenyes (3) s. CO); 24.229 *Drusilla* Samouelle (1 sp., *D. cavicollis* Casey (4) AK); 24.230 *Eburniogaster* Seevers (2 spp. (3) AZ, TX); 24.231 *Ecitonidia* Wasmann (1 sp., *E. wheeleri* Wasmann (3) AZ, TX; (5) CO, KS); 24.232 *Ecitopora* Wasmann (1 sp., *E. nitidiventris* Brues (3) TX); 24.233 *Ecitoxenida* Wasmann (3 spp. (2) NC, AL; (3) TX); 24.234 *Encephalus* Kirby (1 sp., *E. americanus* Seevers (1) IL; (5) MT); 24.235 *Elachistarthron* Notman (1 sp., *E. anomala* Notman (2) FL); 24.236 *Euthorax* Solier (5 spp. (1), (2), (3), (5)); 24.237 *Euvira* Sharp (1 sp., *E. debilis* Sharp (US?)); 24.238 *Evanystes* Gistel (8 spp. (1), (3), (4), (5)); 24.239 *Falagria* Samouelle (8 spp.); 24.240 *Falagriota* Casey (1 sp., *F. occidua* Casey (3) CA); 24.241 *Gaenima* Casey (1 sp., *G. impedita* Casey (3) CA); 24.242 *Gennadota* Casey (2 spp. (1)); 24.243 *Genosema* Notman (2 spp. (2) LA, FL); 24.244 *Gnypeta* Thomson (13 spp.); 24.245 *Gnypetella* Casey (1 sp., *G. laticeps* Casey (3) CA); 24.246 *Goniusa* Casey (1 sp., *G. obtusa* LeConte (1) PA); 24.247 *Gymnusa* Gravenhorst (3 spp. (1), (4)); 24.248 *Gyronycha* Casey (1 sp., *G. valens* Casey (1) IN, NY; (2) NC; (3) s. CA, TX); 24.249 *Gyrophaena* Mannerheim (70 spp); 24.250 *Halobrecta* Thomson (1 sp., *H. algophila* Fenyes (3) s. CA); 24.251 *Homalota* Mannerheim (1 sp., *H. plana* Gyllenhal (1) IN, NY; (3) CA, TX; (4) AK, WA, ID); 24.252 *Homia* Blackwelder (1 sp., *H. gigantula* LeConte (3) TX); 24.253

Homoeusa Kraatz (3 spp. (1), (5)); 24.254 *Hoplandria* Kraatz (2 spp. (1), (2), (3)); 24.255 *Hygropora* Kraatz (1 sp., *H. americana* Fenyes (4) BC)': 24.256 *Hylota* Casey (1 sp., *H. ochracea* Casey (1) NY); 24.257 *Ischnopoda* Stephens (6 spp. (1), (2), (3), (5)); 24.258 *Ityocara* Thomson (1 sp., *I. rubens* Erichson (NA, locality?); 24.259 *Leptobamona* Casey (1 sp., *L. pertenuis* Caset (1) NJ); 24.260 *Liparocephalus* Maeklin (2 spp. (3), (4)); 24.261 *Longipeltina* Bernhauer (1 sp., *L. bakeri* Bernhauer (3) CA); 24.262 *Lophomucter* Notman (1 sp., *L. laevicollis* Notman (2) FL); 24.263 *Lypoglossa* Fenyes (1 sp., *L. fenyesi* Bernhauer (4) AK, BC); 24.264 *Melanalia* Casey (2 spp. (3) CA); 24.265 *Meotica* Mulsant and Rey (2 spp. (1)); 24.266 *Meronera* Sharp (1 sp., *M. venustula* Erichson (1) IN, RI; (2) FL; (3) TX, (4) UT); 24.267 *Microdonia* Casey (4 spp. (3), (5)); 24.268 *Myllaena* Erichson (9 spp.); 24.269 *Myrmecopora* Saulcy (1 sp., *M. vaga* LeConte (5) MN); 24.270 *Nosora* Casey (1 sp., *N. meticola* Casey (3) AZ); 24.271 *Ocalea* Erichson (7 spp. (3), (4)); 24.272 *Ocyusa* Kraatz (4 spp. (1), (3), (4), (5)); 24.273 *Oligota* Mannerheim (11 spp. (1), (3), (5)); 24.274 *Omoschema* Notman (1 sp., *O. laticeps* Notman (2) FL); 24.275 *Orthodiatelus* Notman (1 sp., *O. innotablis* Notman (2) FL); 24.276 *Oxypoda* Mannerheim (90 spp.); 24.277 *Pachycerota* Casey (1 sp., *P. duryi* Casey (1) MA; (5) IA); 24.278 *Parocalea* Bernhauer (1 sp., *P. baicalica* Eppelsheim (NA, locality?); 24.279 *Phanerota* Casey (3 spp. (1), (2), (3)); 24.280 *Philotermes* Kraatz (6 spp. (1), (2)); 24.281 *Phloeopora* Erichson (9 spp. (1), (3), (4), (5)); 24.282 *Phytosus* Curtis (1 sp., *P. littoralis* Horn (1) NJ); 24.283 *Placusa* Erichson (7 spp. (1), (2), (3), (4)); 24.284 *Platandria* Casey (5 spp.); 24.285 *Pontomalota* Casey (5 spp. (3), (4)); 24.286 *Probeyeria* Seevers (1 sp., *P. pulex* Sanderson (2) AK; (3) AZ; (5) KS); 24.287 *Pulicomorpha* Mann (1 sp., *P. coeca* Mann (3) CA); 24.288 *Schistacme* Notman (1 sp., *S. obtusa* Notman (2) FL); 24.289 *Schistoglossa* Kraatz (1 sp., *S. viduata* Erichson (NA, locality?); 24.290 *Silusa* Erichson (9 spp. (1), (3), (5)); 24.291 *Silusida* Casey (1 sp., *S. marginella* Casey (1) NY, PA); 24.292 *Sipalia* Mulsant and Rey (20 spp. (1), (2), (3), (5)); 24.293 *Stichoglossa* Fairmaire and Laboulbene (7 spp. (1), (2), (3)); 24.294 *Strigota* Casey (15 spp.); 24.295 *Strophogastra* Fenyes (1 sp., *S. penicillata* Fenyes (5) MB); 24.296 *Symbiochara* Fenyes (1 sp., *S. lativentris* Fenyes (3) s. CA); 24.297 *Tarphiota* Casey (3 spp. (3), (4)); 24.298 *Teliusa* Casey (2 spp. (1), (3)); 24.299 *Termitonidia* Seevers (1 sp., *T. lunata* Seevers (3) AZ); 24.300 *Tetradonia* Wasmann (1 sp., *T. megalops* Casey (3) TX); 24.301 *Tetralaucopora* Bernhauer (2 spp. (1), (2)); 24.302 [Number not used]; 24.303 *Tetralina* Casey (3 spp. (3), (5)); 24.304 *Tetrallus* Bernhauer (3 spp. (3) CA); 24.305 *Thamiaraea* Thomson (1 sp., *T. americana* Bernhauer (2) LA)); 24.306 *Thecturota* Casey (5 spp. (1), (2), (3)); 24.307 *Thinusa* Casey (2 spp. (3), (4)); 24.308 *Thyasophila* Fairmaiere and Laboulbene (4 spp. (1), (5)); 24.309 *Tinotus* Sharp (10 spp.); 24.310 *Tomoglossa* Kraatz (1 sp., *T. luteicornis* Erichson (4) UT); 24.311 *Trachyota* Casey (2 spp. (3) CA)); 24.312 *Trichiusa* Casey (17 spp.); 24.313 *Xenodusa* Wasmann (5 spp. (1), (3), (4), (5)); 24.314 *Xesturida* Casey (1 sp., *X. laevis* Casey (1) IN; (2) MS) 24.315 *Zyrax* Stephens (19 spp. (1), (2), (3), (5))]

25. PSELAPHIDAE (Antloving Beetle Family)

Length: 0.5–5.5 mm. This family resembles Staphylinidae, but the abdomen is not flexible and is broader than that of most Staphylinidae. Found in rotting logs, in moss, humus, under bark, or in ants' nests. There are 654 species in the U.S. and Canada.

Subfamily Faroninae
Tribe Faronini

[25.1 *Sonoma* Casey (19 spp. (1), (2), (3), (4)); 25.2 *Megarafonus* Casey (5 spp. (3), (4))]

Tribe Byxidicerini

[25.3 *Bythinoplectus* Reitter (1 sp., *B. gloydi* Park (3) AZ)]

Subfamily Pselaphinae
Tribe Mayetini

[25.4 *Mayetia* Mulsant and Rey (18 spp. (2), (3), (4), (5))]

Tribe Speleobamini

[25.5 *Speleobama* Park (1 sp., *S. vana* Park (2) AL); 25.6 *Prespelea* Park (2 spp. (2) TN, NC)]

Tribe Holozodini

[25.7 *Caccoplectus* Sharp (1 sp., *C. spinipes* Schaeffer (3) TX)]

Tribe Euplectini

[25.8 *Abdiunguis* Park and Wagner (1 sp. (4) OR)]

Subtribe Rhinoscepsina

[25.9 *Rhinoscepsis* LeConte (1 sp., *R. bistriatus* LeConte (2) FL)); 25.10 *Morius* Casey (1 sp., *M. occidens* Casey (3) CA)]

Subtribe Trogastrina

[25.11 *Rhexidius* Casey (13 spp. (1), (2), (3)); 25.12 *Oropus* Casey (31 spp. (3), (4)); 25.13 *Tetrascapha* Schuster and Marsh (2 spp. (3), (4)); 25.14 *Foveoscapha* Park and Wagner (1 sp., *F. terracola* Park and Wagner (4) WA, OR); 25.15 *Euboarhexius* Grigarick and Schuster (1 sp., *E. sinus* Grigarick and Schuster (3) CA)]

Subtribe Trichonychina

[25.16 *Trichonyx* Chaudoir (1 sp., *T. sulcicollis* (Reichenbach) (1) NY)]

Subtribe Rhexina

[25.17 *Rhexius* LeConte (8 spp. (1), (2), (5))]

Subtribe Panaphantina

[25.18 *Thesium* Casey (2 spp. (2), (3), (5))]

Subtribe Bibloporina

[25.19 *Bibloporus* Thomson (1 sp., *B. bicanalis* (Casey) (1) NY)); 25.20 *Eutyphlus* LeConte (5 spp. (1), (2)); 25.21 *Hatchia* Park and Wagner (1 sp., *H. carinata* Park and Wagner (4) WA); 25.22 *Ramecia* Casey (7 spp. (1), (2), (3))]

Subtribe Trisignina

[25.23 *Trisignis* Park and Schuster (2 spp. (3) CA)]

Subtribe Euplectina

[25.24 *Cropodes* Casey (2 spp. (3) CA; (4) OR); 25.25 *Acolonia* Casey (1 sp., *A. cavicollis* (LeConte) (2) FL); 25.26 *Trigonoplectus* Bowman (2 sp. (1) PA); 25.27 *Bibloplectus* Reitter (5 spp. (1), (2), (3)); 25.28 *Trimioplectus* Brendel (2 spp. (1), (5)); 25.29 *Thesiastes* Casey (4 spp. (1), (2)); 25.30 *Euplectus* Leach (16 spp. (1), (2), (3), (5)); 25.31 *Pycnoplectus* Casey (11 spp. (1), (2), (3)); 25.32 *Leptoplectus* Casey (1 sp. *L. pertenuis* (Casey) (1), (2), (5))]

Subtribe Trimiina

[25.33 *Actium* Casey (33 spp. (1), (3), (4), (5); 25.34 *Actiastes* Casey (8 spp.); 25.35 *Pseudactium* Casey (4 spp. (1)); 25.36 *Pilactium* Grigarick and Schuster (1 sp., *P. summersi* Grigatick and Schuster (3) CA); 25.37 *Pygmactium* Schuster and Grigarick (2 spp. (2)); 25.38 *Simplona* Casey (1 sp., *S. arizonica* Casey (3) AZ); 25.39 *Cupila* Casey (3 spp. (3), (4)); 25.40 *Basolum* Casey (2 spp. (1), (2), (5)); 25.41 *Melba* Casey (14 spp. (1), (2), (5)); 25.42 *Dalmosella* Casey (1 sp., *D. tenuis* Casey (1) PA)]

Fig. 24.60.

25.43 *Trimiomelba* Casey

Three species are found in (1), (2), including the following:

T. dubia (LeConte). L. 0.8 mm. Dull brownish, very finely pubescent. Elytra each with two basal foveae, the discal line reaching the middle. Found under stones. (See Fig. 24.60.) (1) IN; (2) GA.

[25.44 *Lemelba* Park (1 sp., *L. davisi* Park (2) FL)]

Tribe Brachyglutini

Subtribe Eupseniina

[25.45 *Eupsenius* LeConte (2 spp. (1), (2), (5))]

Subtribe Brachyglutina

[25.46 *Rybaxis* Saulcy (11 spp. (1), (2), (4), (5)); 25.47 *Nisaxis* Casey (4 spp. (1), (3), (5)); 24.48 *Brachygluta* Thomson (22 spp. (1), (2), (3), (5)); 25.49 *Reichenbachia* Leach (78 spp.); 25.50 *Briaraxis* Brendel (1 sp., *B. depressa* Brendel (2) FL); 25.51 *Anchylarthron* Brendel (3 spp. (1), (2), (5)); 25.52 *Eutrichites* LeConte (1 sp., *E. zonatus* (Brendel) (1), (2), (3)); 25.53 *Scalenarthrus* LeConte (1 sp., *S. horni* LeConte (3)); 25.54 *Pselaptus* LeConte (1 sp., *P. belfragei* LeConte (3))]

Subtribe Decarthronina

[25.55 Decarthron (26 spp. (1), (2), (3), (5))]

Tribe Tychini

[25.56 *Hesperotychus* Schuster and Marsh (12 spp. (3), (4), (5)); 25.57 *Hylotychus* Grigarick and Schuster (10 spp. (3), (4)); 25.58 *Lucifotychus* Park and Wagner (12 spp.); 25.59 *Cylindrarctus* Schaufuss (5 spp. (1), (2), (4), (5))]

Tribe Valdiini

[25.60 *Valda* Casey (1 sp., *V. frontalis* Casey (3) CA)]

Tribe Bythinini

[25.61 *Machaerodes* Brendel (1 sp., *M. carinatus* (Brendel) (1), (2)); 25.62 *Machaerites* Mueller (6 spp. (2) AL); 25.63 *Bythinopsis* Raffray (4 spp. (1), (2)); 25.64 *Pselaptrichus* Brendel (33 spp. (3), (4))]

Tribe Batrisini

Subtribe Batrisina

[25.65 *Arthmius* LeConte (5 spp. (1), (2), (3)); 25.66 *Batriasymmodes* Park (1), (2)); 25.67 *Batrisodes* Reitter (73 spp.); 25.68 *Euphalepsus* Reitter (1 sp., *E. dentipes* Raffray (2) LA); 25.69 *Texamaurops* Barr and Steeves (3) TX)]

Tribe Amauropsini

[25.70 *Arianops* Brendel (31 spp. (1), (2))]

Tribe Pselaphini

[25.71 *Pselaphus* Herbst (5 spp. (1), (2), (4), (5))]

Tribe Tyrini

[25.72 *Tyrus* Aubé (5 spp.); 25.73 *Cedius* LeConte (4 spp. (1), (2), (5)); 25.74 *Mipseltyrus* Park (3 spp. (2), (3)); 25.75 *Anitra* Casey (1 sp., *A. glaberula* Casey (3) AZ)]

Tribe Hamotini

[25.76 *Hamotus* Aubé (4 spp. (3)); 25.77 *Cercocerus* LeConte (1 sp., *C. batrisoides* LeConte (1), (2))]

Tribe Ceophyllini

[25.78 *Ceophyllus* LeConte (1 sp., *C. monilis* LeConte (1))]

Tribe Tmesiphorini

[25.79 *Tmesiphorus* LeConte (2 spp. (1), (2), (3), (5))]

Tribe Ctenisini

[25.80 *Ctenisis* Raffray (1 spp., *C. raffrayi* Casey (3) CA, AZ); 25.81 *Pilopius* Casey (14 spp. (1), (2), (3), (5)); 25.82 *Atinus* Horn (2 spp. (2), (3)); 25.83 *Biotus* Casey (1 sp., *B. formicarius* Casey (3) CA, AZ)]

Subfamily Clavigerinae
Tribe Fustigerini

[25.84 *Fustiger* LeConte (2 spp. (1), (2), (3), (5))]

Tribe Adraniini

[25.85 *Adranes* LeConte (6 spp.)]

Superfamily Histeroidea

26. HISTERIDAE (Clown Beetle Family)

Length: 0.5–18 mm (usually 5–10 mm) Body hard, compact, usually black and shiny, with some marked with red, yellow, or orange and others metallic blue, green, or bronze; antennae elbowed, clubbed; prosternum with a keel; elytra short in the majority of species. Usually these beetles are oval, but some are cylindrical and others are flat. They are found on carrion, in fungus, under bark, and in ants' nests. Most species are difficult to identify without the aid of specialized literature. There are 499 species recorded in the U.S. and Canada.

Subfamily Abraeinae
Tribe Abraeini

[26.1 *Abraeus* Leach (1 sp., *A. bolteri* LeConte (3) CA)]

Tribe Plegaderini

[26.2 *Plegaderus* Erichson (15 spp.)]

Tribe Acritini

[26.3 *Acritus* LeConte (17 spp.); 26.4 *Aeletes* Horn (4 spp. (1?), (2)); 26.5 *Halacritus* Schmidt (3 spp. (2), (3))]

Subfamily Teretriinae

[26.6 *Teretrius* Erichson (6 spp. (1), (3)); 26.7 *Teretriosoma* Horn (8 spp. (1), (2), (3), (5))]

Subfamily Saprininae

[26.8 *Hypocaccus* Thomson (18 spp.); 26.9 *Baechmanniolus* Reichardt (3 spp. (1), (2), (3)); 26.10 *Pachylopus* Erichson (4 spp. (1), (2), (3));

Fig. 24.61.

26.11 *Reichardtia* Wenzel (1 sp., *R. pedator* Sharp (locality?)); 26.12 *Neopachylopus* Reichardt (2 spp. (3), (4)); 26.13 *Geomysaprinus* Ross (4 spp. (2), (3), (5)); 26.14 *Xerosaprinus* Wenzel (4 spp. (3), (4), (5))]

26.15 *Saprinus* Erichson

One hundred and three species, the following of which are common:

S. assimilis Paykull. L. 4–5.5 mm. Broadly oval; black, shiny; elytra coarsely punctate on apical third. Found on carrion, especially dead fish and amphibians. (See Fig. 24.61.) (1) n.e. US; (2) s.e. US; (3) TX.

S. fimbriatus LeConte (Carrion Clown Beetle). L. 4.5–5 mm. Black; thorax and elytra rather coarsely punctate; elytral striae short, not reaching apex of elytra. Found on carrion, especially dead fish and frogs along the shore of lakes and streams. (See A&J 95.) (3) CA, AZ, TX.

[26.16 *Euspilotus* Lewis (28 spp.); 26.17 *Chelyoxenus* Hubbard (1 sp., *C. xerobatis* Hubbard (2) FL); 26.18 *Aphelosternus* Wenzel (1 sp., *A. interstitialis* LeConte (3) CA); 26.19 *Gnathoncus* Jacquelin du Val (8 spp. (1), (3), (4)); 26.20 *Eremosaprinus* Ross (4 spp. (3) CA)]

Subfamily Dendrophilinae

[26.21 *Carcinops* Marseul (14 spp.); 26.22 *Xestipyge* Marseul (2 spp. (1), (2), (3)); 26.23 *Dendrophilus* Leach (5 spp. (2), (3), (5)); 26.24 *Anapleus* Horn (1 sp., *A. marginatus* LeConte (1) IL; (3) CA, TX); 26.25 *Bacanius* LeConte (8 spp.); 26.26 *Geocolus* Wenzel (1 sp., *G. caecus* Wenzel (2) GA); 26.27 *Platylomalus* Cooman (1 sp., *P. aequalis* Erichson (1), (2), (3), (5)); 26.28 *Paromalus* Erichson (11 spp.)]

Subfamily Tribalinae

[26.29 *Epierus* Erichson (12 spp. (1), (2), (3)); 26.30 *Pseudepierus* Casey (1 sp., *P. duplicatus* Casey (2) LA; (5) KS); 26.31 *Stictostix* Marseul (2 spp. (3)); 26.32 *Onthophilus* Leach (4 spp. (1), (2), (3), (5)); 26.33 *Peploglyptus* LeConte (1 sp., *P. belfragei* LeConte (3) TX); 26.34 *Caerosternus* LeConte (1 sp., *C. americanus* LeConte (1) IL, MD; (3) TX); 26.35 *Idolia* Lewis (1 sp., unidentified (3) TX)]

Subfamily Histerinae
Tribe Histerini

[26.36 *Atholus* Thomson (2 spp. (2) FL); 26.37 *Peranus* Lewis (3 spp. (1), (2), (3)); 26.38 *Margarinotus* Marseul (30 spp.); 26.39 *Hister* Linnaeus (58 spp.); 26.40 *Spilodiscus* Lewis (19 spp.); 26.41 *Pseudister* Bickhardt (1 sp., *P. hospes* Lewis (1) NY)]

Tribe Platysomini

[26.42 *Omalodes* Erichson (2 spp. (2) FL; (3) AZ); 26.43 *Platysoma* Leach (8 spp. (1), (2), (3)); 26.44 *Cylistix* Marseul (4 spp. (1), (2), (3), (5))]

Tribe Hololeptini
26.45 *Hololepta* Paykull

These flat beetles are usually found under bark. There are nineteen species, including the following:

H. aequalis Say. L. 7–11 mm. Black; flat, broadly oblong; shiny, without punctations; elytra with three very short striae; mandibles project forward. Found under bark of fallen trees in damp woods. (1) n.e. US; (2) FL, LA; (3) TX; (5) MB.

H. populnea LeConte (Flat Clown Beetle). L. 7–9.5 mm. Nearly quadrate and flattened; black; surface sparsely punctate; head recessed into thorax; mandibles prominent. Adults and larvae are both found under the bark of felled poplar and willow. The larvae are predacious on other beetle larvae. (See A&J 94.) (3) CA, AZ; (4) UT.

[26.46 *Ilionota* Carnochan (1 sp., *I. cacti* LeConte (3) (CA, AZ, TX)]

Tribe Exosternini

[26.47 *Phelister* Marseul (18 spp. (1), (2), (3)); 26.48 *Tribalister* Horn (2 spp. (1), (3))]

Subfamily Hetaeriinae
Tribe Hetaeriini

[26.49 *Hetaerius* Erichson (24 spp.); 26.50 *Echinodes* Zimmermann (2 spp. (2), (3) AZ); 26.51 *Yarmister* Wenzel (1 sp., *Y. barberi* Wenzel (2) FL); 26.52 *Reninus* Lewis (1 sp., *R. salvini* Lewis (3) TX); 26.53 *Ulkeus* Horn (1 sp., *U. intricatus* Horn (3) TX; (4) KS); 26.54 *Terapus* Marseul (2 spp. (3) CA, AZ); 26.55 *Chrysetaerius* Reichensperger (1 sp., unidentified (3) AZ)]

27. SPHAERITIDAE (False Clown Beetle Family)

Length: 3.5–6 mm. Oval, convex; black with green or blue reflections; elytra truncate; antennae clubbed. Found under bark, in fungus, moss, dung, or around sap.

27.1 *Sphaerites* Duftschmid

One species, as follows:

S. politus Mannerheim. L. 3.5–5.6 mm. Subquadrate; black, shining; faintly punctate; pronotum twice as wide as long, side punctate, strongly margined; elytra as wide as pronotum, sides feebly arcuate, apices truncate, disc with eleven nearly entire striae of moderately impressed punctures. Found on and near compost and in bear dung. (See Fig. 24.62.) (4) Pacific n.w.

Fig. 24.62.

Series SCARABAEIFORMIA

Superfamily SCARABAEOIDEA

The three families in this superfamily are distinguished by their antennae, which have an apical club composed of flattened plates.

28. LUCANIDAE (Stag Beetle Family)

Length: 8–60 mm. Black or reddish brown; males often with large mandibles, which are sometimes branched or toothed. Antennal plates do not close to form a compact club; antennae are usually elbowed, but if not, beetles are large and flattened, without deep striae on elytra. They are found along sandy beaches, on the ground in woods, or in towns about lights at night. The larvae breed in or beneath decaying logs and stumps. There are 31 species in the U.S. and Canada.

Subfamily Lucaninae

28.1 *Pseudolucanus* Hope

Four species are found in (1), (2), (3), (4), of which the following is common:

P. capreolus Linnaeus (Pinching Beetle). L. 22–35 mm. Brown; male without giant mandibles. Attracted to lights. (See Fig. 24.63.) (1) n.e. US.

28.2 *Lucanus* Scopoli

One species, as follows:

L. elaphus Fabricius (American Stag Beetle). L. male, 45–60 mm; female, 30–35 mm. Dark brown and shiny; legs and antennae nearly black; males with mandibles nearly as long as the body; female mandibles short, not as long as the head. Adults may be found in decaying oak stumps; sometimes they are attracted to lights at night. (See A&J 96.) (1) n.e. US.; (2) KY, VA, NC; (3) OK.

Subfamily Dorcinae

[28.3 *Dorcus* MacLeay (4 spp. (1), (2))]

Subfamily Platycerinae

[28.4 *Platycerus* Geoffroy (5 spp. (1), (3), (4), (5)); 28.5 *Platyceroides* Benesh (7 spp. (3) CA; (4) WA, OR); 28.6 *Platyceropsis* Benesh (1 sp., *P. keeni* Casey (3) CA; (4) BC)]

Subfamily Aesalinae

[28.7 *Diphyllostoma* (3 spp. (3) CA)]

28.8 *Ceruchus* MacLeay

Four species are found in (1), (2), (4), (5), including the following:

C. piceus (Weber). L. 10–15 mm. Antennae not elbowed; dark reddish brown to black; mandibles of males as long as head; of females one-half length of head. Larvae in decayed wood of beech, white birch, elm, oak, hemlock, maple, and butternut. (1) n.e. US.

[28.9 *Nicagus* LeConte (1 sp., *N. obscurus* LeConte (1) IN, NY)]

Subfamily Sinodendrinae

[28.10 *Sinodendron* Hellwig (1 sp., *S. rugosum* Mannerheim (3) CA; (4) WA, OR.)]

29. PASSALIDAE (Peg or Bess Beetle Family)

Length: 30–40 mm. These beetles are easily recognized by their shape and antennae, the latter not elbowed and only slightly lamellate. There is a small horn (the "peg") on the head. There are three species in the U.S., as follows:

Subfamily Passalinae

Tribe Proculini

29.1 *Odontotaenius* Kuwert

One species, the Bess Beetle, as follows:

O. disjunctus (Illiger) (Horned Passalus; Pegbug). L. 32–36 mm. Shiny black; head with short, forward bent horn; elytra deeply striate. This species is subsocial. Adults can make a squeaking sound by rubbing the abdomen against the wings. The larvae respond by rubbing the middle coxae with their short hind legs to make a faint sound. Adults and larvae live together in old logs of deciduous trees, the former chewing the wood and feeding it to the larvae. (See Fig. 24.64 and A&J 97.) (1) n.e. US; (2) s.e. US; (3) TX, OK; (5) KS, IA, MO.

Tribe Passalini

[29.2 *Passalus* Fabricius (2 spp., *P. interruptus* Linnaeus (3) s. TX and *P. punctiger* Lepeletier and Serville (3) s. TX)]

Fig. 24.63.

Fig. 24.64.

30. SCARABAEIDAE (Lamellicorn Beetle Family)

Length: 2–100+ mm. All that is needed to recognize the thousands of species that belong to this very large beetle family are the antennae, which are composed of three to seven leaves or plates that form an apical club that can be expanded or completely folded together. Their shape is rather uniformly convex dorsally-ventrally and obovate anteriorly-posteriorly. They vary in color from a drab black or brown to a brilliant metallic blue or green. They are often marked with bright colors; sometimes the entire body may be a bright red or yellow.

The larvae, C-shaped white grubs, have a brown, sclerotized head with prominent mandibles. Many of them live in the soil and feed on roots. Others live in excrement, nests of burrowing vertebrates, carrion, with social insects, under bark, and in humus and fungus. The adults of many species are leaf feeders and cause great loss of crops, forest trees, and ornamentals.

The group has attracted man's attention since ancient times, either as pests, of which there are many, or as objects of wonderment. The sacred scarab of Egypt has become a common model for artifacts in many parts of the globe. With over 12,000 species worldwide, they are commonly collected. The generic classification is well understood. Except for the very large genera, the species are rather easy to identify. There are 1395 species in 135 genera in the U.S. and Canada.

Subfamily Scarabaeinae

Most of the species of this subfamily are excrement or fungus feeders. They are characterized by the enlarged clypeus that covers the mandibles and posterior tibiae with a single apical spur (rarely with two). The males of some species have a horn on the head, on the pronotum, or both. Included among these beetles is the Sacred Scarab of Egypt, *Scarabaeus sacer* Linnaeus, a dung-ball roller, as are many of our North American species. Each dung ball has an egg inside. The larvae that hatch out feed on this dung.

Tribe Scarabaeini

[30.1 *Deltochilum* Eschscholtz (2 spp. (2) FL; (3) TX)]

30.2 *Canthon* Hoffmansegg

Eight species, including the following:

C. pilularius Linnaeus (Eastern Tumblebug). L. 11–19 mm. Black; legs slender, somewhat curved, with middle and hind tibiae only slightly enlarged. Adults of both sexes (See Fig. 24.65, with female in foreground) make balls of dung that they roll to a suitable site, where a pit is dug and the ball buried after an egg has been laid inside. (1) n.e. US; (2) s.e. US; (3) TX.

C. imitator Brown (Western Tumblebug). L. 10–18 mm. Black to bronze or green; pronotum and elytra coarsely granular; clypeus sharply, deeply emarginate. Adults of both sexes roll dung balls. (See A&J 98.) (3) OK, TX.

[30.3 *Boreocanthon* Halffter (9 spp. (3), (4), (5)); 30.4 *Melanocanthon* Halffter (4 spp. (1), (2), (5)); 30.5 *Glaphyrocanthon* Martinez (1 sp., *G. viridis* (Beauvois) (1), (2), (3) TX, OK; (5) IA, KS, MO); 30.6 *Pseudocanthon* Bates (1 sp., *P. perplexus* (LeConte) (1), (2), (3) AZ, NM, TX; (5) MO); 30.7 *Malagoniella* Martinez (1 sp., *M. astyanax yucateca* Harold (3) TX)]

Tribe Coprini

[30.8 *Ateuchus* Weber (3 spp. (1), (2), (3))]

Fig. 24.65.

30.9 *Dichotomius* Hope

Three species [found in (1); (2); (3) AZ, TX, OK; (5) NE, IA, KS, MO], the following of which is widely distributed:

D. carolinus (Linnaeus). L. 20–28 mm. Black, shiny; elytra with seven striae; males with a blunt horn on the head and an elevation on the pronotum. Adults dig holes in the ground under or near dung, but do not roll the dung into balls. (1), (2), (3) TX, OK; (5) NE, IA, KS, MO.

30.10 *Copris* Geoffroy

Ten species [found in (1), (2), (3)], including the following:

C. minutus (Drury) (Small Black Dung Beetle). L. 8–12.5 mm. Shiny black; head horn often well developed in both sexes. (1) n.e. US; (2) s.e. US; (3) TX, OK; (5) IA, MO, NE.

30.11 *Phanaeus* MacLeay

Eleven species [found in (1), (2), (3)], including the following:

P. vindex MacLeay (Splendid Dung Beetle). L. 14–22 mm. Head bronze, pronotum coppery bronze, elytra green, often tinged with blue; head of males with a horn, of females with a tubercle; first segment of antennal club forms a cover for the other segments; tarsi absent on front legs. Adults dig deep burrows beneath excrement in which to place a ball of dung containing an egg. (See Fig. 24.66.) (1) n.e. US; (2) s.e. US; (3) e. TX, OK; (5) MN, SD, NE, IA, KS, MO.

Tribe Onthophagini

30.12 *Onthophagus* Latreille

Thirty-four species, including the following:

O. hecate Panzer. L. 6.5–9 mm. Body black with bronze reflections; pronotal disc with conspicuous tubercles. Found on dung. (1) n.e. US; (2) s.e. US; (3) TX; (5) MO.

Fig. 24.66.

O. gazella Fabricius (African Dung Beetle). Much larger than the preceding, with metallic pronotum, brown elytra. Introduced for fly control. (3) TX.

Tribe Oniticellini

[30.13 *Oniticellus* Serville (2 spp. (2) FL?; (3) CA; (4) BC)]

Subfamily Aphodiinae

Members of this subfamily are similar to the preceding but are smaller as a rule (usually not over 5 mm in length), less convex, and more elongate. The hind tibiae have two spines. Adults burrow into piles of excrement, which is used as food for both themselves and their larvae.

Tribe Aegialiini

[30.14 *Aegialia* Latreille (19 spp.); 30.15 *Micraegialia* Brown (1 sp., *M. Pusilla* (Horn) (4) BC, WA); 30.16 *Annegialia* Howden (1 sp., *A. ataeniformis* Howden (4) UT)]

Tribe Aphodiini
30.17 *Aphodius* Illiger

There are 211 species in this genus, which is often referred to as the lesser dung beetles. The following is one of the larger of the U.S. species:

A. fimetarius Linnaeus. L. 5–8.5 mm. Elytra red, pronotum black, the front corners with a red spot; head with three tubercles. Common in horse and cow dung, even in winter. (1) n.e. NA; (2) s.e. US; (3) n.e. TX, OK, CA; (4) Pacific n.w.; (5) n. Central States and Provinces.

[30.18 *Oxyomus* Laporte (1 sp., *O. silvestris* Scopoli (4) WA, OR); 30.19 *Xeropsamobeus* Saylor (1 sp., *X. desertus* Van Dyke (3) CA); 30.20 *Euparia* Serville (1 sp., *E. castanea* Serville (2) LA, FL); 30.21 *Myrmecaphodius* Martinez (1 sp., *M. excavaticollis* (Blanchard) (2) NC, GA, LA, MS, AL, FL; (3) TX); 30.22 *Euparixia* Brown (2 spp. (2) LA; (3) AZ); 30.23 *Ataenius* Harold (66 spp.); 30.24 *Saprosites* Redtenbacher (1 sp., *S. ventralis* Horn (1) FL); 30.25 *Pseudataenius* Brown (2 spp. (2) GA, LA, FL; (3) TX, OK; (5) NE, KS); 30.26 *Dialytes* Harold (5 spp. (1) n.e. US; (5) MB); 30.27 *Dialytellus* Brown (2 spp. (1), (2)); 30.28 *Psammodius* Fallen (16 spp.)); 30.29 *Rhyssemus* Mulsant (4 spp. (1), (2), (3), (5)); 30.30 *Trichiorhyssemus* Clouet (2 spp. (3), (5)); 30.31 *Pleurophorus* Mulsant (10 spp. (1), (3), (?4)); 30.32 *Aphotaenius* Cartwright (1 sp., *A. carolinus* Van Dyke (1) IN, OH; (2) VA, NC, SC, FL); 30.33 *Diastictus* Mulsant (2 spp. (3) CA)]

Subfamily Ochodaeinae

[30.34 *Ochodaeus* Serville (19 spp.); 30.35 *Pseudochodaeus* Carlson and Ritcher (1 sp., *P. estriatus* (Schaeffer) (3) CA; (4) OR)]

Subfamily Hybosorinae

[30.36 *Hybosorus* MacLeay (1 sp., *H. illigeri* Reiche (1) IN; (2) s.e. US); 30.37 *Pachyplectrus* LeConte (1 sp., *P. laevis* LeConte (3) CA, AZ); 30.38 *Phaeochrous* Laporte (1 sp., *P. emarginatus* Laporte (3) CA)]

Subfamily Pleocominae

The head of these beetles has a perpendicular horn between the eyes; antennae are nine- to eleven-segmented, with the club three- to seven-segmented.

30.39 *Pleocoma* LeConte (Rain Beetles)

These are called Rain Beetles because they appear in abundance during light rains; they are usually seen crawling on the ground at night. The species have very restricted ranges, often to only a single canyon. All females are wingless. Twenty-nine species [found in (3) CA; (4) UT, OR], including the following:

P. hirticollis Schauss. L. 18–28 mm. Oval, slightly elongate, black to reddish-orange, shiny above, chestnut below, with yellowish, hairlike setae. Males are winged and smaller than females but have larger antennal clubs and an erect horn on the front of the head between the eyes; females may be reddish-brown and are wingless. (See A&J 99.) (3) CA.

[30.40 *Acoma* Casey (8 spp. (3) CA, AZ, TX); (no. 30.41)]

Subfamily Glaphyrinae
30.42 *Lichnanthe* Burmeister

Seven species [found in (1), (2), (3), (4)], including the following:

L. rathvoni LeConte (Rathvon's Scarab). L. 11–16 mm. Black, with head, pronotum, and part of thorax greenish and shiny; elytra brownish; long, erect, hairlike yellow setae dorsally, black setae ventrally. Larvae feed on decaying leaves and other organic debris near streams. Adults are attracted to lights at night. (See A&J 100.) (4) BC, WA, OR, ID, NV.

Subfamily Troginae

These beetles, often called Skin Beetles, are roughly sculptured and usually covered with a crust of soil. They live in carrion, especially old carcasses, feeding primarily on the hide.

30.43 *Trox* Fabricius

Forty-two species are found throughout the U.S. and Canada, including the following:

T. suberosus Fabricius. L. 12–15 mm. These beetles are found on carrion and stridulate or squeak when handled. (1), (2), (3), (4), (5).

[30.44 *Glaresis* Erichson (9 spp. (3), (4), (5))]

Subfamily Geotrupinae

This group of species live in burrows, feeding on dung and fungus. Antennae are eleven-segmented; mandibles are large and exposed.

[30.45 *Bolboceras* Kirby (12 spp.); 30.46 *Bolbocerosoma* Schaeffer (13 spp. (1), (2), (3), (5)); 30.47 *Bradycinetulus* Cockerell (1 sp., *B. rex* Cartwright (3) TX); 30.48 *Bolborhombus* Cartwright (2 spp. (3) AZ, TX); 30.49 *Bolbocerastes* Cartwright (3 spp. (3) CA, AZ, TX; (5) KS); 30.50 *Bolbelasmus* Boucomont (2 spp. (3) CA, TX; (4) OR); 30.51 *Eucanthus* Westwood (3 spp. (1), (2), (3), (5))]

30.52 *Geotrupes* Latreille

Thirteen species [found in (1), (2), (3)], including the following:

G. balyi Jekel (Dorbeetle). L. 10–15 mm. Pronotum and elytra with some blue or purple irridescence on the otherwise black body; antennal club reddish-brown; elytra striae well-developed. Found in stems of toadstools. (1) n.e. US; (2) TN, WV, VA, NC.

G. splendidus (Fabricius). (See Fig. 24.67.) (1) n.e. US; (2) s.e. US.

[30.53 *Peltotrupes* Blanchard (2 spp. (2) FL); 30.54 *Mycotrupes* LeConte (5 spp. (2) GA, SC, FL)]

Fig. 24.67.

Subfamily Ceratocanthinae

[30.55 *Cloeotus* Germar (2 spp. (1), (2), (3)); 30.56 *Acanthocerus* MacLeay (1 sp., *A. aeneus* MacLeay (2) TN, NC, AL, SC, FL)]

Subfamily Melolonthinae (May Beetles and June Bugs)

The species of this group are uniform in having the fifth visible abdominal sternum fused with the next to the last abdominal tergum to form an abdominal ring capped with an exposed terminal plate. These insects are phytophagus, the adults usually found on leaves or flowers and the larvae in the ground where they feed on roots. Many species come to lights at night, often very abundantly. Some are pests of crop, garden, and ornamental plants. They are called May Beetles, June Bugs, or (in Europe) Cockchafers.

[30.57 *Chnaunanthus* Burmeister (2 spp. (3) CA, AZ; (4) OR, VT); 30.58 *Oncerus* LeConte (1 sp., *O. floralis* LeConte (3) CA); 30.59 *Nefoncerus* Saylor (1 sp., *N. convergens* Horn (3) CA); 30.60 *Podolasia* Harold (4 spp. (3) TX)]

30.61 *Serica* MacLeay

L. 6–9 mm. Most species are reddish brown to dark brown, nearly black. Elytra have indistinct, but regularly placed, striae. Adults fly in the evening, coming to lights when distracted from feeding on the leaves of deciduous trees. In the daytime they hide under logs and in leaf litter in woods and orchards. The male genitalia are necessary for distinguishing species, of which there are 109 in the U.S. and Canada. (See Fig. 24.68 for *S. evidens* Blatchley.)

30.62 *Maladera* Mulsant

One species, as follows:

M. castanea (Arrow) (Asiatic Garden Beetle). L. 9–10 mm. Bronzy brown to yellow-brown; elytra with fine striae and a fine, velvety pubescence. Adults are found in weedy areas, but nocturnal adults are often serious pests of garden crops of many kinds. Larvae feed on roots of many weeds. Introduced. (1) CT, s. NY, PA, NJ, MD; (2) VA, NC, SC.

Fig. 24.68.

30.63 *Diplotaxis* Kirby

Brown or black. One hundred and four species, including the following:

D. liberta Germar. L. 12–14mm. Elytra uniformly and finely punctate (or with punctured striae); abdomen with visible sterna connate but sutural lines present; eyes large and prominent; antennal club of males nearly as long as rest of antennae. Adults feed on leaves of trees and shrubs, usually at night; by day, they may be found under stones, bark, and logs. (1) n.e. US; (2) s.e. US.

30.64 *Rhizotrogus* Berthold

[= *Amphimallon* Berthold]

One species, as follows:

R. majalis (Razoumowsky) (European Chafer). L. 10–14 mm. Body dark brown; claws with minute tooth on the basal lobes; pronotum with long hairs, elytra with short. Pests of lawns and roots of ornamentals. Introduced. (1) NY, MA, CT, RI, PA, NJ.

30.65 *Phyllophaga* Harris

L. 10–23 mm, or more. These are the June Bugs or May Beetles. Reddish brown, without markings, they cannot be identified to species without the aid of technical literature that describes features of the male and female genitalia. Eggs are laid in the soil among grass roots. The larvae are the most frequently seen of the white grubs. The adults feed on the leaves of the deciduous trees and are attracted to lights at night. Two hundred and seventeen species, including the following:

P. crenulata Froelich. L. 15–18 mm. (1) n.e. US; (2) s.e. US; (3) OK. (See Fig. 24.69.)

30.66 *Polyphylla* Harris

One of the most colorful genera of the family, with most species marked with broad white lines on the elytra or with white scales, sometimes in punctures. The stripes may appear silvery. Twenty-nine species, including the following:

P. decemlineata (Say) (Ten-lined June Beetle). L. 22–28 mm. Brown; body with yellow and white scales each located within a puncture; elytra with broad white stripes; antennal plates very large. Larvae live in soil; adults are attracted to lights

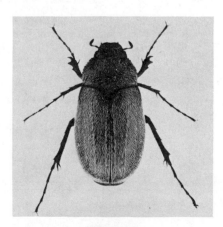

Fig. 24.69.

at night. (2) LA; (3) s.w. US; (4) Pacific n.w.; (5) North Central States. (See A&J 102.)

P. diffracta Casey (Broken-lined Giant Chafer). L. 22–28 mm. Elytral stripes are broken and ragged, or sometimes, when scales are rubbed off, totally absent so that entire body and elytra appear to be brown or black, rarely showing paler elytral stripes. Found in oak and pinon pine canyons. (3) CA, AZ, NM; (4) s. UT. (See A&J 101.)

[30.67 *Polylamina* Hardy (1 sp., *P. pubescens* Cartwright (2) FL); 30.68 *Plectrodes* Horn (1 sp., *P. pubescens* Horn (3) CA); 30.69 *Hypotrichia* LeConte (1 sp., *H. spissipes* LeConte (2) FL); 30.70 *Hypothyce* Howden (1 sp., *H. mixta* Howden (3) TX); 30.71 *Thyce* LeConte (22 spp. (3) CA, NM, TX); 30.72 *Dinacoma* Casey (2 spp. (3) CA); 30.73 *Parathyce* Hardy (6 spp. (3) CA)]

[30.74 *Plectris* Serville (1 sp., *P. aliena* Chapin (2) SC, GA, AL, FL); 30.75 *Gronocarus* Schaeffer (2 spp. (2) AL, FL); 30.76 *Fossocarus* Howden (1 sp., *F. creoleorum* Howden (3) TX); 30.77 *Phobetus* LeConte (9 spp. (3) CA; (4) BC, WA, OR, ID); 30.78 *Benedictia* Sanderson (1 sp., *B. pilosa* Sanderson (3) TX); 30.79 *Isonychus* Mannerheim (1 sp., *I. arizonensis* Howden (3) AZ)]

30.80 *Macrodactylus* Latreille

Three species, found throughout most of the U.S., the first of the following an eastern pest, the second a similar western species:

M. subspinosus (Fabricius) (Rose Chafer). L. 8–10 mm. Dull reddish brown to yellowish brown; densely covered with yellow scales or hairs; elytra in particular covered with elongate, yellowish scales; claws large. These insects feed on roses and grapes in particular, as well as many other fruits, vegetables, cultivated plants, small grains, and a variety of ornamental plants. They are poisonous to poultry that eat them. (1) n.e. US; (2) s.e. US.

M. uniformis Horn (Western Rose Chafer). L. 8–11 mm. Dull yellowish brown to reddish brown; integument covered by yellow scales. Abundant on wild grape, especially along the borders of marshy areas, streams, and lakes, this species is similar to the preceding. (3) s.w. US; (4) Pacific n.w.; (5) Mountain states. (See A&J 103.)

30.81 *Dichelonyx* Harris

Elytra pubescent, not scaly; claws capable of being folded along the last tarsomere. Twenty-nine species, including the following:

D. vicina Fall. L. 9–11 mm. Dark with greenish reflections; pronotum paler with distinct median longitudinal groove. Adults found on various conifers. (4) Pacific n.w.

D. backi (Kirby) (Green Rose Chafer). L. 9–12 mm. Median groove on pronotum lacking; elytra brighter green than those of preceding species. Adults found on conifers, aspen, raspberry, juneberry, and thimbleberry. (1) WI, ON; (4) Pacific n.w.; (5) MT.

D. elongata Schoenherr. (See Fig. 24.70.) (1) n.e. NA; (5) KS.

[30.82 *Coenonycha* Horn (27 spp. (3) (4)); 30.83 *Gymnopyge* Linell (4 spp. (3) CA, AZ; (4) UT); 30.84 *Ceraspis* Serville (1 sp., *C. pilatei* Harold (3) AZ)]

Fig. 24.70.

Tribe Hoplini

30.85 *Hoplia* Illiger

Twelve species, including the following:

H. dispar LeConte (Brown Chafer). L. 7–8.5 mm. Color varies from bright orange to light green—rarely irridescent blue, green, or golden—depending on color of the dense round scales that clothe the body; claws of the front and middle tarsi are unequal in length, the outer one larger and bifid at the apex. Adults are found on various flowers during the day and hide under boards and debris at night. (3) CA; (4) OR, NV. (See A&J 104.)

H. callipyge LeConte (Grapevine Hoplia). Similar to the preceding. Destructive to grapes and many other plants. (3) NM, AZ, CA; (4) IO, UT, WA, OR, BC.

H. trivialis Harold. (See Fig. 24.71.) (1) n.e. US; (2) s.e. U.S.

Subfamily Rutelinae

Similar in appearance to the preceding subfamily, but with the claws, especially on the hind legs, always of unequal length or size, independently movable, and shorter ones always entire.

Tribe Rutelini

[30.86 *Parastasia* Westwood (1 sp., *P. brevipes* LeConte (1) NY, PA, IN, IL; (2) NC, FL; (3) OK, TX; (5) MO)]

30.87 *Cotalpa* Burmeister

Four species, including the following:

C. lanigera Linnaeus (Goldsmith Beetle). L. 20–26 mm. Antennae ten-segmented; wooly pile ventrally; brownish-yellow with green metallic luster; elytral punctures in irregular rows. Taken by beating poplar, willow, and oak. Adults come

Fig. 24.71.

to lights at night; larvae are root feeders and sometimes a pest. (1) n.e. US; (2) s.e. US.

30.88 *Paracotalpa* Ohaus

Four species—found in (3) CA, NM; (4) WA, ID, UT—including the following:

P. ursina Horn (Bear Beetle). L. 14–16.5 mm. Head, pronotum, and ventral surface metallic blue-black, elytra reddish brown; body with long whitish hairs; head and pronotum with coarse punctation. Adults feed on blossoms, buds, and leaves of various trees, particularly those of the rose family. (3) s. CA. (See A&J 109.)

P. granicollis (Haldeman) (Hairy Bear Beetle). L. 13.5–17.5 mm. Head, pronotum, and ventral surface metallic green; elytra brownish red; legs black; body with long whitish hairs; head and pronotum with large confluent punctures. Adults are reported as pests of apple blossoms in some areas; they also feed on buds and leaves of peaches. (3) CA; (4) NV, UT; (5) CO. (See A&J 110.)

[30.89 *Pseudocotalpa* Hardy (1 sp., *P. andrewsi* Hardy (3) CA); 30.90 *Parabrysopolis* Ohaus (2 spp. (3) AZ)]

30.91 *Plusiotis* Burmeister

These are among the most beautiful of beetles. Four species—found in (3) AZ, NM, TX—with perhaps the following two the most striking of all:

P. gloriosa LeConte. L. 25–28 mm. Brilliant green with silver stripes on elytra. Adults feed on juniper leaves at elevations over 4000 ft. Attracted to ultraviolet lights at night, they blend in well with their host plant by day, camouflaged by their color. (3) AZ, TX. (See A&J 108.)

P. beyeri Skinner. L. 28–32 mm. Light green with purple legs; elytra with vague striae. Adults feed on oak at lower elevations. This species is rare in the sense that it is restricted to certain areas in Arizona canyons. It should not be collected since it is in danger of extinction.

30.92 *Pelidnota* MacLeay

Two species, the following of which is a pest:

P. punctata Linnaeus (Spotted Grape Beetle). L. 20–25 mm. Antennae ten-segmented; reddish brown to dark yellow; legs black; thorax and elytra with small marginal black spots. Comes to lights at night. Adults found on grape leaves; larvae, in decaying stumps of oak and hickory. (1) n.e. US; (2) s.e. US; (3) TX. (See A&J 106.)

[30.93 *Rutela* Latreille (1 sp., *R. formosa* Burmeister (2) FL)]

Tribe Anomalini

[30.94 *Leptohoplia* Saylor (1 sp., *L. testaceipennis* Saylor (3) CA)]

30.95 *Popillia* Serville

One species, of which the following is a pest:

P. japonica Newman (Japanese Beetle). L. 10–11 mm. Green with reddish brown or coppery elytra; abdomen with patches of white hairlike setae. This is a very destructive beetle introduced from Asia in 1913. Eggs are laid in the soil in grassy

areas. Larvae feed on the roots of grass and other plants. Adults emerge from midsummer to early fall and infest many plants, particularly members of the rose family, damaging both leaves and flowers. It has spread slowly across much of the eastern U.S. (1) n.e. US; (2) VA; (5) MO. (See A&J 105.)

30.96 *Anomala* Samouelle

[= *Anomalacra* Casey]

Thirty-three species—found in (1), (2), (3), (5)—of which the following two are pests:

A. orientalis Waterhouse (Oriental Beetle). L. 7–10 mm. Straw yellow with black markings; pronotum with pale margins having two metallic magenta spots; antennae nine-segmented. Larvae cause damage to lawns and nursery plants. Introduced. (1) s. NY, MA, CT, RI, e. PA, NJ, DE, e. MD.

A. oblivia Horn (Pine Chafer). L. 8.5–10.5 mm. Elytra without metallic luster, straw yellow to chestnut; pronotum densely punctate. Adults feed on various conifers. (1) n.e. US; (2) s.e. US.

[30.97 *Strigoderma* Burmeister (2 spp. (1), (2), (3), (5))]

Subfamily Dynastinae

Claws on each tarsus about equal in size; mandibles frequently large and dentate externally; sexes freqeuntly dimorphic, the males with tubercles or horns on either head or thorax, or both, and the females of many species similarly equipped but with smaller horns. Many large species belong to this group, commonly known as Rhinoceros, Hercules, and Elephant Beetles, especially the large tropical species. Some are of economic interest.

Tribe Cyclocephalini

[30.98 *Ancognatha* Erichson (1 sp., *A. manca* LeConte (3) AZ, NM); 30.99 *Aspidolea* Bates (1 sp., *A. singularis* Bates (3) ?TX)]

30.100 *Cyclocephala* Latreille

Nine species, the following of which are pests:

C. borealis Arrow (Northern Masked Chafer). L. 11–14 mm. Body pubescent; dull pale yellowish brown; elytra coarsely, densely, and confusedly punctate, sparsely pubescent. Larvae are pests of lawns. (1) n.e. US; (2) s.e. US; (5) MN, IA, NE, MO.

C. immaculata (Olivier) (Southern Masked Chafer). L. 12–14 mm. Similar to the preceding but body is smooth. Common in decaying vegetation and compost and sometimes a lawn pest. (1) IL, IN, OH, PA, NJ, MD, DE; (2) s.e. US; (3) NM, TX.

[30.101 *Dyscinetus* Harold (2 spp. (1), (2), (3), (5)); 30.102 *Coscinocephalus* Prell (1 sp., *C. cribrifrons* Schaeffer (3) AZ)]

Tribe Oryctini

30.103 *Euetheola* Bates

Two speceis [found in (2), (3)], of which the following is a pest:

E. rugiceps (LeConte) (Sugarcane Beetle or Rough-headed Cornstalk Borer). Pest of sugarcane and corn. (See Fig. 24.72.) (2) s.e. US.

Fig. 24.72. (*Courtesy of U.S. Dept. Agric.*)

30.104 *Bothynus* Hope

Ten species, of which the following is a pest:

B. gibbosus (De Geer) (Carrot Beetle). L. 11–16 mm. Mandibles toothed on outer side; reddish brown; elytral striae with umbilicate punctures. Both adults and larvae live in soil. Adults are attracted to lights at night; they feed on the foliage of carrots and sunflowers as well as other plants, including grain crops, beets, and potatoes, but rarely do any serious damage. (1), (2), (3), (4), (5). (See A&J 111.)

[30.105 *Oxygrylius* Casey (2 spp. (3) AZ, TX)]

30.106 *Cheiroplatys* Hope

Three species [found in (3) AZ, NM, TX; (5) CO], including the following:

C. clunalis LeConte. L. 13–18 mm. Reddish brown; front tibiae enlarged; pronotum with coarse punctures. Uncommon (3) AZ, TX.

30.107 *Xyloryctes* Hope

One species, as follows:

X. jamaicensis (Drury) (Rhinoceros Beetle). L. 25–28 mm. Black or reddish black; male pronotum with a median tubercle and head with a rhinoceroslike horn; female pronotum simple and head with a small tubercle. Adults feed on ash; larvae feed on ash roots. (See Fig. 24.73.) (1) n.e. US; (3) TX; (5) MN, NE.

30.108 *Strategus* Hope

Six species, including the following:

S. antaeus Fabricius (Ox Beetle). L. 24–32 mm. Shiny, dark reddish brown; pronotum of male black, with a stout horn

on each side and one in front; female with much reduced front horn. Adults dig tunnels with side chambers in which they place oak leaves; the female lays an egg, and the larvae feed on the decaying leaves and later on roots. (1) n.e. US; (2) s.e. US; (3) TX.

[30.109 *Aphonides* Rivers (1 sp. *A. dunnianus* Rivers (3) AZ, TX); 30.110 *Aphonus* LeConte (5 spp. (1), (2), (3)]

Tribe **Phileurini**

[30.111 *Archophileurus* Kolbe (1 sp., *A. cribrosus* LeConte (3) TX); 30.112 *Hemiphileurus* Kolbe (1 sp., *H. truncatus* Beauvois (3) ?TX); 30.113 *Phileurus* Latreille (3 spp. (1), (2), (3))]

Tribe **Dynastini**

30.114 *Dynastes* Kirby

Two species, as follows:

D. tityus (Linnaeus) (Eastern Hercules Beetle). L. 40–60 mm. Usually greenish gray with brownish to black irregular spots on the elytra, which are sometimes uniformly dark brown. The male has three horns on the thorax; the middle horn, which is the largest and covered ventrally with yellow hairs is curved down to meet a similar, upwardly curved horn on the head. The female has only a slight tubercle on the head. Larvae live in rotting logs and stumps, particularly in hardwoods. Adults feed on rotting fruit and have an offensive odor. Sometimes they congregate in the fall on ash logs. (1) s. IN, s. NY, PA, MD; (2) s.e. US; (3) TX. (See A&J 112.)

D. granti Horn (Southwestern Hercules Beetle). L. 45–55 mm. Similar to the preceding except that lateral horn of pronotum is very short and median horn is much longer than pronotum. (3) AZ.

[30.115 *Megasoma* Kirby (3 spp., (3) CA, AZ, TX)]

Subfamily **Trichiinae**

30.116 *Osmoderma* Lepeletier and Serville

Three species. (1) n.e. US; (2) KY, WV, VA, TN, NC, n. SC, n. GA, AR; (3) OK; (5) MT, MN, IA, NE, KS, MO. The following may serve as an example:

O. eremicola Knoch. L. 25–30 mm. Shiny brown; head deeply excavated between eyes in both sexes, with a tubercle above base of antennae. Larvae found in rotten wood of beech, cherry, apple, and other trees. (See Fig. 24.74.) (1) n.e. US; (2) VA; (3) MO.

Fig. 24.73.

Fig. 24.74.

30.117 *Trichotinus* Casey

Eight species [found in (1), (2), (3), (4), (5)], including the following:

T. affinis (Gory and Percheron) (Flower Beetle). L. 7–10 mm. Head, thorax, ventral side of body, and legs greenish black; elytra greenish with reddish brown stripes; sides with whitish transverse bars (a short whitish bar often present behind scutellum); hind coxae contiguous; pronotum rounded at base. Larvae live in decaying wood; adults are found on flowers of Jersey tea and wild hydrangea. Common. (1) n.e. US; (2) s.e. US. (See A&J 115).

[30.118 *Gnorimella* Casey (1 sp., *G. maculosa* Knoch (1) n.e. US; (2) KY, WV, VA. TN, NC, n. SC, n. AL, n. GA)]

30.119 *Trigonopeltastes* Burmerster

Two species. (1) s. IL, s. IN, s. OH, PA, NJ, MD, DE; (2) s.e. US; (3) e. TX, e. OK; (5) MO, e. KS. The following may serve as an example:

T. delta Forster (Flower Scarab). L. 7–10 mm. Head black; pronotum black with triangular spot on disc, outlined in fine yellow pile; elytra brownish, variegated with black; venter covered with dense yellow pile. The "delta" on the pronotum is typical of this species, but the elytral markings vary. Adults are common on a wide variety of flowers. Distribution as given for the genus. (See A&J 114.)

Subfamily Valginae

[30.120 *Valgus* Scriba (4 spp.)]

Subfamily Cetoniinae

Mandibles of this group are feebly developed, mostly membranous and hidden; their claws are equal and simple. This is the group with many large species in the tropics. The largest of all beetles, and the most massive of all insects, the Goliath Beetle (*Goliathus goliathus* Drury), is one of its members. Prevalent in West Africa, this giant ranges in size from 80 to 115 mm—the size of a mouse.

Many adults are strong flyers, their loud buzz often attracting attention as they visit flowers to feed on nectar and pollen. Apparently they do not open their elytra during flight. The elytra do not cover the side of the abdomen as they do in other lamellicorns. The larvae live in soil and feed on roots.

Tribe Gymnetini

30.121 *Cotinis* Burmeister

Four species, including the following:

C. mutabilis Gory and Percheron (Green June Beetle). L. 24–28.5 mm. Head shiny, somewhat metallic green; pronotum deep green with tawny lateral stripe; elytra usually pale red-brown with sutural margins greenish; ventral surface and legs bright metallic green; body with yellow or pale hairlike setae. Adults feed on ripe fruit, buzzing loudly as they fly from branch to branch. Larvae feed on roots. Abundant. (3) AZ, NM, TX. (See A&J 112.)

C. nitida (Linnaeus) (Eastern Green Fruit Beetle). L. 20–23 mm. Dull velvety green; sides of pronotum and elytra brownish yellow; head and part of ventral surface brilliant metallic green. Larvae feed on roots of grass and other plants and are

Fig. 24.75.

sometimes a pest. Adults eat figs, peaches, and grapes. (1) s. NY, PA, NJ, MD; (2) s.e. US.

[30.122 *Gymnetis* MacLeay (1 sp., *G. flavomarginata* Blanchard [=*sallei* Schaum] (3) AZ, TX); 30.123 *Hologymnetis* Martinez (1 sp., *H argenteola* (Bates) (3) AZ); 30.124 *Gymnetina* Casey (1 sp., *G. cretacea* (LeConte) (3) AZ)]

Tribe Cetoniini

[30.125 *Stephanucha* Burmeister (3 spp.)]

30.126 *Euphoria* Burmeister

Twenty-eight species, including the following:

E. inda (Linnaeus) (Bumble Flower Beetle). L. 13–16 mm. Pronotum triangular; head and pronotum dark, somewhat bronzed, often with yellowish spots; elytra brownish yellow, mottled with black spots that form cross-bands. Adults feed on fruit and green corn. (See Fig. 24.75.) (1) n.e. US; (2) s.e. US; (3) AZ, TX.

[30.127 *Chlorixanthe* Bates (1 sp., *C. chapini* Cartwright (3) TX); 30.128 *Euphoriaspis* Casey (2 spp. (5) NE, KS); 30.129 *Epicometis* Burmeister (1 sp., *E. vestita* Say, introduced, established: (1) ?MA; (4) ?UT); 30.130 *Anatropis* Casey (1 sp., *A. verticalis* Horn (3) CA, NM)]

Tribe Cremastochilini

[30.131 *Genuchinus* Westwood (2 spp. (3) CA, AZ); 30.132 *Lissomelas* Bates (1 sp., *L. flohri* Bates (3) AZ); 30.133 *Psilocnemis* Burmeister (1 sp., *P. leucosticta* Burmeister (1) MD; (2) NC)]

30.134 *Cremastocheilus* Knoch

These are hard-bodied scarabs with tufts of golden trichomes at posterior corners of the thorax that seem to attract ants. Their larvae live in ant nests, apparently on organic debris. The adults are not particularly favored by the ants, but their hard bodies protect them from injury. Although generally distributed throughout the U.S., most of the 32 species occur in the Southwest. (See Fig. 24.76 for *C. castaneae* Knoch.)

Fig. 24.76.

Incertae sedis

[30.135 *Potosia* Mulsant (1 sp., *P. affinis* Andersch, introduced, established: (3) ?CA)]

Superfamily DASCILLOIDEA

31. EUCINETIDAE (Plate-thigh Beetle Family)

Length: 2.5–3 mm. The enlarged hind coxal plates serve to distinguish these small beetles. They live in debris or under fungus-covered bark of trees. There are eight species, as follows:

[31.1 *Eucinetus* Germar (7 spp. (1), (2), (3), (5)); 31.2 *Euscaphurus* Casey (1 sp., *E. saltator* Casey (3) CA)]

32. HELODIDAE (Marsh Beetle Family)

Length: 2–4 mm. These small, soft-bodied beetles are found by beating leaves of trees, shrubs, and low grass near the banks of lakes and streams. There are 37 species in the U.S. and Canada.

Subfamily Helodinae

[32.1 *Elodes* Latreille (10 spp. (1), (2), (3), (4)); 32.2 *Microcara* Thomson (1 sp., *M. explanata* LeConte (1) MI); 32.3 *Cyphon* Paykull (14 spp.); 32.4 *Sarabandus* Leech (1 sp., *S. robustus* LeConte (1) NY); 32.5 *Prionocyphon* Redtenbacher (2 spp. (1), (2), (5)); 32.6 *Ora* Clark (3 spp. (2) FL; (3) TX); 32.7 *Scirtes* Illiger (6 spp. (1), (2), (3))]

33. CLAMBIDAE (Minute Beetle Family)

Length: ±1 mm. These are among the smallest beetles known. They are found in debris or decayed wood. There are 12 species in the U.S. and Canada, as follows:

[33.1 *Calyptomerus* Redtenbacher (1 sp., *C. oblongulus* Mannerheim (3) AZ; (4) AL, BC; (5) CO); 33.2 *Clambus* Fischer von Waldheim (10 spp.); 33.3 *Loricaster* Mulsant and Rey (1 sp. *L. rotundus* Grigarick and Schuster (3) CA)]

34. DASCILLIDAE (Soft-bodied Plant Beetle Family)

Length: 3–9 mm. Elongate and convex, or short and broad; body moderately to densely covered with hairlike setae; antennae subserrate to serrate; tarsi with lobes beneath basal three or four tarsomeres. There are 25 species in the U.S. and Canada, as follows:

Subfamily Dascillinae
Tribe Macropogonini

[34.1 *Macropogon* Motschulsky (3 spp. (1) IL, MI, NH, NB; (3) CA; (4) BC, OR); 34.2 *Eurypogon* Motschulsky (4 spp. (1) IN, MI, PA, PQ; (2) VA; (3) CA; (5) KS); 34.3 *Allopogonia* Cockerell (1 sp., *A. villosus* Horn (3) CA)]

Tribe Anchytarsini

[34.4 *Anchytarsus* Guerin (1 sp., *A. bicolor* Melsheimer (1) NY; (2) GA)]

Tribe Cneoglossini

[34.5 *Odontonyx* Guerin (1 sp., *O. trivittis* Germar (2) s.e. US); 34.6 *Anchycteis* Horn (1 sp., *A. velutina* Horn (3) CA); 34.7 *Stenocolus* LeConte (1 sp., *S. scutellaris* LeConte (3) CA); 34.8 *Araeopidius* Cockerell (1 sp., *A. monachus* LeConte (4) OR)]

Tribe Dascillini

34.9 *Dascillus* Latreille

Two species, including the following:

D. davidsoni LeConte. (3) CA.

Tribe Genecerini

[34.10 *Anorus* LeConte (3 spp. (3) CA, AZ)]

Subfamily Eubriinae

[34.11 *Dicranopselaphus* Guerin (1 sp., *D. variegatus* Horn (1) IL, NY, PA, MD); 34.12 *Ectoparia* LeConte (1 sp., *E. nervosa* Melsheimer (1) n.e. US; (2) s.e. US; (3) OK; (5) IA, MO); 34.13 *Acneus* Horn (4 spp. (3) CA; (4) OR); 34.14 *Alabameubria* Brown (1 sp., *A. starki* Brown (2) AL)]

Subfamily Eubrianacinae
34.15 *Eubrianax* Kiesenwetter

One species, as follows:

E. edwardsi LeConte (False Water Penny). L. 4–6 mm. Body dark brown; head hidden beneath pronotal expansion; each claw with membranous appendage at its base that is nearly as long as the claw; male antennal segments with lateral appendages; those of female filiform. Adults found on bushes hanging over the surface of streams; larvae found in streams. The pupa is aquatic also. (3) CA; (4) OR, NV. (See A&J 116.)

Series ELATERIFORMIA
Superfamily BYRRHOIDEA

35. BYRRHIDAE (Pill Beetle Family)

Length: 5–10 mm. Convex; head deflexed; hind femora fit into grooves in coxae. These rare species live among roots of coarse grasses in sandy places. There are 72 species recorded in the U.S. and Canada, as follows:

Subfamily Byrrhinae
Tribe Simplocariini

[35.1 *Simplocaria* Stephens (4 spp. (1) GR, LB, NH; (4) AK, BC; (5) NW, MN, CO)]

Tribe Morychini

[35.2 *Morychus* Erichson (8 spp. (1) MD; (3) NM; (5) BC, WA, OR; (5) AB MT, NE, CO); 35.3 *Tylicus* Casey (1 sp., *T. subcanus* LeConte (5) MN)]

Tribe Pedilophorini

[35.4 *Listemus* Casey (3 spp. (3) CA; (4) AK); 35.5 *Eusomalia* Casey (1 sp., *E. lecontei* Wickham (4) BC, ID; (5) IA)]

Tribe Byrrhini

[35.6 *Cytilus* Erichson (3 spp. (1) NF, NF, ON NH, IN, PA; (3) CA; (4) BC; (5) MB, MN, CO)]

35.7 *Byrrhus* Linnaeus

Twenty-eight species [found in (1), (4), (5) (see Fig. 24.77 for an example)], including the following:

B. americanus LeConte. L. 7.5–9 mm. (1) n.e. US.

[35.8 *Porcinolus* Mulsant (2 spp. (1) IN, MI, NY, PA; (5) MB, KS)]

Fig. 24.77.

Subfamily **Amphicyrtinae**

Tribe **Amphicyrtini**

[35.9 *Amphicyrta* Erichson (5 spp. (3) CA; (4) NV)]

Tribe **Lioonini**

[35.10 *Lioligus* Casey (5 spp. (4) AK, BC, ID); 35.11 *Lioon* Casey (4 spp. (3) CA; (4) AK, BC)]

Tribe **Exomellini**

[35.12 *Exomella* Casey (1 sp., *E. pleuralis* Casey (4) BC)]

Subfamily **Syncalyptinae**

[35.13 *Curimopsis* Ganglbauer (6 spp. (2) GA; (4) AK, WA; (5) MB, MN, CO); 35.14 *Syncalypta* Stephens (1 sp., *S. spinosa* Rossi (1) NY, CT)]

Superfamily **DRYOPOIDEA**

36. PSEPHENIDAE (Water Penny Beetle Family)

Length: 4–6 mm. The abruptly declivous front of the head, anteriorly narrowed pronotum, and serrate antennae distinguish this family. Adults and larvae are aquatic and found creeping over stones in swiftly flowing water.

36.1 *Psephenus* Haldeman

Eight species, of which the following is common:

P. herricki DeKay (Water Penny Beetle). L. 4–6 mm. Adults may be taken by sweeping vegetation along either running or still water streams or by picking them off the surface of submerged stones. The larvae are circular (hence their common name) and cling to rocks in swift streams in gorges. (See Fig. 24.78.) (1) n.e. US; (2) KY, WV, VA, TN, NC, AR, MS, AL, GA, SC; (3) OK; (5) MN, KS, MO.

37. BRACHYPSECTRIDAE (Texas Beetle)

Length: 5–6 mm. Somewhat resembles a click beetle without the clicking mechanism; antennae serrate. One species, as follows.

37.1 *Brachypsectra* LeConte

B. fulva LeConte (Texas Beetle). (3) CA, TX; (4) UT.

Fig. 24.78.

Fig. 24.79.

38. PTILODACTYLIDAE
(Toed-winged Beetle Family)

Length: 4–6 mm. Males have very long antennae, segments 4 through 10 each with a long basal process; female antennae are long and simple. Adults can be beaten from shrubbery near water and come to lights at night. Larvae live in decaying damp logs or are aquatic. The six species are assigned to two genera, as follows:

Subfamily **Ptilodactylinae**

[38.1 *Lachnodactyla* Champion (2 spp. (3) AZ, TX)]

38.2 *Ptilodactyla* Illiger

Four species—found in (1), (2), (3), (5)—including the following:

P. serricollis serricollis Say. (See Fig. 24.79.) (1) n.e. US; (2) s.e. US; (3) TX; (5) MO.

39. RHIPICERIDAE (Cicada Parasite Beetle Family)

Length: 12–24 mm. Tarsi with large hairy pad between claws; tarsomeres lobed beneath; antennae of males fanshaped, of females serrate; mandibles prominent. Little is known about the biology of this group except what follows. There are six species in the U.S. and Canada.

Tribe **Sandalini**

39.1 *Sandalus* Knoch

Six species. (1) IL, IN, PA; (2) s.e. US; (3) CA, NM, TX; (4) NV. The following may serve as an example:

S. petrophya Knoch. The larvae are parasites of cicada nymphs. Adults are taken flying near ash and elm, usually in the fall. (See Fig. 24.80a for the male; 24.80b for the female.) (1) IL, IN, PA.

40. CALLIRHIPIDAE (Cedar Beetle Family)

Length: 11–15 mm. Similar to preceding family but tarsomeres lack lobes beneath segments and mandibles are smaller. One species, as follows:

Tribe **Zenoini**

40.1 *Zenoa* Say

Z. piceus (Beauvois). Taken from under bark and logs in woods or at lights at night. (See Fig. 24.81.) (1) IN, OH, PA; (2) FL; (5) KS.

Fig. 24.80.

41. CHELONARIIDAE (Turtle Beetle Family)

Length: 4–5 mm. These beetles are extremely compact, the head being completely withdrawn into the pronotum and covered from dorsal view. One rare species, as follows:

41.1 *Chelonarium* Fabricius

C. lecontei Thomson. Pale brown to black; elytra with patches of whitish scales. Adults taken from vegetation near water; larvae aquatic. (2) NC, SC, GA, FL.

42. HETEROCERIDAE (Variegated Mud-loving Beetle Family)

Length: 4–6 mm. Mandibles flattened, protruding; tibiae armed with rows of heavy, flattened spines; body elongate, somewhat flattened. These beetles, which burrow in damp sand and mud flats, may be brought to surface by tramping over the mud. There are 30 species in the U.S. and Canada, as follows:

Tribe Augyliini

[42.1 *Explorator* Pacheco (1 sp., *E. canadensis* (Fall) (5) AB, MB, SA); 42.2 *Centruiatus* Pacheco (2 spp.); 42.3 *Microaugyles* Pacheco (2 spp. (1) IL; (3) s.e. US; (5) MB, NE, CO, KS)]

Tribe Heterocerini

[42.4 *Lanternarius* Pacheco (5 spp.)]

Fig. 24.81.

Fig. 24.82.

42.5 *Neoheterocerus* Pacheco

Ten species, including the following:

N. pallidus (Say). L. ±5 mm. (See Fig. 24.82.) (1) n.e. NA: (2) WV, AR; (3) AZ, NM, OK, TX; (5) MB, SA, CO, IA, KS, MN, NE, MO.

[42.6 *Efflagitatus* Pacheco (1 sp., *E. selanderi* Pacheco (2) FL); 42.7 *Dampfius* Pacheco (4 spp.); 42.8 *Peditatus* Pacheco (2 spp. (1) PA, NJ; (2) LA; (3) TX); 42.9 *Lapsus* Pacheco (1 sp., *L. tristis* (Mannerheim) (1) WI, MI, ON, PQ, IL, NY, CT, NB, PA, NJ; (2) AR, FL; (3) CA; (4) BC, WA, NV, UT, ID; (5) AB, MB, SA, MT, SD, MN, WY, IA)]

Tribe Tropicini

[42.10 *Tropicus* Pacheco (2 spp. (1) IL, IN, OH, PA, MA, NJ, MD, DC; (2) TN, VA, NC, SC, AR, LA, MS, AL, GA, FL; (3) s.w. US; (5) IA, CO, KS)]

43. LIMNICHIDAE (Minute Marsh-loving Beetle Family)

Length: 1–3.6 mm. Oval, convex; brown or black; antennae ten-segmented, short, clavate or pectinate. There are 33 species in the U.S. and Canada:

Subfamily Limnichinae
Tribe Limnichini

[43.1 *Limnichites* Casey (8 spp.); 43.2 *Eulimnichus* Casey (9 spp. (1), (2), (3), (5)); 43.3 *Lichminus* Casey (1 sp., *L. tenuicornis* Casey (3) CA; (4) WA, OR); 43.4 *Limnichoderus* Casey (8 spp. (1), (2), (3))]

43.5 *Lutrochus* Erichson

Three species [found in (1), (3)], including the following:

L. lutens LeConte. L. ±3 mm. (3) TX.

Tribe Bothriophorini

[43.6 *Physemus* LeConte (1 sp., *P. minutus* LeConte (3) CA, AZ, TX)]

Subfamily Cephalobyrrhinae

[43.7 *Throscinus* LeConte (3 spp. (3) CA, TX)]

44. DRYOPIDAE (Long-toed Water Beetle Family)

Length: 1–8 mm. Elongate-oval, convex; short, eleven-segmented antennae with loose, lamellate club; legs, especially

Fig. 24.83.

the tarsi, long with rather long claws. Larvae aquatic; adults either aquatic or terrestrial plant feeders. There are 13 species in the U.S. and Canada, as follows:

[44.1 *Dryops* Olivier (2 spp. (1) PQ; (3) AZ)]

44.2 *Helichus* Erichson

Ten species, including the following:

H. lithophilus (Germar). L. ±5 mm. (See Fig. 24.83.) (1) n.e. US; (2) s.e. US; (3) OK, TX; (5) IA, KS, MO.

[44.3 *Pelonomus* Erichson (1 sp., *P. obscurus* LeConte (1) PQ, IL, IN; (2) KY, TN, LA, AL, GA, SC, FL; (3) OK, TX; (5) KS)]

45. ELMIDAE (Drive or Riffle Beetle Family)

Length: 1–8 mm. Similar to preceding family but shorter, more compact and usually deeply sculptured. Larvae aquatic; adults aquatic or terrestrial, but most species live in rapidly running, cold streams. There are 92 species in the U.S. and Canada, as follows:

Subfamily Larinae

[45.1 *Lara* LeConte (2 spp. (3), (4)); 45.2 *Phanocerus* Sharp (1 sp., *P. clavicornis* Sharp (3) TX)]

Subfamily Elminae

Tribe Ancyronychini

[45.3 *Ancyronyx* Erichson (1 sp., *A. variegata* (1) n.e. US; (2) s.e. US: (3) OK, TX; (5) KS, MO)]

Tribe Elmini

[45.4 *Ampumixis* Sanderson (1 sp., *A. dispar* Fall (3) CA; (4) WA, OR); 45.5 *Atractelmis* Chandler (1 sp., *A. wawona* Chandler (3) CA: (4) OR); 45.6 *Cleptelmis* Sanderson (2 spp. (3), (4), (5)); 45.7 *Cylloepus* Erichson (2 spp. (3) AZ, TX); 45.8 *Huleechius* Brown (1 sp., *H. marroni* subsp. *carolus* Brown (3) AZ); 46.9 *Dubiraphia* Sanderson (10 spp. (1), (2), (3), (5)); 45.10 *Elsianus* Sharp (3 spp. (3) AZ, NM, TX); 45.11 *Gonielmis* Sanderson (1 sp., *G. dietrichi* Musgrave (2) MS, AL, GA, SC, FL); 45.12 *Heterelmis* Sharp (4 spp. (2) AR; (3) AZ; NM, OK, TX; (5) KS); 45.13 *Heterlimnius* Hinton (2) spp. (3), (4), (5)); 45.14 *Hexacylloepus* Hinton (1 sp., *H. ferrugineus* Horn (3) NM, OK, TX); 45.15 *Microcylloepus* Hinton (4 spp.); 45.16 *Narpus* Casey (3 spp. (3), (4), (5)); 45.17 *Neocylloepus* Brown (1 sp., (3) AZ, TX); 45.18 *Neoelmis*

Fig. 24.84.

Musgrave (1 sp., *N. caesa* LeConte (3) OK, TX); 45.19 *Optioservus* Sanderson (13 spp.); 45.20 *Ordobrevia* Sanderson (1 sp., *O. nubifera* Fall (3) CA; (4) WA, OR); 45.21 *Oulimnius* Des Gozis (2 spp. (1), (2)); 45.22 *Promoresia* Sanderson (2 spp. (1), (2)); 45.23 *Rhizelmis* Chandler (1 sp., *R. nigra* Chandler (3) CA)]

45.24 *Stenelmis* Dufour

Twenty-eight species, including the following:

S. lateralis Sanderson. (See Fig. 24.84.) (1) PA; (2) VA, TN, AR, LA, MS, SC; (5) KS, MO.

[45.25 *Xenelmis* Hinton (1 sp., *X. bufo* Sharp (3) AZ); 45.26 *Macronychus* Mueller (1 sp., *M. glabratus* Say (1) n.e. US; (2) s.e. US; (3) OK, TX; (5) ND, MN, IA, KS, MO); 45.27 *Zaitzevia* Champion (2 spp. (3), (4), (5))]

Superfamily BUPRESTOIDEA

46. BUPRESTIDAE (Metallic Wood-boring Beetle Family)

Length: 3–100 mm (usually under 20 mm). These hard-bodied, compact, somewhat flattened, rarely cylindrical, usually metallic-colored beetles have a strongly deflexed head that rests on the prosternum. Some species are marked red or yellow; many are metallic red, blue, or green. The integument is either bare or covered with colored scales. The surface is usually deeply grooved or pitted. The antennae are usually serrate. They somewhat resemble click beetles but lack a clicking mechanism since the thorax and abdomen are tightly joined. The first and second abdominal segments are more solidly united than that of other families. The elytra of some species do not open during flight; the flying wings simply protrude from under the base of the elytra, causing a buzzing noise—a fact long ago reported by foresters who call these insects "buzz beetles." This elimination of the wing drag caused by the open elytra of most flying beetles makes rapid flight possible.

The larvae called "flat-headed borers"—because of their greatly enlarged and flattened thoracic segments—bore into roots and trunks of trees, particularly dead or dying trees; other larvae are leaf miners and stem borers of herbaceous and woody plants. Adults feed on foliage except for the few that feed on fungi. There are many pest species, especially of forest and orchard trees.

Their bright colors make them attractive to collectors, but

in spite of their resulting popularity, there is no easy way to identify them to species. There are 675 species in the U.S. and Canada assigned to 40 genera, as follows:

Subfamily Schizopinae

[46.1 *Schizopus* LeConte (2 spp. (3) CA, AZ); 46.2 *Glyptoscelimorpha* Horn (2 spp. (3) CA); 46.3 *Dystaxia* LeConte (2 spp. (3) CA); 46.4 *Dystaxiella* Knull (2 spp. (3) CA)]

Subfamily Buprestinae

Tribe Thrincopygini

[46.5 *Thrincopyge* LeConte (3 spp. (3) CA, AZ)]

Tribe Chalcophorini

[46.6 *Agaeocera* Waterhouse (3 spp. (3) AZ, NM, TX)]

46.7 *Hippomelas* Castelnau

Nineteen species [found in (2) NC; (3) s.e. US; (4) UT], including the following:

H. sphenica LeConte. L. 18–25 mm. Blackish with a brassy reflection; pubescence sparse and extremely short; prothorax is one-half wider than long; elytra finely punctate; base of elytra and sides of abdomen yellow. Larvae bore into the heartwood of many species of trees. Adults occasionally come to lights at night. They may be collected by beating trees and shrubs. (3) AZ, TX. (See A&J 117.)

46.8 *Chalcophora* Solier

Seven species, of which the following is a pest:

C. angulicollis (LeConte) (Sculptured Pine Borer). (3) s.e. US; (4) BC, WA, OR, ID; (5) SD, NE, CO.

[46.9 *Chalcophorella* Kerreman (4 spp. (1), (2), (3)); 46.10 *Psiloptera* Solier (4 spp. (3) AZ, TX; (5) KS)]

Tribe Buprestini

46.11 *Trachykele* Marseul

Six species, of which the following is a pest:

T. blondeli Marseul (Western Cedar Borer). (3) CA; (4) BC, WA, OR.

[46.12 *Dicerca* Eschscholtz (21 spp.); 46.13 *Poecilonota* Eschscholtz (10 spp., *P. cyanipes* Say (See Fig. 24.85) (1) n.e. NA: (3) AZ, NM); 46.14 *Cinyra* Castelnau (5 spp., *C. gracilipes* (Melsheimer (See Fig. 24.86) (1) n.e. US; (2) s.e. US; (3) AZ, TX)]

46.15 *Buprestis* Linnaeus

Twenty-three species, of which the following are pests:

B. aurulenta Linnaeus (Golden Buprestid). (1) VT: (3) CA, AZ, NM; (4) BC, WA, OR, ID; (5) MT, WY.

B. apricans Herbst (Turpentine Borer). (1) NY, MA; 92) NC, SC, LA, AL, GA, FL; (3) TX; (5) NE.

B. adjecta LeConte (Pine Borer). L. 13–18 mm. Body entirely metallic green to blue-green, with somewhat coppery sides; apices of elytra acute, each with two small apical teeth. Adults are beaten from pine and spruce branches. Larvae infest pine and spruce wood. (See A&J 119.) (3) CA, NM; (4) BC, WA, OR, UT, NV; (5) WY, CO.

B. gibbsi LeConte (Oak Borer). L. 14–20 mm. Elytra greenish to purple with three pairs of yellow spots, the anterior

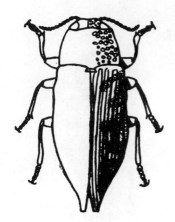

Fig. 24.85.

pair elongate and extending around the sides of the elytra, the two posterior pairs transverse. Adults are found on oak; the larvae probably bore into oak heartwood. (See A&J 118.) (3) CA; (4) WA, OR; (5) CO.

[46.16 *Juniperella* Knull (1 sp., *J. mirabilis* Knull (3) CA); 46.17 *Hesperorhipis* Fall (3 spp. (3) CA, AZ); 46.18 *Xenorhipis* LeConte (3 spp. (3) IL, OH, NY, PA, CT, MA; (2) GA; (3) TX); 46.19 *Trichinorhipis* Barr (1 sp., *T. knulli* Barr (3) CA)]

46.20 *Melanophila* Eschscholtz

Twenty-one species, including the following:

M. consputa LeConte (Charcoal Beetle). (3) CA, AZ; (4) OR, NV; (5) CO.

M. californica Van Dyke (California Flatheaded Borer). (3) CA; (4) OR, ID.

M. drummondi Kirby (Flatheaded Fir Borer). (1) MI; (3) CA, AZ, NM; (4) Pacific n.w.; (5) AB, MT, MN, WY, CO.

M. fulvoguttata Harris (Hemlock Borer). (1) n.e. US; (2) WV, NC.

46.21 *Anthaxia* Eschscholtz

Twenty-three species, including the following:

A. viridifrons Gory. (See Fig. 24.87.) (1) n.e. NA; (2) s.e. US; (3) s.w. US; (4) BC; (5) MB.

[46.22 *Agrilaxia* Kerremans (3 spp. (1) PA; (2), (3) AZ)]

Fig. 24.86.

Fig. 24.87.

Tribe Chrysobothrini

46.23 *Chrysobothris* Eschscholtz

Of the 133 species in this genus, several are pests.

C. tranquebarica (Gmelin) (Australian-pine Borer) (2) FL.

C. mali Horn (Pacific Flatheaded Borer). (3) CA, AZ; (4) OR, NV, UT; (5) AB, CO.

C. femorata (Olivier) (Flatheaded Apple Tree Borer). L. 7.5–16 mm. Dark bronze with sheen of green, copper, or brass; raised areas of elytra sparsely punctate; front tibiae of male with row of small acute teeth. Larvae infest poplar, maple, walnut, willow, oak, elm, apple, pear, and many other trees. (See A&J 120.) (1), (2), (3), (4), (5).

46.24 *Actenodes* Lacordaire

Ten species, including the following:

A. acornis (Say). (See Fig. 24.88.) (1) n.e. US; (2) s.e. US; (3) TX; (5) IA, MO.

Subfamily Acmaeoderinae
Tribe Polycestini

[46.25 *Polycesta* Solier (11 spp. (2), (3), (4))]

Tribe Acmaeoderini

46.26 *Chrysophana* LeConte

One species, as follows:

C. placida LeConte (Flatheaded Cone Borer). Similar to the following species but with scutellum visible and claws simple.

46.27 *Acmaeodera* Eschscholtz

The 128 species in this genus are brightly colored. Most of them are confined to the Southwestern U.S.

A. sparsa Horn. L. 6–8 mm. Scutellum not visible; claws with a basal tooth; dark coppery, with yellow markings. (3) s.e. US; (4) UT; (5) CO.

A. scalaris Mannerheim (Cactus Buprestid). L. 5–10 mm. Head, pronotum, and elytra clothed with setae; black, with a large area of the elytra yellow. Adults are common on cactus blossoms and may be beaten from branches of shrubs and trees. The larvae are wood borers. (See A&J 121.) (3) AZ, NM, TX.

Fig. 24.88.

A. pulchella Herbst. (See Fig. 24.89.) (1) IN, PA; (2) FL; (3) CA, NM, TX; (5) KS.

[46.28 *Acmaeoderoides* Van Dyke (3 spp. (3) CA, AZ)]

Tribe Ptosimini

[46.29 *Potosima* Solier (4 spp. (1), (2), (3), (5)); 46.30 *Paratyndaris* Fisher (14 spp.))]

Tribe Tyndarini

[46.31 *Tyndaris* Thomson (1 sp., *T. balli* Knull (3) AZ)]

Subfamily Agrilinae
Tribe Agrilini

[46.32 *Eupristocerus* Deyrolle (1 sp., *E. cogitans* Weber (See Fig. 24.90) (1) n.e. US; (2) KY, VA; 46.33 *Engyaulus* Waterhouse (1 sp., *E. pulchellus* Bland (3) AZ, NM, TX; (5) CO)]

46.34 *Agrilus* Curtis

Of the 161 species in the U.S. and Canada, most are small (L. 4–9 mm). The following are pests:

A. bilineatus (Weber) (Two-lined Chestnut Borer). L. 4–9 mm. Elytra black, each with a longitudinal stripe of whitish pubescence. Adults are found on the foliage of oak, honey, locust, and chestnut. (1) n.e. US; (2) s.e. US; (3) s.w. US; (5) WY, CO, IA, KS, MO.

A. anixus Gory (Bronze Birch Borer). (1) IL, IN, NY, MA; (5) MN, CO.

Fig. 24.89.

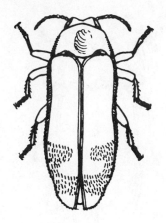

Fig. 24.90.

A. sinuatus Olivier (Sinuate Pear Tree Borer). (1) NY, CT, NJ.

46.35 *Paragrilus* Saunders

Four species [found in (1) IL, NY, PA, NJ; (2) FL; (3) ?AZ], including the following:

P. tenuis LeConte. (See Fig. 24.91.) (1) NY, IL, PA, NJ; (2) FL.

46.36 *Pachyschelus* Solier

Seven species [found in (1), (2), (3), (5)], including the following:

P. laevigatus Say. (See Fig. 24.92.) (1) n.e. US; (2) s.e. US.

46.37 *Brachys* Solier

Eleven described species. They are leaf miners, particularly in oak. The limits of the species are obscure. (1), (2), (3) TX, AZ.

46.38 *Taphrocerus* Solier

Twelve species, including the following:

T. gracilis Say. (See Fig. 24.93.) (1) n.e. NA; (2) NC, GA; (3) s.w. US; (4) WA; (5) MB, MN, IA, MO.

Tribe **Mastogeniini**

46.39 *Mastogenius* Solier

Five species [found in (1), (3), (3)], including the following:

M. subcyaneus (LeConte). (See Fig. 24.94.) (1) n.e. US; (2) s.e. US; (3) TX

Fig. 24.91.

Fig. 24.92.

Fig. 24.93.

[46.40 *Trigonogya* Schaeffer (1 sp., *T. reticulaticollis* Schaeffer (3) TX)]

Superfamily ELATEROIDEA

47. CEBRIONIDAE (Robust Click Beetle Family)

Length: 14–25 mm. These are large, broad species with thin, curved mandibles and usually hairy bodies; they somewhat resemble click beetles. The abdomen has six visible sterna. The larvae are root feeders. The males are attracted to lights at night, but the females are wingless and live in the ground where they are seldom seen. Eighteen species have been recorded in the U.S., all southern.

[47.1 *Selonodon* Latreille (2 spp. (2) AR; (3) AZ); 47.2 *Cebrio* (11 spp. (2) LA, AR, FL; (3) AZ, NM, TX, OK)]

47.3 *Scaptolenus* LeConte

Five species [found in (3) ?CA, TX], including the following:

S. lecontei (Salle). L. 14–17 mm. (3) TX.

Fig. 24.94.

48. ELATERIDAE (Click Beetle Family)

Length: 3–35 mm. Most click beetles are easily recognized by their loosely jointed prothorax. The hind angles of the pronotum are prolonged backward. The middle of the prosternum projects posteriorly and fits into a groove in the mesosternum. This mechanism enables these beetles to produce a clicking sound. When they fall or are turned over on their back, they attempt to land on their feet by flexing the prothorax against the notch in the mesosternum so as to catapult themselves several inches into the air, much to the delight of children and the amazement of any would-be predator. Most species are a drab brown or black, but some have yellow red markings, and a few tropical and subtropical species are brightly colored. Several southern species have phosphorescent spots on the pronotal processes and on the abdomen. In some localities these insects are also called "snap beetles."

The larvae are usually called "wireworms." They are rather hard-bodied, soil-inhabiting species. Many feed on roots and tubers, causing crop loss. Some are carnivorous and live under bark or in decaying logs.

These beetles are difficult to identify to species; the literature for most genera is widely scattered. There are 885 species in the U.S. and Canada, assigned to 73 genera.

Subfamily Pyrophorinae

Tribe Agrypnini

[= Adelocerini]

[48.1 *Lacon* Laporte (13 spp.); 48.2 *Danosoma* Thomson (2 spp.); 48.3 *Agrypnus* Eschscholtz (3 spp. (1), (2), (5), including *A. rectangularis* Say (Fig. 24.95) (1) IN; (2) FL; (5) MO; 48.4 *Meristhus* Candeze (1 sp., *M. cristatus* Horn (3) CA, TX); 48.5 *Rismethus* Fleutiaux (1 sp., *R. scobinula* Candeze (3) TX); 48.6 *Lanelater* Arnett (3 spp. (2), (3))]

Tribe Hemirhipini

48.7 *Alaus* Eschscholtz

Nine species, of which the following are common:

A. oculatus (Linnaeus) (Eyed Click Beetle). L. 23–45 mm. Black, mottled with small patches of white; thorax with two large "eye" spots about as close together as their width; elytra distinctly striated. Adults live beneath loose bark of stumps or logs or in wood piles. Larvae live in decaying wood and are often found in the trunks of old apple trees. (See Fig. 24.96 and A&J 122.) (1) n.e. US; (2) s.e. US; (3) TX.

A. melanops LeConte (Western Eyed Click Beetle). L. 2–35 mm. Dull black with few white marking; "eye" spots on

Fig. 24.95.

Fig. 24.96.

thorax are smaller and more oval than those of preceding species. Adults are found under the bark of rotting logs; larvae usually inhabit the same wood. (See A&J 123.) (3) CA; (4) BC, WA, OR, ID; (5) MT.

[48.8 *Hemirhipis* Berthold (1 sp., *H. fascicularis* Fabricius (1) MD; (2) NC, FL; (3) TX)]

Tribe Chalcolepidiini

48.9 *Chalcolepidius* Eschscholtz

Twelve species [found in (1), (2), (3)], including the following:

C. webbi LeConte (Black and White Click Beetle). L. 36–38 mm. Smooth, polished, clothed rather densely with small, recumbent, and flattened hairlike setae; dark bluish body with black legs; lateral edges of pronotum rather broadly, and elytra very narrowly, clothed with dense, white, recumbent pubescence, the white border abruptly limited. Larvae bore in wood of ponderosa pine and other trees, usually above 5,000-ft elevation. Pupation takes place in the wood after the larve chew open exit holes. Adults emerge from the solid wood with just enough room to allow for a final push to freedom. (See Fig. 24.97 and A&J 125.) (3) CA, AZ.

[48.10 *Oistus* Candez (1 sp., *O. edmonstoni* Hyslop (3) CA; (4) OR)]

Tribe Pyrophorini

48.11 *Pyrophorus* Illiger

Six species, including the following:

P. schotti LeConte (Lantern Click Beetle). L. 20–22 mm. Brown; hind angles of pronotum with small reddish yellow

Fig. 24.97.

Fig. 24.98.

Fig. 24.99.

spots that are luminescent in living specimens. Adults are active at night. In flight, the thoracic light organs glow, and the abdominal light organs cast a light over the ground. The latter organs are hidden when the elytra are closed. The amount of light produced is considerable, enough for a few in a jar to provide a reading lamp. The larvae are also luminescent and carnivorous. They are sometimes beneficial because they prey upon grubs. (See A&J 124.) (3) s. TX.

[48.12 *Deilelater* Costa (1 sp., *D. atlanticus* Hyslop (2) FL); 48.13 *Ignelater* Costa (1 sp., *I. phosphoreus* (Fabricius) (2) FL)]

Tribe Conoderini

48.14 *Conoderus* Eschscholtz

Twenty species, of which the following are pests.

C. amphicollis (Gyllenhal) (Gulf Wireworm). (2) s.e. US.

C. falli Lane (Southern Potato Wireworm). (2) s.e. US.

C. vespertinus (Fabricius) (Tobacco Wireworm). (See Fig. 24.98.) (2) s.e. US.

[48.15 *Heteroderes* Latreille (15 spp. (1), (2), (3), (5)); 48.16 *Aeolus* Eschscholtz (14 spp.)]

Tribe Pseudomelanactini

[48.17 *Pseudomelanactes* Mathieu (1 sp., *P. agrypnoides* (Van Dyke) (3) AZ)]

Subfamily Elaterinae
Tribe Pityobiini

[48.18 *Pityobius* LeConte (2 spp. (1), (2), (3))]

Tribe Dicrepidiini

[48.19 *Dicrepidius* Eschscholtz (3 spp. (1), (2), (3)); 48.20 *Dipropus* Germar (6 spp. (1), (2), (3)); 48.21 *Blauta* LeConte (2 spp. (1), (2), (3)]

Tribe Physorhinini

[48.22 *Physorhinus* Eschscholtz (3 spp. (3) AZ, NM, TX); 48.23 *Anchastus* (19 spp. (1), (2), (3))]

Tribe Ampedini

[48.24 *Megapenthes* Kiesenwetter (28 spp.)]

48.25 *Ampedus* Germar

Sixty-one species, including the following:

A. apicatus (Say) (Black-tailed Click Beetle). L. 9–12 mm. Black; elytra reddish orange with apical black patch not reaching sides or suture except near apex; pronotal vestiture

light yellow. Larvae found in decaying wood; adults on flowers. (See A&J 126.) (3) AZ.

A. linteus (Say). (See Fig. 24.99.) (1) n.e. NA; (2) s.e. US.

[48.26 *Agriotella* Brown (5 spp. (1), (3), (4))]

Tribe Denticollini

[= Lepturoidini]

48.27 *Limonius* Eschscholtz

Sixty-nine species, of which the following are of economic importance:

L. agonus (Say) (Eastern Field Wireworm). (1) n.e. US.

L. californicus Mannerheim (Sugar-beet Wireworm). (3) CA; (4) BC, OR, ID.

L. canus LeConte (Pacific Coast Wireworm). (3) CA; (4) BC, OR, ID; (5) CO.

L. subauratus LeConte (Columbia Basin Wireworm). (4) BC, WA, OR, ID; (5) MT.

L. infuscatus Motschulsky (Western Field Wireworm). (3) CA; WA.

L. dubitans LeConte. (See Fig. 24.100.) (1) n.e. US.

[48.28 *Micrathous* Lane (2 spp. (3) CA; (4) WA, OR); 48.29 *Leptoschema* Horn (2 spp. (3) CA); 48.30 *Elathous* Reitter (5 spp. (1), (5)); 48.31 *Athous* Eschscholtz (50 spp. including *A. scapularis* Say (Fig. 24.101) (1) n.e. US); 48.32 *Hemicrepidius* Germar (13 spp.); 48.33 *Denticollis* Piller and Mitterpacher (3 spp.); 48.34 *Preludius* Lane (1 sp., *P. iaculus* LeConte (3) CA; (4) OR)]

Fig. 24.100.

Fig. 24.101.

Tribe Ctenicerini

[48.35 *Bladus* LeConte (1 sp., *B. quadricollis* Say (1) IN, OH); 48.36 *Perissarthron* Hyslop (1 sp., *P. trapezium* LeConte (3) TX)]

48.37 *Ctenicera* Latreille

This very large genus contains 129 species in the U.S. and Canada, the following being of economic importance:

C. vernalis Hentz. (See Fig. 24.102.) (1) n.e. NA.

C. aeripennis (Kirby) (Puget Sound Wireworm). (4) OR.

C. aeripennis subsp. *destructor* (Brown) (Prairie Grain Wireworm). (5) n. Central States.

C. glauca (Germar) (Dry-land Wireworm). (3) CA.

C. pruninina (Horn) (Great Basin Wireworm). (3) CA; (4) UT; (5) NE.

[48.38 *Eanus* LeConte (8 spp. (1), (4), (5)); 48.39 *Paroedostethus* Van Dyke (1 sp., *P. relictus* Van Dyke (3) CA)]

Tribe Agriotini

48.40 *Agriotes* Eschscholtz

Thirty-seven species, of which the following are of economic importance:

A. lineatus (Linnaeus) (Lined Click Beetle). (1) NF, NS; (4) BC.

A. mancus (Say) (Wheat Wireworm). (1) n.e. NA; (5) n. Pacific States and Provinces.

[48.41 *Dalopius* Eschscholtz (51 spp.); 48.42 *Oxygonus* LeConte (4 spp. (1), (3), (4), (5))]

Fig. 24.102.

Tribe Elaterini

[48.43 *Elater* Linnaeus (4 spp.)); 48.44 *Parallelostethus* Schwarz (1 sp., *P. attenuatus* Say (1) n.e. US; (2) s.e. US; (3) TX); 48.45 *Diplostethus* Schwarz (2 spp. (3) AZ); 48.46 *Neotrichophorus* Jacobson (5 spp. (2), (3)); 48.47 *Orthostethus* Lacordaire (2 spp. (2), (3), (5)); 48.48 *Sericus* Eschscholtz (5 spp.))]

Subfamily Melanactinae

[48.49 *Melanactes* LeConte (7 spp. (1), (2), (3))]

Subfamily Oestodinae

[48.50 *Octinodes* Candeze (12 spp. (3))]

48.51 *Euthysanius* LeConte

Nine species, including the following:

E. pretiosus LeConte. L. 15–19 mm. Body brownish, shiny; antennae twelve-segmented, pectinate; pronotum with posterior-lateral corners attenuated, a curved ventral ridge, and the disk finely, sparsely punctate. (3) s.e. US.

[48.52 *Aplastus* LeConte (15 spp. (3), (4)); 48.53 *Oestodes* LeConte (2 spp. (1), (5)); 48.54 *Anthracopteryx* Horn (1 sp., *A. hiemalis* Horn (5) CO)]

Subfamily Negastriinae

[48.55 *Negastrius* Thomson (7 spp. (1), (3), (4), including *N. choris* (Say) (Fig. 24.103) (1) IN, DC); 48.56 *Neohypdonus* Stibick (13 spp.); 48.57 *Migiwa* Kishii (1 sp., *M. striatulus* (LeConte) (1) IN, OH, PA; (5) MN); 48.58 *Fleutiauxellus* Mequignon (2 spp. (5) MT, SD, NE); 48.59 *Zorochrus* Thomson (2 spp. (3) CA, AZ, OK; (4) UT); 48.60 *Oedostethus* LeConte (1 sp., *O. femoralis* LeConte (1) IN, NJ; (5) CO, MO)]

Subfamily Hypnoidinae

[= Hypolithinae]

[48.61 *Ascolicerus* Mequignon (1 sp., *A. sanborni* (Horn) (1) GR, LB, PQ, NH, ME, NJ; (4) AK, WA; (5) YU, MT, NW, WY); 46.62 *Desolakerrus* Stibick, (1 sp., *D. pallidus* (Becker) (3) CA, AZ; (4) NV); 48.63 *Margaiostus* Stibeck, subgenus *Margaiostus* s. str. (3 spp. (1), (3), (4), (5)); 48.64 *Hypolithus* Eschscholtz (1 sp., *H. littoralis* (Eschscholtz) (4) AK)]

48.65 *Hypnoidus* Dillwyn

Eight species, of which the following is a pest:

H. abbreviatus (Say) (Abbreviated Wireworm). (1) n.e. NA; (2) TN; (3) NM, TX; (4) Pacific n.w.; (5) AB, MB, MN, WY, SD, NE, MO.

Fig. 24.103.

Subfamily Adrastinae

[48.66 *Glyphonyx* Candeze (9 spp. (1), (2), (3))]

Subfamily Melanotinae

48.67 *Melanotus* Eschscholtz

Sixty-seven species, including the following:

M. cribulosus LeConte. L. 9.5–10.5 mm. Body black; elytra and legs dark brown; pronotum densely, coarsely punctate, with carinae on posterior lateral projections not more than one-third distance from base to apex. (1) IL; (3) OK; (5) SD, NE, KA.

M. longulus oregonensis (LeConte) (Oregon Wireworm). (3) CA; (4) BC, WA, OR, NV, UT; (5) MT.

Subfamily Cardiophorinae

[48.68 *Coptostethus* Wollaston (1 sp., *C. americanus* Horn (2) LA); 48.69 *Cardiophorus* Eschscholtz (42 spp.); 48.70 *Aptopus* Eschscholtz (5 spp. (3) AZ, NM, TX)]

48.71 *Horistonotus* Candeze

Fifty-three species, the following of which is a pest:

H. uhleri Horn (Sand Wireworm). (2) GA, FL.

[48.72 *Aphricus* LeConte (7 spp. (3) CA, AZ, NM, TX; (4) UT); 48.73 *Esthesopus* Eschscholtz (11 spp. (1), (2), (3))]

49. THROSCIDAE (False Metallic Wood-boring Beetle Family)

Length: 2–5 mm. The adults of these rare beetles are found on flowers; the larvae, in wood that has been bored by other larvae. They probably are carnivorous. There are 26 species, as follows:

Subfamily Lissominae

[49.1 *Drapetes* Dejean (6 spp. (1), (2), (3))]

Subfamily Throscinae

Tribe Patergini

[49.2 *Pactopus* LeConte (1 sp., *P. horni* LeConte (3) CA; (4) BC, WA, OR, ID)]

Tribe Throscini

[49.3 *Aulonothroscus* Horn (14 spp.)]

49.4 *Trixagus* Kugelann

Five species, including the following:

T. chevrolati Bonvouloir. (See Fig. 24.104.) (1) n.e. US; (2) s.e. US; (3) CA, AZ, TX; (4) BC, UT.

Fig. 24.104.

50. CEROPHYTIDAE (Rare Click Beetle Family)

Length: 7.5–8.5. The very long hind trochanters serve as a good recognition feature for these rare beetles. Two species, as follows.

[50.1 *Cerophytum* Latreille (2 spp., *C. convexicolle* LeConte (3) CA; *C. pulsator* Haldeman (1) PA; (2) NC)]

51. PEROTHOPIDAE (Beech-tree Beetle Family)

Length: 10–18 mm. These beetles closely resemble the Elateridae, but the thorax lacks the clicking mechanism; claws are pectinate. Adults are found on trunks and braches of old beech trees. Three species, as follows:

[51.1 *Perothops* Erichson (*P. mucida* Gyllenhall (1) PA; (2) FL and *P. witticki* LeConte (3) CA; *P. cervina* Lacordaire (3) CA)]

52. EUCNEMIDAE (False Click Beetle Family)

[= Melasidae]

Length: 3–18 mm. These resemble the Elateridae but have a strongly deflexed head that rests on the prosternum, which is lobed. The clicking mechanism is poorly developed and nonfunctional. Adults are found on foliage or on or under bark of beech, maple, and other trees. Larvae frequent rotting wood. Seventy-one species occur in the U.S. and Canada.

Subfamily Gastraulacinae

Tribe Dendrocharini

[52.1 *Dendrocharis* Guerin (1 sp. (2) ?GA, FL)]

Subfamily Eucneminae

[52.2 *Vitellius* Bonvouloir (1 sp., *V. texanus* Knull (3) s. TX); 52.3 *Eucnemis* Ahrens (1 sp., *E. americana* Horn (1) OH; (2) KY; (3) CA); 52.4 *Poecilochrus* Bonvouloir (1 sp., *P. errans* Horn (2) FL); 52.5 *Phaenocerus* Bonvouloir (1 sp., *P. americanus* Horn (4) BC); 52.6 *Stethon* LeConte (1 sp., *S. pectorosus* LeConte (1) IL, IN, OH; (5) MO); 52.7 *Deltometopus* Bonvouloir (2 spp. (1) n.e. US; (2) TN, LA, FL; (3) TX; 52.8 *Dromaeolus* Kiesenwetter (11 spp. (1), (2), (3), (4)); 52.9 *Fornax* Laporte (10 spp. (1) n.e. US; (2) s.e. US; (5) MN)]

Subfamily Dirhaginae

[52.10 *Arrhipis* Bonvouloir (1 sp., *A. laniéri* (Guérin) (2) FL); 52.11 *Entomophthalmus* Bonvoloir (1 sp., *E. rufiolus* LeConte (1) IL; (2) TN); 52.12 *Dirhagus* Latreille (8 spp. (1) n.e. US; (2) s.e. US; (3) TX); 52.13 *Rhagomicrus* Fleutiaux (3 spp. (1) n.e. Us; (2) s.e. US); 52.14 *Adelothyreus* Bonvouloir (1 sp., *A. dejeani* Bonvouloir (1) OH, MD)]

Subfamily Melasinae

[52.15 *Isorhipis* Lacordaire (3 spp. (1) n.e. US; (2) s.e. US; (5) MO); 52.16 *Melasis* Olivier (4 spp. (1), (2), (3), (4)); 52.17 *Euryptychus* LeConte (2 spp. (1) IN, OH, PA, MD); 52.18 *Epiphanis* Eschscholtz (1 sp., *E. cornutus* Eschscholtz (1) NF, NY, PA; (3) NM; (4) AK); 52.19 *Palaeoxenus* Horn (1 sp., *P. dohrni* Horn (3) s. CA); 52.20 *Schizophilus* Bonvouloir (1 sp., *S. subrufus* Randall (1) IN, NY); 52.21 *Hylis* des Gozis (5 spp. (1) IN, PA; (3) CA, AZ; (5) MO); 52.22 *Xylophilus* Mannerheim (1 sp., *X. cylindriformis* Horn (3) CA; (4) NV; 52.23 *Hylochares* Latreille (1 sp. *H. nigricornis* Say (1) IN, OH); 52.24 *Sarpedon* Bonvouloir (1 sp., *S. scabrosus* Bonvouloir (2) TN; (3) s. CA; (5) NE (see Fig. 24.105); 52.25 *Nematodes* Latreille (6 spp. (IN, OH; (2) LA, GA, FL; (3) TX; 52.26 *Diphytaxis* Horn (1 sp., *D. excavata* Horn (3) TX); 52.27 *Anelastes* Kirby (1 sp., *A. druryi* Kirby (1), (2), (3), (4))]

Fig. 24.105.

Superfamily CANTHAROIDEA

53. TELEGEUSIDAE (Long-lipped Beetle Family)

Length: 5–8 mm (up to 35 mm in some tropical species). A very elongate body; large, fan-shaped, non-folding hind wings; short elytra that reach the base of the abdomen at most; and usually flabellate maxillary palpi serve to distinguish these rare beetles. Their habits are poorly known. There are three species in the U.S. and Canada, as follows:

[53.1 *Telegeusis* Horn (2 spp., *T. debilis* Horn (3) AZ and *T. nubifer* Martin (3) AZ); 53.2 *Atractocerus* Beauvois (1 sp., *A. gracilicornis* Schenkling (3) CA)]

54. PHENGODIDAE (Glowworm Beetle Family)

Length: 10–30 mm. All known females are luminous and larviform, that is, without elytra and wings; although they resemble larvae, they are sexually mature. The males have short elytra and twelve-segmented, doubly plumose antennae. The larvae prey upon myripods, soft-bodied insects, and some other invertebrates. They live in leaf litter under forest trees, especially under bark or old boards. There are 25 species in the U.S. and Canada.

Tribe Phengodini

54.1 *Zarhipis* LeConte

Nine species [found in (3) CA; (4) OR], including the following: *Z. integripennis* LeConte (Glowworm). L. 18–20 mm. Elytra of male short, apex pointed, apical half much narrower than basal half; pale yellowish-brown; antennae plumose. Female pale yellow or tan, larviform; abdomen with luminescent lateral spots. Larvae luminescent and predacious on small arthropods. (See A&J 127.) (3) CA; (4) OR.

[54.2 *Phengodes* Illiger (9 spp., including *P. plumosa* (Olivier (1) n.e. US; (2) s.e. US; (5) MT, MN, NE, MO (See Fig. 24.106)); 54.3 *Euryopa* Gorham (1 sp., *E. fusca* Gorham (3) AZ)]

Tribe Mastinocerini

[54.4 *Cenophengus* LeConte (2 spp. (3) CA, TX); 54.5 *Paraptorthodius* Schaeffer (1 sp., *P. mirabilis* Schaeffer (3) TX); 54.6 *Mastinocerus* Solier (3 spp. (3) CA, AZ, TC)]

55. LAMPYRIDAE (Firefly Beetle Family)

Length: 5–20 mm. Brownish, olive, or black sometimes marked with yellow or red. Head more or less completely covered by the prothorax; middle coxae meet at the base; elytra reticulate; abdomen with ventral light organs in both sexes of

Fig. 24.106.

most species. Fireflies (also called lightning bugs) are much in evidence on warm summer nights. A search through forest litter on such nights will reveal the glowing larvae of some of these species, and often the female flashing her light to attract a male of the same species. Sometimes a hungry female of certain species will flash the pattern of yet another species and is soon feasting on one of the latter's amorous, but hapless males.

In most species, adults control their flashing mechanism according to a genetically fixed pattern. The various pattern characteristics of the species result in an isolating barrier between them, that is, males are attracted to females of the same species except in the exceptional case described above. Some adults are predacious; the larvae are also predacious. There are 124 species in the U.S. and Canada, mostly in the East and South.

Subfamily Lampyrinae

Tribe Lampyrini

[55.1 *Lampyris* Geoffroy (2 spp. (2) FL); 55.2 *Microphotus* LeConte (7 spp. (3), (4), (5); 55.3 *Paraphausis* Green (1 sp., *P. eximia* Green (3) AZ)]

Tribe Pleotomini

[55.4 *Pleotomus* LeConte (3 spp. (2) KY; (3) AZ, TX)]

Tribe Lamprocerini

[55.5 *Tenaspis* LeConte (1 sp., *T. angularis* Gorham (2) FL; (3) TX; (4) MO)]

Tribe Cratomorphini

[55.6 *Pyractomena* Melsheimer (16 spp. (1), (2), (3), (5); including *P. angulata* Say (1) n.e. US; (2) s.e. US (See Fig. 24.107)); 55.7 *Micronaspis* Green (1 sp., *M. floridana* Green (2) FL)]

Tribe Photinini

55.8 *Photinus* Laporte

There are 33 species in (1), (2), (3), (5), including the following:

P. pyralis Linnaeus (Common Eastern Firefly). L. 10–14 mm. Pitchy brown; thorax with dull yellow margins, the convex disk roseate with a central black spot; elytra with pale suture and narrow side margins. The light organs are always larger in the males. Adults predacious; larvae luminescent and preda-

Fig. 24.107.

cious. Firefly light is produced by a mixture of chemicals similar to enzymes, resulting in "cold" light, that is, the chemical reaction produces nearly all light and very little heat. (See A&J 129.) (1) n.e. US; (2) s.e. US.

[55.9 *Phausis* LeConte (9 spp. (1), (2), (3), (4)); 55.10 *Lamprorhiza* Motschulsky (1 sp., *L. splendidula* Linnaeus (1) IL, MD)]

55.11 *Ellychnia* Blanchard

Fourteen species, including the following:

E. californica Motschulsky (Western Firefly). L. 10–14 mm. Black or rusty black; disk and side margins of thorax black, with a reddish and yellow space or line between them; elytra finely granulate-punctate and covered with a fine, recumbent yellowish pubescence. Common in spring on tree trunks in woods, especially on maple at or near flowing sap; also found on flowers. Attracted to moth bait. (1), (2), (3), (5).

55.12 *Pyropyga* Motschulsky

Four species, including the following:

P. nigricans Say. L. 10–12 mm. Eyes small; light organs feeble. (1) IN, PA; (3) CA, AZ; (4) BC; (5) CO.

[55.13 *Lucidota* Laporte (3 spp., (1), (2), (?3)); 55.14 *Phosphaenus* Laporte (1 sp., *P. hemipterous* Fourcroy (1) ?Canada)]

Subfamily Amydetinae

[55.15 *Pollaclasis* Newman (1 sp., *P. bifaria* Say (1) IL, NY; (2) TN, GA)]

Subfamily Photurinae

55.16 *Photuris* Dejean

Twenty-one species, including the following:

P. pennsylvanicus De Geer (Woods Firefly). L. 12–15 mm. Head and thorax dull yellow; thorax with red disk having a narrow median dark stripe; elytra brown or pitchy black with pale narrow side margins, suture, and narrow stripe on disk; thorax and elytra densely and rather roughly punctate. Members of this genus may be recognized by their large eyes, slightly exposed head, and antennae that are longer than one-half the length of the body. The light organs of both sexes occupy the whole of the fifth and following segments. Adults are found in forests rather than in fields, as most members of the family are. (See Fig. 24.108 and A&J 139.)

Subfamily Luciolinae

Tribe Ototretini

[55.17 *Brachylampis* Van Dyke (2 spp. (3) CA)]

Subfamily Matheteinae

[55.18 *Matheteus* LeConte (1 sp., *M. theveneti* LeConte (3) CA); 55.19 *Ginglymocladus* Van Dyke (3) CA)]

Fig. 24.108.

Subfamily Pterotinae

[55.20 *Pterotus* LeConte (1 sp., *P. obscuripennis* LeConte (3) CA)]

56. CANTHARIDAE (Soldier Beetle Family)

Length: 1–15 mm (usually 7–12 mm). These beetles somewhat resemble fireflies, but the head is not covered by the prothorax and they lack light-producing organs. The body is narrower than that of the fireflies. The prothorax is margined and often quadrate. They are usually black or dark brown but sometimes a bright yellow, orange, or red with black markings. Adults are found on flowers, particularly goldenrod and milkweed, where some feed on pollen and nectar. Larvae are found beneath bark and in debris; they are predacious. Many species are common at lights at night, and some come to moth bait. There are 468 species in the U.S. and Canada, assigned to 20 genera.

Subfamily Chauliognathinae

[= Chauliognathidae]

Tribe Chauliognathini

56.1 *Chauliognathus* Hentz

Eighteen species, including the following:

C. pennsylvanicus De Geer (Goldenrod Soldier Beetle). L. 9–12 mm. Head and ventral parts black; thorax yellow with a broad black spot on the disk; elytra yellow with an oblong-oval blackish spot on the apical third (sometimes more extended); ventral abdominal segments margined behind with yellow. Adults are abundant in the fall on flowers of goldenrod and other composites; they feed on pollen and nectar. Larvae are carnivorous and feed on other insect larvae. (See A&J 131.) (1) n.e. US; (2) s.e. US; (3) TX.

Tribe Ichthyurini

[56.2 *Ichthyurus* Westwood (1 sp., *I. arizonensis* Fender (3) AZ); 56.3 *Trypherus* LeConte (4 spp. (1), (2), (5)); 56.4 *Belotus* Gorham (1 sp., *B. abdominalis* LeConte (2) GA, FL; (3) TX, OK; (5) KS)]

Subfamily Cantharinae

Tribe Podabrini

56.5 *Podabrus* Westwood

One hundred and seven species, including the following:

P. tomentosus Say. (See Fig. 24.109.)

[56.6 *Hatchiana* Fender (1 sp., *H. arizonensis* Fender (3) AZ)]

Fig. 24.109.

Fig. 24.110.

Tribe Cantharini

[56.7 *Cantharis* Linnaeus (36 spp.); 56.8 *Rhagonycha* Eschscholtz (44 spp.)]

Tribe Silini

[56.9 *Polemius* LeConte (15 spp. (1), (2), (3), (5)); 56.10 *Discodon* Gorham (6 spp. (3) AZ, TX, OK)]

56.11 *Silis* Charpentier

Two subgenera [*Ditemnus* LeConte (12 spp.) and *Silis* s. str. (65 spp.)], including the following:

S. (*Ditemnus*) *latilobus* (Blatchley) (1) n.e. US. (See Fig. 24.110.)

[56.12 *Plectonotum* Gorham (1 sp., *P. excisum* Schaeffer (3) AZ)]

Tribe Malthinini

[56.13 *Malthinus* Latreille (18 spp. (1), (2), (3)); 56.14 *Frostia* Fender (5 spp. (3) CA; (4) OR); 56.15 *Malthodes* Kiesenwetter (121 spp.)]

Tribe Tytthonyx

[56.16 *Tytthonyx* LeConte: 2 subgenera; *Tytthonyx* s. str. (5 spp. (2), (3) and *Thinalmus* Gorham (1 sp., (3) AZ)]

Tribe Omethini

[56.17 *Spathizus* LeConte (1 sp., *S. bicolor* LeConte (3) AZ); 56.18 *Omethes* LeConte (1 sp., *O. marginatus* LeConte (1) OH, CT); 56.19 *Blatchleya* Knab (1 sp., *B. gracilis* Blatchley (1) IN (Fig. 24.111)); 56.20 *Troglomathes* Wittmer (2 spp. (3) CA; (4) OR); 56.21 *Symphyomethes* Wittmer (2 spp. (3) CA)]

57. LYCIDAE (Net-winged Beetle Family)

Length: 5–18 mm. The fan-shaped, net-veined elytra, soft body, and large antennae with broad, flat segments distinguish members of this family from the fireflies and soldier beetles, which they otherwise resemble. The body is usually red or yellow with black markings, or black with sides of pronotum reddish. Both larvae and adults are predacious. Adults are protected by body chemicals and have no known predators. There are 83 species in the U.S. and Canada; these may be identified by using the available technical literature.

Subfamily Lycinae

Tribe Lycini

57.1 *Lycus* Fabricius

Thirteen species, the following of which are common:

L. fernandezi Dugès (Desert Net-winged Beetle). L. 10–18 mm. Dull brownish yellow; elytra black in apical fourth or somewhat more; antennae dark except at extreme base; palpi, tibiae, and tarsi black; head either partly or entirely black; elytra of males broad, those of female narrower. Adults and larvae are predacious and are found on desert flowers and foliage, near stock watering tanks, and in lower elevations of mountains. (See A&J 132.) (3) s.e. US.

L. arizonensis Green (Arizona Net-winged Beetle). L. 13–19 mm. Bright reddish brown; black coloration similar to the preceding. Abundant in Arizona on various plants, including clover and roadside weeds. This is a model for various mimics, as are other species, including beetle and moth mimics. (3) AZ.

Tribe Lygistopterini

[57.2 *Lucaina* Dugès (2 spp. (3)); 57.3 *Lygistopterus* Mulsant (2 spp. (3), (5); 57.4 *Caloptognatha* Green (1 sp., *C. beameri* Green (3) AZ); 57.5 *Adoceta* Bourgeois (2 spp. (3) AZ)]

57.6 *Calochromus* Guérin

Five species, including the following:

C. perfacetus Say. (See Fig. 24.112.) (1) n.e. US; (2) s.e. US; (3) TX.

Tribe Platerodini

[57.7 *Dictyopterus* Mulsant (3 spp.); 57.8 *Eros* Newman (1 sp., *E. thoracicus* Randall (1) n.e. US; (4) BC); 57.9 *Platycis* Thomson (3 spp. (1), (2), (5)); 57.10 *Eropterus* Green (4 spp. (1), (2), (3)); 57.11 *Pseudoplateros* Green (1 sp., *P. moleculus* Green (3) TX); 57.12 *Lopheros* LeConte (1 sp., *L. fraternus* Randall (1) n.e. US); 57.13 *Plateros* Bourgeois (34 spp.)]

Tribe Calopterini

57.14 *Calopteron* Guérin

Five species in (1), (2), (4), (5), including the following:

C. reticulatum Fabricius. (See Fig. 24.113.) (1) n.e. US; (2) s.e. US.

[57.15 *Caeniella* Cockerell (2 spp. (1), (2), (3), (5)); 57.16 *Idiopteron* Bourgeois (1 sp., *I. rufulum* Gorham (3) AZ); 57.17 *Celetes* Newman (3 spp. (1), (2), (3))]

Fig. 24.111.

Fig. 24.112.

Fig. 24.113.

58. MICROMALTHIDAE (Telephone-pole Beetle Family)

Length: 1.5–2.5 mm. Members of this family resemble soldier beetles but have a large head and beadlike antennae. One species, as follows:

58.1 *Micromalthus* LeConte

M. debilis LeConte. Larvae are wood borers in decaying oak or chestnut logs and have been reported in telephone poles. An unusual feature is that larvae at a certain stage give birth to living young larvae. Adults may be found in the vicinity of infested logs. (1) n.e. US; (2) s.e. US.

Series BOSTRICHIFORMIA

Superfamily DERMESTOIDEA

59. DERODONTIDAE (Tooth-necked Fungus Beetle Family)

Length: 3–6 mm. Head has dorsal ocelli in addition to compound eyes; pronotum has coarse, lateral teeth. Seven species, as follows:

[59.1 *Laricobius* Rosenhauer (4 spp. (1), (4)); 59.2 *Peltastica* Mannerheim (1 sp., *P. tuberculata* Mannerheim (4) AK, OR)]

59.3 *Derodontus* LeConte

Two species, including the following:

D. maculatus (Melsheimer). Larvae and adults are found together in slime mold, under the bark of willow and tulip trees, and in shelf fungi. Common, but seldom collected. (1) n.e. US.

60. NOSODENDRIDAE (Wounded-tree Beetle Family)

Length: 4–6 mm. These beetles resemble some Histeridae. They are oval, convex, black; the body has rows of short tufts of hairlike setae. The larvae live in hollow stumps, in tree holes—particularly in elm and alder—and under bark.

60.1 *Nosodendron* Latreille

There are two species in the U.S., as follows:

N. californicum Horn. (3) CA; (4) OR.
N. unicolor Say (1) IL, IN; (5) KS.

61. DERMESTIDAE (Skin and Larder Beetle Family)

Length: 1–12 mm. Body is usually dark; scales are white, yellow, brown, or reddish. These beetles are either oval or slightly elongate oval, with clubbed antennae that are received in an antennal groove beneath the head; the hind coxae are excavated for the reception of the femora. Most species are covered with dense hairlike setae or scales, and the head usually has a median ocellus. Most are also scavengers both in the larval and adults stages, feeding on dried animal or plant materials of high protein content. Adults of some species are pollen feeders, however, and may be found on flowers. Several species are of considerable economic importance. There are 129 species in the U.S. and Canada.

Tribe Dermestini

61.1 *Dermestes* Linnaeus

These are a larger species and lack the median ocellus found on the head of many other species. Of the 23 recorded species, the following are of economic importance:

D. ater De Geer (Black Larder Beetle). L. 7–7.5 mm. Body uniformly but sparsely covered with gray pubescence dorsally; ventrally, with two rows of darker spots on each side where the pubescence is thinner and darker. Often a pest in homes, it is also common on dried carrion. Cosmopolitan.

D. lardarius Linnaeus (Larder Beetle). L. 7–8 mm. Similar to the preceding but basal half of pronotum densely yellow-gray pubescent, with a transverse row of black spots and some black spots at the base. Found in stored products feeding on meat, cheese, and the like. Cosmopolitan. (See Fig. 24.114.)

D. maculatus DeGeer (Hide Beetle). L. 6–10 mm. Similar to the preceding but black, the dorsal surface clothed with white hairs, and grayer and denser near the eyes and on the side of the pronotum; pubescence white beneath; each abdominal segment with a black spot on the side. Larvae and adults feed on carrion and stored animal products. Used to clean bones of museum specimens. Cosmopolitan.

Tribe Thorictini

[61.2 *Thorictodes* Motschulsky (1 sp., *T. heydeni* Reitter (3) TX)]

61.3 *Thylodrias* Motschulsky

One species, as follows:

T. contractus Motschulsky (Odd Beetle). L. 2–3 mm. Yellowish and elongate; antennae filiform, without apical club; abdomen with seven sterna; females wingless; only males with elytra. Often a pest in insect collections. Cosmopolitan.

Fig. 24.114.

Fig. 24.115.

Tribe Orphilini

[61.4 *Orphilus* Erichson (5 spp.)]

Tribe Trinodini

[61.5 *Apsectus* LeConte (2 spp. (3) AZ, TX)]

Tribe Attagenini

61.6 *Attagenus* Latreille

Five species, the following of which are of economic importance:

A. megatoma (Fabricius) (Black Carpet Beetle). L. 3–5.5 mm. Antennal club three-segmented, compact, with last segment of male very long; head and pronotum black; elytra pale reddish brown with yellow or gray pubescence, without spots. A pest of carpets; also found in granaries and on flowers. (See Fig. 24.115.) (1), (2), (3), (4), (5).

A. fasciatus (Thunberg) (Wardrobe Beetle). Similar to the preceding; pubescence dark except for very well-defined subbasal band of light pubescence that is usually broad and extends continuously to median suture. Occasionally found in stored products such as dried milk, spices, and drugs. Reported in Buffalo, NY, and Indianapolis, IN. Established in (2) FL.

[61.7 *Novelsis* Casey (9 spp. (3) CA, AZ; (4) NV, UT)]

Tribe Anthrenini

None of the adults of this tribe feed on the same material as the larvae; instead, they feed on pollen and nectar. The larvae are destructive pests of household materials.

61.8 *Anthrenus* Fabricius

Twelve species, all of them pests to some extent, the following of which are of considerable economic importance:

A. flavipes LeConte (Furniture Carpet Beetle). L. 3–4 mm. Black, but body variably covered with white, yellow, orange,

Fig. 24.116.

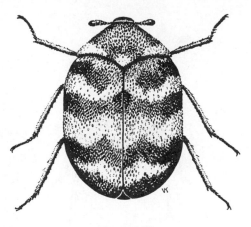

Fig. 24.117.

and black scales; hind tarsi with first tarsomere as long as or longer than second. A household pest in furniture and carpets. Widespread (?cosmopolitan).

A. scrophulariae (Linnaeus) (Carpet Beetle). L. 2.5–3.5 mm. Similar to the preceding except with white scales on the elytra in two or three narrow bands connected by a stripe of orange scales along the suture. Common and serious pest of rugs, upholstered furniture, and other fabrics. Adults often found outside on flowers. Cosmopolitan. (See Fig. 24.116.)

A. verbasci (Linnaeus) (Varied Carpet Beetle). L. 2–3 mm. Convex, oblong oval; thorax black, disk sparsely clothed with yellow scales, more densely covered at the sides by white scales; elytra black with a large basal ring and two transverse zigzag bands of white scales, bordered by yellow ones; ventral surface with fine, long, grayish yellow scales. Adults are common on flowers but may enter homes, lay eggs, and produce destructive larvae that eat wool carpets as well as infest stored food products. Cosmopolitan. (See Fig. 24.117 and A&J 133.)

[61.9 *Thaumaglossa* Redtenbacher (2 spp. (3) AZ, TX); 61.10 *Cryptorhopalum* Guerin (32 spp.); 61.11 *Orphinus* Motschulsky (1 sp., *O. fulvipes* Guerin (2) s. FL); 61.12 *Ctesias* Stephens (1 sp., *C. dusmae* Beal (3) CA)]

61.13 *Trogoderma* Latreille

Fifteen species, many of which are of economic importance. One—*T. granarium* (Everts), the Khapra Beetle (Fig. 24.118

Fig. 24.118. (*U.S. Dept. of Agric.*)

Fig. 24.119.

shows its larvae feeding on dry spaghetti)—is not established in the U.S., but it is the most serious pest of stored grain, grain products, and other agricultural products in other parts of the world. Intercepted frequently at U.S. ports, it must be guarded against constantly to prevent its entrance and establishment in this country.

T. inclusum (LeConte) (Larger Cabinet Beetle). A pest species found in stored cereal products and dried animal matter. Nearly cosmopolitan.

[61.14 *Dearthrus* LeConte (2 spp. (1) MI, IL, IN, OH, PA; (2) GA; (3) CA; (4) OR; 61.15 *Megatoma* Herbst (9 spp. (1) ON; (3) CA, TX; (4) BC, UT, NV; (5) WY); 61.16 *Reesa* Beal (1 sp., *R. vespulae* Milliron (5) MN); 61.17 *Pseudohadrotoma* Kalik (5 spp. (3) CA; (4) BC; (5) YU)]

Superfamily BOSTRICHOIDEA

62. PTINIDAE (Spider Beetle Family)

Length: 2–4 mm. The strongly convex elytra, long legs, and deflexed head with antennae that arise close together from the front serve to characterize this family. The larvae live in dried plant and animal material, in animal nests, and in homes, warehouses, and museums. These are 47 species, several of which are pests.

Subfamily Gibbiinae

62.1 *Gibbium* Scopoli

One species, as follows:

G. psylloides (Czenpinski) (Museum Beetle). L. 2–3 mm. Shiny brown. Often found in museum collections as a pest on specimens. Cosmopolitan. (See Fig. 24.119.)

Fig. 24.120.

Fig. 24.121.

62.2 *Mezium* Curtis

Two species, the following of which is an example:

M. americanum (Laporte) (American Spider Beetle). Similar to the preceding, but with head and thorax covered with yellow scales. Occurs in dwellings, in dried animal products, in warehouses and mills; it also breeds in tobacco, melon seeds, cayene pepper, opium, and grain. Cosmopolitan. (See Fig. 24.120.)

Subfamily Ptininae

62.3 *Trigonogenius* Solier

One species, as follows.

T. globulum Solier (Globular Spider Beetle). (See Fig. 24.121.) (3) CA, AZ; (3) OR.

[62.4 *Sphaericus* Wollaston (1 sp., *S. gibboides* Boieldieu (Introduced, (3) CA; (4) ?); 62.5 *Pitnus* Gorham (1 sp., *P. huesanus* Fisher (2) s. FL)]

62.6 *Niptus* Boieldieu

Four species, including the following:

N. hololeucus (Falderman) (Golden Spider Beetle). L. 3.4–4.5 mm. Pale reddish brown but covered entirely with golden vestiture composed of hairlike setae and scales. Found in households, mills, and warehouses. Cosmopolitan except in tropical region. (See Fig. 24.122.)

[62.7 *Pseudeurostus* Heyden (2 spp. (1) n.e. NA; (4) UT); 62.8 *Tipnus* Thomson (1 sp., *T. unicolor* Piller (?1) "Canada"); 62.9 *Niptinus* Fall (2 spp. (3) s. TX)]

62.10 *Ptinus* Linnaeus

There are 38 species in this genus the U.S. and Canada, assigned to two subgenera: *Ptinus* s. str. (11 spp.) and *Gynopterus*

Fig. 24.122.

Fig. 24.123.

Fig. 24.124.

Mulsant and Rey (27 spp.). The following species have some economic importance:

P. *villiger* Reitter (Hairy Spider Beetle).

P. *clavipes* Panzer (Brown Spider Beetle).

P. *fur* (Linnaeus) (White-marked Spider Beetle). (See Fig. 24.123.)

P. *ocellus* Brown (Australian Spider Beetle).

Subfamily Gnostinae

[62.11 *Gnostus* Westwood (1 sp. *G. floridanus* Blatchley (3) FL)]

63. ANOBIIDAE (Drug Store and Death Watch Beetle Family)

Length: 1–9 mm. The legs are usually short and contractile, that is, capable of being appressed closely to the body; head is deflexed, the pronotum forming a hoodlike cover; antennae eight- to eleven-segmented, with the last three segments often elongate and sometimes flabellate; body dark or reddish brown to black, some species having patches of white scales. The larvae bore into bark, dry wood—including furniture, floors, beams, and wooden walls—twigs, seeds, galls, and fungi. On rare occasions they infest young stems or shoots of growing trees. Several species are found in various stored plant materials and thus the name "drug store beetles." Others have earned the name "death watch beetles" because of their habit in the mating season of striking their vertex against the anterior margin of their pronotum, producing an audible tick that is repeated in periods of seven or eleven strokes; this phenomenon has superstitiously been regarded from ancient times as a portent of death. There are 299 species in the U.S. and Canada in 53 genera.

Subfamily Hedobiinae

[63.1 *Ptilineurus* Reitter (1 sp., *p. marmoratus* Reitter (2) VA); 63.2 *Neohedobia* Fisher (1 sp., *N. texana* Fisher (3) TX; 63.3 *Hedobia* Latreille (3 spp. (3) CA)]

63.4 *Eucrada* LeConte

Two species, as follows;

E. *humeralis* Melsheimer. (See Fig. 24.124.) (1) n.e. US; (2) s.e. US.

E. *robusta* Van Dyke. (4) BC.

Subfamily Dryophilinae

63.5 *Xestobium* Motschulsky

Seven species in (1) n.e. US; (3) CA; (4) BC, WA, OR, the following of which is common:

X. *rufovillosum* (De Geer) (Deathwatch Beetle). Infests old wooden structures (1) n.e. US.

[63.6 *Utobium* Fall (3 spp. (3) CA; (4) OR, NV); 63.7 *Microzogus* Fall (1 sp., *M. insolens* Fall (2) FL); 63.8 *Ozognathus* LeConte (3 spp. (1) NJ, MD, DE; (2) s.e. US; (3) s.w. US; (5) CO); 63.9 *Xarifa* Fall (2 spp. (3) CA); 63.10 *Ernobius* Thomson (29 spp.) 63.11 *Episernus* Thomson (2 spp. (3) CA; (5) CO); 63.12 *Paralobium* Fall (1 sp., *P. mundum* Fall (3) CA)]

Subfamily Anobiinae

[63.13 *Actenobius* Fall (1 sp., *A. pleuralis* Casey (3) CA); 63.14 *Euceratocerus* LeConte (3 spp. ((2) KY, SC; (3) TX); 63.15 *Xeranobium* Fall (5 spp. (3) s.e. US; (4) OR); 63.16 *Oligomerodes* Fall (3 spp. (3) CA); 63.17 *Oligomerus* Redtenbacker (14 spp.)]

63.18 *Stegobium* Motschulsky

One species, as follows:

S. *paniceum* (Linnaeus) (Drugstore Beetle). Infests spices, certain drugs, and other stored products. Probably cosmopolitan. (See Fig. 24.125.)

[63.19 *Gastrallus* Jacquelin du Val (2 spp. (3) CA; (4) UT; (5) CO); 63.20 *Falsogastrallus* Pic [=*Neogastrallus* Fisher] (1 sp., *F. librinocens* (Fisher) (2) FL); 63.21 *Ctenobium* LeConte (1 sp., *C. antennatum* LeConte (2) VA); 63.22 *Trichodesma* LeConte [=*Ptinodes* LeConte] (9 spp.); 63.23 *Nicobium* LeConte (1 sp., *n. castaneum* Olivier (2) s.e. US; (3) TX); 63.24 *Anobiopsis* Fall (1 sp., *A. sericans* Fall (3) CA)]

Fig. 24.125.

63.25 *Anobium* Fabricius

One species, as follows:

A. punctatum (De Geer) (Furniture Beetle; also called Cabinet Beetle). (1) n.e. US; (2) GA; (3) TX; (5) KS.

[63.26 *Hemicoelus* LeConte (8 spp.); 63.27 *Desmatogaster* Knutson (1 sp., *D. subconnata* Fall (1) PQ, ME; (5) MB); 63.28 *Platybregmus* Fisher (1 sp., *P. canadensis* Fisher (1) ON, NY, NJ); 63.29 *Microbregma* Seidlitz (1 sp., *M. emarginatum* Duftschmidt (1) n.e. US; (4) BC); 63.30 *Hadrobregmus* Thomson (5 spp.); 63.31 *Priobium* Motschulsky (3 spp.); 63.32 *Colposternus* Fall (1 sp., *C. tenuilineatus* Horn (3) CA; (4) OR)]

Subfamily Ptilininae

[63.33 *Ptilinus* Mueller (8 spp.)]

Subfamily Xyletininae

[63.34 *Vrilletta* LeConte (12 spp. (1) ON, PQ, PA; (3) CA; (4) Pacific n.w.); 63.35 *Euvrilletta* Fall (4 spp. (1) OH; (2) SC; (3) CA, TX; (4) NV); 63.36 *Xyletomerus* Fall (1 sp., *X. histricus* Fall (3) CA)]

63.37 *Xyletinus* Latreille

X. peltatus Harris (Virginia Creeper Deathwatch Beetle). L. 3.5–6.5 mm. Brown or reddish brown; antennae serrate; eyes large, separated by two to three times the width of the eye; length of the last segment of the maxillary palpi more than twice its width; lateral margins of pronotum very narrow and not reflexed, with sides enlarged. Adults are found on Virginia creeper and also reported on hickory. The larvae have been found in floors and joists of buildings. (1) n.e. US; (2) s.e. US; (3) TX.

63.38 *Lasioderma* Stephens

Four species, the following of which is a pest:

L. serricorne (Fabricius) (Cigarette Beetle). This species is easy to identify by the two ventral pits on the head into which the antennae are curled for protection when the body is contracted. Cosmopolitan.

[63.39 *Megorama* Fall (4 spp. (2) KY; (3) CA)]

Subfamily Dorcatominae

[63.40 *Calymmaderus* Solier (6 spp); 63.41 *Petalium* LeConte (5 spp.); 63.42 *Stagetus* Wollaston (2 spp. (1) MD; (3) CA, AZ; (4) OR)]

63.43 *Tricorynus* Waterhouse

Eighty-two species, including the following:

T. confusum (Fall). (See Fig. 24.126.) (1) PQ; (2) FL; (3) OK, TX.

[63.44 *Mesocoelopus* Jacquelin duVal (1 sp., *M. collaris* Mulsant and Rey (1) OH, DE; (2) VA); 63.45 *Cryptorama* Fall (4 spp. (1) NJ, MD; (2) s.e. US; (3) TX); 63.46 *Cryptoramorphus* White (1 sp., *C. floridanus* White (2) SC, FL); 63.47 *Stichtoptychus* Fall (1 sp., *S. agonus* Fall (3) TX); 63.48 *Protheca* LeConte (1 sp., *P. hispida* LeConte (1) NY; (2) FL; (3) TX); 63.49 *Sculptotheca* Schilsky (1 sp., *S. puberula* (LeConte) (1) WI, MA; (2) FL); 63.50 *Dorcatoma* Herbst (5 spp. (1) n.e. US; (3) s.e. US; (3) CA); 63.51 *Byrrhodes* LeConte (1 sp., *B. setosus* LeConte (2) MS, FL); 63.52 *Priotoma* Gorham (9 spp. (1) n.e. US; (2) s.e. US; (3) CA, TX); 63.53 *Caenocara* Thomson (13 spp.)]

Fig. 24.126.

64. BOSTRICHIDAE (Horned Powder-post Beetle Family)

Length: 2–50 mm (usually 2–20 mm). Most species are black; a few have red elytra. Many resemble the bark beetles (Scolytidae) and might be mistaken for them were it not for their horns and tubercles. Most have a rasplike pronotum. Their antennae are not elbowed but have a three- to four-segmented club. Their tarsi have five tarsomeres. The larvae are wood borers, especially in twigs; a few are found in stored products. Some adults come to light; others are found under bark, on dead limbs, and sometimes emerging from firewood, beams, and other parts of buildings. Sixty-four species are established in the U.S. and Canada, but others species have been intercepted at ports in imported wood products and may eventually become established.

Subfamily Psoinae

Tribe Polycaonini

[64.1 *Melalgus* Dejean (3 spp. (2), (3), (4)); 64.2 *Polycaon* Castelnau (2 spp. (3) CA, AZ, OK; (4) OR, UT)]

Tribe Psoini

[64.3 *Psoa* Herbst (2 spp. (3) CA; (4) WA, OR)]

Subfamily Endecatominae

[64.4 *Endecatomus* Mellie (2 spp. (1) n.e. US; (2) VA, NC; (3) TX; (5) MB)]

Subfamily Dinoderinae

64.5 *Dinoderus* Stephens

Three species, the following of which is a pest:

D. minutus (Fabricius) (Bamboo Powder-post Beetle). Frequently intercepted in bamboo products, it may be established in Florida and perhaps elsewhere.

64.6 *Rhyzopertha* Stephens

One species, as follows:

R. dominica (Fabricius) (Lesser Grain Borer). Cosmopolitan.

64.7 *Prostephanus* Lesne

Four species in (1), (2), (3), CA, AZ, TX, the following of which is a pest:

P. truncatus Horn (Larger Grain Borer). (3) CA.

[64.8 *Stephanopachys* Waterhouse (9 spp.,)]

Subfamily **Bostrichinae**

Tribe **Dinapatini**

[64.9 *Dinapate* (1 sp., *D. wrighti* Horn (3) s. CA)]

Tribe **Bostrichini**

[64.10 *Bostrichus* Geoffroy (1 sp., *B. capucinus* Linnaeus (1) NJ);
64.11 *Sinoxylon* Duftschmid (1 sp., *S. ruficorne* Fahraeus (2) ?FL);
64.12 *Bostrycholites* Lesne (1 sp. *B. cornutus* Olivier (1) VT)]

64.13 *Amphicerus* LeConte

Four species, the following of which are pests:

A. bicaudatus (Say) (Apple Twig Borer). L. 6–12 mm. Reddish brown to very dark brown; male with a large spine on the apex of each elytra; female with a vague callosity in that position; pronotum with two large, hooklike horns and smaller tubercles. Larvae breed in hardwood trees. (1) n.e. US; (2) s.e. US; 93) NM, TX, OK.

A. cornutus Pallas (Powderpost Bostrichid). (2) s.e US; (3) s.w. US; (4) UT; (5) CO.

[64.14 *Lichenophanes* Lesne (7 spp., (1), (2), (3), (5)); 64.15 *Heterobostrychus* Lesne (2 spp. (2) FL; ?elsewhere); 64.16 *Micrapate* Casey (4 spp. (1), (2), (3)); 64.17 *Apatides* Casey (1 sp., *A. fortis* LeConte (3) CA, AZ, NM, TX; (4) UT; see Fig. 24.127)]

Tribe **Xyloperthini**

64.18 *Tetrapriocera* Horn (1 sp., *T. longicornis* Olivier (2) FL)]

64.19 *Scobicia* Lesne

Six species, the following of which is a pest:

S. declivis LeConte (Lead Cable Borer). (3) CA; (4) WA, OR.

[64.20 *Xylomeira* Lesne (1 sp., *X. torquata* Fabricuis (2) FL; (3) TX); 64.21 *Xylobiops* Casey (4 spp. (1), (2), (3), (5)); 64.22 *Dendrobiella* Casey (2 spp. (3) CA, AZ, TX); 64.23 *Xyloblaptus* Lesne (2 spp. (3) s.e US)]

65. LYCTIDAE (Powder-post Beetle Family)

Length: 1–7 mm (usually under 5 mm). Reddish brown to black; head exposed, not hidden like that of the rest of this series of families. The somewhat flattened body and two-segmented antennal club are distinctive. Both larvae and adults live in

Fig. 24.127.

Fig. 24.128.

wood and are of considerable economic importance, particularly as pests of seasoned lumber and tool handles. Fine sawdust produced by the boring process is indicative of this infestation. Eleven species occur in the U.S. and Canada.

Tribe **Lyctini**

65.1 *Lyctus* Fabricius

Seven species, the following of which are common.

L. planicollis LeConte (Southern Lyctus Beetle). (1) IL, IN, OH, RI, NJ, DE; (2) TN, VA, LA, GA, FL; (3) CA, TX; (4) WA, ID; (5) IA, KS, MO.

L. brunneus Stephens. L. 2.2–7 mm. This species is cosmopolitan.

[65.2 *Minthea* Pascoe (1 sp., *M. rugicollis* Walker (Tropicopolitan, probably not established in U.S. except perhaps in (3) s. TX)]

Tribe **Trogoxylini**

65.3 *Trogoxylon* LeConte

Three species, as follows:

T. parallelopipedum Melsheimer. (See Fig. 24.128.) (1) n.e. US; (2) s.e. US; (3) TX; (5) IA, KS.

T. aequale Wollaston. (3) AZ, TX.

T. caseyi Lesne. (3) TX.

Series CUCUJIFORMIA

Superfamily CLEROIDEA

66. TROGOSSITIDAE

Length: 6–18 mm. Shape elongate or oval and flattened (on rare occasions, more or less convex); body usually brown but sometimes blue, green, or black. These are difficult beetles to recognize and might be confused with the Tenebrionidae at first sight except that they have five tarsomeres on every leg; the Tenegrionidae have only four on their hind legs. The first tarsomere is very short. The larvae are carnivorous and hunt their prey under bark, in galleries of wood boring insects (the elongate species), or in fungi (the oval species). A few are stored product pests. There are 64 species in the U.S. and Canada.

Subfamily Peltinae

[66.1 *Calitys* Thomson (2 spp.); 66.2 *Ostoma* Laicharting (3 spp. (1), (3), (4), (5)); 66.3 *Grynocharis* Thomson (2 spp.); 66.4 *Thymalus* Latreille (1 sp., *T. marginicollis* Chevrolate (1), (2), (4), (5)); 66.5 *Eronyxa* Reitter (3 spp. (3) CA; (4) Pacific n.w.); 66.6 *Lophocateres* Olliff (1 sp., *L. pusillus* Klug (Cosmopolitan); 66.7 *Lycoptis* Casey (1 sp., *L. americana* Motschulsky (1) MD; (2) NC, SC, GA)]

Subfamily Trogossitinae

[66.8 *Nemosoma* Latreille (5 spp. (3) CA, AZ; (4) BC, WA, OR); 66.9 *Cylidrella* Sharp (1 sp., *C. championi* Wickham (3) AZ, NM; (5) CO); 66.10 *Corticotomus* Sharp (6 spp.); 66.11 *Euschaefferia* Leng (2 spp. (2) NC; (3) CA, TX); 66.12 *Airora* Reitter (3 spp.); 66.13 *Temnochila* Erichson (10 spp.)]

66.14 *Tenebroides* Piller and Mitterpacher

Eighteen species, the following of which is thought to be a pest:

T. mauritanicus (Linnaeus) (Cadelle). L. 6.5–10 mm. Shiny black with a slight bluish tinge. Found in stored products, but may be a predator. Cosmopolitan. (See Fig. 24.129.)

[7 spp. unplaced.]

67. CLERIDAE (Checkered Beetle Family)

Length: 3–24 mm. Bright contrasting colors, a densely hairy body, and a large head characterize most species of this family. The lobed tarsomeres (all but the fifth on each leg) and the large apical segments of the palpi also serve to distinguish them. Both larvae and adults of most species are predacious. They are found on woody plants, on or under bark, in galleries in wood, in galls, but rarely on foliage. A few species are both stored animal product pests and attracted to carrion. Some adults are often found feeding on pollen, and a few are attracted to lights. There are 266 species in 33 genera in the U.S. and Canada.

Subfamily Thaneroclerinae

[67.1 *Thaneroclerus* LeFebvre (1 sp., *T. buquet* (Introduced; ?localities); 67.2 *Zenodosus* Wolcott (1 sp., *Z.* (1) ON, NY, ME ; (2) NC, AR; (5) CO); 67.3 *Ababa* Casey (1 sp., *A. tantilla* (LeConte) (1) MA, DC; (2) AL, LA; (3) TX; (5) MO)]

Subfamily Clerinae

Tribe Tillini

[67.4 *Callotillus* Wolcott (2 spp (2), (3), (4)); 67.5 *Monophylla* Spinola (5 spp.); 67.6 *Cymatoderella* Barr (2 spp. (1), (2), (3)); 67.7 *Lecontella*

Fig. 24.129.

Fig. 24.130.

Wolcott and Chapin (2 spp. (1), (2), (3), (5)); 67.8 *Araeodontia* Barr (3 spp. (3), (4)); 67.9 *Bostrichoclerus* Van Dyke (1 sp., *B. bicornis* Van Dyke (3) CA); 67.10 *Cymatodera* Gray (71 spp.)]

Tribe Clerini

[67.11 *Priocera* Kirby (5 spp. (1), (2), (3), (5)); 67.12 *Opilo* Latreille (2 spp., (Cosmopolitan)); 67.13 *Perilypus* (1 sp., *P. ornaticollis* (LeConte) (1) IN, OH; (2) TN, AR, LA; (3) TX; 67.14 *Placopterus* Wolcott (3 spp. (1), (2), (3), (5)); 67.15 *Thanasimus* Latreille (5 spp.)]

67.16 *Enoclerus* Gahan

The two subgenera—*Coniferoclerus* Barr (3 spp. (3), (4), (5)) and *Enoclerus* s. str. (32 spp.)—include the following species:

E. (Enoclerus) lecontei (Wolcott) (Black-bellied Clerid). Rare. (1) WI, MI; (3) Ca, AZ; (4) BC, WA, OR, ID; (5) SD.

E. quadrisignatus (Say) (See Fig. 24.130.) (1) IL, IN, OH, PA, NJ; (2) VA, NC; (3) CA, AZ, TX, OK; (5) CO, KS.
[67.17 *Aulicus* Spinola (9 spp. (3), (4))]

67.18 *Trichodes* Herbst

Ten species, several of which are common:

T. nuttalli Kirby. L. 8–10.5 mm. Metallic blue with red or orange bands on elytra. Found flowers of cactus, wild rose, dandelion, daisy, and other plants. (1) n.e. US; (2) VA, TN; (4) BC; (5) MT, ND, MN, WY, SD, AB, MB, SA.

T. ornatus Say (Ornate Checkered Beetle). L. 5–15 mm. Elytra with red to yellow basal, median, and subapical bands that vary to small spots on otherwise metallic, bluish-black body. Adults found on flowers of cactus, yucca, composites, and many other plants where they feed on pollen or prey upon other insects. Larvae prey upon solitary bees and wasps. This species is divided into five subspecies. (See A & J 135.) (3) s.e. US; (4) pacific n.w.; (5) WY, CO.

T. peninsularis Horn (Horn's Checkered Beetle). L. 7–10 mm. Head and pronotum black with greenish luster; elytra brown with yellow and black stripes; abdomen and legs reddish. There are three subspecies, two in (3) CA, AZ, NM. (See A & J 136.)

Subfamily Phyllobaeninae

[67.19 *Phyllobaenus* Dejean (54 spp.); 67.20 *Isohydnocera* Chapin (15 spp. (1), (2), (3), (5)); 67.21 *Wolcottia* Chapin (3 spp. (1), (3), (5))]

Fig. 24.131.

Subfamily Epiphloeinae

[67.22 *Phlogistosternus* Spinola (3 spp. (1), (2), (3)); 67.23 *Neichnea* Wolcott and Chapin (1 sp., *N. laticornis* (Say) (1) ON, PQ, IL, OH, NY, PA, CT, NJ, MD; (2) WV, VA, NC, SC, GA, FL)]

Subfamily Korynetinae
Tribe Enopliini

[67.24 *Neorthopleura* Barr (2 spp. (1), (2), (3), (5)); 67.25 *Pelonides* Kuwert (5 spp.); 67.26 *chariessa* Perty (6 spp.); 67.27 *Cregya* LeConte (3 spp. (1), (2), (3), (5)); 67.28 *Pelonium* Spinola (4 spp.)]

Tribe Korynetini

[67.29 *Lebasiella* Spinola (4 spp. (1), (3)); 67.30 *Loedelia* Lucas (2 spp. (3) CA, AZ, NM)]

67.31 *Necrobia* Olivier

Three cosmopolitan species, the following of which are pests:

N. ruficollis (Fabricius) (Redshouldered Ham Beetle). L. 4–5 mm. Red; head, antennae, and abdomen black; elytra blue or green, with base broadly red. Adults and larvae are found in dry carrion, only rarely in stored meat products. Cosmopolitan. (See Fig. 24.131.)

N. rufipes (De Geer) (Redlegged Ham Beetle). L. 3.5–6 mm. Similar to the preceding but entirely metallic blue except legs and antennae, which are yellowish red. Both larvae and adults feed on smoked meat, cheese skippers, blowflies, and eggs; they are cannibalistic. Cosmopolitan.

[67.32 *Opetiopalpus* Spinola (1 sp., *O. luridus* Spinola (reported in NA but probably in error))]

Subfamily Tarsosteninae Crowson

[67.33 *Tarsostenus* Spinola (1 sp., *T. univttatus* (Rossi) (Cosmopolitan))]

68. MELYRIDAE (Soft-winged Flower Beetle Family)

Length: 2–10 mm. Body soft, often with erect hairs; front coxae large; antennae serrate; elytra usually broader behind. These beetles although carnivorous, are also found on flowers

Fig. 24.132.

feeding on pollen. Some are known to feed on the eggs of other insects. Although fairly common, they are poorly known and rather rare in collections. There are 520 species in the U.S. and Canada assigned to 48 genera, but the genera are poorly defined.

Fig. 24.133.

Subfamily Malachiinae
68.1 *Collops* Erichson

Forty-eight species, the following of which are common:

C. vittatus Say (Two-lined Collops). L. 5–8 mm. Pitchy blue-black; side of pronotum, margin, and suture of the elytra marked with orange-red or yellowish red; disk of the elytra dark bluish; disk of pronotum usually has a large dark spot; basal segments of male antennae are greatly enlarged. Adults are predacious or feed on pollen; larvae are predacious. (1) n.e. US; (2) s.e. US; ((4) Pacific n.w.; (5) n. Central States. (See A & J 134.)

C. quadrimaculatus Fabricius (Four-spotted Egg Eater). L. 4–6 mm. Blue; elytra are crossed near middle by broad orange band and narrow sutural stripe, breaking the blue field into four spots; second segment of male antennae is enlarged. Found on grass and weeds feeding on eggs of other insects. (1) n.e. US; (2) s.e. US; (3) s.w. US. (See Fig. 24.132.)

[68.2 *Trophimus* Horn (1 sp., *T. aeneipennis* Horn (5) CO); 68.3 *Temnopsophus* Horn (2 spp. (2) FL, LA); 68.4 *Endeodes* LeConte (4 spp. (3) CA; 68.5 *Chaetocoelus* LeConte (1 sp., *C. setosus* LeConte (1) MD; (2) FL; (3) TX); 68.6 *Attalusinus* Leng (1 sp., *A. submarginatus* LeConte (3) AZ); 68.7 *Malachius* Fabricius (27 spp., including *M. aeneus* Linnaeus (10 n.e. NA; see Fig. 24.133); 68.8 *Tanaops* LeConte (22 spp. (3)(4), (5)); 68.9 *Nicrolipus* LeConte (9 spp. (3) CA; (4) BC; (5) NE); 68.10 *Hypebaeus* Kiesenwetter (4 spp. (1); (2); (3) AZ, CA; (5) CO); 68.11 *Attalus* Erichson (58 spp.); 68.12 *Nodopus* Marshall (1 sp., *N. caviceps* Marshall (2) MS)]

Subfamily Rhadalinae

[68.13 *Dasyrhadus* Fall (2 spp. (3) CA; (4) WA); 68.14 *Rhadalus* LeConte (2 spp. (3) AZ)]

Subfamily Melyrinae

[68.15 *Melyrodes* Gorham (3 spp. (2) s.e. US); 68.16 *Euryelmis* Casey (3) CA; (4) UT; (5) CO)]

Subfamily Dasytinae

[68.17 *Dolichosoma* Stephens (3 spp., (1), (3), (5)); 68.18 *Pristoscelis* LeConte (2 spp. (3) CA)); 68.19 *Eschatocrepis* LeConte (3 spp. (3) CA;

68.20 *Dasytes* Paykull (25 spp. (1), (3), (4), (5)); 68.21 *Dasytellusi* Casey (9 spp.) (3), (4), (5)); 68.22 *Vecturoides* Fall (1 sp., *V. serrulata* Baisdell (3) CA)); 68.23 *Amphivectura* Blaisdell (1 sp., *A. monticola* Blaisdell (4) BC); 68.24 *Hoppingiana* Blaisdell (2 spp. (4) BC, OR; (5) ?AB); 68.25 *Leptovectura* Casey (1 sp., *L. adspersa* Casey (3) NM); 68.26 *Enallonyx* Wolcott (3 spp. (3) CA); 68.27 *Paeudallonyx* Casey (1 sp., *P. plumbeus* LeConte (3) AZ; (5) CO); 68.28 *Vectura* Casey (4 spp. (3) CA, AZ; (4) UT); 68.29 *Dasytastes* Casey (3) CA); 68.30 *Mecomycter* Horn (4 spp. (3) Ca, AZ, TX; (5) KS); 68.31 *Pseudasydates* Blaisdell (1 sp., *P. inyoensis* Blaisdell (3) CA); 68.32 *Eudasytes* Casey (9 spp. (3) CA, AZ; (4) NV, UT); 68.33 *Asydates* Casey (3 spp. (3) CA); 68.34 *Cradytes* Casey (6 spp. (3) AZ, NM; (5) CO); 68.35 *Eutricholistra* Blaisdell (1 sp., *E. punctata* Blaisdell (3) AZ); 68.36 *Trichochrous* Motschulsky (127 spp. (3), (4), (5)); 68.37 *Trichochronellus* Blaisdell (1 sp., *T. stricticollis* Casey (3) CA); 68.38 *Eutrichopleurus* Blaisdell (5 spp. (4) UT, ID); 68.39 *Byturosoma* Motschulsky (1 sp., *B. fuscus* LeConte (3) CA); 68.40 *Emmenotarsis* Motschyulsky (1 sp., *E. quadricollis* leConte (3) CA); 68.41 *Trichochroides* Blaisdell (10 spp. (3) CA); 68.42 *Sydates* Casey (2 spp. (3) CA, TX); 68.43 *Listromimus* Casey (1 sp., *L. sericatus* Casey (4) NV); 68.44 *Listrimorpha* Blaisdell (1 sp., *L. pallipes* Blaisdell (4) NV); 68.45 *Adasytes* Casey (1 sp., *A. laciniatus* Casey (3) CA); 68.46 *Amecocerus* Soldier (90 spp. (3), (4), (5)); 68.47 *Listropsis* Blaisdell (2 spp. (3) CA); 68.48 *Neodasytes* Hatch (1 sp., *N. testaceus* Hatch (4) ID)]

Superfamily LYMEXYLOIDEA

69. LYMEXYLIDAE (Ship-timber Beetle Family)

Length: 9–14 mm. Body elongate, cylindrical; brown or black with yellowish appendages; antennae serrate; maxillary palpi of male flabellate. Found in decaying wood of chestnut, poplar, and other trees. Two rare species as follows:

69.1 *Hylecoetus* Latreille

H. lugubris Say (Sapwood Timberworm). (1) n.e. US.

69.2 *Melittomma* Murry

M. sericeum (Harris) (Chestnut Timberworm). (See Fig. 24.134.) (1) s. NY, PA, MD; (2) s.e. US.

Superfamily CUCUJOIDEA

70. NITIDULIDAE (Sap-feeding Beetle Family)

Length: 1.5–12 mm. Usually oval, nearly quadrate, rarely elongate; body flattened; pale to black, often with red or yellowish spots on elytra; elytra sometimes shortened, exposing apex of abdomen; antennae with distinct three-segmented club. Adults come to sap flows, moth bait, picnics, flowers, and fungi. They feed on plant juices, nectar, and pollen. A great number are attracted to decaying fruit and even carrion. The larvae of a few lives in seed capsules of various plants. At least one species lives in bumblebee nests. There are 183 species in the U.S. and Canada assigned to 36 genera.

Fig. 24.134.

Subfamily Cateretinae

[70.1 *Cateretes* Herbst (3 spp.); 70.2 *Boreades* Parsons (1 sp., *B. abdominalis* Erichson (1) n.e. NA; (2) s.e. US; (3) TX; (5) MN, NE, KS); 70.3 *Brachypterus* Kugelann (4 spp.)); 70.4 *Brachypterolus* Grouvelle (1 sp., *B. pulicarius* (Linnaeus) (1) n.e. NA; (5) SD, MN, CO); 70.5 *Amartus* LeConte (2 spp. (3) CA, AZ; (4) OR); 70.6 *Anthonaeus* Horn (1 sp., *A. agavensis* Crotch (3) CA)]

Subfamily Carpophilinae

[70.7 *Conotelus* Erichson (4 spp.); 70.8 *Brachypeplus* Erichson (1 sp., *B. glaber* LeConte (2) GA, FL); 70.9 *Colopterus* Erichson (5 spp.)]

70.10 *Carpophilus* Stephens

Thirty-one species, several of which are minor pests:

C. antiquus (Melsheimer) (Antique Sap Beetle). (1) n.e. US; (2) s.e. US.

C. dimidiatus (Fabricius) (Corn Sap Beetle). (2) s.e. US.

C. hemipterus (Linnaeus) (Dried-fruit Beetle). (1), (2), (3), (4), (5).

C. lugubris Murray (Dusky Sap Beetle). (1) n.e. US; (2) s.e. US; (3) TX; (5) CO.

Subfamily Nitidulinae

[70.11 *Haptoncus* Murray (2 spp. (2) s.e. US; (3) CA); 70.12 *Epuraea* Erichson (34 spp.); 70.13 *Aphenolia* Reitter (1 sp., *A. monogama* Crotch (3) CA, TX; (2) WA, ID, NV); 70.14 *Orthopeplus* Horn (1 sp., *O. quadricollis* Horn (3) AZ, NM; (5) CO)]

70.15 *Stelidota* Erichson

Four species, the following of which is sometimes a pest:

S. geminata (Say) (Strawberry Sap Beetle). (1) n.e. US; (2) s.e. US; (3) TX; (5) IA.

[70.16 *Omosita* Erichson (2 spp.); 70.17 *Nitidula* Fabricius (5 spp. (1), (3), (4), (5)); 70.18 *Prometopia* Erichson (2 spp. (1) n.e. US; (5) MN, KS); 70.19 *Lobiopa* Erichson (7 spp.); 70.20 *Soronia* Erichson (4 spp. (1), (3), (4), (5)); 70.21 *Phenolia* Erichson (1 sp., *P. grossa* Fabricius (1) n.e. US; (2) s.e. US; (3) TX; (5) WY, NE, MN); 70.22 *Amphotis* Erichson (2 spp. (1) n.e. US; (2) s.e. US; (3) TX); 70.23 *Thalycra* Erichson (14 spp.); 70.24 *Pseudothalycra* Howden (1 sp., *P. knulli* Howden (3) CA; (4) NV); 70.25 *Pocadius* Erichson (4 spp.); 70.26 *Camptodes* Erichson (5 spp. (3) AZ, TX); 70.27 *Amphicrossus* Erichson (3 spp. (1), (2), (3), (5)); 70.28 *Cychramus* Kugelann (3 spp. (1), (2), (3), (5)); 70.29 *Pallodes* Erichson (2 spp. (1), (2), (3), (5) KS); 70.30 *Cyllodes* Erichson (1 sp., *C. biplagiatus* LeConte (1) n.e. US; (5) MB, MN); 70.31 *Psilopyga* LeConte (4 spp. (1), (2), (3), (5))]

Subfamily Meligethinae

[70.32 *Meligethes* Stephens (8 spp.)]

Subfamily Cryptarchinae

[70.33 *Cryptarcha* Shuckard (6 spp.); 70.34 *Pityophagus* Shuckard (3 spp. (1), (3), (4), (5))]

Fig. 24.135.

70.35 *Glischrochilus* Reitter

Nine species, the following of which are common:

G. obtusus (Say) (Red-spotted Sap Beetles). L. 7.5–14 mm. Body black, shiny; very similar to the following species except that its elytra has only two spots. (1) n.e. US; (2) s.e. US.

G. quadrisignatus (Say) (Red-spotted Sap Beetle). L. 4–7 mm. Body black, shiny; four spots on the elytra, the basal ones usually moon-shaped; the spots may merge. (1), (2), (4), (5).

G. fasciatus (See Fig. 24.135.) (Olivier). (1) n.e. NA; (2) VA, NC, AR; (3) ?NM; (4) BC, ?OR; (5) n. Central States.

Subfamily Cybocephalinae

[70.36 *Cybocephalus* Erichson (2 spp. (1) MI, IN; (2) GA, FL; (3) CA, AZ)]

71. RHIZOPHAGIDAE (Root-eating Beetle Family)

Length: 1.5–3 mm. Body elongate, somewhat flattened, and usually black; two-segmented club on ten-segmented antennae. Most species live under bark; a few are associated with ants. The larvae of some are predacious; some frequent rotten, fungus-infested wood. Very little is known about this group. There are 54 species in the US and Canada in 11 genera.

Subfamily Rhizophaginae

71.1 *Rhizophagus* Herbst

Fourteen species, the following of which is common:

R. bipunctatus (Say). Sometimes common under bark of beech and maple. (See Fig. 24.136.) (1) n.e. NA.

Subfamily Monotominae

[71.2 *Monotoma* Herbst (15 spp.); 71.3 *Phyconomus* LeConte (1 sp., *P. marinus* LeConte (3) CA); 71.4 *Hesperobaenus* LeConte (4 spp. (2), (3), (5)); 71.5 *Leptipsius* Casey (2 spp. (1) IL; (3) CA, AZ); 71.6 *Europs* Wollaston (5 spp. (1), (2), (3); 71.7 *Macreurops* LeConte (8 spp. (1), (2), (3), (5)); 71.8 *Bactridium* LeConte (8 spp. (1), (2), (3), (5)); 71.9 *Pycnotomina* Casey (1 sp., *P. cavicolle* Horn (1) PA, NJ)]

Subfamily Smicripinae

[71.10 *Smicrips* LeConte (2 spp. (2) FL; (3) CA, TX)]

Subfamily Hypocoprinae

[71.11 *Hypocoprus* Motschulsky (1 sp., *H. formicetorum* Motschsulsky (5) CO)]

Fig. 24.136.

72. CUCUJIDAE (Flat Bark Beetle Family)

Length: 2–14 mm. Red to black, flat beetles (some rare species are cylindrical); body rather elongate, with broad, prominent head; antennae eleven-segmented with a two- to four-segmented club, or club absent. Adults and the equally flat larvae occur under loose bark, in decaying plant material, or in stored products. Several species are serious pests of stored flour and other plant products. Eighty-five species occur in the U.S. and Canada.

Subfamily Inopeplinae

[72.1 *Inopeplus* Smith (2 spp. (1), (2), (3))]

Subfamily Silvaninae

72.2 *Oryzaephilus* Ganglbauer

Two species, as follows:

O. mercator (Fauvel) (Merchant Grain Beetle). A cosmopolitan pest of stored products.

O. surinamensis (Linnaeus) (Saw-toothed Grain Beetle). Similar to the preceding; cosmopolitan. (See Fig. 24.137.)

[72.3 *Silvanus* Latreille (5 spp. (Cosmopolitan)); 72.4 *Ahasverus* des Gozis (4 spp. (1), (2), (3))]

72.5 *Cathartus* Reiche

One species, as follows:

C. quadricollis (Guerin) (Square-necked Grain Beetle). Cosmopolitan. (See Fig. 24.138.)

Fig. 24.137.

Fig. 24.138.

[72.6 *Planismus* Casey (1 sp., *P. floridanus* Casey (2) FL [see 24.75.1]); 72.7 *Monanus* Sharp (1 sp., *M. concinnulus* Walker (Cosmopolitan)); 72.8 *Nausibius* Redtenbacher (2 spp. (1), (2), (3))]

Subfamily Passandrinae

[72.9 *Catogenus* Westwood (1 sp., *C. rufus* Westwood (1) IN, PA, MD, DC; (2) NC, FL; (5) IA); 72.10 *Scalidia* Erichson (1 sp., *S. linearis* LeConte (2) FL; (3) TX)]

Subfamily Cucujinae

Tribe Cucujini

[72.11 *Narthecius* LeConte (6 spp. (1), (2), (3), (4)); 72.12 *Pediacus* Schuckard (2 spp. (Cosmopolitan))]

72.13 *Cucujus* Fabricius

One species, as follows:

C. clavipes Fabricius (Red Cucujid). L. 10–14 mm. Bright red to scarlet; flat, easily distinguished from all other bark beetles. Found under loose bark of tulip-poplar and other deciduous trees. (1) n.e. US; (2) VA, NC; (5) n. Central States. (See Fig. 24.139.)

[72.14 *Laemophloeus* Laporte (19 spp.); 72.15 *Placonotus* MacLeay (11 spp.); 72.16 *Leptophloeus* Casey (4 spp.))]

72.17 *Cryptolestes* Ganglbauer

Seven species, the following of which are of economic interest:

C. ferrugineus (Stephens) (Rust Grain Beetle). Cosmopolitan.

Fig. 24.139.

C. pusillus (Schoenherr) (Flat Grain Beetle). Cosmopolitan.

[72.18 *Lathropus* Erichson (5 spp. (1), (2), (3)); 72.19 *Dysmerus* Casey (1 sp., *D. basalis* Casey (1) NJ; (2) FL); 72.20 *Rhinomalus* Gemminger (1 sp., *R. texanus* Schaeffer (3) TX)]

Tribe Uleiotini

[72.21 *Dendrophagus* Schoenherr (1 sp., *D. cygnaei* Mannerheim (1) n.e. NA; (3) NM; (5) MN); 72.22 *Uleiota* Latreille (2 spp. (1), (3) CA)]

Tribe Hemipeplini

[72.23 *Hemipeplus* Latreille (2 spp. (2) GA, FL)]

Tribe Telephanini

[72.24 *Telephanus* Erichson (2 spp. (1) n.e. US; (3) AZ; (5) IA)]

Tribe Cryptamorphini

[72.25 *Psammoecus* Latreille (1 sp., *P. desjardinsi* Guérin (2) FL; (4) WA]

73. SPHINDIDAE (Dry-fungus Beetle Family)

Length: 1–3 mm. Reddish brown, dark brown, to black; oblong, convex; antennae ten-segmented with a three-segmented club; hind tarsi with four tarsomeres. Found living in dry shelf fungi on tree trunks and logs. Relatively rare. Six species, as follows:

73.1 *Odontosphindus* LeConte

Two species in (1), (3), (4), the following of which is relatively common:

O. denticollis LeConte. (1) n.e. US.

[73.2 *Sphindus* Chevrolat (3 spp. (1) n.e. NA; (2) s.e. US; (3) AZ, TX; (5) IA, KS); 73.3 *Eurysphindus* LeConte (1 sp., *E. hirtus* LeConte (1) n.e. US; (2) TN, NC; (3) AZ; (5) MB)]

74. CRYPTOPHAGIDAE (Silken Fungus Beetle Family)

Length: 1–5 mm. Pale brown to black; antennae eleven-segmented with a loose three-segmented club; lateral margin of pronotum often toothed or spined. Many species common on fungi but poorly known. Others found in decayed leaves, in wasp and bumblebee nests, and in nests of semisocial caterpillars where they are scavengers. There are 152 species in the U.S. and Canada in 16 genera.

Subfamily Cryptophaginae

Tribe Cryptophagini

[74.1 *Antherophagus* Latreille (5 spp. (1), (4), (5)); 74.2 *Glyptophorus* Park (1 sp., *G. mycetoecus* Park (5) IA); 74.3 *Emphylus* Erichson (1 sp., *E. americanus* LeConte (3) CA, (4) UT; (5) CO); 74.4 *Crosimus* Casey (2 spp. (1) IN, NY; (5) IA); 74.5 *Salebius* Casey (5 spp.)]

74.6 *Cryptophagus* Herbst

Forty-three species, the following of which are common:

C. acutangulus Gyllenhall (Acute-angled Fungus Beetle). (1), (2), (3), (4), (5). (Fig. 24.140).

C. varus Woodroffe and Coombs (Sigmoid Fungus Beetle). (1), (4), (5).

Fig. 24.140.

[74.7 *Henoticus* Thomson (2 spp. (1), (3), (5)); 74.8 *Pteryngium* Reitter (1 sp., *P. crenatum* Gyllenhal (5) MN); 74.9 *Henoticoides* Hatch (1 sp., *H. lorna* Hatch (4) BC)]

Subfamily Atomariinae

Tribe Caenoscelini

[74.10 *Caenoscelis* Thomson (13 spp.); 74.11 *Macrodea* Casey (1 sp., *M. antennalis* Casey (5) AB)]

Tribe Atomariini

[74.12 *Atomaria* Stephens (41 spp.(1), (3), (4), (5)); 74.13 *Anchicera* Thomson (30 spp.)); 74.14 *Tisactia* Casey (1 sp., *T. subglabra* Casey (1) IN)]

Tribe Ephistemini

[74.15 *Ephistemus* Stephens (4 spp. (1), (2), (3)); 74.16 *Parephistemus* Casey (1 sp., *P. ocularis* Casey (2) NC)]

Tribe Tetmalophilini

[74.17 Telmatophilus Heer (1 sp. *T. americanus* LeConte () IN; (5) CO)]

75. LANGURIIDAE (Lizard Beetle Family)

Length: 2–10 mm. Elongate oval to cylindrical, parallel-sided; usually black, often shiny, sometimes marked with orange; antennae eleven-segmented, with a three- or four-segmented club that is often asymmetrical. The larvae of some species are stem borers in a variety of plants, particularly Compositae and Leguminosae; other live in fungus. Thirty-eight species occur in the U.S. and Canada.

Subfamily Loberinae

Tribe Pharaxonothini

[75.1 *Pharaxonotha* Reitter (2 spp. (1) IL; (2) FL; (3) TX)]

Tribe Loberini

[75.2 *Loberus* LeConte (5 spp. (1), (2), (5)); 75.3 *Hapalips* Reitter (1 sp., *H. texanus* Schaeffer (3) TX)]

Subfamily Toraminae

[75.4 *Toramus* Grouvelle (8 spp. (1), (2), (3))]

Subfamily Cryptophilinae

[75.5 *Cryptophilus* Reiter (3 spp. (1), (2), (3), (5))]

Subfamily Languriinae

Tribe Languriini

75.6 *Languria* Latreille

Fifteen species in (1), (2), (3), (5), the following of which is of economic importance:

L. mozardi Latreille (Clover Stem Borer). L. 5.5–8 mm. Head and thorax reddish orange, the latter with a central black

Fig. 24.141.

spot; elytra bluish black; orange ventrally except that tatsi, tibiae, and apical half of femora are black. Larvae bore in the stems of clover. (See Fig. 24.141.) (1) n.e. US; (2) s.e. US; (5) MN, NE, MO.

[75.7 *Acropteroxys* Gorham (2 spp.); 75.8 *Langurites* Motschulsky (1 sp., *L. lineatus* Laporte (2) FL; (3) AZ); 75.9 *Dasydactylus* Gorham (1 sp., *D. cnici* Schaeffer (3) TX)]

76. EROTYLIDAE (Pleasing Fungus Beetle Family)

Length: 3–20 mm. Elongate, oval, sometimes with a dorsal V- or roofshaped elytra; usually black with reddish yellow markings; antennae eleven-segmented, usually with a three-segmented club; tarsi with five tarsomeres, the fourth often small. The larvae occur on fleshy fungi or within decayed wood debris or moldy stored materials. There are 65 species in the U.S. and Canada in ten genera.

Subfamily Dacninae

[76.1 *Dacne* Latreille (5 spp. (1), (3), (4)); 76.2 *Microsternus* Lewis (1 sp., *M. ulkei* Crotch (1) IN, OH, PA, MD; (2) KY, NC)]

76.3 *Megalodacne* Crotch

Two species in (1), (2), (3), (5), including the following:

M. fasciatus (Fabricius). L. 9–15 mm. Body and appendages black, shiny; elytra with two red cross bars, the basal one irregular in form, enclosing three black spots. Found on fungi. (See Fig. 24.142.) (1) n.e. US; (2) s.e. US; (3) TX; (5) MN, IA, CO.

Subfamily Erotylinae

76.4 *Cypherotylus* Crotch

One species, as follows:

C. californica (Lacordaire) (California Pleasing Fungus Beetle). L. 16–18 mm. Black; elytra yellowish gray with numerous small, irregularly placed black spots. Adults are found in fungus or in fungus-rotted wood. They are also attracted to household products such as powdered milk. (See A&J 136.) (3) CA, AZ, NM; (5) CO, KS.

Subfamily Triplacinae

[76.5 *Triplax* Herbst (25 spp.)); 76.6 *Tritoma* Fabricius (19 spp. (1), (2), (3), (5)); 76.7 *Pseudischyrus* Casey (3 spp. (2) GA, FL); 76.8 *Ischyrus* Lacordaire (6 app. (1), (2), (3), (5)); 76.9 *Haematochiton* Gorham (2 spp. (3) AZ)]

Fig. 24.142.

77. PHALACRIDAE (Shining Flower Beetle Family)

Length: 1–3 mm. Oval, convex; brown to black; head deflexed; antennae eleven-segmented with a loose three-segmented club; tarsi with five tarsomeres, the fourth small. Larvae live on flowers, especially those of Compositae, and in the spikes of grass that has been attacked by grain rust. Adults are found in decaying vegetation. There are 124 species in the U.S. and Canada, assigned to 13 genera. The group is poorly known.

77.1 *Phalacrus* Paykull

Twenty-four species, the following of which is common:

P. politus Melsheimer (Smut Beetle). (See Fig. 24.143.) (1) n.e. US; (2) s.e. US; (5) MO.

[77.2 *Phalacropsis* Casey (1 sp., *P. dispar* (LeConte) (5) CO); 77.3 *Olibrus* Erichson (30 spp.); 77.4 *Tinodemus* Guillebeau (1 sp., *T. grouvellei* Guillebeau (1) MI); 77.5 *Olibroporus* Casey (1 sp., *O. punctatus* Casey (2) FL); 77.6 *Litolibrus* Sharp (2 spp. (2), (3)); 77.7 *Acylomus* Sharp (20 spp.); 77.8 *Stilbus* Seidlitz (34 spp. (1), (2), (3), (5)); 77.9 *Leptostilbus* Casey (3 spp. (2), (3)); 77.10 *Litochrus* Erichson (4 spp. (1), (2), (3)); 77.11 *Gorginus* Guillebeau (1 sp., *G. rubens* LeConte (1) IN; (2) NC, FL); 77.12 *Litochropus* Casey (2 spp. (1) DC; (2) NC, FL); 77.13 *Ochrolitus* Sharp (1 sp., *O. tristriatus* Casey (2) FL)]

78. CERYLONIDAE (Minute Bark Beetle Family)

Length: 2–3 mm. Black or brown, elongate or oval, flat or convex; tarsomeres 4-4-4 or 3-3-3; antennae with ten segments, the apical segment enlarged. Adults and larvae live under bark. There are 17 species in the U.S. and Canada.

Fig. 24.143.

Subfamily Euxestinae

[78.1 *Hypodacne* LeConte (1 sp., *H. punctata* LeConte (1) MI, ON, IN, OH, NY, PA, NJ, MD, DC; (2) VA, KY, TN, NC, SC, AR, MS, FL; (3) TX; (5) IA, KS, MO)]

Subfamily Anommatinae

[78.2 *Anommatus* Wesmael (1 sp., *A. duodecimstriatus* Mueller (1) IL, OH, NY (Introduced))]

Subfamily Murmidiinae

[78.3 *Murmidius* (1 spp. *M. ovalis* Beck (1) ON, NY, IL, MD, DC; (2) AR, LA, FL; (5) KS); 78.4 *Mychocerus* Erichson (2 spp. (1), (2), (3)); 78.5 *Botrodus* Casey (1 sp., *B. estriatus* Casey (2) FL; (3) TX)]

Subfamily Ostomopsinae

[78.5a *Ostomopsis* Scott (1 sp. *O. neotropicalis* Lawrence and Stephan (2) FL)]

Subfamily Ceryloninae

[78.6 *Philothermus* Aubé (3 spp. (1), (2), (3), (5)); 78.7 *Cerylcautomus* Sen Gupta and Crowson (1 sp., *C. floridensis* Sen Gupta and Crowson (2) FL); 78.8 *Lapethus* Casey (2 spp. (2), (3)); 78.9 *Cerylon* Latreille (5 spp.))]

79. CORYLOPHIDAE (Minute Fungus Beetle Family)

Length: 0.5–5 mm (usually under 3 mm). Elongate, cylindrical, or oval; dark, sometimes with pale markings; head covered by expanded pronotum; antennae nine- to eleven-segmented, with a three-segmented club. Adults are found under decaying bark of trees, in rotting fungus-covered plant material, or in excrement. They are either fungus feeders or predacious. Sixty species in 11 genera occur in the U.S. and Canada.

Subfamily Corylophinae

[79.1 *Bathona* Casey (4 spp. (1), (2)); 79.2 *Corylophodes* Matthews (5 spp. (1), (2), (3)); 79.3 *Gronevus* Casey (5 spp. (1), (2), (5))]

Subfamily Orthoperinae

[79.4 *Rypobius* LeConte (2 spp. (1), (2)); 79.5 *Eutrilia* Casey (1 sp., *E. brunnea* Casey (3) CA); 79.6 *Orthoperus* Stephens (12 spp.)]

Subfamily Sericoderinae

[79.7 *Sericoderus* Stephens (5 spp.)]

Subfamily Saciinae

[79.8 *Sacium* LeConte (6 spp. (2), (4), (5)); 79.9 *Molamba* Casey (10 spp. (1), (2), (3), (5), including *M. lunata* LeConte (Fig. 24.144) (1) MA, CT; (2) FL; (5) MD); 79.10 *Arthrolips* Wollaston (8 spp. (1), (2), (3), (5))]

Fig. 24.144.

Subfamily **Aenigmaticinae**

[79.11 *Aenigmaticum* Matthews (2 spp., (2), (3))]

80. COCCINELLIDAE (Ladybird Beetle Family)

Length: 0.8–10 mm. Round, convex; body usually red, orange, brown, or shiny black, with various markings including white spots; head hidden above by the expanded pronotum; tarsi with four tarsomeres, the first and second dilated and the third very small.

The larvae of most species are carnivorous and live exposed on vegetation; a few species are leaf feeders and sometimes become pests—the "black sheep" of the otherwise valuable family. The adults feed voraciously on mites, plant lice, scale insects, thrips, and other insects, including insects eggs (see Fig. 24.145).

The ladybird beetles, or ladybugs as they are often called, are among the most beneficial of all animals because they feed on destructive wild plant bugs as well as "domesticated" crop pests, thus taking part in the proper functioning of an ecosystem. They are rather difficult to identify to species despite their often striking color patterns, because of the great variation of these patterns within any given population. Many species have been imported in an attempt to control crop pests; some of these have become established and others probably not. Those that are established have been given common names. There are 399 species recorded in the U.S. and Canada, assigned to 53 genera.

Subfamily **Sticholotinae**

Tribe **Serangiini**

[80.1 *Dephastus* Casey (4 spp. (1), (2), (3))]

Tribe **Sticholotini**

[80.2 *Microweisea* Cockerell (8 spp. (1), (2), (3)); 80.3 *Nipus* Casey (4 spp. (3) CA, AZ; (4) UT; (5) CO); 80.4 *Gnathoweisea* Gordon (2 spp. (3) CA, AZ)]

Subfamily **Scymninae**

Tribe **Scymnini**

[80.5 *Stethorus* Weise (5 spp. (1), (2), (3)); 80.6 *Scymnus* Kugelann: 2 subgenera: *Scymnus* s. str. (13 spp.) and *Pullus* Mulsant (81 spp.); 80.7 *Nephus* Mulsant: 4 subgenera: *Nephus* s. str. (1 sp., *N. ornatus ornatus* (LeConte, and *N. o. naviculatus* (Casey) (1) n.e. US), *Turboscymnus* Gordon (1 sp., *N. georgei* (Weise) (1) ON; (3) n. CA; (4) OR, ID; (5)

Fig. 24.145.

AB), *Scymnobius* Casey (9 spp.), and *Depressoscymnus* Gordon (1 sp., *N. schwartzi* Gordon (3) s. AZ); 80.8 *Diomus* Mulsant (16 spp. (1), (2), (3), (5)); 80.9 *Selvadius* Casey (3 spp. (3) CA, AZ, NM; (4) UT; 80.10 *Didion* Casey (1 sp., *D. longulum* Casey (4) BC, WA, OR); 80.11 *Blaisdelliana* Gordon (1 sp., *B. vanduzeei* Gordon (4) UT; 80.12 *Nephaspis* Casey (1 sp., *N. amnicola* Wingo (5) IA); 80.13 *Cryptolaemus* Mulsant (1 sp., *C. montrouzieri* Mulsant (3) CA)]

Tribe **Ortalliini**

[80.14 *Cephaloscymus* Crotch (4 spp. (1), (2), (3))]

Tribe **Hyperaspini**

[80.15 *Hyperaspis* Chevrolat (87 spp.); 80.16 *Hyperaspidius* Crotch (28 spp.)); 80.17 *Brachiacantha* Chevrolat (23 spp.)); 80.18 *Thalassa* Mulsant (1 sp., *T. montezumae* Mulsant (2) LA; (3) AZ, NM); 80.19 *Helesius* Casey (2 spp. (3) TX; (5) CO)]

Tribe **Scymnillini**

[80.20 *Zagloba* Casey (1 sp., *Z. ornata* Casey (3) CA); 80.21 *Scymnillus* Horn (2 spp. (2) FL; (3) CA, AZ; (4) WA, OR, ID)]

Subfamily **Chilocorinae**

Tribe **Chilocorini**

[80.22 *Axion* Mulsant (4 spp. (1), (2), (3))]

80.23 *Chilocorus* Leach

Three species in (1), (2), (3), including the following:

C. *stigma* (Say) (Twice-stabbed Lady Beetle).

[80.24 *Exochomus* Redtenbacher (4 spp. (1), (2), (3)); 80.25 *Arawana* Leng (1 sp., *A. arizonica* Casey (3) AZ)]

80.26 *Brumoides* Chapin

Seven species in (3) CA; (4) NV, UT; (5) CO, including the following:

B. *suturalis* (Fabricius) (Threestriped Lady Beetle). (1) ON; (3) TX; (4) NV; (5) MB.

80.27 *Halmus* Mulsant

One species, as follows:

H. *chalybeus* (Boisduval) (Steel-blue Lady Beetle). (3) CA.

Subfamily **Coccidulinae**

Tribe **Coccidulini**

[80.28 *Coccidula* Kugelann (2 spp. (1), (4), (5)); 80.29 *Lindorus* Casey (1 sp., *L. lophantae* Blaisdell (3) CA)]

80.30 *Rhyzobius* Stephens

One species, as follows:

R. *ventralis* (Erichson) (Black Lady Beetle). (3) CA.

Tribe **Exoplectrini**

[80.31 *Exoplectra* Chevrolat (1 sp., *E. subaenescens* Gorham (3) AZ)]

Tribe **Noviini**

[80.32 *Anovia* Casey (1 sp., *A. virginalis* Wickham (3) TX; (4) UT)]

80.33 *Rodolia* Mulsant

One species, as follows:

R. cardinalis Mulsant (Vedalia). Introduced from Australia; feeds on the Cottony-cushion scale (a citrus pest). (2) FL; (3) CA.

[80.34 *Novius* Mulsant (1 sp., *N. koebelei* Coquilett (3) CA)]

Subfamily Coccinellinae

Tribe Coccinellini

[80.35 *Anatis* Mulsand (3 spp.); 80.36 *Myzia* Mulsant (3 spp. (1), (3), (4), (5)); 80.37 *Calvia* Mulsant (1 sp., *C. quatuordecimguttata* Linnaeus (1), (4), (5))]

80.38 *Adalia* Mulsant

One species, as follows:

A. bipunctata (Linnaeus) (Two-spotted Lady Beetle). L. 3.5–5.5 mm. Orange with a black discal spot on each elytron; side margins of the pronotum broadly ivory without an enclosing black spot. Hibernates, often in houses. (1) n.e. US; (4) Pacific n.w.; (5) n. Central States.

[80.39 *Anisosticta* Dejean (2 spp. (1), (4), (5))]

80.40 *Olla* Casey

One species, as follows:

O. sayi (Crotch) (Ash-gray Ladybird Beetle). L. 3–6 mm. Ash-gray to pale yellow with black spots on the pronotum and elytra. Adults and larvae feed on aphids. (See A&J 139.) (1) n.e. US; (2) s.e. US; (3) s.w. US.

80.41 *Cycloneda* Crotch

Four species, including the following:

C. polita Casey (Casey's Ladybird Beetle). L. 4–5 mm. Head of male white; female with black median spot; pronotum black except for front and side margins, which are broadly white, and median posterior region, which is white to varying width; elytra blood red, with small paler area on each side of the scutellum, very rarely entirely yellow. (See A&J 142.) (3) CA, TX; (4) BC, ID; (5) CO.

80.42 *Coccinella* Linnaeus

Thirteen species, including the following:

C. novemnotata Herbst (Nine-spotted Ladybird Beetle). L. 5–8 mm. Head and pronotum black with pale yellowish margins; elytra orange to reddish yellow, each with four black spots; scutellum black, the spot extending onto the elytra. Adults and larvae feed on apids, especially on field crops. (See Fig. 24.146.) (1) n.e. US; (2) VA, NC, SC, GA; (3) TX.

C. septempunctata Linnaeus. L. 5–8 mm. Feeds on apids. (See Fig. 24.147.) Recently established in (1) s.e. CT, s. NY, n. NJ, n. DE.

C. transversoguttata richardsoni Brown (Transverse Lady Beetle). (1) n.e. NA.

80.43 *Hippodamia* Chevrolat

Thirteen species, including the following:

H. convergens Guerin (Convergent Lady Beetle). L. 4.5–6.5 mm. Head, legs, and pronotum black, the latter with a

Fig. 24.146.

whitish margin and the disk with two convergent white lines; elytra red, each with six black spots, the anterior three smaller than the posterior three. Common on stems and foliage of weeds and cultivated crops; hibernates under mullein leaves along borders of cultivated fields. (See A&J 140.) (1) n.e. US; (2) s.e. US; (3) s.w. US.

H. sinuata Mulsant (Sinuate Lady Beetle). (3) CA.

H. tredecimpunctata tibialis (Say) (Thirteen-spotted Lady Beetle). (1) n.e. NA; (3) CA; (4) Pacific n.w. (5) ND, MN.

[80.44 *Ceratomegilla* Crotch (1 sp., *C. ulkei* Crotch (1), (3), (5))]

80.45 *Coleomegilla* Timberlake

One species, as follows:

C. maculata (De Geer). L. 5–6.5 mm. Red; head margined with black; pronotum with two black spots; elytra each with six black spots. Both carnivorous and fungivorous; feeds on weeds and crops; hibernates under rubbish and mullein leaves. (1) n.e. US; (2) s.e. US; (3) CA, TX.

[80.46 *Paranaemia* Casey (1 sp., *P. vittigera* (Mannerheim) (3) CA, AZ, NM, TX; (5) CO, KS); 80.47 *Macronaemia* Casey (1 sp., *M. episcopalis* (Kirby) (1) n.e. US; (3) CA; (5) WY, CO, KS); 80.48 *Mulsantina* Weise (3 spp. (1), (3), (4), (5)); 80.49 *Naemia* Mulsant (1 sp., *N. seriata* (Melsheimer (1) n.e. US; (2) s.e. US; (3) s.w. US); 80.50 *Neoharmonia* Crotch (5 spp. (1), (2), (3), (5))]

Tribe Psylloborini

[80.51 *Psyllobora* Chevrolat (8 spp. (1), (2), (3), (4))]

Fig. 24.147.

Subfamily Epilachninae

Tribe Epilachnini

80.52 *Epilachna* Chevrolat

Three species, as follows:

E. borealis (Fabricius) (Squash Beetle). L. 7–8.5 mm. Pale orange-yellow, shiny; pronotum and elytra with many black spots. Larvae feed on the under surface of the leaves of squash and other cucurbits; adults feed on the upper surface. Hibernates gregariously under leaves. (See Fig. 24.148.) (1) n.e. US; (2) s.e. US.

E. varivestis Mulsant (Mexican Bean Beetle). L. 6–8 mm. Similar to the preceding but pronotum without black spots. A pest on beans. (1) n.e. US; (2) s.e. US; (3) AZ, TX; (4) ID, NV, UT; (5) WY, SC, CO, IA, MO.

E. tredecimnotata Latreille. (3) s. AZ, s. TX.

Tribe Madaini

80.53 *Subcoccinella* Huebner

One species, as follows:

S. vigintiquatuorpunctata (Linnaeus) (Jacques' Beetle). Recently introduced. Found feeding on foliage of bouncing bet and other plants. (1) e. PA, s. NY, n. NJ.

81. ENDOMYCHIDAE (Handsome Fungus Beetle Family)

Length 1–10 mm (usually 4–8 mm). Black with reddish or pale markings; tarsi with four tarsomeres, the third usually minute; antennae eight- to eleven-segmented with a loose three-segmented club; pronotum with two longitudinal grooves. The family somewhat resembles the Coccinelidae, but its pronotal grooves serve to distinguish the two. Found beneath bark in fungus and rotten wood, in dung, and in decayed moldy fruit. There are 32 species in the U.S. and Canada.

Subfamily Mycetaeinae

[81.1 *Anamorphus* LeConte (2 spp. (1) OH; (2) FL); 81.2 *Rhymbomicrus* Casey (1 sp., *R. lobatus* LeConte and Horn (1) DC); 81.3 *Clemmus* Hampe (1 sp., *C. minor* Crotch (1) IL, IN, DC; (2) LA, GA; (5) KS); 82.4 *Bystus* Guérin (1 sp., *B. ulkei* Crotch (1) IN, DC; (2) FL); 81.5 *Mycetaea* Stephens (1 sp., *M. hirta* Marsham (1) MI, NY, MA, PA, MD); 81.6 *Symbiotes* Redtenbacher (3 spp. (1) MI, NY, IN, OH, PA;

(2) FL; (3) CA; (5) KS, CO); 81.7 *Rhanidea* Strohecker (1 sp., *R. unicolor* Ziegler (1) IN; (2) s.e. US); 81.8 *Phymaphora* Newman (2 spp. (1) n.e. US; (2) s.e. US; (3) CA; (5) MB); 81.9 *Stethorhanis* Blaisdell (2 spp., (3) CA; (4) BC)]

Subfamily Xenomycetinae

[81.10 *Xenomycetes* Horn (2 spp. (4) WA, NV))]

Subfamily Eumorphinae

[81.11 *Lycoperdina* Latreille (1 sp., *L. ferruginea* LeConte (1) CT; (2) s.e. US; (5) MN); 81.12 *Aphorista* Gorham (3 spp. (1) CT; (2) s.e. US; (3) s.e. US; (5) MB, CO); 81.13 *Mycetina* Mulsant (3 spp. (1), (3) CA; (4), (5)]

Subfamily Stenotarsinae

[81.14 *Danae* Reiche (1 sp., *D. testacea* Ziegler (1) CT; (2) s.e. US); 81.15 *Stenotarsus* Perty (2 spp. (1) OH, CT; (2) NC, LA, FL)]

81.16 *Epipocus* Germar

Three species in (1), (2), (3), including the following:

E. cinctus LeConte. L. 7–9 mm. Reddish orange; pronotum with dark spots; elytra each with a broad dark stripe and apices truncate, but extending beyond apex of abdomen. Found on fungi. (3) TX.

Subfamily Endomychinae

81.17 *Endomychus* Panzer

Two species in (1), (2), (5), including the following:

E. bigittatus (Say). (See Fig. 24.149.) (1) n.e. US; (2) s.e. US; (5) n. Central States.

Insertis sedis

[81.18 *Eidoreus* Sharp (=*Eupsilobius* Casey) (1 sp., *E. politus* Casey (2) s. FL, tentatively moved from Colydiidae to this family)]

82. LATHRIDIIDAE (Minute Brown Scavenger Beetle Family)

Length: 1–3 mm. Elongate-oval; body brown to black; tarsi with three tarsomeres (some species have front, and some front and middle, legs with two tarsomeres); elytra distinctly striate-punctate. Larvae and adults of most species live in moldy plant or animal materials, often in moldy stored food. There are 120 species reported in the U.S. and Canada.

Fig. 24.148.

Fig. 24.149.

Fig. 24.150.

Subfamily Lathridiinae

[82.1 *Holoparamecus* Curtis (6 spp. (1), (2), (3), (5)); 82.2 *Metophthalmus* Wollaston (6 spp. (2), (3), (4))]

82.3 *Lathridius* Herbst

Eight species, including the following:

L. minutus (Linnaeus) (Squarenosed Fungus Beetle). (See Fig. 24.150.) Cosmopolitan.

[82.4 *Enicmus* Thomson (12 spp.); 82.5 *Microgramme* Walkley (2 spp.); 82.6 *Stephostethus* LeConte (6 spp. (1), (3), (4), (5)); 82.7 *Adistemia* Fall (1 sp., *A. watsoni* Wollaston (1) DC); 82.8 *Eufallia* Muttkowski (1 sp., *E. seminiveus* (Motschulsky) (2) FL); 82.9 *Revelieria* Perris (1 sp., *R. californica* Fall (3) CA)]

82.10 *Cartodere* Thomson

Five species, including the following:

C. constricta (Gyllenhal) (Plaster Beetle). Cosmopolitan.

[82.11 *Aridius* Motschulsky (2 spp. (2), (3), (4))]

82.12 *Thes* Semenov-Tian-Shanski

Two species, including the following:

T. bergrothi (Reitter) (Ridgewinged Fungus Beetle). (1) Greenland; ? elsewhere.

Subfamily Corticariinae

[82.13 *Corticaria* Marsham (35 spp.); 82.14 *Melanophthalma* Motschulsky (32 spp.); 82.15 *Fuchsina* Fall (1 sp., *F. occulata* Fall (3) CA)]

83. BIPHYLLIDAE (False Skin Beetle Family)

Length: 2–4 mm. Brownish; similar to the species of the preceding family but the tarsi have five tarsomeres; pronotum with five raised lines on each side of the disk. These beetles live in fungus or under bark. There are five species in the U.S. and Canada.

[83.1 *Anchorius* Casey (1 sp., *A. lineatus* Casey (3) AZ); 83.2 *Diplocoelus* Guérin (4 spp. (1), (2), (3))]

84. BYTURIDAE (Fruitworm Beetle Family)

Length: 3.5–4.5 mm (rarely to 8 mm). Elongate-oval; pale brown to dark orange; densely covered with fine pubescence; antennae with three-segmented club; tarsi with five tarsomeres. Larvae feed on fruit heads of raspberry, blackberry, and a variety of other flowers; adults also frequent these plants. There are five species in the U.S. and Canada.

[84.1 *Byturellus* Barber (1 sp., *B. grisescens* Janye (3) CA; (4) OR)]

Fig. 24.151.

84.2 *Byturus* Latreille

Four species, the following of which are pests:

B. rubi Barber (Eastern Raspberry Fruitworm). (1) PQ, MD; (5) AB.

B. bakeri Barber (Western Raspberry Fruitworm). (See Fig. 24.151.) (4) ?BC, WA.

Superfamily TENEBRIONOIDEA

85. MONOMMATIDAE (Opossum Beetle Family)

Length: 5–12 mm. Oval; black; antennae with a two- or three-segmented club; pronotum narrowed in front with borders distinctly margined; legs retractile; front and middle tarsi with five tarsomeres, hind tarsi with four. Larvae live under rotten wood; some bore into the roots and stalks of agave. Adults are found on grass, dead twigs, under rotten cactus leaves, or in leaf debris. There are eight species in the U.S.

[85.1 *Hyporhagus* Thomson (7 spp. (2) FL; (3) CA, AZ, TX); 85.2 *Aspathines* Champion (1 sp., *A. ovatus* Champion (2) FL)]

86. CEPHALOIDAE (False Long-horned Beetle Family)

Length: 8–20 mm. These beetles resemble some of the lepturine long-horned beetles; brownish to dark with pale markings; pronotum narrowed in front; tarsi with tarsomeres 5-5-4; tarsal claws pectinate with a fleshy ventral lobe beneath each. Adults are found in flowers. There are ten species in the U.S. and Canada.

Subfamily Cephaloinae

[86.1 *Cephaloon* Newman (6 spp.)]

Subfamily Stenotrachelinae

[86.2 *Stenotrachelus* Latreille (1 sp., *S. aeneus* Fabricius (1) n.e. NA; (4) AK; (5) NW); 86.3 *Anelpistus* Horn (2 spp. (1) NH; (4) BC)]

Subfamily Nematoplinae

[86.4 *Nematoplus* LeConte (1 sp., *N. collaris* LeConte (1) MI)]

87. TENEBRIONIDAE (Darkling Beetle Family)

Length: 2–35 mm. Most species black, some with white or red markings, rarely reddish or brownish; body hard; pronotum margined; tarsi with tarsomeres 5-5-5; tarsomeres usually without large pads; claws simple. Many species may be confused with the Carabidae, but the tarsal formula will serve to separate them.

The adults and larvae are found in almost every kind of habitat except water. None is known to be aquatic, but many species inhabit the exactly opposite environment, the desert. In fact, only about 150 species are found outside the arid southwest. This is characteristic of the species throughout the world. A few are important pests in stored products; some inhabit termite and ant nests; others are found in rotting wood, fungi, debris, under logs and stones, in dung or seeds; a few bore into living plant roots and tubers as larvae; some are found on flowers.

Their classification is complicated by the many subfamilies, tribes, and a large number of genera, the result, no doubt, of the great morphological diversity of the species. Even so, the features used to distinguish genera and species are difficult to recognize. Identification can sometimes be made by shape, but this needs to be carefully checked.

There are 1008 species in the U.S. and Canada, assigned to 176 genera. Some of the subfamilies—for example, Zophorinae—have been treated as separate families by virtue of valid characteristics. For the sake of consistency, however, these are not so treated here, but rather as subfamilies at the end of the classification list.

Subfamily Pimeliinae

Tribe Cnemodinini

[87.1 *Cnemodinus* Cockerell (3 spp. (3) CA, AZ; (4) UT); 87.2 *Polemiotus* Casey (1 sp., *P. submetallicus* (LeConte) (3) AZ, NM); 87.3 *Metopoloba* Casey (3) CA, AZ; (4) NV, UT); 87.4 *Bothrotes* (4 spp.); 87.5 *Lobometopon* Casey (2 spp. (3) AZ, NM, TX; (4) NV, UT; (5) KS, NE); 87.6 *Pechalius* (4 spp. (3) AZ, NM); 87.7 *Epitragodes* Casey (1 sp., *E. tomentosus* (LeConte) (2) GA, FL); 87.8 *Phegoneus* Casey (1 sp., *P. juelichi* (Casey) (3) TX); 87.9 *Schoenicus* LeConte (1 sp., *S. puberlus* LeConte (1) NY; (2) GA, FL); 87.10 *Conoecus* Horn (1 sp., *C. ovipennis* Horn (2) LA; (3) TX)]

Tribe Eurymetopini

[87.11 *Eurymetopon* Eschscholtz (2 spp. (3) CA); 87.12 *Metoponium* Casey: 2 subgenera: *Metoponium* s. str. and *Metoponiopsis* Casey (51 spp. (3) CA, AZ, NM, TX; (4) NV, UT); 87.13 *Telabis* (32 spp. (3) CA, AZ, NM, TX; (4) NV, UT); 87.14 *Cryptadius* LeConte (5 spp. (3) s. CA, TX); 87.15 *Armalia* Casey (2 spp. (3) TX); 87.16 *Hylocrinus* Casey: 3 subgenera: *Hylocrinus* s. str., *Paravius* Casey, and *Locrodes* Casey (12 spp. (3) CA, AZ; (4) NV, UT); 87.17 *Steriphanus* Casey (12 spp. (3) AZ, NM, TX; (5) NE)]

Tribe Auchmobiini

[87.18 *Auchmobius* LeConte (8 spp. (3) CA; (4) NV)]

Tribe Trimytini

[87.19 *Trimytis* LeConte: 2 subgenera *Trimytis* s. str and *Pimalius* Casey (6 spp. (3) AZ, NM, TX; (5) CO); 87.20 *Prometopion* Casey (2 spp. (3) CA, AZ, TX); 87.21 *Chilometopon* Horn (5 spp. (3) CA, TX; (4) NV, UT)]

Tribe Trientomini

[87.22 *Trientoma* Solier (1 sp., *T. wickhami* Casey (2) ?FL)]

Tribe Triorophini

[87.23 *Triorophus* LeConte (21 spp. (3) CA, AZ, TX; (4) NV); 87.24 *Micromes* Casey (2 spp. (3) s. CA); 87.25 *Trichiotes* Casey (1 sp., *T. seriatus* Casey (3) TX); 87.26 *Oxygonodera* Casey (3 spp. (4) UT); 87.27 *Stibia* Horn: subgenus Eutriorophus Casey (4 spp. (3) CA, AZ); 87.28 *Eschatomoxys* Blaisdell (2 spp. (3) CA; (4) UT)]

Tribe Adesmiini

[87.29 *Edrotes* LeConte (4 spp. (3) CA, AZ, NM, TX; (4) UT; (5) CO)]

Tribe Craniotini

[87.30 *Craniotus* LeConte (2 spp. (3) CA, AZ; (4) NV)]

Tribe Stenosini

[87.31 *Araeoschizus* LeConte (12 spp. (3) CA, AZ, NM, TX; (4) UT, NV, ID; (5) WY)]

Tribe Typhlusechini

[87.32 *Typhlusechus* Linell (1 sp., *T. singularis* Linell (3) s. CA)]

Tribe Batuliini

[87.33 *Batulius* LeConte (1 sp., *B. setosus* LeConte (3) s. CA, AZ); 87.34 *Batuliodes* Casey (1 sp., *B. rotundicollis* (LeConte) (3) s. CA)]

Tribe Anepsiini

[87.35 *Anepsius* LeConte (7 spp. (3) CA, AZ; (4) NV, UT; (5) CO)]

Tribe Vacronini

[87.36 *Alaephus* Horn (11 spp. (3) CA, AZ, NM; (4) NV, UT); 87.37 *Eupsophulus* Cockerell (2 spp. (3) CA, AZ); 87.38 *Vacronus* Casey (1 sp., *V. tenuicornis* Casey (3) CA)]

Tribe Belopini

[87.39 *Adelonia* Laporte (1 sp., *A. sulcatulus* (Champion) (3) TX)]

Tribe Nyctoporini

[87.40 *Nyctoporis* Eschscholtz (8 spp. (3) CA)]

Tribe Cryptoglossini

[87.41 *Centrioptera* Mannerheim (10 spp. (3) CA, AZ; (4) NV, UT); 87.42 *Schizillus* Horn (6 spp., (3) CA, AZ; (4) NV); 87.43 *Cryptoglossa* Solier (5 spp. (3) CA, AZ, NM, TX; (4) NV); 87.44 *Threnus* Motschulsky (1 sp., *T. niger* Motschulsky (3) CA); 87.45 *Eschatoporis* Blaisdell (1 sp., *E. numenmacheri* Blaisdell (3) CA)]

Tribe Asidini

[87.46 *Astrotus* LeConte (3 spp. (3) TX); 87.47 *Stenosides* Solier (7 spp. (3) AZ, NM, TX; (5) CO, KS); 87.48 *Microschatia* Solier (4 spp. (3) CA, AZ, NM, TX); 87.49 *Pycnonotida* Casey (5 spp. (3) CA)]

87.50 *Glyptasida* Casey

Twelve species [found in (3) AZ, NM, TX; (4) UT; (5) AB, MT, WY, SD, NE, CO, KS], including the following:

G. costipennis (LeConte) (Desert Darkling Beetle). L. 15–20 mm. Moderately convex; black; surface rough and opaque; prothorax nearly twice as wide as long, with somewhat rounded sides; surface coarsely and confluently punctate throughout. Adults frequent desert areas; they are usually active at night but do not come to lights. (See A&J 143.) (3) AZ.

[87.51 *Philolithus* Lacordaire (23 spp. (3) CA, AZ, NM; (4) BC, WA, OR, NV, UT); 87.52 *Gonasida* Casey (6 spp. (3) AZ, NM, TX; (4) OR, NV, UT, ID; (5) WY, NE, CO, KS); 87.53 *Parasida* Casey (2 spp. (3) AZ, NM); 87.54 *Pycnomorpha* Motschulsky (1 sp., *P. californica* Motschulsky (3) CA); 87.55 *Stenomorpha* Solier (61 spp. (3) CA, AZ, NM, TX; (4) WA, OR, ID; (5) CO, KS, NE); 87.56 *Asidina* Casey (6 spp. (3) CA, AZ, NM; (4) NV); 87.57 *Trichiasida* Casey (11 spp. (3) CA, AZ, TX; (4) NV, UT, ID); 87.58 *Litasida* Casey (1 sp., *L. townsendi* Casey (3) AZ)); 87.59 *Asidopsis* Casey (21 spp. (3) CA, AZ, NM, TX; (4) UT; (5) AB, SA, MT, SD, NE, CO, KS); 87.60 *Megasida* Casey (2 spp. (3) AZ, NM, TX); 87.61 *Stethasida* Casey (18 spp. (3) CA, AZ)]

Tribe Praocini

[87.62 *Praocis* Eschscholtz (1 sp., *P. sellata* Berg, subspecies *bruchi* Kulzer (3) CA)]

Tribe Coniontini

[87.63 *Branchus* LeConte (1 sp., *B. floridanus* LeConte (2) FL; (3) TX)]

87.64 *Coelus* Eschscholtz

Four species in (3) CA; (4) BC, WA, OR, including the following:

C. ciliatus Eschscholtz (Round Darkling Beetle). L. 5.5–7.5 mm. Oval; dark brown to black; sides of body with long, pale, hairlike setae; surface shiny and coarsely punctate. Common in the sand of ocean beaches. (See A&J 144.) (3) CA; (4) BC, WA, OR.

[87.65 *Coniontis* Eschscholtz (51 spp. (3) CA, AZ; (4) BC, WA, OR, UT; (5) MT, CO); 87.66 *Eusattus* LeConte (17 spp. (3) CA, AZ, NM, TX; (4) WA, OR; (5) CO, KS, MO)]

Subfamily Diaperinae

Tribe Bolitophagini

87.67 *Bolitotherus* Candez

One species, as follows:

B. cornutus (Panzer) (Horned Fungus Beetle). L. 6.5–8.5 mm. Brownish to black; body tuberculate; head an thorax of male with horns. Found on woody fungus. (See Fig. 24.152.) (1) IL, IN, OH, PA, CT; (2) NC, MS, FL; (3) TX.

[87.68 *Bolitophagus* Illiger (1 sp., *B. corticola* Say (1), IN, OH, PA, CT); 87.69 *Eleates* Casey (3 spp. (1) MI, ME, PA; (3) CA; (4) BC, WA, OR); 87.70 *Megeleates* Casey (1 sp., *M. sequoiarum* Casey (3) CA)]

Tribe Rhipidandrini

[87.71 *Rhipidandrus* LeConte (2 spp. (1), (2))]

Tribe Diaperini

[87.72 *Diaperis* Mueller (4 spp. (1), (2), (3), (5))]

Fig. 24.152.

Subfamily Phrenapatinae

Tribe Phrenapatini

[87.73 *Dioedus* LeConte (1 sp., *D. punctatus* LeConte (1), (2), (3), (5)); 87.74 *Phthora* Mulsant (1 sp., *P. americana* Horn (3) CA; (4) BC, WA; 95) MT)]

Subfamily Tenebrioninae

Tribe Tenebrionini

87.75 *Alobates* Motschulsky

Two species, including the following:

A. pennsylvanica (De Geer) (False Mealworm). L. 20–23 mm. Elongate-oval and subconvex; black; surface barely shiny; pronotum nearly square; elytra marked with five rows of punctures. Adults and larvae are found throughout the year beneath bark and logs where they feed upon other insects. (See Fig. 24.153 and A&J 147.) (1), (2), (3), (4), (5).

[87.76 *Biomorphus* Motschulsky (1 sp., *B. tuberculatus* Motschulsky (3) CA); 87.77 *Bius* Mulsant (1 sp., *B. estriatus* (LeConte) (3) CA, AZ, NM; (4) UT); 87.78 *Centronopus* Solier (2 spp. (1), (2), (5)); 87.79 *Cibdelis* Mannerheim (5 spp. (3) CA); 87.80 *Coelocnemis* Mannerheim (6 spp. (3), (4), (5)); 87.81 *Glyptotus* LeConte (1 sp., *G. cribratus* LeConte (2) FL; (3) TX); 87.82 *Haplandrus* LeConte (5 spp. (1, (2)); 87.83 *Idiobates* Casey (1 sp., *I. casteneus* (Knoch)); 87.84 *Iphthiminus* Spilman (1 sp., *I. laevissimus* (Casey) (3) CA)); 87.85 *Merinus* LeConte (1 sp., *M. laevis* (Olivier) (1) MI, IN, OH, NJ; (2) GA, FL); 87.86 *Metaclisa* Jacquelin du Val (1 sp., *M. marginalis* Horn (3) CA); 87.87 *Neatus* LeConte (1 sp., *N. tenebrioides* Beauvios) (1) WI, MI, ON, IL, IN, OH, PA, NJ, MD; (2) WV, NC, FL; (3) CA; (4) MO); 87.88 *Oenopion* Champion (1 sp., *O. zopheroides* (Horn)); 87.89 *Polopinus* Casey (2 spp. (2) GA, FL); 87.90 *Polypleurus* Eschscholtz (2 spp. (1), (2), (3)); 87.91 *Scotobaenus* LeConte (4 spp. (3) CA)]

87.92 *Tenebrio* Linnaeus

Two species, as follows:

T. molitor Linnaeus (Yellow Mealworm). L. 13–16 mm. Body dark reddish brown to black and shiny; pronotal punctures more or less distinct; elytral striae and punctures indistinct. Found in stored grain and grain products. Cosmopolitan.

T. obscurus Fabricius (Dark Mealworm). Similar to the preceding but pronotal punctures very dense and confluently punctate. Found in granaries, storehouses, and barns. Cosmopolitan.

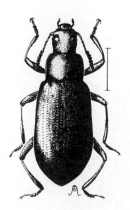

Fig. 24.153.

[87.93 *Upis* Fabricius (1 sp., *U. ceramboides* (Linnaeus) (1) WI, MI, NY, VT, NM, ME; (4) AK; (5) MT, WY, SD)); 87.94 *Xylopinus* LeConte (2 sp. (1), (2), (3), (5)); 87.95 *Zophobas* Blanchard (2 spp. (2), (3))]

Tribe Platydemini

[87.96 *Neomida* Latreille (2 spp.); 87.97 *Palembus* Casey (1 sp., *P. ocularis* Casey (2) FL); 89.98 *Platydema* Laporte and Brulle (18 spp.); 87.99 *Scaphidema* Redtenbacher (1 sp., *S. aeneolum* (LeConte) (1) MI, NY, NH, ON, PQ, LB, NB, IL, PA, CT; (4) AK, BC; (5) MB, AB, MN); 87.100 *Liodema* Horn (1 sp., *L. laeve* (Haldeman) (2) NC, GA, FL; (3) TX); 87.101 *Apsida* Lacordaire (1 sp., *A. belti* Bates (3) TX)]

87.102 *Alphitophagus* Stephens

One species, as follows:

A. bifasciatus (Say) (Two-banded Fungus Beetle). (1) ON, IL, IN, OH, PA, NY, NJ, MD,; (2) TN, VA, NC, GA, AR; (3) CA, TX; (4) WA, OR, ID; (5) SD, MN, IA, KS, NE, MO.

[87.103 *Pentaphyllus* Dejean (2 spp. (1), (2), (3) CA)]

Tribe Phaleriini

[87.104 *Phaleria* Latreille (7 spp. (1), (2), (3)); 87.105 *Phaleromela* Reitter (5 spp. (3), (4))]

Tribe Ulomini

87.106 *Gnatocerus* Thunberg

Four species in (1), (2), (3), including the following:

G. cornutus (Fabricius) (Broad-horned Flour Beetle).

G. maxillosus (Fabricius) (Slenderhorned Flour Beetle). (See Fig. 24.154.)

87.107 *Cynaeus* LeConte

Two species in (1), (3), (5), including the following:

C. angustus (LeConte) (Larger Black Flour Beetle).

87.108 *Latheticus* Waterhouse

Two species, including the following:

L. oryzae Waterhouse (Longheaded Flour Beetle). Cosmopolitan.

[87.109 *Lyphia* Mulsant and Rey (1 sp., *L. tetraphylla* Fairmaire (Cosmopolitan)]

87.110 *Tribolium* MacLeay

A few species of this genus have been the subject of intensive genetic studies that show that there are many strains of each. Although some have been common names, their taxonomy is

difficult. They are common pests in flour. Many are cosmopolitan. Five species, including the following:

T. audax Halstead (American Black Flour Beetle).

T. castaneum (Herbst) (Red Flour Beetle).

T. confusum J. Duval (Confused Flour Beetle). (See Fig. 24.155.)

87.111 *Palorus* Mulsant

Two species, as follows:

P. ratzeburgi (Wissmann) (Small-eyed Flour Beetle).

P. subdepressus (Wollaston) (Depressed Flour Beetle).

[87.112 *Mycotrogus* Horn (3 spp. (3) CA, AZ); 87.113 *Tharsus* LeConte (1 sp., *T. seditiosus* LeConte (2) NC, AL, FL); 87.114 *Uloma* Dejean (6 spp. (1), (2))]

87.115 *Alphitobius* Stephens

Two species, as follows:

A. diaperinus (Panzer) (Lesser Mealworm). Cosmopolitan.

A. laevigatus (Fabricius) (Black Fungus Beetle). (1) MI, OH, PA, CT; (2) LA, FL; (3) CA, AZ; (4) AK; (5) SD.

[87.116 *Eutochia* LeConte (2 sp, (1), (2), (3)); 87.117 *Sitophagus* Mulsant (1 sp., *S. hololeptoides* (Laporte) (3) TX); 87.118 *Adelina* Dejean (3 spp. (1), (2), (3)); 87.119 *Doliodesmus* Spilman (1 sp., *D. charlesi* Spilman (3) AZ); 87.120 *Hypogena* Laporte (1 sp., *H. marginata* (LeConte)); 87.121 *Corticeus* Piller and Mitterpacher (15 spp.)]

Tribe Helopini

[87.122 *Tarpela* Bates (3 spp. (1), (2)); 87.123 *Nautes* Pascoe (1 sp., *N. viridimicans* Horn (3) FL); 87.124 *Helops* Fabricius (39 spp.); 87.125 *Stenotrichus* LeConte (1 sp., *S. rufipes* (LeConte) (3) CA)]

Tribe Talanini

[87.126 *Talanus* Jacquelin du Val (4 spp. (2), (3)); 87.127 *Meracantha* Kirby (1 sp., *M. contracta* (Beauvois))]

Tribe Amarygmini

[87.128 *Cymatothes* Dejean (2 spp. (2), (3))]

Tribe Strongyliini

[87.129 *Strongylium* Kirby (10 spp. (1), (2), (3), (5))]

Tribe Trachyscelini

[87.130 *Trachyscelis* Latreille (1 sp., *T. flavipes* Melsheimer (2) MS, AL, FL)]

Fig. 24.154.

Fig. 24.155.

Tribe Scaurini

[87.131 *Cerenopus* LeConte (1 sp., *C. concolor* LeConte (3) CA, AZ; (4) NV); 87.132 *Argoporis* Horn (4 spp. (3) AZ, TX); 87.133 *Apsena* LeConte (7 spp. (3) CA); 87.134 *Epantius* LeConte (1 sp., *E. obscurus* LeConte (3) CA); 87.135 *Eulabis* Eschscholtz (1 sp., *E. bicarinata* Eschscholtz (3) CA)]

Tribe Amphidorini

[87.136 *Trichoderulus* Blaisdell (2 spp. (3) AZ); 87.137 *Amphidora* Eschscholtz (3 spp. (3) CA); 87.138 *Cratidus* LeConte (3 spp. (3) CA)]

Tribe Blaptini

[87.139 *Blaps* Fabricius (2 spp. (1), (2))]

Tribe Eleodini

87.140 *Eleodes* Eschscholtz

Adults of this usually desert genus [found in (3), (4), (5)] lift their abdomen to a 45-degree angle and emit a foul, defensive fluid. All species are similar. Of the 121 species, one is of economic importance.

The genus is divided into the following subgenera: *Melaneleodes* Blaisdell, *Litheleodes* Blaisdell, *Tricheleodes* Blaisdell, *Pseudeleodes* Blaisdell, *Promus* LeConte, *Heteropromus* Blaisdell, *Eleodes* s. str., *Blapylis* Horn *Metablapylis* Blaisdell, *Steneleodes* Balisdell, *Holeleodes* Blaisdell, *Discogenia* LeConte. The following species may be noted:

E. (*Pronmus*) *opacus* (Say) (Plains False Wireworm). A pest of wheat seed and young plants, particularly during droughts. (3) AZ, NM, OK, TX; (5) SK, MT, SD, NE, IA, CO, KS.

E. (*Eleodes*) *armatus* LeConte (Desert Skunk Beetle). L. 15–35 mm. Black with a smooth body; apex of elytra attenuate; anterior angles of prothorax acute, prominent, and toothed; femora with long acute teeth. Adults are scavengers; larvae live on the roots of grasses and other plants. (See A&J 146.) (3) CA, AZ; (4) NV, UT.

[87.141 *Trogloderus* LeConte (1 sp., *T. costatus* LeConte (3) CA, AZ; (4) NV, ID); 87.142 *Neobaphion* Blaisdell (2 spp. (3) AZ, NM; (4) NV, UT; (5) CO); 87.143 *Embaphion* Say (7 spp. (3) CA, AZ, NM; (4) NV, UT; (5) WY, ND, NE, CO, KS); 87.144 *Eleodimorpha* Blaisdell (1 sp., *E. bolcan* Blaisdell (3) CA); 87.145 *Lariversius* Blaisdell (1 sp., *L. tibialis* Blaisdell (4) NV)]

Tribe Pedinini

[87.146 *Opatrinus* Latreille (3 spp. (1), (2), (3), (5)); 87.147 [Number not used]; 87.148 *Ulus* Horn (6 spp. (2), (3)); 87.149 *Cybotus* Casey (1 sp., *C. estriatus* (LeConte) (2) FL); 87.150 *Mecysmus* Horn (5 spp. (3)): 87.151 *Aconobius* Casey (3 spp. (3) AZ, NM, TX); 87.152 *Blapstinus* Sturm (28 spp.); 87.153 *Conibius* LeConte (7 spp. (3)); 87.154 *Notibius* LeConte (2 spp. (3), (4)); 87.155 *Nocibiotes* Casey (6 spp. (3)); 87.156 *Tonibius* Casey (1 sp., *T. sulcatus* (LeConte)); 87.155 *Nocibiotes* Casey (6 spp. (3)); 87.156 *Tonibius* Casey (1 sp., *T. sulcatus* (LeConte)); 87.157 *Conibiosoma* Casey (1 sp., *C. elongata* (Horn) (3) CA); 87.158 *Trichoton* Hope (1 sp., *T. sordidum* (LeConte) (3) CA, AZ)]

Tribe Opatrini

[87.159 *Lepidocnemeplatia* Kaszab (1 sp., *L. sericea* (Horn) (3) CA, AZ)); 87.160 *Alaudes* Horn (6 spp. (3) (4)); 87.161 *Cheirodes* Gene (1

sp., *C. californica* (Horn) (3) CA; (4) NV); 87.162 *Gonocephalum* Chevrolat (1 sp., *G. bilineatum* Walker (4) BC (Introduced)); 87.163 *Ephalus* LeConte (1 sp., *L. latimanus* (LeConte) (1), (2)); 87.164 *Cyclosattus* Casey (1 sp., *C. websteri* Casey (5) CO); 87.165 *Pseudephalus* Casey (1 sp., *P. brevicornis* Casey (2) AL); 87.166 *Ammodonus* Mulsant and Rey (2 spp. (1), (3), (5)); 87.167 *Leichenum* Blanchard (1 sp., *L. canaliculatum* (Fabricius), subspecies *variegatum* (Klug) (2) NC, MS, AL, GA, FL (Introduced))]

Subfamily Archaeocrypticinae

[87.168 *Uloporus* Casey (1 sp., *U. ovalis* Casey (2) FL; (3) TX)]

Subfamily Dacoderinae

[= Tretothoracidae]

Tribe Dacoderini

[87.169 *Dacoderus* LeConte (2 spp. (3) CA, AZ, TX)]

Subfamily Zopherinae

[= Zopheridae]

Tribe Usechini

[87.170 *Usechus* Motschulsky (4 spp. (3) CA; (4) OR); 87.171 *Usechimorpha* Blaisdell (2 spp. (3) CA; (4) OR)]

Tribe Zopherini

[87.172 *Zopherus* Gray (11 spp. (3) CA, AZ, NM, TX; (4) NV, UT)]

87.173 *Noserus* LeConte

Six species, including the following:

N. plicatus LeConte (Rugged Darkling Beetle). L. 14–18 mm. Body elongate and very hard; black, but covered with mud, with a rough surface; apical segments of antennate fused; elytra fused; hind wings absent. Adults and larvae live under oak bark. (3) CA.

[87.174 *Phellopsis* LeConte (4 spp. (1), (3), (4)); 87.175 *Phloeodes* LeConte (8 spp. (3) CA)]

88. ALLECULIDAE (Comb-clawed Bark Beetle Family)

Length: 5–15 mm. Black or brown, elongate, subdepressed; antennae filiform, serrate, rarely pectinate; tarsomeres 5-5-4; claws pectinate. These soft-bodied beetles resemble the Tenebrionidae; in fact, they are probably only a subfamily of that large group. As with the tiger beetles and other families that form a satellite group around the large families, however, these are kept separate. Adults and larvae occur under bark, in leaf litter, or in fungi. Adults are common on flowers, probably feed on pollen, and are attracted to UV lights at night. Species belonging to the large genera are difficult to identify. There are 185 species in the U.S. and Canada, assigned to 18 genera.

Subfamily Alleculinae

[88.1 *Lobopoda* Solier (6 spp. (1), (2), (3)); 88.2 *Stenochidus* LeConte (3 spp. (3) CA; (4) NV); 88.3 *Alethia* Champion (1 sp., *A. carbonaria* Schaeffer (3) AZ); 88.4 *Charisius* Champion (1 sp., *C. floridanus* Linell (2) FL); 88.5 *Hymenorus* Mulsant (100 spp.); 88.6 *Menoeceus* Champion (1 spp., *M. texanus* Champion (3) TX); 88.7 *Phedius* Champion (2

spp. (3) CA, AZ); 88.8 *Telesicles* Champion (2 spp. (3) AZ, TX; (4) WA); 88.9 *Tedinus* Casey (1 sp., *T. angustus* Casey (2) GA); 88.10 *Pseudocistela* Crotch (7 spp. (1), (3), (4), (5)); 88.11 *Isomira* Mulsant (16 spp.); 88.12 *Capnochroa* LeConte (1 sp., *C. fuliginosa* Melsheimer (1) IN, NY, CT; (2) VA)); 88.13 *Mycetochara* Berthold (30 spp., including *M. foveata* LeConte (Fig. 24.156) (1) MI, IN; (5) IA); 88.14 *Lystrony-chus* Latreille (3 spp. (3) AZ, TX); 88.15 *Prostenus* Latreille (1 sp., *P. californicus* Horn (3) CA; 88.16 *Anamphidora* Casey (1 sp., *A. campbelli* Marshall (3) TX)]

Subfamily Omophlinae

[88.17 *Andrimus* Casey (7 spp. (2) GA, FL); 88.18 *Androchirus* LeConte (2 spp. (1) IN; (2) NC, SC, GA, FL)]

89. LAGRIIDAE (Long-jointed Beetle Family)

Length: 5.5–15 mm. Body metallic blue, green or reddish; antennae with apical segment usually very long. Similar to the Tenebrionidae but distinguished by having the next to the last tarsomere on each tarsus enlarged. Adults are often found beneath bark but feed on leaves at night; larvae breed in vegetable litter or under bark. There are many species in the tropics, but only 33 occur in the U.S. and Canada.

Subfamily Statirinae

[89.1 *Statira* Serville (16 spp.)]

Subfamily Lagriinae
89.2 *Arthromacra* Kirby

Three species, including the following:

A. aenea Say (See Fig. 24.157.) (1) n.e. US; (2) s.e. US; (5) MB, IA, MO.

Subfamily Lupropinae

[89.3 *Anaedus* Blanchard (5 spp. (1), (2), (3)); 89.4 *Prateus* LeConte (1 sp., *P. fusculus* LeConte (1) NY, OH; (2) SC, FL); 89.5 *Paratenetus* Spinola (5 spp. (1), (2), (4), (5))]

Subfamily Apocryphinae

[89.6 *Apocrypha* Eschscholtz (3 spp. (3) CA)]

90. SALPINGIDAE (Narrow-waisted Bark Beetle Family)

Length: 2–15 mm. Dark brown or black; antennae usually slightly clubbed, sometimes serrate; pronotum without lateral margins, narrowed at base; tarsomeres 5-5-4, head rarely

Fig. 24.156.

Fig. 24.157.

produced into a beak. Adults are found in various environments, including under bark, under rocks, in debris, and on flowers; a few species frequent intertidal zones among rocks. There are 33 species in the U.S. and Canada.

Subfamily Aegialitinae

The species of this subfamily are principally found in the intertidal zone along the Pacific coast.

[90.1 *Aegialites* Mannerheim (3 spp. (3) CA; (4) AK)]

Subfamily Salpinginae
Tribe Pythini

[90.2 *Trimitomerus* Horn (1 sp., *T. riversi* Horn (3) AZ); 90.3 *Boros* Herbst (1 sp., *B. unicolor* Say (1) n.e. NA); 90.4 *Lecontia* Champion (1 sp., *L. discicollis* LeConte (1) n.e. US; (5) MN); 90.5 *Sphalma* Horn (1 sp., *S. quadricollis* Horn (3) CA); 90.6 *Pytho* Latreille (5 spp. (1), (2), (5), including *P. niger* Kirby (Fig. 24.158) (1) n.e. NA); 90.7 *Priognathus* LeConte (1 sp., *P. monilicornis* LeConte (1) n.e. NA; (4) AK, BC, WA)]

Tribe Salpingini

[90.8 *Sphaeriestes* Stephens (3 spp. (1), (3), (4), (5)); 90.9 *Salpingus* Illiger (1 sp., *S. picatorum* Seidlitz (1) SP)); 90.10 *Rhinosimus* Latreille (1 sp., *R. viridiaeneuis* Randall (1) n.e. NA; (3) ?CA; (4) AK, BC, see (Fig. 24.159); 90.11 *Vincenzellus* Reitter (1 sp., *V. elongatus* Mannerheim (4) AK)]

Subfamily Mycterinae
90.12 *Mycterus* Clairville

Six species, including the following:

M. scaber Haldemann. (See Fig. 24.160.) (1) n.e. US; (2) s.e. US.

Fig. 24.158.

Fig. 24.159.

Subfamily Lacconotinae

[90.13 *Lacconotus* LeConte (2 spp. (1), (3), (4), (5))]

Subfamily Cononotinae

[90.14 *Cononotus* LeConte (6 spp. (3) CA, AZ; (4) ID, UT)]

91. MYCETOPHAGIDAE (Hairy Fungus Beetle Family)

Length: 1.5–6 mm. Elongate-ovate; brownish to black, often with orange or reddish markings; vestiture short to moderate in length, sparse to dense, suberect; antennae with segments through 7 through 11 enlarged or with two- to three-segmented loose club; tarsomeres 4-4-4, 5-5-5, or of some males, 3-4-4. Most species feed on bark fungi; some (for example, *Berginus* spp.) feed on pine pollen; one (see below) is found in moldy stored grain. Twenty-six species occur in the U.S. and Canada.

Tribe Mycetophagini

91.1 *Mycetophagus* Hellwig

Fifteen species, including the following:

M. quadriguttatus Mueller (Spotted Hairy Fungus Beetle). (1) n.e. NA; (2) NC, AR; (3) CA, TX; (4) BC, OR, ID; (5) AB, MB, SA, NE, IA.

M. punctatus Say. (See Fig. 24.161.) (1) n.e. US; (2) s.e. US; (3) CA, TX; (4) ID; (5) MB, KS, MO.

91.2 *Typhaea* Stephens

One species, as follows:

T. stercorea Linnaeus (Hairy Fungus Beetle). Pest in moldy grain. Cosmopolitan.

Fig. 24.160.

Fig. 24.161.

[91.3 *Litargus* Erichson (6 spp.); 91.4 *Thrimolus* Casey (1 sp., *T. minutus* Casey (1) IN, OH, PA, DC; (2) FL; (3) TX); 91.5 *Berginus* Erichson (3 spp. (1) PA; (2) FL; (3) CA, TX)]

92. CIIDAE (Minute Tree-fungus Beetle Family)

Length: 1–3 mm. Brown to black; head hidden from dorsal view; antennae with a loose three-segmented club; tarsomeres 4-4-4; resemble Scolytidae. Both larvae and adults live gregariously in shelf fungi and in rotten wood. Eighty-five species in the U.S. and Canada.

Subfamily Sphindociinae

[92.1 *Sphindocis* Fall (1 sp., *S. denticollis* Fall (3) CA)]

Subfamily Ciinae

Tribe Ciini

[92.2 *Cis* Latreille (43 spp., including *C. fuscipes* Mellie (Fig. 24.162) (1) n.e. NA; (2) s.e. US; (3) CA, TX; (4) Pacific n.w.; (5) n. Central States); 92.3 *Ennearthron* Mellie (2 spp. (1) OH; (2) KY, BC; (4) BC); 92.4 *Dolichocis* Dury (2 spp. (1) n.e. NA; (3) CA, AZ; (4) BC, OR, ID, UT; (5) NT, AB, MB, SD, WY, CO); 92.5 *Orthocis* Casey (5 spp.); 92.6 *Strigocis* Dury (3 spp. (1), (2), (3), (5)); 92.7 *Hadraule* Thomson (3 spp.); 92.8 *Plesiocis* Casey (1 sp., *P. cribrum* Casey (1) n.e. US; (2) VA; (3) s.e. US; (4) Pacific n.w.; (5) MT, MB, WY, CO); 92.9 *Ceracis* Mellie (21 spp.); 92.10 *Sulcacis* Dury (2 spp. (1) n.e. US; (2) VA, NC, SC; (3) CA, AZ, TX; (4) Pacific n.w.; (5) AB, SK, MB, WY, CO, ND, NE, KS, MO); 92.11 *Malacocis* Gorham (1 sp., *M. brevicollis* Casey (1) n.e. US; (2) s.e. US; (3) TX; (5) MB, KS)]

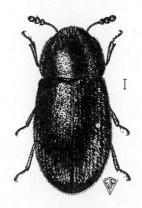

Fig. 24.162.

Tribe **Orophiini**

[92.12 *Rhopalodontus* Mellie (1 sp., *R. americanus* Lawrence (1) WI); 92.13 *Octotemnus* Mellie (1 sp., *O. laevis* Casey (1) n.e. US; (2) WV, VA, TN, MC, AL; (3) CA; (4) AK, BC, WA, OR; (5) AB, SK, MB, MN, IA, KS)]

93. COLYDIIDAE (Cylindrical Bark Beetle Family)

Length: 1–8 mm (usually under 8 mm). Brown to black and hard, usually elongate; tarsomeres 4-4-4, rarely 3-3-3. Many species are predacious, living under bark; others are fungus feeders. There are 87 species in the U.S. and Canada, assigned to 28 genera.

Subfamily **Colydiinae**
Tribe **Orthocerini**

[93.1 *Rhagodera* Erichson (3 spp. (3) s.w. US)]

Tribe **Corticini**

[93.2 *Anchomma* LeConte (1 sp., *A. costatum* LeConte (3) CA)]

Tribe **Coxelini**

[93.3 *Coxelus* Latreille (1 sp., *C. serratus* (Horn) (3) CA); 93.4 *Megataphrus* Casey (2 spp. (3), (4))]

Tribe **Synchitini**

[93.5 *Synchita* Hellwig (5 spp.); 93.6 *Endeitoma* Sharp (1 sp., *E. granulata* (Say)); 93.7 *Eucicones* Sharp (2 spp. (1), (2), (5)); 93.8 *Acolobius* Sharp (1 sp., *A. lineaticollis* (Horn)); 93.9 *Bitoma* Herbst (10 spp.); 93.10 *Eudesmula* Cockerell (1 sp., *E. undulata* Melsheimer (1) IN, OH, PA; (2) VA); 93.11 *Eulachus* Erichson (2 spp. (2) s.e. US); 93.12 *Phloeonemus* Erichson (2 spp. (3) CA, AZ, TX); 93.13 *Namunaria* Reitter (2 spp. (1), (2), (3), (4)); 93.14 *Endophloeus* Erichson (1 sp., *E. nosodermoides* Horn (3) CA; (4) OR); 93.15 *Lobogestoria* Reitter (1 sp., *L. gibbicollis* Reitter (2) LA, AL, GA, SC, FL); 93.16 *Lasconotus* LeConte (21 spp.)]

Tribe **Colydiini**

[93.17 *Aulonium* Erichson (5 spp.); 93.18 *Colydium* Fabricius (Fig. 24.163) (4 spp., including *C. lineola* Say (1) n.e. US; (2) s.e. US; (3) s.w. US; (4) Pacific n.w.; (5) MO)]

Tribe **Nematidiini**

[93.19 *Nematidium* Erichson (1 sp., *N. filiforme* LeConte (2) s.e. US)]

Tribe **Aglenini**

[93.20 *Aglenus* Erichson (1 sp., *A. brunneus* (Schuckard) (1) ON, IL; (2) NC; (3) CA; (5) MO)]

Tribe **Pycnomerini**

[93.21 *Pycnomerus* Erichson (5 spp. (1), (2), (3))]

Fig. 24.163.

Subfamily **Bothriderinae**
Tribe **Deretaphrini**

[93.22 *Deretaphrus* Newman (1 sp., *D. oregonensis* Horn (3) CA; (4) Pacific n.w.)); 93.23 *Oxylaemus* Erichson (2 spp. (1), (2), (3), (4)); 93.24 *Sosylus* Erichson (3 spp. (2), (3))]

Tribe **Bothriderini**

[93.25 *Bothrideres* Erichson (5 spp. (1), (2), (3), (5)); 93.26 *Lithophorus* Sharp (1 sp., *L. ornatus* Arrow (3) TX); 93.27 *Prolyctus* Zimmerman (1 sp., *P. exaratus* (Melsheimer)]

Subfamily **Monoedinae**

[93.28 *Monoedus* Horn (1 sp., *M. guttatus* LeConte (2) FL)]

Subfamily **Myrmechixeninae**

[93.29 *Myrmechixenus* Chevrolat (1 sp., *M. lathridiodes* Crotch (2) SC; (3) CA, AZ, TX)]

94. PYROCHROIDAE (Fire-colored Beetle Family)

Length: 6–20 mm. Broad, rather depressed; pale brown to black with red or yellow thorax, or all red; head narrowed behind eyes; eyes large; antennae serrate to pectinate, in some males plumose; thorax narrowed in front; tarsomeres 5-5-4; elytra soft. Adults are found on shrubs and flowers. Larvae, found under bark, are carnivorous. There are 15 species in the U.S. and Canada.

Subfamily **Ischaliinae**

[94.1 *Ischalia* Pascoe (3 spp. (1), (2), (3), (4))]

Subfamily **Pyrochroinae**

[94.2 *Schizotus* Newman (2 spp. (1), (4), (5)); 94.3 *Neopyrochroa* Blair (4 spp. (1), (2), (3), (5))]

94.4 *Dendroides* Latreille

Six species in (1), (2), (4), (5), including the following:

D. concolor (Newman) (Fire-colored Beetle). L. 9–13 mm. Elongate and slender; fire-red except for eyes and antennae, which are darker; antenna segments each with a lateral branch, those of the male longer than those of the female; eyes very large, those of the males touching dorsally. Adults live on flowers or vegetation. Larvae live under bark; they are carnivorous. (See A&J 148.) (1) n.e. US; (2) VA, TN, NC; (5) MN, KS.

D. canadensis Latreille. (see Fig. 24.164.) (1) n.e. NA; (2) s.e. US; (5) MB, ND, MN, NE, IA, KS, MO.

95. OTHNIIDAE (False Tiger Beetle Family)

Length: 5–9 mm. Slender, somewhat resembling tiger beetles; brown to black, often mottled with gray; tarsomeres 5-5-4. Both larvae and adults live on rotting leaves or under bark, where they may be carnivorous. Five species in the U.S. and Canada, as follows:

[95.1 *Elacatis* Pascoe (5 spp. (2) VA; (3) CA; (4) OR; (5) NE, CO)]

96. PROSTOMIDAE (Jugular-horned Beetle Family)

Length: 5–6 mm. Elongate, somewhat flattened; brown, shiny; antennae with a three-segmented club; underside of head with two horns (see Fig. 24.13). One species, as follows:

Fig. 24.164.

[96.1 *Prostomis* Latreille (1 sp., *P. mandibularis* (Fabricius) (3) CA; (4) BC, OR, NV)]

97. OEDEMERIDAE (Pollen Feeding Beetle Family)

Length: 5–20 mm. Elongate; soft-bodied; usually pale tan to reddish, but also black, often with orange pronotum with black markings; pronotum broad anteriorly, narrower than elytra at base, and without lateral margins; antennae long, filiform; tarsomeres 5-5-4. All adults are obligate pollen feeders. Larvae live in the soil, usually where it is moist, or in rotting stumps; they are rarely stem borers. Some can be pests because of the blistering that results if they are squashed against the skin. There are 86 species in the U.S. and Canada, assigned to 16 genera.

Subfamily Calopodinae

[97.1 *Calopus* Fabricius (1 sp., *C. angustus* LeConte (1) WI, MI, ON, PQ, NB, PA; (3) CA, AZ, NM; (4) BC, WA, OR, ID, NV, UT; (5) AB, MT, CO); 97.2 *Sparedrus* Dejean (2 spp. (3) TX)]

Subfamily Nacerdinae

Tribe Nacerdini

[97.3 *Xanthochroa* Schmidt (6 spp. (1), (2), (3))]

97.4 *Nacerdes* Dejean

One species, as follows:

N. melanura (Linnaeus) (Wharf Borer). Yellow; elytra with black tips. Larvae bore into wharf pilings, both in sea water and fresh water. Cosmopolitan.

Subfamily Oedemerinae

Tribe Ditylini

[97.5 *Ditylus* Fischer (3 spp. (1), (3), (4), (5))]

Tribe Asclerini

[97.6 *Asclera* Dejean (6 spp.)]

Tribe Oxycopiini (new tribe)

[97.7 *Sisenes* Champion (1 sp., *S. championi* Horn (3) AZ)]

97.8 *Oxycopis* Arnett

Twelve species, the following of which is a common pest:

O. mcdonaldi (Arnett) (False Blister Beetle). L. ±7 mm. Dark blue with orange-red pronotum marked with an indefi-

Fig. 24.165.

nite, blackish median longitudinal stripe. Adults are attracted to lights at night near shore resorts; if crushed against body, they will cause blistering. (See Fig. 24.165.) (2) FL.

[97.9 *Copidita* LeConte (1 sp., *C. quadrimaculata* (Motschulsky) (3) CA; (4) BC, WA, OR); 97.10 *Eumecomera* Arnett (3 spp. (3), (4), (5)); 97.11 *Vasaces* Champion (4 spp. (3) AZ, TX)]

Tribe Oedemerini

[97.12 *Heliocis* Arnett (1 sp., *H. repanda* (Horn) (2) FL; (3) TX)]

Tribe Oxaciini (new tribe)

[97.13 *Oxacis* LeConte (29 spp.); 97.14 *Rhinoplatia* Horn (2 spp. (3) CA, AZ; (4) NV); 97.15 *Paroxacis* Arnett (4 spp. (2), (3)); 97.16 *Xanthochroina* Ganglbaur (1 sp., *X. bicolor* (LeConte) (3) CA, AZ, NM, TX; (4) BC, WA, OR, ID, NV, UT; (5) WY, NE, CO)]

Tribe Hypasclerini (new tribe)

[97.17 *Hypasclera* Kirsch (9 spp. (1), (2), (3))]

98. MELANDRYIDAE (False Darkling Beetle Family)

Length: 3–20 mm. Elongate, convex, slender to somewhat broadened; many species hard-bodied; brown to black, rarely with pale markings; antennae long and slender; palpi often large, with a triangular apical segment; pronotum often with two basal impressions; tarsomeres 5-5-4. Larvae and adults are found in dry wood, under bark, or in dry fungi; adults often on flowers. There are 142 species in the U.S. and Canada, assigned to 52 genera.

Subfamily Tetratominae

Tribe Tetratomini

[98.1 *Tetratoma* Fabricius (2 spp. (1), (5)); 98.2 *Abstrulia* Casey (2 spp. (1), (2)); 98.3 *Incolia* Casey (1 sp., *I. longipennis* Casey (1) IN); 98.4 *Eupisenus* Casey (1 sp., *E. elongatus* LeConte (4) AK); 98.5 *Pisenus* Casey (2 spp. (1), (2))]

98.6 *Penthe* Newman

Two species, the following of which is common:

P. pimelia (Fabricius). Found on fungi and rotting wood. (1) n.e. UA; (2) s.e. US; (3) TX.

[98.7 *Synchroa* Newman (1 sp., *S. punctata* Newman (1) IN, NY, CT; (2) FL); 98.8 *Mallodrya* Horn (1 sp., *M. subaenea* Horn (1) OH)]

Tribe Hallomenini

[98.9 *Eustrophinus* Seidlitz (5 spp.); 98.10 *Eustrophus* Illiger (1 sp., *E. tomentosus* Say (1) n.e. US; (5) SD, IA)); 98.11 *Synstrophus* Seidlitz (1 sp., *S. repandus* Horn (1) n.e. US; (4) Pacific n.w.)); 98.12 *Holostrophus* Horn (3 spp. (1), (2), (4)); 98.13 *Hallomenus* Panzer (7 spp. (1), (2), (4))]

Tribe Orchesiini

[98.14 *Orchesia* Latreille (6 spp. (1), (2), (4)); 98.15 *Microscapha* LeConte (1 sp., *M. clavicornis* LeConte (1) IL; (2) GA); 98.16 *Lederia* Reitter (1 sp., *L. arctica* Horn (4) AK)]

Subfamily Melandryinae
Tribe Serropalpini

[98.17 *Amblyctis* LeConte (1 sp., *A. praeses* LeConte (1) NY); 98.18 *Xylita* Paykull (4 spp. (1), (4), (5)); 98.19 *Rushia* Forel (3 spp. (2), (3)); 98.20 *Spilotus* LeConte (1 sp., *S. quadripustulatus* Melsheimer (1) IN, NY); 98.21 *Scotochroa* LeConte (3 spp. (1), (4), (5)); 98.22 *Scotochroides* Mank (1 sp., *S. antennatus* Mank (1) PA, NH); 98.23 *Enchodes* LeConte (1 sp., *E. sericea* Haldemann (1) IN, PA, NY, ME); 98.24 *Serropalpus* Hellenius (3 spp.); 98.25 *Mystaxus* Kugelann (1 sp., *M. simulator* Newman (1) ON, NY, OH); 98.26 *Dircaea* Fabricius (2 spp. (4) BC); 98.27 *Phloeotrya* Stephens (4 spp. (1), (2), (3)); 98.28 *Abdera* Stempens (2 spp. (3) CA; (4) BC); 98.29 *Anisoxya* Mulsant (1 sp., *A. glaucula* LeConte (1) ON, NY, PA; (3) ?AZ)]

Tribe Hypulini

[98.30 *Polypria* Chevrolat (1 sp., *P. cruxrufa* Chevrolat (3) TX); 98.31 *Zilora* Mulsant (5 spp. (1), (2), (3), (4)); 98.32 *Hypulus* Paykull (5 spp. (1), (2), (3)); 98.33 *Microtonus* LeConte (1 sp., *M. sericans* LeConte (1) IN, NY; (2) GA); 98.34 *Symphora* LeConte (2 spp. (1), (2))]

Tribe Melandryini

[98.35 *Prothalpia* LeConte (2 spp. (2), (4)); 98.36 *Melandrya* Fabricius (7 spp. (1), (3), (4)); 98.37 *Phryganophilus* Sahlberg (1 sp., *P. collaris* LeConte (4) WA, OR)]

Subfamily Osphyinae
Tribe Osphyini

[98.38 *Osphya* Illiger (3 spp. (1), (3), including *O. varians* LeConte (Fig. 24.166) (1) IN; (3) TX)]

Subfamily Scraptiinae

[98.39 *Allopoda* LeConte (3 spp. (1), 92), (3)); 98.40 *Scraptia* Latreille (3 spp. (1), (2), (3)); 98.41 *Neoscraptia* Fender (1 sp., *N. testacea* Fender (4) OR); 98.42 *Canifa* LeConte (4 spp. (1), (2)); 98.43 *Pectotoma* Hatch (1 sp., *P. hoppingi* Hatch (4) BC; (5) AB)]

Subfamily Anaspidinae

[98.44 *Diclidia* LeConte (9 spp. (1), (3), (5)); 98.45 *Pentaria* Mulsant (10 spp. (1), (3), (5)); 98.46 *Naucles* Champion (3 spp. (3), (4)); 98.47 *Sphingocephalus* Liljeblad (1 sp., *S. ovalis* Liljeblad (2) FL); 98.48 *Anaspis* Geoffroy (13 spp.); 98.49 *Silaria* Mulsant (1 sp., *S. revelstokei* Liljeblad (4) BC); 98.50 *Larisia* Emery (1 sp., *L. nigricolor* Liljeblad (5) AB); 98.51 *Nassipa* Emergy (1 sp., *N. hoppingi* Liljeblad (4) BC)]

99. MORDELLIDE (Tumbling Flower Beetle Family)

Length: 1.5–15 mm (usually under 8 mm). Wedgeshaped beetles, with short antennae, entire elytra, long, pointed abdomen, and long hind legs often with enlarged femora; head deflexed, not visible from above; usually black or brown, often with white, red, or yellow coarse hairlike setae or scales. Adults are phytophagous, feeding especially on umbelliferous flowers. Some larvae are carnivorous; others frequent rotten wood or are leaf and stem miners; rarely are they parasitic on wasps. The species are difficult to identify without technical references. There are 207 species in the U.S. and Canada, assigned to seven genera.

Tribe Mordellini

[99.1 *Glipodes* LeConte (2 spp. (1), (2)); 99.2 *Conalia* Mulsant and Rey (2 spp. (1), (2), (5)); 99.3 *Isotrilophus* Liljeblad (1 sp., *I. erratica* Smith (2) AR, FL; (3) TX); 99.4 *Glipa* LeConte (6 spp. (1), (2), (3))]

99.5 *Mordella* Linnaeus

Thirty-seven species, including the following:

M. marginata Melsheimer. L. 5–7 mm. Found on many flowers. (See Fig. 24.167.) (1) n.e. US; (2) FL.

M. atrata Melsheimer (Tumbling Flower Beetle). L. 3–6 mm. Dark velvety black; base of elytra and body ventrally covered with a somewhat iridescent pubescence; base of the dorsal exposed portion of the abdomen covered with gray pubescence. Often found on wild-rose blossoms. (See A&J 149.) (1) n.e. US; (2) s.e. US; (3) CA, AZ, TX.

[99.6 *Tomoxia* Costa (10 spp. (1), (2), (3), (5)); 99.7 *Mordellistena* Costa (145 spp.)]

100. RHIPIPHORIDAE (Wedge-shaped Beetle Family)

Length: 4–15 mm. Similar in appearance to the preceding family but distinguished by the pectinate or flabellate antennae and the blunt abdomen; black and orange. These insects are infrequently seen. Adults occur on flowers; larvae are internal parasites of various wasps during the first larval stage but later

Fig. 24.166.

Fig. 24.167.

Fig. 24.168.

emerge and feed on leaves. There are 44 species in the U.S. and Canada.

Subfamily Pelecotominae

[100.1 *Pelecotoma* Fischer (1 sp., *P. flavipes* Melsheimer (2) SC); 100.2 *Trigonodera* Dejean (2 spp. (3) TX)]

Subfamily Ptilophorinae

[100.3 *Toposcopus* LeConte (1 sp., *T. wrighti* LeConte (3) NM)]

Subfamily Rhipiphorinae

Tribe Macrosiagonini

[100.4 *Macrosiagon* Hentz (9 spp. (1), (2), (3), (5) (*M.* sp., Fig. 24.168)]

Tribe Rhipiphorini

100.5 *Rhipiphorus* Bosc

Thirty species, including the following:

R. fasciatus Say. Adults found on goldenrod. (1) IL, IN, PA, CT; (5) MO.

[100.6 *Ripidius* Thunberg (1 sp. *R. pectinicornis* Thornberg, NA (?)]

101. MELOIDAE (Blister Beetle Family)

Length: 3–30 mm (usually 10–15 mm). Black or brown but sometimes orange or marked with red, yellow, or white; soft-bodied; usually rather elongate (some species have globular elytra); head deflexed, with a narrow neck; pronotum without lateral margins; tarsomeres 5-5-4; legs long; tarsal claws each with a lower thin blade, tooth, or spine. Adult blister beetles are phytophagous, and some are serious crop pests. Larvae are parasitic on wild bees and the egg cases of grasshoppers. The blood of the adults contains a vesicating substance, cantharidin—the "Spanish fly" of commerce—that causes human skin to blister. Once thought of an aphrodisiac, it is now used to treat certain urogenital diseases (see *Lytta vesicatoria* below). (While this book was in press, it was learned that certain species of these beetles, trapped in baled hay, were eaten by several extremely valuable Florida race horses. Even though the beetles were dead, the horses died from the poison.) There are 310 species in the U.S. and Canada.

Subfamily Electicinae

[101.1 *Thambospasta* Werner (1 sp., *T. howdeni* Werner (3) TX))]

Subfamily Meloinae

Tribe Meloini

[101.2 *Spastonyx* Selander (2 spp. (3) CA, AZ))]

101.3 *Meloe* Linnaeus

Twenty species, including the following:

M. impressus Kirby. L. 8–24 mm. Bluish black, sometimes with a purplish or greenish hue; elytra short, not covering abdomen. Adults appear on warm days in early spring; they feed on buttercups. Larvae live in bee's nests. (1) n.e. US; (2) s.e. US.

Tribe Lyttini

Subtribe Eupomphina

[101.4 *Cordylospasta* Horn (2 spp., (3) CA, AZ; (4) OR, ID, NV, UT; (5) CO)]

101.5 *Cysteodemus* LeConte

Two species in (3) CA, AZ, NM, including the following:

C. wislizeni LeConte (Desert Blister Beetle). L. 10–15 mm. Pronotum with short lateral spines; elytra greatly inflated, resembling a large spider; dark metallic blue to purplish; surface with dense, deep, coarse, partly confluent punctures. Adults, sometimes seen on flowers, are usually found crawling on the desert floor. (See A&J 150.) (3) AZ, NM.

[101.6 *Eupompha* LeConte (8 spp. (3) CA, AZ, NM, TX; (4) UT; (5) CO); 101.7 *Megetra* LeConte (3 spp. (3) AZ, NM, TX); 101.8 *Negalius* Casey (1 sp., *N. marmoratus* Casey (3) AZ, TX); 101.9 *Phodaga* Wellman (2 spp. (3) CA, AZ, NM; (4) UT); 101.10 *Pleurospasta* Wellman (2 spp. (3) CA, AZ, NM; (4) CT); 101.11 *Tegrodera* LeConte (3 spp. (3) CA, AZ)]

Subtribe Pyrotina

101.12 *Pyrota* Dejean

Twenty-seven species in (1) IL, IN, MA; (2) VA, NC, SC, LA, MS, FL; (3) s.w. US; (4) NV, UT; (5) MT, WY, NE, CO, KS. The following are noteworthy:

P. postica LeConte (Creosote Bush Beetle). L. 15–18 mm. Yellow to brownish yellow and shiny; black markings on head, pronotum, elytra (where they are quadrate, not much longer than broad), and legs. Adults found on creosote bushes and other plants. (3) AZ, NM, TX.

P. palpalis Champion (Fire Blister Beetle). L. 10–15 mm. Shiny surface with only small and inconspicuous punctures dorsally; head, prothorax, venter, and legs pale red or rusty brown; pronotum sometimes with a pair of small black spots in the center; elytra usually whitish yellow with three wide black bands. Adults are found on flowers feeding on pollen and nectar. Larvae probably live in the nests of solitary bees. (See A&J 152.) (3) CA, AZ, NM, TX; (4) UT.

Subtribe Lyttina

101.13 *Lytta* Fabricius

Fifty species, including the following:

L. vesicatoria (Linnaeus) (Spanish Fly). This European species is the source of commercial cantharidin.

L. nuttallii Say (Nuttall Blister Beetle). (3) CA, AZ, NM; (4) ID, UT; (5) AB, SK, MT, ND, MN, SD, NE.

L. sayi (LeConte) (Say's Blister Beetle). (1) n.e. US; (5) MN, WY, IA.

Fig. 24.169.

L. vulnerata LeConte (American Spanish Fly). L. 12–20 mm. Head and thorax shiny; elytra with somewhat raised reticulations; head—except between eyes—and pronotum—except for a pair of spots in the middle—orange; elytra, abdomen, and legs black. Adults are attracted to lights at night; larvae are found in wild bee nests. (See A&J 151.) (4) BC, WA, ID, UT.

Subtribe Epicautina

101.14 *Epicauta* Dejean

This very large genus of 111 species is divided into two subgenera: *Epicauta* s. str. and *Macrobasis* LeConte. Several species are of economic importance, as follows:

E. vittata (Fabricius) (Striped Blister Beetle). L. 9–15 mm. Black, marked with dull yellow; head with two black spots on the top; pronotum with two discal stipes; elytra variable, with two or three black stripes, the outer stripe fused or partly fused with the middle stripe. Larvae feed on the egg masses of grasshoppers. Adults feed on tomato and potato plants and a variety of weeds. (See Fig. 24.169.) (1) n.e. US; (2) s.e. US; (5) IA.

E. maculata Say (Spotted Blister Beetle). (1) IL; (3) AZ, NM, TX.

E. pennsylvanica (De Geer) (Black Blister Beetle). (1) n.e. US; (2) FL; (3) TX; (5) MT.

E. cinerea Forster (Clematis Blister Beetle). (See Fig. 24.170.) (1) n.e. NA; (2) SC; (5) MB, MN, IA.

E. fabricii (LeConte) (Ash-gray Blister Beetle). (1) n.e. NA; (2) GA; (3) AZ, NM.

E. subglabra Fall (Caragana Blister Beetle). (3) AZ; (4) ID.

Fig. 24.170.

E. pestifera Werner (Margined Blister Beetle). (1) n.e. US; (2) s.e. US; (5) n. Central States.

[101.15 *Linsleya* MacSwain (5 spp. (3) CA, AZ, NM, TX; (4) BC; (5) MB); 101.16 *Pleuropompha* LeConte (2 spp. (3) AZ, NM, TC)]

Subfamily Nemognathinae

Tribe Tetraonycini

[101.17 *Tetraonyx* Latreille (5 spp. (2) NC, AL, FL; (3) AZ, NM, TX)]

Tribe Nemognathini

Subtribe Nemognathina

[101.18 *Hornia* Riley (2 spp. (1) DC; (3) CA, NM, TX, OK; (4) UT; (5) MT, CO, KS, MO)]

101.19 *Nemognatha* Illiger

These beetles have the galeae of the mouthparts extended to form a long sucking tube similar to that of butterflies. With this tube they are able to ingest nectar, and with their mandibles, which are retained, they can also eat pollen. Eighteen species, including the following:

N. lurida LeConte (Nectar-sucking Blister Beetle). L. 7–15 mm. Shiny; surface with small but distinct and moderately dense punctures; dorsally reddish brown to yellow with scutellum reddish or black; tips of elytra sometimes black or entire elytra black; body clothed with moderately dense, erect pubescence. (See A&J 153.) (3) CA, AZ, TX; (4) BC, WA, OR, NV, UT; (5) AB, CO.

[101.20 *Rhyphonemognatha* Enns (1 sp., *R. rufa* (LeConte) (1) IL; (3) AZ, TX); 101.21 *Tricrania* LeConte (3 spp. (1) IN, PA, CT; (3) CA, AZ; (4) BC, OR; (5) KS)]

Subtribe Zonitina

[101.22 *Gnathium* Kirby (14 spp. (1) IL; (2) GA, LA; (3) CA, AZ, NM, TX; (4) OR; (5) AB, MT, CO, NE, KS); 101.23 *Pseudozonitis* Dillon (13 spp. (1) IL; (2) LA, FL; (3) CA, AZ, NM; (4) NV, UT; (5) KS); 101.24 *Zonitis* Fabricius (15 spp. (1) ON, IN, OH; (2) VA, LA; (3) CA, AZ, TX, OK; (4) WA, ID, NV, UT)); (5) MB, MT, WY, SD, MN, NE, CO, KS)]

102. ANTHICIDAE (Antlike Flower Beetle Family)

Length: 2–12 mm. Elongate, cylindrical, somewhat depressed; brown to black, sometimes marked with red or yellow; head usually deflexed; pronotum narrowed behind, and in some species a projecting horn present; tarsomeres 5-5-4. Adults are found on flowers and foliage; larvae, in decaying vegetation. The 157 species in the U.S. and Canada are rather difficult to identify.

Subfamily Notoxinae

[102.1 *Mecynotarsus* LaFerte (3 spp.); 102.2 *Notoxus* Fabricius (46 spp., including *N. subtilis* LeConte (Fig. 24.171) (1) WI, MI, IL, IN, OH; (3) AZ, OK, TX; (5) MT, ND, MN, NE, IA, KS, MO)]

Subfamily Anthicinae

[102.3 *Amblyderus* LaFerte (4 spp. (1), (2), (3), including *A. pallens* (LeConte) (Fig. 24.172) (1) n.e. US; (2) s.e. US; (3) NM, TX); 102.4 *Tanarthrus* LeConte (13 spp. (3), (4)); 102.5 *Leptanthicus* Werner (1 sp., *L. staphyliniformis* Werner (3) CA; (4) NV); 102.6 *Sapintus* Casey (9 spp.); 102.7 *Anthicus* Paykull (40 spp.)]

Fig. 24.171.

102.8 *Omonadus* Mulsant and Ray

Two species, of which the following is a pest:

O. floralis (Linnaeus) (Narrownecked Grain Beetle). Found in stored grain and food products (unlike other members of the family). Cosmopolitan.

[102.9 *Thicanus* Casey (4 spp.); 102.10 *Malporus* Casey (3 spp. (1), (2), (3), (5)); 102.11 *Euvacusus* Casey (1 sp., *E. coloradanus* Casey (4) BC; (5) MT, CO); 102.12 *Vacusus* Casey (5 spp. (2), (3), (4), (5)); 102.13 *Baulius* Casey (1 sp., *B. tenuis* (LeConte) (3) CA, AZ, TX; (4) UT); 102.14 *Acanthinus* LaFerte (7 spp. (1), (2), (3), (5)); 102.15 *Formicilla* LeConte (1 sp., *F. munda* LeConte (2) AR, LA; (3) s.w. US); 102.16 *Ischyropalpus* LaFerte (13 spp.)]

Subfamily Tomoderinae

[102.17 *Tomoderus* LaFerte (4 spp. (1), (2), (3), (5))]

103. PEDILIDAE (False Antlike Flower Beetle Family)

Length: 4–12 mm. Elongate, cylindrical, or slightly flattened; brown to black, sometimes with pale or red markings; head prominent, neck narrow; pronotum narrowed in front; tarsomeres 5-5-4. Larvae live in decaying plant debris; adults, on flowers and foliage. The group is poorly known. Seventy-seven species are recorded in the U.S. and Canada.

Tribe Pedilini

103.1 *Pedilus* Fischer

Thirty-seven species, including the following:

P. lugubris Say. Found on leaves of horse chestnut, hawthorn, and other plants. (See Fig. 24.173.) (1) n.e. US.

Fig. 24.172.

Fig. 24.173.

Tribe Eurygeniini

[103.2 *Rilettius* Abdullah (3 spp., (3) AZ, TX); 103.3 *Eurygenius* LaFerte (10 spp., (1), (2), (3), (4)); 103.4 *Neoeurygenius* Abdullah (1 sp., *N. grahami* Abdullah (3) AZ); 103.5 *Stereopalpus* Laferte (11 spp.); 103.6 *Duboisius* Abdullah (5 spp. (3) AZ, TX); 103.7 *Leptoremus* Casey (1 sp., *L. argenteus* Casey (3) CA); 103.8 *Mastoremus* Casey (3 spp. (3) AZ; (4) ID)); 103.9 *Quadrius* Abdullah (2 spp. (3) AZ, NM)]

Tribe Macratriini

[103.10 *Macratria* Newman (4 spp. (1) n.e. US; (3) TX)]

104. EUGLENIDAE (Antlike Leaf Beetle Family)

Length: 1.5–3 mm. Similar in appearance to ants and to many Anthicidae, but the eyes are notched by the antennal bases; reddish yellow to dark; long, erect hairs often on the body; tarsomeres 5-5-4. Adults are found on foliage and flowers; larvae are poorly known. There are 40 species in the U.S. and Canada.

Tribe Phytobaenini

[104.1 *Ganascus* Casey (3 spp. (2) NC, ?FL; (3) TX)]

Tribe Emilinini

[104.2 *Emelinus* Casey (4 spp. (1) IL, IN, PA; (2) FL; (3) AZ)]

Tribe Syzetonini

[104.3 *Elonus* Casey (3 spp. (1), (2), including *E. basalis* (LeConte) (Fig. 24.174.) (1) n.e. US; (2) VA, FL); 104.4 *Pseudanidorus* Pic (12 spp. (1), (2), (3), (5)); 104.5 *Syzeton* Blackburn (10 spp. (1), (2), (3), (5))]

Fig. 24.174.

Tribe Aderini

Subtribe Euglenina

[104.6 *Axylophilus* Casey (1 sp., *A. yuccae* Casey (2) FL)]

Subtribe Cnopina

[104.7 *Cnopus* Champion (2 spp. (2) FL; (3) CA, TX)]

Subtribe Aderina

[104.8 *Phomalus* Casey (2 spp. (1) IN, DC; (3) CA)]

Subtribe Olotelina

[104.9 *Scanylus* Casey (2 spp. (2) FL; (3) AZ)]

Incertae sedis

[104.10 *Sandytes* Casey (1 sp., *S. ptinoides* Schwarz (2) FL)]

Series STREPSIPTERIFORMIA

Superfamily STYLOPOIDEA

105. STYLOPIDAE (Parasitic Beetle Family)

Length: 0.5–4 mm. Males black; antennae with four to seven segments, flabellate and often thickly covered with large sensory pits; elytra very short, fleshy flaps; hind wings large, fanlike with reduced venation, and not foldable; two, three, four, or five tarsomeres on each leg. The adult female is larvalike and continues to be a parasite of bees and leafhoppers as she was throughout the larval stage. The larvae hatch as free agents from eggs laid on flowers. When a suitable host visits the flower, the first-stage larvae attach themselves to it and become parasitic. Males live only long enough to find a female and fertilize her when she protrudes her abdomen from between the abdominal terga of the host. One way to collect these interesting insects is to cage hosts infected with adult female parasites; males will come to the cage at night. Many authors treat this family as a separate order, the Strepsiptera. Although 109 species are recorded in the U.S. and Canada, the group is still poorly known.

Subfamily Mengeinae

[105.1 *Triozocera* Pierce (1 sp., *T. texana* Pierce (3) TX)]

Subfamily Stylopinae

105.2 *Stylops* Kirby

Thirty-eight species, including the following:

S. vandykei Bohart (Bee Parasite Beetle). L. 1–1.5 mm. Male black; antennae and legs brownish, sometimes with yellowish abdominal segments. Female is parasitic on bees, usually *Andrena* bees. (See Fig. 24.175 and A&J 154.) (3) CA.

[105.3 *Eurystylops* Bohard (2 spp. (3) CA: (5) WY); 105.4 *Halictoxenos* Pierce (9 spp. (1), (2), (3), (5)); 105.5 *Crawfordia* Pierce (7 spp. (1), (3) (5)); 105.6 *Hylecthrus* Saunders (1 sp., *H. californicus* Bohart (3) CA)]

Subfamily Xeninae

[105.7 *Xenos* Rossius (13 spp., (1), (2), (3), (5)); 105.8 *Pseudoxenos* Saunders (21 spp.); 105.9 *Membracixenos* Pierce (1 sp., *M. jordani* Pierce (?locality))]

Subfamily Halictophaginae

[105.10 *Halictophagus* Curtis (13 spp. (1), (2), (3), (5)); 105.11 *Stenocranophilus* Pierce (1 sp., *S. anomalocerus* Pierce (5) SK)]

Fig. 24.175.

Subfamily Elenchinae

[105.12 *Elenchus* Curtis (2 spp. (1) OH, MD)]

Series CHRYSOMELIFORMIA

Superfamily CHRYSOMELOIDEA

106. CERAMBYCIDAE (Long-horned Beetle Family)

Length: 3–150 mm. Antennae usually half as long as body and often much longer and usually inserted so that their base is partially surrounded by the eyes. Although their shape is variable, the Cerambycidae may be recognized by these two features alone. In addition, they have the characteristic tarsi of the superfamily—that is, 5-5-5—although the fourth is usually very small and hidden within the bilobed third. A few species with short elytra somewhat resemble the Staphylinidae, but the antennae and tarsi distinguish them. Others that greatly resemble certain leaf beetles may usually be differentiated by the length and manner of their antennae.

Adults feed on wood, roots, leaves, pollen, and (rarely) other insects. The larvae of most species bore into bark and wood. A few species are stem borers. Many are destructive pests of orchard and shade trees. A few are timber pests in houses and barns.

The family is very large and dominant throughout the world. Many of the species, being large and brightly colored, are favorites of collectors. Although species identification is difficult without the aid of the technical literature, the great number of distinctively marked species allows them to be correctly identified merely by comparing them with specimens in classified collections or with the many illustrations available. The family is divided into numerous subfamilies and tribes. Only the main subfamilies and some of the common species will be described and illustrated here. There are 956 species in the U.S. and Canada, assigned to 303 genera.

Subfamily Parandrinae

Tribe Parandrini

[106.1 *Parandra* Latreille (2 spp. (1), (2), (3))]

Subfamily Prioninae

Pronotum with elevated lateral margin, often toothed; usually large and somewhat flattened; brown or black. Face in profile oblique or flat; antennae usually long, sometimes with as many as 25 segments, which overlap tilelike.

Tribe Macrotomini

[106.2 *Strongylaspis* Thomson (1 spp., *S. corticaria* Erichson (2) FL); 106.3 *Archodontes* Lameere (1 sp., *A. melanopus* Linnaeus (2) FL; (3) TX)]

106.4 *Stenodontes* Serville

Three species in three subgenera in (2), (3): *Stenodontes* s. str., *Orthomallodon* Linsley, and *Mallodon* Serville. The following species may serve as an example:

S. (*Orthomallodon*) *dasytomus* Say. L. 23–47 mm. Antennae short, not reaching beyond basal third of elytra; reddish brown to dark brown or black; disk of pronotum with large, shiny spots and sides serrate. Larvae live in a variety of hardwoods and are sometimes a pest of shade trees. (See A&J 155.) (2) s.e. US; (3) s.w. US.

[106.5 *Neomallodon* Linsley (2 spp. (3) AZ)]

Tribe Ergatini

[106.6 *Ergates* Serville (2 spp. (3) CA; (5) CO)]

Tribe Mallaspini

106.7 *Derancistrus* Serville

Two species in two subgenera: *Elateropsis* Chevrolat (1 sp., *D. scabrosus* Gahan (2) FL) and *Sphenostethus* Haldeman, with one species, as follows:

D. taslei Buquet (See Fig. 24.176.) (1) n.e. US; (2) s.e. US; (3) TX.

Tribe Prionini

[106.8 *Orthosoma* Serville (1 sp., *O. brunneum* Forster (Fig. 24.177) (1) n.e. US; (2) s.e. US); 106.9 *Derobrachus* (4 spp. (2) s.e. US; (3) CA, AZ, TX; (4) NV)]

106.10 *Prionus* Fabricius

Thirteen species in four subgenera: *Prionellus* Casey, *Neopolyarthron* Semenov, *Antennalia* Casey, and *Homaesthesis* LeConte; the following species may serve as examples:

P. (*Prionellus*) *laticollis* (Drury) (Broad-necked Root Borer). L. 22–44 mm. Dark brown; antennae as long as body in male, half the length of body in female; pronotum with three stout teeth laterally. Adults attracted to lights at night. Larvae bore in roots of trees and shrubs, often damaging fruit trees and grape vines and other woody plants. (1) n.e. US; (2) s.e. US; (3) OK.

Fig. 24.176.

Fig. 24.177.

P. (*Neopolyarthron*) *imbricornis* Linnaeus (Tile-horned Prionus). L. 24–50 mm. Dark brown to black; antennae with 15 to 20 tilelike segments; pronotum twice as wide as long, narrower than elytra at base. Larvae live in roots of oak and chestnut and probably other plants; sometimes a pest. (See Fig. 24.178.) (1) n.e. US; (2) s.e. US; (3) TX.

P. (*Prionellus*) *californicus* Motschulsky (California Prionus). L. 24–55 mm. Similar to the preceding; antennae with 12 segments, tilelike in male, shorter and more slender in female. Larvae feed on roots of deciduous trees and also live in dead wood of both deciduous and coniferous trees. (3) s.w. US; (4) Pacific n.w.

Tribe Tragosomini

[106.11 *Tragosoma* Serville (4 spp. (1), (3), (4), (5) MT, WY, CO)]

Subfamily Spondylinae

[106.12 *Spondylis* Fabricius (1 sp., *S. upiformis* Mannerheim (1) MI; (2) CA, AZ, NM; (4) BC, WA, OR, ID, NV, UT; (5) AB, MT, WY, SD, NE, CO); 106.13 *Scaphinus* LeConte (1 sp., *S.* (2) VA, AR, AL, GA, SC, FL)]

Subfamily Aseminae

Head short, not narrowed behing eyes; face in profile oblique; second antennal segment longer than broad and nearly one-half as long as third segment.

Fig. 24.178.

Tribe Asemini

106.14 *Arhopalus* Serville

Four species in (1), (3), (4), (5), including the following:

A. productus (LeConte) (New-house Borer). L. 12–25 mm. Black; elongate, slender; surface clothed with short, pale, hairlike setae; front tibiae with one apical spur. Sometimes a pest that emerges from lumber in new buildings. (3) s.w. US.

[106.15 *Megasemum* Kraatz (1 sp., *M. asperum* LeConte (3) s.e. US; (4) Pacific n.w.); 106.16 *Asemum* Eschscholtz (4 spp. (1), (3), (4))]

106.17 *Tetropium* Kirby

Six species in (1), (3), (4), including the following:

T. abietis Fall (Roundedheaded Fir Borer). L. 13–18 mm. Brown to dark brown; elongate, moderately slender; eyes completely divided by antennal bases; pronotum coarsely granulate. Larvae bore in white and red fir and some other conifers. (3) CA; (4) WA, OR.

Tribe Atimiini

[106.18 *Atimia* Haldeman (6 spp. (3), (4))]

106.19 *Paratimia* Fisher

One species, as follows:

P. conicola Fisher (Roundheaded Cone Borer). L. 8–13 mm. Reddish brown; elongate, slender, somewhat cylindrical; vesture coarse, evenly distributed on elytra and pronotum; clytra with narrow, white sutural stripe. Larvae feed on cones of pine. (3) n. CA; (4) OR, coastal.

Tribe Michthisomini

[106.20 *Michthisoma* LeConte (1 sp., *M. heterodoxum* LeConte (2) NC, GA)]

Subfamily Cerambycinae

Pronotum without lateral margins; front tibia without groove on inner side; last segment of maxillary palpi usually more or less triangular; eyes usually notched for base of antennae.

Tribe Opsimini

[106.21 *Opsimus* Mannerheim (1 sp., *O. quadrilineatus* Mannerheim (3) CA; (4) WA, OR); 106.22 *Dicentrus* LeConte (2 spp. (3) CA; (4) WA, OR)]

Tribe Smodicini

[106.23 *Smodicum* Haldeman (3 spp. (1), (2), (3))]

Tribe Methiini

[106.24 *Malacopterus* Serville (1 sp., *M. tenellus* Fabricius (3) s.w. US); 106.25 *Eudistenia* Fall (1 sp. *E. cstipennis* Fall (3) CA); 106.26 *Vandykea* Linsley (1 sp., *V. tuberculata* Linsley (3) CA); 106.27 *Paranoplium* Casey (1 sp. *P. gracile* LeConte (3) CA); 106.28 *Oeme* Newman (2 spp. (1); (2); (3) CA, AZ; (4) UT; (5) CO), including *O. rigida* (Say) (Fig. 24.179) (1) n.e. US; (2) s.e. US); 106.29 *Methia* Newman (17 spp. (2), (3), (4), (5)); 106.30 *Styloxus* LeConte (2 spp. (3), (4)); 106.31 *Pseudomethia* Linsley (1 sp., *P. arida* Linsley (3) CA, AZ); 106.32 *Coleomethia* Linsley (1 sp., *C. evaniiformis* Knull (3) TX); 106.33 *Haplidoeme* Chemsak and Linsley (1 sp., *H. schlingeri* Chemsak

Fig. 24.179.

Fig. 24.180.

and Linsley (3) CA); 106.34 *Tessaropa* Haldeman (1 sp., *T. tenuipes* Haldeman (Fig. 24.180) (1) n.e. US; (2) s.e. US)]

Tribe Achrysonini

[106.35 *Achryson* Serville (1 sp., *A. surinamum* Linnaeus (2) s.e. US; (3) s.e. US); 106.36 *Geropa* Casey (1 sp., *G. concolor* (LeConte) (3) TX)]

Tribe Graciliini

[106.37 *Gracilia* Serville (1 sp., *G. minuta* Fabricius (See Fig. 24.181) (1) n.e. US; (2) s.e. US); 106.38 *Perigracilia* Linsely (1 sp., *P. delicata* Knull (3) AZ); 106.39 *Hypexilis* Horn (1 sp., *H. pallida* Horn (3) TX)]

Fig. 24.181.

Fig. 24.182.

Tribe Hesperophanini

[106.40 *Malobidion* Schaeffer (1 sp., *M. brunneum* Schaeffer (3) AZ); 106.41 *Eucrossus* LeConte (1 sp., *E. villicornis* LeConte (3) s.e. US); 106.42 *Osmidus* LeConte (1 sp., *O. guttatus* LeConte (4) NV); 106.43 *Cacophrissus* Bates (1 sp., *C. pauper* Bates (3) AZ); 106.44 *Xeranoplium* Linsley (2 spp. (3) AZ; (5) CO); 106.45 *Haplidus* LeConte (2 spp. (3) s.w. US; (4) Pacific n.w.); 106.46 *Hesperanoplium* Linsley (2 spp. (3) CA); 106.47 *Meganoplium* Linsely (1 sp., *M. imbelle* LeConte (3) CA); 106.48 *Penichroa* Stephens (1 sp., *P. fasciata* Stephens (1) IN, PA; (4) ID); 106.49 *Tylonotus* Haldeman (2 spp. (1) n.e. US; (2) s.e. US; (3) s.e. US, including *T. bimaculatus* Haldeman (Fig. 24.182) (1) n.e. US; (2) s.e. US; (3) AZ); 106.50 *Zamodes* LeConte (1 sp. *Z. obscurus* LeConte (1) PA); 106.51 *Brothylus* LeConte (2 spp. (3) s.w. US; (4) OR); 106.52 *Hesperophanes* Mulsant (1 sp., *H. pubescens* Haldeman (See Fig. 24.183) (1) n.e. US; (2) s.e. US); 106.53 *Stromatium* Serville (1 sp., *S. fulvum* Villers (?locality))]

106.54 *Eburia* Serville

Ten species that are easily recognized by the shiny, ivory-colored raised markings on the elytra, including the following:

E. quadrigeminata (Say) (Four-marked Ash Borer). L. 12–24 mm. Ivory spots of elytra prominent, four of them basal, four midway. Larvae bore into the heartwood of many kinds of deciduous trees. (See Fig. 24.184.) (1) n.e. US; (2) s.e. US; (3) TX.

Tribe Elaphidionini

[106.55 *Aneflus* LeConte (6 spp. (2) s.e. US); 106.56 *Curtomerus* Stephens (2 spp. (2) FL); 106.57 *Nesostizocera* Linsley (1 sp., *N.*

Fig. 24.183.

Fig. 24.184.

floridana Linsley (2) FL); 106.58 *Pseudoperiboeum* Linsley (1 sp., *P. lengi* Schaeffer (3) AZ)]

106.59 *Psyrassa* Pascoe

Four species, including the following:

P. texana Schaeffer (Slender Texas Longhorn). L. 11–13 mm. Slender, tapered body, uniformly chestnut brown; head coarsely but sparsely and irregularly punctate; thorax shallowly punctate and clothed with sparse, long, erect hairlike setae; elytra coarsely and somewhat densely punctate and clothed with a few scattered, long, erect hairlike setae, antennae longer than body in males, shorter in females. Adults can be beaten from acacias and are attracted to lights at night. Larval host unknown. (See A&J 156.) (3) TX.

[106.60 *Stenosphenus* Haldeman (15 spp. (1) n.e. US; (2) s.e. US; (4) UT, including *S. notatus* Oliver (Fig. 24.185) (1) n.e. US; (2) s.e. US); 106.61 *Atylostagma* White (1 sp., *A. glabrum* Schaeffer (3) AZ); 106.62 *Stenelaphus* Linsley (1 sp., *S. alienus* (LeConte) (3) AZ); 106.63 *Neaneflus* Linsley (2 spp. (2) s.e. US; (4) UT); 106.64 *Anopliomorpha* Linsely (1 sp., *A. rinconium* (Casey) (3) AZ); 106.65 *Axestinus* LeConte (1 sp., *A. obscurus* LeConte (3) AZ, TX); 106.66 *Micraneflus* Linsley (1 sp., *M. imbellis* Casey (3) CA, AZ); 106.67 *Romulus* Knull (1 sp., *R. globosus* Knull (2) FL); 106.68 *Sphaerion* Serville (1 sp., *S. exutum* Newman (3) TX); 106.69 *Aneflomorpha* Casey (20 spp. (1) n.e. US; (2) s.e. US; (3) s.w. US; (4) OR, NV, UT, including *A. subpubescens* (LeConte) (Fig. 24.186) (1) n.e. US; (2) s.e. US.)]

106.70 *Enaphalodes* Haldeman

Eight species, the following of which are common:

E. niveitectus Schaeffer (Barklike Longhorn). L. 23–27 mm. Brown or reddish black; sparsely pubescent except for

Fig. 24.185.

Fig. 24.186.

dense patches of white pubescence on head, pronotum, and most of elytra; head coarsely, sparsely punctate between eyes; antennae longer than body, each segment with a spine; pronotum coarsely and densely punctate; elytra coarsely but not densely punctate, with punctures finer toward apex and apices prominently bisponose. Adults found on branches and trunks of oak; larvae bore in oak. (See A&J 157.) (3) s. AZ.

 E. rufulus (Haldeman) (Red Oak Borer). (1) n.e. US; (2) s.e. US; (3) TX, OK; (5) MN, MO.

 E. cortiphagus Craighead. (See Fig 24.187.) (1) n.e. US; (3) AZ.

[106.71 *Eustromula* Cockerell (2 spp. (3) s.w. US); 106.72 *Astromula* Chemsak and Linsley (1 sp., *A. nitidum* Chemsak and Linsley (3) CA)]

106.73 *Elaphidionoides* Linsley

Nine species—found in (1) n.e. US; (2) s.e. US; (3) s.w. US—the following of which is common:

 E. villosus Fabricius (Twig Pruner). (1) n.e. US; (2) s.e. US; (3) AZ, TX, OK; (5) MB, KS.

[106.74 *Gymnopsyra* Linsley (3 spp. (3) AZ, NM, TX); 106.75 *Anelaphus* Linsely (14 spp. (1), (2), (3)); 106.76 *Micranoplium* Linsley (1 sp., *M. unicolor* (Haldeman) (1) n.e. US; (2) s.e. US); 106.77 *Elaphidionopsis* Linsley (1 sp., *E. fasciatipennis* Linsley (3) TX); 106.78 *Peranoplium* Linsley (5 spp. (3) CA, AZ); 106.79 *Anoplocurius* Fisher (3 spp. (3) CA, AZ, NM)]

106.80 *Elaphidion* Serville

Eight species in (2) SC, FL; (3) TX, including the following:

 E. mucronatum (Say). L. 13–19 mm. Reddish brown to dark brown; pubescence dense, irregular, mottled; antennae longer than body in male, about as long in female. Larvae feed on bark and sapwood of various hardwoods. (1) n.e. NA; (2) s.e. US; (3) TX; (5) MN, KS.

Tribe Piezocerini

[106.81 *Piezocera* Serville (1 sp., *P. serraticollis* Linell (3) TX)]

Tribe Ibidionini

[106.82 *Neocompsa* Martins (2 spp. (3) AZ, TX; 106.83 *Heterachthes* Newman (6 spp. (1) n.e. US; (2) s.e. US; (3) AZ, TX, including *H. ebenus* Newman (Fig. 24.188) (1) n.e. US; (2) s.e. US; (3) TX)]

Fig. 24.187.

Fig. 24.188.

Tribe Curiini

[106.84 *Curius* Newman (1 sp., *C. dentatus* Newman (1) MD; (2) s.e. US); 106.85 *Plectromerus* Haldeman (1 sp., *P. dentipes* Oliver (2) LA, MS, AL, FL)]

Tribe Obriini

[106.86 *Obrium* Dejean (10 spp. (1), (2), (3), (4), including *O. rubidum* LeConte (Fig. 24.189) (1) n.e. US; (2) s.e. US)]

Tribe Hyboderini

[106.87 *Hybodera* LeConte (2 spp. (3) CA; (4) OR); 106.88 *Lampropterus* Mulsant (2 spp. (3) CA; (4) WA, OR); 106.89 *Pseudopilema* Linsley (1 sp., *P. hoppingi* Van Dyke (3) CA); 106.90 *Megobrium* LeConte (1 sp., *M. edwardsi* LeConte (3) CA)]

Fig. 24.189.

Fig. 24.190.

Fig. 24.192.

Tribe Eumichthini

[106.91 *Eumichthus* LeConte (1 sp., *E. oedipus* LeConte (3) CA; (4) WA, OR); 106.92 *Poecilobrium* Horn (1 sp., *P. chalybeum* LeConte (3) CA; (4) BC; (5) CO)]

Tribe Nathriini

[106.93 *Nathrius* Bréthes (1 sp., *N. brevipennis* Mulsant (3) s. CA)]

Tribe Molorchini

[106.94 *Molorchus* Fabricius (3 spp. (1), (2), (3), (4), including *M. bimeculatus* Say (Fig. 24.190) (1) n.e. US; (2) s.e. US)]

Tribe Stenopterini

[106.95 *Callimoxys* Kraatz (2 spp. (1), (2), (3) CA; (4) WA, OR, including *C. sanguinicollis* Olivier (Fig. 24.191) (1) n.e. US; (2) s.e. US)]

Tribe Rhinotragini

[106.96 *Odontocera* Serville (1 sp., *O. aurocincta arizonensis* Linsley (3) AZ)]

Tribe Callichromatini

[106.97 *Plinthocoelium* Shmidt (2 spp. *P.* (1), (2), (3))]

Tribe Rosaliini

106.98 *Rosalia* Serville

One species, as follows:

R. funebris Motschulsky (Bander Alder Borer). L. 23–28 mm. Elongate, somewhat flattened, sides nearly parallel; black

with patches and bands of dense white or bluish-white pubescence; antennae of male longer than body, of female somewhat shorter than body; surface of head and pronotum finely, closely punctate; elytra roughly punctate, more coarsely at the base. Adults are found near their host plant after emerging. Larvae infest alder, oak, willow, and other trees, often causing serious damage. (See A&J 158.) (3) CA; (4) AK, BC, WA, OR.

Tribe Dryobiini

[106.99 *Dryobius* LeConte (1 sp., *D. sexnotatus* Linsley (24.192) (1) n.e. US; (2) s.e. US); 106.100 *Ornithia* Thomson (1 sp., *O. mexicana* Sturm (3) TX)]

Tribe Callidiini

[106.101 *Pronocera* Motschulsky (1 sp., *P. collaris* Kirby (24.193) (1) n.e. NA; (4) AK, WA)]

106.102 *Hylotrupes* Serville

One species, as follows:

H. bajulus (Linnaeus) (Old-house Borer). Larvae in dry coniferous wood in building roofs and attics and sometimes in walls. (1) n.e. US; (2) s.e. US; (3) TX; (5) MN, KS.

[106.103 *Callidiellum* Linsley (2 spp. (3) CA, AZ)]

106.104 *Semanotus* Mulsant

Four species, of which the following are pests:

S. litigiosus (Casey) (Fir Tree Borer). Found throughout coniferous tree area of North America.

Fig. 24.191.

Fig. 24.193.

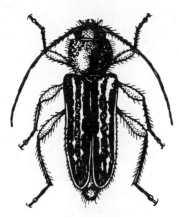

Fig. 24.194.

S. ligneus (Fabricius) (Cedar Tree Borer). Found throughout coniferous tree area of North America.

[106.105 *Meriellum* Linsley (1 sp., *M. proteus* Kirby (Fig. 24.194) (1) n.e. US; (5) CO)]

106.106 *Callidium* Mulsant

Nineteen species, including the following:

C. antennatum hesperum Casey (Black-horned Pine Borer). (3) CA: (4) BC, WA, OR, UT; (5) WY, CO, SD.

[106.107 *Phymatodes* Mulsant (24 spp.); 106.108 *Physocnemum* Haldeman (3 spp. (1) n.e. US; (2) s.e. US); 106.109 *Ropalopus* Mulsant (1 sp., *R. sanguinicollis* Horn (Fig. 24.195) (1) n.e. NA; (2) s.e. US); 106.110 *Elatotrypes* Fisher (1 sp., *E. hoferi* Fisher (5) CO); 106.111 *Xylocrius* LeConte (2 spp. (3) CA, NM; (4) NV)]

Tribe Clytini

106.112 *Megacyllene* Casey

Nine species, the following are pests:

M. robiniae Forester (Locust Borer). (1) n.e. US; (2) s.e. US.

M. caryae (Gahan) (Painted Hickory borer). (1) n.e. US; (2) s.e. US; (3) TX.

[106.113 *Placosternus* Hopping (2 spp. (2) FL; (3) AZ, NM, TX)]

106.114 *Glycobius* LeConte

One species, as follows:

G. speciosus Say (Sugarmaple Borer). (1) ne.e NA.

[106.115 *Calloides* LeConte (2 spp. (1) n.e. NA; (2) s.e. US; (3) CA, AZ; (4) OR, NV, UT); 106.116 *Ochraethes* Chevrolat (1 sp., *O. citrinus*

Fig. 24.195.

Chevrolat (3) TX); 106.117 *Megacheuma* Michel (1 sp., *M. brevipennis* LeConte (4) UT); 106.118 *Tylcus* Casey (1 sp., *T. hartwegi* White (3) AZ, TX); 106.119 *Triodoclytus* Casey (1 sp., *T. lanifer* LeConte (3) CA; (4) OR); 106.120 *Sarosesthes* Thomson (1 sp., *S. fulminans* Fabricius (1) n.e. US; (2) s.e. US); 106.121 *Tanyochraethes* Chemsak and Linsley (1 sp., *T. tildeni* Chemsak and Linsley (3) TX); 106.122 *Euryscelis* Dejean (1 sp., *E. suturalis* Olivier (2) FL)]

106.123 *Xylotrechus* Chevrolat

Twenty-two species, including the following:

X. colonus Fabricius (Rustic Borer). (1) n.e. US; (2) s.e. US.

X. insignis LeConte (Willow Longhorn). L. 12–18 mm. Cylindrical; male reddish brown with coarse brown and yellow vestiture; head with conspicuous V-shaped frontal ridge; surface roughly punctate; elytra with yellow pubescence forming a pair of basal spots and transverse, subapical, and apical bands. Female larger and black, with broad yellow band at base and apex of pronotum; elytra with five transverse bands, incomplete basally, complete apically. A pest of willow, poplar, and other trees. (See A&J 159.) (1) CA: (3) WA, OR.

X. longitarsis Casey. L. 10–19 mm. Black; vestiture above patterned white, grayish, or sometimes yellowish, forming a band along anterior margin of pronotum, a patch on the scutellum, a short, oval, transverse, or lunate bar behind the shoulders, an undulating, transverse median line extending forward along the suture, a subapical bar directed backward toward the suture, and an apical patch. Larvae are found under bark of dead and dying Douglas fir. (4) Pacific n.w.

X. aceris Fisher (Gallmaking Maple Borer). (1) n.e. US.

106.124 *Neoclytus* Thomson

Twenty-six species, including the following:

N. acuminatus Fabricius (Red-headed Ash Borer). (1) n.e. NA; (3) NM, s. TX; (5) MB, MN, CO.

106.125 *Clytus* Laicharting

Eight species, including the following:

C. blaisdelli VanDyke (Douglas Fir Borer). L. 9–11 mm. Elongate and moderately slender; black, with legs and antennae reddish and body distinctly margined with a band of yellow or whitish hairlike setae; pubescence pattern of elytra consists of an oval, slightly oblique spot on the shoulder, a transverse band at the apical third, and a vague apical patch; antennae only about half as long as the body. The larvae infest Douglas fir. (See A&J 160.) (3) CA.

C. marginicollis Laporte and Gory. (See Fig. 24.196.) (1) n.e. US; (2) s.e. US.

106.126 *Cyltoleptus* Casey

One species, as follows:

C. albofasciatus Laporte and Gory (Grape Trunk Borer). (See Fig. 24.197.) (1) n.e. NA; (2) s.e. US.

Tribe Tillomorphini

[106.127 *Euderces* LeConte (4 spp. (3) s.e. US); 106.128 *Tetranodus* Linell (1 sp., *T. niveicollis* Linell (3) TX); 106.129 *Pentanodes* Schaeffer (3) TX)]

Fig. 24.196.

Tribe Anaglyptini

[106.130 *Tilloclytus* (1 sp., *T. geminatus* Haldeman (1) n.e. NA); 106.131 *Crytophorus* LeConte (1 sp., *C. verrucosus* Olivier (Fig. 24.198) (1) n.e. US; (2) s.e. US; 106.132 *Microclytus* LeConte (2 spp. (1) n.e. NA)]

Tribe Cleomenini

[106.133 *Dihammaphora* Chevrolat (1 sp., *D. dispar* Chevrolat (3) TX)]

Tribe Rhopalophorini

[106.134 *Rhopalophora* Serville (6 spp. (1) n.e. US: (3) s.e. US; (3) s.w. US)]

Tribe Heteropsini

[106.135 *Heterops* Blanchard (1 sp., *H. dimidiata* Chevrolat (2) FL)]

Tribe Agallissini

[106.136 *Agallissus* Dalman (1 sp., *A. lepturoides* Chevrolat (3) TX); 106.137 *Zagymnus* LeConte (1 sp., *Z. clerinus* LeConte (2) GA, FL); 106.138 *Osmopleura* Linsley (1 sp., *O. chamaeropis* Horn (2) GA, FL)]

Tribe Ancylocerini

[106.139 *Ancylocera* Serville (1 sp., *A. bicolor* Olivier (2) s.e. US)]

Tribe Purpuricenini

[106.140 *Perarthrus* LeConte (2 spp. (3) CA, AZ); 106.141 *Mannophorus* LeConte (2 spp. (3) AZ, TX); 106.142 *Taranomis* Casey (1 sp., *T. bivittata* Dupont (3) AZ, TX); 106.143 *Lophalia* Casey (1 sp., *L. cyanicollis* Dupont (3) TX); 106.144 *Gnaphalodes* Thomson (1 sp., *G. trachyderoides* Thomson (3) TX); 106.145 *Stenaspis* Serville (2 spp. (3) s.w. US)]

Fig. 24.197.

Fig. 24.198.

106.146 *Callona* Waterhouse

One species, as follows:

C. rimosa Buquet (Mesquite Longhorn). L. 30–38 mm. Male brown; femora frequently reddish orange except at base and apex; elytra green with brassy reflection; dorsal surface bare, ventral surface pubescent; antennae somewhat shorter than body; pronotum coarsely, densely punctate; elytral surface crinkled. Female somewhat larger than male and completely black; antennae reach beyond middle of elytra. Adults are found on mesquite, where they emerged from the wood. Larvae bore into the sapwood about an inch below the surface. As they grow, the gallery is enlarged and waste material discarded through a small opening at the surface; this opening is otherwise kept plugged to prevent ant invasions. (See A&J 161.) (3) s. TX.

[106.147 *Crioprosopus* Serville (2 spp. (3) AZ, TX); 106.148 *Purpuricenus* Dejean (5 spp. (1) n.e. NA: (3) CA, AZ, TX); 106.149 *Deltaspis* Serville (2 spp. (3) CA, AZ)]

106.150 *Knulliana* Linsley

One species, as follows:

K. cincta (Drury) (Banded Hickory Borer). (1) n.e. NA; (2) s.e. US.

106.151 *Tragidion* Serville

Six species, in (1), (2), (3), including the following:

T. annulatum LeConte (Wasplike Longhorn). L. 15–32 mm. Males dark brown or reddish brown; elytra dull brownish yellow margined at base with brown; pubescence golden on elytra except at base; other parts of body black with bluish or violet reflections; antennae longer than body, broadly ringed with orange or brownish yellow. Female black at base; antennae shorter than body. Adults are found on various flowers. Larvae bore into branches of *Baccharis sergilloides*, which grows at elevations between 2000 and 5500 ft. (See A&J 162.) (3) AZ, TX.

[106.152 *Metaleptus* Bates (1 sp., *M. batesi* Horn (3) CA, AR); 106.153 *Rhodoleptus* Linsley (1 sp., *R. femoratus* Schaeffer (3) CA, AZ); 106.154 *Aethecerinus* Fall and Cockerell (3 spp. (2) FL; (3) s.w. US); 106.155 *Chrotoma* Casey (1 sp., *C. dunniana* Casey (3) TX); 106.156 *Amannus* LeConte (3 spp. (3) CA, AZ, NM, TX: (4) NV, UT); 106.157 *Batyle* Thomson (4 spp. (1), (3), (4), (5)); 106.158 *Schizax* LeConte (1 sp., *S. senex* LeConte (3) CA, AZ); 106.159 *Plionoma* Casey (2 spp. (3) CA, AZ, NM, TX); 106.160 *Tylosis* LeConte (4 spp. (3) TX; 106.161

Chlorida (1 sp., *C. festiva* Linnaeus (2) FL); 106.162 *Crossidius* LeConte (12 spp. (3), (4), (5); 106.163 *Elytroleptus* Dugès (8 spp. (3); 106.164 *Parevander* Aurivillius (1 sp., *P. xanthomelas* Guérin (3) TX)]

Tribe Holopleurini

[106.165 *Holopleura* LeConte (1 sp., *H. marginata* LeConte (3) CA; (4) BC, WA, OR)]

Tribe Trachyderini

106.166 *Dendrobias* Serville

One species, as follows:

D. mandibularis Serville (Horse-bean Longhorn). L. 17–32 mm. Body shiny black; elytra yellow with base dark and usually an arcuate median band that divides yellow area but which is sometimes reduced or broken; suture and lateral margins sometimes predominantly dark; mandibles very large in male; antennae very long, extending beyond length of body. Adults sometimes come to lights at night. Larvae infest gorse-bean, willow, and citrus trees, feeding on dry, dead branches. (See A&J 163.) (3) AZ, NM, TX.

Tribe Lissonotini

[106.167 *Lissonotus* Dalman (1 sp., *L. flavocinctus* Dupont (3) CA, AZ, NM, TX)]

Tribe Magaderini

[106.168 *Megaderus* Dejean (1 sp., *M. bifasciatus* Dupont (3) AZ, TX)]

Subfamily Lepturinae

Head elongate, narrowed behind the eyes; face in profile oblique; second antennal segment much less than one-half as long as third; apical segment of maxillary palpi blunt at tip; eyes usually oval with at most only a slight antennal notch; elytra usually narrows apically. This large and difficult subfamily contains many colorful beetles, often found on flowers.

Tribe Desmocerini

106.169 *Desmocerus* Serville

Three species, the folloiwng of which is common:

D. palliatus Forster (Elderberry Longhorn). L. 18–26 mm. Elongate and subcylindrical; metallic bluish except for yellow basal half of elytra, which has two black spots; surface rather finely and densely punctate, coarser on elytra; antennae extends to about middle of the elytra in both sexes; male antennae slightly longer than female antennae. Adults are often found flying around elderberry bushes, where they feed on the flowers. Larvae bore in the roots or base of the stems of the elderberry. When they are mature, they work their way into the hollow pith of the branches and excavate an pupal cell. Adults emerge in the spring and early summer. (See A&J 164.) (1) n.e. NA; (2) s.e. US.

Tribe Necydalini

106.170 *Necydalis* Linnaeus

Seven species, including the following:

N. cavipennis LeConte (Hornet Longhorn). L. 13–24 mm. Reddish brown to black; surface dull; pubescence dense and golden; antennae stout, black, reddish basally, and much shorter than body; elytra very short, with apices narrowed; legs

Fig. 24.199.

elongate, femora swollen. Adults are found by beating oak branches. Larvae bore in several species of oaks, eucalyptus, and other trees. (3) CA, AZ; (4) WA, OR.

N. mellita Say. Similar to the preceding. Flies and sounds like a large bee. (See Fig. 24.199.) (1) n.e. US; (2) s.e. US.

106.171 *Ulochaetes* LeConte

One species, as follows:

U. leoninus LeConte (Lion Beetle). L. 17–32 mm. Black; apical third of elytra and tibiea, except apices, pale yellowish brown; pronotum densely covered with ochreous hairs; elytra very short, hardly reaching base of abdomen; antennae with third segment as long as fourth and fifth combined. This beetle is similar to the preceding, but the hairy pronotum serves to distinguish the two genera. Although it resembles the bumble-bee in appearance as well as in action and flight, it has been given the common name Lion Beetle, probably because of its habits when disturbed. It raises its elytra, curves the abdomen upward, and buzzes (or "roars") loudly without flying away. Larvae bore in the heart and sapwood of various conifers. (3) CA; (4) WA, OR.

Tribe Lepturini

Note: *Anoplodera* Mulsant, a generic name frequently used for North American species of Lepturini, is no longer applied to North American species. Instead, these species may be found in the following genera: 106.205 *Judolia* Mulsant, 106.216 *Ortholeptura* Casey, 106.218 *Strangalepta* Casey, 106.221 *Xestoleptura* Casey, 106.223 *Trigonarthris* Haldeman, 106.225 *Brachyleptura* Casey, and 106.226 *Strophiona* Casey.

[106.172 *Xylosteus* Frivaldszku (1 sp., *X. ornatus* LeConte (3) CA: (4) OR); 106.173 *Leptorhabdium* Kaatz (1 sp., *L. pictum* Haldeman (1) n.e. US: (2) s.e. US)]

106.174 *Centrodera* LeConte

Eleven species [found in (1) n.e. US; (2) s.e. US; (3) CA], including the following:

C. spurca LeConte (Stump Borer). L. 19–30 mm. Stout; pale brownish, shiny surface; tips of mandibles, eyes, and two marginal spots at middle of elytra black; head densely punctate; pubescence sparse; male antennae longer than body; pronotum and elytra with coarse punctures; female antennae shorter than

Fig. 24.200.

Fig. 24.202.

body. Adults are collected by beating branches and nocturnally at lights. Larvae live in soil and feed in rotting stumps and roots. (See A&J 166.) (3) CA; (4) WA, OR, NV, UT.

[106.175 *Piodes* LeConte (1 sp., *P. coriacea* LeConte (4) Pacific n.w.)]

106.176 *Stenocorus* Fabricius

Twelve species, including the following:

S. vestitus Haldemann (Flower Lepturine). L. Males, 9–16 mm; females, 11–21 mm. Males elongate; elytra broad at base, tapering posteriorly; black with brownish yellow elytra, usually pale appendages, and often pale abdomen; pubescence dense, recumbent, and usually golden; surface generally densely punctate; antennae about as long as body. Females broader, with less tapering elytra; antennae extend to about middle of elytra. Frequently found on flowers of many kinds. Larvae breed in Douglas fir. (See A&J 167.) (3) CA; (4) WA, OR.

S. nubifer LeConte (Variable Flower Lepturine). L., Males, 9–17 mm; females, 12–21 mm. Male body strongly tapered posteriorly; all black to brownish yellow with head black; pronotum, legs, and ventral surface pale; elytra often with pale shoulders or pale stripes; pubescence varies from very sparse to dense and recumbent; surface finely punctate; antennae about as long as body. Sides of elytra of females less tapered than those of males; antennae extend a little beyond middle of elytra. Adults frequent flowers of many kinds. (See A&J 168.) (3) CA; (4) WA, OR, ID, NV, UT.

S. cylindricollis (Say). (See Fig. 24.200.) (1) n.e. US; (2) s.e. US.

[106.177 *Encyclops* Newman (2 spp. (1) n.e. NA; (2) s.e. US; (3) CA; (4) OR, including *E. coarulea* (Say) (Fig. 24.201) (1) n.e. US; (2) s.e. US; 106.178 *Pyrotrichus* LeConte (1 sp., *P. vitticollis* LeConte (3) CA; (4) BC, WA, OR, w. NV); 106.179 *Pachyta* Dejean (2 spp. (1) n.e. NA; (3) CA; (4) Pacific n.w.; (5) n. Central States and Provinces); 106.180 *Evodinus* LeConte (2 spp. (1) n.e. NA; (2) VA, NC; (3) CA; (4) Pacific n.w. (5) MT, MN); 106.181 *Anthophylax* LeConte (4 spp. (1), (2), including *A. quadrimaculatus* Champlain and Knull (Fig. 24.202) (1) OH; 106.182 *Neanthophylax* Linsley and Chemsak (4 spp. (3) CA; (4) BC, WA, OR, ID, UT; (5) CO); 106.183 *Rhagium* Fabricius (1 sp., *R. inquisitor* Linnaeus (1) n.e. NA; (4) Pacific n.w.; (5) n. Central Provinces); 106.184 *Comacmaeops* Linsely and Chemack (1 sp., *C. brunnea* Knull (3) TX); 106.185 *Sachalinobia* Jacobson (1 sp., *S. rugipennis* Newman (1) n.e. NA; 106.186 *Gaurotes* LeConte (2 spp. (1) n.e. NA: (2) s.e. US); 106.187 *Acmaeops* LeConte (2 spp., including *A. discoideus* (Haldeman) (Fig. 24.203) (1) n.e. US; (2) s.e. US; 106.188 *Leptalia* LeConte (1 sp., *L. macilenta* Mannerheim (3) CA; (4) WA, OR)]

106.189 *Cortodera* Mulsant

Twenty species in (3), (4), (5), including the following:

C. subpilosa LeConte (Western Mountain Flower Longhorn). L. Males, 7–11 mm; females, 8–13 mm. Male elytra slightly tapered; black, often with elytra, legs, antennae, and abdomen brownish yellow; pubescence usually dense, long, and erect; punctation usually fine and dense; antennae shorter than to much longer than body; female stouter; antennae extend to about middle of elytra. Adults fly about many species of mountain flowers. (4) BC, WA, OR, UT. (See A&J 169.)

[106.190 *Pseudogaurotina* Plavilstshikov (2 spp. (1) n.e. NA; (3) CA; (4) WA, OR); 106.191 *Brachysomida* Casey (5 spp.); 106.192 *Gnathac-*

Fig. 24.201.

Fig. 24.203.

Fig. 24.204.

Fig. 24.205.

maeops Linsley and Chemsak (1 sp., *G. pratensis* Laicharting (1) n.e. NA; (4) Pacific n.w.; (5) n. Central Provinces); 106.193 *Metacmaeops* Linsley and Chemsak (1 sp., *M. vittata* Swederus (1) n.e. US); (2) s.e. US); 106.194 *Megachoriolaus* Linsley (5 spp. (3) s.e. US); 106.195 *Choriolaus* Bates (1 sp., *C. sabinoensis* Knull (3) AZ); 106.196 *Neobellamira* Swaine and Hopping (1 sp., *N. delicata* LeConte (3) CA; (4) OR); 206.197 *Strangalia* Serville (10 spp., including *S. acuminata* (Fig. 24.204) (Olivier). (1) n.e. US; (2) s.e. US; 106.198 *Bellamira* LeConte (1 sp., *B. scalaris* Say (1) n.e. NA; (2) s.e. US); 106.199 *Analeptura* Linsley and Chemsak (1 sp., *A. lineola* Say (1) n.e. NA; (2) s.e. US); 106.200 *Charisalia* Casey (1 sp., *C. americana* Haldeman (1) n.e. US; (2) s.e. US); 106.201 *Alosternida* Podany (1 sp., *A. chalybea* Haldeman (1) n.e. US; (2) s.e. US); 106.202 *Lycochoriolaus* Linsley and Chemsak (1 sp., *L. lateralis* Olivier (2) s.e. US; (3) TX); 106.203 *Orthochoriolaus* Linsely and Chemsak (1 sp., *O. chihuahuae* Bates (3) AZ); 106.204 *Grammoptera* Serville (6 spp. (1), (3), (4), (5)); 106.205 *Judolia* Mulsant (2 spp. (1), (3), (4), (5)); 106.206 *Pygoleptura* Linsley and Chemsak (3 spp. (1), (3), (4), (5)); 106.207 *Dorcasina* Casey (2 spp. (3) CA; (4) WA, OR); 106.208 *Idiopidonia* Swaine and Hopping (1 sp., *I. pedalis* LeConte (1) n.e. NA; (2) s.e. US); 106.209 *Typocerus* Leconte (15 spp.); 106.210 *Neoalosterna* Podany (2 spp. (1) n.e. NA; (2) s.e. US; (3) CA; (4) BC, WA, OR); 106.211 *Pseudostrangalia* Swaine and Hopping (1 sp., *P. cruentata* Haldemann (1) n.e. NA; (2) s.e. US)]

106.212 *Leptura* linnaeus

Fourteen species in (1), (3), (4), (5), including the following:

L. obliterata Haldeman (Flower Long-horned Beetle). L. 9–17 mm. Black; elytra yellowish brown except for black median and apical bands and usually two black median, subbasal spots. Several subspecies are distinguished on the basis of their color variation and other features. Adults occur on many species of flowers; larvae live in wood of various conifers. (3) CA; (4) WA, OR; (5) CO.

L. emarginata Fabricius. (See Fig. 24.205.) (1) n.e. US; (2) s.e. US.

106.213 *Stenostrophia* Casey

Three species [found in (3) CA; (4) BC, WA, OR, ID, NV, UT; (5) WY], including the following:

S. tribalteata LeConte (Tiger-spotted Flower Lepturine). L. 7–12 mm. Sides are tapered in male; female more robust; black, with appendages often pale; elytra with four yellow transverse bands; elytral pubescence yellow and black and dense, short, and recumbent; punctations fine and shallow;

antennae shorter than body. The two-colored pubescence is distinctive of this species. (See A&J 170.) (3) CA; (4) NV.

[106.214 *Trachysida* Casey (2 spp. (3), (4), (5)); 106.215 *Pidonia* Mulsant: 3 subgenera: *Pidonia* s. str., *Thesalia* Casey, and *Ceratopidonia* Linsley and Chemsak (6 spp. (1), (2), (3), (4)); 106.216 *Ortholeptura* Casey (3 spp. (3), (4)); 106.217 *Cyphonotida* Casey (1 sp., *C. laevicollis* Bates (3) AZ, TX); 106.218 *Strangalepta* Casey (2 spp. (1), (2)); 106.219 *Stictoleptura* Casey (1 sp., *S. canadensis* Oliver (1) n.e. NA; (3) CA; (4) BC; (5) MB); 106.220 *Anastrangalia* Casey (3 spp. (1) n.e. NA; (3) CA, AZ, NM; (4) BC, WA, OR)]

106.221 *Xestoleptura* Casey

Six species in (1), (3), (4), (5), including the following:

X. crassipes LeConte (Banded Long-horned Beetle). L. 8–15 mm. Black; legs, except front and middle tarsi, and often the abdomen yellowish; elytra yellowish with two black median spots that usually do not reach the suture, a broader black band at apical third, and black apices, but color pattern is variable; antennae of female usually yellowish. Larvae bore in moist, decomposed wood. (3) CA; (4) BC, WA, OR; (5) CO.

X. octonotata (Say). (See Fig. 24.206.) (1) n.e. US; (2) s.e. US.

[106.222 *Lepturopsis* Linsley and Chemsak (2 spp. (1) n.e. NA; (2) s.e. US; (3) CA; (4) BC, WA, OR); 106.223 *Trigonarthris* Haldeman (3 spp. (1) n.e. NA; (2) s.e. US; (5) KS); 106.224 *Acmaeopsoides* Linsley and Chemsak (1 sp., *A. rufula* Haldeman () WI, MI, ON; (5) MB, MN); 106.225 *Brachyleptura* Casey (7 spp. (1) n.e. NA; (2) s.e. US; (3) CA; (4) AK, BC, WA, OR); 106.226 *Strophiona* Casey (3 spp. (1) n.e. NA; (2) s.e. US; (3) CA; (4) AK, WA, OR; 106.227 *Cosmosalia* Casey (2 spp. (1), (3), (4), (5))]

Fig. 24.206.

Subfamily Lamiinae

Face vertical in profile; front tibiae usually with a more or less distinct, oblique groove on inner side; apical segment of maxillary palpi cylindrical, pointed at tip. Many of the species of this large and varied group are difficult to identify because of their similar appearance; others, however, are very distinctive.

Tribe Parmenini

[106.228 *Parmenosoma* Schaeffer (1 sp., *P. griseum* Schaeffer (3) TX); 106.229 *Ipochus* LeConte (1 sp., *I. fasciatus* LeConte (3) CA); 106.230 *Plectrura* Mannerheim (1 sp., *P. spinicauda* Mannerheim (3) CA; (4) AK, BC, WA, OR)]

Tribe Moneilemini

106.231 *Moneilema* Say

Six species in (3), (4), (5), including the following:

M. armatum LeConte (Black Cactus Longhorn). L. 13–33 mm. Elongate; black; surface shiny; head sparsely punctate with small and medium punctures intermixed; thorax slightly wider than long, with surface minutely punctate on disk and larger punctures along base and beneath lateral spine; elytra sparsely, irregularly punctate to within one-third of apex, the remaining portion densely punctate. Adults feed on cactus; they first appear in May or June and emerge continuously until the end of September. During the day, they hide on the lower part of the cactus for protection from the hot rays of the sun. After copulation takes place on the plant, the female lays her eggs in a fresh wound she has made with her mandibles at a point where the stem branches. The larvae bore into the cactus. Pupation takes place within the plant; emergent adults gnaw their way out. (See A&J 171.) (5) CO, KS.

Tribe Monochamini

106.232 *Neoptychodes* Dillon and Dillon

One species, as follows:

N. trilineatus (Linnaeus) (White-fringed Longhorn). L. 21–25 mm. Elongate-cylindrical, slightly flattened; reddish brown to black; elytra sometimes lighter; head with broad white stripe and a double orange stripe; pronotum with three white stripes; each elytron with two white stripes and a disk and with two rows, more or less distinct, of very small orangish dots, which sometimes fuse to form two lines; surface covered with yellowish gray scales; ventrally black with moderately long, fine, yellowish hairlike setae and irregular patches of dense, yellowish white scales. Larvae feed on fig, alder, and mulberry. (See A&J 172.) (2) SC, GA, LA, MS, AL, FL; (3) AZ, NM, TX.

106.233 *Plectrodera* Thomson

One species, as follows:

P. scalator (Fabricius) (Cottonwood Borer). (2) s.e. US; (3) s.w. US.

106.234 *Goes* LeConte

Seven species in (1), (2), (3), the following of which are pests:

G. tigrinus (De Geer) (White Oak Borer). (1) n.e. US; (2) s.e. US.

G. tessulatus (Haldeman) (Oak Sapling Borer). (1) n.e. US; (2) s.e. US.

[106.235 *Microgoes* Casey (1 sp., *M. oculatus* LeConte (1) n.e. NA; (2) s.e. US); 106.236 *Hebestola* Haldeman (1 sp., *H. nebulosa* Haldeman (1) n.e. NA; (2) s.e. US)]

106.237 *Monochamus* Guérin

Eight species, including the following:

M. carolinensis Olivier (Carolina Sawyer). L. 13–23 mm. Elongate, robust, subcylindrical; brownish; elytra irregularly mottled with patches of brown; pubescence black, gray, or white; males with extremely long antennae, sometimes four and one-half times as long as those of the female and never less than one and one-half times the length of the body. Larvae bore in pine, spruce, and fir. Adults are attracted to lights at night. (See A&J 173.) (1) n.e. US; (2) s.e. US.

M. marmorator Kirby (Balsam-fir Sawyer). (1) n.e. NA; (2) VA, NC.

M. scutellatus scutellatus Say (White-spotted Sawyer). (1) n.e. NA; (2) s.e. US; (3) NM; (4) AK, BC.

M. scutellatus oregonensis LeConte (Oregon Fir Sawyer). (3) CA; (4) BC, WA, OR, NV.

M. titillator Fabricius (Southern Pine Sawyer). (1) n.e. US; (2) s.e. US; (3) TX; (5) ND.

M. mutator LeConte (Spotted Pine Sawyer). (1) ON, PQ; (5) MN.

Tribe Mesosini

[106.238 *Synaphaeta* Thomson (1 sp., *S. guexi* LeConte (3) CA)]

Tribe Dorcaschematini

[106.239 *Dorcaschema* LeConte (3 spp. (1) n.e. NA; (2) s.e. US); 106.240 *Hetoemis* Haldeman (1 sp., *H. cinerea* Olivier (1) n.e. NA; (2) s.e. US; (5) KS)]

Tribe Adetini

[106.241 *Adetus* LeConte (1 sp., *A. brousi* Horn (3) TX; (5) KS); 106.242 *Parmenonta* Thomson (1 sp., *P. wickhami* Schaeffer (3) TX)]

Tribe Ataxiini

[106.243 *Ataxia* Haldeman (5 spp. (1), (2), (3)); 106.244 *Esthlogena* Thomson (2 spp. (3) s.w. US)]

Tribe Desmiphorini

[106.245 *Desmiphora* Serville (2 spp. (3) TX)]

Tribe Apodasyini

[106.246 *Eupogonius* (6 spp. (1), (2), (3)); 106.247 *Psenocerus* LeConte (1 sp., *P. supernotatus* Say (1) n.e. NA; (2) s.e. US)]

Tribe Estolini

[106.248 *Estoloides* Breuning (1 sp., *E. sordida* LeConte (3) AZ); 106.249 *Oplosia* Mulsant (1 sp., *O. nubila* (1) n.e. US)]

Tribe Pogonocherini

[106.250 *Pogonocherus* (6 spp.); 106.251 *Poliaenus* Bates (9 spp. (3) CA, AZ; (4) Pacific n.w.); 106.252 *Ecyrus* LeConte (3 spp. (1), (2), (3) TX); 106.253 *Callipogonius* Linsley (1 sp., *C. cornutus* Linsley (3) TX); 106.254 *Lophopogonius* Linsley (1 sp., *L. crinitus* LeConte (1), (2), (3), (4), (5)); 106.255 *Zaplous* LeConte (1 sp., *Z. annulatus* Chevrolat (2) FL); 106.256 *Pygmaeopsis* Schaeffer (1 sp., *P. viticola* Schaeffer (3)

TX); 106.257 *Lypsimena* LeConte (1 sp., *L. fuscata* LeConte (2) FL; (3) CA)]

Tribe Onciderini

106.258 *Lochmaeocles* Bates

Two species, including the following:

L. marmoratus Casey (Marbled Sawyer). L. 21–29 mm. Elongate-ovate, robust, subcylindrical; dark brown, covered with whitish pubescence; head with white and orange pubescence; pronotum sometimes with indistinct orange markings on each side; elytra with extreme base white and usually with an oblique, broken band at middle of denser white, with small, irregular reddish-orange spots, usually outlined in white and scattered over the disk; antennae of males about twice the length of body, of female only slightly longer than body. Adults are twig girdlers. Larvae feed on bark and sapwood. (3) AZ.

[106.259 *Cacostola* Fairmaire and Germain (2 spp. (3) TX)]

106.260 *Oncideres* Serville

Four species, the following of which is a pest:

O. cingulata Say (Twig Girdler). (1) n.e. US; (2) s.e. US.

Tribe Hippopsini

[106.261 *Hippopsis* Serville (1 sp., *H. lemniscata* (Fabricius) (1) n.e. US; (2) s.e. US)]

Tribe Spalacopsini

[106.262 *Spalacopsis* Newman (5 spp. (2) FL; (3) TX); 106.263 *Dorcasta* Pascoe (1 sp., *D. cinerea* Horn (3) TX)]

Tribe Anisocerini

[106.264 *Thryallis* Thomson (1 sp., *T. undatus* Chevrolat (3) TX)]

Tribe Acanthoderini

[106.265 *Aegomorphus* Haldeman (5 spp. (1), (2), (3)); 106.266 *Peritapnia* Horn (1 sp., *P. fabra* Horn (3) AZ); 106.267 *Steirastoma* Lacordaire (1 sp., *S. brevis* Sulzer (2) FL)]

Tribe Acanthocini

106.268 *Canonura* Casey

Three species in (3), (4), (5), the following of which is a pest:

C. princeps (Walker) (Ponderosa Pine Bark Borer). (3) CA; (4) BC, WA, OR.

Fig. 24.207.

[106.269 *Tylocerina* Casey (1 sp., *T. nodosus* Fabricius (1) n.e. US; (2) s.e. US); 106.270 *Neacanthocinus* Dillon (3 spp.); 106.271 *Trichocanonura* Dillon (1 sp., *T. linearis* Skinner (3) AZ); 106.272 *Ceratographis* Gahan (1 sp., *C. biguttata* LeConte (1) n.e. NA; (2) s.e. US); 106.273 *Graphisurus* Kirby (3 spp. (1), (2), (3) TX; (4) ID, including *G. triangulifer* Haldeman (Fig. 24.207) (1) n.e. US; (2) s.e. US)]

106.274 *Coenopoeus* Horn

One species, as follows:

C. palmeri LeConte (Cactus Longhorn). L. 18–24 mm. Black, densely covered with fine, dark brown pubescence; pronotum and elyta usually marked with ashy or yellowish gray pubescence in spots, or occasionally over the entire area, sometimes forming bands; antennae about as long as body in both sexes, all segments broadly annulate with ashy pubescence at base. Adults come to lights at night. Larvae are wood borers. (See A&J 175.) (3) s.w. US.

106.275 *Lagocheirus* Dejean

Two species in (3) TX, the following of which is a pest of frangipan:

L. undatus (Voet) (Plumeria Borer). (3) s. TX.

[106.276 *Eutrichillus* Bates (3 spp. (3) s.w. US); 106.277 *Glaucotes* Casey (1 sp., *G. yuccivorus* (Fall) (3) AZ); 106.278 *Astylidius* Casey (2 spp. (1) IN, PA, MD, DC; (2) LA, MS; (3) TX); 106.279 *Amniscus* Haldeman (5 spp. (1), (2)); 106.280 *Leptostylus* LeConte (3 spp. (1), (2), (3) TX; (5) ND, SD, NE, KS); 106.281 *Leptostylopsis* Dillon (4 spp. (2) s.e. US; (3) TX); 106.282 *Trichastylopsis* Dillon (2 spp. (3) CA, AZ, NM); 106.283 *Styloleptus* Dillon (2) s.e. US); 106.284 *Sternidius* LeConte (16 spp. (1), (2), (3), (5)); 106.285 *Astyleiopus* Dillon (1 sp., *A. variegatus* Haldeman (1) n.e. NA; (2) s.e. US; (3) AZ); 106.286 *Pseudastylopsis* Dillon (2 spp., (3) CA, AZ); 106.287 *Valenus* Casey (1 sp., *V. inornatus* Casey (3) s.w. US); 106.288 *Sternidocinus* Dillon (1 sp., *S. barbarus* Van Dyke (3) CA); 106.289 *Dectes* LeConte (2 spp. (1) n.e. US; (2) s.e. US; (3) TX); 106.290 *Lepturges* Bates (7 spp. (1) n.e. NA; (2) s.e. US; (3) AZ, TX); 106.291 *Maculurges* Dillon (1 sp., *M. regularis* (LeConte) (1) n.e. US; (2) s.e. US); 106.292 *Urgleptes* Dillon (8 spp. (1), (2), (3) TX); 106.293 *Hyperplatys* Haldeman (6 spp.); 106.294 *Probatius* White (1 sp., *P. umbraticus* Jacquelin du Val (2) FL)]

Tribe Cyrtinini

[106.295 *Cyrtinus* LeConte (2 spp. (1), (2), (3) TX)]

Tribe Saperdini

106.296 *Saperda* Fabricius

Seventeen species, the following of which are pests:

S. candida bipunctata Hopping (Saskatoon Borer). (5) SK, MB.

S. candida candida Fabricius (Roundheaded Apple Tree Borer). (See Fig. 24.208.) (1) n.e. NA; (2) s.e. US.

S. tridentata Olivier (Elm Borer). (1) n.e. NA; (2) s.e. US.

Fig. 24.208.

Fig. 24.209.

S. *vestita* Say (Linden Borer). (1) n.e. NA; (2) s.e. US.

S. *calcarata* Say (Poplar Borer). (See Fig. 24.209.) (1), (2), (3), (4), (5).

Tribe Phytoecini

106.297 *Oberea* Mulsant

Eight species (1), (2), the following of which are pests:

O. *bimaculata* Olivier (Raspberry Cane Borer). L. 8–12 mm. Elongate, slender, cylindrical; black, shiny; pronotum yellow to orange with two round black spots on disk, often with small black spot in front of scutellum; lower sides of thorax black; head and thorax rather sparsely, deeply, and coarsely punctate; elytra with rows of coarse punctures. Adults are collected by sweeping along the margins of marshes. Larvae bore in the canes of raspberries and blackberries. (1) n.e. NA; (2) s.e. US. (See A&J 176.)

O. *tripunctata* (Swederus) (Dogwood Twig Borer). (1) n.e. NA; (2) s.e. US.

[106.298 *Mecas* LeConte: 3 subgenera: *Mecas* s. str., *Pannychis* Thomson, and *Dylobolus* Thomson (4 spp. (3) s.w. US; (4) Pacific n.w.)]

Tribe Tetraopini

106.299 *Tetraopes* Schoenherr

Eyes divided into two on each side. Thirteen species, the following of which are common:

T. *tetrophthalmus* (Forster) (Red Milkweed Beetle). L. 9–15 mm. Body red; antennae blackish; pronotum with four black spots; each elytron with three discal spots, the median one the largest. Larvae breed in milkweed; adults common on milkweed. (1) n.e. US; (2) VA, NC, SC; (5) KS.

T. *basalis* LeConte (Western Milkweed Longhorn). L. 12–15 mm. Stout, short; head, prothorax, and elytra red; ventral surface, tibiae, and tarsi black; marked with round black dots: four on pronotum, one on scutellum, and three on each elytron; antennae black and annulate; pronotum finely, irregularly punctate; elytra finely punctate at base, obsolete apically; male antennae nearly as long as body; female antennae somewhat shorter. Adults feed on milkweed; larvae bore into stems and roots of the same plant. (See A&J 177.) (3) CA; (4) OR.

[106.300 *Phaea* Newman (2 spp. (1) n.e. US; (2) s.e. US; (3) NM; (5) KS)]

Fig. 24.210.

Tribe Hemilophini

[106.301 *Cathetopteron* Hamiloton (1 sp., *C. amoena* Hamilton (3) TX); 106.302 *Hemierana Aurivillius* (2 spp. (1) n.e. US; (2) s.e. US; (3) TX)]

Subfamily Disteniinae

[106.303 *Distenia* Serville (1 sp., *D. undata* Fabricius (Fig. 24.210) (1) IN, CT; (2) FL)]

107. CHRYSOMELIDAE (Leaf Beetles)

Length: 1–20 mm (some tropical species larger). Body elongate, cylindrical to oval and flat; many species brightly colored. Tarsomeres 5-5-5, third tarsomere enlarged, fourth very small, sometimes minute, surrounded by dorsal depression of the third; antennae short, usually filiform, sometimes serrate or with a slight club (clavate), their base not, or on rare occasions slightly, surrounded by eyes; legs usually short; hind femora of many species (the flea beetles, Alticinae, and others) enlarged, fitted for jumping.

Both larvae and adults are leaf, stem, and root feeders. No green plant is immune from their attack. Many species are host specific, and often both adults and larvae are found feeding together on the same plant. As might be expected, many of our worst crop pests are leaf beetles. Consequently, many species have been given common names.

There are 1481 species in the U.S. and Canada, assigned to 188 genera. The subfamilies are rather distinctive. The species can often be "spot" identified because of distinctive shapes and color patterns; however, because of the large number of species in many of the genera, specific identifications can be difficult.

Subfamily Aulacoscelinae

[107.1 *Aulacoscelis* Duponchel and Chevrolat (2 spp. (3) CA, TX); 107.2 *Janbechynea* Monrós, subgenus *Bothroscelis* (1 sp., *J. fulvipes* Jacoby (3) AZ)]

Subfamily Donaciinae

Slender; antennae closely inserted on front of head; prothorax nearly square, much narrower than elytra, without lateral margins; legs long; abdomen with first visible abdominal sternum as long as the remaining four combined. Larvae of these species are aquatic. Adults live on exposed parts of aquatic plants.

[107.3 *Macroplea* Samouelle (1 sp., *M. nigrocornis* Kirby (1), (2), (3), (4), (5))]

Fig. 24.211.

107.4 *Donacia* Fabricius

Thirty-one species, including the following:

D. palmata Olivier (Water Lily Beetle). (1) NS; (2) NC; (3) OK.

D. piscatrix Lacordaire. (See Fig. 24.211.) (1) ME; (2) FL; (3) TX; (5) MN.

[107.5 *Sominella* Jacobson (1 sp., *S. harrisi* LeConte (1) MI, MA, NJ); 107.6 *Plateumaris* Thomson (16 spp.)]

Subfamily **Orsodacninae**

[107.7 *Orsodacne* Latreille (1 sp., *O. atra* Ahrens (Fig. 24.212) (1), (2), (3), (4), (5))]

Subfamily **Zeugophorinae**

[107.8 *Zeugophora* Kunze (9 spp., including *Z. varians* Crotch (Fig. 24.213) (1) PA; (4) WA)]

Subfamily **Synetinae**

[107.9 *Syneta* Dejean (8 spp.); 107.10 *Thricolema* Crotch (1 sp., *T. anomala* Crotch (3) CA; (4) OR)]

Subfamily **Criocerinae**

Length: 5–10 mm; oblong or elongate; antennae rather stout, insertions widely separated; prothorax narrower than elytra at base, usually strongly constricted at middle; abdomen with first visible abdominal sternum as long as following two combined. These beetle are all leaf feeders.

107.11 *Crioceris* Fabricius

Two species, as follows:

C. asperagi (Linnaeus) (Asparagus Beetle). L. 6–7 mm. Body metallic blackish blue; pronotum red; elytra dark with

Fig. 24.212.

Fig. 24.213.

Fig. 24.214.

three yellow spots on each side that vary in size. Larvae feed on asparagus shoots. Introduced. (See Fig. 24.214.) (1) n.e. US; (2) GA; (3) CA; (4) WA, OR; (5) MT, CO.

C. duodecimpunctata (Linnaeus) (Spotted Asparagus Beetle). L. 6–7 mm. Reddish yellow; antennae, legs in part, ventral surface, and scutellum black; elytra with six small black spots. Larvae feed on asparagus berries. Introduced. (1) n.e. US; (4) WA, OR.

[107.12 *Lilioceris* Reitter (1 sp., *L. lilii* Scopoli (1) PQ)]

107.13 *Lema* Fabricius

Twenty-five species, including the following:

L. trilineata (Olivier) (Three-lined Potato Beetle). L. 6–7.5 mm. Body yellow; elytra yellow or reddish yellow, each with a sutural and submarginal black stripe; pronotum usually with two small black spots on anterior half. Found on potato and other solanaceous plants. (See Fig. 24.215.) (1) n.e. US; (2) FL; (3) AZ; (5) MB.

L. sexpunctata Olivier. (See Fig. 24.216.) (1) n.e. US; (2) s.e. US.

107.14 *Oulema* Gozis

One species, as follows:

O. melanopus (Linnaeus) (Cereal Leaf Beetle). L. 4–5.5 mm. Body bluish black; elytra shiny; pronotum and sides of prothorax, femora, and tibiae except for apices reddish or reddish yellow. Adults and larvae feed on grasses; pest of small grains. Introduced. (1) n.e. NA.

Fig. 24.215.

Fig. 24.216.

Subfamily Megascelinae

[107.15 *Megascelis* Sturm (1 sp., *M. texana* Linell (3) TX)]

Subfamily Clytrinae

Usually stout, compact, medium-sized beetles; head usually inserted well into thorax; antennae serrate apically; pronotum narrowly margined on sides, fitted closely to elytra; elytra with lateral lobes short, exposing pygidium.

Tribe Megalostomini

[107.16 *Megalostomis* Chevrolat (1 sp., *M. dimidiata* Lacordaire (3) ?AZ, TX); 107.17 *Coscinoptera* Lacordaire (7 spp.); 107.18 *Euryscopa* Moldenke (7 spp. (3), (4))]

Tribe Babiini

[107.19 *Urodera* Lacordaire (2 spp. (3) AZ, NM, TX)]

107.20 *Babia* Chevrolat

Two species, including the following:

B. quadriguttata (Olivier) (Four-spotted Baboon Beetle). L. 3.5–4 mm. Convex, shining; black with two reddish-yellow spots on each elytron. (1), (2), (3), (4), (5).

107.21 *Saxinis* Lacordaire

Nine species, including the following:

S. knausi Schaeffer (Knaus' Saxinis). L. 3–4 mm. Dark metallic blue to green, with orange-red shoulder spots. Adults and larvae occur on a variety of plants, particularly *Ceanothus* species and redroot. (See A&J 179.) (3) AZ, TX; (5) NE, MO.

Tribe Clytrini

[107.22 *Smaragdina* Chevrolat (1 sp., *S. militaris* LeConte (3) NM, TX; (5) MO)]

107.23 *Anomoea* Lacordaire

Four species, including the following:

A. laticlavia (Forster) (Claycolored Leaf Beetle). (1) PQ; (2) FL; (3) ?CA, NM; (5) MB.

Subfamily Cryptocephalinae

Body usually small, robust, more or less cylindrical; head inserted in prothorax nearly or actually to the eyes; antennae long, slender, usually longer than head and thorax; thorax often

Fig. 24.217.

narrowly margined; elytra somewhat shortened leaving apex of abdomen exposed.

[107.24 *Lexiphanes* Gistl (5 spp. (1), (2), (3), (5))]

107.25 *Cryptocephalus* Mueller

Very difficult to identify to species, many of which feed on the leaves of trees. Seventy-five species, including the following:

C. mutabilis Melsheimer. Occurs commonly on birch, oak sprouts, hazel, and flowers of spiraea, New Jersey tea, and others. (1) n.e. US; (2) VA; (3) TX.

C. venustus Fabricius. (See Fig. 24.217.) (1) PQ; (2) FL; (3) TX.

[107.26 *Bassareus* Haldeman (8 spp. (1), (2), (3), (5), including *B. clathratus* Melsheimer (Fig. 24.218) (1) PA, NJ; (2) TN; (5) NE)]

107.27 *Diachus* LeConte

Ten species, including the following:

D. auratus (Fabricius) (Bronze Leaf Beetle). L. 1.5–2 mm. Uniformly metallic blue, green, or bronze; claws each with an inner basal lobe or appendage. Feeds on flowers of dogwood, yarrow, spiraea, and aster. (1) n.e. US; (2), FL; (3) CA.

[107.28 *Triachus* LeConte (4 spp. (1), (2), (3), (5)); 107.29 *Griburius* Haldeman (4 spp. (1), (2), (3))]

107.30 *Pachybrachis* Chevrolat

These species are the case-bearing leaf beetles. They live in a camouflaging case, which is composed of excreta, and are almost impossible to identify to species even with the aid of extremely technical literature. There are 151 species in the U.S. and Canada, including the following:

P. subfasciatus LeConte. Common on flowers of chokecherry and hawthorn. (1) n.e. US; (2) LA.

P. tridens Melsheimer. (See Fig. 24.219.) Found on hickory and elm. (1) IN, CT; (2) FL.

Fig. 24.218.

Fig. 24.219.

Subfamily Chlamisinae

Shape robust, ovate cylindrical, usually covered with tubercles; body contractile; length 2–5 mm, rarely longer; head small, set into prothorax; antennae short, serrate, and received in grooves on side of prosternum. When disturbed, these beetles draw their legs and antennae in against the body and feign death. In this position they resemble excrement from certain caterpillars and pass unnoticed by predators and collectors alike. The larvae feed on leaves and live in cases which are eventually attached to a twig and become the pupal case.

[107.31 *Pseudochlamys* Lacordaire (1 sp., *P. semirufescens* Karren (3) AZ); 107.32 *Chlamisus* Rafinesque (8 spp. (1), (2), (3), (5)); 107.33 *Diplacaspis* Jacobson (1 sp., *D. prosternalis* Schaeffer (3) AZ, TX)]

107.34 *Neochlamisus* Karren

Sixteen species, including the following is an example.

N. cribripennis (LeConte) (Blueberry Case Beetle). L. 2.7–3.3 mm. Dark coppery red; antennae serrate from fourth or fifth segment apically; elytral tubercles not strongly developed. Common on *Vaccinium* spp. (1) n.e. NA.

N. gibbosus (Fabricius). (See Fig. 24.220.) (1) MI, MD; (2) FL; (3) NM.

[107.35 *Exema* Lacordaire (9 spp.)]

Subfamily Lamprosomatinae

[107.36 *Oomorphus* Curtis (1 sp., *O. floridanus* Horn (2) FL); 107.37 *Lamprosoma* Kirby (1 sp., *L. opulentum* Lacordaire (3) ?CA)]

Subfamily Eumolpinae

Oblong, convex beetles, seldom rounded or oval; color often bright metallic or irridescent; antennae usually long, filiform, insertions widely separate; prothorax usually margined; elytra rounded apically, entire; apex of abdomen covered by elytra; tarsi broad, third segment deeply bilobed.

Fig. 24.220.

Fig. 24.221.

Tribe Eumolpini

[107.38 *Spintherophyta* Dejean (2 spp. (1), (2), (3)); 107.39 *Metaparia* Crotch (3 spp. (3) AZ, TX)]

107.40 *Notonota* Lefevre

Seven species in (1), (2), (3), (5), including the following:

N. puncticollis (Say) (Rose Leaf Beetle). (See Fig. 24.221.) (1) n.e. US; (2) NC; (5) MT.

[107.41 *Euphrytus* Jacoby (3 spp. (3) AZ); 107.42 *Metaxyonycha* Chevrolat (2 spp. (3) AZ, including *M. godmani* Jacoby, Guatemala (See A&J 178)]

107.43 *Colaspia* Fabricius

Thirty-six species, the following of which are pests:

C. brunnea (Fabricius) (Grape Colaspis). (See Fig. 24.222.) (1), (2), (3), (5).

C. pini Barber (Pine Colaspis). (2) LA, MS, AR.

107.44 *Rhabdopterus* Lefevre

Six species, the following of which is a pest:

R. picipes (Olivier) (Cranberry Rootworm). (1) n.e. US; (2) FL.

[107.45 *Eumolpus* Weber (1 sp., *E. robustus* Horn (3) AZ); 107.46 *Tymnes* Chapuis (3 spp. (1), (2), (3))]

107.47 *Chrysochus* Redtenbacher

Two species, as follows:

C. auratus Fabricius (Dogbane Beetle). L. 8–11 mm. Metallic green with coppery luster; pronotum bluish. Found on

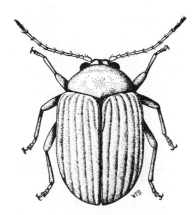

Fig. 24.222.

dogbane (Indian Hemp) and milkweeds. Very common. (1) n.e. US; (2) s.e. US; (5) n. Central States.

C. colbaltinus LeConte (Blue Milkweed Beetle). L. 6.5–11.5 mm. Oblong-convex; shiny, colbalt blue, occasionally with a greenish tinge, or varies to black; ventrally bluish black to black; head and thorax with coarse, very sparse, deep punctures intermingled with minute ones; elytra finely and irregularly punctate. Adults and larvae common on dogbane and less common on milkweed. (See A&J 180.) (3) s.w. US; (4) Pacific n.w.; (5) n. Central States.

[107.48 *Metachroma* Chevrolat (39 spp.)]

107.49 *Typophorus* Erichson

Two species in (1), (2), (3), the following of which is a pest:

T. nigritus viridicyaneus (Crotch) (Sweetpotato Leaf Beetle). (1) n.e. US; (2) NC; (3) s.w. US.

107.50 *Paria* LeConte

Eighteen species in (1), (2), (3), including the following:

P. fragariae Wilcox (Strawberry Rootworm). (1), (2), (3), (5) MO.

P. quadrinotata (Say). (See Fig. 24.223.) (1) n.e. US; (2) s.e. US.

Tribe Adoxiini

[107.51 *Myochrous* Erichson (13 spp.); 107.52 *Graphops* LeConte (20 spp., including *G. pubescens* Melsheimer (Fig. 24.224) (1), (2), (3), (4), (5), widespread; 107.53 *Xanthonia* Balby (4 spp.)]

107.54 *Fidia* Walsh

Six species in (1), (2), (3), (5), the following of which is a pest:

F. viticida Walsh (Grape Rootworm). (1), (2), (3), (5) ND, SD.

107.55 *Bromius* Chevrolat

One species, as follows:

B. obscurus (Linnaeus) (Western Grape Rootworm). (1), (2), (3), (4), (5).

[107.56 *Glyptoscelis* Chevrolat (23 spp.); 107.57 *Colaspides* Laporte (3 spp. (3) CA)]

Subfamily Chrysomelinae

Round or oval, convex; usually brightly colored; head inserted into prothorax to the eyes, only partly visible dorsally;

Fig. 24.223.

Fig. 24.224.

antennae moderately long, the apical segments somewhat enlarged; antennal insertions widely separated; side margins of pronotum well defined; elytra convex, covering the abdomen; tarsi broad, third tarsomere entire, not bilobed.

Tribe Timarchini

[107.58 *Timarcha* Latreille, subgenus *Americanotimarcha* Jolivet (3 spp. (3) CA; (4) BC, WA, OR, ID)]

Tribe Doryphorini

[=Zygogrammini]

107.59 *Zygogramma* Chevrolat

Thirteen species, including the following:

Z. exclamationis (Fabricius) (Sunflower Beetle). L. 7–8 mm. Oval, convex; head brown; pronotum brown with white anterior margin; sutural and adjacent stripe of elytra dark, both reaching apex. (See A&J 181.) (3) AZ, TX; (4) UT; (5) ND, SD.

107.60 *Leptinotarsa* Stål

Twelve species, including the following:

L. juncta (Germar) (Horse-nettle Beetle). L. 10–12 mm. Body reddish orange; elytra each with five black stripes (excluding the sutural), the third and fourth of which are almost always united at the base, sometimes throughout; intervals paler than thorax. Larvae and adults feed on horse-nettle. This species is sometimes called the False Potato Beetle. (1) MD; (2) s.e. US.

L. decemlineata (Say) (Colorado Potato Beetle). L. 5.5–11 mm. Similar to the preceding; elytra with third and fourth stripes entirely distinct. A pest on leaves of potatoes, tomatoes, and eggplant; spread by commerce. (See Fig. 24.225 and A&J 182.) (1), (2), (3), (4), (5).

Fig. 24.225.

Fig. 24.226.

107.61 *Labidomera* Chevrolat

Two species in (1), (2), (3), (5), including the following:

L. clivicolis Kirby. (See Fig. 24.226.) (1) ME; (2) FL; (5) IA.

107.62 *Calligrapha* Chevrolat

Thirty-five species in the following six subgenera: *Graphicallo* Monrós, *Bidensomela* Monrós, *Calligramma* Monrós, *Acalligrapha* Monrós, *Coreopsomela* Monrós, and *Calligrapha* s. str. The following will serve as examples:

C. rowena Knab (Rowena Calligrapha). L. 6.5–8.5 mm. Pronotum dark metallic blue-green; elytra (in life; color fades in preserved specimens) bright orange-red to gold; margins of elytra with broad common sutural stripe with three side branches, the third usually represented by a detached curved spot, and a series of three to eight small spots that tend to form a single row. Adults come to lights at night. They feed on dogwood. (See Fig. 24.227.) (1) n.e. US; (2) GA.

C. scalaris (LeConte) (Elm Calligrapha). L. 8–10 mm. Similar to the preceding; dark metallic green, shiny; elytra creamy white with broad greenish common sutural stripe that projects three short spurs on each side, and each shoulder with large, curved, moon-shaped spot enclosing round greenish spot, and 10 to 15 small spots behind the moon-shaped spot. Occurs on willow, birch, elm, buttonwood, and alder. Uncommon. (1) PQ; (2) GA; (3) TX.

C. wickhami Bowditch (Wickham's Calligrapha). L. 7–8 mm. Oval, convex; reddish brown; pronotum with pale anterior and lateral margins with two pale median spots; elytra pale, marked with irregular patterns of reddish brown; tarsal claws widely separated. Host plant of adults and larvae unknown; they probably feed on various shrubs. (See A&J 184.) (3) TX.

107.63 *Chrysolina* Motschulsky

Sixteen species, including the following:

C. quadrigemina (Suffrian) (Klamathweed Beetle). (3) CA; (4) BC; (5) CO.

Fig. 24.227.

***Tribe* Chrysomelini**

[= Phaedonini]

107.64 *Chrysomela* Linnaeus

Seventeen species in two subgenera (subgenus *Chrysomela* s. str. and *Microdera* Stephens), including the following:

C. crotchi Brown (Aspen Leaf Beetle). (1) n.e. NA; (2) VA; (3) NM; (4) AK.

C. scripta Fabricius (Cottonwood Leaf Beetle). L. 5.5–9 mm. Elongate-oval; blackish with a greenish tinge except on elytra; head dark; antennae either black or with pale middle segments; pronotum varies from entirely dark to pale anteriorly with reddish lateral margins; each elytron yellowish brown with narrow sutural stripe and seven elongated dark spots that vary in size from specimen to specimen. Adults and larvae feed on willow and poplar. (See A&J 183.) (1) n.e. US; (2) FL; (3) AZ; (4) BX; (5) n. Central States.

107.65 *Phaedon* Latreille

Eight species, the following of which is a pest:

P. viridis (Melsheimer) (Watercress Leaf Beetle). (1) n.e. US; (2) FL; (3) NM.

[107.66 *Gastrophysa* Chevrolat (4 spp.)]

107.67 *Plagiodera* Chevrolat

Four species in (1), (3), (4), (5), the following of which is a pest:

P. versicolora (Laicharteg) (Imported Willow Leaf Beetle). (1) n.e. US.

***Tribe* Phratorini**

[107.68 *Phratora* Chevrolat (7 spp.)]

***Tribe* Entomoscelini**

107.69 *Entomoscelis* Chevrolat

One species, as follows:

E. americana Brown (Red Turnip Beetle). (4) AK, WA; (5) MN.

107.70 *Microtheca* Stål

One species, as follows:

M. ochroloma Stål (Yellow-margined Leaf Beetle). (2) LA, AL.

***Tribe* Prasocurini**

[107.71 *Prasocuris* Latreille (1 sp., *P. phellandrii* Linnaeus (1) PQ, OH; (4) BC; (5) CO); 107.72 *Hydrothassa* Thomson (4 spp. (1), (5))]

***Tribe* Gonioctenini**

107.73 *Gonioctena* Chevrolat

Four species in (1), (4), (5), the following of which is a pest:

G. americana Schaeffer (American Aspen Beetle). (1) NY; (5) AB.

***Subfamily* Galerucinae**

Oval or oblong, usually with a soft-appearing body; head exposed; antennae usually long, slender, inserted on front of

head between eyes and close together, third segment usually smaller than fourth (but not in *Galerucella* spp.); pronotum usually margined; elytra entire.

Tribe Galerucini

107.74 *Monocesta* Clark

One species, as follows.

M. coryli (Say) (Larger Elm Leaf Beetle). (1) PA; (2) FL; (5) KS.

[107.75 *Coraia* Clark (1 sp., *C. subcyanescens* Schaeffer (3) TX); 107.76 *Detrospidea* Blake (2 spp. (1), (2), (3), (5)); 107.77 *Trirhabda* LeConte (27 spp.); 107.78 *Miraces* Jacoby (3 spp. (2), (3))]

107.79 *Galerucella* Crotch

Three species in two subgenera (*Galerucella* s. str. and *Neogalerucella* Chujo), the following of which is a pest:

G. (Galerucella) nymphaeae (Linnaeus) (Waterlily Leaf Beetle). (See Fig. 24.228.) (1), (2), (3), (4), (5).

107.80 *Tricholochmaea* Laboissiere

Thirteen species, including the following:

T. cavicollis (LeConte) (Cherry Leaf Beetle). (1) n.e. US; (5) AB.

T. decora decora (Say) (Gray Willow Leaf Beetle). (1) n.e. NA.

T. decora carbo (LeConte) (Pacific Willow Leaf Beetle). (3) NM; (4) BC; (5) MB, KS.

107.81 *Xanthogaleruca* Laboissiere

One species, as follows:

X. luteola Mueller (Elm Leaf Beetle). (1), (2), (3), (4), (5).

[107.82 *Brucita* Wilcox (1 sp., *B. marmorata* (Jacoby) (3) TX)]

107.83 *Erynephala* Blake

Four species in (1), (2), (3), the following of which is a pest:

E. puncticollis (Say) (Beet Leaf Beetle). (3) TX; (5) MB.

[107.84 *Monoxia* LeConte (16 spp. (2), (3), (4), (5)); 107.85 *Ophraella* Wilcox (9 spp.)]

107.86 *Galeruca* Mueller

Five species in (1), (3), (4), (5), including the following:

G. browni Blake (Peppergrass Beetle). (5) AB, MB.

Fig. 24.228.

Fig. 24.229.

Tribe Metacyclini

[107.87 *Malacorhinus* Jacoby (3 spp. (3) CA, AZ, TX)]

Tribe Sermylini

[107.88 *Sermylassa* Reitter (1 sp., *S. halensis* (Linnaeus) (1) ?locality); 107.89 *Agelastica* Chevrolat (1 sp., *A. alni* (Linnaeus) (1) ?locality)]

Tribe Luperini
Subtribe Diabroticina

107.90 *Diabrotica* Chevrolat

Six species, the following of which are pests:

D. undecimpunctata howardi Barber (Southern Corn Rootworm; Spotted Cucumber Beetle). L. 6–7.5 mm. Body yellow to yellowish red with 12 large, distinct black spots on elytra; pronotum greenish yellow; head, legs, and antennae entirely black. Adults feed on citrus as well as many other plants. Larvae are pests on the roots of many forage and truck crops, including cucurbits, corn, and goldenrod. (See Fig. 24.229 and A&J 186.) (1) n.e. NA; (2) s.e. US; (3) s. CA, AZ, NM; (4) s. NA; (5) n. Central States.

D. undecimpunctata undecimpunctata Mannerheim (Western Spotted Cucumber Beetle). L. 6–7.5 mm. Basic color greenish yellow; head, much of the legs and antennae, and central part of the undersurface are black; elytra with eleven black spots. Adults feed on the foliage of cucumbers, corn, and many other plants; larvae feed on the roots of corn and grasses. (See A&J 185.) (3) CA; (4) WA.

D. longicornis (Say) (Northern Corn Rootworm). (See Fig. 24.230.) (3) AZ, TX; (5) KS.

D. virgifera LeConte (Western Corn Rootworm). (1) MI; (3) AZ; (4) UT; (5) MT.

Fig. 24.230.

Fig. 24.231.

D. balteata LeConte (Banded Cucumber Beetle). (2) GA, FL; (3) CA.

[107.91 *Paranapiacaba* Bechyne (2 spp. (3) TX; (5) CO, KS); 107.92 *Amphelasma* Barber (1 sp., *A. cavum vicinum* Jacoby (3) AZ)]

107.93 *Acalymma* Barber

Six species, the following of which are pests:

A. vittatum (Fabricius) (Striped Cucumber Beetle). L. 4.5–6 mm. Body yellow to reddish yellow; elytra with sutural and median stripe black; abdomen black; pronotum with two depressions on disk. Found on cucumber and melon vines. (See Fig. 24.231.) (1) n.e. US; (2) s.e. US; (3) s.w. US; (5) n. Central States.

A. trivittata (Mannerheim) (Western Striped Cucumber Beetle). (3) CA, TX; (4) OR.

[107.94 *Paratriarius* Schaeffer (1 sp., *P. dorsatus* (Say) (1) OH; (2) AR); 107.95 *Neobrotica* Jacoby (2 spp. (3) AZ, TX); 107.96 *Cyclotrypema* Blake (1 sp., *C. furcata* Olivier (3) TX)]

107.97 *Cerotoma* Chevrolat

Three species, the following of which is a pest:

C. trifurcata (Forster) (Bean Leaf Beetle). (1), (2), (3), (5).

[107.98 *Phyllecthris* Dejean (3 spp. (1) NY; (2) GA; (3) TX, including *P. gentilis* LeConte (Fig. 24.232) (1) NY; (2) GA; (3) TX; (5) MT; 107.99 *Luperosoma* Jacoby (3 spp. (2) LA; (3) AZ, TX; (5) KS); 107.100 *Trachyscelida* Horn (1 sp., *T. bicolor* LeConte (3) AZ)]

Subtribe Luperina

[107.101 *Synetocephalus* Fall (9 spp. (3) CA; (4) OR); 107.102 *Pseudoluperus* Beller and Hatch (12 spp. (3), (4), (5)); 107.103 *Keitheatus* Wilcox (1 sp. *K. blakeae* (White) (3) TX); 107.104 *Lygistus* Wilcox (1 sp., *L. streptophallus* Wilcox (3) AZ); 107.105 *Triarius* Jacoby (6 spp. (3)); 107.106 *Scelida* Chapuis (2 spp. (3) AZ); 107.107

Androlyperus Crotch (5 spp. (3), (4)); 107.108 *Scelolyperus* Crotch (27 spp.); 107.109 *Phyllobrotica* Chevrolat (16 spp.); 107.110 *Pteleon* Jacoby (2 spp. (3), (4)); 107.111 *Eusattodera* Schaeffer (6 spp. (1), (2), 93), (5))]

107.112 *Metrioidea* Fairmaire

Eleven species in (1), (3), (4), (5), the following of which is a pest:

M. brunneus (Crotch) (Corn Silk Beetle). (2) NC, FL; (3) TX.

[107.113 *Luperus* Mueller (1 sp., *anonymus* Weise (3) ?CA))]

Subfamily Alticinae (Flea Beetles)

Oval or elongate; head exposed; antennae long, slender, inserted on front of head between eyes and rather close together, with third segment usually equal to, or longer than, fourth; pronotum usually broad, distinctly margined; elytra longer than abdomen. Hind femora are usually enlarged for jumping. This is the largest group of leaf beetles in number of species and number of pests, but the smallest in size and the most difficult to identify. Most species are 1.5 to 4 mm long, but a few are as large as 6 to 7 mm.

107.114 *Phyllotreta* Chevrolat

Thirty-eight species, the following of which are pests:

P. armoraciae (Koch) (Horseradish Flea Beetle). (See Fig. 24.233.) (1) n.e. US.

P. pusilla Horn (Western Black Flea Beetle). (3) CA; (4) WA, OR, ID; (5) WY, KS.

P. ramosa (Crotch) (Western Striped Flea Beetle). (1) NY; (3) CA; (4) NV.

P. striolata (Fabricius) (Striped Flea Beetle). (1), (2), (3), (4), (5).

P. bipustulata (Fabricius). (See Fig. 24.234.) (1) n.e. US; (2) s.e. US; (5) KS.

[107.115 *Tanygaster* Blatchley (2 spp. (1) IN, OH); 107.116 *Aphthona* Chevrolat (5 spp. (1), (2), (3), (5)); 107.117 *Glyptina* LeConte (12 spp. (1), (2), (3), (5)); 107.118 *Lupraea* Jacoby (3 spp. (1), (2), (3)); 107.19 *Longitarsus* Latreille (37 spp.); 107.120 *Dysphenges* Horn (1 sp., *D. elongatulus* Horn (3) TX)]

107.121 *Systena* Chevrolat

Eighteen species, the following of which are pests:

S. elongata (Fabricius) (Elongate Flea Beetle). (1), (2), (3), (5).

Fig. 24.232.

Fig. 24.233.

Fig. 24.234.

Fig. 24.235.

S. frontalis (Fabricius) (Red-headed Flea Beetle). (1), (2), (3), (5).

S. blanda Melsheimer (Pale Flea Beetle). See Fig. 24.235.) (1), (2), (3), (4), (5).

107.122 *Agasicles* Jacoby

One species, as follows:

A. hygrophila Selman and Vogt (Imported Klamathweed Beetle). (See Fig. 24.236 for beetles eating Klamathweed). Introduced. (2), SC, FL; (3) CA.

107.123 *Disonycha* Chevrolat

Thirty-five species, the following of which are pests or common examples:

D. triangularis (Say) (Threespotted Flea Beetle). (1), (2), (3), (4), (5).

Fig. 24.236. (*U.S. Dept. of Agric.*)

Fig. 24.237.

D. xanthomelas (Dalman) (Spinach Flea Beetle). (1), (2), (3), (4), (5).

D. glabrata (Fabricius). (See Fig. 24.237.) (1) n.e. NA; (2) s.e. US; (3) AZ.

[107.124 *Luperaltica* Crotch (4 spp., (1), (2), (3), (5); 107.125 *Phynocephala* Baly (1 sp., *P. intermedia* Jacoby (3) AZ, TX); 107.126 *Syphrea* Baly (4 spp. (2), (3))]

107.127 *Altica* Mueller

Sixty species, the following of which are pests:

A. canadensis Gentner (Prairie Flea Beetle). (1) MI; (5) AB.

A. chalybea Illiger (Grape Flea Beetle). (1) n.e. NA; (2) FL; (3) TX.

A. sylvia Mallock (Blueberry Flea Beetle). (1) ME, MA.

A. ulmi Woods (Elm Flea Beetle). (1) NY; (2) KY.

[107.128 *Macrohaltica* Bechyne (8 spp.); 107.129 *Lysathia* Bechyne (1 sp., *L. ludoviciana* Fall (2) FL; (3) TX); 107.130 *Strabala* Chevrolat (2 spp. (1), (2), (3)); 107.131 *Monomacra* Chevrolat (5 spp. (1), (2), (3), (5) MO); 107.132 *Orestioides* Hatch (2 spp., (1), (3), (4), (5))]

107.133 *Derocrepis* Weisse

Four species in (1), (2), (4), (5), the following of which is a pest:

D. erythropus (Melsheimer) (Red-legged Flea Beetle). (1) NY; (2) NC; (5) CO.

[107.134 *Hippuriphila* Foudras (3 spp. (1), (4), (5)); 107.135 *Crepidodera* Chevrolat (4 spp.); 107.136 *Trichaltica* Harold (2 spp. (1) OH; (3) AZ, TX)]

107.137 *Epitrix* Foudras

Twelve species, the following of which are pests:

E. cucumeris (Harris) (Potato Flea Beetle). (See Fig. 24.238.) (1) NH, ME; (2) FL.

E. fuscula Crotch (Eggplant Flea Beetle). (See Fig. 24.239.) (1) NY; (2) FL; (3) OK.

E. hirtipennis (Melsheimer) (Tobacco Flea Beetle). (1) NY; (2) NC; (3) CA; (4) OR; (5) n. Central States.

E. subcrinita (LeConte) (Western Potato Flea Beetle). (3) AZ; (4) OR.

E. tuberis Gentner (Tuber Flea Beetle). (4) WA; (5) NE.

[107.138 *Hemiglyptus* Horn (1 sp., *H. basalis* Crotch (3) CA); 107.139 *Glenidion* Clark (1 sp., *G. flexicaulis* Schaeffer (3) TX); 107.140 *Orthaltica* Crotch (4 spp.); 107.141 *Pseudorthygia* Csiki (1 sp., *P. nigritarsis* Jacoby (3) TX); 107.42 *Hornaltica* Barber (2 spp. (1), (2),

Fig. 24.238.

Fig. 24.239.

(3)); 107.143 *Mantura* Stephens (1 sp., *M. chrysanthemi floridana* Crotch (1) MA; (2) FL; (3) CA; (4) OR; (5) AB)]

107.144 *Chaetocnema* Stephens

Thirty-one species, the following of which are pests:

C. confinis Crotch (Sweet Potato Flea Beetle). (1) CT; (2) FL; (3) CA; (4); (5).

C. denticulata (Illiger) (Toothed Flea Beetle). (1); (2); (3) TX.

C. ectypa Horn (Desert Corn Flea Beetle). (3) CA, AZ.

C. pulicaria Melsheimer (Corn Flea Beetle). (See Fig. 24.240.) (1) CT; (2) FL; (5) CO.

[107.145 *Blepharida* Chevrolat (1 sp., *B. rhois* Forster (Fig. 24.241) (1) MA; (2) FL; (3); (5)); 107.146 *Phydanis* Horn (1 sp., *P. bicolor* Horn (3) TX); 107.147 *Omophoita* Chevrolat (1 sp., *O. cyanipennis octomaculata* Crotch (2) FL; (3) TX); 107.148 *Asphaera* Chevrolat (2 spp. (3) AZ, TX; (5) KS); 107.149 *Pachyonychis* Clark (1 sp., *P. paradoxus* Clark (1) NJ; (2) AL, FL); 107.150 *Kuschelina* Bechyne (27 spp., including *K. vians* (Illiger (Fig. 24.242) (1) ME; (2) FL; (5) AB; 107.151 *Capraita* Bechyne (16 spp. (1),(2),(3),(5), including *C. sexmaculata* (Illiger) (Fig. 24.243) (1) MA; (2) FL; (3) OK; 107.152 *Phaedromus* Clark (1 sp.,

P. waterhousii Clark (2) ?SC); 107.153 *Hypolampsis* Clark (1 sp., *H. mellyi* Crotch (5) ?KS); 107.154 *Distigmoptera* Blake (9 spp. (1), (2), (3), (5)); 107.155 *Pseudolampsis* Horn (1 sp., *P. guttata* LeConte (2) LA, SC); 107.156 *Pachyonychus* Crotch (1 sp., *P. paradoxus* Melsheimer (1) IN, DC; (2) AL); 107.157 *Dibolia* Latreille (13 spp.); 107.158 *Sphaeroderma* Stephens (1 sp., *S. opima* LeConte (1) OH, MD; (2) NC; (3) TX); 107.159 *Argopistes* Motschulsky (1 sp., *A. scyrtoides* LeConte (2) FL)]

107.160 *Psylliodes* Latreille

Ten species, the following of which is a pest:

P. punctulatus Melsheimer (Hop Flea Beetle). (1), (2), (3), (4), (5).

Subfamily Hispinae

Wedge-shaped, usually brightly colored; surface smooth to deeply punctate, or with elevated costae; head almost always exposed; antennae short, straight, insertions between eyes close together; elytra broad apically, truncate. Larvae of most species are leaf miners.

Tribe Cephaloleiini

[107.161 *Stenispa* Baly (2 spp. (1) MI, MA; (2) LA, FL; (3) TX)]

Tribe Chalepini

[107.162 *Anisostena* Weise (13 spp.); 107.163 *Sumitrosis* Butte (6 spp.); 107.164 *Chalepus* Thumberg (5 spp. (1), (2) (3), (5)); 107.165 *Xenochalepus* Weise (4 spp. (1), (2), (3))]

Fig. 24.241.

Fig. 24.242.

Fig. 24.240.

Fig. 24.243.

Fig. 24.244.

107.166 *Odontota* Chevrolat

Seven species in (1), (2), (3), (5), the following of which is a pest:

O. dorsalis (Thunberg) (Locust Leaf Miner). (See Fig. 24.244.) (1) ON, MA, IL; (2) GA.

107.167 *Baliosus* Weise

Two species, including the following:

B. nervosus Panzer (Basswood Leaf Miner). L. 5–7 mm. Yellowish red with irregular darker markings on elytra; sides of pronotum narrowly dark; legs yellow; abdomen reddish. Found on basswood and other trees. (See Fig. 24.245.) (1) n.e. US; (2) s.e. US.

Tribe Uroplatini

107.168 *Octotoma* Dejean

Two species in (1), (2), (3), the following of which is a pest abroad:

O. scabripennis Guérin (Lantana Leaf Beetle). Mexico and Hawaii.

[107.169 *Stenopodius* Horn (7 spp. (3), (5)); 107.170 *Brachycoryna* Guérin (8 spp. (1), (3), (5)); 107.171 *Glyphuroplata* Uhmann (2 spp. (1), (2), (3), (5)); 107.172 *Pentispa* Chapuis (3 spp. (3) AZ, TX); 107.173 *Microrhopala* Chevrolat (10 spp. (1), (2), (3), (5))]

Subfamily Cassidinae (Tortise Beetles)

Broadly oval, often nearly circular; head with mouth deflexed posteriorly, hidden beneath expanded pronotum; pronotum with lateral margins expanded; elytra wide, almost completely hiding legs; both pronotum and elytra may be armed with prolongations or spines. Larvae have a forklike tail that is nearly as long as the body. This is covered with excrement and cast skins from molts, forming an umbrella-like covering or camouflage. Most species feed on milkweeds, sweet potatoes, and other Convolvulaceae, sometimes on raspberries.

Tribe Hemisphaerotini

107.174 *Hemisphaerota* Chevrolat

One species, as follows:

H. cyanea (Say) (Florida Tortise Beetle). (2) GA, FL.

Tribe Stolaini

[107.175 *Hilarocassis* Spaeth (1 sp., *H. exclamationis* (Linnaeus) (3) AZ)]

107.176 *Chelymorpha* Boheman

Two species, the following of which is common:

C. cassidea (Fabricius) (Argus Tortise Beetle). (1), (2), (3), (4), (5).

Tribe Physonotini

107.177 *Physonota* Boheman

Five species in (1), (2), (3), (5), including the following:

P. arizonae Schaeffer (Arizona Gold Beetle). L. 11–13 mm. Elongate-oval; pale greenish yellow; pronotum with three dark longitudinal marks, the median one four to six times longer than wide; abdomen yellow with short transverse dark mark on each segment near lateral margin. Adults and larvae feed on flowers of burr sage and gentians. (See A&J 187.) (3) AZ.

P. unipunctata (Say). (See Fig. 24.246.) (1) n.e. US; (2) s.e. US.

[107.178 *Eurypepla* Boheman (1 sp., *E. calochroma floridensis* Blake (2) FL)]

Tribe Cassidini

[107.179 *Cassida* Linnaeus (2 spp. (1) IL, NY, MD; (5) NT)]

107.180 *Jonthonota* Spaeth

Two species in (1), (2), (3), (5), the following of which is common:

J. nigripes (Olivier) (Blacklegged Tortise Beetle). (See Fig. 24.247.) (1) NJ; (2) FL; (3) CA, TX; (5) CO, SD.

[107.181 *Agroiconota* Spaeth (1 sp., *A. bivittata* (Say) (1), (2), (3), (5)); 107.182 *Parorectis* Spaeth (2 spp. (2) SC, FL; (3) TX)]

107.183 *Deloyala* Chevrolat

Four species in (1), (2), (3), (5), the following of which is common:

Fig. 24.245.

Fig. 24.246.

Fig. 24.247.

Fig. 24.248.

D. guttata (Olivier) (Mottled Tortise Beetle). (Fig. 24.248.) (1), (2), (3), (5).

[107.184 *Coptocycla* (Chevrolat (3 spp. (2) AL, FL; (3) TX; 107.185 *Plagiometriona* Spaeth (1 sp., *P. clavata* (Fabricius) (1), (2), (3), (5))]

107.186 *Metriona* Weise

Six species in (1), (2), (3), (5), the following of which is common:

M. bicolor (Fabricius) (Goldbug). L. 5.5–6 mm. Brilliant burnished gold, color changeable on its host plant but fades in preserved specimens. Found on sweet potato, morning glory, and bittersweet. Also called Golden Tortise Beetle, but Goldbug is the much older name. (See Fig. 24.249.) (1), (2), (3), (5).

[107.187 *Charidotella* Weise (3 spp. (1), (2), (3), (5))]

Tribe Charidotini

[107.188 *Microctenochira* Spaeth (1 sp., *M. bonvouloiri* Boheman (3) TX)]

Superfamily CURCULIONOIDEA

108. BRUCHIDAE (Pea and Bean Weevils)

Length: 1–6 mm (rarely larger). Black, brown, or tan to yellowish, sometimes variously marked or mottled with light patches of hairlike setae or scales. The body of these beetles is compact, oval; head small, with antennae clavate, serrate, pectinate, or flabellate; mouthparts forming a short beak; elytra shortened, exposing apical segment of abdomen; hind femora enlarged. Larvae develop in seeds, usually those of leguminous plants. Adults are taken by beating vegetation. They feign death when they drop off and resemble seeds. There are 134 species in the U.S. and Canada, assigned to 20 genera.

Subfamily Pachymerinae

[108.1 *Caeybruchus* Bridwell (2 spp.)]

Subfamily Amblycerinae

[108.2 *Amblycerus* Thumberg (2 spp. (1) n.e. US; (2) FL)]

108.3 *Zabrotes* Horn

Seven species in (1), (2), (3), (4, (5), the following of which is a pest:

Z. subfasciatus (Boheman) (Mexican Bean Weevil) (1), (2), (3), (4, (5).

Subfamily Kytorhininae

[108.4 *Kytorhinus* Fischer (1 sp. *K. prolixus* Fall (4) AK; (5) SD)]

Subfamily Bruchinae

[= Mylabrinae]

[108.5 *Megacerus* Fåhraeus: 3 subgenera: *Megacerus.* S. str., *Pachybruchus Pachybruchus* Pic, and *Serratibruchus* Teran and Kingsolver (9 spp. (1), (2), (3)]

108.6 *Callosobruchus* Pic

Four species in (1), (2), (3), including the following:

C. maculatus (Fabricius) (Cowpea Weevil). L. 2.5–4.5 mm. Antennae serrate, with apical segments longer than wide; pale brown; dark to black apical segments; legs pale brown; head black, thorax black, and elytra brown, with intermixed brown and whitish pubescence; each elytron with a large lateral spot with black apex, but the color is variable. Larvae live in black-eyed cowpeas. Adults are often found on flowers. (See Fig. 24.250 and A & J 188.) (1) n.e US; (2) s.e. US; (3) TX.

C. chinensis (Linnaeus). (See Fig. 24.251.) (1) DC; (2) VA.

[108.7 *Stylantheus* Bridwell (1 sp., *S. macrocerus* Horn (1) IN, NJ, DC; (2) TN); 108.8 *Gibbobruchus* Pic (3 spp. (1) IN; (2) s.e. US; (3) TX); 108.9 *Meibomeus* Bridwell (2 spp. (1) MI, IN, MA; (2) GA, FL; (3) AZ, TX)]

Fig. 24.249.

Fig. 24.250.

Fig. 24.251.

108.10 *Acanthoscelides* Schilsky

Sixty-one species, including the following:

A. obtectus (Say) (Bean Weevil). L. 2.5–3.5 mm. Black with yellowish pubescence; first five and last antennal segments orange-brown, the others darker, usually black; front femora entirely black, hind femora blackish beneath, reddish brown above. Injurious to all varieties of garden beans by feeding, making them unfit for marketing. (See Fig. 24.252.) (1) n.e. US; (2) VA, NC, SC, GA; (3) TX.

108.11 *Algarobius* Bridwell

Two species in (3) CA, AZ, NM, TX, the following of which is a pest:

A. bottimeri Kingsolver (Kiawe Bean Weevil (3) NM, TX.

[108.12 *Neltumious* Bridwell (3 spp. (3) CA, AZ; (4) UT); 108.13 *althaeus* Bridwell (1 sp., *a. hibisci* (Olivier) (1) n.e. US); 108.14 *Abutiloneus* Bridwell (1 sp., *A. idoneus* Bridwell (3) TX)]

108.15 *Bruchus* Linnaeus

Four species, of which the following are pests:

B. brachialis Fåhraeus (Vitch Bruchid). (1) n.e. US; (2) s.e. US; (4) Pacific n.w.

B. pisorum Linnaeus (Pea Weevil). (See Fig. 24.253.) (1), (2), (3), (4), (5).

B. rufimanus Boheman (Broadbean Weevil). (1) NJ.

[108.16 *Bruchidius* Schilsky (2 spp. (1) n.e. US; (2) s.e. US; (4) BC); 108.17 *Mimosestes* Bridwell (5 spp.); 108.18 *Merobrachus* Bridwell (4 spp. (3) AZ, TX); 108.19 *Sennius* Bridwell (10 spp. (1), (2), (3))]

Fig. 24.253.

108.20 *Stator* Bridwell

Ten species (1), (2), (3), the following of which is a pest:

S. pruininus Horn (Pruinouse Bean Weevil). (3) n.w. US; (4) Pacific n.w.

109. ANTHRIBIDAE (Fungus Weevil Family)

Length: 1–30 mm. Similar to snout beetles but the beak is broad, the antennae straight and usually clubbed. Many species are brownish, with hairlike scales usually forming patches in mixed shades of white, gray, straw brown, or black. Adults may be collected by beating dead or diseased branches of trees, clumps of dead twigs or leaves, or tangles of dead vines. In general, adults may be found on larval food plants. Some larvae are stem borers, others feed on pollen, and still others are fungus feeders. A few are pests of seeds and beans. There are 79 species in the U.S. and Canada, assigned to 24 genera.

Subfamily Choraginae

109.1 *Araecerus* Schoenherr

One species, as follows:

A. fasciculatus De Geer (Coffee Bean Weevil). L. 2–5 mm. Dark brown, mottled with whitish to yellowish scalelike setae, with variable patterns. Adults feed on mold. Larvae infest stored products but sometimes fresh citrus fruit. Eggs are laid on fruit and larvae bore into skin, but not the flesh. (See Fig. 24.254.) (1, (2), (3), (4), (5), spread by commerce.

[109.2 *Araeocorynus* Jekel (1 sp., *A. cumingi* Jekel (1) OH; (3) CA, AZ); 109.3 *Acaromimus* Jordan (1 sp., *A. americanus* Motschulsky (2) AL,

Fig. 24.252.

Fig. 24.254.

Fig. 24.255.

FL; (3) TX); 109.4 *Choragus* Kirby (4 spp. (1) n.e. US): 109.5 *Euxenulus* Valentine (1 sp., *E. piceus* (LeConte) (2) FL); 109.6 *Euxenus* LeConte (3 spp. (10, (2))]

Subfamily Anthribinae

[109.7 *Discotenes* Labram and Imhoff (2 spp. (3) AZ, TX); 109.8 *Ischnocerus* Schoenherr (3 spp. (1), (2), (3)); 109.9 *Allandrus* LeConte (4 spp.); 109.10 *Stenocerus* Schoenherr (1 sp., *S. longulus* Jekel ((3) TX); 109.11 *Gymnognathus* Schenherr (1 sp., *G. chiricahuae* Sleeper (3) AZ); 109.12 *Piesocorynus* Dejean (5 spp. (1), (2), (3), (5)); 109.13 *Brevibarra* Jordan (1 sp., *B. rectus* (LeConte) (1), (2), (3)); 109.14 *Tropideres* Schoenherr (4 spp.); 109.15 *Trachytropis* Jordan (1 sp., *T. arizonicus* Sleeper (3) AZ); 109.16 *Goniocloeus* Jordan (1 sp., *G. bimaculatus* (Olivier) (1), (2), (3) TX); 109.17 *Phoenicobiella* Cockerell (2 spp. (2), (3) TX); 109.18 *Toxonotus* Lacordaire (6 spp. (1), (2), (3), (5), including *T. cornutus* Say (Fig. 24.255.) (1) n.e. US; (2) s.e. US; (3) TX; (5) KS, MO); 109.19 *Euparius* Schoenherr (5 spp. (1), (2), (3), (5)); 109.20 *Trigonorhinus* Wollaston (9 spp.); 109.21 *Eugonus* Schoenherr (1 sp., *E. bicolor* Valentine (3) AZ); 109.22 *Phaenithon* Schoenherr (1 sp., *P. platanum* Schaeffer (3) AZ); 109.23 *Araeoderes* Shaeffer (1 sp., *A. texanus* Schaeffer (3) TX); 109.24 *Ormiscus* Waterhouse (20 spp. (1), (2), (3), (5))]

110. BRENTHIDAE (Straight-snouted Weevil Family)

Length: 6.5–30 mm. Reddish with black markings to entirely black; sometimes marked with yellow. This group is characterized by a weevillike appearance, but with a greatly elongate body and a snout that projects forward instead of downward. Females tunnel into wood to deposit their eggs. Larve feed on fungi in logs of oak, poplar, maple, and beech. Adults have been found at sap flows and on moth bait. They often live in a subsocial relationship; a few are associated with ants, but not in North America. There are five speices in the U.S. and Canada.

Subfamily Brenthinae

Tribe Brenthini

110.1 *Brenthus* Fabricius

One species, as follows:

B. anchorago (Linnaeus). (2) FL.

Tribe Trachelizini

[110.2 *Parathrachelizus* Kleine (1 sp., *P. uncimanus* (Boheman) (2) FL)]

Fig. 24.256.

Tribe Arrhenodini

110.3 *Arrhenodes* Schoenherr

One species, as follows:

A. minutus (Drury) (Oak Timberworm). (See Fig. 24.256 for the male; Fig. 24.257 for the female.) (1) n.e. US; (2) s.e. US; (3) TX; (5) MN, IA, KS, MO.

[110.4 *Heterobrenthus* Sharp (1 sp., *H. texanus* Schaeffer (3) TX)]

Tribe Stereodermini

[110.5 *Stereodermus* Lacordaire (1 sp., *S exilis* Suffrian (2) FL)]

111. PLATYPODIDAE (Ambrosia Beetle Family)

Length: 2–8 mm. These beetles are very similar to the next family, the bark beetles, but they have a broad, more noticeable head and are elongate, longer, and more slender. The antennae either are scarcely elbowed or not at all. The first tarsomeres are longer than the combined length of the other four. They infest both coniferous and hardwood trees of many kinds, usually those injured by fire, lighting, or disease. Larvae feed on fungi grown in the tunnels they bore. There are seven species, as follows:

Subfamily Platypodinae

111.1 *Platypus* Herbst

Seven species, including the following:

P. wilsoni Swaine. (See Fig. 24.258.) (3) CA; (4) Pacific n.w.

Fig. 24.257.

Fig. 24.258.

112. SCOLYTIDAE (Bark Beetle Family)

Length: 1–9 mm (usually under 4 mm). Body punctate and striate; brown to black; tarsomeres 5-5-5, the fourth minute, the third slender or broad; very stout to moderately elongate, cylindrical; elbowed antennae with distinct club. Bark beetles cause considerable damage to forest trees but usually infest weakened, dying, or dead trees or recently cut logs. They bore under the bark, leaving distinctive patterns or "engravings" (see Fig. 24.259), or into the heartwood, where they live on fungi that grows in their tunnels. They carry spores in special pockets on head or prothorax. Most species noted here infest coniferous trees. A few, including a root borer, are found in other plants. Usually host specific, these beetles are difficult to identify. There are 48 species in the U.S. and Canada, arranged in 67 genera.

Subfamily Hylesininae
Tribe Bothrosternini

[112.1 *Cnesinus* LeConte (1 sp., *C. strigicollis* LeConte (1) n.e. US; (2) s.e. US; (3) TX; (5) MO)); 112.2 *Pagiocerus* Eichhoff (1 sp., *P. frontalis* Fabricius (2) NC, SC, GA, FL; (3) TX)]

Tribe Hylastini

[112.3 *Scierus* LeConte (2 spp.); 112.4 *Hylurgops* LeConte (7 spp.); 112.5 *Hylastes* Erichson (13 spp.)]

Fig. 24.259.

Tribe Hylesinini
112.6 *Hylastinus* Bedel
One species, as follows:

H. obscurus Marsham (Clover Root Borer). (1), (3), (4).

[112.7 *Xylechinus* Chapuis (2 spp. (1), (4), (5)); 112.8 *Dendrosinus* Chapuis (1 sp., *D. bourreriae* Schwarz (2) FL; 112.9 *Pseudohylesinus* Swaine (11 spp. (3), (4), (5));]

112.10 *Hylurgopinus* Swaine
One species, as follows:

H. rufipes (Eichhoff) (Native Elm Bark Beetle). (1), (2), (5).

112.11 *Dendroctonus* Erichson
Thirteen species, all of them pests, as follows:

D. brevicomis LeConte (Western Pine Beetle). (3) CA, AZ, NM; (4) Pacific n.w.; (5) AB, MT, CO.

D. frontalis Zimmerman (Southern Pine Beetle). (1), (2), (3), (5).

D. approximatus Dietz (Mexican Pine Beetle). (3) AZ, NM; (4) UT; (5) CO.

D. adjunctus (Hopkins) (Roundheaded Pine Beetle). (3), AZ, NM; (4) UT; (5) CO.

D. ponderosae Hopkins (Mountain Pine Beetle). (3), (4), (5).

D. jeffreyi Hopkins (Mountain Pine Beetle). (3) CA; (4) OR.

D. terebrans (Olivier) (Black Turpentine Beetle). (1), (2), (3) TX.

D. valens LeConte (Red Turpentine Beetle). (1), (2), (3), (4), (5).

D. punctatus LeConte (Allegheny Spruce Beetle). (1) (2) WV; (4) AK; (5).

D. murrayanae Hopkins (Lodgepole Pine Beetle). (1), (4), (5).

D. rufipennis (Kirby) (Spruce Beetle). (1), (3), (4), (5).

D. simplex LeConte (Eastern Larch Beetle.) (See Fig. 24.260.) (1), (4), (5).

Fig. 24.260.

D. pseudotsugae Hopkins (Douglas Fir Beetle). (3), (4), (5).

112.12 *Phloeosinus* Chapuis

Twenty-five species, the following of which is a pest:

P. punctatus LeConte (Cedar Bark Beetle). (4), (5).

[112.13 *Leperisinus* Reitter (7 spp.)]

112.14 *Alniphagus* Swaine

Two species (3), (4), the following of which is a pest:

A. aspericollis (LeConte) (Alder Bark Beetle). (3) CA; (4).

112.15 *Phloeotribus* Latreille

Eight species, the following of which is a pest:

P. liminaris (Harris) (Cedar Bark Beetle). (1), (2), (3), (5).

[112.16 *Chramesus* LeConte (7 spp. (1), (2), (3), (5)]

Tribe Hypoborini

[112.17 *Chaetophloeus* LeConte (9 spp. (2), (3), (4), (5)); 112.18 *Liparthrum* Wollaston (2 spp. (2) MS; (3) AZ)]

Tribe Polygraphini

[112.19 *Carphoborus* Eichhoff. (1 sp., *C. arizonicus* Blackman (3) AZ); 112.20 *Carphoborus* Eichhoff (19 spp.); 112.21 *Polygraphus* Erichson (3 spp., including *P. rufipennis* (Kirby) (Fig. 24.261) (1) n.e. NA; (2) TN, NC; (3) NM; (4) Pacific n.w.; (5) n. Central States and Prorinces)]

Subfamily Scolytinae
Tribe Scolytini

[112.22 *Cnemonyx* Eichhoff (2 spp. (2) FL)]

112.23 *Scolytus* Geoffroy

Eighteen species, the following of which are pests:

S. mali (Bechstein) (Larger Shot-hole Borer). (1) n.e. US.

S. multistriatus (Marsham) (Smaller European Elm Bark Beetle). (1), (2), (3), (4), (5).

S. muticus Say (Hackberry Engraver). (1, (2), (3), (5).

S. quadrispinosus Say (Hickory Bark Beetle). (1), (2), (3), (5).

S. rugulosus (Ratzeburg) (Shot-hole Borer). (1). (2), (3), (4), (5).

Fig. 24.261.

S. unispinosus LeConte (Douglas Fir Engraver). (3), (4), (5).

S. ventralis LeConte (Fir Engraver). (3), (4), (5).

Tribe Hexacolini

[112.24 *Pycnarthrum* Eichhoff (1 sp., *P. hispidum* Ferrari (2) FL; (3) TX); 112.25 *Scolytodes* Ferrari (1 sp., *S. schwarzi* Hopkins (2) FL)]

Tribe Micracini

[112.26 *Pseudothysanoes* Blackman (15 spp. (1), (2), (3)); 112.27 *Stenocleptus* Blackman (1 sp., *S. sulcatus* Bruck (3) CA; 112.28 *Thysanoes* LeConte (7 spp. (1), (2), (3)); 112.29 *Micracis* LeConte (4 spp. (1), (2), (3)); 112.30 *Micracisella* Blackman (5 spp. (1), (2), (3), (5)); 112.31 *Hylocurus* Eichhoff (13 spp. (1), (2), (3), (4))]

Tribe Cactopinini

[112.32 *Cactopinus* Schwarz (5 spp. (3) CA, AZ; (4) NV, UT)]

Tribe Cryphalini

[112.33 *Trypophloeus* Fairmaire (4 spp. (1), (3), (4), (5)); 112.34 *Ernoporus* Thomson (1 sp., *E. kanawhae* Hopkins (2) WV); 112.35 *Procryphalus* Hopkins (2 spp. (3), (4), (5)); 112.36 *Cryphalomorphus* Schaufuss (1 sp., *C. knabi* Hopkins (2) FL)); 112.37 *Cryphalus* Erichson (4 spp.)]

112.38 *Hypocryphalus* Hopkins

One species, as follows:

H. mangiferae Stebbing (Mango Bark Beetle). (2) FL.

[112.39 *Trischidias* Hopkins (3 spp. (1), (2), (5))]

112.40 *Hypothenemus* Westwood

Twenty-one species in (1), (2), (3), (5), the following of which are pests:

H. obscurus (Fabricius) (Apple Twig Beetle). Host? Intercepted in Brazil nuts.

H. pubescens Hopkins (2) FL; (3) TX.

[112.41 *Cryptocarenus* Eggers (2 spp. (2) FL; (3) TX)]

Tribe Dryocoetini

[112.42 *Crypturgus* Erichson (3 spp.); 112.43 *Dolurgus* Eichhoff (1 sp., *D. pumilus* Mannerheim (3) CA; (4)); 112.44 *Lymantor* Lovendal (1 sp., *L. decipiens* LeConte (1), (2), (5)0; 112.45 *Dendrocranulus* Schedl (3 spp. (2), (3), (4), (5))]

112.46 *Dryocoetes* Eichhoff

Seven species, the following of which are pests:

D. betulae Hopkins (Birch Bark Beetle). (1), (2), (4), (5).

D. confusus Swaine (Western Balsam Bark Beetle). (3), (4), (5).

D. autographus Ratzeburg. (See Fig. 24.262.) (1) n.e. NA; (2) WV, VA, TN, NC; (3) CA, NM; (4) Pacific n.w.; (5) n. Central States and Provinces.

[112.47 *Coctrypes* Eichhoff. (5 spp. (1) NJ, DC; (2) LA, FL; (3)]

Tribe Ipini

[112.48 *Pityogenes* Bedel (6 spp., including *P. hopkinsi* Swaine (Fig. 24.263.) (1) n.e. NA; (2) WV, VA, TN, NC; (5) MN); 112.49 *Pityoketeines* Fuchs (6 spp.); 1112.50 *Orthotomicus* Ferrari (1 sp., *O. caelatus* Eichhoff (10, (2), (3), (4), (5))]

Fig. 24.262.

112.51 *Ips* De Geer

Twenty-four species, the following of which are pests:

I. pini (Say) (Pine Engraver). (1), (2), (3), (4), (5).

I. avulsus (Erichhoff) (Small Southern Pine Engraver). (1), (2), (3).

I. confusus (LeConte) (California Five-spined Ips). (3) CA, AZ, NM, TX; (4) NV, UT; (5) WY, CO.

Tribe Xyloterini

[112.52 *Xylorerinus* Swine (1 sp., *X. politus* (Say) (1), (2), (5) MN)]

112.53 *Trypodendron* Stephens

Five species, the following of which is a pest:

T. lineatum (Olivier) (Stribed Ambrosia Beetle). (1), (2), (3), (4), (5).

Tribe Xyleborini

[112.54 *Premnobius* Eichhoff (1 sp., *P. cavipennis* Eichhoff (2) FL)]

112.55 *Xylosandrus* Reitter

Four species in (1), (2), the following of which is a pest:

X. compactus (Erichhoff) (Black Twig Borer). (2) MS, FL.

[112.56 *Xyleborus* Eichhoff (17 spp.); 112.57 *Xyleborinus* Reitter (2 spp. (1), (2), (3), (4))]

Tribe Corthylini

[112.58 *Dendroterus* Blandford (2 spp. (3) CA, TX); 112.59 *Araptus* Erichhoff (1 sp., *A. politus* Blandford (2) FL); 112.60 *Pseudopityoph-*

Fig. 24.263.

thorus Swaine (10 spp. (1), (2), (3), (5)); 112.61 *Pityoborus* Blackman (2 spp. (2), (3), (4) UT); 112.62 *Pityotrichus* Wood (2 spp. (3) AZ, NM)]

112.63 *Conophthrous* Hopkins

Nine species, the following of which are pests:

C. banksianae McPherson (Jack Pie Tip Beetle) (1) MI, ON; (5) MN.

C. coniperda (Schwarz) (White Pine Cone Beetle). (1), (2), WV, VA; (4) MN.

C. edulis Hopkins (Pinon Cone Beetle). (3) AZ, NM; (4) UT; (5) CO.

C. ponderosae Hopkins (Ponderosa Pine Cone Beetle). (3), (4), (5).

C. radiatae Hopkins (Monterey Pine Cone Beetle). (3) CA.

C. resinosae Hopkins (Red Pine Cone Beetle). (1), (4) MN.

[112.64 *Pityophthorus* Eichhoff (105 spp.); 112.65 *Gnathotrichus* Eichhoff (7 spp.); 112.66 *Monarthrum* Kirsch (5 spp.)]

112.67 *Corthylus* Erichson

Four species in (1), (2), (5), the following of which is a pest:

C. columbianus Hopkins (Columbian Timber Beetle). (1) DC; (2); (5) KS.

113. CURCULIONIDAE
(Snout Beetle and Weevil Family)

Length: 1–35 mm. This is the largest family of all, larger than most phyla even, with over 40,000 species in the world and more to be discovered and named. Fortunately, most species are readily recognized as members of the family by the distinct, usually long and slender snout (see Fig. 24.24). The antennae are almost always elbowed and, unlike those of other beetles, are inserted on the snout itself instead of what would otherwise be considered the head. The snout is actually the drawn-out head, the small mouthparts being located at its end. Its length varies greatly from species to species. In some, it is very short and rather broad; others have a long, very thin, curved "beak" that may even be longer than the rest of the body. The antennae of most species are clubbed. The tarsi are of the phytophagous beetle type, that is, the tarsomeres are 5-5-5, with the fourth segment minute and usually concealed within the depression formed by the bilobed third.

Weevils are phytophagous except for the very few species associated with ants. Larvae attack all parts of plants, roots, stems, leaves, flowers, seeds, and fruit. The total amount of crop loss from weevil damage per year is staggering. No flowering plant is immune. In addition, hundreds of species live under the bark and wood of dead tree trunks and limbs. A few species are aquatic; all stages of some of them live under water and feed on aquatic plants. The majority of weevil larvae live within the tissues of the host plant.

Weevils and snout beetles are the same, the two common names being used interchangeably. However, the ancient word, weevil, refers to any small beetle infesting grain; hence this name sometimes refers to species other than those of this family.

The family is divided into many subfamilies and tribes, and many of the genera are very large and difficult to identify to

Fig. 24.264.

Fig. 24.265.

species. There is no recent publication dealing with the weevil fauna of the U.S. and Canada and the existing literature is widely scattered. Because of its large size and certain technical characteristics, many recent workers divide the group into several families. For the sake of consistency within the order, these are treated here as subfamilies, but the text indicates which of them are elsewhere treated as families. There are 2614 species in 401 genera in the U.S. and Canada.

Subfamily Attelabinae

[= Attelabidae]

Tribe Pilolabini

[113.1 *Pilolabus* Jekel (1 sp., *P. californicus* Voss (3) CA)]

Tribe Attelabini

113.2 *Homoeolabus* Jekel

One species, as follows:

H. analis (Illiger). L. 5–6 mm. Body bright red except legs, which are blue-black; proboscis short. Female rolls leaves of oak, sumac, hickory, or walnut to form a nest for her eggs. (See Fig. 24.264.) (1) n.e. NA; (2) s.e. US; (3) TX.

[113.3 *Attelabus* Linnaeus (8 spp. (1), (2), (3), (5))]

Subfamily Rhynchitinae

[= Cimberinae; Rhynchitidae]

Tribe Auletini

[113.4 *Auletobius* Desbrochers (9 spp.); 113.5 *Eugnamptis* Schoenherr (7 spp. (1), (2), (3), (5))]

Tribe Rhynchitini

[113.6 *Rhynchites* Schneider, subgenus *Dicranognathus* Redtenbacher (1 sp., *R. velatus* LeConte (1) NY; (3) CA)]

113.7 *Merhynchites* Sharp

Nine species, the following of which is a pest:

M. bicolor (Fabricius) (Rose Curculio). L. 5–6.5 mm. Body convex and broad; head with moderately long snout; elytra, thorax, and head behind the eyes bright red (head of some all black); ventrally black; legs black. Beaks of males longer and more slender than those of females. Found on blossoms and leaves of roses, sometimes damaging the buds. (See Fig. 24.265 and A&J 189.) (1) n.e. US; (2) s.e. US.

[113.8 *Haplorhynchites* Voss (5 spp.); 113.9 *Involvulus* Seidlitz (1 sp., *I. hirtus* Fabricius (1), (2), (3), (5)); 113.10 *Pselaphorhynchites* Schilsky (14 spp.)]

Tribe Deporaini

[113.11 *Deporaus* Leach (1 sp., *D. glastinus* LeConte (3) CA, AZ; (4) WA, OR; (5) CO)]

Tribe Pterocolini

[113.12 *Pterocolus* Schoenherr (1 sp., *P. ovatus* Fabricius (Fig. 24.266) (1) MI, ME; (2) FL; (3) AZ, TX; (5) MO))]

Subfamily Nemonychinae

[= Nemonychidae]

Tribe Rhinomacerini

[= Cinberini]

[113.13 *Neocimberus* O'Brien and Wibmer (6 spp.)); 113.14 *Doydirhynchus* Dejean (2 spp. (3) CA; (4) WA, OR)]

Subfamily Oxycoryninae

[= Oxycorynidae; Allocoryninae]

[113.15 *Rhopalotria* Chevrolat (2 spp. (2) FL; (3) AZ, including *R. slossoni* (Schaeffer) (Fig. 24.267) (2) FL)]

Subfamily Apioninae

[= Apionidae]

Tribe Cyladini

113.16 *Cylas* Latreille

One species, as follows:

C. formicarius (Fabricius) (Sweet Potato Weevil). L. 4–6 mm. Bright blue with orange to red thorax. Found on sweet potatoes. (See Fig. 24.268.) (2) LA, MS, FL; (3) TX.

Tribe Nanophylini

[113.17 *Nanophyes* Schoenherr (4 spp.)]

Fig. 24.266.

Fig. 24.267.

Fig. 24.269.

Tribe Aplemonini

[113.18 *Perapion* Wagner (3 spp. (1), (2), (4), (5))]

113.19 *Podapion* Riley

One species, as follows:

P. gallicola Riley (Pine Gall Weevil). (1) n.e. US; (2) s.e. US; (3) CA; (4) AK, OR; (5) MN.

[113.20 *Chrysapion* Kissinger (2 spp. (3) CA, AZ, TX)]

Tribe Apionini
113.21 *Apion* Herbst

This genus may be the largest genus of animals in the world, with over 1100 species, of which 145 are recorded in the U.S. and Canada. Many of them are pests of legumes. The following are common:

A. longirostre Olivier (Hollyhock Weevil). Common on hollyhock. (1) n.e. US; (2) s.e. US; (3) CA.

A. ulicis (Forster) (Gorse Seed Weevil). (See Fig. 24.269.) (3) CA; (4) WA, OR.

Subfamily Ithycerinae

[= Ithyceridae]

113.22 *Ithycerus* Schoenherr

One species, as follows:

I. novaboracensis Forster (New York Weevil). L. 12–18 mm. Elongate-oblong; robust; black, shiny, sparsely clothed with a mixture of ash-gray and pale brown hairlike setae forming stripes on elytra. Found on oak, hickory, and beech; a

pest on some fruit trees in the spring. (See Fig. 24.270.) (1). n.e. NA; (2) s.e. US; (3) TX; (5) NE.

[The remaining subfamilies constitute the family Curculionidae, s. str.]

Subfamily Brachyderinae

[= Thylacitinae]

Tribe Naupactini
113.23 *Graphognathus* Buchanan

Three species in (2). These comprise the White-fringe Beetle complex. They feed on the leaves, stems, and taproots of many kinds of crop plants and weeds, including peanuts, corn, sugarcane, cotton, and cabbage.

113.24 *Pantomorus* Schoenherr

Ten species, the following of which is a pest:

P. cervinus (Boheman) (Fuller Rose Beetle). (1), (2), (4), (5).

[113.25 *Mesagroicus* Schoenherr (10 spp.); 113.26 *Artipus* Schoenherr (1 sp., *A. floridanus* Horn (2) FL); 113.27 *Ericydeus* Pascoe (2 spp. (3) CA, AZ, NM); 113.28 *Glaphyrometopus* Pierce (1 sp., *G. ornithodorus* Pierce (3) TX)]

Tribe Barynotini

[113.29 *Trigonoscuta* Motschulsky (64 spp. (3) CA; (4) WA, OR); 113.30 Stereogaster Van Dyke (1 sp., *S. globosa* Van Dyke (3) CA); 113.31 *Calyptillus* Horn (1 sp., *C. cryptops* Horn (3) NM; (5) CO, KS); 113.32 *Cryptolepidus* Van Dyke (7 spp. (3) CA, AZ; (4) NV); 113.33 *Lachnopus* Schoenherr (3 spp. (2) FL); 113.34 *Omileus* Horn (1 sp., *O. epicaeroides* Horn (3) TX); 113.35 *Stamoderes* Casey (2 spp. (3) CA; (4) BC, WA, OR); 113.36 *Graphorhinus* Say (1 sp., *G. vadosus* Say (3) TX; (5) CO, KS); 113.37 *Bradyrhyncoides* Pierce (1 sp., *B. constrictus* Pierce (3) TX)]

Fig. 24.268.

Fig. 24.270.

Fig. 24.271.

113.38 *Epicaerus* Schoenherr

Eleven species, the following of which is a pest:

E. impricatus (Say) (Imbricated Snout Beetle). (See Fig. 24.271.) (1) IN, NJ; (2) NC, LA, GA; (3) TX; (5) MN, NE, IA, KS, MO.

[113.39 *Barynotus* Germar (3 spp. (1) n.e. NA)]

Tribe Polydrusini

[113.40 *Polydrusus* Germar (5 spp. (1), (2), (3), (5)); 113.41 *Scythropus* Schoenherr (8 spp. (1), 93), (4), (5)); 113.42 *Liophloeus* Germar (1 sp., *L. tessulatus* Mueller (1) NY)]

Tribe Brachyderini

[= Thylacitini]

[113.43 *Thylacites* Germar (1 sp., *T. incanus* Linnaeus (1) n.e. NA; (5) MO); 113.44 *Barypeithes* Jacquelin du Val (1 sp., *B. pellucidus* Boheman (1), (3), (4)); 113.45 *Mitostylus* Horn (4 spp. (3)); 113.46 *Sciaphilus* Schoenherr (1 sp., *S. asperatus* Bonsdorff (1) n.e. NA; (4) BC, ID); 113.47 *Brachysomus* Schoenherr (1 sp., *B. echinatus* Bonsdorff (1) MA)]

Tribe Strophosomini

[113.48 *Strophosoma* Billberg (1 sp., *S. melanogrammus* Forster (1) n.e. NA; (4) BC, WA)]

Tribe Cneorhinini

[113.49 *Philopedon* Stephens (1 sp., *P. plagiatus* Schaller (1) NB, PE)]

Tribe Sitonini

113.50 *Sitona* Germar

Twelve species, the following of which are pests:

S. cylindricollis Fåhraeus (Sweetclover Weevil). (1), (3), (4), (5).

S. hispidula (Fabricius) (Clover Root Weevil). (See Fig. 24.272.) (1), (3), (4), (5).

S. lineata (Linnaeus) (Pea Leaf Weevil). (4) Pacific n.w.

Subfamily Petalochilinae

[113.51 *Notolmus* LeConte (2 spp. (2) GA, FL)); 113.52 *Nanus* Schoenherr (1 sp., *N. uniformis* Boheman (2) FL)]

Subfamily Amalactinae

Tribe Amalactini

[113.53 *Amalactus* Schoenherr (6 spp. (1), (3), (4), (5))]

Fig. 24.272.

Tribe Tanymecini

[113.54 *Isodrusus* Champion (1 sp., *I. debilis* Champion (3) TX); 113.55 *Isodacrys* Sharp (2 spp. (3) TX); 113.56 *Minyomerus* Horn (7 spp. (3), (5)); 133.57 *Piscatopus* Sleeper (1 sp., *P. griseus* Sleeper (3) TX); 113.58 *Tanymecus* Germar (3 sp. (2), (3))]

113.59 *Pachnaeus* Schoenherr

Two species in (1), NJ; (2) FL, the following of which is a pest:

P. litus (Germar) (Citrus Root Weevil). (2) FL.

[113.60 *Amotus* Casey (3 spp. (3) CA); 113.61 *Hadromeropsis* Pierce (1 sp., *H. opalinus* Horn (3) AZ); 113.62 *Polydacrys* Schoenherr (1 sp., *P. depressifrons* Boheman (3) TX); 113.63 *Pandeleteinus* Champion (3 spp. (3), (4) UT; (5) CO); 113.64 *Scalaventer* Howden (1 sp., *S. subtropicus* Fall (2) FL); 113.65 *Pandeleteius* Schoenherr (12 spp., including *P. hilaris* Herbst (Fig. 24.273) (1) IN, OH, MA, CT; (2) MS, FL; (3) TX; (5) MO; 113.66 *Miloderoides* Van Dyke (3 spp. (4) NV, UT; (5) WY, CO); 113.67 *Trigonoscutoides* O'Brien (1 sp., *T. texanus* O'Brien (3) TX)]

Subfamily Otiorrhynchinae

Tribe Otiorrhinini

113.68 *Otiorhynchus* Germar

Sixteen species, the following of which are pests:

O. cribricollis Gyllenhal (Cribrate Weevil). (3) s.w. US.

O. ligustici (Linnaeus) (Alfalfa Snout Beetle). (1) NY.

O. ovatus (Linnaeus) (Strawberry Root Weevil). (1), (2), (3), (4), (5).

O. sulcatus (Fabricius) (Black Vine Weevil). (1), (3), (4), (5).

[113.69 *Stomodes* Schoenherr (1 sp., *S. gryosicollis* Boheman (1) ME); 113.70 *Neoptochus* Horn (1 sp., *N. adspersus* Boheman (2) GA, FL);

Fig. 24.273.

113.71 *Myllocerus* Schoenherr (1 sp., *M. hilleri* Faust (1) MD, DC; (2) VA; (5) KS)]

113.72 *Sciopithes* Horn

Six species in (3) CA; (4) WA, OR, the following of which is a pest:

S. obscurus Horn (Obscure Root Weevil). (3) CA; (4) WA, OR.

[113.73 *Agronus* Horn (3 spp. (3) CA; (4) BC; (5) AB, MT)]

Tribe Peritelini

[113.74 *Omias* Germar (6 spp. (3) CA; (4) BC, WA, OR, ID); 113.75 *Eucilinus* Buchanan (3 spp. (3) CA; (4) UT, ID); 113.76 *Rhypodillus* Cockerell (2 spp. (3), (5) CO); 113.77 *Dysticheus* Horn (2 spp. (3) CA); 113.78 *Eucyllus* Horn (7 spp. (3), (4)); 113.79 *Thinoxenus* Horn (1 sp., *T. squalens* Horn (3) CA); 113.80 *Thricolepis* Horn (2 spp. (3), (4), (5)); 113.81 *Peritelinus* Cascy (3 spp. (3), (4), (5)); 113.82 *Geodercodes* Casey (1 sp., *G. latipennis* Casey (3) CA; (4) BC, WA, OR, ID; (5) MT); 113.83 *Aragnomus* Horn (3 spp. (3) CA; (4) WA); 113.84 *Anchitelus* Van Dyke (3) CA); 113.85 *Orthoptochus* Casey (1 sp., *O. squamiger* Casey (3) CA); 113.86 *Peritelopsis* Horn (1 sp., *P. globiventris* LeConte (3) CA); 113.87 *Stenoptochus* Casey (2 spp. (3) CA)]

113.88 *Nemocestes* Van Dyke

Nine species in (1), (3), (4), (5), the following of which is a pest:

N. incomptus (Horn) (Woods Weevil). (3) CA; (4) WA, OR.

[113.89 *Paraptochus* Seidlitz (3 spp. (3) CA; (4) BC, OR); 113.90 *Peritelodes* Casey (1 sp., *P. obtectus* Casey (3) CA)]

Tribe Trachyphloeini

[113.91 *Trachyphloeus* Germar (3 spp. (1), (4)); 113.92 *Chaetechidius* Sleeper (1 sp., *C. speciosus* Sleeper (5) CO); 113.93 *Cercopeus* Schoenherr (11 spp.); 113.94 *Pseudocercopeus* Sleeper (1 sp., *P. setosus* Sleeper (3) AZ); 113.95 *Cercopedius* Sleeper (1 sp., *C. artemisiae* Pierce (4), (5) MT, CO)]

Tribe Agraphini

[113.96 *Agraphus* Say (1 sp., *A. bellicus* Say (1) PA, NJ; (2) FL); 113.97 *Paragraphus* Blatchley (1 sp., *P. setosus* Blatchley (2) FL)]

Tribe Eustylini

[113.98 *Brachystylus* Schoenherr (1 sp., *B. acutus* Say (1), (2), (5)); 113.99 *Achrastenus* Horn (1 sp., *A. griseus* Horn (3) TX)]

Tribe Hormorini

[113.100 *Hormorus* Horn (1 sp., *H. vadulatus* Uhler (1) n.e. NA)]

113.101 *Agasphaerops* Horn

One species, as follows:

A. nigra Horn (Lily Weevil). (3) CA; (4) BC, WA, OR.

[113.102 *Lupinicolus* Van Dyke (1 sp., *L. blaisdelli* Van Dyke (3) CA)]

Tribe Phyllobiini

113.103 *Phyllobius* Germar

Three species in (1), the following of which are pests:

P. intrusus Kôno (Arborvitae Weevil). Introduced. (1) ME, RI.

P. glaucus scopoli. (See Fig. 24.274.) (1) ON.

Fig. 24.274.

[113.104 *Pseudocyphus* Schaeffer (1 sp., *P. flexicaulis* Schaeffer (3) TX); 113.105 *Compsus* Schoenherr (1 sp., *C. auricephalus* Say (2) GA; (3) TX; (5) C); 113.106 *Evotus* LeConte (1 sp., *E. naso* LeConte (4), (5)); 113.107 *Aphrastus* Say (3 spp. (1), (2), (3), (5, including *A. taeniatus* Say (Fig. 24.275) (1) n.e. US; (2) s.e. US; (5) MO; 113.108 *Diaprepes* Schoenherr (1 sp., *D. abbreviata* Linnaeus (2) FL)]

Subfamily Leptiinae
Tribe Promecopini

[113.109 *Colecerus* Schoenherr (2 spp. (3) AZ, TX); 113.110 *Aracanthus* Say (1 sp., *A. pallidus* Say (1) IL, OH; (2) MS; (3) TX; (5) IA); 113.111 *Eudiagogus* Schoenherr (2 spp. (2), (3) TX, including *E. pulcher* Fåhraeus (Fig. 24.276) (3) TX)]

Tribe Leptopiini

[113.112 *Sapotes* Casey (2 spp. (3)); 113.113 *Phyxelis* Schoenherr (2 spp. (1), (2), (5)); 113.114 *Dirotognathus* Horn (2 spp. (3) CA, AZ; (4) OR); 113.115 *Rhigopsis* LeConte (2 spp. (3) CA); 113.116 *Lepidophorus* Kirby (9 spp. (1), (2), (4), (5)); 113.117 *Cimbocera* Horn (4 spp. (3), (4), (5)); 113.118 *Paracimbocera* Van Dyke (3 spp. (3), (4), (5)); 113.119 *Miloderes* Casey (4 spp. (3) CA, AZ; (4) NV); 113.120 *Plinthodes* LeConte (2 spp. (1) OH; (2) NC; (4) WA, OR); 113.121 *Triglyphulus* Cockerell (2 spp. (3) CA; (4) WA, NV); 113.122 *Acmaegenius* LeConte (2 spp. (4) OR, ID; (5) WY); 113.123 *Trichalophus* LeConte (9 spp. (3), (4), (5)); 113.124 *Adaleres* Casey (3 spp. (3) CA); 113.125 *Lepesoma* Motschulsky (32 spp. (3), (4), (5)); 113.126 *Panscopus* Schoenherr (28 spp., including *P. maculosus* Blatchley (Fig. 24.277) (1) ON, NY; (2) KY; (5) IA); 113.127 *Diamimus* Horn (1 sp., *D. subsericeus* Horn (3) AZ, NM; (4) UT; (5) MT, WY, CO); 113.128 *Orimodema* Horn (1 sp., *O. protracta* Horn (3) CA, AZ, NM; (5) CO); 113.129 *Paranametis* Burke (1 sp., *P. distincta* Burke (3) TX); 113.130 *Dichoxenus* Horn (4 spp. (1), (2), (3), (5)); 113.131 *Anametis* Horn (2 spp. (1), (2), (3), (5)); 113.132 *Peritaxia* Horn (7 spp. (3), (5)); 113.133 *Crocidema* Van Dyke (6 spp. (3), (4)); 113.134 *Pseudorimus* Van Dyke (2 spp. (3) AZ, NM); 113.135 *Melanolemma* Van Dyke (1 sp., *M. montana* Van Dyke (5) Co)); 113.136 *Tropiphorus* Schoenherr (3 spp. (1) NF, NS, PQ)]

Fig. 24.275.

Fig. 24.276.

Tribe Ophryastini

113.137 *Ophryastes* Schoenherr

Thirty-six species in (3), (4), (5), including the following:

O. argentatus LeConte (Silver Twig Weevil). L. 9.5–15.5 mm. Body convex; snout short and broad; antennae inserted toward apex of snout; color usually pearly gray with brown intervals on elytra, but varying to nearly uniformly black in some specimens. Usually found by beating deadwood and shrubbery. (See A&J 190.) (3) CA, AZ; (4) NV, UT.

Subfamily Eremninae

113.138 *Cyrtepistomis* Marshall

One species, as follows:

C. castaneus (Roelofs) (Asiatic Oak Weevil). (1), (2), (5).

113.139 *Calomycterus* Roelofs

One species, as follows:

C. setarius Roelofs (Imported Longhorned Weevil). (1) n.e. US; (5) NE, IA, KS, MO.

[113.140 *Pseudocneorrhinus* Roelofs (1 sp., *P. bifasciatus* Roelofs (1) CT, MD; (2) NC)]

Subfamily Cylindrorhininae

[112.141 *Hormops* LeConte (1 sp., *H. abducens* LeConte (1) OH, DC; (2) FL; (3) TX)]

113.142 *Listroderes* Schoenherr

Two species in (2), (3), the following of which is a pest:

L. obliquus (Klug) (Vegetable Weevil). (2) MS; (3) CA.

Fig. 24.277.

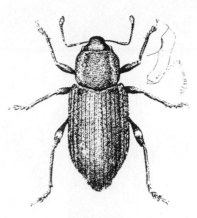

Fig. 24.278.

113.143 *Listronotus* Jekel

Sixty-five species, the following of which are pests:

L. palustris Blatchley. (See Fig. 24.278.) (2) GA. FL.

L. oregonensis LeConte (Carrot Weevil). (4) OR.

[113.144 *Lixellus* LeConte (5 spp.)]

Subfamily Thecesterninae

[113.145 *Thecesternus* Say (8 spp. (1), (2), (3), (5))]

Subfamily Hyperinae

Tribe Hyperini

113.146 *Hypera* Germar

The larvae feed externally on leaves along with the adults. Sixteen species, the following of which are pests:

H. brunneipennis (Boehman) (Egyptian Alfalfa Weevil). (3) CA, AZ.

H. meles (Fabricius) (Clover Head Weevil). (1) NY, CT, NJ; (2) AR, MS, GA.

H. punctata (Fabricius) (Clover Leaf Weevil). (1), (2), (3), (4), (5).

H. nigrirostris (Fabricius) (Lesser Clover Leaf Weevil). (1), (3), (4), (5).

H. postica (Gyllenhal) (Alfalfa Weevil). (1), (3), (4), (5).

[113.147 *Vitavitus* Kissinger (1 sp., *V. thulius* Kissinger (5) NT)]

Subfamily Cleoninae

Tribe Lepyrini

[113.148 *Lepyrus* Germar (5 spp.)]

Tribe Cleonini

113.149 *Cleonus* Schoenherr

Forty-five species, including the following:

C. piger (Scopoli) (Sluggish Weevil). L. 10–16 mm. Body with white pubescence; pronotum with four narrow black stripes; beak with three deep grooves. Larvae stem borers. Introduced. (1) s. ON, w. NY.

C. quadrilineatus Chevrolat. (See Fig. 24.279.) (3) AZ, TX; (4) WA, OR.

Fig. 24.279.

Tribe Lixini

113.150 *Lixus* Fabricius

Twenty-nine species (plus three *incertae sedis*), the following of which is a pest:

L. concavus Say (Rhubarb Curculio). (See Fig. 24.280.) (1), (2), (3), (4), (5).

113.151 *Microlarinus* Hochhuth

Two species (3), (4), both common:

M. lareyniei (Jacquelin du Val) (Puncturevine Seed Weevil). (3) CA, AZ, NM, TX; (4) WA.

M. lypriformis Wollaston (Puncturevine Stem Weevil). (3) CA, AZ; (4) WA.

Subfamily Hylobiinae
Tribe Hylobiini

[113.152 *Heilipodus* Kuschel (1 sp., *H. choicus* (Germar) (3) CA)]

113.153 *Hylobius* Germar

Seven species, the following of which are pests:

H. aliradicus Warner (Southern Pine Root Weevil). (2) NC, GA FL; (3) TX.

H. pales (Herbst) (Pales Weevil). (1), (2), (3), (5).

H. radicus (Pine Root Collar Weevil). (1) MI, NY; (5) MN.

H. rhizophagus Millers, Benjamin, and Warner (Pine Root Tip Weevil). (1) WI, MN; (5) MN.

Fig. 24.280.

113.154 *Pachylobius* LeConte

One species, as follows:

P. picivorus Germar (Pitch-eating Weevil). (1), (2), (3).

[113.155 *Heilipus* Germar (1 sp., *H. apiatus* (Olivier) (2) TN, GA, FL); 113.156 *Eudociminus* Leng (1 sp., *E. mannerheimii* (Boheman) (1), (2))]

Tribe Plinthini

[113.157 *Steremnius* Schoenherr (3 spp. (2), (3), (4)); 113.158 *Sthereus* Motschulsky (2 spp. (4)); 113.159 *Philostratus* Zimmerman (1 sp., *P. ptinoides* (Germar) (1), (3), (4)); 113.160 *Lobosoma* Buchanan (1 sp., *L. horridum* (Mannerheim) (4) AK, BC, WA, OR); 113.161 *Gastrotaphrus* Buchanan (1 sp., *G. barberi* Buchanan (3) CA; (4) BC, WA, OR)]

Tribe Anchonini

[113.162 *Anchonus* Schoenherr (3 spp. (2) FL); 113.163 *Gononotus* LeConte (1 sp., *G. angulicollis* (Suffrian) (2) FL); 113.164 *Metopotoma* Casey (1 sp., *M. repens* Casey (4) WA, OR); 113.165 *Lymantes* Schoenherr (4 spp. (1), (2), (3), (5))]

Tribe Sternechini

113.166 *Sternechus* Schoenherr

Two species in (1), (2), (3), the following of which is a pest:

S. paludatus (Casey) (Bean Stalk Weevil). (3) AZ.

Subfamily Acicnemidinae

[113.167 *Trachodes* Germar (1 sp., *T. hispidus* (Linnaeus) (1) NF)]

Subfamily Raymondionyminae

[113.168 *Schizomicrus* Casey (1 sp., *S. caecus* Casey (3) CA); 113.169 *Gilbertia* Osella (2 spp. (3) CA; (4) OR); 113.170 *Alaocybites* Gilbert (2 spp. (3) CA)]

Subfamily Pissodinae

113.171 *Pissodes* Germar

There are 22 species, many of them pests of pine, spruce, and other conifers, with common names varying according to their host plant. It is necessary to know the host tree and its breeding site to identify the species. The following have common names:

P. approximatus Hopkins (Northern Pine Weevil). (1), (2), (5).

P. nemorensis Germar (Deodar Weevil). (1), (2), (3).

P. radiatae Hopkins (Monterey Pine Weevil). (3), (4).

P. schwarzi Hopkins (Yosemite Bark Weevil). (3), (4), (5).

P. strobi Peck (Engelmann Spruce Weevil; Sitka Spruce Weevil; White Pine Weevil). (1), (2), (3), (4), (5).

P. terminalis Hopping (Lodgepole Terminal Weevil). (3), (4), (5).

Subfamily Erirhininae
Tribe Erirhinini

[113.172 *Dorytomus* Germar (22 spp.); 113.173 *Grypus* Germar (3 spp. (1), (3), (4), (5)); 113.174 *Notaris* Germar (5 spp. (1), (3), (4), (5)); 113.175 *Pachytychius* Jekel (1 sp., *P. haematocephalus* Gyllenhal (1) NY); 113.176 *Procas* Stephens (1 sp., *P. lecontei* Bedel) (1) ON, PQ, MI)]

Fig. 24.281.

Tribe Smicronychini

113.177 *Smicronyx* Schoenherr

Seventy species, the following of which are common:

S. scapalis LeConte. (See Fig. 24.281.) (1) MA; (3) TK; (5) SD, MN, CO, KS.

S. sculpticollis Casey (Dodder Gall Weevil). (1), (2), (3), (5).

[113.178 *Promecotarsus* Casey (3 spp. (3), (4), (5))]

Tribe Tanysphyrini

[113.179 *Tanysphyrus* Germar (1 sp., *T. lemnae* Fabricius (1), (2), (4), (5))]

Tribe Bagoini

[113.180 *Phycocoetes* LeConte (1 sp., *P. testaceus* LeConte (3), (4); 113.181 *Bagous* Germar (28 spp.); 113.182 *Pnigodes* LeConte (4 spp. (2), (3), (5))]

113.183 *Lissorhopturus* LeConte

Six species in (1), (2), (3), (5), the following of which are common:

L. simplex (Say). (See Fig. 24.282.) (1) IN; (2) VA, NC, SC, LA, FL; (5) AB.

L. oryzophilus Kuschel (Lesser Water Weevil). (1), (2), (3), (5).

[113.184 *Brachybamus* Germar (1 sp., *B. electus* Germar (1), (2), (3)); 113.185 *Endalus* Laporte (12 spp.); 113.186 *Onychylis* LeConte (6 spp.); 113.187 *Stenopelmus* Schoenherr (1 sp., *S. rufinasus* Gyllenhal (2), (3), (4)); 113.188 *Cyrtobagous* Hustache (1 sp., *C. singularis* Hustache (2) FL); 113.189 *Neochetina* Hustache (2 spp. (2) LA, FL; (3) TX)]

Fig. 24.282.

Tribe Derelomini

[113.190 *Hypoleschus* Fall (1 sp., *H. atratus* Fall (3) NM; (5) CO); 113.191 *Euclyptus* Dietz (8 spp.)); 113.192 *Acalyptus* Schoenherr (1 sp., *A. carpini* Herbst (1) n.e. US; (5) AB, KS)]

Subfamily Otidocephalinae
Tribe Otidocephalini

[113.193 *Myrmex* Strum (31 spp.); 113.194 *Micromyrmex* Sleeper (1 sp., *M. cavirostris* (Casey) (2) FL)); 113.195 *Oopterinus* Casey (1 sp., *O. perforatus* (Horn) (1) MD; (2) TN, AR GA; (5) IA, MO)]

Tribe Erodiscini

[113.196 *Erodiscus* Schoenherr (1 sp., *E. tinamus* LeConte (2) FL)]

Subfamily Magdalinae
Tribe Magdalini

113.197 *Magdalis* Germar

Twenty-five species, the following of which are pests:

M. aenescens LeConte (Bronze Apple Tree Weevil). (3), (4), (5).

M. armicollis (Say) (Red Elm Bark Weevil). (1), (2), (3), (5).

M. barbita (Say) (Black Elm Bark Weevil). (1), (2), (3), (5).

[113.198 *Trichomagdalis* Fall (3 spp. (3) CA))]

Tribe Laemosaccini

[113.199 *Laemosaccus* Schoenherr (2 spp. (1), (2), (3), (5))]

Subfamily Curculioninae

113.200 *Curculio* Linnaeus

Of the 30 species, several are of economic importance. It is said that squirrels open acorns just enough to look for the larvae of *Curculio*, which commonly infest these nuts. If larvae are not present, they discard the acorn without eating the meat inside.

C. proboscideus Fabricius (Larger Chestnut Weevil). L. 8–11 mm. Dark brown with dense golden or clay-yellow, scalelike setae; thorax with darker stripes; abdomen with brownish black spots; beak very long, usually about twice length of body. Larvae feed inside of chestnuts (now rarely) and chinquapins. When the nut falls, the larvae leave and burrow into the soil to pupate. (See A&J 191.) (1) NH; (2) FL; (3) TX; (5) MO.

C. caryae (Horn) (Pecan Weevil) (1), (2), (3) TX, OK; (5) NE, IA, KS, MO.

C. caryatrypes (Boheman) (Large Chesnut Weevil). (1), (2), (5) KS.

C. neocorylus Gibson (Hazelnut Weevil). (1) ME; (2) GA; (3) TX; (5) MB, NE.

C. occidentis (Casey) (Filbert Weevil). (3) CA, AZ, NM; (4) BC, UT.

C. sayi (Gyllenhal) (Small Chestnut Weevil). (1), (2) FL; (3) TX; (5) KS, MO.

C. victorensis Chittenden. (See Fig. 24.283.) (2) LA; (3) AZ, NM, OK, TX; (5) KS.

Fig. 24.283.

Fig. 24.285.

Tribe Anthonomini

[113.201 *Magdalinops* Dietz (1 sp., *M. vittipennis* Dietz (3) CA); 113.202 *Brachyogmus* Linell (1 sp., *B. ornatus* Linell (3)); 113.203 *Smicraulax* Pierce (2 spp. (3) AZ, TX); 113.204 *Nanops* Dietz (1 sp., *N. schwarzii* Dietz (2) FL); 113.205 *Anthonomopsis* Dietz (1 sp., *A. mixtus* LeConte (1), (3), (5)); 113.206 *Chelonychus* Dietz (1 sp., *C. longipes* Dietz (3), (4), (5))]

113.207 *Tachypterellus* Fall and Cockerell

Two species, the following of which is a pest:

T. quadrigibbus (Say) (Apple Curculio). (1), (3), (5) MO.

113.208 *Anthonomus* Germar

This large genus, with 117 species in the U.S. and Canada, is of considerable economic importance, particularly in the southern states. Identification is difficult. The following species are pests:

A. grandis grandis Boheman (Cotton Boll Weevil). L. 4–7.5 mm. Reddish brown to piceous, covered with coarse, pale yellow scales, forming small spots on the elytra; beak about one-half length of body. Found only on cotton. (See Fig. 24.284.) (2) NC, TN, MS, GA; (3) AZ, NM, TX.

A. grandis thurbeiriae Pierce (Thurberia Weevil). (3) AZ.

A. eugenii Cano (Pepper Weevil). (2), (3).

A. musculus Say (Cranberry Weevil). (1), (2), (5).

A. signatus Say (Strawberry Weevil). (1), (2), (3).

Fig. 24.284.

113.209 *Coccotorus* LeConte

Four species in (1), (2), (3), (5), the following of which are pests:

C. hirsutus Bruner (Sandcherry Weevil). (5).

C. scutellaris LeConte. (See Fig. 24.285.) (1), (2), (3), (5).

[113.210 *Neomastix* Dietz (1 sp., *N. solidaginis* Dietz (1), (2)); 113.211 *Ephelops* Dietz (1 sp., *E. triguttatus* Dietz (2) FL); 113.212 *Epimechus* Dietz (15 spp. (3), (4), (5)); 113.213 *Dietzianus* Sleeper (2 spp. (1))]

Tribe Bradybatini

[113.214 *Cionomimus* Marshall (1 sp., *C. insolens* Dietz (2), (3), (4))]

113.215 *Pseudanthonomus* Dietz

Fourteen species in (1), (2), (3), (5), the following of which are pests:

P. crataegi Walsh. (See Fig. 24.286.) (1) IN, NY, CT; (2) FL; (5) WI.

P. validus Dietz (Currant Fruit Weevil). (1) n.e. NA; (3) NM.

[113.216 *macrorhoptus* LeConte (6 spp. (1), (3), (4), (5))]

Subfamily Rhynchaeninae
113.217 *Rhynchaenus* Clairville-Schellenberg

Sixteen species, the following of which are pests:

R. pallicornis (Say) (Apple Flea Weevil). (1), (3), (5).

Subfamily Prionomerinae
Tribe Prionomerini

[113.218 *Odontopus* Say (1 sp., *O. calceatus* Say (Fig. 24.287) (1), (2), (5))]

Tribe Piazorrhinini

[113.219 *Piazorrhinus* Schoenherr (4 spp. (1), (2), (5))]

Fig. 24.286.

Fig. 24.287.

Subfamily Tychiinae
Tribe Elleschini

[113.220 *Elleschus* Stephens (4 spp.); 113.221 *Proctorus* LeConte (2 spp. (1), (3), (4), (5))]

Tribe Endaeini

[113.222 *Ochyromera* Pascoe (1 sp., *O. ligustri* Warner (2) NC, SC, GA)]

Tribe Lignyodini

[113.223 *Plocetes* LeConte (1 sp. *P. ulmi* LeConte (1), (2)); 113.224 *Neotylopterus* Hustache (3 spp. (1), (3), (5)); 113.225 *Lignyodes* Dejean (11 spp. (1), (3), (4), (5)); 113.226 *Chionanthobius* Pierce (1 sp., *C. schwarzi* Pierce (1) MD; (2) FL); 113.227 *Hamaba* Casey (1 sp., *H. minima* Blatchley (2) FL)]

Tribe Tychiini
113.228 *Tychius* Schoenherr

Fourteen species, the following of which is a pest:

T. stephensi Schoenherr (Red Clover Seed Weevil). (1), (2), (3), (4), (5).

113.229 *Microtrogus* Schoenherr

One species, as follows:

M. picirostris Fabricius (Clover Seed Weevil). (1), (2), (3), (4), (5).

[113.230 *Sibinia* Germar (22 spp. (3), (4), (5))]

Tribe Gymnaetrini

[113.231 *Gymnaetron* Schoenherr (4 spp., including *G. teter* (Fabricius) (Fig. 24.288) (1) WI, MI, ON, IL, IN CT; (2) VA, GA; (3) CA, TX; (4) BC, WA, ID, UT; (5) MN, KS)]

Tribe Mecinini

[113.232 *Miarus* Schoenherr (1 sp., *M. hispidulus* LeConte (1), (5)); 113.233 *Mecinus* Germar (1 sp., *M. pyraster* Herbst (1), (2), (4))]

Subfamily Cioninae

[113.234 *Cionus* Clairville (1 sp., *C. scrophulariae* (Linnaeus) (2) ?LA)]

Subfamily Cholinae

[113.235 *Cholus* Germar (2 spp. (1)); 113.236 *Erethistes* Pascoe (1 sp. *E. arizonicus* Sleeper (3) AZ)]

Fig. 24.288.

Subfamily Cryptorhynchinae
Tribe Ithyporini

[113.237 *Rhyssomatus* Schoenherr (15 spp. (1), (2), (3), (5))]

113.238 *Conotrachelus* Dejean

The 59 species are extremely difficult to identify. The following are pests:

C. nenuphar (Herbst) (Plum Curculio). L. 4.5–6.5 mm. Dark brown varied with black; pubescence brownish yellow, forming a curved bifurcate line on each side of thorax; a band behind middle of elytra composed of yellow and white hairlike setae; beak curved, slightly longer then head and thorax. Adults are common on various fruit trees; larvae infest young fruit, causing extensive crop loss, especially of plum, peach, cherry, and apple. (1), (2), (3), (4), (5).

C. crataegi Walsh (Quince Curculio). (See Fig. 24.289.) (1), (2), (3), (5).

C. juglandis LeConte (Butternut Curculio). (1), (2), (3), (5).

C. retentus Say (Black Walnut Curculio). (1), (2), (3), (5).

C. anaglyptus Say. (See Fig. 24.290.) (1), (?), (3), (5).

[113.239 *Pheloconus* Roelofs (3 spp. (1), (2), (3), (5)); 113.240 *Micralcinus* LeConte (4 spp. (2) LA, MS, AL, FL)]

113.241 *Chalcodermus* Schoenherr

Seven species in (1), (2), (3), (5), the following of which is a pest:

C. aeneus Boheman (Cowpea Curculio). (See Fig. 24.291.) (1), (2), (3), (5).

[113.242 *Chaleponotus* Casey (1 sp., *C. elusus* Casey (1) IN); 113.243 *Micromastus* LeConte (1 sp., *M. gracilis* Boheman (3) CA); 113.244 *Microhyus* LeConte (1 sp., *M. setiger* LeConte (1), (2), (5))]

Fig. 24.289.

Fig. 24.290.

Tribe Cryptorhynchini

Subtribe Tylodina

[113.245 *Canistes* Casey (1 sp., *C. schusteri* Casey (1), (2), (5)); 113.246 *Eurhoptus* LeConte (3 spp. (1), (2), (3), (5)); 113.247 *Lembodes* Schoenherr (1 sp., *L. soliterius* Boheman (2) FL); 113.248 *Paracamptus* Casey (2 spp. (2) FL); 113.249 *Calles* Kissinger (1 sp., *C. cladotrichus* Pierce (3) TX, NM); 113.250 *Peracales* Kissinger (2 spp. (1), (2), (5)); 113.251 *Gerstaeckeria* Champion (18 spp. (2), (3), (4), (5)); 113.252 *Pseudomus* Schoenherr (2 spp. (2) SC, GA, FL); 113.253 *Epacalles* Kissinger (1 sp., *E. inflatus* Blatchley (1), (2)); 113.254 *Pseudoacalles* Blatchley (2 spp. (2) SC, FL); 113.255 *Acalles* Schoenherr (11 spp. (1), (2), (3), (5)); 113.256 *Faustinus* Berg (2 spp. (2) FL)]

Subtribe Cryptorhynchina

[113.257 *Phyrdenus* LeConte (2 spp. (1), (2), (3), (5))]

113.258 *Tyloderma* Say

Thirteen species, the following of which is a pest:

T. fragariae (Riley) (Strawberry Crown Borer). (1) IL, NJ, DC; (5) KS.

[113.259 *Liometophilus* Fall (1 sp., *L. manni* Fall (3) AZ, TX)]

113.260 *Euscepes* Schoenherr

Four species in (2), (3), the following of which is a pest:

E. postfasciatus Fairmaire (West Indian Sweet Potato Weevil). (3) CA.

[113.261 *Ulosomus* Schoenherr (1 sp., *U. laticaudus* Suffrian (2) FL); 113.262 *Maemactes* Schoenherr (1 sp., *M. cribratus* LeConte (3) TX; (5) KS); 113.263 *Zascelis* LeConte (4 spp. (3), (4), (5)]

113.264 *Cryptorhynchus* Illiger

Twelve species, the following of which is a pest:

C. lapathi (Linnaeus) Poplar-and-Willow Borer). (1), (4), (5).

[113.265 *Sternochetus* Pierce (1 sp., *S. manigerae* (Fabricius) (2) FL; (3) CA); 113.266 *Apteromechus* Faust (4 spp. (1), (2), (3)); 113.267 *Pseudomopsis* Champion (1 sp., *P. inflatus* LeConte (2) FL); 113.268 *Sudus* Kissinger (1 sp., *S. floridanus* Kissinger (2) FL); 113.269 *Cophes* Champion (6 spp. (1), (2), (3)); 113.270 *Hohonus* Kissinger (1 sp., *H. lacteicollis* Champion (3) AZ, TX); 113.271 *Rhynchus* Kissinger (1 sp., *R. apiculatus* Gyllenhal (2) VA, FL); 113.272 *Episcirrus* Kuschel (1 sp., *E. branchialis* LeConte (3) AZ, TC); 113.273 *Macromerus* Schoenherr (1 sp., *M. moestus* LeConte (2) GA)]

Subfamily Zygopinae

Tribe Zygopini

[113.274 *Peltophorus* Schoenherr (2 spp. (3) AZ, TX))]

113.275 *Cylindrocopturus* Heller

Twenty-nine species, the following of which is a pest:

C. furnissi Buchanan (Douglas Fir Twig Weevil). (3) CA; (4) WA, OR.

Tribe Lechriopini

[= Mecopini]

[113.276 *Lechriops* Schoenherr (4 spp., including *L. oculatus* Say (Fig. 24.292) (1), (2), (3), (5); 113.277 *Eulechriops* Faust (1 sp., *E. minutus* LeConte (1), (2), (5)); 113.278 *Cylindrocopturinus* Sleeper (1 sp., *C. pictus* Schaeffer (3) AZ); 113.279 *Acoptus* LeConte (1 sp., *A. suturalis* LeConte (1), (2)); 113.280 *Psomus* Casey (1 sp., *P. armatus* Dietz (1))]

Subfamily Tachygoninae

[113.281 *Tachygonus* Schoenherr (9 spp. (1), (2), (3))]

Subfamily Ceutorhynchinae

Tribe Mononychini

[113.282 *Monoychus* Germar (1 sp., *M. vulpeculus* (Fabricius) (1), (2))]

Tribe Coeliodini

113.283 *Craponius* LeConte

One species, as follows:

C. inaequalis (Say) (Grape Curculio). (1), (2), (5) MO.

[113.284 *Cnemogonus* LeConte (1 sp., *C. epilobii* LeConte (1), (4), (5)); 113.285 *Acanthoscelidius* Dalla Torre and Hustache (13 spp.); 113.286 *Hypocoeliodes* Faust (2 spp. (1) NY; (3) TX); 113.287 *Auleutes* Dietz (13 spp.); 113.288 *Pelenosomus* Dietz (1 sp., *P. cristatus* Dietz (1) DC; (2) AL); 133.289 *Coeliodes* Schoenherr (2 spp. (1), (3)); 113.290 *Acallodes* LeConte (1 sp., *A. lysimachiae* Fall (1), (2), (5)); 113.291 *Dietzella* Champion (2 spp.)]

Fig. 24.291.

Fig. 24.292.

Fig. 24.293.

Tribe Ceutorhynchini

113.292 *Ceutorhynchus* Germar

Seventy-eight species, the following of which are pests:

C. *assimilis* (Paykull) (Cabbage Seedpod Weevil). (3), (4), (5).

C. *quadridens* (Panzer) (Cabbage Seedstalk Curculio). (1) MA, NY.

C. *rapae* Gyllenhal (Cabbage Curculio). (3), (4), (5).

C. *ovalis* Dietz. (See Fig. 24.293.) (1) IL, OH; (5) MN.

[113.293 *Rileyonymus* Dietz (1 sp., *R. relictus* Dietz (3) CA; 113.294 *Phrydiuchus* Gozis (2 spp. (4) OR)]

Tribe Phytobiini

[113.295 *Litodactylus* Redtenbacher (1 sp., *L. griseomicans* Schwarz (1), (2), (3), (4), (5)); 113.296 *Euhrychiopsis* Dietz (2 spp. (1), (4), (5)); 113.297 *Rhinoncus* Schoenherr (5 spp.); 113.298 *Perigaster* Dietz (4 spp.); 113.299 *Amalus* Schoenherr (1 sp., *A. haemorrhous* Herbst (1), (3), (4), (5)); 113.300 *Phytobius* Schoenherr (9 spp.); 113.301 *Perenthis* Dietz (1 sp., *P. vestitus* Dietz (1), (2)); 113.302 *Mecopeltus* Dietz (9 spp.)]

Subfamily Baridinae

Tribe Baridini

Subtribe Baridina

[113.303 *Baris* Germar (97 spp., including *B. interstitialis* Say (Fig. 24.294) (1) n.e. US; (2) s.e. US; (3) TX; (5) CO, KS); 113.304 *Cosmobaris* Casey (1 sp., *C. americana* Casey (1), (3), (4), (5)); 113.305 *Plesiobaris* Casey (5 spp. (1), (2), (5)); 113.306 *Stenobaris* Linell (1 sp., *S. avicenniae* Linell (2) FL); 113.307 *Pycnobaris* Casey (4 spp. (3), (5)); 113.308 *Stictobaris* Casey (4 spp. (3) AZ, TX); 113.309 *Trepobaris* Casey (1 sp., *T. elongata* Casey (3) AZ, TX); 113.310 *Aulobaris* LeConte (9 spp. (1), (2), (3), (5))]

Fig. 24.294.

Fig. 24.295.

113.311 *Ampeloglypter* LeConte

Three species in (1), (2), (5), the following of which are pests:

A. *sesostris* (LeConte) (Grape Cane Gall Maker) (See Fig. 24.295.) (1), (2), (5).

A. *ater* LeConte. (See Fig. 24.296.) (1) n.e. US.

[113.312 *Desmoglyptus* Casey (2 spp. (1), (2), (3)); 113.313 *Pseudobaris* LeConte (31 spp. (1), (2), (3), (5)); 113.314 *Microbaris* Casey (1 sp., *M. galvestonica* Casey (3) TX); 113.315 *Hesperobaris* Casey (2 spp. (3), (5))]

113.316 *Trichobaris* LeConte

Nine species in (2), (3), (5), the following of which are pests:

T. *mucorea* (LeConte) (Tobacco Stalk Borer). (3) CA, AZ.

T. *trinotata* (Say) (Potato Stalk Borer). (1), (2), (3), (5).

[113.317 *Rhoptobaris* LeConte (1 sp., *R. canescens* LeConte (4), (5)); 113.318 *Orthoris* LeConte (7 spp. (3) CA, AZ, TX; (4) BC, (5) NE)]

Tribe Madarini

[113.319 *Glyptobaris* Casey (1 sp., *G. lecontei* Champion (1), (2), (5)); 113.320 *Onychobaris* LeConte (35 spp. (1), (3), (4), (5)); 113.321 *Madarellus* Casey (6 spp. (1), (2), (3), (5))]

113.322 *Orchidophilus* Buchanan

Three species in (1), (3), the following of which is a pest:

O. *pereginator* Buchanan (Lesser Orchid Weevil). (1) DC.

Tribe Centrinini

[113.323 *Geraeus* Pascoe (3 spp. (3) AZ, TX)); 113.324 *Pycnogeraeus* Casey (3 spp. (1), (2), (3); 113.325 *Centrinaspis* Casey (32 spp. (1), (2),

Fig. 24.296.

Fig. 24.297.

Fig. 24.298.

(3), (5), including *C. penicellus* Herbst (Fig. 24.297) (1), (2), (3), (5); 113.326 *Pachygeraeus* Casey (2 spp. (1), (5)); 113.327 *Pseudocentrinus* Champion (1 sp., *P. ochraceus* Boheman (3) TX)]

113.328 *Odontocorynus* Schoenherr

Fifty species in (1), (2), (3), (5), the following of which is common:

O. denticornis Casey (White-scaled Flower Weevil). L. 5–6 mm. Oblong and stout; black with sparse white scales above, denser below. Adults are found on various composites, often on goldenrod. (See A&J 192.) (5) CO.

[113.329 *Centrinopus* Casey (5 spp. (1), (3), (5)); 113.330 *Centrinites* Casey (2 spp. (1), (2), (5)); 113.331 *Nicentrus* Casey (22 spp. (1), (2), (3), (5)); 113.332 *Centrinogyna* Casey (5 spp. (3), (4), (5)); 113.333 *Acentrinops* Casey (1 sp., *A. brevicollis* Casey (3) NM, TX); 113.334 *Calandrinus* LeConte (4 spp. (3), (5)); 113.335 *Microcholus* LeConte (2 spp. (1), (2)); 113.336 *Pachybaris* LeConte (1 sp., *P. porosa* LeConte (2) LA, FL); 113.337 *Diorymeropsis* Champion (1 spp., *D. xanthoxyli* Linell (3) TX); 113.338 *Eisonyx* LeConte (3 spp. (2) TN; (3) TX); 113.339 *Oomorphidius* Casey (2 spp. (1), (2), (5)); 113.340 *Cholinobaris* Casey (1 sp., *C. rhomoidea* Casey (2) NC); 113.341 *Zygobaris* LeConte (1 sp., *Z. nitens* LeConte (2) FL); 113.342 *Zygobarella* Casey (1 sp., *Z. xanthoxyli* (Pierce) (3) TX); 113.343 *Zygobarinus* Pierce (1 sp., *Z. coelestinus* (Linell) (2) FL); 113.344 *Amercedes* Casey (1 sp., *subulirostris* Casey (2) LA; (3) TX); 113.345 *Catapastus* Casey (7 spp. (1), (2), (3), (5)); 113.346 *Oligolochus* Casey (8 spp. (1), (2), (3), (5)); 113.347 *Cylindridia* Casey (5 spp. (1), (2), (3), (5)); 113.348 *Sibariops* Casey (42 spp. (1), (2), (3), (5)); 113.349 *Dirabius* Casey (9 spp. (1), (2), (3), (5)); 113.350 *Trichodirabius* Casey (2 spp. (2) LA, FL; (3) TX); 113.351 *Anacentrinus* Buchanan (14 spp.); 113.352 *Barilepsis* Casey (3 spp. (1), (2), (3)); 113.353 *Barinus* Casey (14 spp. (1), (2), (3), (5)); 113.354 *Barilepton* LeConte (4 spp.); 113.355 *Stethobaris* LeConte (10 spp. (1), (2), (3), (5)); 113.356 *Idiostethus* (18 spp. (1), (2), (5)); 113.357 *Haplostethops* Casey (7 spp. (1), (3), (5)); 113.358 *Plocamus* LeConte (2 spp. (1)); 113.359 *Eunyssobia* Casey (1 sp., *E. echidna* LeConte (1) IN, OH; (5) NE, IA); 113.360 *Buchananius* Kissinger (2 spp. (1), (2) AL)]

Subtribe Madopterina

[113.361 *Madopterus* Schoenherr (1 sp., *M. parallela* Champion (3) AZ, TX)]

Subfamily Rhynchophorinae

[= Calendrinae]

Tribe Rhynchophorini

[113.362 *Rhynchophorus* Herbst (2 spp. (2), (3))]

Tribe Sipalini

[113.363 *Yuccaborus* LeConte (1 sp., *Y. frontalis* LeConte (3) CA, AZ, TX); 113.364 *Orthognathus* Schoenherr (1 sp., *O. subparallelus* Chevrolat (3) AZ)]

Tribe Sitophilini

113.365 *Sitophilus* Schoenherr

Four species, the following of which are pests:

S. granarius (Linnaeus) (Granary Weevil). (See Fig. 24.298.) Cosmopolitan.

S. linearis Herbst (Tamarind Weevil). (1) n.e. US; (2) s.e. US.

S. oryzae (Linnaeus) (Rice Weevil). (See Fig. 24.299.) Cosmopolitan.

S. oryzae zeamais Motschulsky (Maise Weevil). (2) FL; (3) TX.

Tribe Sphenophorini

[= Calandrini]

113.366 *Sphenophorus* Schoenherr

[= *Calendra* Clairville and Schellenberg]

Seventy-one species, the following of which are pests.

S. aegualis Gyllenhal (Clay-colored Billbug). (1), (2), (3), (5).

S. callosus (Olivier) (Southern Corn Billbug). (1), (2), (3), (5).

Fig. 24.299.

S. cariosus (Olivier) (Nutgrass Billbug). (1), (2), (3), (5).

S. maidis Chittenden (Maise Billbug). (2), (3), (5).

S. parvulus Gyllenhal (Bluegrass Billbug). (1), (2), (3), (5).

S. venatus vestitus Chittenden (Hunting Billbug). (1), (2), (3), (5).

113.367 *Metamasius* Horn

Three species (localities in the U.S. not certain); the following are pests in the West Indies and Central America:

M. hemipterus (Linnaeus) (West Indian Cane Weevil.)

M. hemipterus sericeus (Olivier) (Silky Cane Weevil).

M. ritchiei Marshall (Pineapple Weevil).

113.368 *Cosmopolites* Chevrolat

One species, as follows:

C. sordida (Germar) (Banana Root Borer). (3) FL.

113.369 *Rhodobaenus* LeConte

Two species in (2), (3), the following of which is common:

R. tredecimpunctatus (Illiger) (Cocklebur Weevil). (2) NC, FL; (3) CA, AZ.

113.370 *Scyphophorus* Schoenherr

Two species in (2), (3), (5), the following of which is common:

S. acuipunctatus Gyllenhal (Agave Weevil). L. 12–15 mm. Body stout and broad; surface sparsely punctate; beak stout and deflexed; elytra lightly striated. Feeds on agave. (See A&J 193.) (2) AL, FL; (3) CA, AZ, NM, TX; (5) CO, KS.

Subfamily Cossoninae
Tribe Acamptini

[113.371 *Acamptus* LeConte (3 spp. (1), (2), (3))]

Tribe Cossonini

[113.372 *Apotrepus* Casey (1 sp., *A. densicollis* Casey (3) AZ); 113.373 *Himatinum* Cockerell (2 spp. (1), (2)); 113.374 *Carphonotus* Casey (1 sp., *C. testaceus* Casey (1), (4), (5)); 113.375 *Cossonus* Clairville (18 spp., including *C. platalea* Say (Fig. 24.300) (1), (2), (5); 113.376 *Caecossonus* Gilbert (1 sp., *C. dentipes* Gilbert (2) FL); 113.377 *Macrancylus* LeConte (2 spp. (1), (2)); 113.378 *Trichacorynus* Blatchley (2 spp. (1) IN; (2) FL; (3) CA); 113.379 *Stenancylus* Casey (2 spp. (2) FL)]

Fig. 24.300.

Fig. 24.301.

113.380 *Caulophilus* Wollaston

Two species in (2), (3), the following of which is a pest:

C. oryzae (Gyllenhal) (Broad Nosed Grain Weevil). (See Fig. 24.301.) (2) NC, SC, GA, FL; (3) CA.

[113.381 *Stenomimus* Wollaston (1 sp., *S. oallidus* Boheman (1), (2)); 113.382 *Mesites* Schoenherr (2 spp. (1), (2)); 113.383 *Rhinanisus* Broun (1 sp., *R. chisosensis* O'Brien (3) TX); 113.384 *Dynatopechus* Marshall (1 sp., *D. aureopilosus* Fairmaire (3) CA; (4) OR)]

Tribe Dryophthorini

[113.385 *Dryophthorus* Schoenherr (1 sp., *D. americanus* Bedel (1), (2), (4)); 113.386 *Dryotribus* Horn (1 sp., *D. mimeticus* Horn (2) FL)]

Tribe Aphelini

[113.387 *Emphyastes* Mannerheim (1 sp., *E. fucicola* Mannerheim (3) CA; (4)]

Tribe Rhyncolini

[113.388 *Tomolips* Wollaston (1 sp., *T. quercicola* Boheman (1), (2), (3), (5)); 113.389 *Nyssonotus* Casey (1 sp., *N. seriatus* Casey (3) CA, AZ, TX), 113.390 *Pentarthrum* Wollaston (1 sp., *P. huttoni* Wollaston (1) PQ); 113.391 *Pentarthrinus* Casey (8 spp. (1), (2)); 113.392 *Pseudopentarthrum* Wollaston (3 spp. (1), (2), (3), (5)); 113.393 *Hexarthrum* Wollaston (2 spp. (1), (2), (4)); 113.394 *Elassoptes* Horn (1 sp., *E. marinus* Horn (3) CA); 113.395 *Stenoscelis* Wollaston (2 spp. (1), (2), (5)); 113.396 *Rhamphocolus* Casey (1 sp., *R. tenuis* Casey (2), AL; (3) TX); 113.397 *Pselactus* Broun (1 sp., *P. spadix* Herbst (1), (3)); 113.398 *Phloeophagus* Schoenherr (5 spp.); 113.399 *Rhyncolus* Germar (15 spp.)]

Incertae sedis

[113.400 *Pactorrhinus* Ancey (1 sp., *P. grisescens* Ancey (3) AZ)]

BIBLIOGRAPHY

[Note: The following citations include some major works that have appeared since Arnett, 1963; the latter work includes references to all publications useful for identification published to that date.]

Arnett, Ross H., Jr. 1963, *The beetles of the United States (A manual for identification).* Catholic University of America Press, xi+1112 pp. [Out of print.]

Arnett, Ross H., Jr., ed. 1978 *Bibliography of Coleoptera of North America north of Mexico* 1758–1948. Gainesville, FL: Flora and Fauna Publications, 180 pp.

Barron, J. R. 1971. A revision of the Trogositidae of America north of Mexico (Coleoptera: Cleroidea). *Mem. Ent. Soc. Canada*, No. 75, 143 pp.

Blatchley, W. S. 1910. *An illustrated descriptive catalogue of the Coleoptera or beetles known to occur in Indiana.* Published by author, 1385 pp. [Out of print.]

Blatchley, W. S., and Leng, C. W. 1916. *Rhynchophora or weevils of North Eastern America.* Published by authors, 682 pp. [Out of print]

Boyd, Howard P. 1982. *Checklist of Cicindelidae, the tiger beetles.* Gainesville, FL: Flora and Fauna Publications, 31 pp.

Chemsak, John A., and Linsley, E. G. 1982. *Checklist of the beetles of Canada, United States, Mexico, Central America, and the West Indies.* Vol. 7, The longhorn beetles and the family Disteniidae. Gainesville FL: Flora and Fauna Publications, 138 pp.

Crowson, R. A. 1955. *The natural classification of the families of Coleoptera.* London: Nathaniel Lloyd, 187 pp.

Crowson, R. A. 1981. *The biology of the Coleoptera.* New York: Academic Press, xii+802 pp.

Erwin, Terry L., Ball, George E., and Whitehead, Donald R., eds. 1979. *Carabid beetles: their evolution, natural history, and classification.* The Hague: Dr. W. Junk bv Publishers, 635 pp.

Erwin, Terry L., Whitehead, Donald R., and Ball, George E. 1977. *Checklist of the beetles of Canada, United States, Mexico, Central America, and the West Indies*, Family 4. Carabidae, the ground beetles. Gainesville, FL: Flora and Fauna Publications, 68 pp.

Hatch, M. H. 1953-1971. *The beetles of the Pacific Northwest.* Part I: Introduction and Adephaga, 340 pp.; Part II: Staphyliniformia, 384 pp.; Part III: Pselaphidae and Diversicornia I, 503 pp.; Part IV: Marcrodactyles, Palpicornes, and Heteromera, 268 pp.; Part V: Rhipiceroidea, Sternoxi, Phylophaga, Rhynchophora, and Lamellicornia, 662 pp. Seattle: University of Washington Press.

Kissinger, David G. 1964. *Curculionidae of America north of Mexico, a key to the genera.* Publ. by author, 143 pp.

Lindroth, Carl H. 1961-1969. *The ground-beetles of Canada and Alaska.* Part 1, I-XLVIII; Part 2, pp. 1-200; Part 3, pp. 201-408; Part 4, pp. 409-648; Part 5, pp. 649-944; Part 6, pp. 945-1192. Lund: Entomologiska Sällskapet.

Linsley, E. Gordon and Chemsak, John A. 1961-1976. *The Cerambycidae of North America.* Part I: Introduction, 97 pp., 35 pls.; Part II: Taxonomy and classification of the Parandrinae, Prioninae, Spondy-linae, and Aseminae, v+102 pp., 1 pl.; Part III: Taxonomy and classification of the subfamily Cerambycinae, tribes Opsimini through Megaderini, ix+188 pp.; Part IV: Taxonomy and classification of the subfamily Cerambycinae, tribes Elaphidionini through Rhinotragini, ix+165 pp.; Part V: Taxonomy and classification of the subfamily Cerambycinae, tribes Callichromini through Ancylocerini, viii+197 pp.; Part VI, No. 1: Taxonomy and classification of the subfamily Lepturinae, viii+138 pp., 2 pls.; Part IV, No. 2. Taxonomy and classification of the subfamily Lepturinae, ix+186 pp. Berkley: University of California Press.

Moore, Ian and Legner, E. F. 1974. Bibliography (1758-1972) to the Staphylinidae of America north of Mexico (Coleoptera). *Hilgardia,* vol. 42:511-547.

Moore, Ian and Legner, E. F. 1974. Keys to the genera of the Stephylinidae of America north of Mexico exclusive of the Aleocharinae (Coleoptera: Staphylinidae). *Hilgardia,* vol. 42:548-563.

Moore, Ian and Legner, E. F. 1975. A *catalogue of the Staphylinidae of America north of Mexico (Coleoptera).* Berkeley: Division of Agricultural Sciences, University of California. Special publication 3015, 514 pp.

Moore, Ian and Legner, E. F. 1979. *An illustrated guide to the genera of the Staphylinidae of America north of Mexico, exclusive of the Aleocharinae (Coleoptera).* Berkeley: Division of Agricultural Sciences, University of California, 332 pp.

Perkins, Philip E. 1980. Aquatic beetles of the family Hydraenidae in the Western Hemisphere: classification, biogeography, and inferred phylogeny (Insecta: Coleoptera). *Questiones Entomologicae,* vol. 16, 554 pp.

Seevers, Charles H. 1978. Generic and tribal revision of the North American Aleocharinae. *Fieldiana: Zoology,* vol. 17, pp. 1-289.

Wilcox, John A. 1975. *Checklist of the beetles of Canada, United States, Mexico, Central America, and the West Indies.* Part 7, The leaf beetles (Chrysomelidae). Gainesville, FL: Flora and Fauna Publications, 166 pp.

Woodruff, Robert E. 1973. *The scarab beetles of Florida. Arthropods of Florida and neighboring land areas.* Vol. 8. Florida Department of Agriculture, xi+220 pp.

Section **Panorpida**

Order 25

HYMENOPTERA (Wasps, Ants, and Bees)

The hymenopterous insects range from solitary species to species with as highly developed a social system as that exhibited by the Honey Bee. This range is one of the most remarkable of biological phenomena and the subject of intensive study by many students of nature. The Latin name of the order comes from the Greek word *hymen,* meaning "membrane"—in reference to the wing structure of these insects—combined with *pteron* ("wing"), as in many other orders.

The order is the third largest group of insects, and, as might be expected, its members occupy a large number of habitats. They are chiefly associated with plant life either as pests or pollinators, or with other insects as external or internal parasites or as predators. As such, they play a significant role in the control of insect populations. Many ants are scavengers and also play an important role in the turnover of the soil.

Diagnosis: L. 0.2-115 mm (usually 2 to 30 mm). Soft-bodied, leathery to extremely hard; shape usually elongate, sometimes compressed; color brown or dark, often marked with yellow, but sometimes red, white, metallic blue, or green, with other colors rare. Antennae are moderate in length, but

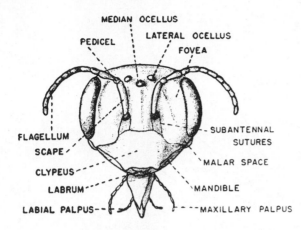

Fig. 25.1. General features of adult head. (*From Mitchell, 1960*)

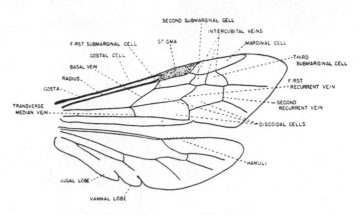

Fig. 25.3. Wing venation. (*From Mitchell, 1960*)

long in some parasitic groups, with 13 segments in the male and 12 segments in the female of most wasps and bees, but in others, especially the parasitic groups, with as few as 3 or as many as 60 segments. (See Fig. 25.1 for general features of adult head.) Mouthparts are basically mandibulate, but in many species (for example, the bee in Fig. 25.2) there is a tongue for lapping nectar from flowers. There are two pairs of wings, the hind pair smaller than the front. Venation is unique and distinctive for the order: the few cross veins are angled to form closed cells (see Fig. 25.3). Many small species have very few veins. Many others are wingless in one or both sexes or certain castes (for example, ant workers and female velvet ants). Legs are usually moderate in length; with few exceptions, the tarsi have five tarsomeres. Parts of the legs may be modified—in bees, to gather pollen, or in Drynidae, for catching hosts or digging in aculeates. The apex of the female abdomen is modified into an ovipositor in many species. In most bees and predatory wasps, and some ants, the ovipositor is modified to form a stinger. (See Figs. 25.4 and 25.5 for general body features.)

A great variety of larvae is found in this order. Some are caterpillarlike (see Fig. 25.6a) but most lack legs (see Fig. 25.6b). The pupal stage is passed either in a silken or parchment-like coccon or naked, either in some sort of isolated cell, or, in the case of the social wasps and bees, in specially constructed cells in a nest that is cared for by the worker caste. One of the most remarkable features of the Hymenoptera, and possibly a reason for the development of their social life, is the fact that

males are usually produced from unfertilized eggs. Thus, some species can control the sex of offspring by permitting or withholding fertilization.

Since some flies, moths, and beetles mimic species of Hymenoptera, close attention must be paid to the features of this order. Probably the typical arrangement of the veins in the two pairs of wings is the best way to distinguish these insects from their mimes.

Metamorphosis: Holometabolous, with egg, larval, pupal, and adult stages.

Habits and habitats: The biology of these insects is so diverse that few generalizations may be made. Many details about their habits and habitats are given in the discussion of individual families and species. A great number of species, probably the majority of them, are parasitic in the larval stage on other insects, but a significant number are plant feeders. As adults, many are predators, usually for the purpose of providing food for their developing larvae. A large number of adults feed on pollen and nectar and are thus involved in the pollination of plants. Many plants are entirely dependent upon bees for pollination, and hence for their survival.

Reproductive behavior: Mating behavior in the Hymenop-

Fig. 25.2. Adult head with sucking mouthparts (posterior view).

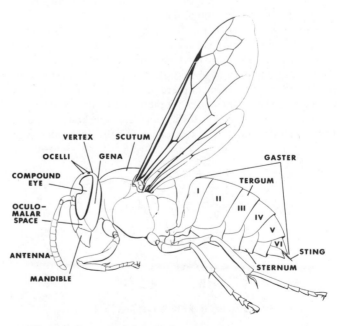

Fig. 25.4. General adult body features. (*U.S. Dept. of Agric.*)

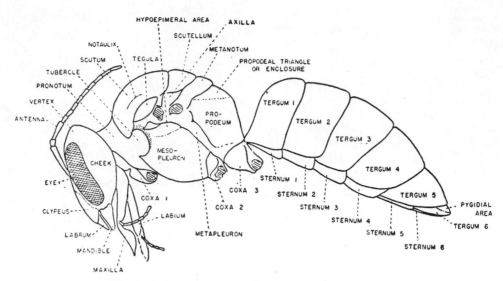

Fig. 25.5. General adult body features. (*From Britton, 1966*)

tera has been poorly studied, relative to other groups, probably because it is relatively simple compared to other aspects of the reproduction of these insects. It is known that virgin female Honey Bees (the queens) will fly upwards to mating stations where up to a hundred males (drones) have gathered. The queen is pursued and captured in flight by a drone. As copulation is completed, the male propels his genitalia into the female and then dies. Certain male bees (Megachilidae) guard clumps of flowers and force females visiting these flowers into copulation. Females may visit many such flower territories and copulate with each resident male in turn. Other reproductive strategies have been reported.

The most advanced kinds of social structure, which are in fact related to reproductive behavior, are found in this order. Nest building, colony housing, and the caste system are extremely varied and highly developed in several families of Hymenoptera, particularly the ants, social wasps, and bees. These structures constitute the subject of many books and articles and cannot be elaborated upon here. Some details are provided in the discussion of individual groups.

Economic importance: Some hymenopterous larvae are leaf and conifer needle feeders, and a few of these are economic pests of fruit and forest trees and nursery plants. Others are wood borers and damage trees in this manner. Compared to other orders, the Hymenoptera are of less importance as economic pests. Unlike the Diptera, none are involved in disease transmission, but their stings are well known, and in some allergic individuals can cause severe illness and even

death. The principal economic value of hymenopterans is threefold: their role in population control through parasitism of other insects, including crop pests; their role as pollinators, and hence the increased production of plant life, including crops; and their production of honey and wax. Certainly they rank as the most beneficial group of insects; without them, life on earth would be much different for man, for many other animals, and for many plants.

Collecting and preserving: Many species are easily collected on flowers or taken from nests. The parasitic species are difficult to find in the wild but may be reared from infested hosts. The use of black Malaise traps is productive in capturing Ichneumonidae and many other groups. Predatory sand wasps may be netted in fields and forests. Nest robbing will yield workers of ants, social wasps, and bees. Sometimes, it is necessary to destroy the nest to find the queens and males of social species. Opening a nest provides the opportunity to collect the other kinds of insects that may inhabit the colony as "guests." These may be welcomed ("invited") guests because they produce something desired by the host, or they may be uninvited predators or scavengers. Most of all, both social and solitary species should be carefully observed and collected. The biology of many of them is still unknown, and data on their activities may be a valuable addition to our knowledge of the order.

Specimens are usually pinned; some will need to be mounted on points because of their small size. Since bees are covered with dense hairlike setae and these hairs tend to mat down, alcohol preservation is not a good way to preserve them. Larvae should be stored in 70-percent alcohol.

Rearing: Honey Bees, as everyone knows, are reared with relative ease in large colonies. Although usually thought to be domesticated, they are not entirely dependent upon man. They often escape and form wild colonies. Rearing ants is sometimes successful but must be carefully performed. Other than these exceptions, rearing of Hymenoptera is difficult. Capturing emerging parasites is far from culturing a species. Mass rearing of wasp parasites of the immature stages of insect pests is possible, however, and is being pursued as a means of biological control of certain crop pests.

Fig. 25.6. Larvae: (a) sawfly larva, and (b) bee larva.

Distribution: About 103,000 species of Hymenoptera have been described. Some entomologists claim that all other species of insects have at least one hymenopterous parasite. If so, then many hundreds of thousands of species remain to be discovered, which would suggest that the Hymenoptera are the largest order of insects. A different parasite for every host, however, is undoubtedly an exaggeration. The species in the U.S. and Canada have been recently cataloged. According to this *Catalog of Hymenoptera in American North of Mexico* (see Krombein, *et al.,* 1979), and with some more recent updating (parts of the catalog are as much as ten years out-of-date), there are 2034 genera and 17,777 species in the U.S. and Canada.

Identification. The identification of many groups is difficult, especially the parasitic species, not only because of the great number of species and their small size but because of the lack of suitable comprehensive literature. The solitary and social wasps and bees are somewhat less difficult to identify because more comprehensive work has been done, and some of the literature on these groups is more readily available in public libraries and book stores. The *Catalog of Hymenoptera* cites much of the usable taxonomic literature. Some additional works are cited in the references at the end of this section.

Following are some hints on how to recognize the major groups:

Sawflies These primitive plant-feeding Hymenoptera are usually easily recognized by the broad connection of the abdomen to the thorax. Their larvae (see Fig. 25.6a) resemble the caterpillars of Lepidoptera, and many of them are plant pests. The first 12 families of Hymenoptera are sawflies and their relatives.

Parasitic wasps A majority of the species of Hymenoptera are parasitic in the larval stage. The species vary in size from extremely minute (under 1 mm) to very large (over 20 mm), but the abdomen of most is constricted near the base, giving the appearance of being attached by a narrow segment. Such is the structure of the abdomen of all remaining groups as well. To recognize this group, consult the accompanying Key to the Families, beginning with couplet 13, and the table of superfamilies (Table 25.1) that follows. It should be noted that the text indicates which of these "parasitic" wasps revert back to plant feeding as gall makers. In many species, the venation of the wings is greatly reduced.

Ants These insects belong to the family Formicidae. They are easily recognized by their characteristic shape and by the node, or pair of nodes, formed by the first, or the first and second, abdominal segments. It is doubtful if ants in the wingless stage can be confused with any other group of insects, although the layman may, and often does, think the winged forms are termites. Female velvet ants (family Mutillidae) are wingless, lack the abdominal nodes, and are usually very "Hairy" and brightly colored.

Wasps, hornets, yellowjackets, and bees Since their ovipositor is modified into a stinger, the females of these species must be treated with care to avoid being stung. They lay their eggs by discharging them directly from the body, rather than from the ovipositor (sting).

Wasps The solitary wasps include both parasitic and predatory species, among which are potter wasps, digger wasps, spider wasps, and others, comprising a large and interesting

Table 25.1 Classification of the Order Hymenoptera

Suborder SYMPHYTA

 Superfamily MEGALODONTOIDEA

1. XYELIDAE (Xyelid Sawfly Family)
2. PAMPHILIIDAE (Web-spinning and Leaf-rolling Sawfly Family)

 Superfamily TENTHREDINOIDEA

3. PERGIDAE (Pergid Sawfly Family)
4. ARGIDAE (Argid Sawfly Family)
5. CIMBICIDAE (Cimbicid Sawfly Family)
6. DIPRIONIDAE (Conifer Sawfly Family)
7. TENTHREDINIDAE (Common Sawfly Family)

 Superfamily SIRICOIDEA

8. ANAXYELIDAE (Cedar Wood Wasp Family)
9. SIRICIDAE (Horntail Family)
10. XIPHYDRIIDAE (Wood Wasp Family)
11. ORUSSIDAE (Parasitic Wood Wasp Family)

 Superfamily CEPHOIDEA

12. CEPHIDAE (Stem Sawfly Family)

Suborder APOCRITA

 Infraorder PARASITICA

 Superfamily ICHNEUMONOIDEA

13. BRACONIDAE (Braconid Family)
14. APHIDIIDAE (Aphidiid Family)
15. HYBRIZONTIDAE (Hybrizontid Family)
16. ICHNEUMONIDAE (Ichneumonfly Family)
17. STEPHANIDAE (Stephanid Family)

 Superfamily CHALCIDOIDEA

18. TORYMIDAE (Torymid Wasp Family)
19. PTEROMALIDAE (Pteromalid Wasp Family)
20. EURYTOMIDAE (Seed Chalcid Family)
21. CHALCIDIDAE (Chalcidid Wasp Family)
22. LEUCOSPIDAE (Leucospid Wasp Family)
23. EUCHARITIDAE (Eucharitid Wasp Family)
24. EUPELMIDAE (Eupelmid Wasp Family)
25. ENCYRTIDAE (Encyrtid Wasp Family)
26. EULOPHIDAE (Eulophid Wasp Family)
27. MYMARIDAE (Fairyfly Family)
28. TRICHOGRAMMATIDAE (Trichogrammatid Wasp Family)

 Superfamily CYNIPOIDEA

29. IBALIIDAE (Ibaliid Wasp Family)
30. LIOPTERIDAE (Liopterid Wasp Family)
31. FIGITIDAE (Figitid Wasp Family)
32. EUCOILIDAE (Eucoilid Wasp Family)
33. CHARIPIDAE (Charipid Wasp Family)
34. CYNIPIDAE (Gall Wasp Family)

 Superfamily EVANIOIDEA

35. EVANIIDAE (Ensign Wasp Family)
36. AULACIDAE (Aulacid Wasp Family)
37. GASTERUPTIIDAE (Gasteruptiid Wasp Family)

 Superfamily PELECINOIDEA

38. PELECINIDAE (Pelecinid Wasp Family)

 Superfamily PROCTOTRUPOIDEA or SERPHOIDEA

39. SERPHIDAE (Serphid Wasp Family)
40. ROPRONIIDAE (Roproniid Wasp Family)
41. HELORIDAE (Helorid Wasp Family)

Table 25.1 (Contd.)

42. DIAPRIIDAE (Diapriid Wasp Family)
43. SCELIONIDAE (Scelionid Wasp Family)
44. PLATYGASTRIDAE (Platygastrid Wasp Family)

Superfamily CERAPHRONOIDEA
45. CERAPHRONIDAE (Ceraphronid Wasp Family)
46. MEGASPILIDAE (Megaspilid Wasp Family)

Superfamily TRIGONALOIDEA
47. TRIGONALIDAE (Trigonalid Wasp Family)

Infraorder ACULEATA

Superfamily CHRYSIDOIDEA
48. BETHYLIDAE (Bethylid Wasp Family)
49. SCLEROGIBBIDAE (Sclerogibbid Wasp Family)
50. CHRYSIDIDAE (Cuckoo Wasp Family)
51. DRYINIDAE (Pincher Wasp Family)
52. EMBOLEMIDAE (Embolemid Wasp Family)

Superfamily SCOLIOIDEA
53. TIPHIIDAE (Tiphiid Wasp Family)
54. SIEROLOMORPHIDAE (Sierolomorphid Wasp Family)
55. MUTILLIDAE (Velvet Ant Family)
56. SCOLIIDAE (Scoliid Wasp Family)
57. SAPYGIDAE (Sapygid Wasp Family)

Superfamily FORMICOIDEA
58. FORMICIDAE (Ant Family)

Superfamily VESPOIDEA
59. VESPIDAE (True Wasp Family)

Superfamily POMPILOIDEA
60. POMPILIDAE (Spider Wasp Family)
61. RHOPALOSOMATIDAE (Rhopalosomatid Wasp Family)

Superfamily SPHECOIDEA
62. SPHECIDAE (Digger Wasp Family)

Superfamily APOIDEA
63. COLLETIDAE (Yellow-faced and Plasterer Bee Family)
64. OXAEIDAE (Oxaeid Bee Family)
65. ANDRENIDAE (Andrenid Bee Family)
66. HALICTIDAE (Sweat Bee Family)
67. MELITTIDAE (Melittid Bee Family)
68. MEGACHILIDAE (Leafcutting and Mason Bee Family)
69. ANTHOPHORIDAE (Cuckoo Bee, Digger Bee, and Carpenter Bee Family)
70. APIDAE (Bumble Bee and Honey Bee Family)

group of hymenopterans. The female solitary wasp builds a few separate cells or digs small holes and lays each egg next to or on paralyzed insects, which serve as food for the hatched larvae.

Hornets and yellowjackets These social wasps belong to the family Vespidae. They are brightly marked with yellow, orange, or white on their otherwise black or brown bodies. The queen starts a nest by building a few cells of comb and laying eggs in each. These hatch into workers that continue to build a "paper" nest large enough for many residents. Hornets and yellowjackets sting.

Bees The body of bees is densely covered with hairlike setae whereas that of wasps lacks hairlike setae. The hind tibiae are somewhat enlarged and usually modified for holding pollen, although some have pollen brushes on the abdomen. Parasitic species lack pollen baskets.

CLASSIFICATION

The classification of the Hymenoptera is stable at the superfamily level, but limits of some of the families continue to be debated, especially in the Chalcidoidea, Cynipoidea, Vespoidea, Sphecoidea, and Apoidea, where suprageneric taxa are shifted from tribe to subfamily, to family, and back again according to the opinions of various authors. Most of these changes reflect subjective rankings rather than conceptual changes of the groups. Since the *Catalog of Hymenoptera* is computerized, it may be expected to be kept up-to-date and will help unify the classification of the order.

The following treatment of the taxa of the Hymenoptera follows much of the *Catalog of Hymenoptera*, with more current information added to some groups; moreover, the families Bethylidae, Serphidae, Chrysididae, Mutillidae, Vespidae, and Spheoidae have been changed to follow more recent literature. (See Table 25.2 for an index to the families and higher taxa.)

Suborder SYMPHYTA (Sawflies and Horntails)

The base of the abdomen of the adults of Symphyta is broadly joined to the thorax. The caterpillars of almost all of them are similar to those of the Lepidoptera but usually have six or more abdominal prolegs (always on the fifth segment, in contrast to the Lepidoptera), although these lack the circles of hooklets found on "true" caterpillars. (One family, the Orussidae, have legless larvae.) They also have only one pair of large ocelli on the head. (Moth larvae have more.) The adults of most Symphyta are called "sawflies" because the ovipositor is often somewhat sawlike and used for making cuts in plant tissue. The following four superfamilies (see Table 25.3) belong to this suborder.

Key to the Families of Hymenoptera in the U.S. and Canada

1. Thorax and abdomen broadly joined, with no constriction between them, the second abdominal segment joined broadly to first without a socket joint and at most a shallow dorsoventral constriction; first abdominal tergum distinctly separated from metathorax (Suborder Symphyta) ... *2*
 Body separated into alitrunk (mesothorax, metathorax, and first abdominal segment), second abdominal segment narrowly constricted basally and articulating by a socket joint with the first abdominal segment, which is fused solidly with the metathorax (see Fig. 25.11). (Suborder Apocrita) *13*

2(1). Antennae inserted on lower surface of head, below level of lower margins of eyes ...**11. Orussidae**
 Antennae inserted on anterior surface of head between eyes *3*

Key to the Families of Hymenoptera in the U.S. and Canada (*Contd.*)

3(2).	Antennal flagellum composed of a single unsegmented piece, sometimes forked ..**4. Argidae**	
	Antennal flagellum many segmented ...	*4*
4(3).	Antennal segment 3 elongate, 9 to 25 apical segments forming a more slender apical filament ..**1. Xyleidae**	
	Antennae without such differentiation into elongate segment 3 and slender, segmented apical filament ...	*5*
5(4).	Antennae capitate, 1 or 2 apical segments conspicuously widened ...**5. Cimbicidae**	
	Antennae never capitate (except in a few *Tenthredo* spp.), at most clavate (gradually widened from base of flagellum), usually filiform, serrate, or pectinate	*6*
6(5).	Antennae 6-segmented; scutellum with anterior margin sinuate.**3. Pergidae**	
	Antennae with more than 6 segments; scutellum with anterior margin inverted V-shaped ...	*7*
7(6).	Front tibiae with 2 apical spurs, 1 of which may be considerably shorter and hidden ...	*8*
	Front tibiae with 1 apical spur only ..	*10*
8(7).	Antennae with 7 to 12 segments**7. Tenthredinidae**	
	Antennae with 13 or more segments ..	*9*
9(8).	Antennae slender and simple**2. Pamphilidae**	
	Antennae serrate or pectinate**6. Diprionidae**	
10(7).	Mesoscutum with pair of diagonal furrows from lateral margins mesocaudad to anterior border of scutellum**9. Siricidae**	
	Mesoscutum without such furrows ...	*11*
11(10).	Pronotum greatly narrowed on middorsal line and represented as a narrow collar ...**10. Xiphydriidae**	
	Pronotum not greatly narrowed on middorsal line	*12*
12(11).	Apical spur of front tibiae with inner margin pectinate; cenchrus, a membranous lobe on each side of the mesonotum, present**8. Anaxyelidae**	
	Apical spur of front tibae with inner margin simple; cenchrus absent **12. Cephidae**	
13(1).	Both pairs of wings absent or at most represented by stubs	*14*
	Mesothoracic wings fully developed, possibly with reduced venation but always with distinct membrane; metathoracic wings usually well developed, often with reduced venation, rarely reduced to stubs ..	*35*
14(13).	An erect scale or 1 or 2 knotlike swellings on petiole between thorax and swollen part of abdomen (gaster) (See Fig. 25.32), the segments bearing these separated by dorsal and ventral membranes; antennae elbowed; (in part)**58. Formicidae**	
	Petiole without such scale or knoblike swellings; gaster may have 1 or 2 segments strongly constricted but without dorsal and ventral membranes separating them	*15*
15(14).	Second abdominal tergum (first postpetiolar) with lateral longitudinal "felt line"—short recumbent hairlike setae arranged in linear fashion; (in part) **55. Mutillidae**	
	Second abdominal tergum without "felt line"	*16*
16(15).	Thorax with only pronotum set off by a suture dorsally, other parts fused; scutellum not apparent; (in part)**53. Tiphiidae**	
	Thorax clearly divided into 3 parts by sutures or sharply defined constrictions, or into 2 parts by a constriction; scutellum usually distinct	*17*
17(16).	Pronotum in lateral view more or less quadrate; caudolateral angle of pronotum not quite reaching tegula (scale at base of front wing), being separated from it by a distinct sclerite, the prepectus; antennae usually elbowed; (in part) [see text for Key to Families] ...**Chalcidoidea**	
	Pronotum in lateral view more or less triangular; caudolateral angle of pronotum reaching tegula, or tegula absent; prepectus absent; antennae usually not elbowed ...	*18*
18(17).	Gastral sterna 2 and 3 membranous, more or less concave, and with a longitudinal fold in dried specimens ..	*19*
	Gastral sterna 2 and 3 sclerotized, without a longitudinal fold	*20*
19(18).	Gaster with a distinct curved or elbowed petiole; (in part)**16. Ichneumonidae**	
	Gaster without a distinct petiole, or if petiolate, then petiole not curved or elbowed; (in part) ...**13. Braconidae**	
20(18).	Front tarsi raptorial, with pincers; antennae 10-segmented**51. Dryinidae**	
	Front tarsi normal, without pincers ..	*21*
21(20).	Gaster usually strongly compressed laterally and covered largely by 1 tergum; (in part) [see text for Key to Families]**Cynipoidea**	
	Gaster depressed or cylindrical, at most slightly compressed and then not covered by 1 tergum ..	*22*

Key to the Families of Hymenoptera in the U.S. and Canada (*Contd.*)

22(21). Mesopleuron divided by an oblique sulcus into upper and lower parts; coxae very long; (in part) ...**60. Pompilidae**
Mesopleuron not divided by a transverse sulcus as above; coxae not unusually long ... *23*

23(22). Antennae with 22 or more segments; (in part)**49. Sclerogibbidae**
Antennae with at most 15 segments *24*

24(23). Gastral segments with sharp lateral margins *25*
Gastral segments rounded laterally *26*

25(24). Antennae 10-segmented, or if less, then without an unsegmented apical club; (in part) ..**44. Platygastridae**
Antennae 11- or 12-segmented, or if 7- or 8-segmented, then with an unsegmented apical club; (in part)**43. Scelionidae**

26(24). Antennae 13- to 15-segmented *27*
Antennae 10- to 12-segmented *29*

27(26). Antennae inserted near clypeus; (in part)**48. Bethylidae**
Antennae inserted near middle of face *28*

28(27). Gaster produced caudally into a pointed tube; antennae 13-segmented; (in part) ..**39. Serphidae**
Gaster not produced into a pointed tube; antennae 14- or 15-segmented; (in part) ..**42. Diapriidae**

29(26). Antennae 11-segmented; (in part)**45. Ceraphronidae**
Antennae 10- or 12-segmented *30*

30(29). Antennae 10-segmented .. *31*
Antennae 12-segmented .. *32*

31(30). Antennae inserted near clypeus; (in part)**45. Ceraphronidae**
Antennae inserted on a frontal prominence in middle of face; (in part) ..**51. Dryinidae**

32(30). Mesosternum with 2 horizontal plates between and partially overlapping the middle coxae ventrally, or with 2 minute erect teeth between coxae; (in part) ..**53. Tiphiidae**
Mesosternum without such plates or teeth *33*

33(32). Antennae inserted near clypeus; (in part)**48. Bethylidae**
Antennae inserted on middle of face *34*

34(33). Antennae elbowed; (in part)**42. Diapriidae**
Antennae not elbowed; (in part)**53. Tiphiidae**

35(13). Posterior margin of pronotum projecting ventrad to form a rounded lateral lobe (tubercle) that usually does not touch tegula (see Fig. 25.6), or this area densely covered with hairlike setae, preventing lobe from being seen *36*
Pronotum without such rounded lobe (see Fig. 25.4), and never densely covered with hairlike setae *38*

36(35). Basal hind tarsomere usually as long as or longer than the others combined and usually broadened or flattened; at least some hairs of thorax plumose, barbed, or spirally twisted; body usually very hairy but sometimes almost bare and metallic green or blue [see text for Key to Families]**Apoidea**
Basal hind tarsomere shorter than the others combined and slender; all body hairs simple and usually sparse *37*

37(36). Prothorax in form of long narrow neck; mesonotum with sharp, high ridge anterior medianally of tegula; metasternum with long thin plate projecting over base of hind coxae (Ampulicinae, *Ampulex* spp.)**62. Sphecidae**
Prothorax usually broader than long; if somewhat elongate, then mesonotum and metasternum not as above (other genera)**62. Sphecidae**

38(35). Antennae with 13 or fewer segments; ovipositor usually issuing at tip of gaster as a sting without long sheaths *39*
Antennae with 14 or more segments; ovipositor usually issuing on ventral surface of gaster some distance from apex and surrounded by a pair of long sheaths; last sternum of gaster of female usually cleft longitudinally on underside *51*

39(38). Hind wing with at least 1 cell completely surrounded by sclerotized veins; trochanters not subdivided *40*
Hind wing without a single cell completely surrounded by sclerotized veins; trochanters composed of 2 distinct segments *57*

40(39). First segment of gaster in the form of a scale or node, or the first and second segments both nodelike and both clearly separated dorsally and ventrally by membranes; (in part) ..**58. Formicidae**
First segment of gaster not in the form of a scale; if in the form of a node and separated from the second by constriction, then latter is not separated from adjacent segments by membranes ventrally and dorsally *41*

Key to the Families of Hymenoptera in the U.S. and Canada (*Contd.*)

41(40).	Front wing with cell 1M longer than cell 1Cu; wings usually longitudinally pleated	*42*
	Front wing with cell 1M shorter than cell 1Cu, or cross vein 1 m-cu absent and hence cell 1M open; wings not longitudinally pleated	*43*
42(41).	Middle tibiae with 1 apical spur; tarsal claws toothed or bifid (Eumeninae) ...**59. Vespidae**	
	Middle tibiae with 2 apical spurs; tarsal claws simple; (in part)**59. Vespidae**	
43(41).	Mesopleuron divided by an oblique sulcus into upper and lower parts; legs unusually long, hind femora almost reaching tip of gaster; (in part)**60. Pompilidae**	
	Mesopleuron not divided by a longitudinal sulcus into upper and lower parts; legs usually shorter ..	*44*
44(43).	Meso- and metasternum forming a continuous plate ventrally overlapping bases of middle and hind coxae, but separated by suture**56. Scoliidae**	
	Meso- and metasternum not forming a continuous plate; mesosternum sometimes developed into thin plates overlapping middle coxae ventrally	*45*
45(44).	Antennae clavate; front wings with two submarginal cells, or if three cells, apex of second discal cell produced above, and jugal lobe of hind wing about half as long as submedial cell (Masarinae) ..**59. Vespidae**	
	Antennae not clavate; other characteristics variable	*46*
46(48).	Each flagellar segment of antennae with a pair of slender apical spines; female with tarsomeres 2 and 3 dilated and lobed**61. Rhopalosomatidae**	
	Flagellar segments of antennae without such spines; female tarsomeres simple	*47*
47(46).	Gastral tergum 2 with lateral longitudinal "felt line"; short recumbent hairlike setae arranged in a streak; (in part)**55. Mutillidae**	
	Gaster without "felt lines" ..	*48*
48(47).	Mesosternum with a pair of thin plates overlapping or projecting over bases of middle coxae ventrally; (in part)**53. Tiphiidae**	
	Mesosternum simple or at most with a pair of minute toothlike spines between middle coxae ..	*49*
49(48).	Hind wings with a distinctly separated jugal lobe**54. Sierolomorphidae**	
	Hind wings without distinctly separated jugal lobe	*50*
50(49).	Gaster with several segments separated by strong constrictions; (in part) ...**53. Tiphiidae**	
	Gaster without such constrictions, except between segments 1 and 2 **57. Sapygidae**	
51(38).	Antennae with 17 or more segments (rarely with as few as 15)	*52*
	Antennae with 16 or fewer segments	*57*
52(51).	Front wing with cells between C and R sclerotized or these veins fused, no clear cell C present ..	*53*
	Front wing with cell C distinct, not sclerotized, but sometimes very narrow	*55*
53(52).	Front wings with cross vein 2 m-cu present; (in part)**16. Ichneumonidae**	
	Front wings with cross veing 2 m-cu absent	*54*
54(53).	Gaster very long and slender and strongly compressed; (in part) **16. Ichneumonidae**	
	Gaster neither long and slender nor strongly compressed; (in part) **13. Braconidae**	
55(52).	Hind femora swollen and toothed before apex; gaster long and slender, ovipositor long; head spherical and borne on a long neck**17. Stephanidae**	
	Hind femora not swollen and without teeth	*56*
56(55).	Head quadrate ...**47. Trigonalidae**	
	Head elongate; (in part)**49. Sclerogibbidae**	
57(51, 39).	Gaster attached to alitrunk dorsally, a considerable distance above and away from bases of hind coxae ..	*58*
	Gaster attached to alitrunk near bases of hind coxae	*60*
58(57).	Gaster with a narrow cylindrical petiole and a short ovoid, compressed distal part ...**35. Evaniidae**	
	Gaster not differentiated into a distinct petiole and a short ovoid, compressed distal part ..	*59*
59(58).	Hind tibiae strongly swollen distally**37. Gasteruptiidae**	
	Hind tibiae not swollen distally**36. Aulacidae**	
60(57).	Hind wing with a deep jugal notch	*61*
	Hind wing without a distinct jugal notch	*65*
61(60).	Antennae 10-segmented; front tarsus of female often pincerlike; (in part)**51. Dryinidae**	
	Antennae 11- to 13-segmented; front tarsi always normal	*62*
62(61).	Pronotum elongate and with a median longitudinal furrow. **52. Embolemidae**	
	Pronotum not elongate and without a median longitudinal furrow	*63*
63(62).	Gaster with 7 or 8 visible terga; (in part)**48. Bethylidae**	
	Gaster with 2 to 6 visible terga ...	*64*

Key to the Families of Hymenoptera in the U.S. and Canada (*Contd.*)

64(63).	Venter of gaster strongly concave, the entire gaster capable of being rolled up into a ball; body brilliant metallic green, blue, or gold; usually 2 to 4 visible terga in gaster; (in part) .. **50. Chrysididae**
	Venter of gaster convex; usually 6 visible terga in gaster; (in part). **50. Chrysididae**
65(60).	Pronotum in lateral view more or less quadrate; caudolateral margin of pronotum not quite reaching tegula (the scale at base of front wings), sometimes separated from it by a distinct sclerite, the prepectus; front wings with only 1 distinct vein; (in part) [see text for key to families] **Chalcidoidea**
	Pronotum in lateral view more or less triangular; caudolateral margin of pronotum reaching tegula ... *66*
66(65).	Wings longitudinally pleated in repose; ovipositor carried on middorsal line [see Chalcidoidea] .. **22. Leucospididae**
	Wings not longitudinally pleated in repose; ovipositor not carried on middorsal line .. *67*
67(66).	Gaster more or less laterally compressed and polished, often covered largely by one tergum, which is keeled or swollen; vein C not developed in front wings; (in part) [see text for Key to Families] **Cynipoidea**
	Gaster cylindrical or dorsoventrally depressed; if compressed, then vein C present in front wing ... *68*
68(67).	Antennae arising far above clypeus on a frontal prominence or shelf. *69*
	Antennae not arising on a frontal prominence or shelf but either just above the clypeus or near middle of face .. *70*
69(68).	Venation of front wings moderately complete, with cell R_1 large but not always complete and vein Rs+M well developed, except at apex; (in part) **51. Dryinidae**
	Venation of front wings very incomplete, with cell R_1 if present, very small and vein Rs+M entirely absent; (in part) **42. Diapriidae**
70(68).	Basal hind tarsomere 1/4 as long as 2nd; female gaster very long; male gaster clavate; length 25–50 mm. .. **38. Pelecinidae**
	Basal hind tarsomere at least as long as 2nd; length under 11 mm *71*
71(70).	Mandibles with apex directed laterad (Vanhorniinae) **39. Serphidae**
	Mandibles with apex directed mesad *72*
72(71).	Antennae 14- or 15-segmented ... *73*
	Antennae 13-segmented or less .. *74*
73(72).	Antennae 14-segmented **40. Roproniidae**
	Antennae 15-segmented **41. Heloridae**
74(72).	Antennae inserted at middle of face **39. Serphidae**
	Antennae inserted close to clypeus .. *75*
75(76).	Gaster with lateral margins rounded *76*
	Gaster with lateral margins sharp or with a carinae *77*
76(75).	Costa vein with stigma; antennae 11-segmented in both sexes ... **46. Megaspilidae**
	Costa vein without stigma; male antennae with 12 segments, female with 11 **45. Ceraphronidae**
77(75).	Antennae usually 10-segmented, rarely 8- or 9-segmented; front wing without Costa vein and often completely veinless **44. Platygastridae**
	Antennae usually 12- or 11-segmented; if, rarely, 7- or 8-segmented, then apical club unsegmented ... **43. Scelionidae**

Table 25.2 Index to the Families and Higher Taxa of Hymenoptera

Aculeatea; *supra* 48	Aulacidae, 36
Agaonidae; *see* Torymidae (18)	Bethylidae, 48
Alloxystidae; *see* Charipidae (33)	Bethyloidea; *see* Chrysidoidea (*supra* 48)
Ampulicidae; *see* Sphecidae (62)	Braconidae, 13
Anaxyelidae, 8	Cephidae, 12
Andrenidae, 65	Cephoidea; *supra* 12
Anthophoridae, 69	Ceraphronidae, 45
Aphidiidae, 14	Ceraphronoidea; *supra* 45
Apidae, 70	Chalcedectidae; *see* Pteromalidae (19)
Apocrita; *supra* 13	Chalcididae, 21
Apoidea; *supra* 63	Chalcidoidea; *supra* 18
Argidae, 4	Charipidae, 33
Astatidae; *see* Sphecidae (62)	Chrysididae, 51

Table 25.2 (*Contd.*)

Chrysidoidea; *supra* 48	Orussidae, 11
Cimbicidae, 5	Oxaeidae, 64
Cleptidae; *see* Chrysididae (50)	Pamphiliidae, 2
Colletidae, 63	Pelecinidae, 38
Crabronidae; *see* Sphecidae (62)	Pelecinoidea; *supra* 38
Cynipidae, 34	Pemphredonidae; *see* Sphecidae, 62
Cynipoidea; *supra* 29	Pergidae, 3
Diapriidae, 42	Perilampidae; *see* Pteromalidae (19)
Dirpionidae, 6	Philanthidae; *see* Sphecidae (62)
Dryinidae, 51	Platygastridae, 44
Embolemidae, 52	Pompilidae, 60
Encyrtidae, 25	Pompiloidea; *supra* 60
Eucharitidae, 23	Proctotrupidae; *see* Serphidae (39)
Eucoilidae, 32	Proctotrupoidea; *supra* 39
Eulophidae, 26	Pteromalidae, 19
Eumenidae; *see* Vespidae (59)	Rhopalosomatidae, 61
Eupelmidae, 23	Roproniidae, 40
Eupelmidae, 24	Sapygidae, 57
Eurytomidae, 20	Scelionidae, 43
Eutrichosomalidae; *see* Pteromalidae (19)	Sclerogibbidae, 49
Evaniidae, 35	Scoliidae, 56
Evanioidea; *supra* 35	Scolioidea; *supra* 53
Figitidae, 31	Serphidae, 39
Formicidae, 58	Serphoidea, *supra*, 39
Formicoidea; *supra* 58	Sierolomorphidae, 54
Gasteruptiidae, 37	Siricoidea; *supra* 8
Halictidae, 66	Sphecidae, 62
Heloridae, 41	Sphcoidea, supra 62
Hybrizontidae, 15	Stephanidae, 17
Ibaliidae, 29	Symphyta; *supra* 1
Ichneumonidae, 16	Syntexidae; *see* Anaxyelidae (8)
Ichneumonoidea; *supra* 13	Tanaostigmatidae; *see* Eupelmidae (24)
Larridae; *see* Sphecidae (62)	Tenthredinidae, 7
Leucospidae, 22	Tenthredinoidea; *supra* 3
Liopteridae, 30	Thysanidae; *see* Encyrtidae (25)
Masaridae; *see* Vespidae (59)	Tiphiidae, 53
Megachilidae, 68	Torymidae, 18
Megalodontoidea; *supra* 1	Trichogrammatidae, 28
Megaspilidae, 46	Trigonalidae, 47
Mellinidae; *see* Sphecidae (62)	Trigonaloidea; *supra* 47
Melittidae, 67	Vanhorniidae; *see* Serphidae (39)
Mutillidae, 55	Vespidae, 59
Mymaridae, 27	Vespoidea; *supra* 59
Nyssonidae; *see* Sphecidae (62)	Xiphydriidae, 10
Ormyidae; *see* Pteromalidae (19)	Xyelidae, 1

Fig. 25.7.

Superfamily MEGALODONTOIDEA

Two families are assigned to this superfamily, as follows:

1. XYELIDAE (Xyelid Sawfly Family)

L. 5–10 mm. The third antennal segment is long, with slender, many-segmented terminal filament. (See Fig. 25.7.) Larvae feed chiefly on staminate pine cones, new pine shoots, and tree leaves. There are 29 species in the U.S. and Canada.

Subfamily Xyelinae
Tribe Xyelini

[1.1 *Xyela* Delman (17 spp.)]

Tribe Pleroneurini
1.2 *Pleroneura* Konow

Five species, including the following:

P. brunneicornis Rohwer (Balsam Shootboring Sawfly). Larvae live in the developing shoots of *Abies* spp.

Table 25.3 Features of the Superfamilies and Families of the Suborder Symphyta

Base of abdomen of all families broadly joined to thorax and not slender.

Group	Foretibial apical spurs	Prothorax	Antennae	Length, in. mm
Megalodontoidea				
1. Xyelidae	2	Posterior margin straight or nearly so	Many-segmented; apical segment very long	Under 10
2. Pamphiliidae	2	Posterior margin straight or nearly so.	13 or more segments	Under 15
Tenthredinoide				
3. Pergidae	2	U-spaced, posterior margin deeply curved.	6 segments	Under 10
4. Argidae	2	U-shaped, posterior margin deeply curved	3 segments, third segment very long	Under 15
5. Cimbicidae	2	U-shaped, posterior margin deeply curved	7 or fewer segments; clubbed	16–25
6. Diprionidae	2	U-shaped, posterior margin deeply curved	13 or more segments; female serrate; male pectinate	Under 12
7. Tenthredinidae	2	U-shaped, posterior margin deeply curved	7–10 segments	4.5–20+
Siricoidea				
8. Anaxyelidae	1	Trapezoidal	13 or more segments	7–8
9. Siricidae	1	Wider than long, narrowest in middle	13 or more segments	24–34+
10. Xiphydriidae	1	U-shaped, posterior margin deeply curved	13 or more segments	12–21
11. Orussidae	2	U-shaped, posterior margin deeply curved	Inserted under ridge below eyes, above base of mandibles	7.5–14
Cephoidea				
12. Cephidae	1	Longer than wide	20–30 segments; filiform or chavate	±8.5

Subfamily Macroxyelinae

Tribe Xyeleciini

[1.3 *Xyelecia* Ross (1 sp., *X. nearctica* Ross)]

Tribe Macroxyelini

[1.4 *Macroxyela* Kirby (3 spp.); 1.5 *Megaxyela* Ashmead (3 spp.)]

2. PAMPHILIIDAE
(Web-spinning and Leaf-rolling Sawfly Family)

Length: 8–15 mm. The adult is stout, dorsoventrally flattened; hind margin of pronotum nearly or actually straight; antennae slender, many-segmented. Larvae have seven-segmented antennae; only thoracic legs present. Some larvae are gregarious; some fasten leaves together with silk; some roll individual leaves; others feed openly. Although most of the 72 species are uncommon, a number are widely distributed and are occasionally of some economic importance.

Subfamily Cephalciinae

Tribe Cephalciini

[2.1 *Cephalcia* Panzer (10 spp.)]

2.2 *Acantholyda* Costa

This genus is divided into two subgenera—*Acantholyda* s. str. (8 spp.) and *Itycorsia* Konow (26 spp.)—including the following species:

A. (Acantholyda) erythrocephala (Linnaeus) (Pine False Web-worm). L. 8–15 mm. This is a robust, introduced species that infests pine. (1) n.e. NA.

Subfamily Pamphiliinae

These species are found on deciduous trees and shrubs.

Tribe Neurotomini

These sawflies are confined to members of the Rosaceae.

2.3 *Neurotoma* Konow

Four species, the following of which is a pest:

N. inconspicua (Norton) (Plum Web-spinning Sawfly). L. ±9 mm. Body dull black with mandibles and legs reddish brown. Larvae feed on plum and sand cherries. (1) n.e. US; (2) AR; (4) BC; (5) MT, SD, KS.

Tribe **Pamphiliini**

[2.4 *Pamphilius* Latreille (16 spp.)]

2.5 *Onycholyda* Takeuchi

Eight species, including the following:

O. amplectus (Fabricius) L. 8–10 mm. Wings smoky; head, legs, and abdomen mostly yellow, thorax black. Larve feed on *Rubus* spp. (1) IL, IN, OH, PA, NJ, MD, DE; (2) s.e. US; (3) TX.

Superfamily **TENTHREDINOIDEA**

Five families belong in this subfamily, as follows:

3. PERGIDAE (Pergid Sawfly Family)

Length: 7–10 mm. Antennae short, six-segmented. Larvae found on oak, walnut, chestnut, and hickory, but poorly known. Five species, mostly east of the Rocky Mountains, and (3) AZ.

Subfamily **Acordulecerinae**

[3.1 *Acordulecera* Say (4 spp.)]

Subfamily **Loboceratinae**

[3.2 *Skelosyzygonia* Malaise (1 sp., *S. spinipes* Malaise (3) ?TX)]

4. ARGIDAE (Argid Sawfly Family)

Length: 8–15 mm. Antennae with only three segments, the third very long (see Fig. 25.8), sometimes U-shaped or Y-shaped in the male. Larvae feed on leaves of trees and shrubs; one species feeds on poison ivy, another on sweet potatoes; one leaf miner on portulaca is known. Fifty-nine species occur in the U.S. and Canada, the majority in the southwestern U.S.

Subfamily **Arginae**

4.1 *Arge* Schrank

Ten species, the following of which is a pest:

A. pectoralis (Leach) (Birch Sawfly). A pest on birch.

Subfamily **Atomacerinae**

[4.2 *Atomacera* Say (3 spp.)]

Fig. 25.8.

Subfamily **Sterictiphorinae**

[4.3 *Sterictiphora* Billberg (6 spp.); 4.4 *Aprosthema* Konow (2 spp.); 4.5 *Neoptilia* Ashmead (2 spp.); 4.6 *Ptenus* Kirby (13 spp.); 4.7 *Schizocerella* Forsius (1 sp., *S. pilicornis* (Holmgren)); 4.8 *Sphacophilus* Provancher: 3 subgenera: *Sphacophilus* s. str. (2 spp.), *Litocolus* Smith (6 spp.), and *Ceocolus* Smith (14 spp.)]

5. CIMBICIDAE (Cimbicid Sawfly Family)

Length: 18–25 mm. Antennae club-shaped. The larvae feed on leaves. There are 12 species in the U.S. and Canada.

Subfamily **Abiinae**

5.1 *Zaraea* Leach

Four species, the following of which is common:

Z. inflata Norton (Honeysuckle Sawfly). (1) IL, IN, OH, PA, NJ, MA; (5) CO, NE.

Subfamily **Cimbicinae**

[5.2 *Trichiosoma* Leach (4 spp.)]

5.3 *Cimbex* Olivier

Four species, the following of which is a pest.

C. americana Leach (Elm Sawfly). L. 22–25 mm. This is the largest sawfly in the U.S., easily recognized by its club-shaped antennae. When disturbed, the larvae spurt fluid from glands above the spiracles. Adults fly from May through June. Larvae feed on elm, willow, poplar, maple, alder, and basswood. (1) n.e. NA; (4) Pacific n.w.; (5) n. Central States.

6. DIPRIONIDAE (Conifer Sawfly Family)

Length: 6–12 mm. Antennae serrate in female, pectinate in male. Larvae feed on conifers, and many cause economic loss throughout the U.S. and Canada. Forty-one species occur in the U.S. and Canada, all confined to coniferous forests.

Subfamily **Monocteninae**

[6.1 *Monoctenus* Dahlbom (3 spp.); 6.2 *Augomonoctenus* Rohwer (2 spp.)]

Subfamily **Diprioninae**

[6.3 *Zadiprion* Rohwer (2 spp.)]

6.4 *Neodiprion* Rohwer

Thirty-five species are assigned to this genus, most of them of economic importance, including the following pest:

N. excitans Rohwer (Blackheaded Pine Sawfly). L. 6–7 mm. Body dusky; wings clear. Larvae feed on pine, causing economic loss, particularly in the South, where they attack timber forests. (See Fig. 25.9.) (1) n.e. US; (2) s.e. US; (3) TX.

In addition to the effects of defoliation, these insects also weaken the trees and make them susceptible to viral diseases. The following species are similar to the preceding:

N. abietis (Harris) (Balsam Fir Sawfly).

N. burkei Middleton (Lodgepole Sawfly).

N. dubiosus Schedl (Brownheaded Jack Pine Sawfly).

Fig. 25.9. (*U.S. Dept. of Agric.*)

N. rugifrons Middleton (Redheaded Jack Pine Sawfly).

N. lecontei (Fitch) (Redheaded Pine Sawfly).

N. merkeli Ross (Slash Pine Sawfly).

N. nanulus nanulus Schedl (Red Pine Sawfly).

N. pinetum (Norton) (White Pine Sawfly).

N. pratti banksianae Rohwer (Jack Pine Sawfly).

N. pratti pratti (Dyar) (Virginia Pine Sawfly).

N. sertifer (Geoffroy) (European Pine Sawfly).

N. swainei Middleton (Swaine Jack Pine Sawfly).

N. taedae linearis Ross (Loblolly Pine Sawfly).

N. tsugae Middleton (Hemlock Sawfly).

6.5 *Diprion* Schrank

One species, as follows:

D. similis (Hartig) (Introduced Pine Sawfly).

[6.6 *Gilpinia* Benson (2 spp.)]

7. TENTHREDINIDAE (Common Sawfly Family)

Length: 5–20 mm. Usually black or brownish; some with red or yellow markings. Antennae slender, with seven to ten segments of varying length. Adults may be found around vegetation, some visiting flowers. Larvae resemble those of Lepidoptera, but they have more prolegs as well as the six thoracic legs. Most feed on leaves, but a few are leaf miners or stem borers. Some fold the edges of leaves; others are gall makers. The family is very large, with 731 species in the U.S. and Canada, many of them of economic importance

Subfamily Selandriinae
Tribe Strongylogastrini

[7.1 *Eriocampidea* Ashmead (1 sp., *E. arizonensis* Ashmead); 7.2 *Hemitaxonus* Ashmead (4 spp.); 7.3 *Strongylogaster* Dahlbom (11 spp.)]

Tribe Aneugmenini

[7.4 *Aneugmenus* Hartig (4 spp.); 7.5 *Birka* Malaise (1 sp., *B. nordica* Smith); 7.6 *Nesoselandria* Rohwer (1 sp., *N. morio* (Fabricius)); 7.7 *Eustromboceros* Rohwer (1 sp., *rufocaudatus* Smith); 7.8 *Stromboceridea* Rohwer (1 sp., *S. nigricans* (Norton))]

Tribe Selandriini

[7.9 *Brachythops* Haliday (2 spp.)]

Tribe Adelestini

[7.10 *Adelesta* Ross (1 sp., *A. nova* (Norton))]

Tribe Heptamelini

[7.11 *Heptamelus* Haliday (1 sp., *H. ochroleucus* (Stephens))]

Subfamily Dolerinae

[7.12 *Dolerus* Panzer (41 spp.); 7.13 *Loderus* Konow (4 spp.)]

Subfamily Susaninae

[7.14 *Susana* Rohwer and Middleton (7 spp.)]

Subfamily Nematinae
Tribe Cladiini

7.15 *Cladius* Illiger

One species, as follows:

C. difformis (Panzer) (Bristly Roseslug).

[7.16 *Priophorus* Dahlbom (4 spp.); 7.17 *Trichiocampus* Hartig (3 spp.)]

Tribe Nematini

7.18 *Hoplocampa* Hartig

Twenty-one species, the following of which are pests:

H. cookei (Clarke) (Cherry Fruit Sawfly).

H. testudinea (Klug) (European Apple Sawfly).

7.19 *Caulocampus* Rohwer

Two species, the following of which is a pest:

C. acericaulis (McGillivray) (Maple Petiole Borer).

7.20 *Hemichroa* Stephens

Two subgenera, *Hemichroa* s. str. (1 sp. *H. crocea* (Geoffroy) (Striped Alder Sawfly) and *Varna* Ross (2 spp.).

[7.21 *Craterocercus* Rohwer (5 spp.); 7.22 *Platycampus* Schiødte (6 spp.); 7.23 *Anoplonyx* Marlatt (4 spp.); 7.24 *Adelomos* Ross (1 sp., *A. cleone* Ross); 7.25 *Neopareophora* MacGillivray (2 spp.); 7.26 *Nematinus* Rohwer (4 spp.)]

7.27 *Pachynematus* Konow

Forty-four species, the following of which is a pest:

P. extensicornis (Norton) (Grass Sawfly). A pest of wheat and other grasses. (1) n.e. US; (5) n. Central States.

7.28 *Pikonema* Ross

Three species, two of which are pests:

P. alaskensis (Rohwer) (Yellowheaded Spruce Sawfly). A pest of many species of *Picea*. (1) n.e. NA; (4) Pacific n.w.; (5) n. Central States and Provinces.

P. dimmockii (Cresson) (Greenheaded Spruce Sawfly). Similar to the preceding; same hosts and distribution.

[7.29 *Eitelius* Kontuniemi (1 sp., *E. gregarius* (Marlatt)]

7.30 *Pristiphora* Latreille

Forty-five species, the following of which are pests:

P. *abbreviata* (Hartig) (California Pear Sawfly).

P. *erichsonii* (Hartig) (Larch Sawfly).

P. *geniculata* (Hartig) (Mountain Ash Sawfly).

7.31 *Croesus* Leach

Four species, the following of which is a pest:

C. *latitarsus* Norton (Dusky Birch Sawfly).

7.32 *Nematus* Panzer

Sixty species, the following of which are pests:

N. *ribesii* (Scopoli) (Imported Currantworm). L. ± 6 mm. Body orange to brownish, with black markings on body and legs. Larvae feed on *Ribes* spp. Cosmopolitan wherever host grows.

N. *ventralis* Say (Willow Sawfly). (1) n.e. US; (5) n. Central States.

7.33 *Pontania* Costa

Forty-two species, the following of which is a pest:

P. *proxima* (Lepeletier) (Willow Redgall Sawfly). Probably introduced. (1) ON, NY, ME.

7.34 *Phyllocolpa* Bensen

Twenty-six species, the following of which is a pest:

P. *bozemani* (Cooley) (Poplar Leaffolding Sawfly).

[7.35 *Euura* Newman: 2 subgenera: *Euura* s. str. (29 spp.) and *Gemmura* Smith (3 spp.); 7.36 *Amauronematus* Konow (50 spp.); 7.37 *Decanematus* Malaise (1 sp., *D. dulichus* Wong)]

Tribe Pseudodineurini

[7.38 *Pseudodineura* Konow (4 spp); 7.39 *Kerita* Ross (3 sp.)]

Tribe Pristolini

[7.40 *Pristola* Ross (2 spp.); 7.41 *Melastola* Wong (2 spp.); Unplaced species of Nematinae (29 spp.)]

Subfamily Heterarthrinae
Tribe Caliroini

7.42 *Endelomyia* Ashmead

One species, as follows:

E. *aethiops* (Fabricius) (Roseslug).

7.43 *Caliroa* Costa

Fifteen species, the following of which are pests:

C. *cerasi* (Linnaeus) (Pear Sawfly).

C. *quercuscoccineae* (Dyar) (Scarlet Oak Sawfly).

Tribe Heterarthrini

[7.44 *Heterarthrus* Stephens (1 sp., *H. nemoratus* (Fallén))]

Tribe Fenusini

[7.45 *Metallus* Forbes (3 spp.); 7.46 *Messa* Leach (5 spp.); 7.47 *Setabara* Ross (1 sp., *S. histrionica* (MacGillivray)); 7.48 *Bidigitus* Smith (1 sp.,

Fig. 25.10. (*Conn. Agric. Exp. Sta.*)

B. *platani* (Burks)); 7.49 *Profenusa* MacGillivray (5 spp.); 7.50 *Nefusa* Ross (1 sp., *N. ambigua* (Norton)); 7.51 *Prolatus* Smith (1 sp., *P. artus* Smith)]

7.52 *Fenusa* Leach

Three species, as follows:

F. *dohrnii* (Tischbein) (European Alder Leafminer).

F. *pusilla* (Lepeletier) (Birch Leafminer). (See Fig. 25.10.)

F. *ulmi* Sundevall (Elm Leafminer).

[7.53 *Fenella* Westwood (1 sp., *F. nigrita* Westwood)]

Subfamily Blennocampinae
Tribe Lycaotini

[7.54 *Blennogeneris* MacGillivray (3 spp.); 7.55 *Lycaota* Konow (3 spp.)]

Tribe Tomostethini

7.56 *Tomostethus* Konow

One species, as follows:

T. *multicinctus* (Rohwer) (Brownheaded Ash Sawfly).

7.57 *Tethida* Ross

One species, as follows:

T. *barda* (Say) (Blackheaded Ash Sawfly).

Tribe Phymatocerini

[7.58 *Phymatocera* Dahlbom (7 spp.); 7.59 *Paracharactus* MacGillivray (3 spp.); 7.60 *Rhadinoceraea* Konow: 2 subgenera: *Rhadinoceraea* s. str. (4 spp.) and *Veratra* Smith (4 spp.); 7.61 *Lagonis* Ross (1 sp., *L. nevadensis* (Cresson)); 7.62 *Monophadnus* Hartig (7 spp.); 7.63 *Stethomostus* Benson (1 sp., *S. fuliginosus* (Schrank)); 7.64 *Eutomostethus* Enslin (2 spp.)]

Tribe Blennocampini

[7.65 *Ardis* Konow (2 spp.); 7.66 *Monardis* Enslin (1 sp., *M. pulla* Smith); 7.67 *Apareophora* Sato (2 spp.); 7.68 *Eupareophora* Enslin (1 sp., *E. parca* (Cresson)); 7.69 *Periclista* Konow: 2 subgenera: *Periclista* s. str. (15 spp.) and *Neocharactus* MacGillivray (4 spp.)]

7.70 *Monophadnoides* Ashmead

Seventeen species, the following of which is a pest:

M. *geniculatus* (Hartig) (Raspberry Sawfly).

Tribe Ceratulini

[7.71 *Ceratulus* MacGillivray (1 sp., *C. spectabilis* MacGillivray)]

Tribe **Waldheimiini**

[7.72 *Waldheimia* Brullé (1 sp., *W. bedeae* Smith)]

7.73 *Erythraspides* Ashmead

Two species, the following of which is a pest:

E. vitis (Harris) (Grape Sawfly).

[7.74 *Halidamia* Benson (1 sp., *H. affinis* (Fallén)]

Subfamily **Allantinae**

Tribe **Eriocampini**

[7.75 *Pseudosiobla* Ashmead (2 spp.); 7.76 *Eriocampa* Hartig (2 spp.); 7.77 *Dimorphopteryx* Ashmead (5 spp.)]

Tribe **Empriini**

[7.78 *Empria* Lepeletier (11 spp.); 7.79 *Phrontosoma* MacGillivray (3 sp.); 7.80 *Monosoma* MacGillivray (1 sp., *M. inferentia* (Norton)); 7.81 *Monostegia* Costa (1 sp., *M. abdominalis* (Fabricius)); 7.82 *Somanica* Smith (1 sp., *S. occua* Smith); 7.83 *Haymatus* Smith (1 sp., *H. blassus* Smith)]

7.84 *Ametastegia* Costa

Fifteen species, the following of which are pests.

A. glabrata (Fallén) (Dock Sawfly). Larvae will bore into apples and other fruits if dock is nearby.

A. pallipes (Spinola) (Violet Sawfly).

[7.85 *Aphilodyctium* Ashmead (1 sp., *A. fidum* (Cresson))]

Tribe **Allantini**

7.86 *Allantus* Panzer

Eight species, the following of which is a pest:

A. cinctus (Linnaeus) (Curled Rose Sawfly).

[7.87 *Macremphytus* MacGillivray (4 spp.); 7.88 *Taxonus* Hartig (9 spp.)]

Subfamily **Tenthredininae**

Tribe **Perineurini**

[7.89 *Leucopelmonus* MacGillivray (1 sp., *L. annulicornis* (Harrington)]

Tribe **Sciapterygini**

[7.90 *Zaschizonyx* Ashmead (2 spp.)]

Tribe **Tenthredopsini**

[7.91 *Aglaostigma* Kirby (7 spp.)]

Tribe **Tenthredinini**

[7.92 *Lagium* Konow (2 spp.); 7.93 *Rhogogaster* Konow (4 spp.); 7.94 *Ischyroceraea* Kiaer (1 sp., *I. arctica* (Thomson)]

7.95 *Tenthredo* Linnaeus

There are 118 species, the following of which is an example:

T. basilaris Say. L. 11–12 mm. Body black with small, yellow markings. Adults fly from May to July. (See A&J 266.) (1) n.e. US; (5) n. Central States.

Tribe **Macrophyini**

7.96 *Macrophya* Dahlbom

Forty-six species in two subgenera—*Macrophya* s. str. (45 spp.) and *Pseudomacrophya* Enslin (1 sp., *M. punctumalbum* (Linnaeus)—including the following:

M. trisyllaba (Norton). L. 10–11 mm. Black, marked with white at antennal apex, clypeus, labrum, mandibles at base, anterior portion of thorax, scutellum, front legs beyond basal third, tarsal segments at base, middle femora at apex, middle tibiae in part, middle tarsal segments, hind femora beneath, and apical margins of abdominal segment. Larvae infest elderberry. (1) n.e. NA; (2) VA, NC, SC, GA; (4) Pacific n.w.; (5) n. Central States.

[7.97 *Deda* Gibson (3 spp.); 7.98 *Pachyprotasis* Hartig (1 sp., *P. rapae* (Linnaeus); unplaced taxa of Tenthredinidae (2 spp.)]

Superfamily SIRICOIDEA (Horntails and Wood Wasps)

Four small families of mostly uncommon species belong here. They are wood borers in the larval stage instead of leaf feeders, although there are species of one family, the rare Orussidae, that are reported to parasitize Buprestid Beetles.

8. ANAXYELIDAE (Anaxyelid Wood Wasp Family)

Subfamily **Syntexinae**

One species, as follows:

8.1 *Syntexis* Rohwer

S. libocedri Rohwer (Incense Cedar Wasp). Bores into *Libocedrus* sp. (3) CA; (4) OR.

9. SIRICIDAE (Horntail Wasp Family)

Length: 20–35 mm. Adults have a triangular or spearlike point at the apex of the abdomen. They are called Horntails because the last dorsal abdominal segment of the female bears a more or less hornlike prolongation. The larvae are wood borers. Pupation takes place in the burrows. At times they may emerge in homes from wood stored by a fireplace; they have also been known to emerge from wooden furniture. There are nineteen species in the U.S. and Canada.

Subfamily **Siricinae**

9.1 *Sirex* Linnaeus

Nine species, the following of which is common:

S. cyaneus Fabricius (Blue Horntail). Hind tibiae with two apical spurs. These insects are found in wood and wood products and are spread by commerce. (1), (2), (3), (4), (5), generally distributed.

9.2 *Urocerus* Geoffroy

Five species, the following of which is common:

U. californicus Norton (California Horntail). L. 32–36 mm. Black; antennae yellow; legs with yellow bands; patches of yellow on side of head; wings amber; ovipositor slightly longer than abdominal horn. Larvae infest fir and sometimes pine.

Fig. 25.11. (*After Comstock*)

(See A&J 265.) (3) n. CA, n. NV; (4) Pacific n.w.; (5) MT, WY, CO.

[9.3 *Xeris* Costa (3 spp.)]

Subfamily Tremicinae

9.4 *Tremex* Jurine

One species, as follows:

T. columba (Linnaeus) (Pigeon Tremex). L. 25–35 mm. Brown or reddish brown, sometimes with black abdomen with yellow spots or bands, and wings uniformly smoky. Hind tibiae with one apical spur. Thorax and abdomen bare. Larvae bore into trunks of diseased trees, particularly maple, elm, and oak. (See Fig. 25.11.) (1), (2), (3), (4), (5), generally distributed.

9.5 *Eriotremex* Benson

One species, as follows:

E. formosanus (Matsumura) (Asian Horntail). L. ±30 mm. Black, slightly violet tinge; pronotum and abdomen with yellow or amber markings. Hind tibiae with one apical spur. Thorax and abdomen with yellowish hair. Larvae found in oak. (2) AL, GA, FL [accidently introduced].

10. XIPHYDRIIDAE (Wood Wasp Family)

Similar to the horntails but without hard point at abdominal apex. Larvae bore into wood of dead or dying angiosperm trees. There are nine species, as follows:

Subfamily Xiphydriinae

[10.1 *Xiphydria* Latreille (9 spp.)]

11. ORUSSIDAE (Parasitic Wood Wasp Family)

Length: 8–14.5 mm. Antennae inserted under ridge below eyes, above base of mandible. Larvae probably parasitize wood-boring buprestid beetles. These wasps, in many respects, are intermediate between the Symphyta and the Apocrita. The reduced wing venation is characteristic of small, parasitic wasps. There are five known species, as follows:

Subfamily Orussinae

11.1 *Orussus* Latreille

Four species, including the following:

O. sayii (Westwood). May be collected in forests. (1) n.e. US.

Subfamily Ophrynopinae

[11.2 *Ophrynopus* Konow (1 sp., *O. nigricans* (Cameron) (3) TX); 11.3 *Kulcania* Benson (1 sp., unidentified, (2) FL?)]

Superfamily CEPHOIDEA

One family, as follows:

12. CEPHIDAE (Stem Sawfly Family)

Length: 9–18 mm. Black; pronotum at most weakly indented behind and its front surface not vertical; abdomen rather compressed. Larvae bore in plant tissue, particularly grasses, grains, roses, willow, raspberries, currents, and similar plants. The twelve species are classified as follows:

Subfamily Cephinae

Tribe Hartigiini

[12.1 *Caenocephus* Konow (1 sp., *C. aldrichi* Bradley)]

12.2 *Hartigia* Schiφdte

Three species, the following of which is a pest:

H. trimaculata (Say). L. 15–18 mm. Body shining black, sometimes with yellow spots on head and a yellow spot on each side of fourth abdominal tergite; light markings on legs. Larvae bore in stems of blackberry and roses. An important economic pest.

12.3 *Janus* Stephens

Four species, the following of which are pests:

J. abbreviatus (Say) (Willow Shoot Sawfly).

J. integer (Norton) (Currant Stem Girdler).

Tribe Cephini

12.4 *Cephus* Latreille

Two species, both of them pests:

C. pygmaeus (Linnaeus) (European Wheat Stem Sawfly).

C. cinctus Norton (Wheat Stem Sawfly). L. 9–11 mm. black with yellow banding on abdomen. Larvae feed on stems of wheat, boring into and eventually killing stem and plant. Because they eventually bore into the stem base, they are missed by the combine during harvest. Mature larvae spend winter in stubble left behind unless field is plowed in fall. (See Fig. 25.12 and A&J 267.) (1) n.e. US; (4) Pacific n.w.; (5) n. Central States.

[12.5 *Calameuta* Konow (1 sp., *C. clavata* (Norton)]

Fig. 25.12. (*U.S. Dept. of Agric.*)

12.6 *Trachelus* Jurine

One species, as follows:

T. tabidus (Fabricius) (Black Grain Stem Sawfly). Infests only cultivated grains such as wheat, barley, rye, and oats. (1) MI, OH, NY, NJ, PA, MD, DE; (2) WV, VA.

Suborder APOCRITA

The abdomen of wasps, ants, and bees is constricted at the base, and therefore the main part of the abdomen is separated from the thorax. The first abdominal segment, however, is firmly fused to the thorax. The term *alitrunk* is applied to this combination of thorax and abdomen. The remaining segments of the abdomen are distinct, the term *gaster* being applied to them.

Most of the species are parasitic in the larval stage, but many are predacious and others are social, living on and feeding upon a great variety of foods, as described in the following discussion of the families. Great numbers of species of parasitic wasps are extremely small, and many of these are seldom seen.

The families of two of the superfamilies—the Chalcidoidea and Cynipoidea—are not included in the main Key to the Families, but each of these 17 families is keyed and briefly mentioned in the text. Many of these are of economic interest as gall makers, seed infestors, and stem borers.

The species that are most often seen and attract considerable attention are the solitary and social wasps and the bees. Many of these make nests, and many of them sting. The larvae of the nesting species feed on food provided by the parent, either as stung prey or as honey or pollen.

The suborder is divided into two infraorders—Parasitica and Aculeata—15 superfamilies, and 69 families. Table 25.4 shows some of the features of the superfamilies of each infraorder.

Infraorder PARASITICA

No consistent features distinguish this group from the aculeate families; its separate classification is used more as a matter of convenience and tradition. Many of the species assigned to the superfamilies of this infraorder are endo- or exoparasitic on

Table 25.4 Features of the Superfamilies and Families of the Suborder Apocrita

Base of abdomen of all families constricted into a narrow pedicel.				
Superfamilies	**Antennal segments**	**Hind trochanters**	**Pronotum**	**Front wings**
PARASITICA				
Ichneumonoidea	16 or more	2	Laterally triangular*	Usually 6 or more closed cells
Chalcidoidea	5–13	2	Laterally quadrate	No closed cells
Cynipoidea	13–16	Usually 1	Laterally triangular*	Several closed cells
Evanioidea	13–14	2	As above	Usually 6 or more closed cells
Pelecinoidea	14	1	As above	5 or fewer closed cells
Proctotrupoidea, Ceraphronoidea, and Trigonaloidea	7–15	1 or 2	As above	Various; may be reduced
ACULEATA				
Bethyloidea	10 or more	Usually 1	Laterally quadrate	Various; may be reduced
Scolioidea	12–13	Usually 1	As above†	Usually 6 or more closed cells
Formicoidea	12–13	1	As above	As above
Vespoidea	12–13	1	Laterally quadrate*	As above
Pompiloidea	12–13	1	As above	As above
Sphecoidea	12–13	1	Distinct lobe laterally‡	As above
Apoidea	12–13	1	As above	As above

*See Fig. 27.11.
†Hind coxae separate or approximate to middle coxae.
‡See Fig. 27.12.

other insects, and a few make galls or feed on seeds. None are nest builders. The parasitism exhibited by these species is somewhat different than that of the parasitic worms. These parasites always kill their victim. Their life and development, usually inside the larva or pupa of the host, is atuned to the host's growth and development. Food selection inside the host is programmed to consume the least vital organs first. It is not until the parasite has become fully developed, or nearly so, that the vital organs of the host are consumed. At this time the host has become fully developed itself, and perhaps even pupated. Once the parasite finishes eating the vital organs, it too pupates and finally leaves the host as an adult. Most females are incapable of stinging humans because of their small size. Many do, however, sting their host, and most will try to sting if given the opportunity. Larger species are capable of inflicting a painful sting and must be handled with caution. The ovipositor of all females is used for egg laying and remains unmodified for stinging.

The term "parasitoid" should be applied to the type of parasitism found in these insects because a true parasite does not usually kill its host. Some entomologists, however, decline to use the term as a means of distinguishing this phenomenon from that of other parasites. The phenomenon may be far more complicated in some species than the one just described. Sometimes more than one parasite may infest the host, or the parasite may even multiply in the embryonic stage, one egg originally inserted in the host producing many adults. Furthermore, some species are parasitic on their fellow parasites, that is, the original parasite may itself have parasites, and eventually a third species emerges instead of the original one. This is termed *hyperparasitism.*

The classification of these groups is difficult. Most of the species are so small that identification is possible only after careful study by specialists. The following discussion of the various families is intended more for the biological information than as an aid to specific or even family identification.

Superfamily ICHNEUMONOIDEA

The five families of this group can be distinguished by using the Key to the Families.

13. BRACONIDAE (Braconid Family)

Length: Usually 2–4 mm (some to 15 mm). Distinguished from other members of this superfamily by the absence of a long, slender, compressed abdomen. Similar to the Ichneumonidae, but with different details of wing venation (see Key). Most species are internal primary parasites, infesting many species of Lepidoptera caterpillars. (See Fig. 25.13 for adults emerging from cocoons on parasitized caterpillar.) Of the 1,937 species in the U.S. and Canada, very few are easy to recognize without the aid of technical literature.

Subfamily Doryctinae

[13.1 *Acrophasmus* Enderlein (7 spp.); 13.2 *Aivalykus* Nixon (1 sp., *A. nearcticus* Marsh); 13.3 *Allorhogas* Gahan (4 spp.); 13.4 *Aptenobracon* Marsh (1 sp., *A. formicoides* Marsh); 13.5 *Callihormius* Ashmead (4 spp.); 13.6 *Curtisella* Spinola (1 sp., *C. lignicola* (Muesebeck)); 13.7 *Dendrosoter* Wesmael (6 spp.); 13.8 *Doryctes* Haliday (15 spp.); 13.9 *Doryctinus* Roman (2 spp.); 13.10 *Ecphylus* Foerster (22 spp.); 13.11 *Glyptocolastes* Ashmead (2 spp.); 13.12 *Hecabolus* Curtis (1 sp., *H.*

Fig. 25.13. (*Courtesy Robert Gossington and* Insect World Digest)

sulcatus Curtis); 13.13 *Heterospilus* Haliday (31 spp.); 13.14 *Histeromerus* Wesmael (1 sp., *H. canadensis* Ashmead); 13.15 *Leluthia* Cameron (3 spp.); 13.15 *Liobracon* Szepligeti (1 sp., *L. aquilonius* Marsh); 13.17 *Monolexis* Foerster (1 sp., *M. fuscicornis* Foerster); 13.18 *Odontobracon* Cameron (6 spp.); 13.19 *Ontsira* Cameron (8 spp.); 13.20 *Pambolidea* Ashmead (2 spp.); 13.21 *Pedinotus* Szépligeti (1 sp., *P. ferrugineus* (Enderlein); 13.22 *Pioscelus* Muesebeck and Walkley (2 spp.); 13.23 *Ptesimogaster* Marsh (2 spp.); 13.24 *Rhaconotus* Ruthe (9 spp.); 13.25 *Rhoptrocentrus* Marshall (1 sp., *R. piceus* Marshall); 13.26 *Spathius* Nees (23 spp.); 13.27 *Stenocorse* Marsh (1 sp., *S. bruchivora* (Crawford))]

Subfamily Braconinae

[13.28 *Atanycolimorpha* Viereck (5 spp.); 13.29 *Atanycolus* Foerster (36 spp.); 13.30 *Bracon* Fabricius (94 spp.); 13.31 *Coeloides* Wesmael (9 spp.); 13.32 *Compsobracon* Ashmead (1 sp., *C. magnificus* (Ashmead)); 13.33 *Cyanopterus* Haliday (1 sp., *C. laevis* (Provancher)); 13.34 *Iphiaulax* Foerster (21 spp.); 13.35 *Vipio* Latreille (9 spp.)]

Subfamily Exothecinae
Tribe Exothecini

[13.36 *Acrisis* Foerster (2 spp.); 13.37 *Allobracon* Gahan (1 undescribed sp.); 13.38 *Colastes* Haliday (3 spp.); 13.39 *Gnaptodon* Haliday (7 spp.); 13.40 *Oncophanes* Foerster (5 spp.); 13.41 *Phanomeris* Foerster (5 spp.); 13.42 *Pseudognaptodon* Fischer (2 spp.); 13.43 *Rhysipolis* Foerster (1 sp., *R. pallipes* (Provancher)); 13.44 *Xenarcha* Foerster (1 sp., *X. hopkinsi* (Ashmead)); 13.45 *Xenosternum* Muesebeck (1 sp., *X. ornigis* Muesebeck)]

Tribe Hormiini

[13.46 *Cantharoctonus* Viereck (2 spp.); 13.47 *Hormius* (8 spp.); 13.48 *Monitoriella* Hedqvist (1 sp., *M. elongata* Hedqvist); 13.49 *Pymatogelasma* Arnett, new name for *Noserus* Foerster not LeConte (homonym) (1 sp., *P. pomifoliellae* (Ashmead)); 13.50 *Parahormius* Nixon (4 spp.)]

Tribe Pambolini

[13.51 *Chremylus* Haliday (1 sp., *C. elaphus* Haliday); 13.52 *Pambolus* Haliday (1 sp., *P. americanus* (Ashmead)]

Subfamily Rogadinae

[13.53 *Aleiodes* Wesmael (3 spp.); 13.54 *Bucculatriplex* Viereck (1 sp., *B. bucculatricis* (Ashmead); 13.55 *Clinocentrus* Haliday (3 spp.); 13.56 *Pelecystoma* Wesmael (2 spp.); 13.57 *Petalodes* Wesmael (2 spp.); 13.58 *Polystenidea* Viereck (2 spp.); 13.59 *Rogas* Nees (38 spp.); 13.60

Tetrasphaeropyx Ashmead (1 sp., *T. pilosis* (Cresson); 13.61 *Yelicones* Cameron (1 sp., *Y. delicatus* (Cresson))]

Subfamily Meteorideinae

[13.62 *Meteoridea* Ashmead (2 spp.)]

Subfamily Helconinae

Tribe Helconini

[13.63 *Eumacrocentrus* Ashmead (1 sp., *E. americanus* (Cresson); 13.64 *Helcon* Nees (4 spp.); 13.65 *Wroughtonia* Cameron (8 spp.)]

Tribe Cenocoeliini

[13.66 *Cenocoelius* Westwood (8 spp.)]

Tribe Diospilini

[13.67 *Baeacis* Foerster (1 undescribed sp.); 13.68 *Diospilus* Haliday (5 spp.); 13.69 *Dyscoletes* Westwood (1 sp., *D. canadensis* Mason); 13.70 *Taphaeus* Wesmael (1 sp., *T. polydrusi* (Gahan))]

Subfamily Zeleinae

[13.71 *Zele* Curtis (2 spp.); 13.72 *Zemiotes* Foerster (7 spp.)]

Subfamily Macrocentrinae

[13.73 *Macrocentrus* Curtis (41 spp.)]

Subfamily Agathidinae

[13.74 *Aenigmostomus* Ashmead (1 sp., *A. longipalpus* (Cresson)); 13.75 *Agathirsia* Westwood (3 spp.)]

13.76 *Agathis* Latreille

Fifty-eight species, including the following:

A. texana (Cresson). L. ±8 mm. Black; abdomen and hind legs orange. (1) n.e. US; (2) s.e. US; (3) TX; (5) KS.

[13.77 *Crassomicrodes* Ashmead (8 spp.); 13.78 *Cremnops* Foerster (14 spp.); 13.79 *Earinus* Wesmael (2 spp.); 13.81 *Megagathis* Kriechbaumer (1 sp., *M. cressoni* (Cameron)); 13.81 *Zelomorpha* Ashmead (2 spp.)]

Subfamily Opiinae

Tribe Ademonini

[13.82 *Ademon* Haliday (3 spp.); 13.83 *Euopius* (4 spp.)]

Tribe Desmiostomatini

[13.84 *Desmiostoma* Foerster (2 spp.); 13.85 *Doryctobracon* Enderlein (2 spp.)]

Tribe Opiini, Subtribe Biosterina

13.86 *Biosteres* Foerster

Twenty-two species, including the following:

B. longicaudatus Ashmead (Longtailed Fruit Fly Parasite).

[13.87 *Diachasma* Foerster (5 spp.)]

Subtribe Opiina

[13.88 *Eurytenes* Foerster (1 sp., *E. abnormis* (Wesmael)); 13.89 *Opius* (113 spp.)]

Subfamily Alysiinae

Tribe Dacnusini

[13.90 *Chaenusa* Haliday (2 spp.); 13.91 *Chorebus* Haliday (16 spp.); 13.92 *Coelinidea* Viereck (5 spp.); 13.93 *Dacnusa* Haliday (4 spp.);

13.94 *Exotela* Foerster (1 undescribed sp.); 13.95 *Symphya* Foerster (6 spp.)]

Tribe Alysiini

[13.96 *Alysia* Latreille (9 spp.); 13.97 *Aphaereta* Foerster (11 spp.); 13.98 *Asobara* Foerster (2 spp.); 13.99 *Aspilota* Foerster (52 spp.); 13.100 *Dapsilarthra* Foerster (3 spp.); 13.101 *Dinostigma* Fischer (1 sp., *D. muesebecki* Fischer); 13.102 *Glyphogaster* Muesebeck and Walkley (1 sp., *G. tachinae* (Ashmead)); 13.103 *Hoplitalysia* Ashmead (1 sp., *H. slossonae* Ashmead); 13.104 *Idiasta* Foerster (3 spp.); 13.105 *Oenonogastra* Ashmead (1 sp., *O. microrhopalae* (Ashmead)); 13.106 *Orthostigma* Ratzeburg (8 spp.); 13.107 *Pentapleura* Foerster (3 spp.); 13.108 *Phaenocarpa* Foerster (76 spp.); 13.109 *Pneumosema* Fischer (1 sp., *P. stigmaticum* Fischer); 13.110 *Synaldis* Foerster (22 spp.)]

Subfamily Sigalphinae

[13.111 *Sigalphus* Latreille (1 sp., *S. bicolor* (Cresson)]

Subfamily Cheloninae

[13.112 *Ascogaster* Wesmael (8 spp.); 13.113 *Chelonus* Panzer: 2 subgenera: *Chelonus* s. str. (28 spp.) and *Microchelonus* Szepligeti (111 spp.); 13.114 *Phanerotoma* Wesmael (14 spp.)]

Subfamily Adeliinae

[13.115 *Adelius* Haliday (3 spp.)]

Subfamily Microgastrinae

Tribe Microgastrini

13.116 *Apanteles* Foerster

L. 2–4 mm. The larvae are internal parasites of Lepidoptera. Many are of importance in the biological control of lepidopterous pests. (See A&J 269 lower.) The 197 species in this genus include the following:

A. melanoscelus (Ratzeberg). (See Fig. 25.14.)

[13.117 *Dirrhope* Foerster (1 sp., *D. americana* Muesebeck); 13.118 *Hypomicrogaster* Ashmead (4 spp.); 13.119 *Microgaster* Latreille (19 spp.); 13.120 *Microplitis* Foerster (33 spp.); 13.121 *Mirax* Haliday (7 spp.); 13.122 *Protomicroplitis* Ashmead (8 spp.)]

Tribe Cardiochilini

[13.123 *Cardiochiles* Nees (32 spp.)]

Subfamily Ichneutinae

Tribe Ichneutini

[13.124 *Ichneutes* Nees (7 spp.); 13.125 *Ichneutidea* Ashmead (2 spp.); 13.126 *Proterops* Wesmael (1 sp., *P. californicus* Cresson)]

Fig. 25.14. (*From Crossman*)

Tribe Muesebeckiini

[13.127 *Muesebeckia* Mason (1 sp., *M. eximia* Mason); 13.128 *Oligoneurus* Szepligeti (1 undescribed sp.); 13.129 *Paroligoneurus* Muesebeck (1 sp., *P. johnsoni* Muesebeck)]

Subfamily Blacinae

Tribe Blacini

[13.130 *Blacus* Nees: 6 subgenera: *Blacus* s. str. (13 spp.), Ganychorus Haliday (4 spp.), *Hysterobolus* Viereck (3 spp.), *Leioblacus* van Achterberg (1 sp., *B. compressiventris* van Achterberg), *Neoblacus* Ashmead (1 sp., *B. koenigi* Fischer), and *Tarpheion* van Achterberg); 13.131 *Centistes* Haliday (4 spp.); 13.132 *Pygostolus* Haliday (1 sp., *P. falcatus* (Nees)); 13.133 *Syrrhizus* Foerster (2 spp.)]

Tribe Brachistini

[13.134 *Aliolus* Say (15 spp.); 13.135 *Allodorus* Foerster (4 spp.); 13.136 *Eubazus* Nees: 2 subgenera: *Eubazus* s. str. (3 spp.) and *Brachistes* Wesmael (5 spp.); 13.137 *Nealiolus* Mason (7 spp.); 13.138 *Schizoprymnus* Foerster (4 spp.); 13.139 *Triaspis* Haliday (19 spp.); 13.140 *Urosigalphus* Ashmead: 5 subgenera: *Bruchiurosigalphus* Gibson (5 spp.), *Microurosigalphus* Gibson (5 spp.), *Neourosigalphus* Gibson (6 spp.), *Paraurosigalphus* Gibson (4 spp.), and *Urosigalphus* s. str. (16 spp.)]

Tribe Orgilini

[13.141 *Charmon* Haliday (2 spp.); 13.142 *Microtypus* Ratzeburg (1 sp., *M. dioryctriae* Rohwer); 13.143 *Orgilus* Haliday (107 spp.); 13.144 *Stantonia* Ashmead (1 sp., *S. carocapsae* Muesebeck)]

Subfamily Neoneurinae

[13.145 *Elasmosoma* Ruthe (5 spp.); 13.146 *Neoneurus* Haliday (1 undescribed sp.)]

Subfamily Euphorinae

Tribe Meteorini

[13.147 *Meteorus* Haliday (39 spp.)]

Tribe Euphorini

[13.148 *Aridelus* Marshall (3 spp.); 13.149 *Chrysopophthorus* Goidanich (1 sp., *C. americanus* Mason); 13.150 *Cryptoxilos* Viereck (1 sp., *C. convergens* Muesebeck); 13.151 *Euphoriella* Ashmead (10 spp.); 13.152 *Holdawayella* Loan (2 spp.); 13.153 *Leiophron* Nees (19 spp.); 13.154 *Microctonus* Wesmael (25 spp.); 13.155 *Myiocephalus* Marshall (1 sp., *M. boops* (Wesmael)); 13.156 *Perilitus* Nees (2 spp.); 13.157 *Peristenus* Foerster (25 spp.); 13.158 *Ropalophorus* Curtis (1 sp., *R. wisconsinensis* Shenefelt); 13.159 *Streblocera* Westwood (1 sp., *S. pulvillicornis* Walley and MacKay); 13.160 *Syntretus* Foerster (3 spp.); 13.161 *Wesmaelia* Foerster (1 sp., *W. pendula* Foerster)]

Tribe Cosmophorini

[13.162 *Cosmophorus* Ratzeburg (5 spp.)]

14. APHIDIIDAE (Aphid Parasite Family)

Length: ±2.5 mm. Almost any group of aphids on a leaf will show some dead ones with a hole in their abdomen where the parasite, a member of this family, emerged. Before pupating, the aphid parasite makes a hole in the underside of the host and briefly emerges from it to fasten the skin of the aphid to the leaf. There are 114 species in this family in the U.S. and Canada.

Fig. 25.15. (*Courtesy of* Insect World Digest)

Subfamily Ephedrinae

14.1 *Ephedrus* Haliday

Seven species, including the following:

E. incompletus (Provancher). L. ±2.5 mm. Black, with legs and abdomen somewhat yellowish. (1) n.e. US; (2) s.e. US; (5) KS, MO.

E. plagiator (Nees). Introduced. (See Fig. 25.15.) (1) IL?; (3) CA.

[14.2 *Toxares* Haliday (1 sp., *T. deltiger* (Haliday))]

Subfamily Prainae

[14.3 *Praon* Haliday (17 spp.)]

Subfamily Aphidiinae

Tribe Aphidiini, *Subtribe* Lysiphlebina

[14.4 *Lysiphlebus* Foerster: 2 subgenera: *Adialytus* Foerster (3 spp.) and *Phlebus* Stary (7 spp., including *L. testaceipes* (Cresson) (Fig. 25.16)]

Subtribe Protaphidiina

[14.5 *Chaetopauesia* Mackauer (2 spp.); 14.6 *Pauesia* Quilis (13 spp.); 14.7 *Xenostigmus* Smith (1 sp., *X. bifasciatus* (Ashmead))]

Subtribe Aphidiina

[14.8 *Euphidius* Mackauer (2 spp.); 14.9 *Aphidius* Nees (29 spp.); 14.10 *Lysaphidus* Smith (4 spp.); 14.11 *Diaeretiella* Stary (1 sp., *D. rapae* (M'Intosh)]

Tribe Trioxini, *Subtribe* Monoctonina

[14.12 *Monoctonus* Haliday: 2 subgenera: *Monoctonus* s. str. (3 spp.) and *Harkeria* Haliday (1 sp., *M. rufus* (Cameron))]

Fig. 25.16. (*From Crossman*)

Subtribe Trioxina

[14.13 *Boreogalba* Machauer (1 sp., *B. gladifer* Machauer); 14.14 *Trioxys* Haliday: 2 subgenera: *Betuloxys* Machauer (1 sp., *T. compressicornis* Ruthe) and *Trioxys* s. str. (10 spp.); 14.15 *Binodoxys* Machauer (8 spp.); 14.16 *Acanthocaudus* Smith (3 spp.)]

15. HYBRIZONTIDAE (Hybrizontid Parasite Family)

Very little is known about the species that comprise this family. They have been found around ants and may parasitize them, or they may be aphid parasites. Two species occur in the U.S. and Canada.

[15.1 *Hydrizon* Fallen (2 spp., *H. flavocinctus* (Ashmead), (2) VA, and *H. rileyi* (Ashmead), (1) MI, IN; (2) VA; (5) IA)]

16. ICHNEUMONIDAE (Ichneumon Family)

L. 3–40 mm. Antennae at least half as long as body. Ovipositors of most females protrude from the tip of their body and are sometimes very much longer than the body; abdomen often long and slender, sometimes compressed.

All ichneumons are parasites on other holometabolous insects (those with complete metamorphosis). A few species parasitize spiders and spider eggs, or eggs of pseudoscorpions. Some are host specific, but it seems that they are more likely to be habitat specific, parasitizing larvae of several kinds found in a particular situation, as for example, leaf feeding larvae, and so on. These wasps prefer moist areas and are scarce in arid regions.

This is the largest family of the Hymenoptera. In the U.S. and Canada there are 3,322 described species and about 5,000 more undescribed. No species seems to have a common name. Identification is often difficult and requires the use of specialized literature.

Subfamily Pimplinae

Some important revisions have been published since the "Catalog of Hymenoptera," including works on Lissonstini, Banchini, Coremastinae, Anomaloninal, and Hemitelini. These recent papers are not considered in the treatment that follows.

Tribe Pimplini

[16.1 *Exeristes* Foerster (3 spp.); 16.2 *Scambus* Hartig: 5 subgenera: *Endromopoda* Hellen (4 spp.), *Lissoscambus* Walley (1 sp., *S. arizonensis* Walley), *Ateleophadnus* Cameron (3 spp.), *Scambus* s. str. (18 spp.), and *Erythroscambus* Walley (1 sp., *E. hirticauda* (Provancher)); 16.3 *Calliephialtes* Ashmead (4 spp.); 16.4 *Pimpla* Fabricius (4 spp.); 16.5 *Liotryphon* Ashmead (10 spp.); 16.6 *Townesia* Ozols (1 sp., *T. tenuiventris* (Holmgren)); 16.7 *Anastelgis* Townes (1 sp., *A. terminalis* Townes); 16.8 *Dolichomitus* Smith (19 spp.); 16.9 *Acropimpla* Townes (1 sp., *A. alboricta* (Cresson)); 16.10 *Gregopimpla* Momoi (1 sp., *G. inquisitor* (Scopoli)); 16.11 *Iseropus* Foerster (3 spp.); 16.12 *Tromatobia* Foerster (5 spp.); 16.13 *Zaglyptus* Foerster (3 spp.); 16.14 *Clistopyga* Gravenhorst (7 spp.); 16.15 *Alophosternum* Cushman (1 sp., *A. foliicola* Cushman)]

Tribe Polysphinctini

[16.16 *Dreisbachia* Townes (2 spp.); 16.17 *Schizopyga* Gravenhorst (3 spp.); 16.18 *Zabrachypus* Cushman (1 sp., *Z. primus* Cushman); 16.19 *Acrodactyla* Haliday (3 spp.); 16.20 *Colpomeria* Holmgren (1 sp., *C. quadrisculpa* (Gravenhorst)); 16.21 *Eruga* Townes (3 spp.); 16.22 *Piogaster* Perkins (1 sp., *P. maculata* Townes); 16.23 *Oxyrrhexis*

Foerster (1 sp., *O. carbonator texana* (Cresson)); 16.24 *Polysphincta* Gravenhorst (5 spp.); 16.25 *Acrotaphus* Townes (1 sp., *A. wiltii* (Cresson)); 16.26 *Sinarachna* Townes (2 spp.); 16.27 *Zatypota* Foerster (13 spp.)]

Tribe Echthromorphini

[16.28 *Itoplectis* Foerster (9 spp.); 16.29 *Ephialtes* Schrank (6 spp.); 16.30 *Coccygomimus* Saussure (22 spp.)]

Tribe Theroniini

[16.31 *Theronia* Holmgren: subgenus *Theronia* s. str. (2 spp.); 16.32 *Neotheronia* Krieger (2 spp.)]

Tribe Delomeristini

[16.33 *Perithous* Holmgren: 2 subgenera: *Perithous* s. str. (3 spp.) and *Hybomischos* Baltazar (1 sp., *P. septencinctorius* (Thunberg)); 16.34 *Delomerista* Foerster (7 spp.); 16.35 *Pseudorhyssa* Merrill (1 sp., *P. maculicoxis* (Kriechbaumer))]

Tribe Diacritini

[16.36 *Diacritus* Foerster (1 sp., *D. muliebris* (Cresson))]

Tribe Neoxoridini

[16.37 *Poemenia* Holmgren (5 spp.); 16.38 *Podoschistus* Townes (1 sp., *P. vittifrons* (Cresson)); 16.39 *Neoxorides* Clement (3 spp.)]

Tribe Rhyssini

16.40 *Rhyssa* Gravenhorst

Seven species (See A&J 268, *R*. sp.), including the following:

R. lineolata (Kirby). L. ±15 mm. Black; antennae with small annulations of white; abdomen black with white marks; legs reddish orange. Female bores into wood and lays her eggs in Coleoptera larvae. (1), (2), (3), (4), (5), throughout.

[16.41 *Rhyssella* Rohwer (2 spp.)]

16.42 *Megarhyssa* Ashmead

Five species, including the following:

M. macrurus macrurus (Linnaeus). L. ±25 mm. Body yellowish to yellowish brown; female with very long ovipositor that is used to lay eggs in dead or dying maple and other deciduous trees infested with the Pigeon Tremex larvae (*Tremex columba* (Linnaeus)). (1) n.e. US; (2) VA, NC; (5) NE.

[16.43 *Epirhyssa* Cresson (1 sp., *E. dietrichi* Townes)]

Subfamily Labeninae
Tribe Labenini

[16.44 *Labena* Cresson (2 spp.)]

Tribe Groteini

[16.45 *Grotea* Cresson (3 spp.)]

Tribe Brachycyrtini

[16.46 *Brachycyrtus* Kriechbaumer (2 spp.)]

Subfamily Tryphoninae
Tribe Phytodietini

[16.47 *Phytodietus* Gravenhorst: 2 subgenera: *Neuchorus* Uchida (2 spp.) and *Phytodietus* s. str. (9 spp.); 16.48 *Netelia* Gray: 6 subgenera: *Paropheltes* Cameron (11 spp.), *Parabates* Foerster (1 sp., *N. johnsoni*

(Ashmead)), *Toxochilus* Townes (7 spp.), *Prosthodocis* Enderlein (1 sp., *N. exserta* (Cushman)), *Netelia* s. str. (58 spp.), and *Bessobates* Townes (7 spp.)]

Tribe Oedemopsini

[16.49 *Eclytus* Holmgren (1 sp., *E. ornatus* Holmgren); 16.50 *Hercus* Townes (2 spp.); 16.51 *Neliopisthus* Thomson (4 spp.); 16.52 *Thymaris* Foerster (1 sp., *T. negligere* (Davis)); 16.53 *Zagryphus* Cushman (1 sp., *Z. nasutus* Davis); 16.54 *Oedemopsis* Tschek (1 sp., *O. davisi* Carlson); 16.55 *Atopotrophos* Cushman (1 sp., *A. bucephalus* (Cresson))]

Tribe Tryphonini

[16.56 *Grypocentrus* Ruthe (6 spp.); 16.57 *Polyblastus* Hartig: 3 subgenera: *Polyblastus* s. str. (8 spp.), *Cophenchus* Townes (2 spp.), and *Labroctonus* Foerster (13 spp.); 16.58 *Ctenochira* Foerster (23 spp.); 16.59 *Erromenus* Holmgren (18 spp.); 16.60 *Aderaeon* Townes (1 sp., *A. bedardi* (Provancher)); 16.61 *Monoblastus* Hartig (14 spp.); 16.62 *Thibetoides* Davis (1 sp., *T. flosamoris* Davis); 16.63 *Lagoleptus* Townes (1 sp., *L. palans* Townes); 16.64 *Boethus* Foerster (4 spp.); 16.65 *Dyspetes* Foerster (1 sp., *D. rufus* (Provancher)); 16.66 *Cosmoconus* Foerster (3 spp.); 16.67 *Tryphon* Fallen: 2 subgenera: *Noemon* Foerster (6 spp.) and *Symboethus* Foerster (10 spp.)]

Tribe Exenterini

[16.68 *Orthomiscus* Mason (2 spp.); 16.69 *Excavarus* Davis (4 spp.); 16.70 *Exyston* Schiφdte (20 spp.); 16.71 *Smicroplectrus* Thomson (8 spp.); 16.72 *Acrotomus* Holmgren (1 sp., *A. succinctus* (Gravenhorst)); 16.73 *Cteniscus* Haliday (17 spp.); 16.74 *Scapnetes* Townes (2 spp.); 16.75 *Exenterus* Hartig (15 spp.); 16.76 *Eridolius* Foerster (8 spp.)]

Tribe Idiogrammatini

[16.77 *Idiogramma* Foerster (6 spp.)]

Subfamily Eucerotinae

[16.78 *Euceros* Gravenhorst (12 spp.)]

Subfamily Adelognathinae

[16.79 *Adelognathus* Holmgren (5 spp.)]

Subfamily Xoridinae

[16.80 *Ischnoceros* Gravenhorst (1 sp., *I. clivulus* Townes); 16.81 *Aplomerus* Provancher (5 spp.); 16.82 *Odontocolon* Cushman (24 spp.); 16.83 *Xorides* Latreille: 2 subgenera: *Exomus* Townes (1 sp., *X. humeralis* (Say)) and *Xorides* s. str. (22 spp.)]

Subfamily Cryptinae

Tribe Hemitelini, Subtribe Chiroticina

[16.84 *Chirotica* Foerster (4 spp.)]

Subtribe Acrolytina

[16.85 *Cormobius* Townes (1 sp., *C. tenuis* Townes); 16.86 *Encrateola* Strand (1 sp., *E. laevigata longicornis* (Provancher)); 16.87 *Eudelus* Foerster (2 spp.); 16.88 *Isdromas* Foerster (1 sp., *I. lycaenae* (Howard)); 16.89 *Acrolyta* Foerster (4 spp.); 16.90 *Indovia* Seyrig (1 sp., *I. maculithorax* (Ashmead)); 16.91 *Neopimpla* Ashmead (1 sp., *N. bicarinata* (Riley)); 16.92 *Diaglyptidea* Viereck (1 sp., *D. lavoiei* (Provancher)); 16.93 *Lysibia* Foerster (1 sp., *L. mandibularis* (Provancher))]

Subtribe Hemitelina

[16.94 *Pleurogyrus* Townes (2 spp.); 16.95 *Obisophaga* Morley (1 undescribed sp.); 16.96 *Arotrephes* Townes (2 spp.); 16.97 *Xiphulcus* Townes (undescribed species); 16.98 *Hemiteles* Gravenhorst (1 sp., *H.*

humeralis Provancher); 16.99 *Aclastus* Foerster (5 spp.); 16.100 *Polyaulon* Foerster (9 spp.)]

Subtribe Gnypetomorphina

[16.101 *Anurotropus* Cushman (1 sp., *A. minutus* Cushman)]

Subtribe Gelina

[16.102 *Xenolytus* Foerster (2 spp.); 16.103 *Dichrogaster* Doumerc (4 spp.); 16.104 *Gelis* Thunberg (80 spp.); 16.105 *Agasthenes* Foerster (2 undescribed species)]

Subtribe Mastrina

[16.106 *Pygocryptus* Roman (7 spp.); 16.107 *Mastrus* Foerster (24 spp.); 16.108 *Amydraulax* Cushman (1 sp., *A. pulchra* Cushman); 16.109 *Apotemnus* Cushman (1 sp., *A. truncatus* Cushman); 16.110 *Helicostizus* Foerster (7 spp.); 16.111 *Lochetica* Kriechbaumer (1 undescribed sp.)]

Subtribe Ethelurgina

[16.112 *Rhembobius* Foerster (2 spp.); 16.113 *Ethelurgus* Foerster (1 sp., *E. syrphicola* (Ashmead))]

Subtribe Endaseina

[16.114 *Charitopes* Foerster (4 spp.); 16.115 *Adiastola* Foerster (1 sp., *A. columbiae* (Viereck)); 16.116 *Medophron* Foerster (2 spp.); 16.117 *Endasys* Foerster (10 spp.); 16.118 *Glyphicnemis* Foerster (1 sp., *G. mandibularis* (Cresson))]

Subtribe Bathytrichina

[16.119 *Bathythrix* Foerster (11 spp.)]

Subtribe Phygadeuontina

[16.120 *Oecotelma* Townes (1 sp., *O. cushmani* (Butcher)); 16.121 *Sulcarius* Townes (3 spp.); 16.122 *Orthizema* Foerster (1 sp., *O. testaceipes* (Cushman)); 16.123 *Uchidella* Townes (undescribed spp.); 16.124 *Gnotus* Foerster (1 sp., *G. chionops* (Gravenhorst)); 16.125 *Hedylus* Foerster (2 spp.); 16.126 *Stibeutes* Foerster (1 sp., *S. yuasai* (Bradley)), 16.127 *Theroscopus* Foerster (3 spp.); 16.128 *Megacara* Townes (1 sp., *M. lucens* (Rovencher)); 16.129 *Phygadeuon* (35 spp.); 16.130 *Ceratophygadeuon* Viereck (4 spp.)]

Subtribe Stilpnina

[16.131 *Stilpnus* Gravenhorst (3 spp.); 16.132 *Mesoleptus* Gravenhorst (6 spp); 16.133 *Atractodes* Gravenhorst (22 spp.)]

Subtribe Cremnodina

[16.134 *Cremnodes* Forester (1 sp., *C. nigripes* (Ashmead)); Unplaced taxa (1 sp.)]

Tribe Aptesini

[16.135 *Demopheles* Foerster (2 spp.); 16.136 *Javra* Cameron (2 spp.); 16.137 *Parmortha* Townes (5 spp.); 16.138 *Cratocryptus* Thomson (1 sp., *C. petilus* Townes); 16.139 *Cubocephalus* Ratzeburg (52 spp.); 16.140 *Oresbius* Marshall (28 spp.); 16.141 *Polytribax* Foerster (6 spp.); 16.142 *Giraudia* Foerster (10 spp.); 16.143 *Schenkia* Foerster (7 spp.); 16.144 *Megaplectes* Foerster (2 spp.); 16.145 *Pleolophus* Townes (14 spp.); 16.146 *Rhytura* Townes (1 sp., *R. pendens* Townes); 16.147 *Aptesis* Foerster (18 spp.); 16.148 *Oxytaenia* Foerster (1 sp., *O. barda carolina* (Townes)); 16.149 *Echthrus* Gravenhorst (5 spp.)]

Tribe Cryptini, Subtribe Agrothereutina

[16.150 *Apsilops* Foerster (3 spp.); 16.151 *Agrothereutes* Foerster (10 spp.); 16.152 *Gambrus* Foerster (10 spp.); 16.153 *Aritranis* Foerster (13

spp.); 16.154 *Pycnocryptus* Thomson (4 spp.); 16.155 *Hidryta* Foerster (2 spp.); 16.156 *Idiolispa* Foerster (4 spp.); 16.157 *Trychosis* Foerster (21 spp.)]

Subtribe Cryptina

[16.158 *Camera* Townes (1 sp., *C. euryaspis* (Cameron)); 16.159 *Ischnus* Gravenhorst (13 spp.); 16.160 *Glabridorsum* Townes (1 sp., *G. stokesii* (Cameron); 16.161 *Chromocryptus* Ashmead (4 spp.); 16.162 *Joppidium* Cresson (9 spp.); 16.163 *Caenocryptus* Thomson (10 spp.); 16.164 *Lanugo* Townes (13 spp.); 16.165 *Buathra* Cameron (6 spp.); 16.166 *Cryptus* Fabricius (20 spp.); 16.167 *Xylophrurus* Foerster (9 spp.); 16.168 *Reptatrix* Townes (1 sp., *R. crassipes* (Pratt)); 16.169 *Meringopus* Foerster (15 spp.); 16.170 *Compsocryptus* Ashmead (14 spp.)]

Subtribe Hemigastrina

[16.171 *Baryceros* Gravenhorst (5 spp.); 16.172 *Whymperia* Cameron (1 sp., *W. tricolor* Townes)]

Subtribe Mesostenina

[16.173 *Cryptanura* Brulle (3 spp.); 16.174 *Mesostenus* Gravenhorst (11 spp.); 16.175 *Polycyrtus* Spinola (1 sp., *P. neglectus* Cushman)]

Subtribe Goryphina

[16.176 *Diapetimorpha* Viereck (9 spp.); 16.177 *Listrognathus* Tschek: 2 subgenera: *Fenestula* Townes (3 spp.) and *Listrognathus* s. str. (12 spp.); 16.178 *Hylophasma* Townes (1 sp., *H. debile* (Townes))]

Subtribe Lymeonina

[16.179 *Mallochia* Viereck (4 spp.); 16.180 *Lymeon* Foerster (4 spp.); 16.181 *Acerastes* Cushman (1 sp., *A. pertinax* (Cresson)); 16.182 *Polycyrtidea* Viereck (2 spp.); 16.183 *Pachysomoides* Strand (3 spp.)]

Subtribe Ceratocryptina

[One unplaced genus and species]

Subtribe Osprynchotina

[16.184 *Messatoporus* Cushman (3 spp.); 16.185 *Acroricnus* Ratzburg (6 spp.)]

Subtribe Gabuniina

[16.186 *Agonocryptus* Cushman (1 sp., *A. discoidaloides* (Viereck)); 16.187 *Cryptohelcostizus* Cushman (10 spp.)]

Subtribe Sphecophagina

[16.188 *Sphecophaga* Westwood (1 sp., *S. vesparum burra* (Cresson))]

Subfamily Acaenitinae
Tribe Coleocentrini

[16.189 *Coleocentrus* Gravenhorst (9 spp.); 16.190 *Mesoclistus* Foerster (1 sp., *M. cushmani* Townes)]

Tribe Acaenitini

[16.191 *Arotes* Gravenhorst (4 spp.); 16.192 *Spilopteron* Townes (4 spp.); 16.193 *Yezoceryx* Uchida (1 sp., *Y. rupinsulensis* (Cresson))]

Subfamily Lycorininae

[16.194 *Toxophoroides* Viereck (5 spp.)]

Subfamily Collyriinae

[16.195 *Collyria* Schiodte (1 sp., *C. coxator* (Villers))]

Subfamily Orthopelmatinae

[16.196 *Orthopelma* Taschenberg (6 spp.)]

Subfamily Ichneumoninae
Tribe Phaeogenini, Subtribe Heterischnina

[16.197 *Heterischnus* Wesmael (2 spp.)]

Subtribe Phaeogenina

[16.198 *Stenodontus* Berthoumieu (2 spp., undescribed); 16.199 *Dicaelotus* Wesmael (6 spp.); 16.200 *Oronotus* Wesmael (1 sp., *O. vincibilis* (Cresson)); 16.201 *Diadromus* Wesmael (4 spp.); 16.202 *Terebraella* Heinrich (1 sp., *T. culiciops* Heinrich); 16.203 *Colpognathus* Wesmael (1 sp., *C. helvus* (Cresson)); 16.204 *Centeterus* Wesmael (4 spp.); 16.205 *Aethecerus* Wesmael (2 spp.); 16.206 *Jethsura* Cameron (1 sp., *J. pyriformis* (Provancher)); 16.207 *Phaeogenes* Wesmael (26 spp.)]

Tribe Gyrodontini, Subtribe Gyrodontina

[16.208 *Cratichneumon* Thomson (64 spp.); 16.209 *Crypteffigies* Heinrich (2 spp.); 16.210 *Homotherus* Foerster (7 spp.); 16.211 *Eupalamus* Wesmael (2 spp.); 16.212 *Anisopygus* Kriechbaumer (2 spp.); 16.213 *Melanichneumon* Thomson (18 spp.); 16.214 *Barichneumon* Thomson (18 spp.); 16.215 *Vulgichneumon* Heinrich (9 spp.); 16.216 *Richtichneumon* Heinrich (3 spp.); 16.217 *Stenobarichneumon* Heinrich (6 spp.); 16.218 *Menkokia* Heinrich (1 sp., *M blandii* (Cresson)); 16.219 *Rubicundiella* Heinrich (6 spp.); 16.220 *Limonethe* Townes (1 sp., *L. maurator* (Brulle)); 16.221 *Carinodes* Hancock (2 spp.); 16.222 *Aoplus* Tischbein (17 spp.); 16.223 *Hemihoplis* Heinrich (1 sp., *H. teres* (Swift)); 16.224 *Platylabops* Heinrich (7 spp.)]

Subtribe Amblytelesina

[16.225 *Ectopimorpha* Viereck (10 spp.); 16.226 *Exephanes* Wesmael (3 spp.); 16.227 *Limerodops* Heinrich (2 spp.); 16.228 *Neamblymorpha* Heinrich (1 sp., *N. milva* (Cresson)); 16.229 *Eutanyacra* Cameron (18 spp.); 16.230 *Setanta* Cameron (1 sp., *S. compta* (Say)); 16.231 *Netanyacra* Heinrich (3 spp.); 16.232 *Diphyus* Kriechbaumer (29 spp.); 16.233 *Ctenichneumon* Thomson (14 spp.); 16.234 *Probolus* Wesmael (2 spp.); 16.235 *Tricholabus* Thomson (6 spp.); 16.236 *Spilichneumon* Thomson (10 spp.); 16.237 *Obtusodonta* Heinrich (4 spp.); Unplaced taxa (10 spp.)]

Subtribe Pterocormina

[16.238 *Stenichneumon* Thomson (4 spp.); 16.239 *Patrocloides* Heinrich (3 spp.); 16.240 *Patroclus* Cresson (1 sp., *P. homocerus homocerus* (Wesmael)); 16.241 *Protopelmus* Heinrich (1 sp., *P. atrocaeruleus* (Cresson)); 16.242 *Orgichneumon* Heinrich (1 sp., *O. calcatorius* (Thunberg)); 16.243 *Thyrateles* Perkins (7 spp.); 16.244 *Pterocormus* Foerster (142 spp.); 16.245 *Chasmias* Ashmead (1 sp., *C. scelestus* (Cresson))]

Subtribe Hoplismenina

[16.246 *Hybophorellus* Schulz (3 spp.); 16.247 *Hoplismenus* Gravenhorst (9 spp.)]

Tribe Ichneumonini, Subtribe Ichneumonina

[16.248 *Syspasis* Townes (1 sp., *S. tauma* (Heinrich)]

16.249 *Ichneumon* Linnaeus

Forty-nine species. Common in undergrowth of rich woodlands, they parasitize Lepidoptera pupae.

[16.250 *Coelichneumonops* Heinrich (4 spp.); 16.251 *Protichneumon* Thomson (4 spp.); 16.252 *Amblyjoppa* Cameron (1 sp., *A. magna* (Cresson)); 16.253 *Catadelphops* Heinrich (1 sp., *C. buccatus* (Cresson)); 16.254 *Neamblyjoppa* Heinrich (1 sp., *N. nasuta* Heinrich); 16.255 *Catadelphus* Wesmael (4 spp.)]

Tribe Trogusini, *Subtribe* Callajoppina

[16.256 *Gnamptopelta* Hopper (2 spp.); 16.257 *Callajoppa* Cameron (1 sp., *C. cirrogaster cirrogaster* (Schrank)); 16.258 *Tricyphus* Kriechbaumer (3 spp.); 16.259 *Tmetogaster* Hopper (1 sp., *T. nubilipennis* (Haldemann)); 16.260 *Conocalama* Hopper (12 spp.)]

Subtribe Trogusina

[16.261 *Macrojoppa* Kriechbaumer (1 sp., *M. fascipennis* (Cresson)); 16.262 *Trogus* Panzer (6 spp.)]

Tribe Joppocryptini

[16.263 *Plagiotrypes* Ashmead (1 sp., *P. concinnus* (Say)); 16.264 *Narthecura* Townes (1 sp., *N. invadens* Heinrich); 16.265 *Lobaegis* Townes (1 sp., *L. septentrionalis* Heinrich); 16.266 *Pseudoplatylabus* Smits van Burgst (2 spp.)]

Tribe Listrodromini, *Subtribe* Listrodromina

[16.267 *Trogomorpha* Ashmead (2 spp.); 16.268 *Neotypus* Foerster (1 sp., *N. nobilitator nobilitator* (Gravenhorst)); 16.269 *Anisobas* Wesmael (7 spp.); 16.270 *Diacantharius* Schmiedeknecht (1 undescribed sp.); 16.271 *Dilopharius* Townes (1 undescribed sp.)]

Tribe Platylabini

[16.272 *Apaeleticus* Wesmael (2 spp.); 16.273 *Carlsonia* Heinrich (1 sp., *C. perturbator* (Heinrich)); 16.274 *Linycus* Cameron (5 spp.); 16.275 *Neolinycus* Heinrich (1 sp., *N. michaelis* Heinrich); 16.276 *Cyclolabus* Heinrich (12 spp.); 16.277 *Platylabus* Wesmael (40 spp.); 16.278 *Dentilabus* Heinrich (2 spp.); 16.279 *Asthenolabus* Heinrich (3 spp.); 16.280 *Pristiceros* Gravenhorst (2 spp.); 16.281 *Tropicolabus* Heinrich (1 sp., *T. foxi* (Davis)); 16.282 *Ambloplisus* Heinrich (1 sp., *A. ornatus* (Cresson)); 16.283 *Hypomecus* Wesmael (1 sp., *H. quadriannulatus* (Gravenhorst))]

Subfamily Metopiinae

[16.284 *Pseudometopius* Davis (1 sp., *P. hagenii* (Cresson)); 16.285 *Chorinaeus* Holmgren (11 spp.); 16.286 *Trieces* Townes (29 spp.); 16.287 *Metopius* Panzer: 4 subgenera: *Metopius* s. str. (9 spp.), *Cultrarius* Davis (11 spp.), *Peltales* Townes (5 spp.), and *Tylopius* Townes (6 spp.); 16.288 *Triclistus* Foerster (13 spp., including *T. propinquus* (Cresson) (Fig. 25.17); 16.289 *Colpotrochia* Holmgren, subgenus *Colpotrochia* s. str. (4 spp.); 16.290 *Periope* Haliday (1 sp., *P. aethiops* (Cresson)); 16.291 *Spudaeus* Gistal (2 spp.); 16.292 *Bothromus* Townes (4 spp.); 16.293 *Apolophus* Townes (1 sp., *A. borealis* Townes); 16.294 *Leurus* Townes (1 sp., *L. caeruliventris borealis* Townes); 16.295 *Seticornuta* Morely (2 spp.); 16.296 *Carria* Schmiedeknecht (4 spp.); 16.297 *Macromalon* Townes (1 sp., *M. montanum* Townes); 16.298 *Hypsicera* Latreille (4 spp.); 16.299 *Stethoncus* Townes (1 sp., *S.

Fig. 25.17. (*From Britton, 1916*)

arcticus Townes); 16.300 *Synosis* Townes (1 sp., *S. clepsydra* Townes); 16.301 *Exochus* Gravenhorst (55 spp.)]

Subfamily Banchinae
Tribe Stilbopini

[16.302 *Stilbops* Foerster (1 sp., undescribed)]

Tribe Glyptini

[16.303 *Sphelodon* Townes (2 spp.); 16.304 *Apophua* Morley (1 sp., *A. simplicipes* (Cresson)); 16.305 *Glypta* Gravenhorst (44 spp.); 16.306 *Cephaloglypta* Obrtel (2 spp.)]

Tribe Lissonotanini

[16.307 *Mnioes* Townes (1 sp., *M. lunatus* Kennedy); 16.308 *Lissonota* Gravenhorst (40 spp.); 16.309 *Loxodocus* Townes (1 sp., *L. palloranus* (Davis)); 16.310 *Alloplasta* Foerster (3 spp.); 16.311 *Arenetra* Holmgren (6 spp.); 16.312 *Cryptopimpla* Taschenberg (4 spp.); 16.313 *Isomeris* Townes (1 sp., *I. marginata* (Provancher)); 16.314 *Syzeuctus* Foerster (5 spp.); 16.315 *Eudeleboea* Lopez Cristobal (3 spp.); 16.316 *Diradops* Townes (1 sp., *D. bethunei* (Cresson))]

Tribe Banchini

[16.317 *Exetastes* Gravenhorst (49 spp.); 16.318 *Agathilla* Westwood (1 sp., *A. bradleyi* (Viereck)); 16.319 *Ceratogastra* Ashmead (1 sp., *C. ornata* (Say)); 16.320 *Banchus* Fabricius (11 spp.)]

Subfamily Neorhacodinae

[16.321 *Neorhacodes* Hedicke (2 spp.)]

Subfamily Ctenopelmatinae
Tribe Ctenopelmatini

[16.322 *Ctenopelma* Holmgren (6 spp.); 16.323 *Xenoschesis* Foerster: 2 subgenera: *Xenoschesis* s. str. (1 sp., *X. cinctiventris* (Ashmead) and *Polycinetis* Foerster (4 spp.); 16.324 *Notopygus* Holmgren (4 spp.); 16.325 *Homaspis* Foerster (5 spp.)]

Tribe Pionini

[16.326 *Lethades* Davis (2 spp.); 16.327 *Hodostates* Foerster (1 sp., *H. rotundatus* (Davis)); 16.328 *Trematopygus* Holmgren (1 sp., *T. semirufus* (Cresson)); 16.329 *Glyptorhaestus* Thomson (1 sp., *G. tomostethi* (Cushman)); 16.330 *Rhorus* Foerster (10 spp.); 16.331 *Sympherta* Foerster (5 spp.); 16.332 *Synoecetes* Foerster (1 sp., *S. festivus* (Cresson)); 16.333 *Coelorhachis* Townes (1 undescribed sp.); 16.334 *Zaplethocornia* Schmiedeknecht (3 spp.); 16.335 *Nanium* Townes (1 sp., *N. capitatum* (Cresson)); 16.336 *Trematopygodes* Aubert (3 spp.); 16.337 *Aechmeta* Townes (2 spp.); 16.338 *Oetophorus* Foerster (3 spp.); 16.339 *Perilissus* Holmgren (6 spp.); 16.340 *Absyrtus* Holmgren (3 spp.); 16.341 *Lophyroplectus* Thomson (1 sp., *L. oblongopunctatus* (Hartig)); 16.342 *Opheltes* Holmgren (1 sp., *O. glaucopterus barberi* Cushman); 16.343 *Lathrolestes* Foerster (15 spp.)]

Tribe Scolobatini

[16.344 *Physotarsus* Townes (1 undescribed sp.); 16.345 *Scolobates* Gravenhorst (1 sp., *S. auriculatus* (Fabricius)]

Tribe Mesoleiini

[16.346 *Otlophorus* Foerster (2 spp.); 16.347 *Atithasus* Foerster (1 sp., *A. bimaculatus* (Ashmead)); 16.348 *Barytarbes* Foerster (4 spp.); 16.349 *Alexeter* Foerster (7 spp.); 16.350 *Protarchus* Foerster (4 spp.); 16.351 *Lamachus* Foerster (9 spp.); 16.352 *Neostroblia* Heinrich (1 sp., *N. incessans* (Davis)); 16.353 *Scopesis* Foerster (2 spp.); 16.354 *Himerta* Foerster (4 spp.); 16.355 *Rhinotorus* Foerster (1 sp., *R. ovalis* (Davis)); 16.356 *Arbelus* Townes (3 spp.); 16.357 *Campodorus* Foerster (11 spp.);

16.358 *Smicrolius* Thomson (2 undescribed spp.); 16.359 *Mesoleius* Homgren (13 spp.); 16.360 *Hyperbatus* Foerster (3 undescribed spp.); 16.361 *Saotis* Foerster (3 spp.); 16.362 *Anoncus* Townes (4 spp.)]

Tribe Euryproctini

[16.363 *Synomelix* Foerster (4 spp.); 16.364 *Synodites* Foerster (6 spp.); 16.365 *Pantorhaestes* Foerster (3 spp.); 16.366 *Mesoleptidea* Viereck (4 spp.); 16.367 *Anisotacrus* Schmiedeknecht (3 spp.); 16.368 *Hadrodactylus* Foerster (12 spp.); 16.369 *Syndipnus* Foerster (10 spp.); 16.370 *Hypamblys* Foerster (3 spp.); 16.371 *Phobetes* Foerster (4 spp.); 16.372 *Hyperallus* Foerster (1 sp., *H. caliroae* Viereck); 16.373 *Occapes* Townes (1 sp., *O. sierrae* Townes); 16.374 *Euryproctus* Holmgren (14 spp.)]

Subfamily Anomaloninae
Tribe Gravenhorstiini

[16.375 *Habronyx* Foerster: 3 subgenera: *Habronyx* s. str. (2 spp.), *Camposcopus* Foerster (1 sp., *H. aclerivorus* (Rohwer)), and *Habrocampulum* Gauld (1 undescribed sp.); 16.376 *Aphanistes* Foerster (2 spp.); 16.377 *Barylypa* Foerster (6 spp.); 16.378 *Corsoncus* Townes (6 spp.); 16.379 *Liopterna* Townes (1 sp., *L. schlingeri* Townes); 16.380 *Therion* Curtis (11 spp.); 16.381 *Heteropelma* Wesmael (1 sp., *H. datanae* Riley); 16.382 *Gravenhortia* Boie, subgenus *Erigorgus* Foerster (13 spp.); 16.383 *Trichomma* Wesmael (3 spp.); 16.384 *Agrypon* Foerster (14 spp.); 16.385 *Parania* Morley (3 spp.); 16.386 *Metoa* Townes (2 spp.); 16.387 *Calcaneum* Townes (1 sp., *C. oporinum* Townes); 16.388 *Ophionellus* Westwood (4 spp.); 16.389 *Ophiopterus* Brullé (1 sp., *O. cincticornis* (Cresson)); Unplaced taxa (1 sp.)]

Tribe Anomalonini

[16.390 *Anomalon* Panzer (5 spp.); 16.391 *Neogreeneia* Viereck (1 sp., *N. picticornis* Viereck)]

Subfamily Campopleginae
Tribe Campoplegini

[16.392 *Sinophorus* Foerster (10 spp.); 16.393 *Sesioplex* Viereck (1 sp., *S. depressus* (Viereck)); 16.394 *Campoplex* Gravenhorst (35 spp.); 16.395 *Porizon* Fallén (6 spp.); 16.396 *Venturia* Schrottky (6 spp.); 16.397 *Casinaria* Holmgren (21 spp.); 16.398 *Charops* Holmgren (1 sp., *C. annulipes* Ashmead); 16.399 *Dusona* Cameron (77 spp.); 16.400 *Leptocampoplex* Horstmann (1 sp., *L. cremastoides* (Holmgren)); 16.401 *Pyracmon* Holmgren (1 sp., *P. sepiella* (Holmgren)); 16.402 *Rhimphoctona* Foerster (8 spp.); 16.403 *Nemeritis* Holmgren (1 sp., *N. macrurus* (Viereck)); 16.404 *Bathyplectes* Foerster (8 spp.); 16.405 *Campoletis* Foerster (49 spp.); 16.406 *Callidora* Foerster (2 spp.); 16.407 *Cymodusa* Holmgren (5 spp.); 16.408 *Cymodusopsis* Viereck (1 sp., *C. aristoteliae* Viereck); 16.409 *Spudastica* Foerster (1 sp., *S. canadensis* Walley); 16.410 *Meloboris* Holmgren (1 sp., *M. alopha* (Townes)); 16.411 *Nepiera* Foerster (7 spp.); 16.412 *Phobocampe* Foerster (12 spp.); 16.413 *Tranosema* Foerster (2 spp.); 16.414 *Dolophron* Foerster (1 sp., *D. pedella* (Holmgren)); 16.415 *Synetaeris* Foerster (1 sp., *S. tenuifemur* (Walley)); 16.416 *Philositus* Townes (1 sp., *P. enchophorus* Townes); 16.417 *Macrus* Gravenhorst (1 sp., *M. parvulus solenobiae* (Ashmead)); 16.418 *Enytus* Cameron (6 spp.); 16.419 *Diadegma* Foerster (44 spp.); 16.420 *Eriborus* Foerster (2 spp.); 16.421 *Lathrostizus* Foerster (2 spp.); 16.422 *Olesicampe* Foerster (36 spp.); 16.423 *Lemophagus* Townes (1 sp., *L. curtus* Townes); 16.424 *Hyposoter* Foerster (27 spp.); 16.425 *Benjaminia* Viereck (2 spp.); 16.426 *Echthronomas* Foerster (2 spp.); 16.427 *Campoctonus* Viereck (5 spp.); 16.428 *Xanthocampoplex* Morley (1 sp., *X. orbitalis* (Walley)); 16.429 *Microcharops* Roman (2 spp.); Unplaced taxa (1 sp.)]

Subfamily Cremastinae

[16.430 *Xiphosomella* Szepligeti (2 spp.); 16.431 *Pristomerus* Curtis (7 spp.); 16.432 *Dimophora* Foerster (1 sp., *D. prima* (Cushman)); 16.433

Eiphosoma Cresson (5 spp.); 16.434 *Pseuderipternus* Viereck (3 spp.); 16.435 *Tanychela* Townes (1 undescribed sp.); 16.436 *Cremastus* Gravenhorst (26 spp.); 16.437 *Dolichopselephus* Ashmead (1 sp., *D. cockerelli* Ashmead); 16.438 *Trathala* Cameron (17 spp.); 16.439 *Neleothymus* Foerster (1 sp., *N. attenuatus* (Cushman)); 16.440 *Neocremastus* Cushman (2 spp.); 16.441 *Temelucha* Foerster (26 spp.)]

Subfamily Phrudinae

[16.442 *Earobia* Townes (1 sp., *E. minor* Townes); 16.443 *Phrudus* Foerster (3 spp.); 16.444 *Peucobius* Townes (2 spp.)]

Subfamily Tersilochinae

[16.445 *Allophroides* Horstmann (undescribed spp.); 16.446 *Probles* Foerster (1 sp., *P. maturus* (Provancher)); 16.447 *Barycnemis* Foerster (7 spp.); 16.448 *Pectinolochus* Aubert (undescribed spp.); 16.449 *Tersilochus* Holmgren (3 spp.); 16.450 *Stethantyx* Townes (1 sp., *S. nearctica* Townes); 16.451 *Allophrys* Foerster (1 undescribed sp.); 16.452 *Phradis* Foerster (5 undescribed spp.); 16.453 *Diaparsis* Foerster (3 spp.); 16.454 *Aneuclis* Foerster (1 undescribed sp.); Unplaced taxa (8 spp.)]

Subfamily Ophioninae
Tribe Ophionini
16.455 *Ophion* Fabricius

Eleven species, including the following:

O. nigrovarius Provancher. L. ±16 mm. Body reddish or dark yellowish brown; wings tinted with brown. Parasite of *Phyllophaga fusca* (Froelich) [Scarabaeidae]. (1) n.e. US; (2) VA, NC, SC, GA; (3) TX; (5) MN, CO, KS, MO.

[16.456 *Clistorapha* Cushman (1 sp., *C. subfuliginosa* (Ashmead)); 16.457 *Boethoneura* Cushman (1 sp., *B. arida* Cushman); 16.458 *Trophophion* (1 sp., *T. tenuiceps* Cushman); 16.459 *Apatophion* Shestakov (2 undescribed spp.); 16.460 *Genophion* Felt (2 spp.)]

Tribe Enicospilini

[16.461 *Rhynchophion* Enderlein (1 sp., *R. flammipennis* (Ashmead)); 16.462 *Thyreodon* Brullé (4 spp.); 16.463 *Simophion* Cushman (1 sp., *S. excarinatus* Cushman); 16.464 *Enicospilus* Stephens (9 spp.)]

Subfamily Mesochorinae

[16.465 *Cidaphus* Foerster (4 spp.); 16.466 *Astiphromma* Foerster (18 spp.); 16.467 *Mesochorus* Gravenhorst (98 spp.); 16.468 *Stictopisthus* Thomson (9 spp.)]

Subfamily Diplazontinae

[16.469 *Syrphoctonus* Foerster (43 spp.); 16.470 *Xestopelta* Dasch (1 sp., *X. vertebrata* (Cushman)); 16.471 *Enizemum* Foerster (8 spp.); 16.472 *Woldstedtius* Carlson (3 spp.); 16.473 *Campocraspedon* Uchida (2 spp.); 16.474 *Phthorima* Foerster (6 spp.); 16.475 *Syrphophilus* Dasch (5 spp.); 16.476 *Tymnophorus* Schmiedeknecht (6 spp.); 16.477 *Diplazon* Viereck (17 spp.); 16.478 *Promethes* Foerster (4 spp.); 16.479 *Sussaba* Cameron (13 spp.)]

Subfamily Oxytorinae

[16.480 *Microleptes* Gravenhorst (1 sp., *M. splendidulus* Gravenhorst); 16.481 *Oxytorus* Foerster (3 spp.); 16.482 *Hyperacmus* Holmgren (1 sp., *H. crassicornis* (Gravenhorst)); 16.483 *Entypoma* Foerster (1 undescribed sp.); 16.484 *Allomacrus* Foerster (1 sp., *A. arcticus* (Holmgren)); 16.485 *Apoclima* Foerster (1 undescribed sp.); 16.486 *Cylloceria* Schiødte (3 spp.); 16.487 *Aniseres* Foerster (2 spp.); 16.488 *Pantisarthrus* Foerster (1 sp., *P. inaequalis* Foerster); 16.489 *Proclitus* Foerster (2 spp.); 16.490 *Dialipsis* Foerster (1 undescribed sp.); 16.491

Plectiscidea Viereck (12 spp.); 16.492 *Aperileptus* Foerster (2 spp.); 16.493 *Blapticus* Foerster (1 or more undescribed spp.); 16.494 *Symplecis* (2 spp.); 16.495 *Catastenus* Foerster (1 undescribed sp.); 16.496 *Eusterinx* Foerster (6 spp.); 16.497 *Helictes* Haliday (1 sp., *H. ruficornis* Davis); 16.498 *Megastylus* Schiødte (2 spp.)]

Subfamily Orthocentrinae

[16.499 *Orthocentrus* Gravenhorst (11 spp.); 16.500 *Picrostigeus* Foerster (4 undescribed spp.); 16.501 *Stenomacrus* Foerster (15 spp.); 16.502 *Leipaulus* Townes (2 spp.); 16.503 *Plectiscus* Gravenhorst (undescribed species); 16.504 *Neurateles* Ratzeburg (2 spp.); Unplaced taxa (22 spp.)]

17. STEPHANIDAE (Stephanid Wasp Family)

Length: 5–19 mm. Uncommon wasps with slender antennae of 30 or more segments; head with a crown of five teeth around the median ocellus; neck long; hind femora swollen and spined beneath; ovipositor long. Of the six species in the U.S. and Canada, all except one are western and southern. These wasps are parasites of coleopterous and hymenopterous wood borers.

[17.1 *Schlettererius* Ashmead (1 sp., *S. cinctipes* (Cresson), (3) CA, AZ; (4) BC, WA, ID, OR, NV, UT; (5) SD)]

17.2 *Megischus* Brulle

Five species, including the following:

M. bicolor (Westwood). (1) n.e. US; (2) s.e. US; (3) s.w. US; (4) UT; (5) n. central states.

Superfamily CHALCIDOIDEA

This superfamily contains 11 families of very small, mostly parasitic wasps, rarely over 4 mm in length. They are extremely important as agents of biological control. The chalcidoids may be distinguished from the remainder of the Parasitica by the presence of a prepectus, an area along the anterior margin of the episternum of the mesothorax that is separated by a suturelike furrow (See Fig. 25.25)—a feature shared with the bees and digger wasps. Their antennae are usually elbowed, with at most 13 segments.

The classification of the superfamily has been revised considerably since the *Catalog of Hymenoptera* was compiled, but these changes have not been incorporated in the following discussion of genera and species. The accompanying Key to the Families has been adapted from old literature and is only a partial aid for their identification. Despite the great difficulty in making identifications even to the family level, as much information as space permits is provided here.

Key to the Families of Chalcidoidea

1.	Tarsi with 3 tarsomeres; wing pubescence usually in rows**28. Trichogrammatidae**	
	Tarsi with 4 or 5 tarsomeres; wing pubescence usually not in rows	*2*
2(1).	Hind wings very narrow, linear, with long stalk at base; wings with long fringe of setae; front wings without a stigmal vein; antennal scape short and compressed, flagellum without a ring segment**27. Mymaridae**	
	Hind wings not narrow and without long stalk at base; wing fringe setae usually short; antennal scape long, flagellum usually with 1 to 3 minute ring segments	*3*
3(2).	Apical spur of front tibia small and straight; tarsi usually with 4 tarsomeres; antennae usually with 9 or fewer segments**26. Eulophidae**	
	Apical spur of front tibia large and curved; tarsi usually with 5 tarsomeres; antennae usually with more than 9 segments ..	*4*
4(3).	Head long, oblong, with deep, longitudinal dorsal groove; occipital margin usually with small tubercle or spine; front and hind legs stout, with tibiae much shorter than femora; middle legs slender (females); (Agaoninae)**18. Torymidae**	
	Head and legs not as above ...	*5*
5(4).	Mesopleura large and convex, usually without femoral groove; apical spur of middle tibia usually very large and stout ...	*6*
	Mesopleura with groove for reception of femora; apical spur of middle tibia not enlarged ...	*9*
6(5).	Mesonotum more or less convex, with parapsidal sutures lacking or indistinct ...**25. Encyrtidae**	
	Mesonotum rarely convex, usually flattened, with parapsidal sutures present and usually distinct; marginal vein usually long ..	*7*
7(6).	Mesonotum of female flattened or slightly concave, with median anterior triangular elevation; parapsidal sutures often not sharply defined; mesonotum of male slightly convex, with parapsidal sutures usually incomplete, not curved laterally ..**24. Eupelmidae**	
	Mesonotum convex in both sexes; parapsidal sutures complete and curved laterally ...	*8*
8(7).	First antennal segment of female slender, not dilated or compressed; flagellum of male antennae filiform, without branches; (part)**19. Pteromalidae**	
	First antennal segment of female more or less dilated or compressed; flagellum of male antennae with 4 branches; (in part)**24. Eupelmidae**	
9(5).	Mandibles cultriform, with 1 or 2 teeth on inner side; thorax strongly elevated, pronotum with only anterior face not visible from above; scutellum large and produced posteriorly; abdomen compressed, with second segment very large; stigmal vein not developed ..**23. Eucharitidae**	
	Mandibles stout, not cultriform, and with 3 or 4 teeth at apex; thorax not elevated ...	*10*

Key to the Families of Chalcidoidea (*Contd.*)

10(9). Hind tibiae with 1 apical spur; pronotum in dorsal view more or less conical, narrowed anteriorly; hind coxae rarely larger than front coxae; ovipositor usually short, or if long, then stigma small; (in part)**19. Pteromalidae**

Hind tibiae with 2 apical spurs (one may be small); pronotum in dorsal view usually quadrate and not distinctly narrowed anteriorly; ovipositor generally long *11*

11(10). Hind femora greatly swollen and usually toothed or denticulate beneath; hind tibiae usually arcuate .. *12*

Hind femora not swollen, or but slightly, and either not toothed beneath or with only 1 or 2 teeth ... *15*

12(11). Hind coxae considerably larger than front coxae *13*

Hind coxae little if any larger than front coxae; (in part) **19. Pteromalidae**

13(12). Hind coxae sharply ridged above .. *14*

Hind coxae somewhat oval or rounded, not sharply ridged above**21. Chalcididae**

14(13). Front wings folded longitudinally at rest; ovipositor usually long and curved upward and forward over dorsal side of abdomen; usually black and yellow; l. ±10 mm

...**22. Leucospidae**

Front wings not folded longitudinally at rest; ovipositor short and not upcurved; usually metallic green; l. 7 mm or less; (Podagrioninae)**18. Torymidae**

15(11). Hind coxae considerably larger than front coxae *16*

Hind coxae subequal to front coxae .. *17*

16(15). Parapsidal sutures present; ovipositor exserted and usually very long; abdomen not pitted or punctate; body metallic; (in part)**18. Torymidae**

Parapsidal sutures absent or very indistinct; ovipositor short and hidden; abdomen of female conical and elongate, of male oblong, and usually with rows of deep pits or punctures in both sexes; (part)**19. Pteromalidae**

17(15). Pronotum more or less quadrate and as wide as mesonotum; mesonotum usually very coarsely sculptured .. *18*

Pronotum short, transversely linear, rarely as wide as mesonotum; mesonotum usually finely sculptured; (in part)**19. Pteromalidae**

18(17). Pronotum short, much wider than long; abdomen of female subtriangular, with 2nd tergum, or fused 2nd and 3rd terga, covering most of its surface; thorax very robust, often metallic; (Perilampinae)**19. Pteromalidae**

Pronotum more or less quadrate, nearly as long as wide; abdomen of female rounded or ovate, more or less compressed, with 2nd tergum never very large; thorax of more normal proportions; black or yellowish; thorax not metallic**20. Eurytomidae**

18. TORYMIDAE (Torymid Wasp Family)

L. 1–2.5 mm. Although divided into several subfamilies as indicated below, the majority of the species of this large family belong to the Toryminae. These have stout mandibles with three to four teeth, a hind coxa that is several times larger than the front coxa, and an ovipositor that is exserted. Many species are metallic green. Most species are parasites of gall-inducing Diptera and Hymenoptera. Some are reared from the nests of bees and wasps and a few from caterpillars and beetle larvae. Two groups are phytophagous. There are 175 species in the U.S. and Canada.

***Subfamily* Agaoninae** (Fig Wasps)

18.1 *Blastophaga* Gravenhorst

The genus is divided into two subgenera: *Blastophaga* s. str. and *Secundeisenia* Schultz. The two included species follow.

B. (Blastophaga) psenes (Linnaeus) (Fig Wasp). L. ±1 mm. Females winged, males wingless; black; front and hind legs thickened, middle pair slender; antennae filiform but apical segments somewhat thickened; head of female with dorsal, longitudinal groove. This introduced species pollinates the commercial Smyrna fig that is grown extensively in California. This fig will produce fruit only when pollinated by pollen from the wild Caprifig since it does not produce pollen itself. This task can be accomplished only by this species of fig wasp—a symbiotic relationship that is one of the most remarkable

associations among living things. The Fig Wasp larvae develop in a gall in the wild fig flowers. The wingless males are the first to emerge from the gall and mate with the females as soon as the latter emerge. The females then collect pollen in the male flowers of the Caprifig and fly to the Smyrna Fig to pollinate its female flowers; they also pollinate other varieties of figs. Since they are able to oviposit only in the shorter flowers of the Caprifig, however, these figs along with their pollen are necessary for the survival of the commercial Smyrna Fig. (See 25.18 and A&J 270.) (3) CA, AZ.

Fig. 25.18. (*U.S. Dept. of Agric.*)

429

B. (Secundeisenia) mexicana (Ashmead). Similar to the preceding. (2) FL.

Subfamily **Idarninae**

Members of this subfamily are also associated with figs, but little is known about them.

[18.2 *Colyostichus* Mayr (1 sp., *C. brevicaudis* Mayr); 18.3 *Neosycophila* Grandi (2 spp.); 18.4 *Idarnes* Walker (1 sp., *I. carme* Walker)]

Subfamily **Toryminae**

[18.5 *Allotorymus* Huber (1 sp., *A. splendens* (Provancher)]

18.6 *Torymus* Dalman

Ninety-nine species, including the following:

T. varians (Walker). Reared from seeds of apple and other Roseaceae. (See Fig. 25.19.) (1) n.e. NA; (2) VA, NC; (4) BC; (5) MB.

[18.7 *Diomorus* Walker (2 spp.); 18.8 *Physothorax* Mayr (3 spp.)]

Subfamily **Erimerinae**

Members of this subfamily are parasitic on insects infesting grass stems.

[18.9 *Erimerus* Crawford (1 sp., *E. wickhami* (Ashmead)); 18.10 *Pseuderimerus* Gahan (3 spp.)]

Subfamily **Monodontomerinae**

[18.11 *Liodontomerus* Gahan (3 spp.); 18.12 *Idiomacromerus* Crawford (1 sp., *I. bimaculipennis* Crawford); 18.13 *Platykula* (1 sp., *P. albihirta* (Ashmead)); 18.14 *Dimeromicrus* Crawford (2 spp.); 18.15 *Monodontomerus* Westwood (13 spp.); 18.16 *Zaglyptonotus* Crawford (2 spp.); 18.17 *Glyphomerus* Foerster (1 sp., *G. stigma* (Fabrocius)); 18.18 *Eridontomerus* Crawford (1 sp., *E. isosomatis* (Riley)); 18.19 *Pseudotorymus* Masi (1 sp., *P. lazulellus* (Ashmead)); 18.20 *Cryptopristus* Foerster (1 sp., *C. harrisii* (Fitch)); 18.21 *Ditropinotus* Crawford (1 sp., *D. aureoviridis* Crawford); 18.22 *Antistrophoplex* Crawford (1 sp., *A. bicoloripes* Crawford); 18.23 *Microdontomerus* Crawford (3 spp.); 18.24 *Roptrocerus* Ratzeberg (1 sp., *R. xylophagorum* (Ratzeburg))]

Subfamily **Megastigminae**

Members of this subfamily are phytophagous species, largely in rosaceous and coniferous seeds.

[18.25 *Megastigmus* Dalman (28 spp.); 18.26 *Eumegastigmus* Hussey (1 sp., *E. transvaalensis* Hussey)]

Fig. 25.19. (*U.S. Dept. of Agric.*)

Subfamily **Podagrioninae**

Members of this subfamily are parasitic on mantid eggs.

[18.27 *Podagrion* Spinola (4 spp.)]

[Unplaced taxa]

One species.

19. PTEROMALIDAE (Pteromalid Wasp Family)

Length: 1–8 mm. Body black, metallic blue, or metallic green. Features diverse, some (Perilampinae) having thorax with large punctures; abdomen small; hind coxae not enlarged; hind femora not toothed; tarsi with five tarsomers. This is the largest family of the superfamily. Most species are parasitic and some are hyperparasites; a few are gall makers; and a few are phytophagous. Some are known to prey as larvae on the eggs or larvae found in stems of grasses and other plants. There are 395 species in the U.S. and Canada.

Subfamily **Ormyrinae**

[19.1 *Monobaeus* Foerster (1 sp., *M. hegeli* Girault); 19.2 *Ormyrus* Westwood (12 spp.)]

Subfamily **Perilampinae**

[19.3 *Euperilampus* Walker (2 spp.)]

19.4 *Perilampus* Latreille

Twenty-four species, including the following:

P. hyalinus Say. L. ±5 mm. Bluish; legs greenish-golden, tarsi brownish. Visits goldenrod in the late summer. Larvae are hyperparasites of the parasites of Lepidoptera and a variety of flies and parasitic wasps. (1), (2), (3), (4), (5), generally distributed.

[19.5 *Chrysolampus* Spinola (5 spp.)]

Subfamily **Brachyscelidiphaginae**

19.6 *Hemadas* Crawford

One species, as follows:

H. nubilipennis (Ashmead). Produces stem galls on *Vaccinium* spp.

Subfamily **Eutrichosomatinae**

[19.7 *Eutrichosoma* Ashmead (1 sp., *E. mirabile* Ashmead)]

Subfamily **Cleonyminae**

Tribe **Cleonymini**

[19.8 *Heydenia* Foerster (1 sp., *H. unica* Cook and Davis); 19.9 *Cleonymus* Latreille (2 spp.)]

Tribe **Chalcedectini**

[19.10 *Chalcedectus* Walker (1 sp., *C. texanus* Brues); 19.11 *Euchrysia* Westwood (3 spp.)]

Tribe **Trigonoderini**

[19.12 *Epistenia* Westwood (6 spp.); 19.13 *Ptinobius* Ashmead (5 spp.); 19.14 *Platygerrhus* Thomson (2 spp.); 19.15 *Plutothrix* Foerster (1 sp., *P. unguttus* (Girault)); 19.16 *Trigonoderus* Westwood (3 spp.); 19.17 *Ogloblinisca* Hedqvist (1 sp., *O. americana* Hedqvist); 19.18 *Janssoniella* Kerrich (2 spp.); 19.19 *Gastracanthus* Westwood (1 sp., *G. conicus* (Girault))]

Subfamily Colotrechninae

[19.20 *Colotrechnus* Thomson, subgenus *Zanonia* Masi (1 sp., *C. ignotus* Burks)]

Subfamily Macromesinae

[19.21 *Macromesus* Walker (1 sp., *M. americanus* Hedqvist)]

Subfamily Spalangiinae

[19.22 *Spalangia* Latreille (9 spp.)]

Subfamily Cerocephalinae

[19.23 *Choetospila* Westwood (1 sp., *C. elegans* Westwood); 19.24 *Choetospilisca* Hedqvist (1 sp., *C. tabida* (Gahan)); 19.25 *Cerocephala* Westwood (2 spp.); 19.26 *Acerocephala* Gahan (2 spp.); 19.27 *Theocolaxia* Girault (2 spp.)]

Subfamily Diparinae

[19.28 *Dipara* Walker (2 spp.); 19.29 *Spalangiolaelaps* Girault (1 sp., *S. argenticoxa* Girault); 19.30 *Trimicrops* Kieffer (1 undescribed sp.)]

Subfamily Eunotinae

[19.31 *Moranila* Cameron (1 sp., *M. californica* (Howard)); 19.32 *Eunotus* Walker (3 spp.); 19.33 *Mesopeltita* Ghesquiere (1 sp., *M. atrocyanea* (Masi)); 19.34 *Scutellista* Motschulsky (1 sp., *S. cyanea* Motschulsky); 19.35 *Tomocerodes* Girault (1 sp., *T. americana* Girault)]

Subfamily Asphinae

[19.36 *Asaphes* Walker (4 spp.); 19.37 *Bairamlia* Waterston (1 sp., *B. marylandensis* (Girault)); 19.38 *Hyperimerus* Girault (1 sp., *H. corvus* Girault)]

Subfamily Panstenoninae

[19.39 *Panstenon* Walker (1 sp., *P. columbianum* Ashmead); 19.40 *Brachycaudonia* Ashmead (1 sp., *B. californica* Ashmead)]

Subfamily Miscogasterinae

Tribe Sphegigasterini

[19.41 *Sphegigaster* Spinola (2 spp.); 19.42 *Syntomopus* Walker (2 spp.); 19.43 *Cyrtogaster* Walker (2 spp.); 19.44 *Lophocomodia* Ashmead (1 sp., *L. americana* Ashmead)]

Tribe Miscogasterini

[19.45 *Halticoptera* Spinola (5 spp.); 19.46 *Merismus* Walker (1 sp., *M. rufipes* Walker); 19.47 *Seladerma* Walker (1 sp., *S. diaeus* (Walker)); 19.48 *Bubekia* Dalla Tore (4 spp.); 19.49 *Paracarotomus* Ashmead (1 sp., *P. cephalotes* Ashmead); 19.50 *Miscogaster* Walker (8 spp.); 19.51 *Lamprotatus* Westwood (3 spp.)]

Tribe Ormocerini

[19.52 *Elachertodomyia* Girault (1 sp., *E. phloeotribi* (Ashmead); 19.53 *Ormocerus* Walker (2 spp.); 19.54 *Parasyntomocera* Girault (1 sp., *P. hillmedia* Girault); 19.55 *Erixestus* Crawford (1 sp., *E. winnemana* Crawford); 19.56 *Systasis* Walker (2 spp.); 19.57 *Gastrancistrus* Westwood (13 spp.)]

Tribe Pirenini

[19.58 *Pirene* Haliday (2 spp.); 19.59 *Spathopus* Ashmead (1 sp., *S. anomalipes* Ashmead); 19.60 *Herbertia* Howard (1 sp., *H. wallacei* Burks); 19.61 *Dipachystigma* Crawford (2 spp.); 19.62 *Morodora* Gahan (1 sp., *M. armata* Gahan); 19.63 *Parecrizotes* Girault (1 sp., *P. marylandensis* Girault); 19.64 *Stigmatocrepis* Ashmead (1 sp., *americana* Ashmead)]

Subfamily Pteromalinae

Tribe Cratomini

[19.65 *Cratomus* Dalman (3 spp.)]

Tribe Pachyneurini

[19.66 *Coruna* Walker (1 sp., *C. clavata* Walker); *19.67 Euneura* Walker (1 sp., *E. lachni* (Ashmead)); 19.68 *Pachyneuron* Walker (13 spp.); 19.69 *Pachycrepoideus* Ashmead (1 sp., *P. vindemiae* (Rondani))]

Tribe Rhaphitelini

[19.70 *Rhaphitelus* Walker (1 sp., *R. maculatus* Walker) 19.71 *Metacolus* Foerster (2 spp.)]

Tribe Pteromalini

[19.72 *Dinotiscus* Ghesquiére (6 spp.); 19.73 *Rhopalicus* Foerster (2 spp.); 19.74 *Cheiropachus* Westwood (4 spp.); 19.75 *Habritys* Thomson (2 spp.); 19.76 *Acaenacis* Girault (1 sp., *A. lausus* (Walker)); 19.77 *Megatrydymus* Girault (2 spp.); 19.78 *Perniphora* Ruschka (1 sp., *P. americana* Miller); 19.79 *Oxysychus* Delucchi (3 spp.); 19.80 *Anisopteromalus* Ruschka (1 sp., *A. calandrae* (Howard); 19.81 *Dinarmus* Thomson (2 spp.); 19.82 *Norbanus* Walker (3 spp.); 19.83 *Homoporus* Thomson (12 spp.); 19.84 *Callitula* Spinola (2 spp.); 19.85 *Psilocera* (2 spp.); 19.86 *Catolaccus* Thomson (7 spp.); 19.87 *Entomychobius* Ashmead (1 sp., *E. flavipes* Ashmead); 19.88 *Psychophagus* Mayr (2 spp.); 19.89 *Capellia* Delucchi (2 spp.); 19.90 *Sceptrothelys* (3 spp.); 19.91 *Pteromalus* Swederus (11 spp.); 19.92 *Habrocytus* Thomson (29 spp., including *H. cerealellae* (Ashmead) (Fig. 25.20)); 19.93 *Lonchetron* Graham (1 sp., *L. giraulti* (Peck); 19.94 *Belonura* Ashmead (1 sp., *B. singularis* Ashmead); 19.95 *Caenacis* Foerster (2 spp.); 19.96 *Psilonotus* Walker (1 sp., *P. achaeus* Walker); 19.97 *Karpinskiella* Boucek (1 sp., *K. paratomicobia* Hagen and Caltagirone); 19.98 *Mesopolobus* Westwood (15 spp.); 19.99 *Meraporus* Walker (1 sp., *M. requisitus* Tucker); 19.100 *Pseudocatolaccus* Masi (1 sp., *P. americanus* Gahan); 19.101 *Peridesmia* Foerster (1 sp., *P. discus* (Walker)); 19.102 *Spaniopus* Walker (2 spp.); 19.103 *Trichomalus* Thomson (6 spp.); 19.104 *Eupteromalus* Kurdjumov (10 spp.); 19.105 *Gyrinophagus* Ruschka (1 sp., *G. dineutis* (Ashmead)); 19.106 *Sisyridivora* Gahan (1 sp., *S. cavigena* Gahan); 19.107 *Nasonia* Ashmead (1 sp., *N. vitripennis* (Walker)); 19.108 *Urolepis* Walker (1 sp., *U. rufipes* (Ashmead)); 19.109 *Diglochis* Foerster (1 sp., *D. occidentalis* (Ashmead)); 19.110 *Tomicobia* Ashmead (2 spp.); 19.111 *Arthrolytus* Thomson (2 spp.); 19.112 *Cyclogastrella* Bukovskij (1 sp., *C. deplanata* (Nees)); 19.113 *Epipteromalus* Ashmead (1 sp., *E. algonquinensis* Ashmead); 19.114 *Tritneptis* Girault (6 spp.)]

Fig. 25.20. (*After Fulton*)

19.115 *Dibrachys* Foerster

This genus is divided into two subgenera, one of which, *Dibrachys* s. str., occurs in the U.S. and Canada. There are four species, the following of which is very common:

D. (Dibrachys) cavus (Walker). This species parasitizes an immense number of insects as a primary, secondary, or tertiary parasite. Cosmopolitan.

[19.116 *Dibrachoides* Kurdjumov (1 sp., *D. dynastes* (Forester)); 19.117 *Paradibrachys* Girault (1 sp., *P. guizoti* Girault); 19.118 *Neocatolaccus* Ashmead (3 spp.); 19.119 *Hypopteromalus* Ashmead (3 spp.); 19.120 *Heteroschema* Gahan (3 spp.); 19.121 *Schizonotus* Ratzeburg (2 spp.); 19.122 *Coelopisthia* Foerster (5 spp.); 19.123 *Muscidifurax* Girault and Sanders (2 spp.); 19.124 *Lariophagus* Crawford (3 spp.); 19.125 *Systellogaster* Gahan (1 sp., *S. ovivora* Gahan); 19.126 *Trimeromicrus* Gahan (1 sp., *T. maculatus* Gahan); 19.127 *Zatropis* Crawford (14 spp.); 19.128 *Hemitrichus* Thomson (1 sp., *H. seniculus* (Nees)); 19.129 *Metastenus* Walker (1 sp., *M. townsendi* (Ashmead))]

20. EURYTOMIDAE (Seed Chalcid Family)

L. 1–4 mm. Hind coxae not enlarged; hind femur not toothed. Many of these insects are phytophagous; some are parasitic; some start as parasitic larvae but mature as phytophagous insects. There are 244 species, a number of which are of economic importance.

Subfamily Rileyinae

[20.1 *Macrorileya* Ashmead (1 sp., *M. oecanthi* (Ashmead); 20.2 *Rileya* Ashmead (9 spp.)]

Subfamily Harmolitinae

20.3 *Harmolita* Motschulsky

Sixty-three species, of which the following are pests:

H. grandis (Riley) (Wheat Strawworm).

H. hordei (Harris) (Barley Jointworm).

H. tritici (Fitch) (Wheat Jointworm). (See Fig. 25.21.)

[20.4 *Gahaniola* Erdos (2 spp.); 20.5 *Cathilaria* Burks (1 sp., *C. opuntiae* (Muesebeck)); 20.6 *Isosomodes* Ashmead (1 sp., *I. giganteus* (Ashmead); 20.7 *Systole* Walker (3 spp.)]

Subfamily Eudecatominae

[20.8 *Eudecatoma* Ashmead (43 spp.); 20.9 *Sycophila* Walker (1 sp., *S. butcheri* Burks)]

Subfamily Aximinae

[20.10 *Axima* Walker (1 sp., *A. zabriskiei* Howard); 20.11 *Bephratoides* Brues (2 spp.); 20.12 *Ipideurytoma* Boucek and Novicky (1 sp., *I. polygraphi* (Ashmead)); 20.13 *Chryseida* Spinola (2 spp.)]

Subfamily Heimbrinae

[20.14 *Heimbra* Cameron (1 sp., *H. opaca* (Ashmead)]

Subfamily Prodecatominae

[20.15 *Prodecatoma* Ashmead (2 spp.)]

20.16 *Bephratelloides* Girault

One species, as follows:

B. cubensis (Ashmead). Develops in seeds of *Annona* spp., including custard apple. (3) FL.

Fig. 25.21. (*U.S. Dept. of Agric.*)

Subfamily Eurytominae

[20.17 *Tenuipetiolus* Bugbee (4 spp.); 20.18 *Phylloxeroxenus* Ashmead (1 sp., *P. phylloxerae* (Ashmead)); 20.19 *Eurytomocharis* Ashmead (10 spp.)]

20.20 *Evoxysoma* Ashmead

Two species, of which the following is a pest:

E. vitis (Saunders) (Grape Seed Chalcid). Develops in seeds of wild and cultivated grapes and causes their fruits to wither.

20.21 *Bruchophagus* Ashmead

These insects develop in leguminous seeds and are not parasitic as the generic name implies. Eight species, the following of which are pests:

B. platypterus (Walker) (Clover Seed and Trefoil Seed Chalcid).

B. roddi (Gussakovsky) (Alfalfa Seed Chalcid).

20.22 *Eurytoma* Illiger

This genus is poorly known taxonomically. A few are phytophagus, some are parasitic, and some are both. There are 103 species, the following of which is a pest:

E. orchidearum (Westwood) (Orchidfly).

21. CHALCIDIDAE (Chalcidid Wasp Family)

L. 2–11 mm. Hind femora greatly enlarged and toothed; hind coxae much larger than front coxae; dark, sometimes with yellow or white markings. These are parasites of many Lepidoptera, Coleoptera, and Diptera, and some are hyperparasites of tachinid flies and ichneumonflies. There are 102 species in the U.S. and Canada.

Subfamily Haltichellinae

[21.1 *Haltichella* Spinola (3 spp.); 21.2 *Hockeria* Walker (5 spp.); 21.3 *Schwarzella* Ashmead (1 sp., *S. arizonensis* Ashmead); Unplaced taxa (1 sp.)]

Subfamily Dirhininae

[21.4 *Dirhinus* Dalman (3 spp.)]

Subfamily Chalcidinae

21.5 *Metadontia* Ashmead

One species, as follows:

M. amoena (Say). (See fig. 25.22). Parasite of the Lycaenid butterflies, *Calycopis cecrops* (Fabricius) and *Strymon melinus* Huebner.

Fig. 25.22. (*U.S. Dept. of Agric.*)

[21.6 *Chalcis* Fabricius (9 spp.); 21.7 *Spilochalcis* Thomson (38 spp.); 21.8 *Ceratosmicra* Ashmead (6 spp.)]

Subfamily Brachymeriinae

21.9 *Acanthochalcis* Cameron: 2 subgenera: *Acanthochalcis* s. str. (1 sp., *A. nigricans* Cameron) and *Belochalcis* Steffan (1 sp., *A. unispinosa* Girault); 21.10 *Phasgonophora* Westwood (1 sp., *P. sulcata* Westwood); 21.11 *Trigonura* Sichel (7 spp.); 21.12 *Brachymeria* Westwood: 3 subgenera: *Brachymeria* s. str. (18 spp.), *Gahanula* Burks (2 spp.), and *Pseudobrachymeria* Burks (6 spp.)]

22. LEUCOSPIDAE (Leucospid Wasp Family)

Length: 2.3–16.5 mm. Hind femora greatly enlarged; hind coxae much larger than front coxae; black, often marked with yellow; front wings fold lengthwise; female with ovipositor curved upward and anteriorly over the abdomen. These are primary parasites of aculeate Hymenoptera. There are five species in the U.S. and Canada.

22.1 *Leucospis* Fabricius

Five species, including the following:

L. affinis affinis Say. L. 4–12 mm. Head tinged with green or purple; prothorax marked with yellow; body black. Adults visit umbelliferous flowers throughout the summer. Larvae are parasites of Megachiline bees. (1), (2), (3), (4), (5), generally distributed.

23. EUCHARITIDAE (Eucharitid Wasp Family)

Length: 2–4 mm. Black or iridescent green; thorax humpbacked, a few with scutellum extending back over abdomen; abdomen attached very low on thorax. Eggs are laid on leaves where the newly hatched larvae attach themselves to a passing ant and ride to its nest, where they parasitize the ant pupae. Twenty-eight species, nearly all southern in distribution.

Subfamily Oraseminae

[23.1 *Orasema* Cameron (16 spp.)]

Subfamily Eucharitinae

[23.2 *Pseudochalcura* Ashmead (3 spp.); 23.3 *Stilbula* Spinola (3 spp.); 23.4 *Lophyrocera* Cameron (2 spp.); 23.5 *Kapala* Cameron (2 spp.); 23.6 *Pseudometagea* Ashmead (2 spp.)]

24. EUPELMIDAE (Eupelmid Wasp Family)

Length: 2–5 mm. Black to brownish; body elongate; margin of prepectus projecting over margin of metepisternum; front and middle coxae widely separated; middle coxae may

rotate either anteriorly or posteriorly. There are 95 species in the U.S. and Canada.

Subfamily Tanaostigmatinae

[24.1 *Tanaostigmodes* Ashmead (4 spp.); 24.2 *Calosota* Curtis (2 spp.); 24.3 *Eusandalum* Ratzeburg (11 spp.)]

Subfamily Eupeliminae

[24.4 *Metapelma* Westwood (2 spp.)]

24.5 *Eupelmus* Dalman

Thirty-eight species, including the following:

E. allyni (French). A parasite of many insects, including the Hessian Fly and other pests. (1), (2), (3), (4), (5), generally distributed.

[24.6 *Arachnophaga* Ashmead (10 spp.); 24.7 *Eupelmella* Masi (4 spp.); 24.8 *Merostenus* Walker (1 sp., *M. excavatus* Dalman); 24.9 *Anastatus* Motschulsky (15 spp.); 24.10 *Phlebopenes* Perty (2 spp.); 24.11 *Zaischnopsis* Ashmead (1 sp., *Z. schwarzii* (Ashmead)); 24.12 *Encyrtaspis* Ashmead (3 spp.); 24.13 *Lecaniobius* Ashmead (3 spp.)]

25. ENCYRTIDAE (Encyrtid Wasp Family)

Length: 1–2 mm. Some species are gallmakers; others are parasitic on snout beetles, Homoptera, and other insects. A few species are polyembryonic, producing several to over 1,000 individuals from a single egg. There are 509 species in the U.S. and Canada.

Subfamily Aphelininae

Tribe Aphelinini

25.1 *Aphelinus* Dalman

These are internal parasites of aphids, some of which are used in the biological control of the latter. There are 17 species in the U.S. and Canada, including the following:

A. lapisligni Howard (Clover Aphid Parasite). (4) OR, ID.

A. mali (Haldeman). (See Fig. 25.23.)

[25.2 *Aphytis* Howard (20 spp.); 25.3 *Centrodora* Foerster (1 sp., *C. speciosissima* (Girault)); 25.4 *Marietta* Motschulsky (5 spp.); 25.5 *Marlattiella* Howard (1 sp., *M. prima* Howard); 25.6 *Mesidia* Foerster (2 spp.); 25.7 *Tumidiscapus* Girault (4 spp.)]

Tribe Coccophagini

25.8 *Ablerus* Howard (3 spp.); 25.9 *Aneristus* Howard (2 spp.); 25.10 *Aspidiotiphagus* Howard (3 spp.); 25.11 *Azotus* Howard (2 spp.); 25.12 *Coccophagoides* Girault (4 spp.); 25.13 *Coccophagus* Westwood (31 spp.); 25.14 *Encarsia* Foerster (9 spp.); 25.15 *Lounsburyia* Compere and Annecke (1 sp., *L. trifasciata* (Compere)); 25.16 *Physcus* Howard (6 spp.); 25.17 *Prospaltella* Ashmead (15 spp.)]

Fig. 25.23. (*After Lundie*)

Tribe Eriaporini

[25.18 *Myiocnema* Ashmead (1 sp., *M. comperei* Ashmead)]

Tribe Pteroptricini

[25.19 *Archenomus* Howard (2 spp.); 25.20 *Eretmocerus* Haldeman (5 spp.)]

Subfamily Signiphorinae
Tribe Signiphorini

[25.21 *Signiphora* Ashmead (13 spp.)]

Tribe Thysanini

[25.22 *Chartocerus* Motschulsky (8 spp.); 25.23 *Thysanus* Walker (1 sp., *T. ater* Haliday)]

Subfamily Tetracneminae
Tribe Anagyrini

[25.24 *Anagyrus* Howard (13 spp.); 25.25 *Anathrix* Burks (F1 sp., *A. argyrus* Burks); 25.26 *Anusia* Foerster (1 sp., *A. neomexicana* Ashmead); 25.27 *Apoanagyrus* Compere (f1 sp., *A. californicus* Compere); 25.28 *Leptomastidea* Mercet (2 spp.); 25.29 *Leptomastix* Foerster (1 sp., *L. dactylopii* Howard); 25.30 *Paranusia* Brethes (1 unidentified sp.); 25.31 *Parastenoterys* Girault (1 sp., *P. niveiclava* Girault); 25.32 *Pseudleptomastix* Girault (1 sp., *P. squammulata* Girault); 25.33 *Rhopus* Foerster (2 spp.)]

Tribe Chrysoplatycerini

[25.34 *Chrysoplatycerus* Ashmead (3 spp.)]

Tribe Ericydnini

[25.35 *Clausenia* Ishii (1 sp., *C. purpurea* Ishii)]

Tribe Pauridiini

[25.36 *Pauridia* Timberlake (1 sp., *P. peregrina* Timberlake)]

Tribe Rhinoencyrtini

[25.37 *Rhinoencyrtus* Mercet (1 unidentified sp.); 25.38 *Aenasius* Walker (6 spp.); 25.39 *Chalcaspis* Howard (3 spp.)]

Tribe Tetracnemini

[25.40 *Calcocerinus* Howard (1 sp., *C. floridanus* (Ashmead)); 25.41 *Arhopoideus* Girault (2 spp.); 25.42 *Tetracnemus* Westwood (5 spp.); 25.43 *Anarhopus* Timberlake (1 sp., *A. sydneyensis* Timberlake); [Unplaced taxa follow:] 25.44 *Cirrhencyrtus* Timberlake (1 sp., *C. ehrhorni* (Timberlake); 25.45 *Ectromatopsis* Compere (1 sp., *E. americana* (Howard)); 25.46 *Neodusmetia* Kerrich (1 sp., *N. sangwani* (Subba Rao)); 25.47 *Paraleurocerus* Girault (1 sp., *P. bicoloripes* Girault); 25.48 *Tetracnemopsis* Ashmead (1 sp., *T. westwoodi* (Cockerell))]

Subfamily Encyrtinae
Tribe Aphycini

[25.49 *Acerophagus* (10 spp.); 25.50 *Aenasioidea* Girault (6 spp.); 25.51 *Aphycus* Mayr (8 spp.); 25.52 *Blastothrix* Mayr (4 spp.); 25.53 *Bothriocraera* Timberlake (2 spp.); 25.54 *Erythraphycus* Compere (3 spp.); 25.55 *Melanaphycus* Compere (3 spp.); 25.56 *Metaphycus* Mercet (29 spp.); 25.57 *Pseudaphycus* Clausen (12 spp.); 25.58 *Stemmatosteres* Timberlake (2 spp.); 25.59 *Tachardiobius* Timberlake (1 sp., *T. nigricans* Timberlake); 25.60 *Timberlakia* Mercet (1 sp., *T. europaea* (Mercet))]

Tribe Arrhenophagini

[25.61 *Arrhenophagus* Aurivillius (1 sp., *A. chionaspidis* Aurivillius)]

Tribe Bothriothoracini

[25.62 *Bothriothorax* Ratzeburg (8 spp.); 25.63 *Trjapitzinellus* Viggiani (1 sp., *T. microrphanos* Gordh); 25.64 *Zeteticontus* Silvestri (1 sp., *Z. insularis* (Howard))]

Tribe Cerapterocerini

[25.65 *Ammonoencyrtus* De Santis (1 sp., *A. californicus* (Compere)); 25.66 *Anicetus* Howard (2 spp.); 25.67 *Cerapterocerus* Westwood (1 sp., *C. floridanus* Ashmead); 25.68 *Eusemion* Dahlbom (1 sp., *E. longipennis* (Ashmead))]

Tribe Chalcerinyini

[25.69 *Echthrogonatopus* Perkins (1 sp., *E. pachycephalus* Perkins); 25.70 *Helegonatopus* Perkins (1 sp., *H. pseudophanes* Perkins)]

Tribe Cheiloneurini

[25.71 *Apterencyrtus* Ashmead (1 sp., *A. microphagus* (Mayr)); 25.72 *Boucekiella* Hoffer (1 sp., *B. depressa* Hoffer); 25.73 *Cheiloneurus* Westwood (11 spp.); 25.74 *Chrysopophagus* Ashmead (5 spp.); 25.75 *Diversinervus* Silvestri (1 sp., *D. elegans* Silvestri); 25.76 *Parasyrpophagus* Girault (1 undescribed sp.); 25.77 *Prochiloneurus* Silvestri (3 spp.); 25.78 *Tineophoctonus* Ashmead (2 spp.); 25.79 *Tyndarichus* Howard (1 unidentified sp.)]

Tribe Comperiini

[25.80 *Comperia* Gomes (1 sp., *C. merceti* (Compere))]

Tribe Copidosomatini

[25.81 *Ageniaspis* Dahlbom (1 sp., *A. bucculatricis* (Howard)); 25.82 *Coelopencyrtus* Timberlake (2 spp.); 25.83 *Copidosoma* Ratzeburg (11 spp.); 25.84 *Parablastothrix* Mercet (1 sp., *P. nearctica* Miller); 25.85 *Paralitomastix* Mercet (1 sp., *P. pyralidis* (Ashmead)); 25.86 *Pentalitomastix* Eady (1 sp., *P. plethoricus* Caltagirone); 25.87 *Pentacnemus* Howard (1 sp., *P. bucculatricis* Howard)]

Tribe Discodini

[25.88 *Discodes* Foerster (2 spp.)]

Tribe Encyrtini

[25.89 *Encyrtus* Latreille (16 spp.)]

Tribe Habrolepidini

[25.90 *Adelencyrtus* Ashmead (2 spp.); 25.91 *Anabrolepis* Timberlake (1 sp., *A. zetterstedtii* (Westwood)); 25.92 *Coccidencyrtus* Ashmead (2 spp.); 25.93 *Comperiella* Howard (1 sp., *C. bifasciata* Howard); 25.94 *Habrolepis* Foerster (2 spp.); 25.95 *Neococcidencyrtus* Compere (1 sp., *N. poutiersi* (Mercet)); 25.96 *Plagiomerus* Crawford (2 spp.); 25.97 *Pseudhomalopoda* Girault (1 sp., *P. prima* Girault)]

Tribe Homalotylini

[25.98 *Anisotylus* Timberlake (4 spp.); 25.99 *Homalotylus* Mayr (13 spp.); 25.100 *Isodromus* Howard (5 spp.)]

Tribe Ixodiphagini

[25.101 *Hunterellus* Howard (1 sp., *H. hookeri* Howard); 25.102 *Ixodiphagus* Howard (1 sp., *I. texanus* Howard)]

Tribe Microteryini

[25.103 *Agromyzaphagus* Gahan (1 sp., *A. detrimentosus* Gahan); 25.104 *Aphidencyrtus* Ashmead (2 spp.); 24.105 *Avetianella* Trjapitzin

(1 unidentified sp.); 25.106 *Cerchysius* Westwood (4 spp.); 25.107 *Microterys* Thomson (20 spp.); 25.108 *Oobius* Trajapitzin (1 unidentified sp.); 25.109 *Ooencyrtus* Ashmead (8 spp.); 25.110 *Platencyrtus* Ferrière (1 sp., *P. parkeri* Ferrière); 25.111 *Pseudencyrtus* Ashmead (3 spp.); 25.112 *Pseudencyrtoides* Gordh and Trjapitzin (1 sp., *P. cupressi* Gordh and Trjapitzin); 25.113 *Syrphophagus* Ashmead (2 spp.); 25.114 *Tachinaephagus* Ashmead (1 sp., *T. zealandicus* Ashmead); 25.115 *Trichomasthus* Thomson (5 spp.)]

Tribe Miraini

[25.116 *Baeocharis* Mayr (3 spp.); 25.117 *Mayridia* Mercet (2 spp.); 25.118 *Mira* Schellenberg (1 sp., *M. macrocera* Schellenberg)]

Tribe Neocladini

[25.119 *Carabunia* Waterston (1 sp., *C. myersi* Waterston); 25.120 *Zarhopalus* Ashmead (3 spp.)]

Tribe Prionomasticini

[25.121 *Hexacladia* Ashmead (2 spp.)]

Tribe Pseudorhopini

[25.122 *Pseudorhopus* Timberlake (2 spp.)]

Tribe Psilophrydini

[25.123 *Psilophrys* Mayr (F1 sp., *P. armata* Ashmead)]

Tribe Thomsoniscini

[25.124 *Quaylea* Timberlake (1 sp., *Q. whittieri* (Girault))]

Tribe Trechnitini

[25.125 *Prionomitus* Mayr (2 spp.); 25.126 *Psyllaephagus* Ashmead (4 spp.); 25.127 *Trechnites* Thomson (1 sp., *T. insidiosus* (Crawford)); [Unplaced taxa follow:] 25.128 *Atropates* Howard (1 sp., *A. collinsi* Howard); 25.129 *Aphycoideus* Williams (1 sp., *A. io* Williams); 25.130 *Blepyrus* Howard (2 spp.); 25.131 *Ceraptroceroideus* Girault (1 sp., *C. cinctipes* Girault); 25.132 *Chestomorpha* Ashmead (1 sp., *C. biformis* Ashmead); 25.133 *Epaenasomyia* Girault (1 sp., *E. varicornis* Girault); 25.134 *Forcipestricis* Burks (1 sp., *F. gazeaui* Burks); 25.135 *Gahaniella* Timberlake (2 spp.); 25.136 *Hexacnemus* Timberlake (1 sp., *H. armitagei* Timberlake); 25.137 *Caenocercus* Thomson (2 spp.); 25.138 *Epicerchysius* Girault (1 sp., *E. xanthipes* Girault); 25.139 *Formicencyrtus* Girault (1 sp., *F. thoreauini* Girault); 25.140 *Epanusia* Girault (2 spp.); 25.141 *Epiencyrtus* Ashmead (2 spp.); 25.142 *Euryhopalus* Howard (1 sp., *E. schwarzi* Howard); 25.143 *Habrolepopteryx* Ashmead (3 spp.); 24.144 *Habrolepoidea* Howard (3 spp.); 24.145 *Hambletonia* Compere (1 sp., *H. pseudococcina* Compere); 25.146 *Hemaenasius* Ashmead (1 sp., *H. confusus* Ashmead); 25.147 *Holcencyrtus* Ashmead (2 spp.); 25.148 *Henicopygus* Ashmead (1 sp., *H. subapterus* Ashmead); 25.149 *Meromyzobia* Ashmead (6 spp.); 25.150 *Nebaocharis* Girault (1 sp., *N. hemiptera* Girault); 25.151 *Paraphaenodiscus* Girault (1 sp., *P. subterraneus* Ferrière); 25.152 *Parapsilophrys* Howard (1 sp., *P. gelechiae* Howard); 25.153 *Pentelicus* Howard (1 sp., *P. aldrichi* Howard); 25.154 *Pheidoloxenus* Ashmead (1 sp., *P. wheeleri* Ashmead); 25.155 *Psilophryoidea* Compere (1 sp., *P. comesor* Compere); 25.156 *Rhytidothorax* Ashmead (1 sp., *R. marlatti* Ashmead); 25.157 *Tetralophiellus* Ashmead (1 sp., *T. brevicollis* Ashmead); 25.158 *Tetralophidea* Ashmead (1 sp., T. bakeri Ashmead); 25.159 *Thysanomastix* Perkins (1 sp., *T. koebelei* Perkins); 25.160 *Zaommoencyrtus* Girault (1 sp., *Z. submicans* Girault)]

26. EULOPHIDAE (Eulophid Wasp Family)

Length: 1–3 mm. A few species are important controls of scale insects; many others are parasitic on beetles, moths, and other insects. There are 507 species in the U.S. and Canada.

Subfamily Eulophinae

Tribe Eulophini

[26.1 *Pnigalio* Schrank (9 spp.); 26.2 *Sympiesis* Foerster (14 spp.); 26.3 *Necremnus* Thomson (7 spp.); 26.4 *Hemiptarsenus* Westwood (1 sp., *H. americanus* (Girault)); 26.5 *Pardiaulomella* Girault (1 sp., *P. ibseni* Girault); 26.6 *Diaulomorpha* Ashmead (1 sp., *borrowi* (Girault)); 26.7 *Diglyphus* Walker (4 spp.); 26.8 *Notanisomorpha* Ashmead (8 spp.); 26.9 *Eulophus* Olivier (9 spp.); 26.10 *Dahlbominus* Hincks (1 sp., *D. fuscipennis* (Zetterredt)); 26.11 *Dimmockia* Ashmead (3 spp.); 26.12 *Dicladocerus* Westwood (3 spp.)]

Tribe Euplectrini

26.13 *Euplectrus* Westwood

Thirteen species, including the following:

E. comstockii Howard. External parasites of moth caterpillars, they develop in about a week.

[26.14 *Euplectromorpha* Girault (1 sp., *E. americana* Girault)]

Tribe Elachertini

[26.15 *Diaulinopsis* Crawford (2 spp.); 26.16 *Ardalus* Howard (1 sp., *A. insuetus* (Gahan)); 26.17 *Paraolinx* Ashmead (3 spp.); 26.18 *Stenomesius* Westwood (2 spp.); 26.19 *Miotropis* Thomson (1 sp., *M. melleus* Ashmead); 26.20 *Elachertus* Spinola (13 spp.); 26.21 *Hyssopus* Girault (7 spp.); 26.22 *Pseudolynx* Girault (3 spp.); 26.23 *Mirolynx* Girault (1 sp., *M. flavitibiae* Girault); 26.24 *Grotiusomyia* Girault (1 sp., *G. flavicornis* Girault); 26.25 *Apterolophus* Gahan (1 sp., *A. pulchricornis* Gahan); 26.26 *Giraultia* Gahan and Fagan (3 spp.); 26.27 *Cirrospiloideus* Ashmead (8 spp.); 26.28 *Peckelachertus* Yoshimoto (1 sp., *P. diprioni* Yoshimoto); 26.29 *Cirrospilus* Westwood (20 sp.); 26.30 *Zagrammosoma* Ashmead (8 spp.); 26.31 *Mirzagrammosoma* Girault (1 sp., *M. lineaticeps* Girault); 26.32 *Aulogymnus* Foerster (1 sp., *A. minyas* (Walker)]

Subfamily Entedontinae

Tribe Euderini

[26.33 *Acrias* Walker (1 sp., *A. nileus* Walker); 26.34 *Euderus* Haliday (27 spp.); 26.35 *Astichus* Foerster (5 spp.)]

Tribe Tetrastichini

[26.36 *Ceratoneura* Ashmead (2 spp.); 26.37 *Paraspalangia* Ashmead (1 sp., *P. annulipes* Ashmead); 26.38 *Winnemana* Crawford (1 sp., *W. argei* Crawford); 26.39 *Thriposoma* Crawford (1 sp., *T. grafi* Crawford); 26.40 *Omphalomopsis* Girault (1 sp., *O. marilandia* Girault); 26.41 *Thymus* Girault (1 sp., *T. albocinctus* (Ashmead)); 26.42 *Prothymus* Girault (1 sp., *P. novus* Girault); 26.43 *Galeopsomyia* Girault (2 spp.); 26.44 *Paragaleopsomyia* Girault (2 spp.); 26.45 *Galeopsomopsis* Girault (2 spp.)]

26.46 *Tetrastichus* Haliday

There are 125 species in this genus, including the following:

T. asparagi Crawford. Although several larvae of this wasp may parasitize eggs of the Asparagus Beetle, this does not prevent the eggs from hatching. The wasp parasites then parasitize the larvae of the Asparagus Beetle until the latter make a pupal cell. The parasites then pupate and finally emerge as adults.

[26.47 *Aprostocetus* Westwood (16 spp.); 26.48 *Hypertetrastichus* Moser (1 sp., *H. ithacus* Moser); 26.49 *Crataepus* Foerster (1 sp., *C. marbis* (Walker)); 26.50 *Burksia* Fullaway (1 sp., *B. viridimaculata* Fullaway); 26.51 *Flockiella* Timberlake (1 sp., *F. eucalypti* Timber-

lake); 26.52 *Syntomosphyrum* Foerster (8 spp.); 26.53 *Melittobia* Westwood (2 spp.)]

Tribe Entedontini

[26.54 *Euderomphale* Girault (3 spp.); 26.55 *Ceranisus* Walker (3 spp.); 26.56 *Euophthalmomyia* Ashmead (1 sp., *E. pallidipes* Ashmead); 26.57 *Omphale* Haliday (1 sp., *O. bicincta* Ashmead); 26.58 *Hubbardiella* Ashmead (1 sp., *H. arizonensis* Ashmead); 26.59 *Closterocerus* Westwood (8 spp.); 26.60 *Eprhopalotus* Girault (1 sp., *E. purpureithorax* Girault); 26.61 *Emersonella* Girault (2 spp.); 26.62 *Chrysocharis* Foerster (15 spp.); 26.63 *Neochrysocharis* Kurdjumov (1 sp., *N. imbrasus* (Walker)); 26.64 *Enaysma* Delucchi, subgenus *Pentenaysma* Graham (6 spp.); 25.65 *Moserina* Delucchi (1 sp., *M. maculata* Delucchi); 26.66 *Achrysocharoides* Girault (3 spp.); 26.67 *Rhicnopeltomyia* Girault (7 spp.); 26.68 *Rhicnopeltoidea* Girault (1 sp., *R. amsterdamensis* Girault); 26.69 *Carlyleia* Girault (1 sp., *C. marilandica* Girault); 26.70 *Chrysocharomyia* Girault (5 spp.); 26.71 *Hoplocrepis* Ashmead (1 sp., *H. albiclavus* Ashmead); 26.72 *Parachrysocharis* Girault (1 sp., *P. semiflava* Girault); 26.73 *Achrysocharis* Girault (7 spp.); 26.74 *Achrysocharella* Girault (16 spp.); 26.75 *Lophocomus* Haliday (1 sp., *L. verticillatus* Ashmead); 26.76 *Horismenus* Walker (15 spp.); 26.77 *Pediobius* Walker (24 spp.); 26.78 *Entedon* Dalman (8 spp.); 26.79 *Paracrias* Ashmead (1 sp., *mirus* (Girault)); 26.80 *Chrysonotomyia* Ashmead (1 sp., *C. auripunctata* (Ashmead)); 26.81 *Emersonopsis* Girault (2 spp.); 26.82 *Nesomyia* Ashmead (1 sp., *N. cimbicis* Brues)]

Subfamily Elasminae

[26.83 *Elasmus* Westwood (16 spp.)]

27. MYMARIDAE (Fairyfly Family)

L. 0.21 to 1 mm. These minute insects, probably the smallest of all, are egg parasites. There are 120 species in the U.S. and Canada.

Subfamily Alaptinae

Tribe Anagrini

[27.1 *Anagrus* Haliday (8 spp.); 27.2 *Stethynium* Enock (2 spp.)]

Tribe Alaptini

[27.3 *Alaptus* Westwood (7 spp.); 27.4 *Dicopus* Enock (1 sp., *D. halitus* Girault)]

Subfamily Mymarinae

Tribe Ooctonini

[27.5 *Arescon* Walker (1 sp., *A. aspidioticola* (Ashmead)); 27.6 *Gonatocerus* Nees (27 spp.); 27.7 *Cosmocomoidea* Howard (1 sp., *C. morrilli* Howard); 27.8 *Ooctonus* Haliday (8 spp.); 27.9 *Camptoptera* Foerster (3 spp.)]

Tribe Anaphini

[27.10 *Parallelaptera* Enock (1 sp., *P. rex* (Girault)); 27.11 *Erythmelus* Enock (7 spp.); 27.12 *Anaphes* Haliday (12 spp.); 27.13 *Paracleruchus* Enock (1 sp., *P. pieloui* (Yoshimoto)]

27.14 *Patasson* Walker

Nine species, including the following:

P. conotracheli (Girault). This is an egg parasite of the pest weevil *Conotrachelus nenuphar* (Herbst) and other species.

Tribe Mymarini

[27.15 *Mymar* Curtis (2 spp.); 27.16 *Neomymar* Crawford (1 sp., *N. vierecki* Crawford)]

27.17 *Caraphractus* Walker

One species, as follows:

C. cinctus Walker. This minute wasp hunts the eggs of the water beetle (*Dytiscus* spp.), swimming rapidly under water with its pecular, paddle-shaped wings, and lays its eggs in the water bug eggs, which the wasp larvae then parasitize.

[27.18 *Acmopolynema* Ogloblin (7 spp.); 27.19 *Barypolynema* Ogloblin (3 spp.); 27.20 *Stephanodes* Enock (1 sp., *S. psecas* (Girault)); 27.21 *Polynema* Haliday (23 spp.)]

28. TRICHOGRAMMATIDAE (Trichogrammatid Wasp Family)

L. 0.25–1 mm. These are egg parasites of other insects, some of them being reared in large numbers to control the latter. There are 43 species in the U.S. and Canada.

[28.1 *Oligosita* Walker (7 spp.); 28.2 *Megaphragma* Timberlake (1 sp., *M. mymaripenne* Timberlake); 28.3 *Hydrophylita* Ghesquière (1 sp., *H. aquivolans* (Matheson and Crosby)); 28.4 *Paracentrobia* Howard (9 spp.); 28.5 *Ufens* Girault (3 spp.); 28.6 *Brachyufens* Viggiani (1 sp., *B. osborni* (Dozier); 28.7 *Zagella* Girault (1 sp., *Z. flavipes* (Girault))]

28.8 *Trichogramma* Westwood

Eight species, including the following:

T. minutum Riley (Minute Egg Parasite). Actually this is a complex of species that are reared to control a number of insect pests.

T. evanescens Westwood. (See Fig. 25.24.)

[Unplaced species of *Trichogramma* (6 spp.)]

[28.9 *Trichogrammatomyia* Girault (1 sp., *T. tortricis* Girault); 28.10 *Poropoea* Foerster (1 sp., *P. attelaborum* Girault); 28.11 *Xenufens* Girault (1 sp., *X. ruskini* Girault); 28.12 *Giraultiola* Nowicki (1 sp., *G. fidiae* (Ashmead)); 28.13 *Tumidiclava* Girault (1 sp., *T. pulchrinotum* Girault); 28.14 *Zaga* Girault (1 sp., *Z. latipennis* Girault); 28.15 *Aphelinoidea* Girault (3 spp.); 28.16 *Lathromeroidea* Girault (1 sp., *L. odonatae* (Ashmead)); 28.17 *Uscana* Girault (2 spp.); Unplaced taxa (20 spp.)]

Fig. 25.24. (*U.S. Dept. of Agric.*)

Superfamily CYNIPOIDEA

L. usually under 5 mm. Antennae usually with 13 segments in female and 14 to 15 in male; pronotum extends posteriorly to tegula; front wings with Costa vein and usually without a stigma; hind wings without an anal lobe; abdomen often laterally compressed, the visible part composed almost entirely of terga, the sterna small and concealed. Many species of this superfamily induce gall formation on plants of various kinds, including the common oak. A large number, however, are parasitic on dipterous larvae and other insects. All known eggs are stalked or pedicellate. The accompanying key will separate most species of Cynipoidea into the currently recognized six families.

Key to the Families of Cynipoidea
(Adapted from Arnold S. Menke, *in litt.*)

1. Parasitic species ... **2**
 Gall-inducing species ... **34. Cynipidae**
2(1). Scutellum surmounted by flat teardrop or nearly circular-shaped plate with dimplelike posterior depression ... **32. Eucoilidae**
 Scutellum without elevated flat plate .. **3**
3(2). Hind tarsi with basal tarsomere about twice combined length of tarsomeres 2 through 8; l. 8 mm or more ... **29. Ibaliidae**
 Hind tarsi with basal tarsomere much less than twice combined length of tarsomeres 2 through 5; l. usually less than 7 mm **4**
4(3). Front wing with closed submarginal cell; first two terga of gaster much smaller than third tergum. ... **30. Liopteridae**
 Front wing with submarginal cell open behind; abdomen usually sessile, or if petiolate, then only first tergum small, or first two largest, or first three terga of nearly equal size **5**
5(4). Scutellum rounded (globuse), smooth, usually polished, not margined and without pair of large foveae or pits at base, or if pits present, mesopleuron with horizontal sulcus; l. 2 mm or less .. **33. Charipidae**
 Scutellum variable, but if rounded, then surface rugose, scutellum often margined laterally, sometimes acuminate or with a process apically, always with a pair of large foveae or pits at base; l. often more than 2 mm **31. Figitidae**

29. IBALIIDAE (Ibaliid Wasp Family)

L. 8–16 mm. Abdomen usually red or orange; head and thorax may be extensively orange; wings sometimes banded; abdomen laterally compressed, knifelike. These wasps are parasitic on horntails (Siricidae). Six species occur in the U.S. and Canada.

Subfamily Ibaliinae

29.1 *Ibalia* Latreille

I. scapellator Westwood. A parasite on *Tremex columba* (Linnaeus). L ±14 mm; body mostly yellow. (See Fig. 25.25 for leg structures.) (1) n.e. NA.

30. LIOPTERIDAE (Liopterid Wasp Family)

L. 5–12 mm. Head and thorax very coarsely sculptured; gaster and sometimes entire body reddish; antennae with 14 segments in male and 13 in female; wings often banded, the front wing with submarginal cell usually complete; abdomen with sulcate petiole and tangentially attached to top edge of gaster. Their biology is unknown. Three rare species occur in the U.S. as follows:

Fig. 25.25.

Subfamily Mesocynipinae

[30.1 *Paramblynotus* Cameron (1 sp., *P. zonatus* Weld, (3) TX); 30.2 *Kiefferiella* Ashmead (2 spp., *K. acmaeodera* Weld, (4) ID), and *K. rugosa* (Ashmead); (3) CA)]

31. FIGITIDAE (Figitid Wasp Family)

L. 3–6 mm. Antennae of female with 13 segments, of male with 14 segments; front wing sometimes folds longitudinally; remnant of a posterior veinlet of first submarginal cell present, often only as a crease or fold; second tergum of gaster of female larger than other terga; mesopleuron coarsely sculptured, at least across middle; scutellum sometimes with a posterior spine. These insects (Anacharitinae) are parasites of lacewings, diptera larvae (such as muscoid flies in rotting meat or dung), and predacious Syrphidae and Chamaemyiidae. There are 60 species in the U.S. and Canada.

Subfamily Aspicerinae

[31.1 *Paraspicera* Kieffer (3 spp.); 31.2 *Prosaspicera* Kieffer (2 spp.); 31.3 *Omalaspis* Giraud (1 sp., *O. nigra* (Hartig)); 31.4 *Callaspidia* Dahlbom (1 sp., *C. provancheri* Ashmead)]

Subfamily Anacharitinae

[31.5 *Xyalaspis* Hartig (2 spp.); 31.6 *Acothyreus* Ashmead (2 spp.); 31.7 *Anacharis* Dalman (9 spp.); 31.8 *Hexacharis* Kieffer (1 sp., *H. flavipes* Kieffer); 31.9 *Aegilips* Walker (8 spp.)]

Subfamily Figitinae

[31.10 *Neralsia* Cameron (3 spp.)]

31.11 *Xyalophora* Kieffer

Three species, including the following:

X. quinquelineata (Say). A parasite of *Sarcophaga* spp. (1), (2), (3), (4), (5), generally distributed.

[31.12 *Paraschiza* Weld (1 sp., *P. cupressana* Weld); 31.13 *Lonchidia* Thomson (1 sp., *L. hirta* Provancher); 31.14 *Melanips* Walker (7 spp.); 31.15 *Sarothrus* Hartig (3 spp.); 31.16 *Trischiza* Foerster (2 spp.); 31.17 *Zygosis* Foerster (1 sp., *Z. laevicsutum* (Provancher)); 31.18 *Figites* Latreille (10 spp.)]

32. EUCOILIDAE (Eucoilid Wasp Family)

L. 0.8–5 mm; black or brown, sometimes with gaster and appendages pale colored; antennae of female with 13 segments, of male with 15 segments; raised, flat plate on scutellum (characteristic of family). There are 80 species in the U.S. and Canada.

[32.1 *Kleidotoma* Westwood: 4 subgenera: *Kleidotoma* s. str. (5 spp.), *Tetrarhoptra* Foerster (3 spp.), *Kleidotomidea* Rohwer and Fagan (1 sp., *K. californica* Kieffer), and *Heptameris* Foerster (4 spp.); unplaced species (3 spp.); 32.2 *Hexacola* Foerster (3 spp.); 32.3 *Eutrias* Foerster (1 sp., *E. tritoma* (Thomson))]

32.4 *Eucoila* Westwood

Nine species, the following of which are parasites of pests:

E. impatiens (Say). Parasites of dung fly larvae.

E. rufocincta (Kieffer). Parasites of maggots in cow dung and blow fly larvae in carrion. (3) s.e. US; (4) Pacific n.w.

[32.5 *Aporeucoela* Kieffer (2 spp.); 32.6 *Trybliographa* Foerster: 5 subgenera: *Tetraplasta* Ashmead (2 spp.), *Pentaplastidia* Weld (1 sp., *T. clarimontis* (Kieffer), *Didyctium* Riley (5 spp.), *Trybliographa* s. str. (4 spp.), *Macrocereucoila* Ashmead (1 sp., *T. ashmeadiana* (Dalla Torre and Kieffer)), and undetermined (6 spp.); 32.7 *Psichacra* Foerster (2 spp.); 32.8 *Ganaspis* Foerster (3 spp.); 32.9 *Ganaspidium* Weld (1 sp., *G. pusillae* Weld); 32.10 *Hypolethria* Foerster (1 sp., *H. vitellinipes* (Kieffer)); 32.11 *Rhoptromeris* Foerster (1 sp., *R. nigroclavata* (Kieffer)); 32.12 *Glauraspidia* Thomson (1 sp., *G. texana* Crawford); 32.13 *Pseudoeucoila* Ashmead: 2 subgenera: *Hexamerocera* Kieffer (3 spp.) and *Pseudoeucoila* s. str. (4 spp.); 32.14 *Cothonaspis* Hartig (2 spp.); 32.15 *Eucoilidea* Ashmead (6 spp.)]

33. CHARIPIDAE (Charipid Wasp Family)

[= Alloxystidae]

L. 2 mm or less. Body smooth; antennae of some species (33.1 *Lytoxysta*) with 13 segments in both sexes, or 13 in female and 14 in male. These are hyperparasites of braconid or chalcidoid primary parasites of aphids or psyllids (33.4 *Dilyta*). There are 31 species in the U.S. and Canada.

Subfamily Alloxystinae

[33.1 *Lytoxysta* Kieffer (2 spp.)]

33.2 *Alloxysta* Foerster

Twenty-five species, including the following:

A. brassicae (Ashmead). A hyperparasite of *Brevicornye brassicae* (Linnaeus). L. ±1.2 mm. (1), (2), (3), (4), (5).

[33.3 *Phaenoglyphis* Foerster (3 spp.)]

Subfamily Charipinae

[33.4 *Dilyta* Foerster (1 sp., *D. necans* (Kieffer)]

34. CYNIPIDAE (Gall Wasp Family)

L. 2–8 mm. First segment of hind tarsi about as long as following two or three combined; most species humpbacked; abdomen with two segments visible dorsally, the remainder telescoped beneath. These are plant-inhabiting wasps, mostly gall makers, but some are inquilines in galls. They are very difficult to identify. There are 636 species in the U.S. and Canada.

Subfamily Synerginae

[34.1 *Saphonecrus* Dalla Torre and Kieffer (4 spp.); 34.2 *Synergus* Haetig (52 spp.); 34.3 *Synophrus* Hartig (1 sp., *S. mexicanus* (Gillette); 34.4 *Synophromorpha* Ashmead (3 spp.); 34.5 *Periclistus* Foerster (7 spp.); 34.6 *Myrtopsen* Rubsaamen (1 sp., *M. mimosae* Weld); 34.7 *Ceroptres* Hartig (16 spp.); 34.8 *Euceroptres* Ashmead (3 spp.)]

Subfamily Cynipinae

[34.9 *Gonaspis* Ashmead (1 sp., *G. potentillae* (Bassett); 34.10 *Antistrophus* Walsh (8 spp.); 34.11 *Diastrophus* (13 spp.); 34.12 *Liposthenes* Foerster (1 sp., *L. glechomae* (Linnaeus)); 34.13 *Aylax* Hartig (2 spp.)]

34.14 *Phanacis* Foerster

Two species, including the following:

P. taraxaci (Ashmead) (Dandelion Gall Wasp). Causes galls on Dandelion. (1) n.e. NA; (5) MN.

[34.15 *Aulacidea* Ashmead (7 spp.)]

34.16 *Diplolepis* Geoffroy

Thirty-six species, including the following:

D. radicum (Osten Sacken) (Rose Root Gall Wasp). Forms galls on the roots of roses. (1) n.e. US; (2) VA.

D. rosae (Linnaeus) (Mossy Rose Gall Wasp). Introduced species; very common on Sweetbrier Roses. (1) n.e. US; (2) VA; (5) KS, MO.

34.17 *Neuroterus* Hartig

Seventy-four species, including the following:

N. clavensis Weld (Oak Gall). Length: ±2 mm. Humpbacked; abdomen with two segments visible dorsally as in other species of family; black. This species causes a characteristic gall formation on stems of oak. (3) AZ, NM.

[34.18 *Trichoteras* Ashmead (7 spp.); 34.19 *Phylloteras* Ashmead (3 spp.); 34.20 *Xystoteras* Ashmead (3 spp.); 34.21 *Xanthoteras* Ashmead (14 spp.); 34.22 *Paracraspis* Weld (3 spp.); 34.23 *Acraspis* Mayr (33 spp.); 34.24 *Philonix* Fitch (12 spp.); 34.25 *Liodora* Foerster (3 spp.); 34.26 *Dros* Kinsey (5 spp.); 34.27 *Adleria* Rohwer and Fagan (7 spp.)]

34.28 *Amphibolips* Reinhard

Twenty-four species, including the following:

A. confluenta (Harris) (Spongy Oak Apple Gall). Common on oak leaves. (See Fig. 25.26.) (1) n.e. NA; (2) VA; (5) KS, MO.

[34.29 *Andricus* Hartig (95 spp.); 34.30 *Besbicus* Kinsey (8 spp.); 34.31 *Atrusca* Kinsey (15 spp.); 34.32 *Disholcaspis* Dalla Torre and Kieffer

Fig. 25.26. (*From Felt, 1918*)

(39 spp.); 34.33 *Antron* Kinsey (13 spp.); 34.34 *Belonocnema* Mayr (3 spp.); 34.35 *Sphaeroteras* Ashmead (15 spp.); 34.36 *Zopheroteras* Ashmead (6 spp.); 34.37 *Loxaulus* Mayr (13 spp.); 34.38 *Bassettia* Ashmead (9 spp.); 34.39 *Eumayria* Ashmead (4 spp.); 34.40 *Trisoleniella* Rohwer and Fagan (4 spp.); 34.41 *Odontocynips* Kieffer (1 sp., *O. nebulosa* Kieffer); 34.42 *Holocynips* Kieffer (4 spp.); 34.43 *Plagiotrochus* Mayr (1 sp., *P. suberi* Weld); 34.44 *Dryocosmus* Giraud (20 spp.); 34.45 *Heteroecus* Kinsey (13 spp.); 34.46 *Callirhytis* Foerster (116 spp.); Unplaced taxa (41 spp.)]

Superfamily EVANIOIDEA

35. EVANIIDAE (Ensign Wasp Family)

L. 3–7 mm. Abdomen short, compressed, resembling a small flag, attached to the thorax dorsally by slender stalk. Larvae are egg parasites of cockroaches. There are 11 species in the U.S. and Canada, widely distributed in the East and Southwest.

35.1 *Evania* Fabricius

One species, as follows:

E. appendigaster (Linnaeus). L. 5.5–7 mm. Black. Larva develop in cockroach eggs. Introduced with home-infesting cockroaches, this is the largest species in the family, the others being under 5 mm. (1) s. MA, s.e. NY,, s.e. PA, NJ, e. MD, DE, DC; (2) s.e. US; (3) AZ, NM, TX.

35.2 *Prosevania* Kieffer

One species, as follows:

P. fuscipes (Illiger). Parasite of the cockroaches *Blatta orientalis* Linnaeus and *Periplaneta americana* (Linnaeus). There is come confusion in the literature between this species and the preceding species. (1) OH, PA, s. NY. w. MA, NJ, MD, DE; (2) VA, NC, SC, GA.

[35.3 *Evaniella* Bradley (3 spp.); 35.4 *Hyptia* Illiger (6 spp.)]

36. AULACIDAE (Aulacid Wasp Family)

L. 6–17 mm. Abdomen slender, elongate, attached to thorax dorsally; antennae long, extending to abdomen. Larvae are parasites of wood-boring Xiphydriidae and Coleoptera. Twenty-eight species in the U.S. and Canada.

36.1 *Pristaulacus* Kieffer

Twenty-one species, widely distributed, including the following:

P. rufitarsis (Cresson). Parasite of beetles of the genera *Saperda, Chrysobothris,* and *Melanophila.* (1), (2), (3), (4), (5), generally distributed.

[36.2 *Aulacus* Jurine (7 spp.)]

37. GASTERUPTIIDAE
(Gasteruptiid Wasp Family)

L. 13–40 mm. Abdomen slender, attached to thorax dorsally, and much longer than it; antennae short, not extending beyond thorax. Adults are found flying around flowers, posts, stumps, and nesting sites of the hosts of their larvae, which are predators or predator-inquilines in the nests of bees and wasps that nest in twigs and wood. There are 15 species in the U.S. and Canada.

37.1 *Gasteruption* Latreille

Fifteen species, including the following:

G. assectator (Linnaeus). L. 11–12 mm. Black; wings with dark veins; hind tibiae club-shaped. Front wings are held folded lengthwise much like that of social wasps. Adults are found on umbelliferous flowers in open fields during the late summer. (See A&J 272.) (1) n.e. NA; (2) VA, NC; (3) n. CA, n. AZ; (4) Pacific n.w.; (5) n. central states.

Superfamily PELECINOIDEA

38. PELECINIDAE (Pelecinid Wasp Family)

L. Female, ±50 mm; male, ±25 mm. Female abdomen very long and slender; male abdomen club-shaped, shorter; males rarely seen. One genus and species only, as follows:

38.1 *Pelecinus* Latreille

P. polyturator (Drury). Black; antennae often with white annulus; male tarsomeres whitish. There is some indication that this may be a complex of species. According to some reports, the larvae are parasites of soil-inhabiting Scarabaeidae, but they may also infest larvae in decaying wood. (See Fig. 25.27.) (1) n.e. NA; (2) s.e. US; (3) s.w. US.

Superfamily PROCTOTRUPOIDEA OR
SERPHOIDEA

39. SERPHIDAE (Serphid Wasp Family)

[= Proctotrupidae]

L. 3–10 mm. Black; wings hyaline to black; antennae 13-segmented; mandibles with one, two, or sometimes several teeth; trochanters single; middle and hind tibiae with two apical spurs. Abdominal sterna 1 through 4 and terga 2 through 4

Fig. 25.27. (*After Comstock*)

fused together to form a synsternum and a syntergum (that is, this region appears to be a single solid segment); base of abdomen a solid stalk composed of sternum 1 and tergum 2 but sometimes so short as to be essentially absent. Most species are found in damp habitats. There are 46 species in the U.S. and Canada.

Subfamily Vanhorniinae

One genus and species, as follows:

39.1 *Vanhornia* Crawford

V. eucnemidarum Crawford. Larvae parasites of species of the beetle family Eucnemidae. Rare. (1) PQ, ME, NH, MA, CT, NY, PA, MA; (2) VA.

Subfamily Serphinae

Most species are parasites of several beetle families, with one genus (*Cryptoserphus*) parasitizing flies.

Tribe Disogmini

[39.2 *Disogmus* Foerster (3 spp.)]

Tribe Cryptoserphini

[39.3 *Fustiserphus* Townes and Townes (1 sp., *F. reticulatus* Townes and Townes); 39.4 *Tretoserphus* Townes and Townes (2 spp.); 39.5 *Cryptoserphus* Kieffer (8 spp.); 39.6 *Mischoserphus* Townes and Townes (4 spp.); 39.7 *Pschornia* Townes and Townes (1 sp., *P. striata* Townes and Townes); 39.8 *Brachyserphus* Hellén (7 spp.)]

Tribe Serphini

[39.9 *Phaenoserphus* Kieffer (12 spp.)]

39.10 *Serphus* Schrank

[= *Proctotrupes* Latreille]

Five species, including the following is an example.

S. caudatus (Say) L. 7–10 mm. Reddish brown to almost entirely black. (1) n.e. NA; (2) s.e. US; (3) NM; (4) Pacific n.w.; (5) n. central states and provinces.

[39.11 *Phaneroserphus* Pschorn-Walcher (2 spp.); 39.12 *Exallonyx* Kieffer: 2 subgenera: *Eocodrus* Pschorn-Walcher (1 sp., *E. brevicornis* Haliday) and *Exallonyx* s. str. (28 spp.); *Codrus* Panzer: not New World]

40. ROPRONIIDAE (Roproniid Wasp Family)

L. 8–10 mm. Parasites of sawflies. Three rare species are known in the U.S. and Canada, as follows:

40.1 *Ropronia* Provancher

R. californica Ashmead. (3) CA; (4) OR.

R. garmani Ashmead. (1) n.e. US; (2) VA, NC, SC, GA; (5) IA.

R. pediculata Provancher. (1) ON, NY.

41. HELORIDAE (Helorid Wasp Family)

L. 4–5 mm. These rare wasps are parasitic on lacewings (Chrysopidae). One genus and species, as follows:

41.1 *Helorus* Latreille

H. paradoxus (Provancher). (1) n.e. US; (2) s.e. US; (3) s.w. US; (4) BC, WA, OR, ID, NV, UT; (5) n. central states.

42. DIAPRIIDAE (Diapriid Wasp Family)

L. 1–7 mm. Antennae arise from protuberance on front of head; first segment of antennae longer than second and third combined. Larvae are parasites of Diptera. There are 303 species in the U.S. and Canada.

Subfamily Ambositrinae

[42.1 *Propsilomma* Kieffer (1 sp., *P. columbianum* (Ashmead))]

Subfamily Ismarinae

[42.2 *Ismarus* Haliday (2 spp.)]

Subfamily Belytinae

[42.3 *Cinetus* Junine (8 spp.); 42.4 *Miota* Foerster (17 spp.); 42.5 *Scorpioteleia* Ashmead (1 sp., *S. mirabilis* Ashmead); 42.6 *Macrohynnis* Foerster (1 sp., *M. americanus* Kieffer); 42.7 *Aclista* Foerster (41 spp.); 42.8 *Pantoclis* Foerster (26 spp.); 42.9 *Zygota* Foerster (22 spp.); 42.10 *Acropiesta* Foerster (7 spp.); 42.11 *Belyta* Jurine (31 spp.); 42.12 *Diphora* Foerster (1 sp., *D. nearctica* Whittaker); 42.13 *Oxylabis* Foerster (6 spp.); 42.14 *Acanosema* Kieffer (1 sp., *A. sylvanum* Whittaker); 42.15 *Rhynchopsilus* Kieffer (1 sp., *R. conicus* (Ashmead)); 42.16 *Polypeza* Foerster (3 spp.); 42.17 *Synacra* Foerster (3 spp.)]

Subfamily Diapriinae

[42.18 *Paramesius* Westwood (10 spp.); 42.19 *Entomacis* Foerster (7 spp.); 42.20 *Hoplopria* Ashmead (undescribed species); 42.21 *Spilomicrus* Westwood (11 spp.); 42.22 *Pentapria* Kieffer (3 spp.); 42.23 *Aneurhynchus* Westwood (5 spp.); 42.24 *Psilus* Panzer (10 spp.); 42.25 *Monelata* Foerster (3 spp.); 42.26 *Basalys* Westwood (14 spp.); 42.27 *Idiotypa* Foerster (1 sp., *I. pallipes* Fouts); 42.28 *Trichopria* Ashmead (57 spp.)]

42.29 *Diapria* Latreille

Three species, including the following:

D. conica (Fabrocius). L. 2.5–3 mm. Black; more or less "woolly." Abdomen longer than head and thorax combined. Parasitic on the Drone Fly (*Eristalis tenax*). (1) n.e. NA; (5) CO, KS, MO.

[42.30 *Acanthopria* Ashmead (1 undescribed sp.); 42.31 *Doliopria* Kieffer (1 sp., *D. americana* Fouts); 42.32 *Auxopaedeutes* Brues (6 spp.); 42.33 *Lepidopria* Kieffer (1 sp., *L. aberrans* Brues); 42.34 *Bruesopria* Wing (2 spp.); 42.35 *Myrmecopria* Ashmead (1 sp., *M. mellea* (Ashmead))]

43. SCELIONIDAE (Scelionid Wasp Family)

L. 0.45–4 mm. Antennae elbowed; wing venation reduced. These wasps live in the eggs of other insects and of spiders. The female of one European species settles on an adult female Mantid and sheds her wings, remaining on the host until the latter lays her eggs. The Scelionid then lays her own eggs in the Mantid eggs. Other species are egg parasites of grasshoppers. There are 275 species in the U.S. and Canada.

Subfamily Scelioninae

[43.1 *Sparasion* Latreille (8 spp.); 43.2 *Sceliomorpha* Ashmead (1 unnamed sp.); 43.3 *Scelio* Latreille (19 spp.); 43.4 *Synoditella* Muese-

beck (2 spp.); 43.5 *Govinda* Nixon (1 unnamed sp.); 43.6 *Baryconus* Foerster (2 spp.); 43.7 *Macroteleia* Westwood (9 spp.); 43.8 *Calotelea* Westwood (5 spp.); 43.9 *Cremastobaeus* Ashmead (2 unnamed spp.); 43.10 *Probaryconus* Kieffer (3 spp.); 43.11 *Oethecoctonus* Ashmead (1 sp., *O. oecanthi* (Riley)); 43.12 *Leptoteleia* Kieffer (1 sp., *L. oecanthi* (Riley)); 43.13 *Holoteleia* Kieffer (3 spp.); 43.14 *Duta* Nixon (1 unnamed spp.); 43.15 *Opisthacantha* Ashmead (2 spp.); 43.16 *Psilanteris* Kieffer (1 sp., *P. reticulatus* (Fouts)); 43.17 *Paridrius* Kieffer (4 spp.); 43.18 *Pseudanteris* Fouts (1 sp., *P. insignis* Fouts); 43.19 *Gryon* Haliday (17 spp.); 43.20 *Mirotelenomus* Dodd (1 undescribed sp.); 43.21 *Embidobia* Ashmead (1 undescribed spp.); 43.22 *Tiphodytes* Bradley (1 sp., *T. gerriphagus* (Marchal)); 43.23 *Thoron* Haliday (1 sp., *T. metallicus* Haliday); 43.24 *Idris* Foerster (8 spp.); 43.25 *Ceratobaeus* Ashmead (2 spp.); 43.26 *Baeus* Haliday (7 spp.)]

Subfamily Teleasinae

[43.27 *Teleas* Latreille (6 spp.); 43.28 *Trimorus* Foerster (97 spp.); 43.29 *Trisacantha* Ashmead (6 spp.)]

Subfamily Telenominae

[43.30 *Aradophagus* Ashmead (1 sp., *A. fasciatus* Ashmead); 43.31 *Eumicrosoma* Gahan (2 spp.)]

43.32 *Telenomus* Haliday

Fifty-three species, including the following:

T. clisiocampae Riley. L. 0.6 mm. Parasitic on eggs of the Tent Caterpillar, *Malacosoma americanum* (Fabricius) and other species. (1) n.e. US; (4) Pacific n.w.; (5) n. central states.

[43.33 *Dissolcus* Ashmead (1 sp., *D. nigricornis* Ashmead); 43.34 *Trissolcus* Ashmead (11 spp.)]

44. PLATYGASTRIDAE (Platygastrid Wasp Family)

L. 1–2 mm. Wings without veins; some females with a long process extending from first abdominal segment forward over head. (See Fig. 25.28 for general body form.) These are mostly parasites of Diptera (Cecidomyiidae) and Homoptera (Mealybugs and Whiteflies). There are 192 species in the U.S. and Canada.

Subfamily Inostemmatinae
Tribe Inostemmatini

[44.1 *Metaclisis* Foerster (2 spp.); 44.2 *Inostemma* Haliday (10 spp.); 44.3 *Isostasius* Foerster (2 spp.); 44.4 *Tetrabaeus* Kieffer (1 sp., *T. americanus* (Brues)); 44.5 *Acerotella* Masner (1+ unnamed spp.); 44.6 *Allotropa* Foerster (6 spp.)]

Tribe Iphitrachelini

[44.7 *Iphitrachelus* Walker (1 sp., *I. foutsi* Jackson)]

Subfamily Sceliotrachelinae

[44.8 *Fidiobia* Ashmead (3 spp.); 44.9 *Amitus* Halderman (3 spp.)]

Subfamily Platygastrinae

[44.10 *Metanopedias* Brues (1 sp., *M. brunneipes* (Ashmead)); 44.11 *Trichacis* Foerster (6 spp.); 44.12 *Isocybus* Foerster (2 spp.)]

44.13 *Platygaster* Latreille

There are 101 species in this genus, including the following:

P. hiemalis Forbes. L. 0.8–1.4 mm. Parasite of the Hessian Fly (*Mayetiola desctructor* (Say). (See Fig. 25.29.)

[44.14 *Euxestonotus* Fouts (4 spp.); 44.15 *Eritrissomerus* Ashmead (4 spp.); 44.16 *Piestopleura* Foerster (1 sp., *P. platygaster* (Fouts)); 44.17 *Synopeas* Foerster (30 spp.); 44.18 *Gastrotrypes* Brues (1 sp., *G. caudatus* Brues); 44.19 *Leptacis* Foerster (11 spp.); 44.20 *Amblyaspis* Foerster (3 spp.)]

Superfamily CERAPHRONOIDEA
45. CERAPHRONIDAE

L. 1.2–4 mm. Antennae elbowed. Some of these species are parasites on aphid parasites and Cecidomyiidae. Of the 48 species recorded in the U.S. and Canada, all have a very limited distribution so far as is known; in no case is more than one or two states or provinces listed.

[45.1 *Ceraphron* Jurine (31 spp.); 45.2 *Neoceraphron* Ashmead (1 sp., *N. macroneurus* (Ashmead)); 45.3 *Aphanogmus* Thomson (13 spp.); 45.4 *Ecitonetes* Brues (1 sp., *E. subapterus* Brues); 45.5 *Synarsis* Foerster (1 undescribed sp.); 45.6 *Homaloceraphron* Dessart and Masner (2 spp.)]

46. MEGASPILIDAE (Megaspilid Wasp Family)

L. 1.5–4 mm. All 61 species in the U.S. and Canada are parasites, mostly of flies and Homoptera. Very little is known about the group.

Subfamily Megaspilinae

[46.1 *Trichosteresis* Foerster (2 spp.); 46.2 *Megaspilus* Westwood (5 spp.); 46.3 *Conostigmus* Dahlbom (30 spp.); 46.4 *Dendrocerus* Ratze-

Fig. 25.28.

Fig. 25.29. (*After Hill*)

burg (22 spp.); 46.5 *Ecnomothorax* Dessert and Masner (1 sp., *E. muesebecki* Dessert and Masner)]

Subfamily Lagynodinae

[46.6 *Lagynodes* Foerster (3 spp.)]

Superfamily TRIGONALOIDEA

47. TRIGONALIDAE (Trigonalid Wasp Family)

L. 10–12 mm. Black or reddish brown with yellowish or white markings; antennae long, reaching beyond thorax, with 16 or more segments. These insects, which resemble solitary wasps, are secondary parasites of social Vespidae and of caterpillar parasites. They lay minute eggs on foliage; these are eaten by the caterpillars. Parasites of the larval parasites of social wasps are probably brought to the vespid larvae with their caterpillar food. There are 4 species, widely distributed, in the U.S. and Canada.

[47.1 *Orthogonalys* Schultz (1 sp., *O. pulchella* (Cresson)); 47.2 *Lycogaster* Shuchard (1 sp., *L. pullata* Schuckard (with 2 subspecies))]

47.3 *Poecilogonalos* Schulz

One species, as follows:

P. costalis (Cresson). (1) OH, PA, NY, MA, NJ, MD, DE; (2) s.e. US. Secondary parasite of *Automeris io* and other insects.

[47.4 *Bareogonalos* Schulz (1 sp., *B. canadensis* (Harrington))]

Infraorder ACULEATA

This group contains the wasps, ants, and bees but is biologically inseparable from the Parasitica since there are parasitic species in some of the families.

Superfamily CHRYSIDOIDEA

48. BETHYLIDAE (Bethylid Wasp Family)

L. 2–5 mm (rarely 10+ mm). Usually black or brown; head prognathous, usually elongate; antennae with 12 or 13 segments; front femora thickened in middle; hind wing with anal lobe and without closed cells; abdomen with seven or eight visible segments. Females of many species resemble ants; they are often wingless. Many species parasitize wood-boring beetle larvae, including some pest species, such as grain pests and the larvae of microlepidoptera. There are 196 species in the U.S. and Canada.

[Note: The following classification is based on Evans (1978), not on the *Catalog of Hymenoptera* of Krombein, *et. al.* (1979), which does not include Evan's revision.]

Subfamily Pristocerinae

48.1 *Pristocera* Klug

The nine species in the U.S. and Canada belong to the subgenus *Acrepyris* Kieffer, including the following:

P.(Acrepyris) armifera (Say). L. ±8 mm. Head and thorax black; antennal flagellum, legs, and abdomen dark reddish brown; wings subhyaline; veins and stigma brown. (1) n.e. US; (2) s.e. US; (3) TX; (5) SD.

[48.2 *Apenesia* Westwood (10 spp.); 48.3 *Parascleroderma* Kieffer (3 spp.); 48.4 *Dissomphalus* Ashmead (8 spp.); 48.5 *Pseudisobrachium* Kieffer (31 spp.)]

Subfamily Epyrinae

Tribe Epyrini

[48.6 *Rhabdepyris* Kieffer: 3 subgenera: *Rhabdepyris* s. str. (4 spp.), *Trichotepyris* Kieffer (7 spp.), and *Chlorepyris* Kieffer (1 sp., *R. fulgens* (Brues)); 48.7 *Anisepyris* Kieffer (16 spp.); 48.8 *Epyris* Westwood (24 spp.); 48.9 *Bakeriella* Kieffer (1 sp., *B. floridana* Evans); 48.10 *Holepyrus* Kieffer (18 spp.); 48.11 *Laelius* Ashmead (5 spp.)]

Tribe Cephalonomiini

[48.12 *Plastanoxus* Kieffer (5 spp.); 48.13 *Prorops* Waterston (2 spp.)]

48.14 *Cephalonomia* Westwood

Nine species, including the following:

C. watersoni Gahan (Parasitic Grain Wasp). L. ±1.6 mm. Black; mouthparts brownish; antennae brown; legs brown except for yellowish brown tarsi; wings hyaline. This is a parasite of the grain pest, *Cryptolestes ferrugineus* (Stephens), wherever that pest, the Rust Grain Beetle of the beetle family Cucujidae, is present, worldwide.

Tribe Sclerodermini

[48.15 *Nesepyris* Bridwell (2 spp.); 48.16 *Glenosmea* Kieffer (1 sp., *G. crandalli* Evans); 48.17 *Sclerodermus* Latreille (3 spp.)]

Subfamily Bethylinae

Tribe Bethylini

[48.18 *Bethylus* Latreille (2 spp.)]

Tribe Sierolini

[48.19 *Sierola* Cameron (1 sp., *S. larifuga* Evans); 48.20 *Prosierola* Kieffer (1 sp., *P. bicarinata* (Brues)); 48.21 *Goniozus* Foerster (36 spp.)]

49. SCLEROGIBBIDAE (Sclerogibbid Wasp Family)

L. 2–4 mm. Antennae with 20 or more segments. One rare species, parasitic on Embioptera.

49.1 *Probethylus* Ashmead

P. schwarzi Ashmead. External parasite. (3) AZ.

50. CHRYSIDIDAE (Cuckoo Wasp Family)

L. 6–12 mm. Body usually brilliantly metallic blue or green, or reddish; integument very hard; antennae with 12 or 13 segments, two to six (usually three) of them visible and concave or hollowed out beneath; body of some capable of curling into a ball for protection. Most of these insects are inquilines or cleptoparasites, that is, parasites that kill the host larvae so that their own larvae may utilize the food stored in the nests of solitary bees and wasps (especially those of ground-nesting or twig-nesting species) or in Mud Dauber nests. The Cleptinae parasitize Tenthredinoidea saw-fly larvae; the Amiseginae attack walking stick (Phasmatodea) eggs. There are 227 species in the U.S. and Canada.

[Note: The following classification is based on Bohart and Kimsey (1982) not the *Catalog of Hymenoptera* of Krombein, *et al.* (1979).]

Subfamily Cleptinae

[50.1 *Cleptes* Latreille: 3 subgenera: *Cleptes* s. str. (3 spp.), *Leiocleptes* Moczar (3 spp.), and *Melanocelptes* Moczar (3 spp.)]

Subfamily Amiseginae

[50.2 *Mesitiopterus* Ashmead (2 spp.); 50.3 *Microsega* Krombein (1 sp., *M. bella* Krombein); 50.4 *Adelphe* Mocsary (1 sp., *A. anisomorphae* Krombein)]

Subfamily Elampinae

[50.5 *Holopyga* Dahlbom (6 spp.); 50.6 *Muesebeckidium* Krombein (2 spp.); 50.7 *Minymischa* Kimsey (3 spp.); 50.8 *Pseudolopyga* Krombein (2 spp.); 50.9 *Microchridium* Bohart (1 sp., *M. minutum* Bohart); 50.10 *Xerochrum* Bohart (1 sp., *X. rubeum* Bohart); 50.11 *Omalus* Panzer: 3 subgenera; *Omalus* s. str. (4 spp.), *Pseudomalus* Ashmead (4 spp.), and *Diplorrhos* Aaron (9 spp.); 50.12 *Elampus* Spinola (6 spp.); 50.13 *Hedychridium* Abeille de Perrin (31 spp.); 50.14 *Hedychreides* Bohart (1 sp., *H. mirum* Bohart); 50.15 *Hedychrum* Latreille (9 spp.)]

Subfamily Chrysididinae

Tribe Chrysididini

50.16 *Chrysis* Linnaeus

There are 77 species, including the following:

C. fuscipennis Brullé. Parasite of the Mud Dauber, *Sceliphron caementarium* (Drury). (1) NJ, MD, DC; (2) VA, TN, KY; (3) CA; (4) NV; (5) MO.

[50.17 *Chrysura* Dahlbom, subgenus *Olochrysis* Lichenstein (10 spp.)]

50.18 *Trichrysis* Lichtenstein

The genus is divided into two subgenera: *Caenochrysis* Kimsey and Bohart (4 spp.) and *Larochrysis* Kimsey and Bohart (3 spp.). The following species may be taken as an example:

T. (Caenochrysis) tridens (Lepeletier). L. 7–11 mm. Metallic blue-green, sometimes with a reddish cast; abdomen hollowed out ventrally, the third abdominal segment with submarginal grooves. Parasite of *Trypargilum politum* (Say), a mud wasp. (1) n.e. US; (2) s.e. US; (3) AZ, NM, TX; (4) NV; (5) ND, SC, MN, WY, NE, IA, CO, KS, MO. (A&J 273).

[50.19 *Ceratochrysis* Cooper (26 spp.); 50.20 *Argochrysis* Kimsey and Bohart [=*Spintharosoma* Zimmerman (in part)] (15 spp.)]

Tribe Euchroeini

[50.21 *Pseudospinola* Linsenmaier (1 sp., *P. neglecta* (Shuckard)); 50.22 *Neochrysis* Linsenmaier: 3 subgenera: *Neochrysis* s. str. (2 spp.), *Ipsiura* Linsenmaier (2 spp.), and *Exochrysis* Bohart (1 sp., *N. alabamensis* (Mocsary))]

Subfamily Parnopinae

[50.23 *Parnopes* Latreille (7 spp.)]

51. DRYINIDAE (Pincher Wasp Family)

L. 2–5 mm. Antennae 10-segmented; head large; front legs of females usually pincerlike, their front tarsi and claws modified to grasp leafhoppers (see Fig. 25.30). The females are either winged or wingless. These wasps are parasites of nymphs and adults of Homoptera. Most of the 139 species in the U.S. and Canada occur in Texas and Arizona, with others scattered across the rest of the U.S. and southern Canada. The group is poorly known.

Fig. 25.30.

Subfamily Anteoninae

[51.1 *Anteon* Jurine: 2 subgenera: *Anteon* s. str. (12 spp.) and *Chelogynus* Haliday (9 spp.); 51.2 *Deinodryinus* Perkins (10 spp.); 51.3 *Prenanteon* Kieffer (3 spp.); 51.4 *Trisanteon* Kieffer (1 sp., *T. rugosus* (Ashmead)); 51.5 *Hesperodryinus* Perkins (2 spp.); 51.6 *Bocchus* Ashmead (4 spp.)]

Subfamily Dryininae

[51.7 *Mesodryinus* Kieffer (3 spp.); 51.8 *Tetradryinus* Kieffer (1 sp., *T. flavipes* (Kieffer)); 51.9 *Thaumatodryinus* Perkins (1 sp., *T. perkinsi* Krombein); 51.10 *Perodryinus* Perkins (1 sp., *P. amoenus* Perkins)]

Subfamily Gonatopodinae

51.11 *Neodryinus* Perkins

This genus is represented in the U.S. and Canada by the subgenus *Prodryinus* Kieffer (4 spp.). The typical subgenus does not occur in our area. The following species is an example:

N. (Prodryinus) typhlocybae (Ashmead). Parasite of the Homopterans *Metcalfa pruinosa* (Say) and *Anormenis spetentrionalis* (Spinola). (1) n.e. US; (2) AR; (3) TX; (4) KS.

[51.12 *Cyrtogonatopus* Kieffer (1 sp., *C. clavicornis* Fenton); 51.13 *Pristogonatopus* Kieffer (1 sp., *P. sjodtedti* (Kieffer)); 51.14 *Dicondylus* Haliday (3 spp.); 51.15 *Pseudogonatopus* Perkins (7 spp.); 51.16 *Agonatopoides* Perkins (1 sp., *A. synchromus* Perkins); 51.17 *Haplogonatopus* Perkins (1 sp., *H. americanus* Perkins); 51.18 *Eucamptonyx* Perkins (2 spp.); 51.19 *Apterodryinus* Perkins (1 sp., *A. torvus* Perkins); 51.20 *Pachygonatopus* Perkins (2 spp.); 51.21 *Chalcogonatopus* Perkins (21 spp.); 51.22 *Gonatopus* Ljungh (13 spp.); 51.23 *Neogonatopus* Perkins (8 spp.); 51.24 *Agonatopus* Perkins (7 spp.); 51.25 *Epigonatopus* Perkins (3 spp.); 51.26 *Digonatopus* Kieffer (1 sp., *D. haplothorax* (Perkins))]

Subfamily Aphelopinae

[51.27 *Aphelopus* Dalman (16 spp.)]

52. EMBOLEMIDAE (Embolemid Wasp Family)

Length: 5–8 mm. Two rare species, as follows:

[52.1 *Ampulicomorpha* Ashmead (1 sp., *A. confusa* Ashmead (1) WI, ON, MD; (2) VA, NC, GA; (3) CA; (4) BC; (5) SK, CO, MO.)]

52.2 *Embolemus* Westwood

E. nearcticus (Brues). L. 5–8 mm. Parasite of Fulgoridae. (1) MA, NY; (2) ?VA.

Superfamily SCOLIOIDEA
53. TIPHIIDAE (Tiphiid Wasp Family)

L. 6–26 mm. Male usually with uncurved spine at end of abdomen; last abdominal tergite hoodlike; coxae well separated; mesosternum with two posterior lobelike extensions that project between and partly cover bases of middle coxae; some females wingless. Larvae parasitize beetle larvae, particularly white grubs, including larvae of Japanese beetles, tiger beetles, and various bees and wasps occurring in soil and rotting wood. There are 225 species in the U.S. and Canada.

Subfamily Tiphiinae
53.1 *Tiphia* Fabricius

This genus is divided into subgenera, but only this typical subgenus is present in the U.S. and Canada. There are 95 species, of which the following is an example.

T. intermedia Malloch. L. ±11 mm. A common species on flowers of wild carrots and other umbelliferae during June to August. The larvae are parasitic on larvae of *Phyllophaga* spp. (Coleoptera: Scarabaeidae). (1) n.e. US; (2) s.e. US; (3) s.w. US; (5) ND, SD, MN, IA, MO.

[53.2 *Krombeinia* Pate (4 spp.); 53.3 *Neotiphia* Malloch (12 spp.); 53.4 *Paratiphia* Sichel (27 spp.); 53.5 *Epomidiopteron* Romand (1 sp., *E. julii* Romand)]

Subfamily Myzininae
53.6 *Myzinum* Latreille

Seventeen species, including the following:

M. maculatum (Fabricius). L. 11–12 mm. Black body; legs black; wings pale; abdominal segments with pale yellow apical margins. (1) MA, NY, NJ, MD, DE; (2) s.e. US; (3) s.e. US; (4) NV.

M. quinquecinctum (Fabricius). L. ±18 mm. Similar to the preceding; body black; female with yellow legs; male with yellow wings. Adults fly from August to September. (1) n.e. US; (2) s.e. US; (3) s.w. US; (5) WY.

[53.7 *Pterombrus* Smith (3 spp.)]

Subfamily Anthoboscinae

[53.8 *Lalapa* Pate (1 sp., *L. lusa* Pate (3) CA; (4) WA, OR, ID)]

Subfamily Brachycistidinae

[53.9 *Brachycistis* Fox (32 spp.); 53.10 *Colocistis* Krombein (7 spp.); 53.11 *Acanthetropis* Wasbauer (4 spp.); 53.12 *Brachycistina* Malloch (1 sp., *B. acuta* (Malloch); 53.13 *Hadrocistis* Wasbauer (2 spp.); 53.14 *Brachycistellus* Baker (1 sp., *B. figitiformis* Baker); 53.15 *Quemaya* Pate (5 spp.); 53.16 *Glyptacros* Mickel and Krombein (2 spp.); 53.17 *Xeroglypta* Mickel and Krombein (1 sp., *X. egregia* Mickel and Krombein); 53.18 *Aulacros* Mickel and Krombein (1 sp., *A. latior* Mickel and Krombein); 53.19 *Bruesiella* Mann (1 sp., *B. furtivus* (Michel and Krombein); 53.20 *Aglyptacros* Mickel and Krombein (4 spp.)]

Subfamily Methocinae

[53.21 *Methocha* Latreille, subgenus *Methocha* s. str. (4 spp.)]

54. SIEROLOMORPHIDAE

L. 4–7 mm. Little is known about members of this family. There are six species in the U.S. and Canada.

54.1 *Sierolomorpha* Ashmead

S. canadensis (Provancher). (1) n.e. US; (2) s.e. US; (3) AZ, NM, TX; (5) AB.

55. MUTILLIDAE (Velvet Ant Family)

L. 3–23 mm. Very hairy, usually brightly colored; wingless females resemble ants. Body usually dark but covered with black, yellow, or red hairlike setae—the "velvet." Some species in the Southwest have long white hairlike setae. The winged male cannot sting, but the females are fierce stingers. Males of some species are often found about flowers; others are nocturnal. Females scurry about in the open, especially in sandy places. The two sexes of a given species usually have dissimilar markings. Most of the species are parasites on the larvae of ground-nesting bees and wasps and a few other insects. There are 483 species in the U.S. and Canada.

Subfamily Apterogyninae

[Note: This and the following subfamily were placed in a separate family, Bradynobaenidae, by Brothers (1975), but this classification has yet to be generally accepted.]

Tribe Chyphotini

[55.1 *Chyphotes* Blake: 2 subgenera: *Chyphotes* s. str. (24 spp.) and *Pitanta* Pate (23 spp.)]

Subfamily Typhoctinae

[55.2 *Typhoctes* Ashmead (4 spp.)]

Subfamily Myrmosinae

[This subfamily was moved by Brothers (1975) to the Mutillidae from the Tiphiidae.]

[55.3 *Myrmosa* Latreille: 2 subgenera: *Myromosa* s. str. (4 spp.) and *Myrmosina* Krombein (3 spp.); 55.4 *Leiomyrmosa* Washbauer (1 sp., *L. spilota* Washbauer); 55.5 *Myrmosula* Bradley (8 spp.)]

Subfamily Sphaeropthalminae
Tribe Sphaeropthalmini

[55.6 *Morsyma* Fox (1 sp., *M. ashmeadii* Fox); 55.7 *Acrophotopsis* Schuster (2 spp.); 55.8 *Dilophotopsis* Schuster (5 spp.); 55.9 *Acanthophotopsis* Schuster (6 spp.); 55.10 *Sphaeropthalma* Blake: 5 subgenera: *Micromutilla* Ashmead (17 spp.), *Physetapsis* Schuster (5 spp.), *Photopsis* Blake (68 spp.), *Photopsioides* Schuster (4 spp.), and *Sphaeropthalma* s. str. (6 spp.); 55.11 *Photomorphus* Viereck: 2 subgenera: *Photomorphina* Schuster (27 spp.) and *Photomorphus* Viereck (8 spp.); 55.12 *Odontophotopsis* Viereck: 2 subgenera: *Odontophotopsis* s. str. (51 spp.) and *Periphotopsis* Schuster (1 sp., *O. mamata* Schuster); 55.13 *Protophotopsis* Schuster, subgenus *Protophotopsis* s. str. (2 spp.)]

Tribe Pseudomethocini

[55.14 *Pseudomethoca* Ashmead (44 spp.); 5.15 *Myrmilloides* Andre (1 sp., *M. grandiceps* (Blake))]

Tribe Dasymutillini
55.16 *Dasymutilla* Ashmead

There are 141 species in this genus, including the following:

D occidentalis occidentalis (Linnaeus) (Common Eastern Velvet Ant). L. 16–18 mm. Body black, marked with red hairlike setae; male with red setae on pronotum and dorsal part

of thorax; abdomen with red setae except on basal segment; female black with red setae except on black extreme apex of metathorax and first and third abdominal segments. Parasitic on the bumble bee, *Bombus fraternus* Smith. (1) CT, s. NY, NJ, MD; (2) s.e. US; (3) TX; (5) MO.

D. sackenii (Cresson) (Western Velvet Ant). L. 12–13 mm. Body black, covered with pale yellowish hairlike setae except for legs and underside of body, which are covered with black setae. Parasite of the wasp *Bembix occidentalis* Fox. (See A&J 275.) (3) CA; (4) OR, NV.

[55.17 *Lomachaeta* Mickel (6 spp.); 55.18 *Smicromutilla* Mickel (1 sp., *S. powelli* Mickel)]

Subfamily Mutillinae

Tribe Ephutini

[55.19 *Timulla* Ashmead, subgenus Timulla s. str. (38 spp.); 55.20 *Ephuta* Say: 2 subgenera: *Ephuta* s. str. (41 spp.); and *Xenochile* Schuster (1 sp., *E. krombeini* Schuster)]

56. SCOLIIDAE (Scoliid Wasp Family)

Length: 20–50 mm. Body very hard, usually black, with bright patterns of red, yellow, white, or combinations of these. The widely separated hind coxae, broad thoracic sternum, and many fine, parallel wrinkles on the wing tips are characteristic of the family. Most of the genera are separated on the basis of wing venation characteristics, and many of the species may be identified by their distinctive abdominal color patterns. The male abdomen is sharply constricted at the base; that of the female, evenly tapered.

The larvae are parasitic on the white grub larvae of scarab beetles, especially the species of *Phyllophaga*. The female flies low over the ground seeking a suitable place to dig for a grub; on finding it, she alights and begins digging with mandibles and legs. After locating a suitable host, she lays her egg on it. The wasp larva that eventually hatches parasitizes the grub. Twenty two species occur in the U.S. and Canada.

Subfamily Campsomeridinae

Tribe Trielidini

[56.1 *Trielis* Saussure, subgenus *Trielis* s. str. (2 spp.); 56.2 *Crioscolia* Bradley (2 spp.)]

Tribe Campsomeridini

56.3 *Campsomeris* Guerin

The genus is divided into three subgenera—*Dielis* Saussure and Sichel (3 spp.), *Xanthocampsomeris* Bradley (3 spp.), and *Pygodasis* Bradley (2 spp.)—and includes the following species:

C. (*Dielis*) *plumipes fossulana* (Fabricius). L. 15–25 mm. Body dark; abdomen with four segments having complete apical bands somewhat emarginate on their basal margin. Adults are found at various flowers. (1) MD; (2) s.e. US; (3) TX.

C. (*Pygodasis*) *quadrimaculata* (Fabricius). L. 15–30 mm. Similar to the preceding except that yellow bands are present on abdominal segments 2 and 3 of some males, interrupted at the middle; some males have five segments with yellow bands, nearly interrupted in most cases; females have two large orange spots on abdominal segments 2 and 3 only. (1) CT, s. NY, NJ, MD; (2) s.e. US; (3) TX, OK.

[56.4 *Micromeriella* Betrem (1 sp., *M. marginella modesta* (Smith) (introduced; probably not established)); 56.5 *Campsomeriella* Betrem, subgenus *Annulimeris* Betrem (1 sp., *C. annulata* (Fabricius) (introduced; probably not established))]

Subfamily Scoliinae

56.6 *Scolia* Fabricius

The seven species in the United States and Canada belong to the subgenus *Discolia* Saussure and include the following:

S. (*Discolia*) *dubia dubia* Say. Abdomen with the second basal segment black and the remaining four reddish brown; the third usually has two large dorsal yellow spots. (1) n.e. US; (2) s.e. US; (3) AZ, NM, TX, OK; (5) CO.

56.7 *Triscolia* Saussure

One species, as follows:

T. ardens (Smith). L. 25–30 mm. Robust, hairy; black with red markings; apical portion of wings with numerous longitudinal wrinkles. Adults are found on flowers. (3) s.w. US. (A&J 276.)

57. SAPYGIDAE (Sapygid Wasp Family)

Length: 10–15 mm. Eyes deeply notched; legs short; body without hairlike setae; integument hard; some entirely black but others spotted or banded with yellow; both sexes winged. Larvae are parasites of other aculeate larvae, mostly of leafcutting bees that nest in hollow twigs. Some are cleptoparasites, that is, they kill the host larvae and their own larvae utilize the stored food. There are 16 species in the U.S. and Canada.

Subfamily Fedtschenkiinae

[57.1 *Fedtschenkia* Saussure (1 sp., *F. anthracina* (Ashmead))]

Subfamily Sapyginae

57.2 *Sapyga* Latreille

Eleven species, including the following:

S. angustata Cresson. Parasite on the bee, *Osmia atrocyanea* Cockerell. (3) CA, AZ; (4) WA, OR, NV, UT; (5) WY, CO.

[57.3 *Eusapyga* Cresson (7 spp.)]

Superfamily FORMICOIDEA

Only the ant family belongs to this superfamily.

58. FORMICIDAE

Length: 1–20 mm. Abdomen with first, or first and second, segment (of gaster) in the form of dorsal humps, or nodes; antennae with 6 to 13 segments, elbowed; most species brownish or black.

All ants are social insects with castes. Most eggs develop into nonreproductives, wingless females, and workers. The queens and males are winged on first emerging from the pupal case. (See Fig. 25.31 for general body form of winged male.) They swarm for a nuptial flight in the same manner as termites; after mating, the females shed their wings and the males die. As a result of this complexity, and various specializations, ants are of constant interest to students of animal behavior and the

Fig. 25.31. (*N.Y. S. Agric. Exp. Sta.*)

Fig. 25.32. Adult worker: (a) Lateral view, and (b) tarsal claw, showing tooth. (*U.S. Dept. of Agric.*)

subject of many books and papers. Very little space is available for this aspect of formicology, but a few examples are given.

Ant nests are the site of any number of invaders. Since the eyesight of ants is not particularly good, shape and color assist in mate recognition only to a limited degree. Pheromones—odorous chemical substances more or less unique to a species—are important aids. Nest guests are often beetles, many of which have evolved shapes similar to those of their hosts. Although not able to supply the proper odors, they can survive in the nest when other invaders would be torn to shreds and eaten, because they secrete substances that the ants like to lick. It is thought that some of these substances may have the effect of a drug since some colonies become so "addicted" to them that the ants spend more time tending the beetles than they do their own young. As a result, the colony begins to deteriorate and finally dies out.

Although ants cannot be identified easily to species without the aid of technical literature, much of this is readily available. A few of the most common species are described and illustrated here. Some species are pests and invade homes as well as picnics. A few may weaken wooden buildings by chewing wood to form tunnels but rarely is this damage very serious. They are sometimes confused with termites, but the two are easily distinguished by their wing venation (See Fig. 15.2 for termite wings). There are 696 species in the U.S. and Canada.

Subfamily Dorylinae

The dorylines, or army ants, of the New World have much the same habits as the famous Old World driver ants. They are predacious, forming long lines of foraging workers. Twenty-nine species have been recorded in the U.S., almost all of them confined to the extreme southern parts, mostly in the Southwest.

Tribe Ecitonini
58.1 *Labidus* Jurine

One species, as follows:

L. coecus (Latreille). (See Fig. 25.32.) (2) s. AR, LA; (3) OK, TX.

[58.2 *Nomamyrmex* Borgmier (1 sp., *N. esenbeckii wilsoni* (Santschi))]

58.3 *Neivamyrmex* Borgmeier

Twenty-four species, the following of which is common:

N. nigrescens (Cresson) (Legionary Ant). L. 3–5 mm (worker). Dark; antennae 12-segmented, short; head broad.

These predacious insects feed on immature stages of the Secondary Screw-worm (Diptera), among other insects. (See Fig. 25.33.) (2) s.e. US; (3) s.w. US; (5) CO, IA, KS, MO.

Subfamily Ponerinae

Members of this group nest in small colonies and are thought to be primitive. Most of our species occur in the southern U.S., where they prey upon a variety of insects.

Tribe Cerapachyini

[58.4 *Cerapachys* Smith (2 spp.)]

Tribe Acanthostichini

[58.5 *Ctenopyga* Ashmead (1 sp., *C. texanus* (Forel))]

Tribe Amblyoponini
58.6 *Amblyopone* Erichson

Three species, including the following:

A. pallipes (Haldeman). Found in wet, wooded areas, they feed upon Chilopods. (1) n.e. NA; (2) s.e. US; (3) AZ, NM, TX; (5) IA, CO.

[58.7 *Prionopelta* Mayr (1 sp., *P. antillana* Forel)]

Tribe Platythyreini

[58.8 *Platythyrea* Roger (1 sp., *P. punctata* (Smith))]

Tribe Ectatommini

[58.9 *Ectatomma* Smith (1 sp., *E. tuberculatum* (Olivier)); 58.10 *Gnamptogenys* Roger (1 sp., *G. hartmani* (Wheeler)); 58.11 *Proceratium* Roger (5 spp.); 58.12 *Discothyrea* Roger (1 sp., *D. testacea* Roger)]

Fig. 25.33. Adult worker: (a) Lateral view, and (b) right mandible. (*U.S. Dept. of Agric.*)

Tribe Ponerini

[58.13 *Pachycondyla* Smith (3 spp.); 58.14 *Brachyponera* Emery (1 sp., *B. solitaria* (Smith)); 58.15 *Cryptopone* Emery (1 sp., *C. gilva* (Roger)); 58.16 *Ponera* Latreille (2 spp.); 58.17 *Hypoponera* Santschi (5 spp.); 58.18 *Leptogenys* Roger, subgenus *Lobopelta* Mayr (2 spp.)]

Tribe Odontomachini

[58.19 *Odontomachus* Latreille (4 spp.)]

Subfamily Pseudomyrmecinae

The five species that belong to this subfamily are plant-inhabitating, with colonies in culms of sedges and grasses, stems of plants, and twigs and branches of trees.

[58.20 *Pseudomyrmex* Lund (5 spp.)] [1 sp. unplaced.]

Subfamily Myrmicinae

This largest subfamily in our region with over 500 species of diverse form and habits may be recognized easily by its two-segmented gaster stalk. Since many of the species are found in or near human habitations, they are commonly seen.

Tribe Myrmicini

[58.21 *Myrmica* Latreille (22 spp.); 58.22 *Paramyrmica* Cole (6 spp.); 58.23 *Manica* Jurine (4 spp.)]

58.24 *Pogonomyrmex* Mayr

These are the harvester ants. The genus is divided into two subgenera: *Pogonomyrmex* s. str. (19 spp.) and *Ephebomyrmex* Wheeler (3 spp.). The following species are common:

P. (Pogonomyrmex) barbatus (Smith) (Red Harvester Ant). L. 6–7 mm. Head, thorax, and abdomen usually red. The workers gather and store seeds and sometimes dead insects. They build their mounds in sandy areas. (2) AR, LA; (3) AZ, NM, TX, OK; (4) NV; (5) CO, w. KS.

P. (Pogonomyrmex) rugosus Emery. (See A&J 277.)

P. (Pogonomyrmex) occidentalis (Cresson) Western Harvester Ant).

P. (Pogonomyrmex) californicus (Buckley) (California Harvester Ant).

P. (Pogonomyrmex) badius (Latreille) (Florida Harvester Ant).

Tribe Pheidolini

[58.25 *Stenamma* Westwood (18 spp.); 58.26 *Aphaenogaster* Mayr (30 spp.); 58.27 *Veromessor* Forel (8 spp.)]

58.28 *Pheidole* Westwood

Seventy-four species, including the following:

P. dentata Mayr. (See Fig. 25.34 for adult worker.) (2) s.e. US; (3) TX; (5) KS.

P. megacephala (Fabricius) (Big-headed Ant). (2) FL.

Tribe Cardiocondylini

[58.29 *Cardiocondyla* Emery (5 spp.)]

Fig. 25.34. (*U.S. Dept. of Agric.*)

Tribe Crematogastrini

58.30 *Crematogaster* Lund

Thirty-one species, including the following:

C. lineolata (Say) (Lined Acrobatic Ant). L. 2.5–3.5 mm. (worker). Easily recognized by its heart-shaped abdomen, this species lives under stones in open places or under bark. It attends aphids and also infests houses, nesting in woodwork. (See Fig. 25.35 for adult worker.) (1) n.e. US; (2) s.e. US; (3) TX; (5) ND, CO.

Tribe Solenopsidini

58.31 *Monomorium* Mayr

Seven species, including the following:

M. minimum (Buckley) (Little Black Ant). L. 1.5–2 mm (worker). This is the common ant in houses throughout its range. (See Fig. 25.36 for adult worker.) (1), (2), (3), (4), (5), generally distributed.

M. pharaonis (Linnaeus) (Pharaoh Ant). L. ±2 mm (worker). A pest in homes and public buildings throughout the year. (See Fig. 25.37 for adult workers.) Introduced. Cosmopolitan.

[58.32 *Xenomyrmex* Forel (1 sp., *X. floridanus floridanus* Emery)]

58.33 *Solenopsis* Westwood

This genus contains 18 species of fire ants, several of which are pests. Their sting can cause large, painful welts on the skin (Fig. 25.38). Many are mound builders (Figs. 25.39 and 25.40) and create difficulties both in cultivated fields and in pastures. Some colonies are composed of mixed species because of the invasion of one species into the nests of another. The following species are the most common:

Fig. 25.35. (*U.S. Dept. of Agric.*)

Fig. 25.36. (*U.S. Dept. of Agric.*)

Fig. 25.39. (*U.S. Dept. of Agric.*)

S. geminata (Fabricius) (Fire Ant). L. 2.4–6 mm (worker). Head of majors (a worker caste) very large. This species is predacious on other insects. The workers produce a severe sting and have become a pest in many places. Attempts to control the ant by airplane spraying have proved futile. Hand control may sometimes be effected by slightly pressing small jars of alcohol into the mound. The ants stream out, enter the jar, and are killed. The colony may soon die out. (See Fig. 25.41.) (2) SC, GA, FL, LA, MS, AL; (3) TX.

S. molesta (Say) (Thief Ant). L. 1.3–1.8 mm (worker). These ants feed on a wide variety of materials; they can be crop pests, destroying seed and seedlings, as well as very common household pests. They are lestobiotic, that is, they nest in or near nests of other ants, from which they rob food and brood. (See Fig. 25.42 for adults worker.) (1), (2), (3), (4), (5), generally distributed.

S. invicta Buren (Red Imported Fire Ant). Imported into Alabama in 1945, from which it has spread throughout the

southeastern U.S. and has become an important pest. (2) TN, NC, SC, GA, LA, MS, AL, AR, FL; (3) TX.

S. richteri Florel (Black Imported Fire Ant). This species, a native of Argentina and Uruguay, was imported into the U.S. in 1920 and is now established into several localities. (2) n. AL, n. MS.

S. xyloni McCook (Southern Fire Ant). L. 1.6–5.8 mm (worker). This is a mound-building pest of lawn and field; it also has a painful sting. (See A&J 270.) (2) SC, GA, LA, MS, AL, FL; (3) s.w. US.

[58.34 *Oligomyrmex* Mayr (1 sp., *O. longii* (Wheeler)]

Tribe **Leptothoracini**

[58.35 *Macromischa* Roger (3 spp.); 58.36 *Rogeria* Emery (2 spp.); 58.37 *Leptothorax* Mayr: 4 subgenera: *Nesomyrmex* Wheeler (1 sp., *L. wilda* Smith), *Myrafant* Smith (33 spp.), *Dichothorax* Emery (2 spp.), and *Leptothorax* s. str. (6 spp.); 58.38 *Symmyrmica* Wheeler (1 sp., *S. chamberlini* Wheeler); 58.39 *Harpagoxenus* Forel 2 spp.)]

Tribe **Myrmecinini**

[58.40 *Myrmecina* Curtis (1 sp., *M. americana* Emery)]

Fig. 25.37. (*U.S. Dept. of Agric.*)

Fig. 25.38. (*U.S. Dept. of Agric.*)

Fig. 25.40. (*U.S. Dept. of Agric.*)

Fig. 25.41. Adult worker: (a) Lateral view, and (b) right mandible. (*U.S. Dept. of Agric.*)

Fig. 25.43. (*U.S. Dept. of Agric.*)

Tribe Tetramoriini

[58.41 *Triglyphothrix* Forel (1 sp., *T. lanuginosa* (Mayr))]

58.42 *Tetramorium* Mayr

Seven species, the following of which are pests:

T. bicarinatum (Nylander) (Guinea Ant). L. 3–3.5 mm (worker). Nests in soil but sometimes a house pest. Introduced. (2) GA, LA, MS, AL, FL; (3) TX.

T. caespitum (Linnaeus) (Pavement Ant). L. 2.5–3 mm (worker). Infests houses and is a pest in gardens. Introduced. (See Fig. 25.43 for adult workers.) (1) n.e. US; (2) KY, TN; (3) CA; (4) WA, NV: (5) NE, MO.

[58.43 *Anergates* Forel (1 sp., *A. atratulus* (Schenck)]

Tribe Ochetomyrmicini

58.44 *Ochetomyrmex* Mayr

One species, as follows:

O. auropunctata (Roger) (Little Fire Ant). L. ±1.5 mm (worker). Nests in soil, infests houses, and stings; often an important pest. (See Fig. 25.44.) Introduced. (2) FL; (3) CA.

Tribe Cephalotini

[58.45 *Zacryptocerus* Wheeler (3 spp.)]

Tribe Dacetini

[58.46 *Strumigenys* Smith (4 spp.); 58.47 *Smithistruma* Brown (25 spp.); 58.48 *Trichoscapa* Emery (1 sp., *T. membranifera* (Emery)); 58.49 *Quadristruma* Brown (1 sp., *Q. emmae* (Emery)]

Tribe Basicerotini

[58.50 *Eurhopalothrix* (1 sp., *E. floridana* Brown and Kempf)]

Tribe Attini

[58.51 *Cyphomyrmex* Mayr (2 spp.); 58.52 *Mycetosoritis* Wheeler (1 sp., *M. hartmanni* (Wheeler)); 58.53 *Trachymyrmex* florel (8 spp.); 58.54 *Acromyrmex* Mayr (2 spp.)]

58.55 *Atta* Fabricius

Two species, the following of which is common:

A. texana (Buckley) (Texas Leaf Cutting Ant). L. 1.5–12 mm (workers). Brownish red; head large; easily recognized by the large nests into which lines of workers bring pieces of leaves cut from nearby plants. The ants feed on the fungus gardens that grow on these leaves, each species cultivating its own species of fungus. (2) LA; (3) e. TX.

[Unplaced taxa of Myrmicinae (18 spp.)]

Subfamily Dolichoderinae

This small subfamily is mostly found in the southern U.S. The species are soil nesting; they emit a foul, smoky odor.

Tribe Dolichoderini

[58.56 *Dolichoderus* Lund, subgenus *Hypoclinea* Mayr (4 spp.)]

Tribe Tapinomini

[58.57 *Liometopum* Mayr (3 spp.)]

58.58 *Iridomyrmex* Mayr

Five species, the following of which is common:

I. humilis (Mayr) (Argentine Ant). L. 2.2–2.6 mm (workers). Nests in soil in large colonies; destroys other ant nests; infests houses; a pest of crops and poultry. (See Fig. 25.45 for adult worker.) Introduced. (1) IL, IN, OH, PA, NJ, MD; (2) s.e. US; (3) s.w. US.

[58.59 *Forelius* Emery (1 sp., *F. foetidus* (Buckley)]

Fig. 25.42. (*U.S. Dept. of Agric.*)

Fig. 25.44. (*U.S. Dept. of Agric.*)

Fig. 25.45. (*U.S. Dept. of Agric.*)

Fig. 25.47. (*U.S. Dept. of Agric.*)

58.60 *Conomyra* Forel

Three species, the following of which is common:

C. insana (Burkley) (Pyramid Ant). This ant builds pyramid-shaped mounds in open, sunny areas. They emit a disagreeable odor from anal glands and are predacious on other insects. (1) IL, IN, OH, PA, MD; (2) s.e. US; (3) CA; (4) OR; (5) ND.

58.61 *Tapinoma* Foerster

Three species, the following of which is common:

T. sessile (Say) (Odorous House Ant). L. 2.4–3.5 mm (workers). Nests in soil; cultivates aphids for honeydew; also infests houses. (See Fig. 24.46 for adults worker.) (1), (2), (3), (4), (5), generally distributed.

[Unplaced taxa (3 spp.)]

Subfamily Formicinae

The remainder of our species of ants belong in this subfamily. The abdominal stalk is one-segmented, that is, there is one node. The majority of species are northern.

Tribe Plagiolepidini
58.62 *Plagiolepis* Mayr

One species, as follows:

P. alluaudi Emery (Little Yellow Ant). This is an introduced species found only on Catalina Island, CA.

[58.63 *Acropyga* Roger (1 sp., *A. epedana* Snelling)]

Tribe Myrmelachistini

[58.64 *Myrmelachista* Roger (1 sp., *M. ramulorum* Wheeler)]

Tribe Brachymyrmecini

[58.65 *Brachymyrmex* Mayr (2 spp.)]

Fig. 25.46. (*U.S. Dept. of Agric.*)

Tribe Camponotini
58.66 *Camponotus* Mayr

These are carpenter ants. The genus is divided into seven subgenera: *Camponotus* Mayr (9 spp.), *Tanaemyrmex* Ashmead (14 spp.), *Myrmothrix* Forel (1 sp., *C. abdominalis* (Buckley), *Myrmentoma* (11 spp.), *Colobopsis* Mayr (8 spp.), *Myrmaphaenus* Emery (2 spp.), and *Myrmobrachys* Forel (3 spp.). The following species are common:

C. (Camponotus) ferrugineus (Fabricius) (Red Carpenter Ant). L. 6–13 mm (workers). This large black and red ant nests in rotted logs and stumps, the soil beneath, and in dead trees. (See Fig. 25.47 for adult worker and A&J 281.) (1) n.e. US; (5) NE, KS.

C. (Camponotus) pennsylvanicus (De Geer) (Black Carpenter Ant). L. 6–13 mm (workers). This large black ant nests in dead wood. It is a pest of buildings, but usually only in old wood. (See Fig. 25.48 for adult worker.) (1) n.e. NA; (2) s.e. US; (5) ND, SD, MN.

C. (Myrmothrix) abdominalis floridanus (Buckley) (Florida Carpenter Ant). L. 5–10 mm (workers). Nests in wood; infests bee hives and houses; many damage woodwork. (2) NC, SC, GA, FL, AL, MS.

Tribe Lasiini
58.67 *Lasius* Fabricius

This genus is divided into three subgenera *Lasius* s. str. (6 spp.), *Cautolasius* Wilson (3 spp.), and *Chthonolasius* Ruzsky (8 spp.). The following species is a pest:

L. (Lasius) alienus (Foerster) (Cornfield Ant). L. 2–2.5 mm. (workers). Nests in rotting logs and stumps and under stones. Cultivates root aphids in its nest and takes them to roots to feed. (1), (2), (3), (4), (5), spotty distribution throughout. (See Fig. 25.49 for adult worker.)

Fig. 25.48. (*U.S. Dept. of Agric.*)

Fig. 25.49. (*U.S. Dept. of Agric.*)

58.68 *Acanthomyops* Mayr

Fifteen species, the following of which are pests:

A. interjectus (Mayr) (Larger Yellow Ant). L. 4–4.5 mm (workers). Nests in exposed soil, making mounds, or under stones and other objects. (1) NY, PA, NJ, MD, DE; (2) s.e. US; (3) NM; (4) NV, UT; (5) n. Central States.

A. claviger (Roger) (Smaller Yellow Ant). L. 3–4 mm (workers). Nests in soil, especially under stones or other objects, and in rotting wood of logs and stumps. (1) ON, NY, MA, PA, NJ, MD; (2) s.e. US; (5) MN, NE, KS.

58.69 *Paratrechina* Motschulsky

This genus is divided into two subgenera: *Paratrechina* s. str. (1 sp.) and *Nylanderia* Emery (8 spp.). The following species is common:

P. (Paratrechina) longicornis (Latreille) (Crazy Ant). L. 2.2–3 mm (workers). Very long legs. Nests in trash, refuse, cavities in plants, trees, rotten wood, and in soil under stones, bricks, and so on. (See Fig. 25.50 for adult worker.) Introduced; found in towns and cities. (1) n.e. US [in greenhouses]; (2) SC, LA, MS, AL, GA, FL; (3) TX, CA.

[58.70 *Prenolepis* Mayr (3 spp.)]

58.71 *Myrmecocystus* Wesmael

Twenty-three species (see A&J 282, top), including the following:

M. melliger Forel (Honey Ant). L. 6–12 mm (workers). Golden to brown body covered with a fine pubescence; antennae 12-segmented, without a club, covered with fine pubescence; storage castes have very large gasters. This species in diurnal. Workers collect nectar and honeydew, which is stored in their distended crops or honey stomachs until they reach their nests. There it is distributed by regurgitation to their larvae and

Fig. 25.50. (*U.S. Dept. of Agric.*)

sister ants. Some of them serve as a storage caste, that is, they eat large quantities of honey that is kept undigested in the gaster. They then cling to the ceiling of the nest and hang downward, serving as living honey pots. Honey ants have long been esteemed as food by the Indians of Arizona and Mexico. (See A&J 280.) (3) w. TX.

Tribe **Formicini**

58.72 *Formica* Linnaeus

Ninety-seven species (see A&J 282, bottom), including the following:

F. pallidefulva pallidefulva Latreille. L. 3.5–6.5 (workers). Mandibles with broad dentate apical border; gaster yellowish or reddish brown; numerous hairlike setae on petiole. They form colonies, ranging in size from small to very large, in the soil, where they pile sticks and wood chips into piles. Their food is largely honeydew, but they also prey upon small arthropods.

Docile and easily enslaved by *Formica pergandei,* they have long been of interest to biologists because of this peculiarity. Briefly, another species raids their nests to carry larvae and pupae back to their own nests. These develop into worker slaves and become a part of the colony; although of a different species, they are similar enough to their captors to be accepted by them. Because this addition to the work force helps the colony as a whole, raids are made not only for food but to obtain still more slaves. (1) NY, NJ, PA, MD, DE; (2) s.e. US; (3) OK, TX; (5) CO, KS, MO.

F. fusca Linnaeus (Silky Ant). L. 3.5–6.5 mm (workers). Black or dark brown or gray, a common blackish ant. Nests in soil in many different situations and also under stones. (1) n.e. NA; (2) KY, WV, VA, TN, NC; (3) NM; (5) YK, SD, IA.

F. exsectoides Forel (Allegheny Mound Ant). L. 3–7 mm (workers). Builds large mounds; damages bark and cambium of small trees and shrubs. (1) n.e. NA; (2) KY, WV, VA, TN, NC, SC, GA; (3) NM; (5) IA, CO, KS.

F. obscuripes Forel (Western Thatching Ant). L. 3.5–7.5 mm (workers). A mound-building ant that constructs its nest out of twigs, grass, and other vegetation. (4) Pacific n.w.; (5) MT, ND.

[58.73 *Polyergus* Latreille (2 spp.)]

[Unplaced taxa in Formicidae (18 spp.)]

Superfamily VESPOIDEA

59. VESPIDAE (True Wasp Family)

Yellow Jackets and Hornets are as well known as bees for the ability of the females to sting with their modified ovipositor. Their powerful venom is a mixture of enzymes and proteins. (In contrast, the different venom of the solitary wasps and bees results in no more than a momentary, and usually slight, pain.) Most species of the Vespidae have taken advantage of the reputation of these few painful stingers and adopted their yellow or red warning markings.

Most members of this family fold their front wings longitudinally in repose (except Masarinae). The first discoidal cell is usually very long, longer than the submedian cell. The eyes are always emarginate. They vary in length from 8 to 25 mm.

Although some authors have treated the subfamily Eumeni-

nae as a separate group, the recent work of Carpenter (1982) has reunited these two groups as a single family. The subfamilies may be distinguished by the accompanying key. There are 415 species in 31 genera in the U.S. and Canada.

Key to the Subfamilies of Vespidea
(Adapted from Carpenter, 1982)

1. Anal lobe of hind wing short, one-third or less length of $M+Cu_1$ cell, or absent; recurrent veins of front wing variable; second discoidal cell (Cu_{1b}) not projecting apically; cu-a straight and much shorter than 1A side of second discoidal cell . **2**

 Anal lobe of hind wing long, one-half length of $M+Cu_1$ cell; recurrent veins of front wing received in different submarginal cells; second discoidal cell apically projecting; cu-a curved and about as long as 1A side of second discoidal cell **Euparagiinae**

2(1). Marginal cell ($3R_1$) of front wing narrowly rounded away from costa; no carina on mesoscutum opposite tegula; middel femur without basal ring (Masarini)
 . **Masarinae**

 Marginal cell of front wings narrowly rounded toward or along costa; mesoscutum either with a carina opposite tegula or with projecting lobe from posterolateral corner; middle femur usually with basal ring . **3**

3(2). Parategula (lobe projecting from posterolateral corner of mesoscutum) present; claws usually bifid; posterior lingula plate longer than broad; solitary or subsocial . **Eumeninae**

 Parategula absent; claws simple; posterior lingula plate as broad as long; eusocial **4**

4(3). Hind coxae with dorsal carina on posterior surface; hind wing without anal lobe; metasoma sessile with first tergum having abrupt declivity . **Vespinae**

 Hind coxae without dorsal carina; hind wing usually with anal lobe; metasoma petiolate or subsessile . **Polistinae**

Subfamily Euparagiinae

Characteristics as given in the key.

[59.1 *Euparagia* Cresson (6 spp.)]

Subfamily Masarinae
Tribe Masarini

Length: 8–18 mm. Characteristics as given in the key; in addition, the antennae are clubbed. These species make nests of mud attached to twigs or sometimes rocks and provision them with pollen and nectar rather than with insect prey as do other members of this family.

59.2 *Pseudomasaris* Ashmead

Fourteen species, including the following:

P. vespoides (Cresson). This species makes a nest of 2 to 13 hard cells attached to rocks and provisioned with pollen. (See A&J 268.) (3) CA, AZ, NM; (4) WA, OR, ID; (5) MT, ND, SD, WY, CO.

Subfamily Eumeninae (Potter Wasps)

L. 10–20 mm. Black with yellow or white markings; front wings with three submarginal cells; mandibles elongate, knifelike (except in *Zethus*, where they are short and broad with apex obliquely truncate and toothed); tarsal claws cleft. This largest group of Vespoid wasps makes nests of mud, either as mud pots or in burrows. *Zethus* Species nest in wood cavities, but some may construct a colony of cells composed of plant material glued together with a resinous material. Potter wasps feed their larvae caterpillars.

[59.3 *Odynerus* Latreille, subgenus *Odynerus* s. str. (4 spp.); 59.4 *Pterocheilus* Klug: 3 subgenera: *Megapterocheilus* (15 spp.), *Onchopterocheilus* Bohart (11 spp.), and *Micropterocheilus* Bohard (12 spp.); 59.5 *Leptochiloides* Bohart (3 spp.); 59.6 *Hypalastoroides* Saussure (2

spp.); 59.7 *Microdymerus* Thomson (15 spp.); 59.8 *Leptochilus*, subgenus *Leptochilus* s. str. (38 spp.); 59.9 *Cephalodynerus* Parker (5 spp.); 59.10 *Smeringodynerus* Snelling (1 sp., *S. morelios* (Saussure)); 59.11 *Dolichodynerus* Bohart (3 spp.); 59.12 *Maricopodynerus* Vierick (7 spp.); 59.13 *Stenodynerus* Saussure (60 spp.); 59.14 *Parancistrocerus* Bequart (37 spp.); 59.15 *Pseudepipona* Saussure (1 sp., *P. herrichii aldrichi* (Fox); 59.16 *Euodynerus* Dalla Torre (58 spp.)]

59.17 *Monobia* Saussure

Two species, including the following:

M. quadridens (Linnaeus). L. ±20 mm. Whitish markings. It lives in hollow stems, old Mud Dauber and potter wasp nests, and elsewhere. (1) n.e. US; (2) s.e. US; (3) NM; (5) KS.

[59.18 *Montezumia* Saussure (1 sp., *M. arizonensis* Bequaert)]

59.19 *Pachodynerus* Saussure

Three species, as follows:

P. nasidens (Latreille) (Keyhole Wasp). L. 8–12 mm. This species is confined to (2) FL; (3) s. AZ, TX.

P. astraeus (Cameron). Nests in cavities in wood, elderberry stems, and Mud Dauber cells.

P. erynnis (Lepeletier). These wasps make mud nests under siding boards of buildings, provisioning them with pyralid moth caterpillars. They also used old Mud Dauber nests.

[59.20 *Pseudodynerus* Saussure (1 sp., *P. quadrisectus* (Say)); 59.21 *Paranortonia* Bequaret (3 spp.)]

59.22 *Ancistrocerus* Wesmael

Thirty-one species, including the following:

A. antilope antilope (Panzer). L. ±15 mm. Black, head, thorax, and abdomen marked with narrow yellow bands; legs yellow. These wasps nest in sumac twigs, making mud parti-

tions. They are provisioned with larvae of the skipper *Epargyreus clarus* (Cramer). (1), (2), (3), (4), (5), generally distributed.

[59.23 *Symmorphus* Wesmael, subgenus *Symmorphus* s. str. (7 spp.)]

59.24 *Eumenes* Latreille

Eighteen species, all in the subgenus *Eumenes* s. str. The following are common:

E. fraternus Say (Potter Wasp). L. 13–17 mm. Body black with yellow markings on thorax and abdomen; wings smoky with violet iridescence. Adults fly from June to October to visit flowers. They make a nest of clay in the form of a pot and provision it with moth and beetle larvae that have been paralized by stinging. Their eggs are suspended from slender threads attached to the top or sides of the pot. (1) n.e. NA; (2) s.e. US; (3) TX, OK; (5) MN, NE, KS.

E. bollii bollii Cresson. Similar to the preceding and common in the West. (3) CA, AZ, MN; (4) Pacific n.w.; (5) n. Central States.

59.25 *Zethus* Fabricius

This genus is divided into three subgenera: *Zethus* s. str. (4 spp.), *Zethusculus* Saussure (1 sp., *Z. slossonae* Fox), and *Zethoides* Fox (2 spp.). The following species may serve as an example:

Z. (Zethus) spinipes variegatus Saussure. L. 13–18 mm. Black; thorax marked with yellow; very narrow apical band of yellow on abdominal segment 3; wings brownish to violet. Nests in mud cells attached to twigs. (1) n.e. US; (2) s.e. US; (3) TX.

[Unplaced taxa (9 spp.)]

Subfamily Vespinae (Hornets and Yellowjackets)

This advanced group of the vespids contains the Hornets— species that nest above ground—and the Yellowjackets— species that nest in the ground. In all cases, the nest is composed of paper, with several to many combs of hexagonal cells that are usually enclosed in a paper envelope. A new nest is made each year, construction being started in the spring by the fertilized queen that hibernated over the winter.

59.26 *Vespa* Linnaeus

In these large brown species, the distance from the ocelli to the top of the head is more than twice the width of the group of ocelli. We have only the following species, which was introduced from Europe in the last century.

V. crabro germanica Christ (European Hornet). L. ±25 mm. Brown with yellow markings; abdominal tergum 1 almost all black, tergum 2 about half black, and the remaining terga basally margined with black, with two lateral spots usually connected to black basal margin (see Fig. 25.51). Nest is constructed in hollow trees, attics, or walls of houses, with several to many tiers of hexagonal cells covered with a paper envelope. This is principally a forest species and therefore seldom encountered, although attracted to lights at night. Adults capture insects to feed their young. They may girdle twigs and stems to drink the sap. (1) n.e. US; (2) s.e. US; (5) ND, SD, MN, IA.

Fig. 25.51. (*U.S. Dept. of Agric.*)

59.27 *Vespula* Thomson

Somewhat smaller than the species of the preceding genus, these Yellowjackets and Hornets have a narrower vertex, and the distance form the ocelli to the top of the head is less than the width of the ocelli group. The genus is divided into two subgenera: *Vespula* s. str. (12 spp.) and *Dolichovespula* Rohwer (5 spp.). The latter is sometimes treated as a separate genus. In *Vespula* s. str., the distance from the bottom of the eye to the base of the mandible is very narrow, being less than half the width of the antennal flagellum, In *Dolichovespula*, this distance is as wide or wider than the width of the flagellum. The following are some common species:

V. (Vespula) austriaca (Panzer) (Parasitic Yellowjacket). L. ±18 mm (queen). Black with yellow on head, thorax, and bands on abdomen; long erect hairs scattered over entire upper side of hind tibiae. This species has no workers; queens lay eggs in nests of closely related species, particularly *V. acadica* (Sladen) (see following species). (1) ON, QU, NB, NC, NF, PE, ME, e. NY, VT, NH, MS, CT, RI, WI, MI; (3) n. CA, n. AZ, n. NM; (4) Pacific n.w.; (5) KE, MC, NT, YK, AB, SK, MT, w. MT, w. WY, w. CO.

V. (Vespula) acadica (Sladen). Similar to the preceding; gaster with two yellow spots on tergum 2 (variable). Distribution as given for the preceding.

V. (Vespula) germanica (Fabricius) (German Yellowjacket). L. ±25 mm (queen); 12–14 mm (workers). Brown with yellow markings on head, thorax, and bands on abdomen; basal black band of abdominal tergum 2 parallel-sided laterally but with posteriomedian lobe that is either narrowly triangular or parallel-sided with apex acumenate, apex of lobe attaining hind margin of tergum, or nearly so (see Fig. 25.52). The nest is built inside walls or under clapboards of old houses as a series of horizontal combs connected by pedicels and surrounded by a paper envelope. It is attached only at the top. This species, introduced in the late 1800s, is a common uninvited guest at picnics. (1) WI, MI, NY, VT, e. IN, OH, PA, NJ, MD, DE; (2) n. VA; (5) MB.

V. (Vespula) maculifrons (Buysson). L. ±18 mm (queen); ±12 mm (workers). Very similar to the preceding; basal black band of tergum 2 triangular. (See Fig. 25.53.) The nest is underground, usually along creek banks but also in yards and golf courses. This species often visits picnics in search of food, and, although aggressive near its nest, seldom stings at the

Fig. 25.52. (*U.S. Dept. of Agric.*)

picnic table unless accidentally contacted on food. The workers visit flowers, fruits, and are attracted to sweets as well as other food substances, including meat. They also gather insects and sometimes help reduce pest populations. (1) n.e. US; (2) s.e. US; (3) n. and e. TX, OK; (5) ND, SD, MN, NB, IA, KS, MO.

V. (*Vespula*) *pensylvanica* (Saussure) (Western Yellow-jacket). L. ±18 mm (queen); 12–14 mm (workers). Dark brown with yellow markings; similar to the preceding but distinguished by the irregular, usually triangular, pale mark on hind margin of the pronotum (See Fig. 25.54). The nest is underground, usually in rodent burrows. Workers prey upon a wide variety of insects. (1) WS; (3) CA, AZ, NM; (4) s. BC, WA, OR, ID, NV, UT; (5) AB, SK, MT, WY, w. CO, ND, SD, MN.

V. (*Dolichovespula*) *maculata* (Linnaeus) (Baldfaced Hornet; Whitefaced Hornet). L. 18–20 mm (queen); 12–14 mm (workers). Black with white markings; male with white margin on first abdominal segment; both sexes with white markings on head and terminal segments of abdomen (see Fig. 25.55.) This species is very common on flowers. Its nest is aerial, usually suspended high in trees or tall bushes, but a few near the ground. Males appear in the fall; the colony disintegrates and does not overwinter. The fertilized queen hibernates until spring and then starts a new colony. This species is the more widespread of the group. (1) n.e. NA; (2) s.e. US; (3) e. TX, e. OK, n. AZ, n. NM, n. CA; Pacific n.w.; (5) n. Central States and Provinces.

V. (*Dolichovespula*) *arenaria* (Fabricius) (Aerial Yellow-jacket). L. ±18 mm (queen); 11–13 mm (workers). Similar to the preceding except that it is marked with yellow and with much less black on abdomen. (See Fig. 25.56 and A&J 284.) The nest is aerial, anywhere from a few inches above ground to high in trees. Nests are also built in garages and sheds. (1) n.e. NA; (2) WV, VA, KY, TN; (3) CA, AZ, NM; (4) Pacific n.w.; (5) MT, WY, CO, MN, IA, AB, SK, MB, KE, MC, NT, YK.

Fig. 25.54. (*U.S. Dept. of Agric.*)

Subfamily **Polistinae** (Paper Wasps)

These wasps are long-legged and usually brown with fewer yellow markings than Yellow Jackets or hornets; their middle tibia has two apical spurs. Their nest lacks an outer paper covering and has only one comb attached to a support by a pedicel. Most of the species occur in the southern U.S.

59.28 *Polistes* Latreille

Eighteen species, the following of which are common:

P. annularis (Linnaeus). L. ±18 mm. Blackish brown, with a conspicuous yellow margin on abdominal tergum 1. The nest is a single horizontal comb of hexagonal paper cells attached to a support by a pedicel. The adults are predacious. (1) CT, s. NY, NJ, MD, DE; (2) s.e. US; (3) TX; (5) SD.

P. fuscatus bellicosus Cresson. L. ±18 mm. Similar to the preceding; abdominal terga 1 and 2 with narrow apical yellow margin. Nest similar to the preceding. (2) SC, GA, FL, LA, MS, AL; (3) TX.

P. fuscatus aurifer Saussure (Golden Paper Wasp). L. 16–20 mm. Similar to the preceding, with golden pile. Adults are abundant on flowers, especially on goldenrod in the fall.

Fig. 25.53. (*U.S. Dept. of Agric.*)

Fig. 25.55. (*U.S. Dept. of Agric.*)

Fig. 25.56. (*U.S. Dept. of Agric.*)

Both males and females fly from May to October. Not an aggressive species. (3) CA; (4) BC, WA, OR, ID, NV; (5) MT.

P. dorsalis dorsalis (Fabricius). L. 17–18 mm. Reddish brown; antennae dark; abdomen dark with tergum 1 narrowly outlined with yellow; tarsi yellow. Nest similar to the preceding. (See A&J 285.) (2) s.e. US; (3) NM, TX, OK; (5) CO, KS, MO.

P. gallicus (Linnaeus). Recently introduced from Europe into the Boston area; now common in Cambridge.

[59.29 *Mischocyttarus* Saussure, subgenus *Kappa* Saussure (2 spp.)]

59.30 *Brachygastra* Perty

One species, as follows:

B. mellifica (Say) (Honey Wasp). These wasps make perennial nests in low trees, each with as many as 50,000 cells. Adults collect and store honey but do not cap the cells as do Honey Bees. (3) s. TX, s. AZ.

[59.31 *Polybia* Lepeletier (2 spp.)]

Superfamily POMPILOIDEA
60. POMPILIDAE (Spider Wasp Family)

Length: 5–40 mm. Long-legged solitary wasps; wings not folded when at rest; hind femora long, extending beyond abdomen; body usually black or blue, some with orange bands, rarely marked with yellow; wings usually black or bluish and jerked continuously when the insect runs about on ground in search of spider prey. Female antennae are frequently held curled. These wasps can sting. Most species burrow in the ground and form branching tunnels that are stocked with paralyzed spiders. The female attaches an egg to each spider, which serves as host for the larva to feed on after hatching. After the larva pupates, the adult emerges from the ground to repeat the process. A few species construct mud cells under stones or in holes in wood. Some are parasitic in the burrows of other spider wasps. There are 288 species in the U.S. and Canada.

Subfamily Pepsinae
Tribe Pepsini

[60.1 *Chirodamus* Haliday (8 spp.)]

60.2 *Pepsis* Fabricius

This genus is divided into four subgenera—*Pepsis* s. str. (6 spp.), *Stenopepsis* Banks (1 sp., *P. venusta* Smith), *Dinopepsis* Banks (2 spp.), and *Gigantopepsis* Lucas (3 spp.)—and the unassigned (6 spp.). The following species may serve as an example:

P. (Dinopepsis) formosa (Say). L. ±40 mm. Body black, satiny with a greenish reflection; wings orange, smoky near margins. Adults frequent flowers of woody shrubs and milkweeds. They prey upon tarantulas. Their sting is severe, even violent. (See A&J 287.) (3) AZ, NM, TX, OK; (4) NV; (5) KS, MO.

[60.3 *Hemipepsis* Dahlbom (4 spp.); 60.4 *Priocnessus* Banks (6 spp.); 60.5 *Entypus* Dahlbom (11 spp.); 60.6 *Cryptocheilus* Panzer (8 spp.); 60.7 *Priocnemis* Schiodte: 3 subgenera: *Sphictostethus* Kohl (1 sp., *P. pretiosa* Banks), *Priocnemissus* Huapt (3 spp.), and *Priocnemis* s. str. (13 spp.); 60.8 *Calicurgus* Pate (4 spp.); 60.9 *Dipogon* Fox: 3 subgenera: *Deuteragenia* Sustera (15 spp.), *Dipogon* s. str. (11 spp.), and *Winnemanella* Krombein (1 sp., *D. fulleri* Krombein)]

Tribe Ageniellini

[60.10 *Phanagenia* Banks (1 sp., *P. bombycina* (Cresson)); 60.11 *Auplopus* Spinola (15 spp.); 60.12 *Ageniella* Banks: 5 subgenera: *Leucophrus* Townes (4 spp.), *Nemagenia* Banks (1 sp., *A. longula* (Cresson)), *Priophanes* Banks (11 spp.), *Ageniella* s. str. (19 spp.), and *Ameragenia* Banks (3 spp.); 60.13 *Priocnemella* Banks (1 sp., *P. tabascoensis* (Cameron))]

Subfamily Pompilinae
Tribe Aporini

[60.14 *Epipompilus* Kohl (1 sp., *E. pulcherrimus* (Evans)); 60.15 *Aporus* Spinola: 2 subgenera: *Aporus* s. str. (9 spp.) and *Plectraporus* Bradley (1 sp., *A. hirsutus* (Banks)); 60.16 *Chelaporus* Bradley (1 sp., *C. anomalus* (Banks)); 60.17 *Allaporus* Banks (5 spp.); 60.18 *Psorthaspis* Banks (15 spp.)]

Tribe Pompilini

[60.19 *Tastiotenia* (1 sp., *T. festiva* Evans); 60.20 *Chalcochares* Banks (2 spp.); 60.21 *Evagetes* Lepeletier (12 spp.); 60.22 *Agenioideus* Ashmead: 3 subgenera: *Ridestus* Banks (1 sp., *A. biedermani* (Banks)), *Agenioideus* s. str. (1 sp., *A. humilis* (Cresson)), and *Gymnochares* Banks (1 sp., *A. birkmanni* (Banks)); 60.23 *Sericopompilus* Howard (3 spp.)]

60.24 *Episyron* Schiødte

Eight species, including the following:

E. biguttatus biguttatus (Fabricius) (Tornado Wasp). L. 9–18 mm. Scales on parts of thorax and first abdominal tergum; body black, marked with pale buff; pubescence reflecting a somewhat bluish color. These very active wasps hunt orbweaver spiders to provision their burrows, visiting flowers of many kinds, but especially umbelliferous plants. They usually nest in sand or gravel banks. Adults are found during June and July. (1) n.e. NA; (2) s.e. US; (3) TX; (5) n. Central States.

[60.25 *Poecilopompilus* Howard (8 spp.); 60.26 *Tachypompilus* Ashmead (6 spp.); 60.27 *Anoplius* Dufour: 5 subgenera: *Lophopompilus* Radoszkowski (5 spp.), *Notiochares* Banks (2 spp.), *Anopliodes* Banks (2 spp.), *Arachnophroctonus* Howard (13 spp.), and *Anoplius* s. str. (14 spp.); 60.28 *Pompilus* Fabricius: 7 subgenera: *Hesperopompilus* Evans (6 spp.), *Xenopompilius* Evans (1 sp., *P. tiahuicanus* Evans), *Perissopompilus* Evans (2 spp.), *Xerochares* Evans (1 sp., *P. expulsus* Schultz),

Ammosphex Wilcke (12 spp.), *Arachnospila* Kincaid (4 spp.), and *Anoplochares* Banks (2 spp.); 60.29 *Aporinellus* Banks (10 spp.); 60.30 *Allochares* Banks (1 sp., *A. azureus* (Cresson)); 60.31 *Paracyphnonyx* Gribodo (1 sp., *P. funereus* (Lepeletier))]

Subfamily Ceropalinae

Tribe Minageniini

[60.32 *Minagenia* Banks (10 spp.)]

Tribe Notocyphini

[60.33 *Notocyphus* Smith (2 spp.)]

Tribe Ceroplaini

60.34 *Ceropales* Latreille

Members of this genus have their hind tarsal claws bent at right angles. Twenty-one species, including the following:

C. bipunctata Say. Wingspan: 10–16 mm. Black, marked with creamy white on head and thorax; front and middle femora usually black, but reddish in the southern subspecies, *C. b. tibialis* Banks (2) NC, FL) and *C. b. bipunctata* s. str. (1) n.e. NA; (2) s.e. US; (3) TX; (5) ND, SD, MN, NE, IO, KS, MO.

61. RHOPALOSOMATIDAE (Rhopalosomatid Wasp Family)

Length: 6–17 mm. These wasps are parasites of cricket nymphs. There are three species, as follows:

61.1 *Rhopalosoma* Cresson

One species, as follows:

R. nearcticum Brues. 13.5–17 mm. Adults fully winged; enlarged ocelli; nocturnal. (1) MD; (2) s.e. US; (5) MO.

61.2 *Olixon* Cameron

One species, as follows:

O. banksii (Brues). L. ±6 mm. Wings brachypterous in both sexes; ocelli very small; diurnal. (1) OH, NY; DC; (2) NC, GA, FL; (5) MN, KS.

61.3 *Liosphex* Townes

One species, as follows:

L. varius Townes. (2) LA, FL.

Superfamily SPHECOIDEA

Although authorities differ in their treatment of this group, the comprehensive review of these wasps by Bohart and Menke (1976) considers all genera to belong to the single family Sphecidae. Other authors elevate many of the subfamilies to family status, as is the case in the *Catalog of Hymenoptera*. The following review of the group follows Bohart and Menke.

62. SPHECIDAE (Digger Wasp Family)

L. 2–40 mm. Body usually black to reddish brown, some steel blue, a few metallic greenish, sometimes marked with yellow or rusty red; body setae sparse, simple; pronotum immovably joined with mesothorax, its posterior margin nearly straight in dorsal view and usually separated from scutum by a constriction that forms a characteristically raised collar; posterior margin of the pronotum always with a rounded pronotal lobe laterally, almost always well separated from tegula (See Fig. 25.6); hind tarsi without flattened first tarsomere but with cleaning brush in a slight depression.

In North America, these wasps are all solitary, although they have complicated behavioral patterns that certainly point toward sociality. In some species, the female feeds larvae from day to day instead of merely laying her eggs on full supplies of food and leaving the larvae to shift for themselves (as, for example, Spider Wasps do). The food is often, but not always, buried at the end of tunnels dug in the soil. Although this group is known as the Digger Wasps, some nest in habitats above ground, such as hollowed out twigs, abandoned beetle larvae borings, and rotten wood, and a few are mason wasps, building various kinds of mud cells. All species use animal food, mostly insects and spiders. These may be stung and either paralyzed or killed. When killed, the prey apparently is partially preserved by the venom because it does not decay as rapidly as might be expected. There are 1139 species in the U.S. and Canada. The accompanying Key distinguishes the subfamilies and tribes that occur in the U.S. and Canada.

Key to the Subfamilies of Tribes of Sphecidae of the U.S. and Canada
(Adapted from Bohart and Menke, 1976)

1.	Gaster with cylindrical petiole composed of sternum only, tergum 1 removed to apex of sternum 1, or if tergum 1 slender and petiole-like, it is displaced to apex of sternum 1 (see Ammophilini); jugal lobe of hind wing comprising nearly all of anal area (Sphecinae) .	2
	Gaster without a petiole composed of sternum only; if with petiole, jugal lobe of hind wing comprising not much more than half of anal area .	4
2(1).	Tarsal claws of front leg and middle leg with two or more basal teeth along inner margin . **Sphecini**	
	Tarsal claws of front leg and middle leg simple or each with single tooth on inner margin .	3
3(2).	Tarsal claws simple or rarely with basal tooth . **Ammophilini**	
	Tarsal claws with one mesal tooth . **Sceliphronini**	
4(1).	Middle tibiae with two apical spurs (rarely none) .	5
	Middle tibiae with one apical spur (rarely none) .	12
5(4).	Claws with one inner tooth or bifid (Ampulicinae) .	6
	Claws simple or with basal lobe, not tooth (62.82 *Pseudoplisus*)	7

Key to the Subfamilies of Tribes of Sphecidae of the U.S. and Canada
(Adapted from Bohart and Menke, 1976) (*Contd.*)

6(5). Gaster petiolate ..**Ampulicini**
Gaster sessile ..**Dolichurini**

7(5). Mandible toothed or notched externoventrally; jugal lobe of hind wing small (Xenosphecinae) ..**Xenosphecini**
Mandible simple externoventrally ... *8*

8(7). Hind wing with jugal lobe more than half length of anal area (Astatinae)**Astatini**
Hind wing with jugal lobe less than half length of anal area (Nyssoninae) *9*

9(8). Front wing with prestigmal length of first submarginal cell much more than length of wing behind marginal cell; (in part)**Stizini**
Front wing with prestigmal length of first submarginal cell not distinctly more than length of wing beyond marginal cell, or propodeum with lateral tooth or prong *10*

10(9). Pronotal collar low and longer than scutellum in dorsal view; (in part)**Alyssonini**
Pronotal collar shorter than scutellum in dorsal view *11*

11(10). Mesoscutum with median lines fused to form single furrow; propodeum with lateral tooth or prong ..**Nyssonini**
Mesoscutum with median lines well separated; propodeum not toothed nor prolonged *12*

12(11). Front wing with second submarginal cell receiving at least second recurrent vein ...**Gorytini**
Front wing with second submarginal cell receiving at most first recurrent vein ...**Mellinini**

13(12). Gaster with petiole composed of sternum only, tergum 1 removed to distal end of sternum 1 (Pemphredoninae) ... *14*
Gaster not petiolate, or petiole composed of both tergum and sternum *15*

14(13). Front wing with three submarginal cells**Psenini**
Front wing with no more than two submarginal cells; (in part)**Pemphredonini**

15(14). Front wing either with one discoidal cell, at most two submarginal cells, and much enlarged stigma, or, two to three submarginal cells, stigma nearly as large as first discoidal cell, two sessile submarginal cells, mandible simple externoventrally, inner orbits not angulate, and hind wing with media diverging at or before cu-a; (in part) ..**Pemphredonini**
Without either combination above .. *16*

16(15). Hind ocelli deformed, usually scarlike, or greatly reduced *17*
Hind ocelli normal .. *18*

17(16). Hind wing with jugal lobe subequal to length of anal area (Larrinae)**Larrini**
Hind wing with jugal lobe at most a little more than half as long as anal area (Nyssoninae) ..**Bembicini**

18(16). Scutal carina oblique posterolaterally; metapleuron broad below, not tapering (Nyssoninae); (in part) ...**Stizini**
Scutum without oblique carina .. *19*

19(18). Propodeum with small, sharp dorsal tooth posterolaterally (Nyssoninae); (in part) ..**Alyssonini**
Propodeum not distinctly toothed .. *20*

20(19). Antennal sockets placed above clypeus by at least one-third of a socket diameter; front wing with three submarginal cells (Philanthinae) *21*
Antennal sockets touching clypeus, or if not, then front wing with fewer than three submarginal cells (Larrinae) ... *23*

21(20). Hind femur ending in flattened plate or truncation**Cercerini**
Hind femur ending normally ... *22*

22(21). Inner orbits of eye sharply angulate or notched**Philanthini**
Inner orbits of eye straight or smoothly curved**Aphilanthopini**

23(20). Inner orbits of eye angulate; front wing often with only one submarginal cell ...**Trypoxylini**
Inner orbits of eye not angulate .. *24*

24(23). Front wing with more than one submarginal cell, or more than two discoidal cells, or both (subdiscoidal cell counted as discoidal cell) *25*
Front wing with one submarginal cell and one or two discoidal cells *26*

25(24). Inner orbits of eyes converging strongly below**Bothynostethini**
Inner orbits of eyes not converging strongly below**Miscophini**

26(24). Front wing with two well-defined discoidal cells in addition to submarginal cell ...**Crabronini**
Front wing with only one discoidal cell**Oxybelini**

Fig. 25.57. (*From Ent. Soc. America*)

Subfamily Ampulicinae

L. 5–15 mm. These wasps nest in twigs, under bark, and under leaf litter on the ground and capture cockroach nymphs for larval food. Unlike other sphecids, they carry their prey backward, on foot, as most pompilid wasps do.

Tribe Dolichurini

[62.1 *Dolichurus* Latreille (1 sp., *D. greenei* Rohwer (1) n.e. US; (2) s.e. US, (5) MO); 62.2 *Paradolichurus* Williams (1 sp., *P. californicus* (Williams), (3) s. CA)]

Tribe Ampulicini
62.3 *Ampulex* Jurine

Two species, as follows:

A. canaliculata Say. Nests in cavities in twigs and in borings in wood. (1) n.e. US; (2) s.e. US; (5) KS, MO.

A. ferruginea Bradley. (See Fig. 25.57.) (2) FL; (3) TX.

Subfamily Sphecinae (Thread-waisted Wasps)

L. 18–30 mm. These wasps, which are often also called Digger Wasps, use spiders, grasshoppers, katydids, crickets, and caterpillars for larval food stores, but usually a single kind, according to species or genus. The advanced behavior of the females of many species of this group has been the subject of numerous studies by animal behaviorists. Some use "tools" in the form of pebbles employed as a hammer or soil tamper. This seemingly unique feature of the world of nonhuman animals has attracted much speculation as a sign of intelligence. However, since it is a fixed part of the instinctive behavior of several species of *Ammophila* (62.14), it probably evolved from their carrying behavior and use of the front of the head for pounding purposes. It should not be confused with similar behavior in man.

Tribe Sceliphronini
62.4 *Chlorion* Latreille

Two, species as follows:

C. aerarium Patton (Blue Mud Dauber). L. ±25 mm. Bronze to purplish blue. Nests in sand, probably constructing several cells that are provisioned with crickets. (1), (2), (3), (4), (5), generally distributed.

C. cyaneum Dahlbom. Similar to the preceding. (3) AZ, NM, TX.

[62.5 *Podium* Fabricius (3 spp.)]

62.6 *Chalybion* Dahlbom

Two species, the following being widespread:

C. californicum (Saussure) (Blue Mud Wasp). L. 22–24 mm. Entirely metallic blue or violaceous; petiole about same length as rest of abdomen. This species sometimes takes over old nests of Mud Daubers. They visit pools to fetch water to soften the old nest, which they then remodel for their own use. (1), (2), (3), (4), (5), generally distributed.

62.7 *Sceliphron* Klug

Two species, the following being widely distributed:

S. caementarium (Drury) (Black and Yellow Mud Dauber). L. 24–28 mm. Body black, with yellow markings; pedicel about twice length of rest of abdomen. This species builds mud nests attached to ceiling and walls of sheds, other out-buildings, sides of buildings, old cars, and many other sites. These are stocked with spiders. Adults are common at flowers of parsnip, water parsnip, and others. They are often seen collecting mud at edges of puddles and pools. (See A&J 292.) (1), (2), (3), (4), (5), generally distributed.

Tribe Sphecini
62.8 *Sphex* Linnaeus

This genus is divided into two subgenera: *Sphex* s. str. (11 spp.) and *Fernaldina* Bohart and Menke (1 sp., *S. lucae* Saussure). The following species are common:

S. ichneumoneus (Linnaeus) (Great Golden Digger Wasp). L. ±24 mm. Black; abdomen (in part) and legs red or reddish with golden pile; wings smoky yellow. Nest made in hard-packed soil or sand and provisioned with grasshoppers. Visits flowers of sumac, *Clematis* sp., milkweed, ceanothus, and others. (See A&J 289.) (1), (2), (3), (4), (5), generally distributed.

S. pensylvanicus Linnaeus (Great Black Wasp). L. ±28 mm. Similar to the preceding except entirely black; wings dark, smoky. Nests are made in soft earth in sheltered areas and provisioned with grasshoppers. (1) n.e. US; (2) s.e. US; (3) s.e. US; (5) n. Central States.

[62.9 *Isodontia* Patton: 2 subgenera: *Isodontia* s. str. (3 spp.) and *Murrayella* Bohart and Menke (3 spp.); 62.10 *Palmodes* Kohl (10 spp.); 62.11 *Prionyx* Vander Linden (7 spp.)]

Tribe Ammophilini
62.12 *Podalonia* Fernald

Nineteen species, the following of which is common:

P. luctuosa (Smith) (Cutworm Wasp). L. ±25 mm. Abdominal stalk short; head and thorax black; abdomen beyond stalk yellowish orange except for dorsal-apical black spot; wings black. Before building their nests, these insects capture and sting caterpillars, usually cutworms, using one for each cell. (1)

n.e. NA; (4) Pacific n.w.; (5) n. Central States and Provinces. (A&J 293).

62.13 *Eremnophila* Menke

One species, as follows:

E. aureonotata (Cameron). L. 20–22 mm. Steel blue; head and thorax with silvery patches of pubescence. Nest is provisioned with skipper larvae. (1) n.e. US; (2) s.e. US; (3) TX; (5) ND, SD, MN, NE, IA, KS, MO.

62.14 *Ammophila* Kirby

Sixty-one species, including the following:

A. azteca azteca Cameron (Aztec Thread-waisted Wasp). L. ±25 mm. Black; abdomen either with patches of red or nearly all red; wings transparent; legs long and black. Nest is provisioned with "hairless" larvae, usually butterfly or geometrid larvae. (1), (2), (3), (4), (5), generally distributed.

A. procera Dehlbom (Common Thread-waisted Wasp.). L. 22–24 mm. Similar to the preceding but much larger; thorax with transverse ridging; abdomen red in part. This species flies along roadsides and paths to visit flowers from June to September. It has been observed by the author using stones (as do other species of this family) to tap down the soil surface after covering its nesting hole, and once using a twig. This instinctive habit is the result of a series of plastic behavioral patterns, each released in proper succession by genetic programming. (See A&J 290.) (1), (2), (3), (4), (5), generally distributed.

A. wrightii (Cresson) (Wright's Thread-waisted Wasp). L. 11–13 mm. Abdominal petiole much longer than gaster; head, thorax, and abdomen orange, the latter with black basal bands; wings transparent. Nest is provisioned with geometrid larvae. (See A&J 291.) (3) CA, AZ, NM, w. TX; (4) WA, OR, ID, NV, UT.

Subfamily Pemphredoninae (Aphid Wasps)

Length: 2–15 mm. These wasps build their nests in cavities in wood or in soil and provision them with aphids and other Homoptera. The group is poorly known biologically.

Tribe Psenini

[62.15 *Ammopsen* Krombein (1 sp., *A. masoni* Krombein); 62.16 *Mimesa* Schuckard (22 spp.); 62.17 *Mimumesa* Malloch (16 spp.); 62.18 *Pseneo* Mallach (3 spp.)]

62.19 *Psen* Latreille

Four species, including the following:

P. barthi Viereck. Nests are made in dead wood and provisioned with species of Membracidae. (1) QU, WI, PA, CT, MD; (2) GA.

[62.20 *Pluto* Pate (16 spp.); 62.21 *Psenulus* Kohl (4 spp.)]

Tribe Pemphredonini

[62.22 *Diodontus* Curtis (27 spp.); 62.23 *Pemphredon* Latreille: 2 subgenera: *Pemphredon* s. str. (8 spp.) and *Cemonus* Panzer (4 spp.); 62.24 *Passaloecus* Shuckard (11 spp.); 62.25 *Polemistus* Saussure (1 sp., *P. pusillus* Saussure); 62.26 *Stigmus* Panzer: 2 subgenera: *Stigmus* s. str. (7 spp.) and *Atopostigmus* Krombein (2 spp.); 62.27 *Spilomena* Shuckard (5 spp.); 62.28 *Xysma* Pate (1 sp., *X. ceanothae* (Viereck));

62.29 *Pulverro* Pate (7 spp.); 62.30 *Ammoplanops* Gussakovskij (7 spp.); 62.31 *Ammoplanus* Giraud (7 spp.); 62.32 *Ammoplanellus* Gussakovij; 2 subgenera: *Ammoplanellus* s. str. (2 spp.) and *Parammoplanus* Pate (3 spp.); 62.33 *Timberlakena* Pate (5 spp.)]

Subfamily Astatinae (Astatid Wasps)

Length: 12–16 mm. These wasps nest in the ground and use various nymphal Hemiptera, such as stink bugs, for larval provisions. Most species are western; a few, transcontinental.

Tribe Astatini

[62.34 *Diploplectron* Fox (13 spp.)]

62.35 *Astata* Latreille

Fourteen species, including the following:

A. occidentalis Cresson. (1), (2), (3), (4), (5), generally distributed.

[62.36 *Dryudella* Spinola (10 spp.)]

Subfamily Larrinae (Larrid Wasps)

L. 10–25 mm. The group is rather poorly known biologically. Many species provide their nests with spiders, grasshoppers, katydids, crickets, mantids, or cockroaches. They usually nest in sandy places.

Tribe Larrini

[62.37 *Larra* Fabricius (1 sp., *L. analis* Fabricius); 62.38 *Liris* Fabricius, subgenus *Leptolarra* Cameron (9 spp.); 62.39 *Larropsis* Patton (24 spp.); 62.40 *Ancistromma* Fox (11 spp.)]

62.41 *Tachytes* Panzer

Thirty-two species, including the following:

T. distinctus distinctus Smith (Sand-Loving Tachytes). L. 10–20 mm. Eyes green, very large; body black with yellow hairlike setae on thorax; wings transparent. Nests are built in sandy soil, lizard holes, or abandoned nests of the Cicada Killer (*Sphecius speciosus*) and provisioned with nymphal grasshoppers.

[62.42 *Tachysphex* Kohl (43 spp.); 62.43 *Prosopigastra* Costa (1 sp., *P. nearctica* Bohart)]

Tribe Miscophini

62.44 *Lyroda* Say

Two species, the following being common:

L. subita (Say). L. ±8 mm. Wings yellowish, apex dusky; abdominal base with dorsal carina; clypeus tridentate laterally. This species, a ground nester, is often seen flying about just above the ground in search of field crickets (*Nemobius* spp.); it also visits flowers from July to September. (1), (2), (3), (4), (5), generally distributed.

[62.45 *Plenoculus* Fox (18 spp.); 62.46 *Solierella* Spinola (37 spp.); 62.47 *Miscophus* Jurine, subgenus *Miscophus* s. str. (1 sp., *M. americanus* Fox), subgenus *Nitelopterus* Ashmead (15 spp.); 62.48 *Nitela* Latreille, subgenus *Nitela* s. str. (5 spp.)]

Tribe Trypoxylini

All of these species are black or black marked with red. Some of the large ones make nests in the form of parallel tubes

that resemble the pipes of a pipe organ. Small species nest in hollows of cut straw, burrows of wood-boring beetles, and chinks in masonry. If a chink is too large, they make it smaller by using mud to partition it into cells able to contain a single egg and sufficient food for one larva. Some species repair abandoned nests of their own or some other species and provision them with spiders. Males of some species stand guard at the nest while the female is out hunting food.

[62.49 *Pisonopsis* Fox (5 spp.); 62.50 *Pison* Jurine: 2 subgenera: *Pison* s. str. (1 sp., *P. laeve* Smith (in US?)) and *Krombeiniellum* Richards (1 sp., *P. agile* (Smith)]

62.51 *Trypoxylon* Latreille

This genus is divided into two subgenera: *Trypoxylon* s. str. (15 spp.) and *Trypargilum* Richards (15 spp.). The following species may serve as examples:

T. frigidum frigidum Smith. L. ±mm. Entirely black; abdominal base straight, with median groove. Nests in elder stems or abandoned beetle burrows; visits flowers from June to August. (1) n.e. NA; (2) WV, VA, NC; (3) NM; (4) Pacific n.w.; (5) n. Central States.

T. (Trypargilum) politum (Say) (Pipe-organ Wasp). L. ±14 mm. Pubescence white; hind tarsi partly pale. This species builds linear series of mud cells in parallel rows that resemble the pipes of an organ. These nests are provisioned with spiders, usually 3 to 18 per cell.

Tribe Bothynostethini

[62.52 *Bothynostethus* Kohl (1 sp., *B. distinctus* Fox)]

Subfamily Crabroninae

L. 6–20 mm (usually under 10 mm). Nests are made in soil, wood, or hollow stems. A variety of insects are used as prey. Soil-resting species use flies; others may use bugs. Adults visit flowers.

Tribe Oxybelini

[62.53 *Enchemicrum* Pate (1 sp., *E. australe* Pate); 62.54 *Belomicrus* Costa (25 spp.)]

62.55 *Oxybelus* Latreille

Nineteen species, including the following:

O. uniglumis Linnaeus. L. 5–9 mm. Abdomen with last two or three terga dark brown to black; pronotal carina sharp, not interrupted or round at pronotal angle. Adults fly during July and August, visiting flowers of wild carrot, parsnip, and other weeds. Their nests are built in sandy places and provisioned with male Brachycera flies (rarely with females). (1), (2), (3), (4), (5), generally distributed.

Tribe Crabronini

62.56 *Anacrabro* Packard

Three species, including the following:

A. ocellatus ocellatus Packard. L. 6–8 mm. Black, marked on thorax and legs with yellow; abdominal segments 1 through 5 with a large yellow spot; wings yellow, basally and apically brownish. Adults are common on wild carrot flowers. They make their nests in sand banks and provision them with bugs of various species.

[62.57 *Encopognathus* Kohl (3 spp.); 62.58 *Entomognathus* Dahlbom, subgenus *Tonchahua* Pate (4 spp.); 62.59 *Lindenius* Lepeletier and Brulle (10 spp.); 62.60 *Rhopalum* Stephens: 2 subgenera: *Rhopalum* s. str. (2 spp.) and *Corynopus* Lepeletier and Brulle (5 spp.); 62.61 *Moniaecera* Ashmead (5 spp.); 62.62 *Huavea* Pate (1 sp., *H. pima* Court and Bohart); 62.63 *Crossocerus* Lepeletier and Brulle: 5 subgenera: *Crossocerus* s. str. (13 spp.), *Ablepharipus* Perkins (1 sp., *C. unicus* (Patton)), *Epicrossocerus* Ashmead (1 sp., *C. insolens* (Fox)), *Hoplocrabro* Thomson (1 sp., *C. angelicus* (Kincaid)), and *Blepharipus* Lepeletier and Brullé (14 spp.); 62.64 *Tracheliodes* Morawitz (3 spp.); 62.65 *Crabro* Fabricius (29 spp.); 62.66 *Enoplolindenius* Rohwer: 2 subgenera: *Iskutana* Pate (1 sp., *E. robertsoni* (Rohwer)) and *Enoplindenius* s. str. (1 sp., *E. clypeatus* (Rohwer)); 62.67 *Ectemnius* Dohlbom (31 spp.); 62.68 *Lestica* Billberg (4 spp.)]

Subfamily Xenosphecinae

[62.69 *Xenosphex* Williams (3 spp., (3) CA, AZ; (4) NV)]

Subfamily Nyssoninae (Sand Wasps)

L. 5–40 mm. All members of this subfamily nest in the ground. Some invade the nests of other wasps, or certain bees that nest in the soil, to live as inquilines; some are predators on Homptera, including cicadas; others form colonies (tribe Bembicini) and feed flies to their larvae.

Tribe Mellinini

62.70 *Mellinus* Fabricius

Four species, including the following:

M. bimaculatus Packard. L. 8–9 mm. Black, with yellow markings on head, pronotum, and abdomen; legs yellow. These wasps nest in the ground and use flies as provision for their larvae. (1) MI, NY, NH, ME, OH, PA, MJ, MA.

Tribe Alyssonini

[62.71 *Alysson* Panzer (9 spp.); 62.72 *Didineis* Wesmael (7 spp.)]

Tribe Nyssonini

[62.73 *Nysson* Latreille (24 spp.); 62.74 *Hyponysson* Cresson (2 spp.); 62.75 *Synnevrus* Costa (5 spp.); 62.76 *Epinysson* Pate (13 spp.); 62.77 *Zanysson* Rohwer (4 spp.); 62.78 *Foxia* Ashmead (3 spp.); 62.79 *Metanysson* Ashmead (5 spp.)]

Tribe Gorytini

[62.80 *Ochleroptera* Holmberg (1 sp., *O. bipunctata* (Say)); 62.81 *Argogorytes* Ashmead (2 spp.); 62.82 *Dienoplus* Fox (4 spp.); 62.83 *Hapalomellinus* Ashmead (3 spp.); 62.84 *Trichogorytes* Rohwer (2 spp.); 62.85 *Gorytes* Latreille (19 spp.); 62.86 *Pseudoplisus* Ashmead (20 spp.); 62.87 *Lestiphorus* Lepeletier (3 spp.); 62.88 *Oryttus* Spinola (6 spp.); 62.89 *Psammaletes* Pate (3 spp.)]

62.90 *Sphecius* Dahlbom

Only the typical subgenus, *Sphecius* s. str. (4 spp.), occurs in the U.S. The following is a common species:

S. speciosus (Drury) (Cicada Killer). Length: ±50 mm. Black with reddish orange legs; yellow markings on thorax and abdominal segments 1 through 3. This very large species provisions its nests with various species of cicadas. (See Fig. 25.58 and A&J 294.) (1), (2), (3), (5), widely distributed east of Rocky Mountains.

[62.91 *Tanyoprymnus* Cameron (1 sp., *T. moneduloides* (Packard)); 62.92 *Arigorytes* Rohwer (5 spp.); 62.93 *Xerogorytes* Bohart (1 sp., *X. anaetis* (Pate)); 62.94 *Hoplisoides* Gribodo (20 spp.)]

Fig. 25.58. (*Courtesy of Robert Gossington and* Insect World Digest)

Tribe Stizini

[62.95 *Stizus* Latreille (4 spp.); 62.96 *Stizoides* Guerin, subgenus *Tachystizus* Pate (2 spp.); 62.97 *Bembecinus* Costa (8 spp.)]

Tribe Bembicini

[62.98 *Bicyrtes* Lepeletier (8 spp.); 62.99 *Microbembex* Patton (7 spp.); 62.100 *Stictia* Illiger (3 spp.)]

62.101 *Bembix* Fabricius

Twenty-one species, including the following:

B. americana spinolae Lepeletier (Common Sand Wasp). L. 16–20 mm. Stout-bodied; labrum long are triangular; yellow with black markings on vertex of head, thorax, and abdomen; wings smoky brown, Not only this species but other *Bembix* species nest gregariously and maintain their colonies from year to year. Not social in the usual sense, they nevertheless take part in mass "flights of intimidation" against intruders. Because they provision their nests with flies, they are thought to have some effect on local fly populations, but it is probably not much. They readily become accustomed to human presence and are not truly aggressive or dangerous. The sexes meet in the air, but copulation takes place on a plant or on the ground. Their nests are built in sandy soils or gravel and consist of a mound of excavated earth, a sloping tunnel of several feet in depth, and a horizontal terminal branch, or cell burrow. There is also a vertical spur for a resting area. Males pass the night in shallow burrows that they construct for this purpose. Provisioning of cells is progressive. Flies are seized and paralyzed either in flight or at rest and carried by the wasp's middle legs to the nest. The fly is released at the entrance to the burrow, grasped with the wasp's hind legs, and dragged inside. At or near larval maturity, the wasp closes the cell, and its occupant spins a cocoon. Overwintering is spent in the prepupal stage, and the life cycle is completed in the spring. These wasps may congregate on the branches of trees and shrubs and appear at times to be sleeping. (See A&J 295). (1) n.e. US; (2) s.e. US; (3) AZ, NM, TX, OK; (4) ID, NV, UT; (5) n. Central States.

[62.102 *Stictiella* Parker (15 spp.); 62.103 *Glenostictia* Gillaspy (11 spp.); 62.104 *Xerostictia* Gillaspy (1 sp., *X. longilabris longilabris* Gilaspy); 62.105 *Steniolia* Say (12 spp.)]

Subfamily Philanthinae (Bee-wolf Wasps)

L. 12–18 mm. These wasps nest in soil in tunnels that they stock with bees (hence their common name), wasps, beetles, or winged ants (Aphilanthopini). Cercerini store beetles in their nests for larval food. Adults visit flowers and feed on nectar.

Tribe Philanthini

62.106 *Philanthus* Fabricius

The species of this genus stock their nests with wild bees and other Hymenoptera. They are colorful, marked with white or yellow; some have reddish legs. Common around flowers. Thirty-one species, including the following:

P. gibbosus (Fabricius). (1), (2), (3), (4), (5), widely distributed.

[62.107 *Trachypus* Klug (1 sp., *T. mexicanus* Saussure)]

Tribe Aphilanthopini

Members of this tribe prey upon winged ants.

[62.108 *Aphilanthops* Patton (4 spp.); 62.109 *Clypeadon* Patton (8 spp.); 62.110 *Listropygia* Bohart (1 sp., *L. bechteli* (Bohart))]

Tribe Cercerini

Members of this tribe prey upon Coleoptera.

62.111 *Cerceris* Latreille

There are 101 species and subspecies in the U.S. and Canada, including the following:

C. clypeata Dahlbom. L. 12–16 mm. Hind femora pale at base and black at apex; six to eight teeth on hind tibiae; black, with yellow markings on head and thorax; abdominal terga narrowly margined with yellow, the sixth of the male and the second of the female with much broader margin. Adults fly from June to October and are common on umbelliferous flowers. They dig their nests in the ground. (See Fig. 25.59.) (1) n.e. US; (2) s.e. US; (3) TX; (5) ND, SD, MN, NE, IA, KS, MO.

62.112 *Eucerceris* Cresson

Twenty-eight species and subspecies, including the following:

E. canaliculata (Say) (Beetle Wasp). L. ±25 mm. Head brown; thorax dark brown with yellow markings; wings brown. Their nests are built in hard-packed soil, gravel, or mud and

Fig. 25.59. (*From American Ent. Soc.*)

provisioned with beetle larvae. (See A&J 296.) (2) AR; (3) s.w. US; (5) MT, SD, NE, KS.

Superfamily APOIDEA

This superfamily of eight families contains the remainder of the Hymenoptera and probably the most advanced forms of all. Bees, as these insects are commonly called, have the first segment of the hind tarsi more or less enlarged and flattened for the purpose of carrying pollen. The exception is the Megachilidae (68), which has brushes of hairlike setae on the abdomen to hold pollen. Body hairlike setae are numerous and usually branched, except in the Nomadinae. Mouthparts are modified into a tongue for feeding on nectar. (See Fig. 25.2) When not in use, the tongue is folded flat against the undersurface of the head.

Bees eat only plant materials, mainly nectar and pollen;

almost without exception, they also store this food in nests for their larvae to eat. As a result, they serve as the major pollinators of a great many plant species. Most of them are diurnal; only a few rare species are nocturnal. These have very large ocelli.

The sex of individual bees may be determined by counting antennal segments: 13 in the male, 12 in the female. Males, moreover, have seven visibly abdominal terga; females, only six. As a rule, and contrary to the impression most people have that all of them make hives as the Honey bees do, most bees are solitary and nest in the ground. Some—for example, the Nomadinae [a sumfamily of the Anthophoridae (69)]—are parasitic "cuckoo" bees; their females lay eggs in the nest of other bees.

The accompanying key and Table 25.5 are aids for identifying the members of this large group collectively known as bees.

Key to the Families of Apoidea of the U.S. and Canada

1. Hind wing with jugal lobe as long as or longer than submedian cell (see Fig. 25.60); galeae and glossa short .. **2**
 Hind wing with jugal lobe shorter than submedian cell or absent; galeae and glossa usually long .. **7**

2(1). Front wing with basal vein strongly arched and usually 3 submarginal cells; glossa pointed; 1 subantennal suture below each antennal socket **66. Halictidae**
 Front wing with basal vein straight or only slightly arched and 2 or 3 submarginal cells; glossa pointed, truncate, or slightly bilobed; 1 or 2 subantennal sutures below each antennal socket .. **3**

3(2). Front wing with 2 submarginal cells .. **4**
 Front wing with 3 submarginal cells .. **5**

4(3). Front wing with apex of marginal cell pointed and second submarginal cell smaller than first; glossa truncate of bilobed; 1 subantennal suture below each antennal socket; black bees, usually with white or yellow markings on face; (Hylaeinae) **63. Colletidae**
 Front wing with apex of marginal cell more or less truncate (Panurginae) (see Fig. 25.61); or if pointed (some Andreninae), then submarginal cells are equal in length; glossa pointed; 2 subantennal sutures below each antennal socket; color variable, but usually not as above. .. **65. Andrenidae**

5(3). Front wing with second recurrent vein sigmoid; glossa truncate or bilobed; 1 subantennal suture below each antennal socket; (Colletinae) **63. Colletidae**
 Front wing with second recurrent vein straight, not sigmoid; glossa pointed; 2 subantennal sutures below each antennal socket **6**

6(5). Front wing with apex of marginal cell on costal margin; stigma well developed; (Andreninae) .. **65. Andrenidae**
 Front wing with apex of marginal cell bent away from costal margin; stigma very small or absent .. **64. Oxaeidae**

7(1). Labial palpi with segments similar and cylindrical; galeae and glossa short **67. Melittidae**

Fig. 25.60.

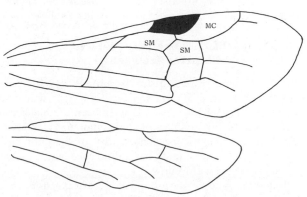

Fig. 25.61.

Key to the Families of Apoidea of the U.S. and Canada (*Contd.*)

Labial palpi with first 2 segments long and somewhat flattened; galeae and glossa elongate
.. *8*

8(7). Front wings with 2 submarginal cells, the second nearly as long as the first; subantennal suture
extending from outer margin of antennal socket **68. Megachilidae**
Front wings usually with 3 submarginal cells; subantennal suture extending from middle of
antennal socket ... *9*

9(8). Hind tibiae without apical spurs (Apinae), or if with apical spurs (Bombinae and
Euglossinae), then hind wing with jugal lobe absent; genae broad **70. Apidae**
Hind tibiae with apical spurs; hind wing with a jugal lobe; genae very narrow
.. **69. Anthophoridae**

Table 25.5 Families of Apoidea of U.S. and Canada

Family	Body Features	Wings
Colletidae (63)	Hairs usually sparse, some nearly hairless; tongue short, bilobed	Forewings with two or three submarginal cells
Oxaeidae (64)	Robust, with thick, pale pubescence on thorax; antennal sockets below middle of eyes; two subantennal sutures; antennae short, elbowed; flagellum shorter than length of eye; hind femora with brush of orange bristles	Stigma small or absent; front wings with three submarginal cells
Andrenidae (65)	Recognized by two sutures below each antenna; females and most males with flat, triangular area on apical abdominal tergum	Panurginae with two submarginal cells on front wing; Andreninae with three
Halictidae (66)	Females and most males with triangular area on apical abdominal tergum; only a single suture below antennal socket	Two submarginal cells in some, three in others; basal vein curved
Melittidae (67)	Facial foveae and subantennal areas absent; two subantennal sutures; mouthparts with glossa short and acutely pointed; triangular area on apical abdominal tergum well developed	Two or three submarginal cells
Megachilidae (68)	Tongue long, threadlike; pollen collecting apparatus on ventral side of abdomen	Two submarginal cells
Anthophoridae (69)	Hairy, or usually with some hair (Anthophorinae) or in Nomadinae sparsely hairy or even bare; females and most males with flat triangular area on apical abdominal tergum; male antennae often long; hind tibia with apical spurs	Two submarginal cells in some, three in others, rarely only one
Apidae (70)	No facial pits; apical abdominal tergum without a triangular plate; hind tibia and first tarsal segment usually forming a pollen basket; hind tibia without apical spurs in Apinae, present in Bombinae and Euglossini	Three submarginal cells

63. COLLETIDAE (Yellow-faced and Plasterer Bee Family)

L. 3.5–12 mm. (rarely up to 20 mm). Wing with three submarginal cells (Colletinae; see Fig. 25.62) or with two (Hylaeinae). The Colletinae, or plasterer bees, are black and unmarked, but their body hairs are light colored. The body of the Hylaeinae, or yellow-faced bees, may or may not have sparse hairlike setae; the thorax has unbranched hairlike setae. The head is marked with yellow.

Plasterer bees nest in the ground or in crevices in bricks and stones. They plaster the sides of the nest with a secretion that dries into a cellophanelike substance.

The yellow-faced bees mix the pollen they eat with nectar inside their crop. The product is regurgitated and stored in the nest for the larvae to feed upon. They make simple nests in plant stalks, insect burrows, and similar cavities.

There are 153 species in the U.S. and Canada.

Subfamily Colletinae

Tribe Paracolletini

[63.1 *Eulonchopria* Brethés (1 sp., *E. punctatissima* Michener)]

Tribe Colletini

63.2 *Colletes* Latreille

There are 114 species and subspecies (see Fig. 25.62), including the following:

Fig. 25.62. *(From Mitchell, 1960)*

C. compactus compactus Cresson (Common Plasterer Bee). L. ±12 mm. Head marked with yellow; body black with white markings on apical portion of each abdominal tergum; body covered with rather sparse pile; wings transparent; antennae black. These bees nest in the ground or crevices in bricks and stones. (See A&J 297.) (1) n.e. US; (2) WV, VA, NC, SC, GA; (3) AZ, NM, TX, OK; (5) CO, KS, MO.

C. nudus Robertson. L. 9–12 mm. Pubescence whitish; eyes convergent below. Adults fly from April (in the South) or June (in the North) to August. (1) n.e. US; (2) NC, LA; (5) CO.

Subfamily Diphaglossinae
Tribe Caupolicanini

[63.3 *Ptiloglossa* Smith (2 spp.); 63.4 *Caupolicana* Spinola: 2 subgenera: *Caupolicana* s. str. (3 spp.) and *Zikanapis* Moure (1 sp., *C. elegans* Timberlake)]

Subfamily Hylaeinae
63.5 *Hylaeus* Fabricius

This genus is divided into seven subgenera: *Prosopis* Fabricius (18 spp.), *Paraprosopis* Popov (15 spp.), *Prosopella* Snelling (1 sp., *H. hurdi* Snelling), *Hylaeana* Michener (1 sp., *H. panamensis* Michener), *Hylaeus* s. str. (13 spp.), *Cephalylaeus* Michener (2 spp.), *Metziella* Michener (1 sp., *H. sparsus* (Cresson)), and Unassigned (4 spp.). The following species may serve as an example:

H. (Prosopis) modestus Say. L. 4.5–7 mm. Black; antennae dark above, reddish beneath; yellow markings on head below antennae, on tibiae, and on thoracic collar. Adults visit parsnip, meadow-sweet, and other flowers from June to August. (1) n.e. US; (2) s.e. US; (5) MN, IA, MO.

64. OXAEIDAE (Oxaeid Bee Family)

Length: 12–22 mm. Robust bees with thick, pale pubescence on the thorax; abdomen dark with sparser pubescence; wing yellowish or brownish black. Four species in the southern part of the U.S., as follows.

64.1 *Protoxaea* Cockerell and Porter

One species, as follows:

P. gloriosa (Fox). (3) AZ, NM, TX.

[64.2 *Mesoxaea* Hurd and Linsley (3 spp.)]

65. ANDRENIDAE (Andrenid Bee Family)

L. 4–15 mm. Body brown, reddish brown, yellow, or otherwise marked; easily recognized by the two sutures under each antenna in combination with the features listed in the Table of Families. These bees nest in tunnels in the soil,

sometimes in large groups. The family is divided into two subfamilies: the Andreninae, with wings having three submarginal cells (See Fig. 25.60), and the Panurginae, with wings having two submarginal cells (See Fig. 25.61). The body of these bees is often marked with yellow; some are entirely yellow; some are white and others entirely black.

This largest family of bees has 1,199 species in the U.S. and Canada and many subspecies, most of them belonging to the genus *Andrena*.

Subfamily Andreninae
65.1 *Andrena* Fabricius

This genus contains the following thirty-eight subgenera: *Andrena* s. str. (60 spp.), *Aporandrena* Lanham (1 sp., *A. coactipostica* Viereck), *Belandrena* Ribble (3 spp.), *Callandrena* Cockerell (52 spp.), *Chaulandrena* LaBerge (1 sp., *A. porterae* Cockerell), *Cnemidandrena* Hedicke (24 spp.), *Conandrena* Viereck (5 spp.), *Dactylandrena* Viereck (3 spp.), *Derandrena* Ribble (9 spp.), *Diandrena* Cockerell (25 spp.), *Eremandrena* LaBerge (2 spp.), *Euandrena* Hedicke (15 spp.), *Geissandrena* LaBerge (1 sp., *A. trevoris* Cockerell), *Gonandrena* Viereck (6 spp.), *Hesperandrena* Timberlake (5 spp.), *Iomelissa* Robertson (1 sp., *A. violae* Robertson), *Larandrena* LaBerge (1 sp., *A. miserabilis* Cresson), *Leucandrena* Hedicke (14 spp.), *Melandrena* Perez (34 spp.), *Micrandrena* Ashmead (17 spp.), *Nemandrena* LaBerge (3 spp.), *Oligandrena* Lanham (5 spp.), *Onagrandrena* Linsley and MacSwain (28 spp.), *Opandrena* Robertson (5 spp.), *Parandrena* Robertson (9 spp.), *Pelicandrena* LaBerge and Ribble (1 sp., *A. atypica* (Cockerell)), *Plastandrena* Hiedicke (6 spp.), *Ptilandrena* Robertson (3 spp.), *Rhaphandrena* LaBerge (2 spp.), *Scaphandrena* Lanham (24 spp.), *Scoliandrena* Lanham (3 spp.), *Scrapteropsis* Viereck (18 spp.), *Simandrena* Perez (17 spp.), *Taeniandrena* (1 sp., *A. wilkella* (Kirby)), *Thysandrena* Lanham (26 spp.), *Trachandrena* Robertson (25 spp.), *Tylandrena* LaBerge (14 spp.), *Xiphandrena* LaBerge (1 sp., *A. mendica* Mitchell), and Unassigned (59 spp.). The following species may serve as an example:

A. (Melandrena) vicina Smith. L. 11–13 mm. Dark, with yellow markings on clypeus only. Commonly found visiting flowers of apple, *Cretaegus* spp., wild cherry, and many others, this species nests in the soil, usually in large numbers, and sometimes damages lawns. They fly from April to October. (See A&J 298.) (1) ON, NS, CT.

[65.2 *Megandrena* Cockerell: 2 subgenera: *Megandrena* s. str. (1 sp., *M. enceliae* (Cockerell) and *Erythrandrena* Zovortink (1 sp., *M. mentzeliae* Zavortink); 65.3 *Ancylandrena* Cockerell (4 spp.)]

Subfamily Panurginae

[65.4 *Protandrena* Cockerell (22 spp.); 65.5 *Pangurinus* Nylander (18 spp.); 65.6 *Pseudopanurgus* Cockerell (13 spp.); 65.7 *Anthemurgus* Robertson (1 sp., *A. passiflorae* Robertson); 65.8 *Heterosarus* Robertson (16 spp.); 65.9 *Pterosarus* Timberlake (43 spp.); 65.10 *Metapsaenythia* Timberlake (2 spp.); 65.11 *Nomadopsis* Ashmead: 4 subgenera: *Nomadopsis* s. str. (10 spp.), *Macronomadopsis* Rozen (7 spp.), *Micronomadopsis* Rozen (22 spp.), and unassigned subgenus (6 spp.); 65.12 *Calliopsis* Smith: 4 subgenera: *Colliopsis* s. str. (7 spp.), *Perissander* Michener (5 spp.), *Calliopsima* Shinn (11 spp.), and *Verbenapis* Cockerell and Atkins (5 spp.); 65.13 *Hypomacrotera* Cockerell and Porter (4 spp.); 65.14 *Xenopanurgus* Michener (1 sp., *X. readioi* Michener)]

65.15 *Perdita* Smith

This genus is divided into the following twenty subgenera: *Allomacrotera* Timberlake (1 sp., *P. stephanomeriae* Timberlake), *Alloperdita* Viereck (7 spp.), *Cockerellia* Ashmead (31 spp.), *Cockerellula* Strand (5 spp.), *Epimacrotera* Timberlake (11 spp.), *Glossoperdita* Cockerell (7 spp.), *Hesperoperdita* Timberlake (3 spp.), *Heteroperdita* Timberlake (12 spp.), *Hexaperdita* Timberlake (29 spp.), *Macrotera* Smith (3 spp.), *Macroterella* Timberlake (7 spp.), *Macroteropsis* Ashmead (8 spp.), *Pentaperdita* Cockerell and Porter (10 spp.), *Perdita* s. str. (414 spp.), *Perditella* Cockerell (4 spp.), *Procockerellia* Timberlake (4 spp.), *Pseudomacrotera* Timberlake (1 sp., *P. turgiceps* Timberlake), *Pygopterdita* Timberlake (54 spp.), *Xeromacrotera* Timberlake (1 sp., *P. cephalotes* (Cresson), and *Xerophasma* Cockerell (2 spp.). The following species may serve as an example:

P. (*Perdita*) *octomaculata octomaculata* (Say). L. 6–7 mm. Head and thorax green; female abdomen black with bright yellow markings except on fifth tergum; male similar but dark brown; yellow markings on face; tubercles and a pair of spots on pronotal collar bright yellow. Adults fly from July to October, particularly visiting composite blossoms. (1) n.e. US; (2) VA, NC, SC, GA: (5) MN.

66. HALICTIDAE (Sweat Bee Family)

Length: 4–10 mm. These species have a reputation of stinging perspiring individuals. Only about 12 of the species are attracted to sweat, but the name "sweat bee" sticks with the whole family. These bees will sting if pressed by clothing or by a bent arm or leg, but usually it is not very painful. They are black or brownish, but some have metallic green or bluish reflections. Nests are formed in clay, sand banks of streams, and other locations. There are 502 species in the U.S. and Canada.

Subfamily Dufoureinae

[66.1 *Dufourea* Lepeletier: 2 subgenera: *Dufourea* s. str. (3 spp.) and *Halictoides* Nylander (66 spp.); 66.2 *Micralictoides* Timberlake (3 spp.); 66.3 *Protodufourea* Timberlake (2 spp.); 66.4 *Conanthalictus* Cockerell: 2 subgenera: *Conanthalictus* s. str. (2 spp.) and *Phaceliapis* Michener (11 spp.); 66.5 *Sphecodosoma* Crawford (2 spp.); 66.6 *Michenerula* Bohart (1 sp., *M. beameri* Bohart); 66.7 *Xeralictus* Cockerell (1 sp., *X. timberlake* Cockerell)]

Subfamily Nomiinae

66.8 *Nomia* Latreille

This genus is divided into the following five subgenera: *Curvinomia* Michener (8 spp.), *Acunomia* Cockerell (4 spp.), *Epinomia* Ashmead (6 spp.), *Dieunomia* Cockerell (7 spp.), and Unassigned (1 sp.). Front wing venation is shown in Fig. 25.63. The following species may serve as an example:

N. melanderi Cockerell (Alkali Bee). This species is an important pollinator, especially of alfalfa. It is reared and encouraged to populate areas near many kinds of crops. (See A&J 300.) (3) n. CA; (4) WA, OR, ID; (5) WY, SD.

N. nortoni nortoni Cresson. L. 16–18 mm. Male with hind tibiae enormously produced at apex; abdomen with conspicuous, greenish apical integumental bands. (1) PA, NJ, MD, DE; (2) s.e. US; (3) NM; (4) ID; (5) CO.

Subfamily Halictinae

Tribe Augochlorini

66.9 *Augochloropsis* Cockerell

This genus is divided into various subgenera, the following of which occurs in the U.S. and Canada: *Paraugochloropsis* Schrottky (4 spp.). The following species may serve as an example:

A. metallica metallica (Fabricius). L. ±9 mm. Entire body brilliant green; abdomen shiny; abdominal terga with conspicuous fringe of pale vibrissae. (1) ON, VT, NH, ME, MA, CT, NY, PA, NJ, MD, DE; (2) s.e. US; (3) AZ, NM, TX.

[66.10 *Augochlora* Smith: 3 subgenera: *Augochlora* s. str. (4 spp.), *Oxystoglossella* Eickwort (1 sp., *A. aztecula* Cockerell), and Unassigned (1 sp.); 66.11 *Augochlorella* Sandhouse (7 spp.); 66.12 *Pseudaugochloropsis* Schrottky (1 sp., *P. graminea* (Fabricius)); 66.13 *Temnosoma* Smith (1 sp., *T. smaragdinum* Smith)]

Tribe Halictini

66.14 *Agapostemon* Guerin-Meneville

Fourteen species, including the following:

A. texanus Cresson. L. 9–11 mm. Body brilliant blue-green scutum shining, double punctate, with sparse, coarse punctures superimposed upon a surface of finer and closer punctures; wings transparent. (See A&J 299.) (1), (2), (3), (4), (5), generally distributed.

A. splendens (Lepeletier). L. ±10 mm. Brilliant blue-green; female abdominal terga more or less tinged with blue or purple; male abdomen black apically, more yellow basally; scutum coarsely rugoso-punctate. Adults fly from April to October. (1) n.e. US; (2) s.e. US; (3) AZ, MN, TX; (5) n. Central States.

66.15 *Halictus* Latreille

This genus is divided into two subgenera: *Halictus* s. str. (4 spp.) and *Seladonia* Robertson (5 spp.). (For front wing venation of former, see Fig. 25.64.) The following species may serve as an example:

H. (*Halictus*) *ligatus* Say. L. 7–10 mm. Black; pubescence yellowish white above, more whitish below; wings with first

Fig. 25.63. (*From Mitchell, 1960*)

Fig. 25.64. (*From Mitchell, 1960*)

submarginal cell equal to second and third combined; head with cheeks angulate below; male with yellowish markings on head. (1), (2), (3), (4), (5), generally distributed.

[66.16 *Lasioglossum* Curtis (19 spp.); 66.17 *Evylaeus* Robertson (67 spp.); 66.18 *Hemihalictus* Cockerell (1 sp., *H. lustrans* (Cockerell)); 66.19 *Sphecodogastra* Ashmead (2 spp.); 66.20 *Dialictus* Robertson (200 spp.); 66.21 *Paralictus* Robertson (5 spp.)]

66.22 *Sphecodes* Latreille

Seventy-seven species, including the following:

S. dichrous Smith. L. 9–10 mm. Black; abdomen red in female only; vertex of head with pronounced median tubercle. Adults visit goldenrod, sunflowers, parsnip, meadow-sweet, and other flowers from May through October. This species is a parasite in the nests of other Halictidae and also a predator. (1) n.e. US; (2) VA, NC, SC, GA: (5) MN, IA, MO.

67. MELITTIDAE (Melittid Bee Family)

Length: 7–12 mm. Black, sometimes with yellow markings on head and yellow or white marking on abdomen. These bees nest in the ground in burrows. There are 30 species in the U.S. and Canada, most of them uncommon.

Subfamily Melittinae

[67.1 *Melitta* Kirby: 2 subgenera: *Melitta* s. str. (4 spp.) and *Dolichochile* Viereck (1 sp., *M. melittoides* (Viereck))]

Subfamily Dasypodinae

[67.2 *Hesperapis* Cockerell: 4 subgenera: *Hesperapis* s. str. (3 spp.), *Amblyapis* Cockerell, (1 sp., *H. ilicifoliae* (Cockerell)), and *Panugomia* Viereck (17 spp.)]

Subfamily Macropidinae
67.3 *Macropis* Panzer

Only the nominal subgenus occurs in the U.S. and Canada. There are seven species, including the following:

M. ciliata Patton. L. 7–8 mm. Visits flowers. (1) n.e. US; (2) VA, NC, SC, GA.

68. MEGACHILIDAE (Leaf-cutting and Mason Bee Family)

L. 7–18 mm. Front wings always with two submarginal cells; abdomen with pollen collecting basket ventrally (absent in parasitic species); tongue and other mouthparts greatly elongate. Most of the species are leaf-cutting bees; a few (*Stelis* spp. and *Coelioxys* spp.) are parasitic. The leaf cutters nest in the ground, in natural cavities, or in wood. Parasitic species lay their eggs in the nests of other leaf-cutting bees. There are 682 species in the U.S. and Canada.

Subfamily Lithurginae

[68.1 *Lithurge* Latreille, subgenus *Lithurgopsis* Fox (7 spp.)]

Subfamily Megachilinae
Tribe Anthidiini

[68.2 *Trachusa* Panzer (3 spp.); 68.3 *Heteranthidium* Cockerell (11 spp.); 68.4 *Paranthidium* Cockerell and Cockerell: 2 subgenera: *Paranthidium* s. str. (1 sp., with 4 subspp.) and *Mecanthidium*

Michener (1 sp., *P. sonorum* Michener); 68.5 *Adanthidium* Moure (2 spp.)]

68.6 *Anthidium* Fabricius

Species of this genus use down from woolly leaved plants for nests in burrows or other cavities. There is only one subgenus in the U.S. and Canada: *Anthidium* s. str. (25 spp.).

[68.7 *Callanthidium* Cockerell (2 spp.)]

68.8 *Dianthidium* Cockerell

Species of this genus make nests of resin (sometimes mixed with small pebbles) on rocks and other surfaces. There are 30 species in the U.S. and Canada.

[68.9 *Anthidiellum* Cockerell (7 spp.); 68.10 *Heterostelis* Timberlake (7 spp.); 68.11 *Stelis* Panzer: 7 subgenera: *Protostelis* Friese (6 spp.), *Microstelis* Robertson (7 spp.), *Pavostelis* Sladen (8 spp.), *Chelynia* Provancher (26 spp.), *Melanostelis* Ashmead (2 spp.), *Stelidium* Robertson (6 spp.), and *Stelidina* Timberlake (6 spp.); 68.12 *Dioxys* Lepeletier and Serville (9 spp.)]

Tribe Megachilini

[68.13 *Heriades* Spinola: 2 subgenera: *Neotrypetes* Robertson (7 spp.) and *Physostetha* Michener (5 spp.); 68.14 *Prochelostoma* Robertson (1 sp., *P. philadelphi* (Robertson)); 68.15 *Chelostoma* Latreille (9 spp.); 68.16 *Chelostomopsis* Cockerell (1 sp., *C. rubifloris* (Cockerell); 68.17 *Proteriades* Titus: 6 subgenera: *Cephalapis* Cockerell (1 sp., *P. jacintana* (Cockerell), *Proteriades* s. str. (22 spp.), *Xerosmia* Michener (1 sp., *P. xerophila* (Cockerell), *Penteriades* Michener and Sokal (4 spp.), *Hoplitina* Cockerell (6 spp.), and *Acrosomia* Michener (3 spp.); 68.18 *Hoplitis* Klug: 8 subgenera: *Hoplitis* s. str. (1 sp., *H. anthocopoides* (Schenck)), *Andronicus* Cresson (1 sp., *H. cylindrica* (Cresson)), *Monumetha* Cresson (7 spp.), *Dasyosmia* Michener (2 spp.), *Cyrtosmia* Michener (1 sp., *H. hypocrita* (Cockerell), *Alcidamea* Cresson (16 spp.), *Formicapis* Sladen (1 sp., *H. robusta* (Nylander)), *Robertsonella* Titus (3 spp.), and Unassigned (2 spp.); 68.19 *Anthocopa* Lepeletier: 4 subgenera: *Atoposmia* Cockerell (14 spp.), *Hexosmia* Michener (4 spp.), *Eremosmia* Michener (15 spp.), and *Isosmia* Michener and Sokal (4 spp.); 68.20 *Ashmeadiella* Cockerell: 4 subgenera: *Chilosima* Michener (2 spp.), *Ashmeadiella* s. str. (30 spp.), *Arogochila* Michener (21 spp.), *Cubitognatha* Michener (1 sp., *A. xenomastax* Michener)]

68.21 *Osmia* Panzer

L. 7–19 mm. Usually metallic blue or green; usually short and broad; pollen brush under abdomen; membranous appendage between claws. These are the mason bees, so called because they construct small, earthen cells on or under stones, in burrows dug in the earth, on twigs or decaying wood, in plant galls, and elsewhere. The genus is divided into 12 subgenera as follows: *Osmia* s. str. (5 spp.), *Chalcosmia* Schmiedeknecht (4 spp.), *Cephalosmia* Sladen (6 spp.), *Centrosmia* Robertson (10 spp.), *Acanthosmioides* Ashmead (22 spp.), *Nothosmia* Ashmead (21 spp.), *Chenosmia* Sinha (41 spp.), *Euthosmia* Sinha (1 sp., *O. glauca* (Fowler)), *Mystacosmia* Snelling (1 sp., *O. nemoris* Sandhouse), *Monilosmia* Robertson (24 spp.), *Trichinosmia* Sinha (1 sp., *O. latisulcata* Michener), and *Diceratosmia* Robertson (4 spp.). The following species may serve as examples:

O. (*Osmia*) *cornifrons* (Radoszkowski). This species occurs in Utah and the Old World but has been introduced into Maryland, where it has become established as a pollinator.

O. (*Osmia*) *lignaria lignaria* Say. This species pollinates apple flowers and many others.

O. (*Chalcosmia*) *coerulescens* (Linnaeus). Pollinates lilac and others.

O. (*Nothosmia*) *pumila* Cresson. Found on red raspberry flowers.

O. (*Chenosmia*) *cobaltina* Cresson. L. 7–18 mm. Metallic blue. (See A&J 301.) (3) CA; (4) BC, WA, OR, ID; (5) C).

68.22 *Megachile* Latreille

These are the leaf cutters, so named because the females snip more or less circular pieces out of leaves or petals. Then they skillfully fit these pieces together to form tight, thimble-shaped cells that snugly fill some suitable space in wood or earth. Examination of one nest with 30 cells, arranged in nine rows under a board contained at least 1,000 pieces of leaves. This large genus is divided into the following 17 subgenera: *Litomegachile* Mitchell (9 spp.), *Neomegachile* Mitchell (2 spp.), *Cressoniella* Mitchell (1 sp., *M. zapoteca* Cresson), *Megachile* s. str. (5 spp.), Entricharaea Thomson (3 spp.) *Delomegachile* Viereck (13 spp.), *Phaenosarus* Mitchell (2 spp.), *Megachiloides* Mitchell (3 spp.), *Derotropis* Mitchell (12 spp.), *Xeromegachile* Mitchell (45 spp.), *Argyropile* Mitchell (7 spp.), *Xanthosarus* Robertson (6 spp.), *Leptorachis* Mitchell (1 sp., *M. petulans* Cresson), *Pseudocentron* Mitchell (5 spp.), *Acentron* Mitchell (1 sp., *M. albitarsis* Cresson), *Melanosarus* Mitchell (2 spp.), *Sayapis* Titus (13 spp.). The following species may serve as examples:

M. (*Litomegachile*) *brevis brevis* Say (Leaf-cutting Bee). L. 7–12 mm. Body black; mandibles four-dentate; abdominal tergum 6 concave in profile; pollen basket pale; abdominal terga with slight amount of black pubescence. (1), (2), (3), (4), (5), generally distributed.

M. (*Megachile*) *centuncularis* (Linnaeus) (Alfalfa Leaf-cutting Bee). L. 7–9 mm. Similar to the preceding but abdomen with black, hairlike setae visible at sides of terga 2 through 6 in dorsal view and tergum 6 with pale tomentum. These bees fly from April through September. Introduced (1) n.e. US; (2) s.e. US; (3) AZ; (4) NV; (5) CO, MO.

M. (*Eutricharaea*) *concinna* Smith (Pale Leaf-cutting Bee). L. 7–9 mm. Similar to the preceding, but with distinct, entire, white apical spots beneath abdomen. Introduced. OH, PA, MD; (2) VA, NC, GA, FL, AL; (3) CA, AZ, OK; (4) WA, NV, UT; (5) KS.

M. (*Megachiloides*) *pascoensis* Mitchell (Northwestern Leaf-cutting Bee). L. 7–9 mm. Black, with dense white pile. Pollinates species of plant genus *Clarkia* (Onagraceae) (Farewell-to-Spring). (See A&J 302.) (3) CA; (4) WA, OR, ID; (5) MT.

[68.23 *Chalicodoma* Lepeletier: 2 subgenera: *Chelostomoides* Robertson (20 spp. and *Pseudomegachile* Friese (1 sp., *C. lanata* (Fabricius)]

68.24 *Coelioxys* Latreille

These bees are usually cleptoparasites (parasites that remove the eggs of another species and lay their own on the provisions left for the former) in in the nests of *Megachile* spp. The genus is divided into ten subgenera, as follows: *Coelioxys* s. str. (5 spp.), *Boreocoelioxys* Mitchell (10 spp.), *Xerocoelioxys* Mitchell (10 spp.), *Schizocoelioxys* Mitchell (1 sp., *C. funeraria* Smith), *Synocoelioxys* Mitchell (5 spp.), *Neocoelioxys* Mitchell (3 spp.), *Melanocoelioxys* Mitchell (1 sp., *C. dolichos* Fox). *Haplocoelioxys* Mitchell (1 sp., *C. mexicana* Cresson), *Glyptocoelioxys* Mitchell (1 sp., *C. germana* Cresson), and *Cyrtocoelioxys* Mitchell (8 spp.).

C. (*Boreocoelioxys*) *sayi* Robertson. L. 9–12 mm. Black; clypeus bilobed; abdomen with white apical spots. (1) n.e. US; (2) s.e. US; (3) AZ, NM, TX, OK; (5) CO, NE, IA, KS, MO.

69. ANTHOPHORIDAE (Cuckoo Bee, Digger Bee, and Carpenter Bee Family)

L. 5–20 mm. Maxillary palpi well developed; genae very narrow; hind wing with jugal lobe; hind tibiae with apical spurs. The family is divided into three distinctive subfamilies. There are 920 species in the U.S. and Canada.

Subfamily Nomadinae (Cuckoo Bees)

These are cleptoparasites in the nests of all families of bees except the Megachilidae and the Apidae. They lack hairlike setae and pollen baskets and resemble small wasps.

Tribe Biastini

[69.1 *Neopasites* Ashmead: 2 subgenera: *Neopasites* s. str. (2 spp.) and *Micropasites* Linsley (3 spp.)]

Tribe Townsendiellini

[69.2 *Townsendiella* Crawford: 3 subgenera: *Townsendiella* s. str. (1 sp., *T. pulchra* Crawford), *Xeropasites* Linsley (1 sp., *T. rufiventris* Linsley), and *Eremopasites* Linsley (1 sp., *T. californica* Michener)]

Tribe Neolarrini

[69.3 *Neolarra* Ashmead: 2 subgenera: *Neolarra* s. str. (9 spp.) and *Phileremulus* Cockerell (4 spp.)]

Tribe Holcopasitini

[69.4 *Holcopasites* Ashmead: 2 subgenera: *Trichopasites* Linsley (3 spp.) and *Holcopasites* Ashmead (14 spp.)]

Tribe Ammobatini

[69.5 *Oreopasites* Cockerell (9 spp.)]

Tribe Protepeolini

[69.6 *Protepeolus* Linsley and Michener (2 spp.)]

Tribe Epeoloidini

[69.7 *Epeoloides* Giraud (2 spp.)]

Tribe Epeolini

69.8 *Epeolus* Latreille

Fifty-one species, including the following:

E. compactus Cresson (Brown and White Cuckoo Bee). L. 12–20 mm. Brown, marked with white pubescence on thorax and abdomen. (See A&J 304.) (3) s.w. US; (4) NV; (5) CO.

[69.9 *Triepeolus* Robertson (111 spp.)]

Tribe Nomadini

69.10 *Nomada* Scopoli

These bees resemble wasps. The genus is divided into the following 11 subgenera: *Nomada* s. str. (123 spp.), *Gnathias*

Fig. 25.65. (*From Mitchell, 1960*)

Robertson (35 spp.), *Phor* Robertson (5 spp.), *Heminomada* Cockerell and Atkins (67 spp.), *Holonomada* Robertson (14 spp.), *Laminomada* Rodeck (2 spp.), *Pachynomada* Rodeck (9 spp.), *Callinomada* Rodeck (7 spp.), *Micronomada* Cockerell and Atkins (29 spp.), *Centrias* Robertson (1 sp., *N. erigeronis* Robertson), and *Nomadula* Cockerell (20 spp.). Front wing venation is shown in Fig. 25.65. The following species may serve as examples:

N. (*Heminomada*) *luteola* Olivier. L. 9–14 mm. Head and thorax marked with red and yellow, very little black; antennae with segment 2 of flagellum less than twice length of segment 1 on its shorter side. Cleptoparasite in nests of other Anthophoridae. (1) n.e. US; (2) s.e. US.

N. (*Micronomada*) *fervida* Smith. L. ±10 mm. Black, marked with red bands and with yellow markings. Adults visit wild cherry and fruit tree flowers and fly low over the ground in woodlands. Cleptoparasite in nests of other Anthophoridae. (2) SC, GA, LA, MS, AL, FL.

[69.11 *Hexepeolus* Lindsley and Michener (2 spp.); 69.12 *Paranomada* Linsely and Michener (3 spp.); 69.13 *Hesperonomada* Linsley (1 sp., *H. melanantha* Linsley); 69.14 *Triopasites* Linsley (5 spp.); 69.15 *Melanomada* Cockerell (3 spp.)]

Subfamily Anthophorinae (Digger Bees)

These bees store a mixture of honey and pollen for larval food in burrows in the ground that are lined with a waxlike substance. These species have pollen-collecting setae located on the hind tibiae and basal tarsal segments. A few are cleptoparasites on other members of the family.

Tribe Exomalopsini

[69.16 *Exomalopsis* Spinola: 4 subgenera: *Exomalopsis* s. str. (4 spp.), *Phanomalopsis* Michener and Moure (3 spp.), *Anthophorula* Cockerell (15 spp.), and *Anthophorisca* Michener and Moure (9 spp.); 69.17 *Ancyloscelis* Latreille (2 spp.)]

Tribe Melitomini

69.18 *Ptilothrix* Smith

Two species, including the following:

P. bombiformis (Cresson) (Eastern Digger Bee). L. 12–18 mm. Black, without markings except for pale hairlike setae on head, thorax, legs, and apex of each abdominal segment; tarsi lack pulvilli. These bees, which resemble small bumble bees, store pollen from *Hibiscus* spp. but also visit a variety of other flowers. (See A&J 303.) (1) IL, IN, OH, PA, NJ, MD, DE; (2) s.e. US; (3) TX; (5) KS.

[69.19 *Diadasia* Patton (31 spp.)]

69.20 *Melitoma* Lepeletier and Serville

Three species, the following of which is common:

M. taurea (Say). L. 9–12 mm. Black; basal segment of flagellum of antennae elongate, nearly as long as the scape and flagellomeres 2 through 4 combined. Adults principally visit *Ipomoea* spp. (1) IL, IN, OH, PA, NJ, MD, DE; (2) s.e. US; (5) KS, MO.

Tribe Eucerini

[69.21 *Synhalonia* Patton (59 spp.); 69.22 *Syntrichalonia* LaBerge (1 sp., *S. exquisita* (Cresson); 69.23 *Eucera* Scopoli (1 sp., *E. maculata* Lepeletier); 69.24 *Xenoglossa* Smith: 2 subgenera: *Eoxenoglossa* Hurd and Linsley (2 spp.) and *Xenoglossa* s. str. (3 spp.); 69.25 *Cemolobus* Robertson (1 sp., *C. ipomoeae* (Robertson)); 69.26 *Anthedonia* Michener (2 spp.); 69.27 *Svastra* Holmberg: 3 subgenera: *Brachymelissodes* LeBerge (1 sp., *S. cressonii* (Dalla Torre)), *Epimelissodes* Ashmead (20 spp.), and *Idiomelissodes* LaBerge (1 sp., *S. duplocincta* (Cockerell)); 69.28 *Xenoglossodes* Ashmead (19 spp.)]

69.29 *Peponapis* Robertson

This genus is divided into four subgenera, as follows: *Eopeponapis* Hurd and Linsley (2 spp.), *Peponapis* s. str. (2 spp.), *Xeropeponapis* Hurd and Linsley (1 sp., *P. timberlakei* Hurd and Linsley), and *Xenopeponapis* Hurd and Linsley (1 sp., *P. crassidentata* (Cockerell)). The following species may serve as an example:

P. (*Peponapis*) *pruinosa* (Say). L. 11–14 mm. Black; clypeus of female black, that of male yellowish apically; antennae short, with length of flagomeres not more than twice as long as wide. Visits flowers of squash. (1) n.e. US; (2) VA, NC, SC, GA, LA, MS, AL; (3) s.e. US; (4) ID; (5) n. Central States.

[69.30 *Melissodes* Latreille: 7 subgenera: *Melissodes* s. str. (16 spp.), *Apomelissodes* LaBerge (4 spp.), *Heliomelissodes* LaBerge (1 sp., *M. desponsa* Smith), *Tachymelissodes* LaBerge (3 spp.), *Eumelissodes* LaBerge (62 spp.), *Psilomelissodes* LaBerge (1 sp., *M. intorta* Cresson), *Callimelissodes* LaBerge (14 spp.), and Unassigned (5 spp.); 69.31 *Florilegus* Robertson, subgenus *Florilegus* s. str. (1 sp., *F. condignus* (Cresson)); 69.32 *Gaesischia* Michener, LaBerge, and Moure, subgenus *Gaesischiana* Michener, LaBerge, and Moure (1 sp., *G. exul* Michener, LaBerge, and Moure); 69.33 *Simanthedon* Zavortink (1 sp., *S. linsleyi* Zavortink); 69.34 *Martinapis* Cockerell, subgenus *Martinapis* s. str. (2 spp.); 69.35 *Melissoptila* Holmberg, subgenus *Ptilomelissa* Moure (1 sp., *M. otomita* (Cresson))]

Tribe Anthophorini

[69.36 *Anthophora* Latreille: 3 subgenera: *Anthophora* s. str. (59 spp.), *Clisodon* Patton (5 spp.), *Micranthophora* Cockerell (22 spp.); 69.37 *Emphoropsis* Ashmead (22 spp.)]

Tribe Melectini

[69.38 *Melecta* Latreille: 2 subgenera: *Melecta* s. str. (11 spp.) and *Melectomimus* Linsley (1 sp., *M. edwardsii* Cresson); 69.39 *Xeromelecta* Linsley: 2 subgenera: *Xeromelecta* s. str. (1 sp., *X. larreae* (Cockerell) and *Melectomorpha* Linsley (2 spp.); 69.40 *Brachymelecta* Linsley (1 sp., *B. mucida* (Cresson)); 69.41 *Zacosmia* Ashmead (2 spp.)]

Tribe Centridini

[69.42 *Centris* Fabricius: 5 subgenera: *Xerocentris* Snelling (5 spp.), *Paracentris* Cameron (10 spp.), *Acritocentris* Snelling (1 sp., *C. ruthannae* Snelling), *Centris* s. str. (4 spp.), *Hemisiella* Moure (2 spp.), and Unassigned (1 sp., *C. limbata* Friese)]

Tribe Ctenioschelini

[69.43 *Ericrocis* Cresson (2 spp.); 69.44 *Mesoplia* Lepeletier (1 sp., *M. dugesi* (Cockerell))]

Subfamily Xylocopinae (Carpenter Bees)

L. 3.5–8 mm (*Ceratina*), 14–27 mm (*Xylocapa*). Body black, bluish green, or blue, usually with yellow or whitish markings; second submarginal cell triangular, or first and second elongate; abdomen black and shiny, or with a greenish tinge. The two genera belonging to this subfamily are easily distinguished by the size difference. Most species collect pollen and make their nests in wood of various kinds; none are cleptoparasites.

Tribe Ceratinini

69.45 *Ceratina* Latreille

This genus is divided into three subgenera: *Ceratina* s. str. (2 spp.), *Zadontomerus* Ashmead (18 spp.), and *Euceratina* Hirashima, Moure, and Daly (1 sp., *C. dallatorreana* Friese). The following species may serve as an example:

C. (Zadontomerus) dupla (Say) (Little Carpenter Bee). L. 6–8 mm. Body bluish green; clypeus with oblong, median, ivory maculation; antennae brownish basally; legs greenish basally, spurs pale yellowish. Adults visit raspberry and goldenrod flowers particularly, but also many others. They nest in sumac and elder stems. (1) n.e. NA; (2) s.e. US; (3) TX; (5) MB, MN.

Tribe Xylocopini

69.46 *Xylocopa* Latreille

This genus is divided into five subgenera: *Xylocopa* s. str. *Schoenherria* Lepeletier (2 spp.), *Notoxylocopa* Hurd (3 spp.), *Xylocopoides* Michener (6 spp.), *Neoxylocopa* Michener (2 spp.), and *Stenoxylocopa* Hurd and Moure (1 sp., *X. artifex* Smith). Front wing venation is shown in Fig. 25.66. The following are examples of the large carpenter bees:

X. (Schoenherria) micans Lepeletier (Southern Carpenter Bee). L. 14–27 mm. Head and thorax black; abdomen black and shiny; whitish pile at base of abdominal segments; sparse, short golden pile on thorax. Males and females overwinter as adults in nests constructed in fence posts, wooden rails, tree stumps, and eaves of buildings. Adults visit flowers of various weeds and take nectar, often simply by biting through the base of the flower instead of sipping from the top. (See A&J 305.) (2) s.e. US; (3) TX.

X. (Xylocopoides) virginica virginica (Linnaeus) (Common Carpenter Bee). L. 19–23 mm. Body somewhat metallic; males with yellow spots on face; wings with very small stigma; marginal cell very narrow; second submarginal cell elongate, mostly beneath first submarginal cell; pubescence of scutum entirely pale yellow in male, black in female. Adults visit apple

Fig. 25.66. (*From Mitchell, 1960*)

blossoms and other flowers. They nest in wood in old buildings and in sound dead wood of trees. (1) n.e. US; (2) s.e. US; (3) TX, OK; (5) NE, KS, MO.

70. APIDAE (Bumble Bees and Honey Bees)

L. 12–27 mm. Body black, usually with yellow markings, or brownish; pubescence yellow or yellow and black, or sometimes partly reddish brown to nearly orange. The wide range of habits exhibited by this family is discussed under the appropriate genus. There are 57 species in the U.S. and Canada.

Subfamily Bombinae

Tribe Euglossini

Only one representative of this large tropical group is found in the U.S. Brightly colored in the tropics, both males and females visit flowers, usually only a single species; that is, they are host specific.

[70.1 *Eulaema* Lepeletier, subgenus *Apeulaema* Moure (1 sp., *E. polychroma* (Mocsary), (3) s. TX]

Tribe Bombini

70.2 *Bombus* Latreille (Bumble Bees)

L. 17–27 mm. Black and yellow, hairy bees, sometimes with orangish markings; front wings with second submarginal cell rectangular. Young queens mate in the autumn and pass the winter in hibernation in the ground or some other protected place. Remaining members of the nest die before winter sets in. The next year each queen starts a new nest by herself, usually in some ready-made hollow such as a deserted mouse nest; some species prefer underground burrows. After arranging a mat of dried grass or similar plant material, she builds an egg cell, primes it with honey-moistened pollen, lays her first eggs, and then closes the cell. She also makes a waxen honey pot and fills it with rather liquid honey for use during inclement weather, meanwhile guarding her eggs. After hatching, the larvae feed on the honey-pollen mixture, which is supplemented with special meals furnished by the queen. In about ten days, the larvae reach full size and each makes a thin, papery, but tough cocoon in which to pupate. The queen continues to brood her young and sips from her honey pot. A week or two later, the first of the offspring—all small-sized females—emerge and take up their duties as workers. These workers do not mate. Males and mating females hatch later in the season.

Bumble Bees are important pollinators, Red clover, for example, depends upon them for its existence, and according to legend, so does the British Empire! "Old maids keep cats; cats catch field mice that otherwise would destroy humblebees [the British name for Bumble Bees] nests; humblebees enable red clover to set seed; red clover is good food for cattle; and roast beef gives strength to men who are the support of the British Empire." Might an empire fall through ecological perturbation? It is worth considering.

The genus is divided into the following ten subgenera: *Bombus* s. str. (5 spp.), *Fraternobombus* Skorikov (1 sp., *B. fraternus* (Smith)), *Bombias* Robertson (2 spp.), *Separatobombus* Frison (2 spp.), *Crotchiibombus* Franklin (1 sp., *B. crotchii* Cresson), *Cullumanobombus* Vogt (1 sp., *B. rufocinctus* Cresson), *Pyrobombus* Dalla Torre (28 spp.), *Alpinobombus* Skorikov (4 spp.), *Subterraneobombus* Vogt (2 spp.), and *Fervido-*

Fig. 25.67. (*From Mitchell, 1960*)

bombus Dkorikov (3 spp.). Front wing venation is shown in Fig. 25.67. The following are common species of Bumble Bees:

B. (*Bombus*) *terricola occidentalis* Greene (Western Bumble Bee). L. 17–27 mm. Black; pubescence yellow on anterior portion of thorax; abdomen with two terga with white pubescence and one with orange-yellow pubescence. (See A&J 306.) (3) n. CA, AZ, NM; (4) Pacific n.w.; (5) SD.

B. (*Pyrobombus*) *ternarius* Say. L.: 17–19 mm (queen); 8–13 mm (worker); 9–13 mm (male). Queen is black, including wing veins, with membrane brownish; pubescence of head black; thorax yellow with fringe of black hairs; abdominal terga 1 and 2 yellow pubescent, with reddish brown band and remainder black. Workers are the same color as the queen. Males with pubescence of head mostly yellow, that of thorax yellow, that of abdominal terga 1 and 2 yellow, remainder black intermixed with yellow. (1) n.e. NA; (2) VA, NC, SC, GA; (4) BC; (5) n. Central States.

B. (*Pyrobombus*) *bimaculatus* Cresson. L.: 17–22 mm (queen); 13–14.5 mm (male); 11–16 mm (worker). Queen is black, including wing veins, with membrane dark; pubescence bright yellow on pronotum, scutum, and abdominal tergum 1, with varying amounts on tergum 2. Workers resemble the queen except for size. Male thorax with yellow pubescence; abdomen may have yellow pubescence on terga 1 through 5, black pubescence on terga 6 and 7 except for a yellow fringe, and yellow or black terga 2 through 5. Very common. (1) n.e. US; (2) s.e. US; (5) KS.

70.3 *Psithyrus* Lepeletier

The species in this genus are obligate social parasites in nests of *Bombus* spp. They resemble Bumble Bees, but lack a worker caste, and their queens lack pollen-collecting baskets on the hind legs. There are 6 species, including the following:

P. citrinus (Smith) (Usurper Bee). L.: 17–21 mm (female); 13–15 mm (male). Females black; pubescence of head mostly black, interspersed with yellow on vertex; that of thorax and abdomen black. Males with abdominal terga 1 and 2 yellow pubescent, remainder black. Adults fly from May through August and parasitize Bumble Bee nests, laying their own eggs in the nest and killing the Bumble Bee queen. (1) n.e. NA; (2) s.e. US; (5) ND, SD, MN.

Subfamily Apinae (Honey Bees)

Tribe Apini

70.4 *Apis* Linnaeus

There is only one species in this genus in the U.S. and Canada (four in the world)—the Honey Bee, introduced from the Old

Fig. 25.68. (*U.S. Dept. of Agric.*)

World by man. There are, however, several subspecies, as will be described.

A. mellifera Linnaeus (Honey Bee). L.: 16–20 mm (queen); ±12 mm (workers); 15–16 mm (male drone). Body dark, abdomen reddish brown with apical segments black. Lives in man-made hives but also escapes into woods (the so-called wild bees). (See Fig. 25.68.)

Much may be written about the Honey Bee, and no other insect has as large a literature file as this species. The individuals usually seen are the workers, all sterile females. Their legs are modified for various tasks. The front legs are used for cleaning the antennae; the hind legs are fitted with the pollen-gathering apparatus (see Fig. 25.68). The basal tarsal segment has pollen combs on the inner side for scraping pollen from the abdomen and the second pair of legs. Pollen is removed from these combs by a row of stiff hairs at the end of the tibia and then pushed upward into the corbicula (pollen basket) by means of a projection just below the tibial comb at the basal tarsal segment. The long hairs on each side of the corbicula prevent the load from slipping sideways. The notch between the tibia and tarsus has been called the pollen press and is used to manipulate the pollen.

The swarming of the Honey Bee brings about an increase in the number of colonies, but it is the queen of the old colony, not one of her daughters, who goes out to form the new colony. A swarm sometimes starts without a queen. In fact, if she is detained by a trap or in some other way, the bees may destroy her and swarm with a young queen. Swarming bees usually cluster on a branch or some other support before proceeding to a cavity of some kind, such as a hollow tree, where they can start the new colony. The old-fashioned idea that ringing bells or beating tin pans hastens this clustering is a mistaken one; in fact, vibrations at certain frequencies may cause hive activity to cease. If difficulties arise in finding a suitable cavity, an

Fig. 25.69. (*National Science Foundation*)

unprotected comb will be made on the branch where the bees have clustered. Shortly after the original swarm has departed the old hive, a young queen that has been left behind in a sealed-up cradle eats her way out, takes her mating flight several days later, and settles down to her work of rebuilding the colony.

More details may be found in the many books available, including details about raising these insects, harvesting the honey, and other aspects of this fascinating species. Several magazines and journals are devoted to the subject. We cannot conclude this discussion, however, without mentioning the work of Karl von Frisch, who has devoted much of his life to the study of bee language and other behavioral aspects of bee life. As a result of his studies, confirmed by many others, it is now known that Honey Bees can give directions and otherwise communicate with one another by means of a dance they perform upon returning to the hive after foraging for pollen and nectar. The form and orientation of this dance provides the direction and distance from the hive to the flowers that constitute their food. With this information, other workers are able to gather it. (See Fig. 25.69.)

Finally, the so-called African Bee needs explanation. In Africa there is an interesting triumvirate: a bird, the honey bee, and man. The bird is the Honeyguide, a robin-sized relative of the woodpeckers. It is a cuckoo type bird that parasitizes the nests of other birds, but it also has an appetite for beeswax. When these birds find a wild bee hive, they fly to the nearest native village and set up such a racket that the villagers realize that they are being directed to a honey store. They follow the bird, smoke out the bees, and gather the honey. The birds then receive a generous supply of wax for their efforts. This kind of cooperation has been going on for thousands of years—no one knows how long, but long enough for the bees to have developed a great "hatred" for man, "hate" being expressed in the form of a genetic change, through selection, that makes them unusually aggressive (for bees) if their hive is approached.

Nothing apparently disturbed this satisfactory state of affairs until some South American beekeepers decided to try to cross their domesticated Honey Bee (the European race) with these wild bees (the same species, but an African race). The result was far from satisfactory in South America. The African Bee inbred the aggressive behavior that it needed in Africa in the hives of the usually docile domesticated Honey Bee. Introduced

in 1957 in Brazil, these bees spread from hive to hive throughout much of South America and are now headed for North America. Because they are so aggressive, they sometimes attack man and livestock and can even cause death.

The African Bee is *A. mellifera adansonii*. The usual Honey Bee of commerce is *A. mellifera ligustica*. As a result of the crossbreeding of these two subspecies into various races, what now appears to be taking place in South America is a gradual dilution of the aggressiveness of the African subspecies. It may well be that in the long run this merger will improve honey production. The story has not ended, but it seems certain that the threat of disaster prompted by the public media will not take place. Man and the Honey Bee will continue their mutually beneficial alliance.

BIBLIOGRAPHY

[Note: The *Catalog of Hymenoptera* (see Krombein, *et. al.* 1979) lists many works useful for the identification of the species of Hymenoptera, as well as biological and other references. The following works are meant to call attention to additional works on these insects, including references not included in this Catalog.]

Akre, Roger D., *et al.* 1981. *The yellowjackets of American North of Mexico.* U.S. Dept. of Agric., Agric. Handbook No. 552, 102 pp.

Bohart, R. M., and Kimsey, L. S. 1982. A synopsis of the Chrysididae in America north of Mexico. *Mem. American Ent. Institute*, No. 33, 266 pp.

Bohart, R. M., and Menke, A. S. 1976. *Sphecid wasps of the world, a generic revision.* Berkeley: Univ. of California Press, ix+695 pp.

Brothers, Dennis J. 1975. Phylogeny and classification of the aculeate Hymenoptera with special reference to Multillidae. *Univ. Kansas Sci. Bull.* 50(11):483–648.

Carpenter, James M. 1982. The phylogenetic relationships and natural classification of the Vespoidea (Hymenoptera). *Syst. Ent.* 7: 11–38 (Dec. 1981).

Crane, Eva. 1975. *Honey, a comprehensive survey.* New York: Crane, Russak and Co., xvi+608 pp.

Creighton, W. S. 1950. The ants of North America. *Bull. Mus. Comp. Zool.*, 104: 585 pp.

Evans, Howard E. 1963. *Wasp farm.* New York: Natural History Press, viii+178 pp.

Evans, Howard E. 1966. *The comparative ethology and evolution of the sand wasps.* Cambridge: Harvard Univ. Press, xviii+526 pp.

Evans, Howard E. 1978. The Bethylidae of America north of Mexico. *Mem. American Entom. Inst.*, No. 27, 332 pp.

Evans, Howard E., and Eberhard, Mary Jane. 1970. *The wasps.* Ann Arbor: Univ. of Michigan Press, vi+265 pp.

Heinrich, Bernd. 1979. *Bumblebee economics.* Cambridge: Harvard Univ. Press, ix+245 pp.

Iwata, Kunio. 1976. *Evolution of instinct, comparative ethology of Hymenoptera.* New Delhi, India: Amerind Publishing Co., xi+535 pp.

Krombein, Karl V. 1967. *Trap-nesting wasps and bees: life histories, nests, and associates.* Washington: Smithsonian Press, vi+570 pp.

Krombein, Karl V.; Hurd, Paul D., Jr.; Smith, David R.; Burks, B. D.; and others. 1979. *Catalog of Hymenoptera in America north of Mexico.* Washington: Smithsonian Institution Press. Vol. 1: Symphyta and Apocrita (Parasitica), xvi+1–1198; vol. 2: Apocrita (Aculeata), 1199–2209; vol. 3: Indexes, xxx+2211–2735.

Michener, Charles D. 1974. *The social behavior of the bees.* Cambridge: Harvard Univ. Press, xii+404 pp.

Mitchell, Theodore B. 1960. Bees of Eastern United States. *North Carolina Agric. Exp. Sta., Tech. Bull.* No. 141, vol. 1, 538 pp.; vol. 2 (*ibid* 1962), 557 pp.

Morse, Roger A. 1975. *Bees and beekeeping*. Ithaca: Cornell Univ. Press, 295 pp.

Smith, M. R. 1943. A generic and subgeneric synopsis of the male ants of the United States. *American Midl. Nat.*, 30: 273–321.

Smith, M. R. 1947. A generic and subgeneric synopsis of the United States ants, based on workers (Hymenoptera, Formicidae). *American Midl. Nat.*, 37: 521–647.

Smith, Marion R., 1965. House-infesting ants of the Eastern United States. *U.S. Dept. Agric. Tech. Bull.* No. 1326, 105 pp.

Spradbery, J. Philip. 1973. *Wasps*. Seattle: Univ. of Washington Press, xvi+408 pp.

Townes, Henry, and Townes, Marjorie, 1981. A revision of the Serphidae (Hymenoptera) *Mem. American Ent. Institute.*, No. 32, iv+541 pp.

Viereck, N. L., *et al.* 1916. The Hymenoptera, or wasp-like insects of Connecticut. *Connecticut State Geol. Nat. Hist. Surv. Bull.* No. 22, 824 pp.

von Frisch, Karl. 1967. *The dance language and orientation of bees*. Cambridge: Harvard Univ. Press, xiv+566 pp.

Wilson, Edward O. 1971. *The social insects*. Cambridge: Harvard Univ. Press, x+548 pp.

Subsection **Amphiesmenoptera**

Order 26

TRICHOPTERA (Caddisflies)

Unique to this order is the ability of many of its aquatic larvae to construct cases of unusual and distinctive designs. Although a few aquatic larvae of some other insects also make cases, none can be confused with these marvelous architects. Many caddisfly larval cases are so characteristic of the group that it is possible to infer something of the evolution of the order by this feature alone.

The caddis is familiar to fishermen and others interested in aquatic life; the adults are less noticeable to most other people, although they are sometimes abundant at lights at night. Their Latin name is formed from *trichos*, meaning "hair," and *pteron*, "wing," indicating that their wings are covered with fine, short setae instead of the scales that typify their relatives, the Lepidoptera. Otherwise, they resemble certain moths in many details and are believed to be a part of the same evolutionary branch as the Lepidoptera. The common name, "caddis," is obscure in origin; it was in use at least as early as 1400, and, since 1651, it has been applied to the larvae of the Trichoptera, at least those used as fish bait.

The larvae of nearly all species are aquatic, although, a rare few frequent moss at the base of trees. Most adults are nocturnal; a few are diurnal. The females usually return to the water to lay their eggs. Some larvae are general filter feeders, eating small particles of plants, algal cells, and organic debris of all kinds; some are predators; many are herbivorous or detritivorous.

Diagnosis: L. 1.5–40 mm. Body rather soft, elongate, cylindrical; large wings that are held tentlike over abdomen when not is use; usually dull brown or yellowish. The many-segmented antennae of some are very long and slender, extending well beyond the end of the abdomen, but many species have antennae shorter than the length of the body. The mouthparts are very dipteralike—that is, of a lapping, sponging type—but they are poorly developed and are used mostly to drink water or nectar. The two pair of wings (vestigial or absent

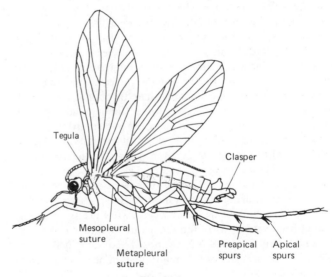

Fig. 26.1.

in females of a few rare species) are rather similar, but the hind pair is frequently wider than the front pair; their surface is covered with hairs and, rarely, with a few scales. The legs are slender and often long, with rather long and stout spurs on the tibia. The abdomen lacks cerci. (See Fig. 26.1 for the principal body features of Rhyacophilidae.) Although these insects resemble various moths, the lack of scales on the wings and the more slender, scaleless antennae and sponging mouthparts easily separate them from the Lepidoptera.

The larvae are somewhat caterpillarlike, but with terminal hooklike prolegs. The true legs are used for walking under water, or, in some species, for swimming. Some species have external gills. (See Fig. 26.2 for a Lymnephilidae larva.)

Metamorphosis: Holometabolous, with egg, larval, pupal, and adult stages.

Fig. 26.2.

Habits and habitats: Eggs are laid in the water (See Fig. 26.3 for *Hydropsycha* sp. egg mass), sometimes near it on overhanging branches (See Fig. 26.4 for *Phryganea* sp. egg ring), or even in dry areas where temporary pools form. The eggs are enclosed in a gelatinous matrix. In some species, this greatly swells in the water. The aquatic larvae of many species construct, and live in, cases made of wood, leaves, stones, sand, or even shells. The case is held together by a fine silk secreted by the salivary glands located in the labium of the larvae. Pupation takes place in the water either under suitable stones or floating logs or in the bottom silt. The pupa in the case remains active because breathing movements continue throughout the entire pupation period. (See Fig. 26.5 for a Limnephilidae pupa.) When its transformation is complete, the pupa crawls or swims to shore and emerges. As soon as the adult leaves its pupal skin, it flies about in search of a mate. Many genera can be recognized by their larval food-gathering habits. They either spin a net to trap food particles, form a silken tube to be used as a retreat from which to dash out to gather food, or construct a case to live in as they crawl about in search of it. A few are free-ranging without nets or cases. Most families exhibit a rather wide range of case construction, and it is not possible to identify them by their nets and cases alone. The major types of nets and cases are listed in Table 26.1.

Not only the great variety of cases and methods of case construction but also the diversity of aquatic habitats and

Fig. 26.4. (*From Betten, 1934*)

feeding habits of these insects provide rewarding studies for anyone willing to spend time observing them.

Reproductive behavior: As soon as the adult emerges from the aquatic pupa, it seeks a mate. Mating may be preceded by a mating dance, which is centered around some "marker" object, such as a log, stump, or rock. Mating itself takes place on the ground or on a bush or shrub. Females lay their eggs either by swimming underwater and placing them on the substrate, by dropping egg balls into the water, by forming an egg mass over or beside the water, or by depositing them in a dry pool that will be flooded later.

Economic importance: Caddisfly larvae are often gathered for use as fish bait. Trout are said to swallow the larvae even when they are in cases made of wood particles, pebbles, or shells. Since many species occur in great abundance in bodies of water harboring fish and other carnivorous aquatic animals, caddisflies have an important role in the food chains of such habitats. Since they supply an important part of the food for many of our game fish, they are of concern to fishermen. Nevertheless, they are not entirely beneficial. Some may destroy growing rice, and large adult swarms can cause allergic reactions in man or block water flow in irrigation or power projects.

Collecting and preserving: Larvae are collected from their aquatic habitat and reared to the adult stage in large vials or jars. Collection data should be kept for each larva; associating these data with the adults that emerge can provide valuable records for specialists, who will be able to add this information to the growing body of knowledge about these insects. Adults can frequently be gathered at lights at night. It is best to preserve

Fig. 26.3. (*From Betten, 1934*)

Antenna case

Hook plate
Wing case

gill

Anal process

Fig. 26.5.

all stages in 80-percent alcohol, although many specialists spread and pin the adults.

Rearing: Caddisfly larvae may be reared in the same manner as larvae of the stoneflies, mayflies, and Odonata.

Distribution: Cooler waters seem to be somewhat preferred by many of the approximately 7,000 described species of the order. At the present time, 1,261 species in 141 genera have been recorded in the U.S. and Canada; since the larvae of only

about 400 of these species are known, the need for further study is self-evident.

Though many excellent works are available for the specialist and many regional guides are available and useful for the identification of both larvae and adults, identification is not easy. Keys, including the accompanying one, make use of wing venation, palpi, and male genitalia features, among other characteristics.

Key to the Adult Trichoptera of the U.S. and Canada (Adapted from Ross, 1944)

1.	Scutellum with posterior part forming a triangular flat area with steep sides	*2*
	Scutellum evenly convex, without a triangular portion set off by sharp sides	*3*
2(1).	Mesoscutum without warts	**7. Hydroptilidae**
	Mesoscutum with warts	*3*
3(1).	Ocelli present	*4*
	Ocelli absent	*10*
4(3).	Maxillary palpi 3-segmented (males); (in part)	**10. Limnephilidae**
	Maxillary palpi 4- or 5-segmented	*5*
5(4).	Maxillary palpi 4-segmented (males); (in part)	**8. Phryganeidae**
	Maxillary palpi 5-segmented	*6*
6(5).	Maxillary palpi with 5th segment 2 or 3 times as long as fourth	**1. Philopotamidae**
	Maxillary palpi with 5th segment not more than 1.75 times as long as 4th	*7*
7(6).	Maxillary palpi with segment 2 short, subequal to segment 1; labrum evenly rounded and fairly wide	*8*
	Maxillary palpus with segment 2 much longer that segment 1; labrum with a wide basal part set off by a crease from long, tonguelike apex	*9*
8(7).	Front tibiae without apical spurs or with 2 apical spurs but without subapical spurs; discoidal cell in front wing sometimes closed; body 3–10 mm in length; wings usually brown with mottling	**6. Glossosomatidae**
	Front tibiae each with 2 apical and 1 subapical spurs; discoidal cell in front wing open; body 9–15 mm in length, usually brownish or bluish gray; mottled wings	**5. Rhyacophilidae**
9(7).	Front tibiae with 2 or more spurs; middle tibiae with 4	**8. Phrygaenidae**
	Front tibiae with 1 or no spur; middle tibiae with 2 or 3 spurs; (in part)	**10. Limnephilidae**
10(3).	Maxillary palpi with 5 or more segments	*11*
	Maxilllary palpi with less that 5 segments	*4*
11(10).	Terminal segment of maxillary palpi with close, suturelike cross striae, these absent from other segments	*12*
	Terminal segment of maxillary palpi without such striae	*14*
12(11).	Front tibiae with 1 preapical spur	**3. Polycentropodidae**
	Front tibae without preapical spur	*13*
13(12)	Hind wing with R almost or entirely normal in its course, stem separate from Sc, 4 or 5 branches distinct; mesoscutum without warts	**4. Hydropsychidae**
	Hind wing with R much reduced, stem either absent or fused with Sc, with 3 or 4 branches; mesoscutum with a pair of small warts.	**2. Psychomyiidae**
14(11).	Middle tibiae without preapical spurs and with row of black spines	*15*
	Middle tibiae with preapical spurs and with or without row of black spines	*19*
15(14).	Pronotum with pair of lateral platelike warts widely separated by median excavated collar, which is usually hidden by produced angulated margin of mesonotum	**18. Leptoceridae**
	Pronotum with warts much closer together, not platelike and usually exposed	*16*
16(15).	Hind wing with anterior margin cut away beyond middle, with row of hamuli along straight basal margin	**16. Helicopsychidae**
	Hind wing with anterior margin straight or evenly rounded	*17*
17(16).	Middle and hind tarsi with crown of 4 black spines at apex of each tarsomere, only a few preapical spines arranged in single row on basal segment	**12. Beraeidae**
	Middle and hind tarsi with apical spines more separated and not forming crown, with numerous preapical spines on all segments, arranged in double row on basal tarsomere	*18*
18(17).	Mesonotum with deep anterior median fissure and approximated warts	**13. Sericostomatidae**

Key to the Adult Trichoptera of the U.S. and Canada (*Contd.*)

Mesonotum with only shallow anterior median crease and more widely spaces warts .. **9. Brachycentridae**

19(14). Middle femora with row of 6 to 10 black spines on anteroventral face **15. Molannidae**

Middle femora with 2 or no black spines on anteroventral face *20*

20(19). Mesonotum with small rectangular scutellum and with scutal warts represented by linear area of small, setate spots extending its full length **17. Calamoceratidae**

Mesonotum with longer and pointed scutellum and with scutal warts oval or lanceolate and short .. *21*

21(20). Scutellum with single large oval or round median wart extending its full length and sometimes width .. *22*

Scutellum with 2 smaller lateral warts, confined to anterior half *23*

22(21). Scutellum round and domelike, with wart appearing to occupy most of its area .. **14. Odontoceridae**

Scutellum triangular, only slightly convex, with wart elongate and occupying only the median area; (Goerinae) **10. Limnephilidae**

23(2). Middle tibia with irregular row of spines; middle tarsus with long double row .. **9. Brachycentridae**

Middle tibia without spines; middle tarsus with only a scattered few in addition to apical ones ... **11. Lepidostomatidae**

Key to the Larval Trichoptera of the U.S. and Canada (Adapted from Wiggins, 1977)

1. Anal claw of larvae with comb of teeth, not hooked-shaped; portable case of sand grains that resembles a snail shell **16. Helicopsychidae**

Anal claw with apex forming stout hook; case otherwise *2*

2(1). Dorsum of each thoracic segment largely covered by sclerotized plate *3*

Metanotum, and sometimes mesonotum, entirely membranous or largely so, with several pairs of smaller sclerites or hairs ... *4*

3(2). Abdomen with ventrolateral rows of branched gills and with prominent brush of long hairs at base of anal claw; posterior margin of meso- and metanotal plates lobate; usually net spinners. **4. Hydropsychidae**

Abdomen without ventrolateral gills and with only 2 or 3 hairs at base of anal claw; posterior margin of meso- and metanotal plates straight; minute forms usually less than 6 mm long; cases often purse- or barrel-shaped **7. Hydroptilidae**

4(2). Antennae very long and prominent, at least 6 times as long as wide, and/or sclerotized plates on mesonotum lightly pigmented except for pair of dark curved lines on posterior half; cases various **18. Leptoceridae**

Antennae no more than 3 times as long as wide, or not apparent; mesonotum never with pair of dark curved lines ... *5*

5(4). Mesonotum largely covered by sclerotized plates, variously subdivided and usually pigmented, although sometimes lightly; pronotum sometimes with prominent antero-lateral lobe .. *11*

Mesonotum usually without sclerotized plates and occasionally with small sclerites covering not more than half of notum; pronotum never with anterolateral lobe *6*

6(5). Abdominal segment 9 with sclerotized plate on dorsum *7*

Abdominal segment 9 with dorsum entirely membranous *9*

7(6). Metanotum usually with cluster of anterolateral setae arising from small, rounded sclerite; prosternal horn present; case tubular, portable, mainly of plant material ... **8. Phryganeidae**

Metanotum with anterolateral seta single, not arising from sclerite; prosternal horn absent; case either constructed of stones and tortoiselike, or none *8*

8(7). Basal half of anal proleg broadly joined with segment 9; anal claw with at least one dorsal accessory hook; case constructed of stones and tortoiselike **6. Glossosomatidae**

Most of anal proleg free from segment 9; anal claw without dorsal accessory hooks, although secondary lateral claw may be present; larvae free-living, without case or fixed retreat **5. Rhyacophilidae**

9(6). Labrum membranous and T-shaped, often withdrawn from view in preserved specimens; larvae construct fixed, sack-shaped nets of silk **1. Philopotamidae**

Labrum sclerotized, rounded, and articulated in normal way *10*

10(9). Trochantin of prothoracic leg with apex acute, fused completely with episternum without separating suture; larvae construct funnel-shaped capture nets, flattened retreats, or tubes in substrate **3. Polycentropodidae**

Key to the Larval Trichoptera of the U.S. and Canada (*Contd.*)

 Trochantin of prothoracic leg broad and hatchet-shaped, separated from episternum by dark suture line; larvae construct tubular retreats on rocks and logs**2. Psychomyiidae**

11(5). Abdominal segment 1 lacking both dorsal and lateral humps, metanotal anterolateral seta entirely lacking or represented by only a single seta without sclerite; case of various materials and arrangements **9. Brachycentridae**

 Abdominal segment 1 always with lateral hump on each side although not always prominent, and usually with median dorsal hump; metanotal anterolateral seta always present, usually represented by sclerite bearing several setae; case of various materials and arrangements. .. *12*

12(11). Tarsal claw of hind leg modified to form short setose stub, or slender filament; case of sand grains with lateral flanges **15. Molannidae**

 Tarsal claws of hind legs no different in structure from those of other legs *13*

13(12). Labrum with transverse row of approximately 16 long setae across central part; case of plant materials variously arranged **17. Calamoceratidae**

 Labrum with only 6 long setae across central part *14*

14(13). Anal proleg with lateral sclerite much reduced in size and produced posteriorly as lobe around base of stout apical seta; base of anal claw with mesial membranous surface giving rise to prominent brush of 25 to 30 fine setae; case of sand grains **12. Beraeidae**

 Anal proleg with lateral sclerite not produced posteriorly as lobe around base of apical seta; base of anal claw with mesial face largely sclerotized and lacking prominent brush of fine setae ... *15*

15(14). Antenna situated very close to anterior margin of eye; median dorsal hump of segment 1 lacking; case of various materials and arrangements **11. Lepidostomatidae**

 Antenna situated at least as close to anterior margin of head capsule as to eye, or closer; median dorsal hump of segment 1 almost always present *16*

16(15). Antenna situated approximately mid-way between anterior margin of head capsule and eye; prosternal horn present, although sometimes short; chloride epithelia (ovoid area of modified cuticle bordered by a thin sclerotized line) usually present on some abdominal segments; case of various materials and construction**10. Limnephilidae**

 Antenna situated at or close to anterior margin of head capsule; prosternal horn and chloride epithelia never present; case only of mineral materials *17*

17(16). Dorsum of anal proleg with cluster of approximately 30 or more setae posteromesiad of lateral sclerite; front trochantin relatively large, with apex hood-shaped ...**13. Sericostomatidae**

 Dorsum of anal proleg with approximately 5 setae posteromesiad of lateral sclerite, sometimes with short spines; front trochantin small, with apex not hood-shaped ...**14. Odontoceridae**

Superfamily HYDROPSYCHOIDEA

1. PHILOPOTAMIDAE (Finger-net Caddisfly Family)

L. 6–9 mm. Ocelli present; maxillary palpi with fifth segment two or three times as long as fourth; one species has wingless females. Larvae form finger-shaped fishing-nets attached to stones and live in rapidly flowing water in streams and rivers. Pupation takes place in cases made of pebbles. The 42 species recorded in the U.S. and Canada are widely distributed and often locally abundant.

1.1 *Chimarra* Stephens

Twenty species, including the following:

C. aterrima Hagen. Dark brown. Found throughout (1) n.e. US; (2) KY, VA, TN, NC.

[1.2 *Dolophilodes* Ulmer (9 spp.); 1.3 *Wormaldia* McLachlan (13 spp.)]

2. PSYCHOMYIIDAE (Tube-net Caddisfly Family)

L. 4–6 mm. Mesoscutum with warts with setae; front tibia without preapical spur; tarsi with basal tarsomere at least two times length of longer apical spur. Larvae make a silk tube that may be branched, but not a portable case. Widespread in flowing water. There are 17 species in the U.S. and Canada.

Subfamily Psychomyiinae

[2.1 *Lype* McLachlan (1 sp., *L. diversa* (Banks); 2.2 *Tinodes* Stephens (11 spp.); 2.3 *Psychomyia* Pictet (3 spp.)]

Subfamily Paduniellinae

[2.4 *Paduniella* Latreille (1 sp., *P. nearctica* Flint)]

Subfamily Xiphocentroninae

[2.5 *Xiphocentron* Brauer (1 sp., *X. mexico* Ross)]

3. POLYCENTROPODIDAE (Trumpet-net and Tube-making Caddisfly Family)

L. 5–10 mm. Mesoscutum with warts with setae; front tibia with preapical spur, or if absent, tarsi with length of basal tarsomere less than two times length of longer apical spur. Larvae make silk tubes, trumpet-shaped silk nets, or branched, silt-buried tubes. There are 68 species, many of them wide-

Table 26.1 Trichoptera Families in the U.S. and Canada and Their Larval Nets and Cases

Family	Nets and Cases
Hydropsychoidea	
1. Philoptamidae	Sacklike silk net makers (Fig. 26.6)
2. Psychomyiidae	Silk tube retreat makers
3. Polycentropodidae	Silk tube retreat makers (Fig. 26.7)
4. Hydropsychidae	Net spinners (Fig. 26.8)
Rhyacophiloidea	
5. Rhyacophilidae	Clingers to stones; free-ranging larvae.
6. Glossosomatidae	Saddle or turtle-shell case markers (*Glossosoma* sp., Fig. 26.9)
7. Hydroptilidae	Most species purse case markers (*Agraylea* sp., Fig. 26.10).
Limnephiloidea	Portable tube case makers of many types
8. Phyrganeidae	Cases tubular (*Phryanea* sp., Fig. 26.11).
9. Brachycentridae	Cases often square in cross-section (*Brachycentrus* sp. Fig. 26.12)
10. Limnephilidae	Cases various (*Pychopsyche* sp., Fig. 26.13; *Platycentropus* sp., 26.14).
11. Lepidostomatidae	Cases cylindrical, log-cabin type, or square
12. Beraeidae 13. Sericostomatidae 14. Odontoceridae	Cases curved, surface smooth, constructed of sand or coarse stones (*Psilotreta* sp., Fig. 26.15).
15. Molannidae	Cases flat with dorsal projections and flanges (*Molanna* sp., Fig. 26.16)
16. Helicopsychidae	Cases snail-shell shaped (*Helicopsyche boralis*, Fig. 26.17).
17. Calamoceratidae	Cases various: flat tubes of large leaf pieces; hollowed-out sticks or pieces of bark or bark pieces (*Heteroplectron americanum*, Fig. 26.18)
18. Leptoceridae	Wide variety of cases

spread throughout the U.S. and Canada in most aquatic habitats.

Subfamily Polycentropodinae

[3.1 *Cernotina* Ross (7 spp.); 3.2 *Cyrnellus* Banks (1 sp., *C. fraternus* (Banks)); 3.3 *Neureclipsis* McLachlan (5 spp.); 3.4 *Nyctiophylax* Brauer (7 spp.); 3.5 *Polycentropus* Curtis (42 spp.); 3.6 *Polyplectropus* Ulmer (1 sp., *P. charlesi* (Ross)]

Subfamily Dipseudopsinae

[3.7 *Phylocentropus* Banks (5 spp.)]

Fig. 26.6.

Fig. 26.7.

Fig. 26.8.

4. HYDROPSYCHIDAE (Common Net-spinning Caddisfly Family)

L. 7–18 mm. Ocelli absent; maxillary palpi with fifth segment elongate; warts on pronotum only. Larvae are filter feeders; a few are predators living in swift currents and common in rivers. They build silk nets between stones, or on stones where the current is swift, to snare food particles. The larva itself hides nearby in a silken retreat embedded with pebbles and debris. When the developed pupa leaves this protective case, it swims to the surface of the stream, and the adult emerges and flies away. Widespread in rivers, streams, and lakes. There are 130 species in the U.S. and Canada.

Subfamily Arctopsychinae

[4.1 *Arctopsyche* McLachlan (4 spp.); 4.2 *Parapsyche* Betten (7 spp.)]

Fig. 26.9. (*From Betten, 1934*)

Fig. 26.10. (*From Betten, 1934*)

Fig. 26.11. (*From Betten, 1934*)

Subfamily Diplectroninae

[4.3 *Aphropsyche* Ross (2 spp.); 4.4 *Diplectrona* Westwood (3 spp.); 4.5 *Homoplectra* Ross (8 spp.); 4.6 *Oropsyche* Ross (1 sp., *O. howellae* Ross)]

Subfamily Hydropsychinae

[4.7 *Cheumatopsyche* Wallengren (40 spp.)]

4.8 *Hydropsyche* Pictet

Fifty-seven species, including the following:

H. simulans Ross. Various shades of brown forming light and dark areas. Adult flies from April to late September. Pupal case is

Fig. 26.12. (*From Betten, 1934*)

Fig. 26.13. (*From Betten, 1934*)

Fig. 26.14. (*From Betten, 1934*)

shown in Fig. 26.19. (3) TX; (5) MN, WY, NE, IA, CO, KS, MO.

[4.9 *Potamyia* Banks (1 sp., *P. flava* (Hagen); 4.10 *Smicridea* McLachlan (4 spp.)]

Subfamily Macronematinae

4.11 *Macronema* Pictet

Three species, the following is a common example:

M. zebratum (Hagen). L. 15–18 mm. Head and thorax metallic bluish brown; antennae brown, paler apically; legs and

Fig. 26.15. (*From Betten, 1934*)

Fig. 26.16. (*From Betten, 1934*)

Fig. 26.17. (*From Betten, 1934*)

Fig. 26.19. (*From Betten, 1934*)

Fig. 26.20.

mouthparts yellow. Adults emerge in late May to early September. (See Fig. 26.20.)

Superfamily RHYACOPHILOIDEA

5. RHYACOPHILIDAE (Free-living Caddisfly Family)

L. 8–13 mm. Ocelli present; maxillary palpi five-segmented, the second segment short, about equal to the first; front tibia usually with preapical spur. Larvae are predacious, without cases, and cling to rock and stones in parchmentlike cocoons. Adults frequent rapid streams. There are 128 species in the U.S. and Canada, many of them abundant and widespread.

Subfamily Rhyacophilinae

[5.1 *Himalopsyche* Banks (1 sp., *H. phryganea* (Ross))]

5.2 *Rhyacophila* Picet

One hundred and twenty-four species in the U.S. and Canada, including the following:

R. fuscula (Walker). Adult various shades of brown with light and dark markings. Larvae prefer running, clear streams; predacious. Adults emerge May to August. (See Fig. 26.21 for pupal case; Fig. 26.22 for adult.)

Subfamily Hydrobiosinae

[5.3 *Atopsyche* Banks (3 spp.)]

6. GLOSSOSOMATIDAE (Saddle Casemaker Caddisfly Family)

L. 3–10 mm. Maxillary palpi five-segmented, with second segment short, rounded, about equal to basal segment. Front

Fig. 26.18. *Heteroplectron americanum* (Walker). (*From Betten, 1934*)

Fig. 26.21. (*From Betten, 1934*)

Fig. 26.22.

tibia without preapical spurs. Larvae make turtle-shaped cases of small pebbles attached to the underside of stones in swift-flowing streams and rivers. There are 76 species in the U.S. and Canada.

Subfamily Glossosomatinae

[6.1 *Anagapetus* Ross (6 spp.); 6.2 *Glossosoma* Curtis (23 spp.)]

Subfamily Agapetinae

[6.3 *Agapetus* Curtis (29 spp.)]

Subfamily Protoptilinae

[6.4 *Culoptila* Mosely (4 spp.); 6.5 *Matrioptila* Ross (1 sp., *M. jeanae* (Ross))]

6.6 *Protoptila* Banks

Thirteen species, the following of which is common:

P. maculata (Hagen). (1) n.e. US.

7. HYDROPTILIDAE (Purse Casemaker Caddisfly Family)

L. 1.5–6.0 mm. Ocelli absent or present; maxillary palpi five-segmented. This family is distinctive because of its dense covering of hairy setae and wings that have a fringe of setae longer than their own width. Larvae make parchmentlike silk cases that are flattened, purse-shaped, and open at both ends; some are covered with small stones. These species are common and widespread in rivers and lakes. There are 201 species in the U.S. and Canada.

Subfamily Ptilocolepinae

[7.1 *Palaeagapetus* Ulmer (3 spp.)]

Subfamily Hydroptilinae
Tribe Hydroptilini

[7.2 *Agraylea* Curtis (3 spp.); 7.3 *Dibusa* Ross (1 sp., *D. angata* Ross); 7.4 *Hydraptila* Dalman (61 spp.)]

Tribe Ochrotrichini

[7.5 *Ochrotrichia* Mosely (47 spp.); 7.6 *Oxyethira* Eaton (6 spp.)]

Tribe Stritobiini

[7.7 *Stactobiella* Martynov (5 spp.)]

Tribe Orthotrichiini

[7.8 *Ithytrichia* Eaton (2 spp.); 7.9 *Orthotrichia* Eaton (47 spp.)]

Tribe Leucotrichiini

[7.10 *Alisotrichia* Flint (1 sp., *A.* new species Flint); 7.11 *Leucotrichia* Mosely (3 spp.); 7.12 *Zumatrichia* Mosely (1 sp., *Z. notosa* (Ross)); 7.13 *Rioptila* Blickle and Denning (1 sp., *R. arizonica* Blickle and Denning)]

Tribe Neotrichini

[7.14 *Mayatrichia* Mosely (4 spp.); 7.15 *Neotrichia* Morton (16 spp.)]

Superfamily LIMNEPHILOIDEA

8. PHRYGANEIDAE (Giant Casemaker Caddisfly Family)

L. 12–25 mm. Ocelli present; maxillary palpi with four segments in the male, five in the female; front tibia with two or more spurs and middle tibia with four. Larvae usually live in still water such as that found in marshes and ponds, but some frequent flowing water. The larval case is made of light plant materials, including leaves; it is often spirally arranged and long and slender; sometimes small pebbles are used. Twenty-six species occur in the U.S. and Canada.

Subfamily Yphriinae

[8.1 *Yphria* Milne (1 sp., *Y. californica* (Banks)]

Subfamily Phryganeinae

[8.2 *Agrypnia* Curtis (8 spp.)]

8.3 *Banksiola* Martynov

Five species, the following being common:

B. dossuaria (Say). Larval cases are made of pieces of plant material arranged spirally. Adults emerge in July and frequent lakes, marshes, and sluggish streams. (See Fig. 26.23.) (1) n.e. NA.

[8.4 *Fabria* Milne (2 spp.); 8.5 *Hagenella* Martynov (1 sp., *H. canadensis* (Banks)]

8.6 *Oligostomis* Kolenati

Two species, the following being common:

O. pardalis (Walker). L. 15–18 mm. Brightly marked with orange and black, this is the most highly colored species in the U.S. (See Fig. 26.24.) (1) n.e. NA.

[8.7 *Oligotricha* Rambur (1 sp., *O. lapponica* (Hagen))]

Fig. 26.23.

Fig. 26.24.

8.8 *Phryganea* Linnaeus

Two species, the following being common:

P. cinerea Walker. L. 21–25 mm. Mostly gray or brown; front wings with irregular pattern of various shades of brown and light gray patches along posterior margin, which form triangular marks there when wings are folded; hind wings uniformly gray with a few slightly darker darts along extreme tips of veins. Larvae make a spiral case (see Fig. 26.25). (1) n.e. NA; (5) AB, SK, MB, MT, MN, WY, SD, CO.

[8.9 *Ptilostomis* Kolenati (4 spp.)]

9. BRACHYCENTRIDAE (Humpless Casemaker Caddisfly Family)

L. 6–11 mm. Ocelli absent; maxillary palpi three-segmented in males, five-segmented in females; scutellum with two lateral warts; middle tibia with irregular row of spines. Larval cases long, round, or square in cross-section, made of sand or pieces of plant debris, and found in running water, including slowly flowing rivers and cold mountain streams. There are 34 species in the U.S. and Canada; they are widespread, but only a few species are commonly collected.

[9.1 *Adicrophleps* Flint (1 sp., *A. hitchcocki* Flint); 9.2 *Amiocentrus* Ross (1 sp., *A. aspilus* (Ross))]

9.3 *Brachycentrus* Curtis

Twelve species, including the following:

B. americanus (Banks). Larval case is square and made of narrow pieces of plant material arranged transversely. Common. (1) n.e. NA.

[9.4 *Eobrachycentrus* Wiggins (1 sp., *E. gelidae* Wiggins); 9.5 *Micrasema* McLachlan (18 spp.); 9.6 *Oligoplectrum* McLachlan (1 sp., *O. echo* Ross)]

10. LIMNEPHILIDAE (Northern Casemaker Caddisfly Family)

L. 7–23 mm. Ocelli present; male maxillary palpi three-segmented, female five-segmented. Larvae live in most aquatic habitats—both still and flowing water—in cases of many types; the latter may be made of sticks of various sizes (these being known as "log cabin" cases), pebbles, stones, sand, or even small shells. This large family has 311 widespread species, many of them common.

Subfamily Dicosmoecinae

[10.1 *Allocosmoecus* Banks (1 sp., *A. partitus* Banks); 10.2 *Amphicosmoecus* Schmid (1 sp., *A. canax* (Ross)); 10.3 *Cryptochia* Ross (7 spp.); 10.4 *Dicosmoecus* McLachlan (5 spp.); 10.5 *Ecclisomyia* Banks (3 spp.); 10.6 *Ironoquia* Banks (4 spp.); 10.7 *Ecclisocosmoecus* Schmid (1 sp., *E. scylla* (Milne)); 10.8 *Onocosmoecus* Banks (8 spp.)]

Subfamily Pseudostenophylacinae

[10.9 *Pseudostenophylax* Martynov (3 spp.); 10.10 *Homophylax* Banks (10 spp.)]

Subfamily Limnephilinae

Tribe Limnephilini

10.11 *Anabolia* Banks

Four species, including the following:

A. bimaculata (Walker). (See Fig. 26.26. for pupal case.) (1) n.e. US; (5) CO, NE, IA.

[10.12 *Arctopora* Thompson (2 spp.); 10.13 *Asynarchus* McLachlan (10 spp.); 10.14 *Clistoronia* Banks (4 spp.); 10.15 *Grammotaulius* Kolenati (6 spp.)]

[10.16 *Nemotaulius* Banks (1 sp., *N. hostilis* (Hagen)); 10.17 *Halesochila* Banks (1 sp., *H. taylori* (Banks))]

Fig. 26.25. (*From Betten, 1934*)

Fig. 26.26. (*From Betten, 1934*)

Fig. 26.27. (*From Betten, 1934*)

10.18 *Hesperophylax* Banks

Six species, including the following:

H. designatus (Walker). L. ±20 mm. Brown; wings with definite pattern of light and dark brown, plus a silver stripe through cell 1R$_5$. (See Fig. 26.27 for pupal case.) (1) n.e. NA.

[10.19 *Lenarchus* Martynov (9 spp.); 10.20 *Leptophylax* Banks (1 sp., *L. gracillis* Banks))]

10.21 *Limnephilus* Leach

This genus contains 93 species, including the following:

L. consocius Walker. L. ±20 mm. Almost entirely rich reddish brown; front wings finely marbled with darker shade of brown without a definite pattern. (See Fig. 26.28 for pupal case (a) and its cross section (b). (1) n.e. NA.

L. rhombicus (Linnaeus). L. ±20 mm. Head, thorax, and legs yellowish brown with scattered brown dots; head with distinct brown area down the center of the front, a pair of brown lines on each side of the front, and an irregular brown area over much of the lateral and ventral portions; pronotum sometimes with anterior half dark. (See Fig. 26.29 for pupal case.) (1) n.e. NA.

[10.22 *Philarctus* McLachlan (1 sp., *P. quaeris* (Milne)]

10.23 *Platycentropus* Ulmer

Three species, the following being common:

P. radiatus (Say). L. 20–23 mm. Body medium shade of brown; wings with very distinct pattern of various shades of brown ranging from almost cream to chocolate. Larvae case made of fiber and wood fragments ("log cabin" construction), round, thick, fuzzy in appearance. Adults appear in June. (1 n.e. NA; (2) s.e. US.

[10.24 *Psychoronia* Banks (2 spp.)]

Fig. 26.28. (*From Betten, 1934*)

Fig. 26.29. (*From Betten, 1934*)

Tribe Stenophylacini

[10.25 *Chyranda* Ross (1 sp., *C. centralis* (Banks)); 10.26 *Clostoeca* Banks (1 sp., *C. disjuncta* (Banks)); 10.27 *Desmona* Denning (1 sp., *D. bethula* Denning)]

10.28 *Hydatophylax* Wallengren

Four species, including the following:

H. argus (Harris). Wingspread 50–55 mm. Head yellow; ocelli prominent because of black margins; antennae with basal segment yellow and others black, somewhat lighter toward apex; prothorax with two large warts covered with long yellow hair; mesothorax dark brown in front with two longitudinal yellow stripes, posteriorly yellow; legs yellow with black spines and spurs, the latter somewhat reddish toward tips; front wing with anterior margin almost white, apex (except veins) white, remainder largely brown with conspicuous white stripes; hind wing transparent, with dark area over tip of Sc and apex very narrowly margined with brown, the veins somewhat darker toward tip. (See Fig. 26.30 for pupal case.) (1) n.e. US.

[10.29 *Philocasca* Ross (7 spp.)]

10.30 *Pycnopsyche* Banks

Fifteen species, including the following:

P. gentilis (McLachlan). L. ±11 mm. Testaceous; tibiae and tarsi with black spines; eyes black. (1) n.e. US.

Fig. 26.30. (*From Betten, 1934*)

Tribe Chilostigmini

[10.31 *Chilostigma* McLachlan (1 sp., *C. itascae* Wiggins); 10.32 *Chilostigmodes* Martynov (1 sp., *C. areolata* (Walker)); 10.33 *Frenesia* Betten and Mosely (2 spp.); 10.34 *Glyphopsyche* Banks (2 spp.); 10.35 *Grensia* Ross (1 sp., *G. preterita* (Walker)); 10.36 *Phanocelia* Banks (1 sp., *P. canadensis* (Banks))]

10.37 *Psychoglypha* Ross

Fifteen species, including the following:

P. subborealis (Banks). L. ±20 mm. Wings yellow-brown with red stigma and silvery streak running across; antennae about as long as body. Larval case constructed of small rock fragments and pieces of wood combined into straight tube of slight taper. Found in cool-water habitats, including springs, larger streams, and marginal pools. (See A&J 196.) (1) n.e. NA; (4) Pacific Northwest; (5) northern Plains States.

Subfamily Apataniinae

[10.38 *Apatania* Kolenati (17 spp.)]

Subfamily Neophylacinae

[10.39 *Farula* Milne (7 spp.); 10.40 *Neophylax* McLachlan (18 spp.); 10.41 *Neothremma* Banks (6 spp.); 10.42 *Oligophlebodes* Ulmer (7 spp.)]

Subfamily Goerinae

[10.43 *Goera* Stephens (6 spp.); 10.44 *Goeracea* Denning (2 spp.); 10.45 *Goereilla* Denning (1 sp., *G. baumanni* Denning); 10.46 *Goerita* Ross (2 spp.); 10.47 *Lepania* Ross (1 sp., *L. cascada* Ross)]

Incertae Sedis

[10.48 *Imania* Martynov (12 spp.); 10.49 *Manophylax* Wiggins (1 sp., *M. annulatus* Wiggins); 10.50 *Moselyana* Denning (1 sp., *M. comosa* Denning); 10.51 *Pedomoecus* Ross (1 sp., *P. sierra* Ross); 10.52 *Rossiana* Denning (1 sp. *R. montana* Denning)]

11. LEPIDOSTOMATIDAE (Bizarre Caddisfly Family)

L. 8–10 mm. Ocelli absent; maxillary palpi of male with only three segments, or fused single segment, and of female with five-segments; scutellum with two lateral warts; middle tibia without spines. Males of many species have unusual modifications of maxillary palpi and legs, or unusually widened wings. Larvae cases may be the square, "log cabin" type—composed of wood fragments, round stones, or both—or the chimney type—composed of leaf or bark panels. The 74 species are widespread in distribution and frequent streams or springs.

[11.1 *Lepidostoma* Rambur (69 spp.); 11.2 *Theliopsyche* Banks (5 spp.)]

12. BERAEIDAE (Small Eastern Caddisfly Family)

This family of small species (L. About 5 mm) is represented in the eastern part of the U.S. only. Larvae make cylindrical, slightly curved cases of sand; they live in wet soil of spring seepage areas. One genus only.

[12.1 *Beraea* Stephens (3 spp.)]

13. SERICOSTOMATIDAE (Bushtailed Caddisfly Family)

This family is represented by 12 rare species found in the mountains of the eastern and western U.S. Larvae are found in running water and along lake shores, where they make cylindrical cases of sand.

Subfamily Sericostomatinae

[13.1 *Agarodes* Banks (9 spp.); 13.2 *Fattigia* Ross and Wallace (1 sp., *F. pele* (Ross)); 13.3 *Gumaga* Tsuda (2 spp.)]

14. ODONTOCERIDAE (Mortarjoint Casemaker Caddisfly Family)

This family is known to contain 16 rare, moderate-sized (L. 12–14 mm) species, equally distributed east and west. The larvae of one, *Psilotreta frontalis* Banks, make a cylindrical case of sand, slightly curved and open at both ends, but closed with pebbles and silk before pupation. Cases of known species lack a silk lining but employ a "mortar" of small pebbles between larger stones held in place by silk bracing. Larvae live in running water.

Subfamily Odontocerinae

[14.1 *Marilia* Mueller (2 spp.); 14.2 *Namamyia* Banks (1 sp., *N. plutonis* Banks); 14.3 *Nerophilus* Banks (1 sp., *N. californicus* (Hagen)); 14.4 *Parthina* Denning (2 spp.); 14.5 *Psilotreta* Banks (9 spp.)]

Subfamily Pseudogoerinae

[14.6 *Pseudogoera* Carpenter (1 sp., *P. singularis* Carpenter)]

15. MOLANNIDAE (Hood Casemaker Caddisfly Family)

L. 10–17. Ocelli absent; maxillary palpi five-segmented in both sexes; middle femora with row of 6 to 10 black spines. Bottom of larval cases with five grains of sand; tip with lateral expansions of coarser grains. Found in large rivers and lakes, rarely in streams with sandy bottoms, this small family contains only the following seven species.

15.1 *Molanna* Curtis

Six species, including the following:

M. uniophila Vorhies. L. 16–17 mm. Body and appendages various shades of brown and gray; wings with light areas in middle forming more or less checkered pattern. Larval case is made of small grains of sand with margin of larger pebbles and a dorsal lip. Adults fly during May and June. They form large colonies on gravel bars in cold lakes and connecting streams. (1) n.e. NA.

M. ulmerina Navás. Similar to the preceding; larvae unknown. (1) n.e. US; (3) OK.

[15.2 *Molannodes* McLachlan (1 sp., *M. tinctus* Zetterstedt)]

16. HELICOPSYCHIDAE (Snail Casemaker Caddisfly Family)

L. 5–7 mm. Ocelli absent; maxillary palpi with five segments; hind wing with front margin cut away beyond middle and with row of very small hooks along straight basal half. Larval cases are constructed of small pebbles in the shape of a spiraled snail shell. They live in clear, cool, slowly flowing streams, usually those with a sandy bottom; in relatively swift streams; or in wave-washed shores of cold lakes. One genus only, with four species in the U.S. and Canada.

16.1 *Helicopsyche* von Siebold

Of the four species, the following appears to be the most common:

H. boralis (Hagen). L. 5–7 mm. Head, body, and appendages straw-colored; body and wings suffused with varying shades of brown. Adults fly from May into September. Common in forested regions, but rare in the Great Plains area. (1) n.e. NA; (2) KY, WV, VA, AR, GA, FL; (3) CA, OK, TX; (4) OR; (5) SK, MT, MN, WY, SD, CO, MO.

17. CALAMOCERATIDAE (Comblipped Casemaker Caddisfly Family)

L. 10–15 mm. Scutellum elongate with longitudinal row of small warts on each side. Larval cases consist of large leaf pieces or hollowed twigs. Found in slowly flowing stretches of small streams. Five species in the U.S. and Canada.

17.1 *Anisocentropus* McLachlan

One species, as follows:

A. pyraloides (Walker). Adult orange brown; maxillary palpi six-segmented. Larva cuts two pieces of leaves and fastens them together to make its case. (2) GA.

17.2 *Heteroplectron* McLachlan

Two species, including the following:

H. californicum McLachlan. Larva hollows out piece of dead twig to make its case. (3) CA; (4) OR, WA, BC.

[17.3 *Phylloicus* Mueller (2 spp.)]

18. LEPTOCERIDAE (Longhorned Casemaker Caddisfly Family)

L. 5–17 mm. Ocelli absent; maxillary palpi five-segmented; antennae very much longer than wings. Larval case usually made of sand, either somewhat cone-shaped or of "log cabin" type. They occur in streams, rivers, ponds, and lakes. One hundred and eight species in the U.S. and Canada.

Subfamily Leptocerinae

[18.1 *Ceraclea* Stephens (38 spp.); 18.2 *Leptocerus* Leach (1 sp., *L. americanus* (Banks)); 18.3 *Mystacides* Berthold (3 spp.)]

18.4 *Nectopsyche* Mueller

Fourteen species, including the following:

N. exquisita (Walker). L. 10–17 mm. Head and thorax tawny, covered with white hair; front wings with cross bands of brownish yellow and series of four quadrate black spots on posterior margin near apex. Larval case made of wood fragments. (1) n.e. NA; (2) s.e. US; (3) OK; (5) MO.

18.5 *Oecetis* McLachlan

Twenty species, of which the following is representative:

O. cinerascens (Hagen). L. 11–13 mm. Medium shades of brown; wing membrane with several dark spots situated at vein fork. Larval case of a beautiful "log cabin" type. Adults fly from May to late September. (1) n.e. NA; (2) VA, TN, AR, GA; (3) OK, TX; (5) SK, MN, SD, MO.

[18.6 *Setodes* Rambur (7 spp.); 18.7 *Triaenodes* McLachlan (25 spp.)]

BIBLIOGRAPHY

Anderson, N. H. 1976. The distribution and biology of the Oregon Trichoptera. *Tech. Bull. 134*. Agric. Exper. Stat. Oregon State Univ. 152 pp.

Betten, Cornelius. 1934. The caddisflies or Trichoptera of New York State. *N.Y.S. Museum Bull.* No. 292. 576 pp., 67 pls.

Flint, O. S. 1960. Taxonomy and biology of Nearctic limnephilid larvae (Trichoptera), with special reference to species in eastern United States. *Entomologica Americana*, n.s. 40: 1–117.

Marshall, J. E. 1979. A review of the genera of the Hydroptilidae (Trichoptera). *Entom. Ser. Bull.* British Mus. (Nat. Hist.), 39(3): 135–239.

McCafferty, W. Patrick, and Provonsha, Arwin. 1981. *Aquatic entomology*. Boston: Science Books International, xv+448 pp.

Merritt, R. W., and Cummins, K. W. eds. 1978. *An introduction to the aquatic insects of North America*. Dubuque: Kendall/Hunt Publ. Co., xiii+441 pp.

Ross, H. H. 1956. *Evolution and classification of the mountain caddisflies*. Urbana: Univ. Ill. Press, 213 pp.

——. 1972. *The caddisflies or Trichoptera of Illinois*. Los Angeles: Entomological Reprint Specialists (reprint of 1944 edition), 326 pp.

Wiggins, G. B. 1977. *Larvae of the North American caddisfly genera (Trichoptera)*. Toronto: Univ. of Toronto Press, xi+401 pp.

Order 27

LEPIDOPTERA (Moths, Butterflies, and Skippers)

Moths, butterflies, and skippers always have been the most popular group of insects among amateur collectors. The brilliant colors of many of the species make them unusually attractive to display. Since many species are of economic importance and a knowledge of them is a practical necessity, they have been intensely studied. Rearing from egg to adult is not only a fascinating pasttime for many, it is also likely to provide data that will make an original contribution to the knowledge of the group.

The Latin name Lepidoptera means "scaly wings" and comes from two Greek words, *lepidos* and *pteron*. Sometimes a group name, Rhopalocera, is used to designate the families of butterflies. This word, which combines the Greek *rhopalon*, meaning "club," and *keras*, meaning "horn," refers to the fact that butterfly antennae are enlarged at the tips and hence "clubbed." The origin of the English word *butterfly* is unknown; it has been in use for at least 1,000 years with many different spellings.

The larvae of almost all Lepidoptera feed on the flowers, fruit, leaves, stems, and roots of the flowering plants, but a few are found in stored products and some on animal matter; a very few are carnivorous, and a few are even internal parasites of other insects. Adults feed on nectar, sap, fruit, and decaying animal or plant products; a few exotic species are blood suckers on cattle and other animals; many adult species do not feed at all.

Diagnosis: Wingspan (measured as distance between wing tips of outspread front wings, including body), 2 to 250 mm (usually at least 5 to not over 80 mm); texture of integument soft to leathery. A full range of colors is found among the species, including gold, silver, and other metallic colors. Most Lepidoptera are more or less of the same shape. (See Fig. 27.1.) The head is usually rather small, and the proboscis (sucking mouthparts), if present, forms a coiled tube beneath it. The

antennae are usually only about half the length of the body and of various shapes, from slender with many segments to featherlike (plumose) or clubbed (clavate). The thorax is stout because of the large wing muscles. The wings are large—the front wings often triangular or trapezoidal, but lanceolate in many of the very small moths. The hind wings are usually more oval, at least in the higher groups, and also somewhat smaller and with fewer veins. (See Fig. 27.2 for Hepialidae and Fig. 27.3 for Zygaenidae.) A few species have wingless females. The abdomen is slender, elongate, and either cylindrical or more oval and stout (the latter particularly if the females are filled with eggs). The abdomen lacks obvious cerci, and the copulatory organs and ovipositor are retracted into the abdomen.

The larvae of Lepidoptera may be confused with some larvae of the Hymenoptera. The latter have prolegs (stout, unsegmented lobes) on at least six, and as many as eight abdominal segments. They also have only one pair of ocelli. Conversely, the larvae of the Lepidoptera, usually called *caterpillars,* have prolegs only on abdominal segments 3 to 6, at most, and the last segment (See Fig. 27.4 for Sphingidae.) These prolegs have a circle of hooklets at the foot end. Some moth larvae (called *loopers*) have one or more pairs of prolegs missing. (See Fig. 27.5 for Noctuidae and Fig. 27.6 for Geometridae.) Lepidoptera larvae have at least three pairs of ocelli and usually six.

Even the smallest adults would be difficult to confuse with any other group of insects. The wings, body, and legs are covered with scales, one of the most characteristic and nearly exclusive features. Even in those species that have a predominantly transparent wing surface, both the surface of the veins and the base are covered with scales. Some Caddisflies have scales on their wings but not on their legs.

Metamorphosis: The metamorphosis of the Lepidoptera is complete, that is, holometabolous. Many species have distinc-

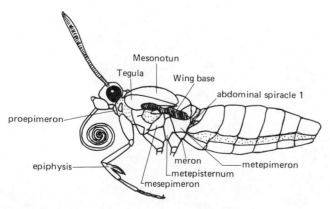

Fig. 27.1. (*Redrawn from Belkin, 1976*)

Fig. 27.2.

Fig. 27.3.

Fig. 27.6.

Fig. 27.7.

tive eggs, laid singly or in clusters. Their shape, sculpturing, and color are characteristic of their species, although the eggs of a great many species are unknown. They are usually glued to the larval food plant, but some are left loose beneath it or even on debris near by. Many species lay eggs on flowers, and the emerging larvae enter the developing fruit. Others lay eggs in stored material such as grain, flour, nuts, dried fruit, and even clothing and fur. Some are known to infest the fur and horns of living animals. Although the larvae are of a great variety of shapes, most are cylindrical, elongate, and of the "typical" caterpillar shape. newly hatched larvae often feed on the egg shell from which they emerge. As it grows, it usually molts five to seven times. Most species have five instars; some have only four, and a few have as many as nine. The pupal stage is passed either in a cocoon (see Fig. 27.7), in a pupal cell that is often lined with silk, or as a chrysalis (see Fig. 27.8). The chrysalis—characteristic of butterflies—is often brightly colored and shiny as a result of the hardened secretion covering the pupa, within which pupa it transforms into an adult. In shape, it most resembles the adult, and, as it matures, the wings of the adult may be seen through the case. The chrysalis is suspended by a pad of silk attached to a leaf or twig; in some species, in addition to the pad, there is a girdle of silk that holds the suspended chrysalis parallel to the surface of the twig or leaf (Fig. 27.8).

Habits and habitats: Most adult Lepidoptera are free fliers and usually frequent vegetation. Adult moths are nocturnal for the most part, but adult butterflies and skippers are diurnal. There are exceptions, of course; some brilliantly colored moths (see Uraniidae) and others are day fliers. These are often confused with butterflies by the uninformed (including many major advertisers, whose agents seem to like these moths and always call them butterflies in their ads). Egg laying habits have already been discussed. Since only the larvae feed in the ordinary sense—adults suck nectar or feed on pollen, but little

else—the larval habitat is the most varied and is usually determined by the food supply. Table 27.1 lists all major habitats of the larvae and indicates the major superfamilies and families in each. Larvae are protected from predators in various ways, depending, of course, on their feeding habits. The major forms of protection are shown in Table 27.2.

Reproductive behavior: Various courtship patterns have been described for the larger moths and butterflies. Adult butterflies are known to buzz their wings, a habit that may be related to courtship and that usually occurs after hibernation. The female of *Parnassius* spp. may scrape the external face of its hind wing with the spines of the tarsi and spurs of the hind legs. The noise created sounds much the same as that of needles scratching on parchment and may be heard for some distance. It occurs *after fertilization,* however, and its significance is unknown. (See also section on butterflies.) The larvae of large moths such as Sphingidae and others stridulate, probably by means of their mandibles, but this phenomenon does not seem to be related to any aspect of "family" life and is therefore unrelated to reproduction. It may be for protection. The same or similar sounds emit from certain pupae in cocoons, undoubtedly to ward off any predators.

The sex attractants emitted by the females of a great number of moths are of considerable practical value. Chemicals known as *pheromones*—special substances secreted from special glands—can lure males from relatively long distances. Obviously this is an easy and efficient means for the sexes to find one another and improve the mixing of genetic strains. The male detects the pheromone by means of sensory structures on its antennae. Pheromones were presumed to be distinct for each species, but it is now known that the differences are not chemical but rather the result of a relationship between these

Fig. 27.4.

(above Fig. 27.4)

Silk girdle

Cremaster

Fig. 27.8.

Fig. 27.5.

Table 27.1 Food Sources of Lepidoptera Larvae

1. Plant material

 A. Terrestrial flowering plants
 1. External leaf feeders (all families except Aegeriidae and Cossidae)
 2. Borers
 a. Leaves (Tineoidea, Gelechioidea, and Copromorphoidea)
 b. Herbaceous stems (Tineoidea, Gelechioidea, Copromorphoidea, Pyralidoidea, and Noctuidae)
 c. Woody stems (Aegeriidae, Carposinidae, Copromorphidae, Tortricidae, and Cossidae)
 d. Fruits and nuts (Tineoidea, Torticidae, Gelechioidea, Pyralidoidea, and Noctuidae)

 B. Aquatic plants
 1. External leaf feeders (Pyralidoidea)
 2. Borers, leaf rollers, or web makers (Pyralidoidea and Noctuidae)

 C. Dead plant material
 1. Dried: grain, flour, fruits, nuts (Tineoidea, Gelechioidea, and Pyralidoidea)
 2. Decayed: leaf mold, fruit, vegetables, wood (Tineoidea and others)

 D. Fungi (some Noctuidae)

 E. Lichens (some Noctuidae, Alucitidae)

2. Animal material

 A. Blood sucking (some Noctuidae)

 B. Living as parasites or predators

 1. On invertebrates (Tineoidea, Pyralidoidea, and Geometroidea) Zygaenoidea
 2. On vertebrates (Pyralidae)

 C. Dead: meat, cheese, fats (Tineoidea and Pyralidoidea)

 D. Dried: wool, fur, homeycomb (Tineoidea and Zygaenoidea)

 E. Decayed: dung, carrion (Papilionidae and Pieridae)

substances and materials extracted from the larval food plant. Although much remains to be learned about them, attempts have already been made to use synthetic pheromones as a means of pest control by attracting males and disposing of them to prevent their fertilization of the female's eggs.

Economic importance: Many species of Lepidoptera are pests of crops, ornamentals, and stored products, as might be expected considering variety of larval habitats. Species of Noctuidae, Pyralidae, and Tineidae, in particular, are serious pests.

Collecting and preserving: Most Lepidoptera are obtained for collections by any of three methods: (1) attraction by light, especially ultraviolet (UV) or black light to lure nocturnal species; (2) laying out bait trails, that is, painting tree trunks and bushes with a sugary material (see Chap. 5) to attract moths

and other species; and (3) use of aerial nets for daytime collecting of butterflies, skippers, and some species of day-flying moths. Once the catch is killed, it should be papered or mounted immediately. Fresh specimens are often kept briefly in refrigerators until they can be mounted to prevent them from drying out and reduce the chance of their scales rubbing off. Pinned specimens are "set" on a spreading board until dry (see Chap. 5) and then labeled and stored in boxes or trays. Usually specimens are stored slightly tilted so that wings may be partially overlapped for storage economy.

Rearing: Many serious collectors search for larvae, cocoons, and even eggs. Larvae are fed until they pupate and the pupae stored until the adult emerges. Adults should be associated with their larval skins; if enough specimens are reared form eggs, a few larvae may be preserved for future association with the adults. Adults obtained from rearing are killed only after their wings have fully expanded and hardened. Such specimens will be perfect condition and make attractive specimens for any collection. To preserve larvae, follow the directions given in Chap. 3.

Distribution: Found worldwide, the Lepidoptera constitute the second largest order of insects, with approximately 112,000 described species. The species of North America are well known compared to those of most other orders. At the

Table 27.2 Means of Protection in Lepidoptera Larvae

1. Structural protection

 A. Hairy integument
 1. Nonpoisonous spines (Notodontidae, Saturnioidea, and Papilionidae)
 2. Poisonous spines (Zygaenoidea, Lymantridae, and Saturnioidea)

 B. Eversible glands (many groups, particularly butterflies; Lymantridae, and Notodontidae)

 C. Sting or bite (None)

 D. Defensive coloration (Most groups)

 E. Conspicuous coloration (A few species in many families probably have poisonous internal substances such as those found in the larvae of Monarch Butterflies and Tomato Worms)

2. External protection

 A. Natural external shelters
 1. Leaves (mines) (Tineoidea and others)
 2. Leaves (rollers) (Tortricidae, Pyralidoidea, and Hesperioidea)
 3. Stems (borers) (see Table 27.1)
 4. Fruit and nuts (see Table 27.1)
 5. Soil (Noctuidae)

 B. Internally manufactured shelters
 1. Silk web or cocoon (Most moths)
 2. Case of silk mixed with foreign materials (Tineoidea, Pyralidoidea, and Gelechioidea)
 3. Nest containing many larvae (Tortricidae, Pyralidoidea, Lasiocampidae, Lymantriidae, and some Geometriodae)

present time, 11,286 species in 2,332 genera and 75 families have been recorded in the U.S. and Canada. Of these, 5,493 are microlepidoptera, 761 are butterflies and skippers, and 5,032 are macrolepidoptera.

Identification of Lepidoptera

Without the aid of illustrated manuals and guides, Lepidoptera are difficult to identify. The following "spot" identification hints will help identify the larger groups of moths and butterflies in their larval stage. They are followed by a detailed discussion of the anatomy of adults, including that of the male and female genitalia, and the system of wing venation used in this order.

Sphingidae (Sphinx Moth) larvae are over 75 mm in length when mature. Most have a caudal "horn" or at least an eyelike spot on the eight abdominal segment. Larvae of Saturniidae (Giant Silkworm Moths), which are also over 75 mm in length when mature, usually lack both caudal "horn" and eyespots. These two families have the largest caterpillars in the order. Arctiidae (Tiger Moth family) larvae are very hairy and of a moderate size, 10–30 mm. Geometridae larvae lack prolegs on abdominal segments 3 through 5 and some Noctuidae on segments 3 and 4 and therefore move with a looping movement. Butterfly caterpillars are usually recognized by their lack of long hair, although all have velvety microscopic setae and many are spiny. Larvae of the Monarch Butterfly and its relatives (Danaidac) have a pair of fleshy filaments on the front and another near the head, whereas those of the Swallowtail Butterflies (Papilionidae) always have a slit behind the head from which is everted a yellowish or reddish, V-shaped scent organ, the *osmeterium*. The larvae of the Microlepidoptera are often either leaf miners, their mines being characteristic of the species, or web makers, the later being gregarious and either feeding together in the web or resting there during the night. Webs are made by a few of the larvae of the large moths such as the Tent Caterpillars. Many other species of Microlepidoptera are leaf folders or leaf rollers (see Table 27.1). These characteristics "nests" will yield some interesting specimens if the larvae are reared to the adult stage.

"Spot" identification of many adults in many groups is relatively easy because of the profusion of full-color illustrations available. All such sight identifications must be confirmed by checking them against written descriptions and using identification keys, and particularly, by comparing the structure of the male genitalia with that which has already been illustrated and described. Microlepidoptera are the most difficult to identify because of their ordinarily small size and the relatively more uniform coloration of their many species.

Technical keys are useful only after one has a knowledge of wing venation and other anatomical features such as those described here. Particular attention must be given not only to wing venation but to the presence, or absense, and the position of ocelli; to the shape and size of the palpi, proboscis, spines, and spurs on the legs; and to the structure of the genitalia.

The External Morphology of Adult Lepidoptera

It is suggested that the following discussion be studied with an actual specimen on hand. Almost any fairly large moth will

Fig. 27.9.

be suitable for this purpose. Because moths are very hairy, it will be necessary to remove the hairs to some extent to make the parts visible. The whole moth can be boiled in 5-percent KOH (potassium hydroxide solution) for about five or ten minutes. Doing so will remove some of the hairs, and the remainder will rub off with a brush or can be pulled out with fine forceps.

Head: The most conspicuous features of the head are the large, nearly hemispherical compound eyes, the antennae, and the proboscis (see Fig. 27.9). In either side of the proboscis is a labial palpus. The proboscis itself is composed of the maxillae (see the moth proboscis in Fig. 27.10); the mandibles (except in certain primitive groups) have disappeared. The compound eyes are frequently bordered by rows of bristles or hairlike scales, which may come over the eye from behind or from below the antennae. Such "lashes" are common in the Noctuidae.

Some moths have a pair of ocelli located near the eyes and just behind the insertion of the antennae. Ocelli are not always present. Sometimes they are replaced by a pair of patches, usually setiferous, called *chaetosemata* (singlar *chaetosema*); these appear to be sensory and are found in all butterflies and many moths. Scales may be mixed with the setae. Most Noctuidae have ocelli and these are used to identify as few of the higher taxa of that family.

Lepidoptera antennae vary considerably from group to group and often between the sexes. In many groups, sex may be determined by the shape of the antennae alone, especially in the Saturniidae, whose males have broadly plumose, and females less broadly plumose, antennae. As previously mentioned, antennae of butterflies are knobbed; of skippers; hooked.

Many moths and all butterflies and skippers have a relatively long proboscis that is used for sucking nectar and other liquids. It is absent in some groups, and a few species of primitive moths have mandibles. Sometimes rudimentary mandibles have been retained in some of the higher moths

Fig. 27.10.

(some species of Sphingidae) and a few butterflies, but they are not functional. Muscles are used to coil the proboscis; blood pressure, to extend it. Features of the anatomy of the proboscis, except for the presence or absence of scales at the base, are seldom used in identification. However, features of the associated labial palpi, particularly their size and position, are used to separate groups.

Cervix: The region that connects the head to the thorax is termed the *cervix.* The paired sclerites imbedded in the membrane of the cervix are known as the *cervical sclerites.*

Thorax: The structure of the thorax is used in the classification of some of the higher taxa as well as for the identification of genera in the Noctuidae. After the dense hair and scales have been removed from the thorax, the relatively narrow prothorax, which is usually not sclerotized dorsally, may be seen. Projecting backward from the pronotum, on each side of the median line, is a sclerotized flap that lies on the anterior border of the mesonotum. These flaps are the *patagia* (sing, *patagium*) outgrowths from the pronotum; they must not be confused with the *tegulae,* which belong to the mesothorax. The mesothorax is large; from the base of each mesothoracic wing, a large tegula projects backward, with the pair of patagia usually overlying the bases of the two tegulae. Most of the tegula lies over the base of the wing, but a special tegular arm projects from its own base, which is forward and beneath the wing base, and rests upon the dorsal edge of the pleuron. The nature of these structures varies considerably from family to family.

The prescutum, although visible at the sides of the large scutum, is very narrow in the middle. The scutellum is distinct behind the scutum and extends laterally into the posterior wing process and the axillary cord on each side. The metathorax is narrow compared to the mesothorax, but its scutum and scutellum are easily recognizable; the axillary cords of the latter run out to the posterior margin of the jugal lobe of the posterior wing in most groups.

The metathorax of many species of moths belonging to the families Noctuidae, Notodontidae, Arctiidae, and Lymantridae is equipped with a very shallow (at most) cavity having a typmanum inside. This "ear," which is usually located behind the wing and close to the abdomen, apparently serves to detect the ultrasonic emissions of predatory bats. In some species, particularly members of Pyralidae, Geometridae, Drepanidae, and related families, this "ear" is located on the first abdominal segment.

As in most insects, there are two pairs of thoracic spiracles. The first lies in the membrane between the pro- and mesothorax, in a line between the middle of the compound eye and the top edge of the meso-episternum. The second lies between the meso- and metathorax, just in front of the top edge of the metepisternum.

Legs: Front legs are present in all species, but in some they are highly modified, particularly in those butterflies whose family classification partially depends upon their structure. The front tibiae in some butterflies (Papilionidae) and most moths exhibit a structure on the inner side termed the *epiphysis.* This is variously shaped and probably used to clean off foreign material when the antennae and possibly the proboscis are pulled through it. It is sometimes referred to in classifications. The remainder of the front legs and the middle and hind legs are unmodified except for differences in the tibial spurs—a feature frequently used for identification and classification. The

middle and hind tibiae of the males of many species bear tufts of scales termed *scent scales*; these may be protected in grooves in the tibiae (see discussion of the *androconia*).

Wings: The wing-coupling apparatus differs from group to group. In many, the *frenulum,* consisting of one or more spines (one in the male—although what appears to be one is sometimes really a few fused together—and two or more in the female of many groups) projects from the anterior margin of the hind wing at its base (see Fig. 27.3); the *retinaculum* projects from the underside of the front wing. In the male, the *retinaculum* is sclerotized as a flap attached to the subcostal vein, but in the female it is a tuft of hairs attached to the cubital vein and projecting forward. Several other types of wing-coupling apparatus occur. The most primitive is the *fibula,* a small lobe at the base of the front wing that rests on the top of the hind wing and presses against small costal spines. In other primitive moths, there is a *jugum*—fibula that overlaps the spineless hind wing (see Fig. 27.2). Among some of the rest of the Lepidoptera—for example, all butterflies—an expanded humeral angle of the hind wing is the only form of wing coupling. This expanded area is stiffened by one or more humeral veins and broadly underlaps the front wing.

Wings are attached to the thorax by a membrane with axillary sclerites, small sclerotized areas at the base of the wing. There are usually only three of these, although some insects have four—for example, Hemiptera. The first sclerite is supported by the anterior wing process of the notum, and its anterior extremity is usually associated with the base of the subcostal vein. Its outer margin articulates along an oblique margin with the second sclerite; the latter is continuous with the end of the radial vein. Below the wing, it rests upon the wing process of the pleuron when the wing is extended. The third sclerite articulates with the posterior wing process of the notum, and the bases of the anal veins are associated with its outer side. The fourth sclerite, when present, lies between the outer extreme of the third and the wing process with which the third would otherwise be in contact.

The *scales* of the wing are modified setae, of which there are two types in the Lepidoptera. *Macrotrichia* are larger, articulated setae that vary from the hairlike to the flattened form, or scales. Different parts of the body and different parts of the wings bear different kinds of scales. Scales are responsible for nearly all of the colors of the Lepidoptera, most of them produced by pigments, but some, especially the blue shades, produced by minute striations on the surface of each scale that serve to break up light rays and thus reflect a particular color (at the same time that the inner part absorbs other colors of the spectrum).

Many male butterflies have specialized scent scales called *androconia* that are probably outlets of the scent glands. These are either scattered over the wing or concentrated in difinite areas; in some butterflies they are located on the hind wing. Many skippers have a patch of androconia, known as the *stigma,* located in a fold near the costal margin of the front wing or near the discal cell (see discussion of wing veins). It has also been noted that scent glands of a few species produce a fluid from the abdomen that is deposited in a scent pouch in the wing.

Wing venation: Since the arrangement of the wing veins is fundamental for the classification of Lepidoptera, a knowledge of the variations involved is essential. Actually, the venation is

relatively simple compared to that of other orders. (Note: To make the veins on dry specimens visible wet the lower surface of the wing with alcohol. For permanent wing mounts, follow the directions given in Chap. 5)

Many different systems of vein naming have been used in the past but the Comstock-Needham system, used throughout the rest of this book, is followed here (see Figs. 27.2 and 27.3).

The venation of the front and hind wings of most Lepidoptera differs—that of the hind wing showing a fustion of the subcosta and the radial sector (see below) to form a single vein as well as a coalescence of the first and second anals. Because of the absence of most cross veins in the Lepidoptera, as compared with other orders, there are very few closed cells. The most conspicuous is the discal cell, a compound cell formed by the atrophy of the stem of R_{4+5} and the main stem of the media.

Each vein, cross vein, and cell has a name and a symbol which are listed below and illustrated on the wing plate (see Introduction).

Veins in order from front to rear (main longitudinal wing structure from the base of the wing outwardly) are as follows:

Costal—C

Subcostal—Sc

Radials—R_1, R_2, R_3, R_4, R_5, (Radials may coalesce near the base or elsewhere, a condition indicated by R_{2+3}, or R_{4+5}, etc.)

Radial sector—Rs (The main radial vein after vein R_1 has branched off.)

Medial—M (There may be a total of four branches, that is, M_1, M_2, M_3, M_4, and these may coalesce, producing M_{1+2}, M_{3+4}, etc.)

Cubital—CuA (there are never more than two anterior cubitals, CuA_1 and CuA_2) and CuP.

Anals—A (Anal veins may be indefinite in number, but there are usually no more than four in Lepidoptera. There are indicated as 1A, 2A, 3A, and 4A.)

Cross veins—the wing braces between the longitudinal veins—are as follows:

Humeral—h (between C and Sc).

Radial—r (between R_1 and R_2 or R_{2+3})

Sectorial—s (between R_{2+3} and R_{4+5})

Radio-medial—r-m (between R_5 and M_1)

Medial—m (between M_2 and M_3 (or M_{1+2} and M_{3+4})

Medio-cubital—m-cu (between M_4 and Cu_1)

Cells—those spaces enclosed by the longitudinal and cross veins—take the name of the longitudinal vein immediately anterior to the cell in question. The discal cell, as mentioned above, is the large, sometimes open cell in the center of the wing that usually extends from the base to just beyond the middle of the wing.

The terms "trifid" and "quadrifed" have been used for the association of veins M_2, M_3, CuA_1 and CuA_2. The medial vein of Lepidoptera is nearly always three-branched, with the basal stalk usually lost, M_4 missing or fused with Cu, and M_1 always free or attached to the radius. If only M_3 is associated with the cubitus, then the cubital system is called "trifid"; if both M_3 and M_2 are associated with the cubitus, the system is called "quadrifid." It is sometimes difficult to decide whether a wing is

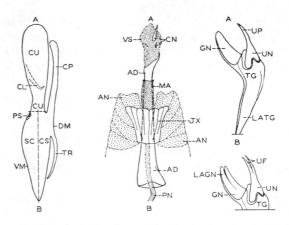

Fig. 27.11. Male genitalia of a moth: Left, right harpe and associated structures (lateral aspect); center, aedeagus and associated structures (ventral aspect); right upper, tegumen and associated structures (dorsolateral aspect); right lower, bifurcated uncus and paired gnathos (dorsolateral aspect). Key to abbreviations: A, apex; AD, aedeagus; AN, anellus; B, base; CL, clasper on surface of cucullus; CN, cornutus; CP, dorsal process of costa (=costal process or dorsal process); CS, costa of harpe; CU, cuculus of harpe; DM, dorsal margin; GN, gnathos; HP, harpe; JX, juxta; LAGN, lateral arm of gnathos; LATG, lateral arm of tegumen; MA, manica (uniting anellus and aedeagus); PN, penis; PS, punctate, setose area near ventrocaidal extremity of sacculus; SC, sacculus of harpe; TG, tegumen; TR, arm of transtilla; UF, furcae of uncus; UN, uncus; UP, uncal process; VM, ventral margin; VN, vinculum; VS, vesica. (*From Hasbrouch, 1964*)

trifid or quadrifid, but if M_2 is connected to the Cu system by a weak vein and arises a third or more above the lower angles of the discal cell, the wing is trifid. If M_2 is connected to the Cu system by a full-strength vein arising only slightly above the lower angle of the discal cell, the wing is quadrifid.

In the higher Lepidoptera, the first Anal (=CuP) is usually missing or represented by only a fold or very short spur; the second anal (=1A) is present, and the third anal (=2A) is variable.

Abdomen: The abdomen consists of ten segments. The first is reduced and the sternum may be membranous or absent. In some moths, the first segment bears the tymanum mentioned previously. Abdominal segments 2 through 6 are usually unmodified, but segments 7 through 10 in females and 8 through 10 in males may be partially or completely modified into the genitalia. There are usually six abdominal spiracles located in the pleural membrane of the segment between the tergum and the sternum.

Male genitalia (Fig. 27.11) are often used for species identification. Since the terminology used for the parts of these structures is voluminous, it would be best to examine actual genitalia while following this description (see Chap. 5 for the preparation of genitalia for study). Keep in mind that these structures vary considerably from species to species and family to family.

Two converging pointed processes will be seen projecting from the posterior end of the male abdomen. (If the relaxed abdomen is held with a pair of forceps, and one of these processes is pulled gently with forceps, it will be easy to extend the genitalia to its full length and thus exposed the whole armature.) The pointed processes are the apices of two large

lateral lobes, the *harpes* (HP*), also called *valves*. These harpes are thought to be the coxites of the ninth segment and are, therefore, homologous to the basal piece of the Coleoptera, the subgenital plates of the Homoptera, and the claspers of the Hemiptera. The apical portion, or *cucullus* (CU), is frequently greatly enlarged and modified in various ways. Tracing the harpes to their attachment to the sides of the basal half of the ninth segment, the *vinculum* (VN), note that at the point of attachment is a joint, above which is the *tegumen* (TG) and below which is the *vinculum* (VN) [=*sternum*]. The vinculum, located in the median area, sometimes extends into a globular structure, the *saccus*.

Attached to the median line of the tegumen is a curved, backwardly projecting process, the *uncus* (UN), and beneath it the *anal tube* with the anus at its apex. The uncus either represents all that is present of a tenth segment or is an appendage of that segment, the segment itself having been reduced to membrane within the ninth. The uncus may be forked apically to form a *furca* (UF).

In many species, a sclerotized ring, either complete or broken, projects downward on each side from the base of the uncus. In its complete state, it surrounds the anal tube. Called the *gnathos* (GN) or *scaphium*, it is either the sternum of the tenth segment or an appendage of the absent sternum.

Passing through the middle of the ninth segment and lying beneath the anal tube and between the bases of the harpes is a sclerotized structure, the base of the *aedeagus* (AD). The membrane surrounding this structure at the point of attachment to the body is the *manica* (MA), and the funnellike cone, the *anellus* (AN). The aedeagus contains an eversible portion, the *intromissive organ*, in which runs the *ductus ejaculatorius*. The *vesica* (VS) or internal sac—an eversible, membranous apical portion of the aedeagus—can be drawn out from the apex of the tube. This sac may have various spines, *cornuti* (CN), on its everted surface. Note that the aedeagus prossesses no recognizible basal piece, unless the sheath is its homolog, an unlikely possibility. A structure known as the *juxta* (JX), or basal ring-wall, that has been described for some species is not homologous with the basal piece. There are no structures corresponding to the parameres of other insects.

Along the dorsal edge of the harpes (Fig. 27.12) is a slight thickening that ends posteriorly in a small inwardly projecting point. This is the *costa* (CS), a part often elaborately modified. On the inner side of each harpe there is a large part often projecting upward from the ventral edge, called the *sacculus* (SC). It is often greatly developed, and the two sacculi may be united to form a median dorsal *transtilla* (TR). The inner side of the harpe frequently possesses tufts of spiny processes termed the *claspers* (CL).

The female abdomen resembles that of the male except that the sternum of the seventh segment is often excised in the median line. The eighth is partly membranous; when at rest, this segment and the rest of the abdomen behind it is completely withdrawn within the seventh. A small sclerotized ring surrounding an oval hole is visible. If this ring is pulled up with a pair of fine forceps, segments 8, 9, and 10 of the abdomen will be exposed. The boundary between th eighth and ninth segments are easily recognized, but the ninth and tenth segments are so

*Letters in parentheses indicate the abbreviations used to label those parts in Figs. 27.11 and 27.12.

Fig. 27.12. Male genitalia of a moth: Left, entire male genital capsule (ventral aspect); right, entire male genital capsule (dorsal aspect). See Key in Fig. 27.11. (*From Hasbrouch, 1964*)

reduced that they cannot be identified separately. They form the sclerotized ring already mentioned, on each side of which a long sclerotized strut projects toward the eighth segment. The ring has two separate openings, a dorsal and ventral. The dorsal is the anus; the ventral is the posterior or ovipositing *gonopore*. The sternum of the eighth segment is irregularly sclerotized with a separate median sclerotized plate. Between the ring and the plate is the anterior or copulatory gonopore. The female genital structures are much used in keys and especially in descriptions.

CLASSIFICATION

Of the various classifications of Lepidoptera that have been used, none seems to have universal acceptance. The one followed here reflects some of the evolutionary trends shown by the wing venation and agrees fairly well with the probable evolution of the larvae. As pointed out by the famous insect morphologist, Robert E. Snodgrass, however, the larvae of the higher insects have sometimes evolved in a direction that is different from that of the adults because of their entirely different lives.

Many amateur lepidopterists would prefer to separate the moths from the butterflies and skippers, as was once the custom. The moths were then grouped in the suborder *Heterocera* and the butterflies and skippers in the suborder *Rhopalocera*. The Heterocera rarely have knobbed antennae, although some are clavate (enlarged apically, but not at the end). Most female moths have slender antennae, whereas male moths have enlarged and feathery or plumelike antennae. Butterfly antennae, on the other hand, have a knob at the end, and some have a recurved hook at the end of the knob.

Another big difference between the two groups is the manner in which the pupa is protected. The larvae of moths either spin a silken cocoon or make a silk-lined pupal cell in the ground or under bark to protect the pupa, whereas butterflies form a chrysalis protected by a secreted transparent covering over the developing larva; the chrysalis is exposed to the elements. The skippers form a cocoon or pupal cell. With all of these differences, it is easy to see how there can be both butterfly specialists and moth specialists. The distinction, however, does not exactly agree with most modern classification schemes. Table 27.3 shows the arrangement of families currently adopted by most professional lepidopterists. An index to these families and the higher taxa is given in Table 27.4 and identification features of the major groups in Table 27.5. A Key to the Families follows.

Key to the Families of Lepidoptera of the U.S. and Canada (Modified from Forbes, 1923)

Adults

1.	Wings absent or rudimentary	*2*
	Wings well-developed	*6*
2(1).	Legs absent; females never leave cocoon; (in part) **11. Psychidae**	
	Legs present, normal	*3*
3(2).	Cocoon seedlike, with valve at one end, formed from larval case; females, less than 6 mm long, normally do not leave cocoon; (in part) **11. Psychidae**	
	Cocoon normally felted by larval hairlike setae, or rudimentary and underground; more than 6 mm long	*4*
4(3).	Ocelli present; (in part) **75. Noctuidae**	
	Ocelli absent	*5*
5(4).	Abdomen closely scaled or spined, or with bristling, dark gray, hairlike setae (some females) **61. Geometridae**	
	Abdomen smoothly clothed with fine, light, woolly, hairlike setae; females normally do not leave cocoon, which is composed of larval hairlike setae; (in part) **74. Lymantriidae**	
6(1).	Hind wing with 4 or 5 free branches of R, with at least 10 veins in anterior part of wing anterior to vannal fold	*7*
	Hind wing with only 1 free branch of R (rarely 2), with at most 7 veins in anterior part of wing anterior to vannal fold	*10*
7(6).	Wings broad (over 25 mm); fringe of wings narrow **4. Hepialidae**	
	Wings about 12 mm; fringe almost or fully as long as breadth of wings	*8*
8(7).	Middle tibiae with spur; mouthparts elongate into a proboscis; front wing with vein Sc forking near apex	*9*
	Middle tibiae without spur; mouthparts mandibulate; front wing with vein Sc forking near middle **1. Micropterigidae**	
9(8).	Ocelli present **2. Eriocraniidae**	
	Ocelli absent **3. Acanthoptcroctetidae**	
10(6).	One or both pairs of wings deeply cleft into narrow strips	*11*
	Wings entire or only one pair moderately cleft	*12*
11(10).	Each wing deeply cleft into 6 narrow strips **25. Alucitidae**	
	Front wing moderately cleft into 2, and hind wing deeply cleft into 3 narrow strips **58. Pterophoridae**	
12(10).	Posterior margin of front wing and veins Sc and R of hind wing with series of recurved spines; front wing at least 4 times as long as wide; hind wing with at least base transparent **35. Sesiidae**	
	Wings without such series of spines, not interlocking at middle, and rarely transparent; if so, then with broader front wing	*13*
13(12).	Hind wing much broader than length of its fringe, never lanceolate and rarely trapezoidal with produced apex	*14*
	Hind wing narrower than, or almost as narrow as, length of its fringe, usually lanceolate, without marked anal angle, or notched below apex and trapezoidal or cleft	*70*
14(13).	Hind wing with ventral surface of vein Cu with double series of enlarged and divergent scales; wings, body, and legs very long (Agdistinae) **58. Pterophoridae**	
	Hind wing without such scales	*15*
15(14).	Front wing with vein P developed at least in middle of its course in broad-winged species and sometimes only near margin in narrower-winged species	*16*
	Front wing with vein P absent completely or represented by fold	*23*
16(15).	Hind wing with vein Sc arising separately from stem of R and running closely parallel to it well beyond discal cell, or fused with it beyond end of discal cell, but then base of R either complete or represented by spur (Schoenobiinae) **55. Pyralidae**	
	Hind wing with vein Sc fused with stem of R, or separate but not closely parallel to R beyond apex of discal cell	*17*
17(16).	Hind wing with vein Sc fused with R for most of distance, separating from it a short distance before apex of discal cell	*18*
	Hind wing with vein Sc entirely separate from stem of R along discal cell, or fused with it for short distance	*19*
18(17).	Front wing with vein R_5 arising from discal cell; proboscis present **50. Zygaenidae**	
	Front wing with vein R_5 stalked; proboscis absent **51. Megalopygidae**	
19(17).	Accessory cell ($1R_3$) not developed	*20*
	Accessory cell ($1R_3$) well marked	*21*

Key to the Families of Lepidoptera of the U.S. and Canada (*Contd.*)

20(19). Front wing with vein R_5 running to outer margin, base of vein M distinct, running through center of cell; hind wing with veins Sc and R connected by strong cross vein or anastomosing; proboscis absent**52. Limacodidae**

With a different combination of characters *70*

21(19). Front wing about 1½ times as long as wide; body short and slender ...**54. Dalceridae**

Front wing usually twice as long as wide; body either short and slender or very heavy .. *22*

22(21). Front wing lanceolate; body very heavy, far exceeding hind wing; mouthparts rudimentary; size usually over 25 mm; (in part)**37. Cossidae**

Front wing more or less oblong, lightly veined; body small and slender; mouthparts usually developed, with scaled proboscis *70*

23(15). Front wing with vein 1A with a recurving spur near its middle (in part) ..**11. Psychidae**

Front wing with vein 1A without spur *24*

24(23). Hind wing with vein P developed, but fading at base *25*

Hind wing with vein P at most represented by short apical spur, usually not developed at all ... *26*

25(24). Hind wing with veins Sc and Rs closely parallel or fused beyond apex of discal cell; (in part) ... **55. Pyralidae**

Hind wing with veins Sc and Rs strongly divergent anterior to end of discal cell ... *70*

26(24). Antennae distinctly swollen toward apex (or apically hooked) and frenulum absent (butterflies and skippers) ... *27*

Antennae not swollen toward tip or hooked, or, if swollen, then strong frenulum present ... *37*

27(26). Front wing with vein R 5-branched and all branches arising directly from discal cell; antennal bases separated by distance greater than half width of eye; antennae usually strongly hooked at apex**40. Hesperiidae**

Front wing with vein R with some branches absent or not arising directly from discal cell (stalked); antennal bases separated by distance less than half width of eye; antennae usually simply clubbed .. *28*

28(27). Front wing with vein 2A ending on margin; hind wing with vein 2A absent ..**41. Papilionidae**

Front wing with vein 2A ending on 1A near base, or not developed; hind wing with veins 1A and 2A both developed *29*

29(28). Labial palpi much longer than thorax**45. Libytheidae**

Labial palpi shorter than thorax ... *30*

30(29). Front wing with R 5-branched; front legs usually reduced in size *31*

Front wing with R 3- or 4-branched; front legs usually of normal size *34*

31(30). Front wing with 3A present but short and 2A appearing forked at base; antennae not scaled above; relatively large, brownish species**49. Danaidae**

Front wing without 3A and 2A not appearing forked at base; antennae usually scaled above ... *32*

32(31). Front wing with several veins swollen at base; antennae enlarged apically but not knobbed; small species, often with eyespots on wings**48. Satyridae**

Front wings with wing veins not greatly swollen at base *33*

33(32). Both wings with M_2 arising from middle of apical margin of discal cell or obsolete *34*

Vein M_2 associated with R in one wing and usually in both *35*

34(30, 33). Hind wing with cross vein h**44. Riodinidae**

Hind wing without cross vein h**43. Lycaenidae**

35(33). Front wing with M_1 associated with R; R usually 3- or 4-branched but if 5-branched, then front leg (only) slightly reduced in size; claws usually bifid ...**42. Pieridae**

Front wing with M_1 arising from discal cell, not associated with R; R always 5-branched; front leg greatly reduced; claws when present not bifid *36*

36(35). Hind wing with humeral vein arising from vein Sc distad of point where veins Rs and Sc+R_1 part**47. Apaturidae**

Hind wing with humeral vein arising otherwise**46. Nymphalidae**

37(26). Body very stout; wings over 50 mm in expanse; hind wings rarely extending beyond middle of abdomen; veins Sc and Rs of hind wing connected at middle or anterior of middle of discal cell by a strong vein R_1; beyond this point, Sc and Rs closely parallel to end of discal cell or beyond; both wings sometimes clear centrally ...**70. Sphingidae**

Key to the Families of Lepidoptera of the U.S. and Canada (*Contd.*)

	Body and wings differently proportioned; veins Sc and Rs of hind wing rarely connected by a strong R_1, or, if so, then Sc and Rs strongly divergent beyond this point ..	*38*
38(37).	Cell $1R_3$ either separated by a distinct vein R_{4+5} from discal cell or completely absent ..	*39*
	Cell $1R_3$ indistinct, the line of separation from discal cell indicated by a slight thickening that starts at angulation of stem of R; hind wing with veins Sc and Rs separate but connected by more or less distinct cross vein; wing expanse under 30 mm ..	*70*
39(3).	Front wings with Cu apparently 3-branched	*40*
	Front wing with Cu apparently 4-branched	*55*
40(39).	Frenulum normal, well-developed	*41*
	Frenulum absent or rudimentary, less than 1/15 of length of hind wing	*48*
41(40).	Hind wing with Sc and Rs sharply divergent from base of wing and not approximated all the way to apex**62. Epiplemidae**	
	Hind wing with Sc and Rs fused or approximated some distance before reaching apex ..	*42*
42(41).	Hind wing with Sc and Rs fused from base to beyond middle, then sharply divergent and swollen at base; (in part)**73. Arctiidae**	
	Hind wing with Sc and Rs separated at extreme base, then closely parallel or fused for a short or long distance ...	*43*
43(42).	Hind wing with Sc sharply angled toward C near base and connected to it by strong humeral cross vein; (in part)**61. Geometridae**	
	Hind wing with Sc moderately curved or straight near base	*44*
44(43).	Hind wing with Cu apparently 4-branched, Sc and Rs closely parallel beyond apex of discal cell ...**59. Thyatiridae**	
	Hind wing with Cu apparently 3-branched, Sc and R_5 separating before apex of discal cell ..	*45*
45(44).	Body stout; no tympanic hood; vein P not developed	*46*
	Body usually slender, or, if rather stout, then well-marked lateral hood on first abdominal segment ..	*47*
46(45).	Galea of maxillae developed into a proboscis, often weak; front wing fully scaled, usually with cell $1R_3$ or R_3 and R_4 stalked for considerable distance ...**71. Notodontidae**	
	Galea of maxilla not developed into a proboscis; front wing with branches of Rs all stalked together; hyaline dots present**66. Apatelodidae**	
47(45).	Hind wing with Sc straight and only slightly swollen at base; no trace of tympanic hood ...**72. Dioptidae**	
	Hind wing with Sc strongly sinuous and strongly swollen at base; (in part) ...**61. Geometridae**	
48(40).	Hind wing with Sc strongly divergent from Rs at extreme base, then sharply bent and touching or fusing or closely parallel to it, or connected by a strong cross vein (R_1); tympanic hood conspicuous, lateral; (in part)**61. Geometridae**	
	Hind wing with Sc fused with Rs for a very short distance, then sharply divergent, or separate from base, or connected by weak cross vein; tympanic hood absent	*49*
49(48).	Antennae without any scales or with but a few inconspicuous scales on shaft ...**69. Saturniidae**	
	Antennae closely scaled on upper side	*50*
50(49).	Hind wing with Sc sharply divergent from Rs from near base	*51*
	Hind wing with Sc and R parallel at base, connected by weak cross vein	*54*
51(50).	Front wing with R_{4+5} widely separated from R_3 all the way from discal cell to margin ...**65. Mimallonidae**	
	Front wing with R_4 arising from discal cell closely associated with R_3	*52*
52(51).	Front wing with R_5 and M_1 stalked or closely approximate at base and separated from R_4 ..	*53*
	Front wing with R_5 separate from M_1**69. Saturniidae**	
53(51).	With tympanal organs ...**64. Uraniidae**	
	Without tympanal organ ...**63. Sematuridae**	
54(50).	Frenulum about 1/16 of hind wing length; R with four branches in front wing; (in part) ...**66. Apatelodidae**	
	Frenulum absent, or, if present, not exceeding humeral angle of hind wing ...**67. Bombycidae**	

Key to the Families of Lepidoptera of the U.S. and Canada (*Contd.*)

55(39).	Front wing with Cu_2 arising from discal cell about 1/3 of way or less from base .**68. Lasiocampidae**	
	Front wing with Cu_2 arising well beyond middle of discal cell	*56*
56(55).	Front wing with all 12 veins present and all R, M, or Cu branches arising separately from discal cell, or with R_2 and R_3 stalked for short distance; (in part) .**56. Thyrididae**	
	Front wing with some veins absent, or with R_3 and R_4 or R_4 and R_5 stalked for some distance .	*57*
57(56).	Hind wing with Sc and Rs parallel to a point beyond separation of R from discal cell and then approaching very closely or fusing for short distance	*58*
	Hind wing with Sc fused with Rs or completely independent from it	*59*
58(57).	First abdominal segment with sclerotized subventral blister and subdorsal cavity opening caudad .**60. Drepanidae**	
	First abdominal segment unmodified (Chrysauginae)**55. Pyralididae**	
59(58).	Hind wing with Sc apparently absent, being fused with Rs except at extreme base .**75. Noctuidae**	
	Hind wing with Sc and Rs separating anteriorly to end of discal cell	*60*
60(59).	Antennae swollen toward apex .**75. Noctuidae**	
	Antennae regularly tapering toward apex .	*61*
61(60).	Ocelli present .	*62*
	Ocelli absent .	*67*
62(61).	Hind wing with Sc and Rs fused from base to at least middle of discal cell; (in part) .**63. Arctiidae**	
	Hind wing with Sc and Rs fusion not reaching middle of discal cell	*63*
63(62).	Hind wing with Sc and Rs fused for more than 1/5 length of discal cell	*64*
	Hind wing with Sc and Rs fused for less than 1/5 length of discal cell, fusion sometimes incomplete .	*65*
64(63).	Hind tarsi usually not more than 3 times as long as thick; tibiae often with reduced spurs; body often stout; M_2 usually a strong vein; tympanic hood above spiracle; (in part) .**73. Arctiidae**	
	Hind tarsi usually much more slender; tibiae with long spurs; body usually slender; tympanic hood usually surrounding spiracle; (in part)**75. Noctuidae**	
65(63).	Tympanic hood enlarged dorsally, the two hooks showing from dorsal aspect as two rounded projections on the 1st abdominal segment, separated by 1/3 of width of abdomen; brilliantly marked species .**73. Arctiidae**	
	Tympanic hoods less conspicuous dorsally, separated by 1/2 width of abdominal segment .	*66*
66(65).	White or yellow species with labial palpi not reaching middle of smoothly scaled front and Cu apparently 4-branched in both wings; hood above spiracle, conspicuous; (in part) .**73. Arctiidae**	
	Species with gray ground color, or labial palpi longer and Cu apparently 3-branched in hind wing; hood lateral; (in part) .**75. Noctuidae**	
67(61).	Front wing with raised scale tufts; small species with Sc and Rs ordinarily fused to near middle of discal cell but free in hind wing; (in part)**75. Noctuidae**	
	Front wing smoothly scaled .	*68*
68(67).	Hind wing with Sc and Rs fused from base to middle of discal cell; (in part) (see also 75.28 *Hypenodes* spp.) .**73. Arctiidae**	
	Hind wing with Sc and Rs not fused from base to middle of discal cell	*69*
69(68).	Hind wing with Sc sharply divergent from Rs at base, then angulate and becoming closely approximate or fusing; (in part)**61. Geometridae**	
	Hind wing with Sc and Rs fused at point about middle of discal cell, or connected by cross vein or closely parallel; (in part) .**74. Lymantriidae**	
70(13, 20, 22, 25, 38).	Maxillary palpi conspicuous, folded in resting position .	*71*
	Maxillary palpi straight, projecting, or rudimentary .	*76*
71(70).	Antennae with eye cap larger than eye .	*72*
	Antennae without or with rudimentary eye cap .	*73*
72(71).	Front wing with branched veins .**5. Nepticulidae**	
	Front wing with 3 or 4 unbranched veins .**6. Opostegidae**	
73(71).	Head smooth-scaled .**10. Tineidae**	
	Head with a few erect hairs or tufted with scales .	*74*
74(73).	Head with a few erect hairlike setae; front wing with R_5 (when present) ending in costa .**33. Acrolepiidae**	

Key to the Families of Lepidoptera of the U.S. and Canada (*Contd.*)

	Head tufted with scales, at least on vertex; front wing with R_5 ending beyond apex ..	*75*
75(74, 90).	Wing membrane with spinules (aculeae); hind wing with Sc and Rs usually strongly divergent from base, R_1 appearing as basal fork of Sc; vertex with very rough scales ...**8. Incurvariidae**	
	Wing membrane without spinules (aculeae absent); hind wing with R_1 strongly developed, and then several times shorter than stem of R; (in part) ..**10. Tineidae**	
76(70).	Front wing with discal cell set obliquely, its apex twice as far from costal as from outer margin, veins Cu_1 and sometimes Cu_2 very short and running transversely to outer margin (if Cu_2 long, them proboscis scaled)	*77*
	Front wing with discal cell in center of wing, or, if rarely oblique, then both Cu_1 and Cu_2 long longitudinal veins ...	*81*
77(76)	Hind wing lanceolate (if broad, then proboscis scaled); Rs and M_1 widely separated, parallel ..	*78*
	Hind wing linear, Rs and M_1 fused or stalked	*80*
78(77).	Ocelli very large and conspicuous; usually with metabolic spots or colorful	*79*
	Ocelli small or absent; usually dull motns **17. Blastobasidae**	
79(78).	Front wing truncated; hind wings rounded, but a little longer than wide; proboscis scaled ... **36. Choreutidae**	
	Front wing pointed; hind wings usually more or less elongate, distinctly longer than wide; proboscis naked **28. Glyphipterigidae**	
80(77).	Front tibiae exceptionally slender, with rudimentary apical epiphysis or none; antennae held forward at rest**18. Coleophoridae**	
	Front tibiae usually stout, epiphysis conspicuous and at middle; antennae folded back at rest; (in part)**21. Cosmopterigidae**	
81(76).	Membrane of hind wing distinctly cut out to form a narrow pointed apex, rarely bifid; (in part) ...**23. Gelechiidae**	
	Membrane not cut out to form a narrow pointed apex	*82*
82(81).	Hind wing rounded at apex or trapezoidal, often broader than fringe; vannus developed ..	*83*
	Hind wing lanceolate and pointed or linear, much narrower than fringe	*101*
83(82).	Hind wing with both M_1 and M_3 undeveloped; front wing without P	*84*
	Hind wing with at most one vein undeveloped	*85*
84(83).	Hind wing with all 3 branches of M present**24. Copromorphidae**	
	Hind wing with 1, or more often 2, branches of M absent**26. Carposinidae**	
85(83).	Vestiture of thorax and legs composed of deep, spatulate hair; proboscis rudimentary; body usually stout; venation complete, with base of M preserved	*86*
	Vestiture of thorax and front and middle tibiae mostly of normal scales; body slender ..	*87*
86(85).	Labial palpi upturned beyond middle of front, usually beyond vertex, or long and extending forward; eyes usually with hairlike setae; (in part)**10. Tineidae**	
	Labial palpi short, not reaching middle of front; eyes bare; (in part) **37. Cossidae**	
87(85).	Front wing with Cu_2 rising less than 3/4 of way from base of discal cell; labial palpi beaklike, with 2nd segment rough and usually extending straight forward or obliquely, and 3rd segment small**38. Tortricidae**	
	Front wint with Cu_2 arising more than 3/4 of way from base of discal cell, or, if less, then palpi smooth and upturned beyond vertex	*88*
88(87).	Labial palpi rough-scaled and beaklike, with 2nd segment roughly scaled dorsally and 3rd projecting and inconspicuous; vein P undeveloped; hind wing with Rs and M_1 approximate or stalked**39. Cochylidae**	
	Labial palpi either weak, not projecting beyond front, or, if long, then without rough scaling dorsally on 2nd segment	*89*
89(88).	Labial palpi weak and hardly projecting beyond front, or rudimentary; proboscis rudimentary ...	*90*
	Labial palpi better developed, conspicuous	*91*
90(89).	Male antennae simple or bristled; female with abdomen heavily tufted at apex; (in part) ...**11. Psychidae**	
	Male antennae plumose; female unknown**53. Epipyropidae**	
91(90).	Labial palpi bristled on outer side of 2nd segment; 3rd segment ovoid, well set off ..	*75*
	Labial palpi not bristled as above, upturned to middle of front or beyond; 2nd segment long and slender, usually tapering	*92*

Key to the Families of Lepidoptera of the U.S. and Canada (*Contd.*)

92(91). Hind wing with R_5 and M_1 closely approximated or stalked; proboscis usually present .. *93*

Hind wing with R_5 and M_1 well separated at origin, usually 1/2 as far as at wing margin .. *96*

93(92). Wings heavy and stiff, closely scaled, with all veins usually present and separate; front wing with R_5 ending beyond apex and vein P undeveloped; maxillary palpi absent; (in part) **56. Thyrididae**

Wings and veins light, lightly scaled; maxillary palpi perceptible, folded or outstanding .. *94*

94(93). Front wing with R_4 and R_5 stalked or united, both ending at C, and vein P undeveloped; (in part)**23. Gelechiidae**

Front wing with R_4 and R_5 separate, or, if united, then forking so that R_4 ends before apex and R_5 beyond .. *95*

95(94). Front wing blunt apically; maxillary palpi folded; proboscis scaled; (in part) **15. Oecophoridae**

Front wing distinctly pointed apically; maxillary palpi small; proboscis naked; (in part) .. **30. Yponomeutidae**

96(92). Front wing with R_5 ending at or before apex *97*

Front wing with R_5 ending beyond apex, or not more than 9 veins arising from discal cell .. *100*

97(96). Vertex more or less tufted; M_1 and M_2 in hind wing stalked *98*

Vertex smooth; usually no branches of M in hind wing stalked **22. Scythrididae**

Vertex extremely rough; Rs and M_1 of hind wing either forked near apex or completely fused **12. Ochsenheimeriidae**

98(97). Front wings narrowly rounded or pointed apically *99*

Front wings broadly rounded or blunt apically**15. Oecophoridae**

99(98). Ocelli present ..**29. Plutellidae**

Ocelli absent ..**31. Argyresthiidae**

100(96). Front wing with R_4 and R_5 stalked and chaetosema absent; (in part) **15. Oecophoridae**

Front wing with R_4 and R_5 separate and chaetosema present; (in part) **30. Yponomeutidae**

101(82). Antennae with eye cap that covers major part of eye when folded back *102*

Antennae with rudimentary eye cap, or none *103*

102(101). Labial palpi small and drooping, or absent**13. Lyonietiidae**

Labial palpi reaching beyond middle of front; (in part)**14. Gracilariidae**

103(101). Head with long, bristly vestiture covering vertex and front; proboscis and maxillary palpi undeveloped; (in part)**10. Tineidae**

Head with at least front smoothly scaled *104*

104(103). Hind wing with stem of R central, sending off 2 branches to C, one near middle and another just anterior to apex**32. Douglasiidae**

Hind wing with stem of R sending no branch to C, or with only one branch anterior to apex .. *105*

105(104). Hind wing lanceolate, at least 1/6 as wide as long, with stem of R running through its center .. *106*

Hind wing linear, with veins crowed, or sterm of R closely associated with Sc toward base or undeveloped *108*

106(105). Maxillary palpi distinct, outstanding; (in part)**14. Gracilariidae**

Maxillary palpi not developed, or indistinct *107*

107(106). Hind wing with stem of Cu at least 2-branched and discal cell usually distinct; labial palpi usually distinct; labial palpi usually upturned beyond middle of front; antennal pecten and ocelli usually present; maxillary palpi small (1- to 2-segmented) .. **16. Elachistidae**

Hind wing with stem of Cu simple and discal cell not formed; labial palpi small, drooping; antennal pecten and ocelli absent; maxillary palpi 5-segmented; (in part) .. **9. Heliozelidae**

108(105). Front wing without developed discal cell *109*

Front wing with distinct discal cell *110*

109(108). Front wing linear, with 3 or 4 simple veins only; proboscis naked **34. Heliodinidae**

Front wing lanceolate, with branched veins; proboscis scaled; (in part) **9. Heliozelidae**

110(108). Front wing lanceolate, with branched veins; proboscis scaled; (in part) **9. Heliozelidae**

Key to the Families of Lepidoptera of the U.S. and Canada (*Contd.*)

	Front wing with only 4 veins running to C and 5 or 6 to inner margin or hind wing, with M_1 widely separated from Rs at origin and often stalked with M_2; proboscis naked; (in part)**30. Yponomeutidae** Front wing with 5 veins running to C, or only 3 or 4 to inner margin; R and M_1 approximate or stalked in hind wing*111*
111(110).	Head entirely smooth scaled ...*112* Head with vertex rough scaled or with a rough anterior crest*113*
112(111).	Hind tibiae with stiff bristles, usually in tufts at the spurs; ocelli absent; proboscis naked ...**27. Epermeniidae** Hind tibiae without tufts of bristles; ocelli present or absent; proboscis scaled**19. Mompiidae, 20. Agonoxenidae, 21. Cosmopterigidae**
113(111).	Front wing with cell $1R_3$ small, or, more often, absent; hind tibiae moderately hairy, often smooth or bristled; proboscis naked; (in part) **14. Gracillariidae** Front wing with cell $1R_3$ very long, extending halfway to base; hind tibiae with large mass of hair; proboscis scaled**7. Tischeriidae**

Table 27.3 Classification of the Order Lepidoptera

Suborder ZEUGLOPTERA

Superfamily MICROPTERIGOIDEA

1. MICROPTERIGIDAE (Mandibulate Moth Family)

Suborder DACNONYPHA

Superfamily ERIOCRANIOIDEA

2. ERIOCRANIIDAE (Eriocraniid Moth Family)
3. ACANTHOPTEROCTETIDAE (Acanthopteroctetid Moth Family)

Suborder EXOPORIA

Superfamily HEPIALOIDEA

4. HEPIALIDAE (Ghost Moth Family; Swifts)

Suborder MONOTRYSIA

Superfamily NEPTICULOIDEA

5. NEPTICULIDAE (Minute Leaf Miner Moth Family)
6. OPOSTEGIDAE (Opostegid Moth Family)
7. TISCHERIIDAE (Tischeriid Moth Family)

Superfamily INCURVARIOIDEA

8. INCURVARIIDAE (Yucca and Fairy Moth Family)
9. HELIOZELIDAE (Shield Bearer Moth Family)

Suborder DITRYSIA

"Division MICROLEPIDOPTERA"

Superfamily TINEOIDEA

10. TINEIDAE (Clothes Moth Family)
11. PSYCHIDAE (Bagworm Moth Family)
12. OCHSENHEIMERIIDAE (Ochsenheimeriid Moth Family)
13. LYONETIIDAE (Lyonetiid Moth Family)
14. GRACILLARIIDAE (Gracillariid Moth Family)

Superfamily GELECHIOIDEA

15. OECOPHORIDAE (Oecophorid Moth Family)
16. ELACHISTIDAE (Elachistid Moth Family)
17. BLASTOBASIDAE (Blastobasid Moth Family)
18. COLEOPHORIDAE (Casebearer Moth Family)

19. MOMPHIDAE (Momphid Moth Family)
20. AGONOXENIDAE (Agonoxenid Moth Family)
21. COSMOPTERIGIDAE (Cosmopterigid Moth Family)
22. SCYTHRIDIDAE (Scythridid Moth Family)
23. GELECHIIDAE (Gelechiid Moth Family)

Superfamily COPROMORPHOIDEA

24. COPROMORPHIDAE (Copromorphid Moth Family)
25. ALUCITIDAE (Many-plume Moth Family)
26. CARPOSINIDAE (Carposinid Moth Family)
27. EPERMENIIDAE (Epermeniid Moth Family)
28. GLYPHIPTERIGIDAE (Sedge Moth Family)

Superfamily YPONOMEUTOIDEA

29. PLUTELLIDAE (Diamondback Moth Family)
30. YPONOMEUTIDAE (Ermine Moth Family)
31. ARGYRESTHIIDAE (Needle Miner Moth Family)
32. DOUGLASIIDAE (Douglasiid Moth Family)
33. ACROLEPIIDAE (Acrolepiid Moth Family)
34. HELIODINIDAE (Heliodinid Moth Family)

Superfamily SESIOIDEA

35. SESIIDAE (Clear-winged Moth Family)
36. CHOREUTIDAE (Choreutid Moth Family)

Superfamily COSSOIDEA

37. COSSIDAE (Carpenter and Goat Moth Family)

Superfamily TORTRICOIDEA

38. TORTRICIDAE (Tortricid Moth Family)
39. COCHYLIDAE (Cochylid Moth Family)

"Division RHOPALOCERA"

Superfamily HESPERIOIDEA

40. HESPERIIDAE (Skipper Family)

Superfamily PAPILIONOIDEA

41. PAPILIONIDAE (Swallowtail and Parnassian Butterfly Family)
42. PIERIDAE (Sulphur, White, and Orange-tip Butterfly Family)
43. LYCAENIDAE (Hairstreak, Copper, and Blue Butterfly Family)
44. RIODINIDAE (Metal-mark Butterfly Family)

Table 27.3 Classification of the Order Lepidoptera (*Contd.*)

45. LIBYTHEIDAE (Snout Butterfly Family)
46. NYMPHALIDAE (Brush-footed Butterfly Family)
47. APATURIDAE (Apaturid Butterfly Family)
48. SATYRIDAE (Nymph, Satyr, and Arctic Butterfly Family)
49. DANAIDAE (Milkweed Butterfly Family)

"Division MICROLEPIDOPTERA" (Cont.)

　Superfamily ZYGAENOIDEA

50. ZYGAENIDAE (Smoky Moth Family)
51. MEGALOPYGIDAE (Flannel Moth Family)
52. LIMACODIDAE (Slug Caterpillar Moth Family)
53. EPIPYROPIDAE (Epiplemid Moth Family)
54. DALCERIDAE (Dalcerid Moth Family)

　Superfamily PYRALOIDEA

55. PYRALIDAE (Snout Moth Family)
56. THYRIDIDAE (Window-winged Moth Family)
57. HYBLAEIDAE (Hyblaeid Moth Family)

　Superfamily PTEROPHOROIDEA

58. PTEROPHORIDAE (Plume Moth Family)

"Division MACROLEPIDOPTERA"

　Superfamily DREPANOIDEA

59. THYATIRIDAE (Thyatirid Moth Family)
60. DREPANIDAE (Hook-tip Moth Family)

Superfamily GEOMETROIDEA

61. GEOMETRIDAE (Geometer Moth Family)
62. EPIPLEMIDAE (Epiplemid Moth Family)
63. SEMATURIDAE (Sematurid Moth Family)
64. URANIIDAE (Uraniid Moth Family)

　Superfamily MIMALLONOIDEA

65. MIMALLONIDAE (Mimallonid Moth Family)

　Superfamily BOMBYCOIDEA

66. APATELODIDAE (Apatelodid Moth Family)
67. BOMBYCIDAE (Silkworm Moth Family)
68. LASIOCAMPIDAE (Lappet Moth Family)
69. SATURNIIDAE (Giant Silkworm Moth Family)

　Superfamily SPHINGOIDEA

70. SPHINGIDAE (Hawk Moth Family)

　Superfamily NOCTUOIDEA

71. NOTODONTIDAE (Prominent Moth Family)
72. DIOPTIDAE (Oak Moth Family)
73. ARCTIIDAE (Tiger Moth Family)
74. LYMANTRIIDAE (Tussock Moth Family)
75. NOCTUIDAE (Noctuid Moth Family)

Table 27.4 Index to the Families and Higher Taxa of Lepidoptera

(Numbers refer to family numbers, not pages)

Acanthopteroctetidae, 3
Acragidae; see Dalceridae (54)
Acrolepiidae, 33
Acrolophidae; *see* Tineidae (10)
Adelidae; *see* Incurvariidae (8)
Aegeriidae; *see* Sesiidae (35)
Aegyreidae; *see* Nymphalidae (46)
Agaristidae; *see* Noctuidae (75)
Agdistidae; *see* Pterophoridae (58)
Agonoxenidae, 20
Alucitidae, 25
Amatidae; *see* Arctiidae (73)
Amydriidae; *see* Tineidae (10)
Apatelodidae; 66
Apaturidae, 47
Arctiidae, 73
Argyresthiidae, 31
Ascelidae; *see* Pieridae (42)
Blastobasidae, 17
Bombycidae, 67
Bombycoidea; *supra* 66
Castniidae; not in the U.S. and Canada
Carposinidae, 26
Ceratocampidae; *see* Saturnidae, (69)
Ceruridae; *see* Notodontidae (71)
Citheroniidae; *see* Saturniidae (69)
Cochlidiidae; *see* Limacodidae (52)
Cochylidae, 39
Coleophorida, 18
Conchylidae; *see* Cochylidae (39)
Copromorphidae (24)
Corpromorphoidea; *supra* 24
Cosmopterigidae, 21
Cosmopterygidae; *see* Cosmopterigidae (21)

Cossidae, 37
Crambidae; *see* Pyralidae (55)
Ctenuchidae; *see* Noctuidae (75)
Cupidinidae; *see* Lycaenidae (43)
Cymatophoridae; *see* Thyatridae (59)
Cycnodiidae, *see* Elachistidae (16)
Dacynonypha; *supra* 2
Dalceridae, 54
Danaidae, 49
Depressariidae; *see* Oecophoridae (15)
Dioptidae, 72
Ditrysia; *supra* 10
Douglasiidae, 32
Drepanidae, 60
Elachistidae, 16
Epermeniidae, 27
Epipaschiidae; *see* Pyralidae (55)
Epiplemidae, 62
Epipyropidae, 53
Eriocephalidae; *see* Micropterigidae (1)
Eriocraniidae, 2
Ericranioidea; *supra* 2
Ethmiidae; *see* Oecophoridae (15)
Erycinidae; *see* Riodinidae (44)
Eucleidae; *see* Limacodidae (52)
Euchromiidae; *see* Noctuidae (75)
Eupterotidae; *see* Apatelodidae (66)
Exoporia; *supra* 2
Frenatae; *see* Macrolepidoptera (*supra* 59)
Galleriidae; *see* Pyralidae (55)
Gelechiidae, 23
Gelechoiidea; *supra* 15
Geometridae, 61
Geometroidea; *supra* 59

Glyphipterigidae, 28
Glyphipterygidae; *see* Glyphipterigidae (28)
Gracillariidae, 14
Heliconiidae; *see* Nymphalidae (46)
Heliodinidae, 34
Heliozelidae, 9
Hemerophilidae; *see* Glyphipterigidae (28)
Hepialidae, 4
Hepialoidea; *supra* 4
Hespiriidae, 40
Hesperioidea; *supra* 40
Hyblaeidae, 57
Hypoptidae; *see* Cossidae (37)
Hypsidae; *see* Arctiidae (73)
Incurvariidae, 8
Incurvarioidea; *supra* 8
Jugatae; *see* Zeugloptera (*supra* 1), Dacnonypha (*supra* 2), and Monotrysia (*supra* 5)
Lacosomidae; *see* Mimallonidae (65)
Lagoidae; *see* Megalopygidae (51)
Lasiocampidae, 68
Lavernidae; *see* Cosmopterigidae (21)
Lemoniidae; *see* Apatelodidae (66)
Libytheidae, 45
Limacodidae, 52
Liparidae; *see* Lymantriidae (74)
Liphyridae; *see* Lycaenidae (43)
Lithosiidae; *see* Arctiidae (73)
Lonomiidae; *see* Saturniidae (69)
Lycaenidae, 43
Lymnadidae; *see* Danaidae (49)
Lymantriidae, 74
Lyonetiidae, 13

Table 27.4　Index to the Families and Higher Taxa of Lepidoptera (*Contd.*)

Macrolepidoptera; *supra* 59
Manidiidae; *see* Semanturidae (63)
Megalopygidae, 51
Megathymidae; *see* Hesperiidae (40)
Microlepidoptera; *supra* 10 and 50
Micropterigidae, 1
Micropterigoidea; *supra* 1
Mimallonidea, 65
Mimallonoidea; *supra* 65
Momphidae, 19
Monotrysia; *supra* 5
Nepticulidae, 5
Nepticuloidea; *supra* 5
Noctuidae, 75
Noctuoidea; *supra* 71
Nolidae; *see* Noctuidae (75)
Notodontidae, 71
Nymphalidae, 46
Ochsenheimeriidae, 12
Oecophoridae, 15
Oenophilidae; *see* Tineidae (10)
Oinophilidae; *see* Tineidae (10)
Olethreutidae; *see* Tortricidae (38)
Opostegidae, 6
Orneodidae; *see* Alucitidae (25)
Papilionidae, 41
Papilionoidea; *supra* 41
Parnassiidae; *see* Papilionidae (41)

Periocopidae; *see* Arctiidae (73)
Perophoridae; *see* Mimallonidae (65)
Phalaenidae; *see* Noctuidae (75)
Phaloniidae; *see* Cochylidae (39)
Phycitidae; *see* Pyralidae (55)
Phyllocnistidae; *see* Gracilariidae (14)
Plusiidae; *see* Noctuidae (75)
Platypterygidae; *see* Drypanidae (60)
Plutellidae, 29
Prodoxidae; *see* Incurvariidae (8)
Psychidae, 11
Pterophoridae, 58
Pterophoroidea; *supra* 58
Pyralidae, 55
Pyralididae; see Pyralidae (55)
Pyraloidea; *supra* 55
Pyraustidae; *see* Pyralidae (55)
Pyromorphidae; *see* Zygaenidae (50)
Rhopalocera; *supra* 40
Riodinidae, 44
Ruralidae; *see* Lycaenidae (43)
Saturniidae, 69
Satyride, 48
Scythridae; *see* Scythrididae (22)
Scythrididae, 22
Sematuridae, 63
Sesiidae, 35
Sesioidea; *supra* 35

Setomorphidae; *see* Tineidae (10)
Smerinthidae; *see* Sphingidae (70)
Sphingidae, 70
Sphingoidea; *supra* 70
Stenomatidae; *see* Oecophoridae (15)
Stenomidae; *see* Oecophoridae (15)
Syntomidae; *see* Arctiidae (73)
Talaeporiidae; *see* Psychidae (11)
Thyatiridae, 59
Thyridae; *see* Thyrididae (56)
Thyrididae, 56
Tinaegeriidae; *see* Heliodinidae (34)
Tineidae, 10
Tineoidea; *supra* 10
Tischeriidae, 7
Tortricidae, 38
Tortricoidea; *supra* 38
Uraniidae, 64
Uzuchidae; *see* Oecophoridae (15)
Xylorictidae; *see* Oecophoridae (15)
Yponomeutidae, 30
Yponomeutoidea; *supra* 29
Zanolidae; *see* Apatelodidae (66)
Zeugloptera; *supra* 1
Zeuzeridae; *see* Cossidae (37)
Zygaenidae, 50
Zygaenoidea; *supra* 50

Table 27.5(a)　Features of the Major Groups of Lepidoptera

I. *Front wings and hind wigns of same shape and venation*

Suborder Zeugloptera, superfamily Micropterigoidea

1. *Micropterygidae*	Small; wingspan, 6–12 mm; mouthparts with mandibles; rare

Suborder Dacnonypha, superfamily Eriocranioidea

2. *Eriocraniidae*	Moderate size; wingspan 6–13.5 mm; mandibulate mouthparts greatly reduced, functionless; 13 uncommon species
3. *Acanthopteroctetidae*	Similar to preceding; vary rare.

Suborder Exoporia, superfamily Hepialoidea

4. *Hepialidae*	Large; wingspan, 25–75 mm; brown or ashy gray, usually with silvery white spots on wings

Suborder Monotrysia

　Superfamily Nepticuloidea

5. *Nepticulidae*	Very small; wingspan, under 3 mm; wings with aculae; basal segment of antennae forms an eye cap; antennae rough; female without ovipositior

Superfamily Incurvarioidea [also includes *Heliozilidae* (9)]

8. *Incurvariidae*	Wings with aculae on wing surface in addition to scales; antennal basal segment not forming an eye cap; antennae smooth, usually long; female with piercing ovipositor

II. *Suborder Ditrysia*

　A. *Wingless or wings greatly reduced (some females of the following families):*

55. *Pyralidae*	Ocelli absent; proboscis absent or greatly reduced; aquatic
38. *Tortricidae*	Ocelli absent; proboscis present
74. *Lymantriidae*	Ocelli present; proboscis absent or greatly reduced; legs short; body stout, densely covered with wool-like setae
61. *Geometridae*	Ocelli usually absent; legs of normal length; body slender, covered with hairlike setae or scales
11. *Psychidae*	Adult females resembles larvae; case made of silk and evergreen needles, leaves, or twigs

Table 27.5(A) (Contd.)

B. *Front wings and hind wings differently shaped; fringe on anal angles of hind wings not longer than elsewhere or only slightly so; spurs of tibiae about as long as width of tibiae* ["Microlepidoptera" in part; *see* Table 27.5(B)]

C. *Front wings and hind wings differently shaped; fringe on inner angle of hind wings usually as long as, or longer than, width of wing; spurs of tibiae more than twice as long as width of tibia* ["Microlepidoptera" in part; *see* Table 27.5(C)]

D. *Usually large; hind wings usually with very short, stout, curved frenulum* ["Macrolepidoptera," superfamilies Mimallonoidea and Bombycoidea; *see* Table 27.5(D)]

E. *Stout, curved frenulum on hind wings* ["Macrolepidoptera"; *see* Table 27.5(E)]

F. *Antennae clubbed; ocelli absent; frenulum absent; usually diurnal* ["Rhopalocera" (Skippers and Butterflies); *see* Table 27.5(F)]

Table 27.5(B) Features of the Major Groups of Lepidoptera

Wings with short fringe of scales in anal area

Superfamily Zygaenoidea [Families noted below as well as Epipyropidae (53) and Dalceridae (54)] Front wing venation with all veins complete and no open discal cell; maxillary palpi minute or absent

52. *Limacodidae*	Small to medium size; wings short, brownish, often marked with silver or green spots of various size, or pale wings with brown bands; vesture often woolly in appearance; proboscis absent
51. *Megalopygidae*	Fairly large; wingspan, to 40 mm; antennae of male and some females pectinate at tip; front wing with vesture often crinkly, more or less hairlike scales giving them the appearance of bits of flannel; proboscis absent
50. *Zyaenidae*	Small; wingspan, to 25 mm; wings smoky black, translucent, sometimes marked with metallic colors; proboscis well-developed

Superfamily Pyralidoidea [Including Thyrididae (56) and Hyblaeidae (57)] Wings normally with three anal veins; maxillary palpi, if present, extending forward, that is, porrect; proboscis sometimes with scales at base

55. *Pyralidae*	Wings narrow or broad, with heavy, closely packed scales; large anal area; body slender; head prominent; ocelli usually present; palpi moderate or long (snout moths); front wings usually with two anals only; ears present on underside of base of abdomen; proboscis scaled

Superfamily Pterophoroidea

58. *Pterophoridae*	Front wing distally divided into two narrow lobes, hind wing into three (except in *Agdistis* spp.); no "ears" on underside of base of abdomen

Superfamily Copromorphoidea

25. *Alucitidae*	Each wing divided into six narrow, plume-like lobes

Table 27.5(C) Features of the Major Groups of Lepidoptera

Wings usually with fringe of scales in anal area as long as wing is wide

Superfamily Tortricoidea Small; head and body with rough textured scales; palpi rough, triangular, or narrow and projecting forward; maxillary palpi minute; proboscis scaled

38. *Tortricidae*	Small; square-tipped wings, with or without fringe of long hairlike setae near base of hind wings
39. *Cochylidae*	Usually small (rarely with wingspan up to 25 mm); rough scales; head with small ocelli; proboscis weak or absent; wings usually long and narrow, rounded, usually bent down at apex

Superfamily Cossoidea

37. *Cossidae*	Large, stout; wings spotted or mottled; frenulum sometimes obsolete; palpi small; proboscis rudimentary

Superfamily Copromorphoidea [Families noted below a well as Alucitidae (25), Copromorphidae (24), Epermeniidae (27), and Glyphipterigidae (28)] Similar to Tortricoidea, distinguished by difference in wing venation

26. *Carposinidae*	Ocelli absent; proboscis weak; antennae heavily ciliated in male; palpi strongly dimorphic, long in female, short in male

Superfamily Gelechioidea [Families noted below and Elachistidae (16), Blastobasidae (17), Momphidae (19), Cosmopterigidae (21), Scythrididae (22), and Agonoxendiae (20)] Proboscis densely scaled basally; labial palpus upturned, head smooth scaled; wings with variable radius

15. *Oecophoridae*	Small to moderate; wingspan, 8–30 mm; head with smooth scales; ocelli usually present; scape often with pecten of stiff hairlike scales; front wings usually with IA present
18. *Coleophoridae*	Antennae much shorter than front wing; scales of head smooth; maxillary palpi moderate, usually a tuft, with third segment often set at an angle; antennae directed forward when at rest
23. *Gelechiidae*	Usually small; wingspan, 8–12 mm (some to 22 mm); head with smooth scales; ocelli often present; scape seldom with pecten; front wings usually with vein IA absent; apex of hind wings often produced

Superfamily Yponomeutoidea [Families noted below as well as Heliodinidae (34), Argyresthiidae (31), Douglasiidae (32), Acrolepiidae (33), and Plutellidae (29)] Proboscis naked; maxillary palpi rarely four-segmented, usually small, three-segmented, or rudimentary

30. *Yponomeutidae*	Wings fully scaled, coupled by frenulum only; ocelli small or absent; not wasplike

Table 27.5(C) (Contd.)

Superfamily Sesioidea (Including Choreutidae (36)]

| 35. *Sesiidae* | Wings partly transparent, coupled by series of recurved bristles and frenulum; ocelli prominent; usually resemble wasps |

Superfamily Tineoidea [Families noted below as well as Ochsenheimeriidae (12) and Lyonetiidae (19)] With characteristics variable, best defined on basis of wing venation; front wing usually with R_5 reaching costa; hind wing with R and M_1 separate, Sc and R typically approximate at base; wingspan, 8–30+ mm; ocelli present or absent; chaetosemata (paired sense organs above eyes) absent (distinguishing this group from Tortricoidea, Zygaenoidea, and some Pyraloidea); maxillary palpi drooping.

14. *Gracillariidae*	Antennae nearly as long as or longer than front wings; scales of head smooth except for dorsal fringe of erect hairlike setae; maxillary palpi porrect or obsolete; antennae directed backward when at rest
11. *Psychidae*	Females wingless [*See* Table 27.5 (A)]; males with scales of head all rough; scale (basal segment) of antennae without pecten (stiff hairlike scales); maxillary palpi rudimentary or absent
10. *Tineidae*	Scales of head usually all rough; scape (basal segment) of antennae often with pecten of stiff hairlike scales; maxillary palpi five-segmented, folded, may be reduced

Table 27.5(D) Features of the Major Groups of Lepidoptera

Superfamily Mimallonoidea

| 65. *Mimallonidae* | Very similar to Bombycoidea; front wings falcate, that is, tips somewhat projected, sickle-shaped; frenulum reduced or absent; antennae of males without third segment abruptly narrowed |

Superfamily Bombycoidea Head small, retracted; ocelli absent; proboscis greatly reduced or vestigial; palpi variously developed but very small; wings large, body large; vesture deep, hairlike scales, sometimes mixed with ordinary scales; frenulum usually vestigial or absent

66. *Apatelodidae*	Distinguished from most other macrolepidoptera by reduced proboscis and large body size; wings slightly falcate (sickle-shaped); frenulum well developed
67. *Bombycidae*	Not native to North America, the silkworm is reared only in domestication; not found in the wild
68. *Lasiocampidae*	Antennae bipectinate to apex in both sexes; proboscis vestigial or absent; labial palpi small to large and prominent

Table 27.5(D) (Contd.)

| 69. *Saturniidae* | Antennae quadripectinate or bipectinate, either extremely broad and tapering or narrowing abruptly one-half to three-quarters of the way out, leaving tip simple except for short bristlelike setae; female antennae simple to quadripectinate, narrower than male's, or absent |

Table 27.5(E) Features of the Major Groups of Lepidoptera

Wings with a frenulum (see also Apatelodidae (66))

Superfamily Sphingoidea

| 70. *Sphingidae* | Large, stout bodied moths with front wings usually nearly twice as long as hind wings; antennae usually thickened, sometimes tapering or hooked apically; proboscis well-developed; maxillary palpi one-segmented |

Superfamily Geometroidea [Including Epiplemidae (62), Sematuridae (63), and Uraniidae (64)] Tympanum large, double, subventral on abdomen; chaetosemata usually prominent; ocelli absent; proboscis without scales, may be reduced or absent

59. *Thyatiridae*	Frenulum of hind wing well-developed, knobbed at tip in male antennae deeply laminate; vesture deep, hairy, or mixed with scales, with truncate mass of hairlike scales on disc of thorax; legs with hairlike scales
60. *Drepanidae*	Wings broad, front wings usually falcate (sickle-shaped); body short and stout; frenulum absent or vestigial
61. *Geometridae*	Wings broad; body slender; ocelli usually absent; chaetosemata (sense organs above eyes) usually present; maxillary palpi minute or vestigial; proboscis without scales; antennae simple or pectinate; ears on ventrolateral part of base of abdomen
59. *Thyatiridae*	Frenulum of hind wing well-developed, knobbed at tip of male; antennae deeply laminate; vesture deep, hairy or mixed with scales, with truncate mass of hairlike scales on disc of thorax; legs with hairlike scales
60. *Drepanidae*	Wings broad, front wingss usually falcate (sickle-shaped); body short and stout; frenulum absent or vestigial

Superfamily Noctuoidea [Families noted below as well as Dioptidae (72)] A complex of large families with varying characteristics; ocelli

Table 27.5(E) (Contd.)

often present; maxillary palpi very small, one- to four-segmented, or absent; chaetosemata (sense organs above eyes) absent; proboscis often well-developed, but may be reduced or absent; "ears" dorsal, on metathorax (absent in Ctenuchinae)

73. *Arctiidae*	Tympanal organs as in Lymantriidae; small to medium size; ocelli usually present; proboscis usually reduced; maxillary palpi one-segmented; front and hind wings quadrifid; closely resemble Noctuidae except that they are often brightly colored
75. *Noctuidae*	Tympanal organs as in Lymantriidae; ocelli usually present; proboscis usually strong; maxillary palip one-segmented; front and hind wings quadrifid; in some, hind wing trifid
71. *Notodontidae*	Metathorax with auditory tympanal organs near wing base directed downward; medium to large moths; ocelli reduced or absent; front and hind wings trifid
74. *Lymantriidae*	Tympanal organs near wing base directed obliquely backwards; ocelli absent; proboscis usually absent; maxillary palpi one-segmented or absent; front and hind wings quadrifid

Table 27.5(F) · Features of the Major Groups of Lepidoptera (Butterfly and Skipper Families)

Superfamily Papilionoidea Antennae approximate at base, club without apical hook; chaetosemata prominent; proboscis without scales; maxillary palpi minute, one-segmented, or absent; front wing sometimes with R three- or four-branched, or, if five-branched, branches separate beyond discal cell

49. *Danaidae*	Front legs greatly reduced; antennae without scales; large, brownish red with black markings; R five-branched
48. *Satyridae*	Front legs greatly reduced; some veins of front wings greatly swollen at base; wings broad, brown, usually with small circular "eye spots"; R five-branched
46. *Nymphalidae*	Front legs greatly reduced; palpi not elongate; front wings usually without swollen veins; wings broad, or if narrow, elongate, and black with yellow, red, or blue markings, sometimes with irregular outer margins, usually brown with dark markings; R five-branched
47. *Apaturidae*	Similar to Nymphalidae, but palpi blade-like; front wings with R_1 and R_2 free and R_4 and R_5 long stalked

Table 27.5(F) (Contd.)

45. *Libytheidae*	Front legs greatly reduced; labial palpi very long, longer than thorax, with vestiture of thick, hairlike scales forming a "snout"; R five-branched
43. *Lycaenidae*	Front legs (males only) greatly reduced; body slender; wings delicate and often brightly colored; antennae nearly always ringed with white; front wing with R four-branched
44. *Riodinidae*	Small; wings short, broad; antennae elongate; color dull brown, orange, and black, sometimes checkered with white, rarely marked strongly with red and orange; front wings with R four-branched; hind wing with C very stout at base
42. *Pieridae*	Medium; wings white, yellow, or orange, usually marked with black; front wing with R four- or five-branched; front legs not reduced, without epiphysis
41. *Papilionidae*	Hind wings usually with tail-like projections, or, if not, white or gray colors and usually with two reddish spots on hind wing; front legs not reduced; front tibia with epiphysis; front wings with R four- or five-branched

Superfamily Hesperioidea Antennae widely separate at base; front wings with R-five-branched

40. *Hesperiidae*	Antennae clubbed, usually with apical hooks; if not, large (40 to 60 mm); ocelli absent; proboscis without scales; maxillary palpi absent

Suborder ZEUGLOPTERA

The wing venation of the front and hind wings of these moths is almost exactly the same; five radials are present in both. A frenulum is not present; instead, the wings are hooked together in flight by a *jugum*, a stong lobe on the posterior margin of the front wing. The middle tibia has apical bristles rather than spurs. There is one superfamily. Micropterigoidea, as follows.

Superfamily MICROPTERIGOIDEA

There is only one family in this superfamiliy, as follows.

1. MICROPTERIGIDAE (Mandibulate Moth Family)

Wingspan: 6–12 mm. Wings moderately narrow, lanceolate; head with functional mandibles; two ocelli present, at some distance from the eyes; maxillary palpi five-segmented, long; antennae moniliform. Middle tibiae with a tuft of hair at apex and no spurs. Adult moths feed freely on the pollen of various flowers, using their mandibles to crush and eat it. Their spherical eggs are laid in small clusters in and under wet moss.

Larvae feed on moss and liverworts and spin cocoons from which adults emerge in the spring. About 35 species of these primitive and rather rare moths occur in the world, only two of them in the U.S., in one genus, as follows:

1.1 *Epimartyria* Walsingham

[=*Micropteryx* Hubner]

E. auricrinella Walsingham. Wingspan: ±8 mm. Body purple; head with golden gloss; base of front wings with golden scales. Found in sunny glades in April and May; often on flowers of *Caltha palustris* (Marsh Marigold; Cowslips) feeding on pollen. (See Fig. 27.13) Rare throughout (1) n.e. US and Canada.

E. pardella Walsingham. Wingspan: ±8 mm. Wings with large yellow spots. (3) CA; (4) OR, BC, VS.

Suborder DACNONYPHA

The venation of the front and hind wings is similar, as it is in the preceding suborder, and both sets of wings are constructed in much the same way. The middle tibia, however, has at least one spur. There is one superfamily, as follows.

Superfamily ERIOCRANIOIDEA

Wingspan: 6–16 mm. Head often broader than long; vestiture rather sparse; chaetosemata present as an elongate pair of raised areas extending transversely across occiput and nearly meeting; ocelli present or absent; antennae simple, of moderate length, with narrow, long, appressed scales; mandibles vestigial; functional haustellum present; maxillary palpi five-segmented; labial palpi two- to three-segmented; front wing relatively narrow, somewhat lanceolate; prominent jugum. Two families occur in North America.

2. ERIOCRANIIDAE (Eriocraniid Moth Family)

Wingspan: 6–13.5 mm. Moderately slender; head with lateral ocelli well separated from eyes; mandibles vestigial but relatively large; maxillary palpi five-segmented, relatively long. Caterpillars are leaf miners on oaks and other trees. There are four genera and 12 species in the U.S. and Canada, all species having an extremely local distribution.

Fig. 27.14.

2.1 *Dyseriocrania* Spuler

[=*Mnemonica* Meyrick]

The genus contains two U.S. species, *D. aurosparsella* Walsingham, (3) CA, and the following:

D. griseocapitella (Walsingham). Wingspan: 9–12.5 mm. Head and thorax grayish with slight iridescence; front wings golden bronze with scattered, small, purple spots and larger blotches near margins; hind wings paler, grayish, with a slight purplish luster. (Fig. 27.14.) Adults in April and May. (1) NY to DC, w. to MI and IL; (2) SC, FL, AL.

[2.2 *Eriocrania* Zeller (2 spp.)]

2.3 *Eriocraniella* Viette

Seven species, including the following:

E. falcata Davis. Wingspan: 7–10 mm. Wings sparsely covered with bronzy brown, hairlike scales above, and whitish ventrally. (See Fig. 27.15.) (3) s. CA, VS.

[2.4 *Neocrania* Davis (1 sp., *N. bifasciata* Davis (3) CA)]

3. ACANTHOPTEROCTETIDAE (Acanthopteroctetid Moth Family)

Wingspan: 11–16 mm. Wings very slender; head without ocelli; mandibles vestigial, nearly absent; maxillary palpi five-segmented.

Fig. 27.13.

Fig. 27.15.

3.1 *Acanthopteroctetes* Braun

Three named species—confined to (3) CA, (4) OR, (5) MT—all extremely local and known from very few specimens. Habits of larvae unknown.

A. tripunctata Braun. (5) MT (known only from Glacier National Park).

Suborder EXOPORIA

Wings of these moths are large, the fringe is narrow, and there is a jugum present. Females have two genital openings, and the anus is on or behind the ninth sternum. There is one superfamily, as follows.

Superfamily HEPIALOIDEA

One family only in North America.

4. HEPIALIDAE (Ghost Moth Family; Swifts)

Wingspan: 25–100 mm. Mouthparts rudimentary, but both mandibles and maxillae present; front and hind wings with similar venation; jugum on front wing overlaps hind wing; legs without tibial spurs. These large, fast-flying moths appear mostly at dusk, but a few of the approximately 200 species are diurnal. They are sometimes called *swifts* because of their rapid diurnal flight. Known larvae are root or stem borers. There are 20 species assigned to two genera in the U.S. and Canada.

4.1 *Sthenopis* Packard

Five species in the U.S. and Canada, including the following:

S. argenteomaculatus Harris (Silver Spotted Ghost Moth). Wingspan: 45–100 mm. Brownish with darker brown, pale-edged, irregular bands on wings and two irregular, small light spots near base of front wing. Hind wing light brown to pale gray. Larvae bore into roots and stems of alder. Males swarm. (See Fig. 27.16.) (1) n.e. US.

S. thule Strecker. Larvae bore into willow. (1) n.e. NA.

S. purpurascens Packard. (1) ON, PQ.

S. quadriguttatus Grote. (1) n.e. US.

Fig. 27.16.

4.2 *Hepialus* Fabricius

Fifteen species in the U.S. and Canada, including the following:

H. mustelinus Packard (Graceful Ghost Moth). Wingspan: male, ±30 mm; female, ±40 mm. Brownish gray; wings with irregular gray mottling. Males swarm. Larvae bore into fern rhizomes. (1) n.e. NA; (5) CO, KS, MO.

H. hyperboreus Moeschler. (1) n.e. NA.

H. lembertii Dyar (Lembert's Ghost Moth). (3) CA.

Suborder MONOTRYSIA

The front and hind wings of these moths have dissimilar venation, with radials in the hind wing reduced to R_1 and Rs; there is a jugum present. There are two superfamilies, Nepticuloidea and Incurvarioidea, as follows.

Superfamily NEPTICULOIDEA

Three families of this superfamily occur in North America. The scape of the antennae is expanded into a broad eye cap; the front wings usually lack a closed discal cell.

5. NEPTICULIDAE (Minute Leaf Miner Moth Family)

Wingspan: Usually 3–5 mm (some up to 10 mm). Head with erect hairlike scales; proboscis very short or rudimentary; wings lanceolate, venation reduced, but with branched R and M in front wing. These moths are not usually collected at lights at night, but if they happen to be attracted, they may be easily overlooked because of their small size. They are very rapid flyers, darting in an irregular pattern or racing over the leaves of the larval food plants where they lay single eggs. Larvae, so far as known, are leaf miners or gall makers; they are often host specific. The mines of each species have a characteristic appearance. There are 82 species in eight genera in the U.S. and Canada, three of which have some economic importance.

5.1 *Stigmella* Schrank
[=*Nepticula* von Heyden]

Fifty species are found in the U.S. and Canada, the following two being of economic interest:

S. juglandifoliella (Clemens) (Pecan Serpentine Leaf Miner). Larvae infest Pecan leaves. (1) OH; (2) s.e. US.

S. gossypii (Forbes and Leonard) (Cotton Leaf Miner). Larvae infest Cotton leaves in (2) s. FL.

Fig. 27.17.

Fig. 27.18.

5.2 *Ectoedemia* Busck

Twenty species, the following of which is common:

E. virgulae (Braun). Wingspan: ±4 mm. Brown with silver bands. (See Fig. 27.17.) (2) FL; (3) TX.

5.3 *Obrussa* Braun

Two species, the following of which is common:

O. ochrefasciella (Chambers) (Hard Maple Bud Miner). Wingspan: 6.5–8 mm. Front wing blackish brown with olive-brown markings. (See Fig. 27.18.) (1) e. NY.

[5.4 *Glaucolepis* Braun (1 sp., *G. saccharella* Braun); 5.5 *Microcalyptris* Braun (5 spp.); 5.6 *Fomoria* Beirne (2 spp.); 5.7 *Manoneura* Davis (1 sp., *M. basidactyla* (Davis)); 5.8 *Artaversala* Davis (1 sp., *A. gilvafascia* Davis)]

6. OPOSTEGIDAE (Opostegid Moth Family)

Wingspan: 8–9 mm. Head smooth except for tuft of long hair-scales on vertex; antennae frequently short; haustellum very short; legs with long stiff bristles on hind tibiae; wings lanceolate, with venation greatly reduced; adults usually white with dark markings. These moths resemble the Nepticulidae but may be distinguished by the unbranched venation of their front wings. Known larvae mine in leaves or bore into bark. Most species of the family are found in the Orient. Seven species occur in North America, all in the following genus:

6.1 *Opostega* Zeller

O. albogalleriella Clemens. Larvae mine leaves of gooseberries and currents. (1) (2) MA to TX.

7. TISCHERIIDAE (Tischeriid Moth Family)

Wingspan: 5–9 mm. Head without ocelli; maxillary palpi absent; proboscis weak, scaled; antennae with scape small, a third of the width of the eye; vertex with smooth, spreading, flat tuft of scales covering base of antennae; wings narrow, lanceolate, with venation primitive, all radials present; hing wings with frenulum. Larvae of this obscure family are blotch leaf-miners, tunneling trumpet-shaped mines in oak and apple leaves. The family contains one genus, as follows:

7.1 *Tischeria* Zeller

Forty-eight species, including the following:

T. malifoliella Clemens (Apple Leaf Trumpet Miner). Wingspan: 5–6 mm. Front wing dark brown; hind wing pale. Larvae are of slight economic importance since they feed on apple leaves. (1) NY, NJ, PA.

Fig. 27.19.

T. badiiella Chambers. (Fig. 27.19.) (3) TX.

T. zelleriella Clemens. Larvae mine leaves of oak. Widespread. (1), (2), (3), (4), (5).

Superfamily INCURVARIOIDEA

These are small moths without ocelli and a short proboscis with scales near the base; their hind wings have a strong frenulum. Larvae are leaf miners when small but later cut out flattened cases to be used as shelters and pupal cases; some larvae form cases from flower parts. There are two families, as follows.

8. INCURVARIIDAE
(Yucca and Fairy Moth Family)

Wingspan: 6–33 mm. Head with vestiture of rough, hairlike scales; antennae, which are similar in both sexes, either short, about half the length of the wings (Prodoxinae), or as long as the wings (Incurvariinae), or very long, much longer than the wings—the longest antennae of any Lepidoptera (Adelinae); scape of antennae without expanded eye cap. Wings aculeate; front wing with closed discal cell and hind wing with venation similar to that of front wing, but with R venation reduced to Rs. Females have a piercing ovipositor. The 56 species of this family are divided into three subfamilies (families by some authors) and 16 genera.

Subfamily Incurvariinae

Small, usually dark-colored moths with five-segmented, folded maxillary palpi; antennae short, not much longer than front wing, or shorter. This subfamily contains eight genera and 22 species.

Fig. 27.20.

8.1 *Incurvaria* Haworth

One species only, as follows:

I. rubiella (Bjerkaund) (Raspberry Bud Moth). Wingspan: 10–12 mm. Front wings brown with three incomplete pale bands; hind wings pale brown. Larvae are a pest of raspberries. (See Fig. 27.20.) (1) n.e. US; (2) KY, NC.

8.2 *Lampronia* Stephens

Six species, including the following:

L. reticulata (Riley). Wingspan: ±12 mm. Front wing white with broad dark "W" covering much of it and a narrower subbasal and an apical band. Larvae found in Yucca seeds. (5) CO.

8.3 *Paraclemensia* Busck

One species only, as follows:

P. acerifoliella Fitch (Maple Leaf Cutter). Wingspan: ±9 mm. Front wings deep purple-blue overlaid with peacock green; hind wings pale, translucent; head orange, with black antennae. Larvae feed on maple (rarely on leaves of other trees) and huckleberry. (See Fig. 27.21.) (1) n.e. US; (2) VA, WV, NC.

[8.4 *Vespina* Davis (1 sp., *V. quercivora* (Davis)); 8.5 *Phylloporia* Heinemann (1 sp., *P. bistrigella* (Haworth)); 8.6 *Tanysaccus* Davis (3 spp.); 8.7 *Greya* Busck (8 spp.); 8.8 *Tridentaforma* Davis (1 sp., *T. fuscoleuca* (Braun))]

Subfamily Prodoxinae

Wingspan: 8–33 mm. Head with rough, hairlike scales; antennae simple in both sexes, approximately one-half the length of front wing; scale without pecten; ocelli absent; chaetosema absent; proboscis short, not coiled when not in use, and galea not appressed to form a sucking tube; mandibles present but greatly reduced, not functional; maxillary palpi very long, nearly as long as haustellum, folded against head. Wings white in most species, but with dark markings; dark in some species. Larvae bore into seeds and stems of Yucca and Agave.

8.9 *Tegeticula* Zeller

Of the three species of Yucca Moths in this genus, the most widespread is described below. The other two species are confined to (3) s. CA, w. AZ; (4) s. NV.

T. yuccasella (Riley) (Yucca Moth). Wingspan: 20–25 mm. Front wings white, without spots; hind wings gray. Larvae infest the fruit and seeds of Yucca, a plant dependent upon the adult moths of this species for pollination. Emergence of the adult from a pupal cell in the ground occurs in the spring during the flowering period of the Yuccas. Upon reaching the Yucca flower, the nearly emerged female moth immediately begins gathering pollen, scraping it from the anther with her specially modified maxillary tentacles. She then forms the pollen into a ball with the aid of her front legs and stores it in a depression or pocket located beneath her head. Her gathering completed, she climbs a pistil and begins the egg-laying process. Her long ovipositor is capable of penetrating the pistil into the carpel of the ovary. After laying one to several eggs on or near an ovule, she withdraws the ovipositor and climbs to the top of the pistil; here, with the aid of her mouthparts, she works the pollen she has stored into the stigmatic cavity, actually forcing it into the stigmatic tube by using her maxillary tentacles as plungers. This activity effectively assures the developing larvae of a food source—the seeds of the developing Yucca fruit. Yuccas cultivated in areas lacking these moths will not set fruit. (See Fig. 27.22.) (1) WI, MI, ON, s. NY, CT, RI, IL, IN, OH, PA, NJ, MD, DE, DC; (2) s.e. US; (3) s.w. US; (4) s. NV, UT; (5) MN, WY, SD, NE, IA, CO, KS, MO.

[8.10 *Parategeticula* Davis (1 sp., *P. pollenifera* Davis)]

8.11 *Prodoxus* Riley

The ten species included in this genus are sometimes called the *Bogus Yucca Moths* since they closely resemble the Yucca Moth but do not pollinate Yucca or Agave flowers. Eggs are inserted into the tissue of the Yucca by the female ovipositor, which is spearlike with a dorsal serrate ridge. When the larvae emerge, they bore into the flower stem but do little actual damage.

P. quinquepunctellus (Clemens). Wingspan: male, 12–19 mm; female, 13–23 mm. Body entirely white; front wings white, sometimes with as many as 12 fuscous spots; hing wings darker. Larvae found in flower stems of Yucca. (See Fig. 27.23.) (1) n.e. US; (2) s.e. US; (3) s.w. US; (4) UT, ID; (5) n. Central states.

P. marginatus Riley. (3) s. CA.

P. y-inversum Riley. (3) s.e. AZ, s.w. NM.

P. coloradensis Riley. (3) s.w. TX, NM, AZ, s. CA, s. NV, s. UT; (5) s. CO.

P. cinereus Riley. (3) s. CA.

[8.12 *Mesepiola* Davis (1 sp., *M. specca* Davis); 8.13 *Agavenema* Davis (2 spp.)]

Fig. 27.21.

Fig. 27.22.

Fig. 27.23.

Subfamily Adelinae

The Adelinae are presumably called Fairy Moths because of the very long antennae of the males (usually more than twice as long as their wings). Their maxillary palpi are greatly reduced. Larvae mine leaves when they first hatch but later make cases and feed on leaves of trees and shrubs. The subfamily contains the following three genera:

[8.14 *Chalceopla* Braun (6 spp.); 8.15 *Nemophora* Leach (1 sp, *N. bellela* (Walker) (5) CO]

8.16 *Adela* Latreille

Of the ten species in the U.S. and Canada, the following is one of the most beautiful and relatively common:

A. purpurea Walker (Willow Fairy Moth). Wingspan: ±14 mm. Antennae of male three times as long as front wing; front wings greenish to bronzy purple with white bar at apical two-thirds (the center third) and narrow, wavy subapical lobe, both edged with black. Adult moth is found on willow blossoms in April. (Fig. 27.24.) (1) n.e. NA, s. to NJ.

9. HELIOZELIDAE (Shield Bearer Moth Family)

Wingspan: 5–9 mm. Scales of head smooth, shining; antennae shorter than wings; maxillary palpi very small but five-segmented. Wings lanceolate, not aculeate, with venation reduced in both wings. Larvae mine leaves of trees and form a pupal case cut from the leaf upon which they have fed. Adults are often covered with metallic scales; they fly during the day and may be found resting on flowers. The group, as a whole poorly known, contains three genera and 31 species.

[9.1 *Heliozela* Herrich-Schäffer (2 spp.)]

Fig. 27.24.

9.2 *Antispila* Huebner

Twelve species, including the following:

A. nysaefoliella Clemens (Tupelo Leaf Miner). Wingspan: 6–8 mm. Front wing brown with conspicuous silver spots; hind wing completely brown. (1) n.e. US.

9.3 *Coptodisca* Walsingham

This, the largest genus of the family, has 17 species, including the following:

C. splendoriferella (Clemens) (Resplendent Shield Bearer). Wingspan: 4–5 mm. Wings brown with basal portion of front wing pale. Larvae mine leaves of wild cherry, apple, and hawthorn. (1) through (5)? Throughout US?

Suborder DITRYSIA

The rest of the order is contained in the single suborder Ditrysia. Its wing venation is extremely diverse, that of the front and hind wings differing considerably. The hind wings not only have reduced radials, they are usually smaller than the front wings. Mouthparts never have functional mandibles. The coiled proboscis found in many groups is often rudimentary.

"Division MICROLEPIDOPTERA"

The name of this division is somewhat misleading, for, although a great many "micros" are very small, size alone does not distinguish them from the rest of the moths, skippers, and butterflies. The wing shape is variable: long and narrow; short and broad, with the hind wing as wide or wider than the front; or deeply lobed. Larvae of many microlepidoptera are leaf miners. A great number of species are of economic importance, some causing damage to crops and a few infesting stored food. The families are difficult to distinguish without careful examination and often then only by collating features of the head, wings, and abdomen. The following discussion lists all families usually recognized in the U.S. and Canada, including all known pest species with both their common and Latin names and their larval hosts.

Superfamily TINEOIDEA

Moths belonging to this superfamily are small to moderate in size. Head with or without ocelli; chaetosemata absent; scale of antenna sometimes forming an eye cap; haustellum present, without scales, and often reduced in size; maxillary palpi 1 through 5 segmented. Wings various, either narrow, lanceolate, with reduced venation, or broad, with hind wing of some broader than front wing; M retained in the discal cell. Larvae are concealed feeders living in leaf mines; they bore into bark or stems and frequently form silken tubes or portable cases. The five families assigned to this superfamily contain a total of 595 species.

10. TINEIDAE (Clothes Moth Family)

Wingspan: 8–14 mm (some to 25 mm). Usually dull brown; head usually with rough, hairlike scales; ocelli absent; antennae usually simple, with some dentate or bipectinate; scape usually with pecten; proboscis short or absent; maxillary palpi five-segmented, sometimes reduced, often drooping. Wings gener-

ally rather narrow, usually lanceolate; discal cell distinct but may have portions of M retained. Larvae of many species feed on rotten wood, fungi, dry animal products, and similar materials. Some tineids are obligate fungus feeders; some are case makers. The most abundant species ordinarily seen are the clothes moths; they are of great concern to most people living in cold climates because of the damage they do to wool clothing stored for the summer months. At present, 175 species have been reported in the U.S. and Canada. These are assigned to 51 genera, as follows:

10.1 *Nemapogon* Schrank

Fifteen species in the U.S. and Canada, including the following:

N. granella (Linnaeus) (European Grain Moth). Wingspan: ±12 mm. Front wings white with a black basal bar and more or less mottled with dark bronzy brown patches and spotted with black. Larvae feed on grain, dried fruit, bracket fungi, and detritus. Introduced from Europe. (1) n.e. NA; (2) s.e. US.

[10.2 *Doleromorpha* Braun (1 sp., *D. porphyris* Braun); 10.3 *Eudarcia* Clemens (2 spp.); 10.4 *Diachorisia* Clemens (1 sp., *D. velatella* Clemens); 10.5 *Bathroxena* Meyrick (1 sp., *B. heteropalpella* (Dietz); 10.6 *Augolychna* Meyrick (1 sp., *A. septemstrigella* (Chambers); 10.7 *Leucomele* Dietz (1 sp., *L. miriamella* Dietz); 10.8 *Oenoe* Chambers (1 sp., *O. hybromella* Chambers); 10.9 *Homosetia* Clemens (12 spp.); 10.10 *Stenoptinea* Dietz (2 spp.); 10.11 *Isocorypha* Dietz (2 spp.); 10.12 *Hybroma* Clemens (1 sp., *H. servulella* Clemens); 10.13 *Homostinea* Dietz (1 sp., *H. curviliniella* Dietz); 10.14 *Pompostolella* Fletcher (1 sp., *P. charipepla* (Meyrick)); 10.15 *Erechthias* Meyrick (1 sp., *E. zebrina* (Butler)); 10.16 *Lepidobregma* Zimmermann (1 sp., *L. minuscula* (Walsingham)); 10.17 *Mea* Busck (2 spp.); 10.18 *Chloropleca* Durrant (1 sp., *C. visaliella* (Chambers)); 10.19 *Scardia* Treitschke (3 spp.); 10.20 *Fernaldia* Grote (2 spp.); 10.21 *Morophagoides* Peterseon (2 spp.); 10.22 *Diataga* Walsingham (1 sp., *D. leptosceles* Walsingham); 10.23 *Xylesthia* Clemens (2 spp.); 10.24 *Phryganeopsis* Walsingham (1 sp., *P. brunnea* Walsingham); 10.25 *Kearfottia* Fernald (1 sp., *K. albifasciella* Fernald); 10.26 *Hypoplesia* Busck (2 spp.); 10.27 *Dyotopasta* Busck (1 sp., *D. yumaella* Kearfot); 10.28 *Tenaga* Clemens (1 sp., *T. pomiliella* Clemens); 10.29 *Cephitinea* Zagulajer (1 sp., *C. obscurostrigella* Chambers); 10.30 *Episcardia* Ragonot (1 sp., *E. insectella* Fabricius); 10.31 *Apreta* Dietz (1 sp., *A. paradoxella* Dietz); 10.32 *Amydria* Clemens (11 spp.)]

10.33 *Acrolophus* Poey

Wingspan: 15–35 mm. Of the 49 species in the U.S. and Canada, about 10 are found in the East, the remainder in the South and West.

A. popeanellus Clemens. Wingspan: 15–16 mm. Front wings with pale fold and inner margin and mottled with dark reddish brown patches (rarely purplish). (See Fig. 27.25.) (1) IL, IN, OH, PA, NJ, MD, DE, DC; (2) s.e. US; (3) TX.

A. morus Grote. Larvae feed on birch and some reported as destructive to young corn seedling. (1) MA, CT, RL, PA, NJ, MD, DE, DC; (2) VA, NC.

A. plumifrontellus Clemens. Wingspan: ±35 mm. Wings light reddish gray, with irregular, dark striations gathered into patches at end and near middle of discal cell and also basad of and near middle of fold, sometimes connected to form a zigzag pattern but sometimes partly or wholly absent, especially in female. (1) s. NY, w. PA, NJ, DE, MD, DC; (2) s.e. US.

[10.34 *Dorata* Busck (3 spp.)]

Fig. 27.25.

10.35 *Phereoeca* Hinton and Bradley

One species, as follows:

P. walsinghami Busck (Household Casebearer). Larvae found in various stored materials. (2) FL.

[10.36 *Tryptodema* Dietz (1 sp., *T. sepulchrella* Dietz)]

10.37 *Tinea* Linnaeus

Nineteen species, the most important being the following:

T. pellionella (Linnaeus) (Casemaking Clothes Moth). Wingspan: 15–18 mm. Wings pale brownish gray with vague dark spots. Larvae make a case instead of webbing. As they feed on woolen clothing and grow, they have to enlarge the case and do so in a unique and interesting manner. Without emerging from the case, they cut a slit about halfway down one of its sides to form a triangular opening. Into this opening they insert a triangular gore of the woolen material upon which they feed. They then repeat the process on the opposite side and continue to repeat it from side to side, continually enlarging the diameter. The case is also lengthened bit by bit by adding to each end. Although the outside of the case is composed of fibers of wool, the inside is lined with silk. Having hibernated in the winter in some secluded place, often high on walls or ceilings, larvae pupate in the larval case during the spring. Adults emerge, mate, and fly about to lay their eggs on some suitable food material. Cosmopolitan. (See A&J 197).

Note: The three species of clothes moths commonly found in homes are all Old World species long associated with man and were introduced into the U.S. and Canada. They can be distinguished by the type of damage they do. The preceding species is very common. The other two (see following accounts) are *Tineola bisselliella* and *Trichophaga tapetzella*.

10.38 *Niditinea* Peterson

Two species in the U.S. and Canada, including the following:

N. fuscipunctella (Haworth) (Poultry House Moth). Wingspan: 11–17 mm. Pale fuscous, tending to clay color, with a somewhat reddish head; antennae blackish; wings with black bar at base of costa; front of thorax and basal half of tegulae with transverse, dark band extending to costa. Larvae breed in nest debris in pigeon nests and poultry houses. (1) n.e. US; (2) s.e. US.

10.39 *Trichophaga* Ragonot

One species only, as follows:

T. tapetzella (Linnaeus) (Carpet Moth). Wingspan: 12–14 mm. Front wing with base black, apex whitish gray; hind wing light gray; head with long white hairs. Larvae feed on wide variety of animal matter—including wool, fur, and even owl pellets—burrowing into it to make silk-lined galleries. Not as common as other clothes moths but cosmopolitan.

[10.40 *Ceratophaga* Peterson (1 sp., *C. vicinella* (Dietz))]

10.41 *Monopis* Huebner

Seven species, including the following:

M. spilotella Tengstrom. Wingspan: 15–16 mm. Front wings mottled with dark reddish brown patches tinged with violet and with triangular cream white patches. (1), (2), (3), (4), (5).

M. biflarimaculella Clemens. Wingspan: 15–16 mm. Head pale white; thorax dark brown with pale spote in front; front wings mottled with umber brown patches tinged with violet and with triangular cream white patch on middle of costa and smaller one farther out on inner margin. (See Fig. 27.26.) (1) n.e. NA; (2) s.e. US; (3) TX; (4) WA.

[10.42 *Eccritothrix* Bradley and Hinton (1 sp., *E. trimaculella* (Chambers)); 10.43 *Praeacedes* Amsel (2 spp.); 10.44 *Elatobia* Herrich-Schaeffer (1 sp., *E. martinella* Walker)]

10.45 *Tineola* Herrich-Schaeffer

One species, as follows:

T. bisselliella (Hummel) (Webbing Clothes Moth). Wingspan: 12–15 mm. Front wings yellowish, without spots; hind wings pale. Larvae feed in folds or crevices of woolen material and spin a web of silk wherever they go. They also feed on fur and other stored material of animal origin. The cocoon formed may somewhat resemble the case of *Tinea pellionella*. Cosmopolitan.

[10.46 *Tiquadra* Walker (1 sp., *T. inscitella* Walker); 10.47 *Setomorpha* Zeller (1 sp., *S. rutella* Zeller); 10.48 *Lindera* Blanchard (1 sp., *L. tessellatella* (Blanchard)]

10.49 *Phaeoses* Forbes

One species only, as follows:

P. sabinella Forbes. Wingspan: 7.5–10.5 mm. Wings slender, uniformly pale grayish brown to stramineous. Eyes

Fig. 27.26.

emarginate near antennal sockets. Larvae unknown. (2) LA, MS, AL, FL; (3) e. TX.

10.50 *Opogona* Zeller

Of the large number of species throughout the world—especially the tropics, where some are known to infest sugar cane—only the folloiwng three occur in the U.S.:

O. arizonensis Davis (3) s.e. AZ, s. TX.

O. floridensis Davis (2) s. FL.

O. omoscopa (Meyrick). (2) CA.

10.51 *Oinophila* Stephens

One species only, as follows:

O. v-flavum (Haworth). Wingspan: 8.5–10 mm. Wings slender; front wings fuscous with two irregular, oblique, pale ochreous bands. Larvae are scavengers, feeding on a wide variety of plant and animal materials. In Europe, but rarely in the U.S., it has become a pest in cellars, feeding on fungi and wine corks. (3) central CA.

Note: These preceding three genera are sometimes placed in a separate family—the Onophilidae—but have not been so treated by recent revisors. For a key to the genera and species, see Davis (1978).

11. PSYCHIDAE (Bagworm Moth Family)

Wingspan: 8–25 mm. Adult males of this family are winged and resemble some of the primitive moths such as the carpenter-worms. Most females are wingless and sometimes scaleless, resembling larvae. The larvae form a bag, a portable case made of bits of twigs and leaves, which they carry with them as they feed; eventually they form a pupa, if they are males, or mature as a larviform female. The male leaves the pupal case behind after maturing. The female spends her entire life within the bag, leaving only after egg laying (the male fertilizes her through an opening in one of its ends). The eggs, which are stored in the bag to overwinter, hatch in May. Young larvae then leave the old bag to start a new one. Both ends of the bag are open, the top for feeding and the bottom for fecal waste discharge. Pupation takes place in the fall. Males emerge in about three weeks and fly to a female case. Both adults die shortly after the female lays her eggs. There are 26 species in 12 genera in the U.S. and Canada.

Subfamily Taleporiinae

[11.1 *Solenobia* Duponchel (2 spp.)]

Subfamily Psychinae

[11.2 *Psyche* Schrank (1 sp., *P. castra* (Pallas)); 11.3 *Apterona* Milliere (1 sp., *A. crenulella helix* (Siebold)); 11.4 *Prochalia* Barnes and McDunnough (1 sp., *P. pygmaea* Barnes and McDunnough); 11.5 *Zamopsyche* Dyar (1 sp., *Z. commentella* Dyar); 11.6 *Cryptothelea* Duncan (2 spp.); 11.7 *Astala* Davis (3 spp.); 11.8 *Hyaloscotes* Butler (4 spp.); 11.9 *Basicladus* Davis (2 spp.); 11.10 *Coloneura* Davis (1 sp., *C. fragilis* (Barnes and McDunnough))]

Fig. 27.27.

Fig. 27.29.

Subfamily Oiketicinae

11.11 *Oiketicus* Guilding

Three species, the following of which is common:

O. abbotii Grote (Log Cabin Bagworm). Wings dark, the front wing with narrow, irregular, white subapical band. Larvae insert short pieces of twigs across the bag, giving it a log cabin appearance; they also include leaves. (See Fig. 27.27.) (2) FL.

11.12 *Thyridopteryx* Stephens

Three species, the following of which is the most common:

T. ephemeraeformis (Haworth) (Evergreen Bagworm). Male wingspan: ±25 mm. Wings transparent and smoky; body dark. Larvae attack both evergreen and deciduous trees, the most common being firs, junipers, pines, spruce, black locust, maple, sweet gum, and sycamore. (See Fig. 27.28.) (1) n.e. US; (2) s.e. US.

The position of the two other species included in this family is uncertain.

12. OCHSENHEIMERIIDAE (Ochsenheimeriid Moth Family)

Wingspan: 9–17 mm. Vertex extremely rough, densely covered with long, divergent, hairlike scales; front very broad, smooth; eyes rounded, small; ocelli well developed, narrowly separated from margin of eyes. Antennae simple, short (less than six-tenths of length of front wing); base roughly scaled

Fig. 27.28.

above; scape greatly lengthened; pectin absent. Maxillary palpi short, two-segmented; galeae short, mostly naked; labial palpi three-segmented, porrect; apical segment slender, nearly covered by enlarged, triangular brush of scales from apical half of second segment. Front wings usually with 11 veins, sometimes with 12; M_1 either separate or stalked with R_4 and R_5; accessory cell normally present; discal cell elongate, with or without evidence of base of M; CuA_2 usually absent; 1A and 2A separate at base and fused for outer half. Hind wings variable, ranging from six to eight veins; Rs and M_1 either forked near apex or completely fused. Of the 23 species of this Palearctic family (all of which have narrow and pointed wings), one has been introduced into North America.

12.1 *Ochsenheimeria* Huebner

One species, as follows:

O. vacculella F. von Roeslerstamm (Cereal Stem Moth). Wingspan: 11–14 mm. Wings brownish gray, somewhat mottled with light brown. Larvae feed on wild grasses and crop grasses, including rye and wheat. (See Fig. 27.29.) (1) OH, PA, NY.

13. LYONETIIDAE (Lyonetiid Moth Family)

Wingspan: 4–11 mm. Wings lanceolate. The species of several genera are either leaf miners, skeletonizers, or make social nests in dirty, frass-filled mines. They live on a variety of plants, mostly trees and shrubs. Larvae of the genus *Bucculatrix* are known as the ribbed-cocoon makers because their cocoons are usually composed of longitudinal ridges, with silk threads forming a regular pattern between them. The family is represented by 122 species in 12 genera in the U.S. and Canada.

[13.1 *Euprora* Busck (1 sp., *E. argentiliniella* Busck); 13.2 *Philonome* Chambers (3 spp.)]

13.3 *Bedellia* Stainton

Two species, as follows:

B. somnulentella (Zeller) (Morning-glory Leaf Miner). Wingspan: 10–12 mm. Antennae long. (See Fig. 27.30.) (1) n.e. NA; (2) s.e. US; (3) s.w. US; (4) WA, OR, UT; (5) MO.

B. minor Busck. (2) LA, FL; (3) OK.

[13.4 *Eulyonetia* Chambers (1 sp., *E. inornatella* Chambers); 13.5 *Lyonetia* Huebner (5 spp.); 13.6 *Acanthocnemes* Chambers (1 sp., *A. fuscoscapulella* Chambers); 13.7 *Proleucoptera* Busck (1 sp., *smilaciella*

Fig. 27.30.

Fig. 27.31.

(Busck)); 13.8 *Paraleucoptera* Heinrich (1 sp., *albella* (Chambers)); 13.9 *Coryrhophora* Braun (1 sp., *C. aurea* Braun); 13.10 *Leucoptera* Huebner (6 spp.); 13.11 *Exegetia* Braun (1 sp., *E. crocea* Braun); 13.12 *Bucculatrix* Zeller (99 spp.)]

14. GRACILLARIIDAE (Leaf Blotch Miner Moth Family)

Wingspan: 4–21 mm (rarely over 15 mm). Head usually smooth-scaled; ocelli absent; antennae nearly as long as, or longer than front wing, with simple, slender scape, usually without pectin; proboscis present; maxillary palpi slender, porrect or ascending, four-segmented; labial palpi slender, porrect or ascending; legs with epiphysis present; tibial spurs absent on front tibiae, two on middle tibiae, four on hind tibiae; front wing lanceolate or linear-lanceolate, with R_5 reaching costa; hind wings lanceolate, with venation often reduced. Since adults are very difficult to identify, it is often better to collect leaves and rear them, the host plant being helpful for identification. Some larvae mine leaves and feed on the parenchyma; their inflated mines are partially lined with silk. Others skeletonize leaves. Still others mine a leaf to begin with and, when partly grown, form a nest by folding it. Most species found on trees and shrubs make bloth mines. A few species live on herbaceous plants. There are 275 described species in 23 genera in the U.S. and Canada.

Subfamily Gracillariinae

14.1 *Caloptilia* Huebner

All species of this genus are leaf miners as young larvae, but many leave their mine when half grown and form a cone by twisting and rolling the end of the leaf. Of the 63 species, the following are of economic interest:

C. *azaleella* Brants (Azalea Leaf Miner).

C. *fraxinella* (Ely) (Privet Leaf Miner).

C. *negundella* (Chambers) (Box Elder Leaf Roller).

C. *murtfeldtella* (Busck) (Poison Ivy Leaf Miner). Wingspan: 17–21 mm. (See Fig. 27.31.) (1) n.e. US; (2) s.e. US; (3) s.w. US; (5) MO.

[14.2 *Gracillaria* Haworth (1 sp., *G. syringella* (Fabricius) (Lilac Leaf Miner)); 14.3 *Neurostrota* Ely (1 sp., *N. gunniella* (Busck)); 14.4

Micrurapteryx Spuler (1 sp., *M. salicifoliella* (Chambers)); 14.5 *Parectopa* Clemens (11 spp.); 14.6 *Neurolipa* Ely (1 sp., *N. randiella* (Busck)); 14.7 *Apophthisis* Braun (2 spp.); 14.8 *Neurobathira* Ely (2 spp.); 14.9 *Callisto* Stephens (1 sp., *C. denticulella* (Thunberg)); 14.10 *Parornix* Spuler (22 spp.); 14.11 *Chilocampyla* Busck (1 sp., *C. dyariella* Busck); 14.12 *Acrocercops* Wallengren (10 spp.); 14.13 *Leucospilapteryx* Spuler (1 sp., *L. venustella* (Clemens)); 14.14 *Metriochroa* Busck (1 sp., *M. psychotriella* Busck); 14.15 *Leucanthiza* Clemens (2 spp.); 14.16 *Marmara* Clemens (17 spp.)]

Subfamily Lithocolletinae

[14.17 *Protolithocolletis* Braun (1 sp., *P. lathyri* Braun); 14.18 *Cremastobombycia* Braun (5 spp.)]

14.19 *Phyllonorycter* Huebner

Of the 79 species, all of them leaf miners, the following is common:

P. *tremuloidiella* (Braun) (Aspen Blotch Miner).

14.20 *Cameraria* Chapman

Thirty-nine species, several of which are common:

C. *cincinnatiella* (Chambers) (Gregarious Leaf Miner).

C. *hamadryadella* (Clemens) (Solitary Oak Leaf Miner).

C. *guttifinitella* (Clemens). Wingspan: ±4 mm. Found on poison ivy. (See Fig. 27.32; leaf blotch in Fig. 27.33.)

[14.21 *Chrysaster* Kumata (1 sp., *C. ostensackenella* (Fitch)); 14.22 *Porphyrosela* Braun (1 sp., *P. desmodiella* (Clemens))]

Fig. 27.32.

Fig. 27.33.

Fig. 27.35.

Subfamily Phyllocnistinae

[14.23 *Phyllocnistis* Zeller (11 spp.)]

Superfamily GELECHIOIDEA

The nine families that belong to this superfamily are of considerable economic importance. All have a densely scaled proboscis, the base of which is clasped by small, four-segmented maxillary palpi (reduced in some). Ocelli present or absent; chaetosemata absent; scape often with pecten. All larvae are concealed feeders.

15. OECOPHORIDAE (Oecophorid Moth Family)

Wingspan: 9–27 mm. Wing shape variable; front wing usually rounded but may be lanceolate; hind wing often broader than front wing except in lanceolate-winged species. Wing color varies from plain brown to spotted and brightly marked. Larvae are plant and fungus feeders or scavengers. Relatively few species of this large family are of economic importance. Larvae of many species are unknown. There are 44 genera and 225 species in the U.S. and Canada.

Subfamily Depressariinae

Tribe Depressariini

[15.1 *Agonopterix* Huebner (45 spp.); 15.2 *Depressariodes* Turati (12 spp.); 15.3 *Bibarrambla* Clarke (1 sp., *B. allenella* (Walsingham))]

Fig. 27.34.

15.4 *Semioscopis* Huebner

Six species, the following of which is widespread:

S. packardella Clemens. Wingspan: 10–25 mm. Front wing grayish with sinuous dark line across discal area that may broaden to reach anterior edge of the wing. Adults fly in April and May. (See Fig. 27.34.) (1) n.e. NA; (3) CA; (4) Pacific n.w.; (5) n. Central States.

15.5 *Depressaria* Haworth

Twenty-four species, the following being of economic importance:

D. pastinacella (Duponchel) (Parsnip Webworm). Wingspan: 20–29 mm. Front wing brown with small, dark spots. Adults on the wing from late June through August. Larvae found on flowers and seeds of umbelliferous plants. (See Fig. 27.35.) (1) n.e. NA; (3) s.w. AZ; (4) Pacific n.w.; (5) n. Central States.

[15.6 *Nites* Hodges (5 spp.); 15.7 *Apachea* Clarke (1 sp., *A. barberella* (Busck)); 15.8 *Himmacia* Clarke (3 spp.)]

Tribe Amphisbatini

[15.9 *Machimia* Clemens (2 spp.); 15.10 *Eupragia* Walsingham (2 spp.); 15.11 *Psilocorsis* Clemens (7 spp.)]

Subfamily Ethmiinae

[15.12 *Pyramidobela* Braun (3 spp.); 15.13 *Ethmia* Huebner (46 spp.); 15.14 *Pseudethmia* Clarke (1 sp., *P. protuberans* Clarke)]

Subfamily Peleopodinae

[15.15 *Pseuderotis* Clarke (1 sp., *P. obiterella* (Busck)); 15.16 *Durrantia* Busck (1 sp., *D. piperatella* (Zeller))]

Subfamily Stenomatinae

15.17 *Antaeotricha* Zeller

[=*Ide* Chambers]

Fifteen species, including the following:

A. leucillana Zeller [=*algidella* Walker]. Wingspan: 15–23 mm. Head white, sprinkled with brown; thorax white dorsally with brownish black tuft posteriorly. (See Fig. 27.36.) (1) NY,

Fig. 27.36.

NH, MA, IL, OH, PA, NJ, MD, DC; (2) WV, VA, NC, AR, LA, GA, SC, FL; (3) TX; (4) OR; (5) MB, IA, KS, MO.

[15.18 *Setiostoma* Zeller (2 spp.); 15.19 *Menestomorpha* Walsingham (2 spp.); 15.20 *Menesta* Clemens (2 spp.); 15.21 *Gonioterma* Walsingham (2 spp.)]

Subfamily Oecophorinae
Tribe Oecophorini

[15.22 *Inga* Busck (8 spp.); 15.23 *Decantha* Busck (4 spp.); 15.24 *Callima* Clemens (2 spp.); 15.25 *Dafa* Hodges (1 sp., *D. formosella* (Denis and Schiffermueller)); 15.26 *Batia* Stephens (1 sp., *B. lunaris* (Haworth)); 15.27 *Fabiola* Busck (5 spp.); 15.28 *Brymblia* Hodges (1 sp., *B. quadrimaculella* (Chambers)); 15.29 *Denisia* Huebner (1 sp., *C. haydenella* (Chambers)); 15.30 *Esperia* Huebner (1 sp., *E. sulphurella* (Fabricius)); 15.31 *Polix* Hodges (1 sp., *P. coloradella* (Walsingham)); 15.32 *Mathildana* Clarke (2 spp.); 15.33 *Borkhausenia* Huebner (1 sp., *B. nefrax* Hodges)); 15.34 *Carolana* Clarke (2 spp.)]

15.35 *Hofmannophila* Spuler

One species only, as follows:

H. pseudospretella (Stainton) (Brown House Moth).

[15.36 *Martyinga* Busck (2 spp.)]

15.37 *Endrosis* Huebner

One species only, as follows:

E. sarcitrella (Linnaeus) (White-shouldered House Moth). Wingspan: 9–18 mm. Head and thorax white; front wings gray. (1) IL, PA, NY, GR; (3) CA; (4) AK, BC, WA, OR, NV.

[15.38 *Eido* Chambers (1 sp., *E. trimaculella* (Fitch)); 15.39 *Carcina* Huebner (1 sp., *C. quercana* (Fabricius))]

Tribe Stathmopodini

[15.40 *Stathmopoda* Herrick-Schaeffer (2 spp.); 15.41 *Idioglossa* Walsingham (1 sp., *I. miraculosa* (Frey)); 15.42 *Cyphacma* Meyrick (1 sp., *C. tragiae* Braun)]

Tribe Pleurotini

[15.43 *Pleurota* Huebner (1 sp., *P. albastrigulella* (Kearfott))]

Subfamily Chimabachinae
Tribe Chimabachini

[15.44 *Cheimophila* Huebner (1 sp., *C. salicella* (Huebner))]

16. ELACHISTIDAE (Elachistid Moth Family)

Wingspan: 6–14 mm. Wings lanceolate. This small family is comprised of eight genera and 57 species in the U.S. and Canada.

Subfamily Coelopoetinae

[16.1 *Coelopoeta* Walsingham (1 sp., *C. glutinosi* Walsingham)]

Subfamily Elachistinae

[16.2 *Onceroptila* Braun (2 spp.); 16.3 *Stephensia* Stainton (1 sp., *S. cunilae* Braun); 16.4 *Hemiprosopa* Braun (1 sp., *H. albella* (Chambers))]

16.5 *Elachista* Treitschke

Forty-three species, the following of which is common:

E. orestella Busck. Wingspan: 12–14 mm. Wings white. Larvae are leaf miners on *Hystrix* spp. (1) n.e. US.

[16.6 *Biselachista* Traugot-Olsen and Nielsen (5 spp.); 16.7 *Cosmiotes* Clemens (3 spp.); 16.8 *Dicranoctetes* Braun (1 sp., *D. angularis* Braun)]

17. BLASTOBASIDAE (Blastobasid Moth Family)

Wingspan: 8–25 mm. Wings usually lanceolate; antennae long. Most known larvae live in nuts, some live in seeds, a few in buds, and some are scavengers in galls. Twenty-one genera with 121 species are recorded in the U.S. and Canada.

Subfamily Symmocinae

[17.1 *Symmoca* Huebner (1 sp., *S. signatella* (Herrich-Schaeffer)); 17.2 *Oegoconia* Stainton (1 sp., *O. quadripuncta* (Haworth)); 17.3 *Sceptea* Walsingham (1 sp., *S. aequepulvella* (Chambers)); 17.4 *Glyphidocera* Walsingham (8 spp.); 17.5 *Gerdana* Busck (1 sp., *G. caritella* Busck))]

Subfamily Blastobasinae
Tribe Blastobasini

[17.6 *Blastobasis* Zeller (10 spp.); 17.7 *Blastobasoides* McDunnough (1 sp., *B. differtellus* McDunnough); 17.8 *Hypatopa* Walsingham (1 sp., *H. titanella* McDunnough); 17.9 *Zenodochium* Walsingham (2 spp.)]

17.10 *Valentinia* Walsingham

Eight species, the following of which is common:

V. glanduella (Riley). Wingspan: 15–25 mm. Light gray, more or less powdery and mottled with discal dots and bars. Adults fly in July, before sunset. Larvae found in acorns. (1), (2), (3), (4), (5), generally distributed.

[17.11 *Euresia* Dietz (1 sp., *E. pulchella* Dietz); 17.12 *Calosima* Dietz (2 spp.); 17.13 *Asaphocrita* Meyrick (1 sp., *A. protypica* Meyrick); 17.14 *Holcocera* Clemens (49 spp.); 17.15 *Holcocerina* McDunnough (4 spp.); 17.16 *Eubolepia* Dietz (2 spp.)]

Tribe Pigritiini

[17.17 *Ploiophora* Dietz (2 spp.); 17.18 *Pigritia* Clemens (11 spp.); 17.19 *Epigritia* Dietz (1 sp., *E. ochrocomella* Clemens); 17.20 *Dryoperia* Coolidge (10 spp.); 17.21 *Pseudopigritia* Dietz (4 spp.)]

18. COLEOPHORIDAE (Casebearer Moth Family)

Wingspan: 7–12 mm (rarely 15 mm). Head smooth-scaled; ocelli absent; scape usually with scale tuft; maxillary palpi minute, two-segmented; labial palpi long, recurved; hind tibiae with roughened, hairlike scales; front wings linear-lanceolate.

This group is easily recognized since most larvae make cases out of their food plant, each species constructing its own distinctive case: small, flattened cylinders; triangular "cigars"; "pistols"; "holsters"; or clusters of plant parts. Larvae mine a leaf before constructing the case in which they live. A great variety of plants are infested with these interesting pests, a few of them of economic importance. Eggs are laid in the summer; many larvae overwinter in their cases and resume feeding in the spring. After pupation takes place, the tiny adults emerge. There are 169 described species in the U.S. and Canada assigned to the following five genera.

Subfamily Coleophorinae

18.1 *Coleophora* Huebner

One hundred and forty-five species, including the following:

C. atromarginata Braun (Pistol Case Bearer). Front wings with white scales except at extreme apex. Very common locally. (1) MA; (2) NC; AR.

C. spissicornis Haworth. Metallic wings. (1) MI, NY, MA, OH, PA, NJ; (2) VA, MS; (5) SD, IA.

C. laticornella Clemens (Pecan Cigar Casebearer).

C. laricella (Huebner) (Larch Casebearer).

C. ulmifoliella McDunnough (Elm Casebearer).

C. malivorella Riley (Apple Pistol Casebearer).

C. pruniella Clemens (Cherry Casebearer).

C. serratella (Linnaeus) (Birch Casebearer; Cigar Casebearer).

Subfamily Batrachedrinae

[18.2 *Batrachedra* Herrich-Schaeffer (18 spp.); 18.3 *Chedra* Hodges (2 spp.); 18.4 *Duospina* Hodges (2 spp.); 18.5 *Homaledra* Busck (2 spp.)]

19. MOMPHIDAE (Momphid Moth Family)

Wingspan: 8–18 mm. Front wing with apical wing tufts; hind wings very narrow with long fringes of hairlike scales on all margins; wing varies from brown with dark brown mottling to pale cream with small brown spots or cream with wide brown bands. Thirty-seven species in two genera are recorded in the U.S. and Canada.

19.1 *Mompha* Huebner

[=*Laverna* Curtis, and others]

Thirty-six species, some of the more common being as follows:

M. brevivittella (Clemens). Wingspan: 10–12 mm. Wings mottled brown. (1) ON; IL, OH, PA, NJ, MD, DC; (5) SD.

M. stellella Busck. Wingspan: ±10 mm. Wings dark cream with large dark brown spots. (1) PA, NJ; (5) MO.

M. eloisella (Clemens). Wingspan: 12–14 mm. Wings cream with small brown spots. (1) ON, IL, PA, MD, DC.

M. circumscriptella (Zeller). Wingspan: 8–10 mm. Wings cream with large brown spots and bands. (1) IL, MD; (2) VA; (5) CO, KS, IA, WN, MO.

M. pecosella Busck. Wingspan: ±9 mm. Wings dark brown with pale brown mottling. (2) CA, AZ, NM.

Fig. 27.37.

M. edithella Busck. Wingspan: 15–18 mm. Brown. Front wing orange with large golden patches, tufts brown; hind wing brown with brown fringe. (See Fig. 27.37.) (5) CO.

19.2 *Synallagma* Busck

One species, as follows:

S. busckiella Engelhardt. Wingspan: ±8 mm. Pale brown with darker brown front wing tips and three small white subapical spots. (1) PA.

20. AGONOXENIDAE (Agonoxenid Moth Family)

Wingspan: 8–12 mm. Head scales smooth; ocelli absent; front very oblique; scape without pecten; maxillary palpi with one segment; hind tibiae with long hairlike scales; front wing lanceolate. Adults run about rapidly; when at rest, their wings are folded tightly alongside the body, with antennae elevated and front legs extended anteriorly. The six species are assigned to three genera in the U.S. and Canada.

Subfamily Blastodacninae

Tribe Blastodacnini

[20.1 *Blastodacne* Wocke (2 spp.)]

20.2 *Glyphipteryx* Curtis

[=*Chrysoclista* Stainton]

Three species, of which the following is common:

G. linneella (Clerck). Wingspan: ±9 mm. Front wings yellowish orange with dark brown basal spot, brown subbasal and apical patches, and three small white spots on wing. Hind wings grayish brown. (See Fig. 27.38.)

Tribe Parametriotini

[20.3 *Aetia* Clemens (1 sp., *A. bipunctella* Chambers)]

21. COSMOPTERIGIDAE (Cosmopterigid Moth Family)

Wingspan: 2–20 mm. Head smooth-scaled; ocelli present or absent; antennae simple or ciliated, scape long and slender, pecten sometimes present; maxillary palpi three- to four-

Fig. 27.38.

segmented, folded over base of proboscis; labial palpi long, recurved. Front wing linear to lanceolate, with R_2 arising well anterior to end of discal cell, R_4 and R_5 stalked, and R_5 running to costa. Legs with hind tibiae having long hairlike scales. Larvae of some are internal parasites of Oak Soft Scale [see *Euclemensia* spp. (21.2)]; others are leaf miners, web or tube spinners, or fruit borers. Adults diurnal. There are 26 genera and 180 species in the U.S. and Canada.

Subfamily Antequerinae

[21.1 *Antequera* Clarke (1 sp., *A. acertella* (Busck)]

21.2 *Euclemensia* Grote

Two species, the following of which is common.

E. bassettella (Clemens). Wingspan: ±15 mm. Brown-black; palpi yellow. Larvae are internal parasites of Oak Soft Scale (*Kermes* spp.). (1) n.e. NA; (2) s.e. US; (3) TX.

Subfamily Cosmopteriginae

[21.3 *Cosmopterix* Huebner (30 spp.); 21.4 *Pebops* Hodges (1 sp., *P. ipomoeae* (Busck)); 21.5 *Tanygona* Braun (1 sp., *T. lignicolorella* Braun); 21.6 *Eralea* Hodges (2 spp.); 21.7 *Melanocinclis* Hodges (5 spp.); 21.8 *Stagmatophora* Herrich-Schaeffer (4 spp.)]

21.9 *Pyroderces* Herrich-Schaeffer

Three species, the following of which is a pest:

P. rileyi (Walsingham) (Pink Scavenger Caterpiller). Wingspan: 10–12 mm. Bright yellow-brown; front wings with irregular and incomplete black bands located one-fourth and one-half of the way to apex; yellow-green, pale, and black markings and bars. Larvae found on stored fruits, corn, rotting cotton bolls, and other materials. (2) s.e. US.

21.10 *Limnaecia* Stainton

One species, as follows:

L. phragmitella Stainton (Cattail Moth). Wingspan: ±20 mm. Clay-colored; front wings with small black discal dots ringed with white. Larvae found in seed heads of cattails. (1) n.e. NA; (2) VA; (3) OK; (5) WY, CO, KS, MO.

[21.11 *Teladoma* Busck (8 spp.); 21.12 *Triclonella* Busck (5 spp.); 21.13 *Anoncia* Clarke (31 spp.)]

Subfamily Chrysopeleiinae

[21.14 *Periploca* Braun (27 spp.); 21.15 *Siskiwitia* Hodges (3 spp.); 21.16 *Pristen* Hodges (1 sp., *P. corusca* (Hodges)); 21.17 *Synploca*

Hodges (1 sp., *S. gumia* Hodges); 21.18 *Stilbosis* Clemens (20 spp.); 21.19 *Chrysopeleia* Chambers (1 sp., *C. purpuriella* Chambers)]

21.20 *Walshia* Clemens

Eight species, the following of which is a pest:

W. miscecolorella (Chambers) (Sweetclover Root Borer). (2) s.e. US; (3) s.w. US; (4) Pacific n.w.; (5) CO, KS, MO.

[21.21 *Nepotula* Hodges (1 sp., *N. secura* Hodges); 21.22 *Afeda* Hodges (1 sp., *A. biloba* Hodges); 21.23 *Perimede* Chambers (10 spp.); 21.24 *Sorhagenia* Spuler (8 spp.)]

21.25 *Ithome* Chambers

Seven species, the following of which is a pest:

I. concolorella Chambers (Kiawe Flower Moth). Wingspan: 2.5–4.3 mm. Found on mesquite. A pest in Hawaii. (2) s.e. US; (3) s.w. US.

[21.26 *Obithome* Hodges (1 sp., *O. punctiferella* (Busck))]

22. SCYTHRIDIDAE (Scythrid Moth Family)

Wingspan: 12–18 mm. Head smooth-scaled; ocelli sometimes present; scape sometimes with pecten; maxillary palpi four-segmented; labial palpi recurved, smooth-scaled. Front wing lanceolate, with R_1 stalked from beyond middle of discal cell but remote from R_2, R_4 and R_5, hind tibiae with long hairlike scales. Moths are diurnal. Thirty-five species in two genera in the U.S. and Canada.

22.1 *Scythris* Huebner

Thirty-four species, the following of which are common:

S. eburnea Walsingham. Wingspan: 12–15 mm. Wings light tan. (3) AZ.

S. basilaris Zeller. Wingspan: ±12 mm. Wings dark brown; front wings with pale apical spot. (See Fig. 27.39.) (1) n.e. US.

[22.2 *Areniscythris* Powell [1 sp., *A. brachypteris* Powell)]

23. GELECHIIDAE (Gelechid Moth Family)

Wingspan: 8–25 mm. Head smooth-scaled; ocelli often present; antennae simple or with short cilia, scape rarely with pecten; maxillary palpi four-segmented, folded over the probos-

Fig. 27.39.

cis; labial palpi recurved, the second segment often tufted beneath, or rough-scaled. Front wing with R_4 and R_5 usually stalked and R_5 reaching costa; wings lanceolate, hind wing usually with an anteriorly projecting apex and a concave front margin. Hind tibiae with long hairlike scales. This large family has 91 genera with 630 species in the U.S. and Canada, many of them of economic interest.

Subfamiliy Anomologinae

[23.1 *Nealyda* Dietz (4 spp.); 23.2 *Metzneria* Zeller (2 spp.); 23.3 *Megacraspedus* Zeller (1 sp., *M. plutella* (Chambers)); 23.4 *Isophrictis* Meyrick (18 spp.); 23.5 *Monochroa* Heinemann (11 spp.); 23.6 *Chrysoesthia* Huebner (4 spp.); 23.7 *Enchrysa* Zeller (1 sp., *E. dissectella* Zeller); 23.8 *Theisoa* Chambers (3 spp.)]

Subfamily Gelechiinae

[23.9 *Stereomita* Braun (1 sp., *S. andropogonis* Braun); 23.10 *Aristotelia* Huebner (39 spp.); 23.11 *Numata* Busck (1 sp., *N. bipunctella* Busck); 23.12 *Glauce* Chambers (1 sp., *G. pectenalaeella* Chamers); 23.13 *Naera* Chambers (1 sp., *N. fuscocristatella* Chambers); 23.14 *Evippe* Chambers (4 spp.); 23.15 *Agnippe* Chambers (4 spp.); 23.16 *Tosca* Heinrich (3 spp.); 23.17 *Argyrolacia* Keifer (1 sp., *A. bifida* Keifer)]

23.18 *Recurvaria* Haworth

Seven species, the following of which is a pest:

R. nanella (Denis and Schiffermueller) (Lesser Bud Moth).

23.19 *Coleotechnites* Chambers

Forty-seven species, the following of which is a pest:

C. milleri (Busck) (Lodgepole Needle Miner).

[23.20 *Sinoe* Chambers (1 sp., *S. robiniella* (Fitch))]

23.21 *Exoteleia* Wallengren

Six species, two of which are of economic interest as pests of pine:

E. pinifoliella (Chambers) (Pine Needle Miner). Wingspan: ±9 mm. Front wing a shining, deep yellow-brown, with three white bands dusted with gray-brown. Larvae are leaf miners in pine needles. (1) n.e. US; (2) s.e. US.

E. nepheos Freeman (Pine Candle Moth). Similar to the preceding.

[23.22 *Trypanisma* Clemens (1 sp., *T. prudens* Clemens); 23.23 *Taygete* Chambers (6 spp.); 23.24 *Leucogoniella* Fletcher (3 spp.); 23.25 *Arogalea* Walsingham (1 sp., *A. cristifasciella* Chambers); 23.26 *Athrips* Billberg (3 spp.); 23.27 *Telphusa* Chambers (5 spp.); 23.28 *Pseudochelaria* Dietz (5 spp.); 23.29 *Neotelphusa* Janse (2 spp.); 23.30 *Pseudotelphusa* Janse (8 spp.); 23.31 *Xenolechia* Meyrick (6 spp.); 23.32 *Teleiodes* Sattler (1 sp., *T. sequax* Haworth); 23.33 *Teleiopsis* Sattler (1 sp., *T. baldiana* (Barnes and Busck)); 23.34 *Lita* Ti (21 spp.); 23.35 *Arla* Clarke (2 spp.); 23.36 *Neodactylota* Busck (4 spp.); 23.37 *Eudactylota* Walsingham (4 spp.); 23.38 *Friseria* Busck (4 spp.); 23.39 *Rifseria* Hodges (1 sp., *R. fuscotaeniaella* (Chambers)); 23.40 *Sriferia* Hodges (3 spp.); 23.41 *Bryotropha* Heinemann (4 spp.); 23.42 *Deltophora* Janse (3 spp.); 23.43 *Gelechia* Huebner (39 spp.)]

23.44 *Gnorimoschema* Busck

Forty-three species, the following of which is common:

G. gallaesolidaginis Riley (Goldenrod Gall Moth). Wingspan: ±22 mm. Powdery gray; scales basally black with white

Fig. 27.40.

tips, shaded with dark brown. Larvae form a linear gall in stems of goldenrod. (See Fig. 27.40.) (1), (2), (3), (4), (5), generally distributed.

23.45 *Phthorimaea* Meyrick

One species, as follows:

P. operculella (Zeller) (Potato Tubeworm). A pest of stored potatoes. (2) s.e. US.

[23.46 *Scrobipalpula* Povolny (12 spp.); 23.47 *Scrobipalpa* Janse (7 spp.); 23.48 *Exceptia* Povolny (1 sp., *E. neopetrella* (Keifer)); 23.49 *Symmetrischema* Povolny (11 spp.); 23.50 *Caryocolum* Gregor and Povolny (3 spp.); 23.51 *Ptycerata* Ely (4 spp.)]

23.52 *Keiferia* Busck

One species, a pest, as follows:

K. lycopersicella (Walsingham) (Tomato Pinworm). A pest of tomatoes. (1), (2), (3), (4), (5), throughout US.

23.53 *Tildenia* Povolny

Three species, the following a pest:

T. inconspicuella (Murtfeldt) (Eggplant Leaf Miner). Larvae mine leaves of eggplant in particular but other plants as well. (2) s.e. US.

[23.54 *Frumenta* Busck (2 spp.); 23.55 *Agonochaetia* Povolny (1 sp., *A. conspersa* (Braun)); 23.56 *Chionodes* Huebner (72 spp.); 23.57 *Neofaculta* Gozmany (1 sp., *N. infernella* (Herrich-Schaeffer)); 23.58 *Filatima* Busck (55 spp.)]

23.59 *Aroga* Busck

Twenty-one species, the following of which is common.

A. websteri (Clarke) (Sagebush Defoliator).

[23.60 *Fascista* Busck (3 spp.)]

23.61 *Faculta* Busck

Two species, one a pest of ornamentals, as follows:

F. cercerisella (Chambers) (Redbud Leaffolder).

[23.62 *Mirificarma* Gozmany (1 st., *M. flamella* (Huebner))]

23.63 *Stegasta* Meyrick

One species, as follows:

S. bosqueella Chambers (Red-necked Peanutworm). Wingspan: ±27 mm. Thorax and front wing rich chocolate

brown, front yellowish white; palpi dark brown with two pale rings on both the second and third segments. Front wing mixed brownish and bluish black, with large, irregular, bilobed yellow or orange dorsal patch, usually extending to costa a third of the way out, and a white, postmedial costal spot; black spot in the discal cell. Larvae found on *Cassia* spp. and peanuts.

[23.64 *Polyhymno* Chambers (2 spp.); 23.65 *Calliprora* Meyrick (1 sp., *C. sexstrigella* (Chambers)); 23.66 *Sophronia* Huebner (3 spp.); 23.67 *Ymeldia* Hodges (1 sp., *Y. janae* Hodges)]

Subfamily **Anacampsinae**

[23.68 *Aproaerema* Durrant (1 sp., *A. anthyllidella* (Huebner)); 23.69 *Syncopacma* Meyrick (5 spp.); 23.70 *Untomia* Busck (2 spp.); 23.71 *Battaristis* Meyrick (5 spp.)]

23.72 *Anacampsis* Curtis

Twenty-two species, the following of which is a pest:

A. fragariella Busck (Strawberry Crown Miner).

[23.73 *Compsolechia* Meyrick (1 sp., *C. crescentifasciella* (Chambers)); 23.74 *Strobisia* Clemens (2 spp.); 23.75 *Holophysis* Walsingham (1 sp., *H. emblemella* (Clemens))]

Subfamily **Chelariinae**

[23.76 *Prostomeus* Busck (1 sp., *P. brunneus* Busck)]

23.77 *Anarsia* Zeller

One species, as follows:

A. lineatella Zeller (Peach Twig Borer). A pest of peach and plum.

[23.78 *Hypatima* Huebner (1 sp., *H. zesticopa* (Meyrick)); 23.79 *Epilechia* Busck (1 sp., *E. catalinella* (Busck))]

23.80 *Sitotroga* Heinemann

One species, as follows:

S. cerealella (Olivier) (Angoumois Grain Moth). Wingspan: ±22 mm. Front wing silky brownish yellow, either with small black spots or without markings. Adults and larvae found in stored grain, including ear corn. Cosmopolitan.

23.81 *Pectinophora* Busck

One species, as follows:

P. gossypiella (Saunders) (Pink Bollworm). Wingspan: 15–20 mm. Dark brown, with irregular blackish markings; hind wings silvery gray. Larvae feed upon the pollen and fleshy parts of cotton flowers and can cause great economic loss. Pantropical. (2) s.e. US; (3) s.w. US.

23.82 *Platyedra* Meyrick

One species, as follows:

P. subcinerea (Haworth) (Cotton Stem Moth). Larvae bore into cotton plants and destroy them.

Subfamily **Dichomeridinae**

[23.83 *Brachmia* Huebner (9 spp.); 23.84 *Brachyacma* Meyrick (1 sp., *B. palpigera* (Walsingham))]

23.85 *Dichomeris* Huebner

Fifteen species, the following of which are pests:

D. ligulella Huebner (Palmerworm). Wingspan: ±15 mm. Front wing four and a half times as long as wide; hind wing much shorter; wings bluish between veins; ground color yellow-brown with discal dots and bands. Larvae are leaf rollers on apple, oak, and other trees.

D. marginella (Fabricius) (Juniper Webworm). Wingspan: ±15 mm. Front wing pale pinkish brown, margined with cream color. Larvae form a communal web in juniper. Introduced. (1) n.e. US; (2) s.e. US.

[23.86 *Anorthosia* Clemens (1 sp., *A. punctipennella* Clemens); 23.87 *Trichotaphe* Clemens (18 spp.); 23.88 *Thelyasceta* Meyrick (2 spp.); 23.89 *Carbatina* Meyrick (1 sp., *C. picrocarpa* Meyrick); 23.90 *Epicorthylis* Zeller (1 sp., *E. inversella* Zeller)]

Subfamily **Lecithocerinae**

[23.91 *Deoclona* Busck (1 sp., *D. yuccasella* Busck)]

Superfamily **COPROMORPHOIDEA**

Five families are included in this superfamily.

24. COPROMORPHIDAE (Copromorphid Moth Family)

Head with ocelli present or absent; maxillary palpi one-segmented, or, in some species, four-segmented and surrounding base of proboscis scaleless; antennae various, simple, unipectinate (rarely bipectinate); legs with hind tibiae smooth or with long hairlike scales. Larvae bore into leaf veins, fruit, and twigs. Primarily a tropical family with five species in the U.S.

24.1 *Lotisma* Busck

L. trigonana Walsingham. Wingspan: 14–22 mm. Front wing brown with diagonal pale stripe that may enlarge to include base as pale triangle and with apical half usually pale brown; hind wing pale brown. (See Fig. 27.41.) (1) DC; (3) CA; (4) WA, OR.

[24.2 *Ellabella* Busck (4 spp.)]

25. ALUCITIDAE (Many-plume Moth Family)

Wingspan: 12–22 mm. Slender moths with each wing divided into six plumes nearly to base. Only one genus and one species in the U.S.

Fig. 27.41.

Fig. 27.42.

Fig. 27.44.

25.1 *Alucita* Linnaeus

A. hexadactyla Linnaeus. Wingspan: 14–22 mm. Dull gray, each plume barred with black and white bands on each side of bars. (See Fig. 27.42.) (1) n.e. US; (4) Pacific n.w.; (5) n. Central States.

Note: *A. huebneri* (Walker) is sometimes treated as a separate species, although most authors consider it a synonym of the above.

26. CARPOSINIDAE (Carposinid Moth Family)

Wingspan: 10–38 mm. Wing rather narrow; front wing with five radials coming from discal cell; front and vertex smooth; mandibles present, minute; proboscis present, weak, usually about one and one-half to two times length of labial palpi, the latter three-segmented; maxillary palpi minute, usually one-segmented. Eleven species in three genera are recorded in the U.S. and Canada.

26.1 *Carposina* Herrich-Schaeffer

Four species, the following of which is common:

C. fernaldana Busck. Wingspan: ±36 mm. Front wing powdery gray, mottled with darker gray concentrated in costa area. Larvae are pests of nearly ripe currants. (See Fig. 27.43.) (1) n.e. US; (5) MO.

[26.2 *Bondia* Newman (6 spp.); 26.3 *Tesuquea* Klots (1 sp., *T. hawleyana* Klots)]

27. EPERMENIIDAE (Epermeniid Moth Family)

Wingspan: 6–20 mm. Head with smooth scales; no ocelli; no chaetosemata; scape with pecten; proboscis without scales;

Fig. 27.43.

maxillary palpi three-segmented, surrounding base of proboscis; front wing lanceolate with small scale tufts on inner margin; hind tibiae with long stiff bristles. Young larvae are leaf miners but later feed on leaf surface after spinning a thin web covering. Eleven species in three genera are recorded in the U.S. and Canada.

Subfamily Epermeniinae

Tribe Epermeniini

27.1 *Epermenia* Huebner

Nine species, the following of which is common:

E. stolidota Meyrick. Wingspan: ±19 mm. Front wings pale brown, long, narrow with apical notch, tip margined with dark brown, and two small dark spots on hind margin. (See Fig. 27.44.) (3) AZ.

Subfamily Ochromolopinae

[27.2 *Ochromolopis* Huebner (1 sp., *O. ramapoella* (Kearfott)); 27.3 *Parochromolopis* Gaedike (1 sp., *P. floridana* Gaedike)]

28. GLYPHIPTERIGIDAE (Sedge Moth Family)

Wingspan: 5–10 mm. Head without raised scales; ocelli prominent; chaetosemata absent in most species, scape without pecten; proboscis scales absent; maxillary palpi two- to four-segmented, very small or reduced to single segment. Wings marked with bright metallic colors; venation with closed discal cell; stigma present. Larvae, rarely gregarious, are stem and leaf axil borers. All adults are diurnal. Sixteen species reported in the U.S. and Canada.

[28.1 *Abrenthia* Busck (1 sp., *A. cuprea* Busck); 28.2 *Neomachlotica* Heppner (1 sp., *N. spirala* Heppner); 28.3 *Glyphipterix* Huebner (8 spp.)]

28.4 *Diploschizia* Heppner

Six species, the following of which is common:

D. impigritella Clemens. Wingspan: ±7 mm. Front wing olive brown, fringe paler, grayer, and glistening; apex of membrane with black spot; markings silvery white, edged more or less with black, especially on inner sides; basal half of costa immaculate; outer half with five transverse bars: the first two converging in middle of wing and nearly meeting a very large crescentic one from before middle of inner margin and another

Fig. 27.45.

running directly across from inner margin; third costal bar smaller, solitary, opposite a small one at anal angle; fourth and fifth bars close together, near apical spot, with a single corresponding one in dorsal fringe; fringe white with heavy black line in base. (See Fig. 27.45.) (1) n.e. US; (2) s.e. US; (3) s.w. US.

Superfamily YPONOMEUTOIDEA

Most of the six families in this group are poorly known.

29. PLUTELLIDAE (Diamondback Moth Family)

Wingspan: 10–20 mm. A poorly defined family related to the Yponomeutidae. Ocelli present (rarely absent); porrect, four-segmented (rarely one- to two-segmented) maxillary palpi; wings narrow, with apices broadly rounded to rounded lanceolate. Eight genera with 52 species in the U.S. and Canada.

[29.1 *Araeolepia* Walsingham (1 sp., *A. subfasciella* Walsingham); 29.2 *Eucalantica* Busck (1 sp., *E. polita* (Walsingham)); 29.3 *Euceratia* Walsingham (2 spp.)]

29.4 *Homadaula* Lower

One species, as follows:

H. anisocentra Meyrick. Wingspan: 10–14 mm. Front wings lustrous gray, with conspicuous black spots sparsely distributed. Larvae feed on mimosa. (1) PA, DE, MD, DC; (2) s.e. US; (3) CA; (5) CO, KS, MO.

[29.5 *Melitonympha* Meyrick (1 sp., *M. heteraula* Meyrick); 29.6 *Pliniaca* Busck (2 spp.)]

29.7 *Plutella* Schrank

Ten species, the following of which is common:

P. xylostella (Linnaeus) (Diamondback Moth). Wingspan: ±13 mm; wings narrow and lanceolate; mouse gray anteriorly to pale posteriorly. Thorax with central white diamond marking. Larvae feed on cabbage and other cruciferous plants. Cosmopolitan. (See Fig. 27.46.)

29.8 *Ypsolopha* Latreille

Thirty-four species, the following of which is common:

Y. dentella Fabricius (European Honeysuckle Leaf Roller). Wingspan: ±18 mm. Front wing brown with distinct yellowish hind margin and narrow yellow stripe; apex sharply hooked; hind wings dark grayish brown. Introduced. (1) WS, NY, MA, CT.

Fig. 27.46.

30. YPONOMEUTIDAE (Ermine Moth Family)

Wingspan: 10–30 mm. Wings usually brightly marked; head scales usually smooth, some with long hairlike scales; ocelli always absent; chaetosemata rarely present; scape rarely with pecten; proboscis without scales; maxillary palpi porrect, with one to two segments, sometimes rudimentary. Front wing often with stigma, variously marked, including some with black spots (Ermine Moths), others with bright markings, and still others drab. Hind tibiae usually with smooth scales. Larvae, often gregarious, feed on leaves and flowers under a slight webbing; others tunnel in stems, mine, or feed on leaf surfaces. Nine genera with 32 species in the U.S. and Canada. The following arrangement of genera is tentative because the group is poorly defined:

30.1 *Atteva* Walker

One species, as follows:

A. punctella (Cramer) (Ailanthus Webworm). Wingspan: 25–30 mm. Front wing reddish with four bands of pale spots surrounded by black borders. Larvae found in webs in ailanthus. (See Fig. 27.47 and A&J 198.) (1) IL, IN, OH, NY, PA, MD; (2) s.e. US; (3) s.e. US.

[30.2 *Eucatagma* Busck (1 sp., *E. amyridella* Meyrick); 30.3 *Lactura* Walker (6 spp.); 30.4 *Ocnerostoma* Zeller (2 spp.); 30.5 *Orinympha* Meyrick (1 sp., *O. aetherias* Meyrick); 30.6 *Podiasa* Busck (1 sp., *P. chiococcella* Busck); 30.7 *Swammerdamia* Huebner (2 spp.); 30.8 *Urodus* Herrich-Schaeffer (1 sp., *U. parvula* Edwards)]

Fig. 27.47.

Fig. 27.48.

30.9 *Yponomeuta* Latreille

Eight species, the following of which is common:

Y. padella (Linnaeus) (Ermine Moth). Wingspan: ±20 mm. White with black spots on thorax and rows on wings. Larvae feed on *Euonymus* spp. (See Fig. 27.48.) (1) n.e. NA; (2) s.e. US.

30.10 *Zelleria* Stainton

Nine species, the following of which is a pest:

Z.˙ haimbachi Busck (Pine Needle Sheathminer). Wingspan: ±18 mm; wings pale brown. (1) WN, MI, IL, NY; (5) MT, WY.

31. ARGYRESTHIIDAE (Needle Miner Moth Family)

Wingspan: 6–12 mm. Difficult to distinguish from Yponomeutidae. Adults rest with wings and abdomen elevated; wings narrow, lanceolate, with venation not reduced and often with markings and reflective scales. One genus and 52 species in the U.S. and Canada.

31.1 *Argyresthia* Huebner

Fifty-two species, the following of which are common:

A. conjugella Zeller (Apple Fruit Moth). Wingspan: ±10 mm. Wings brown with posterior margin of front wing having pearl-like reflective scales. (See Fig. 27.49.) (1) n.e. US; (3) CA.

A. thuiella (Packard) (Arborvitae Leaf Miner). Wingspan: ±7 mm. Front wing with shiny pearl-like reflective scales. (1) OH.

Fig. 27.49.

Fig. 27.50.

32. DOUGLASIIDAE (Douglasiid Moth Family)

Wingspan: ±9 mm. Ocelli very large; head with smooth scales; chaetosemata absent; proboscis without scales; scape without pecten; labial palpi intermediate in size, stout, and drooping. Front wings lanceolate; hind wing narrow, lanceolate. Larvae are leaf miners on Rosaceae species and related plants. One genus and five species in the U.S. and Canada of this poorly known group.

32.1 *Tinagma* Zeller

Five species, the following of which is common:

T. obscurofasciella Chambers. Wingspan: ±9 mm. Larvae are leaf miners on various species of Rosaceae. (See Fig. 27.50.) (1) n.e. US.

33. ACROLEPIIDAE (Acrolepiid Moth Family)

Wingspan: ±12 mm. Very similar to Yponomeutidae and sometimes considered a part of that family. Head scales moderately rough above; ocelli present; maxillary palpi porrect; hind tibiae smooth-scaled. Larvae are poorly known, although one species bores into bulbs and others are leaf tiers or skeletonizers. One genus and three species in the U.S. and Canada.

33.1 *Acrolepiopsis* Gaedike

Three species, the following of which is common:

A. incertella (Chambers). Wingspan: ±25 mm. Front wing gray-brown, somewhat iridescent with red bronze and with vague darker streaks and patches, especially one at middle of costa; oblique white streak extending up from inner margin near base to about middle of wing; hind wing pale. Larvae tie and skeletonize leaves of *Smilax* spp. or bore into lily bulbs. (See Fig. 27.51.) (1) n.e. NA; (2) s.e. US; (3) s.w. US.

Note: *A. assectella* (Zeller) (Leek Moth) is European; its larvae bore into leeks.

34. HELIODINIDAE (Heliodinid Moth Family)

Wingspan: 14–30 mm. Wings lanceolate; ventation entire to greatly reduced. Head scales smooth; maxillary palpi obsolete; proboscis without scales; ocelli present or absent. Hind tibiae smooth-scaled or with stiff bristles. The group is poorly known, with generic assignments uncertain; the following six genera with a total of 20 species are currently assigned as follows:

Fig. 27.51.

[34.1 *Cycloplasis* Clemens (1 sp., *C. panicifoliella* Clemens); 34.2 *Scelorthus* Busck (1 sp., *S. pisoniella* Busck); 34.3 *Lamprolophus* Busck (1 sp., *L. lithella* Busck); 34.4 *Heliodines* Stainton (11 spp.)]

34.5 *Schreckensteinia* Huebner

Three species, the following of which is common:

S. festaliella (Huebner) (Blackberry Skeletonizer). Wingspan: ±27 mm. Deep bronze brown. Larvae found on leaves of *Rubus* spp. in a slight web; sometimes of minor economic importance as pest of blackberries. (See Fig. 27.52.)

[34.6 *Lithariapteryx* Chambers (3 spp.)]

Superfamily SESIOIDEA

35. SESIIDAE (Clear-winged Moth Family)

[=Aegeriidae]

Wingspan: 15–40 mm. Wings of most species transparent with scales confined to veins. In appearance and their flight pattern, many resemble bees and wasps, even to the extent of pretending to sting. Diurnal, they are often seen around flower beds; their shape and color patterns of dark brown or black with yellow or orange warning colors appear to be effective. Larvae bore into roots, stems, vines, tree branches, and tree trunks. Many species are pests of ornamental trees, crop trees, and a few field crops. There are 19 genera with 115 species recorded in the U.S. and Canada.

Subfamily Tinthiinae
Tribe Pennisetiini
35.1 *Pennisetia* Dehne

One species, as follows:

P. marginata (Harris) (Raspberry Crown Borer). Wingspan: male, ±25 mm; female, 30–35 mm. Front wings transparent except for brown margins, tips, and a band across wing about two-thirds of distance to apex; hind wings entirely transparent except for veins and fringe; abdomen banded with brownish black and yellow, more yellow at base, less so apically; legs nearly all yellow. Adults fly August to mid-September. Larvae bore into roots and canes of blackberry, raspberry, and other *Rubus* spp. (1), (2), (3), (4), (5), generally distributed.

Fig. 27.52.

Tribe Tinthiini

[35.2 *Zenodoxus* Grote and Robinson (7 spp.)]

Subfamily Paranthreninae
Tribe Cissuvorini

[35.3 *Cissuvora* Engelhardt (1 sp., *C. ampelopsis* Engelhardt)]

Tribe Paranthrenini

[35.4 *Paranthrene* Huebner (6 spp.)]

35.5 *Vitacea* Engelhardt

Four species, the following of which is a pest:

V. polistiformis (Harris) (Grape Root Borer). Wingspan: 22–40 mm. Front wings opaque, dark brown; hind wings transparent, somewhat yellowish in male; abdomen brown with yellow lines on second and fourth segments; legs and sides of thorax reddish, particularly in males. Larvae bore in grape roots, taking two years to develop. Adults emerge in July and August. Common. (1) n.e. US.

[35.6 *Albuna* Edwards (2 spp.); 35.7 *Euhagena* Edwards (2 spp.)]

Subfamily Sesiinae
Tribe Melittiini
35.8 *Melittia* Huebner

Six species, the following of which are pests:

M. cucurbitae (Harris) (Squash Vine Borer). Wingspan: 25–30 mm. Black with green iridescence; hind wings transparent; abdomen and legs reddish, with abdomen marked with black and bronze and hind legs with long black fringe of scales. This is one of the most common species of the family. Its larvae infest vines of squash, pumpkins, and other species of cucurbites. (See Fig. 27.53.) (1), (2), (3), (4), (5), generally distributed.

M. gloriosa Edwards (Vine Borer). Wingspan: 40–45 mm. Front wings pale green; hind wings transparent, without scales except on veins; hind legs with heavy fringe of orange scales. Larvae bore into bark, stems, and roots of cucurbites. (See A&J 199.) (3) AZ.

Tribe Sesiini
35.9 *Sesia* Fabricius

Two species, the following of which is common:

S. apiformis (Clerck) (Hornet Moth). Wingspan: 30–40 mm. Brown with yellow markings, resembling a hornet. Adults fly from June to July. Larvae found in trunks and roots of

Fig. 27.53.

Fig. 27.55.

popular and willow. Common. (Fig. 27.54.) (1), (2), (3), (4), (5), generally distributed.

Tribe Osminiini

[35.10 *Calasesia* Beutenmüller (1 sp., *C. coccinea* (Beutenmuller)); 35.11 *Osminia* LeCerf (1 sp., *O. ruficornis* (Edwards))]

Tribe Synanthedonini

35.12 *Synanthedon* Huebner

Forty-one species, the following of which are pests:

S. exitiosa (Say) (Peach Tree Borer). Wingspan: 20–30 mm. Female dark blue with reddish tint; hind wings transparent; fourth and fifth abdominal segments orange. Male with front wings and hind wings transparent; wings and body blue; abdomen with narrow bands of white or pale yellow. Larvae bore into peach trunks near ground and do considerable damage. (See Fig. 27.55.) Found wherever peaches are grown in (1) n.e. US; (2) s.e. US; (3) CA?, AZ?; (4) Pacific n.w.; (5) n. Central states. [Note: A western subspecies, *S. e. graefi* Edwards, called the Western peach Tree Borer, is sometimes recognized, but it is doubtful if it is a distinct subspecies.]

S. pictipes (Grote and Robinson) (Lesser Peach Tree Borer). Similar to the preceding, but somewhat smaller. Both sexes resemble the male of *S. exitiosa*. Larvae work higher up in the trunk and infest other trees as well.

Fig. 27.54.

S. tipuliformis (Clerck) (Currant Borer). Female with three and the male with four yellow bands on the abdomen. Adults fly during June and July. Larvae attack current and gooseberry stems. Introduced.

S. acerni (Clemens) (Maple Callus Borer).

S. novaroensis (Edwards) (Douglas-fir Pitch Moth).

S. pyri (Harris) (Apple Bark Borer).

S. scitula (Harris) (Dogwood Moth).

S. rhododendri (Beutenmueller) (Rhododendron Borer).

[35.13 *Palmia* Beutenmüller (1 sp., *P. praecedens* (Edwards)]

35.14 *Podosesia* Möschler

Two species, as follows:

P. syringae (Harris) (Ash Borer; Lilac Borer).

35.15 *Sannina* Walker

One species, including the following:

S. uroceriformis (Walker) (Persimmon Borer).

[35.16 *Carmenta* Edwards (28 spp.); 35.17 *Penstemonia* Engelhardt (4 spp.); 35.18 *Alcathoe* Edwards (4 spp.); 35.19 *Hymenoclea* Engelhardt (1 sp., *H. palmii* (Beutenmüller))]

36. CHOREUTIDAE (Choreutid Moth Family)

Wingspan: 10–14 mm. Proboscis with scales over base; wings broad instead of lanceolate. Nine genera with 29 described species in the U.S. and Canada.

Subfamily Millieriinae

[36.1 *Phormoestes* Heppner (1 sp., *P. palmettovora* Heppner)]

Subfamily Brenthiinae

[36.2 *Brenthia* Clemens (1 sp., *B. pavonacella* Clemens)]

Subfamily Choreutinae

[36.3 *Anthophila* Haworth (1 sp., *A. apinella* (Busck))]

36.4 *Prochoreutis* Diakonoff and Heppner

Five species, the following of which is common:

P. pariana (Clerck) (Apple-and-thorn Skeletonizer). Wingspan: ±12 mm. Wings brown, with pale mottling; apex of front wing darker. (See Fig. 27.56.)

Fig. 27.56.

[36.5 *Caloreas* Heppner (8 spp.); 36.6 *Tebenna* Billberg (8 spp.); 36.7 *Choreutis* Huebner (3 spp.); 36.8 *Tortyra* Walker (1 sp., *T. slossonia* (Fernald)); 36.9 *Hemerophila* Huebner (2 spp.)]

Superfamily COSSOIDEA

One family only, as follows:

37. COSSIDAE (Carpenter Moth or Goat Moth Family)

Wingspan: 20–70 mm. Wing venation primitive with radius five-branched with veins in discal cell; proboscis rudimentary. These moths somewhat resemble sphinx moths and are good flyers. Larvae are wood borers. There has been no recent taxonomic revision, but 45 species are presently assigned to 11 genera in the U.S. and Canada.

Subfamily Hypoptinae

[37.1 *Hypopta* Huebner (1 sp., *H. palmata* Barnes and McDunnough); 37.2 *Inguromorpha* Edwards (3 spp.); 37.3 *Givira* Walker (14 spp.)]

Subfamily Cossulinae
37.4 *Cossula* Bailey

One species, as follows:

C. magnifica (Strecker) (Pecan Carpenterworm). Wingspan: ±37 mm. Grayish with brown markings. Adults fly in May and June. Larvae bore into twigs and tunnel in pitch of pecan, oak, and hickory. (2) s.w. US.

Subfamily Cossinae

[37.5 *Acossus* Dyar (4 spp.); 37.6 *Comadia* Barnes and McDunnough (12 spp.); 37.7 *Fania* Barnes and McDunnough (1 sp., *F. nanus* Strecker)]

37.8 *Prionoxystus* Grote

Three species, the following two of which are pests:

P. macmurtrei (Guérin-Méneville) (Little Carpenterworm). Wingspan ±30 mm; female, ±60–75 mm. Front wing with transverse reticulations. Adults fly in June. Larvae bore into oak. (1) n.e. NA; (2) s.e. US; (5) MN.

P. robiniae (Peck) (Carpenterworm). Wingspan: 50–75 mm. Front wing nearly white with irregular black striations. Hind wings of female pale; male translucent with dark markings at base. Larvae are woodborers in locust, oak, chestnut, poplar, willow, maple, and ash. (See Fig. 27.57 for male; Fig. 27.58 for female.) (1), (2), (3), (4), (5), generally distributed.

[37.9 *Miacora* Dyar [=*Toronia* Barnes and McDunnough (2 spp.)]

Fig. 27.57.

Subfamily Zeurerinae

[37.10 *Hamilcara* Barnes and McDunnough (3 spp.)]

37.11 *Zeuzera* Latreille

One species, as follows:

Z. pyrina (Linnaeus) (Leopard Moth). Wingspan: 45–70 mm. White, similar to *Prionoxystus robininae*, but with regular blue-black spots, hence its common name. Adults on the wing in June and July. Larvae are woodborers in various trees and shrubs. Introduced from Europe. (See Fig. 27.59 for male; Fig. 27.60 for female.) (1) MA, NY, PA, NJ.

Superfamily TORTRICOIDEA

This superfamily contains two closely related families that may be distinguished by the features given in the Key to the Families. The family Tortricidae is the fourth largest of the order.

38. TORTRICIDAE (Tortricid Moth Family)

Wingspan: 9–35 mm. Head usually rough-scaled; ocelli usually present; chaetosemata present; maxillary palpi two- to four-segmented; labial palpi short to very long, porrect, rarely

Fig. 27.58.

Fig. 27.59.

ascending. Front wing with C usually strongly arched, sometimes with costal fold in male, and CuA$_2$ arising from anterior three-fourths of discal cell; wing somewhat square-tipped in most species. Larvae bore into stems, leaves, and fruit. Some make webs on leaves; others are leaf rollers or leaf tiers. About a third of the genera are pests of fruit, seeds, forest trees, and ornamentals. Distinguishing between the genera is based almost entirely on features of the genitalia; these correlate to a considerable extent with features of wing venation. Although the species may be identified by various color patterns, an examination of male genitalia is required for confirmation. There are 1053 species in 91 genera in the U.S. and Canada.

Subfamily Olethreutinae
Tribe Olethreutini

[38.1 *Episimus* Walsingham (3 spp.); 38.2 *Cacocharis* Walsingham (1 sp., *C. cymotoma* (Meyrick))]

38.3 *Bactra* Stephens

Six species, the following of which is common:

B. venosoma (Zeller) (Nutgrass Borer Moth).

38.4 *Endopiza* Clemens

Seventeen species, the following of which is a pest:

E. viteana Clemens (Grape Berry Moth). Wingspan: ±10 mm. Brown with blue-gray and umber-brown markings. Adults

Fig. 27.60.

fly in June. Larvae bore into grapes but pupate on a leaf within a chamber made by cutting a flap of leaf; the leaf drops to the ground in the fall. Adults emerge form the pupae in June. (1), (2), (3), (4), (5), generally distributed.

[38.5 *Lobesia* Guenée (2 spp.); 38.6 *Ahmosia* Heinrich (2 spp.)]

38.7 *Endothenia* Stephens

Sixteen species, the following of which are pests:

E. albolineana (Kearfott) (Spruce Needle Miner).

E. hebesana (Walker) (Verbena Bud Moth).

[38.8 *Aterpia* Guenee (1 sp., *A. approximana* (Heinrich)); 38.9 *Eumarozia* Heinrich (1 sp., *E. malachitana* (Zeller)); 38.10 *Zomaria* Heinrich (3 spp.); 38.11 *Apotomis* Huebner (16 spp.); 38.12 *Pseudosciaphila* Oberthuer (1 sp., *P. duplex* (Walsingham)); 38.13 *Orthotaenia* Stephens (1 sp., *O. undulana* (Dyar and Smith)); 38.14 *Phaecasiophora* Grote (3 spp.); 38.15 *Olethreutes* Huebner (85 spp.)]

38.16 *Hedya* Huebner

Five species, the following of which is common:

H. nubiferana (Haworth) (Green Budworm). Wingspan: ±13 mm. Front wings white or yellow at base, outer part dark, yellowish to nearly black. Adults fly in July. Larvae on many trees and shrubs feeding on the buds and making a webbing. (1) n.e. US.

[38.17 *Tsinilla* Heinrich (1 sp., *T. lineana* (Fernald)); 38.18 *Evora* Heinrich (1 sp., *E. hemidesma* (Zeller))]

Tribe Eucosmini
38.19 *Rhyacionia* Huebner

Twenty-two species, several of which infest the growing tips of various conifers and cause considerable damage.

R. buoliana (Denis and Schiffermueller). Wingspan: 18–26 mm. Bright orange, usually shaded with yellow, with six to eight narrow, anastomosing pale silver-gray transverse lines. Larvae bore into pine shoots and cause crooked growth. (1) n.e. US; (4) Pacific n.w; (5) n. Central states.

R. frustrana (Comstock) (Nantucket Pine Tip Moth). Wingspan: 10–13 mm. Deep red shading to reddish brown, mottled with yellow; outer part of wing with four broad bands of silver gray scales. Larvae bore into shoots of scrub pine. (1) s. MA, s. NY, NJ, PA, MD; (s.e. US); (3) TX.

R. rigidana (Fernald) (Pitch-pine Tip Moth).

R. neomexicana (Dyer) (Southern Pine-tip Moth).

R. subtropica Miller (Subtropical Pine-tip Moth).

38.20 *Petrova* Heinrich

Fourteen species, the following of which are pests:

P. comstockiana (Fernald) (Pitch Twig Moth).

P. albicapitana (Busck) (Northern Pitch Twig Moth).

38.21 *Barbara* Heinrich

Three species, the following of which is common:

B. colfaxiana (Kearfott) (Douglas-fir Cone Moth).

38.22 *Spilonota* Stephens

One species, as follows:

S. ocellana (Denis and Schiffermueller) (Eyespotted Bud Moth).

[38.23 *Strepsicrates* Meyrick (1 sp., *S. smithiana* (Walsingham)); 38.24 *Phaneta* Stephens (100 species)]

38.25 *Eucosma* Huebner

Several of the 141 species are of economic importance, including the following:

E. cocana Kearfott (Shortleaf Pine Cone Borer).

E. tocullionana Heinrich (White Pine Cone Borer).

E. gloriola Heinrich (Pine Shoot Borer).

[38.26 *Pelochrista* Lederer (22 spp.)]

38.27 *Epiblema* Huebner

Thirty-seven species, the following of which are pests:

E. otiosana (Clemens) (Bidens Borer).

E. strenuana (Walker) (Ragweed Borer).

[38.28 *Notocelia* Huebner (4 spp.)]

38.29 *Suleima* Heinrich

Six species, the following of which is a pest:

S. helianthana (Riley) (Sunflower Bud Moth).

[38.30 *Sonia* Heinrich (5 spp.)]

38.31 *Gypsonoma* Meyrick

Seven species, the following of which is a pest:

G. haimbachiana (Kearfott) (Cottonwood Twig Borer).

38.32 *Proteoteras* Riley

Eight species, the following of which is common:

P. willingana (Kearfott) (Boxelder Twig Borer).

38.33 *Zeiraphera* Treitschke

Eight species, the following of which is a severe pest:

Z. canadensis Mutuura and Freeman (Spruce Bud Moth).

[38.34 *Pseudexentera* Heinrich (13 spp.)]

38.35 *Gretchena* Heinrich

Ten species, the following of which is a pest:

G. bolliana (Slingerland) (Pecan Bud Moth).

[38.36 *Griselda* Heinrich (1 sp., *G. radicana* Heinrich); 38.37 *Chimoptesis* Powell (4 spp.); 38.38 *Crocidosema* Zeller (1 sp., *C. plebejana* Zeller); 38.39 *Hendecaneura* Walsingham (1 sp., *H. shawianum* (Kearfott))]

38.40 *Rhopobota* Lederer

Three species, the following of which is common:

R. naevana naevana (Huebner) (Black-headed Fireworm).

38.41 *Epinotia* Huebner

Seventy-five species, the following of which are pests:

E. meritana Heinrich (White-fir Needle Miner).

E. aceriella (Clemens) (Maple Trumpet Skeletonizer).

38.42 *Ancylis* Huebner

Thirty-five species, the following of which is a pest:

A. comptana fragariae (Walsh and Riley) (Strawberry Leaf Roller).

[38.43 *Hystrichophora* Walsingham (11 spp.)]

Tribe Laspeyresiini

[38.44 *Goditha* Heinrich (1 sp., *G. bumeliana* Heinrich); 38.45 *Dichrorampha* Guenee (14 spp.); 38.46 *Satronia* Heinrich (1 sp., *S. tantilla* Heinrich); 38.47 *Ricula* Heinrich (1 sp., *R. maculana* (Fernald)); 38.48 *Talponia* Heinrich (1 sp., *T. plummeriana* (Busck)); 38.49 *Pammene* Huebner (5 spp.); 38.50 *Larisa* Miller (1 sp., *L. subsolana* Miller); 38.51 *Ethelgoda* Heinrich (1 sp., *E. texanana* (Walsingham)); 38.52 *Sereda* Heinrich (1 sp., *S. tautana* (Clemens))]

38.53 *Grapholita* Treitschke

Eighteen species, many of which are important economic pests. The larvae infest fruit.

G. packardi Zeller (Cherry Fruitworm). Wingspan: ±10 mm. Dull blackish. Larvae found in cherries and other fruits in fruit growing areas. (1), (2), (3), (4), (5), generally distributed.

G. prunivora (Walsh) (Lesser Appleworm). Wingspan: ±9 mm. Black-brown marked with yellow-gray. Larvae found in apples, plums, and related fruits. (1), (2), (3), (4), (5), generally distributed.

G. molesta (Busck) (Oriental fruit moth). Wingspan: 10–15 mm. Dark, yellowish brown with some white-tipped scales. Larvae bore into the end of peach twigs, causing them to die; later they bore into the fruit itself, particularly peaches, but also apple and several others in fruit growing areas. Introduced into the U.S. in 1915. (1), (2), (3), (4), (5), generally distributed.

G. interstinctana (Clemens) (Clover-head Caterpillar). Larvae found in the flower heads of clover.

[38.54 *Ofatulena* Heinrich (2 spp.); 38.55 *Corticivora* Clarke (1 sp., *C. clarki* Clarke)]

38.56 *Cydia* Heubner

Forty-seven species, a great many of which are pests of fruit and seeds. The most important species are the following:

C. pomonella (Linnaeus) (Codling Moth). Wingspan: 15–20 mm. Dark gray with pale markings. Larvae found in apples (the usual worm of wormy apples) and other fruit. This very serious pest, introduced into North America in the mid 1700s, now lives wherever apples are grown. (See Fig. 27.61.) (1), (2), (3), (4), (5).

C. caryana (Fitch) (Hickory Shuckworm). Wingspan: 10–12 mm. Dark brown with lead-colored stripes. Larvae found in hickory and walnut and also in galls. (1) n.e. NA; (2) VA, NC, SC, GA.

C bracteatana (Fernald) (Fir Seed Moth). Infests fir tree seeds in cones.

C. nigricana (Stephens) (Pea Moth). Found in pods and seeds of leguminose plants.

C. youngana Kearfott (Spruce Seed Moth). Larvae found in seeds of spruce.

C. saltitans Westwood (Mexican Jumping Bean Borer). Larvae of this native of Mexico, now established in Arizona and Florida, live in seeds of Croton, creating the famous jumping bean. The wriggling of larvae inside the beans causes them to move so violently that they literally appear to "jump".

The following three species are of little economic importance:

C. anaranjada Miller (Slash Pine Seedworm).

C. toreuta Grote (Eastern Pine Seedworm).

C. ingens Heinrich (Longleaf Pine Seedworm).

38.57 *Melissopus* Riley

One species, as follows:

M. latifereanus (Walsingham) (Filbertworm).

38.58 *Ecdytolopha* Zeller

Five species, the following being a twig borer that sometimes forms a gall:

E. insiticiana Zeller (Locust Twig Borer).

[39.59 *Pseudogalleria* Ragonot (1 sp., *P. inimicella* (Zeller).]

Subfamily Tortricinae
Tribe Tortricini
38.60 *Croesia* Heubner

Five species, the following of which is common:

C. semipurpurana (Kearfott) (Oak Leaftier).

38.61 *Acleris* Huebner

Several of the 58 species of this genus are pests:

A. minuta (Robinson) (Yellowheaded Fireworm). Wingspan: 9–18 mm. Orange, reticulate with darker scales. Larvae are leafrollers on cranberry and apple. (1) n.e. US.

A variana (Fernald) (Blackheaded Budworm). Wingspan: 17–20 mm. Mottled gray with various brown, white, or gray ragged bands across the wings, sometimes with white, orange, or yellow stripes down each wing. Larvae found on spruce. (1) n.e. US; (2) s.e. US.

A. gloverana (Walsingham) (Western Blackheaded Budworm). Often a pest.

[38.62 *Apotoforma* Busck (1 sp., *A. rotundipennis* (Walsingham)]

Tribe Cnephasiini

[38.63 *Eulia* Huebner (1 sp., *E. ministrana* (Linnaeus)); 38.64 *Cnephasia* Curtis (2 spp.); 38.65 *Eana* Billberg (5 spp.); 38.66 *Decodes* Oberthuer (8 spp.); 38.67 *Dorithia* Powell (2 spp.); 38.68 *Anopina* Oberthuer (7 spp.); 38.69 *Acroplectis* Meyrick (2 spp., *A. haemanthes* Meyrick and, *incertae sedis*, *A. dorsistriatana* Walsingham, 1884)]

Tribe Archipini
38.70 *Pandemis* Heubner

Five species, the following of which is common:

P. limitata (Robinson) (Threelined Leafroller).

38.71 *Argyrotaenia* Stephen

Thirty-four species, most of them leaf rollers, among which are the following:

A. velutinana (Walker) (Redbanded Leafroller). Wingspan: 12–16 mm. White streaked with gray, shaded with pale and marked with reddish brown and black. Adults fly from April to October. Larvae are leaf rollers on many plants but not on conifers. (1), (2), (3), (4), (5), generally distributed.

A. mariana (Fernald) (Graybanded leafroller). Wingspan: ±20 mm. White shaded with light gray and light brown with large blackish triangle on outer part of front wing. Larvae are leaf rollers on *Vaccinium* spp. (1) n.e. NA; (2) s.e. US.

A. juglandana (Fernald) (Hickory Leafroller). Wingspan: 15–25 mm. Dark brown crossed by two narrow, parallel, oblique blackish spots. Adults fly in June and July. Larvae are leaf rollers on hickory and viburnum. (1) n.e. NA; (5) MN.

A. citrana (Fernald) (Orange Tortrix). Found on citrus trees.

A. pinatubana (Kearfott) (Pine Tube Moth). Wingspan: 10–15 mm. White with dark markings and outer dark patch on front wings. Adults fly from April to October. Larvae continue to make new tubes on white pine needles to feed on until they mature, pupating in the last tube. Found in white pine areas. (1), (2), (3), (4), (5), generally distributed.

38.72 *Choristoneura* Lederer

Sixteen species, the following of which are budworms or leaf rollers:

C. fumiferana (Clemens) (Spruce Budworm). Wingspan: 20–25 mm. Mottled with a clay color and a yellowish or reddish brown. Larvae do enormous damage to spruce buds and foliage. (See Fig. 27.62.) (1) n.e. NA; (4) Pacific n.w.; (5) n. Central states.

C. occidentalis Freeman (Western Spruce Budworm).

C. pinus Freeman (Jack Pine Budworm). Larvae found on pine.

C. conflictana (Walker) (Large Aspen Tortrix). Wingspan: 25–35 mm. Dull light gray with diffuse darker markings. Larvae

Fig. 27.61.

Fig. 27.62.

feed on aspen leaves and related plants. (1) WI, MI, ON. PQ, NY; (4) UT; (5) MT, ND, MN, WY, SD, NE, IA, CO, KS, MO.

C. rosaceana (Harris) (Oblique banded Leafroller). Wingspan: 20–28 mm. Strongly reticulate with brown; vividly contrasting median patch. Larvae found on many trees, shrubs, and herbaceous plants, including apple and clover. (1), (2), (3), (4), (5), generally distributed.

[38.73 *Cudonigera* Obraztsov and Powell (1 sp., *C. houstonana* (Grote))]

38.74 *Archips* Huebner

Twenty-one species, including several pests—particularly webworms that nest on trees and leaf rollers.

A. fervidanus (Clemens) (Oak Webworm). Wingspan: 15–22 mm. Brown on basal half and gray on outer half with heavy and sparse brownish-yellow striae, partly edged with cream with blackish center. Adults on the wing in July and August. Larvae feed on oak leaves and are gregarious nest webbers. (1), (2), (3), (4), (5), generally distributed.

A. cerasivoranus (Fitch) (Uglynest Caterpillar Moth). Wingspan: 18–25 mm. Front wing orange with purple iridescence, spotted and speckled with dark red-brown. Larvae live on wild cherry in large nests of mixed silk and grass. Adults appear in late June and early July. (1), (2), (3), (4), (5), generally distributed.

A. semiferana (Walker) (Oak Leafroller). Wingspan: ±20 mm. Light red, more or less shaded with gray and somewhat mottled with straw yellow. Larvae found on oak, maple, negundo, and other trees. (1), (2), (3), (4), (5), generally distributed.

A. argyrospila (Walker) (Fruit Tree Leafroller). Wingspan: ±20 mm. Irregularly mottled with cream, straw-yellow, red-brown, and often black-brown scales, forming quadrate patches. Adults lay eggs in June. Larvae feed on many plants, including apples. (1), (2), (3), (4), (5), generally distributed.

A. rosana Linnaeus. Larvae feed on current and other small fruits and orchard and shade trees. (1) IL, IN, OH, PA, NY, MA; (5) MO.

[38.75 *Archepandemis* Mutuura (3 spp.); 38.76 *Syndemis* Huebner (1 sp., *S. afflictana* (Walker)); 38.77 *Lozotaenia* Stephens (2 spp.); 38.78 *Aphelia* Huebner (3 spp.); 38.79 *Cacoecimorpha* Oberthuer (1 sp., *C. pronubana* (Huebner)); 38.80 *Clepsis* Guenée (1 spp.); 38.81 *Ptycho-*

loma Stephens (2 spp.); 38.82 *Adoxophyes* Meyrick (2 spp.); 38.83 *Ditula* Stephens (1 sp., *D. angustiorana* (Haworth)); 38.84 *Xenotemna* Powell (1 sp., *X. pallorana* (Robinson))]

Tribe Niasomini

[38.85 *Niasoma* Busck (1 sp., *N. metallicana* (Walsingham))]

Tribe Sparganothidini

[38.86 *Sparganothis* Huebner (37 spp.); 38.87 *Platynota* Clemens (14 spp.); 38.88 *Synnoma* Walsingham (1 sp., *S. lynosyrana* Walsingham); 38.89 *Coelostathma* Clemens (1 sp., *C. discopunctana* Clemens)]

38.90 *Amorbia* Clemens

Three species, the following of which is a minor pest:

A. emigratella Busck (Mexican Leaf Roller).

Subfamily Chlidanotinae
Tribe Hilarographini

[38.91 *Hilarographa* Zeller (3 spp.)]

39. COCHYLIDAE (Cochylid Moth Family)

[=Phaloniidae]

Wingspan: 9–28 mm. Wings long, narrow, rounded, usually bent down at apex. Most larvae are either stem borers or feed in seeds, usually of herbaceous plants. The family is uncommon, although a few species have some economic importance. There are 110 U.S. species assigned to the following nine genera.

39.1 *Aethes* Billberg

[=*Phalonia* Huebner]

Six species, the following two of economic interest:

A. rutilana (Huebner) (Pale Juniper Webworm). Wingspan: 9–12 mm. Bright yellow with four even, deep red bands. Adults lay eggs in June. Larvae live in tubular webs between needles of juniper. (See Fig. 27.63.) (1) WI, MI, ON, NY, PA, NJ.

A. hospes (Walsingham) (Banded Sunflower Moth). Wingspan: 10–15 mm.

[39.2 *Cochylis* Treitschke (9 spp.); 38.3 *Thyrazlia* Walsingham (1 sp., *T. bunteana* (Robinson)); 38.4 *Henricus* Busck (8 spp.); 39.5 *Irazona* Razowski (1 sp. *I. comes* (Walsingham)); 39.6 *Phalonidia* LeMarch (2 spp.)]

Fig. 27.63.

39.7 *Lorita* Busck

One species, as follows:

L. abornana Busck (Chrysanthemum Flower Borer). Infests composites.

[39.8 *Carolella* Busck (10 spp.); 38.9 *Hysterosia* Stephens (72 spp.)]

"Division RHOPALOCERA*"*

As explained in the introduction, this division no longer has taxonomic standing and is used here only as a means of simplifying reference to the earlier literature. It comprises the skippers and butterflies.

Superfamily HESPERIOIDEA

One family only, the Hesperiidae, or skippers, including the former family Megathymidae, or giant skippers.

40. HESPERIIDAE (The Skippers)

Skippers are closely related to, but distinct from the butterflies. In general, they are heavy-bodied and somewhat less brightly colored—usually a dull brown, often marked with orange or white; a few nearly all white; others marked with green or blue or having a bluish or purplish tinge. The antennae are almost always hooded at the tip and clubbed; the Giant Skippers (subfamily Megathyminae) lack the antennal hook. Several species have tails similar to those of the papilios, but only one of these occurs north of the extreme southern part of Texas [see *Urbanus proteus* (40.12)]. Although many species of this large family—290 species in 89 genera—occur within the political limits of the U.S., many of those reported are either strays or established only in small colonies in extreme southern Florida, Texas, New Mexico, Arizona, and California. A large number of these have two or more subspecies that are not listed or counted in the following checklist. Most species can be "spot" identified by means of their color pattern alone, but some can be identified with certainty only by comparing their dissected genitalia with descriptions. It should be noted further that various authors disagree about whether certain species are to be considered as species or subspecies; as a result, species counts vary from work to work. The list given here agrees with the Miller and Brown catalog (1981).

Subfamily Pyrrhopyginae

40.1 *Pyrrhopyge* Huebner

One species, as follows:

P. araxes (Hewitson) (Large Brown Skipper). Wingspan: 45–60 mm. Antennal club curved back, a feature unique to this genus; head partly to entirely yellowish; abdomen sometimes banded with yellow; wings with white marginal spots; front wings with several large white spots. Larvae feed on oak. (See A&J 202.) (2) s.e. US; (3) s.w. US.

Subfamily Pyrginae

[40.2 *Phocides* Huebner (3 spp.); 40.3 *Proteides* Huebner (1 sp., *P. mercurius* (Fabricius), a stray in (2) s. FL; (3) s. TX.

40.4 *Epargyreus* Huebner

Three very similar species occur in the U.S., but only the following is widespread:

Fig. 27.64.

E. clarus (Cramer) (Silver-spotted Skipper). Wingspan: 44–60 mm. Light marks are yellowish except for a large silver spot on each hind wing. Larvae feed on locust and other trees. (See Fig. 27.64.) (1), (2), (3), (4), (5), throughout US and s. Canada.

[40.5 *Polygonus* Huebner (2 spp.); 40.6 *Chioides* Lindsey (2 spp.); 40.7 *Aguna* Williams (2 spp., strays in (3) s. TX, s. AZ); 40.8 *Typhedanus* Butler (1 sp., *T. undulatus* (Hewitson), a stray in (3) s. TX); 40.9 *Polythrix* Watson (3 spp. strays in (3) s. TX, s. AZ); 40.10 *Zestura* Lindsey (1 sp., *Z. dorus* Edwards); 40.11 *Codatractus* Lindsey (3 spp.)]

40.12 *Urbanus* Huebner

Ten species, all with tailed hind wings. The following is the most widespread, the others being confined to the extreme southern U.S.:

U. proteus (Linaeus) (Long-tailed Skipper; Bean Leaf Roller). Wingspan ±45 mm. Hind wings with a long tail; greenish on hind wings, expecially in males. Larvae feed on legumes; sometimes a minor pest. (See Fig. 27.65.) (1) CT, s. NY, PA, NJ, MD, DE, DC; (2) s.e. US; (3) s.w. US.

40.13 *Astraptes* Huebner

Six species, most of them strays in (3) s. TX. The following is established in Texas:

A. fulgerator (Walsh). Wingspan: ±45 mm. Wings black with basal half iridescent; front wings with large, irregular white

Fig. 27.65.

Fig. 27.66.

band diagonally across middle of wing and a small series of white spots near its apex. (See Fig. 27.66.)

[40.14 *Autochton* Huebner (2 spp.)]

40.15 *Achalarus* Scudder

Five species, two of which are strays in (3) s. TX. The following is Widespread:

A. lyciades (Geyer). Wingspan: 38–46 mm. Dark brown with hyline spots forming a broad band across center of front wing; margin of apex of each wing with small yellowish spots; hind wing with broad white marginal band ventrally. Larvae feed on legumes. (See Fig. 27.67.) (1) WIS, MI, NY, NH, IL, IN, OH, PA, NJ, MD, DE, DC; (2) s.e. US; (3) TX.

40.16 *Thorybes* Scudder

Seven widespread species in the U.S., the following of which is common:

T. bathyllus (Smith) (Southern Cloudy Wing). Wingspan: 30–40 mm. Dark brown; front wing with narrow central band with numerous hyaline spots; hyaline spots also near apex; apical margin of wings with small whitish spots. Larvae feed on legumes. (1) n.e. US; (2) s.e. US; (3) TX.

[40.17 *Cabares* Godman and Salvin (1 sp., *C. potrillo* (Lucas) (3) s. TX); 40.18 *Celaenorrhinus* Huebner (2 spp., strays in (3) s. TX); 40.19 *Dyscophellus* Godman and Salvin (1 sp., *D. euribates* (Stoll), a stray in

(3) s. TX); 40.20 *Spathilepia* Butler (1 sp., *S. clonius* (Cramer) (3) s. TX); 40.21 *Cogia* Butler (4 spp.); 40.22 *Nisoniades* Huebner (1 sp., *N. rubescens* Moeschler (3) s. TX); 40.23 *Pellicia* Herrich-Schaeffer (2 spp. (3) s. TX); 40.24 *Bolla* Mabille (2 spp. (3) s. TX); 40.25 *Staphylus* Godman and Salvin (3 spp.); 40.26 *Gorgythion* Godman and Salvin (1 sp., *G. begga* (Kirby) (3) s. TX); 40.27 *Sostrata* Godman and Salvin (1 sp., *S. bifasciata* (Ménétries) (3) s. TX); 40.28 *Carrhenes* Godman and Salvin (1 sp., *C. canescens* (Felder) (3) s. TX); 40.29 *Xenophanes* Godman and Salvin (1 sp., *X. tryxus* (Stoll) (3) s. TX); 40.30 *Systasea* Edwards (2 spp.); 40.31 *Achlyodes* Huebner (1 sp., *A. thraso* (Huebner) (3) s. TX); 40.32 *Grais* Godman and Salvin (1 sp., *G. stigmaticus* (Mabille) (3) s. TX, migrating to (5) KS); 40.33 *Timochares* Godman and Salvin (1 sp., *C. ruptifasciatus* (Ploetz)); 40.34 *Chiomara* Godman and Salvin (1 sp., *C. asychis* (Stoll)); 40.35 *Gesta* Evans (1 sp., *G. gesta* (Herrich-Schaeffer) (3) s. TX); 40.36 *Ephyriades* Huebner (1 sp., *E. brunnea* (Herrich-Schaeffer) (2) s. FL)]

40.37 *Erynnis* Schrank

Seventeen species, all but one widely distributed and difficult to distinguish. The following is common:

E. juvenalis (Fabricius) (Juvenal's Dusky Wing). Wingspan: ±40 mm. Blackish brown with mottlings and white, semitransparent dots. Larvae feed on leaves of oaks. (1) n.e. US; (2) s.e. US; (3) TX, NM; (5) WY, SD, IA, CO, KS, MO.

40.38 *Pyrgus* Huebner

Eight species, most of them western. The following are common:

P. communis Grote (Checkered Skipper). Wingspan: 20–32 mm. Unlike most skippers, this species is nearly white, marked with black. Larvae feed on species of Malvaceae. (See Fig. 27.68.) (1), (2), (3), (4), (5), generally distributed.

P. oileus (Linnaeus). (See Fig. 27.69 and A&J 201.) (2) s. FL, MS, AR: (3) e. TX.

40.39 *Heliopetes* Billberg

Five species, one of them a stray in (3) s. TX. The following is common:

H. ericetorum (Boisduval). Wingspan: ±32 mm. White, base of wings dusky; apical margins of wings marked with zigzag narrow band of black. Larvae on various species of Malvaceae. (See Fig. 27.70.) (3) s.w. US; (4) WA, OR, NV.

40.40 *Celotes* Godman and Salvin

Two species, one a stray in (3) s.w. TX, and the other common, as follows:

Fig. 27.67.

Fig. 27.68.

Fig. 27.69.

Fig. 27.71.

C. nessus (Edwards). Wingspan: 20–26 mm. Brownish; front wing with long, narrow, V-shaped dark markings projecting inward form margin. (See Fig. 27.71.) (2) LA; 93) s.w. US.

40.41 *Pholisora* Scudder

Five species, widely distributed throughout US, the following of which is common:

P. catullus (Fabricius) (Sooty-wing). Wingspan: 22–30 mm. Very dark with rows of fine white dots near outer margin of wing. Larvae feed on lamb's quarters, other Chenopodeaceae, and Amaranthaceae. (See Fig. 27.72) (1) n.e. NA: (2) VA, NC, SC, GA; (3) s.w. US; 94) s. BC, WA, OR, ID, NV; (5) WY, SD, NE, IA, CO, KS, MO.

Subfamily Heteropterinae

[40.42 *Carterocephalus* Lederer (1 sp., *C. palaemon* (Pallas)); 40.43 *Piruna* Evans (4 spp.)]

Subfamily Hesperiinae

[40.44 *Synapte* Mabille (2 spp., strays in (3) s. TX); 40.45 *Corticea* Evans (1 sp., *c. corticea* (Ploetz), a stray in (3) s. TX); 40.46 *Callimormus* Scudder (1 sp., *C. saturnus* (Herrich-Schaeffer), a stray in (3) s. TX); 40.47 *Vidius* Evans (1 sp., *V. perigenes* (Godman) (3) s. TX); 40.48 *Monca* Evans (1 sp., *M. tyrtaeus* (Ploetz) (3) s. TX); 40.49 *Nastra* Evans (3 spp.); 40.50 *Cymaenes* Scudder (2 spp.)]

40.51 *Lerema* Scudder

Two species, one a stray in (3) s. TX, and the other as follows:

L. accius (Smith) (Clouded Skipper). Wingspan: 26–36 mm. Dark brown or blackish with a few subapical spots on front wing. Larvae feed on grass. (1). n.e. US; (2) s.e. US; (3) TX.

[40.52 *Perichares* Schudder (1 sp., *P. philetes* (Gmelin), a stray in (3) s. TX); 40.53 *Rhinthon* Godman (1 sp., *R. osca* (Ploetz), a stray in (3) s.

TX); 40.54 *Decinea* Evans (1 sp., *D. percosius* (Godman) (3) s. TX); 40.55 *Conga* Evans (1 sp., *C. chydaea* (Butler), a stray in (3) s. TX)]

40.56 *Ancyloxypha* Felder

Two species, the following of which is widespread:

A. numitor (Fabricius) (Fiery Skipper). Wingspan: 20–26 mm. Varies from entirely black to nearly entirely orange with black markings. Larvae feed on grass. (1), (2), (3), (4), (5), throughout s. Canada and US.

[40.57 *Oarisma* Scudder (3 spp.); 40.58 *Copaeodes* Scudder (2 spp.); 40.59 *Adopaeoides* Godman (1 sp., *A. prittwitzi* (Ploetz), known only in (3) s.w. TX, extreme s. AZ); 40.60 *Thymelicus* Huebner (1 sp., *T. lineola* (Ochsenheimer), introduced in (1) n.e. NA; (4) s. BC)]

40.61 *Hylephila* Billberg

One species, as follows:

H. phyleus (Drury) (Least Skipper). Wingspan: 24–32 mm. Bright yellow-orange with deeply dentate borders on wings of male; females less yellow-orange. Larvae found on grass, including sugarcane. (1) IL, IN, OH, PA, NJ, CT; (2) s.e. US; (3) s.w. US; (5) CO, KS, MO.

[40.62 *Yvretta* Hemming (2 spp.); 40.63 *Pseudocopaeodes* Skinner and Williams (1 sp., *P. eunus* (Edwards) (3) CA: (4) NV); 40.64 *Stinga* Evans (1 sp., *S. morrisoni* (Edwards) (3) w. TX, NM, AZ; (5) CO)]

40.65 *Hesperia* Fabricius

Eighteen species, all but six widely distributed. The following may serve as examples:

H. sassacus Harris (Indian Skipper). Wingspan: ±30 mm. Bright orange with a broad, well-defined, slightly dentate dark border; male with black stigma on costal margin near apex of front wing. Larvae found on *Panicum* spp. and Crabgrass. (1) n.e. NA; (2) VA.

H. dacotae (Skinner). (See Fig. 27.73.) (5) SD, IA.

Fig. 27.70.

Fig. 27.72.

Fig. 27.73.

Fig. 27.74.

40.66 *Polites* Scudder

Ten species, all but two widespread and the following common:

P. coras (Cramer) (Peck's Skipper). Wingspan: 20–26 mm. Brown with orange markings on front wing; short bars on hind wing; underside of hind wing mostly orange. Larvae feed on grasses. (1), (2), (3), (4), (5), throughout all of U.S. except extreme southern portion.

P. themistocles (Latreille). Wingspan: 20–26 mm. Similar to the preceding but hind wings lack orange markings. Larvae found on *Panicum* spp. (1), (2), (3), (4), (5), throughout s. Canada and the U.S.

40.67 *Wallengrenia* Berg

Two species, as follows:

W. otho (Smith) (Broken Dash). Wingspan 24–32 mm. Brown, yellow-orange areas on upper surface of discal cell and along costal margin of male front wing; female with only a few small patches of yellow-orange on front wing. Larvae (casebearers) found on St. Augustine grass. (1) MD; (2) s.e. US; (3) TX.

W. egeremet (Scudder). Similar to the preceding, but darker and with some tawny coloration. Larvae (casebearers) found on *Panicum* spp. (1) n.e. NA; (2) s.e. US; 93) TX.

[40.68 *Pompeius* Evans (1 sp., *P. verna* Edwards (1) n.e. US; (2) s.e. US); 40.69 *Atalopedes* Scudder (1 sp., *A. campestris* (Boisduval) (2) s.e. US; (3) s.e. US); 40.70 *Atrytone* Scudder (2 spp.); 40.71 *Problema* Skinner and Williams (2 spp.)]

40.72 *Ochlodes* Scudder

Four species, all western, including the following:

O. sylvanoides (Boisduval). Wingspan: 20–28 mm. Reddish-orange wings; males with prominent stigma across front wing; females with more dark areas. Larvae feed on grass. (3) s.e. US; (4) Pacific n.w.; (5) MT, CO.

40.73 *Poanes* Scudder

Seven species, mostly eastern but one in (3) AZ. The following may serve as an example:

P. hobomok (Harris) (Hobomok Skipper). Wingspan: 25–34 mm. Varies from brown with white markings on front wing to predominately yellowish orange. Larvae feed on grass. (See Fig. 27.74.) (1) n.e.NA; (2) VA, NC, SC, GA; (5) MN.

40.74 *Paratrytone* Godman

One species, as follows:

P. melane (Edwards). Wingspan: 28–34 mm. Brown; front wing of male with orange spots, of female with several diffuse, hyline spots; hind wings brown with dusting of orange scales. (See A&J 200.) (3) s.e. US.

[40.75 *Choranthus* Scudder (2 spp., strays in (2) s. FL); 40.76 *Mellana* Hayward (2 spp., strays in (3) s. TX, s. AZ); 40.77 *Euphyes* Scudder (10 spp., widespread); 40.78 *Asbolis* Mabille (1 sp., *A. capucinus* (Lucas) (2) FL); 40.79 *Atrytonopsis* Godman (9 spp.)]

40.80 *Amblyscirtes* Scudder

Twenty-two species, composing the largest genus of this family in the U.S. and Canada. Difficult to distinguish, most of them are found in (3) s.w. US, but a few range north to (2) VA and (5) MO. The following is the most widely distributed:

A. vialis (Edwards). Wingspan: 22–26 mm. All brown except for slight white stigma on front wings near apex and broad, brownish-blue margins on their ventral side. Adults fly along stream banks and woody ravines and in open areas in forests. Larvae feed on various grasses. (1), (2), (3), (4), (5), generally distributed.

40.81 *Lerodea* Scudder

Three species, the following a minor pest:

L. eufala (Edwards) (Rice Leaf Roller). Wingspan: 22–28 mm. Gray-brown with three to five white hyaline spots on front wings. Larvae found on Johnson grass and sorghum in the U.S. (a pest of sugarcane in Cuba). (2). s.e. US; (3) s.w. US.

[40.82 *Oligoria* Scudder (1 sp., *O. maculata* (Edwards) (2) FL, GA, AL, MS, LA; 93) TX)]

40.83 *Calpodes* Huebner

One species, as follows:

C. ethlius (Stoll) (Large Canna Leaf Roller). Wingspan: 44–56 mm. Brown with white spots on all wings. Larvae feed on canna; sometimes a pest. (1) a stray to NY; (2) s.e. US: (5) a stray to MO.

[40.84 *Panoquina* Hemming (7 spp.); 40.85 *Nyctelius* Hayward (1 sp., *N. nyctelius* (Latreille) (3) TX, s. CA); 40.86 *Thespieus* Godman (1 sp., *T. macareus* (Herrich-Schaeffer), a stray in (3) s. TX)]

Fig. 27.75.

Fig. 27.76.

Subfamily Megathyminae (Giant Skippers)

[=Megathymidae of many authors]

The antennae of this group clubbed but usually not hooked. Since all larvae feed on Agavaceae, most species are restricted to arid southwestern regions. Some occur in southeastern parts of the U.S., however, and one, *M. yuccae*, extends north.

Tribe Aegialini

40.87 *Agathymus* Freeman

Twenty species, all of them large, with wingspans up to 90 mm. All larvae feed on species of *Agave*. The following may serve as an example:

A. alliae (Stallings and Turner). (See Fig. 27.75.) (3) CA, AZ; (4) WA, NV, UT.

Tribe Megathymini

40.88 *Megathymus* Scudder

Seven species, the most common being the following:

M. yuccae (Boisduval and LeConte) (Gusanos de Maguey; Maguey Worm). Wingspan: ±70 mm. Dark brown; front wings with quandrangular yellow spots and hind wings with yellow to orange marginal bond. Larvae feed on yucca. This is the species found as larvae in bottles of tequilla; they are also deep fried and eaten as hors d'oeuvres. (See Fig. 27.76.) (2) s.e. US; (3) s.w. US; (5) ND, SD, MT, NE, IO, MO.

40.89 *Stallingsia* Freeman

One species, as follows:

S. maculosus (Freeman). Wingspan: 45–50 mm. Brown with marginal and submarginal rows of orange spots. Larvae feed on *Manfreda maculosa*. (3) s. TX.

Superfamily PAPILIONOIDEA (Butterflies)

The butterflies are the best known of the Lepidoptera and probably of all insects. They are not only attractive, they also do interesting things. For example, they fly in the daytime and show a certain amount of curiosity about the people who are out to collect them, as indicated by their habit of flying just out of the net's reach time and time again. Some click their wings to attract attention, only to give the would-be collector a merry chase—a chase that ends when they disappear behind a camouflage of barklike coloration. Some even form an interesting triad with ants and lupines [see *Celastrina* spp. (43.41) and others].

Adults usually feed on nectar of a great variety of plants, but they also visit dung, carrion, and decaying fruit; many are often seen clustered around mud puddles sucking water, and probably salts, from the muddy soil. Some probably feed on pollen by ejecting a fluid into the anthers and then sucking up the liquid-pollen mixture with their proboscis. Adults of several species congregate, apparently for mutual protection. Among their various behaviorial patterns is a mating behavior that is often distinctive for each species. For example, some males seemingly stake out a territory and patrol that area looking for females of their own species. Others remain on a single perch and dart out at passing butterflies in search of a mate. The behavior of butterflies, in fact, has not been extensively reported and deserves more study.

Larvae of the majority of species are host specific, although some feed on a variety of plants. Adults usually select closely related genera of plant families. It is known from the combined work of entomologists and botanists that butterflies apparently evolved as the flowering plants evolved. At the same time, many plants generated various mechanisms to prevent larvae from feeding and are therefore devoid of butterfly pests. Those with tough leaves or heavy spines are usually protected. Others contain resins or similar substances, or even poisonous chemicals, that make them unpalatable.

Migration of insects has not been studied in the depth it deserves. Insects of many groups are known to migrate, but the most noted examples are found among the butterflies. The principle migratory species include the famous Monarch butterfly, *Danaus plexippus* (49.1). This species has attracted the attention of many entomologists. Over many years they have marked, released, and recovered individual butterflies in various parts of the continent to learn about their flight patterns. During their migrations, butterflies have the habit of congregating in trees in large numbers to "sleep." Some of these trees are used year after year, making them famous as "butterfly trees." When marked specimens are found in these trees, it is possible to learn where they came from. Only recently, however, did entomologists discover the location of the final winter resting

grounds: in Mexico. In the spring, the adults migrate once again, flying north and laying eggs as they go. Two or three generations, each lasting from four to six weeks, are produced, the old adults dying off and the young taking over. In the fall, it is the young replacements that migrate south, flying entirely by instinct. A few other species of butterflies [for example, the Snout Butterfly, *Libytheana bachmannii* (45.1)]migrate, but few as precisely as the Monarch.

The following resumé of the butterflies of North America north of Mexico includes the usual listing of all genera, but, in addition, all *established* species are listed. This compact checklist will enable the users of this book to determine what species may be expected to breed in various localities in each state. As a result, one may easily search for local species and be on the lookout for new records, new host plant data, and information on migration. Although a considerable number of books are now available that help identify butterfly species, one should remember that the color patterns of many species vary considerably, particularly in the family Pieridae. Before a positive identification can be made, the technical literature must be consulted, and usually the aid of specialists is necessary as well. Before publishing data on collected specimens, even informally, such identification is essential. There are many subspecies of butterflies, and the exact limit of their distribution is often uncertain. Since butterflies are still a rapidly evolving group, the boundaries between subspecies, and often species as well, are vague. As a result, synonyms have proliferated, and many misidentifications have not only been made but the data published. Amateurs should be aware of this fact and take extreme care in making identifications. They should note in particular that even though the illustrations for this section are of accurately identified specimens, each represents only one specimen selected from a series; only with a long series to study can one be certain of the identification of a single specimen.

This superfamily is composed of eight currently recognized families. Sometimes fewer are recognized, since some of these are treated as subfamilies. This list of families, genera, and species follows the Miller and Brown (1981) checklist with one exception; Heliconiinae are treated as a subfamily of Nymphalidae (46) instead being given full family status.

41. PAPILIONIDAE
(Swallowtail Butterfly Family and Allies)

Most species of this family have long "tails" on the posterior of the hind wings, but not all. Not all species of butterflies with "tails" are swallowtails (see various Hesperiidae), but there is little difficulty in recognizing the large and colorful members of this group. The larvae have fleshy horns, the *osmeterium*, which secrete malodorous substances to ward off predators; these may be withdrawn at will. Two subfamilies, eight genera, and 35 species comprise the family as represented in the U.S. and Canada, with a great number of subspecies. About half of the latter may be considered rare because of their restricted distribution or because they are strays from Mexico or the West Indies.

Subfamily Parnassiinae
Tribe Parnassiini

There is only one tribe and one genus in this subfamily in the U.S. and Canada. The species of these "tailless" papilionids

Fig. 27.77.

recorded here are invasions from Asia; many species occur in Europe as well as Asia. Adults are of moderate size and so thinly scaled that their wings are more or less translucent. During mating, the male deposits on the abdomen of the female a waxy secretion, called the *sphragis*, that prevents her from mating again. Since the sphragis is distinctive in size and shape, it is often used for identification of the species. The many subspecies and geographic variations of the family make an interesting study. The ground color is white, sometimes suffused with gray, and for all the variations in their markings, most species bear two red or yellowish spots on each hindwing.

41.1 *Parnassius* Latreille

Three species, as follows:

P. eversmanni Ménétries. (4) AK, n. BC; (5) KE, MC, NT, YK.

P. clodius Ménétries. (3) CA; (4) AK, BC, WA, OR, UT; (5) n. MT.

P. phoebus (Fabricius) (Parnassian Butterfly). Wingspan: 60–65 mm. Color as described for the genus; antennae with alternately black and white segments, particularly noticeable at base. Adults are found in the U.S. at high altitudes. Larvae feed on *Sedium* spp. (See Fig. 27.77 and A&J after 77.) (3) n. CA, n. AZ, n. NM; (4) Pacific n.w.; (5) YK.

Subfamily Papilioninae
Tribe Troidini
41.2 *Parides* Huebner

One species, as follows:

P. eurimedes (Stoll). (3) a stray in s. TX.

41.3 *Battus* Scopoli

Three species, as follows:

B. philenor (Linnaeus) (Pipevine Swallowtail). Wingspan: ±100 mm. Male with row of bright spots near margin of hind wing; female with row of distinct spots on each front wing corresponding to those of hind wing. Inner margins of male's hind wings are folded over and contain scales that give off a faint odor, presumably for attracting females. Larvae feed on

Fig. 27.78.

Dutchman's pipe, wild ginger, and other plants. (See Fig. 27.78.) (1) n.e. US; (2) s.e. US; (3) TX, OK, NM, AZ; (5) NE, IA, MO.

 B. polydamas (Linnaeus). (2) s. FL; (3) s. TX.

 B. devilliers (Godart). (2) s. FL.

Tribe Leptocircini

41.4 *Eurytides* Huebner

[=*Graphium* of authors]

Three species, as follows:

 E. marcellus (Cramer) (Zebra Swallowtail). Wingspan: 60–75 mm. Easily recognized because of its long, slender tails (nearly twice as long as those of other swallowtails); black and white striped with red spot and two blue spots on hind wing near tail. Larvae feed on papaw. (See Fig. 27.79.) (1) n.e. NA; (2) s.e. US; (5) NM.

 E. philolaus (Boisduval). (3) a stray in s. TX.

 E. celadon (Lucas). (2) a stray in s. FL.

Fig. 27.79.

Tribe Papilionini

41.5 *Papilio* Linnaeus

Ten species, as follows:

 P. polyxenes Fabricius (Black Swallowtail; Parselyworm; Celeryworm). Wingspan: 90 mm. Black; male with yellow band across middle, female without. Larvae feed on Umbelliferae and Rutaceae and are sometimes a pest on celery and parsley. (See Fig. 27.80.) (1) n.e. US; (2) s.e. US; (3) AZ, NM, OK, TX; (5) MT, ND, MN, WT, SD, NE, IA, CO, KS, MO.

 P. joanae Heitzman. (5) MO.

 P. rudkini F. and R. Chermock. (3) s. CA, w. AZ (desert region).

 P. kahli F. and R. Chermock. (5) MB.

 P. brevicauda Saunders. (1) s.e. Canada.

 P. bairdii Edwards. (3) s. CA, n. AZ, n. NM; (4) NV, UT; (5) w. SD, WY, w. NE.

 P. oregonius Edwards. (4) s. BC, e. WA, e. OR, ID; (5) s. AB, w. MT, w. ND.

 P. machaon Linnaeus. (Old World Swallowtail). Wingspan: 80–85 mm. Hind wing with dark area along inner margin not extending into discal cell area and tails only two or three times as long as wide; basic color that of Tiger Swallowtail, yellow with black markings. Larval food unknown in NA, but in Europe reported to be Compositae. Rare. (See A&J 203.) (1) n.e. Canada; (4) AK, AI; (5) n. Central Canada.

 P. zelicaon Lucas (Anise Swallowtail). Wingspan: 70 mm. Similar to Black Swallowtail but with more extensive yellow, especially on hind wings. Larvae found on Umbelliferae and Rutaceae. (3) CA; (4) Pacific n.w.; (5) AB, MT, WY, CO.

 P. indra Reakirt. (3) CA, n. AZ, n.w. NM; (4) WA, OR, s.e. UT; (5) MT, SD, c. CO.

41.6 *Heraclides* Huebner

[=*Papilio* of authors]

Seven species, as follows:

 H. thoas (Linnaeus). (3) s. TX, rarely strays n.

Fig. 27.80.

H. cresphontes (Cramer) (Orange-dog; Giant Swallowtail). Wingspan: ±110 mm. Black above with two broad yellow bands that seem to cross; more yellow below than above. Larvae feed on citrus (sometimes as a pest), prickly ash, rue, and others. (See Fig. 27.81 and A&J 204.) (1) n.e. US; (2) s.e. US; (3) TX, NM, AZ.

H. aristodemus (Esper). (Subspecies *H. a ponceanus* Schaus known as Schaus Swallowtail) (2) s. FL.

H. andraemon Huebner (Subspecies *bonhotei* Sharp known as Bahaman Swallowtail) (2) a stray in s. FL.

H. ornythion (Boisduval). (3) a stray in s. TX, s. AZ.

H. astyalus (Godart). (3) a stray in (3) s. TX, s. TX.

H. androgeus (Cramer). (2) introduced into s. FL.

41.7 *Pterourus* Scopoli

[=*Papilio* of authors]

Seven species, as follows:

P. glaucus (Linnaeus) (Eastern Tiger Swallowtail). Wingspan: 70–120 mm. Normal color of this, perhaps our most common swallowtail, is yellow with black markings; apex of hind wings with blue spots from inner margin to tails, or in some populations, across entire apex. No other tailed swallowtail has as much yellow at base of front wing, except for the following (see below for means of distinction). A dark variety is known that lacks yellow except for a narrow row of spots near outer margin of wings. The larvae feed on *Prunus* spp., *Betula* spp., *Sorbus* sp., *Populus* spp., *Salix* spp., *Liriodendron* sp., *Fraxinus* sp., *Tilia* sp., *Malus* sp., *Acer* spp., and *Magnolia* sp. (See Fig. 27.82 and A&J 205.) (1) n.e. NA; (2) s.e. US; (3) e. TX; (4) AK, AI; (5) SK, MB, e. MT, WY, SD, NE, IA, CO, KS, MO.

P. rutulus (Lucas) (Western Tiger Swallowtail). Wingspan: 90–110 mm. Very similar to the preceding except that hind wings lack marginal orange spots ventrally. Larvae feed on willow, alder, sycamore, and aspen. Prefers canyon bottoms. (See A&J 206.) (3) CA, AX, NM; (4) Pacific n.w.; (5) AB, MT, WY, CO.

P. multicaudata (Kirby) (Twin-tailed Tiger Swallowtail). Wingspan: ±100 mm. Similar to the preceding, but often larger,

Fig. 27.82.

with reduced black; hind wings each have two tails. Larvae feed on choke-cherry, hop-tree, ash, and *Ligustrum* spp. (3) CA, w. TX; (4) Pacific n.w.; (5) MT, w. NE, CO.

P. eurymedon (Lucas) (White Tiger Swallowtail). Wingspan: 75–90 mm. Wings black with white background but otherwise similar to the preceding; tails narrow, usually entirely black or very narrowly white on inner margin. The only other white swallowtail is *Eurytides marcellus* (Zebra Swallowtail), which has very long tails with white margins on both edges. Larvae feed on *Ceanothus* spp. and Holly-leaved Cherry. (See A&J 207.) (3) CA, NM; (4) BC, WA, OR; (5) MT, WY, CO.

P. pilumnus (Boisduval). (3) s. AZ, s. TX.

P. troilus (Linnaeus) (Spicebush Swallowtail). Wingspan: ±100 mm. Dorsally black or very dark blue with 2 few yellow dots; red spot at base of hind wings; distal half of hind wings greenish; hind wings with two rows of red spots separated by greenish blue ventrally. Larvae feed on spicebush, sassafras, sweet bay, and prickly ash. (See Fig. 27.83.) (1) n.e. NA; (2) s.e. US; (3) e. TX; (5) e. KS, MO.

P. palamedes (Drury). Wingspan: ±100 mm. Similar to *Papilio polyxenes*, with inner row of yellow spots near front

Fig. 27.81.

Fig. 27.83.

Fig. 27.84.

Fig. 27.85.

between two rows on front wings. Larvae feed on red bay, magnolia, and sassafras. (1) NJ; (2) s.e. US; (5) MO.

41.8 *Priamides* Huebner

[=*Papilio* of authors]

One species, as follows:

P. anchisiades (Esper). (3) s.e. TX; (5) strays to KS.

42. PIERIDAE (Sulphur, White, and Orange-tip Butterfly Family)

This family of medium-sized butterflies is easily recognized by its white, orange, or yellow wings, sometimes marked with black or with orange and black but rarely entirely orange. Of the 63 species assigned to 21 genera reported in the U.S. and Canada, at least 20 species are strays.

Subfamily Pierinae

Tribe Pierini

42.1 *Catasticta* Butler

One species, as follows:

C. nimbice (Boisduval). (3) s. TX.

42.2 *Neophasia* Behr

Two species, as follows. Larvae feed on conifers.

N. menapia C. and R. Felder (Pine Butterfly). Wingspan: ±50 mm. Easily recognized by the white-dotted black tips on white front wings and narrow black costal stripe hooked toward apex; hind wings white in male, with submarginal band in female; female markings brownish; wing veins slightly darkened. (See Fig. 27.84.) (3) CA, AZ, NM; (4) BC, WA, OR, ID, NV, UT; (5) AB, SD, NE, MN.

N. terlootii Behr. (3) AZ.

42.3 *Appias* Huebner

One species, as follows:

A. drusilla (Cramer). (1) strays to NY; (2) s. FL, strays n.; (3) s. TX; (5) strays to CO, NE.

42.4 *Pontia* Fabricius

[=*Pieris* of authors]

Four species, as follows:

P. beckerii (Edwards). (3) CA; (4) BC, WA, OR, ID, NV, UT; (5) WY, CO.

P. sisymbrii (Boisduval). (3) CA, AZ, NM; (4) BC, WA, OR, ID, NV, UT; (5) YK, AB, SK, MB, ND, SD, WY, CO.

P. protodice (Boisduval and LeConte) (Southern Cabbageworm). Wingspan: ±50 mm. White with black markings; veins on underside of female's wings, especially hind ones, are tinged with greenish yellow. Larvae found on crucifers; sometimes a pest. (See Fig. 27.85.) (1), (2), (3), (4), OR; (5).

P. occidentalis (Reakirt). (3) CA, AZ, NM; (4), (5) AB, MB, MT, WY, CO.

42.5 *Artogeia* Verity

Three species, as follows:

A. napi (Linnaeus) (Mustard White). Wingspan: ±50 mm. White with black markings. Larvae on many crucifers (See Fig. 27.86.) (1), (2), (4), (5), generally distributed.

A. virginiensis (Edwards). (1) n.e. US; (2) KY, WV, VA, TN, NC, GA; (5) MN.

Fig. 27.86.

Fig. 27.87.

Fig. 27.89.

A. rapae (Linnaeus) (Imported Cabbageworm; Cabbage Butterfly). Wingspan: ±30 mm. White with black front tips and two or three black spots beyond discal cell. Larvae feed on crucifers, particularly cabbage (a common pest throughout its range). (See Fig. 27.87.) Introduced. (1) n.e. NA; (2) KY, WV, VA, TN, NC, n. GA; (5) MN.

42.6 *Ascia* Scopoli

One species, as follows:

A. monuste (Linnaeus). Wingspan: ±50 mm. Male whitish above except for narrow brown outer margin on front wings; female with broad brown outer margin on front wings, as well as narrow brown outer margin on hind wings above. Larvae feed on crucifers. (See Fig. 27.88.) (2) GA, FL, LA; (3) s.c. TX.

42.7 *Ganyra* Billberg

One species, as follows:

G. josephina (Godart). (3) s. TX, stray in s. AZ.

Subfamily Anthocharinae

Tribe Anthocharini

42.8 *Euchloe* Huebner

Four species, as follows:

E. ausonides (Lucas). (1) ON; (3) CA, n. NM; (4) Pacific n.w.; (5) YT, AB, SK, MD.

Fig. 27.88.

E. creusa (Doubleday). (4) AK, BC; (5) YK, NT.

E. hyantis (Edwards). (3) CA, AZ, NM; (4) BC, OR, ID, NV, UT; (5) w. WY, w. CO.

E. olympia (Edwards). (See Fig. 27.89.) (1) n.e. US; (2) KY, WV; (3) n. TX; (5) MT, ND, MN, e. WY, e. CO, KS, IA, NE, MO.

42.9 *Anthocharis* Boisduval, Rambur, and Graslin

Four species, as follows:

A. cethura C. and R. Felder. (3) s. CA, w. AZ; (4) s. NV.

A. pima Edwards. (3) s. AZ; (4) s. NV.

A. dammersi Comstock. (3) s. CA.

A. sara Lucas (Orange-tip). Wingspan: 45–50 mm. Both yellow and white forms are known; front wing tips reddish orange but males of white forms may lack these. Larvae found on various crucifers. (See Fig. 27.90 and A&J 214.) (3) CA, AZ, NM; (4) AK, BC, OR, UT; (5) ID, WY, CO.

42.10 *Falcapica* Klots

Two species, as follows:

F. midea (Huebner) (Falcate Orange-tip). Wingspan: 35–40 mm. White; front wings with black wing tips mottled with white; hind wing white to greenish or brownish yellow mottled with white. Larvae found on various crucifers. (See Fig. 27.91.) (1) NY, MA, IL, IN, OH, PA, NJ, MD; (2) KY, WV, VA, TN, NC, AR, LA, MS, AL, GA; (3) TX; (5) KS.

F. lanceolata (Lucas). (3) CA; (4) s. OR, NV.

Fig. 27.90.

Fig. 27.91.

Subfamily Coliadinae
Tribe Coliadini
42.11 *Colias* Fabricius

Sixteen species. The larvae food of *C. philodice* through *C. nastes* are legume feeders; *C. scudderi* and *C. gigantea* are willow feeders; the remainder are health feeders.

C. philodice Godart (Clouded Sulphur). Wingspan: ±50 mm. Yellow with black margins and black spot on front wing, orange spot on hind wing; some white forms. Adults frequent mud puddles. (See Fig. 27.92 and A&J 27.92.) (1) n.e. NA; (2) s.e. US (except FL); (3) s.w. US (nondesert regions); (4) Pacific n.w. (rare); (5) n. Central States.

C. eurytheme Boisduval (Alfalfa Caterpillar). Wingspan: ±60 mm. Very similar to the preceding, usually with broader marginal markings, and probably hybridizes with it. Usually recognizable by strong orange tint of the yellow on upper side and marginal markings. Larvae found on herbaceous legumes, particularly alfalfa, where it is sometimes a pest. (Fig. 27.93 & A&J 209.) (1), (2), (3), (4), (5), generally distributed.

C. harfordii Edwards. (3) s. CA.

C. occidentalis Scudder. (3) n. CA; (4) Pacific n.w.

C. alexandra Edwards. (3) AZ, NM; (4) BC, OR, UT, ID; (5) MT, WY, NE, ND, AB, SK, MB, NT, SD, CO.

C. meadii Edwards. (See Fig. 27.94.) (3) n. NM; (4) BC, UT; (5) WY, AB.

Fig. 27.93.

C. hecla Lefèbvre. (1) GR; (4) AK; (5) KE, MC, NT, YK.

C. boothii Curtis. (5) NT.

C. thula Hovanitz. (4) AK.

C. nastes Boisduval. (4) AK, BC; (5) KE, MC, NT, YK.

C. scudderi Reakirt. Larvae on willow. (3) NM; (4) UT; (5) CO, WY.

C. gigantea Strecker. Larvae on willow. (4) AK, BC, ID; (5) YK, MT, WY.

C. pelidne Boisduval and LeConte. Larvae on heath. (1) LB, NF, PQ; (4) BC, ID; (5) AB, MT, WY.

C. interior Scudder. Larvae on heath. (See Fig. 27.95 for male; Fig. 27.96 for female.) (1) PQ, LB, NF, PE; (4) BC, OR, WA; (5) AB, SK, MD, MT.

C. palaeno (Linnaeus). Larvae on heath. (1) n. LB; (4) AK, BC; (5) YK, AB, MT.

C. behrii Edwards. Larvae on heath. (1) LB, NY; (4) AK, BC; (5) YK, AB, MB, SK.

42.12 *Zerene* Huebner

Two species, as follows:

Z. eurydice (Boisduval) (California Dogface). Wingspan: ±60 mm. Easily recognized by the "dogface" on front wings; front wings with pink or rose at base. Larvae feed on false indigo. (3) CA, AZ.

Fig. 27.92.

Fig. 27.94.

Fig. 27.95.

Fig. 27.97.

Z. cesonia (Stoll) (Dogface). Wingspan: 40–60 mm. Similar to the preceding but without rose at base of front wings. Larvae feed on false indigo and other herbaceous legumes. (See Fig. 27.97.) (1) WI, MI, ON, NY, PA, MD; (2) s.e. US; (3) s.w. US; (5) WY, ND, MT, IA, MN. (A&J 210). (Fig. 27.97).

42.13 *Anteos* Huebner

Two species, as follows.

A. clorinde (Godart) (Clorinde). Wingspan: 80–90 mm. White with irregular yellow spots in middle of margin of front wing. Larvae feed on *Cassia spectabilis*. (See Fig. 27.98 and A&J 211.) (3) AZ, TX; (5) CO, KS. Rare.

A. maerula (Fabricius). Similar to the preceding, but entirely yellow. (See Fig. 27.99.) (2) a stray in FL; (3) a stray in TX; (5) strays as far n. as NE. Rare.

42.14 *Phoebis* Huebner

Five species, as follows:

P. sennae (Linnaeus) (Cloudless Sulphur). Wingspan: ±60 mm. Male entirely yellow above; female with row of dark brown spots along outer margin of front wings and somewhat similar spot in their center. Larvae feed on *Cassia* spp. and other legumes. (See Fig. 27.100 for female.) (2) s.e. US; (3) s.w. US; (5) strays to CO.

Fig. 27.98.

P. philea (Johansson) (Orange Barred Sulphur). Wingspan: 65–70 mm. Yellow with irregular orange spot on anterior middle of front wing; hind wings with orange apical margins gradually merging with yellow basally. Larvae feed on *Cassia* spp. (See A&J 212.) (2) FL, strays to VA, AL; (3) strays to TX; (5) strays to CO.

P. argante (Fabricius). (3) a stray in s. TX.

Fig. 27.96.

Fig. 27.99.

Fig. 27.100.

Fig. 27.101.

P. agarithe (Boisduval). (2) s. FL; (3) a strays in TX, AZ; (5) strays to KS.

P. neocypris (Huebner) (Giant Tailed Sulphur). Wingspan: ±55 mm. Yellow; hind wings with short, broad tails. Migrates in large numbers. (3) a stray in s. Ax, s. TX.

42.15 *Aphrissa* Buetler

One species, as follows:

A. statira (Cramer). (2) a stray in s. FL.

42.16 *Kricogonia* Reakirt

One species, as follows:

K. lyside (Godart) [=*K. castalia* of authors, not Fabricus]. (2) a stray in s. FL; (3) s. AZ, s. TX; (5) strays to CO, KS, NE.

42.17 *Eurema* Huebner

Four species, as follows:

E. daira (Godart). (2) NC, SC, GA, FL, MS, AR, LA, strays to VA; (3) e. TX.

E. boisduvaliana (C. and R. Felder). (2) a stray in s. FL; (3) s. TX, a stray in s. AZ.

E. mexicana (Boisduval). (1) a stray in ON, MI; (2) a stray in LA; (3) CA, AZ, OK; (5) CO, strays to WY, ND, MN.

E. salome (C. and R. Felder). (3) a stray in s. AZ, s. TX.

42.18 *Pyrisitia* Butler

Six species, as follows:

P. proterpia (Fabricius). (3) s. AZ, s. TX.

P. lisa (Boisduval and LeConte) (Little Sulphur). Wingspan: 30–35 mm. Yellow with extensive black tip on front wing; narrow marginal black band on hind wing, in female sometimes reduced to a spot; white forms rarely found. Larvae feed on various legumes, particularly *Cassia* spp. (See Fig. 27.101.) (1) n.e. NA; (2) s.e. US; (3) TX; (5) CO.

P. chamberlaini (Butler). (2) s. FL?; (3) s. AZ, s. TX.

P. messalina (Fabricius). (2) s. FL.

P. nise (Cramer). (3) s. AZ.

P. dina (Poey). (2) a stray in s. FL; (3) a stray in s. AZ, s. TX.

42.19 *Abaeis* Huebner

One species, as follows:

A. nicippe (Cramer) (Sleepy Orange). Wingspan: 40–50 mm. Orange with black wing margins resembling a sulphur (*Colias* spp.), but much smaller. This is one of many similarly colored orange species, but black margin of wing is relatively narrow, even throughout, and complete; front wing with small black spot near margin, midway. (See Fig. 27.102 and A&J 213.) (1) n.e. US; (2) s.e. US; (3) s.w. US; (5) CO, NE.

42.20 *Nathalis* Boisduval

One species, as follows:

N. iole Boisduval (Dainty Sulphur). Wingspan: 22–30 mm. Yellow with prominent black tips and black extending across center of front wing and anterior part of hind wing. Larvae feed on fetid marigold, garden marigold, chickweed, sneezeweed, and burr marigold. (See Fig. 27.103.) (1) n.e. US; (2) s.e. US; (3) s.w. US; (5) ND, MN, IA.

Subfamily Dismorphiinae
42.21 *Enantia* Huebner

One species, as follows:

E. melite (Johansson). (3) a stray in s. TX.

Fig. 27.102.

Fig. 27.103.

Fig. 27.104.

43. LYCAENIDAE
(Hairstreak, Copper, and Blue Butterfly Family)

Members of this family are rather small, usually attractively marked with irridescent copper or blue colored scales, and often have short, narrow, curved tails on the hind wings. Fragile and difficult to handle without breaking they may be recognized as Lycaenidae by the notch in the eye margin near the antennae. There are 52 genera with 136 species and a large number of subspecies recorded in the U.S. and Canada. Many subspecies have such restricted distribution that they are nearing extinction; some of them are actually known to be extinct although specimens exist in collections. Warning: Some Lycaenidae are protected by federal regulations. Before collecting, find out which species are endangered.

Subfamily Miletinae
Tribe Spalgini
43.1 *Feniseca* Grote

One species, as follows:

F. tarquinius (Fabricius) (The Harvester). Wingspan: 30–35 mm. Sometimes placed in a separate family—Liphyridae—this species can be recognized by the extent of orange on front and hind wings with large circles within it and the dark margins. Larvae are carnivorous, feeding on Wooly Aphids on older ash, beech, currant, Witch Hazel, hawthorn, maple, and elm. (Fig. 27.104). (1) n.e. US; (2) s.e. US; (3) e. TX.

Subfamily Lycaeninae
43.2 *Tharsalea* Scudder

One species, as follows:

T. arota (Boisduval). (3) CA, AZ, NM; (4) s. OR, NV, UT; (5) MT, WY, CO.

43.3 *Lycaena* Fabricius

Two species, as follows:

L. phlaeas (Linnaeus) (American Copper). Wingspan: ±24 mm. Front wings orange with black dots and dark markings; hind wing dark with submarginal band of orange; front wings pink ventrally; hind wings gray or brownish beneath; wings with black dots beneath. Larvae feed on sheep sorrel and other *Rumex* spp. (See Fig. 27.105.) (1) n.e. US; (2) s.e. US; (3) CA; (4) OR; (4) n. Central States.

L. cupreus (Edwards). (3) n. CA; (4) OR, NV, UT; (5) WY.

43.4 *Gaeides* Scudder

Three species, as follows:

G. xanthoides (Boisduval). (1) n.w. IL; (3) CA; (4) s. OR; (5) n. Central States.

G. editha (Mead). (3) CA; (4) Pacific n.w.; (5) MT, WY, CO.

G. gorgon (Boisduval) (Smartweed Cooper). Wingspan: 25–32 mm. Males are bright coppery purple; hind wings of both sexes with series of submarginal bright orange spots or crescents on ventral side. Larvae feed on species of smartweed (Polygonaceae). (See A&J 219.) (3) CA; (4) OR. (A&J 219).

43.5 *Hyllolycaena* Miller and Brown

One species, as follows:

H. hyllus (Cramer) (Bronze Copper). Wingspan: ±35 mm. Female reddish brown dorsally; hind wing with orange band near margin; male differs by having front wing almost as dark as base of hind wing and with a violet reflection; underside of front wing light orange and of hind wing white; both wings with black dots; hind wing with orange. Larvae feed on yellow dock. (1) n.e. US; (2) stray to FL; (5) AB, SK, MB, MT, ND, MN, WY, SD, NE, IA, CO, KS, MO.

43.6 *Chalceria* Scudder

Three species, as follows:

C. rubidus (Behr) (Meadow Copper). Wingspan: 28–32 mm. Males metallic copper dorsally, pale cream ventrally; females either orange or yellow in discal portion of each wing dorsally; submarginal area or wing orange. Adults visit flowers of composites at edge of mountain meadows and along streams, especially in sagebush regions. Larvae feed on dock. (See A&J

Fig. 27.105.

220.) (3) CA, AZ; (4) BC, WA, OR, ID; (5) MT, WY, CO, ND, SD, NE.

C. ferrisi (Johnson and Balogh). (3) s. AZ.

C. heteronea (Boisduval). (3) CA, AZ; (4) s. BC, ID, NV, UT; (5) MT, WY, CO.

43.7 *Epidemia* Scudder

Five species, as follows:

E. epixanthe (Boisduval and LeConte). (1) n.e. NA.

E. dorcas (Kirby). (See Fig 27.106.) (1) n.e. NA; (4) Pacific n.w.; (5) n. Central States.

E. helloides (Boisduval) (Purplish Copper). Wingspan: 28–32 mm. Males metallic purple dorsally and hind wings with orange submarginal band; females yellow above, also with orange submarginal band. Larvae feed on dock, knotweed, baby's breath, and other plants. (See A&J 221.) (1) n.e. NA; (3) CA, n. NM; (4) Pacific n.w.; (5) n. Central States.

E. nivalis (Boisduval). (3) CA; (4) Pacific n.w.; (5) MT, WY, CO.

E. mariposa (Reakirt). (3) n. CA; (4) Pacific n.w.; (5) WY, CO.

43.8 *Hermelycaena* Miller and Brown

H. hermes (Edwards). (3) s. CA.

Subfamily Theclinae
Tribe Theclini
43.9 *Hypaurotis* Scudder

One species, as follows:

H. crysalus (Edwards). (3) AZ, NM; (4) e. VT; (5) CO.

43.10 *Habrodais* Scudder

One species, as follows:

H. grunus (Boisduval). (3) s. CA; (4) s. VN.

Tribe Eumaeini
43.11 *Eumaeus* Huebner

Two species, as follows:

E. atala (Poey). (2) s. FL.

E. minijas (Huebner). (3) s. TX.

Fig. 27.106.

43.12 *Atlides* Huebner

One species, as follows:

A. halesus (Cramer) (Great Blue Hairstreak). Wingspan: 37–50 mm. Iridescent bluish green above on thorax and basal half of wings; below, front wings nearly plain except for small patch of blue; all wings with crimson spot near base; three rows of green spots on each hind wing. Larvae feed on mistletoe. (See A&J 217.) (1) PA, NJ; (2) s.e. US; (3) s.w. US; (4) OR.

43.13 *Chlorostrymon* Clench

Three species, as follows:

C. maesites (Herrich-Schaeffer) (Maesites Hairstreak). Wingspan: 18–20 mm. Brilliant purplish blue above, brown ventrally; hind wing below with apical patch extending three-fourths the distance to front margin; females dark brown above, with base of front wing and most hind wing dark blue, dark green ventrally. Larval habitat unknown. (See A&J 215.) (2) s. FL.

C. telea (Hewitson). (3) s. TX.

C. simaethis (Drury). (3) s. CA, s. TX.

43.14 *Phaeostrymon* Clench

One species, as follows:

P. alcestis (Edwards). (3) OK, TX; (5) KS.

43.15 *Harkenclenus* dos Passos

One species, as follows:

H. titus (Fabricius) (Coral Hairstreak). Wingspan: ±30 mm. Dark brown with row of coral-red spots on underside of hind wings. Larvae feed on plum and wild cherry; attended by ants. (1) n.e. NA; (2) KY, WV, VA, TN, NC, AR, SC, GA; (3) n. CA, n. TX; (4) BC, WA, OR, NV, UT; (5) n. Central States.

43.16 *Satyrium* Scudder

Thirteen species, as follows:

S. behrii (Edwards). (3) CA, n. NM; (4) BC, WA, OR; (5) WY, CO.

S. fuliginosum (Edwards). (3) n. CA; (4) BC, WA; (5) WY, CO.

S. acadica (Edwards). (1) n.e. US; (4) Pacific n.w.; (5) n. Central States.

S. californica (Edwards). (3) CA; (4) BC, WA, OR.

S. sylvinus (Boisduval). (3) CA, AZ; (4) NV, UT.

S. edwardsii (Grote and Robinson). (1) n.e. NA; (2) s.e. US; (3) TX; (5) n. Central States.

S. calanus (Huebner) (Banded Hairstreak). Wingspan: ±20 mm. Brown above; double row of close, dark, blue-edged spots just beyond middle. Larvae feed on oak, hickory, and walnut. (See Fig. 27.107.) (1) n.e. US: (2) s.e. US; (3) TX; (5) n. Central States.

S. caryaevorum (McDunnough). (1) n.e. US; (5) MN, IA.

S. kingi (Klots and Clench). (2) s.e. US.

S. liparops (LeConte) (Striped Hairstreak). Wingspan: ±28 mm. Brown above; numerous broken, white cross-lines on

Fig. 27.107.

underside. Larvae on oak, willow, shadbush, apple, plum, blueberry, and blackberry. Uncommon to rare. (1) n.e. US; (2) s.e. US; (5) n. Central States.

S. auretorum (Boisduval). (3) CA.

S. tetra (Edwards). (3) CA; (4) NV.

S. saepium (Boisduval). (3) CA; (4) BC, WA, OR, ID; (5) MT, WY, CO.

43.17 *Ocaria* Clench

One species as follows:

O. ocrisia (Hewitson). (3) s. TX.

43.18 *Ministrymon* Clench

Two species as follows:

M. clytie (Edwards). (3) s. AZ, s. TX.

M. leda (Edwards). (3) s. CA, s. AZ.

43.19 *Tmolus* Huebner

Two species, as follows:

T. echion (Linnaeus) (Larger Lantana Butterfly). (3) a stray in s. TX (this species introduced into Hawaii to control lantana).

T. azia (Hewitson). (3) TX.

43.20 *Oenomaus* Huebner

One species, as follows:

O. ortygnus (Cramer). (3) s. TX.

43.21 *Thereus* Huebner

Three species, as follows:

T. zebina (Hewitson). (3) s. TX.

T. spurina (Hewitson). (3) s. TX?

T. palegon (Stoll). (3) s. TX.

43.22 *Allosmaitia* Clench

One species, as follows:

A. pion (Godman and Salvin). (3) s. TX.

43.23 *Calycopis* Scudder

Two species, as follows:

C. cecrops (Fabricius). Wingspan: ±25 mm. Hind wings with long tails; red band across lower surface of wings just beyond middle. Larvae feed on *Croton* spp. and dwarf sumac. (1) n.e. US; (2) s.e. US; (3) TX; (5) KS, MO.

C. isobeon (Butler and Druce). (3) TX; (5) strays to KS.

43.24 *Callophrys* Billberg

Seven species, as follows:

C. dumetorum (Boisduval). Wingspan: ±23 mm. Brown above, but a beautiful pale to dark green below; hind wing slightly pointed apically. Larvae feed mainly on *Lotus* spp., but also other plants. (3) CA; (4) Pacific n.w.

C. comstocki Henne. (3) CA.

C. lemberti Tilden. (3) CA.

C. apama (Edwards). (3) AZ, NM; (4) s. UT; (5) s. WY, CO.

C. affinis (Edwards). (4) Pacific n.w.; (5) MT, WY, CO.

C. viridis (Edwards). (3) CA.

C. sheridanii (Edwards). (3) CA, AZ, NM; (4) Pacific n.w.; (5) MT.

43.25 *Cyanophrys* Clench

Two species, as follows:

C. miserabilis (Clench). (3) s. TX.

C. goodsoni (Clench). (3) s. TX.

43.26 *Mitoura* Scudder

Ten species, as follows:

M. spinetorum (Hewitson). (3) CA; (4) Pacific n.w.; (5) MT, WY, CO.

M. johnsoni (Skinner). (3) CA; (4) BC, WA, OR.

M. rosneri Johnson. (4) BC.

M. barryi Johnson (4) OR.

M. byrnei Johnson (4) ID.

M. nelsoni (Boisduval). (3) CA: (4) Pacific n.w.

M. siva (Edwards). (3) CA, AZ, NM; (4) Pacific n.w.; (5) MT, ND, WY, CO.

M. loki (Skinner). (3) s. CA.

M. gryneus (Heubner) (Olive Hairstreak. Wingspan ±25 mm. Orange to reddish brown above with dark margins; beneath dark green, with three rows of whitish dashes on each side. Larvae on red cedar. (See Fig. 27.108.) (1) n.e. US; (2) s.e. US; (3) NM, OK, TX.

M. hesseli Rawson and Ziegler. (1) NH, NY, PA, NJ, MD; (2) VA, NC.

43.27 *Xamia* Clench

One species, as follows:

X. xami (Reakirt). (3) s. AZ, s. TX.

43.28 *Sandia* Clench and Ehrlich

One species, as follows:

S. mcfarlandi Ehrlich and Clench. (3) NM, TX.

Fig. 27.108.

43.29 *Incisalia* Scudder

Eight species, as follows:

I. augustus (Kirby) (Brown Elfin). Wingspan: ±20 mm. Brown to brownish green above; unifrom rusty brown below except for darker basal area of hind wings. Larvae feed on *Kalmia* spp. and *Vaccinium* spp. (3) CA, AZ; (4) BC, NV, UT.

I. fotis (Strecker). (3) CA, AZ; (4) BC, NV, UT. One of the several subspecies, which follows, has a common name; restricted to very small habitats, it is threatened with extinction.

I. f. bayensis (Brown) (San Bruno Elfin). Wingspan: 22–24 mm. Light brown above with brownish orange at lower edge of hind wing; basal half of wing and outer margins reddish brown, irregularly separated from brown remainder by irregular, narrow pale line; hind wings each with short, blunt tail; antennae with alternately black and white segments and dark brown antennal club. (3) CA, San Bruno nr. San Francisco.

I. polios Cook and Watson. (1) n.e NA; (2) VA; (3) NM; (4) Pacific n.w.; (5) n. Central States.

I. irus (Godart). (See Fig. 27.109.) (1). n.e. US; (2) s.e. US; (3) TX.

I. henrici (Grote and Robinson). (1) n.e. US; (2) s.e. US; (3) TX.

I. lanoraieensis Sheppard. (1) PQ, ME.

I. niphon (Huebner) (Banded Elfin). Wingspan: ±28 mm. Olive-brown with veins black; fringe of upper side of wings alternately brown and white; underside of wings rich, mottled brown, with distinct wavy white lines. Larvae feed on pine. (1) n.e. NA; (2) s.e. US; (5) MT, MN.

I. eryphon (Boisduval). (1) MI; (3) CA, AZ, NM; (4) Pacific n.w.; (5) MT.

43.30 *Arawacus* Kaye

[=*Dolymorpha* of authors]

One species, as follows:

A. jada (Hewitson). (3) s. AZ.

43.31 *Euristrymon* Clench

Three species, as follows:

E. favonius (Smith). (2) s.e. GA, n.e. FL.

E. ontario (Edwards). (1) n.e. US; (2) s.e. US; (3) TX; (5) KS, MO.

E. polingi (Barnes and Benjamin). (3) s.w. TX.

43.32 *Hypostrymon* Clench

One species, as follows:

H. critola (Hewitson). (3) s. AZ.

43.33 *Parrhasius* Huebner

[=*Panthiades* of authors]

P. m-album (Boisduval and LeConte). Wingspan: ±35 mm. Bluish on inner half of upper surface; below, each front wing crossed by two white lines, one of which continues on hind wing and is M-shaped at rear. Larvae feed on oak. (1) CT, PA, NJ, MD; (2) s.e. US; (3) TX.

43.34 *Strymon* Huebner

Thirteen species, most of which have tails and are brown or a delicate blue above, with various patterns ventrally.

S. melinus (Huebner) (Gray Hairstreak; Cotton Square Borer). Wingspan: ±18 mm. Hind wings with two tails; dull velvety green or brown above; ventrally with two bright red spots near tails. Larvae feed on many different plants including buds, flowers, and pods of hairy bush clover and developing seeds of hops, beans, and cotton. (See Fig. 27.110 and A&J 218.) (1) n.e. NA; (2) s.e. US; (3) s.w. US; (4) Pacific n.w.; (5) n. Central States.

S. avalona (Wright). (3) Santa Catalina Is. CA.

S. rufofusca (Hewitson). (3) s. TX.

S. bebrycia (Hewitson). (3) s. TX.

Fig. 27.109.

Fig. 27.110.

S. martialis (Herrich-Schaeffer). (2) s. FL.

S. yojoa (Reakirt). (3) s. TX.

S. albata (C. and R. Felder). (3) s. TX.

S. acis (Drury). (2) s. FL.

S. alea (Godman and Salvin). (3) s. TX.

S. columella (Fabricius). (2) s. FL; (3) s. TX.

S. limenia (Hewitson). (2) s. FL.

S. cestri (Hewitson). (2) s. TX.

S. bazochii (Godart) (Smaller Lantana Butterfly). (3) a stray in s. TX. (Introduced into Hawaii from Mexico to control lantana.)

43.35 *Erora* Schudder

Two species, as follows:

E. laeta (Edwards). (1) n.e. US; (2) WV, VA, TN.

E. quaderna (Hewitson). (3) AZ, NM, TX; (4) s. UT.

43.36 *Electrostrymon* Clench

Two species, as follows:

E. endymion (Fabricius). (3) s. TX.

E. angfelia (Hewitson). (2) s. FL.

Subfamily **Polyommatinae**
Tribe **Lampidini**
43.37 *Brephidium* Scudder

Two species as follows:

B. exilis (Boisduval) (Western Pigmy Blue). Wingspan: 16–18 mm. The smallest species of butterfly known. Males dorsally brown, with margins of wings black and bases with extensive purple area but ventrally grayish white at bases of wings to dark tan apically; females lighter in color. Larvae feed on various Chenopodiaceace and *Petunia parviflora*. (See A&J 222.) (3) s.w. US; (4) OR; (5) CO, KS, NE.

B. isophthalma (Herrich-Schaeffer). (2) AL, GA, FL.

43.38 *Leptotes* Scudder

Two species, as follows:

L. cassius (Cramer). (2) FL; (3) s. TX; (5) strays to KS, MO.

L. marina (Reakirt). (1) IL; (3) s.e. US; (5) NE, IA, CO, KS, MO.

43.39 *Zizula* Chapman

One species, as follows:

Z. cyna (Edwards). (3) AZ, NM, TX.

43.40 *Hemiargus* Huebner

Three species, as follows:

H. thomasi Clench. (2) s. FL.

H. ceraunua (Fabricius). (2) FL, AL, GA; (3) s.w. US.

H. isola (Reakirt). (1) MI, IL, IN, OH; (3) s.w. US; (4) BC, WA, OR; (5) n. Central States.

Fig. 27.111.

Tribe **Everini**
43.41 *Everes* Huebner

Two species, as follows:

E. comyntas (Godart) (Eastern Tailed Blue). Wingspan: 20–28 mm. Hind wings with delicate hairlike tails and white tip; female largely dark brown above. Larvae feed on clover and other legumes. (See Fig. 27.111.) Abundant. (1) n.e. NA; (2) s.e. US; (3) TX.

E. amyntula (Boisduval) (Western Tailed Blue). Wingspan: 20–28 mm. Dorsal color of this species varies from brood to brood, from light blue to brownish blue, with females darker; ventrally they are a very bright bluish white with black spots and one submarginal orange spot on hind wing. Larvae feed on cultivated clover and many other legumes. They are attended by ants; the pupae stridulate to get the attention of the ants to protect them. (See A&J 223.) (3) CA, AZ, NM; (4) Pacific n.w.; (5) MT, ND, MN, SD.

Tribe **Celastrini**
43.42 *Celastrina* Tutt

Two species, as follows:

C. ladon (Cramer) (Spring Azure) [=*C. argiolus* of authors]. Wingspan: 23 mm. Small; blue above; hind wings without tails. Many variations are caused by sexual differences and seasonal brood changes. Larvae feed on flowers of various plants, including dogwood, spirea, and ceanothus. Ants that attend the larvae touch them with their antennae to induce them to excrete a sweet fluid from their abdominal glands so that the ants may drink. (See Fig. 27.112.) (1), (2), (3), (4), (5), generally distributed.

C. ebenina Clench. (2) WV.

Fig. 27.112.

Tribe Scolitantidini

43.43 *Philotes* Scudder

One species, as follows:

P. sonorensis (C. and R. Felder). (3) CA.

43.44 *Euphilotes* Mattoni

Four species, as follows:

E. battoides (Behr). (3) s.w. US; (4) WA, OR, ID, NV. The typical subspecies, *E. b. battoides* (Behr) (El Segundo Blue), is an endangered species restricted to (2) San Joaquin River, CA, in a single colony.

E. enoptes (Boisduval). (3) CA, AZ; (4) WA, OR, ID, NV, UT; (5) MT, WY, CO. One subspecies, *E. e. smithi* (Mattoni) (Smith's Blue), is restricted to coastal fog belt of Monterey Co., CA, where it is an endangered species.

E. pallescens (Tilden and Downey). (3) CA; (4) NV, UT.

E. rita (Barnes and McDunnough). (3) AZ, NM; (4) NV, UT; (5) CO.

43.45 *Philotiella* Mattoni

One species, as follows:

P. speciosa (Edwards). (3) CA.

43.46 *Glaucopsyche* Scudder

Three species, as follows:

G. piasus (Boisduval). (3) CA; (4) BC, WA, OR; (5) AB.

G. lygdamus (Doubleday). (1) n.e. US; (2) s.e. US, except FL; (3) AZ, NM, TX; (4) Pacific n.w.; (5) n. Central States.

G. xerces (Boisduval) (Xerces Blue). Extinct. Wingspan: 27–30 mm. Male light blue; black spots on wing round, surrounded with white, or absent; ventrally pale; female brownish with black wing spots. Larvae reported to feed on *Lotus* spp., *Lupinus* spp. The last specimen was taken in 1943 from its only known habitat, the sand dunes on the San Francisco Peninsula in CA, an area destroyed by population encroachment. The species is now "preserved" by the name of the Xerces Society, an organization devoted to the preservation of rare and threatened insects and other arthropods. (See Fig. 27.113.)

Fig. 27.113.

Fig. 27.114.

Tribe Polyommatini

43.47 *Lycaeides* Huebner

Two species as follows:

L. argyrognomon (Bergstraesser). (1) n.e. US; (4) Pacific n.w.; (5) n. Central States. One subspecies, *L. a. lotis* (Lintner) (Lotus Blue), known only from Mendocino and Point Arena, CA, is threatened.

L. melissa (Edwards). (1) n.e. US; (2) s.w. US; (4) Pacific n.w.; (5) n. Central States. One subspecies, *L. m. samuelis* Nabokov (Karner Blue Butterfly), is also threatened in some areas. Wingspan: ±25 mm. Male bright blue above with narrow black margin and white fringe; ventrally light bluish gray with black spots and series of red submarginal spots; female with dark wings except at base; hind wings with red submarginal spots. Larvae feed on *Lupinus* spp., attended by ants. Usually confined to sand pine areas, the typical locality of this subspecies is the Pine Bush area near Albany, New York. Since this area has been taken over almost entirely by housing and shopping centers, the topotypical material is threatened with extinction, although the subspecies is abundant elsewhere. This is a characteristic example of the fate of many species of insects throughout the world; type localities of thousands of species have been similarly destroyed. (See Fig. 27.114.) (1) n.e. US.

43.48 *Plebejus* Kluk

One species, as follows:

P. saepiolus (Boisduval). (1) n.e. US; (3) CA; (4) Pacific n.w.; (5) n. Central states.

43.49 *Plebulina* Nabokov

One species, as follows:

P. emigdionis (Grinnell). (3) s. CA.

43.50 *Icaricia* Nabokov

Five species, as follows:

I. icarioides (Boisduval). (3) CA, AZ; (4) Pacific n.w.; (5) MT. One of the 12 subspecies, *I. i. missionensis* Hovanitz (Mission Blue), is of particular interest because it, too, is threatened. Wingspan: 25 mm. Male a beautiful pale blue with narrow black wing margins dorsally, and ventrally bluish white with many black dots; female brown with bluish wing bases dorsally, pale ventrally. Larvae feed on *Lupinus* spp. and are

Fig. 27.115.

attended by ants. This subspecies, restricted to Twin Peaks on the San Francisco Peninsula, CA, is another threatened by population encroachment.

I. shasta (Edwards). (3) CA; (4) WA, OR, ID, NV, UT; (5) MT, AB.

I. acmon (Westwood) (Acmon Blue). Wingspan: 22–25 mm. Males bright blue above, with front wing with narrow black apical margin and hind wing with submarginal orange stripe; females brown above, with front wing sometimes with bluish white underneath with black spots and orange subapical stripe. Larvae feed on various legumes. (See Fig. 27.115 and A&J 224.) (3) CA; (4) s. BC, WA, OR, ID; (5) MT, ND, MN, WY, CO, NE, KS.

I. lupini (Boisduval). (3) CA; (4) OR, WA.

I. neurona (Skinner). (3) s. CA.

43.51 *Vacciniina* Tutt

One species, as follows:

V. optilete (Knoch). (4) AK; (5) MT.

43.52 *Agriades* Huebner

One species, as follows:

A. franklinii (Curtis) [=*A. aquilo* of authors]. (1) LB; (3) CA, n. AZ, n. NM; (4) Pacific n.w.; (5) AB, SK, MB, MT.

44. RIODINIDAE (Metalmark Butterfly Family)

Wingspan: 20–35 mm. Wings short, broad; antennae elongate. Many species with metallic marks on wings and hence their common name. Wing marking resembles that of the preceding family. This large tropical family is represented by only 25 species in seven genera in the U.S., with all but three species confined to the southern portion.

Subfamily Euselasiinae

44.1 *Euselasia* Huebner

One species, as follows:

E. abreas (Edwards). (3) AZ?

Subfamily Riodininae

44.2 *Calephelis* Grote and Robinson

Ten species, as follows:

C. virginiensis (Guérin-Méneville). (2) s.e. US; (3) e. TX.

C. borealis (Grote and Robinson) (Northern Metalmark). Wingspan: 25–30 mm. Brown with two very narrow wavy blue

Fig. 27.116.

bands across wings toward apex; underside orange with small black spots. Larvae feed on *Senecio obovatus.* (See Fig. 27.116.) (1) IN, OH, PA, s. NY, NJ, MD; (2) KY, WV, VA.

C. nemesis (Edwards). (3) CA, AZ, NM, TX.

C. perditalis Barnes and McDunnough. (3) s. TX.

C. wrighti Holland. (3) s. CA.

C. muticum McAlpine. (1) MI, ME, IL, IN, OH, PA.

C. rawsoni McAlpine. (3) s. TX.

C. freemani McAlpine. (3) s. TX.

C. arizonensis McAlpine. (3) s. AZ.

C. dreisbachi McAlpine. (3) s. AZ.

44.3 *Caria* Huebner

One species, as follows:

C. ino Godman and Salvin. (3) s. TX.

44.4 *Lasaia* Bates

One species, as follows:

L. sula Staudinger. (3) s. TX.

44.5 *Melanis* Huebner

One species, as follows:

M. pixe (Boisduval). (3) s. TX.

44.6 *Emesis* Fabricius

Three species, as follows:

E. zela Butler. (3) s. AZ.

E. ares (Edwards). (3) s. AZ.

E. emesia (Hewitson). (3) s. TX.

44.7 *Apodemia* C. and R. Felder

Eight species, as follows:

A. mormo (C. and R. Felder). (See Fig. 27.117.) (3) s.w. US; (4) WA, OR, ID; (5) WY.

A. multiplaga Schaus. (3) s. TX.

A. hepburni Godman and Salvin. (3) s. TX.

A. palmerii (Edwards). (3) s.w. US; (4) NV, UT.

A. walkeri Godman and Salvin. (3) s. TX.

Fig. 27.117.

A. phyciodoides Barnes and Benjamin. (3) s. AZ.

A. nais (Edwards). (3) AZ, NM; (5) CO.

A. chisosensis Freeman. (3) s. TX.

45. LIBYTHEIDAE (Snout Butterfly Family)

Wingspan: 40–45 mm. Palpi greatly elongate, forming a "snout" that projects forward, a distinctive feature of this butterfly family. Only one species is common in the U.S.; the other two are either strays or not actually present in the U.S.

45.1 *Libytheana* Michener

Three species, as follows:

L. bachmannii (Kirtland) (Snout Butterfly). Wingspan: 40–45 mm. Wings dark with orange markings and white spots toward apex of front wings; underside of hind wings paler, brownish gray. Migrates in the south in August, sometimes in vast numbers. Larvae live on hackberry. (See Fig. 27.118 and A&J 240.) (1) n.e. US; (2) s.e. US (rare north of NC); (3) e. TX.

L. carinenta (Cramer). (3) s. TX, s. AZ; (5) strays to KS.

L. motya (Boisduval and LeConte). (3) s. TX? Probably not in the U.S.

46. NYMPHALIDAE
(Brush-footed Butterfly Family)

This, the largest family of butterflies, is so-named because of the greatly reduced front legs, which are useless in the male but apparently serve a sensory function in the female, that of detecting the chemicals that identify the larval food plant. Since the ventral wing surface of many species are marked much differently than the dorsal surface, these areas offer some of the best recognition features. There are 138 species and a great many subspecies assigned to 44 genera in the U.S. and Canada. As is true of most families, a considerable number are confined to the extreme southern part of the U.S., although many species stray north, sometimes for hundreds of miles, and therefore may be encountered long distances from their breeding ground. A considerable number of species have a very wide distribution, sometimes encircling the globe. Many of our common species are rather drab compared to the tropical strays.

Subfamily Heliconiinae

Many authors consider this a separate family, including Miller and Brown (1981).

46.1 *Agraulis* Boisduval and LeConte

One species, as follows:

A. vanillae (Linnaeus). One subspecies is represented in the US: *A. v. nigrior* Michener (Gulf Fritillary). Wingspan: 65–70 mm. Reddish brown above, with black spots, a row of which along margin of each hind wing are circles enclosing a brown dot and three of which near middle of front margin of front wings are circles enclosing a white dot; spangled with silver below. Larvae feed on passion flowers. (See Fig. 27.119.) (2) s.e. US; (3) CA, TX.

46.2 *Dione* Huebner

One species, as follows:

D. moneta Huebner. (3) a stray in s. TX.

46.3 *Dryadula* Michener

One species, as follows:

D. phaetusa (Linnaeus). (3) s. TX?

46.4 *Dryas* Huebner

One species, as follows:

D. iulia (Fabricius). (2) s. FL; (3) s. TX.

Fig. 27.118.

Fig. 27.119.

Fig. 27.120.

46.5 *Eueides* Huebner

One species, as follows:

E. isabella (Stoll). (3) s. TX?

46.6 *Heliconius* Kluk

Two species, as follows:

H. charitonius (Linnaeus) (Zebra Butterfly). Wingspan: 75–85 mm. Brownish black striped with yellow. Larvae feed on passion flowers. (See Fig. 27.120 and A&J 238.) (2) LA, MS, AL, FL; (3) a stray in TX; (5) a stray in KS.

H. erato (Linnaeus). (3) s. TX.

Subfamily Argynninae (Fritillaries and Silverspots)

46.7 *Euptoieta* Doubleday

Two species, as follows:

E. claudia (Cramer) (Variegated Fritillary). Wingspan: 48–65 mm. Brown with black markings, underside not spotted with silver. Larvae feed on pansies, violets, mandrake, passion flower, and other low plants. (2) s.e. US; (3) s.w. US; (5) strays to MT, MN, WY.

E. hegesia (Cramer). (3) s. TX.

46.8 *Speyeria* Scudder

Thirteen species, most of which are western and rather difficult to identify correctly.

S. diana (Cramer). Wingspan: 80–100 mm. Male brown with outer third of upper side of wings orange; female black with blue spots. (See Fig. 27.121 for male and A&J 235.) (2) s.e. US.

S. cybele (Fabricius) (Great Spangled Fritillary). Wingspan: 60–75 mm. Broad yellowish band near edge of underside of hind wings. Larvae feed on violets at night and hide in leaves beneath them by day. (See Fig. 27.122.) (1) n.e. US; (2) KY, WV, VA, TN, NC, AR, GA; (3) NM, OK; (4) UT; (5) AB, MB, MT, ND, CO.

S. aphrodite (Fabricius). Wingspan: 60–70 mm. Distinguished by absence of broad yellowish submarginal band on underside of hind wing, but since there is usually a narrow one, it is often difficult to tell this species from the preceding.

Fig. 27.121.

Absence of sex scaling on veins of front wing distinctive of the species. (1) n.e. US; (2) VA; (5) n. Central states.

S. idalia (Drury) (Regal Fritillary). Wingspan: 75–110 mm. Male differs from female in having submarginal row of spots orange instead of cream, and black margin of front wings less pronounced. Adults usually prefer swampy meadows. Larvae feed on violets. (See Fig. 27.123.) (1) n.e. US; (2) VA; (3) OK; (5) ND, e. CO.

S. nokomis (Edwards). (See Fig. 27.124.) (3) CA, AZ, NM; (4) NV, UT; (5) CO.

S. edwardsii (Reakirt). (5) AB, MT, SD, WY, CO.

S. coronis (Behr). (3) CA; (4) UT, OR, WA; (5) WY, CO.

S. zerene (Boisduval). (3) CA; (4) BC, WA, OR, NV, ID; (5) AB, MT, WY, CO.

S. callippe (Boisduval). (3) CA; (4) BC, WA, OR, NV; (5) MT, AB, CO.

S. egleis (Behr). (3) CA; (4) OR, NV, UT, ID; (5) MT, WY, CO.

S. atlantis (Edwards) (Mountain Silverspot). Wingspan: ±55 mm. Much like *S. aphrodite*, but smaller and darker at base of wings both above and below and with submarginal

Fig. 27.122.

Fig. 27.123.

Fig. 24.124.

yellow band on lower side of hind wings paler; narrow black border usually present on upper side of all wings; hind wings with black spots in middle connected to form a very narrow irregular band. Males with strong sex scaling on front wing veins and decided odor of sandalwood. (1) n.e. NA; (2) VA; (3) CA, AZ, NM; (4) OR, UT, NV, ID; (5) AB, MB, MT, SD, MN, WY, CO.

S. hydaspe (Boisduval). (3) CA, NM; (4) BC, WA, OR.

S. mormonia (Boisduval). (3) CA, AZ, NM; (4) AK, BC, WA, OR, NV, UT, ID; (5) WY, CO.

46.9 *Boloria* Moore

One species, as follows:

B. napaea (Hoffmansegg). (4) AK; (5) AB, SK, MB, WY.

46.10 *Proclossiana* Reuss

[=*Boloria* of authors]

One species, as follows:

P. eunomia (Esper). (1) ON; (4) AK, BC; (5) KE, MC, NT, YK, AB, SK, MB, MT.

46.11 *Clossiana* Reuss

[=*Boloria* of authors]

Twelve species, as follows:

C. selene (Denis and Schiffermueller) (Silver Bordered Fritillary). Wingspan: ±40 mm. Rich in silver spots on underside of wings. Adults found in bogs, marshy areas, and forest meadows. Larvae feed at night on violets and hide by day in dead leaves nearby. (See Fig. 27.125.) (1) n.e. NA; (4) AK, BC; (5) n. Central states.

C. bellona (Fabricius) (Meadow Fritillary). Wingspan: 35–45 mm. Very similar to the preceding, without silver spots on ventral surface. Larvae feed on violets. (1) n.e. NA; (2) WV, VA, TN; (4) Pacific n.w.; (5) AB, SK, MB, MT, WY, CO.

C. frigga (Thunberg). (4) AK, BC; (5) YK, NT, CO.

C. improba (Butler). (1) LB; (4) AK; (5) AB, SK, MB, KE, MC, NT, YK.

C. kriemhild (Strecker). (4) UT, ID; (5) MT.

C. epithore (Edwards). (3) CA; (4) WA, OR; (5) WY.

C. polaris (Boisduval). (1), (2), (3), (4), (5), generally distributed.

C. freija (Thunberg). (1) LB, ON, WI; (3) n. NM; (4) AK, BC, n. WA; (5) KE, MC, NT, YK, MT, ND, MN.

C. alberta (Edwards). (4) BC; (5) AB.

C. astarte (Doubleday and Hewitson). (4) AK, BC, WA; (5) YK.

C. t. titania (Esper) (White Mountain Fritillary). (1) NH; (4) AK, BC, WA; (5) AB, YK, CO. One subspecies, *C. t. mountina* (Scudder) (White Mountain Fritillary), is found in White Mts. of NH. Wingspan: 35–40 mm. Underside darker than in subspecies described above, without distinct silver spots. Larvae feed on violets, willow, and smartweed.

C. chariclea (Schneider). (1) GR, LB; (4) AK; (5) YK.

Subfamily Melitaeinae

Tribe Melitaeini

46.12 *Poladryas* Bauer

Two species, as follows:

P. minuta (Edwards). (3) TX.

P. arachne (Edwards). (3) CA, AZ, NM, OK, TX; (5) WY, NE.

Fig. 24.125.

46.13 *Thessalia* Scudder

Five species, as follows:

T. theona (Ménétries) (White-patched Butterfly). Wing-span: 30–38 mm. Dark brown with very wide transverse rows of brownish orange spots and brownish yellow in center; row of white submarginal spots on each wing. (See A&J 232.) (3) AZ, TX.

T. chinatiensis (Tinkham). (3) w. TX.

T. cyneas (Godman and Salvin). (3) s.e. AZ.

T. fulvia (Edwards). (3) e. AZ, w. TX; (5) s. CO.

T. leanira (C. and R. Felder). (3) CA; (4) OR, NV, UT; (5) CO.

46.14 *Chlosyne* Butler

Seven species, as follows:

C. californica (Wright). (3) CA; (4) NV.

C. lacinia (Geyer). (3) s.w. US; (4) NV, UT; (5) NE, CO, KS. Subspecies *C. l. adjutrix* Scudder (Scudder's Patched Butterfly). Wingspan: 50–55 mm. Wings, especially hind wings, dorsally with broad orange band and margins heavily black. Larvae feed on sunflowers and a variety of weeds. (3) TX, NM.

C. definita (Aaron). (3) AZ, NM, TX.

C. endeis (Godman and Salvin). (3) s. TX.

C. erodyle (Godman and Salvin)

C. janais (Drury). (3) s. TX, strays to AZ.

C. rosita Hall. (3) s. TX.

46.15 *Charidryas* Schudder (The Checkerspots)
[=*Chlosyne* of authors]

Nine species, as follows:

C. gorgone (Huebner) (Gorgone Checkerspot). Wingspan: male, ±30 mm; female, ±40 mm. Underside of hind wing mostly pale silvery gray, without orange markings. Larvae feed on many composites. (2) NC, SC, GA; (3) NM, OK, TX; (5) MB, MT, ND, SD, WY, NE, CO, KS.

C. nycteis (Doubleday and Hewitson) (Silvery Checkerspot). Wingspan: 30–50 mm. Wings tawny orange, lighter on underside and marked with black; below, hind wings silvery white but with orange markings. Larvae feed on sunflowers and other composites. (See Fig. 27.126.) (1) n.e. US; (2) VA, NC, SC, GA, AL, MS, LA; (3) TX. (A&J 231.)

C. harrisii (Scudder) (Harris Checkerspot). Wingspan: ±40 mm. Resembles the preceding species on upperside, but underside darker, with continuous row of silver spots along outer margin of hind wings. Larvae feed on asters. (1) n.e. US; (2) WV, VA; (5) MB, MT, ND, SD.

C. palla (Boisduval). (3) CA; (4) WA, OR, ID, NV, UT; (5) CO.

C. acastus (Edwards). (3) CA, NM; (4) OR; (5) MT, NE.

C. neumoegeni (Skinner). (3) CA, AZ; (4) NV, UT.

C. gabbi (Behr). (3) CA.

Fig. 25.126.

C. damoetas (Skinner). (3) CA; (4) BC, NV, UT; (5) AB, WY, CO.

C. hoffmanni (Behr). (3) CA; (4) BC, OR.

46.16 *Microtia* Bates

One species, as follows:

M. elva Bates. (3) s. AZ, s. TX.

46.17 *Dymasia* Higgins

One species, as follows:

D. dymas (Edwards). (3) TX, s. NM, s.e. VA.

46.18 *Texola* Higgins

One species, as follows:

T. elada (Hewitson). (3) s. AZ, s. TX.

46.19 *Anthanassa* Scudder

Four species, as follows:

A. texana (Edwards). (2) FL, GA, LA; (3) TX, AZ; (5) strays to KS, NE.

A. frisia (Poey). (2) s. FL; (3) s. TX.

A. ptolyca (Bates). (3) s. TX.

A. tulcis (Bates). (3) s. TX.

46.20 *Phyciodes* Huebner

Nine species, as follows:

P. vesta (Edwards). (3) s. TX; (5) strays to KS.

P. phaon (Edwards). (2) s.e. US; (3) s.w. US; (5) KS.

P. tharos (Drury) (Pearl Crescent). Wingspan: 30–35 mm. Wings dorsally orange with black borders; ventrally with large, unmarked orange-brown base and towards outer margin of front wing. Adults from over-wintered larvae brighter and with more distinct light markings on underside than those from summer broods. Larvae feed on asters. (1), (2), (3), (4), (5), generally distributed.

P. batesii (Reakirt). Wingspan: ±45 mm. Differs from *P. tharos* by having heavier black markings above and by lack of conspicuous dark markings on lower side of hind wings, these being almost uniformly pale yellow. Larvae feed on asters. (1) n.e. US; (5) NE, IA.

P. pratensis (Behr). (3) CA, AZ, NM; (4) NV; (5) CO.

P. picta (Edwards). (3) AZ, NM, OK, TX; (4) CO, w. NE, KS.

P. orseis (Edwards). (3) CA; (4) OR, NV.

P. pallida (Edwards). (3) CA, AZ; (4) BC, WA, OR, ID, NV; (5) MT, WY.

P. mylitta (Edwards). (3) AZ, NM; (4) BC, WA, OR, NV; (5) CO.

46.21 *Hypodryas* Higgins

One species, as follows:

H. gilletti (Barnes). Wingspan: ±50 mm. Very distinct with red-orange submarginal wing bands. Larvae feed on twin-berried honeysuckle. (4) ID; (5) AB, MT, WY.

46.22 *Occidryas* Higgins

[=*Euphydryas* of some authors]

Four species, as follows:

O. anicia (Doubleday and Hewitson). This species extremely variable, with 22 subspecies recognized. (3) CA, AZ, NM; (4) AK, WA, OR, NV, UT; (5) AB, MT, YK, WY, NE, CO.

O. chalcedona (Doubleday) (Checkerspot). Wingspan: 50–56 mm. Wings variable, usually black to red-brown with light yellow spots. Larvae feed on Scrophulariaceae. Very common. (See A&J 233.) (3) CA, AZ, NM, TX; (4) OR, NV.

O. colon (Edwards). (3) CA; (4) BC, WA, OR, NV, UT, ID; (5) MT.

O. editha (Boisduval). (3) CA, AZ, NM; (4) BC, WA, OR, NV; (5) MT, AB, WY, CO.

46.23 *Euphydryas* Scudder

One species, as follows:

E. phaeton (Drury) (The Baltimore). Wingspan: 45–60 mm. Wings nearly black, marked with red and pale yellow. Larvae feed chiefly on Scrophulariaceae, especially Turtlehead (*Chelone glabra*). Adults found in swampy meadows during June and July. (See Fig. 27.127.) (1) n.e. NA; (2) KY, WV, VA, TN, NC, AR; (5) KS, MO.

Subfamily **Nymphalinae (Anglewings, Tortoise-shells, Mourning-cloaks, etc.)**

Tribe **Nymphalini**

46.24 *Polygonia* Huebner

These are the Anglewings, so-called because of their wings' ragged edges. They are tawny, with darker markings above and a combination of brown and gray below that corresponds closely with the color of dead leaves. Ten species, as follows:

P. interrogationis (Fabricius) (Question Mark). Wingspan: ±65 mm. Underside of hind wing with vague silver spots forming question mark; tips of hind wings violet. Summer form with dark markings on upper side clouded; typical winter form paler. Larvae feed chiefly on hop and elm. Common. (See Fig. 27.128.) (1) n.e. US; (2) s.e. US; (3) TX.

Fig. 27.127.

P. comma (Harris) (Hop Merchant; Comma). Wingspan: ±50 mm. Similar to the preceding but with silver comma on underside of hind wings. Larvae feed on hops, nettles, and related plants, slightly rolling the leaves for its protection while eating. (See Fig. 27.129.) (1) n.e. US; (2) VA, NC, SC, GA; (5) KS, NE, IA.

P. satyrus (Edwards). Very similar to *P. comma*, but paler. Larvae feed on stinging nettles. Rare in east. (1) WI, MI, ON, NY, NF; (3) AZ; (5) MT, ND, SD, WY, MN.

P. faunus (Edwards). (Green Comma). Wingspan: ±50 mm. Wings deeply notched and underside of hind wings, each with silver comma; strongly tinted with green along outer third. Larvae feed on birch, willow, currant, and gooseberry. (See Fig. 27.130.) (1) n.e. NA; (2) WV, VA, TN, NC, GA.

P. hylas (Edwards). (3) CA, AZ, NM; (4) ID; (5) MT, WY, CO.

P. silvius (Edwards). (3) CA.

P. zephyrus (Edwards) (Zephyr Anglewing). Wingspan: 50–55 mm. Dorsally light orange with narrow marginal brown band and submarginal row of pale yellow lunules; ventrally

Fig. 27.128.

Fig. 27.129.

Fig. 27.131.

gray or gray-brown. Larvae feed on squaw currant only. (3) CA, NM; (4) BC, WA, OR, ID.

P. gracilis (Grote and Robinson). (1) n.e. NA; (4) Pacific n.w.; (5) AB, SK, MB, MT.

P. oreas (Edwards). (3) CA; (4) OR.

P. progne (Cramer) (Gray Comma). Wingspan: ±50 mm. Underside grayish with comma tapering at ends. Larvae feed on currant, gooseberry, and elm. (1) n.e. NA; (2) VA, NC; (3) KS, NE.

46.25 *Nymphalis* Kluk

Three species, as follows:

N. vau-album (Dennis and Schiffermueller). (1) n.e. NA; (2) VA, NC; (4) Pacific n.w.; (5) MT, WY, ND, SD, MN. Subspecies, *N. v. j-album* (Boisduval and LeConte) (Compton Tortoise Shell). Wingspan: 70 mm. Tawny orange above, with three large black patches and spot of white along front margin, among other markings; below, ashy brown with white J or L on hind wings. Adults hibernate during winter. Larvae feed on willow, poplar, and birch. (See Fig. 27.131.)

N. californica (Boisduval) (California Tortoise Shell). Wingspan: ±60 mm. Similar to the preceding but confined to West Coast. (3) CA; (4) Pacific n.w.; (5) MT, WY, CO.

N. antiopa (Linnaeus) (Mourning Cloak). Wingspan: 55–85 mm. Easily recognized by uniformly dark brown, nearly black wings with series of submarginal blue spots and straw-yellow marginal bands on both pairs; underside of wings without blue spots. Larvae feed on willow, poplar, elm, and hackberry. Adults fly year around on warm days, hibernate in winter when it is cold. (See Fig. 27.132 and A&J 236.) (1), (2), (3), (4), (5), generally distributed.

46.26 *Aglais* Dalman

One species, as follows:

A. milberti (Godart). Similar to *N. californica* but with broad orange submarginal wing bands. Found in cooler parts of both eastern and western NA. (See Fig. 27.133.) (1) n.e. NA; (2) WV, VA; (4) Pacific n.w.; (5) n. Central States.

46.27 *Vanessa* Fabricius

Four species, as follows:

V. virginiensis (Drury) (American Painted Lady; Painted Beauty). Wingspan: ±50 mm. Upper surface tawny orange and

Fig. 27.130.

Fig. 27.132.

Fig. 27.133.

brownish black, except for large white spots; underside of each hind wing with two eyespots. Larvae feed on various plants. (See Fig. 27.134.) (1), (2), (3), (4), (5), generally distributed.

V. cardui (Linnaeus) (Painted Lady; Cosmopolite). Wingspan: 50–60 mm. Hind wings ventrally with row of four or more small postmedian eyespots. Larvae feed on burdock, thistle, sunflower, hollyhock, and other plants. Permanent resident of Sonoran desert and nearby areas in the U.S. but migrates over most of NA; nearly cosmopolitan. (See Fig. 27.135.)

V. annabella (Field) (West Coast Lady). Wingspan: 50–55 mm. Smaller than *V. cardui* but otherwise similar. Larvae feed on Malvaceae. Adults fly throughout year in warm regions. (See Fig. 27.136.) (3) CA, AZ, NM, TX; (4) BC, WA, OR, ID, NV, UT; (5) AB, MT, WY, CO.

V. atalanta (Linnaeus), *V. a. rubria* (Fruhstorfer) (Red Admiral). Wingspan: ±50 mm. Upper surface purplish black with lightly shaded areas bright orange and apical spots white; undersurface of hind wings marbled and marked with wavy lines of intricate pattern and also with green-dusted submarginal series of obscure eyespots. Larvae feed on nettle and hops. [See Figs. 27.137 (dorsal view) and 27.138 (ventral); see also A&J 234.] (1), (2), (3), (4), (5), generally distributed.

46.28 *Hypanartia* Huebner

One species, as follows:

H. lethe (Fabricius). (3) s. TX?

Fig. 27.134.

Fig. 27.135.

Tribe Hypolimnini
46.29 *Hypolimnas* Huebner

One species, as follows:

H. misippus (Linnaeus). (2) s. FL.

46.30 *Junonia* Huebner [=*Precis* of authors]

Three species, as follows:

J. coenia Huebner (The Buckeye). Wingspan: ±50 mm. Dorsally dark brown; conspicuous peacocklike eyespots, small orange spots, and dull whitish band on each front wing; each hind wing ventrally gray-brown with much the same markings except for narrow but conspicuous band of yellowish orange and considerably reduced eyespots. Larvae feed on plantain, snapdragon, and *Gerardia* spp. (See Fig. 27.139 and A&J 230.) (1), (2), (3), (4), (5), generally distributed.

J. nigrosuffusa Barnes and McDunnough. (3) s. AZ, s. TX.

J. evarete (Cramer). (2) s. FL; (3) s. TX.

46.31 *Anartia* Huebner

Three species, as follows:

A. jatrophae (Johansson). (1) strays to MA; (2) s. FL.

A. chrysopelea Huebner. (2) s. FL?

A. fatima (Fabricius). (3) s. TX; (5) strays to KS.

Fig. 27.136.

Fig. 27.137.

Fig. 27.139.

46.32 *Siproeta* Huebner

One species, as follows:

S. stelenes (Linnaeus). (2) s. FL; (3) s. TX.

Subfamily Limenitidinae
Tribe Limenitidini
46.33 *Basilarchia* Scudder (The Admirals)
[=*Limenitis* of authors]

Four species, as follows:

B. arthemis (Drury) (White Admiral; Banded Purple). Wingspan: ±60 mm. Dorsally with broad white band across each wing; ventrally dark brown with similar markings and some orange spots in addition. Adults fly June through September. Larvae feed on birch, willow, poplar, and other trees. (See Fig. 27.140 & A&J 226.) (1) n.e. NA; (2) s.e. US; (3) TX, (4) Pacific n.w.; (5) n. Central states.

B. arthemis astyanax (Fabricius) (Red Spotted Purple). Wingspan: 60–80 mm. Dorsally black and pale blue or green with three or four red spots in row near margin of front wings; ventrally brown with submarginal row of red spots, two at base of front wings, four at base of hind wings. Larvae feed on wild cherry, willow, poplar, and other trees. (See Fig. 27.141 and A&J 227.) (1) n.e. US; (2) s.e. US; (5) MN.

Fig. 27.140.

B. archippus (Cramer) (Viceroy). Wingspan: 60–75 mm. Orange with black veins; differs from Monarch [see *Danaus plexippus* (49.1)] by presence of narrow black band across hind wing. Larvae prefer wet areas where poplar, willow, and aspen grow. (See Fig. 27.142 and A&J 228.) (1), (2), (3), (4), (5), generally distributed.

Fig. 27.138.

Fig. 27.141.

Fig. 27.142.

B. weidemeyerii (Edwards). (3) CA, AZ, NM; (4) WA, OR, ID; (5) MT, SD, WY, CO, NE, strays in KS.

B. lorquini (Boisduval) (Lorquin's Admiral). Wingspan: ±60 mm. Similar to *B. arthemis* but smaller and with orange apical patches dorsally on front wing tips. Larvae feed on willow, cottonwood, and poplar. (See Fig. 27.143 and A&J 229.) (3) CA; (4) Pacific n.w.; (5) MT, AB, WY.

46.34 *Adelpha* Huebner

Two species, as follows:

A. fessonia (Hewitson). (3) s.e. TX.

A. bredowii Geyer (California Sister). Wingspan: ±75 mm. Resembles *B. lorquini* except that orange patch on front wing is separated from margin by dark band. Larvae feed on oak. (See A&J 225.) (3) CA, AZ, NM, TX; (4) UT.

Tribe Epicaliini

46.35 *Myscelia* Doubleday

Four species, as follows:

M. ethusa (Boisduval). (3) s.e. TX.

M. skinneri Mengel. (3) s. TX?

Fig. 27.143.

M. streckeri Skinner. (3) s. CA?

M. cynanthe C. and R. Felder. (3) a stray in s. TX.

46.36 *Eunica* Huebner

Two species, as follows:

E. monima (Stoll). (2) s. FL; (3) s. TX.

E. tatila (Herrich-Schaeffer). (2) s. FL; (5) a stray in KS.

46.37 *Dynamine* Huebner

One species, as follows:

D. dyonis Geyer. (3) s. TX.

46.38 *Diaethria* Billberg

Two species, as follows:

D. clymena (Cramer). (2) s. FL.

D. asteria (Godman and Salvin). (3) s.e. TX.

Tribe Eurytelini

46.39 *Mestra* Huebner

Two species, as follows:

M. amymone (Ménétries). (3) s. TX; (5) a stray in CO, KS, NE.

M. cana (Erichson). (2) s. FL.

46.40 *Biblis* Fabricius

One species, as follows:

B. hyperia (Cramer). (3) a stray in s. TX.

Tribe Ageroniini

46.41 *Hamadryas* Huebner (Calico Butterflies)

Five species, probably all of them strays in the U.S., although members of this genus abound in the tropics. They are peculiar in that they rest head down on the bark of a tree. On taking flight, they click their wings, circle around at some distance, and return to the same spot on the tree.

H. fornax (Huebner). (3) a stray in s. TX.

H. feronia (Linnaeus). (3) a stray in s. TX.

H. februa (Huebner). (3) a stray in s. TX.

H. ferox (Staudinger). (3) a stray in s. TX?

H. amphinome (Linnaeus). (3) a stray in s. TX?

Tribe Coloburini

46.42 *Historis* Huebner

Two species, as follows:

H. odius (Fabricius). (2) stray is s. FL.

H. archeronta (Fabricius). (2) stray in s. FL.

46.43 *Smyrna* Huebner

One species, as follows:

S. karwinskii Geyer. (3) s. TX.

Subfamily Marpesiinae

46.44 *Marpesia* Huebner (The Dagger-tails)

Four species, all with long, slender tails on hind wing. Larvae feed on Moraceae.

M. coresia (Godart). (3) s. TX.

M. chiron (Fabricius). (2) s. FL; (3) s. TX.

M. petreus (Cramer). (2) FL; (3) s.e. TX.

M. eleuchea Huebner. (2) s. FL?

47. APATURIDAE (Apaturid Butterfly Family)

Wingspan: 45–60 mm. Very similar to the Nymphalidae, differing only in features of wing venation and larvae. There are 17 species assigned to four genera in the U.S., most of them in extreme southern parts. Larvae feed on hackberry and goatweed.

Subfamily Charaxinae

47.1 *Anaea* Huebner

Three species, as follows:

A. aidea (Guérin-Méneville). (3) s. CA, s. AZ, s. NM, s. TX; (5) a stray in KS, CO.

A. floridalis Johnson and Comstock. (2) s. FL.

A. andria Scudder. (See Fig. 27.144.) (1) IL, IN, OH; (2) KY, TN, AL, MS, AR, LA; (3) OK, TX; (5) e. CO, KS.

47.2 *Memphis* Huebner

Two species, as follows:

M. glycerium (Doubleday). (3) s. AZ.

M. pithyusa (Felder). (3) s. TX.

Subfamily Apaturinae

47.3 *Asterocampa* Roeber

Ten species, as follows:

A. celtis (Boisduval and LeConte). Wingspan: 45–55 mm. Gray-olive to olive-brown with dark markings; front wing with silver spots toward apex; ventrally much lighter. (See Fig. 27.145.) (1) n.e. US; (2) s.e. US; (3) c. TX; (5) MN.

Fig. 27.144.

Fig. 27.145.

A. antonia (Edwards). (3) c. TX, c. OK, AZ; (4) UT; (5) s. CO.

A. montis (Edwards). (3) s. AZ, s. NM.

A. subpallida (Barnes and McDunnough). (3) s. AZ.

A. leila (Edwards). (3) s. AZ, s. NM, w. TX.

A. alicia (Edwards). (2) SC, GA, FL, AL, MS, LA; (3) e. TX.

A. clyton (Boisduval and LeConte). (1) n.e. US; (2) VA, NC, SC, GA, AL, MS, LA; (3) e. TX; (5) NE, IA, MO.

A. flora (Edwards). (2) s. GA, FL.

A. texana (Skinner). (3) TX; (5) a stray in KS.

A. louisa Stallings and Turner. (3) s. TX.

47.4 *Doxocopa* Huebner

Two species, as follows:

D. pavon (Latreille). (3) s.e. TX.

D. laurae (Drury). (3) s. TX.

48. SATYRIDAE (Nymph, Satyrs, and Arctic Butterfly Family)

Wingspan: 30–70 mm. Brownish or gray butterflies with several eyespots on wing margins. Adults fly in an erratic path, bobbing back and forth in a characteristic manner. Larvae feed on monocotyledons, particularly grasses and sedges. Most of the 50 species are found either in the North or in the high mountains of the West. There are 13 genera in the U.S. and Canada.

Subfamily Elymniinae

Tribe Parargini

48.1 *Enodia* Huebner

[=*Lethe* of authors]

Three species, as follows:

E. portlandia (Fabricius) (Pearly Eye). Wingspan: 45–55 mm. Yellowish brown with black eyespots, four on front wing and five on hind wing dorsally; spots on ventral surface distinctly eyed; front wing with conspicuous pearly violet

Fig. 27.146.

Fig. 27.147.

markings. Larvae feed on grasses. (See Fig. 27.146 and A&J 337.) (1) n.e. US; (2) s.e. US; (3) TX; (5) n. Central States.

E. anthedon Clark. (1) n.e. US; (2) AR; (3) MN, IA, MO.

E. creola (Skinner). (1) IL, IN; (2) KY, WV, VA, TN, NC, AR, LA, MS, AL, GA; (3) TX.

48.2 *Satyrodes* Scudder

[=*Lethe* of authors]

Two species, as follows:

S. eurydice (Johansson). Wingspan: 40–50 mm. Four small eyespots on front wing and six on hind wing; upper side mouse brown; ventrally slate brown with larger eyespots. Larvae feed on coarse grasses and sedges and are active during the day unlike many other larvae. (See Fig. 27.147.) (1) n.e. NA.

S. appalachia (Chermock). (1) n.e. US; (2) s.e. US; (5) MN, SD, IA, MO.

***Subfamily* Satyrinae**

***Tribe* Euptychiini**

48.3 *Cyllopsis* Felder

[=*Euptychia* of authors]

Four species, as follows:

C. pyracmon (Butler). (3) AZ.

C. henshawi (Edwards). (See Fig. 27.148.) (3) AZ, w. TX; (5) w. CO.

C. pertepida (Dyar). (3) AZ, TX.

C. gemma (Huebner). (1) s. IL, s. IN; (2) s.e. US; (3) TX.

48.4 *Hermeuptychia* Foerster

[=*Euptychia* of authors]

Two species, as follows:

H. hermes (Fabricius) ?(3) TX.

H. sosybius (Fabricius). (1) NJ, MD; (2) s.e. US; (3) TX.

48.5 *Neonympha* Huebner

[=*Euptychia* of authors]

Two species, as follows:

N. areolatus (Smith). Wingspan: 30–35 mm. Yellowish brown, without spots above and three or four spots on underside of hind wing narrow-elongate. Larvae feed on coarse grass. A Coastal Plain species. (1) NJ, DE, MD; (2) VA, NC, SC, GA, FL; (3) TX.

N. mitchellii French (1) MI, IN, OH, PA, NJ.

48.6 *Megisto* Huebner

[=*Euptychia* of authors]

Two species, as follows:

M. cymela (Cramer) (Little Wood Nymph). Wingspan: 35–50 mm. Dark brown above; two eyespots on each wing above; eyespots larger ventrally, two on front and six on hind wings, each distinctly ringed with yellow. Larvae feed on grasses. (See Fig. 27.149.) (1) n.e. US; (2) s.e. US; (3) TX; (4) MN, IA, MO.

M. rubricata (Edwards). (3) AZ, NM, TX, OK.

Fig. 27.148.

Fig. 27.149.

Fig. 27.151.

48.7 *Paramacera* Butler

One species, as follows:

P. allyni Miller. (3) AZ.

Note: P. xicaque of authors is a misidentification.

Tribe Coenonymphini

48.8 *Coenonympha* Huebner

Six species, as follows:

C. haydenii (Edwards). (4) ID; (5) MT, WY.

C. kodiak Edwards. (4) AK; (5) YK, MC.

C. inornata Edwards. (See Fig. 27.150.) (1) ON, QU, NB, NF, NY; (4) BC; (5) AB, MB, SK.

C. ochracea Edwards. (3) AZ, NM; (4) ID, NV; (5) MT, WY, CO, SD, w. NE, MC.

C. ampelos Edwards (3) CA; (4) BC, WA, OR.

C. california Westwood. (3) CA; (4) OR.

Tribe Maniolini

48.9 *Cercyonis* Scudder

Four species, as follows:

C. pegala (Fabricius) (Common Wood-nymph). Wingspan: 60–70 mm. Dark brown, often with large yellow area on outer part of front wing, with narrow brown border and two eyespots within yellow area; hind wing dark brown with two small eyespots. Yellow area of front wing varies in many

Fig. 27.150.

subspecies, sometimes being reduced to a pale brown area. Larvae feed on grass. (See Fig. 27.151.) (1), (2), (3), (4), (5), generally distributed in wooded areas.

C. meadii (Edwards). (3) AZ, NM; (4) UT; (5) ND, WY, CO.

C. sthenele (Boisduval). (3) CA, AZ, NM; (4) WA, OR, NV, UT; (5) MT, WY, CO.

C. oetus (Boisduval). (3) CA, AZ, NM; (4) BC, OR, ID; (5) AB, MT, WY, CO, SD.

Tribe Erebiini

48.10 *Erebia* Dalman

Eleven species, as follows:

E. vidleri Elwes. (4) WA, OR.

E. rossii (Curtis). (4) AK, BC; (5) KE, MC, NT, YK, MT.

E. disa (Thunberg). (1) ON; (4) AK; (5) KE, MC, NT, YK.

E. magdalena Strecker. (4) AK, UT; (5) WY, CO, YK.

E. fasciata Butler. (4) AK; (5) KE, MC, NT, YK.

E. discoidalis (Kirby). (4) AK; (5) KE, MC, NT, YK, AB, MB, SK, MT.

E. theano (Tauscher). (4) AK; (5) KE, MC, NT, YK, AB, MB, SK, MT, WY, CO.

E. youngi Holland. (4) AK; (5) YK.

E. epipsodea Butler. (See Fig. 27.152.) (3) NM; (4) AK, BC, WA, OR; (5) YK, AB, MB, SK, MT, WY, CO.

E. callias Edwards. (5) WY, CO.

E. dabanensis Erschoff. (4) AK.

Tribe Pronophilini

48.11 *Gyrocheilus* Butler

One species, as follows:

G. patrobas (Hewitson). (3) s.e. AZ.

Tribe Satyrini

48.12 *Neominois* Scudder

One species, as follows:

N. ridingsii (Edwards). (3) CA, AZ; NM; (4) NV, UT; (5) WY, CO.

Fig. 27.152.

Fig. 27.153.

48.13 *Oeneis* Huebner

Eleven species, as follows:

O. ivallda (Mead). (3) c. CA.

O. nevadensis (C. and R. Felder). (3) CA; (4) BC, WA, OR, NV.

O. macounii (Edwards). (1) w. ON, MI; (4) BC; (5) NT, AB, MB, MN.

O. chryxus (Doubleday and Hewitson). (1) ON, MI, QU, LB; (3) CA, AZ, NM; (4) BC, WA, OR; (5) AB, MB, SK.

O. uhleri (Reakirt). (5) AB, SK, MB, MT, ND, WY, SD, w. NE, CO, KE, MC, NT, YK.

O. alberta Elwes. (3) AZ; (5) AB, MB, SK, CO.

O. taygete Geyer. (1) MI, ON, QU, GR, LB; (4) BC, AK; (5) AB, MB, SK, MT, MN, WY.

O. bore (Schneider). (4) AK; (5) YK, MC, NT, KE.

O. jutta (Huebner). (1) ON, QU, LB, NF; (4) AK; (5) KE, MC, NT, YK, AB, MB, MT, ND, MN, WY, CO.

O. melissa (Fabricius). (See Fig. 27.153.) (1) ON, QU, NH, LB, NF; (3) NM; (4) AK; (5) AB, SK, MB, MT, WY, CO, KE, MC, NT, YK.

O. polixenes (Fabricius). (1) ME, LB, ON, QU; (3) NM; (4) AK; (5) KE, MC, NT, YK, AB, MB, SK, MT, WY, CO.

49. DANAIDAE (Milkweed Butterfly Family)

Since the large butterflies of this small family are distasteful to birds and lizards, they are mimicked by various species in other families. Larvae of the Danaidae found in the U.S. and Canada feed on milkweed of various species. There are four species in two genera in the U.S. and Canada.

Subfamily Danainae

49.1 *Danaus* Kluk

Three species, as follows:

D. plexippus (Linnaeus) (Monarch Butterfly; Milkweed Butterfly). Wingspan: ±100 mm. Brownish red shading to dark yellow at base; veins and wing tips black, with white spots on latter, hind wings without black line across wing. Both larvae

and adults are poisonous to birds. Recently it has been determined that the poisonous material is located only in the exoskeleton, something that birds have apparently learned only recently as well, for they now scoop out the soft tissue in the interior of the butterfly's body and leave the poisonous exoskeleton untouched. (See 27.154 and A&J 239.) (1), (2) (3), (4), (5), generally distributed wherever milkweed grows.

Note: Many butterflies migrate, some as "strays" and others following a more or less fixed pattern. Adults of this species migrate south at the end of the summer, congregating on trees in CA, TX, and FL and eventually reaching Mexico, where they pass the winter. In the spring, they migrate north, laying eggs on milkweed as they go. The eggs hatch, larvae feed, and new adults emerge to continue the northward migration. Those arriving in the far north of the U.S. and Canada represent the latest brood, and it is these that head south again in the fall.

D. gilippus (Cramer). (2) GA, FL, AL, MS, LA; (3) s.e. TX.

D. eresimus (Cramer). (2) s. FL; (3) s. TX.

Subfamily Ituninae

49.2 *Lycorea* Doubleday and Hewitson

One species, as follows:

L. cleobaea (Godart). (2) s. FL; (3) TX.

Fig. 27.154.

Division "MICROLEPIDOPTEA" (Cont.)

Superfamily ZYGAENOIDEA

The Zygaenoidea include the following five small families.

50. ZYGAENIDAE (Smoky Moth Family)

Wingspan: 16–28 mm. A few species with metallic scales; many brightly colored tropical species; some species with a red collar; others mimics of lycid beetles. Smoky gray, translucent wings, the front ones rounded. Antennae usually thickened and pectinate; head prominent, with small or rudimentary maxillary palpi; proboscis stout, scales absent; ocelli well separated from eyes and sometimes very small. Larvae are leaf skeletonizers. Six genera and 22 species are recorded in the U.S. and Canada.

50.1 *Harrisina* Packard

Seven species, of which the following are of some economic importance:

H. americana (Guérin-Méneville) (Grape Leaf Skeletonizer). Wingspan: 18–25 mm. Black, slightly iridescent, with orange collar. Adults on the wing from May to August. Larvae—characterized by black tufts and a pale body—feed on grape or Virginia Creeper. (1) MA, NY, PA, NJ, MD, DE; (2) VA.

H. brillians Barnes and McDunnough (Western Grape Leaf Skeletonizer). Similar to the preceding, replacing that species in the West. (3) s.e. US; (4) Pacific n.w.; (5) n. Central states.

50.2 *Seryda* Walker

Two species, including the following:

S. constans Edwards. (See Fig. 27.155.)

[50.3 *Acoloithus* Clemens (3 spp.); 50.4 *Triprocris* Grote (2 spp.)]

50.5 *Tetraclonas* Jordan

Two species, both lycid beetle mimics:

T. dyari (Jordon). Wingspan: 18–23 mm. Wings orange with black tips. (3) AZ.

T. latercula (Edwards). Very similar to the preceding, but somewhat darker. (3) AZ.

50.6 *Pyromorpha* Herrich-Schaeffer

Six species, the following of which is common:

P. dimidiata Herrich-Schaeffer. Wingspan: 20–26 mm. Wings dark brown, front wings with orange on basal half. (1) n.e. US; (2) s.e. US.

51. MEGALOPYGIDAE (Flannel Moth Family)

Wingspan: 25–50 mm. The crinkly hairlike scales near the anterior border of the front wings differentiate most species of this family from all others. The frenulum is rudimentary in the species included here. Wings are white, orange-yellow, or marked with brown spots and margined with brown, some with broad brown bands. Larvae have seven pairs of abdominal prolegs; stinging hairs are mixed with soft hair in diffuse tufts. Eleven species in four genera are recorded in the U.S. and Canada.

[51.1 *Trosia* Huebner (1 sp., *T. obsolescens* Dyar)]

51.2 *Lagoa* Harris

Four species, the following of which is common:

L. crispata (Packard) (Crinkled Flannel Moth). Wingspan: 25–35 mm. Cream white; crinkly, hairlike, black and brown setae, mostly along costa. Larvae are cream white, turning darker as they mature, and feed on various shrubs and trees. (1) n.e. US: (2) s.e. US.

51.3 *Megalopyge* Huebner

Three species, the following of which are common:

M. opercularis (Smith) (Puss Caterpillar Moth). Wingspan: 25–40 mm. Thorax and abdomen with basal tufts of pale yellow, hairlike setae; wings with sparse, crinkly, hairlike, chocolate brown and white setae, blackish on Costa; outer margin of wings yellow; front legs blackish with white at apex of tibiae. Larvae feed on a variety of plants, including crops such as orange, pecan, almond, and persimon. (See Fig. 27.156 for male; Fig. 27.157 for female.) (1) NY (rare), PA, MD; (2) s.e. US.

M. lapena heteropuncta Barnes and McDunnough. (See Fig. 27.158.)

[51.4 *Norape* Walker (3 spp.)]

Fig. 27.155.

Fig. 27.156.

Fig. 27.157.

Fig. 27.158.

52. LIMACODIDAE
(Slug Caterpillar Moth Family)

Wingspan: 12–30 mm (usually 20–25 mm). Stumpy winged moths, usually brown or gray, but some species yellow or green. Larvae are sluglike caterpillars that crawl about on their flattened bodies instead of on legs. Some have spines that can be irritating to human skin if handled. They feed on the leaves of shrubs and trees. Of the 400 species known, 52 are reported in the U.S. and Canada, assigned to 21 genera.

[52.1 *Epiperola* Dyar (1 sp., *E. perornata* Dyar); 52.2 *Tortricidia* Packard (3 spp.); 52.3 *Slossonella* Dyar (1 sp., *S. tenebrosa* Dyar); 52.4 *Kronaea* Reakirt (1 sp., *K. minuta* Reakirt); 52.5 *Heterogenea* Knoch (1 sp., *H. shurtleffi* Packard); 52.6 *Packardia* Grote and Robinson (4 spp.); 52.7 *Lithacodes* Packard (4 spp.); 52.8 *Apoda* Haworth [=*Limacodes* Latreille] (4 spp.)]

52.9 *Prolimacodes* Schaus

Two species, the following of which is common:

P. badia Huebner. Wingspan: 25–30 mm. Front wings dark anteriorly, with pale posterior half distinctly separated by irregular border; hind wings dark. (See Fig. 27.159.) (1) n.e. US; (2) s.e. US.

52.10 *Cnidocampa* Dyar

One species, as follows:

C. flavescens (Walker) (Oriental Moth). Wingspan: ±30 mm. Outer half of front wings light fawn, with two oblique, brown lines and lemon yellow base. Introduced. (1) MA.

[52.11 *Alarodia* Moeschler (1 sp., *A. slossoniae* Packard); 52.12 *Cryptophobetron* Dyar (1 sp., *C. oropeso* Barnes); 52.13 *Isochaetes* Dyar (1 sp., *I. beutenmuelleri* Edwards)]

52.14 *Phobetron* Huebner

Two species, the following of which is common:

P. pithecium (Smith) (Hag Moth). Wingspan: 20–25 mm. Male with translucent, smoky wings, veins, and borders, especially inner margin of hind wing, which is smoky gray with darker, vague transverse bands. Female with opaque wings; front wings light to dark brown mixed with a few blue scales, thin borders dark and markings clear-cut; hind wings dark. Larvae with eight relatively long, fleshy, hairy, brown append-

ages that cover the back and project from the sides with a backward twist that makes them resemble locks of disheveled hair. These fleshy hooks are covered with feathery, brown hairlike setae, among which are longer, black, stinging hairlike setae. The bullet-shaped cocoon, which is protected by the stinging setae left behind from the larval skin, is attached to leaves or twigs and fully exposed to view but at the same time hidden because camouflaged to blend with its surroundings. The larvae feed on a great variety of leaves. (1) n.e. NA; (2) s.e. US.

[52.15 *Natada* Walker (2 spp.); 52.16 *Isa* Packard [=*Sisyrosea* Grote] (2 spp.); 52.17 *Adoneta* Clemens (4 spp.); 52.18 *Monoleuca* Grote and Robinson (8 spp.)]

52.19 *Euclea* Huebner

Five species, the following of which is common:

E. delphinii Boisduval. Wingspan: 25–30 mm. Brown, shading to purplish brown and tawny, and marked with green that may be edged with white. Larvae feed on trees and shrubs. Adults fly in June. (See Fig. 27.160.) (1) n.e. NA; (2) s.e. US.

52.20 *Parasa* Moore

Two species, as follows:

P. indetermina (Boisduval) (Stinging Rose Caterpillar Moth). Wingspan: 20–25 mm. Head and thorax green above,

Fig. 27.159.

Fig. 27.160.

Fig. 27.162.

brown beneath; front wings green with brown patch at base and brown and slightly irregular border, which is about one-fifth as broad as length of wing, and usually with darker shade at middle of outer margin. Male antennae serrate at middle. Larvae without hump but with strong stinging spines on second, fifth, and last segments of abdomen; body red or yellow, purple, and white. Found on apple, other trees, and roses. (See Fig. 27.161.) (1) n.e. US; (2) s.e. US.

P. chloris (Herrich-Schaeffer) (Green Slug Moth). Wingspan: 20–25 mm. Similar to the preceding except that veins of front wings are darker and center is without dark patch. Male antennae broadly pectinate. Larvae humped anteriorly, with spines reduced and a pointed tail. (1) s. NY, PA, NJ, MD; (2) s.e. US.

52.21 *Sibine* Herrich-Schaeffer

Two species, the following of which is common:

S. stimulea Clemens (Saddleback Caterpillar Moth). Wingspan: ±30 mm. Front wings shining, deep seal brown shaded with black and with three white points; hind wings paler. Body of larvae is brown, with strikingly marked green saddle, a central brown patch, and sharp spines on both anterior and posterior dorsal lobes. These spines can sting painfully. The cocoon is smooth, oval, and retains the larval hairlike setae for protection. Adults fly in July and August in the North and

throughout the year (except in December) in the extreme South. Larvae feed on apple, pear, cherry, corn, and a variety of other plants. (1) n.e. US; (2) s.e. US.

53. EPIPYROPIDAE (Epipyropid Moth Family)

This family contains only one species in the U.S.

53.1 *Fulgoraecia* Newman

One species only, as follows:

F. exigua Edwards. Wingspan: 8–13 mm. Wings dark mottled brownish purple. Larvae are parasites of certain fulgorid bugs. (See Fig. 27.162.) (1) DE, MD, PA; (2) AR, FL, GA, MS; (3) AZ, NM, TX.

54. DALCERIDAE (Dalcerid Moth Family)

One species only in the U.S., as follows:

54.1 *Dalcerides* Neumoegen and Dyar

D. ingenita Edwards. Wingspan: 18–24 mm. Front wings dark yellow; hind wings orange. (See Fig. 23.163.) (3) s. AZ.

Superfamily PYRALOIDEA

There are three families in this superfamily, most of the species belonging to the following very large family.

Fig. 27.161.

Fig. 27.163.

55. PYRALIDAE (Snout Moth Family)

Wingspan: 10–40 mm. These are moths of diverse shapes and colors, often resembling those of "macrolepidoptera" families. They are distinguished by small maxillary palpi of three to four segments or palpi that are only rudimentary; a proboscis with scales at base; ocelli usually present (although sometimes small) but sometimes absent; chaetosemata present in some subfamilies; antennae simple or filiform, rarely pectinate. Larvae are stem borers, leaf skeletonizers, or may roll and tie leaves, but are rarely leaf miners; a number are scavengers, including those that infest stored products. Some species are carnivorous and some aquatic or subaquatic, boring into the stems and roots of submerged plants.

This very large family has well over 11,000 species in the world, many of which are very common and a considerable number economically important. The Pyralidae represent the second largest family of the order and are divided into about 18 subfamilies. Some of these are treated as separate families by some authors. The following key to currently recognized subfamilies is adapted from Munroe, 1972. Some groups have been recently revised, and others still need study. There are 423 genera and 1374 species currently recorded in the U.S. and Canada.

Key to the Subfamilies of Pyralidae of the U.S. and Canada
(Adapted from Munroe, 1972)

Adults

1.	Median, longitudinal, chitinous flap (the *praecinctorium*) extends into the cavity between thorax and abdomen; tympanic bullae medially fused	*2*
	Praecinctorium absent; tympanic bullae separate or approximate	*12*
2(1).	Chaetosema present	*3*
	Chaetosema absent	*8*
3(2).	Front wing with distal part of 1st A developed as tubular vein	*4*
	Front wing with 1st A represented only by fold	*5*
4(3).	Proboscis present; R_2 of front wing stalked with R_{3+4}; M_2 of hind wing lost; outer margin of wing between apex and hind angle usually with series of black and metallic spots; (in part) **Nymphulinae**	
	Proboscis absent; R_2 of front wing either stalked with or separate from R_{3+4}; M_2 of hind wing present; outer margin of wing between apex and hind angle without series of black and metallic spots **Schoenobiinae**	
5(3).	Vein R_2 of front wing at least closely apposed to and usually stalked with R_{3+4}; labial palpi usually upturned and with basal segment relatively long; wings mostly with conspicuous pattern of transverse bands on pale ground; (in part) **Nymphulinae**	
	Vein R_2 of front wings well separated from R_{3+4}; labial palpi always porrect, with 2nd segment much longer than basal segment; maxillary palpi with prominent terminal tuft of scales connecting plane of vertex and front with dorsal plane of terminal part of labial palpi	*6*
6(5).	Front wings usually with weakly raised patches of black scales; Cu of hind wings usually not distinctly pectinated with hairlike scales **Scopariinae**	
	Front wings without raised patches of black scales; Cu of hind wings usually distinctly pectinated with hairlike scales	*7*
7(6).	Hind wings with cell closed, M_1 widely separated from Rs **Ancylolomiinae**	
	Hind wing with cell open, M_1 basally approximated to Rs **Crambinae**	
8(2).	Valve of male genitalia with costal process; uncus simple; gnathos well developed **Cybalomiinae**	
	Valve of male genitalia without costal process, or uncus bilobed and laterally decurved and setose, or gnathos absent	*9*
9(8).	Uncus of male genitalia bilobed and laterally setose; gnathos well developed **Odontiinae**	
	Uncus of male genitalia simple or gnathos rudimentary or absent	*10*
10(9).	Male genitalia with gnathos well developed, slender, dorsally toothed near apex; uncus narrow and distally pointed; valve usually without clasper, at most with simple hooklike clasper **Evergestinae**	
	Male genitalia with gnathos almost always weak and rudimentary or absent; gnathos, if well developed, not toothed dorsally and uncus broadly triangular, not long and slender	*11*
11(10).	Hind wings with areas of spatulate setae in cubital and anal regions of upperside; praecinctorium (see couplet 1) simple **Glaphyriinae**	
	Hind wings without areas of spatulate setae in cubital and anal regions of upperside; praecinctorium distally bilobed, often strongly so **Pyraustinae**	
12(1).	Veins R_3 and R_4 of front wings completely fused	*13*
	Veins R_3 and R_4 of front wings stalked	*14*
13(12).	Proboscis rudimentary or absent; uncus of male with prominent laterally or posterolaterally directed, spinelike process; ovipositor of female with deep, compressed lobes **Peoriinae**	

Key to the Subfamilies of Pyralidae of the U.S. and Canada (*Contd.*)
(Adapted from Munroe, 1972)

Proboscis usually well developed, but sometimes rudimentary or absent; if the latter, uncus of male simple and rounded and ovipositor of female with small, shallow lobes ..**Phycitinae**

14(12). Male genitalia with gnathos prominent, usually slender and distally hooked; uncus various .. *15*

Male genitalia without gnathos; uncus broad and rounded**Galleriinae**

15(14). Maxillary palpi absent; first A of hind wings absent**Chrysauginae**

Maxillary palpi present, often conspicuous; first A of hind wings well developed *16*

16(15). Front wing above tufted with scales; male with labial palpus or basal segment of antennae often produced upward and backward over vertex; Sc and Rs of hind wings anastomosed ..**Epipaschiinae**

Front wings above not tufted with scales; labial palpi and basal segment of antennae not produced upward and backward over vertex; Sc and Rs of hind wings usually only approximated ..**Pyralinae**

Subfamily Scopariinae

Small to medium-sized moths; wings triangular; front wings with tufts of scales; usually powdery gray to brown. Most species inhabit northern regions or mountains of the West.

[55.1 *Gesneria* Huebner (2 spp.); 55.2 *Cosipara* Munroe (3 spp.); 55.3 *Scoparia* Haworth (14 spp.); 55.4 *Eudonia* Billberg (18 spp.)]

Subfamily Nymphulinae

Small to medium-sized, slender, often pale moths, usually with definite, complicated patterns of transverse bands on front wings; hind wings sometimes with shining metallic spots. Larvae semiaquatic, feeding on aquatic plants.

Tribe Ambiini

[55.5 *Undulambia* Lange (3 spp.)]

Tribe Nymphulini

[55.6 *Neocatachysta* Lange (1 sp., *N. magnificalis* (Huebner)); 55.7 *Chrysendeton* Grote (3 spp.); 55.8 *Nymphula* Schrank (1 sp., *N. ekthlipsis* (Grote)); 55.9 *Munroessa* Lange (4 spp.); 55.10 *Contiger* Lange (1 sp., *C. vittatalis* (Dyar)); 55.11 *Nymphuliella* Lange (1 sp., *N. daeckealis* (Haimbach))]

55.12 *Synclita* Lederer

Four species, the following of which is a pest:

S. obliteralis (Walker) (Waterlily Leaf Cutter). Wingspan: male, 11–14 mm; female, 15–20 mm. Male front wings brownish gray—obscurely variegated with brown—with whitish spot; female paler, dull brownish gray to orange-brown. Larvae feed on waterlilies, pondweed, and duckweed. (1) n.e. US; (2) s.e. US; (3) e. TX.

[55.13 *Langessa* Munroe (1 sp., *L. nomophilalis* Dyar); 55.14 *Parapoynx* Huebner (6 spp.); 55.15 *Oligostigmoides* Lange (1 sp., *O. cryptale* (Druce))]

Tribe Argyractini

[55.16 *Usingeriessa* Lange (2 spp.); 55.17 *Neargyractis* Lange (1 sp., *N. slossonalis* (Dyar)); 55.18 *Petrophila* Guilding (15 spp.); 55.19 *Eoparargyractis* Lange (3 spp.); 55.20 *Oxyelophila* Forbes (1 sp., *O. callista* (Forbes))]

Subfamily Odontiinae

Minute to medium-sized moths with robust bodies; proboscis and maxillary palpi usually well-developed; ocelli present; eyes may be reduced; front prominent or armed with sclerotized processes. Wings usually relatively small, front wings often with scaled prominence of posterior margin near base. Larvae include leaf webbers, leaf miners, and seed feeders. Inhabitants of dry temperate regions throughout the U.S. and Canada. No species is of more than minor economic importance.

Tribe Dichogamini

[55.21 *Metrea* Grote (1 sp., *M. ostreonalis* Grote); 55.22 *Dichogama* Lederer (3 spp.); 55.23 *Alatuncusia* Amsel (1 sp., *A. bergii* (Moeschler)); 55.24 *Eustixis* Huebner (1 sp., *E. pupula* Huebner)]

Tribe Odontiini

[55.25 *Microtheoris* Meyrick (2 spp.); 55.26 *Rhodocantha* Munroe (1 sp., *R. diagonalis* Munroe); 55.27 *Frechinia* Munroe (6 spp.); 55.28 *Procymbopteryx* Munroe (1 sp., *P. belialis* (Druce)); 55.29 *Cymbopteryx* Munroe (2 spp.); 59.30 *Neocymbopteryx* Munroe (1 sp., *N. heitzmani* Munroe); 59.31 *Edia* Dyar (2 spp); 55.32 *Dichozoma* Munroe (1 sp., *D. parvipicta* (Barnes and McDunnough)); 55.33 *Cuneifrons* Munroe (1 sp., *C. coloradensis* Munroe); 55.34 *Gyros* Edwards (3 spp.); 55.35 *Anatralata* Munroe (1 sp., *A. versicolor* (Warren)); 55.36 *Eremantha* Munroe (1 sp., *E. chemsaki* Munroe); 55.37 *Metaxmeste* Huebner (1 sp., *M. nubicola* Munroe); 55.38 *Pogonogenys* Munroe (3 spp.); 55.39 *Chrismania* Barnes and McDunnough (1 sp., *C. pictipennalis* Barnes and McDunnough); 55.40 *Plumipalpia* Munroe (1 sp., *P. martini* Monroe); 55.41 *Nannobotys* Munroe (1 sp., *N. commortalis* (Grote)); 55.42 *Porphyrorhegma* Munroe (1 sp., *P. fortunata* Munroe); 55.43 *Psammobotys* Munroe (2 spp.).]

55.44 *Mimoschinia* Warren

One species, as follows:

M. rufofascialis (Stephens) (Barberpole Caterpillar Moth). Small to medium-sized; front wings light yellow, greenish, or buff above, sometimes heavily marked with reddish brown, with outwardly oblique band beyond middle and somewhat wavy postmedial band, both dark reddish brown. Several subspecies in the U.S. and Canada. Larvae of *M. r. novalis* (Grote) are white with wine-red band on each segment, but sometimes the entire thorax is red; they feed on various malvaceous plants. (3) s.e. US; (4) Pacific n.w.; (5) AB; WY.

[55.45 *Jativa* Munroe (1 sp., *J. castanealis* (Hulst)); 55.46 *Pseudoschinia* Munroe (1 sp., *P. elautalis* (Grote)); 55.47 *Odontivalvia* Munroe (1 sp., *O. radialis* Munroe); 55.48 *Noctueliopsis* Munroe (9 spp.); 55.49 *Mojavia* Munroe (1 sp., *M. achemonalis* (Barnes and McDunnough)); 55.50 *Mojaviodes* Munroe (1 sp., *M. blanchardae* Munroe); 55.51

Heliothelopsis Munroe (3 spp.); 55.52 *Chlorobapta* Barnes and McDunnough (1 sp., *C. rufistrigalis* Barnes and McDunnough); 55.53 *Glaucodontia* Munroe (1 sp., *G. pyraustoides* Munroe)]

Subfamily Glaphyriinae

Small, broad-winged moths; body slender to stout. Antennae short, somewhat thickened in male, and ventrally pilose or ciliated, dorsally scaled. Labial palpi usually short, three-segmented. Proboscis well-developed in most species but may be reduced or absent; eyes large; ocelli present, reduced, or absent; chaetosemata absent, but prominent tufts of radiating scales behind dorsal-lateral angle of eyes. Occurs throughout the U.S. and Canada.

55.54 *Hellula* Guenée

Five species, the following of which is a minor pest of cabbage:

H. rogatalis (Hulst) (Cabbage Webworm). Wingspan: 30–38 mm. Variegated from olive-brown on buff background to yellowish buff on whitish background. Larvae feed on cabbage, radish, and other cruciferous plants, as well as beets and relatives. (2) NC, SC, GA, FL, AL, MS, LA; (3) s.w. US.

[55.55 *Upiga* Capps (1 sp., *U. virescens* (Hulst)); 55.56 *Paregesta* Munroe (1 sp., *P. californiensis* Munroe); 55.57 *Scybalistodes* Munroe (4 spp.); 55.58 *Nephrogramma* Munroe (2 spp.); 55.59 *Stegea* Munroe (7 spp.); 55.60 *Abegesta* Munroe (3 spp.); 55.61 *Glaphyria* Huebner (6 spp.); 55.62 *Aethiophysa* Munroe (4 spp.); 55.63 *Xanthophysa* Munroe (1 sp., *X. psychialis* (Hulst)); 55.64 *Plumegesta* Munroe (1 sp., *P. largalis* Munroe); 55.65 *Lipocosma* Lederer (7 spp.); 55.66 *Lipocosmodes* Munroe (1 sp., *L. fuliginosalis* (Fernald)); 55.67 *Dicymolomia* Zeller (6 spp.); 55.68 *Chalcoela* Zeller (2 spp.)]

Subfamily Evergestinae

Small to medium-size, with triangular, usually broad front wings and broadly rounded hind wings; vertex roughly scaled; chaetosemata absent; labial palpi porrect or obliquely upturned; maxillary palpi prominent; proboscis well-developed; eyes may be reduced; ocelli present. Larvae are web makers and feed on cruciferous plants or Capparidaceae. Two species of the following genus are of some economic importance.

55.69 *Evergestis* Huebner

Nineteen species, the following two of which are pests:

E. pallidata (Hufnagel) (Purple-backed Cabbageworm). Wingspan: 20–25 mm. Straw yellow, sometimes dusted with brown, and with fine but distinct middle and lateral lines across wings. Adults fly May to September. Larvae feed on Cruciferae but are of minor economic importance. (1) n.e. NA; (2) KY, VA; (3) AZ; (4) Pacific n.w.; (5) n. Central states and provinces.

E. rimosalis (Guenée) (Cross-striped Cabbageworm). Wingspan: ±27 mm. Similar to the preceding but with obliquely brown shading along front of wing. Larvae feed on cabbage. (1) s. NY, IL, IN, OH, PA, NJ, MD; (2) s.e. US; (3) TX; (4) WA, OR, ID; (5) MT, WY, CO.

[55.70 *Prorasea* Grote (6 spp.); 55.71 *Cornifrons* Lederer (2 spp.); 55.72 *Cylindrifrons* Munroe (1 sp., *C. succandidalis* (Hulst)); 55.73 *Orenaia* Duponchel (7 spp.); 55.74 *Evergestella* Munroe (1 sp., *E. evincalis* (Moeschler)); 55.75 *Trischistognatha* Warren (1 sp., *T. pyrenealis* (Walker))]

Fig. 27.164.

Subfamily Pyraustinae

Species in this group are usually yellow or white. Larvae are web makers and leaf rollers, living gregariously, or they bore into stems and fruit.

Tribe Pyraustini

[55.76 *Munroeodes* Amsel (1 sp., *M. thalesalis* (Walker)); 55.77 *Saucrobotys* Munroe (2 spp.); 55.78 *Nascia* Curtis (1 sp., *N. acutella* (Walker)); 55.79 *Epicorsia* Huebner (1 sp., *E. oedipodalis* (Guenée)); 55.80 *Pseudopyrausta* Amsel (1 sp., *P. santalis* (Barnes and McDunnough)); 55.81 *Oenobotys* Munroe (2 spp.); 55.82 *Triuncidia* Munroe (1 sp., *T. eupalusalis* (Walker)); 55.83 *Crocidophora* Lederer (3 spp.)]

55.84 *Ostrinia* Huebner

Four species, the following of which are pests:

O. obumbratalis (Lederer) (Smartweed Borer). Wingspan: 20–27 mm. Pale buff with brownish transverse lines. Adults appear in June, frequenting meadows and lights at night. Larvae usually bore into *Polygonum* spp. but may also infest other plants bordering marshy areas, including corn. (1) n.e. NA; (2) s.e. US; (5) n. Central states and provinces.

O. nubilalis (Huebner) (European Corn Borer). Wingspan: 30–35 mm. Similar to the preceding but usually darker brown. Adults emerge from pupae in May and lay eggs on newly planted corn; larvae feed on the stalks and leaves. Introduced from Europe about 1909 and spread rapidly through NA. (See Fig. 27.164 for male; Fig. 27.165 for female.) (1) n.e. NA; (2) s.e.

Fig. 27.165.

US; (3) s.w. US; (5) MB, SK, MT, ND, MN, WY, NE, IA, CO, KS, MO.

[55.85 *Fumibotys* Munroe (1 sp., *F. fumalis* (Guenée)); 55.86 *Perispasta* Zeller (1 sp., *P. caeculalis* Zeller); 55.87 *Eurrhypara* Huebner (1 sp., *E. hortulata* (Linnaeus)); 55.88 *Phlyctaenia* Huebner (3 spp.); 55.89 *Nealgedonia* Munroe (1 sp., *N. extricalis* (Guenée)); 55.90 *Mutuuraia* Munroe (1 sp., *N. mysippusalis* (Walker)); 55.91 *Anania* Huebner (2 spp.); 55.92 *Hahncappsia* Munroe (14 spp.)]

55.93 *Achyra* Guenée

Three species, the following of which is a pest:

A. rantalis (Guenée) (Garden Webworm). Wingspan: ±20 mm. Yellowish with grayish brown markings. Web-making larvae are yellow with black spots and feed on weeds as well as garden plants, skeletonizing leaves. Pupae live in silk-lined cases in the ground. (1), (2), (3), (4), (5), widespread.

[55.94 *Neohelvibotys* Munroe (3 spp.); 55.95 *Helvibotys* Munroe (5 spp.); 55.96 *Sitochroa* Huebner (3 spp.); 55.97 *Arenochroa* Munroe (1 sp., *A. flavalis* (Fernald)); 55.98 *Xanthostege* Munroe (2 spp.); 55.99 *Sericoplaga* Warren (1 sp., *S. externalis* Warren)]

55.100 *Uresiphita* Huebner

One species, as follows:

U. reversalis (Guenée) (Genista Caterpillar Moth). Wingspan: ±30 mm. Front wings brown with faint markings; hind wings bright yellow with blackish apex. Adults fly in June and July. Larvae feed on *Baptisia* spp., *Lonicera* spp., and others; sometimes a pest of ornamentals. (1) n.e. US; (2) s.e. US; (3) s.w. US; (5) n. Central States.

55.101 *Loxostege* Huebner

Twenty-five species, the following of which are pests:

L. sticticalis (Linnaeus) (Beet Webworm). Wingspan: ±25 mm. Yellowish with light brown markings. Larvae general feeders, including on cultivated plants. (1), (2), (3), (4), (5), generally distributed.

L. cereralis (Zeller) (Alfalfa Webworm). Similar to the preceding but nearly white, heavily streaked with brown, especially on veins. Larvae feed on alfalfa.

[55.102 *Pyrausta* Schrank (59 spp.); 55.103 *Hyalorista* Warren (1 sp., *H. taeniolalis* (Guenée)); 55.104 *Portentomorpha* Amsel (1 sp., *P. xanthialis* (Guenée))]

Tribe Spilomelini

55.105 *Udea* Guenée

Twenty-three species, all of them leaf tiers. The following are pests:

U. rubigalis (Guenée) (Celery Leaf Tier; Greenhouse Leaf Tier).

U. profundalis (Packard) (False Celery Leaf Tier).

[55.106 *Neoleucinodes* Capps (1 sp., *N. prophetica* (Dyar)); 55.107 *Lamprosema* Huebner (3 spp.); 55.108 *Lineodes* Guenée (4 spp.); 55.109 *Zellerina* Torre y Callejas (1 sp., *Z. solanalis* (Barnes and McDunnough)); 55.110 *Ercta* Walker (1 sp., *E. vittata* (Fabricius)); 55.111 *Apilocrocis* Amsel (2 spp.); 55.112 *Diaphantania* Moeschler (1 sp., *D. impulsalis* (Herrich-Schaeffer); 55.113 *Loxostegopsis* Dyar (5 spp.); 55.114 *Sufetula* Walker (1 sp., *S. diminutalis* (Walker)); 55.115 *Falcimorpha* Amsel (1 sp., *F. philogelos* (Dyar)); 55.116 *Eurrhyparodes* Snellen (1 sp., *E. lygdamis* Druce); 55.117 *Deuterophysa* Warren (1 sp., *D. fernaldi* Munroe); 55.118 *Hydropionea* Hampson (2 spp.)]

55.119 *Geshna* Dyar

One species, as follows:

G. cannalis (Quaintance) (Lesser Canna Leaf Roller).

[55.120 *Hydriris* Meyrick (1 sp., *H. ornatalis* (Duponchel)); 55.121 *Choristostigma* Warren (7 spp.); 55.122 *Mecyna* Doubleday (4 spp.); 55.123 *Mimorista* Warren (3 spp.); 55.124 *Diacme* Warren (4 spp.); 55.125 *Epipagis* Huebner (3 spp.); 55.126 *Sameodes* Snellen (1 sp., *S. albiguttalis* (Warren)); 55.127 *Samea* Guenée (3 spp.); 55.128 *Somatania* Moeschler (1 sp., *S. pellucidalis* Moeschler); 55.129 *Loxomorpha* Amsel (2 spp.); 55.130 *Nomophila* Huebner (1 sp., *nearctica* Munroe); 55.131 *Pilemia* Moeschler (1 sp., *P. periusalis* (Walker)); 55.132 *Ategumia* Amsel (1 sp., *A. ebulealis* Guenée)]

55.133 *Desmia* Westwood

Ten species, the following of which is a pest:

D. funeralis (Huebner) (Grape Leaf Roller). Wingspan: 20–28 mm. Brownish black with two white spots on each front wing and one on each hind wing. Adults fly May to October. Larvae feed on grape leaves, folding and fastening them with strands of silk, then feeding on upper surface within fold that protects them from most predators. (See Fig. 27.166.) (1), (2), (3), (4), (5), widespread.

55.134 *Hymenia* Huebner

One species, as follows:

H. perspectalis (Huebner) (Spotted Beet Webworm). Wingspan: ±22 mm. Brown mottled with yellow and translucent white or yellowish markings. Adults fly in late autumn. Larvae feed on beets, chard, often in greenhouses. (1) n.e. US; (2) s.e. US.

55.135 *Spoladea* Guenée

One species, as follows:

S. recurvalis (Fabricius) (Hawaiian Beet Webworm). Similar to the preceding. (1) NY, PA, MD; (2) s.e. US.

[55.136 *Diasemiopsis* Munroe (1 sp., *D. leodocusalis* (Walker)); 55.137 *Diasemiodes* Munroe (2 spp.); 55.138 *Diathrausta* Lederer (2 spp.); 55.139 *Anageshna* Munroe (1 sp., *A. primordialis* (Dyar)); 55.140 *Apogeshna* Munroe (1 sp., *A. stenialis* (Guenée)); 55.141 *Steniodes*

Fig. 27.166.

Snellen (1 sp., *S. mendica* (Hedemann)); 55.142 *Penestola* Moeschler (1 sp., *P. simplicialis* Barnes and McDunnough)); 55.143 *Antigastra* Lederer (1 sp., *A. catalaunalis* (Duponchel)); 55.144 *Blepharomastix* Lederer (12 spp.); 55.145 *Araschnopsis* Amsel (1 sp., *A. subulalis* (Guenée)); 55.146 *Elepte* Huebner (1 sp., *E. anticostalis* (Grote)): 55.147 *Synclera* Lederer (1 sp., *S. jarbusalis* (Walker)); 55.148 *Glyphodes* Guenée (3 spp.); 55.149 *Colomychus* Munroe (1 sp., *C. talis* (Grote))]

55.150 *Diaphania* Huebner

Eight species, the following of which are pests:

D. nitidalis (Stoll) (Pickleworm). Larvae on cucumber and related plants. (1) strays to NY; (2) s.e. US.

D. hyalinata (Linnaeus) (Melonworm). Wingspan: ±28 mm. White with dark edges on front and hind wings. Larvae feed on various melons. (1) strays to s. Canada; (2) s.e. US.

[55.151 *Hoterodes* Guenée (1 sp., *H. ausonia* (Cramer)); 55.152 *Leucochroma* Guenée (1 sp., *L. corope* (Stoll)); 55.153 *Omiodes* Guenée (4 spp.); 55.154 *Condylorrhiza* Lederer (1 sp., *C. vestigialis* (Guenée)); 55.155 *Stemorrhages* Lederer (1 sp., *S. costata* (Fabricius)); 55.156 *Palpita* Huebner (11 spp.); 55.157 *Polygrammodes* Guenée (4 spp.); 55.158 *Azochis* Walker (1 sp., *A. rufidiscalis* Hampson); 55.159 *Compacta* Amsel (3 spp.); 55.160 *Laniifera* Hampson (1 sp., *L. cyclades* (Druce)); 55.161 *Mimophobetron* Munroe (1 sp., *M. pyropsalis* (Hampson)); 55.162 *Liopasia* Moeschler (1 sp., *L. teneralis* (Lederer)); 55.163 *Terastia* Guenée (1 sp., *T. meticulosalis* Guenée); 55.164 *Agathodes* Guenée (1 sp., *A. designalis* Guenée)]

55.165 *Pantographa* Lederer

One species, as follows:

P. limata Grote and Robinson (Basswood Leaf Roller). Wingspan: ±37 mm. White, shaded with yellow, marked with dull brown. Adults fly June through August. Larvae feed on basswood (linden). (1) n.e. US; (2) s.e. US.

[55.166 *Pleuroptya* Meyrick (3 spp.); 55.167 *Syllepte* Huebner (1 sp., *S. diacymalis* (Hampson)); 55.168 *Phaedropsis* Warren (2 spp.)]

55.169 *Lygropia* Lederer

Four species, the following of which is a pest:

L. tripunctata (Fabricius) (Sweetpotato Leaf Roller). Wingspan: 25–30 mm. Larvae feed on sweetpotato. (2) s.e. US.

[55.170 *Lypotigris* Huebner (1 sp., *L. reginalis* (Stoll)); 55.171 *Diastictis* Huebner (9 spp.); 55.172 *Framinghamia* Strand (1 sp., *F. helvalis* (Walker)); 55.173 *Microthyris* Lederer (2 spp.); 55.174 *Phostria* Huebner (2 spp.); 55.175 *Asciodes* Guenée (1 sp., *A. gordialis* Guenée); 55.176 *Psara* Snellen (2 spp.); 55.177 *Sathria* Lederer (1 sp., *S. internitalis* (Guenée)); 55.178 *Bicilia* Amsel (1 sp., *B. iarchasalis* (Walker))]

55.179 *Herpetogramma* Lederer

Nine species, the following of which are pests:

H. phaeopteralis Guenée (Tropical Sod Webworm).

H. bipunctalis (Fabricius) (Southern Beet Webworm). Wingspan 25 mm. Dull yellow-brown with black kidney-shaped spot and smaller, circular spot on front wing. Larvae feed on beets and many other herbaceous plants. (1) IL, IN, OH, PA, NJ, MD; (2) s.e. US.

[55.180 *Pilocrocis* Lederer (1 sp., *P. ramentalis* Lederer); 55.181 *Cryptobotys* Munroe (1 sp., *C. zoilusalis* (Walker)); 55.182 *Syllepis* Poey (1 sp., *S. hortalis* (Walker)); 55.183 *Syngamia* Guenée (1 sp., *S. florella* (Stoll)); 55.184 *Salbia* Guenée (3 spp.); 55.185 *Marasmia* Lederer (2 spp.); 55.186 *Conchylodes* Guenée (4 spp.); 55.187 *Ommatospila* Lederer (1 sp., *O. narcaeusalis* (Walker)); 55.188 *Daulia* Walker (2 spp.); 55.189 *Palpusia* Amsel (1 sp., *P. goniopalpia* (Hampson)); 55.190 *Maracayia* Amsel (1 sp., *M. chlorisalis* (Walker))]

Subfamily Schoenobiinae

A small group, mostly of aquatic species. Wings loosely rolled in repose; proboscis weak or absent. Adults frequent wet places. Larvae are borers in marsh and aquatic plants. Twenty-six species in the following genera.

[55.191 *Acentria* Stephens (1 sp., *A. nivea* (Olivier)); 55.192 *Patissa* Moore (7 spp.); 55.193 *Scirpophaga* Treitschke (2 spp.); 55.194 *Carectocultus* Blanchard (1 sp., *C. dominicki* Blanchard); 55.195 *Rupela* Walker (3 spp.); 55.196 *Donacaula* Meyrick (12 spp.)]

Subfamily Cybalomiinae

Only one species, as follows:

[55.197 *Cybalomia* Lederer (1 sp., *C. extorris* Warren)]

Subfamily Ancylolomiinae

Front wing frequently notched at middle and twisted in the resting position. Only 15 species in the U.S and Canada; most species are Old World.

55.198 *Surattha* Walker

Two species, the following of which is a pest:

S. indentella Kearfott (Buffalograss Webworm).

[55.199 *Mesolia* Ragonot (4 spp.); 55.200 *Prionapteryx* Stephens (5 spp.); 55.201 *Pseudoschoenobius* Fernald (1 sp., *P. opalescalis* (Hulst)); 55.202 *Eufernaldia* Hulst (1 sp., *E. cadarella* (Druce))]

Subfamily Crambinae

These are the grass moths, often very common; many species occur throughout the U.S. and Canada. When at rest, most species wrap wings tightly around body, thereby emphasizing their long palpi, making them appear to have a "snout." Larvae of many feed on grasses at night.

Tribe Crambini

55.203 *Crambus* Fabricius

Fifty species, of which those listed are pests. Larvae are known as "sodworms"; they feed on grasses at night, retreating to tubes made of silk and cut grass.

C. agitatellus Clemens (Grass Webworm). Wingspan: 20–35 mm. Front wings pale yellow with darker markings and silver streaks. Adults appear in July. Larvae make webbings in grass. (See Fig. 27.167.) (1), (2), (3), (4), (5), generally distributed.

C. teterrellus (Zincken) (Bluegrass Webworm). A light brown species.

C. caliginosellus Clemens (Corn Root Webworm). A smoky brown to dusty brown species. Larvae are pests of corn, tobacco, and a variety of grasses.

C. vulgivagellus Clemens (Vagabond Crambus). Clay-colored species with front part and outer margins of front wings shading to pale yellow. Larvae common on grass and sorrel. (1) n.e. NA.

[55.204 *Fernandocrambus* Aurivillius (2 spp.)]

Fig. 27.167.

55.205 *Chrysoteuchia* Huebner

One species, as follows:

C. topiaria (Zeller) (Cranberry Girdler). Wingspan: ±18 mm. Clay-colored to clear yellow toward outer margin of front wings, with dark brown and five more or less shining stripes between veins. Adults fly during June and July. Larvae are minor pest of cranberry but feed on great variety of low-growing plants. (1), (2), (3), (4), (5), generally distributed.

[55.206 *Arequipa* Walker (1 sp., *A. turbatella* Walker); 55.207 *Raphiptera* Hampson (1 sp., *R. argillaceella* (Packard)); 55.208 *Platytes* Guenée (1 sp., *P. vobisne* Dyar); 55.209 *Agriphila* Huebner (11 spp.); 55.210 *Catoptria* Huebner (4 spp.); 55.211 *Pediasia* Huebner (8 spp.); 55.212 *Microcrambus* Bleszynski (9 spp.); 55.213 *Loxocrambus* Forbes (3 spp.); 55.214 *Fissicrambus* Morrison (12 spp.); 55.215 *Thaumatopsis* Morrison (12 spp.); 55.216 *Parapediasia* Bleszynski (3 spp.); 55.217 *Tehama* Hulst (1 sp., *T. bonifatella* (Hulst)); 55.218 *Euchromius* Guenée (2 spp.); 55.219 *Microcausta* Hampson (2 spp.); 55.220 *Diptychophora* Zeller (2 spp.)]

Tribe Argyriini

[55.221 *Argyria* Huebner (4 spp.); 55.222 *Urola* Walker (1 sp., *U. nivalis* (Drury)); 55.223 *Vaxi* Bleszynski (3 spp.)]

Tribe Chilini

[55.224 *Epina* Walker (2 spp.)]

55.225 *Chilo* Zincken

Three species, the following of which is a pest:

C. plejadellus Zincken (Rice Stalk Borer). Pest of rice in South and wild rice in North.

[55.226 *Thopeutis* Huebner (1 sp., *T. forbesellus* (Fernald)); 55.227 *Acigona* Huebner (1 sp., *A. comptulatalis* (Hulst))]

55.228 *Diatraea* Guilding

Seven species, the following of which are pests:

D. saccharalis (Fabricius) (Sugarcane Borer).

D. grandiosella (Dyar) (Western Corn Borer).

D. crambidoides (Grote) (Southern Cornstalk Borer).

[55.229 *Haimbachia* Dyar (10 spp.); 55.230 *Eoreuma* Ely (7 spp.); 55.231 *Xubida* Schaus (8 spp.); 55.232 *Hemiplatytes* Barnes and Benjamin (3 spp.)]

Subfamily Pyralinae

Species with well-developed, prominent, linear maxillary palpi that appear snoutlike; front wings without tufts of scales; antennal socket rarely separated from eye by scales.

55.233 *Pyralis* Linnaeus

Six species, the following of which is a pest:

P. farinalis (Linnaeus) (Meal Moth). Wingspan: 15–35 mm. Pale brown with darker brown markings and irregular white lines across wings. Larvae and adults found in stored grain and hay. (See Fig. 27.168.) (1), (2), (3), (4), (5), generally distributed.

[55.234 *Aglossa* Latreille (8 spp.)]

55.235 *Hypsopygia* Huebner

One species, as follows:

H. costalis (Fabricius) (Clover Hayworm). Wingspan: 13–18 mm. Light dull rose with fine, pale yellow lines across wings and anterior wing patches. Larvae found in stored hay; a minor pest. (1), (2), (3), (4), (5), generally distributed.

[55.236 *Herculia* Walker (9 spp.); 55.237 *Uscodys* Dyar (2 spp.); 55.238 *Neodavisia* Barnes and McDunnough (1 sp., *N. singularis* (Barnes and McDunnough))]

Subfamily Chrysauginae

Maxillary palpi completely absent; labial palpi normal, not elongate, and fully scaled; proboscis well-developed; ocelli usually present. Larvae are usually leaf rollers.

[55.239 *Caphys* Walker (1 sp., *C. arizonensis* Munroe); 55.240 *Parachma* Walker (3 spp.); 55.241 *Acallis* Ragonot (3 spp.); 55.242 *Zaboba* Dyar (2 spp.); 55.243 *Anemosella* Dyar (4 spp.); 55.244 *Lepidomys* Guenée (1 sp., *L. irrenosa* Guenée); 55.245 *Negalasa* Barnes and McDunnough (1 sp., *N. fumalis* Barnes and McDunnough); 55.246 *Galasa* Walker (2 spp.); 55.247 *Tetraschistis* Hampson (1 sp., *T. leucogramma* Hampson); 55.248 *Penthesilea* Ragonot (1 sp., *P. sacculalis* (Ragonot)); 55.249 *Tosale* Walker (3 spp.); 55.250 *Salobrena* Walker (2 spp.); 55.251 *Epitamyra* Ragonot (1 sp., *E. birectalis* Hampson); 55.252 *Salole* Dyar (1 sp., *S. ligniperdalis* Dyar); 55.253 *Clydonopteron* Riley (1 sp., *C. tecomae* Riley); 55.254 *Bonchis* Walker (1 sp., *B. munitalis* (Lederer)); 55.255 *Streptopalpia* Hampson (1 sp., *S.*

Fig. 27.168.

minusculalis (Moeschler)); 55.256 *Arta* Grote (3 spp.); 55.257 *Xantippe* Ragonot (2 spp.); 55.258 *Condylolomia* Grote (1 sp., *C. participalis* Grote); 55.259 *Blepharocerus* Blanchard (2 spp.); 55.260 *Heliades* Ragonot (1 sp., *H. mulleolella* (Hulst))]

Subfamily Epipaschiinae

Front wings with tufts of scales. Species may be distinguished from the Pyralinae by antennal sockets that are completely surrounded by scales.

[55.261 *Macalla* Walker (2 spp.); 55.262 *Epipaschia* Clemens (3 spp.); 55.263 *Cacozelia* Grote (2 spp.); 55.264 *Jocara* Walker (6 spp.); 55.265 *Oneida* Hulst (2 spp.); 55.266 *Pococera* Zeller (1 sp., *P. atramentalis* Lederer); 55.267 *Tallula* Hulst (4 spp.)]

55.268 *Tetralopha* Zeller

Twenty-six species, the following of which are pests:

T. robustella Zeller (Pine Webworm). Wingspan: 22–25 mm. Antennae with basal segment much enlarged; male with yellow maxillary plumes; wings with basal third black, remainder gray with white markings. Larvae feed on pine. (1), (2), (3), (4), (5), generally distributed.

T. scortealis (Lederer) (Lespedeza Webworm). (See Fig. 27.169.) Similar to the preceding. Larvae feed on various legumes.

[55.269 *Coenodomus* Walsingham (1 sp., *C. hockingii* Walsingham)]

Subfamily Galleriinae

These few species are best known as scavengers (in larval stage) in nests of various bees.

Tribe Galleriini

55.270 *Galleria* Fabricius

One species, as follows:

G. mellonella (Linnaeus) (Greater Wax Moth). Wingspan: 25–35 mm. Purplish brown, mottled front wings and pale brown or yellowish hind wings. Female lays eggs at night in hives of Honey Bees. Larvae feed at night to prevent being stung and thrown out of hive and hide by day in silken tubes of their construction. Poorly kept hives are seriously damaged by larval webbing and destruction of combs. (See Fig. 27.170.) Cosmopolitan.

Fig. 27.169.

Fig. 27.170.

55.271 *Achroia* Huebner

One species, as follows:

A. grisella (Fabricius) (Lesser Wax Moth). Wingspan: 17–21 mm. Similar to the preceding but smaller; head yellow; similar habits, but larvae also feed on dried stored food and dead insects. Cosmopolitan.

[55.272 *Trachylepidia* Ragonot (1 sp., *T. fructicassiella* Ragonot)]

Tribe Megarthridini

[55.273 *Omphalocera* Lederer (3 spp.); 55.274 *Thyridopyralis* Dyar (1 sp., *T. gallaerandialis* Dyar)]

Tribe Tirathabini

55.275 *Aphomia* Huebner

Three species, the following of which is a pest:

A. gularis (Zeller) (Stored Nut Moth).

[55.276 *Paralipsa* Butler (2 spp.)]

55.277 *Corcyra* Ragonot

One species, as follows:

C. cephalonica (Stainton). Common pest of stored products in Europe now introduced into U.S.

Tribe Macrothecini

[55.278 *Macrotheca* Ragonot (10 spp.); 55.279 *Alpheias* Ragonot (4 spp.); 55.280 *Alpheioides* Barnes and McDunnough (1 sp., *A. parvulalis* Barnes and McDunnough); 55.281 *Decaturia* Barnes and McDunnough (1 sp., *D. pectinalis* Barnes and McDunnough)]

Subfamily Phycitinae

Usually silky gray; proboscis usually well developed; head with antennal socket separated from eyes by complete line of scales; wings without tufts of scales; wingspan seldom over 30 mm. This large subfamily has many species of economic importance.

55.282 *Acrobasis* Zeller

Forty-four species, very difficult to identify and with a wide variety of feeding habits but usually host specific.

A. juglandis (LeBaron) (Pecan Leaf Casebearer).

A. nuxvorella Neunzig (Pecan Nut Casebearer).

A. betulella Hulst (Birch Tube Maker).

Z. indigenella (Zeller) (Leaf Crumpler).

A. vaccinii Riley (Cranberry Fruitworm).

A. comptoniella Hulst (Sweetfern Leaf Casebearer).

A. demotella Grote (Walnut Shoot Moth).

[55.283 *Rhodophaea* Guenée (8 spp.); 55.284 *Trachycera* Ragonot (1 sp., *T. pallicornella* (Ragonot)); 55.285 *Anabasis* Heinrich (1 sp., *A. ochrodesma* (Zeller)); 55.286 *Hypsipyla* Ragonot (1 sp., *H. grandella* (Zeller)); 55.287 *Crocidomera* Zeller (1 sp., *C. turbidella* Zeller); 55.288 *Cuniberta* Heinrich (1 sp., *C. subtinctella* (Ragonot)); 55.289 *Adanarsa* Heinrich (1 sp., *A. intransitella* (Dyar)); 55.290 *Bertelia* Barnes and McDunnough (2 spp.); 55.291 *Hypargyria* Ragonot (1 sp., *H. slossonella* (Hulst)); 55.292 *Chararica* Heinrich (3 spp.); 55.293 *Myelois* Huebner (1 sp., *M. grossipunctella* Ragonot); 55.294 *Myelopsis* Heinrich (5 spp.); 55.295 *Apomyelois* Heinrich (1 sp., *A. bistriatella* (Hulst)); 55.296 *Ectomyelois* Heinrich (2 spp.)]

55.297 *Amyelois* Amsel

One species, as follows:

A. transitella (Walker) (Navel Orangeworm).

55.298 *Fundella* Zeller

Two species, the following of which is a pest:

F. pellucens Zeller (Caribbean Pod Borer).

[55.299 *Promylea* Ragonot (1 sp., *P. lunigerella* Ragonot); 55.300 *Anadelosemia* Dyar (2 spp.); 55.301 *Dasypyga* Ragonot (2 spp.); 55.302 *Davara* Walker (1 sp., *D. caricae* (Dyar)); 55.303 *Sarasota* Hulst (1 sp., *S. plumigerella* Hulst); 55.304 *Atheloca* Heinrich (1 sp., *A. subrufella* (Hulst)); 55.305 *Triozosneura* Blanchard (1 sp., *T. dorsonotata* Blanchard)]

55.306 *Monoptilota* Hulst

One species, as follows:

M. pergratialis (Hulst) (Lima-bean Vine Borer).

[55.307 *Zamagiria* Dyar (3 spp.); 55.308 *Anegcephalesis* Dyar (1 sp., *A. arctella* (Ragonot)); 55.309 *Ancylostomia* Ragonot (1 sp., *A. stercorea* (Zeller)); 55.310 *Caristanius* Heinrich (2 spp.)]

55.311 *Etiella* Zeller

One species, as follows:

E. zinckenella (Treitschke) (Lima-bean Pod Borer).

[55.312 *Glyptocera* Ragonot (1 sp., *G. consobrinella* (Zeller)); 55.313 *Pima* Hulst (8 spp.); 55.314 *Pimodes* Blanchard (1 sp., *P. insularis* Blanchard); 55.315 *Interjectio* Heinrich (4 spp.); 55.316 *Ambesa* Grote (3 spp.); 55.317 *Catastia* Huebner (3 spp.); 55.318 *Glyphocystis* Blanchard (1 sp., *G. viridivallis* Blanchard); 55.319 *Immyrla* Dyar (1 sp., *I. nigrovittella* Dyar); 55.320 *Oreana* Hulst (1 sp., *O. unicolorella* (Hulst)); 55.321 *Olybria* Heinrich (2 spp.); 55.322 *Salebriacus* Heinrich (1 sp., *S. odiosellus* (Hulst)); 55.323 *Salebriaria* Heinrich (7 spp.); 55.324 *Salebria* Zeller (1 sp., *S. nigricans* Hulst); 55.325 *Quasisalebria* Heinrich (1 sp., *Q. admixta* Heinrich); 55.326 *Ortholepia* Ragonot (4 spp.); 55.327 *Polopeustis* Ragonot (1 sp., *P. arctiella* (Gibson)); 55.328 *Meroptera* Grote (4 spp.)]

55.329 *Nephopterix* Huebner

Nineteen species, the following of which is a pest:

N. subcaesiella (Clemens) (Locust Leaf Roller).

[55.330 *Tlascala* Hulst (1 sp., *T. reductella* (Walker)); 55.331 *Tulsa* Heinrich (3 spp.); 55.332 *Telethusia* Heinrich (2 spp.); 55.333 *Phobus*

Heinrich (4 spp.); 55.334 *Actrix* Heinrich (2 spp.); 55.335 *Stylopalpia* Hampson (1 sp., *S. scobiella* (Grote)); 55.336 *Hypochalcia* Huebner (1 sp., *H. hulstiella* Ragonot); 55.337 *Pyla* Grote (18 spp.); 55.338 *Phycitopsis* Ragonot (1 sp., *P. flavicornella* Ragonot)]

55.339 *Dioryctria* Zeller

Twenty-three species, the following of which are pests:

D. disclusa Heinrich (Webbing Coneworm). Wingspan: 23–27 mm. Front wing bright reddish, orange-brown, or yellowish, usually with whitish or pale buff dusting, orange band, and pale lines and streaks. Larvae feed on pine cones. (See Fig. 27.171.) (1) n.e. US; (2) s.e. US.

D. zimmermani (Grote) (Zimmerman Pine Moth). Larvae bore in pine, usually under bark of small branches, causing pitch to ooze out. (1) n.e. NA.

D. reniculelloides Mutuura and Munroe (Spruce Coneworm). Larvae feed on young cones of spruce and fir but rarely on balsam fir and tamarack. (1) n.e. NA; (4) Pacific n.w.; (5) n. Central state and provinces.

D. amatella (Hulst) (Southern Pine Coneworm).

D. clarioralis (Walker) (Blister Coneworm).

[55.340 *Oryctometopia* Ragonot (1 sp., *O. fossulatella* Ragonot); 55.341 *Sarata* Ragonot (20 spp.); 55.342 *Philodema* Heinrich (1 sp., *P. rhoiella* (Dyar)); 55.343 *Lipographis* Ragonot (4 spp.); 55.344 *Adelphia* Heinrich (2 spp.); 55.345 *Ufa* Walker (4 spp.)]

55.346 *Elasmopalpus* Blanchard

One species, as follows:

E. lignosellus (Zeller) (Lesser Cornstalk Borer).

[55.347 *Acroncosa* Barnes and McDunnough (2 spp.); 55.348 *Passodena* Hulst (1 sp., *P. flavidorsella* (Ragonot)); 55.349 *Ulophora* Ragonot (1 sp., *U. groteii* Ragonot); 55.350 *Tacoma* Hulst (3 spp.); 55.351 *Ragonotia* Grote (1 sp., *R. dotalis* (Hulst)); 55.352 *Martia* Ragonot (1 sp., *M. arizonella* Ragonot); 55.353 *Eumysia* Dyar (5 spp.); 55.354 *Divitiaca* Barnes and McDunnough (3 spp.); 55.355 *Macrorrhinia* Ragonot (2 spp.); 55.356 *Ocala* Hulst (1 sp., *O. dryadella* Hulst); 55.357 *Valdivia* Ragonot (1 sp., *V. lativittella* (Ragonot)); 55.358 *Heterographis* Ragonot (1 sp., *H. morrisonella* Ragonot); 55.359 *Staudingeria* Ragonot (1 sp., *S. albipenella* (Hulst))]

55.360 *Hulstia* Ragonot

One species, as follows:

H. undulatella (Clemens) (Sugarbeet Crown Borer).

Fig. 27.171.

[55.361 *Honora* Grote (7 spp.); 55.362 *Canarsia* Hulst (1 sp., *C. ulmiarrosorella* (Clemens); 55.363 *Eurythnidia* Ragonot (1 sp., *E. ignidorsella* (Ragonot)); 55.364 *Wunderia* Grossbeck (1 sp., *W. neaeriatella* Grossbeck); 55.365 *Diviana* Ragonot (1 sp., *D. eudoreella* Ragonot); 55.366 *Palatka* Hulst (1 sp., *P. nymphaeella* (Hulst))]

55.367 *Psorosina* Dyar

One species, as follows:

P. hammondi (Riley) (Apple Leaf Skeletonizer).

[55.368 *Patriciola* Heinrich (1 sp. *P. semicana* Heinrich); 55.369 *Anderida* Heinrich (1 sp., *A. sonorella* (Ragonot)); 55.370 *Mescinia* Ragonot (1 sp., *M. estrella* Barnes and McDunnough)]

55.371 *Homoeosoma* Curtis

Eleven species, the following of which is a pest:

H. electellum (Hulst) (Sunflower Moth).

[55.372 *Phycitodes* Hampson (1 sp., *P. albatella* (Ragonot)); 55.373 *Unadilla* Hulst (2 spp.); 55.374 *Laetilia* Ragonot (5 spp.); 55.375 *Rostrolaetillia* Blanchard (10 spp.); 55.376 *Welderella* Blanchard (1 sp., *W. parvella* (Dyar)); 55.377 *Baphala* Heinrich (1 sp., *B. basimaculatella* (Ragonot)); 55.378 *Rhagea* Heinrich (2 spp.)]

55.379 *Zophodia* Huebner

Two species, the following of which is a pest:

Z. convulutella (Huebner) (Gooseberry Fruitworm).

55.380 *Melitara* Walker

Two species, the following of which is common:

M. dentata (Grote) (Blue Cactus Borer).

[55.381 *Olycella* Dyar (2 spp.); 55.382 *Alberada* Heinrich (3 spp.); 55.383 *Cahela* Heinrich (1 sp., *C. ponderosella* (Barnes and McDunnough)); 55.384 *Rumatha* Heinrich (3 spp.); 55.385 *Yosemitia* Ragonot (3 spp.); 55.386 *Eremberga* Heinrich (3 spp.); 55.387 *Ozamia* Ragonot (2 spp.); 55.388 *Cactobrosis* Dyar (3 spp.); 55.389 *Lascelina* Heinrich (1 sp., *L. canens* Heinrich); 55.390 *Metephestia* Ragonot (1 sp., *M. simplicula* (Zeller)); 55.391 *Selga* Heinrich (1 sp., *S. arizonella* (Hulst))]

55.392 *Euzophera* Zeller

Four species, the following of which is a pest:

E. semifuneralis (Walter) (American Plum Borer).

55.393 *Eulogia* Heinrich (1 sp., *E. ochrifrontella* (Zeller)); 55.394 *Ephestiodes* Ragonot (5 spp.); 55.395 *Moodna* Hulst (2 spp.)]

55.396 *Vitula* Ragonot

Three species, the following of which is a pest:

V. edmandsae serratilinella Ragonot (Dried-fruit Moth). Stored product pest also found in bumble bee nests. (1), (2), (3), (4), (5), generally distributed.

55.397 *Manhatta* Hulst (2 spp.); 55.398 *Caudellia* Dyar (3 spp.); 55.399 *Sosipatra* Heinrich (4 spp.)]

55.400 *Plodia* Guenée

One species, as follows:

P. interpunctella (Huebner) (Indian Meal Moth). wingspan: ±15 mm. Very distinctive with front wings dark at extreme base, then wide, creamy white band extending to middle, followed by three or four narrow bands on a reddish brown ground, hind wings dingy gray, fringed with long hairs. Both larvae and adults are common in stored grain and cereal products, including those in homes. Larval feeding is characterized by webbing constructed over and in food material. Cosmopolitan.

55.401 *Anagasta* Heinrich

One species, as follows:

A. kuehniella (Zeller) (Mediterranean Flour Moth). Wingspan: ±22 mm. Dark gray crossed by wavy lines, the "v"-shaped mark near base of each wing making a "w" when wings are closed; hind wings silvery gray. Larvae and adults are found in meal, flour, and other processed grains; probably their most widespread and serious pest. Introduced into the U.S. about 1889. (1), (2), (3), (4), (5), generally distributed.

55.402 *Ephestia* Guenée

One species, as follows:

E. elutella (Huebner) (Tobacco Moth). Wingspan: ±15 mm. Similar in appearance to *Cadra cautella* (55.403) except that entire front wing is pale gray to brownish with narrow bands and streaks. Larvae feed on stored tobacco leaves and other products, particularly chocolates, seeds, and prepared cereals, less commonly in grains and flour; also found in rotten wood. Widespread.

55.403 *Cadra* Walker

Two species, both of them pests:

C. cautella (Walker) (Almond Moth). Wingspan: ±15 mm. Brownish or blackish gray; similar to the following except for direct, rather distinct, pale antemedial line. Larvae infest dried fruits, especially figs and nuts. Widespread.

C. figulilella (Gregson) (Raisin Moth). Wingspan: ±20 mm. Antemedial line oblique from costa to Cu₁, then upright to inner margin. Dark gray. Larvae found in dried fruit.

[55.404 *Bandera* Ragonot (3 spp.); 55.405 *Wakulla* Schaeffer (1 sp., *W. carneella* (Barnes and McDunnough)); 55.406 *Tampa* Ragonot (1 sp., *T. dimediatella* Ragonot); 55.407 *Varneiria* Dyar (2 spp.); 55.408 *Eurythmia* Ragonot (3 spp.); 55.409 *Erelieva* Heinrich (2 spp.); 55.410 *Barberia* Dyar (1 sp., *B. affinitella* Dyar); 55.411 *Cabnia* Dyar (1 sp., *C. myronella* Dyar); 55.412 *Anerastia* Huebner (1 sp., *A. lotella* (Huebner)); 55.413 *Coenochroa* Ragonot (3 spp.)]

Subfamily Peoriinae

Very similar to the preceding subfamily; palpi frequently porrect; wing markings usually longitudinal; ocelli present; proboscis weak.

[55.414 *Peoria* Ragonot (15 spp.); 55.415 *Tolima* Ragonot (1 sp., *T. cincaidella* Dyar); 55.416 *Navasota* Ragonot (1 sp., *N. hebetella* Ragonot); 55.417 *Anacostia* Shaffer (1 sp., *A. tribulella* Shaffer); 55.418 *Arivaca* Shaffer (7 spp.); 55.419 *Atascosa* Shaffer (1 sp., *A. glareosella* (Zeller)); 55.420 *Homosassa* Hulst (4 spp.); 55.421 *Reynosa* Shaffer (1 sp., *R. floscella* (Hulst)); 55.422 *Goya* Ragonot (2 spp.); 55.423 *Uinta* Hulst (1 sp., *U. oreadella* Hulst)]

56. THYRIDIDAE (Window-Winged Moth Family)

Wingspan: 15–45 mm. Heavy-bodied, body densely clothed with scales; wings often with transparent discal spots and of diverse shapes, some resembling sphingids, other

Fig. 27.172.

Fig. 27.173.

geometers, and others lycaenids. The following seven genera and 12 species are recorded in the U.S. and Canada.

Subfamily Thyridinae

56.1 *Thyris* Laspeyres

Two species, the following of which is common:

T. sepulchralis Guérin. Wingspan: 15–23 mm. Black with translucent white markings. Larvae feed on grape. Adults diurnal and fly in June. (See Fig. 27.172.) (1) n.e. US; (2) s.e. US.

[56.2 *Dysodia* Clemens (4 spp.); 56.3 *Hexeris* Grote (1 sp., *H. enhydris* Grote)]

Subfamily Siculodinae

[56.4 *Belonoptera* Herrich-Schaeffer (1 sp., *B. fratercula* (Pagenstecher)); 56.5 *Rhodoneura* Guenée (1 sp., *R. terminalis* (Walker))]

56.6 *Meskea* Grote

One species, as follows:

M. dyspteraria Grote. Wingspan: 30–45 mm. wings long, narrow, pale tan; vein markings darker brown. (3) TX.

Subfamily Striglininae

[56.7 *Banisia* Walker (2 spp.)]

57. HYBLAEIDAE (Hyblaeid Moth Family)

This family is often treated as a subfamily of the Noctuidae. Only the following species occurs in the U.S.

57.1 *Hyblaea* Fabricius

H. puera Cramer. Wingspan: 28–35 mm. Front wing grayish brown; hind wings orange with two wavy, dark brown bands. Larvae feed on flowers of Day Jessamine (*Cestrum diurum*). (See Fig. 27.173.) (2) FL.

Superfamily PTEROPHOROIDEA

Only the following family is included in this superfamily in the U.S. and Canada.

58. PTEROPHORIDAE (Plume Moth Family)

Wingspan: 15–30 mm. These long-legged moths may be recognized by wings that are split into plumes, that is, at least hind wings are split by deep clefts reaching nearly to base, except in *Agdistis* sp. (58.1). Wings are held tightly rolled and at sharp angle from body when not in use. Legs are distinctive because of long, projecting spines. Larvae of some species are densely hairy, somewhat resembling small wooly-bears [Arctiidae (73)], but are easily distinguished by their small size, silk tubes, and loose webs. Pupae are soft and hairy and hang head down in a way somewhat resembling the chrysalids of butterflies. Some species make very thin cocoons. Twenty genera and 146 species are recorded in the U.S. and Canada.

Subfamily Agdistinae

[58.1 *Agdistis* Huebner (1 sp., *A. americana* Barnes and Lindsey)]

Subfamily Platyptiliinae

[58.2 *Sphenarches* Meyrick (1 sp., *S. ontario* McDunnough); 58.3 *Geina* Tutt (3 spp.); 58.4 *Capperia* Tutt (3 spp.); 58.5 *Oxyptilus* Zeller (1 sp., *O. delawaricus* Zeller); 58.6 *Trichoptilus* Walsingham (6 spp.); 58.7 *Megalorrhipida* Amsel (1 sp., *M. defectalis* (Walder)); 58.8 *Cnaemidophorus* Wallengran (1 sp., *C. rhododactylus* (Dennis and Schiffermueller)]

58.9 *Platyptilia* Huebner

Eleven species, the following of which is a minor pest.

P. carduidactyla (Riley) (Artichoke Plume Moth). Wingspan: 20–27 mm. Front wings dark wood-brown or tawny brown with irregular oblique shading basally and darker, triangular distal spot. Front wings only moderately cleft; hind wings divided into three plumes. Adults fly from May to September. Larvae form webs and live gregariously on flower heads of thistle and other plants, including artichoke. (See Fig. 27.174.) (1), (2), (3), (4), (5), generally distributed.

[58.10 *Anstenoptilia* Zimmerman (1 sp., *A. marmarodactyla* (Dyar); 58.11 *Amblyptilia* Huebner (1 sp., *A. pica* (Walsingham))]

58.12 *Lantanophaga* Zimmerman

One species only, as follows:

L. pusillidactyla (Walker) (Lantana Plume Moth).

[58.13 *Lioptilodes* Zimmerman (1 sp., *L. parvus* (Walsingham)); 58.14 *Stenoptilodes* Zimmerman (22 spp.); 58.15 *Stenoptilia* Huebner (10 spp.)]

Fig. 27.174.

Fig. 27.175.

Subfamily Pterophorinae
58.16 *Pterophorus* Shaeffer

One species, as follows:

P. walsinghami (Fernald) (Grape Plume Moth). Wingspan: ±18 mm. Similar wing clefting as in *Platyptilia carduidactyla*; tawny or pale yellow barred with white and brown lines across wings. Adults are found around damp meadows in rank growth from May to July. Larvae fold grape leaves with webbing and live gregariously in this shelter. (1), (2), (3), (4), (5), generally distributed.

[58.17 *Pselnophorus* Wallengren (1 sp., *P. belfragei* (Fish)); 58.18 *Adaina* Tutt (6 spp.); 58.19 *Oidaematophorus* Wallengren (73 spp.); 58.20 *Emmelina* Tutt (1 sp., *E. monodactyla* (Linnaeus))]

Division "MACROLEPIDOPTERA"

The remaining moth families are generally termed the "Macros." Although many species are as small as many of the so-called "Micros," they are usually of a larger size, with wingspans over 20 mm. Moreover, none of the "Macros" have lanceolate wings or a fringe of scales on the hind wing as long or longer than the wing width. The division is merely one of convenience and has no taxonomic significance. There are 17 families in six superfamilies in this group. It includes the largest family of moths, the Noctuidae, and the second largest family, the Geometridae.

Superfamily DREPANOIDEA

Only two families belong to this small group.

59. THYATIRIDAE (Thyatirid Moth Family)

The North American species, which resemble the Noctuidae, may be recognized by their deeply laminate antennae and special wing venation, with the radials distinct and R_5 and M_1 stalked at the base. The proboscis is well-developed but not very strong. Larvae feed on oak, cornel, and various species of Rosaceace. Sixteen species assigned to six genera occur in the U.S. and Canada.

Subfamily Thyatirinae
Tribe Habrosynini
59.1 *Habrosyne* Huebner

Two species, the following of which is common:

H. scripta Gosse. Wingspan; 30–35 mm. Light brown with zig-zag pattern of pale markings on front wings. (See Fig. 27.175.) (1) n.e. NA; (5) n. Central states and provinces.

[59.2 *Pseudothyatira* Grote (1 sp. *P. cymatophoroides* Guenée)]

Tribe Thyatirini

[59.3 *Thyatira* Oschsenheimer (1 sp., *T. mexicana* Edwards)]

Tribe Macrothyatirini

[59.4 *Euthytira* Smith (3 spp.)]

Subfamily Polyplocinae
Tribe Ceranemotini

[59.5 *Ceranemota* Clarke (8 spp.); 59.6 *Bycombia* Benjamin (1 sp., *B. verdugoensis* Hill)]

60. DREPANIDAE (Hook-tip Moth Family)

Wingspan: 25–35 mm. Front wings usually sickle-shaped, hence hook-tipped; their discal cell sometimes open; ocelli absent; chaetosemata reduced or absent; proboscis small or absent; maxillary palpi minute. These moths resemble some Geometridae but are usually distinguishable by stumpy body and outer margin of hind wings. Larvae feed on variety of plants, including birch, alder, viburnum, and cornel. There are five species in three genera in the U.S. and Canada.

Subfamily Drepaninae
60.1 *Drepana* Schrank

Two species, including the following:

D. arcuata Walker (Hook-tip Moth). Wingspan: ±30 mm. Pale yellow with dark brown markings. Larvae feed on birch and alder. (See Fig. 27.176.) (1) n.e. NA; (2) s.e. US.

[60.2 *Eudeilinia* Packard (2 spp.)]

Subfamily Oretinae

[60.3 *Oreta* Walker (1 sp., *O. rosea* Walker)]

Fig. 27.176.

Superfamily GEOMETROIDEA

This superfamily contains the very large family Geometridae along with three small, similar families.

61. GEOMETRIDAE (Geometer Moth Family)

Wingspan: 15–40 mm. Most species are rather easy to recognize by shape alone. They are slender-bodied; both wings are broad, with some angled. Distal pattern of lines on front wings is usually continued on hind wings. Ocelli usually absent; chaetosemata present; proboscis present; maxillary palpi usually one-segmented, rarely two-segmented.

Larvae are equally easy to recognize. These are the inchworms, measuringworms, spanworms, or loopers (their common name depends upon the region in which they live). Since most lack several prolegs on the abdomen, their locomotion is achieved by drawing the hind part of the body up to the thorax and then extending the front portion, thereby seeming to measure or span a surface. This feature is shared by a few species of other families, especially the Noctuidae. Some larvae resemble twigs when they rest because they grasp a real twig with their hind prolegs and stiffen the rest of the body to hold it away from the branch; their coloration also blends in with that of the bark of the twig. Still others fasten bits of flowers on their back as a concealment. Larvae of certain tree-feeding species may decend to the ground on a long strand of silk; upon reaching it, they may migrate to another tree or hibernate in ground debris. Should one of these larvae alight upon a person instead of the ground, it walks in a looping motion across the person's body. From this action stems the old saying that one is being measured for a new set of clothes, a story familiar to nearly everyone.

This is the third largest family of the order, with 254 genera and 1404 species, assigned to six subfamilies, in the U.S. and Canada. Identification of subfamilies is difficult, and there are no readily available keys based on the present arrangement of genera. The species are difficult to identify also; to do so, both the male genitalia and details of the wing venation must be correlated with the color patterns of the adults.

Subfamily Archiearinae

[61.1 *Archiearis* Huebner (1 sp., *A. infans* (Moeschler)); 61.2 *Leucobrephos* Grote (1 sp., *L. brephoides* (Walker))]

Subfamily Oenochrominae
61.3 *Alsophila* Huebner

One species, as follows:

A. pometaria (Harris) (Fall Cankerworm). Wingspan: male, ±30 mm; female, wingless. Light gray with light and dark markings on wings of male. Adult females found on tree trunks on warm days and nights in November and December. Larvae feed on apple, elm, maple, and other trees in spring. Eggs resemble a tiny gray flower pot with gray cover decorated with dark central spot and dark ring near edge. Female lays several hundred eggs in regular rows in a flat mass on tree bark in November (rarely in spring) The leaf-skeletonizing larvae, a considerable pest, hatch out in spring after leaves appear. They may be recognized by the yellow stripes on each side below, and three narrower whitish stripes above, the spiracles on an otherwise black body. They let themselves down by means of silken threads, which enable them to go from leaf to leaf. If they miss a leaf, they may go back up the thread and try once more. By the first of June, they are ready to drop to the ground. Then they crawl two or three inches into the soil and spin a thin but tough cocoon in which to pupate. Adults emerge in late August; rarely do they hibernate until spring. Wingless females emerge and crawl up a tree trunk to mate and lay their eggs. (See Fig. 27.177.) (1), (2), (3), (4), (5), generally distributed.

[61.4 *Ametris* Huebner (1 sp., *A. nitocris* (Cramer)); 61.5 *Almodes* Guenée (1 sp., *A. terraria* Guenée)]

Subfamily Ennominae
Tribe Abraxini

[61.6 *Heliomata* Grote and Robinson (4 spp.); 61.7 *Protitame* McDunnough (7 spp.)]

Tribe Semiothisini

[61.8 *Eumacaria* Packard (1 sp., *E. latiferrugata* (Walker))]

61.9 *Itame* Huebner

Forty-eight species, the following of which is a minor pest:

I. ribearia (Fitch) (Currant Spanworm). Wingspan: ±30 mm. Yellow with dark brown markings. Adults fly in early July. Larvae hatch in spring as leaves come out and feed on black currant and gooseberry. (1) s. ON, s. QU, WI, MI, NY, VT, NH, ME, MA, CT, RI, IL, IN, OH, PA, NJ; (5) CO, NE, IA, MO.

Fig. 27.177.

Fig. 27.178.

Fig. 27.179.

[61.10 *Epelis* Hulst) 1 sp., *E. truncataria* (Walker); 61.11 *Mellilla* Grote (1 sp., *M. xanthometata* (Walker)); 61.12 *Elpiste* Gumppenberg (3 spp.)]

61.13 *Semiothisa* Huebner

Ninety-three species, the following of which is typical:

S. fissinotata Walker. Wingspan: ±30 mm. Pale with blackish markings, Larvae feed on various trees. (See Fig. 27.178.) (1), (2), (3), (4), (5), generally distributed.

[61.14 *Enconista* Lederer (1 sp., *E. dislocaria* (Packard)); 61.15 *Narraga* Walker (2 spp.); 61.16 *Sperrya* Rindge (1 sp., *S. cervula* Rindge); 61.17 *Xenoecista* Warren (3 spp.)]

Tribe **Boarmiini**

[61.18 *Dasyfidonia* Packard (2 spp.); 61.19 *Orthofidonia* Packard (3 spp.); 61.20 *Hesperumia* Packard (4 spp.); 61.21 *Neoalcis* McDunnough (1 sp., *N. californiaria* (Packard)); 61.22 *Ematurga* Lederer (1 sp., *E. amitaria* (Guenée)); 61.23 *Hypomecis* Huebner (4 spp.); 61.24 *Pimaphera* Cassino and Swett (2 spp.); 61.25 *Glenoides* McDunnough (2 spp.); 61.26 *Glena* Hulst (10 spp.)]

61.27 *Stenoporpia* McDunnough

Twenty-three species, including the following:

S. excelsaria Strecker. Wingspan: ±30 mm. Grayish with dark markings. Larvae feed on Ponderosa Pine and Douglas Fir. (See Fig. 27.179.) (3) s.e. US; (4) Pacific n.w.; (5) MT, WY, CO.

[61.28 *Exelis* Guenée (3 spp.); 61.29 *Tornos* Morrison (7 spp.); 61.30 *Glaucina* Hulst (31 spp.); 61.31 *Synglochis* Hulst (1 sp., *S. perumbraria* Hulst); 61.32 *Eubarnesia* Cockerell (1 sp., *E. ritaria* (Grossbeck)); 61.33 *Paraglaucina* Rindge (1 sp., *P. hulstinoides* (Grossbeck)); 61.34 *Nepterotaea* McDunnough (7 spp.); 61.35 *Chesiadodes* Hulst (11 spp.); 61.36 *Hulstina* Dyar (8 spp.); 61.37 *Pterotaea* Hulst (22 spp.); 61.38 *Aethalura* McDunnough (1 sp., *A. intertexta* Walker); 61.39 *Anacamptodes* McDunnough (17 spp.); 61.40 *Iridopus* Warren (2 spp.)]

61.41 *Anavitrinelia* McDunnough

Four species, the following of which is a pest:

A. pampinaria (Guenée) (Cranberry Spanworm). Wingspan: 25–30 mm. Powdery gray with blackish markings. Larvae are general feeders. (1), (2), (3), (4), (5), generally distributed.

[61.42 *Cleora* Curtis (2 spp.); 61.43 *Gnophos* Treitschke (1 sp., *T. macguffini* Smiles)]

61.44 *Ectropis* Huebner

One species, as follows:

E. crepuscularia Dennis and Schiffermueller) (Small Engrailed Geometer). Wingspan: 30–35 mm. Powdery, whitish gray with blackish, indistinct lines. Adults fly from May to early September. Larvae feed on hemlock and other trees. (See Fig. 27.180.) (1) n.e. NA; (4) Pacific n.w.; (5) n. Central States.

[61.45 *Protoboarmia* McDunnough (1 sp., *P. porcelaria* (Guenée); 61.46 *Epimecis* Huebner (6 spp.); 61.47 *Mericisca* Hulst (3 spp.); 61.48 *Parapheromia* McDunnough (5 spp.); 61.49 *Prionomelia* Warren (2 spp.); 61.50 *Tracheops* Hulst (1 sp., *T. bolteri* Hulst); 61.51 *Melanochroia* Huebner (2 spp.)]

Tribe **Melanolophiini**

[61.52 *Melanolophia* Hulst (5 spp.); 61.53 *Carphoides* McDunnough (3 spp.); 61.54 *Paraphoides* Rindge (1 sp., *P. errantaria* (McDunnough)); 61.55 *Galenara* McDunnough (7 spp.); 61.56 *Vinemina* McDunnough (3 spp.); 61.57 *Eufidonia* Packard (3 spp.)]

Tribe **Bistonini**

61.58 *Biston* Leach

Two species, the following of which is common:

B. betularia cognataria (Guenée) (Pepper-and-salt Moth). Wingspan: ±30 mm. White, densely and finely dotted with

Fig. 27.180.

Fig. 27.181.

Fig. 27.182.

black and dark markings. Larvae are general feeders. (See Fig. 27.181.) (1) n.e. NA; (4) Pacific n.w.; (5) n. Central states.

[61.59 *Cochisea* Barnes and McDunnough (9 spp.); 61.60 *Lycia* Huebner (3 spp.); 61.61 *Hypagyrtis* Huebner (4 spp.); 61.62 *Phigalia* Duponchel (4 spp.)]

61.63 *Paleacrita* Riley

Three species, the following of which is a pest:

P. vernata (Peck) (Spring Cankerworm). Wingspan: male, 20–32 mm; female, wingless. Ash gray with blackish lines and hind wings with single, small central spot. Frequent at lights as early as April. Larvae feed on apple, elm, and many other trees. Females lay as many as 400 eggs in irregular clusters in crevices of bark of host tree. Adults are ovoid, slightly ridged, and iridescent purple. The species is of considerable economic importance. When the English Sparrow was introduced to control it, the bird itself became a pest, preferring city to forest life and at best exerting only minor control of the Cankerworm infesting city shade trees. (1) n.e. NA; (2) WV, w. VA, KY, w. NC, n. GA; (3) n. CA, n. AZ, n. NM; (4) Pacific n.w.; (5) n. Central States.

61.64 *Erannis* Riley

Three species, the following of which is a minor pest:

E. tiliaria (Harris) (Linden Looper). Wingspan: male, ±40 mm; female, wingless. Male pale straw or fawn color with brownish markings. Larvae feed on various trees, including Linden, elm, and apple. (1) n.e. NA; (4) Pacific n.w.; (5) n. Central States.

Tribe Baptini

[61.65 *Lomographa* Huebner (5 spp.); 61.66 *Palyas* Guenée (1 sp., *P. auriferaria* (Hulst)); 61.67 *Phrygionis* Huebner (1 sp., *P. argentata* (Drury))]

Tribe Caberini

[61.68 *Sericosema* Warren (4 spp.); 61.69 *Cabera* Treitschke (5 spp.); 61.70 *Eudrepanulatrix* Rindge (1 sp., *E. rectifascia* (Hulst); 61.71 *Drepanulatrix* Gumppenberg (11 spp.) 61.72 *Apodrepanulatrix* Rindge (2 spp.); 61.73 *Ixala* Hulst (4 spp.); 61.74 *Numia* Guenée (1 sp., *N. terebintharia* Guenée); 61.75 *Chloraspilates* Packard (2 spp.); 61.76 *Erastria* Huebner (4 spp.); 61.77 *Pterospoda* Dyar (3 spp.); 61.78

Stergamataea Hulst (2 spp.); 61.79 *Thysanopyga* Herrich-Schaeffer (1 sp., *T. intractata* (Walker)); 61.80 *Episemasia* Hulst (2 spp.)]

Tribe Angeronini

[61.81 *Aspitates* Treitschke (5 spp.); 61.82 *Lytrosis* Hulst (4 spp.)]

61.83 *Euchlaena* Huebner

Sixteen species, the following of which is common:

E. serrata Drury (Saw-wing). Wingspan: ±50 mm. Bright straw yellow with dark brown markings at apex of each wing. Adults on the wing in June and July. Larvae feed on maple and apple. (See Fig. 27.182.) (1) n.e. NA; (5) n. Central States.

61.84 *Xanthotype* Warren

Five species, of which the following is common:

X. urticaria Swett. Wingspan: 30–40 mm. Bright yellow with delicate light brown bands and spots outlined with darker brown. Adults fly June to August. Larvae feed on dogwood. (See Fig. 27.183.) (1) n.e. NA; (5) n. Central States.

[61.85 *Cymatophora* Huebner (1 sp., *C. approximaria* Huebner)]

Tribe Azelinini

[61.86 *Stenaspilatodes* Franclemont and Poole (1 sp., *S. antidiscaria* (Walker))]

Fig. 27.183.

Fig. 27.184.

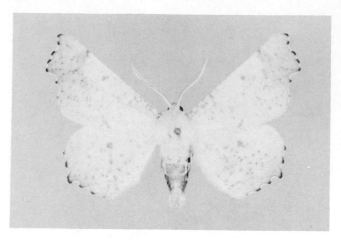

Fig. 27.185.

61.87 *Pero* Herrich-Schaeffer

Sixteen species, including the following:

P. honestaria Walker. Wingspan: ±35 mm. Male blackish with pale outer margins; female brownish with black markings. Adults fly from April to September. Larvae feed on wild cherry. (See Fig. 27.184.) (1), (2), (3), (4), (5), generally distributed.

Tribe Nacophorini

[61.88 *Nacophora* Hulst (9 spp.); 61.89 *Thyrinteina* Moeschler (1 sp. and subsp. *T. arnobia phala* Rindge); 61.90 *Holochroa* Hulst (1 sp., *A. dissociaria* (Hulst)); 61.91 *Aethaloida* McDunnough (1 sp., *A. packardaria* (Hulst)); 61.92 *Hemimorina* McDunnough (1 sp., *H. dissociata* McDunnough); 61.93 *Hemnypia* McDunnough (1 sp., *H. baueri* McDunnough); 61.94 *Parexcelsa* Pearsell (1 sp., *P. ultraria* Pearsell); 61.95 *Ceratonyx* Guenée (3 spp.); 61.96 *Gabriola* Taylor (5 spp.); 61.97 *Yermoia* McDunnough (2 spp.); 61.98 *Animomyia* Dyar (7 spp.)]

Tribe Gonodontini

[61.99 *Colotois* Huebner (1 sp., *C. pennaria* (Linnaeus))]

Tribe Campaenini

[61.100 *Campaea* Lamark (1 sp., *C. perlata* (Guenée))]

Tribe Ennomini

61.101 *Ennomos* Treitschke

Two species, both of them of some economic importance:

E. subsignarius (Huebner) (Elm Spanworm; Snow-white Linden Moth). Wingspan: ±40 mm. White; yellow on antennae. Common at lights at night from late June through July. Larvae on apple, elm, maple, and many other trees and shrubs. (1) n.e. NA; (2) s.e. US.

E. margnarius Guenée (Maple Spanworm; Notch-wing). Wingspan: 50–55 mm. Bright, light orange-yellow with brown, reddish brown, and dark markings. This is the largest of our common species. Adults fly from August to November. Larvae feed on maple and many other trees. (See Fig. 27.185.) (1) n.e. NA; (4) Pacific n.w.; (5) n. Central States.

Tribe Epirranthini

[61.102 *Epirranthis* Huebner (1 sp., *E. substriataria* (Hulst))]

Tribe Sphacelodini

[61.103 *Sphacelodes* Guenée (2 spp.)]

Tribe Lithinini

[61.104 *Philedia* Hulst (1 sp., *P. punctomacularia* (Hulst)); 61.105 *Petrophora* Huebner (2 spp.); 61.106 *Tacparia* Walker (3 spp.); 61.107 *Thallophaga* Hulst (3 spp.); 61.108 *Homochlodes* Hulst (3 spp.); 61.109 *Nyctiphanta* Hulst (1 sp., *N. laetula* Hulst); 61.110 *Gueneria* Packard (1 sp., *G. similaria* (Walker))]

Tribe Anacogini

[61.111 *Slossonia* Hulst (1 sp., *S. rubrotincta* Hulst); 61.112 *Selenia* Huebner (2 spp.)]

61.113 *Metanema* Guenée

Two species, the following of which is common:

M. inatomaria Guenée. Wingspan: ±35 mm. Pale gray with red, blue, and dark brown markings. Adults fly June to August. Larvae feed on poplar. (See Fig. 27.186.) (1) s. ON, s. QU, NY, NH, VT, MA, RI, CT, IL, IN, OH, PA, NJ; (3) n. AZ; (5) n. Central States.

[61.114 *Metarranthis* Warren (13 spp.); 61.115 *Cepphis* Huebner (2 spp.); 61.116 *Anagoga* Huebner (1 sp., *A. occiduaria* (Walker)); 61.117 *Probole* Herrich-Schaeffer (3 spp.)]

Fig. 27.186.

Fig. 27.187.

61.118 *Plagodis* Huebner

Five species, the following of which is common:

P. phlogosaria Herrich-Schaeffer. Wingspan: 27–30 mm. Light straw yellow, with light brown markings. Adults fly May and June; some species to August. Larvae feed on basswood, white birch, apple, black, and choke cherry. (*P. keuzingaria* Packard is illustrated in Fig. 27.187.) (1) n.e. NA; (4) Pacific n.w.; (5) n. Central States.

Tribe Ourapterygini

[61.119 *Philtraea* Hulst (7 spp.); 61.120 *Eriplatymetra* (3 spp.); 61.121 *Melemaea* Hulst (2 spp.); 61.122 *Lychnosea* Grote (2 spp.); 61.123 *Neoterpes* Hulst (4 spp.); 61.124 *Caripeta* Walker (12 spp.); 61.125 *Snowia* Neumoegen (1 sp., *S. montanaria* Neumoegen); 61.126 *Nemeris* Rindge (3 spp.); 61.127 *Meris* Hulst (5 spp.); 61.128 *Destutia* Grossbeck (4 spp.); 61.129 *Besma* Capps (4 spp.)]

61.130 *Lambdina* Capps

Nine species, the following of which is a pest:

L. fiscellaria fiscellaria (Guenée) (Hemlock Looper; Western Hemlock Looper; Western Oak Looper). Wingspan: ±35 mm. Cream, buff, or mouse gray with dark markings, usually edged with orange. Adults fly August to October. Eggs overwinter. Larvae feed on oak, spruce, balsam, and hemlock. (See Fig. 27.188.) (1), (2), (3), (4), (5), generally distributed.

[61.131 *Evita* Capps (1 sp., *E. hyalinaria* (Grossbeck))]

Fig. 27.188.

Fig. 27.189.

61.132 *Cingilia* Walker

One species, as follows:

C. catenaria (Drury) (Chain-spotted Geometer). Wingspan: 30–40 mm. Pure white with distinct black spots along outer margin of each wing and indistinct wavy black line across both wings. Adult fly September and October. Larvae feed on sweet fern and many other low plants as well as trees, especially arbor vitae. (See Fig. 27.189.) (1) n.e. NA; (5) MT, ND, SD, WY, NE, IA, MN, CO, KS, MO.

61.133 *Nepytia* Hulst

Twelve species, the following of which are pests:

N. phantasmaria (Strecker) (Phantom Hemlock Looper). Feeds on hemlock. (4) BC, WA.

N. canosaria (Walker) (False Hemlock Looper). Larvae feed on pine, spruce, fir, and hemlock. (1) s. ON, QU, WI, MI, NY, NH, VT, ME, IL, IN, OH, PA.

N. semiclusaria (Walker) (Pine Conelet Looper). Feeds on needles of many conifers. (1) n.e. US.

Related species are pests in (2) FL; (3) s.w. US; (4) Pacific n.w.; (5) n. Central States.

61.134 *Sicya* Guenée

Six species, including the following:

S. snoviaria Hulst. (See Fig. 27.190.)

S. morsicaria Hulst. Wingspan: 25–30 mm. Pale with brownish to black markings. Larvae feed on mistletoe, *Phoradendron juniperinum* (growing on juniper), and resemble the plant, the leaves of which are reduced to small scales. (1), (2), (3), (4), (5), widely distributed.

S. macularia Harris. (See Fig. 27.191.) (1) n.e. NA; (3) CA; (4) Pacific n.w. (5) n. Central States.

[61.135 *Euaspilates* Packard (1 sp., *E. spinataria* Packard); 61.136 *Eucaterva* Grote (2 spp.); 61.137 *Acanthotoca* Fletcher (1 sp., *A. graefi* (Hulst)); 61.138 *Plataea* Herrich-Schaeffer (6 spp.); 61.139 *Eusarca* Huebner (16 spp.); 61.140 *Somatolophia* Hulst (10 spp.); 61.141 *Pherne* Hulst (4 spp.); 61.142 *Synaxis* Hulst (10 spp.); 61.143 *Tetracis* Guenée (2 spp.); 61.144 *Eugonobapta* Warren (1 sp., *E. nivosaria* (Guenée));

Fig. 27.190.

Fig. 27.192.

61.145 *Eutrapela* Huebner (1 sp., *clemataria* (Smith)); 61.146 *Oxydia* Guenée (6 spp.); 61.147 *Phyllodonta* Warren (1 sp., *P. peccataria* (Barnes and McDunnough)); 61.148 *Patalene* Herrich-Schaeffer (3 spp.)]

61.149 *Prochoerodes* Grote

Seven species, the following of which is a pest:

P. transversata Drury (Large Maple Spanworm). Wingspan: ±50 mm. Fawn color with dark brown and black markings. Larvae feed on oak and maple and other trees. (See Fig. 27.192.) (1), (2), (3), (4), (5), generally distributed.

[61.150 *Pityeja* Walker (1 sp., *P. ornata* Rindge); 61.151 *Nepheloleuca* Butler (2 spp.); 61.152 *Antepione* Packard (7 spp.); 61.153 *Sericoptera* Herrich-Schaeffer (1 sp., *S. virginaria* (Hulst))]

61.154 *Sabulodes* Guenée

Ten species, including the following:

S. niveostriata Cockerell. Wingspan: ±50 mm. Front wings dark with white slashes of varying length; hind wings pale. (See Fig. 27.193.) Larvae feed on pine. (3) AZ, NM; (5) CO.

S. aegrotata Guenée [=*caberata* of authors] (Omnivorous Looper). Wingspan: ±50 mm. Similar to the preceding. Larvae found on great variety of plants. (3) CA; (4) OR.

[61.155 *Enypia* Hulst (4 spp.)]

61.156 *Nematocampa* Guenée

Three species, the following of which is a pest.

N. filamentaria Guenée (Filament Bearer; Horned Spanworm). Wingspan: 19–25 mm. Male light straw color; female cream white, veined with brown. Larvae feed on hops and various herbs, less often on trees. Eggs overwinter. (1), (2), (3), (4), (5), generally distributed.

Subfamily Geometrinae

Tribe Nemoriini

[61.157 *Chlorosea* Packard (4 spp.)]

61.158 *Nemoria* Huebner

Thirty-five species, including the following:

N. mimosaria Guenée. Wingspan: 20–25 mm. Wings grass green with two delicate lines running across both pair of wings. Larvae feed on oak, alder, hemlock, and fir. (See Fig. 27.194.) (1) n.e. US; (5) n. Central States.

[61.159 *Phrudocentra* Warren (2 spp.); 61.160 *Dichorda* Warren (4 spp.)]

Tribe Dichordophorini

[61.161 *Dichordophora* Prout (1 sp., *D. phoenix* (Prout))]

Fig. 27.191.

Fig. 27.193.

Fig. 27.194.

Fig. 27.195.

Tribe Synchlorini

61.162 *Synchlora* Guenée

Seven species, including the following:

S. aerata Fabricius. Wingspan: 15–22 mm. Grass green with pale lines on both wings. Maxillary palpi reddish. Larvae feed on flowers of various low plants, particularly raspberry and blackberry; they fasten bits of flower petals and leaves to their bodies for camouflage. Adults commonly attracted to lights at night. (See A&J 241.) (1) n.e. US; (2) s.e.

[61.163 *Cheteoscelis* Prout (4 spp.)]

Tribe Lophochoristini

[61.164 *Lophochorista* Warren (1 sp., *L. lesteraria* (Grossbeck)); 61.165 *Eueana* Prout (1 sp., *E. niveociliaria* (Herrich-Schaeffer))]

Tribe Hemitheini

[61.166 *Chlorochlamys* Hulst (4 spp.); 61.167 *Chloropteryx* Hulst (3 spp.); 61.168 *Xerochlora* Ferguson (5 spp.); 61.169 *Hemithea* Duponchel (1 sp., *H. aestivaria* (Huebner)); 61.170 *Hethemia* Ferguson (1 sp., *H. pistasciaria* (Guenée)); 61.171 *Mesothea* Warren (1 sp., *M. incertata* (Walker))]

Subfamily Sterrhinae

Tribe Sterrhini

[61.172 *Eumacrodes* Warren (1 sp., *E. yponomeutaria* (Guenée)); 61.173 *Euacidalia* Packard (5 spp.); 61.174 *Protoproutia* McDunnough (2 spp.); 61.175 *Lobocleta* Warren (7 spp.); 61.176 *Idaea* Treitschke (19 spp.); 61.177 *Paota* Hulst (1 sp., *P. fultaria* (Grote))]

61.178 *Pigia* Guenée

Two species, including the following:

P. multilineata Hulst. Wingspan: ±30 mm. Pale ground color with diagonal brownish markings. (See Fig. 27.195.) (3) AZ.

[61.179 *Odontoptila* Warren (1 sp., *O. obrimo* (Druce)); 61.180 *Ptychamalia* Prout (1 sp., *P. doreraria* (Barnes and McDunnough))]

Tribe Cosymgiini

[61.181 *Pleuroprucha* Moeschler (2 spp.); 61.182 *Cyclophora* Huebner (7 spp.); 61.183 *Semaeopus* Herrich–Schaeffer (5 spp.)]

Tribe Timandrini

61.184 *Haematopis* Huebner

One species, as follows:

H. grataria (Fabricius) (Chickweed Geometer). Wingspan: 20–25 mm. Wings yellow-brown with diagonal band of reddish orange across both pair near middle and two narrow brown bands near apex; single small reddish orange spot on front wings. Larvae feed on chickweed and other low plants. (See Fig. 27.196.) (1) n.e. NA; (2) s.e. US; (3) TX.

[61.185 *Calothysanis* Huebner (1 sp., *C. amaturaria* (Walker))]

Tribe Scopulini

[61.186 *Acratodes* Guenée (1 sp., *A. suavata* (Hulst))]

61.187 *Scopula* Schrank

Twenty-four species, including the following:

S. limboundata Haworth. Wingspan: ±28 mm. Cream white with buff and blackish markings. Larvae feed on variety of low plants. (See Fig. 27.197.) (1) n.e. NA; (5) n. Central States.

[61.188 *Leptostales* Moeschler (8 spp.); 61.189 *Lophosis* Hulst (1 sp., *L. labeculata* (Hulst))]

Fig. 27.196.

Fig. 27.197.

Fig. 27.199.

Subfamily Larentiinae
Tribe Hydriomenini

[61.190 *Dysstroma* Huebner (14 spp.)]

61.191 *Eulithis* Huebner

Thirteen species, the following of which are pests:

E. gracilineata Guenée (Greater Grapevine Looper). Wingspan: 35–40 mm. Pale yellow with darker shading. Adults appear in late June and fly until early September. Larvae feed on grape and Virginia Creeper. (See Fig. 27.198.) (1) n.e. US; (2) s.e. US; (5) MT, ND, MN, WY, NE, IA, CO, KS, MO.

E. diversilineata (Huebner) (Lesser Grapevine Looper). Wingspan: ±30 mm. Orange-yellow shaded with light brown. Larvae feed on grape and Virginia Creeper. (1), (2), (3), (4), (5), generally distributed.

[61.192 *Eurhinosea* Packard (1 sp., *E. flavaria* Packard; 61.193 *Eustroma* Huebner (3 spp.); 61.194 *Ecliptopera* Warren (2 spp.); 61.195 *Colostygia* Huebner (1 sp., *C. turbata* Huebner)); 61.196 *Plemyria* Huebner (1 sp., *P. georgii* Hulst); 61.197 *Thera* Stephens (4 spp.); 61.198 *Ceratodalia* Packard (1 sp., *C. gueneata* Packard); 61.199 *Hydriomena* Huebner (56 spp.); 61.200 *Hymenodria* McDunnough (1 sp., *H. mediodentata* (Barnes and McDunnough)); 61.201 *Ersephila* Hulst (2 spp.); 61.202 *Carptima* Pearsell (1 sp., *C. hydriomenata* Pearsell); 61.203 *Cyclica* Grote (1 sp., *C. frondaria* Grote)]

Fig. 27.198.

61.204 *Grossbeckia* Barnes and McDunnough

One species, as follows:

G. semimaculata Barnes and McDunnough. Wingspan: 30–35 mm. Front wings fold, the part posterior to fold without markings. (See Fig. 27.199.) (1) AZ.

[61.205 *Eutrepsia* Herrich-Schaeffer (1 sp., *E. inconstans* (Dyer)); 61.206 *Triphosa* Stephens (4 spp.); 61.207 *Monostoecha* Fletcher (1 sp., *M. semipectinata* (Hulst)); 61.208 *Coryphista* Hulst (1 sp., *C. meadii* (Packard))]

61.209 *Hydria* Huebner

Two species, the following of which is common:

H. undulata Huebner (Scallop-shell Moth). Wingspan: ±30 mm. Clay-colored with wavy brown lines. Adults fly from May through July. Larvae feed on wild cherry. (1) n.e. NA; (2) VA, NC; (4) Pacific n.w.; (5) n. Central States.

[61.210 *Rheumaptera* Huebner (2 spp.); 61.211 *Archirhoe* Herbulot (4 spp.); 61.212 *Pterocypha* Herrich-Schaeffer (1 sp., *P. floridata* (Walker)); 61.213 *Entephria* Huebner (7 spp.); 61.214 *Mesoleuca* Huebner (2 spp.); 61.215 *Spargania* Guenée (5 spp.); 61.216 *Hammaptera* Herrich-Schaeffer (1 sp., *H. parinotata* (Zeller)); 61.217 *Psaliodes* Guenée (1 sp., *P. fervescens* Dyar); 61.218 *Perizoma* Huebner (13 spp.); 61.219 *Anticlea* Stephens (4 spp.)]

Tribe Stamnodini

[61.220 *Stamnodes* Guenée (23 spp.); 61.221 *Stamnoctenis* Warren (7 spp.) 61.222 *Marmopteryx* Packard (4 spp.); 61.223 *Heterusia* Huebner (1 sp., *H. atalantata* (Guenée))]

Tribe Xanthorhoini

[61.224 *Xanthorhoe* Huebner (26 spp.); 61.225 *Epirrhoe* Huebner (4 spp.)]

61.226 *Euphyia* Huebner

Four species, including the following:

E. intermediata Guenée. Wingspan: ±23 mm. Ground color light gray; front wings heavily marked with blackish lines and bands; hind wings lighter in color but with blackish markings. Larvae feed on chickweed and related plants. (See Fig. 27.200.) (1), (2), (3), (4), (5), generally distributed.

Fig. 27.200.

[61.227 *Enchoria* Hulst (3 spp.); 61.228 *Loxofidonia* Packard (1 sp., *L. acidaliata* (Packard)); 61.229 *Zenophleps* Hulst (4 spp.); 61.230 *Psychophora* Kirby (4 spp.); 61.231 *Orthonama* Huebner (3 spp.); 61.232 *Disclisioprocta* Wallengren (1 sp., *D. stellata* (Guenée)); 61.233 *Herreshoffia* Sperry (1 sp., *H. gracea* Sperry)]

Tribe Asthenini

[61.234 *Hydrelia* Huebner (6 spp.); 61.235 *Venusia* Curtis (5 spp.); 61.236 *Trichodezia* Warren (3 spp.)]

Tribe Operophterini

[61.237 *Epirrita* Huebner (3 spp.)]

61.238 *Operophtera* Huebner

Four species, the following of which are pests:

O. bruceata Hulst (Bruce's Spanworm). Wingspan: male, 30 mm; female with rudimentary wings. Gray with light brown lines on front wings of male and veins with dashed black markings; hind wings longer than front wings, pale and lightly marked with brown on veins, small dark spots at apex. Adults fly September to November. Larvae feed on apple, maple, and other trees in early spring. (See Fig. 27.201.) (1) s. ON, s. QU, WI, MI, NY, NH, VT, ME, MA, RI, CT, IL, IN, OH, PA, NJ; (5) AB, MB, SK, MT, ND, MN, WY, SD, IA, CO, NE, KS, MO.

O. brumata (Linnaeus) (Winter Moth). Similar to the preceding, a late fall species, and a serious pest of forest, shade, and orchard trees. Introduced into eastern Canada and the West Coast from Europe.

Tribe Eudulini

[61.239 *Eubaphe* Huebner (5 spp.)]

Tribe Eupitheciini

[61.240 *Horisme* Huebner (4 spp.)]

61.241 *Eupithecia* Curtis

This is the largest genus of the family with 157 species, including the following:

E. ravocostaliata Packard. Wingspan: ±23 mm. White, shaded with pale gray and black dots and lines. Larvae feed on willow. (See Fig. 27.202.) (1) n.e. NA; (4) Pacific n.w.; (5) n. Central States.

E. spermaphaga (Dyar) (Fir Cone Looper). Wingspan: ±25 mm. Gray with black and red-brown markings. Larvae bore into seeds and cones of various conifers. (3) CA; (4) Pacific n.w.

[61.242 *Nasusina* Pearsell (4 spp.); 61.243 *Prorella* Barnes and McDunnough (16 spp.); 61.244 *Chloroclystis* Huebner (1 sp., *C. rectangulata* (Linnaeus))]

Tribe Lobophorini

[61.245 *Carsia* Huebner (1 sp., *C. sororiata* (Huebner)); 61.246 *Aplocera* Stephens (1 sp., *A. plagiata* (Linnaeus)); 61.247 *Lithostege* Huebner (6 spp.); 61.248 *Scelidacantha* Hulst (1 sp., *S. triseriata* (Packard)); 61.249 *Acasis* Duponchel (1 sp., *A. viridata* (Packard)); 61.250 *Trichopteryx* Huebner (1 sp., *T. veritata* Pearsell); 61.251 *Cladara* Hulst (3 spp.); 61.252 *Lobophora* Curtis (5 spp.); 61.253 *Heterophleps* Herrich-Schaeffer (3 spp.); 61.254 *Dyspteria* Huebner (1 sp., *D. abortivaria* (Herrich-Schaeffer))]

62. EPIPLEMIDAE (Epiplemid Moth Family)

Wingspan: 15–20 mm. These moths may be confused with the geometers unless distinguished by wing venation features. Close examination will show discal cell to be open distally, that is, no cross veins set it off from rest of wing, and outer margin of hind wing is irregular unlike that of the Drepanidae,

Fig. 27.201.

Fig. 27.202.

Fig. 27.203.

which they also resemble. Seven genera with eight species are recorded in the U.S. and Canada.

[62.1 *Epiplema* Herrich-Schaeffer (1 sp., *incolorata* Guenée))]

62.2 *Callizzia* Packard

Two species, the following of which is common:

C. amorata Packard. Wingspan: 15–20 mm. Grayish tan with mottled brown wing markings. Larvae feed on honeysuckle. (See Fig. 27.203.) (1) n.e. US; (2) Pacific n.w.; (5) n. Central States.

[62.3 *Antiplecta* Warren (1 sp., *A. triangularis* Warren); 62.4 *Calledapteryx* Grote (1 sp., *C. dryopterata* Grote); 62.5 *Philagraula* Haulst (1 sp., *P. slossoniae* Hulst); 62.6 *Erosia* Guenée (1 sp., *E. incendiata* Guenée); 62.7 *Schidax* Huebner (1 sp., *S. coronaria* Strecker)]

63. SEMATURIDAE (Sematurid Moth Family)
63.1 *Anurapteryx* Hampson

One species, as follows:

A. crenulata Barnes and Linsley. Wingspan: 40–45 mm. Wings brown with dark brown markings; outer third with wavy band resembling that of a geometrid. (See Fig. 27.204.) (3) AZ.

64. URANIIDAE (Uranid Moth Family)

This is a tropical family of day-flying moths, some species of which migrate. Only one species, a very colorful insect that resembles a swallowtail butterfly, has been recorded in the U.S. All records are probably of strays from migrations.

64.1 *Urania* Fabricius

One species, as follows:

U. fulgens (Walker). Wingspan: ±80 mm. Migrates to US. (1) s. FL (one record); (3) s. TX (several records).

Superfamily MIMALLONOIDEA

One family, as follows:

65. MIMALLONIDAE (Sack-bearer Moth Family)

These moths closely resemble the Bombycidae (67). Front wings with irregular margins, tending toward a sickle shape. Larvae feed on oak and make a portable case of leaves (chiefly oak) and silk (compare with larvae of the Trichoptera and Psychidae). Four species occur in the U.S., one widely distributed in e. U.S., one from Brownsville, TX, and two from s.e. AZ.

[65.1 *Lacosoma* Grote (2 spp.)]

65.2 *Cicinnus* Blanchard

One species, as follows:

C. melsheimeri (Harris). Wingspan: 34–42 mm. Brownish gray with dark brown submarginal line across both pairs of wings. Larvae feed on oak, particularly scrub oak. (See Fig. 27.205.) (1) n.e. NA: (2) s.e. US; (3) AZ, NM, TX.

[65.3 *Naniteta* Franclemont (1 sp., *N. elassa* Franclemont)]

Superfamily BOMBYCOIDEA
66. APATELOIDIDAE (Apatelodid Moth Family)

[=Zanolidae]

This small family of moths resemble the silkworm moth. Front wings in the species in the U.S. and Canada are notched apically; hind wings are irregular. Larvae feed on wide variety of trees and shrubs. There are five species in two genera.

Fig. 27.204.

Fig. 27.205.

Fig. 27.206.

66.1 *Apatelodes* Packard

Two species, the following of which is common:

A. pudefacta Dyar. Wingspan: 38–40 mm. Gray-brown with pale markings and distinct black spots. Larvae feed on sunflowers. (See Fig. 27.206.) (3) s.e. AZ.

[66.2 *Olcecostera* Butler (3 spp.)]

67. BOMBYCIDAE (Silkworm Moth Family)

About 100 species of this family occur in the world. Only the Silkworm Moth is known in the U.S.

67.1 *Bombyx* Linnaeus

One species, which exists only in domestication:

B. mori (Linnaeus) (Silkworm Moth). Wingspan: 35–45 mm. White with veins brown; front wing notched apically, somewhat sickle-shaped. Larvae are reared on Red Mulberry and produce commercial silk in the Orient. (See Fig. 27.207 for male; Fig. 27.208 for cocoon.)

68. LASIOCAMPIDAE (Lappet Moth Family)

This moderate-sized, world-wide family is mainly tropical. Many species are rather large (100-mm wingspan or more);

Fig. 27.208.

none are really brightly colored. Larvae feed on leaves of various trees. Thirty-five species, in 11 genera occur in the U.S. and Canada, a few of them of economic importance.

Subfamily Macromphaliinae

[68.1 *Hypopacha* Neumoegen and Dyar (1 sp., *H. grisea* (Neumoegen))]

68.2 *Tolype* Huebner

Eleven species, the following of which is common:

T. velleda (Stoll). Wingspan: 35–50 mm. Dark gray with white lines. Larvae feed on apple, aspen, oak, birch, elm, basswood, and ash. (See Fig. 27.209.) (1) ne.e NA; (2) s.e. US; (3) TX; (5) MN.

[68.3 *Apotolype* Franclemont (2 spp.); 68.4 *Artace* Walker (2 spp.)]

Subfamily Gastropachinae

[68.5 *Heteropacha* Harvey (1 sp., *H. rileyana* Harvey)]

68.6 *Phyllodesma* Huebner

Three species, the following of which is common:

P. americana (Harris) (Lappet Moth). Wingspan: 28–40 mm. Pale to dark brown with pale bands on front wings edged with darker brown. Larvae feed on oak, poplar, aspen, willow, birch, and shrubs of the Rosaceae. (1) n.e. US; (3) AZ; (4) ID; (5) n. Central states.

Fig. 27.207.

Fig. 27.209.

Fig. 27.210.

Fig. 27.211.

Subfamily Lasiocampinae

[68.7 *Caloecia* Barnes and McDunnough (2 spp.); 68.8 *Quadrina* Grote (1 sp., *Q. diazoma* Grote); 68.9 *Dicogaster* Barnes and McDunnough (1 sp., *D. coronada* (Barnes)); 68.10 *Gloveria* Packard (5 spp.)]

Tribe Malacosomatini

68.11 *Malacosoma* Huebner

Six species, of which the following are pests:

M. disstria Huebner (Forest Tree Caterpillar Moth). Wingspan: 28–38 mm. Yellowish brown with two dark lines across front wing, sometimes uniting to form broad band. Found at lights in July. Larvae prefer aspen but feed on maple and many other trees as well (unlike following species, they do not make tents). (See Fig. 27.210.) (1), (2), (3) CA, TX; (4), (5), generally distributed.

M. americana (Fabricius) (Eastern Tent Caterpillar). Wingspan: 30–42 mm. Similar to the preceding but usually darker, with lines on wings more distinct. Larvae form an extensive community tent of silk in which to spend the night and forage out from it by day. (See A&J 242.) They feed on apple, wild cherry, and witch hazel. (1) n.e. NA; 92) s.e. US.

M. constrictum (Edwards) (Pacific Tent Caterpillar Moth). Larvae do not make tents.

M. tigris (Dyar) (Sonoran Tent Caterpillar).

M. californicum (Packard) (Western Tent Caterpillar).

M. incurvum (Edwards) (Southwestern Tent Caterpillar).

69. SATURNIIDAE (Giant Silkworm Moth Family)

These moths are among the largest in North America, often brightly colored and almost always strikingly marked. The sexes are easily distinguished by the structure of the antennae, those of the males broadly plumose, of the females narrowly so. Many species are easily reared from eggs laid by captive females. Larvae of the saturniids form cocoons, but those of the citheronids (sometimes treated as a separate family) pupate in cells formed in soil.

Of the approximately 1,100 species in the world, there are 69 assigned to 18 genera in the U.S. and Canada. Because of the great interest in this group among collectors and the advanced state of our knowledge about it, all species and subspecies known to occur in the U.S. and Canada are listed here, the more common species being described and illustrated.

Unfortunately, many species of these beautiful moths have been threatened by environmental degradation in recent years. One of the principle causes in the use of mercury vapor lights in rural areas that attract them and other moths in enormous numbers at night. They congregate around the lights, far from their larval food plants, and die without leaving progeny. (Refer to the discussion of UV light collecting in Chap. 5.)

Subfamily Citheroniinae

69.1 *Eacles* Huebner

Two species, as follows:

E. imperialis imperialis (Drury) (Imperial Moth). Wingspan: 100–130 mm. Rich yellow, with large, reddish brown patches at base and apex of each wing of the male, reduced in the female to heavy bar across wings, which may have purplish tinge; each wing with one small whitish dot near center, surrounded by brown ring; front wings sometimes with two spots. Larvae are hairy, with four thoracic horns varying from green to very dark brown, and feed on a great variety of trees. (See Fig. 27.211 for female.) (1) n.e. NA; (2) s.e. US.

E. i. pini Michener. (1) NI, ON, NY.

E. i. nobilis Neumoegen. (3) TX.

E. oslari Rothschild. (See Fig. 27.212 for male; Fig. 27.213 for female.) (3) s. AZ.

Fig. 27.212.

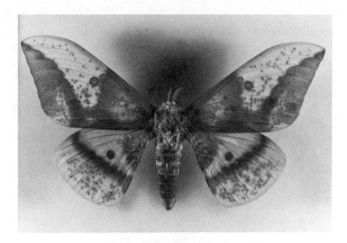

Fig. 27.213.

69.2 *Citheronia* Huebner

Three species, as follows:

C. regalis (Fabricius) (Hickory Horned Devil; Regal Moth; Royal Walnut Moth). Wingspan: 120–140 mm. Front wings black, broadly marked with rusty red on veins, a series of seven to nine white spots in a row near outer margin, a discal spot, and a basal spot; hind wings yellowish brown with paler yellow markings; thorax and abdomen rusty red, narrowly banded with yellowish brown. Larvae feed on walnut, hickory, butternut, ash, persimmon, sweet gum, and sumac. There are two pair of horns on second and third thoracic segments; these are reddish, tipped with black, and harmless. (See Fig. 27.214 for male; Fig. 27.215 for female.) (1) n.e. US; (2) s.e. US.

C. sepulcralis Grote and Robinson (Pine-devil Moth). Wingspan: 80–100 mm. Black, dusted with rusty brown; wing veins narrowly outlined with rusty brown; small rusty brown spot at base of front wings; base of hind wings also rusty brown. Larvae are brown and have only one pair of horns on second and third thoracic segment; these are shorter that those of the preceding. They feed on pine. (1) s. ME, MA, CT, RI, s. NY, NJ, DE, e. MD; (2) VA, NC, SC, GA, FL.

C. splendens sinaloensis Hoffman. (3) AZ.

Fig. 27.215.

69.3 *Sphingicampa* Walsh

Seven species, as follows:

S. bicolor (Harris) (Honey Locust Moth). Wingspan: 50–68 mm. Front wings yellowish brown to yellow-gray, variously sprinkled with black, usually with narrow, vague bar or color demarcation across wing near apex and often with two very small silver spots near apex of discal cell; hind wings vary from yellowish brown to rosy pink, with vague color demarcations. Larvae feed on honey locust and coffee bean trees. (5) n. Central states.

S. helligbrodti (Harvey). (3) s. TX.

S. hubbardi (Dyar). (3) s. AZ.

S. bisecta (Lintner). (See Fig. 27.216.) (1) WI, MI, IL, IN, OH; (2) AR, LA; (3) e. TX, e. OK; (5) MN, IA, MO.

S. montana (Packard). (3) s. AZ.

S. blanchardi Ferguson. (3) TX.

S. albolineata (Grote and Robinson). (3) s. TX.

69.4 *Dryocampa* Harris

One species, as follows:

D. rubicunda rubicunda (Fabricius) (Green-striped Mapleworm; Rosy Maple Moth). Wingspan: 35–50 mm. Color varies from nearly pure white with purple wing base to nearly all

Fig. 27.214.

Fig. 27.216.

Fig. 27.217.

purple with broad central bands of white or brownish yellow; body pale to brownish yellow. Larvae with green stripes on body, head orange-brown, horns black; they feed on maple and oak. (1) n.e. NA; (2) s.e. US.

D. r. alba Grote. (See Fig. 27.217.) (1) IL; 95) NE, KS, MO.

69.5 *Anisota* Huebner

Eight species, as follows:

A. stigma stigma (Fabricius) (Spiny Oakworm). Wingspan: 42–58 mm. Bright rusty orange tinged with pink, sprinkled by darker brown; wing bars narrow; single small silver spot in discal cell of front wings. Larvae feed on oak and hazel. (See Fig. 27.218.) (1) n.e. US; (2) s.e. US; (5) KS, MO.

A. s. fuscosa Ferguson. (3) TX.

A. senatoria (Smith) (Orange-striped Oakworm). Wingspan: 32–50 mm. Females similar to males and females of *A. stigma stigma,* but males with sharply angular hind wings. (1) n.e. NA: (2) s.e. US.

A. virginiensis virginiensis (Drury) (Pink-striped Oakworm). Wingspan: male, 33–40 mm; female, 50–55 mm. Female

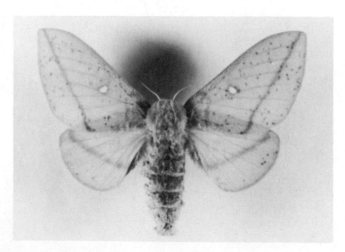

Fig. 27.218.

much like that of the preceding but more thinly scaled and with definite violet band along outer margin of each front wing; male like male of the preceding but darker and with central areas of front wings transparent and with definite boundaries. Larvae are dark green with two purplish red stripes and three rows of black spines on each side; second segment covered with white granules and long lashes; they feed on oak. (1) n.e. US; (2) s.e. US; 93) TX.

A. v. pellucida (Smith). (2) SC, GA, FL.

A. v. discolor Ferguson. (3) TX.

A. consularis Dyar. (2) FL.

A. finlaysoni Riotte. (1) s. ON, WI; (5) MN.

A. peigleri Riotte. (3) TX.

A. oslari Rothschild. (3) AZ, NM, TX.

A. manitobensis McDunnough. (5) MB.

Subfamily Hemileucinae
69.6 *Coloradia* Blake

Four species, as follows:

C. pandora pandora Blake (Pandora Moth). Wingspan: 80–90 mm. Front wings pale with irregular black markings; hind wings pale with very light black scaling. Larvae feed on pine. (3) CA, AZ, MB; (4) OR, UT, NV; (5) CO.

C. p. lindseyi Barnes and Benjamin. (3) CA; (4) OR.

C. p. davisi Barnes and Benjamin. (3) AZ, MN, w. TX.

C. luski Barnes and Benjamin. (3) AZ, NM.

C. doris Barnes. (3) CA, AZ, NM; (4) WA, OR, ID, NV, UT; (5) MT, WO, CO.

C. velda Johnson and Walter.

69.7 *Hemileuca* Walker

Eighteen species, as follows:

H. oliviae Cockerell (Range Caterpillar). Wingspan: 50–70 mm. White, lightly dusted with brownish gray to nearly all brownish gray; darker specimens with narrow, pale line across front wings. Larvae feed on range grasses. (3) NM, TX, OK; (5) CO.

H. maia (Drury) (Buck Moth). Wingspan: 55–70 mm. Black, with definite, narrow, yellowish white bands across wings and with moonspot of white surrounded by black at distal end of each discal cell; tip of abdomen reddish brown. Larvae feed on scrub oak and chinquapin oak from May through July. Adults fly in late September during Indian summer. (See Fig. 27.219.) (1) n.e. US; (2) s.e. US.

H. nevadensis Stretch. (1) MI, IL; (4) Pacific n.w.; (5) n. Central states.

H. lucina Edwards. (1) WI, MI, NH, MA, ME.

H. chinatiensis (Tinkham). (3) ?TX.

H. h. hera (Harris). (See Fig. 27.220.) (3) CA: (4) Pacific n.w.; (5) CO.

H. h. marcata (Neumoegen). (3) CA; (4) OR.

H. magnifera (Rotger). (5) CO.

Fig. 27.219.

Fig. 27.221.

H. eglanterina eglanterina (Boisduval). (See Fig. 27.221 and A&J 244.) (3) CA; (4) Pacific n.w.; (5) AB, MT, WY.

H. e. shastaensis (Grote). (3) CA: (4) OR.

H. e. annulata Ferguson. (4) UT; (5) WY, CO.

H. nuttalli nuttalli (Strecher). (3) AZ, NM; (4) Pacific n.w.; (5) WY, CO.

H. n. uniformis (Cockerell). (3) CA; (4) OR, UT; (5) CO.

H. neumoegeni Edwards. (See Fig. 27.222.) (3) AZ.

H. burnsi Watson. (3) CA, AZ; (4) NV, UT.

H. grotei Grote and Robinson. (3) NM, TX.

H. diana Packard. (3) AZ, TX; (5) CO.

H. electra electra Wright. (3) CA.

H. e. clio Barnes and McDunnough. (3) AZ.

H. tricolor (Packard). (See Fig. 27.223.) (3) AZ, NM.

H. juno Packard. (3) NM, AZ, CA; (4) ID; (5) UT.

H. hualapai (Neumoegen). (3) NM, TX, OK; (5) CO.

H. griffini Tuskes. (3) AZ; (4) UT.

Fig. 27.222.

69.8 *Automeris* Huebner

Five species, as follows:

A. randa Druce. (3) AZ.

A. io io (Fabricius) (Io Moth). Wingspan: 56–80 mm. Bright yellow-orange with large eyespots on hind wings. Adults appear at lights from end of May through July. Larvae have spines that secrete an irritating fluid when handled; they feed on a great variety of plants, including corn. (See Fig. 27.224.) (1) n.e. NA; (2) s.e. US; (3) TX, OK; (5) n. Central States.

A. io lilith (Strecker). (2) SC, GA, FL.

A. io neomexicana Barnes and Benjamin. (3) NM, TX.

A. zephyria Grote. (See Fig. 27.225.) (3) NM, w. TX.

A. cecrops pamina (Neumoegen). (3) AZ, NM.

A. iris hesselorum Ferguson (3) s. AZ.

Fig. 27.220.

Fig. 27.223.

Fig. 27.224.

Fig. 27.226.

69.9 *Hylesia* Huebner

One species, as follows:

H. coinopus Dyar. (3) s. AZ.

Subfamily Saturniinae

Tribe Saturniini

69.10 *Saturnia* Schrank

Three species, as follows:

S. mendocino Behrens. Wingspan: 45–60 mm. Rich brown with dark brown spot on each discal cell, that of front wings particularly surrounded by white; moderate dark brown band across hind wings. Larvae feed on Manzanita, *Rhus* spp., and *Ceanothus* spp. (See Fig. 27.226 and A&J 247.) (3) CA.

S. walterorum Hogue and Johnson. (See A&J 247.) (3) CA (very rare).

S. albofasciata (Johnson). (See A&J 247.) (3) CA (very rare).

69.11 *Agapema* Neumoegen and Dyar

Moths of this genus are all rather similar in appearance, very dark chocolate brown with striking white bands and bars;

eyespots on each wing are narrowly white in center of a dark spot, which in turn is surrounded by an orange ring and then by a black ring. Larvae apparently feed on greasewood, *Laria* spp. Three species, as follows:

A. galbina galbina (Clemens). (See Fig. 27.227 and A&J 245.) (3) AZ.

A. g. anona (Ottolengui). (3) AZ.

A. solita Ferguson. (3) s. TX.

A. homogena Dyar. (3) AZ, NM, TX.

69.12 *Antheraea* Huebner

One species, as follows:

A. polyphemus polyphemus (Cramer) (Polyphemus Moth). Wingspan: 100–130 mm. This well-known large brown moth is easily recognized. Larvae feed on leaves of many trees and shrubs. (See Fig. 27.228 and A&J 250.) (1), (2), (3), (4), (5), generally distributed.

A. p. olivacea (Cockerell). (5) CO.

A. p. oculea (Neumoegen). (See A&J 250.) (3) AZ, NM.

Fig. 27.225.

Fig. 27.227.

Fig. 27.228.

69.13 *Actias* Leach

One species, as follows:

A. luna (Linnaeus) (Luna Moth). Wingspan: 100–120 mm This moth cannot be confused with any other species; its beautiful green color unfortunately fades in a collection; hind wings have long curved tails. Larvae feed on many trees and shrubs. (See Fig. 27.229 and A&J 243.) (1) n.e. US; (2) s.e. US.

Tribe Attacini
69.14 *Samia* Huebner

One species, as follows:

S. cynthia (Drury) (Cynthia Moth; Ailanthus Silkmoth). Wingspan: 130–140 mm. Brown, with base of wings darker; each wing with pale half moon in center, with pale V-mark to base and pale band across vertically. Introduced into the U.S. in 1861 for silk production. Larvae usually feed on ailanthus but are attracted to many other trees. They are confined to city areas. (See Fig. 27.230.) (1) n.e. US; (2) VA, NC, SC, GA.

69.15 *Rothschildia* Grote

Larvae are poorly known but apparently feed on a variety of plants. Three species, as follows:

Fig. 27.229.

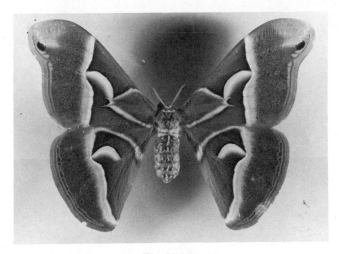

Fig. 27.230.

R. cincta (Tepper) [=*R. jorulla* of authors (not Westwood)]. (See Fig. 27.231 and A&J 249.) (3) AZ, s. TX.

R. forbesi Benjamin. (3) s. TX.

R. orizabra (Westwood).

69.16 *Eupackardia* Cockerell

One species, as follows:

E. calleta (Westwood). Wingspan: 85–110 mm. Very dark moth similar to the following in appearance. Larvae feed on a variety of desert shrubs. (3) s. TX, s. AZ.

69.17 *Callosamia* Packard

Three species, as follows:

C. promethea (Drury) (Promethea Moth). Wingspan: 80–95 mm. Male very dark with clay-colored borders; female brown with well-developed pattern. Larvae feed on great variety of deciduous shrubs and trees, particularly Lauraceae, *Lirodendron* spp., liquidambar, and wild cherry. (See Fig. 27.232 for male; Fig. 27.233 for female.) (1) n.e. NA; (2) s.e. US; (5) MN, IA, NE, KS, MO.

C. angulifera (Walker). Wingspan: ±100 mm. Larger than the preceding; males with wood brown wings; V-marks on

Fig. 27.231.

Fig. 27.232.

Fig. 27.234.

wings of both sexes. Larvae feed chiefly on tulip trees. (1) n.e. NA; (2) TN, s. MS.

C. securifera (Maassen). Wingspan: ±95 mm. Similar to the preceding but wing margins much lighter. Larvae feed on sweet bay. Rare (2) SC, GA, FL, AL, MS.

69.18 *Hyalophora* Duncan

Four species, as follows:

H. cecropia (Linnaeus) (Cecropia Moth). Wingspan: 80–130 mm. Head, body, and bases of front wings rich red with white bands; ground color of wings dusky reddish brown; crescents on wings vary from white to reddish, bordered with red and black; a reddish band beyond prominent white band; outer border of both pair of wings light clay-brown. Larvae green with bluish tints and with two rows of blue tubercles along each side, two rows of yellow ones along back, and two pairs of red ones on thorax; they feed on a great variety of trees and shrubs. (See Fig. 27.234 for male and A&J 248.) (1) n.e. NA; (2) s.e. US; (4) BC, WA, UT; (5) MT, ND, SD, MN, WY, NE, IA, CO, KS, MO.

H. euryalus (Boisduval) (California Silkmoth). (See A&J 246.) (3) CA; (4) Pacific n.w.

H. columbia (Smith). (1) n. ON, s. QU, MI, WI.

H. gloveri gloveri (Strecker). (See Fig. 27.235 for female.) (3) AZ, TX; (4) NV, UT: (5) MT, WY, CO.

H. g. nokomis (Brodie). (5) AB, MB, MT, ND.

Superfamily SPHINGOIDEA

70. SPHINGIDAE (Hawk Moth Family)

About 1,100 species of these easily recognized moths populate the world. Their characteristic shape cannot be confused with that of any other insect (except for a few mimics). Hawk moths look so very much like hummingbirds when in flight that some are often confused with these birds by laymen. They lack ocelli but have a well-developed proboscis, sometimes extremely long to be suitable for sucking up nectar from flowers with long corollas. Many species are diurnal, some nocturnal, some crepuscular, and others both nocturnal and crepuscular.

Larvae of some species are pests. Their large size and soft candal spine (absent only in some species such as those of *Lapara* and *Eumorpha*) are characteristic. The common Tomato Hornworm is a good example of a hawk moth larva. After the fully grown larva decends to the ground, it forms an earthen cell and transforms into a pupa. Adults may be reared

Fig. 27.233.

Fig. 27.235.

Fig. 27.236.

Fig. 27.238.

by collecting mature larvae and providing them with a container of soil in which to pupate.

The 124 species in 42 genera that live in the U.S. and Canada are favorites of collectors because most of them are colorful, all are fairly large, and most are relatively easy to identify to species.

Subfamily **Sphinginae**

Tribe **Sphingini**

70.1 *Agrius* Huebner

One species, as follows:

A. cingulatus (Fabricius) (Sweetpotato Hornworm; Pink Spotted Hawk Moth). Wingspan: ±110 mm. Front wings dark, mottled with gray; hind wings with pink ground color; abdomen rose with black bands. (See Fig. 27.236.) Larvae feed on sweet potato. (2) s.e. US.

[70.2 *Cocytius* Huebner (2 spp.); 70.3 *Neococytius* Hodges (1 sp., *N. cluentius* (Cramer))]

70.4 *Manduca* Huebner

Nine species, the following of which are pests:

M. sexta (Linnaeus) (Tobacco Hornworm; Carolina Sphinx; Hornblower). Wingspan: ±120 mm. Wings dark mottled with gray; abdomen with six orange-yellow spots on

each side. Larvae feed on tobacco, tomato, potato, and other solanaceous plants. (See Fig. 27.237 and A&J 253.) (1) n.e. US; (2) s.e. US.

M. quinquemaculata (Haworth) (Tomato Hornworm; Five Spotted Hawk Moth). Wingspan: 110 mm. Gray; wings with brown mottling; abdomen with five yellow spots on each side. Larvae feed on tomato and other plants. (See Fig. 27.238.) (1) n.e. US; (2) s.e. US.

M. rustica (Fabricius) (Rustic Sphinx; Jasmine Sphinx). Larvae feed on jasmine and begonia. (See Fig. 27.239.)

M. jasminearum (Guerin) (Ash Sphinx). Larvae feed on ash. (See Fig. 27.240.)

70.5 *Dolba* Walker

One species, as follows:

D. hyloeus (Drury) (Pawpaw Sphinx). Larvae feed on possum haw, inkberry, and littleleaf sweetfern. (See Fig. 27.241.)

[70.6 *Dolbogene* Rothschild and Jordan (1 sp., *D. hartwegii* (Butler))]

70.7 *Ceratomia* Harris

Five species, the following of which are common:

C. amyntor (Geyer) (Elm Sphinx). Wingspan: ±105 mm. Brown and dark brown bands and bars and small white

Fig. 27.237.

Fig. 27.239.

Fig. 27.240.

Fig. 27.242.

Fig. 27.243.

markings on wings. Larvae have four short thoracic horns in addition to the caudal horn (they are often known as the Four Horned Sphinx). Larvae feed on elm. (See Fig. 27.242.) (1) n.e. US; (2) s.e. US.

C. catalpae (Boisduval) (Catalpa Sphinx). Wingspan: 55–90 mm. Brown with faint purple tinge, dark brown bars, and light brown spots. Larvae on catalpa. (See Fig. 27.243.) (1) n.e. US; (2) s.e. US.

[70.8 *Isoparce* Rothschild and Jordan (1 sp., *I. cupressi* (Boisduval)); 70.9 *Sagenosoma* Jordan (1 sp., *S. elsa* (Strecker)); 70.10 *Paratrea* Grote (1 sp., *P. plebeja* (Fabricius))]

70.11 *Sphinx* Linnaeus

Twenty-two species, the following of which are common:

S. chersis (Huebner) (Great Ash Sphinx). Wingspan: 110–115 mm. Ash gray with dark markings; abdomen with pale lateral spots. Larvae feed on lilac, ash, privet, cherry, and trembling aspen. (See Fig. 27.244.) (1), (2), (3), (4), (5), generally distributed.

S. eremitus (Huebner) (Hermit Sphinx). Larvae feed on beebalm, mint, bugleweed, and sage.

S. kalmiae Smith (Laurel Sphinx). Larvae feed on laurel, lilac, privet, ash, poplar, and fringe tree.

[70.12 *Lapara* Walker (2 spp.)]

Tribe Smerinthini

[70.13 *Protambulyx* Rothschild and Jordan (2 spp.); 70.14 *Amplypterus* Huebner with one species, *A. donysa* of authors (not Druce), included in MONA checklist.]

70.15 *Smerinthus* Latreille

Three species, the following of which are common:

S. jamaicensis (Drury) (Twin-spot Sphinx): Wingspan: 60–80 mm. Front wings with irregular outer edge and brown, dark brown, and light gray markings; hind wings distinctive tan

Fig. 27.241.

Fig. 27.244.

Fig. 27.245.

Fig. 27.247.

and rose, each with blue eye-spot ringed with black and with black bar through the spot (hence "twin-spot"). Larvae feed on poplar, birch, willow, elm, ash, apple, peach, and plum. (See Fig. 27.245.) (1), (2), (3), (4), (5), generally distributed.

S. cerisyi Kirby. Wingspan: 55–65 mm. Similar to the preceding, but wing veins set off by pale scales and eye-spots of hind wings with dark center instead of bar. Larvae feed on willow and poplar. (See Fig. 27.246 and A&J 252.) (1) n.e US; (4) Pacific n.w.; (5) n. Central States.

[70.16 *Paonias* Huebner (3 spp.)]

70.17 *Laothoe* Fabricius

[=*Cressonia* Grote and Robinson]

One species, as follows:

L. juglandis (Smith) (Walnut Sphinx). Wingspan: 55–70 mm. Pale brown with brown or gray lines and small brown spot at apex of discal cell. Larvae feed on walnut, hickory, butternut, and beech. (See Fig. 27.247.) (1) n.e. US; (2) s.c. US; (5) ND, SD, MN, NE, IA, KS, MO.

70.18 *Pachysphinx* Huebner

Two species, the following of which is common:

P. modesta (Harris) (Modest Sphinx; Big Poplar Sphinx). (See Fig. 27.248.) (1) n.e. US; (2), s.e. US; (3) TX; (4) Pacific n.w.; (5) n. Central States.

Fig. 27.248.

Subfamily Macroglossinae
Tribe Dilophonotini

[70.19 *Pseudosphinx* Burmeister (1 sp., *P. tetrio* (Linnaeus)); 70.20 *Isognathus* C. and R. Felder (1 sp., *I. rimosus* (Grote)); 70.21 *Erinnyis* Huebner (8 spp.); 70.22 *Phryxus* Huebner (1 sp., *P. caicus* (Cramer)); 70.23 *Pachylia* Walker (1 sp., *P. ficus* (Linnaeus)); 70.24 *Pachylioides* Hodges (1 sp., *P. resumens* (Walker)); 70.25 *Madoryx* Boisduval (1 sp., *M. pseudothyreus* (Grote)); 70.26 *Callionima* Lucas (2 spp.); 70.27 *Perigonia* Herrich-Schaeffer (1 sp., *P. lusca* (Fabricius))]

70.28 *Aellopos* Huebner

Four species, the following of which is common:

A. titan (Cramer). (See Fig. 27.249.) (1) n.e. US; (2) AR; (3) TX; (5) MO.

70.29 *Enyo* Huebner

Two species, including the following:

E. lugubris (Linnaeus). (See Fig. 27.250.) (2) SC, GA, FL, AL, MS, LA; (3) AZ, NM, TX.

70.30 *Hemaris* Dalman

These are the Hummingbird Moths, with abdomen blunt or tufted at the apex and wings with large transparent areas. Four species, the following of which is common:

Fig. 27.246.

Fig. 27.249.

Fig. 27.252.

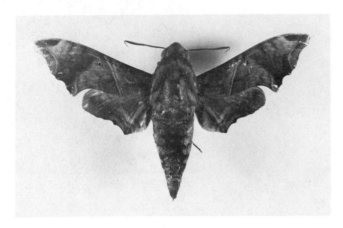

Fig. 27.250.

H. thysbe (Fabricius) (Common Clear-wing). Wingspan: 45–55 mm. Reddish brown with large clear areas in each wing; undersurface of thorax not banded with dark scales; (other species of genus have black or red bands); abdomen with dull yellow markings. Larvae feed on cranberry, hawthorn, cherry, plum, honeysuckle, and snowberry. (See Fig. 27.251.) (1) n.e. NA; (2) s.e. US; (4) Pacific n.w.; (5) n. Central States.

Tribe Philampelini

70.31 *Eumorpha* Huebner

Ten species, of which the following are common:

E. pandorus (Huebner). Wingspan: 110–115 mm. Beautiful greenish-tinged sphinx; front wings with narrow pink dash. Adults fly at dusk and thereafter from June to November. Larvae feed on ampelopsis, grape, and Virginia creeper. (See Fig. 27.252.) (1) n.e. US; (2) s.e. US. (A&J 251).

E. fasciata (Sulzer). (See Fig. 27.253.) (2) SC, GA, FL, AL, MS, LA; (3) s.w. US.

E. achemon (Drury) (Achemon Sphinx). Wingspan: ±95 mm. Brown; similar to *E. pandorus* but without green tint or pink dash on front wing; hind wings pale rose with brown margins. Larvae feed on grape and ampelopsis. (See Fig. 27.254.) (1), (2), (3), (4), (5), generally distributed.

E. labruscae (Linnaeus) (Gaudy Sphinx). Wingspan: ±130 mm. Front wings deep green with sparse brown markings and vaguely defined yellow-orange discal and hind marginal spots; hind wings marked with blue, red, brown, and tan. Larvae feed on ampelopsis, cissus, grape, and christmasbush. (See Fig. 27.255.) (3) FL, strays to ME, MI, and s. SK.

Tribe Macroglossini

[70.32 *Cautethia* Grote (3 spp.)]

Fig. 27.251.

Fig. 27.253.

Fig. 27.254.

Fig. 27.257.

70.35 *Arctonotus* Boisduval

One species, as follows:

A. lucidus Boisduval. (See Fig. 27.257.) (3) CA; (4) WA, ID, OR.

70.36 *Amphion* Huebner

One species, as folllows:

A. nessus (Cramer). (See Fig. 27.258) (1) n.e. NA; (2) s.e. US; (5) n. Central states.

70.37 *Proserpinus* Huebner

Six species, the following of which are common:

P. juanita (Strecker). (See Fig. 27.259.) (3) AZ, NM, TX; (5) CO, KS, MO.

P. clarkiae (Boisduval) (Clark's Day Sphinx). (See Fig. 27.260.) (3) CA; (4) Pacific n.w.; (5) AB, WY, CO.

P. flavofasciata (Walker) (Yellow-banded Day Sphinx). (See Fig. 27.261.) (1) n.e. NA; (4) Pacific n.w; (5) n. Central States.

Fig. 27.255.

70.33 *Sphecodina* Blanchard

One species, as follows:

S. abbottii (Swainson) (Abbott's Sphinx). (See Fig 27.256.) (1) n.e. US; (2) s.e. US.

[70.34 *Deidamia* Clemens (1 sp., *D. inscripta* (Harris))]

70.38 *Euproserpinus* Grote and Robinson

Three species, the following of which is common:

E. phaeton Grote and Robinson. (See Fig. 27.262.) (3) s. CA.

[70.39 *Macroglossum* Scopoli (1 sp., *M. stellatarum* (Linnaeus))]

Fig. 27.256.

Fig. 27.258.

Fig. 27.259.

Fig. 27.262.

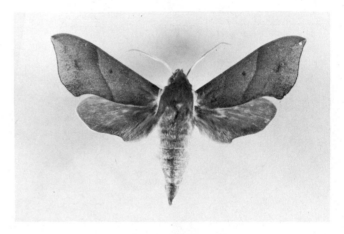

Fig. 27.263.

70.40 *Darapsa* Walker

Three species, the following of which are common:

D. myron (Cramer) (Virginia-creeper Sphinx; Grape-vine Sphinx; Hog Caterpillar). (See. Fig. 27.263.) (1) n.e. US; (2) s.e. US; (3) NM, TX.

D. pholus (Cramer) (Azalea Sphinx). (See Fig. 27.264.) (1) n.e. US; (2) s.e. US; (3) TX; (4) Pacific n.w.; (5) n. Central States.

70.41 *Xylophanes* Huebner

Five species, the following of which are common:

X. pluto (Fabricius). (See Fig. 27.265.) (2) s. FL; (3) s. TX.

X. tersa (Walker). (See Fig. 27.266.) (3) AZ, w. TX.

70.42 *Hyles* Huebner

Three species, the following of which are common:

H. lineata (Fabricius) (White-lined Sphinx). Wingspan: 65–75 mm. Similar to *Eumorpha labruscae* above, but with veins of front wings outlined with pale scales. Larvae feed on many plants, particularly garden varieties and apple. (See Fig. 27.267.) (1), (2), (3), (4), (5), generally distributed.

H. gallii (Rottenberg). Wingspan: 65–75 mm. Similar to preceding, but front wing without white lines; costal margin of front wing dash olive green. (See Fig. 27.268.) (1), (4), (5).

Fig. 27.261.

Fig. 27.264.

Fig. 27.265.

Fig. 27.266.

Superfamily NOCTUOIDEA

This superfamily is an exceedingly large complex of rather similar moths. Five families are assigned to it, including the largest family of the Lepidoptera, the Noctuidae, which concludes the order.

Fig. 27.267.

Fig. 27.268.

71. NOTODONTIDAE (Prominent Moth Family)

These moths superficially resemble the Noctuidae. They too are abundant at lights at night and often on sugar bait. Larvae of some genera lack claspers at the end of the abdomen and wave the latter in the air in a characteristic manner. The classification of the family is confused. Forbes divides the genera into subfamilies and tribes, but this treatment is not generally agreed on, and no comprehensive work establishes the arrangement of the genera. There are 41 genera and 136 species in the U.S. and Canada.

71.1 *Clostera* Samouelle

Seven species, the following of which are common:

C. apicalis (Walker). Wingspan: 25–35 mm. Light dirty gray to mouse gray, shaded with brown. Larvae feed on poplar in the east and willow in the west. (See Fig. 27.269.) (1), (2), (3), (4), (5), generally distributed.

C. inclusa (Huebner) (Poplar Tentmaker). Wingspan: 30–35 mm. Similar to the preceding, but paler in color. Larvae feed on poplar and willows. (1) n.e. US; (2) VA, NC, GA; (5) SD, MN, CO, KS, MO.

71.2 *Datana* Walker

Thirteen species, the following of which are common:

D. ministra (Drury) (Yellow-necked Caterpillar Moth). Wingspan: 40–50 mm. Front wings reddish brown with dark

Fig. 27.269.

Fig. 27.270.

fine lines; hind wings pale. Adults fly from June to August. The yellow and red striped larvae are destructive of apple and other trees. They rest with both head and tip of the abdomen in the air. (See Fig. 27.270.) (1) n.e. US; (2) s.e. US; (5) n. Central States.

D. integerrima Grote and Robinson (Walnut Caterpillar Moth). Wingspan: 35–50 mm. Bands of light red-brown and yellow-green on wings. Frequently taken at lights at night from June to August. Larvae feed on walnut and hickory. (1) n.e. US; (2) VA, NC, SC, GA, AR.

71.3 *Nadata* Walker

Two species, the following of which is common:

N. gibbosa (Smith). Wingspan: 45–55 mm. Light yellow, dusted with rusty red, with silver dots. Larvae usually feed on oak but also infest maple and other trees. (See Fig. 27.271.) (1), (2), (3), (4), (5), generally distributed.

[71.4 *Hyperaeschra* Butler (2 spp.); 71.5 *Peridea* Stephan (3 spp.); 71.6 *Pheosia* Huebner (2 spp.); 71.7 *Odontosia* Huebner (2 spp.); 71.8 *Notodonta* Ochsenheimer (3 spp.); 71.9 *Nerice* Walker (1 sp., *N. bidentata* Walker); 71.10 *Ellida* Grote (1 sp., *E. caniplaga* Walker)]

71.11 *Gluphisia* Boisduval

Five species, the following of which is common:

G. septentrionis Walker. Wingspan: 28–32 mm. Gray to blackish with dark lines and some yellowish shading. Larvae

Fig. 27.272.

feed on poplar. (See Fig. 27.272.) (1) (2), (3), (4), (5), generally distributed.

71.12 *Furcula* Lamarck

Six species, including the following:

F. scolopendrina (Boisduval). Wingspan: 35–45 mm. Cream white with gray hour-glass markings and black dots. Larvae feed on willow. (See Fig. 27.273.) (1) n.e. NA.

[71.13 *Cerura* Schrank (3 spp.); 71.14 *Nystalea* Guenée (3 spp.); 71.15 *Elymiotis* Walker (1 sp., *E. notodontoides* Walker); 71.16 *Hippia* Moeschler (2 spp.)]

71.17 *Symmerista* Huebner

Five species, the following of which is common:

S. leucitys Franclemont (Orange-humped Mapleworm Moth). Wingspan: 34–38 mm. Ash gray, marked with dark and light lines and black dashes; body yellow to yellow mixed with chestnut. Larvae feed on maple. (1) n.e. NA; (5) MN.

[71.18 *Pentobesa* Schaus (1 sp., *P. valta* Schaus); 71.19 *Dasylophia* Packard (3 spp.); 71.20 *Notela* Schaus (1 sp., *N. jaliscana* Schaus); 71.21 *Didugua* Druce (1 sp., *D. argentilinea* Druce); 71.22 *Afilia* Schaus (1 sp., *A. oslari* Dyar); 71.23 *Skewesia* Dyar (1 sp., *S. angustiora* Barnes and McDunnough); 71.24 *Cargida* Schaus (1 sp., *C. pyrrha* Druce); 71.25 *Rifargia* Walker (3 spp.); 71.26 *Litodonta* Harvey (6 spp.); 71.27 *Misogada* Walker (1 sp., *M. unicolor* Packard); 71.28 *Macrurocampa* Dyar (2 spp.)]

Fig. 27.271.

Fig. 27.273.

Fig. 27.274.

Fig. 27.275.

71.29 *Heterocampa* Doubleday

Twenty-one species, the following of which are common:

H. umbrata Walker. Wingspan: 45–50 mm. Male gray and pale green dusted with white at base; female darker with brownish gray shading. Larvae feed on oak. (See Fig. 27.274.) (1) n.e. US; (5) ND, SD, MN, NE, IA, KS, MO.

H. guttivitta (Walker) (Saddled Prominent; also called Maple Prominent). Wingspan: 35–42 mm. Green with heavy gray dusting marked with dark lines and spots. Larvae feed on beech, maple, apple, and other trees; sometimes a pest. (1) n.e. US; (2) s.e. US; (5) ND, SD, MN, NE, IA, KS, MO.

71.30 *Lochmaeus* Doubleday

Two species, the following of which is a pest:

L. manteo Doubleday (Variable Oak Leaf Caterpillar Moth). Wingspan: 40–50 mm. Powdery gray, shaded with brownish gray, with dark lines and dark spots. Larvae feed on oak. (1) n.e. US; (2) s.e. US; (5) ND, SD, MN, NE, IA, KS, MO.

[71.31 *Theroa* Schaus (1 sp., *T. zethus* Druce); 71.32 *Praeschausia* Benjamin (1 sp., *P. zapata* (Schaus)); 71.33 *Ursia* Barnes and McDunnough (2 spp.)]

71.34 *Schizura* Doubleday

Eight species, the following of which are pests:

S. concinna (Smith) (Red-humped Caterpillar Moth). Wingspan: 30–35 mm. Front wing gray with brown and black markings. Larvae have red hump and feed on apple and many other plants, especially Rosaceae. (1), (2), (3), (4), (5), generally distributed.

S. unicornis (Smith) (Unicorn Caterpillar Moth). Wingspan: 28–30 mm. Dark gray shaded and mottled with pale gray-green; base solid green with pale markings. Larvae found on various trees. (See Fig. 27.275.) (1) n.e. US; (5) ND, SD, MN, NE, IA, KS, MO.

71.35 *Oligocentria* Herrich-Schaeffer

Nine species, the following of which is common:

O. perangulata (Edwards). Wingspan: 38–48 mm. Wings with white streaks mixed with brown and red-brown. Larvae feed on oak. (See Fig. 27.276.) (3) s.w. US.

[71.36 *Euhyparpax* Beutenmueller (1 sp., *E. rosea* Beutenmueller); 71.37 *Hyparpax* Huebner (5 spp.); 71.38 *Lirimiris* Walker (1 sp., *L. truncata* Herrich-Schaeffer); 71.39 *Astylis* Boisduval (1 sp., *A. biedermani* Skinner); 71.40 *Pseudhapigia* Schaus (1 sp., *P. brunnea* Schaus); 71.41 *Hemiceras* Guenée (1 sp., *H. cadmia* Guenée)]

72. DIOPTIDAE (Oak Moth Family)

Most species are brightly marked, resembling certain butterflies. Only two species occur in the U.S.

72.1 *Phryganidia* Packard

P. californica Packard (California Oakworm Moth). Wingspan: ±30 mm. Pale brown, with veins dark. (See Fig. 27.277.) (3) CA.

72.2 *Zunacetha* Walker

Z. annulata Guerin. Wingspan: ±30 mm. Wings white; veins dark brown in front wing with orange front margin on basal half; wavy, narrow, vertical band at middle of wing and irregular brown circle with white interior in basal third of wing. (See Fig. 27.278.) (3) a stray in s. TX.

73. ARCTIIDAE (Tiger Moth Family)

The Tiger Moths are often brightly colored with white, red, or yellow and with the spots or stripes that give them their common name. Most species have a wingspan of 25–30 mm.

Fig. 27.276.

Fig. 27.277.

The larvae are covered with tufts of hair; they, too, are often brightly colored. Well over 2,000 species are known, many of them tropical. There are 89 genera and 264 species recorded in the U.S. and Canada.

Subfamily Pericopinae

[=Pericopidae of authors]

Tribe Pericopini

73.1 *Gnophaela* Walker

Five species, the following of which are common:

G. latipennis (Boisduval). Wingspan: 25–30 mm. Wings dark with pale markings. (See Fig. 27.279.) (3) s. AZ, s. TX.

G. vermiculata Grote and Robinson. Wingspan: 40–45 mm. Brown with yellow markings on wings. Larval food unknown. (See A&J 255.) (3) s.w. US.

73.2 *Composia* Huebner

One species, as follows:

C. fidelissima Herrich-Schaeffer, subspecies *C. f. vagrans* Bates. Winspan: 25–30 mm. Dark blue with red and white markings. Larvae feed on *Echites umbellata* and cultivated oleander. (2) s. FL.

[73.3 *Phaloesia* Walker (1 sp., *P. saucia* Walker); 73.4 *Daritis* Walker (1 sp., *D. howardi* (Edwards))]

Tribe Doaini

[73.5 *Doa* Neumoegen and Dyar (1 sp., *D. ampla* Grote); 73.6 *Leuculodes* Dyar (1 sp., *L. lacteolaria* Hulst)]

Fig. 27.278.

Fig. 27.279.

Subfamily Lithosiinae

Tribe Lithosiini

[73.7 *Eilema* Huebner (2 spp.); 73.8 *Crambidia* Packard (10 spp.); 73.9 *Agylla* Walker (1 sp., *A. septentrionalis* Barnes and McDunnough); 73.10 *Inopsis* Felder (2 spp.); 73.11 *Gnamplonychia* Hampson (1 sp., *G. ventralis* Barnes and Lindsey); 73.12 *Gardinia* Kirby (1 sp., *G. anopla* Hering)]

73.13 *Cisthene* Walker

Twenty species, the following of which is common:

C. barnesii (Dyar) (Barne's Tiger Moth). Wingspan: 25–30 mm. Front wings with distinct cream stripes; hind wings almost entirely black except for an irregular subapical orange spot; hind margin of wing slightly produced. Larval food plant not recorded. (See A&J 258.) (3) AZ.

[73.14 *Ptychoglene* Felder (3 spp.); 73.15 *Propyria* Hampson (1 sp., *P. schausi* (Dyar))]

73.16 *Lycomorpha* Harris

Six species, the following of which is common:

L. pholus (Drury). Wingspan: 25–30 mm. Resembles lycid beetles. (see Coleoptera); wings orange with apical fifth black. Larvae feed on lichens. (See A&J 260.) (1), (2), (3), (4) (5), widely distributed.

73.17 *Hypoprepia* Huebner

Four species, the following of which is common:

H. miniata (Kirby). Wingspan: 28–40 mm. Wings deep pink or scarlet with gray markings. Larvae feed on lichens. (See Fig. 27.280.) (1) n.e. US; (2) s.e. US; (5) ND, SD, MN, NE, IA, KS, MO.

[73.18 *Haematomis* Hampson (1 sp., *H. mexicana* Druce); 73.19 *Bruceia* Neumoegen (2 spp.); 73.20 *Eudesmia* Huebner (2 spp.); 73.21 *Clemensia* Packard (1 sp., *C. albata* Packard); 73.22 *Pagara* Walker (2 spp.); 73.23 *Neoplynes* Hampson (1 sp., *N. eudora* Dyar)]

Tribe Afridini

[73.24 *Afrida* Moescher (2 spp.); 73.25 *Comachara* Franclemont (1 sp., *cadburyi* Franclemont)]

Tribe Acsalini

[73.26 *Acsala* Benjamin (1 sp., *A. anomala* Benjamin); (4) AK; (5) YK)]

Fig. 27.280.

Fig. 27.282.

Subfamily Arctiinae
Tribe Callimorphini
73.27 *Utetheisa* Huebner

Two species, the following of which is common:

U. bella (Linnaeus) (Bella Moth). Wingspan: 35–45 mm. Front wings yellow with transverse white stripes, each with row of small black dots within stripe; hind wings pink with narrow, irregular black border. Larvae feed on *Crotalaria* sp. (or rattlebox; hence the frequent name, the Rattle-box Moth), *Lespedesa* spp., and other legumes. (See Fig. 27.281.) (1) n.e. US; (2) s.e. US; (3) TX; (5) KS. (A&J 259)

73.28 *Haploa* Huebner

Six species, the following of which is common:

H. lecontei Guérin-Méneville. Wingspan: 40–55 mm. Front wings and thorax creamy white, marked with black; hind wings, abdomen, and head yellow. Larvae are general feeders. (See Fig. 27.282.) (1) IL, IN, OH, s. ON, NY, MA; PA, NJ, MD, DE; (2) VA, NC, SC, GA, LA, MS, AL, AR; (3) TX; (5) KS, MO.

73.29 *Tyria* Huebner

One species, as follows:

T. jacobaeae (Linnaeus) (Cinnabar Moth). This species has been introduced into n. CA to control Klamathweed; established in some areas.

Tribe Arctini

[73.30 *Holomelina* Herrich-Schaeffer (12 spp.); 73.31 *Leptarctia* Stretch (1 sp., *L. californiae* Walker); 73.32 *Parasemia* Huebner (1 sp., *P. plantaginis* (Linnaeus))]

73.33 *Dodia* Dyar

One species, as follows:

D. albertae Dyar. (See Fig. 27.283.)

73.34 *Pyrrharctia* Packard

One species, as follows:

P. isabella (Smith and Abbot) (Banded Woollybear Moth). Wingspan: ±50 mm. Buff to light brown with darker stripes and spots; abdomen with a dorsal row of dark spots. Larvae are covered with stiff hairlike setae, chestnut in center, ends black; they feed on grasses and many other plants. In the fall, they migrate to a suitable place to hibernate and overwinter. This is the common "woollybear" caterpillar that is said to foretell the extent of the coming winter. The relative amount of black "fur" on the ends of the caterpillar varies both with its age and the wetness of the fall weather. The wetter the weather, the more the black "fur," and the younger the caterpillar, the greater the extent of it. Therefore, the younger caterpillars forecast an earlier winter, and thus, a longer one. These larvae pass the winter in hybernation. They pupate in the spring, emerge as adults in late May, and lay eggs for the first of their

Fig. 27.281.

Fig. 27.283.

Fig. 27.284.

two broods, the second appearing in August; this is the one usually seen. (See Fig. 27.284.) (1), (2), (3), (4), (5), generally distributed.

[73.35 *Seirarctia* Packard (1 sp., *S. echo* Abbott and Smith)]

73.36 *Estigmene* Huebner

Two species, the following of which is common:

E. acrea (Drury) (Salt Marsh Caterpillar Moth). Wingspan: ±55 mm. Front wings white with small black spots; hind wings of male yellow, of female, white. Larvae are general feeders, especially on low plants; not particularly associated with marshy areas. (See Fig. 27.285.) (1), (2), (3), (5), generally distributed.

73.37 *Spilosoma* Curtis

Seven species, the following of which is common:

S. virginica (Fabricius) (Yellow Woollybear Moth). Wingspan: 35–45 mm. Wings and body entirely white with a few small black spots on wings and two rows of dark spots on abdomen dorsally. Larvae are general feeders and often found in gardens, they vary from yellow to white and even reddish. (See Fig. 27.286.) (1), (2), (3), (4), (5), generally distributed.

Fig. 27.285.

Fig. 27.286.

73.38 *Hyphantria* Harris

One species, as follows:

H. cunea (Drury) (Fall Webworm Moth). Wingspan: 25–42 mm. Front wings entirely white (Fig. 27.287) varying to heavily speckled with black dots (Fig. 27.288); hind wings white; abdomen white to dark. Larvae make large nests in many different kinds of trees, particularly apple, ash, and oak. The nests enlarge and become very noticeable in the early fall. They are seldom of economic importance in the U.S. but are always

Fig. 27.287.

Fig. 27.288.

Fig. 27.289.

Fig. 27.291.

unsightly in shade trees. Since being introduced to Europe and Japan, however, they have caused serious damage to forests. (See A & J 261.) (1) n.e. US; (2) s.e. US.

[73.39 *Euerythra* Harvey (2 spp.); 73.40 *Alexicles* Grote (1 sp., *A. aspersa* Grote); 73.41 *Turuptiana* Walker (2 spp.)]

73.42 *Ecpantheria* Huebner

Four species, including the following:

E. *scribonia* (Stoll). (See Fig. 27.289.)

73.43 *Arachnis* Geyer

Six species, including the following:

A. *zuni* Neumoegen. (See Fig. 27.290.)

73.44 *Phragmatobia* Stephens

Three species, the following of which is common:

P. *fuliginosa* (Linnaeus), subspecies *P. f. rubricosa* Harris (Ruby Tiger Moth). Wingspan: 25–35 mm. Front wings dark brown to smoky, pink at base, veins darker; hind wings pale. Larvae are general feeders. (See Fig. 27.291.) (1) ON, PQ, n. NY.

[73.45 *Neoarctia* Neumoegen and Dyar (3 spp.); 73.46 *Platarctia* Packard (1 sp., *P. parthenos* (Harris))]

73.47 *Platyprepia* Dyar

One species, as follows:

P. *virginalis* (Boisduval) (Ranchman's Tiger Moth). Wingspan: 50–60 mm. Front wings black with large pale yellow spots; hind wings yellow with black markings varying to almost entirely black with some submarginal yellow spots. Larval food unknown. (See A & J 256.) (3) s.w. US; (4) Pacific n.w.

[73.48 *Acerbia* Sotavalta (2 spp.); 73.49 *Pararctia* Sotavalta (1 sp., *P. lapponica* (Thunberg))]

73.50 *Arctia* Schrank

One species, as follows:

A. *caja* (Linnaeus), subsp. *A. c. americana* Harris (Great Tiger Moth). Wingspan: ±55 mm. Front wings fawn brown with broad off-white markings; hind wings yellowish to orange with large black spots. Larvae are general feeders. (See Fig. 27.292.) (1) n.e. NA; (4) Pacific n.w.; (5) n. Central States.

73.51 *Kodiosoma* Stretch

Two species, including the following:

K. *fulvum* Stretch. (See Fig. 27.293.)

73.52 *Apantesis* Harris

A number of species of this genus are also called Tiger Moths because of the striking markings on their wings. Front wings

Fig. 27.290.

Fig. 27.292.

Fig. 27.293.

Fig. 27.295.

Fig. 27.296.

dark with white stripes; hind wings reddish orange with black spots. Thirty-one species, the following of which are common:

A. ornata (Packard) (Tiger Moth). Wingspan: 40–45 mm. Front wings black with white, sometimes pinkish, stripes; hind wings reddish orange with black spots and broad stripes; abdomen reddish with black markings. Larvae feed on a wide variety of low plants. (See Fig. 27.294.) (3) CA; (4) BC, WA, OR.

A. virgo (Linnaeus). Similar to the preceding. (See Fig. 27.295.) (1) n.e. US; (2) s.e. US.

A. phalerata (Harris) (Harnessed Moth). Wingspan: 30–40 mm. Straw yellow with black markings. Larvae feed on a great variety of plants. (See Fig. 27.296 and A & J 257.) (1) n.e. US; (2) s.e. US; (5) ND, SD, MN, NE, IA, KS, MO.

A. placentia (Smith). (See Fig. 27.297.)

A. proxina (Guérin-Méneville). (See Fig. 27.298.)

A. vittata (Fabricius). (See Fig. 27.299 for male; Fig. 27.300 for female.)

A. radians (Walker). (See Fig. 27.301.)

[73.53 *Hyperborea* Grum-Grshimalo (1 sp., *H. czekanowskii* Grum-Grshimalo)]

Tribe **Phaegopterini**

[73.54 *Hypocrisias* Hampson (1 sp., *H. minima* Neumoegen)]

73.55 *Halysidota* Huebner

Seven species, the following of which are common:

H. tessellaris (Smith) (Pale Tussock Moth; Banded Tussock Moth). Wingspan: ±50 mm. Cream white with light brown marking edged with black. Larvae feed on various flowers as well as alder, hickory, and sycamore. (See Fig. 27.302.) (1), (2), (3), (4), (5), generally distributed.

Fig. 27.294.

Fig. 27.297.

Fig. 27.298.

Fig. 27.301.

Fig. 27.299.

Fig. 27.302.

H. harrisii Walsh (Sycamore Tussock Moth). Very similar to the preceding but lighter in color. Larvae apparently feed only on sycamore. (1), (2), (3), (4), (5), widely distributed.

73.56 *Lophocampa* Harris

Eleven species, the following of which are common:

L. argentata Packard (Silver-spotted Tiger Moth). Wingspan: 35–40 mm. Similar to the other tussock moths but with silver spots. Larvae feed on fir needles and other conifers. (3) s.w. US; (4) Pacific n.w.

L. maculata (Harris) (Spotted Tussock Moth). Wingspan: ±40 mm. Front wings light yellow with four broad, irregular, merging light brown bands, narrowly edged with darker brown; hind wings whitish; abdomen pale to dark. Larvae feed on poplar, maple, and other trees. (See Fig. 27.303.) (1) n.e. NA; (4) Pacific n.w.; (5) n. Central States.

Fig. 27.300.

Fig. 27.303.

Fig. 27.304.

Fig. 27.306.

L. caryae (Harris) (Hickory Tussock Moth). Wingspan: 37–50 mm. Front wing yellow-brown to cream, with rows of cream-colored spots outlined with brown. Larvae feed on various trees, including hickory. (See Fig. 27.304.) (1) n.e. NA; (2) s.e. US; (5) ND, SD, MN, NE, IA, KS, MO.

[73.57 *Leucanopsis* Rego-Barros (3 spp.)]

73.58 *Aemilia* Kirby

One species, as follows:

A. ambigna Strecker. Wingspan: ±45 mm. Wings pale cream with veins of front wings broadly marked with brown. Larvae are general feeders. (See Fig. 27.305.) (5) MT, WY, CO.

[73.59 *Apocrisias* Franclemont (1 sp., *A. thaumasta* Franclemont)]

73.60 *Hemihyalea* Hampson

Four species, including the following:

H. edwardsi Packard. Wingspan: ±50 mm. Wings pale brown with veins and a few spots dark brown, edges of spots speckled with black dots. (See Fig. 27.306.) (3) CA.

[73.61 *Calidota* Dyar (1 sp., *C. laqueata* Edwards); 73.62 *Opharus* Walker (1 sp., *O. muricolor* (Dyar); 73.63 *Carales* Walker (1 sp., *C. arizonensis* (Rothschild)); 73.64 *Pareuchaetes* Grote (1 sp., *P. insulata* (Walker))]

73.65 *Cycnia* Huebner

Four species, including the following:

C. tenera Huebner. Wingspan: 32–37 mm. Wings white with yellow on front margin; body yellow with black spots. Larvae feed on dogbane and milkweed. (See Fig. 27.307.) (1), (2), (3), (4), (5), generally distributed.

73.66 *Euchaetes* Harris

Twelve species, the following of which is common:

E. egle (Drury) (Milkweed Tussock Moth). Wingspan: 35–40 mm. Mouse gray with yellow abdomen with black spots. Larvae on milkweed. (See Fig. 27.308.) (1) n.e. US; (2) s.e. US.

[73.67 *Pygoctenucha* Grote (2 spp.); 73.68 *Lerina* Walker (1 sp., *L. incarnata* Walker)]

73.69 *Ectypia* Clemens

Three species, including the following:

E. clio (Packard) (Clio Moth). Wingspan: 45–50 mm. Entirely white except for black veins on front wings and slight markings on hind wings; abdomen pale yellow with dorsal median row of black spots. Larval food unknown. Rare. (See Fig. 27.309 and A&J 254.) (3) s. CA.

Fig. 27.305.

Fig. 27.307.

Fig. 27.308.

Fig. 27.310.

73.70 *Pygarctia* Grote

Eight species, including the following:

P. murina Stretch. Wingspan: ±25 mm. Front wings and thorax mouse gray; hind wings paler; abdomen orange. Larvae are general feeders. (See Fig. 27.310.) (3) TX.

[73.71 *Eupseudosoma* Grote (1 sp., *E. involutum* Sepp); 73.72 *Bertholdia* Schaus (1 sp., *B. trigona* Grote); 73.73 *Trichromia* Huebner (1 sp., *T. prophaea* (Schaus))]

Subfamily Ctenuchinae

[=Amatidae of authors]

These moths are mostly day-flying, tropical species that mimic wasps, other Hymenoptera, and some beetles. Relatively few of the more than 2,000 species reach the U.S., and those that do are mostly southern. The body may be marked with yellow and often has a ground color of metallic blue-black scales. Adults are common on flowers. Larvae have hairlike setae in tufts arising from warts or as long tufts of hair. They feed on a wide variety of plants, and some are pests.

73.74 *Ctenucha* Kirby

Six species, the following of which are common:

C. cressonana Grote. Wingspan: ±50 mm. Wings and body dark metallic blue-black; wing veins and margins white; head

red. Larvae feed on grasses and sedges. (See Fig. 27.311.) (2) s.e. US; (3) s.w. US.

C. virginica (Esper). Wingspan: 40–50 mm. Wings brown-black to black; head and thorax orange; abdomen peacock blue. Adults on flowers of blackberry, spiraea, and others. Larvae feed on grass. (See Fig. 27.312.) (1) n.e. US; (2) VA; (5) ND, SD, MN, NE, IA, KS, MO.

[73.75 *Dahana* Grote (1 sp., *D. atripennis* Grote)]

73.76 *Cisseps* Franclemont

Three species, including the following:

C. fulvicollis (Huebner). Wingspan: ±35 mm. Front wings brownish, darker at margins; head and thorax yellow; abdomen

Fig. 27.311.

Fig. 27.309.

Fig. 27.312.

Fig. 27.313.

blue-black. Larvae feed on grass. (See Fig. 27.313.) (1) n.e. US; (2) s.e. US.

[73.77 *Lymire* Walker (1 sp., *L. edwardsii* Grote); 73.78 *Eucereon* Huebner (1 sp., *E. carolina* Edwards); 73.79 *Empyreuma* Huebner (1 sp., *E. affinis* Rothschild); 73.80 *Macrocneme* Huebner (1 sp., *M. chrysitis* Guérin-Méneville); 73.81 *Antichloris* Huebner (1 sp., *A. viridis* Druce); 73.82 *Episcepsis* Butler (1 sp., *E. inornata* (Walker)); 73.83 *Psilopleura* Hampson (1 sp., *P. vittatum* (Walker)); 73.84 *Pseudosphex* Huebner (1 sp., *P. strigosa* (Druce)); 73.85 *Cosmosoma* Huebner (3 spp.); 73.86 *Didasys* Grote (1 sp., *D. belae* Grote)]

73.87 *Syntomeida* Harris

Four species, including the following:

S. ipomoeae Harris (Yellow-banded Wasp Moth). Wingspan: ±40 mm. Metallic blue-black with yellow markings; mimics a wasp. Larvae feed on morning glory. (See Fig. 27.314.) (2) LA, MS, AL, FL; (3) TX.

[73.88 *Pseudocharis* Druce (1 sp., *P. minima* Grote); 73.89 *Horama* Huebner (2 spp.)]

74. LYMANTRIIDAE
(Tussock Moth Family)

Although this is a fairly large family of about 2,500 species, only six genera and 32 species are native to the U.S. and Canada. Three additional genera and four species have been

Fig. 27.314.

introduced. Larvae with front and rear tufts of hairlike setae are characteristic of the group. They feed on the foliage of trees and shrubs, avoiding herbaceous plants.

Subfamily Orgyiinae
Tribe Orgyiini
74.1 *Gynaephora* Huebner

Two species, one from the far north and the other as follows:

G. rossii (Curtis). (1) LB, NF; (4) AK; (5) KE, MC, NT, YK, AB, MT, WY, CO.

74.2 *Dasychira* Huebner

Sixteen species, including the following:

D. pinicola (Dyar) (Pine Tussock Moth). Wingspan: 35–45 mm. Front wings very dark brown to nearly white, with two dark, wavy, rather narrow bars across wings; hind wings pale brown, nearly unmarked. Larvae feed on pine. (1) n.e. US; (5) MN.

74.3 *Orgyia* Ochsenheimer

Ten species, the following of which are pests:

O. vetusta (Boisduval) (Western Tussock Moth). Wingspan: 28–30 mm. Female wingless; front wings of males vary from very pale yellowish brown to reddish brown, marked with white patches and darker brown lines; hind wings rusty, without marks. Larvae feed on oak and lupine. (3) CA.

O. antigua (Linnaeus) [typical subspecies not in the U.S. or Canada; our subspecies are *O. a. nova* Fitch, *O. a. badia* Edwards, and *O. a. argillacea* Ferguson] (Rusty Tussock Moth). Wingspan: 24–35 mm. Female wingless; male front wings rusty brown to pale yellow with brownish markings and small white spot near rear apex of wing; hind wings without distinct markings. Larvae with pair of black anterior hair pencils behind head, another pair on first abdominal segment, and another pair of lateral pencils on second abdominal segment, a feature unique to this species; body black with orange and yellow spots; four dorsal abdominal tufts light brown or white; body covered with white, hairlike setae. Larvae feed on most trees and shrubs. (1) n.e. US; (2) VA, NC, SC, GA; (3) CA; (4) Pacific n.w.; (5) n. Central States.

O. pseudotsugata (McDunnough) (Douglas Fur Tussock Moth). Wingspan: 30–35 mm. Females wingless; front wings of male dark brown, usually with prominent white scales and wavy dark bands across wings; hind wings nearly uniformly brownish red. Larvae with whitish hairlike setae, dark skin, red tubercles, and large, brown-tipped dorsal tufts. They feed on Douglas fir, fir, spruce, hemlock, pine, and larch. (See Fig. 27.315.) (3) CA, AZ; (4) Pacific n.w.; (5) AB, MT, WY, CO.

O. leucostigma (Smith) (White-marked Tussock Moth). Wingspan: 30–35 mm. Female wingless; front wings of male dark brown with prominent center band of white in most species; hind wings uniformly dark brown. Larvae with black dorsal band, two long, black anterior hair pencils and a single posterior pencil, and four white dorsal abdominal tufts; head red; abdominal warts yellow. They feed on many kinds of trees and shrubs, often letting themselves down on silk lines. (1) n.e. US; (2) s.e. US.

Fig. 27.315.

Fig. 27.317.

Tribe Lymantriini

74.4 *Lymantria* Huebner

One species, as follows:

L. dispar (Linnaeus) (Gypsy Moth). Wingspan: Male, 33–40 mm; female, 55–58 mm. Male brown with dark markings (See Fig. 27.316); female white with dark markings (See Fig. 27.317). The female cannot fly. Larvae yellow with red and blue tubercles and with long hairs but without pencils. Eggs are laid in egg masses with hairs from the female abdomen (Fig. 27.318). Shortly after laying them (Fig. 27.319), the females die. The larvae (Fig. 27.320) feed on the leaves of forest trees. The pupae are formed in a very light silken covering. This serious pest of shade trees (Fig. 27.321) was introduced in 1858 and has now spread throughout (1) n.e. US; (2) VA; (3) CA.

74.5 *Leucoma* Stephens

One species, as follows:

L. salicis (Linnaeus) (Satin Moth). Wingspan: 45–48 mm. White moths without markings. Larvae feed on poplar and willow. Introduced into (1) n.e. US; (4) BC.

74.6 *Euproctis* Huebner

Two species, as follows:

E. chrysorrhoea (Linnaeus) (Brown–tailed Moth). Wingspan: 28–38 mm. Wings and thorax white; abdomen with apical

Fig. 27.318. (*U.S. Dept. of Agric.*)

tuft. Larvae feed on apple, cherry, oak, maple, and a variety of other trees. Introduced. (1) ME, MA, CT, RI.

E. similis (Fuessly) (Goldtail Moth). Similar to the preceding, but with yellow abdomen. Introduced. (1), ON, NJ; (4) BC.

Fig. 27.316.

Fig. 27.319. (*U.S. Dept. of Agric.*)

Fig. 27.320. *(U.S. Dept. of Agric.)*

75. NOCTUIDAE (Noctuid Moth Family)

This very large family of moderate-size insects (wingspan usually 20–45 mm, but sometimes larger) are the most common moths found at sugar bait trails and at lights at night. Most species are rather obscurely marked and rarely display bright colors (some exceptions are the underwing moths, *Catocala* spp. (75.148). For the most part, noctuid colors are subtle, delicate greens, grays, brown, or black, and white in intricate patterns.

Larvae of many noctuids, including cutworms, are serious agriculture pests. Cutworms feed at about ground level on the stem of the plant host, cutting into, and often cutting off, the plant stem at the base. Most noctuid larvae are plant leaf feeders and stem borers; a few mine leaves; a few are carnivorous on scale insects; and some feed on fungi, lichens, and algae on trees and rocks. The larvae of most species have a single seta on each wart. Some are semiloopers because they lack some abdominal prolegs on segments three and four, or these legs may be reduced; they might thus be confused with some larvae of the Geometridae.

Only a brief sample of the species of this difficult group are given here, with emphasis on those that are of economic interest. No simple key to the subfamilies is available at present,

Fig. 27.321. *(U.S. Dept. of Agric.)*

although the group is divided into 16 subfamilies as well as many tribes. Each of the subfamilies is briefly characterized, followed by brief descriptions of some representative species. Most species must be identified by referring to the technical literature, which depends a great deal on the characteristics of the male and female genitalia. Some other identification features follow: Eyes hairy or naked, which refers to the presence or absence of hairlike setae on the eyes between the facets. Lashed eyes have long setae or narrow hairlike scales before and behind eyes that may be detected under fairly low power. The extremely minute setae, however, may be seen only under very high magnification. Ocelli are present in all species except members of the subfamily Hypenodinae and in one species of Sarrothripinae. The entire family and its respective subfamilies may be divided into two major groups based on the venation of the hind wing. One group is referred to as the "trifid noctuids" because the M_2 vein (of the hind wing) is at the middle or above and the last is very weak or absent, leaving only three veins that arise from the posterior part of the discal cell. The "quadrifid noctuids" that form the second group have four veins that arise from the posterior part of the discal cell because vein M_2 is well-developed. This feature alone is extremely useful for placing species. Unfortunately, two subfamilies have species that exhibit both characteristics, as described below. Spines on the shaft of the tibiae, especially the middle tibiae, are peculiar to some subfamilies: the Heliothidinae, the Noctuinae, and the Catocalinae. They are also present, however, in some Plusiinae. Various kinds of scales are present that have some value in distinguishing the subfamilies, but they vary considerably.

The family currently contains 2,925 species assigned to 607 genera, but these numbers are constantly increasing as new species are discovered inhabiting the U.S. and Canada.

Subfamily Herminiinae

This is a large subfamily of mainly tropical, not very distinctive, moths. Eyes naked; ocelli present; hind wings quadrifid; tibiae unarmed; palpi large in North American species. Most larvae have all of their prolegs.

75.1 *Idia* Huebner

Fifteen species, including the following:

I. lubricalis Geyer. Wingspan: 25–35 mm. Front wings deep black-brown with pale lines; hind wings lighter with dark, narrow bands. Larvae feed on lichens. (See Fig. 27.322.) (1) n.e. US; (2) s.e. US.

[75.2 *Reabotis* Smith (1 sp., *R. immaculalis* (Hulst)); 75.3 *Phalaenophana* Grote (2 spp.)]

75.4 *Zanclognatha* Lederer

Fifteen species, including the following:

Z. ochreipennis Grote. Wingspan: ±28 mm. Front wings dull yellow-green marked with dull brownish gray, with dark and pale lines. Adults fly in July. Larvae feed on dead leaves in forests. (See Fig. 27.323.) (1) n.e. NA.

[75.5 *Chytolita* Grote (2 spp.); 75.6 *Hormisa* Walker (5 spp.); 75.7 *Phalaenostola* Grote (4 spp.); 75.8 *Tetanolita* Grote (4 spp.); 75.9 *Bleptina* Guenée (6 spp.); 75.10 *Hypenula* Grote (2 spp.); 75.11 *Renia* Guenée (12 spp.); 75.12 *Aristaria* Guenée (1 sp., *A. theroalis* (Walker)); 75.13 *Carteris* Dognin (1 sp., *C. oculatalis* (Moeschler)); 75.14 *Phylc-*

Fig. 27.322.

Fig. 27.324.

taina Moeschler (1 sp., *P. irrigualis* Moeschler); 75.15 *Lascoria* Walker (4 spp.); 75.16 *Palthis* Huebner (2 spp.); 75.17 *Rejectaria* Guenee (1 sp., *R. albisinuata* (Smith)); 75.18 *Redectis* Nye (2 spp.); 75.19 *Macristis* Schaus (2 spp.)]

Subfamily Rivulinae

This subfamily is currently inadequately defined. The group is quadrifid and considered to be primitive, closely allied to the preceding subfamily.

[75.20 *Rivula* Guenée (1 sp., *R. propinqualis* Guenée); 75.21 *Oxycilla* Grote (5 spp.); 75.22 *Zelicodes* Grote (1 sp., *Z. linearis* Grote); 75.23 *Colobochyla* Huebner [=*Salia* Huebner] (1 sp., *C. interpuncta* Grote); 75.24 *Melanomma* Grote (1 sp., *M. auricinctaria* Grote); 75.25 *Mycterophora* Hulst (5 spp.); 75.26 *Parascotia* Huebner (1 sp., *P. fuliginaria* (Linnaeus)); 75.27 *Prosoparia* Grote (1 sp., *P. perfuscaria* Grote)]

Subfamily Hypenodinae

These very small moths (wingspan of 10–20 mm) are easily confused with the microlepidoptera. Eyes naked; ocelli absent; hind wings quadrifid; tibiae unarmed. Most of the species are uncommon or rare. Known larvae feed on fungus.

[75.28 *Hypenodes* Doubleday (5 spp.); 75.29 *Dasyblemma* Dyar (1 sp., *D. straminea* Dyar)]

75.30 *Dyspyralis* Warren

Four species, the following of which is rather common:

D. illocata Warren. Life history unknown. (1) n.e. US; (2) s.e. US.

Fig. 27.323.

[75.31 *Parahypenodes* Barnes and McDunnough (1 sp., *P. quadralis* Barnes and McDunnough); 75.32 *Schrankia* Huebner (1 sp., *S. macula* (Druce); 75.33 *Quandara* Nye (1 sp., *Q. brauneata* (Swett); 75.34 *Sigela* Hulst (3 spp.); 75.35 *Abablemma* Nye (3 spp.); 75.36 *Phobolosia* Dyar (1 sp., *P. anfracta* (Edwards); 75.37 *Nigetis* Walker (1 sp., *N. formosalis* Walker)]

Subfamily Hypeninae

Eyes naked and lashed, ocelli present; hind wings quadrifid but M_2 well separated from M_3; tibia unarmed; palip twice as long as head, projecting forward. Larvae are semiloopers and feed high on plants.

75.38 *Bomolocha* Huebner

Fourteen species, including the following:

B. baltimoralis Guenée. Wingspan: ±30 mm. Shading from grayish white to wood brown with large dark patch and whitish lines. Larvae feed on maple. (See Fig. 27.324.) (1) n.e. US; (2) VA, NC, SC, GA.

[75.39 *Lomanaltes* Grote (1 sp., *L. eductalis* (Walker); 75.40 *Ophiuche* Huebner (5 spp.)]

75.41 *Hypena* Schrank

Four species, the following of which is a pest:

H. humuli (Harris) (Hop Looper). Wingspan: 27–30 mm. Dull yellowish green (female) or brownish gray (male) shaded with brownish gray and with black markings. Larvae a pest on hops. (1), (2), (3), (4), (5), generally distributed.

75.42 *Platypena* Grote

One species, as follows:

P. scabra (Fabricius) (Green Cloverworm Moth). Wingspan: 25–33 mm. Dark brown with paler mottling and faint whitish markings; hind wings rather large compared to those of other noctuids. Adults fly all year. Larvae feed on alfalfa, soybeans, and other legumes. (See Fig. 27.325.) (1) n.e. NA; (2) s.e. US; (5) ND, SD, MN, NE, IA, KS, MO.

[75.43 *Tathorhynchus* Hampson (1 sp., *T. exsiccatus* Lederer)); 75.44 *Hemeroplanis* Huebner (11 spp.); 75.45 *Glympis* Walker (1 sp., *G. concors* (Huebner)); 75.46 *Spargaloma* Grote (1 sp., *S. sexpunctata* Grote); 75.47 *Phytometra* Haworth (5 spp.); 75.48 *Nychioptera* Franclemont (3 spp.); 75.49 *Hormoschista* Moerschler (1 sp., *H. latipalpis* (Walker)); 75.50 *Ommatochila* Butler (1 sp., *O. mundula* (Zeller))]

Fig. 27.325.

Subfamily Catocalinae

Eyes naked; ocelli present; hind wings quadrifid; tibiae spined or not. This subfamily includes the most popular species among amateur collectors, the *Catocala* (75.148), or Underwing Moths, particularly attractive because of the striking patterns on their hind wings. Front wings are held over the hind wings when at rest. Their mottled color offers protective camouflage when a moth alights on a tree trunk. In flight, the hind wings are displayed in a flash pattern. These species are among the largest of the noctuids. Some larvae may lack one or two pair of prolegs, these are semiloopers. In addition, many are tapered front and rear, giving them a fairly characteristic shape. They feed on the leaves of trees and shrubs; some feed on herbs. Since the color patterns of the adults are variable, it is difficult to spot identify species with accuracy.

[75.51 *Pangrapta* Huebner (1 sp., *P. decoralis* Huebner); 75.52 *Ledaea* Druce (1 sp., *L. peditalis* (Walker)); 75.53 *Isogona* Guenée (7 spp.)]

75.54 *Metalectra* Huebner

Ten species, including the following:

M. discalis Grote. Wingspan: 23–28 mm. Powdery, dark reddish brown mixed with yellowish green, gray, and black. Larvae feed on dry fungus. (See Fig. 27.326.) (1) n.e. NA: (2) s.e. US.

[75.55 *Arugisa* Walker (3 spp.); 75.56 *Pseudorgyia* Harvey (2 spp.); 75.57 *Scolecocampa* Guenée (2 spp.); 75.58 *Pharga* Walker (1 sp., *P.*

Fig. 27.326.

pallens (Barnes and McDunnough)); 75.59 *Palpidia* Dyar (1 sp., *P. pallidior* Dyar); 75.60 *Gabara* Walker (7 spp.); 75.61 *Phyprosopus* Grote (2 spp.); 75.62 *Hypsoropha* Huebner (2 spp.); 75.63 *Psammathodoxa* Dyar (1 sp., *P. cochlidioides* Dyar); 75.64 *Cecharismena* Moeschler (3 spp.); 75.65 *Matiloxis* Schaus (1 sp., *M. anartoides* Walker)); 75.66 *Plusiodonta* Guenée (2 spp.); 75.67 *Calyptra* Ochsenheimer (1 sp., *C. canadensis* (Bethune)); 75.68 *Gonodonta* Huebner (6 spp.); 75.69 *Eudocima* Billberg (1 sp., *E. materna* (Linnaeus)); 75.70 *Goniapteryx* Perty (1 sp., *C. servia* (Cramer)); 75.71 *Anomis* Huebner (9 spp.)]

75.72 *Alabama* Grote

One species, as follows:

A. argillacea (Huebner) (Cotton Leafworm). Wingspan: 30–35 mm. Light fawn brown with fine dark bars and spots with a few white scales. Adults often migrate from the South in huge numbers, attracting attention in metropolitan centers lying in their path. Larvae feed on leaves, buds, and even new twigs of cotton. They pupate in a cocoon made in a folded leaf. (See Fig. 27.327.) (1) a stray in NY (in October); (2) s.e. US.

Fig. 27.327.

75.73 *Scoliopteryx* Germar

One species, as follows:

S. libatrix (Linnaeus) (Herald Moth). Wingspan: 40–45 mm. Front wings light wood brown with irregular yellow and orange patch and spot, and whitish and red-brown bars across patch; hind wings brownish gray. Adults fly from July to May, overwintering as adults. Larvae feed on willow and poplar. (See Fig. 27.328.) (1) n.e. NA; (2) VA; (3) NM; (5) n. Central States.

[75.74 *Litoprosopus* Grote (4 spp.); 75.75 *Diphthera* Huebner (1 sp., *D. festiva* (Fabricius)); 75.76 *Raparna* Moore (1 sp., *R. melanosipla* (Grote)); 75.77 *Concana* Walker (1 sp., *C. mundissima* Walker); 75.78 *Asticta* Huebner (1 sp., *A. victoria* (Grote)); 75.79 *Rhosologia* Walker (1 sp., *R. stigmaphiles* Dyar; 75.80 *Obrima* Walker (1 sp., *O. rinconada* Schaus); 75.81 *Bandelia* Lindsey (1 sp., *B. angulata* (Barnes and Lindsey)); 75.82 *Euanotia* Barnes and McDunnough (2 spp.); 75.83 *Eulepidotus* Huebner (4 spp.); 75.84 *Metallata* Moeschler (1 sp., *M. absumens* (Walker))]

75.85 *Anticarsia* Huebner

One species, as follows:

A. gemmatalis Huebner (Velvetbean Caterpillar Moth). Wingspan: 35–40 mm. Color variable, dull gray, gray-brown, or

Fig. 27.328.

Fig. 27.330.

reddish mottled with yellowish green and black. Adults migrate in the pattern of *Alabama argillacea* (75.72) but more sporadically. (Fig. 27.329.) Larvae feed on velvet bean, alfalfa, peanuts, and other legumes. (2) s.e. US.

[75.86 *Azeta* Guenée (2 spp.); 75.87 *Antiblemma* Huebner (3 spp.); 75.88 *Goniocarsis* Hampson (1 sp., *G. electrica* (Schaus)); 75.89 *Epitausa* Walker (1 sp., *E. prona* (Moeschler)); 75.90 *Ephyrodes* Guenée (1 sp., *E. cacata* Guenée); 75.91 *Athyrma* Huebner (1 sp., *A. adjutrix* (Cramer)); 75.92 *Syllectra* Huebner (1 sp., *S. erycata* (Cramer)); 75.93 *Epidromia* Guenée (1 sp., *E. poaphilodes* (Guenée)); 75.94 *Massala* Walker (1 sp., *M. obvertens* (Walker)); 75.95 *Panopoda* Guenée (4 spp.); 75.96 *Phoberia* Huebner (1 sp., *P. atomaris* Huebner); 75.97 *Cissusa* Walker (5 spp.); 75.98 *Litocala* Harvey (1 sp., *L. sexsignata* (Harvey))]

75.99 *Melipotis* Huebner

[=*Heliothis* Huebner]

Thirteen species, including the following:

M. jucunda Huebner. Wingspan: 35–40 mm. Front wing shaded with gray and with white markings and fine black lines; hind wing dirty white with broad brownish gray outer band. (See Fig. 27.330.) (1) IL, IN, OH, PA, NJ, MD, DE; (2) s.e. US; (5) MB, ND, SD, IA.

[75.100 *Ianius* Richards (1 sp., *I. mosca* (Dyar)); 75.101 *Panula* Guenée (1 sp., *P. inconstans* (Guenée); 75.102 *Forsebia* Richards (1 sp., *F. perlaeta* (Edwards)); 75.103 *Bulia* Walker (2 spp.)]

75.104 *Drasteria* Huebner

Five species, including the following:

D. graphica Huebner. Wingspan: 30–35 mm. Light gray with yellowish to blackish markings. (See Fig. 27.331.) (1) n.e. US; (2) s.e. US.

[75.105 *Synedoida* Edwards (21 spp.); 75.106 *Hypocala* Guenée (1 sp., *H. andremona* (Cramer)); 75.107 *Boryzops* Richards (1 sp., *B. purissima* (Dyar)); 75.108 *Orodesma* Herrich-Schaeffer (1 sp., *O. apicina* Herrich-Schaeffer); 75.109 *Hemeroblemma* Huebner (1 sp., *H. opigena* Drury)); 75.110 *Latebraria* Guenée (1 sp., *L. amphigyroides* Guenée); 75.111 *Thysania* Dalman (2 spp.)]

75.112 *Ascalapha* Huebner

[=*Erebus* of authors.]

One species, as follows:

A. odorata (Linnaeus) (Black Witch). Wingspan: 110–115 mm. This, one of the largest and most beautiful of the noctuids, resembles a saturnid. Broad, triangular wings with irregular outer margins; dark brown, dusted with yellow-green, with wavy white band traversing both wings; some blue dusting;

Fig. 27.329.

Fig. 27.331.

large, poorly defined eyespot inside band near front margin of front wing and equally poorly defined eyespot on lower outer margin of hind wing. Larvae feed on legumes; sometimes a pest. A tropical species that strays as far north as Canada.

[75.113 *Tyrissa* Walker (1 sp., *T. multilinea* Barnes and McDunnough); 75.114 *Lesomone* Huebner (5 spp.); 75.115 *Bendisodes* Hampson (1 sp., *B. aeolia* (Druce)); 75.116 *Helia* Huebner (1 sp., *H. agna* (Druce)); 75.117 *Selenisa* Hayward (1 sp., *S. sueroides* (Guenée)); 75.118 *Heteranassa* Smith (3 spp.); 75.119 *Coxina* Guenée (1 sp., *C. cinctipalpis* (Smith)); 75.120 *Euclystis* Huebner (2 spp.); 75.121 *Coenipeta* Huebner (1 sp., *C. bibitrix* (Huebner)); 75.122 *Metria* Huebner (3 spp.); 75.123 *Kakopoda* Smith (1 sp., *K. cincta* Smith); 75.124 *Toxonprucha* Moeschler (7 spp.); 75.125 *Zaleops* Hampson (2 spp.); 75.126 *Matigramma* Grote (4 spp.); 75.127 *Pseudanthracia* Grote (1 sp., *P. coracias* (Guenée))]

75.128 *Zale* Huebner

Thirty-five species, including the following:

Z. lunata Drury. Wingspan: ±50 mm. Dull wood brown, shaded and tinted with dull yellow-green, rarely with pale yellow markings. Larvae are general feeders on leaves of trees. (See Fig. 27.332 for male.) (1), (2), (3), (4), (5), generally distributed.

[75.129 *Euparthenos* Grote (1 sp., *E. nubilis* (Huebner)); 75.130 *Eubolina* Harvey (1 sp., *E. impartialis* Harvey); 75.131 *Allotria* Huebner (1 sp., *A. elonympha* (Huebner)); 75.132 *Ophisma* Guenée (1 sp., *O. tropicalis* Guenée); 75.133 *Mimophisma* Hampton (1 sp., *M. delunaris* (Guenée)); 75.134 *Dysgonia* Huebner (3 spp.); 75.135 *Parallelia* Huebner (1 sp., *P. bistriaris* Huebner); 75.136 *Cutina* Walker (2 spp.); 75.137 *Focillidia* Hampson (1 sp., *F. texana* Hampson).]

75.138 *Euclidia* Ochsenheimer

Two species, including the following:

E. cuspidea Huebner. Wingspan: 30–40 mm. Purple-gray shaded with brown, with pale lines. Larvae feed on clover and grass. (See Fig. 27.333.) (1) n.e. US; (2) s.e. US; (3) AZ, NM, TX.

75.139 *Caenurgia* Walker (2 spp.)]

75.140 *Caenurgina* McDunnough

Five species, the following of which are pests:

C. erechtea (Cramer) (Forage Looper). Wingspan: 30–40 mm. Front wing mouse gray with two distinct bars nearly black

Fig. 27.333.

and with fine black lines and dots; hind wing yellowish green with broad dark band and paler, brownish lines. Larvae feed on clover; rarely a pest. (1), (2), (3), (4), (5), widely distributed in US.

C. crassiuscula (Haworth) (Clover Looper). Wingspan: 30–40 mm. Front wing with two poorly defined bars; otherwise similar to the preceding. Larvae feed on clover and sometimes grass. (See Fig. 27.334.) (1) n.e. US; (2) s.e. US.

[75.141 *Callistege* Huebner (3 spp.); 75.142 *Mocis* Huebner (4 spp.); 75.143 *Celiptera* Guenée (2 spp.); 75.144 *Ptichodis* Huebner (6 spp.); 75.145 *Argyostrotis* Huebner (10 spp.); 75.146 *Doryodes* Guenée (4 spp.); 75.147 *Spiloloma* Grote (1 sp., *S. lunilinea* Grote)]

75.148 *Catocala* Schrank

One hundred and ten species, the following of which are common:

C. vidua Smith. Wingspan: ±80 mm. Front wing gray, shaded with darker, brownish gray and black; hind wings black with fairly broad white margins. Larvae feed on walnut, butternut, hickory, and oak. Adults fly in August and September. (1) n.e. US; (2) s.e. US.

C. neogama Smith. Wingspan: 70–80 mm. Greenish gray shaded with blackish; hind wing deep yellow with two heavy, wavy black bands. Larvae feed on walnut and hickory. (See Fig. 27.335.) (1), (2), (3), (4), (5), generally distributed.

Fig. 27.332.

Fig. 27.334.

Fig. 27.335.

Fig. 27.337.

C. ilia Cramer. Wingspan: 70–80 mm. Front wing gray, mottled with gray; hind wing reddish orange with central black band narrower than marginal band. Larvae feed on oak.

C. relicta Walker (White Underwing). Wingspan: 75–80 mm. White with gray and black markings. Larvae feed on poplar aspen, and probably willow. (See Fig. 27.336.) (1), (2), (3), (4), (5), generally distributed.

C. concumbena Walker (Pink Underwing). Wingspan: 60–70 mm. Front wings light gray with white markings and brown tints; hind wings light pink with two broad black bands. Larvae feed on willow and poplar. (1) n.e. NA; (5) n. Central states.

C. cara Guenée (Bronze Underwing). Wingspan: 70–80 mm. Front wing smooth gray-brown with black lines; hind wings deep pink with two even black bands. Larvae feed on willow and poplar. (See Fig. 27.337.) (1) n.e. US; (2) s.e. US.

C. ultronia Huebner (Plum Tree Underwing). Wingspan: ±55 mm. Front wings dark brown streaked and shaded with yellow-green or green-gray tint; hind wings deep red with two more or less even black bands. Larvae feed on plum, apple, and cherry leaves. Adults fly from late July to October. (1) n.e. US; (2) s.e. US; (3) TX; (5) CO, KS, MO.

C. mira Grote. Wingspan: 45–50 mm. Front wings green-gray with dark markings; hind wing deep orange-yellow with two black bands. Larvae feed on *Crataegus* spp. (See Fig. 27.338.) (1) n.e. US; (2) s.e. US.

C. grynea Cramer. Wingspan: 42–50 mm. Front wing even greenish-gray with pale and black markings; hind wings deep orange-yellow with broad outer black band and irregular narrower inner band that may curve around back to base of wing. Larvae feed on apple, plum, and *Crataegus* spp. (1) n.e. US; (2) VA, NC; (5) KS, MO.

C. aholibah Strecker. Wingspan: ±60 mm. Front wings brownish with dark markings and a few scattered white patches; hind wings red with broad outer black band reaching margin and narrower inner band not reaching inner margin of wing. Larvae feed on oak. (See Fig. 27.339.) (3) s.w. US; (4) Pacific n.w.

C. amica Huebner. Wingspan: 35–40 mm. Front wings bluish white shaded with brown and dusted with black; hind wings broad marginal black band and small black dot near lower margin in place of inner band. Larvae feed on oak. (1) n.e. US; (2) s.e. US; (3) AZ, NM, TX.

Subfamily Plusiinae

This is a moderate-sized subfamily of worldwide distribution. Eyes naked, but some with heavy lashes; ocelli present; hind wings quadrifid; some with spined tibiae. A few species are of economic importance; the larvae of these lack some of their prolegs and must loop to walk as do the larvae of geometers.

Fig. 27.336.

Fig. 27.338.

Fig. 27.339.

Tribe Abrostolini

[75.149 *Abrostola* Ochsenheimer (4 spp.); 75.150 *Mouralia* Walker (1 sp., *M. tinctoides* (Guenée))]

Tribe Plusiini

[75.151 *Argyrogramma* Huebner (2 spp.);

75.152 *Trichoplusia* McDunnough

Two species, the following of which is a pest:

T. ni Huebner, subsp. *T. n. brassicae* Riley (Cabbage Looper). Wingspan: ±35 mm. Yellowish green shaded with gray and black, with some brown markings. Larvae feed on low, succulant plants and are injurious to cabbage. (See Fig. 27.340.) (1), (2), (3), (4), (5), generally distributed.

[75.153 *Agrapha* Huebner (1 sp., *A. oxygramma* (Geyer))]

75.154 *Pseudoplusia* McDunnough

One species, as follows:

P. includens (Walker) (Soybean Looper). Wingspan: ±35 mm. Dull brownish gray with strong bronzy tint and with black markings. Larvae feed on many plants and may cause some economic loss on soybeans. (1) n.e. US; (2) s.e. US.

75.155 *Autoplusia* McDunnough

Four species, the following of which is a pest:

A. egena (Guenée) (Bean Leaf Skeletonizer). Wingspan: ±35 mm. Yellow-brown with darker brown markings. Larvae feed on beans and other lelgumes. (2) LA, MS, AL, FL; (3) TX.

[75.156 *Rachiplusia* Hampson (1 sp., *R. ou* (Guenee)); 75.157 *Diachrysia* Huebner (2 spp.); 75.158 *Allagrapha* Franclemont (1 sp., *A. aerea* (Huebner)); 75.159 *Pseudeva* Hampson (2 spp.); 75.160 *Polychrysia* Huebner (2 spp.); 75.161 *Euchalcia* Huebner (1 sp., *E. albavitta* (Ottolengui)); 75.162 *Chrysanympha* Grote (1 sp., *C. formosa* (Grote)); 75.163 *Eosphoropteryx* Dyar (1 sp., *E. thyatyroides* (Guenée))]

75.164 *Autographa* Huebner

Eighteen species, the following of which is a pest:

A. californica (Speyer) (Alfalfa Looper). Wingspan: ±40 mm. Gray or brown with pale markings and one or more silver spots. Larvae feed on cabbage and other low succulents. (See Fig. 27.341 and A&J 262.) (1), (2), (3), (4), (5), generally distributed.

75.165 *Anagrapha* McDunnough

One species, as follows:

A. falcifera (Kirby) (Celery Looper). Wingspan: 35–40 mm. Light gray, shaded with brown, but showing considerable color variation. Larvae a general feeder on low plants, including celery; sometimes of economic importance. (See Fig. 27.342.) (1), (2), (3), (4), (5), generally distributed.

[75.166 *Syngrapha* Huebner (25 spp.); 75.167 *Plusia* Ochsenheimer (4 spp.)]

Subfamily Euteliinae

A small group that rests with its front wings crumpled and partly rolled around its hind wings. Eyes naked; ocelli present; hind wings quadrifid; tibiae unarmed.

[75.168 *Aon* Neumoegen (1 sp., *A. noctuiformis* Neumoegen)]

75.169 *Marathyssa* Walker

Two species, including the following:

M. inficita Walker. Wingspan: 25–28 mm. Dark gray shaded with chocolate brown, crimson, and white. Larvae feed

Fig. 27.340.

Fig. 27.341.

Fig. 27.342.

on *Rhus* spp. (See Fig. 27.343.) (1), (2), (3), (4), (5), generally distributed.

[75.170 *Paectes* Huebner (11 spp.)]

75.171 *Eutelia* Huebner

Two species, including the following:

E. pulcherrima Grote. Wingspan: ±36 mm. Front wings light red-brown to light gray, marked with black and white. Larvae feed on *Rhus* spp. (See Fig. 27.344.) (1) s. NY, PA, MD; (2) s.e. US; (3) AZ, NM, TX.

Subfamily Sarrothripinae

This subfamily consists of small species resembling some of the microlepidoptera, especially the Tortricidae. Eyes hairy; ocelli almost always present; hind wings quadrifid to trifid; tibiae unarmed.

Tribe Risobini

75.172 *Baileya* Grote

Five species, including the following:

B. ophthalmica Guenée. Wingspan: ±25 mm. Ash gray with gray-brown and white markings. Larvae feed on ironwood. (See Fig. 27.345.) (1) n.e. US; (2) s.e. US.

Tribe Sarrothripini

[75.173 *Characoma* Walker (1 sp., *C. nilotica* (Rogenhofer)); 75.174 *Nycteola* Huebner (5 spp.); 75.175 *Iscadia* Walker (1 sp., *I. asperta* Walker)]

Fig. 27.344.

Tribe Collomenini

[75.176 *Motya* Walker (1 sp., *M. abseuzalis* Walker); 75.177 *Collomena* Moeschler (1 sp., *C. filifera* (Walker))]

Subfamily Nolinae

The moths of this subfamily resemble the arctiids, from which they are distinguished by wing features. They are moderate in size with a wingspan of 12–14 mm and ridges and tufts of scales on the front wings. Little is known of the larvae. Some writers say they feed on lichen. At least one species feeds on flowers and seeds of grasses, including sorghum.

[75.178 *Meganola* Dyar (6 spp.)]

75.179 *Nola* Leach

Ten species, including the following:

N. sorghiella Riley. Feeds on grasses and sorgham. (2) s.e. US.

N. triquetrana Fitch. Reported in witch hazel. Distribution?

Subfamily Acontiinae

Larvae of this subfamily are semiloopers resembling the geometers because their first pair or two of prolegs are much reduced or absent. Eyes naked; ocelli present; hind wings trifid or quadrifid; tibiae unarmed. They feed mostly on low plants.

Tribe Cydosiini

[75.180 *Cydosia* Westwood (3 spp.)]

Fig. 27.343.

Fig. 27.345.

Fig. 27.346.

Fig. 27.347.

Tribe Eustrotiini

[75.181 *Tripudia* Grote (10 spp.); 75.182 *Cobubatha* Walker (9 spp.)]

75.183 *Exyra* Grote

Four species, including the following:

E. rolandiana Grote (Pitcher Plant Moth). Wingspan: 16–26 mm. Head and thorax crimson and deep yellow; front wings usually deep purple-brown with crimson base and yellow markings. Larvae feed on pitcher plants. (See Fig. 27.346.) (1) n.e. US; (2) s.e. US.

[75.184 *Oruza* Walker (2 spp.); 75.185 *Homocerynea* Barnes and McDunnough (1 sp., *H. cleoriformis* Barnes and McDunnough)); 75.186 *Phoenicophanta* Hampson (2 spp.); 75.187 *Ozarba* Walker (4 spp.); 75.188 *Amiana* Dyar (1 sp., *A. niama* Dyar); 75.189 *Hyperstrotia* Hampson (6 spp.); 75.190 *Sexserrata* Barnes and Benjamin (1 sp., *S. hampsoni* Barnes and Benjamin); 75.191 *Grotellaforma* Barnes and Benjamin (1 sp., *G. lactea* (Stretch)); 75.192 *Homolagoa* Barnes and McDunnough (1 sp., *H. grotelliformis* Barnes and McDunnough); 75.193 *Thioptera* Franclemont (2 spp.); 75.194 *Lithacodia* Huebner (10 spp.); 75.195 *Homophoberia* Morrison (2 spp.); 75.196 *Neotarache* Barnes and Benjamin (1 sp., *N. deserticola* Barnes and Benjamin); 75.197 *Capis* Grote (1 sp., *C. curvata* Grote); 75.198 *Argillophora* Grote (1 sp., *A. furcilla* Grote); 75.199 *Cerma* Huebner (3 spp.); 75.200 *Cerathosia* Smith (1 sp., *C. tricolor* Smith); 75.201 *Leuconycta* Hampson (2 spp.); 75.202 *Diastema* Guenée (2 spp.); 75.203 *Amyna* Guenée (2 spp.); 75.204 *Aleptina* Dyar (1 sp., *A. inca* Dyar); 75.205 *Paracretona* Dyar (1 sp., *P. aleptivoides* (Barnes and McDunnough)); 75.206 *Copibryophila* Smith (1 sp., *C. angelica* Smith); 75.207 *Metaponpneumata* Moeschler (1 sp., *M. rogenhoferi* Moeschler); 75.208 *Airamia* Barnes and Benjamin (1 sp., *A. albiocula* (Barnes and McDunnough))]

Tribe Eublemmini

[75.209 *Eumicremma* Berio (1 sp., *E. minima* Guenee)); 75.210 *Eumestleta* Butler (3 spp.); 75.211 *Proroblemma* Hampson (1 sp., *P. testa* Barnes and McDunnough); 75.212 *Araeopteron* Hampson (1 sp., *A. vilhelmina* Dyar)]

Tribe Acontiini

75.213 *Tarachidia* Hampson

Twenty species, including the following:

T. candefacta (Huebner). Wingspan: ± 22 mm. White, marked with black, brown, violet, gray, and olive. Larvae feed on *Ambrosia elatior*. (See Fig. 27.347.) (1), (2), (3), (4), (5), generally distributed.

[75.214 *Fruva* Grote (3 spp.); 75.215 *Conochares* Smith (6 spp.); 75.216 *Therasea* Grote (4 spp.); 75.217 *Ponometia* Herrich-Schaeffer (5 spp.); 75.218 *Hemispragueia* Barnes and Benjamin (1 sp., *H. idella* (Barnes)); 75.219 *Spragueia* Grote (12 spp.)]

75.220 *Acontia* Ochsenheimer

Thirty-three species, the following of which is a pest:

A. dacia Druce (Brown Cotton Leafworm).

[75.221 *Eusceptis* Huebner (1 sp., *E. flavifrimbriata* Todd); 75.222 *Pseudalypia* Edwards (1 sp., *P. crotchii* Edwards)]

Tribe Bagisarini

[75.223 *Bagisara* Walker (9 spp.)]

Subfamily Pantheinae

Unlike most noctuids, larvae of the species of this subfamily are densely clothed with tufts of hair and secondary hair. Eyes hairy or naked; ocelli present; hind wings quadrifid; tibiae unarmed.

75.224 *Panthea* Huebner

Seven species, including the following:

P. furcilla Packard. Wingspan: 35–50 mm. Light gray, marked with white and black. Larvae feed on pine and larch. (See Fig. 27.348.) (1) n.e. US; (2) s.e. US.

[75.225 *Colocasia* Ochsenheimer (2 spp.); 75.226 *Pseudopanthea* McDunnough (1 sp., *P. palata* (Grote)); 75.227 *Lichnoptera* Herrich-Schaeffer (1 sp., *L. decora* (Morrison))]

Fig. 27.348.

Fig. 27.349.

75.228 *Charadra* Walker

Three species, including the following:

C. deridens Guenêe. Wingspan: 40–45 mm. Light gray with distinct black powdering and distinct black lines and markings. Larvae feed on oak, birch, and elm, forming a nest between leaves. (See Fig. 27.349.) (1) n.e. US; (2) s.e. US.

[75.229 *Meleneta* Smith (1 sp., *M. antennata* Smith); 75.230 *Raphia* Huebner (7 spp.)]

Subfamily Acronictinae

Adults of this small subfamily are difficult to characterize. Larvae have hairlike setae in tufts. The following few examples will indicate the general appearance of the group.

Tribe Acronictini

75.231 *Acronicta* Ochsenheimer

Seventy-five species, including the following:

A. lepusculina Guenêe (Cottonwood Dagger Moth). Wingspan: 40–50 mm. White dusted with gray, with gray or blackish shading. Larvae feed on poplar (cottonwood). (See Fig. 27.350.) (1), (2), (3), (4), (5), generally distributed.

A. hamamelis Guenêe. Similar to the preceding. Larvae feed on witch hazel and various forest trees. (1) n.e. US; (2) s.e. US.

Fig. 27.350.

A. oblinita (Smith) (Smeared Dagger Moth; Smartweed Caterpillar). Wingspan: 35–50 mm. Pale gray dusted with white, with white and gray streaks; hind wings pale. Larvae feed on smartweed. (See Fig. 27.351.) (1) n.e. US; (2) s.e. US; (4) BC, WA, OR; (5) n. Central States.

A. americana (Harris) (Dagger Moth). Wingspan: 50–62 mm. Front wings light gray with fine pattern of brownish scales, some resembling daggers; hind wings brownish. Larvae with body hairlike setae and long tufts of hairlike setae, but no tubercles. Larvae feed on maple, elm, oak, and other forest trees. (1), (2), (3), (4), (5), generally distributed.

A. hastulifera Smith. Similar to the preceding, but with wings pale to chocolate brown and wing spears instead of daggers. Larvae feed on alder and maple. (1) n.e. US; (2) VA, NC, SC, GA.

[75.232 *Merolonche* Grote (5 spp.); 75.233 *Simyra* Ochsenheimer (1 sp., *S. henrici* (Grote)); 75.234 *Agriopodes* Hampson (4 spp.); 75.235 *Polygrammate* Huebner (1 sp., *P. hebraeicum* Huebner); 75.236 *Harrisimemna* Grote (1 sp., *H. trisignata* (Walker))]

Tribe Bryophilini

[75.237 *Cryphia* Huebner (11 spp.)]

Subfamily Agaristinae

[=Agaristidae of authors]

Most species are western; a few occur in the east, one of these, *Eudryas unio*, being common. Eyes not hairy; ocelli present; hind wings trifid; tibiae unarmed; vesture of front part of head rough.

[75.238 *Xerociris* Cockerell (1 sp., *X. wilsoni* (Grote))]

75.239 *Eudryas* Boisduval

Three species, the following of which is common:

E. unio Huebner (Pearly Wood Nymph). Wingspan: 30–35 mm. Metallic blue-black mottled with violet gray, central portion of wings cream; hind wings bordered with reddish. Larvae feed on *Epilobium* spp., *Oenothera* spp., and *Lythrum* spp. (See Fig. 27.352.) (1) n.e. US; (2) s.e. US; (3) NM, TX; (4) UT.

[75.240 *Gerra* Walker (2 spp.); 75.241 *Gerrodes* Hampson (1 sp., *G. minatea* Dyar); 75.242 *Neotuerta* Kiriakoff (1 sp., *N. hemicycla* (Hampson)); 75.243 *Caularis* Walker (1 sp., *C. lunata* Hampson)]

Fig. 27.351.

Fig. 27.352.

Fig. 27.354.

75.244 *Euscirrhopterus* Grote

[=*Copidryas* of authors]

Two species, the following of which is common:

E. gloveri Grote and Robinson. Wingspan: ±38 mm. Front wing brown with extensive markings; hind wing straw yellow, margin broadly banded with brown. Larvae feed on purslane. (See Fig. 27.353.) (3) s.w. US (5) NE, KS.

[75.245 *Psychomorpha* Harris (2 spp.); 75.246 *Eupseudomorpha* Dyar (1 sp., *E. brillians* (Neumoegen)); 75.247 *Alypiodes* Grote (2 spp.)]

75.248 *Alypia* Huebner

Seven species, the following of which is common:

A. octomaculata (Fabricius) (Eight-spotted Forester). Wingspan: ±30 mm. Black; front wings with vague blue bordering and two large yellow spots; hind wing with two large white spots. Adults are diurnal and fly in June. Larvae feed on grape, woodbine, and Japanese ivy. (See Fig. 27.354.) (1) n.e. US; (2) s.e. US; (3) e. TX.

[75.249 *Androloma* Grote (3 spp.)]

Subfamily Amphipyrinae

This very large subfamily contains 532 species in the U.S. and Canada. Eyes naked; ocelli present; hind wing trifid; tibiae unarmed. Adults are nearly uniform in external appearance, making it necessary to examine male genital apparatus for accurate identification. Larvae have a variety of feeding habits. Many are cutworms and eat low to the ground; others are stem borers; a few are leaf skeletonizers. A great many are serious pests of various crops.

Tribe Apameini
75.250 *Apamea* Ochsenheimer

Forty species, the following of which is a pest:

A. amputatrix (Fitch) (Yellow-headed Cutworm Moth). Wingspan: 45–50 mm. Crimson, shaded with greenish gray and some brownish gray. Larvae feed on garden and field crops. (See Fig. 27.355.) (1) n.e. US; (2) VA; (3) NM; (4) Pacific n.w.; (5) n. Central States.

[75.251 *Agroperina* Hampson (9 spp.); 75.252 *Protagrotis* Hampson (4 spp.)]

75.253 *Crymodes* Guenée

Eight species, the following of which is a pest:

C. devastator (Brace) (Glassy Cutworm Moth). Wingspan: ±40 mm. Dark brownish gray, more or less powdery or with mixture of lighter gray with darker patches. Larvae feed on a variety of plants, including garden and field crops. (See Fig. 27.356.) (1) WI, MI, ON, QU, NY, VT, NH, ME, MA, RI, CT, IL, IN, OH, PA, NJ; (4) Pacific n.w.; (5) n. Central States.

Fig. 27.353.

Fig. 27.355.

Fig. 27.356.

Fig. 27.358.

[75.254 *Luperina* Boisdural (8 spp.); 75.255 *Trichoplexia* Hampson (1 sp., *T. exornata* (Moeschler)); 75.256 *Ommatostola* Grote (1 sp., *O. lintneri* Grote); 75.257 *Eremobina* McDunnough (5 spp.)]

75.258 *Oligia* Huebner

Twenty species, the following of which are pests:

O. fractilinea (Grote) (Lined Stalk Borer Moth). Wingspan: 28–30 mm. Larvae bore into grass stems, occasionally into young corn. (1) WI, MI, ON, QU, NY, VT, NH, ME, MA, RI, CT, IL, IN, OH, PA, NJ; (5) CO, NE, IO, KS, MO.

O. modica Guenée (Black-banded Hadena). Wingspan: ±28 mm. Wings dark brown with pale apical markings. Larvae feed on a variety of plants. (See Fig. 27.357.) (1) n.e. US; (2) s.e. US; (5) ND, SD, MN, NE, IA, KS, MO.

[75.259 *Euros* Edwards (2 spp.), 75.260 *Cobalos* Smith (2 spp.); 75.261 *Meropleon* Dyar (4 spp.); 75.262 *Lemmeria* Barnes and Benjamin (1 sp., *L. digitalis* (Grote)); 75.263 *Selicanis* Smith (1 sp., *S. cinereola* Smith); 75.264 *Parastichtis* Huebner (1 sp., *P. discivaria* (Walker)); 75.265 *Xylomoia* Staudinger (2 spp.); 75.266 *Spartiniphaga* McDunnough (3 spp.); 75.267 *Hypocoena* Hampson (7 spp.); 75.268 *Phragmatiphila* Hampson (1 sp., *P. interrogans* (Walker)); 75.269 *Benjaminiola* Strand (1 sp., *B. colorada* (Smith)); 75.270 *Mammifrontia* Benjamin and Lindsey (2 spp.); 75.271 *Archanara* Walker (4 spp.); [75.272–75.274 not used]

75.275 *Macronoctua* Grote

One species, as follows:

M. onusta Grote (Iris Borer). Wingspan: 40–45 mm. Front wing dull wood brown with black shading; hind wings whitish shaded with yellow-gray. Larvae bore into rootstock and crown of iris, sometimes into gladiolus. (See Fig. 27.358.) (1) n.e. US; (5) IA.

[75.276 *Helotropha* Lederer (1 sp., *H. reniformis* (Gote))]

75.277 *Amphipoea* Billberg

Nine species, including the following:

A. sensilis Smith. (Fig. 27.359.)

[75.278 *Parapamea* Bird (1 sp., *P. buffaloensis* (Grote))]

75.279 *Papaipema* Smith

Forty-six species, the following of which are common:

P. marginidens Guenée. Wingspan: 30–40 mm. Shaded and dusted with tawny orange and brown on yellow base; purple-brown markings contrasting with orange patches and pale yellow areas. Larvae feed on Umbelliferae but also on many other plants. (See Fig. 27.360.) (1) ON, QU, n. NY.

P. leucostigma (Harris) [=*P. purpurifascia* (Grote and Robinson)] (Columbine Borer Moth). Wingspan: 30–40 mm.

Fig. 27.357.

Fig. 27.359.

Fig. 27.360.

Fig. 27.361.

Bright yellow marked with deep red and black. Larvae feed on columbine. (1) n.e. NA; (5) ND, SD, MN, CO, NE, IA, KS, MO.

P. cataphracta (Grote) (Burdock Borer). Wingspan: 30–35 mm. Straw yellow, scaled and marked with brownish gray or gray, with yellow spots. Larvae bores in a great variety of thick-rooted herbs. (1) n.e. NA; (5) ND, SD, MN, CO, NE, IA.

P. nebris (Guenée) (Stalk Borer Moth). Wingspan: 30–40 mm. Dull brown with slight olive tint, frosted with white, and with brown lines and white and yellow spots. Larvae bore in soft-stemmed herbs, including wheat, corn, tomatoes, and potatoes. (1) n.e. NA; (2) VA, NC, SC, GA, LA, MS, AL, AR; (3) TX.

75.280 *Hydraecia* Grote

Ten species, the following of which is common:

H. micacea (Esper) (Potato Stem Borer; Rosy Rustic Moth). Wingspan: 32–40 mm. Olive brown with darker brown or olive shading and with pale lines. Larvae general feeders, including potatoes as well as equisetum. Introduced. (1) n.e. NA.

75.281 *Achatodes* Guenée

One species, as follows:

A. zeae (Harris) (Elder Shoot Borer Moth). Wingspan: 25–30 mm. Front wings crimson, shading to pinkish brown with blackish and ash gray markings; hind wings light brownish gray with faint dark discal spot. Larvae bore into elder shoots. (1) n.e. US; (2) s.e. US; (3) TX; (5) ND, SD, MN, NE, IA, KS, MO.

[75.282 *Peraniana* Strand (1 sp., *P. dissociata* (Barnes and McDunnough)); 75.283 *Iodopepla* Franclemont (1 sp., *I. u-album* (Guenée)); 75.284 *Bellura* Walker (4 spp.); 75.285 *Aseptis* McDunnough (17 spp.)]

75.286 *Euplexia* Stephens

Two species, the following of which is common:

E. benesimilis McDunnough. Wingspan: ±30 mm. Dark purplish gray, mottled with blackish, marked with pale gray and dark gray bands. Larvae feed on viburnum. (See Fig. 27.361.) (1) n.e. NA; (2) VA, NC; (4) Pacific n.w.; (5) n. Central states.

[75.287 *Phlogophora* Treitschke (2 spp.); 75.288 *Conservula* Grote (1 sp., *C. anodonta* (Guenée); 75.289 *Enargia* Huebner (3 spp.); 75.290 *Ipimorpha* Huebner (3 spp.)]

75.291 *Chytonix* Grote

Four species, including the following:

C. sensilis Grote. Wingspan: 25–32 mm. Dull brown with some coppery shades, median area greenish gray shading to yellow gray; diffuse white spot in male; female with white scaling. Larval food unknown. (1) n.e. US; (2) VA, NC. Uncommon.

C. palliatricula Grote. Larvae feed on fungus.

[75.292 *Dypterygia* Stephens (3 spp.); 75.293 *Andropolia* Grote (12 spp.); 75.294 *Rhizagrotis* Smith (2 spp.); 75.295 *Pseudohadena* Alpheraky (1 sp., *P. vulnerea* (Grote))]

75.296 *Hyppa* Duponchel

Four species, the following of which is common:

H. xylinoides Guenée. Wingspan: 33–42 mm. Front wings light gray, shaded with paler blue and darker brown tints and black spots, some filled with white; hind wings light brownish gray. Larvae cutworms eat a variety of plants, including cranberry. (See Fig. 27.362.) (1) MA, RI, CT, s. NY, NJ, MD, DE; (2) VA.

[75.297 *Nedra* Clarke (4 spp.); 75.298 *Agrotisia* Hampson (1 sp., *A. evelinae* Benjamin); 75.299 *Properigea* Barnes and Benjamin (10 spp.);

Fig. 27.362.

Fig. 27.363.

Fig. 27.365.

75.300 *Hemibryomima* Barnes and Benjamin (1 sp., *H. chryselectra* (Grote)); 75.301 *Pseudobryomima* Barnes and Benjamin (3 spp.)]

75.302 *Pseudanarta* Grote

Thirteen species, the following of which is common:

P. flavidens Grote. Wingspan: 25–30 mm. Front wings dark with pale markings; hind wings yellow with wide, dark brown apical band. Larvae feed on a variety of plants. (See Fig. 27.363.) (3) CA; (4) Pacific n.w.

[75.303 *Homoanarta* Barnes and Benjamin (3 spp.); 75.304 *Pseudanthoecia* Smith (1 sp., *P. tumida* (Grote)); 75.305 *Phosphila* Huebner (2 spp.); 75.306 *Miracavira* Franclemont (2 spp.); 75.307 *Cropia* Walker (2 spp.); 75.308 *Speocropia* Hampson (2 spp.); 75.309 *Trachea* Ochsenheimer (1 sp., *T. delicata* (Grote)); 75.310 *Paratrachea* Hampson (1 sp., *P. viridescens* (Barnes and McDunnough)); 75.311 *Neophaenis* Hampson (1 sp., *N. respondens* (Walker)); 75.312 *Fagitana* Walker (1 sp., *F. littera* (Guenée))]

75.313 *Callopistria* Huebner

Four species, the following of which is common:

C. floridensis (Guenée) (Florida Fern Caterpillar). Wingspan: 28–35 mm. Female red-brown; male shaded with yellowish green (See Fig. 27.364.) (2) s.e. US.

[75.314 *Phuphena* Walker (2 spp.); 75.315 *Acherdoa* Walker (1 sp., *A. ferraria* Walker)]

Tribe Amphipyrini

[75.316 *Magusa* Walker (1 sp., *M. orbifera* (Walker))]

Fig. 27.364.

75.317 *Amphipyra* Ochsenheimer

Four species, the following of which is common:

A. pyramidoides Guenée (Copper Underwing). Wingspan: 38–50 mm. Front wings gray, shaded with brownish gray, marked with heavy black spots; hind wings coppery orange. Larvae feed on grape, maple, walnut, and apple. (See Fig. 27.365.) (1), (2), (3), (4), (5), generally distributed.

[75.318 *Protoperigea* McDunnough (2 spp.); 75.319 *Micrathetis* Hampson (3 spp.)]

75.320 *Proxenus* Herrich-Schaeffer

Three species, the following of which is a pest:

P. mindara Barnes and McDunnough (Rough-skinned Cutworm Moth). Wingspan: ±25 mm. Front wings glossy, dark brownish gray with very small yellowish green dots; hind wings white, shaded to gray at margins. Larvae feed on dandelion. (1), (2), (3), (4), (5), generally distributed.

[75.321 *Anorthodes* Smith (3 spp.); 75.322 *Caradrina* Ochsenheimer (1 sp., *C. morpheus* (Hufnagel)); 75.323 *Platyperigea* Smith (7 spp.); 75.324 *Crambodes* Guenée (1 sp., *C. talidiformis* Guenée)]

75.325 *Balsa* Walker

Three species, the following of which is a pest:

B. malana Fitch (Many-dotted Apple Worm). Wingspan: ±25 mm. Dull gray, with faint violet tint, black lines. Larvae feed on apple. (See Fig. 27.366.) (1) n.e. US; (2) VA, NC, SC, GA, LA, MS, AL, AR; (3) OK; (5) KS, MO.

Fig. 27.366.

Fig. 27.367.

Fig. 27.369.

75.326 *Spodoptera* Guenêe

Nine species, the following of which are pests:

S. ornithogalli Guenêe (Yellow-striped Armyworm Moth). Wingspan: 35–40 mm. Front wings with very complex pattern of dull brown, blue-gray, yellow-gray, and white; hind wings with fine, blackish veins and very narrow border. Larvae feed on cotton and a variety of other plants. (See Fig. 27.367.) (1) s. NY, PA, NJ, MD, DE; (2) s.e. US.

S. praefica (Grote) (Western Yellow-striped Armyworm). Very similar to the preceding. (3) s.w. US; (4) Pacific n.w.

S. exigua (Huebner) (Beet Armyworm Moth; Small Mottled Willow Caterpillar; Pigweed Caterpillar). Wingspan: 25–28 mm. Grayish with black markings; hind wings paler. Larvae feed on a variety of plants. (See Fig. 27.368.) (1) WI; (3) s.w. US; (4) Pacific n.w.; (5) KS.

S. eridania (Cramer) (Southern Armyworm).

S. frugiperda (Smith) (Fall Armyworm). Infests almost any field crop; often of economic importance.

S. mauritia (Boisduval) (Lawn Armyworm). Distribution?

S. exempta (Walker) (Nutgrass Armyworm). Distribution?

[75.327 *Leucochlaena* Hampson (1 sp., *L. hipparis* (Druce)]

Fig. 27.368.

75.328 *Elaphria* Huebner

Ten species, including the following:

E. festivoides Guenêe. Wingspan: 22–27 mm. Pale grayish green, shading from pale red to dull brown, with pale lines. (See Fig. 27.369.) Larvae are general feeders. (1), (2), (3), (4), (5), generally distributed.

[75.329 *Bryolymnia* Hampson (2 spp.); 75.330 *Gonodes* Druce (1 sp., *G. liquida* (Moeschler)); 75.331 *Galgula* Guenêe (1 sp., *G. partita* Guenêe); 75.332 *Perigea* Guenêe (1 sp., *P. xanthioides* Guenêe); 75.333 *Platysenta* Grote (14 spp.); 75.334 *Draudita* Barnes and Benjamin (9 spp.); 75.335 *Condica* Walker (2 spp.); 75.336 *Stibaera* Walker (2 spp.); 75.337 *Emarginea* Guenêe (3 spp.); 75.338 *Ogdoconta* Butler (5 spp.); 75.339 *Stiriodes* Hampson (4 spp.); 75.340 *Azenia* Grote (2 spp.); 75.341 *Narthecophora* Smith (1 sp., *N. pulverea* Smith); 75.342 *Lythrodes* Smith (3 spp.); 75.343 *Heminocloa* Barnes and Benjamin (1 sp., *H. mirabilis* (Neumoegen)); 75.344 *Bistica* Dyar (1 sp., *B. noela* (Druce)); 75.345 *Neumoegenia* Grote (3 spp.)]

Tribe Stiriini

[75.346 *Stibadium* Grote (12 spp.); 75.347 *Plagiomimicus* Grote (3 spp.); 75.348 *Polenta* Morrison (6 spp.); 75.349 *Chrysoecia* Hampson (4 spp.); 75.350 *Cirrhophanus* Grote (4 spp.); 75.351 *Hoplolythra* Hampson (2 spp.); 75.352 *Xanthothrix* Edwards (2 spp.); 75.353 *Eulithosia* Edwards (1 sp., *E. composita* Edwards); 75.354 *Cyptonychia* Druce (1 sp., *C. thoracica* (Edwards); 75.355 *Chalcopasta* Hampson (5 spp.); 75.356 *Basilodes* Guenêe (3 spp.)]

75.357 *Stiria* Grote

Five species, including the following:

S. rugifrons Grote. Wingspan: 35–40 mm. Yellow with contrasting light brown thorax and wing markings. Larvae are general feeders. (See Fig. 27.370.) (1), (2), (3), (4), (5), generally distributed.

[75.358 *Fala* Grote (1 sp., *F. ptychophora* Grote); 75.359 *Chamaeclea* Grote (2 spp.)]

Tribe Nocloini

[75.360 *Oslaria* Dyar (2 spp.); 75.361 *Nocloa* Smith (9 spp.); 75.362 *Paramiama* Barnes and Benjamin (5 spp.); 75.363 *Euamiana* Barnes and Benjamin (3 spp.); 75.364 *Ruacodes* Hampson (1 sp., *R. tela* (Smith)); 75.365 *Petalumaria* Buckett and Bauer (1 sp., *P. californica* (Buckett and Bauer)); 75.366 *Redingtonia* Barnes and McDunnough (1 sp., *R. alba* Barnes and McDunnough); 75.367 *Amolita* Grote (6 spp.); 75.368 *Hemioslaria* Barnes and Benjamin (1 sp., *H. pima* Barnes and

Fig. 27.370.

Fig. 27.371.

Benjamin); 75.369 *Acopa* Harvey (2 spp.); 75.370 *Nacopa* Barnes and Benjamin (2 spp.); 75.371 *Prothrinax* Hampson (1 sp., *P. luteomedia* (Smith)); 75.372 *Walterella* Dyar (1 sp., *W. ocellata* (Barnes and McDunnough)); 75.373 *Escaria* Grote (2 spp.); 75.374 *Fotella* Grote (4 spp.); 75.375 *Cephalospargeta* Moeschler (1 sp., *C. elongata* Moeschler); 75.376 *Prochloridea* Barnes and McDunnough (1 sp., *P. modesta* Barnes and McDunnough); 75.377 *Aleptinoides* Barnes and McDunnough (1 sp., *A. ochrea* Barnes and McDunnough); 75.378 *Anycteola* Barnes and Benjamin (1 sp., *A. fotelloides* (Barnes and McDunnough)); 75.379 *Afotella* Barnes and Benjamin (1 sp., *A. cylindrica* (Grote)); 75.380 *Fota* Grote (2 spp.); 75.381 *Gloanna* Nye (1 sp., *G. grisescens* (Barnes and Lindsey)); 75.382 *Podagra* Smith (1 sp., *P. crassipes* Smith); 75.383 *Policocnemis* Benjamin (1 sp., *P. ungulatus* Benjamin); 75.384 *Minofala* Smith (1 sp., *M. instans* Smith); 75.385 *Eviridemas* Barnes and Benjamin (1 sp., *E. minuta* (Barnes and McDunnough)); 75.386 *Axenus* Grote (1 sp., *A. arvalis* Grote); 75.387 *Annaphila* Grote (23 spp.)]

Subfamily Cuculliinae

Larvae of this subfamily feed above ground, often on tree leaves. Adults fly very late in the fall or very early in the spring. Eyes naked, lashed; ocelli present; hind wings trifid; tibiae unarmed.

Tribe Xylenini

75.388 *Xylena* Ochsenheimer

Five species, the following of which is common:

X. nupera Lintner (Red Swordgrass Moth). Wingspan: ±55 mm. Wood brown shaded and streaked with black. Larvae feed on grasses. (Fig. 27.371.) (1) n.e. NA; (4) UT; (5) n. Central States.

[75.389 *Lithomoia* Huebner (1 sp., *L. solidaginis* (Huebner)); 75.390 *Homoglaea* Morrison (5 spp.); 75.391 *Litholomia* Grote (1 sp., *L. napaea* (Morrison))]

75.392 *Lithophane* Huebner

Forty-four species, the following of which are common:

L. antennata Walker (Green Fruitworm). Wingspan: 35–40 mm. Light gray with blue-violet tint marked with darker gray and black spots. Larvae feed on apple and other trees, including choke cherry. (1) n.e. US; (4) Pacific n.w.; (5) n. Central States.

L. laticinerea Grote. Similar to the preceding, but with more brownish tints. Larvae feed on choke cherry. (1) n.e. NA; (5) NE, IA.

[75.393 *Pyreferra* Franclemont (4 spp.); 75.394 *Eupsilia* Huebner (8 spp.); 75.395 *Sericaglaea* Franclemont (2 spp.); 75.396 *Xystopeplus* Franclemont (1 sp., *X. rufago* (Huebner)); 75.397 *Metaxaglaea* Franclemont (5 spp.); 75.398 *Epiglaea* Grote (2 spp.); 75.399 *Chaetaglaea* Franclemont (3 spp.); 75.400 *Psectraglaea* Hampson (1 sp., *P. carnosa* (Grote)); 75.401 *Eucirroedia* Grote (1 sp., *E. pampina* (Guenée)); 75.402 *Pseudoglaea* Grote (1 sp., *P. olivata* (Harvey)); 75.403 *Agrochola* Huebner (3 spp.); 75.404 *Sunira* Franclemont (4 spp.); 75.405 *Anathix* Franclemont (4 spp.); [75.406 not used]; 75.407 *Achytonix* McDunnough (2 spp.); 75.408 *Cosmia* Ochsenheimer (1 sp., *C. calami* (Harvey)); 75.409 *Zotheca* Grote (1 sp., *z. tranquilla* Grote); 75.410 *Thurberiphaga* Dyar (1 sp., *T. diffusa* (Barnes)); [75.411–75.415 not used]; 75.416 *Xanthia* Ochsenheimer (1 sp., *X. togata* (Esper)); 75.417 *Hillia* Grote (2 spp.); 75.418 *Fishia* Grote (8 spp.); 75.419 *Platypolia* Grote (3 spp.); 75.420 *Xylotype* Hampson (2 spp.); 75.421 *Dryotype* Hampson (1 sp., *D. opina* (Grote)); 75.422 *Mniotype* Franclemont (7 spp.); 75.423 *Sutyna* Todd (3 spp.); 75.424 *Pachypolia* Grote (1 sp., *P. atricornis* Grote); 75.425 *Brachylomia* Hampson (8 spp.); 75.426 *Lomilysis* Franclemont (1 sp., *L. discolor* (Smith)); 75.427 *Epipemas* Smith (3 spp.)]

Tribe Feraliini

75.428 *Feralia* Grote

Six species, the following of which is common:

F. comstocki Grote. Wingspan: ±35 mm. Apple green with white lines and rings with solid black between (one of the most beautiful of the noctuids). Larvae feed on hemlock. (See Fig. 27.373.) (1) n.e. NA; (2) WV, VA, KY, TN, NC; (4) Pacific n.w.; (5) n. Central states.

Fig. 27.372.

Fig. 27.373.

Fig. 27.374.

Tribe Psaphidini

[75.429 *Brachionycha* Huebner (1 sp., *B. borealis* (Smith)); 75.430 *Eutolype* Grote (4 spp.); 75.431 *Copipanolis* Grote (1 sp., *C. styracis* (Guenée)); 75.432 *Pseudocopivaleria* Buckett and Bauer (2 spp.); 75.433 *Psaphida* Walker (2 spp.); 75.434 *Copivaleria* Grote (1 sp., *C. grotei* (Morrioson)); 75.435 *Apsaphida* Franclemont (1 sp., *A. eremna* Franclemont); 75.436 *Viridemas* Smith (1 sp., *V. galena* Smith)]

Tribe Oncocnemidini

[75.437 *Supralathosea* Barnes and Benjamin (1 sp., *S. baboquivariensis* Barnes and Benjamin); 75.438 *Provia* Barnes and McDunnough (1 sp., *P. argentata* Barnes and McDunnough); 75.439 *Pleromella* Dyar (1 sp., *P. opter* Dyar); 75.440 *Pleromelloida* Nye (5 spp.); 75.441 *Neogalea* Hampson (1 sp., *N. esula* (Druce)); 75.442 *Catabena* Walker (6 spp.); 75.443 *Oxycnemis* Grote (10 spp.); 75.444 *Leucocnemis* Hampson (4 spp.); 75.445 *Tristyla* Smith (1 sp., *T. alboplagiata* Smith); 75.446 *Hemistilbia* Barnes and Benjamin (1 sp., *H. apposita* (Barnes and McDunnough)); 75.447 *Apharetra* Grote (4 spp.); 75.448 *Homohadena* Grote (8 spp.); 75.449 *Adita* Grote (1 sp., *A. chionanthi* (Smith)); 75.450 *Homoncocnemis* Hampson (1 sp., *H. fortis* (Grote)); 75.451 *Oncocnemis* Lederer (85 spp.); 75.452 *Lepipolys* Guenée (2 spp.); 75.453 *Sympistis* Huebner (7 spp.); 75.454 *Stylopoda* Smith (6 spp.); 75.455 *Copanarta* Grote (2 spp.); 75.456 *Pseudacontia* Smith (3 spp.); 75.457 *Triocnemis* Grote (1 sp., *T. saporis* Grote); 75.458 *Crimona* Smith (1 sp., *C. pallimedia* Smith); 75.459 *Cerapoda* Smith (1 sp., *C. stylata* Smith); 75.460 *Calophasia* Stephens (1 sp., *C. lunula* (Hufnagel); 75.461 *Behrensia* Grote (2 spp.)]

Tribe Cuculliini

[75.462 *Lathosea* Grote (3 spp.); 75.463 *Rancora* Smith (8 spp.)]

75.464 *Cucullia* Schrank

Seventeen species, including the following:

C. intermedia Speyer. Wingspan. ±50 mm. Front wings dark gray streaked with black; hind wings yellow-gray to whitish. Larvae feed on flowers. (See Fig. 27.374.) (1) n.e. US; (2) VA; (5) ND. SD, MN, NE, IA.

[75.465 *Nycterophaeta* Smith (1 sp., *N. luna* (Morrison)); 75.466 *Copicucullia* Smith (10 spp.); 75.467 *Opsigalea* Hampson (1 sp., *O. blanchardi* Todd); 75.468 *Emariannia* Benjamin (1 sp., *E. cucullidea* Benjamin)]

Subfamily Hadeninae

A great number of species in this subfamily are of economic importance. Eyes hairy; ocelli present; hind wings trifid; tibiae unarmed. Larvae of this group also called armyworms and cutworms.

Tribe Hadenini

[75.469 *Sparkia* Nye (1 sp., *S. immacula* (Grote)); 75.470 *Trichocosmia* Grote (2 spp.); 75.471 *Hadenella* Grote (1 sp., *H. pergentilis* Grote)]

75.472 *Discestra* Hampson

Fifteen species, the following of which is a pest:

D. trifolii (Hufnagel) (Nutmeg Moth: Clover Cutworm). Wingspan: ±35 mm. Dull powdery gray with greenish tint; front wings with well marked "W" on veins. Larvae feed on various plants; injurious to cabbage and clover. (See Fig. 27.375.) (1), (2), (3), (4), (5), generally distributed.

[75.473 *Trudestra* McDunnough (1 sp., *T. hadeniformis* (Smith)); 75.474 *Scotogramma* Edwards (15 spp.); 75.475 *Tridepia* McDunnough (1 sp., *T. nova* (Smith)); 75.476 *Trichoclea* Grote (11 spp.); 75.477 *Sideridis* Huebner (4 spp.); 75.478 *Admetovis* Grote (2 spp.)]

75.479 *Mamestra* Ochsenheimer

Two species, the following of which is a pest:

M. configurata Walker (Bertha Armyworm Moth). Wingspan: ±40 mm. Brown shaded with black. Larvae feed on a variety of plants. (3) CA; (4) Pacific n.w. (5) MT, WY, CO.

M. curialis Smith. Wingspan: ±42 mm. Dull brown shaded with black. (See Fig. 27.376.) (1) n.e. NA; (5) n. Central States and Provinces.

Fig. 27.375.

Fig. 27.376.

Fig. 27.378.

75.480 *Polia* Ochsenheimer

Ten species, including the following:

P. pupurissata Smith. Wingspan: 40–55 mm. Purplish gray. (Fig. 27.377.) (1), (2), (3), (4), (5), widespread.

75.481 *Melanchra* Huebner

Four species, including the following:

M. adjuncta Guenée. Wingspan: 35–40 mm. Ground color nearly black, formed of mixture of very deep green and black scales, with some white scales. (See Fig. 27.378.) (1) n.e. NA; (2) WV, VA, KY; (5) MB, ND, SD, MN.

M. picta (Harris) (Zebra Caterpillar Moth). Wingspan: 35–42 mm. Deep shading to paler red-brown with dark patches. Larvae feed on most low plants. (See Fig. 27.379.) (1) n.e. US.

[75.482 *Lacanobia* Billberg (4 spp.)]

Fig. 27.379.

75.483 *Trichordestra* McCabe

Eight species, including the following:

T. legitima (Grote) (Striped Garden Caterpillar Moth). Wingspan: 30–35 mm. Light violet-gray shaded with brown. Larvae feed on a variety of plants. (1) n.e. NA; (2) VA, NC, SC, GA; (3) s.w. US; (4) Pacific n.w. (5) n. Central States.

75.484 *Spiramater* McCabe

Two species, including the following:

S. lutra (Guenée). Wingspan: 40–50 mm. Dull gray marked with velvety black and white. (See Fig. 27.380.) (1) n.e. US; (2) VA, NC; (3) CA; (4) BC, WA, OR, ID, NV, UT; (5) n. Central States.

Fig. 27.377.

Fig. 27.380

Fig. 27.381.

Fig. 27.383.

[75.485 *Papestra* Sukhareva (5 spp.); 75.486 *Anartomima* Boursin (1 sp., *A. secendens* (Walker)); 75.487 *Hadena* Schrank (1 sp., *H. ectypa* (Morrison)); 75.488 *Anepia* Hampson (7 spp.); 75.489 *Hecatera* Guenée (1 sp., *H. sutrina* (Grote)); 75.490 *Miselia* Ochsenheimer (2 spp.); 75.491 *Anarta* Ochsenheimer (7 spp.); 75.492 *Lasiestra* Hampson (18 spp.); 75.493 *Lasionycta* Aurivillius (16 spp.)]

75.494 *Lacinipolia* McDunnough

Fifty-seven species, including the following:

L. renigera (Stephens) (Bristly Cutworm Moth). Wingspan: 22–30 mm. Deep purple-brown; wings with green patches and bars; thorax grayer. Larvae feed on a variety of plants. (See Fig. 27.381.) (1), (2), (3), (4), (5), generally distributed.

[75.495 *Trichocerapoda* Benjamin (3 spp.); 75.496 *Dargida* Walker (2 spp.)]

75.497 *Faronta* Smith

Six species, including the following:

F. diffusa (Walker) (Wheat Head Armyworm Moth). Wingspan: ±30 mm. Front wings pale yellow with dark markings. Larvae feed on grasses only, including wheat. (See Fig. 27.382.)

[75.498 *Aletia* Huebner (2 spp.)]

75.499 *Pseudaletia* Franclemont

Two species, the following of which is a pest:

P. unipuncta (Haworth) (Armyworm Moth). Wingspan: 35–40 mm. Dull brown, often with reddish tinge, dusted with

yellowish gray. Adults appear in June, lay yellowish eggs in rows at base of grass leaves. Larvae feed on various grasses at night, hide during day. At irregular intervals they become sufficiently numerous to eat everything in one area and then migrate as a group to new feeding grounds, thereby attracting the attention of the general public and causing great concern. In the North, there may be two broods a year; in the South, as many as six. (See Fig. 27.383.) (1), (2), (3), (4), (5), generally distributed.

75.500 *Leucania* Ochsenheimer

Twenty-five species, including the following:

L. multilinea Walker. Wingspan: 30–35 mm. Pale yellow-green marked with brownish gray and with black dots. Larvae feed on a wide variety of plants. (See Fig. 27.384.) (1), (2), (3), (4), (5), generally distributed.

[75.501 *Perigonica* Smith (6 spp.); 75.502 *Acerra* Grote (1 sp., *A. normalis* Grote); 75.503 *Stretchia* Edwards (6 spp.)]

75.504 *Orthosia* Ochsenheimer

Twenty-four species, including the following:

O. hibisci (Guenée). Wingspan: 35–40 mm. Front wings dull gray-brown, sometimes shaded with reddish, markings dark and light gray. Larvae feed on a wide variety of hosts. (See Fig. 27.385.) (1) n.e. NA; (4) Pacific n.w.; (5) n. Central States.

Fig. 27.382.

Fig. 27.384.

Fig. 27.385.

[75.505 *Crocigrapha* Grote (1 sp., *C. normani* (Grote)); 75.506 *Himella* Grote (1 sp., *H. intractata* (Morrison)); 75.507 *Egira* Duponchel (15 spp.); 75.508 *Achatia* Huebner (1 sp., *A. distincta* Huebner); 75.509 *Morrisonia* Grote (3 spp.); 75.510 *Cerapteryx* Curtis (1 sp., *C. graminis* (Linnaeus)); 75.511 *Tholera* Huebner (1 sp., *T. americana* (Smith))]

75.512 *Nephelodes* Guenée

Five species, the following of which is a pest.

N. minians Guenée (Bronzed Cutworm). Wingspan: 35–50 mm. Color varies from dull yellow to olive, rose, or purple, with dark, diffuse marking. Larvac feed on a variety of plants. (See Fig. 27.386.) (1) n.e. NA; (2) VA, NC, GA.

Tribe Eriopygini

[75.513 *Anhimella* McDunnough (3 spp.); 75.514 *Homorthodes* McDunnough (14 spp.); 75.515 *Protorthodes* McDunnough (21 spp.); 75.516 *Ulolonche* Smith (9 spp.); 75.517 *Hyperepia* Barnes and Lindsey (2 spp.); 75.518 *Pseudorthodes* Morrison (7 spp.)]

75.519 *Orthodes* Guenée

Five species, including the following:

O. crenulata (Butler). Wingspan: 30–35. Mouse gray marked with white, black, and dark brown; hind wings paler. Larvae feed on a variety of plants. (See Fig. 27.387.) (1) n.e. US.

Fig. 27.386.

[75.520 *Synorthodes* Franclemont (2 spp.); 75.521 *Hexorthodes* McDunnough (13 spp.); 75.522 *Eriopyga* Guenée (1 sp., *E. crista* (Walker)); 75.523 *Ursogastra* Smith (5 spp.); 75.523a *Zosteropoda* Grote (2 spp.); 75.523b *Neleucania* Smith (5 spp.); 75.524 *Trichorthosia* Grote (4 spp.); 75.525 *Trichopolia* Grote (2 spp.); 75.526 *Trichagrotes* McDunnough (1 sp., *T. spinosa* (Barnes and McDunnough)); 75.527 *Trichofeltia* McDunnough (1 sp., *T. circumdata* (Grote)); 75.528 *Mimobarathra* Barnes and McDunnough (1 sp., *M. antonito* (Barnes); 75.529 *Miodera* Smith (2 spp.); 75.530 *Engelhardtia* Barnes and Benjamin (1 sp., *E. ursina* (Smith))]

Fig. 27.387.

75.531 *Tricholita* Grote

Eight species, including the following:

T. signata Walker. Wingspan: 28–38 mm. Dull reddish-brown, varying to purple, with orange patch and yellowish to white markings. Larvae feed on a variety of plants. (See Fig. 27.388.) (1) n.e. US; (4) Pacific n.w.; (5) n. Central States.

[75.532 *Lophoceramica* Dyar (1 sp., *L. artega* (Barnes)); 75.533 *Hydroeciodes* Hampson (5 spp.)]

Tribe Glottulini

[75.534 *Xanthopastis* Huebner (1 sp., *X. timais* (Cramer))]

Subfamily Noctuinae

[=Agrotinae of authors]

This subfamily includes a number of serious pests. Eyes usually naked, sometimes sparsely hairy, never lashed; hind wings trifid; tibiae armed.

Fig. 27.388.

Tribe Agrotini

75.535 *Agrotis* Ochsenheimer

Twenty-nine species, the following of which are pests:

A. orthogonia Morrison (Pale Western Cutworm Moth). Wingspan: 30–35 mm. Brownish gray with dark markings. Larvae feed on many plants. (1) IL; (4) Pacific n.w.; (5) n. Central States.

A. gladiaria Morrison (Clay-backed Cutworm Moth). Wingspan: ±35 mm. Similar to the preceding, usually grayer. Adults is diurnal, flying in September. Larvae cause great economic loss by feeding on clover, corn, tobacco, hemp, onion, strawberries, blackberries, raspberries, alfalfa, barley, beans, cabbage, oats, peas, potatoes, sweetpotatoes, tomato, garden flowers, and grasses. (1) n.e. NA; (3) AZ, NM, TX; (4) UT; (5) n. Central States.

A. malefida Guenée (Pale-sided Cutworm Moth; Shagreened Cutworm). Wingspan: 40–45 mm. Male clay-colored dusted with brownish gray; female medium gray to blackish. Larvae feed on almost any kind of leaf. (1), (2), (3), (4), (5), generally distributed.

A. venerabilis Walker (Dusky Cutworm Moth). Wingspan: 35–40 mm. Dark brown; front wings gray-brown to yellowish with green tint, markings blackish; hind wings brownish gray. Larvae feed on alfalfa, corn, oats, strawberries, and many other kinds of crop and garden plants and weeds. (1), (2), (3), (4), (5), generally distributed.

A. ipsilon (Hufnagel) (Black Cutworm Moth; Greasy Cutworm Moth). Wingspan: 40–55 mm. Male clay-colored, shaded with reddish; female darker; hind wings off-white. Larvae cause great damage to corn and other plants by cutting off stems. Cosmopolitan. (See Fig. 27.389.)

A. subterranea (Fabricius) (Granulate Cutworm Moth). Wingspan: 32–40 mm. Male clay-colored, similar to the preceding. (1), (2), (3), (4), (5), widely distributed.

[75.536 *Onychagrotis* Hampson (1 sp., *O. rileyana* (Morrison))]

75.537 *Feltia* Walker

Eleven species, the following of which is a pest:

F. jaculifera (Guenée) [=*ducens subgothica* of authors] (Dingy Cutworm Moth). Wingspan: ±35 mm. Light gray with

Fig. 27.390.

white and dark brown and black markings. Larvae feed on corn and other field and garden crops. (See Fig. 27.390.) (1), (2), (3) AZ, NM, TX, OK; (4), (5), widespread.

[75.538 *Copablepharon* Harvey (13 spp.); 75.539 *Eucoptocnemis* Grote (3 spp.); 75.540 *Manruta* Smith (1 sp., *M. elingua* Smith); 75.541 *Trichosilia* Hampson (1 sp., *T. acarnea* (Smith)); 75.542 *Proragrotis* McDunnough (2 spp.); 75.543 *Mesembragrotis* Barnes and Benjamin (1 sp., *M. ruckesi* Barnes and Benjamin)]

75.544 *Euxoa* Huebner

This very large genus contains the following five subgenera:

Subgenus *Longivesica* Hardwick. Four species, the following of which is a pest:

E. (L.) messoria (Harris) (Dark-sided Cutworm Moth). Wingspan: 35–40 mm. Light powdery yellow-brown, with faint gray tint and dark and light bands. Larvae feed on a wide variety of plants. (See Fig. 27.391.) (1) n.e. US; (4) Pacific n.w.; (5) n. Central States.

Subgenus *Pleonectopoda* Grote. Twenty-four species, the following of which is a pest:

E. (P.) scandens (Riley) (White Cutworm Moth). Wingspan: ±35 mm. Pale gray with a few black scales and obscure markings. Larvae frequent sandy areas; sometimes injurious to

Fig. 27.389.

Fig. 27.391.

Fig. 27.392.

Fig. 27.393.

young apple trees by eating buds. (1) n.e. US; (5) ND, SD, NE, IA, KS, MO.

Subgenus *Chorizagrotis* Smith. Four species, the following of which is a pest:

E. (C.) auxiliaris Grote (Army Cutworm Moth). Wingspan: 35–45 mm. Wings basically brownish gray, shading from pale toward middle of inner margin to entirely blackish brown. Larvae feed on a great variety of hosts; often a serious pest of winter wheat. (See Fig. 27.392.) (3) s.w. US; (4) Pacific n.w.; (5) n. Central States.

Subgenus *Euxoa* s. str. One hundred and twenty-two species, the following of which are pests:

E. (E.) detersa (Walker) (Sandhill Cutworm Moth). Wingspan: ±26 mm. Pale with light brown markings. Larvae feed on many crop plants; usually not a serious pest. (1) n.e. NA; (2) VA, KY, TN, NC, SC; (4) Pacific n.w.; (5) n. Central States.

E. (E.) tessellata (Harris) (Striped Cutworm Moth). Wingspan: 30–35 mm. Front wings dull yellow-brown with black spots and dashes; hind wings light brown with dark markings. Larvae feed on a wide variety of plants. (1) n.e. US; (4) WA, OR, ID; (5) n. Central States.

E. (E.) ochrogaster (Guenée) (Red-backed Cutworm Moth). Wingspan: 37–42 mm. Front wings usually brownish yellow, shaded with red-brown and black. Larvae feed on a wide variety of plants. (1) n.e. NA; (4) Pacific n.w.; (5) n. Central States.

Subgenus *Orosagrotis* Hampson. Thirteen species.

Tribe Aniclini
75.545 *Loxagrotis* McDunnough

Twelve species, the following of which is a pest:

L. albicosta (Smith) (Western Bean Cutworm). A pest of beans and other plants. (3) AZ, NM; (4) UT, ID; (5) SD, NE, CO.

[75.546 *Richia* Grote (8 spp.); 75.547 *Pseudorthosia* McDunnough (1 sp., *P. variabilis* Grote); 75.548 *Pseudoseptis* McDunnough (1 sp., *P. grandipennis* (Grote)); 75.549 *Ochropleura* Huebner (1 sp., *O. plecta* (Linnaeus)); 75.550 *Protogygia* McDunnough (9 spp.); 75.551 *Euagrotis* McDunnough (10 spp.)]

75.552 *Anicla* Grote

Two species, including the following:

A. infecta Ochsenheimer. Wingspan: ±35 mm. Light gray, marked with strongly contrasting deep brown or black. Larvae prefer grasses. (See Fig. 27.393.) (1) n.e. US; (2) s.e. US.

[75.553 *Crassivesica* Hardwick (1 sp., *C. bocha* (Morrison)); 75.554 *Hemieuxoa* McDunnough (1 sp., *H. rudens* (Harvey))]

75.555 *Peridroma* Huebner

One species, as follows:

P. saucia (Huebner) (Variegated Cutworm Moth). Wingspan: 45–55 mm. Variable, from clay-colored to light brownish gray; double lines on wings. Larvae feed on most crops other than grasses. (See Fig. 27.394.)

[75.556 *Diarsia* Huebner (7 spp.)]

Tribe Noctuini

[75.557 *Protexarnis* McDunnough (1 sp., *P. balanitis* (Grote))]

75.558 *Actebia* Stephens

One species, as follows:

A. fennica (Tauscher) (Black Army Cutworm Moth; Finnish Dart); Wingspan: 38–45 mm. Very dark gray or black with yellowish green and gray markings. Larvae feed on

Fig. 27.394.

Fig. 27.395.

Fig. 27.397.

blueberry and many other plants. (1) n.e. NA; (4) Pacific n.w.; (5) n. Central States.

[75.559 *Rhyacis* Huebner (1 sp., *R. quadrangula* (Zetter))]

75.560 *Spaelotis* Boisduval

Two species, both of them pests:

S. clandestina (Harris) (W-marked Cutworm Moth). Wingspan: ±40 mm. Smoky brown with traces of white markings; hind wings pale. Larvae on many plants. (See Fig. 27.395.) (1) n.e. NA; (2) VA; (5) ND, SD, MN, NE, IA, KS, MO.

S. havilae (Grote) (Western W-marked cutworm Moth). Similar to the preceding. (4) Pacific n.w.; MT, WY, CO.

75.561 *Graphiphora* Ochsenheimer

One species, as follows:

G. haruspica Grote. Wingspan: 45–50 mm. Brownish gray, marked with black. Larvae feed on many plants. (See Fig. 27.396.) (1) n.e. NA; (4) Pacific n.w.; (5) n. Central States.

75.562 *Eurois* Huebner (5 spp.); 75.563 *Barrovia* Barnes and McDunnough (1 sp., *B. fasciata* (Skinner)); 75.564 *Parabarrovia* Gibson (1 sp., *P. keelei* Gibson); 75.565 *Pachnobia* Guenée (5 spp.)]

75.566 *Xestia* Huebner

Sixteen species, the following of which is a pest:

X. adela Francelemont [=*c-nigrum* of authors] (Spotted Cutworm Moth). Wingspan: ±40 mm. Vestitute coarse; front wing of male dark brown marked with reddish yellow; female darker; hind wings pale. Larvae feed on a wide variety of plants. (See Fig. 27.397.) (1) n.e. NA; (2) VA, NC, SC, GA.

[75.567 *Anomogyna* Staudinger (17 spp.); 75.568 *Setagrotis* Smith (6 spp.); 75.569 *Agrotiphila* Grote (3 spp.); 75.570 *Epipsiliamorpha* Barnes and Benjamin (2 spp.); 75.571 *Archanarta* Barnes and Benjamin (3 spp.); 75.572 *Eugraphe* Huebner (1 sp., *E. subrosea* (Stephens); subsp. *E. s. opacifrons* (Grote)); 75.573 *Adelphagrotis* Smith (3 spp.); 75.574 *Paradiarsia* McDunnough (1 sp., *P. littoralis* (Packard)); 75.575 *Hemipachnobia* McDunnough (1 sp., *H. subporphyea* (Walker)); 75.576 *Cerastis* Ochsenheimer (1 sp., *C. tenebrifera* (Walker)); 75.577 *Metalepsis* Grote (3 spp.); 75.578 *Choephora* Grote and Robinson (1 sp., *C. fungorum* Grote and Robinson); 75.579 *Aplectoides* Butler (1 sp., *A. condita* (Guenée)); 75.580 *Anaplectoides* McDunnough (3 spp.); 75.581 *Chersotis* Boisduval (1 sp., *C. juncta* (Grote))]

75.582 *Protolampra* McDunnough

Three species, including the following:

P. rufipectus Morrison. Wingspan: ±35 mm. Front wing light brownish gray with reddish tint; hind wings pale. Larvae feed on many plants. (See Fig. 27.398.) (1) n.e. NA; (3) CA; (4) Pacific n.w.; (5) n. Central States.

Fig. 27.396.

Fig. 27.398.

[75.583 *Eueretagrotis* Smith (3 spp.); 75.584 *Heptagrotis* McDunnough (1 sp., *H. phyllophora* (Grote)); 75.585 *Hemigraphiphora* McDunnough (1 sp., *H. plebeia* (Smith)); 75.586 *Cryplocala* Benjamin (1 sp., *C. acadiensis* (Bethune))]

75.587 *Abagrotis* Smith

Thirty species, the following of which is a pest:

A. alternata Grote (Greater Red Dart Moth; Mottled Gray Cutworm). Wingspan: 35–40 mm. Yellowish green to dull light brown, dotted with blackish scales, dark maculations. Larvae feed on a wide variety of plants. (See Fig. 27.399.) (1) n.e. NA; (2) s.e. US.

[75.588 *Rhynchagrotis* Smith (6 spp.); 75.589 *Pronoctua* Smtih (2 spp.)]

Tribe Ufeini

[75. 590 *Ufeus* Grote (4 spp.)]

Subfamily Heliothinae

Members of this subfamily are similar in size and appearance and are difficult to identify without technical keys and illustrations; they include bollworms and cutworms. Eyes naked; ocelli present; hind wings trifid; tibia spined. Larvae of most species feed on a wide variety of plants; larvae of many species may cause considerable crop damage. Only some of the more common pests are listed here. The term "armyworm" refers to those larvae that migrate in large numbers from one host plant to another, not necessarily to a specific insect. As noted previously, the term "cutworm" refers to the manner of feeding; such larvae cut through plant stems at ground level. In constrast, "bollworms" concentrate on flower heads, damaging the seeds.

[75.591 *Derrima* Walker (1 sp., *D. stellata* Walker); 75.592 *Microhelia* Hampson (2 spp.); 75.593 *Heliothodes* Hampson (3 spp.); 75.594 *Baptarma* Smith (1 sp., *B. felicita* Smith); 75.595 *Eutricopis* Morrison (1 sp., *E. nexilis* Morrison); 75.596 *Pyrrhia* Huebner (2 spp.); 75.597 *Rhodoecia* Hampson (1 sp., *R. aurantiago* (Guenée)); 75.598 *Erythroecia* Hampson (2 spp.)]

75.599 *Heliothis* Ochsenheimer

Thirteen species, several of which are serious pests, as follows:

H. ononia (Fabricius) (Flax Bollworm). Wingspan: 25–30 mm. Yellowish with greenish tinge, dark markings. Larvae feed

Fig. 27.400.

on flowers of flax and other low plants. (4) Pacific n.w.; (5) n. Central States.

H. virescens (Fabricius) (Tobacco Budworm). Wingspan: 28–35 mm. Front wings light olive with three oblique dark bands, sometimes outlined in white; hind wing white with brownish border. Larvae feed on tobacco flowers and other Solanaceae. (1) n.e. US; (2) s.e. US; (3) s.w. US.

H. subg. *Helicoverpa* Hardwick, *H. H. zea* (Boddie) (Corn Earworm; Bollworm; Tomato Fruitworm). Larvae feed on corn, tomatoes, cotton, and tobacco, as well as many wild plants; a serious pest causing great crop loss each year. (See Fig. 27.400 and A&J 263.) (1), (2), (3), (4), (5), generally distributed.

[75.600 *Protoschinia* Hardwick (1 sp., *P. scutosa* (Fabricius))]

75.601 *Schinia* Huebner

One hundred and twenty-two species, including the following:

S. jaguarina Guenée. Wingspan: ±30 mm. Front wing yellow with greenish tint; lines fine and distinct; hind wing with black border. Larvae feed on flowers and seeds. (See Fig. 27.401.) (1), (2), (3), (4), (5), generally distributed.

S. arcigera Guenée. Wingspan: ±25 mm. Front wings chocolate brown with gray brown bands, fine white lines.

Fig. 27.399.

Fig. 27.401.

Fig. 27.402.

Larvae feed on asters. (See Fig. 27.402.) (1) n.e. US; (2) s.e. US; (3) TX; (5) ND, SD, MN, NE, IA, KS, MO.

[75.602 *Thyreion* Smith (2 spp.); 75.603 *Heliolonche* Grote (5 spp.); 75.604 *Melaporphyria* Grote (1 sp., *M. immortua* Grote)]

Tribe Grotellini

[75.605 *Grotella* Harvey (17 spp.); 75.606 *Hemigrotella* Barnes and McDunnough (1 sp., *H. argenteostriata* Barnes and McDunnough); 75.607 *Neogrotella* Barnes and Benjamin (3 spp.)]

BIBLIOGRAPHY

Miller, Lee D., and Brown, F. Martin. 1981. *A catalogue/checklist of the butterflies of America north of Mexico.* The Lepidopterists' Society, Memoir No. 2, vii+280 pp.

Ferguson, Douglas C., *in* Dominick, R. B. *et al.* 1971–1972. *The moths of America north of Mexico.* Fascicle 20.2, Bombycoidea, Saturniidae, xxi+277 pp., 22 c/pls.

Ibid 1978. Fascicle 22.2. Noctuoidea, Lymantriidae, x+110 pp., pl. A, 8 c/pls.

Forbes, William T. M. 1923. [1969 reprint]. *The Lepidoptera of New York and neighboring states. Primitive forms. Microlepidoptera, Pyraloids, Bombyces.* Los Angeles: Entomological Reprint Specialists, 729 pp.

Ibid. 1948. Part II. Memoir 274. Ithaca: Cornell University Agricultural Experiment Station, 263 pp.

Ibid. 1954. Part III. Memoir 329. *Loc cit,* 433 pp.

Ibid. 1960. Part IV. Memoir 371. *Loc cit,* 188 pp.

Franclemont, John G. *in* Dominick, R. B., *et al.* 1973. *The moths of America north of Mexico.* Fascicle 20.1. Mimallonoidea; Bombycoidea (in part), viii+86 pp., 11 c/pls.

Hodges, Ronald W., *in* Dominick, R. B., *et al.* 1971. *The moths of America north of Mexico.* Fascicle 21. Spingoidea, xii+158 pp., 14 c/pls.

Ibid. 1974. Fascicle 6.2. Gelechioidea, Oecophoridae, x+142 pp., pl. A, 7 c/pls.

Ibid. 1978. Fascicle 6.1. Gelechioidea, Introduction and Cosmopterigidae, x+166 pp., 6 pls.

Hodges, Ronald W., *et al.* 1983. *Checklist of the Lepidoptera of America North of Mexico.* Oxfordshire, England: E. W. Classey, xxiv+284 pp.

Holland, W. J. 1968 [reprint]. *The moth book.* New York: Dover, xxiv+479 pp., 48 c/pls.

Howe, William H. 1975. *The butterflies of North America.* New York: Doubleday, xiii+633 pp., 97 c/pls.

Munroe, Eugene, *in* Dominick, R. B., *et* al. 1972. *The moths of America north of Mexico.* Fascicle 13.1A. Pyraloidea, Pyralidae (in part), pp. 1–136.

Ibid. 1972. Fascicle 13.1B, pp. 137–250.

Ibid. 1973. Fascicle 13.1C, xx+pp. 251–304, pls. A–K, 13 c/pls.

Ibid. 1976. Fascicle 13.2A, pp. 1–78, pls. A–H, 4 c/pls.

Ibid. 1976. Fascicle 13.2B, xvii+pp. 79–150, pls. I–U, 9 c/pls.

Subsection **ANTHIOPHORA**

Order 28
MECOPTERA (Scorpionflies and their Allies)

Scorpionflies and other members of this order are usually found in shaded low shrubs and herbs of forest borders or within forests with a canopy sufficiently open to permit such undergrowth. They are found in other habitats, too. The large *Panorpa nuptialis*, with deep yellow wings broadly banded with brown, and the black-winged *Panorpa lugubris* (see Fig. 28.5) venture from wood borders out into nearby fields of such crops as cotton and soybeans or into grassy pastures and swales. Here they may most often be seen in the evening or early morning of autumn days in the southern states. This inconspicuous portion of our fauna deserves to be better understood and appreciated. The mecopteran ancestors of present-day scorpionflies were almost surely also the ancestors of the Diptera and Siphonaptera.

The Latin name *Mecoptera* is derived from Greek—*meco*, meaning "long," and *pteron*, "wing." It is scarcely appropriate for all of our North American species, as some have more oval wings and in others the wings are greatly reduced or even absent. The common name *scorpionfly*, refers to the resemblance of males of *Panorpa* spp. to Scorpions because of the enlarged abdominal tip carried above their back.

Although adults of scorpionflies and some of the related

hangingflies are active during the day, most mate at night and some feed during darkness. Both adults and larvae of scorpionflies feed chiefly on dead insects; adult hangingflies are predacious, capturing soft-bodied insects by means of their enlarged hind tarsi. The boreids, or snow scorpionflies, feed on mosses, both as larvae and as adults. The adults of panorpodidae feed upon leaf epidermis. Most larval Mecoptera live in the soil.

Diagnosis: L. 3–30 mm (most scorpionflies, 10–15 mm; hangingflies, 15–25 mm; boreids, 3–8 mm). Body usually elongate, cylindrical, not hardened except in boreids; usually light to dark brown or dark reddish brown (blackish in boreids); wings yellowish brown, banded or spotted with brown in scorpionflies, paler but with dark tips in one common species of hangingfly, reduced in boreids. Head prolonged into beak in nearly all species (Fig. 28.1) with well developed mandibles at tip of beak. Antennae simple, with 14 or more segments, about half length of body, or longer. Front and hind pairs of wings similar in shape and marking; long, extending well beyond end of abdomen in scorpionflies and hangingflies; slender, hardened, and hooklike in male boreids; small, hardened, oval pads in female boreids; absent altogether in *Apterobitticus apterus*, a West Coast hangingfly. Legs long and slender. In male scorpionflies, genital claspers enlarged (Fig. 28.2), terminal portions resembling cerci of earwigs; abdomen of female tapers to slender tip with two-segmented cerci. In hangingflies, end of male abdomen is somewhat enlarged, with tiny claspers. Females possess elongate, nearly tubular ovipositors.

Larvae are of two types; those of the boreids and panorpodids somewhat resemble larvae of the beetle family Scarabaeidae. The front pair of thoracic legs are directed ventrally beneath the thorax, whereas the middle and hind pair of legs extend out to the side. Larvae of the other families resemble the caterpillars of the Lepidoptera, with or without abdominal prolegs. The larval abdomen is nine- or ten-segmented. If prolegs are present, they appear on the first eight segments.

Scorpionflies are sometimes confused with wasps, and some hangingflies resemble large crane flies; the rarely seen *Merope tuber* is remarkably like a cockroach in appearance and behavior. The presence of four wings, of course, separates Mecoptera from the true flies, and the wing venation and shape of the head are quite unlike those of wasps or cockroaches.

Fig. 28.2.

Metamorphosis: Holometabolous with egg, larval, pupal, and adult stages.

Habits and habitats: Eggs are laid in moist, protected places. Larvae pass through four molts in the soil, where they feed on dead insects. Pupation usually occurs in an earthen cell. Adults emerge in approximately two weeks and live and mate in or near wooded areas.

Reproductive behavior: Mating takes place a few days after emergence from the pupal cell. Some species have a complicated mating behavior pattern that requires the gift of suitable prey to the female before she will permit mating. Males of certain species take advantage of this action and mimic females in order to get a free meal!

Collecting and preserving: Adults are usually obtained by netting them in flight. Larvae occasionally appear in Berlese funnel extractions from soil. Adults may be pinned, or both larvae and adults may be preserved in 80-percent alcohol.

Rearing: Adult Mecoptera should be captured alive and carefully transported to the rearing area. Individual adult females are placed either in glass jars or cages of about one cubic foot that have been supplied with twigs from which they can suspend themselves. The container should be covered with cheese cloth held by a rubber band and kept at the right moisture level to prevent the growth of mold. The females are fed small freshly killed flies or other soft bodied insects until their eggs are laid. These are collected from the bottom of the containers and placed on a slightly moist pad of paper tissue in glass Stender dishes. Rich garden soil may be placed in the larval container, but it is not absolutely necessary since the paper tissue seems to work as well. Moisture must be checked daily and carefully controlled. Tiny pieces of meat or freshly killed house flies are the proper larval food. If there is soil in which to pupate, the larvae will eventually enter it, but if they have been reared on tissue paper, they will pupate without it. Less moisture is now required, but they should not be allowed to dry out. Adults will emerge after several days.

Distribution: Most of the 480 species of the world are found in temperate regions. The hangingflies are most diverse in the tropics. The greatest density of species appears to be in southeastern Asia, but 68 species in ten genera have been recorded in the U.S. and Canada.

Identification: The most recently published key to the species of the U.S. and Canada is that of Carpenter (1931). Most North American species belong to the genus *Panorpa*. The literature on the group is widely scattered.

Economic importance: No pest species are known. The role that species of this order play in their various ecosystems has not been evaluated.

CLASSIFICATION

This small order is divided into nine families, five of which occur in the U.S. and Canada. These five may be distinguished by using the accompanying key.

Fig. 28.1.

Key to the Families of Mecoptera in the U.S. and Canada

1. Tarsi each with single claw ... 1. **Bittacidae**
 Tarsi each with 2 claws .. *2*
2(1). Wings greatly reduced, without veins (male) or nearly absent (female); female with elongate ovipositor ... 2. **Boreidae**
 Wings rarely reduced in size, with veins *3*
3(2). Ocelli absent; wings short and broad, functional 3. **Meropeidae**
 Ocelli present; wings usually elongate .. *4*
4(3). Face short; Rs four-branched; wings of female very short, nonfunctional
 ... 5. **Panorpodidae**
 Face elongate; Rs five-branched (Fig. 28.3); female with elongate wings
 ... 4. **Panorpidae**

Fig. 28.3.

1. BITTACIDAE (Hangingfly Family)

These insects resemble large crane flies when they hang by their front and middle legs from leaves or stems of low plants. Tarsi with only one claw. There are four genera and 11 species, as follows:

1.1 *Apterobittacus* MacLachlan

One species only, as follows:

A. apertus (MacLachlan) (Wingless Hangingfly). L. 15–20 mm. Wingless; body yellow-brown to dull olive green; legs very long. Adults prey upon crane flies and other insects. (3) CA.

1.2 *Bittacus* Latreille

Eight species, the following of which is common:

B. strigosus Hagen. L. 12–15 mm. Pale yellowish brown; wings yellowish with cross veins usually margined with gray. Widespread woodland species often attracted to lights at night: (1) n.e. NA; (2) s.e. US; (3) TX.

1.3 *Hylobittacus* Byers

One species, as follows:

H. apicalis (Hagen) (Black-tipped Hangingfly). L. 10–15 mm. Active by day; rests with wings outspread; body yellowish to pale tan; wings hyaline with darkened tips. (1) n.e. US; (2) s.e. US.

1.4 *Orobittacus* Villegas and Byers

One species, as follows:

O. obscurus Villegas and Byers. L. 12–16 mm. Nocturnal; rests with wings folded at sides, as does *Bittacus* spp.; antennae

very long; body brown; wings yellowish brown. Adults prey upon fungus gnats and other small flies. (3) CA.

2. BOREIDAE (Snow Scorpionfly Family)

These insects are sometimes seen on melting snow in early spring, usually near mossy rocks, banks, tree bases. Wings reduced, narrow, and hooklike (male) or small flaps (female) in *Boreus*. Despite their small size (±3 mm), they are conspicuous on snow because of their dark color and walking or jumping movement. There are three genera and 13 species, as follows:

Subfamily Caurininae

[2.1 *Caurinus* Russell (1 sp., *C. dectes* Russell (4) OR)]

Subfamily Boreinae

2.2 *Boreus* Latreille

Ten species, two of which occur in the east, the remainder in the west. The following is a common eastern species:

B. brumalis Fitch. L. ±3 mm. Black. The most common eastern species. (See Fig. 28.4.) (1) n.e. NA.

[2.3 *Hesperoboreus* Penny (2 spp. (3) CA; (4) WA, OR)]

3. MEROPEIDAE (Forcepsfly Family)

Wings broad, brownish; ocelli absent; male with long, slender claspers. One genus and one species only, as follows:

3.1 *Merope* Newman

M. tuber Newman (Forcepfly). L. 10–12 mm. Occasionally taken at lights at night. (1) n.e. NA; (2) VA, NC, SC, GA; (5) MN, MO.

Fig. 28.4.

Fig. 28.5. (*Courtesy of* Insect World Digest)

Fig. 28.6.

4. PANORPIDAE (Common Scorpionfly Family)

Wings elongate, somewhat narrowed, marked with dark brown bands or spots (or nearly black throughout in one species); males with bulbous genital segments preceded by two slender segments and abdominal tip curved forward over back, giving appearance of a scorpion (hence the common name); abdomen of female narrowed to slender tip. Thirty-nine species recorded in the U.S. and Canada, all in the following genus:

4.1 *Panorpa* Linnaeus

The following species are typical representatives:

P. lugubis Swederus. L. 12–25 mm. Males larger than females. Wings black with a few white spots. Locally common. (See Fig. 28.5.) (2) VA, NC, SC, GA, FL, AL, MS, LA; (3) TX.

P. isolata Carpenter. L. 9–11 mm. Wings yellowish with dark brown bands and spots. Locally common. (2) s.e. US.

P. rufescens Rambur. L. 10–12 mm. Reddish brown; wings slightly reddish yellow with large apical spots and smaller spots towards base. Found in woodlands. Uncommon. (See A&J 194.) (2) s.e. US.

P. helena Byers. Widespread. (1) n.e. US; (2) VA, NC, SC, LA, MS, AL, GA; (5) e. KS, MO.

P. nuptialis Gerstacher. (See Fig. 28.6.) (1), (2), (3), (4), (5), widespread.

5. PANORPODIDAE (Short-faced Scorpionfly Family)

Similar to the Panorpidae but of uniform yellowish brown; abdomen of male not curved above back; female with reduced wings. One genus, as follows:

[5.1 *Brachypanorpa* Carpenter (4 spp.)]

BIBLIOGRAPHY

Byers, G. W. 1954. Notes on North American Mecoptera. *Ann. Ent. Soc. America*, 47: 484–510.

——. 1965. Families and genera of Mecoptera. *Proc. 12 Int. Congress Ent.* London (1964): 123.

——. 1973. Zoogeography of the Meropeidae (Mecoptera). *Journ. Kansas Ent. Soc.* 46(4): 511–516.

——. 1973. Descriptions and distributional records of American Mecoptera. *Journ. Kansas Ent. Soc.* 46(3): 362–375.

——. 1974. Synonymy in North American Panorpidae (Mecoptera). *Journ. Kansas Ent. Soc.* 47(1): 22–25.

Carpenter, F. M. 1931. Revision of Nearctic Mecoptera *Bull. Mus. Comp. Zool.*, Harvard Univ. 72: 205–277.

Penny, N. D. 1975. A systematic study of the family Boreidae (Mecoptera). *Univ. Kansas Sci. Bull.* 51: 139–217.

Penny, N. D., and Byers, G. W. 1979. A check-list of the Mecoptera of the world. *Acta Amazonica.* 9(2): 365–388.

Russell, Loren K. 1979. A new genus and a new species of Boreidae from Oregon (Mecoptera). *Proc. Ent. Soc.* Washington. 81: 22–31.

Setty, L. R. 1940. Biology and morphology of some North American Bittacidae. *American Midl. Nat.* 23: 257–353.

Order 29

DIPTERA (The Flies)

Few animals surpass the flies in intricate detail of construction, and few exceed their freedom of movement and diversity of activity. No animals, except perhaps people themselves, are responsible for greater loss of human life and economic loss than they are. More than 50 percent of the world's population is diseased from fly-borne pathogens and parasites. Crop losses suffered each year because of pest flies are exceeded by those of few other insects. At the same time, extremely beneficial species exist, the parasitic and predatory habits of which aid in the population control of many pest insects; they rank in value with the parasitic wasps. The role of flies in the detritus cycle—processing dead plant and animal material—is exceeded only by that of bacteria and fungi.

The Latin name for flies, Diptera, was taken from two Greek words: *di*, meaning "two," and *pteron*, meaning "wing," indicating their major characteristic of having two wings, that is, only one pair. The second, or hind, pair either has been reduced to small balancing organs called *halteres* or are entirely absent.

Flies often occur in extremely large numbers. They are difficult to differentiate and are consequently treated as harmful regardless of their kind. For a long time in the course of human development, their role in disease transmission went unrecognized. Much of recent human history has been affected by their transmission of such diseases as malaria and typhoid, resulting in epidemics that have changed the course of battle and retarded the economic development of many societies.

Diagnosis: L. 0.5–40 mm (rarely up to 75 mm). Usually soft-bodied or leathery; surface with spines, setae, and sometimes scales. The setae usually are arranged in definite patterns, which have been named (see Figs. 29.1, 29.3, and 29.5). Their position is useful for the identification of families, genera, and sometimes even species. The shape of flies is surprisingly uniform. The head is more or less globular; the thorax more or less oval and humpbacked to a greater or lesser degree; and the abdomen is either elongate, cylindrical, or oval. Usually, flies are dull in color—black, brownish, or pale. They rarely exhibit bright colors, although many species are metallic blue or green.

The head is an intricate structure with many features used in identification of families, genera, and species. (See Figs. 29.1; 29.2, for mouth parts; 29.3, for lateral view.) Compound eyes and often ocelli are present. The latter vary in number and position. The front of the head (termed "frons" by many authors) is simple in the lower families and usually without specialized sclerites and bristles. In the Muscomorpha Schizophora, there is a modification, the *ptilinum*, an invaginated, saclike organ located slightly dorsal to the bases of the antennae. During emergence from the puparium, this sac is everted and used to push off the puparium cap and help the newly formed adult work through soil and leaves to the surface. When it is withdrawn, it leaves a slit, the *ptilinal fissure*, which

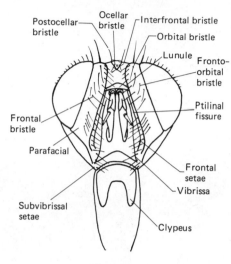

Fig. 29.1. (*Modified from Hall and Townsend, 1977*)

may be seen as an inverted "U" on the front. The portion above and nearly connecting the two antennal bases is termed the *lunule*. Many different types of antennae (Fig. 29.4) are found throughout the order. The first two segments are named, the basal one being the *scape* and the next, the *pedicel;* the remaining segment, or segments, is termed the *flagellum*. The flagellum is variously modified. In primitive flies (suborder Nematocera), it is divided into at least four *flagellomeres*, and usually more. The flagellomeres are not true segments,

Fig. 29.2. (*Courtesy of E. J. Gerberg*)

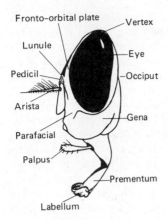

Fronto-orbital plate — Vertex
Lunule — Eye
Pedicil — Occiput
Arista
Parafacial — Gena
Palpus
— Prementum
Labellum

Fig. 29.3. (*Modified from Hall and Townsend, 1977*)

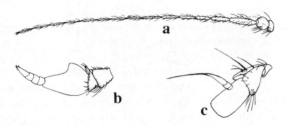

a

b

c

Fig. 29.4. Antennal types: (a) Filiform, (b) stylate, and (c) aristate.

h C Rs Sc R_1 R_{2+3}
c sc r_1 R_4
bm br r-m r_3
upper d r_5 r_4
cup m-m m_1 R_5
lower alula m-cu M_1
calypter A_2 A_1 cua$_1$ m_3 m_2 M_2
alular a_1 M_3 M_3
incision CUA$_1$
anal CUA$_{2}+A_1$
lobe CUP

Fig. 29.6. (See Introduction for abbreviations.)

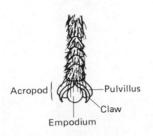

Acropod — Pulvillus
Claw
Empodium

Fig. 29.7.

although they are usually so termed in the older literature. The antennae of the suborder Brachycera consist of only three segments, but segment 3 is variously modified; it usually has a terminal or dorsal *arista*, or spine, which is a modification of the flagellomeres of the Nematocera. In rare instances this structure is annulated, giving the appearance of flagellomeres. Mouthparts too are much modified. Some are greatly elongate for blood sucking (mosquitoes, etc.); others are short and fitted for sponging (house flies; see Fig. 29.2); others for stabbing (horse flies); others for sucking nectar; and still others are nonfunctional

The prothorax is small. (For a lateral view of the thorax, see Fig. 29.5, in which the circles indicate the positions of the setae.) The mesothorax is large and bears the only pair of wings. The metathorax is smaller, with at most a pair of halteres, the greatly reduced hind pair of wings. These have a balancing

function in many flies. The flying wings have wing veins (see Fig. 29.6) comparable to those of the other orders of insects, but their patterns are distinctive and vary greatly from group to group. Different for most families, they are used extensively in family definition. One must be familiar with wing venation in order to identify flies. The comparative wing venation of the Diptera provides an excellent study in the evolution of the order. It is possible to trace vein modifications from group to group and arrive at a phylogenetic picture of their evolution.

Legs also vary considerably from family to family. In general, they are of moderate size, although in some groups (e.g., mosquitoes and crane flies) they may be greatly elongated; in others fitted for grasping prey; and so on. The tarsi of almost all flies consist of five tarsomeres. Tarsal claws and pads are present in shapes and sizes that vary from group to group. These structures are located at the end of the fifth tarsomere and are termed the *acropod*. (See Fig. 29.7.) Variations of the acropod are also indicative of the evolutionary development of any group. In addition to the claws, this structure may bear a membranous, saclike *acrolium* and a median process, the *empodium*, which in turn is variously modified according to the group.

Copulatory and egg laying apparatus is usually withdrawn into the abdomen, but in some species these structures may be exposed.

Eggs of flies are not well known and usually not distinctive. The larvae, or maggots, are legless. (See Fig. 29.8.) The head may be greatly reduced or even apparently absent in some groups; in others, for example mosquito larvae (Fig. 29.9), it is

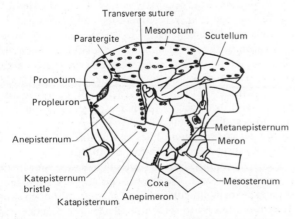

Transverse suture
Paratergite Mesonotum
Scutellum
Pronotum
Propleuron
Anepisternum
Metanepisternum
Meron
Katepisternum bristle
Coxa
Mesosternum
Katapisternum Anepimeron

Fig. 29.5. (*Modified from Hall and Townsend, 1977*)

a

b

Fig. 29.8. Legless larva: (a) Lateral view, and (b) caudal view, showing apical spiracles.

Fig. 29.9. (*From Johannsen, 1969*)

large and well developed. The larvae of many groups are well known and may be identified with existing keys and descriptions. Pupae of many species inhabit a special protective case, the *puparium* (Fig. 29.10). These are found in soil, debris, or other habitats. The pupae of aquatic species are often active swimmers (e.g., mosquito pupae, shown in Fig. 29.11).

Flies are seldom confused with other insects not only because of their single pair of wings but also because of their distinctive wing venation. Since some species mimic bees and wasps, the two groups might be confused without a close look. Some of the wingless ectoparasites, for example, the sheep keds and beelice, are similar in appearance to lice or ticks (the latter are not insects) but are distinctively shaped and, of course, have only three pairs of legs (ticks have four, except when newly hatched).

Metamorphosis: Holometabolous, with egg, larval, and pupal stages.

Habits and habitats: Flies occur almost everywhere. Many groups are aquatic in the larval stage. Some species are found in brine, others even in oil. Many are stem, leaf, and fruit borers, and others form plant galls. They are often found on, or flying

Fig. 29.10.

Fig. 29.11. (*From Johannsen, 1969*)

about, flowers, sap, garbage, feces, dead animals, or living animals (as blood suckers or as feeders on mucus and other body exudates). In homes as infesters of food and garbage, they are among our most noticed "guests" and our most annoying pests whether they bite or just "buzz around." The larvae of some are internal parasites of other insects; the larvae of others are predators of insects and other small organisms. Some are extensively used for the biological control of crop pests, and some for the control of disease vectors. A few are external parasites of birds and mammals, but none of these ectoparasites has chosen man as their permanent host, although some are reported as accidental internal parasites of man, and one, the so-called *Human Bot Fly* (see *Dermatobia hominis*) does infest the internal tissues of human beings, although its primary hosts are larger mammals, including cattle.

Reproductive behavior: Because of the small size of most flies, their behavior patterns have not been intensively studied. It is known, however, that the buzzing or humming of mosquitoes serves to attract the sexes. These and other species of flies are known to swarm for their mating dances. Egg laying habits are as varied as feeding habits. In most cases, eggs are laid on, or very near to, the food needed by the larvae.

Collecting and preserving: Some species are attracted to lights at night. Others can be collected by using various baits or with nets. An air net used around flowers, vegetation, debris, or the like will capture many species. The larger specimens may be pinned, but care must be taken not to destroy the spines and setae needed for identification purposes. Since most flies are rather small (under 10 mm), they are usually glued to triangular paper points or mounted on minuten nadeln. Larvae are preserved in 80-percent alcohol or mounted on slides.

Rearing: Larvae of aquatic species may be reared by simulating the aquatic habitat. Techniques for rearing mosquitoes have been well described. Other species may be reared on decaying meat, and so on. The most famous fly of all, the laboratory Fruit Fly, species of *Drosophila*, is reared under standardized conditions; it is used in classrooms for teaching genetics as well as in the laboratory for genetic and related research. The mass rearing of sterlized male Screwworm Flies in an attempt to control this pest is, no doubt, the most massive insect-rearing project of all time. As a by-product of rearing wild moth and butterfly caterpillars, parasitic flies will often appear instead of their victim—the adult lepidopteran. Many species of flies may be obtained in this way, and the host skin should be retained for host-parasite records.

Distribution: The order is worldwide in distribution. About 98,500 species have been described and cataloged, but since more species are added every year, especially in the parasitic groups, the actual number is probably considerably larger. At any rate, the Dipterans comprise the fourth largest order. The catalog of the flies of the United States and Canada listed 16,130 species in 1965; since then, the number of recorded and newly described species has increased to 16,914 in 2,222 genera and is still increasing.

Notes on identification: Flies can be difficult to identify accurately to species. In some cases, identification characteristics are not only complex but very difficult to see except with the best optical instruments. The absence of color patterns in most species makes them difficult to "spot" identify, although some family groups are easy to recognize after a little practice. The amateur might need to become a specialist in certain groups and

depend upon the help of specialists for specific identification of others.

Economic importance: The importance of flies as vectors of disease has already been mentioned. As crop pests, several have caused enough damage to attract the attention of the press. Medfly outbreaks cause alarm in the citrus-producing areas of the country. The Hessian Fly is the cause of great grain crop losses from time to time. There are other pest species, including root maggots, seed maggots, and leaf miners. The role of flies as parasites of other insects and in the detritus cycle is of great importance, as is their role in the transmission of disease, although they are no longer serious disease carriers in the U.S. and Canada.

During the writing of this book, the first part of a comprehensive and extremely valuable monograph on the families of flies (with keys to the genera) was published (McAlpine, *et al.*, 1981). The new and revised classification given in that book is followed here, and the genera and species it cited have been added to the list in this book. The remainder of the families are listed as they appear in the catalog of the Diptera of United States and Canada (Stone, *et al.* 1965). The figures given above for the number of species and genera recorded in the U.S. and Canada will not agree with those in the following text because of the unpublished catalog information. For the accurate identification of flies, one must make use of the references to additional literature in these two works.

The accompanying Key to the Families is modified from that given in McAlpine to make it somewhat simpler, but the classification synopsis in Table 29.1 and Table 29.2 is exactly as it is in that work.

Table 29.1 Classification of the Diptera

Suborder NEMATOCERA

Infraorder **TIPULOMORPHA**

Superfamily **TANYDEROIDEA**

1. TANYDERIDAE (Primitive Crane Fly Family)

Superfamily **TIPULOIDEA**

2. TIPULIDAE (Crane Fly Family)

Infraorder **BLEPHARICEROMORPHA**

Superfamily **BLEPHARICEROIDEA**

3. BLEPHARICERIDAE (Net-winged Midge Family)

Superfamily **DEUTEROPHLEBIOIDEA**

4. DEUTEROPHLEBIIDAE (Mountain Midge Family)

Superfamily **NYMPHOMYIOIDEA**

5. NYMPHOMYIIDAE (Nymphomyiid Fly Family)

Infraorder **AXYMYIOMORPHA**

Superfamily **AXYMYIOIDEA**

6. AXYMYIIDAE (Axymyiid Fly Family)

Infraorder **BIBIONOMORPHA**

Superfamily **PACHYNEUROIDEA**

7. PACHYNEURIDAE (Pachyneurid Gnat Family)

Superfamily **BIBIONOIDEA**

8. BIBIONIDAE (March Fly Family)

Superfamily **SCIAROIDEA**

9. MYCETOPHILIDAE (Fungus Gnat Family)
10. SCIARIDAE (Dark-winged Fungus Gnat Family)
11. CECIDOMYIIDAE (Gall Midge Family)

Infraorder **PSYCHODOMORPHA**

Superfamily **PSYCHODOIDEA**

12. PSYCHODIDAE (Moth and Sand Fly Family)

Superfamily **TRICHOCEROIDEA**

13. TRICHOCERIDAE (Winter Crane Fly Family)

Superfamily **ANISOPODOIDEA**

14. ANISOPODIDAE (Wood Gnat Family)

Superfamily **SCATOPSOIDEA**

15. SCATOPSIDAE (Minute Black Scavenger Fly Family)
16. SYNNEURIDAE (Synneurid Gnat Family)

Infraorder **PTYCHOPTEROMORPHA**

Superfamily **PTYCHOPTEROIDEA**

17. PTYCHOPTERIDAE (Phantom Crane Fly Family)

Infraorder **CULICOMORPHA**

Superfamily **CULICOIDEA**

18. DIXIDAE (Dixid Midge Family)
19. CHAOBORIDAE (Phantom Midge Family)
20. CULICIDAE (Mosquito Family)

Superfamily **CHIRONOMOIDEA**

21. THAUMALEIDAE (Solitary Midge Family)
22. SIMULIIDAE (Black Fly Family)
23. CERATOPOGONIDAE (Biting Midge Family)
24. CHIRONOMIDAE (Midge Family)

Suborder BRACHYCERA

Infraorder **TABANOMORPHA**

Superfamily **TABANOIDEA**

25. PELECORHYNCHIDAE (Pelecorhynchid Fly Family)
26. TABANIDAE (Horse Fly and Deer Fly Family)
27. ATHERICIDAE (Athericid Fly Family)
28. RHAGIONIDAE (Snipe Fly Family)

Superfamily **STRATIOMYOIDEA**

29. XYLOPHAGIDAE (Xylophagid Fly Family)
30. XYLOMYIDAE (Xylomyid Fly Family)
31. STRATIOMYIDAE (Soldier Fly Family)

Infraorder **ASILOMORPHA**

Superfamily **ASILOIDEA**

32. THEREVIDAE (Stiletto Fly Family)
33. SCENOPINIDAE (Window Fly Family)
34. VERMILEONIDAE (Vermileonid Fly Family)
35. MYDIDAE (Mydas Fly Family)
36. APIOCERIDAE (Flower Fly Family)
37. ASILIDAE (Robber Fly Family)

Superfamily **BOMBYLIOIDEA**

38. ACROCERIDAE (Small-headed Fly Family)
39. NEMESTRINIDAE (Tangle-veined Fly Family)

Table 29.1 Classification of the Diptera (*Contd.*)

40. BOMBYLIIDAE (Bee Fly Family)
41. HILARIMORPHIDAE (Hilarimorphid Fly Family)

Superfamily EMPIDOIDEA

42. EMPIDIDAE (Dance Fly Family)
43. DOLICHOPODIDAE (Long-legged Fly Family)

Infraorder MUSCOMORPHA ASCHIZA

Superfamily LONCHOPTEROIDEA

44. LONCHOPTERIDAE (Pointed-winged Fly Family)

Superfamily PLATYPEZOIDEA

45. PLATYPEZIDAE (Flat-footed Fly Family)
46. PHORIDAE (Humpbacked Fly Family)

Superfamily SYRPHOIDEA

47. SYRPHIDAE Flower (Fly Family)
48. PIPUNCULIDAE (Big-headed Fly Family)

Infraorder SCHIZOPHORA ACALYPTRATAE

Superfamily CONOPOIDEA

49. CONOPIDAE (Thick-headed Fly Family)

Superfamily NERIOIDEA

50. CYPSELOSOMATIDAE (Cypselosomatid Fly Family)
51. MICROPEZIDAE (Stilt-legged Fly Family)
52. NERIIDAE (Nerid Fly Family)

Superfamily DIOPSOIDEA

53. TANYPEZIDAE (Tanypezid Fly Family)
54. STRONGYLOPHTHALMYIIDAE (Strongylophthalmyiidae Fly Family)
55. PSILIDAE (Rust Fly Family)
56. DIOPSIDAE (Stalk-eyed Fly Family)

Superfamily TEPHRITOIDEA

57. LONCHAEIDAE (Lonchaeid Fly Family)
58. OTITIDAE (Picture-winged Fly Family)
59. PLATYSTOMATIDAE (Platystomatid Fly Family)
60. PYRGOTIDAE (Light Fly Family)
61. TEPHRITIDAE (Fruit Fly Family)
62. RICHARDIIDAE (Richardiid Fly Family)
63. PALLOPTERIDAE (Pallopterid Fly Family)
64. PIOPHILIDAE (Skipper Fly Family)

Superfamily OPOMYZOIDEA

65. CLUSIIDAE (Clusiid Fly Family)
66. ACARTOPHTHALMIDAE (Acartophthalmid Fly Family)
67. ODINIIDAE (Odiniid Fly Family)
68. AGROMYZIDAE (Leaf Fly Family)
69. OPOMYZIDAE (Opomyzid Fly Family)
70. ANTHOMYZIDAE (Anthomyzid Fly Family)

71. AULACIGASTRIDAE (Aulacigastrid Fly Family)
72. PERISCELIDIDAE (Periscelidid Fly Family)
73. ASTEIIDAE (Asteiid Fly Family)
74. MILICHIIDAE (Milichiid Fly Family)
75. CARNIDAE (Carnid Fly Family)
76. BRAULIDAE (Bee Louse Fly Family)

Superfamily SCIOMYZOIDEA

77. COELOPIDAE (Seaweed Fly Family)
78. DRYOMYZIDAE (Dryomyzid Fly Family)
79. SCIOMYZIDAE (Marsh Fly Family)
80. ROPALOMERIDAE (Ropalomerid Fly Family)
81. SEPSIDAE (Sepsid Fly Family)

Superfamily LAUXANIOIDEA

82. LAUXANIIDAE (Lauxaniid Fly Family)
83. CHAMAEMYIIDAE (Chamaemyiid Fly Family)

Superfamily SPHAEROCEROIDEA

84. HELEOMYZIDAE (Heleomyzid Fly Family)
85. TRIXOSCELIDIDAE (Trixoscelidid Fly Family)
86. CHYROMYIDAE (Chyromyid Fly Family)
87. RHINOTORIDAE (Rhinotorid Fly Family)
88. SPHAEROCERIDAE (Small Dung Fly Family)

Superfamily EPHYDROIDEA

89. CURTONOTIDAE (Curtonotid Fly Family)
90. DROSOPHILIDAE (Pomace Fly Family)
91. DIASTATIDAE (Diastatid Fly Family)
92. CAMILLIDAE (Camillid Fly Family)
93. EPHYDRIDAE (Shore Fly Family)
94. CHLOROPIDAE (Frit Fly Family)
95. CRYPTOCHETIDAE (Cryptochetid Fly Family)
96. TETHINIDAE (Tethinid Fly Family)
97. CANACIDAE (Beach Fly Family)

Infraorder SCHIZOPHORA CALYPTRATE

Superfamily MUSCOIDEA

98. SCATOPHAGIDAE (Dung Fly Family)
99. ANTHOMYIIDAE (Anthomyiid Fly Family)
100. MUSCIDAE (House Fly Family)

Superfamily OESTROIDEA

101. CALLIPHORIDAE (Blow Fly Family)
102. OESTRIDAE (Bot and Warble Fly Family)
103. SARCOPHAGIDAE (Flesh Fly Family)
104. RHINOPHORIDAE (Rhinophorid Fly Family)
105. TACHINIDAE (Parasitic Fly Family)

Superfamily HIPPOBOSCOIDEA

106. HIPPOBOSCIDAE (Louse Fly Family)
107. NYCTERIBIIDAE (Wingless Bat Fly Family)
108. STREBLIDAE (Bat Fly Family)

Table 29.2 Index to the Families and Family Synonyms of Diptera in the U.S. and Canada

Acartophthalmidae, 66
Acroceridae, 38
Agromyzidae, 68
Anisopodidae, 14
Anthomyiidae, 99
Anthomyzidae, 70
Apioceridae, 36

Asilidae, 37
Asteiidae, 73
Athericidae, 27
Aulacigastridae, 71
Axymyiidae, 6
Bibionidae, 8
Blephariceridae, 3

Bombyliidae, 40
Borboridae; *see* Sphaeroceridae (88)
Braulidae, 76
Calliphoridae, 101
Calobatidae; *see* Micropezidae (51)
Camillidae, 92
Canacidae, 97

Table 29.2 (*Contd.*)

Carnidae, 75
Cecidomyiidae, 11
Ceratopogonidae, 23
Chamaemyiidae, 83
Chaoboridae, 19
Chironomidae, 24
Chloropidae, 94
Chyromyidae, 86
Clusiidae, 65
Clusiodidae; *see* Clusiidae (65)
Coelopidae, 77
Coenomyiidae; *see* Xylophagidae (29)
Conopidae, 49
Cordiluridae; *see* Scathophagidae (98)
Corynoscelididae; *see* Synneuridae (16)
Cryptochetidae, 95
Culicidae, 20
Curtonotidae, 89
Cuterebridae; *see* Oestridae (102)
Cyrtidae; *see* Acroceridae (38)
Cypselosomatidae, 50
Deuterophlebiidae, 4
Diastatidae, 91
Diopsidae, 56
Dixidae, 18
Dolichopodidae, 43
Dorilaidae; *see* Pipunculidae (48)
Drosophilidae, 90
Dryomyzidae, 78
Empidae; *see* Empididae (42)
Empididae, 42
Ephydridae, 93
Erinnidae; *see* Xylophagidae (29)
Fungivoridae; *see* Mycetophilidae (9)
Gasterophilidae; *see* Oestridae (102)
Geomyzidae; *see* Opomyzidae (69)
Helcomyzidae; *see* Dryomyzidae (78)
Heleidae; *see* Ceratopogonidae (23)
Heleomyzidae, 84
Helomyzidae; *see* Heleomyzidae (84)
Hilarimorphidae, 41
Hippoboscidae, 106
Hypotidae; *see* Empididae (42)
Hyperoscelididae; *see* Synneuridae (16)
Hypodermatidae; *see* Oestridae (102)
Itonididae; *see* Cecidomyiidae (11)
Larvaevoridae; *see* Tachinidae (105)
Lauxaniidae, 82

Leptidae; *see* Rhagionidae (28)
Liriopeidae; *see* Ptychopteridae (17)
Lonchaeidae, 57
Lonchopteridae, 44
Lycoriidae; *see* Sciaridae, 10
Melusinidae; *see* Trichoceridae (13)
Metopiidae; *see* Sarcophagidae (103)
Micropezidae, 51
Milichiidae, 74
Muscidae, 100
Musidoridae; *see* Lonchopteridae (44)
Mycetophilidae, 9
Mydidae, 35
Mydasidae; *see* Mydidae (35)
Nemestrinidae, 39
Neottiophilidae; *see* Pallopteridae (63)
Neriidae, 52
Nycteribiidae, 107
Nymphomyiidae, 5
Ochtiphilidae; *see* Chamaemyiidae (83)
Odiniidae, 67
Oestridae, 102
Omphralidae; *see* Scenopinidae (33)
Opomyzidae, 69
Orphnephilidae; *see* Thaumaleidae (21)
Ortalidae; *see* Otitidae (58)
Otitidae, 58
Pachyneuridae, 7
Palloptcridac, 63
Pelecorhynchidae, 25
Periscelididae, 72
Petauristidae; *see* Trichoceridae (13)
Phoridae, 46
Phryneidae; *see* Anisopodidae (14)
Phycodromidae; *see* Coelopidae (77)
Phyllomyzidae; *see* Milichiidae (74)
Piophilidae, 64
Pipunculidae, 48
Platypezidae, 45
Platystomatidae, 59
Platystomidae; *see* Platystomatidae (59)
Psilidae, 55
Psychodidae, 12
Pterocallidae; *see* Otitidae (58)
Ptychopteridae, 17
Pyrgotidae, 60
Rhagionidae, 28

Rhinophoridae, 104
Rhinotoridae, 87
Rhopalomeridae; *see* Ropalomeridae (80)
Rhyphidae; *see* Anisopodidae (14)
Richardiidae, 62
Ropalomeridae, 80
Sapromyzidae; *see* Lauxaniidae (82)
Sarcophagidae, 103
Scathophagidae, 98
Scatomyzidae; *see* Scathophagidae (98)
Scatophagidae; *see* Scathophagidae (98)
Scatopsidae, 15
Scenopinidae, 33
Sciaridae, 10
Sciomyzidae, 79
Scopeumatidae; *see* Scathophagidae (98)
Sepsidae, 81
Simuliidae, 22
Sphaeroceridae, 88
Stephanostomatidae; *see* Sarcophagidae (103)
Stratiomyidae, 31
Streblidae, 108
Strongylophthalmyiidae, 54
Sylvicolidae; *see* Anisopodidae (14)
Synneuridae, 16
Syrphidae, 47
Tabanidae, 26
Tachinidae, 105
Tanyderidae, 1
Tanypezidae, 53
Tendipedidae; *see* Chironomidae (24)
Tephritidae, 61
Tetanoceridae; *see* Sciomyzidae (79)
Tethinidae, 96
Thaumaleidae, 21
Therevidae, 32
Thyreophoridae; *see* Richardiidae (62)
Tipulidae, 2
Trichoceridae, 13
Trixoscelididae, 85
Trupaneidae; *see* Tephritidae (61)
Trypetidae; *see* Tephritidae (61)
Tylidae; *see* Micropezidae (51)
Ulidiidae; *see* Otitidae (58)
Vermileonidae, 34
Xylomyidae, 30
Xylophagidae, 29

Key to the Families of Diptera in the United States and Canada

[Adapted from McAlpine, *et al.* (1981)]

The following set of keys is divided into parts for ease in using . It is somewhat simplified by the elimination of a few extremely small and rare families or parts of families. All families are discussed in the text, and all genera recognized in Stone, *et al.* (1965), and McAlpine, *et al.* (1981) are listed. Where families have not been separated, all of them that will key to that point are listed.

Table of Keys

Key A: Wings greatly reduced, nonfunctional for flying, or entirely absent. (Families from both suborders and several infraorders have wingless, or nearly wingless, species. Frequently, these are ectoparasites or aquatic.)

Key B: Antennal flagellum with four or more freely articulated flagellomeres, usually with apical

Key to the Families of Diptera in the
United States and Canada (*Contd.*)

Table of Keys (*Contd.*)

flagellomere not forming a stylus or arista. Palpi generally three- to five-segmented. Ptilinal fissure and lunule absent. **Suborder NEMATOCERA.**

Key C: Antennal flagellum forms a single compound segment, usually with a terminal or dorsal stylus and arista; palpi with not more than two segments. Ptilinal fissure and lunule absent. Wing with vein CuA$_2$ usually short, usually joining A$_1$ near wing base. **Suborder BRACHYCERA**; *Infraorders* **TABANOMORPHA, ASILOMORPHA,** and **MUSCO-MORPHA ASCHIZA.**

Key D: Antennal flagellum forms a single compound segment with a dorsal arista; palpi with not more than two segments. Ptilinal fissure and lunule present. Antennal pedicel always with a complete dorsal seam. head with vibrissae present. Greater ampulla present as a distinct, bulbous swelling below wing base. **Suborder BRACHYCERA**; *Infraorder* **SCHIZO-PHORA–CALYPTRATAE** (see also Key F, *Superfamily* **HIPPOBOSCOIDEA**).

Key E: Antennal flagellum forms a single compound segment with a dorsal arista; palpi with not more than two segments. Ptilinal fissure and lunule present. Antennal pedicel without, or with greatly reduced, dorsal seam. Greater ampulla as a distinct, bulbous swelling below wing base absent, or if present, then vibrissa of front absent. **Suborder BRACHYCERA;** *Infraorder* **SCHIZOPHORA–ACALYPTRATAE.**

Key F: Antennal flagellum forms a single compound segment with a dorsal arista; palpi with not more than two segments. Ptilinal fissure and lunule present. Antennal pedicel always with a complete dorsal seam. Thorax usually strongly flattened, with venter greatly broadened and widely separating mid and hind coxae medially. Claws strongly recurved and toothed. Adults ectoparasitic on birds and mammals. **Suborder BRACHYCERA;** *Infraorder* **SCHIZOPHORA–CALYPTRATAE;** *Superfamily* **HIPPOBOSCOIDEA**

Key A: Wingless Adult Flies

1. Flagellum with two or more distinctly separate flagellomeres, exclusive of stylus or arista . *2*

Flagellum with single consolidated segment, exclusive of stylus or arista *8*

2(1). Ocelli absent . *3*

At least one ocellus present . *5*

3(2). Mesoscutum with complete V-shaped suture (in 8 genera) **2. Tipulidae**

Mesoscutum without complete V-shaped suture . *4*

4(3). Eyes minute; wings and halteres absent (see *Baeonotus*). **11. Cecidomyiidae**

Eyes well-developed; vestiges of wings and halteres present (see *Clunio* and *Eretmoptera*) . **24. Chironomidae**

5(2). Tibiae without apical spurs (some genera) . **11. Cecidomyiidae**

Tibiae with apical spurs; the latter sometimes short . *6*

6(5). Eyes meeting dorsally, forming an eye bridge (some females of *Bradysia* and *Epidapus*) . **10. Sciaridae**

Eye bridge absent . *7*

7(6). Palpi one-segmented; length ±2 mm (female of *Pnyxia scabiei*) **10. Sciaridae**

Palpi with 3 or more segments; length at least ±4 mm (females of *Baeopterogyna* and some *Boletina*) . **9. Mycetophilidae**

8(1). Length less than 2 mm, flagellum with elongate annulated stalk and inflated knob; compound eyes joined on ventral surface of head behind vestigial mouthparts; usually slender, pale, and weakly sclerotized flies (*Palaeodipteron walkeri*) . **5. Nymphomyiidae**

Length more than 2 mm; flagellum without elongate annulated stalk; compound eyes not meeting on ventral surface of head; stouter, darker, more strongly sclerotized flies . . . *9*

9(8). Pedicel swollen; flagellum at least twice as long as broad and with a minute apical seta; remnant of larval eye strongly apparent; abdomen about 3 times as long as remainder of body (*Oreadomyia albertae*) . **24. Chironomidae**

Pedicel not swollen; flagellum less than twice as long as broad, and usually with elongate stylus or arista; remnant of larval eye not apparent; abdomen less than twice as long as remainder of body . *10*

10(9). Thorax unusually short (in dorsal view, less than half as long as head) and closely adjoining and rather similar in shape to abdominal tergite 1+2; tarsi without claws but bearing inflexed comb of many microscopic teeth (*Braula coeca,* associated with honey bees) . **76. Braulidae**

Thorax at least as long as head, strongly separated from abdominal tergite 1+2 and differing greatly from it in shape; each tarsus with 2 claws . *11*

11(10). Middle and hind coxae widely separated ventromedially; tarsal claws strongly recurved and toothed; ectoparasites of bats, birds, or mammals . *12*

Key to the Families of Diptera in the
United States and Canada (*Contd.*)

Key A: Wingless Adult Flies (*Contd.*)

Coxae not widely separated ventromedially; tarsal claws simple; usually not ectoparasites of bats or other mammals; sometimes associated with nestling birds **14**

12(11). Head vertically oriented, folded back into groove on mesoscutum; first tarsomere of each tarsus very elongate, at least as long as remainder of tarsus; ectoparasites of bats (*Basilia*) ... **107. Nycteribiidae**

Head horizontally oriented, not folded back; first tarsomere of each tarsus short, subequal to 2nd tarsomere; parasites of bats, other mammals, or birds **13**

13(12). Compound eyes always present and relatively large, vertically oval, at least three-fourths as high as head, with at least 100 very small facets; ectoparasites of birds and mammals other than bats (*Melophagus* and females of *Lipoptena*) **106. Hippoboscidae**

Compound eyes sometimes absent, but if present, small and round, never more than half as high as head, with less than 40 relatively large beadlike facets; ectoparasites of bats (several genera) ... **108. Streblidae**

14(11). Lunule absent .. **15**
Lunule present ... **17**

15(14). Arista with 3 aristomeres (females of several genera) **46. Phoridae**
Arista with 2 aristomeres ... **16**

16(15). Proboscis short and retracted; vextex excavated; compound eyes pubescent (females of some *Campsicnemus*) **43. Dolichopodidae**

Proboscis elongate and projecting; vertex convex; compound eyes base (*Chersodromia*) .. **42. Empididae**

17(14). First tarsomere of hind leg swollen, shorter than 2nd tarsomere (*Carolinaptera,* some *Leptocera*) .. **88. Sphaeroceridae**

First tarsomere of hind leg not swollen, longer than 2nd tarsomere **18**

18(17). Propleuron with vertical ridge (some *Conioscinella*) **94. Chloropidae**
Propleuron without vertical ridge **19**

19(18). Face strongly convex; subcranial cavity unusually large (females of some *Hyadina* and *Nostima*) **93. Ephydridae**

Face concave; subcranial cavity normal **20**

20(19). Postocellar bristles absent; front with single, reclinate orbital bristle; reduced wings with apical spot (some *Geomyza*) **69. Opomyzidae**

Postocellar bristles present; front with at least 2 orbital bristles; reduced wing, if present, without apical spot **21**

21(20). Postocellar bristles subparallel; gena with row of strong bristles in middle; associated with nestling birds (*Carnus hemapterus*) **75. Carnidae**

Postocellar bristles convergent; gena without row of bristles in middle; not associated with birds ... **22**

22(21). All tibiae without preapical dorsal bristle; front femur with strong ctenidial bristle; front with two strong, reclinate fronto-orbital bristles on lower half (some *Anthomyza*) ...
... **70. Anthomyzidae**

Some or all tibiae with preapical dorsal bristle; front femur without ctenidial bristle; front without strong fronto-orbital bristles on lower half (some *Lutomyia*)
... **84. Heleomyzidae**

KEY B: Suborder NEMATOCERA

1. Wings extremely narrow, with greatly reduced venation and extraordinarily long fringes (*see* wingless aquatic species, Key A) **5. Nymphomyiidae**

2(1). Antennae pectinate, otherwise with features of the suborder Brachycera.
... **30. Xylomyidae**

Antennae rarely pectinate, always without stylus or arista or other features of the suborder Brachycera .. **3**

3(2). Wings with network of fine, creaselike lines between true veins and with number of main veins more or less reduced; anal lobe strongly projecting **4**

Wings without network of creaselike lines between main veins, and not with venation particularly reduced nor anal lobe strongly projecting **5**

4(3). Wings unusually broad and fanlike; flagellum with 4 flagellomeres, the terminal one excessively lengthened in male. **4. Deuterophlebiidae**

Wings longer and narrower than above; flagellum with 11 to 13 flagellomeres, the terminal one not lengthened **3. Blephariceridae**

5(3). Halteres with a basal appendage, the prehalter **17. Ptychopteridae**
Halteres without prehalter .. **6**

6(5). Wings with two strong anal veins, A_1 and A_2, reaching wing margin; legs long and slender
... **7**

**Key to the Families of Diptera in the
United States and Canada** (*Contd.*)

KEY B: Suborder NEMATOCERA (*Contd.*)

Wings with at least A_2 absent or fading out before reaching wing margin; legs variable *8*

7(6). Scutum with complete V-shaped suture; ocelli absent or rudimentary; A_2 usually more than half as long as A_1 and relatively straight. **2. Tipulidae**

Scutum with V-shaped suture incompletely developed in middle; ocelli present; A_2 much less than half as long as A_1 and strongly curved at apex **13. Trichoceridae**

8(6). R with 5 free branches reaching wing margin; cell d present; anal lobe well-developed .. **1. Tanyderidae**

R usually with fewer than 5 free branches, but if five free radial branches present (some Psychodidae), then cell d absent and anal lobe undeveloped *9*

9(8). C continuing around wing, though weaker along hind margin *10*

C ending just beyond insertion of last branch of R, usually near wing tip; if this character is indistinct (see *Cramptonomyia*), then R with 3 branches and with supernumerary cross vein r-r forming a closed cell, br_3 between R_{2+3} and R_{4+5} *16*

10(9). First tarsomere much shorter than 2nd and both more or less fused, each tarsus thus appearing to be, at most, 4-segmented; ocelli absent; C usually with break just beyond insertion of R_{4+5}; small fragile midges with weakly veined wings (Cedidomyliinae and Porricondylinae) .. **11. Cecidomyiidae**

First tarsomere longer than 2nd; each tarsus clearly 5-segmented *11*

11(10). Ocelli usually present, but if not (see females of some *Conarete*), then C with break just beyond insertion of R_{4+5}; small fragile midges with weakly veined wings (Lestremiinae) .. **11. Cecidomyiidae**

Ocelli absent; C with break just beyond insertion of R_{4+5}; small to relatively large midges and gnats .. *12*

12(11). Antennae short, about as long as head; flagellum unusually short and slender for Nematocera, with 2 or 3 outstanding bristles at apex of terminal flagellomere; wing with 6 or 7 veins reaching margin **21 Thaumaleidae**

Antennae at least as long as head; flagellum not unusually reduced, usually with whorls of long, hairlike setae on all flagellomeres; wing with 9 to 11 veins reaching margin ... *13*

13(12). Sc incomplete or ending in C or R_1 before middle of wing; therefore one long vein (R_1) reaching C in apical half of wing in front of first forked vein (R_2 and R_3); M with 3 branches; cells bm and br, if present, not more than half as long as wing; pedicel usually smaller than scape and not cup-shaped; very hairy, mothlike flies ...**12. Psychodidae**

Sc complete, ending C at or beyond middle of wing; therefore 2 long veins (Sc and R_1) reaching C in apical half of wing in front of first forked vein (R_2 and R_3); M with 2 branches; cells br and bm usually more than half as long as wing; pedicel usually larger than scape and cup-shaped; sparsely to moderately hairy, mosquitolike flies *14*

14(13). Scales present on wing veins, head, and legs and usually on other parts of body; proboscis long, extending far beyond clypeus **20. Culicidae**

Scales absent from wing veins and other parts of body, though conspicuous hairs frequently present; proboscis short, barely extending beyond clypeus *15*

15(14). Wing veins with very short, relatively sparse, inconspicuous, hairlike setae; stem of R_{2+3} strongly forwardly arched; antennae with relatively short, sparse, indistinctly arranged, hairlike setae. ... **18. Dixidae**

Wing veins with long, dense, conspicuous hairs; stem of R_{2+3} nearly straight; antennae with abundant, long, hairlike setae in distinct whorls **19. Chaoboridae**

16(9). Ocelli absent .. *17*

Ocelli present (except in *Hesperodes* of Mycetophilidae) *19*

17(16). Antennae short, about as long as head; flagellum shortly setulose in both sexes; wings broad, with posterior veins weak **22. Simuliidae**

Antennae much longer than head, and distinctly hairy, typically more so in male than in female; wings usually narrow, with posterior veins usually strong *18*

18(17). Two branches of M present, M_2 usually distinct, sometimes weakened ast base, rarely obsolescent never more than 2 branches of R reaching wing margin; R_{2+3}, if present, crossveinlike and forming a closed cell r_1 (first radial cell); anterior thoracic spiracle rarely round, separated (sometimes narrowly) from postspiracular membrane by dorsal extension of anepisternum and situated nearly level with lower margin of paratergite; mouthparts of female with bladelike mandibles usully present; postnotum usually without longitudinal groove **23. Ceratopogonidae**

One branch of M present; M_2 never apparent; usually 3 branches of R reaching wing margin; R_{2+3}, if present, ending in wing margin; anterior thoracic spiracle distinctly oval, open posteriorly to postspiracular membrane and situated well below level of lower margin of paratergite; mouthparts of both sexes lacking functional mandibles; postnotum usually with longitudinal groove **24. Chironomidae**

<div align="center">

**Key to the Families of Diptera in the
United States and Canada** (*Contd.*)

KEY B: Suborder NEMATOCERA (*Contd.*)

</div>

19(16). Wings with R 3-branched and with supernumerary cross vein r-r forming cell, br$_3$, between R$_{2+3}$ and R$_{4+5}$; cell dm (=d in Fig. 29.6) usually closed; M 3-branched; A$_1$ complete (*Cramptonomyia*) ... **7. Pachyneuridae**
 Wings with R sometimes with 3 branches, but never with supernumerary cross vein or closed cell between R$_{2+3}$ and R$_{4+5}$; cell d present or absent; M with 2 or 3 branches; A$_1$ complete or incomplete ... *20*

20(19). Wings with cell d present; M with 3 branches (Anisopodinae) **14. Anisopodidae**
 Wing with cell d absent; M never with more than 2 free branches *21*

21(20). Wings with cells br and bm confluent and with 6 veins arising from composite basal cell; Sc and A$_1$ complete (*Mycetobia*) **14. Anisopodidae**
 Wing venation differing from the preceding in one or more respects; if cells br and bm confluent, then with at most 5 veins arising from composite basal cell; Sc and A$_1$ complete or incomplete .. *22*

22(21). R with 4 branches; R$_2$ and R$_3$ occurring as 2 separate veins; R$_2$ short, oblique, and joining R$_1$ close to wing margin; scutum with pair of shiny oval spots near middle; tibiae without apical spirs. .. **6. Axymyiidae**
 R with 3 branches or fewer branches; R$_2$ and R$_3$ never occurring as 2 separate veins; scutum without shiny spots; tibiae with or without spurs *23*

23(22). Wings with two closed basal cells, that is, with cells br and bm separate and closed distally; pulvilli and empodium strongly and equally developed; acropod with 3 relatively similar pads ... **8. Bibionidae**
 Wings with only one closed basal cell, that is, either with cells br and bm confluent or with cell bm open to wing margin, except in a few Mycetophilidae (*Paleoplatyura* and *Platyura*); pulvilli at most weakly developed; acropod never with 3 similar pads *24*

24(23). Eyes nearly meeting below antennae, and holoptic above; small scatopsidlike flies
 ... **16. Synneuridae**
 Eyes widely separated below antennae, with or without narrow eye bridge above antennae; size and form variable ... *25*

25(24). Tibiae without apical spurs; wing with c ending far from wing apex and usually with only C and R darkly pigmented **15. Scatopsidae**
 Tibiae with apical spurs; wing with C ending at or near wing apex and usually with all veins darkly pigmented .. *26*

26(25). Eyes meeting in narrow eye bridge above antennae (except in *Pnyxia,* in which eyes are reduced in both sexes and wings and halteres are lacking in female; *see* Key A); wings with stem and fork of M subequal in length, and with fork distinctly bell-shaped; all mesothoracic pleural sclerites bare **1. Sciaridae**
 Eyes never meeting above antennae; wings usually with fork of m much longer than stem, and lanceolate rather than bell-shaped; usually some mesothoracic pleural sclerites at least weakly haired **9. Mycetophilidae**

<div align="center">

**KEY C: Suborder BRACHYCERA; Infraorders TABANOMORPHA,
ASILOMORPHA, and MUSCOMORPHA ASCHIZA**

</div>

1. Empodia pulvilliform; each acropod with 3 similar flattened pads below tarsal claws; CuA$_2$ free or meeting A$_1$ in acute angle near wing margin *2*
 Empodia usually setiform or absent; if acropod with 3 pads, then empodium much narrower and more tapered than pulvilli; if empodia somewhat pulvilliform (some Empididae and Dolichopodidae), then CuA$_2$ joining A$_1$ at obtuse angle far from wing margin .. *12*

2(1). Head usually small, rarely more than half as wide as thorax; eyes holoptic or nearly so in both sexes; lower lobe of calypter extremely large, wider than head **38. Acroceridae**
 Head more than half as wide as thorax; eyes never holoptic in female; lower lobe of calypter smaller, not as wide as head *3*

3(2). Venation peculiar with branches of R and M more or less converging to apex of wing, the latter branches curving forward and ending before or scarcely behind apex of wing, and with a composite "diagonal vein" running from distal end of cell br to posterior margin of wing ... **39. Nemestrinidae**
 Venation more normal than above; branches of R and M diverging to apical wing margin; branches of M joining margin far behind apex of wing; without a composite diagonal vein ... *4*

4(3). C ending near apex of wing ... *5*
 C continuing around wing, though usually weaker along posterior margins *7*

5(4). C usually ending well before, on rare ocassions nearly at, wing apex; branches of R more

**KEY C: Suborder BRACHYCERA; Infraorders TABANOMORPHA,
ASILOMORPHA, and MUSCOMORPHA ASCHIZA** (*Contd.*)

or less crowded anteriorly, with all ending in margin well before wing apex; cell d (or dm) short, usually little longer than wide; tibial spurs usually absent **31. Stratiomyidae**

C extending beyond wing apex; branches of R not crowded anteriorly, with R$_5$ ending at or beyond wing apex; cell d at least twice as long as broad; tibial spurs present on at least middle and hind tibiae .. **6**

6(5). Front tibiae with ventral apical spur; precoxal bridge absent; antennae of some pectinate .. **29. Xylophagidae**

Front tibiae without ventral apical spur; precoxal bridge present; antennae not pectinate .. **30. Xylomyidae**

7(4). Subscutellum strongly developed; posterior thoracic spiracle with scalelike elevation immediately behind it (reduced in *Glutops*) **8**

Subscutellum absent or very weakly developed; posterior thoracic spiracle never with scalelike elevation immediately behind it **10**

8(7). Flagellum with slender nonannulated arista; wing with cell r$_1$ closed by vein R$_{2+3}$ meeting C at end of R$_1$.. **27. Athericidae**

Flagellum with coarse annulated stylus; wing with cell r$_1$ open and vein R$_{2+3}$ meeting C far beyond end of R$_1$.. **9**

9(8). Both upper and lower calypteres large, subequal in size; first abdominal tergite deeply notched in middle of posterior margin and with median suture **26. Tabanidae**

Upper caltypter moderately large; lower one scarcely developed; first abdominal tergite without a median notch or suture **15. Pelecorhynchidae**

10(7). Wing with anal lobe and alula undeveloped, and with C in this area strong; alular incision absent; scutellum small, with flat bare disc **34. Vermileonidae**

Wing usually with anal lobe and alula well-developed, but if not (*Xylophagus*), C in this area weak or absent; alular incision present (weak in *Xylophagus*); scutellum large, with convex hairy disc .. **11**

11(10). Clypeus exposed and strongly convex, in profile with anterior surface bulging beyond parafacial and usually reaching dorsally to bases of antennae; flagellum usually with not more than 7 flagellomeres, and with distal ones frequently forming a slender stylus or arista .. **28. Rhagionidae**

Clypeus recessed in a deep facial groove and more or less flattened, in profile with anterior surface depressed below level of parafacial and not reaching dorsally to bases of antennae; flagellum usually with at least 8 gradually smaller flagellomeres, and with apical ones not forming a slender stylus or arista, except in *Dialysis* **30. Xylophagidae**

12(1). Palpi with 5 segments; flagellum with 10 flagellomeres; terminal flagellomere with 2 or 3 outstanding bristles at apex; wing with 6 or 7 veins reaching wing margin; pulvilli absent (Nematocera with short slender antennae) **21. Thaumaleidae**

Palpi with at most 2 segments; flagellum with 3 or 4 flagellomeres; terminal flagellomere not as above; wing venation otherwise; pulvilli usually present **13**

13(12). CuA$_2$ reaching wing margin near A$_1$ or joining A$_1$ near wing margin; if joining A$_1$, then CuA$_2$ at least 1.5 times longer than apical section of A$_1$, except in a few Bombyliidae **14**

CuA$_2$ absent, vestigial, or joining A$_1$ far from wing margin; if joining A$_1$, then CuA$_2$ not or scarcely longer than apical section of A$_1$, except in a few Empididae and Platypezidae (*Polyporivora* spp.) .. **21**

14(13). Branches of M peculiarly curved forward, more or less parallel to posterior wing margin; at least M$_1$ ending freely in wing margin before wing apex; large asilidlike flies **15**

Branches of M not curved as in the preceding, but if forwardly bent, then not ending freely in wing margin; size and form variable **16**

15(14). Flagellum unusually long, with slender stalklike base and strongly clubbed apex; stalk at least twice as long as combined length of scape and pedicel; single ocellus present **35. Mydidae**

Flagellum shorter than head, without stalklike base; entire flagellum not much longer than combined length of scape and pedicel; 3 ocelli present **36. Apioceridae**

16(14). Spurious vein (see Fig. 29.39) evident as strong veinlike fold between Rs and M; M$_1$ curved forward, more or less in line with cross vein dm-cu and joining unbranched R$_{4+5}$ in a cross-veinlike manner .. **47. Syrphidae**

Spurious vein undeveloped; M$_1$ usually not curved forward in cross-veinlike manner, but if so (some Bombyliidae), then joining a furcate R$_{4+5}$ **17**

KEY C: Suborder BRACHYCERA; Infraorders TABANOMORPHA, ASILOMORPHA, and MUSCOMORPHA ASCHIZA (*Contd.*)

17(16). Head strongly hemispherical, with compound eyes unusally large and almost meeting on midline both above and below antennae; flagellum with dorsal arista; R_{4+5} unbranched; C ending at wing apex **48. Pipunculidae**
Head usually not hemispherical, but if so (some Bombyliidae), then flagellum without dorsal arista; R_{4+5} usually furcate; C usually continuing around wing *18*

18(17). Vextex usually distinctly excavated between eyes; ocellar tubercle below dorsal level of eyes; eyes never holoptic; face relatively long, with cluster row of long bristles called the *mystax;* proboscis stout, polished; labella reduced and inconspicuous; hypopharynx protrusible, strongly developed for piercing **37. Asilidae**
Vertex not or only slightly concave; ocellar tubercle usually elevated above dorsal level of eyes; eyes usally holoptic in male; face relatively short, sometimes hairy, but without mystax; proboscis short and stout to long and slender, usually dull pruinose; labella usually well-developed and conspicuous; hypopharynx not protrusible nor developed for piercing ... *19*

19(18). Wings with cell bm truncate distally with four corners from which arise four separate veins, namely M_{1+2}, M_3, CuA_1 and CuA_2; base of cell m_3 truncate ...**32. Therevidae**
Wing with cell bm, when present, pointed distally and with three corners from which arise three separate veins, namely M_{1+2}, M_3, $+ CuA_1$, and CuA_2; base of cell m_3, when present, pointed .. *20*

20(19). Wing with cell dm absent, and with R_{4+5} and M_{1+2} rather similarly forked, each fork not longer than its stem; small, blackish, empididlike flies, 3 to 5 mm long, with dusky wings .. **41. Hilarimorphidae**
Wing with cell dm usually present, but if not, then R_{4+5} and M_{1+2} not similarly forked; small to large, yellowish to blackish flies, with marked or unmarked wings **40. Bombyliidae**

21(13). Flagellum with minute stylus concealed in subapical pit; cross vein r-m at or beyond middle of wing; M unbranched and curved forward, joining R_{4+5} or closely approaching it in wing margin **33. Scenopinidae**
Flagellum usually with elongate, fully exposed stylus or arista (absent in empidid *Allanthalia*); cross vein r-m well before middle of wing or absent; M branched or unbranched, sometimes curved forward but not as in the preceding *22*

22(4). Wings pointed at apex, with peculiar linear venation; main veins except Sc and R_3 with black setulae above; flagellum rounded, with terminal arista; slender, brownish or yellowish flies, 2 to 5 mm long **44. Lonchopteridae**
Wings rounded at apex and with radiating venation; veins at least in posterior half of wing not setose; flagellum, body size, and color variable *23*

23(22). Wings with branches of R strongly thickened and crowded into anterior base, and with four other weak and peculiarly aligned veins in remainder of wing blade; C ending near middle of anterior margin; small humpbacked flies, 1 to 4 mm long **46. Phoridae**
Wings with branches of R not strongly thickened and crowded anterobasally, and with other veins normal; C extending at least to wing apex *24*

24(23). Antennae with pedical much longer than flagellum; flagellum with dorsal three-segmented arista; mid-coxal prong strongly developed (suborder SCHIZOPHORA, but lacking a ptilinum; *Sepedon*) .. **79. Sciomyzidae**
Antennae with pedicel not, or scarcely, as long as flagellum; if arista three-segmented (Platypezidae), then terminally situated; mid-coxal prong absent *25*

25(24). Wings with both A_1 and Sc reaching wing margin, and with cell cup acute at posterior apex; hind tarsi, at least in male, with one or more basal tarsomeres expanded and flattened; arista three-segmented, terminally situated **45. Platypezidae**
Wings rarely with A_1 reaching wing margin (some Empididae), but if so, either Sc incomplete or cell cup obtuse or rounded at posterior apex; hind tarsi not modified as above; arista or stylus two-segmented, terminally or dorsally situated (absent in empidid genus *Allanthalia*) ... *26*

26(25). Rs orginating at, or near, level of cross vein h, distal to cross vein h by, at most, length of cross vein h; cross vein r-m in basal fourth or wing; cells bm and dm confluent, that is, cross vein bm-cu absent; Sc usually abruptly curved posteriorly and fused with R_1, except in Hydrophorinae **45. Dolichopodidae**
Rs orginating well distal to level of cross vein h, usually distal to it by more than length of cross vein h; cross vein r-m distal to basal fourth of wing; cell bm usually separated from cell dm (when cell dm present) by cross vein bm-cu; Sc usually joining C or ending freely, never abruptly joining R_1 **42. Empididae**

**Key to the Families of Diptera in the
United States and Canada** (*Contd.*)

KEY D: Suborder BRACHYCERA, Infraorder SCHIZOPHORA CALYPTRATAE

1. Large, heavy-bodied flies with hairlike setae, but bristleless, resembling honeybees, carpenter bees, or bumble bees; head inflated, with reduced or atrophied mouthparts, no vibrissae, and small sunken antennae; meron usually with cluster of long hairlike setae; 9 to 25 mm long ... **102. Oestridae**
 Usually smaller, trimmer, ordinarily bristled flies; head almost always with well-developed mouthparts, vibrissae, and antennae; meron bare or with row of bristles, sometimes with scattered, fine, hairlike setae in addition to bristles; 1 to 15 mm long ... *2*

2(1). Meron with row of bristles, and sometimes with additional hairlike setae *3*
 Meron without bristles .. *10*

3(2). Subscutellum strongly developed, prominently and evenly convex in profile **105. Tachinidae**
 Subscutellum absent or weakly developed, but if weakly developed (as in Rhinophoridae), upper half more or less membranous and concave in profile *4*

4(3). Abdomen and usually thorax with distinct metallic blue or green luster; palpi usually orange yellow; (most species) **101. Calliphoridae**
 Abdomen usually dull, variegated gray, brown, or black, sometimes shining black, but never metallic blue or green; palpus blackish to yellowish *5*

5(3). Thorax with silky, wavy, yellowish hairlike setae in addition to normal black bristles and hairs (*Pollenia*) .. **102. Calliphoridae**
 Thorax without silky, yellowish, hairlike setae *6*

6(5). Scutum usually with three conspicuous black stripes on gray background; notopleuron usually with three or four bristles; hind coxae usually with hairlike setae on posterior surface; arista usually plumose (most Sarcophaginae) **103. Sarcophagidae**
 Scutum with or without black stripes; notopleuron always with only 2 bristles; hind coxae always without hairs on posterior surface; arista bare to plumose *7*

7(6). Coxopleural streak absent (Opsodexiinae) **101. Calliphoridae**
 Coxopleural streak present ... *8*

8(7). Second abdominal sternite overlapping margins of 2nd abdominal tergite; lower calypter with inner base expanded, impinging on scutellum (Miltogramminae) **103. Sarcophagidae**
 Second abdominal sternite not overlapping margins of 2nd abdominal tergite; lower calypter with inner base not expanded, widely removed from scutellum *9*

9(8). M complete and joining R_{4+5} **104. Rhinophoridae**
 Apical portion of M atrophied (*Bezzimyia*) **105. Tachinidae**

10(2). A_2 curved forward beyond apex of A_1, with course of A_1 (if extended) intersecting A_2 before wing margin; Sc always nearly straight on apical two-thirds; hind tibiae always with strong bristle near middle of dorsal surface in addition to preapical dorsal bristle (Fanniinae) ... **100. Muscidae**
 A_2 not curved as in the preceding; with coarse of A_1 not intersecting A_2 before wing margin; Sc usually distinctly curved forward on apical half or less; hind tibiae rarely with strong bristle near middle of dorsal surface (though similar bristle called the *calcar* sometimes present on posterodorsal surface) ... *11*

11(10). Palpi absent; cross veins r-m and dm-cu separated by distance not or scarcely greater than length of cross vein dm-cu; cross vein bm-cu partially atrophied (*Acridomyia*) **99. Anthomyiidae**
 Palpi present; cross veins r-m and dm-cu usually more widely separated; cross vein bm-cu usually complete ... *12*

12(11). A_1 never attaining wing margin even as a fold; lower calypter broad, never linear (most species) .. **100. Muscidae**
 A_1 usually traceable to wing margin at least as a creaselike fold, but if not (as in some Scathophagidae), then lower calypter linear *13*

13(12). Scutellum usually with fine, pale, hairlike setae on apicovenral surface, and front usually narrower in male than in female; if scutellum bare on ventral surface and front wide in male (Fucelliinae, some Myopinini), the front with strong interfrontal bristles; occiput with coarse black bristles and hairlike setae only, never with fine, pale, hairlike setae; katepisternum usually with 2 to 4 bristles; lower calypter linear to broadly expanded .. **99. Anthomyiidae**
 Scutellum bare on ventral surface; front wide in both sexes, and without interfrontal bristles; occiput almost always with rather numerous fine, pale, hairlike setae, sometimes interspersed with additional black bristles and hairlike setae; katepisternum usually with one bristle; lower calypter always linear **98. Scathophagidae**

Key to the Families of Diptera in the
United States and Canada (*Contd.*)

KEY E: Suborder BRACHYCERA, Infraorder SCHIZOPHORA ACALYPTRATAE

1. Proboscis usually very long and slender, frequently 2 or more times longer than head; pedicel usually longer than 1st flagellomere; cross vein sc-r present or cell cup distinctly longer than cell bm, or with both characters present simultaneously; M joining R_{4+5} or closely approaching it .. **49. Conopidae**
 Proboscis usually shorter and stouter, not longer than head except in some Milichiidae, where it is elbowed; pedicel usually shorter than 1st flagellomere, but if longer (some Neriidae, most Sciomyzidae, and some Piophilidae), then cross vein sc-r absent and cell cup shorter than cell bm; M approaching R_{4+5} or not **2**

2(1). Ocelli absent; medium to large flies, with heavily marked wings **60. Pyrgotidae**
 Ocelli present; size variable, with wings marked or unmarked **3**

3(2). Eye at end of stout stalk; antennae widely displaced laterally; scutellum with only 2 subapical bristles, each arising from an elongate process **56. Diopsidae**
 Eye not on stalk; antennae not displaced; scutellum usually with 4 bristles not arising from elongate process ... **4**

4(3). Arista minute, situated apically on very large 1st flagellomere; compound eye very large and pubescent; scutellum large, convex, uniformly setose **95. Cryptochetidae**
 Arista well-developed; compound eyes and scutellum variable **5a**

5a(5). Hind tarsus with 1st tarsomere distinctly swollen and usually shorter than 2nd tarsomere; Sc always incomplete; CuA_1 usually incomplete. **88. Sphaeroceridae**
 Hind tarsus with 1st tarsomere not swollen and longer than 2nd tarsomere; Sc complete or incomplete; CuA_1 usually complete **6**

6(5). Sc abruptly bent forward at nearly 90°, weakened beyond bend and ending at subcostal break; wing almost always with markings; pedicel with dorsal cleft; vibrissae absent; greater ampulla usually weakly distinguishable; anepimeron always with bristles or hairs or both .. **61. Tephritidae**
 Sc less abruptly bent; disagreeing with the preceding in one or more of remaining characters ... **7**

7(6). Slender-bodied flies, with long slender legs; R_{4+5} and M meeting or strongly converging at wing margin; Sc always complete (includes **53. Tanypezidae** and **52. Neriidae**)
 .. **51. Micropezidae**
 Usually stouter flies, with shorter more robust legs; R_{4+5} and M usually subparallel or divergent at wing margin, but if these veins converging (**80. Ropalomeridae**), then legs not long and slender; Sc complete or incomplete **8**

8(7). Sc complete, or nearly so, ending in C or just short of it and free from R_1 distally **9**
 Sc incomplete, not reaching C, often fusing with R_1 distally **25**

9(8). C without subcostal break (includes **80. Ropalomeridae**) **10**
 C with subcostal break (includes **87. Rhinotoridae** and **97. Canacidae**) **17**

10(9). Posterior thoracic spiracle with one or more fine bristles on lower margin; form usually antlike; head subspherical; palpi vestigial (except in *Orygma*); abdomen usually elongate and basally constricted **81. Sepsidae**
 Posterior thoracic spiracle without bristles or outstanding hairlike setae; form usually not antlike; palpi usually well-developed (includes **77. Coelopidae**) **11**

11(10). Face broadly membranous and sunken in middle; vibrissa present
 **65. Clusiidae** and **66. Acartophthalmidae**
 Face uniformly sclerotized and convex in middle; vibrissa absent **12**

12(11). Some or all tibiae with preapical dorsal bristle **13**
 All tibiae without preapical dorsal bristle **15**

13(12). Postocellar bristles distinctly convergent **82. Lauxaniidae**
 Postocellar bristles almost parallel, divergent, or absent **14**

14(13). Clypeus large and prominent, in profile distinctly bulging beyond lower margin of face; pedicel always short **78. Dryomyzidae**
 Clypeus small and withdrawn, in profile more or less concealed under lower margin of face; pedicel usually elongate **79. Sciomyzidae**

15(12). Costal section between apices of Sc and R_1 as long as cell c; adjacent membrane entirely blackish; remainder of wing whitish hyaline; small flies, 3 mm long; female with membranous tubular ovipositor **83. Chamaemyiidae**
 Costal section between apices of Sc and R_1 shorter than cell c; adjacent membrane usually not entirely blackish; if this area blackish, then remainder of wing with additional markings; usually larger flies; female with rigid, shaftlike ovipositor **16**

16(15). Postocellar bristles distinctly developed, divergent; katepisternal bristle present (except in *Mymecothea*, an antlike genus with 2 scutellar setae); (in part) **58. Otitidae**
 Postocellar bristles absent or very weakly developed; katepisternal bristles absent, though

**Key to the Families of Diptera in the
United States and Canada** (*Contd.*)

KEY E: Suborder BRACHYCERA, Infraorder SCHIZOPHORA ACALYPTRATAE (*Contd.*)

hairlike setae or pile commonly present; form never antlike, always with 4 scutellar setae .. **59. Platystomatidae**

17(9). Vibrissa present, but sometimes weak in **96. Tethinidae** *18*

Vibrissa absent, but subvibrissal bristles sometimes vibrissalike in **86. Chyromyidae** and **57. Lonchaeidae** *24*

18(17). C with distinct humeral break in addition to subcostal break *19*

C with subcostal break only (includes **65. Clusiidae**) *21*

19(18). Arista broadly plumose; C extensively and strongly spinose; all tibiae with strong preapical dorsal bristle; medium-sized, yellowish flies, with strongly arched scutum .. **89. Curtonotidae**

Arista bare or with short hairlike setae; C not spinose; tibiae without preapical dorsal bristle; small to very small, mostly shining black flies, with normally arched scutum .. *20*

20(19). Gena broad, and with row of bristles in middle; proboscis with stout bulbous prementum and short inconspicuous labella; (in part) **75. Carnidae**

Gena usually narrow, but if broad, bristles confined to lower margin; proboscis with slender prementum and long conspicuous labella folded back along prementum; (in part) ... **74. Milichiidae**

21(20). Postocellar bristles divergent ... *22*

Postocellar bristles convergent or absent *23*

22(21). Front always with 3 to 5 strong, inclinate frontal bristles that are relatively similar to the 2 reclinate orbital bristles in size and spacing; (in part) **68. Agromyzidae**

Front seldom with any strong, inclinate frontal bristles, but if 1 or 2 present (*Actenoptera*), then these positioned distant from and inclined oppositely to the 2 lateroclinate orbital bristles ... **64. Piophilidae**

23(22). All tibiae without preapical dorsal bristle; C not spinose; A_1 fading out on apical third or more, never traceable to wing margin; vibrissa and postocellar bristles weakly differentiated to virtually absent; (in part) **96. Tethinidae**

All tibiae with preapical dorsal bristle; C spinose, except in some Heleomyzidae (*Borboropsis* and *Oldenbergiella*), in which A is traceable to wing; vibrissa and postocellar bristles strong **84. Heleomyzidae** and **85. Trixoscelididae**

24(17). Halteres black; anepisternum with row of strong bristles posteriorly; front, face, thorax, abdomen, and legs (exclusive of tarsi) black, usually with metallic reflections; stout, bristly flies with broad flat abdomen; female with lancelike ovipositor **57. Lonchaeidae**

Halteres usually whitish, but if blackish, then anepisternum without row of strong bristles, and/or head, thorax, abdomen, and legs not as extensively black; form variable; (includes **83. Chyromyidae, 63. Pallopteridae,** and **62. Richardiidae**); (in part) **58. Otitidae**

25(8). C without subcostal or humeral break; (includes **71. Aulacigastridae** (*Stenomicra*), **72. Periscelididae, 73. Asteiidae,** and **83. Chamaemyiidae** (*Paraleucopis*).

C with at least subcostal break present *26*

26(25). CuA_2 and A_1 absent or vestigial, never forming closed cell cup; cross vein bm-cu absent, making cells bm and dm confluent .. *27*

CuA_2 and A_1 present, always forming closed cell cup; cross vein bm-cu usually present, making cells bm and dm usually separate *29*

27(26). C with subcostal break only, without humeral break; CuA_1 usually with kink marking position of atrophied cross vein bm-cu; arista bare or micropubescent, plumose **94. Chloropidae**

C with both subcostal and humeral breaks; CuA_1 without kink; arista bare to long plumose .. *28*

28(27). Face strongly convex; subcranial cavity usually very large; postocellar bristles, if present, divergent ... **93. Ephydridae**

Face concave; subcranial cavity normal; postocellar bristles convergent or subparallel (includes *Carnus* and *Meoneura* of **75. Carnidae**) **92. Camillidae**

29(26). Vibrissa absent and gena without vibrissalike bristle; katepisternum without an outstanding bristle, though frequently setulose; mostly slender, rather fragile flies, with elongate wings .. *30*

Vibrissa present or gena with vibrissalike bristle; in either case, katepisternum always with one or more outstanding bristles; form variable (includes **71. Aulacigastridae**) *31*

30(29). Notopleuron usually with 2 bristles; anepisternum with an outstanding bristle, in addition to fine, hairlike setae; ocelli situated far forward, with anterior one about midway between vertex and antennae **54. Strongylophthalmyiidae**

Key to the Families of Diptera in the
United States and Canada *Contd.*)

KEY E: Suborder BRACHYCERA, Infraorder SCHIZOPHORA ACALYPTRATAE (*Contd.*)

Notopleuron with 1 bristle, the posterior one; anepisternum without bristle, with fine,
 hairlike setae only; ocelli situated near vertex, with anterior one on dorsal third of front
 .. **55. Psilidae**

31(29). C with both humeral and subcostal break ... *32*
 C with subcostal break only (includes **67. Odiniidae** and **69. Opomyzidae**) *35*

32(31). Long axis of antennae strongly elbowed, with flagellum distinctly decumbent; arista
 frequently long plumose (includes *Cinderella* of **84. Heleomyzidae, 91. Diastatidae**)
 .. **90. Drosophilidae**
 Long axis of antennae nearly straight, with flagellum more or less porrect; arista bare or
 shortly pubescent .. *33*

33(32). All fronto-orbital bristles uniformly oriented, essentially reclinate; interfrontal bristles
 weak and scattered; middle of face membranous and sunken, bearing some fine setulae
 on upper portion .. **50. Cypselosomatidae**
 Fronto-orbital bristles not uniformly directed, usually with some inclinate, some
 lateroclinate, some proclinate, and some reclinate; interfrontal bristles usually stronger
 and serially arranged; middle of face sclerotized and raised, usually bare *34*

34(33). Gena broad, with row of bristles in middle; proboscis with stout bulbous prementum and
 short inconspicuous labella; (in part) **75. Carnidae**
 Gena usually narrow, but if broad, then bristles confined to lower margin; proboscis with
 slender prementum and long, conspicuous labella folded back along prementum; (in
 part) ... **74. Milichiidae**

35(31). Postocellar bristles divergent, always present; (part) **86. Agromyzidae**
 Postocellar bristles convergent or absent .. *36*

36(35). Anepisternum bare; front femora usually with strongly developed ctenidial spine
 .. **70. Anthomyzidae**
 Anepisternum setulose; front femora usually without distinct ctenidial spine; (includes **96.**
 Tethinidae, in part) .. **86. Chyromyidae**

KEY F: Suborder BRACHYCERA, Infraorder SCHIZOPHORA-CALYPTRATAE

Superfamily HIPPOBOSCOIDEA

1. Wingless; head vertically oriented, folded back into groove on mesoscutum; 1st tarsomere of
 each tarsus very elongate, at least as long as remainder of tarsus; ectoparasites of bats
 .. **107. Nycteribiidae**
 Winged, wings either short or vestigial; head horizontally oriented, not folded back; 1st
 tarsomere of each tarsus short, subequal to 2nd tarsomere *2*

2(1). Compound eye large, horizontally oval, at least three-fourths as high as head, with at least 100
 very small facets; posterior wing veins weaker, less crowded, and more divergent than
 anterior ones; ectoparasitic on birds and mammals other than bats
 .. **106. Hippoboscidae**
 Compound eyes small or absent, but if present, rounded, never more than half as high as head,
 and with less than 40 relatively large, beadlike facets; wing veins relatively uniform in
 strength, dispersal, and arrangement; ectoparasitic on bats **108. Steblidae**

Suborder NEMATOCERA

These are the so-called "primitive" flies, characterized by longer
antennae with several flagellomeres and additional features as
cited in the preceding Key.

Infraorder TIPULOMORPHA

The following two families comprise this infraorder, each in a
separate superfamily:

Superfamily TANYDEROIDEA

1. TANYDERIDAE (Primitive Crane Fly Family)

Wingspan: 20–42 mm. Some resemblance to Crane Flies
but distinguished on the basis of wing venation characters (see
Key) and presumably not closely related to that family; wings

banded with brown. Larvae live in wet, sandy soil along larger
streams.

[1.1 *Protoplasa* Osten Sacken (1 sp., *P. fitchii* Osten Sacken [(1) n.e.
US; (2) s.e. US]); 1.2 *Protanyderus* Handlirsch (3 spp.)]

Superfamily TIPULOIDEA

2. TIPULIDAE (Crane Fly Family)

Length: Usually 10–25 mm (some only 6 mm and others
with wingspan up to 75 mm). Long-legged flies, somewhat
resembling mosquitoes, but without body scales. Usually
brownish, some with brown or black on wings. Mesothorax
with prominent V-shaped suture between wings, which is very
characteristic of the family and usually easily visible.

The larvae (called *leatherjackets*) are aquatic, semiaquatic,

or live in decaying vegetation; a few live under bark, some in fungi, and others are leaf feeders, particularly on violets.

The family—the largest family of Diptera—consists of 64 genera, numerous subgenera, and 1517 species in the U.S. and Canada. Few are pests and those that are are generally minor. Because few species are easy to recognize and few marked with distinctive patterns, no particular species may be termed common, although any particular region always offers a few that are frequently collected at lights at night.

Subfamily Tipulinae

Tribe Tipulini

[2.1. *Leptotarsus* Guérin-Meneville, subgenus *Longurio* Loew (4 spp.); 2.2 *Megistocera* Wiedemann (1 sp., *M. longipennis* (Macquart)); 2.3 *Brachypremna* Osten Sacken (1 s., *B. dispellens* (Walker))]

2.4 *Holorusia* Loew

One species, as follows:

H. rubiginosa Loew. The largest species of Crane Fly, with a wingspan of 75 mm. (3) CA.

[2.5 *Prionocera* Loew (16 spp.); 2.6 *Ctenophora* Meigen, with 3 subgenera: *Ctenophora* s. str. (2 spp.), *Tanyptera* Latreille (1 sp., *C. dorsalis* Walker), and *Phoroctenia* Coquillett (1 sp., *C. vittata angustipennis* Loew); 2.7 *Nephrotoma* Meigen (40 spp.); 2.8 *Dolichopeza* Curtis, with 2 subgenera: *Dolichopeza* s. str. (2 spp.) and *Oropeza* Needham (13 spp.)]

2.9 *Tipula* Linnaeus

This large genus is divided into the following 27 subgenera:

Trichotipula Alexander (30 spp.); *Schummelia* Edwards (7 spp.); *Nobilotipula* Alexander (2 spp.); *Bellardina* Edwards (5 spp.); *Triplicitipula* Alexander (23 spp.); *Nippotipula* Matsumura (1 sp., *T. abdominalis* (Say)); *Tipula* s. str. (1 sp., *T. paludosa* Meigen); *Setitipula* Alexander (3 spp.); *Platytipula* Matsumura (11 spp.); *Yamalotipula* Matsumura (51 spp.); *Tipulodinodes* Alexander (1 sp., *T. lacteipes* Alexander); *Beringotipula* Savtshenko (22 spp.); *Arctotipula* Alexander (17 spp.); *Pterelachisus* Rondani (39 spp.); *Angarotipula* Savtshenko (3 spp.); *Serratipula* Alexander (5 spp.); *Vestiplex* Bezzi (17 spp.); *Savtshenkia* Mannheims (9 spp.); *Odonatisca* Savlshenko (5 spp.); *Sinotipula* Alexander (17 spp.); *Nesotipula* Alexander (1 sp., *T. pribilovia* Alexander); *Labiotipula* Alexander (3 spp.); *Eremotipula* Alexander (25 spp.); *Eumicrotipula* Alexander (2 spp.); *Lunatipula* Edwards (160 spp.); *Hesperotipula* Alexander (18 spp.); *Lindneria* Mannheims (6 spp.).

T. cunctans Say (Smoky Crane Fly). L. 14–18 mm. Gray, thorax with brownish gray stripes; abdomen dark brown; wings lightly clouded. Larvae feed on roots of legumes; sometimes a pest. (1) n.e. US; (2) s.e. US; (5) CO, NE, IA, KS, MO.

T. illustris Doane (North Western Crane Fly). L. 15–22 mm. (See A&J 309.)

T. trivittata Say. L. 18–26 mm. Brownish; wings tinged with brown, particularly anteriorly. Larvae live in streams, debris, under stones, or in mud and gravel along shore. Adults common on woodland foliage near streams. (See Fig. 29.12.) (1) n.e. US; (2) s.e. US.

T. paludosa Meigen (European Crane Fly). L. 14–25 mm. This species invaded Washington state as a pest on lawns,

Fig. 29.12. (*From Curran, 1934*)

pastures, grains, and other crops in 1970. Also established in British Columbia, Newfoundland, and Nova Scotia, but apparently not a serious pest.

T. simplex Doane (Range Crane Fly). L. ±10 mm. Female nearly wingless, resembles a spider or daddy longlegs. Larvae a pest of range grasses, grain, and alfalfa.

Subfamily Cylindrotominae

[2.10 *Cylindrotoma* Macquart (3 spp.); 2.11 *Phalacrocera* Schiner (4 spp.); 2.12 *Liogma* Osten Sacken (1 sp., *L. nodicornis* (Osten Sacken)); 2.13 *Triogma* Schiner (1 sp., *T. exsculpta* Osten Sacken)]

Subfamily Limoniinae

Tribe Limoniini

[2.14 *Limonia* Meigen, with 9 subgenera: *Limonia* s. str., (12 spp.); *Idioglochina* Alexander (1 sp., *L. marmorata* (Osten Sacken)), *Metalimnobia* Matsumura (9 spp.), *Hesperolimonia* Alexander (1 sp., *L. infuscata* (Doane)), *Discobola* Osten Sacken (3 spp.), *Melanolimonia* Alexander (4 spp.); *Rhipidia* Meigen (8 spp.), *Dicranomyia* Stephens (72 spp.), *Alexandriaria* Garrett (4 spp.), and *Geranomyia* Haliday (14 spp.); 2.15 *Helius* Lepeletier and Serville (2 spp.); 2.16 *Antocha* Osten Sacken (7 spp.); 2.17 *Thaumastoptera* Mik (1 sp., *T. hynesi* Alexander; 2.18 *Elliptera* Schiner (6 spp.); 2.19 *Dicranoptycha* Osten Sacken (23 spp.); 2.20 *Orimarga* Osten Sacken, with 2 subgenera: *Orimarga* s. str. (4 spp.) and *Diotrepha* Osten Sacken (1 sp., *O. mirabilis* (Osten Sacken))]

Tribe Pediciini

[2.21 *Ula* Haliday (3 spp.); 2.22 *Pedicia* Latreille, with 3 subgenera: *Pedicia* s. str. (11 spp.), *Pentacyphona* Alexander (10 spp.), and *Tricyphona* Zetterstedt (44 spp.); 2.23 *Ornithodes* Coquillett (2 spp.); 2.24 *Nasiternella* Wahlgren (1 sp., *N. hyperborea* (Osten Sacken); 2.25 *Dicronota* Zetterstedt, with 7 subgenera: *Eudicranota* Alexander (4 spp.), *Rhaphidolabina* Alexander (1 sp., *D. flaveola* (Osten Sacken)), *Polyangaeus* Doane (4 spp.), *Dicranota* s. str. (11 spp.), *Paradicranota* Alexander (3 spp.), *Plectromyia* Osten Sacken (10 spp.), and *Rhaphidolabis* Osten Sacken (28 spp.)]

Tribe Hexatomini

[2.26 *Paradelphomyia* Alexander (11 spp.); 2.27 *Polymera* Wiedemann (2 spp.); 2.28 *Phyllolabis* Osten Sacken (12 spp.); 2.29 *Epiphragma* Osten Sacken (4 spp.); 2.30 *Austrolimnophila* Alexander, with 2 subgenera: *Austrolimnophila* s. str. (3 spp.) *Archilimnophila* Alex-

ander (3 spp.); 2.31 *Dactyloabis* Osten Sacken, with 2 subgenera: *Dactylolabis* s. str. (17 spp.) and *Eudactylolabis* Alexander (3 spp.); 2.32 *Pseudolimnophila* Alexander (5 spp.); 2.33 *Prolimnophila* Alexander (1 sp., *P. areolata* (Osten Sacken)); 2.34 *Limnophila* Macquart, with 14 subgenera: *Lasiomastix* s. str. (3 spp.), *Eutonia* Wulp (3 spp.), *Prionolabis* Osten Sacken (22 spp.), *Idiolimnophila* Alexander (1 sp., *L. emmelina* Alexander), *Eloeophila* Rondani (19 spp.), *Dicranophragma* Osten Sacken (2 spp.), *Afrolimnophila* Alexander (2 spp.), *Idioptera* Macquart (2 spp.), *Prionolabis* Osten Sacken (21 spp.), *Phylidorea* Bigot (40 spp.), *Arctolimnophila* Alexander (2 spp.), *Dendrolimnophila* Alexander (1 sp., *L. albomanicata* (Alexander), *Brachylimnophila* Alexander (2 spp.), and *Hesperolimnophila* Alexander (3 spp.); 2.35 *Shannonomyia* Alexander (3 spp.); 2.36 *Pilaria* Sintenis (11 spp.); 2.37 *Ulomorpha* Osten Sacken (8 spp.); 2.38 *Hexatoma* Latreille, with 2 subgenera: *Hexatoma* s. str. (2 spp.) and *Eriocera* Macquart (33 spp.); 2.39 *Ataba* Osten Sacken (4 spp.); 2.40 *Elephantomyia* Osten Sacken (2 spp.)]

Tribe Eriopterini

[2.41 *Cladura* Osten Sacken (5 spp.); 2.42 *Chionea* Dalman (8 spp.); 2.43 *Neolimnophila* Alexander (4 spp.); 2.44 *Gnophomyia* Osten Sacken (3 spp.); 2.45 *Eugnophomyia* Alexander (2 spp.); 2.46 *Idiognophomyia* Alexander (2 spp.); 2.47 *Gonomyia* Meigen, subgenus *Progonomyia* Alexander (4 spp.), with 7 subgenera: *Idiocera* Dale (17 spp.), *Euptilostena* Alexander (2 spp.), *Teuchogonomyia* Alexander (4 spp.), *Lipophleps* Bergroth (5 spp.), *Paralipophleps* Alexander (1 sp., *G. pleuralis* (Williston), *Neolipophleps* Alexander (3 spp.), and *Gonomyia* s. str. (25 spp.); 2.48 *Teucholabis* Osten Sacken (7 spp.); 2.49 *Rhabdomastix* Skuse, with 2 subgenera: *Rhabdomastic* s. str. (1 sp., *R. nuttingi* Alexander), and *Sacandaga* Alexander (25 spp.); 2.50 *Lipsothrix* Loew (6 spp.); 2.51 *Hesperoconopa* Alexander (5 spp.); 2.52 *Cryptolabis* Osten Sacken, subgenus *Cryptolabis* s. str. (11 spp.); 2.53 *Phantolabis* Alexander (1 sp., *P. lacustris* (Alexander)); 2.54 *Cheilotrichia* Rossi, with 2 subgenera: *Cheilotrichia* s. str. (1 sp., *C. alicia* (Alexander) and *Empeda* Osten Sacken (11 spp.); 2.55 *Gonempeda* Alexander (3 spp.); 2.56 *Gonomyodes* Alexander (4 spp.); 2.57 *Arctoconopa* Alexander (9 spp.); 2.58 *Empedomorpha* Alexander (1 sp., *E. empedoides* (Alexander)); 2.59 *Erioptera* Meigen, with 7 subgenera: *Trimicra* Osten Sacken (1 sp., *E. pilipes* (Fabricius)), *Symplecta* Meigen (4 spp.), *Erioptera* s. str. (29 spp.), *Mesocyphona* Osten Sacken (15 spp.), *Ilisia* Osten Sacken (5 spp.), *Hoplolabis* Osten Sacken (4 spp.), and *Psiloconopa* Zetterstedt (30 spp.); 2.60 *Ormosia* Rondani, with 5 subgenera: *Rhypholophus* Kolenati (10 spp.), *Scleroprocta* Edwards (3 spp.), *Ormosia* s. str. (75 spp.), *Oreophila* Lackschewitz (6 spp.), and *Parormosia* Alexander (7 spp.); 2.61 *Tasiocera* Skuse, subgenus *Dasymolophilus* Goetghebuer (5 spp.); 2.62 *Molophilus* Curtis, with 2 subgenera: *Promolophilus* Alexander (5 spp.) and *Molophilus* s. str. (40 spp.); 2.63 *Toxorhina* Loew (2 spp.); 2.64 *Gonomyopsis* Alexander (1 sp., *G. doaneiana* Alexander)]

Infraorder BLEPHARICEROMORPHA
Superfamily BLEPHARICEROIDEA

One family, as follows:

3. BLEPHARICERIDAE
(Net-winged Midge Family)

Length: 3–13 mm. Eye usually divided into upper region of larger facets and lower region of smaller facets. Legs long and slender, hind legs stouter than others. Larvae live attached by ventral suckers to rocks in rapidly flowing streams. Adults live near such streams. Some have a network of fine, veinlike lines on wings and hence their common name. The 24 U.S. species are nearly all western in distribution and rather uncommon.

Fig. 29.13. (*From Curran, 1934*)

3.1 *Agathon* Roeder

Three species, including the following:

A. elegantula Roeder. (See Fig. 29.13.) (4) NV, ID; (5) CO.

3.2 *Bibiocephala* Osten Sacken

One species, as follows:

B. grandis Osten Sacken. (5) MT, WY, CO.

3.3 *Blepharicera* Macquart

Eleven species, the following of which is fairly common:

B. separata Alexander. (1) n.e. US.

[3.4 *Dioptopsis* Enderlein (5 spp.); 3.5 *Philorus* Kellogg (4 spp.)]

Superfamily DEUTEROPHLEBIOIDEA

One family, as follows:

4. DEUTEROPHLEBIIDAE (Mountain Midge Family)

Length: 2–4 mm. Antennae of male about four times as long as body, minute in female, with four flagellomeres. Of the four species in the U.S., perhaps only one could be termed common.

4.1 *Deuterophlebia* Edwards

Four species, including the following:

D. coloradensis Pennack. Dark brown to black, with abdomen light brown in male and dark green in female. Mouthparts lacking. Wings silvery blue, nearly veinless but with fanlike folds. Larvae live in shallow portions of rapidly flowing, well-aerated mountain streams. (4) UT; (5) AB, MT, WY, CO.

Superfamily NYMPHOMYIOIDEA

One family, as follows:

5. NYMPHOMYIIDAE (Nymphomyiid Fly Family)

Length: 1.5–2.5 mm. Wings vestigial. Body long, slender, weakly sclerotized, sparsely setose; pale. Antennae with clavate

flagellum, annulated basally. One species of this very rare family of flies is known in U.S. and Canada.

5.1 *Palaeodipteron* Ide

One species only, as follows:

P. walkeri Ide. (1) QU, NB, ME.

Infraorder AXYMYIOMORPHA
Superfamily AXYMYIOIDEA

One family only, as follows:

6. AXYMYIIDAE (Axymyiid Fly Family)

[From Pachyneuridae of authors]

Length: ±7mm. Characteristics as given in the Key to Families. Family contains seven species with large eyes and short antennae and legs. Larvae live in rotting wood partially submerged in water and free of moss and bark. Extremely rare, with only one species described.

6.1 *Axymyia* McAtee

Two species, one in (4) AK, undescribed, and the second as follows:

A. furcata McAtee. (1) ON, QU, NY, PA, MD; (2) WV, VA, KY, TN, NC; (5) MN.

Infraorder BIBIONOMORPHA
Superfamily PACHYNEUROIDEA

One family only, as follows:

7. PACHYNEURIDAE (Pachyneurid Gnat Family)

Length: 5–6 mm. Body slender; legs long; wings long; resemblance to Crane Flies. Adults lay eggs on alder; larvae bore into rotten wood. The only species in the U.S. and Canada is very rare and poorly known.

7.1 *Cramptonomyia* Alexander

One species only, as follows:

C. spenceri Alexander. (4) BC, WA, OR.

Superfamily BIBIONOIDEA

One family only, as follows:

8. BIBIONIDAE (March Fly Family)

Length: 5–12 mm. Body usually dark, covered with long setae; characteristics as given in the Key. These flies frequent flowers, often in large numbers, in spring and summer. Although called *March flies*, they rarely appear in March, at least in the north unless an exceptional warm spell causes early blooming. Larvae feed on excrement, decaying roots, and logs; A few are of economic importance as root feeders. The 78 species are assigned to six genera, as follows:

Subfamily Hesperininae

[8.1 *Hesperinus* Walker (1 sp., *H. brevifrons* Walker)]

Subfamily Pleciinae

[8.2 *Penthetria* Meigen (1 sp., *P. heteroptera* (say)]

8.3 *Plecia* Wiedemann,

Two species, the following of which is locally a pest:

P. nearctica Hardy (Love Bug). L. 13–15 mm. Entirely black except thorax, which is dorsally reddish brown. Larvae occur in decaying vegetation, especially in hardwood hammocks. Adults (see Fig. 29.14.) fly in May and September. At times, large numbers flying in copula (see Fig. 29.15) and attracted to highways by car exhausts may smash on car windshields. When females hit a windshield, their eggs smear and impair driver's vision. This has become a great problem in many parts of the South. (See A&J 316.) (2) s.e. US.

Subfamily Bibioninae
8.4 *Bibio* Geoffroy

This is the largest genus, with 53 species in the U.S. and Canada. The following is a common example.

B. albipennis Say. L. 10–12 mm. Legs long and white. These insects are clumsy fliers, on the wing from May to August. They also visit flowers and are often taken by sweeping these plants, especially in gardens; occasionally they form clusters at windows. (1), (2), (3), (4), (5), generally distributed.

[8.5 *Bibiodes* Coquillett (3 spp.); 8.6 *Dilophus* Meigen (18 spp.)]

Superfamily SCIAROIDEA

Three families, as follows:

9. MYCETOPHILIDAE (Fungus Gnat Family)

Length: 2.2–13.5 mm. Bristles of the tibiae are often stout, usually with strong spurs. Body usually dull yellow, brown, or black, but a few brightly marked. Usually distinguished by very long coxae. Antennae, often sexually dimorphic, vary from

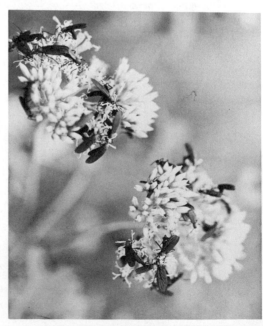

Fig. 29.14. (*Fla. Dept. of Agric.*)

Fig. 29.15. (*Fla. Dept. of Agric.*)

extremely short to extremely long, those of the male being long. Adults are found in shaded, humid woods.

Larvae of all of known species except those of the subfamily Keroplatinae live on forest fungus. All Keroplatinae larvae spin webs to trap prey. In New Zealand, one species produces such webs in caves. The famous Glowworm Cave, a well-known tourist attraction—has vast numbers of larvae—so many, in fact, that they light up this dark place with their glowing bodies. The light, apparently attracts insects to their web and provides their food. Some North American species also glow.

The 714 species are classified as follows:

Subfamily Bolitophilinae

[9.1 *Bolitophila* Meigen, with 2 subgenera: *Cliopisa* Enderlein (12 spp.) and *Bolitophila* s. str. (8 spp.)]

Subfamily Diadocidiinae

[9.2 *Diadocidia* Ruthe, with 2 subgenera: *Adidocidia* Lastovka and Matile (2 spp.) and *Diadocidia* s. str. (2 spp.)]

Subfamily Ditomyiinae

[9.3 *Ditomyia* Winnertz (2 spp.); 9.4 *Symmerus* Walker, with 2 subgenera: *Symmerus* s. str. (1 sp., *S. lautus* (Loew), and *Psilosymmerus* Munroe (3 spp.)]

Subfamily Keroplatinae

[9.5 *Asindulum* Latreille (1 sp., *A. montanum* Roeder); 9.6 *Fenderomyia* Shaw (1 sp., *F. smithi* Shaw); 9.7 *Hesperodes* Coquillett (1 sp., *H. johnsoni* Coquillett); 9.8 *Cerotelion* Rondani (1 sp., *C. johannseni* (Fisher)); 9.9 *Euceroplatus* Edwards (3 spp.); 9.10 *Heteropterna* Skuse (1 sp., *H. cressoni* (Fisher))]

9.11 *Keroplatus* Bosc

Four species, including the following:

K. carbonarius Bosc. L. 10–12 mm. Dark, with pale markings on legs; wings with a few dark patches. Larvae spin mucus webs to snare small insects and other small invertebrates for food. (1) IN, OH, PA, NJ, MD; (2) VA, NC.

[9.12 *Macrocera* Meigen (24 spp.)]

9.13 *Orfelia* Costa

Thirty-four species, including the following:

O. fultoni (Fisher). Larvae of this species produce luminescent webs. (2) VA, NC, SC.

[9.14 *Paleoplatyura* Meunier (3 spp.)]

Subfamily Lygistorrhininae

[9.15 *Platyura* Meigen (7 spp.); 9.16 *Robsonomyia* Matile and Vockeroth (1 sp., *R. reducta* Matile and Vockeroth); 9.17 *Macrorrhyncha* Winnertz (2 spp.); 9.18 *Lygistorrhina* Skuse (1 sp., *L. sanctaecatharinae* Thompson)]

Subfamily Manotinae

[9.19 *Manota* Williston (1 sp., unnammed)]

Subfamily Mycetophilinae

[9.20 *Allodia* Winnertz (17 spp.); 9.21 *Allodiopsis* Tuomikoski (4 spp.); 9.22 *Anatella* Winnertz (5 spp.); 9.23 *Tarnania* Tuomikoski (1 sp., *T. tarnanii* (Dziedzicki)); 9.24 *Brachypeza* Winnertz (3 spp.); 9.25 *Exechia* Winnertz (48 spp.); 9.26 *Exechiopsis* Tuomikoski (4 spp.); 9.27 *Rymosia* Winnertz (22 spp.); 9.28 *Stigmatomeria* Tuomikoski (1 sp., *S. crassicornis* (Stannius)); 9.29 *Pseudobrachypeza* Tuomikoski (1 sp., *P. bulbosa* (Johannsen)); 9.30 *Cordyla* Meigen (10 spp.); 9.31 *Brevicornu* Marshall (4 spp.); 9.32 *Dynatosoma* Winnertz (8 spp.); 9.33 *Macrobrachius* Dziedzicki (1 sp., *M. productus* (Johannsen)); 9.34 *Epicypta* Winnertz (2 spp.); 9.35 *Mycetophila* Meigen (97 spp.); 9.36 *Phronia* Winnertz (49 spp.); 9.37 *Sceptonia* Winnertz (2 spp.); 9.38 *Trichonta* Winnertz (46 spp.); 9.39 *Zygomyia* Winnertz (9 spp.)]

Subfamily Sciophilinae

[9.40 *Aphrastomyia* Coher and Lane (1 sp., unnamed); 9.41 *Boletina* Staeger (36 spp.); 9.42 *Coelosia* Winnertz (6 spp.); 9.43 *Dziedzickia* Johannsen (8 spp.); 9.44 *Gnoriste* Meigen (4 spp.); 9.45 *Hadroneura* Lundstroem (4 spp.); 9.46 *Speolepta* Edwards (1 sp., unnamed); 9.47 *Synapha* Meigen (3 spp.); 9.48 *Aglaomyia* Vockeroth (1 sp., *A. gatineau* Vockeroth); 9.49 *Acomoptera* (1 sp., *A. plexipus* (Garrett)); 9.50 *Drepanocercus* Vockeroth (1 sp., *D. ensifer* Vockeroth); 9.51 *Saigusaia* Vockeroth (1 sp., *S. cincta* Johannsen)); 9.52 *Mycomya* Rondani (61 spp.); 9.53 *Novakia* Strobl (1 sp., unnamed); 9.54 *Neoempheria* Osten Sacken (7 spp.); 9.55 *Loicia* Vockeroth (1 sp., *L. basifurca* Vockeroth); 9.56 *Acnemia* Winnertz (3 spp.); 9.57 *Allocotocera* Mik (1 sp., *A. pulchella* (Curtis)); 9.58 *Anaclileia* Winnertz (3 spp., unnamed)); 9.59 *Azana* Walker (1 sp., unnamed); 9.60 *Eudicrana* Loew (1 sp., *E. obumbrata* Loew); 9.61 *Adicroneura* Vockeroth (1 sp., *A. biocellata* Vockeroth); 9.62 *Leptomorphus* Curtis (7 spp.); 9.63 *Garrettella* Vockeroth (1 sp., *G. shermani* (Garrett)); 9.64 *Megalopelma* Enderlein (2 spp.); 9.65 *Apolephthisa* Grzegorzek (1 sp., unnamed); 9.66 *Monoclona* Mik (5 spp.); 9.67 *Greenomyia* Brunetti (2 spp.); 9.68 *Neuratelia* Rondani (14 spp.); 9.69 *Paratinia* Mik (1 sp., *P. recurva* Johannsen)); 9.70 *Phthinia* Winnertz (3 spp.); 9.71 *Polylepta* Winnertz (3 spp.); 9.72 *Sciophila* Meigen (23 spp.); 9.73 *Baeopterogyma* Vockeroth (1 sp., *B. nudipes* Vockeroth); 9.74 *Coelophthinia* Edwards (1 sp., *C. curta* (Johannsen)); 9.75 *Decosia* Winnertz (15 spp.); 9.76 *Acadia* Vockeroth (1 sp., *A. polypori* Vockeroth); 9.77 *Ectrepesthoneura* Enderlein (1 sp., *E. bicolor* (Coquillett)); 9.78 *Leia* Meigen (19 spp.); 9.79 *Megophthalmida* Dziedzicki (1 sp., *M. occidentalis* Johannsen); 9.80 *Rondaniella* Johannsen (1 sp., *R. dimidiata* (Meigen)); 9.81 *Tetragoneura* Winnertz (11 spp.); 9.82 *Syntemna* Winnertz (3 spp.); 9.83 *Cluzobra* Edwards (1 sp., unnamed)]

10. SCIARIDAE (Dark-winged Fungus Fly Family)

Length: 1–11 mm. Very similar to preceding family, but distinguished by position of the eyes, which meet above antennae, except in 10.18 (see below). Larvae live wherever fungus grows, including potted plants in homes. Some are pests of commercially grown mushrooms. Sometimes abundant enough to form a crawling mass of several inches across and several feet long, similar to armyworm migrations. The family contains 137 species assigned to 20 genera as follows:

[10.1 *Metangela* Ruebsaamen (1 sp., *M. toxoneura* (Osten Sacken); 10.2 *Odontosciara* Ruebsaamen (1 sp., *O. nigra* (Wiedemann)); 10.3 *Phytosciara* Frey, with 2 subgenera: *Dolichosciara* Tuomikoski (1 sp., *P. flavipes* (Meigen)) and *Prosciara* Frey (1 sp., unnamed); 10.4 *Sciara* Meigen (25 spp.); 10.5 *Eugnoriste* Coquillett (3 spp.); 10.6 *Rhynchosciara* Ruebsaamen (1 sp., *R. proboscidea* (Lengersdorf)); 10.7 *Pseudosciara* Schiner (1 sp., *P. forceps* (Pettey)); 10.8 *Zygoneura* Meigen (2 spp.); 10.9 *Corynoptera* Winnertz (6 spp.)]

10.10 *Lycoriella* Frey

The 14 species of this genus are known as Mushroom Flies. (See Fig. 29.16 for *Lycoriella* spp.) It is uncertain which species are of economic importance. This group was previously known as *Sciara* of authors, not Meigen (see 10.4 above).

[10.11 *Chaetosciara* Frey (1 sp., *C. joffrei* (Pettey))]

10.12 *Bradysia* Winnertz

Sixty-five species, including the following:

B. picea (Ruebsaamen). L. ±5 mm. Dark with large dusky wings. Larvae live in fungus. (2) s.e. US.

[10.13 *Scatopsciara* Edwards (5 spp.); 10.14 *Plastosciara* Berg (1 sp., *P. johnstoni* (Shaw)); 10.15 *Niadina* Rapp (1 sp., *N. jauva* Rapp); 10.16 *Epidapus* Haliday (2 spp.); 10.17 *Moehnia* Pritchard (1 sp., *M. erema* Pritchard)]

10.18 *Pnyxia* Johannsen

One species, as follows:

P. scabiei (Hopkins). (Potato Scab Gnat). L. ±4 mm. Body dark; eyes do not meet above antennae; compound eyes distinctly separated dorsally. Females wingless. Larvae bore into potatoes grown on low ground. (1), (2), (3), (4), (5), generally distributed.

[10.19 *Schwenkfledina* Frey (3 spp.); 10.20 *Scythropochroa* Enderlein (1 sp., unnamed)]

11. CECIDOMYIIDAE (Gall Midge Family)

Length: 1–5 mm (sometimes up to 8 mm). Frail flies with long legs and antennae; wings with reduced venation.

Larvae of at least 540 of the 1059 species known from the U.S. and Canada make galls on various plants. Many other species live in decaying organic matter; some are fungus feeders; some are predacious; a few are reported to be parasitic. Some may live as inquilines with ants and termites. Several species, as indicated, are destructive pests.

An interesting process termed *paedogenesis* occurs in the larvae of some of these flies. The larvae are capable of

Fig. 29.16. (*From Curran, 1934*)

reproducing themselves. A mature larva will form inside itself several daughter larvae, thereby multiplying in the larval stage. This phenomenon, which seems to occur only in fungus-feeding species, is a means of maximizing the production of adults to overcome some of the perils of not finding suitable fungus.

The gall-forming species are of considerable interest, not only because they are pests, but because of the complex relationships between the Gall Midges and the plant. The form of the gall is often characteristic of the species of fly causing the deformation. Other species of insects may invade the gall, moveover, and take over as a parasite on the Gall Midge larvae, or as a predator, and so on.

[Note: The arrangement of taxa in this list, which follows the key in McAlpine (1981), is not necessarily phylogenetic.]

Subfamily Lestremiinae

Tribe Baeonotini

[11.1 *Baenotus* Byers (1 sp., *B. microps* Byers)]

Tribe Micromyini

[11.2 *Monardia* Kieffer, with 3 subgenera: *Monardia* s. str. (4 spp.), *Xylopriona* Kieffer (4 spp.), and *Polyardis* Prichard (6 spp.); 11.3 *Mycophila* Felt (4 spp.); 11.4 *Bryomyia* Kieffer (4 spp.); 11.5 *Peromyia* Kieffer (5 spp.); 11.6 *Campylomyza* Meigen (7 spp.); 11.7 *Cordylomyia* Felt (6 spp.); 11.8 *Corinthomyia* Felt (1 sp., *C. brevicornis* (Felt)); 11.9 *Micromya* Rondani (2 spp.); 11.10 *Aprionus* Kieffer (4 spp.); 11.11 *Trichopteromyia* Williston (1 sp., *T. modesta* Williston)]

Tribe Lestremiini

[11.12 *Anarete* Haliday (11 spp.); 11.13 *Conarete* Pritchard (4 spp.); 11.14 *Wasmanniella* Kieffer (1 sp., *W. clauda* Pritchard); 11.15 *Gongromastix* Enderlein (2 spp.); 11.16 *Allarete* Pritchard (2 spp.); 11.17 *Anaretella* Enderlein (3 spp.); 11.18 *Lestremia* Macquart (3 spp.); 11.19 *Pararete* Pritchard (1 sp., *P. elongata* (Felt))]

Tribe Forbesomyiini

[11.20 *Forbesomyia* Malloch (1 sp., *F. atra* Malloch)]

Tribe Catotrichini

11.21 *Catotricha* Edwards

Two species, including the following:

C. americana (Felt). (See Fig. 29.17.) (1) NH.

Tribe Strobliellini

[11.22 *Strobliella* Kieffer (1 sp., *S. intermedia* Kieffer)]

Tribe Catochini

[11.23 *Anocha* Pritchard (2 spp.); 11.24 *Neocatocha* Felt (1 sp., *N. marilandica* Felt); 11.25 *Tritozyga* Loew (1 sp., *T. sackeni* Felt); 11.26 *Eucatocha* Edwards (2 spp.); 11.27 *Catocha* Haliday (1 sp., *C. slossonae* Felt)]

Subfamily Porricondylinae

Tribe Heteropezini

[11.28 *Henria* Wyatt (2 spp.); 11.29 *Miastor* Meinert (1 sp., *M. metroloas* Meinert); 11.30 *Heteropezina* Pritchard (1 sp., *H. cathistes* Pritchard); 11.31 *Heteropeza* Winnertz (2 spp.)]

Tribe Winnertziini

[11.32 *Kronomyia* Felt (1 sp., *K. populi* Felt); 11.33 *Winnertzia* Rondani (9 spp.); 11.34 *Parwinnertzia* Felt (1 sp., *P. notmani* Felt)]

Fig. 29.17. (*From Curran, 1934*)

Tribe Diallactini

[11.35 *Haplusia* Karsch (2 spp.)]

Tribe Asynaptini

[11.36 *Colomyia* Kieffer (1 sp., *C. hordei* Barnes); 11.37 *Camptomyia* Kieffer (8 spp.); 11.38 *Feltomyina* Alexander (3 spp.); 11.39 *Pseudo-camptomyia* Parnell (1 sp., *P. photophila* (Felt)); 11.40 *Asynapta* Loew (12 spp.); 11.41 *Parasynapta* Panelius (1 sp., *P. canadensis* (Felt))]

Tribe Dirhizini

[11.42 *Dirhiza* Loew (1 sp., *D. papillata* (Felt))]

Tribe Dicerurini

[11.43 *Dicerura* Kieffer (1 sp., *D. oregonensis* (Felt)); 11.44 *Tetraneuromyia* Mamaev (3 spp.); 11.45 *Neosynepidosis* Parnell (1 sp., *N. furcata* (Felt))]

Tribe Porricondylini

[11.46 *Solntsevia* Mamaev (1 sp., *S. maculata* (Felt)); 11.47 *Parepidosis* Kieffer (2 spp.); 11.48 *Holoneurus* Kieffer (3 spp.); 11.49 *Coccopsis* de Meijere (1 sp., *C. marginata* de Meijere); 11.50 *Didactylomyia* Felt (1 sp., *D. longimana* (Felt)); 11.51 *Porricondyla* Rondani (21 spp.); 11.52 *Claspettomyia* Grover (3 spp.); 11.53 *Neocolpodia* Mamaev (1 sp., *N. pinea* (Felt)); 11.54 *Isocolpodia* Parnell (3 spp.); 11.55 *Monepidosis* Mamaev (1 sp., *M. carolina* (Felt)); 11.56 *Schistoneurus* Mamaev (1 sp., *S. pectinata* (Felt)); 11.57 *Basicondyla* Parnell (1 sp., *B. fultonensis* (Felt)]

Subfamily Cecidomyiinae

Tribe Lasiopterini

[11.58 *Ozirhincus* Rondani (1 sp., *O. millefolii* (Wachtl)); 11.59 *Hybolasioptera* Ruebsaamen (1 sp., *H. elymi* Gagné); 11.60 *Lasioptera* Meigen (34 spp.); 11.61 *Protaplonyx* Felt (1 sp., *P. sarcobati* (Felt); 11.62 *Calamomyia* Gagné (18 spp.); 11.63 *Edestosperma* Gagné (1 sp., *E. aristidae* Gagné); 11.64 *Astictoneura* Gagné (1 sp., *A. muhlenbergiae* (Marten)); 11.65 *Edestochilus* Gagné (1 sp., *E. allioides* (Pritchard)); 11.66 *Chilophaga* Gagné (4 spp.); 11.67 *Asteromyia* Felt (8 spp.)]

11.68 *Neolasioptera* Felt

Fifty-seven species, the following of which is a pest:

N. murtfeldtiana (Felt) (Sunflower Seed Midge).

Tribe Stomatosematini

[11.69 *Stomatosema* Kieffer (3 spp.); 11.70 *Rhizomyia* Kieffer (8 spp.); 11.71 *Epimyia* Felt (1 sp., *E. carolina* Felt); 11.72 *Brachineura* Rondani (3 spp.)]

Tribe Asphondylliini

11.73 *Schizomyia* Kieffer

Twelve species, the following of which is a pest:

S. vitispomum (Osten Sacken) (Grape Apple Gall).

11.74 *Asphondylia* Loew

Fifty-four species, the following of which is a pest:

A. websteri Felt (Alfalfa Gall Midge).

[11.75 *Polystepha* Kieffer (16 spp.); 11.76 *Stephomyia* Taveres (1 sp., *S. eugeniae* Tavares); 11.77 *Bruggmannia* Tavares (1 sp., *B. pisonifolia* (Felt))]

Tribe Cecidomyiini

[11.78 *Coccidomyia* Felt (1 sp., *C. pennsylvanica* Felt); 11.79 *Aphidoletes* Kieffer (3 spp.); 11.80 *Harmandia* Kieffer (4 spp.); 11.81 *Tanaodiplosis* Gagné (1 sp., *T. androgynes* (Felt)); 11.82 *Dicrodiplosis* Kieffer (3 spp.); 11.83 *Feltiella* Ruebsaamen (14 spp.); 11.84 *Lobodiplosis* Felt (6 spp.); 11.85 *Karschomyia* Felt (10 spp.); 11.86 *Kalodiplosis* Felt (1 sp., *K. floridana* Felt); 11.87 *Diadiplosis* Felt (3 spp.)]

11.88 *Resseliella* Seitner

Fifteen species, the following of which is a pest:

R. clavula (Beutemueller) (Dogwood Clubgall Midge).

[11.89 *Plectrodiplosis* Gagné (1 sp., *P. fascipennis* Gagné); 11.90 *Bremia* Rondani (8 spp.); 11.91 *Ctenodactylomyia* Felt (1 sp., *C. watsoni* Felt); 11.92 *Pitydiplosis* Gagné (1 sp., *P. packardi* (Felt)); 11.93 *Homobremia* Kieffer (1 sp., *H. insolens* (Felt)); 11.94 *Youngomyia* Felt (1 sp., *Y. podophylli* (Felt)); 11.95 *Ancylodiplosis* Gagné (1 sp., *A. bryanti* (Felt)); 11.96 *Coquillettomyia* Felt (3 spp.); 11.97 *Glenodiplosis* Gagné (1 sp., *G. callipus* Gagné); 11.98 *Mycodiplosis* Ruebsaamen (7 spp.); 11.99 *Clinodiplosis* Kieffer (48 spp.); 11.100 *Planetella* Westwood (22 spp.); 11.101 *Parallelodiplosis* Ruebsaamen (15 spp.); 11.102 *Sequoiomyia* Moehn (1 sp., *S. taxodii* (Felt)); 11.103 *Taxodiomyia* Gagné (2 spp.); 11.104 *Silvestrina* Kieffer (1 sp., *S. cincta* (Felt)); 11.105 *Aphodiplosis* Gagné (1 sp., *A. triangularis* (Felt)); 11.106 *Cartodiplosis* Gagné (1 sp., *C. nyssaecola* (Beutenmueller)); 11.107 *Caryomyia* Felt (13 spp.)]

11.108 *Contarinia* Rondani

Sixty-one species, the following of which are pests:

C. catalpae (Comstock) (Catalpa Midge).

C. johnoni Felt (Grape Blossom Midge).

C. pyrivora (Riley) (Pear Midge).

C. sorghicola (Coquillett) (Sorghum Midge).

C. bromicola (Marikovskij and Agafonova) (Bromegrass Seed Midge).

C. vaccinii Felt (Blueberry Tip Midge).

C. juniperina Felt (Juniper Midge).

11.109 *Monarthropalpus* Ruebsaamen

One species, as follows:

M. buxi (Laboulbene) (Boxwood Leaf Miner).

[11.110 *Pinyonia* Gagné (1 sp., *P. edulicola* Gagné); 11.111 *Olpodiplosis* Gagné (1 sp., *O. helianthi* (Brodie)); 11.112 *Halodiplosis* Kieffer (1 sp., *H. sarcobati* (Felt))]

11.113 *Cecidomyia* Meigen

Eight species, the following of which is a pest:

　　C. resinicoloides Williams (Monterey-pine Resin Midge).

[11.114 *Pilodiplosis* Gagné (1 sp., *P. helianthibulla* (Walsh))]

11.115 *Thecodiplosis* Kieffer

Four species, the following of which is a pest:

　　T. pini resinosae Kearby (Red Pine Needle Midge).

[11.116 *Zeuxidiplosis* Kieffer (1 sp., *Z. giardi* (Kieffer))]

11.117 *Paradiplosis* Felt

Two species, the following of which are pests:

　　P. tumifex Gagné (Balsam Gall Midge).

[11.118 *Lobopteromyia* Felt (1 sp., *L. filicis* (Felt))]

11.119 *Prodiplosis* Felt

Six species, the following of which is a pest:

　　P. citrulli (Felt) (Cucurbit Midge).

[11.120 *Tropidiplosis* Gagné (1 sp., *T. pectinata* Gagné); 11.121 *Odontodiplosis* Felt (3 spp.); 11.122 *Adiplosis* (1 sp., *A. toxicodendri* (Felt)); 11.123 *Trisopsis* Kieffer (4 spp.); 11.124 *Dentifibula* Felt (1 sp., *D. viburni* (Felt)); 11.125 *Thamadiplosis* Gagné (1 sp., *T. magnicauda* Gagné); 11.126 *Pectinodiplosis* Felt (1 sp., *P. erratica* (Felt)); 11.127 *Endaphis* Kieffer (1 sp., unnamed); 11.128 *Thripsobremia* Barnes (1 sp., *T. quercifolia* (Felt)); 11.129 *Epidiplosis* Felt (1 sp., *E. sayi* Felt); 11.130 *Arthrocnodax* Ruebsaamen (3 spp.); 11.131 [number not used]; 11.132 *Lestodiplosis* Kieffer (47 spp.); 11.133 *Apagodiplosis* Gagné (1 sp., *A. papyriferae* (Gagné)); 11.134 *Putoniella* Kieffer (1 sp., *P. marsupialis* (Loew)); 11.135 *Blaesodiplosis* Gagné (3 spp.); 11.136 *Macrodiplosis* Kieffer (10 spp.); 11.137 *Obolodiplosis* Felt (1 sp., *O. robiniae* (Haldeman)); 11.138 *Ametrodiplosis* Ruebsaamen (1 sp., *A. dulichii* (Felt)); 11.139 *Hyperdiplosis* Felt (4 spp.); 11.140 *Giardomyia* Felt (5 spp.); 11.141 *Gongrodiplosis* Gagné (1 sp., *G. latipes* (Felt)); 11.142 *Platydiplosis* Gagné (1 sp., *P. nigricauda* Gagné); 11.143 *Cordylodiplosis* Gagne (1 sp., *C. molliterga* Gagné)]

11.144 *Sitodiplosis* Kieffer

One species, as follows:

　　S. mosellana (Géhin) (Wheat Midge).

Tribe Ledomyini

[11.145 *Ledomyia* Kieffer (16 spp.)]

Tribe Oligotrophini

[11.146 *Janetiella* Kieffer (8 spp.)]

11.147 *Mayetiola* Kieffer

Ten species, the following of which is of great economic importance:

　　M. destructor (Say) (Hessian Fly). L. ±3 mm. Body and wings dark. Larvae bore into grain stems, causing great economic loss in wheat, rye, and barley fields. Recently resistant varieties of these grains have been grown that seems to

Fig. 29.18. (*From Curran, 1934*)

minimize the loss. (See Fig. 29.18.) Occurs throughout (5) n. Central states, and wherever grain is grown.

　　M. rigidae (Osten Sacken) (Willow-beaker Gall Midge).

[11.148 *Trotteria* Kieffer (2 spp.); 11.149 *Camptoneuromyia* Felt (6 spp.); 11.150 *Procystiphora* Felt (2 spp.)]

11.151 *Rhabdophaga* Westwood

Thirty-eight species, the following of which are of some economic importance:

　　R. salicisbatatas (Osten Sacken) (Willow Stem Gall).

　　R. strobiloides (Osten Sacken) (Willow Cone Gall).

　　R. swainei Felt (Spruce Bud Midge).

11.152 *Dasineura* Rondani

Ninety-five species, the following of which are pests:

　　D. gibsoni Felt. (See Fig. 29.19.) (1) ON, IN.

　　D. leguminicola (Lintner) (Clover Seed Midge).

　　D. rhodophaga (Coquillett) (Rose Midge).

　　D. trifolii (Loew) (Clover Leaf Midge).

Fig. 29.19. (*From Curran, 1934*)

[11.153 *Lygocecis* Gagné (2 spp.); 11.154 *Sackenomyia* Felt (3 spp.); 11.155 *Cystiphora* Kieffer (1 sp., *C. canadensis* Felt); 11.156 *Ficiomyia* Felt (2 spp.); 11.157 *Walshomyia* Felt (5 spp.)]

11.158 *Rhopalomyia* Ruebsaamen

This genus is divided into two subgenera: *Rhopalomyia* s. str. (56 spp.) and *Diarthronomyia* Felt (30 spp). The following are of economic importance:

R. solidaginis (Loew) (Goldenrod Gall Midge).

R. chrysanthemi (Ahlberg) (Chrysanthemum Gall Midge).

[11.159 *Iteomyia* Kieffer (1 sp., *I. salicifolia* (Felt))]

11.160 *Oligotrophus* Latreille

One species, as follows:

O. betheli Felt (Juniper Tip Midge).

[11.161 *Semudobia* Kieffer (5 spp.)]

Infraorder PSYCHODOMORPHA
Superfamily PSYCHODOIDEA

One family, as follows:

12. PSYCHODIDAE (Moth and Sand Fly Family)

Length: 1.5–4 mm. Body and wings covered with hairlike setae. These very "hairy" flies hold their wings rooflike over the body and at first sight might be confused with tiny moths. They are weak, erratic fliers that live in shady places but are also attracted to lights at night and may enter homes. Adults of some are bloodsuckers and disease vectors. Some larvae live in decaying vegetation; others in water, particularly in drains and sewers, including household sink drains and septic tanks. Ninety species occur in the U.S. and Canada.

Subfamily Trichomyiinae

[12.1 *Trichomyia* Haliday (3 spp.)]

Subfamily Phlebotominae

12.2 *Lutzomyia* Franca

Nine species, the following of which is common:

L. vexator Coquillett. A common blood-sucking species. (1) MD; (2) s.e. US; (3) s.w. US.

Subfamily Bruchomyiinae

[12.3 *Nemopalpus* Macquart (1 sp., *N. nearcticus* Young)]

Subfamily Psychodinae

[12.4 *Maruina* Mueller (3 spp.)]

12.5 *Telmatoscopus* Eaton

Seventeen species, the following of which is a common pest:

T. albipunctatus (Williston). L. ±4 mm. Resembles a tiny grayish moth, with white antennae and white spots on edges of wings and tips of leg segments. Larvae frequently found breeding in sinks, drains, and other containers filled with decaying debris.

[12.6 *Brunettia* Annandale (2 spp.); 12.7 *Trichopsychoda* Tonnoir (1 sp., *T. insulicola* (Quate)); 12.8 *Philosepedon* Eaton (5 spp.); 12.9

Threticus Eaton (2 spp.); 12.10 *Eurygarka* Quate (1 sp., *E. helicis* (Dyar)); 12.11 *Psychoda* Latreille (21 spp.); 12.12 *Pericoma* Walker, with 2 subgenera: *Pericoma* s. str. (23 spp.) and *Clytocerus* Eaton (1 sp., *P. americana* Kincaid); 12.13 *Breviscapus* Quate (1 sp., *B. trilobus* (Kincaid))]

Superfamily TRICHOCEROIDEA

One family only, as follows:

13. TRICHOCERIDAE (Winter Crane Fly Family)

Wingspan: 5–12 mm. Resemblance to true Crane Flies (Tipulidae), but head with ocelli, which are absent in Tipulidae. Common name refers to their habit of swarming in late winter (early spring). Larvae are saprophytic on decaying vegetation; some are reported to infest stored potatoes. Most of the 29 species have a northern distribution.

[13.1 *Diazosoma* Bergroth (1 sp., *D. hirtipennis* (Siebke)]

13.2 *Trichocera* Meigen

Twenty-seven species, including the following:

T. bimacula Walker. Common. (1) n.e. NA.

[13.3 *Paracladura* Brunetti (1 sp., *P. trichoptera* (Osten Sacken))]

Superfamily ANISOPODOIDEA

One family, as follows:

14. ANISOPODIDAE (Wood Gnat Family)

Length: 2–10 mm. Body slender with long slender legs; head with 3 ocelli; antennae relatively long. These flies somewhat resemble mosquitoes but have spots on their wings and lack scales. They may be found on tree trunks in forests and sometimes fly in swarms. Larvae of some live in fermenting sap, others in manure, but most in decaying vegetation. Nine species in the U.S. and Canada, as follows:

Subfamily Anisopodinae

14.1 *Sylvicola* Harris

Five species, including the following:

S. fenestralis (Scopoli) (Wood Gnat). Very common in wooded areas. (1), (2), (3), (4), (5), widespread.

14.2 *Olbiogaster* Osten Sacken

Three species, the following of which is common:

O. taeniata (Bellardi). (1) FL; (3) TX.

Subfamily Mycetobiinae

[14.3 *Mycetobia* Meigen (1 sp., *M. divergens* Walker)]

Superfamily SCATOPSOIDEA

Two families, as follows:

15. SCATOPSIDAE (Minute Black Scavenger Fly Family)

Length: 0.6–4 mm. Brown, gray, or black, sometimes yellow, dull to shining. Widely distributed in the U.S. and

Canada, only a few of these little known flies are known from their larvae. These are found in decaying animal and plant vegetation, in manure, and under bark. The 72 species in 16 genera are classified as follows:

Subfamily Scatopsinae

Tribe Rhegmoclematini

[15.1 *Rhegmoclema* Enderlein (6 spp.); 15.2 *Rhegmoclemina* Enderlein, with 2 subgenera: *Rhegmoclemina* s. str. (3 spp.) and *Neorhegmoclemina* Cook (2 spp.); 15.3 *Parascatopse* Cook (3 spp.)]

Tribe Scatopsini

[15.4 *Colobostema* Enderlein (4 spp.)]

15.5 *Scatopse* Geoffroy

Three species, including the following:

S. fuscipes Meigen. Cosmopolitan. (See Fig. 29.20.)

[15.6 *Reichertella* Enderlein (3 spp.); 15.7 *Apiloscatopse* Cook (3 spp.); 15.8 *Swammerdamella* Enderlein (10 spp.)]

15.9 *Coboldia* Melander

One species, as follows:

C. fuscipes (Meigen). Very common; larvae found in all kinds of decaying plant and animal material. Cosmopolitan.

[15.10 *Quateiella* Cook (2 spp.); 15.11 *Rhexoza* Enderlain (10 spp.)]

Subfamily Aspistinae

[15.12 *Aspistes* Meigen (4 spp.); 15.13 *Arthria* Kirby (3 spp.)]

Subfamily Ectaetiinae

[15.14 *Ectaetia* Enderlein (2 spp.)]

Subfamily Psectrosciarinae

[15.15 *Psectrosciara* Kieffer (10 spp.); 15.16 *Anapsusis* Enderlein (3 spp.)]

16. SYNNEURIDAE (Synneurid Gnat Family)

Length: 2–3.5 mm. Dark brown to black; palpi erect, four-segmented; antennae with 10 to 14 beadlike flagellomeres. Larvae live in decaying wood. The family consists of the following two species:

[16.1 *Exiliscelis* Hutson (1 sp., *E. californiensis* Hutson); 16.2 *Synneuron* Lundstroem (1 sp., *S. decipiens* Hutson)]

Fig. 29.20. (*From Curran, 1934*)

Infraorder PTYCHOPTEROMORPHA
Superfamily PTYCHOPTEROIDEA

One family only, as follows:

17. PTYCHOPTERIDAE
(Phantom Crane Fly Family)

Length: 6.14 mm. Head without ocelli; antennae long, with multisegmented flagellum; legs long, sometimes with conspicuous bands of white; body and legs long and slender. These flies resemble Crane Flies but are far removed from that family on basis of wing venation. Larvae are aquatic or semiaquatic, found in debris in stagnant or nearly stagnant water. The 16 species are assigned to two genera as follows:

Subfamily Ptychopterinae

[17.1 *Ptychoptera* Meigen (10 spp.)]

Subfamily Bittacomorphinae

[17.2 *Bittacomorphella* Alexander (4 spp.)]

17.3 *Bittacomorpha* Westwood

Two species, as follows:

B. occidentalis Aldrich. L. ±8 mm. Legs black with white bands; hind tarsi swollen. Adults fly about swampy places along gorges; on the wing from May to September. Larvae are aquatic. (See A&J 310.) (3) CA; (4) WA, OR.

B. clavipes Fabricius. L. 10–14 mm. Similar to the preceding. (1) n.e. NA; (2) s.e. US; (3) AZ, NM, TX, OK; (5) MB, SK, MT, ND, SD, MN, WY, NE, IA, CO, KS, MO.

Infraorder CULICOMORPHA

Two superfamilies, as follows:

Superfamily CULICOIDEA

Three closely related families, as follows:

18. DIXIDAE (Dixid Midge Family)

Length: 4.5–7 mm. Body fragile; brown, black, or yellow; legs and antennae long. These flies closely resemble mosquitoes but lack the long proboscis and body scales. Larvae are aquatic. (See Fig. 29.21 for *Dixia* spp.) The 42 species known from the

Fig. 29.21. (*From Curran, 1934*)

U.S. and Canada are mostly northern in distribution and not widespread.

18.1 *Dixella* Dyar and Shannon

Nineteen species, the following being widespread:

 D. nova Walker. (1) n.e. NA; (4) Pacific n.w.; (5) n. Central States.

[18.2 *Meringodixa* Nowell (1 sp., *M. chalonensis* Nowell); 18.3 *Dixa* Meigen (22 spp.)]

19. CHAOBORIDAE (Phantom Midge Family)

Length: 1.5–10 mm. Body fragile; pale yellow, gray, or brown; ocelli absent; antennae plumose in male, simple in female. This family also closely resembles the mosquitoes but lack a proboscis and have only marginal wing scales. The aquatic larvae are transparent, hence their common name, and predacious. Many species are northern in distribution. The 19 species are classified in five genera as follows:

Subfamily Chaoborinae

19.1 *Chaoborus* Lichtenstein

This genus is divided into three subgenera: *Chaoborus* s. str. (3 spp.), *Schadonophasma* Dyar and Shannon (2 spp.), and *Sayomyia* Coquillett (5 spp.). The following two species are common:

 C. flavicans (Meigen). (1) n.e. NA; (3) n. CA; (4) Pacific n.w.; (5) n. Central states.

 C. astictopus Dyar and Shannon (Clear Lake Gnat). (3) CA; (4) OR.

19.2 *Mochlonyx* Loew

Three species, including the following:

 M. cinctipes (Coquillett). (See Fig. 29.22.) (1) n.c. NA; (2) s.e. US; (4) WA, OR.

Subfamily Eucorethrinae

[19.3 *Eucorethra* Underwood (1 sp., *E. underwoodi* Underwood)]

Subfamily Corethrellinae

[19.4 *Lutzomiops* Lane (1 sp., *L. kerrvillensis* Stone); 19.5 *Corethrella* Coquillett (4 spp.)]

Fig. 29.22. (*From Curran, 1934*)

20. CULICIDAE (Mosquito Family)

Length: 3–9 mm. Mosquitoes are easily recognized by their long proboscis, scaly wings and body, and plumose (male; see Fig. 29.28) or hairy (female; see Fig. 29.29) antennae. Many tropical species (where the greatest number of species occur) are beautifully marked with white, silver, green, or iridescent blue, rarely red, scales. Several species in the U.S. and Canada are brightly marked.

Larvae of all species are aquatic, most of them algae feeders but some predacious, the latter feeding on other mosquito larvae, other insects, and other small invertebrates in aquatic situations. They occupy all aquatic habits, mostly pools and quiet water, but also flowing water, leaf bracts, tree holes, and even sea water along the shore, including crab holes and holes in rocks. Unlike those of most insects, the pupae are active aquatic organisms, capable of submerging in water and swimming with a characteristic bobbing motion; they do not feed.

Adults are notorious disease transmitters. Males do not take blood but feed apparently on nectar and sap. Females of most species "bite" (suck blood of) animals, including reptiles, amphibians, birds, and mammals. A few species, as indicated, do not take blood meals. Females also feed on nectar and sap; their blood meals are apparently for use in the manufacture of eggs.

The 150 species recorded in the U.S. and Canada are arranged in 13 genera as follows:

Subfamily Anophelinae

20.1 *Anopheles* Meigen

This genus contains several subgenera, the following two of which occur in North America: *Anopheles* Meigen (13 spp.) and *Nyssorhynchus* Blanchard (1 sp., *A. albimanus* Weidemann). The following species are important disease vectors.

 A. quadrimaculatus Say (Common Malaria Mosquito). Wingspan: ±10 mm. Easily recognized by its tilted stance and four patches of dark scales on each wing. Adults hide in dark outbuildings and cellars and may be found flying during the winter even in the North in these locations if they are warm. Females bite at night. Larvae live in permanent fresh water streams, ponds, lakes, and similar habitats with vegetation present. Adults appear in July and fly until it is cold enough to hibernate. This species is the vector of malaria in the U.S., although at present this disease has been eliminated in our country. Common. (See A&J 313.) (1) n.e. NA; (2) s.e. US; (3) AZ, MN, TX, OK; (5) MT, ND, MN, SD, WY, NE, IA, CO, KS, MO.

 A. albimanus Wiedemann. Similar to the preceding but with different wing markings. A vector of malaria in Central America, this species reaches the U.S. (2) FL; (3) s. TX.

 A. punctipennis (Say). (See Fig. 29.23 for the female.) (1), (2), (3), (4), (5).

Subfamily Toxorhynchitinae

20.2 *Toxorhynchites* Theobald

These large mosquitoes do not take blood meals. Their proboscis is curved downward and is inflexible. The one species in the U.S. and Canada is assigned to the subgenus *Lynchiella* Lahille.

Fig. 29.23. (*From Matheson, 1944*)

T. rutilus (Coquillett) (Elephant Mosquito). Length: ±12 mm. Body is covered with shiny metallic blue scales. Larvae live in tree holes, artificial containers, and bracts of bromeliads. Larvae predacious on other mosquitoes and have been used for the biological control of certain species on an experimental basis. (See A&J 312.) (2) SC, GA, FL.

Subfamily Culicinae

Tribe Sabethini

20.3 *Wyeomyia* Theobald

This genus is the only representative in the U.S. and Canada of a large group of tropical species that live in leaf and flower bracts, tree holes, palm spathes, and similar organic aquatic habitats. Our species are in the subgenus *Wyeomyia* s. str. and live in pitcher plants. There are four species, the most common of which follows:

W. (W.) smithii (Coquillett) (Pitcher-plant Mosquito). L. ±4 mm. This tiny mosquito is brightly colored with silver scales on the thorax. The female is a painful biter, seemingly preferring knuckles, which then swell and ache instead of itch. Larvae live in the water in pitcher plants and are not harmed by the digestive fluids secreted by the plant.

Tribe Culicini

20.4 *Mansonia* Blanchard

Two species belong in this genus, assigned to the subgenus *Mansonia* s. str. Larvae attach themselves to aquatic plants and obtain their oxygen from plant tissues instead of rising to the surface for air as do other mosquito larvae.

[20.5 *Coquillettidia* Dyar, subgenus *Coquillettidia* s. str. (1 sp., *C. perturbans* (Walker)); 20.6 *Uranotaenia* Lynch Arribalzaga (3 spp.)]

20.7 *Orthopodomyia* Theobald

Four species. Larvae usually live in tree holes but may be found in foul water such as sewerage.

20.8 *Psorophora* Robineau-Desvoidy

The genus is divided into three subgenera as follows: *Psorophora* s. str. (2 spp), *Janthinosoma* Lynch Arribalzaga (7 spp.),

and *Grabhamia* Theobold (4 spp.). The following species is common:

P. ciliata (Fabricius) (Gallinipper). Wingspan: 8–9 mm. Body dark; head and thorax with patches of white and yellow scales; abdomen with patches of purplish blue, iridescent scales. Adult females are ferocious biters. Larvae develop rapidly in temporary rain pools. This species is sometimes a serious pest mosquito. (1) n.e. US; (2) s.e. US; (3) AZ, NM, TX, OK; (5) NE, IA, KS, MO.

20.9 *Aedes* Meigen

This large genus is divided into the following six subgenera: *Aedes* s. str. (1 sp., *A. cinereus* Meigen), *Stegomyia* (1 sp., *A. aegypti* (Linnaeus), *Finlaya* Theobald (5 spp.), *Aedimorphus* (1 sp., *A vexans* (Meigen), *Ochlerotatus* Lynch Arribalzaga (59 spp.), and *Kompia* Aitken (1 sp., *A. purpureipes* Aitken). The following species are common:

A. (Ochlerotatus) sticticus (Meigen) (Floodwater Mosquito). Wingspan: 7–9 mm. Body dark with front legs dark with white scales; head, thorax, and hind legs light; abdomen with narrow basal bands of white scales. Adults fly from May to October. Eggs laid on dry margins of pools; larvae hatch when these pools are flooded. Common in wooded areas, especially in river valleys. (1), (2), (3), (4), (5), throughout U.S.

A. (Ochlerotatus) taeniorhynchus (Wiedemann) (Black Salt Marsh Mosquito). Wingspan ±7 mm. Brown; proboscis black with white ring at middle; abdomen black, each segment with narrow basal band of yellowish white scales and small white patch on each side near middle; legs black with hind tarsal segments each with broad basal white band and last segment usually entirely white; middle and front tarsi with narrow basal bands, the last two segments entirely black. A pest mosquito along coastal areas. (See A&J 311.) (1) n.e. US; (2) s.e. US; (3) CA.

Additional *Aedes* that are pest mosquitoes follow:

A. (Ochlerotatus) aboriginis Dyar (Northwest Coast Mosquito).

A. (Ochlerotatus) cantator (Coquillett) (Brown Salt Marsh Mosquito).

A. (Ochlerotatus) sierrensis (Ludlow) (Western Treehole Mosquito).

A. (Ochlerotatus) sollicitans (Walker) (Salt Marsh Mosquito).

A. (Ochlerotatus) squamiger (Coquillett) (California Salt Marsh Mosquito).

A. (Stegomyia) aegypti (Linnaeus) (Yellowfever Mosquito). One of the best known insects since it is the vector of yellow fever. At present, both this disease and mosquito have been eradicated from the U.S. and Canada, but it continues to transmit the disease elsewhere. It is cosmopolitan. Larvae live only in artificial containers near habitations. Until recently, it was widely used as an experimental mosquito in various laboratories. (See Fig. 29.24 for female.)

A. (Aedimorphus) vexans (Meigen) (Vexans Mosquito). (See Fig. 29.25 for male; Fig. 29.26 for female.)

[20.10 *Haemagogus* Williston, subgenus *Longipalpifer* Levi-Costillo (1 sp., *H. equinus* Theobald); 20.11 *Culisetia* Felt (9 spp.)]

Fig. 29.24. (*From Matheson, 1944*)

Fig. 29.25. Adult male: MXP, Maxillary palpus; PB, proboscis; ANT, antenna. (*From Matheson, 1944*)

Fig. 29.26. Adult female. (*From Matheson, 1944*)

20.12 *Culex* Linnaeus

This genus is divided into several subgenera. Our species are in following three subgenera: *Culex* s. str. (13 spp.), *Neoculex* Dyar (5 spp.), and *Melanoconion* Theobald (9 spp.). The following species are common:

C. pipiens pipiens Linnaeus (Northern House Mosquito). Wingspan: 8–9 mm. Brownish; abdomen dark with pale basal bands broadly joined to white lateral patches. Larvae found in foul water in artificial containers, sewage, and waste contaminated run-off. Common pest mosquito. (1) n.e. NA; (4) Pacific n.w.; (5) n. Central States.

C. pipiens quinqufasciatus Say (Southern House Mosquito). Wingspan: 8–9 mm. Very similar to the preceding but pale bands on abdominal tergites are narrowly joined or entirely disconnected from lateral patches. Larvae in same situations as the preceding. Common pest mosquito. (2) s.e. US; (3) s.w. US.

20.13 *Deinocerites* Theobald

Larvae live in crab holes along ocean beaches. Three species, as follows:

D. cancer Theobald (Crab-hole Mosquito). (2) FL.

D. pseudes Dyar and Knab. (3) TX.

D. mathesoni Belkin and Hogue. (3) TX.

Superfamily CHIRONOMOIDEA

Four families, as follows:

21. THAUMALEIDAE (Solitary Midge Family)

Length: 2–4.5 mm. Shiny yellow to dark brown. Rather rare flies, with distribution limited to the northern U.S. and Canada. Larvae occur on rocks in flowing water; adults often found nearby. Seven species in the U.S. and Canada, as follows.

21.1 *Thaumalea* Ruthe

Six species, the following of which is common:

T. americana Bezzi. (1) n.e. NA; (2) VA, NC.

[21.2 *Trichothaumalea* Edwards (1 sp., *T. pluvialis* Dyar and Shannon)]

22. SIMULIIDAE (Black Fly Family)

Length: 1–5.5 mm. Variously called Black Flies, Buffalo Gnats, and Turkey Gnats, these flies are usually black or dark brown, stout, with short antennae, humpbacked, short-legged; wings with anterior veins strong, posterior veins weak. Adult females of many species bite people.

Groups of black larvae are found on rocks, sticks, and leaves in shallow, swift-flowing water and cling by means of hooks at hind end of body; they also have a front pair of appendages to use when crawling.

In tropical Africa and Central America, they are the vectors of onchocerciasis, or river blindness, a disease that has inflicted a large proportion of the population of West Africa. Not involved in human disease transmission in the U.S. but often severe pests in some parts of this country and in Canada. The 143 species belong to the following 11 genera:

Subfamily **Parasimuliinae**

[22.1 *Parasimulium* Malloch, with 2 subgenera: *Parasimulium* s. str. (3 spp.) and *Astoneomyia* Peterson (1 sp., *P. melanderi* Stone)]

Subfamily **Simuliinae**

[22.2 *Gymnopais* Stone (5 spp.); 22.3 *Twinnia* Stone and Jamnback (3 spp.)]

22.4 *Prosimulium* Roubaud

The genus is divided into the following four subgenera: *Prosimulium* s. str. (32 spp.), *Helodon* Enderlein (6 spp.), *Parahelodon* Peterson (3 spp.), and *Distosimulium* Peterson (1 sp., *P. pleurale* Malloch). The following species is common:

P. exigens Dyar and Shannon. L. 2–4.5 mm. These flies crawl over the face, neck, and hands, and may bite. They are found flying over streams in May and June. (4) Pacific n.w.

22.5 *Simulium* Latreille

The genus is divided into the following 11 subgenera: *Eusimulium* Roubaud (20 spp.), *Byssodon* Enderlein (1 sp., *S. meridionale* Riley), *Psilopelmia* Enderlein (6 spp.), *Psilozia* Enderlein (3 spp.), *Hemicnetha* Enderlein (2 spp.), *Phosterodoros* Stone and Snoddy (12 spp.), *Simulium* s. str. (17 spp.), *Parabyssodon* Rubtzov (1 sp., *S. transiens* Rubtzov), *Ectemnaspis* Enderlein (1 sp., unnamed), *Shewellomyia* Peterson (2 spp.), and *Hearlea* Vargas, Martinez, and Diaz (1 sp., *S. canadense* Hearle). The following species are common:

S. meridionale Riley (Turkey Gnat). L. ±2 mm. A pest of turkeys and other fowl. Common. (1), (2), (3), (4), (5), throughout US.

S. vittatum Zetterstedt. Common. (1), (2), (3), (4), (5), throughout US.

S. nigricoxum stone. (See Fig. 29.27.) (4) AK; (5) NT.

S. aureum Fries. L. 3–4 mm. Common. (1), (2), (3), (4), (5). throughout US. (A&J 315).

S. pictipes Hagen. Does not bite humans but is very common in certain areas. (1) n.e. US; (2) s.e. US.

[22.6 *Greniera* Doby and David (4 spp.); 22.7 *Mayacnephia* Wygodzinsky and Coscaron (4 spp.); 22.8 *Stegopterna* Enderlein (2 spp.); 22.9 *Metacnephia* Crosskey (7 spp.); 22.10 *Ectemnia* Enderlein (4 spp.)]

22.11 *Cnephia* Enderlein

Four species, the following of which is a pest:

C. pecuarum (Riley) (Southern Buffalo Gnat). L. ±2.5 mm. A pest of poultry. (1) IL, IN, OH, PA, NJ, MD; (2) s.e. US; (3) TX.

23. CERATOPOGONIDAE (Biting Midge Family)

Length: 1–6 mm (rarely larger). Females bite vertebrates, other insects, or are predatory. Abundant near water, these flies are vectors of such human diseases as filariasis and a number of diseases of domestic animals. They are sometimes called Punkies, No-see-'ums (because of their small size), or Sand Flies. Some species are ectoparasitic on large insects such as dragonflies; a few visit flowers for nectar. Larvae breed in decaying plant material or are aquatic or semiaquatic. The

Fig. 29.27. (*From Cameron, 1918*)

family contains 463 species in 36 genera in the U.S. and Canada, as follows:

Subfamily **Leptoconopinae**

[23.1 *Leptoconops* Skuse, with 4 subgenera: *Leptoconops* s. str. (6 spp.), *Holoconops* Kieffer (15 spp.), *Brachyconops* Wirth and Atchley (1 sp., *L. californiensis* Wirth and Atchley), and *Magaconops* Wirth and Atchley (1 sp., *L. floridensis* Wirth)]

Subfamily **Forcipomyiinae**

[23.2 *Atrichopogon* Kieffer, with 3 subgenera: *Atrichopogon* s. str. (18 spp.), *Meloehelea* Wirth (3 spp.), and *Psilokempia* Enderlein (3 spp.); 23.3 *Forcipomyia* Meigen, with 12 subgenera: *Pterobosca* Macfie (1 sp., *F. fusicornis* (Coquillett), *Lasiohelea* Kieffer (1 sp., *F. fairfaxensis* Wirth), *Thyridomyia* Saunders (7 spp.), *Synthyridomyia* Saunders (4 spp.), *Metaforcipomyia* Saunders (1 sp., *F. pluvialis* Malloch), *Caloforcipomyia* Saunders (1 sp., *F. glauca* Macfie), *Forcipomyia* s. str. (30 spp.), *Warmkea* Saunders (2 spp.), *Blantonia* Wirth and Dow (1 sp., *F. caribbea* Wirth and Dow), *Trichohelea* Goetghebuer (9 spp.), *Euprojoannisia* Bréthes (14 spp.), and *Microhelea* Kieffer (2 spp.)]

Subfamily **Dasyheleinae**

[23.4 *Dasyhelea* Kieffer (37 spp.)]

Subfamily **Ceratopogoninae**

Tribe **Culicoidini**

23.5 *Culicoides* Latreille

This genus contains several pests. It is divided into the following subgenera: *Culicoides* s. str. (15 spp.), *Hoffmania* Fox (2 spp.), and *Avaritia* Fox (8 spp.), as well as the following nine subgenera that contain a total of 93 spp.: *Wirthomyia* Vargas, *Oecacta* Poey, *Callotia* Vargas and Kremer, *Drymodesmyia* Vargas, *Haematomyidium* Goeldi, *Diphaomyia* Vargas, *Beltranmyia* Vargas (8 spp.), *Monoculicoides* Khalaf (3 spp.), and *Selfia* Khalaf (7 spp.).

One common pest species, as follows:

C. furens (Poey) (Salt Marsh Punkie). L. 2–2.5 mm. Dark with white markings on thorax; wing "pictured," dark with transparent spots. Adults are severe biters and a serious pest. Larvae occur in salt marshes. (See Fig. 29.28 for female.) (1) MA, RI, CT, s. NY, NJ, DE, MD; (2) VA, NC, SC, GA, FL, AL, MS, LA; (3) TX.

[23.6 *Paradasyhelea* Macfie (1 sp., *C. olympiae* Wirth and Blanton)]

Tribe **Ceratopogonini**

[23.7 *Ceratopogon* Meigen (4 spp.); 23.8 *Isohelea* Kieffer (3 spp.); 23.9 *Brachypogon* Kieffer (2 spp.); 23.10 *Rhynchohelea* Wirth and Blanton (1 sp., *R. monilicornis* Wirth and Blanton); 23.11 *Alluaudomyia* Kieffer (8 spp.); 23.12 *Ceratoculicoides* Wirth and Ratanaworabhan (3 spp.)]

Fig. 29.28. (*From Blanton and Wirth, 1979*)

Tribe Stilobezzini

[23.13 *Stilobezzia* Kieffer, with 3 subgenera: *Stilobezzia* s. str. (14 spp.), *Neostilobezzia* Goetghebuer (3 spp.), and *Eukraiohelea* Ingram and Macfie (1 sp., *E. elegantula* (Johannsen)); 23.14 *Echinohelea* Macfie (1 sp., *E. lanei* Wirth); 23.15 *Monohelea* Kieffer, with 2 subgenera: *Monohelea* s. str. (15 spp.) and *Schizohelea* Kieffer (1 sp., *M. leucopeza* (Meigen); 23.16 *Serromyia* Meigen (3 spp.); 23.17 *Parabezzia* Malloch (14 spp.)]

Tribe Heteromyiini

[23.18 *Clinohelea* Kieffer (7 spp.); 23.19 *Heteromyia* Say (2 spp.); 23.20 *Neurohelea* Kieffer (2 spp.); 23.21 *Neurobezzia* Wirth and Ratanaworabhan (1 sp., *N. granulosa* (Wirth)); 23.22 *Pellucidomyia* Macfie (1 sp., *P. wirthi* (Lane))]

Tribe Sphaeromiini

[23.23 *Johannsenomyia* Malloch (2 spp.); 23.24 *Jenkinshelea* Macfie (4 spp.); 23.25 *Probezzia* Kieffer (19 spp.); 23.26 *Sphaeromias* Curtis (2 spp.); 23.27 *Nilobezzia* Kieffer (4 spp.); 23.28 *Mallochohelea* Wirth (11 spp.); 23.29 *Macropeza* Meigen (1 sp., *M. blantoni* Wirth and Ratanaworabhan)]

Tribe Stenoxenini

[23.30 *Stenoxenus* Coquillett (1 sp., *S. johnsoni* Coquillett); 23.31 *Paryphoconus* Enderlein (1 sp., *P. sonorensis* Wirth and Ratanaworabhan)]

Tribe Palpomyiini

[23.32 *Pachyhelea* Wirth (1 sp., *P. pachymera* (Williston)); 23.33 *Palpomyia* Meigen (31 spp.); 23.34 *Bezzia* Kieffer (42 spp.); 23.35 *Phaenobezzia* Haeselbarth (1 sp., *P. opaca* (Loew))]

24. CHIRONOMIDAE (Midge Family)

Length: 1–10 mm. Antennae of male plumose, of female filiform; proboscis lacking; wings narrow; male abdomen long and slender, female stouter. These midges are often seen, especially in early spring or in autumn, in immense swarms, dancing in the air. Although doubtless thought by many to be mosquitoes, which they resemble, they do not bite. While at rest, they usually raise their front legs and keep them constantly vibrating.

Most larvae are aquatic, and many live in tubes in soft mud. A few species live in the littoral zone of the sea, but most are confined to fresh water habitats, ranging from swift flowing mountain streams to lakes. A few species are leaf miners of aquatic plants.

The classification of the family has been somewhat confused, and there are many undescribed species. The following classification, which includes 817 species in 139 genera, is the most recent, given in McAlpine (1981).

Subfamily Podonominae

Tribe Podonomini

[24.1 *Parochlus* Enderlein (1 sp., *P. kiefferi* (Garrett))]

Tribe Boreochlini

[24.2 *Lasiodiamesa* Kieffer (4 spp.); 24.3 *Trichotanypus* Kieffer (5 spp.); 24.4 *Boreochlus* Edwards (3 spp.)]

Subfamily Tanypodinae

Tribe Coelotanypodini

[24.5 *Clinotanypus* Kieffer (5 spp.); 24.6 *Coelotanypus* Kieffer (6 spp.)]

Tribe Tanypodini

[24.7 *Tanypus* Meigen (11 spp.)]

Tribe Macropelopiini

[24.8 *Procladius* Skuse (42 spp.); 24.9 *Parapelopia* Roback (1 sp., *P. serta* Roback); 24.10 *Macropelopis* Thienemann (1 sp., *M. decedens* (Walker)); 24.11 *Alotanypus* Roback (2 spp.); 24.12 *Derotanypus* Roback (2 spp.); 24.13 *Natarsia* Fittkau (2 spp.); 24.14 *Psectrotanypus* Kieffer (7 spp.)]

Tribe Pentaneurini

[24.15 *Ablabesmyia* Johannsen (18 spp.); 24.16 *Conchapelopia* Fittkau (11 spp.); 24.17 *Telopelopia* Roback (1 sp., *T. okoboji* (Walley)); 24.18 *Thienemannimyia* Fittkau (7 spp.); 24.19 *Xenopelopia* Fittkau (1 sp., *X. tincta* Roback); 24.20 *Arctopelopia* Fittkau (4 spp.); 24.21 *Cantopelopia* Roback (1 sp., *C. gesta* Roback); 24.22 *Nilotanypus* Kieffer (2 spp.); 24.23 *Guttipelopia* Fittkau (2 spp.); 24.24 *Larsia* Fittkau (6 spp.); 24.25 *Trissopelopia* Kieffer (1 sp., *T. ogemawi* Roback); 24.26 *Pentaneura* Philippi (2 spp.); 24.27 *Zavrelimyia* Fittkau (3 spp.); 24.28 *Krenopelopia* Fittkau (1 sp., *K. narda* Roback); 24.29 *Paramerina* Fittkau (5 spp.); 24.30 *Monopelopia* Fittkau (2 spp.); 24.31 *Labrundinia* Fittkau (6 spp.)]

Subfamily Diamesinae

[24.32 *Protanypus* Kieffer (3 spp.); 24.33 *Boreoheptagyia* Brundin (1 sp., *B. lurida* (Garrett)); 24.34 *Pseudodiamesa* Goetghebuer (3 spp.); 24.35 *Pagastia* Oliver (2 spp.); 24.36 *Hesperodiamesa* Sublette (1 sp., *H. sequax* (Garrett)); 24.37 *Diamesa* Meigen (30 spp.); 24.38 *Potthastia* Kieffer (2 spp.); 24.39 *Sympotthastia* Pagast (1 sp., *S. fulva* (Johannsen)); 24.40 *Odontomesa* Pagast (1 sp., *O. lutosopra* (Garrett)); 24.41 *Prodiamesa* Kieffer (2 spp.); 24.42 *Monodiamesa* Kieffer (4 spp.)]

Subfamily Chironominae

Tribe Chironomini

[24.43 *Xenochironomus* Kieffer (6 spp.)]

24.44 *Glyptotendipes* Kieffer

Thirteen species, including the following:

G. paripes (Edwards). L. ±6 mm. Body gray. Adults found on vegetation near water; fly from May to August. Larvae are blood red with black eye spots; found in polluted water. Very common. (1) n.e. US; (2) s.e. US.

[24.45 *Cryptochironomus* Kieffer (6 spp.); 24.46 *Demicryptochironomus* Lenz (1 sp., *D. cuneata* (Townes)); 24.47 *Microchironomus* Kieffer (1 sp., *M. nigrovittatus* (Mallock)); 24.48 *Cryptotendipes* Lenz (3 spp.); 24.49 *Parachironomus* Lenz (16 spp.); 24.50 *Paracladopelma* Harnisch (11 spp.); 24.51 *Harnischia* Kieffer (2 spp.); 24.52 *Cladopelma* Kieffer (7 spp.); 24.53 *Kiefferulus* Goetghebuer (1 sp., *K. dux* (Johannsen)); 24.54 *Dicrotendipes* Kieffer (9 spp.); 24.55 *Einfeldia* Kieffer (7 spp.)]

24.56 *Chironomus* Miegen

Twenty-five species, including the following:

C. attenuatus Walker (Common Midge). L. 5–5.5 mm. Pale green to light brown; thorax and abdomen marked with dark bands; wings pale brown. Larvae are scavengers. Adults are attracted to lights at night in great numbers. One of the most common and widespread species of this family. (See A&J 314.) (1), (2), (3), (4), (5), generally distributed.

[24.57 *Goeldichironomus* Fittkau (1 sp., *G. holoprasinus* (Goeldi)); 24.58 *Microtendipes* Kieffer (4 spp.); 24.59 *Paralauterborniella* Lenz (3 spp.); 24.60 *Pseudochironomus* Malloch (11 spp.); 24.61 *Omisus* Townes (1 sp., *O. pica* Townes); 24.62 *Paratendipes* Kieffer (6 spp.); 24.63 *Nilothauma* Kieffer (3 spp.); 24.64 *Lauterborniella* Bause (3 spp.); 24.65 *Stenochironomus* Kieffer (11 spp.); 24.66 *Endochironomus* Kieffer (2 spp.); 24.67 *Graceus* Goetghebuer (1 sp., unnamed); 24.68 *Polypedilum* Kieffer (40 spp.); 24.69 *Phaenopsectra* Kieffer (8 spp.); 24.70 *Stictochironomus* Kieffer (13 spp.); 24.71 *Pagastiella* Brundin (1 sp., *P. ostansa* (Webb)); 24.72 *Tribelos* Townes (6 spp.); 24.73 *Pedionomus* Sublette (1 sp., *P. beckae* Sublette)]

Tribe Tanytarsini

[24.74 *Corynocera* Zetterstedt (2 spp.); 24.75 *Lenziella* Kieffer (1 sp., *L. cruscula* Saether); 24.76 *Zavrelia* Kieffer (1 sp., unnamed); 24.77 *Micropsectra* Kieffer (15 spp.); 24.78 *Stempellina* Bause (4 spp.); 24.79 *Rheotanytarsus* Bause (3 spp.); 24.80 *Lauterbornia* Kieffer (2 spp.); 24.81 *Paratanytarsus* Bause (5 spp.); 24.82 *Cladotanytarsus* Kieffer (1 sp., *C. viridiventris* Malloch); 24.83 *Tanytarsus* Wulp (20 spp.)]

Subfamily Orthocladiinae

[24.84 *Oreadomyia* Kevan and Cutten-Ali-Khan (1 sp., *O. albertae* Kevan and Cutten-Ali-Khan); 24.85 *Thalassosmittia* Strenzke and Remmert (3 spp.); 24.86 *Clunio* Haliday (1 sp., *C. marshalli* Stone and Wirth); 24.87 *Eretmoptera* Kellogg (1 sp., *E. browni* Kellogg); 24.88 *Tethymyia* Wirth (1 sp., *T. aptena* Wirth); 24.89 *Corynoneura* Winnertz (20 spp.); 24.90 *Thienemanniella* Kieffer (4 spp.); 24.91 *Symbiocladius* Kieffer (1 sp., *S. equitans* Claassen); 24.92 *Heleniella* Gowin (1 sp., *H. curtistila* Saether); 24.93 *Acricotopus* Kieffer (2 spp.); 24.94 *Plecopteracoluthus* Steffan (1 sp., *P. downsi* Steffan); 24.95 *Diplocladius* Kieffer (1 sp., *D. cultriger* Kieffer); 24.96 *Smittia* Holmgren (20 spp.); 24.97 *Eukiefferiella* Thienemann (9 spp.); 24.98 *Paratrichocladius* Santos Abreu (2 spp.); 24.99 *Mesocricotopus* Brundin (1 sp., *M. thienemanni* (Goetghebuer); 24.100 *Nanocladius* Kieffer (13 spp.); 24.101 *Rheocricotopus* Thienemann and Harnisch (9 spp.); 24.102 *Paracricotopus* Thienemann and Harnisch (1 sp., unnamed); 24.103 *Paracladius* Hirvenoja (2 spp.); 24.104 *Halocladius* Wulp (50 spp.); 24.105 *Cricotopus* Wulp (50 spp.); 24.106 *Eurycnemus* (1 sp., *E. annuliventris* (Malloch); 24.107 *Brillia* Kieffer (6 spp.); 24.108 *Paraphaenocladius* Thienemann (5 spp.); 24.109 *Heterotrissocladius* Spaerck (6 spp.);

24.110 *Metriocnemus* Wulp (14 spp.); 24.111 *Parametriocnemus* Goetghebuer (5 spp.); 24.112 *Pseudorthocladius* Goetghebuer (3 spp.); 24.113 *Heterotanytarsus* Spaerck (2 spp.); 24.114 *Gymnometriocnemus* Goetghebuer (2 spp.); 24.115 *Cardiocladius* Kieffer (3 spp.); 24.116 *Abiskomyia* Edwards (1 sp., unnamed); 24.117 *Psectrocladius* Kieffer (19 spp.); 24.118 *Limnophyes* Eaton (20 spp.); 24.119 *Parachaetocladius* Wuelker (2 spp.); 24.120 *Synorthocladius* Thienemann (1 sp., *S. semivirens* (Kieffer)); 24.121 *Clinocladius* Sublette (1 sp., *C. subparallelus* (Malloch)); 24.122 *Chaetocladius* Kieffer (6 spp.); 24.123 *Platycladius* Sublette (1 sp., *P. pleuralis* (Malloch)); 24.124 *Baeoctenus* Saether (1 sp., *B. bicolor* Saether); 24.125 *Orthocladius* Wulp (20 spp); 24.125a *Psilometriochemus* Saether (1 sp., *P. triannulatus* Saether); 24.126 *Oliveria* Saether (1 sp., *O. tricornis* (Oliver)); 24.127 *Zalutschia* Lipina (7 spp.); 24.128 *Hydrobaenus* Fries (13 spp.); 24.129 *Bryophaenocladius* Thienemann (5 spp.); 24.130 *Chasmatonotus* Loew (12 spp.); 24.131 *Krenosmittia* Thienemann (2 spp.); 24.132 *Pseudosmittia* Goetghebuer (1 sp., *P. setavena* Saether); 24.133 *Physoidella* Saether (1 sp., *P. dentolatens* Saether); 24.134 *Parakiefferiella* Thienemann (2 spp.); 24.135 *Epoicocladius* Zavrel (1 sp., *E. flavens* (Malloch)); 24.136 *Mariocladius* Sublette (1 sp., *M. subaterrumus* (Malloch))]

Subfamily Telomatogetoninae

[24.137 *Thalassomyia* Schiner (1 sp., *T. bureni* Wirth); 24.138 *Paraclunio* Kieffer (3 spp.); 24.139 *Telmatogeton* Schiner (2 spp.)]

Suborder BRACHYCERA

The remaining families, which represent the majority of the species, belong in this suborder. These are the flies with no more than three antennal segments but with an arista (terminal or dorsal) or a stylus.

Infraorder TABANOMORPHA

Two superfamilies, the Tabanoidea and Stratiomyoidea, belong to this infraorder, as follows:

Superfamily TABANOIDEA

The following four families are assigned to this superfamily. They are stocky flies, including the horse flies and similar kinds.

25. PELECORHYNCHIDAE (Pelecorhynchid Fly Family)

Length: 4–18 mm. Brown to black; clypeus and parafacial usually strongly swollen and convex; antennae porrect with stylate flagellum; legs with empodia pulvilliform. Larvae found in wet soil; predacious. Adults known to feed on nectar. This rare family contains eight species, as follows:

[25.1 *Glutops* Burgess (7 spp.)]

25.2 *Bequaertomyia* Brennan

One species, as follows:

B. jonesi (Cresson). Coal black; wings smoky; antennae and palpi orange. (3) CA; (4) BC, WA, OR.

26. TABANIDAE (Horse Fly and Deer Fly Family)

Length: 6–30 mm (rarely larger). Body without bristles; antennae with flagellum annulated; calpyteres large; legs with empodia pulvilliform. The distinctive shape of members of this family make them easy to recognize. Their habit of flying around one's head, always just beyond reach, and biting one's back is within the experience of most people. They range in

color from black to pale yellow, usually with stripes on the abdomen, and often with green (whence the frequent name "greenheads") or purple eyes. The eyes, which are very large, and comprise most of the head, are separated above in the female but meet dorsally in the male. Males feed on nectar and are seldom seen. Most adult females feed on the blood of mammals and birds. They may become a serious pest of livestock.

The larvae are predacious, and if not aquatic, live in moist soil near water. They hibernate as mature larvae, pupate, and emerge in late spring and early summer.

It is said that the Declaration of Independence was signed by July 4, 1776 instead of at a later date that would have permitted further discussion because the horse flies in Philadelphia were biting so fiercely at the time that the delegates decided to adjourn just to get away from them.

The 350 species occurring in the U.S. and Canada are classified as follows:

Subfamily Pangoniinae

Tribe Scionini

[26.1 *Goniops* Aldrich (1 sp., *G. chrysocoma* (Osten Sacken))]

Tribe Pangoniini

[26.2 *Asaphomyia* Stone (2 spp.); 26.3 *Brennania* Philip (2 spp.); 26.4 *Apatolestes* Williston (13 spp.); 26.5 *Esenbeckia* Rondani (4 spp.); 26.6 *Pilimas* Brennan (3 spp.); 26.7 *Stonemyia* Brennan (5 spp.)]

Subfamily Chrysopsinae

Tribe Bouvieromyiini

[26.8 *Merycomyia* Hine (2 spp.)]

Tribe Chrysopsini

[26.9 *Neochrysops* Walton (1 sp., *N. globosus* Walton); 26.10 *Silvius* Meigen, with 4 subgenera: *Silvius* s. str., (2 spp.), *Griseosilvius* Philip (9 spp.), *Assipala* Phillip (1 sp., *S. ceras* (Townsend), and *Zeuximyia* Philip (1 sp., *S. philipi* Pechuman)]

26.11 Chrysops Meigen

These are the Deer Flies. The genus is divided into two subgenera: *Chrysops* s. str. (100 spp.) and *Liochrysops* Philip (1 sp., *C. hyalinus* Shannon). The following species are common:

C. callidus Osten Sacken. L. 7–9 mm. Black, with middorsal yellow triangles on abdomen and large pale yellow spots on sides near base; wings with characteristic brown markings. Adults, which fly from May to September, are found in damp woodlands, buzzing about and biting warm-blooded animals. (1), (2), (3), (4), (5), generally distributed.

C. carbonarius Walker. L. 7–9 mm. Black with yellow-gray and green-gray markings; wings with characteristic black markings. Habits similar to the preceding species. (1), (2), (3), (4), (5), generally distributed.

C. niger Macquart (Black Deer Fly). L. 6.5–8.5 mm. Black with some white pubescence; wings with characteristic black markings. (1) n.e. US; (2) s.e. US; (5) ND, SC, MN, CO, NE, KS, MO.

C. vittatus Wiedemann. L. 6.5–10 mm. Yellow; abdomen with four dorsal black stripes; wings with characteristic black markings. (1) n.e. US; (2) s.e. US; (5) MN.

C. flavidus Wiedemann. L. 8–12 mm. Brown to black with light tan markings; wings with characteristic black markings.

Bite is painful. (See A&J 321.) (1), MI, ON, VT, NH, MA, OH, PA, NY, NJ, MD; (2) s.e. US; (3) TX.

Tribe Haematopotini

[26.12 *Haematopota* Meigen (5 spp.)]

Tribe Diachlorini

[26.13 *Bolbodimyia* Bigot (1 sp., *B. atrata* (Hine)); 26.14 *Holcopsis* Enderlein (4 spp.); 26.15 *Microtabanus* Fairchild (1 sp., *M. pygmaeus* (Williston)); 26.16 *Chlorotabanus* Lutz (1 sp., *C. crepuscularis* (Bequaert)); 26.17 *Diachlorus* Osten Sacken (1 sp., *D. ferrugatus* (Fabricius)); 26.18 *Leucotabanus* Lutz (2 spp.); 26.19 *Anacimas* Enderlein (2 spp.); 26.20 *Stenotabanus* Lutz, with 2 subgenera: *Stenotabanus* s. str. (3 spp.) and *Aegialomyia* Philip (4 spp.)]

Tribe Tabanini

[26.21 *Agkistrocerus* Philip (2 spp.); 26.22 *Hamatabanus* Philip (3 spp.)]

26.23 Hybomitra Enderlein

These are the "greenheaded" horse flies. Sixty species, including the following:

H. lasiophthalma (Macquart). L. 13–14 mm. Eyes purple with green bands; head brown; apical half of the abdomen brown; wings with small brown spots. Adults fly from May to September, usually near water; males may be found on flowers. These flies bite wet skin in particular. (1), (2), (3), (4), (5), widespread.

[26.24 *Atylotus* Osten Sacken (12 spp.); 26.25 *Whitneyomyia* Bequaert (1 sp., *W. beatifica* (Whitney))]

26.26 Tabanus Linnaeus

The genus is divided into two subgenera in the U.S. and Canada: *Tabanus* s. str. (100 spp.) and *Glaucops* Szilady (1 sp., *T. fratellus* Williston). The following species, which usually lack wing markings, are common:

T. americanus Forester. L. 22–28 mm. Thorax and abdomen reddish brown; wings clear except along costal cell. (A&J 320.) (1) n.e. US; (2) s.e. US; (3) TX.

T. atratus Fabricius (Black Horse Fly). L. 20–25 mm. Entirely black. (1), (2), (3), (4), (5), throughout US.

T. lineola Fabricius (Striped Horse Fly). L. ±12 mm. Gray; head brown; abdomen with narrow, median dorsal, pale stripe. (1) n.e. US; (2) s.e. US; (3) TX.

T. nigrovittatus Macquart (Greenhead). (1) NB, NF, ME, MA, RI, CT, s. NY, NJ, DE, MD; (2) VA, NC, SC, GA, FL, AL, MS, LA, TX.

T. punctifer Osten Sacken. L. ±10 mm. Pale gray; mesonotum with fine grayish pile; abdomen and wings black. Adults are blood suckers and prey upon horses, mules, and pack donkeys, but not man (See A&J 319.) (3) s.w. US; (4) Pacific n.w.; (5) MT, WY, CO.

T. sulcifrons Macquart. (See Fig. 29.29.)

27. ATHERICIDAE (Athericid Fly Family)

[From Rhagionidae of authors]

Length: 7–8 mm. Fuscous to black with fasciated abdomen. Found on vegetation near streams. Female of *Suragina* a

Fig. 29.29. (*U.S. Dept. of Agric.*)

bloodsucker on cattle and man. Larvae aquatic. Six species, as follows:

[27.1 *Atherix* Meigen (3 spp., widely distributed.); 27.2 *Suragina* Walker (3 spp., (3) s. w. TX)]

28. RHAGIONIDAE (Snipe Fly Family)

L. 2–25 mm. Black or gray, sometimes with yellow thoracic markings and sometimes with dark spots on wings; antennae with single terminal bristle (stylus); legs rather long; abdomen cone-shaped, tapering toward apex. Adults are predacious, found on grass stems and tree trunks resting head down. A few species bite man. Larvae found in decaying wood, under bark, in burrows of wood-boring insects, in moss, and occasionally in water. They are predacious. Most of the 104 species that occur in the U.S. and Canada have rather restricted distribution; less than half are eastern. Many are locally common, and most of these are quite similar in appearance.

[28.1 *Litoleptis* Chillcott (1 sp., *L. alaskensis* Chillcott); 28.2 *Bolbomyia* Loew (4 spp.); 28.3 *Ptiolina* Zetterstedt (12 spp.); 28.4 *Spania* Meigen (1 sp., *S. nigra americana* Johnson); 28.5 *Arthroceras* Williston (4 spp.); 28.6 *Symphoromyia* Frauenfeld (29 spp., unassigned to the following five subgenera: *Symphoromyia* s. str., *Axinicera* Turner, *Paraphoromyia* Becker, *Pogonaria* Becker, and *Ochleromyia* Turner)]

28.7 *Rhagio* Fabricius

Twenty-five species; the following of which is common:

R. mystacea (Macquart) (Snipe Fly). L. 7–16 mm. Yellow; eyes large and reddish brown; pronotum yellow with four dark brown stripes; basal portion of each segment of abdomen dark brown; apical portion of each segment of legs dark. Adults common in woods, especially near moist places, and may be found on foliage, in long grass, and on tree trunks. (See A&J 322.) (1) n.e. US; (2) s.e. US.

28.8 *Chrysopilus* Macquart

Thirty-two species; the following of which is common:

C. ornatus (Say). Found in damp woods on foliage of undergrowth during June and July. (1) n.e. US; (2) s.e. US; (5) MN, KS.

Superfamily STRATIOMYOIDEA

Three families are assigned to this superfamily.

29. XYLOPHAGIDAE (Xylophagid Fly Family)

Length: 2–25 mm. Slender, somewhat resembling some parasitic wasps; body without bristles or noticeable hairlike setae; black, sometimes marked with yellow, or completely yellow. Adults, which are extremely variable in size, live in forested areas and feed on sap, nectar, and other liquids. Known larvae feed on decaying vegetation and live under bark, or in decaying logs; they are scavengers or predators. Of the 27 species in the U.S. and Canada, most are northern in distribution.

Subfamily Coenomyiinae

[29.1 *Dialysis* Walker (9 spp.)]

29.2 *Coenomyia* Latreille

One species, as follows:

C. ferruginea Scopoli. Widespread. (1) n.e. US; (2) s.e. US.

[29.3 *Arthropeas* Loew (2 spp.)]

Subfamily Xylophaginae

[29.4 *Rachicerus* Walker (5 spp.); 29.5 *Xylophagus* Meigen, with 3 subgenera: *Anarylophagus* Malloch (1 sp., *X. nitidus* Adams), *Xylophagus* s. str. (4 spp.), and *Archimyia* Enderlein (5 spp.)]

30. XYLOMYIDAE (Xylomyid Fly Family)

Length: 5–15 mm. Usually brightly colored or with distinct pale markings against a blackish background; body with inconspicuous hairlike setae but without bristles; antennae stout, not pectinate. Adults found in forested or wooded areas. Larvae are predacious or saprophagous and live under bark. Most of the ten species are confined to the eastern U.S. with restricted distribution.

30.1 *Solva* Walker

Two species, the following of which is widely distributed but uncommon:

S. pallipes (Loew). (1) n.e. US; (2) s.e. US; (3) s.w. US.

[30.2 *Xylomya* Rondani (8 spp.)]

31. STRATIOMYIDAE (Soldier Fly Family)

Length: 2–18 mm. Usually green, yellow, blue, or black, a few metallic, often with variegated pattern on abdomen consisting of yellow or green and black stripes; abdomen broad and flat, often extending on each side of the folded wings. These are chiefly forest species, or they fly around sedges and grasses near meadows. Often they visit umbelliferous flowers for pollen and nectar.

Larvae have various habits. Those that are aquatic (e.g. *Stratiomys* and *Odontomyia* spp.) have a circlet of bristles on the apex of the abdomen that opens out flat when they are at the surface taking air into the tracheal system through tail spiracles. The bristles fold together when the larva submerges. Most aquatic larvae pupate in mud at the water's edge. Larvae also mature in cow dung (e.g. *Chloromyia* and *Hermetia* spp.), under stones, in tree sap, in decaying wood (e.g. *Pachygaster* spp.), in moss, and on vegetables, such as potato tubers and growing lettuce. Some are carnivorous; others herbivorous. Pupation occurs in the last larval skin.

The 254 species are classified as follows:

Subfamily Chiromyzinae

[31.1 *Inopus* Walker (1 sp., *I. rubiceps* (Macquart))]

Subfamily Beridinae

[31.2 *Allognosta* Osten Sacken (4 spp.); 31.3 *Actina* Meigen (1 sp., *A. viridis* (Say)); 31.4 *Beris* Latreille (3 spp.)]

Subfamily Sarginae

[31.5 *Chloromyia* Duncan (1 sp., *C. formosa* (Scopoli) [(1) NY, introduced])]

31.6 *Sargus* Fabricius

This genus is divided into two subgenera: *Pedicellina* James (1 sp., *S. fasciatus* Fabricius) and *Sargus* s. str. (5 spp.). The following are examples of the latter:

S. cuprarius (Linnaeus). L. ±13 mm. Head, thorax, and base of abdomen pale brown; legs pale brown except front tarsi dark brown, nearly black; apical segments of abdomen dark. Found around flowers, especially umbelliferous species and on leaves in wet places during June and July. (1) n.e. US; (3) CA, AZ, NM; (5) CO, KS, MO.

S. decorus Say. L. ±12. Common. (1), (2), (3), (4), (5), generally distributed.

[31.7 *Microchrysa* Loew (2 spp.); 31.8 *Cephalochrysa* Kertész (4 spp.)]

31.9 *Ptecticus* Loew

Four species, including the following:

P. trivittatus (Say) (Yellow Soldier Fly). L. 6–7 mm. Body metallic blue covered with dense golden yellow pubescence; eyes black; abdomen yellow with darker reddish brown basal band on each segment; wings unmarked. Adults are found in wooded areas visiting flowers, particularly those of the Umbelliferae. (See A&J 318.) (1) n.e. US; (2) s.e. US; (3) TX; (5) CO, KS, MO.

[31.10 *Merosargus* Loew (2 spp.)]

Subfamily Clitellariini
Tribe not assigned.

[31.11 *Antissa* Walker [=*Exodontha* Rondani of Stone, *et al.*, 1965] (2 spp.)]

Tribe Hermetiini
31.12 *Hermetia* Latreille

Twelve species, including the following:

H. illucens (Linnaeus) (Black Soldier Fly). L. ±20 mm. Dark; wings dusky, second abdominal tergite with two pale yellow spots. Larvae found in manure along with house fly larvae, in decaying vegetation, waste animal matter, bees' wax, and similar materials. It is reputed to cause intestinal myiasis. Spread by commerce. (1) n.e. US; (2) s.e. US; (3) s.w. US.

Tribe Clitellariinni

[31.13 *Brachycara* Thompson (2 spp.); 31.14 *Dieuryneura* James (1 sp., *D. stigma* (Giglio-Tos)); 31.15 *Adoxomyia* Kertesz (11 spp.); 31.16 *Euryneura* Schiner (1 sp., *E. propinqua* Schiner); 31.17 *Dicyphoma* James (1 sp., *D. schaefferi* (Coquillett)); 31.18 *Cyphomyia* Wiedemann (2 spp.)]

Subfamily Chrysochlorinae

[31.19 *Chrysochlorina* James (1 sp., *C. quadrilineata* (Bigot))]

Subfamily Pachygastrinae

[31.20 *Cosmariomyia* Kertész (1 sp., *C. pallidipennis* (Williston)); 31.2 *Artemita* Walker (1 sp., *A. inornata* (Williston)); 31.22 *Berkshiri* Johnson (1 sp., *B. albistylum* Johnson); 31.23 *Borboridea* Kertész (1 sp *B. microcephala* (Kraft and Cook)); 31.24 *Zabrachia* Coquillett (1 spp.); 31.25 *Neopachygaster* Austen (4 spp.); 31.26 *Pachygaster* Meige (3 spp.); 31.27 *Gowdeyana* Curran (1 sp., *G. punctifera* (Malloch) 31.28 *Eidalimus* Kertész (2 spp.)]

Subfamily Nemotelinae

[31.29 *Akronia* Hine (1 sp., *A. frontosa* Hine); 31.30 *Nemotelus* Geof froy, with 2 subgenera: *Nemotelus* s. str. (12 spp.) and *Camptopeltu* Williston (26 spp.)]

Subfamily Stratiomyinae
Tribe Oxycerini

[31.31 *Oxycera* Meigen (7 spp.); 31.32 *Glariopsis* Lindner (1 sp., *G. decemmaculatus* (Osten Sacken)); 31.33 *Euparyphus* Gerstaecher, with 4 subgenera: *Aochletus* Osten Sacken (5 spp.), *Parochletus* Quist (2 spp.), *Nigriparyphus* Quist (7 spp.), and *Euparyphus* s. str. (9 spp.); 31.34 *Caloparyphus* James (9 spp.)]

Tribe Myxosargini

[31.35 *Myosargus* Brauer (4 spp.); 31.36 *Anoplodonta* James (1 sp., *A. nigrirostris* (Loew))]

Tribe Odontomyiini
31.37 *Hedriodiscus* Enderlein

Seven species, including the following:

H. trivittatus (Say) (Soldier Fly). L. 8–10 mm. Head green or yellow between antennae and oral margin; thorax yellowish brown with prominent pale stripes on mesonotum; wings without markings; abdomen flat and broad. Larvae found in moist areas. Adults attracted to flowers. (See A&J 317.) (1) n.e. US; (2) s.e. US; (3) TX; (5) CO, KS, MO.

[31.38 *Odontomyia* Meigen, with 3 subgenera: *Odontomyia* s. str. (15 spp.), *Catatasina* Enderlein (9 spp.), and *Odontomyiina* Enderlein (7 spp.)]

Tribe Stratiomyini
31.39 *Stratiomys* Geoffroy

Twenty-six species, including the following:

S discalis Loew. L. ±12 mm. Black; abdomen with yellow markings; pile pale yellow. Found around leaves and flowers of umbelliferous plants growing in wet places. (1) n.e. US.

S. lativentris Loew. (See Fig. 29.30.) (1) n.e. NA.

[31.40 *Hoplitimyia* James (3 spp.); 31.41 *Labostigmina* Enderlein (18 spp.)]

Infraorder ASILOMORPHA

Three superfamilies—the Asiloidea, Bombylioidea, and Empidoidea—belong to this infraorder.

Superfamily ASILOIDEA

This superfamily consists of six families, as follows:

Fig. 29.30. (*Courtesy of J. E. V. Gerberg*)

Fig. 29.31. (*From Curran, 1934*)

[32.27 *Schlingeria* Irwin (1 sp., *S. ammobata* Irwin); 32.28 *Phycus* Walker (1 sp., unnammed); 32.29 *Parapherocera* Irwin (3 spp.); 32.30 *Pherocera* Cole (4 spp.)]

32. THEREVIDAE (Stiletto Fly Family)

Length: 2.5–15 mm. Body with pile that may cover all or part of body in varying densities; setae usually prominent. These delicate, long-legged flies are similar to the Asilidae except that the head is not hollowed out between the eyes; it may even be convex, and the eyes of the males may meet dorsally. Adults are found on blossoms, dry ground, or along sandy beaches or dunes. They are rapid fliers, usually for only very short distances, and apparently not predacious. Larvae, which are predacious, are found in sand or decaying wood. They may feed on root-feeding larvae of other insects. The 145 species found in the U.S. and Canada are widespread but not very common.

Subfamily Therevinae

[32.1 *Apsilocephala* Kroeber (1 sp., *A. longistyla* Kroeber); 32.2 *Nebritus* Coquillett (2 spp.); 32.3 *Megalinga* Irwin and Lyneborg (1 sp., *M. insignata* Irwin and Lyneborg); 32.4 *Arenigena* Irwin and Lyneborg (3 spp.); 32.5 *Dialineura* Rondani (1 sp, *D. gorodkovi* Zaitzev); 32.6 *Pallicephala* Irwin and Lyneborg (5 spp.); 32.7 *Litolinga* Irwin and Lyneborg (3 spp.); 32.8 *Rhagioforma* Irwin and Lyneborg (1 sp., *R. maculipennis* (Kroeber)); 32.9 *Pandivirila* Irwin and Lyneborg (3 spp.); 32.10 *Lysilinga* Irwin and Lyneborg (3 spp.); 32.11 *Brachylinga* Irwin and Lyneborg (10 spp.); 32.12 *Ammonaios* Irwin and Lyneborg (1 sp., *A. niveus* (Kroeber)); 32.13 *Acrosathe* Irwin and Lyneborg (6 spp.); 32.14 *Thereva* Latreille (29 spp.); 32.15 *Tabuda* Walker (3 spp.); 32.16 *Tabudamima* Irwin and Lyneborg (1 sp., *T. melanophleba* (Loew)); 32.17 *Viriliricta* Irwin and Lyneborg (3 spp.); 32.18 *Dichoglena* Irwin and Lyneborg (4 spp.); 32.19 *Spiriverpa* Irwin and Lyneborg (9 spp.); 32.20 *Chromolepida* Cole (2 spp.); 32.21 *Penniverpa* Irwin and Lyneborg (1 sp., *P. festina* (Coquillett)); 32.22 *Breviperna* Irwin (1 sp., *B. placida* (Coquillett)); 32.23 *Ozodiceromya* Bigot (34 spp.)]

Subfamily Phycinae

[32.24 *Cyclotelus* Walker (6 spp.)]

32.25 *Psilocephala* Zetterstedt

Three species, including the following:

P. haemorrhoidalis (Macquart). L. 9–10 mm. Adults prey upon wasps. (1) n.e. US; (3) s.e. US; (3) TX.

32.26 *Henicomyia* Coquillett

One species, as follows:

H. hubbardii Coquillett (See Fig. 29.31.) (3) AZ.

33. SCENOPINIDAE (Window Fly Family)

Length: 1–7 mm. Usually black, sometimes with white markings. Larvae are predacious; found in decaying wood, some in fungi, one in households. All but two species have a western distribution, and that restricted to rather limited areas, mainly in the arid Southwest. Of the 136 species, only two are common, as described below.

33.1 *Scenopinus* Latreille

Forty-eight species, the following of which are cosmopolitan:

S. fenestralis (Linnaeus) (Window Fly). L. 4–5.5 mm. Blue, with reddish yellow legs; front rough; halteres vary from white to dark brown. Larvae prey on stored food pests. On emerging from the food, adults fly to windows to get into the open. Spread by commerce. Cosmopolitan.

S. glabrifrons Meigen. L. 4–5.5 mm. Similar to the preceding, except front is polished; white knobs on halteres; legs orange-brown. Habits similar to the preceding. Cosmpolitan.

[33.2 *Brevitrichia* Hardy (43 spp.); 33.3 *Metatrichia* Coquillett (1 sp., *M. bulbosa* (Osten Sacken)); 33.4 *Pseudatricha* Osten Sacken (37 spp.); 33.5 *Belosta* Hardy (7 spp.)]

34. VERMILEONIDAE

[From Rhagionidae of authors]

(Vermileonid Fly Family)

Length: 5–6 mm. Body nearly hairless; head moderate; antennae stylate; legs slender; wings with nearly complete venation; abdomen slightly petiolate. Larvae are termed "wormlions" because they construct pitfall traps in much the same manner as antlions (see Neuroptera) in order to capture prey. Only one genus with two species occurs in the U.S. as follows:

[34.1 *Vermileo* Macquart (2 spp. [(3) CA, AZ, NM; (4) NV; (5) CO.])]

35. MYDIDAE (Mydas Fly Family)

Length: 9–60 mm. These flies somewhat resemble wasps, with last segment of the antennae enlarged and slightly club-

shaped; hind legs longer and stouter than others; hind tibiae with heavy apical spur or with bristles. Almost all adults are black, some with yellow-orange markings on second abdominal tergite. They are predacious. Known larvae live in decaying wood or soil; at least one species is predacious on beetle larvae in stumps and logs or in sandy soil. Of the 45 species, most are uncommon and have restricted distribution, primarily in the southwestern U.S.

Subfamily Ectyphinae

35.1 *Opomydas* Curran

Three species, including the following:

O. limbatus (Williston) (Juice Mydas Fly). L. 20–25 mm. Head and thorax almost entirely dark reddish brown to black; antennal club orange-red; abdomen yellowish; male aedeagus is large, the apical portion bent down and forward. Adults predacious on other insects. Larvae prey upon beetle larvae in rotting logs and stumps. (See A&J 325.) (3) CA, AZ.

[35.2 *Heteromydas* Hardy (1 sp., *H. bicolor* Hardy]

Subfamily Mydinae

[35.3 *Messiasia* d'Andretta (2 spp.)]

35.4 *Mydas* Fabricius

Seventeen species, including the following:

M. clavatus (Drury). L. ±30 mm. Black; second abdominal segment orange. Common. (1), (2), (3), (4), (5), generally distributed.

[35.5 *Phyllomydas* Bigot (7 spp.)]

Subfamily Leptomydinae

[35.6 *Pseudonomoneura* Bequaert (4 spp.); 35.7 *Nemomydas* Curran (11 spp.)]

36. APIOCERIDAE (Flower-loving Fly Family)

Length: 7.5–35 mm (usually 12–20 mm). Similar to the preceding family but with the wing venation differences given in the Key. Adults hover and buzz in flight. Larvae of very few species are known; they live in sand and are carnivorous. Of the 29 species of these uncommon desert flies, only two are found outside the southwestern U.S.

36.1 *Rhaphiomidas* Osten Sacken

Nine species, including the following:

R. trochilus (Coquillett) (Flower-loving Fly). L. 10–14 mm. Dusty brown; eyes dark green; abdomen dark with light posterior bands on each segment; wings brownish; proboscis long and swordlike; thorax with fine dusty pile. (3) CA.

36.2 *Apiocera* Westwood

Twenty species, the following two being found outside the Southwest:

A. haruspex Osten Sacken. (3) s.w. US; (4) BC, WA, OR; (5) WY.

A. martinorum Painter. (4) OR, ID.

37. ASILIDAE (Robber Fly Family)

Length: 3–50+ mm (usually 9–15 mm). Body either long and slender or short and stout (beelike). Slender species are without hairlike setae; beelike species are covered with long hairy setae. Both forms are predacious, with the latter's resemblance to bumblebees possibly helping them get close to their prey, although this mimicking may be a protection against enemies that fear bee stings. Bulging of eyes makes head seem to be hollowed between them; proboscis stout rather than long; face bearded; abdomen of a few very long, slender, and wasplike; legs strong and usually bristled. Adults may bite. Larvae are predacious, feeding upon other insect larvae in rotting wood, under bark or fallen leaves, or in loose soil. Of the 883 species in the U.S. and Canada, most have restricted ecological requirements and hence are rather locally distributed. The family is predominantly southwestern U.S.

Subfamily Leptogastrinae

Tribe Leptogastrini

[37.1 *Leptopteromyia* Williston (1 sp., *L. americana* Hardy)]

37.2 *Leptogaster* Meigen

This genus contains the following five subgenera: *Psilonyx* Aldrich (1 sp., *L. annulatus* (Say)), *Beameromyia* Martin (15 spp.), *Apachekolos* Martin (5 spp.); *Tipulogaster* Cockerell (1 sp., *L. glabrata* Wiedemann), and *Leptogaster* s. str. (30 spp.). The following is a common species:

L. flavipes Loew. L. 9–13 mm. Adults, which resemble wasps, are on the wing in June and July and may be taken by sweeping rank vegetation; they may also be found resting on dead weeds or twigs. (1) n.e. US; (2) s.e. US; (5) MN, KS.

[37.3 *Lestomyia* Williston (6 spp.); 37.4 *Saropogon* (19 spp.); 37.5 *Diogmites* Loew (26 spp.); 37.6 *Blepharepium* Rondani (1 sp., *B. secabile* (Walker)); 37.7 *Comantella* Curran (4 spp.); 37.8 *Taracticus* Loew (3 spp.); 37.9 *Nicocles* Jaennicke (14 spp.); 37.10 *Cophura* Osten Sacken (24 spp.); 37.11 *Hodophylax* James (4 spp.); 37.12 *Omniablautus* Pritchard (5 spp.); 37.13 *Parataracticus* Cole (5 spp.); 37.14 *Lasiopogon* Loew (38 spp.); 37.15 *Townsendia* Williston (3 spp.); 37.16 *Stichopogon* Loew (10 spp.); 37.17 *Willistonina* Back (1 sp., *W. bilineata* (Williston)); 37.18 *Stenopogon* Loew, with 3 subgenera: *Stenopogon* s. str. (48 spp.), *Scleropogon* Loew (15 spp.), and *Ospriocerus* Loew (22 spp.); 37.19 *Microstylum* Macquart (2 spp.); 37.20 *Archilestris* Loew (1 sp., *A. magnifica* (Walker)); 37.21 *Itolia* Wilcox (93 spp.)]

Tribe Laphystiini

[37.22 *Laphystia* Loew (30 spp.); 37.33 *Psilocurus* Loew (7 spp.); 37.24 *Zabrops* Hull (2 spp.); 37.25 *Perasis* Hermann (1 sp., *P. argentifacies* (Williston))]

Tribe Damalini

[37.26 *Holcocephala* Jaennicke (3 spp.); 37.27 *Haplopogon* Engel (7 spp.); 37.28 *Orrhodops* Hull (1 sp., *O. americanus* (Curran)); 37.29 *Bromleyus* Hardy (1 sp., *B. flavidorsus* Hardy); 37.30 *Plesiomma* Macquart (1 sp., *P. unicolor* Loew)]

Tribe Diochiini

[37.31 *Dioctria* Meigen, with 2 subgenera: *Nannodioctria* Wilcox and Martin (2 spp.) and *Dioctria* s. str. (6 spp.); 37.32 *Myelaphus* Bigot (2 spp.); 37.33 *Dicolonus* Loew (5 spp.); 37.34 *Echthodopa* Loew (3 spp.); 37.35 *Eudioctria* Wilcox and Martin (14 spp.); 37.36 *Metadioctria* Wilcox and Martin (3 spp.); 37.37 *Bohartia* Hull (6 spp.); 37.38 *Ablautus* Loew (13 spp.); 37.39 *Prolepsis* Walker (1 sp., *P. tristis* (Walker)); 37.40 *Callinicus* Loew (4 spp.); 37.41 *Ceraturgus* Wiedemann (9 spp.); 37.42 *Metapogon* Coquillett (11 spp.); 37.43 *Eucyrtopogon* Curran (11 spp.); 37.44 *Backomyia* Wilcox and Martin (5 spp.); 37.45 *Cyrtopogon* Loew (70 spp.); 37.46 *Coleomyia* Wilcox and Martin (7 spp.); 37.47 *Nan-*

nocyrtopogon Wilcox and Martin (28 spp.); 37.48 *Holopogon* Loew (17 spp.); 37.49 *Hadrokolos* Martin (3 spp.); 37.50 *Heteropogon* Loew (24 spp.); 37.51 *Prichardomyia* Martin (1 sp., *P. vespoides* (Bigot)); 37.52 *Sintoria* Hull (4 spp.); 37.53 *Wilcoxia* James (5 spp.)]

Subfamily Asilinae

Tribe Atomosiini

[37.54 *Atomosia* Macquart (9 spp.); 37.55 *Cerotainia* Schiner (3 spp.); 37.56 *Atomosiella* Wilcox (1 sp., *A. antennata* (Banks)); 37.57 *Antonio-myia* Hermann (2 spp.)]

Tribe Laphriini

[37.58 *Dasylechia* Williston (1 sp., *D. atrox* (Williston)); 37.59 *Lampria* Macquart (3 spp.)]

37.60 *Laphria* Meigen

Sixty-three species, including the following:

L. flavicollis Say. L. ±16 mm. Body black, covered with long, dense, yellow hairs. (2) s.e. US.

[37.61 *Orthogonis* Hermann (1 sp., *O. stygia* (Bromley)); 37.62 *Cerotainiops* Curran (6 spp.); 37.63 *Andrenosoma* Rondani, with 2 subgenera: *Andrenosoma* s. str. (4 spp.) and *Pogonosoma* Rondani (2 spp.)]

Tribe Ommatiini

[37.64 *Ommatius* Wiedemann (8 spp.)]

Tribe Asilini

37.65 *Efferia* Coquillett

One hundred species, including the following:

E. aestuans (Linnaeus). L. ±27 mm. Brown; thorax grayish; abdomen darker with large pale yellow apical spots. Adults frequent open places, resting on the ground or on dead weeds and twigs during June through August. (See A&J 326.) (1) n.e. NA; (2) s.e. US; (3) TX, OK; (5) ND, SD, MN, NE, IA, KS, MO.

[37.66 *Promachus* Loew (21 spp., including *P. vertebratus* (Say) (see Fig. 29.32 [(1) WI, IL, OH; (5) CO, KS, MO]; 37.67 *Promachella* Cole and Pritchard (1 sp., *P. pilosa* (Wilcox)); 37.68 *Promachina* Bromley (1 sp., *P. trapezoidalis* (Bellardi)); 37.69 *Mellophora* Macquart (14 spp.); 37.70 *Mallophorina* Curran (15 spp.); 37.71 *Proctacanthus* Macquart (18 spp.; common and often collected); 37.72 *Eccritosia* Schiner (1 sp., *E. zamon* (Townsend)); 37.73 *Proctacanthella* Bromley (5 spp.)]

37.74 *Asilus* Linnaeus

Seventy-four species, in the following seven subgenera: *Machimus* Loew, *Negasilus* Curran, *Prolatiforceps* Martin, *Polacan-*

tha Martin, *Dicropaltum* Martin, *Neomochtherus* Osten Sacken, and *Cerdistus* Loew). The following species is an example:

A. sericeus Say. L. 20–28 mm. Brown; wings brown; legs pale brown. Adults, which fly from June through August, are seen resting on open ground or on dead weeds and twigs in open places. (1) IL, IN, OH, PA, NY, MA, CT, RI; (5) KS, MO.

[37.75 *Neoitamus* Osten Sacken (8 spp.); 37.76 *Wyliea* Martin (1 sp., *W. mydas* (Brauer)); 37.77 *Philonicus* Loew (6 spp.); 37.78 *Rhadiurgus* Loew (1 sp., *R. variabilis* (Zetterstedt))]

Superfamily BOMBYLIOIDEA

This superfamily contains the following four families.

38. ACROCERIDAE (Small-headed Fly Family)

Length: 2.5–21 mm. Thorax and abdomen appear inflated, thus dwarfing head, which is deflected; calypteres very large. Often bright metallic green, blue, red, or purple; some brown, black, orange, yellow, or even white. Abdomen may be spotted; mesonotum may be striped. Some are beelike, others wasplike, a few beetlelike, many apparently mimics. Body without bristles. Legs with empodia pulvilliform. Although rarely collected, these flies may be found near spider webs. All known larvae are internal parasites of spiders. Of the 59 species, most are confined to the southwestern states.

Subfamily Panopinae

[38.1 *Lasia* Wiedemann (2 spp.); 38.2 *Eulonchus* Gerstaecker (7 spp.); 38.3 *Ocnaea* (9 spp.)]

38.4 *Pterodontia* Gray

Six species, the following of which is widespread:

P. flavipes Gray. (1) n.e. NA; (3) CA; (4) OR, WA, ID; (5) MT, ND, SD, MN, WY.

Subfamily Acrocerinae

[38.5 *Ogcodes* Latreille, with 2 subgenera: *Ogcodes* s. str. (16 spp.) and *Neogcodes* Schlinger (1 sp., *O. albiventris* Johnson)]

38.6 *Turbopsebius* Schlinger

Three species, including the following:

T. sulphuripes Loew. (See Fig. 29.33.) (1) n.e. NA; (2) s.e. US; (3) TX; (5) MN.

[38.7 *Acrocera* Meigen (16 spp.)]

Fig. 29.32. (*From Sweetman, after Walton*)

Fig. 29.33. (*From Curran, 1934*)

Fig. 29.34. (*From Curran, 1934*)

39. NEMESTRINIDAE
(Tangle-veined Fly Family)

Length: 7–14 mm. The six rare species assigned to this family have a beelike appearance and buzz loudly. Bristles lacking but body covered with hairlike setae. They are called Tangle-veined Flies because of the way the branches of the median vein join before the apical margin and end toward the front margin of the wing before the apex. Most known larvae are parasites of grasshoppers.

39.1 *Hirmoneura* Meigen

Three species, including the following:

H. bradleyi Bequaert. (See Fig. 29.34.) (3) TX.

[39.2 *Neorhynchocephalus* Lichtwardt (2 spp. [(2) FL; (3) s.w. US]); 39.3 *Trichopsidea* Westwood (1 sp., *T. clausa* Osten Sacken [(2) AR, AL, FL; (3) s.w. US; (4) BC, WA, OR, ID; (5) MT, MB, ND, SD, WY, CO, KS])]

40. BOMBYLIIDAE (Bee Fly Family)

Length: 4–40 mm. Body covered with hairlike setae; brightly colored, wings often with maculations. Face not hollowed out; eyes, especially of the male, almost touching above; proboscis, if short, with broad tip, and if long (often) used by many species to sip nectar or feed on pollen. These fuzzy flies hover in mid-air and suddenly dart a few feet away to hover elsewhere, very much like Syrphid Flies. Larvae feed upon the eggs or young stages of grasshoppers, beetles, and often of tiger beetles, Lepidoptera, bees, and wasps. Of the 797 species recorded in the U.S. and Canada, many are confined to the sandy regions of the Southwest.

[Division Homoeophthalmae]

Subfamily Cylleniinae

[40.1 *Amphicosmus* Coquillett (4 spp.); 40.2 *Metacosmus* Coquillett (3 spp.); 40.3 *Paracosmus* Osten Sacken (5 spp.)]

Subfamily Toxophorinae

[40.4 *Lepidophora* Meigen (7 spp.); 40.5 *Toxophora* Meigen (7 spp.)]

Subfamily Systropinae

[40.6 *Dolichomyia* Wiedemann (1 sp., *D. gracilis* Williston); 40.7 *Systropus* Wiedemann (4 spp.)]

Subfamily Bombyliinae

[40.8 *Aldrichia* Coquillett (2 spp.); 40.9 *Triploechus* Edwards (4 spp.); 40.10 *Heterostylum* Macquart (6 spp.)]

40.11 *Bombylius* Linnaeus

Thirty-five species, including the following:

B. major Linnaeus (Black-tailed Bee Fly). Length: 7–12 mm. Very distinctive, with long proboscis; front half of wings dark brown; vestiture pale. Adults, which fly from May to August, are seen hovering over open, sunny, and, especially, sandy ground. Larvae parasitic in nests of various wild bees. (See A&J 328.) (1), (2), (3), (4), (5), widespread.

40.12 *Systoechus* Loew

Five species, the following of which are common:

S. vulgaris Loew (Grasshopper Bee Fly). L. 9–10 mm. Beelike; proboscis short. Larvae parasitic in egg cases of certain grasshoppers. (1), (2), (3), (4), (5), generally distributed.

S. slitus (Walker). L. ±10 mm. Beelike; body black, covered with long, dense, pale yellow pile. (1) NJ, MD, DE; (2) s.e. US.

S. oreas Osten Sacken (Common Bee Fly). L. ±10 mm. Black to pale with light gray pile covering thorax and abdomen; wings without maculations. Larvae parasitic on bees. (See A&J 327.) (3) CA; (4) Pacific n.w.

[40.13 *Anastoechus* Osten Sacken (3 spp.); 40.14 *Conoshorus* Meigen (19 spp.); 40.15 *Sparnopolius* Loew (5 spp.), including *S. lherminierii* (Macquart) (see Fig. 29.35.) [(1) n.e. NA; (2) s.e. US; (3) TX; (5) MT]); 40.16 *Parabombylius* Williston (9 spp.); 40.17 *Geminaria* Coquillett (2 spp.); 40.18 *Lordotus* Loew (22 spp.)]

Subfamily Cythereinae

[40.19 *Pantarbes* Osten Sacken (3 spp.)]

Subfamily Ecliminae

[40.20 *Thevenemyia* Bigot, with 2 subgenera: *Thevenemyia* s. str. (23 spp.) and *Arthroneura* Hull (1 sp., *T. tridentata* (Hull))]

Subfamily Crytosiinae

[40.21 *Platypygus* Loew (1 sp., *P. americanus* Melander)]

Subfamily Mythicomyiinae

[40.22 *Empidideicus* Becker (5 spp.); 40.23 *Mythicomyia* Coquillett (130 spp.); 40.24 *Glabellula* Bezzi (6 spp.)]

Subfamily Phthiriinae

[40.25 *Apolysis* Loew (8 spp.); 40.26 *Desmatomyia* Williston (1 sp., *D. anomala* Williston); 40.27 *Oligodranes* Loew (52 spp.); 40.28 *Phthiria*

Fig. 29.35. (*From Sweetman*)

Meigen, with 2 subgenera: *Pthiria* s. str. (10 spp.) and *Poecilognathus* Jaennicke (21 spp.)]

Subfamily Geroninae

[40.29 *Geron* Meigen, with 2 subgenera: *Geron* s. str. (16 spp.) and *Empidigeron* Painter (6 spp.)]

Subfamily Heterotropinae

[40.30 *Prorates* Melander (6 spp.); 40.31 *Heterotropus* Loew (1 sp., *H. senex* Melander); 40.32 *Apystomyia* Melander (1 sp., *A. elinguis* Melander); 40.33 *Coenotoides* Hall (2 spp.); 40.34 *Coenotus* Cole (4 spp.)]

[Division Tomophthalmae]

Subfamily Lomatiinae

[40.35 *Epacmus* Osten Sacken (13 spp.); 40.36 *Desmatoneura* Williston (1 sp., *D. argentifrons* Williston); 40.37 *Exepacmus* Coquillett (1 sp., *E. johnsoni* Coquillett); 40.38 *Aphoebantus* Loew (54 spp.); 40.39 *Eucessia* Coquillett (1 sp., *E. rubens* Coquillett); 40.40 *Bryodemina* Hull (2 spp.); 40.41 *Ogcodocera* Macquart (2 spp.)]

Subfamily Anthracinae

[40.42 *Dicranoclista* Bezzi (2 spp.)]

40.43 *Anthrax* Scopoli

Thirty-seven species, the following of which are common:

A. analis Macquart. L. ±8 mm. Black; tip of abdomen of male white, of female black; basal half of wing black. Larvae parasitic on tiger beetle larvae. (1) ME, MA, RI, CT, s. NY, NJ, MD, DE; (2) VA, NC, SC, GA, FL; (4) WA, OR, UT.

A. tigrinus (DeGeer). Parasitic on Carpenter Bees. (1) n.e. US; (2) s.e. US; (3) s.w. US; (5) KS.

Subfamily Exoprosopinae

[40.44 *Exoprosopa* Macquart (43 spp.); 40.45 *Ligyra* Newman (2 spp.); 40.46 *Astrophanes* Osten Sacken (1 sp., *A. adonis* Osten Sacken); 40.47 *Dipalta* Osten Sacken (2 spp.); 40.48 *Paradiplocampta* Hall (1 sp., *P. tabeti* Hall); 40.49 *Neodiplocampta* Curran (4 spp.); 40.50 *Mancia* Coquillett (1 sp., *M. nana* Coquillett); 40.51 *Stonyx* Osten Sacken (1 sp., *S. clelia* Osten Sacken); 40.52 *Lepidanthrax* Osten Sacken (34 spp.); 40.53 *Rhynchanthrax* Painter (4 spp.); 40.54 *Oestranthrax* Bezzi (1 sp., *O. farinosus* Johnson and Maughan); 40.55 *Poecilanthrax* Osten Sacken (33 spp.); 40.56 *Hemipenthes* Loew (25 spp.); 40.57 *Villa* Lioy (37 spp.); 40.58 *Paravilla* Painter (24 spp.); 40.59 *Diochanthrax* Hall (1 sp., *D. morulus* Hall); 40.60 *Thyridanthrax* Osten Sacken (7 spp.); 40.61 *Chrysanthrax* Osten Sacken (27 spp.)]

41. HILARIMORPHIDAE (Hilarimorphid Fly Family)

Length: 1.8–7.2 mm. Body dark; head with ocelli; antennae with aical, two segmented stylus; wings hyaline, usually with pterostigma. The 30 species in the U.S. and Canada are all assigned to the following genus.

41.1 *Hilarimorpha* Schiner

Thirty species, including the following:

H. pusilla Johnson. (1) VT, NH.

Superfamily EMPIDOIDEA

42. EMPIDIDAE (Dance Fly Family)

Length: 1.5–12 mm. Body rather elongate; dark to black, often yellow or light brown, but not metallic; legs slender, or thickened and modified for catching prey.

Adults are predacious. Some species have a curious habit as part of their mating dance. The male brings gifts of captured insects to the female. These are "wrapped" in a frothy bubble, or web covering made from a secretion of the glands in the front tarsi. The female keeps these presents during the mating process. Larvae are probably predacious as well. They are aquatic, semi-aquatic, or dung dwellers. A few have been described as living in owl's nests, roots, and fungi. The 728 species recorded in the U.S. and Canada are classified as follows.

Subfamily Tachydromiinae

[42.1 *Tachypeza* Meigen (17 spp.); 42.2 *Tachydromia* Meigen (13 spp.); 42.3 *Tachyempis* Melander (6 spp.); 42.4 *Charadrodromia* Melander (3 spp.) 42.5 *Chersodromia* Walker (8 spp.); 42.6 *Micrempis* Melander (4 spp.); 42.7 *Megagrapha* Melander (2 spp.); 42.8 *Symballophthalmus* Becker (1 sp., *S. masoni* Chillcott); 42.9 *Platypalpus* Macquart (100) spp.); 42.10 *Stilpon* Loew (6 spp.); 42.11 *Drapetis* Meigen (40 spp.), subgenus *Crossopalpus* Bigot, and subgenus *Drapetis* s. str.)]

Subfamily Hemerodromiinae

Tribe Cehlipodini

[42.12 *Chelipoda* Macquart (6 spp.); 42.13 *Phyllodromis* Zetterstedt (1 sp., *P. americana* Melander)]

Tribe Hemerodromiini

[42.14 *Hemerodromia* Meigen (16 spp.); 42.15 *Chelifera* Macquart (12 spp.); 42.16 *Thanategia* Melander (3 spp.); 42.17 *Metachela* Coquillet (2 spp.); 42.18 *Neoplasta* Coquillett (2 spp.)]

Subfamily Brachystomatinae

[42.19 *Anomalemis* Melander (2 spp.); 42.20 *Brachystoma* Meigen (4 spp.)]

Subfamily Clinocerinae

[42.21 *Niphogenia* Melander (1 sp., *N. eucera* Melander); 42.22 *Ceratempis* Melander (1 sp., *C. longicornis* Melander); 42.23 *Oreothalia* Melander (2 spp.); 42.24 *Boreodromia* Coquillett (1 sp., *B. bicolor* (Loew)); 42.25 *Heleodromia* Haliday (1 sp., *H. pullata* (Melander)); 42.26 *Proclinopyga* Melander (5 spp.); 42.27 *Roederiodes* Coquillett (7 spp.); 42.28 *Dolichocephala* Macquart (2 spp.); 42.29 *Wiedemannia* Zetterstedt (6 spp.); 42.30 *Clinocera* Meigen (16 spp.); 42.31 *Trichoclinocera* Collin (6 spp.)]

Subfamily Empidinae

[42.32 *Microphorella* Becker (5 spp.); 42.33 *Microphorus* Macquart (15 spp.); 42.34 *Oreogeton* Schiner (8 spp.); 42.35 *Brochella* Melander (1 sp., *B. monticola* Melander); 42.36 *Empis* Linnaeus (80 spp.)]

42.37 *Rhamphomyia* Meigen

One hundred and fifty species, including the following:

R. weedi (Coquillett). (See Fig. 29.36.) (2) MS.

[42.38 *Toreus* Melander (1 sp., *T. neomexicanus* (Melander)); 42.39 *Hilara* Meigen (50 spp.); 42.40 *Philetus* Walker (1 sp., *R. primigenia* Melander); 42.41 *Hesperempis* Melander (2 spp.); 42.42 *Ragus* Walker (1 sp., *R. primigenia* Melander); 42.43 *Parathalassius* Mik (3 spp.); 42.44 *Hormopeza* Zetterstedt (7 spp.); 42.45 *Anthepiscopus* Becker (7 spp.); 42.46 *Iteaphila* Zetterstedt (12 spp.); 42.47 *Apalocnemis* Philippi (2 spp.); 42.48 *Gloma* Meigen (3 spp.)]

Subfamily Ocydromiinae

[42.49 *Holocyrtoma* Melander (2 spp.); 42.50 *Bicellaria* Macquart (11 spp.); 42.51 *Leptopeza* Macquart (5 spp.); 42.52 *Ocydromia* Meigen (1 sp., *O. glabricula* (Fallén)); 42.53 *Oedalea* Meigen (4 spp.); 42.54 *Euthyneura* Macquart (6 spp.); 42.55 *Allanthalia* Melander (1 sp., *A. padilla*

Fig. 29.36. (*From Curran, 1934*)

(Zetterstedt)): 42.56 *Anthalia* Zetterstedt (11 spp.); 42.57 *Trichina* Meigen (7 spp.)]

Subfamily Hybotinae

[42.58 *Meghyperus* Loew (2 spp.)]

42.59 *Syneches* Walker

Fourteen species, including the following:

S. thoracicus (Say). L. ±4.5 mm. Body brown; wing with prominent stigma. (1) n.e. US; (5) MN, KS.

[42.60 *Syndyas* Loew (6 spp.); 42.61 *Hybos* Meigen (1 sp., *H. reversus* Walker); 42.62 *Euhybus* Coquillett (12 spp.)]

43. DOLICHOPODIDAE (Long-legged Fly Family)

Length: 0.8–3 mm (some to 9 mm). Slender, tapering, usually metallic green abdomens; legs long, tarsi often relatively long. Males of some species are ornamented with tufts of scales, expecially on the tarsi, which are displayed before the females during their courtship rituals, much as certain ornamental birds display their finery. These enlargements may occur not only on the tarsi, but also on the antennae, arista of the antennae, palpi, and other locations depending upon the species. Both adults and larvae are predacious. The former are common along streams and in wet meadows. The latter live in moist earth rich in vegetation; some live under bark; a few are leaf miners; many are aquatic. This large family contains 1227 species in the U.S. and Canada. [Note: the following list of genera follows that given in Stone, *et al.* (1965), with an update from McAlpine, *et al.* (1981).]

Subfamily Sciapodinae

[43.1 *Mesorhaga* Schiner (11 spp.)]

43.2 *Condylostylus* Bogot

Forty species, including the following:

C. chrysoprasi (Walker). L. ±5.5 mm. Entirely coppery green with bluish reflections; eyes separate, somewhat projecting. Larvae predacious, living in semiaquatic situations (See Fig. 29.37 and A&J 329.) (2) s.e. US; (3) TX.

[43.3 *Chrysosoma* Guérin-Méneville (3 spp.); 43.4 *Sciapus* Zeller (24 spp.); 43.5 *Psilopiella* Van Duzee (1 sp., *P. rutila* Van Duzee.]

Subfamily Dolichopodinae

[43.6 *Dolichopus* Latreille (311 spp.); 43.7 *Hercostomus* Loew (26 spp.); 43.8 *Gymnopternus* Loew (74 spp.); 43.9 *Paraclius* Bigot (17 spp.);

Fig. 29.37. (*From Curran, 1934*)

43.10 *Pelastoneurus* Loew (29 spp.); 43.11 *Tachytrechus* Haliday (33 spp. [includes *Polymedon* Osten Sacken])]

Subfamily Plagioneurinae

[43.12 *Plagioneurus* Loew (1 sp., *P. univittatus* Loew)]

Subfamily Hydrophorinae

[43.13 *Hydrophorus* Fallén (54 spp.); 43.14 *Scellus* Loew (12 spp.); 43.15 *Melanderia* Aldrich, with 2 subgenera: *Melanderia* s. str. (2 spp.) and *Wirthia* Arnaud (1 sp., *M. curvipes* (Van Duzee)); 43.16 *Liancalus* Loew (5 spp.); 43.17 *Thinophilus* Wahlberg (24 spp.); 43.18 *Diostracus* Loew (2 spp.); 43.19 *Hypocharassus* Mik (2 spp.)]

Subfamily Aphrosylinae

[43.20 *Paraphrosylus* Becker (6 spp.)]

Subfamily Medeterinae

[43.21 *Medetera* Fischer von Waldheim (52 spp.); 43.22 *Thrypticus* Gerstaecker (13 spp.)]

Subfamily Rhaphiinae

[43.23 *Rhaphium* Meigen (79 spp.); 43.24 *Nematoproctus* Loew (7 spp.); 43.25 *Keirosoma* Van Duzee (1 sp., *K. slossonae* Van Duzee); 43.26 *Syntormon* Loew (20 spp.); 43.27 *Parasyntormon* Wheeler (20 spp.); 43.28 *Peloropeodes* Wheeler (8 spp.); 43.29 *Neurigonella* Robinson (2 spp.); 43.30 *Systenus* Loew (6 spp.)]

Subfamily Neurigoninae

[43.31 *Neurigona* Rondani (40 spp.)]

Subfamily Diaphorinae

[43.32 *Diaphorus* Meigen (15 spp.); 43.33 *Chrysotus* Meigen (120 spp.); 43.34 *Asyndetus* Loew (21 spp.); 43.35 *Argyra* Macquart (46 spp.)]

Subfamily Sympycninae

[43.36 *Campsicnemus* Haliday (21 spp.); 43.37 *Sympycnus* Loew (32 spp.); 43.38 *Calyxochaetus* Bigot (15 spp.); 43.39 *Sympycnidelphus* Robinson (3 spp.); 43.40 *Neoparentia* Robinson (1 sp., *N. caudata* (Van Duzee)); 43.41 *Chrysotimus* Loew (9 spp.); 43.42 *Achradocera* Becker (2 spp.); 43.43 *Xanthochlorus* Loew (1 sp., *X. helvinus* Loew); 43.44 *Harmstonia* Robinson (2 spp.); 43.45 *Teuchophorus* Loew (4 spp.); 43.46 *Telmaturgus* Mik (1 sp., *T. parvus* (Van Duzee)); 43.47 *Achalcus* Loew (2 spp.); 43.48 *Enlinia* Aldrich (6 spp.); 43.49 *Micromorphus* Mik (7 spp.); 43.50 *Nanomyina* Robinson (1 sp., *N. litorea* Robinson); 43.51 *Lamprochromus* Mik (3 spp.)]

Infraorder MUSCOMORPHA ASCHIZA

Three superfamilies in this infraorder: the Lonchopteroidea, Platypezoidea, and Syrphoidea. [Note: The genera and species given follow the classification of Stone, *et al.* (1965).]

Superfamily LONCHOPTEROIDEA

There is only one family in this superfamily.

44. LONCHOPTERIDAE (Pointed-winged Fly Family)

Length: 2–5 mm. Only four species of this family of slender, yellowish to brownish flies are recorded in the U.S. They are found in moist, shady places. Larvae live under leaves and in decaying vegetation.

44.1 *Lonchoptera* Meigen

Four species, the following of which is cosmopolitan (other species are northern in distribution):

L. furcata (Fallén).

Superfamily PLATYPEZOIDEA
45. PLATYPEZIDAE (Flat-footed Fly Family)

Length: 2–5 mm. Usually black or brown; hind tarsi enlarged. Adults are sometimes common in damp woods, especially in sunny glades, where they run about on broad-leaved plants with a zigzag movement, often stopping; some hover. Males may dance in swarms. Some of these flies are called Smoke Flies because they are attracted to open fires as are certain other insects. The latter have special smoke detection organs, but it is not known if these flies also have them. All larvae apparently infest fungi. The 67 species are classsified as follows:

[45.1 *Melanderomyia* Kessel (1 sp., *M. kahli* Kessel)]

45.2 *Microsania* Zetterstedt

These are the smoke flies. The following two species occur in the U.S. and Canada:

M. imperfecta (Loew) (Eastern Smoke Fly). (1) n.e. US; (2) s.e. US.

M. occidentalis Malloch (Western Smoke Fly). (3) CA; (4) Pacific n.w.

[45.3 *Callomyia* Meigen (9 spp.); 45.4 *Agathomyia* Verrall (28 spp.); 45.5 *Platypezina* Wahlgren (3 spp.); 45.6 *Protoclythia* Kessel (4 spp.); 45.7 *Platypeza* Meigen (16 spp.); 45.8 *Metaclythia* Kessel (1 sp., *M. currani* Kessel); 45.9 *Calotarsa* Townsend (3 spp.)]

46. PHORIDAE (Humpbacked Fly Family)

Length: 1–5 mm. Humpbacked flies are usually black, with some brown, others yellow. Deflected head gives them a humpbacked appearance. Wing veins reduced to a few; hind femora flattened. Adults, common around decaying vegetation or animal matter, move in quick, jerky movements. Some larvae are scavengers, infesting carrion and sometimes fungi; others are parasites of wasps, beetles, caterpillars, land mollusks, or millipeds. Medical records show cases of larvae infesting wounds, working under the skin, and even invading the human digestive tract. Some infest social insect nests where they parasitize ants, termites, and bees. There are 226 species in the U.S. and Canada.

Subfamily Phorinae

[46.1 *Anevrina* Lioy (11 spp.); 46.2 *Chaetopleurophora* Schmitz (6 spp.); 46.3 *Spiniphora* Malloch (5 spp.); 46.4 *Triphleba* Rondani (14 spp.); 46.5 *Hypocera* Lioy (2 spp.); 46.6 *Diplonevra* Lioy (5 spp.); 46.7 *Dohrniphora* Dahl (6 spp.); 46.8 *Borophaga* Enderlein (4 spp.); 46.9 *Abaristophora* Schmitz (1 sp., *A. diversipennis* Borgmeier); 46.10 *Stichillus* Enderlein (5 spp.); 46.11 *Conicera* Meigen, with 2 subgenera: *Conicera* s. str. (1 sp., *C. dauci* (Meigen) and *Hypocerina* Malloch (2 spp.); 46.12 *Coniceromyia* Borgmeier (2 spp.); 46.13 *Phora* Latreille (11 spp.)]

Subfamily Aenigmatiinae
46.14 *Aenigmatias* Meinert

Five species that live in ant nests. Females are wingless.

Subfamily Metopininae
Tribe Beckerinini

[46.15 *Beckerina* Malloch (4 spp.)]

Tribe Metopinini

[46.16 *Woodiphora* Schmitz (1 sp., *W. velutinipes* (Brues)]

46.17 *Megaselia* Rondani

The genus is divided into two subgenera: *Megaselia* s. str. (49 spp.) and *Aphiochaeta* Brues (42 spp.). The following species is common:

M. scataris (Loew). (See Fig. 29.38.) (1) IN, OH, PA, s. NY, MA, MD: (2) s.e. US; (3) TX.

[46.18 *Physoptera* Borgmeier (1 sp., *P. apicinebula* (Malloch)); 46.19 *Gymnophora* Macquart (3 spp.); 46.20 *Plastophora* Brues (3 spp.); 46.21 *Phalacrotophora* Enderlein, with 2 subgenera: *Phalacrotophora* s. str. (2 spp.) and *Omapantia* Schmitz (1 sp., *P. longifrons* (Brues)); 46.22 *Syneura* Brues (1 sp., *S. cocciphila* (Coquillett)); 46.23 *Rhyncophoromyia* Malloch (1 sp., *R. conica* (Malloch)); 46.24 *Trophithauma* Schmitz (1 sp., *T. rostratum* (Melander and Brues)); 46.25 *Apocephalus* Coquillett, with 2 subgenera: *Apocephalus* s. str. (8 spp.) and *Mesophora* Borgmeier (2 spp.); 46.26 *Cremersia* Schmitz (3 spp.); 46.27 *Myrmosicarius* Borgmeier (2 spp.); 46.28 *Auxanommatidia* Borgmeier (1 sp., *A.* unnamed); 46.29 *Pseudacteon* Coquillett (5 spp.); 46.30 *Metopina* Macquaret (1 sp., *M. fenyesi* Malloch); 46.31 *Cataclinusa* Schmitz (1 sp., *C. pachycondylae* (Brues)); 46.32 *Puliciphora* Dahl (7 spp.); 46.33 *Acontistoptera* Brues (1 sp., *A. melanderi* Brues)]

46.34 *Xanionotum* Brues

Three species, including the following:

X. sp. (2) MS, AL; (3) AZ, TX. (See Fig. 29.39)

[45.35 *Ecitomyia* Brues (1 sp., *E. wheeleri* Brues); 46.36 *Commoptera* Brues (1 sp., *C. solenopsidis* Brues); 46.37 *Trophodeinus* Borgmeier (2 spp.); 46.38 *Lecanocerus* Borgmeier (1 sp., *L. compressiceps* Borgmeier)]

Fig. 29.38. (*From Curran, 1934*)

Fig. 29.39. (*From Curran, 1934*)

Superfamily SYRPHOIDEA

This superfamily contains the following two families.

47. SYRPHIDAE (Flower Fly Family)

Length: 1–35 mm (usually 10–20 mm). Body often with black and yellow bands. These flies are almost always easily recognized by the presence of a spurious wing vein (see SP in Fig. 29.40) that runs lengthwise across the middle of the wing. It has no beginning or ending at any of the other veins.

Many species can be recognized by their hovering, although hovering is not an eclusive trait of this family. Some species may be collected at flowers. Adults feed on nectar and pollen, and many are pollinators. Many species are almost bare of hairlike setae and resemble wasps; others are hairy and resemble bees, even to the buzzing noise, which they seem to imitate. Some of these seem curious about human beings and will "look one straight in the eye" as they hover a short distance from one's face; the uninitiated, thinking them dangerous, will try to avoid them. They are all harmless, however, and do not bite or sting.

Many larvae feed on decaying vegetation; others are predacious, especially on aphids. Some are plant feeders and pests; a few are aquatic in the larval stage.

There are 91 genera, with a total of 874 species in the U.S. and Canada.

The generic classification used here is based on a manuscript prepared by J. R. Vockeroth (Biosystematic Research Institute, Agriculture Canada, Ottawa) and F. C. Thompson (Systematic Entomology Laboratory, U.S. Department of Agriculture, Washington), the use of which is gratefully acknowledged.

Subfamily Microdontinae

47.1 *Microdon* Meigen

Thirty-one species, including the following:

M. fulgens Weidemann. L. ±15 mm. Antennae black; head blue with pale yellow pile; thorax and abdomen golden green; wings brown; legs green or blue (1) NJ, e. PA, MD, DE; (2) VA, NC, SC, FL.

[47.2 *Rhopalosyrphus* Giglio-Tos (1 sp., *R. carolae* Capelle); 47.3 *Mixogaster* Macquart (3 spp.)]

Subfamily Syrphinae
Tribe Paragini

[47.4 *Paragus* Latreille, with 2 subgenera: *Paragus* s. str. (±5 spp.) and *Pandasyopthalmus* Stuckenberg (2 spp.)]

Tribe Toxomerini
47.5 *Toxomerus* Macquart

Seventeen species, including the following:

T. marginatus (Say). L. 5–6 mm. Head light yellow, sides black; antennae reddish yellow; thorax greenish black; scutellum yellow; legs yellow; abdomen black with narrowly yellow margin. (1), (2), (3), (4), (5), generally disturbed.

[47.6 *Baccha* Fabricius (1 sp., *B. elonga* Fabricius)): 47.7 *Leucopodella* Hull (1 sp., *L. marmorata* (Bigot)]

Tribe Melanostomatini

[47.8 *Xanthandrus* Verrall (1 sp., *X. mexicanus* Curran); 47.9 *Melanostoma* Schiner (16 spp.)]

47.10 *Platycheirus* Lepeletier and Serville

Sixty species, including the following:

P. quadratus (Say). L. ±7 mm. Head deep shining green covered with yellow pile; antennae brownish black; thorax deep shining green; legs reddish brown; abdomen black with yellow spots. (1) n.e. NA, (2) VA, NC, SC; (3) CA; (4) Pacific n.w.; (5) Central states.

Tribe Syrphini
47.11 *Chrysotoxum* Fabricius

Seventeen species, the following of which are common:

C. ventricosum Loew. L. ±10 mm. Eyes hairy; body black with bright yellow markings on head, thorax, and abdomen. (1) n.e. NA; (3) AZ, NM; (4) Pacific n.w.; (5) n. Central states.

C. integre Williston (Yellowjacket Fly). L. ±10 mm. Black with yellow markings, that resemble those of wasps. (3) CA, AZ; (4) Pacific n.w. (A&J 333).

47.12 *Syrphus* Fabricius

Seventeen species, including the following:

S. rectus Osten Sacken. L. 7–14 mm. Eyes without hair; head yellow, with brown antennae; thorax greenish; abdomen black with yellow crossbands; hind femora of female yellow and black, of male black except at tip. Adults visit almost any flower from April through August. (1) n.e. NA; (2) s.e. US.

S. torvus Osten Sacken. L. 10–13 mm. Yellow on head with faint gray spot under eyes; eyes hairy; thorax dull green; abdomen with three prominent yellow crossbands. Adults feed on pollen, nectar and honeydew from aphids (See Fig. 29.40.)

Fig. 29.40. SP: Spurious vein. (*From Metcalf*)

(1) n.e. NA; (2) s.e. US; (3) CA; (4) Pacific n.w.; (5) n. Central states.

[47.13 *Epistrophe* Dusek and Láska, with 2 subgenera: *Epistrophe* s. str. (5 spp.) and *Epistrophella* Dušek and Láska (5 spp.)]

47.14 *Metasyrphus* Matsumura

The genus includes two subgenera: *Metasyrphus* s. str. (35 spp.) and *Lapposyrphus* Dušek and Láska (2 spp.). The following species may serve as an example:

M. americanus (Wiedemann) (American Flower Fly). L. ±10 mm. Metallic, greenish; three yellow abdominal crossbands, that of the first reaching the lateral margins but not those of the second or third. Front of head with median black stripe; sides of head black. Adults frequent flowers. Larvae are predacious on aphids. (1), (2), (3), (4), (5), generally distributed.

[47.15 *Eupeodes* Osten Sacken (1 sp., *E. volucris* Osten Sacken); 47.16 *Scaeva* Fabricus (1 sp., *S. pyrastri* (Linnaeus)); 47.17 *Dasysyrphus* Enderlein (13 spp.); 47.18 *Leucozona* Schiner, with 2 subgenera: *Leucozona* s. str (1 sp., *L. lucorum* (Linnaeus)) and *Ischyrosyrphus* Mik (2 spp.); 47.19 *Melangyna* Verrall, with 2 subgenera: *Melangyna* s. str. (13 spp.) and *Meligramma* Frey (3 spp.); 47.20 *Parasyrphus* Matsumura (7 spp.); 47.21 *Xanthogramma* Schiner (1 sp., *X. flavipes* (Loew)); 47.22 *Doros* Meigen (1 sp., *D. aequalis* Loew); 47.23 *Dideomima* Vockeroth (1 sp., *D. coquilletti* (Williston)); 47.24 *Didea* Macquart (2 spp.); 47.25 *Megasyrphus* Dušek and Láska (1 sp., *M. anniulipes* (Zetterstedt)); 47.26 *Meliscaeva* Frey (1 sp., *M. cinctella* (Zetterstedt))]

47.27 *Ocyptamus* Macquart

Twelve species, including the following:

O. fuscipennis Say. L. 10–11 mm. Wings almost entirely dark brown; thorax metallic greenish black; abdomen bronze-brown and black. (1) n.e. NA; (2) s.e. US; (3) TX; (5) CO, KS, MO.

[47.28 *Pseudodoros* Becker (1 sp., *P. clavatus* Fabricius); 47.29 *Salpingogaster* Schiner, with 2 subgenera: *Salpingogaster* s. str. (2 spp.) and *Eosalpingogaster* Hull (1 sp., *S. nepenthe* (Hull))]

47.30 *Allograpta* Osten Sacken

Six species, including the following:

A. obligua (Say). L. 6–7 mm. Head yellow with brown and black markings; antennae brown to black; thorax deeply shining green with yellow stripe on side; abdomen black with yellow stripes. (1), (2), (3), (4), (5), generally distributed.

47.31 *Sphaerophoria* Lepeletier and Serville

Thirteen species, the following of which is common:

S. contigua Macquart. L. ±8 mm. Head yellow, shining; antennae reddish yellow; thorax dark greenish, shiny, with short yellow stripe on side; abdomen black with yellow crossbands. Found on flowers from May to October. (1), (2), (3), (4), (5), generally distributed.

Subfamily Eristalinae

Tribe Pipizini

[47.32 *Pipiza* Fallén (16 spp.); 47.33 *Heringia* Rondani (30 spp.); 47.34 *Trichopsomyia* Williston (8 spp.)]

Tribe Rhingiini

[47.35 *Cheilosia* Meigen (77 spp.); 47.36 *Hiatomyia* Shannon (22 spp.); 47.37 *Ferdinandea* Rondani (5 spp.); 47.38 *Rhingia* Scopoli (1 sp., *R.*

nasica Say)); 47.39 *Chamaesyrphus* Mik (3 spp.); 47.40 *Pelecocera* Meigen (1 sp., *P. pergandei* (Williston))]

Tribe Volucellini

47.41 *Volucella* Geoffroy

One species, as follows:

V. bombylans (Linnaeus) (Hover Fly). L. 10–11 mm. Very hairy species resembling a bee; black with red and/or yellow markings; wings with a distinct band. Larvae are scavengers in nests of bumble bees. (See A&J 330.) (1) n.e. US; (2) s.e. US; (3) TX; (5) KS.

47.42 *Ornidia* St. Fargeau and Serville

One species, as follows:

O. obesa (Fabricius). L. ±9.5 mm. Brilliant green; legs black; wings with faint brown tinge and brown spots. (2) LA, MS, AL, FL; (3) NM, TX.

[47.43 *Copestylum* Macquart (39 spp.)]

Tribe Callicerini

[47.44 *Callicera* Panzer (4 spp.)]

Tribe Sericomyiini

[47.45 *Sericomyia* Meigen (11 spp.); 47.46 *Arctophila* Schiner (2 spp.); 47.47 *Pyritis* Osburn (2 spp.)]

Tribe Brachyopini

[47.48 *Neoascia* Williston (10 spp.); 47.49 *Sphegina* Meigen, with 2 subgenera: *Sphegina* s. str. (±20 spp.) and *Asiosphegina* Stackelberg (±5 spp.); 47.50 *Brachyopa* Meigen, with 2 subgenera: *Brachyopa* s. str. (13 spp.) and *Hammerschmidtia* Schummel (2 spp.); 47.51 *Orthonevra* Meigen (2 spp.); 47.52 *Chrysogaster* Meigen (2 spp.); 47.53 *Chrysosyrphus* Sedman (8 spp.); 47.54 *Myolepta* Newman (7 spp.); 47.55 *Lepidomyia* Loew (1 sp., *L. micheneri* Fluke))]

Tribe Merodontini

47.56 *Merodon* Meigen

One species, as follows:

M. equestris (Fabricius) (Narcissus Bulb Fly).

47.57 *Eumerus* Meigen

Three species, the following of which are pests:

E. strigatus (Fallén) (Onion Blub Fly).

E. tuberculatus Rondani (Lesser Blub Fly).

[47.58 *Psilota* Meigen (3 spp.); 47.59 *Nausigaster* Williston (8 spp.)]

Tribe Eristalini

[47.60 *Helophilus* Meigen (10 spp.); 47.61 *Parhelophilus* Girschner (8 spp.); 47.62 *Lejota* Rondani, with 5 subgenera: *Anasimyia* Schiner (10 spp.), *Asemosyrphus* Bigot (1 sp., *L. polygrammus* (Loew)), *Arctosyrphus* Frey (1 sp., *L. willingii* (Smith)), *Lunomyia* Curren and Fluke (1 sp., *L. cooleyi* (Seamans)), and *Polydontomyia* Williston (1 sp., *L. curvipes* (Wiedemann))]

47.63 *Mallota* Meigen

Nine species, including the following:

M. bautias (Walker). L. 13–16 mm. Thorax and base of abdomen with yellow hairlike setae, elsewhere black; wings with pale brown bands. (1) n.e. US; (2) s.e. US; (3) TX.

47.64 *Meromacrus* Rondani

Four species, including the following:

M. acutus (Fabricius). L. ±18 mm. Body dark; head, thorax, and abdomen with narrow bright yellow markings. (2) s.e. US.

47.65 *Eristalis* Latreille

Two subgenera: *Eristalis* s. str. (1 sp., *E. tenax* (Linnaeus), described below) and *Eoseristalis* Kenervo (21 spp.).

E. tenax (Linnaeus) (Drone Fly; Rat-tailed Maggot). L. 12–14 mm. Resembles a honey bee. Adults fly from May to September, visiting flowers. Larvae live in polluted water (where they are able to breathe by extending their long tapering tails to the surface) and in wet, decaying carcasses. Cosmopolitan. (See A&J 331.)

[47.66 *Eristalinus* Rondani (1 sp., *E. aeneus* (Scopoli)); 47.67 *Palpada* Macquart (10 spp.)]

Tribe Cerioidini
47.68 *Ceriana* Rafinesque

Five species, including the following:

C. willistoni (Kahl). L. ±14 mm. Wasp mimic; black with yellow spot on head, yellow stripes on thorax; legs yellow; wings black in front, hyaline in back; abdomen with yellow crossbands. (1) n.e. US; (2) s.e. US; (3) TX; (5) MN.

[47.69 *Sphiximorpha* Rondani (8 spp.); 47.70 *Polybiomyia* Shannon (9 spp.); 47.71 *Monoceromyia* Shannon (1 sp., *M. floridensis* (Shannon))]

Tribe Milesiini

[47.72 *Criorhina* Meigen (14 spp.); 47.73 *Sphecomyia* Latreille (8 spp.); 47.74 *Merapioidus* Bigot (1 sp., *M. villosus* Bigot); 47.75 *Blera* Billberg (16 spp.); 47.76 [Number not used]; 47.77 *Somula* Macquart (2 spp.)]

47.78 *Temnostoma* Lepeletier and Serville

Ten species, including the following:

T. alternans Loew. L. 12–15 mm. Wasp mimic; body black; antennae yellow to reddish; thorax with yellow stripes; abdomen with yellow crossbands. (1) n.e. US; (2) VA, NC, SC, GA; (5) CO, KS, MO.

[47.79 *Pterallastes* Loew (1 sp., *P. thoracicus* Loew); 47.80 *Palumbia* Rondani (1 sp., *?P. inflata* (Macquart)); 47.81 *Teuchocnemis* Osten Sacken (2 spp.)]

47.82 *Milesia* Latreille

Three species, including the following:

M. virginiensis (Drury). L. 18–21 mm. Wasp mimic; body brownish black; abdomen with large yellow spots; legs yellow. (1) n.e. US; (2) s.e. US; (3) TX.

[47.83 *Spilomyia* Meigen (11 spp.); 47.84 *Tropidia* Meigen (8 spp.); 47.85 *Syritta* Lepeletier and Serville (1 sp., *S. pipiens* (Linnaeus)); 47.86 *Xylota* Meigen (29 spp.); 47.87 *Chalcosyrphus* Curran, subgenus *Chalcosyrphus* s. str. (1 sp., *C. depressus* (Shannon)), with 2 subgenera: *Xylotomima* Shannon (25 spp.) and *Neplas* Porter (1 sp., *C. pauxillus* (Williston)); 47.88 *Brachypalpus* Macquart, with 2 subgenera: *Brachypalpus* s. str. (1 sp., *B. oarus* (Walker)) and *Crioprora* Osten Sacken (4 spp.); 47.89 *Hadromyia* Williston, with 2 subgenera: *Hadromyia* s. str. (1 sp., *H. grandis* (Williston)) and *Chrysosomidia* Curran (5 spp.); 47.90

Pocota Lepeletier and Serville (1 sp., *P. bomboidea* Hunter)); 47.91 *Cynorhinella* Curran (2 spp.)]

48. PIPUNCULIDAE (Big-headed Fly Family)

Length: 1.5–9.5 mm. Adults cannot be mistaken for any other fly because of their very large heads, larger than their thorax. Although uncommon, they may be collected in fields near woods where their larvae parasitize various species of Homoptera. The 105 species are widely distributed throughout the U.S. and Canada.

Subfamily Chalarinae

[48.1 *Chalarus* Walker (2 spp.); 48.2 *Verrallia* Mik (2 spp.); 48.3 *Jassidophaga* Aczel (2 spp.)]

Subfamily Pipunculinae
Tribe Nephrocerini

[48.4 *Nephrocerus* Zetterstedt (2 spp.)]

Tribe Pipunculini
48.5 *Pipunculus* Latreille

This genus is divided into three subgenera: *Pipunculus* s. str. (10 spp.), *Eudorylas* Aczel (36 spp.), and *Cephalosphaera* Enderlein (8 spp.). The following species may serve as an example:

P. (Pipunculus) ater Meigen. L. 3.5–4 mm. Entirely dark with large red eyes. Collected by sweeping foliage in woodlands. June and July. (1) n.e. NA; (2) KY, WV, VA, TN, NC, AR, LA, MS, AL, GA; (3) s.w. US; (5) ND, SD, MN, NE, IA, KS, MO.

[48.6 *Allomethus* Hardy (2 spp.); 48.7 *Tomosvaryella* Aczel (32 spp.); 48.8 *Dorylomorpha* Aczel (9 spp.)]

Infraorder SCHIZOPHORA ACALYPTRATAE

This large group contains nine superfamilies and forty-nine families, many of which are small in size as well as number of species and often very rare.

Superfamily CONOPOIDEA

Only one family belongs to this superfamily, as follows.

49. CONOPIDAE (Thick-headed Fly Family)

Length: 4–18 mm. The head of most species of this family is wider than the thorax. They are wasplike or beelike, usually brown. The antennae may be fairly long, with the terminal segment somewhat enlarged. Adults feed on nectar and pollen. Larvae parasitize bumblebees, wasps, and grasshoppers. There are 67 species in the U.S. and Canada; widely distributed.

Subfamily Conopinae
Tribe Conopini

[49.1 *Conops* Linnaeus, subgenus *Asiconops* Chen (1 sp., *C. bermudensis* Parsons [Bermuda])]

49.2 *Physoconops* Szilady

This genus is divided into three subgenera: *Pachyconops* s. str. (6 spp.), *Gyroconops* Camras (1 sp., *P. sylvosus* (Williston), and *Physoconops* Szilady (5 spp.). The following species may serve as an example:

P. (*Pachyconops*) *excisus* (Wiedemann). L. ±16 mm. Wasplike; brown with pale brown markings; wings with front half brown. (1) n.e. US; (2) s.e. US; (5) CO, KS, MO.

Tribe Physocephalini

49.3 *Physocephala* Schiner

Seven species, including the following:

P. burgessi (Williston) (Wasp Fly). L. ±5 mm. Black to reddish brown; facial grooves yellow; sides of head reddish yellow; hind femora thickened at base. Larvae are internal parasites of the Bumble Bee, *Bombus sonorus*. Adults visit flowers for pollen and nectar. (See A&J 335.) (3) s.w. US; (4) Pacific n.w.; (5) AB, MT, WY, CO.

Subfamily Myopinae

[49.4 *Zodion* Latreille (14 spp.); 49.5 *Robertsonomyia* Malloch (2 spp.); 49.6 *Myopa* Fabricius (14 spp.)]

49.7 *Thecophora* Rondani

Eight species, including the following:

T. occidensis (Walker) (Common Thick-headed Fly). L. ±5 mm. Black with reddish brown markings; head narrower than most species of this family; antennae long, with enlarged terminal segment. Adults feed on pollen and nectar of flowers. Larvae are endoparasites of bees. (See A&J 334.) (1) n.e. NA; (2) KY, WV, VA, TN, NC, AR, LA, MS, AL, GA; (3) s.w. US.

Subfamily Dalmanniinae

[49.8 *Dalmannia* Robineau-Desvoidy (6 spp.)]

Subfamily Stylogastrinae

[49.9 *Stylogaster* Macquart (3 spp.)]

[1 sp., unplaced]

Superfamily NERIOIDEA

50. CYPSELOSOMATIDAE (Cypselosomatidae Fly Family)

This family apparently contains the following two species, treated in the Stone, *et al.* (1965) catalog as Acalyptrates of uncertain position. L. 2.5–3.0 mm.

[50.1 *Latheticomyia* Wheeler: *L. tricolor* Wheeler ((3) AZ; (4) UT) and *L. lineata* Wheeler ((3) AZ)]

51. MICROPEZIDAE (Stilt-legged Fly Family)

Length: 4–15 mm. Abdomen narrowly attached to thorax, wasplike. Middle and hind legs very long, each longer than body. Adults found in marshes or moist woods on leaves, stems, and tree trunks. Known larvae are saprophagous. There are 31 species in the U.S. and Canada.

Subfamily Calobatinae

[51.1 *Cnodacophora* Czerny (1 sp., *C. nasoni* (Cresson))]

51.2 *Compsobata* Czerny

Of the two subgenera, *Compsobata* s. str. contains one species, as follows:

Fig. 29.41. (*From Curran, 1934*)

C. univittata (Walker). (See Fig. 29.41.) (1) n.e. NA; (3) s. CA, AZ, NM; (4) BC, WA, OR, ID; (5) n. Central states.

Subgenus *Trilophyrobata* Hennig (4 spp.).

Subfamily Micropezinae

[51.3 *Micropeza* Meigen, with 2 subgenera: *Micropeza* s. str. (9 spp.) and *Neriocephalus* Enderlein (6 spp.)]

Subfamily Taeniapterinae

[51.4 *Calobatina* Enderlein (3 spp.); 51.5 *Grallipeza* Rondani (1 sp., *C. nebulosa* (Loew)); 51.6 *Hoplocheiloma* Cresson (1 sp., *H. fasciatum* Cresson)]

51.7 *Rainieria* Rondani

One species, as follows:

R. antennaepes (Say). Very common. (1) n.e. US; (2) s.e. US.

51.8 *Taeniaptera* Macquart

Two species, including the following:

T. trivittata Macquart. L. ±10 mm. Body chestnut brown; wings extensively patterned with brown. Adults fly during May and June. (1) n.e. US; (2) s.e. US.

[2 spp. unplaced]

52. NERIIDAE (Neriid Fly Family)

Length: 10–12 mm. Head elongate, cylindrical, projecting anteriorly; antennae stout, projecting anteriorly; eyes not much taller than broad and equidistant in both sexes; arista apical; ocellar bristles absent; wing with R_1 not setose. Two uncommon species occur in the U.S. Their larvae live in decaying roots of papaya and in necrotic tissues of various cacti.

[52.1 *Odontoloxozus* Enderlein (1 sp., *O. longicornis* (Coquillett), (3) s.w. US); 52.2 *Glyphidops* Enderlein (1 sp., *G. flavifrons* (Bigot), (3) s. AZ)]

Superfamily DIOPSOIDEA

53. TANYPEZIDAE (Tanypezid Fly Family)

Length: 5–7 mm. Eyes very large, distinctly deeper than wide, and closer together in male than in female; ocellar bristles

present; legs long, tarsi longer than tibiae. There are two species in the U.S. of these rare and poorly known flies.

[53.1 *Tanypeza* Fallén; *T. luteipennis* Knab and Shannon [(1) n.e. US] and *T. picticornis* Knab and Shannon [(1) MI, NY, MD; (2) VA]]

54. STRONGYLOPHTHALMYIIDAE
(Strongylophthalamyiid Fly Family)

[From Psilidae of authors]

Very little is known about the one species assigned to this family. The larvae are unknown. L. ±5 mm.

[54.1 *Strongylophthalmyia* Heller (1 sp., *S. angustipennis* Melander [(1) ON, QU, NS, MI, NY, VA, NH, ME, MA; (3) NM; (4) BC; (5) AB, MB, SK, MT, ND, SD, WY, NE])]

55. PSILIDAE (Rust Fly Family)

Length: 3–8 mm. Antennae with third segment three or four times as long as second. Adults live in moist areas and in woods. Larvae either are root and stem borers or live under bark of various trees and shrubs. There are 34 species, as follows.

Subfamily Psilinae

[55.1 *Loxocera* Meigen (6 spp.)]

55.2 *Psila* Meigen

The genus is divided into three subgenera: *Chamaepsila* Hendel (8 spp.), *Pseudopsila* Johnson (6 spp.), and *Tetrapsila* Frey (1 sp., *P. frontalis* Coquillett). The following is a pest:

P. (Chamaepsila) rosae (Fabricius) (Carrot Rust Fly). L. ±4 mm. Shiny black with reddish-yellow head and yellow legs. Larvae infest carrots. (1) n.e. US; (3) n. CA; (4) Pacific n.w.; (5) WY, n. CO.

Subfamily Chylizinae

[55.3 *Chyliza* Fallén (10 spp.)]

[3 spp., unplaced]

56. DIOPSIDAE (Stalk-eyed Fly Family)

Length: 3.5–6 mm. Head considerably wider than thorax. Eye stalks in our species broad; much longer, narrower stalks in tropical species, some 3 or 3.5 times as long as thorax is wide. Only one species reaches our region.

56.1 *Sphyracephala* Say

One species, as follows:

S. brevicornis Say. L. ±4 mm. Body bare; wings with two broad, pale brown stripes; easily recognized by eye stalks. Found on rocks near water or on skunk cabbage and similar vegetation. Larvae apparently breed in decaying vegetation. (See Fig. 29.42.) (1) n.e. US; (2) VA, NC; (5) CO, KS, MO.

Superfamily TEPHRITOIDEA

57. LONCHAEIDAE (Lonchaeid Fly Family)

Length: 5–6 mm. Shiny black; wings not pictured. Adults common in woods. Larvae of most species secondary invaders

Fig. 29.42. (*From Curran, 1934*)

of injured or diseased plants, under bark, or in decaying fruit and other plant material. Thirty-eight species occur in the U.S. and Canada.

[57.1 *Dasiops* Rondani (7 spp.); 57.2 *Chaetolonchaea* Czerny (1 sp., *C. pallipennis* (Zetterstedt))]

57.3 *Earomyia* Zetterstedt

Eight species, the following of which is common:

E. aberrans (Malloch). A pest of cones of conifers. (1) n.e. US; (2) FL.

57.4 *Lonchaea* Fallén

Twenty species, of which the following is the most common:

L. polita Say. (1), (2), (3), (4), (5), widespread.

[57.5 *Silba* Macquart (1 sp., *S. glaberrima* (Wiedemann))]

58. OTITIDAE (Picture-winged Fly Family)

Length: 3.5–12 mm. Wings of most species pictured; costa not broken where Sc reaches it; Sc slightly curved at tip; body usually quite bright and often metallic. Larvae feed on decaying vegetable matter except for the few that live in roots and are pests. There are 127 species in the U.S. and Canada.

Subfamily Otitinae

[58.1 *Callopistromyia* Hendel (1 sp., *C. annulipes* (Macquart)); 58.2 *Cephalia* Meigen (4 spp.); 58.3 *Ceroxys* Macquart (1 sp., *C. latiusculus* (Loew)); 58.4 *Curranops* Harriot (2 spp.)]

58.5 *Delphinia* Robineau-Desvoidy

One species, as follows:

D. picta (Fabricius). L. ±8 mm. Head and thorax brown; abdomen dark brown, nearly black; heavy, long black bristles on thorax; wings pictured. (1) n.e. US; (2) s.e. US; (5) MN, NE, IA, KS, MO.

[58.6 *Diacrita* Gerstaecker (2 spp.); 58.7 *Dyscrasis* Aldrich (1 sp., *D. hendeli* Aldrich); 58.8 *Haiga* Steyskal (1 sp., *H. nevadana* Steyskal); 58.9 *Herina* Robineau-Desvoidy (4 spp.); 58.10 *Hiatus* Cresson (1 sp., *H. fulvipes* Cresson); 58.11 *Idana* Loew (1 sp., *I. marginata* (Say)); 58.12 *Melieria* Robineau-Desvoidy (6 spp.); 58.13 *Myiomyrmica* Steyskal (1 sp., *M. fenestrata* (Coquillett)); 58.14 *Myrmecothea* Hendel (1 sp., *M. myrmecoides* (Loew)); 58.15 *Notogramma* Loew (2 spp.); 58.16 *Otites* Latreille (5 spp.); 58.17 *Pseudotephritis* Johnson, subgenus *Pseudotephritis* s. str. (3 spp.); subgenus *Pseudotephritina* Malloch (2 spp.); 58.18 *Pterocalla* Rondani (1 sp., *P. strigula* Loew); 58.19 *Seioptera* Kirby (5 spp.)]

58.20 *Tetanops* Fallén

The genus is divided into three subgenera: *Tetanops* s. str. (5 spp.), *Eurycephalomyia* Hendel (1 sp., *T. myopaeformis* (Roeder) [see below]), and *Psaeropterella* Hendel (2 spp.). The following is a pest:

T. (Eurycephalomyia) myopaeformis (Roeder) (Sugarbeet Root Maggot). (3) CA, AZ, NM; (4) BC, WA, OR, ID; (5) MB, MT, WY, CO.

[58.21 *Tetropismenus* Loew (1 sp., *T. hirtus* Loew); 58.22 *Tritoxa* Loew (5 spp.); 58.23 *Tujunga* Steykal (1 sp., *T. mackenziei* Steykal); 58.24 *Ulidiotites* Steyskal (1 sp., *U. dakotana* Steyskal)]

Subfamily Ulidiinae

[58.25 *Acrosticta* Loew (6 spp.); 58.26 *Axiolgina* Hendel (1 sp., *A. ferrumequinum* Hendel [(2)s. FL]); 58.27 *Chaetopsis* Loew (7 spp.); 58.28 *Eumtopiella* Hendel (2 spp.); 58.29 *Euxesta* Loew (31 spp.); 58.30 *Homalocephala* Zetterstedt (4 spp.); 58.31 *Oedopa* Loew (2 spp.); 58.32 *Paroedopa* Coquillett (1 sp., *P. punctigera* Coquillett); 58.33 *Physiphora* Fallén (2 spp.); 58.34 *Steneretma* Loew (1 sp., *S. laticauda* Loew); 58.35 *Stenomyia* Loew (4 spp.); 58.36 *Stictomyia* Bigot (2 spp.); 58.37 *Texasa* Steyskal (1 sp., *T. chaetifrons* Steyskal); 58.38 *Zacompsia* Coquillett (1 sp., *Z. fulva* Coquillett)]

[Unplaced genus: 58.39 *Prionella* Robineau-Desvoidy (2 spp.)]

[Unplaced species, 1 sp.]

59. PLATYSTOMATIDAE (Platystomatid Fly Family)

Length: 3.5–12 mm. Pictured wings with Sc slightly bent; costa not broken at juncture of C and Sc. Known larvae found on decaying vegetation. There are 41 species in the U.S. and Canada.

[59.1 *Amphicnephes* Loew (2 spp.); 59.2 *Pogonortalis* Hendel (1 sp., *P. doclea* (Walker))]

59.3 *Rivellia* Robineau-Desvoidy

Thirty-four species, of which the following is relatively common:

R. quadrifasciata (Macquart). (1) n.e. NA; (2) s.e. US; (3) TX; (5) n. Central states.

[59.4 *Senopterina* Macquart (4 spp.)]

60. PYRGOTIDAE (Light Fly Family)

Length: 6–18 mm. Usually brown, with brown pictured wings; head elongate. Adults attracted to lights at night, particularly lanterns and campfires. Larvae parasitize scarab beetle larvae. All five of our species are confined to eastern North America.

60.1 *Pyrgota* Wiedemann

Two species, the following of which is common:

P. undata Wiedemann. L. ±12 mm. Body brown; head somewhat elongate; wings with anterior half dark brown. (See Fig. 29.43.) (1) n.e. NA; (2) s.e. US; (5) n. Central states.

[60.2 *Pyrgotella* Curran (1 sp., *P. chagnoni* (Johnson)); 60.3 *Sphecomyiella* Hendel (2 spp.)]

Fig. 29.43. (*From Sweetman*)

61. TEPHRITIDAE (Fruit Fly Family)

Length: 2–12 mm (rarely up to 25 mm, including long ovipositor). Most species with characteristic pictured wings. Costa vein broken at subcostal junction; subcosta bent at right angles unlike that of other pictured-winged flies; calypters very small; ocelli present. Adult males, of the common species at least, court females by walking about with their colored wings raised, often only one wing at a time, and moving back and forth in a characteristic fashion. Larvae of many species live in fruit; others develop in seeds of composites, are leaf miners, or cause galls. True fruit flies are among the most destructive of insects and therefore the most feared by growers, especially citrus fruit growers. A total of 280 species is known in the U.S. and Canada.

[Note: *Dacus cucurbitae* Coquillett (Melon Fly), *D. dorsalis* Hendel (Oriental Fruit Fly), and *Ceratitis capitata* (Wiedemann) (Mediterranean Fruit Fly; see Fig. 29.44) are very serious pests in tropical regions and in Hawaii but have not become permanently established in the U.S. or Canada. Since it is always possible that they may be imported with produce, constant inspection of these imports is necessary. At times, the Mediterranean Fruit Fly becomes temporarily established in the citrus region of California.]

61.1 *Toxotrypana* Gerstaecker

One species, as follows:

T. curvicauda Gerstaecker (Papaya Fruit Fly). (2) s. FL; (3) s. TX.

Fig. 29.44. (*From U.S. Dept. of Agric.*)

[61.2 *Rhynencina* Johnson (1 sp., *R. longirostris* Johnson); 61.3 *Urophora* Robineau-Desvoidy (8 spp.); 61.4 *Callachna* Aldrich (1 sp., *C. gibba* (Loew)); 61.5 *Peronyma* Loew (1 sp., *P. sarcinata* (Loew)); 61.6 *Procecidochares* Hendel (11 spp.); 61.7 *Procecidocharoides* Foote (4 spp.); 61.8 *Cecidocharella* Hendel (1 sp., *C. borrichia* Bush and Huettel); 61.9 *Eutreta* Loew (15 spp.); 61.10 *Cryptotreta* Blanc and Foote (1 sp., *C. pallida* (Cole)); 61.11 *Paracantha* Coquillett (6 spp.)]

61.12 *Eurosta* Loew

Nine species, including the following:

E. conspurcata Doane. L. ±7 mm. Body brown; wings covered with brown patterns. Adults found in low vegetation. (1) n.e. US.

E. solidaginis (Fitch) (Goldenrod Gall Fly). L. ±7.5 mm. Body brown; thorax with dark, longitudinal stripes; wings with dense brown picturing. Larvae form stem galls in goldenrod, where they overwinter. Related species also make galls in goldenrod. (1) n.e. US; (5) KS, MO.

[61.13 *Acidogona* Loew (1 sp., *A. melanura* (Loew)); 61.14 *Jamesomyia* Quisenberry (1 sp., *J. geminata* (Loew)); 61.15 *Xanthomyia* Phillips (2 spp.); 61.16 *Xenochaeta* Snow (2 spp.)]

61.17 *Acinia* Robineau-Desvoidy

One species, as follows:

A. picturata (Snow) (Sourbush Seed Fly).

[61.18 *Icterica* Loew (2 spp.); 61.19 *Acrotaenia* Loew (1 sp., *A. testudinea* (Loew)); 61.20 *Oxyna* Robineau-Desvoidy (3 spp.)]

61.21 *Euaresta* Loew

Eight species, including the following:

E. bella (Loew). L. 2–3 mm. Head yellow; thorax black with some light areas, entirely covered with golden yellow pile; legs yellow; abdomen light with dark brown tinge; wings pictured with open transparent spots along margins. Adults fly from June to August; taken by sweeping vegetation in bottomlands. (1), (2), (3), (4), (5), generally distributed.

[61.22 *Paroxyna* Hendel (22 spp.); 61.23 *Dioxyna* Frey (2 spp.); 61.24 *Trupanea* Schrank (20 spp.); 61.25 *Tephritis* Latreille (18 spp.); 61.26 *Gonioxyna* Hendel (1 sp., *G. fuscata* Foote); 61.27 *Dyseuaresta* Hendel (1 sp., *D. mexicana* (Wiedemann)); 61.28 *Neotephritis* Hendel (3 spp.); 61.29 *Euarestoides* Benjamin (4 spp.); 61.30 *Mylogymnocarena* Foote (1 sp., *M. apicata* (Thomas)); 61.31 *Metatephritis* Foote (1 sp., *M. fenestrata* Foote); 61.32 *Hexachaeta* Loew (3 spp.); 61.33 *Myoleja* Rondani (4 spp.); 61.34 *Aciurina* Curran (10 spp.); 61.35 *Valentibulla* Foote and Blanc (5 spp.); 61.36 *Xanthaciura* Hendel (4 spp.); 61.37 *Stenopa* Loew (2 spp.); 61.38 *Orellia* Robineau-Desvoidy (3 spp.); 61.39 *Paraterellia* Foote (4 spp.); 61.40 *Neaspilota* Osten Sacken (11 spp.); 61.41 [number not used]; 61.42 *Chaetostomella* Hendel (1 sp., *C. undosa* (Coquillett))]

61.43 *Anastrepha* Schiner

Twenty species, the following of which are pests:

A. ludens (Loew) (Mexican Fruit Fly). This is a serious pest in Mexico and Central America. (See Fig. 29.45 for larvae-infested pear.) It invades south Texas from time to time and infests grapefruit and other citrus.

A. pallens (Coquillett) (Bumelia Fruit Fly). (3) TX.

Fig. 29.45. (*From U.S. Dept. of Agric.*)

61.44 *Rhagoletis* Loew

Twenty-one species, several of which are severe pests:

R. pomonella (Walsh) (Apple Maggot). L. 4–4.5 mm. Head yellow; thorax dark brown to black, paler ventrally; legs yellow; abdomen dark brown with white cross bands on posterior margins of first three segments in male and first four in female; wings with four dark bars, the basal one united posteriorly with the second; bars 2 through 4 united anteriorly; wing without apical spot. Adults fly from July to September. Females lay eggs under skin of developing apples or in the fruit of *Crataegus* spp. (1) n.e. US; (2) s.e. US; (3) TX; (4) OR; (5) ND, SD, MN, NE, IA, KS, MO.

R. cingulata (Loew) (Cherry Fruit Fly). L. 3.5–4 mm. Head yellow; thorax dark brown with irregular, lateral white stripe; legs yellow tinged with brown; abdomen as in preceding species; wing pattern of four bars, with apical two united anteriorly and small apical spot in addition. Larvae infest cherries. (See Fig. 29.46.) (1) n.e. US; (2) s.e. US; (5) IA, NE.

R. indifferens Curran (Western Cherry Fruit Fly). Similar to the preceding. (3) CA; (4) Pacific n.w.; (5) n. Central states.

R. completa Cresson (Walnut Husk Fly).

R. fausta (Osten Sacken) (Black Cherry Fruit Fly).

R. mendax Curran (Blueberry Maggot).

Fig. 29.46. *Rhafoletis cingulata* (Loew). (*Fla. Dept. of Agric.*)

61.45 *Zonosemata* Benjamin

Two species, the following of which is a pest:

Z. electa (Say) (Pepper Maggot). L. 6.5–7.5 mm. Head and antennas yellow, tinted with rufous brown; thorax bright yellow, marked with brown and black; legs yellowish; abdomen yellowish with small black apical spot. Larvae infest solanaceous fruit, especially eggplant. (1) n.e. US; (2) s.e. US; (3) TX, OK, NM, AZ.

[61.46 *Rhagoletotrypeta* Aczel (2 spp.); 61.47 *Oedicarena* Loew (2 spp.); 61.48 *Gymnocarena* Hering (3 spp.)]

61.49 *Strauzia* Robineau–Desvoidy

One species, as follows:

S. longipennis (Wiedemann) (Sunflower Maggot).

[61.50 *Trypeta* Meigen (7 spp.); 61.51 *Euleia* Walker (2 spp.)]

61.52 *Epochra* Loew

One species, as follows:

E. canadensis (Loew) (Currant Fruit Fly).

[61.53 *Chetostoma* Rodani (2 spp.); 61.54 *Tomoplagia* Coquillett (2 spp.)]

62. RICHARDIIDAE (Richardiid Fly Family)

Length: 3.5–15 mm. Ocelli present; wings with subcosta present, but not at right angles to costa; costa broken near Sc; second abdominal segment with lateral bristles; femora often thickened and spined; wings usually patterned. Larvae and adult habits poorly known. Only one of the nine species is widely distributed (see below).

[62.1 *Omomyia* Coquillett (2 spp.); 62.2 *Automola* Loew (1 sp., *A. rufa* Cresson); 62.3 *Coniceps* Loew (1 sp., *C. niger* Loew)]

62.4 *Odontomera* Macquart

Two species, the following of which is common:

O. ferruginea Macquart. (1) n.e. US; (2) s.e. US; (3) TX.

[62.5 *Sepsisoma* Johnson (3 spp.)]

63. PALLOPTERIDAE (Pallopterid Fly Family)

Length: 4.7 mm. Scutum with one or more presutural dorsocentral bristles; cell cup without angular extension at posterior apex; disc of proepisternum always bare; wings usually with brown markings. Adults are found in woods. Larval habits in this country are unknown. They may be flower and stem feeders or beetle larvae predators, occurring under bark, if they follow the habits of their European relatives. Nine species, all in the following genus:

63.1 *Palloptera* Fallén

The following species is common:

P. superba Loew. Rows of black spots at base of bristles along apex of abdominal segments. (1) n.e. US; (2) VA, NC.

64. PIOPHILIDAE (Skipper Fly Family)

Length: 1–9.5 mm. Black, usually metallic, possibly with bluish reflection. Adults are found around decaying animal matter or fungi where their larvae live. There are 31 species.

Subfamily Piophilinae
64.1 *Piophila* Fallén

The genus is divided into nine subgenera: *Piophila* s. str. (1 sp., *P. casei* (Linnaeus) [see below]), *Allopiophila* Hendel (9 spp.), *Amphipogon* Wahlberg (1 sp., *P. hyperborea* (Guene)), *Arctopiophila* Duda (1 sp., *P. nigerrima* Lundbeck), *Lasiopiophila* Duda (1 sp., *P. pilosa* Staeger), *Liopiophila* Duda (6 spp.), *Mycetaulus* Loew (7 spp.), *Prochyliza* Walker (2 spp.), *Protopiophila* Duda (1 sp., *P. foveolata* Meigen), [2 spp., unplaced]. The following species is a pest:

P. (*Piophila*) *casei* (Linnaeus) (Cheese Skipper). L. 4–5 mm. The jumping larvae infest cheese and sometimes human intestines. They are also pests of smoked meats and meat products. Cosmopolitan. (See Fig. 29.47.)

Subfamily Neottiophilinae

[64.2 *Actenoptera* Czerny (1 sp., *A. hilarella* (Zetterstedt))]

Superfamily OPOMYZOIDEA

65. CLUSIIDAE (Clusiid Fly Family)

Length: 2–6 mm. Arista subapical; pedicel with an angular though sometimes weak projection on outer side; metepisternum bare; face broadly membranous and sunken in middle; vibrissa present; front with pair of cruciate interfrontal bristles and two to five strong, more or less equally spaced, mostly reclinate front-orbital bristles, with at most only the lowest one inclinate; C without humeral break; all tibiae with preapical dorsal bristle. These rare flies are sometimes found around rotting wood or on grass in meadows. Larvae probably occur in decaying wood; like Cheese Skippers, they are capable of leaping. Most of the 27 species occur in the eastern U.S.

Subfamily Clusiinae

[65.1 *Chaetoclusia* Coquillett (1 sp., *C. affinis* Johnson); 65.2 *Clusia* Haliday (3 spp.); 65.3 *Heteromeringia* Czerny (3 spp.); 65.4 *Sobarocephala* Czerny (6 spp.)]

Subfamily Clusiodinae
65.5 *Clusiodes* Coquillett

This genus is divided into two subgenera: *Clusiodes* s. str. (9 spp.) and *Columbiella* Malloch (5 spp.). The following species is common.

C. (*Clusiodes*) *melanostoma* (Loew). (1) n.e. NA; (4) WA; (5) AB.

Fig. 29.47. (*From Curran, 1934*)

66. ACARTOPHTHALMIDAE
(Acartophthalmid Fly Family)

Length: 2–2.5 mm. Arista dorsobasal; front broadly membanous and sunken in middle, without cruciate interfrontal bristles; vibrissae present; C with humeral break; all tibiae without preapical dorsal bristle; metepisternum bare; black; yellow front coxae and halteres. Larvae found in rotten fungi and carrion. Two species in the following genus.

66.1 *Acartophthalmus* Czerny

The following species may serve as an example:

A. nigrinus (Zetterstedt). (1) n.e. US; (4) Pacific n.w.; (5) n. Central States.

67. ODINIIDAE (Odiniid Fly Family)

Length: 2–5 mm. Adults are attracted to sap flows on wounded trees, fungi, and rotting wood. Larvae are probably scavengers. Eleven rare species with very limited distribution.

[67.1 *Odinia* Robineau-Desvoidy (8 spp.); 67.2 *Neoalticomerus* Hendel (1 sp., *N. seamansi* Shewell)]

67.3 *Traginops* Coquillett

Two species, the following of which is widely distributed.

T. irroratus Coquillett. Wings spotted. (1) n.e. US; (2) s.e. US.

68. AGROMYZIDAE
(Leaf Miner Fly Family)

Length: 1–5 mm. Black or gray, often marked with yellow; wings usually transparent, possibly tinged with white or brown; costa broken and indented slightly at apex of Sc. Adults are common around vegetation of many kinds. Most larvae are leaf miners; some are stem and seed borers. Some species are of economic importance. There are 188 species in the U.S. and Canada.

68.1 *Agromyza* Fallén

Nineteen species, the following of which are pests:

A. parvicornis Loew (Corn Blotch Leaf Miner).

A. frontella (Rondani) (Alfalfa Blotch Leaf Miner).

[68.2 *Japanagromyza* Sasakawa (1 sp., *J. viridula* (Coquillett)); 69.3 *Melanagromyza* Hendel (17 spp.)]

68.4 *Ophiomyia* Braschnikov

Seven species, the following of which is of interest:

O. lantanae Froggatt (Lantana Seed Fly). This species has been released in Hawaii as a means of controlling lantana. It has been introduced into (2) FL; (3) TX, s. CA.

[68.5 *Tylomyza* Hendel (1 sp., *T. nasuta* (Melander)]

Subfamily Phytomyzinae

[68.6 *Phytobia* Lioy, with 10 subgenera: *Phytobia* s. str. (7 spp.), *Nemorimyza* Frey (1 sp., *p. posticata* (Meigen), *Amauromyza* Hendel (2 spp.), *Cephalomyza* Hendel (3 spp.), *Poemyza* Hendel (6 spp.), *Dizygomyza* Hendel (6 spp.), *Icteromyza* Hendel (3 spp.), *Trilobomyza* Hendel (3 spp.), *Praspedomyza* Hendel (3 spp.), *Calycomyza* Hendel (14 spp.)]

68.7 *Cerodontha* Rondani

The genus is divided into two subgenera: *Cerodontha* s. str. (1 sp., *C. dorsalus* (Loew) [see below]), *Xenophytomyza* Frey (1 sp., *C. illinoensis* (Malloch). The following species is a pest.

C. (Cerodontha) dorsalis (Loew) (Grass Sheath Miner).

68.8 *Liriomyza* Mik

Thirty-five species, the following of which are pests:

L. brassicae (Riley) (Serpentine Leaf Miner).

L. sativae Blanchard (Vegetable Leaf Miner).

[68.9 *Metopomyza* Enderlein (1 sp., *M. interfrontalis* (Melander)); 68.10 *Haplomyza* Hendel (3 spp.); 68.11 *Phytoliriomyza* Hendel (3 spp.); 68.12 *Xyraeomyia* Frick (1 sp., *X. conjunctimontis* Frick); 68.13 *Phytagromyza* Hendel (5 spp.); 68.14 *Pseudonapomyza* Hendel (2 spp.); 68.15 *Napomyza* Westwood (3 spp.); 68.16 *Phytomyza* Fallén (40 spp.).]

69. OPOMYZIDAE (Opomyzid Fly Family)

Length: 1–5 mm. Adults found on grass in moist areas; larvae are probably stem borers. Thirteen rare species occur in the U.S. and Canada.

[69.1 *Opomyza* Fallén (2 spp.)]

69.2 *Anomalochaeta* Frey

One species, as follows:

A. guttipennis (Zetterstedt). (1) n.e. Canada; (4) AK; (5) n. Central Provinces.

[69.3 *Geomyza* Fallén (10 spp.)]

70. ANTHOMYZIDAE (Anthomyzid Fly Family)

Length: 2–4 mm. Yellow or black. Adults occur on grass and low vegetation in marshy areas; larvae found on marsh plants. Fourteen species, as follows:

70.1 *Anthomyza* Fallén

Five species, the following of which is common:

A. gracilis Fallén. (1), (2), (3), (4), (5), generally distributed.

[70.2 *Ischnomyia* Loew (2 spp.); 70.3 *Mumetopia* Melander (3 spp.); 70.4 *Stenomicra* Coquillett (1 sp., *S. angustata* Coquillett); 70.5 *Cyamops* Melander (3 spp.)]

71. AULACIGASTRIDAE
(Aulacigastrid Fly Family)

Length: ±2.5 mm. Dark brown with reddish areas on legs, yellow markings on body; ocellar bristles extremely weak, minute; front with bright orange band near anterior margin; costa without subcostal or humeral break. One rare species only, found at sap flows from wounded trees.

[71.1 *Aulacigaster* Macquart (1 sp., *A. leucopeza* (Meigen) [(1), (2), (3), (4), (5), throughout NA])]

72. PERISCELIDIDAE
(Periscelidid Fly Family)

Length: ±3 mm. Wing with R_1 joining C near middle, R_{4+5} and M not convergent; postocellar setae strong. These rare flies

are attracted to sap oozing from wounded trees. There are 3 species.

72.1 *Periscelis* Loew

Three species, the following of which is probably the most common:

P. annulata (Fallén).

73. ASTEIIDAE (Asteiid Fly Family)

Length: 1–2 mm. Wing with R_1 joining C in Basal third, R_{4+5} and M distinctly convergent distally; postocellar setae weak or absent. Nineteen rare species occur in the U.S. and Canada. Larvae are unknown.

Subfamily Sigaloessinae

73.1 *Leiomyza* Macquart

Four species, the following of which is considered to be widespread, despite its spotty distribution:

L. curvinervis (Zetterstedt).

[73.2 *Phlebosotera* Duda (3 spp.); 73.3 *Astiosoma* Duda (4 spp.); 73.4 *Sigaloessa* Loew (4 spp.)]

Subfamily Asteiinae

[73.5 *Asteia* Meigen (3 spp.); 73.6 *Loewimyia* Sabrosky (1 sp., *L.* unnamed sp.)]

74. MILICHIIDAE (Milichid Fly Family)

Length: 1–5 mm. Adults usually shiny black. Larvae live in decaying vegetation, manure, or carrion; few have been found in debris in ant nests and bird nests. There are 36 species in the U.S. and Canada.

Subfamily Madizinae

[74.1 *Phyllomyza* Fallén (3 spp.); 74.2 *Neophyllomyza* Melander (2 spp.); 74.3 *Paramyia* Williston (1 sp., *P. nitens* (Loew)); 74.4 *Stomosis* Melander (2 spp.); 74.5 *Aldrichiomyza* Hendel (1 sp., *A. agromyzina* (Hendel)); 74.6 *Madiza* Fallén (1 sp., *M. glabra* Fallén); 74.7 *Leptometopa* Becker (2 spp.)]

74.8 *Desmometopa* Loew

Three species, the following of which is common:

D. m-nigrum (Zetterstedt). (1) n.e. US; (2) s.e. US; (3) s.w. US.

Subfamily Milichiinae

[74.9 *Pholeomyia* Bilimek (12 spp.); 74.10 *Eusiphona* Coquillett (3 spp.); 74.11 *Milichia* Meigen (1 sp., *M. aethiops* Malloch); 74.12 *Michiella* Giglio-Tos (5 spp.)]

75. CARNIDAE (Carnid Fly Family)

[From Milichiidae of authors]

Length: 1–2 mm. Arista micropubescent; M_1 weak and unpigmented; mid-tibiae without preapical dorsal bristle. Little is known about the sixteen species in this family except that one is an ectoparasite of birds, as follows:

[75.1 *Hemeromyia* Coquillett (2 spp.); 75.2 *Meoneura* Rondani (13 spp.)]

75.3 *Carnus* Nitzsch

One species, as follows:

C. hemapterus Nitzsch. An ectoparasite of nestling birds. (1) n.e. NA; (2) s.e. US; (3) s.w. US.

76. BRAULIDAE (Bee Louse Fly Family)

Length: 1–1.5 mm. These are louselike insects with short, thick legs, vestigial eyes, and without wings or halteres. Each tarsal segment has a pair of comblike appendages. One species only, as follows:

76.1 *Braula* Nitzsch

B. coeca Nitzsch (Bee Louse). Eggs are laid among the brood of honey bees. Larvae feed on the bee's food. Adults attach themselves to the bee host. (See Fig. 29.48. (1), (2), (3), (4), (5), wherever bees are kept.

Superfamily SCIOMYZOIDEA

This superfamily contains five families, as follows.

77. COELOPIDAE (Seaweed Fly Family)

Length: 3–10 mm. Metepisternum setose below posterior thoracic spiracle, the later without bristles or outstanding hairlike setae; thorax distinctly flattened. Our five species of these strongly bristled flies are confined to the seacoast, where the larvae breed in seaweed wrack.

77.1 *Coelopa* Meigen

This genus is divided into three subgenera: *Coelopa* s. str. (1 sp., *C. stejnegeri* Aldrich), *Fucomyia* Haliday (2 spp.), and *Neocoelopa* Mallach (1 sp., *C. vanduzeei* Cresson). The following species are common:

C. (Fucomyia) frigida (Fabricius). The only eastern species. (1) LB, NF, ME, MA, RI.

C. (Neocoelopa) vanduzeei Cresson. (3) CA; (4) AK, BC, WA, OR.

[77.2 *Coleopina* Malloch (1 sp., *C. anomala* (Cole) (3) CA.)]

78. DRYOMYZIDAE (Dryomyzid Fly Family)

Length: 4.5–12 mm. Adults of some are often abundant in moist wood, sometimes on dung; others are found along sea-

Fig. 29.48. (*From Curran, 1934*)

shore. Known larvae live in rotting seaweed of shore wrack. Thirteen species, as follows:

Subfamily Dryomyzinae

[78.1 *Dryomyza* Fallen (7 spp.); 78:2 *Oedoparena* Curran (2 spp.), 78.3 *Cinderella* Steyskal (1 sp., *C. lampra* Steskal)]

Subfamily Helcomyzinae

78.4 *Helcomyza* Curtis

One species, as follows:

H. mirabilis Melander. (4) WA, OR.

[78.5 *Heterocheila* Rondani (2 spp.)]

79. SCIOMYZIDAE (Marsh Fly Family)

Length: 2–12 mm. Usually brownish or gray, possibly with spots on wings. All known larvae are parasites or predators of fresh water or terrestrial snails. There are 140 species in the U.S. and Canada.

Subfamily Sciomyzinae

[79.1 *Atrichomelina* Cresson (1 sp., *A. pubera* (Loew)); 79.2 *Colobaea* Zetterstedt (1 sp., *C. americana* Steyskal); 79.3 *Oidematops* Cresson (1 sp., *O. ferrugineus* Cresson); 79.4 *Pherbellia* Robineau-Desvoidy (23 spp.); 79.5 *Pteromicra* (14 spp.); 79.6 *Sciomyza* Fallén (4 spp.)]

Subfamily Tetanocerinae

[79.7 *Antichaeta* Haliday, with 2 subgenera: *Antichaeta* s. str. (6 spp.) and *Parantichaeta* Enderlein (1 sp., *A. johnsoni* (Cresson))]

79.8 *Dictya* Meigen

Nineteen species, the following of which is common:

D. umbroides Curran (Swale Fly). Common on vegetation along streams and ponds from June to August. (1) n.e. Canada, MI; (4) AK; (5) Central Provinces.

[79.9 *Dictyacium* Steyskal (2 spp.); 79.10 *Elgiva* Meigen (2 spp.)]

79.11 *Euthycera* Latreille

One species, as follows:

E. arcuata (Loew). L. ±7.5 mm. Body and wings brown; thorax dark gray with brown spots of two sizes; wings with small pale spots forming rows; spines of thorax large, black. (1) n.e. NA; (2) KY, VA, NC, TN, AR; (3) TX.

[79.12 *Hedria* Steyskal (1 sp., *H. mixta* Steyskal); 79.13 *Hoplodicta* Cresson (3 spp.); 79.14 *Limnia* Robineau-Desvoidy (13 spp.); 79.15 *Pherbecta* Steyskal (1 sp., *P. limenitis* Steyskal)]

79.16 *Poecilographa* Melander

One species, as follows:

P. decora (Loew) (Marsh Fly). L. 6–7 mm. Yellow with brown patches on wings; body with a few bristles; antennae aristate, the arista with bristles; proboscis rather large; bristles of head and thorax arise from conspicuous dark brown spots. Adults commonly fly about banks of ponds and streams. (See A&J 336.) (1) n.e. US; (5) CO, KS, MO.

[79.17 *Renocera* Hendel (7 spp.)]

79.18 *Sepedon* Latreille

Twelve species, the following of which is an example:

S. armipes Loew. Found on vegetation along streams and ponds. (1) n.e. US; (2) KY, WV, VA, NC, SC, GA, AR, LA, MS, AL; (3) AZ, NM, TX, OK; (4) Pacific n.w.; (5) n. Central states.

[79.19 *Tetanocera* Dumeril (29 spp.); 79.20 *Trypetoptera* Hendel (1 sp., *T. canadensis* (Macquart)); unplaced species (2 spp.)]

80. ROPALOMERIDAE (Ropalomerid Fly Family)

Length: ±7 mm. C without subcostal break; apical section of M bent sharply forward in line with cross vein dm-cu and ending near R_{4+5} before wing apex. One species only, as follows:

80.1 *Rhytidops* Lindner

R. floridensis (Aldrich). Adults are attracted to fresh exudates of various palms. (2) FL.

81. SEPSIDAE (Black Scavenger Fly Family)

Length: 3.5–6.5 mm. Shining black, sometimes purple; round and narrow heads; somewhat wasplike abdomens. Both adults and larvae of most species are found on or near carrion, manure, and decaying vegetation. There are 34 species in the U.S. and Canada.

[81.1 *Decachaetophora* Duda (1 sp., *D. aeneipes* (Meijere))]

81.2 *Meroplius* Rondani

One species, as follows:

M. stercorarius (Robineau-Desvoidy). (See Fig. 29.49.) (1) n.e. NA; (2) s.e. US; (4) Pacific n.w.

[81.3 *Nemopoda* Robineau-Desvoidy (4 spp.); 81.4 *Orygma* Meigen (1 sp., *O. luctuosum* Meigen); 81.5 *Palaeosepsis* Duda (2 spp.); 81.6 *Saltella* Robineau-Desvoidy (1 sp., *S. sphondylii* (Schrank))]

81.7 *Sepsis* Fallén

Twelve species, including the following:

S. punctum (Fabricius). Adults fly from June to September. Found on maure. (1), (2), (3), (4), (5), generally distributed.

Fig. 29.49. (*From Curran, 1934*)

[81.8 *Thermira* Robineau-Desvoidy, with 3 subgenera: *Themira* s. str. (9 spp.), *Enicita* Westwood (2 spp.), and *Enicomira* Duda (1 sp., *T. minor* (Haliday))]

Superfamily LAUXANIOIDEA
82. LAUXANIIDAE (Lauxaniid Fly Family)

Length: 2–7 mm. Body usually yellow, sometimes gray or black; wings often spotted. Adults are found in shaded woods or on vegetation and flowers near streams. Larvae live on decaying vegetation or leaf litter; some in bird nests; a few are leaf miners. There are 135 species in the U.S. and Canada, many widely distributed.

[82.1 *Calliopum* Strand (6 spp.); 82.2 *Camptoprosopella* Hendel (22 spp.); 82.3 *Deutominettia* Hendel (1 sp., *D. geniseta* (Malloch))]

82.4 *Homoneura* Wulp

Twenty-nine species, many of which are very common and recognizable by their yellow bodies and wings (usually) with a few black spots.

[82.5 *Lauxania* Latrielle (3 spp.); 82.6 *Lauxaniella* Malloch (5 spp.); 82.7 *Lyciella* Collin (12 spp.)]

82.8 *Minettia* Robineau-Desvoidy

Sixteen species, the following of which is common:

M. lupulina (Fabricius). L. 3.5–4 mm. Head and thorax purplish gray; abdomen brown; wings pale brownish yellow; thorax very large. Found on flowers and often collected by sweeping. Adults fly during June and July. (1) n.e. US; (2) KY, WV, VA, NC, AR; (3) AZ, NM, TX, OK.

[82.9 *Neodeceia* Malloch (1 sp., *N. cineracea* (Coquillett)); 82.10 *Neogriphoneura* Malloch (1 sp., *N. sordida* (Wiedemann)); 82.11 *Pachycerina* Macquart (1 sp., *P. flavida* (Wiedemann)); 82.12 *Physegenua* Macquart (1 sp., *P. nasalis* (Thomson)); 82.13 *Physoclypeus* Hendel (1 sp., *P. coquilletti (Hendel))*; 82.14 *Poecilominettia* Hendel (5 spp.); 82.15 *Pseudocalliope* Malloch (4 spp.); 82.16 *Pseudogriphoneura* Hendel (7 spp.); 82.17 *Sapromyza* Fallén (10 spp.); 82.18 *Steganopsis* Meijere, subgenus *Steganolauxania* Frey (1 sp., *S. latipennis* (Coquillett)); 82.19 *Trigonometopus* Macquart (2 spp.); 82.20 *Trivialia* Malloch (1 sp., *T. fuscocapitata* (Malloch)); 82.21 *Trypetisoma* Malloch (1 sp., *T. sticticum* (Loew)); 82.22 *Xenochaetina* Malloch (1 sp., *X. muscaria* (Loew)); 82.23 *Xenopterella* Malloch (1 sp., *X. costalis* Curran); Unplaced species (3 spp.)]

83. CHAMAEMYIIDAE (Chamaemyiid Fly Family)

Length: 1–4 mm. Body covered with dense gray pile; wing with CuA$_2$ and A$_1$ strong; cell cup complete; antennae with arista bare or micropubescent; ocellar bristles present, though sometimes weakly so. The larvae of some of this poorly known group are predacious, feeding on soft scales and aphids. One species has been reared from a bird's nest. There are 36 species in the U.S. and Canada.

Subfamily Cremifaniinae

[83.1 *Cremifania* Czerny (2 spp.)]

Subfamily Chamaemyiinae
Tribe Chamaemyini
83.2 *Plunomia* Curran

Four species, including the following:

P. elegans Curran. (1) n.e. US; (4) Pacific n.w.; (5) n. Central states.

[83.3 *Acrometopia* Schiner (1 sp., *A. punctata* Coquillett); 83.4 *Chamaemyia* Meigen (6 spp.); 83.5 *Paraleucopis* Malloch (1 sp., *P. corvina* Malloch); 83.6 *Pseudodinia* Coquillett (4 spp.); 83.7 *Pseudoleucopis* Malloch (1 sp., *P. benefica* Malloch [introduced])]

Tribe Leucopini

[83.8 *Lipoleucopis* Meijere (1 sp., *L. praecox* Meijere [introduced]); 83.9 *Leucopis* Meigen, with 4 subgenera: *Neoleucopis* Malloch (2 spp.), *Leucopomyia* Malloch (1 sp., *L. pulvinariae* Malloch), *Xenoleucopis* Malloch (1 sp., unnamed), and *Leucops* s. str. (18 spp.)]

Superfamily SPHAEROCEROIDEA
84. HELEOMYZIDAE (Heleomyzid Fly Family)

Length: 2–7.5 mm. Body yellow, orange, or reddish brown; vibrissa and postocellar bristle strong; face tuberculate; ocellar bristles arising on ocellar triangle above anterior ocellus; wings with spots and C spinose, except in species of *Borboropsis* and *Oedenbergiella*, in which A$_1$ is traceable to wing margin; middle tibiae with preapical dorsal bristle. Adults usually occur in shaded areas. Larvae breed either in fungus or decaying plant and animal matter, including that in bird nests and mammal burrows. There are 113 species in the U.S. and Canada.

Subfamily Suilliinae

[84.1 *Porsenus* Darlington (1 sp., *P. johnsoni* Darlington); 84.2 *Suilla* Robineau-Desvoidy (9 spp); 84.3 *Allophyla* Loew (2 spp.)]

Subfamily Helomyzinae

[84.4 *Borboropsis* Czerny (1 sp., *B. fulviceps* (Strobl)); 84.5 *Oldenbergiella* Czerny (1 sp., *O. brumalis* Czerny); 84.6 *Orbellia* Robineau-Desvoidy (3 spp.); 84.7 *Heteromyza* Fallén (1 sp., *H. oculata* Fallén); 84.8 *Tephrochlamys* Loew (2 spp.); 84.9 *Aecothea* Haliday (3 spp.); 84.10 *Eccoptomera* (7 spp.); 84.11 *Lutomyia* Aldrich (4 spp.); 84.12 *Pseudoleria* Garrett (12 spp.); 84.13 *Anorostoma* Loew (16 spp.); 84.14 *Neoleria* Malloch (8 spp.); 84.15 *Spanoparea* Czerny (3 spp.); 84.16 *Morpholeria* Garrett (1 sp., *M. tristis* (Loew)); 84.17 *Acantholeria* Garrett (3 spp.); 84.18 *Schroederella* Enderlein (2 spp.); 84.19 *Scoliocentra* Loew (3 spp.); 84.20 *Anypotacta* Czerny (2 spp.); 84.21 *Amoebaleria* Garrett (15 spp.)]

84.22 *Heleomyza* Fallén

Twelve species, including the following:

H. serrata (Linnaeus). L. 3–5 mm. Head yellow; thorax ash gray with four brown stripes; legs yellowish orange; wings transparent but with faint brownish tinge; abdomen yellow to reddish brown. Larvae found in bird nests, dung, and fungi. Common. (1) n.e. US; (2) KY, TN; (4) Pacific n.w.; (5) n. Central states.

[84.23 *Trichochlamys* Czerny (1 sp., *T. borealis* Czerny); unplaced species (1 sp, *Helomyza fasciata* Walker)]

85. TRIXOSCELIDIDAE (Trixoscelidid Fly Family)

Length: 2–3 mm. Head with vibrissa and postocellar bristles strong; ocellar bristles arising just outside ocellar triangle beside or slightly below anterior ocellus; all tibiae with preapical dorsal bristles. These flies occur in sandy or arid areas. Larvae of most are unknown; one has been reared from a bird's nest. Of the 30 species, only two are eastern; most of the rest are in the arid Southwest.

85.1 *Neossos* Malloch

Two species, the following of which is widespread:

N. marylandicus Malloch (1) n.e. NA; (4) BC; (5) ?n. Central states.

[85.2 *Paraneossos* Wheeler (1 sp., *P. arizonicus* Wheeler); 85.3 *Spiloshroa* Williston (5 spp.); 85.4 *Trixoscelis* Rondani (20 spp.); 85.5 *Zagonia* Coquillett (2 spp.)]

86. CHYROMYIDAE (Chyromyid Fly Family)

Length: 1–3 mm. Light yellow with golden green, rust red, or purple eyes; postocellar bristles convergent; halteres usually whitish. Adults may be found on various plants or at windows attracted to the light after emerging from firewood. Larvae have been reared from bird nests, mammal burrows, and rotting wood. Nine species occur in the U.S. and Canada; their distribution is mostly northern, but many species do not have precise distributional records.

[86.1 *Aphaniosoma* Becker 93 spp.)]

86.2 *Chyromya* Robineau-Desvoidy

Three species, the following of which is widespread:

C. flava (Linnaeus). (1) n.e. NA; (2) s.e. US.

[86.3 *Gymnochiromyia* Hendel (3 spp.)]

87. RHINOTORIDAE (Rhinotorid Fly Family)

Length: 6–8 mm. Wing with one to many supernumerary cross veins between C and R_{2+3}; C with a subcostal break; vertex strongly excavated. Only one species, as follows:

87.1 Rhinotora Schiner

R. diversa Giglio-Tos (3) AZ. NM

88. SPHAEROCERIDAE (Small Dung Fly Family)

Length: 1.5–5 mm. Black; wings with costa interrupted, Sc incomplete, not reaching costa. Adults found near manure or other decaying matter. Larvae live as scavengers in excrement and decaying vegetable matter, seaweed, or fungi. Of the 117 species recorded in the U.S. and Canada, many are very common.

[88.1 *Sphaerocera* Latreille, with 2 subgenera: *Sphaerocera* s. str., (4 spp.) and subgenus *Lotobia* Lioy (5 spp.)]

88.2 *Copromyza* Fallén

The genus is divided into five subgenera: *Copromyza* s. str. (5 spp.), *Olinea* Richard (1 sp., *C. atra* (Meigen)), *Fungobia* Lioy (2 spp.), *Crumomyia* Macquart (3 spp.), and *Borborillus* Duda (6 spp.). The following species may serve as an example:

C. equina Fallén. Adults found on manure in July and August. (1), (2), (3), (4), (5), widespread.

[88.3 *Leptocera* Oliver, with 13 subgenera: *Leptocera* s. str. (5 spp.), *Rachispoda* Lioy (22 spp.), *Opacifrons* Duda (7 spp.), *Pteremis* Rondani (3 spp.), *Thoracochaeta* Duda (4 spp.), *Poecilosomella* Duda (1 sp., *L. angulata* (Thomson)), *Pterogramma* Spuler (2 spp.), *Bromeloecia* Spuler (1 sp., *L. winnemana* Malloch), *Limosina* Macquart (37 spp.)., *Trachyopella* Duda (1 sp., *L. lineafrons* Spuler), *Halidayina* Duda (1 sp., *L. spinipennis* (Haliday)), *Elachisoma* Rondani (1 sp., *L. approximata* Malloch), *Coproica* Rondani (7 spp.)]

Superfamily EPHYDROIDEA

This superfamily contains the following nine families.

89. CURTONOTIDAE (Curtonotid Fly Family)

Length: ±7 mm. Grayish, humpbacked, similar to the Pomace Flies. Only one species, as follows:

89.1 *Curtonotum* Macquart

C. helvum (Loew). (1) n.e. US; (2) KY, WV, VA, NC, SC, GA.

90. DROSOPHILIDAE (Pomace Fly Family)

Length: 2.5–4.5 mm. Adults are recognized by break in costal vein near junction of subcosta; C without erect spinules, with ordinary reclinate setulae only; proclinate orbital bristles usually arising ventromedially to reclinate orbital bristles; eyes usually red. Common species of Pomace Flies are found around decaying fruit and other rotting vegetation; others live on fresh sap, nectar from flowers, and in fungi. Larvae feed on bacteria and fungi in the same places. A few species are leaf miners; others are ectoparasitic on nymphs of plant bugs. There are 117 species in the U.S. and Canada, and many more species of this famous family inhabit the tropics.

Subfamily Steganinae

[90.1 *Stegana* Meigen, subgenus *Steganina* Wheeler (2 sp.); 90.2 *Amiota* Loew (8 spp.), with 3 subgenera: *Amiota* s. str. (8 spp.), *Phortica* Schiner (1 sp., *A. huachucae* Wheeler), and *Sinophthalmus* Coquillett (1 sp., *A. picta* (Coquillett); 90.3 *Leucophenga* Mik, with 2 subgenera: *Leucophenga* s. str. (3 spp.) and *Neoleucophenga* Oldenberg (4 spp.); 90.4 *Pseudiastrata* Coquillet, with 2 subgenera: *Pseudiastata* s. str. (1 sp., *P. nebulosa* Coquillett) and *Hyalistata* Wheeler (1 sp., *P. pictiventris* Wheeler); 90.5 *Gitona* Meigen (3 spp.); 90.6 *Paracacoxenus* Hardy (1 sp., *P. guttatus* Hardy and Wheeler); 90.7 *Rhinoleucophenga* Hendel (1 sp., *R. obesa* (Loew)); 90.8 *Trachyleucophenga* Hendel (1 sp., unnamed)]

Subfamily Drosophilinae

90.9 *Drosophila* Fallén

This genus is divided into seven subgenera: *Drosophila* s. str. (75 spp.), *Hirtodrosophila* Duda (10 spp.), *Lordiphosa* Basden (1 sp., *D. basdeni* Wheeler), *Phloridosa* Sturtevant (2 spp.), *Pholadoris* Sturtevant (3 spp.), *Siphlodora* Patterson and Mainland (1 sp., *D. sigmoides* Loew), and *Sophophora* Sturtevant (15 spp.). The following species is the best known of the family:

D. (*Siphlodora*) *melanogaster* Meigen (Laboratory Fruit Fly). L. ±3 mm. These common flies are widely used for laboratory studies of genetics. Larvae feed on ripe or overripe bananas and other fruit, and on vinegar, stale beer, and similar fermenting materials as well. They complete their life cycle in about two weeks—one of the reasons they are laboratory favorites. Another is that they easily reared. Commercially available containers and food preparations are available for this purpose. Cosmopolitan. (See (A&J 338.)

[90.10 *Scaptomyza* Hardy, with 4 subgenera: *Scaptomyza* s. str. (5 spp.), *Hemiscaptomyza* Hackman (7 spp.), *Mesoscaptomyza* Hackman (6 spp.), and *Parascaptomyza* Duda (1 sp., *S. pallida* (Zetterstedt)); 90.11 *Chymomyza* Czerny (8 spp.); 90.12 *Mycodrosophila* Oldenberg (3 spp.); 90.13 *Cladochaeta* Coquillett (1 sp., *C. nebulosa* Coquillet); 90.14 *Clastopteromyia* Malloch (3 spp.); 90.15 *Dettopsomyia* Lamb (1 sp., *D. nigrovillata* (Malloch)); 90.16 *Paramycodrosophila* Duda (2 spp.); 90.17 *Microdrosophila* Malloch (1 sp., *M. quadrata* (Sturtevant)); Unplaced species (5 spp.)]

91. DIASTATIDAE (Diastatid Fly Family)

Length: 2–4 mm. Wings with small, evenly spaced, erect spinules in C beyond subcosta break; proclimate orbital bristles arising dorsolaterally to lowermost reclinate orbital bristle. Very little is known about these flies. There are six species in the U.S. and Canada, as follows:

[91.1 *Diastata* Meigen (4 spp.)]

91.2 *Campichoeta* Macquart

Two species, the following of which is widely distributed.

C. griseola (Zetterstedt). (1) n.e. US; (2) VA; (3) CA, AZ, NM; (4) Pacific n.w.; (5) n. Central states.

92. CAMILLIDAE (Camillid Fly Family)

Length: 1.5–2.5 mm. Face concave; subcranial cavity normal; postocellar bristles convergent or subparallel; arista plumose; M_1 strong and normally pigmented; middle tibiae with preapical dorsal bristle. Only one species in North America, as follows:

92.1 *Camilla* Haliday

C. glabra (Fallén). Nothing is known about the biology of this species. (1) ON.

93. EPHYDRIDAE (Shore Fly Family)

Length: 2.5–9 mm. Adults are found on or near water, in mud or low vegetation. Larvae are aquatic or semiaquatic, often found in great numbers, providing food for fish and waterfowl. Some (*Ephydra cinera;* see below) are able to live in very high concentrations of salt. Some larvae are leaf miners of aquatic and semiaquatic plants and may become minor pests on watercress and rice and other irrigated cereals. There are 426 species in the U.S. and Canada.

Subfamily Psilopinae

Tribe Gymnopini

[93.1 *Mosillus* Latreille (3 spp.); 93.2 *Athyroglossa* Loew, with 3 subgenera: *Arthyroglossa* s. str. (3 spp.), *Parathyroglossa* Hendel (1 sp., *A. ordinata* Becker), and *Ochtheroidea* Williston (3 spp.)]

Tribe Atissini

[93.3 *Atissa* Haliday (2 spp.); 93.4 *Ptilomyia* Coquillett (6 spp.); 93.5 *Allotrichoma* Becker (7 spp.); 93.6 *Pseudohecamede* Hendel (3 spp.); 93.7 *Hecamede* Haliday (1 sp., *H. albicans* (Meigen)); 93.8 *Glenanthe* Haliday (2 spp.); 93.9 *Pelignus* Cresson (1 sp., *P. salinus* Cresson); 93.10 *Diphuia* Cresson (1 sp., *D. nitida* Sturtevant and Wheeler); 93.11 *Pelignellus* Sturtevant and Wheeler (1 sp., *P. subnudus* Sturtevant and Wheeler)]

Tribe Discocerinini

[93.12 *Discocerina* Macquart, with 3 subgenera: *Discocerina* s. str. (4 spp.), *Basila* Cresson (1 sp., *D. nadineae* (Cresson)), and *Lamproclasiopa* Hendel (2 spp.); 93.13 *Hecamedoides* Hendel (1 sp., *H. glaucellus* (Stenhammar)); 93.14 *Hydrochasma* Hendel (4 spp.); 93.15 *Diclasiopa* Hendel (1 sp., *D. lacteipennis* (Loew)); 93.16 *Ditrichophora* Cresson (15 spp.); 93.17 *Polytrichophora* Cresson (4 spp.); 93.18 *Paratissa* Coquillett (1 sp., *P. semilutea* (Loew))]

Tribe Discomyzini

[93.19 *Discomyza* Meigen (2 spp.); 93.20 *Clanoneurum* Becker (1 sp., *C. americanum* Cresson)]

Tribe Psilopini

[93.21 *Psilopa* Fallén (6 spp.); 93.22 *Helaeomyia* Cresson (2 spp.); 93.23 *Leptopsilopa* Cresson (4 spp.); 93.24 *Ceropsilopa* Cresson (7 spp.); 93.25 *Cressonomyia* Arnaud (4 spp.); 93.26 *Clasiopella* Hendel (1 sp., *C. uncinata* Hendel); 93.27 *Neopsilopa* Mathis and Wirth (1 sp., *N. wirthi* Mathis and Friedberg) 93.28 *Trimerina* Macquart (1 sp., *T. madizans* (Fallén)); 93.29 *Trimerinoides* Cresson (1 sp., *T. adfinis* (Cresson)); 93.30 *Rhysophora* Cresson (1 sp., *R. robusta* Cresson)]

Subfamily Notiphilinae

Tribe Typopsilopini

[93.31 *Typopsilopa* Cresson (4 spp.)]

Tribe Hydrelliini

93.32 *Hydrellia* Robineau-Desvoidy

Fifty-seven species, the following of which is a pest:

H. griseola (Fallén) (Cereal Leaf Miner). Pest of irrigated cereal crops. (1), (2), (3), (4), (5), widespread.

Tribe Philygriini

[93.33 *Philygria* Stenhammar (4 spp.); 93.34 *Nostima* Coquillett (8 spp.); 93.35 *Lemnaphila* Cresson (1 sp., *L. scotlandae* Cresson)]

Tribe Ilytheini

[93.36 *Ilythea* Haliday (3 spp.); 93.37 *Zeros* Cresson (5 spp.)]

Tribe Notiphilini

[93.38 *Notiphila* Fallén, with 2 subgenera: *Notiphila* s. str. (25 spp.) and *Dichaeta* Meigen (24 spp.); 93.39 *Paralimna* Loew, with 2 subgenera: *Paralimna* s. str. (3 spp.) and *Phaiosterna* Cresson (2 spp.); 93.40 *Oedenops* Becker (1 sp., *O. nudus* (Coquillett))]

Subfamily Parydrinae

Tribe Parydrini

[93.41 *Parydra* Stenhammar, with 3 subgenera; *Parydra* Stenhammar (25 spp.), *Chaetoapinaea* Hendel (21 spp., including *P. Chaetoapnaea humilis* Williston; see Fig. 29.50); and *Callinapaea* Sturtevant and Wheeler); 93.42 *Eutaenionotum* Olenberg (1 sp., *E. guttipennis* (Stenhammar)); 93.43 *Rhinonapaea* Wirth (1 sp., *R. metallica* Cole))]

Tribe Lipochaetini

[93.44 *Lipochaeta* Coquillett (1 sp., *L. slossonae* Coquillett); 93.45 *Asmeringa* Becker (1 sp., *A. lindsleyi* Sturtevant and Wheeler)]

Tribe Hyadinini

[93.46 *Hyadina* Haliday (9 spp.); 93.47 *Axysta* Haliday (3 spp.); 93.48 *Lytogaster* Becker (7 spp.); 93.49 *Pelina* Haliday (7 spp.); 93.50 *Gastrops* Williston (2 spp.)]

Fig. 29.50. (*Courtesy of* Insect World Digest)

93.51 *Ochthera* Latreille

Thirteen species, including the following:

O. exsculpta Loew. L. ±3.5 mm. Body black; eyes orange; front femora greatly enlarged, spined, raptorial. Adults prey upon other flies and fly larvae, including mosquito larvae. (2) NC, GA, FL.

O. mantis (DeGeer). Similar to the preceding. Cosmopolitan.

[93.52 *Brachydeutera* Loew (2 spp.)]

Subfamily Ephydrinae

Tribe Ephydrini

[93.53 *Cirrula* Cresson (2 spp.)]

93.54 *Ephydra* Fallén

Sixteen species, including the following:

E. cinera Jones (Brine Fly). L. ±4 mm. Opaque gray with shining, silky, green front. Sometimes this fly is so abundant in Great Salt Lake, Utah, that the beach is covered with pupal skins (Fig. 29.51); and the water is black with adults and pupae on the surface (Fig. 29.52). (See A&J 337.) (3) CA, AZ, NM, TX; (4) UT.

[93.55 *Setacera* Cresson (8 spp.); 93.56 *Dimecoenia* Cresson (12 spp.)]

Tribe Scatellini

[93.57 *Coenia* Robineau-Desvoidy (2 spp.); 93.58 *Paracoenia* Cresson, with 3 subgenera; *Paracoenia* s. str. (6 spp.), *Leptocoenia* (1 sp., *P. paurosoma* (Sturtevant and Wheeler), and *Thiomyia* Wirth (1 sp., *P. quatei* (Wirth)); 93.59 *Philotelma* Becker (1 sp., *P. alaskense* Cresson); 93.60 *Lamproscatella* Hendel, with 5 subgenera; *Lamproscatella* s. str. (4 spp.), *Haloscatella* Mathis (5 spp.), *Thinoscatella* Mathis (2 spp.); 93.61 *Scatella* Robineau-Desvoidy, *Scatella* Robineau-Desvoidy (15 spp.), and *Neoscatella* Malloch (3 spp.); 93.62 *Limnellia* Malloch (10 spp.); 93.63 *Scatophila* Becker (22 spp.); Unplaced species (6 spp.)]

Fig. 29.51. (*Courtesy of* Insect World Digest)

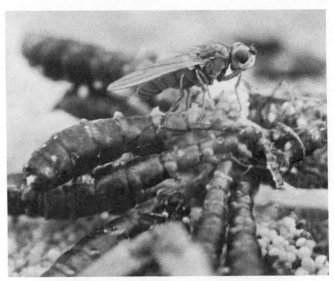

Fig. 29.52. (*From Curran, 1934*)

94. CHLOROPIDAE (Frit Fly Family)

Length: 1–4 mm. Usually black with yellow markings, or gray. Adults are common in grass and other low plants; some are in flowers. A species of *Liohippelates* (see below), the Eye Gnats, are annoying to man and animals and are disease carriers. Larvae live in decaying plant and animal material; some are grass feeders, others form galls; some are predacious on aphids or eggs of spiders, mantids, or Lepidoptera. Frit Flies are sometimes called Grass Flies. There are 273 species in the U.S. and Canada.

Subfamily Oscinellinae

[94.1 *Apotropina* Hendel [=*Lasiopleura* Becker] (8 spp.); [*Hippelates* Loew (not in U.S. and Canada)]]

94.2 *Liohippelats* Duda

Ten species, the following of which is a pest:

L. pusio Loew (Eye Gnat). This serious pest of man and domestic animals is the vector of an eye disease resulting from the transfer of bacteria on the feet of the females from open, infected wounds and from excrement to the eyes and open wounds of man and other animals. In some regions, these bacteria can cause blindness if prompt attention is not given to the first signs of the disease. Males feed on nectar. Common. (1) n.e. NA; (2) s.e. US; (3) s.w. US; (4) UT; (5) ND, SD, MN, NE, IA, KS, MO.

[94.3 *Apallates* Sabrosky (10 spp.); 94.4 *Biorbitella* Sabrosky (5 spp.); 94.5 *Cadrema* Walker (1 sp., *C. pallida* (Loew)); 94.6 *Ceratobarys* Coquillett (1 sp., *C. eulophus* (Loew)); 94.7 *Elachiptera* Macquart (18 spp.); 94.8 *Melanochaeta* Bezzi (3 spp.); 94.9 *Eribolus* Becker (4 spp.); 94.10 *Oscinisoma* Lioy (1 sp., *O. alienum* (Becker)); 94.11 *Hapleginella* Duda (1 sp., *H. conicola* (Greene); 94.12 *Monochaetoscinella* Duda (2 spp.); 94.13 *Stenoscinis* Malloch (3 spp.); 94.14 *Rhopalopterum* Duda (10 spp.)]

94.15 *Oscinella* Becker

Three species, the following of which is common:

O. frit (Linnaeus) (Frit Fly). (1) n.e. US; (2) KY, WV, VA, TN, NC, SC, AR, LA, MS, AL, GA; (3) s.w. US; (4) Pacific n.w.; (5) n. Central states.

[94.16 *Oscinoides* Malloch (1 sp., *O. arpidia* Malloch); 94.17 *Rhodesiella* Adams (1 sp., *R. brimleyi* Sabrosky); 94.18 *Gaurax* Loew (24 spp.); 94.19 *Pseudogaurax* Malloch (3 spp.); 94.20 *Dicraeus* Loew (6 spp.); 94.21 *Opetiophora* Loew (1 sp., *O. straminea* Loew); 94.22 *Eugaurax* Malloch (1 sp., *E. floridensis* Malloch); 94.23 *Conioscinella* Duda (10 spp.); 94.24 *Dasyopa* Malloch (1 sp., *D. latifrons* (Loew); 94.25 *Olcella* Enderlein (9 spp.); 94.26 *Tricimba* Lioy (7 spp.); 94.27 *Aphanotrigonum* Duda (2 spp.); 94.28 *Chaetochlorops* Malloch (1 sp., *C. inquilinus* (Coquillett)); 94.29 *Goniopsita* Duda (2 spp.); 94.30 *Lipara* Meigen (1 sp., *L. lucens* Meigen); 94.31 *Calamoncosis* Enderlein (1 sp., unnamed); 94.32 *Siphonella* Macquart (1 sp., *S. oscinina* (Fallén)); 94.33 *Incertella* Sabrosky (7 spp.); 94.34 *Malloewia* Sabrosky (8 spp.); 94.35 *Neoscinella* Sabrosky (3 spp.); 94.36 *Speccafrons* Sabrosky (1 sp., *S. mallochi* (Sabrosky))]

Subfamily Chloropinae
94.37 *Thaumatomyia* Zenker

Thirteen species, the following of which is common:

T. glabra (Meigen). Larva are predacious on root aphids. (1), (2), (3), (4), (5), generally distributed.

[94.38 *Trigonomma* Enderlein (1 sp., *T. fossulatum* (Loew)); 94.39 *Cetema* Hendel (2 spp.); 94.40 *Anthracophaga* Loew (1 sp., *A. declinata* Becker); 94.41 *Chlorops* Meigen (44 spp.); 94.42 *Epichlorops* Becker (3 spp.); 94.43 *Ectecephala* Macquart (5 spp.); 94.44 *Lasiosina* Becker (4 spp.); 94.45 *Parectecephala* Becker (6 spp.); 94.46 *Diplotoxa* Loew (7 spp.); 94.47 *Elliponeura* Loew (2 spp.); 94.48 *Neodiplotoxa* Malloch (2 spp.); 94.49 *Homaluroides* Sabrosky (9 spp.)]

94.50 *Meromyza* Meigen

Three species catalogued, and more have been described recently; the following is a pest.

M. americana Fitch (Wheat Stem Maggot). A minor pest of small grains. Larvae bore in upper part of stems, causing the heads to die. (1) n.e. US; (2) VA, NC, SC; (3) TX; (5) SD, MN.

[Unplaced species (1 sp., *Chlorops ater* Macquart)]

95. CRYPTOCHETIDAE (Cryptochetid Fly Family)

Length: 1.5–2 mm. One species has been intentionally introduced into California.

95.1 *Cryptochetum* Rondani

C. iceryae (Williston). Parasite on the Cottony-cushion Scale. It is deep blue, with abdomen blue-green; wings short, rounded, grayish. (3) CA, introduced.

96. TETHINIDAE (Tethinid Fly Family)

Length: 2–3 mm. All tibiae without preapical dorsal bristle; wings with C not spinose, A_1 fading out on apical third or more, never traceable to wing margin; head with vibrissa and postocellar bristles weakly differentiated to virtually absent. Most of species live along seashore; those living elsewhere are usually in alkaline areas. Larvae are unknown. There are 22 species in the U.S. and Canada.

[96.1 *Pelomyia* Williston (4 spp.)]

96.2 *Pelomyiella* Hendel

Three species, the following of which is common:

P. mallochi (Sturtevant). (1) n.e. NA; (3) CA; (4) Pacific n.w.; (5) MB, CO.

[96.3 *neopelomyia* Hendel (1 sp., *N. rostrata* Hendel); 96.4 *Phycomyza* Melander (1 sp., *P. milichioides* (Melander)); 96.5 *Tethinia* Haliday (13 spp.)]

97. CANACIDAE (Beach Fly Family)

Length: 1–3.5 mm. Subcranial cavity usually large; gena with one to several strong up-curved (anaclinate) bristles immediately below compound eye; front usually broad with three to five pairs of lateroclinate fronto-orbital bristles; wings with costa broken; SC incomplete. These rather rare flies are found along seashore in intertidal zone. Larvae feed on algae on wave-splashed rocks or sandy beaches. There are five species in the U.S. and Canada.

Subfamily Canacinae
Tribe Dynomiellini
97.1 *Canacea* Cresson

Two species, the following of which is common:

C. macateei (Malloch). (1) PE, ME, MA, RI, CT, s. NY, NJ, MD, DE; (2) VA, NC, SC, GA, FL; (3) TX.

Subfamily Nocticanacinae

[97.2 *Canaceoides* Cresson (1 sp., *C. nudatus* (Cresson); 97.3 *Nocticanace* Malloch (2 spp.)]

Infraorder SCHIZOPHORA CALYPTRATAE

This infraorder contains the remaining three superfamilies and 11 families of Diptera.

Superfamily MUSCOIDEA

The three families of flies of the House Fly type comprise this superfamily.

98. SCATOPHAGIDAE (Dung Fly Family)

[From Anthomyiidae of authors]

Length: 4–13 mm. Differentiated from the Anthomyiidae by the characters given in the Key to the Families, particularly by the bare ventral surface of the scutellum. In addition, the costa usually does not have spinules. Many species are yellow and covered with hairlike setae. Some of the larva live in dung; others are leaf miners. The 148 species in the U.S. and Canada are arranged as follows. [Note: This family contains many more species than are given here. This list follows that in Stone, *et al.* (1965).]

Tribe Scatophagini

[98.1 *Norellia* Robineau-Desvoidy, subgenus *Norellisoma* Wahlgren (1 sp., *N. spinimana* (Fallén)); 98.2 *Cordilura* Fallén, with 5 subgenera: *Cordilura* s. str. (22 spp.), *Achaetella* Malloch (2 spp.), *Cordilurina* James (13 spp.), *Pseudacicephala* Malloch (3 spp.), and *Scoliaphleps* Becker (1 sp., *C. ustulata* Zetterstedt; 98.3 *Gonatherus* Rondani (1 sp., *G. planiceps* (Fallén); 98.4 *Nanna* Becker (9 spp.); 98.5 *Orthacheta* Becker (4 spp.); 98.6 *Gonarcticus* Becker (2 spp.); 98.7 *Bucephalina* Malloch, with 2 subgenera: *Bucephalina* s. str. (2 spp.) and *Neogimnomera* Malloch (1 sp., *B. amans* (Cresson)); 98.8 *Megaphthalma* Becker (1 sp., *M. pallida americana* Malloch); 98.9 *Megaphthalmoides* Ringdahl (1 sp., *M. unilineatus* (Zetterstedt); 98.10 *Pogonota* Zetterstedt, with 2 subgenera: *Pogonota* s. str. (3 spp.) and *Lasioscelus* Becker (2 spp.); 98.11 *Okeniella* Hendel (1 sp., *O. dasyprocta* (Loew));

98.12 *Cosmetopus* Becker (1 sp., *C. longus* (Walker)); 98.13 *Pleurochaetella* Vockeroth (1 sp., *P. simplicipes* (Becker)); 98.14 *Allomyella* Malloch (6 spp.); 98.15 *Microprosopa* Becker (7 spp.); 98.16 *Acanthocnema* Becker (3 spp.); 98.17 *Staegeria* Rondani (1 sp., unnamed); 98.18 *Spaziphora* Rondani (1 sp., *S. cincta* (Loew)); 98.19 *Cordylurella* Malloch (3 spp.); 98.20 *Trichopalpus* Rondani (3 spp.); 98.21 *Chaetosa* Coquillett (2 spp.); 98.22 *Ernoneura* Becker (1 sp., *E. argus* (Zetterstedt))]

98.23 *Scatophaga* Meigen

Twenty-eight species, the following of which is common:

S. stercoraria (Linnaeus) (Dung Fly). L. ±9 mm. Grayish brown, clothed with yellow to reddish hairlike setae; thorax with long, heavy, black spines. Males bright yellow because of longer, heavier covering of pile. Adults fly from April to October around fresh cow manure. Larvae live in the manure. (See A&J 340.) (1), (2), (3), (4), (5), generally distributed.

[98.24 *Ceratinostoma* Meade (1 sp., *C. ostiorum* (Curtis)); 98.25 *Gimnomera* Rondani (5 spp.); 98.26 *Hydromyza* Fallén (1 sp., *H. confluens* Loew)]

Tribe Delinini

[98.27 *Parallelomma* Becker (1 sp., *P. vittatum* (Meigen)); 98.28 *Americina* Malloch (1 sp., *A. adusta* (Loew)); 98.29 *Delina* Robineau-Desvoidy (1 sp., *D. nigrita* (Fallén); 98.30 *Hexamitocera* Becker (3 spp.); 98.31 *Plethochaeta* Coquillett (2 spp.); 98.32 *Neochirosia* Malloch (3 spp.); Unplaced species (3 spp.)]

99. ANTHOMYIIDAE (Anthomyiid Fly Family)

Length: 7–9 mm. These flies, like the Scatophagidae, resemble House Flies but are differentiated by their wing venation and antennal characters as given in the Key to the Families. Usually black, with black setae; slender; legs long. Adults of many species are predacious, and even catch bees. Larvae of some live in plant stems, and some are parasitic on caterpillars; a few are aquatic (see subfamily Fucelliinae), and some live in decaying plant material. Among the pest species are many called Root Maggots and Seed Maggots. Seed Maggots (see *Hylemya* below) may destroy soybeans and other seed plants before they germinate or kill the young plants before they emerge from the soil. The 412 species assigned to this family are difficult to identify.

Subfamily Fucelliinae

[99.1 *Fucellia* Robineau-Desvoidy (17 spp.); 99.2 *Circia* Malloch (1 sp., *C. tinctipennis* Malloch)]

Subfamily Anthomyiinae
Tribe Myopinini

[99.3 *Myopina* Robineau-Desvoidy (3 spp.); 99.4 *Pseudochirosia* Ringdahl (2 spp.); 99.5 *Chirosia* Rondani (2 spp.); 99.6 *Chiastocheta* Pokorny (1 sp., *C. glauca* (Coquillett))]

Tribe Chelisiini

[99.7 *Chelisia* Rondani (1 sp., *C. elegans* Stein)]

Tribe Anthomyiini
99.8 *Hylemya* Robineau-Desvoidy

This genus is divided in 13 subgenera: *Hylemya* s. str. (2 spp.), *Pycnoglossa* Coquillett (9 spp.), *Phorbia* Robineau-Desvoidy (10 spp.), *Delia* Robineau-Desvoidy (84 spp.), *Botanophila* Lioy (17 spp.), *Pegohylemyia* Schnabl (23 spp.), *Egle* Robineau-

Desvoidy (9 spp.), *Craspedochaeta* Macquart (5 spp.), *Lasiomma* Stein (5 spp.), *Acrostilpna* Ringdahl (7 spp.), *Hylemyza* (1 sp. *H. lasciva* (Zetterstedt), *Paregle* Schnable (4 spp.), and *Crinurina* Karl. The following species are of economic importance.

H. (*Delia*) *antiqua* (Meigen) (Onion Maggot). Larvae bore into roots of onions, causing the plants to die.

H. (*Delia*) *brassicae* Wiedemann (Cabbage Maggot). A root borer.

H. (*Delia*) *brunnescens* (Zellerstedt) (Carnation Maggot). Their root boring kills carnation plants.

H. (*Delia*) *floralis* (Fallén) (Turnip Maggot). These maggots bore into the roots of turnips, causing them to weaken and die.

[99.9 *Macrophorbia* Malloch (1 sp., *M. houghi* Malloch); 99.10 *Alliopsis* Schnabl and Dziedzicki (2 spp.); 99.11 *Eremomyia* Stein (10 spp.); 99.12 *Eremomyioides* Malloch (6 spp.); 99.13 *Emmesomyia* Malloch (2 spp.)]

99.14 *Pegomya* Robineau-Desvoidy

This genus is divided into two subgenera: *Pegomya* s. str. (94 spp.) and *Nupedia* Karl (10 spp.). The following species are of economic importance:

P. (*Pegomya*) *betae* (Curtis) (Beet Leaf Miner; Spinach Leaf Miner). This species mines the leaves of beets, spinach, and similar plants.

P. (*Pegomya*) *rubivora* (Coquillett) (Raspberry Cane Maggot). Larvae girdle inner bark of tips of young raspberry and blackberry shoots and weakens the plants.

[99.15 *Hydrophoria* Robineau-Desvoidy (29 spp.); 99.16 *Anthomyia* Meigen (2 spp.); 99.17 *Anthomyiella* Malloch (1 sp., *A. pratincola* (Panzer)); 98.18 *Calythea* Schnabl and Dziedzicki (4 spp.); 99.19 *Paraprosalpia* Villeneuve (20 spp.); 99.20 *Neohylemyia* Malloch (3 spp.); 99.21 *Leucophora* Robineau-Desvoidy (10 spp.); 99.22 *Proboscimyia* Bigot (2 spp.); 99.23 *Macateeia* Malloch (2 spp.); 99.24 *Eustalomyia* Kowarz (3 spp.)]

100. MUSCIDAE (House Fly Family)

Length: 2–12 mm. Most species are grayish or brown; others are black or yellow. They are differentiated from the previous family by the features given in the Key to the Families. Many are attracted to excrement and decaying animal matter; some of these are predacious. Some species suck blood and others are commensals; many are vectors of disease. Adults may be found around flowers. Larvae feed on living plants as well as dung, carrion, and the inhabitants of decaying vegetation. A few are aquatic. The family contains 622 species in the U.S. and Canada.

Subfamily Coenosiinae

[100.1 *Schoenomyza* Haliday (4 spp.); 100.2 *Coenosia* Meigen, with 4 subgenera: *Coenosia* s. str. (2 spp.), *Limosia* Robineau-Desvoidy (54 spp.), *Hoplogaster* Rondani (12 spp.), and *Neodexiopsis* Malloch (11 spp.); 100.3 *Bithoracochaeta* Stein (1 sp., *B. leucoprocta* (Wiedemann)); 100.4a *Allognota* Pokorny (1 sp., *A. semivitta* Malloch); 100.4b *Atherigona* Rondani, subgenus *Acritochaeta* Grimshaw (1 sp., *A. orientalis* Schiner); 100.5 *Macrorchis* Rondani (3 spp.); 100.6 *Pseudocoenosia* Stein (4 spp.); 100.7 *Phyllogaster* Stein (8 spp.); 100.8 *Limnospila* Schnabl (1 sp., *L. albifrons* (Zetterstedt)); 100.9 *Lispocephala* Pokorny (7 spp.); 100.10 *Pentacricia* Stein (1 sp., *P. aldrichii* Stein); Unplaced species (6 spp.)]

Subfamily Lispinae

[100.11 *Lispe* Latreille (23 spp.)]

Subfamily Limnophorinae

[100.12 *Lispoides* Malloch (1 sp., *L. aequifrons* (Stein)); 100.13 *Spilogona* Schnabl (86 spp.); 100.14 *Mydaeina* Malloch (1 sp., *M. obscura* Malloch); 100.15 *Gymnodia* Robineau-Desvoidy (4 spp.); 100.16 *Limnophora* Robineau-Desvoidy (6 spp.); 100.17 *Pseudolimnophora* Strobl (2 spp.); 100.18 *Bucephalomyia* Malloch (1 sp., *B. femorata* (Malloch))]

Subfamily Mydaeinae

[100.19 *Helina* Robineau-Desvoidy (53 spp.); 100.20 *Quadrularia* Huckett (3 spp.); 100.21 *Ariciella* Malloch (1 sp., *A. rubripalpis* (Wulp)); 100.22 *Hebecnema* Schnabl (5 spp.); 100.23 *Myospila* Rondani (1 sp., *M. meditabunda* (Fabricius)); 100.24 *Mydaea* Robineau-Desvoidy (19 spp.); 100.25 *Xenomydaea* Malloch (7 spp.)]

Subfamily Fanniinae

100.26 *Fannia* Robineau-Desvoidy

Ninety-nine species, the following of which are of medical importance:

F. canicularis (Linnaeus) (Little House Fly). L. 5–6 mm. Gray, resembling the House Fly but noticeably smaller. Adults often enter houses, weaving back and forth in the air without settling. They are also seen around excrement. Larvae breed in decaying animal and plant material. They have been reported to cause myiasis in the human urethra. Cosmopolitan.

F. pusio (Wiedemann) (Chicken Dung Fly). Similar to the preceding; common in barnyards. (1) n.e. US; (2) s.e. US; (3) AZ, NM, TX.

F. scalaris (Fabricius) (Latrine Fly). L. 5–6 mm. Very close in appearance to the preceding two flies. Larvae live in excrement and sometimes cause myiasis. (1), (2), (3), (4), (5), generally distributed.

[100.27 *Coelomyia* Haliday (2 spp.); 100.28 *Euryomma* Stein (2 spp.); 100.29 *Piezura* Rondani (2 spp.); 100.30 *Platycoenosia* Strobl (1 sp., *P. mikii* Strobl); 100.31 *Azelia* Robineau-Desvoidy (5 spp.)]

Subfamily Phaoniinae

[100.32 *Hydrotaea* Robineau-Desvoidy (24 spp.); 100.33 *Neohydrotaea* Malloch (1 sp., *N. hirtipes* Malloch); 100.34 *Trichopticoides* Ringdahl (1 sp., unnamed); 100.35 *Ophyra* Robineau-Desvoidy (4 spp.); 100.36 *Pogonomyia* Rondani (8 spp.); 100.37 *Eupogonomyia* Malloch (3 spp.); 100.38 *Pogonomyioides* Malloch (1 sp., *P. segnis* (Holmgren)); 100.39 *Bebryx* Gistel (1 sp., unnamed); 100.40 *Lasiops* Meigen, with 2 subgenera: *Lasiops* s. str. (13 spp.) and *Alloeostylus* Schnabl (2 spp.); 100.41 *Dialyta* Meigen (2 spp.); 100.42 *Dendrophaonia* Malloch (3 spp.); 100.43 *Coenosopsia* Malloch (1 sp., *C. prima* Malloch); 100.44 *Phaonia* Robineau-Desvoidy, with 3 subgenera: *Phaonia* s. str. (65 spp.), *Lophosceles* Ringdahl (3 spp.), and *Wahlgrenia* Ringdahl (1 sp., *P. magnicornis* (Zetterstedt)); 100.45 *Bigotomyia* Malloch (2 spp.); 100.46 *Pseudophaonia* Malloch (2 spp.); 100.47 *Muscina* Robineau-Desvoidy (5 spp.)]

Subfamily Muscinae

[100. 48 *Pararicia* Brauer and Bergenstamm (2 spp.); 100.49 *Mesembrina* Meigen (1 sp., *M. latreillii* Robineau-Desvoidy); 100.50 *Hypodermodes* Townsend (1 sp., *H. solitarius* Knab); 100.51 *Graphomya* Robineau-Desvoidy (1 sp., *G. maculata* (Scopoli)); 100.52 *Synthesiomyia* Brauer and Bergenstamm (1 sp., *S. nudiseta* (Wulp)); 100.53 *Neomuscina* Townsend, with 2 subgenera: *Neomuscina* s. str. (1 sp., *N. tripunctata* (Wulp)) and *Spilopteromyia* Malloch (2 spp.); 100.54

Philornis Meinert (2 spp.); 100.55 *Morellia* Robineau-Desvoidy (3 sp.); 100.56 *Pyrellia* Robineau-Desvoidy (2 spp.); 100.57 *Orthellia* Robineau-Desvoidy (1 sp., *O. caesarion* (Meigen))]

100.58 *Musca* Linnaeus

Two species, both of which are pests and are of medical importance:

M. domestica Linnaeus (House Fly). L. 7–8 mm. Thorax black with stripes of gray pile; head and abdomen with brown markings. This fly is recognized by almost everyone because of its abundance around homes and barnyards. Several subspecies have been distinguished and appear to have somewhat differing distributions. (See Fig. 29.53 and A&J 341.) Cosmopolitan.

M. autumnalis De Geer (Face Fly) L. 6.5–7 mm. This is a common species around the face of cattle. Larvae live in cow manure and other excrement. Unintentionally introduced about 1952. (1) n.e. NA; (2) s.e. US; (3) s.w. US.

Subfamily Stomoxyinae

Members of the subfamily are blood suckers as adults.

100.59 *Haematobia* Lepeletier and Serville

One species as follows:

H. irritans (Linnaeus) (Horn Fly). L. ±4 mm. Resembles the House Fly except for size. Adults are blood suckers and very injurious to cattle but rarely bite man. Larvae found in manure or decaying vegetable matter. (1), (2), (3), (4), (5), generally distributed wherever cattle are.

[100.60 *Lyperosiops* Townsend (1 sp., *L. alcis* (Snow))]

100.61 *Stomoxys* Geoffroy

One species, a pest, as follows:

S. calcitrans (Linnaeus) (Stable Fly; Biting House Fly). L. 7–8 mm. Body gray with black markings and abdomen broad, but otherwise very similar to the House Fly. This species, a severe biter of man and animals, is abundant around stables and cow barns during summer, flying near manure, but it also frequents cabbage, both in the field and stored. Larvae live in manure. It is this fly that arrives during humid weather and invades homes. One often hears the expression: "It must be going to rain, the flies are biting." People have the mistaken idea that the House Fly will bite before it rains, when in reality it is this fly. (See Fig. 29.54.)

[100.62 *Acridomyia* (2 spp.); unplaced species (9 spp.)]

Fig. 29.53. (*U.S. Dept. of Agric.*)

Fig. 29.54. (*From Knox*)

Superfamily **OESTROIDEA**

101. CALLIPHORIDAE (Blow Fly Family)

Length: 7–14 mm. Metallic blue, green, or black flies distinguished by their plumose antennal arista and lack of a pronounced postscutellum. Adults feed on nectar, pollen, and decaying plant and animal matter. Larvae live in carrion, dung, and decaying plant material. A few species are intestinal parasites of invertebrates. Others transmit human diseases. The 78 species in the U.S. and Canada are widely distributed.

Subfamily Rhiniinae

[101.1 *Stomorhina* Rondani (1 sp., *S. lunata* (Fabricius))]

Subfamily Chrysomyinae
Tribe Chrysomyini

[101.2 *Chloroprocta* Wulp (1 sp., *C. fuscanipennis* (Macquart))]

101.3 *Cochliomyia* Townsend

Four species, the following two of which are serious pests:

C. hominivorax (Coquerel) (Screw-worm Fly). L. 8–10 mm. Metallic black body with shining greenish-black legs. Larvae are severe pests of cattle and other domestic animals, and sometimes of man. Females lay their eggs in open wounds. Larvae feed on tissues and exudates, causing secondary infection. Recent attempts to bring it under control by sterilizing males have been successful. It is capable of spreading throughout the U.S.

C. macellaria (Fabricius) (Secondary Screw-worm Fly). L. 6–9 mm. Body bluish green; head orange; legs reddish; thorax with three black stripes. Larvae live principally on decaying carcasses but may enter wounds with the preceding species. (1), (2), (3), (4), throughout US.

[101.4 *Paralucilia* Brauer and Bergenstamm (1 sp., *P. wheeleri* (Hough))]

Tribe Phormiini
101.5 *Phormia* Robineau-Desvoidy

One species, as follows:

P. regina (Meigen) (Black Blow Fly). L. 6–11 mm. Olive or greenish body. Larvae live in carcasses or in bloody wounds. (1) n.e. NA; (2) s.e. US; (3) s.w. US.

[101.6 *Boreellus* Aldrich and Shannon (1 sp., *B. atriceps* (Zellerstedt)); 101.7 *Protophormia* Townsend (1 sp., *P. terraenovae* (Robineau-Desvoidy)); 101.8 *Protocalliphora* Hough (10 spp.)]

Subfamily Calliphorinae
Tribe Luciliini

[101.9 *Francilia* Shannon (1 sp., *F. fuscipalpis* (Zetterstedt)); 101.10 *Bufolucilia* Townsend (3 spp.)]

101.11 *Lucilia* Robineau-Desvoidy

One species, as follows:

L. illustris (Meigen). L. 6–9 mm. Blue-green. Adults frequent open woodlands and meadows and are attracted to wild parsnips and fresh meat. Larvae live on carrion. They can cause myiasis in animals. (See A&J 342.) (1), (2), (3), (4), (5), generally distributed.

101.12 *Phaenicia* Robineau-Desvoidy

Seven species, the following of which is very common:

P. sericata (Meigen). L. 6–9.5 mm. Yellow-green to bluish or coppery green. Larvae found on carrion; fresh meat attracts adults, on which the females immediately lay eggs. Cosmopolitan.

[Unplaced species (1 sp., *Somomyia rectinervis* Bigot)]

Tribe Calliphorini

[101.13 *Acronesia* Hall (7 spp.); 101.14 *Eucalliphora* Townsend (1 sp., *E. lilaea* (Walker)); 101.15 *Aldrichina* Townsend (1 sp., *A. grahami* (Aldrich))]

[Note: *Chrysomya rufifacies* (Macquart) (Hairy Maggot Blow Fly), a species common in Hawaii, should not be confused with *Calliphora rufifacies* Macquart, which is a synonym of *C. vicina* Robineau-Desvoidy.]

101.16 *Calliphora* Robineau-Desvoidy

Ten species, the following of which is very common:

C. vomitoria (Linnaeus). L. 10–14 mm. Blue-black with tawny red beard on face. Adults fly early in the year. (1) n.e. NA; (2) VA; (3) CA; (4) Pacific n.w.; (5) n. Central states.

[101.17 *Onesia* Robineau-Desvoidy (2 spp.)]

101.18 *Cynomyopsis* Townsend

One species, as follows:

C. cadaverina (Robineau-Desvoidy) (Blow Fly; Shiny Bluebottle Fly). L. 9–14 mm. Black with gray markings; head with gray or yellow to brownish pile; abdomen shining blue-green. Adults fly from April to October. Larvae infest carrion and are sometimes found in cured meat. (1), (2), (3), (4), (5), generally distributed.

[101.19 *Cyanus* Hall (1 sp., *C. elongatus* (Hough)); 101.20 *Cynomya* Robineau-Desvoidy (3 spp.); unplaced species (1 sp., *Cynomyia flavipalpis* Macquart)]

Subfamily Polleniinae
Tribe Polleniini

101.21 *Pollenia* Robineau-Desvoidy

Two species, the following of which is common:

P. rudis (Fabricius) (Cluster Fly). L. 8–10 mm. Larger and darker than a House Fly; thorax black, its sides and often its top with short, golden, crinkly, hairlike setae; abdomen black and silver. Adults on shrubbery around homes and in fields; attracted to flowers. Larvae parasitize earthworms. Adults fly

April to June in the North, and throughout the year in the South. In the fall, many enter dwellings to hibernate. Eggs are deposited in soil. Larvae hatch in four to six days and infest earthworms for two weeks. (See Fig. 29.55.) (1), (2), (3), (4), (5), generally distributed.

Tribe Melanodexiini

[101.22 *Melanodexia* Williston (8 spp.)]

Tribe Melanomyini

[101.23 *Opelousia* Townsend (5 spp.); 101.24 *Opsodexia* Townsend (4 spp.); Unplaced species (1 sp., *Calliphora splendida* Macquart)]

102. OESTRIDAE (Bot and Warble Fly Family)

[=Gastrophilidae, Cuterebridae, and Oestridae of authors]

Length: 8–25 mm. Heavy-bodied, with hairlike setae but no bristles; resemblance to honeybees, carpenter bees, or bumble bees; head inflated; mouthparts reduced or atrophied; vibrissae absent; antennae small. Larvae are endoparasites of mammals, including man. There are 41 species in the U.S. and Canada.

Subfamily Gastrophilinae

Larvae develop in the intestines of species of Equidae and are called Horse Bots.

102.1 *Gasterophilus* Leach

Four species, as follows:

G. haemorrhoidalis (Linnaeus) (Nose Bot Fly). L. 15–18 mm. Abdomen red-tipped. Larvae are blood red and infest the nasal cavity and pharynx of a horse briefly before progressing to its stomach. Cosmopolitan.

G. intestinalis (De Geer) (Horse Bot Fly). L. ±18 mm. Adults with dark, irregular transverse band across wings. The reddish larvae infest a horse's tongue before descending to its stomach. Cosmopolitan.

G. nasalis (Linnaeus) (Throat Bot Fly). L. 9–16 mm. Adults similar to the preceding. The pale yellow larvae infest the pylorus and duodenum of a horse. Cosmopolitan.

G. inermis Brauer. Larvae, unlike those of the other three species, lack spines. Introduced. (1) IL.

Subfamily Cuterebrinae

The adults of these flies are rarely seen. The larvae are subcutaneous parasites of rodents and rabbits in the U.S. and Canada, but in Central and South America they also parasitize cattle and even man. The so-called Human Bot Fly, or Torsalo (*Dermatobia hominis* (Linnaeus, Jr.)), is really a parasite of cattle, sheep, dogs, cats, rabbits, and other animals, including man. The female lays her eggs on the side of the abdomen of certain female mosquitoes. When the mosquito alights on an animal for a blood meal, the Bot Fly larvae that are in their fully developed first stage leave the eggs and penetrate the skin of their prospective host. They then migrate through the body, finally coming to rest near the surface of the skin. The small breathing hole they make in the skin usually becomes infected, and swelling and pain occur as the larvae develop. The heavy spines that cover their bodies are used to keep the chamber open and insure a supply of blood nad serum to feed upon. When the larvae have completed their development, they emerge from the cell, drop to the ground, and pupate in the soil. The adults emerge some time later. This species does not occur as far north as the U.S.

102.2 *Cuterebra* Clark

Twenty-six species, including the following two common species (Fig. 29.56):

C. buccata (Fabricius). Larvae live under the skin of rabbits. (1) n.e. US; (2) s.e. US; (3) TX.

C. cuniculi (Clark) (Rabbit Bot Fly). L. 20–25 mm. Black, stout flies, covered with a short pile that is light gray on the thorax, white on sides; antennal arista plumose. Life cycle is similar to that described above for *Dermatobia hominis* except that the eggs are laid directly on the rabbit's skin. (See A&J 350.) (2) s.e. US; (3) s.e. US.

Subfamily Oestrinae

Length: 8–13 mm. The uncommon adults of these flies somewhat resemble Blow Flies; their bodies are covered with short, sometimes appressed, hairlike setae, and they lack heavy spines. The larvae are endoparasitic on sheep, cattle, and other mammals.

Tribe Oestrini

102.3 *Oestrus* Linnaeus

One species, as follows.

O. ovis Linnaeus (Sheep Bot Fly). Larvae live in the nasal cavities of sheep, rarely goats. Adults are dark gray with small black spots, particularly on thorax; setae are light brown. They may be found resting in the corners and crevices of buildings where sheep are kept. Cosmopolitan.

Tribe Cephenemyiinae

[102.4 *Cephenemyia* Latreille (6 spp.)]

Fig. 29.55. (*From Hall, 1948*)

Fig. 29.56. (*From Curran, 1934*)

Tribe Hypodermatinae

102.5 *Hypoderma* Latreille

Two subgenera, as follows: *Hypoderma* s. str. (2 spp.) and *Oedemagena* Latreille, (1 sp., *H. tarandi* (Linnaeus)). The following two species are common pests:

H. (Hypoderma) bovis (Linnaeus) (Northern Cattle Grub). (1) n.e. NA; (2) VA, NC; (3) n. TX, n. CA; (4) Pacific n.w.; (5) n. Central states.

H. lineatus (de Villers) (Common Cattle Grub). Cosmopolitan.

[102.6 *Suioestrus* Townsend (1 sp., *S. cookii* Townsend)]

103. SARCOPHAGIDAE (Flesh Fly Family)

Length: 2.8–22 mm (usually 6–11 mm). Black or gray flies, never metallic, often with yellow hairs; postscutellum not developed; antennal arista plumose on basal half only. Adults feed on nectar, tree sap, fruit juices, and honeydew from aphids. Males have the interesting habit of establishing a territorial position, from which they fly out to capture a passing female. Larvae feed on a wide range of animal flesh. A few are parasites of other insects—grasshoppers, for example. Many rob wasp nests by first destroying the eggs of the wasp host and then feeding on the insects stored in the nest. Others live under the skin of turtles, in the stomachs of frogs, and in other animals. Some are "aquatic," living as predators in the leaves of pitcher plants. Since the eggs of most species hatch in the female's body, she lays living and rather large larvae. There are 327 species in the U.S. and Canada.

Subfamily Miltogramminae

Tribe Miltogrammini

[103.1 *Amobia* Robineau-Desvoidy, with 2 subgenera: *Amobia* s. str. (2 spp.) and *Sarcomacronychia* Townsend (4 spp.)]

103.2 *Eumacronychia* Townsend

Fifteen species, the following of which is common:

E. scitula Reinhard (Banded Flesh Fly). L. 4–9 mm. Body grayish; thorax with dark longitudinal stripes; abdomen with white and black crossbands; tip of abdomen orange. This species lays its eggs in the nests of wasps. They presumably follow the wasp back to her nest as she provisions it with prey. Once she has left the nest, the fly enters, destroys the eggs, and lays her own in their place. The fly larvae then feed on the food provided by the wasp for her own young. (3) CA. (A&J 344).

[103.3 *Euphyto* Townsend (6 spp.); 103.4 *Gymnoprosopa* Townsend (7 spp.); 103.5 *Hilarella* Rondani (1 sp., *H. hilarella* (Zetterstedt)); 103.6 *Macronychia* Rondani (2 spp.); 103.7 *Metopia* Meigen, with 2 subgenera; *Metopia* s. str. (6 spp.) and *Allenanicia* Townsend (4 spp.); 103.8 *Opsidia* Coquillet (2 spp.); 103.9 *Opsidiotrophus* Reinhard (1 sp., *O. micidus* Reinhard); 103.10 *Phrosinella* Robineau-Desvoidy (5 spp.); 103.11 *Ptychoneura* Brauer and Bergenstamm (1 spp., *P. aristalis* (Coquillett)); 103.12 *Senotainia* Macquart (13 spp.); 103.13 *Sphenometopa* Townsend (5 spp.); 103.14 *Taxigramma* Perris (1 sp., *T. heteroneura* (Meigen))]

Tribe Paramacronychiini

[103.15 *Brachicoma* Rondani (4 spp.); 103.16 *Cattasoma* Reinhard (2 spp.); 103.17 *Erythrandra* Brauer and Bergenstamm (2 spp.); 103.18 *Pseudosarcophaga* Kramer (1 sp., unnamed); 103.19 *Sarcofahrtia* Parker (2 spp.); 103.20 *Wohlfahrtia* Brauer and Bergenstamm (1 sp., *W. vigil* (Walker))]

Subfamily Sarcophaginae

[103.21 *Anolisimyia* Dodge (1 sp., *A. blakeae* Dodge); 103.22 *Archimimus* Reinhard (2 spp.); 103.23 *Argoravinia* Townsend (1 sp., *A. modesta* (Wiedemann))]

103.24 *Blaesoxipha* Loew

This genus is divided into eight subgenera: *Acanthodotheca* Townsend (18 spp.), *Acridiophaga* Townsend (6 spp.), *Blaesoxipha* s. str. (7 spp.), *Fletcherimyia* Townsend (4 spp.), *Kellymyia* Townsend (5 spp.), *Servaisia* Robineau-Desvoidy (14 spp.), *Speciosa* Roback (1 sp., *B. speciosa* (Lopes), and *Spirobolomyia* Townsend (4 spp.); unplaced species (1 sp., *Sarcophaga hetaera* (Reinhard)).

The various species of this genus, known as Grasshopper Maggots, are similar in appearance and size to House Flies but have a larger head and eyes that point forward. The larvae infest grasshoppers throughout the U.S. and Canada.

[103.25 *Boettcheria* Parker (5 spp.); 103.26 *Camptops* Aldrich (1 sp., *C. unicolor* Aldrich); 103.27 *Cistudinomyia* Townsend (1 sp., *C. cistudinis* (Aldrich)); 103.28 *Colcondamyia* Reinhard (1 sp., *C. falcifera* Reinhard); 103.29 *Comasarcophaga* Hall (2 spp.); 103.30 *Emblemasoma* Aldrich (3 spp.); 103.31 *Erucophaga* Reinhard (1 sp., *E. triloris* Reinhard); 103.32 *Helicobia* Coquillett (2 spp.); 103.33 *Johnsonia* Coquillett, with 2 subgenera: *Johnsonia* s. str. (4 spp.) and *Sthenopyga* (3 spp.); 103.34 *Mecynocorpus* Roback (1 sp., *M. salvum* (Aldrich)); 103.35 *Metoposarcophaga* Townsend (10 spp.); 103.36 *Microcerella* Macquart (4 spp.); 103.37 *Neophyto* Townsend (5 spp.); 103.38 *Oxysarcodexia* Townsend, with 2 subgenera: *Oxysarcodexia* s. str. (10 spp.) and *Dexosarcophaga* Townsend (1 sp., *O. transita* (Townsend)); 103.39 *Pachygraphia* Brauer and Bergenstamm (1 sp., unnamed); 103.40 *Peckia* Robineau-Desvoidy (2 spp.); 103.41 *Ravinia* Robineau-Desvoidy, with 2 subgenera: *Chaetoravinia* Townsend (8 spp.) and *Ravinia* s. str. (9 spp.); 103.42 *Sarcodexia* Townsend, with 4 subgenera: *Rafaelia* Townsend (4 spp.), *Sarcodexia* s. str. (1 sp., *S. sternodontis* Townsend), *Sarcodexiopsis* Townsend (2 spp.), and *Titanogrypa* Townsend (3 spp.); 103.43 *Sarcofahrtiamyia* Hall (1 sp., *S. tenta* Hall); 103.44 *Sarcofahrtiopsis* Hall (1 sp., unnamed)]

103.45 *Sarcophaga* Meigen

Seventy-four species, the following of which may serve as common examples:

S. bullata Parker. L. 7.5–15 mm. Body dark brown with prominent gray stripes on thorax and gray spots on abdomen. Larvae found in decaying animal matter. (1), (2), (3), (4), (5), generally distributed.

S. haemorrhoidalis (Fallén). L. 10–14 mm. Similar to the preceding species, this fly is the most common cause of myiasis in humans. Larvae normally feed on decaying animal matter but will develop in the human digestive tract if the eggs are ingested with food. Cosmopolitan. (See A&J 343.)

[103.46 *Tricharaea* Thomson (3 spp.); 103.47 *Udamopyga* Hall (1 sp., *U. niagarana* (Parker)); 103.48 *Tephromyiopsis* Townsend (1 sp., *T. rufocaudata* (Bigot)); unplaced species (13 spp.)]

104. RHINOPHORIDAE (Rhinophorid Fly Family)

[From Tachinidae, Rhinophorinae of authors]

Length: ±5 mm. Postscutellum is distinctly, though narrowly, developed. Larvae are parasitic on insects and isopods. There are four species in the U.S. and Canada.

[104.1 *Bezzimyia* Townsend (2 spp.)]

104.2 *Melanophora* Meigen

One species, as follows:

M. roralis (Linnaeus). This is the most widespread species of this family in the U.S. (1) n.e. US; (2) s.e. US; (5) KS.

[104.3 *Styloneuria* Brauer and Bergenstamm (1 sp., *S. discrepans* (Pandelle))]

105. TACHINIDAE (Parasitic Fly Family)

Length: 5–15 mm. These flies are fairly easy to recognize by their well-developed postscutellum (best visible from the side) and their usually bare antennal arista, combined with heavy body bristles (present in some other muscoid flies as well), particularly on the posterior portion of the abdomen. Adults are strong fliers; their relatively large, stout bodies make them noticeable when they visit flowers, or buzz by. The larvae of all species are internal parasites of other insects, especially caterpillars, but also the larvae of beetles, sawflies, and the nymphs of bugs and grasshoppers (of isopods as well, although rarely). Some also parasitize the adults of these groups. They are extremely beneficial as population regulators of many species of insects, including many severe crop pests. Along with the parasitic Hymenoptera, they regulate many, if not most, terrestrial ecosystems.

The adult female lays eggs of two types. Some place a very tiny egg on a plant leaf that is the food of the caterpillar or nymph of the host species. After the egg is consumed by the host, it hatches in the digestive tract. The larva then enters the body of the victim and slowly consumes its tissues without killing it until it is mature (at which time the host has been totally consumed). Other species lay large eggs directly on the host; these hatch and the larvae penetrate the integument. Still others inject maggots into the host; once inside, they too feed slowly on the host without killing it until they are mature.

This would probably be the largest family of flies if the many undescribed species were included with the 1277 species now known from the U.S. and Canada.

Subfamily Phasiinae

Flies in this subfamily are parasites of adult Hemiptera and some adult Coleoptera.

Tribe Cymnosomatini

[105.1 *Cistogaster* Latreille (1 sp., *C. amplifrons* (Brooks); 105.2 *Gymnoclytia* Brauer and Bergenstamm (7 spp.); 105.3 *Gymnosoma* Meigen (5 spp.)]

Tribe Trichopodini

[105.4 *Eutrichopoda* Townsend (1 sp., unnamed [not in U.S. or Canada but erroneously reported in FL])]

105.5 *Trichopoda* Berthold

This genus is divided into two subgenera: *Galactomyia* townsend (3 spp.) and *Trichopoda* s. str. (3 spp.). The following species are common:

T. (*Galactomyia*) *pennipes* (Fabricius). Parasite of Squash Bugs.

T. (*Trichopoda*) *indivisa* Townsend (Hairy-legged Fly). L. 9–11 mm. Reddish brown; eyes brown; abdomen with patches of yellow; wings brown; hind tibiae with wide, leaflike expansions fringed with long, stout setae. Females fasten unin-

cubated eggs externally on adults of various bugs. Adult flies visit flowers and feed on pollen and nectar. Larval host records include rearing from Cicadas. (See A&J 346.) (3) s.w. US.

[105.6 *Xanthomelanodes* Townsend (5 spp.)]

Tribe Phasiini

[105.7 *Alophorella* Townsend (11 spp.); 105.8 *Euclytia* Townsend (1 sp., *E. flava* (Townsend)); 105.9 *Hyalomya* Robineau-Desvoidy (4 spp.); 105.10 *Paraphorantha* Townsend (3 spp.); 105.11 *Phasia* Latreille (3 spp.)]

105.12 *Phasiomyia* Townsend

One species, as follows:

P. splendida (Coquillett) (Orange-spotted Tachinid). L. 8–9 mm. Black; eyes red; legs black; wings smoky; tip of abdomen with large orange spot. Larvae unknown. (See A&J 349.) (1) n.e. US; (4) Pacific n.w.; (5) n. Central states.

[105.13 *Phoranthella* Brooks (1 sp., *P. punctigera* (Townsend)); 105.14 *Tricholytia* Townsend (3 spp.); unplaced species (2 spp.)]

Tribe Freraeini

The known hosts of these species are carabid beetles.

[105.15 *Eugymnogaster* Townsend (1 sp., *E. monyana* (Coquillett))]

Tribe Catharosiini

Species of this tribe are parasites of adult Hemiptera of the family Lygaeidae.

[105.16 *Catharosia* Rondani (3 spp.); 105.17 *Procatharosia* Villeneuve (2 spp.)]

Tribe Cylindromyiini

[105.18 *Apinops* Coquillett (1 sp., *A. ater* Coquillett); 105.19 *Apostrophus* Loew (2 spp.); 105.20 *Beskia* Brauer and Bergenstamm (1 sp., *B. aelops* (Walker)); 105.21 *Bessaria* Robineau-Desvoidy (1 sp., *B. brevipennis* (Loew)); 105.22 *Cylindromyia* Meigen, with 3 subgenera: *Apinocyptera* Townsend (2 spp.), *Cylindromyia* s. str. (10 spp.), and *Neocyptera* Townsend (2 spp.) [unplaced spp. (2 spp.)]; 105.23 *Epigrimyia* Townsend (2 spp.); 105.24 *Euscopolia* Townsend (1 sp., *E. dakotensis* Townsend); 105.25 *Hemyda* Robineau-Desvoidy (1 sp., *H. aurata* Robineau-Desvoidy); 105.26 *Ichneumonops* Townsend (1 sp., *I. mirabilis* Townsend)]

Tribe Imitomyiini

[105.27 *Imitomyia* Townsend (1 sp, *I. sugens* (Loew))]

Tribe Cinochirini

[105.28 *Cinochira* Xetterstedt (1 sp., *C. mitis* (Reinhard))]

Tribe Leucostomatini

[105.29 *Calyptrosomus* Reinhard (1 sp., *C. dapsilis* Reinhard); 105.30 *Clairvillia* Robineau-Desvoidy (3 spp.); 105.31 *Leucostoma* Meigen (7 spp.)]

Tribe Strongygastrini

The species of this tribe are parasites of adult Coleoptera.

[105.32 *Campogaster* Rondani (1 sp., *C. exigua* (Meigen) [introduced]); 105.33 *Clistomorpha* Townsend 91 sp., *C. didyma* (Loew)); 105.34 *Hyalomyodes* Townsend (3 spp.)]

Tribe Hesperophasiini

[105.35 *Coleophasia* Townsend (1 sp., *C. pacifica* (Curran)); 105.36 *Hesperophasia* Townsend (1 sp., *H. setosa* Townsend); 105.37 *Hesperophasiopsis* Townsend (3 spp.)]

Tribe Eutherini

Parasites of the Hemiptera family Pentatomidae.

[105.38 *Euthera* Loew (3 spp.)]

Tribe Chiricahuiini

[105.39 *Chiricahuia* Townsend (1 sp., *C. cavicola* Townsend)]

Tribe Palpostomatini

Parasites of Scarabaeidae beetles.

[105.40 *Eutrixopsis* Townsend (1 sp., *E. javana* Townsend [introduced]; 105.41 *Hamaxia* Walker (1 sp., *H. incongrua* Walker [introduced])]

Subfamily Proseninae

Most species parasitize Coleoptera larvae, but some parasitize Lepidoptera or Orthoptera.

Tribe Glaurocarini

[105.42 *Cenosoma* Wulp (1 sp., *C. signiferum* Wulp); 105.43 *Oestrophasia* Bauer and Bergenstamm (2 spp.)]

Tribe Ormiini

Parasites of nocturnal Orthoptera.

[105.44 *Euphasiopteryx* Townsend (4 spp.); 105.45 *Ormia* Robineau-Desvoidy (3 spp.)]

Tribe Trixodini

[105.46 *Trixodes* Coquillett (1 sp., *T. obesus* Coquillett)]

Tribe Trixini

[105.47 *Eumegaparia* Townsend (3 spp.); 105.48 *Phasiops* Coquillett (1 sp., *P. flavus* Coquillett)]

Tribe Aulacephalini

[105.49 *Eutrixa* Coquillett (2 spp. [parasites of adult *Phyllophaga* spp. Coleoptera: Scarabaeidae]); 105.50 *Isidotus* Reinhard (1 sp., *I. incanus* Reinhard)]

Tribe Dexillini

Parasites of larvae of Scarabaeidae.

[105.51 *Dexilla* Westwood (3 spp.); 105.52 *Megaparia* Townsend (1 sp., *M. venosa* (Wulp)); 105.53 *Megapariopsis* Townsend (1 sp., *M. opaca* (Coquillett)); 105.54 *Microphthalma* Macquart (5 spp.)]

Tribe Myiophasiini

Parasites of weevil grubs; females larviposit at weevil punctures in plant tissues.

[105.55 *Myiophasia* Brauer and Bergenstamm (13 spp.)]

Tribe Melisoneurini

[105.56 *Microchaetina* Wulp (4 spp.); 105.57 *Orestilla* Reinhard (1 sp., *O. primoris* Reinhard); 105.58 *Orthosimyia* Reinhard (2 spp.); 105.59 *Phalacrophto* Townsend (1 sp., *P. sarcophagina* (Coquillett)); 105.60 *Reinhardiana* Arnaud (1 sp., *R. petiolata* (Townsend)); 105.61 *Steveniopsis* Townsend (3 spp.); 105.62 *Websteriana* Walton (1 sp., *W. costalis* (Coquillett))]

Tribe Prosenini

Parasites of larvae of Scarabaeidae and other Coleoptera.

[105.63 *Arctophyto* (9 spp.); 105.64 *Ateloglossa* Coquillett (3 spp.); 105.65 *Dinera* Robineau-Desvoidy (1 sp., *D. grisescens* (Fallén)); 105.66 *Dolichocodia* Townsend (2 spp.); 105.67 *Hesperodinera* Townsend (1 sp., *H. cinerea* Townsend); 105.68 *Mochlosoma* Brauer and Bergenstamm (5 spp.); 105.69 *Nimioglossa* Reinhard (2 spp.); 105.70 *Prosena* Lepeletier and Serville (1 sp., *P. siberita* (Fabricius)); 105.71 *Prosenoides* Brauer and Bergenstamm (3 spp.); 105.72 *Ptilodexia* Brauer and Bergenstamm (22 spp.); unplaced species 92 spp.)]

Tribe Theresiini

Parasites of wood-boring Coleoptera, Lepidoptera, and Tabanidae.

[105.73 *Carinosillus* Reinhard (5 spp.); 105.74 *Euchaetogyne* Townsend (1 sp., *E. roederi* (Williston)); 105.75 *Eutheresia* Townsend (7 spp.); 105.76 *Nicephorus* Reinhard (1 sp., *N. floridensis* Reinhard); 105.77 *Opsotheresia* Townsend (2 spp.); 105.78 *Paratheresia* Townsend (1 sp., *P. claripalpis* (Wulp)); 105.79 *Theresia* Robineau-Desvoidy (1 sp. *T. rutilans* (Fabricius)); 105.80 *Ursophyto* Aldrich (1 sp., *U. nigriceps* (Bigot)); 105.81 *Vibrissotheresia* Reinhard (1 sp., *V. pechumani* Reinhard)]

Subfamily Tachininae

Members of this subfamily are parasites of Lepidoptera.

Tribe Macromyini

[105.82 *Bombyliomyia* Brauer and Bergenstamm (1 sp., *B. sorer* (Williston))]

105.83 *Bombyliopsis* Townsend

One species, as follows:

B. abrupta (Wiedemann). L. 12–14 mm. A common species found flying in swampy glades in woods or on flowers and foliage from June to September. (1) n.e. US; (2) s.e. US; (3) s.w. US.

[105.84 *Chlorohystricia* Townsend (1 sp., *C. cyaneiventris* (Wulp)); 105.85 *Macromya* Robineau-Desvoidy (1 sp., unnamed)]

Tribe Tachinini

[105.86 *Metopotachina* Townsend (5 spp.); 105.87 *Nowickia* Wachtl, with 4 subgenera: *Echinomyodes* Townsend (17 spp.), *Fabriciella* Bezzi (6 spp.), *Nowickia* s. str. (6 spp.), and *Rhachogaster* Townsend (7 spp.); 105.88 *Peleteria* Robineau-Desvoidy, with 4 subgenera: *Oxydosphyra* Townsend (2 spp.), *Panzeriopsis* Townsend (5 spp.), *Peleteria* s. str. (12 spp.), and *Sphyromyia* Bigot (19 spp.) [unplaced species (2 spp.)]; 105.89 *Tachina* Meigen (1 sp., [introduced]) [unplaced species (1 sp., *Echinomyia victoria* Townsend)]]

Tribe Dejeaniini

[105.90 *Adejeania* Townsend (1 sp., *A. vexatrix* (Osten Sacken))]

105.91 *Archytas* Jaennicke

This genus is divided into two subgenera: *Archytas* s. str. (8 spp.) and *Nemochaeta* Wulp (5 spp.). The following species is common:

A. (Archytas) apicifer (Walker). Parasite of tent caterpillars. (1), (2), (3), (4), (5), generally distributed.

105.92 *Jurinella* Brauer and Bergenstamm

One species, as follows:

J. lutzi Curran. (Brown Tachinid). L. 9–11 mm. Robust brown body with coarse, long black bristles; abdomen black; wings brown; eyes red; arista prominent and black. Larvae parasitize various species of armyworms. (See A&J 348.) (3) s.w. US.

[105.93 *Juriniopsis* Townsend (4 spp.); 105.94 *Microtrichomma* Giglio-Tos (2 spp.)]

105.95 *Paradejeania* Brauer and Bergenstamm

One species, as follows:

P. rutilioides nigrescens Arnaud. L. ±14 mm. Body orange-yellow; thorax darker above; abdomen with long, dense black spines. Larvae parasitize various lepidopterous larvae. (See A&J 345.) CA; (4) WA, OR.

[105.96 *Pararchytas* Brauer and Bergenstamm (2 spp.); 105.97 *Protodejeania* Townsend (2 spp.)]

Tribe Juriniini

[105.98 *Epalpus* Rodani (3 spp.); 105.99 *Parepalpus* Coquillett (1 sp., *P. flavidus* Coquillett); 105.100 *Rhachoepalpus* Townsend (1 sp., unnamed)]

105.101 *Xanthoepalpus* Townsend

One species, as follows:

X. bicolor (Williston) (Yellow and Black Tachinid). L. 9–11 mm. Black; body robust, with coarse, black bristles; basal segments of abdomen yellow; wings smoky. Larvae are parasites of caterpillars of Lepidoptera. Adults visit flowers. (See A&J 347.) (3) s.w. US; (4) BC, WA, OR.

Tribe Cuphocerini

[105.102 *Copecrypta* Townsend (1 sp., *C. ruficauda* (Wulp)); 105.103 *Deopalpus* Townsend (11 spp.)]

Tribe Linnaemyini

[105.104 *Bonnetia* Robineau-Desvoidy (1 sp., *B. comta* (Fallén)); 105.105 *Chrysotachina* Brauer and Bergenstamm (2 spp.); 105.106 *Gymnocheta* Robineau-Desvoidy (4 spp.); 105.107 *Hineomyia* Townsend (1 sp., *H. setigera* (Coquillett)); 105.108 *Linnaemya* Robineau-Desvoidy (4 spp.); 105.109 *Nigrobonellia* Brooks (3 spp.); 105.110 *Spilochaetosoma* Smith (1 sp., *S. californicum* Smith); 105.111 *Tenuirostra* Ringdahl (1 sp., *T. actica* (Sack)); 105.112 *Thompsonomyia* Brooks (1 sp., *T. anthracina* (Thompson)); 105.113 *Trafoia* Brauer and Bergenstamm (1 sp., *T. rufipalpis* (Bigot))]

Tribe Ernestiini

[105.114 *Appendicia* Stein (1 sp., *A. frontalis* (Tothill)); 105.115 *Melinocera* Townsend (2 spp.); 105.116 *Mericia* Robineau-Desvoidy (20 spp.); 105.117 *Metaphyto* Coquillett (3 spp.); 105.118 *Ostracophyto* Townsend (1 sp., *O. aristalis* Townsend); 105.119 *Promericia* Brooks (1 sp., *P. fasciventris* (Curran)); 105.120 *Pseudomeriania* Brooks (1 sp., *P. nigrocornea* (Tothill)); *105.121 Xanthophyto* Townsend (2 spp.)]

Tribe Melanophryini

[105.122 *Atropharista* Townsend (1 sp., *A. insolita* (Walker)); 105.123 *Melanophrys* Williston (1 sp., *M. flavipennis* Williston)]

Tribe Aphriini

[105.124 *Apachemyia* Townsend (1 sp., *A. pallida* (Coquillett)); 105.125 *Aphria* Robineau-Desvoidy (2 spp.); 105.126 *Neofischeria* Townsend (1 sp., *N. flava* Townsend); 105.127 *Neosolieria* Townsend (1 sp., *N. sila* (Reinhard)); 105.128 *Parademoticus* Townsend (1 sp., *P. piperi* (Coquillett)); 105.129 *Parafischeria* Townsend (1 sp., *P. eucerata* (Bigot)); 105.130 *Pyraustomyia* Townsend (1 sp., *P. penitalis* (Coquillett))]

Tribe Lyphini

[105.131 *Lypha* Robineau-Desvoidy (7 spp.)]

Tribe Germariini

[105.132 *Asseclamyia* Reinhard (1 sp., *A. sphenofrons* Reinhard); 105.133 *Bigonicheta* Rondani (1 sp., *B. spinipennis* (Meigen)); 105.134 *Cacozelus* Reinhard (1 sp., *C. riederi* Reinhard); 105.135 *Chromatocera* Townsend (2 spp.); 105.136 *Cockerelliana* Townsend 91 sp., *C. capitata* Townsend); 105.137 *Dichocera* Williston (2 spp.); 105.138 *Exoristoides* Coquillett (2 spp.); 105.139 *Helioplagia* Townsend (1 sp., *H. slossonae* (Coquillett)); 105.140 *Homalactia* Townsend (3 spp.); 105.141 *Impeccantia* Reinhard (1 sp., *I. claterna* Reinhard); 105.142 *Lydina* Robineau-Desvoidy (3 spp.); 105.143 *Mactomyia* Reinhard (1 sp., *M. fracida* Reinhard); 105.144 *Mauromyia* Coquillett (1 sp., *M. pulla* Coquillett); 105.145 *Metatachina* Townsend (1 sp., *M. mellifrons* Townsend); 105.146 *Neodichocera* Walton (1 sp., *N. orientalis* (Coquillett)); 105.147 *Paradmontia* Coquillett (1 sp., *P. brevis* Coquillett); 105.148 *Petinarctia* Villeneuve (1 sp., *P. stylata* (Brauer and Bergenstamm)); 105.149 *Plagiosippus* Reinhard (1 sp., *P. invasor* Reinhard); 105.150 *Trochilodes* Coquillett (2 spp.)]

Tribe Campylochetini

[105.151 *Chaetophlepsis* Townsend (10 spp.); 105.152 *Parahypochaeta* Brauer and Bergenstamm (1 sp., *P. heteroneura* Brauer and Bergenstamm)]

Tribe Voriini

[105.153 *Anzamyia* Reinhard (1 sp., *A. cordata* (Reinhard)); 105.154 *Athrycia* Robineau-Desvoidy (1 sp., *A. cinera* (Coquillett)); 105.155 *Catalinovoria* Townsend (2 spp.); 105.156 *Chaetoplagia* Coquillett (1 sp., *C. atripennis* Coquillett); 105.157 *Cyrtophleba* Rondani (2 spp.); 105.158 *Eucyrtophloeba* Townsend (1 sp., *E. horrida* (Giglio-Tos)); 105.159 *Euptilopareia* Townsend (2 spp.); 105.160 *Ginglychaeta* Aldrich (1 sp., *G. seriata* Aldrich); 105.161 *Goniochaeta* Townsend (2 spp.); 105.162 *Meleterus* Aldrich (2 spp.); 105.163 *Menetus* Aldrich (1 sp., *M. macropogen* (Bigot); 105.164 *Metaplagia* Coquillett (1 sp., *M. occidentalis* Coquillett); 105.165 *Metavoria* Townsend (4 spp.); 105.166 *Plagiomima* Brauer and Bergenstamm, with 2 subgenera; *Plagiomima* s str (7 spp) and *Siphoplagiopsis* Townsend (3 spp.); 105.167 **Psi**, new name of *Psilopleura* Reinhard (1 sp., *P. arida* Reinhard); 105.168 *Uclesia* Girschner (3 spp.); 105.169 *Voria* Robineau-Desvoidy (2 spp.); 105.170 *Wagneria* Robineau-Desvoidy (5 spp.)]

Subfamily Dexiinae

Members of this subfamily are parasites of many Lepidoptera, some beetle larvae, and some other insects.

Tribe Thelairini

[105.171 *Spathidexia* Townsend (6 spp.); 105.172 *Thelaira* Robineau-Desvoidy (2 spp.)]

Tribe Dexiini

[105.173 *Dexia* Meigen (3 spp.)]

Tribe Macquartiini

[105.174 *Alaskophyto* Townsend (1 sp., *A. obscura* (Coquillett)); 105.175 *Anthomyiopsis* Townsend (1 sp., *A. cypseloides* Townsend); 105.176 *Athanatus* Reinhard (1 sp., *A. californicus* (Coquillett)); 105.177 *Dyscolomyia* Reinhard (1 sp., *D. lucina* Reinhard); 105.178 *Eubrachymera* Townsend (1 sp., *E. debilis* Townsend); 105.179 *Eulasiona* Townsend, with 2 subgenera: *Eulasiona* s. str. (2 spp.) and *Paramuscopteryx* Townsend (2 spp.); 105.180 *Gibsonomyia* Curran (1 sp., *G. washingtoniana* (Bigot)): 105.181 *Grisdalemyia* Curran (3 spp.); 105.182 *Ictericophyto* Townsend (3 spp.); 105.183 *Lasionalia* Curran (1 sp., *L. cinerea* Curran); 105.184 *Meledonus* Aldrich (3 spp.); 105.185 *Metopomuscopteryx* Townsend (3 spp.); 105.186 *Minella* Robineau-Desvoidy (1 sp., *M. americana* Reinhard); 105.187 *Muscopteryx* Townsend (8 spp.); 105.188 *Myioclonia* Reinhard (3 spp.); 105.189 *Ochrocera* Townsend (1 sp., *O. vaginalis* Townsend); 105.190 *Pelatachina* Meade

(3 spp.); 105.191 *Pseudomorina* Wulp (1 sp., *P pictipennis* Wulp); 105.192 *Xanthocera* Townsend (3 spp.)]

Tribe Hyalurgini

[105.193 *Hyualurgus* Brauer and Bergenstamm (1 sp., *H. lucidus* (Meigen) [introduced])]

Tribe Iceliini

[105.194 *Ervia* Robineau-Desvoidy (1 sp., *E. triquetra* (Olivier))]

Tribe Zeliini

[105.195 *Metadexia* Coquillett (1 sp., *M. tricolor* Coquillett); 105.196 *Minthozelia* Townsend (7 spp.); 105.197 *Zelia* Robineau-Desvoidy (4 spp.)]

Tribe Uramyini

[105.198 *Anaporia* Townsend (3 spp.); 105.199 *Paraporia* Townsend (1 sp., *P. quadrimaculata* (Macquart)); 105.200 *Pseudeuantha* Townsend (2 spp.); 105.201 *Uramya* Robineau-Desvoidy (1 sp., *U. halisidotae* (Townsend))]

Tribe Urodexiini

[105.202 *Chaetonodexodes* Townsend (1 sp., *C. vanderwulpi* (Townsend)); 105.203 *Cholomyia* Bigot (1 sp., *C. inaequipes* Bigot); 105.204 *Phyllophilopsis* Townsend (2 spp.)]

Tribe Ebeniini

[105.205 *Chaetonopsis* Townsend (1 sp., *C. spinosa* (Coquillett))]

Tribe Sophiini

[105.206 *Euantha* Wulp (1 sp. *E. litturata* (Olivier)); 105.207 *Eucordyligaster* Townsend (1 sp., *E. septentrionalis* (Townsend))]

Tribe Eriothrixini

[105.208 *Atrophopalpus* Townsend (2 spp.); 105.209 *Catemophrys* Townsend (1 sp., *C. sequens* (Townsend))); 105.210 *Ceratomyiella* Townsend (2 spp.); 105.211 *Epidexia* Townsend (2 spp.); 105.212 *Micromintho* Townsend (1 sp., *M. melania* Townsend); 105.213 *Paradidyma* Brauer and Bergenstamm (11 spp.); 105.214 *Periscepsia* Gistel (7 spp.); 105.215 *Vanderwulpia* Townsend (1 sp., *V. atrophopodoides* Townsend)]

Tribe Leskiini

[105.216 *Dejeaniopalpus* Townsend (1 sp., *D. texensis* Townsend); 105.217 *Eumyobia* Townsend (1 sp., unnamed); 105.218 *Genea* Rondani (1 sp., *G. aurea* James); 105.219 *Jaynesleskia* Townsend (1 sp., unnamed); 105.220 *Leskiella* James (1 sp., *L. brevirostris* James); 105.221 *Leskiomima* Brauer and Bergenstamm (2 spp.); 105.222 *Myobiopsis* Townsend (2 spp.); 105.223 *Siphoclytia* Townsend (1 sp., *S. robertsonii* Townsend); 105.224 *Sipholeskia* Townsend (2 spp.)]

Tribe Telothyriini

[105.225 *Leskiopsis* Townsend (1 sp., *L. Thecata* (Coquillett))]

Subfamily Goniinae

Tribe Acemyini

Parasites of Orthoptera.

[105.226 *Acemya* Robineau-Desvoidy (2 spp.); 105.227 *Ceracia* Rondani (1 sp., *C. dentata* (Coquillett); 105.228 *Euhalidaya* Walton (1 sp., *E. genalis* (Coquillett)); 105.229 *Hemithrixion* Brauer and Bergenstamm (2 spp.)]

Tribe Blondeliini

Parasites of Lepidoptera, Coleoptera, and tenthredinid Hymenoptera.

[105.230 *Adoryphorophaga* Townsend (2 spp.); 105.231 *Anoxynops* Townsend (1 sp., *A. aldrichi* (Curran)); 105.232 *Apacheprospherysa* Townsend (1 sp., *A. orbitalis* Townsend); 105.233 *Aplomyiopsis* Villeneuve (8 spp.); 105.234 *Aporatachina* Meade (3 spp.); 105.235 *Blondelia* Robineau-Desvoidy (6 spp.); 105.236 *Celatoria* Coquillett (2 spp.); 105.237 *Charasoma* Reinhard (3 spp.); 105.238 *Compsiluria* Bouché (1 sp., *C. concinnata* (Meigen)); 105.239 *Crytomeigenia* Brauer and Bergenstamm (19 spp.); 105.240 *Dolichotarsus* Brooks (3 spp.); 105.241 *Doryphorophaga* Townsend (3 spp.); 105.242 *Elephantocera* Townsend (1 sp., *E. greeni* Townsend); 105.243 *Eribella* Mesnil (2 spp.); 105.244 *Erynniopsis* Townsend (2 spp.); 105.245 *Eucelatoria* Townsend (2 spp.); 105.246 *Eucelatoriopsis* Townsend (1 sp., *E. dimmocki* (Aldrich)); 105.247 *Lixophaga* Townsend (12 spp.); 105.248 *Lydellohoughia* Townsend (1 sp., *L. tenela* (Reinhard)); 105.249 *Lydinolydella* Townsend (1 sp., *L. metallica* Townsend [introduced]); 105.250 *Meigenia* Robineau-Desvoidy (2 spp.); 105.251 *Meigenielloides* Townsend (1 sp., *M. cinerea* Townsend); 105.252 *Metadoria* Brauer and Bergenstamm (1 sp., *M. levis* (Aldrich and Webber)); 105.253 *Myiopharus* Brauer and Bergenstamm (3 spp.); 105.254 *Opsomeigenia* Townsend (2 spp.); 105.255 *Oswaldia* Robineau-Desvoidy, with 2 subgenera: *Dexodes* Brauer and Bergenstamm (3 spp.); and *Oswaldia* Robineau-Desvoidy (5 spp.); 105.256 *Oxynops* Townsend (1 sp., *O. anthracinus* (Bigot)); 105.257 *Panacemyia* Townsend (3 spp.); 105.258 *Paralispe* Brauer and Bergenstamm (1 sp., *P. infernalis* (Townsend)); 105.259 *Phoeniciomyina* Townsend (1 sp., *P. arizonica* Townsend); 105.260 *Phrynofrontia* Townsend (1 sp., *P. discalis* (Coquillett)); 105.261 *Pseudomyothyria* Townsend (1 sp., *P. ancilla* (Walker)); 105.262 *Schizocerophaga* Townsend (1 sp., *S. leibyi* Townsend); 105.263 *Sitophaga* Gistel (12 spp.); 105.264 *Spathimeigenia* Townsend (13 spp.); 105.265 *Tachinophyto* Townsend (1 sp., *T. floridensis* Townsend); 105.266 *Thelairodoria* Townsend (1 sp., *T. setinervis* (Coquillett)); 105.267 *Thematheca* Reinhard (1 sp., *T. medeola* Reinhard); 105.268 *Tinalydella* Townsend (1 sp., *T. procincta* (Reinhard)); 105.269 *Torynotachina* Townsend (1 sp., *T. quinteri* Townsend); 105.270 *Trypheromyia* Reinhard (1 sp., *T. pallens* Reinhard); 105.271 *Urophyllopsis* Townsend (1 sp., *U. retiniae* Townsend); 105.272 *Velocia* Robineau-Desvoidy (1 sp., *V. barbata* (Coquillett)); 105.273 *Vibrissina* Rondani (1 sp., *V. turrita* (Meigen) [introduced]); 105.274 *Xiphomyia* Townsend (2 spp.)]

Tribe Neominthoini

[105.275 *Eupelecotheca* Townsend (1 sp., *E. celer* Townsend); 105.276 *Pelecotheca* Townsend (1 sp., *P. curulis* (Reinhard))]

Tribe Exoristini

[105.277 *Bessa* Robineau-Desvoidy (2 spp.); 105.278 *Chaetexorista* Brauer and Bergenstamm (1 sp., *C. javana* Brauer and Bergenstamm); 105.279 *Diplostichus* Brauer and Bergenstamm (2 spp.); 105.280 *Epiplagiops* Blanchard (1 sp., *E. littoralis* Blanchard [introduced]); 105.281 *Euphorocera* (11 spp.)]

105.282 *Exorista* Meigen

Three species, including the following:

E. mella (Walker). L. ±12 mm. Body black with dark gray stripes on thorax and spots on abdomen; long stout, black spines on body, especially tip of abdomen. Larvae parasitize caterpillars, including the destructive Gypsy Moth (See Fig. 29.57) (1), (2), (3), (4), (5), generally distributed.

[105.283 *Guerinia* Robineau-Desvoidy (3 spp.); 105.284 *Gueriniopsis* Reinhard (1 sp., *G. setipes* (Coquillett)); 105.285 *Palpexorista* Townsend (9 spp.); 105.286 *Parasetigena* Brauer and Bergenstamm (1 sp., *P. agilis* (Robineau-Desvoidy)); 105.287 *Phorocera* Robineau-Desvoidy (1 sp., *P. obscura* (Fallén) [introduced]); 105.288 [number not used]; 105.289 *Pseudotachinomyia* Smith (4 spp.); 105.290 *Spoggosia* Rondani (1 sp., *S. gelida* (Coquillett)); 105.291 *Stomatomyia* Brauer and Bergenstamm (2 spp.); 105.292 *Tachinomyia* Townsend (10 spp.)]

Fig. 29.57. (*From Curran, 1934*)

Tribe Siphonini, *subtribe* Coronimyiina

[105.293 *Clausicella* Rondani (6 spp.); 105.294 *Coronimyia* Townsend (2 spp.); 105.295 *Crocinosoma* Reinhard (1 sp., *C. cornuale* Reinhard); 105.296 *Drepanoglossa* Townsend (2 spp.); 105.297 *Ginglymia* Townsend (1 sp., *G. acrirostris* Townsend); 105.298 *Lasioneura* Coquillett (2 spp.); 105.299 *Philocalia* Reinhard (1 sp., *P. tenuirostris* Reinhard)]

Subtribe Siphonia

[105.300 *Actia* Robineau-Desvoidy (9 spp.); 105.301 *Aphantorhapha* Townsend (3 sp.); 105.302 *Chaetostigmoptera* Townsend (1 sp., *C. crassinervis* (Walton)); 105.303 *Eucoronimyia* Townsend (1 sp., *E. hastata* (Coquillett)); 105.304 *Evidomyia* Reinhard (1 sp., *E. infida* Reinhard); 105.305 *Lispideosoma* Reinhard (1 sp., *L. flavipes* Reinhard); 105.306 *Messiomyia* Reinhard (1 sp., *M. triconis* Reinhard); 105.307 *Paralispidea* Townsend (2 spp.); 105.308 *Phantasiomyia* Townsend (2 spp.); 105.309 *Phasiostoma* Townsend (1 sp., *P. aristale* (Coquillett)); 105.311 *Siphona* Meigen (8 spp.); 105.312 *Slossonaemyia* Townsend (2 spp.)]

Subtribe Nearina

[105.313 *Acronarista* Townsend (2 spp.); 105.314 *Acronaristopsis* Townsend (1 sp., unnamed); 105.315 *Apheloglutus* Green (1 sp., *A. latifrons* (Greene); 105.316 *Dichaetoneura* Johnson (1 sp., *D. leucoptera* Johnson); 105.317 *Elfia* Robineau-Desvoidy (14 spp.); 105.318 *Euryceromyia* Townsend (1 sp., *E. robertsonii* Townsend); 105.319 *Phytomyptera* Rondani (1 sp., *P. walleyi* Brooks); 105.320 *Pseudapinops* Coquillett (2 spp.); 105.321 *Schizactia* Townsend (2 spp.); 105.322 *Schizotachina* Walker (3 spp.)]

Tribe Graphogastrini

[105.323 *Clastoneuriopsis* Reinhard (3 spp.); 105.324 *Psalidopteryx* Townsend (12 spp.)]

Tribe Admontiini

Parasites of Tipulid larvae.

[105.325 *Admontia* Brauer and Bergenstamm (10 spp.)]

Tribe Hyperecteinini

[105.326 *Cartocometes* Aldrich (1 sp., *C. io* Aldrich); 105.327 *Euthyprosopa* Townsend (1 sp., *E. petiolata* Townsend); 105.328 *Gilvella* Mesnil (2 spp.); 105.329 *Gremlinotrophus* Reinhard (1 sp., *G. derisus* Reinhard); 105.330 *Hyperecteina* Schiner (1 sp., *H. aldrichi* Mesnil [2 spp. introduced]); 105.331 *Miamimyia* Townsend (1 sp., *M. cincta* Townsend); 105.332 *Oedematocera* Townsend (1 sp., *O. flaveola* (Coquillett)); 105.333 *Oraphasmophaga* Reinhard (1 sp., *O. pictipennis* (Reinhard)); 105.334 *Phasmophaga* Townsend (2 spp.); 105.335 *Roeseliopsis* Townsend (2 spp.); 105.336 *Stenoneura* Reinhard (1. sp., *S. serotina* Reinhard)]

Tribe Erythrocerini

[105.337 *Canelomyia* Reinhard (1 sp., *C. fumator* Reinhard); 105.338 *Elodia* Robineau-Desvoidy (3 spp. [introduced]); 105.339 *Erynnia* Robineau-Desvoidy (1 sp., *E. tortricis* (Coquillett)); 105.340 *Ocytata* Gistel (1 sp., *O. pallipes* (Fallén) [introduced])]

Tribe Frontinini

[105.341 *Cloacina* Reinhard (1 sp., *C. filialis* Reinhard); 105.342 *Eleodiphaga* Walton (3 spp.); 105.343 *Hypertrophocera* Townsend (1 sp., *H. parvipes* Townsend); 105.344 *Istocheta* Rondani (1 sp., *I. claripennis* Reinhard); 105.345 *Organomyia* Townsend (1 sp., *O. frontalis* Townsend); 105.346 *Paraphasmophaga* Townsend (2 spp.)]

Tribe Goniini, *Subtribe* Goniina

[105.347 *Acroglossa* Williston (3 spp.); 105.348 *Aravaipa* Townsend (1 sp., *A. atrophopoda* Townsend); 105.349 *Chaetocrania* Townsend (1 sp., *C. antennalis* (Coquillett)); 105.350 *Distichona* Wulp (1 sp., *D. georgiae* (Brauer and Bergenstamm)); 105.351 *Eucnephalia* Townsend (1 sp., *E. gonoides* Townsend); 105.352 *Gonia* Meigen (29 spp.); 105.353 *Imaguncula* Reinhard (1 sp., *I. tabida* Reinhard); 105.354 *Olenochaeta* Townsend (1 sp., *O. kansensis* Townsend); 105.355 *Onychogonia* Brauer and Bergenstamm (5 spp.); 105.356 *Spallanzania* Robineau-Desvoidy (2 spp.); 105.357 [number not used]]

Subtribe Chaetogaediina

[105.358 *Chaetogaedia* Brauer and Bergenstamm (6 spp.); 105.359 *Chaetoglossa* Townsend (2 spp.); 105.360 *Gaediophana* Brauer and Bergenstamm (1 sp., *G. lugubris* (Wulp)); 105.361 *Gaediopsis* Brauer and Bergenstamm, with 2 subgenera: *Gaediopsis* Brauer and Bergenstamm (3 spp.) and *Eugaediopsis* Townsend (5 spp.); 105.362 *Hesperomyia* Brauer and Bergenstamm (2 spp.); 105.363 *Torosomyia* Reinhard (1 sp., *T. parallela* Reinhard)]

Tribe Belvosiini

[105.364 *Atacta* Schiner (2 spp.); 105.365 *Atactopsis* Townsend (1 sp., *A. reinhardi* Sabrosky and Arnaud); 105.366 *Belvosia* Robineau-Desvoidy (11 spp.); 105.367 *Triachora* Townsend (4 spp.)]

Tribe Harrisiini

[105.368 *Leschenaultia* Robineau-Desvoidy (8 spp.); 105.369 *Parachaeta* Coquillett (2 spp.)]

Tribe Sturmiini

[105.370 *Blepharipa* Rondani (1 sp., *B. scutellata* (Robineau-Desvoidy)); 105.371 *Bolomyia* Brauer and Bergenstamm (1 sp., *B. rufata* (Robineau-Desvoidy)); 105.372 *Drino* Robineau-Desvoidy (11 spp.); 105.373 *Gymnoerycia* Townsend (1 sp., *G. rubra* Townsend); 105.374 *Masiphyomyia* Reinhard (4 spp.); 105.375 *Microsillus* Aldrich (1 sp., *M. baccharis* (Reinhard)); 105.376 *Milonius* Reinhard (1 sp., *M. scordalus* Reinhard); 105.377 *Mimologus* Reinhard (1 sp., *M. effetus* Reinhard); 105.378 *Myothyriopsis* Townsend (1 sp., *M. picta* (Wulp)); 105.379 *Mystacella* Wulp (2 spp.); 105.380 *Pales* Robineau-Desvoidy (1 sp., *P. parvida* (Meigen) [introduced]); 105.381 *Siphosturmia* Coquillett (7 spp.); 105.382 *Sturmia* Robineau-Desvoidy (2 spp); 105.383 *Townsendiellomyia* Baranov (1 sp., *T. nidicola* (Townsend)); 105.384 *Zizyphomyia* Townsend (1 sp., *Z. limata* (Coquillett)]

Tribe Winthemiini

[105.385 *Hemisturmia* Townsend (1 sp., *H. tortricis* (Coquillett)); 105.386 *Nemorilla* Rondani (3 spp.); 105.387 *Omotoma* Lioy (1 sp., *O. fumiferanae* (Tothill)); 105.388 *Orasturmia* Reinhard (1 sp., *O. vallicola* Reinhard); 105.389 *Pseudolomyia* Reinhard (1 sp, *P. scissilis* Reinhard)]

105.390 *Winthemia* Robineau-Desvoidy

Twenty-four species, including the following:

W. quadripustilata (Fabricius) (Red-tailed Tachina). Parasite of armyworms and probably responsible for keeping them in check; reports show that at least 50 percent of the larvae of this moth are parasitized by this fly. (1) n.e. US; (2) s.e. US; (3) s.w. US; (4) Pacific n.w. (5), n. Central states.

Tribe Masiphyini

[105.391 *Ignotomyia* Reinhard (1 sp., *I. cunina* Reinhard); 105.392 *Phasiopsis* Townsend (1 sp., *P. floridana* Townsend); 105.393 *Promasiphya* Townsend (2 spp.)]

Tribe Carceliini

[105.394 *Angustiopsis* Reinhard (1 sp., *A. saginata* Reinhard); 105.395 *Carcelia* Robineau-Desvoidy (2 spp.); 105.396 *Eusisyropa* Townsend (5 spp.); 105.397 *Gymnocarcelia* Townsend (1 sp., *G. ricinorum* Townsend); 105.398 *Hubneria* Robineau-Desvoidy (1 sp., *H. estigmenensis* (Sellers)); 105.399 *Hyphantrophaga* Townsend (3 spp.); 105.400 *Sisyropa* Brauer and Bergenstamm (2 spp.)]

Tribe Eumasicerini

[105.401 *Eumasicera* Townsend (1 sp., *E. sternalis* (Coquillett)); 105.402 *Houghia* Coquillett (1 sp., *H. setipennis* Coquillett); 105.403 *Hypertrophomma* Townsend (1 sp., *H. opacum* Townsend); 105.404 *Metopiops* Townsend (1 sp., *M. pyralidis* (Coquillett)); 105.405 *Pacidianus* Reinhard (2 spp.); 105.406 *Phaenopsis* Townsend (1 sp., *P. venusta* Reinhard); 105.407 *Pseudochaeta* Coquillett (9 spp.)]

Tribe Eryciini

[105.408 *Angustia* Sellers (1 sp., *A. angustivitta* (Aldrich and Webber)); 105.409 *Aplomyia* Robineau-Desvoidy (16 spp.); 105.410 *Buquetia* Robineua-Desvoidy (1 sp., *B. obscura* (Coquillett)); 105.411 *Catagoniopsis* Townsend (3 spp.); 105.412 *Ceromasia* Rondani (3 spp.); 105.413 *Chrysoexorista* Townsend (5 spp.); 105.414 *Clemelis* Robineau-Desvoidy (1 sp., *C. unipilum* (Aldrich and Webber)); 105.415 *Cyzenis* Robineau-Desvoidy (2 spp.); 105.416 *Euceromasia* Townsend (4 spp.); 105.417 *Euexorista* Townsend (1 sp., *E. futilis* (Oosten Sacken)); 105.418 *Eufrontina* Brooks (2 spp.); 105.419 *Frontiniella* Townsend (1 sp., *F. parancilla* Townsend); 105.420 *Lespesia* Robineau-Desvoidy (20 spp.); 105.421 *Lydella* Robineau-Desvoidy (3 spp.); 105.422 *Madremyia* Townsend (1 sp., *M. saundersii* (Williston)); 105.423 *Masicera* Macquart (1 sp., *M. silvatica* (Fallén) [introduced]); 105.424 *Metagonistylum* Townsend (1 sp., *M. minense* Townsend [introduced]); 105.425 [number not used]; 105.426 *Nilea* Robineau-Desvoidy (4 spp.); 105.427 *Obolocera* Townsend (1 sp., *O. rapae* (Smith)); 105.428 *Patelloa* Townsend (8 spp.); 105.429 *Phryxe* Robineau-Desvoidy (2 spp.); 105.430 *Pilatea* Townsend (12 spp.); 105.431 *Prophryno* Townsend (2 spp.); 105.432 *Pseudoperichaeta* Brauer and Bergenstamm (2 spp.); 105.433 *Thelymyia* Brauer and Bergenstamm (4 spp.); 105.434 *Tsugaea* Hall (1 sp., *T. nox* Hall); 105.435 *Zenillia* Robineau-Desvoidy (4 spp.) [unplaced species (13 spp.)]; 105.436 Unplaced genus; 105.437 *Otomasicera* Townsend (1 sp., *O. patella* Townsend [Unplaced species (24 spp.)]

Superfamily HIPPOBOSCOIDEA

106. HIPPOBOSCIDAE (Louse Fly Family)

Length: 4–7 mm. Usually flattened; palpi slender; eyes round or oval; tarsal claws strong and often armed with a series of small teeth; wings usually present but often broken off, rarely vestigial. All species are blood suckers and ectoparasites, mostly on birds but also on mammals, usually with restricted host specificity. There are 28 species in the U.S. and Canada, many widely distributed.

Subfamily Ornithoicnae

[106.1 *Ornithoica* Rondani (2 spp.)]

Subfamily Ornithomyiinae
Tribe Ornithomyiini

[106.2 *Ornithomyia* Latreille (1 sp., *O. fringillina* Curtis); 106.3 *Myiophthiria* Rondani, subgenus *Brachypteromyia* Williston (1 sp., *M. fimbriata* (Waterhouse)); 106.4 *Ornithoctona* Speiser (2 spp.); 106.5 *Stilbometopia* Coquillett (3 spp.); 106.6 *Lynchia* Wyenbergh (7 spp.); 106.7 *Microlynchia* Lutz, Neiva, and Lima (1 sp., *pusilla* (Speiser))]

106.8 *Pseudolynichia* Bequaert

Two species, including the following:

P. canariensis (Macquart) (Pigeon Fly). Infests pigeons. (1) n.e. US; (2) s.e. US; (3) s.w. US; (5) MN.

Tribe Olfersiini
106.9 *Olfersia* Leach

Four species, including the following:

O. spinifera (Leach) (Frigate Bird Fly). Frigate Birds and other birds are infested by these flies (2) LA, FL.

O. sordida Bigot. (2) LA, FL; (3) TX; (4) OR, UT.

Subfamily Melophaginae
Tribe Lipoptenini

[106.10 *Neolipoptena* Bequaert (1 sp., *N. ferrisi* (Bequaert))]

106.11 *Lipoptena* Nitzsch

This genus is divided into two subgenera: *Lipoptena* s. str. (1 sp., *L. cervi* (Linnaeus) and *Lipoptenella* Bequaert (2 spp.). The following is a common species.

L. (*Lipoptennella*) *depressa* (Say) (Deer Keds). Found on Mule Deer and other deer throughout the year. Winged individuals may fly to barns in the fall. They sometimes bite man. (3) s.w. US; (4) Pacific n.w.; (5) n. Central States.

Tribe Melophagini
106.12 *Melophagus* Latreille

One species, as follows:

M. ovinus (Linnaeus) (Sheep Ked; Sheep Tick). L. 6–7 mm. Body brown; spines short, dense, dark brown; wingless. These ooviparous flies are ectoparasites of sheep. Their maggots attach to the wool with a sticky substance; within 12 hours they change to brown "seeds" or "eggs" which are

Fig. 29.58. (*U.S. Public Health Serv.*)

Fig. 29.59. (*From Curran, 1934*)

really pupae. The adults that emerge remain on the sheep. During their life span of about six months, the female produces about 15 young per week. Cosmopolitan. (See Fig. 29.58.)

107. NYCTERIBIIDAE (Wingless Bat Fly Family)

Length: ±3 mm. Wingless, spiderlike ectoparasites of bats. There are five species in the U.S., mostly all southwestern.

107.1 *Basilia* Ribeiro

Five species, the following of which is most widespread:

B. antrozoi (Townsend). (See Fig. 29.59.) (2) LA; (3) s.w. US; (4) OR; (5) KS.

108. STREBLIDAE (Bat Fly Family)

Length: 2–3 mm. These insects resemble spiders but are usually winged. (See Fig. 29.60.) They are obligate ectoparasitic blood suckers on bats. Adult females deposit the young, as pupae, in caves with bat roosts or on trunks of trees nearby. They are uncommon in collections. Of the five species in the U.S., most are in the Southwest.

Subfamily Trichobiinae

[108.1 *Nycterophilia* Ferris (1 sp., *N. coxata* Ferris)]

108.2 *Trichobius* Gervais

Four species, the most widespread being the following:

T. corynorhini Cockerell. (2) s.e. US; (3) s.w. US; (4) WA, OR; (5) CO, KS.

[108.3 *Paratrichobius* Lima (1 sp., *P. americanus* Peterson and Ross.]

Fig. 29.60. (*From Curran, 1934*)

Unplaced Diptera

Unplaced genus: *Scatophora* Robineau-Desvoidy. Unplaced species: 6 spp.

BIBLIOGRAPHY

[Note: See McAlpine, *et al.* (1981) and Stone *et al.* (1965) for references to family and generic revisions and monographs.]

Arnaud, Paul H. 1978. A host-parasite catalog of North American Tachinidae (Diptera), *Misc. Publ.* No. 1319, United States Dept. Agric., 860 pp.

Atchley, William R., *et al.* 1981. A bibliography and keyword index of the biting midges (Diptera: Ceratopogonidae). *Bibliography and Literature of Agriculture*, No. 13, United States Dept. of Agric., 544 pp.

Blanton, Franklin S., and Wirth, Willis W. 1979. The sand flies (*Culicoides*) of Florida (Diptera: Ceratopogonidae). *Arthropods of Florida*, vol. 10, 204 pp.

Cole, Frank R. 1960. *The flies of western North America.* Berkeley: Univ. of California Press, xi + 693 pp.

Curran, C. H. 1934. *The families and genera of North American Diptera.* 512 pp.

Hall, David G. 1947. *The blowflies of North America.* Entomological Society of America, 477 pp.

Hall, Robert D. and Townsend, Lee H., Jr., 1977. The blow flies of Virginia (Diptera: Calliphoridae). Blacksburg: *Research Div. Bull.* 123, Virginia Polytechnic Institute and State University.

Harbach, Ralph E. and Kenneth L. Knight, 1980. *Taxonomists' glossary of mosquito anatomy.* Marlton, NJ: Plexus Publishing, Inc., xi + 415 pp.

McAlpine, J. F., *et al.* 1981. *Manual of Nearctic Diptera,* vol. 1. Research Branch Agriculture Canada, Monog. 27, vi + 674 pp.

Stone, Alan, *et al.* 1965. A catalog of the Diptera of America north of Mexico. *Agriculture Handbook*, No. 276, United States Dept. of Agric., 1696 pp.

Order 30

SIPHONAPTERA (Fleas)

The exact relationship of this small, specialized order of wingless, laterally compressed insects to the other orders of winged insects is uncertain, mainly because not one of its species has wings. Fleas may or may not be specialized descendants of the Mecoptera, but they unmistakably comprise a distinct order. All are obligate ectoparasites that live on certain mammals and birds in their nests.

The Latin name for fleas comes from the Greek word *siphon*, meaning "pipe"—which refers, of course, to their sucking mouthparts—and *apteron*, meaning "wingless." The common English name, flea, is a very old word, dating back to at least the year 700. This should not be surprising because fleas have probably been man's steady companion throughout his entire existence.

Many fleas are very strong in spite of their small size. Except for a few species, they can jump distances that are hundreds of times their length. In times past, flea "circuses" were very popular in Europe. By fashioning minute pieces of gold wire around their bodies to inhibit their jumping ability, fleas in these circuses were forced to crawl. A favorite stunt was to have them pull tiny hand-curved wagons. For a few pennies, the spectator could watch their antics through a magnifying glass. Since fleas do their best to avoid light, they are easily "trained" to perform by regulating light. The author has not found any records of American flea circuses.

Diagnosis: L. 1 to 5 mm (rarely to 9 mm). All fleas are characteristically shaped, having been highly modified for an ectoparasitic life that consists of moving through a dense "forest" of hair or feathers. Body brown to black, strongly compressed laterally, with head fused to a small thorax; abdomen more or less oval and modified apically, showing small claspers and other copulatory structures. Most species are hard-bodied with numerous spines and setae that are uniformly placed (a feature they share with flies) and that are useful for the differentiation of species and higher taxa. Antennae are short and held in grooves at the side of the head; mouthparts are a modified, piercing-sucking type, usually short and stout. (See Fig. 30.1). No species shows any evidence of wings or wing pads. Legs are moderate in size, fitted with spines and setae, and with the hind femora somewhat enlarged in most spines so that they may be used for jumping.

The larvae are elongate, cylindrical, with chewing mouthparts, but without legs or ocelli.

Fleas might be confused with lice by the uninformed, but their body shape, particularly by being compressed instead of flattened, is distinctive and uniform throughout the order.

Metamorphosis: Holometabolous with egg, larval, pupal, and adult stages. The eggs vary in size, shape, and color from group to group, but in most species for which this stage is known they are white, ovoid, and nonadhesive. Frequently deposited while the adult is feeding, they soon fall into the nest or lair of

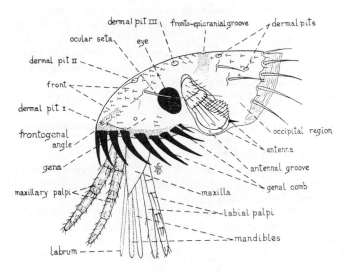

Fig. 30.1.

the host animal. Those species that deposit adhesive eggs usually attach them to the nesting material or other debris. As is true of other insects, the incubation period is temperature-dependent and may require from a few days to months.

Flea larvae are structurally rather uniform throughout the order. The three instars differ little from one another except in terms of size and are best distinguished by using the width of the head capsule. None of the body segments except the head is sclerotized, and that only lightly so; the rest are white or cream colored. Both thoracic legs and abdominal prolegs are lacking, locomotion being accomplished by reflexing the head to pull the body forward as well as by pushing movements that a pair of blunt terminal appendages called *anal struts* provide.

The larvae spin a silken cocoon that incorporates sand grains and debris; in this it assumes a V-shaped position prior to transforming into the pupal stage. This transformation usually takes place within a few days after the cocoon is completed. Most adult fleas emerge from the cocoon in response to some kind of mechanical stimulation—an increase in CO_2, an increase in temperature, or some combination of these factors. Such stimuli are usually provided by the return of the host to its nest or lair. In their absence, adult fleas may remain quiescent for extended periods, some as long as 450 days. Female fleas are usually larger than males and tend to emerge earlier.

Habits and habitats: Adult fleas feed on the blood of their hosts. Most larvae feed on debris, including the bloody feces of the adult fleas. Upon emergence from the cocoon, adults immediately seek out their host to take their first blood meal. Unlike lice, most fleas do not spend all their time on the skin of the host; rather, they usually jump off it when it leaves its nest

or lair and jump back on when it returns. Clinging to the host when it leaves, however, is their only means of dispersing the species. Flea larvae lack eyes, but they do possess dermal light receptors and are negatively phototropic. Although highly active creatures, they are seldom observed because they hide themselves in the debris of the nest or lair of their host. Near the end of the third instar, feeding ceases and the contents of the alimentary tract are voided. At the same time, there is a sharp decrease in movement, a shortening of the body, and a color change to creamy yellow in preparation for the coming pupal stage.

In contrast, the larvae of some of the vermipsyllids are essentially free-living; they frequent open pasture lands and feed on whatever organic material is available. At another extreme, a pygiopsyllid, known only from Tasmania, attaches its eggs to the fur of its marsupial host; its larvae live as dermal parasites. Eventually they leave the host to spin a cocoon and pupate on the ground. An even more extreme example of specialization is that of *Tunga monositus*. Adult females of this species are subcutaneous parasites of deer mice in Baja California. Their eggs are very large, and there are only two larval instars, neither of which feeds.

A few species of fleas may be found on a wide variety of hosts, but these are exceptional. Most species exhibit host specificity, at least on an ordinal level. Only about 6 percent of the known species parasitize birds; about 74% are associated with rodent hosts.

Individual interactions between fleas and their hosts show considerable variation. Those species that have lost the ability to jump are restricted to the nest or lair of the host animal, tend to quit the host when it becomes active, and are seldom collected except from the nesting material, where they may be quite numerous. At the other extreme are species that remain on the host at all times; these are usually good jumpers and have well developed eyes. Still others attach themselves firmly to the host with their mouthparts and spend long, sedentary periods before moving to a new feeding site.

The so-called "sand fleas" are really dog or cat fleas that become abundant in houses (a mammal nest) when the host pet is absent, having emerged after its departure. These hungry fleas, in need of a blood meal, will readily feed on the legs and bodies of any human beings available. This is a common phenomenon at the end of a vacation period. It is wise upon returning home to let the pet enter first.

Reproductive behavior: Fleas need blood meals for the formation of eggs. In some species, the reproductive hormone of the mammal host affects the reproductive cycle of the flea, so closely attuned are the two. This dependency assures that the fleas' offspring will be able to find a blood meal when they become adults because the female host must remain in her nest while both the larvae of the fleas and the young of the mammal are developing.

Collecting and preserving: Adult fleas may be collected directly from the body of the host animal or from the host's nest. Those species that are seldom found on the host when the latter is out of the nest must be searched for in the nest. Nesting material frequently continues to yield adult fleas for months if kept slightly moist and warm in the laboratory.

Fleas may be preserved indefinitely in 75 percent ethyl alcohol but must be mounted on microscope slides for accurate identification. Most faunal studies require mounted specimens for verification by specialists.

Rearing: Relatively few species of fleas have been successfully colonized in the laboratory, and most of those that have been are associated with disease transmission. Larvae may be reared on a diet of powdered whole blood and dog food or various synthetic diets. Adults, however, require fresh blood to reproduce, necessitating the presence of live host animals.

Identification: Fleas are difficult to identify except with the aid of technical literature. Since a number of monographs are available for this purpose, carefully prepared specimens may be identified with the aid of a compound microscope. Host records are important aids for identification.

Distribution: Fleas often have the same distribution as their hosts. At the end of 1979, the order Siphonaptera contained 2237 valid names and an additional 420 synonyms. By the end of 1980, an additional 22 species had been described for the world fauna. Although a few of these species are truly cosmopolitan, the distribution of most is restricted to one of the continental land masses. Fleas are known from all continents and major islands of the world, but the variety of genera and species is greatest in the temperate regions, less in the lowland tropics, and least in the Antarctic.

Economic importance: Adult fleas affect their hosts in two ways. Although their feeding activities may be a constant source of irritation, it seldom reaches debilitating proportions. Strong allergic reactions to flea bites are shown by some people, and heavy infestations may result in traumatic dermatitis, even in hosts not otherwise allergic. A more serious attribute of fleas is their ability to transmit disease. They are major vectors of endemic typhus and bubonic plague. The great "black death" (a confused complex of cholera, typhoid, and bubonic plague) is estimated to have killed 25 percent of the population of Europe during its coures in the fourteenth century. They figure in the life cycle of dog and rodent tapeworms. They are also suspected of maintaining reservoirs of a number of microorganisms capable of causing disease in man and wild animals.

Control of the few species infesting domestic animals is easily accomplished by the use of commercial preparations formulated for this purpose. Reinfestation is inevitable, however, unless the larval habitat is eliminated, and good sanitation is essential to keep the population under control.

In the United States and Canada, there are currently 325 recognized species and subspecies of fleas, representing 66 genera in seven families. Few additional species are likely to be discovered in this part of North America in the future, but placement of the species in the family Ceratophyllidae will probably change drastically with the publication of new research.

CLASSIFICATION

The higher classification of the Siphonaptera has undergone considerable modification over the past 30 years (see Lewis, 1972–1975). The key to the superfamilies and families provided by Hopkins and Rothschild (1953–1971) has been adopted for this work.

Key to the Families of Siphonaptera in the U.S. and Canada

1. Outer internal ridge of midcoxae absent; mesonotum lacking pseudosetae under the collar; metanotum and abdominal terga lacking marginal spinelets; spiracles circular; abdominal terga II–VII with at most one row of bristles; sensillium with 8 or 14 pits per side; hind tibia lacking an outer apical tooth (Pulicoidea) **1. Pulicidae**
 Outer internal ridge of midcoxae usually present; apical tooth of hind tibiae usually pointed; sensilium usually with 16 or more pits per side *2*

2(1). Mesopleural rod not bifid; anterior tentorial arm present; no genal or pronotal combs; ventral margin of pronotum never bilobed; 5th tarsomeres always with 4 pairs of plantar bristles (Malacopsylloidea) **2. Rhopalopsyllidae**
 Not with the preceding combination of characters (Ceratophylloidea) *3*

3(2). Combs, spinelets, antepygidial bristles, spiniform bristles on inner surface of hind coxae, and anal stylet of females all absent; ectoparasites of carnivores **3. Vermipsyllidae**
 Some or all of these structures present ... *4*

4(3). Metanotum lacking marginal spinelets; arch of tentorium visible in front; female sensillum usually more or less convex; anal stylet usually with a long apical bristle and 1 or 2 small to minute subapical ones; 1 or 2 spermathecae **4. Hystrichopsyllidae**
 Metanotum with marginal spinelets; tentorium variable; dorsal surface of sensilium straight; anal stylet of female with 1 or 2 long lateral bristles in addition to apical one; 1 spermatheca ... *5*

5(4). Head fracticipit, with a sulcus that extends from antennal groove to dorsum separating the two regions; genal comb of 2 broad spines, which may be pointed or obtuse, arising immediately behind oral angle; parasits of bats **5. Ischnopsyllidae**
 Not with the preceding combination of characters *6*

6(5). Genal comb absent; no arch of tentorium in front of eye; no interantennal suture; eye circular or vestigal; metanotum and some abdominal terga with spinelets
 ... **7. Ceratophyllidae**
 Genal comb present or absent; arch of tentorium present and usually clearly visible; interantennal suture variable; eye often sinuate or vestigial **6. Leptopsyllidae**

Superfamily PULICOIDEA

1. PULICIDAE (Common Flea Family)

Subfamily Tunginae

Tribe Hectopsyllini

1.1 *Hectopsylla* Frauenfeld

Nine species, all native to the Neotropical Region; most are associated with small mammal hosts. Two species are found on birds, including the following:

H. psittaci Frauenfeld. Found on zoo birds, but not indigenous. (3) s. CA.

Tribe Tungini

1.2 *Tunga* Jarocki

Nine species in South and Central America, Southeast Asia, and Africa; these parasitize small mammals, livestock, and human beings. Adult females are subcutaneous, neosomic parasites. The following species may serve as examples:

T. monositus Barnes and Radovsky. Found in Baja California; may be expected in (3) s. CA.

T. penetrans (Linnaeus) (Chigoe Flea). Introduced into Africa and (2) FL.

Subfamily Pulicinae

Tribe Archaeopsyllini

1.3 *Ctenocephalides* Stiles and Collins

Most of the thirteen species and subspecies in this group are native to Africa. The following species that occur in the

U.S. and Canada were probably transported from Africa on pets.

C. felis felis (Bouche) (Cat Flea). L. ±1 mm. Characterized by genal and pronotal combs. Cosmopolitan on cats; rarely a parasite on man. (See Fig. 30.2 and A&J 195.)

C. canis (Curtis) (Dog Flea). Similar to the preceding but distinguishable by its much shorter forehead and by spine I of its head comb being very distinctly shorter than spine II. This species is an important intermediate host of the Dog Tapeworm (*Dipylidium caninum*), a parasite common in dogs and cats and sometimes in man. In tropical regions, it transmits several additional parasites as well. This is probably the most common flea in human habitations throughout the world. (See Fig. 30.3.)

Fig. 30.2.

Fig. 30.3.

Tribe Pulicini

1.4 *Echidnophaga* Olliff

This genus contains 21 species and subspecies in Australia, Africa, Central Asia, and the Middle East, with the following species found in the U.S. and Canada:

E. gallinacea (Westwood) (Sticktight Flea; Hen Flea). Practically cosmopolitan in temperate and semitropical climates, where it may be a pest of domestic poultry. It is also frequently found on hedgehogs and larger carnivores.

1.5 *Pulex* Linnaeus

Three of the six species occur in the U.S. and Canada, as follows:

P. irritans Linnaeus (Human Flea). Although intimately associated with man, it is primarily a parasite of carnivores. Cosmopolitan.

P. porcinus Jordan and Rothschild. Parasite of peccaries. (3) s.w. US.

P. simulans Baker. Parsite of carnivores, ungulates, and large rodents. (2) s.e. US; (3) s.w. US; (4) Pacific n.w.

Tribe Spilopsyllini

[1.6 *Actenopsylla* Jordan and Rothschild (1 sp., *A. suavis* Jordan and Rothschild [on sea birds] (3) CA; (4) Pacific n.w.); 1.7 *Cediopsylla* Jordan (4 spp. [on lagomorphs] (1), (2), (3), (4), (5)); 1.8 *Euhoplopstyllus* Ewing (1 sp., *E. glacialis* (Taschenberg), with 3 supspp. [on rabbits, hares, and lynx] (1), (2), (3), (4), (5)); 1.9 *Hoplopsyllus* Baker (1 sp., *H. anomalus* (Baker) [on ground squirrels and hares] (3) s.w. US)]

Tribe Xenopsyllini

1.10 *Xenopsylla* Glinkiewicz

One species only in the U.S. and Canada, as follows:

X. cheopis (Rothschild) (Oriental Rat Flea). Distributed worldwide and established in the U.S. and Canada, where it is associated with rats. It is a prime vector of plague. (1) n.e. US, coastal; (2) s.e. US, coastal; (3) CA; (4) Pacific n.w.

Superfamily MALACOPSYLLOIDEA

2. RHOPALOPSYLLIDAE (Club Flea Family)

Subfamily Rhopalopsyllinae

2.1 *Polygenis* Jordan

Two species in the U.S., as follows:

P. floridanus Johnson and Layne. Parasite of small rodents. (2) FL.

P. gwyni (Fox). Parasite of small rodents. (2) LA, MS, AL, FL; (3) TX.

Superfamily CERATOPHYLLOIDEA

3. VERMIPSYLLIDAE (Carnivore Flea Family)

[3.1 *Chaetopsylla* Kohaut (5 spp. [on carnivores but uncommon] (1), (2), (3), (4), (5))]

4. HYSTRICHOPSYLLIDAE (Rodent Flea Family)

Subfamily Hystrichopsyllinae

Tribe Hystrichopsyllini

[4.1 *Hystrichopsylla* Taschenberg (11 spp. and subspp. [mainly on small rodents and insectivores] (3) s.w. US; (4) Pacific n.w.; (4) n. Central States); 4.2 *Atyphloceras* Jordan and Rothschild (4 spp. and subspp. [on small rodents] (1), (2), (3), (4), (5))]

Subfamily Stenoponiinae

[4.3 *Stenoponia* Jordan and Rothschild (2 spp. [on small rodents] (1), (2), (3), (5) n. Central states)]

Subfamily Neopsyllinae

Tribe Neopsyllini

[4.4 *Neopsylla* Wagner (1 sp., *N. inopina* Rothschild [on ground squirrels] (4) Pacific n.w.); 4.5 *Tamiophila* Jordan (1 sp., *T. grandis* (Rothschild) [on chipmunks] (1) n.e. NA)]

Tribe Phalacropsyllini

[4.6 *Epitedia* Jordan (7 spp. [on small rodents]); 4.7 *Catallagia* Rothschild (13 spp. [on small rodents]); 4.8 *Delotelis* Jordan (2 spp. [on voles] (4) Pacific n.w.); 4.9 *Phalacropsylla* Rothschild (3 spp. [on woodrats] (3), (4)); 4.10 *Meringis* Jordan (18 spp. [on small rodents, particularly kangaroo rats] (3) s.w. US; (4) NV, UT)]

Subfamily Anomiopsyllinae

Tribe Jordanopsyllini

[4.11 *Jordanopsylla* Traub and Tipton (1 sp., *J. allredi* Traub and Tipton [on deer mice] (4) UT)]

Tribe Anomiopsyllini

[4.12 *Stenistomera* Rothschild (3 spp. [on small rodents] (3) n.w. US; (4) Pacific n.w.); 4.13 *Callistopsyllus* Jordan and Rothschild (3 spp. [on small rodents] (3) s.w. US; (4) Pacific n.w.); 4.14 *Conorhinopsylla* Stewart (2 spp. [on flying squirrels and woodrats] (1) n.e. US; (2) s.e. US; (3) OK; (5) KS, MO); 4.15 *Megarthroglossus* Jordan and Rothschild (13 spp. and subspp. [mainly on woodrats] (3) s.w. US; (4) Pacific n.w.); 4.16 *Anomiopsyllus* Baker (9 spp. [mostly on woodrats])]

Subfamily Radinopsyllinae

Tribe Corypsyllini

[4.17 *Corypsylla* Fox (3 spp. [on insectivores] (3) n. CA; (4) s. BC, WA, OR); 4.18 *Nearctopsylla* Rothschild (11 spp. [on insectivores])]

Tribe Rhadinopsyllini

4.19 *Paratyphloceras* Ewing

One species, as follows:

P. oregonensis Ewing. Specific parasite of the Mountain Beaver, an archaic rodent occurring only in (4) Pacific n.w.

[4.20 *Trichopsylloides* Ewing (1 sp., *T. oregonsis* Ewing [on Mountain Beavers] (4) Pacific n.w.); 4.21 *Rhadinopsylla* Jordan and Rothschild (10 spp. [on small rodents])]

4.22 *Doratopsylla* Jordan and Rothschild

Nine species, the following of which is common:

D. blarinae Fox. Parasite of the short-tailed shrew.

Subfamily Doratopsyllinae

Tribe Doratopsyllini

4.23 *Corrodopsylla* Wagner

Two species, as follows:

C. hamiltoni (Traub). Parasite of shrews (5) n. Central States.

C. curvata curvata (Rothschild). Parasite of shrews. (1), (2), (3), (4), (5).

Subfamily Ctenophthalminae

Tribe Carterettini

[4.24 *Carteretta* Fox (2 spp. [on small rodents] (3) s.w. US; (4) WA, OR, ID, NV, UT; (5) n. Central States)]

Tribe Ctenophthalmini

[4.25 *Ctenophthalmus* Kolenati (1 sp., *C. pseudagyrtes* Baker [on many small mammals] (5) Rocky Mts., with subspecies *C.p. micropus* Traub, (2) GA)]

5. ISCHNOPSYLLIDAE (Bat Flea Family)

Subfamily Ischnopsyllinae

[5.1 *Nycteridopsylla* Oudemans (3 spp. [on vespertilionid bats] (1), (2), (3), (4), (5)); 5.2 *Myodopsylla* Jordan and Rothschild (6 spp. [on bats]); 5.3 *Sternopsylla* Jordan and Rothschild (1 sp., *S. distincta texana* (Fox) [on molossid bats] (3) TX)]

6. LEPTOPSYLLIDAE (Scaled Flea Family)

Subfamily Leptopsyllinae

Tribe Leptopsyllini

[6.1 *Peromyscopsylla* Fox (12 spp. [on small rodents])]

6.2 *Leptopsylla* Jordan and Rothschild

One species, as follows:

L. segnis (Schoenherr) (European Mouse Flea). Transported throughout the world by the House Mouse. Cosmopolitan.

Subfamily Amphipsyllinae

Tribe Dolichopsyllini

[6.3 *Dolichopsyllus* Baker (1 sp., *D. stylosus* (Baker) [on Mountain Beavers] (4) Pacific n.w.)]

Tribe Ornithophagini

[6.4 *Ornithophaga* Mikulin (1 sp., *O. anomala* Mikulin [on woodpeckers] (4) UT)]

Tribe Amphipsyllini

[6.5 *Odontopsyllus* Baker (2 spp. [on rabbits and hares]); 6.6 *Ctenophyllus* Wagner (1 sp., *C. armattus* (Wagner) [on pikas] (3), (4), (5)); 6.7 *Guesibia* Jordan (1 sp., *G. ashcrafti* Augustuson [on pikas] (3) CA)); 6.8 *Amphipsylla* Wagner (2 spp.) [on small rodents] (1) LA, (4) AK, WA; (5) YK, AB)]

Fig. 30.4.

7. CERATOPHYLLIDAE (Bird and Rodent Flea Family)

Subfamily Ceraotphyllinae

[7.1 *Amphalius* Jordan (1 sp., *A. runnatus necopinus* (Jordan) [on pikas] (3), (4), (5))]

7.2 *Ceratophyllus* Curtis

Eighteen species found on various birds, including the following:

C. gallinae (Schrank) (European Chicken Flea).

C. niger Fox (Western Chicken Flea). Sometimes a pest of domestic poultry.

[7.3 *Dasypsyllus* Baker (2 spp. [on birds] (3), (4), (5)); 7.4 *Diamanus* Jordan (1 sp., *D. montanus* (Jordan and Rothschild) [on ground squirrels] (3), (4), (5)); 7.5 *Jellisonia* Traub (2 spp. [on small rodents] (3) TX); 7.6 *Malaraeus* Jordan (8 spp. [on small rodents] (3), (4), (5)); 7.7 *Megabothris* Jordan (11 sp. [on microtine rodents] (1), (2), (3), (4), (5)); 7.8 *Mioctenopsylla* Rothschild (2 spp. [on sea birds] (4) AK); 7.9 *Monopsyllus* Kolenati (13 spp. [on small rodents, including squirrels, pikas, and small carnivores])]

7.10 *Nosopsyllus* Jordan

Two species associated with small rodents, including the following:

N. fasciatus (Bosc) (Northern Rat Flea). Imported through marine commerce. (See Fig. 30.4) (1), (2), (3), (4).

[7.11 *Opisocrostis* Jordan (7 spp. [on ground squirrels] (1) IL; (4) Pacific n.w.; (5) n. Central states); 7.12 *Opisodasys* Jordan (6 spp. [on deer mice, squirrels, and flying squirrels]); 7.13 *Orchopeas* Jordan (18 spp. [on squirels and other small rodents]); 7.14 *Oropsylla* Wagner and Ioff (5 spp. [on woodchucks]); 7.15 *Pleochaetis* Jordan (2 spp. [on small rodents]); 7.16 *Tarsopsylla* Wagner (1 sp., *T. octodecimdentata coloradensis* (Baker) [on tree squirrels and flying squirrels] (5) CO); 7.17 *Thrassis* Jordan (29 spp. [on woodchucks and ground squirrels])]

Subfamily Dactylopsyllinae

[7.18 *Dactylopsylla* Jordan (18 spp. [on pocket gophers] (3), (4), (5)); 7.19 *Foxella* Wagner (1 sp., *F. ignota* (Baker) [on pocket gophers] (3) s.w. US; (4) WA, OR; (5) n. Central States)]

BIBLIOGRAPHY

Benton, Allen H. 1980. *An atlas of the fleas of the Eastern United States*. Fredonia, NY: Marginal Media, xv+177 pp.

Ewing, H. E., and Fox, I. 1943. The fleas of North America. *Misc. Publ.* No. 500, U.S. Dept. of Agric., 128 pp.

Fox, I. 1940. *Fleas of Eastern United States.* Ames: Iowa State College Press, vii+191 pp.

Holland, G. P. 1949. The Siphonaptera of Canada. *Tech. Bull.* No. 70, Canada Dept. of Agric., 306 pp.

Hopkins, G. H. E., and Rothschild, M. 1953–1971. *An illustrated catalogue of the Rothschild collection of fleas (Siphonaptera) in the British Museum* (Natural History). 1953. vol. 1, Tungidae and Pulicidae, xv+361 pp.; 1956, vol. 2, Vermipsyllidae to Xyphiopsyllidae, xi+445 pp.; 1961. vol. 3, Hystrichopsyllidae (in part), viii+560 pp.; 1966. vol. 4, Hystrichopsyllidae (in part), viii+549 pp.; 1971. vol. 5, Leptopsyllidae and Ancistropsyllidae, viii+530 pp. London: British Museum.

Hubbard, C. A. 1947. *Fleas of Western North America.* Ames: Iowa State College Press, vii+533 pp.

Jellison, W. L., and Good, N. E. 1942. Index to the literature of Siphonaptera of North America. *Nat. Inst. Health Bull.* No. 187, U.S. Public Health Service, 193 pp.

Jellison, W. L.; Locher, B.; and Bacon, R. F. 1953. *Ibid.* Supplement I. Hamilton, Montana: Rocky Mountain Lab., 246 pp.

Jellison, W. L., and Glesne, L. 1967. *Ibid.* Supplement 2. Hamilton, Montana: Rocky Mountain Lab., 406 pp.

Lewis, Robert E. 1972–1975. Notes on the geographical distribution and host preferences in the order Siphonaptera. Pts. 1–6, *Journ. Med. Ent.*, 9:511–520; 10:255–260; 11:147–167; 11:403–413; 11:525–540; 11:658–676.

Marshall, A. G. 1981. *The Ecology of ectoparasitic insects.* New York: Academic Press, xvi+459 pp.

Petrischeva, P. A., ed. 1965. *Vectors of diseases of natural foci.* Jerusalem: Israel Program for Scientific Translations.

Glossary

Aberration an individual with some abnormal difference, particularly a color difference; aberrations named as such are no longer recognized by the International Rules of Zoological Nomenclature.

Abdomen the hindmost body region of the three tagmata of the insect body (see Fig. 5 in Chap. 2 and Figs. 16 and 20 in Chap. 3.)

Acropod a small terminal segment on the distal end of the last tarsomere of the tarsus, usually bearing a pair of claws (*see also* Pretarsus and Fig. 29.7).

Adectuous pupa a pupa with appendages glued to the body wall, that is, not free.

Adult the sexually mature stage of Hexapoda; except for certain primitive species, this stage does not molt; usually the winged stage in Insecta.

Alitrunk the fused mesothorax, metathorax, and first abdominal segment of Hymenoptera.

Alula a broad basal wing lobe in some Diptera; also termed the *axillary lobe*.

Ametabolous a type of metamorphosis characterized by no or very little external change except in size; characteristic of primitive Hexapoda.

Ampulla a blisterlike enlargement or bulbous swelling near base of wing in certain Diptera; the greater ampulla

Anal (A) posterior wing veins (Fig. 29.6).

Anal loop in some Odonata, the area between the branches of the cubitus and anal veins that includes a few or many cells (see Fig. 7.4).

Anal ring in scale insects, an elevated ringlike structure surrounding the anus. (see Fig. 21.5).

Anal stylet in Siphonaptera, a long bristle (sometimes with additional short ones) located on the last tergum.

Androconia special scent scales located on the wings of some male butterflies.

Anepimeron the upper division of the mesopleuron (*see* Diptera) when it is divided into two parts by a suture.

Anepisternum the upper portion of the episternum (*see* Diptera) when it is divided into two parts by a suture (see Fig. 29.5).

Antecoxal piece a small inner sclerite between the trochantin and the episternum.

Antenna a sensory organ on the head of almost all Hexapoda always paired and consisting of one or more segments, each with sensory setae or spines.

Antennamere a division of the flagellum of the antenna; not a true segment.

Antenodal cross vein a vein or veins located basally from the node between the costal and subcostal veins.

Antepygidial bristle a long bristle or septa located on the seventh tergum (anterior to the pygidium) of Siphonoptera.

Apical pertaining to the apex or outer end of a structure.

Apodeme a rigid process projecting inward from the body wall of an insect.

Appendiculate with appendages.

Apterous without wings.

Arcuate arched or curved, bowlike.

Arculus a small cross vein near the base between the radius and cubitus in Odonata (see Fig. 7.1).

Areola postica a cell in the front wing of certain Psocoptera located between Cu_{1a} and M_2.

Arista a bristle on the flagellum of the antennae of certain Diptera. (*see* Fig. 9.4).

Aristomeres the divisions of an arista.

Arolium more or less membranous, saclike structure at the end of the acropod of some Diptera.

Asuleae spinules between scales on wings of Lepidoptera.

Auditory organ a special chamber covered with a stretched membrane on the anterior tibia of certain Orthoptera, or the abdomen of other insects that functions as an ear.

Auricle one of a pair of lateral appendages on the second abdominal segment of certain male dragonflies.

Auxillary cord the produced posterior angles of the notum that form the posterior margins of the basal membranes of the wings.

Axillary sclerites part of the wing-flexing sclerites of the basal portion of the wings of some insects.

Banksian line a prominent longitudinal line in the wings of some Neuroptera that is formed by the bending of the branches of vein MP_2.

Beak *see* Snout.

Bifid in two branches.

Bilocular pore in scale insects, a pore with two openings (see Fig 21.5).

Biome a major ecological division of a continent characterized by certain dominant plants.

Biparental having a male and a female parent, as opposed to hermaphroditic or parthenogenetic reproduction.

Brachypterous with short wings or elytra.

Calcar a posterodorsal bristle located on the hind tibia at, or apically away from, the middle (*see* Diptera.)

Calypter a basal lobe or lobes (pl. calypteres) on the posterobasal portion of the axillary membrane of the wings of some Diptera.

Capitate a type of antenna with the terminal segments enlarged to form a spherical mass.

Carnivorous feeding upon animals.

Category a class group or hierarchy to which a taxon belongs; for example, Noctuidae constitute a taxon in the hierarchy of families of Lepidoptera.

Caudal pertaining to the tail, or posterior portion, of an organism.

Caudal filament a thin, usually segmented, median posterior abdominal process.

Cell an area of the wing of insects enclosed by veins.

Cenchrus a membranous lobe on each side of the mesonotum that is present in some Hymenoptera.

Cercus (pl. cerci) a lateral posterior abdominal process, usually slender and sometimes filamentous and segmented.

Cervix a sclerite imbedded in the membrane that connects the head to the thorax.

Chaetosema (pl., chaetosemata) a patch or pair of patches on the head, usually setiferous, that appear to take the place of ocelli and are sensory.

Character a feature, usually a structure that is characteristic of a group.

Chelicera (pl, chelicerae) the pincerlike first pair of appendages of certain Arthropoda.

Chitin a complex nitrogenous carbohydrate forming the main skeletal substance of the arthropods.

Chloride epithelia ovoid area of modified cuticle bordered by a thin sclerotized line on the abdomen of Trichoptera larvae.

Circulius (pl., circuli) in scale insects, a glandular structure, the contents of which are discharged internally (see Fig. 21.5).

Cladistics another term for phylogenetic systematics.

Clasper in Neuroptera, a clasping organ at the apex of the male abdomen.

Class a division of a phylum; a category in the classification hierachy.

Classification the arrangement of species in a hierarchial system of categories and taxa.

Clavate gradually thickened toward the apex; clubbed.

Clavus the club of an antenna.

Claw a hollow, sharp organ, usually paired, at the end of the acropod.

Cline a gradual series of morphological or physiological differences exhibited by a group of species, usually geographically related.

Clubbed (or **club-shaped**) shaped like a club, with the apex or distal portion enlarged (*see also* Capitate).

Cluster pore plate in scale insects, a group of pores located on the surface of the body on a plate near the posterior spiracle.

Clypeus that part of the insect head below the front to which the labrum is attached.

Cocoon a pupal covering composed, in part or entirely, of silk spun by a larvae.

Compound eye an aggregation of separate ommatidia, or visual elements, usually paired, on the head of most adult insects.

Compressed flattened from side to side.

Condyle a process that articulates the base of the mandible to the head capsule of an insect.

Connate with segments or sclerites that are fused and incapable of moving.

Contiguous touching or close together.

Cordate heart-shaped.

Corium the elongate basal section of the front wing of most Hemiptera; the thickened basal portion, or the hemelytra, of Hemiptera.

Cornicle one of a pair of short, tubelike structures on the fifth or sixth abdominal segment of many aphids (Homoptera).

Costa (C) the thickened anterior vein of the insect wing; in the genitalia of male Lepidoptera, the dorsal part of the clasper.

Coxa (pl., coxae) the basal segment of the leg, articulating to the body.

Coxal cavity the cavity or socket into which the coxa articulates.

Coxopleural streak a suture between the meron and katepimeron of the metathorax of some Diptera (some Calliphoridae).

Cross vein a usually short vein between two main veins of the wings of insects.

Cryptic coloration color patterns of insects and other animals that resemble those of part of the habitat and hence tend to "hide" the animal by making it difficult to see when it is not moving; that is, camouflage.

Ctenidal bristles stiff setae arranged in a comblike row on the front femora (*see* Diptera).

Ctenidial spine a prominent, single spine in place of the ctenial bristles on the femora (*see* Diptera).

CuA cubito-anal vein of the wing of an insect.

Cubitus (Cu) a major wing vein that follows the median vein (see Fig. 29.6).

Cultriform shaped like a pruning knife; curved.

Cuneus the small triangular area at the end of the embolium of the hemelytra of the wing of certain Hemiptera (see Fig. 20.1).

CuP cubitus posterior; posterior branch of the cubital vein in the insect wing (see Fig. 29.6).

Cup posterior cubital cross vein in the insect wing (see Fig. 29.6).

Cupule a narrowed sixth segment of the antenna of certain Coleoptera (see Fig. 24.9).

Decticuous pupa pupae with free appendages, that is, appendages not glued to the body wall.

Depressed flattened dorso-ventrally.

Determination the identification of a specimen.

Detritus cycle the part of the ecological cycle that involves the feeding upon, and hence processing of, dead plant and animal material.

Dichotomous divided into two parts.

Discal cell in Lepidoptera, a wing cell in the center of the wing formed by the base of branches of the radial, medial, and cubital veins (see Fig. 27.3).

Distal away from the base or point of attachment.

Diversity different body types and systems present in a taxon.

Dorsal seam a groove on the dorsal surface of the pedicel of the antenna of certain Diptera.

Ducts in scale insects, tubes with slender inner filaments scattered randomly over the dorsum.

Ductus ejaculatorius a duct or tube through which seminal fluid is discharged by the male.

Ectoparasite an insect parasite that feeds on the surface of the body and is usually blood sucking.

Egg the first free-living stage of the life cycle of most insects, usually within a flexible shell.

"8"-shaped pores in scale insects, pores with eight loculars, or openings around the center.

Elytron a modified, thickened, and hardened front wing of an insect, particularly of the Coleoptera.

Emarginate notched, with an obtuse, rounded, or quadrate section cut from the margin.

Empodium (pl. empodia) a median process arising from the ventral region of the arolium of the tarsus.

Endoparasite an internal parasite.

Epicranial suture a suture on the head of an insect separating the vertex and the front.

Epimeron the posterior division of the thoracic pleuron (see Fig. 24.1b).

Epiphysis an antenna cleaner on the front tibia of certain insects; a notch through which the antennae may be drawn.

Epipleural fold the raised lower edge of the deflexed or inflexed portion of the elytra or pronotum (see Fig. 24.14).

Episternum the anterior portion of the pleuron (see Fig. 24.14).

Epistoma the lower face of the head between the mouth and the eyes, immediately behind or above the labium.

Exoskeleton the chitinous, sclerotized covering of the insect body.

Exertible vesicles membranous internal sacs, containing fluids, that may be turned inside out and protruded from the body.

Exuvium (pl. exuvia) the cast skin of larvae or nymphs at molting.

Eye bridge a narrow dorsal connection, across the top of the head, of facets of the compound eyes of certain Diptera.

Eye cap a fringe of setae covering part of the eyes of certain Lepidoptera.

Face in Diptera, the front portion of the head between the antennae and above the clypeus

Falcate sickle-shaped, convexly curved; said of a wing that is deeply excavated below the apex, leaving the apex acute and somewhat curved.

Family a category in the hierarchy of classification; a division of an order.

Felt lines short, recumbent, hairlike setae arranged in a streak in some Hymenoptera.

Femur (pl. femora) the segment of the leg of an insect beyond the trochanter and before the tibia.

Fibula in some Lepidoptera, a small lobe at the base of the front wing that rests on the top of the hind wing and presses against small costal spines.

Filament a long, slender, threadlike, usually segmented process.

File stationary part of the sound-producing surface of a stridulating insect.

Filiform threadlike, slender, and of nearly equal diameter throughout.

Flabellate fan-shaped.

Flagellum the third and succeeding segments of most antennae.

Flagellomere a division of the flagellum of the antenna.

Frontanelle a small, frontal pore on the head of some termites.

Forceps hood or pincerlike processes at the apex of the abdomen in most Dermaptera.

Form sometimes used as a subdivision of a species, but not as a recognized taxon; also refers to a species or a group of species as a general term.

Fossorial fitted for digging.

Fracticipit a type of flea head separated into two regions by a sulcus extending from the antennal groves to the dorsum (see Fig. 30.1).

Frenulum in certain Lepidoptera, the spine, simple in males, compound in females, arising from the base of the hind wings and projecting under the front wing; used to unite the wings in flight.

Frons another term for front (q.v.).

Front the unpaired sclerite of the head between the arms of the epicranial suture; the front, upper part of the head beyond the insertion of the antennae.

Frontal bristles in certain Diptera, bristles situated along the edge of the front near the antennae (see Fig. 29.1).

Fronto-orbital bristles in certain Diptera, setae on the fronto-orbital plate exterior to the frontal bristles.

Furca a fork; in the genitalia of male Lepidoptera, a structure, often consisting of paired harpes, which arises as an elaborate ventral part of the juxta (Fig. 27.11).

Furcula a forked process in the Collembola; the spring or jumping apparatus on the fourth abdominal segment (see Fig. 1.1).

Fuscus brownish grey, dusky.

Galea the outer lobe of the maxilla (see Fig. 27.10).

Gaster abdomen of Hymenoptera beyond first or second segment, that is, beyond the petiole.

Gena (pl. genae) the cheek; the part of the head on each side below the eyes.

Genal comb a row of heavy spines on the latero-ventral border of the head of Siphonaptera (see Ctenidium).

Geniculate elbowed.

Genitalia the modified apical abdominal segments used in copulation.

Genus the category in the classification hierarchy to which species are assigned.

Gill a thin-walled structure with trachae, used for the absorption of oxygen in aquatic insects.

Gill remnant in the adults of Plecoptera, the remains of a gill of the naiad.

Gill tuft a type of gill consisting of tufts of filamentous gills.

Globose spherical; almost perfectly rounded in all directions.

Glossa (pl. glossae) the paired inner lobes of the labium, particularly the coiled sucking tube of many Lepidoptera.

Gonopore the opening of the genital tube of insects.

Graduate series of cross veins a series of cross veins in steps across the posterior portion of the wings of certain Neuroptera (see Fig. 23.12).

Gradual metamorphosis (see Paurometabolous metamorphosis) a metamorphosis usually consisting of egg, nymph, and adult stages.

Greater ampulla see Ampulla.

Group used to refer to a taxon without specifying the Latin name (for example, "This group [referring to a preceding taxon] is large and widely distributed.").

Gula the throat sclerite that forms the central part of the head ventrally and extends from the submentum to the posterior margin.

Gular sutures the sutures bordering the gula.

Haemocoel the major body cavity of insects containing the blood.

Hairlike seta a fine seta, often refered to as a "hair," on the surface of the insect body; a term used in insect anatomy in place of "hair," the latter being a structure characteristic of mammals.

Hair pencil on abdomen of Neuroptera, a patch of long, hairlike setae.

Halter (pl. halteres) the modified, vestigial hind wings of Diptera that functions as sensory, balancing organs.

Harpes the claspers in the male genitalia of Lepidoptera (see Fig. 27.12).

Haustellate having mouthparts adapted for sucking.

Head the foremost body region of insects (see Fig. 5 in Chap. 2).

Hemelytron the basal thickened portion of the wing, typical of Hemiptera.

Hemimetabolous metamorphosis incomplete metamorphosis, with egg, aquatic nymph (termed naiad), and adult stages.

Herbivorous feeding on plants.

Hibernation a period of lethargy or suspension of most bodily activities with a greatly reduced respiration rate, occuring particularly during periods of low temperature.

Holometabolous with complete metamorphosis, including egg, larval, pupal, and adult stages.

Holoptic in Diptera, having the two compound eyes contiguous, so that the front is divided into upper and lower parts.

Holotype the single specimen upon which the description of a species is based and so designated at the time of description; also known as the *type specimen*.

Homothermic having the property of warm-blooded animals, as opposed to *poikilothermic*, or cold-blooded, animals such as insects.

Hooklet a small, hooklike structure.

Humeral break a notched costal vein of the wing at the humeral cross vein.

Humeral cross vein the cross vein near the base of the wing that connects the costal and subcostal veins.

Hyaline transparent or nearly so; glassy.

Hydrofuge pile very fine, closely placed, hairlike setae that cover the surface of some aquatic insects; this pile traps any air carried beneath the water surface.

Hypermetamorphosis a metamorphosis in which an insect passes through more than the normal number of stages, particularly a stage other than the pupal that follows the full grown larval stage.

Hypognathous having the head vertical and the mouth directed ventrad.

Hypopharynx a sensory structure on the inner surface of the labium; a tongue.

Identification the process of finding the correct name of an organism.

Imago the adult stage.

Incisor the cutting surface of a mandible.

Infraorder a division of an order; a category sometimes used between suborder and family (same as *series*)

Instar the stage between molts of the nymph or larva; also called *statium*.

Intercalary sector in Odonota, that sector formed by veins inserted between the principle veins and meeting them at an angle.

Intercalary veins veins inserted between the principle veins.

Interfrontal bristles in Diptera, those bristles on the frontal vitta of the head between the frontal bristles (see Fig. 29.1).

Internal sac an eversible, membranous, apical portion of the aedeagus in Lepidoptera and other insects, usually with small spines or spicules imbedded in the membrane.

Joint an articulation; the area of flexion between sections of an appendage.

Jugal lobe the backwardly projecting area of contact of an insect's front wing with its hind wing (*see* Jugum).

Jugum an enlarged fibula that overlaps the spineless hind wing in certain primitive Lepidoptera (see Fig. 27.2).

Juxta a sclerotization of the inner wall of the phallotheca, often forming a ring or tube about the base of the aedeagus in male Lepidoptera (see Fig. 27.11).

Katepisternal bristle a bristle on the katepisternum (see Fig. 29.5).

Katepisternum the lower part of the episternum (see Fig. 29.5).

Labellum (pl. labella) the sensitive tip of the mouth structures of certain Diptera (see Fig. 29.2).

Labial mask a large ventral structure on the head of naiads of certain Odonata; a modified labium that is capable of shooting outward in front of the head to capture prey.

Labial palpus a segmented sensory appendage of the labium of insects (see Fig. 27.9).

Labium the lower lip of the mouthparts of insects (see Fig. 24.3).

Labrum the upper lip or flap of the mouthparts of insects (see Fig. 24.8).

Law of priority a rule of zoological nomenclature (as prescribed by the International Rules of Zoological Nomenclature) which states that the oldest validly proposed scientific name of an animal must be used and that later names proposed for the same animal must be treated as junior synonyms.

Lamellate formed of thin, overlapping plates.

Laminate formed of thin, flat layers or leaves.

Lanceolate spear-shaped.

Larva the growing stage of the life cycle of holometabolous insects, which feeds after it is hatched from the egg and eventually changes into a pupal stage.

Larviform an adult resembling a larva but sexually mature.

Lash in certain Lepidoptera, a border of setae or bristles over the eyes that arises from behind or below the antennae.

Laterad toward the side.

Lateral at the side.

Lingula a more or less slender tongue or strap-shaped organ at the vasiform orifice of the anal apparatus of the homopteran superfamily Aleyrodoidea.

Lobate with lobes; divided by a deep incision.

Locular pore in scale insects, a pore with two or several openings through the pore plate.

Lunule a small, lunate mark or crescent above the base of the antennae of certain Diptera (see Fig. 29.1).

Luteous yellowish with greenish tinge.

MA the anterior medial vein of the wings of Ephemeroptera (see Fig. 6.5).

Macrotrichia the larger microscopic hairlike setae on the surface of the wings of Diptera and Lepidoptera.

Malphigian tubes long and slender blind tubes in the haemocoel that open into the beginning of the hind intestine of insects; used for excretory functions.

Mandible one of the pair of jaws in insects, stout and toothlike.

Mandibular tusk a projection on the mandibles of naiads of certain Ephemeroptera.

Mandibulate having biting jaws or mandibles.

Manubrium the large, median base of the furcula in certain Collembola (see Fig. 1.1).

Maxilla the second pair of jaws of a mandibulate insect (see Fig. 24.3).

Maxillary palpus a segmented sensory structure located on the maxilla.

Median in, at, or pertaining to the middle.

Median (M) a major wing vein following the radius (see Fig. 18 in Chap. 3).

Median cross vein (m) a cross vein on the wings of most insects that connects the branches of the median vein (see Fig. 29.6).

Mediocubital cross-vein (m-cu) the cross vein connecting a branch of the median vein with a branch of the cubitus vein.

Melanin an organic pigment in the cuticle of insects that produces amber, brown, or black coloration.

Mentum the distal sclerite of the insect labrum.

Meron the lateral, postarticular area of the base of the coxa and the lower region of the epimeron (see Fig. 25.5).

Mesal; mesad pertaining to or directed toward the median plane of the body.

Mesipimeron the sclerite between the humeral and first lateral suture in Odonata; the epimeron of the mesothorax (see Fig. 24.16).

Mesonotal collar the anterior margin of the mesonotum in certain fleas.

Mesonotum the dorsal surface of the mesothorax.

Mesopleural rod an inner chitinous ridge on the mesopleuron in Siphanoptera.

Mesopleuron (pl., mesopleura) the lateral surface of the mesothorax.

Mesoscutum in Hymenoptera and Diptera, the scutum of the mesothorax.

Mesothorax the second, or middle, thoracic segment, which bears the middle pair of legs and, in winged insects, the anterior pair of wings.

Metamorphosis the series of changes through which an insect passes in developing from egg to adult.

Metanotum the upper surface of the metathorax.

Metathorax the third, or last, thoracic segment, which bears the third pair of legs and, in winged insects, the second pair of wings or, in Diptera, the halteres.

Metepimeron in Odonata, the part of the epimeron behind the second lateral suture.

Microseta the component of very fine pile or bloom of microscopic setae.

Microtubular duct in scale insects, a duct with very slender inner filaments.

Mid-coxal prong in certain Diptera, a process extending from the mesocoxa.

Migration a mass movement, usually seasonal, of many individual insects away from or toward their breeding area; in the case of most insects, these movements are random and thus function as a means of species dispersal; in some, they take place in one direction only.

Molar area the roughened or ridged grinding surface of a mandible.

Molt to cast off or shed the outer covering of the integument periodically during growth.

Moniliform beadlike.

MP posterior medial vein of the wing.

Multilocular pore in scale insects, a pore with many openings through the pore plate.

Musciform resembling a fly.
Mystax a cluster or row of long hairlike setae or bristles on the face of some Diptera.

Naiad the nymph of aquatic hemimetabolous insects.
Nasute a soldier cast of termites with a snout on the head through which an irritating defensive substance is extruded.
Nearctic one of the zoogeographical regions of the earth that includes Canada, Alaska, Greenland, the United States, and the temperate northern part of Mexico.
Notopleural sutures in Coleoptera, the suture that separates the protergal region from the pleural region of the prothorax.
Notopleuron in higher Diptera, a clearly delimited, sunken area between the postpronotal lobe and the wing base.
Node; nodus a thickened, dark area of the wing located between the costa and subcosta.
Nomenclature the scientific names of animals and plants and the application of these names.
Numerical taxonomy *see* Phenetics.
Nymph the immature stage of insects with gradual (paurometabolous) metamorphosis.

Obtectus pupa a pupa with appendages glued to the body wall, that is, not free [another term for adectuous pupa (q.v.)].
Occiput the posterior portion of the head of insects between the top of the head at the location of the ocelli.
Ocellar bristle a bristle inserted just behind the median ocellus in certain Diptera.
Ocellus a simple eye in some adult insects that consists of a single, beadlike lens.
Ochre pale yellow to orange-red.
Ommatidium (pl., ommatidia) a facet of the compound eye.
Onychium (pl., onychia) a small process between the tarsal claws of Diptera, or a long, hairy pad between the claws of certain Coleoptera.
Oothecae an egg packet; eggs covered with a hardened case.
Operculum the lidlike structure covering the vasiform orifice of the Homoptera superfamily Aleurodoidea.
Opisthognathous with the head deflexed so that the mouthparts are in a posterior ventral position.
Orbital bristle a usually proclinate or divergent bristle situated on the parafrontals between the frontals and orbits on the head of certain Diptera (see Fig. 29.1).
Order a division of a class in the hierarchy of categories.
Osmeterium V-shaped scent organs behind the head in the larvae of Papilionidae (Lepidoptera).
Ostiole in scale insects, one of the lateral metasternal external openings.
Ovipositor the tubular or valved structure by means of which eggs are deposited.

P *see* Plical vein.
Papilla a minute, soft projection.
Parafacial in Diptera, pertaining to the part of the face between the facial ridges and the eyes (see Fig. 29.1).
Paraglossa one of a pair of structures lying at each side of the ligula of the labium.
Paranotal lobe lobe at the dorsal lateral margin of the pronotum.
Parasite any animal or plant that lives in or on and at the expense of another animal or plant.
Paratergal plates plates along the lateral margin of certain lice.
Paratergite the narrow lateral sclerite beneath the prescutum and scutum on the thorax of Diptera (see Fig. 29.5).
Parthenogenesis reproduction from unfertilized eggs.
Patagia sclerotized flaps projecting backward from the pronotum on each side of the median line and lying on each side of the mesonotum.
Paurometabolous having a metamorphosis in which the change from the immature stage (nymph) to the adult is more or less gradual; that is, the nymph resembles the adult but lacks functional wings and is sexually immature.
Pectinate comblike.
Pedicel second segment of most antennae.
Penes open, slitlike structures from the seminal vesicles to the outer surface.
Penultimate next to the last.
Petiole the narrowed portion of the abdomen of certain Hymenoptera.
Phenetics techniques, expecially the use of mathematical algorithms, that group individual specimens into taxa based on the degree of similarity and differences of their characteristics, usstually without weighting the latter.
Phosphorescent organ a light-producing structure found on the adults or larvae of certain insects, particularly beetles.
Phylogenetic systematics a system of classification that attempts to produce classifications that reflect the evolution of plants and animals.
Phylogeny the arrangement of organisms to show their evolutionary relationships.
Phylum a major division of the animal kingdom; a category.
Phytophagous feeding on plants.
Pile a covering of microsetae or hairlike setae.
Pilula axillaris a small structure at the hind margin of the hind wing of the male of certain Neuroptera, usually consisting of a basal pedicel and a distal knob that bears setae on its dorsal surface.
Plantar bristles bristles on the ventral surface of the tarsi of certain Siphanoptera.
Plantula a flaplike structure at the base of the first tarsomere.
Pleuron The lateral sclera of the thorax.
Pleurosternal suture the suture that separates the pleural region from the sternum in Coleoptera (see Fig. 24.6).
Plical vein (P) a single wing vein or series of veins located between the cubital and the anal veins and associated with the anal furrow (see Fig. 18 in Chap. 3).
Plumose featherlike.
Poikilothermic cold-blooded, or having a body temperature at, or close to, that of the ambient.
Population a group of individuals of a single species living in a particular region and capable of reproducing.
Porrect extending forward horizontally.
Postantennal organ a sensory structure located on the head of some Collembola between the eye and antenna.
Postnotum an intersegmental plate on the dorsum of the thorax that is associated with the tergum of the preceding segment; that is, the pronotum, mesonotum, or metanotum.
Postocellar bristles in Diptera, a pair or more of bristles arising just below the vertex on the occiput and behind the ocellar tubercle (see Fig. 29.1).
Praecincotorium in certain Lepidoptera, a median, longitudinal, chitinous flap extending into the cavity between the thorax and abdomen.
Precosta (PC) a short basal vein of the wing of certain (fossil) primitive insects that joins the costa vein at its base.
Precoxal bridge a sclerotized connection in certain Diptera between the prosternum and proepisternum.
Prehalter in Diptera, a membranous scale in front of the halter.
Prementum distal portion of the Labium to which the labella is attached.
Prepectus an anterior marginal sclerite of the sternopleural areas of a segment; in Hymenoptera, an area along the anterior margin of the episternum of the mesothorax.
Prepupa an active but nonfeeding stage of the nymphs of Thysanoptera and some Homoptera.
Prescutum the anterior area of the mesonotum or metanotum between the antecostal suture and the prescutal suture when the later is present.

Pretarsus in Thysanoptera, the terminal part of the tarsus, usually with claws; *see* Acropod.

Proboscis the elongated mouthparts of many insects.

Process projection.

Prognathous with the head horizontal and the jaws directed forward.

Proleg on unsegmented appendage on the abdomen of many larvae used for walking.

Pronotal comb in Siphonaptera, a row of stout spines on the hind margin of the pronotum.

Pronotum the upper or dorsal surface of the prothorax.

Propleuron (pl., propleura) one of the lateral sclerites of the prothorax.

Propygidium the tergum anterior to the pygidium in Coleoptera.

Protergal pertaining to the first tergum.

Prothorax pertaining to the first thoracic segment.

Proximal pertaining to the part of an appendage nearest the body.

Pruinose covered with fine dust, as if frosted.

Pseudocellus smooth, thin area of cuticle usually outlined by a rim of granules on the head and body of some Collembola.

Pterostigma a thickened, opaque spot on the costal margin of a wing either near its middle or distally from the middle.

Pterothorax the meso- and metathorax, bearing the wings.

Ptilinal fissure the crescentic groove that cuts across the front above the antennal bases (*see* Ptilinum).

Ptilinum an inflatable organ on the head of certain Diptera that is capable of being thrust out through the frontal suture or fissure (*see* Lunule) just above the bases of the antennae.

Pubescence a covering of setae.

Pubescent covered with hairlike setae.

Pulvillus (pl., pulvilli) soft, padlike structures between the tarsal claws.

Punctate set with impressed punctures, or small impressions, pits, or deep depressions.

Pupa the transformational stage between larva and adult in homotabolous insects.

Puparium (pl., puparia) in certain Diptera, the thickened, hardened, larval skin within which the pupa is formed.

Pygidium (pl., pygidia) the tergum of the last abdominal segment.

Quadrangle cell a wing cell in the wing of damselflies bounded by M_4, Cu, the arculus, and a cross vein between M_4 and Cu; similar to the triangle in the wings of dragonflies.

Quadrifid four-branched.

Race a term usually applied to populations to reflect geographical differences; under the International Rules of Zoological Nomenclature, races are no longer given Latin names and have no validity as named taxa.

Radial cross vein (r) a cross vein that connects the branches of the radial vein.

Radial-median cross vein (r-m) a cross vein between the radius and the median (Fig. 29.6).

Radial sector the base of the radius after R_1 has branched off.

Radius (R) the third wing vein (see Fig. 18 in Chap. 3).

Raptorial adapted for seizing prey.

Reclinate; reflexed directed backward.

Recurrent vein a vein at the base of the wing between the costa and the subcosta, extending obliquely from the latter to the former.

Reticulate netlike.

Retractile capable of being drawn back (or extended).

Retinaculum in Lepidoptera, the loop into which the frenulum of the male is fitted

Rhegma in Neuroptera, a small area in the front wing where small branches of Rs, MA, MP, and CuA curve together.

Sacculus in the male genitalia of Lepidoptera, the ventral part of the harpes (see Fig. 27.11).

Saccus in Lepidoptera, a median sclerotized pocket in the female genitalia that is formed by the invaginated sternal region of the ninth abdominal segment; in the male genitalia, a midventral cephalad projection of the ninth abdominal sternum.

Saltatorial capable of jumping.

Saprophagous feeding on dead or decaying animal or vegetable tissue.

Scale a modified, broad, flattened seta.

Scalelike resembling a scale.

Scape basal segment of most antennae.

Scaphium in male Lepidoptera, a ventral process of the tenth abdominal segment that is located below the uncus (see Fig. 27.11).

Scent scales tufts of scales on the middle and hind tibiae of males of certain Lepidoptera, or in some Lepidoptera, on the wings or abdomen.

Scientific name the Latin or Latinized name given to an organism, as opposed to its common or vernacular name.

Scerite a thickened portion of the insect body that is bounded by a suture.

Sclerotin the substance forming the hard parts of the insect skeleton.

Sclerotized having a body wall hardened by sclerotin.

Scraper moving part of the sound-producing surface of the insect body.

Scutellar setae in Diptera, setae along the posterior margin of the scutellum.

Scutellum the posterior division of the notum; in Coleoptera, the triangular piece between the elytra.

Scutum (pl., scuti) the major part of the notum of the meso- and metathorax.

Segment a ring or subdivision of the body or of an appendage between areas of flexibility, with muscles attached for movement (see Fig. 16).

Sensillum a plate or pair of plates (pl., sensillia) on the last abdominal tergum in some Siphonaptera.

Sensorium (pl., sensoria) a sense setae or sense cone on the antennae of thrips in particular and other insects in general.

Series a major group of superfamilies within an order (see Coleoptera); same as *infraorder*.

Serrate sawlike.

Seta (pl., setae) a hollow outgrowth developed as an extension of the epidermal layer of the body wall.

Setiferous tubercles a raised structure bearing a seta or setae.

Setiform bristle- or seta-shaped.

Setula (pl., setulae) a small stiff bristle or seta.

Sexual dimorphosis morphological differences between males and females of a species, for example, size difference, presence of horns on the male, their absence in the female, color pattern differences, etc.

Sinuous undulating; curved in and out.

Snout the prolongation of the head, at the end of which the mouthparts are situated.

Spatulate sword-shaped or spoon-shaped.

Species (pl., species) a group of individuals or populations that are similar in structure and physiology to one another, differ from other such groups, and are capable of interbreeding and producing fertile offspring. [Abbreviated as sp. (singular) or spp. (plural).]

Specific name the two-part name (generic and trivial) either in Latin or a Latinized form that is used to refer to a species.

Spermatheca the sac or reservoir in the female that receives the sperm during coition.

Spermatophore a packet of sperm.

Spiculose with a minute spine or process.

Spiracles external openings of the trachea, usually with valves capable of opening and closing.

Spina (pl. spinae) the unpaired, median apodemal process of a spinasternum; the median apodeme of the posternellum.

Spinasternum one of the spina-bearing, intersegmental sclerites of the thoracic sternum; also called the *intercoxal piece*, especially in Coleoptera.

Spine a more or less thornlike process or outgrowth of the body wall not separated from it by a joint; a large seta.

Spiniform bristles bristles that are spinelike.

Spinneret the larval apparatus by means of which silk is spun.

Spinose covered with spines.

Spurious vein a false, veinlike thickening on the wings of certain Diptera that has no connection at the wing base and ends before the wing margin.

Stage; stadium (pl., stadia) any definite period between molts of developing insects.

Stemmata (sing., stemma) larval ocelli.

Sternum the ventral plate of a body segment.

Stigma scent scales located in a fold near the costal margin of the front wing or near the discal cell of skippers (Lepidoptera).

Stria (pl., striae) a groove or depressed line, usually on the elytra.

Striate with striae.

Stridulation production of sound by rubbing one part of the insect body against another, usually as a file and scraper.

Stylet a needlelike structure, especially the elongated portions . of the piercing-sucking type of insect mouthparts.

Stylus (pl., styli) a short, slender process, which in aphids may be a tubular appendage located at the end of the abdomen; in scale insects, a long spinelike appendage at the end of the abdomen of the male (the genital spike); in Diptera, the ovipositor or a thickened, segmented arista at or near the tip of the third antennamere (flagellum); or, finally, any group of small, usually pointed, exarticulate appendages that are most frequently found on the terminal segments of the abdomen (in this sense, the term equals *cerci*).

Subclass a subdivision of the class category in the classification heirarchy.

Subcosta (Sc) the second major wing vein (Fig. 29.6).

Subcostal break a break in the subcostal vein near the base, usually at the point of the humeral cross vein junction.

Subcranial cavity [= *oral cavity*] the depression on the ventral side of the head from which the mouthparts extend.

Subfamily a division of the family category in the classification hierarchy.

Subgenus (pl., subgenera) a subdivision of the genus category in the classification heirarchy.

Submentum the basal part of the labium.

Subscutellum a bulge behind the scutellum of the metathorax of Diptera [= *postscutellum*].

Subspecies a subdivision of the species category in the classification hierarchy; the only division of a species that may be validly given a Latin or Latinized name.

Subvibrissal bristles setae along the anteroventral margin of the gena of the head of Diptera.

Sulcus a furrow or groove.

Superclass a division of a phylum above the category of class in the classification hierarchy.

Superfamily a division of an order above the category of family in the classification hierarchy.

Suture a seam or impressed line between sclerites of the body wall; also in Coleoptera, the line of juncture of the closed elytra.

Synonym another name used for a species, or other taxon, invalid because it is either of a more recent date or invalidly proposed.

Systematics the science of the taxonomy and evolution of species of plants and animals.

Tagma (pl., tagmata) a major body region, for example, the head.

Tarsomeres the parts of the tarsi of insects.

Tarsus (pl., tarsi) the portion of the leg of insects distal to the tibia.

Taxon a named group of organisms arranged in any one category in the classification hierarchy.

Taxonomy the naming and arranging of species and groups into a system of classification.

Tegula a small scale between the pronotum and the base of the front wing of Fulgoroidea (Homoptera) and of some Hymenoptera.

Tegmen (pl., tegmina) the thickened front wings of Orthoptera and related insects, or the basal thickened portion of the front wings of Hemiptera.

Telson the primitive terminal body segment of Arthropoda; in insects, the terminal region of the abdomen.

Tenaculum the clasp or catch in Collembola spring apparatus (see Fig. 1.1).

Teneral the condition of the newly emerged adult before it is hardened and fully pigmented.

Tentorial arm part of the internal skeleton of the head.

Tergum the dorsal sclera of the body segments.

Thorax the middle body region of the three tagmata of the insect body (see Fig. 5 in Chap. 2).

Thysanuriform resembling or shaped like a silverfish.

Tibia the section of the insect leg between the femur and the tarsus.

Tibial spur a spur or heavy spine at the apex or distal end of the tibia.

Tomentose covered with matted, woolly, hairlike setae.

Trachea an internal respiratory tube.

Tracheal gill the flattened or hairlike process in aquatic larvae through which oxygen is absorbed from the water.

Triangle a portion of the wing veins in dragonflies.

Tribe a division of the subfamily; a category in the classification hierarchy.

Trichosors on the wings of some Neuroptera, small enlargements or expensions of the costa between veinlets present between the termination of veins.

Trifid three-branched.

Trilocular pore in scale insects, a pore with three openings.

Trochanter the portion of the leg between the coxa and the femur.

Trochantin the basal part of the trochanter when it is two-segmented; in Coleoptera, a sclerite often present on the outer side of, and sometimes moveable on, the coxa.

Truncate cut off squarely.

Tympanal organ the ear or auditory organ of an insect.

Tympanic bullae a bulbous or blisterlike tympanic structure.

Tympanic hood in Lepidoptera, one of a pair of tubercles or rounded prominences on the dorsal surface of the first abdominal segment.

Tympanic membrane the membrane stretched across the surface of the tympanic cavity as a part of the tympanum.

Tympanum a cavity (the ear) on the metathorax of certain moths, or on the abdomen or legs of other insects.

Type specimen usually the holotype; if some other specimen designed to replace a lost holotype, it is termed the *neotype* or *lectotype*.

Umber dark reddish brown.

Uncus the curved hook directed downward from a triangular basal plate in the male genitalia of Lepidoptera (Fig. 27.11).

Valve a lid or cover for an aperture or opening in the male genitalia, or harpes, of Lepidoptera.

Valvula the central part of the harpe in the male genitalia of Lepidoptera.

Vannal area the area of hind wing that folds fanlike in certain insects.

Variation individual differences found in populations and species.

Variety a term applied to a specimen showing some variation from the majority of the members of its species; a named variety is no longer valid in zoological nomenclature.

Vasiform vase-shaped; having the form of a hollow tube.

Vein a tube running through the membrane of the wings of insects.

Veinlet a small vein in the wing of an insect.

Ventral tubular duct see Ducts.

Verrica (pl., verrucae) a wart or wartlike prominence of the insect body wall.

Vertex the top of the head.

Vibrissa a heavy, elongate, curved spine on the head of Diptera (see Fig. 29.1).

Vitta a stripe or stripes on the body; *vittae*, striped.

Vouchered specimen a specimen whose identification is verified by comparison with the type specimens, or specimens previously compared with the type, and found to belong to that species.

Wart a spongy excrescence, more or less cylindric, on the body of an insect; in Trichoptera, a pitted elevation.

Wing the paired membranous flight organ, or modifications of same, located on the mesothorax and the metathorax of most insects.

Wing pad the encased, underdeveloped wings of the nymphs of insects.

Wing scales the stumps of the wings of winged termites after the wings have been shed.

INDEX

Both Latin and English (common) names of insects and terms are included in the following index. Terms defined in the glossary are not separately indexed, but their first use in the text of Part I, is indicated by *page* number. When only a single number appears after an index entry, it always refers to a *page number* in the first six chapters that comprise the Introduction (Part I). All indexed names in Part II carry a compound number composed of three parts (for example, 25.17.26). The first set of digits refers to the order number in Part II. This same number appears on the running heads of each left-hand page as an aid in finding the correct section. The second set of digits refers to the number of the family within the order (found on the right-hand running head), and the third set, to the number of the genus within the family (see also page 9 of Chapter 1 for a full explanation of this system). Thus, each order, family, and genus has a distinct number, making it easy to find the desired name on those pages with many numbers. When the word "supra" appears in an entry, the user should look ahead of the genus to find the taxon on the page. In the few cases that the word "infra" appears, the user should look *after* the generic name on the page. Since species are not individually numbered, they are indexed by using the number of the genus to which they belong. Therefore, any species in the index will carry the same number as its genus, the generic name always appearing after the specific name. Illustrations are numbered consecutively within each order. Hence, each figure number starts with the number of the particular order, followed by the specific number of the figure (for example, Fig. 25.67).

A

aaroni, Neoneura 7.10.1
Aaroniella 17.21.1
Ababa 24.67.3
Abablemma 27.75.35
Abachrysa 23.9.10
Abacidus 24.4.86
Abaeis 27.42.19
Abagrotis 27.75.587
Abaristophora 29.46.9
Abax 24.4.87
Abbott's Sphinx 27.70.33
abbotii, Oiketecus 27..11.11
abbottii, Sphecodina 27.70.33 (Fig. 27.256)
abbreviata, Diaprepes 24.113.108
abbreviata, Pristiphora 25.7.30
Abbreviated Wireworm 24.48.65
abbreviations 8(Table 1.1)
abbreviatus, Hypnoidus 24.48.65
abbreviatus, Janus 25.12.3
abbreviatus, Scapteriscus 11.11.3
Abdera 24.98.28
Abdiunguis 24.25.8
abdomen 20
abdominalis, Belotus 24.56.4
abdominalis, Boreades 24.70.2
abdominalis, Brachydella 21.14.175
abdominalis, Camponotus 25.58.66
abdominalis floridanus, Camponotus 25.58.66
abdominalis, Graptocorixa 20.35.5 (Fig. 20.65)
abdominalis, Microcephalothrips 22.4.44
abdominalis, Monostegia 25.7.81

abdominalis, Tipula 29.2.9
abducens, Hormops 24.113.141
Abedus 20.37.2
Abraeus 24.26.1
Abraxini, supra 27.61.6
abreas, Euselasia 27.44.1
Abrenthia 27.28.1
Abrocomophagidae 18.8.1
Abrostola 27.75.149
Abrostolini, supra 27.75.149
abrupta, Bombyliopsis 29.105.83
abrupta, Empoasca 21.14.77
abseuzalis, Motya 27.75.176
Abstrulia 24.98.2
absumens, Metallata 27.75.84
Absyrtus 25.16.340
abutilonea, Trialeurodes 21.18.17
Abutiloneus 24.108.14
Acacia Psyllid 21.17.27
Acadia 29.9.76
acadica, Satyrium 27.43.16
acadica, Vespula 25.59.27
acadiensis, Cryplocala 27.75.586
Acaenacis 25.19.76
Acaenitinae, supra 25.16.189
Acaenitini, supra 25.16.191
Acalles 24.113.255
Acalligrapha 24.107.62
Acallis 27.55.241
Acallodes 24.113.290
Acalophaena 24.24.48
Acalymma 24.107.93
Acalypta 20.14.1
Acalyptratae, supra 29.49.1
Acalyptus 24.113.192
acalyptus, Matsucoccus 21.23.2

Acamptini, supra 29.113.371
Acamptus 24.113.371
Acanalonia 21.7.1
Acanaloniid Planthopper Family, supra 21.7.1
Acanaloniidae, supra 21.7.1
Acanosema 25.42.14
Acanthaclisinae, supra 23.14.11
Acanthametropodinae, supra 6.1.6
Acanthametropus 6.1.6
Acantherus 11.5.29
Acanthetropis 25.53.11
Acanthinus 24.102.14
Acanthocaudus 25.15.16
Acanthocephala 20.4.2
Acanthocephalini, supra 20.4.2
Acanthocerus 24.30.56
Acanthochalcis 25.21.9
Acanthocheila 20.14.2
Acanthocini, supra 24.106.268
Acanthocnema 29.98.16
Acanthocnemes 27.13.6
Acanthoderini, supra 24.106.265
Acanthodotheca 29.103.24
Acantholeria 29.84.17
Acantholoma 20.3.5
Acantholomidea 20.3.5
Acantholyda 25.2.2
Acanthomyops 25.58.68
Acanthophotopsis 25.55.9
Acanthophysa 20.12.5
Acanthopria 25.42.30
Acanthopteroctetid Moth Family, supra 27.3.1
Acanthopteroctetidae, supra 27.3.1
Acanthopteroctetes 27.3.1

Acanthoscelides 24.108.10
Acanthoscelidius 24.113.285
Acanthosmioides 25.68.21
Acanthosomatidae 20.3.1
Acanthosomatinae, supra 20.3.62
Acanthostichini, supra 25.58.5
Acanthotoca 27.61.137
Acanthothrips 22.5.25
Acaricoris 20.13.4
acarnea, Trichosilia 27.75.541
Acaromimus 24.109.3
Acartophthalmid Fly Family, supra 29.66.1
Acartophtalmidae, supra 29.66.1
Acartophthalmus 29.66.1
Acasis 27.61.249
acastus, Charidryas 27.46.15
Acaudus 21.19.28
accerra, Thyanta 20.3.45
accius, Lerema 27.40.51
Acemya 29.105.226
Acemyini, supra 29.105.226
Acentria 27.55.191
Acentrinops 24.113.333
Acentron 25.68.22
Acerastes 25.16.181
Aceratagallia 21.14.15
Acerbia 27.73.48
Acercaria, supra 17.1.1
Acerella 2.3.3
Acerentomidae, supra 2.3.1
Acerentomoidea, supra 2.2.1
Acerentulus 2.3.1
acericaulis, Caulocampus 25.7.19
acericola, Pulvinaria 21.26.19
aceriella, Epinotia 27.38.41
acerifoliae, Drepanaphis 21.19.64
acerifoliella, Paraclemensia 27.8.3 (Fig. 27.21)
aceris, Neoprociphilus 21.19.149
aceris, Phenacoccus 21.25.32
aceris, Xylotrechus 24.106.123
acerni, Synanthedon 27.35.12
Acerocephala 25.19.26
Acerophagus 25.25.49
Acerntella 25.44.5
Acerra 27.75.502
acertella, Antequera 27.21.1
aceto-orcein stain 45
Actropis 20.23.138
Acheatella 29.98.2
achaeus, Psilonotus 25.19.96
Achalarus 27.40.15
Achalcus 29.43.47
Achatia 27.75.508
achatina, Clastoptera 21.12.7
Achatodes 27.75.281
achemon, Eumorpha 27.70.31 (Fig. 27.254)
Achemon Sphinx 27.70.31
achemonalis, Mojavia 27.55.49
Achenomorphus 24.24.49
Acherdoa 27.75.315
Acherontiella 1.2.9
Acheta 11.10.6
Achilid Planthopper Family, supra 2.4.1
Achilidae, supra 21.4.1
Achilinae, supra 21.4.1
Achlyodes 27.40.31
Acholerops 24.20.19
Acholla 20.17.11
Achorotile 21.2.7
Achradocera 29.43.42
Achrastenus 24.113.99
Achroia 27.55.271
achromata, Micrisotoma 1.4.17

Achrysocharella 25.26.74
Achrysocharis 25.26.73
Achrysocharoides 25.26.66
Achryson 24.106.35
Achrysonini, supra 24.106.35
Achurum 11.5.25
Achyra 27.55.93
Achytonix 27.75.407
Acicephala 29.98.2
Acicnemidinae, supra 24.113.167
acidaliata, Loxofidonia 27.61.228
Acidogona 29.61.13
Acidoproctus 18.1.1
Acidota 24.24.102
Acigona 27.55.227
Acilius 24.7.37
Acinaca 21.11.11
Acinia 29.61.17
Acinocoris 20.9.3
Acinopterini, supra 21.14.93
Acinopterus 21.14.93
acis, Strymon 27.43.34
Aciurina 29.61.34
Aclastus 25.16.99
Aclerda 21.27.1
Acleridae, supra 21.27.1
Acleris 27.38.61
aclerivorus, Habronyx 25.16.375
acletus, Scapteriscus 11.11.3
Aclista 25.42.7
Acmaegenius 24.113.122
Acmaeodera 24.46.27
acmaeodera, Kiefferiella 25.30.2
Acmaeoderinae, supra 24.46.25
Acmaeoderini, supra 24.46.26
Acmaeoderoides 24.46.28
Acmaeops 24.106.187
Acmaeopsoides 24.106.224
Acmon Blue 27.43.50
acmon, Icaricia 27.43.50 (Fig. 27.115)
Acmopolynema 25.27.18
Acnemia 29.9.56
Acneus 24.34.13
Acolobius 24.93.8
Acoloithus 27.50.3
Acolonia 24.25.25
Acoma 24.30.40
Acomoptera 29.9.49
Acompocoris 20.21.7
Aconobius 24.87.151
Acontia 27.75.220
Acontiinae, supra 27.75.180
Acontiini, supra 27.75.213
Acontistoptera 29.46.33
Acopa 37.75.369
Acoptus 24.113.279
Acordulecera 25.3.1
Acordulecerinae, supra 25.3.1
acornis, Actenodes 24.46.24 (Fig. 24.88)
Acossus 27.37.5
Acothyreus 25.31.6
Acraspis 25.34.23
Acratodes 27.61.186
Acratrichis 24.15.18
Acratrichini, supra 24.15.14
acrea, Estigmene 27.73.36 (Fig. 27.285)
Acrepyris 25.48.1
Acrias 25.26.33
Acricotopus 29.24.93
Acrididae, Supra 11.5.1 (Fig. 11.10)
Acridinae, supra 11.5.33
Acridiophaga 29.103.24
Acridomyia 29.100.62
Acrimea 24.24.193
acrirostris, Ginglymia 29.105.297

Acrisis 25.13.36
Acritini, supra 24.26.3
Acritocentris 25.69.42
Acritochaeta 29.100.4A
Acritus 24.26.3
Acrobasis 27.55.282
Acrocera 29.38.7
Acrocercops 27.14.12
Acroceridae, supra 29.38.1
Acrocerinae, supra 29.38.5
Acrodactyla 25.16.19
Acrodectes 11.7.25
Acroglossa 29.105.347
Acrolepiid Moth Family, supra 27.33.1
Acrolepiidae, supra 27.33.1
Acrolepiopsis 27.33.1
Acrolophitus 11.5.30
Acrolophus 27.10.33
Acrolyta 25.16.89
Acrolytina, supra 25.16.85
Acromctopia 29.83.3
Acromyrmex 25.58.54
Acronarista 29.105.313
Acronaristopsis 29.105.314
Acroncosa 27.55.347
Acronesia 29.101.13
Acroneuria 8.9.1
Acroneuriinae, supra 8.9.1
Acroneuriini, supra 8.9.1
Acronicta 27.75.231
Acronictinae, supra 27.75.231
Acronictini, supra 27.75.231
Acrophaea 21.8.3
Acrophasmus 25.13.1
Acrophga 25.58.63
Acrophotopsis 25.55.7
Acropiesta 25.42.10
Acropimpla 25.16.9
Acroplectis 27.38.69
Acropteroxys 24.75.7
Acroricnus 25.16.185
Acrosathe 29.32.13
Acrosomia 25.68.17
Acrosothrips 22.5.26
Acrosternum 20.3.52
Acrosticta 29.58.25
Acrostilicus 24.24.50
Acrostilpna 29.99.8
Acrotaenia 29.61.19
Acrotaphus 25.16.25
Acrotelsa 5.3.1
Acrotomus 25.16.72
Acrulia 24.24.103
Acrythosiphon 21.19.2
Acsala 27.73.26
Acsalini, supra 27.73.26
Actebia 27.75.558
Actenodes 24.46.24
Actenobius 24.63.13
Actenopsylla 31.1.6
Actenoptera 29.64.2
Actia 29.105.300
Actias 27.69.13
Actiastes 24.25.34
actica, Tenuirostra 29.105.111
Actidium 24.15.7
Actina 29.31.3
Actinopteryx 24.15.22
Actitocoris 20.23.193
Actium 24.25.33
Actornithophilus 18.6.1
Actrix 27.55.334.
acuductus, Agabetes 24.7.27
acuipunctatus, Scyphophorus 24.113.370
Aculeata, infra 25.48.1

aculeatum, Doru 13.5.1 (Figs. 13.8, 13.9)
acuminata, Kilifia 21.26.8
acuminata, Strangalia 24.106.197 (Fig. 24.204)
Acuminate Scale 21.26.8
acuminatus, Neoclytus 24.106.124
Acunomia 25.66.81
Acupalpus 24.4.118
Acusana 21.14.24
acuta, Brachycistina 25.53.12
acuta, Oracella 21.25.27
Acutalini, supra 21.15.20
Acutalis 21.15.20
acutangulus, Cryptophagus 24.74.6 (Fig. 24.140)
acutangulus, Thasus 20.4.8 (Fig. 20.22)
Acutaspis 21.38.2
Acute-angled Fungus Beetle 24.74.6
acutella, Nascia 27.55.78
Acuticauda 21.19.1
acuticephala, Penehuleria 21.14.89
Acutifrons 18.1.2
acutissimus, Podisus 20.3.74 (Fig. 20.17)
acutus, Aradus 20.13.1
acutus, Brachystylus 24.113.98
acutus, Meromacrus 29.47.64
Acylomus 24.77.7
Acylophorus 24.24.20
ada, Viehoperla 8.6.6
Adaina 27.58.18
Adaleres 24.113.124
Adalia 24.80.38
Adamontia 29.105.325
Adanarsa 27.55.289
Adanthidium 25.68.5
Adasytes 24.68.45
addendus, Mesonoterus 24.8.5
Adejeania 29.105.90
Adela 27.8.16
adela, Xestia 27.75.566 (Fig. 27.397)
Adelencyrtus 25.25.90
Adelesta 25.7.10
Adelestini, supra 25.7.10
Adelges 21.10.1
Adelgidae, supra 21.20.1
Adeliinae, supra 25.13.115
Adelina 24.87.118
Adelinae, supra 27.8.14
Adelius 25.13.115
Adelocerini, supra 24.48.1
Adelognathinae, supra 25.16.79
Adelognathus 25.16.79
Adelomos 25.7.24
Adelonia 24.87.39
Adelopsis 24.22.6
Adelothrips 22.5.61
Adelothyreus 24.52.14
Adelpha 27.46.34
Adelphagrotis 27.75.573
Adelphe 25.50.4
Adelphia 27.55.344
Adelphocoris 20.23.139
Ademon 25.13.82
Ademonini, supra 25.13.82
Adephaga, supra 24.2.1
Aderaeon 25.16.60
Aderina, supra 24.104.8
Aderini, supra 24.104.6
Adesmiini, supra 24.87.29
Adetini, supra 24.106.241
Adetus 24.106.241
adfinis, Trimerinoides 29.93.29
Adialytus 25.14.4
Adiastola 25.16.115
Adicroneura 29.9.61

Adicrophleps 26.9.1
Adidocidia 29.9.2
Adiplosis 29.11.122
Adistemia 24.82.7
Adita 27.75.449
adjecta, Buprestis 24.46.15
adjuncta, Melanchra 27.75.481 (Fig. 27.378)
adjunctus, Dendroctonus 24.112.11
adjutrix, Athyrma 27.75.91
adjutrix, Chlosyne 27.46.14
adjuvans, Aspidaphis 21.19.19
Adleria 25.34.27
Admetovis 27.75.478
Admirals 27.46.33
admixta, Quasisalebria 27.55.325
Admontiini, supra 29.105.325
adnixa, Raphidia 23.3.1 (Fig. 23.8)
Adoceta 24.57.5
Adoneta 27.52.17
adonis, Astrophanes 29.40.46
Adopaeoides 27.40.59
adoptiva, Paraleptophlebia 6.7.6
Adoryphorophaga 29.105.230
Adoxiini, supra 24.107.51
Adoxomyia 29.31.15
Adoxophyes 27.38.82
Adraneothrips 22.5.27
Adranes 24.25.85
Adraniini, supra 24.25.85
Adrastinae, supra 24.48.66
adspersa, Leptovectura 24.68.25
adspersus, Neoptochus 24.113.70
adult stage 15
adusta, Americina 29.98.28
aechmeae, Gymnaspis 21.38.37
Aechmeta 25.16.337
Aecothea 29.84.9
Aedeas 29.20.9
Aedimorphus 29.20.9
Aegeriidae, supra 27.35.1
Aegialia 24.30.14
Aegialiini, supra 24.30.14
Aegialini, supra 27.40.87
Aegialites 24.90.1
Aegialites 24.90.1
Aegialitinae, supra 24.90.1
Aegilips 25.31.9
Aegomorphus 24.106.265
aegrotata, Sabulodes 27.61.154
aegualis, Sphenophorus 24.113.366
aegypti, Aedes 29.20.9 (Fig. 29.24)
Aeletes 24.26.4
Aelia 20.3.39
Aellopos 27.70.28
aelops, Beskia 29.105.20
Aelothripinae, supra 22.1.4
Aemilia 27.73.58
Aenasioidea 25.25.50
Aenasius 25.25.38
aenea, Arthomacra 24.89.2 (Fig. 24.157)
aeneipennis, Trophimus 24.68.2
aeneipes, Decachaetophora 29.81.1
aeneolum, Scaphidema 24.87.99
aenescens, Magdalis 24.113.197
aenescens, Micratopus 24.4.59
aeneus, Acanthocerus 24.30.56
aeneus, Chalcodermus 24.113.241 (Fig. 24.291)
aeneus, Eristalinus 29.47.66
aeneus, Malachius, 24.68.7 (Fig. 24.133)
aeneus, Stenotrachelus 24.86.2
Aenigimaticum 24.79.11
Aenigmatias 29.46.14
Aenigmaticinae, supra 24.79.11

Aenigmatiinae, supra 29.46.14
Aenigmostomus 25.13.74
aeolia, Bendisodes 27.75.115
Aeolophides 11.5.89
Aeolothripidae, supra 22.1.1
Aeolothripini, supra 22.1.8
Aeolothripoidea, supra 22.1.1
Aeolothrips 22.1.8
Aeolus 24.48.16
aequabile, Calopteryx 7.8.1 (Fig. 7.19)
aequale, Camptozygum 20.23.145
aequale, Trogoxylon 24.65.3
aequalis, Doros 29.47.22
aequalis, Hololepta 24.26.45
aequalis, Platylomalus 24.26.27
aequepulvella, Sceptea 27.17.8
aequifrons, Lispoides 29.100.12
aequipunctatus, Lispinus 24.24.93
aerarium, Chlorion 25.62.4
aerata, Coptodera 24.4.146
aerata, Synchlora 27.61.162
aerea, Allagrapha 27.75.158
Aerial Yellowjacket 25.59.27
aeripennis, Ctenicera 24.48.37
Aerochoreutes 11.5.66
aerodromia, Siphlonisca 6.1.4
Aeropedellus 11.5.5
Aesalinae, supra 24.28.7
Aeshna 7.4.1
Aeshnidae, supra 7.4.1
aestivaria, Hemithea 27.61.169
aestuans, Efferia 29.37.65
Aetalion 21.16.1
Aetalionid Treehopper Family, supra 21.16.1
Aetalionidae, supra 21.16.1
Aethaloida 27.61.91
Aethalura 27.61.38
Aethecerinus 24.106.154
Aethecerus 25.16.205
aetherias, Orinympha 27.30.5
Aethes 27.39.1
Aethiophysa 27.55.62
aethiops, Endelomyia 25.7.42
aethiops, Milichia 29.74.11
aethiops, Periope 25.16.290
Aetia 27.20.3
Afeda 27.21.22
affiguratus, Hoplomachus 20.23.45
affinis affinis, Leucospis 25.22.1
affinis, Callophrys 27.43.24
affinis, Chaetoclusia 29.65.1
affinis, Empyreuma 27.73.79
affinis, Halidamia 25.7.74
affinis, Potosia 24.30.135
affinis, Thecabius 21.19.208
affinis, Trichiotinus 24.30.117
affinitella, Barberia 27.55.410
afflictana, Syndemis 27.37.76
Afilia 27.71.22
Aflexia 21.14.194
Afotella 27.75.379
African Dung Beetle 24.30.12
African Migratory Locust 11.5.94
Afrida 27.73.24
Afridini, supra 27.73.24
Afrolimnophila 29.2.34
Agabetes 24.7.27
Agabetini, supra 24.7.27
Agabini, supra 24.7.24
Agabinus 24.7.23
Agabus 24.7.24
Agaeocera 24.46.6
Agallaria 21.14.12
Agallia 21.14.13
Agalliinae, supra 21.14.12

Agalliini, supra 21.14.12
Agalliopsis 21.14.12
Agallissini, supra 24.106.136
Agallissus 24.106.136
Agaoninae, supra 25.18.1
Agapema 27.69.11
Agapetinae, supra 26.6.3
Agapetus 26.6.3
Agapostemon 25.66.14
Agaristidae, supra 27.75.238
Agaristinae, supra 27.75.238
agarithe, Phoebis 27.42.14
Agarodes 26.13.1
Agasicles 24.107.122
Agasphaerops 24.113.101
Agasthenes 25.16.105
Agasthodes 27.55.164
Agathidiinae, supra 24.19.9
Agathidinae, supra 25.13.74
Agathidium 24.19.10
Agathilla 25.16.318
Agathirsia 25.13.75
Agathis 25.13.76
Agathomyia 29.45.4
Agathon 29.3.1
Agathymus 27.40.87
Agave Weevil 24.113.370
Agavenema 27.8.13
agavensis, Anthonaeus 24.70.6
Agdistinae, supra 27.58.1
Agdistis 27.58.1
Ageneotettix 11.5.17
Ageniaspis 25.25.81
Ageniella 25.60.12
Ageniellini, supra 25.60.10
Agenioideus 25.60.22
Ageroniini, supra 27.46.41
Agelastica 24.107.89
Aegialomyia 29.26.20
agile, Pison 25.62.50
agilis, Edmundsius 6.1.2
agilis, Parasetigena 29.105.286
agitatellus, Crambus 27.55.203
Agkistrocerus 29.26.21
Aglais 27.46.26
Aglaomyia 29.9.48
Aglaopteryx 14.5.8
Aglaostigma 25.7.91
Aglaothorax 11.7.39
Aglenini, supra 24.93.20
Aglenus 24.93.20
Aglossa 27.55.234
Aglyptacros 25.53.20
Aglyptinus 24.19.12
agna, Helia 27.75.116
Agnippe 27.23.15
Agnocoris 20.23.140
Agonatopus 25.52.24
Agonatopoides 25.51.16
Agonochaetia 27.23.55
Agonocrybites 25.16.186
Agonopterix 27.15.1
Agonoxenid Moth Family, supra 27.20.1
Agonoxenidae, supra 27.20.1
Agonum 24.4.74
agonus, Limonius 24.48.27
agonus, Stichtoptychus 24.63.47
Agra 24.4.151
Agrapha 27.75.153
Agraphini 24.113.96
Agraphus 24.113.96
Agraulis 27.46.1
Agraylea 26.7.2
Agrenia 1.4.21
Agriades 27.43.52
agrifoliae, Atarsaphis 21.19.21

Agrilaxia 24.46.21
Agrilinae, supra 24.46.32
Agrilini, supra 24.46.32
Agrilus 24.46.34
Agrion 7.8.1
Agrionidae 7.11.1
Agriopodes 27.75.234
Agriotella 24.48.26
Agriotes 24.48.40
Agriotini, supra 24.48.40
Agriphila 27.55.209
Agrius 27.70.1
Agrochola 27.75.403
Agroecotettix 11.5.84
Agroiconota 24.107.181
Agromyza 29.68.1
Agromyzaphagus 25.25.103
Agromyzidae, supra 29.68.1
agromyzina, Aldrichiomyza 29.74.5
Agronus 24.113.73
Agroperina 27.75.251
Agrothereutes 25.16.151
Agrothereutina, supra 25.16.150
Agrothrips 22.5.28
Agrotinae, supra 27.75.535
Agrotiphila 27.75.469
Agrotis 27.75.535
Agrotisia 27.75.298
Agrtoini, supra 27.75.535
Agrypnia 26.8.2
Agrypnini, supra 24.48.1
agrypnoides, Pseudomelanactes 24.48.17
Agrypnus 24.48.3
Agrypon 25.16.384
Aguna 27.40.7
Agylla 27.73.9
Agymnastus 11.5.44
Agyrtes 24.21.4
Agyrtinae, supra 24.21.3
Agyrtini, supra 24.21.3
Ahasverus 24.72.4
Ahautlea, supra 20.35.7
Ahmosia 27.38.6
aholibah, Catocala 27.75.148 (Fig. 27.339)
aidea, Anaea 27.47.1
Aidemona 11.5.111
Ailanthus Silkmoth 27.69.14
Ailanthus Webworm 27.30.1 (Fig. 27.47)
aimotofus, Salpingothrips 22.4.34
ainsliei, Orchesella 1.5.2
air sac 12
Airamia 27.75.208
Airora 24.66.12
Aivalykus 25.13.2
Aknisus 20.12.1
Akronia 29.31.29
Alabama Grote 27.75.72
alabamensis, Neochrysis 25.50.22
Alabameubria 24.34.14
Alaephus 24.87.36
Alaocybites 24.113.170
Alaptinae, supra 25.27.1
Alptini, supra 25.27.3
Alaptus 25.27.3
Alapus 21.14.197
Alarodia 27.52.11
alaskana, Isotoma 1.4.23
alaskense, Philotelma 29.93.59
alaskensis, Litoleptis 29.28.1
alaskensis, Pikonema 25.7.28
Alaskophyto 29.105.174
Alatuncusia 27.55.23
Alaudes 24.87.160
Alaus 24.48.7
alba, Dryocampa 27.69.4 (Fig. 27.217)
alba, Hypochlora 11.5.86

alba, Redingtonia 37.75.366
albastrigulella, Pleurota 27.15.43
albata, Clemensia 27.73.21
albatella, Phycitodes 27.55.372
albavitta, Euchalcia 27.75.161
albella, Hemiprosopa 27.16.4
albella, Paraleucoptera 27.13.8
Alberada 27.55.382
alberta, Clossiana 27.46.11
alberta, Oeneis 27.48.13
albertae, Dodia 27.73.33. (Fig. 27.283)
albertae, Oreadomyia 29.24.84
albicans, Hecamede 29.93.7
albicapitana, Petrova 27.38.20
albiclavus, Hoplocrepis 25.26.71
albiscosta, Loxagrotis 27.75.545
albida, Hebardacris 11.5.113
albifrons, Limnospila 29.100.8
albiguttalis, Sameodes 27.55.127
albifasciella, Kearfottia 27.10.25
albihirta, Platykula 25.18.13
albimanus, Anopheles 29.20.1
albiocula, Airamia 27.75.208
albipenella, Staudingeria 27.55.359
albipennis, Bibio 29.8.4
albipunctatus, Telmatoscopus 29.12.5
albisinuata, Rejectaria 27.75.17
albistylum, Berkshiria 29.31.22
albistylus, Stylogomphus 7.3.11
albitarsis, Megachile 25.68.22
albiventris, Ogcodes 29.38.5
albocinctus, Thymus 25.26.41
albofasciata, Saturnia 27.69.10
albofasciatus, Cyltoleptus 24.106.126
albofasciatus, Spanagonicus 20.23.69
albogalleriella, Opostega 27.6.1
albolineana, Endothenia 27.38.7
albolineata, Sphingicampa 27.69.3
albolineata Trimerotropis 11.5.62
albomanicata, Limnophila 29.2.34
alboplagiata, Tristyla 27.75.445
albopunctatus, Arvelius 20.3.55
alboricta, Acropimpla 25.16.9
albostriella, Alebra 21.14.67
Albuna 27.35.6
Alcaeorrhynchus 20.3.66
Alcathoe 27.35.18
alcestis, Phaeostrymon 27.43.14
Alcidamea 25.68.18
alcis, Lyperosiops 29.100.60
alcohol collections 39
Alconeura 21.14.69
Alder Bark Beetle 24.112.14
Alder Spittle Bug 21.12.7
Alderfly Family, supra 23.1.1
aldrichi, Anoxynops 29.105.231
aldrichi, Caenocephus 25.12.1
aldrichi, Hyperecteina 29.105.330
aldrichi, Pentelicus 25.25.153
aldrichi, Pseudepipona 25.59.15
Aldrichia 29.40.8
aldrichii, Pentacricia 29.100.10
Aldrichina 29.101.15
Aldrichiomyza 29.74.5
alea, Strymon 27.43.34
Alebra 21.14.67
Alebrini, supra 21.14.67
Aleiodes 25.13.53
Alena 23.3.2
Aleochara 24.24.194
Aleocharinae 24.24.193
Aleodorus 24.24.195
Alepidia 20.23.125
Alepidiella 20.23.126
Aleptina 27.75.204

Aleptinoides 27.75.377
aleptivoides, Paracretona 27.75.205
Alethia 24.88.3
Aletia 27.75.498
Aleurocanthus 21.18.1
Aleurochiton 21.18.2
Aleurocybotus 21.18.3
Aleurodicus 21.18.18
Aleurodicinae, supra 21.18.18
Aleurodothrips 22.5.29
Aleuroglandulus 21.18.4
Aleurolobus 21.18.5
Aleuroparadoxus 21.18.6
Aleuroplatus 21.18.7
Aleuropleurocelus 21.18.8
Aleuropteryginae, supra 21.18.8
Aleuropterygini, supra 23.5.1
Aleuropteryx 23.5.1
Aleurothrixus 21.18.9
Aleurotulus 21.18.10
Aleyrodes 21.18.11
Aleyrodidae, supra 21.18.1
Aleyrodinae, supra 21.18.1
Aleyrodoidea, supra 21.18.1
Alfalfa Blotch Leaf Miner 29.68.1
Alfalfa Caterpillar 27.42.11
Alfalfa Gall Midge 29.11.74
Alfalfa Leaf-cutting Bee 25.68.22
Alfalfa Looper 27.75.164
Alfalfa Plant Bug 20.23.139
Alfalfa Seed Chalcid 25.20.21
Alfalfa Snout Beetle 24.113.68
Alfalfa Webworm 27.55.101
Alfalfa Weevil 24.113.146
Algarobius 24.108.11
algidella, Antaeotricha 27.15.17
algonquinensis, Epipteromalus 25.19.113
algophila, Halobrecta 24.24.250
alicia, Asterocampa 27.47.3
alicia, Cheilotrichia 29.2.54
aliena, Plectris 24.30.74
alienum, Oscinisoma 29.94.10
alienus, Lasius 25.58.67 (Fig. 25.49)
alienus, Stenelaphus 24.106.62
Aligia 21.14.134
Aliolus 25.13.134
aliradicus, Hylobius 24.113.153
Alisalia 24.24.196
Alisotrichis 26.7.10
Alkai Bee 25.66.8
Allacma 1.7.9
Allacrotelsa 5.3.2
Allagrapha 27.75.158
Allandrus 24.109.9
Allanthalia 29.42.55
Allantinae, supra 25.7.75
Allantini, supra 25.7.86
Allantus 25.7.86
Allaporus 25.60.17
Allarete 29.11.16
Alleculidae, supra 24.87.1
Alleculinae, supra 24.88.1
Allegheny Mound Ant 25.58.72
Allegheny Spruce Beetle 24.112.11
Allenanicia 29.103.7
allenella, Bibarrambla 27.15.3
alleni, Hygronemobius 11.10.16
alliae, Agathymus 27.40.87 (Fig. 27.75)
allii, Labopidicola 20.23.109
allioides, Edestochilus 29.11.65
Alliopsis 29.99.10
Alloambria 21.19.3

Allobracon 25.13.37
Allocapnia 8.3.1
Allochares 25.60.30
Allocoryninae, supra 24.113.15
Allocosmoecus 26.10.1
Allocotocera 29.9.57
Allodia 29.9.20
Allodiopsis 29.9.21
Allodorus 25.13.135
Alloeorrhynchus 20.18.3
Alloeostylus 29.100.40
Allognosta 29.31.2.
Allognota 29.100.4
Allograpta 29.47.30
Allomacrotera 25.65.15
Allomacrus 25.16.484
Allomethus 29.48.6
Allomyella 29.98.14
Allonarcys 8.5.1
Allonemobius 11.10.13
Alloperdita 25.65.15
Alloperla 8.8.1
Allophroides 25.16.445
Allophyla 29.84.3
Allophys 25.16.451
Allopiophila 29.64.1
Alloplasta 25.16.310
Allopoda 24.98.39
Allopodops 20.3.20
Allopogonia 24.34.3
Allorhinocoris 20.23.141
Allorhogas 25.13.3
Allosmaitia 27.43.22
Allothrips 22.5.1
Allotorymus 25.18.5
Allotria 27.75.131
Allotrichoma 29.93.5
Allotropa 25.44.6
Alloxysta 25.33.2
Alloxystidae, supra 25.33.1
Alloxystinae, supra 25.33.1
allredi, Jordanopsylla 30.4.11
alluaudi, Plagiolepis 25.58.62
Alluaudomyia 29.23.11
Allygianus 21.14.123
Allygiella 21.14.124
Allygus 21.14.105
allyni, Eupelmus 25.24.5
allyni, Paramacera 27.48.7
Allysson 25.62.71
Almodes 27.61.5
Almond Moth 27.55.403
almus, Eulonus 21.14.84
alni, Agelastica 24.107.89
Alniphagus 24.112.14
Aloephagus 21.19.4
Alohini, supra 21.2.3
alopha, Meloboria 25.16.410
Alophorella 29.105.7
Alophosternum 25.16.15
Alosternida 24.106.201
Alotanypus 29.24.11
Alpheias 27.55.279
Alpheioides 27.55.280
Alphina 21.3.4
Alphitoaphis 21.19.5
Alphitobius 24.87.115
Alphitophagus 24.87.102
Alpinobombus 25.70.2
Alsophila 27.61.3 (Fig. 27.177)
alternans, Temnostoma 29.47.78
alternata, Abagrotis 27.75.587 (Fig. 27.399)
alternata, Eurygaster 20.3.11 (Fig. 20.6)
alternata, Sigara 20.35.18
alternatus, Nabis 20.18.5

alternatus, Trigoniophthalmus 4.1.6
althaeae, Brooksetta 20.23.92
Althaeus 24.108.13
Altica 24.107.127
Alticinae, supra 2.107.114
altus, Derallus 23.12.12
Alucita 27.25.1
Alucitidae, supra 27.25.1
Alveotingis 20.14.3
Alydidae, supra 20.5.1
Alydinae, supra 20.5.6
Alydus 20.5.9
Alypia 27.75.248
Alypiodes 27.75.247
Alysia 25.13.96
Alysiinae, supra 25.13.90
Alysiini, supra 25.13.96
Alyssonini, supra 25.62.71
amabilis, Anomopsocus 17.14.2 (Fig. 17.6)
Amalactinae, supra 24.113.53
Amalactini 24.113.53
Amalactus 24.113.53
Amalopota 21.9.10
Amalus 24.113.299
amanda, Eusama 21.14.117
Amannus 24.106.156
amans, Bucephalina 29.98.7
Amara 24.4.95
Amarochara 24.24.197
Amarodytes 24.7.7
Amartus 24.70.5
Amarygmini, supra 24.87.128
Amastrini, supra 21.15.32
Amastris 21.15.34
amatella, Dioryctria 27.55.339
Amatidae, supra 27.73.74
amaturaria, Calothysanis 28.61.185
Amaurochrous 20.3.17
Amauromyza 29.68.6
Amauronematus 25.7.36
Amauropsini, supra 24.25.70
Ambaraphis 21.19.6
Amber-spot 7.7.13
Ambesa 27.55.316
ambigna, Aemilia 27.73.58 (Fig. 27.305)
ambigua, Neanura 1.2.16
ambigua, Nefusa 25.7.50
Ambiini, supra 27.55.5
ambitiosus, Pictonemoblius 11.10.17
Ambloplisus 25.16.282
Amblopusa 24.24.198
Amblyapis 25.67.2
Amblyaspis 25.44.20
Amblycera, supra 18.3.1
Amblycerinae, supra 24.108.2
Amblycerus 24.108.2
Amblychila 24.3.1
Amblycorypha 11.7.1
Amblyctis 24.98.17
Amblyderus 24.102.3
Amblyjoppa 25.16.252
Amblyomia 20.4.7
Amblyopone 25.58.6
Amblyoponini, supra 25.58.6
Amblyptilia 27.58.11
Amblyscirtes 27.40.80
Amblysellus 21.14.219
Amblytelesina, supra 25.16.225
Amblytropidia 11.5.21
Amblytylus 20.23.31
Ambositrinae, supra 25.42.1
Ambrosia Beetle Family, supra 24.111.1
Ambryinae, supra 20.38.4
Ambrysus 20.38.4
Ambush Bug 20.16.1

Ambush Bug Family 20.16.1
Ambylgnathus 24.4.130
Amecocerus 24.68.46
Ameletus 6.1.
Amelinae, supra 14.1.1
Ameragenia 25.60.12
Amercedes 24.113.344
Amerentulus 2.3.2
American Aspen Beetle 24.107.73
American Bird Grasshopper 11.5.114
American Black Flour Beetle 24.87.110
American Cockroach 14.3.2
American Cockroach Family 14.3.1
American Copper 27.43.3
American Flower Fly 29.47.14
American Ground Mealybug 21.25.38
American Painted Lady 27.46.27
American Plum Borer 27.55.392
American Ruby Spot 7.8.2
American Spanish Fly 24.101.13
American Spider Beetle 24.62.2
American Stag Beetle 24.28.2
americana, Acetropis 20.23.138
americana, Acronicta 27.75.231
americana, Aelia 20.3.39
americana, Agdistis 27.58.1
americana, Arctia 27.73.50 (Fig. 27.292)
americana, Catotricha 29.11.21 (Fig. 29.17)
americana, Charisalia 24.106.200
americana, Chionaspis 21.38.14
americana, Cimbex 24.4.3
americana, Colobaea 29.79.2
americana, Cosmobaris 24.113.304
americana, Cymatia 20.35.2
americana, Deinopsis 24.24.221
americana, Dirrhope 25.13.117
americana, Dolania 6.1.1
americana, Doliopria 25.42.31
americana, Ectromatopsis 25.25.45
americana, Entomoscelis 24.107.69
americana, Eucnemis 24.52.3
americana, Euplectromorpha 25.26.14
americana, Gonioctena 24.107.73
americana, Harrisina 27.50.1
americana, Heoclisis 23.14.12
americana, Hetaerina 7.8.2 (Fig. 7.20)
americana, Hygropora 24.24.255
americana, Leptopteromyia 29.37.1
americana, Lophocomodia 25.19.44
americana, Lycoptis 24.66.6
americana, Malacosoma 27.68.11
americana, Meromyza 29.94.50
americana, Microvelia 20.28.4
americana, Minella 29.105.186
americana, Myrmecina 25.58.40
americana, Ogloblinisca 25.19.17
americana, Pericoma 29.12.12
americana, Periplaneta 14.3.2 (Fig. 14.16)
americana, Perniphora 25.19.78
americana, Phthora 24.87.74
americana, Phyllodesma 27.68.6
americana, Phyllodromis 29.42.13
americana, Phymata 20.16.1
americana, Ranatra 20.36.1 (Figs. 20.67, 20.68)
americana, Schistocerca 11.5.114 (Fig. 11.23)
americana, Silpha 24.21.7 (Fig. 24.54)
americana, Spania 29.28.4
americana, spinolae, Bembix 25.62.101
americana, Stigmatocrepis 25.19.64
americana, Tomocerodes 25.19.35
americana, Thamiaraea 24.24.305
americana, Thaumalea 29.21.1
americana, Tholera 27.75.511

Americanotimarcha 24.107.58
americanum, Clanoneurum 29.93.20
americanum, Eriosoma 21.19.74
americanum, Mezium 24.62.2 (Fig. 24.120)
americanum, Omophron 24.4.2
americanus, Acaromimus 24.109.3
americanus, Acerentulus 2.3.2
americanus, Anapus 20.23.82
americanus, Atlanticus 11.7.29 (Fig. 11.35)
americanus, Brachycentrus 26.9.3
americanus, Byrrhus 24.35.7
americanus, Caerosternus 24.26.34
americanus Chrysopophthorus 25.13.149
americanus, Conostethus 20.23.40
americanus, Coptostethus 24.48.68
americanus, Cycloptiloides 11.10.2
americanus, Dryophthorus 24.113.385
americanus, Emphylus 24.74.3
americanus, Encephalus 24.24.234
americanus, Eumacrocentrus 25.13.63
americanus, Haplogonatopus 25.51.17
americanus, Hemiptarsenus 25.26.4
americanus, Leptocerus 26.18.2
americanus, Lethocerus 20.37.1 (Fig. 20.71)
americanus, Macrohynnis 25.42.6
americanus, Macromesus 25.19.21
americanus, Metabletus 24.4.164
americanus, Metasyrphus 29.47.14
americanus, Miscophus 25.62.47
americanus, Nallachius 23.10.1
americanus, Nicrophorus 24.21.9 (Fig. 24.55)
americanus, Ochterus 20.40.1
americanus, Omoglymmius 24.2.1
americanus, Orrhodops 29.37.28
americanus, Pambolus 25.13.52
americanus, Paratrichobius 29.108.3
americanus, Phaenocerus 24.52.5
americanus, Platypygus 29.40.21
americanus, Pseudocatolaccus 25.19.100
americanus, Rhacognathus 20.3.70
americanus, Rhizoecus 21.25.38
americanus, Rhopalodomtus 24.92.12
americanus, Smicrus 24.15.19
americanus, Tabanus 29.26.26.
americanus, Telmatophilus 24.74.17
americanus, Tetrabaeus 25.44.4
americanus, Zeluroides 20.17.30
Americina 29.98.28
americoferus, Nabis 20.18.5 (Fig. 20.46)
Amerinus 24.4.116
Ameroduvalius 24.4.44
ametabolous 13
Ametastegia 25.7.84
Ametor 24.12.16
Ametris 27.61.4
Ametrodiplosis 29.11.138
Ametropodidae, supra 6.3.1
Ametropus 6.3.1
Amiana 27.75.188
amica, Catocala 27.75.148
Amiocentrus 26.9.2
Amiota 29.90.2
Amischa 24.24.199
Amiseginae, supra 25.50.2
amitaria, Ematurga 27.61.22
Amitermes 15.4.2
Amitermitinae, supra 15.4.1
Amitus 25.44.9
Ammobaenetes 11.9.18
ammobata, Schlingeria 29.32.27
Ammobatini, supra 25.69.5
Ammodonus 24.87.166

Ammonaios 29.32.12
Ammonoencyrtus 25.25.65
Ammophila 25.62.14
Ammophilini, supra 25.62.12
Ammoplanellus 25.62.32
Ammoplanops 25.62.30
Ammoplanus 25.62.31
Ammopsen 25.62.15
Ammosphex 25.60.28
Amnegialia 24.30.16
Amnestinae, supra 20.1.8
Amnestus 20.1.8
amnicola, Nephaspis 24.80.12
Amniscus 24.106.279
Amobia 29.103.1
Amoebaleria 29.84.21
amoena, Cathetopteron 24.106.301
amoena, Metadontia 25.21.5
amoenus, Closterocoris 20.23.146
amoenus, Perodryinus 25.51.10
amoenus, Tropidosteptes 20.23.190
Amolita 27.75.367
Amonostherium 21.15.1
amorata, Callizzia 27.62.2 (Fig. 27.203)
Amorbia 27.38.90
Amotus 24.113.60
Ampedini, supra 24.48.24
Ampedus 24.48.25
Ampeloglypter 24.113.311
ampelopsis, Cissuvora 27.35.3
ampelos, Coenonympha 27.48.8
Amphalius 30.7.1
Amphasia 24.4.112
Amphelasma 24.107.92
Amphiagrion 7.11.1
Amphiareus 20.21.21
Amphibolips 25.34.28
Amphibolothrips 22.5.30
Amphicercidus 21.19.7
Amphicerus 24.64.13
Amphicnephes 29.59.1
amphicollis, Conoderus 24.48.14
Amphicosmoecus 26.10.2
Amphicosmus 29.40.1
Amphicrossus 24.70.27
Amphicroum 24.24.104
Amphicyrta 24.35.9
Amphicyrtinae, supra 24.35.9
Amphicyrtini, supra 24.35.9
Amphidora 24.87.137
Amphidorini, supra 24.87.136
Amphientometae, supra 17.5.1
Amphientomidae, supra 17.5.1
Amphientominae, supra 17.5.1
Amphiesmenoptera, supra 26.1.1
Amphigerontia 17.23.1
Amphigerontiinae, supra 17.23.1
amphigyroides, Latebraria 27.75.110
Amphimallon 24.30.64
Amphinemuia 8.1.1
Amphinemurinae, supra 8.1.1
amphinome, Hamadryas 27.46.41
Amphion 27.70.36
Amphipoea 27.75.277
Amphipogon 29.64.1
Amphipsocidae, supra 17.12.1
Amphipsylla 30.6.8
Amphipsyllinae, supra 30.6.3
Amphipsyllini, supra 30.6.5
Amphipyga 21.14.175
Amphipyra 27.75.317
Amphipyrinae, supra 27.75.250
Amphipyrini, supra 27.75.316
Amphisbatini, supra 27.15.9
Amphitornus 11.5.12
Amphivectura 24.68.23

Amphizoa 24.5.1
Amphizoidae, supra 24.5.1
Amphorinophora 21.19.105
Amphorophora 21.19.8
Amphotis 24.70.22
ampla, Doa 27.73.5
amplectus, Onycholyda 25.2.5
ampliata, Uniptera 21.4.2
Amplicephalus 21.14.223
amplifrons, Cistogaster 29.105.1
amplipennis, Treherniella 22.5.73
amplus, Sporothrips 22.5.21
Amplypterus 27.70.14
Ampulex 25.62.3
Ampulicinae, supra 35.62.1
Ampulicini, supra 25.62.3
Ampulicomorpha 25.52.1
Ampumixis 24.45.4
amputatrix, Apamea 27.75.250 (Fig. 27.355)
amsterdamensis, Rhicnopeltoidea 25.26.68
Amycle 21.3.5
Amyclinae, supra 21.3.5
Amyclini, supra 21.3.5
Amydetinae, supra 24.55.15
Amydraulax 25.16.108
Amydria 27.10.32
Amyelois 27.55.297
amymone, Mestra 27.46.39
Amyna 27.75.203
Amynothrips 22.5.24
amyntor, Ceratomia 27.70.7 (Fig. 27.242)
amyntula, Everes 27.43.41
amyridella, Eucatagma 27.30.2
Amyrsidea 18.6.2
Anabasis 27.55.285
Anabolia 26.11.1
Anabrolepis 25.25.91
Anabrus 11.7.26
Anacaena 24.12.19
Anacampsinae, supra 27.23.68
Anacampsis 27.23.72
Anacamptodes 27.61.39
Anacentrinus 24.113.351
Anacharis 25.31.7
Anacharitinae, supra 25.31.4
Anacimas 29.26.19
Anaclileia 29.9.58
Anacogini, supra 27.61.111
Anacostia 27.55.417
Anacrabro 25.62.56
Anacyptus 24.24.189
Anadelosemia 27.55.300
Anaea 27.47.1
Anaedus 24.89.3
anaetis, Xerogorytes 25.62.93
Anagapetus 26.6.1
Anagasta 27.55.401
Anageshna 27.55.139
Anaglyptini, supra 24.106.130
anaglyptus, Conotrachelus 24.113.238 (Fig. 24.290)
Anagoga 27.61.116
Anagrapha 27.75.165
Anagrini, supra 25.27.1
Anagrus 25.27.1
Anagyrini, supra 25.25.24
Anagyrus 25.25.24
Anajapygid Entotroph Family 3.3.1
Anajapygidae, supra 3.3.1
Anajapyx 3.3.1
Analeptura 24.106.199
analis, Anthrax 29.40.43
analis, Homoeolabus 24.113.2 (Fig. 24.264)
analis, Larra 25.62.37

Anametis 24.113.131
Anamorphus 24.81.1
Anamphidora 24.88.16
Anania 27.55.31
Anaphini, supra 25.27.10
Anaphes 25.27.12
Anaphothrips 22.4.19
Anaplectoides 27.75.580
Anapleus 24.26.24
Anaporia 29.105.198
Anapsusis 29.15.16
Anapus 20.23.82
Anaquedius 24.24.21
anaranjada, Cydia 27.38.56
Anareolatae, supra 10.1.1
Anarete 29.11.12
Anaretella 29.11.17
Anarhopus 25.25.43
Anarsia 27.23.77
Anarta 27.75.491
Anartia 27.46.31
anartoides, Matiloxis 27.75.65
Anartomima 27.75.486
Anarylophagus 29.29.5
Anasa 20.4.27
Anasimyia 29.47.62
Anaspidinae, supra 24.98.44
Anaspis 24.98.48
Anastatus 25.24.9
anastelgis 25.16.7
Anastoechus 29.40.13
Anastrangalia 24.106.220
Anastrepha 29.61.43
Anatella 29.9.22
Anathix 27.75.405
Anathrichus 24.4.101
Anathrix 25.25.25
Anaticola 18.1.3
Anatis 24.80.35
Anatoecus 18.1.4
Anatralata 27.55.35
Anatropis 24.30.130
Anavitrinelia 27.61.41
Anax 7.4.2
Anaxipha 11.10.20
Anaxyelid Wood Wasp Family, supra 25.8.1
Anaxyelidae, supra 25.8.1
Ancepaspis 21.38.3
Anchastus 24.48.23
Anchicera 24.74.13
anchisiades, Priamides 27.41.8
Anchitelus 24.113.84
Anchomma 24.93.2
Anchonini, supra 24.113.162
Anchonoderus 24.4.78
Anchonus 24.113.162
Anchor Stink Bug 20.3.64 (Fig. 20.14)
anchorago, Brenthus 24.110.1
anchorago, Stiretus 20.3.64 (Fig. 20.14)
Anchorius 24.83.1
Anchycteis 24.34.6
Anchylarthron 24.25.51
Anchytarsini, supra 24.34.4
Anchytarsus 24.34.4
Ancient Barklice Family 17.19.1
ancilla, Herrera 21.13.13
ancilla, Pseudomyothyria 29.105.261
Ancistroceruw 25.59.22
Ancistromma 25.62.40
Ancistrona 18.6.3
Ancognatha 24.30.98
Anconatus 21.19.9
Anconia 11.5.67
Ancylandrena 25.65.3
Ancylis 27.38.42
Ancylocera 24.106.139

Ancylocerini, supra 24.106.139
Ancylodiplosis 29.11.95
Ancylolomiinae, supra 27.55.198
Ancyloscelis 25.69.7
Ancylostomia 27.55.309
Ancyloxypha 27.40.56
ancylus, Diaspidiotus 21.38.24
Ancyronychini, supra 24.45.3
Ancyronyx 24.45.3
Andaspis 21.38.4
Anderida 27.55.369
andersoni, Amynothrips 22.5.24
andraemon, Heraclides 27.41.6
Andrallus 20.3.69
andrae, Dysdercus 20.8.1 (Fig. 20.32)
andrei, Nipponentomon 2.3.4
andremona, Hypocala 27.75.106
Andrena 25.65.1
Andrenid Bee Family, supra 25.65.1
Andrenidae, supra 25.65.1
Andreninae, supra 25.65.1
Andrenosoma 29.37.63
andrewsi, Pseudocotalpa 24.30.89
andria, Anaea 27.47.1 (Fig. 27.144)
Andricus 25.34.29
Andrimus 24.88.17
Androchirus 24.88.18
androgeus, Heraclides 27.41.6
androgynes, Tanaodiplosis 29.11.81
Androloma 27.75.249
Androlyperus 24.107.107
Andronicus 25.68.18
andropogonis, Stereomita 27.23.9
Andropolia 27.75.293
Aneflomorpha 24.206.69
Aneflus 24.106.55
Anegcephalesis 27.55.308
Anelaphus 24.106.75
Anelastes 24.52.27
Anelpistus 24.86.3
Anemosella 27.55.243
Anepeorinae, supra 6.6.11
Anepeorus 6.6.11
Anepia 27.75.488
Anepsiini, supra 24.87.35
Anepsius 24.87.35
Anerastia 27.55.412
Anergates 25.58.43
Aneristus 25.25.9
Aneuclis 25.16.454
Aneugmenini, supra 25.7.4
Aneugmenus 25.7.4
Aneurhynchus 25.42.23
Aneurota 24.24.200
Aneurus 20.13.3
Anevrina 29.46.1
anfracta, Phobolosia 27.75.36
Angarotipula 29.2.9
angata, Dibusa 26.7.3
Angel Insects 16.11
Angel Insect Family 16.1.1
angelia, Electrostrymon 27.43.36
angelica, Copibryophila 27.75.206
angelicus, Crossocerus 25.62.63
Angeronini, supra 27.61.81
Anglewings 27.46.24
Angora Goat Chewing Louse 18.2.1
Angoumois Grain Moth 27.23.80
angraeci, Conchaspis 21.36.1
angularis, Dicranoctetes 27.16.8
angularis, Tenaspis 24.55.5
angulata, Bandelia 27.75.81
angulata, Leptocera 29.88.3
Angulate Leafhopper 21.14.93
angulatus, Acinopterus 231.14.93
angulatus, Blepharidopterus 20.23.90

angulatus, Scaphinotus 24.4.16
angulicollis, Chalcophora 24.46.8
angulicollis, Dasycerus 24.17.1
angulicollis, Gononotus 24.113.163
angulifera, Callosamia 27.69.17
angulifera, Draeculacephala 21.14.47 (Fig. 21.20)
angustata, Orochares 24.24.124
angustata, Prosapia 21.12.1
angustata, Sapyga 25.57.2
angustata, Stenomicra 29.70.4
angustatus, Scolops 21.11.5 (Fig. 21.10)
Angustia 29.105.408
angusticollis, Scaphinotus 24.4.16
angusticollis, Zootermopsis 15.1.1
Angustiopsis 29.105.394
angustiorana, Dirula 27.38.83
angustiora, Skewesia 27.71.23
angustipennis, Ctenophora 29.2.6
angustipennis, Strongylophthalmyia 29.53.1
angustipennis, Tenodera 14.1.10 (Figs. 14.11, 14.12)
angustivitta, Angustia 29.105.408
angustus, Calopus 24.97.1
angustus, Catalinus 24.20.11
angustus, Cynaeus 24.87.107
angustus, Ferrisicoccus 21.25.20
angustus, Tedinus 24.88.9
Anhimella 27.75.513
Anicetus 25.25.66
anicia, Occidryas 27.46.22
Anicla 27.75.552
Ancilini, supra 27.75.545
Aniferella 21.19.10
Anillaspis 24.4.63
Anillinus 24.4.62
Anillodes 24.4.60
Animal lice 18.8.1
Animomyia 27.61.98
Anise Swallowtail 27.41.5
Anisembia 9.1.2
Anisembiidae, supra 9.1.1
Anisepyrus 25.48.7
Aniseres 25.16.487
Anisobas 25.16.269
anisocentra, Homadaula 27.29.4
Anisocentropus, supra 26.17.1
Anisocerini, supra 24.106.264
Anisococcus 21.25.3
Anisodactylus 24.4.110
Anisolabis 13.1.3
Anisomorpha 10.4.1
anisomorphae, Adelphe 25.50.4
Anisomorphinae 10.4.1
Anisomorphini, supra 10.4.1
Anisopilothrips 22.4.1
Anisopinae, supra 20.33.1
Anisopodidae, supra 29.14.1
Anisopodinae, supra 29.14.1
Anisopodoidea, supra 29.14.1
Anisoptera, supra 7.1.1
Anisopteromalus 25.19.80
Anisopygus 25.16.212
Anisoscelini, supra 20.4.4
Anisostena 24.107.162
Anisosticta 24.80.39
Anisostylus 21.15.27
Anisota 27.69.5
Anisotacrus 25.16.367
Anisotoma 24.19.9
Anisotylus 25.25.98
Anisoxya 24.98.29
Anitra 24.25.75
anixus, Agrilus 24.46.34
Ankothrips 22.1.1
Ankylotylus 20.23.32

annabella, Vanessa 27.46.27 (Fig. 27.135)
Annaphila 27.75.387
anniulipes, Megasyrphus 29.47.25
annularis, Polistes 25.59.28
Annulaspis 21.38.5
annulata, Annulimeris 25.56.5
annulata, Hemileuca 27.69.7
annulata, Periscelis 29.72.1
annulata, Pronotacantha 20.12.4
annulata, Zunacetha 27.72.2 (Fig. 27.278)
annulatum, Tragidion 24.106.151
annulatus, Loptogaster 29.37.2
annulatus, Manophylax 26.10.49
annulatus, Tuberculatus 21.19.217
annulatus, Zaplous 24.106.255
annulicornis, Leucopelmonus 25.7.89
annulicornis, Namacus 20.4.21
annulicornis, Rocconota 20.17.20
Annulimeris 25.56 5
annulipes, Callopistromyia 29.58.1
annulipes, Charops 25.16.398
annulipes, Euborellia 13.1.2 (Fig. 13.2, 13.3)
annulipes, Paraspalangia 25.26.37
annuliventris, Eurycnemus 29.24.106
Anobiidae, supra 24.63.1
Anobiinae, supra 24.63.13
Anobiopsis 24.63.24
Anobium 24.63.25
Anocha 29.11.23
Anodocheilus 24.7.8
anodonta, Conservula 27.75.288
Anoecia 21.19.11
Anogdus 24.19.4
Anolisimyia 29.103.21
Anomala 24.30.96
anomala, Acsala 27.73.26
anomala, Coleopina 29.77.2
anomala, Desmatomyia 29.40.26
anomala, Elachistarthron 24.24.235
anomala, Ornithophaga 30.6.4
anomala, Thriscolema 24.107.10
Anomalacra 24.30.96
Anomalagrion 7.11.2
Anomalemis 29.42.19
Anomalini, supra 29.30.94
anomalipes, Spathopus 25.19.59
anomalocerus, Stenocranophilus 24.105.1
Anopmalochaeta 29.69.2
Anomalon 25.16.290
Anomaloninae, supra 25.16.375
Anomalonini, supra 25.16.390
anomalus, Chelaporus 25.60.16
anomalus, Hoplopsyllus 30.1.9
anomaly 23
Anomiopsyllinae, supra 30.4.11
Anomiopsyllini, supra 30.4.12
Anomiopsyllus 30.4.16
Anomis 27.75.71
Anommatinae, supra 24.78.2
Anommatus 24.78.2
Anomocera 21.17.3
Anomognathus 24.24.201
Anomogyna 27.75.567
Anomologinae, supra 27.23.1
Anomoea 24.107.23
Anomopsocus 17.14.2
anona, Agapema 27.69.11
Anoncia 27.21.13
Anoncus 25.16.362
anonymus, Luperus 24.107.113
Anopheles 29.20.1
Anophelinae, supra 29.20.1
Anopina 27.38.68
Anopius 25.60.27
anopla, Gardinia 27.73.12

Anopliodes 25.60.27
Anopliomorpha 24.106.64
Anoplochares 25.60.28
Anoplocurius 24.106.79
Anoplodera, supra 24.106.172
Anoplodonta 29.31.36
Anoplonyx 25.7.23
Anopolotermes 15.4.1
Anoplura, supra 19.1.1
Anormenis 21.8.4
Anorostoma 29.84.13
Anorthodes 27.75.321
Anorthosia 27.23.86
Anorus 24.34.10
Anotia 21.9.11
Anotylus 24.24.141
Anovia 24.80.32
Anoxynops 29.105.231
anqulata, Pyractomena 24.55.6 (Fig. 24.107)
anserinus, Trinoton 18.6.35
anseris, Anaticola 18.1.3
Anstenoptilia 27.58.10
Ant Bug 20.23.153
Ant Mimic Bug Family 20.9.1
Antaeotricha, 27.15.17
antaeus, Strategus 24.30.108
Antarctophthirus 19.1.1
antenna 12.20
antennaepes, Rainieria 29.51.7
antennameres 10
antennal segments 10
Antennalia 24.106.10
antennalis, Chaetocrania 29.105.349
antennalis, Macrodea 24.74.11
antennata, Atomosiella 29.37.56
antennata, Melenenta 27.75.229
antennata, Lithophane 27.75.392
antennatum, Ctenobium 24.63.21
antennatum, Paducia 21.19.157
antennatum hesperum, Callidium 24.106.106
antennatus, Numidicola 18.6.28
antennatus, Scotochroides 24.98.22
Anteon 25.51.1
Anteoninae, supra 25.51.1
Anteos 27.42.13
Antepione 27.61.152
Antequera 27.21.1
Antequerinae, supra 27.21.1
Anthalia 29.42.56
Anthanassa 27.46.19
Anthaxia 24.46.21
anthedon, Enodia 27.48.1
Anthedonia 25.69.26
Anthelococcus 21.25.2
Anthemurgus 25.65.7
Anthepiscopus 29.42.45
Antheraea, 27.69.12
Antherophagus 24.74.1
Anthicidae, supra 24.102.1
Anthicinae, supra 24.102.3
Anthicus 24.102.7
Anthidiellum 25.68.9
Anthidiini, supra 25.68.2
Anthidium 25.68.6
Anthiitae, supra 24.4.168
Anthiophora, supra 28.1.1
Anthobium 24.24.105
Anthoboscinae, supra 25.53.8
Anthocharinae, supra 27.42.8
Anthocharini, supra 27.42.8
Anthocharis 27.42.9
Anthocopa 25.68.19
anthocopoides, Hoplitis 25.68.18
Anthocoridae, supra 20.21.1
Anthocorinae, supra 20.21.1

Anthocorini, supra 20.21.1
Anthocoris 20.21.5
Anthomyia 29.99.16
Anthomyiella 29.99.17
Anthomyliid Fly Family, supra 29.99.1
Anthomyiidae, supra 29.98.1;
 supra 29.99.1
Anthomyiinae, supra 29.99.3
Anthomyiini, supra 29.99.8
Anthomyiopsis 29.105.175
Anthomyza 29.70.1
Anthomyzid Fly Family 29.70.1
Anthomyzidae, supra 29.70.1
Anthonaeus 24.70.6
Anthonomini, supra 24.113.201
Anthonomopsis 24.113.205
Anthonomus 24.113.208
Anthophagus 24.24.106
Anthophila 27.36.3
Anthophora 25.69.36
Anthophoridae, supra 25.69.1
Anthophorinae, supra 25.69.16
Anthophorini, supra 25.69.36
Anthophorisca 25.69.16
Anthophorula 25.69.16
Anthophylax 24.106.181
anthracina, Fedtschenkia 25.57.1
anthracina, Thompsonomyia 29.105.112
Anthracinae, supra 29.40.42
anthracinus, Ectopiocerus 20.23.158
Anthracophaga 29.94.40
Anthracopteryx 24.48.54
Anthracosiphon 21.19.12
Anthrax 29.40.43
Anthrenini, supra 24.61.8
Anthrenus 24.61.8
Anthribidae, supra 24.109.1
Anthribinae, supra 24.109.7
anthyllidella, Aproaerema 27.23.68
Antianthe 21.15.43
Antiblemma 27.75.87
Anticarsia 27.75.85
Antichaeta 29.79.7
Antichloris 27.73.81
Anticlea 27.61.219
anticostalis, Eulepte 27.55.146
antidiscaria, Strenaspilatodes 27.61.86
Antigastra 27.55.143
antigua, Orgyia 27.74.3
antillana, Prionopelta 25.58.7
antillanus, Myopsocus 17.24.2
Antillocorini, supra 20.7.32
Antillocoris 20.7.32
Antillormenis 21.8.5
Antillothrips 22.5.31
antilope antilope, Ancistrocerus 25.59.22
antiopa, Nymphalis 27.46.25 (Fig. 27.132)
Antiplecta 27.62.3
antiqua, Hylemya 29.99.8
Antique Sap Beetle 24.70.10
antiquus, Carpophilus 24.70.10
Antispila 27.9.2
Antissa 29.31.11
Antistrophoplex 25.18.22
Antistrophus 25.34.10
Antlike Flower Beetle Family,
 supra 24.102.1
Antlike Leaf Beetle Family, supra 24.104.1
Antlike Stone Beetle Family, supra 24.20.1
Antlion Family, supra 23.14.1
Antlions 23.1.1
Antloving Beetle Family, supra 24.25.1
Ant-loving Crickets 11.10.1
antonia, Asterocampa 27.47.3
Antonina 21.25.4
Antoninoides 21.25.5

Antoniomyia 29.37.57
antonito, Mimobaratha 27.75.528
Antocha 29.2.16
Antron 25.45.44
antrozoi, Basilia 29.107.1 (Fig. 29.59)
Ants, supra 25.1.1
Anuraphis 21.19.13
Anurapteryx 27.63.1
Anurida 1.2.12
Anuridella 1.2.12
Anurogryllus 11.10.7
Anurophorus 1.4.3
Anurotropus 25.16.101
Anusia 25.25.26
Anycteola 27.75.378
Anypotacta 29.84.20
Anzamyia 29.105.153
Aochletus 29.31.33
Aon 27.75.168
Aonidia 21.38.6
Aonidiella 21.38.7
Aonidomytilus 21.38.8
aonidum, Chrysomphalus 21.38.16
Aoplus 25.16.222
Apache 21.9.13
Apachea 27.15.7
Apachekolos 29.37.2
Apachemyia 29.105.124
Apacheprospherysa 29.105.232
Apaeleticus 25.16.272
Apagodiplosis 29.11.133
Apallates 29.94.3
Apalocnemis 29.42.47
apama, Callophrys 27.43.24
Apamea 27.75.250
Apameini, supra 27.75.250
Apanisagrion 7.11.3
Apanteles 25.13.116 (Fig. 25.14)
Apantesis 27.73.52
Apareophora 25.7.67
Apatania 26.10.38
Apataniinae, supra 26.10.38
Apatelodes 27.66.1
Apatelodid Moth Family, supra 27.66.1
Apatelodidae, supra 27.66.1
Apateticus 20.3.73
Apatides 24.64.17
Apatolestes 29.26.4
Apatophion 25.16.459
Apaturid Butterfly Family, supra 27.47.1
Apaturidae, supra 27.47.1
Apaturinae, supra 27.47.3
Apenes 24.4.142
Apenesia 26.48.2
Aperileptus 25.16.492
apertus, Apterobittacus 28.1.1
Apeulaema 25.70.1
Apezococcus 21.31.1
Aphaenogaster 25.58.26
Aphaerata 25.13.97
Aphalara 21.17.2
Aphalarini, supra 21.17.2
Aphalaroida 21.17.4
Aphaniosoma 29.86.1
Aphanistes 25.16.376
Aphanogmus 25.45.3
Aphanotrechus 24.4.42
Aphanotrigonum 29.94.27
Aphantorhapha 29.105.301
Apharetra 27.75.447
Aphelia 27.38.78
Aphelini, supra 24.113.387
Aphelininae 25.25.1
Aphelinini, supra 25.25.1
Aphelinoidea 25.28.15
Aphelinus 25.25.1

Apheloglutus 29.105.315
Aphelonema 21.6.3
Aphelopinae, supra 25.51.27
Aphid Parasite Family, supra 25
Aphid Wasp 25.62.15
Apheloplastus 24.19.15
Aphelopus 25.51.27
Aphidencyrtus 25.25.104
Aphelosternus 24.26.18
Aphenolia 24.70.13
Aphididae, supra 21.19.1
Aphidiidae, supra 25.14.1
Aphidiina, supra 25.14.8
Aphidiinae, supra 25.14.4
Aphidiini, supra 25.14.4
Aphidius 25.14.9
Aphidoidea, supra 21.19.1
Aphidoletes 29.11.79
Aphidopsis 21.19.14
Aphids, supra 21.1.1
Aphilodyctium 25.7.85
Aphilanthops 25.62.108
Aphilanthopini, supra 25.62.108
Aphiochaeta 29.46.17
Aphis, 21.19.15
Aphleboderrhis 20.13.10
Aphodiinae, supra 24.30.14
Aphodiini, supra 24.30.17
Aphodiplosis 29.11.105
Aphodius 24.30.17
Aphoebantus 29.40.38
Aphomia 27.55.275
Aphonides 24.30.109
Aphonus 24.30.110
Aphorista 24.81.12
Aphotaenius 24.30.32
Aphrastomyia 29.9.40
Aphrastus 24.113.107
Aphria 29.105.125
Aphricus 24.48.72
Aphriini, supra 29.105.124
Aphrissa 27.42.15
Aphrodes 21.14.36
Aphrodinac, supra 21.14.36
Aphrodini, supra 21.14.36
aphrodite, Speyeria 27.46.8
Aphrophora 21.12.5
Aphrophorinae, supra 21.12.2
Aphropsyche 26.4.3
Aphrosylinae, supra 29.43.20
Aphthargelia 21.19.16
Aphthona 24.107.116
Aphycini, supra 25.25.49
Aphycoideus 25.25.129
Aphycus 25.25.51
Aphylla 7.3.3
Aphytis 25.25.2
apiatus, Heilipus 24.113.155
apicalis, Clostera 27.71.1 (Fig. 27.269)
apicalis, Diestrammena 11.9.4
apicalis, Ficana 20.4.25
apicalis, Hylobittacus 28.1.3
apicalis, Neotridactylus 11.6.1
apicalis, Stachycnemus 20.5.11
apicata, Mylogymnocarena 29.61.30
apicatus, Ampedus 24.48.25
apicatus, Bidessus 24.7.11
apicedentatus, Spongovostox 13.3.2
apicifer, Archytas 29.105.91
apicina, Orodesma 27.75.108
apicinebula, Physoptera 29.46.18
apiculata, Nepa 20.36.2 (Fig. 20.69)
apiculatus, Nissoscolopocerus 20.4.23
apiculatus, Rhynchus 24.113.271
Apidae, supra 25.70.1
apiifolia, Dysaphis 21.19.67

apiformis, Sesia 27.35.9 (Fig. 27.54)
Apilocrocis 27.55.111
Apiloscatopse 29.15.7
Apimela 24.24.202
Apinae, supra 25.70.4
apinella, Anthophila 27.36.3
Apini, supra 25.70.4
Apinocyptera 29.105.22
Apinops 29.105.18
apiocera 29.36.2
Apioceridae, supra 29.36.1
Apiomerinae, supra 20.17.1
Apiomerus 20.17.1
Apion 24.113.21
Apionidae, supra 24.113.16
Apioninae, supra 24.113.16
Apoinini, supra 24.113.21
Apis 25.70.4
Aplanus 21.14.139
Aplastus 24.48.52
Aplectoides 27.75.579
Aplemonini, supra 24.113.18
Aplocera 27.61.246
Aploderus 24.24.142
aplodontiae, Leptinillus 24.18.2
Aplomerus 25.16.81
Aplomyia 29.105.409
Aplomyiopsis 29.105.233
Aplopus 10.2.1
Apoanagyrus 25.25.27
Apobaetis 6.4.1
Apocellus 24.24.143
Apocephalus 29.46.25
Apoclima 25.16.485
Apocrisias 27.73.59
Apocrita, supra 25.13.1
Apocrypha 24.89.6
Apocryphinae, supra 24.89.6
Apoda 27.52.8
Apodasyini, supra 24.106.246
apodemes 10
Apdoemia 27.44.7
Apodrepanulatrix 27.61.72
Apogeshna 27.55.140
Apoidea, supra 25.63.1
Apolephthisa 29.9.65
Apolophus 25.16.293
Apolysis 29.40.25
Apomelissodes 25.69.30
Apomyelois 27.55.295
Apophthisis 27.14.7
Apophua 25.16.304
Aporandrena 25.65.1
Aporatachina 29.105.234
Aporeucoela 25.32.5
Aporinellus 25.60.29
Aporini, supra 25.60.14
Aporus 25.60.15
Apostrophus 29.105.19
Apote 11.7.27
Apotemnus 25.16.109
Apotoforma 27.38.62
Apotolype 27.68.3
Apotomis 27.38.11
Apotrepus 24.113.372
Apotropina 29.94.1
Appalachia 11.5.96
appalachia, Satyrodes 27.48.2
Appelia 21.19.28
Appendicia 29.105.114
appendiculatus, Neuroptynx 23.15.1 (Fig. 23.14)
appendigaster, Evania 25.35.1
Appendiseta 21.19.17
Appendisotoma 1.4.12
Appias 27.42.3

Apple Aphid 21.19.15
Apple Bark Borer 27.35.12
Apple Curculio 24.113.207
Apple Flea Weevil 24.113.217
Apple Fruit Moth 27.31.1
Apple Grain Aphid 21.19.186
Apple Leaf Skeletonizer 27.55.367
Apple Leaf Trumpet Miner 27.7.1
Apple Maggot 29.61.44
Apple Pistol Casebearer 27.18.1
Apple Red Bug 20.23.164
Apple Sucker 21.17.27
Apple Twig Beetle 24.112.40
Apple Twig Borer 24.64.13
Apple-and-thorn Skeletonizer 27.36.4
Apple Leafhopper 21.14.77
Apple Mealybug 21.25.32
approximana, Aterpia 27.38.8
approximaria, Cymatophora 27.61.85
approximata, Leptocera 29.88.3
approximatus, Dendroctonus 24.112.11
approximatus, Kalotermes 15.2.5
approximatus, Pissodes 24.113.171
apposita, Hemistilbia 27.75.446
Apreta 27.10.31
apricans, Buprestis 24.46.15
Aprionus 29.11.10
Apristus 24.4.161
Aproaerema 27.23.68
Aprosthema 25.4.4
Aprostocetus 25.26.47
Apsaphida 27.75.435
Apsena 24.87.133
Apsida 24.87.101
Apsilocephala 29.32.1
Apsilops 25.16.150
aptena, Tethymyia 29.24.88
Aptenobracon 25.13.4
Aptenopedes 11.5.104
Apteralipus 24.6.3
aptera, Myrmicodipnella 17.2.3
Apterencyrtus 25.25.71
Apterobittacus 28.1.1
Apterodryinus 25.51.19
Apterogyninae, supra 25.55.1
Apteroloma 24.21.1
Apterolophus 25.26.25
Apteromechus 24.113.266
Apterona 27.11.3
Apteronina 24.24.203
Apterothrips 22.4.20
apterum, Odontoxiphidium 11.7.22
apterus, Pyrrhocoris 20.8.1
Aptesini supra 25.16.135
Aptesis 25.16.147
Aptinothripina, supra 22.4.19
Aptinothrips 22.4.21
Aptopus 24.48.70
Apystomyia 29.40.32
Aquanirmus 18.1.5
aquatica, Cavariella 21.19.45
aquatica, Podura 1.1.1
aquilo, Agriades 27.43.52
aquilonius, Liobracon 25.13.16
aquivolans, Hydrophylita 25.28.3
Aracanthus 24.113.110
arachidis, Marava 13.3.5
arachne, Poladryas 27.46.12
Arachnis 27.73.43
Arachnocoris 20.18.4
Arachnophaga 25.24.6
Arachnophroctonus 25.60.27
Arachnospila 25.60.28
Aradidae, supra 20.13.1
Aradinae, supra 20.13.1
Aradophagus 25.43.30

Aradus 20.13.1
Araecerus 24.109.1
Araeocerus 24.24.77
Araeocorynus 24.109.2
Araeoderes 24.109.23
Araeodontia 24.67.8
Araeolepia 27.29.1
Araeopidae 21.2.1
Araeopidius 24.34.8
Araeopini, supra 21.2.6
Araeopteron 27.75.212
Araeoschizus 24.87.31
Aragnomus 24.113.83
aramatus, Psomus 24.113.280
Araptus 24.112.59
Araschnopsis 27.55.145
Araucaria Aphid 21.19.148
araucariae, Neophyllaphis 21.19.148
araucariae, Eriococcus 21.31.4
Aravaipa 29.105.348
Arawacus 27.43.30
Arawana 24.80.25
araxes, Pyrrhopyge 27.40.1
Arbelus 25.16.356
arborea, Brenda 21.14.10
Arborvitae Leaf Miner 27.31.1
Arborvitae Weevil 24.113.103
Archaecoccoidea, supra 21.22.1
Archaeocrypticinae, supra 24.87.168
Archaeognatha, supra 4.1.1
Archaeopsyllini, supra 30.1.3
Archanara 27.75.271
Archanarta 27.75.571
Archaphorura 1.3.3
Archenomus 25.25.19
Archepandemis 27.38.75
archeronta, Historis 27.46.42
Archiearinae, supra 27.61.1
Archiearis 27.61.1
Archilestes 7.9.1
Archilestris 29.37.20
Archilimnophila 29.2.30
archimedia, Palaeoaphis 21.19.158
Archimerus 20.4.11
Archimimus 29.103.22
Archimyia 29.29.5
Archipini, supra 27.38.70
archippus, Basilarchia 27.46.33 (Fig. 27.142)
Archips 27.38.74
Archipsocidae, supra 17.19.1
Archipsocopsis 17.19.2
Archipsocus 17.19.1
Archirhoe 27.61.211
Archisotoma 1.4.13
Archodontes 24.106.3
Archophileurus 24.30.111
Archostemata, supra 24.1.1
Archytas 29.105.91
arcigera, Schinia 27.75.601 (Fig. 27.402)
arctella, Anegecphalesis 27.55.308
Arctia 27.73.50
Arctic Butterfly Family 27.48.1
arctica, Ischyroceraea 25.7.94
arctica, Lederia 24.98.16
arctica, Miscodera 24.4.32
arcticus, Allomacrus 25.16.484
arcticus, Petridiobus 4.1.1
arcticus, Stethoncus 25.16.299
arctiella, Polopeustis 27.55.327
Arctiidae, supra 27.73.1
Arctiinae, supra 27.73.27
Arctini, supra 27.73.30
Arctoclinidium 24.2.2
Arctoconopa 29.2.57
Arctocorisa 20.35.8

Arctocorixa 20.35.8
Arctolimnophila 29.2.34
Arctonotus 27.70.35
Arctopora 26.10.12
Arctoperlaria, supra 8.1.1
Arctophila 29.47.46
Arctophyto 29.105.63
Arctopiophila 29.64.1
Arctoprlopia 29.24.20
Arctopsyche 26.4.1
Arctopsychinae, supra 26.4.1
Arctorthezia 21.22.2
Arctosyrphus 29.47.62
Arctotipula 29.2.9
arcuata, Corythycha 20.14.7
arcuata, Drepana 27.60.1 (Fig. 27.176)
arcuata, Euthycera 29.79.11
arculata, Peltoperla 8.6.1 (Fig. 8.9)
Arcynopteryx 8.7.5
Ardalus 25.26.16
ardens, Triscolia 25.56.7
Ardeicola 18.1.6
Ardeiphilus 18.6.4
Ardis 25.7.65
Ardistomis 24.4.29
arenaria, Disamara 24.4.94
arenaria, Halocoryza 24.4.26
arenaria, Leucolepisma 5.3.5
arenaria, Vespula 25.59.27 (Fig. 25.56)
arenarius, Misericoccus 21.25.25
Arenetra 25.16.311
Arenigena 29.32.4
Areniscythris 27.22.2
Arenivaga 14.4.1
Arenochroa 27.55.37
areolata, Chilostigmodes 26.10.32
areolata, Platypedia 21.13.21
areolata, Prolimnophila 29.2.33
Areolatae, supra 10.3.1
areolatus, Neonympha 27.48.5
Arequipa 27.55.206
ares, Emesis 27.44.6
Arescon 25.27.5
Arethaea 11.7.2
argante, Phoebis 27.42.14
Arge 25.4.1
argei, Winnemana 25.26.38
argentata, Lophocampa 27.73.56
argentata, Phryionis 27.61.67
argentata, Provia 27.75.438
argentatus, Athysanus 21.14.163
argentatus, Bootettix 11.5.31 (Fig. 11.14)
argentatus, Ophryastes 24.113.137
argenteola, Hologymnetis 24.30.123
argenteomaculatus, Sthenopis 27.4.1
argenteostriata, Hemigrotella 27.75.606
argenteus, Leptoremus 24.103.7
argenticoxa, Spalangiolaelaps 25.19.29
argentifasies, Perasis 29.37.25
argentifrons, Desmatoneura 29.40.36
argentilinea, Didugua 27.71.21
argentiliniella, Euprora 27.13.1
Argentine Ant 25.58.58
Argia 7.11.4
Argiacris 11.5.100
Argiallagma 7.11.5
Argid Sawfly Family 25.4.1
Argidae, supra 25.4.1 (Fig. 25.8)
argillacea, Alabama 27.75.72; 27.75.85
argillacea, Orgyia 27.74.3
argillaceella, Raphiptera 27.55.207
Argillophora 27.75.198
Arginae, supra 25.4.1
argiolus, Celastrina 27.43.42
Argochrysis 25.50.20
Argogorytes 25.62.81

Argopistes 24.107.159
Argoporis 24.87.132
Argoravinia 29.103.23
argus, Ernoneura 29.98.22
argus, Hydatophylax 26.10.28 (Fig. 26.30)
Argus Tortise Beetle 24.107.176
Argynninae, supra 27.46.7
Argyostrotis 27.75.145
Argyra 29.43.35
Argyractini, supra 27.55.16
Argyresthia 27.31.1
Argyresthiidae, supra 27.31.1
Argyria 27.55.221
Argyriini, supra 27.55.221
Argyrocoris 20.23.87
Argyrogramma 27.75.151
argyrognomon, Lycaeides 27.43.47
Argyrolacia 27.23.17
Argyropile 25.68.22
argyrospila, Archips 27.38.74
Argyrotaenia 27.38.71
argyrus, Anathrix 25.25.25
Arhaphe 20.9.4
Arhopalus 24.106.14
Arhopoideus 25.25.41
Arhyssus 20.6.2
Arianops 24.25.70
Ariciella 29.100.21
Aridia 21.11.12
arida, Boethoneura 25.16.457
arida, Janetschekbrya 1.5.5 ·
arida, Pseudomethia 24.106.31
arida, Psilopluera 29.105.167
Aridelus 25.13.148
aridifolia sinensis, Tenodera 14.1.10 (Figs. 14.9, 14.10)
Aridius 24.82.11
Arigomphus 7.3.9
Arigorytes 25.62.92
Arilus 20.17.12
aristale, Phasiostoma 29.105.309
aristalis, Ostracophyto 29.105.118
aristalis, Ptcyhoneura 29.103.11
Aristaria 27.75.12
aristidae, Edestosperma 29.11.63
aristodemus, Heraclides 27.41.6
Aristotelia 27.23.10
aristotliae, Cymodusopsis 25.16.408
Aritranis 25.16.153
Arivaca 27.55.418
Arizona Gold Beetle 24.107.177
Arizona Cotton Stainer 20.8.1
Arizona Net-winged Beetle 24.57.1
arizonae, Gryllita 11.10.8
arizonae, Physonota 24.107.177
arizonae, Pseudovates 14.1.13
arizonella, Martia 27.55.352
arizonella, Selga 25.55.391
arizonensis, Baileyothrips 22.4.23
arizonensis, Calephelis 27.44.2
arizonensis, Caphys 27.55.239
arizonensis, Carales 27.73.63
arizonensis, Eriocampidea 25.7.1
arizonensis, Hatchiana 24.56.6
arizonensis, Hubbardiella 25.26.58
arizonensis, Ichthyurus 24.56.2
arizonensis, Isonychus 24.30.79
arizonensis, Lycus 24.57.1
arizonensis, Montezuma 25.59.18
arizonensis, Odontocera 24.106.96
arizonensis, Opogona 27.10.50
arizonensis, Scambus 25.16.2
arizonensis, Schwarzella 25.21.3
arizonensis, Ululodes 23.15.2 (Fig. 23.15)
arizonica, Arawana 24.80.25
arizonica, Phoeniciomyia 29.105.259

arizonica, Riotila 26.7.13
arizonica, Simplona 24.25.38
arizonicus, Carphobius 24.112.19
arizonicus, Erethistes 24.113.236
arizonicus, Paraneossos 29.85.2
arizonicus, Pseudozelurus 20.17.28
arizonicus, Trachytropis 24.109.15
Arla 27.23.35
Armalia 24.87.15
armata, Morodora 25.19.62
armata, Odontella 1.217
armata, Oplonaeschna 7.4.10
armata, Psilophrys 25.25.123
armattus, Ctenophyllus 30.6.6
armatum, Moneilema 24.106.231
armatus, Eleodes 24.87.140
armicollis, Magdalis 24.113.197
armifera, Pristocera 25.48.1
armigera, Anasa 20.4.27
armipes, Sepedon 29.79.18
armitagei, Hexacnemus 25.25.136
armoraciae, Phyllotreta 24.107.114 (Fig. 24.233)
Armored Louse Family 19.6.1
Armored Mayfly Family 6.17.1
Armored Scale Insect Family, supra 21.38.1
Army Cutworm Moth 27.75.544
Armyworm Moth 27.75.499
arnobia phala, Thyrinteina 27.61.89
Aroga 27.23.59
Arogalea 27.23.25
Arogochila 25.68.20
arota, Tharsalea 27.43.2
Arotes 25.16.191
Arotrephes 25.16.96
Arpediothrips 22.4.22
Arpedium 24.24.107
Arphia 11.5.34
Arphnus 20.7.14
arpidia, Oscinoides 29.94.16
arranging collections 41
Arrhenodes 24.110.3
Arrhenodini, supra 24.110.3
Arrhenophagini, supra 25.25.61
Arrhenophagus 25.25.61
Arrhipis 24.52.10
Arrhopalites 1.7.3
Arta 27.55.256
Artace 27.68.4
Artaversala 27.5.8
artega, Lophoceramica 27.75.532
Artemisaphis 21.19.153
artemisiae, Cercopedius 24.113.95
artemisiae, Titanosiphon 21.19.213
artemisicola, Obtusicauda 21.19.153
Artemita 29.31.21
Arthaldeus 21.14.185
arthemis astyanax,
Basilarchia 27.46.33 (Fig. 27.141)
arthemis, Basilarchia 27.46.33 (Fig. 27.140)
Arthmius 24.25.65
Arthria 29.15.13
Arthroceras 29.289.5
Arthrocnodax 29.11.120
Arthrolips 24.79.10
Arthrolytus 25.19.111
Arthromacra 24.89.2
Arthroneura 29.40.20
Arthropeas 29.29.3
Arthroplea 6.6.9
Arthropleinae, supra 6.6.9
Arthropleona, supra 1.1.1
Arthropoda 10
Arthyroglossa 29.93.2
Artichoke Plume Moth 27.58.9

articulatus, Selenaspidus 21.38.78
artifex, Xylocopa 25.69.46 (Fig. 25.66)
artipennis, Chaetoplagia 29.105.156
Artipus 24.113.26
Artochia 24.24.108
Artogeia 27.42.5
artus, Prolatus 25.7.51
Arugisa 27.75.55
Arundanus 21.14.225
arundinariae, Geodiaspis 21.38.36
arundineus, Crumbana 21.14.209
arvalis, Axenus 27.75.386
Arvelius 20.3.55
Arytaina 21.17.25
Arytainini, supra 21.17.24
Asaphes 25.19.36
Asaphidion 24.4.66
Asaphocrita 27.17.13
Asaphomyia 29.26.2
Asarcopus 21.6.4
Asbolis 27.40.78
Ascalapha 27.75.112
Ascalaphidae, supra 23.15.1
Ascalaphinae, supra 23.15.2
ascalonicus, Myzus 21.19.144
Aschiza, supra 29.44.1
Ascia 27.42.6
Asciodes 27.55.175
Ascius 21.14.91
Asclera 24.97.6
Asclerini, supra 24.97.6
Ascogaster 25.13.112
Ascolicerus 24.48.61
Aseminae, supra 24.106.14
Asemini, supra 24.106.14
Asemobius 24.24.84
Asemoplus 11.5.99
Asemosyrphus 29.47.62
Asemum 24.106.16
Aseptis 27.75.285
Ash Borer 27.35.14
Ash Plant Bug 20.23.190
Ash Sphinx 27.70.4
Ash-gray Blister Beetle 24.101.14
Ash-gray Ladybird Beetle 24.80.40
Ash-gray Leaf Bug Family 20.10.1
ashcrafti, Guesibia 30.6.7
Ashlockaria 20.7.61
Ashmeadea 21.15.46
ashmeadiana, Trybliographa 25.32.6
Ashmeadiella 25.68.20
ashmeadii, Morsyma 25.55.6
Asiatic Garden Beetle 24.30.62
Asiatic Oak Weevil 24.113.138
Asiatic Red Scale 21.38.7
Asiconops 29.49.1
Asidina 24.87.56
Asidini, supra 24.87.46
Asidopsis 24.87.59
Asilidae, supra 29.37.1
Asilinae, supra 29.37.54
Asilini, supra 29.37.65
Asiloidea, supra 29.32.1
Asilomorpha 29.32.1
Asilus 29.37.74
Asindulum 29.9.5
asini, Haematopinus 19.3.1
Asiosphegina 29.47.49
Asiphonaphis 21.19.18
Asiracinae, supra 21.2.1
Asmeringa 29.93.45
Asobara 25.13.98
Asopinae, supra 20.3.64
Asopini, supra 20.3.65
asparagi, Brachycorynella 21.19.30
asparagi, Tetrastichus 25.26.46

Asparagus Beetle 24.107.11
Aspathines 24.85.2
Aspectus 24.61.5
Aspen Beetle, American 24.107.73
Aspen Leaf Beetle 24.107.64
asperagi, Crioceris 24.107.11 (Fig. 24.214)
asperatus, Sciaphilus 24.113.46
aspersa, Alexicles 27.73.40
asperta, Iscadia 27.75.175
aspericollius, Alniphagus 24.112.14
asperum, Megasenum 24.106.15
Asphaera 24.107.148
Asphinae, supra 25.19.36
Asphondylia 29.11.74
Asphondylliini, supra 29.11.73
Aspicerinae, supra 25.31.1
Aspidaphis 21.19.19
Aspidaphium 21.19.20
Aspidaspis 21.38.9
Aspidiella 21.38.10
aspidioticola, Arescon 25.27.5
Aspidiotiphagus 25.25.10
Aspidiotus 21.38.11
aspidistrae, Pinnaspis 21.38.64
Aspidoglossa 24.4.30
Aspidolea 24.30.99
aspilota 25.13.99
aspilus, Adicrophleps 26.9.2
Aspistes 29.15.12
Aspistinae, supra 29.15.12
Aspitates 27.61.81
Assassin Bug Family 20.17.1
Asseclamyia 29.105.132
assectator, Gasteruption 25.37.1
assectella, Acrolepiopsis 27.33.1
assimilis, Ceutorhynchus 24.113.292
assimilis, Helenomus 218.6.18
assimilis, Gryllus 11.10.10 (Fig. 11.44)
assimilis, Saprinus 24.26.15 (Fig. 24.61)
Assipala 29.26.10
associatus, Chlamydatus 20.23.38
Astala 27.11.7
astarte, Clossiana 27.46.11
Astata 25.62.35
Astatid Wasp, supra 25.62.34
Astatinae, supra 25.62.34
Astatini, supra 25.62.34
Asteia 29.73.5
Asteiid Fly Family, supra 29.73.1
Asteiidae, supra 29.73.1
Asteiinae, supra 29.73.5
Astenus 24.24.51
asteria, Diaethria 27.46.38
Asterolecaniidae, supra 21.35.1
Asterolecanium 21.35.1
Asterocampa 27.47.3
Asteromyia 29.11.67
Asthenesita 24.24.204
Asthenolabus 25.16.279
Asthenini, supra 27.61.234
Astichus 25.26.35
Asticta 27.75.78
Astictoneura 29.11.64
astictopus, Chaoborus 29.19.1
Astiosoma 29.73.3
Astiphromma 25.16.466
Astoneomyia 29.22.1
astraeus, Pachodynerus 25.59.19
Astraptes 27.40.13
Astromula 24.106.72
Astrophanes 29.40.46
Astrotus 24.87.46
astyalus, Heraclides 27.41.6
astyanax yucateca, Malagoniella 24.30.7
Astyleiopus 24.106.285
Astylidius 24.106.278

Astylis 27.71.39
asychis, Chiomara 27.40.34
Asydates 24.68.33
asymmetricus, Acrosothrips 22.5.26
asynamorus, Tachyeines 11.9.5 (Fig. 11.40)
Asynapta 29.11.40
Asynaptini, supra 29.11.36
Asynarchus 26.10.13
Asyndetus 29.43.34
Ataba 29.2.39
Atacta 29.105.364
Atactopsis 29.105.365
ataeniformis, Annegialia 24.30.16
Ataenius 24.30.23
atala, Eumaeus 27.43.11
atalanta, Vanessa 27.46.27
atalantata, Heterusia 27.61.223
Atalopedes 28.40.69
Atanus 21.14.132
Atanycolimorpha 25.13.28
Atanycolus 25.13.29
Atanygnathus 24.24.22
Atarsaphis 21.19.21
Atarsos 21.19.22
atascasus, Mexara 21.14.216
Atascosa 27.55.419
Ataxia 245.106.243
Ataxiini, supra 24.106.243
Ategumia 27.55.132
Ateleophadnus 25.16.2
Ateloglossa 29.105.64
Atelophus 11.7.28
Aster Leafhopper 21.14.97
ater, Ampeloglypter 24.113.311 (Fig. 24.296)
ater, Apinops 29.105.18
ater, Chlorops 29.94.50
ater, Dermestes 24.61.1
ater, Dufouriellus 20.21.24
ater, Pipunculus 29.48.5
ater, Thysanus 25.25.23
Aterpia 27.38.8
aterrima, Chimarra 26.1.1
Ateuchus 24.30.8
Athanatus 29.105.176
Atheas 20.14.4
Atheloca 27.55.304
Athericia Fly Family, supra 29.27.1
Athericidae, supra 29.27.1
Atherigona 29.100.4a
Atherix 29.27.1
Atheroides 21.19.123
Atheta 24.24.205
Atholus 24.26.36
Athous 24.48.31
Athrips 27.23.26
Athrycia 29.105.154
Athyrma 27.75.91
Athysanella 21.14.175
Athysanus 21.14.163
Atimia 24.106.18
Atimiini, supra 24.106.18
Atinus 24.25.82
Atissa 29.93.3
Atissini, supra 29.93.3
Atithasus 25.16.347
atlantica, Alloperla 8.8.1
atlantica, Cinara 21.19.53
Atlanticus 11.7.29, 11.7.39
atlanticus, Deilelater 24.48.12
atlantis, Speyeria 27.46.8
Atlenuipyga 21.14.2
Atlides 27.43.12
Atomacera 25.4.2
Atomacerinae, supra 25.4.2

Atomaria 24.74.12
Atomariinae, supra 24.74.10
Atomariini, supra 24.74.12
atomaris, Phoberia 27.75.96
atomarius, Hyidiothrips 22.5.48
Atomoscelis 20.23.33
Atomosia 29.37.54
Atomosiella 29.37.56
Atomosiini, supra 29.37.54
Atoposmia 25.68.19
Atopostigmus 25.62.26
Atopotrophos 25.16.55
Atopsyche 26.5.3
Atyphloceras 30.4.2
atra, Forbesomyia 29.11.20
atra, Galgupha 20.2.1
atra, Olinea 29.88.2
atra, Orsodacne 24.107.7 (Fig. 24.212)
Atrachelus 20.17.13
Atracodes 21.8.14
Atractelmis 24.45.5
Atractocerus 24.53.2
Atractodes 25.16.133
Atractothrips 22.5.2
Atractotomus 20.23.34
atramentalis, Pococera 27.55.266
Atranus 24.4.79
atrata, Bolbodimyia 29.26.13
atrata, Mordella 24.99.5
atratus, Hypoleschus 24.113.190
atratus, Tabanus 29.26.26
atratulus, Anergates 25.58.43
Atrecus 24.24.39
atriceps, Boreellus 29.101.6
Atrichomelina 29.79.1
Atrichopogon 29.23.2
atricornis, Pachypolia 27.75.424
atricornus, Elasmostethus 20.3.63
atripennis, Dahana 27.73.75
atripennis, Zacycloptera 11.7.46
Atriplicia 21.31.2
atriplicis, Hayhurstia 21.19.95
atrocaeruleus, Protopelmus 25.16.241
atrocyanea, Mesopeltita 25.19.33
atromarginata, Coleophora 27.18.1
Atropates 25.25.128
Atropetae, supra 17.1.1
Atropharista 29.105.122
Atrophopalpus 29.105.208
atrophopoda, Aravaipa 29.105.348
atrophopodoides, Vanderwulpia 29.105.215
atrox, Dasylechia 29.37.58
Atrytone 27.40.70
Atrytonopsis 27.40.79
Atrusca 25.34.31
Atta 25.58.55
Atta Ant Cockroach 14.6.8
Attacini, supra 27.69.14
Attagenini, supra 24.61.6
Attagenus 24.61.6
Attalus 24.68.11
Attalusinus 24.68.6
Attaneuria 8.9.2
Attaphila 14.6.8
Attaphilinae, supra 14.6.8
Attelabidae, supra 24.113.1
Attelabinae, supra 24.113.1
Attelabini, supra 24.113.2
attelaborum, Poropoea 25.28.10
Attelabus 24.113.3
Attenella 6.13.2
attenuatus, Chironomus 29.24.56
attenuatus, Neleothymus 25.16.439
attenuatus, Parallelostetus 24.48.44
Atteva 27.30.1
Attini, supra 25.58.51

Atylostagma 24.106.61
Atylotus 29.26.24
Atymna 21.15.44
atypica, Andrena 25.65.1
Auchenorrhyncha, supra 21.1.1 (Fig. 21.4)
Auchmobiini, supra 24.87.18
Auchmobius 24.87.18
audax, Tribolium 24.87.110
Aufeius 20.6.5
Augochlora 25.66.10
Augochorella 25.66.11
Augochlorini, supra 25.66.9
Augochioropsis 25.66.9
Augolychna 27.10.6
Augomonoctenus 25.6.2
augusta, Despaxia 8.4.1
augustus, Incisalia 27.43.29
Augyliini, supra 24.42.1
Aulacaspis 21.38.12
Aulacephalini, supra 29.105.49
Aulacid Wasp Family, supra 25.36.1
Aulacidae, supra 25.36.1
Aulacidea 25.34.15
Aulacigaster 29.71.1
Aulacigastrid Fly Family, supra 29.71.1
Aulacigastridae, supra 29.71.1
Aulacizes 21.14.40
Aulacorthum 21.19.24
Aulacoscelinae, supra 24.107.1
Aulacoscelis 24.107.1
Aulacros 25.53.18
Aulacus 25.36.2
Auletini, supra 24.113.4
Auletobius 24.113.4
Auleutes 24.113.287
Aulicus 24.67.17
Aulobaris 24.113.310
Aulocara 11.5.18
Aulogymnus 25.26.32
Aulonium 24.93.17
Aulonothroscus 24.49.3
Auplopus 25.60.11
aurantiacus, Machilinus 4.2.1
aurantiago, Rhodoecia 27.75.597
aurantii, Aonidiella 21.38.7
aurantii, Toxoptera 21.19.214
aurata, Danbara 21.14.131
aurata, Hemyda 29.105.25
auratus, Chrysochus 24.107.47
auratus, Diachus 24.107.27
aurea, Coryrhophora 27.13.9
aurea, Genea 29.105.218
aurea, Perlinoides 8.7.18
arueitarsus, Nipponentomon 2.3.4
aureonotata, Eremnophila 25.62.13
aureopilosus, Dynatopechus 24.113.384
aureoviridis, Ditropinotus 25.18.21
auretorum, Satyrium 27.43.16
aureum, Simulium 29.22.5
aureus, Heterotermes 15.3.2
auricephalus, Compsus 24.113.105
auricrinella, Epimartyia 27.1.1
auricinctaria, Melanomma 27.75.24
auricularia, Forficula 13.5.2 (Figs. 13.10, 13.11)
auriculata, Tingis 20.14.22
auriculatus, Capaneus 20.4.10
auriculatus, Scolobates 25.16.345
Auridius 21.14.181
aurifasciata, Fregatiella 18.6.16
aurifer, Polistes 25.59.28
auriferaria, Palyas 27.61.66
auripunctata, Chrysonotomyia 25.26.80
aurivillii, Notapictinus 20.13.9
aurocincta arizonensis,
 Odontocera 24.106.96

auropunctata, Ochetomyrmex 25.58.44
 (Fig. 25.44)
aurosparsella, Dyseriocrania 27.2.1
aurulenta, Buprestis 24.46.15
ausonia, Hoterodes 27.55.151
ausonides, Euchloe 27.42.8
australe, Enchemicrum 25.62.53
australasiae, Periplaneta 14.3.2
Australian Cockroach 14.3.2
Australian Dog Louse 18.3.1
Australian Spider Beetle 25.62.10
Australian-pine Borer 24.46.23
australis, Haldorus 21.14.210
australis, Isoneurothrips 22.4.43
austriaca, Vespula 25.59.27
Austrolimnophila 29.2.30
Austromenopon 18.6.5
Autalia 24.24.206
Autochton 27.40.14
Autographa 27.75.164
autographus, Dryocoetes 24.112.46
Automeris 27.69.8
Automola 29.62.2
Autoplusia 27.75.155
autumnalis, Episcopellus 24.4.125
autumnalis, Musca 29.100.58
Auxanommatidia 29.46.28
Auxopaedeutes 25.42.32
auxiliaris, Euxoa 27.75.544 (Fig. 27.392)
avalona, Strymon 27.43.34
Avaritia 29.23.5
avenae, Macrosiphum 21.19.122
Avetianella 25.25.105
avicenniae, Stenobaris 24.113.306
Avocado Whitefly 21.18.17
avulsus, Ips 24.112.51
Axelsonia 1.4.19
Axenus 27.75.386
Axestinus 24.106.65
Axima 25.20.10
Aximinae, supra 25.20.10
Axinicera 29.28.6
Axinopalpus 24.4.162
Axiolgina 29.58.26
Axion 24.80.22
Axylophilus 24.104.6
Axymyia 29.6.1
Axymyiid Fly Family 29.6.1
Axymyiidae, supra 29.6.1
Axymyiodea, supra 29.6.1
Axymyiomorpha, supra 29.6.1
Axysta 29.93.47
Aylax 25.34.13
Azana 29.9.59
Azalea Bark Scale 21.31.4
Azalea Lace Bug 20.14.20
Azalea Leaf Miner 27.14.1
Azalea Sphinx 27.70.40
Azalea Whitefly 21.18.15
azaleae, Eriococcus 21.31.4
azaleae, Pealius 21.18.15
azaleella, Caloptilia 27.14.1
Azelia 29.100.31
Azelinini, supra 27.61.86
Azenia 27.75.340
Azeta 27.75.86
Aztec Thread-waisted Wasp 25.62.14
azteca, Aidemona 11.5.111
azteca azteca, Ammophila 25.62.14
azteca, Gonolabis 13.1.1
azteca, Platylactisca 11.5.52
Aztecacria 11.5.112
Aztecarpalus 24.4.133
aztecula, Augochlora 25.66.10
azia, Tmolus 27.43.19
Azochis 27.55.158

Azotus 25.25.11
azureus, Allochares 25.60.30

B

babia 24.107.20
Babiini, supra 24.107.19
baboquivariensis, Supralathosea 27.75.437
Bacanius 24.26.25
Baccha 29.47.6
baccharis, Microsillus 29.105.375
bachmannii, Libytheana 27.41.1, 27.45.1
backi, Dichelonyx 24.30.81
Backomyia 29.37.44
Backswimmer 20.33.3
Backswimmer Bug Family, supra 20.33.1
Bactra 27.38.3
Bactridium 24.71.8
Bacunculinae 10.1.1
badia, Orgyia 27.74.3
badia, Prolimacodes 27.52.9 (Fig. 27.159)
badiiella, Tischeria 27.7.1
Badister 24.4.107
badius, Pogonomyrmex 25.58.24
Baeacis 25.13.67
baebarae, Thalassotrechus 24.4.46
Baechmanniolus 24.26.9
Baenotus 29.11.1
Baeocharis 25.25.116
Baeoctenus 29.24.124
Baeonotini, supra 29.11.1
Baeopterogyma 29.9.73
Baetidae, supra 6.4.1
Baetis 6.4.2
Baetisca 6.17.1
Baetiscidae 6.17.1
Baetodes 6.4.3
Baetoidea, supra 6.1.1
Baeus 25.43.26
Bagisara 27.75.223
Bagisarini, supra 27.75.223
Bagnalliella 22.5.32
Bagoini, supra 24.113.180
Bagous 24.113.181
Bagworm Moth Family, supra 27.11.1
Bahaman Swallowtail 27.41.6
baicalica, Parocalea 24.24.278
Baileya 27.75.172
Baileyothrips 22.4.23
Bairamlia 25.19.37
bairdii, Papilio 27.41.5
bait 34
bajula, Bajulata 21.15.32
BajulataєNM21.15.32
bajulus, Hylotrupes 24.106.102
Bakerella 21.2.13
bakeri, Byturus 24.84.2 (Fig. 24.151)
bakeri, Longipeltina 24.24.261
bakri, Nearctaphis 21.19.146
bakeri, Tetralophidea 25.25.158
Bakeriella 25.48.9
balanitis, Protexarnis 27.75.557
Balclutha 21.14.95
Balcluthini, supra 21.14.93
Baldfaced Hornet 25.59.27
baldiana, Teleiopsis 27.23.33
Baldulus 21.14.96
Baliosus 24.107.167
Baliothrips 22.4.35
Ballana 21.14.121
Ballella 20.23.88
balli, Pazu 21.14.204
balli, Tyndaris 24.46.31
ballii, Thripsaphis 21.19.210
Ballistura 1.4.12
Balsa 27.75.325

Balsam Fir Sawfly 25.6.4
Balsam-fir Sawyer 24.106.237
Balsam Gall Midge 29.11.117
Balsam Shootboring Sawfly 25.1.2
Balsam Twig Aphid 21.19.135
Balsam Woolly Adelgid 21.20.1
balteata, Diabrotica 24.107.90
balteata, Macrodiplax 7.7.14
Baltimore 27.46.23
baltimoralis, Bomolocha 27.75.38 (Fig. 27.324)
balyi, Geotrupes 24.30.52
Bamboo Powder-post Beetle 24.64.5
bambusae, Melanaphis 21.19.128
Bamona 24.24.207
Banana Aphid 21.19.163
Banana Root Borer 24.113.368
Banasa 20.3.53
Banchinae, supra 25.16.302
Banchini, supra 25.16.317
Banchus 25.16.320
BandaraєN21.14.130
Banded Alder Borer 24.106.98
Banded Cucumber Beetle 24.107.90
Banded Elfin 27.43.29
Banded Flesh Fly 29.103.2
Banded Greenhouse Thrips 22.4.5 (Fig. 22.4)
Banded Hairstreak 27.43.16
Banded Hickory Borer 24.106.150
Banded Long-horned Beetle 24.106.221
Banded Purple 27.46.33
Banded Sunflower Moth 27.39.1
Banded Tussock Moth 27.73.55
Banded Woollybear 27.73.34
Band-winged Grasshoppers 11.5.34
Band-winged Whitefly 21.18.17
Bandelia 27.75.81
Bandera 27.55.404
Banisia 27.56.7
banksi, Machiloides 4.2.2
banksianae, Conophthorus 24.112.63
banksii, Olixon 25.61.2
Banksiola 26.8.3
Baphala 27.55.377
Baptarma 27.75.594
Baptini, supra 27.61.65
Barbara 27.38.21
barbara, Oroperla 8.7.16
barbarus, Sternidocinus 24.106.288
barbata, Velocia 29.105.272
barbtus, Pogonomyrmex 25.58.24
barberella, Apachea 27.15.7
Barberia 27.55.410
barberi, Acerella 2.3.3 (Fig. 2.1)
barberi, Gastrotaphrus 24.113.161
barberi, Opheltes 25.16.342
barberi, Sympherobius 23.8.4
barberi, Yarmister 24.26.51
Barberiella 20.23.152
Barberpole Caterpillar Moth 27.55.44
Barber's Brown Lacewing 23.8.4
Barber's fluid 37
barbita, Magdalis 24.113.197
Barchyusa 24.24.212
barda carolina, Oxytaenia 25.16.149
barda, Tethida 25.7.57
Bareogonalos 25.47.4
Barichneumon 25.16.214
Baridina, supra 24.113.303
Baridinae, supra 24.113.303
Baridini, supra 24.113.303
Barilepsis 24.113.352
Barilepton 24.113.354
Barinus 24.113.353
Baris 24.113.303

Bark Beetle Family, supra 24.112.1
Bark Crevice Scale Insect Family, supra 21.30.1
Barklice 17.1.1
Barklike Longhorn 24.106.70
Barley Jointworm 25.20.3
Barnacle Scale 21.26.1
Barn's Tiger Moth 27.73.13
barnesii, Cisthene 27.73.13
barretti, Conwentzia 23.5.6
Barrovia 27.75.563
barryi, Mitoura 27.43.26
barthi, Psen 25.62.19
Baryceros 25.16.171
Barycnemis 25.16.447
Baryconus 25.43.6
Barylypa 25.16.377
Barynotini, supra 24.113.29
Barynotus 24.113.39
Barypeithes 24.113.44
Barypolynema 25.27.19
Barytarbes 25.16.348
Barytettix 11.5.110
Barythrips 22.5.3
basalis, Dysmerus 24.72.19
basalis, Elonus 24.104.3 (Fig. 24.174)
basalis, Hemiglyptus 24.107.138
basalis, Tetraopes 24.106.299
Basalys 25.42.26
basdeni, Drosophila 29.90.9
Basiaeschna 7.4.3
Basicerotini, supra 25.58.50
Basicladus 27.11.9
Basicondyla 29.11.57
basicornis, Ballella 20.23.88
basidactyla, Manoneura, 27.5.7
basifurca, Loicia 29.9.55
Basila 29.93.12
Basilarchia 27.46.33
basilaris, Catops 24.22.7 (Fig. 24.56)
basilaris, Harpalellus 24.4.132
basilaris, Scythris, 27.22.1
basilaris, Tenthredo 25.7.95
Basilia 29.107.1
Basilodes 27.75.356
basimaculatella, Baphala 27.55.377
Basolum 24.25.40
Bassareus 24.107.26
bassettella, Euclemensia 27.21.2
Bassettia 25.34.38
Basswood LaceBug 20.14.11
Basswood Leaf Miner 24.107.167
Basswood Leaf Roller 27.55.165
Bat Bug Family 20.19.1
Bat Flea Family, supra 30.5.1
Bat Fly Family, supra 29.108.1
batesi, Metaleptus 24.106.152
batesii, Phyciodes 27.46.20
Bathon 24.79.1
Bathroxena 27.10.5
bathyllus, Thorybes 27.450.16
Bathyplectes 25.16.404
Bathysciinae, supra 24.22.1
bathyscioides, Glacicavicola 24.19.17
Bathytrichina, supra 25.16.119
Bathythrix 25.16.119
Batia 27.15.26
Batrachedra 27.18.2
Batrachedrinae, supra 27.18.2
Batrachideinae, supra 11.1.5
Batriasymmodes 24.25.66
Batrisina, supra 24.25.65
Batrisini, supra 24.25.65
Batrisodes 24.25.67
batrisoides, Cercocerus 24.25.77
Battaristis 27.23.71

Battigrassiella 5.2.1
battoides, Euphilotes 27.43.44
Battus 27.41.3
Batuliini, supra 24.87.33
Batuliodes 24.87.34
Batulius 24.87.33
Batyle 24.106.157
baueri, Hemnypia 27.61.93
Bauluis 24.102.13
baumanni, Georeilla 26.10.45
bautias, Mallota 29.47.63
bayensis, Incisalia, f. 27.43.29
bazochii, Strymon 27.43.34
Beach Fly Family 29.97.1
Beaded Lacewing Family, Supra 23.11.1
Beamerella 20.23.35
beameri, Caloptognatha 24.57.4
beameri, Dictyssonia 21.6.15
beameri, Dikraneuroidea 21.14.76
beameri, Michenerula 25.66.6
beameri, Pseudocorixa 20.35.16
Beameria 21.13.8
Beameromyia 29.37.2
Bean Aphid 21.19.15
Bean Capsid 20.23.6
Bean Leaf Beetle 24.107.97
Bean Leafroller 27.40.12
Bean Leaf Skeletonizer 27.75.155
Bean Stalk Weevil 24.113.166
Bean Thrips 22.4.2
Bean Weevil 24.108.10
Bear Beetle 24.30.88
Beardsley Leafhopper 21.14.95
beardsleyi, Balclutha 21.14.95
beatifica, Whitneyomyia 29.26.25
Beaver Parasite 24.18.3
bebrycia, Strymon 27.43.34
Bebryx 29.100.39
bechteli, Listropygia 25.62.110
beckae, Pedionomus 29.24.73
beckerii, Pontia 27.42.4
Beckerina 29.46.15
beckii, Lepidosaphes 21.38.45
Beckerinini, supra 29.46.15
Beckocoris 20.23.36
Bed Bug 20.20.2
Bed Bug Family 20.20.1
bedardi, Aderaeon 25.16.60
bedeae, Waldheimia 25.7.72
Bedellia 27.13.3
Bee Fly Family, supra 29.40.1
Bee Louse 29.76.1
Bee Louse Fly Family, supra 29.76.1
Bee Parasite Family 24.105.2
Beech Blight Aphid 21.19.80
Beech Scale 21.30.1
Beech-tree Beetle Family, supra 24.51.1
Beeria 24.24.2
Bees, supra 25.1.1
Bee-wolf Wasp 25.62.106
Beet Armyworm Moth 27.75.326
Beet Leaf Beetle 24.107.83
Beet Leaf Miner 29.99.14
Beet Leafhopper 21.14.149
Beet Webworm 27.55.101
Beetles, supra 24.1.1
begga, Gorgythion 27.40.26
behavior 24
Behningidae, supra 6.8.1
Behrensia 27.75.461
behrii, Colias 27.42.11
behrii, Satyrium 27.43.16
belae, Didasys 27.73.86
Belandrena 25.65.1
Belaphotroctes 17.6.1
belfragei, Peploglyptus 24.26.33

belfragei, Protenor 20.5.1
belfragei, Pselaptus 24.25.54
belfragei, Pslenophorus 27.58.17
belialis, Procymbopteryx 27.55.28
bella, Euaresta 29.61.21
bella, Microsega 25.50.3
Bella Moth 27.73.27
bella, Nannothemis 7.7.18
bella, Saileria 20.23.121
bella, Utetheisa 27.73.27 (Fig. 27.281)
Bellamira 24.106.198
Bellardina 29.2.9
bellela, Nemophora 27.8.15
bellicosum, Daihiniella 11.9.16
bellicosus, Polistes 25.59.28
bellicus, Agraphus 24.113.96
bellona, Clossiana 27.46.11
bellula, Corythucha 20.14.7 (Fig. 20.36)
bellula, Menkeleon 23.14.4
Bellura 27.75.284
Belocephalus 11.7.17
Belochalcis 25.21.9
Belomicrus 25.62.54
Beloneura 8.9.3
Belonia 7.7.1
Belonochilus 20.7.10
Belonocnema 25.34.34
Belonoptera 27.56.4
Belonuchus 24.24.1
Belonura 25.19.94
Belopini, supra 24.87.39
Belosta 29.33.5
Belostoma 20.37.3
Belostomatidae, supra. 20.37.1
Belostomatinae, supra 20.37.2
Belotus 24.56.4
Belpharipus 25.62.63
Belted Skimmer Family 7.5.1
belti, Apsida 24.87.101
Beltranmyia 29.23.5
Belvosia 29.105.366
Belvosiini, supra 29.105.364
Belyta 25.42.11
Belytinae, supra 25.42.3
Bembecinus 25.62.97
Bembicini, supra 25.62.98
Bembidiini, supra 24.4.51
Bembidion 24.4.67 (Fig. 24.36)
Bembix 25.62.101
Bemisia 21.18.12
Benedictia 24.30.78
Bendisodes 27.75.115
benfica, Pseudoleucopis 29.83.7
benesimilis, Euplexia 27.75.286 (Fig 27.361)
Benjaminia 25.16.425
Benjaminiola 27.75.269
Bephratelloides, supra 25.20.16
Bephratoides 25.20.11
Bequaertomyia 29.25.2
Beraea 26.12.1
Beraeidae, supra 26.12.1
berberidis, Liosomaphis 21.19.115
bergii, Alatuncusia 27.55.23
Berginus 24.91.5
Bergmathothrips 22.4.24
bergrothi, Thes 24.82.12
Beridinae, supra 29.31.2
Beringotipula 29.2.9
Beris 29.31.4
Berkshiria 29.31.22
Berlese funnel 35
bermudensis, Conops 29.49.1
Berosinae, supra 24.12.10
Berosus 24.12.10
Berothidae, supra 23.11.1

Berothoidea, supra 23.10.1
Bertelia 27.55.290
Bertha Armyworm Moth 27.75.479
Bertholdia 27.73.72
Berytidae, supra 20.12.1
Berytinae, supra 20.12.6
Bertinus 20.12.7
besametsa, Prostoia 8.1.1 (Fig. 8.4)
Besbicus 25.34.30
Beskia 29.105.20
Besma 27.61.129
Bess Beetle 24.29.1
Bessaria 29.105.21
besselsi, Archisotoma 1.4.13
Bessobates 25.16.48
betae, Pegomya 29.99.14
betae, Smynthurodes 21.19.199
betheli, Oligotrophus 29.11.160
bethula, Desmona 26.10.27
bethunei, Diradops 25.16.316
Bethylid Wasp Family, supra 25.48.1
Bethylidae, supra 25.48.1
Bethylinae, supra 25.48.18
Bethylini, supra 25.48.18
Bethylus 25.48.18
betulae, Dryocoetes 24.112.46
Betulaphis 21.19.25
betularia Cognataria, Biston 27.61.58 (Fig. 27.181)
betulella, Acrobasis 27.55.282
Betuloxys 25.14.14
beutenmuelleri, Isochaetes 27.52.13
Beyeria 24.24.208
beyeri, Plusiotis 24.30.91
Bezzia 29.23.34
Bezzimyia 29.104.1
Biastini, supra 25.69.1
Bibarrambla 27.15.3
Bibio 29.8.4
Bibiocephala 29.3.2
Bibiodes 29.8.5
Bibionidae, supra 29.8.1
Bibioninae, supra 29.8.4
Bibionoidea, supra 29.8.1
Bibionomorpha, supra 29.7.1
bibitrix, Coenipeta 27.75.121
Biblical story 18
Biblis 27.46.40
Bibliplectus 24.25.27
Bibloporina, supra 24.25.19
Bibloporus 24.25.19
bicanalis, Bibloporus 24.25.19
bicarinata, Eulabis 24.87.135
bicarinata, Neopimpla 25.16.91
bicrinata, Prosierola 25.48.20
bicarinatum, Tetramorium 25.58.42
bicaudatus, Amphicerus 24.64.13
Bicellaria 29.42.50
biceps, Systelloderes 20.15.2
Bicilia 27.55.178
bicincta, Omphale 25.26.57
bicincta, Prosapia 21.12.1
biclavis, Howardia 21.38.41
bicolor, Anchytarsus 24.34.4
bicolor, Ancylocera 24.106.139
bicolor, Anurida 1.2.12
bicolor, Baeotenus 29.24.124
bicolor, Boreodromia 29.42.24
bicolor, Bryobiota 24.24.213
bicolor, Ectreperthoneura 29.9.77
bicolor, Eugonus 24.109.21
bicolor, Heteromydas 29.35.2
bicolor, Isonchia 6.1.7 (Fig. 6.5)
bicolor, Megischus 25.17.2
bicolor, Merhynchites 24.113.7 (Fig. 24.265)

bicolor, Metriona 24.107.186 (Fig. 24.249)
bicolor, Nanothrips 22.5.69
bicolor, Neoephemera 6.15.1
bicolor, Phydanis 24.107.146
bicolor, Rhopalothrips 22.5.63
bicolor, Sigalphus 25.13.111
bicolor, Spathizus 24.56.17
bicolor, Sphingicampa 27.69.3
bicolor, Trachyscelida 24.107.100
bicolor, Xamthochroina 24.97.16
bicolor, Xanthoepalpus 29.105.101
bicolor variegatum,
 Dactylotum 11.5.106 (Fig. 11.22)
bicoloripes, Antistrophoplex 25.18.22
bicoloripes, Paraleurocerus 25.25.47
bicoloripes, Williamsiella 22.5.76
bicornis, Bostrichocleurus 24.67.9
Bicyrtes 25.62.98
Biddie Family 7.2.1
Bidens Borer 27.38.27
bidens, Picomerus 20.3.76
Bidensomela 24.107.62
bidentata, Nerice 27.71.9
bidentatus compar, Campanulotes 18.1.8
bidenticulata, Agrenia 1.4.21
Bidessini, supra 24.7.7
Bidessonotus 24.7.9
Bidessus 24.7.11
Bidigitus 25.7.48
biedermani, Agenioideus 25.60.22
biedermani, Astylis 27.71.39
bifaria, Pollaclasis 24.55.15
bifascia, Prosapia 21.12.1
bifasciata, Amblyomia 20.4.7
bifasciata, Comperiella 25.25.93
bifasciata, Neocrania 27.2.4
bifasciata, Sostrata 27.40.27
bifasciatus, Alphitophagus 24.87.102
bifasciatus, Mefaderus 24.106.168
bifasciatus, Pseudocneorrhinus 24.113.140
bifasciatus, Xenostigmus 25.14.7
bifida, Argyrolacia 27.23.17
Bifidungulus 20.23.89
bifidus, Helocombus 24.12.23
biflarimaculella, Monopis 27.10.41 (Fig.
 27.26)
biformis, Chestomorpha 25.25.132
biformis, Furcaspis 21.38.33
bifurea, Tylaniura 21.6.20
Big Green Darner 7.4.2
Big Green Pine-tree Katydid 11.7.49
Big Poplar Sphinx 27.70.18
Bigeyed Bug 20.7.18
Big-head Ant 25.58.28
Big-headed Fly Family, supra 29.48.1
bigittatus, Endomychus 24.81.17 (Fig.
 24.149)
Bigonicheta 29.105.133
Bigotomyia 29.100.45
biguttatus biguttatus, Episyron 25.60.24
biguttatus, Ceratographis 24.106.272
biguttatus, Rasahus 20.17.26
bilineata, Hexagenia 6.11.2
bilineata, Isoperla 8.7.2
bilineata, Willistonina 29.37.17
bilineatum, Gonocephalum 24.87.162
bilineatus, Agrilus 24.46.34
biloba, Afeda 27.21.22
bilobatus, Remenus 8.7.20
bimacula, Trichocera 29.13.2
bimaculata, Anabolia 26.11.1 (Fig. 26.26)
bimaculata, Cosmopepla 20.3.41 (Fig.
 20.11)
bimaculata, Oberea 24.106.297
bimaculata, Thelia 21.15.348
bimaculatus, Atithasus 25.16.347

bimaculatus, Bombus 25.70.2
bimaculatus, Goniocloeus 24.109.16
bimaculatus, Lemellus 21.14.190
bimaculatus, Mellinus 25.62.70
bimaculatus, Molorchus 24.106.94 (Fig.
 24.190)
bimaculatus, Tylonotus 24.106.49 (Fig.
 24.182)
bimaculipennis, Idiomacromerus 25.18.12
Binodoxys 25.14.15
binotata, Enchenopa 21.15.8
binotatus, Stenotus 20.23.186
biocellata, Adicroneura 29.9.61
Biocrypta 24.24.52
bioculatus, Perillus 20.3.68 (Fig. 20.15)
biome 26,27 (Table 4.2)
Biomorphus 24.87.76
Biorbitella 29.94.4
Biosteres 25.13.86
Biosterina, supra 25.13.86
Biotus 24.25.83
Bipersona 21.19.26
Biphyllidae, supra 24.83.1
biplagiatus, Cyllodes 24.70.30
bipunctalis, Herpetogramma 27.55.179
bipunctata, Adalia 24.80.38
bipunctata, Arthroplea 6.6.9
bipunctata, Ceropales 25.60.34
bipunctata, Ochleroptera 25.62.80
bipunctata, Saperda 24.106.296
bipunctata, Tetyra 20.3.1
bipunctatus, Rhizophagus 24.71.1 (Fig.
 24.136)
bipunctella, Aetia 27.20.3
bipunctella, Numata 27.23.11
bipustulata, Phyllotreata 24.107.114 (Fig.
 24.234)
Birch Bark Beetle 24.112.46
Birch Casebearer 27.18.1
Birch Leafminer 25.7.52
Birch Sawfly 25.4.1
Birch Tube Maker 27.55.282
Bird Flea Family, supra 30.7.1
Bird Lice Family 18.1.1
Bird Nest Barklice Family 17.3.1
birectalis, Epitamyra 27.55.252
Birka 25.7.5
birkmanni, Agenioideus 25.60.22
bisecta, Sphingicampa 27.69.3 (Fig.
 27.216)
Biselachista 27.16.6
bisetosus, Matsucoccus 21.23.2
bisonia, Stictocephala 21.23.2
bisonia, Stictocephala 21.15.24
bispina, Schizoptera 20.25.3
bisselliella, Tineola 27.10.45, see
 also 27.10.37
Bistica 27.75.344
bistriaris, Parallelia 27.75.135
bistriatella, Apomyelois 27.55.295
bistriatus, Rhinoscepsis 24.25.9
bistrigella, Phylloporia 27.8.5
Biston 27.61.58
Bistonini, supra 27.61.58
bisulcatus, Protachys 24.4.57
Bithoracochaeta 29.100.3
Biting House Fly 29.100.61
Biting Midge Family, supra 29.23.1
Bitoma 24.93.9
Bittacidae, supra 28.1.1
Bittacomorphella 29.17.2
Bittacomorpha 29.17.3
Bittacomorphinae, supra 29.17.2
Bittacus 28.1.2
Bius 24.87.77
bivittata, Acanalonia 21.7.1

bivittata, Agroiconota 24.107.181
bivittata, Taranomis 24.106.142
bivittatus, Melanoplus 11.5.94
Bizarre Caddisfly Family, supra 26.11.1
Blaberidae, supra 14.6.1
Blaberinae, supra 14.6.1
Blaberoidea, supra 14.4.1
Blaberus 14.6.1
Blacinae, supra 25.13.130
Blacini, supra 25.13.130
Black Army Cutworm Moth 27.75.558
Black Blister Beetle 24.101.14
Black Blow Fly 29.101.5
Black Cactus Longhorn 24.106.231
Black Carpenter Ant 25.58.66
Black Carpet Beetle 24.61.6
Black Cherry Aphid 21.19.144
Black Cherry Fruit Fly 29.61.44
Black Citrus Aphid 21.19.214
Black Cutworm Moth 27.75.535
Black Deer Fly 29.26.11
Black Earwing Family 13.4.1
Black Elm Bark Weevil 24.113.197
Black Fly Family, supra 29.22.1
Black Fungus Beetle 24.87.115
Black Grain Stem Sawfly 25.12.6
Black Horse Fly 29.26.26
Black Imported Fire Ant 25.58.33
Black Lady Beetle 24.80.30
Black Larder Beetle 24.61.1
black lights 33
Black Peach Aphid 21.19.28
Black Pineleaf Scale 21.38.56
Black Salt Marsh Mosquito 29.20.9
Black Scale 21.26.20
Black Scavenger Fly Family, supra 29.81.1
Black Soldier Fly 29.31.12
Black Swallowtail 27.41.5
Black Thread Scale 21.38.42
Black Twig Borer 24.112.55
Black Vine Weevil 24.113.68
Black Walnut Curculio 24.113.238
Black and White Click Beetle 24.48.9
Black and White Cuckoo Bee 25.69.8
Black Witch 27.75.112
Black and Yellow Mud Dauber 25.62.7
Black-banded Hadena 27.75.258
Black-bellied Clerid 24.67.1
Black-headed Fireworm 27.38.40
Black-horned Pine Borer 24.106.106
Black-horned Tree Cricket 11.10.19
Black-tailed Bee Fly Family 29.40.11
Black-tipped Hangingfly 28.1.3
Black-wing 7.8.1
Blackberry Skeletonizer 27.34.5
Blackfaced Leafhopper 21.14.220
Blackheaded Ash Sawfly 25.7.57
Blackheaded Budworm 27.38.61
Blackheaded Pine Sawfly 25.6.4
Blackmargined Aphid 21.19.137
Blacus 25.13.130
Bladus 24.48.35
Blaesodiplosis 29.11.135
Blaesoxipha 29.103.24
blaisdelli, Clytus 24.106.125
blaisdelli, Lupinicolus 24.113.102
Blaisdelliana 24.80.11
blakeae, Anolisimyia 29.103.21
blakeae, Keitheatus 24.107.103
blanchardae, Mojaviodes 27.55.50
blanchardi, Opsigalea 27.75.467
blanchardi, Parlatoria 21.38.62
blanchardi, Sphingicampa 27.69.3
blanda, Systena 24.107.121 (Fig. 24.235)
blandii, Menkokia 25.16.218
Blantonia 29.23.3

blantoni, Macropeza 29.23.29
Blaps 24.87.139
Blapsitinus 24.87.152
Blapticus 25.16.493
Blaptini, supra 24.87.139
blarinae, Doratopsylla 30.4.22
blassus, Haymatus 25.7.83
Blaste 17.23.2
Blastobasid Moth Family, supra 27.17.1
Blastobasidae, supra 27.17.1
Blastobasinae, supra 27.17.6
Blastobasini 27.17.6
Blastobasis 27.17.6
Blastobasoides 27.17.7
Blastodacne 27.20.1
Blastodacninae, supra 27.20.1
Blastodacnini, supra 27.20.1
Blastophaga 25.18.1
Blastopsocus 17.23.3
Blastothrix 25.25.52
Blatta 14.3.1
Blattaria, supra 14.2.1 (Fig. 14.13)
Blatchleya 24.56.19
Blattella 14.5.1
Blattellidae, supra 14.5.1
Blattellinae, supra 14.5.1
Blattidae, supra 14.3.1
Blattinae, supra 14.3.1
Blattoidea, supra 14.2.1
Blauta 24.48.21
Blapylis 24.87.140
Bledionotinae, supra 20.7.20
Bledius 24.24.144
Blennocampinae, supra 25.7.54
Blennocampini, supra 25.7.64
Blennogeneris 25.7.54
Blephartcpium 29.37.6
Blepharhymenus 24.24.209
Blepharicera 29.3.3
Blephariceridae, supra 29.3.1
Blephariceroidea, supra 29.3.1
Blephariceromorpha, infra 29.3.1
Blepharida 24.107.145
Blepharidopterus 20.23.90
Blcpharipa 29.105.370
Blepharocerus 27.55.259
Blepharomastix 27.55.144
Bleptina 27.75.9
Blepyrus 25.25.130
Blera 29.47.75
Blethisa 24.4.19
Blind Springtail Family, supra 1.3.1
Blissinae, supra 20.7.16
Blissus 20.7.16
Blister Beetle Family, supra 24.101.1
Blister Coneworm 27.55.339
Blitophaga 24.31.8
blondeli, Trachykele 24.46.11
Blondelia 29.105.235
Blondeliini, supra 29.105.230
Bloodsucking Conenose 20.17.39
Blow Flies, supra 29.102.3
Blow Fly 29.101.18
Blow Fly Family, supra 29.101.1
Blue Butterfly Family 27.43.1
Blue Cactus Borer 27.55.380
Blue Horntail 25.9.1
Blue Milkweed Beetle 24.107.47
Blue Mud Dauber 25.62.4
Blue Mud Wasp 25.62.6
Blueberry Case Beetle 24.107.34
Blueberry Flea Beetle 24.107.127
Blueberry Maggot 29.61.44
Blueberry Thrips 22.4.41
Blueberry Tip Midge 29.11.108
Bluegrass Billbug 24.113.366

Bluegrass Webworm 27.55.203
Blunt-nosed Cranberry Leafhopper 21.14.165
Boarmiini, supra 27.61.18
Bocchus 25.51.6
bocha, Crassivesica 27.75.553
Body Louse 19.8.1
Body Louse Famiy 19.8.1
Boernerina 21.19.27
Boernerinella 21.19.27
Boethoneura 25.16.457
Boethus 25.16.64
Boettcheria 29.103.25
Bogus Yucca Moths 27.8.11
Bohartia 29.37.37
bohemani, Monosynamma 20.23.54
Boisduval Scale 21.38.25
boisduvaliana, Eurema 27.42.17
boisduvalli, Diaspis 21.38.25
Bolbelasmus 24.30.50
Bolboceras 24.30.45
Bolbocerastes 24.30.49
Bolbocerosoma 24.30.46
Bolbodimyia 29.26.13
Bolbomyia 29.28.2
Bolborhombus 24.30.48
bolcan, Eleodimorpha 24.87.144
Boletina 29.9.41
Bolitobius 24.24.175
Bolitochara 24.24.210
Bolitophagini, supra 24.87.67
Bolitophagus 24.87.68
Bolitophila 29.9.1
Bolitophilinae, supra 29.9.1
Bolitotherus 24.87.67
Bolla 27.40.24
bolliana, Arenivaga 14.4.1 (Fig. 14.177)
bolliana, Gretchena 27.38.35
bollii bollii, Eumenes 25.59.24
Boll's Sand Cockraoch 14.4.1
bollworm 27.75.599
Bolomyia 29.105.371
Boloria 27.46.10, 27.46.12
Bolothrips 22.5.4
Bolotoperla 8.2.1
Bolshecapnia 8.3.2
bolteri, Abraeus 24.26.1
bolteri, Tracheops 27.61.50
Bolteria 20.23.142
Bombardier Beetle 24.4.4
BombiasALLA 25.70.2
bombiformis, Ptilothrix 25.69.18
Bombinae, supra 25.70.1
Bombini, supra 25.70.2
Bomblyiidae, supra 29.40.1
bomboidea, Pocota 29.47.90
Bombus 25.70.2
Bombycidae, supra 27.67.1
bombycina, Phanagenia 25.60.10
Bombycoidea, supra 27.66.1
bombylans, Volucella 29.47.41
Bombyliinae, supra 29.40.8
Bombyliomyia 29.105.82
Bombyliopsis 29.105.83
Bombylioidea 29.32.1, 29.38.1
Bombylius 29.40.11
Bombyx 27.67.1
Bomolocha 27.75.38
bonasia, Callicentrus 21.15.3
Bonchis 27.55.254
Bondia 27.26.2
boneti, Bonetrura 1.4.11
Bonetrura 1.4.11
bonhotei, Heraclides 27.41.6
bonifatella, Tehama 27.55.217
boninsis, Dysmicoccus 21.15.16
Bonnetia 29.105.104

bonnevillensis, Brachyungius 21.19.32
Bonneyana 21.14.114
Bonomiella 18.6.6
book dealers, 51 (Table 5.4)
Booklice 17.1.1
Booklouse 17.6.3
Booklouse Family 17.6.1
Boopedon 11.5.20
Boopidae, supra 18.3.1
boops, Myiocephalus 25.13.155
Bootettix 11.5.31
boothii, Colias 27.42.11
bonvouloiri, Microctenochira 24.107.188
boralis, Helicopsyche 26.16.1
Borboridea 29.31.23
Borborillus 29.88.2
Borboropora 24.24.211
Borboropsis 29.84.4
Bordeades 24.70.2
boreale, Hopolsphyrum 11.10.5
borealis, Apolphus 25.16.293
borealis, Brachionycha 27.75.429
borealis, Brunneria 14.1.11
borealis, Calephelis 27.44.2 (Fig. 27.116)
borealis, Corynothrix 1.5.1
borealis, Cyclocephala 24.30.100
borealis, Epilachna 24.80.52 (Fig. 24.148)
borealis, Leurus 25.16.294
borealis, Metretopus 6.2.1
borealis, Trichochlamys 29.84.23
Boreaphilus 24.24.109
Boreellus 29.101.6
Boreidae, supra 28.2.1
Boreinae, supra 28.2.2
bore, Oeneis 27.48.13
Boreocanthon 24.30.3
Boreochus 29.24.4
Boreocoelioxys 25.68.24
Boreoheptagyia 29.24.33
Boreochlini, supra 29.24.2
Boreodromia 29.42.24
Boreogalba 25.14.13
Boreus 28.2.2
Borophaga 29.46.8
Boros 24.90.3
Boriomyia 23.8.6
Borkhausenia 27.15.33
borrichia, Cecidocharella 29.61.8
borrowi, Diaulomorpha 25.26.6
Borrowing Water Beetle Family,
 supra 24.8.1
Boryzops 27.75.107
bosqueella, Stegasta 27.23.63
Bostaera 21.2.14
Bostrichidae, supra 24.64.1
Bostrichiformia, supra 24.59.1
Bostrichinae, supra 24.64.9
Bostrichini, supra 24.64.10
Bostrichoclerus 24.67.9
Bostrichoidea, supra 24.62.1
Bostrichus 24.64.10
bostoni, Aniferella 21.19.10
Bostrycholites 24.64.12
bostrychophilus, Liposcelis 17.6.3 (Fig.
 17.4)
Bot Fly Family, supra 29.102.1
Botanophila 29.99.8
Bothrideres 24.93.25
Bothriderinae, supra 24.93.22
Bothriderini, supra 24.93.25
Bothriocera 21.1.10
Bothriocerini, supra 21.1.11
Bothriocraera 25.25.53
Bothriophorini, supra 24.43.6
Bothriothoracini, supra 25.25.62
Bothriothorax 25.25.62

Bothriovulsus 1.7.10
Bothromus 25.16.292
Bothroscelis 24.107.2
Bothrosternini, supra 24.112.1
Bothrotes 24.87.4
Bothynostethini, supra 25.62.52
Bothynostethus 25.62.52
Bothynotus 20.23.9
Bothynus 24.30.104
Botocudo 20.7.33
Botrodus 24.78.5
bottimeri, Algarobius 24.1087.11
Boucekiella 25.25.72
Bourletiella 1.7.6
bourreriae, Dendrosinus 24.112.8
Bouvieromyiini, supra 29.26.8
Bovicola 18.2.1
bovis, Bovicola 18.2.1 (Fig. 18.3)
bovis, Hypoderma 29.102.5
bowreyi, Pseudischnaspis 21.38.70
box 42
Box Elder Leaf Roller 27.14.1
Boxelder Aphid 21.19.165
Boxelder Bug 20.6.8 (Fig. 20.26)
Boxelder Psyllid 21.17.27
Boxelder Twig Borer 27.38.32
Boxwood Leaf Miner 29.11.109
Boxwood Psyllid 21.17.27
Boyeria 7.4.4
bozemanii, Phyllocolpa 25.7.34
brachialis, Bruchus 24.108.15
Brachiacantha 24.80.17
Brachicoma 29.103.15
Brachineura 29.11.72
Brachinini, supra 24.4.4
Brachinitae, supra 24.4.4
Brachinus 24.4.4
Brachionycha 27.75.429
Brachistes 25.13.136
Brachistini, supra 25.13.134
Brachmia 27.23.83
Brachyacma 27.23.84
Brachybamus 24.113.184
Brachycara 29.31.13
Brachycaudonia 25.19.40
Brachycaudus 21.19.28
Brachycentridae, supra 26.9.1
Brachycentrus 26.9.3
Brachycepsis 24.20.10
Brachycera, supra 29.25.1
Brachyceratocoris 20.23.37
Brachycercus 6.16.1
brachychaeta, Uroleucon 21.19.219
Brachycistellus 25.53.14
Brachycistidinae, supra 25.53.9
Brachycistina 25.52.12
Brachycistis 25.53.9
Brachycolus 21.19.29
Brachyconops 29.23.1
Brachycoryna 24.107.170
Brachycorynella 21.19.30
Brachycyrtini, supra 25.16.46
Brachycyrtus 25.16.46
Brachydella 21.14.175
Brachyderinae, supra 24.113.23
Brachyderini, supra 24.113.43
Brachydeutera 29.93.52
Brachygastra 25.59.30
Brachygluta 24.25.48
Brachyglutina, supra 24.25.45
Brachyglutini, supra 24.25.45
Brachylampis 24.55.17
Brachyleptura, supra 24.106.172,
 24.106.225
Brachylimnophila 29.2.34
Brachylinga 29.32.11

Brachylomia 27.75.425
Brachymelecta 25.69.40
Brachymelissodes 25.69.27
Brachymeria 25.21.12
Brachymeriinae, supra 25.21.9
Brachymesia 7.7.2
Brachymyrmecini, supra 25.58.65
Brachymyrmex 25.58.65
Brachynemurini, supra 23.14.2
Brachynemurus 23.14.2
Brachynotocoris 20.23.91
Brachyogmus 24.113.202
Brachyopa 29.47.50
Brachyopini, supra 29.47.48
Brachypalpus 29.47.88
Brachypanorpa 28.5.1
Brachypeplus 24.70.8
Brachypeza 29.9.24
Brachypogon 29.23.9
Brachyponera 25.58.14
Brachypremna 29.2.3
Brachypsectra 24.37.1
Brachypsectridae, supra 24.37.1
brachyptera, Pseudopomala 11.5.24
Brachypterinae, supra 8.2.1
brachypteris, Areniscythris 27.22.2
Brachypterolus 24.70.4
Brachypteromyia 29.106.3
Brachypterus 24.70.3
Brachys 24.46.37
Brachyscelidiphaginae, supra 25.19.6
Brachyserphus 25.39.8
Brachysiphym 21.19.31
Brachysomida 24.106.191
Brachysomus 24.113.47
Brachystola 11.4.7
Brachystolini, supra 11.4.7
Brachystoma 29.42.20
Brachystomatinae, supra 29.42.19
Brachystomella 1.2.13
Brachystylus 24.113.98
Brachythops 25.7.9
Brachyufens 25.28.6
Brachyungius 21.19.32
Bracon 25.13.30
Braconid Family, supra 25.13.1
Braconidae, supra 25.13.1
Braconinae, supra 25.13.28
bractatus, Halticus 20.23.83 (Figs. 20.51,
 20.52)
bracteatan, Cydia 27.38.56
bradleyi, Agathilla 25.16.318
bradleyi, Atractothrips 22.5.2
bradleyi, Hirmoneura 29.39.1 (Fig. 29.34)
bradleyi, Setvena 8.7.21
Bradybatini, supra 24.113.214
Bradycellus 24.4.115
Bradycinetulus 24.30.47
Bradynotes 11.5.101
Bradysia 29.10.12
Bradyrhyncoides 24.113.37
Braggia 21.19.33
branchialis, Episcirrus 24.113.272
Branchus 24.87.63
Brasiella 24.3.4
brasiliensis, Picturaphis 21.19.169
brassicae, Alloxysta 25.33.2
brassicae, Brevicoryne 21.19.34
brassicae, Hylemya 29.99.8
brassicae, Liriomyza 29.68.8
brassicae, Trichoplusia 27.75.152 (Fig.
 27.340)
Brathininae, supra 24.24.140
Brathinus 24.24.140
Braula 29.76.1
Braulidae, supra 29.76.1

brauneata, Quandara 27.75.33
braythripoides, Eschatothrips 22.5.38
Brechmorhoga 7.7.3
bredowii, Adelpha 27.46.34
breeding population 18
Bremia 29.11.90
Brenda 21.14.10
Brennania 29.26.3
Brenthia 27.36.2
Brenthidae, supra 24.110.1
Brenthiinae, supra 27.36.2
Brenthinae, supra 24.110.1
Brenthini, supra 24.110.1
Brenthus 24.110.1
Brephidium 27.63.37
brephoides, Leucobrephos 27.61.2
Brepholoxa 20.3.59
Brevennia 21.25.6
Brevibarra 24.109.13
brevicauda, Eucapnopsis 8.3.4
brevicauda, Papilio 27.41.5
brevicaudis, Colyostichus 25.18.2
brevicephalus, Esthiopterum 18.1.24
brevicollis, Acentrinops 24.113.333
brevicollis, Malacocis 24.92.11
brevicollis, Neothrips 22.5.14
brevicollis, Tetralophiellus 25.25.157
brevicomis, Dendroctonus 24.112.11
brevifrons, Hesperinus 29.8.1
brevicornis, Corinthomyia 29.11.8
brevicornis, Sphyracephala 29.56.1
brevicornis, Pseudephalus 24.87.165
brevicornis, Metaleptea 11.5.33
brevicornis, Exallonyx 25.39.12
Brevicornu 29.9.31
Brevicoryne 21.19.34
brevirostris, Leskiella 29.105.220
brevirostris, Pseudosiphona 29.105.310
brevipennis, Bessaria 29.105.21
brevipennis, Emesaya 20.17.3
brevipennis, Megacheuma 24.106.117
brevipennis, Nathrius 24.106.93
Breviperna 29.32.22
brevipes, Daihinia 11.9.17
brevipes, Dysmicoccus 21.25.16
brevipes, Parastasia 24.30.86
brevis brevis, Megachile 25.68.22
brevis, Paradmontia 29.105.147
brevis, Steirastoma 24.106.267
Breviscapus 29.12.13
brevistylis, Petrobius 4.1.4 (Fig. 4.1)
brevistylus, Hagenius 7.3.4 (Fig. 7.4)
Brevitrichia 29.33.2
brevivittella, Mompha 27.19.1
Briaraxia 24.25.50
Brillia 29.24.207
brillians, Eupseudomorpha 27.75.246
brillians, Harrisina 27.50.1
brimleyi, Rhodesiella 29.94.17
Bristletails 4.1.1
Bristly Cutworm Moth 27.75.494
Bristly Roseslug 25.7.15
britannicus, Dynaspidiotus 21.38.27
Broad nosed Grain Weevil 24.113.380
Broad-headed Bug Family 20.5.1
Broad-horned Flour Beetle 24.87.106
Broad-necked Root Borer 24.106.10
Broad-winged Damselfly Family 7.8.1
Broad-winged Katydid 11.7.6
Broadbean Weevil 24.108.15
Brochella 29.42.35
Brochymena 20.3.25
Broken Dash 27.40.67
Broken-lioned Giant Chafer 24.30.66
Bromegrass Seed Midge 29.11.108
bromeliae, Diaspis 21.38.25

bromeliae, Sclerosococcus 21.35.4
Bromeloecia 29.88.3
bromicola, Contarinia 29.11.108
Bromius 24.107.55
Bromleyus 29.37.29
Bronze Apple Tree Weevil 24.113.197
Bronze Birch Borer 24.46.34
Bronze Copper 27.43.5
Bronze Leaf Beetle 24.107.27
Bronze Tiger Beetle 24.3.4
Bronze Underwing 27.75.148
Bronzed Cutworm 27.75.512
Brooksetta 20.23.92
Broscodera 24.4.33
Broscini, supra 24.4.32
Broscitae, supra 24.4.32
Brothylus 24.106.51
brousi, Adetus 24.106.241
Brown Chafer 24.30.85
Brown Chicken Louse 18.1.28
Brown Citrus Aphid 21.19.214
Brown Cockroach 14.3.2
Brown Cotton Leafworm 27.75.220
Brown Elfin 27.63.23
Brown House Moth 27.15.35
Brown Lacewing Family, supra 23.8.1
Brown Salt Marsh Mosquito 29.20.9
Brown Soft Scale
Brown Spider Beetle 24.62.10
Brown Stink Bug 20.3.34
Brown Tachinid 29.105.92
Brown-banded Cockroach 14.5.10
Brownheaded Ash Sawfly 25.7.56
Brownheaded Jack Pine Sawfly 25.6.4
Brown-hooded Cockroach Family 14.2.1
browni, Eretmoptera 29.24.87
browni, Galeruca 24.107.86
Brown-tailed Moth 27.74.6
bruceata, Operophtera 27.61.238 (Fig.
 27.201)
Bruceia 27.73.19
Bruce's Spanworm 27.61.238
bruchi 24.87.62
Bruchidae, supra 24.108.1
Bruchidius 24.108.16
Bruchinae, supra 24.108.5
Bruchiurosigalphus 25.13.140
bruchivora, Stenocorse 25.13.27
Bruchomorpha 21.6.2
Bruchomyiinae, supra 29.12.3
Bruchophagus 25.20.21
Bruchus 24.108.15
Brucita 24.107.82
Bruelia 18.1.7
bruesi, Tylothrips 22.5.75
Bruesiella 25.53.19
Bruesopria 25.42.34
Bruggmannia 29.11.77
brumalis, Boreus 28.2.2 (Fig. 28.4)
brumalis, Oldenbergiella 29.84.5
brumata, Operophtera 27.61.238
Brumoides 24.80.26
brunnea, Climaciella 23.7.5
brunnea, Colaspia 24.107.43 (Fig. 24.222)
brunnea, Comacmaeops 24.106.184
brunnea, Ephyriades 27.40.36
brunnea, Eutrilia 24.79.5
brunnea, Periplaneta 14.3.2
brunnea, Phryganeopsis 27.10.24
brunnea, Pseudhapigia 27.71.40
brunnea, Rhabdocephala 21.3.7
brunneicornis, Pleroneura 25.1.2
brunneipennis, Hypera 24.113.146
Bruneria 11.5.4
Brunettia 29.12.6
Brunneria 14.1.11

brunnescens, Hylemya 29.99.8
brunneum, Malobidion 24.106.40
brunneum, Orthosoma 24.106.8 (Fig.
 24.177)
brunneus, Aglenus 24.93.20
brunneus, Lyctus 24.65.1
brunneus, Metrioidea 24.107.112
brunneus, Prostomeus 27.23.76
Brush-footed Butterfly Family,
 supra 27.46.1
Brushlegged Mayfly Family 6.5.1
bryanti, Ancylodiplosis 29.11.95
Bryantopsis 21.15.53
Brychius 24.6.4
Brymblia 27.15.28
Bryobiota 24.24.213
Bryocorinae, supra 20.23.20
Bryocorini, supra 20.23.20
Bryodemina 29.40.40
Bryolymnia 27.75.329
Bryomyia 29.11.4
Bryophaenocladius 29.24.129
Bryophilini, supra 27.75.237
Bryoporus 24.24.176
Bryothinusa 24.24.214
Bryotropha 27.23.41
Buathra 25.16.165
Bubekia 25.19.48
buccata, Cuterebra 29.102.2
buccatus, Catadelphops 25.16.253
bucculatricis, Ageniaspis 25.25.81
bucculatricis, Bucculatriplex 25.13.54
bucculatricis, Pentacnemus 25.25.87
Bucculatriplex 25.13.54
Bucculatrix 27.13.12
buccatus, Catadelphops 25.16.253
Bucephalina 29.98.7
Bucephalomyia 29.100.18
bucephalus, Atopotrophos 25.16.55
buchanani, Colpodes 24.4.76
Buchananius 24.113.360
Buck Moth 27.69.7
Buckellacris 11.5.107
buckelli, Cycphoderris 11.8.1
Buckell's Hump-winged Cricket 11.8.1
Buckeye 27.46.30
Buckthorn Aphid 21.19.15
Bucrates 11.7.18
Buenoa 20.33.1
Buffalo Treehopper 21.15.24
buffaloensis, Parapamea 27.75.278
Buffalograss Webworm 27.55.198
Bufolucilia 29.101.10
bufo, Xenelmis 24.45.25
Bugs 20.1.1
Bulbana 21.14.28
bulbosa, Metatrichia 29.33.4
bulbosa, Pseudobrachypeza 29.9.29
Bulia 27.75.103
bullata, Sarcophaga 29.103.45
bullatus, Geocoris 20.7.18
Bumble Bees, supra 25.70.1, 25.70.2
Bumble Flower Beetle 24.30.126
Bumelia Fruit Fly 29.61.43
bumeliae, Nicholiella 21.38.54
bumeliana, Goditha 27.38.44
bunteana, Thyrazlia 27.39.3
buoliana, Rhyacionia 27.38.19
Buprestidae, supra 24.46.1
Buprestinae, supra 24.46.5
Buprestini, supra 24.46.11
Buprestis 24.46.15
Buprestoidea, supra 24.46.1
buprestoides, Anisomorpha 10.4.1 (Figs.
 10.4, 10.5)
buquet, Thaneroclerus 24.67.1

Buquetia 29.105.410
Burdock Borer 27.75.279
bureni, Thalassomyia 29.24.137
burgessi, Physocephala 29.49.3
burkei, Neodiprion 25.6.4
Burksia 25.26.50
burnneipes, Metanopedias 25.44.10
burnsi, Hemileuca 27.69.7
burra, Sphecophaga 25.16.1
Burrower Bug Family 20.1.1
Burrowing Ground Beetle 24.4.111 (Fig.
 24.40)
Burrowing Mayflies 6.8.1
Bursaphis 21.19.35
bursarius, Pemphigus 21.19.162
Burtinus 20.5.8
busckiella, Synallagma 27.19.2
Bush Katydids 11.7.1
Bushtailed Caddisfly Family, supra 26.13.1
butcheri, Sycopila 25.20.9
Butternut Curculio 24.113.238
buxi, Monarthropalpus 29.11.109
buxi, Psylla 21.17.27
Bycombia 27.59.6
byrnei, Mitoura 27.43.26
Byrrhidae, supra 24.35.1
Byrrhinae, supra 24.35.1
Byrrhini, supra 24.35.6
Byrrhodes 24.63.51
Byrrhoidea, supra 24.35.1
Byrrhus 24.35.7 (Fig. 24.77)
Byrsocryptoides 21.19.36
Byssodon 29.22.5
Bystus 24.81.4
Bythinini, supra 24.25.61
Bythinoplectus 24.25.3
Bythinopsis 24.25.63
Byturellus 24.84.1
Byturidae, supra 24.84.1
Byturosoma 24.68.39
Byturus 24.84.2
Byxidicerini, supra 24.25.3

C

cabares 27.40.17
Cabbage Aphid 21.19.34
Cabbage Curculio 24.113.292
Cabbage Looper 27.75.152
Cabbage Maggot 29.99.8
Cabbage Seedpod Weevil 24.113.292
Cabbage Seedstalk Curculio 24.113.292
Cabbage Webworm 27.55.54
Cabera 27.61.69
caberata, Sabulodes 27.61.154
Caberini, supra 27.61.68
Cabinet Beetle 24.63.25
Cabnia 27.55.411
Cabrulus 21.14.208
Cacama 21.13.6
cacata, Ephyrodes 27.75.90
Caccoplectus 24.25.7
Cachryphora 21.19.37
Cacocharis 27.38.2
Cacoecimorpha 27.38.79
Cacostola 24.106.259
Cacozelia 27.55.263
Cacozelus 29.105.134
cacti, Ilionota 24.26.46
cacti, Xanthopygus 24.24.19
Cactobrosis 27.55.388
cactocaetes, Chloroplus 11.5.88
Cactopinini, supra 24.122.32
Cactopinus 24.112.32
Cactus Felt Scale EM 21.3.4

Cactus Buprestid 24.46.27
Cactus Longhorn 24.106.274
Cactus scale 21.38.25
cadarella, Eufernaldia 27.55.202
cadaverina, Cynomopsis 29.101.18
cadburyi, Comachara 27.73.25
Caddisflies, supra 26.1.1
Cadelle 24.66.14
cadmia, Hemiceras 27.71.41
Cadra 27.55.403
Cadrema 29.94.5
Caeciliidae, supra 17.10.1
Caeciliitae, supra 17.10.1
Caecilius 17.10.1
Caecossonus 24.113.376
caecus, Geocolus 24.26.26
caeculalis, Perispasta 27.55.86
caecus, Schizomicrus 24.113.168
caelatus, Asemobius 24.24.84
caelatus, Orthotomicus 24.112.50
caementarium, Sceliphron 25.62.7
Caenacis 25.19.95
Caenidae 6.16.1
Caeniella 24.57.15
Caenis 6.16.2
Caenocara 24.63.53
Caenocephus 25.12.1
Caenocercus 25.25.137
Caenochrysis 25.50.18
Caenocryptus 25.16.163
Caenocyrta 24.19.14
Caenoidea, supra 6.15.1
Caenopamera 20.7.46
Caenoscelini, supra 24.74.10
Caenoscelis 24.74.10
Caenotoides 29.40.33
Caenurgia 27.75.139
Caenurgina 27.75.140
Caerosternus 24.26.34
caerulea, Encyclops 24.106.177 (Fig. 24.201)
caerulea, Zicrona 20.3.75
caesa, Neoelmis 24.45.18
caesarion, Orthellia 29.100.57
caespitum, Tetramorium 25.58.42 (Fig. 25.43)
Caeybruchus 24.108.1
Cafius 24.24.3
Cahela 27.55.383
caicus, Phryxus 27.70.22
Cainosternum 24.19.5
Cainotyphlus 24.24.164
caja, Arctia 27.73.50
Calacanthia 20.32.6
Caladonus 21.14.110
Calameuta 25.12.5
calami, Cosmia 27.75.408
Calamoceratidae, supra 26.17.1
Calamomyia 29.11.62
Calamoncosis 29.94.31
Calanana 21.14.152
calandrae, Anisopteromalus 25.19.80
Calandrini, supra 24.113.366
Calandrinus 24.113.334
calanus, Satyrium 27.43.16 (Fig. 27.107)
Calaphis 21.19.38
Calesesia 27.35.10
Calathus 24.4.93
Calcaneum 25.16.387
calcarata, Anurida 1.2.12
calcarata, Saperda 24.106.296 (Fig. 24.209)
calcaratus, Petrobius 4.1.5
Calcaritermes 15.2.7
calcatorius, Origichneumon 25.16.242

calceatus, Odontopus 24.113.218 (Fig. 24.287)
calceolariae, Pseudococcus 21.25.35
calcitrans, Stomoxys 29.100.61 (Fig. 29.54)
Calcocerinus 25.25.40
Calendra 24.113.366
Calendrinae, supra 24.113.362
Calephelis 27.44.2
Calico Bug 20.3.48 (Fig. 20.12)
Calico Butterfly 27.46.41
Calico Scale 21.26.6
Calicurgus 25.60.8
Calidota 27.73.61
calidum, Calosoma 24.4.13 (Fig. 24.32)
california, Coenonympha 27.48.8
California Dogface 27.42.12
California Five-spined Ips 24.112.51
California Flatheaded Borer 24.46.20
California Harvester Ant 25.58.24
California Horntail 25.9.2
California Oakworm Moth 27.72.1
California Pear Sawfly 25.7.30
California Pleasing Fungus Beetle 24.76.4
California Prionus 24.106.10
California Red Scale 21.38.7
California Salt Marsh Mosquito 29.20.9
california, Satyrium 27.43.16
California Silkmoth 27.69.18
California Sister 27.46.34
California Timemas 10.3.1
California Tortoise Shell 27.46.25
californiae, Leptarctia 27.73.31
californica, Archilestes 7.9.1
califronica, Autographa 27.75.164 (Fig. 27.341)
californica, Brachycaudonia 25.19.40
californica, Cheirodes 24.87.161
californica, Chlosyne 27.46.14
californica, Coccivora 20.21.4
californica, Conwentzia 23.5.6
californica, Cypherotylus 24.76.4
californica, Ellychnia 24.55.11
californica, Kleidotoma 25.32.1
californica, Leposoma 24.113.400
californica, Melanophila 24.46.20
californica, Moranila 25.19.31
califronica, Nothochrysa 23.9.1
californica, Nuculaspis 21.38.56
californica, Nymphalis 27.46.25
californica, Petalumaria 27.75.365
californica, Phryganidia 27.72.1 (Fig. 27.277)
californica, Platylyra 11.7.10
californica, Pteronarcys 8.5.3
californica, Pycnomorpha 24.87.54
californica, Revieria 24.82.9
californica, Ropronia 25.40.1
californica, Timema 10.3.1
californica, Townsendiella 25.69.2
californica, Yphira 26.8.1
californiaria, Neoalcia 27.61.21
californiensis, Exiliscelis 29.16.1
californiensis, Leptoconops 29.23.1
californiensis, Paregesta 27.55.56
californicum, Chalybion 25.62.6
californicum, Heteroplectron 26.17.2
californicum, Malacosoma 27.68.11
californicum, Nosodendron 24.60.1
californicum, Nipponentomon 2.3.4
californicum, Spilchastosoma 29.105.110
californicus, Ammonoencyrtus 25.25.64
californicus, Apoanagyrus 25.25.27
califronicus, Athanatus 29.105.176
californicus, Georissus 24.14.1
californicus, Hylecthrus 24.105.6

californicus, Kormus 21.2.21
californicus, Limonius 24.48.27
californicus, Neoleptotyphlus 24.24.167
californicus, Nerophilus 26.14.3
californicus, Notholopus 20.23.172
californicus, Paradolichurus 25.62.2
californicus, Parothius 24.24.43
californicus, Petrobius 4.1.5
californicus, Philabus 24.113.1
californicus, Pogonomyrmex 25.58.24
californicus, Prionus 24.106.10
californicus, Prostenus 24.88.15
californicus, Proterops 25.13.126
californicus, Sticthippus 11.5.43
californicus, Urocerus 25.9.2
caligineus, Cyrtocapsus 20.23.21
caliginosellus, Crambus 27.55.203
Caliothrips 22.4.2
Caliroa 25.7.43
caliroae, Hyperallus 25.16.372
Caliroini, supra 25.7.42
Caliscelinae, supra 21.6.1
Caliscelini, supra 21.6.1
Calisiinae, supra 20.13.2
Calitys 24.66.1
Callachna 29.61.4
Callajoppa 25.16.257
Callajoppina 25.16.256
Callandrena 25.65.1
Callanthidium 25.68.7
Callaphis 21.19.39
Callaspidia 25.31.4
Calledapteryx 27.62.4
Calles 24.113.249
calleta, Eupackardia 27.69.16
callias, Erebia 27.48.10
Callibaetis 6.4.4
Callicentrus 21.15.3
Callicera 29.47.44
Callicerini, supra 29.47.44
Callichromatini, supra 24.106.97
Callicorixa 20.35.9
Callida 24.4.147
Callidiellum 24.106.103
Callidiini, supra 24.106.101
Callidium 24.106.106
Callidora 25.16.406
callidus, Chrysops 29.26.11
Calliephialtes 25.16.3
Calligramma 24.107.62
Calligrapha 24.107.62
Callihormius 25.13.5
Callima 27.15.24
Callimelissodes 25.69.30
Callimormus 27.30.46
Callimorphini, supra 27.73.27
Callimoxys 24.106.95
Callinapaea 29.93.41
Callinicus 29.37.40
Callinomada 25.69.10
Calliodis 20.21.17
Callionima 27.70.26
Calliopsima 25.65.12
Calliopum 29.82.1
Calliperla 8.7.1
Calliphora 29.101.16
Calliphoridae, supra 29.101.1
Calliphorinae, supra 29.101.9
Calliphorini, supra 29.101.13
Callipogonius 24.106.253
callippe, Speyeria 27.46.8
Calliprora 27.23.65
Callipsis 25.65.12
Callipterenella 21.19.40
callipterus, Callipterenella 21.19.40
callipus, Glenodiplosis 29.11.97

callipyge, Hoplia 24.30.85
Callirhipidae, supra 24.40.1
Callirhytis 25.34.46
callista, Oxyelophila 27.55.20
Callistege 27.75.141
Callistini, supra 24.4.98
Callistitae, supra 24.4.98
Callisto 27.14.9
Callistopsyllus 30.4.13
Callitula 25.19.84
Callizzia 27.62.2
Calloides 24.106.115
Callomyia 29.45.3
Callona 24.106.146
Callopistria 27.75.313
Callopistromyia 29.58.1
Callophrys 27.43.24
callorhini, Antarctophthirus 19.1.1
Callosamia 27.69.17
Callosobruchus 24.108.6
callosus, Sphenophorus 24.113.366
Callotia 29.23.5
Callotillus 24.67.4
Calobatina 29.51.4
Calobatinae, supra 29.51.1
calochroma floridensis,
 Eurypepla 24.107.178
Calochromus 24.57.6
Calocoris 20.23.143
Calodera 24.24.215
Caloecia 27.68.7
Caloforcipomyia 29.23.3
Calomycterus 24.113.130
Caloneurodea, supra 10.1.1
Calonia 21.14.87
Caloparyphus 29.31.34
Calophasia 27.75.460
Calophyla 21.17.8
Calopodinae, supra 24.97.1
Calopterini, supra 24.57.14
Calopteron 24.57.14
Calopterygidae, supra 7.8.1
Calopteryx 7.8.1
Caloptilia 27.14.1
Caloptognatha 24.57.4
Caloreas 27.36.5
Calosima 27.17.12
Calosoma 24.4.13
Calosota 25.24.2
Calotarsa 29.45.9
Calotelea 25.43.8
Calothysanis 27.61.185
Calotingis 20.14.5
Calpodes 27.40.83
calva, Banasa 20.3.53
Calvia 24.80.37
calvus, Platycixius 21.1.8
Calx 1.5.3
Calycomyza 29.68.6
Calycopis 27.43.23
Calymmaderus 24.63.40
Calyptillus 24.113.31
Calyptodera 20.23.144
Calyptomerus 24.33.1
Calyptoproctus 21.3.2
Calyptra 27.75.67
Calyptratae, supra 29.98.1
Calyptrosomus 29.105.29
Calythea 29.99.18
Calyxochaetus 29.43.38
Camel Cricket 11.9.1, 11.9.4
Camellia Mining Scale 21.38.26
Camellia Parlatoria Scale 21.38.62
Camellia Scale 21.38.45
camelliae, Lepidosaphes 21.38.45
camelliae, Parlatoria 21.38.62

camellifolia, Pterophylla 11.7.6, 11.7.16
Camelopsocus 17.23.6
Camera 25.15.158
Cameraria 27.14.20
Camilla 29.92.1
Camillid Fly Family, supra 29.92.1
Camillidae, supra 29.92.1
Camirus 20.3.4
Camnula 11.5.38
Campaea 27.61.100
Campaenini, supra 27.61.99
Campanulotes 18.1.8
campbelli, Anamphidora 24.88.16
campbelli, Thermobia 5.3.8
campestris, Atalopedes 27.40.69
campestris, Lyctocoris 20.21.14 (Fig. 20.49)
Camphor Scale 21.39.68
Camphor Thrips 22.5.49
Campichoeta 29.91.2
Campocraspedon 25.16.473
Campoctonus 25.16.427
Campodea 3.1.1
Campodeidae, supra 3.1.1
campodeiformis, Grylloblatta 12.1.1 (Fig. 12.1)
Campodeinae, supra 3.1.1
Campodorus 25.16.357
Campogaster 29.105.32
Campoletis 25.16.405
Camponotini, supra 25.58.66
Camponotus 25.58.66
Campopleginae, supra 25.16.392
Campoplegini, supra 25.16.392
Campoplex 25.16.394
Camposcopus 25.16.375
Campsicnemus 29.43.36
Campsomeridinae, supra 25.56.1
Campsomeridini, supra 25.56.3
Campsomeriella 25.56.5
Campsomeris 25.56.3
Campsurinae, supra 6.10.2
Campsurus 6.10.2
Camptodes 24.70.26
Camptomyia 29.11.37
Camptoneuromyia 29.11.149
Camptonotus 11.9.1
Camptopelta 29.31.30
Camptoprosopella 29.81.82
Camptops 29.103.26
Camptoptera 25.27.9
Camptozygum 20.23.145
Campylacantha 11.5.87
Campylenchia 21.15.7
Campylochetini, supra 29.105.151
Campylomma 20.23.39
Campylomyza 29.11.6
cana, Mestra 27.46.39
Canacea 29.97.1
Canaceoides 29.97.2
Canacidae 29.97.1
Canacinae, supra 29.97.1
Canada balsam 44
Canadaphis 21.19.41
canadense, Gruimenopon 18.6.17
canadense, Simulium 29.22.5
canadensis, Acerella 2.3.3
canadensis, Altica 24.107.127
canadensis, Bareogonalos 25.47.4
canadensis, Calyptra 27.75.67
canadensis, Cystiphora 29.11.155
canadensis, Delphiniobium 21.19.61
canadensis, Dendroides 24.94.4 (Fig. 24.164)
canadensis, Dyscoletes 25.13.69
canadensis, Epochra 29.61.52

canadensis, Explorator 24.42.1
canadensis, Hagenella 26.8.5
canadensis, Histeromerus 25.13.14
canadensis, Parasynapta 29.11.41
canadensis, Phanocelia 26.10.36
canadensis, Platybregmus 24.63.28
canadensis, Protopterocallis 21.19.173
canadensis, Pseudocnemodus 20.7.60
canadensis, Sierolomorpha 25.54.1
canadensis, Spudastica 25.16.409
canadensis, Stictoleptura 24.106.219
canadensis, Trypetoptera 29.79.20
canadensis, Zeiraphera 27.38.33
canaliculata, Ampulex 25.62.3
canaliculata, Eucerceris 25.62.112
canaliculatum, Leichenum 24.87.167
canariensis, Pseudolynchia 29.106.8
Canarsia 27.55.362
canax, Amphicosmoecus 26.10.2
cancer, Deinocerites 29.20.13
candefacta, Tarachidia 27.75.213 (Fig. 27.347)
candida bipunctata, Saperda 24.106.296
candida candida, Saperda 24.106.296 (Fig. 24.208)
Candy-stripe Leafhopper 21.14.51
Canelomyia 29.105.337
canens, Lascelina 27.55.389
canescens, Carrhenes 27.40.28
canescens, Rhoptobaris 24.113.317
canicularis, Fannia 29.100.26
canicularis, Tibicen 21.13.4
Canifa 24.98.42
caniplaga, Ellida 27.71.10
canis, Ctenocephalides 30.1.3 (Fig. 30.3)
canis, Tetragoneuria 7.6.7
canis, Trichodectes 18.2.9
Canistes 24.113.245
cannalis, Geshna 27.55.119
Cannaphila 7.7.4
Canonura 24.106.268
canosaria, Nepytia 27.61.133
cantator, Aedes 29.20.9
Cantharidae, supra 24.56.1
Cantharinae, supra 24.56.5
Cantharini, supra 24.56.7
Cantharis 24.56.7
Cantharoctonus 25.13.46
Cantharoidea, supra 24.53.1
Canthon 24.30.2
Cantopelopia 29.24.21
Cantura 21.14.100
canus, Limonius 24.48.27
Capaneus 20.4.10
Capellia 25.19.89
Caphys 27.55.239
capillatum, Pelosoma 24.12.28
Capis 27.75.197
capitata, Ceratits, supra 29.61.1 (Fig. 29.44)
capitata, Cockereiana 29.105.136
capitata, Phaeganophora,
 supra 8.1.1, 8.9.12 (Fig. 8.1)
capitata, Symploce 14.5.3
capitatum, Nanium 25.16.335
Capitophorus 21.19.42
capizzii, Fenderia 24.24.97
Capnia 8.3.3
Capniidae, supra 8.3.1
Capnobotes 11.7.30
Capnochroa 24.88.12
caponis, Lipeurus 18.1.35
Capperia 27.58.4
caprae, Bovicola 18.2.1
Capraita 24.107.151
capreolus,
 Pseudolucanus 24.28.1 (Fig. 24.63)

Caprithrips 22.4.32
capsiformis, Nabis 20.18.5
capucinus, Asbolis 27.40.78
capucinus, Bostrichus 24.64.10
cara, Catocala 27.75.148 (Fig. 27.337)
cara, Protoneura 7.10.2
Carabidae, supra 24.4.1
Carabinae, supra 24.4.7
Carabini, supra 24.4.12
Carabitae, supra 24.4.12
Carabunia 25.25.119
Carabus 24.4.12
Caradrina 27.75.322
caraganae, Acrythosiphon 21.19.2
Caragana Aphid 21.19.2
Caragana Blister Beetle 24.101.14
Caragana Plant Bug 20.23.110
Carales 27.73.63
Caraphractus 25.27.17
Carbatina 27.23.89
carbo, Tricholochmaea 24.107.80
carbonaria, Alethia 24.88.3
carbonarius, Chrysops 29.26.11
carbonarius, Keroplatus 29.9.11
carbonator texana, Oxyrrhexis 25.16.23
Carbro 25.62.65
Carbroninae, supra 25.62.53
Carcelia 29.105.395
Carceliini, supra 29.105.395
Carcina 27.15.39
Carcinophoridae, supra 13.1.1
Carcinops 24.26.21
Cardiastethini, supra 20.21.20
Cardiastethus 20.21.23
cardinalis, Rodolia 24.80.33
Cardiochiles 25.13.123
Cardiochilini, supra 25.13.123
Cardiocladius 29.24.115
Cardiocondyla 25.58.29
Cardiocondylini, supra 25.58.29
Cardiophorinae, supra 24.48.68
Cardiophorus 24.48.69
cardui, Brachycaudus 21.19.28
cardui, Vanessa 27.46.27 (Fig. 27.135)
Carduiceps 18.1.9
carduidactyla, Platyptilia 27.58.9 (Fig. 27.274)
Carectocultuds 27.55.194
Cargida 27.71.24
Caria 27.44.3
caribbea, Forcipomyia 29.23.3
Caribbean Black Scale 21.26.20
Caribbean Pod Borer 27.55.298
Cariblatta 14.5.9
caricae, Davara 27.55.302
caricis, Cyrtorhinus 20.23.94
caricis, Vesiculaphis 21.19.221
carinata, Ashmeasea 21.15.46
carinata, Hatchia 24.25.21
carinata, Neduba 11.7.39
carinata, Opuntiaspis 21.38.58
carinata, Sirthenea 20.17.27
Carinated Shield-back Katydid 11.7.39
carinatum, Achurum 11.5.25 (Fig. 11.12)
carinatus, Machaerodes 24.25.61
carinenta, Libytheana 27.42.1
Carinetini, supra 21.13.13
Carinodes 25.16.221
Carinosillus 29.105.73
cariosa, Brochymena 20.3.25 (Fig. 20.8)
cariosus, Sphenophorus 24.113.366
Caripeta 27.61.124
Caristanius 27.55.310
caritella, Gerdana 27.17.5
carlinianus, Aerochoreutes 11.5.66
Carlsonia 25.16.273

Carlyleia 25.26.69
carme, Idarnes 25.18.4
Carmenta 27.35.16
Carnation Maggot 29.99.8
carneella, Wakulla 27.55.405
carneia, Chrysopa 23.9.9
Carneocephala 21.14.48
Carnid Fly Family, supra 29.75.1
Carnidae, supra 29.75.1
Carniotini, supra 24.87.30
Carnivore Flea Family, supra 30.3.1
carnivorous 24
carnosa, Psectraglaea 27.75.400
Carnoy's A 45
Carnus 29.75.3
carocapsae, Stantonia 25.13.144
carolae, Rhopalosyrphus 29.47.2
Carolana 27.15.34
Carolella 27.39.8
Carolina Conifer Aphid 21.19.53
carolina, Dissosteira 11.5.47 (Fig. 11.17)
carolina, Epimyia 29.11.71
carolina, Eucereon 27.73.78
Carolina Grasshopper 11.5.47
Carolina Mantis 14.1.8
carolina, Nemocapnia 8.3.7
carolina, Monepidosis 29.11.5
carolina, Oxytaenia 25.16.149
Carolina Sawyer 24.106.237
Carolina Sphinx 27.70.4
carolina, Stagmomantis 14.1.8 (Figs. 14.5, 14.6)
Carolinaia 21.19.43
carolinensis, Camptonotus 11.9.1 (Fig. 11.38)
carolinensis, Dasycerus 24.17.1
carolinensis, Monochamus 24.106.237
carolinensis, Narvesus 20.17.34 (Fig. 20.44)
carolinus, Aphotaenius 24.30.32
carolinus, Dichotomius 24.30.9
carolus, Huleechius 24.35.8
Carpelimus 24.24.145
Carpenter Bee Family, supra 25.69.1
Carpenter Bees 25.69.45
Carpenter Moth Family, supra 27.37.1
carpenteri, Canadaphis 21.19.41
Carpenterworm 27.37.8
Carpet Beetle 24.61.8
Carphobius 24.112.20
Carphoborus 24.112.20
Carphoides 27.61.53
Carphonotus 24.113.374
Carpilis 20.7.49
carpini, Acalyptus 24.113.192
Carpocoris 20.3.30
Carpophilinae, supra 24.70.7
Carpophilus 24.70.10
Carposinia 27.26.1
Carposinid Moth Family, supra 27.26.1
Carposinidae, supra 27.26.1
Carptima 27.61.202
Carrhenes 27.40.28
Carrhydrus 24.7.25
Carria 25.16.296
carribeanus, Symphylus 20.3.10
Carrion Beetle Family, supra 24.21.1
Carrion Clown Beetle 24.26.15
Carrot Beetle 24.30.104
Carrot Rust Fly 29.55.2
Carrot Weevil 24.113.143
Carsia 27.61.245
Carsidarinae, supra 21.17.9
Carsonus 21.14.62
Carteretta 30.4.24
Carterettini, supra 30.4.24

Carteris 27.75.13
Carterocephalus 27.40.42
Carthasis 20.18.11
Cartocometes 29.105.326
Cartodere 24.82.10
Cartodiplosis 29.11.106
Carulaspis 21.38.13
Carventinae, supra 20.13.4
caryae, Curculio 24.113.200
caryae, Eulecanium 21.26.6
caryae, Longistigma 21.191.119
caryae, Lygocoris 20.23.165
caryae, Magacyllene 24.106.112
caryaefoliae, Melanocallis 21.19.129
caryaevorum, Satyrium 27.43.16
caryana, Cydia 27.38.56
caryatrypes, Curculio 24.113.200
carye, Lophocampa 27.73.56 (Fig. 27.304)
Caryocolum 27.23.50
Caryomyia 29.11.107
Carynota 21.15.35
cascada, Lepania 26.10.47
Cascadoperla 8.7.4
Case Barklice Family 17.4.1
Casebearer Moth Family, supra 27.18.1
casei, Piophila 29.64.1 (Fig. 29.47)
Casemaking Clothes Moth 27.10.37
caseyi, Trogoxylon 24.65.3
Casey's Ladybird Beetle 24.80.41
Casinaria 25.16.397
Cassida 24.107.179
cassidea, Chelymorpha 24.107.176
Cassidinae, supra 24.107.174
Cassidini, supra 24.107.179
cassius, Leptotes 27.43.38
casta, Hydrobiomorpha 24.12.8 (Fig. 24.51)
castaeneus, Infernophilus 24.4.148
castalia, Kricogonia 27.42.16
castenea, Euparia 24.30.20
castanea, Maladera 24.30.62
castaneae, Cremastocheilus 24.30.134 (Fig. 24.76)
castanealis, Jativa 27.55.45
castaneum, Nicobium 24.63.23
castaneum, Tribolium 24.87.110
castaneus, Cyrtepistomis 24.113.138
castaneus, Idiobates 24.87.83, 24.87.147
castanipes, Scaphiumm 24.23.1
Castolus 20.17.14
castoris, Platypsyllus 24.18.3
castra, Psyche 27.11.2
Cat Flea 30.1.3
Cat Louse 18.2.3
Catabena 27.75.442
Catacanthus 24.4.135
Cataclinusa 29.46.31
Catadelphops 25.16.253
Catadelphus 25.16.255
Cataenococcus 21.25.8
Catagoniopsis 29.105.411
Catajapyx 3.4.5
catalaunalis, Antigastra 27.55.143
catalinae, Bryothinusa 24.24.214
catalinella, Epilechia 27.23.79
Catalinovoria 29.105.155
Catalinus 24.20.11
catalinus, Penestirellus 21.14.168
Catallagia 30.4.7
Catalpa Midge 29.11.108
Catalpa Sphinx 27.70.7
catalpae, Ceratomia 27.70.7 (Fig. 27.243)
catalpae, Contarinia 29.11.108
Catamergus 21.19.44
Catapastus 24.113.345
cataphracta, Papaipema 27.75.279

cataractae, Visoka 8.1.11
Catastenus 25.16.495
Catastia 27.55.317
Catasticta 27.42.1
Catasina 29.31.38
category 15
Catemophrys 29.105.209
catenaria, Cingilia 27.61.132 (Fig. 27.189)
Cateretes 24.70.1
Cateretinae, supra 24.70.1
Caterpillar Hunter 24.4.13
Catharosia 29.105.16
Catharosiini, supra 29.105.16
Cathartus 24.72.5
Cathetopteron 24.106.301
Cathilaria 25.20.5
cathistes, Heteropezina 29.11.30
Catinathrips 22.4.36
Catocala, supra 27.75.1, 27.75.148
Catocalinae, supra 27.75.51
Catocha 29.11.27
Catogenus 24.72.9
Catolaccus 25.19.86
Catonia 21.4.1
Catopocerinae, supra 24.19.18
Catopinae, supra 24.22.2
Catopini, supra 24.22.7
Catopocerus 24.19.18
Catops 24.22.7
Catoptria 27.55.210
Catoptrichus 24.22.9
Catorhintha 20.4.24
Catotrichini, supra 29.11.21
Cattail Moth 27.21.10
Cattasoma 29.103.16
Cattle Chewing Louse 18.2.1 (Fig. 18.3)
Cattle-tail Louse 19.3.1
catullus, Pholisora 237.40.41 (Fig.27.72)
caudata, Alloambria 21.19.3
caudata, Neoparentia 29.43.40
Caudatella 6.13.3
caudatus, Gastrotrypes 25.44.18
caudatus, Serphus 25.39.10
Caudellia 27.55.398
Caularis 27.75.243
Caulocampus 25.7.19
Caulophilus 24.113.380
Caulotops 20.23.20
Caupolicana 25.63.4
Caupolicanini, supra 25.63.3
Cauririnae, supra 28.2.1
Caurinus 28.2.1
cautella, Cadra 27.55.403
Cautethia 27.70.32
Cautolasius 25.58.67
Cavaraiellia 21.19.45
Cavariella 21.19.45
cavernis, Primicimex 20.20.1
caviceps, Hyalochloria 20.23.105
caviceps, Nodopus 24.68.12
cavicola, Chiricahuia 29.105.39
cavicolle, Pycnotomina 27.71.9
cavicollis, Acolonia 24.25.25
cavicollis, Drusilla 24.24.229
cavicollis, Tricholochmaea 24.107.80
cavigena, Sisyridivora 25.19.106
cavipennis, Necydalis 24.106.170
cavipennis, Premnobius 24.112.54
cavirostris, Micromyrmex 24.113.194
cavum vicinum, Amphelasma 24.107.92
cavus, Dibrachys 25.19.115
Cazenus 21.14.188
ceanothae, Xysma 25.62.28
Cebrio 24.47.2
Cebrionidae, supra 24.47.1
Cecharismena 27.75.64

Cecidocharella 29.61.8
Cecidomyia 29.11.113
Cecidomyiidae, supra 29.11.1
Cecidomyiinae, supra 29.11.58
Cecidomyiini, supra 29.11.78
cecropia, Hyalophora 27.69.18 (Fig. 27.234)
Cecropia Moth 27.69.18
cecrops, Calycopis 27.43.23
cecrops pamina, Automeris 27.69.8
Cedar Bark Beetle 24.112.15
Cedar Beetle Family, supra 24.40.1
Cedar Tree Borer 24.106.104
Cediopsylla 30.1.7
Cedius 24.25.73
Cedoaphis 21.19.46
Cedusa 21.9.8
Cehlipodini, supra 29.42.12
celadon, Eurytides 27.41.4
Celaenorrhinus 27.40.18
Celastrina 27.43.42
Celatoria 29.105.236
Celastrini, supra 27.43.42
celer, Eupelocotheca 29.105.275
Celery Aphid 21.19.29
Celery Leaf Tier 27.55.105
Celery Looper 27.75.165
Celeryworm 27.41.5
Celetes 24.57.17
Celina 24.7.14
Celinini, supra 24.7.14
Celiptera 27.75.143
Celithemis 7.7.5
Celotes 27.40.40
celtidis, Corythucha 20.14.7
celtidismamma, Pachypsylla 21.17.21
celtis, Asterocampa 27.47.3 (Fig. 27.145)
celtis, Pelliculaspis 21.38.63
Cemolobus 25.69.25
Cemonus 25.62.23
Cenchreini, supra 21.9.4
Cenocoeliini, supra 25.13.66
Cenocoelius 25.13.66
Cenocorixa 20.35.10
Cenophengus 24.54.4
Cenosoma 29.105.42
Centeterus 25.16.204
Centistes 25.13.131
centralis, Chyranda 26.10.25
Centrias 25.69.10
Centridini, supra 25.69.42
Centrinaspis 24.113.325
Centrinini, supra 24.113.323
Centrinites 24.113.330
Centrinogyna 24.113.332
Centrinopus 24.113.329
Centrioptera 24.87.41
Centris 25.69.42
Centrocorisa 20.35.11
Centrodera 24.106.174
Centrodontini, supra 21.15.14
Centrodontus 21.15.14
Centrodora 25.25.3
Centronopus 24.87.78
Centroptilum 6.4.5
Centrosmia 25.68.21
Centrotinae, supra 21.15.1
Centruiatus 24.42.2
centuncularis, Megachile 25.68.22
Ceocolus 25.4.8
Ceophyllini, supra 24.25.78
Ceophyllus 24.25.78
Cephalapis 25.68.17
Cephalciinae, supra 25.2.1
Cephalciini, supra 25.2.1
Cephalia 29.58.2

Cephalica 25.2.1
Cephalobyrrhinae, supra 24.43.7
Cephalochrysa 29.31.8
Cephalodynerus 25.59.9
Cephaloglypta 25.16.306
Cephaloidae, supra 24.86.1
Cephaloinae, supra 24.86.1
Cephalomyza 29.68.6
cephalonica, Corcyra 27.55.277
Cephalonomia 25.48.14
Cephalonomiini, supra 25.48.12
Cephaloon 24.86.1
Cephaloscymus 24.80.14
Cephalosmia 25.68.21
Cephalospargeta 27.75.375
Cephalosphaera 29.48.5
cephalotes, Paracarotomus 25.19.49
cephalotes, Perdita 25.65.15
Cephalothrips 22.5.33
Cephalotini, supra 25.58.45
Cephalylaeus 25.63.5
Cephenemyia 29.102.4
Cephenemyiinae, supra 29.102.4
Cephenniini, supra 24.20.12
Cephennium 24.20.12
Cephidae, supra 25.12.1
Cephinae, supra 25.12.1
Cephini, supra 25.12.4
Cephitinea, 27.10.29
Cephoidea, supra 25.12.1
Cephus 25.12.4
Cepphis 27.61.115
Ceracia 29.105.227
Ceracis 24.92.9
Ceraclea 26.18.1
Ceraleptus 20.4.32
ceramboides, Upis 24.87.93
Cerambycidae, supra 24.106.1
Cerambycinae, supra 24.106.21
Ceramphis 24.20.20
Ceranemota 27.59.5
Ceranemotini, supra 27.59.5
Ceranisus 25.26.55
Ceraotphyllinae, supra 30.7.1
Cerapachyini, supra 25.58.4
Cerapachys 25.58.4
Ceraphron 25.45.1
Ceraphronidae, supra 25.45.1
Ceraphronoidea, supra 25.45.1
Cerapoda 27.75.459
Ceraptericerini, supra 25.25.65
Cerapterocerus 25.25.67
Cerapteryx 27.75.510
Ceraptroceroideus 25.25.131
ceras, Assipala 29.26.10
cerasi, Caliroa 26.7.43
cerasi, Myzus 21.19.144
cerasivoranus, Archips 27.38.74
cerasorum, Elecanium 21.26.6
Ceraspis 24.30.84
Cerastipsocinae, supra 17.23.4
Cerastipsocini, supra 17.23.4
Cerastipsocus 17.23.4
Cerastis 27.75.576
Ceratagallia 21.14.14
Cerataphis 21.19.48
Ceratempis 29.42.22
Cerathosia 27.75.200
Ceratina 25.69.45
Ceratinini, supra 25.69.45
Ceratinostoma 29.98.24
Ceratobaeus 25.43.25
Ceratobarys 29.94.6
Ceratocapsini, supra 20.23.130
Ceratocapsus 20.23.130
Ceratochrysis 25.50.19

Ceratocanthinae, supra 24.30.54
Ceratoculicoides 29.23.12
Ceratocombus 20.24.1
Ceratocryptina, supra 25.16.184
Ceratodalia 27.61.198
Ceratographis 24.106.272
Ceratogastra 25.16.319
Ceratomegilla 24.80.44
Ceratomia 27.70.7
Ceratomyiella 29.105.210
Ceratonsura 25.26.36
Ceratonyx 27.61.95
Ceratophaga 27.10.40
Ceratophygadeuon 25.16.130
Ceratophyllidae, supra 30.7.1
Ceratophylloidea, supra 30.3.1
Ceratophyllus 30.7.2
Ceratophysella 1.2.1
Ceratopidea 20.23.93
Ceratopidonia 24.106.215
Ccratopogon 29.23.7
Ceratopogonidae, supra 29.23.1
Ceratopogoninae, supra 29.23.5
Ceratopogonini, supra 29.23.7
Ceratosmicra 25.21.8
Ceratothrips 22.4.37
Ceratulini, supra 25.7.71
Ceratulus 25.7.71
Ceraturgus 29.37.41
ceraunua, Hemiargus 27.43.40
Cerceris 25.62.111
cercerisella, Faculta 27.23.61, in *Fascista* 27.23.61
Cerchysius 25.25.106
Cercocerus 24.25.77
Cercopedius 24.113.95
Cercopeus 24.113.93
Cercopidae 21.12.1
Cercopinae, supra 21.12.1
Cercopini, supra 21.12.1
Cercopoidea 21.12.1
Cercyon 24.12.30
Cercyonini, supra 24.12.28
Cercyonis 27.48.9
Cerdistus 29.37.74
Cereal Leaf Beetle 24.107.14
Cereal Leaf Miner 29.93.32
cerealella, Sitotroga 27.23.80
cerealellae, Habrocytus 25.19.92 (Fig. 25.20)
cerealium, Limothrips 22.4.18
Cerecerini, supra 25.62.111
Cerenopus 24.87.131
cereralis, Loxostege 27.55.101
Ceresa 21.15.23
Ceresini, supra 21.15.22
Ceriana 29.47.68
ceriferus, Ceroplastes 21.26.1 (Fig. 21.27)
Cerioidini, supra 29.47.68
cerisyi, Smerinthus 27.70.15 (Fig. 27.246)
Cerma 27.75.199
Cernotina 26.3.1
Cerobasis 17.2.1
Cerocephala 25.19.25
Cerocephalinae, supra 25.19.23
Cerococcidae, supra 21.34.1
Cerococcus 21.34.1
Cerodontha 29.68.7
Ceromasia 29.105.412
Ceropales 25.60.34
Ceropalinae, supra 25.60.32
Cerophytidae, supra 24.50.1
Cerophytum 24.50.1
Ceroplaini, supra 25.60.34
Ceroplastes 21.26.1
Ceroplastodes 21.26.2.

Ceropsilopa 29.93.24
Ceropsylla 21.17.16
Ceroptres 25.34.7
Cerotainia 29.37.55
Cerotainiops 29.37.62
Cerotelion 29.9.8
Cerotoma 24.107.97
Ceroxys 29.58.3
Cerpegillettea 21.19.47
Ceruchus 24.28.8
Cerura 27.71.13
Ceruraphis 21.19.49
cervi, Lipoptena 29.106.11
cervina, Perothops 24.51.1
cervinus, Pantomorus 24.113.24
cervula, Sperrya 27.61.16
Cerylcautomus 24.78.7
Cerylon 24.78.9
Cerylonidae, supra 24.78.1
Ceryloninae, supra 24.78.6
cesonia, Zerene 27.42.12 (Fig. 27.97)
cestri, Strymon 27.43.34
Cetema 29.94.39
cethura, Anthocharis 27.42.9
Cetoniinae, supra 24.30.120
Cetoniini, supra 24.30.125
Ceuthophilini, supra 24.30.125
Ceuthophilini, supra 11.9.9
Ceuthophilus 11.9.10, 11.9.4
Ceutorhynchinae, supra 24.113.282
Ceutorhynchini, supra 24.113.292
Ceutorhynchus 24.113.292
Ceuthothrips 22.5.5
Chaenusa 25.13.90
Chaetaglaea 27.75.399
Chaetanophothrips 22.4.25
Chaetarthria 24.12.9
Chaetarthriinae, supra 24.12.9
Chaetechidius 24.113.92
Chaetexoeista 29.105.278
chaetifrons, Texasa 29.58.37
Chaetoapnaea 29.93.41
Chaetochlorops 29.94.28
Chaetocladius 29.24.122
Chaetoclusia 29.65.1
Chaetocnema 24.107.144
Chaetocoelus 24.68.5
Chaetocrania 29.105.349
Chaetofoveolocoris 20.23.194
Chaetogaedia 29.105.358
Chaetogaediina, supra 29.105.358
Chaetoglossa 29.105.359
Chaetolonchaea 29.57.2
Chaetonodexodes 29.105.202
Chaetonopsis 29.105.205
Chaetopauesia 25.14.5
Chaetophlepsis 29.105.151
Chaetophloeus 24.112.17
Chaetophylidea 20.23.74
Chaetoplagia 29.105.156
Chaetopleurophora 29.46.2
Chaetopsis 29.58.27
Chaetopsylla 30.3.1
Chaetoravinia 29.103.41
Chaetosa 29.98.21
Chaetosciara 29.10.11
Chaetosiphon 21.19.50
Chaetostigmoptera 29.105.302
Chaetostomella 29.61.42
Chaff Scale 21.38.62
chagnoni, Pyrgotella 29.60.2
Chain-spotted Geometer 27.61.132
Chaitophorus 21.19.51
Chalarinae, supra 29.48.1
Chalarus 29.48.1

Chalcaspis 25.25.39
Chalcedectini, supra 25.19.10
Chalcedectus 25.19.10
chalcedona, Occidryas 27.46.22
Chalceopla 27.8.14
Chalceria 27.43.6
Chalcerinyini, supra 25.25.69
Chalcidid Wasp Family, supra 25.21.1
Chalcididae, supra 25.21.1
Chalcidinae, supra 25.21.5
Chalcidoidea, supra 25.18.3
Chalcis 25.21.6
Chalcochares 25.60.20
Chalcodermus 24.113.241
Chalcoela 27.55.68
Chalcogonatopus 25.51.21
Chalcolepidiini, supra 24.48.9
Chalcolepidius 24.48.9
Chalcopasta 27.75.355
Chalcophora 24.46.8
Chalcophorella 24.46.9
Chalcophorini, supra 24.46.6
Chalcosmia 25.68.21
Chalcosyrphus 29.47.87
Chalepini, supra 24.107.162
Chaleponotus 24.113.242
Chalepus 24.107.164
Chalicodoma 25.68.23
chalonensis, Meringodixa 29.18.2
chalybea, Alospernida 24.106.201
chalybea, Altica 24.107.127
chalybeum, Poecilobrium 24.106.92
chalybeus, Halmus 24.80.27
Chalybion 25.62.6
Chamaeclea 27.75.359
Chamaemyia 29.83.4
Chamaemyiid Fly Family, supra 29.83.1
Chamaemyiidae, supra 29.83.1
Chamaemyiinae, supra 29.83.2
Chamaemyini, supra 29.83.2
Chamaepsila 29.55.2
chamaeropis, Osmopleura 24.106.138
Chamaesyrphus 29.47.39
chamberlaini, Pyrisitia 27.42.18
chamberlini, Symmyrmica 25.58.38
championi, Cylidrella 24.66.9
championi, Proarna 21.13.7
championi, Sisenes 24.97.7
Changa 11.11.3
Chaoboridae, supra 29.19.1
Chaoborinae, supra 29.19.1
Chaoborus 29.19.1
chaparral 28
chapini, Chlorixanthe 24.30.127
Characoma 27.75.173
Charadra 27.75.228
Charadrodromia 29.42.4
Chararica 27.55.292
Charasoma 29.105.237
Charaxinae, supra 27.47.1
Charcoal Beetle 24.46.20
Charhyphus 24.24.85
charlesi, Doliodesmus 24.87.119
charichlea, Clossiana 27.46.11
Charidotella 24.107.187
Charidotini, supra 24.107.188
Charidryas 27.46.15
Chariessa 24.67.26
Chariesterini, supra 20.14.17
Chariesterus 20.4.17
charipepla, Pompostolella 27.10.14
Charipid Wasp Family Supra 25.33.1
Charipidae, supra 25.33.1
Charipinae, supra 25.33.4
Charisalia 24.106.200
Charisius 24.88.4

charitonius, Heliconius 27.46.6 (Fig. 27.120)
Charitopes 25.16.114
charlesi, Polyplectropus 26.3.6
Charmon 25.13.141
Charops 25.16.398
Chartocerus 25.25.22
Chasmatonotus 29.24.130
Chasmias 25.16.245
Chauiiodinae, supra 23.2.2
Chaulandrena 25.65.1
Chauliodes 23.2.2
Chauliognathidae, supra 24.56.1
Chauliognathinae, supra 24.56.1
Chauliognathini, supra 24.56.1
Chauliognathus 24.56.1
Checkered Beetle Family, supra 24.67.1
Checkered Skipper 27.40.38
Checkerspot 27.46.22
Checkerspots 27.46.15
Chedra 27.18.3
Cheese Skipper 29.64.1
Cheiloneurini, supra 25.25.71
Cheiloneurus 25.25.73
Cheilosia 29.47.35
Cheilotrichia 29.2.54
Cheimophila 27.15.44
Cheirodes 24.87.161
Cheiropachus 25.19.74
Cheiroplatys 24.30.106
Cheirotoma 1.4.23
Chelaporus 25.60.16
Chelariinae, supra 27.23.76
Chelicerca 9.1.1
Chelifera 29.42.15
Chelinidea 20.4.18
Chelinidini, supra 20.4.18
Chelipoda 29.42.12
Chelisia 29.99.7
Chelisiini, supra 29.99.7
Chelisoches 13.4.1
Chelisochidae, supra 13.4.1
Chelogynus 25.51.1
Chelonariidae, supra 24.41.1
Chelonarium 24.41.1
Cheloninae, supra 25.13.112
Chelonus 25.13.113
Chelonychus 24.113.206
Chelopistes 18.1.10
Chelostoma 25.68.15
Chelostomoides 25.68.23
Chelostomopsis 25.68.16
Chelymorpha 24.107.176
Chelynia 25.68.11
Chelyoxenus 24.26.17
Chelysoma 20.3.3
chemskia, Eremantha 27.55.36
Chenosmia 25.68.21
cheoha, Schaefferia 1.2.2
cheopis, Xenopsylla 30.1.10
Chermidae 21.17.1, 21.20.1
Chernokrilus 8.7.6
Cherry Casebearer 27.18.1
Cherry Fruit Fly 29.61.44
Cherry Fruit Sawfly 25.7.18
Cherry Fruitworm 27.38.53
Cherry Leaf Beetle 24.107.80
chersis, Sphinx 27.70.11 (Fig. 27.244)
Chersodromia 29.42.5
Chersotis 27.75.581
Chesiadodes 27.61.35
Chestnut Timberworm 24.69.2
Chestomorpha 25.25.132
Cheteoscelis 27.61.163
Chetostoma 29.61.53
Cheumatopsyche 26.4.7

chevrolati, Trixagus 24.49.4 (Fig. 24.104)
Chevrolatia 24.20.16
Chevrolatiini, supra 24.20.16
Chewing Lice 18.1.1
Chiastocheta 29.99.6
Chicken Body Louse 18.6.24
Chicken Dung Fly 29.100.26
Chicken Head Louse 18.1.17
Chickweed Geometer 27.61.184
Chigoe Flea 30.1.2
chihuahuae, Orthochoriolaus 24.106.203
chilensis, Abrocomophaga 18.8.1
Chilini, supra 27.55.224
Chilo 27.55.225
Chilocampyla 27.14.11
Chilocorinae, supra 24.80.22
Chilocorini, supra 24.80.22
Chilocorus 24.80.23
Chilmetopon 24.87.21
Chilophaga 29.11.66
Chilopoda 10
Chilosima 25.68.20
Chilostigma 26.10.31
Chilostigmini, supra 26.10.30
Chilostigmodes 26.10.32
Chilothrips 22.4.26
Chiloxanthinae, supra 20.32.1
Chiloxanthus 20.32.2
Chimabachinae, supra 27.15.44
Chimabachini, supra 27.15.44
Chimarocephala 11.5.36
Chimarra 26.1.1
Chimoptesis 27.38.37
chinatiensis, Hemileuca 27.69.7
chinatiensis, Thessalia 27.46.13
Chinch Bug 20.7.16 (Fig. 20.29
chinensis, Callosobruchus 24.108.6 (Fig. 24.251)
chinensis, Parlatoreopsis 21.38.61
Chinese Mantis 14.1.10
Chinese Obscure Scale 21.38.61
Chinese Wax Scale 21.26.1, 21.26.22
chiococella, Podiasa 27.30.6
Chioides 27.40.6
Chiomara 27.40.34
chionanthi, Adita 27.75.449
Chionanthobius 24.113.226
chionaspidis, Arrhenophagus 25.25.61
Chionaspis 21.38.14
Chionea 29.2.42
Chionodes 27.23.56
chionops, Gnotus 25.16.124
chiragrus, Megalonotus 20.7.70
chiricahuae, Gymnognathus 24.109.11
Chiricahuia 29.105.39
Chiricahuiini, supra 29.105.39
Chirodamus 25.60.1
Chiromyzinae, supra 29.31.1
chiron, Marpesia 27.46.44
Chironomidae, supra 29.24.1
Chironominae, supra 29.24.43
Chironomini, supra 29.24.43
Chironomoidea, supra 29.21.1
Chironomus 29.24.56
Chirosia 29.99.5
Chirothripini, supra 22.4.17
Chirothripoides 22.5.34
Chirothrips 22.4.17
Chirotica 25.16.84
Chiroticina 25.16.84
chisos, Cicada 21.13.12
chisosensis, Apodemia 27.44.7
chisosensis, Rhinanisus 24.113.383
chitin 10
chittendeni, Dialeurodes 21.18.14
Chlaenius 24.4.98

Chlamisinae,supra 24.107.31
Chlamisus 24.107.32
Chlamydatus 20.23.38
Chlidanotinae, supra 27.38.91
Chloealtis 11.5.1
Chloraspilates 27.61.75
Chlorepyris 25.48.6
Chlorida 24.106.161
Chlorion 25.62.4
Chloriona 21.2.23
chlorionis, Diaphnocoris 20.23.97
chloris Parasa 27.52.20
chlorisalis, Maracayia 27.55.190
Chlorixanthe 24.30.127
Chlorobapta 27.55.52
Chlorochlamys 27.61.166
Chlorochroa 20.3.29
Chloroclystis 27.61.244
Chlorocoris 20.3.46
Chlorohystricia 29.105.84
Chloromyia, supra 29.31.1, 29.31.5
Chloroperlidae, supra 8.8.1
Chloroperlinae, supra 8.8.1
chlorophaea, Phyllovates 14.1.12
Chloropidae, supra 29.94.1
Chloropinae, supra 29.94.37
Chloropleca 27.10.18
Chloroplus 11.8.88
Chloroprocta 29.101.2
Chlorops 29.94.41
Chloropteryx 27.61.167
Chlorosea 27.61.157
Chlorostrymon 27.43.13
Chlorotabanus 29.26.16
Chlorotettix 21.14.106
chlorum, Cyrtophyllicus 11.7.32
Chlosyne 27.46.14, 27.46.15
Chnaunanthus 24.30.57
Chnaurococcus 21.25.7
Choephora 27.75.578
Choetospila 25.19.23
Choetospilisca 25.19.24
choicus, Heilipodus 24.113.152
Cholinae, supra 24.113.235
Cholinobaris 24.113.340
Cholomyia 29.105.203
Cholus 24.113.235
Chondrocera 20.4.3
Choraginae, supra 24.109.1
Choragus 24.109.4
Choranthus 27.40.75
Chorebus 25.13.91
choreutes, Lophognathella 1.3.1
Choreutid Moth Family, supra 27.36.1
Choreutidae, supra 27.36.1
Choreutinae, supra 27.36.3
Choreutis 27.36.7
Chorinaeus 25.16.285
Choriolaus 24.106.195
choris, Negastrius 24.48.55(Fig. 24.103)
Chorisoneura 14.5.7
Choristoneura 27.38.72
Choristostigma 27.52.121
Chorizagrotis 27.75.544
Chorizococcus 21.25.9
Chorosomini, supra 20.6.6
Choroterpes 6.7.1
Chorthippus 11.5.3
Chortinaspis 21.38.15
Chortophaga 11.5.35
Chramesus 24.112.16
Chremylus 25.13.51
Chrismania 27.52.39
christianseni, Eosentomon 2.1.1
Chromagrion 7.11.6
Chromaphis 21.19.52

Chromatocera 29.105.135
Chromocryptus 25.16.161
Chromolepida 29.32.20
chromosome counts 45
Chrotoma 24.106.155
chrysanthemi floridana, Mantura 24.107.143
chrysanthemi, Rhopalomyia 29.11.158
Chrysanthemum Aphid 21.19.121
Chrysanthemum Flower Borer 27.39.7
Chrysanthemum Gall Midge 29.11.158
Chrysanthemum Lace Bug 20.14.7
Chrysanthemum Thrips 22.4.53
Chrysanthrax 29.40.61
Chrysanympha 27.75.162
Chrysapion 24.113.20
Chrysaster 27.14.21
Chrysauginae, supra 27.55.239
Chryseida 25.20.13
chryselectra, Hemibryomima 27.75.300
Chrysendeton 27.55.7
Chrysetaerius 24.26.55
Chrysididae, supra 25.50.1
Chrysididinae, supra 25.50.16
Chrysididini, supra 25.50.16
Chrysidoidea, supra 25.48.1
Chrysis 25.50.16
chrysitis, Macrocneme 27.73.80
Chrysobothrini, supra 24.46.23
Chrysobothris 24.46.23
Chrysocharis 25.26.62
Chrysocharomyia 25.26.70
Chrysochlorina 29.31.19
Chrysochlorinae, supra 29.31.19
Chrysochraon 11.5.2
Chrysochus 24.107.47
Chrysoclista 27.20.2
chrysocoma, Goniops 29.26.1
Chrysoecia 27.75.349
Chrysoesthia 27.23.6
Chrysoexorista 29.105.413
Chrysogaster 29.47.52
Chrysolampus 25.19.5
Chrysolina 24.107.63
Chrysomela 24.107.64
Chrysomelidae, supra 24.107.1
Chrysomeliformia, supra 24.106.1
Chrysomelinae, supra 24.107.58
Chrysomelini, supra 24.107.64
Chrysomeloidea, supra 24.106.1
Chrysomphalus 21.38.16
Chrysomyinae, supra 29.101.2
Chrysomyini, supra 29.101.2
Chrysonotomyia 25.26.80
Chrysopa 23.9.9
chrysopelea, Anartia 27.46.31
Chrysopeleia 27.21.19
Chrysopeleiinae, supra 27.21.14
Chrysoperla 23.9.9
Chthonolsius 25.58.67
chydaea, Conga 27.40.55
Chyliza 29.55.3
Chylizinae, supra 29.55.3
Chymomyza 29.90.11
Chyphotes 25.55.1
Chyphotini, supra 25.55.1
Chyranda 26.10.25
Chyromya 29.86.2
Chyromyid Fly Family, supra 29.86.1
Chyromyidae, supra 29.86.1
Chytolita 27.75.5
Chytonix 27.75.291
Cibalacris 11.5.72
Cibdelia 24.87.79
Cicada 21.13.12
Cicada Family, supra 21.13.1
Cicada Killer 25.62.90 (Fig. 25.58)

Cicada Parasite Beetle Family, supra 24.39.1
Cicadas, supra 21.1.1
Cicadella 21.14.79
Cicadellidae, supra 21.14.1
Cicadellinae, supra 21.14.67
Cicadellini, supra 21.14.79
Cicadelloidea, supra 21.14.1
Cicadette 21.13.19
Cicadettini, supra 21.13.19
Cicadidae, supra 21.13.1
Cicadinae, supra 21.13.11
Cicadini, supra 21.13.11
Cicadoidea, supra 21.13.1
Cicadula 21.14.151
Cicindela 24.3.4
Cicindelidae, supra 24.3.1 (Figs. 24.27, 24.28)
Cicindelidia 24.3.4
Cicindelina, supra 24.3.4
Cicindelinae, supra 24.3.1
Cicindelini, supra 24.3.4
cicindeloides, Arhaphe 20.9.4 (Fig. 20.34)
Cicinnus 27.65.2
Ciconiphilus 18.6.7
Cidaphus 25.16.465
Cigar Casebearer 27.18.1
Cigarette Beetle 24.63.38
Ciidae, supra 24.92.1
Ciinae, supra 24.92.2
Ciini, supra 24.92.2
Cilea 24.24.177
ciliata, Corythucha 20.14.7
ciliata, Ctenolepisma 5.3.3
ciliata, Macropis 25.67.3
ciliata, Psorophora 29.20.8
ciliatus, Coelus 24.87.64
Cimberinae, supra 24.113.4
Cimberini, supra 24.113.13
Cimbex 25.5.3
Cimbicid Sawfly Family, supra 25.5.1
Cimbicidae, supra 25.5.1
Cimbicinae, supra 5.5.2
cimbicis, Nesomyia 25.26.82
Cimbocera 24.113.117
Cimex 20.20.2
Cimexopsis 20.20.5
Cimicidae, supra 20.20.1
Cimicinae, supra 20.20.2
cimicoides, Macrocephalus 20.16.2
Ciminius 21.14.44
Cimolus 20.4.26
Cinara 21.19.53
cincaidella, Tolima 27.55.415
cincinnatiella, Cameraria 27.14.20
cincta, Knulliana 24.106.150
cincta, Kokopoda 27.75.123
cincta, Miamimyia 29.105.331
cincta, Rothschildia 27.69.15 (Fig. 27.231)
cincta, Saigusaia 29.9.51
cincta, Spaziphora 29.98.18
cincta, Silvestrina 29.11.104
cinctella, Meliscaeva 29.47.26
cincticornis, Ophiopterus 25.16.389
cinctipalpis, Coxina 27.75.119
cinctipes, Amaurochrous 20.3.17
cinctipes, Ceraptroceroideus 25.25.131
cinctipes, Mochlonyx 29.19.2 (Fig. 29.22)
cinctipes, Schlettererius 25.17.1
cinctiventris, Rhiginia 20.17.2
cinctiventris, Xenoschesis 25.16.323
cinctus, Allantus 25.7.8
cinctus, Caraphractus 25.27.17
cinctus, Cephus 25.12.4
cinctus, Epipocus 24.81.16
cinctus, Largus 20.9.1

cinctus, Pselliopus 20.17.17 (Fig. 20.40)
cinctus, Sehirus 20.1.1 (Fig. 20.3)
Cinderella 29.78.3
cinera, Athrycia 29.105.154
cinera, Ephydra, supra 29.93.1, 29.93.54 (Figs. 29.51, 29.52)
cineracea, Neodeceia 29.82.9
cinerascens, Oecetis 26.18.5
cinerea, Dorcasta 24.106.263
cinerea, Epicauta 24.101.14 (Fig. 24.170)
cinerea, Hesperodinera 29.105.67
cinerea, Hetoemis 24.106.240
cinerea, Lasionalia 29.105.183
cinerea, Meigenielloides 29.105.251
cinerea, Nauphoeta 14.6.7
cinerea, Phryganea 26.8.8 (Fig. 26.25)
cinereola, Selicanis 27.75.263
Cinereous Cockroach 14.6.7
cinereum, Piesma 20.10.1
cinereus, Aedes 29.20.9
cinereus, Atrachelus 20.17.13
cinereus, Horesidotes 11.5.15
cinereus, Prodoxus 27.8.11
Cinetus 25.42.3
Cingilia 27.61.132
cingulata, Oncideres 24.106.260
cingulata, Rhagoletis 29.61.44 (Fig. 29.46)
cingulata, Ticida 21.11.14
cingulatus, Agrius 27.70.1 (Fig. 27.236)
cingulatus, Antillothrips 22.5.31
Cinnabar Moth 27.73.29
cinnamomeus, Oliarus 21.1.1 (Fig. 21.6)
Cinochira 29.105.28
Cinochirini, supra 29.105.28
Cinygma 6.6.1
Cinygmula 6.6.2
Cinyra 24.46.14
Cioninae, supra 24.113.234
Cionimimus 24.113.214
Cionus 24.113.234
Circaputo 21.25.10
Circia 29.99.2
Circotettix 11.5.65
Circulaspis 21.38.17
Circulifer 21.14.149
circumdata, Trichodeltia 27.75.527
circumflexum, Aulacorthum 21.19.24
circumscriptella, Mompha 27.19.1
Cirrhencyrtus 25.25.44
Cirrhophanus 27.75.350
cirripediformis, Ceroplastes 21.26.1
cirrogaster cirrogaster, Callajoppa 25.16.257
Cirrophthirius 18.1.11
Cirrospiloideus 25.26.27
Cirrospilus 25.26.29
Cirrula 29.93.53
Cis 24.92.2
Cisseps 27.73.76
Cissusa 27.75.97
Cissuvora 27.35.3
Cissuvorini, supra 27.35.3
Cistalia 20.7.28
Cisthenea 27.73.13
Cistogaster 29.105.1
cistudinis, Cistudinomyia 29.103.27
Cistudinomyia 29.103.27
Citheronia 27.69.2
Citheroiniinae, supra 27.69.1
citrana, Argyrotaenia 27.38.71
citri, Dialeurodes 21.18.14
citri, Planococcus 21.25.33
citri, Scirtothrips 22.4.15
citri, Unaspis 21.38.83
citricauda, Priesneriella 22.5.17
citricida, Toxoptera 21.19.214
citricola, Aphis 21.19.15

Citricola scale 21.26.4
citrifolii, Dialeurodes 21.18.14
Citrina, Aonidiella 21.38.7
citrinus, Ochraethes 24.106.116
citrinus, Psithyrus 25.70.3
Citrophilus Mealybug 21.25.35
citrulli, Prodiplosis 29.11.119
Citrus Blackfly 21.18.1
Citrus Mealybug 21.25.33
Citrus Planthopper 21.8.8
Citrus Root Weevil 24.113.59
Citrus Snow Scale 21.38.83
Citrus Thrips 22.4.15
Citrus Whitefly 21.18.14
Civil Bluet 7.11.8
civile, Enallagma 7.11.8 (Fig. 7.23)
cixiforma, Myiomma 20.23.4
Cixiid Planthopper Family, supra 21.1.1
Cixiidae, supra 21.1.1
Cixiini, supra 21.1.1
Cixius 21.1.5
Claassenia 8.9.10
Cladara 27.61.251
Cladiini, supra 25.7.15
cladistics 17
Cladius 25.7.15
Cladochaeta 29.90.13
Cladomorphinae, supra 10.2.1
Cladopelma 29.24.52
Cladotanytarsus 29.24.82
cladotrichus, Calles 24.113.249
Cladura 29.2.41
Clairvillia 29.105.30
Clambidae, supra 24.33.1
Clambus 24.33.2
clandestina, Opistheurista 20.23.205
clandestina, Spaelotis 27.75.560 (Fig. 27.395)
Clanoneurum 29.93.920
clara, Oliarces 23.6.1
clarimontis, Trybliographa 25.32.6
clarioralis, Dioryctria 27.55.339
claripalpis, Paratheresia 29.105.78
claripennis, Istocheta 29.105.344
claripennis, Labobella 20.23.134
claripennis, Scotothrips 22.5.23
clarki, Corticivora 27.38.55
clarkiae, Proserpinus 27.70.37 (Fig. 27.260)
Clark's Day Sphinx 27.70.37
clarus, Epargyreus 27.40.4 (Fig. 27.64)
Clasiopella 29.93.26
claspers 22
Claspettomyia 29.11.53
classification 10
classifying 4
Clastoneuriopsis 29.105.323
Clastoptera 21.12.7
Clastopterinae, supra 21.12.7
Clastopterini, supra 21.12.7
Clastopteromyia 29.90.14
claterna, Impeccantia 29.105.141
clathratus, Allygiella 21.14.124
clathratus, Bassareus 24.107.26 (Fig. 24.218)
clauda, Wasmanniella 29.11.14
claudia, Euptoieta 27.46.7
clausa, Trichopsidea 29.39.3
Clausenia 25.25.35
Clausicella 29.105.293
Clavaspis 21.38.18
clavata, Calameuta 25.12.5
clavata, Coruna 25.19.66
clavata, Plagiometriona 24.107.185
clavatus, Mydas 29.35.4
clavatus, Pseudodoros 29.47.28

clavensis, Neuroterus 25.34.17
clavicornis, Cyrtogonatopus 25.51.12
clavicornis, Microscapha 24.98.15
clavicornis, Oncozygia 20.3.16
clavicornis, Phanocerus 24.45.2
claviger, Acanthomyops 25.58.68
claviger, Duplaspidiotus 21.38.26
Clavigerinae, supra 24.25.84
Clavilispinus 24.24.91
clavipes, Bittacomorpha 29.17.3
clavipes, Cucujus 24.72.13 (Fig. 24.139)
clavipes, Ptinus 24.62.10
clavula, Ressiliella 29.11.88
Clay-backed Cutworm Moth 27.75.535
Clay-colored Billbug 24.113.366
Claycolored Leaf Beetle 24.107.23
Clayia 18.6.8
cleaning specimens 40
Clear Lake Gnat 29.19.1
Clear-0winged Grasshopper 11.5.38
Clear-winged Moth Family, supra 27.35.1
Cleftfooted Minnow Mayfly Family 6.2.1
clelia, Stonyx 29.40.51
clemataria, Eutrapela 27.61.145
Clematis Blister Beetle 24.101.14
Clematodes 11.5.78
Clemelis 29.105.414
Clemensia 27.73.21
Clemmus 24.81.3
cleobaea, Lycorea 27.49.2
Cleomenini, supra 24.106.133
cleone, Adelomos 25.7.24
Cleoninae, supra 24.113.148
Cleonini, supra 24.113.149
Cleonus 24.113.149
Cleonyminae, supra 25.19.8
Cleonymini, supra 25.19.8
Cleonymus 25.19.9
Cleora 27.61.42
cleoriformis, Homocerynea 27.75.185
Clepsis 27.38.80
clepsydra, Synosis 25.16.300
Cleptelmis 24.45.6
Cleptes 25.50.1
Cleptinae, supra 25.50.1
Cleridae, supra 24.67.1
Clerinae, supra 24.67.4
Clerini, supra 24.67.11
clerinus, Zagymnus 24.106.137
Click Beetle Family, supra 24.48.1
Clidicinae, supra 24.20.21
Clidicini, supra 24.20.21
Clidophleps 21.13.17
Cligenes 20.7.34
Climacia 23.13.1
Climaciella 23.7.5
Clindium 24.2.2
cline 18.23
Clinocentrus 25.13.55
Clinocera 29.42.30
Clinocerinae, supra 29.42.21
Clinocladius 29.24.121
Clinodiplosis 29.11.99
Clinohelea 29.23.18
Clinopleura 11.7.31
Clinotanypus 29.24.5
clio, Ectypia 27.73.69 (Fig. 27.309)
clio, Henileuca 27.69.7
Clio Moth 27.73.69
Cliopisa 29.9.1
clisiocampae, Telenomus 25.43.32
Clisodon 25.69.36
Clistomorpha 29.105.33
Clistopyga 25.16.14
Clistorapha 25.16.456
Clistoronia 26.10.14

Clitellariini, supra 29.31.11, 29.31.13
clitellarius, Colladonus 21.14.108
clivicolis, Labidomera 24.107.61 (Fig. 24.226)
Clivina 24.4.25
Clivinema 20.23.10
Clivinemini, supra 20.23.9
clivulus, Ischnoceros 25.16.80
Cloacina 29.105.341
Cloanthanus 21.14.92
clodius, Parnassius 27.41.1
Cloeon 6.4.6
Cloeotus 24.30.55
clonius, Spathilepia 27.40.20
Clorinde 27.42.13
clorinde, Anteos. 27.42.13 (Fig. 27.98)
Clostera 27.71.1
Clossiana 27.46.11
Closterocoris 20.23.146
Closterocerus 25.26.59
Clostoeca 26.10.26
Clothes Moth Family, supra 27.10.1
Clouded Plant Bug 20.23.171
Clouded Skipper 27.40.51
Clouded Sulphur 27.42.11
Cloudless Sulphur 27.42.14
Cloudywinged Whitefly 21.18.14
Clover Aphid 21.19.146
Clover Aphid Parasite 25.25.1
Clover Cutworm 27.75.472
Clover Hayworm 27.55.235
Clover Head Weevil 24.113.146
Clover Leaf Midge 29.11.152
Clover Leafhopper 21.14.15
Clover Leaf Weevil 24.113.146
Clover Looper 27.75.140
Clover Root Borer 24.112.6
Clover Root Weevil 24.113.50
Clover Seed Chalcid 25.20.21
Clover Seed Midge 29.11.152
Clover Seed Weevil 24.113.229
Clover Stem Borer 24.75.6 (Fig. 24.141)
Clover-head Caterpillar 27.38.53
Clown Beetle Family, supra 24.26.1
Club Flea Family, supra 30.2.1
Clubtail Family 7.3.1
cluentius, Neococytius 27.70.3
clunalis, Cheiroplatys 24.30.106
Clunio 29.24.87
Clusia 29.65.2
Clusiid Fly Family, supra 29.65.1
Clusiidae, supra 29.65.1
Clusiinae, supra 29.65.1
Clusiodes 29.65.5
Clusiodinae, supra 29.65.5
Cluster Fly 29.101.21
Cluzobra 29.9.83
Clydonopteron 27.55.253
clymena, Diaethria 27.46.38
Clypeadon 25.62.109
clypealis, Leptoglossus 20.4.4
clypeata, Cerceris 25.62.111 (Fig. 25.59)
clypeatus, Enoplolindenius 25.62.66
clypeus 20
clytie, Ministrymon 27.43.18
Clytini, supra 24.106.112
Clytocerus 29.12.12
clyton, Asterocampa 27.47.3
Clytrinae, supra 24.107.16
Clytrini, supra 24.107.22
Clytus 24.106.125
Cnaemidophorus 27.58.8
Cnemidandrena 25.65.1
Cnemodinini, supra 24.87.1
Cnemodinus 24.87.1
Cnemodus 20.7.63

Cnemogonus 24.113.284
Cnemonyx 24.112.22
Cnemotettix 11.9.2
Cneoglossini, supra 24.34.5
Cneorhinini, supra 24.113.49
Cnephasia 27.38.64
Cnephasiini, supra 27.38.63
Cnephia 29.22.11
Cnesinus 24.112.1
cnici, Dasydactylus 24.75.9
c-nigrum, Xestia 27.75.566
Cnodacophora 29.50.1
Cnopia, supra 24.104.7
Cnopus 24.104.7
coactipostica, Andrena 25.65.1
coalingaensis, Bourletiella 1.7.6
Cobalos 27.75.260
cobaltina, Osima 25.68.21
Coboldia 29.15.9
Cobubatha 27.75.182
cocana, Eucosma 27.38.25
Coccidae, supra 21.26.1
Coccidencyrtus 25.25.92
Coccidomyia 29.11.78
Coccidula 24.80.28
Coccidulinae, supra 24.80.28
Coccidulini, supra 24.80.28
coccinea, Calasesia 27.35.10
coccinea, Graphocephala 21.14.51
Coccinella 24.80.42
Coccinellidae, supra 24.80.1
Coccinellinae, supra 24.80.35
Coccinellini, supra 24.80.35
coccineus, Eriococcus 21.31.4
cocciphila, Syneura 29.46.22
Coccivora 20.21.4
Coccobaphes 20.23.147
Coccoidea, supra 21.22.1
Coccophagini, supra 25.25.8
Coccophagoides 25.25.12
Coccophagus 25.25.13
Coccopsis 29.11.49
Coccotorus 24.113.209
Coccus 21.26.4
coccus, Dactylopius 21.28.1
Coccygomimus 25.16.30
Cochineal Insect 21.28.1
Cochineal Scale Insect Family,
 supra 21.28.1
Cochisea 27.61.59
cochlidioides, Psammathodoxa 27.75.63
Cochliomyia 29.101.3
Cochlorhinini, supra 21.14.84
Cochlorhinus 21.14.86
Cochylid Moth Family, supra 27.39.1
Cochylidae, supra 27.39.1
Cochylis 27.39.2
cockerelli, Dolichopselephus 25.16.437
cockerelli, Paratrioza 21.17.11
cockerelli, Pseudaulacaspis 21.38.69
Cockerellia 25.65.15
Cockerellian 29.105.136
Cockerellula 25.65.15
Cockerell's Blue-winged
 Grasshopper 11.5.45
Cocklebur Weevil 24.113.369
Cockroaches 14.1.1, 14.2.1
Coconut Mealybug 21.25.26
Coconut Scale 21.38.11
Coctrypes 24.112.47
Cocytius 27.70.2
Codatractus 27.40.11
codens, state and province 5
Codling Moth 27.38.56
Codrus 25.39.12

coeca, Braula 29.76.1 (Fig. 29.48)
coeca, Pulicomorpha 24.24.287
coecus, Labidus 25.58.1 (Fig. 25.32)
coelestinus, Zygobarinus 24.113.343
Coelichneumonops 25.16.250
Coelidia 21.14.33
Coelidiinae, supra 21.14.33
Coelidiini, supra 21.14.33
Coelinidae 25.13.92
Coeliodes 24.113.289
Coeliodini, supra 24.113.283
Coelioxys 25.68.24
Coelocnemis 24.87.80
Coeloides 25.13.31
Coelomyia 29.100.27
Coelopa 29.77.1
Coelopencyrtus 25.25.82
Coelophthinia 29.9.74
Coelopidea, supra 29.77.1
Coelopisthia 25.19.122
Coelopoeta 27.16.1
Coelopoetinae, supra 27.16.1
Coelorhachis 25.16.333
Coelosia 29.9.42
Coelosthathma 28.38.89
Coelotanypodini, supra 29.24.5
Coelotanypus 29.24.6
Coelus 24.87.64
Coenagrion 7.11.7
Coenagrionidae, supra 7.11.1
Coenia 29.93.57
coenia, Junonia 27.46.30 (Fig. 27.139)
Coenipeta 27.75.121
Coenochroa 27.55.413
Coenodomus 27.55.269
Coenomyia 29.29.2
Coenomyiinae, supra 29.29.1
Coenonycha 24.30.82
Coenonympha 27.48.8
Coenonymphini, supra 27.48.8
Coenopoeus 24.106.274
Coenosia 29.100.2
Coenosiinae, supra 29.100.1
Coenosopsia 29.100.43
Coenotus 29.40.34
Coenus 20.3.37
coerulescens, Osmia 25.68.21
coffeae, Saissetia 21.26.20
Coffee Bean Weevil 24.109.1
Cogia 27.40.21
cogitans, Euprostocerus 24.46.32 (Fig.
 24.90)
cognatus, Prosopothrips 22.4.30
coinopus, Hylesia 27.69.9
Colaspia 24.107.43
Colaspides 24.107.57
Colastes 25.13.38
colbaltinus, Chrysochus 24.107.47
Colcondamhia 29.103.28
Colecerus 24.113.109
Colenis 24.19.6
Coleocentrini, supra 25.16.189
Coleocentrus 25.16.189
Coleomegilla 24.80.45
Coleomethia 24.106.32
Coleomyia 29.37.46
Coleophasia 29.105.35
Coleophora 27.18.1
Coleophoridae, supra 27.18.1
Coleophorinae, supra 27.18.1
Coleopina 29.77.2
Coleoptera, supra 24.1.1
coleoptrata, Lepyronia 21.12.3
Coleotechnites 27.23.19
colfaxiana, Barbara 27.38.21
Coliadinae, supra 27.42.11

Coliadini, supra 27.42.11
Colias 27.42.11
Colimona 21.14.54
Colinicola 18.1.12
Colladonus 21.14.108
collare, Spharagemon 11.5.48
Collaria 20.23.195
collaris, Acrotelsa 5.3.1
collaris, Diplozona 20.23.15
collaris, Mesocoelopus 24.63.44
collaris, Nematoplus 24.86.4
collaris, Phryganophilus 24.98.37
collaris, Pronecera 24.106.101 (Fig.
 24.193)
collecting areas 27
collecting equipment 50 (Table 5.2)
collecting goals 31
collecting insects 31
collecting obligations 31
collecting places; forbidding 30
collection, arrangement and storage of 41
Collembola, supra 1.1.1 (Fig. 1.1)
Colletes 25.63.2
Colletidae, supra 25.63.1
Colletinae, supra 25.63.1 (Fig. 25.62)
Colletini, supra 25.63.2
collinisi, Atropates 25.25.128
Colliuris 24.4.140
Collomena 27.75.177
Collomenini, supra 27.75.176
Collophora 1.7.2
Collops 24.68.1
Collyria 25.16.195
Collyriinae, supra 25.16.195
Colobaea 29.70.2
Colobochyla 27.75.23
Colobopsis 25.58.66
Colobostema 29.15.4
Coloburella 1.4.5
Coloburini, supra 27.46.42
Colocasia 27.75.225
Coloceras 18.1.13
Colocistis 25.53.10
Colomychus 27.55.148
Colomyia 29.11.36
Colon 24.22.10
colon, Occidryas 27.46.22
Coloneura 27.11.10
Colonae, supra 24.22.10
colonus, Xylotrechus 24.106.123
Colopha 21.19.54
Colopterus 24.70.9
color 23
colorada, Benjaminiola 27.75.269
coloradanus, Euvacusus 24.102.11
coloradella, Polix 27.15.31
coloradensis, Cuneifrons 27.55.33
coloradensis, Deuterophlebia 29.4.1
coloradensis, Prodoxus 27.8.11
coloradensis, Scaphinotus 24.4.16
coloradensis, Tarsopsylla 30.7.16
Coloradia 27.69.6
Colorado Potato Beetle 24.107.60
Coloradoa 21.19.55
Colostygia 27.61.195
Colotois 27.61.99
Colotrechninae, supra 25.19.20
Colotrechnus 25.19.20
Colpocephalum 18.6.9
Colpodes 24.4.76
Colpognathus 25.16.203
Colpomeria 25.16.20
Colposternus 24.63.32
Colpotrochia 25.16.289
columba, Tremex 25.9.4, 25.16.42
columbae, Columbicola 18.1.14

Columbia Basin Wireworm 24.48.27
columbia, Hyalophora 27.69.18
columbiae, Adiastola 25.16.115
columbianum, Panstenon 25.19.39
columbianum, Propsilomma 25.42.1
Columbian Timber Beetle 24.112.67
columbianus, Corthylus 24.112.67
Columbicola 18.1.14
Columbiella 29.65.5
Columbine Borer Moth 27.75.279
columella, Strymon 27.43.34
Colydiidae, supra 24.93.1
Colydiinae, supra 24.93.1
Colydiini, supra 24.93.17
Colydium 24.93.18 (Fig. 24.163)
Colymbetes 24.7.33
Colymbetinae, supra 24.7.24
Colymbetini, supra 24.7.31
Colyostichus 25.18.2
Comachara 27.73.25
Comacmaeops 24.106.184
Comadia 27.37.6
Comantella 29.37.7
Comasarcophaga 29.103.29
Comatomenopon 18.6.10
Comb-clawed Bark Beetle Family 24.88.1
Comblipped Casemaker Caddisfly Family,
 supra 26.17.1
comes, Irazona 27.39.5
comesor, Psilophryoidea 25.25.155
Comma 27.46.24
comma, Polygonia 27.46.24 (Fig. 27.129)
comma, Stenolophus 24.4.114
Commellus 21.14.207
commentella, Zamopsyche 27.11.5
Common Barklice Family 17.23.1
Common Bee Fly 29.40.12
Common Blue 7.11.8
Common Burrower Mayfly Family 6.11.1
Common Carpenter Bee 25.69.46
Common Carrion Beetle 24.21.7
Common Cattle Grub 29.102.5
Common Cave Cricket 11.9.8
Common Clear-wing 27.70.30
Common Damsel Bug 20.18.5
Common Earwig Family 13.5.1
Common Eastern Firefly 24.55.8
Common Eastern Velvet Ant 25.55.16
Common Flea Family, supra 30.1.1
Common Forktail 7.11.10
Common Malaria Mosquito 29.20.1
Common Meadow Katydid 11.7.23
Common Midge 29.24.56
Common Mole Cricket 11.11.2
common names 16
Common Net-spinning Caddisfly
 Family 26.4.1
Common Plasterer Bee 25.63.2
Common Sawfly Family, supra 25.7.1
Common Scorpionfly Family, supra 28.4.1
Common Skimmer Family 7.7.1
Common Spongefly 23.13.2
Common Stilt Bug 20.12.6
Common Stonefly Family 8.9.1
Common Thick-headed Fly 29.49.7
Common Thread-waisted Wasp 25.62.14
Common Walkingstick 10.1.4
Common Walkingstick Family 10.1.1
Common Wood-nymph 27.48.9
Commoptera 29.46.36
commortalis, Nannobotys 27.55.41
communa, Isotoma 1.4.23
commune, Crenidorsum 21.18.13
communis, Lygocoris 20.23.165
communis, Pyrgus 27.40.38 (Fig. 27.68)
comosa, Moselyana 26.10.50

comosus, Synxenoderus 20.20.6
Compacta 27.55.159
compacta, Acalophaena 24.24.48
compacta, Arcynopteryx 8.7.5
compacta, Pachygontha 20.7.24
compactus compactus Colletes 25.63.2
compactus, Epeolus 25.69.8
compactus, Xylosandrus 24.112.55
comperei, Myiocnema 25.25.18
Comperia 25.25.80
Comperiella 25.25.93
Comperiini, supra 25.25.80
completa, Rhagoletis 29.61.44
Composia 27.73.2
composita, Eulithosia 27.75.353
Composite Thrips 22.4.44
compound eyes 12
compressiceps, Lecanocerus 29.46.38
compressicornis, Trioxys 25.14.14
compressiventris, Blacus 25.13.130
Compsilura 29.105.238
Compsobata 29.51.2
Compsobracon 25.13.32
Compsocryptus 25.16.170
Compsolechia 27.23.73
Compsus 24.113.105
compta, Setanta 25.16.230
comptana, Ancylis 27.38.42
comptoniella, Acrobasis 27.55.282
comptulatalis, Acigona 27.55.227
comptulus, Plochiocoris 20.21.12
Compsodes 14.4.3
Comstock Mealybug 21.25.35
comstocki, Callophrys 27.43.24
comstocki, Feralia 27.75.428 (Fig. 27.373)
comstocki, Pseudococcus 21.25.35
comstockiana, Petrova 27.38.20
Comstockiella 21.38.19
comstockii, Euplectrus 25.26.13
comta, Bonnetia 29.105.104
comyntas, Everes 27.43.41 (Fig. 27.111)
Conahaspsis 21.36.1
Conalcaea 11.5.85
Conalia 24.99.2
Conandrena 25.65.1
Conanthalictus 25.66.4
Conarete 29.11.13
Concana 27.75.77
concanus, Fridonus 21.14.119
concavus, Lixus 24.113.150 (Fig. 24.280)
concentricus, Pasaremus 21.14.178
Conchapelopia 29.24.16
Conchaspididae, supra 21.36.1
conchiformis, Lepidosaphes 21.38.45
Conchylodes 27.55.186
concinna, Megachile 25.68.22
concinna, Schizura 27.71.34
concinnata, Compsilura 29.105.238
concinnulus, Moranus 24.72.7
concinnus, Plagiotrypes 25.16.263
concolor, Cerenopus 24.87.131
concolor, Cupes 24.1.1 (Fig. 24.25)
concolor, Dendroides 24.94.4
concolor, Geropa 24.106.35
concolorella, Ithome 27.21.25
concors, Glympis 27.75.45
concumbena, Catocala 27.75.148
condei, Acerella 2.3.3
Condica 27.75.335
condignus, Florilegus 25.69.31
condita, Aplectoides 27.75.579
conditum, Chromagrion 7.11.6
Condylognatha, supra 20.1.1
Condylolomia 27.55.258
Condylorrhiza 27.55.154
Condylostylus 29.43.2

Cone-heads 11.7.17
configurata, Mamestra 27.75.479
configuratus, Diplicolenus 21.14.192
confinis, Acerentulus 2.3.1
confinis, Chaetocnema 24.107.144
conflictana, Choristoneura 27.38.72
confluens, Hydromyza 29.98.26
confluenta, Amphibolips 25.34.28 (Fig.
 25.26)
confluenta, Lopidea 20.23.110 (Fig. 20.53)
confusa, Ampulicomorpha 25.52.1
confusa, Isoperla 8.7.2
Confused Flour Beetle 24.87.110
confusum, Tribolium 24.87.110 (Fig.
 24.155)
confusum, Tricorynus 24.63.43 (Fig.
 24.126)
confusus, Dryocoetes 24.112.46
confusus, Hemaenasius 25.25.146
confusus, Ips 24.112.51
Conga 27.40.55
Coniana 11.5.68
Conibiosoma 24.87.157
Conibius 24.87.153
conica, Diapria 25.42.29
conica, Rhyncophoromyia 29.46.23
Coniceps 29.62.3
Conicera 29.46.11
Coniceromyia 29.46.12
conicola, Hapleginella 29.94.11
conicola, Paratimia 24.106.19
conicus, Gastracanthus 25.19.19
conicus, Rhynchopsilus 25.42.15
Conifer Sawfly Family, supra 25.6.1
Coniteroclerus 24.67.16
coniferous forest 28
Coniontini, supra 24.87.63
Coniontis 24.87.65
Coniopterygidae, supra 23.5.1
Coniopteryginae, supra 23.5.4
Coniopterygini, supra 23.5.1
Coniopterygoidea, supra 23.5.1
Coniopteryx 23.5.4
Conioscinella 29.94.23
coniperda, Conophthorus 24.112.63
conjugella Argyresthia 27.31.1 (Fig. 27.49)
conjunctimontis, Xyraeomyia 29.68.12
Conocalama 25.16.260
Conocephalinae, supra 11.7.21
Conocephalocoris 20.23.19
Conocephalus 11.7.21
Conochares 27.75.215
Conoderini, supra 24.48.14
Conoderus 24.48.14
Conoecus 24.87.10
Conomyra 25.58.60
Conontinae, supra 24.90.14
Cononotus 24.90.14
Conophthorus 24.112.63
Conopidae, supra 29.49.1
Conopinae, supra 29.49.1
Conopini, supra 29.49.1
Conopoidea, supra 29.49.1
Conops 29.49.1
Conorhinopsylla 30.4.14
Conoshorus 29.40.14
Conostethus 20.23.40
Conostigmus 25.46.3
Conotelus 24.70.7
conotracheli, Patasson 25.27.14
Conotrachelus 24.113.238
Conozoa 11.5.61
Conservula 27.75.288
consobrinella, Glyptocera 27.55.312
consocius, Limnephilus 26.10.21 (Fig.
 26.28)

consors, Hoplomachidea 20.23.44
conspersa, Agonochaetia 27.23.55
conspersa, Chloealtis 11.5.1
conspersus, Alydus 20.5.9
conspersus, Pachypeltocoris 20.23.174
conspurcata, Eurosta 29.61.12
consputa, Melanophila 24.46.20
constans, Seryda 27.50.2 (Fig. 27.155)
constricta, Cartodere 24.82.10
constrictum, Malacosoma 27.68.11
constrictus, Amphiareus 20.21.21
constrictus, Bradyrhynooides 24.113.37
consularis, Anisota 27.69.5
contaminata, Antillormenis 21.8.5
Contarinia 29.11.108
conterminus, Teliapsocus 17.12.1
Contiger 27.55.10
contigua, Sphaerophoria 29.47.31
contracta, Meracantha 24.87.127
contractus, Thylodrias 24.61.3
Convelinus 21.14.92
convergens, Cryptoxilos 25.13.150
convergens, Hippodamia 24.80.43
convergens, Nefoncerus 24.30.59
Convergent Lady Beetle 24.80.43
convexicolle, Cerophytum 24.50.1
convulutella, Zophodia 27.55.379
Conwentzia 23.5.6
Conwentzini, supra 23.5.6
cookei, Hoplocampa 25.7.18
cookei, Plusiocampa 3.1.8 (Fig. 3.3)
cookei, Stenometopiellus 21.14.172
cookii, Suioestrus 29.102.6
Cooley Spruce Gall Adelgid 21.20.1
cooleyi, Adelges 21.10.1
cooleyi, Lejota 29.47.62
Copablepharon 27.75.538
Copaeodes 27.40.58
Copanarta 27.75.455
Copecrypta 29.105.102
copelandi, Traicanthella 1.2.5
Copelatini, supra 24.7.29
Copelatus 24.7.29
Copestylum 29.47.43
Cophenchus 25.16.57
Cophes 24.113.269
Cophura 29.37.10
Copibryophila 27.75.206
Copicerus 21.2.1
Copicucullia 27.75.466
Copidita 24.97.9
Copidonoma 25.25.83
Copidosomatini, supra 25.25.81
Copidryas 27.75.244
Copipanolis 27.75.431
Copiphorinae, supra 11.7.17
Copivaleria 27.75.434
Copper Butterfly Family, supra 27.43.1
Copper Underwing 27.75.317
Coprini, supra 24.30.8
Copris 24.30.10
Coproica 29.88.3
Copromorphid Moth Family, supra 27.24.1
Copromorphidae, supra 27.24.1
Copromorphoidea, supra 27.24.1
Copromyza 29.88.2
Coprophilus 24.24.146
Coproporus 24.24.178
Coptocycla 24.107.184
Coptodera 24.4.146
Coptodisca 27.9.3
Coptostethus 24.48.68
Coptotermes 15.3.4
Coptotermitinae, supra 15.3.4
Coptotomini, supra 24.7.30
Coptotomus 24.7.30

Coquillettia 20.23.75
coquilletti, Caladonus 21.14.110
coquilletti, Dideomima 29.47.23
coquilletti, Physoclypeus 29.82.13
Coquillettidia 29.20.5
Coquillettomyia 29.11.96
cora, Sierraperla 8.6.2 (Fig. 8.10)
coracias, Pseudanthracia 27.75.127
Coraia 24.107.74
Coral Hairstreak 27.43.15
coras, Polites 27.40.66
Corcyra 27.55.277
Cordalia 24.24.216
cordata, Anzamyia 29.24.216
cordatus, Rotundiceps 18.1.55
Cordillacris 11.5.28
Cordilura 29.98.2
Cordilurina 29.98.2
Cordulaia 7.6.2
Cordulegaster 7.2.1
Cordulegasteridae, supra 7.2.1
Corduliidae, supra 7.6.1
Cordyla 29.9.30
Cordylodiplosis 29.11.143
Cordylomyia 29.11.7
Cordylospasta 24.101.4
Cordylurella 29.98.19
Corecorini, supra 20.4.15
Corecoris 20.4.15
Coreinae, supra 20.4.2
Coreini, supra 20.4.19
Coreopsomela 24.107.62
coresia, Marpesia 27.46.44
Corethrella 29.19.5
Corethrellinae, supra 29.19.4
coriacea, Piodes 24.106.175
Corimelaenidae, supra 20.2.1
Corinthomyia 29.11.9
Coriomeris 20.4.33
Coriscidae, supra 20.5.1
Corisella 20.35.12
Corixidae, supra 20.35.1
Corixidea 20.25.2
Corixinae, supra 20.35.3
Corixini, supra 20.35.7
Corizidae, supra 20.6.1
Cormelaena 20.2.3
Cormobius 25.16.85
Corn Blotch Leaf Miner 29.68.1
Corn Earworm 27.75.599
Corn Field Ant 25.58.67
Corn Hopper 21.2.18
Corn Leaf Aphid 21.19.186
Corn Root Aphid 21.19.13
Corn Root Webworm 27.55.203
Corn Sap Beetle 24.70.10
Corn Silk Beetle 24.107.112
Cornaphis 21.19.56
corni, Chionaspis 21.38.14
corni, Parthenolecanium 21.26.14
corni, Pseudasiphonaphis 21.19.176
Cornifrons 27.55.71
cornifrons, Osmia 25.68.21
corniger, Nasutiterms 15.4.4 (Fig. 15.6)
Cornonoculus 21.31.3
cornuale, Crocinosoma 29.105.295
cornuparvum, Neolecanium 21.26.12
Cornuplura 21.13.5
cornutus, Amphicerus 24.64.13
cornutus, Bolitotherus 24.87.67
cornutus, Bostrycholites 24.64.12
cornutus, Callipogonius 24.106.253
cornutus, Corydalus 23.2.1 (Fig. 23.6)
cornutus, Epiphanis 24.52.18
cornutus, Gnatocerus 24.87.106
cornutus, Multareis 21.15.16

cornutus, Toxonotus 24.109.18 (Fig. 24.255)
coronada, Dicogaster 27.68.9
coronaria, Schidax 27.62.7
Coronimyia 29.105.294
Coronimyiina, supra 29.105.293
coronis, Speyeria 27.46.8
corope, Leucochroma 27.55.152
Corrodopsylla 30.4.23
corrugata, Euptychodera 20.3.14
corrugatans, Prociphilus 21.19.172
corruptus, Polypsocus 17.13.1
Corsoncus 25.16.378
Corthylini, supra 24.112.58
Corthylus 24.112.67
Corticaria 24.82.13
corticaria, Strongylaspis 24.106.2
Corticariinae, supra 24.82.13
Corticea 27.40.45
corticea, Corticea 27.40.45
Corticeus 24.87.121
Corticini, supra 24.93.2
corticinus, Achenomorphus 24.24.49
corticis, Neothrips 22.5.54
Corticivora 27.38.55
corticola, Bolitophagus 24.87.68
Corticoris 20.23.2
Corticotomus 24.66.10
cortiphagus, Enaphalodes 24.106.70 (Fig. 24.187)
Cortodera 24.106.189
Coruna 25.19.66
corusaca, Pristen 27.21.16
corvina, Paraleucopis 29.83.5
corvus, Hyperimerus 25.19.38
Corydalidae, supra 23.2.1
Corydalinae, supra 23.2.1
Corydalus 23.2.1
coryli, Monocesta 24.107.74
coryli, Myzocallis 21.19.142
coryli, Trialeurodes 21.18.17 (Fig. 21.23)
Corylophidae, supra 24.79.1
Corylophinae, supra 24.79.1
Corylophodes 24.79.2
Corynocera 29.24.74
Corynoneura 29.24.89
Corynoptera 29.10.9
Corynopus 25.62.60
corynorhini, Trichobius 29.108.2
Corynothrix 1.5.1
corynothrix, Decorosiphon 21.19.60
Coryphaeschna 7.4.5
Coryphista 27.61.208
Corypsylla 30.4.17
Corypsyllini, supra 30.4.17
Coryrhophora 27.13.9
Corythaica 20.14.6
Corythucha 20.14.7
Coscinocephalus 24.30.102
Coscinoptera 24.107.17
Cosipara 27.55.2
Cosmariomyia 29.31.20
Cosmetopus 29.98.12
Cosmia 27.75.408
Cosmiotes 27.16.7
Cosmocomoidea 25.27.7
Cosmoconus 25.16.66
Cosmopepla 20.3.41
Cosmophorini, supra 25.13.162
Cosmophorus 25.13.162
Cosmoplites 24.113.368
Cosmopolite 27.46.27
Cosmopolitan Grain Barklouse 17.14.1
Cosmopterigid Moth Family, supra 27.21.1
Cosmopterigidae, supra 27.21.1
Cosmopteriginae, supra 27.21.3

Cosmopterix 27.21.3
Cosmosalia 24.106.227
Cosmosoma 27.73.85
Cosmobaris 24.113.304
Cossidae, supra 27.37.1
Cossinae, supra 27.37.5
Cossoidea, supra 27.37.1
Cossoninae, supra 24.113.371
Cossonini, supra 24.113.372
Cossonus 24.113.375
Cossula 27.37.4
Cossulinae, supra 27.37.4
costa 21
costalis, Ambaraphis 21.19.6
costalis, Hypsopygia 27.55.235
costalis, Monellia 21.19.137
costalis, Poecilogonalos 25.47.3
costalis, Webesteriana 29.105.62
costalis, Xenopterella 29.82.23
costata, Stemorrhages 27.55.155
costatum, Anchomma 24.93.2
costatus, Pemelus 24.12.34
costatus, Trogloderus 24.87.141
costipennis, Eudistenia 24.106.25
costipennis, Glyptasida 24.87.50
Cosymbiini, supra 27.61.181
Cotalpa 24.30.87
Cothonaspis 25.32.14
Cotinis 24.30.121
Cotton Aphid 21.19.15
Cotton Boll Weevil 24.113.208
Cottonwood Borer 24.106.233
Cotton Fleahopper 20.23.64
Cotton Lace Bug 20.14.7
Cotton Leaf Miner 27.5.1
Cotton Leafworm 27.75.72 (Fig. 27.327)
Cotton Square Borer 27.43.34
Cotton Stainer 20.8.1
Cotton Stainer Family 20.8.1
Cotton Stem Moth 27.23.82
Cottonwood Dagger Moth 27.75.231
Cottonwood Leaf Beetle 24.107.64
Cottonwood Twig Borer 28.38.31
Cottony Camellia Scale 21.26.19
Cottony Cushion Scale 21.23.8
Cottony Grape Scale 21.26.19
Cottony Hydrangea Scale 21.26.19
Cottony Maple Leaf Scale 21.26.19
Cottony Maple Scale 21.26.19
Coulee Cricket 11.7.41
couloniana, Stilpnochlora 1.7.12
Cowpea Aphid 21.19.15
Cowpea Curculio 24.113.241
Cowpea Weevil 25.108.6
coxata, Nycterphilia 29.108.1
coxator, Collyria 25.16.195
Coxelini, supra 24.93.3
Coxelus 24.93.3
Coxina 27.75.119
coxa 20.22
coypus, Pitrufquenia 18.4.4
Crab Louse 19.9.1
Crab-hole Mosquito 29.20.13
crabo germanica, Vespa 25.59.26 (Fig. 25.51)
Crabronini, supra 25.62.56
craccivora, Aphis 21.19.15
Cracker Grasshopper 11.5.62
Cradytes 24.68.34
craigheadi, Mixothrips 22.5.68
Crambidia 27.73.8
crambidoides, Diatraea 27.55.228
Crambinae, supra 27.55.203
Crambini, supra 27.55.203
Crambodes 27.75.324
Crambus 27.55.203

Cramptonomyia 29.7.1
Cranberry Fruitworm 27.55.282
Cranberry Girdler 27.55.205
Cranberry Rootworm 24.107.44
Cranberry Spanworm 27.61.41
Cranberry Weevil 24.113.208
crandalli, Glenosmea 25.48.16
Crane Fly Family, supra 29.2.1
craniifer, Blaberus 14.6.1 (Fig. 14.20)
Craniotus 24.87.30
Crapemyrtle 21.19.212
Craponius 24.113.283
Craspedochaeta 29.99.8
Craspedolepta 21.17.5
Craspedonirmus 18.1.15
Craspedorrhynchus 18.1.16
Craspeduchus 20.7.1
Crassana 21.14.137
Crassaspis 21.38.20
crassicornis, Anaticola 18.1.3 (Fig. 18.1)
crassicornis, Eudectus 24.24.112
crassicornis, Hyperacmus 25.16.482
crassicornis, Lampracanthia 20.32.5
crassicornis, Neoxus 24.24.150
crassicornis, Stictopleurs 20.6.7
crassicornis, Umbonia 21.15.4
crassidentata, Peponapis 25.69.29
crassinervis, Chaetostigmoptera 29.105.302
crassipes, Carrhydrus 24.7.25
crassipes, Podagra 27.75.382
crassipes, Reptatrix 25.16.168
crassipes, Xestoleptura 24.106.221
crassiuscula, Caenurgina 27.75.140 (Fig. 27.334)
Crassivesica 27.75.553
crassocornis, Stigmatomeria 29.9.28
Crassomicrodes 25.13.77
crassus, Hadrotes 24.24.15
crataegarius, Ovatus 21.19.155
crataegi, Conotrachelus 24.113.238 (Fig. 24.289)
crataegi, Glossonotus 21.15.36
crataegi,
 Pseudanthonomus 24.113.215 (Fig. 24.286)
Crataepus 25.26.49
Crataraea 24.24.217
Craterocercus 25.7.21
Cratichneumon 25.16.208
Cratidus 24.87.138
Cratocryptus 25.16.138
Cratomini, supra 25.19.65
Cratomorphini, supra 24.55.6
Cratomus 25.19.65
Cratypedes 11.5.42
Crawfordia 24.105.5
Crawfordiella 21.17.19
Crawling Water Beetle Family, supra 24.6.1
Crazy Ant 25.58.69
Creeping Water Bug Family, supra 20.38.1
Cregya 24.67.27
Cremastinae, supra 25.16.430
Cremastobaeus 25.43.9
Cremastobombycia 27.14.18
Cremastocheilus 24.30.134
Cremastochilini, supra 24.30.131
cremastoides, Leptocampoplex 25.16.400
Cremastus 25.16.436
Crematogaster 25.58.30
Crematogastrini, supra 25.58.30
Cremersia 29.46.26
Cremifania 29.83.1
Cremifaniinae, supra 29.83.1
Cremnodes 25.16.134
Cremnodina, supra 25.16.134
Cremnops 25.13.78

crenatum, Pteryngium 24.74.8
Crenidorsum 21.18.13
Crenitis 24.12.18
Crenontiades 20.23.148
Crenulaspidiotus 21.38.21
crenulata, Anurapteryx 27.63.1 (Fig. 27.204)
crenulata, Orthodes 27.75.519 (Fig 27.387)
crenulata, Phyllophaga 24.30.65 (Fig. 24.69)
crenulella helix, Apterona 27.11.3
creola, Enodia 27.48.1
creoleorum, Fossocarus 24.30.76
Creophilus 24.24.14
Creosote Bush Beetle 24.101.12
Crepiododera 24.107.135
crepuscularia, Ectropis 27.61.44 (Fig. 27.180)
crepuscularis, Chlorotabanus 29.26.16
crescentifasciella, Compsolechia 27.23.73
Crescent-marked Lily Aphid 21.19.24
Cresote Bush Beetle 24.101.12
cresphontes, Heraclides 27.41.6 (Fig. 27.81)
cressonana, Ctenucha 27.73.74 (Fig 27.311)
Cressonia 27.70.17
cressoni, Heteropterna 29.9.10
cressoni, Megagathis 25.13.80
cressonii, Svastra 25.69.27
Cressoniella 25.68.22
Cressonomyia 29.93.25
cretacea, Gymnetina 24.30.124
creusa, Euchloe 27.42.8
cribipennis, Neochlamisus 24.107.34
Cribrate Weevil 24.113.68
cribratus, Glyptotus 24.87.81
cribratus, Macmactes 24.113.262
cribricollis, Otiorhynchus 24.113.68
cribrifrons, Coscinocephalus 24.30.102
cribrosus, Archophileurus 24.30.111
cribrum, Plesiocis 24.92.8
Cribrus 21.14.193
cribulosus, Melanotus 24.48.67
Cricket Family 11.10.1
Crickets 11.1.1
Crimalia 24.24.218
Crimona 27.75.458
Criomorphus 21.2.24
crinitus, Lophopogonius 24.106.254
Crinkled Flannel Moth 27.51.2
Crinurina 29.99.8
Criocerinae, supra 24.107.11
Crioceris 24.107.11
Criocoris 20.23.41
Crioprora 29.47.88
Crioprosopus 24.106.147
Criorhina 29.47.72
Crioscolia 25.56.2
Crisicoccus 21.25.11
crispata, Lagoa 27.51.2
cristifasciella, Arogalea 27.23.25
crista, Eriopyga 27.75.522
cristatus, Arilus 20.17.12 (Fig. 20.39)
cristatus, Meristhus 24.48.4
cristatus, Pelenosomus 24.113.288
cristicola, Ollifiella 21.29.1
critola, Hypostrymon 27.43.32
crocea, Exegetia 27.13.11
crocea, Hemichroa 25.7.20
Crocidema 24.113.133
Crocidomera 27.55.287
Crocidophora 27.55.83
Crocidosema 27.38.38
Crocigrapha 27.75.505

Crocinosoma 29.105.295
Croesia 27.38.60
Croesus 25.7.31
crookiae, Nelaspis 21.38.52
Crophius 20.7.21
Cropia 27.75.307
Cropodes 24.25.24
Crosimus 24.74.4
cross veins 21
Crossidius 24.106.162
Crossocerus 25.62.63
Crossodonthina 1.2.16
Crossopalpus 29.42.11
Cross-striped Cabbageworm 27.55.69
crotchi, Chrysomela 24.107.64
crotchii, Bombus 25.70.2
crotchii, Pseudalypia 27.75.222
Crotchiibombus 25.70.2
Croton Mussel Scale 21.38.45
cruciatus, Graphopsocus 17.11.1
cruentata, Pseudostrangalia 24.106.211
Crumbana 21.14.209
Crumomyia 29.88.2
cruscula, Lenziella 29.24.75
Crustacea 10
cruxrufa, Polypria 24.98.30
Crymodes 27.75.253
Cryotomyzus 21.19.58
Cryphalini, supra 24.112.33
Cryphalomorphus 24.112.36
Cryphalus 24.112.37
Cryphia 27.75.237
Cryphocricinae, supra 20.38.5
Cryphocricos 20.38.5
Cryphula 20.7.29
Cryplocala 27.75.586
Cryptadius 24.87.14
cryptale, Oligostigmoides 27.55.15
Cryptanura 25.16.173
Cryptaphis 21.19.57
Cryptarcha 24.70.33
Cryptarchinae, supra 24.70.33
Crypteffigies 25.16.209
Crypticerya 21.23.7
Cryptina, supra 25.16.158
Cryptinae, supra 25.16.84
Cryptini, supra 25.16.150
Cryptobotys 27.55.181
Cryptocarenus 24.112.41
Cryptocephalinae, supra 24.107.24
Cryptocephalus 24.107.25
Cryptocercidae, supra 14.2.1
Cryptocercus 14.2.1
Cryptocheilus 25.60.6
Cryptochetid Fly Family, supra 29.95.1
Cryptochetidae, supra 29.95.1
Cruyptochetum 29.95.1
Cryptochia 26.10.3
Cryptochironomus 29.24.45
Cryptococcidae, supra 21.30.1
Cryptococcus 21.30.1
Cryptoglossa 24.87.43
Cryptoglossini, supra 24.87.40
Cryptohelcostizus 25.16.187
Cryptolabis 29.2.52
Cryptolaemus 24.80.13
Cryptolepidus 24.113.32
Cryptolestes 24.72.17
Cryptomeigenia 29.105.239
Cryptophagidae, supra 24.74.1
Cryptophaginae, supra 24.74.1
Cryptophagini, supra 24.74.1
Cryptophagus 24.74.6
Cryptophilinae, supra 24.75.5
Cryptophilus 24.75.5
Cryptophobetron 27.52.12

Cryptophorus 24.106.131
Cryptopimpla 25.16.312
Cryptopleurum 24.12.32
Cryptopristus 25.18.20
cryptomeriae, Ectopsoscopis 17.16.1
Cryptopone 25.58.15
cryptops, Calyptillus 24.113.31
Cryptopygus 1.4.14
Cryptorama 24.63.45
Cryptoramorphus 24.63.46
Cryptorhopalum 24.61.10
Cryptorhynchina, supra 24.113.257
Cryptorhynchinae, supra 24.113.237
Cryptorhynchinini, supra 24.113.245
Cryptorhynchus 24.113.264
Cryptoripersia 21.25.12
Cryptoserphini, supra 25.39.3
Cryptoserphus, supra 25.39.2, 25.39.5
Cryptostemma 20.24.2
Cryptotermes 15.2.8
Cryptothelea 27.11.6
Cryptotreta 29.61.10
Cryptothrips 22.5.6
Cryptoxilos 25.13.150
Crypturgus 24.112.42
Cryptus 25.16.166
crysalus, Hypaurotis 27.43.9
crystleae, Illinoia 21.19.105
crytobium, Subacyrosiphon 21.19.202
Crytosiinae, supra 29.40.21
Crytotendipes 29.24.48
Cteniscus 25.16.73
Ctenicera 24.48.37
Ctenicerini, supra 24.48.35
Ctenichneumon 25.16.233
Ctenioschelini, supra 25.69.43
Ctenisini, supra 24.25.80
Ctenisis 24.25.80
Ctenobium 24.63.21
Ctenocallis 21.19.59
Ctenocephalides 30.1.3
Ctenochira 25.16.58
Ctenodactylini, supra 24.4.136
Ctenodactylitae, supra 24.4.136
Ctenodactylomyia 29.11.91
Ctenolepisma 5.3.3
Ctenopelma 25.16.322
Ctenopelmatinae, supra 25.16.321
Ctenopelmatini, supra 25.16.322
Ctenophora 29.2.6
Ctenophthalminae, supra 30.4.24
Ctenophthalmini, supra 30.4.25
Ctenophthalmus 30.4.25
Ctenophyllus 30.6.6
Ctenopyga 25.58.5
Ctenothrips 22.4.38
Ctenotrachelus 20.17.33
Ctenucha 27.73.74
Ctenuchinae, supra 27.73.74
Ctesias 24.61.12
Cuban Cockroach 14.6.5
Cuban Laurel Thrips 22.5.43
cubensis, Bephratelloides 25.20.16
cubensis, Idiataphe 7.7.9
cubital 22
Cubitognatha 25.68.20
Cubocephalus 25.16.139
Cuckoo Bee 25.69.1
Cuckoo Bee Family, supra 25.69.1
Cuckoo Wasp Family, supra 25.50.1
Cuclotogaster 18.1.17
Cucujidae, supra 24.72.1
Cucujinae, supra 24.72.11
Cucujini, supra 24.72.11
Cucujoidea, supra 24.70.1
Cucujus 24.72.13

Cuculicola 18.1.18
Cuculiphilus 18.6.11
Cucullia 27.75.464
cucullidea, Emariannia 27.75.468
Cuculliinae, supra 27.75.388
Cucullini, supra 27.75.462
Cucullococcus 21.25.13
Cuculoecus 18.1.19
cucumeris, Epitrix 24.107.137 (Fig. 24.238)
Cucurbit Midge 29.11.119
cucurbitae, Dacus, supra 29.61.1
cucurbitae, Melittia 27.35.8 (Fig. 27.53)
Cudonigera 27.38.73
Cuerna 21.14.43
Culex 29.20.12
Culicidae, supra 29.20.1 (Figs. 29.28, 29.29)
Culicinae, supra 29.20.3
Culicini, supra 29.20.4
culiciops, Terebraella 25.16.202
Culicoidea, supra 29.18.1
Culicoides 29.23.5
Culicoidini, supra 29.23.5
Culicomorpha, supra 29.18.1
Culisetia 29.20.11
Cullumanobombus 25.70.2
Culoptila 26.6.4
cultellatum, Neoerythromma 7.11.12
Cultrarius 25.16.287
cultriger, Diplocladius 29.24.95
Cultus 8.7.7
cumingi, Araeocorynus 24.109.2
Cummingsiella 18.1.20
cunctans, Tipula 29.2.9
cunea, Hyphantria 27.73.38 (Figs. 27.287, 27.288)
cuneatus, Neocapsus 20.23.170
Cuneifrons 27.55.33
Cuniberta 27.55.288
cuniculi, Cuterebra 29.102.2
cunilae, Stephensia 27.16.3
cunina, Ignotomyia 29.105.391
Cupedidae, supra 24.1.1
Cupes 24.1.1
Cuphocerini, supra 29.105.102
Cupidaspis 21.38.22
Cupila 24.25.39
cuprarius, Sargus 29.31.6
cuprea, Abrenthia 27.28.1
cupressana, Paraschiza 25.31.12
cupressi, Ehrhornia 21.25.17
cupressi, Isoparce 27.70.8
cupressi, Pseudencyrtoides 25.25.112
cupreus, Lycaena 27.43.3
cupripenne, Agonum 24.4.74
Curculio 24.113.200
Curculionidae, supra 24.113.1
Curculioninae, supra 24.113.200
Curculionoidea, supra 24.108.1
curialis, Mamestra 27.75.479 (Fig. 27.376)
Curicta 20.36.3
Curictini, supra 20.36.3
Curinini, supra 24.106.84
Curimopsis 24.35.13
Curius 24.106.84
Curled Rose Sawfly 25.7.86
currani, Metaclythia 29.45.8
Curranops 29.58.4
Currant Aphid 21.19.58
Currant Borer 27.35.12
Currant Fruit Fly 29.61.52
Currant Fruit Weevil 24.113.215
Currant Spanworm 27.61.9
Currant Stem Girdler 25.12.3
curta, Coelophthinia 29.9.74

curtipennis, Chorthippus 11.5.3
Curtisella 25.13.6
curtisii, Amblysellus 21.14.219
curtistila, Heleniella 29.24.92
Curtomerus 24.106.56
Curtonotid Fly Family, supra 29.89.1
Curtonotidae, supra 29.89.1
Curtonotum 29.89.1
curtus, Lemophagus 25.16.243
curulis, Pelecotheca 29.105.276
curvata, Capis 27.75.197
curvata curvata, Corrodopsylla 30.4.23
curvicauda, Toxotrypana 29.61.1
curviliniella, Homostinea 27.10.13
curvinervis, Leiomyza 29.73.1
Curvinomia 25.66.8
curvipes, Lejota 29.47.62
curvipes, Melanderia 29.43.15
cushmani, Mesoclistus 25.16.190
cushmani, Oecotelma 25.16.120
cuspidata, Anomognathus 24.24.201
cuspidea, Eculidia 27.75.138 (Fig. 27.333)
Cuterebra 29.102.2
Cuterebridae, supra 29.102.1
Cuterebrinae, supra 29.102.2
Cutina 27.75.136
Cutworm Wasp 25.62.12
Cyamops 29.70.5
cyanea, Hemisphaerota 24.107.174
cyanea, Scutellista 25.19.34
cyaneiventris, Chlorohystricia 29.105.84
cyaneous, Leprus 11.5.45 (Fig. 11.16)
cyaneum, Chlorion 25.62.4
cyaneus, Sirex 25.9.1
cyanicollis, Lophalia 24.106.143
cyanide jar 36
cyanipennis octomaculata,
 Omophoita 24.107.147
cyanipes, Poecilonota 24.46.13 (Fig. 24.85)
Cyanophrys .27.43.25
cyanophylli, Abgrallaspis 21.38.1
Cyanophyllum, Scale 21.38.1
Cyanopterus 25.13.33
Cyanus 29.101.19
Cyarda 21.8.11
Cybalomia 27.55.197
Cybalomiinae, supra 27.55.197
cybele, Speyeria 27.46.8 (Fig. 27.122)
Cybister 24.7.42
Cybisterinae 24.7.41
Cybocephalinae, supra 24.70.36
Cybocephalus 24.70.36
Cybotus 24.87.149
cycadis, Poliaspis 21.38.65
Cychramus 24.70.28
Cychrini, supra 24.4.14
Cychrus 24.4.15
cyclades, Laniifera 27.55.160
Cyclica 27.61.203
Cyclocephala 24.30.100
Cyclocephalini, supra 24.30.98
Cyclogastrella 25.19.112
Cyclolabus 25.16.276
Cycloneda 24.80.41
Cyclophora 27.61.182
Cycloplasis 27.34.1
Cycloptiloides 11.10.2
Cycloptilum 11.10.1, 11.10.3
Cyclosattus 24.87.164
Cyclotelus 29.32.24
Cyclotrypema 24.107.96
Cycnia 27.73.65
Cydamus 20.5.3
Cydia 27.38.56
Cydnidae, supra 20.1.1

Cydninae, supra 20.1.1
Cydnoides 20.2.2
cydoniae, Corythucha 20.14.7
Cydosia 27.75.180
Cydosiini, supra 27.75.180
cygnaei, Dendrophagus 24.72.21
Cylapinae, supra 20.23.6
Cyladini, supra 24.113.16
Cylapus 20.23.6
Cylas 24.113.16
Cylidrella 24.66.9
Cylindera 24.3.4
Clindarctus 24.25.59
cylindrica, Afotella 27.75.379
cylindrica, Hoplitis 25.68.18
Cylindrical Bark Beetle Family,
 supra 24.93.1
cylindricollis, Sitona 24.113.50
cylindricollis, Stenocorus 24.106.176 (Fig. 24.200)
Cylindridia 24.113.347
cylindriformis, Xylophilus 24.52.22
Cylindrifrons 27.55.72
Cylindrocopturinus 24.113.278
Cylindrocopturus 24.113.275
Cylindromyia 29.105.22
Cylindromyiini, supra 29.105.18
Cylindronotum 24.4.155
Cylindrorhininae, supra 24.113.141
Cylindrotoma 29.2.10
Cylindrotominae, supra 29.2.10
Cylistix 24.26.44
Cylleniinae, supra 29.40.1
Cylloceria 25.16.486
Cyllodes 24.70.30
Cylloepus 24.45.7
Cyllopsis 27.48.3
Cyltopeptus 24.106.126
Cymaenes 27.40.50
Cymatia 20.35.2
Cymatiinae, supra 20.35.2
Cymatodera 24.67.10
Cymatoderella 24.67.6
Cymatophora 27.61.85
cymatophoroides, Pseudothyatira 27.59.2
Cymatothes 24.87.128
Cymbiodyta 24.12.24
Cymbopteryx 27.55.29
cymela, Megisto 27.48.6 (Fig. 27.149)
Cyminae, suprsa 20.7.14
Cymindis 24.4.141
Cymini, supra 20.7.14
Cymnosomatini, supra 29.105.1
Cymodusa 25.16.407
Cymodusopsis 25.16.408
cymotoma, Cacocharis 27.38.2
Cymus 20.7.15
cyna, Zizula 27.43.39
Cynaeus 24.87.107
cynanthe, Myscelia 27.46.35
cyneas, Thessalia 27.46.13
cynicus, Apateticus 20.3.73 (Fig. 20.16)
Cynipidae, supra 25.34.1
Cynipinae, supra 25.34.9
Cynipoidea, supra 25.29.1
Cynomya 29.101.20
Cynomyopsis 29.101.18
Cynorhinella 29.47.91
Cynthia Moth 27.69.14
cynthia, Samia 27.69.14 (Fig. 27.230)
Cyparium 24.23.3
Cypha 24.24.190
Cyphacma 27.15.42
Cyphea 24.24.219
Cypherotylus 24.76.4
Cyphoderris 11.8.1

Cyphomyia 29.31.18
Cyphomyrmex 25.58.51
Cyphon 24.32.3
Cyphonotida 24.106.217
Cyphopelta 20.23.149
cypseloides, Anthomyiopsis 29.105.175
Cypselosomatidea, suprae 29.50.1
Cypselosomatidae Fly Family 29.50.1
Cyptonychia 27.75.354
Cyrnellus 26.3.2
Cyrpoptus 21.3.3
Cyrtacanthacridinae, supra 11.5.114
Cyrtepistomis 24.113.138
Cyrtinini, supra 24.106.295
Cyrtinus 24.106.295
Cyrtobagous 24.113.188
Cyrtocapsus 20.23.21
Cyrtocoelioxys 25.68.24
Cyrtogaster 25.19.43
Cyrtogonatopus 25.51.12
Cyrtomenus 20.1.5
Cyrtopeltis 20.23.28
Cyrtopeltocoris 20.23.137
Cyrtophleba 29.105.158
Cyrtophyllicus 11.7.32
Cyrtopogon 29.37.45
Cyrtorhinus 20.23.94
Cyrtoscydmus 24.20.10
Cyrtosmia 26.68.18
Cyrtoxipha 11.10.21
Cysteodemus 24.101.5
Cystiphora 29.11.155
Cythereinae, supra 29.40.19
Cytilus 24.35.6
Cyzenis 29.105.415
czekanowskii, Hyperborea 27.73.53

D

dabanensis, Erebia 27.48.10
Dacerla 20.23.153
Dacetini, supra 25.58.46
dacia, Acontia 27.75.220
Dacne 24.76.1
Dacninae, supra 24.76.1
Dacnochilus 24.24.53
Dacnonypha, supra 27.2.1
Dacnusa 25.13.93
Dacnusini, supra 25.13.90
Dacoderinae, supra 24.87.169
Dacoderini, supra 24.87.169
Dacoderus 24.87.169
dacotae, Hesperia 27.40.65 (Fig. 27.73)
Dactuliothrips 22.1.2
Dactylandrena 25.65.1
Dactylaobis 27.2.31
Dactylaspis 21.38.23
Dactylobaetis 6.4.7
dactylopii, Leptomastix 25.25.29
Dactylopiidae, supra 21.28.1
Dactylopius 21.28.1
Dactylopsylla 30.7.19
Dactylopsyllinae, supra 30.7.18
Dactylosternum 24.12.26
Dactylotum 11.5.106
daeckealis, Nymphuliella 27.55.11
Dagamaea 1.4.9
Dagbertus 20.23.154
Dagger Moth 27.75.231
Dagger-tails 27.46.44
Dahana 27.73.75
Dahlbominus 25.26.10
Daihinia 11.9.17
Daihiniella 11.9.16
Daihiniodes 11.9.15
Dainty Sulphur 27.42.20

daira, Eurema 27.42.17
dakota, Lopidea 20.23.110
dakotana, Ulidiotites 29.58.24
dakotensis, Euscopolia 29.105.24
Dalcerid Moth Family, supra 27.54.1
Dalceridae, supra 27.54.1
Dalcerides 27.54.1
daleae, Ceratopidea 20.23.93
Daleapidea 20.23.95
Dallasiellus 20.1.7
dallatorreana, Ceratina 25.69.45
Dalmannia 29.49.8
Dalmanniinae, supra 29.49.8
Dalmosella 24.25.42
Dalopius 24.48.41
Daltonia 21.14.218
Damalini, supra 29.37.26
dammersi, Anthocharis 27.42.9
damnifica, Schistocerca 11.5.114 (Fig.
 11.24)
damoctas, Charidryas 27.46.15
Damp Barklice Family 17.8.1
Dampfius 24.42.7
Damsel Bug Family 20.18.1
Damselflies 7.1.1, 7.8.1
Danae 24.81.14
Danaidae, supra 27.49.1
Danainae 27.49.1
Danaus 27.49.1
Danbara 21.14.131
Dance Fly Family, supra 29.42.1
Dandelion Gall Wasp 25.34.14
Danepteryx 21.6.17
Dannella 6.13.4
Danosoma 24.48.2
Dapsilarthra 25.13.100
dapsilis, Calyptrosomus 29.105.29
Darapsa 27.70.40
Dargida 27.75.496
Daritis 27.73.4
Dark Fishfly 23.2.5
Dark Mealworm 24.87.92
Dark-sided Cutworm Moth 27.75.544
Dark-winged Fungus Fly Family,
 supra 29.10.1
Darlingtonea 24.4.43
Darkling Beetle Family, supra 24.87.1
Darmistus 20.5.2
Darner Family 7.4.1
Darninae 21.15.17
Darnini, supra 21.15.17
Darnis 21.15.18
Dascillidae, supra 24.34.1
Dascillinae, supra 24.34.1
Dascillini, supra 24.34.9
Dascilloidea, supra 24.31.1
Dascillus 24.34.9
Dasineura 29.11.152
Dasiops 29.57.1
Dasyblemma 27.75.29
Dasyceridae, supra 24.17.1
Dasycerus 24.17.1
Dasychira 27.74.2
Dasycorixa 20.35.4
Dasydacytlus 24.75.9
Dasydemellinae, supra 17.12.1
Dasydemellini, supra 17.12.1
Dasyfidonia 27.61.18
Dasyhelea 29.23.4
Dasyheleinae, supra 29.23.4
Dasylechia 29.37.58
Dasylophia 27.71.19
Dasymolophilus 29.2.61
Dasymutilla 25.55.16
Dasymutillini, supra 25.55.16
Dasyopa 29.94.23

Dasyosmia 25.68.18
Dasypodinae, supra 25.67.1
dasyprocta, Okeniella 29.98.11
Dasypsyllus 30.7.3
Dasypyga 27.55.301
Dasyrhadus 24.68.13
Dasysyrphus 29.47.17
Dasytastes 24.68.29
Dasytellus 24.68.21
Dasytes 24.68.20
Dasytinae, supra 24.68.17
dasytomus, Stenodontes 24.106.4
Datana 27.71.2
datanae, Heteropelma 25.16.382
Date Bug 21.6.4
dauci, Conicera 29.46.11
dauci, Semiaphis 21.19.195
Daulia 27.55.188
Davara 27.55.302
davidsoni, Dascillus 24.34.9
davisi, Chelicerca 9.1.1
davisi, Coloradia 27.69.6
davisi, Landisaphis 21.19.113
davisi, Lemelba 24.25.44
davisi, Lopidea 20.23.110
davisi, Oedemopsis 25.16.54
Davisonia 21.14.97
dearnessi, Phenacoccus 21.25.32
dearnessi, Rhizaspidiotus 21.38.76
Dearthrus 24.61.14
Death's Head Cockroach 14.6.1
Death Watch Beetle Family, supra 24.63.1
Deathwatch Beetle 24.63.5
debile, Hylophasma 25.16.178
debilis, Eubrachymera 29.105.178
debilis, Euvira 24.24.237
debilis, Isodrusus 24.113.54
debilis, Micromalthus 24.58.1
debilis, Telegeusis 24.53.1
Decachaetophora 29.81.1
Decanematus 25.7.37
Decantha 27.15.23
Decarthron 24.25.55
Decarthronina, supra 24.25.55
Decaturia 27.55.281
decedens, Macropelopsis 29.24.10
decemlineata, Leptinotarsa 24.107.60 (Fig.
 24.225)
decemlineata, Polyphylla 24.30.66
decemmaculatus, Glariopsis 29.31.32
deciduous forest 28
Decinea 27.40.54
decipiens, Lymantor 24.112.44
decipiens, Synneuron 29.16.2
decisus, Deltella 21.14.217
declinata, Anthracophaga 29.94.40
declivis, Scobicia 24.64.19
Decodes 27.38.66
decolor, Lopus 20.23.79
decoloratus, Campsurus 6.10.2
decora carbo, Tricholochmaea 24.107.80
decora decora, Tricholochmaea 24.107.80
decora, Ecertobia 20.23.157
decoralis, Pangrapta 27.75.51
Decorosiphon 21.19.60
decorus, Protacanthus 20.12.3
decorus, Sargus 29.31.6
Decosia 29.9.75
Dectes 24.106.289
dectes, Caurinus 28.2.1
Decticinae, supra 11.7.25
Decticita 11.7.33
Decua 21.14.56
Decusa 24.24.220
Deuteragenia 25.60.9
Deda 25.7.97

Deer Fly Family, supra 29.26.1
Deer keds 29.106.11
Defa 27.15.25
defectalis, Megalorrhipida 27.58.7
definita, Chlosyne 27.46.14
deformata, Ceramphis 24.20.20
degeeri, Apache 21.9.13
Degeeriella 18.1.21
Deidamia 27.70.34
Deilelater 24.48.12
Deinocerites 29.20.13
Deinodryinus 25.51.2
Deinopsis 24.24.221
dejeani, Adelothyreus 24.52.14
dejeani, Omus 24.3.2
Dejeaniini, supra 29.105.90
Dejeaniopalpus 29.105.216
Dejean's Omus 24.3.2
delawaricus, Oxyptilus 27.58.5
Deleaster 24.24.147
Delia 29.99.8
delicata, Neobellamira 24.106.196
delicata, Perigracilia 24.106.38
delicata, Trachea 27.75.309
delicatus, Yelicones 25.13.61
Delina 29.98.29
Delinini, supra 29.98.27
Delius 24.20.8
delius, Coenus 20.3.37
Delochilocoris 20.7.72
Delomegachile 25.68.22
Delomerista 25.16.34
Delomeristini, supra 25.16.33
Delotelis 30.4.8
Deloyala 24.107.183
Delphacid Planthopper Family, supra 21.2.1
Delphacidae, supra 21.2.1
Delphacinae, supra 21.2.3
Delphacodes 21.2.26
Delphinia 29.58.5
delphinii, Euclea 27.52.19 (Fig. 27.160)
Delphiniobium 21.19.61
delta, Trigonopeltastes 24.30.119
Deltanus 21.14.222
Deltaspis 24.106.149
Deltella 21.14.217
deltiger, Toxares 25.14.2
Deltocephalini, supra 21.14.98
Deltocephalinae, supra 21.14.84
Deltocephalus 21.14.211
Deltochilum 24.30.1
Deltometopus 24.52.7
Deltophora 27.23.42
delunaris, Mimophisma 27.75.133
Demicryptochironomus 29.24.46
Demopheles 25.16.135
demotella, Acrobasis 27.55.282
Dendrobias 24.106.166
Dendrobiella 24.64.22
Dendrocerus 25.46.4
Dendrocharini, supra 24.52.1
Dendrocharis 24.52.1
Dendrocoris 20.3.57
Dendroctonus 24.112.11
Dendroctranulus 24.112.45
Dendroides 24.94.4
Dendroleon 23.14.1
Dendroleontinae, supra 23.14.1
Dendroleontini, supra 23.14.1
Dendrolimnophila 29.2.34
Dendrophagus 24.72.21
Dendrophaonia 29.100.42
Dendrophilinae, supra 24.26.21
Dendrophilus 24.26.23
dendropogonus, Chirothripoides 22.5.34
Dendrosinus 24.112.8

Dendrosoter 25.13.7
Dendroterus 24.112.58
Dendrotettix 11.5.95
Dendrothripini, supra 22.4.9
Dendrothrips 22.4.9
Denigastrura 1.2.3
Denisia 27.15.29
Denisiella 1.7.1
Dennyus 18.6.12
densicollis, Apotrepus 24.113.372
dentata, Cercia 29.105.227
dentata, Hardya 21.14.171
dentata, Melitara 27.55.380
dentata, Pheidole 25.58.28 (Fig. 25.34)
dentatus, Curius 24.106.84
dentella, Ypsolopha 27.29.8
Denticollini, supra 24.48.27
Denticollis 24.48.33
denticollis, Odontosphindus 24.73.1
denticollis, Sphindocis 24.92.1
denticornis, Goniothrips 22.5.41
denticornis, Odontocorynus 24.113.328
denticrus, Megaphasma 10.1.5
denticulata, Chaetocnema 24.107.144
denticulela, Callisto 27.14.9
Dentifibula 29.11.124
Dentilabus 25.16.278
dentipes, Caecossonus 24.113.376
dentipes, Euphalepsus 24.25.68
dentipes, Plectromerus 24.106.85
dentolatens, Phycoidella 29.24.133
Deoclona 27.23.91
Deodar Weevil 24.113.171
Deopalpus 29.105.103
Dephastus 24.80.1
deplanata, Cyclogastrella 25.19.112
Deporaini, supra 24.113.11
Deporaus 24.113.11
depressa, Boucekiella 25.25.72
depressa, Briaraxis 24.25.50
depressa, Lipoptena 29.106.11
Depressaria 27.15.5
Depressariinae, supra 27.15.1
Depressariini 27.15.1
Depressariodes 27.15.2
Depressed Flour Beetle 24.87.111
depressifrons, Polydacrys 24.113.62
Depressoscymnus 24.80.7
depressus, Chalcosyrphus 29.47.87
depressus, Pasimachus 24.4.22
depressus, Sesioplex 25.16.393
Deraeocapsus 20.23.13
Deraeocorinae, supra 20.23.9
Deraeocorini, supra 20.23.13
Deraeocoris 20.23.14
Derallus 24.12.12
Derancistrus 24.106.7
Derandrena 25.65.1
Derbid Planthopper Family, supra 21.9.1
Derbidae, supra 21.9.1
Dercylinus 24.4.103
Derelomini, supra 24.113.190
Deretaphrini, supra 24.93.22
Deretaphrus 24.93.22
deridens, Charadra 27.75.228 (Fig. 27.349)
derisus, Gremlinotrophus 29.105.329
Dermaptera, supra 13.1.1 (Fig. 13.1)
Dermestes 24.61.1
Dermestidae, supra 24.61.1
Dermeslini, supra 24.61.1
Dermestoidea, supra 24.59.1
Derobrachus 24.106.9
Derocrepis 24.107.133
Derodontidae, supra 24.59.1
Derodontus 24.59.3
Deronectes 24.7.17

deropeltiformis, Ischnoptera 14.5.2
Derophthalma 20.23.155
Derotanypus 29.24.12
Derotmema 11.5.54
Derotropis 25.68.22
Derovatellus 24.7.3
Derrima 27.75.591
desert 28
Desert Blister Beetle 24.101.5
Desert Cockroach Family 14.4.1
Desert Corn Flea Beetle 24.107.144
Desert Darkling Beetle 24.87.50
Desert Locust 11.5.114
Desert Long-horned Grasshopper
 Family 11.3.1
Desert Net-winged Beetle 24.57.1
Desert Skunk Beetle 24.87.140
Desert Termite Family 15.4.1
Deserta 21.11.7
deserticola, Mirolepisma 5.3.6
deserticola, Neotarache 27.75.196
deserticola, Spaniacris 11.4.4
desertus, Xeropsamobeus 24.30.19
deshaisiana, Cydia, see saltitans,
 Cydia 27.38.56
designalis, Agathodes 27.55.164
designatus, Hesperophylax 26.10.18 (Fig.
 26.26)
desjardinsi, Psammoecus 24.72.25
Desmatogaster 24.63.27
Desmatomyia 29.40.26
Desmatoneura 29.40.36
Desmia 27.55.133
Desmiostoma 25.13.84
Desmiostomatini, supra 25.13.84
Desmiphora 24.106.245
Desmiphorini, supra 24.106.245
Desmocerini, supra 24.106.169
Desmocerus 24.106.169
Desmococcus 21.23.11
desmodiella, Porphyrosela 27.14.22
Desmoglyptus 24.113.312
Desmometopa 29.74.8
Desmona 26.10.27
Desmopachria 24.7.5
Desolakerrus 24.48.62
Desoria 1.4.23
Despaxia 8.4.1
desponsa, Melissodes 25.69.30
Destria 21.14.221
destructor, Aspidiotus 21.38.11
destructor, Ctenicera 24.48.37
destructor, Mayetiola 29.11.147 (Fig.
 29.18)
Destutia 27.61.128
detersa, Euxoa 27.75.544
detrimentosus, Agromyzaphagus 25.25.103
Detrospidea 24.107.76
Dettopsomyia 29.90.15
Deuteronectes 24.7.18
Deuterophlebia 29.4.1
Deuterophlebiidae, supra 29.4.1
Deuterophlebioidea, supra 29.4.1
Deuterophysa 27.52.117
Deuterosminthurus 1.7.6
Deutominettia 29.82.3
Devastating Grasshopper 11.5.94
devastator, Crymodes 27.75.253 (Fig.
 27.356)
devastator, Melanoplus 11.5.94
devastatrix, Phylloxera 21.21.1
Devia 24.24.222
devilliers, Battus 27.41.3
Dexia 29.105.173
Dexiinae, supra 29.105.171
Dexiini, supra 29.105.173

Dexilla 29.105.51
Dexillini, supra 29.105.51
Dexodes 29.105.255
Dexosarcophaga 29.103.38
Diabrotica 24.107.90
Diabroticina, supra 24.107.90
Diachasma 25.13.87
Diacheila 24.4.18
Diachlorini, supra 29.26.13
Diachlorus 29.26.17
Diachorisia 27.10.4
Diachrysia 27.75.157
Diachus 24.107.27
Diacme 27.22.124
Diacnatharius 25.16.270
Diacrita 29.58.6
Diacritini, supra 25.16.36
diacritus 25.16.36
diacymalis, Syllepte 27.55.167
Diadasia 25.69.19
Diadegma 25.16.419
diadema, Sinea 20.17.21 (Fig. 20.41)
Diadiplosis 29.11.87
Diadocidia 29.9.2
Diadocidiinae, supra 29.9.2
Diadromus 25.16.201
Diaeretiella 25.14.11
Diaethria 27.46.38
diaeus, Selanderma 25.19.47
Diaglyptidea 25.16.92
diagnosis 4
diagonalis, Rhodocantha 27.55.26
Dialeurodes 21.18.14
Dialictus 25.66.20
Dialineura 29.32.4
Dialipsis 25.16.490
Diallactini, supra 29.11.25
Dialysis 29.29.1
Dialyta 29.100.41
Dialytellus 24.30.27
Dialytes 24.30.26
Diamanus 30.7.4
Diamesa 29.24.37
Diamesinae, supra 29.24.32
Diamimus 24.113.127
Diamondback Moth 27.29.7
Diamnodback Moth Family, supra 27.29.1
diana, Hemileuca 27.69.7
diana, Speyeria 27.46.8 (Fig. 27.121)
Diandrena 25.65.1
dianthi, Pezothrips 22.4.47
dianthi Rhizoecus 21.25.38
Dianthidium 25.68.8
Dianous 24.24.191
Diaparsis 25.16.453
Diaperinae, supra 24.87.67
Diaperini, supra 24.87.72
diaperinus, Alphitobius 24.87.115
Diaperis 24.87.72
Diapetimorpha 25.16.176
Diaphania 27.55.150
Diaphanopterodea, supra 6.1.1
Diaphantania 27.55.112
Diapheromera 120.1.4
Diaphnidia 20.23.96
Diaphnocoris 20.23.97
Diaphorinae, supra 29.43.32
Diaphorus 29.43.32
Diaprepes 24.113.108
Diapria 25.42.29
Diapriid Wasp Family, supra 25.42.1
Diapriidae, supra 25.42.1
Diapriinae, supra 25.42.18
Diarsia 27.75.556
Diarthronomyia 29.11.158
Diasemiodes 27.55.137

Diasemiopsis 27.55.136
Diaspididae, supra 21.38.1
Diaspidiotus 21.38.24
Diaspis 21.38.25
Diastata 29.91.1
Diastatid Fly Family, supra 29.91.1
Diastatidae, supra 29.91.1
Diastema 27.75.202
Diastictis 27.55.171
Diastictus 24.30.33
Diastrophus 25.34.11
Diataga 27.10.22
Diathrausta 27.55.138
Diatraea 27.55.228
Diaulinopsis 25.26.15
Diaulota 24.24.223
Diaulomorpha 25.26.6
diazoma, Quadrina 27.68.8
Diazosoma 29.13.1
Dibolia 24.107.157
Dibolocelus 24.12.5
Dibrachys 25.19.115
Dibrauchoides 25.19.116
Dibusa 26.7.3
Dicaelotus 25.16.199
Dicaelus 24.4.105
Dicentrus 24.106.22
Diceratosmia 25.68.21
Diceratothrips 22.5.7
Dicerca 24.46.12
Diceroprocta 21.13.3
Dicerura 29.11.43
Dicerurini, supra 29.11.43
differtellus, Blastobasoides 27.17.7
Dichaeta 29.93.38
Dichaetocoris 20.23.98
Dichaetoneura 29.105.316
Dicheirus 24.4.113
Dichelonyx 24.30.81
Dichocera 29.105.137
Dichocysta 20.14.8
Dichogama 27.55.22
Dichogamini, supra 27.55.21
Dichoglena 29.32.18
Dichomeridinae, supra 27.23.83
Dichomeris 27.23.85
Dichopetala 11.7.3
Dichorda 28.61.160
Dichordophora 27.61.161
Dichordophorini, supra 27.61.161
Dichothorax 25.58.37
Dichotomius 24.30.9
Dichoxenus 24.113.130
Dichozoma 27.52.32
Dichrogaster 25.16.103
Dichromorpha 11.5.9
Dichrooscytus 20.23.156
Dichrorampha 27.38.45
dichrous, Sphecodes 25.66.22
Dicladocerus 25.26.12
Diclasiopa 29.93.15
Diclidia 24.98.44
Dicogaster 27.68.9
Dicolonus 29.37.33
Dicondylia, supra 5.1.1
Dicondylus 25.51.14
Dicopus 25.27.4
Dicosmoecinae 26.10.1
Dicosmoecus 26.10.4
dicotylis, Macrogyropus 18.4.3
Dicraeus 29.94.20
Dicranoclista 29.40.42
Dicranoctetes 27.16.8
Dicranognathus 24.113.6
Dicranomyia 29.2.14
Dicranophragma 29.2.34

Dicranopselaphus 24.34.11
Dicranoptycha 29.2.19
Dicranotropis 21.2.16
Dicrepidiini, supra 24.48.19
Dicrepidius 24.48.19
Dicrodiplosis 29.11.82
Dicropaltum 29.37.74
Dicrotendipes 29.24.54
Dictya 29.79.8
Dictyacium 29.79.9
Dictyla 20.14.9
Dictyobia 21.6.14
Dictyonia 21.6.9
Dictyonissus 21.6.13
Dictyonota 20.14.23
Dictyopharid Planthopper Family,
 supra 21.11.1
Dictyopharidae, supra 21.11.1
Dictyopharinae, supra 21.11.1
Dictyopharini, supra 21.11.1
Dictyoptera, supra 14.1.1 (Fig. 14.1)
Dictyopterus 24.57.7
dictyospermi, Chrysomphalus 21.38.16
Dictyospermum Scale 21.38.16
Dictyssa 21.6.12
Dictyssonia 21.6.15
Dicymolomia 27.55.67
Dicyphinae, supra 20.23.28
Dicyphoma 29.31.17
Dicyphonia 21.14.8
Dicyphus 20.23.29
Dicyrtoma 1.7.10
Dicyrtomina 1.7.10
Dicyrtominae, supra 1.7.10
Didactylomyia 29.11.50
Didasys 27.73.86
Didea 29.47.24
Dideomima 29.47.23
Didineis 25.62.72
Didion 24.80.10
Didronota 29.2.25
Didugua 27.71.21
Didyctium 25.32.6
didyma, Clistomorpha 29.105.33
Didymops 7.5.1
Dielis 25.56.3
Dienoplus 25.62.82
Diestota 24.24.224
Diestrammena 11.9.4
dietrichi, Epirhyssa 25.16.43
dietrichi, Gonielmis 24.45.11
Dietrich's fluid 37
Dietrich's glue 39
Dietzella 24.113.291
Dietzianus 24.113.213
Dieuches 20.7.67
Dieunomia 25.66.8
Dieuryneura 29.31.14
Differential Grasshopper 11.5.94
differentialis, Melanoplus 11.5.94
difformis, Cladius 25.7.15
diffracta, Polyphylla 24.30.66
diffusa, Faronta 27.75.498 (Fig. 27.382)
diffusa, Thurberiphaga 27.75.410
Digger Bees 25.69.16
Digger Bee Family, supra 25.69.1
Digger Wasp Family, supra 25.62.1
digitalis, Lemmeria 27.75.262
Diglochis 25.19.109
Diglotta 24.24.225
Diglyphus 25.26.7
Digonatopus 25.51.26
Dihammaphora 24.106.133
Dikraneura 21.14.70
Dikraneurini, supra 21.14.69
Dikraneuroidea 21.14.76

Dikrella 21.14.74
Dilaridae, supra 23.10.1
dilatus, Dicaelus 24.4.105 (Fig. 24.39)
Dilinium 24.15.10
Dilopharius 25.16.271
Dilophonotini, supra 27.70.19
Dilophotopsis 25.55.8
Dilophus 29.8.6
Dilyta 25.33.4
Dimecoenia 29.93.56
dimediatella, Tampa 27.55.406
Dimeromicrus 25.18.14
dimidiata, Heterops 24.106.135
dimidiata, Megalostomis 24.107.16
dimidiata, Pyromorpha 27.50.6
dimidiata, Rondaniella 29.9.80
dimidiatus, Carpophilus 24.70.10
diminutalis, Sufetula 27.55.114
Dimmockia 25.26.11
dimmocki, Eucelatoriopsis 29.105.246
dimmocki, Pikonema 25.7.28
Dimorphopteryx 25.7.77
Dimophora 25.16.432
dina, Pyrisitia 27.42.18
Dinacoma 24.30.72
Dinapate 24.64.9
Dinapatini, supra 24.64.9
Dinardilla 24.24.226
Dinarmus 25.19.81
Dinera 29.105.65
Dineutini, supra 24.9.1
dineutis, Gyrinophagus 25.19.105
Dineutus 24.9.1
Dingy Cutworm Moth 27.75.537
Dinocoryna 24.24.227
Dinoderinae, supra 24.64.5
Dinoderus 24.64.5
Dinopepsis 25.60.2
Dinorothrips 22.4.3
Dinostigma 25.13.101
Dinotiscus 25.19.72
Diochanthrax 29.40.59
Diochinae, supra 24.24.26
Diochiini, supra 29.37.31
Diochus 24.24.26
Dioctria 29.37.31
Diodontus 25.62.22
Dioedus 24.87.73
Diogmites 29.37.5
Diolcus 20.3.6
Diolozona 20.23.15
Diomorus 25.18.7
Diomus 24.80.8
dione 27.46.2
Diopsidae, supra 29.56.1
Diopsoidea, supra 29.53.1
Diopsothrips 22.5.8
Dioptidae 27.72.1
Dioptopsis 29.3.4
Dioryctria 27.55.339
dioryctriae, Microtypus 25.13.142
Diorymeropsis 214.113.337
Diospilini, supra 25.13.67
Diospilus 25.13.68
diospyri, Trioza 21.17.10
Diotrepha 29.2.20
Dioxyna 29.61.23
Dioxys 25.68.12
dioxys, Mitrops 21.11.2
Dipachystigma 25.19.61
Dipalta 29.40.47
Dipara 25.19.28
Diparinae, supra 25.19.28
Diphaglossinae, supra 25.63.3
Diphaomyia 29.23.5
Diphlebini, supra 20.23.1

Diphleps 20.23.1
Diphora 25.42.12
Diphthera 27.75.75
Diphuia 29.93.10
Diphyllaphis 21.19.62
Diphyllostoma 24.28.7
Diphyothrips 22.5.35
Diphytaxis 24.52.26
Diphyus 25.16.232
Diplacaspis 24.107.33
Diplazon 25.16.477
Diplazontinae, supra 25.16.469
Diplectrona 26.4.4
Diplectroninae, supra 26.4.3
Dipljapyx 3.4.2
Diplochaetus 24.4.49
Diplocheila 24.4.104
Diplocladius 29.24.95
Diplocolenus 21.14.192
Diplocoelus 24.83.2
Diplolepis 25.34.16
Diplonevra 29.46.6
Diploperla 8.7.8
Diploplectron 25.62.34
Diplopoda 10
Diplorrhos 25.50.11
Diploschizia 27.28.4
Diplostethus 24.48.45
Diplostichus 29.105.279
Diplotoxa 29.94.46
Diplotaxis 24.30.63
Diplous 24.4.68
Dipogon 25.60.9
Diprion 25.6.5
Diprionidae, supra 25.6.1
Diprioninae, supra 25.6.3
diprioni, Peckelachertus 25.26.28
Dipropus 24.48.20
Dipseudopsinae, supra 26.3.7
Dipsocoridae, supra 20.24.1
Diptera, supra 29.1.1
diptera, Psectra 23.8.9
Diptychophora 27.55.220
Dirabius 24.113.349
Diradops 25.16.316
Dircaea 24.98.26
Dirhagus 24.52.12
Dirhaginae, supra 24.52.10
Dirhininae, supra 25.21.4
Dirhinus 25.21.4
Dirhiza 29.11.42
Dirhizini, supra 29.11.42
Dirotognathus 24.113.114
Dirrhope 25.13.117
disa, Erebia 27.48.10
Disamara 24.4.94
discalis, Metalectra 27.75.54 (Fig. 27.326)
discalis, Phrynofrontia 29.105.260
discalis, Stratiomys 29.31.39
Discestra 27.75.472
discicollis, Lecontia 24.90.4
discivaria, Parastichtis 27.75.254
Disclisioprocta 27.61.232
disclusa, Dioryctria 27.55.339 (Fig. 27.171)
Discobola 29.2.14
Discocephalini, supra 20.3.21
Discocerina 29.93.12
Discocerini, supra 20.3.64
Discocerinini, supra 29.93.12
Discococcus 21.25.14
Discoderus 24.4.127
Discodes 25.25.88
Discodini, supra 25.25.88
Discodon 24.56.10
Discogastrini, supra 20.4.31

Discogenia 24.87.140
discoidalis, Erebia 27.48.10
discoidaloides, Agonocryptus 25.16.186
discoideus, Acmaeops 24.106.187 (Fig. 24.203)
Discolia 25.56.6
discolor, Anisota 27.69.5
discolor, Lomilysis 27.75.426
Discomyza 29.93.19
Discomyzini, supra 29.93.19
discopunctana, Callostathma 27.38.89
Discotenes 24.109.7
Discothyrea 25.58.12
discrepans, Styloneuria 29.104.3
discus, Peridesmia 25.19.101
Disholcaspis 25.34.32
disjuncta, Closoeca 26.10.26
disjunctus, Odontotaenius 24.29.1 (Fig. 24.64)
dislocaria, Enconista 27.61.14
dislocatus, Metriorrhynchomiris 20.23.166
Dismorphiinae, supra 27.42.21
Disogmini, supra 25.39.2
Disogmus 25.39.2
Disonycha 24.107.123
dispar, Ampumixis 24.45.4
dispar, Baliothrips 22.4.35
dispar, Hoplia 24.30.85
dispar, Lymantria 27.74.4 (Figs. 27.316, 27.317, 27.318, 27.319, 27.320, 27.321)
dispar, Phalacropsis 24.77.2
dispellens, Brachpremna 29.2.3
dispersal 25
dispersus, Aleurodicus 21.18.18
dissectella, Enchrysa 27.23.7
dissecting needle 43
dissimilis, Goniodes 18.1.28
Dissochaetus 24.22.3
dissociaria, Holochroa 27.61.90
dissociata, Hemimorina 27.61.92
dissociata, Peraniana 27.75.282
Dissolcus 25.43.33
Dissomphalus 25.48.4
Dissosteira 11.5.47
disstria, Malacosoma 27.68.11 (Fig. 27.210)
Distenia 24.106.303
Disteniinae, supra 24.106.303
Distichlicococcus 21.25.15
distichlium, Paludicoccus 21.25.28
Distichona 29.105.350
Distigmopter 24.107.154
distincta, Achatia 27.75.508
distincta, Micrixys 24.4.97
distincta, Paranametis 24.113.129
distincta texana, Sternopsylla 30.5.3
distinctus, Bothynostethus 25.62.52
distinctus, Cligenes 20.7.34
distinctus distinctus, Tachytes 25.62.41
distinguendus, Salignus 20.23.185
Distosimulium 29.22.4
Distractus 29.43.18
distribution 3, 26
distribution coden 4
Ditemnus 24.56.11
Ditomyia 29.9.3
Ditomyiinae, supra 29.9.3
Ditrichophora 29.93.16
Ditropinotus 25.18.21
Ditrysia, supra 27.10.1
Ditula 27.38.83
Ditylus 24.97.5
Ditylini, supra 24.97.5
Diura 8.7.9
Diuraphis 21.19.63
divalis, Rimulincola 24.24.171

diversa, Lype 26.2.1
diversa, Praecocaspis 21.38.66
diversa, Rhinotora 29.87.1
divergens, Mycetobia 29.14.3
Diversinervus 25.25.75
diversipennis, Abaristophora 29.46.9
diversisquamis, Ctenolepisma 5.3.3
diversity 18
diversiunguis, Catajapyx 3.4.5 (Fig. 3.5)
diversus, Valtissius 20.7.30
Diviana 27.55.365
Divitiaca 27.55.354
Dixa 29.18.3
Dixella 29.18.1
Dixid Midge Family, supra 29.18.1
Dixidae, supra 29.18.1 (Fig. 29.21)
Dixianus 21.14.145
Dizygomyza 29.68.6
DNA 18
Doa 27.73.5
Doaini, supra 27.73.5
doaneiana, Gonomyopsis 29.2.64
Dobsonflies, supra 23.1.1
Dobsonfly 23.2.1
Dobsonfly Family, supra 23.2.1
Docessissophothrips 22.5.36
Dock Sawfly 25.7.84
doclea, Pogonortalis 29.59.2
Docophoroides 18.1.22
Dodder Gall Weevil 24.113.177
Doddsia 8.2.2
Dodia 27.73.33
Dogbane Beetle 24.107.47
Dog Chewing Louse 18.2.9
Dog Flea 30.1.3
Dog Sucking Louse 19.2.1
Dog-day Cicada 21.13.4
Dog's Head 7.6.7
Dogwood Clubgall Midge 29.11.88
Dogwood Moth 27.35.12
Dogwood Scale 21.38.14
Dogwood Spittle Bug 21.12.7
Dogwood Twig Borer 24.106.297
dohrni, Palaeoxenus 24.52.19
dohrnii, Fenusa 25.7.52
Dohrniphora 29.46.7
dolabrata, Leptopterna 20.23.197
Dolania 6.8.1
Dolba 27.70.5
Dolbogene 27.70.6
Doldina 20.17.15
Doleranus 21.14.107
Dolerinae, supra 25.7.12
Doleromorpha 27.10.2
Dolerus 25.7.12
Dolichocephala 29.42.28
Dolichochile 25.67.1
Dolichocis 24.92.3
Dolichocodia 29.105.66
Dolichoderinae, supra 25.58.56
Dolichoderini, supra 25.58.56
Dolichoderus 25.58.56
Dolichodynerus 25.59.11
Dolichomiris 20.23.196
Dolichomitus 25.16.8
Dolichomyia 29.40.6
Dolichonabis 20.18.9
Dolichopeza 29.2.8
Dolichopodidae, supra 29.43.1
Dolichopodinae, supra 29.43.6
Dolichopodini, supra 11.9.8
Dolichoselephus 25.16.437
Dolichopsyllini, supra 30.6.3
Dolichopsyllus 30.6.3
Dolichopus 29.43.6
dolichos, Coelioxys 25.68.24

Dolichosciara 29.10.3
Dolichosoma 24.68.17
Dolichotarsus 29.105.240
Dolichovespula 25.59.27
Dolichurini, supra 25.62.1
Dolichuris 25.62.1
Doliodesmus 24.87.119
Doliopria 25.42.31
Doliponta 24.24.228
Doliotettix 21.14.157
Dolophilodes 26.1.2
Dolophron 25.16.414
Dolurgus 24.112.43
Dolymorpha 27.43.30
domestica, Musca 29.100.58 (Fig. 29.53)
domestica, Thermobia 5.3.8
domesticus, Acheta 11.10.6 (Fig. 11.43)
dominica, Rhyzopertha 24.64.6
dominicki, Carectocultus 27.55.194
Donacaula 27.55.196
Donacia 24.107.4
Donaciinae, supra 24.107.3
Dontonodus 21.15.56
donysa, Amyplypterus 27.70.14
doralis, Dacus, supra 29.61.1
Dorata 27.10.34
Doratopsylla 30.4.22
Doratopsyllinae, supra 30.4.23
Doratopsyllini, supra 30.4.23
Doratura 21.14.173
Dorbeetle 24.30.52
Dorcadothrips 22.4.39
dorcas, Epidemia 2743.7 (Fig. 27.106)
Dorcaschema 24.106.239
Dorcaschematini, supra 24.106.239
Dorcasina 24.106.207
Dorcasta 24.106.263
Dorcatominae, supra 24.63.40
Dorcatoma 24.63.50
Dorcinae, supra 24.28.3
Dorcus 24.28.3
doris, Coloradia 27.69.6
Dorithia 27.38.67
dorneraria, Ptychamalia 27.61.180
Dorocordulia 7.6.3
Doroneuria 8.9.4
Doros 29.47.22
dorsalis, Cicindela 24.3.4
dorsalis, Cordulegaster 7.2.1
dorsalis, Ctenophora 29.2.6
dorsalis dorsalis, Polistes 25.59.28
dorsalis, Odontota 24.107.166 (Fig. 24.244)
dorsalus, Cerodontha 29.68.7
dorsata, Bruchomorpha 21.6.2 (Fig. 21.8)
dorsata, Pteronarcys 8.5.3 (Fig. 8.8)
dorsatus, Paratriarius 24.107.94
dorsistriata, Acroplectis 27.38.69
dorsonotata, Triozosneura 27.55.305
Doru 13.5.1
dorus, Zestura 27.40.10
Dorycephalinae, supra 21.14.2
Dorycephalini, supra 21.14.2
Dorycephalus 21.14.2
Doryctes 25.13.8
Doryctinae, supra 25.13.1
Doryctinus 25.13.9
Doryctobracon 25.13.85
Dorydiella 21.14.144
Dorylinae, supra 25.58.1
Dorylomorpha 29.48.8
Doryodes 27.75.146
Doryphorini, supra 24.107.59
Doryphorophaga 29.105.241
Dorypteryx 17.4.1
Dorytomus 24.113.172

dossuaria, Banksiola 26.8.3 (Fig. 26.23)
dotalis, Ragonotia 27.55.351
Douglas Fir Beetle 24.112.11
Douglas Fir Borer 24.106.125
Douglas-fir Cone Moth 27.38.21
Douglas Fir Engraver 24.112.23
Douglas-fir Pitch Moth 27.35.12
Douglas Fir Tussock Moth 27.74.3
Douglas Fir Twig Weevil 24.113.275
Douglasiid Moth Family, supra 27.32.1
Douglasiidae, supra 27.32.1
downsi, Plecopteracoluthuis 29.24.94
Doxocopa 27.47.4
Doydirhynchus 24.113.14
dracaenae, Parthenothrips 22.4.6
dracontea, Dragonana 21.14.19
Dracotettigini 11.4.1
Dracotettix 11.4.1
Draeculacephala 21.14.47
Dragonana 21.14.19
Dragonflics 7.1.1
drakei, Curicta 20.36.3 (Fig. 20.70)
Drapetes 24.49.1
Drapetis 29.42.11
Drasteria 27.75.104
Drastophus 24.20.5
Draudita 27.75.334
drawer 42
Dreisbachia 25.16.16
dreisbachi, Calephelis 27.44.2
Drepana 27.60.1
Drepanaphis 21.19.64
Drepanidae, supra 27.60.1
Drepaninae, supra 27.60.1
Drepanocercus 29.9.50
Drepanoglossa 29.105.296
Drepanoidea, supra 27.59.1
drepanosiphoides, Toxopterella 21.19.215
Drepanosiphum 21.19.65
Drepanothrips 22.4.14
Drepanulatrix 27.61.71
Drepanura 1.5.3
Dried-fruit Beetle 24.70.10
Dried-fruit Moth 27.55.396
Drino 29.105.372
Drionia 21.14.85
Driotura 21.14.174
Drive Beetle Family, supra 24.45.1
Dromaeolus 24.52.8
Dromius 24.4.160
Dromochorus 24.3.4
Dromogomphus 7.3.6
Drone Fly 29.47.65
Dropsophilidae, supra 29.90.1
Dros 25.34.26
Drosophila 29.90.9
Drosophilinae, supra 29.90.9
Drug Store Beetle Family, supra 24.63.1
Drugstore Beetle 24.63.18
Drumming Katydid 11.7.48
drummondi, Melanophila 24.46.20
Drunella 6.13.5
druryi, Anelastes 24.52.27
Drusilla 24.24.229
drusilla, Appias 27.42.3
dryadella, Ocala 27.55.356
Dryadula 27.46.3
Dryas 27.46.4
Dry-fungus Beetle Family, supra 24.73.1
drying 38
Dryinidae, supra 25.51.1
Dryininae, supra 25.51.7
Dry-land Wireworm 24.48.37
Drymini, supra 20.7.35
Drymodesmyia 29.23.5
Drymus 20.7.35

Dryobiini, supra 24.106.99
Dryobius 24.106.99
Dryocampa 27.69.4
Dryocoetes 24.112.46
Dryocoetini, supra 24.112.42
Dryocosmus 25.34.44
Dryomyza 29.78.1
Dryomyzid Fly Family, supra 29.78.1
Dryomyzidae, supra 29.78.1
Dryomyzinae, supra 29.78.1
Dryoperia 27.17.20
Dryophilinae 24.63.5
Dryophthorini, supra 24.113.385
Dryophthorus 24.113.385
Dryopidae, supra 24.44.1
Dryopoidea, supra 24.36.1
Dryops 24.44.1
dryopterata, Calledapteryx 27.62.4
Dryotribus 24.113.386
Dryotype 27.75.421
Dryptitae, supra 24.4.165
Dryptocephala, infra 20.3.21
Dryudella 25.62.36
dubia, Trimiomelba 24.25.43 (Fig. 24.60)
dubia dubia, Scolia 25.56.6
dubiosus, Neodiprion 25.6.4
Dubiraphia 24.45.9
dubitans, Limonius 24.48.27 (Fig. 24.100)
Dubiosius 24.103.6
ducens, Feltia 27.75.537
Dufourea 25.66.1
Dufoureinae, supra 25.66.1
Dufouriellus 20.21.24
dugesi, Mesoplia 25.69.44
dulichii, Ametrodiplosis 29.11.138
dulichus, Decanematus 25.7.37
dumetorum, Callophrys 27.43.24
Dung Fly 29.98.23
Dung Fly Family 29.98.1
dunniana, Chrotoma 24.106.155
dunnianus, Aphonides 24.30.109
duodecimpunctata, Crioceris 24.107.11
duodecimstriatus, Anommatus 24.78.2
Duospina 27.18.4
dupla, Ceratina 25.69.45
Duplaspidiotus 21.38.26
duplex, Pseudaonidia 21.38.68
duplex, Pseudosciaphila 27.38.12
duplicatus, Pseudepierus 24.26.30
duplocincta, Svastra 25.69.27
Durocapillata 21.19.66
Durrantia 27.15.16
duryi, Pachycerota 24.24.277
duryi, Throscoptilium 24.15.2
Dusky Birch Sawfly 25.7.31
Dusky Cutworm Moth 27.75.535
Dusky Sap Beetle 24.70.10
Dusky Stink Bug 20.3.34
dusmae, Ctesias 24.61.12
Dusona 25.16.399
Dusty-wings Family, supra 23.5.1
Duta 25.43.14
dux, Kiefferulus 29.24.53
dyariella, Chilocampyla 27.14.11
dyari, Tetraclonia 27.50.5
Dycoderus 20.7.22
Dyctia 21.6.16
Dylobolus 24.106.298
dymas, Dymasia 27.46.17
Dymasia 27.46.17
Dynamine 27.46.37
Dynaspidiotus 21.38.27
Dynastes 24.30.114
dynastes, Dibrachoides 25.19.116
Dynastinae, supra 24.30.98

Dynastini, supra 24.30.114
Dynatopechus 24.113.384
Dynatosoma 29.9.32
Dynomiellini, supra 29.97.1
dyonis, Dynamine 27.46.37
Dyotopasta 27.10.27
Dypterygia 27.75.292
Dysaphis 21.19.67
Dyschirius 24.4.24
Dyscinetus 24.30.101
Dyscoletes 25.13.69
Dyscolomyia 29.105.177
Dyscophellus 27.40.19
Dyscrasis 29.58.7
Dysdercus 20.8.1
Dyseriocrania 27.2.1
Dyseuaresta 29.61.27
Dysgonia 27.75.134
Dysimia 21.9.7
Dysmerus 24.72.19
Dysmicoccus 21.25.16
Dysmicohermes 23.2.3
Dysodia 27.56.2
Dyspetes 25.16.65
Dysphenges 24.107.120
dyspteraria, Meskea 27.56.6
Dyspteria 27.61.254
Dyspyralis 27.75.30
Dysstroma 27.61.190
Dystaxia 24.46.3
Dystaxiella 24.46.4
Dysticheus 24.113.77
Dythemis 7.7.6
Dytiscidae, supra 24.7.1
Dytiscinae, supra 24.7.35
Dytiscini, supra 24.7.35
Dytiscus 24.7.35
Dziedzickia 29.9.43

E

eacles 27.69.1
Eana 27.38.65
Eanus 24.48.38
Earinus 25.13.79
Earobia 25.16.442
Earomyia 29.57.3
Earwigs 13.1.1
Earwiglike Entotroph Family 3.4.1
Eastern Blue Darner 7.4.1
Eastern Digger Bee 25.69.18
Eastern Field Wireworm 24.48.27
Eastern Green Fruit Beetle 24.30.121
Eastern Hercules Beetle 24.30.114
Eastern Larch Beetle 24.112.11
Eastern Leaf-footed Bug 20.4.4
Eastern Lubber Grasshopper 11.4.5
Eastern Pine Seedworm 27.38.56
Eastern Raspberry Fruitworm 24.84.2
Eastern Smoke Fly 29.45.2
Eastern Spruce Gall Adelgid 21.20.1
Eastern Subterranean Termite 15.3.1
Eastern Tailed Blue 27.43.41
Eastern Tent Caterpillar Moth 27.68.11
Eastern Tiger Swallowtail 27.41.7
Eastern Tumblebug 24.30.2
ebenina, Celastrina 27.43.42
Ebeniini, supra 29.105.205
ebenus, Heterachthes 24.106.83 (Fig. 24.188)
ebrium, Enallagma 7.11.8
ebulealis, Ategumia 27.55.132
Eburia 24.106.54
eburnea, Scythris 27.22.1
Eburniogaster 24.24.230
ecarinata, Ecarinosphaerula 24.19.8

Ecarinosphaerula 24.19.8
Ecbletus 24.24.172
Ecclisocosmoecus 26.10.7
Ecclisomyia 26.10.5
Eccoptomera 29.84.10
Eccoptura 8.9.5
Eccritosia 29.37.72
Eccritothrix 27.10.42
Ecdytolopha 27.38.58
Ecertobia 20.23.157
Echiaster 24.24.54
echidna, Eunyssobia 24.113.359
Echidnophaga 30.1.4
Echinaphis 21.19.68
echinatus, Brachysomus 24.113.47
echinocacti, Diaspis 21.38.25
Echinodes 24.26.50
Echinohelea 29.23.14
Echinomyodes 29.105.87
Echinophthiriidae, supra 19.1.1
Echinophthirius 19.1.2
Echinothrips 22.4.40
echion 27.43.19
Echmepteryx 17.1.1
echo, Oligoplectrum 26.9.6
echo, Seirarctia 27.73.35
Echthodopa 29.37.34
Echthrogonatopus 25.25.69
Echthromorphini, supra 25.16.28
Echthronomas 25.16.426
Echthrus 25.16.149
Ecitomyia 29.46.35
Ecitonetes 25.45.4
Ecitonidia 24.24.231
Ecitonini, supra 25.58.1
Ecitopora 24.24.232
Ecitoxenida 24.24.233
Ecliminae, supra 29.40.20
Ecliptopera 27.61.194
Eclytus 25.16.49
Ecnomothorax 25.46.5
ecological data label 41
Ecpantheria 27.73.42
Ecphylus 25.13.10
Ectaetia 29.15.14
Ectaetiinae, supra 29.15.14
Ectatomma 25.58.9
Ectatommini, supra 25.58.9
Ectecephla 29.94.43
Ectemnia 29.22.10
Ectemnaspis 29.22.5
Ectemnius 25.62.67
Ectobiinae, supra 14.5.12
Ectobius 14.5.12
Ectoedemia 27.5.2
Ectomyelois 27.55.296
ectoparasitic 24
Ectopimorpha 25.16.225
Ectopiocerus 20.23.158
Ectopsocidae, supra 17.16.1
Ectopsocopis 17.16.1
Ectopsocus 17.16.2
Ectrepesthoneura 29.9.77
Ectrichodiinae, supra 20.17.2
Ectromatopsis 25.25.45
Ectropis 27.61.44
ectypa, Chaetocnema 24.107.144
ectypa, Hadena 27.75.487
Ectyphinae, supra 29.35.1
Ectypia 27.73.69
Ecyrus 24.106.252
Edaphus 24.24.161
Edessa 20.3.60
Edessini, supra 20.3.60
Edestochilus 29.11.65
Edestosperma 29.11.63

Edia 27.55.31
editha, Gaeides 27.43.4
editha, Occidryas 27.46.22
edithella, Mompha 27.19.1 (Fig. 27.37)
edmandsae serratilinella, Vitula 27.55.396, see bombylicolella in "Checklist."
edmonstoni, Oistus 24.48.10
Edmundsius 6.1.2
Edrotes 24.87.39
eductalis, Lomanaltes 27.75.39
edulicola, Pinyonia 29.29.110
edulis, Conophthorus 24.112.63
edwardsi, Eubrianax 24.34.15
edwardsi, Hemihyalea 27.73.60 (Fig. 27.306)
edwardsi, Megobrium 24.106.90
edwardsii, Lymire 27.73.77
edwardsii, Melectomimus 25.69.38
edwardsii, Satyrium 27.43.16
edwardsii, Speyeria 27.46.8
Efferia 29.37.65
effetus, Mimilogus 29.105.377
Efflagitatus 24.42.6
Ega 24.4.82
egena, Autoplusia 27.75.155
egenus, Apheloplastus 24.19.15
egeremet, Wallengrenia 27.40.67
eggs 13
egg laying 24
Eggplant Flea Beetle 24.107.137
Eggplant Lace Bug 20.14.11
Eggplant Leaf Miner 27.23.53
Egira 27.75.507
eglanterina eglanterina, Hemileuca 27.69.7 (Fig. 27.221)
Egle 29.99.8
egle, Euchaetes 27.73.66 (Fig 27.308)
egleis, Speyeria 27.46.8
egregia, Xeroglypta 25.53.17
Egyptian Alfalfa Weevil 24.113.146
ehrhorni, Cirrhencyrtus 25.25.44
ehrhorni, Mycetococcus 21.35.2
Ehrhornia 21.25.17
Eidalimus 29.31.28
Eidmaniella 18.6.13
Eido 27.15.38
Eidoreus 24.81.18
Eight-spotted Forester 27.75.248
Eilema 27.73.7
Einfeldia 29.24.55
Eiphosoma 25.16.433
Eisonyx 24.113.338
Eitelius 25.7.29
ekthlipsis, Nymphula 27.55.8
El Segundo Blue 27.43.44
Elacatis 24.95.1
Elachertini, supra 25.26.15
Elachertodomyia 25.19.52
Elachertus 25.26.20
Elachiptera 29.94.7
Elachisoma 29.88.3
Elachista 27.16.5
Elachistarthron 24.24.235
Elachistid Moth Family, supra 27.16.1
Elachistidae, supra 27.16.1
Elachistinae, supra 27.16.1
elada, Texola 27.46.18
Elampinae, supra 25.50.5
Elampus 25.50.12
Elaphidion 24.106.80
Elaphidionini, supra 24.106.55
Elaphidionoides 24.106.73
Elaphidionopsis 24.106.77
Elaphria 27.75.328
Elaphrini, supra 24.4.18
Elaphritae, supra 24.4.18

Elaphropus 24.4.53
Elaphrothrips 22.5.9
Elaphrus 24.4.20
elaphus, Chremylus 25.13.51
elaphus, Lucanus 24.28.2
Elasminae, supra 25.26.83
Elasmopalpus 27.55.346
Elasmosoma 25.13.145
Elasmostethus 20.3.63
Elasmucha 20.3.62
Elasmus 25.26.83
elassa, Naniteta 27.65.3
Elassoptes 24.113.394
Elater 24.48.43
Elateridae, supra 24.48.1
Elateriformia, supra 24.35.1
Elaterinae, supra 24.48.18
Elaterini, supra 24.48.43
Elateroidea, supra 24.47.1
Elateropsis 24.106.7
Elathous 24.48.30
Elatobia 27.10.44
Elatobium 21.19.69
Elatophilus 20.21.2
Elatotrypes 24.106.110
elautalis, Pseudoschinia 27.55.46
Elder Shoot Borer Moth 27.75.281
Elderberry Longhorn 24.106.169
Eleates 24.87.69
electa, Zonosemata 29.61.45
electellum, Homoeosoma 27.55.371
Electicinae, supra 24.101.1
electra, Hemileuca 27.69.7
electrica, Goniocarsis 27.75.88
Electric-light Bugs, supra 20.37.1
Electrostrymon 27.43.36
electus, Brachybmaus 24.113.184
elegans, Chelisia 29.99.7
elegans, Choetospila 25.19.23
elegans, Diversinervus 25.25.75
elegans, Insara 11.7.4
elegans, Nemotarsus 24.4.158
elegans, Plunomia 29.83.2
elegans, Sipha 21.19.196
elegans, Zikanapis 25.63.4
eleganthulus, Lachnophorus 24.4.80
elegantula, Agathon 29.3.1 (Fig. 29.13)
elegantula, Stilobezzia 29.23.13
elegantulus, Pamphantus 20.7.20
eleganus, Trogoninirmus 18.1.60
Elenchinae, supra 24.105.12
Elenchus 24.105.12
Eleodes 24.87.140
Eleodimorpha 24.87.144
Eleodini, supra 24.87.140
Eleodiphaga 29.105.342
Elephant Louse, infra 18.8.1
Elephant Mosquito 29.20.2
elephantis, Haematomyzus, infra 18.8.1
Elephantocera 29.105.242
Elephantomyia 29.2.40
eleuchea, Maresia 27.46.44
Eleusis 24.24.92
elevatus, Scaphinotus 24.4.16
Elfia 29.105.317
Elgiva 29.79.9
elingua, Manruta 27.75.540
elingius, Apystomyia 29.40.32
Elipsocidae, supra 17.20.1
Elipsocinae, supra 17.20.1
Elipsocus 17.20.1
elisa, Celithemis 7.7.5 (Fig. 7.11)
Ellabella 27.24.2
Elleschini, supra 24.113.220
Elleschus 24.113.220
Ellida 27.71.10

Ellipes 11.6.2
Elliponeura 29.94.47
Ellipsoptera 24.3.4
Elliptera 29.2.18
Elliptical Barklice Family 17.20.1
Ellychnia 24.55.11
Elm Borer 24.106.296
Elm Calligrapha 24.107.62
Elm Casebearer 27.18.1
Elm Cockscomb-gall Aphid 21.19.54
Elm Flea Beetle 24.107.127
Elm Lace bug 20.14.8
Elm Leaf Aphid 21.19.212
Elm Leaf Beetle 24.107.81
Elm Leaf Beetle, Larger 24.107.74
Elm Leafminer 25.7.52
Elm Sawfly 25.5.3
Elm Scurfy Scale 21.38.14
Elm Spanworm 27.61.101
Elm Sphinx 27.70.7
Elmidae, supra 24.45.1
Elminae, supra 24.45.3
Elmini, supra 24.45.4
Elodia 29.105.338
Elodes 24.32.1
Eloeophila 29.2.34
eloisella, Mompha 27.19.1
elongata, Cephalospargeta 27.75.375
elongata, Conibiosoma 24.87.157
elongata, Dichelonyx 24.30.81 (Fig. 24.70)
elongata, Kinonia 21.14.170
elongata, Monitoriella 25.13.48
elongata, Pararete 29.11.19
elongata, Systena 24.107.121
elongata, Trepobaris 24.113.309
Elongate Flea Beetle 24.107.121
Elongate Hemlock Scale 21.38.31
Elongate-Bodied Springtail Family,
 supra 1.2.1
elongatulus, Dysphenges 24.107.120
elongatus, Coccus 21.26.4
elongatus, Cyanus 29.101.19
elongatus, Eupisenus 24.98.4
elongatus, Vincenzellus 24.90.11
Elonium 24.24.110
Elonus 24.104.3
elonympha, Allotria 27.75.131
Elpiste 27.61.12
elsa, Sagenosoma 27.70.9
Elsianus 24.45.10
elusus, Chaleponotus 24.113.242
elutella, Ephestia 27.55.402
elva, Microtia 27.46.16
Elymana 21.14.154
elymi, Hybolasioptera 29.11.59
Elymiotis 27.71.15
Elymniinae, supra 27.48.1
Elytroleptus 24.106.163
emarginata, Leptura 24.106.212 (Fig.
 24.205)
emarginatum, Microbregma 24.63.29
emarginatus, Phaeochrous 24.30.38
Emarginea 27.75.337
Emariannia 27.75.468
Ematurgia 27.61.22
Embaphion 24.87.143
Embidobia 25.43.21
Embidopsocinae, supra 17.6.1
Embidopsocus 17.6.2
Embioptera, supra 9.1.1 (Figs. 9.1, 9.2)
Emblemasoma 29.103.30
emblemella, Holophysis 27.23.7
Emblethis 20.7.73
Embolemid Wasp Family, supra 25.52.1
Embolemidae, supra 25.52.1
Embolemus 25.52.2

Emelinini, supra 24.104.2
Emelinus 24.104.2
Emersonella 25.26.61
Emersonopsis 25.26.81
Emesaya 20.17.3
emesia, Emesis 27.44.6
Emesinae, supra 20.17.3
Emesis 27.44.6
emigdionis, Plebulina 27.43.49
emigratella, Amorbia 27.38.90
emmae, Aleuroglandulus 21.18.4
emmae, Quadristruma 25.58.49
Emmelina 27.58.20
emmelina, Linmophila 29.2.34
Emmenotarsis 24.68.50
Emmesomyia 29.99.13
Empeda 29.2.54
empedoides, Empedomorpha 29.2.58
Empedomorpha 29.2.58
Emphoropis 25.69.37
Empicoris 20.17.4
Emphyastes 24.113.387
Emphylus 24.74.3
Empididae, supra 29.42.1
Empidideicus 29.40.22
Empidigeron 29.40.29
Empidinae, supra 29.42.32
Empidoidea, supra 29.32.1, 29.42.1
Empis 29.42.36
Empoasca 21.14.77
Empria 25.7.78
Empriini, supra 25.7.78
Empyreuma 27.73.79
Enallagma 7.11.8
Enallonyx 24.68.26
Enalosalda 20.32.1
Enantia 27.42.21
Enaphalodes 24.106.70
Enargia 27.75.289
Enaysma 25.26.64
Encarsia 25.25.14
enceliae, Exuviaspis 21.38.29
enceliae, Megandrena 25.65.2
Encephalus 24.24.234
Enchemicrum 25.62.53
Enchenopa 21.15.8
Enchodes 24.98.23
enchophorus, Philositus 25.16.416
Enchoria 27.61.227
Enchrysa 27.23.7
Enconista 27.61.14
Encopognathus 25.62.57
 Encoptolophus 11.5.37
Encrateola 25.16.86
Encyclops 24.106.177
Encyrtid Wasp Family, supra 25.25.1
Encyrtidae, supra 25.25.1
Encyrtinae, supra 25.25.49
Encyrtini, supra 25.25.89
Encyrtaspis 25.24.12
Encyrtus 25.25.89
Endaeini, supra 24.113.222
Endalus 24.113.185
endangered species 26
Endaphis 29.11.127
Endaseina, supra 25.16.114
Endmasys 25.16.117
Endecatominae, supra 24.64.4
Endecatomus 24.64.4
endeis, Chlosyne 27.46.14
Endeitoma 24.93.6
Endelomyia 25.7.42
Endeodes 24.68.4
Enderleinellidae, supra 19.5.1
Enderleinellus 19.5.1
Endochironomus 29.24.66

endocrine system 13
Endomychidae, supra 24.81.1
Endomychinae, supra 24.81.17
Endomychus 24.81.17
Endophloeus 24.93.14
Endopiza 27.38.4
Endothenia 27.38.7
Endria 21.14.214
Endromopoda 25.16.2
Endrosis 27.15.37
endymion, Electrostrymon 27.43.36
enemies 26
Eneopterinae, supra 11.10.24
Engelhardtia 27.75.530
Engelmann Spruce Weevil 24.113.171
English Grain Aphid 21.19.122
Engyaulus 24.46.33
Enhydrinae, supra 24.9.1
Enhydrini, supra 24.9.1
enhydris, Hexeris 27.56.3
Enicita 29.81.8
Enicmus 24.82.4
Enicocephalidae, supra 20.15.1
Enicomira 29.81.8
Enicospilini, supra 25.16.461
Enicospilus 25.16.464
Enizemum 25.16.471
Enlinia 29.43.48
Ennearthron 24.92.3
Ennominae, supra 27.61.6
Ennomini, supra 27.61.101
Ennomos 27.61.101
Enochrus 24.12.20
Enoclerus 24.67.16
Enodia 27.48.1
Enopliini, supra 24.67.24
Enoplolindenius 25.62.66
enoptes, Euphilotes 27.43.44
ensifer, Drepanocerus 29.9.50
ensiger, Neoconocephalus 11.7.19 (Fig.
 11.31)
ensigera, Bryantopsis 21.15.53
Ensign Scale Insect Family, supra 21.22.1
Ensign Wasp Family, supra 25.35.1
Entanoneura 23.7.6
Entedon 25.26.78
Entedontinae, supra 25.26.33
Entedontini, supra 25.26.54
Entephria 27.61.213
Entognatha, supra 1.1.1
Entomacis 25.42.19
Entomobrya 1.5.3
Entomobryidae, supra 1.5.1 (Fig. 1.7)
Entomobryinae, supra 1.5.1
Entomobryoides 1.5.3
Entomobryomorpha, supra 1.4.1
Entomognathus 25.62.58
entomological information 51
Entomological libraries 51
entomological society 20 (Table 5.3)
Entomophthalmus 24.52.11
Entomoscelini, supra 24.107.69
Entomoscelis 24.107.69
Entomychobius 25.19.87
Entotrophi, supra 3.1.1 (Fig. 3.1)
Entotrophs 3.1.1
Entylia 21.15.54
Entypoma 25.16.483
Entypus 25.60.5
environment 3
environmental factors 26
Enyo 27.70.29
Enypia 27.61.155
Enytus 25.16.418
Eobrachycentrus 26.9.4
Eocodrus 25.39.12

Eoessigia 21.19.70
Eojapyx 3.4.4
Eomacrosiphon 21.19.71
Eoparargyractis 27.55.19
Eopeponapis 25.69.29
Eoreuma 27.55.230
Eosalpingogaster 29.47.29
Eosentomidae 2.1.1
Eosentomoidea, supra 2.1.1
Eosentomon 2.1.1
Eoseristalis 29.47.65
Eosphoropteryx 27.75.163
Eotettix 11.5.92
Eoxenoglossa 25.69.24
Epacalles 24.113.253
Epacmus 29.40.35
Epaenasomyia 25.25.133
Epalpus 29.105.98
Epameibaphis 21.19.72
Epantius 24.87.134
Epanusia 25.25.140
Epargyreus 27.40.4
epedana, Acropyga 25.58.63
Epelis 27.61.10
epeolini, supra 25.69.8
Epeoloides 25.69.7
Epeoloidini, supra 25.69.7
Epeolus 25.69.8
Epeorus 6.6.3
Epermenia 27.27.1
Epermeniid Moth Family, supra 27.27.1
Epermeniidae, supra 27.27.1
Epermeniinae, supra . 27.27.1
Epermeniini, supra 27.27.1
Ephalus 24.87.163
Ephebomyrmex 25.58.24
ephedrae, Merinocapsus 20.23.50
ephedrae, Pallulaspsis 21.38.60
ephedrae, Philephedra 21.26.15
Ephedrinae, supra 25.14.1
Ephedrus 25.14.1
Ephelinus 24.24.111
Ephelops 24.113.211
Ephemera 6.11.1
ephemeraeformis,
 Thyridopteryx 27.11.12 (Fig. 27.28)
Ephemeridae, supra 6.11.1
Ephemerella 6.13.1
Ephemerellidae, supra 6.13.1
Ephemerelloidea, supra 6.13.1
Ephemeroidea, supra 6.8.1
Ephemeroptera, supra 6.1.1 (Figs. 6.1,
 6.2, 6.3, 6.4)
Ephestia 27.55.402
Ephestiodes 27.55.394
Ephialtes 25.16.29
Ephistemini, supra 24.74.15
Ephistemus 24.74.15
Ephoron 6.10.1
Ephutini, supra 25.55.19
Ephuta 25.55.20
Ephydra 29.93.54
Ephyriades 27.40.36
Epbydridae, supra 29.93.1
Ephydrinae, supra 29.93.53
Ephydrini, supra 29.93.53
Ephydroidea, supra 29.89.1
ephyra, Perlinella 8.1.1, 8.9.8 (Fig. 8.2)
Ephyrodes 27.75.90
Epiaeschna 7.4.6
Epiblema 27.38.27
epicaeroides, Omileus 24.113.34
Epicaerus 24.112.38
Epicaliini, supra 27.46.35
Epicauta 24.101.14
Epicautina, supra 24.101.14

Epicerchysius 25.25.138
Epichlorops 29.94.42
Epicometis 24.30.129
Epicordulia 7.6.1
Epicorsia 27.55.79
Epicorthylis 27.23.90
Epicrossocerus 25.62.63
Epicyta 29.9.34
Epidapus 29.10.16
Epidemia 27.43.7
Epidexia 29.105.211
Epidiaspis 21.38.28
Epidiplosis 29.11.129
Epidromia 27.75.93
Epiencyrtus 25.25.141
Epierus 24.26.29
Epiglaea 27.75.398
Epigonatopus 25.51.25
Epigrimyia 29.105.23
Epigritia 27.17.19
Epilachna 24.80.52
Epilachninae, supra 24.80.52
Epilachnini, supra 24.80.52
Epilechia 27.23.79
epilobii, Cnemogonus 24.113.284
Epimacrotera 25.65.15
Epimartyria, 27.1.1
Epimecis 27.61.46
Epimechus 24.113.212
Epimelissodes 25.69.27
Epimetopinae, supra 24.12.2
Epimetopus 24.12.2
Epimyia 29.11.71
Epina 27.55.224
Epinomia 25.66.8
Epinotia 27.38.41
Epinysson 25.62.76
Epipagis 27.55.125
Epipaschia 27.55.262
Epipaschiinae, supra 27.55.261
Epipemas 27.75.427
Epiperola 27.52.1
Epiphanis 24.52.18
Epiphloeinae, supra 24.67.22
Epiphragma 29.2.29
Epiplagiops 29.105.280
Epiplema 27.61.1
Epiplemid Moth Family, supra 27.62.1
Epiplemidae, supra 27.62.1
Epipocus 24.81.16
Epipompilus 25.60.14
Epipsiliamorpha 27.75.570
Epipsocetae, supra 17.8.1
Epipsocinae, supra 17.8.1
Epipsocus 17.8.1
epipsodea, Erebia 27.48.10 (Fig. 27.152)
Epiptera 21.4.3
Epipteromalus 25.19.113
Epipyropid Moth Family, supra 27.53.1
Epipyropidae 27.53.1
Epirhyssa 25.16.43
Epirranthini, supra 27.61.102
Epirranthis 27.61.102
Epirrhoe 27.61.225
Epirrita 27.61.237
Episbates 18.1.23
Episcardia 27.10.30
Episcepsis 27.73.82
Episcirrus 24.113.272
episcopalis, Macronaemia 24.80.47
Episcopellus 24.4.125
Episemasia 27.61.80
Episernus 24.63.11
Episimus 27.38.1
Epistenia 25.19.12
Epistrophe 29.47.13

Epistrophella 29.47.13
Episyron 25.60.24
Epitamyra 27.55.251
Epitausa 27.75.89
Epitedia 30.4.6
epithore, Clossiana 27.46.11
Epitragodes 24.87.7
Epitrix 24.107.137
epixanthe, Epidemia 27.43.7
Epochra 29.61.52
Epoicocladius 29.24.135
Epomidiopteron 25.53.5
eponina, Celithemis 7.7.5 (Fig. 7.12)
Eprhopalotus 25.26.60
Epuraea 24.70.12
Epyrinae, supra 25.48.6
Epyrini, supra 25.48.6
Epyris 25.48.8
eques, Taeniopoda 11.4.6
equestris, Merodon 29.47.56
equi, Bovicola 18.2.1
equina, Copromyza 29.88.2
equinus, Haemagogus 29.20.10
equitans, Symbiocladuis 29.24.91
Eralea 27.21.6
Erannis 27.61.64
Erastria 27.61.76
erato, Heliconius 27.46.6
Ercta 27.55.110
Erebia 27.48.10
Erebiini, supra 27.48.10
Erebus 27.75.112
erechtea, Caenurgina 27.75.140
Erechthias 27.10.15
Erelieva 27.55.409
erema, Moehnia 29.10.17
Eremandrena 25.66.1
Eremantha 27.55.36
Eremberga 27.55.386
Eremiacris 11.5.77
Eremiaphilinae, supra 14.1.1
eremicola, Osmoderma 24.30.116 (Fig. 24.74)
Ereminellus 20.7.45
eremitus, Sphinx 27.70.11
eremna, Apsaphida 27.75.435
Eremninae, supra 24.113.138
Eremnophila 25.62.13
Eremobina 27.75.257
Eremoblatta 14.4.2
Eremochrysa 23.9.12
Eremocoris 20.7.36
Eremoleon 23.14.9
Eremomyia 29.99.11
Eremomyiodes 29.99.12
Eremopasites 25.69.2
Eremopedes 11.7.34
Eremosaprinus 24.26.20
Eremosmia 25.68.19
Eremotipula 29.2.9
eresimus, Danaus 27.49.1
Eretes 24.7.40
Erethistes 24.113.236
Eretini, supra 24.7.40
Eretmocerus 25.25.20
Eretmoptera 29.24.87
Ergates 24.106.6
Ergatini, supra 245.106.6
Eriaporini, supra 25.25.18
Eribella 29.105.243
Eribolus 29.94.9
Eriborus 25.16.420
Ericaphis 21.19.73
Ericerus 21.26.22
ericetorum, Heliopetes 27.40.39 (Fig. 27.70)

erichsonii, Pristiphora 25.7.30
Erichsonius 24.24.4
Ericrocis 25.69.43
Ericydeus 24.113.27
Ericydnini, supra 25.25.35
eridania, Spodoptera 27.75.326
Eridolius 25.16.76
Eridontomerus 25.18.18
Erigeron Root Aphid 21.19.15
erigeronis, Nomada 25.69.10
Erigorgus 25.16.382
Erimerinae, supra 25.18.9
Erimerus 25.18.9
Erinnyis 27.70.21
Eriocampa 25.7.76
Eriocampidea 25.7.1
Eriocampini, supra 25.7.75
Eriocera 29.2.38
Eriococcidae, supra 21.31.1
Eriococcus 21.31.4
Eriocrania 27.2.2
Eriocraniella 27.2.3
Eriocraniid Moth Family, supra 27.2.1
Eriocraniidae, supra 27.2.1
Eriocranioidea, supra 27.2.1
eriogoni, Nicholia 20.23.57
Eriopeltis 21.26.3
Erioptera 29.2.59
Eriopterini, supra 29.2.41
Eriopyga 27.75.522
Eriopygini, supra 27.75.513
Eriosoma 21.19.74
Eriotremex 25.9.5
Eriothrixini, supra 29.105.208
Eriplatymetra 27.61.120
Erirrhininae 24.113.172
Erirrhinini, supra 24.113.172
Eristalinae, supra 29.47.32
Eristalini, supra 29.47.60
Eristalinus 29.47.66
Eristalis 29.47.65
Eritettix 11.5.10
Eritrissomerus 25.44.15
Erixestus 25.19.55
Erkosothrips 22.5.37
Ermine Moth 27.30.10
Ermine Moth Family, supra 27.30.1
Ernestiini, supra 29.105.114
Ernobius 24.63.10
Ernoneura 29.98.22
Ernoporus 24.112.34
Erodiscini, supra 24.113.196
Erodiscus 24.113.196
erodyle, Chlosyne 27.46.14
Eronyxa 24.66.5
Eropterus 24.57.10
Erora 27.43.35
Eros 24.57.8
erosa, Phymata 20.16.1 (Fig. 20.37)
Erosia 27.62.6
Erotidothripinae, supra 22.2.1
Erotylidae, supra 24.76.1
Erotylinae, supra 24.76.4
Erpetogomphus 7.3.10
errans, Poecilochrus 24.52.4
errantaria, paraphoides 27.61.54
Errastunus 21.14.199
erratica, Isotrilophus 24.99.3
erratica, Pectinodiplosis 29.11.126
Errhomenellini, supra 21.14.61
Errhomenus 21.14.61
Erromenus 25.16.59
Ersephila 27.61.201
Erucophaga 29.103.31
Eruga 25.16.21
Ervia 29.105.194

erycata, Syllectra 27.75.92
Eryciini, supra 29.105.408
Erynephala 24.107.83
Erynnia 29.105.339
Erynniopsis 29.105.244
Erynnis 27.40.37
erynnis, Pachodynerus 25.59.19
eryphon, Incisalia 27.43.29
erysimi, Lipaphis 21.19.117
Erythemis 7.7.7
Erythmelus 25.27.11
Erythrandrena 25.65.2
Erythraphycus 25.25.54
Erythraspides 25.7.73
Erythrandra 29.103.17
erythrocephala, Acantholya 25.2.2
Erythrocerini, supra 29.105.337
Erythrodiplax 7.7.8
Erythroecia 27.75.598
Erythroneura 21.14.82
erythropus, Derocrepis 24.107.133
Erythroscambus 25.16.2
Erythrothrips 22.1.4
Escaria 27.75.373
Eschatocrepis 24.68.19
Eschatomoxys 24.87.28
Eschatoporis 24.87.45
Eschatothrips 22.5.38
Esenbeckia 29.26.5
esenbeckii wilsoni, Nomamyrmex 25.58.2
Esperanza 20.5.4
Esperia 27.15.30
Esselenia 11.5.7
Essigella 21.19.75
essigi, Campodea 3.1.1
estacadus, Daltonia 21.14.218
Esthesopus 24.48.73
Esthlogena 24.106.244
Estigmene 27.73.36
estigmenensis, Hubneria 29.105.398
Esthiopterum 18.1.24
Estolini, supra 24.106.248
Estoloides 24.106.248
estrella, Mescinia 27.55.370
estriatus, Bius 24.87.77
estriatus, Botrodus 24.78.5
estriatus, Cybotus 24.87.149
estriatus, Pseudochodaeus 24.30.35
esula, Neogalea 27.75.442
Ethelgoda 27.38.51
ethlius, Calpodes 27.40.83
Ethelurgina, supra 25.16.112
Ethelurgus 25.16.113
Ethmia 27.15.13
Ethmiinae, supra 27.15.12
ethusa, Myscelia 27.46.35
ethyl acetate jars 36
Etiella 27.55.311
Euacidalia 27.61.173
Euaesthetinae, supra 24.24.161
Euaesthetus 24.24.162
Euagrotis 27.75.551
Euamiana 27.75.363
Euandrena 25.65.1
Euanotia 27.75.82
Euantha 29.105.206
Euaresta 29.61.21
Euarestoides 29.61.29
Euaspilates 27.61.135
Eubaeocera 24.23.5
Eubaphe 27.61.239
Eubarnesia 27.61.32
Eubazus 25.13.136
Eublemmini, supra 27.75.209
Euboarhexius 24.25.15
Euborellia 13.1.2

Eubolepia 27.17.16
Eubloina 27.75.130
Eubrachymera 29.105.178
Eubrianacinae, supra 24.34.15
Eubrianax 24.34.15
Eubriinae, supra 24.34.11
Eucaerus 24.4.152
Eucalantica 27.29.2
Eucalliphora 29.101.14
Eucallipterus 21.19.76
Eucalymnatus 21.26.5
eucalypti, Flockiella 25.26.51
Eucamptonyx 25.51.18
Eucanthus 24.30.51
Eucapnopsis 8.3.4
Eucatagma 27.30.2
Eucaterva 27.61.136
Eucatocha 29.11.26
Eucelatoria 29.105.245
Eucelatoriopsis 29.105.246
Eucera 25.69.23
eucera, Niphogenia 29.42.21
Euceraphis 21.19.77
eucerata, Parafischeria 29.105.129
Euceratia 27.29.3
Euceratina 25.69.45
Euceratocerus 24.63.14
Eucerceris 25.62.112
Eucereon 27.73.78
Eucerini, supra 25.69.21
Euceromasia 29.105.416
Euceroplatus 29.9.9
Euceroptres 25.34.8
Euceros 25.16.78
Eucerotinae, supra 25.16.78
Eucessia 29.40.39
Euchaetes 27.73.66
Euchactogyne 29.105.74
Euchalcia 27.75.161
Eucharitid Wasp Family, supra 25.23.1
Eucharitidae, supra 25.23.1
Eucharitinae, supra 25.23.2
Euchlaena 27.61.83
Euchloe 27.42.8
Euchroeini, supra 25.50.21
Euchromius 27.55.218
Euchrysia 25.19.11
Eucicones 24.93.7
Eucilinus 24.113.75
Eucinetidae, supra 24.31.1
Eucinetus 24.31.1
Eucirroedia 27.75.401
Euclea 27.52.19
Euclemensia 27.21.2
Euclidia 27.75.138
Euclyptus 24.113.191
Euclystis 27.75.120
Euclytia 29.105.8
Eucnemidae, supra 24.52.1
eucnemidarum, Vanhornia 25.39.1
Eucneminae, supra 24.52.2
Eucnemis 24.52.3
Eucnephalia 29.105.351
Eucoila 25.32.4
Eucoilid Wasp Family, supra 25.32.1
Eucoilidae, supra 25.32.1
Eucoilidea 25.32.15
Eucolpocephalum 18.6.14
Euconnini, supra 24.20.2
Euconnus 24.20.2
Eucoptocnemis 27.75.539
Eucordyligaster 29.105.207
Eucorethra 29.19.3
Eucorethrinae, supra 29.19.3
Eucoronimyia 29.105.303
Eucosma 27.38.25

Eucosmini, supra 27.38.19
Eucrada 24.63.4
Eucrossus 24.106.41
Eucyrtophloeba 29.105.158
Eucyrtopogon 29.37.43
Eucyllus 24.113.78
Eudactylolabis 29.2.31
Eudactylota 27.23.37
Eudarcia 27.10.3
Eudasytes 24.68.32
Eudecatoma 25.20.8
Eudecatominae, supra 25.20.8
Eudectus 24.24.112
Eudeilinia 27.60.2
Eudeleboea 25.16.315
Eudelus 25.16.87
Euderces 24.106.127
Euderini, supra 25.26.33
Euderomphale 25.26.54
Euderus 25.26.34
Eudesmia 27.73.20
Eudesmula 24.93.10
Eudicrana 29.9.60
Eudicranota 29.2.25
Eudioctria 29.37.35
Eudistenia 24.106.25
Eudocima 27.75.69
Eudociminus 24.113.156
Eudonia 27.55.4
eudora, Neoplynes 27.73.23
eudoreela, Diviana 27.55.365
Eudorylas 29.48.5
Eudrepanulatrix 27.61.70
Eudryas 27.75.239
Eudulini, supra 27.61.239
Eueana 27.61.165
Eueides 27.46.5
Eueretagrotis 27.75.583
Euerythra 27.73.39
Euetheola 24.30.103
Euexorista 29.105.417
eufala, Lerodea 27.40.81
Eufallia 24.82.8
Eufernaldia 27.55.202
Eufidonia 27.61.57
Eufrontina 29.105.418
Eugaediopsis 29.105.361
Eugaurax 29.94.22
eugeniae, Stephomyia 29.11.76
eugenii, Anthonomus 24.113.208
Euglenidae, supra 24.104.1
Euglenina, supra 24.104.6
Euglossini, supra 25.70.1
Eugnamptus 24.113.5
Eugnophomyia 29.2.45
Eugnoriste 29.10.5
Eugonobapta 27.61.144
Eugonus 24.109.21
Eugraphe 27.75.572
Eugymnogaster 29.105.15
Euholognatha, supra 8.1.1
Euhoplopsyllus 30.1.8
Euhrychiopsis 24.113.296
Euhybus 29.42.62
Euhyparpax 27.71.36
Euidella 21.2.17
Eukiefferiella 29.24.97
Euklastus 21.9.1
Eukraiohelea 29.23.13
Eulabis 24.87.135
Eulachus 21.19.78
Eulachus 24.93.11
Eulaema 25.70.1
Eulasiona 29.105.179
Eulecanium 21.26.6
Euleia 29.61.51

Eulepidotus 27.75.83
Eulepte 27.55.146
Eulia 27.38.63
Eulimnichus 24.43.2
Eulithis 27.61.191
Eulithosia 27.75.353
Eullechriops 24.113.277
Eulogia 27.55.393
Eulonchopria 25.63.1
Eulonchus 29.38.2
Eulonus 21.14.84
Eulophid Wasp Family, supra 25.26.1
Eulophidae, supra 25.26.1
Eulophinae, supra 25.26.1
Eulophini, supra 25.26.1
Eulophus 25.26.9
eulophus, Ceratobrays 29.94.6
Eulyonetia 27.13.4
Eumacaria 27.61.8
Eumacrocentrus 25.13.63
Eumacrodes 27.61.172
Eumacronychia 29.103.2
Eumaeini, supra 27.43.11
Eumaeus 27.43.11
Eumarozia 27.38.9
Eumasicera 29.105.401
Eumasicerini, supra 29.105.401
Eumastacidae, supra 11.2.1
Eumayria 25.34.39
Eumecomera 24.97.10
Eumegaparia 29.105.47
Eumegastigmus 25.18.26
Eumelissodes 25.69.30
Eumenes 25.59.24
Eumeninae, supra 25.59.3
Eumerus 29.47.57
Eumcsocampa 3.1.5
Eumestleta 27.75.210
Eumetopiella 29.58.28
eumichthini, supra 24.106.91
Eumichthus 24.106.91
Eumicremma 27.75.209
Eumicrosoma 25.43.31
Eumicrotipula 29.2.9
Eumolpinae, supra 24.107.38
Eumolpini, supra 24.107.28
Eumolpus 24.107.45
eumops, Hesperoctenes 20.19.1
Eumorpha, supra 27.70.1, 27.70.31
Eumorphinae, supra 24.81.11
Eumorsea 11.2.3
Eumyobia 29.105.217
Eumysia 27.55.353
Eunemobius 11.10.14
Euneura 25.19.67
Eunica 27.46.36
eunomia, Proclossiana 27.46.9
Eunota 24.3.4
Eunotinae, supra 25.19.31
Eunotus 25.19.32
eunus, Pseudocopaeodes 27.40.63
Eunyssobia 24.113.359
Euodynerus 25.59.16
euonymi, Unaspis 21.38.83 (Fig. 21.34)
Euonymus Scale 21.38.83
Euophthalmomyia 25.26.56
Euopius 25.13.83
Eupackardia 27.69.16
Eupalamus 25.16.211
eupalusalis, Triuncidia 27.55.82
Euparagia 25.59.1
Euparagiinae, supra 25.59.1
Eupareophora 25.7.68
Euparia 24.30.20
Euparius 24.109.19
Euparixia 24.30.22

Euparthenos 27.75.129
Euparyphus 29.31.33
Eupelecotheca 29.105.275
Eupeliminae, supra 25.24.4
Eupelmella 25.24.7
Eupelmid Wasp Family 25.24.1
Eupelmidae, supra 25.24.1
Eupelmus 25.24.5
Eupeodes 29.47.15
Euperilampus 25.19.3
Euphalepsus 24.25.68
Euphalerus 21.17.24
Euphasiopteryx 29.105.44
Euphidius 25.14.8
Euphilotes 27.43.44
euphorbiae, Macrosiphum 21.191.122
Euphoria 24.30.126
Euphoriaspis 24.30.128
Euphoriella 25.13.151
Euphorinae, supra 25.13.147
Euphorini, supra 25.13.148
Euphorocera 29.105.281
Euphorticus 24.4.81
Euphrytus 24.107.41
Euphydryas 27.46.23
Euphyes 27.40.77
Euphyia 27.61.226
Euphyllurini, supra 21.17.22
Euphyto 29.103.3
Eupisenus 24.98.4
Eupithecia 27.61.241
Eupitheciini, supra 27.61.240
Euplectina, supra 24.25.24
Euplectini, supra 24.25.8
Euplectromorpha 25.26.14
Euplectrini, supra 25.26.13
Euplectrus 25.26.13
Euplectus 24.25.30
Euplexia 27.75.286
Eupnigodes 11.5.16
Eupogonius 24.106.246
Eupogonomyia 29.100.37
Eupompha 24.101.6
Eupomphina, supra 24.101.4
Eupragia 27.15.9
Eupristocerus 24.46.32
Euproctinus 24.4.153
Euproctis 27.74.6
Euprojoannisia 29.23.3
Euprora 27.13.1
Euproserpinus 27.70.38
Eupsenius 24.25.45
Eupseniina, supra 24.25.45
Eupseudomorpha 27.75.246
Eupseudosoma 27.73.71
Eupsilia 27.75.394
Eupsilobius 24.81.18
Eupsophulus 24.87.37
Eupteromalus 25.19.104
Eupthchia 27.48.3
Euptilopareia 29.105.159
Euptilostena 29.2.47
Euptoieta 27.46.7
Euptychia 27.48.4, 27.48.5, 27.48.6
Euptychiini, supra 27.48.3
Euptychodera 20.3.14
eureka, Abachrysa 23.9.10
Eurema 27.42.17
Euresia 27.17.11
eureum 18.6.15
Eurhinosea 27.61.192
Eurhopalthrix 25.58.50
Eurhoptus 24.113.246
euribates, Dyscophellus 27.40.19
eurimedes, Parides 27.41.2
Euristrymon 27.43.31

Eurois 27.75.562
europaea, Timberlakia 25.25.60
European Alder Leafminer 25.7.52
European Apple Sawfly 25.7.18
European Chafer 24.30.64
European Chicken Flea 30.7.2
Europenan Corn Borer 27.55.84
European Crane Fly 29.2.9
European Elm Scale 21.31.5
European Fruit Lecanium 21.26.14
European Fruit Scale 21.38.73
European Grain Moth 27.10.1
European Honeysuckle Leaf Roller 28.29.8
European Hornet 25.59.26
European Mantis 14.1.9
European Mole Cricket 11.11.1
European Mouse Flea 30.6.2
European Peach Scale 21.26.14
European Pine Sawfly 25.6.4
European Wheat Stem Sawfly 25.12.4
Europiella 20.23.42
Europs 24.71.6
Euros 27.75.259
Eurosta 29.61.12
Eurphullura 21.17.23
Eurphydryas 27.46.22
Eurrhypara 27.55.87
Eurryhyparodes 27.55.116
euryalus, Hyalophora 27.69.18
euryaspis, Camera 25.16.158
Eurycephalomyia 29.58.20
Euryceromyia 29.105.318
eurychilopterella 20.23.16
Eurycnemus 29.24.106
Eurycoccus 21.25.18
Eurycotis 14.3.4
Euryderus 24.4.122
eurydice, Satyrodes 27.48.2 (Fig. 27.147)
eurydice, Zerene 27.42.12
Euryelmis 24.68.16
Eurygarka 29.12.10
Eurygaster 20.3.11
Eurygeniini, supra 24.103.2
Eurygenius 24.103.3
Euryhopalus 25.25.142
Eurylophella 6.13.6
eurymedon, Pterourus 27.41.7
Eurymetopini, supra 24.87.11
Eurymetopon 24.87.11
Euryneura 29.31.16
Euryomma 29.100.28
Euryopa 24.54.3
Euryophthalminae 290.9.1
Euryophthalmus 20.9.1
Eurypepla 24.107.178
Eurypogon 24.34.2
Euryproctini, supra 25.16.363
Euryproctus 25.16.374
Euryptychus 24.52.17
Eurysa 21.2.5
Euryscelis 24.106.122
Euryscopa 24.107.18
Eurysphindus 24.73.3
eurysternus, Haematopinus 19.3
Eurystylops 24.105.3
Eurytelini, supra 27.46.39
Eurytenes 25.13.88
eurytheme, Colias 27.42.11 (Fig. 27.93)
Eurythmia 27.55.408
Eurythnidia 27.55.363
Eurythrips 22.5.39
Eurytides 27.41.4
Eurytoma 25.20.22
Eurytomidae, supra 25.20.1
Eurytominae, supra 25.20.17
Eurytomocharis 25.20.19

Eusama 21.14.117
Eusandalum 25.24.3
Eusapyga 25.57.3
Eusarca 27.61.139
Eusattodera 24.107.111
Eusattus 24.87.66
Euscaphurus 24.31.2
Euscelidius 21.14.155
Euscepes 24.113.260
Eusceptis 27.75.221
Euschaefferia 24.566.11
Euschistus 20.3.34
Euschizaphis 21.19.191
Euscirrhopterus 27.75.244
Euscopolia 29.105.254
Euselasia 27.44.1
Euselasiinae, supra 27.44.1
Eusemion 25.25.68
eusimulium 29.22.5
Eusiphona 29.74.10
Eusisyropa 29.105.396
Eusomalia 24.35.5
Eusora 21.14.136
Eusphalerum 24.24.113
Euspilotus 24.26.16
Eustalomyia 29.99.24
Eusterinx 25.16.496
Eustictus 20.23.17
Eustixis 27.55.24
Eustroma 27.61.193
Eustromboceros 25.7.7
Eustromuloa 24.106.71
Eustrophinus 24.98.9
Eustrophus 24.98.10
Eustrotiini, supra 27.75.181
Eustylini, supra 24.113.98
Eutaenionotum 29.93.42
Eutanyacra 25.16.229
Eutelia 27.75.171
Euteliinae 27.75.168
Eutettix 21.14.135
Euthagena 27.35.7
Euthalidaya 29.105.228
Eutheia 24.20.13
Eutheliini, supra 24.20.13
Euthera 29.105.38
Eutheresia 29.105.75
Eutherini, supra 29.105.38
Euthiodes 24.20.15
Euthiscia 21.6.6
Euthlastoblatta 14.5.8
Euthochtha 20.4.14
Euthoracaphis 21.19.79
Euthorax 24.24.236
Euthosmia 25.68.21
Euthycera 29.79.11
Euthyneura 29.42.54
Euthyprosopa 29.105.327
Euthyrhynchus 20.3.71
Euthysanius 24.48.51
Euthytira 27.59.4
Eutochia 24.87.116
Eutolype 27.75.430
Eutomostethus 25.7.64
Eutonia 29.2.34
Eutrapela 27.61.145
Eutrepsia 27.61.205
Eutreta 29.61.9
Eutrias 25.32.3
Eutricharaea 25.68.22
Eutrichillus 24.106.276
Eutrichites 24.25.52
Eutricholista 24.68.35
Eutrichophilus 18.2.2
Eutrichopleurus 24.68.38
Eutrichopoda 29.105.4

Eutrichosoma 25.19.7
Eutrichosomatinae, supra 25.19.7
Eutricopis 27.75.595
Eutrila 24.79.5
Eutriorophus 24.87.27
Eutrixa 29.105.49
Eutrixopsis 29.105.40
Eutyphlus 24.25.20
Euura 25.7.35
Euvacusus 24.102.11
Euvira 24.24.237
Euvrilletta 24.63.35
Euxenulus 24.109.5
Euxenus 24.109.6
Euxesta 29.58.29
Euxestinae, supra 24.78.1
Euxestonotus 25.44.14
Euxoa 27.75.544
Euzophera 27.55.392
Evacanthini, supra 21.14.60
Evacanthus 21.14.60
Evagetes 25.60.21
Evalljapyginae, supra 3.4.7
Evalljapyx 3.4.7
evanescens, Trichogramma 25.28.8 (Fig. 25.24)
Evania 25.35.1
Evaniella 25.35.3
Evaniidae, supra 25.35.1
evaniiformis, Coleomethia 24.106.32
Evanioidea, supra 25.35.1
evansi, Verdanus 21.14.191
Evanystes 24.24.238
Evarthrus 24.4.88
evarete, Junonia 27.46.30
evelinae, Agrostisia 27.75.298
Everes 27.43.41
Evergestella 27.55.74
Evergestinae, supra 27.55.69
Evergestis 27.55.69
Evergreen Bagworm 27.11.12
Everini, supra 27.43.41
eversmanni, Parnassius 27.41.1
evidens, Serica 24.30.61 (Fig. 24.68)
Evidomyia 29.105.304
evincalis, Evergestella 27.55.74
Evippe 27.24.14
Eviridemas 27.75.385
Evita 27.61.131
Evodinus 24.106.180
Evolenes 24.4.102
Evora 27.38.18
Evotus 24.113.106
Evoxysoma 25.20.20
Evylaeus 25.66.17
Exllonyx 25.39.12
exarata, Evolenes 24.4.102
exaratus, Prolyctus 24.93.27
excarinatus, Simophion 25.16.463
Excavarus 25.16.69
excavata, Diphytaxis 24.52.26
excavaticollis, Myrmecaphodius 24.30.21
excavatus, Merostenus 25.24.8
excelsa, Helonica 21.15.38
excelsaria, Stenoporpia 27.61.27 (Fig. 27.179)
Exceptia 27.23.48
exchanging specimens 47
excisa, Oligembia 9.2.1
excisum, Plectonotum 24.56.12
excisus, Physoconops 29.49.2
excitans, Neodiprion 25.6.4 (Fig. 25.9)
exclamationis, Hilarocassis 24.107.175
exclamationis, Zoniagrion 7.11.14
exclamationis, Zygogramma 24.107.59
Excultanus 21.14.142

Exechia 29.9.25
Exechiopsis 29.9.26
Exelis 27.61.28
Exema 24.107.35
exempta, Spodoptera 27.75.326
Exenterini, supra 25.16.68
Exenterus 25.16.75
Exepacmus 29.40.37
Exephanes 25.16.226
Exeristes 25.16.1
Exetastes 25.16.317
exigens, Prosimulium 29.22.4
exigua, Campogaster 29.105.32
exigua, Fulgoraecia 27.53.1 (Fig. 27.162)
exigua, Spodoptera 27.75.326 (Fig. 27.368)
Exiguus, Anodocheilus 24.7.8
exilis, Brephidium 27.43.37
exilis, Lutridia 18.2.5
exilis, Stereodermus 24.110.5
Exiliscelis 29.16.1
eximia, Muesebeckia 25.13.127
eximia, Paraphausis 24.55.3
Exitianus 21.14.166
exitiosa, Synanthedon 27.35.12 (Fig. 27.55)
exitiosus, Exitianus 21.14.166
Exochomus 24.80.24
Exochrysis 25.50.22
Exochus 25.16.301
Exodontha 29.31.11
Exomalopsini, supra 25.69.16
Exomalopsis 25.69.16
Exomella 24.35.12
Exomellini, supra 24.35.12
Exomus 25.16.83
Exoplectra 24.80.31
Exoplectrini, supra 24.80.31
Exoporia, supra 27.4.1
Exoprosopa 29.40.44
Exoprosopinae, supra 29.40.44
Exorista 29.105.282
Exoristini, supra 29.105.277
Exoristoides 29.105.138
exornata, Trichoplexia 27.75.255
exoskeleton 10
Exosternini, supra 24.26.47
Exotela 25.13.94
Exoteleia 27.23.21
Exothecinae, supra 25.13.36
Exothecini, supra 25.13.36
expansa, Antianthe 21.15.43
expansa, Decusa 24.24.220
expansa, Pictetiella 8.7.19
explanata, Microcara 24.32.2
Explorator 24.42.1
expulsus, Pomipius 25.60.28
exquisita, Acanthocheila 20.14.2
exquisita, Nectopsyche 26.18.4
exquisita, Syntrichalonia 25.69.22
exsanguis, Zelus 20.17.22
exsculpta, Ochthera 29.93.51
exsculpta, Triogma 29.2.13
exsectoides, Formica 25.58.72
exserta, Netelia 25.16.48
exsiccatus, Tathorhynchus 27.75.43
extensicornis, Pachynematus 25.7.27
extensum, Xenogenus 20.6.6
externa, Fiorinia 21.38.31
externalis, Sericoplaga 27.55.99
extimus, Piestus 24.24.8
extorris, Cybalomia 27.55.197
extricalis, Nealgedonia 27.55.89
Extrusanus 21.14.160
exul, Gaesischiana 25.69.32
exutum, Sphaerion 24.206.68
Exuviaspis 21.38.29

Exyra 27.75.183
Exyston 25.16.70
eye 12
eye, compound 20
Eye Gnats 29.94.2
Eyed Click Beetle 24.48.7
Eysarcoris 20.3.42
Eyespotted Bud Moth 27.38.22

F

fabae, Aphis 21.19.15
fabae, Empoasca 21.14.77
Fabiola 27.15.27
fabra, Peritapnia 24.106.266
Fabria 26.8.4
Fabriciella 29.105.87
fabricii, Epicauta 24.101.14
Faculta 27.23.61
Fagiphagus 21.19.80
fagisuga, Cryptococcus 21.30.1
Fagitana 27.75.312
Fahrrenholzia 19.7.2
fairfaxensis, Forcipomyia 29.23.3
Fairy Moth Family, supra 27.8
Fairyfly Family, supra 25.27.1
Fala 27.75.358
Falagria 24.24.239
Falagriota 24.24.240
Falcapica 27.42.10 (Fig. 27.91)
falcata, Eriocraniella 27.2.3
Falcate Orange-tip 27.42.10
falcatus, Pygostolus 25.13.132
Falcicula 11.10.22
falcifer, Rhizoecus 21.25.38
falcifera, Anagrapha 27.75.165 (Fig. 27.342)
falcifera, Colcondamyia 29.103.28
Falcimorpha 27.55.115
Falcolipeurus 18.1.25
Fall Armyworm 27.75.326
Fall Cankerworm 27.61.3
Fall Webworm Moth 27.73.38
falli, Conoderus 24.48.14
falliana, Bamona 24.24.207
False Antlike Flower Beetle Family, supra 24.103.1
False Armored Scale Insect Family, supra 21.36.1
False Blister Beetle 24.97.8 (Fig. 24.165)
False Celery Leaf Tier 27.55.105
False Chinch Bug 20.7.11
False Click Beetle Family, supra 24.52.1
False Clown Beetle Family, supra 24.27.1
False Darkling Beetle Family, supra 24.97.1
False Hemlock Looper 27.61.133
False Lizard Barklice Family 17.18.1
False Long-horned Beetle Family, supra 24.86.1
False Mealworm 24.87.75
False Metallic Wood-boring Beetle, supra 24.49.1
False Oleander Scale 21.38.69
False Parlatoria Scale 21.38.72
False Potato Beetle 24.107.60
False Skin Beetle Family, supra 24.83.1
False Tiger Beetle Family, supra 24.95.1
False Water Penny 24.34.15
Falsogastrallus 24.63.20
famelicus, Dicyphus 210.23.29
family 15
Fania 27.37.7
Fannia 29.100.26
Fanniinae, supra 29.100.16
farinalis, Pyralis 27.55.233 (Fig. 27.168)
farinosus, Oestranthrax 29.40.54

Faroninae, supra 24.25.1
Faronini, supra 24.25.1
Faronta 27.75.497
Farula 26.10.39
fasciapennis, Aleurodothrips 22.5.29
fasciata, Barrovia 27.75.563
fasciata, Celithemis 7.7.5
fasciata, Erebia 27.48.10
fasciata, Eumorpha 27.70.31 (Fig. 27.253)
fasciata, Helomyza 29.84.23
fasciata, Penichroa 24.106.48
fasciata, Strophopteryx 8.2.4
fasciatipennis, Elaphidionopsis 24.106.77
fasciatum, Hoplocheiloma 29.51.6
fasciatus, Allonemobius 11.10.13 (Fig. 11.45)
fasciatus, Aradophagus 25.43.30
fasciatus, Attagenus 24.61.6
fasciatus, Caliothrips 22.4.2
fasciatus, Conocephalus 11.7.21
fasciatus, Glischrochilus 24.70.35 (Fig. 24.135)
fasciatus, Haliplus 24.6.1 (Fig. 24.46)
fasciatus, Ipochus 24.106.229
fasciatus, Megalodacne 24.76.3 (Fig. 24.142)
fasciatus, Nosopsyllus 30.7.10 (Fig. 30.4)
fasciatus, Oncopeltus 20.7.8 (Fig. 20.28)
fasciatus, Rhipiphorus 24.100.5
fasciatus, Sargus 29.31.6
fascicularis, Hemirhipis 24.48.8
fasciculatus, Araecerus 24.109.1 (Fig. 24.254)
fascifrons, Macrosteles 21.14.97
fascipennis, Macrojappa 25.16.261
fascipennis, Plectrodiplosis 29.11.89
Fascista 27.23.60
fasciventris, Promericia 29.105.119
Fateful Barklice Family 17.14.1
fatima, Anartia 27.46.31
Fattigia 26.13.2
faunal zones 27 (Table 4.2)
faunus, Polygonia 27.46.24 (Fig. 27.130)
fausta, Rhagoletis 29.61.44
Faustinus 24.113.256
favonius, Euristrymon 27.43.31
Feather-winged Beetle Family, supra 24.15.1 (Fig. 24.17)
februa, Hamadryas 27.46.41
Fedtschenkia 25.57.1
Fedtschenkiinae, supra 25.57.1
feeding habitats 24
felicita, Baptarma 27.75.594
Felicola 18.2.3
felis felis, Ctenocephalides 30.1.3 (Fig. 30.2)
Felt Scale Insect Family, supra 21.31.1
Feltia 27.75.537
Feltiella 29.11.83
Feltomyina 29.11.38
femorale, Eucolpocephalum 18.6.14
femoralis, Hercinothrips 22.4.5
femoralis, Oedostethus 24.48.60
femorata, Acanthocephala 20.4.2 (Figs. 20.18, 20.19)
femorata, Bucephalomyia 29.100.18
femorata, Chrysobothris 24.46.23
femorata, Diapheromera 10.1.4 (Fig. 10.2)
femoratus, Pelocoris 20.38.3, (Fig. 20.72)
femoratus, Rhodoleptus 24.106.153
femur (femora) 22
femurrubrum, Melanoplus 11.5.94 (Fig. 11.21)
Fenderia 24.24.97
Fenderomyia 29.9.6
Fenella 25.7.53

fenestrata, Metatephritis 29.61.31
fenestrata, Myiomyrmica 29.58.13
fenestralis, Porrhodites 24.24.129
fenestralis, Scenopinus 29.33.1
fenestralis, Sylvicola 29.14.1
Fenestula 25.16.177
Feniseca 27.43.1
fennica, Actebia 27.75.558
Fenusa 25.7.52
Fenusini, supra 25.7.45
fenyesi, Lypoglossa 24.24.263
fenyesi, Metopina 29.46.30
Feralia 27.75.428
Feraliini, supra 27.75.428
Ferdinandea 29.47.37
Fern Aphid 21.19.104
Fern Scale 21.38.64
fernaldana, Carposinia 27.26.1 (Fig. 27.43)
fernaldi, Deuterophysa 27.55.117
Fernaldia 27.10.20
Fernaldina 25.62.8
fernandezi, Lyus 24.57.1
Fernandocrambus 27.55.204
feronia, Hamadryas 27.46.41
ferox, Brachynemurus 23.14.2
ferox, Castolus 20.17.14
ferox, Hamadryas 27.46.41
ferox, Hemiquedius 24.24.23
ferraria, Acherdoa 27.75.315
ferrisi, Chalceria 27.43.6
ferrisi, Neolipoptena 29.106.10
Ferrisia 21.25.19
Ferrisicoccus 21.25.20
Ferrisidea 21.38.30
ferrugatus, Diachlorus 29.26.17
ferruginea, Ampulex 25.62.3 (Fig. 25.57)
ferruginea, Anisomorpha 10.4.1
ferruginea, Coenomyia 29.29.2
ferruginea, Lycoperdina 24.81.11
ferruginea, Odontomera 29.62.4
ferruginea, Orthemis 7.7.18
ferrugineus, Callibaetis 6.4.4
ferrugineus, Camponotus 25.58.66 (Fig. 25.47)
ferrugineus, Cryptolestes 24.72.17
ferrugineus, Hexacylloepus 24.45.14
ferrugineus, Oidematops 29.79.3
ferrugineus, Pedinotus 25.13.21
ferruginosus, Tomonotus 11.5.53
ferrumequinum, Axiolgina 29.58.26
fervescens, Psaliodes 27.61.217
fervida, Nomada 25.69.10
fervidanus, Archips 27.38.74
Fervidobombus 25.70.2 (Fig. 25.67)
fessonia, Adelpha 27.46.34
festaliella, Schreckensteinia 27.34.5 (Fig. 27.52)
festina, Penniverpa 29.32.21
festinus, Spissistilus 21.15.26
festiva, Chlorida 24.106.161
festiva, Diphthera 27.75.75
festiva, Tastiotenia 25.60.19
festivoides, Elaphria 27.75.328 (Fig. 27.369)
festivus, Synoecetes 25.16.332
Fibla 23.4.1
Ficana 20.4.25
Ficiomyia 29.11.156
ficorum, Gynaikothrips 22.5.43
ficus, Pachylia 27.70.23
fidelissima, Composia 27.73.2
Fidia 24.107.54
Fidicinini, supra 21.13.7
Fidiobia 25.44.8
fidum, Aphilodyctium 25.7.85
Fieberiella 21.14.150

Fieberocapsus 20.23.99
Field Cockroach 14.5.1
Field Cricket 11.10.10
Field Crickets 11.10.6
field records 32
field storage 37
Fiery Hunter 24.4.13
Fiery Skipper 27.40.61
Fig Scale 21.38.45
Fig Wasps, supra 25.18.1
Figites 25.31.18
Figitid Wasp Family, supra 25.31.1
Figitidae, supra 25.31.1
figitiformis, Brachycistellus 25.53.14
Figitinae, supra 25.31.10
figulilella, Cadra 27.55.403
Filament Bearer 27.61.156
filamentaria, Nematocampa 27.61.156, syn. linchata (Haworth) in "Checklist."
Filatima 27.23.58
Filbert Aphid 21.19.142
Filbert Weevil 24.113.200
Filbertworm 27.38.57
filialis, Cloacina 29.105.341
filicis, Loboptercomyia 29.11.118
filifera, Collomena 27.75.177
filiforme, Nematidium 25.93.19
filiformis, Ganocapsus 20.23.159
Fimbriaphis 21.19.81
fimbriata, Myiophthiria 29.106.3
fimbriatus, Neopharnus 20.3.56
fimbriatus, Saprinus 24.26.15
fimetarius, Aphodius 24.30.17
fimetarius, Onychiurus 1.3.3
Finger-net Caddisfly Family, supra 26.1.1
Finlaya 29.20.9
finlaysoni, Anisota 27.69.5
Fiorinia 21.39.31
Fiorinia Scale 21.38.31
fioriniae, Fiorinia 21.38.31
Fir Cone Looper 27.61.241
Fir Engraver 24.112.23
Fir Seed Moth 27.38.56
Fir Tree Borer 24.106.104
Fire Ant 25.58.33
Fire Blister Beetle 24.101.12
Fire Bug 20.3.48 (Fig. 20.12)
Firebrat 5.3.8
Firebrat Family 5.3.1
Fire-colored Beetle 24.94.4
Fire-colored Beetle Family, supra 24.94.1
Firefly Beetle Family, supra 24.55.1
Firgartus 21.14.161
fiscellaria, Lambdina 27.61.130 (Fig. 27.188)
Fishfly 23.2.2
Fishia 27.75.418
Fissicrambus 27.55.214
fissionotata, Semiothisa 27.61.13 (Fig. 27.178)
Fissuraspis 21.38.32
Fitchana 21.14.128
Fitchia 20.17.16
Fitchiella 21.6.1
fitchii, Protoplasa 29.1.1
fitchii, Rhopalosiphum 21.19.186
Five Spotted Hawk Moth 27.70.4
Flabellomicrosiphum 21.19.82
flamella, Mirificarma 27.23.62
flammipennis, Rhynchophion 25.16.461
Flannel Moth Famiuly, supra 27.51.1
Flat Bark Beetle Family, supra 24.72.1
Flat Bug Family 20.13.1
Flat Clown Beetle 24.26.45
Flat Grain Beetle 24.72.17
Flat Grass Scale Insect Family, supra 21.27.1

Flat Pit Scale Insect Family, supra 21.33.1
Flat-footed Fly Family, supra 29.45.1
Flatheaded Apple Tree Borer 24.46.23
Flatheaded Cone Borer 24.46.26
Flatheaded Fir Borer 24.46.20
Flatheaded Mayfly Family 6.6.1
Flatid Planthopper Family, supra 21.8.1
Flatidae, supra 21.8.1
Flatinae, supra 21.8.1
Flatini, supra 21.8.1
Flatoides 21.8.12
Flatoidinae, supra 21.8.12
Flatoidinus 21.8.13
flava, Chyromya 29.86.2
flava, Euclytia 29.105.8
flava, Neofischeria 29.105.126
flava, Oestlundiella 21.19.154
flava, Potamyia 26.4.9
flava, Sipha 21.19.196
flava, Tetragonocephala 21.17.20
flavalis, Arenochroa 27.55.97
flavaria, Eurhinosea 27.61.192
flavescens, Cnidocampa 27.52.10
flavescens, Tomocerus 1.5.13
flavens, Epoicocladius 29.24.135
flaveola, Dicronota 29.2.25
flaveolus, Fieberocapsus 20.23.99
flavescens, Pantala 7.7.22
flavicans, Chaoborus 29.19.1
flavicauda, Miopthachys 24.4.51
flaviceps, Carneocephala 21.14.48
flavicollis, Laphria 29.37.60
flavicornella, Phycitopsis 27.55.338
flavicornis, Grotiusomyia 25.26.24
flavoicornis, Lomamyia 23.11.1 (Fig. 23.11)
flavida, Pachycerina 29.82.11
flavidens, Pseudanarta 27.75.302 (Fig. 27.363)
flavidorsella, Passodena 27.55.348
flavidorsus, Bromleyus 29.37.29
flavidus, Chrysops 29.26.11
flavidus, Parepalpus 20.105.99
flavifrimbriata, Eusceptis 27.75.221
flavifrons, Glyphidops 29.52.2
flaviola, Oedematocera 29.105.332
flavipes, Anthrenus 24.61.8
flavipes, Entomychobius 25.19.87
flavipes, Hexacharis 25.31.8
flavipes, Leptogaster 29.37.2
flavipes, Lispideosoma 29.105.305
flavipes, Pelecotoma 24.100.1
flavipes, Phytosciara 29.10.3
flavipes, Pterodontia 29.38.4
flavipes, Reticulitermes 15.3.1
flavipes, Tetradryinus 25.51.8
flavipes, Trachyscelis 24.87.130
flavipes, Xanthogramma 29.47.21
flavipes, Zagella 25.28.7
flavipalpis, Cynomyia 29.101.20
flavipennis, Melanophrys 29.105.123
flavitibiae, Mirolynx 25.26.23
flavocinctus, Hydrizon 25.15.1
flavocinctus, Lissonotus 24.106.167
flavofasciata, Proserpinus 27.70.37 (Fig. 27.261)
flavomarginta, Gymnetis 24.30.122
flavoscuta, Lopidella 20.23.111
flavus, Phasiops 29.105.48
Flax Bollworm 27.75.599
Flea Beetles, supra 24.107.114
Fleas, supra 30.1.1
Fleckled Mayflies 6.4.4
Flesh Fly Family, supra 29.103.1
Fletcher Scale 21.26.14
fletcheri, Parthenolecanium 21.26.14

Fletcherimyia 29.103.24
Fleutiauxellus 24.48.58
Flexamia 21.14.195
flexicaulis, Glenidion 24.107.139
flexicaulis, Pseudocyphus 24.113.104
Flies, supra 29.1.1
floccifera, Pulvinaria 21.26.19
floccosus, Aleurothrixus 21.18.9
floccosus, Geopemphigus 21.19.86
flocki, Speleketor 17.4.4
Flockiella 25.26.51
flohri, Lissomelas 24.30.132
Floodwater Mosquito 29.20.9
flora, Asterocampa 27.47.3
floralis, Hylemya 29.99.8
floralis, Omonadus 24.102.8
floralis, Oncerus 24.30.58
floralis, Uhleriola 20.7.69
florella, Syngamia 27.55.183
Florida Carpenter Ant 25.58.66
Florida Damp-wood Termite 15.3.3
Florida Fern Caterpillar 27.75.313
Florida Ground Mealybug 21.25.38
Florida Harvester Ant 25.58.24
Florida Red Scale 21.38.16
Florida Tortise Beetle 24.107.174
Florida Wax Scale 21.26.1
floridae, Ardeiphilus 18.6.4
floridalis, Anaea 27.47.1
floridana, Amblycorypha 11.7.1 (Fig. 11.27)
floridana, Bakeriella 25.48.9
floridana, Entanoneura 23.7.6
floridana, Eurhopalothrix 25.58.50
floridana, Kalodiplosis 29.11.86
floridana, Mantura 24.107.143
floridana, Micronaspis 24.55.7
floridana, Nesostizocera 24.106.57
floridana, Onota 24.4.154
floridana, Parochromolopis 27.27.3
floridana, Phasiopsis 29.105.392
floridana, Physopleurella 20.21.20
floridanus, Artipus 24.113.26
floridanus, Branchus 24.87.63
floridanus, Calcocerinus 25.25.40
floridanus, Cerapterocerus 25.25.67
floridanus, Charisius 24.88.4
floridanus, Cryptoramorphus 24.63.46
floridanus, Derovatellus 24.7.3
floridnaus, Euthyrhynchus 20.3.71
floridanus floridanus, Xenomyrmex 25.58.32
floridanus, Gracilentulus 2.3.5
floridanus, Gnostus 24.62.11
floridanus, Neapodops 20.3.16A
floridanus, Oligolinus 24.24.42
floridanus, Oomorphus 24.107.36
floridanus, Planismus 24.72.6 (see 24.75.1)
floridanus, Polygenis 30.2.1
floridanus, Rhizoecus 21.25.38
floridanus, Streprterothrips 22.5.70
floridanus, Sudus 24.113.268
floridanus, Typhloceuthophilus 11.9.19
floridata, Pterocypha 27.61.212
floridensis, Callopistria 27.75.313 (Fig. 27.364)
floridensis, Ceroplastes 21.26.1
floridensis, Cerylauctomus 24.78.7
floridensis, Didymops 7.5.1
floridensis, Eugaurax 29.94.22
floridensis, Lea 11.7.14
floridensis, Leptoconops 29.23.1
floridensis, Liothrips 22.5.49
floridensis, Monoceromyia 29.47.71
floridensis, Nicephorus 29.105.76
floridensis, Opogona 27.10.50
floridensis, Rhytidops 29.80.1

floridensis, Tachinophyto 29.105.265
floridensis, Trialeurodes 21.18.17
Floridonus 21.14.115
florii, Fieberiella 21.14.150
Florilegus 25.69.31
flosamoris, Thibetoides 25.16.62
floscella, Reynosa 27.55.421
Flower Beetle 24.30.117
Flower Fly Family, supra 29.47.1
Flower Lepturine 24.106.176
Flower Long-horned Beetle 24.106.212
Flower Scarab 24.30.119
Flower Thrips 22.4.41
Flower-loving Fly 29.36.1
Flower-loving Fly Family, supra 29.36.1
fluctus, Proechinophthirus 19.1.3
Fluff Louse 18.1.27
Focillidia 27.75.137
foetidus, Forelius 25.58.59
Fokkeria 20.3.12
foliicola, Alophosternum 25.16.15
folsomi, Campodea 3.1.1 (Fig. 3.2)
folsomi, Orchesella 1.5.2 (Fig. 1.8)
Folsomia 1.4.15
Folsomides 1.4.10
Fomoria 27.5.6
fonscolombii, Spanioneura 21.17.28
fontana Grasshopper 11.65.62
fontana, Trimerotropis 11.5.62 (Fig. 11.19)
Fontenelleini, supra 23.5.2
Forage Looper 27.75.140
Forbes Scale 21.38.73
forbesi, Aphis 21.19.15
forbesi, Quadraapidiotus 21.38.73
forbesi, Rothschildea 27.69.15
forbesii, Aleurochiton 21.18.2
Forbesomyia 29.11.20
Forbesomyiini, supra 29.11.20
forbsellus, Thopeutis 27.55.226
forceps, Pseudosciara 29.10.7
Forcepsfly, supra 28.3.1
Forcipata 21.14.72
forcipata, Neaviperla 8.8.3
Forcipestricis 25.25.134
forcipomyia 29.23.3
Forcipomyiinae, supra 29.23.2
Forda 21.19.83
Forelius 25.58.59
forensis, Libellula 7.7.13 (Fig. 7.14)
forests 28, 29
Forest Silverfish Family 5.1.1
Forest Tree Caterpillar Moth 27.68.11
Forficula 13.5.2
Forficulidae, supra 13.5.1
Fork-tailed Bush Katydid 11.67.11
Formica 25.58.72
Formicapis 25.68.18
formicarium, Xenomedon 24.24.76
formicarius, Biotus 24.25.83
formicarius, Cylas 24.113.16 (Fig. 24.268)
formicarius, Megastilicus 24.24.61
Formicencyrtus 25.25.139
formicetorum, Hypocoprus 24.71.11
Formicidae, supra 25.58.1 (Fig. 25.31)
formicina, Hymenocoris 20.15.1
Formicinae, supra 25.58.62
Formicini, supra 25.58.72
Formicoidea, supra 25.58.1
formicoides, Aptenobracon 25.13.4
formicoides, Barberiella 20.23.152
formosa, Chloromyia 29.31.5
formosa, Chrysanympha 27.75.162
formosa generosa, Cicindela 24.3.4
formosa, Pepsis 25.60.2
formosa, Rutela 24.30.93
formosalis, Nigetis 27.75.37

Formosan Subterranean Termite 15.3.4
formosana, Neotoxoptera 21.19.151
formosana, Coptotermes 15.3.4
formosanus, Eriotremex 25.9.5
formosella, Dafa 27.15.25
formosus, Tropidolophus 11.5.46
forms 19
fornax, Hamadrysas 27.46.41
fornacula, Cinara 21.19.53
forreri, Caenopamera 20.7.46
Forsebia 27.75.102
forticornis, Rhinacloa 20.23.67
fortis, Apatides 24.64.17 (Fig. 24.127)
fortis, Homoncocnemis 27.75.450
fortunata, Porphyrorhegma 27.55.42
Fossocarus 24.30.76
fossor, Isoplasuts 24.19.16
fossulatella, Oryctometopia 27.55.340
fossulatum, Trigonomma 29.94.38
Fota 27.75.380
Fotella 27.75.374
fotelloides, Anycteola 27.75.378
fotis, Incisalia 27.43.29
Four horned Sphinx 27.70.7
Four-lined Plant Bug 20.23.180
Four-lined Silverfish 5.3.3
Four-marked Ash Borer 24.106.54
Four-spot 7.7.13
Four-spotted Baboon Beetle 24.107.20
Four-spotted Egg Eater 24.68.71
Four-spotted Sap Beetle 24.70.35
Four-spotted Tree Cricket 11.10.19
foutsi, Iphitrachelus 25.44.7
foveata, Mycetochara 24.88.13 (Fig. 24.156)
foveolata, Piophila 29.64.1
Foveoscapha 24.25.14
Foxella 30.7.19
Foxglove Aphid 21.19.2
foxi, Tropicolabus 25.16.281
Foxia 25.62.78
fracida, Mactomyia 29.105.143
fractilinea, Oligia 27.75.258
fragaefolii, Chaetosiphon 21.19.50
fragariae, Paria 24.107.50
fragariae, Tyloderma 24.113.258
fragariella, Anacampsis 27.13.72
fragilis, Coloneura 27.11.10
Framinghamia 27.55.172
Francilia 29.101.9
franciscanus, Limnogonus 20.27.1
frankenhaeuseri, Catoprichus 24.22.9
Frankliniella 22.4.41
franklinii, Agraiades 27.43.52
Franklinothripini, supra 22.1.7
Franklinothrips 22.1.7
franseriae, Sittocapsus 20.23.187
fratellus, Tabanus 29.26.26
fratercula, Belonoptera 27.56.4
Fraternobombus 25.70.2
fraternus, Bombus 25.70.2
fraternus, Cyrnellus 26.3.2
fraternus, Eumenes 25.59.24
fraternus, Loperos 24.57.12
fraternus, Megadytes 24.7.41
fraternus, Prepos 20.23.20 (Fig. 20.57)
fraxinella, Caloptilia 27.14.1
fraxinifolii, Meliarhizophagus 21.19.131
Frechinia 27.55.27
Free-living Caddisfly Family, supra 26.5.1
freemani, Calephelis 27.44.2
Fregatiella 18.6.16
freija, Clossiana 27.46.11
Frenesia 26.10.33
Freraeini, supra 29.105.15
Fridonus 21.14.119

Friesea 1.2.14
Frigate Bird Fly 29.106.9
frigga, Cloissiana 27.46.11
frigida, Coelopa 29.77.1
frigidum frigidum, Trypoxylon 25.62.51
frigidus, Frigartus 21.14.161
Fringed Orchid Aphid 21.19.48
fringillina, Ornithomyia 29.106.2
Friscanus 21.14.64
friscanus, Friscanus 21.14.64
Friseria 27.23.38
frisia, Anthanatasa 27.46.19
frisoni, Iowana 21.19.106
Frit Fly 29.94.15
Frit Fly Family, supra 29.94.1
frit, Oscinella 29.94.15
Fritillaries, supra 27.46.7
Froeschneria 20.7.56
Fromicilla 24.102.15
frondaria, Cyclica 27.61.203
frons 20
front 20
frontalis, Appendicia 29.105.114
frontalis, Dendroctonus 24.112.11
frontalis, Organomyia 29.105.345
frontalis, Pagiocerus 24.112.2
frontalis, Psila 29.55.2
frontalis, Psilotreta, supra 26.14.1
frontalis, Systena 24.107.121
frontalis, Valda 24.25.60
frontalis, Yuiccaborus 24.113.363
frontella, Agromyza 29.68.1
Frontiniella 29.105.419
Frontinini, supra 29.105.341
frontosa, Akronia 29.31.29
frosti, Grylloprociphilus 21.19.92
Frostia 24.56.14
fructicassiella, Trachylepidia 27.55.272
frugiperda, Spodoptera 27.75.326
Fruit Fly Family, supra 29.61.1
Fruit Tree Leafroller 27.38.74
Fruitworm Beetle Family, supra 24.84.1
Frumenta 27.23.54
frustrana, Rhyacionia 27.38.19
Fruva 27.75.214
Fucellia 29.99.1
Fucelliinae, supra 29.99.1
Fuchsina 24.82.15
fucicola, Emphyastes 24.113.387
fuciocola, Actinopteryx 24.15.22
Fucomyia 29.77.1
fulgens, Microdon 29.47.1
fulgens, Rhabdepyris 25.48.6
fulgens, Urania 27.64.1
fulgerator, Astraptes 27.40.13 (Fig. 27.66)
fulgidus, Gyrohypnus 24.24.30
Fulgoraecia 27.53.1
Fulgorid Planthopper Family 21.3.1
Fulgoridae, supra 21.3.1
Fulgoroidea, supra 21.1.1
Fulicoffula 18.1.26
fuliginaria, Parascotia 27.75.26
fuliginosa, Capnochroa 124.88.12
fuliginosa, Periplaneta 14.3.2
fuliginosa, Phragmatobia 27.73.44
fuliginosalis, Lipocosmodes 27.55.66
fuliginosum, Satyrium 27.43.16
fuliginosus, Stethomostus 25.7.63
Fullawaya 21.19.84
Fuller Rose Beetle 24.113.24
fulleri, Dipogon 25.60.9
fulninans, Sarosesthes 24.106.120
fultaria, Paota 27.61.277
fultonensis, Basicondyla 29.11.57
fultoni, Oecanthus 11.10.19
fultoni, Orfelia 29.9.13

fulva, Brachypsectra 24.37.1
fulva, Sympotthastia 29.24.39
fulva, Zacompsia 29.58.38
fulvia, Thessalia 27.46.13
fulviceps, Borboropsis 29.84.4
fulvipes, Hiatus 29.58.10
fulvicollis, Cisseps 27.73.76 (Fig. 27.313)
fulvipes, Janbechynea 24.107.2
fulvipes, Orphinus 24.61.11
Fulvius 20.23.7
fulvoguttata, Melanophila 24.46.20
fulvum, Kodiosoma 27.73.51 (Fig. 27.293)
fulvum, Stromatium 24.106.53
fulvus, Traxus 21.6.7
fumalis, Fumibotys 27.55.85
fumalis, Negalasa 27.55.245
fumans, Brachinus 24.4.4
fumator, Canelomyia 29.105.337
fumestra, Odopoea 21.13.1
Fumibotys 27.55.85
fumidus, Noctuocoris 20.23.115
fumiferanba, Choristoneura 27.38.72 (Fig. 27.62)
fumiferanae, Omotoma 29.105.387
fumigants 42
fumineum, Belostoma 20.37.3
fumipennis violacea, Argia 7.11.4 (Fig. 7.22)
fumosus, Anopolotermes 15.4.1
Fundella 27.55.298
funebris, Rosalis 24.106.98
funeralis, Desmia 27.52.133 (Fig. 27.166)
funeraria, Coelioxys 25.68.24
funerea, Cannaphila 7.7.4
funereus, Paracyphononyx 25.60.31
funicola, Attaphila 14.6.8
Fungobia 29.88.2
fungorum, Choephora 27.75.578
Fungus Gnat Family, supra 29.9.1
Fungus Weevil Family, supra 24.109.1
fur, Ptinus 24.62.10 (Fig. 24.123)
Furcaspis 21.38.33
furcata, Axymyia 29.6.1
furcata, Cyclotrypema 24.107.96
furcata, Lonchoptera 29.44.1
furcata, Neosynepidosis 29.11.45
furcata, Scudderia 11.7.11 (Fig. 11.29)
Furchadaspis 21.38.34
furcilla, Argillophora 27.75.198
furcilla, Panthea 27.75.224 (Fig. 27.348)
Furcula 27.71.12
furens, Culicoides 29.3.5 (Fig. 29.28)
furfura, Chionaspis 21.38.14
furnissi, Cylindroccopturus 24.113.275
Furniture Beetle 24.63.25
Furniture Carpet Beetle 24.61.8
furtivus, Bruesiella 25.53.19
fusca, Euryopa 24.54.3
fusca, Formica 25.58.72
fusca, Frankliniella 22.4.41
fuscanipennis, Chloroprocta 29.101.2
fuscata, Gonioxyna 29.61.26
fuscata, Lypsimena 24.106.257
fuscatus aurifer, Polistes 25.59.28
fuscatus bellicosus, Polistes 25.59.28
fusciocornis, Monolexis 25.13.17
fuscipalpis, Francilia 29.101.9
fuscipennis, Chrysis 25.50.16
fuscipennis, Dahlbominus 25.26.10
fuscipennis, Parasemidalis 23.5.5
fuscipes, Cis 24.92.2 (Fig. 24.162)
fuscipes, Coboldia 29.15.9
fuscipes, Hydrobius 24.12.14
fuscipes, Prosevani 25.35.2
fuscipes, Scatopse 29.15.5 (Fig. 29.20)
fuscocapitata, Trivialia 29.82.20

fuscocristatella, Naera 27.23.13
fuscoleuca, Tridentaforma 27.8.8
fuscosa, Anisota 27.69.5
fuscoscapulella, Acanthocnemes 27.13.6
fuscotaeniaella, Rifseria 27.23.39
fuscovittata, Saica 20.17.32
fuscula, Epitrix 24.10.137 (Fig. 24.239)
fuscula, Rhyacophila 26.5.2 (Figs. 26.21, 26.22)
fusculus, Prateus 24.89.4
fuscus, Byturosoma 24.68.39
fuscus, Gnophothrips 22.5.42
fuscus, Stenopelmatus 11.9.3 (Fig. 11.39)
Fusedback Mayflies 6.13.1
fusicornis, Forcipomyia 29.23.3
fuscipennis, Ocyptamus 29.47.27
Fustiger 24.25.84
Fustigerini, supra 24.25.84
Fustiserphus 25.39.3
futilis, Euexorista 29.105.417

G

gabara 27.75.60
gabbi, Charidryas 27.46.15
Gabriola 27.61.96
Gabrius 24.24.5
Gabronthus 24.24.6
Gabuniina, supra 25.16.186
Gaediophana 29.105.360
Gaediopsis 29.105.361
Gaeides 27.43.4
Gaenima 24.24.241
Gaesischia 25.69.32
Gaesischiana 25.69.32
gagates, Mallochiola 20.22.1
Gage's stain 44
Gahaniella 25.25.135
Gahaniola 25.20.4
Gahanula 25.21.12
Galactomyia 29.105.5
Galasa 27.55.246
galbina galbina, Agapema 27.69.11 (Fig. 27.227)
galeator, Euthochtha 20.4.14
Galeatus 20.14.10
galena, Viridems 27.75.436
Galenara 27.61.55
galeopitheci, Hamophthirius, infra 19.8.1
Galeopsomopsis 25.26.45
Galeopsomyia 25.26.43
Galerita 24.4.167
Galeritini 24.4.167
Galeruca 24.107.86
Galerucella 24.107.79
Galerucinae, supra 24.107.74
Galerucini, supra 24.107.74
Galgula 27.75.331
Galgupha 20.2.1
Gall Midge Family, supra 29.11.1
Gall Pine Scale 21.23.2
Gall Wasp Family, supra 25.34.1
gallaerandialis, Thyridopyralis 27.55.274
gallaesolidaginis, Gnorimoschema 27.23.44
Galleria 27.55.270
Galleriinae, supra 27.55.270
gallicola, Apezococcus 21.31.2
gallicola, Podapion 24.113.19
gallicolus, Matsucoccus 21.23.2
gallicus, Polistes 25.59.28
gallii, Hyles 27.70.42 (Fig. 27.268)
gallinacea, Echidnophaga 30.1.4
gallinae, Ceratophyllus 30.7.2
gallinae, Goniocotes 18.1.27
gallinae, Menopon 18.6.25 (Fig. 18.4)
Gall-like Scale Insect Family, supra 21.29.1

Gallmaking Maple Borer 24.106.123
galvestonica, Microbaris 24.113.314
Gambrus 25.16.152
Gammarotettigini, supra 11.9.6
Gammarotettix 11.9.6
Ganascus, supra 24.104.1
Ganaspidium 25.32.9
Ganaspis 25.32.8
Ganocapsus 20.23.159
Ganychorus 25.13.130
Ganyra 27.42.7
Garden Fleahopper 20.23.83 (Fig. 20.52)
Garden Webworm 27.55.93
Gardena 20.17.5
Gardinia 27.73.12
Garganus 20.23.160
Gargaphia 20.14.11
garmani, Ropronia 25.40.1
Garrettella 29.9.63
Gasterophilus 29.102.1
Gasteruptiid Wasp Family, supra 25.37.1
Gasteruptiidae, supra 25.37.1
Gasteruption 25.37.1
Gastracanthus 25.19.19
Gastrallus 24.63.19
Gastrancistrus 25.19.57
Gastraulacinae, supra 24.52.1
Gastrodes 20.7.37
Gastropachinae, supra 27.68.5
Gastrophilidae, supra 29.102.1
Gastrophilinae, supra 29.102.1
Gastrophysa 24.107.66
Gastrops 29.93.50
Gastropthrips 22.5.10
Gastrotaphrus 24.113.161
Gastrotrypes 25.44.18
gatineau, Aglaomyia 29.9.48
Gaudy Sphinx 27.70.31
Gaurax 29.94.18
Gaurotes 24.106.186
gazeaui, Forcipestricis 25.25.134
gazella, Onthophagus 24.30.12
Gehringiini, supra 24.4.50
Gehringia 24.4.50
Geina 27.58.3
Geissandrena 25.65.1
Gelastocoridae, supra 20.39.1
Gelastocorinae, supra 20.39.1
Gelastocoris 20.39.1
gelastops, Hesperolabops 20.23.24
Gelechia 27.23.43
gelechiae, Parapsilophrys 25.25.152
Gelechid Moth Family, supra 27.23.1
Gelechiidae, supra 27.23.1
Gelechiinae, supra 27.23.9
Gelechioidea, supra 27.15.1
gelida, Spoggosia 29.105.290
gelidae, Eobrachycentrus 26.9.4
Gelina, supra 25.16.102
Gelis 25.16.104
Geminaria 29.40.17
geminata, Jamesomyia 29.61.14
geminata, Solenopsis 25.58.33 (Fig. 25.41)
geminata, Stelidota 24.70.15
geminatus, Tilloclytus 24.106.130
gemma, Cyllopsis 27.48.3
gemmatalis, Anticarsia 27.75.85 (Fig. 27.329)
Gemmura 25.7.35
genalis, Euhalidaya 29.105.228
Genaparlatoria 21.38.35
Genea 29.105.218
Genecerini, supra 24.34.10
Genesis 18
geniculata, Pristiphora 25.7.30
geniculatus, Monophnadoides 25.7.70

geniseta, Deutominettia 29.82.3
Genista Caterpillar Moth 27.55.100
genitalia, slides 43
Gennadota 24.24.242
Genophion 25.16.460
Genosema 24.24.243
gentilis, Pycnopsyche 26.10.30
gentilis, Phyllecthris 24.107.98 (Fig. 24.232)
Genuchinus 24.30.131
genus (genera) 15
Geocolus 24.26.26
Geocorinae, supra 20.7.18
Geocorini, supra 20.7.18
Geocoris 20.7.18
Geodercodes 24.113.82
Geodiaspis 21.38.36
geographical distribution 23
Geoica 21.19.85
Geometer Moth Family, supra 27.61.1
Geometridae, supra 27.61.1
Geometrinae, supra 27.61.157
Geometroidea, supra 27.61.1
Geomydoecus 18.2.4
Geomysaprinus 24.26.13
Geomyza 29.69.3
Geopemphigus 21.9.86
Geopinus 24.4.111
georgei, Nephus 24.80.7
georgia, Oudemansia 1.2.18
georgiae, Distichona 29.105.350
Georgiaphis 21.19.87
georgii, Plemyria 27.61.196
Georissus 24.14.1
Georyssidae, supra 24.14.1
Geotrupes 24.30.52
Geotrupinae, supra 24.30.45
Geraeus 24.113.323
Geranchon 21.19.88
Geranomyia 29.2.14
Gerdana 27.17.5
German Cockroach 14.5.1
German Cockroach Family 14.5.1
German Yellowjacket 25.59.27 (Fig. 25.52)
germanica, Blattella 14.5.1
germana, Coelioxys 25.68.24
germanica, Vespa 25.59.26
germanica, Vespula 235.59.27
Germariini, supra 29.105.132
Geron 29.40.29
Geroninae, supra 29.40.29
Geropa 24.106.36
Gerra 27.75.240
Gerridae, supra 20.27.1 (Fig. 20.59)
Gerrinae, supra 20.27.1
gerriphagus, Tiphodytes 25.43.22
Gerris 20.27.3
Gerrodes 27.75.241
gerstaecheri, Triatoma 20.17.39 (Fig. 20.45)
Gerstaeckeria 24.113.251
gertschi, Tricholepidion 5.1.1
Geshna 27.52.119
Gesneria 27.55.1
Gesta 27.40.35
gesta, Cantopelopia 29.24.21
gesta, Gesta 27.40.35
Ghilianella 20.17.6
Ghost Moth Family, supra 27.4.1
Giant Casemaker Caddisfly Family, supra 26.8.1
Giant Hawaiian Dragonfly 7.4.1
Giant Lacewing Family, supra 23.12.1
Giant Mayfly 6.11.2
Giant Mealybug Family, supra 21.24.1
Giant Scale Insect Family, supra 21.23.1

Giant Silkworm Moth Family, supra 27.69.1
Giant Skippers, supra 27.40.87
Giant Stonefly Family, supra 8.5.1
Giant Swallowtail 27.41.6
Giant Water Bug Family, supra 20.37.1
Giant Water Bugs 20.37.1
giardi, Zeuxidiplosis 29.11.116
Giardomyia 29.11.140
gibba, Callachna 29.61.4
gibbicollis, Lobogestoria 24.93.15
Gibbiinae, supra 24.62.1
Gibbium 24.62.1
Gibbobruchus 24.108.8
gibboides, Sphaericus 24.62.4
gibbosa, Nadata 27.71.3 (Fig. 27.271)
gibbosus, Atlanticus 11.7.29
gibbosus, Bothynus 24.30.104
gibbosus, Neochlamisus 24.107.34 (Fig. 24.220)
gibbosus, Philanthus 25.62.106
ginndi, Buprestis 24.46.15
gibsoni, Dasineura 29.11.152 (Fig. 29.19)
Gibsonomyia 29.105.180
Giffard's Whitefly 21.18.12
giffardi, Bemisia 21.18.12
gigantea, Colias 27.42.11
gigantea, Oligembia 9.2.1
gigantea, Styifera 5.3.7
giganteus, Isosomodes 25.20.6
Gigantopepsis 25.60.2
gigantula, Homia 24.24.252
gigas, Goniodes 18.1.28
gigas, Protophylus 24.24.168
gigas, Quesada 21.13.10 (Fig. 21.16)
gilaensis, Platyoplus 11.7.44
Gilbertia 24.113.169
gilippus, Danaus 27.49.1
Gillette Felt Scale 21.31.4
gillettei, Eriococcis 21.31.4
gilletti, Hypodryas 27.46.21
gilletti, Thatuna 21.14.65
Gillettiella 21.14.169
Gilpinia 25.6.5
gilva, Cryptopone 25.58.15
gilvafascia, Artaversala 27.5.8
Gilvella 29.105.328
Gimnomera 29.98.25
Ginglychaeta 29.105.160
Ginglymia 29.105.297
Ginglymocladus 24.55.19
Gipurs 21.14.187
Giraudia 25.16.142
giraulti, Lonchetron 25.19.93
Giraultia 25.26.26
Giraultiola 25.28.12
Gitona 29.90.5
Givira 27.37.3
Glabellua 29.40.24
glaber, Brachypeplus 24.70.9
glaberrima, Silba 29.57.5
glaberula, Anitra 24.25.75
glabra, Camilla 29.92.1
glabra, Madiza 29.74.6
glabra, Thaumatomyia 29.94.37
glabrata, Ametastegia 25.7.84
glabrata, Disonycha 24.107.123 (Fig. 24.237)
glabrata, Leptogaster 29.37.2
glabratus, Macronychus 24.45.26
glabricula, Ocydromia 29.42.52
Glabridorsum 25.16.160
glabrifrons, Scenopinus 29.33.1
Glabromyzus 21.19.89
glabrum, Atylostagma 24.106.61
glacialis, Euhoplopsyllus 30.1.8
glacialis, Zubovskya 11.5.97

Glacicavicola 24.19.17
Glacicavicolinae, supra 24.19.17
gladiaria, Agrtotis 27.75.535
gladifer, Boreogalba 25.14.13
Gladiolus Thrips 22.4.53
Gladionura 21.14.175
Glaenocorisa 20.35.3
Glaenocorisini, supra 20.35.3
glanduella, Valentinia 27.17.10
Glaphyria 27.55.61
Glaphyriinae, supra 27.55.54
Glaphyrinae, supra 24.30.42
Glaphyrocanthon 24.30.5
Glaphyrometopus 24.113.18
glareosella, Atascosa 27.55.419
Glaresis 24.30.44
Glariopsis 29.31.32
glastinus, Deporaus 24.113.11
glauca, Alphina 21.3.4
glauca, Chiastocheta 29.99.6
glauca, Ctenicera 24.458.37
glauca, Osmia 25.68.21
Glauce 27.23.12
glaucellus, Hecamedoides 29.93.13
Glaucina 27.61.30
Glaucocarini, supra 29.105.42
Glaucodontia 27.55.53
Glaucolepis 27.5.4
Glaucops 29.26.26
Glaucopsyche 27.43.46
glaucopterus barberi, Opheltes 25.16.342
Glaucotes 24.106.277
glaucula, Anisoxya 24.98.29
glaucus, Phyllobius 24.113.103 (Fig. 24.274)
glaucus, Pterourus 27.41.7 (Fig. 27.82)
Glauraspidia 25.32.12
glechomae, Liposthenes 25.34.12
Glena 27.61.26
Glenanthe 29.93.8
Glendenningia 21.19.90
Glenidion 24.107.139
Glenoides 27.61.25
Glenodiplosis 29.11.97
Glenosmea 25.48.16
Glenostictia 25.62.103
Glenurini, supra 23.14.6
Glenurus 23.14.8
Glipa 24.99.4
Glipodes 24.99.1
Gliricola 18.4.1
Glischrochilus 24.70.35
Gloanna 27.75.381
Globe Trotter 7.7.22
Globiceps 20.23.100
globitheca, Hydnosella 24.15.5
globiventris, Peritelopsis 24.113.86
Globose Scale 21.26.21
globosa, Sterogaster 24.113.30
globosus, Neochrysops 29.26.9
globosus, Romulus 24.106.67
Globular Spider Beetle 24.62.3
Globular Springtail Family, supra 1.7.1
globulum, Trigonogenius 24.62.23 (Fig. 24.121)
Gloma 29.42.48
Gloomy Scale 21.38.49
Gloridonus 21.14.120
gloriola, Eucosma 27.38.25
gloriosa, Melittia 27.35.8
gloriosa, Plusiotis 24.30.91
gloriosa, Protoxaea 25.64.1
gloriosus, Aztecacris 11.5.112
Glosselytrodea, supra 23.1.1
Glossonotus 21.15.36
Glossoperdita 25.65.15

Glossosoma 26.6.2
Glossosomatidae, supra 26.6.1
Glossosomatinae, supra 26.6.1
Glottulini, supra 27.75.534
Glover Scale 21.38.45
gloverana, Acleri%s 27.38.61
gloveri, Euscirrhopterus 27.75.244 (Fig. 27.353)
gloveri gloveri, Hyalophora 27.69.18 (Fig. 27.235)
gloveri, Lepidosaphes 21.38.45
Gloveria 27.68.10
gloydi, Bythinoplectus 24.25.3
gloydi, Paederopsis 24.24.66
Glowworm 24.54.1
Glowworm Beetle Family, supra 24.54.1
Gluphisia 27.71.11
glutinosi, coelopoeta 27.16.1
Glutops 29.25.1
glycerium, Memphis 27.47.2
Glycobius 24.106.114
Glympis 27.75.45
Glyphicnemis 25.16.118
Glyphidocera 27.17.4
Glyphidops 29.52.2
Glyphina 21.19.91
Glyphipterigidae, supra 27.28.1
Glyphipterix 27.28.3
Glyphipteryx 27.20.2
Glyphocystis 27.55.318
Glyphodes 27.55.148
Glyphogaster 25.13.102
Glyphomerus 25.18.17
Glyphonyx 24.48.66
Glyphopsyche 26.10.34
Glyphuroplata 24.107.171
Glypta 25.16.305
Glyptacros 25.53.16
Glyptasida 24.87.50
Glyptina 24.107.117
Glyptini, supra 25.16.303
Glyptobaris 24.113.319
Glyptocera 27.55.312
Glyptocoelioxys 25.68.24
Glyptocombus 20.25.1
Glyptocotastes 25.13.11
Glyptophorus 24.74.2
Glyptorhaestus 25.16.329
Glyptoscelimorpha 24.46.2
Glyptoscelis 24.107.56
Glyptotendipes 29.24.44
Glyptothrips 22.5.40
Glyptotus 24.87.81
Gnamplomychia 27.73.11
Gnamptogenys 25.58.10
Gnamptopelta 25.16.256
Gnaphalodes 24.106.144
Gnaptodon 25.13.39
Gnathacmaeops 24.106.192
Gnathamitermes 15.4.3
Gnathias 25.69.10
Gnathium 24.101.22
Gnathoncus 24.26.19
Gnathotrichus 24.112.65
Gnathoweisea 24.80.4
Gnatocerus 24.87.106
Gnawing Barklice Family 17.13.1
Gnophaela 27.73.1
Gnopholeon 23.14.3
Gnophomyia 29.2.44
Gnophos 27.61.43
Gnophothrips 22.5.42
Gnorimella 24.30.118
Gnorimoschema 27.23.44
Gnoriste 29.9.44
Gnostinae, supra 24.62.11

Gnostus 24.62.11
Gnotus 25.16.124
Gnypeta 24.24.244
Gnypetella 24.24.245
Gnypetomorphina, supra 25.15.101
Goat Chewing Louse 18.2.1
Goat Moth Family, supra 27.37.1
Goat Sucking Louse 19.2.1
Goditha 27.38.44
godmani, Metaxyonycha 24.107.42
Goeldichironomus 29.24.57
Goera 26.10.43
Goeracea 26.10.44
Goereilla 26.10.45
Goerinae, supra 26.10.43
Goerita 26.10.46
Goes 24.106.234
Goldbug 24.107.186
Golden Buprestid 24.46.15
Golden Oak Scale 21.35.1
Golden Paper Wasps 25.59.28
Golden Spider Beetle 24.62.6
Golden Tortise Beetle 24.107.186
Golden-eye Lacewing 23.9.9 (Fig. 23.10)
Goldenglow Aphid 21.19.219
Goldenrod Gall Fly 29.61.12
Goldenrod Gall Midgel 29.11.158
Goldenrod Soldier Beetle 24.56.1
Goldsmith Beetle 24.30.87
Goldtailed Moth 27.74.6
Goliath Beetle 24.30.120
goliathus, Goliathus 24.30.120
Gomphaeschna 7.4.7
Gomphidae, supra 7.3.1
Gomphocerinae, supra 11.5.1
Gomphoides 7.3.2
Gomphurus 7.3.9
Gomphus 7.3.1, 7.3.9
Gonandrena 25.65.1
Gonarcticus 29.98.6
Gonasida 24.87.52
Gonaspis 25.34.9
Gonatheurs 29.98.3
Gonatista 14.1.7
Gonatocerus 25.27.6
Gonatopodinae, supra 25.51.11
Gonatopus 25.51.22
Gonempeda 29.2.55
Gongrodiplosis 29.11.141
Gongromastix 29.11.15
Gonia 29.105.352
goniana, Crassana 21.14.137
Gonianotini, supra 20.7.72
Goniapteryx 27.75.70
Gonielmis 24.45.11
Goniina, supra 29.105.347
Goniinae, supra 29.105.226
Goniini, supra 29.105.347
Goniocarsis 27.75.88
Goniochaeta 29.105.161
Goniocloeus 24.109.16
Goniocotes 18.1.27
Gonioctena 24.107.73
Gonioctenini, supra 24.107.73
Goniodes 18.1.28
goniopalpia, Palpusia 27.55.189
Goniops 29.26.1
Goniopsita 29.94.29
Gonioterma 27.15.21
Goniothrips 22.5.41
Goniotropis 24.4.5
Gonioxyna 29.61.26
Goniozus 25.48.21
Goniusa 24.24.246
Gonocephalum 24.87.162
Gonodes 27.75.330

Gonodonta 27.75.68
Gonodontini, supra 27.61.99
gonoides, Eucnephalia 29.105.351
Gonolabis 13.1.1
Gonomyia 29.2.47
Gonomyodes 29.2.56
Gonomyopsis 29.2.64
Gononotus 24.113.163
goodsoni, Cyanophrrys 27.43.25
Goose Body Louse 18.6.35
Gooseberry Fruitworm 27.55.379
Gooseberry Witchbroom Aphid 21.19.109
gordialis, Asciodes 27.55.175
Gorginus 24.77.11
gorgon, Gaeides 27.43.4
gorgone, Charidryas 27.46.15
Gorgone Checkerspot 27.46.15
Gorgythion 27.40.26
gorodkovi, Dialineura 29.32.5
Gorpini, supra 20.18.11
Gorse Seed Weevil 24.113.21
Goryphina, supra 25.16.176
Gorytes 25.62.85
Gorytini, supra 25.62.80
Gossyparia 21.31.5
gossypiella, Pectinophora 27.23.81
gossypii, Aphis 21.19.15
gossypii, Corythucha 20.14.7
gossyppi, Phenoacoccus 21.25.32
gossypii, Stigmella 27.5.1
Govinda 25.43.5
Gowdeyana 29.31.27
Goya 27.55.422
Grabhamia 29.20.8
gracea, Herreshoffia 27.61.233
Gracefull Ghost Moth 27.4.2
Graceus 29.24.67
gracile, Paranoplium 24.106.27
Gracilentulus 2.3.5
Gracilia 24.106.36
gracilicornis, Atractocerus 24.53.2
Graciliini, supra 24.106.36
gracilineata, Eulithis 27.61.191 (Fig. 27.198)
gracilis, Anthomyza 29.70.1
gracilis, Blatchleya 24.56.19 (Fig. 24.111)
gracilis, Dolichomyia 29.40.6
gracilis, Leptophylax 26.10.20
gracilis, Micromastus 24.113.243
gracilis, Polygonia 27.46.24
gracilis, Taprocerus 24.46.38
Gracillaria 27.14.2
Gracillariidae, supra 27.14.1
Gracillariinae, supra 27.14.1
gracillipes, Ceuthophilus 11.9.10 (Fig. 11.42)
gracilipes, Cinyra 24.46.14 (Fig. 24.86)
gracilipes papago, Arethaea 11.7.2
graecula, Cetexa 21.14.118
graefi, Acanthotoca 27.61.137
graefi, Synanthedon exitiosa 27.35.12
grafi, Thriposoma 25.26.39
grahami, Aldrichina 29.101.15
grahami, Neoeurygenius 24.103.4
Grain Thrips 22.4.18
Grallipeza 29.51.5
graminea, Pseudaugochloropsis 25.66.12
gramineae, Toxonothrips 22.4.54
Graminella 21.14.220
graminum, Schizaphis 21.19.191
graminis, Antonina 21.25.4
graminis, Cerapteryx 27.75.510
graminis, Pentamyzus 21.19.164
graminis, Thesprotia 14.1.5
Grammoptera 24.106.204
Grammotaulius 26.10.15

granarium, Trogoderma 24.61.13 (Fig. 24.118)
granarius, Sitophilus 24.113.365 (Fig. 24.298) QWL Granary Booklice Family 17.2.1
Granary Booklouse 17.2.2
Granary Weevil 24.113.365
grandella, Hypsipyla 27.55.286
grandiceps, Katacephala 21.17.22
grandiceps, Metisotoma 1.4.16
grandiceps, Myrmilloides 25.55.15
grandiosella, Diatraea 27.55.228
grandipennis, Pseudoseptis 27.75.548
grandis, Alcaeorrhynchus 20.3.66
grandis, Archilestes 7.9.1
grandis, Bibiocephala 29.3.2
grandis grandis, Anthonomus 24.113.208 (Fig. 24.284)
grandis, Grandolobus 21.15.47
grandis, Hadromyia 29.47.89
grandis, Haffneria 18.1.29
grandis, Harmolita 25.20.3
grandis, Lebia 24.4.159 (Fig. 24.43)
grandis, Tamiophila 30.4.5
grandis thurbeiriae, Anthonomus 24.113.208
Grandolobus 21.15.47
granella, Nemapogon 27.10.1
granicollis, Paracotalpa 24.30.88
granti, Dynastes 24.30.114
granulata, Endeitoma 24.93.6
Granulate Cutworm Moth 27.75.535
Granulated Grouse Locust 11.1.2
granulosa, Neurobezzia 29.23.21
Grape Apple Gall 29.11.73
Grape Berry Moth 27.38.4
Grape Blossom Midge 29.11.108
Grape Cane Gall Maker 24.113.311
Grape Colaspis 24.107.43
Grape Curculio 24.113.283
Grape Flea Beetle 24.107.127
Grape Leaf Roller 27.55.133
Grape Leaf Skeletonizer 27.50.1
Grape Mealybug 21.25.35
Grape Phylloxera 21.21.1
Grape Plume Moth 27.58.16
Grape Root Borer 27.35.5
Grape Rootworm 24.107.54
Grape Sawfly 25.7.73
Grape Scale 21.38.24
Grape Seed Chalcid 25.20.20
Grape Trunk Borer 24.106.126 (Fig. 24.197)
Grape Whitefly 21.18.17
Grapevine Aphid 21.19.15
Grapevine Hoplia 24.30.85
Grape-vine Sphinx 27.70.40
graphica, Drasteria 27.75.104 (Fig. 27.331)
Graphicallo 24.107.62
Graphiphora 27.75.561
Graphisurus 24.106.273
Graphiun 27.41.4
Graphocephala 21.14.51
Graphoderus 24.7.39
Graphogastrini, supra 29.105.323
Graphognathus 24.113.23
Grapholita 27.38.53
Graphomya 29.100.51
Graphops 24.107.52
Graphopsocus 17.11.1
Graphorhinus 24.113.36
Graptocorixa 20.35.5
Graptocorixini, supra 20.35.5
Grass Flies, supra 29.94.1
Grass Sawfly 25.7.27
Grass Sharpshooter 21.14.47

Grass Sheath Miner 29.68.7
Grass Thrips 22.4.19
Grass Webworm 27.55.203
Grasshopper Bee Fly 29.40.12
Grasshopper Maggots 29.103.24
Grasshoppers 11.1.1
grassland 28
Grass-root Beetle 24.24.140
grataria, Haematopis 27.61.184 (Fig. 27.196)
Gravenhorstiini, supra 25.16.375
Gravenhortia 25.16.382
Gray Comma 27.46.24
Gray Hairstreak 27.43.34
Gray Lawn Leafhopper 21.14.166
Gray Sugarcane Mealybug 21.25.16
Gray Willow Leaf Beetle 24.107.80
Grayback Family 7.1.1
Graybanded Leafroller 27.38.71
Greasy Cutworm Moth 27.75.535
Great Ash Sphinx 27.70.11
Great Basin Wireworm 24.48.37
Great Black Wasp 25.62.8
Great Blue Hairstreak 27.43.12
Great Golden Dipper Wasp 25.62.8
Great Spangled Fritillary 27.46.8
Great Tiger Moth 27.73.50
Greater Grapevine Looper 27.61.191
Greater Red Dart Moth 27.75.587
Greater Wax Moth 27.55.270
Greedy Scale 21.38.39
Green Budworm 27.38.16
Green Bug 21.19.191
Green Cloverworm Moth 27.75.42 (Fig. 27.325)
Green Comma 27.46.24
Green Fruitworm 27.75.392
Green Ground Beetle 24.4.98
Green June Beetle 24.30.121
Green Lacewing Family, supra 23.9.1
Green Peach Aphid 21.19.144
Green Rose Chafer 24.30.81
Green Scale 21.26.4
Green Shield Scale 21.26.19
Green Slug Moth 27.52.20
Green Spruce Aphid 21.19.53
Green Stink Bug 20.3.52
Green Stonefly Family 8.8.1
greenei, Doichurus 25.62.1
Green-eyed Skimmer Family 7.6.1
Greenhead 29.26.26
Greenheaded Spruce Sawfly 25.7.28
Greenhouse Leaf Tier 27.55.105
Greenhouse Orthezia 21.22.1
Greenhouse Stone Cricket 11.9.5
Greenhouse Thrips 22.4.4
Greenhouse Whitefly 21.18.17
greeni, Elephantocera 29.105.242
Greenomyia 29.9.67
Green-striped Grasshopper 11.5.35
Green-striped Mapleworm 27.69.4
Green-winged Stonefly 8.7.2
gregaria, Schistocerca 11.5.114 (Fig.11.26)
Gregarious Leaf Miner 27.14.20
gregarius, Eitelius 25.7.29
Gremlinotrophus 29.105.329
Greniera 29.22.6
Grensia 26.10.35
Gretchena 27.38.35
Greya 27.8.7
Greyopimpla 25.16.10
Griburius 24.107.29
griffini, Hemileuca 27.69.7
grindeliae, Atarsos 21.19.22
Grisdalemyia 29.105.181
grisea, Gonatista 14.1.7

grisea, Hypopacha 27.68.1
Griselda 27.38.36
grisella, Achrois 27.55.271
griseocaptitella, Dyseriocrnia 27.2.1
griseola, Campichoeta 29.91.2
griseola, Hydrellia 29.93.32
griseolus, Myochroocoris 20.23.55
griseomicans, Lotodactylus 24.113.295
Griseosilvius 29.26.10
grisescens, Byturellus 24.84.1
grisescens, Dinera 29.105.65
grisescens, Gloanna 27.75.381
grisescens, Macustus 21.14.157
grisescens, Pactorrhinus 24.113.401
griseum, Parmenosoma 24.106.228
griseus, Achrastenus 24.113.99
griseus, Piscatopus 24.113.57
Gromphadorhina, supra 14.6.8
Gronevus 24.79.3
Gronocarus 24.30.75
grossa, Phenolia 24.70.21
Grossbeckia 27.61.204
grossipunctella, Myelois 27.55.293
grossus, Euryderus 24.4.122
Grotea 25.16.45
grotei, Copivaleria 27.75.434
grotei, Hemileuca 27.69.7
groteii, Ulophora 27.55.349
Groteini, supra 25.16.45
Grotella 27.75.605
Grotellaforma 27.75.191
grotelliformis, Homolagoa 27.75.192
Grotellini, supra 27.75.605
Grotiusomyia 25.26.24
Ground Beetle Family, supra 24.4.1
Ground Cricket 11.9.1, 11.10.13
Ground Mealybug 21.25.38
Ground Plant Bug, supra 20.24.1
Grouse Locust Family 11.1.1
grouvellei, Tinodemus 24.77.4
Gruimenopon 18.6.17
grunus, Habrodais 27.43.10
Gryllacrididae, supra 11.9.1
Grullacridinae, supra 11.9.1
Gryllidae, supra 11.10.1
Gryllinae, supra 11.10.6.
Gryllita 11.10.8
Grylloblatta 12.1.1 (Fig. 12.1)
Grylloblattidae, supra 12.1.1
Gryllodes 11.10.9
Grylloprociphious 21.19.92
Gryllotalpa 11.11.1
gryllotalpa, Gryllotalpa 11.11.1
Gryllotalpidae, supra 11.11.1
Gryllotalpinae, supra 11.11.1
Gryllus 11.10.1, 11.10.10
grynea, Catocala 27.75.148
gryneus, Mitoura 27.43.26
Grynocharis 24.66.3
Gryon 25.45.19
gryosicollis, Stomodes 24.113.69
Grypocenturus 25.16.56
Grypus 24.113.173
gueneata, Ceratodalia 27.61.198
Gueneria 27.61.110
Guerinia 29.105.283
Gueriniopsis 29.105.284
Guesibia 30.6.7
guexi, Synaphaeta 24.106.238
Guinea Ant 25.58.42
Guinea Pig Lice Family 18.4.1
Guinea Pig Louse 18.8.1
guizoti, Paradibrachys 25.19.117
gularis, Aphomia 27.55.275, see Paralipsa 27.55.176
Gulf Fritillary 27.46.1

Gulf Wireworm 24.48.14
Gumaga 26.13.3
gumia, Synploca 27.21.17
gunniella, Neurostrota 27.14.3
gurlti, Pseudonirmus 18.1.51
Gusanos De Maguey 27.40.88
guttalatus, Oncotylus 20.23.58
guttata, Cicada 21.13.12
guttata, Deloyala 24.107.183 (Fig. 24.248)
guttata, Pseudolampsis 24.107.155
guttata, Romalea 11.4.5 (Fig. 11.8)
guttatum, Chelysoma 20.3.3
guttatus, Monoedus 24.93.28
guttatus, Osmidus 24.106.42
guttatus, Paracacosenus 29.90.6
guttifinitella, Cameraria 27.14.20 (Figs. 27.32, 27.33)
Guttipelopia 29.24.23
guttipennis, Anomalochaeta 29.69.2
guttipennis, Eutaenionotum 29.93.42
guttivitta, Heterocampa 27.71.29
guttulastus, Paraxenetus 20.23.151
gwyni, Polygenis 30.2.1
Gymnaetron 24.113.231
Gymnaspis 21.38.37
Gymnastrini, supra 24.113.231
Gymnetina 24.30.124
Gymnetini, supra 24.30.121
Gymnetis 24.30.122
Gymnocarcelia 29.105.397
Gymnocarena 29.61.48
Gymnochares 25.60.22
Gymnocheta 29.105.106
Gymnochiromyia 29.86.3
Gymnoclytia 29.105.2
Gymnodia 29.100.15
Gymnoerycia 29.105.373
Gymnognathus 24.109.11
Gymnometriocnemus 29.24.114
Gymnopais 29.22.2
Gymnophora 29.46.19
Gymnopini, supra 29.93.1
Gymnoprosopa 29.103.4
Gymnopsyra 24.106.74
Gymnopternus 29.43.8
Gymnopyge 24.30.83
Gymnoscirtetes 11.5.79
Gymnosoma 29.105.3
Gymnusa 24.24.247
Gynacantha 7.4.8
Gynaephora 27.74.1
Gynaikothrips 22.5.43
gynandromorphs 23
Gynandropus 24.4.131
Gynembia 9.3.2
Gynopterus 24.62.10
Gypona 21.14.25
Gyponana 21.14.22
Gyponini, supra 21.14.19
Gypsoaphis 21.19.93
Gypsonoma 27.38.31
Gypsy Moth 27.74.4
Gyretes 24.9.3
Gyrinidae, supra 24.9.1
Gyrininae, supra 24.9.2
Gyrinus 24.9.2
Gyrinophagus 25.19.105
Gyrocheilus 27.48.11
Gyroconops 29.49.2
Gyrodontina, supra 25.16.208
Gyrodontini, supra 25.16.208
Gyrohypnus 24.24.30
Gyronycha 24.24.248
Gyrophaena 24.24.249
Gyropidae, supra 18.4.1
Gyropsylla 21.17.6

Gyropus 18.4.2
Gyros 27.55.34

H

habitats 25 (Table 4.1)
Habritys 25.19.75
Habrocampulum 25.16.375
Habrocerinae, supra 24.24.185
Habrocerus 24.24.185
Habrocytus 25.19.92
Habrodais 27.43.10
Habrolepidini, supra 25.25.90
Habrolepis 25.25.94
Habrolepoidea 25.25.144
Habrolepopteryx 25.25.143
Habrolinus 24.24.31
Habronyx 25.16.375
Habrophlebia 6.7.2
Habrophlebiodes 6.7.3
Habroscelimorpha 24.3.4
Habrosyne 27.59.1
Habrosynini, supra 27.59.1
Hackberry Engraver 24.112.23
Hackberry Lace Bug 20.14.7
Hackberry Nipplegall Maker 21.17.21
Hacklegill Mayfly Family 6.9.1
Hadena 27.75.487
Hadenella 27.75.471
hadenifromis, Trudfestra 27.75.473
Hadeninae, supra 27.75.469
Hadenini, supra 27.75.469
Hadenoecus 11.9.8
Hadraule 24.92.7
Hadrobregmus 24.63.30
Hadrocistis 25.53.13
Hadrodactylus 25.16.368
Hadrokolos 29.37.49
Hadromeropsis 24.113.61
Hadromyia 29.47.89
Hadronema 20.23.101
Hadroneura 29.9.45
Hadrotes 24.24.15
Hadrotettix 11.5.63
Haemagogus 29.20.10
haemanthes, Acroplectis 27.38.69
Haematobia 29.100.59
haematocephalus, Pachytychius 24.113.175
Haematochiton 24.75.9
Haematomis 27.73.18
Haematomyidium 29.23.5
Haematomyzidae, infra 18.8.1
haematomyzus, infra 18.8.1
haematopinidae, supra 19.3.1
Haematopinoides 19.6.2
haematopinoidinae, supra 19.6.2
Haematopinus 19.3.1
Haematopotini, supra 29.26.12
Haematopis 27.61.184
Haematopota 29.26.12
Haematosiphon 20.20.4
Haematosiphoninae, supra 20.20.1
Haemodipus 19.7.4
haemorrhoidalis, Gasterophilus 29.102.1
haemorrhoidalis, Heliothrips 22.4.4
haemorrhiodalis, Psilocephala 29.32.25
haemorrhoidalis, Sarcophaga 29.103.45
haemorrhous, Amalus 24.113.299
Haffneria 18.1.29
Hag Moth 27.52.14
Hagenella 26.8.5
hageni, Echmepteryx 17.1.1
hageni, Micrathyria 7.7.17
hageni, Tanypteryx 7.1.2
hagenii, Pseudometopius 25.16.284
Hagenius 7.3.4

Hahncappsia 27.55.92
Haida 24.24.114
Haideoporus 24.7.21
Haiga 29.58.8
haimbachi, Zelleria 27.30.10
Haimbachia 27.55.229
haimbachiana, Gypsonoma 27.38.31
Hairstreak Butterfly Family, supra 27.43.1
Hairy Bear Beetle 24.30.88
Hairy Chinch Bug 20.7.16
Hairy Fungus Beetle 24.91.2
Hairy Fungus Beetle Family, supra 24.91.1
Hairy Maggot Blow Fly 29.101.15
Hairy Rove Beetle 24.24.14
Hairy Spider Beetle 24.62.10
Hairy-legged Fly 29.105.5
Hairy-veined Barklice Family 17.9.1
Hairy-winged Barklice Family 17.12.1
Halacritus 24.26.5
Haldorus 21.14.210
halensis, Sermylassa 24.107.88
Halesochila 26.10.17
halesus, Atlides 27.43.12
Haliaspis 21.38.38
Halictidae, supra 25.66.1
Halictinae, supra 25.66.9
Halictini, supra 25.66.14
Halictoides 25.66.1
Halictophaginae, supra 24.105.10
Halictophagus 24.105.10
Halictoxenos 24.105.4
Halictus 25.66.15 (Fig. 25.64)
Halidamia 25.7.74
Halidayina 29.88.3
Halipeurus 18.1.30
Haliplidae, supra 24.6.1
Haliplus 24.6.1
halisidotae, Uramya 29.105.201
halitus, Dicopus 25.27.4
Halmus 24.80.27
Hallodapini, supra 20.23.74
Hallomenini, supra 24.98.9
Hallomenus 24.98.13
Halobates 20.27.5
Halobatinae, supra 20.27.5
Halobrecta 24.24.250
Halocladius 29.24.104
Halocoryza 24.4.26
Halodiplosis 29.11.112
halophilus, Neomachilis 4.8
Haloscatella 29.93.60
Haltichella 25.21.1
Haltichellinae, supra 25.21.1
Halticini, supra 20.23.82
Halticoptera 25.19.45
Halticotoma 20.23.22
Halticus 20.23.83
Halyini, supra 20.3.25
Halysidota 27.73.55
Hamaba 24.113.227
hamadryadella, Cameraria 27.14.20
Hamadryas 27.46.41
hamamelidis, Hormaphis 21.19.97
hamamelis, Acronicta 27.75.231
Hamamelistes 21.19.94
Hamana 21.14.23
Hamatabsanus 29.26.22
hamatus, Omoglymmius 24.2.1
Hamaxia 29.105.41
Hambletonia 25.25.145
Hamilcara 27.37.10
hamiltoni, Corrodopsylla 30.4.23
Hammaptera 27.61.216
Hammerschmidtia 29.47.50
hammondi, Psorosina 27.55.367
Hamophthiriidae, infra 19.8.1

Hamophthirius, infra 19.8.1
Hamotini, supra 24.25.76
Hamotus 24.25.76
hampsoni, Sexserrata 27.75.190
hamula, Leuctra 8:4.2 (Fig. 8.7)
Handsome Fungus Beetle Family, supra 24.81.1
Hangingfly Family, supra 28.1.1
Hapalaraea 24.24.115
Hapalomellinus 25.62.83
Hapithus 11.10.24
Haplandrus 24.87.82
Hapleginella 29.94.11
Haplidoeme 24.106.33
Haplidus 24.106.45
Haplips 24.75.3
Haploa 27.73.28
Haplocampas 3.1.6
Haplocoelioxys 25.68.24
Haploembia 9.3.3
Haplogleniinae, supra 23.15.1
Haplogonatopus 25.51.17
Haplomyza 29.68.10
Haplopogon 29.37.27
Haplorhynchites 24.113.8
Haplostethops 24.113.357
haplothorax, Digonatopus 25.51.26
Haplothrips 22.5.44
Haplusia 219.11.35
Haptoncus 24.70.11
Hardya 21.14.171
harfordii, Colias 27.42.11
Harkenclenus 27.43.15
Harkeria 25.14.12
Harlequin Bug 20.3.48 (Fig. 20.12)
Harlequin Cockroach 14.3.3
Harlomillsia 1.5.11
Harmandia 29.11.80
Harmolita 25.20.3
Harmolitinae, supra 25.20.3
Harmostini, supra 20.6.4
Harmostes 20.6.4
Harmstonia 29.43.44
Harnessed Moth 27.73.52
Harnischia 29.24.51
Harpactorinae, supra 20.17.11
Harpagoxenus 25.58.39
Harpalellus 24.4.132
Harpalitae, supra 24.4.108
Harpalini, supra 24.4.108
Harpalobrachys 24.4.123
Harpalus 24.4.124
harperi, Neopinnaspis 21.38.53
Harris Checkerspot 27.46.15
harrisi, Dytiscus 24.7.35 (Fig. 24.47)
harrisi, Sominella 24.107.5
harrisii, Charidryas 27.46.15
harrisii, Cryptopristus 25.18.120
harrisii, Halysidota 27.73.55
Harrisiini, supra 29.105.368
Harrisimemna 27.75.236
Harrisina 27.50.1
Harrisoniella 18.1.31
harti, Euklastus 21.9.1
harti, Syncerothrips 22.5.22
Hartigia 25.12.2
Hartigiini, supra 25.12.1
hartmani, Gnamptogenys 25.58.10
hartmanni, Mycetosoritis 25.58.52
Hartomymus 24.4.128
hartwegi, Tylcus 24.106.118
hartwegii, Dolbogene 27.70.6
haruspex, Apiocera 29.36.2
haruspica, Graphiphora 27.75.561 (Fig. 27.396)
Harvester 27.43.1

Hastaperla 8.8.2
hastata, Eucoronimyia 29.105.303
hastatum, Anomalagrion 7.11.2
hastatus, Malirekus 8.7.14
hastulifera, Acronicta 27.75.231
Hatchia 24.25.21
Hatchaiana 24.56.6
havilae, Spaelotis 27.75.560
Hawaiian Beet Webworm 27.55.135
Hawk Lice Family 18.5.1
Hawk Louse 18.5.1
Hawk Moth Family, supra 27.70.1
hawleyi, Taedia 20.23.188
hawleyana, Tesuquea 27.26.3
Hawthorn Lace Bug 20.14.7
haydenella, Denisia 27.15.29
haydenii, coenonympha 27.48.8
Hayhurstia 21.19.95
Haymatus 25.7.83
Hazelnut Weevil 24.113.200
head 20
Head Louse 19.8.1
Hearlea 29.22.5
Heath Spittle Bug 21.12.7
Hebardacris 11.5.113
hebardi, Falcicula 11.10.22
Hebata 21.14.77
Hebecephalus 21.14.203
Hebecnema 29.100.22
hebesana, Endothenia 27.38.7
Hebestola 24.106.236
hebetella, Navasota 27.55.416
Hebexa 21.14.184
hebraeicum, Polygrammate 27.75.235
Hebridae, supra 20.30.1
hebriodes, Merragata 20.30.2
Hebrus 20.30.1
Hecabolus 25.113.12
hecadactyla, Neocurtilla 11.11.2 (Fig. 11.48)
Hecalinae, supra 21.14.4
Hecalini, supra 21.14.4
Hecalus 21.14.5
Hecamede 29.93.7
Hecamedoides 29.93.13
Hecatera 27.75.489
hecate, Onthophagus 24.30.12
hecla, Colias 27.42.11
Hectopsylla 30.1.1
Hectopsyllini, supra 30.1.1
hecuba, Timpanoga 6.13.8
Hecullus 21.14.4
hederae, Aphis 21.19.15
Hedobia 24.63.3
Hedobiinae, supra 24.63.1
Hedria 29.79.12
Hedriodiscus 29.31.37
Hedya 27.38.16
Hedychreides 25.50.14
Hedychridium 25.50.13
Hedychrum 25.50.15
Hedylus 25.16.125
hegeli, Monobaeus 25.19.1
hegesia, Euptoieta 27.46.7
heidemann, Lidopus 20.23.3
heidemanni, Alepidiella 20.23.126
heidemanni, Brepholoxa 20.3.59
heidemanni, Neocenchrea 21.9.6
Heidemanniella 20.23.43
Heilipodus 24.113.152
Heilipus 24.113.155
Heimbra 25.20.14
Heimbrinae, supra 25.20.14
heitzmani, Neocymbopteryx 27.55.30
Helaeomyia 29.93.22
Helcomyza 29.78.4

Helcomyzinae, supra 29.78.4
Helcon 25.13.64
Helconinae, supra 25.13.63
Helconini, supra 25.13.63
Helegonatopus 25.25.70
helena, Panorpa 28.4.1
helenae, Macrophthalmothrips 22.5.52
helenae, Xenicopoda 24.24.138
Heleniella 29.24.92
Helenomus 18.6.18
Heleodromia 29.42.25
Heleomyza 29.84.22
Heleomyzid Fly Family, supra 29.84.1
Heleomyzidae, supra 29.84.1
Helesius 24.80.19
helferi, Trimerotropis 11.5.62
Helfer's Dune Grasshopper 11.5.62
Helia 27.75.116
Heliades 27.55.260
helianthana, Suleima 27.38.29
helianthi, Olpodiplosis 29.11.111
helianthibulla, Pilodiplosis 29.11.114
Heliastus 11.5.69
Heliaula 11.5.19
helichrysi, Brachycaudus 21.19.28
Helichus 24.44.2
helidis, Eurygarka 29.12.10
Helicobia 20.103.32
Heliconis 23.5.2
Heliconiinae, supra 27.46
Heliconius 27.46.6
Helicopsyche 26.16.1
Helicopsychidae, supra 26.16.1
Helicostizus 25.16.110
Helicoverpa 27.75.599
Helictes 25.16.497
Helina 29.100.19
Heliocis 24.97.12
Heliococcus 21.25.21
Heliodinid Moth Family, supra 27.34.1
Heliodinidae, supra 27.34.1
Heliodines 27.34.4
Heliolonche 27.75.603
Heliomata 27.61.6
Heliomelissodes 25.69.30
Heliopetes 27.40.39
Helioplagia 29.105.139
Heliothelopsis 27.55.51
Heliothinae, supra 27.75.591
Heliothis 27.75.99, 27.75.599
Heliothodes 27.75.593
Heliothrips 22.4.4
Heliozela 27.9.1
Heliozelidae, supra 27.9
Heliria 21.15.37
Helius 29.2.15
helligbrodti, Sphingicampa 27.69.3
helloides, Epidemia 27.43.7
Hellula 27.55.54
Helluomorphoides 24.4.168
Helluonini, supra 24.4.168
helmani, Pseudoseopsis 17.5.1
Helobata 24.12.22
Helochara 21.14.49
Helocharini, supra 24.12.20
Helochares 24.12.21
Helocombus 24.12.23
Helocordulia 7.6.4
Helodidae, supra 24.32.1
Helodinae, supra 24.32.1
Helodon 29.22.4
Helomyzinae, supra 29.84.4
Helonica 21.15.38
Helophilus 29.47.60
Helophorinae, supra 24.12.1
Helophorus 24.12.1

Helopicus 8.7.10
Helopini, supra 24.87.122
Helops 24.87.124
Helorid Wasp Family, supra 25.41.1
Heloridae, supra 25.41.1
Helorus 25.41.1
Helotropha 27.75.276
helvalis, Framinghamia 27.55.172
Helvibotys 27.55.95
helvimacula, Reuterella 17.20.3
helvinus, Xanthochlorus 29.43.43
helveum, Curtonotum 29.89.1
helvus, Colpognathus 25.16.203
Hemadas 25.19.6
Hemaenasius 25.25.146
hemapterus, Carnus 29.75.3
Hemaris 27.70.30
Hemerobiidae, supra 23.8.1
Hemeroblemma 27.75.209
Hemerobioidea, supra 23.8.1
Hemerobius 23.8.1
Hemerodromia 29.42.14
Hemerodromiinae, supra 29.42.12
hemerodromiini, supra 29.42.14
Hemeromyia 29.75.1
Hemerophila 27.36.09
Hemeroplanis 27.75.44
Hemiargus 27.43.40
Hemiberlesia 21.38.39
Hemiblabera 14.6.2
Hemibryomima 27.75.300
Hemiceras 27.71.41
Hemichroa 25.7.20
Hemicnetha 29.22.5
Hemicoelus 24.63.26
Hemicrepidus 24.48.32
hemicryphus, Physokermes 21.26.16 (Fig. 21.28)
hemicycla, Neotuerta 27.75.242
hemidesma, Evora 27.38.18
Hemierana 24.106.302
Hemieuxa 27.75.553
Hemigastrina, supra 25.16.171
Hemiglyptus 24.107.138
Hemigymnaspis 21.38.40
Hemigraphiphora 27.75.585
Hemigrotella 27.75.606
Hemihalictus 25.66.18
hemihoplis 25.16.223
Hemihyalea 27.73.60
Hemileuca 27.69.7
Hemileucinae, supra 27.69.6
Hemilophini, supra 24.106.301
hemimetabolous 13
Hemimorina 27.61.92
Heminocloa 27.75.343
Heminomada 25.69.10
Hemioslaria 27.75.368
Hemiosus 24.12.11
Hemipachnobia 27.75.575
Hemipenthes 29.40.56
Hemipeplini, supra 24.72.23
Hemipeplus 24.72.23
Hemipepsis 25.60.3
Hemiphileurus 24.30.112
Hemiplatytes 27.55.232
Hemiprosopa 27.16.4
Hemipsocidae 17.17.1
Hemipsocus 17.17.1
Hemiptarsenus 25.26.4
Hemiptera, supra 20.1.1, 29.105.1 (Figs. 20.1, 20.2)
hemiptera, Nebaocharis 25.25.150
hemipterous, Phosphaenus 24.55.14
hemipterus, Carpophilus 24.70.10
hemipterus, Metamasius 24.113.367

hemipterus sericeus, Metamasius 24.113.367
Hemiquedius 24.24.23
Hemirhipini, supra 24.48.7
Hemirhipis 24.48.7
Hemiscaptomyza 29.90.10
Hemisiella 25.69.42
Hemisphaerodella 20.23.23
Hemisphaerota 24.107.174
Hemisphaerotini, supra 24.107.174
Hemispherical Scale 21.26.20
Hemispragueia 27.75.218
Hemistilbia 27.75.446
Hemisturmia 29.105.385
Hemitaxonus 25.7.2
Hemiteles 25.16.98
Hemitelina, supra 25.16.94
hemitelini, supra 25.16.84
Hemithea 27.61.169
Hemitheini, supra 27.61.166
Hemithrixion 29.105.229
Hemitrichus 25.19.128
Hemitrioza 21.17.17
Hemlock Borer 24.46.20
Hemlock Looper 27.61.130
Hemlock Sawfly 25.6.4
Hemlock Scale 21.38.1
Hemnypia 27.61.93
Hemyda 29.105.25
Hen Flea 30.1.4
Hendecaneura 27.38.39
hendeli, Dyscrasis 29.58.7
Henicinae, supra 11.9.2
Henicomyia 29.32.26
Henicopygus 25.25.148
Henoticoides 24.74.9
Henoticus 24.74.7
Henria 29.11.28
henrici, Inscisalia 27.43.29
henrici, Simyra 27.75.233
Henricus 27.39.4
henroti, Litocampa 3.1.2
henshawi, Cyllopsis 27.48.3 (Fig. 27.148)
Heoclisis 23.14.12
hepburni, Apodemia 27.44.7
Hepialidae, supra 27.4.1
Hepialoidea, supra 27.4.1
Hepialus 27.4.2
Heptagenia 6.6.4
Heptageniidae, supra 6.6.1
Heptageniinae, supra 6.6.1
Heptagrotis 27.75.584
Heptamelini, supra 25.7.11
Heptamelus 25.7.11
Heptameris 25.32.1
Heptasogasteridae, infra 18.2.10
hera, Hemileuca 27.69.7 (Fig. 27.220)
heraclei, Brachycolus 21.19.29
Heraclides 27.41.6
Heraeus 20.7.65
Herald Moth 27.75.73
Herbertia 25.19.60
Hercinothrips 22.4.5
Hercostomus 29.43.7
Herculean Scale 21.38.1
herculeana, Clavaspis 21.38.18
Herculia 27.55.236
Hercus 25.16.50
Heriades 25.68.13
Herina 29.58.9
Heringia 29.47.33
Hermelycaena 27.43.8
hermes, Hermelycaena 27.43.8
hermes, Hermeuptychia 27.48.4
Hermetia, supra 29.31.1; 29.31.12
Hermetiini, supra 29.31.12
Hermeuptychia 27.48.4

Herminiinae, supra 27.75.1
Hermit Sphinx 27.70.11
hermosa, Anajapyx 3.3.1
hermsi, Hesperoctenes 20.19.1
heros, Epiaeschna 7.4.6 (Fig. 7.7)
Herpetogramma 27.55.179
Herrera 21.13.13
Herreshoffia 27.61.233
herrichii aldrichi, Pseudepipona 25.59.15
herricki, Psephenus 24.36.1
Hersoniini, supra 20.23.150
hesione, Neogeriris 20.27.2
Hesperagrion 7.11.9
Hesperandrena 25.65.1
Hesperanoplium 24.106.46
Hesperapis 25.67.2
Hesperempis 29.42.41
Hesperentominae, supra 2.2.1
Hesperentomon 2.2.1
Hesperia 27.40.65
hesperidum, Coccus 21.26.4
Hesperiidae, supra 27.40.1
Hesperiinae, supra 27.40.44
Hesperininae, supra 29.8.1
Hesperinus 29.8.1
Hesperioidea, supra 27.40.1
Hesperobaenus 24.71.4
Hesperobaris 24.113.315
Hesperoboreus 28.2.3
Hesperocapsus 20.23.102
Hesperocimex 20.20.7
Hesperoconopa 29.2.51
Hesperocorixa 20.35.131
Hesperoctenes 20.19.1
Hesperodes 29.9.7 .
Hesperodiamesa 29.24.36
Hesperodinera 29.105.67
Hesperodryinus 25.51.5
Hesperolabops 20.23.24
Hesperolimonia 29.2.14
Hesperolimnophila 29.2.34
Hesperolinus 24.24.32
Hespcromyia 29.105.362
Hesperonomada 25.69.13
Hesperoperdita 25.65.15
Hesperoperla 8.9.6
Hesperophanes 24.106.52
Hesperophanini, supra 24.106.40
Hesperophantia 21.8.1
Hesperophasia 29.105.36
Hesperophasiini, supra 29.105.35
Hesperophasiopsis 29.105.37
Hesperophasmatini, supra 10.2.1
Hesperophylax 26.10.18
Hesperophylum 20.23.18
Hesperopompilus 25.60.28
Hesperorhipis 24.46.17
Hesperotettix 11.5.91
Hesperotingis 20.14.12
Hesperotipula 29.2.9
Hesperotychus 24.25.56
hesperum, Callidium 24.106.106
Hesperumia 27.61.20
hesperus 24.24.7
hesperus, Ceratocombus 20.24.1
hesperus, Podisma 11.5.98
hesperus, Reticulitermes 15.3.1
hesseli, Mitoura 27.43.26
hesselorum, Automeris 27.69.8
Hessian Fly 29.11.147
hetaera, Sarcophaga 29.103.24
Hetaeriinae, supra 24.26.49
Hetaeriini, supra 24.26.49
Hetaerina 7.8.2
Hetaerius 24.26.49
Heterachthes 24.106.83

Heteranassa 27.75.118
Heteranthidium 25.68.3
heterarthrinae, supra 25.7.42
Hetararthrini, supra 25.7.44
Heterarthrus 25.7.44
heteraula, Melitonympha 27.29.5
Heterelmis 24.45.12
Heterischnina, supra 25.16.197
Heterischnus 25.16.197
Heterlimnius 24.45.13
Heterobostrychus 24.64.15
Heterobrenthus 24.110.4
Heterocampa 27.71.29
Heteroceridae, supra 24.42.1
Heterocerini, supra 24.42.4
Heterocheila 29.78.5
Heterocloen 6.4.8
Heterococcus 21.25.22
Heterocordylus 20.23.102
Heteroders 24.48.15
heterodoxum, Hespoeragrion 7.11.9
heterodoxum, Michthisom 24.106.20
Heterodoxus 18.3.1
Heteroecus 25.34.45
Heterogaster 20.7.26
Heterogastrinae, supra 20.7.26
Heterogenea 27.52.5
Heterographis 27.55.358
heterographis, Cuclotogaster 18.1.17
Heteroleptotyphlus 24.24.165λQ
heteromeringia 29.65.3
Heteromurus 1.5.9
Heteromydas 29.35.2
Heteromyia 29.23.19
Heteromyiini, supra 29.23.18
Heteromyza 29.84.7
heteronea, Chalceria 27.43.6
Hctcronemia 10.1.6
Heteronemiidae, supra 10.1.1
Heteronemiinae, supra 10.1.1
Heteronemiini, supra 10.1.1
heteroneura, Parahypochaeta 29.105.152
heteroneura, Taxigramma 29.103.14
Heteropacha 27.68.5
heteropalpella, Bathroxena 27.10.5
Heteropelma 25.16.381
Heteroperdita 25.65.15
Heteropeza 29.11.31
Heteropezina 29.11.30
Heteropezini, supra 29.11.28
Heterophleps 27.61.253
heterophyllae, Chionaspis 21.38.14
Heteroplectron 26.17.2
heteropogon 29.37.50
Heteropromus 24.87.140
Heterops 24.106.135
Heteropsini, supra 24.106.135
Heteropsylla 21.17.7
heteroptera, Penthetria 29.8.2
Heteropterinae, supra 27.40.42
Heteropterna 29.9.10
heteropuncta, Megalopyge 27.51.4 (Fig. 27.15)
heteropygus, Neophilopterus 18.1.39
Heterosarus 25.65.8
Heterosceloides 20.3.65
Heteroschema 25.19.120
Heterosminthurus 1.7.6
Heterospilus 25.13.13
Heterostelis 25.68.10
Heterostylum 29.40.10
Heterotanytarsus 29.24.113
Heterotermes 15.3.2
Heterotermitinae, supra 15.3.1
Heterothops 24.24.24
Heterothripidae, supra 22.3.1

Heterothripini, supra 22.3.1
Heterothrips 22.3.1
Heterotoma 20.23.104
Heterotrissocladius 29.24.109
Heterotropinae, supra 29.40.30
Heterotropus 29.40.31
Heterusia 27.61.223
Hethemia 27.61.170
Hetoemis 24.106.240
Hexachaeta 29.61.32
Hexacharis 25.31.8
Hexacladia 25.25.121
Hexacnemus 25.25.136
Hexacola 25.32.3
Hexacolini, supra 24.112.24
Hexacylloepus 24.45.14
hexadactyla, Alucita 27.25.1 (Fig. 27.42)
Hexagenia 6.11.2
Hexamcrocera 25.32.13
Hexamitocera 29.98.30
Hexaperdita 25.65.15
Hexapoda, supra 1.1.1, 10
Hexarthrum 24.113.393
Hexatoma 29.2.38
Hexatomini, supra 29.2.25
Hexepeolus 25.69.11
Hexeris 27.56.3
Hexorthodes 27.75.521
Hexosmia 25.68.19
heydeni, Thorictodes 24.61.2
Heydenia 25.19.8
Hiatus 29.58.10
Hiatomyia 29.47.36
hibisci, Althaeus 24.108.13
hibisci, Orthosia 27.75.504 (Fig. 27.385)
hibisci, Pealius 21.18.15
Hibiscus Whitefly 21.18.15
Hickory Bark Beetle 24.112.23
Hickory Horned Devil 27.69.1
Hickory Leafroller 27.38.71
Hickory Plant Bug 20.23.165
Hickory Shuckworm 27.38.56
Hickory Tussock Moth 27.73.56
Hide Beetle 24.61.1
Hidryta 25.16.155
hiemalis, Anthracopteryx 24.48.54
hiemalis, Platygaster 25.44.13 (Fig. 25.29)
hiemalis, Stenogastrura 1.2.7
hierarchy of categories 16 (Table 2.2)
hieroglyphica, Neocicada 21.13.11
Hilara 29.42.39
hilare, Acrosternum 20.3.52 (Fig. 20.13)
Hilarella 29.103.5
hilarella, Actenoptera 29.64.2
hilarella, Hilarella 29.103.5
Hilarimorpha 29.41.1
Hilarimorphid Fly Family, supra 29.41.1
Hilarimorphidae, supra 29.41.1
hilaris, Pandeleteius 24.113.65 (Fig. 24.273)
Hilarocassis 24.107.175
Hilarographa 27.38.91
Hilarographini, supra 27.38.91
hilleri, Myllocerus 24.113.71
Hillia 27.75.417
hillmeadia, Parasyntomocera 25.19.54
Himalopsyche 26.5.1
Himatinum 24.113.373
Himella 27.75.506
Himerta 25.16.354
Himmacia 27.15.8
Hincomyia 29.105.107
Hindsiothrips 22.5.45
hipparis, Leucochlaena 27.75.327
Hippelates 29.94.1
Hippia 27.71.16

Hippiscus 11.5.39
Hippoboscidae, supra 29.106.1
Hippoboscoidea, supra 29.106.1
Hippodamia 24.80.43
Hippomelas 24.46.7
Hippopsini, supra 24.106.261
Hippopsis 24.106.261
Hippuriphila 24.107.134
Hirmoneura 29.30.1
hirsuta, Chaetofoveolocoris 20.23.194
hirsuta, Paratriatoma 20.17.38
hirsutus, Aporus 25.60.15
hirsutus, Circaputo 21.245.10
hirsutus, Coccotorus 24.113.209
hirta, Lonchidia 25.31.13
hirta, Mycetaea 24.81.5
hirticauda, Erythrocambus 25.16.2
hirticollis, Pleocoma 24.30.39
hirtipennis, Diazosoma 29.13.1
hirtipennis, Epitrix 24.107.137
hirtipes, Neohydrotaea 29.100.33
Hirtodrosophila 29.90.9
hirtus, Eurysphindus 24.73.3
hirtus, Involvulus 24.113.9
hirtus, Tetropismenus 29.58.21
hispida, Parantonae 21.15.31
hispida, Protheca 24.63.48
hispidula, Sitona 24.113.50 (Fig. 24.272)
hispidulus, Miarus 24.113.232
hispidum, Pycnarthrum 24.112.24
hispidum, Trimenopon 18.8.1
hispidus, Trachodes 24.113.167
Hispinae, supra 24.107.161
Hister 24.26.29
Histeridae, supra 24.26.1
Histerinae, supra 24.26.36
Histerini, supra 24.26.36
Histeroidea, supra 24.26.1
Histeromerus 25.13.14
Historis 27.46.42
histricus, Xyletomerus 24.63.36
histrionica, Aphelonema 21.6.3 (Fig. 21.9)
histrionica, Murgantia 20.3.48 (Fig. 20.12)
histrionica, Setabara 25.7.47
hitchcocki, Adicrophleps 26.9.1
hobomok, Poanes 27.40.73
Hobomok Skipper 27.40.73
Hockeria 25.21.2
hockingii, Coenodomus 27.55.269
Hodophylax 29.37.11
Hodostates 25.16.327
Hodotermitidae, supra 15.1.1
hoferi, Elatotrypes 24.106.110
Hoffmania 29.23.5
hoffmanni, Charidryas 27.46.15
Hofmannophila 27.15.35
Hog Caterpillar 27.70.40
Hog Louse 19.3.1
Hohonus 24.113.270
Hohorstiella 18.6.19
Holcaphis 21.19.63
Holcencyrtus 25.25.147
Holcocephala 29.37.26
Holcocera 27.17.14
Holcocerina 27.17.15
Holcopasites 25.69.4
Holcopasitini, supra 25.69.4
Holcopsis 29.26.14
Holcostethus 20.3.26
Holdawayella 25.13.152
Holeleodes 24.87.140
Holepyrus 25.48.10
Hollyhock Plant Bug 20.23.92
Hollyhock Weevil 24.113.21
Holly Scale 21.38.27
Holocampa 3.1.7

Holochroa 27.61.90
Holocompsa 14.4.4
Holocompsinae, supra 14.4.4
Holoconops 29.23.1
Holocynips 25.34.42
Holocyrtoma 29.42.49
Hologymnetis 24.30.123
Hololepta 24.26.45
Hololeptini, supra 24.26.45
hololeptoides, Sitophagus 24.87.117
hololeucus, Niptus 24.62.6 (Fig. 24.122)
Holomelina 27.73.30
Holomenopon 18.6.20
Holometabola, supra 23.1.1
holometabolous 13
Holoneurus 29.11.48
Holonomada 25.69.10
Holoparamecus 24.82.1
Holophysis 27.23.75
Holopleura 24.106.165
Holopleurini, supra 24.106.165
Holopogon 29.37.48
holoprasinus, Goeldichironomus 29.24.57
Holopyga 25.50.5
Holorusia 29.2.4
Holostrophus 24.98.12
Holoteleia 25.43.13
holotype 6
Holozodini, supra 24.25.7
Homadaula 27.29.4
Homaemus 20.3.9
Homaeotarsus 24.24.55
Homaesthesis 24.106.10
Homalactia 29.105.140
Homaledra 27.18.5
Homalocephala 29.58.30
Homaloceraphron 25.45.6
Homalocoris 20.17.23
Homalodisca 21.14.41
Homalota 24.24.251
Homalotylus 25.25.99
Homaluroides 29.94.9
Homaspis 25.16.325
Homeotyphlus 24.24.166
Homia 24.24.252
Homidia 1.5.3
Homilopsocidea, supra 17.14.1
hominis, Dermatobia, supra 29.102.2, 29.102.2
hominivorax, Cochliomyia 29.101.3
Homoanarta 27.75.303
homobremia 29.11.93
homocerus homocerus, Patroclus 25.16.240
Homocerynea 27.75.185
Homochlodes 27.61.108
Homoeolabus 24.113.2
Homoeoneuria 6.5.2
Homoeophthalmae, supra 29.40.1
homoeosoma 27.55.371
homoeusa 24.24.253
homogena, Agapema 27.69.11
Homoglaea 27.75.390
Homohadena 27.75.448
Homolagoa 27.75.192
Homoncocnemis 27.75.450
Homoneura 29.82.4
Homophoberia 27.75.195
Homophylax 26.10.10
Homoplectra 26.4.5
Homoporus 25.19.83
Homoptera, supra 21.1.1
Homorthodes 27.75.514
Homosassa 27.55.420
Homosetia 27.10.9
Homostinea 27.10.13
homothermic 12

Homotherus 25.16.210
Homothraulus 6.7.4
honestaria, Pero 27.61.87 (Fig. 27.184)
Honey Ant 25.58.71
Honey Bee 25.70.4
Honey Bees, supra 25.70.1, supra 25.70.4
Honey Locust Moth 27.69.3
Honeylocust Plant Bug 20.23.97
Honeysuckle Sawfly 25.5.1
Honey Wasp 25.59.30
Honora 27.55.361
Hood Casemaker Caddisfly Family,
 supra 26.15.1
hookeri, Hunterellus 25.25.101
Hook-tip Moth 27.60.1
Hook-tip Moth Family, supra 27.60.1
Hop Aphid 21.19.167
Hop Flea Beetle 24.107.160
Hop Looper 27.75.41
Hop Merchant 27.46.24
Hop Plant Bug 20.23.188
Hoperius 24.7.34
hopkinsi, Haematomyzus, infra 18.8.1
hopkinsi, Pityogenes 24.112.48 (Fig.
 24.263)
hopkinsi, Xenarcha 25.13.44
Hoplandria 24.24.254
Hoplandrothrips 22.5.46
Hoplia 24.30.85
Hoplini, supra 24.30.85
Hoplismenia, supra 25.16.246
Hoplismenus 25.16.247
Hoplisoides 25.62.94
Hoplistoscelis 20.18.7
Hoplitalysa 25.13.103
Hoplitimyia 29.31.40
Hoplitina 26.68.17
Hoplitis 25.68.18
Hoplocampa 25.7.18
Hoplochaitophorus 21.19.96
Hoplocheiloma 29.51.6
Hoplocrabro 25.62.63
Hoplocrepis 25.26.71
Hoplodicta 29.79.13
Hoplogaster 29.100.2
Hoplolabis 29.2.59
Hoplolythra 27.75.351
Hoplomachidea 20.23.44
Hoplomachus 20.23.45
Hoplophorionini, supra 21.15.4
Hoplopleura 19.6.1
Hoplopleuridae, supra 19.6.1
Hoplopleurinae, supra 19.6.1
Hoplopria 25.42.20
Hoplopsyllus 30.1.9
Hoplosphyrum 11.10.5
Hoplothrips 22.5.47
hoppingi, Nassipa 24.98.51
hoppingi, Pectotmoma, 24.98.43
hoppingi, Pseudopilema 24.106.89
Hoppingiana 24.68.24
Horama 27.73.89
hordei, harmolita 25.20.3
hordei, Colomyia 29.11.36
Hordnia 21.14.52
Horesidotes 11.5.15
Horicas 20.23.167
Horisme 27.61.240
Horismenus 25.26.76
Horistonotus 24.48.71
Hormaphi 21.19.97
Hormiini, supra 25.13.46
Hormorini, supra 24.113.100
Hormisas 27.75.6
Hormius 25.13.47
Hormopeza 29.42.44

Hormops 24.113.141
Hormorus 24.113.100
Hormoschista 27.75.49
Horn Fly 29.100.59
Hornaltica 24.107.142
Hornblower 27.70.4
Horned Fungus Beetle 24.87.67 (Fig.
 24.152
Horned Passalus 24.29.1
Horned Powder-post Beetle Family,
 supra 24.64.1
Horned Spanworm 27.61.156
Horned Squash Bug 20.4.27
Hornet Longhorn 24.106.170
Hornet Moth 27.35.9
Hornets, supra 25.59.26
horni, Pactopus 24.49.2
horni, Scalenarthrus 24.25.53
Hornia 24.101.18
hornii, Macrovelia 20.29.2
Horn's Checkered Beetle 24.67.18
Horntail Wasp Family 25.9.1
Horntails, supra 25.1.1, supra 25.8.1
Horologion 24.4.64
horrida, Eucyrtophlobea 29.105.158
horridum, Lobosoma 24.113.160
Horse Bot Fly 29.102.1
Horse Chewing Louse 18.2.1
Horse Fly Family, supra 29.26.1
Horse Lubber 11.4.6
Horse Sucking Louse 19.43.1
Horse-bean Longhorn 24.106.166
Horse-nettle Beetle 24.107.60
Horseradish Flea Beetle 24.107.114
Horseshoe Crab Beetle Family,
 supra 24.16.1
hortalis, Syllepis 27.55.182
Hortensia 21.14.50
hortensis, Bourletiella 1.7.6 (Fig. 1.9, Fig.
 1.10)
hortulata, Eurrhypara 27.55.87
hospes, Acrostilicus 24.24.50
hospes, Aethes 27.39.1, see Hysterosia in
 ''Checklist.''
hospes, Balclutha 21.14.95
hospes, Pseudister 24.26.41
hostilis, Neomotaulius 26.10.16
Hoterodes 27.55.151
hottesi, Thripsaphis 21.19.210
houghi, Macrophorbia 29.9.9
Houghia 29.105.402
houghtonensis, Kakimia 21.19.109
House Cricket 11.10.6
House Fly Family, supra 29.100.1
houstonana, Cudonigera 27.38.73
Hover Fly 29.47.41
howardi, Daritis 27.73.4
howardi, Diabrotica 24.107.90
Howardia 21.38.41
howdeni, Taambospasta 24.101.1
howdeni, Tullbergia 1.3.4
howellae, Oropsyche 26.4.6
Hoyer's Mounting Media 45
huachuca, Knullana 21.14.104
huacnucae, Amiota 29.90.2
hualapai, Hemileuca 27.69.7
Huavea 25.62.62
hubbardi, marginitermes 15.2.2
hubbardi, Oligembia 9.2.1
hubbardi, Sphingicampa 27.69.3
hubbardi, Zorotypus 16.1.1 (Fig. 16.2)
Hubbardiella 25.26.58
hubbardii, Henicomyia 29.32.26
Hubbard's Angel Insect 16.1.1
Hubbellia 11.7.49
Hubneria 29.105.398

Huckleberry Planthopper 21.1.2
huebneri, Alucita 27.25.1
huesanus, Pitnus 24.62.5
Huleechius 24.45.8
Huleria 21.14.88
Hulstia 27.55.360
hulstiella, Hypochalcia 27.55.336
Hulstina 27.61.36
hulstinoides, Paraglaucina 27.61.33
Human Bot Fly, supra 29.102.2
Human Flea 30.1.5
humanus capitis, Pediculus 19.8.1
humanus humanus, Pediculus 19.1.1,
 19.8.1 (Fig. 19.2)
humeralis, Eucrada 24.63.4 (Fig. 24.124)
humeralis, Hemiteles 25.16.98
humeralis, Xorides 25.16.83
humilis, Agenioideus 25.60.22
humilis, Hyalopteroides 21.19.100
humilis, Iridomyrmex 25.58.58 (Fig.
 25.45)
humilis, Parydra 29.93.41 (Fig. 29.50)
Hummingbird Lice Family 18.7.1
Humococcus 21.25.23
Humpbacked Fly Family, supra 29.46.1
Humpless Casemaker Caddisfly Family,
 supra 26.9.1
Hump-winged Cricket Family 11.8.1
humuli, Hypena 27.75.41
humuli, Phorodon 21.19.167
Hunch-backed Beetle 24.4.2
hungerfordi, Cryphocricos 20.38.5
Hunterellus 25.25.101
Hunting Billbug 24.113.366
hurdi, Hylaeus 25.63.5
Husseyella 20.28.3
huttoni, Pentarthrum 24.113.390
Hyadaphis 21.19.98
Hyadina 29.93.46
Hyadinini, supra 29.93.46
hyalinaria, Evita 27.61.131
hyalinata, Diaphania 27.55.150
Hyaline Grass Bug 20.6.3
hyalinus, Chrysops 29.26.11
hyalinus, Japananus 21.14.90
hyalinus, Liorhyssus 20.6.3
hyalinus, Perilampus 25.19.4
Hyaliodes 20.23.12
Hyaliodini, supra 20.23.12
Hyalistata 29.90.4
Hyalochloria 20.23.105
Hyalomya 20.105.9
Hyalomyodes 29.105.34
Hyalomyzus 21.19.99
Hyalophora 27.69.18
Hyalopsocus 17.23.7
Hyalopteroides 21.19.100
Hyalopterus 21.19.101
Hyalorista 27.55.102
Hyaloscotes 27.11.8
Hyalurgini, supra 29.105.193
Hyalurgus 29.105.193
Hyalymenus 20.5.6
Hyantiini, supra 21.13.10
hyantis, Euchloe 27.42.8
Hyblaea 27.57.1
Hyblaeid Moth Family, supra 27.57.1
Hyblaeidae, supra 27.57.1
Hybodera 24.106.87
Hyboderini, supra 24.106.87
Hybolasioptera 29.11.55
Hybomischos 25.16.33
Hybomitra 29.26.23
Hybophorellus 25.16.246
Hybophthiridea, infra 19.8.1
Hybophthirus, infra 19.8.1

Hybos 29.42.61
Hybosorinae, supra 24.30.36
Hybosorus 24.30.36
Hybotinae, supra 29.42.58
Hybrizontid Parasite Family, supra 25.15.1
Hybrizontidae, supra 25.15.1
Hybroma, 27.10.12
hybromella, Oenoe 27.10.8
hydaspe, Speyeria 27.46.8
Hydaticinae, supra 24.7.36
Hydaticini, supra 24.7.36
Hydaticus 24.7.36
Hydatophylax 26.10.28
Hydnobius 24.19.2
Hydnosella 24.15.5
Hydraecia 27.75.280
Hydraena 24.13.2
Hydraeninae, supra 24.13.1
hydrangeae, Pulvinaria 21.26.19
Hydraptila 26.7.4
Hydrelia 27.61.234
Hydrellia 29.93.32
Hydrelliini, supra 29.93.32
Hydria 27.61.209
Hydriomena 27.61.199
hydriomenata, Carptina 27.61.202
Hydriomenini, supra 27.61.190
Hydriris 27.22.120
Hydrizon 25.15.1
Hydrobaenus 29.24.128
Hydrobiinae, supra 24.12.12
Hydrobiini, supra 24.12.12
Hydrobiomorpha 24.12.8
Hydrobiosinae, supra 26.5.3
Hydrobius 24.12.14
Hydrocanthus 24.8.6
Hydrocanthini, supra 24.8.6
Hydrochara 24.12.7
Hydrochasma 29.93.1
Hydrochinae, supra 24.12.3
Hydrochus 24.12.3
Hydroecioedes 27.75.533
Hydroisotoma 1.4.20
Hydrometra 20.26.1
Hydrometridae, supra 20.26.1
Hydromyza 29.98.26
Hydroperla 8.7.11
Hydrophilidae, supra 24.12.1
Hydrophilinae, supra 24.12.4
Hydrophiloidea, supra 24.12.1
Hydrophilus 24.12.6
Hydrophoria 29.99.15
Hydrophorineae, supra 29.43.13
Hydrophorus 29.43.13
Hydrophylita 25.28.3
Hydroporinae, supra 24.7.3
Hydroporini, supra 24.7.15
Hydroporus 24.7.16
Hydropsyche 26.4.8
Hydropsychidae, supra 26.4.1
Hydropsychinae, supra 26.4.7
Hydropsychoidea, supra 26.1.1
hydroptilidae, supra 26.7.1
Hydroptilinae, supra 26.7.2
Hydroptilini, supra 26.7.2
Hydroscapha 24.11.1
Hydroscaphidae, supra 24.11.1
Hydrotaea 29.100.32
Hydrothassa 24.107.72
Hydrotrupes 24.7.22
Hydrovatini, supra 24.7.4
Hydrovatus 24.7.4
Hygronemobius 11.10.15
hygrophila, Agasicles 24.107.122 (Fig. 24.236)
Hygropora 24.24.255

Hygrotus 24.7.15
Hyidiothrips 22.5.48
Hylacinae, supra 25.63.5
Hylaeana 25.63.5
Hylaeus 25.63.5
hylas, Polygonia 27.46.24
Hylastes 24.112.5
Hylastini, supra 24.112.3
Hylastinus 24.112.6
Hylecoetus 24.69.1
Hylecthrus 24.105.6
Hylemya, supra 29.99.1, 29.99.8
Hylemyza 29.99.8
Hylephila 27.40.61
Hyles 27.70.42
Hylesia 27.69.9
Hylesininae, supra 24.112.1
Hylesinini, supra 24.112.6
Hylis 24.52.21
Hyllolycaena 27.43.5
hyllus, Hyllolycaena 27.43.5
Hylobiinae, supra 24.113.152
Hylobiini, supra 24.113.152
Hylobittacus 28.1.3
Hylobius 24.113.153
Hylochares 24.52.23
Hylocrinus 24.87.16
Hylocurus 24.112.31
hyloeus, Dolba 27.70.5 (Fig. 27.241)
Hylogomphus 7.3.9
Hylophasma 25.16.178
Hylota 24.24.256
Hylotrupes 24.106.102
Hylotychus 24.25.57
Hylurgopinus 24.112.10
Hylurgops 24.112.4
hymenaea, Pantala 7.7.22
Hymenarcys 20.23.38
Hymenia 27.55.134
Hymeniphera 20.4.13
Hymenoclea 27.35.19
Hymenocoris 20.15.1
Hymenodria 27.61.200
Hymenoptera, supra 25.1.1
Hymenorus 24.88.5
Hymetta 21.14.83
hynesi, Thaumastoptera 29.2.17
Hypagyrtis 27.61.61
Hypalastoroides 25.59.6
Hypamblys 25.16.370
Hypanartia 27.46.28
Hypargyria 27.55.291
Hyparpax 27.71.37
Hypasclera 24.97.17
Hypasclerini, supra 24.97.17
Hypatima 27.23.78
Hypatopa 27.17.8
Hypaurotis 27.43.9
Hypdoropha 27.75.62
Hypebaeus 24.68.10
Hypena 27.75.41
Hypeninae, supra 27.75.38
Hypenodes 27.75.28
Hypenodinae, supra 27.75.28
Hypenula 27.75.10
Hypera 24.113.146
Hyperacmus 25.16.482
Hyperaeschra 27.71.4
Hyperallus 25.16.372
Hyperaspidius 24.80.16
Hyperaspini, supra 24.80.15
Hyperaspis 24.80.15
Hyperbatus 25.16.360
Hyperborea 27.73.53
hyperborea, Nasiternella 29.2.24
hyperborea, Piophila 29.64.1

hyperboreus, Hepialus 27.4.2
Hypercampa 3.1.1
Hyperdiplosis 29.11.139
Hyperecteina 29.105.330
Hyperecteinini, supra 29.105.326
Hyperepia 27.75.517
hyperia, Biblis 27.46.40
hyperici, Brachysiphum 21.19.31
hyperici, Hypericicoccus 21.31.6
Hypericicoccus 21.31.6
Hyperimerus 25.19.38
Hyperinae, supra 24.113.146
Hyperini, supra 24.113.146
Hyperomyzus 21.19.102
Hyperplatys 24.106.293
Hyperstrotia 27.75.189
Hypertetrastichus 25.26.48
Hypertrophocera 29.105.343
Hypertrophomma 29.105.403
Hypcxilis 24.106.39
Hyphantria 27.73.38
Hyphantrophaga 29.105.399
Hypnoidinae, supra 24.48.61
Hypnoidus 24.48.65
Hypoborini, supra 24.112.17
Hypocaccus 24.26.8
Hypocala 27.75.106
Hypocera 29.46.5
Hypocerina 29.46.11
Hypochalcia 27.55.336
Hypocharassus 29.43.19
Hypochlora 11.5.86
Hypoclinea 25.58.56
Hypocoeliodes 24.113.286
Hypocoena 27.75.267
Hypocoprinae, supra 24.71.11
Hypocoprus 24.71.11
Hypocrisias 27.73.54
hypocrita, Hoplitis 25.68.18
Hypocryphalus 24.112.38
Hypocyphtinae, supra 24.24.189
Hypodacne 24.78.1
Hypoderma 29.102.5
Hypodermatinae, supra 29.102.5
Hypodermodes 29.100.50
Hypodryas 27.46.21
Hypogastrura 1.2.1
Hypogastruridae, supra 1.2.1
Hypogastrurinae, supra 1.2.1
Hypogena 24.87.120
Hypogeococcus 21.25.24
Hypogeocoris 20.7.19
Hypolampsis 24.107.153
Hypoleschus 24.113.190
Hypolethria 25.32.10
Hypolimnas 27.46.29
Hypolimnini, supra 27.46.29
Hypolithinae 24.48.61
Hypolithus 24.48.64
Hypomachilodes 4.2.4
Hypomacrotera 25.65.13
hypomecis 27.61.23
Hypomecus 25.16.283
Hypomicrogaster 25.13.118
Hyponeura 7.11.4
Hyponygrus 24.24.33
Hyponysson 25.62.74
Hypopacha 27.68.1
Hypoplesia 27.10.26
Hypoponera 25.58.17
Hypoprepia 27.73.17
Hypopta 27.37.1
Hypopteromalus 25.19.119
Hypoptinae, supra 27.37.1
Hyporhagus 24.85.1
Hyposoter 25.16.424

Hypostrymon 27.43.32
Hypotelus 24.24.86
Hypothenemus 24.112.40
Hypothyce 24.30.70
Hypotrichia 24.30.69
Hyppa 27.75.296
Hypselonotus 20.4.29
Hypsicera 25.16.298
Hypsipla 27.55.286
Hypsoprora 21.15.11
Hypsoprorini, supra 21.15.10
Hypsopygia 27.55.235
Hyptia 25.35.4
Hypulini, supra 24.98.30
Hypulus 24.98.32
Hyropionea 27.55.118
Hyselosomatinae, supra 20.25.1
Hyssopus 25.26.21
Hysterobolus 25.13.130
Hysterŏneura 21.19.103
Hysteropterini, supra 21.6.6
Hysteropterum 21.6.8
Hysterosia 27.39.9
Hystrichophora 27.38.43
Hystrichopsylla 30.4.1
Hystrichopsyllinae, supra 30.4.1
Hystrichopsyllini, supra 30.4.1
Hystrichopsyolidae, supra 30.4.1

I

iaculus, Preludius 24.48.34
Ianius 27.75.100
iarchasalis, Bicilia 27.55.178
Iassinae, supra 21.14.19
Iassini, supra 21.14.29
Ibalia 25.29.1
Ibaliid Wasp Family 25.29.1
Ibaliidae, supra 25.29.1
Ibaliinae, supra 25.29.1
Ibidionini, supra 24.106.82
Ibidoecus 18.1.32
ibseni, Pardiaulomella 25.26.5
Icaricia 27.43.50
icarioides, Icaricia 27.43.50
Iceliini, supra 29.105.194
Icerya 21.23.8
iceryae, Cryptochetum 29.95.1
Ichneumon 25.16.249
Ichneumon Family, supra 25.16.1
ichneumoneus, Sphex 25.62.8
Ichneumonidae, supra 25.16.1
Ichneumonina, supra 25.16.248
Ichneumoninae, supra 25.16.197
Ichneumonini, supra 25.16.248
Ichneumonoidea, supra 25.13.1
Ichneumonops 29.105.26
Ichneutes 25.13.124
Ichneutidea 25.13.125
Ichneutinae, supra 25.13.124
Ichneutini, supra 25.13.124
Ichthyurini, supra 24.56.2
Ichthyurus 24.56.2
Icodema 20.23.46
Icterica 29.61.18
Ictericophyto 29.105.182
Icteromyza 29.68.6
Idaea 27.61.176
idahoensis, Knowltonella 1.2.4
idalia, Speyeria 27.46.8 (Fig. 27.123)
Idana 29.58.11
Idarnes 25.18.4
Idarninae, supra 25.18.2
Ide 27.15.17
idella, Hemispragueia 27.75.218
identification label 41

identification specialists 42
identification, species 5, 6
identifying 4
Idia 27.75.1
Idiasta 25.13.104
idiastes, Apezococcus 21.31.1
Idiataphe 7.7.9
Idiobates 24.87.83
Idiocera 29.2.47
Idiocerinae, supra 21.14.18
Idiocerini, supra 21.14.18
Idiocerus 21.14.18
Idiodonus 21.14.111
Idioglochina 29.2.14
Idioglossa 27.15.41
Idiognophomyia 29.2.46
Idiogramma 25.16.77
Idiogrammatini, supra 25.16.77
Idiolimnophila 29.2.34
Idiolispa 25.16.156
Idiomacromerus 25.18.12
Idiomelissodes 25.69.27
Idionotus 11.7.35
Idiopidonia 24.106.208
Idioptera 29.2.34
Idiopteron 24.57.16
Idiopterus 21.19.104
Idiostatus 11.7.36
Idiostethus 24.113.356
Idiotypa 25.42.27
Idolia 24.26.35
Idolothripinae, supra 22.5.1
Idona 21.14.75
idoneus, Abutiloneus 24.108.14
Idris 25.43.24
Ignelater 24.48.13
ignidorsella, Eurythnidia 27.55.363
ignipecta, Prosapia 21.12.1
ignota, Foxella 30.7.19
Ignotomyia 29.105.391
ignotus, Acaricoris 20.13.4
Iherminierii, Sparnopolius 29.40.15 (Fig. 29.35)
ilia, Catocala 27.75.148
ilicifoliae, Hesperapis 25.67.2
ilicis, Gyropsylla 21.17.6
ilicis, Kermes 21.29.1
ilicis, Nibeapis 21.38.55
Ilionota 24.26.46
Ilisia 29.2.59
Ilithucia 21.15.22
illigeri, Hybosorus 24.30.36
illinoensis, Cerodontha 29.68.7
Illinoia 21.19.105
illinoisensis, Aphis 21.19.15
Illinothrips 22.5.11
illocata, Dyspyralis 27.75.30
illucens, Hermetia 29.31.12
illumina, Nigridonus 21.14.109
illustrations 4, 16
illustris, Lucilia 29.101.11
illustris, Tipula 29.2.9
Ilnacora 20.23.106
Ilnacorella 20.23.107
Ilybius 24.7.26
Ilythea 29.93.36
Ilytheini, supra 29.93.36
Imaguncula 29.105.353
Imania 20.10.48
imbelle, Meganoplium 24.106.47
imbellis, Micraneflus 24.106.66
imbrasus, Neochrysocharis 25.26.63
Imbricated Snout Beetle 24.113.38
imbricator, Fagiphagus 21.19.80
imbricatum, Cainosternum 24.19.5
imbricornis, Prionus 24.106.10 (Fig. 24.178)

imitator, Canthon 24.30.2
Imitomyia 29.105.27
Imitomyini, supra 29.105.27
immacula, Sparkia 27.75.469
immaculalis, Reabotis 27.75.2
immaculara, Cyclocephala 24.30.100
immortua, Helaporphyria 27.75.604
Immyrla 27.55.319
impartialis, Eubolina 27.75.130
impatiens, Eucoila 25.32.4
Impeccantia 29.105.141
impedita, Gaenima 24.24.241
imperfecta, Microsania 29.45.2
Imperial Moth 27.69.1
imperialis imperialis, Eacles 27.69.1 (Fig. 27.212)
impigritella, Diploschizia 27.28.4 (Fig. 27.45)
Imported Cabbageworm 27.42.5
Imported Currantworm 25.7.32
Imported Klamathweed Beetle 24.107.122
Imported Longhorned Weevil 24.113.139
Imported Mealybug 21.25.35
Imported Willow Leaf Beetle 24.107.67
importus, Pseudococcus 21.25.35
impressicollis, Aufeius 20.6.5
impressifrons, Clivina 24.4.25
impressus, Dercylinus 24.4.103
impressus, Meloe 24.101.3
impricatus, Epicaerus 24.113.38 (Fig. 24.271)
improba, Clossiana 27.46.11
impulsalis, Diahantania 27.55.112
impunctata, Colenis 24.19.6
impunctiventris, Euschistus 20.3.34
inaequalis, Craponius 24.113.283
inaequalis, Pantisarthrus 25.16.488
inaequipes, Cholomyia 29.105.203
inatomaria, Metanema 27.61.113 (Fig. 27.186)
inca, Aleptina 27.75.204
incanus, Isidotus 29.105.50
incanus, Thylacites 24.113.43
incarnata, Lerina 27.73.67
incendiata, Erosia 27.62.6
Incense Cedar Wasp 25.8.1
incerta, Dicranotropis 21.2.16
incertata, Mesothea 27.61.171
Incertella 29.94.33
incertella, Arcolepiopsis 27.33.1 (Fig. 27.51)
incessans, Neostroblia 25.16.352
Incidifrons 18.1.33
Incisalia 27.43.29
Incisitermes 15.2.4
includens, Pseudoplusia 27.75.154
inclusa, Clostera 27.71.1
inclusum, Trogoderma 24.61.13
incognita, Hebexa 21.14.184
Incolia 24.98.3
incolorata, Epiplema 27.62.1
incompletus, Ephedrus 25.14.1
incomptus, Nemocestes 24.113.88
incongrua, Hamaxia 29.105.41
inconsequens, Taeniothrips 22.4.52 (Fig. 22.1)
inconspicua, Neurotoma 25.2.3
inconspicuella, Tildenia 27.23.53
inconstans, Eutrepsia 27.61.205
inconstans, Panula 27.75.101
incrassatus, Geopinus 24.4.111
Incurvaria 27.8.1
Incurvariidae, supra 27.8.1
Incurvariinae, supra 27.8.1
Incurvarioidea, supra 27.8.1
incurvum, Malacosoma 27.68.11

inda, Euphoria 24.30.126 (Fig. 24.75)
indentella, Surattha 27.55.198
indeprensus, Apobaetis 6.4.1
indetermina, Parasa 27.52.20 (Fig. 27.161)
index numbering system 9
Indian Meal Moth 27.55.400
Indian Skipper 27.40.65
Indian Wax Scale 21.26.1
indica, Notonecta 20.33.3(Fig. 20.64)
indica, Radionaspis 21.38.75
indifferens, Rhagoletis 29.61.44
indigenella, Acrobasis 27.55.282
Indiopsocus 17.23.11
indivisa, Trichopoda 29.105.5
Indovia 25.16.90
indra, Papilio 27.41.5
inermis, Gasterophilus 29.102.1
infans, Archiearis 27.61.1
infecta, Anicla 27.75.552
inferentia, Monosoma 25.7.80
infernalis, Paralispe 29.105.258
infernella, Neofaculta 27.23.57
Infernophilus 24.4.148
inficita, Marathyssa 27.75.169 (Fig. 27.343)
infida, Evidomyia 29.105.304
inflata, Inocellia 23.4.1
inflata, Palumbia 29.47.80
inflata, Zaraea 25.5.1
inflatus, Epacalles 24.113.253
inflatus, Pseudomopsis 24.113.267
inflatus, Suphis 24.8.2
information sequence 4
infraorder 15
infumata, Sialis 23.1.1
infuscata, Calodera 24.24.215
infuscata, Limonia 29.2.14
infuscata, Moselia 8.4.3
infuscatus, Limonius 24.48.27
Inga 27.15.22
ingenitus, Dalcerides 27.54.1 (Fig. 27.163)
ingens, Coryphaeschna 7.4.5
ingens, Cydia 27.38.56
Inglisia 21.26.7
Inguromorpha 27.37.2
inimica, Endria 21.14.214
inimicella, Pseudogalleria 27.38.59
inland waters 29
Inna 24.4.150
innotablis, Orthodiatelus 24.24.275
innumerabilis, Pulvinaria 21.26.19 (Fig. 21.29)
ino, Caria 27.44.3
Inocellia 23.4.1
Inocelliidae, supra 23.4.1
inodorus, Haematosiphon 20.20.4
Inopeplinae, supra 24.72.1
Inopeplus 24.72.1
inopina, Neopsylla 30.4.4
Inopsis 27.73.10
Inopus 29.31.1
inornata, Aonidiella 21.38.7
inornata, Artemita 29.31.21
inornata, Coenonympha 27.48.8 (Fig. 27.150)
inornata, Episcepsis 27.73.82
Inornate Scale 21.38.7
inornatella, Eulyonetia 27.13.4
inornatus, Valenus 24.106.287
Inostemma 25.44.2
Inostemmatinae, supra 25.44.1
Inostemmatini, supra 25.44.1
inquilinus, Chaetochlorops 29.94.28
inquilinus, Lepinotus 17.2.2
inquisitor, Gregopimpla 25.16.10
inquisitor, Rhagium 24.106.183
insana, Conomyra 25.58.60

Insara 11.7.4
inscitella, Tiquadra 27.10.46
inscripta, Deidamia 27.70.34
inscriptus, Puren 23.14.7
Inscudderia 11.7.5
insect(s)
 abdomen 11
 body regions 11
 circulatory system 11
 classification 10
 distinguished from other animals 3
 heart 11
 identification 3
 legs 11
 methods of study 4
 mouth parts 20
 number of species 7, 8 (Table 1.1)
 numbers compared 7
 orders 4
 pins 38
 respiratory systems 12
 sinuses 11
 size 11
 wing trembling 12
 wings 11
Insecta, supra 4.1.1
insectella, Episcardia 27.10.30
insertus, Menecles 20.3.43
insidiosus, Trechnites 25.25.127
insignata, Megalinga 29.32.3
insignis, Broscodera 24.4.33
insignis, Eriococcus 21.31.4
insignis, Mimoceps 20.23.191
insignis, Orthezia 21.22.1
insignis, Pseudanteris 25.43.18
insignis, Xylotrechus 24.106.123
insiticiana, Ecdytolopha 27.38.58
insolens, Cionomimus 24.113.214
insolens, Epicrossocerus 25.62.63
insolens, Homobremia 29.11.93
insolens, Microzogus 24.63.7
insolita, Atropharista 29.105.122
instans, Minofala 27.75.384
instar 14
insuetus, Ardalus 25.26.16
insularis, Blissus 20.7.16
insularis, Caprithrips 22.4.32
insularis, Pimodes 27.55.314
insularis, Zeteticontus 25.25.64
insulata, Notonecta 20.33.3
insulata, Pareuchaetes 27.73.64
insulicola, Trichopsychoda 29.12.7
intacta, Leucorrhinia 7.7.12
integer, Cryptophilus 24.83.3
integer, Dyschirius 24.4.24
integer, Janus 25.12.3
integerrima, Datana 27.71.2
integre, Chyrysotoxum 29.47.11
integripennis, Zarhipis 24.54.1
intercepta, Oxycrepis 24.4.90
interfrontalis, Metopomyza 29.69.9
intergressus, Eysarcoris 30.3.42
interior, Colias 27.42.11 (Figs. 27.95, 27.96)
Interjectio 27.55.315
interjectus, Acanthomyops 25.58.68
intermedia, Cucullia 27.75.464 (Fig. 27.374)
intermedia, Phynocephala 24.107.125
intermedia, Strobliella 29.11.22
intermedia, Tiphia 25.53.1
intermediata, Euphyia 27.61.226 (Fig. 27.200)
International Commission of Zoological Nomenclature 17
internitalis, Sathria 27.55.177

interpuncta, Colobochyla 27.75.23
interpunctella, Plodia 27.55.400
interrogans, Phragmatiphila 27.75.268
interrogantionis, Polygonia 27.46.24 (Fig. 27.128)
interrupta, Hesperocorixa 20.35.13 (Fig. 20.66)
interrupta, Mantispa 23.7.4 (Fig. 23.9)
interruptus, Passalus 24.29.2
interstinctana, Grapholita 27.38.53
interstitialis, Aphelosternus 24.26.18
interstitialis, Baris 24.113.303 (Fig. 24.294)
intertexta, Aethalura 27.61.38€QL
intestinalis, Gasterophilus 29.102.1
intorta, Melissodes 25.69.30
intractata, Himella 27.75.506
intractata, Thysanopyga 27.61.79
intransitella, Adanarasa 27.55.289
intricatus, Ulkcus 24.26.53
Introduced Pine Sawfly 25.6.5
intrusus, Phyllobius 24.113.103
invadens, Narthecura 25.16.264
invasor, Plagiosippus 29.105.149
invaria, Ephemerella 6.13.1 (Fig. 6.10)
inversella, Epicorthylis 27.23.90
investigator, Nicrophorus 24.21.9
invicta, Solenopsis 25.58.33
involutum, Eupseudosoma 27.73.71
Involvulus 24.113.9
Inyodectes 11.7.37
inyoensis, Pseudasydates 24.68.31
io, Aphycoideus 25.25.129
io, Cartocometes 29.105.326
io io, Automeris 27.69.8 (Fig. 27.224)
io lilith, Automeris 27.69.8
Io Moth 27.69.8
io neomexicana, Automeris 27.69.8
Iodopepla 27.75.283
iole, Nathalis 27.42.20 (Fig. 27.103)
Iomelissa 25.65.1
Ionia 21.14.15
Ioscytus 20.32.9
iowaense, Proturentomon 2.2.2
Iowana 21.19.106
Iowanus 21.14.142
Iphiaulax 25.13.34
Iphitrachelini, supra 25.44.7
Iphitrachelus 25.44.7
Iphthiminus 24.87.84
Ipideurytoma 25.20.12
Ipimorpha 27.75.290
Ipini, supra 24.112.48
Ipochus 24.106.229
ipomoeae, Cemolobus 25.69.25
ipomoeae, Pebops 27.21.4
ipomoeae, Syntomeida 27.73.87 (Fig. 27.314)
Ips 24.112.51
ipsilon, Agrotis 27.75.535 (Fig. 27.389)
Ipsiura 25.50.22
Irazona 27.39.5
Irbisia 20.23.161
iricolor, Hydrocanthus 24.8.6 (Fig. 24.49)
iridis, Iridothrips 22.4.42
Iridomyrmex 25.58.58
Iridopus 27.61.40
Iridothrips 22.4.42
Iris 14.1.6
iris, Automeris 27.69.8
Iris Borer 27.75.275
Iris Thrips 22.4.42
Iron 6.6.3
Ironodes 6.6.5
Ironopsis 6.6.3
Ironoquia 26.10.6

irrenosa, Lepidomys 27.55.244
irrigualis, Phylctaina 27.75.14
irritans, Haematobia 29.100.59
irritans, Pulex 30.1.5
irroratus, Copicerus 21.2.1
irroratus, Traginops 29.67.3
irus, Incisalia 27.43.29 (Fig. 27.109)
Isa 27.52.16
isabella, Eueides 27.46.5
isabella, Pyrrharctia 27.73.34 (Fig. 27.284)
Iscadia 27.75.175
Ischalia 24.94.1
Ischaliinae, supra 24.94.1
Ischnaspis 21.38.42
Ischnocera, supra 18.1.1
Ischnoceros 25.16.80
Ischnocerus 24.109..8
Ischnodemus 20.7.17
Ischnomyia 29.70.2
Ischnonyctes 20.17.7
Ischnopoda 24.24.257
Ischnopsyllidae, supra 30.5.1
Ischnopsyllinae, supra 30.5.1
Ischnoptera 14.5.2
Ischnorhynchinae, supra 20.7.13
Ischnura 7.11.10
Ischnus 25.16.159
Ischyroceraea 25.7.94
Ischyropalpus 24.102.16
Ischyrosyrphus 29.47.18
Ischyrus 24.76.8
Isdromas 25.16.88
Iseropus 25.16.11
ishidae, Orientus 21.14.143
Isidotus 29.105.50
Iskutana 25.62.66
islands 27
isleta, Shotwellia 11.5.64
Ismarinae, supra 25.42.2
Ismarus 25.42.2
isobeon, Calycopis 27.43.23
Isocapnia 8.3.5
Isochaetes 27.52.13
Isocolpodia 29.11.54
Isocorypha 27.10.11
Isocybus 25.44.12
Isodontia 25.62.9
Isodromus 25.25.100
Isadrusus 24.113.54
Isogenoides 7.8.12
Isognathus 27.70.20
Isogona 27.75.53
Isohelea 29.23.8
Isohydnocera 24.67.20
isola, Hemiargus 27.43.40
isolata, Panorpa 28.4.1
Isomeris 25.16.313
Isometopinae, supra 29.23.1
Isometopini, supra 20.23.2
Isomira 24.88.11
Isoneurothrips 22.4.43
Isonychia 6.1.7
Isonychiinae, supra 6.1.7
Isonychus 24.30.79
Isoparce 27.70.8
Isoperla 8.7.2
Isoperlinae, supra 8.7.1
Isophrictis 27.23.4
isophthalma, Brephidium 27.43.37
Isoplastus 24.16.1
Isoptera, supra 15.1.1 (Figs. 15.1, 15.2, 15.5)
Isorhipis 24.52.15
isosomatis, Eridontomerus 25.18.18
Isosomia 25.68.19
Isosomodes 25.20.6

Isostasius 25.44.3
Isotoma 1.4.23
Isotomidae, supra 1.4.1
Isotomiella 1.4.18
Isotomodes 1.4.8
Isotomurus 1.4.20
Isotrilophus 24.99.3
Issidae, supra 21.6.1
Issinae, supra 21.6.6
Issini, supra 21.6.19
Istocheta 29.105.344
Italian Pear Scale 21.38.28
Itame 27.61.9
itascae, Chilostigma 26.10.31
Iteaphila 29.42.46
Iteomyia 29.11.159
ithacae, Abgrallaspis 21.38.1
ithacus, Hypertetrastichus 25.26.48
Ithome 27.21.25
Ithonidae, supra 23.6.1
Ithyceridae, supra 24.113.22
Ithycerinae, supra 24.113.22
Ithycerus 24.113.22
Ithyporini, supra 24.113.237
Ithytrichia 26.7.8
Itolia 29.37.21
Itoplectis 25.16.28
Ituninae, supra 27.49.2
Itycorsia 25.2.2
Ityocara 24.24.258
iulia, Dryas 27.46.4
ivallda, Oeneis 27.48.13
Ivy Aphid 21.19.15
Ixala 27.61.73
Ixodiphagini, supra 25.25.101
Ixodiphagus 25.25.102
Iziphya 21.19.107

J

Jacintanta, Proteriades 25.68.17
Jack Pine Budworm 27.38.72
Jack Pine Sawfly 25.6.4
Jack Pine Tip Beetle 24.112.63
Jacksonia 21.19.108
jacobaeae, Tyria 27.73.29
Jacques'' Beetle 24.80.53
jaculifera, Feltia 27.75.537(Fig. 27.390)
jada, Arawacus 27.43.30
Jadera 20.6.9
jaguarina, Schinia 27.75.601 (Fig. 27.401)
j-album, Nymphalis 27.46.25 (Fig. 27.131)
jaliscana, Notela 27.71.20
Jalysus 20.12.2
jamaicensis, Smerinthus 27.70.15 (Fig. 27.245)
jamaicensis, Xyloryctes 24.30.107 (Fig. 24.73)
Jamesomyia 29.61.14
janae, Ymeldia 27.23.67
janais, Chlosyne 27.46.14
janata, Basiaeschna 7.4.3
Janbechynea 24.107.2
Janetiella 29.11.146
Janetschekbrya 1.5.5
Janssoniella 25.19.18
Janthinosoma 29.20.8
Janus 25.12.3
janus, Galerita 24.4.167 (Fig. 24.44)
Japanagromyza 29.68.2
Japanese Maple Scale 21.38.48
Japananus 21.14.90
Japanese Beetle 24.30.95
Japetus 20.9.5
japonica, Lopholeucaspis 21.38.48
japonica, Popillia 24.30.95

japonicum, Stimulopalpus 17.5.2
Japygidae, supra 3.4.1
Japyginae, supra 3.4.1
Japyx 3.4.1
jarbusalis, Synclera 27.55.147
Jasmine Sphinx 27.70.4
jasminearum, Manduca 27.70.4(Fig. 27.240)
Jassidae 21.14.1
Jassidophaga 29.48.3
Jativa 27.55.45
jatrophae, Anartia 27.46.31
jauva, Niadina 29.10.15
javalii, Pecaroecus 19.4.1
javana, Chaetexorista 29.105.278
javana, Eutrixopsis 29.105.40
Javra 25.16.136
Jaynesleskia 29.105.219
jeanae, Matrioptila 26.6.5
jeaneli, Ameroduvalius 24.4.44
Jeffrey Pine Beetle 24.112.11
jeffreyi, Dendroctonus 24.112.11
Jellisonia 30.7.5
Jenkinshelea 29.23.24
Jerusalem Cricket 11.9.3
jessopae, Hemigymnaspis 21.38.40
Jethsura 25.16.206
joanae, Papilio 27.41.5
Jocara 27.55.264
joffrei, Chaetosciara 29.10.11
johannseni, Certelion 29.9.8
Johannsenomyia 29.23.23
Johnny White-face 7.7.12
johnoni, Contarinia 29.11.108
Johnsonia 29.103.33
johnsoni, Exepacmus 29.40.37
johnsoni, Hesperodes 29.9.7
johnsoni, Mitoura 27.43.26
johnsoni, Netelia 25.16.48
johnsoni, Parantichaeta 29.79.7
johnsoni, Paroligoneurus 25.13.129
johnstoni, Plastosciara 29.10.14
johnsoni, Porsenus 29.84.1
johnsoni, Stenoxenus 29.23.30
jonesi, Bequaertomyia 29.25.2
Jonthonota 24.107.180
Joppidium 25.16.162
Joppocryptini, supra 25.16.263
jordani, Membracixenos 24.105.9
Jordanopsylla 30.4.11
Jordanopsyllini, supra 30.4.11
jorulla, Rothschildia 27.69.15
Joruma 21.14.78
Jorumini, supra 21.14.78
josephina, Ganyra 27.42.7
juanita, Proserpinus 27.70.37 (Fig. 27.259)
jucunda, Melipotis 27.75.99 (Fig. 27.330)
Judenkoa 21.19.184
Judolia, supra 24.106.172, 24.106.205
juelichi, Phegoneus 24.87.8
juglandana, Argyrotaenia 27.38.71
juglandicola, Chromaphis 21.19.52
juglandifoliella, Stigmella 27.5.1
juglandis, Acrobasis 27.55.282
juglandis, Callaphis 21.19.39
juglandis, Conotrachelus 24.113.238
juglandis, Laothoe 27.70.17 (Fig. 27.247)
juglansregiae, Quadraspidiotus 21.38.73
Jugular-horned Beetle Family, supra 24.96.1
Juice Mydas Fly 29.35.1
julii, Epomidiopteron 25.53.5
Jumping Bristletail Family 4.1.1
Jumping Bush Cricket 11.10.25
Jumping Plantlice Family, supra 21.17.1
Jumping Soil Bug Family, supra 20.25.1
Jumping Thrips Family, supra 22.2.1
juncta, Chersotis 27.75.581

juncta, Leptinotarsa 24.107.60
June Bug, supra 24.30.57
Juniper Midge 29.11.108
Juniper Scale 21.38.13
Juniper Tip Midge 29.11.160
Juniper Webworm 27.23.85
Juniperella 24.46.16
juniperina, Contarinia 29.11.108
juniperina, Trichaetipyga 21.15.30
juniperi, Carulaspis 21.38.13
juniperi, Sanbornia 21.19.188
junius, Anax 7.4.2 (Fig. 7.6)
juno, Hemileuca 27.69.7
Junonia 27.46.30
Jurinella 29.105.92
Juriniini 29.105.98
Juriniopsis 29.105.93
jurgiosus, Saxius 20.4.31
jutta, Oeneis 27.48.13
juvenalis, Erynnis 27.40.37
Juvenal's Dusky Wing 27.40.37

K

KAAD 37
kahawaluokalani, Sarucallis 21.19.189
kahli, Melanderomyia 29.45.1
kahli, Papilio 27.41.5
Kakimia 21.19.109
Kakopoda 27.75.123
Kalissus 24.24.81
kalmiae, Neoamphorophora 21.19.147
kalmiae, Sphinx 27.70.11
kalmii, Lygaeus 20.7.3 (Fig. 20.27)
Kalodiplosis 29.11.86
Kalotermes 15.2.5
Kalotermitidae, supra 15.2.1
Kaltenbachiella 21.19.110
kanawhae, Ernoporus 24.112.34
kansensis, Olenochaeta 29.105.354
Kapala 25.23.5
Kappa 25.59.29
Karner Blue Butterfly 27.43.47
Karnyothrips 22.5.44
Karpinskiella 25.19.97
Karschomyia 29.11.85
karwinskii, Smyrna 27.46.43
Katacephala 21.16.22
Kathroperla 8.8.8
Katiannina 1.7.4
Katianninae, supra 1.7.2
Katydid Family 11.7.1
Katydids 11.1.1
Kearfottia 27.10.25
keelei, Parabarrovia 27.75.564
keeni, Haida 24.24.114
keeni, Platyceropsis 24.28.6
Keiferia 27.23.52
Keirosoma 29.43.25
Keitheatus 24.107.103
Kelisia 21.2.11
kelloggi, Pteroxanium 17.1.2
kelloggi, Radicoccus 21.25.37
kelloggi, Stramenaspis 21.38.80
Kellymyia 29.103.24
Keltonia 20.23.47
kempi, Monilothrips 22.4.7
kentuckensis, Darlingtonea 24.4.43
Keonella 21.14.59
Kerita 25.7.39
Kermes 21.29.1
Kermesidea, supra 21.29.1
Keroplarinae, supra 29.9.5
Keroplatus 29.9.11
Kerriidae, supra 21.32.1

kerrivillensis, Lutzomips 29.19.4
Keyhole Wasp 25.59.19
keys, use of 6
key to orders 53
Khapra Beetle 24.61.13
Kiawe Bean Weevil 24.108.11
Kiawe Flower Moth 27.21.25
kiefferi, Parochlus 29.24.1
Kiefferiella 25.30.2
Kiefferulus 29.24.53
Kilifia 21.26.8
killing 36
Kimminsia 23.8.2
kingi, Satyrium 27.43.16
Kinnarid Planthopper Family, supra 21.10.1
Kinnaridae, supra 21.10.1
Kinonia 21.14.170
kirbyi, Otiocerus 21.9.12
kirkaldyi, Dialeurodes 21.18.14
Kirkaldy's Whitefly 21.18.14
Kirzousacorixa 20.35.7
Kissing Bug 20.17.29
Klamathweed Beetle 24.107.63
Kleidocerys 20.7.13
Kleidotoma 25.32.1
Kleidotomidea 25.32.1
Klopicoris 20.23.162
knabi, Cryphalomorphus 24.112.36
knausi, Saxinis 24.107.21
Knaus'' Saxinis 24.107.21
knighti, Calotingis 20.14.5
Knowltonella 1.2.4
knowltoni, Tullbergia 1.3.4
Knullana 21.14.104
Knulliana 24.106.150
knulli, Pseudothalycra 24.70.24
knulli, Trichinorhipis 24.46.19
kodiak, Coenonympha 27.48.8
Kodiosoma 27.73.51
koebelei, Novius 24.80.34
koebelei, Thysanomastix 25.25.159
Koebelia 21.14.32
Koebeliinae, supra 21.14.32
Koebeliini, supra 21.14.32
koenigi, Blacus 25.13.130
Kogotus 8.7.13
Kolenetrus 20.7.44
kollarii, Centrocorisa 20.35.12
Kompia 29.20.9
Kondo Ground Mealybug 21.25.38
kondonis, Rhizoecus 21.25.38
Kormus 21.2.21
Korynetinae, supra 24.67.24
Korynetini, supra 24.67.29
kosztarabi, Torovothrips 22.5.72
Krenopelopia 29.24.28
Krenosmittia 29.24.131
Kricogonia 27.42.16
kriemhild, Clossiana 27.46.11
krombeini, Ephuta 25.55.20
Krombeinia 25.53.2
Krombeiniellum 25.62.50
Kronomyia 29.11.32
Kronaea 27.52.4
kuehniella, Anagasta 27.55.401
Kulcania 25.11.3
Kunzeana 21.14.73
Kurodaia 18.6.21
Kurtomathrips 22.4.27
Kuschelina 24.107.150
Kuwanaspis 21.38.43
Kuwania 21.23.5
Kuwaniini, supra 21.32.4
Kuwayama 21.17.12
Kybos 21.14.77
Kytorhininae, supra 24.108.4

Kytorhinus 24.108.4

L

labeculata, Lophosis 27.61.189
labeling 40
Labena 25.16.44
Labeninae, supra 25.16.44
Labenini, supra 25.16.44
Labia 13.3.4
Labidomera 24.107.61
Labidura 13.2.1
Labiduridae, supra 13.2.1
Labidus 25.58.1
Labiidae, supra 13.3.1
Labiinae, supra 13.3.4
Labiotipula 29.2.9
labium 20
Labopella 20.23.134
Labopidea 20.23.108
Labopidicola 20.23.109
Labopini, supra 20.23.134
Labops 20.23.135
Laboratory Fruit Fly 29.90.9
Labostigmina 29.31.41
Labroctonus 25.16.57
labrum 20
Labrundinia 29.24.31
labruscae, Eumorpha 27.70.31 (Fig. 27.255)
Lac Insect 21.32.1
Lac Scale Insect Family supra 21.32.1
Lacanobia 27.75.482
lacca, Laccifer 21.32.1
Laccifer 21.32.1
Lacciferidae, supra 21.32.1
Laccobius 24.12.13
Laccocera 21.2.6
Laccodytes 24.7.2
Lacconotinae, supra 24.90.13
Lacconotus 24.90.13 QWL Laccophilinae, supra 24.7.1
Laccophilini, supra 24.7.1
Laccophilus 24.7.1
Laccornis 24.7.20
Lace Bug Family 20.14.1
Lacewings 23.1.1
Lachesilla 17.14.1
Lachesillidae, supra 17.14.1
Lachlania 6.5.1 (Fig. 6.4)
lachni, Euneura 25.19.67
Lachnochaitophorus 21.19.111
Lachnodactyla 24.38.1
Lachnophorus 24.4.80
Lachnopus 24.113.33
Lachnus 21.19.112
lacinia, Chlosyne 27.46.14
laciniatus, Adasytes 24.68.45
Lacinipolia 27.75.494
Lacon 24.49.1
Lacosoma 27.65.1
lactea, Grotellaforma 27.75.191
lacteicollis, Hohonus 24.113.270
lacteipennis, Diclasiopa 29.93.15
lacteipes, Tipula 29.2.9
lacteolaria, Leuculodes 27.73.6
Lactista 11.5.51
lactucae, Nasonovia 21.19.145
Lactura 27.30.3
lacustris, Brachycercus 6.16.1
lacustris, Phantolabis 29.2.53
lacustris, Platpatrobus 24.4.71
ladon, Celastrina 27.43.42
Ladona 7.7.10
Ladybird Beetle Family, supra 24.80.1
Laelius 25.48.11

Laemobothriidae, supra 18.5.1
Laemobothrion 18.5.1
Laemophloeus 24.72.141
Laemosaccini, supra 24.113.199
Laemosaccus 24.113.199
laeta, Erora 27.43.35
Laetilia 27.55.374
laetula, Nyctiphanta 27.61.109
Laetulonthus 24.24.8
laetulus, Lactulonthus 24.24.8
laetus, Pachyopsis 21.14.30
laeve, Liodema 24.87.100
laeve, Pison 25.62.50
Laevicephalus 21.14.189
laevicollis, Cyphonotida 24.106.217
laevicollis, Drastophus 24.20.5
laevicollis, Lophomucter 24.24.262
laevicsutum, Zygosis 25.31.17
laevigata, Encrateola 25.16.86
laevigata, Gromphadorhina,
 infra 14.6.7 (Figs. 14.21, 14.22)
laevigatus, Alphitobius 24.87.115
laevigatus, Pachyschelus 24.46.36 (Fig.
 24.,92)
laevisculus, Parathriphleps 20.21.9
laeviscutatus, Rhasis 20.23.184
laevissimus, Iphthiminus 24.87.84
laevis, Aglyptinus 24.19.12
laevis, Cyanopterus 25.13.33
laevis, Merinus 24.87.85
laevis, Octotemnus 24.92.13
laevis, Pachyplectrus 24.30.37
laevis, Xesturida 24.24.314
lagacei, Megourina 21.19.126
Lagium 25.7.92
Lagriidae, supra 24.89.1
Lagriinae, supra 24.89.2
Lagoa 27.51.2
Lagocheirus 24.106.275
Lagoleptus 25.16.63
Lagonis 25.7.61
Lagopoecus 18.1.34
laguna, Entomobrya 1.5.3
Lagynodes 25.46.6
Lagynodinae, supra 25.46.6
laingi, Margarodes 21.23.6
lais, Apanisagrion 7.11.3
Lalapa 25.53.8
Lamachus 25.16.351
Lambdina 27.61.130
Lambersius 21.19.219
Lamellicorn Beetle Family, supra 24.30.1
Lamiinae, supra 24.106.228
Laminomada 25.69.10
Lampethusa 20.23.163
Lampidini, supra 27.43.37
lampra, Cinderella 29.78.3
Lampracanthia 20.32.5
Lampria 29.37.59
Lamprocerini, supra 24.55.5
Lamprochromus 29.43.51
Lamproclasiopa 29.93.12
Lamprolophus 27.34.3
Lampronia 27.8.2
Lampropterus 24.106.88
Lamprorhiza 24.55.10
Lamproscatella 29.93.60
Lamprosema 27.55.107
Lamprosoma 24.107.37
Lamprosomatinae, supra 24.107.36
Lamprotatus 25.19.51
Lampyridae, supra 24.55.1
Lampyrinae, supra 24.55.1
Lampyrini, supra 24.55.1
Lampyris 24.55.1
lanata, Chalicodoma 25.68.23

lanceolata, Falcapica 27.42.10
Landisaphis 21.19.113
lanei, Echinohelea 29.23.14
Lanelater 24.48.6
Langessa 27.55.13
longimana, Didactylomyia 29.11.50
Languria 24.75.6
Languriidae, suprra 24.75.1
Languriinae, supra 24.75.6
Languriini, supra 24.75.6
Langurites 24.75.8
lanieri, Arrhipis 24.52.10
lanifer, Triodoclytus 24.106.119
lanigera, Cotalpa 24.30.87
lanigerum, Eriosoma 21.19.74
Laniifera 27.55.160
lanoraieensis, Incisalia 27.43.29
Lantana Lace Bug 20.14.21
Lantanta Leaf Beetle 24.107.168
Lantana Plume Moth 27.58.12
Lantana Seed Fly 29.68.4
lantanae, Ophiomyia 29.68.4
Lantanophaga 27.58.12
Lantern Click Beetle 24.48.11
Lanternarius 24.42.4
Lanternfly, supra 21.1.1
Lanthus 7.3.7
lanuginosa, Triglypbothrix 25.58.41
Lanugo 25.16.164
Laothoe 27.70.17
Lapara 27.70.12
Lapara, supra 27.70.1
lapathi, Crytorhynchus 24.113.264
Lapazia 21.38.44
lapena heteropuncta, ·
 Megalopyge 27.51.3 (Fig. 27.158)
Lapethus 24.78.8
Laphria 29.37.60
Laphriini, supra 29.37.58
Laphystia 29.37.22
Laphystiini, supra 29.37.22
lapisligni, Aphelinus 25.25.1
Lappet Moth 27.68.6
Lappet Moth Family, supra 27.68.1
lapponica, Oligotricha 26.8.7
lapponica, Pararctia 27.73.49
lapponica, Silpha 24.21.7
lapponicus, Ectobius 14.5.12
Lapposyrphus 29.47.14
Laprobia 13.3.3
Lapsus 24.42.9
laqueata, Calidot 27.73.61
Lara 24.45.1
Larandrena 25.65.1
Larch Aphid 21.19.53
Larch Casebearer 27.18.1
Larch Sawfly 25.7.30
lardarius, Dermestes 24.61.1 (Fig. 24.114)
Larder Beetle 24.61.1
Larentiinae, supra 27.61.190
lareyniei, Microlarinus 24.113.151
largalis, Plumegesta 27.55.64
Large Aspen Tortrix 27.38.72
Large Brown Skippers 27.40.1
Large Canna Leafroller 27.40.83
Large Chicken Louse 18.1.28
Large Duck Louse 18.6.35
Large-headed Grasshopper 11.5.102
Large Hickory Lecanium 21.26.6
Large Kissing Bug 20.17.39
Large Maple Spanworm 27.61.149
Large Sand Cricket 11.6.1
Large Squaregill Mayfly Family 6.15.1
Large Turkey Louse 18.1.10
Larfer Black Flour Beetle 24.87.107
Larger Brown Bush Cricket 11.10.24

Larger Cabinet Beetle 24.61.13
Larger Chestnut Weevil 24.113.200
Larger Elm Leaf Beetle 24.107.74
Larger Grain Borer 24.64.7
Larger Lantana Butterfly 27.43.19
Larger Pale Booklouse 17.2.4
Larger Shot-hole Borer 24.112.23
Larger Yellow Ant 25.58.68
Largidae, supra 20.9.1
Largidea 20.23.11
Larginae, supra 20.9.1
Largus 20.9.1
laricella, Coleophora, 27.18.1
laricis, Cinara 21.19.53
Laricobius 24.59.1
larifuga, Sierola 25.48.19
Larinae, supra 24.45.1
Lariophagus 25.19.124
Larisa 27.38.50
Larisia 24.98.50
Lariversius 24.87.145
Larochrysis 25.50.18
Larra 25.62.37
larreae, Clematodes 11.5.78
larreae, Pseudodiaspis 21.38.71
larreae, Xeromelecta 25.69.39
Larrid Wasp 25.62.37
Larrinae, supra 25.62.37
Larrini, supra 25.62.37
Larropsis 25.62.39
Larsia 29.24.24
larva 13
Lasaia 27.44.4
Lascelina 27.55.389
lasciva, Hylemyza 29.99.8
Lasconotus 24.93.16
Lascoria 27.75.15
Lasia 29.38.1
Lasiestra 27.75.492
Lasiini, supra 25.58.67
Lasiocampidae, supra 27.68.1
Lasiocampinae 27.68.7
Lasiochilinae, supra 20.21.12
Lasiochiloides 20.21.19
Lasiochilus 20.21.13
Lasioderma 24.63.38
Lasiodiamesa 29.24.2
Lasioglossum 25.66.16
Lasiohelea 29.23.3
Lasiomastix 29.2.34
Lasiomerus 20.18.8
Lasiomma 29.99.8
Lasionalia 29.105.183
Lasioneura 29.105.298
Lasionycta 27.75.493
lasiophthalma, Hybomitra 29.26.23
Lasiopiophila 29.64.1
Lasiopleura 29.94.1
Lasiopogon 29.37.14
Lasiops 29.100.40
Lasioptera 29.11.60
Lasiopterini, supra 29.11.58
Lasioscelus 29.98.110
Lasiosina 29.94.44
Lasius 25.58.67
Laspeyresiini, supra 27.38.44
Latalus 21.14.198
Latania Scale 21.38.39
lataniae, Hemiberlesia 21.38.39
Latebraria 27.75.110
lateralis, Darnis 21.15.18
lateralis, Elasmucha 20.3.62
lateralis, Lycochoriolaus 24.106.202
lateralis, Stenelmis 24.45.24 (Fig. 24.84)
latercula, Tetraclonia 27.50.5
Latheticomyia 29.50.1

Latheticus 24.87.108
Lathosea 27.75.462
Lathridiidae, supra 24.82.1
Lathridiinae, supra 24.82.1
lathridiodes, Myrmechixenus 24.93.29
Lathridius 24.82.3
Lathriopyga 1.2.16
Lathrobium 24.24.56
Lathrolestes 25.16.343
Lathromeroidea 25.28.16
Lathropinus 24.24.78
Lathropus 24.72.18
Lathrostizus 25.16.421
lathyri, Protolithocolletis 27.14.17
Latiblattella 14.5.11
laticauda, Steneretma 29.58.34
laticaudus, Ulosomus 24.113.261
laticephalus, Beckocoris 20.23.36
laticeps, Gnypetella 24.24.245
laticeps, Omoschema 24.24.274
laticinerea, Lithophane 27.75.392
laticlavia, Anomoea 24.107.23
laticollis, Prionus 24.106.10
laticollis, Stetoliodes 24.19.11
laticornella, Coleophora 27.18.1
laticornis, Chondrocera 20.4.3
laticornis, Neichnea 24.67.23
latifereanus, Melissopus 27.38.57
latiferrugata, Eumecaria 27.61.8
latifrons, Apheloglutus 29.105.315
latifrons, Dasyopa 29.94.24
latilobus, Silis 24.56.11 (Fig. 24.110)
latimanus, Ephalus 24.87.163
latior, Aulacros 25.53.18
latipalpis, Hormoschista 27.75.49
latipennis, Ceratocombus 20.24.1
latipennis, Geodercodes 24.113.82
latipennis, Gnophaela 27.73.1 (Fig. 27.279)
latipennis, Steganolauxania 29.82.18
latipennis, Zaga 25.28.14
latipes, Gongrodiplosis 29.11.141
latisulcata, Osmia 25.68.21
latitarsus, Croesus 25.7.31
latiusculus, Ceroxys 29.58.3
lativentris, Rhaebothrips 22.5.20
lativentris, Stratiomys 29.31.39 (Fig. 29.30)
lativentris, Symbiochara 24.24.296
lativittella, Valdivia 27.55.357
latreillii, Mesembrina 29.100.49
Latrine Fly 29.100.26
latus, Euthiodes 24.20.15
latus, Pelatines 24.21.3
laurae, Doxocopa 27.47.4
Laurel Sphinx 27.70.11
laurentina, Baetisca 6.17.1 (Figs. 6.3, 6.12
lausus, Acaenacis 25.19.76
Lauterbornia 29.24.80
Lauterborniella 29.24.64
lautus, Symmerus 29.9.4
Lauxania 29.82.5
Lauxaniella 29.82.6
Lauxaniid Fly Family, supra 29.82.1
Lauxaniidae, supra 29.82.1
Lauxanioidea, supra 29.82.1
Laverna 27.19.1
lavoiei, Diaglyptidea 25.16.92
Lawn Armyworm 27.75.326
lawrensis, Numidilipeurus 18.1.40
lazulellus, Pseudotorymus 25.18.19
Lea 11.7.14
Lead Cable Borer 24.64.19
Leaf Beetle Family, supra 24.107.1
Leaf Blotch Miner Moth Family, supra 27.14.1

Leaf Crumpler 27.55.282
Leaf Litter Barklice Family 17.17.1
Leaf Miner Fly Family, supra 29.68.1
Leaf-cutting Bee 25.68.22
Leaf-cutting Bee Family, supra 25.68.1
Leaf-footed Bug 20.4.2
Leafhopper, supra 21.1.1
Leafhopper Assassin Bug 20.17.22
Leafhopper Family, supra 21.14.1
Leaf-rolling Crickets 11.9.1
Leaf-rolling Sawfly Family, supra 25.2.1
leanira, Thessalia 27.46.13
Least Sipper 27.40.56
leatherjackets, supra 29.2.1
Lebasiella 24.67.29
Lebia 24.4.159
Lebiini, supra 24.4.141
Lebiitae, supra 24.4.137
Lecalida 24.4.149
Lecaniobius 25.24.13
Lecanocerus 29.46.38
Lecanodiaspididae, supra 21.33.1
Lecanodiaspis 21.33.1
Lechriopini, supra 24.113.276
Lechriops 24.113.276
Lecithocerinae, supra 27.23.91
lecontei, Amphizoa 24.5.1 (Fig. 24.45)
lecontei, Chelonarium 24.41.1
lecontei, Enoclerus 24.67.16
lecontei, Eusomalia 24.35.5
lecontei, Glyptobaris 24.113.319
lecontei, Haploa 27.73.28 (Fig. 27.282)
lecontei, Neodiprion 25.6.4
lecontei, Procas 24.113.176
lecontei, Ptinellodes 24.15.15
lecontei, Scaptolenus 24.47.3
lecontei, Stenolophus 24.4.114
Lecontella 24.67.7
Lecontia 24.90.4
lectularius, Cimex 20.20.2 (Fig. 20.48)
leda, Ministrymon 27.43.18
Ledaea 27.75.52
Ledaria 24.98.16
Lednia 8.1.3
Ledomyia 29.11.145
Ledomyini, supra 29.11.145
Ledrinae, supra 21.14.1
leechi, Ecbletus 24.24.172
Leek Moth 27.33.1
Legionary Ant 25.58.3
legitima, Trichordestra 27.75.483, in Lacanobia in "Checklist-."
legs 22
leguminicola, Dasineura 29.11.152
Leia 29.9.78
leibyi, Schizocerophaga 29.105.262
Leichenum 24.87.167
leila, Asterocampa 27.47.3
Leioblacus 25.13.130
Leiocleptes 25.50.1
Leiodes 24.19.3
Leiodidae, supra 24.19.1
Leiolinus 24.24.34
Leiomyrmosa 25.55.4
Leiomyza 29.73.1
Leiophron 25.13.153
Leioscyta 21.15.6
Leipaulus 25.16.502
leiroides, Harpalobrachys 24.4.123
Leistus 24.4.8
Lejota 29.47.62
Leluthia 25.13.15
Lema 24.107.13
lemberti, Callophrys 27.43.24
lembertii, Hepialus 27.4.2
Lembert's Ghost Moth 27.4.2

Lembodes 24.113.247
Lemelba 24.25.44
Lemellus 21.14.190
lemmae, Tanysphyrus 24.113.179
Lemmeria 27.75.262
Lemnaphila 29.93.35
lemniscata, Hippopsis 24.106.261
Lemophagus 25.16.423
lenae, Bembidion 24.4.67
Lenarchus 26.10.19
Lendomini, supra 24.21.10
Lendomus 24.21.10
lengi, pseudoperiboeum 24.106.58
lengi, Scaphinotus 24.4.16 (Fig. 24.33)
lentus, Derovatellus 24.7.3
Lenziella 29.24.75
leodocusalis, Diasemiopsis 27.55.136
leoninus, Ulochaetes 24.106.171
Leopard Moth 27.37.11
Lepania 26.10.47
leperii, Epidiaspis 21.38.28
Leperisinus 24.112.13
Lepesoma 24.113.125
lepida, Heterosceloides 20.3.65
Lepidanthrax 29.40.52
Lepidobregma 27.10.16
Lepidocnemoplatia 24.87.159
Lepidocyrtus 1.5.8
Lepidomyia 29.47.55
Lepidomys 27.55.244
Lepidophora 29.40.4
Lepidophorus 24.113.116
Lepidopria 25.42.33
Lepidopsallus 20.23.48
Lepidopsocidae, supra 17.1.1
Lepidopsocinae, supra 17.1.1
Lepidoptera, supra 27.1.1
Lepidosaphes 21.38.45
Lepidostoma 26.11.1
Lepidostomatidae, supra 26.11.1
Lepidotrichidae, supra 5.1.1
Lepinotus 17.2.2
Lepipolys 27.75.452
Lepisma 5.3.4
Lepismatidae, supra 5.3.1
Lepolepidinae, supra 17.1.3
Lepolepis 17.1.3
Leprus 11.5.45
Leptacinus 24.24.35
Leptacis 25.44.19
Leptalia 24.106.188
Leptanthicus 24.102.5
Leptarctia 27.73.30
Lepthohypes 6.14.2
Lepthemis 7.7.11
Leptiinae, supra 24.113.109
Leptinidae, supra 24.18.1
Leptinillus 24.18.2
Leptinotarsa 24.107.60
Leptinus 24.18.1
Leptipsius 24.71.5
Leptobamona 24.24.259
Leptocampoplex 25.16.400
Leptocera 29.88.3
Leptoceridae, supra 26.18.1
Leptocerinae, supra 26.18.1
Leptocerus 26.18.2
Leptochiloides 25.59.5
Leptochilus 25.59.8
Leptociecini, supra 27.41.4
Leptocoenia 29.93.58
Leptoconopinae, supra 29.23.1
Leptoconops 29.23.1
Leptocoris 20.6.8
Leptocorisinae, supra 20.5.5
Leptodictya 20.14.13

Leptodiridae, supra 24.22.1
Leptogaster 29.37.2
Leptogastrinae, supra 29.37.1
Leptogenys 25.58.18
Leptoglossus 20.4.4
Leptolarra 25.62.38
Leptomastidea 25.25.28
Leptomastix 25.25.29
Leptometopa 29.74.7
Leptomorphus 29.9.62
Leptomydinae, supra 29.35.6
Leptopeza 29.42.51
Leptopharsa 20.14.14
Leptophlebia 6.7.5
Leptophlebiidae, supra 6.7.1
Leptophlebioidea, supra 6.7.1
Leptophloeus 24.72.16
Leptophoplia 24.30.94
Leptophylax 26.10.20
Leptopiini, supra 24.113.112
Leptoplectus 24.25.32
Leptopodidae, supra 20.31.1
Leptopsilopa 29.93.23
Leptopsylla 30.6.2
Leptopsyllidae, supra 30.6.1
Leptopsyllinae, supra 30.6.1
Leptopsyllini, supra 30.6.1
Leptopterna 20.23.17
Leptorachis 25.68.22
Leptoremus 24.103.7
Leptorhabdium 24.106.173
Leptormenis 21.8.2
leptosceles, Diataga 27.10.22
Leptoscelini, supra 20.4.6
Leptoschema 24.48.19
Leptoscydmini, supra 24.20.17
Leptoscydmus 24.20.17
Leptostales 27.61.188
Leptostilbus 24.77.9
Leptostylopsis 24.106.281
Leptostylus 24.106.280
Leptotarsus 29.2.1
Leptoteleia 25.43.12
Leptotes 27.43.38
Leptothoracini, supra 25.58.35
Leptothorax 25.58.37
Leptothrips 22.5.44
Leptotrachelus 24.4.136
Leptotyphlinae, supra 24.24.164
Leptovectura 24.68.25
Leptoypha 20.14.15
Leptura 24.106.212
Lepturges 24.106.290
Lepturinae, supra 24.106.169
Lepturini, supra 24.106.172
lepturoides, Agallisus 24.106.136
Lepturoidini 24.48.27
Lepturopsis 24.106.222
Leptysma 11.5.73
lepusculina, Acronicta 27.75.231 (Fig.
 27.350)
Lepyrini, supra 24.113.148
Lepyronia 21.12.3
Lepyroniini, supra 21.12.3
Lepyrus 24.113.148
Lerema 27.40.51
Lerina 27.73.68
Lerodea 27.40.81
Leschenaultia 29.105.368
Leskiella 29.105.220
Leskiini, supra 29.105.216
Leskiomima 29.105.221
Leskiopsis 29.105.25
Lesomene 27.75.114
Lespedeza Webworm 27.55.268
Lespesia 29.105.420

Lesser Appleworm 27.38.53
Lesser Bulb Fly 29.47.57
Lesser Bud Moth 27.23.18
Lesser Canna Leaf Roller 27.55.119
Lesser Clover Leaf Weevil 24.113.146
Lesser Cornstalk Borer 27.55.346
Lesser Grain Borer 24.64.6
Lesser Grapevine Looper 27.61.191
Lesser Lawn Leafhopper 21.14.220
Lesser Mealworm 24.87.115
Lesser Orchid Weevil 24.113.322
Lesser Peach Tree Borer 27.35.12
Lesser Snow Scale 21.38.64
Lesser Water Weevil 24.113.183
Lesser Wax Moth 27.55.271
lesteraria, Lophochorista 27.61.164
Lestes 7.9.2
Lesteva 24.24.116
Lestica 25.62.68
Lestidae, supra 7.9.1
Lestiphorus 25.62.87
Lestodiplosis 29.11.132
Lestomyia 29.37.3
Lestremia 29.11.18
Lestremiinae, supra 29.11.1
Lestremiini, supra 29.11.12
Lethades 25.16.326
Lethaeini, supra 20.7.28
Lethe 27.48.1, 27.48.2
lethe, Hypanbartia 27.46.28
Lethemurus 1.5.3
Lethocerinae, supra 20.37.1
Lethocerus 20.37.1
Lettuce Root Aphid 21.19.162
Leucandrena 25.65.1
Leucania 27.75.500
Leucanopsis 27.73.57
Leucanthiza 27.14.15
Leucaspis 21.38.46
leucillana, Antaeotricha 27.15.17 (Fig.
 27.36)
leucitys, Symmerista 27.71.17
Leucobrephos 27.61.2
Leucochlaena 27.75.327
Leucochroma 27.55.152
Leucochrysa 23.9.2
Leucocnemis 27.75.444
Leucogoniella 27.23.24
leucogramma, Tetraschistis 27.55.247
Leucolepisma 5.3.5
Leucoma 27.74.5
Leucomele 27.10.7
Leuconycta 27.75.201
Leucopelmonus 25.7.89
leucopeza, Aulacigaster 29.71.1
leucopeza, Monohelea 29.23.15
Leucophaea 14.6.6
Leucophenga 29.90.3
Leucophora 29.99.21
Leucophrus 25.60.12
leucophthalmus, Philaenus 21.12.4
Leucopini, supra 29.83.8
Leucopis 29.83.9
Leucopodella 29.47.7
Leucopomyia 29.83.9
leucoprocata, Bithoracochaeta 29.100.3
Leucoptera 27.13.10
leucoptera, Dichaetoneura 29.105.316
leucopterus hirtus, Blissus 20.7.16
leucopterus leucopterus,
 Blissus 20.7.16 (Fig. 20.29)
Leucorrhinia 7.7.12
Leucospid Wasp Family, supra 25.21.1
Leucospidae, supra 25.22.1
Leucospilapteryx 27.14.13
Leucospis 25.22.1

leucosticta, Psilocnemis 24.30.133
leucostigma, Orgyia 27.74.3
leucostigma, Papaipema 27.75.279
Leucostoma 29.105.31
Leucostomatini, supra 29.105.29
Leucotabanius 29.26.18
Leucotrichia 26.7.11
Leucotrichiini, supra 26.7.10
Leucothrips 22.4.10
Leucozona 29.47.18
Leuctra 8.4.2
Leuctridae, supra 8.4.1
Leuctrinae, supra 8.4.1
Leuculodes 27.73.6
Leurolestes 14.6.3
Leuronota 21.17.15
Leurus 25.16.294
Levidea 21.17.18
levis, Metadoria 29.105.252
Lexiphanes 24.107.24
Liancalus 29.43.16
Liaphlus 24.6.1
libatrix, Scoliopteryx 27.75.73 (Fig.
 27.328)
Libellula 7.7.13
Libellulidae, supra 7.7.1
liberta, Diplotaxis 24.30.63
libocedrii, Syntexis 25.8.1
libraries, entomological 51
librinocens, Falsogastrallus 24.63.20
Liburnia 21.2.25
Liburniella 21.2.4
Libytheana 27.45.1
Libytheidae, supra 27.45.1
Lichenomima 17.24.1
Lichenophanes 24.64.14
Lichminus 24.43.1
Lichnanthe 24.30.42
Lichnoptera 27.75.227
Lichtenisa 21.26.9
Licinini, supra 24.4.104
Licinus 24.4.106
Lidopus 20.23.3
ligata, Chlorochroa 20.3.29
ligatus, Halictus 25.66.15
Light Fly Family, supra 29.60.1
light production 25
lignaris lignaria, Osmia 25.68.21
ligneus, Semanotus 24.106.104
lignicola, Curtisella 25.13.6
lignicolorella, Tanygona 27.21.5
ligniperdalis, Salole 27.55.252
lignosellus, Elasmopalpus 27.55.346
Lignyodes 24.113.225
Lignyodini, supra 24.113.223
ligulella, Dichmomeris 27.23.85
ligustici, Otriorhynchus 24.113.68
ligustri, Myzus 21.19.144
ligustri, Ochyromera 24.113.222
Ligyra 29.40.45
Ligyrocoris 20.7.55
Lilac Borer 27.35.12
Lilac Leaf Miner 27.14.1
lilaea, Eucalliphora 29.101.14
lilii, Lilioceris 24.107.12
lilii, Macrosiphum 21.19.122
Lilioceris 24.107.12
Lily Bulb Thrips 22.5.49
Lily Weevil 24.113.101
Lima-bean Pod Borer 27.55.311
Lima-bean Vine Borer 27.55.306
Limacodes 27.52.8
Limacodidae, supra 27.52.1
limata, Pantographa 27.55.165
limata, Zizyphomyia 29.105.384
Limbanus 21.14.122

limbata, Centris 25.69.42
limbata, Hexagenia 6.11.2 (Fig. 6.1)
limbatus, Bovicola 18.2.1
limbatus, Gyrinus 24.9.2
limbatus, Opomydas 29.35.1
limboundata, Scopula 27.61.187 (Fig. 27.197)
limenia, Strymon 27.43.34
Limenitidinae, supra 27.46.33
Limenitidini, supra 27.46.33
Limenitis 27.46.33
limenitis, Pherbecta 29.79.15
Limerodops 25.16.227
liminaris, Phloeotribus 24.112.15
limitata, Pandemis 27.38.70
Limnaecia 27.21.10
Limnebiidae, supra 24.13.1
Limnebius 24.13.3
Limnellia 29.93.62
Limnephilidae, supra 26.10.1
Limnephilini, supra 26.11.1
Limnephiloidea, supra 26.8.1
Limnephilus 26.10.21
Limnia 29.79.14
Limnichidae, supra 24.43.1
Limnichinae, supra 24.43.1
Limnichini, supra 24.43.1
Limnichites 24.43.1
Limnichoderus 24.43.4
Limnocorinae, supra 20.38.1
Limnocoris 20.38.2
Limnogonus 20.27.1
Limnophila 29.2.34
Limnophora 29.100.16
Limnophorinae, supra 29.100.12
Limnoporus 20.27.4
Limnophyes 29.24.118
Limnospila 29.100.8
Limonethe 25.16.220
Limonia 29.2.14
Limoniinae, supra 29.2.14
Limoniini, supra 29.2.14
Limonius 24.48.27
Limosia 29.100.2
Limosina 29.88.3
Limotettix 21.14.164
Limothrips 22.4.18
Limulodes 24.16.1
Limulodidae, supra 24.16.1
Linden Borer 24.106.296
Linden Looper 27.61.64
Lindenius 25.62.59
Lindera 27.10.48
Lindingaspis 21.38.47
Lindneria 29.2.9
Lindorus 24.80.29
lindsleyi, Asmeringa 29.93.45
lindseyi, Coloradia 27.69.6
lineafrons, Trachyopella 29.88.3
lineana, Tsinilla 27.38.17
linearis, Dolichomiris 20.23.196
linearis, Scalidia 24.72.10
linearis, Sitophilus 24.113.365
linearis, Trichocanonura 24.106.271
linearis, Zelicodes 27.75.22
Linear-winged Grasshopper 11.5.104
lineata, Ctenolepisma 5.3.3
lineata, Hyles 27.70.42 (Fig. 27.267)
lineata, Latheticomyia 29.50.1
lineata, Levidea 21.17.18
lineata, Sitona 24.113.50
lineatella, Anarsia 27.23.77
lineaticeps, Mirzagrammosoma 25.26.31
lineaticolis, Acolobius 24.93.8
lineatipes, Paltothemis 7.7.21
lineatum, Micridium 24.15.9

lineatum, Trypodendron 24.112.53
lineatus, Agriotes 24.48.40
lineatus, Anchorius 24.83.1
lineatus, Hypoderma 29.102.5
lineatus, Langurites 24.75.8
lineatus, Philaenus 21.12.4
lineatus, Playstoechotes 23.12.2
lineatus, Poecilocapsus 20.23.180 (Fig. 20.55)
Lined Acrobatic Ant 25.58.30 (Fig. 25.35)
Lined Click Beetle 24.48.40
Lined Spittle Bug 21.12.4
Lined Stalk Borer Moth 27.75.258
lineloa, Tabanus 29.26.26
Lineodes 27.55.108
lineola, Analeptura 24.106.199
lineola, Colydium 24.93.18
lineola, Thymelicus 27.40.60
lineolaris, Lygus 20.23.166
lineolata, Crematogaster 25.58.30 (Fig. 25.35)
lineolata, Rhyssa 25.16.40
lineolatus, Adelphocoris 20.23.139
Lineomyzocallis 21.19.142
Lineostethus 20.3.22
Linnaemya 29.105.108
Linnaemyini, supra 29.105.103
linneella, Glyphipteryx 27.20.2 (Fig. 27.38)
Linognathidae, supra 19.2.1
Linognathus 19.2.1
Linosiphon 21.19.114
Linsleya 24.101.15
linsleyi, Simanthedon 25.69.33
linteus, Ampedus 24.48.25 (Fig. 24.99)
lintneri, Ommatostola 27.75.256
Linycus 25.16.274
Liobracon 25.13.16
Liochrysops 29.26.11
Liodema 24.87.100
Liodessus 24.7.10
Liodontomerus 25.18.11
Liodora 25.34.25
Liogma 29.2.12
Liohippelates, supra 29.94.1
Liohippelats 29.94.2
Lioligus 24.35.10
Liometophilus 24.113.259
liometopi, Dinardilla 24.24.226
Liometopum 25.58.57
Lion Beetle 24.106.171
Lionothus 24.19.13
Lioon 24.35.11
Lioonini, supra 24.35.10
Lioon 24.35.11
Liopasia 27.55.162
Liophloeus 24.113.42
Liopiophila 29.64.1
Liopterid Wasp Family, supra 25.30.1
Liopteridae, supra 25.30.1
Liopterna 25.16.379
Lioptilodes 27.58.13
Liorhyssus 20.6.3
Liosomaphis 21.19.115
Liosphex 25.61.3
Liothrips 22.5.49
Liotryphon 25.16.5
Lipamyzodes 21.19.116
Lipaphis 21.19.117
Lipara 29.94.30
Liparocephalus 24.24.260
liparops, Satyrium 27.43.16
Liparthrum 24.112.18
Lipeurus 18.1.35
Lipochaeta 29.93.44
Lipochaetini, supra 29.93.44

Lipocosma 27.55.65
Lipocosmodes 27.55.66
Lipographis 27.55.343
Lipoleucopis 29.83.8
Lipophleps 29.2.47
Lipoptena 29.106.11
Lipoptenella 29.106.11
Lipoptenini, supra 29.106.10
Liposcelidae, supra 17.6.1
Liposcelinae, supra 17.6.1
Liposcelis 17.6.3
Liposthenes 25.34.12
Lipsothrix 29.2.50
liquida, Gonodes 27.75.330
Lirimiris 27.71.38
liriodendri, Macrosiphum 21.19.122
liriodendri, Toumeyella 21.26.22 (Fig. 21.30)
Liriomyza 29.68.8
Liris 25.62.38
lisa, Pyrisitia 27.42.18 (Fig. 27.101)
Lispe 29.100.11
Lispideosoma 29.105.305
Lispinae, supra 29.100.11
Lispininae, supra 24.24.91
Lispinus 24.24.93
Lispocephala 29.100.9
Lispoides 29.100.12
Lispothrips 22.5.50
Lissobiops 24.24.57
Lissohypnus 24.24.36
Lissomelas 24.30.132
Lissominae, supra 24.49.1
Lissonota 25.16.308
Lissonotanini, supra 25.16.307
Lissonotini, supra 24.106.167
Lissonotus 24.106.167
Lissorhopturus 24.113.183
Lissoscambus 25.16.2
Lissothrips 22.5.51
Listemus 24.35.4
Listrimorpha 24.68.44
Listroderes 24.113.142
Listrodromina, supra 25.16.267
Listrodromini, supra 25.16.267
Listrognathus 25.16.177
listromimus 24.68.43
Listronotus 24.113.143
Listropsis 24.68.47
Listropygia 25.62.110
Listroscelinae 11.7.24
Lita 27.23.34
Litaneutria 14.1.3
Litargus 24.91.3
Litasida 24.87.58
Lithacodes 27.52.7
Lithacodia 27.75.194
Litharissapteryx 27.34.6
Litheleodes 24.87.140
lithella, Lamprolophus 27.34.3
Lithinini, supra 27.61.104
lithocharinus, Teropalpus 24.24.156
Lithocharis 24.24.58
Lithocharodes 24.24.37
Lithocolletinae, supra 27.14.17
Litholomia 27.75.391
Lithomoia 27.75.389
Lithophane 27.75.392
lithophilus, Helichus 24.44.2 (Fig. 24.83)
Lithophorus 24.93.26
Lithosiinae, supra 27.73.7
Lithosiini, supra 27.73.7
Lithurge 25.68.1 1L Lithurginae, supra 25.68.1
Lithurgopsis 25.68.1
litigiosus, Semanotus 24.106.104

Litobranchia 6.11.3
Litocala 27.75.98
Litocampa 3.1.2
Litopchropus 24.77.12
Litochrus 24.77.10
Litocolus 25.4.8
Litodactylus 24.113.295
Litodonta 27.71.26
Litoleptis 29.28.1
Litoliburs 24.77.6
Litolinga 29.32.7
Litomegachile 25.68.22
Litomiris 20.23.198
Litoprosopus 27.75.74
litorea, Nanomyia 29.43.50
littera, Fagitana 27.75.312
Little Black Ant 25.58.31
Little Carpenter Bee 25.69.45
Little Carpenterworm 27.37.8
Little Earwig Family 13.3.1
Little Fire Ant 25.58.44
Little Green Leafhopper 21.14.95
Little House Fly 29.100.26
Little Stout Crawler Mayfly Family 6.14.1
Little Sulphur 27.42.18
Little Wingless Grasshopper 11.5.79
Little Wood Nymph 27.48.6
Little Yellow Ant 25.58.62
littoralis, Epiplagiops 29.105.280
littoralis, Hypolithus 24.48.64
littoralis, Paradiarsia 27.75.574
littoralis, Phytosus 24.24.282
litturata, Euantha 29.105.206
Liturgousinae, supra 14.1.7
litus, Pachnaeus 24.113.59
Livia 21.17.1
Liviinae, supra 21.17.1
Liviini, supra 21.17.1
Lixellus 24.113.144
Lixini, supra 24.13.150
Lixophaga 29.105.247
Lixus 24.113.150
Lizard Barklice Family 17.10.1
Lizard Beetle Family, supra 24.75.1
lleae, Parlatoria 21.38.62
Lobaegis 25.16.265
lobata, Dactylaspis 21.38.23
lobata, Hymeniphera 20.4.13
lobata, Oligembia 9.2.1
lobatus, Rhymbomicurs 24.81.2
Lobella 1.2.16
Loberinae, supra 24.75.1
Loberini, supra 24.75.2
Loberus 24.75.2
Lobesia 27.38.5
Lobiopa 24.70.190
Loblolly Pine Sawfly 25.6.4
Loboceratinae, supra 25.3.2
Lobocleta 27.61.175
Lobodiplosis 29.11.84
Lobogestoria 24.93.15
Lobometopon 24.87.5
Lobopelta 25.58.18
Lobophora 27.61.252
Lobophorini, supra 27.561.245
Lobopoda 24.88.1
Lobopteromyia 29.11.118
Lobosoma 24.113.160
Lobrathium 24.24.59
locality label 40
Lochetica 25.16.11
Lochmaeocles 24.106.258
Lochmaeus 27.71.30
Locrodes 24.87.16
Locust Borer 24.106.112
Locust Leaf Miner 24.107.166

Locust Leaf Roller 27.55.329
Locust Treehopper 21.15.48
Locust Twig Borer 27.38.58
Loderus 25.7.13
Lodgepole Needle Miner 27.23.19
Lodgepole Pine Beetle 24.112.11
Lodgepole Sawfly 25.6.4
Lodgepole Terminal Weevil 24.113.171
Loedelia 24.67.30
Loewimyia 29.73.6
Log Cabin Bagworm 27.11.11
Loicia 29.9.55
loki, Mitoura 27.43.26
Lolochrysa 23.9.12
Lomachaeta 25.55.17
Lomamyia 23.11.1
Lomanaltes 27.75.39
Lomatiinae, supra 29.40.35
Lomilysis 27.75.426
Lomographa 27.61.65
Lonatura 21.14.215
Lonchaea 29.57.4
Lonchaeid Fly Family, supra 29.57.1
Lonchaeidae, supra 29.57.1
Lonchetron 25.19.93
Lonchidia 25.31.13
Lonchoptera 29.44.1
Lonchopteridae, supra 29.44.1
Lonchopteroidea, supra 29.44.1
Long Brown Scale 21.26.4
Longheaded Flour Beetle 24.87.108
Long-horned Beetle Family, supra 24.106.1
Longhorned Casemaker Caddisfly Family,
 supra 26.18.1
Long-horned Earwig Family 13.2.1
Long-horned Grasshopper Family 11.7.1
longicauda, Eoessigia 21.19.70
longicaudata, Ctenolepisma 56.3.3
longicaudatus, Biosteres 25.13.86
Longicaudus 21.19.118
longicollis, Nematolinus 24.24.40
longicornis, Ceratempis 29.42.22
longicornis, Diabrotica 24.107.90 (Fig.
 24.230)
longicornis, Odontoloxozus 29.52.1
longicornis, Paratrechina 25.58.69 (Fig.
 25.50)
longicornig, Tetrapriocera 24.64.18
longifrons, Phalacrotophora 29.46.21
longifrons, Wesmaelius 23.8.3
longii, Oligomyrmex 25.58.34
longilabris longilabris, Xerostictia 25.62.104
Longimenopon 18.6.22
Longipalpifer 29.20.10
longipalpus, Aenigmostomus 25.13.74
longipalpus, Supella 14.5.10 (Fig. 14.19)
Longipeltina 24.24.261
longipennis, Dissosteira 11.5.47
longipennis, Eusemion 25.25.68
longipennis, Incolia 24.98.3
longipennis, Megistocera 29.2.2
longipennis, Pachydiplax 7.7.20
longipennis, Strauzia 29.61.49
longipennis, Vellica 24.24.137
longipes, Chelonychus 24.13.206
longipes, Zelus 20.17.22 (Fig. 20.42)
longirostre, Apion 24.113.21
longirostris, Ischnaspis 21.38.42
longirostris, Pseudambia 21.19.175
longirostris, Rhynencina 29.61.2
longispinus, Pseudococcus 21.25.35
Longistigma 21.19.119
longistyla, Apsilocephala 29.32.1
longistylosus, Rhaphidothrips 22.4.50
Longitarsis, Xylotrechus 24.106.123
Longitarsus 24.107.119

Longivesica 27.75.544
Long-jointed Beetle Family, supra 24.89.1
Longleaf Pine Seedworm 27.38.56
Long-legged Fly Family, supra 29.43.1
Long-lipped Beetle Family, supra 24.53.1
Long-nosed Cattle Louse 19.1.1
Longtailed Fruit Fly Parasite 25.13.86
Longtailed Mealybug 21.25.35
Long-tailed Silverfish 5.3.3
Long-tailed Skipper 27.40.12
Long-toed Water Beetle Family,
 supra 24.44.1
longula, Ageniella 25.60.12
longula, Meidea 20.3.24
longulum, Didion 24.80.10
longulus oregonensis, Melanotus 24.48.67
longulus, Paromius 20.7.52
longulus, Stenocerus 24.109.10
Longurio 29.2.1
longus, Cosmetopus 29.98.12
lonicerae, Rhopalomyzus 21.19.184
lonicericola, Alphitoaphis 21.19.5
Lophalia 24.106.143
lophantae, Lindorus 24.80.29
Lopheros 24.57.12
Lophioderini, supra 24.20.1
Lophioderus 24.20.1
Lophocampa 27.73.56
Lophoceramica 27.75.532
Lophocomodia 25.19.44
Lophocomus 25.26.75
Lophochorista 27.61.164
Lophochoristini, supra 27.61.164
Lophognathella 1.3.1
Lopholeucaspis 21.38.48
Lophosceles 29.100.44
Lophosis 27.61.189
Lophyrocera 25.23.4
Lophyroplectus 25.16.341
Lophocateres 24.66.6
Lophomucter 24.24.262
Lophopogonius 24.106.254
Lophopompilus 25.60.27
Lopidea 20.23.110
Lopidella 20.23.111
Lopus 20.23.79
Lordiphosa 29.90.9
Lordithon 24.24.179
Lordotus 29.40.18
Loricaster 24.33.3
loricatus, Scaphytopius 21.14.92
Loricera 24.4.17
Loricerini, supra 24.4.17
Loriceritae, supra 24.4.17
Lorita 27.39.7
lorna, Henoticoides 24.74.9
lorquini, Basilarchia 27.46.33,
 27.46.34 (Fig. 27.143)
lotella, Anerastia 27.55.412
Lotisma 27.24.1
Lotobia 29.88.1
louisa, Asterocampa 27.47.3
lousiianae, Diopsothrips 22.5.78
Lounsburyia 25.25.15
Louse Fly Family, supra 29.106.1
Love Bug 29.8.3
Loving Barklice Family 17.21.1
Loxa 20.3.47
Loxagrotid 27.75.545
Loxandrus 24.4.89
Loxaulus 25.34.37
Loxocera 29.54.1
Loxocrambus 27.55.213
Loxodocus 25.16.309
Loxofidonia 27.61.228
Loxomorpha 27.55.129

Loxophora 21.11.15
Loxostege 27.55.101
Loxostegopsis 27.25.113
Lozotaenia 27.38.77
Lubber Grasshopper 11.4.7
Lubber Grasshopper Family 11.4.1
lubricalis, Idia 27.75.1 (Fig. 27.322)
lucae, Sphex 25.62.8
Lucaina 24.57.2
Lucanidae, supra 24.28.1
Lucaninae, supra 24.28.1
Lucanus 24.28.2
lucens, Lipara 29.94.30
lucens, Megacara 25.16.128
Lucidota 24.55.13
lucidum, Nosopon 18.6.27
lucidus, Arctonotus 27.70.35 (Fig. 27.257)
lucidus, Hyalurgus 29.105.193
Lucifotychus 24.25.58
Lucilia 29.101.11
Luciliini, supra 29.101.9
lucina, Dyscolomyia 29.105.177
lucina, Hemileuca 27.69.7
Luciolinae, supra 24.55.17
lucorum, Leucozona 29.47.18
luctuosa, Calliperla 28.7.1
luctuosa, Libellula 7.7.13 (Fig. 7.13)
luctuosa, Podalonia 25.62.12
luctuosum, Orygma 25.81.4
ludens, Anatrepha 29.61.43 (Fig. 29.45)
ludoviciana, Lysathia 24.107.29
lugens, Mormidea 20.3.32
lugubis, Panorpa 28.4.1 (Fig. 28.5)
lugubris, Carpophilus 24.70.10
lugubris, Enyo 27.70.29 (Fig. 27.250)
lugubris, Gaediophana 29.105.360
lugubris, Hylecoetus 24.69.1
lugubris, Pedilus 24.103.1 (Fig. 24.173)
lugubris, Xestonotus 24.4.108
luna, Actias 27.69.13 (Fig. 27.229)
Luna Moth 27.69.13
luna, Nycterophaeta 27.75.465
Lunacepos 18.1.36
lunaris, Aconocoris 20.9.3
lunaris, Batia 27.15.26
lunata, Caularis 27.75.243
lunata, Molamba 24.79.9 (Fig. 24.144)
lunata, Stomorhina 29.101.1
lunata, Termitonidia 24.24.299
lunata, Zale 27.75.128 (Fig. 27.332)
Lunatipula 29.2.9
lunatus, Mnioes 25.16.307
lunigerella, Promylea 27.55.299
lunilinea, Spiloloma 27.75.147
Lunomyia 29.47.62
lunula, Calophasia 27.75.460
Luperaltica 24.107.124
Luperina 27.75.254
Luperina, supra 24.107.101
Luperini, supra 24.107.90
Luperosoma 24.107.99
Luperus 24.107.113
lupini, Icaricia 27.43.50
Lupinicolus 24.113.102
Lupraea 24.107.118
Lupropinae, supra 24.89.3
lupulina, Minettia 29.82.8
lurida, Acinaca 21.11.11
lurida, Boreoheptagyia 29.24.33
lurida, Nemognatha 24.101.19
lurida, Pycnogypta 24.24.132
lurida, Tafalisca 11.10.26
luridus, Opetiopalpus 24.67.32
lusa, Lalapa 25.53.8
lusca, Perigonia 27.70.27
lusius, Somaphanthus 18.6.34

luski, Coloradia 27.69.6
lustrans, Hemihalictus 25.66.18
lutea, Cariblatta 14.5.9
luteicornis, Tomoglossa 24.24.310
luteipennis, Tanypeza 29.53.1
lutem, Macrosiphum 21.19.122
lutens, Lutrochus 24.43.5
luteola, Nomada 25.69.10
luteola, Xanthogaleruca 24.107.81
luteolus, Scaphoideus 21.14.99
luteolus, Xylastodoris 20.11.1
luteomedia, Prothrinax 27.75.371
Lutomyia 29.84.11
lutosopra, Odontomesa 29.24.40
lutra, Sprimater 27.75.484 (Fig. 27.380, in Lacanobia)
Lutridia 18.2.5
Lutreochus 24.43.5
lutzi, Jurinella 29.105.92
lutzi, Limnocoris 20.38.2
Lutzomiops 29.19.4
Lutzomyia 29.12.2
Luzulaspis 21.26.10
Lycaeides 27.43.47
Lycaena 27.43.3
lycaenae, Isdromas 25.16.88
Lycaenidae, supra 27.43.1
Lycaeninae, supra 27.43.2
Lycaota 25.7.55
Lycaotini, supra 25.7.54
Lychnosea 27.61.122
Lycia 27.61.60
lyciades, Achalarus 27.40.15 (Fig. 27.15)
Lycidae, supra 24.57.1
Lyciella 29.82.7
Lycinae, supra 24.57.1
Lycini, supra 24.57.1
Lycioides 21.14.146
Lycochoriolaus 24.106.202
Lycogaster 25.47.2
Lycomorpha 27.73.16
Lycoperdina 24.81.11
lycopersicella, Keiferia 27.23.52
lycoposugus, Tilihagus 21.19.211
Lycoptis 24.66.7
Lycorea 27.49.2
Lycoriella 29.10.10 (Fig. 29.16)
Lycorininae, supra 25.16.194
Lyvotyocorinae, supra 20.21.14
Lyctidae, supra 24.65.1
Lyctini, supra 24.65.1
Lyctocorini, supra 20.21.14
Lyctocoris 20.21.14
Lyctus 24.65.1
Lycus 24.57.1
Lydella 29.105.421
Lydellohoughia 29.105.248
lydia, Plathemis 7.7.24 (Fig. 7.16)
Lydina 29.105.142
Lydinolydella 29.105.249
Lygaeidae, supra 20.7.1
Lygaeinae, supra 20.7.1
Lygaeospilus 20.7.2
Lygaeus 20.7.3
lygdamis, Eurrhyparodes 27.55.116
lygdamus, Glaucopsyche 27.43.46
Lygidea 20.23.164
Lygistopterus 24.57.3
Lygistopterini, supra 24.57.2
Lygistorrhina 29.9.18
Lygistorrhininae, supra 29.9.15
Lygistus 24.107.104
Lygocecis 29.11.153
Lygocoris 20.23.165
Lygropia 27.55.169
Lygus 20.23.166

Lymantes 24.113.165
Lymantor 24.112.44
Lymantria 27.74.4
Lymantriidae, supra 27.74.1
Lymantriini, supra 27.74.4
Lymeon 25.16.180
Lymeonina, supra 25.16.179
Lymexylidae, supra 24.69.1
Lymexyloidea, supra 24.69.1
Lymire 27.73.77
Lynchia 29.106.6
Lynchiella 29.20.2
lynosyrana, Synnoma 27.38.88
Lyonetia 27.13.5
Lyonetiid Moth Family, supra 27.13.1
Lyonetiidae, supra 27.13.1
Lype 26.2.1
Lyperosiops 29.100.60
Lypha 19.105.131
Lyphia 24.87.109
Lyphini, supra 29.105.131
Lypoglossa 24.24.263
Lypotigris 27.55.170
lypriformis, Microlarinus 24.113.151
Lypsimena 24.106.257
Lyroda 25.62.44
lyropictus, Periphyllus 21.19.165
Lyrosoma 24.21.2
Lyrosomini, supra 24.21.2
Lysaphidus 25.14.10
Lysathia 24.107.129
Lysibia 25.16.93
lyside, Kricogonia 27.42.126
Lysilinga 29.32.10
lysimachiae, Acallodes 24.113.290
Lysiphlebina, supra 25.14.4
Lysiphlebus 25.14.4
Lystridea 21.14.66
Lystronychus 24.88.14
Lythrodes 27.75.342
Lytogaster 29.93.48
Lytoxysta 25.33.1
Lytrosis 27.61.82
Lytta 24.101.13
Lyttina, supra 24.101.13
Lyttini, supra 24.101.4

M

macalla 27.55.261
macareus, Thespieus 27.40.86
macateei, Canacea 29.97.1
Macateeia 29.99.23
Maccevethini, supra 20.6.7
Macchiatiella 21.19.120
macellaria, Cochliolyia 29.101.3
macer, Papusus 24.20.21
macgillivrayi, Sminthurinus 1.7.4
macguffini, Gnophos 27.61.43
Machaerilaemus 18.6.23
Machaerites 24.25.62
Machaerodes 24.25.61
machaon, Papilio 27.41.5
Machilidae 4.1.1
Machilinus 4.2.1
Machilis 4.1.7
Machiloides 4.2.2
Machimia 27.15.9
Machimus 29.37.74
macilenta, Leptalia 24.106.188
mackenziei, Tujunga 29.58.23
macmurtrei, Prionoxystus 27.37.8
macounii, Oeneis 27.48.13
Macquartiini, supra 29.105.174
Macrancylus 24.113.377
Macratria 24.103.10

Macratriini, supra 24.103.10
Macremphytus 25.7.87
Macreurops 24.71.7
Macristis 27.75.19
Macrobaenetes 11.9.20
Macrobasis 24.101.14
Macrobrachius 29.9.33
Macrocentrinae, supra 25.13.73
Macrocentrus 25.13.73
Macrocephalinae, supra 20.16.2
Macrocephalus 20.16.2
macrocephalus, mulcticola 18.1.37
Macrocera 29.9.12
macrocera, Mira 25.25.118
Macrocereucoila 25.32.6
macrocerus, Stylantheus 24.108.7
Macrocneme 27.73.80
Macrodactylus 24.30.80
Macrodea 24.74.11
Macrodiplax 7.7.14
Macrodiplosis 29.11.36
Macroglossinae, supra 27.70.19
Macroglossini, supra 27.70.32
Macroglossum 27.70.39
Macrogyropus 18.4.3
Macrohaltica 24.107.128
Macrohynnis 25.42.6
Macrojappa 25.16.261
Macrolepidoptera, supra 27.59.1
Macrolophus 20.23.30
Macromalon 25.16.297
Macromerus 24.113.273
Macromesinae, supra 25.19.21
Macromesus 25.19.21
Macromia 7.5.2
Macromiidae 7.5.1
Macromischa 25.58.35
macromphaliinae, supra 27.68.1
Macromya 29.105.85
Macromyini, supra 29.105.82
Macronaemia 24.80.47
Macronema 26.4.11
Macronematinae, supra 26.4.11
macroncurus, Neoceraphron 25.45.21
Macronoctua 27.75.275
Macronomadopsis 25.65.11
Macronychia 29.103.6
Macronychus 24.45.26
Macropelopiini, supra 29.24.8
Macropelopsis 29.24.10
Macropeza 29.23.29
Macrophorbia 29.99.9
Macrophthalmothrops 22.5.52
Macrophya 25.7.96
Macrophyini, supra 25.7.96
Macropidinae, supra 25.67.3
Macropis 25.67.3
Macroplea 24.107.3
macropogen, Menetus 29.105.163
Macropogon 24.34.1
Macropogonini, supra 24.34.1
Macropsinae, supra 21.14.16
Macropsini, supra 21.14.16
Macropsis 21.14.17
Macrorchis 29.100.5
Macrorileya 25.20.1
Macrorhoptus 24.113.216
Macrorhinia 27.55.355
Macrorrhyncha 29.9.17
Macrosiagon 24.100.4 (Fig. 24.168)
Macrosiagonini, supra 24.100.4
Macrosiphoniella 21.19.121
Macrosiphum 21.19.122
Macrosteles 21.14.97
Macrostelini, supra 21.14.96
Macroteleia 25.43.7

Macrotella 25.65.15
Macrotera 25.65.15
Macroteropsis 25.65.15
Macrotheca 27.55.278
Macrothecini, supra 27.55.278
Macrothemis 7.7.15
Macrothyatirini, supra 27.59.4
Macrotomini, supra 24.106.2
Macrotracheliella 20.21.10
Macrotyloides 20.23.112
Macrotylus 20.23.80
Macrovelia 20.29.2
Macroxyela 25.1.4
Macroxyelinae, supra 25.1.3
Macroxyelini, supra 25.1.4
Macrurocampa 27.71.28
macrurus macrurus, Megarhyssa 25.16.42
macrurus, Nemeritis 25.16.403
Macrus 25.16.417
macswaini, Hesperentomon 2.2.1
macswaini, Procampodea 3.2.1
Mactomyia 29.105.143
macula, Schrankia 27.75.32
maculana, Ricula 27.38.47
macularia, Sicya 27.61.134 (Fig. 27.191)
maculata, Bakerella 21.2.13
maculata, Calopteryx 7.8.1 (Fig. 7.18)
maculata, Coleomegilla 24.80.45
maculata, Dysimia 21.9.7
maculata, Epicauta 24.101.14
maculata, Eucera 25.69.23
maculata, Graphomya 29.100.51
maculata, Lophocampa 27.73.56 (Fig. 27.303)
maculata, Moscrina 25.26.65
maculata, Oligoria 27.40.82
maculata, Piogaster 25.16.22
maculata, Protoptila 26.6.6
maculata, Solntsevia 29.11.46
maculata, Therioaphis 21.19.209
maculata, Tytthotyle 11.4.3
maculata, Vespula 25.59.27 (Fig. 25.55)
maculatum, Myzinum 25.53.6
maculatus, Callosobruchus 24.108.6 (Fig. 24.250)
maculatus, Cordulegaster 7.2.1
maculatus, Dermestes 24.61.1
maculatus, Derodontus 24.59.3
maculatus, Rhaphitelus 25.19.70
maculatus, Stictothrips 22.5.66
maculatus, Trimeromicrus 25.19.126
maculicolle, Agonum 24.4.74
maculicoxis, Pseudorhyssa 25.16.35
maculifrons, Vespula 25.59.27 (Fig. 25.53)
maculipennis, Acrolophitus 11.5.30 (Fig. 11.13)
maculipennis, Rhagioforma 29.32.8
maculithorax, Indovia 25.16.90
maculiventris, Podisus 20.3.74
Maculolachnus 21.19.123
maculosa, Gnorimella 24.30.118
maculosus, Panscopus 24.113.126 (Fig. 24.277)
maculosus, Stallingsia 27.40.89
maculosus, Staphylinus 24.24.13 (Fig. 24.58)
Maculurges 24.106.291
Macustus 21.14.158
Madagascaran Cockroach 14.6.7
Madaini, supra 24.80.53
Madarellus 24.113.321
Madarini, supra 24.113.319
Madeira Cockroach 14.6.6
maderae, Leucophaea 14.6.6
Madiza 29.74.6
madizans, Trimerina 29.93.28

Madizinae, supra 29.74.1
Madopterina, supra 24.113.361
Madopterus 24.113.361
Madoryx 27.70.25
Madremyia 29.105.422
Madrua 20.4.19
Maemactes 24.113.262
maerkelii, Pithanus 20.23.192
maerula, Anteos 27.42.13 (Fig. 27.99)
maesites, Chlorostrymon 27.43.13
Maesites Hairstreak 27.43.13
Magaconops 29.23.1
Magaderini, supra 24.106.168
magdalena, Erebia 27.48.10
Magdalinae, supra 24.113.197
Magdalini, supra 24.113.197
Magdalinops 24.113.201
Magdalis 24.113.197
Magicicada 21.13.18
magna, Amblyjoppa 25.16.252
magna, Brachystola 11.4.7 (Fig. 11.9)
magna, Ferrisidea 21.38.30
magnafemoralis, Neurothrips 22.5.55
magnicauda, Thamadiplosis 29.11.125
magnicornis, Phaonia 29.100.44
magnifera, Hemileuca 27.69.7
magnifica, Archilestris 29.37.20
magnifica, Cossula 27.37.4
magnifica, Macromia 7.5.2 (Fig. 7.9)
magnificalis, Neocatachysta 27.55.6
Magnificent Skimmer 7.5.2
magnificus, Compsobracon 25.13.32
Magnolia Scale 21.26.12
Maguey Worm 27.40.88
Magusa 27.75.316
maia, Hemileuca 27.69.7 (Fig. 27.219)
maidiradicis, Anuraphis 21.19.13
maidis, Peregrinus 21.2.18
maidis, Rhopalosiphum 21.19.186
maidis, Sphenophorus 24.113.366
Maise Billbug 24.113.366
Maise Weevil 24.113.365
majalis, Rhizotrogus 24.30.64
major, Bombylius 29.40.11
major, Corixidea 20.25.2
Malachiinae, supra 24.68.1
malachitana, Eumarozia 27.38.9
Malachius 24.68.7
Malacocis 24.92.11
Malacopsylloidea, supra 30.2.1
Malacopterus 24.106.24
Malacorhinus 24.107.87
Malacosoma 27.68.11
Malacothrips 22.5.53
Maladera 24.30.62
Malagoniella 24.30.7
malana, Balso 27.75.325 (Fig. 27.366)
Malaraeus 30.7.6
m-album, Parrhasius 27.43.33
malefida, Agrotis 27.75.535
Malenka 8.1.2
Malezonotus 20.7.47
mali, Aphelinus 25.25.1 (Fig. 25.23)
mali, Chrysobothris 24.46.23
mali, Psylla 21.17.27
mali, Scolytus 24.112.23
malifoliella, Tischeria 27.7.1
maligna, Empoasca 21.14.77
Malirekus 8.7.14
malivolans, Bucrates 11.7.18
malivorella, Coleophora 27.18.1
malkini, Porophila 24.15.3
Mallada 23.9.8
Mallaspini, supra 24.106.7
mallochi, Pelomyiella 29.96.2
mallochi, Speccafrons 29.94.36

Mallochia 25.16.179
Mallochiola 20.22.1
Mallochohelea 29.23.28
Mallodon 24.106.4
Mallodrya 24.98.8
Malloewia 29.94.34
Mallophaga, supra 18.1.1
Mallophorina 29.37.70
Mallota 29.47.63
Malobidion 24.106.40
Malphighian Tubes 12
Malporus 24.102.10
Malthinini, supra 24.56.13
Malthinus 24.56.13
Malthodes 24.56.15
mamata, Odontophotopsis 25.55.12
Mamestra 27.75.479
Mammal Chewing Lice Family 18.2.1
Mammal Nest Beetle Family, supra 24.18.1
Mammifrontia 27.75.270
Mamurius 20.4.12
manca, Ancognatha 24.30.98
Mancia 29.40.50
mancus, Agriotes 24.48.40
Manda 24.24.148
mandible 20
mandibularis, Dendrobias 24.106.166
mandibularis, Glyphicnemis 25.16.118
mandibularis, Lysibia 25.16.93
mandibularis, Prostomis 24.96.1
Mandibulate Moth Family, supra 27.1.1
Manduca 27.70.4
mangiferae, Hypocryphalus 24.112.38
mangiferae, Protopulvinaria 21.26.17
Mango Bark Beetle 24.112.38
Mango Shield Scale 21.26.17
Manhatta 27.55.397
Manica 25.58.23
manigerae, Sternochetus 24.113.265
Maniolini, supra 27.48.9
manitobensis, Anisota 27.69.5
mannerheimii, Eudociminus 24.113.156
manni, Liometophilus 24.113.259
Mannophorus 24.106.141
Manomera 10.1.3
Manonerua 27.5.7
Manophylax 26.10.49
Manota 29.9.19
manotinae, supra 29.9.19
Manruta 27.75.540
Mansonia 29.20.4
manteo, Lochmaeus 27.71.30
manteri, Caecilius 17.10.1 (Fig. 17.5)
Mantids 14.1.1
Mantidae, supra 14.1.1
Mantinae, supra 14.1.8
Mantis 14.1.9
Mantislike Lacewing Family supra 23.7.1
Mantispa 23.7.4
Mantispidae, supra 23.7.1
Mantispilla 23.7.3
Mantispinae, supra 23.7.3
Mantispoidea, supra 23.7.1
Mantodea, supra 14.1.1
Mantoida 14.1.1
Mantura 24.107.143
Many-dotted Apple Worm 27.75.325
Many-plume Moth Family, supra 27.25.1
Manzutus 21.14.57
Maple Callus Borer 27.35.12
Maple Leaf Cutter 27.8.3
Maple Petiole Borer 25.7.19
Maple Prominent 27.71.29
Maple Spanworm 27.61.101
Maple Trumpet Skeletonizer 27.38.41
Maracayia 27.55.190

Marasmia 27.55.185
marathonensis, Marathonia 21.14.55
Marathonia 21.14.55
Marathyssa 27.75.169
Marava 13.3.5
marbis, Crataepus 25.26.49
Marbled Sawyer 24.106.258
marcata, Hemileuca 27.69.7
marcella, Miathyria 7.7.16
marcellus, Eurytides 27.41.4, 27.41.7 (Fig. 27.79)
March Fly Family, supra 29.8.1
Margaiostus 24.48.63
Marganana 21.14.26
Margarinotus 24.26.38
margaritacea, Buenoa 20.33.1
Margarodes 21.23.6
Margarodidae, supra 21.23.1
Margarodinae, supra 21.23.4
Margarodini, supra 21.23.6
margarum, Aphidopsis 21.19.14
marginalis, Metaclisa 24.87.86
marginata, Coccopsis 29.11.49
marginata, Holopleura 24.106.165
marginata, Hypogena 24.87.120
marginata, Idana 29.58.11
marginata, Isomeris 25.16.313
marginata, Mordella 24.99.5 (Fig. 24.167)
marginata, Nidicola 20.21.18
marginata, Pennisetia 27.35.1
marginata, Suwallia 8.8.5 (Fig. 8.11)
marginatus, Anapleus 24.26.24
marginatus, Omethes 24.56.18
marginatus, Prodoxus 27.8.11
marginatus, Toxomerus 29.47.5
Margined Blister Beetle 24.101.14
marginella, Dichomeris 27.23.85
marginella modesta, Micromeriella 25.56.4
marginella, Silusida 24.24.291
marginepunctata, Psoquilla 17.3.1
marginicollis, Clytus 24.106.125 (Fig. 24.196)
marginicollis, Thymalus 24.66.4
marginidens, Papaipema 27.75.279 (Fig. 27.360)
marginifera, Hubbellia 11.7.49 (Fig. 11.37)
Marginitermes 15.2.2
margnariua, Ennomos 27.61.101 (Fig. 27.185)
Margus 20.4.20
maria, Tallaperla 8.6.5
mariana, Argyrotaenia 27.38.71
Maricopodynerus 25.59.12
Marietta 25.25.4
marilandia, Omphalomopsis 25.26.40
marilandica, Carlyeia 25.26.69
marilandica, Neocatocha 29.11.24
Marilia 26.14.1
marina, Leptotes 27.43.38
marinus, Elassoptes 24.113.394
marinus, Phyconomus 24.71.3
Mariocladius 29.24.136
mariposa, Epidema 27.43.7
maritima, Anisolabis 13.1.3
maritima, Anurida 1.2.12 (Fig. 1.3)
maritimus, Homeotyphlus 24.24.166
maritimus, Petrobius 4.1.5
maritimus, Pseudococcus 21.25.35
marlatti, Pheonicococcus 21.37.1
marlatti, Rhytidothorax 25.25.156
Marlattiella 25.25.5
Marmara 27.14.16
marmarodactyla, Anstenoptilia 27.58.10
Marmopteryx 27.61.222
marmorata, Brucita 24.107.82
marmorata, Corythucha 20.14.7

marmorata, Leucopodella 29.47.7
marmorata, Limnonia 29.2.14
marmorator, Monochamus 24.106.237
marmoratus, Calyptoproctus 21.3.2
marmoratus, Lochmaeocles 24.106.258
marmoratus, Negalius 24.101.8
marmoratus, Ptilineurus 24.63.1
marmoratus, Stethaulax 20.3.7
marmoratus, Thermonectus 24.7.38 (Fig24.48)
Marpesia 27.46.44
Marpesiinae, supra 27.46.44
marroni, Huleechius 24.45.8
Marsh Fly 29.79.16
Marsh Fly Family, supra 29.79.1
Marsh Treader Bug Family, supra 20.26.1
marshalli, Clunio 29.24.86
marshalli, Sensiphorura 1.3.2
Marsupial Chewing Lice Family 18.3.1
Marsupial Lice Family 18.8.1
marsupials, Putoniella 29.11.134
Martarega 20.33.2
Martia 27.55.352
martialis, Strymon 27.43.34
Martinapis 25.69.34
martinella, Elatobia 27.10.44
martini, Hydrometra 20.26.1 (Fig. 20.58)
martini, Plumipalpia 27.55.40
martinorum, Apiocera 29.36.2
Martyinga 27.15.36
Maruina 29.12.4
marylandensis, Bairamlia 25.19.37
marylandensis, Parecrizotes 25.19.63
marylandicus, Neossos 29.85.1
Masarinae, supra 25.59.2
Masarini, supra 25.59.2
Masicera 29.105.423
Masiphyini, supra 29.105.391
Masiphyomyia 29.105.374
Masked Hunter 20.17.29
maskelli, Pealius 21.18.15
Mason Bee Family, supra 25.68.1
Masonaphis 21.19.105
masoni, Ammopsen 25.62.15
masoni, Symballophthalmus 29.42.8
Masoreini, supra 24.4.138
Massala 27.75.94
Mastinocerini, supra 24.54.4
Mastinocerus 24.54.6
Mastogeniini, supra 24.46.39
Mastogenius 24.46.39
Mastopoda 21.19.124
Mastoremus 24.193.8
Mastrina, supra 25.16.106
Mastrus 25.16.107
materna, Eudocima 27.75.69
mathesoni, Deinocerites 29.20.13
Matheteinae, supra 24.55.18
Matheteus 24.55.18
Mathildana 27.15.32
Matigramma 27.75.126
Matiloxis 27.75.65
Matini, supra 24.7.28
Matriarchal Katydid 11.7.47
Mathrilaeum 24.24.117
Matrioptila 26.6.5
Matsucoccini, supra 21.23.2
Matsucoccus 21.23.2
matthewsi, Zacotus 24.4.34
matthiolae, Lipamyzodes 21.19.116
maturus, Probles 25.16.446
Matus 24.7.28
maurator, Limonthe 25.16.220
mauritanicus, Tenebroides 24.66.14 (Fig. 24.129)
mauritia, Spodoptera 27.75.326

Mauromyia 29.105.144
maxilla 20
maxillosus, Creophilus 24.24.14 (Fig. 24.59)
maxillosus, Gnatocerus 24.87.106 (Fig. 24.154)
maximum, Laemobothrion 18.5.1
May Beetles, supra 24.30.57
maya, Mantoida 14.1.1
maya, Phrixa 11.7.9
Mayacnephia 29.22.7
Mayatrichia 26.7.14
mayeri, Aplopus 10.2.1 (Fig. 10.3)
Mayer's Walkingtick 10.2.1
Mayetia 24.25.4
Mayetini, supra 24.25.4
Mayetiola 29.11.147
Mayflies 6.1.1
Mayridia 25.25.117
mcdanieli, Paradoxococcus 21.25.30
mcdonaldi, Oxycopis 24.97.8
mcfarlandi, Sandia 27.43.28
Mea 27.10.17
meadii, Cercyonis 27.48.9
meadii, Colias 27.42.11 (Fig. 27.94)
meadii, Coryphista 27.61.208
Meadorus 20.3.62
Meadow Copper 27.43.6
Meadow Fritillary 27.46.11
Meadow Katydids 1.7.21
Meadow Planthopper 21.11.5
Meadow Spittle Bug 21.12.4
Meal Moth 27.55.233
Mealy Plum Aphid 21.19.101
Mealybug Family, supra 21.25.1
Mecanthidium 25.68.4
Mecas 24.106.298
Mecidea, supra 20.3.24
Mecidini, supra 20.3.24
Mecinini, supra 24.113.232
Mecinus 24.113.233
Mecomma 20.23.113
Mecomycter 24.68.30
Meconema 117.48
Meconematinae, supra 11.7.48
Mecopini, supra 24.113.276
Mecopeltus 24.113.302
Mecoptera, supra 28.1.1
Mecyna 27.25.122
Mecynocorpus 29.103.34
Mecynotarsus 24.102.1
Mecysmus 24.87.150
medeola, Thematheca 29.105.267
Medetera 29.43.21
Medeterinae, supra 29.43.21
media, Lopidea 20.23.110
median vein 22
medicaginis, Kuwayama 21.17.12
mediodentata, Hymenodria 27.61.200
mediospinosa, Dacerla 20.23.153
Mediterranean Cockroach 14.5.12
Mediterranea Flour Moth 27.55.401
Mediterranean Fruit Fly, supra 29.61.1
Mediterranean Mantis 14.1.6
meditabunda, Myospila 29.100.24
Medon 24.24.60
Medophron 25.16.116
Megabothris 30.7.7
Megacara 25.16.128
Megacephala 24.3.3
megacephala, Pheildoe 25.58.28
Megacephalina, supra 24.3.3
Megacephalini, supra 24.3.1
Megacerus 24.108.5
Megacheuma 24.106.117
Megachile 25.68.22

Megachilidae, supra 25.68.1
Megachilinae, supra 25.68.2
Megachilini, supra 25.68.13
Megachiloides 25.68.22
Megachoriolaus 24.106.194
Megacraspedus 27.23.3
Megacyllene 24.106.112
Megaderus 24.106.168
Megadytes 24.7.41
Megagrahis 25.13.80
Megagrapha 29.42.7
Megaleuctra 8.4.6
Megalgus 24.64.1
Megalinga 29.32.3
Megalinus 24.24.38
Megaloceroea 20.23.199
Megalocoleus 20.23.81
Megalodacne 24.76.3
Megalodontoidea, supra 25.1.1
Megalomus 23.8.5
Megalonotini, supra 20.7.70
Megalonotus 20.7.70
Megalopelma 29.9.64
Megalopinus 24.24.160
megalops, Tetradonia 24.24.300
Megalopsallus 20.23.49
Megalopsidiiane, supra 24.24.160
Megaloptera, supra 23.1.1
Megalopyge 27.51.3
Megalopygidae, supra 27.51.1
Megalorrhipida 27.58.7
Megalostomini, supra 24.107.16
Megalostomis 24.107.16
Megalothorax 1.6.1
Megalothrips 22.5.12
Megalotomus 20.5.7
Megamelanus 21.2.20
Megamelus 21.2.12
Megandrena 25.65.2
Meganola 27.75.178
Meganoplium 24.106.47
Megaparia 29.105.52
Megapariopsis 29.105.53
Megapenthes 24.48.24
Megaphasma 10.1.5
Megaphragma 25.28.2
Megaphthalma 29.98.8
Megaphthalmoides 29.98.9
Megaplectes 25.16.144
Megapterocheilus 25.59.3
Megarafonus 24.25.2
Megarcys 8.7.15
Megarhyssa 25.16.42
Megarthridini, supra 27.55.273
Megarthroglossus 30.4.15
Megarthrus 24.24.100
Megascelinae, supra 24.107.15
Megascelis 24.107.15
Megasecoptera, supra 6.1.1
Megaselia 29.46.17
Megasemum 24.106.15
Megasida 24.87.60
Megasoma 24.30.115
Megaspilid Wasp Family, supra 25.46.1
Megaspilidae, supra 25.46.1
Megaspilinae, supra 25.46.1
Megaspilus 25.46.2
Megasternini, supra 24.12.32
Megasternum 24.12.33
Megastigminae, supra 25.18.25
Megastigmus 25.18.25
Megastilicus 24.24.61
Megastylus 25.16.498
Megasyrphus 29.47.25
Megataphyrus 24.93.4
Megathrips 22.5.13

Megathymidae, supra 27.40.87
Megathyminae, supra 27.40.87
Megathymini, supra 27.40.88
Megathymus 27.40.88
Megatoma 24.61.15
megatoma, Attagenus 24.61.6
Megatrydymus 25.19.77
Megaxyela 25.1.5
Megeleates 24.87.70
Megetra 24.101.7
Meghyperus 29.42.58
Megischus 25.17.2
Megisto 27.48.6
Megistocera 29.2.2
Megistocera 29.2.2
Megobrium 24.106.90
Megophthalmida 29.9.79
Megophthalminae, supra 21.14.10
Megophthalmini, supra 21.14.10
Megorama 24.63.39
Megoura 21.19.125
Megourina 21.19.126
Megouroparsus 21.19.127
Meibomeus 24.108.9
Meigenia 29.105.250
Meigenielloides 29.105.251
Meinertellidae, supra 4.2.1
Meiocampa 3.1.3
Melanactes 24.48.49
Melanactinae, supra 24.48.49
Melanaethus 20.1.3
Melanagomyza 29.68.3
Melanalia 24.24.264
melanantha, Hesperonomada 25.69.13
Melanaphis 21.19.128
Melanaphycus 25.25.55
Melanaspis 21.38.49
Melanchra 27.75.481
melanderi, Acontistoptera 29.46.33
melanderi, Nomia 25.66.8
melanderi, Parasimulium 29.22.1
Melanderia 29.43.15
Melanderomyia 29.45.1
Melandrena 25.65.1
Melandrya 24.98.36
Melandryidae, supra 24.98.1
Melandryinae, supra 24.98.17
Melandryini, supra 24.98.35
melane, Paratrytone 27.40.74
Melaneleodes 24.87.140
Melangyna 29.47.19
melania, Micromintho 29.105.212
Melanichneumon 25.16.213
Melanips 25.31.14
Melanis 27.44.5
Melanocallis 21.19.129
Melanocanthon 24.30.4
Melanocelptes 25.50.1
Melanochaeta 29.94.8
Melanochroia 27.61.51
Melanocinclis 27.21.7
Melanocoelioxys 25.68.24
Melanoconion 29.20.12
Melanocoris 29.21.1
Melanocoryphys 20.7.4
Melanodexia 29.101.22
Melanodexiini, supra 29.101.22
melanogaster, Drosophila 29.90.9
melanogrammus, Strophosoma 24.113.48
Melanolemma 24.113.135
Melanolestes 20.17.25
Melanolimonia 29.2.14
Melanolophia 27.61.52
Melanolophiini, supra 27.61.52
Melanomada 25.69.15
Melanomma 27.75.24
Melanomyini, supra 29.101.23

Melanophila 24.46.20
melanophleba, Tabudamima 29.32.16
Melanophora 29.104.2
Melanophryini, supra 29.105.122
Melanophrys 29.105.123
Melanophthalma 24.82.14
Melanopleurus 20.7.5
Melanoplinae, supra 11.5.73
Melanoplus 11.5.94
melanops, Alaus 24.48.7
melanopus, Archodontes 24.106.3
melanopus, Oulema 24.107.14
Melanorhopala 20.14.16
Melanosarus 25.68.22
melanoscelus, Apanteles 25.13.116
melanosipla, Raparna 27.75.76
Melanostelis 25.68.11
Melanostoma 29.47.9
melanostoma, Clusiodes 29.65.5
Melanostomatini, supra 29.47.8
Melanotinae, supra 24.48.67
Melanotrichus 20.23.114
Melanotus 24.48.67
Melanthripinae, supra 22.1.1
Melanthrips 22.1.3
melanura, Acidogona 29.61.13
melanura, Nacerdes 24.97.4
melanura, Oligembia 9.2.1
Melaphis 21.19.130
Melaporhyria 27.75.604
Melasidae 24.52.1
Melasinae, supra 24.52.15
Melasis 24.52.16
Melastola 25.7.41
Melba 24.25.41
meleagridis, Chelopistes 18.1.10 (Fig. 18.2)
Melecta 25.69.38
Melectini, supra 25.69.38
Melectomimus 25.69.38
Melectomorpha 25.69.39
Meledonus 29.105.184
Melemaea 27.61.121
Meleneta 27.75.229
Meleoma 23.9.3
meles, Hypera 24.113.146
Meleterus 29.105.162
Meliarhizophagus 21.19.131
Melieria 29.58.12
Meligethes 24.70.32
Meligethinae, supra 24.70.32
Meligramma 29.47.19
Melinocera 29.105.115
melinus, Strymon 27.43.34
Melipotis 27.75.99
Meliscaeva 29.47.26
Melisoneurini, supra 29.105.56
melissa, Lycaeides 27.43.47
melissa, Oeneis 27.48.13 (Fig. 27.153)
Melissodes 25.69.30
Melissoptila 25.69.356
Melissopus 27.38.7
Melitaeinae, supra 27.46.12
Melitara 27.55.380
melite, Enantia 27.42.21
Melitoma 25.69.20
Melitomini, supra 25.69.18
Melitonympha 27.29.5
Melitta 25.67.1
Melittia 27.35.8
Melittid Bee Family, supra 25.67.1
Melittidae, supra 25.67.1
Melittinae, supra 25.67.1
Melittiini, supra 27.35.8
Melittobia 25.26.53
melittoides, Melitta 25.67.1

Melittomma 24.69.2
mella, Exorista 29.105.282 (Fig. 29.57)
mella, Myrmecopria 25.42.35
Mellana 27.40.76
melleus, Miotropis 25.26.19
mellifera adansonii, Apis 25.70.4
mellifera, Apis 25.70.4 (Figs. 25.68, 25.69)
mellifera lingustica, Apis 25.70.4
mellifica, Brachygastra 25.59.30
mellifrons, Metatachina 29.105.145
melliger, Myrmecocystu 25.58.71
Mellilla 27.61.11
Mellinini, supra 25.62.70
Mellinus 25.62.70
mellita, Necydalis 24.106.170 (Fig. 24.199)
mellonella, Galleria 27.55.270 (Fig. 27.170)
Mellophora 29.37.69
mellyi, Hypolampsis 24.107.153
Meloboris 25.16.410
Meloe 24.101.3
Meloehela 29.23.2
Meloidae, supra 24.101.1
Meloinae, supra 24.101.2
Meloini, supra 24.101.2
Melolonthinae, supra 24.30.57
Melon Aphid 21.19.15
Melon Fly, supra 29.61.1
Melonworm 27.55.150
Melophaginae, supra 29.106.10
Melophagini, supra 29.106.12
Melophagus 29.106.12
Melormenis 21.8.7
melsheimeri, Cicinnus 27.65.2 (Fig. 27.205)
Melyridae, supra 24.68.1
Melyrinae, supra 24.68.15
Melyrodes 24.68.15
Membracidae, supra 21.15.1
Membracinae, supra 21.15.4
Membracis 21.15.9
Membracixenos 24.105.9
Membracoidea, supra 21.15.1
membranifera, Trichoscapa 25.58.48
Memnonia 21.14.6
Memphis 27.47.2
Menacanthus 18.6.24
menapia, Neophasia 27.42.2 (Fig. 27.84)
mendax, Brechmorhoga 7.7.3
mendax, Lygidea 20.23.164
mendax, Rhagoletis 29.61.44
mendica, Andrena 25.65.1
mendica, Steniodes 27.55.141
mendocino, Saturnia 27.69.10 (Fig. 27.226)
Menecles 20.3.43
Menesta 27.15.20
Menestomorpha 27.15.19
Menetus 29.105.163
Mengeinae, supra 24.105.1
Menkeleon 23.14.4
Menkokia 25.16.218
Menoeceus∈N24.88.6
Menopon 18.6.25
Menoponidae, supra 18.6.1
Menosoma 21.14.176
mentzeliae, Megandrena 25.65.2
Meoneura 29.75.2
Meotica 24.24.265
Meracantha 24.87.127
Merapioidus 29.47.74
Meraporus 25.19.99
mercator, Oryzaephilus 24.72.2
merceti, Comperia 25.25.80

Merchant Grain Beetle 24.72.2
mercuruis, Proteides 27.40.3
Merhynchites 24.113.7
Mericia 29.105.116
Mericisca 27.61.47
meridionale, Simulium 29.22.5
meridionalis, Margarodes 21.23.6
Meriellum 24.106.105
Meringis 30.4.10
Meringodixa 29.18.2
Meringopus 25.16.169
Merinocapsus 20.23.50
Merinus 24.87.85
meriopterum, Heterotoma 20.23.104
Meris 27.61.127
Merismus 25.19.46
Meristhus 24.48.4
meritana, Epinotia 27.38.41
merkeli, Neodiprion 25.6.4
Mermiria 11.5.23
Merobrachus 24.108.18
Merocorinae, supra 20.4.1
Merocoris 20.4.1
Merodon 29.47.56
Merodontini, supra 29.47.56
Merolonche 27.75.232
Meromacrus 29.47.64
Meromyza 29.94.50
Meromyzobia 25.25.149
Meronera 24.24.266
merons 10
Merope 28.3.1
Meropeidae, supra 28.3.1
Meropleon 27.75.261
Meroplius 29.81.2
Meroptera 27.55.328
Merosargus 29.31.10
Merostenus 25.24.8
Merothripidae, supra 22.2.1
Merothrips 22.2.1
Merragata 20.30.2
Merycomyia 29.26.8
Mesachorutes 1.2.3
Mesagroicus 24.113.25
Mesamia 21.14.126
Mescaptomyza 29.90.10
Mescinia 27.55.370
Mescohorinae, supra 25.16.465
Mesembragrotis 27.75.543
Mesembrina 29.100.49
Mesentotoma 1.5.3
Mesepiola 27.8.12
Mesidia 25.25.6
Mesites 24.113.382
Mesitiopterus 25.50.2
Meskea 27.56.6
Mesocapnia 8.3.6
Mesochorus 25.16.467
Mesoclistus 25.16.190
Mesocoelopus 24.63.44
Mesocricotopus 29.24.99
Mesocynipinae, supra 25.30.1
Mesocyphona 29.2.59
Mesodryinus 25.51.7
Mesolecanium 21.26.11
Mesoleiini, supra 25.16.346
Mesoleius 25.16.359
Mesoleptidea 25.16.366
Mesoleptus 25.16.132
Mesoleuca 27.61.214
Mesolia 27.55.199
Mesomachilis 4.1.3
Mesopoterus 24.8.5
mesonotum 21
Mesopeltita 25.19.33
Mesophora 29.46.25

Mesoplia 25.69.44
Mesopolobus 25.19.98
Mesopsocidae, supra 17.22.1
Mesopsocus 17.22.1
Mesorhaga 29.43.1
Mesosini, supra 24.106.238
Mesostenina, supra 25.16.173
Mesostenus 25.16.174
Mesothea 27.61.171
mesothorax 21
Mesovelia 20.29.1
Mesoveliidae, supra 20.29.1
Mesoxaea 25.64.2
Mesquite Katydid 11.7.4
Mesquite Longhorn 24.106.146
Messa 25.7.46
Messatoporus 25.16.184
messalina, Pyrisitia 27.42.18
Messiasia 29.35.3
Messiomyia 29.105.306
messoria, Euxoa 27.75.544 (Fig. 27.391)
Mestobregma 11.5.59
Mestra 27.46.39
Metablapylis 24.87.140
Metabletus 24.4.164
Metacanthinae, supra 20.12.1
Metachela 29.42.17
Metachroma 24.107.48
Metaclisa 24.87.86
Metaclisis 25.44.1
Metaclythia 29.45.8
Metacmaeops 24.106.193
Metacnephia 29.22.9
Metacolus 25.19.71
Metacosmus 29.40.2
Metacyclini, supra 24.107.87
Metadexia 29.105.195
Metadioctria 29.37.36
Metadontia 25.21.5
Metadoria 29.105.252
Metaforcipomyia 29.23.3
Metagonistylum 29.105.424
Metajapyx 3.4.3
Metalectra 27.75.54
Metalepsis 27.75.577
Metaleptea 11.5.33
Metaleptus 24.106.152
Metalimnobia 29.2.14
Metallata 27.75.84
Metallic Wood-boring Beetle Family,
 supra 24.46.1
metallica, Lydinoilydella 29.105.249
metallica metallica, Augochloropsis 25.66.9
metallica, Rhinonapaea 29.93.43
metallicana, Niasoma 27.38.85
metallicus, Thoron 25.43.23
Metallus 25.7.45
Metalmark Butterfly Family, supra 27.44.1
Metalpagia 29.105.164
Metamasius 24.113.367
metamorphosis 13 (Table 2.1)
Metanema 27.61.113
Metangela 29.10.1
Metanopedias 25.44.10
metanotum 21
Metanysson 25.62.70
Metaparia 24.107.39
Metapelma 25.24.4
Metaphorura 1.3.4
Metaphycus 25.25.56
Metaphyto 29.105.117
Metapodiessa 20.4.2
Metapogon 29.37.42
Metaponpneumata 27.75.207
Metapsaenythia 25.65.10
Metapterus 20.17.8

Metarranthis 27.61.114
Metastenus 25.19.129
Metasyrphus 29.47.14
Metatachina 29.105.145
Metatephritis 29.61.31
metathorax 21
Metator 11.5.58
Metatrichia 29.33.3
Metatriozoa 21.17.14
Metatropiphorus 20.18.10
Metavoria 29.105.165
Metaxaglaea 27.75.397
Metaxmeste 27.55.37
Metaxyonycha 24.107.42
Metcalfa 21.8.8
Meteoridea 25.13.62
Meteorideinae, supra 25.13.62
Meteorini, supra 25.13.147
Meteorus 25.13.147
Metephestia 27.55.390
Methia 24.106.29
Methiini, supra 24.106.24
Methocha 25.53.21
Methocinae, supra 25.53.21
meticola, Nosora 24.24.270
meticulosalis, Terastia 27.55.163
Metisotoma 1.4.16
Metoa 25.16.386
Metophthalmus 24.82.2
Metopia 29.103.7
Metopiinae, supra 25.16.284
Metopina 29.46.30
Metopininae, supra 29.46.15
Metopinini, supra 29.46.16
Metopiops 29.105.404
Metopius 25.16.287
Metopoloba 24.87.3
Metopolophium 21.19.2
Metopomuscopteryx 29.105.185
Metopomyza 29.68.9
Metoponiopsis 24.87.12
Metoponium 24.87.12
Metoposarcophaga 29.103.35
Metopotachina 29.105.86
Metopotoma 24.113.164
Metrea 27.55.21
Metretopodidae, supra 6.2.1
Metretopus 6.2.1
Metria 27.75.122
Metriini, supra 24.4.3
Metriitae, supra 24.4.3
Metriocampa 3.1.7
Metriochroa 27.14.14
Metriocnemus 29.24.110
Metrioidea 24.107.112
Metriona 24.107.186
Metrioptera 11.7.38
Metriorrhynchomiris 20.23.167
Metrius 24.4.3
Metrobates 20.27.7
metroloas, Miastor 29.11.29
Metylophorini, supra 17.23.5
Metylophorus 17.23.5
Metziella 25.63.5
Metzneria 27.23.2
Mexara 21.14.216
Mexican Bean Beetle 24.80.52
Mexican Bean Weevil 24.108.3
Mexican Black Scale 21.26.20
Mexican Fruit Fly 29.61.43
Mexican Jumping Bean Borer 27.38.56
Mexican Leaf Roller 27.38.90
Mexican Mealybug 21.25.32
Mexican Pine Beetle 24.112.11
mexicana, Blastophaga 25.18.1
mexicana, Coelioxys 25.68.24

mexicana, Diuraphis 21.19.63
mexicana, Dyseuaresta 29.61.27
mexicana, Eurema 27.42.17
mexicana, Haematomis 27.73.18
mexicana, Martarega 20.33.2
mexicana, Ornithia 24.106.100
mexicana, Sermyle 10.1.2
mexicana, Sphongophorus 21.15.13
mexicana, Tenagobia 20.35.1
mexicana, Tettigades 21.13.20
mexicana, Thyatira 27.59.3
mexicanum, Enalosalda 20.32.1
mexicanus, Pogonodaptus 24.4.120
mexicanus, Synophrus 25.34.3
mexicanus, Trachypus 25.62.107
mexicanus, Xanthandrus 29.47.8
mexico, Xiphocentron 26.2.5
Mezira 20.13.6
Mezirinae, supra 20.13.6
Mezium 24.62.2
Miacora 27.37.9
Miamimyia 29.105.331
Miarus 24.113.232
Miastor 29.11.29
Miathyria 7.7.16
micacea, Hydraecia 27.75.280
micado, Valifictorus 11.10.12
micans, Xylocopa 25.69.46
Miceopezidae, supra 29.51.1
michaelis, Neolinycus 25.16.275
Michellania 1.2.1
micheneri, Lepidomyia 29.47.55
Michenerula 25.66.6
Michiella 29.74.12
Michthisoma 24.106.20
Michthisomini, supra 24.106.20
micidus, Opsidiotrophus 29.103.9
Micracanthia 20.32.11
Micracini, supra 24.112.26
Micracis 24.112.29
Micracisella 24.112.30
Micraegialia 24.30.15
Micralcinus 24.113.240
Micralictoides 25.66.2
Micralymma 24.24.118
Micrandrena 25.65.1
Micraneflus 24.106.66
Micranoplium 24.106.76
Micranthophora 25.69.36
Micranurida 1.2.12
Micranurophorus 1.4.4
Micrapate 24.64.16
Micrasema 26.9.5
Micrathetis 27.75.319
Micrathyria 7.7.17
Micrathous 24.48.28
Micratopus 24.4.59
Micrelytrinae, supra 20.5.1
Micrempis 29.42.6
Micridium 24.15.9
Micrisotoma 1.4.17
Micrixys 24.4.97
Microaugyles 24.42.3
Microbaris 24.113.314
Microbembex 25.62.99
Microbledius 24.24.149
Microbregma 24.63.29
Microcalyptris 27.5.5
Microcara 24.32.2
Microcausta 27.55.219
Microcentini, supra 21.15.55
Microcentrum 11.7.6
Microcentrus 21.15.55
microcephala, Borboridea 29.31.23
microcephala, Suturella 24.15.4
Microcephalothrips 22.4.44

Microcerella 29.103.36
Microchaetina 29.105.56
Microcharops 25.16.429
Microchelonus 25.13.113
Microchironomus 29.24.47
Microcholus 24.113.335
Microchridium 25.50.9
Microchrysa 29.31.7
microcirculus, Pseudococcus 21.25.35
Microclytus 24.106.132
Microcoryphia, supra 4.1.1 (Fig. 4.1)
Microcrambus 27.55.212
Microctenochira 24.107.188
Microctonus 25.13.154
Microcylleopus 24.45.15
Microdera 24.107.64
Microdon 29.47.1
Microdonia 24.24.267
Microdontinae, supra 29.47.1
Microdontomerus 25.18.23
Microdosophila 29.90.17
Microdynerus 25.59.7
Microedus 24.24.119
Microgaster 25.13.119
Microgastrinae, supra 25.13.116
Microgastrini, supra 25.13.116
Microgastrura, 1.2.6
Microgoes 24.106.235
Microgramme 24.82.5
Microhelea 29.23.3
Microhelia 27.75.592
Microhyus 24.113.244
Microlarinus 24.113.151
Microledrida 21.1.7
Microleptes 25.16.480
Microlepidoptera, supra 10.1.1, 27.50.1
Microlestes 24.4.163
Microlinus 24.24.38
Microlipus 24.68.9
Microlophium 21.19.132
Microlynchia 29.106.7
Micromalthidae, supra 24.58.1
Micromalthus 24.58.1
Micromastus 24.113.243
Micromeriella 25.56.4
Micromes 24.87.24
Micromintho 29.105.212
Micromorphus 29.43.49
Micromus 23.8.7
Micromutilla 25.55.10
Micromya 29.11.9
Micromyini, supra 29.11.2
Micromyrmex 24.113.194
Micronaspis 24.55.7
Micronectinae, supra 20.35.1
Micronomada 25.69.10
Micronomadopsis 25.65.11
Microparsus 21.19.133
Micropasites 25.69.1
Micropeplinae, supra 24.24.81
Micropeplus 24.24.82
Micropeza 29.51.3
Micropezinae, supra 29.51.3
microphagus, Apterencyrtus 25.25.71
microphanos, Trjapitzinellus 25.25.63
Microphorella 29.42.32
Microphorus 29.42.33
microphotus 24.55.2
Microphthalma 29.105.54
microphthalmus, Sciocoris 20.3.23 (Fig. 20.7)
Microphthirus 19.5.2
Microphylellus 20.23.51
Microphylidae 20.23.52
Microphysidae, supra 20.22.1
Microplitis 25.13.120

Microporus 20.1.2
Microprosopa 29.98.15
microps, Baenotus 29.11.1
Micropsectra 29.24.77
microptera, Romalea 11.4.5
Micropterigidae, supra 27.1.1
Micropterigoidea, supra 27.1.1
Micropterocheilus 25.59.4
Micropteryx, see 27.1.1
micropus, Ctenophthalmus 30.4.25
Microrhopala 24.107.173
microrhopalae, Oenonogastra 25.13.105
Microsania 29.45.2
Microscapha 24.98.15
Microschatia 24.87.48
microscope slides 43
Microscydmus 24.20.2
Microsega 25.50.3
Microsillus 29.105.375
Microsiphoniella 21.19.134
Microstelis 25.68.11
Microsternus 24.76.2
Microstylum 29.37.19
Microtabanus 29.26.15
Microtendipes 29.24.58
Microteryini, supra 25.25.103
Microterys 25.25.107
Microtes 11.5.50
Microtheca 24.107.70
Microtheoris 27.55.25
Microthoraciidae, infra 19.2.2
Microthoracius, infra 19.2.2
Microthylax 24.3.4
Microthyris 27.55.173
Microtia 27.46.16
Microtominae, supra 20.17.23
Microtomus 20.17.24
Microtonus 24.98.33
microtrema, Diphyllaphis 21.19.62
Microtrichomma 29.105.94
Microtrogus 24.113.229
Microtypus 25.13.142
Micrrourosigalphus 25.13.140
Microvelia 20.28.4
Microveliinae, supra 20.28.3
Microweisea 24.80.2
Microzogus 24.63.7
Micrurapteryx 27.14.4
Micrutalini, supra 21.15.21
Micrutalis 21.15.21
Mictini, supra 20.4.8
Middle Barklice Family 17.22.1
middletonii, Aphis 21.19.15
Midge Family, supra 29.24.1
Migiwa 24.48.57
migration 25
Migratory Bird Locust 11.5.114
Migratory Grasshopper 11.5.94
mikii, Platycoenosia 29.100.30
milberti, Aglais 27.46.26 (Fig. 27.133)
Milesia 29.47.82
Milesiini, supra 29.47.72
Miletinae, supra 27.43.1
Milichia 29.74.11
Milichid Fly Family, supra 29.74.1
Milichiidae, supra 29.74.1, 29.75.1
Milichiinae, supra 29.74.9
milichioides, Phycomyza 29.96.4
militare, Hadronema 20.23.101
militaris, Smaragdina 24.107.22
Milkweed Bug 20.7.8; supra 20.8.1 (Fig. 20.28)
Milkweed Butterfly 27.49.1
Milkweed Butterfly Family, supra 27.49.1
Milkweed Tussock Moth 27.73.66
millefolii, Ozirhincus 29.11.58

milleri, Coleotechnites 27.23.19
Millieriinae, supra 27.36.1
Miloderes 24.113.119
Miloderoides 24.113.66
Milonius 29.105.376
Miltogramminae, supra 29.103.1
Miltogrammini, supra 29.103.1
milva, Neamblymorpha 25.16.228
Mimallonidae, supra 27.65.1
Mimallonoidea, supra 27.65.1
Mimesa 25.62.16
mimeticus, Dryotribus 24.113.386
mimeticus, Japetus 20.9.5
Mimobarathra 27.75.528
Mimocampa 3.1.5
Mimoceps 20.23.191
mimlogus 29.105.377
Mimophisma 27.75.133
Mimophobetron 27.55.161
Mimorista 27.55.123
mimosae, Myrtopsen 25.34.6
mimosaria, Nemoria 27.61.158 (Fig. 27.194)
Mimoschinia 27.55.44
mimosestes 24.108.17
mimudus, Ochrimnus 20.7.6
mimulus, Dysdercus 20.8.1
Mimumesa 25.62.17
Minagenia 25.60.32
Minageniini, supra 25.60.32
minatea, Gerrodes 27.75.241
mindara, Proxenus 27.75.320
Mindarus 21.19.135
Minella 29.105.186
minense, Metagonistylum 20.105.424
Mineocapsus 20.23.53
minerva, Draeculacephala 21.14.47
Minettia 29.82.8
Mineus 20.3.72
minians, Nephelodes 27.75.512 (Fig. 27.385)
mini, Crenulaspidiotus 21.38.21
miniata, Hypoprepia 27.73.17 (Fig. 27.280)
minijas, Eumaeus 27.43.11
minima, Carulaspis 21.38.13
minima, Eumicremma 27.75.209
minima, Hamaba 24.113.227
minima, Hypocrisias 27.73.54
minima, Pseudocharis 27.73.88
minimum, Monomorium 25.58.31 (Fig. 25.36)
Minimus Mealybug 21.25.32
minimus, Mineocapsus 20.23.53
minimus, Phenacoccus 21.25.32
minimus, Xeracris 11.5.70
Mining Scale 21.38.41
ministra, Datana 27.71.2 (Fig. 27.270)
ministrana, Eulia 27.38.63
Ministrymon 27.43.18
Minofala 27.75.384
minor, Bedellia 27.13.3
minor, Berytinus 20.12.7
minor, Clemmus 24.81.3
minor, Earobia 25.16.442
minor, Enicomira 29.81.8
minor, Incisitermes 15.2.4
minor, Isotomiella 1.4.18
minor, Labia 13.3.4 (Fig. 13.5)
minor, Parorgerius 21.11.10
Mint Aphid 21.19.155
Minthea 24.65.2
Minthozelia 29.105.196
minuenda, Idona 21.14.75
minuscula, Lepidobregma 27.10.16
minusculalis, Streptopalia 27.55.255

minuta, Acleris 27.38.61
minuta, Drepanaphis 21.19.64
minuta, Ellipes 11.6.2
minuta, Eviridemas 27.75.385
minuta, Gracilia 24.106.36 (Fig. 24.181)
minuta, Kronaea 27.52.4
minuta, Poladryas 27.46.12
Minute Bark Beetle Family,
supra 24.78.1
Minute Beetle Family, supra 24.33.1
Minute Black Scavenger Fly Family,
supra 29.15.1
Minute Bladder Bug Family 20.22.1
Minute Bog Beetle Family, supra 24.10.1
Minute Brown Scavenger Beetle Family,
supra 24.82.1
Minute Cypress Scale 21.38.13
Minute Egg Parasite 25.28.8
Minute Fungus Beetle Family, supra 24.79.1
Minute Leaf Miner Moth Family,
supra, 27.5.1
Minute Marsh-loving Beetle Family,
supra 24.43.1
Minute Moss Beetle Family, supra 24.13.1
Minute Pirate Bug Family 20.21.1
Minute Scavenger Beetle Family,
supra 24.17.1
Minute Tree-fungus Beetle Family,
supra 24.92.1
minutissma, Microgastrura 1.2.6
minutum, Microchridium 25.50.9
minutum, Trichogramma 25.28.8
minutus, Anurotropus 25.16.101
minutus, Arrhenodes 24.110.3 (Figs.
24.256, 24.257)
minutus, Copris 24.30.10
minutus, Dinoderus 24.64.5
minutus, Eulechriops 24.113.277
minutus, Homalocoris 20.17.23
minutus, Lathridius 24.82.3 (Fig. 24.150)
minutus, Physemus 24.43.6
minutus, Scalmophorus 21.15.12
minutus, Thrimolus 24.91.4
minyas, Aulogmnus 25.26.32
Minymischa 25.50.7
Minyomerus 24.113.56
Mioctenopsylla 30.7.8
Miodera 27.75.529
Miogryllus 11.10.11
Miojapyx 3.4.9
Miomoptera, supra 10.1.1
Mioptachys 24.4.51
Miota 25.42.4
Miotropis 25.26.19
Mipseltyrus 24.25.74
Mira 25.25.118
mira, Crawfordiella 21.17.19
mira, Catocala 27.75.148, (Fig. 27.338)
mirabile, Eutrichosoma ,25.19.7
mirabilis, Helcomyza 29.78.4
mirabilis, Heminocloa 27.75.343
mirabilis, Hemisphaerodella 20.23.23
mirabilis, Ichneumonops 29.105.26
mirabilis, Juniperella 24.46.16
mirabilis, Orimarga 29.2.20
mirabilis, Patraptorthodius 24.54.5
mirabilis, Scorpioteleia 25.42.5
Miracavira 27.75.306
Miraces 24.107.78
miracula, Timodema 21.11.13
miraculosa, Idioglossa 27.15.41
Miraini, supra 25.25.116
miranda, Saissetia 21.26.20
Mirax 25.13.121
miriamella, Leucomele 27.10.7
Miridae, supra 20.23.1 (Fig. 20.2)

Mirificarma (27.23.62)
Mirinae, supra 20.23.138
Mirini, supra 20.23.138
Mirolepisma 56.3.6
Mirolynx 25.26.23
Mirotelenomus 25.43.20
mirum, Hedychreides 25.50.14
mirus, Paracrias 25.26.79
Mirzagrammosoma 25.26.31
miscecolorella, Walshia 27.21.20
Mischievous Bird Grasshopper 11.5.114
Mischocyttarus 25.59.29
Mischoserphus 25.39.6
Miscodera 24.4.32
Miscogaster 25.19.50
Miscogasterinae, supra 25.19.41
Miscogasterini, supra 25.19.45
Miscophini, supra 25.62.44
Miscophus 25.62.47
Miselia 27.75.490
miserabilis, Andrena 25.65.1
miserabilis, Cyanophrus 27.43.25
Misericoccus 21.25.25
misippus, Hypolimnas 27.46.29
Misodema 21.6.10
Misogada 27.71.27
missionensis, Icaricia 27.43.50
mississippiensis, Allopodops 20.3.20
mississippiennis, Mysidia 21.9.3
missus, Tomocerus 1.5.13
Mistharnophantia 21.8.10
Misturaphis 21.19.136
mitchellensis, Adelopsis 24.22.6
mitchellii, Neonympha 27.48.5
mitis, Cinochira 29.105.38
Mitostylus 24.113.45
Mitoura 27.43.26
Mitrops 21.11.2
Mixogaster 29.47.3
Mixomachilis 4.1.4
Mixothrips 22.5.68
mixta, Hedria 29.79.12
mixta, Hypothyce 24.330.70
mixtus, Allygus 21.14.105
mixtus, Anthonomopsis 24.113.205
Mnemonica 27.2.1
m-nigrum, Desmometopa 29.74.8
Mnioes 25.16.307
Mniotype 27.75.422
moapensis, Usingerina 20.38.1
Mochlosoma 29.105.68
Mochlonyx 29.19.2
Mocis 27.75.142
Mocuellus 21.14.182
Modest Sphinx 27.70.18
modesta, Argoravinia 29.103.23
modesta, Cyphopelta 20.23.149
modesta, Micromeriella 25.56.4
modesta, Montezumina 11.7.7
modesta, Pachysphinx 27.70.18 (Fig.
27.248)
modesta, Trichopteromyia 29.11.11
modesta, Prochloridea 27.75.376
modestrum, Stneonema 6.6.8 (Fig. 6.7)
modestus, Agroecotettix 11.5.84
modestus, Atomoscelis 20.23.33
modestus, Cryrtiopeltis 20.23.28
modestus, Hylaeus 25.63.5
modica, Oligia 27.75.258 (Fig. 27.357)
Moehnia 29.10.17
moerens, Chaetophylidea 20.23.74
moerens, Ranzovius 20.23.65
moestus, Macromerus 24.113.273
Mogoplistinae, supra 11.10.2
Mohavacris 11.3.2
mojave, Arpediothrips 22.4.22

Mojavia 27.55.49
Mojaviodes 27.55.50
Molamba 24.79.9
Molanna 26.15.1
Mollannidae, supra 26.15.1
Mollannodes 26.15.2
Mole Cricket Family, supra 11.11.1
moleculus, Pseudoplateros 24.57.11
molesta, Grapholita 27.38.53
molesta, Solenopsis 25.58.33 (Fig. 25.42)
molitor, Tenebrio 24.87.92
molliculus, Megalocoleus 20.23.81
mollipes, Draeculacephala 21.14.47
molliterga, Cordylopsis 29.11.143
Molophilus 29.2.62
Molorchini, supra 24.106.94
Molorchus 24.106.94
Mompha 27.19.1
Momphid Moth Family, supra 27.19.1
Momphidae, supra 27.19.1
monachus, Araeopidius 24.34.8
Monalocoris 20.23.25
Monanus 24.72.7
Monarch Butterfly 27.49.1
Monardia 29.11.2
Monardis 25.7.66
Monarthropalpus 29.11.109
Monarthrum 24.112.66
Monca 27.40.48
moneduloides, Tanyoprymnus 25.62.91
Moneilema 24.106.231
Moneilemini, supra 24.106.231
Monelata 25.42.25
Monellia 21.19.137
Monelliopsis 21.19.138
Monepidosis 29.11.55
moneta, Dione 27.46.2
Moniaecera 25.62.61
monilicornis, Priognathus 24.90.7
monilicornis, Rhynchoheles 29.23.10
monilis, Ceophyllus 24.25.78
Monilosmia 25.68.21
Monilothrips 22.4.7
monima, Eunica 27.46.36
Monitoriella 25.13.48
Monkey Grasshopper Family 11.2.1
Monobaeus 25.19.1
monobasic 4
Monobia 25.59.17
Monoblastus 25.16.61
Monocampa 3.1.1
Monoceromyia 29.47.71
Monocesta 24.107.74
Monochaetoscinella 29.94.12
Monochamini, supra 24.106.232
Monochamus 24.106.237
Monochroa 27.23.5
Monoclona 29.9.66
Monocteninae, supra 25.6.1
Monoctenus 25.6.1
Monoctonia, supra 25.14.12
Monoctonus 25.14.12
Monoculicoides 29.23.5
monodactyla, Emmelina 27.58.20
Monodiamesa 29.24.42
Monodontomerinae, supra 25.18.11
Monodontomerus 25.18.15
Monoedinae, supra 24.93.28
Monoedus 24.93.28
monogama, Aphenolia 24.70.13
Monohelea 29.23.15
Monoleuca 27.52.18
Monolexis 25.13.17
Monomacra 24.107.131
Monommatidae, supra 24.85.1
Monomorium 25.58.31

Mononychini, supra 24.113.282
Monopelopia 29.24.30
Monophadnoides 25.7.70
Monophadnus 25.7.62
Monophlebinae, supra 21.23.7
Monophylla 24.67.5
Monopis 27.10.41
Monopsis 21.5.3
Monopsyllus 30.7.9
Monoptilota 27.55.306
Monorachis 21.1.3
monositus, Tunga 30.1.2
Monosoma 25.7.80
Monostegia 25.7.81
Monostoecha 27.61.207
Monosynamma 20.23.54
Monotoma 24.71.2
Monotominae, supra 24.71.2
Monotrysia, supra 27.5.1
Monoxia 24.107.84
Monoychus 24.113.282
monstrosa, Cyphoderiis 11.8.1
montana, Melanolemma 24.113.135
montana, Rossiana 26.10.52
montana, Sphingicampa 27.69.3
montanaria, Snowia 27.61.125
Montandoniola 20.21.11
montanum, Asindulum 29.9.5
montanum, Macromalon 25.16.297
montanus, Colladonus 21.14.108
montanus, Diamanus 30.7.4
Monterey Pine Cone Beetle 24.112.63
Monterey Pine Weevil 24.113.171
Monterey-pine Resin Midge 29.11.113
montezumae, Thalassa 24.80.18
Montezumia 25.59.18
Montezumina 11.7.7
monticola, Amphivectura 24.68.23
monticola, Brochella 29.42.35
montis, Asterocampa 27.47.3
montrouierii, Cryptolaemus 24.80.13
Monumetha 25.68.18
monuste, Ascia 27.42.6 (Fig. 27.88)
monyana, Eugymnogaster 29.105.15
Moodna 27.55.395
mopsus, Mamurius 20.4.12
moraguesi, Montandoniola 20.21.11
morainensis, Diphyothrips 22.5.35
Moranila 25.19.31
Mordella 24.99.5
Mordellidae, supra 24.99.1
Mordellini, supra 24.99.1
Mordellistena 24.99.7
Mordvilkoja 21.19.139
morelios, Smeringodynerus 25.59.10
Morellia 29.100.55
Morganella 21.38.50
morgani, Campodea 3.1.1
morgani, Phthirothrips 22.5.57
mori, Bombyx 27.67.1 (Figs. 27.207, 27.208)
mori, Pseudodendrothrips 22.4.11
mori, Tetraleurodes 21.18.16
morio, Chelisches 13.4.1 (Figs. 13.6, 13.7)
morio, Nesoselandria 25.7.6
Morion 24.4.31
Morionini, supra 24.4.31
Morius 24.25.10
Mormidea 20.3.32
mormo, Apodemia 27.44.7 (Fig. 27.117)
Mormon Cricket 11.7.26
mormonia, Speyeria 27.46.8
Morning-glory Leaf Miner 27.13.3
Morodora 25.19.62
Moromorpha 20.3.31

Morophagoides 27.10.21
morpheus, Caradrina 27.75.322
Morphocorixa 20.35.14
Morpholeria 29.84.16
morrili, Corythucha 20.14.7
Morrill Lace Bug 20.14.7
morrilli, Cosmocomoidea 25.27.7
morrisonella, Heterographis 27.55.358
morrisoni, Paracolpha 21.19.160
morrisoni, Pygmaeococcus 21.25.36
morrisoni, Stinga 27.40.64
Morrisonia 27.75.509
morsei, Gymnoscirtetes 11.5.79
Morseinae, supra 11.2.1
morsicaria, Sicya 27.61.134
Morsyma 25.55.6
Mortarjoint Casemaker Caddisfly Family, supra 26.14.1
Morulina 1.2.15
morulus, Diochanthrax 29.40.59
morus, Acroplophus 27.10.33
Morychini, supra 24.35.2
Morychus 24.35.2
mosca, Ianius 27.75.100
Moselia 8.4.3
mosellana, Sitodiplosis 29.11.144
Moselyana 26.10.50
Moserina 25.26.65
Mosillus 29.93.1
Mosquito Family, supra 29.20.1
Mossy Rose Gall Wasp 25.34.16
Moth Fly Family, supra 29.12.1
Mothlike Netwing Family, supra 23.6.1
Moths, Butterflies, and Skippers, supra 27.1.1
Motschulskium 24.15.8
Mottled Cupes 24.1.1
Mottled Gray Cutworm 27.75.587
Mottled Sand Grasshopper 11.5.48
Mottled Tortise Beetle 24.107.183
Motya 27.75.176
motya, Libytheana 27.45.1
Mountain Ash Sawfly 25.7.30
Mountain Leafhopper 21.14.108
Mountain Midge Family, supra 29.4.1
Mountain Pine Beetle 24.112.11
Mountian Silverspot 27.46.8
mountains 29
mountaina, Clossiana 27.46.11
Mouralia 27.75.150
Mourning-cloak 27.46.25
Mourning-cloaks 27.46.24
Mouselike Barklice Family 17.24.1
mozardi, Languria 24.75.6
Mozena 20.4.9
mucida, Brachymelecta 25.69.40
mucida, Perothops 24.51.1
mucorea, Trichobaris 24.113.316
mucronatum, Elaphidion 24.106.80
Mud-backed Beetle Family, supra 24.14.1
muescbecki, Dinostigma 25.13.101
muesebecki, Eunomothorax 25.46.5
Muesebeckia 25.13.127
Muesebeckidium 25.50.6
Muesebeckiini, supra 25.13.127
muhlenbergiae, Astictoneura 29.11.64
Mula 21.9.2
Mulberry Whitefly 21.18.16
Mulcticola 18.1.37
muliebris, Discritus 25.16.36
mulleolella, Heliades 27.55.260
mulsanti, Mesovelia 20.29.1
Mulsantina 24.80.48
Multareis 21.15.16
Multareoides 21.15.125

multicaudata, Pterourus 27.41.7
multicinctus, Tomostethus 25.7.56
multilinea, Leucania 27.75.500 (Fig. 27.384)
multilinea, Tyrissa 27.75.113
multilineata, Pigia 27.61.178 (Fig. 27.195)
multiplaga, Apodemia 27.44.7
multipora, Crassaspis 21.38.20
multispinosa, Acholla 20.17.11
multistriatus, Scolytus 24.112.23
Mumetopia 29.70.3
munda, Fomricilla 24.102.15
mundissima, Concana 27.75.77
mundula, Ommatochila 27.75.50
mundum, Paralopbium 24.63.12
munitalis, Bonchis 27.55.254
Munroeodes 27.55.76
Munroessa 27.55.9
Murgantia 20.3.48
muricolork, Opharus 27.73.62
murina, Pygarctia 27.73.70 (Fig. 27.310)
murinus, Neelus 1.6.1
Murmidiinae, supra 24.78.3
Murmidius 24.87.3
murrayanae, Dendroctonus 24.112.11
Murrayella 25.62.9
murtfeldtiana, Neolasioptera 29.11.68
murtfeldtlla, Caloptilia 27.14.1 (Fig. 27.31)
Musca 19.100.58
Muscaphis 21.19.140
muscaria, Xenochaetina 29.82.22
musci, Micranurophorus 1.4.4
musci, Muscaphis 21.19.140
Muscidae, supra 29.100.1
Muscidifurax 25.19.123
Muscina 29.100.47
Muscinae, supra 29.100.48
muscles 10
Muscoidea, supra 29.98.1
Muscomorpha, supra 29.44.1
Muscopteryx 29.105.187
musculus, Anthonomus 24.113.208
Museum Beetle 24.62.1 (Fig. 24.119)
Mushroom Flies 29.10.10
Mustard White 27.42.5
mustelinus, Hepialus 27.4.2
mutabilis, Cotinis 24.30.121
mutabilis, Cryptocephalus 24.107.25
mutator, Monchamus 24.106.237
muticum, Calephelis 27.44.2
muticus, Neides 20.12.6
muticus, Scolytus 24.112.23
Mutillidae 25.55.1
Mutillinae, supra 25.55.19
mutus, Pterostichus 24.4.85 (Fig. 24.37)
Mutuuraia 27.55.90
Myas 24.4.83
Mycetaea 24.81.5
Mycetaeinae, supra 24.81.1
Mycetaspis 21.38.51
Mycetaulus 29.64.1
Mycetina 24.81.13
Mycetobia 29.14.3
Mycetobiinae, supra 29.14.3
Mycetococcus 21.35.2
Mycetochara 24.88.13
mycetoecus, Glyptophorus 24.74.2
Mycetophagidae, supra 24.91.1
Mycetophagini, supra 24.91.1
Mycetophagus 24.91.1
Mycetophila 29.9.35
Mycetophilidae, infra 29.9.1
Mycetophilinae, supra 29.9.20
Mycetoporus 24.24.180
Mycetoseoritis 25.58.52
Mychocerus 24.78.4

Mycodiplosis 29.11.98
Mycodrosophila 29.90.12
Mycomya 29.9.52
Mycophila 29.11.3
Mycotrogus 24.87.112
Mycotrupes 24.30.54
Mycterinae, supra 24.90.12
Mycterophora 27.75.25
Mycterothrips 22.4.45
Mycterus 24.90.12
Mydaea 29.100.24
Mydaeina 29.100.14
Mydaeinae, supra 29.100.19
Mydas 29.35.4
Mydas Fly Family, supra 29.35.1
mydae, Wyliea 29.37.76
Mydidae, supra 29.35.1
Mydinae, supra 29.35.3
Myelaphus 29.37.32
Myelois 27.55.293
Myelopsis 27.55.294
myersi, Aloephagus 21.19.4
myersi, Carabunia 25.25.119
Myiocephalus 25.13.155
Myioclonia 29.105.188
Myiocnema 25.25.18
Myiomma 20.23.4
Myiomyrmica 29.58.13
Myiopharus 29.105.253
Myiophasia 29.105.55
Myiophasiini, supra 29.105.55
Myiophthiria 29.106.3
Mylabrinae, supra 24.108.5
mylitta, Phyciodes 27.46.20
Myllaena 24.24.268
Myllocerus 24.113.71
Mylogymnocarena 29.61.30
Mymar 25.27.15
Mymaridae, supra 25.27.1
Mymarinae, supra 25.27.5
Mymarini, supra 25.27.15
mymaripenne, Megaphragma 25.28.2
Myndus 21.1.4
Myobiopsis 29.105.222
Myochroocoris 20.23.55
Myochrous 24.107.51
Myodocha 20.7.66
Myodochini, supra 20.7.44
Myodopsylla 30.5.2
Myoleja 29.61.33
Myolepta 29.47.54
Myopa 29.49.6
myopaeformis, Eurycephalomyia 29.58.20
Myopia 1.4.23
Myopina 29.99.3
Myopinae, supra 29.49.4
Myopinini, supra 29.99.3
Myopsocidae, supra 17.24.1
Myopsocus 17.24.2
Myosargus 29.31.35
Myospila 29.100.23
Myothyriopsis 29.105.378
Myrafant 25.58.37
Myrmaphaenus 25.58.66
Myrmecaphodius 24.30.21
Myrmechixeninae, supra 24.93.29
Myrmechixenus 24.93.29
Myrmecina 25.58.40
Myrmecinini, supra 25.58.40
Myrmecocystus 25.58.71
myrmeciodes, Myrmecothea 29.58.14
Myrmecophila 11.10.1
Myrmecophilinae, supra 11.10.1
Myrmecopora 24.24.269
Myrmecopria 25.42.35
Myrmecothea 29.58.14

Myrmelachista 25.58.64
Myrmelachistini, supra 25.58.64
Myrmeleon 23.14.10
Myrmeleontidae, supra 23.14.1
Myrmeleontinae, supra 23.14.10
Myrmeleontini, supra 23.14.10
Myrmeleontoidea, supra 23.14.1
Myrmentoma 25.58.66
Myrmex 24.113.193
Myrmica 25.58.21
Myrmicinae, supra 25.58.21
Myrmicini, supra 25.58.21
Myrmicodipnella 17.2.3
Myrmilloides 25.55.15
Myrmobrachys 25.58.66
Myrmosa 25.55.3
Myrmosicarius 29.46.27
Myrmosina 25.55.3
Myrmosinae, supra 25.55.3
Myrmosula 25.55.5
Myrmothrix 25.58.66
myronella, Cabnia 27.55.411
myron, Darapsa 27.70.40 (Fig. 27.263)
Myrsidea 18.6.26
Myrtopsen 25.34.6
Myscelia 27.46.35
Mysidia 21.9.3
mysippusalis, Mutuuraia 27.55.90
mystacea, Rhagio 29.28.7
Mystacella 29.105.379
Mystacides 26.18.3
Mystacosmia 25.68.21
Mystaxus 24.98.25
mysteca, Amblytropidia 11.5.21
Mythicomyia 29.40.23
Mythicomyiinae, supra 29.40.22
Myxophaga, supra 24.10.1
Myxosargini, supra 29.31.35
Myzaphis 21.19.141
Myzia 24.80.36
Myzininae 25.53.6
Myzinum 25.53.6
Myzocallis 21.19.142
Myzodium 21.19.143
Myzosiphon 21.19.185
Myzus 21.19.144

N

nabicula 20.18.6
Nabidae, supra 20.18.1
Nabinae, supra 20.18.4
Nabini, supra 20.18.4
Nabis 20.18.5
Nacaeus 24.24.94
Nacarina 23.9.5
Nacerdes 24.97.4
Nacerdinae, supra 24.97.3
Nacerdini, supra 24.97.3
Nacopa 27.75.370
Nacophora 27.61.88
Nacophorini, supra 27.61.88
Nadata 27.71.3
nadineae, Discocerina 29.93.12
Naemia 24.80.49
Naera 27.23.13
Naevana naevana, Rhopobota 27.38.40,
 changed in "Checklist" to unipunctana
naiads 13, 14
nais, Apodemia 27.44.4
Nallachius 23.10.1
Namacus 20.4.21
Namamyia 26.14.2
Namunaria 24.93.13
nana, Mancia 29.40.50
nanella, Recurvaria 27.23.18

Naniteta 27.65.3
Nanium 25.16.334
Nanna 29.98.4
Nannium 20.13.8
Nannobotys 27.55.41
Nannocyrtopogon 29.37.47
Nannodioctria 29.37.31
Nannothemis 7.7.18
Nanocladius 29.24.100
Nanomyina 29.43.50
Nanophyes 24.113.17
Nanophylini, supra 24.113.17
Nanoips 24.113.203
Nanopsocetae, supra 17.6.1
Nanopsocus 17.7.2
Nanosella 24.15.1
Nanosellinae, supra 24.15.1
Nanothrips 22.5.69
Nantucket Pine Tip Moth 27.38.19
nanulus nanulus, Neodiprion 25.6.4
Nanus 24.113.52
nanus, Fania 27.37.7
napaea, Boloria 27.46.9
napaea, Litholomia 27.75.391
napi, Artogeia 27.42.5(Fig. 27.86)
Napochus 24.20.3
Napomyza 29.68.15
naranjal, Paraleyrodes 21.18.19
narcaeusalis, Ommatospila 27.55.187
Narcissus Bulb Fly 29.47.56
narda, Krenopelopia 29.24.28
Narnia 20.4.5
Narpus 24.45.16
Narraga 27.61.165
Narrow Barklice Family 17.11.1
Narrow Snail Eater 24.4.16
Narrownecked Grain Beetle 24.102.8
Narrow-waisted Bark Beetle Family,
 supra 24.90.1
Narrow-winged Bush Grasshopper 11.5.89
Narrow-winged Damselfly Family 7.11.1
Narrow-winged Mantis 14.1.10
Narthecius 24.72.11
Narthccophora 27.75.341
Narthecura 25.16.264
Narvesus 20.17.34
nasalis, Gasterophilus 29.102.1
nasalis, Physeghenua 29.82.12
Nascia 27.55.78
Nasiaeschna 7.4.9
nasica, Rhingia 29.47.39
nasicus, Conocephalocoris 20.23.19
nasidens, Pachodynerus 25.59.19
Nasiternella 29.2.24
naso, Evotus 24.113.106
nasoni, Cnodacophora 29.51.1
Nasonia 25.19.107
Nasonovia 21.19.145
Nassipa 24.98.51
nastes, Colias 27.42.11
Nastra 27.40.49
nasturtii, Aphis 21.19.15
Nasusina 27.61.242
nasuta, Bostaera 21.2.14
nasuta, Neamblyjoppa 25.16.254
nasuta, Tylomyza 29.68.5
Nasutitermes 15.4.4
Nasutitermitinae, supra 15.4.4
nasutus, Amblytylus 20.23.31
nasutus, Zagryphus 25.16.53
Natada 27.52.15
natans, Hydroscapha 24.11.1
Natarsia 29.24.13
Nathalis 27.42.20
Nathriini, supra 24.106.93
Nathrius 24.106.93

Native Elm Bark Beetle 24.112.10
Naubates 18.1.38
Naucles 24.98.46
Naucoridae, supra 20.38.1
Naucorinae, supra 20.38.3
Naupactini, supra 24.113.23
Nauphoeta 14.6.7
Nausibius 24.72.8
Nausigaster 29.47.59
Naustiform Termites 15.4.1
Nautes 24.87.123
Navasota 27.55.416
Navel Orangeworm 27.55.297
naviculatus, Nephus 24.80.7
Neacanthocinus 24.106.270
Neaethus 21.6.11
Nealgedonia 27.55.89
Nealiolus 25.13.137
Nealyda 27.23.1
Neamblyjoppa 25.16.254
Neamblymorpha 25.16.228
Neanefulus 24.106.63
Neanthophylax 24.106.182
Neanura 1.2.16
Neanurinae, supra 1.2.12
Neaphaenops 24.4.40
Neapodops 20.3.16a
Nearctaphis 21.19.146
nearctica, Diphora 25.42.12
nearctica, Manda 24.24.148
nearctica, Nomophila 27.55.130
nearctica, Paduniella 26.2.4
nearctica, Parablostothrix 25.25.84
nearctica, Plecia 29.8.3 (Fig. 29.14; 29.15)
nearctica, Prosopigastra 25.62.43
nearctica, Stethantyx 25.16.450
nearctica, Xyelecia 25.1.34
nearcticum, Rhopalosma 25.61.1
nearcticus, Nemopalpus 29.12.3
nearcticus, Aivalykus 25.13.2
nearcticus, Calcaritermes 15.2.7
nearcticus, Embolemus 25.52.2
nearcticus, Mesomachilis 4.1.3
nearcticus, Nemopalpus 29.12.3
Nearctopsylla 30.4.18
neareiatella, Wunderia 27.55.364
Neargyractis 27.55.17
Nearina, supra 29.105.312
Neaspilota 29.61.40
Neatus 24.87.87
Neaviperla 8.8.3
Nebaocharis 25.25.150
nebrascensis, Phoetaliotes 11.5.102
Nebria 24.4.10
Nebriini, supra 24.4.8
Nebriitae, supra 24.4.7
nebris, Papaipema 27.75.279
Nebritus 29.32.2
nebulosa, Cladochaeta 29.90.13
nebulosa, Grallipeza 29.51.5
nebulosa, Hebestola 24.106.236
nebulosa, Leptophlebia 6.7.5 (Fig. 6.8)
nebulosa, Odontocynips 25.34.41
nebulosa, Pseudiastata 29.90.4
neublosus, Brachynemurus 23.14.2 (Fig. 23.13)
neublosus, Deraeocoris 20.23.14
necans, Dilyta 25.33.4
necopinus, Amphalius 30.7.1
Necrobisa 24.67.31
Necrodes 24.21.6
Necrodini, supra 24.21.6
Necrophilini, supra 24.21.5
Necrophilus 24.21.5
Nectarosiphon 21.19.144
Nectar-sucking Blister Beetle 24.101.19

Nectopsyche 26.18.4
Necremnus 25.26.3
Necydalini, supra 24.106.170
Necydalis 24.106.170
Nedra 27.75.297
Neduba 11.7.39
Needle Miner Moth Family, supra 27.31.1
Neelidae, supra 1.6.1
Neelides 1.6.1
Neelus 1.6.1
Nefoncerus 24.30.59
nefrax, Borkhausenia 27.15.33
Nefusa 25.7.50
Negalasa 27.55.245
Negasilus 29.37.74
Negalius 24.101.8
Negastriinae, supra 24.48.55
Negastrius 24.48.55
neglecta, Pseudospinola 25.50.21
neglecta, Saissetia 21.26.20
neglectus, Cratypedes 11.5.42
neglectus, Polycyrtus 25.16.175
negligere, Thymaris 25.16.51
Negosiana 21.14.21
Negro Bug 20.2.3
Negro Bug Family 20.2.1
negundella, Caloptilia 27.14.1
negundinis, Periphyllus 21.19.165
negundinis, Psylla 21.17.27
Nehalennia 7.11.11
Neichnea 24.67.23
Neides 20.12.6
Neididae 20.12.1
Neivamyrmex 25.58.3
Neladius 24.20.9
Nelaspis 21.38.52
Neleothymus 25.16.439
Neliopisthus 25.16.51
nelsoni, Mitoura 27.43.26
Nelsonites 24.4.39
Neltumius 24.108.12
Nelucania 27.75.523b
Nemadini, supra 24.22.2
Nemadus 24.22.2
Nemagenia 25.60.12
Nemandrena 25.65.1
Nemapogon 27.10.1
Nematidiini, supra 23.93.19
Nematidium 24.93.19
Nematinae, supra 25.7.15, 25.7.41
Nematini, supra 25.7.18
Nematinus 25.7.26
Nematocampa 27.61.156
Nematocera, supra 29.1.1
Nematodes 24.52.25
Nematolinus 24.24.40
Nematoplinae, supra 24.86.4
Nematoplus 24.86.4
Nematoproctus 29.43.24
Nematus 25.7.32
Nemeris 27.61.126
Nemeritis 25.16.403
nemesis, Calephelis 27.44.2
Nemestrinidae, supra 29.39.1
Nemobiinae, supra 11.10.13
Nemocapnia 8.3.7
Nemocestes 24.113.88
Nemochaeta 129.105.91
Nemognatha 24.101.19
Nemognathina, supra 24.101.18
Nemognathinae, supra 24.101.17
Nemognathini, supra 24.101.18
Nemomydas 29.35.7
Nemonychidae, supra 24.113.13
Nemonychinae, supra 24.113.13
Nemopalpus 29.12.3

Nemophora 27.8.13
Nemopoda 29.81.3
nemoratus, Heterarthrus 25.7.44
nemorensis, Pissodes 24.113.171
Nemoria 27.61.158
Nemoriini, supra 27.61.157
Nemorilla 29.105.386
Nemorimyza 29.68.6
nemoris, Osmai 25.68.21
Nemosoma 24.66.8
Nemotarsus 24.4.158
Nemotaulius 26.10.16
Nemotelinae, supra 29.31.29
Nemotelus 29.31.30
Nemoura 8.1.4
Nemouridae, supra 8.1.1
Nemourinae, supra 8.1.3
Nemouroidea, supra 8.1.1
nenuphar, Conotrachelus 24.113.238
Neoalcis 27.61.21
Neoalticomerus 29.67.2
Neoalosterna 24.106.210
Neoamphorophora 21.19.147
Neoarctia 27.73.45
Neoascia 29.47.48
Neobaphion 24.87.142
Neobarrettia 11.7.24
Neobellamira 24.106.196
Neobidessus 24.7.12
Neobisnius 24.24.9
Neoblacus 25.13.130
Neoborella 20.23.168
Neoborops 20.23.169
Neobrotica 24.107.95
Neocapsus 20.23.170
Neocatachysta 27.55.6
Neocatocha 29.11.24
Neocatolaccus 25.19.118
Neocenchrea 21.9.6
Neoceraphron 25.45.2
Neocharactus 25.7.69
Neochetina 24.113.189
Neochirosia 29.98.32
Neochlamisus 24.107.34
Neochrysis 25.50.22
Neochrysocharis 25.26.63
Neochrysops 29.26.9
Neocicada 21.13.11
Neocimberis 24.113.13
Neocladini, supra 25.25.119
Neoclypeodytes 24.7.13
Neoclytus 24.106.124
Neococcidencyrtus 25.25.95
Neococcoidea, supra 21.24.1
Neococytius 27.70.3
Neocoelidia 21.14.38
Neocoelidiinae, supra 21.14.38
Neocoelidiini, supra 21.14.38
Neocoelioxys 25.68.24
Neocoelpa 29.77.1
Neocolpodia 29.11.53
Neocompsa 24.106.82
Neoconis 23.5.3
Neoconocephalus 11.7.19
Neocorixa 20.35.6
Neocorylobium 21.19.122
neocorylus, Curculio 24.113.200
Neocrania 27.2.4
Neocremastus 25.16.440
Neoculex 29.20.12
Neocurtilla 11.11.2
Neocylloepus 24.45.17
Neocymbopteryx 27.55.30
neocypris, Phoebis 27.42.14
Neocyptera 29.105.22
Neocyrtus 24.19.7

Neodactylota 27.23.36
Neodasytes 24.68.48
Neodeceia 29.82.9
Neodexiopsis 29.100.2
Neodichocera 29.105.146
Neodiplocampta 29.40.49
Neodiplotoxa 29.94.48
Neodiprion 25.6.4
Neodonus 21.14.113
Neodryinus 25.51.11
Neodusmetia 25.25.46
Neoelmis 24.45.18
Neoephemera 6.15.1
Neoephemeridae, supra 6.15.1
Neoerythromma 7.11.12
Neoeurygenius 24.103.4
Neofaculta 27.23.57
Neofischeria 29.105.126
Neogalea 27.75.441
Neogalerucella 24.107.79
neogama, Catoclala 27.75.148 (Fig. 27.335)
Neogastrallus 24.63.20
Neogcodes 29.38.5
Neogerris 20.27.2
Neogimnomera 29.98.7
Neogonatopus 25.51.23
Neogreeneia 25.16.391
Neogriphoneura 29.82.10
Neogrotella 27.75.607
Neohaematopinus 19.7.3
Neoharmonia 24.80.50
Neohedobia 24.63.2
Neoheegeria 22.5.44
Neohelvibotys 27.55.94
Neohermes 23.2.4
Neoheterocerus 24.42.5
Neohydrotaea 29.100.33
Neohylemyia 29.99.20
Neohypdonus 24.48.56
Neoitamus 29.37.75
Neokakimia 21.19.145
Neokolla 21.14.58
Neolarra 25.69.3
Neolarrını, supra 25.69.3
Neolasioptera 29.11.68
Neolecanium 21.26.12
Neoleptotyphlus 24.24.167
Neoleria 29.84.14
Neoleucinodes 27.55.106
Neoleucophenga 29.90.3
Neoleucopis 29.83.9
Neolimnophila 29.2.43
Neolinognathidae, infra 19.8.1
Neolinognathus, infra 19.8.1
Neolinycus 25.16.275
Neolipoptena 29.106.10
Neomachilellus 4.2.3
Neomachilis 4.1.8
Neomachlotica 27.28.2
Neomallodon 24.106.5
Neomastix 24.113.210
Neomedon 24.24.62
Neomegachile 25.68.22
neomexicana, Anusia 25.25.26
neomexicana, Rhyacionia 27.38.19
neomexicanus, Scaphinotus 24.4.16
neomexicanus, Toreus 29.42.38
Neomida 24.87.96
Neominois 27.48.12
Neominthoini, supra 29.105.275
Neomochtherus 29.37.74
Neomon 25.16.67
Neomuscina 29.100.53
Neomymar 25.27.16
Neomyzocallis 21.19.142

Neomyzus 21.19.24
Neonaphorura 1.3.4
Neonasonovia 21.19.102
Neonemobius 11.10.16
Neoneura 7.10.1
Neoneurinae, supra 25.13.145
Neoneurus 25.13.146
Neonympha 28.48.5
Neopachygaster 29.31.25
Neopachylopus 24.26.12
Neopamera 20.7.64
Neoparacletus 21.19.172
Neoparentia 29.43.40
Neopareophora 25.7.25
neopasites 25.69.1
Neopelomyia 29.96.3
Neopeltodytes 24.6.2
Neoperla 8.9.9
Neoperlini, supra 8.9.9
neopetrella, Exceptia 27.23.48
Neophaenis 27.75.311
Neopharnus 20.3.56
Neophasia 27.42.2
Neophiloptuers 18.1.39
Neophylacinae, supra 26.10.39
Neophylax 26.10.40
Neophyllaphis 21.19.148
Neophyllomyza 29.74.2
Neophyto 29.103.37
Neopimpla 25.16.91
Neopinnaspis 21.38.53
Neoplastia 29.42.18
Neoplatypedia 21.13.22
Neoplea 20.34.1
Neoplynes 27.73.23
Neopolyarthron 24.106.10
Neoprocciphillus 21.19.149
Neopsilopa 29.93.27
Neopsylla 30.4.4
Neopsyllinae, supra 30.4.4
Neopsyllini, supra 30.4.4
Neoptera, supra 8.1.1
Neoptilia 25.4.5
Ncoptochus 24.113.70
Neoptychodes 24.106.232
Neopyrochroa 24.94.3
Neorhacodes 25.16.321
Neorhacodinae, supra 25.16.321
Neorhegmoclemina 29.15.2
Neorhynchocephalus 29.39.2
Neorthopleura 24.67.124
Neoscatella 29.93.61
Neoscinella 29.94.35
Neoscraptia 24.98.41
Neoscutopterus 24.7.31
Neoslossonia 21.14.3
Neosminthurus 1.7.8
Neosolieria 29.105.127
Neososos 29.85.1
Neosteingelia 21.23.4
Neosthrips 22.5.14
Neostilobezzia 29.23.13
Neostroblia 25.16.352
Neostylopyga 14.3.3
Neosuris 20.7.42
Neosycophila 25.18.3
Neosymydobius 21.19.150
Neosynepidosis 29.11.45
Neotarache 27.75.196
Neotelphusa 27.23.29
Neotephritis 29.61.28
Neotermes 15.2.6
Neoterpes 27.61.123
Neotettix 11.1.3
Neotheronia 25.16.32
Neothremma 26.10.41

Neothrips 22.5.54
Neotiphia 25.53.3
Neotoxoptera 21.19.151
Neotrichia 26.7.15
Neotrichini, supra 26.7.14
Neotrichodectes 18.2.6
Neotrichophorus 24.48.46
Neotridactylus 11.6.1
Neotriozella 221.17.13
Neotrochus 24.24.98
neotropicalis, Ostomopsis 24.78.5a
Neotrypetes 25.68.13
Neottiglossa 20.3.40
Neottiophilinae, supra 29.64.2
Neotuerta 27.75.242
Neotylopterus 24.113.224
Neotypus 25.16.268
Neourosigalphus 25.13.140
Neoxabea 11.10.18
Neoxorides 25.16.39
Neoxoridini, supra 25.16.37
Neoxus 24.24.150
Neoxylocopa 25.69.46
Nepa 20.36.2
nepenthe, Salpingogaster 29.47.29
Nephanes 24.15.21
Nephaspis 24.80.12
Nephelodes 27.75.512
Nepheloleuca 27.61.151
nepheos, Exoteleia 27.23.21
Nephesini, supra 21.8.2
Nephopterix 27.55.329
nephrelepidis, Idiopterus 21.19.104
Nephrocerini, supra 29.48.4
Nephrocerus 29.48.4
Nephrogramma 27.55.58
nephrolepidus, Aleurotulus 21.18.10
Nephrotoma 29.2.7
Ncphus 24.80.7
Nepidae, supra 20.36.1
Nepiera 25.16.411
Nepinae, supra 20.36.2
Nipini, supra 20.36.2
Nepiomorpha 17.20.4
Nepiomorphinae, supra 17.20.4
Neplas 29.37.87
Nepomorpha, supra 20.26.1
Nepotula 27.21.21
Nepterotaea 27.61.34
Nepticula 27.5.1
Nepticulidae, supra, 27.5.1
Nepticuloidea, supra 27.5.1
Nepytia 27.61.133
Neralsia 25.31.10
Nerice 27.71.9
nerii, Aphis 21.19.15
nerii, Aspidiotus 21.38.11
Neriid Fly Family, supra 29.52.1
Neriidae, supra 29.52.1
Neriocephalus 29.51.3
Nerioidea, supra 29.50.1
Nerophilus 26.14.3
Nersia 21.11.1
Nerthra 20.39.2
Nerthrinae, supra 20.39.2
nervatus, Phyllodinus 21.2.9
nervosa, Ectoparia 24.34.12
nervosa, Gynacantha 7.4.8
nervosonpunctatum, Aetalion 21.16.1
nervosus, Baliosus 24.107.167 (Fig. 24.245)
Nesepyris 25.48.15
Nesomyia 25.26.82
Nesomyrmex 25.58.37
Nesoselandria 25.7.6
Nesosteles 21.14.94

Nesostizocvera 24.106.57
Nesotipula 29.2.9
Nessorhininae, supra 21.15.3
Nessorhinini, supra 21.15.3
nessus, Amphion 27.70.36 (Fig. 27.258, floridensis in "Checklist")
nessus, Celotes 27.40.40 (Fig. 27.71)
Netanyacra 25.16.231
Netelia 25.16.48
Netrosoma 11.5.80
nets 32
Net-winged Beetle Family, supra 24.57.1
Net-winged Midge Family, supra 29.3.1
Neuchorus 25.16.47
Neumoegenia 27.75.345
neumoegeni, Charidryas 27.46.15
neumoegeni, Hemileuca 27.69.7 (Fig. 27.222)
Neuraphini, supra 24.20.10
Neurateles 25.16.504
Neuratelia 29.9.68
Neureclipsis 26.3.3
Neurigona 29.43.31
Neurigonella 29.43.29
Neurigioninae, supra 29.43.31
Neurobathra 27.14.8
Neurobezzia 29.23.21
Neurocolpous 20.23.171
Neurocordulia 7.6.5
Neuroctenus 20.13.7
Neurohelea 29.23.20
Neurolipa 27.14.6
neurona, Icaricia 27.43.50
Neuroptera, supra 23.1.1
Neuropterida, supra 23.1.1
Neuroptynx 23.15.1
Neurostrota, 27.14.3
Neuroterus 25.34.17
Neurothrips 22.5.55
Neurotneta 21.5.1
Neurotoma 25.2.3
Neurotomini, supra 25.2.3
Nevada Sage Grasshopper 11.5.94
nevadana, Haiga 29.58.8
Nevadaphis 21.19.152
nevadensis, Brachyceratocoria 20.23.37
nevadensis, Hemileuca 27.69.7
nevadensis, Lagonis 25.7.61
nevadensis, Machilinus 4.2.1
nevadensis, Oeneis 27.48.13
Nevadocoris 20.23.56
New House Borer 24.106.14
new storage methods 48
New York Weevil 24.113.22
Newcomer's fixing fluid 45
Newsteadia 21.22.2
nexilis, Eutricopis 27.75.595
Nezara 20.3.51
ni, Trichoplusia 27.75.152
Niadina 29.10.15
niagarana, Udamopyga 29.103.47
niama, Amiana 27.75.188
Niasoma 27.38.85
Niasomini, supra 27.38.85
Nicagus 24.28.9
Nicentrus 24.113.331
Nicephorus 29.105.76
Nicholia 20.23.57
Nicholiella 21.38.54
nicippe, Abaeis 27.42.19 (Fig. 27.102)
Nicobium 24.63.23
Nicocles 29.37.9
Nicoletia 5.2.2
Nicoletiidae 5.2.1
Nicrophorinae, supra 24.21.9
Nicrophorini, supra 24.21.9

Nicrophorus 24.21.9
Nidicola 20.21.18
nidicola, Townsendiellomhia 29.105.383
nidicornis, Liogma 29.2.12
Niditinea 27.10.38
Niesthrea 20.6.1
Niesthrini, supra 20.6.1
niger, Ceratophyllus 30.7.2
niger, Chrysops 29.26.11
niger, Coniceps 29.62.3
niger, Pytho 24.90.6 (Fig. 24.158)
niger, Threnus 24.87.44
nigerrima, Piophila 29.64.1
Nigetis 27.75.37
nigra, Agasphaerops 24.113.101
nigra americana, Spania 29.28.4
nigra, Drionia 21.14.85
nigra, Odontosciara 29.10.2
nigra, Oligotoma 9.3.1
nigra, Omalaspis 25.31.3
nigra, Parasaissetia 21.26.13
nigra, Rhizelmis 24.45.23
Nigra Scale 21.26.13
nigra, Zeropamera 20.7.62
nigrescens, Neivamyrmex 25.58.3 (Fig. 25.33)
nigricana, Cydia 27.38.56
nigricans, Acanthochalcis 25.21.9
nigricans, Ophrynopus 25.11.2
nigricans, Pyropyga 24.55.12
nigricans, Salebria 27.55.324
nigricans, Stromboceridea 25.7.8
nigricans, Tachardiobius 25.25.59
nigricauda, Platydiplosis 29.11.142
nigriceps, Perigona 24.4.137
nigriceps, Ursophyto 29.105.80
nigricolor, Larisia 24.98.50
nigricornis, Dissolcus 25.43.33
nigricornis, Hylochares 24.53.23
nigricornis, Oecanthus 11.10.19 (Fig. 11.46)
nigricoxum, Simulium 29.22.5 (Fig. 29.27)
Nigridonus 21.14.109
nigrifrons, Graminella 21.14.220
nigrina, Oligembia 9.2.1
nigrinus, Acartophthalmus 29.66.1
Nigriparyphus 29.31.33
nigripes, Cremnodes 25.16.134
nigrior, Agraulis 27.46.1 (Fig. 27.119)
nigrior, Dineutus 24.9.1 (Fig. 24.50)
nigrirostris, Anoplodonta 29.31.36
nigrirostris, Hypera 24.113.146
nigrita, Delina 29.98.29
nigrita, Fenella 25.7.53
nigritarsis, Pseudorthygia 24.107.141
nigritus viridicyaneus, Typophorus 24.107.49
Nigrobonellia 29.105.109
nigroclavata, Rhoptromeris 25.32.11
nigrocornea, Pseudomeriania 29.105.120
nigrocornis, Macroplea 24.107.3
nigrofasciatum, Mesolecanium 21.26.11
nigrolineatum, Icodema 30.23.46
nigromaculosum, Eomacrosiphon 21.19.71
nigronervosa, Pentalonia 21.19.163
Nigronia 23.2.5
nigropilosus, Thrips 22.4.53
nigrosuffusa, Junonia 27.46.30
nigrovarius, Ophion 25.16.455
nigrovillata, Dettopsomyia 29.90.15
nigrovittatus, Microchironomus 29.24.47
nigrovittatus, Tabanus 29.26.26
nigrovittella, Immyrla 27.55.319
Nilea 29.105.426
nileus, Acrias 25.26.33
Nilobezzia 29.23.27

Nilotanypus 29.24.22
Nilothauma 29.24.63
nilotica, Characoma 27.75.173
nimbice, Catasticta 27.42.1
Nimioglossa 29.105.69
Nine-spotted Ladybird Beetle 24.80.42
Nineta 23.9.6
Nionia 21.14.35
Nioniinae, supra 21.14.35
Nioniini, supra 21.14.35
nipae, Nipaecoccus 21.25.26
Nipaecoccus 21.25.26
Niphogenia 29.42.21
niphon, Insisalia 27.43.29
Nipponentomon 2.3.4
Nipponorthezia 21.22.4
Nippotipula 29.2.9
Niptinus 24.62.9
Niptus 24.62.6
Nipus 24.80.3
Nisaxis 24.25.47
nise, Pyrisitia 27.42.18
Nisoniades 27.40.22
Nisquallia 11.5.109
Nissoscolopocerus 20.4.23
nitela 25.62.48
Nitelopterus 25.62.47
nitens nitens, Schistocerca 11.5.114 (Fig. 11.25)
nitens, Paramyia 29.74.3
nitens, Xestocoris 20.7.31
nitens, Zygobaris 24.113.341
Nites 27.15.6
nitida, Cotinis 24.30.121
nitida, Diphuia 29.93.10
nitidalis, Disphania 27.55.150
nitidiventris, Ecitopora 24.24.232
Nitidula 24.70.17
Nitidulidae, supra 24.70.1
Nitidulinae, supra 24.70.11
nitidulus, Thylochromus 20.7.39
nitidum, Astromula 24.106.72
nitidus, Brathinus 24.24.140
nitidus, Edaphus 24.24.161
nitidus, Heteromurus 1.5.19
nitidus, Kalissus 24.24.81
nitidus, Xylophagus 29.29.5
nitocris, Ametris 27.61.54
nivalis, Urola 27.55.222
nivea, Acentria 27.55.191
nivea, Panchlora 14.6.5
Niveapis 21.38.55
niveiclava, Parastenoterys 25.25.31
niveicollis, Tetranodus 24.106.128
niveitectus, Enaphalodes 24.106.70
niveociliaria, Eueana 27.61.165
niveostriata, Sabulodes 27.61.154 (Fig. 27.193)
niveus, Ammonaios 29.32.12
nivicola, Hypogastrura 1.2.1 (Fig. 1.2)
nivosaria, Eugonobapta 27.61.144
nobilis, Eacles 27.69.1
nobilitator nobilitator, Neotypus 25.16.268
Nobilotipula 29.2.9
Noble Tiger Beetle 24.3.4
Nocibiotes 24.87.155
Nocloa 27.75.361
Nocloini, supra 27.75.360
Nocticanace 29.97.3
Nocticanacinae, supra 29.97.1
Noctophus 24.20.4
Noctueliopsis 27.55.48
Noctuid Moth Family, supra 27.75.1
Noctuidae, supra 27.75.1
noctuiformis, Aon 27.75.168
Noctuinae, supra 27.75.535

Noctuini, supra 27.75.557
Noctuocoris 20.23.115
Noctuoidea, supra 27.71.1
Nodita 23.9.4
Nodopus 24.68.12
nodosa, Ptochiomera 20.7.48
nodosus, Tylocerina 24.106.269
Noedavisia 27.55.238
noela, Bistica 27.75.344
nokomis, Hyalophora 27.69.18
nokomis, Speyeria 27.46.8 (Fig. 27.124)
Nola 27.75.179
Nolima 23.7.2
Nolimini, supra 23.7.2
Nolinae, supra 27.75.178
Nomada 25.69.10
Nomadinae, supra 25.69.1
Nomadini, supra 25.69.10
Nomadopsis 25.65.11
Nomadula 25.69.10 (Fig. 25.65)
Nomamyrmex 25.58.2
Nomia 25.66.8 (Fig. 25.63)
Nomiinae, supra 25.66.8
Nomiini, supra 24.4.35
Nomius 24.4.35
Nomophila 27.25.130
nomophilalis, Langessa 27.55.13
Norape 27.51.4
Norbanus 25.19.82
nordica, Birka 25.7.5
Norellia 29.98.1
Norellisoma 29.98.1
Norfolk Island Pine Felt Scale 21.31.4
normalis, Acerra 27.75.502
normani, Crocigrapha 27.75.505
North Western Crane Fly 29.2.9
Northern Casemaker Caddisfly Family,
 supra 26.10.1
Northern Cattle Grub 29.102.5
Northern Corn Rootworm 24.107.90
Northern House Mosquito 29.20.12
Northern Masked Chafer 24.30.100
Northern Metalmark 27.44.2
Northern Pine Weevil 24.113.171
Northern Pitch Twig Moth 27.38.20
Northern Rat Flea 30.7.10
Northern Rock Crawler 12.1.1
Northwest Coast Mosquito 29.20.9
Northwestern Leaf-cutting Bee 25.68.22
nortoni nortoni, Nomia 25.66.8
Norway Maple Aphid 21.19.165
Norvellina 21.14.138
Nose Bot Fly 29.102.1
Noserus 24.87.173, 25.13.49 (Homonym)
Nosodendridae, supra 24.60.1
Nosodendron 24.60.1
nosodermoides, Endophloeus 24.93.14
Nosopon 18.6.27
Nosopsyllus 30.7.10
Nosora 24.24.270
Nossidium 24.15.6
Nostima 29.93.34
notabilis, Phylloxera 21.21
notabilis, Wetmorea 20.23.5
Notanisomorpha 25.26.8
Notapictinus 20.13.9
Notaris 24.113.174
notatipennis, Burtinus 20.5.8
notatus, Cyrtopeltis 20.23.28
notatus, Stenosphenus 24.106.60 (Fig.
 24.185)
Notela 27.71.20
Noteridae, supra 24.8.1
Noterini, supra 24.8.4
Nothochrysa 23.9.1
Notholopus 20.23.172

Nothosmia 25.68.21
Notibius 24.87.154
Notiobis 24.4.109
Notiochares 25.60.27
Notiophilini, supra 24.4.11
Notiophilus 24.4.11
Notiphila 24.93.38
Notiphiliane, supra 29.93.31
Notiphilini 29.93.38
notmani, Parwionnertzia 29.11.34
Notocelia 27.38.28
Notocyphini, supra 25.60.33
Notocyphus 25.60.33
Notodonta 27.71.8
Notodontidae, supra 27.71.1
notodontoides, Elymiotis 27.71.15
Notogramma 29.58.15
Notolmus 24.113.51
Notomicrini, supra 24.8.1
Notomicrus 24.8.1
Notonecta 20.33.3
Notonectidae, supra 20.33.1
Notonectinae, supra 20.33.2
Notonota 24.107.40
Notopodops 20.3.19
notopygus 25.16.324
notosa, Zumatrichia 26.7.12
Notoxinae, supra 24.102.1
Notoxus 24.102.2
Notoxylocopa 25.69.46
Notus 21.14.71
nova, Adelesta 25.7.10
nova, Dixella 29.18.1
nova, Orgyia 27.74.3
nova, Tridepia 27.75.475
novaboracensis, Ithycerus 24.113.22 (Fig.
 24.270)
Novakia 29.9.53
novaroensis, Synanthedon 27.35.12
Noviini, supra 24.80.32
Novius 24.80.34
novus, Prothymus 25.26.42
Novelsis 24.61.7
novemnotata, Coccinella 24.80.42(Fig.
 24.146)
Nowickia 29.105.87
nox, Tsugaea 29.105.434
nubicola, Metaxmeste 27.55.37
nubifera, Ordobrevia 24.45.20
nubifer, Stenocorus 24.106.176
nubifer, Tetegeusis 24.53.1
nubiferana, Hedya 27.38.16
nubila, Microtes 11.5.50
nubila, Oplosia 24.106.249
nubilalis, Ostrinia 27.55.84 (Figs. 27.164;
 27.165)
nubilipennis, Hemadas 25.19.6
nubilipennis, Tmetogaster 25.16.259
nubilis, Euparthenos 27.75.129
nubilus, Neurocolpus 20.23.171
Nuculaspis 21.38.56
nudatus, Canaceoides 29.97.2
nudipes, Baeopterogyma 29.9.73
nudiseta, Synthesiomyia 29.100.52
Nudobius 24.24.41
nudus, Colletes 25.63.2
nudus, Oedenops 29.93.40
Numata 27.23.11
numbering system 9
numenius, Belonochilus 20.7.10
numenmacheri, Eschatoporis 24.87.45
numerical taxonomy 17
Numia 27.61.74
numidae, Lipeurus 18.1.35
Numidicola 18.6.28
Numidilipeurus 18.1.40

numitor, Ancyloxypha 27.40.56
Nupedia 29.99.14
nupera, Xylena 27.75.388 (Fig. 27.371)
nuptialis, Panorpa 28.4.1 (Fig. 28.6)
Nurenus 21.14.112
Nutgrass Armyworm 27.75.326
Nutgrass Billbug 24.113.366
Nutgrass Borer Moth 27.38.3
Nutmeg Moth 27.75.472
Nuttall Blister Beetle 24.101.13
nuttalli nuttalli, Hemileuca 27.69.7
nuttalli, Trichodes 24.67.18
nuttalli, Lytta 24.101.13
nuttingi, Rhabdomastix 29.2.49
nuxvorella, Acrobasis 27.55.282
Nychioptera 27.57.48
nyctalus, Cimexopsis 20.20.5
nycteis, Charidryas 27.46.15 (Fig. 27.126)
Nyctelius 27.40.85
nyctelius, Nyctelius 27.40.85
Nycteola 27.75.174
Nycteribiidae, supra 29.107.1
Nycteridopsylla 30.5.1
Nycterophaeta 27.75.465
Nycterophilia 29.108.1
Nyctiophylax 26.3.4
Nyctiphanta 27.61.109
Nyctoporini, supra 24.87.40
Nyctoporis 24.87.40
Nylanderia 25.58.69
nymph 13
Nymph Butterfly Family, supra 27.48.1
nymphaea, Galerucella 24.107.79 (Fig.
 24.228)
nymphaea, Rhopalosiphum 21.19.186
nymphaeella, Palatka 27.55.366
Nymphalidae, supra 27.46.1
Nymphalinae, supra 27.46.24
Nymphalini, supra 27.46.24
Nymphalis 27.46.25
Nymphocixia 21.1.9
Nymphomyiid Fly Family, supra 29.5.1
Nymphomyiidae, supra 29.5.1
Nymphomyioidea, supra 29.5.1
Nymphula 27.55.8
Nymphuliella 27.55.11
Nymphulinae, supra 27.52.5
Nymphulini, supra 27.55.6
nysaefoliella, Antispila 27.9.2
Nysius 20.7.11
nyssaecola, Cartodiplosis 29.11.106
Nysson 25.62.73
Nyssoninae, supra 25.62.70
Nyssonini, supra 25.62.73
Nyssonotus 24.113.389
nyssorhynchus 29.20.1
nystalea 27.71.14

Oak Borer 24.46.15
Oak Felt Scale 21.31.4
Oak Gall 25.34.17
Oak Lace Bug 20.14.7
Oak Leafroller 27.38.74
Oak Leaftier 27.38.60
Oak Lecanium 21.26.14
Oak Moth Family, supra 27.72.1
Oak Sapling Borer 24.106.234
Oak Timberworm 24.110.3
Oak Webworm 27.38.74
oallidus, Stenomimus 24.113.381
Oarisma 27.40.57
oarus, Brachypalpus 29.47.88
Oberea 24.106.297
obesa, Mozena 20.4.9

obesa, Ornidia 29.47.42
obesa, Paxilla 11.1.6 (Fig. 11.7)
obesa, Rhagovelia 20.28.2 (Figs. 20.61, 20.62)
obesa, Rhinoleucophenga 29.90.7
Obese Pygmy Grasshopper 11.1.6 (Fig. 11.7)
obesus, Trixodes 29.105.46
Obisophaga 25.16.95
obiterella, Pseuderotis 27.15.15
Obithome 27.21.26
obligua, Allograpta 29.47.30
oblinita, Acronicta 27.75.231 (Fig. 27.351)
Oblique Banded Leafroller 27.38.72
obliquus, Listroderes 24.113.142
obliteralis, Synclita 27.55.12
obliterata, Leptura 24.106.212
oblivia, Anomalla 24.30.96
oblongifolia, Ambloycorypha 11.7.1
oblongopunctata, Agra 24.4.151
oblongopunctatus, Lophyroplectus 25.16.341
oblongulus, Calyptomerus 24.33.1
Oblong-winged Katydid 11.7.1
obniger, Pachydrus 24.7.6
Obolocera 29.105.427
Obolodiplosis 29.11.137
Obriini, supra 24.106.86
Obrima 27.75.80
obrimo, Odontopila 27.61.179
Obrium 24.106.86
Obrussa 27.5.3
obscura, Alaskiphyto 29.105.174
obscura, Buquetia 29.105.410
obscura, Cordalia 24.24.216
obscura, Dictyonia 21.6.9
obscura, Lapazia 21.38.44
obscura, Melanaspis 21.38.49
obscura, Myudaeina 29.100.14
obscura, Phorocera 29.105.287
Obscure Mealybug 21.25.35
Obscure Root Weevil 24.113.72
Obscure Scale 21.38.49
obscuripennis, Pterotus 24.55.20
obscuripes, Formica 25.58.72
obscurofasciella, Tinagma 27.32.1 (Fig. 27.50)
obscurostrigella, Cephitinea 27.10.29
obscurus, Anaphothrips 22.4.19
obscurus, Axestinus 24.106.65
obscurus, Bromius 24.107.55
obscurus, Cimolus 20.4.26
obscurus, Epantius 24.87.134
obscurus, Hylastinus 24.112.6
obscurus, Hypothenemus 24.112.40
obscurus, Nicagus 24.28.9
obscurus, Orobittacus 28.1.4
obscurus, Pelonomus 24.44.3
obscurus, Progomphus 7.3.1
obscurus, Pseudococcus 21.25.35
obscurus, Sciopithes 24.113.72
obscurus, Tenebrio 24.87.92
obscurus, Zamodes 24.106.50
obsolescens, Trosia 27.51.1
obsoletus, Dendroleon 23.14.1
obtectus, Acanthoscelides 24.108.10 (Fig. 24.252)
obtectus, Peritelodes 24.113.90
obtusa, Clastoptera 21.12.7
obtusa, Goniusa 24.24.246
obtusa, Schistacme 24.24.288
obtusatus, Hydrochara 24.12.7
Obtusicauda 21.19.153
obtusifrons, Paramesus 21.14.177
Obtusodonta 25.16.237
obtusus, Glischrochilus 24.70.35
obumbratalis, Ostrinia 27.55.84

obumbrata, Eudicrana 29.9.60
obvertens 27.75.94
Ocala 27.55.356
Ocalea 24.24.271
Ocaria 27.43.17
Occapes 25.16.373
Occasjapyx 3.4.6
occatoria, Sibovia 21.14.53
occidens, Morius 24.25.10
occidensis, Thecophora 29.49.7
occidentalis, Astata 25.62.35
occidentalis, Bittacomorpha 29.17.3
occidentalis, Boernerinella 21.19.27
occidentalis, Bombus 25.70.2
occidentalis, Choristoneura 27.38.72
occidentalis, Colias 27.42.11
occidentalis, Dieuches 20.7.67
occidentalis, Diglochis 25.19.109
occidentalis, Doddsia 8.2.2
occidentalis, Frankliniella 22.4.41
occidentalis, Lepolepis 17.1.3
occidentalis, Megophthalmida 29.9.79
occidentalis, Microsnaia 29.45.2
occidentalis, Metaplagia 29.105.164
occidentalis occidentalis, Dasymutilla 25.55.16
occidentalis, Pogonomyrmex 25.58.24
occidentalis, Pontia 27.42.4
occidentis, Curculio 24.113.200
occidentis, Pterotermes 15.2.1
Occidryas 27.46.22
occidua, Falagriota 24.24.240
occiduaria, Anagoga 27.61.116
occiduus, Blissus 20.7.16
Occiephelinus 24.24.120
occua, Somanica 25.7.81
occulata, Fuhsina 24.82.15
Oceanic Field Cricket 11.10.12
oceanicus, Nanopsocus 17.7.2
oceanicus, Teleogryllus 11.10.12
oceans 27
ocellana, Spilonota 27.38.22
ocellata, Walterella 27.75.372
ocellatus ocellatus, Anacrabro 25.62.56
ocellus (ocelli) 12.20
ocellus, Ptinus 24.62.10
Ochetomyrmex 25.58.44
Ochetomyrmicini, supra 25.58.44
Ochleromyia 29.28.6
Ochleroptera 25.62.80
Ochlerotatus 29.20.9
Ochlodes 27.40.72
Ochodaeiniae, supra 24.30.34
Ochodaeus 24.30.34
ochoterenai, Trochiliphagus 18.7.2
ochracea, Coenonympha 27.48.8
ochracea, Hylota 24.24.256
ochraceus, Pseudocentrinus 24.113.327
Ochraethes 24.106.116
ochrea, Aleptinoides 27.75.377
ochrefasciella, Obruss 27.5.3 (Fig. 27.18)
ochreipennis, Zanclognatha 27.75.4 (Fig. 27.323)
ochrifrontella, Eulogia 27.55.393
Ochrimnus 20.7.6
Ochrocera 29.105.189
ochrocomella, Epigritia 27.17.19
ochrodesma, Anabasis 27.55.185
ochrogaster, Euxoa 27.75.544
ochroleucus, Heptamelus 25.7.11
Ochrolitus 24.77.13
ochroloma, Microtheca 24.107.70
Ochromolopinae, supra 27.27.2
Ochromolopis 27.27.2
Ochropleura 27.75.549
Ochrostomus 20.7.7

Ochrotrichia 26.7.5
ochrotrichini, supra 26.7.5
Ochsenheimeria 27.12.1
Ochsenheimeriid Moth Family, supra 27.12.1
Ochsenheimeriidae, supra 27.12.1
Ochteridae, supra 20.40.1
Ochterus 20.40.1
Ochthebius 24.13.1
Ochthephilus 24.24.151
Ochthephilum 24.24.63
Ochthera 29.93.51
Ochtheroidea 29.93.2
Ochyromera 24.113.222
Ocnaea 29.38.3
Ocnerostoma 27.30.4
ocrisia, Ocaria 27.43.17
octa, Weberacantha 1.4.7
Octinodes 24.48.50
octodecimdentata coloradensis, Tarsopsylla 30.7.16
octogeneria, Coloburella 1.4.5
Octogomphus 7.3.8
octomaculata, Alypia 27.75.248 (Fig. 27.354)
octomaculata octomaculata, Perdita 25.65.15
octomaculata, Omophoita 24.107.147
octonotata, Xestoleptura 24.106.221 (Fig. 24.206)
Octotemnus 24.92.13
Octotoma 24.107.168
ocularis, Palembus 24.87.97
ocularis, Parephistemus 24.74.16
oculata, Chrysopa 23.9.9
oculata, Harlomillsia 1.5.11
oculata, Heteromyza 29.84.7
oculatalis, Carteris 27.75.13
oculatus, Alaus 24.48.7 (Fig. 24.96)
oculatus, Gelastocoris 20.39.1 (Fig. 20.74)
oculatus, Lechriops 24.113.276 (Fig. 24.292)
oculatus, Microgoes 24.106.235
oculea, Antheraea 27.69.12
Ocydromia 29.42.52
Ocydromiinae, supra 29.42.49
Ocyptamus 29.47.27
Ocypus 24.24.10
Ocytata 29.105.340
Ocyusa 24.24.272
Odacanthini, supra 24.4.140
Odd Beetle 24.61.3
Odinia 29.67.1
Odiniidae, supra 29.67.1
Odiniid Fly Family, supra 29.67.1
odiosellus, Salebriacus 27.55.322
odius, Historis 27.46.42
Odmalea 20.3.58
Odonaspis 21.38.57
Odonata, supra 7.1.1 (Figs. 7.1, 7.2, 7.3)
odonatae, Lathromeroidea 25.28.16
Odonatisca 29.2.9
Odontella 1.2.17
Odontiinae, supra 27.55.21
Odontiini, supra 27.55.25
Odontivalvia 27.55.47
Odontobracon 25.13.18
Odontocera 24.106.96
Odontoceridae, supra 26.14.1
Odontocerinae, supra 26.14.1
Odontocolon 25.16.82
Odontocorynus 24.113.328
Odontocynips 25.34.41
Odontodiplosis 29.11.121
Odontoloxozus 29.52.1
Odontomachini, supra 25.58.19
Odontomachus 25.58.19

Odontomera 29.62.4
Odontomesa 29.24.40
Odontomyia, supra 29.31.1, 29.31.38
Odontomyiina 29.31.38
Odontomyiini, supra 29.31.37
Odontonyx 24.34.5
Odontophotopsis 25.55.12
Odontopsyllus 30.6.5
Odontoptila 27.61.179
Odontopus 24.113.218
Odontosciara 29.10.2
Odontosia 27.71.7
Odontosphindus 24.73.1
Odontota 24.107.166
Odontotaenius 24.29.1
Odontotarsini, supra 20.3.11
Odontothrips 22.4.46
Odontoxiphidium 11.7.22
Odopoea 21.13.1
odorata, Ascalapha 27.75.112
Odorous House Ant 25.58.61
Odynerus 25.59.3
Oebalus 20.3.33
Oecacta 29.23.5
oecanthi, Leptoteleia 25.43.12
oecanthi, Macrorileya 25.20.1
oecanthi, Oethecoctonus 25.43.11
Oecanthinae, supra 11.10.18
Oecanthus 11.10.19
Oecetis 26.18.5
Oeciacus 20.20.3
Oecleus 21.1.6
Oeclidius 21.10.1
Oecophorid Moth Family, supra 27.15.1
Oecophoridae 27.15.1
Oecophorinae, supra 27.15.22
Oecophorini, supra 27.15.22
Oecotelma 25.16.120
Oedalea 29.42.53
Oedaleonotus 11.5.90
Oedaleothrips 22.5.15
Oedancala 20.7.23
Oedemagena 29.102.5
Oedematocera 29.105.332
Oedemeridae, supra 24.97.1
Oedemerinae, supra 24.97.5
Oedemerini, supra 24.97.12
Oedemopsini, supra 25.16.49
Oedemopsis 25.16.54
Oedenops 29.93.40
Oedicarena 29.61.47
oedipodalis, Epicorsia 27.55.79
oedipodinae, supra 11.5.34
oedipus, Eumichthus 24.106.91
Oedopa 29.58.31
Oedoparena 29.78.2
Oedostethus 24.48.60
Oegoconia 27.17.2
Oeme 24.106.28
Oemopteryx 8.2.3
Oeneis 27.48.13
Oenobotys 27.55.81
Oenochrominae, supra 27.61.3
Oenoe 27.10.8
Oenomaus 27.43.20
Oenonogastra 25.13.105
Oenopion 24.87.88
oestlundi, Gypsoaphis 21.19.93
Oestlundia 21.19.105
Oestlundiella 21.19.154
Oestodes 24.48.53
Oestodinae, supra 24.48.50
Oestranthriax 29.40.54
Oestridae, supra 29.102.1
Oestrinae, supra 29.102.3
Oestrini, supra 29.102.3

Oestroidea, supra 29.101.1
Oestrophasia 29.105.43
Oestrus 29.102.3
Oethecoctonus 25.42.11
Oetophorus 25.16.338
oetus, Cercyonis 27.48.9
Ofatulena 27.38.54
Ogcodes 29.38.5
Ogcodocera 29.40.41
Ogdoconta 27.75.338
ogemawi, Trissopelopia 29.24.25
Ogloblinisca 25.19.17
oidaematophorus 27.58.19
Oidematops 29.79.3
Oiketicinae, supra 27.11.11
Oiketicus 27.11.11
oileus, Pyrgus 27.40.38 (Fig. 27.69)
oinophila 27.10.51
Oistus 24.48.10
Okanagana 21.13.15
Okanagodes 21.13.16
Okeniella 29.98.11
okoboji, Telopelopia 29.24.17
Olbiogaster 29.14.2
Olceclostera 27.66.2
Olcella 29.94.25
Oldenbergiella 29.84.5
Old-house Borer 24.106.102
Old World Swallowtail 27.41.5
oleae, Saissetia 21.26.20
Oleaneder Aphid 21.19.15
Oleander Pit Scale 21.35.1
Oleander Scale 21.38.11
Olenochaeta 29.105.354
Olesicampe 25.16.422
Olethreutinae, supra 27.38.1
Olethreutini, supra 27.38.1
Olethreutes 27.38.15
Olfersia 29.106.9
Olfersiini, supra 29.106.9
Oliarces 23.6.1
Oliaronus 21.1.11
Oliarus 21.1.2
Olibroporus 24.77.5
Olibrus 24.77.3
Oligacanthopus 11.10.4
Oligandrena 25.65.1
Oligembia 9.2.1
Oligembiidae, supra 9.2.1
Oligia 27.75.258
Oligocentria 27.71.35
Oligodranes 29.40.27
Oligolinus 24.24.42
Oligolochus 24.113.346
Oligomerodes 24.63.16
Oligomerus 24.63.17
Oligomyrmex 25.58.34
Oligoneuriidae, supra 6.5.1
Oligoneurus 25.13.128
Oligonicella 14.1.4
Oligonicinae, supra 14.1.4
Oligophlebodes 26.10.42
Oligoplectrum 26.9.6
Oligoria 27.40.82
Oligosita 25.28.1
Oligostigmoides 27.55.15
Oligostomis 26.8.6
Oligota 24.24.273
Oligothrips 22.3.2
Oligotoma 9.3.1
Oligotomidae, supra 9.3.1
Oligotricha 26.8.7
Oligotrophini, supra 29.11.146
Oligotrophus 29.11.160
Olinea 29.88.2
Olisthaerinae, supra 24.24.174

Olisthaerus 24.24.174
Olisthopus 24.4.75
olivacea, Antheraea 27.69.12
olivacea, Campylacantha 11.5.87
olivata, Pseudoglaea 27.75.402
Olive Hairstreak 27.43.26 (Fig. 27.108)
Olive Scale 21.38.62
Oliveria 29.24.126
oliviae, Hemileuca 27.69.7
Olixon 25.61.2
Olla 24.80.40
Ollarianus 21.14.133
Ollifiella 21.29.1
Olochrysis 25.50.17
Olophrum 24.24.121
Olotelina, supra 24.104.9
Olpodiplosis 29.11.111
Olybria 27.55.321
Olycella 27.55.381
olympia, Euchloe 27.42.8 (Fig. 27.89)
olympiae, Paradasyhelea 29.23.6
olympica, Gehringia 24.4.50
olympica, Nisquallia 11.5.109
Omalaphora 21.12.6
Omalaspis 25.31.3
Omaliinae, supra 24.24.102
Omalium 24.24.122
Omalodes 24.26.42
Omalus 25.50.11
Omanana 21.14.103
omani, Notopodops 20.3.19
Omapantia 29.46.21
Omethes 24.56.18
Omethini, supra 24.56.17
Omias 24.113.74
Omicrus 24.12.31
Omileus 24.113.34
Omina 24.3.1
Omiodes 27.55.153
Omisus 29.24.61
Ommatidiotini, supra 21.6.4
Ommatiini, supra 29.37.64
Ommatius 29.37.64
Ommatochila 27.75.50
Ommatospila 27.55.187
Ommatostola 27.75.256
Omniablautus 29.37.12
Omnivorous Looper 27.61.154
Omoglymmius 24.2.1
Omomyia 29.62.1
Omonadus 24.102.8
Omophlinae, supra 24.88.17
Omophoita 24.107.147
Omophron 24.4.2
Omophroninae, supra 24.4.2
Omophronini, supra 24.4.2
Omoschema 24.24.274
omoscopa, Opogona 27.10.50
Omosita 24.70.16
Omotoma 29.105.387
Omphale 25.26.57
Omphalocera 27.55.273
Omphalomopsis 25.26.40
Omus 24.3.2
Onagrandrena 25.65.1
Oncerometopus 20.23.204
Onceroptila 27.16.2
Oncerotrachelus 20.17.31
Oncerus 24.30.58
Onchopterocheilus 25.59.4
Onciderini, supra 24.106.258
Oncidrees 24.106.260
Oncocephlus 20.17.35
Oncocnemidini, supra 27.75.437
Oncocnemis 27.75.451
Oncometopia 21.14.42

Oncopeltus 20.7.8
Oncophanes 25.13.40
Oncopodura 1.5.12
Oncopodurinae, supra 1.5.11
Oncopsis 21.14.16
Oncotylini, supra 20.23.79
Oncotylus 20.23.58
Oncozygia 20.3.16
Oneida 27.55.265
Onesia 29.101.17
Onion Aphid 21.19.151
Onion Bulb Fly 29.47.57
Onion Maggot 29.99.8
Onion Plant Bug 20.23.109
Onion Thrips 22.4.53 (Fig. 22.3)
Oniticellini, supra 24.30.13
Oniticellus 24.30.13
Onocosmoecus 26.10.8
onoia, Heliothis 27.75.599
Onota 24.4.154
ontario, Euristryomon 27.43.31
ontario, Sphenarches 27.58.2
Ontholestes 24.24.11
Onthophagini, supra 24.30.12
Onthophagus 24.30.12
Onthophilus 24.26.32
Ontsira 25.13.19
onusta, Macronoctua 27.75.275 (Fig. 27.358)
onusta, Tramea 7.7.28 (Fig. 7.17)
Onychagrotis 27.75.536
Onychiuridae, supra 1.3.1 (Fig. 1.4)
Onychiurus 1.3.3. (Fig. 1.5)
Onychobaris 24.113.320
Onychogonia 29.105.355
Onycholyda 25.2.5
Onychylis 24.113.186
Oobius 25.25.108
Ooctonini, supra 25.27.5
Ooctonus 25.27.8
Oodes 24.4.99
Oodini, supra 24.4.99
Ooencyrtus 25.25.109
Oomorphidus 24.113.339
Oomorphus 24.107.36
Oopterinus 24.113.195
Oosternum 24.12.29
opaca, Heimbra 25.20.14
opaca, Megapariopsis 29.105.53
opaca, Phaenobezzia 29.23.25
opaca, Prionochaeta 24.22.8
Opacifrons 29.88.3
opacifrons, Eugraphe 27.75.572
opacum, Hypertrophomma 29.105.403
opacum, Lyrosoma 24.21.2
opacus, Eleodes 24.87.140
opalescalis, Pseudoschoenobius 27.55.201
opalinus, Hadromeropsis 24.113.61
Opandrena 25.65.1
Opatrini, supra 24.87.159
Opatrinus 24.87.146
Opeia 11.5.11
Opelousia 29.101.23
opercularis, Megalopyge 27.51.3 (Figs. 27.156, 27.157)
operculella, Phthorimaea 27.23.45 (Fig. 27.40)
Operophtera 27.61.238
Operophterini, supra 27.61.234
Opetiopalpus 24.67.32
Opetiophora 29.94.21
Opharus 27.73.62
Opheltes 25.16.342
Ophiderma 21.14.59
Ophiogomphus 7.3.5

Ophiomyia 29.68.4
Ophion 25.16.455
Ophionellus 25.16.388
Ophioninae, supra 25.16.455
Ophionini, supra 25.16.455
Ophioomma 24.24.27
Ophiopterus 25.16.389
Ophisma 27.75.132
Ophiuche 27.75.40
Ophraella 24.107.85
Ophryastes 24.113.137
Ophryastini, supra 24.113.137
Ophryonpinae, supra 25.11.2
Ophrynopus 25.11.2
ophtahalmica, Baileya 27.75.172 (Fig. 27.345)
Ophyra 29.100.35
opigena, Hemeroblemma 27.75.109
Opiina, supra 25.13.88
Opiinae, supra 25.13.82
Opiini, supra 25.13.86
Opila 24.67.12
opima, Sphaeroderma 24.107.158
opina, Dryotype 27.75.421
Opisocrostis 30.7.11
Opisodasys 30.7.12
Opisthacantha 25.43.15
Opistheurista 20.23.205
Opisthiini, supra 24.4.7
Opisthius 24.4.7
Opius 25.13.89
Oplomus 20.3.67
Oplonaeschna 7.4.10
Oplosia 24.106.249
Opogona 27.10.50
Opomydas 29.35.1
Opomyza 29.69.1
Opomyzid Fly Family, supra 29.69.1
Opomyzidae, supra 29.69.1
Opomyzoidea, supra 29.65.1
oporinum, Calcaneum 25.16.387
Opossum Beetle Family, supra 24.85.1
Opostega 27.6.1
Opostegid Moth Family, supra 27.6.1
Opostegidae, supra 27.6.1
Opresini, supra 24.20.7
Opresus 24.20.7
Opshomala 11.5.74
Opsidia 29.103.8
Opsidiotroophus 29.103.9
Opsigalea 27.75.467
Opsimini, supra 24.106.21
Opsimus 24.106.21
Opsius 21.14.148
Opsodexia 29.101.24
Opsoltheriea 29.105.77
Opsomeigenia 29.105.254
opter, Pleromella 27.75.439
optilete, Vacciniina 27.43.51
Optioservus 24.45.219
opulentum, Lamprosoma 24.107.37
opuntiae, Cathilaria 25.20.5
Opuntiaspis 21.38.58
Ora 24.32.6
Oracella 21.25.27
Orange Barred Suphur 27.42.14
Orange Tortrix 27.38.71
Orange-dog 27.41.6
Orange-humped Mapleworm Moth 27.72.17
Orange-spotted Tachinid 29.105.12
Orange-striped Oakworm 27.69.5
Orange-tip Butterfly Family, supra 27.42.1
Oraphasmophaga 29.105.333
Orasema 25.23.1
Oraseminae, supra 25.23.1

Orasturmia 29.105.388
oratoria, Iris 14.1.6 (Figs. 14.2, 14.3, 14.4)
Oravelia 20.29.3
Orbellia 29.84.6
orbifera, Magusa 27.75.316
orbitalis, Apacheprosperysa 29.105.232
orbitalis, Xanthocampoplex 25.16.428
Orchard Cicada 21.13.21
Orchelimum 11.7.23
Orchesella 1.5.2
Orchesia 24.98.14
Orchesiini, supra 24.98.14
Orchid Aphid 21.19.122
Orchid Mealybug 21.25.35
Orchid Soft Scale 21.26.4
orchidearum, Cerataphis 21.19.48
orchidearum, Eruytoma 25.20.22
Orchidfly 25.20.22
orchidii, Chaetanophothrips 22.4.25
Orchidophilus 24.113.322
Orchopeas 30.7.13
ordinata, Arthyroglossa 29.93.2
Ordobrevia 24.45.20
oreadella, Uinta 27.55.423
Oreadomyia 29.24.84
Oreana 27.55.320
oreas, Polygonia 27.46.24
oreas, Systoechus 29.40.12
Orectoderus 20.23.76
Oregmopyga 21.31.7
Orgeon Fir Sawyer 24.106.237
Oregon Wireworm 24.48.67
oregonensis, Deretaphrus 24.93.22
oregonensis, Dicerura 29.11.43
oregonensis, Listronotus 24.113.143
oregonensis, Monochamus 24.106.237
oregonensis, Paratyphloceras 30.4.19
oregonensis, Trichopsylloides 30.4.20
oregonius, Papilio 27.41.5
oreios, Oligothrips 22.3.2
Orellia 29.61.38
Orenaia 27.55.73
Oreodytes 24.7.19
Oreogeton 29.42.34
Oreopasites 25.69.5
Oreophila 29.2.60
Oreothalia 29.42.23
Oresbius 25.16.140
orestella, Elachista 27.16.5
Orestilla 29.105.57
Orestiodes 24.107.132
Oreta 27.60.3
Oretinae, supra 27.60.3
Oretochilinae, supra 24.9.3
Orfelia 29.9.13
Orgamara 21.11.6
Organomyia 29.105.345
Orgeriinae, supra 21.11.6
Orgeriini, supra 21.11.6
Orgerius 21.11.9
Orgichneumon 25.16.242
Orgilini, supra 25.13.141
Orgilus 25.13.143
Orgyia 27.74.3
Orgyiinae, supra 27.74.1
Orgyiini, supra 27.74.1
Oriental Beetle 24.30.96
Oriental Cockroach 14.3.1
Oriental Fruit Fly, supra 29.61.1
Oriental Fruitworm 27.38.53
Oriental Moth 27.52.10
Oriental Rat Flea 30.1.10
orientalis, Anomala 24.30.96
orientalis, Aonidiella 21.38.7

orientalis, Atherigona 29.100.4b
orientalis, Blatta 14.3.1 (Fig. 14.15)
orientalis, Neodichocera 29.105.146
Orientus 21.14.143
Oriini, supra 20.21.8
Orima 29.105.45
Orimarga 29.2.20
Orimodema 24.113.128
Orinympha 27.30.5
Orius 20.21.8
orizabra, Rothschildia 27.69.15
Ormenaria 21.8.9
Ormenoides 21.8.6
Ormiini, supra 29.105.44
Ormiscus 24.109.24
Ormocerini, supra 25.19.52
Ormocerus 25.19.53
Ormosia 29.2.60
Ormyrinae, supra 25.19.1
Ormyrus 25.19.2
ornata, Apantesis 27.73.52 (Fig. 27.294)
ornata, Ceratogastra 25.16.319
ornata, Liburniella 21.2.4
ornata, Pityeja 27.61.150
ornata, Sigara 20.35.18
ornata, Umoka 21.14.212
ornata, Zagloba 24.80.20
Ornatae Aphid 21.19.144
ornatalis, Hydriris 27.55.120
Ornate Checkered Beetle 24.67.18
Ornate Pit Scale Insect Family,
 supra 21.34.1
ornaticollis, Perilypus 24.67.13
ornatus, Ambloplisus 25.16.282
ornatus, Brachyogmus 24.113.202
ornatus, Chrysopilus 29.28.8
ornatus, Dendrothrips 22.4.9
ornatus, Eclytus 25.16.49
ornatus, Lithophorus 24.93.26
ornatus, Myzus 21.19.144
ornatus ornatus, Nephus 24.80.7
ornatus, Trichodes 24.67.18
ornatus, Xylosteus 24.106.172
Urnidia 29.47.42
ornigis, Xenosternum 25.13.45
ornithia 24.106.1
Ornithobius 18.1.41
Ornithoctona 29.106.4
Ornithodes 29.2.23
ornithodorus, Glaphyrometopus 24.113.28
ornithogalli, Spodoptera 27.75.326 (Fig.
 27.367)
Ornithoica 29.106.1
Ornithoicinae, supra 29.106.1
Ornithomyia 29.106.2
Ornithomyiinae, supra 29.106.2
Ornithomyiini, supra 29.106.2
Ornithophaga 30.6.4
Ornithophagini, supra 30.6.4
ornythion, Heraclides 27.41.6
Orobanus 24.24.123
Orobittacus 28.1.4
Orocastus 21.14.180
Orochares 24.24.124
Orocharis 11.10.25
Orodesma 27.75.208
Oronotus 25.16.200
Oroperla 8.7.16
oropeso, Cryptophobetron 27.52.12
Oropeza 29.2.8
Orophiini, supra 24.92.12
Oropsyche 26.4.6
Oropsylla 30.7.14
Oropus 24.25.12
Orosagrotis 27.75.544
Orothripini, supra 22.1.4

Orothrips 22.1.5
Orphilini, supra 24.61.4
Orphilus 24.61.4
Orphinus 24.61.11
Orphulella 11.5.8
Orrhodops 29.37.28
Orseis, Phyciodes 27.46.20
Orsillacis 20.7.9
Orsillinae, supra 20.7.10
Orsillini, supra 20.7.10
Orsodacne 24.107.7
Orsodacninae, supra 24.107.7
Ortalliini, supra 24.80.14
Orthacheta 29.98.5
Orthaltica 24.107.140
Orthellia 29.100.57
Orthemis 27.7.19
Orthezia 21.22.1
Ortheziidae, supra 21.22.1
Orthizema 25.16.122
Orthocephalus 20.23.84
Orthocentrinae, supra 25.16.499
Orthocentrus 25.16.499
Orthocerini, supra 24.93.1
Orthochoriolaus 24.106.203
Orthocis 24.92.5
Orthocladiinae, supra 29.24.84
Orthocladius 29.24.125
Orthodes 27.75.519
Orthodiatelus 24.24.275
Orthofidonia 27.61.19
Orthognathus 24.113.364
Orthogonalys 25.47.1
orthogonia, Agrotis 27.75.535
Orthogonis 29.37.61
Ortholepia 27.55.326
Ortholeptura, supra 24.106.172,
 24.106.216
Ortholomus 20.7.12
Orthomallodon 24.106.41
Orthomiscus 25.16.68
Orthonama 27.61.231
Orthonevra 29.47.51
Orthopelma 25.16.196
Orthopelmatinae, supra 25.16.196
Orthopeplus 24.70.14
Orthoperinae, supra 24.79.4
Orthoperus 24.79.6
Orthopodomyia 29.20.7
Orthops 20.23.173
Orthoptera, supra 11.1.1 (Figs. 11.1, 11.2,
 11.3, 11.4, 11.5)
Orthoptochus 24.113.85
Orthoris 24.113.318
Orthosia 27.75.504
Orthosimyia 29.105.58
Orthosoma 24.106.8
Orhtostethus 24.48.47
Orthostigma 25.13.106
Orthotaenia 27.38.13
Orthotomicus 24.112.50
Orthotrichia 26.7.9
Orthotrichiini, supra 26.7.8
Orthotylinae, supra 20.23.82
orthotylini, supra 20.23.87
Orthotylus 20.23.116
ortygnus, Oenomaus 27.43.20
Orus 24.24.64
Orussidae, supra 25.11.1
Orussinae, supra 25.11.1
Orussus 25.11.1
Oruza 27.75.184
orycteropodis, Hybophthirus, Infra 19.8.1
Oryctini, supra 24.30.103
Oryctometopia 27.55.340
Orygma 29.81.4

Oryttus 25.62.88
oryzae, Caulophilus 24.113.380 (Fig.
 24.301)
oryzae, Latheticus 24.87.108
oryzae, Sitophilus 24.113.365 (Fig.
 24.299)
oryzae zeamais, Sitophilus 24.113.365
Oryzaephilus 24.72.2
oryzophilus, Lissorhopturus 24.113.183
Osborn Scale 21.38.24
Osbornellus 21.14.101
osborni, Brachyufens 25.28.6
osborni, Diaspidiotus 21.38.24
Osbornia 21.6.18
Osborniella 18.6.29
osca, Rhinthon 27.40.53
Oscinella 29.94.15
Oscinellinae, supra 29.94.1
oscininia, Siphonella 29.94.32
Oscinisoma 29.94.10
Oscinoides 29.94.16
oslari, Afilia 27.71.22
oslari, Anisota 27.69.5
oslari, Eacles 27.69.1 (Figs. 27.213,
 27.214)
Oslaria 27.75.360
Osmia 25.68.21
Osmidus 24.106.42
Osminia 27.35.11
Osminiini, supra 27.35.10
Osmoderma 24.30.116
Osmopleura 24.106.138
osmundae, Zonothrips 22.4.13
Osmyloidea, supra 23.6.1
Osobenus 8.7.17
Osoriinae, supra 24.24.97
Osorius 24.24.99
Osphya 24.98.38
Osphyinae, supra 24.98.38
Osphyini, supra 24.98.38
Osprioserus 29.37.18
Osprynchotina, supra 25.16.184
ostansa, Pagastiella 29.24.71
ostensackenella, Chrysaster 27.14.21
ostiorum, Ceratinostoma 29.98.24
Ostoma 24.66.2
Ostomopsinae, supra 24.78.5a
Ostomopsis 24.78.5a
Ostracophyto 29.105.118
ostreaeformis, Quadraspidiotus 21.38.73
ostreonalis, Metrea 27.55.21
Ostrinia 27.55.84
Ostrocerca 8.1.5
Oswaldia 29.105.255
Othniidae, supra 24.95.1
otho, Wallengrenia 27.40.67
Otidocephalinae, supra 24.113.193
Otidocephalini, supra 24.113.193
Otiocerini, supra 21.9.10
Otiocerus 21.9.12
Otiorhyrhinini, supra 24.113.68
Otiorhynchus 24.113.68
Otiorrhynchinae, supra 24.113.68
otiosana, Epiblema 27.38.27
Otites 29.58.16
Otitidae, supra 29.59.1
Otitinae, supra 29.58.1
Otlophorus 25.16.346
Otomasicera 29.105.437
otomita, Melissoptila 25.69.35
Ototretini, supra 24.55.17
ou, Rachiplusia 27.75.156
Oudemansia 1.2.8
Oulema 24.107.14
Oulimnius 24.45.21
Ourapterygini, supra 27.61.119

Outer Barklice Family 17.16.1
Oval Guinea Pig Louse 18.4.2
ovalis, Ceutorhynchus 24.113.292 (Fig. 24.293)
ovalis, Gyropus 18.4.2
ovalis, Murmidius 24.78.3
ovalis, Rhinotorus 25.16.355
ovalis, Sphingocephalus 24.98.47
ovalis, Uloporus 24.87.168
Ovaticoccus 21.31.8
Ovatus 21.19.155
ovatus, Aspathines 24.85.2
ovatus, Otiorhynchus 24.113.68
ovatus, Pterocolus 24.113.12 (Fig. 24.266)
ovinus, Melophagus 29.106.12 (Fig. 29.58)
ovipennis, Conoecus 24.87.10
ovis, Bovicola 18.2.1
ovis, Oestrus 29.102.3
ovivora, Systellogaster 25.19.125
Ovoviviparous Cockroach Family 14.6.1
Owlfly Family, supra 23.15.1
Ox Beetle 24.30.108
Oxaciini, supra 24.97.13
Oxacis 24.97.13
Oxaeid Bee Family, supra 25.64.1
Oxaeidae, supra 25.64.1
Oxalis Whitefly 21.18.11
Oxybelini, supra 25.62.53
Oxybelus 25.62.55
Oxycareninae, supra 20.7.21
Oxycera 29.31.31
Oxycerini, supra 29.31.31
Oxycilla 27.75.21
Qxycnemis 27.75.443
Oxycopiini, supra 24.97.7
Oxycopis 24.97.8
Oxycorynidae, supra 24.113.15
Oxycoryninae, supra 24.113.15
Oxycrepis 24.4.90
Oxydia 27.61.146
Oxydosphyra 29.105.88
Oxydrepanus 24.4.28
Oxyelophila 27.55.20
Oxyethira 26.6.6
Oxygonodera 24.87.26
Oxygonus 24.48.42
oxygramma, Agrapha 27.75.153
Oxygrylius 24.30.105
Oxyhaloinae, supra 14.6.6
Oxylabis 25.42.13
Oxylaemus 24.93.23
Oxylipeurus 18.1.42
Oxyna 29.61.20
Oxynops 29.105.256
Oxyomus 24.30.18
Oxypoda 24.24.276
Oxyporinae, supra 24.24.159
Oxyporus 24.24.159
Oxyptilus 27.58.5
Oxyrrhexis 25.16.23
Oxysarcodexia 29.103.38
Oxystoglossella 26.66.10
Oxysychus 25.9.79
Oxytaenia 25.16.148
Oxytelliane, supra 24.24.141
Oxytelus 24.24.152
Oxythrips 22.4.28
Oxytorinae, supra 25.16.480
Oxytorus 25.16.481
Oyster Shell Scale 21.38.45
Ozaenini, supra 24.4.5
Ozamia 27.55.387
Ozarba 27.75.187
Ozirhincus 29.11.58
Ozodiceromya 29.32.23

Ozognathus 24.63.8
Ozophora 20.7.41
Ozophorini, supra 20.7.41

P

Pachnaeus 24.113.59
Pachnobia 27.75.565
Pachodynerus 25.59.19
Pachybaris 24.113.336
Pachybrachis 24.107.30
Pachybruchus 24.108.5
pachycephalus, Echthrogonatopus 25.25.69
Pachycerina 29.82.11
Pachycerota 24.24.277
Pachycondyla 25.58.13
pachycondylae, Catacljinusa 29.46.31
Pachyconops 29.49.2
Pachycoris 20.3.2
Pachycrepoideus 25.19.69
Pachydiplax 7.7.20
Pachydrini, supra 24.7.5
Pachydrus 24.7.6
Pachygaster, supra 29.31.1, 29.31.26
Pachygastrinae, supra 29.31.20
Pachygeraeus 24.113.326
Pachygonatopus 25.51.20
Pachygraphia 29.103.39
Pachygrontha 20.7.24
Pachygronthinae, supra 20.7.23
Pachygronthini, supra 20.7.23
Pachyhelea 29.23.32
Pachylia 27.70.23
Pachyliodes 27.70.24
Pachylobius 24.113.154
Pachylopus 24.26.10
pachymera, Pachyhelea 29.23.32
Pachymerinae, supra 24.108.1
Pachymorphinae, supra 10.1.7
Pachynematus 25.7.27
Pachyneuroidea, supra 29.7.1
Pachyneurid Gnat Family, supra 29.7.1
Pachyneuridae, supra 29.6.1; supra 29.7.
Pachyneurini, supra 25.19.66
Pachyneuron 25.19.68
Pachynomada 25.69.10
Pachyonychis 24.107.149
Pachyonychus 24.107.156
Pachyopsis 21.14.30
Pachypappa 21.19.156
Pachypeltocoris 20.23.174
Pachyplectrus 24.30.37
Pachypolia 27.75.424
Pachyprotasis 25.7.98
Pachypsylla 21.17.21
Pachypsyllini, supra 21.17.19
Pachyschelus 24.46.36
Pachysphinx 27.70.18
Pachysomoides 25.16.183
Pachystilicus 24.24.65
Pachyta 24.106.179
Pachyteles 24.4.6
Pachytroctidae, supra 17.7.1
Pachytychius 24.113.175
Pacidianus 29.105.405
Pacific Coast Wireworm 24.48.27
Pacific Dampwood Termite 15.1.1
Pacific Flatheaded Borer 24.46.23
Pacific Pelagic Water Strider 20.27.5
Pacific Tent Caterpillar Moth 27.68.11
Pacific Willow Leaf Beetle 24.107.80
pacifica, Chimarocephala 11.5.36
pacifica, Coleophasia 29.105.35
pacifica, Diglotta 24.24.225
Pacificallis 21.19.217
pacificata, Ilithucia 21.15.22

pacificus, Hemerobius 23.8.1
Packard Grasshopper 11.5.94
packardaria, Aethaloida 27.61.91
packardella, Semioscopis 27.15.4 (Fig. 27.34)
packardi, Grapholita 27.38.53
packardi, Melanoplus 11.5.94
packardi, Pitydiplosis 29.11.92
packardi, Trialeurodes 21.18.17
Packardia 27.52.6
Pactopus 24.49.2
Pactorrhinus 24.113.401
Padaeus 20.3.35
padella, Yponomeuta 27.30.9 (Fig. 27.48)
padiilla, Allanthalia 29.42.55
Paducia 21.19.157
Paduniella 26.2.4
Paduniellinae, supra 26.2.4
Paectes 27.75.170
Paederopsis 24.24.66
Paederus 24.24.67
paeoniae, Pseudaonidia 21.38.68
Paeudallonyx 24.68.27
Pagara 27.73.22
Pagaronia 21.14.63
Pagasa 20.18.1
Pagastia 29.24.35
Pagastiella 29.24.71
Pagiocerus 24.112.2
Painted Beauty 27.46.27
Painted Hickory Borer 24.106.112
Painted Lady 27.46.27
Painted Leafhopper 21.14.214
Painted Maple Aphid 21.19.64
Palaeagapetus 26.7.1
palaemon, Carterocephalus 27.40.42
palaeno, Colias 27.42.11
Palaeoaphis 21.19.158
Palaeodipteron 29.5.1
Palaeoptera, supra 6.1.1
Palaeosepsis 29.81.5
Paleoxenus 24.52.19
palamedes, Pterourus 27.41.7
Palaminus 24.24.79
palans, Lagoleptus 25.16.63
palata, Pseudopanthea 27.75.226
Palatka 27.55.366
Pale Damsel Bug 20.18.5
Pale Flea Beetle 24.107.121
Pale Juniper Webworm 27.39.1
Pale Leaf-cutting Bee 25.68.22
Pale Louse Family 19.2.1
Pale-sided Cutworm Moth 27.75.535
Pale Tussock Moth 27.73.55
Pale Western Cutworm Moth 27.75.535
Paleacrita 27.61.63
palegon, Thereus 27.43.21
Palembus 24.87.97
Paleodictyoptera supra 6.1.1
Paleoplatyura 29.9.14
Pales 29.105.380
pales, Hylobius 24.113.153
Pales Weevil 24.113.153
Palinaspis 21.38.59
Palingeniidae, supra 6.12.1
palla, Charidryas 27.46.15
Pallacocoris 20.23.175
pallens, Amblyderus 24.102.3 (Fig. 24.172)
pallens, Anastrepha 29.61.43
pallens, Asthanesita 24.24.204
pallens, Doliotettix 21.14.157
pallens, Geocoris 20.7.18
pallens, Pharga 27.75.58
pallens, Trypheromyia 29.105.270
pallescens, Atranus 24.4.79

pallescens, Euphilotes 27.43.44
palliatricula, Chytonix 27.75.291
palliatus, Desmocerus 24.106.169
Pallicephala 29.32.6
pallicornella, Trachycera 27.55.284
pallicornis, Rhynchaenus 24.113.217
pallida americana, Megaphthalma 29.98.8
pallida, Apachemyia 29.105.124
pallida, Cadrema 29.94.5
pallida, Cryptotreta 29.61.10
pallida, Hypexilis 24.106.39
pallida, Phyciodes 27.46.20
pallida, Scaptomyza 29.90.10
pallidata, Evergestis 27.55.69
pallidefulva pallidefulva, Formica 25.58.72
pallidior, Palpidia 27.75.59
pallidipennis, Cosmariomyia 29.31.20
pallidipes, Euophthalmomyia 25.26.56
pallidulus, Taylorilygus 20.23.189
pallidulum, Argiallagma 7.11.6
pallidum, Eosentomon 2.1.1
pallidus, Aracanthus 24.113.110
pallidus, Desolakerrus 24.48.62
pallidus, Neoheterocerus 24.42.5 (Fig. 24.82)
pallidus, Phoetalia 14.6.3
pallimedia, Crimona 27.75.458
palliolata, Sobata 21.14.129
pallipennis, Chaetolonchaea 29.57.2
pallipes, Amblyopone 25.58.6
pallipes, Ametastegia 25.7.84
pallipes, Ankylotylus 20.23.32
pallipes, Idiotypa 25.42.27
pallipes, Listrimorpha 24.68.44
pallipes, Nebria 24.4.10
pallipes, Ocytata 29.105.340
pallipes, Rhysipolis 25.13.43
pallipes, Saldula 20.32.10
pallipes, Solva 29.30.1
Pallodes 24.70.29
Palloptera 29.63.1
Pallopterid Fly Family, supra 29.63.1
Pallopteridae, supra 29.63.1
pallorana, Xenotemna 27.38.84
palloranus, Loxodocus 25.16.309
palloris, Sericopsothrips 22.4.16
Pallulaspis 21.38.60
Palm Scale Insect Family, supra 21.37.1
palmata, Donacia 24.107.4
palmata, Hypopta 27.37.1
palmarum, Asarcopus 21.6.4
palmarum, Omicrus 24.12.31
palmeri, Apodemia 27.44.7
palmeri, Coenopoeus 24.106.274
palmeri, Nionia 21.14.35
Palmerworm 27.23.85
Palmetto Scale 21.38.19
palmettovora, Phormoestes 27.36.1
Palmia 27.35.13
Palmicola 17.20.2
palmii, Hymenoclea 27.35.19
Palmocorixa 20.35.15
Palmodes 25.62.10
Palonica 21.15.39
Palorus 24.87.111
Palpada 29.47.67
palpalis, Hydrotrupes 24.7.22
palpalis, Pyrota 24.101.12
Palpexorista 29.105.285
Palpidia 27.75.59
palpigera, Brachyacma 27.23.84
Palpita 27.55.156
Palpomyia 29.23.33
Palpomyiini, supra 29.23.32
Palpostomatini, supra 29.105.40
palpus 20

Palpusia 27.55.189
Palthis 27.75.16
Paltothemis 7.7.21
Paluda 21.14.153
paludatus, Sternechus 24.113.166
Paludicoccus 21.25.28
paludosa, Tipula 29.2.9
Palumbia 29.47.80
Palus 21.14.179
palustris, Isotomurus 1.4.20
palustris, Listronotus 24.11.143 (FIG. 24.278)
Palyas 27.61.66
Palyneoptera, supra 8.1.1
Pambolidea 25.13.20
Pambolini, supra 25.13.51
Pambolus 25.13.52
Pamilla 20.23.131
Pammene 27.38.49
Pamphantini, supra 20.7.20
Pamphantus, supra 20.7.20
Pamphiliidae 25.2.1
Pamphiliinae, supra 25.2.3
Pamphiliini, supra 25.2.4
Pamphilus 25.2.4
pampina, Eucirroedia 27.75.401
pampinaria, Anavitrinella 27.61.41
Panacemyia 29.105.257
Panagaeini, supra 24.4.96
Panagaeitae 24.4.96
Panageus 24.4.96
panamensis, Hylaeus 25.63.5
Panaphantina, supra 24.25.18
Panchaetoma 1.4.23
Panchaetothripinae, supra 22.4.1
Panchlora 14.6.5
Panchlorinae, supra 14.6.5
Pandasyopthalmus 29.47.4
Pandeleteinus 24.113.63
Pandeleteius 24.113.65
Pandemis 27.38.70
Pandivirila 29.32.9
Pandora Moth 27.69.6
pandora pandora, Coloradia 27.69.6
pandorus, Eumorpha 27.70.31 (Fig 27.252)
Pangaeus 20.1.4
Pangoniinae, supra 29.26.1
Pangoniini, supra 29.26.2
Pangrapta 27.75.51
Pangruinus 25.65.5
paniceum, Stegobium 24.63.18 (Fig. 24.125)
panicifoliella, Cycloplasis 27.34.1
panicola, Pseudoregma 21.19.180
Panntoa, supra 6.13.1
Pannychis 24.106.298
Panopinae, supra 29.38.1
Panopoda 27.75.95
Panoquina 27.40.84
Panorpa 28.4.1
Panorpida, supra 25.1.1
Panorpidae, supra 28.4.1
Panorpodidae, supra 28.5.1
Panscopus 24.113.126
Panstenon 25.19.39
Panstenoninae, supra 25.19.39
Pantala 7.7.22
Pantarbes 29.40.19
Panthea 27.75.224
Pantheinae, supra 27.75.224
pantherina, Poecilotettix 11.5.105
Panther-spotted Grasshopper 11.5.106
Panthiades 27.43.33
Pantisarthrus 25.16.488
Pantoclis 25.42.8

Pantographa 27.55.165
Pantomorus 24.113.24
Pantorhaestes 25.16.365
Panugomia 25.67.2
Panula 27.75.101
Panurginae, supra 25.65.4
Panzeriopsis 29.105.88
Paonias 27.70.16
Paota 27.61.177
Papago Thread-legged Katydid 11.7.2
Papagona 21.6.5
Papaipema 27.75.279
Papaya Fruit Fly 29.61.1
Paper Triangle 37
Paper Wasps, supra 25.59.28
Papestra 27.75.485
Papilio 27.41.5, 27.41.6, 27.41.7, 27.41.8
Papilionidae, supra 27.41.1
Papilioninae, supra 27.41.2
Papilionini, supra 27.41.5
Papilionoidea, supra 27.41.1
papillata, Dirhiza 29.11.42
papillata, Jacksonia 21.19.108
Papulaphis 21.19.159
Papusus 24.20.21
papyriferae, Apagodiplosis 29.11.133
Parabacillus 10.1.7
Parabarrovia 27.75.564
Parabates 25.16.48
Parabezzia 29.23.17
Parablastothrix 25.25.84
Parabolocratus 21.14.7
Parabombylius 29.40.16
Parabrysopolis 24.30.90
Parabyssodon 29.22.5
Paracacoxenus 29.90.6
Paracamptus 24.113.248
Paracantha 29.61.11
Paracapnia 8.3.8
Paracarotomus 25.19.49
Paracentris 25.69.42
Paracentrobia 25.28.4
Parachaeta 29.105.369
Parachaetocladius 29.24.119
Paracharactus 25.7.59
Parachrionomus 29.24.49
Parachma 27.55.240
Parachrysocharis 25.26.72
Paracimbocera 24.113.118
Paracladius 29.24.103
Paracladopelma 29.24.50
Paracladra 29.13.3
Paraclemensia 27.8.3
Paracleruchus 25.27.13
Paraclisis 18.1.43
Paraclius 29.43.9
Paracloeodes 6.4.11
Paraclunio 29.24.138
Paracoccus 21.25.29
Paracoelidea 21.14.39
Paracoenia 29.93.58
Paracolletini, supra 25.63.1
Paracolopha 21.19.160
Paracosmus 29.40.3
Paracotalpa 24.30.88
Paracraspis 25.34.22
Paracretona 27.75.205
Paracrias 25.26.79
Paracricotopus 29.24.102
Paracymus 24.12.17
Paracyphononyx 25.60.31
Paracyrtophyllus 11.7.15
Paradacerla 20.23.150
Paradasyhelea 29.23.6
Paradejeania 29.105.95
Paradeliphrum 24.24.125

Paradelphomyia 29.2.26
Parademoticus 29.105.128
Paradiarsia 27.75.574
Paradibrachys 25.19.117
Paradicranota 29.2.25
Paradidyma 29.105.213
Paradiplocampta 29.40.48
Paradiplosis 29.11.117
Paradmontia 29.105.147
Paradolichurus 25.62.2
paradoxella, Apreta 27.10.31
Paradoxococcus 21.15.30
paradoxus, Helorus 25.41.1
paradoxus, Pachyonychis 24.107.149
paradoxus, Pachyonychus 24.107.156
Parafischeria 29.105.129
Paragaleopsomyia 25.26.44
Paragini, supra 29.47.4
Paraglucina 27.61.33
Paragnetina 8.9.11
Paragraphus 24.113.97
Paragrilus 24.46.35
Paragus 29.47.4
Parahelodon 29.22.4
Parahormius 25.13.50
Parahypenodes 27.75.31
Parahypochaeta 29.105.152
Paraidemona 15.5.82
Parajapyginae, supra 3.4.8
Parajapyx 3.4.8
Parakiefferiella 29.24.134
Paralauterborniella 29.24.59
Paraleptophlebia 6.7.6
Paraleucopis 29.83.5
Paraleucoptera 27.13.8
Paraleuctra 8.4.4
Paraleurocerus 25.25.47
Paraleyrodes 21.18.19
Paraliaphilus 24.6.1
Paralictus 25.66.21
Paralimna 29.93.39
Paralimulodes 24.16.2
Paralipophleps 29.2.47
Paralipsa 27.55.276
Paralispe 29.105.258
Paralispidea 29.105.307
Paralitomastix 25.25.85
parallela, Aphrophora 21.12.5
parallela, Madopterina 24.113.361
parallela, Torosomyia 29.105.363
Parallelaptera 25.27.10
parallelepipedus, Aba 24.4.87
Parallelia 27.75.135
Parallelodiplosis 29.11.101
Parallelomma 29.98.27
parallelopipedum,
 Trogoxylon 24.65.3 (Fig. 24.128)
Parallelostethus 24.48.44
Parallothrips 22.5.16
Paralobium 24.63.12
Paralucilia 29.101.4
Paramacera 27.48.7
Paramacronychiini, supra 29.103.15
Paramblynotus 25.30.1
Parameletus 6.1.3
Paramerina 29.24.29
Paramesius 25.42.18
Paramesus 21.14.177
Parametriocnemus 29.24.111
Parametriotini, supra 27.20.3
Paramiama 27.75.362
Parammoplanus 25.62.32
Paramuscopteryx 29.105.179
Paramycodrosophila 29.90.16
Paramyia 29.74.3
Paramyrmica 25.58.22

Paranaemia 24.80.46
Paranametis 24.113.129
Paranapiacaba 24.107.91
parancilla, Frontiniella 29.105.419
Parancistrocerus 25.59.14
Parandra 24.106.1
Parandrena 25.65.1
Parandrinae, supra 24.106.1
Parandrini, supra 24.106.1
Paranemoura 8.1.6
paranensis, Schistocerca 11.5.114
Paraneoptera, supra 16.1.1
Paraneossos 29.85.2
Paraneotermes 15.2.3
Parania 25.16.385
Paranomada 25.69.12
Paranoplium 24.106.27
Paranortonia 25.59.21
Paranthaclisis 23.14.11
Paranthidium 25.68.4
Paranthrene 27.35.4
Paranthreninae, supra 27.35.3
Paranthrenini, supra 27.35.4
Parantichaeta 29.79.7
Parantonae 21.15.31
Paranura 1.2.19
Paranurophorus 1.4.5
Paranusia 25.25.30
Paraolinx 25.26.17
Parapamea 27.75.278
Parapediasia 27.55.216
Parapelopia 29.24.9
Paraperla 8.8.9
Paraperlinae, supra 8.8.8
Paraphaenocladius 29.24.108
Paraphaenodiscus 25.25.151
Paraphasmlophaga 29.105.346
Paraphausis 24.55.3
Parapherocera 29.32.29
Parapheromia 27.61.48
Paraphlepsius 21.14.140
Paraphoides 27.61.54
Paraphorantha 29.105.10
Paraphoromyia 29.28.6
Paraphrosylus 29.43.20
Paraplea 20.34.2
Paraporia 29.105.199
Parapoynx 27.55.14
Paraproba 20.23.117
Paraprociphilus 21.19.172
Paraprosalpia 29.99.19
Paraprosopis 25.63.5
Parapsilophrys 25.25.152
Parapsyche 26.4.2
Paraptochus 24.113.89
Paraptorthodius 24.54.5
Pararchytas 29.105.96
Pararctia 27.73.49
Pararete 29.11.19
Parargini, supra 27.48.1
Pararicia 29.100.48
Pararina 21.13.9
Parasa 27.52.20
Parasaissetia 21.26.13
Parascaptomyza 29.90.10
Parascatopse 29.15.3
Paraschiza 21.19.191
Paraschizaphis 21.19.191
Parascleroderma 25.48.3
Parascotia 27.75.26
Parasemia 27.73.32
Parasemidalis 23.5.5
Parasetigena 29.105.286
Parasida 24.87.53
Parasimuliinae, supra 29.22.1
Parasimulium 29.22.1

Parasitic Beetle Family, supra 24.105.1
Parasitic Fly Family, supra 29.105.1
Parasitic Grain Wasp 25.48.14
Parasitic Wood Wasp Family, supra 25.11.1
Parasitic Yellowjacket 25.59.27
Parasitica, infra 25.13.1
Paraspalangia 25.26.37
Paraspicera 25.31.1
Parastasia 24.30.86
Parastenoterys 25.25.31
Parastichtis 27.75.264
Parasynapta 29.11.41
Parasyntomocera 25.19.54
Parasyntormon 29.43.27
Parasyrphus 29.47.20
Paratachys 24.4.56
Paratanytarsus 29.24.81
Parataracticus 29.37.13
Parategeticula 27.8.10
Paratendipes 29.24.62
Paratenetus 24.89.5
Paraterellia 29.61.39
Paratettix 11.1.4
Parathalassius 29.42.43
Parathecabius 21.19.208
Paratheresia 29.105.78
Parathrachelizus 24.11.02
Parathyce 24.30.73
Parathyroglossa 29.93.2
Paratimia 24.106.19
Paratinia 29.9.69
Paratiphia 25.53.4
Paratissa 29.93.18
paratomicobia, Karpinskiella 25.19.97
Paratrachea 27.75.310
Paratrea 27.70.10
Paratrechina 25.58.69
Paratriarius 24.107.94
Paratriatoma 20.17.38
Paratrichobius 29.108.3
Paratrichocladius 29.24.98
Paratrioza 211.17.11
Paratriphleps 20.21.9
Paratrytone 27.40.74
Paratylotropidia 11.5.93
Paratyndaris 24.46.30
Paratyphloceras 30.4.19
Paraugochloropsis 25.66.9
Paraurosiglalphus 25.13.140
Paravelia 20.28.5
Paravilla 29.40.58
Paravius 24.87.16
Paraxenetus 20.23.151
parca, Eupareophora 25.7.68
parca, Goniotropis 24.4.5
Parcoblatta 14.5.5
pardalis, Oligostomis 26.8.6 (Fig. 26.24)
Pardalophora 11.5.40
pardella, Epimartyria 27.1.1
Pardiaulomella 25.26.5
Parecrizotes 25.19.63
Parectecephala 29.94.45
Parectopa 27.14.5
Paregesta 27.55.56
Paregle 29.99.8
Parepalpus 29.105.99
Parephistemus 24.74.16
Parepidosis 29.11.47
Pareuchaetes 27.73.64
Parevander 24.106.164
Parexcelsa 27.61.94
Parhelophilus 29.47.61
Paria 24.107.50
pariana, Prochoreutis 27.36.4 (Fig. 27.56)
Parides 27.41.2
Paridris 25.43.17

parinotata, Hammaptera 27.61.216
paripes, Glyptotendipes 29.24.44
parkeri, Platencyrtus 25.25.110
Parlatoreopsis 21.38.61
Parlatoria 21.38.62
Parlatoria Date Scale 21.38.62
parlatoriodes, Pseudoparlatoria 21.38.72
Parmenini, supra 24.106.228
Parmenonta 24.106.242
Parmenosoma 24.106.228
Parmorthia 25.16.137
Parnassian Butterfly 27.41.1
Parnassiinae, supra 27.41.1
Parnassiini, supra 27.41.1
Parnassius 27.41.1
Parnopes 25.50.23
Parnopinae, supra 25.50.23
Parocalea 24.24.278
Parochletus 29.31.33
Parochlus 29.24.1
Parochromotopis 27.27.3
Paroedopa 29.58.32
Paroedostethus 24.48.39
Paroligineurus 25.13.129
Paromalus 24.26.28
Paromius 20.7.52
Paronellinae, supra 1.5.10
Paropheltes 25.16.48
Paropomala 11.5.26
Parorectis 24.107.182
Parorgerius 21.11.10
Parormosia 29.2.60
Parornix 27.14.10
Parothius 24.24.43
Paroxacis 24.97.15
Paroxya 11.5.103
Paroxyna 29.61.22
Parrhasius 28.43.33
parrotti, Antoninoides 21.25.5
Parselyworm 27.41.5
Parsnip Webworm 27.15.5
Parthenicus 20.23.118
Parthenolecanium 21.26.14
parthenos, Platarctia 27.73.46
Parthenothrips 22.4.6
Parthina 26.14.4
participalis, Condylolomia 27.55.25
partita, Galgula 27.75.331
partitus, Allocomoecus 26.10.1
parvella, Welderella 27.55.376
parviceps, Cibalacris 11.5.72
parvicornis, Agromyza 29.68.1
parvicornis, Toumeyella 21.26.22
parvida, Pales 29.105.380
parvipes, Hypertrophocera 29.105.343
parvipicta, Dichozoma 27.55.32
parvula, Urodus 27.30.8
parvulalis, Alpheioedes 27.55.280
parvulus, Apteralipus 24.6.3
parvulus solenobiae, Macrus 25.16.417
parvulus, Sphenophours 24.113.366
parvus, Lioptilodes 27.58.13
parvus, Telmaturgus 29.43.46
Parwinnertzia 29.11.34
Parydra 29.93.41
Parydrinae, supra 29.93.41
Parydrini, supra 29.93.41
Paryphes 20.4.30
Paryphoconus 29.23.31
Pasadenus 21.14.125
Pasaremus 21.14.178
pascoensis, Megachile 25.68.22
pascuellus, Arthaldeus 21.14.185
Pasimachus 24.4.22
Passalidae, supra 24.29.1
Passalinae, supra 24.29.1

Passalini, supra 24.29.2
Passaloecus 25.62.24
Passalus 24.29.2
Passandrinae, supra 24.72.9
passiflorae, Anthemurgus 25.65.7
Passodena 27.55.348
pastinacella, Depressaria 27.15.5 (Fig. 27.35)
Patalene 27.61.148
Patapius 20.31.1
Patara 21.9.4
Patasson 25.27.14
Patchia 21.19.161
patella, Otomasicera 29.105.437
Patelloa 29.105.428
Patergini, supra 24.49.1
Patissa 27.55.192
Patrebitae, supra 24.4.68
Patriciola 27.55.368
patrobas, Gyrocheilus 27.48.11
Patrobini, supra 24.4.68
Patrobus 24.4.70
Patrocloides 25.16.239
Patroclus 25.16.240
Pauesia 25.14.6
pauper, Cacophrissus 24.106.43
Pauridia 25.25.36
Pauridini, supra 25.25.35
paurometabolous 13
Pauropoda 10
Pauropsyllinae, supra 21.17.6
paurosoma, Paracoenia 29.93.58
Paussinae, supra 24.4.3
Paussitac, supra 24.4.5
pauxillus, Chalcosyrphus 29.47.87
Pavement Ant 25.58.42
pavon, Doxocopa 27.47.4
pavonacella, Brenthia 27.36.2
Pavostelis 25.68.11
Pawpaw Sphinx 27.70.5
Paxilla 11.1.6
Pazu 21.14.204
Pea Aphid 21.19.2
Pea and Bean Weevil Family, supra 24.108.1
Pea Leaf Weevil 24.113.50
Pea Moth 27.38.56
Pea Weevil 24.108.15
Peach Tree Borer 27.35.12
Peach Twig Borer 27.23.77
Pealius 21.18.15
Peanut Bug, supra 21.1.1 (Fig. 21.3)
Pear Midge 29.11.108
Pear Plant Bug 20.23.165
Pear Psylla 21.17.27
Pear Sawfly 25.7.43
Pear Thrips 22.4.52
Pearl Crescent 27.46.20
Pearly Eye 27.48.1
Pearly Wood Nymph 27.75.239
Pebops 27.21.4
Pecan Bud Moth 27.38.35
Pecan Carpenterworm 27.37.4
Pecan Casebearer 27.55.282
Pecan Cigar Casebearer 27.18.1
Pecan Leaf Phylloxera 21.21.1
Pecan Nut Casebearer 27.55.282
Pecan Phylloxera 21.21.1
Pecan Serpentine Leaf Miner 27.5.1
Pecan Spittle Bug 21.12.7
Pecan Weevil 24.113.200
Pecaroecidae, supra 19.4.1
Pecaroecus 19.4.1
Pecarry Louse Family, supra 19.4.1
pecatonica, Acanthametropus 6.1.6
peccataria, Phyllodonta 27.61.147

Pechalius 24.87.6
pechumani, Vibrissotheresia 29.105.81
Peckelachertus 25.26.28
Peckia 29.103.40
Peck's Skipper 27.40.66
Peconus 21.14.206
pecosella, Mompha 27.19.1
pectenalaeella, Glauce 27.23.12
pectinalis, Decaturia 27.55.281
pectinata, Schistoneurus 29.11.56
poctinata, Tropidiplosis 29.11.120
pectinicornis, Ripidius 24.100.6
Pectinodiplosis 29.11.126
Pectinolochus 25.16.448
Pectinophora 27.23.81
Pectinopygus 18.1.44
pectoralis, Arge 25.4.1
pectorosus, Stethon 24.52.6
pectotoma 24.98.43
pecuarum, Cnephia 29.22.11
pedalis, Idiopidonia 24.106.208
pedator, Reichardtia 24.26.11
pedella, Dolophron 25.16.414
pederifromis, Episbates 18.1.23
Pedetontus 4.1.2
Pediacus 24.72.12
Pediasia 27.55.211
Pedicellina 29.31.6
Pedicia 29.2.22
Pediciini, supra 29.2.21
Pedicinidae, infra 19.8.1
Pedicinus, infra 19.8.1
pedicularia, Lachesilla 17.14.1 (Fig. 17.6)
pediculata, Ropronia 25.40.1
Pediculidae, supra 19.8.1
Pediculus 19.8.1
Pedilidae, supra 24.103.1
Pedilini, supra 24.103.1
Pedilophorini, supra 24.35.4
Pedilus 24.103.1
Pedinini, supra 24.87.146
Pedinotus 25.13.21
Pediobius 25.26.77
Pediodectes 11.7.40
Pedionomus 29.24.73
pedis, Eojapyx 3.4.4
peditalis, Ledaea 27.75.52
Peditatus 24.42.8
pedo, Saga 11.7.47
Pedomoecus 26.10.51
Pedumella 21.14.175
Peg or Bess Beetle Family, supra 24.29.1
pegala, Cercyonis 27.48.9 (Fig. 27.151)
Pegbug 24.19.1
pege, Oravelia 20.29.3
Pegohylemyia 29.99.8
Pegomya 29.99.14
peigleri, Anisota 27.69.5
pela, Ericerus 21.26.22
Pelastoneurus 29.43.10
Pelatachina 29.105.190
Pelatines 24.21.3
Pelaturidae, supra 7.1.1
pele, Fattigia 26.13.2
Pelecinid Wasp Family, supra 25.38.1
Pelecinidae, supra 25.38.1
Pelecinoidea, supra 25.38.1
Pelecinus 25.38.1
Pelecocera 29.47.40
Pelecomalium 24.24.126
Pelecorhynchid Fly Family, supra 29.25.1
Pelecorhynchidae, supra 29.25.1
Pelecotheca 29.105.276
Pelecotoma 24.100.1
Pelecotominae, supra 24.100.1
Pelecystoma 25.13.56

Pelenosomus 24.113.288
Peleopodinae, supra 27.15.15
Peleopodini, supra 27.15.15
Peleteria 29.105.88
Pelicandrena 25.65.1
pelidne, Colias 27.42.11
Pelidnota 24.30.92
Pelignellus 29.93.1
Pelignus 29.93.9
Pelina 29.93.49
Peliococcus 21.25.31
Pelitropis 21.5.2
Pellicia 27.40.23
Pelliculaspis 21.38.63
pellionella, Tinea, 27.10.37; 27.10.45
pellucens, Fundella 27.55.298
pellucida, Anisota 27.69.5
pellucida, Camnula 11.5.38
pellucidalis, Somatania 27.55.128
Pellucidomyia 29.23.22
pellucidus, Barypeithes 24.113.44
Pelochrista 27.38.25
Pelocoris 20.38.3
Pelomyia 29.96.1
Pelomyiella 29.96.2
Pelonides 24.67.25
Pelonium 24.67.28
Pelonomus 24.44.3
Pelophila 24.4.9
Peloropeodes 29.43.28
Pelosoma 24.12.28
Peltales 25.16.287
Peltaphis 21.19.210
Peltastica 24.59.2
peltatus, Xyletinus 24.63.37
Peltinae, supra 24.66.1
Peltodytes 24.6.2
Peltoperla 8.6.1
Peltoperlidae, supra 8.6.1
Peltoperloidea, supra 8.6.1
Peltophorus 24.113.274
Peltotrupes 24.30.53
Pemelus 24.12.34
Pemphiginae 21.19.13
Pemphigus 21.19.162
Pemphredon 25.62.23
Pemphredoninae, supra 25.62.15
Pemphredonini, supra 25.62.22
pendens, Rhytura 25.16.146
pendula, Wasmaelia 25.13.161
Penehuleria 21.14.89
Penenirmus 18.1.45
Penestirellus 21.14.168
Penestola 27.55.142
penetrans, Tunga 30.1.2
penicellus, Centrinaspis 24.113.325 (Fig. 24.297)
Penichroa 24.106.48
penicillata, Strophogastra 24.24.295
peninsularis, Trichodes 24.67.18
penitalis, Pyraustomyia 29.105.130
pennaria, Colotois 27.61.99
pennipes, Trichopoda 29.105.5
Pennisetia 27.35.1
Pennisetiini, supra 27.35.1
Penniverpa 29.32.21
pennsylvania, Coccidomyia 29.11.78
Pennsylvania Wood Cockroach 14.5.5
Penstemonia 27.35.17
pennsylvanica, Alobates 24.87.75 (Fig. 24.153)
pennsylvanica, Epicuata 24.101.14
pennsylvanicus,
 Camponotus 25.58.66 (Fig. 25.48)
pennsylvanicus, Chauliognathus 24.56.1

pennsylvanicus, Photuris 24.55.16 (Fig. 24.108)
pensylvanica, Parcoblatta 14.5.5 (Fig. 14.18)
pensylvanica, Vespula 25.59.27 (Fig. 25.54)
pensylvanicus, Chlaenius 24.4.98
pensylvanicus, Harpalus 24.4.124 (Fig. 24.42)
pensylvanicus, Sphex 25.62.8
pentacantha, Nasiaeschna 7.4.9
Pentacnemus 25.25.87
Pentacora 20.32.3
Pentacricia 29.100.10
Pentacyphona 29.2.22
Pentagenia 6.12.1
pentagona, Pseudaulacaspis 21.38.69
Pentagonica 24.4.139
Pentagonicini, supra 24.4.139
Pentagramma 21.2.2
Pentalitomstix 25.25.86
Pentalonia 21.19.163
Pentamyzus 21.19.164
Pentaneura 29.24.26
Pentaneurini, supra 29.24.15
Pentanodes 24.106.129
Pentaperdita 25.65.15
Pentaphyllus 24.87.103
Pentaplastidia 25.32.6
Pentapleura 25.13.107
Pentapria 25.42.22
Pentaria 24.98.45
Pentarthrinus 24.113.391
Pentarthrum 24.113.390
Pentatomidae, supra 20.3.1
Pentatominae, supra 20.3.16
Pentatomini, supra 20.3.26
Pentatrichopus 21.19.50
Pentelicus 25.25.153
Pentenaysma 25.26.64
Penteriades 25.68.17
Penthe 24.98.6
Penthesilea 27.55.248
Penthetria 29.8.2
Penthimia 21.14.31
Penthimiinae, supra 21.14.31
Penthimiini, supra 21.14.31
Pentispa 24.107.172
Pentobesa 27.71.18
Peony Scale 21.38.68
Peoria 27.55.414
Peoriinae, supra 27.55.414
Peplogyptus 24.26.33
Peponapis 25.69.29
Pepper Maggot 29.61.45
Pepper Weevil 24.113.208
Pepper-and-salt Moth 27.61.58
Peppergrass Beetle 24.107.86
Pepsinae, supra 25.60.1
Pepsini, supra 25.60.1
Pepsis 25.60.2
Peracales 24.113.250
Peranabrus 11.7.41
perangulata, Oligocentria 27.71.35 (Fig. 27.276)
Peraniana 27.75.282
Peranoplium 24.106.78
Peranus 24.26.37
Perapion 24.113.18
Perarthrus 24.106.140
Perasis 29.37.25
percosius, Decinea 27.40.54
Perdita 25.65.15
perdita, Kathroperla 8.8.8
perditalis, Calephelis 27.44.2

Perditella 25.65.15
pereginator, Orchidophilus 24.113.322
peregrina, Pauridia 25.25.36
Peregrinus 21.2.18
Perenthis 24.113.301
perfacetus, Calochromus 24.57.6 (Fig. 24.112)
perfecta, Paranemoura 8.1.6
perpida, Madura 20.4.19
perforatus, Oopterinus 24.113.195
perfuscaria, Prosoparia 27.75.27
pergandei, Formica 25.58.72
pergandei, Pelecocera 29.47.40
pergandii, Parlatoria 21.38.612
pergentilis, Hadenella 27.75.471
Pergid Sawfly Family, supra 25.3.1
Pergidae, supra 25.2.3
pergratialis, Monoptilota 27.55.306
Perichares 27.40.52
Pcriclista 25.7.69
Periclistus 25.34.5
Pericoma 29.12.12
Pericompus 24.4.54
Pericopidae, supra 27.73.1
Pericopinae, supra 27.73.1
Pericopini, supra 27.73.1
Peridea 27.71.5
Peridesmia 25.19.101
Peridroma 27.75.555
Perigaster 24.113.298
Perigea 27.75.332
Perigenes 20.7.57
perigenes, Vidius 27.40.47
Perigona 24.4.137
Perigonia 27.70.27
Perigonica 27.75.501
Perigonini, supra 24.4.137
Perigracilia 24.106.38
Perilampinae, supra 25.19.3
Perilampus 25.19.4
Perilissus 25.16.339
Perilitus 25.13.156
Perillus 20.3.68
Perilypus 24.67.13
Perimede 27.21.23
Perineurini 25.7.89
Perineus 18.1.46
Periodical Cicada 21.13.18
Periope 25.16.290
Periphotopsis 25.55.12
Periphyllus 21.19.165
Periplaneta 14.3.2
Periploca 27.21.14
Peripsocidae, supra 17.15.1
Peripsocinae, supra 17.15.1
peripsocoides, Nepiomorpha 17.20.4
Peripsocus 17.15.1
Periscelidid Fly Family, supra 29.72.1
Periscelididae, supra 29.71.1
Periscelis 29.72.1
Periscepsia 29.105.214
Perispasta 27.55.86
Perissander 25.65.12
Perissarthron 24.48.36
Perissopompilus 26.60.28
Peristenus 25.13.157
Peritapnia 24.106.266
Peritaxia 24.113.132
Peritelini, supra 24.113.74
Peritelinus 24.113.81
Peritelodes 24.113.90
Peritelopsis 24.113.86
Perithemis 7.7.23
Perithous 25.16.33
Peritrechus 20.7.68

Peritropis 20.23.8
periusalis, Pilemia 27.52.131
Perizoma 27.61.218
perkinsi, Thaumatodryinus 25.51.9
perlaeta, Forsebia 27.75.102
perlata, Campaea 27.61.100
Perlesta 8.9.7
Perlidae, supra 8.9.1
Perlinae, supra 8.9.9
Perlinella 8.9.8
Perlini, supra 8.9.10
Perlinoides 8.7.18
Perlodidae, supra 8.7.1
Perloidea, supraeRM8.7.1
Perlodinae, supra 8.7.5
Perlomyia 8.4.7
perniciosus, Quadraspidiotus 21.38.73
Perniphora 25.19.78
Pero 27.61.87
Perodyrinus 25.51.10
Peromyia 29.11.5
Peromyscopsylla 30.6.1
Peronyma 29.61.5
perornata, Epiperola 27.52.1
Perothopidae, supra 24.51.1
Perothops 24.51.1
perplexus, Pseudocanthon 24.30.6
perpusillus, Orocastus 21.14.180
perseae, Acutaspis 21.38.2
perseae, Paraleyrodes 21.18.19
perseae, Pseudacysta 20.14.19
persicae, Brachycaudus 21.19.28
persicae, Myzus 21.19.144
persicae, Parthenolecanium 21.26.14
persimilis, Chlorochroa 20.3.29
Persimmon Borer 27.35.15
Persimmon Psylla 21.17.10
personatus, Reduvius 20.17.29 (Fig. 20.43)
perspectalis, Hymenia 27.55.134
persquamosus, Petrobius 4.1.5
pertenuis, Leptobamona 24.24.259
pertenuis, Leptoplectus 24.25.32
pertepida, Cyllopsis 27.48.3
pertinax, Acerastes 25.16.181
pertiosus, Callibaetis 6.4.4
perturbans, Coquillettidia 29.20.5
perturbator, Carlsonia 25.16.273
perumbraria, Synglochis 27.61.30
pestifera, Epicauta 24.101.14
Petalium 24.63.41
Petalochilinae, supra 24.113.51
Petalodes 25.13.57
Petalumaria 27.75.365
petauristes, Machiloides 4.2.24
Peterson's fluid 37
petilus, Cratocryptus 25.16.138
Petinarctia 29.105.148
petiolata, Euthyprosopa 29.105.327
petiolata, Reinhardiana 29.105.160
petraea, Chrysochraon 11.5.2
petreus, Marpesia 27.46.44
Petridiobus 4.1.1
Petrobius 4.1.5
Petrophila 27.55.18
Petrophora 27.61.105
petrophya, Sandalus 24.39.1 (Figs. 24.80a, 24.80b)
petrorum, Geranchon 21.19.88
Petrova 27.38.20
petulans, Megachile 25.68.22
Peucobius 25.16.444
Pezothrips 22.4.47
Phaceliapis 25.66.4
Phaea 24.106.300
Phaecasiophora 27.37.14

Phaedon 24.107.65
Phaedonini, supra 24.107.64
Phaedromus 24.107.152
Phaedropsis 27.55.168
Phaedrotettix 11.5.81
Phaegopterini, supra 27.73.54
Phaenicia 29.101.12
Phaenithon 24.109.22
Phaenobezzia 29.23.35
Phaenocarpa 25.13.108
Phaenocerus 24.52.5
Phaenoglyphis 25.33.3
Phaenonotum 24.12.27
Phaenopsectra 29.24.69
Phaenopsis 29.105.406
Phaenosarus 25.68.22
Phaenoserphus 25.39.9
Phaeochrous 24.30.38
Phaeogenes 25.16.207
Phaeogenina, supra 25.16.198
Phaeogenini, supra 25.16.197
phaeopteralis, Herpetogramma 27.55.179
Phaeoses 27.10.49
Phaeostrymon 27.43.14
phaeton, Euphydryas 27.46.23 (Fig. 27.127)
phaeton, Euproserpinus 27.70.38 (Fig. 27.262)
phaetusa, Dione 27.46.3
Phaiosterna 29.93.39
Phalacridae, supra 24.77.1
Phalacrocera 29.2.11
phalacrophyto 29.105.59
Phalacropsis 24.77.2
Phalacropsylla 30.4.9
Phalacropsyllini, supra 30.4.6
Phalacrotophora 29.46.21
Phalacrus 34.77.1
Phalaenophana 27.75.3
Phalaenostola 27.75.7
Phalaeopterus 24.24.127
phalerata, Apantesis 27.73.52 (Fig. 27.296)
Phaleria 24.87.104
Phaleriini, supra 24.87.104
Phaleromela 24.87.105
Phaloesia 27.73.3
Phalonia 27.39.1
Phalonidia 27.39.6
Phaloniidae, supra 27.39.1
Phanacis 25.34.14
Phanaeus 24.30.11
Phanagenia 25.60.10
Phaneroptera 11.7.8
Phaneropterinae, supra 11.7.1
Phaneroserphus 25.39.11
Phanerotoma 25.13.114
Phaneta 27.38.24
Phanocelia 26.10.36
Phanocerus 24.45.2
Phanomalopsis 25.69.16
Phanomeris 25.13.41
Phantasiomyia 29.105.308
phantasmaria, Nepytia 27.61.133
Phantolabis 29.2.53
Phantom Crane Fly Family, supra 29.17.1
Phantom Hemlock Looper 27.61.133
phaon, Phyciodes 27.46.20
Phaonia 29.100.44
Phaoniinae, supra 29.100.32
Pharaoh Ant 25.58.31
pharaonis, Monomorium 25.58.31 (Fig. 25.37
Phartorini, supra 24.107.68
Pharaxonotha 24.75.1

Pharaxonothini, supra 24.75.1
Pharga 27.75.58
Phasganophora 8.9.12
Phasgonophora 25.21.10
Phasia 29.105.11
Phasiinae, supra 29.105.1
Phasiini, supra 29.105.7
Phasiomyia 29.105.12
Phasiops 29.105.48
Phasiopsis 29.105.392
Phasiostoma 29.105.309
Phasmida, supra 10.1.1
Phasmatidae 10.2.1
Phasmatodea, supra 10.1.1 (Fig. 10.1)
Phasmophaga 29.105.334
Phaulotettix 11.5.83
Phausis 24.55.9
Phedius 24.88.7
Phegoneus 24.87.8
Pheidole 25.58.28
Pheidolini, supra 25.58.25
Pheidoloxenus 25.25.154
Phelister 24.26.47
phellandrii, Prasocuris 24.107.71
Phellopsis 24.87.174
Pheloconus 24.113.239
Phenacoccus 21.25.32
phenetics 17
Phengodes 24.54.2
Phengodidae, supra 24.54.1
Phengodini, supra 24.54.1
Phenolia 24.70.21
Pheosia 27.71.6 WL Pherbecta 29.79.15
Pherbellia 29.79.4
Phereoeca 27.10.35
Pherne 27.61.141
Pherocera 29.32.30
Phibalosminae 10.2.1
Phigalia 27.61.62
philadelphi, Glenningia 21.19.90
philadelphi, Prochelostoma 25.68.14
Philaenus 21.12.4
Philagruala 27.62.5
Philampelini, supra 27.70.31
Philanthinae, supra 25.62.106
Philanthini, supra 25.62.106
Philanthus 25.62.106
Philarctus 26.10.22
Philaronia 21.12.2
Philbostroma 11.5.6
philea, Phoebis 27.42.14 (Fig. 27.100)
Philedia 27.61.104
philenor, Battus 27.41.3 (Fig. 27.78)
Philephedra 21.26.15
Phileremulus 25.69.3
philetes, Perichares 27.40.52
Philetus 29.42.40
Phileurini, supra 24.30.111
Phileurus 24.30.113
philipi, Silvius 29.26.10
Philocalia 29.105.299
Philocasca 26.10.29
Philoceanus 18.1.47
philococcus, Opuntiaspis 21.38.58
Philodema 27.55.342
philodice, Colias 27.42.11 (Fig. 27.92)
philogelos, Falcimorpha 27.55.115
philolaus, Eurytides 27.41.4
Philolithus 24.87.51
Philonicus 29.37.77
Philonix 25.34.24
Philonome 27.13.2
Philonthus 24.24.12
philopagus, Acrodectes 11.7.25
Philopedon 24.113.49

Philopotamidae, supra 26.1.1
Philopteridae, supra 18.1.1
Philopterus 18.1.48
Philornis 29.100.54
Philorus 29.3.5
Philosepedon 29.12.8
Philositus 25.166.415
Philostratus 24.113.159
Philotarsidae, supra 17.21.1
Philotarsus 17.21.2
Philotelma 29.93.59
Philotermes 24.24.280
Philotes 27.43.43
Philothermus 24.78.6
Philotiella 27.43.45
Philtraea 27.61.119
Philya 21.15.10
philygria 29.93.33
Philygriini, supra 29.93.33
Phimodera 20.3.13
phlaeas, Lycaena 27.43.4 (Fig. 27.104)
Phlaeothripidae, supra 22.5.1
Phlaothripinae, supra 22.5.24
Phlaeothripoidea, supra 22.5.1
Phlaeothrips 22.5.47
Phlebosotera 29.73..22
Phlebotominae, supra 29.12.2
Phlebus 25.14.4
Phlegopenes 25.24.10
Phlegyas 20.7.25
Phlepsanus 21.14.141
Phloeobiothrips 22.5.46
Phloeocharinae, supra 24.24.171
Phloeodes 24.87.175
Phloeomyzus 21.19.166
Phloeonemus 24.93.12
Phloeonous 24.24.128
Phloeophagus 24.113.398
Phloeopora 24.24.281
Phloeosinus 24.112.12
phloeotribi, Elachertodomyia 25.19.52
Phloeotribus 24.112.15
Phloeotrya 24.98.27
Phloeoxena 24.4.144
Phlogistosternus 24.67.22
Phlogophora 27.75.287
phlogosaria, Plagodis 27.61.118 (Fig. 27.187)
Phloridosa 29.90.9
Phlox Plant Bug 20.23.110
Phlyctaenia 27.55.88
Phoberia 27.75.96
Phobertron 27.52.14
Phobetes 25.16.371
Phobetus 24.30.77
Phobocampe 25.16.412
Phobolosia 27.75.36
Phobus 27.55.333
phocae, Echinophthrius 19.1.2
Phocides 27.40.2
Phodaga 24.101.9
Phodesgras Mealybug 21.25.4
Phoebis 27.42.14
phoebus, Parnassius 27.41.1 (Fig. 27.77)
Phoeniciomyia 29.105.259
Phoenicobiella 24.109.17
Pheonicococcidae, supra 21.37.1
Pheonicococcus 21.37.1
Phoenicophanta 27.75.186
phoenix, Dichordophora 27.61.161
Phoetalia 14.6.3
Phoetaliotes 11.5.102
Pholadoris 29.90.9
Pholeomyia 29.74.9
Pholisora 27.40.41
pholus, Darapsa 27.70.40 (Fig. 27.264)

pholus, Lycomorpha 27.73.16
Phomalus 24.104.8
Phor 25.69.10
Phora 29.46.13
Phorantnhella 29.105.13
Phorbia 29.99.8
Phoridae, supra 29.46.1
Phorinae, supra 29.46.1
Phormia 29.101.5
Phormiini, supra 29.101.5
Phormoestes 27.36.1
Phorocera 29.105.287
Phoroctenia 29.2.6
phorodendronea, Klopicoris 20.23.162
Phorodon 21.19.167
Phortica 29.90.2
Phorticus 20.18.2
Phosphaenus 24.55.14
Phosphila 27.75.305
phosphoreus, Ignelater 24.48.13
Phosterodoros 29.22.5
Phostria 27.55.174
Photininae, supra 14.1.11
Photinini, supra 24.55.8
Photinus 24.55.8
Photomorphina 25.55.11
Photomorphus 25.55.11
photophila, Pseudocamptomia 29.11.39
Photopsiodes 25.55.10
Photopsis 25.55.10
Photurinae, supra 24.55.16
Photuris 24.55.16
Phradis 25.16.452
Phragmatiphila 27.75.268
Phragmatobia 27.73.44
phragmitella, Limnaecia 27.21.10
Phrasterothrips 22.5.56
Phratora 24.107.68
Phrenapatinae, supra 24.87.73
Phrenapatini, supra 24.87.73
Phrixa 11.7.9
Phrixocnemis 11.9.14
Phronia 29.9.36
Phrontosoma 25.7.79
Phrosinella 29.103.10
Phrudinae, supra 25.16.442
Phrudocentra 27.61.159
Phrudus 25.16.443
Phrydiuchus 24.113.294
Phryganea 26.8.8
phryganea, Himalopsyche 26.5.1
Phryganeidae, supra 26.8.1
Phryganeinae, supra 26.8.2
Phryganeopsis 27.10.24
Phryganidia 27.72.1
Phryganophilus 24.98.37
Phrygionis 27.61.67
Phrynofrontina 29.105.260
Phrynotettigini, supra 11.4.2
Phrynotettix 11.4.2
Phrypeus 24.4.65
Phryxe 29.105.429
Phryxus 27.70.22
Phthia 20.4.6
Phthinia 29.9.70
Phthiraptera infra 18.8.1
Phthiria 29.40.28
Phthiriinae, supra 29.40.25
Phthirothrips 22.5.57
Phthora 24.87.74
Phthorima 25.16.474
Phthorimaea 27.23.45
Phuphena 27.75.314
Phycinae, supra 29.32.24
Phyciodes 27.46.20
phycioloides, Apodemia 27.44.7

Phycitinae, supra 27.55.282
Phycitodes 27.55.372
Phycitopsis 27.55.338
Phycocoetes 24.113.180
Phycoidella 29.24.133
Phycomyza 29.96.4
Phyconomus 24.71.3
Phycus 29.32.28
Phydanis 24.107.146
Phygadeuon 25.16.129
Phygadeuontina, supra 25.16.120
Phyganeidae 26.8.1
Phylctaina 27.75.14
phyleus, Hylephila 27.40.61
Phylidorea 29.2.34
Phylinae, supra 20.23.31
Phylini, supra 20.23.31
Phyllaphis 121.19.168
Phyllecthris 24.107.98
Phyllobaeninae, supra 24.67.19
Phyllobaenus 24.67.19
Phyllobiini, supra 24.113.103
Phyllobius 24.13.103
Phyllobrotica 24.107.109
Phyllocnistinae, supra 27.14.23
Phyllocnistis, 27.14.23
Phyllocolpa 25.7.34
Phyllodesma 27.68.6
Phyllodictus 21.2.8
Phyllodinus 21.2.9
Phyllodonta 27.61.147
Phyllodromis 29.42.13
Phyllogaster 29.100.7
Phyllogomphoides 7.3.2
Phylloicus 26.17.3
Phyllolabis 29.2.28
Phyllomydas 29.35.5
Phyllomyza 29.74.1
Phyllonorycter, 27.14.19
Phyllopalpus 11.10.23
Phyllophaga 24.30.65
Phyllophilopsis 29.105.204
phyllophora, Heptagrotis 27.75.584
Phyllopidea 20.23.59
Phylloporia 27.8.5
phyllopus, Leptoglossus 20.4.4 (Fig. 20.20)
Phylloscelis 21.11.4
Phylloteras 25.34.19
Phyllotreta 24.107.114
Phyllovates 14.1.12
Phylloxera 21.21.1
Phylloxerid Family, supra 21.21.1
Phylloxeridae, supra 21.21.1
phylloxerae, Phylloxeroxenus, 25.20.18
Phylloxeroxenus 25.20.18
Phylocentropus 26.3.7
phylogenetic systematics 17
Phymacysta 20.14.17
Phymaphora 24.81.8
Phymata 20.16.1
Phymatidae, supra 20.16.1
Phymatinae, supra 20.16.1
Phymatocera 25.7.58
Phymatocerini, supra 25.7.58
Phymatodes 24.106.107
Phymatopsallus 20.23.60
Phynocephala 24.107.125
Phyprosopus 27.75.61
Phyrdenus 24.113.257
Physatocheila 20.14.18
Physconelloiddes 18.1.49
Physcus 25.25.16
Physegenua 29.82.12
Physemus 24.43.6
Physetapsis 25.55.10

Physiphora 29.58.33
Physocephala 29.49.3
Physocephalini, supra 29.49.3
Physoclypeus 29.82.13
Physocnemum 24.106.108
Physoconops 29.49.2
Physokermes 21.26.16
Physonota 24.107.177
Physonotini, supra 24.107.177
Physopleurella 20.21.20
Physoptera 29.46.18
Physorhinini, supra 24.48.22
Physorhinus 24.48.22
Physostetha 25.68.13
Physotarsus 25.16.344
Physothorax 25.18.8
Phytagromyza 29.68.13
Phytobaenini, supra 24.104.1
Phytobia 29.68.6
Phytobius 24.113.300
Phytobiini, supra 24.113.295
Phytocoris 20.23.176
Phytodietini, supra 25.16.47
Phytodietus 25.16.47
Phytoecini, supra 24.106.297
Phytoliriomyza 29.68.11
Phytometra 27.75.47
Phytomyptera 29.105.319
Phytomyza 29.68.16
Phytomyzinae, supra 29.68.6
Phytosciara 29.10.3
Phytosus 24.24.282
Phyxelis 24.113.113
Piagetiella 18.6.30
piasus, Glaucopsyche 27.43.46
Piazorrhinini, supra 24.113.219
Piazorrhinus 24.113.219
pica, Amblyptilia 27.58.11
pica, Omisus 29.24.61
Picatorum, Salpingus 24.90.9
picea, Bradysia 29.10.12
piceae, Adelges 21.20.1
piceae, Physokermes 21.26.16
piceus, Ceruchus 24.28.8
piceus, Euxenulus 24.109.5
piceus, Psydrus 24.4.36
piceus, Rhoptrocenturs 25.13.25
piceus, Zenoa 24.40.1
Picicola 18.1.50
picipennis, Caenocyrta 24.19.14
picipes, Lathropinus 24.24.78
picipes, Melanolestes 20.17.25
picipes, Rhabdopterus 24.107.44
picirostris, Microtrogus 24.113.229
picivorus, Pachylobius 24.113.154
Pickleworm 27.55.150
Picomerus 20.3.76
picrocarpa, Carbatina 27.23.89
Picrostigeus 25.16.500
picta, Amiota 29.90.2
picta, Delphinia 29.58.5
picta, Melanchra 27.75.481 (Fig. 27.379)
picta, Myothyriopsis 29.105.378
picta, Phthia 20.4.6
picta, Phyciodes 27.46.20
Pictetiella 8.7.19
picticornis, Neogreeneia 25.16.391
picitcornis, Tanypeza 29.53.1
pictipennalis, Chrismania 27.55.33
pictipennis, Oraphasmophaga 29.105.333
pictipennis, Pseudomorina 29.105.191
pictipes, Dichocysta 20.14.8
pictipes, Simulium 29.22.5
pictipes, Synanthedon 27.35.12
pictiventris, Pseudiastata 29.94.4
Pictonemobius 11.10.17

pictum, Dactylotum 11.5.106
pictum, Leptorhabdium 24.106.173
Picturaphis 21.19.169
picturata, Acinia 29.61.17
picturatus, Dycoderus 20.7.22
Picture-winged Fly Family, supra 29.58.
Pictured Grasshopper 11.5.106
pictus, Cylindrocopturinus 24.113.278
pictus, Thinopinus 24.24.16
Picumma 21.6.22
Pidonia 24.106.215
pieloui, Paracleruchus 25.27.13
Pieridae, supra 27.42.1
Pierinae, supra 27.42.1
Pierini, supra 27.42.1
Pieris 27.42.4
Piesma 20.10.1
Piesmatidae, supra 20.10.1
Piesocorynus 24.109.12
Piestopleura 25.44.16
Piestinae, supra 24.24.84
Piestus 24.24.87
Piezocera 24.106.81
Piezocerini, supra 24.106.81
Piezodorus 20.3.54
Piezosternum 20.3.61
Pilophorini, supra 20.23.125
Pilophoropsis 20.23.132
Pilophorus 20.23.127
Pilopius 24.25.81
pilosa, Benedictia 24.30.78
pilosa, Piophila 29.64.1
pilosa, Promachella 29.37.67
pilosus, Tetrasphaeropyx 25.13.60
pilularius, Canthon 24.30.2 (Fig. 24.65)
pilumnus, Pterourus 27.41.7
Pima 27.55.313
pima, Anthocharis 27.42.9
pima, Hemioslaria 27.75.368
pima, Huavea 25.62.62
Pimachrysa 23.9.13
Pimalius 24.87.19
Pimaphera 27.61.24
pimelia, Penthe 24.98.6
Pimeliinae, supra 24.87.1
Pimodes 27.55.314
Pimpla 25.16.4
Pimplinae, supra 25.16.1
Pimplini, supra 25.16.1
Pinacodera 24.4.143
Pinalitus 20.23.177
pinatubana, Argyrotaenia 27.38.71
Pincher Wasp Family, supra 25.51.1
Pinching Beetle 24.28.1
Pine Adelgid Family, supra 21.20.1
Pine Bark Adelgid 21.20.2
Pine Borer 24.46.15
Pine Butterfly 27.42.2
Pine Candle Moth 27.23.21
Pine Chafer 24.30.96
Pine Colaspis 24.107.43
Pine Conelet Looper 27.61.133
Pine Engraver 24.112.51
Pine False Web-worm 25.2.2
Pine Gall Weevil 24.113.19
Pine Leaf Adelgid 21.20.2
Pine Needle Miner 27.23.21
Pine Needle Scale 21.38.14
Pine Needle Sheathminer 27.30.10
Pine Root Collar Weevil 24.113.153
Pine Root Tip Weevil 24.113.153
Pine Scale 21.38.14
Pine Shoot Borer 27.38.25
Pine Spittle Bug 21.12.5
Pine Tortoise Scale 21.26.22

Pine Tube Moth 27.38.71
Pine Tussock Moth 27.74.2
Pine Webworm 27.55.268
pinea, Neocolpodia 29.11.53
Pineapple Mealybug 21.25.16
Pineapple Scale 21.38.25
Pineapple Weevil 24.113.367
Pine-devil Moth 27.69.2
pineolae, Dicyrtoma 1.7.10
pineticola, Conwentzia 23.5.6
pinetum, Neodiprion 25.6.4
Pineus 21.20.2
pini, Colaspia 24.107.43
pini, Eacles 27.69.1
pini, Ips 24.112.51
pini resinosae, Thecodiplosis 29.11.115
pini, Toumeyella 21.26.22
pinicola, Dasychira 27.74.2
pinifoliae, Chionaspis 21.38.14
pinifoliae, Pineus 21.20.2
pinifoliella, Exoteleia 27.23.21
Pink Bollworm 27.23.81
Pink Spotted Hawk Moth 27.70.1
Pink Sugarcane Mealybug 21.25.39
Pink Underwing 27.75.148
Pink-striped Oakworm 27.69.5
Pinnaspis 21.38.64
pinning forceps 42
Pinon Cone Beetle 24.112.63
Pinophilinae, supra 24.24.77
Pinophilus 24.24.80
pins, mounting 39
Pintalia 21.1.1
Pinumius 21.14.200
pinus, Choristoneura 27.38.72
Pinyon Pine Scale 21.23.2
Pinyonia 29.11.110
Piodes 24.106.175
Piogaster 25.16.22
pion, Allosmaitia 27.43.22
Pionini, supra 25.16.326
Piophila 29.64.1
Piophilidae, supra 29.64.1
Piophilinae, supra 29.64.1
Pioscelus 25.13.22
Piosoma 24.4.121
pipens, Syritta 29.47.85
Pipe-organ Wasp 25.62.51
piperatella, Durrantia 27.15.16
piperatus, Acantherus 11.5.29
piperatus, Neodonus 21.14.113
piperi, Parademoticus 29.105.128
Pipevine Swallowtail 27.41.3
pipiens quinquifasciatus, Culex 29.20.12
pipiens pipiens, Culex 29.20.12
Pipiza 29.47.32
Pipizini, supra 29.47.32
Pipunculidae, supra 29.48.1
Pipunculinae, supra 29.48.4
Pipunculini, supra 29.48.5
Pipunculus 29.48.5
Piratinae, supra 20.17.25
Pirene 25.19.58
Pirenini, supra 25.19.58
Piruna 27.40.43
Piscatopus 24.113.57
piscatrix, Donacia 24.107.4 (Fig. 24.211)
Pisenus 24.98.5
Pison 25.62.50
pisoniella, Scelorthus 27.34.2
pisonifolia, Bruggmannia 29.11.77
Pisonopsis 25.62.49
pisorum, Bruchus 24.108.15 (Fig. 24.253)
Pissodes 24.113.171
pissodinae, supra 24.113.171
Pissonotus 21.2.19

pistasciaria, Hethemia 27.61.170
Pistol Case Bearer 27.18.1
pisum, Acrythosiphon 21.19.2
Pit Scale Insect Family, supra 21.35.1
Pitanta 25.55.1
Pitch Twig Moth 27.38.20
Pitch-eating Weevil 24.113.154
Pitch-pine Tip Moth 27.38.19
Pitcher Plant Moth 27.75.183
Pitcher-plant Mosquito 29.20.3
Pitedia 20.3.29
Pithanini, supra 20.23.191
Pithanus 20.23.192
pithecium, Phobertron 27.52.14
pithyusa, Memphis 27.47.2
Pitnus 24.62.5
Pitrufquenia 18.4.4
Pitydiplosis 29.11.92
Pityeja 27.61.150
Pityobiini supra 24.48.18
Pityobius 24.48.18
Pityoborus 24.112.61
Pityogenes 24.112.48
Pityoketeines 24.112.49
Pityophagus 24.70.34
Pityophthorus 24.112.64
Pityotrichus 24.112.62
Pityococcinae, supra 21.23.10
Pityococcini, supra 21.23.10
Pityococcus 21.23.10
pixe, Melanis 27.44.5
placentia, Apantesis 27.73.52 (Fig. 27.297)
places forbidding collecting 30
placida, Chrysophana 24.46.26
placida, Previperna 29.32.22
Placoaphis 21.19.170
Placonotus 24.72.15
Placopterus 24.67.14
Placosternus 24.106.113
Placusa 24.24.283
plagiata, Aplocera 27.61.246
plagiator, Ephedrus 25.14.1 (Fig. 25.15)
plagiatus, Philopedon 24.113.49
Plagiodera 24.107.67
Plagiognathus 20.23.61
Plagiolepidini, supra 25.58.62
Plagiolepis 25.58.62
Plagiomerus 25.25.96
Plagiometriona 24.107.185
Plagiomima 29.105.166
Plagiomimicus 27.75.347
Plagioneurinae 29.43.12
Plagioneurus 29.43.12
Plagiosippus 29.105.149
Plagiostira 11.7.42
Plagiotrochus 25.34.43
Plagiotrypes 25.16.263
Plagodis 27.61.118
Plains False Wireworm 24.87.140
plana, Homalota 24.24.251
planatus, Hoperius 24.7.34
planatus, Pogonistes 24.4.48
Planetella 29.11.100
planiceps, Gonatherus 29.98.3
planicollis, Lyctus 24.6,5.1
Planipennis, supra 23.5.1
Planismus 24.72.6(see Pharax, anotha in Languriidae 24.75.1)
Planococcus 21.25.33
Plant Bug Family 20.23.1
plantaginea, Dysaphis 21.19.67
plantaginis, Parasemia 27.73.32
Planthoppers, supra 21.1.1
Plantlice, supra 21.19.1
Plastandrena 25.65.1
Plastanoxus 25.48.12

Plaster Beetle 24.82.10
Plasterer Bee Family, supra 25.63.1
Plastophora 29.46.20
Plastosciara 29.10.14
Plataea 27.61.138
platalea, Cossonus 24.113.375 (Fig. 24.300)
Platandria 24.24.284
platani, Bidigitus 25.7.48
Platarctia 27.73.46
Platencyrtus 25.25.110
Platerodini, supra 24.57.7
Plateros 24.57.13
Plate-thigh Beetle Family, supra 24.31.1
Plateumaris 24.107.6
Plathemis 7.7.13; 7.7.24
Plathpalpus 29.42.9
Platidiolus 24.4.69
Platybregmus 24.63.28
Platycampus 25.7.22
Platycarenus 20.3.21
Platycerinae, supra 24.28.4
Platycentrini, supra 21.15.1
Platycentropus 26.10.23
Platycentrus 21.15.1
Platyceroides 24.28.5
Platyceropsis 24.28.6
platycerus 24.28.4
Platycheirus 29.47.10
Platycholeus 24.22.1
Platycis 24.57.9
Platycixius 21.1.8
Platycladius 29.24.123
Platycleis 11.7.43
Platycoenosia 29.100.30
Platycotis 21.15.5
Platydema 24.87.98
Platydemini, surpa 24.87.96
Platydiplosis 29.11.142
Platyedra 27.23.82
Platygaster 25.44.13
platygaster, Piestopleura 25.44.16
Platygastrid Wasp Family, supra 25.44.1
Platygastridae, supra 25.44.1 (Fig. 25.28)
Platygastrinae, supra 25.44.10
Platygerrhus 25.19.14
Platykula 25.18.13
Platylabini, supra 25.16.272
Platylabops 25.16.224
Platylabus 25.16.277
Platylactista 11.5.52
Platylygus 20.23.178
Platylomalus 24.26.27
Platylyra 11.7.10
Platymantispinae, supra 22.7.1
Platymantispini, supra 23.7.1
Platynota 27.38.87
Platynus 24.4.77
Platyoplus 11.7.44
Platypatrobus 24.4.71
Platypedia 21.13.21
Platypediinae, supra 21.13.21
Platypena 27.75.42
Platyperigea 27.75.323
Platypeza 29.45.7
Platypezidae, supra 29.45.1
Platypezina 29.45.5
Platypezoidea, supra 29.44.1; 29.45.1
Platypodidae, supra 24.111.1
Platypodinae, supra 24.111.1
Platypolia 27.75.419
Platyprepia 27.73.47
Platyprosopinae, supra 24.24.28
Platyprosopus 24.24.28
Platypsyllus 24.18.3
platypterus, Bruchophagus 25.20.21

Platyptilia 27.58.9
Platyptiliinae, supra 27.58.2
Platypus 24.111.1
Platypygus 29.40.21
Platysenta 27.75.333
Platysoma 24.26.43
Platysomini, supra 24.26.42
Platystethus 24.24.153
Platystoechotes 23.12.2
Platystomatid Fly Family, supra 29.59.1
Platystomatidae, supra 29.59.1
Platytes 27.55.208
Platythyrea 25.58.8
Platythyreini, supra 25.58.8
Platytipula 29.2.9
Platyura 29.9.15
Pleasing Fungus Beetle Family, supa 24.7.6.1
Pleasing Lacewing Family, supra 23.10.1
plebeia, Hemigraphiphora 27.75.585
plebeja, Paratrea 27.70.10
plebejana, Crocidosema 27.38.38
Plebejus 27.43.48
plebejus, Stenolophus 24.4.114 (Fig. 24.41)
Plebulina 27.43.49
Plecia 29.8.3
Pleciinae, supra 29.8.2
plecta, Ochropleura 27.75.549
Plecoptera, supra 8.1.1 (Figs. 8.1, 8.2, 8.3)
Plecopteracoluthus 29.24.94
Plectiscidea 25.16.491
Plectiscus 25.16.503
Plectonotum 24.56.12
Plectoptera 14.5.6
Plectopterinae, supra 14.5.6
Plectraporus 25.60.15
Plectris 24.30.74
Plectrodera 24.106.233
Plectrodes 24.30.68
Plectrodiplosis 29.11.89
Plectromerus 24.106.85
Plectromyia 29.2.25
Plectrothrips 22.5.58
Plectrura 24.106.230
Plega 23.7.1
Plegaderini, supra 24.26.2
Plegaderus 24.26.2
Plegadiphilus 18.6.31
Pleidae, supra 20.34.1
plejadellus, Chili 27.55.225
Plemyria 27.61.196
Plenoculus 25.62.45
plenus, Kolenetrus 20.7.44
Pleochaetis 30.7.15
Pleocoma 24.30.39
Pleocominae, supra 24.30.39
Pleolophus 25.16.145
Pleonectopoda 27.75.544
Pleotomini, supra 24.55.4
Pleeotomus 24.55.4
Pleotrichophorus 21.19.171
Pleromella 27.75.439
Pleromelloida 27.75.440
Pleroneura 25.1.2
Pleroneurini, supra 25.1.2
Plesiobaris 24.113.305
Plesiocis 24.92.8
Plesiocoris 20.23.179
Plesiodema 20.23.61
Plesiomma 29.37.30
Plesiommata 21.14.46
Plesiothrips 22.4.48
Plethochaeta 29.98.31
plethoricus, Pentalitomastix 25.25.86

pleurale, Prosimulium 29.22.4
pleuralis, Actenobius 24.63.13
pleuralis, Exomella 24.35.12
pleuralis, Gonomyia 29.2.47
pleuralis, Platycladius 29.24.123
Pleurochaetella 29.98.13
Pleurogyrus 25.16.94
pleuron (pleura) 20
Pleurophorus 24.30.31
Pleuropompha 24.101.16
Pleuroprucha 27.61.181
Pleuroptya 27.55.166
Pleurospasta 24.101.10
Pleurota 27.15.43
Pleutotini, supra 27.15.43
plexippus, Danaus 27.41.1, 27.49.1 (Fig. 27.154)
plexipus, Acompotera 29.9.49
Plical 22
Plicatus, Noserus 24.87.173
Pliniaca 27.29.6
Plinthini, supra 24.113.157
Plinthocoelium 24.106.97
Plinthisini, supra 20.7.27
Plinthisus 20.7.27
Plinthodes 24.113.120
Plinoma 24.106.159
Plitineurus 24.63.1
Plocamus 24.113.358
Plocetes 24.113.223
Plochiocoris 20.21.12
Plochionus 24.4.157
Plodia 27.5.400
Ploiaria 20.17.9
Ploiophora 27.17.17
Plum Curculio 24.113.238
Plum Leafhopper 21.14.17
Plum Tree Underwing 27.75.148
Plum Web-spinning Sawfly 25.2.3
plumbeus, Paeudallonyx 24.68.27
plumbeus, Trochopus 20.28.1
Plume Moth Family, supra 27.58.1
Plumegesta 27.55.64
Plumeria Borer 24.106.275
plumifrontella, Acrolophus 27.10.33
plumigerella, Sarasota 27.55.303
Plumipalpia 27.55.40
plumipes fossulana, Campsomeris 25.56.3
plummeriana, Talponia 27.38.48
plumosa, Phengodes 24.54.2 (Fig. 24.106)
Plunomia 29.83.2
Plusia 27.75.167
Plusiinae, supra 27.75.149
Plusiini, supra 27.75.151
Plusiocampa 3.1.8
Plusiocampinae, supra 3.1.8
Plusiodonta 27.75.66
Plusiotis 24.30.91
Plutella 27.29.7
Plutellidae, supra 27.29.1
Pluto 25.62.20
pluto, Xylophanes 27.70.41 (Fig. 27.265)
Plutomurus 1.5.13
plutonis, Manamyia 26.14.2
Plutothrix 25.19.15
pluvialis, Forcipomyia 29.23.3
Pneumosema 25.13.109
Pnigalio 25.26.1
plutella, Megacraspedus 27.23.3
Pnigodes 24.113.182
Pnirontis 20.17.36
Pnyxia 29.10.18
Poanes 27.40.73
poaphilodes, Epidromia 27.75.93
Poblicia 21.3.1
Pocadius 24.70.25

Pococera 27.55.266
Pocota 29.47.90
Podabrini, supra 24.56.5
Podabrus 25.56.5
Podagra 27.75.382
Podagrion 25.18.27
Podagrioninae, supra 25.18.27
Podalonia 25.62.12
Podapion 24.113.19
Podiasa 27.30.6
Podisma 11.5.98
Podisus 20.3.74
Podium 25.62.5
Podmosta 8.1.7
Podolasia 24.30.60
Podonominae, supra 29.24.1
Podonomini, supra 29.24.1
Podopidae 20.3.1
Podopini, supra 20.3.16
podopioides, Prionosoma 20.3.44
podophylli, Youngomyia 11.29.94
Podops 20.3.17
Podoschistus 25.16.38
Podosesia 27.35.14
Podothrips 22.5.59
Podura 1.1.1
Poduridae, supra 1.1.1
Poduromorpha, supra 1.1.1
Poecilanthrax 29.40.55
Poecilobrium 24.106.92
Poecilocapsus 20.23.80
Poecilochrus 24.52.4
Poecilognathus 20.40.28
Poecilogonalos 25.47.3
Poecilographa 29.79.16
Poecilominettia 29.82.14
Poecilonota 24.46.13
Poecilopompilus 25.60.25
Poecilosomella 29.88.3
Poecilotettix 11.5.105
Poecilothrips 22.5.60
Poemenia 25.16.37
Poemyza 29.68.6
poeyi, Plectoptera 14.5.6
Pogonaria 29.28.6
Pogonini, supra 24.4.46
Pogonistes 24.4.48
Pogonocherini, supra 24.106.250
Pogonocherus 24.106.250
Pogonodaptus 24.4.120
Pogonognathellus 1.5.13
Pogonogenys 27.55.38
Pogonomyia 29.100.36
Pogonomyioides 29.100.38
Pogonomyrmex 25.58.24
Pogonortalis 29.59.2
Pogonosoma 29.37.63
Pogonota 29.98.10
Pogonus 24.4.47
Poiocerinae, supra 21.3.1
Poicerini, supra 21.3.1
Pointed-winged Fly Family, supra 29.44.1
Poison Ivy Leaf Miner 27.14.1
Polacantha 29.37.74
Poladryas 27.46.12
Polana 21.14.27
polaris, Clossiana 27.46.11
Polemiotus 24.87.2
Polemistus 25.62.25
Polemius 24.56.9
Polia 27.75.480
Poliaenus 24.106.251
Poliaspis 21.38.65
Policocnemis 27.75.383
polingi, Euristrymon 27.43.31
polios, Incisalia 27.43.29

Polistes 25.59.28
Polistinae, supra 25.59.28
polistiformis, Vitacea 27.35.5
polita, Acicephala 29.98.2
polita, Cycloneda 24.80.41
polita, Eucalantica 27.29.2
polita, Lonchaea 29.57.4
Polites 27.40.66
politum, Trypoxylon 25.62.51
politus, Araptus 24.112.59
politus, Eidoreus 24.81.18
politus, Lendomus 24.21.10
politus, Phalacrus 24.77.1 (Fig. 24.143)
politus, Philonthus 24.24.12
politus, Sphaerites 24.27.1 (Fig. 24.62)
politus, Sphaerius 24.10.1
politus, Xylorerinus 24.112.52
Polix 27.15.31
polixenes, Oenieis 27.48.13
Pollaclasis 24.55.15
Pollen Feeding Beetle Family, supra 24.97.1
Pollenia 29.101.21
pollenifera, Parategeticula 27.8.10
Polleniinae, supra 29.101.21
Polleniini, supra 29.101.21
Pollinia 21.35.3
pollini, Pollinia 21.35.3
Polopeustis 27.55.327
Polopinus 24.87.89
Polpochila 24.4.119
polunini, Byrsocryptoides 21.19.36
Polyamia 21.14.213
Polyangaeus 29.2.25
Polyardis 29.11.2
Polyaulon 25.16.100
Polybia 25.59.31
Polybiomyia 29.47.70
Polyblastus 25.16.57
Polycaon 24.64.2
Polycentropodiae, supra 26.3.1
Polycentropodinae, supra 26.3.1
Polycentropus 26.3.5
Polycesta 24.46.25
Polycestini, supra 24.46.25
polychroma, Eulaema 25.70.1
Polychrysia 27.75.160
Polycinetis 25.16.323
Polycoanini, supra 24.64.1
Polyctenidae, supra 20.19.1
Polycyrtidea 25.16.182
Polycyrtus 25.16.175
Polydacrys 24.113.62
polydanas, Battus 27.41.3
Polyderis 24.4.58
Polydontomia 29.47.62
polydrusi, Tapaeus 25.13.70
polydrusini, supra 24.113.40
Polydrusus 24.113.40
Polyergus 25.58.73
Polygenis 30.2.1
Polyglyptini, supra 21.15.52
Polygonia 27.46.24
Polygonus 27.40.5
Polygrammate 27.75.235
Polygrammodes 27.55.157
polygrammus, Lejota 29.47.62
polygraphi, Ipideurytoma 25.20.12
Polygraphini, supra 24.112.19
Polygraphus 24.112.21
Polyhymno 27.23.64
Polykatianna 1.7.4
Polylamina 24.30.67
Polylepta 29.9.71
Polymedon 29.43.11
Polymera 29.2.27
Polymerus 20.23.181

Polymitarcyidae, supra 6.10.1
Polymitarcyinae, supra 6.10.1
Polynema 25.27.21
Polyneoptera, supra 8.1.1
Polyommatinae, supra 27.43.37
Polyommatini, supra 27.43.47
Polypedilum 29.24.68
Polypeza 25.42.16
Polyphaga, supra 24.12.1
Polyphagidae, supra 14.4.1
Polyphaginae, supra 14.4.1
Polyphemothrips 22.5.61
Polyphemus Moth 27.69.12
polyphemus polyphemus,
 Antheraea 27.69.12 (Fig. 27.228)
Polyphylla 24.30.66
Polyplacidae, supra 19.7.1
Polyplax 19.7.1
Polyplectropus 26.3.6
Polyplcurus 24.87.90
Polyplocinae, supra 27.59.5
polypori, Acadia 29.9.76
Polyposocus 17.13.1
Polypria 24.98.30
Polypsocidae, supra 17.13.1
polysgona, Annulaspis 21.38.5
Polysphincta 25.16.24
Polysphinctini, supra 25.16.16
Polystenidea 25.13.58
Polystepha 29.11.75
Polystoechotes 23.12.1
Polystoechotidae, supra 23.12.1
Polythrix 27.40.9
polytrapezuius, Oxylipeurus 18.1.42
Polytribax 25.16.141
Polytrichophora 29.93.17
polyturator, Pelecinus 25.38.1 (Fig. 25.27)
polyxenes, Papilio 27.41.5, 27.41.7 (Fig. 27.80)
Polyzosteriinae, supra 14.3.4
Pomace Fly Family, supra 29.90.1
Pomaphis 21.19.67
pomaria, Typhlocyba 21.14.81
pometaria, Alsophila 27.61.3
pomi, Aphis 21.19.15
pomifoliellae, Noserus 25.13.49
pomiliella, Tenaga 27.10.28
pomonella, Cydia 27.38.56 (Fig. 27.61)
pomonella, Rhagoletis 29.61.44
Pompeius 27.40.68
Pompilidae, supra 25.60.1
Pompilinae, supra 25.60.14
Pompilini, supra 25.60.19
Pompiloidea, supra 25.60.1
Pompilus 25.60.28
Pompostolella 27.10.14
Ponana 21.14.28
ponceanus, Heraclides aristodemus 27.41.6
Ponderosa Pine Bark Beetle 24.106.268
Ponderosa Pine Cone Beetle 24.112.63
ponderosae, Conophthus 24.112.63
ponderosae, Dendroctonus 24.112.11
ponderosella, Cahela 27.55.383
Ponera 25.58.16
ponerinae, supra 25.58.4
Ponerini, supra 25.58.13
Ponometia 27.75.217
Pontania 25.7.33
Pontia 27.42.4
Pontomalota 24.24.285
popeanella, Acrolophus 27.10.33 (Fig. 27.25)
Popillia 24.30.95
Poplar Borer 24.106.296
Poplar Leaffolding Sawfly 25.7.34
Poplar Petoileball Aphid 21.19.162

Poplar Tentmaker 27.71.1
Poplar Twig Gall Aphid 21.19.162
Poplar Vagabond Aphid 21.19.139
Poplar-and-Willow Borer 24.113.264
population, breeding 18
population samples 47
populi, Cornaphis 21.19.56
populi, Kronomyia 29.11.32
populiramulorum, Pemphigus 21.19.162
populitransversus, Pemphigus 21.19.162
populivenae, Pemphigus 21.19.162
populnea, Hololepta 24.26.45
porcelaria, Protoboarmia 27.61.45
porcelli, Gliricola 18.4.1
Porcinolus 24.35.8
porcinus, Pulex 30.1.5
Porizon 25.16.395
Pornax 24.52.9
Porophila 24.15.3
Poropoea 25.28.10
porosa, Pachybaris 24.113.336
porosum, Acrythosiphon 21.19.2
porosum, Rhodobium 21.19.183
Porotachys 24.4.57
porphyris, Deleromorpha 27.10.2
Porphyrorhegma 27.55.42
Porphyrosela 27.14.22
Porpomiris 20.23.200
Porrhodites 24.24.129
Porricondyla 29.11.51
Porricondylinae, supra 29.11.28
Porricondylini, supra 29.11.46
Porsenus 29.84.1
portaeureae, Leucaspis 21.38.46
Portentomorpha 27.55.104
porterae, Andrena 25.65.1
portlandia, Enodia 27.48.1 (Fig. 27.146)
postica, Hypera 24.113.146
postica, Pyrota 24.101.12
posticata, Phytobia 29.68.6
postifasciatus, Euscepes 24.113.260
Potamanthidae, supra 6.9.1
Potamanthus 6.9.1
Potamyia 26.4.9
Potato Aphid 21.19.122
Potato Beetle, False 24.107.60
Potato Flea Beetle 24.107.137
Potato Leafhopper 21.14.77
Potato Psyllid 21.17.11
Potato Stalk Borer 24.113.316
Potato Scab Gnat 29.10.18
Potato Stem Borer 27.75.280
Potato Tuberworm 27.23.45
potentillae, Gonaspis 25.34.9
Potosia 24.30.135
Potosima 24.46.29
potrillo, Cabares 27.40.17
Potter Wasp 25.59.24
Potter Wasps 25.59.3
Potthastia 29.24.38
Poultry House Moth 27.10.38
Poultry Lice Family 18.6.1
poutiersi, Neococcidencyrtus 25.25.95
Powder-post Beetle Family, supra 24.65.1
Powderpost Bostrichid 24.64.13
Powder-post Termite Family 15.2.1
powelli, Smicromutilla 25.55.18
Praeacedes 27.10.43
Praecocaspis 21.38.66
praecedens, Palmia 27.35.13
praecox, Lipoleucopis 29.83.8
praefica, Spodoptera 27.75.326
Praeschausia 27.71.32
praeses, Amblyctis 24.98.17
praestans, Hubbellia 11.7.49
praetextatus, Cercyon 24.12.30 (Fig. 24.52)

Prainae, supra 25.14.3
Prairiana 21.14.20
Prairie Flea Beetle 24.107.127
Prairie Grain Wireworm 24.48.37
Praocis 24.87.62
Praocini, supra 24.87.62
praon 25.14.3
Prasocurini, supra 24.107.71
Prasocuris 24.107.71
Praspedomyza 29.68.6
pratensis, Gnathacmaeops 24.106.192
pratensis, Phyciodes 27.46.20
Prateus 24.89.4
pratincola, Anthomyiella 29.99.17
pratti banksiane, Neodiprion 25.6.4
pratti pratti, Neodiprion 25.6.4
Precis 27.46.30
Predacious Diving Beetle, supra 24.7.1
Predacious Thrips Family, supra 22.1.1
Predatory Stink Bug 20.3.66
Predatory Stonefly Family 8.7.1
Preeriella 22.5.62
Preludius 24.49.34
Premnobius 24.112.54
Prenanteon 25.51.3
Prenolepis 25.58.70
Prepops 20.23.20
Prescott Pine Scale 21.23.2
Prescottia 21.14.98
Prespelea 24.25.6
preterita, Grensia 26.10.35
pretiosa, Priocnemis 25.60.7
pretiosus, Euthysanius 24.48.51
Priacma 24.1.2
Priamides 27.41.8
pribilovia, Tipula 29.2.9
Prichardomyia 29.37.51
Priesneriella 22.5.17
prima, Coenosopsia 29.100.43
prima, Dimophora 25.16.432
prima, Marlattiella 25.25.5
prima, Pseudhomalopoda 25.25.97
Primicimex 20.20.1
Primicimicinae, supra 20.20.1
primigenia, Philetus 29.42.40
primigenia, Ragus 29.42.42
Primitive Coccoids 21.22.1
Primitive Crane Fly Family, supra 29.1.1
Primitive Minnow Mayfly Family 6.1.1
primordialis, Anageshna 27.55.139
primoris, Orestilla 29.105.57
primus, Zabrachypus 25.16.18
princeps, Canonura 24.106.268
princeps, Epicordulia 7.6.1 (Fig. 7.10)
Priobium 24.63.31
Priocera 24.67.11
Priocnemella 25.60.13
Priocnemis 25.60.7
Priocnemissus 25.60.7
Priocnessus 24.90.7
Priognathus 24.90.7
Prionapteryx 27.55.200
Prionella 29.58.39
Prionellus 24.106.10
Prioninae, supra 24.106.2
Prionini, supra 24.106.8
Prionocera 29.2.5
Prionochaeta 24.22.8
Prionocyphon 24.32.5
Prionolabis 29.2.34
Prionomasticini, supra 25.25.121
Prionomelia 27.61.49
Prionomerinae, supra 24.113.218
Prionomerini, supra 24.113.218
Prionomitus 25.25.125
Prionopelta 25.58.7

Prionosoma 20.3.44
Prionoxystus 27.37.8
Prionus 24.106.10
Prionyx 25.62.11
Priophanes 25.60.12
Priophorus 25.7.16
Priotoma 24.63.52
Pristaulacus 25.36.1
Pristen 27.21.16
Pristiceros 25.16.290
Pristiphora 25.7.30
Pristocera 25.48.1
Pristocerinae, supra 25.48.1
Pristoceuthophilus 11.9.9
Pristogonatopus 25.51.13
Pristola 25.7.40
Pristolini, supra 25.7.40
Pristomerus 25.16.431
Pristonychus 24.4.92
Pristoscelis 24.68.18
Pritchard Ground Mealybug 21.25.38
prittwitzi, Adopaeoides 27.40.59
Privet Aphid 21.19.144
Privet Leaf Miner 27.14.1
Privet Thrips 22.4.9
Proarna 21.13.7
Proba 20.23.182
Probaryconus 25.43.10
Probatius 24.106.294
Probethylus 25.49.1
Probeyeria 24.24.286
Probezzia 29.23.25
Problema 27.40.71
Probles 25.16.446
Probole 27.61.117
Probolus 25.16.234
proboscidea, Rhynchosciara 29.10.6
proboscideus, Curculio 24.113.200
Proboscimyia 29.99.22
Procampodea 3.2.1
Procampodeid Entotroph Family 3.2.1
Procampodeidae, supra 3.2.1
Procas 24.113.176
Procatharosia 29.105.17
Procecidochares 29.61.6
Procecidocharoides 29.61.7
Procellariphaga 18.6.32
procera, Ammophila 25.62.14
Proceratium 25.58.11
Prochalia 27.11.4
Prochelostoma 25.68.14
Prochiloneurus 25.25.77
Prochloridea 27.75.376
Prochoerodes 27.61.149
Prochoreutis 27.36.4
Prochyliza 29.64.1
procincta, Tinalydella 29.105.268
Prociphilus 21.19.172
Procladius 29.24.8
Proclinopyga 29.42.26
Proclitus 25.16.489
Proclossiana 27.46.10
Procockerellia 25.65.15
Proconiini, supra 21.14.40
Procryphalus 24.112.35
Proctacanthella 29.37.73
Proctacanthus 29.37.71
Proctorus 24.113.221
Proctotrupes 25.39.10
Proctotrupidae, supra 25.39.1
Proctotrupoidea, supra 25.39.1
Proculini, supra 24.29.1
Procymbopteryx 27.55.28
Procystiphora 29.11.150
Predecatoma 25.20.15
Predecatominae, supra 25.20.15

Prodiamesa 29.24.41
Prodiplosis 29.11.119
Prodoxinae, supra 27.8.9
Prodoxus 27.8.11
Prodryinus 25.51.11
producta, Fokkeria 20.3.12
producta, Orsillacis 20.7.9
productilis, Ghilianella 20.17.6
productus, Arhaopalus 24.106.14
productus, Macrobrachius 29.9.33
Proechinophthirus 19.1.3
profundalis, Udea 27.55.105
Profenusa 25.7.49
progne, Polygonia 27.46.24
Progomphus 7.3.1
Progonomyia 29.2.47
prograptus, Oligacanthopus 11.10.4
Proisotoma 1.4.12
Prokelisia 21.2.22
Prolatiforceps 29.37.74
Prolatus 25.7.51
Prolepsis 29.37.39
Proleucoptera 27.13.7
Prolimacodes 27.52.9
Prolimnophila 29.2.33
prolixus, Kytorhinus 24.108.4
Prolyctus 24.93.27
Promachella 29.37.67
Promachina 29.37.68
Promachus 29.37.66
Promasiphya 29.105.393
Promecognathini, supra 24.4.21
Promecognathus 24.4.21
Promecopini, supra 24.113.109
Promecotarsus 24.113.178
Promerica 29.105.119
promethea, Callosamia 27.69.17 (Fig.
 27.232; 27.233)
Promethea Moth 27.69.17
Promethes 25.16.478
Prometopia 24.70.18
Prometopion 24.87.20
Prominent Moth Family, supra 27.71.1
Promolophilus 29.2.62
Promoresia 24.45.22
Promus 24.87.140
Promylea 27.55.299
Prongill Mayfly Family 6.7.1
prona, Epitausa 27.75.89
Pronocera 24.106.101
Pronoctua 27.75.589
Pronophilini, supra 27.48.11
Pronotacantha 20.12.4
Pronoterus 24.8.4
Pronotocrepis 20.23.77
pronotum 21
pronubana, Cacoecimorpha 27.38.79
pronunciation of scientific names 17
Properigea 27.75.299
prophaea, Trichromia 27.73.73
Prophalangopsidae, supra 11.8.1
prophetica, Neoleucinodes 27.25.106
Prophryno 20.105.431
propinqua, Euryneura 29.31.16
propinqualis, Rivula 27.75.20
propinquus, Triclistus 25.16.28
Propsilomma 25.42.1
Propyria 27.73.15
Proragrotis 27.75.542
Prorasea 27.55.70
Prorastriopes 1.7.6
Prorates 29.40.30
Prorella 27.61.243
Prorhinotermes 15.3.3
Proroblemma 27.75.211
Prorocorpha 11.5.27

Prororocorypha 11.5.76
Prorops 25.48.13
Prosapia 21.12.1
Prosaspicera 25.31.2
Prosciara 29.10.3
Prosena 29.105.70
Proseninae, supra 29.105.42
Prosenini, supra 29.105.63
Prosenoides 29.105.71
Proserpinus 27.70.37
Prosevania 25.35.2
Prosierola 25.48.20
Prosimulium 29.22.4
Prosoparia 27.75.27
Prosopella 25.63.5
prosopidis, Lecanodiaspis 21.33.1 (Figs.
 21.32, 21.33)
prosopidis, Xerophilaspis 21.38.85
Prosopigastra 25.62.43
Prosopis 25.63.5
Prosopistomatoidea 6.17.1
Prosopoanaphothrips 22.4.29
Prosopothrips 22.4.30
Prospaltella 25.25.17
prospera, Devia 24.24.222
Prostemminae, supra 20.18.1
Prostenus 24.88.15
Prostephanus 24.64.7
prosternalis, Diplacaspis 24.107.33
Prosthodochis 25.16.48
Prostoia 8.1.8 (Fig. 8.4)
Prostomeus 27.23.76
Prostomidae, supra 25.96.1
Prostomis 245.96.1
Protacanthus 20.12.3
Protagrotis 27.75.252
Protalebra 21.14.68
Protambulyx 27.70.13
Protandrena 25.65.4
Protanyderus 29.1.2
Protaphidiina, supra 25.14.5
Protaphorura 1.3.3
Protaplonyx 29.11.61
Protarchus 25.16.350
Protechorutes 1.2.12
Proteides 27.40.3
Proteininae, supra 24.24.100
Proteinus 24.24.101
Protentomidae, supra 2.2.1
Protentominae, supra 2.2.2
Protentomon 2.2.2
Protenor 20.5.1
Proteoteras 27.38.32
Protepeolini, supra 25.69.6
Protepeolus 25.69.6
proterpia, Pyrisitia 27.42.18
Proteriades 25.68.17
Proterops 25.13.126
proteus, Clastoptera 21.12.7
proteus, Meriellum 24.106.105 (Fig.
 24.194)
proteus, Urbanus, supra 27.40.1, 27.40.12
Protexarnis 27.75.557
Protelytroptera 15.1.1
Prothalpia 24.98.35
Protheca 24.63.48
prothorax 21
Prothrinax 27.75.371
Prothymus 25.26.42
Protichneumon 25.16.251
Protitame 27.61.7
Protoboarmia 27.61.45
Protocalliphora 29.101.8
Protochaulides 23.2.7
Protoclythia 29.45.6
Protodejeania 29.105.97

Protodiaspis 21.38.67
protodice, Pontia 27.42.4(Fig. 27.85)
Protodonata, supra 7.1.1
Protodufourea 25.66.33
Protogygia 27.75.550
Protolampra 27.75.582
Protolithocolletis 27.14.17
Protomicroplitis 25.13.122
Protoneura 7.10.2
Protoneuridae 7.10.1
Protopelmus 25.16.241
Protoperigea 27.75.318
Protophormia 29.101.7
Protophotopsis 25.55.13
Protopiophila 29.64.1
Protoplasa 29.1.1
Protoproutia 27.61.174
Protopterocallis 21.19.173
Protoptila 26.6.6
Protoptilinae, supra 26.6.4
Protopulvinaria 21.26.17
Protorthodes 21.75.515
Protorthoptera, supra 10.1.1
Protoschinia 27.75.600
Protostelis 25.68.11
Prototyphlus 24.24.168
Protoxaea 25.64.1
protracta, Orimodema 24.113.128
protracta, Triatoma 20.17.39
protuberans, Pseudethmia 27.15.14
Protura, supra 2.1.1 (Fig. 2.1)
Proturans 2.1.1
Proturentomon 2.2.2
protypica, Asaphocrita 27.17.13
provancheri, Calaspiddia 25.31.4
Provia 27.75.438
province codens 5
Proxenus 27.75.320
proxima, Pontania 25.7.33
proxima, Runibia 20.3.50
proxina, Apantesis 27.73.52 (Fig. 27.298)
Proxius 20.13.5
Proxys 20.3.36
prudens, Trypanisma 27.23.22
prunastri, Sphaerolecanium 21.26.21
pruininus, Stator 24.108.20
pruinosa, Metcalfa 21.8.8
pruinosa, Peponapis 25.69.29
Pruinouse Bean Weevil 24.108.20
Prumnacris 11.5.108
Prune Leafhopper 21.14.81
pruni, Hyalopterus 21.19.101
prunicola, Typhocyba 21.14.81
pruniella, Coleophora 27.18.1
pruninina, Ctenicera 24.48.37
prunivora, Graphilita 27.38.53
Prytanes 20.7.51
Psaeropterella 29.58.20
Psalidopteryx 29.105.324
Psaliodes 27.61.217
Psallus 20.23.63
Psamathobledius 24.24.54
Psammaletes 25.62.89
Psammathodoxa 27.75.63
Psammobotys 27.55.43
Psammodius 24.30.28
Psammoecus 24.72.25
Psammoleon 23.14.6
Psammotettix 21.14.183
Psaphida 27.75.433
Psaphidini, supra 27.75.429
Psara 27.55.176
Pschornia 25.39.7
psecas, Stephanodes 25.27.20
Psectra 23.8.9
Psectraglaea 27.75.400

Psectrocladius 29.24.117
Psectrosciara 29.15.15
Psectrosciarinae, supra 29.15.15
Psectrotanypus 29.24.14
Pselactus 24.113.397
Pselaphidae, supra 24.25.1
Pselaphinae, supra 24.25.4
Pselaphini, supra 24.25.71
Pselaphorhynchites 24.113.10
Pselaphus 24.25.71
Pselaptrichus 24.25.65
Pselaptus 24.25.54
Pselliopus 20.17.17
Pselnophorus 27.58.17
Psen 25.62.19
Pseneo 25.62.18
psenes, Blastophaga 25.18.1 (Fig. 25.18)
Psenini, supra 25.62.15
Psenocerus 24.106.247
Psenulus 25.62.21
Psephenidae, supra 24.36.1
Psephenus 24.36.1
Psephidonus 24.24.130
Pseudacaudella 21.19.174
Pseudachorudina 1.2.20
Pseudachorutes 1.2.20
Pseudacicephala 29.98.2
Pseudacontia 27.75.456
Pseudacteon 29.46.29
Pseudactium 24.25.35
Pseudacysta 20.14.19
pseudagyrtes, Ctenophthalmus 30.4.25
Pseudaletia 27.75.499
Pseudambia 21.19.175
Pseudanarta 27.75.302
Pseudanidorus 24.104.4
Pseudanophthalmus 24.4.38
Pseudanteris 25.43.18
Pseudanthoecia 27.75.304
Pseudanthonomus 24.113.215
Pseudantonina 21.25.34
Pseudanthracia 27.75.127
Pseudanurophorus 1.4.3
Pseudaonidia 21.38.68
Pseudaphycus 25.25.57
Pseudapinops 29.105.320
Psuedaptinus 24.4.165
Pseudasiphonaphis 21.19.176
pseudaspidiotus, Genaparlatoria 21.38.35
Pseudastylopsis 24.106.286
Pseudasydates 24.68.31
Pseudataenius 24.30.25
pseudatomoscelis 20.23.564
Pseudatricha 29.33.4
pseudaugochloropsis 25.66.12
Pseudaulacaspis 21.38.69
Pseudeleodes 24.87.140
Pseudencyrtoides 25.25.112
Pseudencyrtus 25.25.111
Pseudephalus 24.87.165
Pseudepierus 24.26.30
Pseudepipona 25.59.15
Pseuderimerus 25.18.10
Pseuderipternus 25.16.434
Pseuderotis 27.15.15
pseudes, Deinocerites 29.20.13
Pseudethmia 27.15.14
Pseudeuantha 29.105.200
Pseudeurostus 24.62.7
Pseudeva 27.75.159
Pseudexentera 27.38.34
Pseudhapigia 27.71.40
Pseudhomalopoda 25.25.97
Pseudiastata 29.90.4
Pseudiron 6.6.10
Pseudironinae, supra 6.6.10

Pseudischnaspis 21.38.70
Pseudischyrus 24.76.7
Pseudisobrachium 25.48.5
Pseudisotoma 1.4.23
Pseudister 24.26.41
Pseudleptomastix 25.25.32
Pseudoacalles 24.113.254
Pseudobaris 24.113.313
Pseudobourletiella 1.7.6
Pseudobrachymeria 25.21.12
Pseudobrachypeza 29.9.29
Pseudobryomima 27.75.301
Pseudocaeciliidae, supra 17.18.1
Pseudocaeciliinae, supra 17.18.1
Pseudocaecilius 17.18.1
Pseudocalliope 29.82.15
Pseudocamptomyia 29.11.39
Pseudocanthon 24.30.6
Pseudocatolaccus 25.19.100
Pseudocentrinus 24.113.327
Pseudocentron 25.68.22
Pseudocercidis 21.19.177
Pseudocercopeus 24.113.94
Pseudochaeta 29.105.407
Pseudochalcura 25.23.2
Pseudocharis 27.73.88
Pseudochelaria 27.23.28
Pseudochironomus 29.24.60
Pseudochirosia 29.99.4
Pseudochlamys 24.107.31
Pseudochodaeus 24.30.35
Pseudocistela 24.88.10
Pseudocloeon 6.4.10
Pseudoncnemodus 20.7.60
Pseudococcidae, supra 21.25.1
Pseudocneorrhinus 24.113.140
pseudococcina, Hambletonia 25.25.145
Pseudococcus 21.25.35
Pseudocoenosia 29.100.6
Pseudocopaeodes 27.40.63
Pseudocopivaleria 27.75.432
Pseudocorixa 20.35.16
Pseudocotalpa 24.30.89
Pseudocyphus 24.113.104
Pseudodendrothrips 22.4.11
Pseudodiamesa 29.24.34
Pseudodiaspis 21.39.71
Pseudodineura 25.7.38
Pseudodineurini, supra 25.7.38
Psuedodinia 29.83.6
Pseudodynerus 25.59.20
Pseudodoros 29.47.28
Pseudoeucoila 25.32.7
Pseudoepameibaphis 21.19.178
Pseudofimetarius, Onychiurus 1.3.3
Pseudogalleria 27.38.59
Pseudogaurax 29.94.19
Pseudogaurotina 24.106.190
Pseudoglaea 27.75.402
Pseudognaptodon 25.13.42
Pseudogoera, supra 26.14.6
Pseudogoerinae, supra 26.14.6
Pseudogonatopus 25.51.15
Pseudogriphoneura 29.82.16
Pseudohadena 27.75.295
Pseudohadrotoma 24.61.17
Pseudohaida 24.24.131
Pseudohecamede 29.93.6
pseudohesperidum, Coccus 21.26.4
Pseudohylesinus 24.112.9
Pseudolampsis 24.107.155
Pseudoleon 7.7.25
Pseudoleria 29.84.12
Pseudoleucopis 29.83.7
Pseudolimnophila 29.2.32
Pseudolimnophora 29.100.17

Pseudolomyia 29.105.389
Pseudolopyga 25.50.8
Pseudolucanus 24.28.1
Pseudoluperus 24.107.102
Pseudolynchia 29.106.8
Pseudolynx 25.26.22
Pseudomacrophya 25.7.96
Pseudomacrotera 25.65.15
pseudomagnoliarum, Coccus 21.26.4
Pseudomalus 25.50.11
Pseudomasaris 25.59.2
Pseudomegachile 25.68.23
Pseudomelanactes 24.48.17
Pseudomelanactini, supra 24.48.17
Pseudomenopon 18.6.33
Pseudomeriania 29.105.120
Pseudometagea 25.23.6
Pseudomethia 24.106.31
Pseudomethoca 25.55.14
Pseudomethocini, supra 25.55.14
Pseudometopius 25.16.284
pseudomeyeri, Tsugaspidiotus 21.38.82
Pseudomops 14.5.4
Pseudomopsis 24.113.267
Pseudomorina 29.105.191
Pseudomorpha 24.4.72
Pseudomorphini, supra 24.4.72
Pseudomorphitae, supra 24.4.72
Pseudomus 24.113.252
Pseudomyothyria 29.105.261
Pseudomyrmecinae, supra 25.58.20
Pseudomyrmex 25.58.20
Pseudonapomyza 29.68.14
Pseudonirmus 18.1.51
Pseudonomoneura 29.35.6
Pseudopachybrachius 20.7.53
Pseudopamera 20.7.59
Pseudopanthea 27.75.226
Pseudopanurgus 25.65.6
Pseudoparlatoria 21.38.72
Pseudopdsallus 20.23.119
Pseudopentarthrum 24.113.392
Pseudoperibocum 24.106.56
Pseudoperichaeta 29.105.432
pseudophanes, Helegonatopus 25.25.70
Pseudophaonia 29.100.46
Pseudophasmatidae, supra 10.4.1
Pseudophasmatinae, supra 10.4.1
Pseudophilippia 21.26.18
Pseudophloeinae, supra 20.4.32
Pseudophyllinae, supra 11.7.14
Pseudopigritia 27.17.21
Pseudopilema 24.106.89
Pseudopityophthorus 24.112.60
Pseudoplateros 24.57.10
Pseudoplaylabus 25.16.266
Pseudoplisus 25.62.86
Pseudoplusia 27.75.154
Pseudopomala 11.5.24
Pseudopsila 29.55.2
Pseudopsinae, supra 24.24.83
Pseudopsis 24.24.83
Pseudopsocinae, supra 17.20.1
Pseudopterocomma 21.19.179
Pseudopyrausta 27.55.80
Pseudoregma 21.19.180
Pseudorgyia 27.75.56
Pseudorhopini, supra 25.25.122
Pseudorhopus 25.25.122
Pseudorhyssa 25.16.35
Pseudorimus 24.113.134
Pseudorthocladius 29.24.112
Pseudorthodes 27.75.518
Pseudorthosia 27.75.547
Pseudorthygia 24.107.141
Pseudosarcophaga 29.103.18

Pseudoschinia 27.55.46
Pseudoschoenobius 27.55.201
Pseudosciaphila 27.38.12
Pseudosciara 29.10.7
Pseudoseopsis 17.5.1
Pseudoseptis 27.75.548
Pseudosermyla 10.1.1
Pseudosiobla 25.7.75
Pseudosiphona 29.105.310
Pseudosmittia 29.24.132
Pseudosphex 27.73.84
Pseudosphinx 27.70.19
Pseudospinola 25.50.21
pseudospretella, Hofmannophila 27.15.35
Pseudostenophylacinae, supra 26.10.9
Pseudostenophylax 26.10.9
Pseudostrangalia 24.106.211
Pseudotachinomyia 29.105.289
Pseudotelphusa 27.23.30
Pseudotephritina 29.58.17
Pseudotephritis 29.58.17
Pseudothalycra 24.70.24
Pseudothrips 22.4.49
Pseudothyatira 27.59.2
pseudothyreus, Madoryx 27.70.25
Pseudothysanoes 24.112.26
Pseudotorymus 25.18.19
pseudotsugae, Dendroctonus 24.112.11
pseudotsugata, Orgyia 27.74.3 (Fig. 27.315)
Pseudovates 14.1.13
Pseudoxenetus 20.23.128
Pseudoxenos 24.105.8
Pseudozelurus 20.17.28
Pseudozonitis 24.101.23
Psi 29.105.167
Psichacra 25.32.7
psiddi, Pulvinaria 21.26.19
Psilidae, supra 29.54.1
Psilidae, supra 29.55.1
Psilinae, supra 29.55.1
Psila 29.55.2
Psilanteris 25.43.16
Psilocephala 29.32.25
Psilocera 25.19.85
Psilocnemis 24.30.133
Psiloconopa 29.2.59
Psilocorsis 27.15.9
Psilocurus 29.37.23
Psilokempia 29.23.2
Psilomelissodes 25.69.30
Psilometriocnemus 29.24.125A
Psilonous 25.19.96
Psilonyx 29.37.2
Psilopa 29.93.21
Psilopelmia 29.22.5
Psilophrydini, supra 25.25.123
Psilophryoidea 25.25.155
Psilophrys 25.25.123
Psilopiella 29.43.5
Psilopinae, supra 29.93.1
Psilopini, supra 29.93.21
Psilopleura 27.73.83, 29.105.167 (Homonym)
Psiloptera 24.46.10
Psilopyga 24.70.31
Psilosymmerus 29.9.4
Psilota 29.47.58
Psilothrips 22.4.31
Psilotreta 26.14.5
Psilozia 29.22.5
Psilus 25.42.24
Psinidia 11.5.60
Psithyrus 25.70.3
psittaci, Hectopsylla 30.1.1
Psoa 24.64.3

Psocatropetae, supra 17.4.1
Psocatropos 17.4.2
Psocetae, supra 17.23.1
Psocidae, supra 17.23.1
Psocidus 17.23.8
Psocinae, supra 17.23.6
psociformis, Conwentzia 23.5.6
Psocodea, supra 17.1.1
Psocomorpha, supra 17.8.1
Psocoptera, supra 17.1.1 (Figs. 17.1, 17.2)
Psocus 17.23.9
Psoinae, surpa 24.64.1
Psonini, supra 24.64.3
Psoloessa 11.5.14
Psomophus 24.20.2
Psomus 24.113.280
Psoquilla 17.3.1
Psoquillidae, supra 17.3.1
Psorophora 29.20.8
Psorosina 27.55.367
Psorthaspis 25.60.18
Psyche 27.11.2
psychialis, Xanthophysa 27.55.63
Psychidae, supra 27.11.1
Psychinae, supra 27.11.2
Psychoda 29.12.11
Psychodidae, supra 29.12.1
Psychodinae, supra 29.12.4
Psychodomorpha, supra 29.12.1
Psychoglypha 26.10.37
Psychomastax 11.2.2
Psychomorpha 27.75.245
Psychomyia 26.3.1
Psycohmyiidae, supra 26.2.1
psychomiinae, supra 26.2.1
Psychophagus 25.19.88
Psychophora 27.61.230
Psychoronia 26.10.24
psychotriella, Metriochroa 27.14.14
Psydrini, supra 24.4.36
Psydritae, supra 24.4.35
Psydrus 24.4.36
Psylla 21.17.27
Psyllaephagus 25.25.126
Psyllidae, supra 21.17.1
Psyllinae, supra 21.17.19
Psyllini, supra 21.17.27
Psylliodes 24.107.160
Psyllipsocidae, supra 17.4.1
Psyllipsocus 17.4.3
Psyllobora 24.80.51
Psylloborini, supra 24.80.50
Psylloidea, supra 21.17.1
psylloides, Gibbium 24.62.1
Psyllopsis 21.17.26
Psyassa 24.106.59
Ptecticus 29.31.9
Pteleon 24.107.110
Ptenidium 24.15.12
Ptenothrix 1.7.10
Ptenus 25.4.6
Pterallastes 29.47.79
Pterelachisus 29.2.9
Pteremis 29.88.3
pteridis, Mastopoda 21.19.124
Pterobosca 29.23.3
Pterocalla 29.58.18
Pterocallis 21.19.181
Pterocheillus 25.59.4
Pterocolini, supra 24.113.12
Pterocolus 24.113.12
Pterocomma 21.19.182
Pterocormina, supra 25.16.238
Pterocormus 25.16.244
Pterocypha 27.61.212
Pterodontia 29.38.4

Pterogramma 29.88.3
Pteroloma 24.21.1
Pterolimini, supra 24.21.1
Pterolominae, supra 24.21.1
Pteromalid Wasp Family, supra 25.19.1
Ptermalidae, supra 25.19.1
Pteromalinae, supra 25.19.65
Pteromalini, supra 25.19.72
Pteromalus 25.19.91
Pterombrus 25.53.7
Pteromicra 29.79.5
Pteronarcella 8.5.2
Pteronarcyidae, supra 8.5.1
Pteronarcyoidea, supra 8.5.1
Pteronarcys 8.5.3
Pterophoridae, supra 27.58.1
Pterophorinae, supra 27.58.16
Pterophoroidea, supra 27.58.1
Pterophorus 27.58.16
Pterophylla 11.7.16
Pterophyllinae 11.7.14
Pteroptricini, supra 25.25.19
Pterosarus 25.65.9
Pterospoda 27.61.77
Pterostichini, supra 24.4.73
Pterostichitae, supra 24.4.73
Pterostichus 24.4.85
Pterotaea 27.61.37
Pterotermes 15.2.1
Pterothorax 21
Pterotinae, supra 24.55.20
Pterotus 24.55.20
Pterourus 27.41.7
Pteroxanium 17.1.2
Pterygota, supra 67.1.1
Pteryngium 24.74.8
Pteryx 24.15.14
Ptesimogaster 25.13.23
Pthiridae, supra 19.9.1
Pthirus 19.9.1
Ptichodis 27.75.144
Ptilandrena 25.65.1
Ptiliidae, supra 24.15.1
Ptiliinae, supra 24.15.6
Ptiliini, supra 24.15.6
Ptilininae, supra 24.63.33
Ptilinus 24.63.33
Ptiliodina 24.15.17
Ptiliola 24.15.13
Ptiliopycna 24.15.16
Ptilium 24.15.11
Ptilocolepinae, supra 26.7.1
Ptilodactyla 24.38.2
Ptilodactylidae, supra 24.38.1
Ptilodactylinae, supra 24.38.1
Ptilodexia 29.105.72
Ptiloglossa 26.63.3
Ptilomelissa 25.69.35
Ptilomyia 29.93.4
Ptiloneura 17.91
Ptiloneuridae, supra 17.9.1
Ptilophorinae, supra 24.100.3
Ptilostomis 26.8.9
Ptilothrix 25.69.18
Ptinella 24.15.20
Ptinellodes 24.15.15
Ptinidae, supra 24.62.1
Ptininae, supra 24.62.3
Ptinobius 25.19.13
Ptinodes 24.63.22
ptinoides, Philostratus 24.113.159
ptinoides, Sandytes 24.104.10
Ptinus 24.62.10
Ptiolina 29.28.3
Ptochiomera 20.7.48
ptolyca, Anthanassa 27.46.19

Ptomaphagini, supra 24.22.4
Ptomaphagus 24.22.5
Ptosimini, supra 24.46.29
Ptycerata 27.23.51
Ptychamalia 27.61.180
Ptychoglene 27.73.14
Ptycholoma 27.38.81
Ptychoneura 29.103.11
ptychophora, Fala 27.75.358
Ptychoptera 29.17.1
Ptychopteridae, supra 29.17.1
Ptychopterinae, supra 29.17.1
Ptychopteroidea, supra 29.17.1
Ptychopteromorpha, supra 29.17.1
Ptycta 17.23.12
Ptyelini, supra 21.12.2
pubera, Atrichomelina 29.79.1
puberula, Sculptotheca 24.63.49
puberulus, Volonetus 20.7.47
pubescens, Aphleboderrhis 20.13.10
pubescens, Atranus 24.4.79
pubescens, Graphops 24.107.52 (Fig. 24.224)
pubescens, Hesperophanes 24.106.52 (Fig. 24.183)
pubescens, Hypothenemus 24.112.40
pubescens, Metatriozoa 21.17.14
pubescens, Plectrodes 24.30.68
pubescens, Polylamina 24.30.67
Pubic Louse 19.9.1
Pubic Louse Family 19.9.1
pubis, Pthirus 19.9.1 (Fig. 19.3)
publerus, Schoenicus 24.87.9
Publilia 21.15.52
pudefacta, Apatelodes 27.66.1 (Fig. 27.206)
pudicus, Ambrysus 20.38.4
puella, Pararina 21.13.9 (Fig. 21.15)
puera, Hyblaea 27.57.1 (Fig. 27.173)
puerilis, Tyttholeon 23.14.5
Puget Sound Wireworm 24.48.37
Pugnax, Oebalus 20.3.33
pulchella, Acmaeodera 24.46.27 (Fig. 24.89)
pulchella, Allocotocera 29.9.57
pulchella, Euresia, 27.17.11
pulchella, Libellula 7.7.13
pulchella, Orthogonalis 25.47.1
pulchellus, Engyaulus 24.46.33
pulchellus, Phyllopalpus 11.10.23
pulcher, Eudiagogus 24.113.11
pulcherrima, Eutelia 27.75.171 (Fig. 27.344)
pulcherrimus, Epipompilus 25.60.14
pulchra, Amydraulax 25.16.108
pulchra, Townsendiella 25.69.2
pulchricornis, Apterolophus 25.26.25
pulchrinotum, Tumidiclava 25.28.13
Pulex 30.1.5
pulex, Probeyeria 24.24.286
pulicaria, Chaetocnema 24.107.144 (Fig. 24.240)
pulicaria, Cormelaena 20.2.3 (Fig. 20.5)
pulicarius, Brachypterolus 24.70.4
Pulicidae, supra 30.1.1
Pulicinae, supra 30.1.3
Pulicini, supra 30.1.4
Puliciphora 29.46.32
Pulicoidea, supra 30.1.1
Pulicomorpha 24.24.287
pulla, Mauromyia 29.105.144
pulla, Monardis 25..66
pullata, Heleodromia 29.42.25
pullata, Lycogaster 25.47.2
Pullus 24.80.6
pulsator, Cerophytum 24.50.1

pulsatorium, Trogium 17.2.4
pulverea, Narthecophora 27.75.341
Pulverro 25.62.29
pulvialis, Trichothaumalea 29.21.2
pulvillicornis, Streblocera 25.13.159
pulvillifer, Cnemotettix 11.9.2
pulvillus 22
Pulvinaria 21.26.19
pulvinariae, Leucopomyia 29.83.9
pumicata, Stomis 24.4.84
pumila Osmia 25.68.21
pumilio, Laccodytes 24.7.2
pumilus, Dolurgus 24.112.43
punctata, Acrometopia 29.83.3
punctata, Beeria 24.24.2
punctata, Eutricholista 24.68.35
punctata, Hypera 24.113.146
punctata, Hypodacne 24.78.1
punctata, Pelidnota 24.30.92
punctata, Platythyrea 25.58.8
punctata, Synchroa 24.98.7
punctatissima, Eulonchipria 25.63.1
punctatissimus, Psamathobledius 24.24.154
punctatum, Anobium 24.63.25
punctatus, Dendroctonus 24.112.11
punctatus, Dioedus 24.87.73
punctatus, Mycetophagus 24.91.1 (Fig. 24.161)
punctatus, Olibroporus 24.77.5
punctatus, Phloeosinus 24.112.12
punctatus, Polystoechotes 23.12.1
punctatus, Symphyothrips 22.5.67
punctella, Atteva 27.30.1
puncticeps, Stictocranius 24.24.163
puncticollis, Erynephala 24.107.83
puncticollis, Notonota 24.107.40 (Fig. 24.221)
puncticollis, Tympanophorus 24.24.18
puncticornis, Brachynotocoris 20.23.91
punctiferella, Obithome 27.21.26
punctifer, Tabanus 29.26.26
punctifera, Gowdeyana 29.31.27
punctiger, Passalus 24.29.2
punctigera, Paroedipa 29.58.32
punctigera, Phoranthella 29.105.13
pounctipennella, Anorthosia 27.23.86
punctipennis, Anopheles 29.20.1 (Fig. 29.23)
punctomacularia, Philedia 27.61.104
punctulatus, Cryptocercus 14.2.1 (Fig. 14.14)
punctulatus, Psylliodes 24.107.160
punctum, Sepsis 29.81.7
punctumalbum, Macrophya 25.7.96
Puncturevine Seed Weevil 24.113.151
Puncturevine Stem Weevil 24.113.151
pupa 15
pupula, Eustixis 27.55.24
pupurissata, Polia 27.75.480 (Fig. 27.377)
purchasi, Icerya 21.23.8 (Fig. 21.26)
purcis, Microtomus 20.17.24
Puren 23.14.7
purissima, Boryzops 27.75.107
Purple Scale 21.38.45
Purplebacked Cabbageworm 27.55.69
Purplespotted Lily Aphid 21.19.122
Purplish Cooper 27.43.7
purprueithorax, Eprhopalotus 25.26.60
purpurascens, Sthenopsis 27.4.1
purpurea, Adela 27.8.16 (Fig. 27.24)
purpurea, Clausnia 25.25.35
purpureipes, Aedes 29.20.9
purpurescens, Sminthurus 1.7.9
Purpuricenini, supra 24.106.140
Purpuricenus 24.106.148
purpuriella, Chrysopeleia 27.21.19

purpurifascia, Papaipema 27.75.279
Purse Casemaker Caddisfly Family,
 supra 26.7.1
pusilla, Fenusa 25.7.52 (Fig. 25.10)
pusilla, Hilarimorpha 29.41.1
pusilla, Microlynchia 29.106.7
pusilla, Micraegialia 24.30.15
pusilla, Phyllotreta 24.107.114
pusillae, Ganaspidium 25.32.9
pusillidactyla, Lantanophaga 27.58.12
pusillum, Eosentomon 2.1.1
pusillus, Cryptolestes 24.72.17
pusillus, Georissus 24.14.1
pusillus, Gymnoscirtetes 11.5.79
pusillus, Lophocateres 24.66.6
pusillus, Polemistus 25.62.25
pusillus, Trichinothrips 22.5.74
pusio, Fannia 29.100.26
pusio, Liohippelats 29.94.2
pusio, Microlinus 24.24.39
pusio, Nannium 20.13.8
Puss Caterpillar Moth 27.52.3
pustulans, Asterolecanium 21.35.1
Putnam Scale 21.38.24
putnami, Neoslossonia 21.14.3
Puto 21.14.1
Putoidae, supra 21.24.1
Putoniella 29.11.134
Pycnarthrum 24.112.24
Pycnobaris 24.113.307
Pycnocoris 20.23.183
Pycnocryptus 25.16.154
Pycnoderes 20.23.26
Pycnogeraeus 24.113.324
Pynoglossa 29.99.8
Pycnoglypta 24.24.132
pycnogonida 10
Pycnomerini, supra 24.93.21
Pycnomerus 24.93.21
Pycnomorpha 24.87.54
Pycnonotida 24.87.49
Pycnophus 24.20.6
Pycnoplectus 24.25.31
Pycnoscelinae, supra 14.6.4
Pycnoscelus 14.6.4
Pycnospsyche 26.10.30
Pycnotomina 24.71.9
Pygarctia 27.73.70
Pygidiothrips 22.5.18
Pygmactium 24.25.37
pygmaea, Allocapnia 8.3.1 (Fig. 8.6)
pygmaea, Prochalia 27.11.4
Pygmaeococcus 21.25.36
Pygmaeopsis 24.106.256
pygmaeus, Arrhopalites 1.7.3
pygmaeus, Baetis 6.4.2
pygmaeus, Cephus 25.12.4
pygmaeus, Microtabanus 29.26.15
pygmaeus, Nomius 24.4.35
Pygmy Grasshopper Family 11.1.1
Pygmy Mole Cricket Family 11.6.1
Pygocryptus 25.16.106
Pygodasis 25.56.3
Pygolampis 20.17.37
Pygoleptura 24.106.206
Pygopterdita 25.65.15
Pygoctenucha 27.73.67
Pygostolus 25.13.132
Pygothrips 22.5.19
Pyla 27.55.337
Pymatogelasma 25.13.49
Pyracmon 25.16.401
pyracmon, Cyllopsis 27.48.3
Pyractomena 24.55.6
pyralidis, Metopiops 29.105.404
pyralidis, Paralitomastix 25.25.85

Pyralidae, supra 27.55.1
Pyralinae, supra 27.55.233
Pyralis 27.55.233

Q

Quaderna, Erora 27.43.35
Quadraceps 18.1.52
quadralis, Parahypenodes 27.75.31
quadrangula, Rhyacis 27.75.559
quadrangularis, Lepyronia 21.12.3
Quadraspidiotus 21.38.73
quadrata, Glaenocoris 20.35.3
quadrata, Microdrosophila 29.90.17
quadratus, Platycheirus 29.47.10
quadriannulatus, Hypomecus 25.16.283
quadriceps, Borboropora 24.24.211
quadriceps, Crimalia 24.24.218
quadricollis, Bladus 24.48.35
quadricollis, Cathartus 24.72.5 (Fig.
 24.1380
quadricollis, Emmenotarsis 24.68.40
quadricollis, Orthopeplus 24.70.14
quadricollis, Sphalma 24.90.5
quadridens, Ceutorhynchus 24.113.292
quadridens, Monobia 25.59.17
quadrifasciata, Rivellia 29.59.3
quadrigemina, Chrysolina 24.107.63
quadrigeminata, Eburia 24.106.54 (Fig.
 24.184)
quadrigibbus, Tachypterellus 24.113.207
quadriguttata, Babia 24.107.20
quadriguttatum piceum,
 Scaphidium 24.23.2 (Fig. 24.57)
quadriguttatus, Mycetophagus 24.91.1
quadriguttatus, Sthenopis 27.4.1
quadrililcatus, Opsimus 24.106.21
quadrilineata, Chrysochlorina 29.31.19
quadrilineatus, Cleonus 24.113.149 (Fig.
 24.279)
quadrimaculata, Campsomeris 25.56.3
quadrimaculata, Copicita 24.97.9
quadrimaculata, Libellula 7.7.13
quadrimaculata, Paraporia 29.105.199
quadrimaculatus, Anopheles 29.20.1
quadrimaculatus,
 Anthophylax 24.106.181 (Fig. 24.202)
quadrimaculatus, Collops 24.68.1 (Fig.
 24.132)
quadrimaculatus, Pycnoderes 20.23.26
quadrimaculatum, Philbostroma 11.5.6
quadrimaculella, Brymblia 27.15.28
Quadrina 27.68.8
quadrinotata, Paria 24.107.50 (Fig. 24.223)
quadrinotata, Polana 21.14.27
quadrioculata, Collophora 1.7.2
quadripertusus, Haematopinus 19.3.1
quadripuncta, Oegoconia 27.17.2
quadripunctata, Agallia 21.14.13 (Fig.
 21.18)
quadripunctata, Huleria 21.14.88
quadripunctata, Phaneroptera 11.7.8
quadripunctatus, Oecanthus 11.10.19
quadripustilata, Winthemia 29.105.390
quadripustulata, Brochymena 20.3.25
quadripustulatus, Spilotus 24.98.20
quadrisectis, Pseudodynerus 25.59.20
quadrisignathus, Enocluers 24.67.16 (Fig.
 24.130)
quadrisignathus, Glischrochilus 24.70.35
quadrispinosus, Scolytus 24.112.23
Quadristruma 25.58.49
quadrisculpa, Colpomeria 25.16.20
Quadrius 24.103.9
Quadrularia 29.100.20
quaeris, Philarcuts 26.10.22

quaintancii, Pseudophilippia 21.26.18
Quandara 27.75.33
Quasisalebria 27.55.325
quatei, Paracoenia 29.93.58
Quateiella 29.15.10
quatuordecimguttata, Calvia 24.80.37
Quaylea 25.25.124
Quediinae, supra 24.24.20
Quedius 24.24.25
Quemaya 25.53.15
quercana, Carcina 27.15.39
quercicola, Tomolips 24.113.388
quercifex, Parthenolecanium 21.26.14
quercifolia, Thripsobremia 29.11.128
quercivora, Vespina, 27.8.4
quercus, Eriococcus 21.31.4
quercus, Kuwania 21.23.5
quercuscoccineae, Caliroa 25.7.43
Quernaspis 21.38.74
querquedulae, Trinoton 18.6.35
Quesade 21.13.10
quesneli, Sbenaphis 21.19.190
Question Mark 27.46.24
quiescence 14
Quince Curculio 24.113.238
Quince Treehopper 21.15.36
quinquecinctum, Myzinum 25.53.6
quinquelineata, Xyalophora 25.31.11
quinquemaculata, Manduca 27.70.4 (Fig.
 27.238)
quinquepunctellus, Prodoxus 27.8.11 (Fig.
 27.23)
quinquespinosus, Megalotomus 20.5.7
quinquifasciatus, Culex 29.20.12
quinteri, Torynotachina 29.105.269
quohoqiformis, Palinaspis 21.38.59
Quontus 21.14.201

R

Rabbit Bot Fly 29.102.2
Rabbit Louse 19.7.4
races 19
Rachicerus 29.29.4
Rachiplusia 27.75.156
Rachispoda 29.88.3
radians, Apantesis 27.73.52 (Fig. 27.301)
 vittata in "Checklist."
radiatae, Conophthorus 24.112.63
radiatae, Pissodes 24.113.171
radiatus, Platycentropus 26.10.23
radicana, Griselda 27.38.36
radicum, Diplolepis 25.34.16
radicus, Hylobius 24.113.153
Radinopsyllinae, supra 30.4.16
Radionaspis 21.38.75
radius 21
Rafaelia 29.103.42
raffrayi, Ctenisis 24.25.80
Ragonotia 27.55.351
Ragus 29.42.42
Ragweed Borer 27.38.27
Ragweed Plant Bug 20.23.38
Rain Beetle 24.30.39
Rainbow Grasshopper 11.5.106
rain forest 29
rainierensis, Prumnacris 11.5.108
rainieri, Subhaida 24.24.133
Rainieria 29.51.7
Raisin Moth 27.55.403
Rallicola 18.1.53
ramapoella, Ochromolopis 27.27.2
ramburii, Psyllipsocus 17.4.3 (Fig. 17.3)
Ramecia 24.25.22
ramentalis, Pilocrocis 27.55.180

ramosa, Phyllotreta 24.107.114
Ramphocorixa 20.35.17
Ramulini supra 10.1.7
ramulorum, Myrmelachista 25.58.64
Ranatra 20.36.1
Ranatrinae, supra 20.36.1
Ranchman's Tiger Moth 27.73.47
Rancora 27.75.463
randa, Automeris 27.69.8
randiella, Neurolipa 27.14.6
Range Caterpillar Moth 27.69.7
Ranger Crane Fly 29.2.9
rantalis, Achyra 27.55.93
Ranzovius 20.23.65
rapae, Artogeia 27.42.5 (Fig. 27.87)
rapae, Ceutorhynchus 24.113.292
rapae, Diaeretiella 25.14.11
rapae, Obolocera 29.105.427
rapae, Pachyprotasis 25.7.98
Raparna 27.75.76
rapax, Hemiberlesia 21.38.39
raphanus, Nysius 20.7.11
Raphia 27.75.230
Raphidia 23.3.1
Raphidiidae, supra 23.3.1
Raphidiodea, supra 23.3.1
Raphiptera 27.55.207
Rapid Plant Bug 20.23.139
rapidus, Adelphocoris 20.23.139 (Fig. 20.54)
raptoria, Brachyusa 24.24.212
rara, Trama 21.19.216
rare 26
Rare Click Beetle Family, supra 24.50.1
Rasahus 20.17.26
Raspberry Bud Moth 27.8.1
Raspberry Cane Borer 24.106.297
Raspberry Cane Maggot 29.99.14
Raspberry Crown Borer 27.35.1
Raspberry Sawfly 25.7.70
rastiicornis, Chauliodes 23.2.2
rasus, Pycnophus 24.20.6
Rasvena 8.8.4
Ratemia, infra 19.8.1
Ratemiidae, infra 19.78.1
rathvoni, Lichnanthe 24.30.42
Rathvon's Scarab 24.30.42
Rat-tailed Maggot 29.47.65
Rattle-box Moth 27.73.27
ratzeburgi, Palorus 24.87.111
Ravinia 29.103.41
ravocostaliata, Eupithecia 27.61.241 (Fig. 27.202)
rawsoni, Calephelis 27.44.2
Raymondionyminae, supra 24.113.168
Reabotis 27.75.2
readioi, Xenopanurgus 25.65.14
rearing 48
rectangularis, Agrypnus 24.48.3 (Fig. 24.95)
rectangulata, Chloroclystis 27.61.244
recticornis, Megaloceroea 20.23.199
rectifascia, Eudrepanulatrix 27.61.70
rectinervis, Somomyia 29.101.12
rectus, Brevibarra 24.109.13
rectus, Syrphus 29.47.12
recurva, Paratinia 29.9.69
recurvalis, Spoladea 27.55.135
Recurvaria 27.23.18
recurvata, Litobranchia 6.11.3
Red Admiral 27.46.27
Red Bug 20.9.1
Red Bug Family 20.8.1 20.9.1
Red Carpenter Ant 25.58.66
Red Clover Seed Weevil 24.113.228
Red Cucujid 24.72.13

Red Date Scale 21.37.1
Red Elm Bark Weevil 24.113.197
Red Flour Beetle 24.87.110
Red Harvester Ant 25.58.24
Red Imported Fire Ant 25.58.33
Red Milkweed Beetle 24.106.299
Red Oak Borer 24.106.70
Red Orchid Scale 21.38.33
Red Pine Cone Beetle 24.112.63
Red Pine Needle Midge 29.11.115
Red Pine Sawfly 25.6.4
Red Pine Scale 21.23.2
Red Spotted Purple 27.46.33
Red Swordgrass Moth 27.75.388
Red Turnip Beetle 24.107.69
Red Turpentine Beetle 24.112.11
Red Wax Scale 21.26.1
Red-backed Cutworm Moth 27.75.544
Redbanded Leafroller 27.38.71
Redbanded Thrips 22.4.8
Redbay Scale 21.38.2
Redbud Leaffolder 27.23.61
Redectis 27.75.18
Red-headed Ash Borer 24.106.124
Red-headed Bush Cricket 11.10.23
Red-headed Flea Beetle 24.107.121
Redheaded Jack Pine Sawfly 25.6.4
Redheaded Pine Sawfly 25.6.4
Red-humped Caterpillar Moth 27.71.34
Redingtonia 27.75.366
Red-legged Earwig Family 13.1.1
Red-legged Flea Beetle 24.107.133
Red-legged Grasshopper 11.5.94
Redlegged Ham Beetle 24.67.31
Red-necked Peanutworm 27.23.63
Redshouldered Ham Beetle 24.67.31
Red-shouldered Stink Bug 20.3.45
Red-spotted Sap Beetle 24.70.35
Red-tailed Tachind 29.105.390
reducta, Robsonomyia 29.9.15
reductella, Tlascala 27.55.330
reductus, Tomocerus 1.5.13
Reduviidae, supra 20.17.1
Reduviinae, supra 20.17.28
Reduvius 20.17.29
Reesa 24.61.16
reflexulus, Harmostes 20.6.4 (Fig. 20.25)
Regal Fritillary 27.46.8
Regal Moth 27.69.1
regalis, Citheronia 27.69.2 (Figs. 27.211, 27.215)
regina, Phormia 29.101.5
reginalis, Lypotigris 27.55.170
regions, body 20 (Table 4.2)
regularis, Maculurges 24.106.291
rehi, Brevennia 21.25.6
rehni, Argiacris 11.5.100
Rehnita 11.5.56
Reichenbachia 24.25.49
Reichardtia 24.26.11
Reichertella 29.15.6
reinhardi, Atactopsis 29.105.365
Reinhardiana 29.105.60
Rejectaria 27.75.17
relaxing methods 38
 specimens 43
relicta, Catocala 27.75.148 (Fig. 27.336)
relicta, Leptormenis 21.8.2
religiosa, Mantis 14.1.9. (Figs. 14.7, 14.8)
relictus, Paroedostethus 24.48.39
relictus, Rileyonymuis 24.113.293
Remadosus 21.14.162
Remarkable Felt Scale 21.31.4
Remenus 8.7.20
remigis, Gerris 20.27.3 (Fig. 20.60)
remingtoni, Mixomachilis 4.1.4

Remycampa 3.1.3
Renardia 24.24.95
renardii, Zelus 20.17.22
Renia 27.75.11
reniculelloides, Dioryctria 27.55.339
reniformis, Helotropha 27.75.276
renigera, Lacinipolia 27.75.494 (Fig. 27.381)
Reninus 24.26.52
Renocera 29.79.17
Renodaeus 20.23.129
repanda, Cicindela 24.3.4
repanda, Heliocis 24.97.12
repandus, Synstrophus 24.98.11
repens, Metopotoma 24.113.164
Repipta 20.17.18
reproductive system 13
Reptatrix 25.16.168
requisitus, Meraporus 25.19.99
research projects 48
resh, Tibicen 21.13.4 (Fig. 21.12)
resinicoloides, Cecidomyia 29.11.113
resinosae, Conophthorus 24.112.63
resinosae, Matsucoccus 21.23.2
resinosae, Thecodiplosis 29.11.115
resonans, Mula 21.9.2
Resplendent Shield Bearer 27.9.3
respondens, Neophaenis 27.75.311
Resseliella 29.11.88
Resthenini, surpa 20.23.204
resumens, Pachyliodes 27.70.24
retentus, Conotrachelus 24.113.238
reticulata, Lampronia 27.8.2
reticulata, Misodema 21.6.10
reticulata, Scolopsella 21.3.6
Reticulate Winged Book Louse 17.2.2
Reticulated Beetle Family, supra 24.1.1
reticulatiocollis, Trigonogya 24.46.40
reticulatum, Calopteron 24.57.14 (Fig. 24.113)
reticulatus, Fustiserphus 25.39.3
reticulatus, Lepinotus 17.2.2
reticulatus, Propsopothrips 22.4.29
reticulatus, Psilanteris 25.43.16
Reticulitermes 15.3.1
retinerve, Microcentrum 11.7.6
retiniae, Urophyllopsis 29.105.271
Reuterella 17.20.3
reuteri, Drepanothrips 22.4.14
Reuteria 20.23.120
Reuteroscopus 20.23.66
Revelieria 24.82.9
revelstokei, Anaspis 24.98.49
reversalis, Uresiphita 27.55.100
reversus, Hybos 29.42.61
rex, Bradycinetulus 24.30.47
rex, Parallelaptera 25.27.10
Reynosa 27.55.421
Rhabdepyris 25.48.6
Rhabdocephala 21.3.7
Rhabdomastix 29.2.49
Rhabdophaga 29.11.151
Rhabdopterus 24.107.44
Rhachocnemis 11.9.13
Rhachoepalpus 20.105.100
Rhachogaster 29.105.87
Rhachognathus 20.3.70
Rhaconotus 25.13.24
Rhadalinae, supra 24.68.13
Rhadalus 24.68.14
Rhadinoceraea 25.7.60
Rhadinopsylla 30.4.21
Rhadinopsyllini, supra 30.4.19
Rhadiurgus 29.37.78
Rhaebothrips 22.5.20
Rhagadotarsinae, supra 20.27.6

Rhagea 27.55.378
Rhagio 29.28.7
Rhagioforma 29.32.8
Rhagionidae, supra 29.27.1 29.28.1,
29.34.1
Rhagium 24.106.183
Rhagodera 24.93.1
Rhagoletis 29.61.44
Rhagomicrus 24.52.13
Rhagonycha 24.56.8
Rhagopetotrypeta 29.61.46
Rhagovelia 2.28.2
Rhagoveliinae, supra 20.28.1
Rhammatocerus 11.5.13
rhamni, Macchiatiella 21.19.120
Rhamphocolus 24.113.396
Rhamphomyia 29.42.37
Rhanidea 24.81.7
Rhantus 24.7.32
Rhaphandrena 25.65.1
Rhaphildolabina 29.2.25
Rhaphidolabis 29.2.25
Rhaphidophorinae, supra 11.9.4
Rhaphidophorini, supra 11.9.4
Rhaphidothrips 22.4.50
Rhaphiinae, supra 29.43.23
Rhaphiomidas 29.36.1
Rhaphitelini, supra 25.19.70
Rhaphitelus 25.19.70
Rhaphium 29.43.23
Rhasis 20.23.184
Rhegmoclema 29.15.1
Rhegmoclematini, surpa 29.15.1
Rhegmoclemina 29.15.2
Rhembobius 25.16.112
Rheocricotopus 29.24.101
Rheotanytarsus 29.24.79
Rheumaptera 27.61.210
Rheumatobates 20.27.6
Rhexidius 24.25.11
Rhexina, supra 24.25.17
Rhexius 24.25.17
Rhexoza 29.15.11
Rhicnopeltoidea 25.26.68
Rhicnopeltomyia 25.26.67
Rhiginia 20.17.2
Rhigopsis 24.113.115
Rhimphoctona 25.16.402
Rhinacloa 20.23.67
Rhinanisus 24.113.383
Rhingia 29.47.38
Rhingiini, supra 29.47.35
Rhiniinae, supra 29.101.1
Rhinocapsus 20.23.68
Rhinoceros Beetle 24.30.107
Rhinoencyrtini, supra 25.25.37
Rhinoencyrtus 25.25.37
Rhinoleucophenga 29.90.7
Rhinomacerini, supra 24.113.13
Rhinomalus 24.72.20
Rhinonapea 29.93.43
Rhinoncus 24.113.297
Rhinophorid Fly Family, supra 29.104.1
Rhinophoridae, supra 29.104.1
Rhinophorinae, supra 29.104.1
Rhinoplatia 24.97.14
Rhinopsylla 21.17.9
Rhinoscepsina, supra 24.25.9
Rhinoscepsis 24.25.9
Rhinosimus 24.90.10
Rhinotermitidae, supra 15.3.1
Rhinotermitinae, supra 15.3.3
Rhinotora 29.87.1
Rhinotorid Fly Family, supra 29.87.1
Rhinotoride, supra 29.87.1
Rhinotorus 25.16.355

Rhinotragini, supra 24.106.96
Rhinthon 27.40.53
Rhipiceridae, supra 24.39.1
Rhipidandrini, supra 24.87.71
Rhipidandrus 24.87.71
Rhipidia 29.2.14
Rhipiphoridae, supra 24.100.1
Rhipiphorinae, supra 24.100.4
Rhipiphorini, supra 24.100.5
Rhipiphorus 24.100.5
Rhithrogena 6.6.6
Rhizagrotis 27.75.294
Rhizaspidiotus 21.38.76
Rhizelmis 24.45.23
Rhizoecus 21.25.38
Rhizomyia 29.11.70
Rhizophagidae, supra 24.71.1
Rhizophaginae, supra 24.71.1
Rhizophagus 24.71.1
rhizophagus, Hylobius 24.113.153
Rhizotrogus 24.30.64
rhodeanum, Dilinium 24.15.10
Rhodesiella 29.94.17
RhodobaenuseDM24.113.369
Rhodobium 21.19.183
Rhodocantha 27.55.26
rhododactylus, Cnaemidiphorus 27.58.8
rhododendri, Stephanitis 20.14.20
rhododendri, Synanthedon 27.35.12
Rhododendron Borer 27.35.12
Rhododendron Lace Bug 20.14.20
Rhododendron Whitefly 21.18.14
Rhodoecia 27.75.597
Rhodoleptus 24.106.153
Rhodoneura 27.56.5
Rhodophaea 27.55.283
rhodophaga, Dasincura 29.11.152
Rhogogaster 25.7.93
rhoiella, Philodema 27.55.342
rhois, Blepharida 24.107.145 (Fig. 24.241)
rhois, Melaphis 21.19.130
rhombicus, Limnephilus 26.10.21 (Fig. 26.29)
rhombifolia, Neostylopyga 14.3.3
rhombifolium, Microcentrum 11.7.6 (Fig. 11.28)
Rhombogaster 20.4.9
rhomoidea, Cholinobaris 24.113.340
Rhopalicus 25.19.73
Rhopalidae, supra 20.6.1
Rhopalinae, supra 20.6.1
Rhopalini, supra 20.6.3
Rhopalocera, supra 27.40.1
Rhopalodontus 24.92.12
Rhopalomyia 29.11.158
Rhopalomyzus 21.19.184
Rhopalophora 24.106.134
Rhopalophorini, supra 24.106.134
Rhopalopsyllidae, supra 30.2.1
Rhopalopsyllinae, supra 30.2.1
Rhopalopterum 29.94.14
Rhopalosiphoninus 21.19.185
Rhopalosiphum 21.19.186
Rhopalosomatid Wasp Family 25.61.1
Rhopalosomatidae, supra 25.61.1
Rhopalosyrphus 29.47.2
Rhopalotria 24.113.15
Rhopalothrips 22.5.63
Rhopalum 25.62.60
Rhopobota 27.38.40
Rhoptobaris 24.113.317
Rhoptrocentrus 25.13.25
Rhoptromeris 25.32.11
Rhopus 25.25.33
Rhorus 25.16.330
Rhosologia 27.75.79

Rhubarb Curculio 24.113.150
Rhyacionia 27.38.19
Rhyacis 27.75.559
Rhyacophila 26.5.2
Rhyacophilidae, supra 26.5.1
Rhyacophilinae, supra 26.5.1
Rhyacophiloidea, supra 26.5.1
Rhymbomicrus 24.81.2
Rhynchaeninae, supra 24.113.217
Rhynchaenus 24.113.217
Rhynchagrotis 27.75.588
Rhynchanthrax 29.40.53
Rhynchites 24.113.6
Rhynchitidae, supra 24.113.4
Rhynchitinae, supra 24.113.4
Rhynchitini, supra 24.113.6
Rhynchohelea 29.23.10
Rhynchomitra 21.11.3
Rhynchopsilus 25.42.15
Rhynchophion 25.16.461
Rhynchophorinae, supra 24.113.362
Rhynchophorini, supra 24.113.362
Rhynchophorus 24.113.362
Rhynchophthirina, infra 18.8.1
Rhynchosciara 29.10.6
Rhynchus 24.113.271
Rhyncolini, supra 24.113.388
Rhyncolus 24.113.399
Rhyncophoromyia 29.46.23
Rhynencina 29.61.2
Rhynocoris 20.17.19
Rhynonirmus 18.1.54
Rhyopsocus 17.3.2
Rhyparochrominae, supra 20.7.27
Rhyparochromini, supra 20.7.67
Rhyparopharus 20.4.10
rhyparus, Orgerius 21.11.9
Rhypholophus 29.2.60
Rhyphonemognata 24.101.20
Rhypodillus 24.113.76
Rhysipolis 25.13.43
Rhysodes 24.2.1
Rhysodidae, supra 24.2.1
Rhysophora 29.93.30
Rhyssa 25.16.40
Rhyssella 25.16.41
Rhyssemus 24.30.29
Rhyssini, supra 25.16.40
Rhyssomatus 24.113.237
Rhytidolomia 20.3.28
Rhytidops 29.80.1
Rhytidothorax 25.25.156
Rhytura 25.16.146
Rhyzobius 24.80.30
Rhyzopertha 24.64.6
ribearia, Itame 27.561.9
ribesii, Nematis 26.7.32
ribis, Cryptomyzus 21.19.58
ricanioides, Hesperophantia 21.8.1
Rice Leafroller 27.40.81
Rice Root Aphid 21.19.186
Rice Stalk Borer 27.55.225
Rice Stink Bug 20.3.33
Rice Weevil 24.113.365
Richardiid Fly Family, supra 29.62.1
Richardiidae, supra 29.62.1
richardsi, Docessissophothrips 22.5.36
richardsoni, Opisthius 24.4.7
Richia 27.75.546
richteri, Solenopsis 25.58.33
Richtichneumon 25.16.216
Ricinidae, supra 18.7.1
ricinorum, Gymnocarcelia 29.105.397
Ricinus 18.7.1
Rickera 8.7.3
rickseckeri, Phrypeus 24.4.65

Ricula 27.38.47
Ridestus 25.60.22
Ridgewinged Fungus Beetle 24.82.12
ridingsii, Neominois 27.48.12
riederi, Cacozelus 29.105.134
riehmi, Therioaphis 21.19.209
Rifargia 27.71.25
Riffle Beetle Family, supra 24.45.1
Rifseria 27.23.39
rigida, Oeme 24.106.28 (Fig. 24.179)
rigidae, Mayetiola 29.11.147
rigidana, Rhyacionia 27.38.19
Rilettius 24.103.2
Rileya 25.20.2
rileyana, Heteropacha 27.68.5
rileyana, Onychagrotis 27.75.536
rileyi, Hydrizon 25.15.1
rileyi, Pyroderces 27.21.9
rileyi, Tricampa 3.1.4
Rileyinae, supra 25.20.1
Rileyonymus 24.113.293
rimosa, Callona 24.106.146
rimosalis, Evergestes 27.55.69
rimosus, Isognathus 27.70.20
Rimulincola 24.24.171
rinconada, Obrima 27.75.80
rinconium, Anopliomorpha 24.106.64
Riodinidae, supra 27.44.1
Riodininae, supra 27.44.2
Rioptila 26.7.13
riparia, Labidura 13.2.1 (Fig. 13.4)
Ripidius 25.100.6
Rismethus 24.48.5
Risobini, supra 27.75.172
rita, Euphilotes 27.43.44
ritaria, Eubarnesia 27.61.32
ritchiei, Metamasius 24.113.367
Rivellia 29.59.3
riversi, Trimitomerus 24.90.2
Rivula 27.75.20
Rivulinae, supra 27.75.20
Roachlike Stonefly Family 8.6.1
Robber Fly Family, supra 29.37.1
robertsoni, Enoplolindenius 25.62.66
robertsoni, Fitchiella 21.6.1 (Fig. 21.7)
robertsonii, Euryceromyia 29.105.318
robertsonii, Siphoclytia 29.105.223
Robertsonella 25.68.18
Robertsonomyia 29.49.5
robiniae, Appendiseta 21.19.17
robiniae, Lopidea 20.23.110
robiniae, Megacyllene 24.106.112
robiniae, Oblodiplosis 29.11.137
robiniae, Prionoxystus 27.37.8,
 27.37.11 (Figs. 27.57, 27.58)
robiniella, Sinoe 27.23.20
Robsonomyia 29.9.16
Robust Click Beetle Family, supra 24.47.1
Robust Leafhopper 21.14.29
robusta, Calytodera 20.23.144
robusta, Eucrada 24.63.4
robusta, Hoplitis 25.68.18
robusta, Rhysophora 29.93.30
robusta, Stragania 21.14.29
robusta, Udeopsylla 11.11
robustella, Tetralopha 27.55.268
robustulus, Delius 24.20.8
robustus, Aradus 20.13.1
robustus, Eumolpus 24.107.45
robustus, Sarabandus 24.32.4
Rocconota 20.17.20
Rock Bristletail Family 4.2.1
Rock Crawler Family 12.1.1
Rocky Mountain Grasshopper 11.5.94
roddi, Bruchophagus 25.20.21
Rodent Flea Family, supra 30.4.1; 30.7.1

Rodolia 24.80.33
roederi, Euchaetogyne 29.105.74
Roederiodes 29.42.27
Roeseliopsis 29.105.335
Rogadinae, supra 25.13.53
Rogas 25.13.59
rogatalis, Hellula 27.55.54
rogenhoferi, Metaponpneumata 27.75.207
Rogeria 25.58.36
rohweri, Echinaphis 21.19.68
rolandiana, Exyra 27.75.183 (Fig. 27.346)
Rolled-winged Winter Stonefly Family 8.4.1
Romalea 11.4.5
Romaleidae, supra 11.4.1
Romaleini, supra 11.4.5
Romulus 24.106.67
Rondaniella 29.9.80
Root Maggots, supra 29.99.1
Root-eating Beetle Family, supra 24.71.1
Ropalophorus 25.13.158
Ropalopus 24.106.109
Ropalosoma 25.61.1
Ropalomerid Fly Family, supra 29.80.1
Ropalomeridae, supra 29.80.1
Ropronia 25.40.1
Roproniid Wasp Family, supra 25.40.1
Roproniidae, supra 25.40.1
Roptrocerus 25.18.24
roralis, Melanophora 29.104.2
rosaceana, Choristoneura 27.38.72
rosae, Aulacaspis 21.38.12
rosae, Crypticerya 21.23.7
rosae, Diplolepis 25.34.16
rosae, Macrosiphum 21.19.122 (Fig. 21.2)
rosae, Pseudocercidis 21.19.177
rosae, Psila 29.55.2
rosae, Typhlocyba 21.14.81
Rosalia 24.106.98
Rosaliini, supra 24.106.98
rosana, Archips 27.38.74
Rose Aphid 208, 21.19.122 (Fig. 21.2)
Rose Chafer 24.30.80
Rose Curculio 24.113.7
Rose Leaf Beetle 24.107.40
Rose Leafhopper 21.14.81
Rose Midge 29.11.152
Rose Root Gall Wasp 25.34.16
Rose Scale 21.38.12
rosea, Euhyparpax 27.71.36
rosea, Oreata 27.60.3
Rosenus 21.14.202
Roseslug 25.7.42
rosita, Chlosyne 27.46.14
rosneri, Mitoura 27.43.26
rossi, Bolotoperla 8.2.1
rossi, Illinothrips 22.5.11
Rossiana 26.10.52
rossii, Erebia 27.48.10
rossii, Gynaephora 27.74.1
rostrata, Neopelomyia 29.96.3
rostrata, Turpilia 1.7.13
rostratum, Eosentomon 2.1.1
rostratum, Trophithauma 29.46.24
Rostrolaetillia 27.55.375
Rosy Apple Aphid 21.19.67
Rosy Maple Moth 27.69.4
Rosy Rustic Moth 27.75.280
Rothschildia 27.69.15
Rotten-wood Termite Family 15.1.1
rotulata, Pelitropis 21.5.2
rotunda, Shipsa 8.1.9
rotundatus, Gelastocoris 20.39.1
rotundatus, Hodostates 25.16.327
Rotundiceps 18.1.55
rotundicollis, Batuliodes 24.87.34
rotundipennis, Apotoforma 27.38.62

rotundus, Loricaster 24.33.3
Rough-headed Cornstalk Borer 24.30.103
Rough-skinned Cutworm Moth 27.75.320
Rough Stink Bug 20.3.25
Round Darkling Beetle 23.87.64
Round Fungus Beetle Family, supra 24.19.1
Roundheaded Apple Tree Borer 24.106.296
Roundheaded Cone Borer 24.106.19
Roundheaded Fir Borer 24.106.17
Round-headed Katydids 11.7.1
Roundheaded Pine Beetle 24.112.11
Rove Beetle Family, supra 24.24.1
Rowena Calligrapha 24.107.62
rowena, Calligrapha 24.107.62 ((Fig. 24.227)
Royal Palm Bug Family 20.11.1
Royal Walnut Moth 27.69.1
Ruacodes 27.75.364
rubens, Ceroplastes 21.26.1
rubens, Eucessoa 29.40.39
rubens, Gorginus 24.77.11
rubens, Ityocara 24.24.258
rubescens, Nisoniades 27.40.22
rubeum, Xerochrum 25.50.10
rubi, Byturus 24.84.2
rubiceps, Inopus 29.31.1
rubicunda rubicunda, Dryocampa 27.69.4
Rubicundiella 25.16.219
rubida, Pseudacaudella 21.19.174
rubidum, Obrium 24.106.86 (Fig. 24.189)
rubidus, Chalceria 27.43.6
rubiella, Incurvaria 27.8.1 (Fig. 27.20)
rubifloris, Chelostomopsis 25.68.16
rubigalis, Udea 27.55.105
rubiginosa, Holorusia 29.2.4
rubivora, Pegomya 29.99.14
rubra, Chelicerca 9.1.1
rubra, Gymnoerycia 29.105.373
rubranura, Aflexia 21.14.194
rubria, Vanessa 27.46.27 (Figs. 27.137, 27.138
rubricata, Megisto 27.48.6
rubricosa, Phragmatobia 27.73.44 (Fig. 27.291)
rubripalpis, Ariciella 29.100.21
rubripennis, Stenistoderus 24.24.45
rubrocinctus, Selenothrips 22.4.8
rubrofasciatus, Triatoma 20.17.39
rubromaculatus, Empicoris 20.17.4
rubrotincta, Slossonia 27.61.111
Ruby Tiger Moth 27.73.44
ruckeri, Nicoletia 5.2.2
ruckesi, Mesmbragrotis 27.75.543
rudbeckiae, Uroleucon 21.19.219
rudens, Hemieuxa 27.75.554
rudis, Pollenia 29.101.21 (Fig. 29.55)
rudkini, Papilio 27.41.5
rufa, Automola 29.62.2
rufa, Heliaula 11.5.19
rufa, Ophioomma 24.24.27
rufa, Rhyphonemognatha 24.101.20
rufago, Xystopeplus 27.75.396
rufata, Bolomyia 29.105.371
rufescens, Panorpa 28.4.1
rufiabdominalis, Rhopalosiphum 21.19.186
ruficauda, Copecrypta 29.105.102
ruficollis, Necrobia 24.67.31 (Fig. 24.131)
ruficorne, Sinozylon 24.64.11
ruficornis, Helictes 25.16.497
ruficornis, Osminia 27.35.11
rufidiscalis, Azochis 27.55.158
rufifacies, Calliphora 29.101.15
rufifacies, Chrysomya 29.101.15
rufifascia, Ormenaria 21.8.9
rufimanus, Bruchus 24.108.15
rufinasus, Stenopelmus 24.113.187

rufiolus, Entomophthalmus 24.52.11
rufipalpis, Trafoia 29.105.113
rufipectus, Protolampra 27.75.582 (Fig. 27.399)
rufipes, Hylurgopinus 24.112.10
rufipes, Merismus 25.19.46
rufipes, Necrobia 24.67.31
rufipes, Stentrichus 24.87.125
ruifpes, Urolepis 25.19.108
rufipennis, Dendroctonus 24.112.11
rufipennis, Pollygraphus 24.112.21 (Fig. 24.261)
rufistrigalis, Chlorobapta 27.55.52
rufitarsis, Pristaulacus 25.36.1
rufiventris, Townsendiella 25.69.2
rufocaudata, Tephromyiopsis 29.103.48
rufocaudatus, Eustromboceros 25.7.7
rufocincta, Eucoila 25.32.4
rufocinctus, Bombus 25.70.2
rufofascialis, Mimoschinia 27.55.34
rufofusca, Strymon 27.43.34
rufoscutellatus, Paryphes 20.4.30
Rufous Scale 21.38.78
rufovillosum, Xestobium 24.63.5
rufula, Acmaeopsoides 24.106.224
rufulum, Idiopteron 24.57.16
rufulus, Enaphalodes 24.106.70
rufus, Catogenus 24.72.9
rufus, Dyspetes 25.16.65
rufus, Monoctonus 25.14.12
rufus, Oxydrepanus 24.4.28
Rugaspidiotus 21.38.77
Rugged Darkling Beetle 24.87.173
rugglesi, Melanoplus 11.5.94
rugiceps, Euetheola 24.30.103 (Fig. 24.72)
Rugilus 24.24.68
rugicollis, Minthea 24.65.2
rugicollis, Plesiocoris 20.23.179
rugifrons, Neodiprion 25.6.4
rugifrons, Stiria 27.75.357 (Fig. 27.370)
rugipennis, Sachalinobia 24.106.185
rugosa, Kiefferiella 25.30.2
Rugosana 21.14.22
rugosum, Sinodendron 24.28.10
rugosus, Hippiscus 11.5.39 (Fig. 11.15)
rugosus, Pogonomyrmex 25.58.24
rugosus, Trisanteon 25.51.4
rugulosus, Scolytus 24.112.23
rules of nomenclature 17
Rumatha 27.55.384
Rungsia 21.19.196
Runibia 20.3.50
runnatus necoipinus, Amphalius 30.7.1
Rupela 27.55.195
rupinsulensis, Yezoceryx 25.16.193
ruptifasciatus, Timochares 27.40.33
ruralis, Attaneuria 8.9.2
ruscarius, Elaphrus 24.4.20 (Fig. 24.34)
Rushia 24.98.19
ruskini, Xenufens 25.28.11
Rust Fly Family 29.55.1
Rust Grain Beetle 24.72.17
Rusted Banded Aphid 21.19.67
Rustic Borer 24.106.123
Rustic Sphinx 27.70.4
rustica, Manduca 27.70.4 (Fig. 27.239)
Rusty Plum Aphid 21.19.103
Rusty Tussock Moth 27.74.3
Rutela 24.30.93
Rutelinae, supra 24.30.86
Rutelini, supra 24.30.86
rutella, Setomorpha 27.10.47
ruthannae, Acritocentris 25.69.42
rutila Psilopiella 29.43.5
rutilana, Aethes 27.39.1 (Fig. 27.63)
rutilans, Theresia 29.105.79

rutiloides nigrescens, Paradejeania 29.105.95
rutilus, Toxorhynchites 29.20.2
rutulus, Pterourus 27.41.7
Rybaxis 24.25.46
Rymosia 29.9.27
Rypobius 24.79.4

S

sabalis, Comstockiella 21.38.19
Sabethini, supra 29.20.3
sabina, Acherontiella 1.2.9
sabinella, Phaeoses 27.10.49
sabinoensis, Choriolaus 24.106.195
sabulicola, Entomobrya 1.5.3
Sabulodes 27.61.154
sabulosa, Claassenia 8.9.10
Sacandaga 29.2.49
saccharalis, Diatraea 27.55.228
saccharella, Glaucolepis 27.5.4
sacchari, Aspidiella 21.38.10
sacchari, Melanaphis 21.19.128
sacchari, Saccharicoccus 21.25.39
Saccharicoccus 21.25.39
saccharina, Lepisma 5.3.4 (Fig. 5.2)
saccharivora, Saccharosydne 21.2.15
Saccharosydne 21.2.15
sacculalis, Penthesilea 27.55.248
Sachalinobia 24.106.185
Saciinae, supra 24.79.8
Sacium 29.79.8
Sack-bearer Moth Family, supra 27.65.1
sackeni, Tritozyga 29.11.25
sackenii, Dasymutilla 25.55.16
Sackenomyia 29.11.153
Saddle Casemaker Caddisfly Family, supra 26.6.1
Saddleback Caterpillar Moth 27.52.21
Saddled Leafhopper 21.14.108
Saddled Prominent 27.71.29
Saemundssonia 18.1.56
saepiolus, Plebejus 27.43.48
saepium, Satyrium 27.43.16
Saga 11.7.47
Sagenosoma 27.70.9
Saginae, supra 11.7.47
saginata, Angustiopsis 29.105.394
Saica 20.17.32
Saicinae, supra 20.17.31
Saigusaia 29.9.51
Saileria 20.23.121
St. Andrew's Cotton Bug 20.8.1
saintcyri, Clastoptera 21.12.7
Saissetia 21.26.20
Salbia 27.55.184
Salda 20.32.8
Saldidae, supra 20.32.1
Saldinae, supra 20.32.4
Saldoida 20.32.4
Saldula 20.32.10
Salebius 24.74.5
Salebria 27.55.324
Salebriacus 27.55.322
Salebriaria 27.55.323
Salia 27.75.23
salicariae, Aphis 21.19.15
salicella, Cheimophila 27.15.44
salicis, Leucoma 27.74.5
salicifolia, Iteomyia 29.11.159
salicifoliella, Micrurapteryx 27.14.4
salicis, Omalaphora 21.12.6
salicisbatatas, Rhabdophaga 29.11.151
Salignus 20.23.185
salignus, Tuberolachnus 21.19.218
Salina 1.5.10
salinator, Euconnus 24.20.2

salinus, Pelignus 29.93.9
sallei, Gymnetis 24.30.122
Salmonfly, 8.5.3
Salobrena 27.55.250
Salole 27.55.252
salome, Eurema 27.42.17
Salpingidae, supra 24.90.1
Salpinginae, supra 24.90.2
Salpingini, supra 24.90.8
Salpingogogaster 29.47.29
Salpingothrips 22.4.34
Salpingus 24.90.9
Salt Marsh Caterpillar Moth 27.73.36
Salt Marsh Mosquito 29.20.9
Salt Marsh Punkie 29.23.5
saltator, Euscaphurus 24.31.2
saltator, Glyptocombus 20.25.1
saltator, Orocharis 11.10.25
saltator, Pedetontus 4.1.2
Saltella 29.81.6
saltitans, Cydia 27.38.56
Saltusaphis 21.19.187
salvini, Renius 24.26.52
salvum, Mecynocorpus 29.103.34
Samea 27.55.127
Sameodes 27.55.126
Samia 27.69.14
samples, population 47
sampsoni, Nevadaphis 21.19.152
samuelis, Lycaeides 27.43.47 (Fig. 27.114)
San Bruno Elfin 27.43.29
San Jose Scale 21.38.73
sanborni, Ascolicerus 24.48.61
sanborni, Macrosiphoniella 21.19.121
Sanbornia 21.19.188
sanctaecatharinae, Lygistorrhina 29.9.18
Sanctanus 21.14.224
Sand Cricket 11.9.3
Sand Fly Family, supra 29.12.1
Sand-Loving Tachytes 25.62.41
Sand Minnow Mayfly Family 6.3.1
Sandalini, supra 24.39.1
Sandalus 24.39.1
Sandcherry Weevil 24.113.209
Sandhill Cutworm Moth 27.75.544
Sandia 27.43.28
sandini, Puto 21.24.1
Sandytes 24.104.10
sanguinareus, Coccobaphes 20.23.147
sanguinarium, Linosiphon 21.19.114
sanguinicollis, Callimoxys 24.106.95 (Fig. 24.191)
sanguinicollis, Ropalopus 24.106.109 (Fig. 24.195)
sanguinipes, Melanoplus 11.5.94
sanguinolenta, Aceratagallia 21.14.15
sanguisuga, Triatoma 20.17.39
sangwani, Neodusmetia 25.25.46
Sannina 27.35.15
santatalis, Pseudopyrausta 27.55.80
Saotis 25.16.361
Sap-feeding Beetle Family, supra 24.70.1
Saperda 24.106.296
Saperdini, supra 24.106.296
Saphonecrus 25.34.1
Saintus 24.102.6
saporis, Triocnemis 27.75.457
Sapotes 24.113.112
Saprininae, supra 24.26.8
Saprinus 24.26.15
Sapromyza 29.82.17
Saprophagus 24
Saprosites 24.30.24
Sapwood Timberworm 24.69.1
Sapyga 25.57.2
Sapygid Wasp Family, supra 25.57.1

Sapygidae, supra 25.57.1
Sapyginae, supra 25.57.2
sara, Anthocharis 27.42.9 (Fig. 27.90)
Sarabandus 24.32.4
Sarasota 27.55.303
Sarata 27.55.341
Saratoga Spittle Bug 21.12.5
saratogensis, Aphorphora 21.12.5
sarcinata, Peromyma 29.61.5
sarcitrella, Endrosis 27.15.37
sarcobati, Halodiplosis 29.11.112
sarcobati, Protaplonyx 29.11.671
sarcobati, Tannerocoris 20.23.71
Sarcodexia 29.103.42
Sarcodexiopsis 29.103.42
Sarcofahrtia 29.103.19
Sarcofahrtiamyia 29.103.43
Sarcofahrtiopsis 29.103.44
Sarcomacronychia 29.103.1
Sarcophaga 29.103.45
Sarcophagidae, supra 29.103.1
sarcophagina, Phalacrophyto 29.105.59
Sarcophaginae, supra 29.103.21
Sarginae, supra 29.31.5
Sargus 29.31.6
Saropogon 29.37.54
Sarosesthes 24.106.120
Sarothurs 25.31.15
Sarpedon 24.52.24
Sarrothripinae, supra 27.75.172
Sarrothripini, supra 27.75.173
Sarucallis 21.19.189
Saskatoon Borer 24.106.296
sassacus, Hesperia 27.40.65
Sathria 27.55.177
Satin Moth 27.74.5
sativae, Liromyza 29.68.8
Satronia 27.38.46
Satula 21.19.219
saturata, Libellula 7.7.13 (Fig. 7.15)
Saturnia 27.69.10
Saturniidae, supra 27.69.1
Saturniinae, supra 27.69.10
Saturniini, supra 27.69.10
saturnus, Callimormus 28.40.46
Satyridae, supra 27.48.1
Satyrinae, supra 27.48.3
Satyrini, supra 27.48.12
Satyrium 27.43.16
Satyrodes 27.48.2
Satyrs Butterfly Family, supra 27.48.1
satyrus, Polygonia 27.46.24
saucia, Peridroma 27.75.555 (Fig. 27.394)
saucia, Phaloesia 27.73.3
Saucrobotys 27.55.77
saundersii, Madremyia 29.105.422
saundersii, Oligotoma 9.3.1 (Figs. 9.1, 9.2)
Saurius 23.9.7
Saurohypnus 24.24.44
Savtshenkia 29.2.9
Sawflies, supra 25.1.1
Saw-toothed Grain Beetle 25.72.2
Saw-wing 27.61.83
saxifragae, Nasonovia 21.19.145
Saxinis 24.107.21
Saxius 20.4.31
Sayapis 25.68.22
sayi, Chlorochroa 20.3.29 (Fig. 20.9)
sayi, Coelioxys 25.68.24
sayi, Curculio 24.113.200
sayi, Epidiplosis 29.11.129
Sayi, Lytta 24.101.13
sayi, Olla 24.80.40
sayii, Orussus 25.11.1
sayi, Sayiana 21.9.9

Sayiana 21.9.9
Sayomyia 29.19.1
Say's Blister Beetle 24.101.132
Say's Ground Beetle 24.4.98
Say's Stink Bug 20.3.29
Sbenaphis 21.19.190
scaber, Mycterus 24.90.12 (Fig. 24.160
scabiei, Pnyxia 29.10.18
scabra, Platypena 27.75.42
scabricollis, Peranabrus 11.7.41 (Fig. 11.36)
scabripennis, Octotoma 24.107.168
scabrosus, Derancistrus 24.106.7
scabrosus, Sarpedon 24.52.24 (Fig. 24. 105)
Scaeva 29.47.16
scalaris, Acmaeodera 24.46.27
scalaris, Bellamira 24.106.198
scalaris, Calligrapha 24.,107.62
scalaris, Chaetosiphon 21.19.50
scalaris, Fannia 29.100.26
scalator, Plectrodera 24.106.233
Scalaventer 24.113.64
Scale insects, supra 21.1.1
Scaled Flea Family, supra 30.6.1
Scalenarthus 24.25.53
Scalidia 24.72.10
Scallop-shell Moth 27.61.209
Scalmophorus 21.15.12
Scalponotatus 20.23.85
Scaly Crickets 11.10.2
Scaly-winged Barklice Family 17.1.1
Scaly-winged Barklouse 17.1.1
Scambus 25.16.2
scammelli, Ericaphis 21.19.73
scandens, Euxoa 27.75.544
Scanylus 24.104.9
scapalis, Smicronyx 24.113.177 (Fig. 24. 281)
scapellator, Ibalia 25.29.1
Scaphandrena 25.65.1
Scaphidema 24.87.99
Scaphidiidae, supra 24.23.1
Scaphidiini, supra 24.23.1
Scaphidium 24.23.2
Scaphinotus 24.4.16
Scaphinus 24.106.13
Scaphisoma 24.23.4
Scaphisomini, supra 24.23.4
Scaphium 24.23.1
Scaphoideus 21.14.99
Scaphytopiini, supra 21.14.90
Scaphytopius 21.14.92
Scapnetes 25.16.74
Scapteriscinae, supra 11.11.3
Scapteriscus 11.11.3
Scaptococcus 21.25.40
Scaptolenus 24.47.3
Scaptomyza 29.90.10
scapularis, Athous 24.48.31 (Fig. 24.101)
Scarabaeidae, supra 24.30.1
Scarabaeiformia, supra 24.28.1
Scarabaeinae, supra 24.30.1
Scarabaeini, supra 24.30.1
Scarabaeoidea, supra 24.28.1
Scardia 27.10.19
Scarites 24.4.23
Scaritini, supra 24.4.22
Scarititae, supra 24.4.21
Scarlet Oak Sawfly 25.7.43
scataris, Megaselia 29.46.17 (Fig. 29.38)
Scatella 29.93.61
Scatellini, supra 29.93.57
Scatophaga 29.98.23
Scatophagidae, supra 29.98.1
Scatophagini, supra 29.98.98
Scatophila 29.93.63

Scatophora 29.108.3
Scatopsciara 29.10.13
Scatopse 29.15.5
Scatopsidae, supra 29.15.1
Scatopsinae, supra 29.15.1
Scatopsini, supra 29.15.4
Scatopsoidea, supra 29.15.1
Scaurini, supra 24.87.131
scelestus, Chasmias 25.16.245
Scelida 24.107.106
Scelidacantha 27.61.248
Scelio 25.43.3
Sceliomorpha 25.43.2
Scelionid Wasp Family, supra 25.43.1
Scelionidae, supra 25.43.1
Scelioninae, supra 25.43.1
Sceliphron 25.62.7
Sceliotrachelinae, supra 25.44.8
Scellus 29.43.14
Scclolyperus 24.107.108
Scelorthus 27.34.2
Scenopinidae, supra 29.33.1
Scenopinus 29.33.1
Scentless Plant Bug Family 20.6.1
Sceptea 27.17.3
Sceptonia 29.9.37
Sceptrothelys 25.19.90
Schadonophasma 29.19.1
Schaefferia 1.2.2
schaefferi, Aztecarpalus 24.4.133
Schaefferi, Dicyphoma 29.31.17
schaefferi, Dontonodus 21.15.56
schaefferi, Isotomurus 1.4.20
schaefferi, Odmalea 20.3.58
Schaffneria 20.23.133
Schaus Swallowtail 27.41.6
schausi, Propyria 27.73.15
Schenkia 25.16.143
schenkii, Euscelidius 21.14.155
Schidax 27.62.7
Schinia 27.75.601
Schistacme 24.24.288
Schistoglossa 24.24.289
Schistocerca 11.5.114
Schistoneurus 29.11.56
Schistonota, supra 6.1.1
Schizactia 29.105.321
Schizaphis 21.19.191
Schizax 24.106.158
Schizillus 24.87.42
Schizocerella 25.4.7
Schizocerophaga 29.105.262
Schizocoelioxys 25.68.24
Schizogenius 24.4.27
Schizohelea 29.23.15
Schizolachnus 21.19.192
Schizomicrus 24.113.168
Schizomyia 29.11.73
Schizoneura 21.19.74
Schizoneurata 21.19.193
Schizonotus 25.19.121
Schizophilus 24.52.20
Schizophora Acalyptratae, supra 29.49.1
Schizophora Calyptratae, supra 29.98.1
Schizopinae, supra 24.46.1
Schizoprymnus 25.13.138
Schizoptera 20.25.3
Schizotpteridae, supra 20.25.1
Schizopterinae, supra 20.25.2
Schizopus 24.46.1
Schizopyga 25.16.17
Schizotachina 29.105.322
Schizotus 24.94.2
Schizura 27.71.34
Schlettererius 25.17.1
schlingeri, Haplidoeme 24.106.33

schlingeri, Liopterna 25.16.379
Schlingeria 29.32.27
schmitti, Apteronina 24.24.203
schmitti, Noctophus 24.20.4
Schoenherria 25.69.46
Schoenicus 24.87.9
Schoenobiinae, supra 27.55.191
Schoenomyza 29.100.1
Schoettella 1.2.1
schotti, Pyrophorus 24.48.11
Schoutedenia 21.19.194
Schrankia 27.74.32
Schrecksteinia 27.34.5
Schroederella 29.84.18
schusteri, Canistes 24.113.245
Schwarzella 25.21.3
schwartzi, Nephus 24.80.7
schwarzi, Chionanthobius 24.113.226
schwarzi, Euryhopalus 25.25.142
schwarzi, Pissodes 24.113.171
schwarzi, Probethylus 25.49.1
schwarzi, Scolytodes 24.112.25
schwarzii, Nanops 24.113.204
schwarzii, Zaischnopsis 25.24.11
Schwenkfledina 29.10.19
scia, Anaxipha 11.10.20 (Fig. 11.47)
Sciaphilus 24.113.46
Sciapodinae, supra 29.43.1
Sciapterygini, supra 25.7.90
Sciapus 29.43.4
Sciara 29.10.4, 29.10.10
Sciaridae, supra 29.10.1
Sciaroidea, supra 29.8.1
scientific names 15, 46
scientific observations 46
Scicrus 24.112.3
Sciocorini, supra 20.3.23
Sciocoris 20.3.23
Sciomyza 29.79.6
Sciomyziidae, supra 29.79.1
Sciomyzinae, supra 29.79.1
Sciomyzoidea, supra 29.77.1
Scionini, supra 29.26.1
Sciophila 29.9.72
Sciophilinae, supra 29.9.40
Sciopithes 24.113.72
Scirpophaga 27.55.193
Scirtes 24.32.7
Scirtetica 11.5.49
Scirtothrips 22.4.15
scissilis, Pseudolomyia 29.105.389
scitula, Eumacronychia 29.103.2
scitula, Synanthedon 27.35.12
sclerites 20
Sclerodermini, supra 25.48.15
Sclerodermus 25.48.17
Sclerogibbid Wasp Family 25.49.1
Sclerogibbidae, supra 25.49.1
Scleropogon 29.37.18
Scleroprocta 29.2.60
Scleroracus 21.14.165
Sclerosococcus 21.35.4
sclerotin 10
Scobicia 24.64.19
scobiella, Stylopalpia 27.55.335
scobinula, Rismethus 24.48.5
Scolecocampa 27.75.57
Scolia 25.56.6
Scoliandrena 25.65.1
Scoliaphleps 29.98.2
Scoliid Wasp Family 25.56.1
Scoliidae, supra 25.56.1
Scoliinae, supra 25.56.6
Scoliocentra 29.84.19
Scolioidea, supra 25.53.1
scoliopi, Macrosiphum 21.19.122

Scoliopteryx 27.75.73
Scolitantidini, supra 27.43.43
Scolobates 25.16.345
Scolobatini, supra 24.16.344
scolopendrina, Furcula 27.71.12 (Fig. 27.273)
Scolopini, supra 20.21.16
Scolopocerus 20.4.22
Scoloposcelis 20.21.16
Scolopostethus 20.7.38
Scolops 21.11.5
Scolopsella 21.3.6
Scolothrips 22.4.51
Scolytidae, supra 24.112.1
Scolytinae, supra 24.112.22
Scolytini, supra 24.112.22
Scolytodes 24.112.25
Scolytus 24.112.23
Scopaeothrips 22.5.64
Scopaeus 24.24.69
Scoparia 27.55.3
Scopariinae, supra 27.55.1
Scopesis 25.16.353
Scopophus 24.20.2
Scopula 27.61.187
Scopulini, supra 27.61.186
scordalus, Milonius 29.105.376
Scorpionflies, supra 28.1.1
Scorpioteleia 25.42.5
scortealis, Tetralopha 27.55.268 (Fig. 27.169)
scotlandae, Lemnaphila 29.93.35
Scotobaenus 24.87.91
Scotochroa 24.98.21
Scotochroides 24.98.22
Scotogramma 27.75.474
Scotothrips 22.5.23
Scrapteropsis 25.65.1
Scraptia 24.98.40
Scraptiinae, supra 24.98.39
Screw-worm Fly 29.101.3
scribonia, Ecpantheria 27.73.42 (Fig. 27.289)
scripta, Chrysomela 24.107.64
scripta, Habrosyne 27.59.1 (Fig. 27.175)
scriptanus, Peconus 21.14.206
Scrobipalpa 27.23.47
Scrobipalpula 27.23.46
scrophulariae, Anthrenus 24.61.8 (Fig. 24.116)
scrophulariae, Cionus 24.113.234
scrub, desert 28
scrub, thorn 28
scrupulosa, Teleonemia 20.14.21
scrutator, Calosoma 24.4.13
scudderi, Colias 27.42.11
Scudderia 11.7.11
Scudder's Decticid 11.7.29
Scudder's Patched Butterfly 27.46.14
sculpteile, Clindium 24.22.2 (Fig. 24.26)
sculpticauda, Braythrips 22.5.3
sculpticollis, Smicronyx 24.113.177
Sculptotheca 24.63.49
Sculptured Pine Borer 24.46.8
Scurfy Scale 21.38.14
scurrilis, Argyrocoris 20.23.87
scutatus, Ulixes 21.6.19
scutellaris, Coccotorus 24.113.209 (Fig. 24.285)
scutellaris, Heidemanniella 20.23.43
scutellaris, Saurohypnus 24.24.44
scutellaris, Stenocolus 24.34.7
scutellata, Blepharipa 29.105.37
scutellatus oregonensis, Monochamus 24.106.237
scutellatus, Orthops 20.23.173

scutellatus scutellatus, Monochamus 24.106.237
Scutelleridae 20.3.1
Scutellerinae, supra 20.3.1
Scutellista 25.19.34
scutellum 21
scutosa, Protoschinia 27.75.600
Scybalistodes 27.55.57
Scydmaenidae, supra 24.20.1
Scydmaeninae, supra 24.20.1
Scydmaenini, supra 24.20.18
Scydmaenus 24.20.18
scylla, Ecclisocosmoecus 26.10.7
Scymnillini, supra 24.80.20
Scymnillus 24.80.21
Scymninae, supra 24.80.5
Scymnini, supra 24.80.5
Scymnobius 24.80.7
Scymnus 24.80.6
Scyphophorus 24.113.370
scyrtoides, Argopistes 24.107.159
Scythrid Moth Family, supra 27.22.1
Scythridae, supra 27.22.1
Scythris 27.22.1
Scythropochroa 29.10.20
Scythropus 24.113.41
Seal Louse Family 19.1.1
seamansi, Neoalticomerus 29.67.2
Seashore Springtail 1.2.12
seasonal changes 25
Seaweed Fly Family, supra 29.77.1
secabile, Blepharepium 29.37.6
secedens, Anartomima 27.75.486
Secliohrini, supra 25.62.4
secludis, Texocoris 20.23.124
Secondary Screw-worm Fly 29.101.3
Secopennis 21.14.196
secticornis, Apterothrips 22.4.20
sector, radial 22
secundeisenia 25.18.1
secura, Nepotula 27.21.21
securifera, Callosamia 27.69.17
Sedge Moth Family, supra 27.28.1
seditiosus, Tharsus 24.87.113
Seed Bug Family 20.7.1
Seed Chalcid Family, supra 25.20.1
Seed-corn Beetle 24.4.114
Seed Maggots, supra 29.99.1
Seedling Springtail 1.7.6
segment, parts of 21
segment, true 10
segmentata, Vanduzeea 21.15.33
segnis, Leptopsylla 30.6.2
segnis, Pogonomyioides 29.100.38
Sehirinae, supra 20.1.1
Sehirus 20.1.1
Seioptera 29.58.19
Seira 1.5.7
Seirarctia 27.73.35
Seladerma 25.19.47
Seladonia 25.66.15
selanderi, Efflagitatus 24.42.6
Selandriinae, supra 25.7.1
Selandriini, supra 25.7.9
Selenaspidus 21.38.78
selene, Clossiana 27.46.11 (Fig. 27.122)
Selenia 27.61.112
Selenisa 27.75.117
Selenophorus 24.4.126
Selenothrips 22.4.8
Selfia 29.23.5
Selga 27.55.391
Selicanis 27.75.263
Selizini, supra 21.8.10
sellata, Praocis 24.87.62
Selonodon 24.47.1

Selvadius 24.80.9
Semaeopus 27.61.183
Semanotus 24.106.104
Sematurid Moth Family, supra 27.63.1
Sematuridae, supra 27.63.1
Semiaphis 21.19.195
semicana, Patriciola 27.55.368
Semicerura 1.4.22
semicinctum, Sympetrum 7.7.26
semiclusaria, Nepytia 27.61.133
Semidalis 23.5.7
semifasciata, Libellula 7.7.13
semiferana, Archips 27.38.74
semiflava, Parachrysocharis 25.26.72
semiflavus, Odothrips 22.5.59
semifuneralis, Euzophera 27.55.392
Semiini, supra 20.23.136
semilutea, Paratissa 29.93.18
semimaculata, Grossbeckia 27.61.204 (Fig. 27.199)
semiminiveus, Eufallia 24.82.8
seminole, Pygidiothrips 22.5.18
Semioscopis 27.15.4
Semiothisa 27.61.13
Semiothisini, supra 27.61.8
semipectinata, Monostoecha 27.61.207
semipunctatus, Pronoterus 24.8.4
semipurpurana, Croesia 27.38.60
semirufescens, Pseudochlamys 24.107.31
semirufus, Trematopygus 25.16.328
Semium 20.23.136
semivirens, Synorthocladius 29.24.120
semivitta, Allognota 29.100.4
semivittata, Trichopepla 20.3.27
Semudobia 29.11.161
senatoria, Anisota 27.69.5
seneum, Cylindronotum 24.4.155
senex, Heterotropus 29.40.31
senex, Schizax 24.106.158
seniculus, Hemitrichus 25.109.128
sennae, Phoebis 27.42.14
Sennius 24.108.19
Senopterina 29.59.4
Senotainia 29.103.12
sensilis, Amphipoea 27.75.277 (Fig. 27.359)
sensilis, Chytonix 27.75.291
Sensiphorura 1.3.2
separata, Blepharicera 29.3.3
Separatobombus 25.70.2
separator box 32
Sepedon 29.79.18
Sepedophilus 24.24.181
Sephina 20.4.16
sepiella, Pyracmon 25.16.401
Sepsidae, supra 29.81.1
Sepsis 29.81.7
Sepsisoma 29.62.5
septempunctata, Coccinella 24.80.42 (Fig. 24.147)
septemstrigella, Augolychna 27.10.6
septencinctorius, Perithous 25.16.33
septendecim, Magicicada 21.13.18 (Fig. 21.17)
septentrionalis, Agylla 27.73.9
septentrionalis, Anormenis 21.8.4
septentrionalis, Eucordyligaster 29.105.207
septentrionalis, Lobaegis 25.16.265
septentrionalis, Pseudomops 14.5.4
septentrionis, Gluphisia 27.71.11 (Fig. 27.272)
sepulchralis, Thyris 27.56.1 (Fig. 27.172)
sepulchrella, Tryptodema 27.10.36
sepulcralis, Citheronia 27.69.2
sequax, Hesperodiames 29.24.36
sequax, Teleiodes 27.23.32

sequens, Catemophrys 29.105.209
sequoiarum, Megeleates 24.87.70
Sequoiomyia 29.11.102
Serangiini, supra 24.80.1
Sereda 27.38.52
seriata, Ginglychaeta 29.105.160
seriata, Naemia 24.80.49
seriatus, Nyssonotus 24.113.389
seriatus, Pseudatomoscelis 20.23.64 (Fig. 20.50)
seriatus, Trichiotes 24.87.25
Serica 24.30.61
Sericaglaea 27.75.395
sericans, Anobiopsis 24.63.24
sericans, Microtonus 24.98.33
sericata, Phaenicia 29.101.12
sericatus, Listromimus 24.68.43
sericea, Enchodes 24.98.23
sericea, Lepidocnemeplatia 24.87.159
sericea, Plesiodema 20.23.62
sericeum, Melittomma 24.69.2 (Fig. 24.134)
sericeus, Asilus 29.37.74
sericeus, Chlaenius 24.4.98 (Fig. 24.38)
sericeus, Halobates 20.23.5
sericeus, Metamasius 24.113.367
Sericoda 24.4.73
Sericoderinae, supra 24.79.7
Sericoderus 24.79.7
Sericomyia 29.47.45
Sericomyiini, supra 29.47.45
Sericophanes 20.23.122
Sericoplaga 27.55.98
Sericopompilus 25.60.23
Sericopsothrips 22.4.16
Sericoptera 27.61.153
Sericothripini, supra 22.4.12
Sericothrips 22.4.12
Sericosema 27.61.68
Sericostomatidae, supra 26.13.1
Sericostomatinae, supra 26.12.1
Sericus 24.48.48
Serinethinae, supra 20.6.8
Sermylassa 24.107.88
Sermyle 10.1.2
Sermylini, supra 24.107.86
serotina, Stenoneura 29.105.336
Serpentine Leaf Miner 29.68.8
serpentinum, Lissobiops 24.24.57
Serphid Wasp Family, supra 25.39.1
Serphidae, supra 25.39.1
Serphinae, supra 25.39.2
Serphini, supra 25.39.9
Serphoidea, supra 25.39.1
Serphus 25.39.10
serrata, Euchlaena 27.61.83 (Fig. 27.182)
serrata, Heleomyza 29.84.22
serrata, Priacma 24.1.2
Serratella 6.137
serratella, Coleophora 27.18.1
Serratibruchus 24.108.5
serraticollis, Piezocera 24.106.81
Serratipula 29.2.9
serratus, Coxelus 24.93.3
serricollis serricollis, Ptilodactyla 24.38.2 (Fig. 24.79)
serricorne, Lasioderma 24.63.38
serricornis, Nigronia 23.2.5 (Fig. 23.7)
serripes, Myodocha 20.7.66 (Fig. 20.30)
Serromyia 29.23.16
Serropalpini, surpa 24.98.17
Serropalpus 24.98.24
serrulata, Vecturoides 24.68.22
serrulatus, Atheroides 21.19.23
serta, Parapelopia 29.24.9
sertifer, Neodiprion 25.6.4

Servaisia 29.103.24
servia, Goniapteryx 27.75.70
servulella, Hybroma 27.10.12
servus, Euschistus 20.3.34 (Fig. 20.10)
Seryda 27.50.2
Sesia 27.35.9
Sesiidae, supra 27.35.1
Sesiinae, supra 27.35.8
Sesiini, supra 27.35.9
Sesioidea, supra 27.35.1
Sesioplex 25.16.393
sesostris, Ampelopglypter 24.113.311 (Fig. 24.295)
sessile, Tapinima 25.58.61 (Fig. 25.46)
Setabara 25.7.47
Setacera 29.93.55
Setagrotis 27.75.568
Setanta 25.16.230
setariae, Hysteroneura 21.19.103
setarius, Calomycterus 24.113.139
setavena, Pseudosmittia 29.24.132
Seticornuta 25.15.295
setiger, Echinocloleus 24.22.4
setiger, Microhyus 24.113.244
setigera, Hincomyia 29.105.107
setinervis, Thelairodina 29.105.266
Setiostoma 27.15.18
setipennis, Houghia 29.105.402
setipes, Gueriniopsis 29.105.284
Setitpula 29.2.9
Setodes 26.18.6
Setomorpha 27.10.47
setosa, Hesperophasia 29.205.36
setosa, Neanura 1.2.16
setosum, Piosoma 24.4.121
setosus, Batulius 24.87.33
setosus, Byrrhodes 24.63.51
setosus, Chaetocoelus 24.68.5
setosus, Ctenocallis 21.19.59
setosus, Eutrichophilus 18.2.2
setosus, Linognathus 19.2.1
setosus, Paragraphus 24.113.97
setosus, Pseudocercopeus 24.113.94
Setvena 8.7.21
sexguttata, Cicindela 24.3.4
sexmaculata, Capraita 24.107.151 (Fig. 24.243)
sexmaculatus, Pinumius 21.14.200
sexmaculatus, Scolothrips 22.4.51
sexnotatus, Dryobius 24.106.99 (Fig. 24.192)
sexpinnatus, Sminthurides 1.7.1
sexpunctata, Lema 24.107.13 (Fig. 24.216)
sexpunctata, Spargaloma 27.75.46
sexpunctata, Zabrosa 21.14.116
Sexserrata 27.75.190
sextrigella, Calliprora 27.75.98
sexstrigella, Calliprora, 27.23.65
sexta, Manduca 27.70.4 (Fig. 27.237)
Shaft Louse 18.6.25
Shallot Aphid 21.19.144
Shannonomyia 29.2.35
shasta, Icaricia 27.43.50
shastaensis, Hemileuca 27.69.7
shawianum, Hendecaneura 27.38.39
Sheep Bot Fly 29.102.3
Sheep Chewing Louse 18.2.1
Sheep Ked 29.106.12
Sheep Tick 29.106.12
Shellenius 21.9.14
Shenahweum 21.19.64
sheridanii, Callophrys 27.43.24
shermani, Ctenotrachelus 20.17.33
shermani, Garrettella 29.9.563
Shewellomyia 29.22.5
Shield Bearer Moth Family, supra 27.9.1

Shieldback Mayflies 16.18.1
Shield-backed Katydids 11.7.25
Shieldbacked Pine Seedbug 20.3.1
shiloenisis, Misturaphis 21.19.136
Shining Flower Beetle Family,
　supra 24.77.1
Shining Fungus Beetle Family,
　supra 24.23.1
Shiny Bluebottle Fly 29.101.18
shipping 47
Shipsa 8.1.9
Ship-timber Beetle Family, supra 24.69.1
shizuokensis, Aleyrodes 21.18.11
Shore Bug Family, supra 20.32.1
Shore Fly Family, supra 29.93.1
Short Nosed Cattle Louse 19.3.1
Short-faced Scorpionfly Family,
　supra 28.5.1
Short-horned Grasshopper 11.5.33
Short-horned Grasshopper Family 11.5.1
Short-horned Springtail Family 1.6.1
Shortleaf Pine Borer 27.38.25
Short-winged Mole Cricket 11.11.3
Shot-hole Borer 24.112.23
Shotwellia 11.5.64
shurtleffi, Cordulia 7.6.2
shurtleffi, Heterogenea 27.52.5
Siagonium 24.24.88
Sialidae, supra 23.1.1
Sialis 23.1.1
Sibariops 24.113.348
siberita, Prosena 29.105.70
Sibine 27.52.21
Sibinia 24.113.230
Sibovia 21.14.53
Siculodinae, supra 27.56.4
Sicya 27.61.134
Sideridis 27.75.477
sideroxyli, Ceropsylla 21.17.16
Sierola 25.48.19
Sierolini, supra 25.48.19
Sierolomorpha 25.54.12
Sierolomorphidae, supra 25.54.1
sierra, Pedomoecus 26.10.51
sierrae, Occapes 25.16.373
Sierraperla 8.6.2
sierrensis, Aeses 29.20.9
Sigaloessa 29.73.4
Sigaloessinae, Family 29.73.1
Sigalphinae, supra 25.13.111
Sigalphus 25.13.111
Sigara 20.35.18
Sigela 27.75.34
sigillatus, Gryllodes 11.10.9
Sigmoid Fungus Beetle 24.74.6
sigmoides, Drosophila 29.90.9
signata, Calonia 21.14.87
signata, Phloeoxna 24.4.144
signata, Tricholita 27.75.531 (Fig. 27.388)
signatella, Symmoca 27.17.1
signatus, Actitocoris 20.23.193
signatus, Anthonomus 24.113.208
signiferum, Cenosoma 29.105.42
Signiphora 25.25.21
Signiphorinae, supra 25.25.21
signiphorini, supra 25.25.21
signoreti, Ambrysus 20.38.4 (Fig. 20.73)
Sikaianini, supra 21.9.1
sila, Neosolieria 29.105.127
Silaria 24.98.49
Silba 29.57.5
Silini, supra 24.56.9
Silis 24.56.11
Silken Fungus Beetle Family, supra 24.74.1
Silkworm Moth Family, supra 27.67.1
Silky Ant 25.58.72

Silky Cane Weevil 24.113.367
Silpha 24.21.7
Silphidae, supra 24.21.1
Silphinae, supra 24.21.6
Silphini, supra 24.21.7
silphoides, Cilea 24.24.177
silphoides, Licinus 24.4.106
Silusa 24.24.290
Silusida 24.24.291
Silvaninae, supra 24.72.2
Silvanus 24.72.3
silvatica, Masicera 29.105.423
Silver Bordered Fritillary 27.46.11
Silver Spotted Ghost Moth 27.4.1
Silver Twig Weevil 24.113.137
Silverfish, supra 5.1.1, 5.3.4
Silverfish Family 5.3.1
Silverspots, supra 27.46.7
Silver-spotted Skipper 27.40.4
Silver-spotted Tiger Moth 27.73.56
Silvery Checkerspot 27.46.15
Silvestrina 29.11.104
silvestris, Oxyomus 24.30.18
Silvius 29.26.10
silvius, Polygonia 27.46.24
simaethis, Chlorostrymon 27.43.13
Simandrena 25.65.1
Simanthedon 25.69.33
similaria, Gueneria 27.61.110
similaris, Tibicen 21.13.4 (Fig. 21.13)
similis, Diprion 25.6.5
similis, Euproctis 27.74.6
similis, Hortensia 21.14.50
simondsi, Anthelococcus 21.25.2
simophion 25.16.463
simplex, Anabrus 11.7.26 (Fig. 11.34)
simplex, Coloburella 1.4.5
simplex, Dendroctonus 24.112.1 (Fig. 24.260)
simplex, Lissorhoptrus 24.113.183 (Fig. 24.282)
simplex, Prorhinotermes 15.3.3 (Figs. 15.3, 15.4)
simplex, Pseudachorutes 1.2.20
simplex, Thamnotettix 21.14.156
simplex, Thrips 22.4.53
simplex, Tipula 29.2.9
simplicialis, Penestola 27.55.142
simplicicollis, Erythemis 7.7.7
simplicicornis, Paraneotermes 15.2.3
simplicipes, Apophua 25.16.304
simplicipes, Pleurochaetella 29.98.13
simplicula, Metephestia 27.55.390
Simplocaria 24.35.1
Simplocariini, supra 24.35.1
Simplona 24.25.38
simulans, Ephemera 6.11.1 (Fig. 6.9)
simulans, Hydropsyche 26.4.8 (Fig. 26.19)
simulans, Pulex 30.1.5
simulator, Mystaxus 24.98.25
Simuliidae, supra 29.22.1
Simuliinae, supra 29.22.2
Simulium 29.22.5
Simyra 27.75.233
sinaloensis, Citheronia 27.69.2
Sinarachna 25.16.26
Sinea 20.17.21
Sinella 1.5.4
sinensis, Ceroplastes 21.26.1
singularis, Aspidolea 24.30.99
singularis, Belonura 25.19.94
singularis, Cyrtobagous 24.113.188
singularis, Neodavisia 27.55.238
singularis, Pseudogoera 26.14.6
singularis, Tanyrhinus 24.24.134
singularis, Typhlusechus 24.87.32

Sinodendrinae, supra 24.28.10
Sinodendron 24.28.10
Sinoe 27.23.20
Sinophorus 25.16.392
Sinophthalmus 29.90.2
Sinotipula 29.2.9
Sinoxylon 24.64.11
Sintoria 29.37.52
sinuata, Hippodamia 24.80.43
Sinuate Lady Beetle 24.80.43
Sinuate Pear Tree Borer 24.46.34
sinuatocolle, Motschulskium 24.15.8
sinuatus, Agrilus 24.46.34
sinus, Euboarhexius 24.25.15
Sipalia 24.24.292
Sipalini, supra 24.113.363
Sipha 21.19.196
Siphlodora 29.90.9
Siphlonisca 6.1.4
Siphlonuridae, supra 6.1.1
Siphlonurus 6.1.5
Siphloplecton 6.2.2
Siphoclytia 29.105.223
Sipholeskia 29.105.224
Siphona 29.105.311
Siphonaptera, supra 39.1.1
Siphonatrophia 21.19.197
Siphonella 29.94.32
Siphonina, supra 29.105.300
Siphonini, supra 29.105.293
Siphonophoroides 21.19.198
Siphoplagiopsis 29.105.166
Siphosturmia 29.105.381
siphunculata, Placoaphis 21.19.170
Siproeta 27.46.32
Sirex 25.9.1
Siricidae, supra 25.9.1
Siricinae, supra 25.9.1
Siricoidea, supra 25.8.1
Sirthenea 20.17.27
Sisamnes 20.7.50
Sisenes 24.97.7
Siskiwitia 27.21.15
sisymbrii, Pontia 27.42.4
Sisyra 23.13.2
Sisyridae, supra 23.13.1
Sisyridivora 25.19.106
Sisyropa 29.105.400
Sisyrosea 27.52.16
Sitka Spruce Weevil 24.113.171
Sitobion 21.19.122
Sitochroa 27.55.96
Sitodiplosis 29.11.144
Sitona 24.113.50
Sitonini, supra 24.113.50
Sitophaga 29.105.263
Sitophagus 24.87.117
Sitophilini, supra 24.13.365
Sitophilus 24.113.365
Sitotroga 27.23.80
Sittocapsus 20.23.187
Situlaspis 21.38.79
siva, Mitoura 27.43.26
Sixeonotus 20.23.27
Six-spotted Thrips 22.4.51
Six-spotted Tiger Beetle 24.3.4
sjodtedti, Pristogonatopus 25.51.13
Skelosyzygonia 25.3.2
Skewesia 27.71.23
Skiff Beetle Family, supra 24.11.1
Skin and Larder Beetle Family,
　supra 24.61.1
Skin Beetles 24.30.42
skinneri, Myscelia 27.46.35
Skipper Fly Family, supra 29.64.1
Skippers, supra 27.40.1

Skwala 8.7.22
Slash Pine Flower Thrips 22.5.42
Slash Pine Sawfly 25.6.4
Slash Pine Seedworm 27.38.56
Slaterobius 20.7.54
Slaterocoris 20.23.86
Slender Duck Louse 18.1.3
Slender Entotroph Family 3.1.1
Slender Goose Louse 18.1.3
Slender Guinea Louse 18.1.35
Slender Meadow Katydid 11.7.21
Slender Seedcorn Beetle 24.4.25
Slender Springtail Family 1.5.1
Slender Texas Longhorn 24.106.59
Slender Turkey Louse 18.1.42
Slenderhorned Flour Beetle 24.87.106
Sleepy Orange 27.42.19
sleesmani, Pappulaphis 21.19.159
slides, microscope 43
Sliky Cane Weevil 24.113.367
slitus, Systoechus 29.40.12
slossonae, Catocha 29.11.27
slossonae, Helioplagia 29.105.139
slossonae, Hoplitalysia 25.13.103
slossonae, Keirosoma 29.43.25
slossonae, Lipochaeta 29.93.44
slossonae, Secopennis 21.14.106
slossonae, Zethusculus 25.59.25
Slossonaemyia 29.105.312
slossonalis, Neargyractis 27.55.17
Slossonella 27.52.3
slossonella, Hypargyria 27.55.291
slossoni, Chloriona 21.2.23
slossoni, Rhopalotria 24.113.15 (Fig.
 24.267)
Slossonia 27.61.111
slossonia, Tortyra 27.36.8
slossoniae, Alarodiea 27.52.11
slossoniae, Philagraula 27.62.5
Slug Caterpillar Moth Family, supra 27.52.1
Sluggish Weevil 24.113.149
Small Black Dung Beetle 24.30.10
Small Carrion Beetle Family, supra 24.22.1
Small Chestnut Weevil 24.113.200
Small Dung Fly Family, supra 29.88.1
Small Eastern Caddisfly Family,
 supra 26.12.1
Small Engrailed Geometer 27.61.44
Small Milkweed Bug 20.7.3 (Fig. 20.27)
Small Minnow Mayfly Family 6.4.1
Small Mottled Willow Caterpillar 27.75.326
Small Pigeon Louse 18.1.8
Small Southern Pine Engraver 24.112.51
Small Squaregill Mayfly Family 6.16.1
Small Water Strider Bug Family,
 supra 20.28.1
Small Winter Stonefly Family 8.3.1
Small-eyed Flour Beetle 24.87.111
Small-headed Fly Family 29.38.1
Smaller Angular-winged Katydid 11.7.6
Smaller European Elm Bark
 Beetle 24.112.23
Smaller Lantana Butterfly 27.43.34
Smalle Sand Cricket 11.6.2
Smaller Yellow Ant 25.58.68
Smaragdina 24.107.22
smaragdina, Zammara 21.13.2
smaragdimun, Temnosoma 25.66.13
Smartweed Borer 27.55.84
Smartweed Caterpillar 27.75.231
Smartweed Cooper 27.43.4
Smeared Dagger Moth 27.75.231
Smeringodynerus 25.59.10
Smerinthini, supra 27.70.13
Smerinthus 27.70.15
Smicraulax 24.113.203

Smicridea 26.4.10
Smicripinae, supra 24.71.10
Smicrips 24.71.10
Smicrolius 25.16.358
Smicromutilla 25.55.18
Smicronychini, supra 24.113.177
Smicronyx 24.113.177
Smicroplectrus 25.16.71
Smicrus 25.15.19
smilaciella, Proleucoptera 27.13.7
Smilia 21.15.50
Smiliinae 21.15.35
Smilini, supra 21.15.35
Sminthuridae, supra 1.7.1
Sminthurides 1.7.1
Sminthuridinae, supra 1.7.1
Sminthurinae, supra 1.7.5
Sminthurinus 1.7.4
Sminthurus 1.7.9
smithi, Euphilotes 27.43.44
smithi, Fenderomyia 29.9.6
smithiana, Strepsicrates 27.38.23
smithii, Wyeomyia 29.20.3
Smithistruma 25.58.47
Smittia 29.24.96
Smodicini, supra 24.106.23
Smodicum 24.106.23
Smoky Alderfly 23.1.1
Smoky Crane Fly 29.2.9
Smoky Moth Family, supra 27.50.1
Smoky-brown Cockroach 14.3.2
Smoky-winged Darner 7.4.6
Smooth Springrail Family 1.4.1
Smut Beetle 24.77.1
Smynthurodes 21.19.199
Smyrna 27.46.43
Snail Casemaker Caddisfly Family,
 supra 26.16.1
Snail Eating Ground Beetle 24.4.16
Snakefly Family 23.3.1
Snipe Fly 29.28.7
Snipe Fly Family, supra 29.28.1
Snout Beetle and Weevil Family,
 supra 24.113.1
Snout Butterfly 27.41.1, 27.45.1
Snout Butterfly Family, supra 27.45.1
Snout Moth Family, supra 27.55.1
snoviaria, Sicya 27.61.134; see morsicaria in
 "Checklist."
Snow Scorpionfly Family 28.2.1
Snowball Aphid 21.19.49
Snowflea 1.2.1
snowi, Coniana 11.5.68
snowi, Neocorixa 20.35.6
snowi, Nurenus 21.14.112
snowi, Prororcorpha 11.5.27
snowi, Prororcorypha 11.5.76
Snowia 27.61.125
Snowy Tree Cricket 11.10.19
snyderi, Zorotypus 16.1.1
Snyder's Angel Insect 16.1.1
Sobarocephala 29.65.4
Sobata 21.14.129
socialis, Lasiochiloides 20.21.19
sodalis, Alofa 20.21.22
Soft Scale Insect Family, supra 21.26.1
Soft-bodied Plant Beetle Family,
 supra 24.34.1
Soft-winged Flower Beetle Family,
 supra 24.68.1
solana, Empoasca 21.14.77
Solanaceous Treehopper 21.15.43
solanalis, Zellerina 27.55.109
solani, Acrythosiphon 21.19.2
solani, Gargaphia 20.14.11
solani, Paracoccus 21.25.29

solani, Phenacoccus 21.25.32
Solanum Mealybug 21.25.32
Soldier Beetle Family, supra 24.56.1
Soldier Fly 29.31.37
Soldier Fly Family, supra 29.31.1
Soldierless Termites 15.4.1
Solenobia 27.11.1
solenobiae, Marcus 25.16.417
Solenopotes 19.2.2
Solenopsidini, supra 25.58.31
solenopsidis, Commoptera 29.46.36
Solenopsis 25.58.33 (Figs. 25.38, 25.39,
 25.40)
solidaginis, Eurosta 29.61.12
solidaginis, Lithomoia 27.75.389
solidaginis, Neomastix 24.113.210
solidaginis, Rhopalomyia 29.11.158
Solierella 25.62.46
solieri, Haploembia 9.3.3
Soliperla 8.6.3
solita, Agepema 27.69.11
solitaria, Brachyponera 25.58.14
solitaria, Bursaphis 21.19.35
solitaria, Timonidia 21.11.16
solitarius, Aleurolobus 21.18.5
solitarius, Hypodermodes 29.100.50
Solitary Midge Family, supra 29.21.1
Solitary Oak Leaf Miner 27.14.20
soliterius, Lembodes 24.113.247
sollicitans, Aedes 29.20.9
Solntsevia 29.11.46
Solubea 20.3.33
Solva 29.30.1
Somanica 25.7.82
Somaphantus 18.6.34
Somatania 27.55.128
Somatochlora 7.6.6
Somatolophia 27.61.140
Sominella 24.107.5
somnulentella, Bedellia 27.13.3 (Fig.
 27.30)
Somotrichus 24.4.145
Somula 29.47.77
Sonia 27.38.30
Sonoma 24.25.1
Sonoran Tent Caterpillar Moth 27.68.11
sonorella, Anderida 27.55.369
sonorensis, Parypoconus 29.23.31
sonorensis, Philotes 27.43.43
sonorum, Mecanthidium 25.68.4
sonorus, Bombus 29.49.3
sonorus, Graminella 21.14.220
Sonronius 21.14.97
Sooty-wing 27.40.41
Sophiini, supra 29.105.206
Sophiothrips 22.5.65
Sophophora 29.90.9
Sophronia 27.23.66
Sorobobium 21.19.215
sordulentus, Monorachis 21.1.3
sordida, Cosmoplites 24.113.368
sordida, Estoloides 24.106.248
sordida, Neogriphonerua 29.82.10
sordida, Olfersia 29.106.9
sordidum, Trichoton 24.87.158
sorer, Bombyliomyia 29.105.82
sorghicola, Contarinia 29.11.108
sorghiella, Nola 27.75.179
Sorghum Midge 29.11.108
Sorhagenia 27.21.24
Sorhoanus 21.14.186
Soronia 24.70.20
sororiata, Carsia 27.61.245
Sosipatra 27.55.399
Sostrata 27.40.27
sosybius, Hermeuptychia 27.48.4

Sosylus 24.93.24
sounds 25
Sourbush Seed Fly 29.61.17
Southern Armyworm 27.75.326
Southern Beet Webworm 27.55.179
Southern Buffalo Gnat 29.22.11
Southern Cabbageworm 27.42.4
Southern Carpenter Bee 25.69.46
Southern Cinch Bug 20.7.16
Southern Cloudy Wing 27.40.16
Southern Corn Billbug 24.113.366
Southern Corn Rootworm 24.107.90
Southern Cornstalk Borer 27.55.228
Southern Fire Ant 25.58.33
Southern Garden Leafhopper 21.14.77
Southern Green Stink Bug 20.3.51
Southern House Mosquito 29.20.12
Southern Lyctus Beetle 24.65.1
Southern Masked Chafer 24.30.100
Southern Mole Cricket 11.11.3
Southern Pine Beetle 24.112.11
Southern Pine Coneworm 27.88.339
Southern Pine Root Weevil 24.113.153
Southern Pine Sawyer 24.106.237
Southern Pine-tip Moth 27.38.19
Southern Potato Wireworm 24.48.124
Southwestern Big Red 7.7.13
Southwestern Hercules Beetle 24.30.114
Southwestern Tent Caterpillar
 Moth 27.68.11
Sow Thistle Aphid 21.19.145
Soybean Looper 27.75.154
Soybean Thrips 22.4.12
Soyedina 8.1.10
spadix, Pselactus 24.113.397
spadix, Sophiothrips 22.5.65
Spaelotis 27.75.560
Spalacopsini, supra 24.106.262
Spalacopsis 24.106.262
Spalangia 25.19.22
Spalangiinae, supra 25.19.22
Spalangiolaelaps 25.19.29
Spalgini, supra 27.43.1
Spallanzania 29.105.356
Spanagonicus 20.23.69
Spangbergiella 21.14.9
Spania 29.28.4
Spaniacris 11.4.4
Spaniarcrini, supra 10.4.4
Spanioneura 21.17.28
Spaniopus 25.19.102
Spanish Fly 24.101.13
Spanoparea 29.84.15
Sparasion 25.43.1
Sparedrus 24.97.2
Spargaloma 27.75.46
Spargania 27.61.215
Sparganothidini, supra 27.38.86
Sparganothis 27.38.86
Sparkia 27.75.469
Sparnopolius 29.40.15
sparsa, Acmaeodera 24.46.27
sparsus, Hylasus 25.63.5
Spartiniphaga 27.75.265
Spastonyx 24.101.2
Spathanus 21.14.102
Spathidexia 29.105.171
Spathilepia 27.40.20
Spathimeigenia 29.105.264
Spathius 25.13.26
Spathizus 24.56.17
Spathopus 25.19.59
spatulata, Isotoma 1.23.4
Spaziphora 29.98.18
specca, Mesepiola 27.8.12
Speccafrons 29.94.36

specialists, identification 6, 42
species 15, 17, 18
species, rare 7
specific name 16
specimens, exchange and shipping of 47
specimen, type 6
Speciosa 29.103.24
speciosa, Blaesoxipha 29.103.24
speciosa, Philotiella 27.43.45
speciosissima, Centrodora 25.25.3
speciosus, Chaetechidius 24.113.92
speciosus, Glycobius 24.106.114
speciosus, Sphecius 25.62.90
spectabilis, Ceratulus 25.7.71
specularis, Octogomphus 7.3.8
Speleketor 17.4.4
Speleobama 24.25.5
Speleobamini, supra 24.25.5
spenceri, Cramptonomyia 29.2.7
spenceri, Meiocampa 3.1.3
Speocropia 27.75.308
speokites, Horologion 24.4.64
Speolepta 29.9.46
Sperchopsis 24.12.15
spermaphaga, Eupithecia 27.61.241
Sperrya 27.61.16
Speyeria 27.46.8
Sphacelodini, supra 27.61.103
Sphacelodes 27.61.103
Sphacophilus 25.4.88
Sphaericus 24.62.4
Sphaeridia 1.7.1
Sphaeridiinae, supra 24.12.25
Sphaeridiini, supra 24.12.25
Sphaeridium 24.12.25
Sphaeriestes 24.90.8
Sphaeriidae, supra 24.10.1
Sphaerion 24.106.68
Sphaeritidae, supra 24.27.1
Sphaerites 24.27.1
Sphaerius 24.10.1
Sphaerocera 29.88.1
Sphaeroceridae, supra 29.88.1
Sphaeroceroidea, supra 29.84.1
Sphaeroderma 24.107.158
Sphaeroderus 24.4.14
Sphaerolecanium 21.26.21
Sphaeromias 29.23.26
Sphaerophoria 29.47.31
Sphaeropthalma 25.5.10
Sphaeropthalmini, supra 25.55.6
Sphaeropthaminae, supra 25.55.6
Sphaeroteras 25.34.35
Sphalma 24.90.5
Spharagemon 11.5.48
Sphecidae, supra 25.62.1
Sphecinae, supra 25.62.4
Sphecini, supra 25.62.8
Sphecius 25.62.90
Sphecodes 25.66.22
Sphecodina 27.70.33
Sphecodogastra 25.66.19
Sphecodosoma 25.66.5
Sphecoidea, supra 25.62.1
Sphecomyia 29.47.73
Sphecomyiella 29.60.3
Sphecophaga 25.16.188
Sphecophagina, supra 25.16.188
Sphegigaster 25.19.41
Sphegigasterini, supra 25.19.41
Sphegina 29.47.49
Sphelodon 25.16.303
Sphenarches 27.58.2
sphenarioides, Aptenopedes 11.5.104
sphenica, Hippomelas 24.46.7
sphenofrons, Asseclamyia 29.105.132

Sphenometopa 29.103.13
Sphenophorus 24.113.366
Sphenophrini, supra 24.111.366
Sphenostethus 24.106.7
Sphex 25.62.8
Sphictostethus 25.60.7
Sphindidae, supra 24.73.1
Sphindociinae, supra 24.92.1
Sphindocis 24.92.1
Sphindus 24.73.2
Sphingicampa 27.69.3
Sphingidae, supra 27.70.1
Sphinginae, supra 27.70.1
Sphingini, supra 27.70.1
Sphingocephalus 24.98.47
Sphingoidea, supra 27.70.1
Sphinx 27.70.11
Sphiximorpha 29.47.69
sphondylii, Saltella 29.81.6
Sphongophorus 21.15.13
Sphragisticus 20.7.71
Sphyracephala 29.56.1
Sphyrocoris 20.3.8
Sphyromyia 29.105.88
Sphyrotheca 1.7.7
Spicebush Swallowtail 27.41.7
Spicotus, Gomphus 7.3.9 (Fig. 7.5)
Spider Beetle Family, supra 24.62.1
Spider Wasp Family, supra 25.60.1
spiders 10
Spilichneumon 25.16.236
Spilochaetosoma 29.105.110
Spilochalcis 25.21.7
Spilococcus 21.25.41
Spilodiscus 24.26.40
Spilogona 29.100.13
Spiloloma 27.75.147
Spilomelini, supra 27.55.105
Spilomena 25.62.27
Spilomicrus 25.42.21
Spilomyia 29.47.83
Spilonota 27.38.22
Spilopsyllini, supra 30.1.6
Spilopteromyia 29.100.53
Spilopteron 25.16.192
Spiloshroa 29.85.3
Spilosoma 27.73.37
spilota, Leiomyrmosa 25.55.4
spilotella, Monopis 27.10.41
Spilotus 24.98.20
Spinach Flea Beetle 24.107.123
Spinach Leaf Miner 29.99.14
Spinadinae, supra 6.6.12
Spinadis 6.6.12
spinata, Bourletiella 1.7.6
spinataria, Euaspilates 27.61.135
spine 22
Spined Assassin Bug 20.17.21
Spined Rat Louse 19.7.1
Spined Soldier Bug 20.3.74
Spined Stilt Bug 20.12.2
Spine-tailed Earwig 13.5.1
spinetorum, Mitoura 27.43.26
spinicauda, Plectrura 24.106.230
spinidens, Andrallus 20.3.69
spinifera, Olfersia 29.106.9
spinifrons, Amnestus 20.1.8 (Fig 20.4)
spinifrons, Galeatus 20.14.10
spiniger, Heterodoxus 18.3.1
spinimana, Norellia 29.98.1
spinipennis, Bigonicheta 29.105.133
spinipennis, Leptocera 29.88.3
spinipes, Skelosyzygonia 25.3.2
spinipes, Caccoplectus 24.25.7
spinipes variegartus, Zethus 25.59.25
Spiniphora 29.46.3

spinolae, Bembix 25.62.10
spinosa, Chaetonopsis 29.105.205
spinosa, Neobarrettia 11.7.24 (Fig. 11.33)
spinosa, Syncalypta 24.35.14
spinosa, Trichagrotes 27.75.526
spinosus, Baetis 6.4.2 (Fig. 6.6)
spinosus, Hamamelistes 21.19.94
spinosus, Jalysus 20.12.2 (Fig. 20.35)
spinosus, Patapius 20.31.1
Spintharosoma 25.50.20
Spintherophyta 24.107.38
spinulata, Allacrotelsa 5.3.2
spinulosa, Polyplax 19.7.1 (Fig. 19.1)
Spiny Crawler Mayfly Family 6.13.1
Spiny Oakworm 27.69.5 (Fig. 27.218)
Spiny Rat Louse Family 19.7.1
Spinyheaded Burrower Mayfly
 Family 6.12.1
Spiny-legged Bug Family, supra 20.31.1
spiracle 12.21.22
spiraea, Neomachlotica 27.28.2
Spiramater 27.75.484, not in "Checklist."
Spirea Aphid 21.19.15
Spiriverpa 29.32.19
Spirobolomyia 29.103.24
Spiroporococcus 21.31.9
spissicornis, Coleophora 27.18.1
spissipes, Hypotrichia 24.30.69
Spissistilus 21.15.26
Spittle Bug Family, supra 21.12.1
splendens, Agapostemon 25.66.14
splendens, Allotorymus 25.18.5
splendens sinaloensis, Citheronia 27.69.2
Splendid Dung Beetle 24.30.11
Splendid Tiger Beetle 24.3.1
splendida, Calliphora 29.101.24
splendida, Cicindela 24.3.23
splendida, Phasiomyia 29.105.12
splendidula, Lamprorhiza 24.55.10
splendidulus, Microleptes 25.16.480
splendidus, Geotrupes 24.30.52 (Fig.
 24.67)
splendoriferella, Coptodisca 27.9.3
Splitback Mayflies 6.1.1
Spodoptera 27.75.326
Spoggosia 29.105.290
Spoladea 27.55.135
Spondylinae, supra 24.106.12
Spondylis 24.106.12
Sponged Treehopper 21.15.13
Spongillafly Family, supra 23.13.1
Spongiphorinae, supra 13.3.1
Spongovostox 13.3.2
Spongy Oak Apple Gall 25.34.28
sponsa, Neurotneta 11.5.1
Sporothrips 22.5.21
spot identification 53
Spotted Alfalfa Aphid 21.19.209
Spotted Asparagus Beetle , 24.107.11
Spotted Beet Webworm 27.55.134
Spotted Blister Beetle 24.101.14
Spotted Cucumber Beetle 24.107.90
Spotted Cutworm Moth 27.75.566
Spotted Grape Beetle 24.30.92
Spotted Hairy Fungus Beetle 24.91.1
Spotted Pine Sawyer 24.106.237
Spotted Tussock Moth 27.73.56
Spottedwinged Antlion 23.14.1
Spragueia 27.75.219
spreading wings 40
spretella (-fuscipunctella), Niditinea 27.10.38
spretus, Melanoplus 11.5.94
Spring Azure 27.43.42
Spring Cankerworm 27.61.63
Spring Stonefly Family 8.1.1
Springtails 1.1.1

Sprinkled Locust 11.5.1
Spruce Adelgid Family, supra 21.20.1
Spruce Aphid 21.19.69
Spruce Beetle 24.112.11
Spruce Bud Midge 29.11.151
Spruce Bud Moth 27.38.33
Spruce Bud Scale 21.26.16.
Spruce Budworm 27.38.72
Spruce Mealybug 21.24.1
Spruce Needle Miner 27.38.7
Spruce Pine Coneworm 27.55.339
Spruce Seed Moth 27.38.56
Spudaeus 25.16.291
Spudastica 25.16.409
spumarius, Philaenus 21.12.4
spurca, Centrodera 24.106.174
spuria, Gossyparia 21.31.5
spurina, Thereus 27.43.21
Spur-throated Grasshoppers 11.5.73
squalens, Thinoxenus 24.113.79
squamiger, Aedes 29.20.9
squamiger, Orthoptochus 24.113.85
squammulata, Pseudleptomastix 25.25.32
Squamocoris 20.23.123
squamosus, Haematopinoides 19.6.2
Square-headed Snake Fly Family,
 supra 23.4.1
Square-necked Grain Beetle 24.72.5
Squarenosed Fungus Beetle 24.82.3
Squash Beetle 24.80.52
Squash Bug 20.4.27 (Fig. 20.24)
Squash Bug Family 20.4.1
Squash Vine Borer 27.35.8
Squirrel Louse Family 19.5.1
Sriferia 27.23.40
Stable Fly 29.100.61
Stachanorema 1.4.6
Stachiella 18.2.7
Stachisma 5.3.2
Stachyocnemus 20.5.11
Stactobiella 26.7.7
stactogalus, Opsius 21.14.148
Staegeria 29.98.17
Stag Beetle Family, supra 24.28.1
Stagetus 24.63.42
Stagmatophora 27.21.8
Stagmomantis 14.1.8
Stagona 21.19.200
Stalk Borer Moth 27.75.279
Stalked-winged Damselfly Family 7.9.1
Stalk-eyed Fly Family 29.56.1
Stallingsia 27.40.89
Stamoderes 24.113.35
Stamnoctenis 27.61.221
Stamnoderus 24.24.70
Stamnodes 27.61.220
Stamnodini, supra 27.61.220
Stantonia 25.13.144
Staphylinidae, supra 24.24.1
Staphyliniformia, supra 24.12.1
staphyliniformis, Leptanthicus 24.102.5
Staphylininae, supra 24.24.1
Staphylinoidea, supra 24.15.1
Staphylinus 24.24.13
Staphylus 27.40.25
starki, Alabameubria 24.34.14
state codens 5
Stathmopoda 27.15.40
Stathmopodini, supra 27.15.40
Statira 24.89.1
statira, Aphrissa 27.42.15
Statirinae, supra 24.89.1
Stator 24.108.20
Staudingeria 27.55.359
Steatococcus 21.23.9
Steel-blue Lady Beetle 24.80.27

Stegana 29.29.1
Steganina 29.90.1
Steganinae, supra 29.90.1
Steganolauxania 29.82.18
Steganopsis 29.82.18
Stegaspinae, supra 21.15.55
Stegasta 27.23.63
Stegea 27.55.53
Stegobium 24.63.18
Stegomyia 29.20.9
Stegophylla 21.19.201
Stegopterna 29.22.8
Steingeliinae, supra 21.23.3
Steingeliini, supra 21.23.3
Steirastoma 24.106.267
Steiroxys 11.7.45
stejnegeri, Coelopa 29.77.1
stelenes, Siproeta 27.46.32
Stelidina 25.68.11
Stelidota 24.70.15
Stelis 25.68.11
stellata, Chiloxanthus 20.32.2
stellata, Derrima 27.75.591
stellata, Disclisioprocta 27.61.232
stellella, Mompha 27.19.1
stellatarum, Macroglossum 27.70.39
Stem Sawfly Family, supra 25.12.1
Stemmatomeinx 21.25.42
Stemmatosteres 25.25.58
Stemorrhages 27.55.155
Stempellina 29.24.78
Stenacidia 1.7.1
Stenacris 11.5.74
Stenacron 6.6.7
Stenamma 25.58.25
Stenancylus 24.113.379
Stenaspilatodes 27.61.86
Stenaspis 24.106.145
Stenelaphus 24.106.62
Steneleodes 24.87.140
Stenelmis 24.45.24
Steneretma 29.58.34
stenialis, Apogeshna 27.55.140
Stenichneumon 25.16.238
Stenichnus 24.20.10
Stenininae, supra 24.24.191
Steniodes 27.55.141
Steniolia 25.62.105
Stenispa 24.107.161
Stenistoderus 24.24.45
Stenistomera 30.4.12
Stenobarichneumon 25.16.217
Stenobaris 24.113.306
Stenobothrus 11.5.4
Stenocerus 24.109.10
Stenochidus 24.88.2
Stenochironomus 29.24.65
Stenocleptus 24.112.27
Stenocolus 24.34.7
Stenocorse 25.13.27
Stenocorus 24.106.176
Stenocranophilus 24.105.11
Stenocranus 21.2.10
Stenocrepis 24.4.100
Stenocris 20.5.5
Stenodema 20.23.201
Stenodemini, supra 20.23.193
Stenodontes 24.106.4
Stenodontus 25.16.198
Stenodynerus 25.59.13
Stenogastrura 1.2.7
Stenolemoides 20.17.10
Stenolophus 24.4.113
Stenomacra 20.9.2
Stenomacrus 25.16.501
Stenomatinae, supra 27.15.17

Stenomesius 25.26.18
Stenometopiellus 21.14.172
Stenomicra 29.70.4
Stenomimus 24.113.381
Stenomorpha 24.87.55
Stenomorphus 24.4.129
Stenomyia 29.58.35
Stenonema 6.6.8
Stenoneura 29.105.336
Stenopa 29.61.37
Stenopelmatinae, supra 11.9.3
Stenopelmatus 11.9.3
Stenopelmus 24.113.187
Stenopepsis 25.60.2
Stenophylacini, supra 26.10.25
Stenopodinae, supra 20.17.33
Stenopodius 24.107.169
Stenopogon 29.37.18
Stenoponia 30.4.3
Stenoponiinae, supra 30.4.3
Stenoporpia 27.61.27
stenopsis, Linognathus 19.2.1
Stenopsocidae, supra 17.11.1
Stenopterini, supra 24.106.95
Stenoptilia 27.58.15
Stenoptilodes 27.58.14
Stenoptinea 27.10.10
Stenoptochus 24.113.87
Stenoscelis 24.113.395
Stenoscinis 29.94.13
Stenosides 24.87.47
Stenosini, supra 24.87.31
Stenosphenus 24.106.60
Stenostrophia 24.106.213
Stenotabanus 29.26.20
Stenotarsinae, supra 24.81.14
Stenotarsus 24.81.15
Stenotrachelinae, supra 24.86.2
Stenotrachelus 24.86.2
Stenotrichus 24.87.125
Stenotus 20.23.186
Stenoxenini, supra 29.23.30
Stenoxenus 29.23.30
Stenoxylocopa 25.69.46
Stenus 24.24.192
Stephanid Wasp Family, supra 25.17.1
Stephanidae, supra 25.17.1
Stephanitis 20.14.20
Stephanodes 25.27.20
stephanomeriae, Perdita 25.65.15
Stephanopachys 24.64.8
Stephanothrips 22.5.30
Stephanucha 24.30.125
stephensi, Tychius 24.113.228
Stephensia 27.16.3
Stephomyia 29.11.76
Stephostethus 24.82.6
sterocoraria, Scatophaga 29.98.23
stercorarius, Meroplius 29.81.2 (Fig.
 29.49)
stercorea, Ancylostomia 27.55.309
stercorea, Typhaea 24.90.2
Steremnius 24.113.157
Stereodermini, supra 24.110.5
Stereodermus 24.110.5
Stereogaster 24.113.30
Stereomita 27.23.9
Stereopalpus 24.103.5
Stergamataea 27.61.78
Sterictiphora 25.4.3
Sterictiphorinae, supra 25.4.3
Steriphanus 24.87.17
sternalis, Eumasicera 29.105.401
Sternechini, supra 24.113.166
Sternechus 24.113.166
Sternidius 24.106.284

Sternidocinus 24.106.288
Sternochetus 24.113.265
sternodontis, Sarcodexia 29.103.42
Sternopsylla 30.5.3
Sternorrhyncha, supra 21.17.1
sternum (sterna) 20
Sterrhinae, supra 27.61.172
Sterrhini, supra 27.61.172
Stethanytyx 25.16.450
Stethasida 24.87.61
Stethaulax 20.3.7
Stethobaris 24.113.355
Stetholiodes 24.19.11
Stethomostus 25.7.63
Stethon 24.52.6
Stethoncus 25.16.299
Stethophyma 11.5.32
Stethorhianis 24.81.9
Stethorus 24.80.5
Stethynium 25.27.2
Steveniopsis 29.105.61
stevensi, Empoasca 21.14.77
Steven's Leafhopper 21.14.77
Sthenarus 20.23.70
sthenele, Cercyonis 27.48.9
Sthenopis 27.4.1
Sthenopyga 29.103.33
Sthereus 24.113.158
Stibaera 27.75.336
Stibedium 27.75.346
Stibeutes 25.16.126
Stibia 24.87.27
Stichillus 29.46.10
Stichoglossa 24.24.293
Sticholotinae, supra 24.80.1
Sticholotini, supra 24.80.2
Stichopogon 29.37.16
Stichtoptychus 24.63.47
Sticktight Flea 30.1.4
Sticthippus 11.5.43
Stictia 25.62.100
sticticalis, Loxostege 27.55.101
sticticum, Trypetisoma 29.82.21
sticticus, Aedes 29.20.9
sticticus, Eretes 24.7.40
Stictiella 25.62.102
Stictobaris 24.113.308
Stictocephala 21.15.24
Stictochironomus 29.24.70
Stictocranius 24.24.163
Stictoleptura 24.106.219
Stictolinus 24.24.46
Stictolobus 21.15.28
Stictomyia 29.58.36
Stictopelta 21.15.19
Stictopisthus 25.16.468
Stictopleurus 20.6.7
Stictostix 24.26.3
Stictothrips 22.5.66
stigma, Chilocorus 24.80.23
stigma, Dieuryneura 29.31.14
stigma, Glyphomerus 25.18.17
stigma stigma, Anistoa 27.69.5
stigmaphiles, Rhosologia 27.75.79
stigmaticus, Grais 27.40.32
stigmaticum, Pneumosema 25.13.109
Stigmatocrepis 25.19.64
Stigmatomeria 29.9.28
Stigmella 27.5.1
Stigmus 25.62.26
Stilbometopia 29.106.5
Stilbopini, supra 25.16.302
Stilbops 25.26.302
Stilbosis 27.21.18
Stilbula 25.23.3
Stilbus 24.77.8

Stiletto Fly Family, supra 29.32.1
Stilicolina 24.24.71
Stilicopsis 24.24.72
Stilobezzia 29.23.13
Stilobezzini, supra 29.23.13
Stilomedon 24.24.73
Stilpnina, supra 25.16.131
Stilpnochlora 11.7.12
Stilpon 29.42.10
Stilpnus 25.16.131
Stilt Bug Family 20.12.1
Stilt-legged Fly Family, supra 29.51.1
stimulea, Sibine 27.52.21
Stimulopalpus 17.5.2
Stinga 27.40.64
Stinging Rose Caterpillar Moth 27.52.20
Stink Beetle 24.4.35
Stink Bug Family 20.3.1
Stirellus 21.14.167
Stiretrus 20.3.64
Stiria 27.75.357
Stiriini, supra 27.75.346
Stiriodes 27.75.339
Stizini, supra 25.62.95
Stizoides 25.62.96
Stizus 25.62.95
Stobaera 21.2.3
stokesii, Glabridorsum 25.16.160
Stolaini, supra 24.107.175
stolidota, Epermenia 27.27.1 (Fig. 27.44)
Stomacoccus 21.23.3
Stomatomyia 29.105.291
Stomatosema 29.11.69
Stomatosematini, supra 29.11.69
Stomatothrips 22.1.6
Stomis 24.4.84
Stomodes 24.113.69
Stomorhina 29.101.1
Stomosis 29.74.4
Stomoxyinae, supra 29.100.59
Stomoxys 29.100.61
Stoneflies 8.1.1
Stonemyia 29.26.7
Stonyx 29.40.51
storage containers 37
Stored Nut Moth 27.55.275
Stout Barklice Family 17.15.1
Strabala 24.107.130
strachani, Pinnaspis 21.38.64
Stragania 21.14.29
Straight-snouted Weevil Family,
 supra 24.110.1
Stramenaspis 21.38.80
straminea, Dasyblemma 27.75.29
straminea, Opetiophora 29.94.21
stramineus, Menacanthus 18.6.24
Strangalepta, supra 24.106.172, 24.106.218
Strangalia 24.106.197
Strategus 24.30.108
Stratiomyidae, supra 29.31.1
Stratiomyhinae, supra 29.31.31
Stratiomyini, supra 29.31.39
Stratiomyoidea, supra 29.25.1, 29.29.1
Stratiomys, supra 29.39.1, 29.31.39
Strauzia 29.61.49
Strawberry Aphid 21.19.50
Strawberry Crown Borer 24.113.258
Strawberry Crown Miner 27.23.72
Strawberry Leaf Roller 27.38.42
Strawberry Root Aphid 21.19.15
Strawberry Root Weevil 24.113.68
Strawberry Rootworm 24.107.50
Strawberry Sap Beetle 24.70.15
Strawberry Weevil 24.113.208
Strawberry Whitefly 21.18.17
Streblidae, supra 29.108.1

Streblocera 25.13.159
streckeri, Mycelia 27.46.35
strenuana, Epiblemema 27.38.27
strenuus, Anax 7.4.1
strenuva, Machilis 4.1.7
Strepsicrates 27.38.23
Strepsipteriformia, supra 24.105.1
Streptanus 21.14.159
Strepterothrips 22.5.70
Streptopalpia 27.55.255
streptophallus, Lygistus 24.107.104
Stretchia 27.75.503
striata, Helobata 24.12.22
striata, Pschornia 25.39.7
striatulus, Migiwa 24.48.57
stricticollis, Trichochronellus 24.68.37
strigatus, Eumerus 29.47.57
strigicollis, Cnesinus 24.112.1
strigipes, Mineus 20.3.72
Strigiphilus 18.1.57
Striglininae, supra 27.56 7
Strigocis 24.92.6
Strigoderma 24.30.97
strigosa, Pseudosphex 27.73.84
strigosus, Bittacus 28.1.2
Strigota 24.24.294
strigula, Pterocalla 29.58.18
striola, Neoplea 20.34.1
striolata, Phyllotreta 24.107.114
Striped Alder Sawfly 25.7.20
Striped Ambrosia Beetle 23.112.53
Striped Cucumber Beetle 24.107.93
Stripped Cutworm Moth 27.75.544
Striped Flea Beetle 24.107.114
Striped Garden Caterpillar Moth 27.75.483
Striped Ground Cricket 11.10.13
Striped Hairstreak 27.43.16
Striped Horse Fly 29.26.26
Striped Mealybug 21.25.19
Striped Pine Scale 21.26.22
Striped Walkingstick Family 10.4.1
Stritobiini, supra 26.7.7
strobi, Cinara 21.19.53
strobi, Pineus 21.20.2
strobi, Pissodes 24.113.171
Strobliella 29.11.22
Strobliellini, supra 29.11.22
stroblioides, Rhabodophaga 29.11.151
Strobisia 27.23.74
Stromatium 24.106.53
Stromboceridea 25.7.8
Strongygastrini, supra 29.105.32
Strongylaspis 24.106.2
Strongyliini, supra 24.87.129
Strongylium 24.87.129
Strongylogaster 25.7.3
Strongylogastrini, supra 25.7.1
Strongylophthalmyia 29.54.1
Strongylophthalmyiid Fly Family,
 supra 29.54.1
Strongylophthalmyiidae, supra 29.54.1
Strophiona, supra 24.106.172, 24.106.226
Strophogastra 24.24.295
Strophopteryx 8.2.4
Strophosoma 24.113.48
Strophosomini, supra 24.113.48
Strumigentys 25.58.46
Strymon 27.43.34
Stump Borer 24.106.174
Sturmia 29.105.382
Sturmiini, supra 29.105.370
Sturnidoecus 18.1.58
stygia, Orthogonis 29.37.61
stygica, Nerthra 20.39.2
stygiatus, Tricorythodes 6.14.1 (Fig. 6.11)
Stylantheus 24.108.7

stylata, Cerapoda 27.75.459
stylata, Doratura 21.14.173
stylata, Petinarctia 29.105.148
stylet 20
Stylifer 55.3.7
Stylogaster 29.49.9
Stylogomphnus 7.3.11
Styloleptus 24.106.283
Stylogastrinae, supra 29.49.9
Styloneuria 29.104.3
Stylopalpia 27.55.335
Stylopoda 27.75.454
Stylopidae, supra 24.105.1
Stylopids, supra 24.1.1
Stylopinae, supra 24.105.1
Stylopoidea, supra 24.105.1
Stylops 24.105.2
stylosus, Dolichopsyllus 30.6.3
Styloxus 24.106.30
Stylurus 7.3.9
styracis, Copipanolis 27.75.431
Styracosceles 11.9.12
suavata, Acratodes 27.61.186
suavis, Actenopsylla 30.1.6
suavis, Pallacocoris 20.23.175
Subacyrosiphon 21.19.202
subaenea, Mallodrya 24.98.8
subaenescens, Exoplectra 24.80.31
subangulata, Aspidoglissa 24.4.30
subapterus, Ecitonetes 25.45.4
subapterus, Henicopygus 25.25.148
subapterus, Tmetothrips 22.4.33
subaterrimus, Mariocladius 29.24.136
subauratus, Limonius 24.48.27
subborealis, Psychoglypha 26.10.37
subcaesiella, Nephopterix 27.55.329
subcanus, Tylicus 24.35.3
subcinerea, Platyedra 27.23.82
Subcoccinella 24.80.53
subcoeruleus, Trigonopselaphus 24.24.17
subcoleopteratus, Nabiclua 20.18.6 (Fig.
 20.47)
subconnata, Desmatogaster 24.63.27
subcosta 21
subcrinita, Epitrix 24.107.137
subcyanescnes, Coraia 24.107.75
subcyaneus, Mastogenius 24.46.39 (Fig.
 24.94)
subdepressus, Palorus 24.87.111
subdiaphanna, Eremoblatta 14.4.2
suberi, Plagiotrochus 25.34.43
suberosus, Trox 24.30.43
subfamily 15
subfasciatus, Pachybrachis 24.107.20
subfasciatus, Zabrotes 24.108.3
subfasciella, Araeolepia 27.29.1
subfuliginosa, Clistorapha 25.16.456
subglabra, Epicauta 24.101.14
subglabra, Tisactia 24.74.14
subgothica, Feltia 27.75.537
Subhaida 24.24.133
subita, Lyroda 25.62.44
submarginatus, Attalusinus 24.68.6
submetallicus, Polemiotus 24.87.2
submicans, Zaommoencyrtus 25.25.160
submutans, Petroibus 4.1.5
subnudus, Pelignellus 29.93.11
suborders 15
subornata, Plathemis 7.7.24
subpallida, Asterocampa 27.47.3
subparallelus 24.113.364
subparallelus, Clinocladius 29.24.121
subpilosa, Cortodera 24.106.189
subporphyea, Hemipachnobia 27.75.575
subpubescens,
 Aneflomorpha 24.106.69 (Fig. 24.186)

subrosea, Eugtaphe 27.75.572
subrostratus, Felicola 18.2.3
subrufella, Atheloca 27.55.304
subrufus, Schizophilus 24.52.20
Subsaltusaphis 21.19.203
subsericeus, Diamimus 24.113.127
subsignarias, Ennomos 27.61.101
subsolana, Larisa 27.38.50
subspecies 18
subspinosus, Macrodactylus 24.30.80
substriataria, Epirranthis 27.61.102
subterranea, Agrotis 27.75.535
Subterranean Silverfish Family 5.2.1
Subterranean Termite Family 15.3.1
Subterraneobombus 25.70.2
subterraneus, Hadenoecus 11.9.8
subterraneus, Paraphaenodiscus 25.25.151
subterraneus, Scarites 24.4.23
subtilis, Notoxus 24.102.2 (Fig. 24.171)
subtinctella, Cuniberta 27.55.288
subtropica, Rhyacionia 27.38.19
Subtropical Pine Tip Moth 27.38.19
subtropicus, Scalaventer 24.113.64
subulalis, Araschnopsis 27.55.145
subulata, Tetrix 11.1.2 (Fig. 11.6)
subulatum, Piezosternum 20.3.61
subulirostris, Amercedes 24.113.344
subvaira, Ephemerella 6.13.1
succandidalis, Cylindrifrons 27.55.72
succinctus, Acrotomus 25.16.72
succinctus, Largus 20.9.1 (Fig. 20.33)
sucifrons, Aneurota 24.24.200
Suckfly 20.23.28
Sucking Lice 19.1.1
Sudus 24.113.268
sueroides, Selenisa 27.75.117
Sufetula 27.55.114
Sugar Beet Root Aphid 21.19.162
Sugar Maple Scale 21.30.1
Sugarbeet Crown Borer 27.55.360
Sugar-beet Root Maggot 29.58.20
Sugar-beet Wireworm 24.48.27
Sugarcane Aphid 21.19.128
Sugarcane Beetle 24.30.103
Sugarcane Borer 27.55.228
Sugarcane Scale 21.38.10
Sugarmaple Borer 24.106.114
sugens, Imitomyia 29.105.27
Suilla 29.84.2
suilla, Marganana 21.14.26
Suilliinae, supra 29.84.1
Suioestrus 29.102.6
suis, Haematopinus 19.3.1
sula, Lasaia 27.44.4
Sulcacis 24.92.10
Sulcarius 25.16.121
sulcata, Phasgonophora 25.21.10
sulcatulus, Adelonia 24.87.39
sulcatus, Hecabolus 25.13.12
sulcatus, Otiorhynchus 24.113.68
sulcatus, Stenocleptus 24.112.27
sulcatus, Tonibius 24.87.156
sulcicollis, Trichonyx 24.25.16
sulcifrons, Tabanus 29.26.26 (Fig. 29.29)
sulcipes, Scolops 21.11.5
Suleima 27.38.29
Sulphur Butterfly Family, supra 27.42.1
sulphurea, Arphia 11.5.34
sulphurella, Esperia 27.15.30
sulphuripes, Turbopsebius 29.38.6 (Fig.
 20.33)
Sulphur-winged Locust 11.5.34
sumichrasti, Achurum 11.5.25
Sumichrast's Toothpick Grasshopper 11.5.25
Sumitrosis 24.107.163
summersi, Pilactium 24.25.36

Sunflower Beetle 24.107.59
Sunflower Bud Moth 27.38.29
Sunflower Maggot 29.61.49
Sunflower Moth 27.55.371
Sunflower Seed Midge 29.11.68
Sunflower Spittle Bug 21.12.7
Sunira 27.75.404
Sunius 24.24.74
Supella 14.5.10
Superb Plant Bug 20.23.139
superba, Palloptera 29.63.1
superbus, Adelphocoris 20.23.139
superbus, Pseudoleon 7.7.25
superbus, Tibicen 21.13.4 (Fig. 21.14)
superfamily 15
superior, Petrobius 4.1.5
supernotatus, Psenocerus 24.106.247
Suphis 24.8.2
Suphisellus 24.8.3
Suphisini, supra 24.8.2
Supralathosea 27.75.437
Suragina 29.27.2
Surattha 27.55.198
Suricatoecus 18.2.8
Surinam Cockroach 14.6.4
surinamensis, Necrodes 24.21.6
surinamensis, Pycnoscelus 14.6.4
surinamensis, Oryzaephilus 24.72.2 (Fig. 24.1237)
suninamum, Achryson 24.106.35
Susana 25.7.14
Susaninae, supra 25.7.14
Sussaba 25.16.479
sutrina, Hectera 27.75.489
suturalis, Acoptus 24.113.279
suturalis, Brumoides 24.80.26
suturalis, Euryscelis 24.106.122
suture 20
Suturella 24.15.4
suturellus, Dysdercus 20.8.1 (Fig. 20.31)
Sutyna 27.75.423
Suwallia 8.8.5
svastra 25.69.27
Swaine Jack Pine Sawfly 25.6.4
swainei, Rhabdophaga 29.11.151
swaineri, Neodiprion 24.6.4
Swale Fly 20.79.8
Swallow Bug 20.20.3
Swallowtail and Allies Butterfly Family, supra 27.41.1
Swammerdamella 29.15.8
Swammerdamia 27.30.7
Sweat Bee Family, supra 25.66.1
Sweetclover Aphid 21.19.209
Sweetclover Root Borer 27.21.20
Sweetclover Weevil 24.113.50
Sweetfern Leaf Casebearer 27.55.282
Sweetpotato Flea Beetle 24.107.144
Sweetpotato Hornworm 27.70.1
Sweetpotato Leaf Beetle 24.107.49
Sweetpotato Leaf Roller 27.55.169
Sweet Potato Weevil 24.113.16
Sweetpotato Whitefly 21.18.12
Sweltsa 28.8.6
Swifts, supra 27.4.1
Sword-bearing Katydid 11.7.19
Sycamore Lace Bug 20.14.7
Sycamore Tussock Moth 27.73.55
Sycophila 25.20.9
Sydates 24.68.42
sydneyensis, Anarhopus 25.25.43
Syllectra 27.75.92
Syllepis 27.55.182
Syllepte 27.55.167
sylvanoides, Ochlodes 27.40.72
sylvanum, Acanosema 25.42.14

sylvia, Altica 24.107.127
Sylvicola 29.14.1
sylvinus, Satyrium 27.43.16
sylvosus, Physoconops 29.49.2
Symballophthalmus 29.42.8
Symbiochara 24.24.296
Symbiocladius 29.24.91
Symbiotes 24.81.6
Symboethus 25.16.67
Symmerista 27.71.17
Symmerus 29.9.4
Symmetrischema 27.23.49
Symmoca 27.17.1
Symmocinae, supra 27.17.1
Symmorphus 25.59.23
Symmyrmica 25.58.38
Sympetrum 7.7.26
Sympherobius 23.8.4
Sympherta 25.16.331
Symphora 24.98.34
symphoricarpi, Aphis 21.19.16
Symphoromyia 29.28.6
Symphya 25.13.95
Symphyla 10
Symphylus 20.3.10
Symphyomethses 24.56.21
Symphyothrips 22.5.67
Symphypleona, supra 1.6.1
Symphyta 25.1.1
Sympiesis 25.26.2
Sympistis 27.75.453
Symplecis 25.16.494
Symplecta 29.2.59
Symploce 14.5.3
Sympotthastia 29.24.39
Sympycnidelphus 29.43.39
Sympycnus 29.43.37
Sympyninae, supra 29.43.36
Symydobius 21.19.204
Synacra 25.42.17
Synaldis 25.13.110
Synallagma 27.19.2
Synanthedon 27.35.12
Synanthedonini, supra 27.35.12
Synapha 29.9.47
Synaphaeta 24.106.238
Synapte 27.40.44
Synarsis 25.45.5
Synaxis 27.61.142
Syncalypta 24.35.14
Syncalyptinae, supra 24.35.13
Syncerothrips 22.5.22
Synchita 24.93.5
Synchitini, supra 24.93.5
Synchlora 27.61.162
Synchlorini, supra 27.61.162
Synchroa 24.98.7
synchromus, Agonatopoides 25.51.16
Synchus 24.4.91
Synclera 27.55.147
Synclita 27.55.12
Syncopacma 27.23.69
Syndemis 27.38.76
Syndipnus 25.16.369
Syndyas 29.42.60
Syneches 29.42.59
Synedoida 27.75.105
Synerginae, supra 25.34.1
Synergs 25.34.2
Syneta 24.107.9
Synetaeris 25.16.415
Synetinae, supra 24.107.9
Synetocephalus 24.107.101
Syneura 29.46.22
Syngamia 27.55.183
Syngrapha 27.75.166

Synglochis 27.61.31
Synhalonia 25.69.21
Synneurid Gnat Family, supra 29.16.1
Synneuridae, supra 29.16.1
Synneuron 29.16.2
Synnevrus 25.62.75
Synnoma 27.38.88
Synocoelioxys 25.68.24
Synoecetes 25.16.332
Synoditella 25.43.4
Synodites 25.16.364
Synomelix 25.16.363
synonyms 17
Synopeas 25.44.17
Synophromorpha 25.34.4
Synophrus 25.34.3
Synorthocladius 29.24.120
Synorthodes 27.75.520
Synosis 25.16.300
Synploca 27.21.17
Synstrophus 24.98.11
Syntames 21.9.5
Syntemna 29.9.82
Syntexinae, supra 25.8.1
Syntexis 25.8.1
Synthesiomyia 29.100.52
Synthyridomyia 29.23.3
Syntomeida 27.73.87
Syntomium 24.24.155
Syntomopus 25.19.42
Syntomosphyrum 25.26.52
Syntormon 29.43.26
Syntretus 25.13.160
Syntrichalonia 25.69.22
Synxenodcrus 20.20.6
Syphrea 24.107.126
Syrmococcus 21.25.43
Syrbula 11.5.22
syringae, Podoscsia 27.35.14
syringella, Gracillaria 27.14.2
Syritta 29.47.85
syrphicola, Ethelurgus 25.16.113
Syrphidae, supra 29.47.1
Syrphinae, supra 29.47.3
Syrphini, supra 29.47.11
Syrphoctonus 25.16.469
Syrphoidea, supra 29.44.1, 29.47.1
Syrphophagus 25.25.113
Syrphophilus 25.16.475
Syrphus 29.47.12
Syrrhizus 25.13.133
Syspasis 25.16.248
Systasea 27.40.30
Systasis 25.19.56
Systelloderes 20.15.2
Systellogaster 25.19.125
Systellognatha, supra 8.5.1
Systellonotini, supra 20.23.137
systematics 7
Systena 24.107.121
Systenus 29.43.30
Systoechus 29.40.12
Systole 25.20.7
Systropinae, supra 29.40.6
Systropus 29.40.7
Syzeton 24.104.5
Syzetonini, supra 24.104.3
Syzeuctus 25.16.314

T

tabaci, Bemisia 21.18.12
tabaci, Thrips 22.4.53
tabacinum, Stilomedon 24.24.73
Tabanidae 29.26.1
Tabanini, supra 29.26.21

Tabanoidea, supra 29.25.1
Tabanomorpha, supra 29.25.1
Tabanus 29.26.26
tabascoensis, Priocnemella 25.60.13
tabeti, Paradiplocampta 29.40.48
tabida, Choetospilisca 25.19.24
tabida, Imaguncula 29.105.353
tabida, Monopsis 21.5.3
tabidus, Trachelus 25.12.6
Tabuda 29.32.15
Tabudamima 29.32.16
Tachardiella 21.32.1
Tachardiidae, supra 21.32.1
Tachardiobius 25.25.59
Tachina 29.105.89
tachinae, Glyphogaster 25.13.102
Tachinaephagus 25.25.114
Tachinidae, supra 29.104.1, 29.105.1
Tachininae, supra 29.105.82
Tachinini, supra 29.105.86
Tachinomorphus 24.24.182
Tachinomyia 29.105.292
Tachinophyto 29.105.265
Tachinus 24.24.183
Tachopteryx 7.1.1
Tachycines 11.9.5
Tachydromia 29.42.2
Tachydromiinae, supra 29.42.1
Tachyempis 29.42.3
Tachygoninae, supra 24.113.281
Tachygonus 24.113.281
Tachymelissodes 25.69.30
Tachypeza 29.42.1
Tachypompilus 25.60.26
Tachyporinae, supra 24.24.175
Tachyporus 24.24.184
Tachypterellus 24.113.207
Tachys 24.24.55
Tachysphex 25.62.42
Tachystizus 25.62.96
Tachyta 24.4.52
Tachytes 25.62.41
Tachytrechus 29.43.11
Tacoma 27.55.350
Tacparia 27.61.105
taedae linearis, Neodiprion 25.6.4
Taedia 20.23.188
Taeniandrena 25.65.1
Taeniaptera 29.51.8
Taeniapterinae, supra 29.51.4
taeniata, Olbiogaster 29.14.2
taeniatum, Doru 13.5.1
taeniatus, Aphrastus 24.113.107
taeniola, Zica 20.4.28
taeniolalis, Hyalorista 27.25.103
taeniolata, Macromia 7.5.2
Taenionema 8.2.5
Taeniopoda 11.4.6
Taeniopterygidae, supra 8.2.1
Taeniopteryginae, supra 8.2.6
Taeniopteryx 8.2.6
taeniorhynchus, Aedes 29.20.9
Taeniothrips 22.4.52
Tafallia 1.2.11
Tafalisca 11.10.26
tahoensis, Habrolinus 24.24.31
taiga 28
Takecallis 21.19.205
Talanini, supra 24.87.126
Talanus 24.87.126
Taleporiinae, supra 27.11.1
talidiformis, Crambodes 27.75.324
talis, Colomychus 27.55.149
Tallaperla 8.6.5
Tallula 27.55.267
Talponia 27.38.48

Tamalia 21.19.206
Tamarind Weevil 24.113.365
Tamarix Leafhopper 21.14.148
Tambiniinae, supra 21.5.1
Tambiniini, supra 21.5.1
Tamiophila 30.4.5
Tampa 27.55.406
Tanaemyrmex 25.58.66
Tanaoceridae, supra 11.301
Tanaocerus 11.3.1
Tanaodiplosis 29.11.81
Tanaops 24.68.8
Tanaostigmatinae, supra 25.24.1
Tanaostigmodes 25.24.1
Tanarthrus 24.102.4
Tangle-veined Fly Family, supra 29.39.1
Tannerocoris 20.23.71
tantilla, Ababa 24.67.3
tantilla, Satronia 27.38.46
Tanychela 25.16.435
Tanyderidae, supra 29.1.1
Tanyderoidea, supra 29.1.1
Tanygaster 24.107.115
Tanygona 27.21.5
Tanymecini, supra 24.113.54
Tanymecus 24.113.58
Tanyochraethes 24.106.121
Tanyoprymnus 25.62.91
Tanypeza 29.53.1
Tanypezid Fly Family, supra 29.53.1
Tanypezidae, supra 29.53.3
Tanypodinae, supra 29.24.5
Tanypodini, supra 29.24.7
Tanyptera 29.2.6
Tanypteryx 7.1.2
Tanypus 29.24.7
Tanyrhinus 24.24.134
Tanysaccus 27.8.6
Tanysphyrini, supra 24.113.179
Tanysphyrus 24.113.179
Tanytarsini, supra 29.24.74
Tanytarsus 29.24.83
tapetzella, Trichophaga 27.10.37, 27.10.39
Taphaeus 25.13.70
Taphrocerus 24.46.38
Tapinella 17.7.1
Tapinoma 25.58.61
Tapinomini, supra 25.58.57
Tarachidia 27.75.213
Taracticus 29.37.8
tarandi, Hypoderma 29.102.5
Taranomis 24.106.142
tarantula hawk 25.60.2
taraxaci, Phanacis 25.34.14
Tardigrada 10
Targionia 21.38.81
targionii, Ctenolepisma 5.3.3
Tarnania 29.9.23
tarnanii, Tarnania 29.9.23
Tarnished Plant Bug 20.23.166
Tarosteninae, supra 24.67.33
Tarpela 24.87.122
Tarpheion 25.13.130
Tarphiota 24.24.297
tarquinius, Feniseca 27.43.1 (Fig. 27.104)
tarsalis, Gynembia 9.3.2
tarsomeres 10
Tarsopsylla 30.7.16
Tarsostenus 24.67.33
tarsus (tarsi) 22
Tasiocera 29.2.61
taslei, Derancistrus 24.106.7 (Fig. 24.176)
Tastionenia 25.60.19
Tathorhynchus 27.75.43
tatila, Eunica 27.46.36
tauma, Syspasis 25.16.248

Taunaya 21.15.17
taurea, Melitoma 25.69.20
Tauriphila 7.7.27
taurus, Repipta 20.17.18
tautana, Sereda 27.38.52
Taxigramma 29.103.14
taxodii, Floridonus 21.14.115
taxodii, Sequoiomyia 29.11.102
Taxodiomyia 29.11.103
taxon (taxa) 7, 15
taxonomy 17
Taxonus 25.7.88
taxus, Aonidiella 21.38.7
Taxus Mealybug 21.25.16
Taygete 27.23.23
taygete, Oeneis 27.48.13
taylori, Halesochila 26.10.17
Taylorilygus 20.23.189
Tea Parlatoria Scale 21.38.62
Tea Scale 21.38.31
Tebenna 27.36.6
Tecnophilus 24.4.156
tecomae, Clydonopteron 27.55.253
Tedinus 24.88.9
Tegeticula 27.8.9
Tegrodera 24.101.11
Tehama 27.55.217
tela, Ruacodes 27.75.364
Telabis 24.87.13
Teladoma 27.21.11
Telamona 21.15.40
Telamonanthe 21.15.42
telea, Chlorostrymon 27.43.13
Teleas 25.43.27
Teleasinae, supra 25.43.27
Telebasis 7.11.13
Telebasis, supra 24.53.1
Telegeusis 24.53.1
Teleiodes 27.23.32
Teleiopsis 27.23.33
Telenominae, supra 25.43.30
Telenomus 25.43.32
Teleogryllus 11.10.12
Teleonemia 20.14.21
Teleorhinus 20.23.78
Telephanini, supra 24.72.24
Telephanus 24.72.24
Telephone-pole Beetle Family, supra 24.58.1
Telesicles 24.88.8
Telethusia 27.55.332
Teliapsocus 17.12.1
Teliusa 24.24.298
tellkampf, Neaphaenops 24.4.40
Telmatophilini, supra 24.74.17
Telmatophilus 24.74.17
Telmatoscopus 29.12.5
Telmaturgus 29.43.46
Teloleuca 20.32.7
Telomatogeton 29.24.139
Telomatogetoninae, supra 29.24.137
Telonaca 21.15.41
Telopelopia 29.24.17
Telothyriini, supra 29.105.225
Telotphlus 24.24.169
Telphusa 27.23.27
Telusus 21.14.205
Temelucha 25.16.441
Temnochila 24.66.13
Temnopsophus 24.68.3
Temnosoma 25.66.13
Temnostethus 20.21.3
Temnostoma 29.47.78
Tempyra 20.7.43
Tenaga 27.10.28
Tenagobia 20.35.1
Tenaspis 24.55.5

tenax, Eristalis 29.47.65
tenebricornis, Lineostethus 20.3.22
tenebricosa, Hemiblabera 14.6.2
tenebricosa, Melanaspis 21.28.49
tenebricosus, Scaphinotus 24.4.16
tenebrifera, Cerastis 27.75.576
Tenebrio 24.87.92
tenebrioides, Neatus 24.87.87
Tenebrionidae, supra 24.87.1
Tenebrioninae, supra 24.87.75
Tenebrionini, supra 24.87.75
Tenebrionoidea, supra 24.85.1
Tenebroides 24.66.14
tenebrosa, Slossonella 27.52.3
tenebrosa, Somatochlora 7.6.6
tenela, Lydellohoughia 29.105.248
tenellus, Circulifer 21.14.149
tenellus, Malacopterus 24.106.24
tenera, Cycnia 27.73.65 (Fig. 27.307)
tenerals 23
teneralis, Liopasia 27.55.162
Ten-lined June Beetle 24.30.66
Tenodera 14.1.10
Ten-spot 7.7.13
tenta, Sarcofahrtiamyia 20.103.43
Tenthredinidae, supra 25.7.1, 25.7.98
Tenthredininae, supra 25.7.89
Tenthredinini, supra 25.7.92
Tenthredinoidea, supra 25.3.1
Tenthredo 25.7.95
Tenthredopsini, supra 25.7.91
tenuiceps, Trophophion 25.16.458
tenuicornis, Cylapus 20.23.6
tenuicornis, Lichminus 24.43.3
tenuicornis, Vacronus 24.87.38
tenuifemur, Synetaeris 25.16.415
tenuilineatus, Colposternus 24.63.32
tenuipennis, Aeolophides 11.5.89
tenuipes, Tessaropa 24.106.34 (Fig. 24.180)
Tenuipetiolus 25.20.17
Tenuirostra 29.105.111
tenuirostris, Philocalia 29.105.299
Tenuirostritermes 15.4.5
tenuis, Baulius 24.102.14
tenuis, Corombius 25.16.85
tenuis, Dagamaea 1.4.9
tenius, Dalmosella 24.25.42
tenuis, Neladius 24.20.9
tenuis, Paragrilus 24.46.35 (Fig. 24.91)
tenuis, Rhamphocolus 24.113.396
tenuiventris, Townesia 25.16.6
Tephritidae, supra 29.61.1
Tephritis 29.61.25
Tephritoidea, supra 29.57.1
Tephrochlamys 29.84.8
Tephromyiopsis 29.103.48
Teracriini, supra 20.7.25
Terapus 24.26.54
Terastia 27.55.163
Teratembiidae 9.2.1
Teratocoris 20.23.202
terebintharia, Numia 27.61.74
Terebraella 25.16.202
terebrans, Dendroctonus 24.112.11
Terebrantia, supra 22.1.1
teres, Hemihoplis 25.16.223
Teretriinae, supra 24.26.6
Teretriosoma 24.26.7
Teretrius 24.26.6
tergata, Nicoletia 5.2.2
tergum (terga) 20
terlootii, Neophasia 27.42.2
Termatophylini, supra 20.23.19
terminalis, Acanthocephala 20.4.2
terminalis, Anastelgis 25.16.7

terminalis, Pissodes 24.113.171
terminalis, Rhodoneura 27.56.5
Termites 15.1.1
Termitidae, supra 15.4.1
Termitonidia 24.24.299
Termopsinae, supra 15.1.1
terna, Rasvena 8.8.4
ternarius, Bombus 25.70.2
Teropalpus 24.24.156
terracola, Foveoscapha 24.25.14
terraenovae, Protophormia 29.101.7
Terrapin Scale 21.26.11
terraria, Almodes 27.61.5
terrarium 49
terricola occidentalis, Bombus 25.70.2
tersa, Xylophanes 27.70.41 (Fig. 27.266)
Tersilochinae, supra 25.16.445
Tersilochus 25.16.449
Tessaratominae, supra 20.3.61
Tessaropa 24.106.34
tesselatum, Omophron 24.4.2 (Fig. 24.30)
tesselatus, Sperchopsis 24.12.15
tessellaris, Halysidota 27.73.55 (Fig. 27.302)
tessellata, Euxoa 27.75.544
tessellata, Platycleis 11.7.43
Tessellated Scale 21.26.5
tessellatella, Lindera 27.10.48
tessellatus, Eucalymnatus 21.26.5
tessellatus, Prociphilus 21.19.172
tessulatus, Goes 24.106.234
tessulatus, Liophloeus 24.113.42
testa, Proroblemma 27.75.211
testacea, Danae 24.81.14
testacea, Discothyrea 25.58.12
testacea, Neoscraptia 24.98.41
testacea, Pachyteles 24.4.6
testaceipennis, Leptohophlia 24.30.94
testaceipes, Lysiphlebus 25.14.4 (Fig. 25.16)
testaceipes, Orthizema 25.16.122
testaceus, Anacyptus 24.24.189
testaceus, Himatinum 24.113.374
testaceus, Leptinus 24.18.1 (Fig. 24.53)
testaceus, Neodasytes 24.68.48
testaceus, Phycocoetes 24.113.180
testudinarius, Cirrophthirius 18.1.11
testudinea, Acrotaenia 29.61.19
testudinea, Hoplocampa 25.7.18
Tesuquea 27.26.3
Tetanocera 29.79.19
Tetanocerinae, supra 20.79.7
Tetanolita 27.75.8
Tetanops 29.58.20
teter, Gymnaetron 24.113.231 (Fig. 24.288)
teterrellus, Crambus 27.55.203, see Parapediasia 27.55.216 in "Checklist."
Tethida 25.7.57
Tethinia 29.96.5
Tethinid Fly Family, supra 29.9.6.1
Tethinidae, supra 29.9.6.1
Tethymyia 29.24.88
tetra, Moromorpha 20.3.31
tetra, Satyrium 27.43.16
Tetrabaeus 25.44.4
Tetracanthella 1.4.1
Tetracis 27.61.143
Tetraclonia 27.50.5
Tetracneminae, supra 25.25.24
Tetracnemini, supra 25.25.40
Tetracnemopsis 25.25.48
Tetracnemus 25.25.42
Tetradonia 24.24.300
Tetradryinus 25.51.8
Tetragoneura 29.9.81

Tetragoneuria 7.6.7
Tetragonocephala 21.17.20
Tetragonoderus 24.4.138
Tetralaucopora 24.24.301
Tetraleurodes 21.18.16
Tetralina 24.24.303
Tetrallus 24.24.304
Tetralopha 27.55.268
Tetralophidea 25.25.157
Tetralophiellus 25.25.157
Tetramorini, supra 25.58.41
Tetramorium 25.58.42
Tetraneura 21.19.207
Tetraneurella 21.19.207
Tetraneuromyia 29.11.44
Tetranodus 24.106.128
Tetraonycini, supra 24.101.17
Tetraonyx 24.101.17
Tetraopes 24.106.299
Tetraopini, supra 24.106.299
Tetraphleps 20.21.6
Tetraplasta 25.32.6
Tetrapriocera 24.64.18
Tetrapsila 29.55.2
tetrapteralis, Xerophilaphis 21.19.223
Tetrarhoptra 25.32.1
Tetrascapha 24.25.13
Tetraschistis 27.55.247
Tetrasphaeropyx 25.13.60
Tetrastichini, supra 25.26.36
Tetrastichus 25.26.46
Tetratoma 24.98.1
Tetratominae, supra 24.98.1
Tetratomini, supra 24.98.1
Tctrigidae, supra 11.1.1
Tetriginae, supra 11.1.1
Tetrix 11.1.2
tetrophthalmus, Tetraopes 24.106.299
Tetropismenus 29.58.21
Tetropium 24.106.17
Tettigades 21.13.20
Tettigadinae, supra 21.13.20
Tettigellinan, supra 21.14.40
Tettigellini, supra 21.14.44
Tettigidea 11.1.5
Tettigoniidae, supra 11.7.1
Tettigoniinae, supra 11.7.49
Tetyra 20.3.1
Tetyrini, supra 20.3.1
Teuchogonomyia 29.2.47
Teucholabis 29.2.48
Teuchonemis 29.47.81
Teuchophorus 29.43.45
Texamaurops 24.25.69
texana, Agathis 25.13.76
texana, Anisembia 9.1.2
texana, Anthanassa 27.46.19
texana, Asterocampa 27.47.3
texana, Atta 25.58.55
texana, Esperanza 20.5.4
texana, Focillidia 27.75.137
texana, Glauraspidia 25.32.12
texana, Inna 24.4.50
texana, Lomamyia 23.11.1
texana, Megascelis 24.107.15
texana, Mermiria 11.5.23 (Fig. 11.11)
texana, Neohedobia 24.63.2
texana, Neosteingelia 21.23.4
texana, Psyrassa 24.106.59
texana, Triozocera 24.105.1
texanana, Ethelgoda 27.38.51
Texananus 21.14.142
texanus, Agapostemon 25.66.14
texanus, Araeoderes 24.109.23
texanus, Chalcedectus 25.19.10

texanus, Ctenopyga 25.58.5
texanus, Deltanus 21.14.222
texanus, Haideoporus 24.7.21
texanus, Hapalips 24.75.3
texanus, Heterobrenthus 24.110.4
texanus, Hypomachilodes 4.2.3
texanus, Ixodiphagus 25.25.102
texanus, Menoeceus 24.88.6
texanus, Platyprosopus 24.24.28
texanus, Pogonus 24.4.47
texanus, Renodaeus 20.23.129
texanus, Rhinomalus 24.72.20
texanus, Sphaerius 24.10.1
texanus, Trigonoscutoides 24.113.67
texanus, Vitellius 24.52.2
Texas Beetle 24.37.1
Texas Beetle Family, supra 24.37.1
Texas Leaf Cutting Ant 25.58.55
Texasa 29.58.37
texensis, Chorisoneura 14.5.7
texensis, Dejenaniopalpus 29.105.216
texensis, Texoreddellia 5.2.3
Texocoris 20.23.124
Texola 27.46.18
Texoreddellia 5.2.3
Thalassa 24.80.18
thalassinum, Meconema 11.7.48
Thalassomyia 29.24.137
Thalassosmittia 29.24.85
Thalassotrechus 24.4.46
thalesalis, Munroeodes 27.55.76
Thallophaga 27.61.107
Thalycra 24.70.23
Thamadiplosis 29.11.125
Thambospasta 24.101.1
Thamiaraea 24.24.305
Thamnoltettix 21.14.156
Thanasimus 24.67.15
Thanategia 29.42.16
Thaneroclerinae, supra 24.67.1
Thaneroclerus 24.67.1
tharos, Phyciodes 27.46.20
Tharsalea 27.43.2
Tharsus 24.87.113
Thasus 20.4.8
Thatuna 21.14.65
Thaumaglossa 24.61.9
Thaumalea 29.21.1
Thaumaleidae, supra 29.21.1
thaumasta, Apocrisias 27.73.59
Thaumastocoridae, supra 20.11.1
Thaumastoptera 29.2.17
Thaumatodryinus 25.51.9
Thaumatomyia 29.94.37
Thaumatopsis 27.55.215
theae, Fiorinia 21.38.31
theae, Parlatoria 21.38.62
theano, Eribia 27.48.10
Thecabius 21.19.208
thecata, Leskiopsis 29.105.225
Theclinae, supra 27.43.9
Theclini, supra 27.43.9
Thecodiplosis 29.11.115
Thecophora 29.49.7
Thecesterninae, supra 24.113.145
Thecesternus 24.113.145
Thecturota 24.24.306
Theisoa 27.23.8
Thelaira 29.105.172
Thelairini, supra 29.105.171
Thelairodoria 29.105.266
Thelia 21.15.48
Theliopsyche 26.11.2
Thelyasceta 27.23.88
Thelymia 29.105.433
Thematheca 29.105.267

themistocles, Polites 27.40.66
Theocolaxia 25.19.27
theona, Thessalia 27.46.13
Thera 27.61.197
Therasea 27.75.216
theresae, Clayia 18.6.8
Theresia 29.105.79
Theresiini, supra 29.105.73
Thereus 27.43.20
Thereva 29.32.14
Therevidae, supra 29.32.1
Therioaphis 21.19.209
Therion 25.16.380
thermarum, Gabronthus 24.24.6
Thermira 29.81.8
Thermobia 5.3.8
Thermonectini, supra 24.7.37
Thermonectus 24.7.38
Theroa 27.71.31
theroalis, Aristaria 27.75.12
Theronia 25.16.31
Theroniini, supra 25.16.31
Theroscopus 25.16.127
Thes 24.82.12
Thesalia 24.106.215
Thesiastes 24.25.29
Thesium 24.25.18
Thespieus 27.40.86
Thesprotia 14.1.5
Thessalia 27.46.13
Thevenemyia 29.40.209
theveneti, Matheteus 24.55.18
Thibetoides 25.16.62
Thicanus 24.102.9
Thick Barklice Family 17.7.1
Thick-headed Fly Family, supra 29.49.1
Thief Ant 25.58.33
thienemanni, Mesocricotopus 29.4.99
Thienemanniella 29.24.90
Thienemannimyia 29.24.18
Thinalmus 24.56.16
Thinobius 24.24.157
Thinocharis 24.24.75
Thinodromus 24.24.158
Thinophilus 29.43.17
Thinopinus 24.24.16
Thinoscatella 29.93.60
Thinoxenus 24.113.79
Thinusa 24.24.307
Thiomyia 29.93.58
Thionia 21.6.21
Thioniini, supra 21.6.21
Thioptera 27.75.193
Thirteen-Spotted Lady Beetle 24.80.43
Thistle Aphid 21.19.28
thoas, Heraclides 27.41.6
Tholera 27.75.511
thomasi, Hemiargus 27.43.40
thomasi, Parallothrips 22.5.16
thomomys, Mesachorutes 1.2.3
Thompsonomyia 29.105.112
Thomsoniscini, supra 25.25.124
Thopeutis 27.55.226
thoracica, Cyptonychia 27.75.354
thoracicus, Eros 24.57.8
thoracicus, Pterallastes 29.47.79
thoracicus, Syneches 29.42.59
Thoracochaeta 29.88.3
Thoracophorus 24.24.96
thorax 20, 21
thoreauini, Formicencyrtus 25.25.139
thoreyi, Tachopteryx 7.1.1
Thorictini, supra 24.61.2
Thorictodes 24.61.2
Thorn Bug 21.15.4
Thoron 25.43.23

Thorybes 27.40.16
Thorybothrips 22.5.71
thraso, Achlyodes 27.40.31
Thrassis 30.7.17
Thraulodes 6.7.7
Thread Bug 20.17.4
Thread-legged Bug 20.17.3 (Fig. 20.38)
Thread-legged Bug Family 20.17.1
Threadtailed Stonefly 8.1.10
Thread-waisted Wasps, supra 25.62.4
Threebanded Leafhopper 21.14.82
Three-cornered Alfalfa Treehopper 21.15.26
Three-lined Potato Beetle 24.107.13
Threelined Leafroller 27.38.70
Threespotted Flea Beetle 24.107.123
Threestriped Lady Beetle 24.80.26
Threnus 24.87.44
Threticus 29.12.9
Thricolema 24.107.10
Thricolepis 24.113.80
Thrimolus 24.91.4
Thrincopyge 24.46.5
Thrincopygini, supra 24.46.5
Thriopidea, supra 22.3.1
Thripidae, supra 22.4.1
Thripina, supra 22.4.35
Thripinae, supra 22.4.9
Thripini, supra 22.4.19
Thriposoma 25.26.39
Thrips, supra 22.1.1, 22.4.53
Thrips Family, supra 22.4.1
Thripsaphis 21.19.210
Thripsobreina 29.11.128
Throat Bot Fly 29.102.1
Throscidae, supra 24.49.1
Throscinae, supra 24.49.2
Throscini, supra 24.49.3
Throscinus 24.43.7
Throscoptilium 24.15.2
Thryallis 24.106.264
Thrypticus 29.43.22
thuiella, Argyresthia 27.31.1
thula, Colias 27.42.11
thule, Sthenopis 27.4.1
Thuleaphis 21.19.28
thulius, Vitavitus 24.113.147
thurbeiriae, Anthonomus 24.113.208
Thurberia Weevil 24.113.208
Thurberiphaga 27.75.10
Thyanta 20.3.45
Thyasophila 24.24.308
Thyatira 27.59.3
Thyatirid Moth Family, supra 27.59.1
Thyatiridae, supra 27.59.1
Thyatirinae, supra 27.59.1
Thyatirini, supra 27.59.3
thyatyroides, Eosphoropteryx 27.75.163
Thyce 24.30.71
Thylacites 24.113.43
Thylacitinae, supra 24.113.23
Thylacitini, supra 24.113.43
Thylochromus 20.7.39
Thylodrias 24.61.3
Thymalus 24.66.4
Thymaris 25.16.52
Thymelicus 27.40.60
Thymus 25.26.41
Thyrateles 25.16.243
Thyrazlia 27.39.3
Thyreion 27.75.602
Thyreocoridae, supra 20.2.1
Thyreodon 25.16.462
Thyridanthrax 29.40.60
Thyrididae, supra 27.56.1
Thyridinae, supra 27.56.1
Thyridomyia 29.23.3

Thyridopteryx 27.11.12
Thyridopyralis 27.55.274
Thyrinteina 27.61.89
Thyris 27.56.1
Thysandrena 25.65.1
Thysania 27.75.111
Thysanini, supra 25.25.22
Thysanoes 24.112.28
Thysanomastix 25.25.159
Thysanoptera, supra 22.1.1
Thysanopyga 27.61.79
Thysanura, supra 5.1.1 (Fig. 5.1)
Thysanus 25.25.23
thysbe, Hemaris 27.70.30 (Fig. 27.251)
tiahuicanus, Pompilus 25.60.28
Tiaja 21.14.11
tibia (tibae) 22
tibialis, Ceropales 25.60.34
tibialis, Lariversius 24.87.145
Tibicen 21.13.4
Tibiceninae, supra 21.13.1
Tibicenini, supra 21.13.3
Tibicininae, supra 21.13.13
Tibicinini, supra 21.13.14
Tibicinoides 21.13.14
Ticida 21.11.14
Tiger Beetle Family, supra 24.3.1
Tiger Moth 27.73.52
Tiger Moth Family, supra 27.73.1
Tiger-spotted Flower Lepturine 24.106.213
tigrinus, Anthrax 29.40.43
tigrinus, Goes 24.106.234
tigris, Malacosoma 27.68.11
tildeni, Tanyochraethes 24.106.121
Tildenia 27.23.53
Tile-horned Prionus 24.106.10
tiliae, Eucallipterus 21.19.76
tiliae, Gargaphia 20.14.11
tiliaria, Erannis 27.61.64
Tiliphagus 21.19.211
Tillini, supra 24.67.4
Tilloclytus 24.106.130
Tillomorphini, supra 24.106.127
timais, Xanthopastis 27.75.534
Timandrini, supra 27.61.184
Timarcha 24.107.58
Timarchini, supra 24.107.58
timberlake, Xeralictus 25.66.7
timberlakei, Mohavacris 11.3.2
timberlakei, Peponapis 25.69.29
Timberlakena 25.62.33
Timberlakia 25.25.60
Timema 10.3.1
Timema Family 10.3.1
Timematidae, supra 10.3.1
Timochares 27.40.33
Timodema 21.11.13
Timonidia 21.11.16
Timpanoga 6.13.8
Timulla 25.55.19
timuqua, Ceuthothrips 22.5.5
Tinagma 27.32.1
Tinalydella 29.105.268
tinamus, Erodiscus 24.113.196
tincta, Xenopelopia 29.24.19
tinctipennis, Circia 29.99.2
tinctoides, Mouralia 27.75.150
tinctus, Molannodes 26.15.2
Tinea 27.10.37
Tineidae, supra 27.10.1
Tineoidea, supra 27.10.1
Tineola 27.10.45
Tineophoctonus 25.25.78
Tingidae, supra 20.14.1
Tinginae, supra 20.14.1
Tingini, supra 20.14.1

Tingis 20.14.33
Tinobregmini, supra 21.14.34
Tinobregmus 21.14.34
Tinocallis 21.19.212
Tinodemus 24.77.4
Tinodes 26.2.2
Tinotus 24.24.309
Tinthiinae, supra 27.35.1
Tinthiini, supra 27.35.2
Tiphia 25.53.1
Tiphiid Wasp Family, supra 25.53.1
Tiphiidae, supra 25.53.1
Tiphiinae, supra 25.53.1
Tipnus 24.62.8
Tipula 29.2.9
Tipulidae, supra 29.2.1
tipuliformis, Synanthedon 27.35.12
Tipulinae, supra 29.2.1
Tipulini, supra 29.2.1
Tipulodinodes 29.2.9
Tipulogaster 29.37.2
Tipuloidea, supra 29.2.1
Tipulomorpha, supra 29.1.1
Tiqiuadra 27.10.46
Tirathabini, supra 27.55.275
Tisactia 24.74.14
Tischeria 27.7.1
Tischeriid Moth Family, supra 27.7.1
Tischeriidae, supra 27.7.1
tissoti, Schizoneurata 21.19.193
titan, Aellops 27.70.28 (Fig. 27.249)
titanella, Hypatopa 27.17.8
titania, Clossiana 27.46.11.
Titanogrypa 29.103.42
Titanosiphon 21.19.213
titillator, Monochamus 24.106.237
Tiphodytes 25.43.22
titus, Harkenclenus 27.43.15
tityus, Dynastes 24.30.114
Tlascala 27.55.330
Tmesiphorini, supra 24.25.79
Tmesiphorus 24.25.79
Tmetogaster 25.16.259
Tmetothrips 22.4.33
Tmolus 27.43.19
Toad Bug 20.39.1
Toad Bug Family, supra 20.39.1
Tobacco Budworm 27.75.599
Tobacco Flea Beetle 24.107.137
Tobacco Hornworm 27.70.4
Tobacco Moth 27.55.402
Tobacco Stalk Borer 24.113.316
Tobacco Thrips 22.4.41
Tobacco Wireworm 24.48.14 (Fig. 24.98)
tocullionana, Eucosma 27.38.25
Toed-winged Beetle Family, supra 24.38.1
togata, Xanthia 27.75.416
Togodolentus 20.7.40
tokionis, Lepidosaphes 21.38.45
Tolima 27.55.415
Tollius 20.5.10
Tolype 27.68.2
Tomato Bug 20.23.28
Tomato Fruitworm 27.75.599
Tomato Hornworm 27.70.4
Tomato Pineworm 27.23.52
Tomato Psyllid 21.17.11
tomentosus, Epitragodes 24.87.7
tomentosus, Eustrophus 24.98.10
tomentosus, Podabrus 24.56.5 (Fig. 24.109)
Tomicobia 25.19.110
Tominotus 20.1.6
Tomocerina 1.5.13
Tomocerinae, supra 1.5.13
Tomocerodes 25.19.35

Tomocerus 1.5.13
Tomoderinae, supra 24.102.17
Tomoderus 24.102.17
Tomoglossa 24.24.310
Tomolips 24.113.388
Tomolonus 1.5.13
Tomonotus 11.5.53
Tomophthalmae, supra 29.40.35
Tomoplagia 29.61.54
tomostethi, Glyptrorhaetus 25.16.329
Tomostethini, supra 25.7.56
Tomostethus 25.7.56
Tomosvaryella 29.48.7
Tomoxia 24.99.6
Tonchahua 25.62.58
Tonginae, supra 21.6.23
Tonibius 24.87.156
tontonus, Oliaronus 21.1.12
Toothed Flea Beetle 24.107.144
Tooth-legged Grasshopper 11.5.1
Tooth-necked Fungus Beetle Family, supra 24.59.1
topiaria, Chrysoteuchia 27.55.205
Toposcopus 24.100.3
Toraminae, supra 24.75.4
Toramus 24.75.4
Toreus 29.42.38
toreuta, Cydia 27.38.56
Tornado Wasp 25.60.24
Tornos 27.61.29
Toronia 27.37.9
Torosomyia 29.105.363
torquata, Xylomeira 24.64.20
torridus, Pachycoris 20.3.2
Torsalo, supra 29.102.2
Tortise Beetle, supra 24.107.174
Tortistilus 21.15.25
Tortoise-Shells 27.46.24
Tortopus 6.10.3
Tortricid Moth Family, supra 27.38.1
Tortricidia 27.52.2
Tortricidae, supra 27.38.1
Tortricinae, supra 27.38.60
Tortricini, supra 27.38.60
tortricis, Erynnia 29.105.339
tortricis, Hemisturmia 29.105.385
tortricis, Trichogrammatomyia 25.28.10
Tortricoidea, supra 27.38.1
Tortyra 27.36.8
Torvothrips 22.5.72
torvus, Apterodryinus 25.51.19
torvus, Syrphus 29.47.12 (Fig. 29.40)
Torymid Wasp Family, supra 25.18.1
Torymidae, supra 25.18.1
Torymus 25.18.6
Torynotachina 29.105.269
Tosale 27.55.249
Tosca 27.23.17
Toumeyella 21.26.22
Townesia 25.16.6
townsendi, Litasida 24.87.58
townsendi, Metastenus 25.19.129
Townsendia 29.37.15
Townsendiellini, supra 25.69.2
Townsendiellomyia 29.105.383
Toxares 25.14.2
toxicodendri, Adiplosis 29.11.122
Toxidium 24.23.6
Toxochilus 25.16.48
Toxomerini, supra 29.47.5
Toxomerus 29.47.5
toxoneura, Metangela 29.10.1
Toxonothrips 22.4.54
Toxonotus 24.109.18
Toxonprucha 27.75.124
Toxophora 29.40.5

Toxophorinae, supra 29.40.4
Toxophoroides 25.16.194
Toxoptera 21.19.214
Toxopterella 21.19.215
Toxorhina 29.2.63
Toxorhynchites 29.20.2
Toxorhynchitinae, supra 29.20.2
Toxotrypana 29.61.1
Trabeculus 18.1.59
Trachandrena 25.65.1
Trachceops 27.61.50
trachea 12, 22
Trachea 27.75.309
Tracheliodes 25.62.64
Trachelizini, supra 24.110.2
Trachelus 25.12.6
Tracheops 24.113.167
Trachusa 25.68.2
Trachycera 27.55.284
Trachyderini, supra 24.106.166
trachyderoides, Gnaphalodes 24.106.144
Trachykele 24.46.11
Trachylepidia 27.55.272
Trachyleucophenga 29.90.8
Trachymyrmex 25.58.53
Trachyopella 29.88.3
Trachyota 24.24.311
Trachypachinae, supra 24.4.1
Tracyhypachini, supra 24.4.1
Trachypachus 24.4.1
Trachyphloeini, supra 24.113.91
Trachyphloeus 24.113.91
Trachypus 25.62.107
Trachyrhachis 11.5.57
Trachyscelida 24.107.100
Trachyscelini, supra 24.87.130
Trachyscelis 24.87.130
Trachysida 24.106.214
Trachythrips 22.5.30
Trachytropis 24.109.15
Trafoia 29.105.113
tragiae, Cyphacma 27.15.42
Tragidion 24.106.151
Traginops 29.67.3
Tragosoma 24.106.11
Tragosomini, supra 24.106.11
Trama 21.19.216
Tramea 7.7.28
Tranosema 25.16.413
tranquebarica, Chrysobothris 24.46.23
tranquilla, Zotheca 27.75.409
transiens, Simulium 29.22.5
transita, Oxysarcodexia 29.103.38
transitans, Protentomon 2.2.2
transitella, Amyelois 27.55.297
transporting live insects 38
transvaalensis, Eumegastigmus 25.18.26
transversa, Didymops 7.5.1 (Fig. 7.8)
transversata,
 Prochoercodes 27.61.149 (Fig. 27.192)
Transverse Lady Beetle 24.80.42
transversoguttata richardsoni,
 Coccinella 24.80.42
trapezoidalis, Promachina 29.37.68
trapezium, Perissarthron 24.48.36
Trapezonotus 20.7.75
traps 35
Trathala 25.16.438
Traverella 6.7.8
Traxus 21.6.7
Trechitae, supra 24.4.37
Trechnites 25.25.127
Trechini, supra 24.4.37
Trechnitini, supra 25.25.125
Trechoblemus 24.4.37
Trechus 24.4.45

tredecimnotata, Epilachna 24.80.52
tredecimpunctata, Hippodamia 24.80.43
tredecimpunctatus, Rhodobaenus 24.113.369
Tree Thrips Family, supra 22.3.1
Treehopper Family, supra 21.15.1
Trefoil Seed Chalcid 25.20.21
Treherniella 22.5.73
Trematopygodes 25.16.336
Trematopygus 25.16.328
Tremex 25.9.4
Tremicinae, supra 25.9.4
tremuloidiella, Phyllonorycter 27.14.19
Trepidulus 11.5.55
Trepobaris 24.113.309
Trepobates 20.27.8
Trepobatinae, supra 20.27.7
Tretoserphus 25.39.4
Tretothoracidae 24.87.169
trevoris, Andrena 25.65.1
Triacanthagyna 7.4.11
Triacanthella 1.2.5
Triachora 29.105.367
Triachus 24.107.28
Triaenodes 26.18.7
Trialeurodes 21.18.17
trianata, Aceratagallia 21.14.15
triangle, paper 37
triangularis, Antipletca 27.62.3
triangularis, Aphodiplosis 29.11.105
triangularis, Ascius 21.14.91
triangularis, Disonycha 24.107.123
triangularis, Hydrophilus 24.12.6
triangulifer, Graphisurus 24.106.273 (Fig. 24.207)
triannulatus, Psilometriocnemus 29.24.125a)
Triarius 24.107.105
Triarthron 24.19.1
Triaspis 25.13.139
Triatoma 20.17.39
Triatominae, supra 20.17.38
Tribalinae, supra 24.26.29
Tribalister 24.26.48
tribalteata, Stenostrophia 24.106.213
tribe 15
Tribelos 29.24.72
Tribolium 24.87.110
tribulella, Anascostia 27.55.417
Tricampa 3.1.4
Trichacis 25.44.11
Trichacorynus 24.113.378
Trichadenotecnum 127.23.10
Trichaetipyga 21.15.30
Trichagrotes 27.75.526
Trichalophus 24.113.123
Trichaltica 24.107.136
Trichareaa 29.103.46
Trichastylopsis 24.106.282
Tricheleodes 24.87.140
Trichiasida 24.87.57
Trichiinae, supra 24.30.116
Trichina 29.42.57
Trichinorhipis 24.46.19
Trichinosmia 25.68.21
Trichinothrips 22.5.74
Trichiocampus 25.7.17
Trichiorhyssemus 24.30.30
Trichiosoma 25.5.2
Trichiotes 24.87.25
Trichiotinus 24.30.117
Trichiusa 24.24.312
Trichobaris 24.113.316
Trichobiinae, supra 29.108.1
Trichobius 29.108.2
Trichocallis 21.19.210
Trichocanonura 24.106.271
Trichocellus 24.4.117

Trichocera 29.13.2
Trichocerapoda 27.75.495
Trichoceridae, supra 29.13.1
Trichoceroidea, supra 29.13.1
Trichochlamys 29.84.23
Trichochroides 24.68.41
Trichochronellus 24.68.37
Trichochrous 24.68.36
Trichoclea 27.75.476
Trichoclinocera 29.42.31
Trichocorixa 20.35.19
Trichocosmia 27.75.470
Trichodectes 18.2.9
Trichodectidae, supra 18.2.1
Trichoderulus 24.87.136
Trichodes 24.76.18
Trichodesma 24.63.22
Trichodezia 27.61.236
Trichodirabius 24.113.350
Trichofeltia 27.75.527
Trichogramma 25.28.8
Trichogrammatid Wasp Family,
 supra 25.28.1
Trichogrammatidae, supra 25.28.1
Trichogrammatomyia 25.28.9
Trichogorytes 25.62.84
Trichohelea 29.23.3
Tricholabus 25.16.235
Tricholepidion 5.1.1
Tricholipeurus 18.2.10
Tricholita 27.75.531
Tricholochmaea 24.107.80
Tricholytia 29.105.14
Trichomagdalis 24.113.198
Trichomalus 25.19.103
Trichomasthus 25.25.115
Trichomma 25.16.383
Trichomyia 29.12.1
Trichomyiinae, supra 29.12.1
Triochonta 29.9.38
Trichonychina, supra 24.25.16
Trichonyx 24.25.16
Trichopalpus 29.98.20
Trichopasites 25.69.4
Trichopepla 20.3.27
Trichophaga 27.10.39
Trichophya 24.24.186
Trichophyinae, supra 24.24.186
Trichoplexia 27.75.255
Trichoplusia 27.75.152
Trichopoda 29.105.5
Trichopodini, supra 29.105.4
Trichopolia 27.75.525
Trichopria 25.42.28
Trichopseniinae, supra 24.24.187
Trichopsenius 24.24.187
Trichopsidea 29.39.3
Trichopsomyia 29.47.34
Trichopsychoda 29.12.7
Trichopsylloides 30.4.20
Trichoptera, supra 26.1.1
trichoptera, Paracladura 29.13.3
Trichopteromyia 29.11.11
Trichopteryx 27.61.250
Trichopticoides 29.100.34
Trichoptilus 27.58.6
Trichordestra 27.75.483, not in
 "Checklist."
Trichorthosia 27.75.524
Trichoscapa 25.58.48
Trichosilia 27.75.541
Trichosteresis 25.46.1
Trichotanypus 29.24.3
Trichotaphe 27.23.87
Trichotepyris 25.48.6
Trichoteras 25.34.18

Trichothaumalea 29.21.2
Trichotichnus 24.4.134
Trichotipula 29.2.9
Trichoton 24.87.158
Trichromia 27.73.73
Trichrysis 25.50.18
Tricimba 29.94.26
tricincta, Erythroneura 21.14.82
Triclistus 25.16.288 (Fig. 25.17)
Triclonella 27.21.12
tricolor, Cerathosia 27.75.200
tricolor, Hemileuca 27.69.7 (Fig. 27.223)
tricolor, Isotomurus 1.4.20 (Fig. 1.6)
tricolor, Latheticomyia 29.50.1
tricolor, Metadexia 29.105.195
tricolor, Whymperia 25.16.172
triconis, Messiomyia 29.105.306
tricornis, Oliveria 29.24.126
Tricorynus 24.63.43
Tricorythidae, supra 6.14.1
Tricorythodes 6.14.1
Tricrania 24.101.21
trictura, Cascadoperla 8.7.4
Tricyphona 29.2.22
Tricyphus 25.16.258
Tridactylidae, supra 11.6.1
tridens, Pachybrachis 24.107.30 (Fig. 24.119)
tridens, Trichrysis 25.50.18
Tridentaforma 27.8.8
tridentata, Arthroneura 29.40.20
tridentata, Saperda 24.106.296
Tridepia 27.75.475
Tridiscus 21.25.44
Trieces 25.16.286
Trielidini, supra 25.56.1
Trielis 25.56.1
Trientoma 24.87.22
Trientomini, supra 24.87.22
Triepeolus 25.69.9
trifasciata, Lounsburyia 25.25.15
trifasciatus, Hadrotettix 11.5.63
trifida, Triacanthagyna 7.4.11
trifolii, Dasineura 29.11.152
trifolii, Discestra 27.75.472 (Fig. 27.375)
trifolii, Therioaphis 21.19.209
trifurcata, Cerotoma 24.107.97
Triglyphothrix 25.58.41
Triglyphulus 24.113.121
trigona, Bertholdia 27.73.72
Trigonalid Wasp Family, supra 25.47.1
Trigonalidae, supra 25.47.1
Trigonaloidea, supra 25.47.1
trigonana, Lotisma 27.24.1
Trigonarthris, supra 24.106.172, 24.106.223
Trigonidiinae, supra 11.10.20
Tritoniophtalmus 4.1.6
Trigonodemus 24.24.135
Trigonodera 24.100.2
Trigonoderini, supra 25.19.12
Trigonoderus 25.19.16
Trigonogenius 24.62.3
Trigonogya 24.46.40
Trigonometopus 29.82.19
Trigonomma 29.94.38
Trigonopeltastes 24.30.119
Trigonoplectus 24.25.26
Trigonopselaphus 24.24.17
Trigonorhinus 24.109.20
Trigonoscuta 24.113.29
Trigonoscutoides 24.113.67
Trigonotylus 20.23.203
Trigonura 25.21.11
Trigonurus 24.24.89
triguttatus, Ephelops 24.113.211
trilineata, Lema 24.107.13 (Fig. 24.215)

trilineatus, Neoptychodes 24.106.232
Trilobe Scale 21.38.68
Trilobita 10
trilobitiformis, Pseudaonidia 21.38.68
Trilobomyza 29.68.6
trilobus, Breviscapus 29.12.13
Trilophyrobata 29.51.2
triloris, Erucophaga 29.103.31
trimaculata, Hartigia 25.12.2
trimaculata, Macropsis 21.14.17
trimaculella, Eccritothrix 27.10.42
trimaculella, Eido 27.15.38
Trimenopon 18.8.1
Trimenoponidae, supra 18.8.1
Trimerina 29.93.28
Trimerinoides 29.93.29
Trimeromicrus 25.19.126
Trimerotropis 11.5.62
Trimicra 29.2.59
Trimicrops 25.19.30
Trimiina, supra 24.25.33
Trimiomelba 24.25.43
Trimioplectus 24.25.28
Trimitomerus 24.90.2
Trimorus 25.43.28
Trimytini, supra 24.87.19
Trimytis 24.87.19
Trinodini, supra 24.61.5
trinotata, Trichobaris 24.113.316
Trinoton 18.6.35
Triocnemis 27.75.457
Triodoclytus 24.106.119
Triogma 29.2.13
Trionymus 21.25.45
Triopasites 25.69.14
Triopsis 29.11.123
Triorophini, supra 24.87.23
Triorophus 24.87.23
Trioxina, supra 25.14.13
Trioxini, supra 25.14.12
Trioxys 25.14.14
Trioza 21.17.10
Triozinae, supra 21.17.10
Triozocera 24.105.1
Triozosneura 27.55.305
Triphleba 29.46.4
Triphosa 27.61.206
Triplacinae, supra 24.76.5
Triplax 24.76.5
Triplicitipula 29.2.9
Triploechus 29.40.9
Triprocris 27.50.4
Tripudia 27.75.181
tripunctata, Acanthopteroctetes 27.3.1
tripunctata, Lygropia 27.55.169
tripunctata, Neomuscina 29.100.53
tripunctata, Oberea 24.106.297
triquetra, Ervia 29.105.194
triquetra, Homalodisca 21.14.41 (Fig. 21.19)
triquetrana, Nola 27.75.179
Trirhabda 24.107.77
trirhodus, Longicaudus 21.19.118
Trisacantha 25.43.29
Trisanteon 25.51.4
Trischidias 24.112.39
Trischistognatha 27.55.75
Trischiza 25.31.16
Triscolia 25.56.7
triseriata, Scelidacantha 27.61.248
trisignata, Harrisimemna 27.75.236
Trisignina, supra 24.25.23
Trisignis 24.25.23
Trisoleniella 25.34.40
trispinosa, Stenodema 20.23.201
Trissolcus 25.43.34

Trissopelopia 29.24.25
tristigmus, Euschistus 20.3.34
tristis, Anasa 20.4.27 (Fig. 20.24)
tristis, Lapsus 24.42.9
tristis, Morpholeria 29.84.16
tristis, Prolepsis 29.37.39
tristriatus, Ochrolitus 24.77.13
Tristyla 27.75.445
trisyllaba, Macrophya 25.7.96
tritici, Brachycolus 21.19.29
tritici, Frankliniella 22.4.41
tritici, Harmolita 25.20.3 (Fig. 25.21)
Tritneptis 25.19.114
Tritoma 24.76.6
tritoma, Eutrias 25.32.3
Tritoxa 29.58.22
Tritozyga 29.11.25
Triuncidia 27.55.82
Trivialia 29.82.20
trivialis, Hoplia 24.30.85 (Fig. 24.71)
trivittata, Acalymma 24.107.93
trivittata, Taeniaptera 29.51.8
trivittata, Tipula 29.2.9 (Fig. 29.12)
trivittatus, Hedeiodiscus 29.31.37
trivittatus, Leptocoris 20.6.8 (Fig. 20.26)
trivittatus, Padaeus 20.3.35
trivittatus, Ptecticus 29.31.9
trivittis, Odontonyx 24.34.5
Trixagus 24.49.4
Trixini, supra 29.105.47
Trixodes 29.105.46
Trixodini, supra 29.105.46
Trixoscelidid Fly Family, supra 29.85.1
Trixoscelididae, supra 29.85.1
Trixoscelis 29.85.4
Triznaka 8.8.7
Trjapitizinellus 25.25.63
trochanter 22
Trochiliphagus 18.7.2
Trochiolodes 29.105.150
Trochiloecetes 18.7.3
trochilus, Rhaphiomidas 29.36.1
Trochopus 20.28.1
Troctomorpha, supra 17.5.1
Trogastrina, supra 24.25.11
Trogidae, supra 17.2.1
Trogiinae, supra 17.2.1
Troginae, supra 24.30.43
Trogiomorpha, supra 17.1.1
Trogium 17.2.4
Troglanillus 24.4.61
Trogloderus 24.87.141
Troglomathes 24.56.20
Trogoderma 24.61.13
Trogomorpha 25.16.267
Trogoninirmus 18.1.60
Trogossitidae, supra 24.66.1
Trogossitinae, supra 24.66.8
Trogoxylini, supra 24.65.3
Trogoxylon 24.65.3
Trogus 25.16.262
Trogusina, supra 25.16.231
Trogusini, supra 25.126.256
Troidini, supra 27.41.2
troilus, Pterourus 27.41.7 (Fig. 27.83)
Tromatobia 25.16.12
Trophimus 24.68.2
Trophithauma 29.46.24
Trophodeinus 29.46.37
Trophophion 25.16.458
Tropical Barklice Family 17.5.1
Tropical Damesfly Family 7.10.1
Tropical Nasutiform Termite 15.4.4
tropical rain forest 29
Tropical Sod Webworm 27.55.179
tropicalis, Ophisma 27.75.132

Tropicanus 21.14.147
Tropicini, supra 24.42.10
Tropicus 24.42.10
Tropicolabus 25.16.281
Tropideres 24.109.14
Tropidia 29.47.84
Tropidiplosis 29.11.120
Tropidischia 11.9.7
Tropidocephalini, supra 21.2.4
Tropidolophus 11.5.46
Tropidosteptes 20.23.190
Tropiduchid Planthopper Family, supra 21.5.1
Tropiduchidae, supra 21.5.1
Tropiphorus 24.113.136
Tropisternus 24.12.4
Trosia 27.51.1
Trotteria 29.11.148
Trout-stream Beetle Family 24.5.1
Trox 24.30.43
Troyminae, supra 25.18.5
truculentus, Phrixocnemis 11.9.14
Trudestra 27.75.473
True Cave Crickets 11.9.8
True Katydid 11.7.16
True Katydids, supra 11.7.14
True Wasp Family 25.59.1
Trumpet-net Caddisfly Family, supra 26.3.1
truncata, Lirimiris 27.71.38
truncataria, Epelis 27.61.10
truncatus, Apotemnus 25.16.109
truncatus, Hemiphileurus 24.30.112
truncatus, Prostephanus 24.64.7
Trunip Aphid 21.19.117
Trupanea 29.61.24
Trybliographa 25.32.6
trybomi, Calacanthia 20.32.6
Trychosis 25.16.157
Trypanisma 27.23.22
Trypargilum 25.62.51
Trypeta 29.61.50
Trypetisoma 29.82.21
Trypetoptera 29.79.20
Trypheromyia 29.105.270
Trypherus 24.56.3
Tryphon 25.16.67
Tryphoninae, supra 25.16.47
Tryphonini, supra 25.16.56
Trypodendron 24.112.53
Trypophloeus 24.112.33
Trypoxylini, supra 25.62.49
Trypoxylon 25.62.51
Tryptodema 27.10.36
tryxus, Xenophanes 27.40.29
Tsinilla 27.38.17
tsugae, Neodiprion 25.6.4
Tsugaea 29.105.434
Tsugaspidiotus 21.38.82
Tube-forming Desert Termite 15.4.3
Tube-making Caddisfly Family, supra 26.3.1
Tube-net Caddisfly Family, supra 26.2.1
Tube-tailed Thrips Family, supra 22.5.1
Tuber Flea Beetle 24.107.137
tuber, Merope 28.3.1
tuberculata, Ethiscia 21.6.6
tuberculata, Peltastia 24.59.2
tuberculata, Vandykea 24.106.26
tuberculatum, Ectatomma 25.58.9
Tuberculatus 21.19.217
tuberculatus, Biomorphus 24.87.76
tuberculatus, Eumerus 29.47.57
Tuberculoides 21.19.217
tuberis, Epitrix 24.107.137
Tuberolachnus 21.19.218
tubifera, Axelsonia 1.4.19

tubiformans, Gnathamitermes 15.4.3 (Fig. 15.5)
Tubulifera, supra 22.5.1
Tujunga 29.58.23
tulcis, Anthanassa 27.46.19
Tule Beetle 24.4.74
Tulip Bulb Aphid 21.19.67
tulipae, Dysaphis 21.19.76
Tuliptree Aphid 21.19.122
Tuliptree Scale 21.26.22
Tullbergia 1.3.4
Tusla 27.55.331
tumana, Lednia 8.1.3
Tumbling Flower Beetle 24.99.5
Tumbling Flower Beetle Family, supra 24.99.1
tumida, Phymacysta 20.14.17
tumida, Pseudanthoecia 27.75.304
Tumidiclava 25.28.13
Tumidiscapus 25.25.7
tumidula, Acrulia 24.24.103
tumifex, Paradiplosis 29.11.117
Tunga 30.1.2
Tunginae, supra 30.1.1
Tungini, supra 30.1.2
Tundra 27
Tupelo Leaf Miner 27.8.2
Tuponia 20.23.72
turbata, Colostygia 27.61.195
turbatella, Arequipa 27.55.206
turbidella, Crocidomera 27.55.287
Turbopsebius 29.38.6
Turboscymnus 24.80.7
turgiceps, Perdita 25.65.15
Turkey Gnat 29.22.5
trumalis, Husseyella 20.28.3
turneri, Eosentoimon 2.1.1
Turnip Maggot 29.99.8
Turpentine Borer 24.46.15
Turpilia 11.7.13
turrita, Vibrissina 29.105.273
Turtle Beetle Family, supra 24.41.1
Turuptiana 27.73.41
Tusked Mayflies 6.8.1
Tuskless Burrower Mayfly Family 6.8.1
Tussock Moth Family, supra 27.74.1
Twice-stabbed Lady Beetle 24.80.23
Twig Girdler 24.106.260
Twig Pruner 24.106.73
Twiningia 21.14.127
Twinnia 29.22.3
Twin-spot Sphinx 27.70.15
Twin-tailed Tiger Swallowtail 27.41.7
Two-banded Fungus Beetle 24.87.102
Two Circuli Mealybug 21.25.32
Two Seta Pine Scales 21.23.2
Two-lined Chestnut Borer 24.46.34
Two-lined Collops 24.68.1
Two-lined Spittle Bug 21.12.1
Two-marked Treehopper 21.15.8
Two-spotted Lady Beetle 24.80.38
Two-spotted Stink Bug 20.3.68
Two-striped Grasshopper 11.5.94
Tychiinae, supra 24.113.220
Tychiini, supra 24.113.228
Tychini, supra 24.25.56
Tychius 24.113.228
Tychocampa 3.1.2
Tylana 21.6.23
Tylandrena 25.65.1
Tylanira 21.6.20
Tylcus 24.106.118
Tylicus 24.35.3
Tylocentrus 21.15.2
Tylocerina 24.106.269

Tyloderma 24.113.258
Tylodina, supra 24.113.245
Tylomyza 29.68.5
Tylonotus 24.106.49
Tylopius 25.16.287
Tylosis 24.106.160
Tylothrips 22.5.75
Tylozygus 21.14.45
Tymnes 24.107.46
Tymnophorus 25.16.476
Tympanophorus 24.24.18
Tyndarichus 25.25.79
Tyndarini, supra 24.46.31
Tyndaris 24.46.31
type specimen 6
Typhaea 24.91.2
typhaeus, Merocoris 20.4.1
Typhedanus 27.40.8
Typhloceuthophilus 11.9.19
Typhlocyba 21.14.81
typhlocybae, Neodryinus 25.51.11
Typhlocybella 21.14.80
Typhlogastrura 1.2.2
Typhlusechini, supra 24.87.32
Typhlusechus 24.87.32
Typhoctes 25.55.2
Typhoctinae, supra 25.55.2
Typocerus 24.106.209
Typophorus 24.107.49
Typopsilopa 29.93.31
Typopsilopini, supra 29.93.31
Tyria 27.73.29
Tyrini, supra 24.25.72
Tyrissa 27.75.113
tyrtaeus, Monca 27.40.48
Tyrus 24.25.72
Tyttholeon 23.14.5
Tytthonyx 24.56.16
Tytthotyle 11.4.3
Tytthus 20.23.73

U

ualbum, Iodopepla 27.75.283
Uchidella 25.16.123
Uclesia 29.105.168
Udamopyga 29.103.47
Udea 27.55.105
Udeocorini, supra 20.7.42
Udeopsylla 11.9.11
Ufa 27.55.345
ufeini, supra 27.75.590
Ufens 25.28.5
Ufeus 27.75.590
Uglynest Caterpillar 27.38.74
uhleri, Ceuthophilus 11.9.10 (Fig. 11.41)
uhleri, Chlorochroa 20.3.29
uhleri, Craspeduchus 20.7.1
uhleri, Horistonotus 24.48.71
uhleri, Oeneis 27.48.13
Uhleriola 20.7.69
Uhler's Camel Cricket 11.9.10
Uinta 27.55.423
Ula 29.2.21
Uleiota 24.72.22
Uleiotini, supra 24.72.21
ulicis, Apion 24.113.21 (Fig. 24.269)
Ulidiinae, supra 29.58.25
Ulidiotites 29.58.24
Ulixes 21.6.19
ulkei, Bystus 24.81.4
ulkei, Ceratomegilla 24.80.44
ulkei, Lihonthus 24.19.13
ulkei, Microsternus 24.76.2
Ulkeus 24.26.53

ulmerina, Molanna 26.15.1
ulmi, Altica 24.107.127
ulmi, Corythucha 20.14.7
ulmi, Fenusa 25.7.52
ulmi, Fissuraspis 21.38.32
ulmi, Lepidospahes 21.38.45
ulmi, Plocetes 24.113.223
ulmi, Tetraneura 21.19.207
ulmiarrosorella, Canarsia 27.55.362
ulmicola, Colopha 21.19.54
ulmifoliella, Coleophora 27.18.1
ulmifolii, Tinocallis 21.19.212
ulmifusa, Kaltenbachiella 21.19.1
Ulochaetes 24.106.171
Ulolonche 27.75.516
Uloma 24.87.114
Ulomini, supra 24.87.106
Ulomorpha 29.2.37
Ulophora 27.55.349
Uloporus 24.87.168
Ulosomus 24.113.261
ultraria, Parexcelsa 27.61.94
ultronia, Catocala 27.75.148
Ululodes 23.15.2
Ulus 24.87.148
umbellulariae, Euthoracphis 21.19.79
Umbonia 21.15.4
umbrata, Heterocampa 27.71.29 (Fig.
 27.274)
umbraticus, Probatius 24.106.294
umbroides, Dictya 29.79.8
Umoka 21.14.212
Unadilla 27.55.373
Unamis 24.24.136
Unaspis 21.38.83
uncatoides, Psylla 21.17.27
uncimanus, Parathrachelizus 24.110.2
uncinata, Clasiopella 29.93.26
uncinata, Pyrgocorypha 11.7.20
uncinatus, Microphthirus 19.5.2
undata, Distenia 24.106.303 (Fig. 24.210)
undata, Pyrgota 29.60.1 (Fig.29.43)
undatus, Lagocheirus 24.106.275
undatus, Thryallis 24.106.264
undecimpunctata howardi,
 Diabrotica 24.107.90 (Fig. 24.229)
undecimpunctata undecimpunctata,
 Diabrotica 24.107.90
underwoodi, Eucorethra 29.19.3
undosa, Chaetostomella 29.61.42
Undulambia 27.55.5
undulana, Orthotaenia 27.38.13
undulata, Eudesmula 24.93.10
undulata, Hydria 27.61.209
undulata, Notonecta 20.33.3 (Fig. 20.63)
undulatella, Hulstia 27.55.360
undulatus, Typhedanus 27.40.8
Ungulate Louse Family, supra 19.3.1
ungulatus, Policocnemis 27.75.383
unguttus, Plutothrix 25.19.15
unica, Diphleps 20.23.1
unica, Heydenia 25.19.8
unicolor, Boros 24.90.3
unicolor, Camptops 29.103.26
unicolor, Micranoplium 24.106.76
unicolor, Misogada 27.71.27
unicolor, Nosodendron 24.60.1
unicolor, Plesiomma 29.37.30
unicolor, Rhanidea 24.81.7
unicolor, Tipnus 24.62.8
unicolorella, Oreana 27.55.320
Unicorn Caterpillar Moth 27.71.34
unicornis, Schizura 27.71.34 (Fig. 27.275)
unicus, Crossocerus 25.62.63
unifasciatus, Somotrichus 24.4.145

uniformis, Hemileuca 27.69.7
uniformis, Macrodactylus 24.30.80
uniformis, Nanus 24.113.52
uniglumis, Oxybelus 25.62.55
unigui ulatus, Lestes 7.9.2 (Fig. 7.21)
unilineatus, Megaphthalmoides 29.98.9
unio, Eudryas 27.75.239 (Fig. 27.352)
uniophila, Molanna 26.15.1
unipilum, Clemelis 29.105.414
Uniptera 21.4.2
unipuncta, Psdeudaletia 27.75.499 (Fig.
 27.383)
unipunctana, Rhopobota, see
 naevana 27.38.40
unipunctata, Cicindela 24.3.4
unipunctata, Nymphocixia 21.1.10
unipunctata, Physonota 24.107.177 (Fig.
 24.146)
Unique-headed Bug Family 20.15.1
unispinosa, Acanthochalcis 25.21.9
unispinosus, Scolytus 24.112.23
univittata, Compsobata 29.51.2 (Fig.
 29.41)
univittatus, Tarsostenus 24.67.33
univittatus, Plagioneurus 29.43.12
Untomia 27.23.70
upiformis, Spondylis 24.106.12
Upiga 27.55.55
Upis 24.87.93
Uramya 29.105.201
Uramyini, supra 29.105.198
Urania 27.64.1
Uranid Moth Family, supra 27.64.1
Uraniidae, supra 27.64.1
Uranotaenia 29.20.6
Urbanus 27.40.12
Uresiphita 27.55.100
Urgleptes 24.106.292
uroceriformis, Sannuna 27.35.15
Urocerus 25.9.2
Urodera 24.107.19
Urodexiini, supra 29.105.202
Urodus 27.30.8
Urola 27.55.222
Urolepis 25.19.108
Uroleucon 21.19.219
Uromelan 21.19.219
Urophora 29.61.3
Urophyllopsis 29.105.271
Uroplatini, supra 24.107.168
Urosigalphus 25.13.140
Ursia 27.71.33
ursina, Engelhardtia 27.75.530
ursina, Paracotalpa 24.30.88
ursinis, Pycnocoris 20.23.183
Ursogastra 27.75.523
Ursophyto 29.105.80
urticaria, Xanthotype 27.61.84 (Fig.
 27.183)
Uscana 25.28.17
Uscodys 27.55.237
Usechimorpha 24.87.171
Usechini, supra 24.87.170
Usechus 24.87.170
Usingeriessa 27.55.16
Usingerina 20.38.1
ustulata, Scoliaphleps 29.98.2
ustulata, Tylana 21.6.23
Usurper Bee 25.70.3
Utacapnia 8.43.9
utahensis, Durocapillata 21.19.66
utahnus, Dixianus 21.14.145
Utamphorophora 21.19.220
Utaperla 8.8.10
Utetheisa 27.73.27

Utobium 24.63.6
UV lights 33
uvae, Diaspidiotus 21.39.24
Uzelia 1.4.2

V

Vacciniina 27.43.51
vaccinii, Acrobasis 27.55.282
vaccinii, Contarinia 29.11.108
vaccinii, Cucullococcus 21.25.13
vaccinii, Frankliliella 22.4.41
vaccinii, Scleroracus 21.14.165
vacculella, Ochsenheimeria 27.12.1 (Fig.
 27.219)
Vacronini, supra 24.87.36
Vacronus 24.87.38
Vacusus 24.102.12
vadosus, Graphorhinus 24.113.36
vadulatus Hormorus 24.113.100
vaga, Blattella 14.5.1
vaga, Myrmecopora 24.24.269
vaga, Schistocerca 11.5.114
Vagabond Crambus 27.55.203
vagabunda, Mordvilkoja 21.19.139
vagans, Ceratocombus 20.24.1
vagans, Composia 27.73.2
Vagrant Grasshopper 11.5.114
Valda 24.25.60
Valdiini, supra 24.25.60
Valdivia 27.55.357
valens, Dendroctonus 24.112.11
valens, Gyronycha 24.24.248
Valentibulla 29.61.35
valentinei, Troglanillus 24.4.61
Valentinia 27.17.10
Valenus 24.106.287
Valginae, supra 24.30.120
valgum, Macrobaenetes 11.9.20
Valgus 24.30.120
valida, Halticotoma 20.23.122
validus, Leptinillus 24.18.2
validus, Pseudanthonomus 24.113.215
validus, Rhachocnemis 11.9.13
Valifictorus 11.10.12
vallicola, Orasturmia 29.105.388
vallicularia, Soyedina 8.1.10 (Fig. 8.5)
valta, Pentobesa 27.71.18
Valtissius 20.7.30
vana, Speleobama 24.25.5
vanderwulpi, Chaetonodexodes 29.105.202
Vanderwulpia 29.105.215
Van Duzee Treehopper 21.15.33
Vanduzeea 21.15.33
vanduzeei, Blaisdelliana 24.80.11
vanduzeei, Coelopa 29.77.1
vanduzeei, Esselenia 11.5.7
vanduzeei, Patara 21.9.4
Vanduzeeina 20.3.15
Vandykea 24.106.26
vandykei, Eumesocampa 3.1.5
vandykei, Occiephelinus 24.24.120
vandykei, Oligembia 9.2.1
vandykei, Platidiolus 24.4.69
vandykei, Stylops 24.105.2 (Fig. 24.175)
vandykei, Vicelva 24.24.173
vaneecki, Liothrips 22.5.49
Vanessa 27.46.27
Vanhornia 25.39.1
Vanhorniinae, supra 25.39.1
vanillae, Agraulis 27.46.1
vannals 22
vaporariorum, Trialeurodes 21.18.17

variabilis, Boernerina 21.19.27
variabilis, Pseudorthosia 27.75.547
variabilis, Rhadiurgus 29.37.78
variabilis, Sericothrips 22.4.12
Variable Flower Lepturine 24.106.176
Variable Oak Leaf Caterpillar
 Moth 27.71.30
varaiana, Acleris 27.38.61
varians, Osphya 24.98.38 (Fig. 24.166)
varians, Torymus 25.18.6 (Fig. 25.19)
varians, Zeugophora 24.107.8 (Fig.
 24.213)
variation 18, 23
varicornis, Epaenasomyia 25.25.133
varicornis, Eucaerus 24.4.152
Varied Carpet Beetle 24.61.8 (Fig. 24.117)
variegata, Ancyronyx 24.45.3
variegata, Derophthalma 20.23.155
Variegated Cutworm Moth 27.75.555
Variegated Fritillary 27.46.7
Varicgated Mud-loving Beetle Family,
 supra 24.42.1
variegatum, Leichenum 24.87.167
variegatus, Astyleiopus 24.106.285
variegatus, Dicranopselaphus 24.34.11
variegatus, Zethus 25.59.25
varieties 19
variolosum, Asterolecanium 21.35.1
varius, Liosphex 25.61.3
varivestis, Epilachna 24.80.52
Varna 25.7.20
Varneria 27.55.407
varus, Cryptophagus 24.74.6
Vasaces 24.97.11
Vatellini, supra 24.7.3
Vatinae, supra 14.1.12
vau-album, Nymphalis 27.46.25
Vaxi 27.55.223
Vectura 24.68.28
Vecturoides 24.68.22
vedalia 24.80.33
Vegetable Leaf Miner 29.68.8
Vegetable Weevil 24.113.142
veins 21
Velataspis 21.38.84
velatella, Diachorisia 27.10.4
velatus, Rhynchites 24.113.6
velda, Coloradia 27.69.6
Veliidae, supra 20.28.1
Veliinae, supra 20.28.5
Vella 23.14.13
velleda, Tolype 27.68.2 (Fig. 27.209)
Vellica 24.24.137
Velocia 29.105.272
velutina, Anchycteis 24.34.6
velutinana, Argyrotaenia 27.38.71
velutinipes, Woodiphora 29.46.16
Velvet Ant Family, supra 25.55.1
Velvet Water Bug Family, supra 20.30.1
Velvetbean Caterpillar Moth 27.75.85
Velvety Shore Bug Family, supra 20.40.1
venatus vestitus, Sphenophorus 24.113.366
venerabilis, Agrotis 27.75.535
venosa, Megaparia 29.105.52
venosoma, Bactra 27.38.3
ventralis, Gnamplonychia 27.73.11
ventralis, Nematus 25.7.32
ventralis, Rhyzobius 24.80.30
ventralis, Saprosites 24.30.24
ventralis, Scolytus 24.112.23
ventricosum, Chrysotoxum 29.47.11
ventricosus, Haemodipus 19.7.4
Venturia 25.16.396
Venusia 27.61.235
venusta, Pepsis 25.60.2
venusta, Phaenopsis 29.105.406

venusta, Rickera 8.7.3
venustella, Leucospilapteryx 27.14.13
venustula, Meronera 24.24.266
venustulus, Anisopilothrips 22.4.1
venustus, Cryptocephalus 24.107.25 (Fig.
 24.217)
Veraphis 24.20.14
Veratra 25.7.60
verbasci, Anthrenus 24.61.8
verbasci, Campylomma 20.23.39
Verbena Bud Moth 27.38.7
Verbenapis 25.65.12
Verdanus 21.14.191
verdugoensis, Bycombia 27.59.6
veris, Doliponta 24.24.228
veritata, Trichopteryx 27.61.250
vermiculata, Gnophaela 27.73.1
vermiforme, Eosentomon 2.1.1
Vermileo 29.34.1
Vermileoid Fly Family, supra 29.34.1
Vermileonidae, supra 29.34.1
Vermipsyllidae, supra 30.3.1
verna, Pompeius 27.40.68
vernalis, Ctenicera 24.48.37
vernata, Paleacrita 27.61.63
vernix, Anaquedius 24.24.21
Vernoniella 18.1.61
Veromessor 25.58.27
Verrallia 29.48.2
verrucosus, Crytophorus 24.106.131 (Fig.
 24.198)
verruculatus, Trimerotropis 11.5.62
versicolor, Anatralata 27.55.35
versicolora, Plagiodera 24.107.67
Vertagopus 1.4.23
vertebrata, Xestopelta 25.16.470
vertebratus, Promachus 29.37.66 (Fig.
 29.32)
verticalis, Aeshna 7.4.1
verticalis, Anatropis 24.30.130
verticalis, Ischnura 7.11.10
verticillatus, Lophocomus 25.26.75
verticis, Potamanthus 6.9.1
vesicatoria, Lytta 24.101.13
Vesicephalus 1.7.5
Vesiculaphis 21.19.221
vesiculosa, Lepthemis 7.7.11
vesiculosus, Anajapyx 3.3.1 (Fig. 3.3)
Vespa 25.59.26
vespa, Beyeria 24.24.208
vesparum, Sphecophaga 25.16.188
vespertinus, Conoderus 24.48.14
Vespidae, supra 25.59.1
Vespiform Thrip 22.1.7
vespiformis, Franklinothrips 22.1.7
Vespina 27.8.4
Vespinae, supra 25.59.26
Vespoidea, supra 25.59.1
vespoides, Prichardomyia 29.37.51
vespoides, Pseudomasaris 25.59.2
Vespula 25.59.27
vespulae, Reesa 24.61.16
vesta, Phyciodes 27.46.20
vestigialis, Condylorhiza 27.55.154
Vestiplex 29.2.9
Vestistilus 21.15.29
vestita, Epicometis 24.30.129
vestita, Saperda 24.106.296
vestitus, Perenthis 24.113.301
vestitus, Sphenophorus 24.113.366
vestitus, Stenocorus 24.106.176
vetusta, Orgyia 27.74.3
vexans, Aedes 29.20.9 (Figs. 29.25,
 29.26)
vexator, Lutzomyia 29.12.2
vexatrix, Adejeania 29.105.90

vexillorum, Matsucoccus 21.23.2
vflavum, Oinophila 27.10.51
vialis, Amblyscirtes 27.40.80
vians, Kuschelina 24.107.150 (Fig.
 24.242)
viatoria, Rhammatocerus 11.5.13
vibrans, Habrophlebia 6.7.2
Vibrissina 29.105.273
Vibrissotheresia 29.105.81
viburni, Dentiflbula 29.11.124
viburnicola, Ceruraphis 21.19.49
vuburniphila, Aphis 21.19.15
Viburnum Aphid 21.19.15
vicaria, Sisyra 23.13.2
vicarius, Emblethis 20.7.73
vicarius, Oeciacus 20.20.3
Vicelva 24.24.173
Viceroy 27.46.33
viciae, Megoura 21.19.125
vicina, Andrena 25.65.1
vicina, Dichelonyx 24.30.81
vicinella, Ceratophaga 27.10.40
vicinum, Amphelasma 24.107.92
vicinus, Scapteriscus 11.11.3 (Fig. 11.49)
victorensis, Curculio 24.113.200 (Fig.
 24.283)
victoria, Asticta 27.75.78
victoria, Echinomyia 29.105.89
Vidius 27.40.47
vidleri, Erebia 27.48.10
vidua, Catocala 27.75.148
viduata, Schistoglossa 24.24.289
viduus, Scaphinotus 24.4.16
Viehoperla 8.6.6
vierecki, Neomymar 25.27.16
vigil, Wohlfahrtia 29.103.20
vigilax, Neoborops 20.23.168
vigintiquatuorpunctata,
 Subcoccinella 24.80.53
vilhelmina, Araeopteron 27.75.212
Villa 29.40.57
villicornis, Eucrossus 24.106.41
villiger, Ptinus 24.62.10
villosus, Allopogonia 24.34.3
villosus, Elaphidionoides 24.106.73
villosus, Merapioidus 29.47.74
Vincenzellus 24.90.11
vincibilis, Oronotus 25.16.200
vinctus, Carabus 24.4.12 (Fig 24.31)
vindemiae, Pachycrepoideus 25.19.69
vindex, Phanaeus 24.30.11 (Fig. 24.66)
Vine Borer 27.35.8
Vinemina 27.61.56
violae, Andrena 25.65.1
violae, Noetoxoptera 21.19.151
violacea, Vulsirea 20.3.49
violaceus, Sminthurides 1.7.1
violaceus, Staphylinus 24.24.13
Violet Aphid 21.19.151
Violet Dancer 7.11.4
Violet Rove Beetle 24.24.13
Violet Sawfly 25.7.84
Vipio 25.13.35
virescens, Heliothis 27.75.599
virescens, Upiga 27.55.55
virgata, Ferrisia 21.25.19
virgifera, Diabrotica 24.107.90
virginalis, Anovia 24.80.32
virginalis, Platyprepia 27.73.47
virginana, Sericoptera 27.61.153
Virginia Creeper Deathwatch
 Beetle 24.63.37
Virginia Creeper Leafhopper 21.14.82
Virginia-creeper Sphinx 27.70.40
Virginia Pine Sawfly 25.6.4
virginica, Ctenucha 27.73.74 (Fig. 27.312)

virginica, Spilosoma 27.73.37 (Fig. 27.286)
virginica virginica, Xylocopa 25.69.46
virginiensis, Artogeia 27.42.5
virginiensis, Calephelis 27.44.2
virginiensis, Milesia 29.47.82
virginiensis, Vanessa 27.46.27 (Fig. 27.134)
virginiensis virginiensis, Anisota 27.69.5
virginicus, Aphanotrechus 24.4.42
virgo, Apantesis 27.73.52 (Fig. 27.295)
virgulae, Ectoedemia 27.5.2 (Fig. 27.17)
viridata, Acasis 27.61.249
Viridemas 27.75.436
viridescens, Paratrachea 27.75.310
viridiaeneus, Rhinosimus 24.90.10 (Fig. 24.159)
viridicyaneus, Typophorus 24.107.49
viridifasciata, Chortophaga 11.5.35
viridifrons, Anthaxia 24.46.21 (Fig. 24.87)
viridimaculta, Burksia 25.26.50
viridimicans Nautes 24.87.122
viridis, Actina 29.31.3
viridis, Antichloris 27.73.81
viridis, Callophrys 27.43.24
viridis, Coccus 21.26.4
viridis, Glaphyrocanthon 24.30.5
viridis, Isotoma 1.4.23
viridis, Phaedon 24.107.65
viridis, Schoutedenia 21.19.194
viridivallois, Glyphocystis 27.55.318
viridiventris, Cladotanytarsus 29.24.82
viridula, Japanagromyza 29.68.2
viridula, Nezara 20.3.51
Viriliricta 29.32.17
visaliella, Chloropleca 27.10.18
Visoka 8.1.11
Vitacea 27.35.5
Vitavitus 24.113.147
vitch, Bruchid 24.108.15
viteana, Endopzia 27.38.4
vitellinipes, Hypolethia 25.32.10
Vitellius 24.52.2
viticida, Fidia 24.107.54
viticola, Pygmaeopsis 24.106.256
vitifoliae, Phylloxera 21.21.1
vitis, Erythraspides 25.7.73
vitis, Evoxysoma 25.20.20
vitis, Pulvinaria 21.26.19
vitispomum, Schizomyia 29.11.73
vitreipennis, Stencris 11.5.74
vitripennis, Hyaliodes 20.23.12
vitripennis, Nasonia 25.19.107
vittata angustipennis, Ctenophora 29.2.6
vittata, Apantesis 27.73.52 (Figs. 27.299, 27.300)
vittata, Epicauta 24.101.14 (Fig. 24.169)
vittata, Ercta 27.55.110
vittata, Metacmaeops 24.106.193
vittata, Trialeurodes 21.18.17
vittatalis, Contiger 27.55.10
vittatum, Acalymma 24.107.93 (Fig. 24.231)
vittatum, Parallelomma 29.98.27
vittatum, Psiolopleura 27.73.83
vittatum, Simulium 29.22.5
vittatus, Chrysops 29.26.11
vittatus, Collops 24.68.1
vitticolis, Pyrotrichus 24.106.178
vittifrons, Podoschistus 25.16.38
vittiger, Chelinidea 20.4.18 (Fig. 20.23)
vittigherta, Paranaemia 24.80.46
vittipennis, Magdalinops 24.113.201
Vitula 27.55.396
vituli, Linognathus 19.2.1
vobisne, Platytes 27.55.208

Volonetus 20.7.47
Volucella 29.47 41
Volucellini, supra 29.47.41
volucris, Eupeodes 29.47.15
vomitoria, Calliphora 29.101.16
Voria 29.105.169
Voriini, supra 29.105.153
Vostox 13.3.1
vouchering 6
Vrilletta 24.63.34
vulgare, Orchelimum 11.7.23 (Fig. 11.32)
vulgaris, Systoechus 29.40.12
Vulgichneumon 25.16.215
vulgivagellus, Crambus 27.55.203, see Agriphila 27.55.206 in "Checklist."
vulnerata, Lytta 24.101.13
vulnerea, Pseudohadena 27.75.295
vulpeculus, Monoychus 24.113.282
Vulsirea 20.3.49

W

Wagneria 29.105.170
Wahlgrenia 29.100.44
Wahlgreniella 21.19.222
Wakulla 27.55.405
Waldheimia 25.7.72
Waldheimiini, supra 25.7.72
walkeri, Apodemia 27.44.7
walkeri, Palaeodipteron 29.5.1
Walkingsticks 10.1.1
wallacei, Herbertia 25.19.60
wallacei, Spinadis 6.6.12
Wallengrenia 27.40.67
walleyi, Phytomyptera 29.105.319
wallisi, Cyphea 24.24.219
wallula, Conozoa 11.5.61 (Fig. 11.18)
Wallula Grasshopper 11.5.61
Walnut Aphid 21.19.52
Walnut Caterpillar Moth 27.71.2
Walnut Husk Fly 29.61.44
Walnut Scale 21.38.73
Walnut Shoot Moth 27.55.282
Walnut Sphinx 27.70.17
Walshia 27.21.20
Walshomyia 29.11.1578
walsinghami, Phereoeca 27.10.35
walsinghami, Pterophorus 27.58.16
Walterella 27.75.372
walteri, Dorcadothrips 22.4.39
walterorum, Saturnia 27.69.10
Warble Fly Family, supra 29.102.1
Wardrobe Beetle 24.61.6
Warmkea 29.23.3
Wart Hog Louse, infra 18.8.1
washingtoniana, Gibsonomyia 29.105.180
wasmanni, Paralimulodes 24.16.2
Wasmanniella 29.11.14
Wasp Family 29.49.3
Wasplike Longhorn 24.106.151
Wasps, supra 25.1.1
Water Boatman Bug Family, supra 20.35.1
Watercress Leaf Beetle 24.107.65
Watercress Sharpshooter 21.14.47
waterhousii, Phaedromnus 24.107.152
Water Lily Aphid 21.19.186
Water Lily Beetle 24.107.4
Waterlily Leaf Beetle 24.107.79
Waterlily Leaf Cutter 27.55.12
Water Penny Beetle 24.36.1 (Fig. 24.78)
Water Penny Beetle Family, supra 24.36.1
Water Prince 7.6.1
Water Scavenger Beetle Family, supra 24.12.1
Waterscorpion Bug Family, supra 20.36.1
Water Springtail 1.1.1

Water Strider Bug Family, supra 20.27.1
Water Treader Bug Family, supra 20.29.1
watersoni, Cephalonomia 25.48.14
watsoni, Adistemia 24.82.7
watsoni, Ctenodactylomyia 29.11.91
wawona, Atractelmis 24.45.5
webbi, Chalcolepidius 24.48.9 (Fig. 24.97)
Webbing Clothes Moth 27.10.45
Webbing Coneworm 27.55.339
Weberacantha 1.4.7
Webspinners 9.1.1
Web-spinning Sawfly Family 25.2.1
websteri, Aroga 27.23.59
websteri, Asphondylia 29.11.74
websteri, Cyclosattus 24.87.164
Websteriana 29.105.62
Weda 20.3.18
Wedge-shaped Beetle Family, supra 24.100.1
weedi, Rhamphomyia 29.42.37 (Fig. 29.35)
Weevillike Planthopper Family, supra 21.6.1
Weevils, supra 24.1.1
weidemeyerii, Basilarchia 27.46.33
Welderella 27.55.376
Wesmaelia 25.13.161
Wesmaelius 23.8.3
West Coast Lady 27.46.27
West Indian Cane Weevil 24.113.367
West Indian Sweet Potato Weevil 24.113.260
westcotti, Trchoblemus 24.4.37
Western Balsam Bark Beetle 24.112.46
Western Bean Cutworm 27.75.545
Western Bigeyed Bug 20.7.18
Western Black Flea Beetle 24.107.114
Western Blackheaded Budworm 27.38.61
Western Bloodsucking Conenose 20.17.39
Western Brown Stink Bug 20.3.34
Western Bumble Bee 25.70.2
Western Cedar Bark Beetle 24.112.12
Western Cedar Borer 24.46.11
Western Cherry Fruit Fly 29.61.44
Western Chicken Flea 30.7.2
Western Chinch Bug 20.7.16
Western Corn Borer 27.55.228
Western Corn Rootworm 24.107.90
Western Damsel Bug 20.18.5
Western Drywood Termite 15.2.4
Western Eyed Click Beetle 24.48.7
Western Field Wireworm 24.48.27
Western Firefly 24.55.11
Western Flower Thrips 22.4.41
Western Grape Leaf Skeletonizer 27.50.1
Western Grape Rootworm 24.107.55
Western Harvester Ant 25.58.24
Western Hemlock Looper 27.61.130
Western Lily Aphid 21.19.122
Western Milkweed Longhorn 24.106.299
Western Mountain Flower Longhorn 24.106.189
Western Oak Looper 27.61.130
Western Peach Tree Borer 27.35.12
Western Pigmy Blue 27.43.37
Western Pine Beetle 24.112.11
Western Plant Bug 20.23.67
Western Potato Flea Beetle 24.107.137
Western Potato Leafhopper 21.14.77
Western Raspberry Fruitworm 24.84.2
Western Rose Chafer 24.30.80
Western Smoke Fly 29.45.2
Western Spotted Cucumber Beetle 24.107.90
Western Spruce Budworm 27.38.72
Western Striped Cucumber Beetle 24.107.93
Western Striped Flea Beetle 24.107.114
Western Subterranean Termite 15.3.1

Western Tailed Blue 27.43.41
Western Tent Caterpillar Moth 27.68.11
Western Thatching Ant 25.58.72
Western Tiger Swallowtail 27.41.7
Western Treehole Mosquito 29.20.9
Western Tumblebug 24.30.2
Western Tussock Moth 27.74.3
Western Velvet Ant 25.55.16
Western Wheat Aphid 21.19.29
Western Widow 7.7.13
Western W-marked Cutworm
 Moth 27.75.560
Western Yellowjacket 25.59.27
Western Yellow-striped Armyworm
 Moth 27.75.326
westwoodi, Tetracnemopsis 25.25.48
Wetmorea 20.23.5
Wharf Borer 24.97.4
Wheat Head Armyworm Moth 27.75.497
Wheat Jointworm 25.20.3
Wheat Midge 29.11.144
Wheat Stem Maggot 29.94.50
Wheat Stem Sawfly 25.12.4 (Fig. 25.12)
Wheat Strawworm 25.20.3
Wheat Wireworm 24.48.40
Wheel Bug 20.17.12
wheeleri, Battigrassiella 5.2.1
wheeleri, Ecitonidia 24.24.231
wheeleri, Eosentomon 2.1.1
wheeleri, Paralucilia 29.101.4
wheeleri, Pheidoloxenus 25.25.154
wheeleri, Xanionotum 29.46.34
Whirligig Beetle Family, supra 24.9.1
White Admiral 27.46.33
White Apple Leafhopper 21.14.81
White-banded Elm Leafhopper 21.14.99
White Beach Tiger Beetle 24.3.4
White Butterfly Family, supra 27.42.1
White Cutworm Moth 27.75.544
White-fir Needle Miner 27.38.41
Whitefaced Hornet 25.59.27
Whitefly Family 21.18.1
White-fringed Longhorn 24.106.232
White-legged Mayflies 6.1.7
White-lined Grasshopper 11.5.62
White-lined Sphinx 27.70.42
White-marked Tussock Moth 27.74.3
Whitemarked Fleahopper 20.23.69
White-marked Spider Beetle 24.62.10
White Mountain Fritillary 27.46.11
White Oak Borer 24.106.234
White-patched Butterfly 27.46.13
White Peach Scale 21.38.69
White Pine Aphid 21.19.53
White Pine Cone Beetle 24.112.63
White Pine Cone Borer 27.38.25
White Pine Sawfly 25.6.4
White Pine Weevil 24.113.171
White-scaled Flower Weevil 24.113.328
White-shouldered House Moth 27.15.37
White-spotted Sawyer 24.106.237
White-tailed Skimmer 7.7.24
White Tiger Swallowtail 27.41.7
White Tree Cricket 11.10.18
White Underwing 27.75.148
Whitneyomyia 29.26.25
whittieri, Quaylea 25.25.124
Whymperia 25.16.172
wickhami, Calligrapha 24.107.62
wickhami, Erimerus 25.18.9
wickhami, Jalysus 20.12.2
wickhami, Parmenonta 24.106.242
wickhami, Trientoma 24.87.22
Wickham's Calligrapha 4.107.62
Widow 7.7.13
Wiedemannia 29.42.29

Wilcoxia 29.37.53
wilda, Leptothorax 25.58.37
wilkella, Andrena 25.65.1
Willemia 1.2.10
willingana, Proteoteras 27.38.32
willingii, Lejota 29.47.62
williamsi, Cryptococcus 21.30.1
Williamsiella 22.5.76
Williamsonia 7.6.8
willistoni, Ceriana 29.47.68
Willistonina 29.37.17
Willow Aphid 21.19.15
Willow-beaker Gall Midge 29.11.147
Willow Cone Gall 29.11.151
Willow Fairy Moth 27.8.16
Willow Leaf Beetle, Gray 24.107.80
Willow Leaf Beetle, Imported 24.107.67
Willow Longhorn 24.106.123
Willow Redgall Sawfly 25.7.33
Willow Sawfly 25.7.32
Willow Shoot Sawfly 25.12.3
Willow Stem Gall 29.11.151
Willowsia 1.5.6
wilsoni, Platypus 24.111.1 (Fig. 24.258)
wilsoni, Xerociris 27.75.238
wiltii, Acrotaphus 25.16.25
Window Fly 29.33.1
Window Fly Family, supra 29.33.1
Window-Winged Moth Family,
 supra 27.56.1
Wing 21
Wing Louse 18.1.35
wing venation 6
Winged Bush Cricket 11.10.20
Winged Walkingstick Family 10.2.1
Wingless Bat Fly Family, supra 29.107.1
Wingless Hangingfly 28.1.1
Wingless Mountain Grasshopper 11.5.97
Winnemana 25.26.38
winnemana, Erixestus 25.19.55
winnemana, Leptocera 29.88.3
Winnemanella 25.60.9
Winnertzia 29.11.33
Winnertziini, supra 29.11.32
Winter Crane Fly Family, supra 29.13.1
Winter Moth 27.61.238
Winter Stonefly Family 8.2.1
Winthemia 29.105.390
Winthemiini, supra 29.105.375
wirthi, Neopsilopa 29.93.27
wirthi, Pellucidomyia 29.23.22
Wirthia 29.43.15
Wirthomyia 29.23.5
wisconsinensis, Rophalophorus 25.13.158
wislizeni, Cysteodemus 24.101.5
wistariae, Dysmiciccus 21.25.16
witticki, Perothops 24.51.1
woglumi, Aleurocanthus 21.18.1
Wohlfahrtia 29.103.20
Wolcottia 24.67.21
Woldstedtius 25.16.472
Wood Gnat 29.14.1
Wood Gnat Family, supra 29.14.1
Wood Wasp Family, supra 25.10.1
Wood Wasps, supra 25.8.1
Woodiphora 29.46.16
Woods Firefly 24.55.16
Woods Weevil 24.113.88
Woolly Alder Aphid 21.19.172
Woolly Apple Aphid 21.19.74
Woolybear Moth 27.73.34
Woolly Elm Aphid 21.19.74
Woolly Pear Aphid 21.19.74
Woolly Pine Scale 21.26.18
Woolly Whitefly 21.18.9
Wormaldia 26.1.3

Wounded-tree Beetle Family, supra 24.60.1
wrighti, Calephelis 27.44.2
wrighti, Dinapate 24.64.9
wrighti, Togodolentus 29.7.40
wrighti, Toposcopus 24.100.3
wrightii, Ammophila 25.62.14
Wright's Thread-waisted Wasp 25.62.14
Wrinkled Bark Beetle Family, supra 24.2.1
Wrinkled Grasshopper 11.5.39
Wroughtonia 25.13.65
Wunderia 27.55.364
Wyeomyia 29.20.3
Wyliea 29.37.76
wyomingensis, Paropomala 11.5.75

X

xami, Xamia 27.43.27
Xamia 27.43.27
Xanionotum 29.46.34 (Fig. 29.39)
Xanthaciura 29.61.36
Xanthandrus 29.47.8
xanthenes, Eccoptura 8.9.5
Xanthia 27.75.416
xanthialis, Portentomorpha 27.55.104
xanthioides, Perigea 27.75.332
xanthipes, Epicerchysius 25.25.138
Xanthippus 11.5.41
Xanthocampoplex 25.16.428
Xanthocampsomeris 25.56.3
xanthocephala, Clastoptera 21.12.7
Xanthocera 29.105.192
Xanthochlorus 29.43.43
Xanthochroa 24.97.3
Xanthochroina 24.97.16
Xanthoepalpus 20.105.101
Xanthogaleruca 24.107.81
Xanthogramma 29.47.21
xanthoides, Gaeides 27.43.4
Xantholininae, supra 24.24.29
Xantholobus 21.15.51
Xanthomelanodes 29.105.6
xanthomelas, Disonycha 24.107.123
xanthomelas, Parevander 24.106.164
xanthometata, Millilla 27.61.11
Xanthomyia 29.61.15
Xanthonia 24.107.53
Xanthopastis 27.75.534
Xanthophysa 27.55.63
Xanthophyto 29.105.121
Xanthopyginae, supra 24.24.14
Xanthopygus 24.24.19
Xanthorhoe 27.61.224
Xanthorhoini, supra 27.61.224
Xanthosuarus 25.68.22
Xanthostege 27.55.98
xanthostoma, Tropidischia 11.9.7
Xanthoteras 25.34.21
Xanthothrix 27.75.352
Xanthotype 27.61.84
xanthoxyli, Diorymeropsis 24.113.337
xanthoxyli, Zygobarella 24.113.342
Xantippe 27.55.257
Xarifa 24.63.9
Xenarcha 25.13.44
Xenelmis 24.45.25
Xenicopoda 24.24.138
Xeninae, supra 24.105.7
Xenistusa 24.24.188
Xenoborus 20.23.190
Xenochaeta 29.61.16
Xenochaetina 29.82.22
Xenochalepus 24.107.165
Xenochile 25.55.20
Xenochironomus 29.24.43
Xenodusa 24.24.313

Xenoecista 27.61.17
Xenogenus 20.6.6
Xenoglossa 25.69.24
Xenoglossodes 25.69.28
Xenolechia 27.23.31
Xenoleurcopis 29.83.9
Xenolytus 25.16.102
xenomastax, Ashmeadiella 25.68.20
Xenomedon 24.24.76
Xenomycetes 24.81.10
Xenomycetinae, supra 24.81.10
Xenomydaea 29.100.25
Xenomyrmex 25.58.32
Xenopanurgus 25.65.14
Xenopelopia 29.24.19
Xenopeponapis 25.69.29
Xenophanes 27.40.29
Xenophytomyza 29.68.7
Xenopompilus 25.60.28
Xenopsylla 30.1.10
Xenopsyllini, supra 30.1.10
Xenopterella 29.82.23
Xenorhipis 24.46.18
Xenos 24.105.7
Xenoschesis 25.16.323
Xenosphecinae, supra 25.62.69
Xenosphex 25.62.69
Xenosternum 25.13.45
Xenostigmus 25.14.7
Xenotemna 27.38.84
Xenotrechus 24.4.41
Xenotyphlus 24.24.170
Xenufens 25.28.11
Xenylla 1.2.8
Xenyllodes 1.2.17
Xeracris 11.5.70
Xeralictus 25.66.7
Xeranobium 24.63.15
Xeranoplium 24.106.44
Xerces Blue 27.43.46
xerces, Glaucopsyche 27.43.46 (Fig.
 27.113)
Xeris 25.9.3
xerobatis, Chelyoxenus 24.26.17
Xerocentris 25.69.42
Xerochares 26.60.28
Xerochlora 27.61.168
Xerochrum 25.50.10
Xerociris 27.75.238
Xerocoelioxys 25.68.24
Xerocoris 20.4.5
Xeroglypta 25.53.17
Xerogorytes 25.62.93
Xeromacrotera 25.65.15
Xeromegachile 25.68.22
Xeromelecta 25.69.39
Xeropasites 25.69.2
Xeropeponapis 25.69.29
Xerophasma 25.65.15
xerophila, Proteriades 25.68.17
Xerophilaphis 21.19.223
Xerophilaspis 21.38.85
Xerophloea 21.14.1
Xerophloeini, supra 21.14.1
Xeropsamobeus 24.30.19
Xerosparinus 24.26.14
Xerosmia 25.68.17
Xerostictia 25.62.104
Xestia 27.75.566
Xestipyge 24.26.22
Xestobium 24.63.5
Xestocephalinae, supra 21.14.37
Xestocephalini, supra 21.14.37
Xestocephalus 21.14.37
Xestocoris 20.7.31
Xestoleptura, supra 24.106.172, 24.106.221

Xestolinus 24.24.47
Xestonotus 24.4.108
Xestopelta 25.16.470
Xestophus 24.20.2
Xesturida 24.24.314
xicaque, Paramacera 27.48.7
Xiphandrena 25.65.1
Xiphocentron 26.2.5
Xiphocentroninae, supra 26.2.5
Xiphomyia 29.105.274
Xiphosomella 25.16.430
Xiphulcus 25.16.97
Xiphydria 25.10.1
Xiphydridae, supra 25.10.1
Xiphydriinae, supra 25.10.1
Xorides 25.16.83
Xoridinae, supra 25.16.80
Xubida 27.55.231
Xuthus 20.4.10
Xyalaspis 25.31.5
Xyalophora 25.31.11
Xyela 25.1.1
Xyelecia 25.1.3
Xyeleciini, supra 25.1.3
Xyelid Sawfly Family, supra 25.1.1
Xyelidae, supra 25.1.1 (Fig. 25.7)
Xyelinae, supra 25.1.1
Xyelini, supra 25.1.1
Xylastodorinae 20.11.1
Xylastodoris, supra 20.11.1
Xyleborini, supra 24.112.54
Xyleborinus 24.112.57
Xyleborus 24.112.56
Xylechinus 24.112.7
Xylena 27.75.388
Xylenini, supra 27.75.388
Xylesthia 27.10.23
Xyletininae, supra 24.63.34
Xyletinus 24.63.37
Xyletomerus 24.63.36
xylinoides, Hyppa 27.75.296 (Fig. 27.362)
Xylita 24.98.18
Xylobiops 24.64.21
Xyloblaptus 24.64.23
Xylococcinae 21.23.1
Xylococcini, supra 21.23.1
Xylococculus 21.23.1
Xylocopa 25.69.46
Xylocopinae, supra 25.69.45
Xylocopoides 25.69.46
Xylocorini, supra 20.21.15
Xylocoris 20.21.15
Xylocopini, supra 25.69.46
Xylocrius 24.106.111
Xylodroomus 24.24.139
Xylomeira 24.64.20
Xylomoia 27.75.265
Xylomya 29.30.2
Xylomyid Fly Family, supra 29.30.1
Xylomyidae, supra 29.30.1
xyloni, Solenopsis 25.58.33
Xyloperthini, supra 24.64.18
Xylophagid Fly Family, supra 29.29.1
Xylophagidae, supra 29.29.1
Xylophaginae, supra 29.29.4
xylophagorum, Roptrocerus 25.18.24
Xylophagus 29.29.5
Xylophanes 27.70.41
Xylophilus 24.52.22
Xylophrurus 25.16.167
Xylopinus 24.87.94
xylopriona 29.11.2
Xylorerinus 24.112.52
Xyloryctes 24.30.107
Xylosandrus 24.112.55
xylostella, Plutella 27.29.7 (Fig. 27.46)

Xylosteus 24.106.172
Xylota 29.47.86
Xyloterini, supra 24.112.52
Xylotomima 29.47.87
Xylotrechus 24.106.123
Xylotype 27.75.420
Xyonysius 20.7.11a
Xyraeomyia 29.68.12
Xysma 25.62.28
Xystopeplus 27.75.396
Xystoteras 25.43.20

Y

yakimae, Osobenus 8.7.17
Yamalotipula 29.2.9
yamaskanensis, Neurocordulia 7.6.5
Yarmister 24.26.51
Yelicones 25.13.61
Yellow and Black Tachinid 29.105.101
Yellow-banded Day Sphinx 27.70.37
Yellow-banded Wasp Moth 27.73.87
Yellow Clover Aphid 21.19.209
Yellow-face Bee Family, supra 25.63.1
Yellow-faced Leafhopper 21.14.92
Yellowfever Mosquito 29.20.9
Yellow-headed Cutworm Moth 27.75.250
Yellowheaded Fireworm 27.38.61
Yellowheaded Leafhopper 21.14.48
Yellowheaded Spruce Sawfly 25.7.28
Yellowjacket Fly 29.47.11
Yellowjackets, supra 25.59.26
Yellow-margined Leaf Beetle 24.107.70
Yellow Mealworm 24.87.92
Yellow-necked Caterpillar Moth 27.71.2
Yellow Rose Aphid 21.19.2
Yellow Scale 21.38.7
Yellow Soldier Fly 29.31.9
Yellow-striped Armyworm Moth 27.75.326
Yellow Sugarcane Aphid 21.19.196
Yellow Woollybear Moth 27.73.37
Yermoia 27.61.97
Yersiniops 14.1.2
Yezoceryx 25.16.193
y-inversum, Prodoxus 27.8.11
Ymeldia 27.23.67
yojoa, Strymon 27.43.34
Yoroperla 8.6.7
Yosemite Bark Weevil 24.113.171
yosemitensis, Eosentomon 2.1.1
Yosemitia 27.55.385
youngana, Cydia 27.38.56
youngi, Erebia 27.48.10
Youngomyia 29.11.94
Yphria 26.8.1
Yphriinae, supra 26.8.1
Yponometua 27.30.9
yponomeutaria, Eumacrodes 27.61.172
Yponomeutidae, supra 27.30.1
Yponomeutoidea, supra 27.29.1
Ypsolopha 27.29.8
Ypsotingini, supra 20.14.23
yuasai, Stibeutes 25.16.126
Yucanda 21.11.8
Yucca Moth 27.8.9
Yucca Moth Family, supra 27.8.1
Yucca Plant Bug 20.23.22
Yuccaborus 24.113.363
yuccae, Axylophilus 24.104.6
yuccae, Megathymus 27.40.88 (Fig. 27.76)
yuccae, Thorybothrips 22.5.71
yuccasella, Deoclona 27.23.91
yuccasella, Tegeticula 27.8.9
yuccivorus, Glaucotes 24.106.277
Yugus 8.7.23

yumaella, Dyoyapsta 27.10.27
Yvretta 27.40.62

Z

Zaboba 27.55.242
Zabrachia 29.31.24
Zabrachypus 25.16.18
zabriskiei, Axima 25.20.10
Zabrops 29.37.24
Zabrosa 21.14.116
Zabrotes 24.108.3
Zacompsia 29.58.38
Zacosmia 25.69.41
Zacotus 24.4.34
Zacryptocerus 25.58.45
Zacycloptera 11.7.46
Zadiprion 25.6.43
Zadontomerus 25.69.45
Zaga 25.28.14
Zagella 25.28.7
Zagloba 24.80.20
Zaglyptonotus 25.18.16
Zaglyptus 25.16.13
Zagonia 29.85.5
Zagrammosoma 25.26.30
Zagryphus 25.16.53
Zagymnus 24.106.137
Zaischnopsis 25.24.11
Zaitzevia 24.45.27
Zale 27.75.128
Zaleops 27.75.125
Zalobius 24.24.90
Zalutschia 29.24.127
Zamagiria 27.55.307
zamiae, Furchadaspis 21.38.34
Zammara 21.13.2
Zammarini, supra 21.13.1
Zamodes 24.106.50
zamon, Eccritosia 29.37.72
Zamopsyche 27.11.5
Zanclognatha 27.75.4
Zanolidae, supra 27.66.1
Zanonia 25.19.20
Zanysson 25.62.77
Zaommoencyrtus 25.25.160
Zapada 8.1.12
zapata, Praeschausia 27.71.32
Zaplethocornis 25.16.334
Zaplous 24.106.255
zapoteca, Megachile 25.68.22
Zaraea 25.5.1
Zarhipis 24.54.1
Zarhopalus 25.25.120
Zascelis 24.113.263
Zaschizonyx 25.7.90
Zatropis 25.19.127
Zatypota 25.16.27

Zavrelia 29.24.76
Zavrelimyia 29.24.27
Zaxenothrips 22.5.77
zea, Heliothis 27.75.599 (Fig. 27.400)
zeae, Achatodes 27.75.281
zealandicus, Tachinaephagus 25.25.114
Zealeuctra 8.4.5
zeamais, Sitophilus 24.113.365
zebina, Thereus 27.43.21
Zebra Butterfly 27.46.6
Zebra Caterpillar Moth 27.75.481
Zebra Swallowtail 27.41.4, 27.41.7
zebratum, Macronema 26.4.11
zebrina, Erechthias 27.10.15
Zeiraphera 27.38.33
zela, Emesis 27.44.6
Zele 25.13.71
Zelia 29.105.197
zelicaon, Papilio 27.41.5
Zelicodes 27.75.22
Zeliini, supra 29.105.194
Zelleria 27.30.10
zelleriella, Tischeria 27.7.1
Zellerina 27.55.109
Zelomorpha 25.13.81
Zeluroides 20.17.30
Zelus 20.17.22
Zemiotes 25.13.72
Zenillia 29.105.435
Zenoa 24.40.1
Zenodochium 27.17.9
Zenodosus 24.67.2
Zenodoxus 27.35.2
Zenoini, supra 24.40.1
Zenophleps 27.61.229
Zephyr Angle Wing 27.46.24
zephyria, Automeris 27.69.8 (Fig. 27.225)
zephyrus, Polygonia 27.46.24
Zerene 27.41.12
zerene, Speyeria 27.46.8
Zeridoneus 20.7.58
Zeropamera 20.7.62
Zeros 29.93.37
zesticopa, Hypatima 27.23.78
Zestura 27.40.10
Zeteticontus 25.25.64
Zethoides 25.59.25
Zethus 25.59.25
zethus, Theroa 27.71.31
Zethusculus 25.59.25
zetterstedtii, Anabrolepis 25.25.91
Zeugloptera, supra 27.1.1
Zeugophora 24.107.8
Zeugophorinae, supra 24.107.8
Zeurerinae, supra 27.37.10
Zeuxidiplosis 29.11.116
Zeuximyia 29.26.10
Zeuzera 27.37.11
Zicca 20.4.28

Zicrona 20.3.75
ziczac, Erythroneura 21.14.82
Zikanapis 25.63.4
Zilora 24.98.31
Zimmerman Pine Moth 27.55.339
zimmermani, Dioryctria 27.55.339
zinckenella, Etiella 27.55.311
Zizula 27.43.39
Zizyphomyia 29.105.384
Zobrini, supra 24.4.94
Zodion 29.49.4
zoilusalis, Cryptobotys 27.55.181
Zomaria 27.38.10
zonatus, Eutrichites 24.25.52
zonatus, Paramblynotus 25.30.1
Zoniagrion 7.11.14
Zonitina, supra 24.101.22
Zonitis 24.101.24
Zonosemata 29.61.45
Zonothrips 22.4.13
Zootermopsis 15.1.1
Zopheridae 24.87.170
Zopherinae, supra 24.87.170
Zopherini, supra 24.87.172
zopheroides, Oenopion 24.87.88
Zopheroteras 25.34.36
Zopherus 24.87.172
Zophobas 24.87.95
Zophodia 27.55.379
Zoraptera, supra 16.1.1 (Fig. 16.1)
Zoraidinae, supra 21.9.1
Zorochrus 24.48.59
Zorotypidae, supra 16.1.1
Zorotypus 16.1.1
Zosteropoda 27.75.532a
Zotheca 27.75.409
Zubovskya 11.5.97
Zumatrichia 26.7.12
Zunacetha 27.72.2
zuni, Arachnis 27.73.43 (Fig. 27.290)
Zuphiini, supra 24.4.165
Zuphium 24.4.166
Zygaenidae, supra 27.50.1
Zygaenoidea, supra 27.50.1
Zygobarella 24.113.342
Zygobarinus 24.113.343
Zygobaris 24.113.341
Zygogramma 24.107.59
Zygogrammini 24.107.59
Zygomyia 29.9.39
Zygoneura 29.10.8
Zygopinae, supra 24.113.274
Zygopini, supra 24.113.274
Zygoptera, supra 7.8.1
Zygosis 25.31.17
Zygota 25.42.9
Zyras 24.24.315
Zyxaphis 21.19.224